Joint Conference on Empirical Methods in Natural Language Processing and Computational Natural Language Learning 2012

(EMNLP 2012)

Jeju Island, Korea
12 – 14 July 2012

Volume 1 of 2

ISBN: 978-1-62276-503-4

Printed from e-media with permission by:

Curran Associates, Inc.
57 Morehouse Lane
Red Hook, NY 12571

Some format issues inherent in the e-media version may also appear in this print version.

Printed by Curran Associates, Inc. (2013)

For permission requests, please contact the Association for Computational Linguistics
at the address below.

Association for Computational Linguistics
209 N. Eighth Street
Stroudsburg, Pennsylvania 18360

Phone: 1-570-476-8006
Fax: 1-570-476-0860

acl@aclweb.org

Additional copies of this publication are available from:

Curran Associates, Inc.
57 Morehouse Lane
Red Hook, NY 12571 USA
Phone: 845-758-0400
Fax: 845-758-2634
Email: curran@proceedings.com
Web: www.proceedings.com

Preface by General and Program Chairs

It is our pleasure to welcome you to the EMNLP-CoNLL 2012 conference, a joint meeting of the Conference on Empirical Methods in Natural Language Learning (EMNLP) and the Conference on Computational Natural Language Learning (CoNLL). After the successful first collaboration in 2007, EMNLP-CoNLL 2012 is being jointly organized by the SIGDAT and SIGNLL special interest groups of the Association of Computational Linguistics.

This time, EMNLP-CoNLL is co-located with, and immediately after ACL's 50th anniversary conference. The choice of the location is an opportunity for the ACL community to return to the beautiful Jeju Island, Korea, following a seven-year hiatus since the Second International Joint Conference on Natural Language Processing (IJCNLP 2005) was held here.

Out of 606 submissions received by EMNLP-CoNLL this year, a total of 36 submissions were eventually withdrawn or rejected without review. From the remaining submissions, 99 were accepted for oral presentation and 40 for poster presentation, for a combined acceptance rate of 24.8%. As in recent editions of EMNLP, authors were given the opportunity to provide supplementary material in conjunction with their submissions, which the program committee could but was not required to take into account during reviewing. Also as in recent editions, authors of accepted papers were offered an additional page in the camera-ready version of their submissions, so that comments received from reviewers could be more easily addressed.

The papers submitted to the conference were subject to a rigorous reviewing process, made possible by efforts of a team of 525 primary and 66 secondary reviewers, acting under the guidance of 22 area chairs. Presence of unsupported claims, or failure to properly compare with previous work, were likely serious obstacles, on the path from initial submission to acceptance and then publication in our proceedings. Luckily, our preface has a guaranteed placement in the proceedings. Therefore, without access to insider data and impressions from previous editions of the conference, we will still go on a limb here, and make the unsupported claim that our team of area chairs has been the greatest. That their expertise, dedication and willingness to go beyond the call of duty had a positive impact on a timely reviewing process and a high-quality conference program, would be an understatement. It has been a pleasure to interact and work with our area chairs.

The schedule of our conference is strengthened by two invited speakers, Eric Xing and Patrick Pantel, who we were very happy to have accept our invitation; and by the CoNLL Shared Task, an annual tradition for the CoNLL conferences. This year's CoNLL Shared Task is Modeling Multilingual Unrestricted Coreference in OntoNotes, and its proceedings and detailed schedule are available separately.

We would like to thank all authors who submitted to our conference, for their willingness to share their knowledge with the rest of us. It may take a few weeks or many years, for the knowledge distilled into the present proceedings to have a measurable impact on our field and beyond. An impact that would not be possible without countless hours spent by authors, from developing ideas to running experiments to building usable systems - steps that often fail, and sometimes succeed.

We would also like to thank all members of the program committee, for their willingness to offer feedback that sometimes reaches extraordinary levels of detail and value to authors. To recognise some of the most dedicated reviewers, we include the Best Reviewer awards a little later in these proceedings.

Naoaki Okazaki, Publications Chair, deserves our special thanks. He brought in a healthy dose of rigor to the planning and preparation of not only this proceedings but also conference materials, matched only by his dedication to deliver under tight scheduling constraints.

If the combination of oral presentations, posters and invited talks that make up EMNLP-CoNLL 2012 is considered a success, it is because it benefited from the touch of many people. Francesco Figari easily kept tabs on our salvos of large and small requests for updates to our conference website. Rich Gerber, Paolo Gai and the larger team managing the conference submission system were quick to offer answers to all our questions. The publication chairs and local arrangements committee of ACL 2012, including Michael White, Maggie Li, Jong Park and especially Gary Geunbae Lee, covered significant tasks on behalf of EMNLP-CoNLL, all with a smile. Chin-Yew Lin, Miles Osborne, Eric Fosler-Lussier, Dekang Lin, Rada Mihalcea, Regina Barzilay, Ulrich Germann and David Yarowsky offered high-level advice or answered detailed questions, drawing upon their experience as organizers of previous ACL-sponsored conferences.

We are grateful to our sponsors (Baidu, Google and Microsoft), for their support of best paper awards and support of student travel in particular, and the financial well-being of the conference in general. It has been an honor to be of service to the conference, for which we would like to thank the community and those who offered us this opportunity. We hope that you enjoy the conference, and have a productive and pleasant stay in South Korea!

Jun'ichi Tsujii, General Chair
James Henderson and Marius Paşca, Program Chairs

General Chair:

Jun'ichi Tsujii, Microsoft Research Asia

Program Chairs:

James Henderson, Xerox Research Centre Europe
Marius Paşca, Google

Area Chairs:

Eugene Agichtein, Emory University
Yejin Choi, Stony Brook University
Hal Daumé III, University of Maryland
Doug Downey, Northwestern University
Chris Dyer, Carnegie Mellon University
Adrià de Gispert, University of Cambridge
Julia Hirschberg, Columbia University
Anna Korhonen, University of Cambridge
Bing Liu, University of Illinois at Chicago
Hwee Tou Ng, National University of Singapore
Patrick Pantel, Microsoft Research
Marco Pennacchiotti, Yahoo! Labs
Slav Petrov, Google
Simone Paolo Ponzetto, Sapienza University of Rome
John Prager, IBM Research
Chris Quirk, Microsoft Research
Sebastian Riedel, University of Massachusetts at Amherst
Hiroya Takamura, Tokyo Institute of Technology
Partha Talukdar, Carnegie Mellon University
Kristina Toutanova, Microsoft Research
Reut Tsarfaty, Uppsala University
Marilyn Walker, University of California at Santa Cruz

Publication Chair:

Naoaki Okazaki, Tohoku University

Program Committee: Reviewers:

Ahmed Abbasi, Robert Abbott, Omri Abend, Meni Adler, Mikhail Ageev, Lars Ahrenberg, Hua Ai, Cem Akkaya, Pranav Anand, Alina Andreevskaia, Ion Androutsopoulos, Eiji Aramaki, Yoav Artzi, Abhishek Arun, Nicholas Asher, Giuseppe Attardi, Necip Fazil Ayan,

Anton Bakalov, Alexandra Balahur, Niranjan Balasubramanian, Timothy Baldwin, Carmen Banea, Ritwik Banerjee, Mohit Bansal, Roy Bar-Haim, Kedar Belare, Anja Belz, Paul Bennett, Stefan Benus, Taylor Berg-Kirkpatrick, Nicola Bertoldi, Justin Betteridge, Chandra Sekhar Bhagavatula, Aditya Bhargava, Jiang Bian, Chris Biemann, Dan Bikel, Alexandra Birch, Arianna Bisazza, Graeme Blackwood, Sasha Blair-Goldensohn, Jim Blevins, Michael Bloodgood, Phil Blunsom, Bernd Bohnet, Ester Boldrini, Antal van den Bosch, Elizabeth Boschee, Jan Botha, Alexandre Bouchard-Côté, Jordan Boyd-Graber, Thorsten Brants, Ulf Brefeld, Chris Brew, Ted Briscoe, Razvan Bunescu, David Burkett, Bill Byrne, Donna Byron,

Chris Callison-Burch, Nicola Cancedda, Marie Candito, Yunbo Cao, Giuseppe Carenini, Michael Carl, Andrew Carlson, Marine Carpuat, Xavier Carreras, Francisco Casacuberta, Dan Cer, Ozlem Cetinoglu, Mauro Cettolo, Joyce Chai, Soumen Chakrabarti, Jason Chang, Ming-Wei Chang, Ciprian Chelba, Hsin-Hsi Chen, Stanley Chen, Colin Cherry, Jackie Cheung, David Chiang, Munmun De Choudhury, Grzegorz Chrupala, Philipp Cimiano, Alex Clark, Steve Clark, Shay Cohen, Trevor Cohn, Bonaventura Coppola, Marta Ruiz Costa-Jussa, Danilo Croce, Tim Van de Cruys, Silviu Cucerzan, Aron Culotta,

Walter Daelemans, Daniel Dahlmeier, Bhavana Dalvi, Dana Dannells, Dipanjan Das, Steve DeNeefe, John DeNero, Vera Demberg, Michael Denkowski, Tejaswini Deoskar, Barry Devereux, Ann Devitt, Mona Diab, Laura Dietz, Mike Dillinger, Nikhil Dinesh, Xiaowen Ding, Bill Dolan, Mark Dras, Mark Dredze, Markus Dreyer, Greg Druck, Kevin Duh, Benjamin van Durme, Marc Dymetman,

Koji Eguchi, Andreas Eisele, Jacob Eisenstein, Jason Eisner, Micha Eisner, Michael Elhadad, Charles Elkan, David Elson, Katrin Erk, Oren Etzioni,

Anthony Fader, Katja Filippova, Radu Florian, George Foster, Jennifer Foster, Anette Frank, Marjorie Freedman, Dayne Freitag, Atsushi Fujita, Sadaoki Furui,

Michael Gamon, Kuzman Ganchev, Juri Ganitkevitch, Jianfeng Gao, Claire Gardent, Matt Gardner, Milica Gasic, Josef van Genabith, Matthew Gerber, Daniel Gildea, Daniel Gillick, Kevin Gimpel, Roxana Girju, Amir Globerson, Yoav Goldberg, Dan Goldwasser, Cyril Goutte, Amit Goyal, João Graça, Spence Green, Ralph Grishman, Joakim Gustafson,

Ryuichiro HIgashinaka, Viet Ha-Thuc, Barry Haddow, Gholamreza Haffari, Patrick Haffner, Jan Hajic, Dilek Hakkani-Tur, David Hall, Keith Hall, Greg Hanneman, Christian Hardmeier, Saša Hasan, Helen Hastie, Jun Hatori, Zhongjun He, Kenneth Heafield, John Henderson, Tsutomu Hirao, Graeme Hirst, Anna Hjalmarsson, Hieu Hoang, Julia Hockenmaier, Liangjie Hong, Mark Hopkins, Veronique Hoste, Edward Hovy, Estevam Hruschka, Yunhua Hu, Fei Huang, Liang Huang, Minlie Huang, Samar Husain,

Francisco Iacobelli, Gonzalo Iglesias, Diana Inkpen, Ann Irvine, Tatsuya Izuha,

Jagadeesh Jagarlamud, Heng Ji, Jing Jiang, Wen Bin Jiang, Richard Johansson, Howard Johnson,

Nobuhiro Kaji, Pallika Kanani, Hiroshi Kanayama, Rohit Kate, Junichi Kazama, Shahram Khadivi, Jin Dong Kim, Irwin King, Tracy King, Brian Kingsbury, Katrin Kirchhoff, Kevin Knight, Philipp

Koehn, Mamoru Komachi, Greg Kondrak, Christian Konig, Terry Koo, Moshe Koppel, Alexander Kotov, Zornitsa Kozareva, Jayant Krishnamurthy, Lun-Wei Ku, Marco Kuhlmann, Roland Kuhn, Seth Kulick, Shankar Kumar, Oren Kurland,

Oier Lopez de Lacalle, Philippe Langlais, Mirella Lapata, Claudia Leacock, John Lee, Yoong Keok Lee, Alessandro Lenci, Gregor Leusch, Abby Levenberg, Chi-Ho Li, Fangtao Li, Mu Li, Shoushan Li, Hui Lin, Thomas Lin, Xiao Ling, Jing Liu, Qun Liu, Yang Liu, Zhanyi Liu, Andrej Ljoje, Adam Lopez, Annie Louis, Bin Lu, Wei Lu, Yue Lu, Michael Lucas, Stephanie Lukin, Yajuan Lv,

Yanjun Ma, Klaus Macherey, Wolfgang Macherey, Nitin Madnani, Wolfgang Maier, Suresh Manandhar, Daniel Marcu, Anna Margolis, Katja Markert, Marie-Catherine de Marneffe, Craig Martell, Andre Martins, Yuval Marton, Spyros Matsoukas, Takuya Matsuzaki, Evgeny Matusov, Mausam, Arne Mauser, Jon May, Andrew McCallum, Diana McCarthy, David McClosky, Ryan McDonald, Kathleen McKeown, Beata Megyesi, Gerard De Melo, Paola Merlo, Haitao Mi, Rada Mihalcea, David Mimno, Yasuhiro Minami, Teru Misu, Yusuke Miyao, Saif Mohammad, Behrang Mohit, Karo Moilanen, Dan Moldovan, Martin Molina, Robert Moore, Paul Morarescu, Pedro Moreno, Shinsuke Mori, Hajime Morita, Alessandro Moschitti, Dana Movshovitz-Attias, Arjun Mukherjee, Vanessa Murdock, Markos Mylonakis, Lluís Mŕrquez,

Tetsuji Nakagawa, Mikio Nakano, Toshiaki Nakazawa, Preslav Nakov, Jason Naradowsky, Vivi Nastase, Roberto Navigli, Mark-Jan Nederhof, Ani Nenkova, Graham Neubig, Alena Neviarouskaya, Vincent Ng, Jian-Yun Nie, John Niekrasz, Hitoshi Nishikawa, Joakim Nivre, Tadashi Nomoto, Scott Nowson,

Brendan O'Connor, Stephan Oepen, Kemal Oflazer, Naoaki Okazaki, Manabu Okumura, Constantin Orasan, Myle Ott,

Sebastian Pado, Shimei Pan, Sinno Jialin Pan, Soo-Min Pantel, Becky Passonneau, Alexandre Passos, Siddharth Patwardhan, Michael Paul, Matthias Paulik, Adam Pauls, Gerald Penn, Sasa Petrovic, Elias Ponvert, Hoifung Poon, Ana-Maria Popescu, Andrei Popescu-Belis, Maja Popovic, Fred Popowich, Matt Post, Peter Prettenhofer, Emily Mower Provost, Sampo Pyysalo,

Yanjun Qi, Silvia Quarteroni,

Dragomir Radev, Altaf Rahman, Bhuvana Ramabhadran, Maya Ramanath, Owen Rambow, Ari Rappoport, Sujith Ravi, Deepak Ravichandran, Emmanuel Rayner, Sravana Reddy, Ines Rehbein, Roi Reichart, Joseph Reisinger, David Reitter, Jason Riesa, Verena Rieser, Stefan Riezler, German Rigau, Ellen Riloff, Laura Rimell, Eric Ringger, Alan Ritter, Brian Roark, Andrew Rosenberg, Paolo Rosso, Dan Roth, Wang Rui, Josef Ruppenhofer, Alexander Rush, Graham Russell,

Stijn De Saeger, Kenji Sagae, Mark Sammons, Sunita Sarawagi, Anoop Sarkar, Christina Sauper, Hassan Sawaf, Frank Schilder, Hinrich Schuetze, Bjoern Schuller, Holger Schwenk, Djamé Seddah, Satoshi Sekine, Hendra Setiawan, Burr Settles, Fei Sha, Libin Shen, Shuming Shi, Ekaterina Shutova, Mário J. Silva, Fabrizio Silvestri, Michel Simard, Sameer Singh, Kairit Sirts, Gabriel Skantze, Jason Smith, Noah Smith, Ronnie Smith, Ben Snyder, Stephen Soderland, Radu Soricut, Lucia Specia, Valentin Spitkovsky, Caroline Sporleder, Vivek Srikumar, Mark Steedman, Benno Stein, Amanda Stent, Svetlana Stoyanchev, Veselin Stoyanov, Carlo Strapparava, Michael Strube, Keh-Yih Su, Michael Subotin, Fabian Suchanek, Katsuhito Sudoh, Ang Sun, Mihai Surdeanu, Idan Szpektor, Diarmuid Ó Séaghdha,

David Talbot, Songbo Tan, Joseph Tepperman, Joel Tetreault, Blaise Thomson, Joerg Tiedemann,

Christoph Tillmann, Ivan Titov, Cigdem Toprak, Kentaro Torisawa, Roy Tromble, Oren Tsur, Yoshimasa Tsuruoka, Peter Turney, Oscar Täckström,

Raghavendra Udupa, Jakob Uszkoreit, Masao Utiyama,

Lucy Vanderwende, Tony Veale, Paola Velardi, Rossano Venturini, Yannick Versley, Jette Viethen, David Vilar, Aline Villavicencio, Andreas Vlachos, Martin Volk,

Sabine Schulte im Walde, Stephen Wan, Xiaojun Wan, Haifeng Wang, Taro Watanabe, Furu Wei, Gerhard Weikum, Ralph Weischedel, Ji-Rong Wen, Chris Wendt, Dominic Widdows, Janyce Wiebe, Derry Wijaya, Shuly Wintner, Kamfai Wong, Frank Wood, Fei Wu, Joern Wuebker,

Yunqing Xia, Deyi Xiong, Peng Xu, Nianwen Xue,

Grace Yang, Muyun Yang, Yi Yang, Alexander Yates, Mark Yatskar, Ainur Yessenalina, Elad Yom-Tov, Jianxing Yu, Yisong Yue,

Wlodek Zadrozny, Fabio Massimo Zanzotto, Richard Zens, Torsten Zesch, Luke Zettlemoyer, Bing Zhang, Congle Zhang, Hao Zhang, Hui Zhang, Joy Zhang, Lei Zhang, Min Zhang, Qi Zhang, Yue Zhang, Bing Zhao, Shiqi Zhao, Tiejun Zhao, Wayne Xin Zhao, Jing Zheng, Liu Zhiyuan, Bowen Zhou, Guodong Zhou, Ming Zhou, Jing-Bo Zhu, Xiaodan Zhu, Chengqing Zong, Geoff Zweig

Program Committee: Secondary Reviewers:

Gabor Angeli, Gerlof Bouma, Steven Burrows, Paula Carvalho, Diego Ceccarelli, Janara Christensen, Eric Corlett, Bart Desmet, Frank Ferraro, Tiziano Flati, Francisco Guzman, Yifan He, Dirk Hovy, Rubén Izquierdo, Jiarong Jiang, Tetsuo Kiso, Effi Levi, Baichuan Li, Nedim Lipka, Lemao Liu, Jeff Lund, Pierre Magistry, Thang Luong Minh, Makoto Miwa, Abdelrahman Mohamed, Taesun Moon, Tanmoy Mukherjee, Ryo Nagata, Franco Maria Nardini, Viet-An Nguyen, Gozde Ozbal, Wang Pidong, Barbara Plank, Quentin Pleple, Natalia Ponomareva, Vladimir Popescu, Daniel Preotiuc, Ju Qi, Kyle Rawlins, Majid Razmara, Nils Reiter, Joseph Le Roux, Benoît Sagot, Mohammad Salameh, Baskaran Sankaran, Uma Sawant, Roy Schwartz, Aliaksei Severyn, Kathrin Spreyer, Gabriele Tolomei, Olga Uryopina, Rakesh Varna, Zhiyang Wang, Zhuoran Wang, Jonny Weese, Michael Wick, Wei Xu, Haiqin Yang, Xuchen Yao, Mo Yu, Yintao Yu, Jiajun Zhang, Bo Zhao, Shanheng Zhao, Tu Zhaopeng, Chao Zhou

Invited Talks:

"On Learning Sparse Structured Input-Output Models"

Eric Xing, Carnegie Mellon University

In many modern problems across areas such as natural language processing, computer vision, and social media inference, one is often interested in learning a Sparse Structured Input-Output Model (SIOM), in which the input variables of the model such as lexicons in a document bear rich structures due to the syntactic and semantic dependences between them in the text; and the output variables such as the elements in a multi-way classification, a parse, or a topic representation are also structured because of their interrelatedness. A SIOM can nicely capture rich structural properties in the data and in the problem, but it also raises severe computational and theoretical challenge on sparse, consistent, and tractable model identification and inference.

In this talk, I will present models, algorithms, and theories that learn Sparse SIOMs of various kinds in very high dimensional input/output space, with fast and highly scalable optimization procedures, and strong statistical guarantees. I will demonstrate application of our approach to problems in large-scale text classification, topic modeling, and dependency parsing.

"The Appification of the Web and the Renaissance of Conversational User Interfaces"

Patrick Pantel, Microsoft Research

The appification of the Web is triggering a fundamental shift in how users access information. We are moving from centralized access points, such as search engines, towards highly specialized, and yet fragmented, functionalities in disconnected apps. This talk explores an entity-centric conversational interface as a mechanism to overcome this fragmentation, highlighting the numerous associated NLP challenges and opportunities that lie ahead.

Consider mobile scenarios, where the traditional search engine paradigm is being cannibalized by search and browse functionalities built directly into specialized apps. For example, while users can search for restaurants and products using their mobile browser, they are increasingly turning directly to applications such as Yelp, Urbanspoon and Amazon. However, interoperability between applications and lacking generalized interfaces to their functionalities pose serious scalability challenges. In this talk, we argue for an entity-centric conversational interface in which natural user interactions with entities are paired with actions that can be performed on the entities, thus enabling the brokering of web pages and applications that can satisfy the intended action. In this vision, the broker is aware of all entities and actions of interest to its users, understands the intent of the user, and provides direct actionable results through APIs with external providers satisfying the intent. The user saves clicks and time to accomplish her intended action and can discover related actions. New revenue streams open up from paid action placement and lead generation opportunities. At the forefront of this direction are a number of NLP challenges in the areas of entity recognition, entity linking, knowledge extraction, intent recognition, and dialog modeling, to name a few.

We end by proposing one particular technique for learning and mapping user intents in a search interface. In an annotation study conducted over a traffic sample of web usage logs, we found that a large proportion of user queries involve actions on entities, calling for an automatic approach to identifying relevant actions for entity-bearing queries. We pose the problem of finding actions that can be performed on entities as the problem of doing probabilistic inference in a graphical model that captures how entity-bearing information requests are generated. Given a large collection of real-world queries and clicks from a commercial search engine, the models are learned efficiently through maximum likelihood estimation using an EM algorithm. Given a new query, inference enables the recommendation of a set of pertinent actions and providers. We propose an evaluation methodology for measuring the relevance of our recommended actions, and show empirical evidence of the quality and the diversity of the discovered actions.

Best Reviewer Awards:

Hua Ai	Ion Androutsopoulos	Yoav Artzi	Mohit Bansal
Aditya Bhargava	Graeme Blackwood	Sasha Blair-Goldensohn	David Burkett
Marie Candito	Marine Carpuat	Xavier Carreras	Soumen Chakrabarti
Colin Cherry	Mark Dredze	Kevin Duh	David Elson
Katja Filippova	Matthew Gerber	Kevin Gimpel	Yoav Goldberg
Spence Green	Greg Hanneman	Saša Hasan	Alexander Kotov
Jayant Krishnamurthy	Marco Kuhlmann	Roland Kuhn	Mirella Lapata
Annie Louis	Andre Martins	Ryan McDonald	Robert Moore
Arjun Mukherjee	Vanessa Murdock	Jason Naradowsky	Roberto Navigli
Vincent Ng	John Niekrasz	Joakim Nivre	Becky Passonneau
Hoifung Poon	Andrei Popescu-Belis	Owen Rambow	Ines Rehbein
Alan Ritter	Alexander Rush	Noah Smith	Oren Tsur
Oscar Täckström	Lucy Vanderwende	Jette Viethen	Gerhard Weikum
Janyce Wiebe	Joern Wuebker	Yue Zhang	

Table of Contents

Conference Program

Thursday, July 12, 2012

	Session 1-AM-0P: Opening
09:00-09:15	Opening Remarks
	Session 1-AM-1P: Plenary Session: Invited Talk Session Chair: James Henderson
09:15-10:30	Invited Talk: On Learning Sparse Structured Input-Output Models (Eric Xing, Carnegie Mellon University)
10:30-11:00	Coffee Break
	Session 1-AM-2A: Machine Translation: Bilingual Lexicons and Alignment Session Chair: David Chiang
11:00-11:30	*Syntactic Transfer Using a Bilingual Lexicon* Greg Durrett, Adam Pauls and Dan Klein
11:30-12:00	*Regularized Interlingual Projections: Evaluation on Multilingual Transliteration* Jagadeesh Jagarlamudi and Hal Daume III
12:00-12:30	*Bilingual Lexicon Extraction from Comparable Corpora Using Label Propagation* Akihiro Tamura, Taro Watanabe and Eiichiro Sumita
	Session 1-AM-2B: Social Media: Author Style and Attribution Session Chair: Janyce Wiebe
11:00-11:30	*Lexical Differences in Autobiographical Narratives from Schizophrenic Patients and Healthy Controls* Kai Hong, Christian G. Kohler, Mary E. March, Amber A. Parker and Ani Nenkova
11:30-12:00	*Streaming Analysis of Discourse Participants* Benjamin Van Durme
12:00-12:30	*Detecting Subgroups in Online Discussions by Modeling Positive and Negative Relations among Participants* Ahmed Hassan, Amjad Abu-Jbara and Dragomir Radev

Thursday, July 12, 2012 (continued)

Session 1-AM-2C: Dialogue and Interactive Systems
Session Chair: Michael White

11:00-11:30 *Generative Goal-Driven User Simulation for Dialog Management*
Aciel Eshky, Ben Allison and Mark Steedman

11:30-12:00 *Optimising Incremental Dialogue Decisions Using Information Density for Interactive Systems*
Nina Dethlefs, Helen Hastie, Verena Rieser and Oliver Lemon

12:00-12:30 *Mixed Membership Markov Models for Unsupervised Conversation Modeling*
Michael J. Paul

Session 1-AM-2D: Information Extraction: Entity Disambiguation
Session Chair: Raymond Mooney

11:00-11:30 *An Entity-Topic Model for Entity Linking*
Xianpei Han and Le Sun

11:30-12:00 *Linking Named Entities to Any Database*
Avirup Sil, Ernest Cronin, Penghai Nie, Yinfei Yang, Ana-Maria Popescu and Alexander Yates

12:00-12:30 *Towards Efficient Named-Entity Rule Induction for Customizability*
Ajay Nagesh, Ganesh Ramakrishnan, Laura Chiticariu, Rajasekar Krishnamurthy, Ankush Dharkar and Pushpak Bhattacharyya

12:30-14:00 Lunch

Session 1-PM-1A: Sentiment Analysis
Session Chair: Bing Liu

14:00-14:30 *Active Learning for Imbalanced Sentiment Classification*
Shoushan Li, Shengfeng Ju, Guodong Zhou and Xiaojun Li

14:30-15:00 *A Weakly Supervised Model for Sentence-Level Semantic Orientation Analysis with Multiple Experts*
Lizhen Qu, Rainer Gemulla and Gerhard Weikum

15:00-15:30 *Collocation Polarity Disambiguation Using Web-based Pseudo Contexts*
Yanyan Zhao, Bing Qin and Ting Liu

Thursday, July 12, 2012 (continued)

Session 1-PM-1B: Semantics: Nouns, Verbs and Predicates
Session Chair: Rada Mihalcea

14:00-14:30 *Aligning Predicates across Monolingual Comparable Texts using Graph-based Clustering*
Michael Roth and Anette Frank

14:30-15:00 *Local and Global Context for Supervised and Unsupervised Metonymy Resolution*
Vivi Nastase, Alex Judea, Katja Markert and Michael Strube

15:00-15:30 *Learning Verb Inference Rules from Linguistically-Motivated Evidence*
Hila Weisman, Jonathan Berant, Idan Szpektor and Ido Dagan

Session 1-PM-1C: Machine Learning: Latent Models
Session Chair: Alexandre Klementiev

14:00-14:30 *Spectral Dependency Parsing with Latent Variables*
Paramveer Dhillon, Jordan Rodu, Michael Collins, Dean Foster and Lyle Ungar

14:30-15:00 *A Phrase-Discovering Topic Model Using Hierarchical Pitman-Yor Processes*
Robert Lindsey, William Headden and Michael Stipicevic

15:00-15:30 *A Bayesian Model for Learning SCFGs with Discontiguous Rules*
Abby Levenberg, Chris Dyer and Phil Blunsom

Session 1-PM-1D: Summarization
Session Chair: Dragomir Radev

14:00-14:30 *Multiple Aspect Summarization Using Integer Linear Programming*
Kristian Woodsend and Mirella Lapata

14:30-15:00 *Minimal Dependency Length in Realization Ranking*
Michael White and Rajakrishnan Rajkumar

15:00-15:30 *Framework of Automatic Text Summarization Using Reinforcement Learning*
Seonggi Ryang and Takeshi Abekawa

15:30-16:00 Coffee Break

Thursday, July 12, 2012 (continued)

Session 1-PM-2A: Machine Translation
Session Chair: Xiong Deyi

16:00-16:30 *Large Scale Decipherment for Out-of-Domain Machine Translation*
Qing Dou and Kevin Knight

16:30-17:00 *N-gram-based Tense Models for Statistical Machine Translation*
Zhengxian Gong, Min Zhang, Chew Lim Tan and Guodong Zhou

17:00-17:30 *Source Language Adaptation for Resource-Poor Machine Translation*
Pidong Wang, Preslav Nakov and Hwee Tou Ng

Session 1-PM-2B: Dependency Parsing
Session Chair: Emily Pitler

16:00-16:30 *Exploiting Reducibility in Unsupervised Dependency Parsing*
David Mareček and Zdeněk Žabokrtský

16:30-17:00 *Improving Transition-Based Dependency Parsing with Buffer Transitions*
Daniel Fernández-González and Carlos Gómez-Rodríguez

17:00-17:30 *Generalized Higher-Order Dependency Parsing with Cube Pruning*
Hao Zhang and Ryan McDonald

Session 1-PM-2C: Phonemes, Words and Speech
Session Chair: Pascale Fung

16:00-16:30 *Universal Grapheme-to-Phoneme Prediction Over Latin Alphabets*
Young-Bum Kim and Benjamin Snyder

16:30-17:00 *Name Phylogeny: A Generative Model of String Variation*
Nicholas Andrews, Jason Eisner and Mark Dredze

17:00-17:30 *Syntactic Surprisal Affects Spoken Word Duration in Conversational Contexts*
Vera Demberg, Asad Sayeed, Philip Gorinski and Nikolaos Engonopoulos

Thursday, July 12, 2012 (continued)

Session 1-PM-2D: Question Answering
Session Chair: Alessandro Moschitti

16:00-16:30 *Why Question Answering using Sentiment Analysis and Word Classes*
Jong-Hoon Oh, Kentaro Torisawa, Chikara Hashimoto, Takuya Kawada, Stijn De Saeger, Jun'ichi Kazama and Yiou Wang

16:30-17:00 *Natural Language Questions for the Web of Data*
Mohamed Yahya, Klaus Berberich, Shady Elbassuoni, Maya Ramanath, Volker Tresp and Gerhard Weikum

17:00-17:30 *Answering Opinion Questions on Products by Exploiting Hierarchical Organization of Consumer Reviews*
Jianxing Yu, Zheng-Jun Zha and Tat-Seng Chua

17:30-18:00 Break

Session 1-PM-3P: Poster Session and Reception (18:00-22:00)

Locally Training the Log-Linear Model for SMT
Lemao Liu, Hailong Cao, Taro Watanabe, Tiejun Zhao, Mo Yu and Conghui Zhu

Iterative Annotation Transformation with Predict-Self Reestimation for Chinese Word Segmentation
Wenbin Jiang, Fandong Meng, Qun Liu and Yajuan Lü

Automatically Constructing a Normalisation Dictionary for Microblogs
Bo Han, Paul Cook and Timothy Baldwin

Unsupervised PCFG Induction for Grounded Language Learning with Highly Ambiguous Supervision
Joohyun Kim and Raymond Mooney

Forced Derivation Tree based Model Training to Statistical Machine Translation
Nan Duan, Mu Li and Ming Zhou

Multi-instance Multi-label Learning for Relation Extraction
Mihai Surdeanu, Julie Tibshirani, Ramesh Nallapati and Christopher D. Manning

An "AI readability" Formula for French as a Foreign Language
Thomas François and Cédrick Fairon

Thursday, July 12, 2012 (continued)

Thursday, July 12, 2012 (continued)

Thursday, July 12, 2012 (continued)

Friday, July 13, 2012

Session 2-AM-1P: Plenary Session: Invited Talk
Session Chair: Marius Pasca

09:15-10:30 Invited Talk: The Appification of the Web and the Renaissance of Conversational User Interfaces (Patrick Pantel, Microsoft Research)

10:30-11:00 Coffee Break

Session 2-AM-2A: Machine Translation: Role of Syntax
Session Chair: Qun Liu

Session 2-AM-2B: Information Extraction: Temporally-Aware Extraction
Session Chair: Jong-Hoon Oh

Friday, July 13, 2012 (continued)

Session 2-AM-2C: Discourse and Generation
Session Chair: Anette Frank

11:00-11:30 *A Novel Discriminative Framework for Sentence-Level Discourse Analysis*
Shafiq Joty, Giuseppe Carenini and Raymond Ng

11:30-12:00 *Using Discourse Information for Paraphrase Extraction*
Michaela Regneri and Rui Wang

12:00-12:30 *Generating Non-Projective Word Order in Statistical Linearization*
Bernd Bohnet, Anders Björkelund, Jonas Kuhn, Wolfgang Seeker and Sina Zarriess

Session 2-AM-2D: CoNLL Shared Task
Session Chair: Sameer Pradhan

11:00-12:30 CoNLL Shared Task Session

12:30-13:45 Lunch

13:45-14:30 SIGDAT and SIGNLL Business Meetings

Session 2-PM-1A: Semantics: Words and Topics
Session Chair: Roi Reichart

14:30-15:00 *Learning Syntactic Categories Using Paradigmatic Representations of Word Context*
Mehmet Ali Yatbaz, Enis Sert and Deniz Yuret

15:00-15:30 *Exploring Topic Coherence over Many Models and Many Topics*
Keith Stevens, Philip Kegelmeyer, David Andrzejewski and David Buttler

Friday, July 13, 2012 (continued)

Session 2-PM-1B: Machine Translation: Pruning
Session Chair: Kevin Knight

14:30-15:00 *Entropy-based Pruning for Phrase-based Machine Translation*
Wang Ling, João Graça, Isabel Trancoso and Alan Black

15:00-15:30 *A Systematic Comparison of Phrase Table Pruning Techniques*
Richard Zens, Daisy Stanton and Peng Xu

Session 2-PM-1C: Evaluation
Session Chair: Billy Tak-Ming Wong

14:30-15:00 *Probabilistic Finite State Machines for Regression-based MT Evaluation*
Mengqiu Wang and Christopher D. Manning

15:00-15:30 *An Empirical Investigation of Statistical Significance in NLP*
Taylor Berg-Kirkpatrick, David Burkett and Dan Klein

Session 2-PM-1D: CoNLL Shared Task
Session Chair: Alessandro Moschitti

14:30-15:30 CoNLL Shared Task Session

15:30-16:00 Coffee Break

Session 2-PM-2A: Information Extraction: Relation and Event Extraction
Session Chair: Mausam

16:00-16:30 *Employing Compositional Semantics and Discourse Consistency in Chinese Event Extraction*
Peifeng Li, Guodong Zhou, Qiaoming Zhu and Libin Hou

16:30-17:00 *Reading The Web with Learned Syntactic-Semantic Inference Rules*
Ni Lao, Amarnag Subramanya, Fernando Pereira and William W. Cohen

17:00-17:30 *Ensemble Semantics for Large-scale Unsupervised Relation Extraction*
Bonan Min, Shuming Shi, Ralph Grishman and Chin-Yew Lin

Friday, July 13, 2012 (continued)

Session 2-PM-2B: Parsing Models and Evaluation
Session Chair: Ivan Titov

16:00-16:30 *Forest Reranking through Subtree Ranking*
Richard Farkas and Helmut Schmid

16:30-17:00 *Parser Showdown at the Wall Street Corral: An Empirical Investigation of Error Types in Parser Output*
Jonathan K. Kummerfeld, David Hall, James R. Curran and Dan Klein

17:00-17:30 *Extending Machine Translation Evaluation Metrics with Lexical Cohesion to Document Level*
Billy T. M. Wong and Chunyu Kit

Session 2-PM-2C: Large-Scale NLP Algorithms
Session Chair: Benjamin van Durme

16:00-16:30 *Fast Large-Scale Approximate Graph Construction for NLP*
Amit Goyal, Hal Daume III and Raul Guerra

16:30-17:00 *Building a Lightweight Semantic Model for Unsupervised Information Extraction on Short Listings*
Doo Soon Kim, Kunal Verma and Peter Yeh

17:00-17:30 *Sketch Algorithms for Estimating Point Queries in NLP*
Amit Goyal, Hal Daume III and Graham Cormode

Session 2-PM-2D: Machine Learning: Inference
Session Chair: Jennifer Gillenwater

16:00-16:30 *Monte Carlo MCMC: Efficient Inference by Approximate Sampling*
Sameer Singh, Michael Wick and Andrew McCallum

16:30-17:00 *On Amortizing Inference Cost for Structured Prediction*
Vivek Srikumar, Gourab Kundu and Dan Roth

17:00-17:30 *Exact Sampling and Decoding in High-Order Hidden Markov Models*
Simon Carter, Marc Dymetman and Guillaume Bouchard

Saturday, July 14, 2012

Session 3-AM-1P: Plenary Session
Session Chair: Jun'ichi Tsujii

09:00-09:30	*PATTY: A Taxonomy of Relational Patterns with Semantic Types* Ndapandula Nakashole, Gerhard Weikum and Fabian Suchanek
09:30-10:00	*Training Factored PCFGs with Expectation Propagation* David Hall and Dan Klein
10:00-10:30	*A Coherence Model Based on Syntactic Patterns* Annie Louis and Ani Nenkova
10:30-11:00	Coffee Break

Session 3-AM-2A: Machine Translation: Decoding
Session Chair: Preslav Nakov

11:00-11:30	*Language Model Rest Costs and Space-Efficient Storage* Kenneth Heafield, Philipp Koehn and Alon Lavie
11:30-12:00	*Document-Wide Decoding for Phrase-Based Statistical Machine Translation* Christian Hardmeier, Joakim Nivre and Jörg Tiedemann
12:00-12:30	*Left-to-Right Tree-to-String Decoding with Prediction* Yang Feng, Yang Liu, Qun Liu and Trevor Cohn

Saturday, July 14, 2012 (continued)

Session 3-AM-2B: Distributional and Compositional Semantics
Session Chair: Bo Pang

11:00-11:30 *Semantic Compositionality through Recursive Matrix-Vector Spaces*
Richard Socher, Brody Huval, Christopher D. Manning and Andrew Y. Ng

11:30-12:00 *Polarity Inducing Latent Semantic Analysis*
Wen-tau Yih, Geoffrey Zweig and John Platt

12:00-12:30 *First Order vs. Higher Order Modification in Distributional Semantics*
Gemma Boleda, Eva Maria Vecchi, Miquel Cornudella and Louise McNally

Session 3-AM-2C: Discourse: Coreference Resolution
Session Chair: Mihai Surdeanu

11:00-11:30 *Learning-based Multi-Sieve Co-reference Resolution with Knowledge*
Lev Ratinov and Dan Roth

11:30-12:00 *Joint Learning for Coreference Resolution with Markov Logic*
Yang Song, Jing Jiang, Wayne Xin Zhao, Sujian Li and Houfeng Wang

12:00-12:30 *Resolving "This-issue" Anaphora*
Varada Kolhatkar and Graeme Hirst

Session 3-AM-2D: Information Retrieval
Session Chair: Jianfeng Gao

11:00-11:30 *Entity based Q&A Retrieval*
Amit Singh

11:30-12:00 *Constructing Task-Specific Taxonomies for Document Collection Browsing*
Hui Yang

12:00-12:30 *Besting the Quiz Master: Crowdsourcing Incremental Classification Games*
Jordan Boyd-Graber, Brianna Satinoff, He He and Hal Daume III

12:30-14:00 Lunch

Saturday, July 14, 2012 (continued)

	Session 3-PM-1A: Machine Learning: Transfer and Biases Session Chair: Benjamin Snyder
14:00-14:30	*Multi-Domain Learning: When Do Domains Matter?* Mahesh Joshi, Mark Dredze, William W. Cohen and Carolyn Rose
14:30-15:00	*Biased Representation Learning for Domain Adaptation* Fei Huang and Alexander Yates
15:00-15:30	*Unambiguity Regularization for Unsupervised Learning of Probabilistic Grammars* Kewei Tu and Vasant Honavar
	Session 3-PM-1B: Opinion Mining: Discovering Opinion Expressions Session Chair: Yejin Choi
14:00-14:30	*Extracting Opinion Expressions with semi-Markov Conditional Random Fields* Bishan Yang and Claire Cardie
14:30-15:00	*Opinion Target Extraction Using Word-Based Translation Model* Kang Liu, Liheng Xu and Jun Zhao
15:00-15:30	*Word Salad: Relating Food Prices and Descriptions* Victor Chahuneau, Kevin Gimpel, Bryan R. Routledge, Lily Scherlis and Noah A. Smith
	Session 3-PM-1C: Part of Speech Tagging Session Chair: Slav Petrov
14:00-14:30	*Learning to Map into a Universal POS Tagset* Yuan Zhang, Roi Reichart, Regina Barzilay and Amir Globerson
14:30-15:00	*Part-of-Speech Tagging for Chinese-English Mixed Texts with Dynamic Features* Jiayi Zhao, Xipeng Qiu, Shu Zhang, Feng Ji and Xuanjing Huang
15:00-15:30	*Wiki-ly Supervised Part-of-Speech Tagging* Shen Li, João Graça and Ben Taskar

Saturday, July 14, 2012 (continued)

Session 3-PM-1D: Word Sense Disambiguation
Session Chair: Marc Dymetman

14:00-14:30 *Joining Forces Pays Off: Multilingual Joint Word Sense Disambiguation*
Roberto Navigli and Simone Paolo Ponzetto

14:30-15:00 *A New Minimally-Supervised Framework for Domain Word Sense Disambiguation*
Stefano Faralli and Roberto Navigli

15:00-15:30 *Grounded Models of Semantic Representation*
Carina Silberer and Mirella Lapata

15:30-16:00 Coffee Break

Session 3-PM-2A: Syntax and Parsing: Joint Parsing Models
Session Chair: Jason Eisner

16:00-16:30 *Improved Parsing and POS Tagging Using Inter-Sentence Consistency Constraints*
Alexander Rush, Roi Reichart, Michael Collins and Amir Globerson

16:30-17:00 *Unified Dependency Parsing of Chinese Morphological and Syntactic Structures*
Zhongguo Li and Guodong Zhou

17:00-17:30 *A Transition-Based System for Joint Part-of-Speech Tagging and Labeled Non-Projective Dependency Parsing*
Bernd Bohnet and Joakim Nivre

Session 3-PM-2B: Social Media
Session Chair: Alan Ritter

16:00-16:30 *Identifying Event-related Bursts via Social Media Activities*
Xin Zhao, Baihan Shu, Jing Jiang, Yang Song, Hongfei Yan and Xiaoming Li

16:30-17:00 *User Demographics and Language in an Implicit Social Network*
Katja Filippova

17:00-17:30 *Revisiting the Predictability of Language: Response Completion in Social Media*
Bo Pang and Sujith Ravi

Saturday, July 14, 2012 (continued)

Session 3-PM-2C: NLP Applications
Session Chair: Chikara Hashimoto

16:00-16:30 *Supervised Text-based Geolocation Using Language Models on an Adaptive Grid*
Stephen Roller, Michael Speriosu, Sarat Rallapalli, Benjamin Wing and Jason Baldridge

16:30-17:00 *A Discriminative Model for Query Spelling Correction with Latent Structural SVM*
Huizhong Duan, Yanen Li, ChengXiang Zhai and Dan Roth

17:00-17:30 *Characterizing Stylistic Elements in Syntactic Structure*
Song Feng, Ritwik Banerjee and Yejin Choi

Session 3-PM-3P: Closing

17:30-17:45 Closing: Closing Remarks

Syntactic Transfer Using a Bilingual Lexicon

Greg Durrett, Adam Pauls, and **Dan Klein**
Computer Science Division
University of California, Berkeley
{gdurrett,adpauls,klein}@cs.berkeley.edu

Abstract

We consider the problem of using a bilingual dictionary to transfer lexico-syntactic information from a resource-rich source language to a resource-poor target language. In contrast to past work that used bitexts to transfer analyses of specific sentences at the token level, we instead use features to transfer the behavior of words at a type level. In a discriminative dependency parsing framework, our approach produces gains across a range of target languages, using two different low-resource training methodologies (one weakly supervised and one indirectly supervised) and two different dictionary sources (one manually constructed and one automatically constructed).

1 Introduction

Building a high-performing parser for a language with no existing treebank is still an open problem. Methods that use no supervision at all (Klein and Manning, 2004) or small amounts of manual supervision (Haghighi and Klein, 2006; Cohen and Smith, 2009; Naseem et al., 2010; Berg-Kirkpatrick and Klein, 2010) have been extensively studied, but still do not perform well enough to be deployed in practice. Projection of dependency links across aligned bitexts (Hwa et al., 2005; Ganchev et al., 2009; Smith and Eisner, 2009) gives better performance, but crucially depends on the existence of large, in-domain bitexts. A more generally applicable class of methods exploits the notion of universal part of speech tags (Petrov et al., 2011; Das and Petrov, 2011) to train parsers that can run on any language with no adaptation (McDonald et al., 2011) or unsupervised adaptation (Cohen et al., 2011). While these universal parsers currently constitute the highest-performing methods for languages without treebanks, they are inherently limited by operating at the coarse POS level, as lexical features are vital to supervised parsing models.

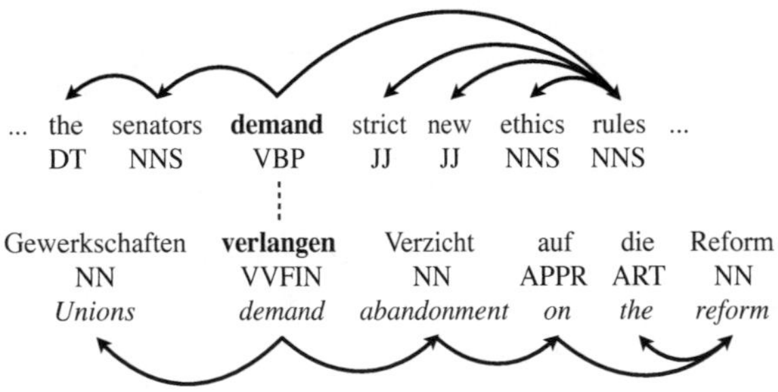

Figure 1: Sentences in English and German both containing words that mean "demand." The fact that the English *demand* takes nouns on its left and right indicates that the German *verlangen* should do the same, correctly suggesting attachments to *Verzicht* and *Gewerkschaften*.

In this work, we consider augmenting delexicalized parsers by transferring syntactic information through a bilingual lexicon at the word type level. These parsers are delexicalized in the sense that, although they receive target language words as input, their feature sets do not include indicators on those words. This setting is appropriate when there is too little target language data to learn lexical features directly. Our main approach is to add features which are lexical in the sense that they compute a function of specific target language words, but are still un-lexical in the sense that all lexical knowledge comes from the bilingual lexicon and training data in the source language.

Consider the example English and German sentences shown in Figure 1, and suppose that we wish to parse the German side without access to a German treebank. A delexicalized parser operating at the part of speech level does not have sufficient information to make the correct decision about, for example, the choice of subcategorization frame for the verb *verlangen*. However, *demand*, a possible English translation of *verlangen*, takes a noun on its left and a noun on its right, an observation that in this case gives us the information we need. We can fire features in our German parser on the attachments of *Gewerkschaften* and *Verzicht* to *verlangen* indicating that similar-looking attachments are attested in English for an English translation of *verlangen*. This allows us to exploit fine-grained lexical cues to make German parsing decisions even when we have little or no supervised German data; moreover, this syntactic transfer is possible even in spite of the fact that *demand* and *verlangen* are not observed in parallel context.

Using type-level transfer through a dictionary in this way allows us to decouple the lexico-syntactic projection from the data conditions under which we are learning the parser. After computing feature values using source language resources and a bilingual lexicon, our model can be trained very simply using any appropriate training method for a supervised parser. Furthermore, because the transfer mechanism is just a set of features over word types, we are free to derive our bilingual lexicon either from bitext or from a manually-constructed dictionary, making our method strictly more general than those of McDonald et al. (2011) or Täckström et al. (2012), who rely centrally on bitext. This flexibility is potentially useful for resource-poor languages, where a human-curated bilingual lexicon may be broader in coverage or more robust to noise than a small, domain-limited bitext. Of course, it is an empirical question whether transferring type level information about word behavior is effective; we show that, indeed, this method compares favorably with other transfer mechanisms used in past work.

The actual syntactic information that we transfer consists of purely monolingual lexical attachment statistics computed on an annotated source language resource.[1] While the idea of using large-scale summary statistics as parser features has been considered previously (Koo et al., 2008; Bansal and Klein, 2011; Zhou et al., 2011), doing so in a projection setting is novel and forces us to design features suitable for projection through a bilingual lexicon. Our features must also be flexible enough to provide benefit even in the presence of cross-lingual syntactic differences and noise introduced by the bilingual dictionary.

Under two different training conditions and with two different varieties of bilingual lexicons, we show that our method of lexico-syntactic projection does indeed improve the performance of parsers that would otherwise be agnostic to lexical information. In all settings, we see statistically significant gains for a range of languages, with our method providing up to 3% absolute improvement in unlabeled attachment score (UAS) and 11% relative error reduction.

2 Model

The projected lexical features that we propose in this work are based on lexicalized versions of features found in MSTParser (McDonald et al., 2005), an edge-factored discriminative parser. We take MSTParser to be our underlying parsing model and use it as a testbed on which to evaluate the effectiveness of our method for various data conditions.[2] By instantiating the basic MSTParser features over coarse parts of speech, we construct a state-of-the-art delexicalized parser in the style of McDonald et al. (2011), where feature weights can be directly transferred from a source language or languages to a desired target language. When we add projected lexical features on top of this baseline parser, we do so in a way that does not sacrifice this generality: while our new features take on values that are language-specific, they interact with the model at a language-independent level. We therefore have the best of

[1] Throughout this work, we will use English as the source language, but it is possible to use any language for which the appropriate bilingual lexicons and treebanks exist. One might expect to find the best performance from using a source language closely related to the target.

[2] We train MSTParser using the included implementation of MIRA (Crammer and Singer, 2001) and use projective decoding for all experiments described in this paper.

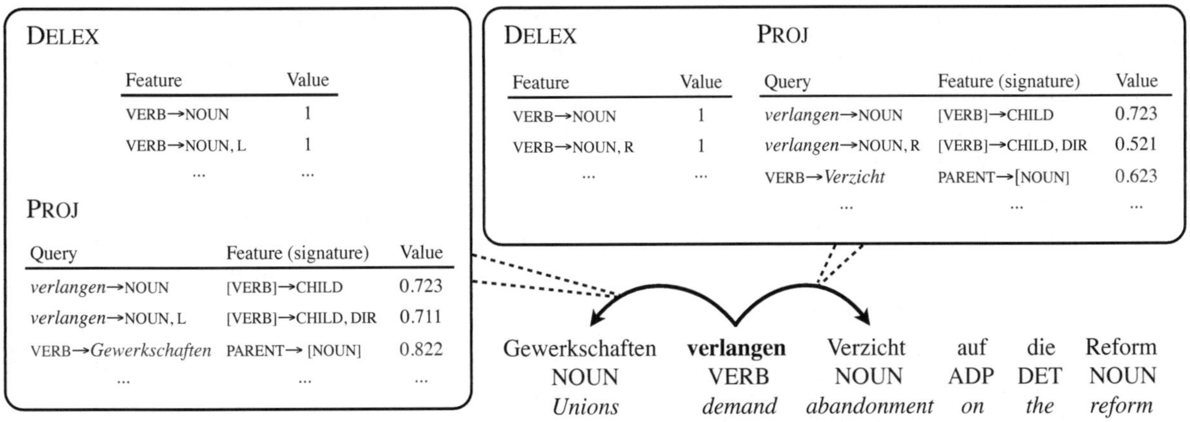

Figure 2: Computation of features on a dependency arc. DELEX features are indicators over characteristics of dependency links that do not involve the words in the sentence. PROJ features are real-valued analogues of DELEX features that do contain words. We form a query from each stipulated set of characteristics, compute the values of these queries heuristically, and then fire a feature based on each query's signature. Signatures indicate which attachment properties were considered, which part of the query was lexicalized (shown by brackets here), and the POS of the query word. This procedure yields a small number of real-valued features that still capture rich lexico-syntactic information.

two worlds in that our features can be learned on any treebank or treebanks that are available to us, but still exploit highly specific lexical information to achieve performance gains over using coarse POS features alone.

2.1 DELEX Features

Our DELEX feature set consists of all of the unlexicalized features in MSTParser, only lightly modified to improve performance for our setting. McDonald et al. (2005) present three basic types of such features, ATTACH, INBETWEEN, and SURROUNDING, which we apply at the coarse POS level. The ATTACH features for a given dependency link consist of indicators of the tags of the head and modifier, separately as well as together. The INBETWEEN and SURROUNDING features are indicators on the tags of the head and modifier in addition to each intervening tag in turn (INBETWEEN) or various combinations of tags adjacent to the head or modifier (SURROUNDING).[3]

MSTParser by default also includes a copy of each of these indicator features conjoined with the direction and distance of the attachment it denotes. These extra features are important to getting good performance out of the baseline model. We slightly modify the conjunction scheme and expand it with additional backed-off conjunctions, since these changes lead to features that empirically transfer better than the MSTParser defaults. Specifically, we use conjunctions with attachment direction (left or right), coarsened distance,[4] and attachment direction and coarsened distance combined.

We emphasize again that these baseline features are entirely standard, and all the DELEX feature set does is recreate an MSTParser-based analogue of the direct transfer parser described by McDonald et al. (2011).

2.2 PROJ Features

We will now describe how to compute our projected lexical features, the PROJ feature set, which constitutes the main contribution of this work. Recall that we wish our method to be as general as possible and work under many different training conditions; in particular, we wish to be able to train our model on only existing treebanks in other languages when no target language trees are available (discussed in Section 3.3), or on only a very small target language treebank (Section 3.4). It would greatly increase the power of our model if we were able to include target-language-lexicalized versions of the ATTACH

[3]As in Koo et al. (2008), our feature set contains more backed-off versions of the SURROUNDING features than are described in McDonald et al. (2005).

[4]Our five distance buckets are $\{1, 2, 3–5, 6–10, 11+\}$.

features, but these are not learnable without a large target language treebank. We instead must augment our baseline model with a relatively small number of features that are nonetheless rich enough to transfer the necessary lexical information.

Our overall approach is sketched in Figure 2, where we show the features that fire on two proposed edges in a German dependency parse. Features on an edge in MSTParser incorporate a subset of observable properties about that edge's head, modifier, and context in the sentence. For sets of properties that do not include a lexical item, such as VERB→NOUN, we fire an indicator feature from the DELEX feature set. For those that do include a lexical item, such as *verlangen*→NOUN, we form a *query*, which resembles a lexicalized indicator feature. Rather than firing the query as an indicator feature directly, which would result in a model parameter for each target word, we fire a broad feature called an *signature* whose value reflects the specifics of the query (computation of these values is discussed in Section 2.2.2). For example, we abstract *verlangen*→NOUN to [VERB]→CHILD, with square brackets indicating the element that was lexicalized. Section 2.2.1 discusses this coarsening in more detail. The signatures are agnostic to individual words and even the language being parsed, so they can be learned on small amounts of data or data from other languages.

Our signatures allow us to instantiate features at different levels of granularity corresponding to the levels of granularity in the DELEX feature set. When a small amount of target language data is present, the variety of signatures available to us means that we can learn language-specific transfer characteristics: for example, nouns tend to follow prepositions in both French and English, but the ordering of adjectives with respect to nouns is different. We also have the capability to train on languages other than our target language, and while this is expected to be less effective, it can still teach us to exploit some syntactic properties, such as similar verb attachment configurations if we train on a group of SVO languages distinct from a target SVO language. Therefore, our feature set manages to provide the training procedure with choices about how much syntactic information to transfer at the same time as it prevents overfitting and provides language independence.

2.2.1 Query and Signature Types

A query is a subset of the following pieces of information about an edge: parent word, parent POS, child word, child POS, attachment direction, and binned attachment distance. It must contain exactly one word.[5] We experimented with properties from INBETWEEN and SURROUNDING features as well, but found that these only helped under some circumstances and could lead to overfitting.[6]

A signature contains the following three pieces of information:

1. The non-empty subset of attachment properties included in the query
2. Whether we have lexicalized on the parent or child of the attachment, indicated by brackets
3. The part of speech of the included word

Because either the parent or child POS is included in the signature, there are three meaningful properties to potentially condition on, of which we must select a nonempty subset. Some multiplication shows that we have $7 \times 2 \times 13 = 182$ total PROJ features.

As an example, the queries

verlangen → NOUN
verlangen → ADP
sprechen → NOUN

all share the signature [VERB]→CHILD, but

verlangen → NOUN,RIGHT
Verzicht → ADP
VERB → *Verzicht*

have [VERB]→CHILD,DIR, [ADP]→CHILD, and PARENT→[NOUN] as their signatures, respectively.

The level of granularity for signatures is a parameter that simply must be engineered. We found some benefit in actually instantiating two signatures for every query, one as described above and one that

[5] Bilexical features are possible in our framework, but we do not use them here, so for clarity we assume that each query has one associated word.

[6] One hypothesis is that features looking at the sentence context are more highly specialized to a given language, since they examine the parent, the child, *and* one or more other parts of speech or words.

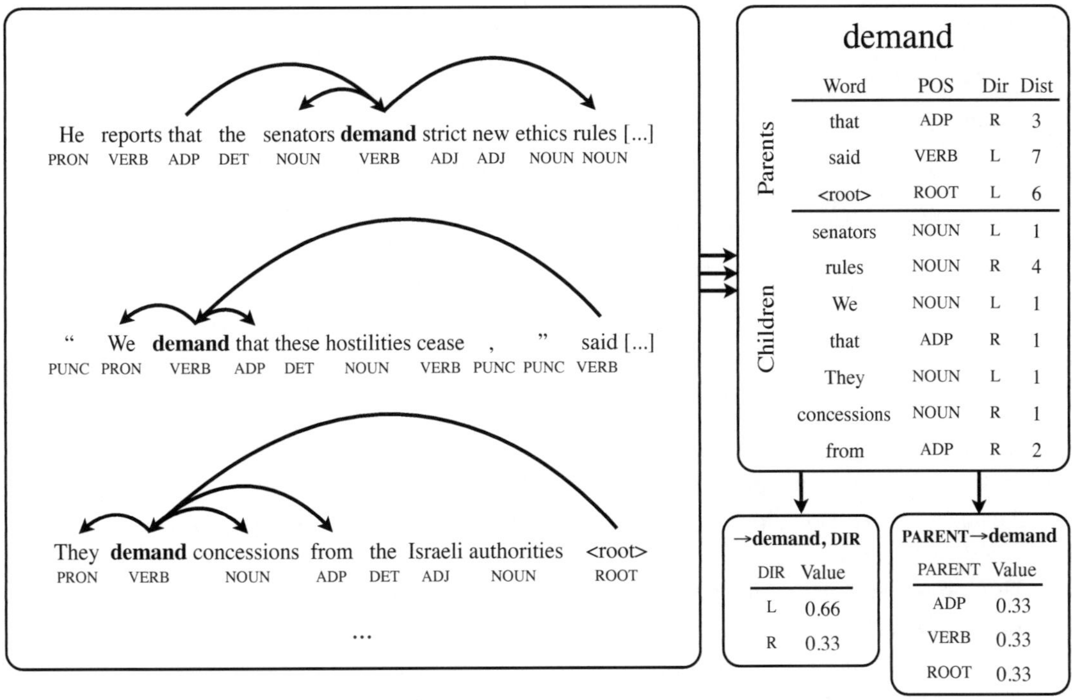

Figure 3: Computation of query values. For each occurrence of a given source word, we tabulate the attachments it takes part in (parents and children) and record their properties. We then compute relative frequency counts for each possible query type to get source language scores, which will later be projected through the dictionary to obtain target language feature values. Only two query types are shown here, but values are computed for many others as well.

does not condition on the part of speech of the word in the signature. One can also imagine using more refined signatures, but we found that this led to overfitting in the small training scenarios under consideration.

2.2.2 Query Value Estimation

Each query is given a value according to a generative heuristic that involves the source training data and the probabilistic bilingual lexicon.[7] For a particular signature, a query can be written as a tuple $(x_1, x_2, \dots, w_t)$ where w_t is the target language query word and the x_i are the values of the included language-independent attachment properties. The value this feature takes is given by a simple generative model: we imagine generating the attachment properties x_i given w_t by first generating a source word w_s from w_t based on the bilingual lexicon, then jointly generating the x_i conditioned on w_s. Treating the choice of source translation as a latent variable to be marginalized out, we have

$$\begin{aligned} \text{value} &= p(x_1, x_2, \dots | w_t) \\ &= \sum_{w_s} p(w_s | w_t) p(x_1, x_2, \dots | w_s) \end{aligned}$$

The first term of the sum comes directly from our probabilistic lexicon, and the second we can estimate using the maximum likelihood estimator over our source language training data:

$$p(x_1, x_2, \dots | w_s) = \frac{c(x_1, x_2, \dots, w_s)}{c(w_s)} \quad (1)$$

where $c(\cdot)$ denotes the count of an event in the source language data.

The final feature value is actually the logarithm of this computed value, with a small constant added before the logarithm is taken to avoid zeroes.

[7] Lexicons such as those produced by automatic aligners include probabilities natively, but obviously human-created lexicons do not. For these dictionaries, we simply assume that each word translates with uniform probability into each of its possible translations. Tweaking this method did not substantially change performance.

3 Experiments

3.1 Data Conditions

Before we describe the details of our experiments, we sketch the data conditions under which we evaluate our method. As described in Section 1, there is a continuum of lightly supervised parsing methods from those that make no assumptions (beyond what is directly encoded in the model), to those that use a small set of syntactic universals, to those that use treebanks from resource-rich languages, and finally to those that use both existing treebanks and bitexts.

Our focus is on parsing when one does not have access to a full-scale target language treebank, but one does have access to realistic auxiliary resources. The first variable we consider is whether we have access to a small number of target language trees or only pre-existing treebanks in a number of other languages; while not our actual target language, these other treebanks can still serve as a kind of proxy for learning which features generally transfer useful information (McDonald et al., 2011). We notate these conditions with the following shorthand:

BANKS: Large treebanks in other target languages

SEED: Small treebank in the right target language

Previous work on essentially unsupervised methods has investigated using a small number of target language trees (Smith and Eisner, 2009), but the behavior of supervised models under these conditions has not been extensively studied. We will see in Section 3.4 that with only 100 labeled trees, even our baseline model can achieve performance equal to or better than that of the model of McDonald et al. (2011). A single linguist could plausibly annotate such a number of trees in a short amount of time for a language of interest, so we believe that this is an important setting in which to show improvement, even for a method primarily intended to augment unsupervised parsing.

In addition, we consider two different sources for our bilingual lexicon:

AUTOMATIC: Extracted from bitext

MANUAL: Constructed from human annotations

Both bitexts and human-curated bilingual dictionaries are more widely available than complete treebanks. Bitexts can provide rich information about lexical correspondences in terms of how words are used in practice, but for resource-poor languages, parallel text may only be available in small quantities, or be domain-limited. We show results of our method on bilingual dictionaries derived from both sources, in order to show that it is applicable under a variety of data conditions and can successfully take advantage of such resources as are available.

3.2 Datasets

We evaluate our method on a range of languages taken from the CoNLL shared tasks on multilingual dependency parsing (Buchholz and Marsi, 2006; Nivre et al., 2007). We make use of dependency treebanks for Danish, German, Greek, Spanish, Italian, Dutch, Portuguese, and Swedish, all from the 2006 shared task.

For our English resource, we use 500,000 English newswire sentences from English Gigaword version 3 (Graff et al., 2007), parsed with the Berkeley Parser (Petrov et al., 2006) and converted to a dependency treebank using the head rules of Collins (1999).[8] Our English test set (used in Section 3.4) consists of the first 300 sentences of section 23 of the Penn treebank (Marcus et al., 1993), preprocessed in the same way. Our model does not use gold fine-grained POS tags, but we do use coarse POS tags deterministically generated from the provided gold fine-grained tags in the style of Berg-Kirkpatrick and Klein (2010) using the mappings of Petrov et al. (2011).[9] Following McDonald et al. (2011), we strip punctuation from all treebanks for the results of Section 3.3. All results are given in terms of unlabeled attachment score (UAS), ignoring punctuation even when it is present.

We use the Europarl parallel corpus (Koehn, 2005) as the bitext from which to extract the AUTOMATIC bilingual lexicons. For each target language, we produce one-to-one alignments on the English-target bitext by running the Berkeley Aligner (Liang et al., 2006) with five iterations of IBM Model 1 and

[8] Results do not degrade much if one simply uses Sections 2-21 of the Penn treebank instead. Coverage of rare words in the treebank is less important when a given word must also appear in the bilingual lexicon as the translation of an observed German word in order to be useful.

[9] Note that even in the absence of gold annotation, such tags could be produced from bitext using the method of (Das and Petrov, 2011) or could be read off from a bilingual lexicon.

	This work					Past work			
		MANUAL		AUTOMATIC		MPH11*		TMU12**	
	DELEX	DELEX+PROJ	Δ	DELEX+PROJ	Δ	Multi-dir	Multi-proj Δ	No clusters	X-lingual Δ
DA	41.3	43.0	1.67 ‡	43.6	2.30 ‡	48.9*	0.6*	36.7**	2.0**
DE	58.5	58.7	0.20	59.5	0.94 †	56.7*	-0.1*	48.9**	1.8**
EL	57.9	59.9	1.99 ‡	60.5	2.55 ‡	60.1*	5.0*	59.5**	3.5**
ES	64.2	65.4	1.20 ‡	65.7	1.52 ‡	64.2*	0.3*	60.2**	2.7**
IT	65.9	66.5	0.58	67.4	1.54 ‡	64.1*	0.9*	64.6**	4.2**
NL	57.0	57.5	0.52	58.8	1.88 ‡	55.8*	9.9*	52.8**	1.5**
PT	75.4	77.2	1.83 ‡	78.7	3.29 ‡	74.0*	1.6*	66.8**	4.2**
SV	64.5	66.1	1.61 ‡	66.9	2.34 ‡	65.3*	2.7*	55.4**	1.5**
AVG	60.6	61.8	1.20	62.6	2.05	61.1*	2.7*	55.6**	2.7**

Table 1: Evaluation of features derived from AUTOMATIC and MANUAL bilingual lexicons when trained on a concatenation of non-target-language treebanks (the BANKS setting). Values reported are UAS for sentences of all lengths in the standard CoNLL test sets, with punctuation removed from training and test sets. Daggers indicate statistical significance computed using bootstrap resampling; a single dagger indicates $p < 0.1$ and a double dagger indicates $p < 0.05$. We also include the baseline results of McDonald et al. (2011) and Täckström et al. (2012) and improvements from their best methods of using bitext and lexical information. These results are not directly comparable to ours, as indicated by * and **. However, we still see that the performance of our type-level transfer method approaches that of bitext-based methods, which require complex bilingual training for each new language.

five iterations of the HMM aligner with agreement training. Our lexicon is then read off based on relative frequency counts of aligned instances of each word in the bitext.

We also use our method on bilingual dictionaries constructed in a more conventional way. For this purpose, we scrape our MANUAL bilingual lexicons from English Wiktionary (Wikimedia Foundation, 2012). We mine entries for English words that explicitly have foreign translations listed as well as words in each target language that have English definitions. We discard all translation entries where the English side is longer than one word, except for constructions of the form "to VERB", where we manually remove the "to" and allow the word to be defined as the English infinitive. Finally, because our method requires a dictionary with probability weights, we assume that each target language word translates with uniform probability into any of the candidates that we scrape.

3.3 BANKS

We first evaluate our model under the BANKS data condition. Following the procedure from McDonald et al. (2011), for each language, we train both our DELEX and DELEX+PROJ features on a concatenation of 2000 sentences from each other CoNLL training set, plus 2000 sentences from the Penn Treebank. Again, despite the values of our PROJ queries being sensitive to which language we are currently parsing, the signatures are language independent, so discriminative training still makes sense over such a combined treebank. Training our PROJ features on the non-English treebanks in this concatenation can be understood as trying to learn which lexico-syntactic properties transfer "universally," or at least transfer broadly within the families of languages we are considering.

Table 1 shows the performance of the DELEX feature set and the DELEX+PROJ feature set using both AUTOMATIC and MANUAL bilingual lexicons. Both methods provide positive gains across the board that are statistically significant in the vast majority of cases, though MANUAL is slightly less effective; we postpone until Section 4.1 the discussion of the shortcomings of the MANUAL lexicon.

We include for reference the baseline results of McDonald et al. (2011) and Täckström et al. (2012) (multi-direct transfer and no clusters) and the improvements from their best methods using lexical information (multi-projected transfer and crosslingual clusters). We emphasize that these results are *not* directly comparable to our own, as we have different training data (and even different training languages) and use a different underlying parsing model (MSTParser instead of a transition-based

AUTOMATIC									
	100 train trees			200 train trees			400 train trees		
	DELEX	DELEX+PROJ	Δ	DELEX	DELEX+PROJ	Δ	DELEX	DELEX+PROJ	Δ
DA	67.2	69.5	2.32 ‡	69.5	72.3	2.77 ‡	71.4	74.6	3.16 ‡
DE	72.9	73.9	0.97	75.4	76.5	1.09 †	77.3	78.5	1.25 ‡
EL	70.8	72.9	2.07 ‡	72.6	74.9	2.30 ‡	74.3	76.7	2.41 ‡
ES	72.5	73.0	0.46	74.1	75.4	1.29 ‡	75.3	77.2	1.81 ‡
IT	73.3	75.4	2.13 ‡	74.7	77.3	2.54 ‡	76.0	78.7	2.74 ‡
NL	63.0	65.8	2.82 ‡	64.7	67.6	2.86 ‡	66.1	69.2	3.06 ‡
PT	78.1	79.5	1.45 ‡	79.5	81.1	1.66 ‡	80.7	82.4	1.63 ‡
SV	76.4	78.1	1.69 ‡	78.1	80.2	2.02 ‡	79.6	81.7	2.07 ‡
AVG	71.8	73.5	1.74	73.6	75.7	2.07	75.1	77.4	2.27
EN	74.4	81.5	7.06 ‡	76.6	83.0	6.35 ‡	78.3	84.1	5.80 ‡
MANUAL									
DA	67.2	68.1	0.88	69.5	70.9	1.44 ‡	71.4	73.3	1.92 ‡
DE	72.9	73.4	0.44	75.4	76.2	0.77	77.3	78.4	1.12 ‡
EL	70.8	71.9	1.06 †	72.6	74.1	1.48 ‡	74.3	75.8	1.56 ‡
ES	72.5	71.9	-0.64	74.1	74.3	0.23	75.3	76.4	1.04 ‡
IT	73.3	74.3	1.01 †	74.7	76.4	1.66 ‡	76.0	78.0	2.01 ‡
NL	63.0	65.4	2.43 ‡	64.7	67.5	2.76 ‡	66.1	69.0	2.91 ‡
PT	78.1	78.2	0.13	79.5	80.1	0.62	80.7	81.5	0.82 ‡
SV	76.4	76.6	0.25	78.1	79.1	1.01 †	79.6	81.0	1.40 ‡
AVG	71.8	72.5	0.70	73.6	74.8	1.25	75.1	76.7	1.60
EN	74.4	81.5	7.06 ‡	76.6	83.0	6.35 ‡	78.3	84.1	5.80 ‡

Table 2: Evaluation of features derived from AUTOMATIC and MANUAL bilingual lexicons when trained on various small numbers of target language trees (the SEED setting). Values reported are UAS for sentences of all lengths on our enlarged CoNLL test sets (see text); each value is based on 50 sampled training sets of the given size. Daggers indicate statistical significance as described in the text. Statistical significance is not reported for averages.

parser (Nivre, 2008)). However, our baseline is competitive with theirs,[10] demonstrating that we have constructed a state-of-the-art delexicalized parser. Furthermore, our method appears to approach the performance of previous bitext-based methods, and because of its flexibility and the freedom from complex cross-lingual training for each new language, it can be applied in the MANUAL case as well, a capability which neither of the other methods has.

3.4 SEED

We now turn our attention to the SEED scenario, where a small number of target language trees are available for each language we consider. While it is imaginable to continue to exploit the other treebanks in the presence of target language trees, we found that training our DELEX features on the seed treebank alone gave higher performance than any attempt to also use the concatenation of treebanks from the previous section. This is not too surprising because, with this number of sentences, there is already good monolingual coverage of coarse POS features, and attempting to train features on other languages can be expected to introduce noise into otherwise accurate monolingual feature weights.

We train our DELEX+PROJ model with both AUTOMATIC and MANUAL lexicons on target language training sets of size 100, 200, and 400, and give results for each language in Table 2. The performance of parsers trained on small numbers of trees can be highly variable, so we create multiple treebanks of each size by repeatedly sampling from each language's train treebank, and report averaged results. Furthermore, this evaluation is not on the standard CoNLL test sets, but is instead on those test sets with a few hundred unused training sentences added, the reason being that some of the CoNLL test sets are very small (fewer than 200 sentences) and appeared

[10]The baseline of Täckström et al. (2012) is lower because it is trained only on English rather than on many languages.

to give highly variable results. To compute statistical significance, we draw a large number of bootstrap samples for each training set used, then aggregate all of their sufficient statistics in order to compute the final p-value. We see that our DELEX+PROJ method gives statistically significant gains at the 95% level over DELEX for nearly all language and training set size pairs, giving on average a 9% relative error reduction in the 400-tree case.

Because our features are relatively few in number and capture heuristic information, one question we might ask is how well they can perform in a non-projection context. In the last line of the table, we report gains that are achieved when PROJ features computed from parsed Gigaword are used directly on English, with no intermediate dictionary. These are not comparable to the other values in the table because we are using our projection strategy monolingually, which removes the barriers of imperfect lexical correspondence (from using the lexicon) and imperfect syntactic correspondence (from projecting). As one might expect, the gains on English are far higher than the gains on other languages. This indicates that performance is chiefly limited by the need to do cross-lingual feature adaptation, not inherently low feature capacity. We delay further discussion to Section 4.2.

One surprising thing to note is that the gains given by our PROJ features are in some cases larger here than in the BANKS setting. This result is slightly counterintuitive, as our baseline parsers are much better in this case and so we would expect diminished returns from our method. We conclude that accurately learning which signatures transfer between languages is important, and it is easier to learn good feature weights when some target language data is available. Further evidence supporting this hypothesis is the fact that the gains are larger and more significant on larger training set sizes.

	AUTOMATIC		MANUAL	
	Voc	OCC	Voc	OCC
DA	324K	0.91	22K	0.64
DE	320K	0.89	58K	0.55
EL	196K	0.94	23K	0.43
ES	165K	0.89	206K	0.74
IT	158K	0.91	78K	0.65
NL	251K	0.87	50K	0.72
PT	165K	0.85	46K	0.53
SV	307K	0.93	28K	0.60

Table 3: Lexicon statistics for all languages for both sources of bilingual lexicons. "Voc" indicates vocabulary size and "OCC" indicates open-class coverage, the fraction of open-class tokens in the test treebanks with entries in our bilingual lexicon.

4 Discussion

4.1 AUTOMATIC versus MANUAL

Overall, we see that gains from using our MANUAL lexicons are slightly lower than those from our AUTOMATIC lexicons. One might expect higher performance because scraped bilingual lexicons are not prone to some of the same noise that exists in automatic aligners, but this is empirically not the case. Rather, as we see in Table 3, the low recall of our MANUAL lexicons on open-class words appears to be a possible culprit. The coverage gap between these and the AUTOMATIC lexicons is partially due to the inconsistent structure of Wiktionary: inflected German and Greek words often do not have their own pages, so we miss even common morphological variants of verb forms in those languages. The inflected forms that we do scrape are also mapped to the English base form rather than the corresponding inflected form in English, which introduces further noise. Coverage is substantially higher if we translate using stems only, but this did not empirically lead to performance improvements, possibly due to conflating different parts of speech with the same base form.

One might hypothesize that our uniform weighting scheme in the MANUAL lexicon is another source of problems, and that bitext-derived weights are necessary to get high performance. This is not the case here. Truncating the AUTOMATIC dictionary to at most 20 translations per word and setting the weights uniformly causes a slight performance drop, but is still better than our MANUAL lexicon. This further demonstrates that these problems are more a limitation of our dictionary than our method. English Wiktionary is not designed to be a bilingual dictionary, and while it conveniently provided an easy way for us to produce lexicons for a wide array

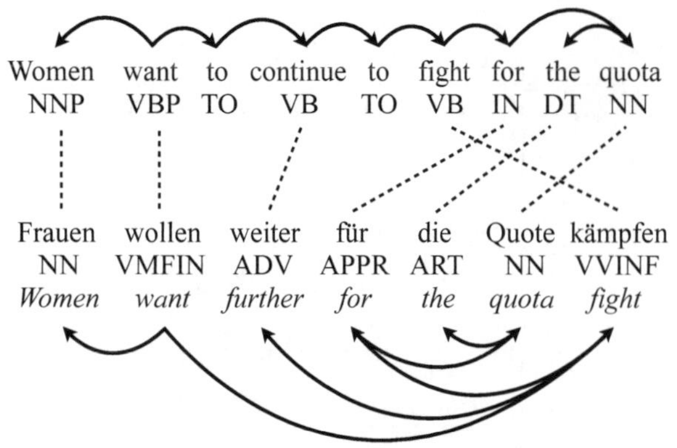

Figure 4: Example of a German tree and a parallel English sentence with high levels of syntactic divergence. The English verb *want* takes fundamentally different children than *wollen* does, so properties of the sort we present in Section 2.2 will not transfer effectively.

of languages, it is not the resource that one would choose if designing a parser for a specific target language. Bitext is not necessary for our approach to work, and results on the AUTOMATIC lexicon suggest that our type-level transfer method can in fact do much better given a higher quality resource.

4.2 Limitations

While our method does provide consistent gains across a range of languages, the injection of lexical information is clearly not sufficient to bridge the gap between unsupervised and supervised parsers. We argued in Section 3.4 that the cross-lingual transfer step of our method imposes a fundamental limitation on how useful any such approach can be, which we now investigate further.

In particular, any syntactic divergence, especially inconsistent divergences like head switching, will limit the utility of transferred structure. Consider the German example in Figure 4, with a parallel English sentence provided. The English tree suggests that *want* should attach to an infinitival *to*, which has no correlate in German. Even disregarding this, its grandchild is the verb *continue*, which is realized in the German sentence as the adverb *weiter*. While it is still broadly true that *want* and *wollen* both have verbal elements located to their right, it is less clear how to design features that can still take advantage of this while working around the differences we have described. Therefore, a gap between the performance of our features on English and the performance of our projected features, as is observed in Table 2, is to be expected in the absence of a more complete model of syntactic divergence.

5 Conclusion

In this work, we showed that lexical attachment preferences can be projected to a target language at the type level using only a bilingual lexicon, improving over a delexicalized baseline parser. This method is broadly applicable in the presence or absence of target language training trees and with bilingual lexicons derived from either manually-annotated resources or bitexts. The greatest improvements arise when the bilingual lexicon has high coverage and a number of target language trees are available in order to learn exactly what lexico-syntactic properties transfer from the source language.

In addition, we showed that a well-tuned discriminative model with the correct features can achieve good performance even on very small training sets. While unsupervised and existing projection methods do feature great versatility and may yet produce state-of-the-art parsers on resource-poor languages, spending time constructing small supervised resources appears to be the fastest method to achieve high performance in these settings.

Acknowledgments

This work was partially supported by an NSF Graduate Research Fellowship to the first author, by a Google Fellowship to the second author, and by the NSF under grant 0643742. Thanks to the anonymous reviewers for their insightful comments.

References

Mohit Bansal and Dan Klein. 2011. Web-scale Features for Full-scale Parsing. In *Proceedings of ACL*, pages 693–702, Portland, Oregon, USA.

Taylor Berg-Kirkpatrick and Dan Klein. 2010. Phylogenetic Grammar Induction. In *Proceedings of ACL*, pages 1288–1297, Uppsala, Sweden.

Sabine Buchholz and Erwin Marsi. 2006. CoNLL-X Shared Task on Multilingual Dependency Parsing. In *Proceedings of CoNLL*, pages 149–164.

Shay B. Cohen and Noah A. Smith. 2009. Shared Logistic Normal Distributions for Soft Parameter Tying in

Unsupervised Grammar Induction. In *Proceedings of NAACL*, pages 74–82, Boulder, Colorado.

Shay B. Cohen, Dipanjan Das, and Noah A. Smith. 2011. Unsupervised Structure Prediction with Non-Parallel Multilingual Guidance. In *Proceedings of EMNLP*, pages 50–61, Edinburgh, UK.

Michael Collins. 1999. Head-Driven Statistical Models for Natural Language Parsing. *Ph.D. thesis, University of Pennsylvania.*

Koby Crammer and Yoram Singer. 2001. Ultraconservative Online Algorithms for Multiclass Problems. *Journal of Machine Learning Research*, 3:2003.

Dipanjan Das and Slav Petrov. 2011. Unsupervised Part-of-Speech Tagging with Bilingual Graph-Based Projections. In *Proceedings of ACL*, pages 600–609, Portland, Oregon, USA.

Kuzman Ganchev, Jennifer Gillenwater, and Ben Taskar. 2009. Dependency Grammar Induction via Bitext Projection Constraints. In *Proceedings of ACL*, pages 369–377, Suntec, Singapore.

David Graff, Junbo Kong, Ke Chen, and Kazuaki Maeda. 2007. English Gigaword Third Edition. Linguistic Data Consortium, Catalog Number LDC2007T07.

Aria Haghighi and Dan Klein. 2006. Prototype-driven Grammar Induction. In *Proceedings of CoLING-ACL*, pages 881–888, Sydney, Australia.

Rebecca Hwa, Philip Resnik, Amy Weinberg, Clara Cabezas, and Okan Kolak. 2005. Bootstrapping Parsers via Syntactic Projection Across Parallel Texts. *Natural Language Engineering*, 11:311–325, September.

Dan Klein and Christopher D. Manning. 2004. Corpus-Based Induction of Syntactic Structure: Models of Dependency and Constituency. In *Proceedings of ACL*, pages 479–486.

Philipp Koehn. 2005. Europarl: A Parallel Corpus for Statistical Machine Translation. In *MT Summit X*, pages 79–86, Phuket, Thailand. AAMT.

Terry Koo, Xavier Carreras, and Michael Collins. 2008. Simple Semi-Supervised Dependency Parsing. In *Proceedings of ACL.*

Percy Liang, Ben Taskar, and Dan Klein. 2006. Alignment by Agreement. In *Proceedings of NAACL*, New York, New York.

Mitchell P. Marcus, Mary Ann Marcinkiewicz, and Beatrice Santorini. 1993. Building a Large Annotated Corpus of English: the Penn Treebank. *Computational Linguistics*, 19:313–330, June.

Ryan McDonald, Koby Crammer, and Fernando Pereira. 2005. Online Large-Margin Training of Dependency Parsers. In *Proceedings of ACL*, pages 91–98, Ann Arbor, Michigan.

Ryan McDonald, Slav Petrov, and Keith Hall. 2011. Multi-Source Transfer of Delexicalized Dependency Parsers. In *Proceedings of EMNLP*, pages 62–72, Edinburgh, Scotland, UK.

Tahira Naseem, Harr Chen, Regina Barzilay, and Mark Johnson. 2010. Using Universal Linguistic Knowledge to Guide Grammar Induction. In *Proceedings of EMNLP*, pages 1234–1244, Cambridge, Massachusetts.

Joakim Nivre, Johan Hall, Sandra Kübler, Ryan Mcdonald, Jens Nilsson, Sebastian Riedel, and Deniz Yuret. 2007. The CoNLL 2007 Shared Task on Dependency Parsing. In *Proceedings of EMNLP-CoNLL*, pages 915–932, Prague, Czech Republic.

Joakim Nivre. 2008. Algorithms for Deterministic Incremental Dependency Parsing. *Computational Linguistics*, 34:513–553, December.

Slav Petrov, Leon Barrett, Romain Thibaux, and Dan Klein. 2006. Learning Accurate, Compact, and Interpretable Tree Annotation. In *Proceedings of ACL*, pages 433–440, Sydney, Australia.

Slav Petrov, Dipanjan Das, and Ryan McDonald. 2011. A Universal Part-of-Speech Tagset. In *ArXiv*, April.

David A. Smith and Jason Eisner. 2009. Parser Adaptation and Projection with Quasi-Synchronous Grammar Features. In *Proceedings of EMNLP*, pages 822–831, Suntec, Singapore.

Oscar Täckström, Ryan McDonald, and Jakob Uszkoreit. 2012. Cross-lingual Word Clusters for Direct Transfer of Linguistic Structure. In *Proceedings of NAACL*, Montreal, Canada.

Wikimedia Foundation. 2012. Wiktionary. Online at http://www.wiktionary.org/.

Guangyou Zhou, Jun Zhao, Kang Liu, and Li Cai. 2011. Exploiting Web-Derived Selectional Preference to Improve Statistical Dependency Parsing. In *Proceedings of ACL*, pages 1556–1565, Portland, Oregon, USA.

Regularized Interlingual Projections: Evaluation on Multilingual Transliteration

Jagadeesh Jagarlamudi
University of Maryland
College Park, USA, 20742
jags@umiacs.umd.edu

Hal Daumé III
University of Maryland
College Park, USA, 20742
hal@umiacs.umd.edu

Abstract

In this paper, we address the problem of building a multilingual transliteration system using an interlingual representation. Our approach uses international phonetic alphabet (IPA) to learn the interlingual representation and thus allows us to use any word and its IPA representation as a training example. Thus, our approach requires only monolingual resources: a *phoneme dictionary* that lists words and their IPA representations.[1] By adding a phoneme dictionary of a new language, we can readily build a transliteration system into any of the existing previous languages, without the expense of all-pairs data or computation. We also propose a regularization framework for learning the interlingual representation, which accounts for language specific phonemic variability, and thus it can find better mappings between languages. Experimental results on the name transliteration task in five diverse languages show a maximum improvement of 29% accuracy and an average improvement of 17% accuracy compared to a state-of-the-art baseline system.

1 Introduction

Because of the wide usage of English, many natural language processing (NLP) tasks have bilingual resources from English into other languages. For example, significantly larger parallel texts are available between English and other languages. Similarly, bilingual dictionaries and transliteration data sets are more accessible from a language into English than into a different language. This situation has caused the NLP community to develop approaches which use a resource rich language (Q say English) as pivot to build resources/applications between a new language pair P and R. Previous studies in machine translation (Utiyama and Isahara, 2007; Paul and Sumita, 2011), transliteration (Khapra et al., 2010), and dictionary mining (Saralegi et al., 2011) show that these bridge language approaches perform competitively with approaches that use resources between P and R. In this paper, we propose a regularization framework for bridge language approaches and show its effectiveness for name transliteration task. The key idea of our approach is that it accounts for language specific variation in the bridge language resources (i.e. between $P \leftrightarrow Q$ and $Q \leftrightarrow R$) and aims to minimize this variation as much as possible. Though our technique is general, for clarity we describe it in the context of named entity (NE) transliteration.

Named entity (NE) transliteration involves transliterating a name in one language into another language and is shown to be crucial for machine translation (MT) (Knight and Graehl, 1998; Al-Onaizan and Knight, 2002; Hermjakob et al., 2008; Li et al., 2009) and cross-lingual information retrieval (CLIR) (AbdulJaleel and Larkey, 2003; Mandl and Womser-Hacker, 2005; Udupa et al., 2009). There exists a large body of literature in transliteration, especially in the bilingual setting, well summarized by Ravi and Knight (2009). We

[1] It is arguable that getting words and their IPA representation require knowledge about both words and IPA symbols, but it still is specific to one language and, in this sense, we refer to it as a monolingual resource.

English		Bulgarian	
Word	IPA	Word	IPA
bashful	/ˈbæʃfəl/	шибам	/ˈʃibəm/
tuesday	/ˈtu:zdeɪ/	лук	/luk/
craft	/kɹæft/	как	/kak/
book	/bʊk/	музей	/mʊˈzej/
head	/hɛd/	спека	/spɛˈkɤ/

Table 1: Example phoneme dictionaries in English and Bulgarian. The English translations for the Bulgarian words are switch, onion, how, museum, and spekle.

summarize the approaches that are most relevant to us in Sec. 5. In this paper, we operate in the context of transliteration mining (Klementiev and Roth, 2006; Sproat et al., 2006) where we assume that we are given a source language name and a list of target language candidate transliterations and the task is to identify the correct transliteration.

Given a set of l languages, we address the problem of building a transliteration system between every pair of languages. A straight forward supervised learning approach would require training data of name pairs between every pair of languages (Knight and Graehl, 1998) or a set of common names transliterated from every language into a pivot language. Though it is relatively easy to obtain names transliterated into a pivot language (such as English), it is unlikely that such data sets contain the same names. Bridge language approaches overcome the need for common names and build transliteration systems for resource poor languages (Khapra et al., 2010). However, such approaches still require training data consisting of bilingual name transliterations (orthographic name-to-name mappings). In this paper, we relax the need for name transliterations by using international phonetic alphabet (IPA) in a manner akin to a "bridge language."

2 IPA for Transliteration

We assume that we have a list of words and their IPA representations in each of the l languages. The words in different languages need not have any relationship to each other. Table 1 shows few words and their IPA representations in English and Bulgarian languages. We refer to the set of (word, IPA) pairs as *phoneme dictionary* in this paper. Notice that the common symbols in the IPA sequences indicate a vague phonetic correspondence between the character sequences of English and Bulgarian. For example, both the words 'bashful' and 'шибам' have the symbol 'ʃ' in their IPA sequences which indicate a possible mapping between the character sequences 'sh' and 'ш'.

The use of IPA as the bridge language offers multiple advantages. As shown in Table 1, it allows us to include any (word, IPA) pair in the training data and thus it relaxes the need for name pairs as the training data. Since we only need a phoneme dictionary in each language, our approach does not require any bilingual resources to build the transliteration system. Moreover, since our training data can contain any word (not only the NEs), it is easier to obtain such a resource, for e.g. the phoneme dictionaries obtained from Wiktionary contain at least 2000 words in 21 languages and we will see in Sec. 6 that we can build a decent transliteration system with 2000 words.[2] Finally, unlike other transliteration approaches, by simply adding a phoneme dictionary of $(l+1)^{st}$ language we can readily get a transliteration system into any of the existing l languages and thus avoid the need for all-pairs data or computation.

Using IPA as the bridge language poses some new challenges such as the language specific phonemic inventory. For example, Mandarin doesn't have /v/, so it is frequently substituted with /w/ or /f/. Similarly, !Xóõ (Southern Khoisan, spoken in Botswana) has 122 consonants, mostly consisting of a large inventory of different word-initial click sounds (Haspelmath et al., 2005), many of which do not exist in any other documented languages. Besides this language specific phonemic inventory, names have different IPA representations in different languages. For example, as shown in Table 2, the IPA sequences for 'China' in English and Dutch have common IPA symbols but the English IPA sequence has additional symbols. Moreover, a name can have multiple pronunciations with in a language, e.g. 'France' has two different IPA sequences in English (Table 2).

In order to handle this phonemic diversity, our method explicitly models language-specific variability and attempts to minimize this phonemic variabil-

[2] In our experiments, we consider languages with small (2000) and big (>30K) phoneme dictionaries.

Word	IPA sequence
China	/ˈtʃaɪ.nə/ (En), /ˈʃina/ (Du), /ˈçi:na:/ (De)
America	/əˈmɛrɪkə/ (En), /aˈme.ri.ka/ (Ro)
France	/ˈfɹɑ:ns/ (En), /ˈfɹænts/ (En), /fʁɑ̃s/ (Fr)

Table 2: IPA sequences of few words in different languages indicated using language codes in the parenthesis ('En' for English, 'Du' for Dutch, 'De' for German, 'Ro' for Romanian, and 'Fr' for French).

ity as much as possible. At a high level, our approach uses the phoneme dictionaries of each language to learn mapping functions into an interlingual representation (also referred as common subspace). Subsequently, given a pair of languages, a query name in one of the languages and a list of candidate transliterations in the other language, we use the mapping functions of those two language to identify the correct name transliteration. The mapping functions explicitly model the language specific variability and thus account for fine grained differences. Our experimental results on four language pairs from two different language families show a maximum improvement of 29% accuracy and an average improvement of 17% accuracy compared to a state-of-the-art baseline approach. An important advantage of our approach is that, it extends easily to more than two languages and in fact adding phoneme dictionary from a different, but related, language improves the accuracies of a given language pair. Our main contributions are: 1) building a transliteration system using (word, IPA) pairs and hence using only monolingual resources and 2) proposing a regularization framework which is more general and applies to other bridge language applications such as lexicon mining (Mann and Yarowsky, 2001).

3 Low Dimensional Projections

Our approach is inspired by the Canonical Correlation Analysis (CCA) (Hotelling, 1936) and its application to transliteration mining (Udupa and Khapra, 2010).

First, we convert the phoneme dictionary of each language into feature vectors, i.e. we convert each word into a feature vector of n-gram character sequences and similarly, we also, convert the IPA representations into feature vectors of n-gram IPA symbol sequences. For example, if we use unigram and bigram sequences as features, then the feature vectors of 'head' and its IPA sequence ˋhɛd' are given by $\{h, e, a, d, \#h, he, ea, ad, d\$\}$ and $\{h,\varepsilon, d, \#h, h\varepsilon, \varepsilon d, d\$\}$. For brevity, we refer to the spaces of n-gram character and IPA symbol sequences as character and phonemic spaces respectively. The character space is specific to each language while the phonemic space is shared across all the languages. Since we use IPA as bridge, even though two languages share orthography (e.g. English and French) it is irrelevant for our approach.

Then, for each language, we find mappings (A_i and U_i) from the character and phonemic spaces into a common k-dimensional subspace such that the correct transliterations lie closer to each other in this subspace. Before moving into the details of our approach, we will describe the notation and then give an overview of the process by which our approach finds the transliteration.

3.1 Notation

Let $\mathbf{x}_i^{(m)} \in \mathbb{R}^{d_i}$ and $\mathbf{p}_i^{(m)} \in \mathbb{R}^c$ be the feature vectors of the mth word and its IPA sequence in the $i^{th}(1 \cdots l)$ language, where d_i is the size (i.e. no. of features) of the character space of the language and c is the size of the common phonemic space. Let X_i $(d_i \times n_i)$ and P_i $(c \times n_i)$ denote the ith language data matrices with $\mathbf{x}_i^{(m)}$ and $\mathbf{p}_i^{(m)}$ $m = 1 \cdots n_i$ as the columns respectively. We consistently use subscript to indicate the language and superscript to indicate the index of an example point.

3.2 Method Overview

During the training stage, for each language, we find mappings (or projection directions) $A_i \in \mathbb{R}^{(d_i \times k)}$ and $U_i \in \mathbb{R}^{(c \times k)}$ from the character and phonemic spaces into a k-dimensional subspace (or an interlingual representation) such that a name gets mapped to the *same* k-dimensional vector irrespective of the language. That is, given a name $\mathbf{x}_i$ it gets mapped to the vector $A_i^T \mathbf{x}_i$ and similarly its IPA sequence $\mathbf{p}_i$ gets mapped to $U_i^T \mathbf{p}_i$. During the testing stage, given a name $\mathbf{x}_i$ in the source (i^{th}) language, we find its transliteration in the target (j^{th}) language $\mathbf{x}_j$ by solving the following decoding problem:

$$\arg\min_{\mathbf{x}_j} L(\mathbf{x}_i, \mathbf{x}_j) \tag{1}$$

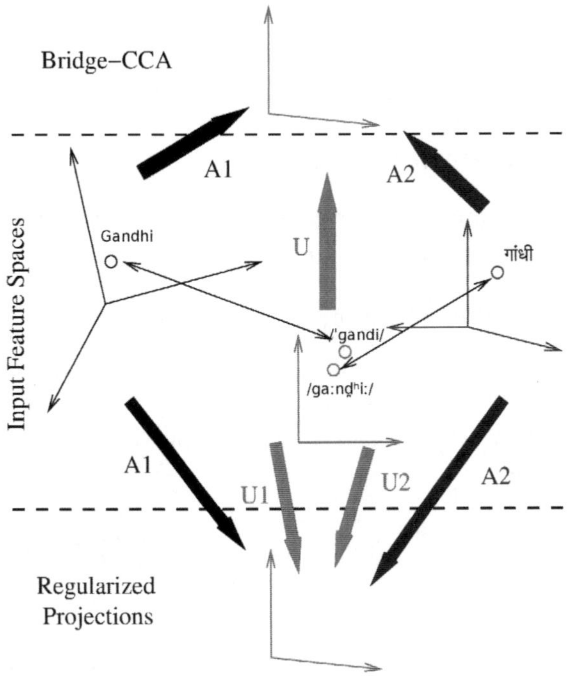

Figure 1: A single name (Gandhi) is shown in all the input feature spaces. The alignment between the character and phonemic space is indicated with double dimensional arrows. Bridge-CCA uses a single mapping function U from the phonemic space into the common subspace (the 2-dimensional green space at the top), where as our approach uses two mapping functions U_1 and U_2, one for each language, to map the IPA sequences into the common subspace.

where $L(\mathbf{x}_i, \mathbf{x}_j)$ is given by

$$\min_{\mathbf{p} \in \mathbb{R}^c} \|A_i^T \mathbf{x}_i - U_i^T \mathbf{p}\|^2 + \|A_j^T \mathbf{x}_j - U_j^T \mathbf{p}\|^2 \quad (2)$$

This formulation uses the source language mappings (A_i and U_i) to find the IPA sequence $\mathbf{p}$ that is closest to the source name and then uses it, along with the target language mappings (A_j and U_j), to identify the correct transliteration from a list of candidate transliterations.

At a high level, existing bridge language approaches such as Bridge-CCA (Khapra et al., 2010) assume that $U_i \equiv U_j$ thus ignoring the language specific variation. To understand its implication consider the example shown in Fig. 1. The middle portion of the Fig. shows the name Gandhi (represented as point) in the character spaces of English and Hindi, three-dimensional spaces, and its IPA sequences in the phonemic space (the two-dimensional space in the middle). Notice that, because of the phonemic variation, the same name is represented by two distinct points in the common phonemic space.[3] Now, since Bridge-CCA uses a single mapping function for both the IPA sequences, it fails to map these two distinct points into a common point in the interlingual subspace.

Our new formulation, as explained above, relaxes this hard constraint and learns different mapping functions (U_i and U_j) and hence our approach can potentially map both the distinct IPA sequences into a single point. As a result our approach successfully handles the language specific phonemic variation. At the same time we constrain the projection directions such that they behave similarly for the phonemic sounds that are observed in majority of the languages. In the example shown in Fig. 1, our model (called Regularized Projections) finds two different mapping functions U_1 and U_2, one for each language, from the phonemic space into the common two-dimensional space at the bottom.

3.3 Regularized Projections

In this section we first formulate the problem of finding the mapping functions (A_i and U_i) of each language as an optimization problem. In the following section (Sec. 4), we develop a method for solving the optimization problem and also derive closed form solution for the prediction problem given in Eq. 1. For simplicity, we describe our approach in terms of single projection vectors, $\mathbf{a}_i \in \mathbb{R}^{d_i}$ and $\mathbf{u}_i \in \mathbb{R}^c$, rather than full matrices, but the generalization is trivial.

Inspired by the Canonical Correlation Analysis (CCA) (Hotelling, 1936), we find projection directions in the character and phonemic spaces of each language such that, after projection, a word is closer to its aligned IPA sequence. To understand this, assume that we have a name (say "Barack Obama") in all the languages[4] and its feature vectors are given by $\mathbf{x}_i$ and $\mathbf{p}_i$ $i = 1 \cdots l$ in the character and phone-

[3] In reality, as explained in the previous section, the phonemic variation that is commonly observed is that different features are triggered for different languages. But for visualization purpose, we showed the IPA sequences as if they differ in the feature values.

[4] Our model does not require same names in different languages; this is used only for easier understanding.

mic spaces respectively. Then, we might try to find projection directions $\mathbf{a}_i$ in each language and $\mathbf{u}$ in the common phonemic space such that:

$$\arg\min_{\mathbf{a}_i,\mathbf{u}} \sum_{i=1}^{l} \Big(\langle \mathbf{x}_i, \mathbf{a}_i \rangle - \langle \mathbf{p}_i, \mathbf{u} \rangle \Big)^2 \quad (3)$$

where $\langle \cdot, \cdot \rangle$ denotes the dot product between two vectors. This model assumes that the projection direction $\mathbf{u}$ is same for the phonemic space of all the languages. This is a hard constraint and does not handle the language specific variability as discussed in the previous section. We model the language specificity by relaxing this hard constraint.

In our model, intuitively, the parameters corresponding to the phonemic sounds that occur in majority of the languages are shared across the languages while the parameters of the language specific sounds are modeled per each language. This is achieved by modeling the projection directions of the ith language phonemic space $\mathbf{u}_i \leftarrow \mathbf{u} + \mathbf{r}_i$. The vector $\mathbf{u} \in \mathbb{R}^c$ is common to the phonemic spaces of all the languages and thus handles sounds that are observed in multiple languages while $\mathbf{r}_i \in \mathbb{R}^c$, the residual vector, is specific to each language and accounts for the language specific phonemic variations. Then the new formulation is given by:

$$\arg\min_{\mathbf{a}_i,\mathbf{u},\mathbf{r}_i} \sum_{i=1}^{l} \|\langle \mathbf{x}_i, \mathbf{a}_i \rangle - \langle \mathbf{p}_i, \mathbf{u} + \mathbf{r}_i \rangle\|^2 + \lambda \langle \mathbf{p}_i, \mathbf{r}_i \rangle^2$$

where λ is the residual parameter. The first term of this summation ensures that a word and its IPA sequence gets mapped to closer points in the subspace while the second term forces the residual vectors to be as small as possible. By enforcing the residual vectors to be small, this formulation encourages the sounds that occur in majority of the languages to be accounted by $\mathbf{u}$ and the sounds that are specific to the given language by $\mathbf{r}_i$. The final optimization problem is obtained by summing these terms over all the examples and all the languages and is given by:

$$\min_{\mathbf{a}_i,\mathbf{u},\mathbf{r}_i} \sum_{i=1}^{l} \Big(\frac{\|X_i^T \mathbf{a}_i - P_i^T(\mathbf{u} + \mathbf{r}_i)\|^2}{n_i} + \lambda \, \|P_i^T \mathbf{r}_i\|^2 \Big) \quad (4)$$

$$\text{s.t.} \sum_{i=1}^{l} \frac{1}{n_i} \|X_i^T \mathbf{a}_i\|^2 = 1 \text{ and } \sum_{i=1}^{l} \frac{1}{n_i} \|P_i^T \mathbf{u}\|^2 = 1$$

The constraints of the above optimization problem avoid the trivial solution of setting all the vectors to zero and are referred to as length constraints.

4 Model Optimization

In this section, we derive the solutions for the optimization problems presented in the previous section.

4.1 Training the Model

We follow the standard procedure of forming the Lagrangian and setting its derivative to zero. The Lagrangian $\mathcal{L}$ of the optimization problem in Eq. 4 is given by:

$$\mathcal{L} = \sum_i \frac{1}{n_i} ||X_i^T \mathbf{a}_i - P_i^T(\mathbf{u}+\mathbf{r}_i)||^2 + \lambda \sum_i \|P_i^T \mathbf{r}_i\|^2$$

$$+\alpha \Big(\sum_i \frac{1}{n_i} \|X_i^T \mathbf{a}_i\|^2 - 1 \Big) + \beta \Big(\sum_i \frac{1}{n_i} \|P_i^T \mathbf{u}\|^2 - 1 \Big)$$

where α and β are Lagrangian multipliers corresponding to the length constraints. Differentiating $\mathcal{L}$ with respect to $\mathbf{a}_i$, $\mathbf{r}_i$ and $\mathbf{u}$ and setting the derivatives to zero yields the following equations, respectively:

$$\begin{aligned} (1+\alpha) X_i X_i^T \mathbf{a}_i - X_i P_i^T \mathbf{r}_i &= X_i P_i^T \mathbf{u} \\ -P_i X_i^T \mathbf{a}_i + (1 + \lambda n_i) P_i P_i^T \mathbf{r}_i &= -P_i P_i^T \mathbf{u} \end{aligned}$$

$$\sum_i \frac{1}{n_i} \Big(P_i X_i^T \mathbf{a}_i - P_i P_i^T \mathbf{r}_i \Big) = (1+\beta) \sum_i \frac{1}{n_i} P_i P_i^T \mathbf{u}$$

We can rewrite these equations in matrix form, as shown in Eqs. 5 and 6, since the solution becomes clear in this form. For brevity, let $E_i = (1 + \alpha) X_i X_i^T$, $F_i = -X_i P_i^T$ and $G_i = (1 + \lambda n_i) P_i P_i^T$. Then, $\mathbf{u}$ can be solved for using the generalized eigenvalue problem shown in Eq. 7. This step involves computing an inverse of a $(d_i + c)$ matrix and an eigenvalue problem of size c which can be expensive since solving each of these problems involve cubic time. This can be reduced further into a problem of smaller size by using inverse of a partitioned matrix as shown in Eq. 8. This identity reduces the matrix inverse computation from a problem of size $d_i + c$ into two smaller problems of size d_i and c each. This reduces the time complexity considerably since the inverse computation is cubic in the size of the matrix.

$$\begin{bmatrix}(1+\alpha)X_iX_i^T & -X_iP_i^T\\ -P_iX_i^T & (1+\lambda n_i)P_iP_i^T\end{bmatrix}\begin{bmatrix}\mathbf{a}_i\\ \mathbf{r}_i\end{bmatrix} = \begin{bmatrix}X_iP_i^T\\ -P_iP_i^T\end{bmatrix}\mathbf{u} \tag{5}$$

$$\sum_i \frac{1}{n_i}\begin{bmatrix}P_iX_i^T & -P_iP_i^T\end{bmatrix}\begin{bmatrix}\mathbf{a}_i\\ \mathbf{r}_i\end{bmatrix} = (1+\beta)\sum_i \frac{1}{n_i}P_iP_i^T\mathbf{u} \tag{6}$$

$$\sum_i \frac{1}{n_i}\begin{bmatrix}-F_i^T & \frac{-G_i}{1+\lambda n_i}\end{bmatrix}\begin{bmatrix}E_i & F_i\\ F_i^T & G_i\end{bmatrix}^{-1}\begin{bmatrix}-F_i\\ \frac{-G_i}{1+\lambda n_i}\end{bmatrix}\mathbf{u} = (1+\beta)\sum_i \frac{1}{n_i}P_iP_i^T\mathbf{u} \tag{7}$$

$$\text{If } M_i = \left(E_i - F_iG_i^{-1}F_i^T\right)^{-1}, \text{ then } \begin{bmatrix}E_i & F_i\\ F_i^T & G_i\end{bmatrix}^{-1} = \begin{bmatrix}M_i & -M_iF_iG_i^{-1}\\ -G_i^{-1}F_i^TM_i & G_i^{-1}+G_i^{-1}F_i^TM_iF_iG_i^{-1}\end{bmatrix} \tag{8}$$

Substituting Eq. 8 into Eq. 7 and further simplifying results in the following eigenvalue problem for solving $\mathbf{u}$:

$$\sum_i \frac{G_i + (\lambda n_i)^2 F_i^T M_i F_i}{n_i(1+\lambda n_i)^2}\mathbf{u} = (1+\beta)\sum_i \frac{P_iP_i^T}{n_i}\mathbf{u}$$

where $M_i = \left(E_i - F_iG_i^{-1}F_i^T\right)^{-1}$. Notice that the term $E_i = (1+\alpha)X_iX_i^T$ depends on the Lagrangian multiplier α. Because of this, we cannot solve for both the parameters and the Lagrangian multipliers at the same time. One possible approach is to do an alternate optimization over the parameters and Lagrangian multipliers, but in this paper we fix α and solve for $\mathbf{u}$. The value of α denotes the correlation and its maximum value is 1. In practice, we often observe that the top few correlations take the value of 1. Based on this observation we fix the value of α to 1 (Sec. 6).

Subsequently, we use $\mathbf{u}$ to solve for $\mathbf{a}_i$ and $\mathbf{r}_i$ as follows:

$$\mathbf{a}_i = -\frac{\lambda n_i M_i F_i}{1+\lambda n_i}\mathbf{u} \tag{9}$$

$$\mathbf{r}_i = \frac{\lambda n_i G_i^{-1} F_i^T M_i F_i - I}{1+\lambda n_i}\mathbf{u} \tag{10}$$

In order to increase the stability of the system we regularize G_i and E_i by adding τI. We use the top k eigenvectors $\mathbf{u}$ and their corresponding $\mathbf{a}_i$ and $\mathbf{r}_i$ vectors as columns and form the mappings U, A_i and R_i respectively. These mappings are used in predicting the transliteration of a name in one language into any other language, which will be described in the following section.

4.2 Transliteration Mining (Prediction)

During the testing phase, given a source name and a list of candidate transliterations, we solve the decoding problem shown in Eq. 1 to find the appropriate target language transliteration. Formally, given a word $\mathbf{x}_i$ in i^{th} language we find its transliteration into j^{th} language $\mathbf{x}_j$, by solving the optimization problem shown in Eq. 1, where $U_i = U + R_i$ and $U_j = U + R_j$. Similar to the previous case, the closed form solution can be found by computing the first derivative with respect to the unknown phoneme sequence and the target language transliteration and setting it to zero. First, the IPA sequence $\mathbf{p}^*$ that minimizes $L(\mathbf{x}_i, \mathbf{x}_j)$ is given by:

$$\mathbf{p}^* = C_{ij}^{-1}\left(U_iA_i^T\mathbf{x}_i + U_jA_j^T\mathbf{x}_j\right) \tag{11}$$

where $C_{ij} = U_iU_i^T + U_jU_j^T$. We substitute this back in Eq. 2 and then solve for $\mathbf{x}_j$, the best transliteration in the jth language, as:

$$A_j\left(I - U_j^TC_{ij}^{-1}U_j\right)A_j^T\mathbf{x}_j = A_jU_j^TC_{ij}^{-1}U_iA_i^T\mathbf{x}_i \tag{12}$$

Since U_i and U_j are not full rank matrices, to increase the numerical stability of the prediction step, we use $C_{ij} = U_iU_i^T + U_jU_j^T + 0.001\, I$ where I is an identity matrix. Notice that this solution doesn't depend on the $\mathbf{p}^*$ and hence we don't need to compute it explicitly.

5 Related Work

There is a large body of the literature in named entity transliteration, so we will describe only the most relevant ones to our approach. In transliteration, generative approaches aim to generate the target language transliteration of a given source name (Knight and Graehl, 1998; Jung et al., 2000; Haizhou et al., 2004; Al-Onaizan and Knight, 2002) while discriminative approaches assume a list of target language names, obtained from other sources, and try to identify the correct transliteration (Klementiev and Roth, 2006; Sproat et al., 2006). The effectiveness of the discriminative approaches depend on the list of target language candidates. Sproat et al. (2006) report an oracle accuracy of 85%, but it depends on the source of the candidate transliterations. Nevertheless, all these approaches require either bilingual name pairs or phoneme sequences to learn to transliterate between two languages. Thus, if we want to build a transliteration system between every pair of languages in a given set of languages then these approaches need resources between every pair of languages which can be prohibitive.

Bridge language approaches propose an alternative and use a resource rich language such as English as common language (Khapra et al., 2010) but they still need bilingual resources. Moreover Bridge-CCA (Khapra et al., 2010) uses a single mapping function for the phonemic space of all the languages and thus it can not handle language specific variability. In the original setting, authors use English as the pivot and since the feature space of English is fixed, irrespective of the target language, this may not be a serious concern but it becomes crucial when we use IPA as the bridge language.

Approaches that map words in different languages into the common phonemic space have also been well studied. But most of these approaches use language specific resources such as CMU pronunciation dictionary (Gao et al., 2004) or a carefully constructed cost matrices for addition, substitution, and deletion of phonemes between a pair of languages (Tao et al., 2006; Yoon et al., 2007). Variants of soundex algorithm (Odel and Russel, 1918) such as Kodex (Kang and Choi, 2000) use hand constructed consonant to soundex code tables for name transliteration. Similar to our approach these variants only require soundex mappings of a new language to build transliteration system, but our model does not require explicit mapping between n-gram characters and the IPA symbols instead it learns them automatically using phoneme dictionaries. Alternatively unsupervised approaches have also been explored (Ravi and Knight, 2009), but their accuracies are fairly low compared to the supervised and weekly supervised approaches.

6 Experiments

Our experiments are designed to evaluate the following three aspects of our model, and of our approach to transliteration in general:

IPA as bridge: Unlike other phonemic based approaches (Sec. 5), we do not *explicitly* model the phoneme modifications between pairs of languages. Moreover, the phoneme dictionary in each language is crawled from Wiktionary (Sec. 6.1), which is likely to be noisy. So, the first aspect we want to evaluate is the effectiveness of using IPA as the bridge language. Here, we also compare our method with other bridge language approaches and establish the importance of modeling language specific variance.

Multilinguality: In our method, simply adding a phoneme dictionary of a new language allows us to extend our transliteration system into any of the existing languages. We evaluate the effect of data from a different, but related, languages on a transliteration system between a given pair.

Complementarity: Using IPA as bridge language allows us to build transliteration system into resource poor languages. But we also want to evaluate whether such an approach can help improving a transliteration system trained directly on bilingual name-pairs.

6.1 Data Sets

We use data sets from five languages in order to evaluate the effectiveness of our approach. The phoneme dictionaries (list of words and their IPA representations as shown in Table 1) are obtained from Wiktionary. The Wiktionary dump downloaded in October 2011 has at least 2000 (word, IPA) pairs in 21 languages which also includes some resource poor languages (e.g. Armenian, Taiwanese, Turkish, etc.).

In principle, our method allows us to build transliteration system into any of these language pairs without any additional information. But, in this paper, we use English (En), Bulgarian (Bg), Russian (Ru), French (Fr), and Romanian (Ro) for eval-

	En.	Bg.	Ru.	Fr.	Ro.
Train	31K	36K	1141	36K	5211
Dev.	–	1264	2000	2717	430
Test	–	1264	2000	2717	431
# Features	5000	3998	2900	5000	3465

Table 3: Statistics of different data sets. Training data is monolingual phoneme dictionaries while development/test sets are bilingual name pairs between English and the respective language.

uation purposes, as they suffice to showcase all the three aspects mentioned in the previous section. Table 3 shows the sizes of phoneme dictionaries used for training the models. The phoneme dictionaries of English, Bulgarian, and Russian contain more than 30K (word,IPA) pairs while the remaining two languages have smaller phoneme dictionaries. The development and test sets between English and the remaining language pairs are obtained from geonames data base.[5] These are geographic location names from different countries written in multiple languages.

6.2 Experimental Setup

We convert the phoneme dictionaries of each language into feature vectors. We use unigram and bigram features in the phonemic space and unigram, bigram and trigram features in the character space. An example for feature generation is shown in Sec. 3. After converting the data into feature vectors, we retain the most frequent 5000 features. We only keep the frequent 5000 features since we observed, elsewhere, that including infrequent features leads CCA based methods to learn projection directions with perfect correlations which are not effective for downstream applications. The last row of Table 3 shows the number of features in the character space of each of the languages. The phonemic space is common to all the languages and has 3777 features. Though the phonemic features are common to all the languages, as discussed in Sec. 2, only a subset of features will be observed in a given language. For example, in our data sets, of the total 3777 common phonetic features only 3312, 882, and 1009 features are observed in English, Bulgarian, and Russian languages respectively. This indicates the diversity in the phonemic inventory of different languages.

[5]http://www.geonames.org/

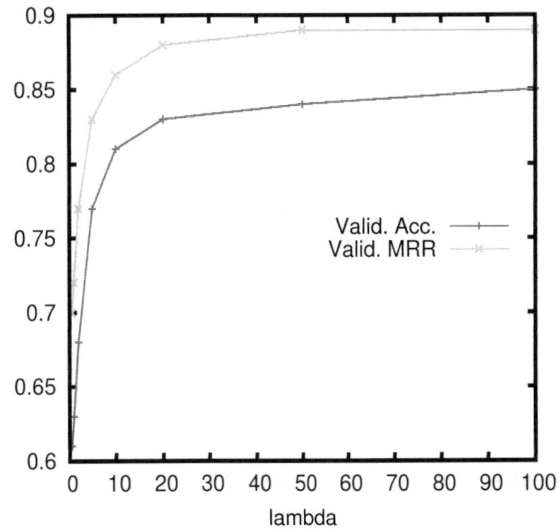

Figure 2: Performance of transliteration system with residual parameter λ on English-Bulgarian development data set.

We compare our approach against Bridge-CCA, a state-of-the-art bridge language transliteration system which is known to perform competitively with other discriminative approaches (Khapra et al., 2010). We use the phoneme dictionaries in each language to train our approach, as well as the baseline system. The projection directions learnt during the training are used to find the transliteration for a test name as described in Sec. 4.2. We report the performance in terms of the accuracy (exact match) of the top ranked transliteration and the mean reciprocal rank (MRR) of the correct transliteration. We find transliterations in both the directions (i.e. target language transliterations given a source name and vice versa) and report average accuracies. The regularization parameter (τ) and the size of the interlingual representation (k) in both our approach and Bridge-CCA are tuned on the development set.

6.3 Description of Results

In this section we report experimental results on the three aspects mentioned above.

6.3.1 IPA as Bridge

Fig. 2 shows the performance of our system with the residual parameter λ (in Eq. 4) on the develop-

		En-Bg		En-Ru		En-Fr		En-Ro	
		Acc.	MRR	Acc.	MRR	Acc.	MRR	Acc.	MRR
1	Bridge-CCA	68.83	77.22	44.50	53.22	41.55	52.89	71.69	79.59
2	Ours (cosine)	67.68	76.52	45.07	53.63	42.45	53.06	74.13	81.28
3	Ours (Eq. 12)	83.70	88.32	63.47	73.01	70.68	78.13	77.38	**84.22**
4	Ours (cosine + Multi.)	68.91	77.44	49.15	57.20	42.55	53.02	77.49	84.04
5	Ours (Eq. 12 + Multi.)	**84.45**	**88.43**	**66.70**	**75.85**	**71.09**	**78.43**	**77.49**	84.04

Table 4: Results of our approach and the baseline system on the test set. The second block shows the results when our approach is trained only on phoneme dictionaries of the language pair, the third block shows results when we include other language data as well.

ment data set. When λ is small, the model does not attempt to constrain the projection directions U_i's and hence they tend to map names to completely unrelated vectors. As we increase the residual parameter, it forces the residual vectors (R_i) to be smaller and thus the subspaces identified for each language are closely tied together. Thus, it models the commonalities across languages and also the language specific variability. Based on the performance curves on the development data, we fix $\lambda = 50$ in the rest of the experiments.

Table 4 shows the results of Bridge-CCA and our approach on the four language pairs. We report the results of our approach with the decoding proposed in Sec. 4.2 and a simple cosine similarity measure in the common-subspace, i.e. $\cos\left(A_i^T \mathbf{x}_i, A_j^T \mathbf{x}_j\right)$. Comparison of the accuracies in rows 1, 2 and 3, shows that simply using cosine similarity performs almost same as the Bridge-CCA approach. However, using the decoding suggested in Eq. 12 gives significant improvements. To understand why the cosine angle between $A_i^T \mathbf{x}_i$ and $A_j^T \mathbf{x}_j$ is not the appropriate measure, assume that the vectors $\mathbf{x}_i$ and $\mathbf{x}_j$ are feature vectors of same name in two languages and let $\mathbf{p}$ be its true IPA representation. Then, since our model learns projection directions such that $A_i^T \mathbf{x}_i \approx U_i^T \mathbf{p}$,

$$\cos(A_i^T \mathbf{x}_i, A_j^T \mathbf{x}_j) = \cos\left((U+R_i)^T \mathbf{p}, (U+R_j)^T \mathbf{p}\right)$$

The additional residual matrices R_i and R_j make the cosine measure inappropriate. At the same time, our model forces the residual matrices to be small and this is probably the reason why it performs competitively with the Bridge-CCA. On the other hand, our decoding method, as shown in Eq. 1, integrates over the best possible phoneme sequence and thus yields significant improvements. In the rest of the paper, we report results with the decoding in Eq. 12 unless specified explicitly. Our approach achieves a maximum improvement of 29.13% accuracy over Bridge-CCA in English-French and on an average it achieves 17.17% and 15.19% improvement in accuracy and MRR respectively. Notice that even though our Russian phoneme dictionary has only 1141 (word, IPA) pairs, our approach is able to achieve an accuracy of 63.47% and an MRR of 73% indicating that the correct name transliteration is, on an average, at rank 1 or 2.

6.3.2 Multilinguality

The fourth and fifth rows of Table 4 also show the multilingual results. In particular, we train our system on data from the three languages En, Bg, and Ru and test it on En-Bg and En-Ru test sets. Similarly, we train a different system on data from En, Fr and Ro and evaluate it on En-Fr and En-Ro test sets. We split the languages based on the language family, Russian and Bulgarian are Slavonic languages while French and Romanian are Romance languages, and expect that languages in same family have similar pronunciations. Comparing the performance of our system with and without the multilingual data set, it is clear that having data from other languages helps improve the accuracy.

6.3.3 Complementarity

In the final experiment, we want to compare the performance of our approach, which uses only monolingual resources, with a transliteration system trained using bilingual name pairs. We train a CCA based transliteration system (Udupa and Khapra,

	En-Bg		En-Fr	
	Acc.	MRR	Acc.	MRR
CCA	95.57	96.76	95.82	96.67
Ours+CCA	95.69	96.90	96.14	96.90
Δ Err	2.7%	4.2%	7.5%	6.8%
Ours+CCA(t)	95.80	96.95	96.34	97.04
Δ Err	5.4%	5.8%	12.3%	11.3%

Table 5: Comparison with a system trained on bilingual name pairs. The (t) in the third row indicates parameters are tuned for test set. We also show the percentage error reduction achieved by a linear combination of our approach and CCA.

2010) on a training data of 3792 and 8151 location name pairs. Notice that the training and test data for this system are from the same domain and thus it has an additional advantage over our approach, which is trained on whatever happens to be on Wiktionary.

The second row of Table 5 shows the results of CCA on English-Bulgarian and English-French language pairs. CCA achieves high accuracies even though the training data is relatively small, most likely because of the domain match between training and test data sets. As another baseline, we tried using Google machine translation API to transliterate the English names of the En-Bg test set. We hoped that since these are names, the translation engine would simply transliterate them and return the result. Of the output, we observed that about 500 names are passed through the MT system unchanged and so we ignore them. On the remaining names, it achieved an accuracy of 76.15% and the average string edit distance of the returned transliteration to the true transliteration is about 3.74. These accuracies are not directly comparable to the results shown in Table 5 because, presumably, it is a transliteration generation system unlike CCA which is a transliteration mining approach. For lack fair comparison, we don't report the accuracies of the Google transliteration output in Table 5.

Table 5 also shows the results of our system when combined with the CCA approach. For a given English word, we score the candidate transliterations using our approach and then linearly combine their scores with the scores assigned by CCA. We perform a line search between $[0, 1]$ for the appropriate weight combination. The third and fourth rows of Table 5 show the results of the linear combination when the weight is tuned for the development and test sets respectively. The improvements, though not significant, are encouraging and suggest that a sophisticated way of combining these different systems may yield significant improvements. This experiment shows that a transliteration system trained on word and IPA representations can actually augment a system trained on bilingual name pairs leading to an improved performance.

7 Conclusion

In this paper we proposed a regularization technique for the bridge language approaches and showed its effectiveness on the name transliteration task. Our approach learns interlingual representation using only monolingual resources and hence can be used to build transliteration system between resource poor languages. We show that, by accounting the language specific phonemic variation, we can get a significant improvements. Our experimental results suggest that a transliteration system built using IPA data can also help improve the accuracy of a transliteration system trained on bilingual name pairs.

Thought we used IPA as a bridge language there are other viable options. For example, as shown in Khapra et al. (2010) we can use English as the bridge language. Since name transliteration problem is being studied for a considerable time, many resources already exist between English and other languages. So, one can argue the appropriateness of IPA as bridge language compared to, say, English. While this is an important question, in this paper, we are primarily interested in showing the importance of handling language specific phenomenon in the bridge language approaches. In future, we would like to study the appropriateness of IPA vs. English as the bridge language and also the generalizability of our technique to other scenarios.

Acknowledgements

This work is partially funded by NSF grant IIS-1153487 and the BOLT program of the Defense Advanced Research Projects Agency, Contract No. HR0011-12-C-0015.

References

Nasreen AbdulJaleel and Leah S. Larkey. 2003. Statistical transliteration for english-arabic cross language information retrieval. In *Proceedings of the twelfth international conference on Information and knowledge management*, CIKM '03, pages 139–146, New York, NY, USA. ACM.

Yaser Al-Onaizan and Kevin Knight. 2002. Machine transliteration of names in arabic text. In *Proceedings of the ACL-02 workshop on Computational approaches to semitic languages*, SEMITIC '02, pages 1–13, Stroudsburg, PA, USA. ACL.

Wei Gao, Kam fai Wong, and Wai Lam. 2004. Phoneme-based transliteration of foreign names for OOV problem. In *Proceedings of the 1st International Joint Conference on Natural Language Processing (IJCNLP)*, pages 374–381.

Li Haizhou, Zhang Min, and Su Jian. 2004. A joint source-channel model for machine transliteration. In *Proceedings of the 42nd Annual Meeting on Association for Computational Linguistics*, ACL '04, Stroudsburg, PA, USA. ACL.

Martin Haspelmath, Matthew Dryer, David Gil, and Bernard Comrie, editors. 2005. *The World Atlas of Language Structures*. Oxford University Press.

Ulf Hermjakob, Kevin Knight, and Hal Daumé III. 2008. Name translation in statistical machine translation - learning when to transliterate. In *Proceedings of ACL-08: HLT*, pages 389–397, Columbus, Ohio, June. ACL.

Harold Hotelling. 1936. Relation between two sets of variables. *Biometrica*, 28:322–377.

Sung Young Jung, SungLim Hong, and Eunok Paek. 2000. An english to korean transliteration model of extended markov window. In *Proceedings of the 18th conference on Computational linguistics - Volume 1*, COLING '00, pages 383–389, Stroudsburg, PA, USA. ACL.

Byung-Ju Kang and Key-Sun Choi. 2000. Two approaches for the resolution of word mismatch problem caused by english words and foreign words in korean information retrieval. In *Proceedings of the 5th international workshop on on Information retrieval with Asian languages*, IRAL '00, pages 133–140, New York, NY, USA. ACM.

Mitesh M. Khapra, Raghavendra Udupa, A. Kumaran, and Pushpak Bhattacharyya. 2010. Pr + rq $\approx$ pq: Transliteration mining using bridge language. In *Proceedings of the Twenty-Fourth AAAI Conference on Artificial Intelligence, AAAI 2010*, Atlanta, Georgia, USA, July. AAAI Press.

Alexandre Klementiev and Dan Roth. 2006. Weakly supervised named entity transliteration and discovery from multilingual comparable corpora. In *Proceedings of the 21st International Conference on Computational Linguistics and the 44th Annual Meeting of the Association for Computational Linguistics*, ACL-44, pages 817–824, Stroudsburg, PA, USA. ACL.

Kevin Knight and Jonathan Graehl. 1998. Machine transliteration. *Computational Linguistics*, 24(4):599–612.

Haizhou Li, A. Kumaran, Vladimir Pervouchine, and Min Zhang. 2009. Report of news 2009 machine transliteration shared task. In *Proceedings of the 2009 Named Entities Workshop: Shared Task on Transliteration*, NEWS '09, pages 1–18, Stroudsburg, PA, USA. ACL.

Thomas Mandl and Christa Womser-Hacker. 2005. The effect of named entities on effectiveness in cross-language information retrieval evaluation. In *Proceedings of the 2005 ACM symposium on Applied computing*, SAC '05, pages 1059–1064, New York, NY, USA. ACM.

Gideon S. Mann and David Yarowsky. 2001. Multipath translation lexicon induction via bridge languages. In *Proceedings of the 2nd meeting of the North American Chapter of the Association for Computational Linguistics on Language technologies*, NAACL '01, pages 1–8, Stroudsburg, PA, USA. ACL.

M. K. Odel and R. C. Russel. 1918. U.s. patent numbers, 1,261,167 (1918) and 1,435,663(1922).

Michael Paul and Eiichiro Sumita. 2011. Translation quality indicators for pivot-based statistical mt. In *Proceedings of 5th International Joint Conference on Natural Language Processing*, pages 811–818, Chiang Mai, Thailand, November. AFNLP.

Sujith Ravi and Kevin Knight. 2009. Learning phoneme mappings for transliteration without parallel data. In *Proceedings of Human Language Technologies: The 2009 Annual Conference of the North American Chapter of the Association for Computational Linguistics*, pages 37–45, Boulder, Colorado, June. ACL.

Xabier Saralegi, Iker Manterola, and Iñaki San Vicente. 2011. Analyzing methods for improving precision of pivot based bilingual dictionaries. In *Proceedings of the 2011 Conference on Empirical Methods in Natural Language Processing*, pages 846–856, Edinburgh, Scotland, UK., July. ACL.

Richard Sproat, Tao Tao, and ChengXiang Zhai. 2006. Named entity transliteration with comparable corpora. In *Proceedings of the 21st International Conference on Computational Linguistics and the 44th annual meeting of the Association for Computational Linguistics*, ACL-44, pages 73–80, Stroudsburg, PA, USA. ACL.

Tao Tao, Su-Youn Yoon, Andrew Fister, Richard Sproat, and ChengXiang Zhai. 2006. Unsupervised named entity transliteration using temporal and phonetic correlation. In *Proceedings of the 2006 Conference on Empirical Methods in Natural Language Processing*, EMNLP '06, pages 250–257, Stroudsburg, PA, USA. ACL.

Raghavendra Udupa and Mitesh M. Khapra. 2010. Transliteration equivalence using canonical correlation analysis. In *ECIR'10*, pages 75–86.

Raghavendra Udupa, Saravanan K, Anton Bakalov, and Abhijit Bhole. 2009. "they are out there, if you know where to look": Mining transliterations of oov query terms for cross-language information retrieval. In *Proceedings of the 31th European Conference on IR Research on Advances in Information Retrieval*, ECIR '09, pages 437–448, Berlin, Heidelberg. Springer-Verlag.

Masao Utiyama and Hitoshi Isahara. 2007. A comparison of pivot methods for phrase-based statistical machine translation. In *Proceedings of Human Language Technologies 2007: The Conference of the North American Chapter of the Association for Computational Linguistics; Proceedings of the Main Conference*, pages 484–491, Rochester, New York, April. ACL.

Su-Youn Yoon, Kyoung-Young Kim, and Richard Sproat. 2007. Multilingual transliteration using feature based phonetic method. In *Proceedings of the 45th Annual Meeting of the Association of Computational Linguistics*, pages 112–119, Prague, Czech Republic, June. ACL.

Bilingual Lexicon Extraction from Comparable Corpora Using Label Propagation

Akihiro Tamura and **Taro Watanabe** and **Eiichiro Sumita**
Multilingual Translation Laboratory, MASTAR Project
National Institute of Information and Communications Technology
3-5 Hikaridai, Keihanna Science City, Kyoto, 619-0289, JAPAN
{akihiro.tamura,taro.watanabe,eiichiro.sumita}@nict.go.jp

Abstract

This paper proposes a novel method for lexicon extraction that extracts translation pairs from comparable corpora by using graph-based label propagation. In previous work, it was established that performance drastically decreases when the coverage of a seed lexicon is small. We resolve this problem by utilizing indirect relations with the bilingual seeds together with direct relations, in which each word is represented by a distribution of translated seeds. The seed distributions are propagated over a graph representing relations among words, and translation pairs are extracted by identifying word pairs with a high similarity in the seed distributions. We propose two types of the graphs: a co-occurrence graph, representing co-occurrence relations between words, and a similarity graph, representing context similarities between words. Evaluations using English and Japanese patent comparable corpora show that our proposed graph propagation method outperforms conventional methods. Further, the similarity graph achieved improved performance by clustering synonyms into the same translation.

1 Introduction

Bilingual lexicons are important resources for bilingual tasks such as machine translation (MT) and cross-language information retrieval (CLIR). Therefore, the automatic building of bilingual lexicons from corpora is one of the issues that have attracted many researchers. As a solution, a number of previous works proposed extracting bilingual lexicons from comparable corpora, in which documents were not direct translations but shared a topic or domain[1]. The use of comparable corpora is motivated by the fact that large parallel corpora are only available for a few language pairs and for limited domains.

Most of the previous methods are based on assumption (I), that a word and its translation tend to appear in similar contexts across languages (Rapp, 1999). Based on this assumption, many methods calculate word similarity using context and then extract word translation pairs with a high-context similarity. We call these methods context-similarity-based methods. The context similarities are usually computed using a seed bilingual lexicon (e.g. a general bilingual dictionary) by mapping contexts expressed in two different languages into the same space. In the mapping, information not represented by the seed lexicon is discarded. Therefore, the context-similarity-based methods could not find accurate translation pairs if using a small seed lexicon.

Some of the previous methods tried to alleviate the problem of the limited seed lexicon size (Koehn and Knight, 2002; Morin and Prochasson, 2011; Hazem et al., 2011), while others did not require any seed lexicon (Rapp, 1995; Fung, 1995; Haghighi et al., 2008; Ismail and Manandhar, 2010; Daumé III and Jagarlamudi, 2011). However, they suffer the problems of high computational cost (Rapp, 1995), sensitivity to parameters (Hazem et al., 2011), low accuracy (Fung, 1995; Ismail and Manandhar, 2010), and ineffectiveness for language pairs with

[1]Although Vulić et al. (2011) regarded document-aligned texts such as texts on Wikipedia as comparable corpora, we do not limit comparable corpora to these kinds of texts.

different types of characters (Koehn and Knight, 2002; Haghighi et al., 2008; Daumé III and Jagarlamudi, 2011).

In face of the above problems, we propose a novel method that uses a graph-based label propagation technique (Zhu and Ghahramani, 2002). The proposed method is based on assumption (II), which is derived by recursively applying assumption (I) to the "contexts": a word and its translation tend to have similar co-occurrence (direct and indirect) relations with all bilingual seeds across languages.

Based on assumption (II), we propose a three-step approach: (1) constructing a graph for each language with each edge indicating a direct co-occurrence relation, (2) representing every word as a seed translation distribution by iteratively propagating translated seeds in each graph, (3) finding two words in different languages with a high similarity with respect to the seed distributions. By propagating all the seeds on the graph, indirect co-occurrence relations are also considered when computing bilingual relations, which have been neglected in previous methods. In addition to the co-occurrence-based graph construction, we propose a similarity graph, which also takes into account context similarities between words.

The main contributions of this paper are as follows:

- We propose a bilingual lexicon extraction method that captures co-occurrence relations with all the seeds, including indirect relations, using graph-based label propagation. In our experiments, we confirm that the proposed method outperforms conventional context-similarity-based methods (Rapp, 1999; Andrade et al., 2010), and works well even if the coverage of a seed lexicon is low.
- We propose a similarity graph which represents context similarities between words. In our experiments, we confirm that a similarity graph is more effective than a co-occurrence-based graph.

2 Context-Similarity-based Extraction Method

The bilingual lexicon extraction from comparable corpora was pioneered in (Rapp, 1995; Fung, 1995). The popular similarity-based methods consist of the following steps: modeling contexts, calculating context similarities, and finding translation pairs.

Step 1. Modeling contexts: The context of each word is generally modeled by a vector where each dimension corresponds to a context word and each dimension has a value indicating occurrence correlation. Various definitions for the context have been used: distance-based context (e.g. in a sentence (Laroche and Langlais, 2010), in a paragraph (Fung and McKeown, 1997), in a predefined window (Rapp, 1999; Andrade et al., 2010)), and syntactic-based context (e.g. predecessors and successors in dependency trees (Garera et al., 2009), certain dependency position (Otero and Campos, 2008)). Some treated context words equally regardless of their positions (Fung and Yee, 1998), while others treated the words separately for each position (Rapp, 1999). Various correlation measures have been used: log-likelihood ratio (Rapp, 1999; Chiao and Zweigenbaum, 2002), tf-idf (Fung and Yee, 1998), pointwise mutual information (PMI) (Andrade et al., 2010), context heterogeneity (Fung, 1995), etc.

Shao and Ng (2004) represented contexts using language models. Andrade et al. (2010) used a set of words with a positive association as a context. Andrade et al. (2011a) used dependency relations instead of context words. Ismail and Manandhar (2010) used only in-domain words in contexts. Pekar et al. (2006) constructed smoothed context vectors for rare words. Laws et al. (2010) used graphs in which vertices correspond to words and edges indicate three types of syntactic relations such as adjectival modification.

Step 2. Calculating context similarities: The contexts which are expressed in two different languages are mapped into the same space. Previous methods generally use a seed bilingual lexicon for this mapping. After that, similarities are calculated based on the mapped context vectors using various measures: city-block metric (Rapp, 1999), cosine similarity (Fung and Yee, 1998), weighted jaccard index (Hazem et al., 2011), Jensen-Shannon divergence (Pekar et al., 2006), the number of overlapping context words (Andrade et al., 2010), SimRank (Laws et al., 2010), euclidean distance (Fung, 1995), etc.

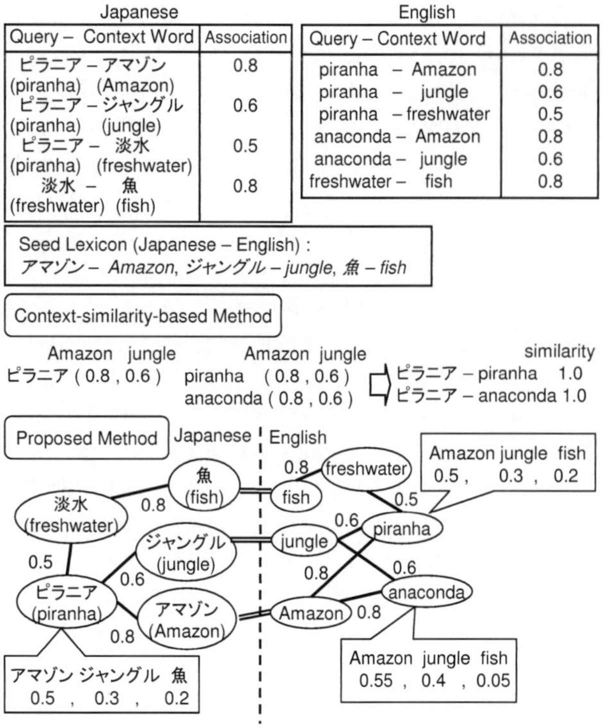

Figure 1: An Example of a Previous Method and our Proposed Method

Andrade et al. (2011b) performed a linear transformation of context vectors in accordance with the notion that importance varies by context positions. Gaussier et al. (2004) mapped context vectors via latent classes to capture synonymy and polysemy in a seed lexicon. Fišer et al. (2011) and Kaji (2005) calculated 2-way similarities.

Step 3. Finding translation pairs: A pair of words is treated as a translation pair when their context similarity is high. Various clues have been considered when computing the similarities: concept class information obtained from a multilingual thesaurus (Déjean et al., 2002), co-occurrence models generated from aligned documents (Prochasson and Fung, 2011), and transliteration information (Shao and Ng, 2004).

2.1 Problems from Previous Works

Most of previous methods used a seed bilingual lexicon for mapping modeled contexts in two different languages into the same space. The mapping heavily relies on the entries in a given bilingual lexicon. Therefore, if the coverage of the seed lexicon is low, the context vectors become sparser and its discriminative capability becomes lower, leading to extraction of incorrect translation equivalents.

Consider the example in Figure 1, where a context-similarity-based method and our proposed method find translation equivalents of the Japanese word "ピラニア (piranha)". There are three context words for the query. However, the information on co-occurrence with "淡水 (freshwater)" disappears after the context vector is mapped, because the seed lexicon does not include "淡水 (freshwater)". The same thing happens with the English word "piranha". As a result, the pair of "ピラニア (piranha)" and "anaconda" could be wrongly identified as a translation pair.

Some previous work focused on the problem of seed lexicon limitation. Morin and Prochasson (2011) complemented the seed lexicon with bilingual lexicon extracted from parallel sentences. Koehn and Knight (2002) used identically-spelled words in two languages as a seed lexicon. However, the method is not applicable for language pairs with different types of characters such as English and Japanese. Hazem et al. (2011) exploited *k*-nearest words for a query, which is very sensitive to the parameter *k*.

Some previous work did not require any seed lexicon. Rapp (1995) proposed a computationally demanding matrix permutation method which maximizes a similarity between co-occurrence matrices in two languages. Ismail and Manandhar (2010) introduced a similarity measure between two words in different languages without requiring any seed lexicon. Fung (1995) used context heterogeneity vectors where each dimension is independent on language types. However, their performances are worse than those of conventional methods using a small seed lexicon. Haghighi et al. (2008) and Daumé III and Jagarlamudi (2011) proposed a generative model based on probabilistic canonical correlation analysis, where words are represented by context features and orthographic features[2]. However, their experiments showed that orthographic features to be important for effectiveness, which means low per-

[2]In Haghighi et al. (2008) and Daumé III and Jagarlamudi (2011), indirect relations with seeds are considered topologically, but our method utilizes degrees of indirect correlations with seeds.

formance for language pairs with different character types.

3 Lexicon Extraction Based on Label Propagation

As described in Section 2, the performance of previous work is significantly degraded when used with a small seed lexicon. This problem could be resolved by incorporating indirect relations with all the seeds when identifying translation pairs. For example, in Figure 1, "ピラニア (piranha)" has some degree of association with the seed "魚 - fish" through "淡水 (freshwater)" in both the Japanese side and the English side, although "ピラニア (piranha)" and "魚 (fish)" do not co-occur in the same contexts. Moreover, "anaconda" has very little association with the seed "魚 - fish" in the English side. Therefore, the indirect relation with the seed "魚 - fish" helps to discriminate from between "piranha" and "anaconda" and could be an important clue for identifying a correct translation pair.

To utilize indirect relations, we introduce assumption (II): a word and its translation tend to have similar co-occurrence (direct and indirect) relations with all bilingual seeds across languages[3]. Based on assumption (II), we propose to identify a word pair as a translation pair when its co-occurrence (direct and indirect) relations with all the seeds are similar.

To obtain co-occurrence relations with all the seeds, including indirect relations, we focus on a graph-based label propagation (LP) technique (Zhu and Ghahramani, 2002). LP transfers labels from labeled data points to unlabeled data points. In the process, all vertices have soft labels that can be interpreted as label distributions. We apply LP to bilingual lexicon extraction by representing each word as a vertex in a graph with each edge encoding a direct co-occurrence relation. Translated seeds are propagated as labels, and seed distributions are obtained for each word. From the seed distributions, we identify translation pairs.

In summary, our proposed method consists of three steps (see Algorithm 1): (1) graph construction for each language, (2) seed propagation in each graph, (3) translation pair extraction.

Algorithm 1 Bilingual Lexicon Extraction

Require: comparable corpora D^e and D^f,
a seed lexicon S consists of S^e and S^f
Ensure: Output translation pairs T
1-1: $G^e = \{E^e, V^e, W^e\} \leftarrow$ construct-graph(D^e)
1-2: $G^f = \{E^f, V^f, W^f\} \leftarrow$ construct-graph(D^f)
2-1: $\tilde{G^e} = \{E^e, V^e, W^e, Q^e\} \leftarrow$ propagate-seed (G^e, S^e)
2-2: $\tilde{G^f} = \{E^f, V^f, W^f, Q^f\} \leftarrow$ propagate-seed (G^f, S^f)
3: $T \leftarrow$ extract-translation (Q^e, Q^f, S)

3.1 Graph Construction

We construct a graph representing the association between words for each language. Each graph is an undirected graph because the association does not have direction. The graphs are constructed as follows:

Step 1. Vertex assignment extracts words from each corpus, and assigns a vertex to each of the extracted words. Let $V = \{v_1, \cdots, v_n\}$ be a set of vertices.

Step 2. Edge weight calculation calculates association strength between two words as the weights of edges. Let E and W be a set of edges and that of the weights respectively, and $e_{ij} \in E$ links v_i and v_j, and $w_{ij} \in W$ is the weight of e_{ij}. Note that $|E| = |W|$.

Step 3. Edge pruning excludes edges whose weights are lower than threshold, in order to reduce the computational cost during seed propagations.

We propose two types of graphs that differ in the association measure used in Step 2: a co-occurrence graph and a similarity graph[4].

3.1.1 Co-occurrence Graph

A co-occurrence graph directly encodes assumption (II). Each edge in the graph indicates correlation strength between occurrences of two linked words. An example is shown in Figure 1.

In **edge weight calculation**, the co-occurrence frequencies are first computed for each word pair in the same context, and then the correlation strength is estimated. There are various definitions of a context or correlation measures that can be used (e.g. the

[3]Assumption (I) indicates direct co-occurrence relations between a word and its context words are preserved across different languages. Therefore, assumption (II) is derived by recursively applying assumption (I) to the "context words".

[4]We can combine the association measures used in a co-occurrence graph and a similarity graph. We will leave this combination approach for future work.

approaches used for modeling contexts in context-similarity-based methods). In this paper, we use words in a predefined window (window size is 10 in our experiments) as the context and PMI as the correlation measure:

$$w_{ij} = PMI(v_i, v_j) = log\frac{p(v_i, v_j)}{p(v_i) \cdot p(v_j)},$$

where $p(v_i)$ (or $p(v_j)$) is the probability that v_i (or v_j) occurs in a context, and $p(v_i, v_j)$ is the probability that v_i and v_j co-occur within the same context. We estimate $PMI(v_i, v_j)$ by the Bayesian method proposed by Andrade et al.(2010). Then, edges with a negative association, $PMI(v_i, v_j) \leq 0$, are pruned in **edge pruning**.

3.1.2 Similarity Graph

Co-occurrence graphs are very sensitive to accidental relation caused by lower frequent co-occurrence. Thus, we propose a similarity graph where context similarities are employed as weights of edges instead of simple co-occurrence-based correlations. Since the context similarities are computed by the global correlation among words which co-occur, a similarity graph is less subject to accidental co-occurrence. The use of a similarity graph is inspired by assumption (III): a word and its translation tend to have similar context similarities with all bilingual seeds across languages[5].

In **edge weight calculation**, we first construct a correlation vector representing co-occurrence relations for each word. The correlation vectors are constructed in the same way as the context vectors used in context-similarity-based methods (see Section 2), where context words are words in a predefined window (window size is 4 in our experiment), the association measure is PMI, and context words are treated separately for each position. A correlation vector for each position is computed separately, then concatenated into a single vector within the window. Secondly, we calculate similarities between correlation vectors. There are various similarity measures that can be used, and cosine similarity is used in this paper:

$$w_{ij} = Cos(\vec{f_i}, \vec{f_j}) = \frac{\vec{f_i} \cdot \vec{f_j}}{||\vec{f_i}||||\vec{f_j}||},$$

where $\vec{f_i}$ (or $\vec{f_j}$) is the correlation vector of v_i (or v_j). Then, in **edge pruning**, we preserve the edges with top 100 weight for each vertex.

3.2 Seed Propagation

LP is a graph-based technique which transfers the labels from labeled data to unlabeled data in order to infer labels for unlabeled data. This is primarily used when there is scarce labeled data but abundant unlabeled data. LP has been successfully applied in common natural language processing tasks such as word sense disambiguation (Niu et al., 2005; Alexandrescu and Kirchhoff, 2007), multi-class lexicon acquisition (Alexandrescu and Kirchhoff, 2007), and part-of-speech tagging (Das and Petrov, 2011). LP iteratively propagates label information from any vertex to nearby vertices through weighted edges, and then a label distribution for each vertex is generated where the weights of all labels add up to 1.

We adopt LP to obtain relations with all bilingual seeds including indirect relations by treating each seed as a label. First, each translated seed is assigned to a label, and then the labels are propagated in the graph described in Section 3.1.

The seed distribution for each word is initialized as follows:

$$q_i^0(z) = \begin{cases} 1 & if \ \ v_i \in V_s \ and \ z = v_i \\ 0 & if \ \ v_i \in V_s \ and \ z \neq v_i \\ u(z) & otherwise \end{cases},$$

where V_s is the set of vertices corresponding to translated seeds, u is a uniform distribution, $q_i^k(i = 1 \cdots |V|)$ is the seed distribution for v_i after k propagation, and $q_i^k(z)$ is the weight of a label (i.e., a translated seed) z in q_i^k.

After initialization, we iteratively propagate the seeds through weighted edges. In each propagation, seeds are probabilistically propagated from linked vertices under the condition that larger edge weights allow seeds to travel through easier. Thus, the closer vertices are, the more likely they have similar seed distributions. In Figure 1, the balloons attached to

[5]This assumption is justified because context similarities are based on co-occurrence relations that are preserved across different languages.

vertices in the graphs show examples of the seed distributions generated by propagations. For example, the English word "piranha" has the seed distribution where the weights of the seeds "Amazon", "jungle", and "fish" are 0.5, 0.3, and 0.2, respectively. Specifically, each of seed distributions is updated as follows:

$$q_i^m(z) = \begin{cases} q_i^0(z) & if\ v_i \in V_s \\ \dfrac{\sum_{v_j \in N(v_i)} w_{ij} \cdot q_j^{m-1}(z)}{\sum_{v_j \in N(v_i)} w_{ij}} & otherwise \end{cases},$$

where $N(v_i)$ is the set of vertices linking to v_i. We ran this procedure for 10 iterations in our experiments.

3.3 Translation Pair Extraction

After label propagations, we treat a pair of words in different languages with similar seed distributions as a translation pair. Seed distribution can be regarded as a vector where each dimension corresponds to each translated seed and each dimension has updated weight through label propagations. A similarity between seed distributions can therefore be calculated in the same way as a context-similarity-based method. In this paper, we use the cosine similarity defined by the following:

$$Cos(q_x^f, q_y^e) = \frac{\sum_{s_i \in S} q_x^f(v_i^f) \cdot q_y^e(v_i^e)}{\sqrt{\sum_{s_i \in S}(q_x^f(v_i^f))^2}\sqrt{\sum_{s_i \in S}(q_y^e(v_i^e))^2}},$$

where q_x^f (or q_y^e) is the seed distribution for a word x (or y) in the source language (or target language), S is the seed lexicon whose i-th entry s_i is a pairing of a translated seed in the source language v_i^f and one in the target language v_i^e.

4 Experiment

4.1 Experiment Data

We used English and Japanese patent documents published between 1993 and 2005 by the US Patent & Trademark Office and the Japanese Patent Office respectively, which were a part of the data used in the NTCIR-8 patent translation task (Fujii et al., 2010). Note that these documents are not aligned.

There are over three million English-Japanese parallel sentences (e.g. training data, test data, and development data used in the NTCIR-8 patent translation task, which is called *NTCIR parallel data* hereafter) in the patent data. However, a preliminary examination showed that the NTCIR parallel data covers less than 3% of all words because there are a number of technical terms and neologisms. Therefore, the patent translation task is a task that requires bilingual lexicon extraction from non-parallel data.

	Pair	Japanese Word	English Word
Lex_S	2,742	2,566	2,326
Lex_L	28,053	18,587	12,893

Table 1: Size of Seed Lexicons

We selected documents belonging to the *physics* domain from each monolingual corpus based on International Patent Classification (IPC) code[6], and then used them as a comparable corpus in our experiments. As a result, we used 1,479,831 Japanese documents and 438,227 English documents. The reason for selecting the *physics* domain is that this domain contains the most documents of all the domains.

The Japanese texts were segmented and part-of-speech tagged by ChaSen[7], and the English texts were tokenized and part-of-speech tagged by TreeTagger (Schmid, 1994). Next, function words were removed since function words with little semantic information spuriously co-occurred with many words. As a result, the number of distinct words in Japanese corpus and English corpus amounted to 1,111,302 and 4,099,825[8], respectively.

We employed seed lexicons from two sources: (1) EDR bilingual dictionary (EDR, 1990), (2) automatic word alignments generated by running GIZA++ (Och and Ney, 2003) with the NTCIR parallel data consisting of 3,190,654 parallel sentences. From each source, we extracted pairs of nouns appearing in our corpus. From (2), we excluded word pairs where the average of 2-way translation proba-

[6] *SECTION G* of IPC code indicates the *physics* domain.

[7] `http://chasen-legacy.sourceforge.jp/`

[8] The English words contain words in tables or mathematical formula but the Japanese words do not because the data format differs between English and Japanese. This is why the number of English words is larger than that of Japanese words, even though the number of English documents is smaller than that of Japanese documents.

bilities was lower than 0.5. The pairs from (1) and (2) amounted to 27,353 and 2,853 respectively, and the two sets were not exclusive. In order to measure the impact of seed lexicon size, we prepared two seed lexicons: Lex_L, a large seed lexicon that is a union of all the extracted word pairs, and Lex_S, a small seed lexicon that is a union of a random sampling one-tenth of the pairs from (1) and one-tenth of the pairs from (2). Table 1 shows the size of each seed lexicon. Note that our seed lexicons include one-to-many or many-to-one translation pairs.

We randomly selected 1,000 Japanese words as our test data which were identified as either a noun or an unknown by ChaSen and were not covered either by the EDR bilingual dictionary or by the NTCIR parallel data. This is because the purpose of our method is to complement existing bilingual dictionaries or parallel data. Note that the Japanese words in our test data may not have translation equivalents in the English side.

4.2 Competing Methods

We evaluated two types of our label propagation based methods against two baselines. $Cooc$ employs co-occurrence graphs and Sim uses similarity graphs when constructing graphs for label propagation as described in Section 3.

$Rapp$ is a typical context-similarity-based method described in Section 2 (Rapp, 1999). Context words are words in a window (window size is 10) and are treated separately for each position. Associations with context words are computed using the log-likelihood ratio (Dunning, 1993). The similarity measure between context vectors is the city-block metric.

$Andrade$ is a sophisticated method in context-similarity-based methods (Andrade et al., 2010). Context is a set of words with a positive association in a window (window size is 10). The association is calculated using the PMI estimated by a Bayesian method, and a similarity between contexts is estimated based on the number of overlapping words (see the original paper for details).

4.3 Experiment Results

Table 2 shows the performance of each method using Lex_S or Lex_L. Hereafter, $Method(L)$ (or $Method(S)$) denotes the $Method$ using Lex_L (or Lex_S). We measure the performance on bilingual lexicon extraction as Top N accuracy (Acc_N), which is the number of test words whose top N translation candidates contain a correct translation equivalent over the total number of test words (=1,000). Table 2 shows Top 1 and Top 20 accuracy. We manually[9] evaluated whether translation candidates contained a correct translation equivalent. We did not use recall because we do not know if the translation equivalents of a test word appear in the corpus.

	Lex_S		Lex_L	
	Acc_1	Acc_{20}	Acc_1	Acc_{20}
$Rapp$	1.5%	3.8%	4.8%	17.6%
$Andrade$	1.9%	4.2%	5.6%	17.6%
$Cooc$	3.2%	8.6%	9.2%	28.3%
Sim	4.1%	11.5%	10.8%	30.6%

Table 2: Performance on Bilingual Lexicon Extraction

Table 2 shows that the proposed methods outperform the baselines both when using Lex_S and using Lex_L. The improvements are statistically significant in the sign-test with 1% significance-level. The results show that capturing the relations with all the seeds including indirect relations is effective.

The accuracies of the baselines in Table 2 are worse than the previous reports: 14% Acc_1 and 46% Acc_{10} (Andrade et al., 2010), and 72% Acc_1 (Rapp, 1999). This is because previous works evaluated only the queries whose translation equivalents existed in the experiment data, which is not always true in our experiments. Moreover, previous works evaluated only high-frequency words: common nouns (Rapp, 1999) and words with a document frequency of at least 50 (Andrade et al., 2010). Our test data, on the other hand, includes many low-frequency words. It is generally true that translation of high-frequency words is much easier than that of low frequency words. We discuss the impact of test word frequencies in detail in Section 5.3.

Table 2 also shows that Sim outperforms $Cooc$ both when using Lex_S and using Lex_L. The improvements of Acc_{20} are statistically significant in the sign-test with 5% significance-level.

[9] We could not evaluate using existing dictionaries because most of the test data are technical terms and neologisms not included in the dictionaries.

	$Sim(L)$ (2)	$Cooc(L)$ (5)	$Andrade(L)$ (181)
1	psychosis	polynephropathy	disease
2	manic-depression	neuroleptic	bowel
3	epilepsy	iridocyclitis	disorder
4	insomnia	Tic	symptom
5	dementia	manic-depression	sclerosis
	$Sim(S)$ (974)	$Cooc(S)$ (1652)	$Andrade(S)$ (1747)
1	ulceration	dyslinesia	bulimia
2	ulcer	encephalomyelopathy	spasticity
3	naphthol	ganglionic	Parkinson
4	dementia	corticobasal	Asymmetric
5	gastritis	praecox	anorexia

Table 3: Translation Candidates for 躁鬱病 (manic-depression)

躁鬱病				
	$Cooc(L)$	$Andrade(L)$	$Cooc(S)$	$Andrade(S)$
1	睡眠薬 (0.12) narcotic	睡眠薬 (7.6) narcotic	痴呆 (0.016) dementia	後天 (5.0) posteriori
2	精神病 (0.11) psychosis	老年 (6.3) old	継子 (0.014) alien,stepchild	痴呆 (3.7) dementia
3	神経症 (0.08) neurosis	精神病 (6.3) psychosis	後天 (0.012) posteriori	潰瘍 (3.2) ulcer
4	ホルモン (0.05) hormone	気管支炎 (5.6) bronchitis	陽性 (0.012) electropositivity	ピリオド (2.9) period
5	不眠症 (0.04) insomnia	後天 (5.0) posteriori	潰瘍 (0.011) ulcer	重度 (2.5) seriousness
manic-depression				
	$Cooc(L)$	$Andrade(L)$	$Cooc(S)$	$Andrade(S)$
1	illness (0.15)	illness (8.6)	ganja (0.012)	galop (7.0)
2	neurosis (0.11)	psychotherapeutics (7.0)	carbanilide (0.011)	madness (5.4)
3	seizure (0.07)	galop (7.0)	paludism (0.011)	libido (5.2)
4	psychosis (0.06)	psychosis (6.8)	resignation (0.010)	vitiligo (4.6)
5	insomnia (0.04)	somnambulism (6.7)	galop (0.009)	dementia (4.3)

Table 4: Seeds with the Highest Weight

5 Discussion

5.1 Effect of Indirect Relations with Seeds

Table 3 shows a list of the top 5 translation candidates for the Japanese word "躁鬱病 (manic-depression)" for each method, where the ranks of the correct translations are shown in parentheses next to method names. Table 4 shows the top 5 translated seeds which characterize the query, where the values in parentheses indicate weight. Table 3 shows that $Cooc(L)$ can find the correct translation equivalent but $Andrade(L)$ cannot. Table 4 shows that $Cooc(L)$ can utilize more seeds closely tied to the query (e.g. "神経症 (neurosis)", "不眠症 (insomnia)"), which did not occur in the context of the query in the experiment data. The result shows that indirectly-related seeds are also important clues, and our proposed method can utilize these.

5.2 Impact of Seed Lexicon Size

Table 2 shows that a reduction of seed lexicon size degrades performance. This is natural for the baseline methods because Lex_S cannot translate most of context words, which are necessary for word characterization. Consider $Andrade(L)$ and $Andrade(S)$ in the example in Section 5.1. Table 4 shows that $Andrade(S)$ uses less relevant seeds with the query, and has to express the query by seeds with less association. For example, "精神病 (psychosis)" cannot be used in $Andrade(S)$ because Lex_S does not have the seed. Therefore, it is more difficult for $Andrade(S)$ to find correct translation pairs.

The proposed methods also share the same tendency, although each word is expressed by all the seeds in the seed lexicon. Consider $Cooc(L)$ and $Cooc(S)$ in the above example. Table 4 shows that $Cooc(S)$ expresses the query by a smooth seed distribution, which is difficult to discriminate from others. This is because Lex_S does not have relevant seeds for the query. This is why $Cooc(S)$ cannot find the correct translation equivalent. On the other hand, $Cooc(L)$ characterizes "躁鬱病" and "manic-depression" by strongly relevant seeds (e.g. "精神病 (psychosis)","神経症 (neurosis)"), and then finds the correct translation equivalent.

To examine the robustness-to-seed lexicon size, we calculated the reduction rate of Acc_{20} with the following expression: (Acc_{20} with Lex_L − Acc_{20} with Lex_S) / Acc_{20} with Lex_L. The reduction rates of *Rapp*, $Andrade$, $Cooc$, and Sim are 78.4%, 76.1%, 69.6%, and 62.4% respectively. Moreover, the difference between degradation in $Cooc$ and that in $Andrade$ is statistically significant in the sign-test with 1% significance-level. These results indicate that the proposed methods are more robust to seed lexicon size than the baselines. This is because the proposed methods can utilize seeds with indirect relations while the baselines utilize only seeds in the context.

To verify our claim, we examined the number of test words which occurred with no seeds in the context. There were 570 such words in *Rapp(S)*, 387 in *Rapp(L)*, 572 in $Andrade(S)$, and 388 in $Andrade(L)$. The baselines cannot find their trans-

	Low Freq.		High Freq.	
	Acc_1	Acc_{20}	Acc_1	Acc_{20}
$Rapp(L)$	0.5%	2.4%	7.2%	25.6%
$Andrade(L)$	0.3%	1.8%	8.6%	26.3%
$Cooc(L)$	0.8%	4.3%	13.9%	40.7%
$Sim(L)$	2.2%	6.7%	15.0%	42.0%

Table 5: Comparison between Performance for High and Low Frequency Words

lation equivalents. Words such as this occur even if using Lex_L, and that number increases when Lex_S is used. On the other hand, the proposed methods are able to utilize all the seeds in order to find equivalents for words such as these. Therefore, the proposed methods work well even if the coverage of a seed lexicon is low.

5.3 Impact of Word Frequencies

Our test data includes many low-frequency words which are not covered by the EDR bilingual dictionary or the NTCIR parallel data. 624 words appear in the corpus less than 50 times. Table 5 shows Acc_N using Lex_L for 624 low-frequency words and 376 high-frequency words. Table 5 shows that performance for low-frequency words is much worse than that for high-frequency words. This is because translation of high-frequency words utilizes abundant and reliable context information, while the context information for low-frequency words is statistically unreliable. In the proposed methods, edges linking rare words are sometimes generated based on accidental co-occurrences, and then unrelated seed information is transferred through the edges. Therefore, even our label propagation based methods, especially for $Cooc$, could not identify the correct translation equivalents for rare words. Sim alleviated the problem by using a similarity graph in which edges are generated based on global correlation among words, as indicated by Table 5. Table 5 also suggests that top 20 translation candidates for high-frequency words have potential to contribute to bilingual tasks such as MT and CLIR although the overall performance is still low.

5.4 Effect of Similarity Graphs

We examined Acc_N for synonyms of translated seeds in Japanese. The Acc_1 and Acc_{20} of $Sim(L)$ are 15.6% and 56.3%, respectively, and those of $Cooc(L)$ are 9.4% and 37.5%, respectively. The results show that similarity graphs are effective for clustering synonyms into the same translation equivalents. For example, $Sim(L)$ extracted the correct translation pair of the English word "iodine" and the Japanese word "イオディン", a synonym of the translated seed "ヨウ素 (iodine)" in Japanese. This is because synonyms tend to be linked in the similarity graph and have similar seed distributions. On the other hand, in the co-occurrence graph, synonyms tend to be indirectly linked through mutual context words, so the seed distributions of the two could be far away from each other.

There are in particular many loanwords in patent documents, which are spelled in different ways from person to person. For example, the loan word for the English word "user" is often written as "ユーザ", but it is sometimes written as "ユーザー", with an additional prolonged sound mark. Therefore, Sim is particularly effective for the experiment data.

5.5 Error Analysis

We discuss errors of the proposed methods except the errors for low-frequency words (see Section 5.3). Our test data includes words whose translation equivalents inherently cannot be found. The first of these types are words whose equivalent does not exist in the English corpus. This is an unavoidable problem for methods based on comparable corpora. The second one are words whose English equivalents are compound words. The Japanese morphological analyzer tends to group a compound word into a single word, while the English text analyzer does not perform a collocation of words divided by the delimiter *space*. For example, the single Japanese word "掌紋" is equivalent to "palm pattern" or "palm print", which is composed of two words. This case was counted as an error even though the proposed methods found the word "palm" as a equivalent of "掌紋".

A main reason of errors other than those above is word sense ambiguity, which is different in every language. For example, the Japanese word "右"

means "right" and "conservatism" in English. The proposed methods merge different senses by propagating seeds through these polysemous words in only one language side. This is why translation pairs could have wrong seed distributions and then the proposed methods could not identify correct translation pairs. We will leave this word sense disambiguation problem for future work.

6 Related Work

Besides the comparable corpora approach discussed in Section 2, many alternatives have been proposed for bilingual lexicon extraction. The first is a method that finds translation pairs in parallel corpora (Wu and Xia, 1994; Fung and Church, 1994; Och and Ney, 2003). However, large parallel corpora are only available for a few language pairs and for limited domains. Moreover, even the large parallel corpora are relatively smaller than comparable corpora.

The second is a method that exploits the Web. Lu et al. (2004) extracted translation pairs by mining web anchor texts and link structures. As an alternative, mixed-language web pages are exploited by first retrieving texts including both source and target languages from the web by using a search engine or simple rules, and then extracting translation pairs from the mixed-language texts utilizing various clues: Zhang and Vines (2004) used co-occurrence statistics, Cheng et al. (2004) used co-occurrences and context similarity information, and Huang et al. (2005) used phonetic, semantic and frequency-distance features. Lin et al. (2008) proposed a method for extracting parenthetically translated terms, where a word alignment algorithm is used for establishing the correspondences between in-parenthesis and pre-parenthesis words. However, those methods cannot find translation pairs when they are not connected with each other through link structures, or when they do not co-occur in the same text.

Transliteration is a completely different way for bilingual lexicon acquisition, in which a word in one language is converted into another language using phonetic equivalence (Knight and Graehl, 1998; Karimi et al., 2011). Although machine transliteration works particularly well for proper names and loan words, it cannot be employed for phonetically dissimilar translations.

All the methods mentioned above may potentially extract translation pairs more precisely than our comparable corpora approach when their underlying assumptions are satisfied. We might improve the performance of our method by augmenting a seed lexicon with translation pairs extracted using the above methods, as experimented with in Section 4, in which additional lexical entries are included from parallel data.

7 Conclusion

We proposed a novel bilingual lexicon extraction method using label propagation for alleviating the limited seed lexicon size problem. The proposed method captures relations with all the seeds including indirect relations by propagating seed information. Moreover, we proposed using similarity graphs in propagation process in addition to co-occurrence graphs. Our experiments showed that the proposed method outperforms conventional context-similarity-based methods (Rapp, 1999; Andrade et al., 2010), and the similarity graphs improve the performance by clustering synonyms into the same translation.

We are planning to investigate the following open problems in future work: word sense disambiguation and translation of compound words as described in (Daille and Morin, 2005; Morin et al., 2007). In addition, indirect relations have also been used in other tasks, such as paraphrase acquisition from bilingual parallel corpora (Kok and Brockett, 2010). We will utilize their random walk approach or other graph-based techniques such as modified adsorption (Talukdar and Crammer, 2009) for generating seed distributions. We are also planning an end-to-end evaluation, for instance, by employing the extracted bilingual lexicon into an MT system.

Acknowledgments

We thank anonymous reviewers of EMNLP-CoNLL 2012 for helpful suggestions and comments on a first version of this paper. We also thank anonymous reviewers of First Workshop on Multilingual Modeling (MM-2012) for useful comments on this work.

References

Andrei Alexandrescu and Katrin Kirchhoff. 2007. Data-Driven Graph Construction for Semi-Supervised Graph-Based Learning in NLP. In *Human Language Technologies 2007: The Conference of the North American Chapter of the Association for Computational Linguistics; Proceedings of the Main Conference*, pages 204–211.

Daniel Andrade, Tetsuya Nasukawa, and Junichi Tsujii. 2010. Robust Measurement and Comparison of Context Similarity for Finding Translation Pairs. In *Proceedings of the 23rd International Conference on Computational Linguistics (COLING 2010)*, pages 19–27.

Daniel Andrade, Takuya Matsuzaki, and Junichi Tsujii. 2011a. Effective Use of Dependency Structure for Bilingual Lexicon Creation. In *Proceedings of the 12th International Conference on Computational Linguistics and Intelligent Text Processing (CICLing 2011) - Volume Part II*, pages 80–92.

Daniel Andrade, Takuya Matsuzaki, and Junichi Tsujii. 2011b. Learning the Optimal Use of Dependency-parsing Information for Finding Translations with Comparable Corpora. In *Proceedings of the 4th Workshop on Building and Using Comparable Corpora*, pages 10–18.

Pu-Jen Cheng, Jei-Wen Teng, Ruei-Cheng Chen, Jenq-Haur Wang, Wen-Hsiang Lu, and Lee-Feng Chien. 2004. Translating Unknown Queries with Web Corpora for Cross-Language Information Retrieval. In *Proceedings of the 27th Annual International ACM SIGIR Conference on Research and Development in Information Retrieval*, pages 146–153.

Yun-Chuang Chiao and Pierre Zweigenbaum. 2002. Looking for candidate translational equivalents in specialized, comparable corpora. In *Proceedings of the 19th International Conference on Computational Linguistics (COLING 2002)*, pages 1–5.

Béatrice Daille and Emmanuel Morin. 2005. French-English Terminology Extraction from Comparable Corpora. In *Proceedings of 2nd International Joint Conference on Natural Language Processing (IJCNLP 2005)*, pages 707–718.

Dipanjan Das and Slav Petrov. 2011. Unsupervised Part-of-Speech Tagging with Bilingual Graph-Based Projections. In *Proceedings of the 49th Annual Meeting of the Association for Computational Linguistics: Human Language Technologies (ACL-HLT 2011)*, pages 600–609.

Hal Daumé III and Jagadeesh Jagarlamudi. 2011. Domain Adaptation for Machine Translation by Mining Unseen Words. In *Proceedings of the 49th Annual Meeting of the Association for Computational Linguistics: Human Language Technologies (ACL-HLT2011)*, pages 407–412.

Hervé Déjean, Éric Gaussier, and Fatia Sadat. 2002. An approach based on multilingual thesauri and model combination for bilingual lexicon extraction. In *Proceedings of the 19th International Conference on Computational linguistics (COLING 2002)*, pages 1–7.

Ted Dunning. 1993. Accurate Methods for the Statistics of Surprise and Coincidence. *COMPUTATIONAL LINGUISTICS*, 19(1):61–74.

EDR. 1990. Bilingual Dictionary. In *Technical Report TR-029*. Japan Electronic Dictionary Research Institute, Tokyo.

Darja Fišer, Nikola Ljubešić, Špela Vintar, and Senja Pollak. 2011. Building and using comparable corpora for domain-specific bilingual lexicon extraction. In *Proceedings of the 4th Workshop on Building and Using Comparable Corpora*, pages 19–26.

Atsushi Fujii, Masao Utiyama, Mikio Yamamoto, Takehito Utsuro, Terumasa Ehara, Hiroshi Echizen-ya, and Sayori Shimohata. 2010. Overview of the Patent Translation Task at the NTCIR-8 Workshop. In *Proceedings of the 8th NTCIR Workshop*, pages 371–376.

Pascale Fung and Kenneth Ward Church. 1994. K-vec: A New Approach for Aligning Parallel Texts. In *Proceedings of the 15th International Conference on Computational Linguistics (COLING 1994)*, pages 1096–1102.

Pascale Fung and Kathleen McKeown. 1997. Finding Terminology Translations from Non-parallel Corpora. In *Proceedings of the 5th Annual Workshop on Very Large Corpora*, pages 192–202.

Pascale Fung and Lo Yuen Yee. 1998. An IR Approach for Translating New Words from Nonparallel, Comparable Texts. In *Proceedings of the 36th Annual Meeting of the Association for Computational Linguistics and 17th International Conference on Computational Linguistics, Volume 1*, pages 414–420.

Pascale Fung. 1995. Compiling Bilingual Lexicon Entries from a Non-Parallel English-Chinese Corpus. In *Proceedings of the 3rd Annual Workshop on Very Large Corpora*, pages 173–183.

Nikesh Garera, Chris Callison-Burch, and David Yarowsky. 2009. Improving Translation Lexicon Induction from Monolingual Corpora via Dependency Contexts and Part-of-Speech Equivalences. In *Proceedings of the 13th Conference on Computational Natural Language Learning (CoNLL 2009)*, pages 129–137.

Eric Gaussier, Jean-Michel Renders, Irina Matveeva, Cyril Goutte, and Herve Déjean. 2004. A Geometric View on Bilingual Lexicon Extraction from Comparable Corpora. In *Proceedings of the 42nd Annual Meeting on Association for Computational Linguistics (ACL 2004)*, pages 526–533.

Aria Haghighi, Percy Liang, Taylor Berg-Kirkpatrick, and Dan Klein. 2008. Learning Bilingual Lexicons from Monolingual Corpora. In *Proceedings of the 46th Annual Meeting of the Association for Computational Linguistics (ACL 2008): the Human Language Technology Conference (HLT)*, pages 771–779.

Amir Hazem, Emmanuel Morin, and Sebastian Peña Saldarriaga. 2011. Bilingual Lexicon Extraction from Comparable Corpora as Metasearch. In *Proceedings of the 4th Workshop on Building and Using Comparable Corpora*, pages 35–43.

Fei Huang, Ying Zhang, and Stephan Vogel. 2005. Mining Key Phrase Translations from Web Corpora. In *Proceedings of Human Language Technology Conference and Conference on Empirical Methods in Natural Language Processing (HLT-EMNLP 2005)*, pages 483–490.

Azniah Ismail and Suresh Manandhar. 2010. Bilingual lexicon extraction from comparable corpora using in-domain terms. In *Proceedings of the 23rd International Conference on Computational Linguistics (COLING 2010)*, pages 481–489.

Hiroyuki Kaji. 2005. Extracting Translation Equivalents from Bilingual Comparable Corpora. *IEICE - Trans. Inf. Syst.*, E88-D:313–323.

Sarvnaz Karimi, Falk Scholer, and Andrew Turpin. 2011. Machine Transliteration Survey. *ACM Computing Surveys*, 43(3):1–46.

Kevin Knight and Jonathan Graehl. 1998. Machine Transliteration. *Computational Linguistics*, 24:599–612.

Philipp Koehn and Kevin Knight. 2002. Learning a Translation Lexicon from Monolingual Corpora. In *Proceedings of ACL Workshop on Unsupervised Lexical Acquisition*, pages 9–16.

Stanley Kok and Chris Brockett. 2010. Hitting the Right Paraphrases in Good Time. In *Proceedings of Human Language Technologies: The 2010 Annual Conference of the North American Chapter of the Association for Computational Linguistics (HLT-NAACL 2010)*, pages 145–153.

Audrey Laroche and Philippe Langlais. 2010. Revisiting Context-based Projection Methods for Term-Translation Spotting in Comparable Corpora. In *Proceedings of the 23rd International Conference on Computational Linguistics (COLING 2010)*, pages 617–625.

Florian Laws, Lukas Michelbacher, Beate Dorow, Christian Scheible, Ulrich Heid, and Hinrich Schütze. 2010. A Linguistically Grounded Graph Model for Bilingual Lexicon Extraction. In *Proceedings of the 23rd International Conference on Computational Linguistics (COLING 2010)*, pages 614–622.

Dekang Lin, Shaojun Zhao, Benjamin Van Durme, and Marius Pasca. 2008. Mining Parenthetical Translations from the Web by Word Alignment. In *Proceedings of the 46th Annual Meeting of the Association for Computational Linguistics (ACL 2008): the Human Language Technology Conference (HLT)*, pages 994–1002.

Wen-Hsiang Lu, Lee-Feng Chien, and Hsi-Jian Lee. 2004. Anchor Text Mining for Translation of Web Queries: A Transitive Translation Approach. *ACM Transactions on Information Systems*, 22(2):242–269.

Emmanuel Morin and Emmanuel Prochasson. 2011. Bilingual Lexicon Extraction from Comparable Corpora Enhanced with Parallel Corpora. In *Proceedings of the 4th Workshop on Building and Using Comparable Corpora*, pages 27–34.

Emmanuel Morin, Béatrice Daille, Koichi Takeuchi, and Kyo Kageura. 2007. Bilingual Terminology Mining - Using Brain, not brawn comparable corpora. In *Proceedings of the 45th Annual Meeting of the Association of Computational Linguistics (ACL 2007)*, pages 664–671.

Zheng-Yu Niu, Dong-Hong Ji, and Chew Lim Tan. 2005. Word Sense Disambiguation Using Label Propagation Based Semi-Supervised Learning. In *Proceedings of the 43rd Annual Meeting of the Association for Computational Linguistics (ACL 2005)*, pages 395–402.

Franz Josef Och and Hermann Ney. 2003. A Systematic Comparison of Various Statistical Alignment Models. *Computational Linguistics*, 29:19–51.

Pablo Gamallo Otero and José Ramom Pichel Campos. 2008. Learning Spanish-Galician Translation Equivalents Using a Comparable Corpus and a Bilingual Dictionary. In *Proceedings of the 9th International Conference on Computational Linguistics and Intelligent Text Processing (CICLing 2008)*, pages 423–433.

Viktor Pekar, Ruslan Mitkov, Dimitar Blagoev, and Andrea Mulloni. 2006. Finding Translations for Low-Frequency Words in Comparable Corpora. *Machine Translation*, 20:247–266.

Emmanuel Prochasson and Pascale Fung. 2011. Rare Word Translation Extraction from Aligned Comparable Documents. In *Proceedings of the 49th Annual Meeting of the Association for Computational Linguistics: Human Language Technologies (ACL-HLT2011)*, pages 1327–1335.

Reinhard Rapp. 1995. Identifying Word Translations in Non-Parallel Texts. In *Proceedings of the 33rd Annual Meeting of the Association for Computational Linguistics (ACL 1995)*, pages 320–322.

Reinhard Rapp. 1999. Automatic Identification of Word Translations from Unrelated English and German Corpora. In *Proceedings of the 37th Annual Meeting of the Association for Computational Linguistics (ACL 1999)*, pages 519–526.

Helmut Schmid. 1994. Probabilistic Part-of-Speech Tagging Using Decision Trees. In *Proceedings of the International Conference on New Methods in Language Processing*, pages 44–49.

Li Shao and Hwee Tou Ng. 2004. Mining New Word Translations from Comparable Corpora. In *Proceedings of the 20th International Conference on Computational Linguistics (COLING 2004)*, pages 618–624.

Partha Pratim Talukdar and Koby Crammer. 2009. New Regularized Algorithms for Transductive Learning. In *Proceedings of the European Conference on Machine Learning and Principles and Practice of Knowledge Discovery in Databases (ECML-PKDD 2009)*, pages 442–457.

Ivan Vulić, Wim De Smet, and Marie-Francine Moens. 2011. Identifying Word Translations from Comparable Corpora Using Latent Topic Models. In *Proceedings of the 49th Annual Meeting of the Association for Computational Linguistics: Human Language Technologies (ACL-HLT 2011)*, pages 479–484.

Dekai Wu and Xuanyin Xia. 1994. Learning an English-Chinese Lexicon from a Parallel Corpus. In *Proceedings of the First Conference of the Association for Machine Translation in the Americas (AMTA 1994)*, pages 206–213.

Ying Zhang and Phil Vines. 2004. Using the Web for Automated Translation Extraction in Cross-Language Information Retrieval. In *Proceedings of the 27th Annual International ACM SIGIR Conference on Research and Development in Information Retrieval*, pages 162–169.

Xiaojin Zhu and Zoubin Ghahramani. 2002. Learning from Labeled and Unlabeled Data with Label Propagation. Technical report, CMU-CALD-02-107.

Lexical Differences in Autobiographical Narratives from Schizophrenic Patients and Healthy Controls

Kai Hong[1], Christian G. Kohler[2], Mary E. March[2], Amber A. Parker[3], Ani Nenkova[1]
University of Pennsylvania
Philadelphia, PA, 19104, USA
[1]{hongkai1,nenkova}@seas.upenn.edu
[2]{kohler,memarch}@mail.med.upenn.edu
[3]{parker}@sas.upenn.edu

Abstract

We present a system for automatic identification of schizophrenic patients and healthy controls based on narratives the subjects recounted about emotional experiences in their own life. The focus of the study is to identify the lexical features that distinguish the two populations. We report the results of feature selection experiments that demonstrate that the classifier can achieve accuracy on patient level prediction as high as 76.9% with only a small set of features. We provide an in-depth discussion of the lexical features that distinguish the two groups and the unexpected relationship between emotion types of the narratives and the accuracy of patient status prediction.

1 Introduction

Recent studies have shown that automatic language analysis can be successfully applied to detect cognitive impairment and language disorders. Our work further extends this line of investigation with analysis of the lexical differences between patients suffering from schizophrenia and healthy controls.

Prior work has reported on characteristic language peculiarities exhibited by schizophrenia patients. There are more repetitions in speech of patients compared to controls (Manschreck et al., 1985). Patients also tend to repeatedly refer back to themselves (Andreasen., 1986). Deviations from normal language use in patients on different levels, including phonetics and syntax, have been documented (Covington et al., 2005), however lexical differences have not been investigated in detail.

In this paper we introduce a dataset of autobiographical narratives told by schizophrenic patients and by healthy controls. The narratives are related to emotional personal experiences of the subjects for five basic emotions: ANGER, SAD, HAPPY, DISGUST, FEAR. We train an SVM classifier to predict subject status. Our good results on the relatively small dataset indicate the potential of the approach. An automatic system for predicting patient status from autobiographical narratives can aid psychiatrists in tracking patients over time and can serve as an easy way to administer large scale screening. The detailed feature analysis we performed also pinpoints key differences between the two populations.

We study a range of lexical features including individual words, repetitions as well as classes of words defined in specialized dictionaries compiled by psychologists (Section 4). We use several approaches for feature analysis to identify statistically significant differences in the two populations. There are 169 significant features among all of the 6057 features we examined. Through feature selection we are able to obtain a small set of 25 highly predictive features which lead to status classification accuracy significantly better than chance (Section 6.3). We also show that differences between patients and controls are revealed best in stories related to SAD and ANGRY narratives, they are decent in HAPPY stories, and that distinctions are poor for DISGUST and FEAR (Section 6.5).

2 Related Work

Research in psychometrics has studied patterns of lexical usage in a large variety of scenarios. A popular tool used for psychometric analysis is Linguistic Inquiry and Word Count (LIWC) (Pennebaker et al., 2007). One of the most interesting discoveries in that line of research is that people with physical or emotional pain are likely to use first-person singular pronouns more often than the general population (Rude et al., 2004). In the view of therapy, Pennebaker discovered that writing emotional experiences can be helpful in therapeutic process (Pennebaker, 1997). It has also been shown that the usage of pronouns and function words can be indicators of writing styles, physical health and other distinctions (Tausczik and Pennebaker, 2010).

The combination of natural language processing (NLP) and machine learning (ML) has been explored in many psychology related projects, and is gaining popularity. It has been shown that features from language models (LMs) can be used to detect impairment in monolingual and bilingual children (Gabani et al., 2009). Even better results are achieved when features derived from LMs are combined with other surface features to predict language impairment. Similarly, studies on child language development and autism have shown that n-gram cross-entropy from LMs representative of healthy and impaired subjects is a highly significant feature predictive of language impairment (Prud'hommeaux et al., 2011). The feasibility of making use of lexical features to analyze language dominance among bilingual children has also been confirmed (Solorio et al., 2011).

In non-medically related research, LIWC and lexical features have been used to recognize different personalities such as *introvert* vs *extrovert*, *openness* vs *experience*, *conscientiousness* vs *unconscientiousness*, etc. (Mairesse et al., 2007). Similar features have been applied to differentiate author personality of e-mails (Gill et al., 2006), blogs (Gill et al., 2009) and other documents.

Speech-related features and interactional aspects of dialog behavior such as pauses, fillers, etc, have also been found helpful in identifying autistic patients (Heeman et al., 2010).

Variables (# Subjects)	Schizophrenia (n=23)	Control (n=16)
Mean age (SD)	33.81 (9.65)	32.29 (6.59)
Mean number of words per story (SD)	192.22 (122.4)	180.79 (95.87)

Table 1: Basic demographic information

Syntax features have been used in approaches of automatic detection of neurological problems. Parsing texts produced by subjects and using bag of rules as features have been applied in analyzing language dominance (Solorio et al., 2011). Methods that quantify syntactic complexity like Yngve score and Fraizer score have been used to analyze autism (Prud'hommeaux et al., 2011). Moreover, there has been research on detecting mild cognitive impairment, which could be an earlier state of Alzheimer's disease: five different ways of evaluating syntactic complexity measures were introduced in their paper (Roark et al., 2011).

In our own work, we focus our analysis exclusively on lexical features. Similarly to prior work, we present the most significant features related to differences between schizophrenic patients and healthy controls. Unlike prior work, instead of doing class ablation studies we perform feature selection from the full set of available features and identify a small set of highly predictive features which are sufficient to achieve the top performance we report. Such targeted analysis is more helpful for medical professionals as they search to develop new therapies and ways to track patient status between visits.

3 Data

For our experiments we collected autobiographical narratives from 39 speakers. The speakers are asked to tell their experience involving the following emotions: HAPPY, ANGER, SAD, FEAR and DISGUST, which comprise the set of the five basic emotions (Cowie, 2000). Most subjects told a single story for each of the emotions, some told two. The total number of stories in the dataset is 201.

The stories were narrated in the doctor's office. The recordings of the narratives were manually transcribed in plain text format. We show age and length in words of the told stories for the two groups in Table 1. There are 23 patients with schizophrenia and 16 healthy controls, telling 120 and 81 stories respectively.

4 Features

Here we introduce the large set of lexical features that we group in three classes: a large class of features computed for individual lexical items, basic features, features derived on the basis of pre-existing dictionaries and language model features. We also detail the way we performed feature normalization and feature selection.

4.1 Surface Features

4.1.1 Basic Features

Basic features include token to type ratio to capture vocabulary diversity, letters per word, words per sentence, sentences per document and words per document. These features describe the general properties of the language used by the subject, without focus on specific words.

Repetitions, revisions, large amount of fillers or disfluencies can be indicators for language impairment. In our basic features we detect the number of repetitions in words, punctuations and sentences for each transcript. Then these three measures are normalized by total number of words or sentences.

We define repetitions as the occurrence of the same token in a sliding window of five items within the same sentence. We count repetitions of words and punctuation separately. The repetition of punctuation, mostly commas and full-stops, are indicative of phrasing in speech which has been indirectly captured in the transcript. Repetition of any word is counted, regardless of which specific word was repeated. For example, for the sentence *I am, am, afraid, that something bad would happen. am* is counted as repeated once, and comma is counted as repeated twice. Finally, sentence repetition captures the amount of overlapping at the beginning of two adjacent sentences, defined as the number of tokens from the beginning of the sentence until the first token where the two sentences differ.

4.1.2 Lexical Features

For words in the vocabulary: we use a real value feature equal to the word frequency for each document. Of particular interest we track the use of pronouns because early research has reported that people with cognitive impairment have a tendency to use subjective words or referring to themselves (Rude et al., 2004).

In addition, for each word in the vocabulary, we apply the presence of the repetition about one particular word.

4.1.3 Perplexity from Language Models

Inspired by the predictive power of language model reported in prior work, we also include several language model features. We build language models on words as well as part-of-speech (POS) tags from Stanford POS-tagger (Toutanova et al., 2003). We tried unigram, bigram and trigram language models by word and POS tag. Experiments showed that bigram performed better than random, and the other two performed below random. Thus in the experiments we report later we train one model for patients and one for controls and use the perplexity of a given text according to the bigram language models on word and POS as features in prediction.

4.2 Dictionaries: LIWC and Diction

Text analysis packages have been widely used in research related to personality analysis, sentimental analysis and psychometric studies. We use two dictionary-based systems, LIWC (Pennebaker et al., 2007)[1] and Diction[2], which both give scores to transcripts based on broad categories.

4.2.1 Linguistic Inquiry&Word Count(LIWC)

LIWC calculates the degree to which people use different categories of words. Several manually compiled dictionaries are at the heart of the application. Each word or word stem could be in one or more word categories or sub-dictionaries. For instance, the word "cried" is part of the following categories: *sadness*, *negative emotion*, *overall affect*, *verb*, and *past tense verb*. When a narrative contains the word "cried", the scale scores corresponding to these five subcategories are incremented. The final output for each narrative is a real value score for each of the 69 categories.

[1]See http://www.liwc.net

[2]See http://www.dictionsoftware.com

Because of the elaborate development of dictionaries and categories, LIWC has been used for predicting emotional and cognitive problems from subject's spoken and written samples. Representative applications include studying attention focus through personal pronouns, studying honesty and deception by emotion words and exclusive words and identifying thinking styles (Tausczik and Pennebaker, 2010). Thus it is reasonable to expect that LIWC derived features would be helpful in identifying schizophrenia patients. In Section 6.4 we discuss in more detail the features which turned out to be significantly different between patients and controls within LIWC.

4.2.2 Diction

We also use Diction to analyze the lexical characteristics of the transcripts. Similar to LIWC, Diction scores are computed with reference to manually compiled dictionaries. The master variable scores in Diction include *activity*, *certainty*, *commonality*, *optimism* and *realism*. These five main scores are computed with 33 dictionaries that define pertinent subcategories. The master variable scores are constructed as follows: $S_m = \sum_{i=1}^{n} a_i - \sum_{j=1}^{m} s_j$, where a_i are additive traits, s_j are subtractive traits (giving positive/negative evidence for the presence of the feature, respectively). For example, Certainty and Realism scores are calculated as follows:

Realism = *[Familiarity + Spatial Awareness + Temporal Awareness + Present Concern + Human Interest + Concreteness] - [Past Concern + Complexity]*

Certainty = *[Tenacity + Leveling + Collectives + Insistence] - [Numerical Terms + Ambivalence + Self Reference + Variety]*

We also give definitions for some important categories. The complete description of categories is available in the *Diction* manual (Hart, 2000).

Cognition: *Words referring to cerebral processes, both functional and imaginative.*

Satisfaction: *Terms associated with positive affective states.*

Insistence: *A measure of code-restriction and contentedness, with the assumption that the repetition of key terms indicates a preference for a limited, ordered world.*

Diversity: *Words describing individuals or groups of individuals differing from the norm.*

Familiarity: *Consisted of the most common words in English.*

Certainty: *Language indicating resoluteness, inflexibility, and completeness and a tendency to speak ex cathedra.*

Realism: *Language describing tangible, immediate, recognizable matters that affect people's everyday lives.*

4.3 Feature normalization

We use two feature normalization approaches: projection normalization and binary normalization. Both of the two approaches are applied to basic features, dictionary features and word features. As for repetition, we don't use normalization, because it is in itself binary. For transcript i, we denote the value of the jth feature as v_{ij}. We denote min_j, max_j, $average_j$ as the minimum, maximum and average value for each feature in the training corpus, respectively. Thus for each feature j, we have: $average_j = \frac{1}{n}\sum_{i=1}^{n} v_{ij}$ $\min_j = \min_i\{v_{ij}\}, \max_j = \max_i\{v_{ij}\}$.

4.3.1 Projection Normalization

Here we simply normalize all feature values to a range of $[0, 1]$, where 0 corresponds to the smallest observed value and 1 to the largest observed value across all transcripts. Then we could have $p_{ij} = \frac{v_{ij} - min_j}{max_j - min_j}$, where p_{ij} is the feature value after normalization.

4.3.2 Binary normalization

Here all features are converted to binary values, reflecting whether the value falls below or above the average value for that feature observed in training. The value p_{ij} of j-th feature for the i-th instance is as below:

$$p_{ij} = \begin{cases} 0 & v_{ij} < \frac{1}{n}\sum_{i=1}^{n} v_{ij} \\ 1 & \text{otherwise} \end{cases}$$

4.3.3 Prediction on the Test Set

All of the previous values, $average_j$, max_j and min_j are derived from the training set. While doing classification, for a new testing instance, we denote the feature vector as $f = (f_1, f_2, \ldots f_n)$.

f_j is then compared with $average_j$ to do binary normalization. We also use $p_j = \frac{f_j - min_j}{max_j - min_j}$ to do projection normalization. If $p_j < 0$, we change p_j into 0; if $p_j > 1$, we change p_j into 1. For the words or features that are not seen in training, we just ignore this dimension.

4.4 Feature selection

All lexically based analysis is plagued by data sparsity problems. In the medical domain this problem is even more acute because collecting patient data is difficult. The number of features we defined outnumbers our samples by orders of magnitude. Therefore, in our classification procedure, we perform feature selection by doing two-sided T-test to compare the values of features in the patient and control groups. The features with p-value ≤ 0.05 are considered as indicative and are selected for later machine learning experiments, in which 169 out of 6057 features have been selected. We discuss the significant features in the full set in Section 6.4 .

Note however that we don't use the features selected on the full dataset for machine learning experiments because when T-tests are applied on the full dataset feature selection decisions would include information about the test set as well. Therefore, we adopt a leave-one-subject-out (LOSO) evaluation approach instead. In each iteration, we set aside one subject as test set. The data from the remaining subjects form the training set. Feature selection is done on the training set only and a model is trained. The predictions are tested on the held out subject. The procedure is repeated for every subject as test set.

The choice of p-value cut-off allows us to relax and tighten the requirement on significance of the features and thus the size of the feature set. We report results with different p-values in Table 3. We also explore alternative feature ranking and feature selection procedures in Section 6.3. In each fold different features may be selected. For ease of discussing feature differences we present a discussion of the 169 significant features on the entire dataset.

5 Our approach

The goal of our system is to classify the person who told a story in one of two categories: Schizophrenia group (SC) and Control group (CO). In order to do this, we give labels to the stories told by each subject. Therefore we could use our model to identify the status of the person who told each individual story, the task is to answer the question "Was the subject who told this story a patient or control?". Then we combine the predictions for stories to predict status of each subject, and the task becomes answering the question "Is this subject a patient or control given that they told these five stories?". Thus in story level prediction we use no information about the fact that subjects told more than one story, while in subject-level prediction we do use this information.

First we present an experiment that relies only on language models for the prediction. Then we present the complete learning-based system that uses the full set of features. Finally, we describe the decision making approach to combine the story level predictions to derive a subject-level prediction.

5.1 Language Model

Language models have been used previously for language impairment on children (Gabani et al., 2009) and language dominance prediction (Solorio et al., 2011). Patients with speaking disorder or cognitive impairment express themselves in atypical ways. Language models (LMs) give a straightforward way of estimating the probability of the productions of a given subject. We expect that the approach would be useful for the study of schizophrenia as well and so start with a description of the LM experiments.

We use LMs on words to recognize the difference between patients and controls in vocabulary use. We also trained a LM on POS tags because it could reduce sparsity and focus more on grammatical patterns. Two separate LMs are trained on transcripts of schizophrenia and controls respectively, using leave-one-subject-out protocol.

Story-level decisions are made by assigning the class whose language model yields lower perplexity:

$$s(t) = \begin{cases} SC & PER_{SC}(t) \leq PER_{CO}(t) \\ CO & \text{otherwise} \end{cases}$$

by Story (%)	SC-F	CO-F	Accuracy	Macro-F
Random	54.4	44.6	50.0	49.5
Majority	74.8	0.0	59.7	37.4
2-gram	62.5	44.4	55.2	53.5
2-gram-Pos	62.2	53.3	58.2	57.8

by Subject (%)	SC-F	CO-F	Accuracy	Macro-F
Random	54.1	45.1	50.0	49.6
Majority	74.2	0.0	59.1	37.1
2-gram	65.2	50.0	58.9	57.6
2-gram-Pos	66.7	54.5	61.5	60.6

Table 2: Language model performance

Here t means a transcript from a subject, while PER_{SC} and PER_{CO} are perplexities for patients and controls, respectively. We experimented with unigram, bigram and trigram LMs on words and POS tags. Laplace smoothing is used when generating word probabilities.

5.2 Classification Phase

Language models are convenient because they summarize information from patterns in lexical and POS use into a single number. However, most of the successful applications of LMs require large amount of training data while our dataset is relatively small. Moreover, we would like to analyze more specific differences between the patient and control group and this would be more appropriately done using a larger set of features.

We have described our features and feature selection process in Section 4. We use SVM-light (Joachims, 1999) for our machine learning algorithm, as its effectiveness has been proved in various learning-based clinical tasks compared to other classifiers (Gabani et al., 2009) .

5.3 Status Decision

Story level predictions are made for each transcript either based on LM perplexity or SVM prediction. The most intuitive way to obtain a subject-level prediction is by voting from story-level predictions between the stories told by the particular subject. The subject-level prediction is simply set to equal the majority prediction from individual stories. On the few occasions where there are equal votes for schizophrenia and control, the system makes a preference towards schizophrenia, because it is more dangerous to omit a potential patient.

P-value cut-off	by Story	by Subject	# Features
0.15	59.0	58.9	450
0.10	61.7	64.1	341
0.05	62.7	**64.1**	169
0.01	57.7	**65.4**	44
0.005	64.2	**71.6**	32
0.001	65.7	**75.6**	18
0.0005	61.7	66.7	14

Table 3: Performance by subject after T-test feature selection in different confidence levels.

6 Experiments and Results

We perform our experiments on the 201 transcripts of the 39 speakers. The two baselines we compare with are doing random assignments and majority class, which for our datasets correspond to predicting all subjects into the Schizophrenia group.

We report precision, recall and F-measure for both patient and control groups, as well as overall accuracy and Macro-F value. We get predictions in leave-one-subject-out fashion and compute the results over the complete set of predictions.

6.1 Language Model Performance

Our first experiment relies only on the perplexity from language models to make the prediction. We use the 1,2,3-gram models on word and POS sequences. From the result in Table 2 we can see bigram LM performed better than random baseline for both story and subject level prediction. 3-gram and 1-gram LM did not give a credible performance, with results worse than that of the baselines. Because of space constraints we do not report the specific numbers.

6.2 Classification Result after Feature Selection

Next we evaluate the performance of classification with different number of features from the classes we define in Section 4. As discussed above, we performed feature selection by choosing different levels of significance for the p-value cut-off. Feature selection is performed 39 times for each LOSO training fold. On the standard cut-off p-value ≤ 0.05, our system could achieve 62.7% accuracy on story and 64.1% on patient level prediction. The best performance is achieved when the cut-off p-value is

	Measurement	Schizophrenia P (%)	Schizophrenia R (%)	Schizophrenia F (%)	Control P (%)	Control R (%)	Control F (%)	General Accuracy (%)	General Macro-F (%)
Story	Random	59.7	50.0	54.4	40.5	50.0	44.6	50.0	49.5
	Majority	59.7	100.0	74.8	NA	0.0	0.0 (NA)	59.7	37.4
	25-Features	68.7	75.0	71.7	57.1	49.4	52.9	64.7	62.3
Subject	Random	59.0	50.0	54.1	41.0	50.0	45.0	50.0	49.6
	Majority	59.0	100.0	74.2	NA	0.0	0.0 (NA)	59.0	37.1
	25-Features	**75.0**	**91.3**	**82.4**	81.8	56.3	66.7	**76.9**	**74.6**

Table 4: Performance on best feature-set by feature ranking using signal to noise

stricter, 0.001, where an accuracy of 75.6% can be reached. In this case only about 18 features are used for the classification. Detailed results are shown in Table 3.

6.3 Performance with Different Feature Size

Next we investigate the relationship between feature set size and accuracy of prediction. We are interested in identifying the smallest possible set of features which gives performance close to the one reported on the full set of significant features. Narrowing the feature set as much as possible will be most useful for clinicians as they understand the differences between the groups and look for indicators of the illness they need to track during regular patient visits. Physicians and psychologists are also interested to know the most significant lexical differences revealed by the stories.

As an alternative to ranking features by p-value, we use the Challenge Learning Object Package (CLOP) [3] (Guyon et al., 2006) . It is a toolkit with a combination of preprocessing and feature selection. We experiment with signal-to-noise (s2n), Gram-Schmidt orthogonalization and Recursive Feature Elimination for finding a subset of indicative features (Guyon and Elisseeff, 2003). The signal-to-noise method gives better results than the other two by at least 6% for the top performance feature set. Thus we pick the best k features according to the s2n result and use only those k features for classification.

Figure 1 shows how prediction accuracy changes with feature sets of different sizes. From the plot we clearly see that our top performance is achieved with 25 to 40 features, after which performance drops. The peak performance is achieved when

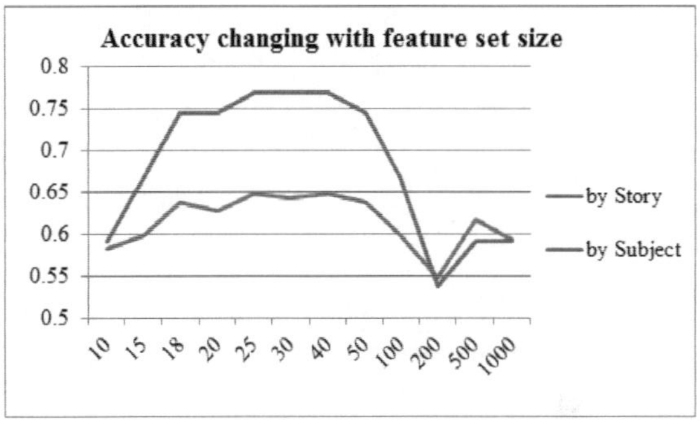

Figure 1: Story and Subject prediction accuracy

there are 25 features, where we could reach 75.0% precision, 91.3% recall, 82.4% F-measure for patient, and 76.9% accuracy for overall, as shown in Table 4. Detailed information about the top 30 features can be found in Table 5. '+' and '-' means more prevalent for patient and control, while '**prj**' and '**01**' correspond to the two normalization approaches in Section 4.3, projection and binary respectively.

6.4 Analysis of Significant Features

In this section we discuss the specific features that were revealed as most predictive by the feature selection methods that we employed. We have seen that it only requires about 25-40 features to obtain peak performance.

First we briefly review the features that turned out to be statistically significant (for 0.05 p-value cut-off). Table 7 provides a list of the features with higher values for Schizophrenia and Control respectively. [4] We group the significant features according to the feature classes we introduced in

[3] See http://clopinet.com/CLOP/

[4] LM1 is defined as the ratio of CO perplexity and SC perplexity from LMs, LM7 comes from projection normalization of LM1. If LM perplexity for CO is smaller than that of SC, then we set LM3 as 1; otherwise we set LM4 as 1.

Rank	Feature	Category	P-value
1	Prj-Self +	Diction	5.33E-06
2	01-Self +	Diction	7.34E-06
3	Prj-punctuation -	Basic	1.33E-05
4	01-I +	LIWC	2.73E-05
5	01-sorry -	Lexical	0.007
6	01-money +	Lexical	6.95E-05
7	01-punctuation -	Basic	4.88E-05
8	prj-I +	LIWC	5.12E-05
9	01-extremely +	Lexical	5.10E-05
10	prj-mildly +	Lexical	0.0006
11	prj-sorry -	Lexical	0.011
12	prj-I +	Lexical	0.0002
13	LM1 +	LM	0.0002
14	LM7 +	LM	0.0002
15	I +	Repeat	0.0003

Rank	Feature	Category	P-value
16	and +	Repeat	0.0002
17	01-mildly +	Lexical	0.0004
18	prj-adverb -	LIWC	0.0006
19	01-relationship -	Lexical	0.024
20	01-late -	Lexical	0.024
21	prj-comma -	Lexical	0.001
22	Repeat word -	Basic	0.001
23	prj-late -	Lexical	0.034
24	prj-very -	Lexical	0.007
25	prj-extremely +	Lexical	0.001
26	01-couldn't +	Lexical	0.001
27	prj-relationship -	Lexical	0.037
28	very -	Repeat	0.007
29	prj-? +	Lexical	0.002
30	prj-moderately +	Lexical	0.006

Table 5: Table of the top 30 features by signal-to-noise ranking

Section 4. Of the 169 significant features, 111 are more prevalent in patients, 58 are more prevalent among the controls. If a feature was significant with both normalizations we use, we list it only once in Table 7.

Among the words indicative of schizophrenia, subjective words such as *I* and LIWC category *self* are among the most significant. This finding conforms with prior research that patients with mental disorders refer to themselves more often than regular people. Patients produce more questions (as indicated by the significance of the question mark as a feature). It is possible that this indicates a disruption in their thought process and they forget what they are talking about. Further work will be needed to understand this difference better.

In terms of words, patients talked more about *money*, *trouble*, and used adverbs like *moderately* and *basically*. Repetition in language is also a revealing characteristic of the patient narratives. There is a substantial difference in the appearance of repetitions between the two groups, as well as repetition of specific words: *I*, *and*, and repetition of filled pauses *um*. As patients focus more on their own feelings, they talked a lot about their family, using words such as *son*, *grandfather* and even *dogs*.

Diction features revealed some unexpected differences. The schizophrenia group scores higher in the *Self*, *Cognition*, *Past*, *Insistence* and *Satisfaction* categories. This indicates that they are more likely to talk about past experience, using cognitive terms and having a repetition of key terms. We were particularly curious to understand why patients score higher on *Satisfaction* ratings. On closer inspection we discovered that patients' stories were rated higher in *Satisfaction* when they were telling SAD stories. This finding has important clinical implications because one of the diagnostic elements for the disease is inappropriate emotion expression. Our study is the first to apply an automatic measure to detect such anomaly in patients' emotional narratives. Prompted by this discovery, we take a closer look at the interaction between the emotion expressed in a story and the accuracy of status prediction in the next section.

The control group exhibited more word complexity, sentence complexity and thoughtfulness in their stories. They use more adverbs and exclusive words (e.g. but, without, exclude) on general trend. They use the word *sorry* significantly more often than patients.

6.5 Status Prediction by Emotion

We also investigate if classification accuracy differs depending on the type of conveyed emotion. Accuracy per emotion with three feature selection methods is shown in Table 6. When using signal-to-noise, we can see that on SAD stories the two groups can be distinguished better. Story-level accuracies on HAPPY stories reach 72.5%, and that the accuracy on HAPPY stories is the next highest one. When applying the 0.05 p-value cut-off to select significant features, ANGER stories become the ones for which the status of a subject

Accuracy (%)	s2n (25)	T-test (0.05)	T-test (0.001)
Happy	66.7	59.0	**71.8**
Disgust	63.4	61.0	51.2
Anger	61.0	**70.7**	**70.7**
Fear	60.0	55.0	67.5
Sad	**72.5**	60.0	67.5
Story	64.7	62.9	65.7
Patient	76.9	64.1	74.4
Majority	59.0	59.0	59.0

Table 6: Accuracy per emotion by different feature-sets

can be predicted most accurately. Using the threshold of 0.001 for selection gives the best overall prediction. In that case, HAPPY and ANGER are the emotions for which recognition is best. The changes in the recognition accuracy depending on feature selection suggests that in future studies it may be more beneficial to perform feature selection only on stories from a given type because obviously indicative features exist at least for the SAD, ANGER and HAPPY stories.

Regardless of the feature selection approach, it is more difficult to tell the two groups apart when they tell DISGUST and FEAR stories. These results seem to indicate that when talking about certain emotions patients and controls look much more alike than when other emotions are concerned. Future data acquisition efforts can focus only on collecting autobiographical narratives relevant to the emotions for which patients and controls differ most.

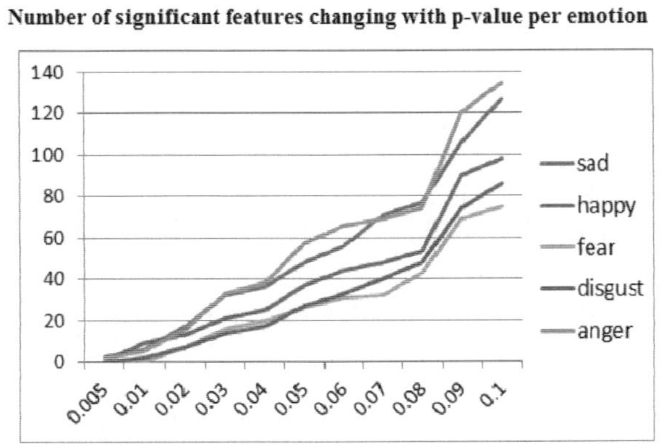

Figure 2: Number of significant features by P-value selection on different thresholds (per emotion)

In future work we would like to use only stories from a given emotion to classify between patients and controls. Doing this with our current dataset is not feasible because there are only about 40 transcripts per emotion. Therefore, we use our data to identify significant features that distinguish patients from controls only on narratives from a particular emotion. For example, we compare the differences of SAD stories told by patients and controls. We count the number of significant features between patients and controls with 11 different p-value cut-offs, and provide a plot that visualizes the results in Figure 2. From the graph, it is clear that there are many more differences between the two groups in ANGER and SAD narratives. HAPPY comes next, then DISGUST and FEAR. However, at lower confidence levels, HAPPY has equal number of significant features as ANGER and SAD, which is in line with the result in Table 6.

The feature analysis performed by emotion reveals more differences between patients and controls, beyond common features such as *self*, *I*, etc. For HAPPY stories, patients talk more about their *friends* and *relatives*; they also have a

Types	Significant features more common in **SCH**
Basic	repeat-word, sentence/document
LIWC	I, insight, personal-pronoun
Diction	self, cognition, past, insistence, satisfaction
Lexical	?, ain't, alone, at, aw, become, before, behind care, chance, confused, couldn't, December, dog dogs, extreme, extremely, feeling, forty, friends god, got, grandfather, guess, guy, hand, hanging hearing, hundred, increased, looking, loved mental, met, mild, mildly, moderate, moderately money, my, myself, outside, paper, passed, piece remember, sister, son, stand, step, story, take taken, throwing, took, trouble, use, wake wanna, way
Repeat	a, and, I, um, was
LM	LM1, LM4, LM7

Types	Significant features more common in **CO**
Basic	length/word, words/sentence
LIWC	≥6-letters, adverb, exclusive words, inhibitive
Diction	certainty, cooperation, diversity familiarity, realism
Lexical	",", able, actually, are, basically, be, being, get's in, late, not, really, relationship, result, she's sleep, sorry, tell, their, there's, very, weeks
Repeat	very, ","
LM	LM3

Table 7: Significant features (p-value ≤ 0.05)

higher tendency of being *ambivalent*. For DISGUST stories, patients are more disgusted with *dogs*, and they talk more about *health*. The control group shows a higher *communication* score, referring to a better social interaction. ANGER is one of the emotions that best reveals the differences between groups, and schizophrenia patients show more *aggression* and *cognition* while talking, according to features derived from Diction. The control group sometimes talks more about *praise*. In FEAR stories patients talk about *money* more often than controls. Meanwhile, the control group uses more *inhibition* words, for instance: block, constrain and stop. An interesting phenomenon happens in SAD narratives. When talking about sad experiences, patients sometimes show *satisfaction* and *insistence*, while the controls talked more about *working* experiences.

7 Conclusion

In this paper, we analyzed the predictive power of different kinds of features for distinguishing schizophrenia patients from healthy controls. We provided an in-depth analysis of features that distinguish patients from controls and showed that the type of emotion conveyed by the personal narratives is important for the distinction and that stories for different emotions give different sets indicators for subject status. We report classification results as high as 76.9% on the subject level, with 75.0% precision and 91.3% on recall for schizophrenia patients.

We consider the results presented here to be a pilot study. We are currently collecting and transcribing additional stories from the two groups which we would like to use as a definitive test set to verify the stability of our findings. We plan to explore syntactic and coherence models to analyze the stories, as well as emotion analysis of the narratives.

References

Nancy C. Andreasen. 1986. Scale for the assessment of thought, language, and communication (TLC). *Schizophrenia Bulletin*, 12:473 – 482.

Michael A. Covington, Congzhou He, Cati Brown, Lorina Naci, Jonathan T. McClain, Bess Sirmon Fjordbak, James Semple, and John Brown. 2005. Schizophrenia and the structure of language: The linguist's view. *Schizophrenia Research*, 77(1):85 – 98.

Roddy Cowie. 2000. Describing the emotional states expressed in speech. In *Proceedings of the ISCA Workshop on Speech and Emotion*.

Keyur Gabani, Melissa Sherman, Thamar Solorio, Yang Liu, Lisa Bedore, and Elizabeth Peña. 2009. A corpus-based approach for the prediction of language impairment in monolingual english and spanish-english bilingual children. In *Proceedings of HLT-NAACL*, pages 46–55.

Alastair J. Gill, Jon Oberlander, and Elizabeth Austin. 2006. Rating e-mail personality at zero acquaintance. *Personality and Individual Differences*, 40(3):497 – 507.

Alastair J. Gill, Scott Nowson, and Jon Oberlander. 2009. What are they blogging about? personality, topic and motivation in blogs. In *Proceedings of the AAAI ICWSM'09*.

Isabelle Guyon and André Elisseeff. 2003. An introduction to variable and feature selection. *J. Mach. Learn. Res.*, 3:1157–1182, March.

Isabelle Guyon, Jiwen Li, Theodor Mader, Patrick A. Pletscher, Georg Schneider, and Markus Uhr. 2006. Feature selection with the CLOP package. Technical report, http://clopinet.com/isabelle/Projects/ETH/TM-fextract-class.pdf.

Rodrick Hart. 2000. Diction 5.0, the text-analysis program user's manual, Scolari Software, Sage Press. http://www.dictionsoftware.com/.

Peter A. Heeman, Rebecca Lunsford, Ethan Selfridge, Lois M. Black, and Jan P. H. van Santen. 2010. Autism and interactional aspects of dialogue. In *Proceedings of the SIGDIAL 2010 Conference*, pages 249–252.

T. Joachims. 1999. Making large–scale SVM learning practical. In B. Schölkopf, C. J. C. Burges, and A. J. Smola, editors, *Advances in Kernel Methods — Support Vector Learning*, pages 169–184, Cambridge, MA. MIT Press.

F. Mairesse, M. A. Walker, M. R. Mehl, and R. K. Moore. 2007. Using Linguistic Cues for the Automatic Recognition of Personality in Conversation and Text. *Journal of Artificial Intelligence Research*, 30:457–500.

Theo C. Manschreck, Brendan A. Maher, Toni M. Hoover, and Donna Ames. 1985. Repetition in schizophrenic speech. *Language & Speech*, 28(3):255 – 268.

J.W. Pennebaker, R.J. Booth, and Francis. 2007. Linguistic inquiry and word count (LIWC

2007): A text analysis program. Austin, Texas. http://www.liwc.net/.

James W. Pennebaker. 1997. Writing about Emotional Experiences as a Therapeutic Process. *Psychological Science*, 8(3):162–166.

Emily T. Prud'hommeaux, Brian Roark, Lois M. Black, and Jan van Santen. 2011. Classification of atypical language in autism. In *Proceedings of the 2nd Workshop on Cognitive Modeling and Computational Linguistics*, CMCL'11, pages 88–96.

Brian Roark, Margaret Mitchell, John-Paul Hosom, Kristy Hollingshead, and Jeffrey Kaye. 2011. Spoken language derived measures for detecting mild cognitive impairment. *IEEE Transactions on Audio, Speech & Language Processing*, 19(7):2081–2090.

Stephanie Rude, Eva-Maria Gortner, and James Pennebaker. 2004. Language use of depressed and depression-vulnerable college students. *Cognition & Emotion*, 18(8):1121–1133.

Thamar Solorio, Melissa Sherman, Y. Liu, Lisa Bedore, Elizabeth Peña, and A. Iglesias. 2011. Analyzing language samples of spanish-english bilingual children for the automated prediction of language dominance. *Natural Language Engineering*, 17(3):367–395.

Yla R. Tausczik and James W. Pennebaker. 2010. The Psychological Meaning of Words: LIWC and Computerized Text Analysis Methods. *Journal of Language and Social Psychology*, 29(1):24–54, March.

Kristina Toutanova, Dan Klein, and Christopher D. Manning. 2003. Feature-rich part-of-speech tagging with a cyclic dependency network. In *Proceedings of HLT-NAACL 03*.

Streaming Analysis of Discourse Participants

Benjamin Van Durme
Human Language Technology Center of Excellence
Johns Hopkins University

Abstract

Inferring attributes of discourse participants has been treated as a *batch*-processing task: data such as all tweets from a given author are gathered in bulk, processed, analyzed for a particular feature, then reported as a result of academic interest. Given the sources and scale of material used in these efforts, along with potential use cases of such analytic tools, discourse analysis should be reconsidered as a *streaming* challenge. We show that under certain common formulations, the batch-processing analytic framework can be decomposed into a sequential series of updates, using as an example the task of gender classification. Once in a streaming framework, and motivated by large data sets generated by social media services, we present novel results in approximate counting, showing its applicability to space efficient streaming classification.

1 Introduction

The rapid growth in social media has led to an equally rapid growth in the desire to mine it for useful information: the content of public discussions, such as found in tweets, or in posts to online forums, can support a variety of data mining tasks. Inferring the underlying properties of those that engage with these platforms, the *discourse participants*, has become an active topic of research: predicting individual attributes such as age, gender, and political preferences (Rao et al., 2010), or relationships *between* communicants, such as organizational dominance (Diehl et al., 2007). This research can benefit areas such as: (A) commercial applications, e.g., improved models for advertising placement, or detecting fraudulent or otherwise unhelpful product reviews (Jindal and Liu, 2008; Ott et al., 2011); and (B) in enhanced models of civic discourse, e.g., inexpensive, large-scale, *passive polling* of popular opinion (O'Connor et al., 2010).

Classification with streaming data has usually been taken in the computational linguistics community to mean individual decisions made on items that are presented over time. For example: assigning a label to each newly posted product review as to whether it contains positive or negative sentiment, or whether the latest tweet signals a novel topic that should be tagged for tracking (Petrovic et al., 2010).

Here we consider a distinct form of stream-based classification: we wish to assign, then *dynamically update*, labels on discourse participants based on their associated streaming communications. For instance, rather than classifying individual reviews as to their sentiment polarity, we might wish to classify the underlying author as to whether they are genuine or paid-advertising, and then update that decision as they continue to post new reviews. As the scale of social media continues to grow, we desire that our model be aggressively space efficient, which precludes a naive solution of storing the full communication history for all users.

In this paper we make two contributions: (1) we make explicit that a standard bag-of-words classification model for predicting latent author attributes can be simply decomposed into a series of streaming updates; then (2) show how the randomized algorithm, *Reservoir Counting* (Van Durme and Lall, 2011), can be extended to maintain approximate averages, allowing for significant space savings in our classification model. Our running example task is gender prediction, based on spoken communication and microblogs/Twitter feeds.

2 Model

Assume that each discourse participant (e.g., speaker, author) a has an associated stream of communications (e.g., tweets, utterances, emails, etc.): $(c_i) = C$. Then let $C_t = (c_1, ..., c_t)$ represent the first t elements of C.

Assume access to a pretrained classifier Φ:[1]

$$\Phi(a) = \begin{cases} 1 & \text{if } w \cdot f(C) \geq 0, \\ 0 & \text{otherwise,} \end{cases}$$

which we initially take to be linear: author labels are determined by computing the sign of the dot product between a weight vector w, and feature vector $f(C)$, each of dimension d. Note that $f(C)$ is a feature vector over the entire set of communications from a given author.

For example, Φ might be trained to classify author gender:

$$\texttt{Gender}(a) = \begin{cases} \texttt{Male} & \text{if } w \cdot f(C) \geq 0, \\ \texttt{Female} & \text{otherwise.} \end{cases}$$

We now make explicit how under certain common restrictions on the feature space, the classification decision can be decomposed into a series of decision *updates* over the elements of C.

Define $\hat{f}(c_i)$ to be the vector containing the local, count-based feature values of communication c_j.[2] For convenience let us assume that $\hat{f}(c_i) \in \mathbb{N}^d$. Where $|v|_1 = \sum_i |v_i|$ is the L1-norm of vector v, let z_t be the *normalizing constant* at t:

$$z_t = \sum_{i=1}^{t} |\hat{f}(c_i)|_1$$

Now define $f_j(C)$, the j-th entry of $f(C)$, as:

$$f_j(C) = \frac{\sum_{i=1}^{n} \hat{f}_j(c_i)}{z_n}$$

Thus $f(C)$ represents the global relative frequency of each local, count-based feature. This allows us to rearrange terms:

$$\begin{aligned} w \cdot f(C) &= \sum_{j=1}^{d} w_j f_j(C) \\ &= \frac{1}{z_n} \sum_{j=1}^{d} w_k (\sum_{i=1}^{n} \hat{f}_j(c_i)) \\ &= \frac{1}{z_n} \sum_{i=1}^{n} (\sum_{j=1}^{d} w_k \hat{f}_j(c_i)) \end{aligned}$$

Let (s_t, z_t) be the current *state* of the classifier:

$$(s_t, z_t) \doteq (\sum_{i=1}^{t} \sum_{k=1}^{d} w_k \hat{f}_k(c_j), z_t)$$

which pairs the observed *rolling sum*, s_t with the feature stream length z_t.

The classifier decision after seeing everything up to and including communication c_t is thus a simple average:

$$\Phi_t(a) = \begin{cases} 1 & \text{if } \frac{s_t}{z_t} \geq 0, \\ 0 & \text{otherwise.} \end{cases}$$

Finally we reach the observation that:

$$\begin{aligned} s_t &= s_{t-1} + w \cdot \hat{f}(c_t) \\ z_t &= z_{t-1} + |\hat{f}(c_t)|_1 \end{aligned}$$

which means that from an engineering standpoint we can process a stream of communication one element at a time, without the need to preserve the history explicitly. That is: for each author, for each attribute being analyzed, an online system only need maintain a state pair (s_t, z_t) by extracting and weighting features locally for each new communication. Beyond the computational savings of not needing to store communications nor explicit feature vectors in memory, there are potential privacy benefits as well: analytic systems need not have a lasting record of discourse, they can instead glean whatever signal is required locally in the stream, and then discard the actual communications.

Log-linear Rather than a strictly linear Φ, such as instantiated via perceptron or SVM with linear kernel, many prefer log-linear models as their classification framework:

$$\Phi(a) = \begin{cases} 1 & \text{if } \frac{1}{1+\exp(-w \cdot f(C))} \geq 0.5, \\ 0 & \text{otherwise.} \end{cases}$$

[1] While here we assume binary decision tasks, dynamic classification in a multiclass, or regression, setting is an interesting avenue of exploration, for which these definitions generalize.

[2] As seen later in Table 1, we have in mind features such as the frequency of the n-gram *my wife*.

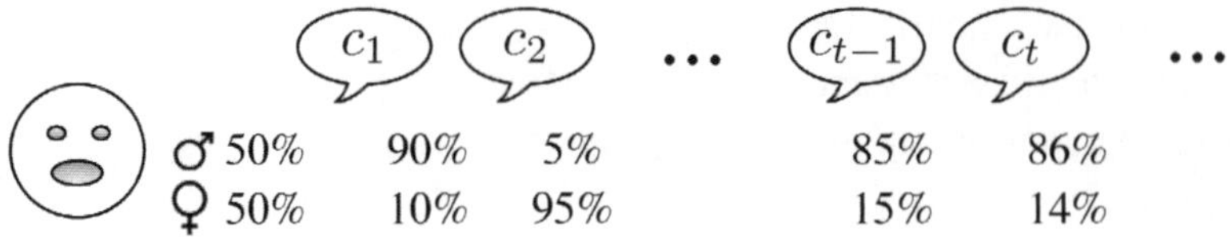

Figure 1: A streaming analytic model should update its decision with each new communication, becoming more stable in its prediction as evidence is acquired.

In either setting, the state of the classifier is sufficiently captured by the pair (s_t, z_t), under the restrictions on f.[3]

2.1 Validation

As an example of a model decomposed into a stream, we revist the task of gender classification based on speech transcripts, as explored by Boulis and Ostendorf (2005) and later Garera and Yarowsky (2009). In the original problem definition, one would collect all transcribed utterances from a given speaker in a corpus such as Fisher (Cieri et al., 2004) or Switchboard (Godfrey et al., 1992), known as a *side* of the conversation. Then by collapsing these utterances into a single document, one could classify it as to whether it was generated by a male or female. Here we define the task as: starting from scratch, report the classifier probability of the speaker being male, as each utterance is presented.

Intuitively we would expect that as more utterances are observed, the better our classification accuracy. Researchers such as Burger et al. (2011) have considered this point, but by comparing the classification accuracy based on the volume of batch data available per author (in that case, tweets): the more prolific the author had been, the better able they were to correctly classify their gender. We confirm here this can be reframed: as a speaker (author) continues to emit a stream of communication, a dynamic model tends to improve its online prediction.

Our collection based on Switchboard consisted of 520 unique speakers (240 female, 280 male), with a total of roughly 400k utterances. Similar to Boulis and Ostendorf, we extracted unigram and bigram counts as features, but without further TFIDF reweighting. Ngrams were required to occur at least 10 times in the training set, recomputed for each split of 10-fold cross validation. Weights were computed under a log-linear model using `LibLinear` (Fan et al., 2008), with 5% of training held out for tuning an L2 regularizing term. Feature extraction and dynamic aspects were handled through additions to the `Jerboa` package (Van Durme, 2012). Similar to previous work, we found intuitive features such as *my husband* to be weighted heavily (see Table 1), along with certain non-lexical vocalizations such as transcribed laughter.

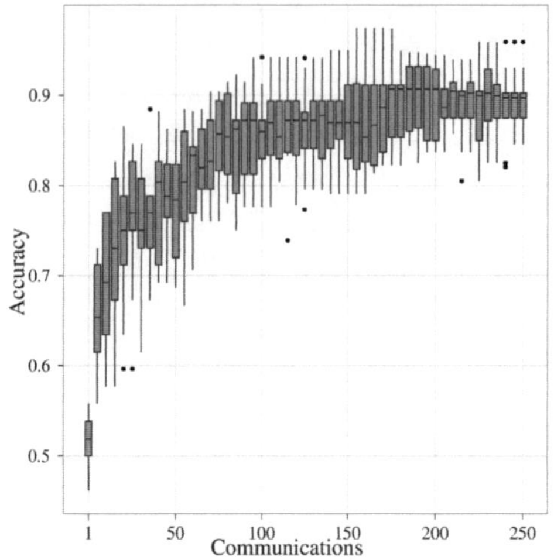

Figure 2: Accuracy on Switchboard gender classification, reported at every fifth utterance, using a dynamic log-linear model with 10-fold cross validation.

Table 1: Top ten features by gender.

Male	a, wife, is, my wife, right, of, the, uh, actually, [vocalized-noise]
Female	have, and, [laughter], my husband, really, husband, children, are, would

[3]Note that some non-linear kernels can be maintained online in a similar fashion. For instance, a polynomial kernel of degree p decomposes as: $(f(C_n) \cdot w)^p = (\frac{s_n}{z_n})^p$.

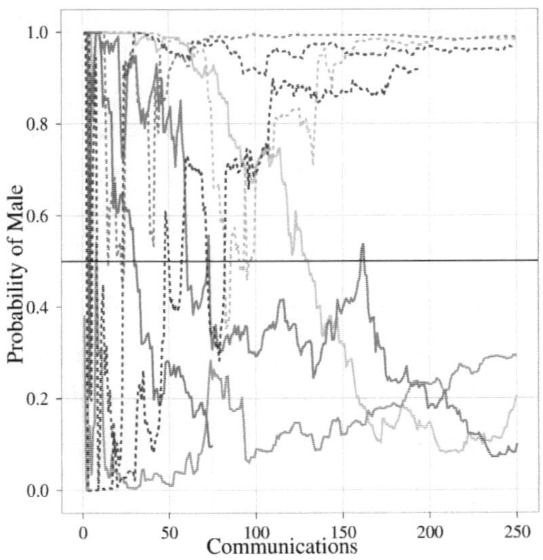

Figure 3: Streaming analysis of eight randomly sampled speakers, four per gender (red-solid: female, blue-dashed: male). Being a log-linear model, the decision boundary is marked at $y = 0.5$.

As seen in Figure 2, accuracy indeed improves as more content is emitted. Figure 3 highlights the streaming perspective: individual speakers can be viewed as distinct trajectories through $[0, 1]$, based on features of their utterances.

3 Randomized Model

Now situated within a streaming context we exact space savings through approximation, extending the approach of Van Durme and Lall (2011), there concerned with online Locality Sensitive Hashing, here initially concerned with taking averages.

When calculating the average over a sequence of values, $X_n = (x_1, ..., x_n)$, we divide the sum of the sequence, $\text{sum}(X_n) = \sum_{i=1}^{n} x_i$, by its length, $\text{length}(X_n) = |X_n|$:

$$\text{avg}(X_n) = \frac{\text{sum}(X_n)}{\text{length}(X_n)}$$

Our goal in this section is to maintain a space efficient approximation of $\text{avg}(X_t)$, as t increases, by using a bit-saving approximation of both the sum, and the length of the sequence.

We begin by reviewing the method of Reservoir Counting, then extend it to a new notion we refer to as Reservoir Averaging. This will allow in the subsequent section to map our analytic model to a form

Figure 4: Social media platforms such as Facebook or Twitter deal with a very large number of individuals, each with a variety of implicit attributes (such as gender). This motivates a desire for online space efficiency.

explicitly amenable to keeping an online average.

3.1 Reservoir Counting

Reservoir Counting plays on the folklore algorithm of reservoir sampling, first described in the literature by Vitter (1985). As applied to a stream of arbitrary elements, reservoir sampling maintains a list (reservoir) of length k, where the contents of the reservoir represents a uniform random sample over all elements $1...t$ observed thus far in the stream.

When the stream is a sequence of positive and negative integers, reservoir counting implicitly views each value as being unrolled into a sequence made up of either 1 or -1. For instance, the sequence: (3, **-2**, 1) would be viewed as:

(1, 1, 1, **-1**, **-1**, 1)

Since there are only two distinct values in this stream, the contents of the reservoir can be characterized by knowing the fixed value k, and then s: how many elements in the reservoir are 1.[4] This led to Van Durme and Lall defining a method, `ReservoirUpdate`, here abbreviated to `ResUp`, that allows for maintaining an approximate sum, defined as $t(\frac{2s}{k} - 1)$, through updating these two parameters t and s with each newly observed element. Expected accuracy of the approximation varies with the size of the sample, k. Reservoir Counting exploits the fact that the reservoir need only be considered implicitly, where s represented as a b-bit unsigned integer can be used to characterize a reservoir of size $k = 2^b - 1$. This allowed those authors to show a 50% space reduction in the task of online

[4]As the number of -1 values is simply: $k - s$.

Locality Sensitive Hashing, at similar levels of accuracy, by replacing explicit 32-bit counting variables with approximate counters of smaller size. See (Van Durme and Lall, 2011) for further details.

3.2 Reservoir Averaging

For a given integer x, let $m = |x|$ be the magnitude of x, and $\sigma = \text{sign}(x)$. For a given sequence, let m^* be the largest such value of m.

Modifying the earlier implicit construction, consider the sequence (3, **-2**, 1), with $m^* = 3$, mapped to the sequence:

(1, 1, 1, 1, 1, 1, **-1**, **-1**, **-1**, **-1**, **-1**, **1**, 1, 1, 1, 1, -1, -1)

where each value x is replaced with $m^* + m$ elements of σ, and $m^* - m$ elements of $-\sigma$. This views x as a sequence of length $2m^*$, made up of 1s and -1s, where each x in the discrete range $[-m^*, m^*]$ has a unique number of 1s.

Now recognize that the average over the original sequence, here $\frac{3-2+1}{3} = \frac{2}{3}$, is proportional to the average over the implicit sequence, $\frac{1+1+...-1-1}{18} = \frac{4}{18} = \frac{2}{3}(\frac{1}{m^*})$.

Generally for a sequence $(x_1, ..., x_n)$, with m^* as defined, the average times $\frac{1}{m^*}$ is equal to:

$$\frac{\sum_{i=1}^{n} x_i}{n}\left(\frac{1}{m^*}\right) = \frac{1}{n2m^*}\sum_{i=1}^{n}\left(\sum_{l=1}^{m^*+m_i}\sigma_i + \sum_{l=1}^{m^*-m_i} -\sigma_i\right)$$
$$= \frac{\sum_{i=1}^{n} m_i \sigma}{nm^*}$$

where $n2m^*$ is the total number of 1s and -1s observed in the implicit stream, up to and including the mapping of element x_n. If applying Reservoir Counting, s would then record the sampled number of 1s, as per norm, where t maintained as the implicit stream length can also be viewed as storing $t = n2m^*$. At any point in the stream, the average over the original value sequence can then be approximated as: (1) the approximate sum of the implicit stream; divided by (2) the implicit stream length; times (3) m^* to cancel the $\frac{1}{m^*}$ term:

$$\left(t\left(\frac{2s}{k} - 1\right)\right)_1 \left(\frac{1}{t}\right)_2 (m^*)_3 = \left(\frac{2s}{k} - 1\right)m^*$$

Granularity As defined this scheme operates on streams of integers. We extend the definition to work with a stream of fixed precision floating point variables. Let g be a positive integer that we refer to as the *granularity*. Modify the mapping of value x from a sequence of length $2m^*$, to a sequence of length g, comprised of $\frac{m^*+m}{2m^*}g$ instances of σ, and $(1 - \frac{m^*-m}{2m^*})g$ instances of -σ. As seen in line 4 of Algorithm 1, a random coin flip determines placement of the remainder.

For example, the value 1.3, with $m^* = 3$, and $g = 10$, would now be represented as a sequence of $\frac{3+1.3}{6}g = 7.16 \in (7, 8)$ instances of 1, followed by however many instances of -1 that lead to a sequence of length g, after probabilistic rounding. The possible sequences are thus:

(1, 1, 1, 1, 1, 1, 1, -1, -1, -1)
(1, 1, 1, 1, 1, 1, 1, 1, -1, -1)

with the former more likely.

At this point we have described the framework captured by Algorithm 1, where Van Durme and Lall (2011) defined `ResUp`.

Algorithm 1 UPDATEAVERAGE$(n, k, m, m^*, \sigma, g, s)$

Parameters:
n : size of stream
k : size of reservoir, also maximum value of s
m : magnitude of update
m^* : maximum magnitude of all updates
σ : sign of update
g : granularity
s : current value of reservoir

1: **if** $m = 0$ or $\sigma = 0$ **then**
2: Return without doing anything
3: $v := \frac{m+m^*}{2m^*}g$
4: $v := \lceil v \rceil$ with probability $v - \lfloor v \rfloor$, $\lfloor v \rfloor$ otherwise
5: $s' :=$ ResUp(ng, k, v, σ, s)
6: $s' :=$ ResUp$((ng + v), k, g - v, -\sigma, s')$
7: Return s'

Log-scale Counting For additional space savings we might approximate the length parameter t with a small bit representation, using the approximate counting scheme of Morris (1978). The method enables counting in log-scale by probabilistically incrementing a counter, where it becomes less and less likely to update the counter after each increment. This scheme is popularly known and used in a variety of contexts, recently in the community by Talbot (2009) and Van Durme and Lall (2009)

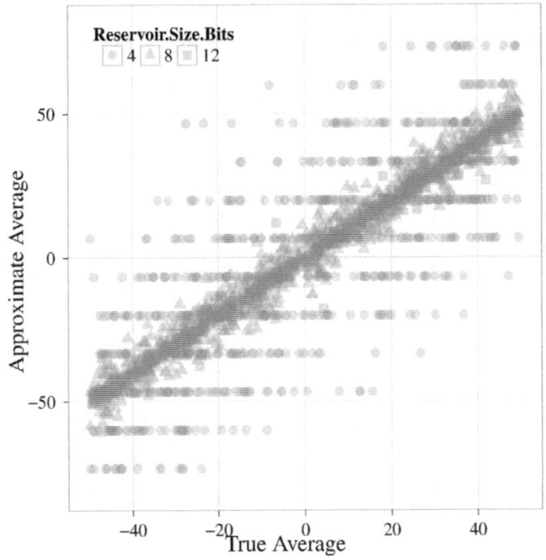

Figure 5: Results on averaging randomly generated sequences, with $m^* = 100, g = 100$, and using an 8 bit Morris-style counter of base 2. Larger reservoir sizes lead to better approximation, at higher cost in bits.

to provide a streaming extension to the Bloom-filter based count-storage mechanism of Talbot and Osborne (2007a) and Talbot and Osborne (2007b). See (Flajolet, 1985) for a detailed analysis of Morris-style counting.

3.3 Experiment

We show through experimentation on synthetic data that this approach gives reasonable levels of accuracy at space efficient sizes of the length and sum parameter. Random sequences of 1,000 values were generated by: (1) fix a value for m^*; (2) draw a polarity bias term μ uniformly from the range [0,1]; then (3) for each value, x: (a) σ was positive with probability μ; (b) m was drawn from [0, m^*]. Figure 5 shows results for varying reservoir sizes (using 4, 8 or 12 bits) when $g = 100$, $m^* = 100$, and the length parameter was represented with an 8 bit Morris-style counter of base 2.

3.4 Justification

Before we close this section, one might ask why this extension is needed in the first place. As Reservoir Counting already allows for keeping an online sum, and pairs it with a length parameter, then this would presumably be what is needed to get the average we are focussed on. Unfortunately that is not the case: the parameter recording the current stream length, here called t, tracks the length of the implicit stream of 1s and -1s, it does not track the length of the original stream of values that gave rise to the mapped version. As an example, consider again the sequence: (3, -2, 1), as compared to: (2,1,-1,-1,1). Both have the same sum, and would therefore be viewed the same under the pre-existing Reservoir Counting algorithm, giving rise to implicit streams of the same length. But critically the sequences have different averages: $\frac{2}{3} \neq \frac{2}{5}$, which we cannot detect based on the original counting algorithm.

Finally, we restate the constraint: for the sequence to averaged, one must know m^* ahead of time.

4 Application to Classification

Going back to our streaming analysis model, we have a situation that can be viewed as a sequence of values, such that we do know m^*. First reinterpret the fraction $\frac{s_t}{z_t}$ equivalently as the normalized sum of a stream of elements sampled from w:

$$\frac{s_t}{z_t} = \frac{1}{z_t} \sum_{i=1}^{t} \sum_{j=1}^{d} \sum_{l=1}^{\hat{f}_j(c_i)} w_j$$

The value m^* is then: $m^* = \max_j |w_j|$, over a sequence of length z_t. Rather than updating s_t and z_t through basic addition, we can now use a smaller bit-wise representation for each variable, and update via Reservoir Averaging.

4.1 Problems in Practice

Reconsidering the earlier classification experiment, we found this approximation method led to terrible results: while our experiments on synthetic data worked well, those sequences were sampled somewhat uniformly over the range of possible values. As seen in Figure 6, sequences arising from observed feature weights in a practical setting may not be so broadly distributed. In brief: the more the maximum possible update, m^*, can be viewed as an outlier, then the more the resulting implicit encoding of g elements per observed weight becomes dominated by "filler". As few observed elements will in that case require the provided range, then the implicit representation will be a mostly balanced set of

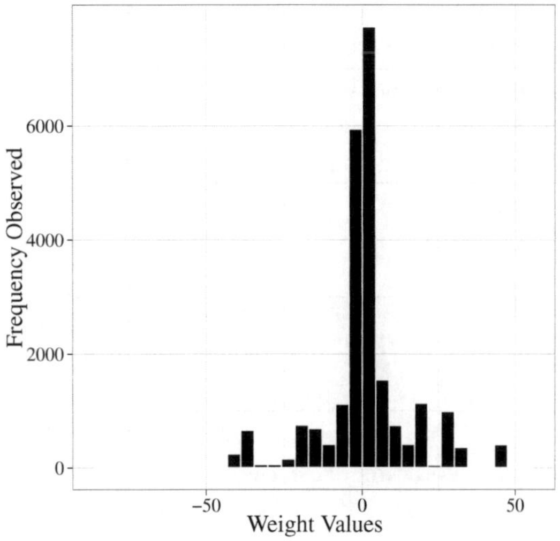

Figure 6: Frequency of individual feature weights observed over a full set of communications by a single example speaker. Most observed features have relatively small magnitude weight. The mean value is 1.3, with $\frac{1}{1+e^{-1.3}} = 0.79 > 0.5$, which properly classifies the speaker as MALE.

1 and -1 values. These mostly balanced encodings make it difficult to maintain an adequate approximation of the true average, when reliant on a small, implicit uniform sample. Here we leave further analysis aside, focusing instead on a modified solution for the classification model under consideration.

4.2 Rewriting History

Practically we would like to restrict our range to the dense region of weight updates, while at the same time not throwing away or truncating larger weights that appear outside a reduced window. We do this by fitting a replacement to m^*: $m' \leq m^*$, based on the classifier's training data, such that too-large elements will be *accommodated* into the stream by implicitly assuming that the portion of a value that falls outside the restricted window is "spread out" over the previously observed values. That is, we modify the contents of the implicit reservoir by *rewriting history*: pretending that earlier elements were larger than they were, but still within the reduced window. As long as we don't see too many values that are overly large, then there will be room to accommodate the overflow without any theoretical damage to the implicit stream: all count mass may still be accounted for. If a moderately high number of overly large elements are observed, then we expect in practice for this to have a negligible impact on downstream performance. If an exceptional number of elements are overly large, then the training data was not representative of the test set.

The newly introduced parameter m' is used in MODIFIEDUPDATEAVERAGE (MUA), which relies on REWRITEHISTORY. Note that MUA uses the same value of n when calling REWRITEHISTORY as it does in the subsequent line calling UPDATEAVERAGE: we modify the state of the reservoir without incrementing the stream length, taking the current overflow and pretending we saw it earlier, spread out across previous elements. This happens by first estimating the number of 1 values seen thus far in the stream: $\frac{s}{k}n$, then adding in twice the overflow value, which represents removing o instances of $-\sigma$ from the stream, and then adding o instances of σ. We probabilistically round the resultant fraction to achieve a modified version of s, which is returned.

Algorithm 2 MUA$(n, k, m, m', \sigma, g, s)$

```
1: if m < m' then
2:     Return UPDATEAVERAGE(n, k, m, m', σ, g, s)
3: s' := REWRITEHISTORY(n, k, m, m', σ, g, s)
4: Return UPDATEAVERAGE(n, k, m', m', σ, g, s')
```

Algorithm 3 REWRITEHISTORY$(n, k, m, m', \sigma, g, s)$

Parameters:
o : overflow to be accommodated

```
1: o := ((m − m')/(2m')) g
2: if σ > 0 then
3:     if s = k then
4:         Return s
5:     p := min(1.0, s/k + 2o/n)
6: else
7:     if s = 0 then
8:         Return s
9:     p := max(0.0, s/k − 2o/n)
10: Return ⌈pk⌉ with prob. pk − ⌊pk⌋, ⌊pk⌋ otherwise
```

4.3 Experiment

Figure 7 compares the results seen in Figure 2 to a version of the experiment when using approximation. Parameters were: $g = 100$; $k = 255$; and a Morris-style counter for stream length using 8 bits

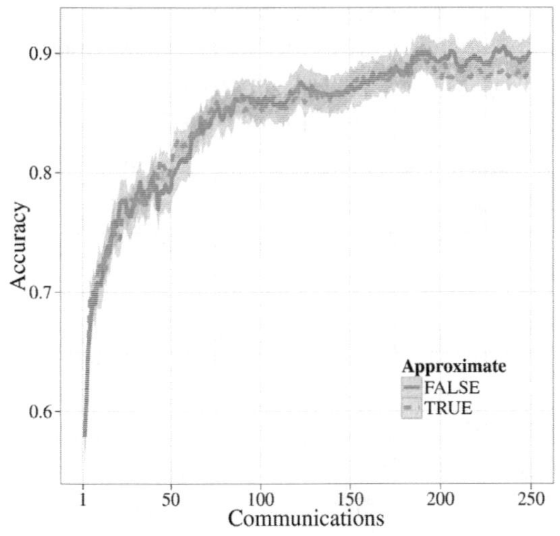

Figure 7: Comparison between using explicit counting and approximation on the Switchboard dataset, with bands reflecting 95% confidence.

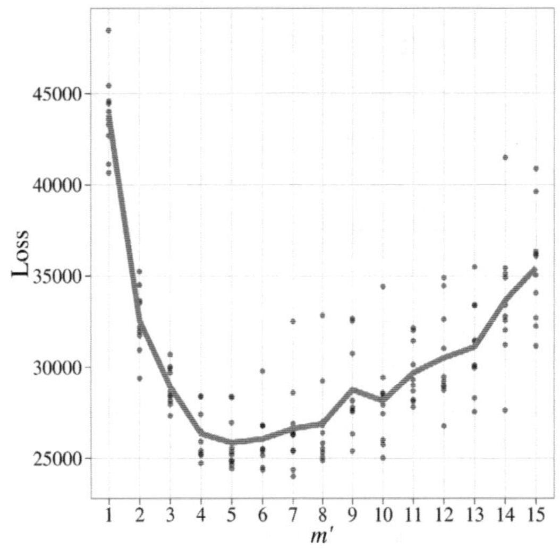

Figure 8: Summed 0/1 loss over all utterances by each speaker in the Switchboard training set, across 10 splits. A value of $m' = 5$ was on average that which minimized the number of mistakes made.

and a base of 1.3. The value m' was fit independently for each split of 10-fold cross validation, by finding through simple line search that which minimized the number of prediction errors on the original training data (see Figure 8). This result shows our ability to replace 2 variables of 32 bits (sum and length) with 2 approximation variables of 8 bits (reservoir status s, and stream length n), leading to a 75% reduction in the cost of maintaining online classifier state, with no significant cost in accuracy.

5 Real World Stream: Twitter

5.1 Setup

Based on the tweet IDs from the data used by Burger et al. (2011), we recovered 2,958,107 of their roughly 4 million original tweets.[5] These tweets were then matched against the gender labels established in that prior work. As reported by Burger et al., the dominant language in the collection is English (66.7% reported), followed by Portuguese (14.4%) then Spanish (6.0%), with a large variety of other languages with small numbers of examples.

Content was lowercased, then processed by regular expression to collapse the following into respective single symbols: emoticons; URLs; usernames (@mentions); and hashtags. Any content deemed to be a retweet (following the characters *RT*) was removed. Text was then tokenized according to a modified version of the Penn TreeBank tokenization standard[6] that was less English-centric.

5.2 Experiment

A log-linear classifier was built using all those authors in the training set[7] with at least 10 tweets. Similar to the previous experiment, unigrams and bigrams features were used exclusively, with the parameter m' fit on the training data.

As seen in Figure 9, results were as in Switchboard: accuracy improves as more data streams in per author, and our approximate model sacrifices perhaps a point of accuracy in return for a 75% reduction in memory requirements per author.

Table 2 gives the top features per gender. We see similarities to Switchboard in terms such as *my*

[5] Standard practice in Twitter data exchanges is to share only the unique tweet identifications and then requery the content from Twitter, thus allowing, e.g., the individual authors the ability to delete previous posts and have that reflected in future data collects. While respectful of author privacy, it does pose a challenge for scientific reproducibility.

[6] Such as codified in `http://www.cis.upenn.edu/~treebank/tokenizer.sed`

[7] The same training, development and test set partitions were used as by Burger et al. (2011), minus those tweets we were unable to retrieve (as previously discussed).

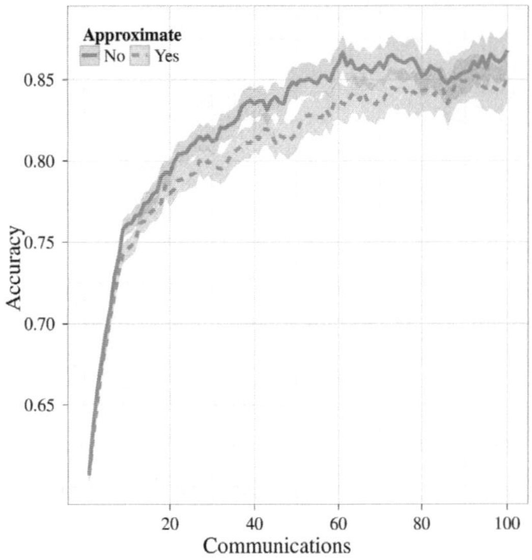

Figure 9: Comparison between using explicit counting and approximation, on the Twitter dataset, with bands reflecting 95% confidence.

wife, along with terms suggesting a more youthful population. Foreign terms are recognized by their parenthetical translation and 1st- or 2nd-person + Male/Female gender marking. For example, the Portuguese *obrigado* can be taken to be literally saying: *I'm obliged (thank you), and I'm male.*

6 Related Work

Streaming algorithms have been developed within the applied communities of networking, and (very large) databases, as well as being a popular topic in the theoretical computer science literature. A summary of the streaming algorithms community is beyond the scope of this work: interested readers are directed to Muthukrishnan (2005) as a starting point.

Within computational linguistics interest in streaming approaches is a more recent development; we provide here examples of representative work, beyond those described in previous sections. Levenberg and Osborne (2009) gave a streaming variant of the earlier perfect hashing language model of Talbot and Brants (2008), which operated in batch-mode. Using a similar decomposition to that here, Van Durme and Lall (2010) showed that Locality Sensitive Hash (LSH) signatures (Indyk and Motwani, 1998; Charikar, 2002) built using count-based feature vectors can be maintained online, as compared to their earlier uses in the community (Ravichandran et al., 2005; Bhagat and Ravichandran, 2008). Finally, Goyal et al. (2009) applied the frequent items[8] algorithm of Manku and Motwani (2002) to language modeling.

For further background in predicting author attributes such as gender, see (Garera and Yarowsky, 2009) for an overview of previous work and (non-streaming) methodology.

Table 2: Top thirty-five features by gender in Twitter.

Male	obrigado (*thank you* [1M]), wife, my wife, bro, cansado (*tired* [1M]), gay, mate, dude, [@username] why, buddy, windows, album, dope, beer, [@username] yo, sir, ps3, comics, galera (*folks/people*), amigo (*friend* [2M]), man !, fuckin, omg omg, cheers, ai n't
Female	obrigada (*thank you* [1F]), hubby, husband, cute, my husband, ?, cansada (*tired* [1F]), hair, dress, soooo, lovely, etsy, boyfriend, jonas, loved, book, sooo, girl, sé (*I*), lindo (*cute*), shopping, amiga (*friend* [2F]), yummy, ppl, cupcakes

7 Conclusions and Future Work

We have taken the predominately batch-oriented process of analyzing communication data and shown it to be fertile territory for research in large-scale streaming algorithms. Using the example task of automatic gender detection, on both spoken transcripts and microblogs, we showed that classification can be thought of as a continuously running process, becoming more robust as further communications become available. Once positioned within a streaming framework, we presented a novel approximation technique for compressing the streaming memory requirements of the classifier (per author) by 75%.

There are a number of avenues to explore based on this framework. For instance, while here we assumed a static, pre-built classifier which was then applied to streaming data, future work may consider the interplay with online learning, based on methods such as by Crammer et al. (2006). In the appli-

[8] See the survey by Cormode and Hadjieleftheriou (2009) for approaches to the *frequent items* problem, otherwise known as finding *heavy hitters*.

cations arena, one might take the savings provided here to run multiple models in parallel, either for more robust predictions (perhaps "triangulating" on language ID and/or domain over the stream), or predicting additional properties, such as age, nationality, political orientation, and so forth. Finally, we assumed here strictly count-based features; streaming log-counting methods, tailored Bloom-filters for binary feature storage, and other related topics are assuredly applicable, and should give rise to many interesting new results.

Acknowledgments I thank the reviewers and my colleagues at Johns Hopkins University for helpful feedback, in particular Matt Post, Mark Dredze, Glen Coppersmith and David Yarowsky. Thanks to David Yarowsky and Theresa Wilson for their assistance in collecting data.

References

Rahul Bhagat and Deepak Ravichandran. 2008. Large Scale Acquisition of Paraphrases for Learning Surface Patterns. In *Proceedings of ACL*.

Constantinos Boulis and Mari Ostendorf. 2005. A quantitative analysis of lexical differences between genders in telephone conversations. In *Proceedings of ACL*.

John D. Burger, John Henderson, George Kim, and Guido Zarrella. 2011. Discriminating gender on twitter. In *Proceedings of EMNLP*.

Moses Charikar. 2002. Similarity estimation techniques from rounding algorithms. In *Proceedings of STOC*.

Christopher Cieri, David Miller, and Kevin Walker. 2004. The fisher corpus: a resource for the next generations of speech-to-text. In *Proceedings of LREC*.

Graham Cormode and Marios Hadjieleftheriou. 2009. Finding the frequent items in streams of data. *Communications of the ACM*, 52(10):97–105.

Koby Crammer, Ofer Dekel, Joseph Keshet, Shai Shalev-Shwartz, and Yoram Singer. 2006. Online passive-aggressive algorithms. *Journal of Machine Learning Research*, 7:551–585.

Christopher P. Diehl, Galileo Namata, and Lise Getoor. 2007. Relationship identification for social network discovery. In *Proceedings of AAAI*.

Rong-En Fan, Kai-Wei Chang, Cho-Jui Hsief, Xiang-Rui Wang, and Chih-Jen Lin. 2008. Liblinear: A library for large linear classification. *Journal of Machine Learning Research*, (9).

Philippe Flajolet. 1985. Approximate counting: a detailed analysis. *BIT*, 25(1):113–134.

Nikesh Garera and David Yarowsky. 2009. Modeling latent biographic attributes in conversational genres. In *Proceedings of ACL*.

John J. Godfrey, Edward C. Holliman, and Jane McDaniel. 1992. Switchboard: Telephone speech corpus for research and development. In *Proceedings of ICASSP*.

Amit Goyal, Hal Daumé III, and Suresh Venkatasubramanian. 2009. Streaming for large scale NLP: Language Modeling. In *Proceedings of NAACL*.

Piotr Indyk and Rajeev Motwani. 1998. Approximate nearest neighbors: towards removing the curse of dimensionality. In *Proceedings of STOC*.

Nitin Jindal and Bing Liu. 2008. Opinion spam and analysis. In *Proceedings of the International Conference on Web Search and Wed Data Mining*, pages 219–230.

Abby Levenberg and Miles Osborne. 2009. Stream-based randomised language models for smt. In *Proceedings of EMNLP*.

Gurmeet Singh Manku and Rajeev Motwani. 2002. Approximate frequency counts over data streams. In *Proceedings of the 28th international conference on Very Large Data Bases (VLDB)*.

Robert Morris. 1978. Counting large numbers of events in small registers. *Communications of the ACM*, 21(10):840–842.

S. Muthu Muthukrishnan. 2005. Data streams: Algorithms and applications. *Foundations and Trends in Theoretical Computer Science*, 1(2).

Brendan O'Connor, Ramnath Balasubramanyan, Bryan R. Routledge, and Noah A. Smith. 2010. From tweets to polls: Linking text sentiment to public opinion time series. In *Proceedings of ICWSM*.

Myle Ott, Yejin Choi, Claire Cardie, and Jeffrey Hancock. 2011. Finding deceptive opinion spam by any stretch of the imagination. In *Proceedings of ACL*.

Sasa Petrovic, Miles Osborne, and Victor Lavrenko. 2010. Streaming first story detection with application to twitter. In *Proceedings of NAACL*.

Delip Rao, David Yarowsky, Abhishek Shreevats, and Manaswi Gupta. 2010. Classifying latent user attributes in twitter. In *Proceedings of the 2nd International Workshop on Search and Mining User-generated Contents (SMUC)*.

Deepak Ravichandran, Patrick Pantel, and Eduard Hovy. 2005. Randomized Algorithms and NLP: Using Locality Sensitive Hash Functions for High Speed Noun Clustering. In *Proceedings of ACL*.

David Talbot and Thorsten Brants. 2008. Randomized language models via perfect hash functions. In *Proceedings of ACL*.

David Talbot and Miles Osborne. 2007a. Randomised language modelling for statistical machine translation. In *Proceedings of ACL*.

David Talbot and Miles Osborne. 2007b. Smoothed Bloom filter language models: Tera-Scale LMs on the Cheap. In *Proceedings of EMNLP*.

David Talbot. 2009. Succinct approximate counting of skewed data. In *Proceedings of IJCAI*.

Benjamin Van Durme and Ashwin Lall. 2009. Probabilistic Counting with Randomized Storage. In *Proceedings of IJCAI*.

Benjamin Van Durme and Ashwin Lall. 2010. Online Generation of Locality Sensitive Hash Signatures. In *Proceedings of ACL*.

Benjamin Van Durme and Ashwin Lall. 2011. Efficient Online Locality Sensitive Hashing via Reservoir Counting. In *Proceedings of ACL*.

Benjamin Van Durme. 2012. Jerboa: A toolkit for randomized and streaming algorithms. Technical Report 7, Human Language Technology Center of Excellence, Johns Hopkins University.

Jeffrey S. Vitter. 1985. Random sampling with a reservoir. *ACM Trans. Math. Softw.*, 11:37–57, March.

Detecting Subgroups in Online Discussions by Modeling Positive and Negative Relations among Participants

Ahmed Hassan
Microsoft Research
Redmond, WA
hassanam@microsoft.com

Amjad Abu-Jbara
University of Michigan
Ann Arbor, MI
amjbara@umich.edu

Dragomir Radev
University of Michigan
Ann Arbor, MI
radev@umich.edu

Abstract

A mixture of positive (friendly) and negative (antagonistic) relations exist among users in most social media applications. However, many such applications do not allow users to explicitly express the polarity of their interactions. As a result most research has either ignored negative links or was limited to the few domains where such relations are explicitly expressed (e.g. Epinions trust/distrust). We study text exchanged between users in online communities. We find that the polarity of the links between users can be predicted with high accuracy given the text they exchange. This allows us to build a signed network representation of discussions; where every edge has a sign: positive to denote a friendly relation, or negative to denote an antagonistic relation. We also connect our analysis to social psychology theories of balance. We show that the automatically predicted networks are consistent with those theories. Inspired by that, we present a technique for identifying subgroups in discussions by partitioning singed networks representing them.

1 Introduction

Most online communities involve a mixture of positive and negative relations between users. Positive relations may indicate friendship, agreement, or approval. Negative relations usually indicate antagonism, opposition, or disagreement.

Most of the research on relations in social media applications has almost exclusively focused on positive links between individuals (e.g. friends, fans, followers, etc.). We think that one of the main reasons, of why the interplay of positive and negative links did not receive enough attention, is the lack of a notion for explicitly expressing negative interactions. Recently, this problem has received increasing attention. However, all studies have been limited to a handful of datasets from applications that allow users to explicitly label relations as either positive or negative (e.g. trust/distrust on Epinion (Leskovec et al., 2010b) and friends/foes on Slashdot (Kunegis et al., 2009)).

Predicting positive/negative relations between discussants is related to another well studied problem, namely debate stance recognition. The objective of this problem is to identify which participants are supporting and which are opposing the topic being discussed. This line of work does not pay enough attention to the relations between participants, rather it focuses on participant's stance toward the topic. It also assumes that every participant either supports or opposes the topic being discussed. This is a simplistic view that ignore the nature of complex topics that has many aspects involved which may result in more than two subgroups with different opinions.

In this work, we apply Natural Language Processing techniques to text correspondences exchanged between individuals to identify the underlying signed social structure in online communities. We present a method for identifying user attitude and for automatically constructing a signed social network representation of discussions. We apply the proposed methods to a large set of discussion posts. We evaluate the performance using a manually labeled dataset. We also conduct a large scale evaluation by showing that predicted links are consistent with the principals of social psychology theories, namely the Structural Balance Theory (Heider, 1946). The balance theory has been shown to hold both theoretically (Heider, 1946) and empirically (Leskovec et al., 2010c) for a variety of social community settings. Finally, we present a method for identifying subgroups in online discussions by identifying groups with high density of intra-group positive relations and high density of inter-group negative relations. This method is capable of identifying subgroups even if the community splits into more than two subgroups which is more general than stance recognition which assumes that only two groups exist.

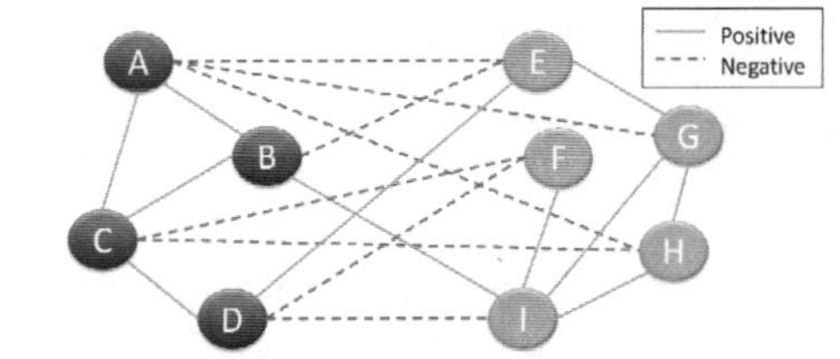

Source	Target	Sign	Evidence from Text
A	E	-	I have to disagree with what you are saying.
G	A	-	You are missing the entire point, he is putting lives at risk.
D	I	-	and you manufacture lies for what reason?
E	G	+	you have explained your position very well.
C	H	+	I am neutral on this, but I agree with your assessment!

Figure 1: An example showing a signed social network along with evidence from text that justifies edge signs.

The input to our algorithm is a set of text correspondences exchanged between users (e.g. posts or comments). The output is a *signed network* where edges signify the existence of an interaction between two users. The resulting network has polarity associated with every edge. Edge polarity is a means for indicating positive or negative affinity between two individuals.

Figure 1 shows a signed network representation for a subset of posts from a long discussion thread. The thread discussed the November 2010 Wikileaks cable release. We notice that participants split into two groups, one supporting and one opposing the leak. We also notice that most negative edges are between groups, and most positive edges are within groups. It is worth mentioning that networks generated from larger datasets (i.e. with thousands of posts) have much more noise compared to this example.

The rest of the paper is structured as follows. In section 2, we review some of the related prior work on mining sentiment from text, mining online discussions, extracting social networks from text, and analyzing signed social networks. We define our problem and explain our approach in Section 3. Section 4 describes our dataset. Results and discussion are presented in Section 5. We present a method for identifying subgroups in online discussions in Section 3.3. We conclude in Section 6.

2 Related Work

In this section, we survey several lines of research that are related to our work.

2.1 Mining Sentiment from Text

Our general goal of mining attitude from one individual toward another makes our work related to a huge body of work on sentiment analysis. One such line of research is the well-studied problem of identifying the polarity of individual words (Hatzivassiloglou and McKeown, 1997; Turney and Littman, 2003; Kim and Hovy, 2004; Takamura et al., 2005). Subjectivity analysis is yet another research line that is closely related to our general goal of mining attitude. The objective of subjectivity analysis is to identify text that presents opinion as opposed to objective text that presents factual information (Wiebe, 2000; Hatzivassiloglou and Wiebe, 2000; Banea et al., 2008; Riloff and Wiebe, 2003). Our work is different from subjectivity analysis because we are not only interested in discriminating between opinions and facts. Rather, we are interested in identifying the polarity of interactions between individuals. Our method is not restricted to phrases or words, rather it generalizes this to identifying the polarity of an interaction between two individuals based on several posts they exchange.

2.2 Stance Classification

Perhaps the closest work to this paper is the work on stance classification. We notice that most of these methods focus on the polarity of the written text assuming that anyone using positive text belongs to one group and anyone using negative text belongs to another. This works well for single-aspect topics or entities like the ones used in (Tan et al., 2011) (e.g. Obama, Sara Palin, Lakers, etc.). In this simple notion of topics, it is safe to assume that text polarity is a good enough discriminator. This unfortunately is not the case in online discussions about complex topics having many aspects (e.g. abortion, health care, etc.). In such complex topics, people use positive and negative text targeting different aspects of the topic, for example in the health care bill topic, discussants expressed their opinion regarding many aspects including: the enlarged coverage, the insurance premiums, Obama, socialism, etc. This shows that simply looking at text polarity is not enough to identify groups.

Tan et al. (2011) studied how twitter following relations can be used to improve stance classification. Their main hypothesis is that connected users are more likely to hold similar opinions. This may be correct for the twitter following relations, but it is not necessarily correct for open discussions where no such relations exist. The only criterion that can be used to connect discussants is how often they reply to each other's posts. We will show later that while many people reply to people with similar opinions, many others reply to people with different opinions as well.

Thomas et al. (2006) address the same problem of determining support and opposition as applied to congressional floor-debates. They assess the agreement/disagreement between different speakers by training a text classifier and applying it to a window surrounding the names of other speakers. They construct their training data by assuming that if two speaker have the same vote, then every reference connecting them is an agreement and vice versa. We believe this will result in a very noisy training/testing set and hence we decided to recruit human annotators to create a training set. We found out that many instances with references to other discussants were labeled as neither agreement nor disagreement regardless of whether the discussants have similar or opposing positions. We will use this system as a baseline and will show that the existence of positive/negative words close to a person name does not necessarily show agreement or disagreement with that person.

Hassan et al. (2010) use a language model based approach for identifying agreement and disagreement sentences in discussions. This work is limited to sentences. It does not consider the overall relation between participants. It also does not consider subgroup detection. We will use this method as a baseline for one of our components and will show that the proposed method outperforms it.

Murakami and Raymond (2010) present another method for stance recognition. They use a small number of hand crafted rules to identify agreement and disagreement interactions. Hand crafted rules usually result in systems with very low recall causing them to miss many agreement/disagreement instances (they report 0.26 recall at the 0.56 precision level). We present a machine learning system to solve this problem and achieve much better performance. Park et al. (2011) propose a method for finding news articles with different views on contentious issues. Mohit et al. (2008) present a set of heuristics for including disagreement information in a minimum cut stance classification framework. Galley et al. (2004) show the value of using durational and structural features for identifying agreement and disagreement in spoken conversational speech. They use features like duration of spurts, speech rate, speaker overlap, etc. which are not applicable to written language.

Our approach is different from agreement/disagreement identification because we not only study sentiment at the local sentiment level but also at the global level that takes into consideration many posts exchanged between participants to build a signed network representation of the discussion. Research on debate stance recognition attempts to perform classification under the "supporting vs. opposing" paradigm. However such simple view might not always be accurate for discussions on more complex topics with many aspects. After building the signed network representation of discussions, we present a method that can detect how the large group could split into many subgroups (not necessarily two) with coherent opinions.

2.3 Extracting Social Networks from Text

Little work has been done on the front of extracting social relations between individuals from text. Elson et al. (2010) present a method for extracting social networks from nineteenth-century British novels and serials. They link two characters based on whether they are in conversation or not. McCallum et al. (2007) explored the use of structured data such as email headers for social network construction. Gruzd and Hyrthonthwaite (2008) explored the use of post text in discussions to study interaction patterns in e-learning communities. Extracting social power relations from natural language (i.e. who influences whom) has been studied in (Bramsen et al., 2011; Danescu-Niculescu-Mizil et al., 2011).

Our work is related to this line of research because we employ natural language processing techniques to reveal embedded social structures. Despite similarities, our work is uniquely characterized by the fact that we extract signed social networks with both positive and negative links from text.

2.4 Signed Social Networks

Most of the work on social networks analysis has only focused on positive interactions. A few recent papers have taken the signs of edges into account.

Brzozowski et al. (2008) study the positive and negative relationships between users of Essembly. Essembly is an ideological social network that distinguishes between ideological allies and nemeses. Kunegis et al. (2009) analyze user relationships in the Slashdot technology news site. Slashdot allows users of the website to tag other users as friends or foes, providing positive and negative endorsements. Leskovec et al. (2010b) study signed social networks generated from Slashdot, Epinions, and Wikipedia. They also connect their analysis to theories of signed networks from social psychology. A similar study used the same datasets for predicting positive and negative links given their context (Leskovec et al., 2010a).

All this work has been limited to analyzing a handful of datasets for which an explicit notion of both positive and negative relations exists. Our work goes beyond this limitation by leveraging the power of natural language processing to automate the discovery of signed social networks using the text embedded in the network.

The research presented in this paper extends this previous work in a number of ways: (i) we present a method based on linguistic analysis that finds instances of showing positive or negative attitude between participants (ii) we propose a technique for representing discussions as signed networks where a sign is associated with every edge to denote whether the relation is friendly or antagonistic (iii) we evaluate the proposed methods using human annotated data and also conduct a large scale evaluation based on social psychology theories; (iv) finally we present a method for identifying subgroups that globally splits the community involved in the discussion by utilizing the dynamics of the local interactions between participants.

3 Approach

3.1 Identifying Attitude from Text

To build a signed network representation of discussants, we start by trying to identify sentences that show positive or negative attitude from the writer to the addressee. The first step toward identifying attitude is to identify words with positive/negative semantic orientation. The semantic orientation or polarity of a word indicates the direction the word deviates from the norm (Lehrer, 1974). We use OpinionFinder (Wilson et al., 2005a) to identify words with positive or negative semantic orientation. The polarity of a word is also affected by the context where the word appears. For example, a positive word that appears in a negated context should have a negative polarity. Other polarized words sometimes appear as neutral words in some contexts. To identify contextual polarity of words, a large set of features is used including words, sentences, structure, and other features similar to the method described in (Wilson et al., 2005b).

Our overall objective is to find the direct attitude between participants. Hence after identifying the semantic orientation of individual words, we move on to predicting which polarized expressions target the addressee and which do not.

Text polarity alone cannot be used to identify attitude between participants. Sentences that show an attitude are different from subjective sentences. Subjective sentences are sentences used to express opinions, evaluations, and speculations (Riloff and Wiebe, 2003). While every sentence that shows an attitude is a subjective sentence, not every subjective sentence shows an attitude toward the recipient.

In this method, we address the problem of identifying sentences with attitude as a relation detection problem in a supervised learning setting. We study sentences that has mentions to the addressee and polarized expressions (negative/positive words or phrases). Mentions could either be names of other participants or second person pronouns (you, your, yours) used in text posted as a reply to another participant. Reply structure (i.e. who replies to whom) is readily available in many discussion forums. In cases where reply structure is not available, we can use a method like the one in (Lin et al., 2009) to recover it.

We predict whether the mention is related to the polarized expression or not. We regard the mention and the polarized expression as two entities and try to learn a classifier that predicts whether the two entities are related or not.

The text connecting the two entities offers a very condensed representation of the information needed to assess whether they are related or not. For example the two sentences *"you are completely unqualified"* and *"you know what, he is unqualified ..."* show two different ways the words *"you"*, and *"unqualified"* could appear in a sentence. In the first case the polarized word "unqualified" refers to the word "you". In the second case, the two words are not related. The information in the shortest path between two entities in a dependency tree can be used to assert whether a relationship exists between them (Bunescu and Mooney, 2005).

The sequence of words connecting the two entities is a very good predictor of whether they are related or not. However, these paths are completely lexicalized and consequently their performance will be limited by data sparseness. To alleviate this problem, we use higher levels of generalization to represent the path connecting the two tokens. These representations are the part-of-speech tags, and the shortest path in a dependency graph connecting the two tokens. We represent every sentence with several representations at different levels of generalization. For example, the sentence "*your ideas are very inspiring*" will be represented using lexical, polarity, part-of-speech, and dependency information as follows:

LEX: "*YOUR ideas are very POS*"
POS: "*YOUR NNS VBP RB JJ_POS*"
DEP: "*YOUR poss nsubj POS*"

The set of features we use are the set of unigrams, and bigrams representing the words, part-of-speech tags, and dependency relations connecting the two entities. For example the following features will be set for the previous example:

YOUR_ideas, YOUR_NNS, YOUR_poss, poss_nsubj, ..., etc.

We use Support Vector Machines (SVM) as a learning system because it is good with handling high dimensional feature spaces.

3.2 Extracting the Signed Network

In this subsection, we describe the procedure we used to build the signed network given the component we described in the previous subsection. This procedure consists of two main steps. The first is building the network without signs, and the second is assigning signs to different edges.

To build the network, we parse our data to identify different threads, posts and senders. Every sender is represented with a node in the network. An edge connects two nodes if there exists an interaction between the corresponding participants. We add a directed edge $A \rightarrow B$, if A replies to B's posts at least n times in m different threads. We set m, and n to 2 in all of our experiments. The interaction information (i.e. who replies to whom) can be extracted directly from the thread structure. Alternatively, as mentioned earlier, we can use a method similar to the one presented in (Lin et al., 2009) to recover the reply structure if it is not readily available.

Once we build the network, we move to the more challenging task in which we associate a sign with every edge. We have shown in the previous section how sentences with positive and negative attitude can be extracted from text. Unfortunately the sign of an interaction cannot be trivially inferred from the polarity of sentences. For example, a single negative sentence written by A and directed to B does not mean that the interaction between A and B is negative. One way to solve this problem would be to compare the number of negative sentences to positive sentences in all posts between A and B and classify the interaction according to the plurality value. We will show later, in our experiments section, that such a simplistic method does not perform well in predicting the sign of an interaction.

Participant Features
Number of posts per month for A (B)
Percentage of positive posts per month for A (B)
Percentage of negative posts per month for A (B)
gender
Interaction Features
Percentage/number of positive (negative) sentences per post
Percentage/number of positive (negative) posts per thread
Discussion Domain (e.g. politics, science, etc.)

Table 1: Features used by the Interaction Sign Classifier.

As a result, we decided to pose the problem as a classical supervised learning problem. We came up with a set of features that we think are good predictors of the interaction sign, and we trained a classifier using those features on a labeled dataset. Our features include numbers and percentages of positive/negative sentences per post, posts per thread, and so on. A sentence is labeled as positive/negative if a relation has been detected in this sentence between a mention referring to the addressee and a positive/negative expression. A post is considered positive/negative based on the majority of relations detected in it. We use two sets of features. The first set is related to A only or B only. The second set is related to the interactions between A and B. The features are summarized in Table 1.

3.3 Sub-Group Detection

In any discussion, different subgroups may emerge. Members of every subgroup usually have a common focus (positive or negative) toward the topic being discussed. Each member of a group is more likely to show positive attitude to members of the same group, and negative attitude to members of opposing groups. The signed network representation could prove to be very useful for identifying those subgroups. To detect subgroups in a discussion thread, we would like to partition the corresponding signed network such that positive intra-group links and negative inter-group links are dense.

This problem is related to the constrained clustering (Wagstaff et al., 2001) and the correlation clustering problem (Bansal et al., 2004). In constrained clustering, a pairwise similarity metric (which is not available in our domain), and a set of must-link/cannot-link constraints are used with a standard data clustering algorithm. Correlation clustering operates in a scenario where given a signed graph $G = (V, E)$ where the edge label indicates whether two nodes are similar (+) or different (-), the task is to cluster the vertices so that similar objects are grouped together. Bansal et. al (2004) proved NP-hardness and gave constant-factor approximation algorithms for the special case in which the graph is complete (full information) and every edge has weight +1 or -1 which is not the case in our network. Alternatively, we can use a greedy optimization algorithm to find partitions. A criterion function for a local optimization partitioning procedure is constructed such that positive links are dense within groups and negative links are dense between groups.

For any potential partition C, we seek to optimize the following function: $P(C) = \alpha \sum_n + (1-\alpha) \sum_p$ where $\sum_n$ is the number of negative links between nodes in the same subgroup, $\sum_p$ is the number of positive links between nodes in different subgroups, and α is a trade factor that represents the importance of the two terms. We set α to 0.5 in all our experiments.

Clusters are selected such that: $C^* = \arg\min P(C)$. A greedy optimization framework is used to minimize $P(C)$. Initially, nodes are randomly partitioned into t different clusters and the criterion function P is evaluated for that cluster. Every cluster has a set of neighbors in the cluster space. A neighbor cluster is obtained by moving one node from one cluster to another, or by exchanging two nodes in two different clusters. Neighbor partitions are evaluated, and if one with a lower value for the criterion function is found, it is set as the current partition. This greedy procedure is repeated with random restarts until a minimal solution is found. To determine the number of subgroups t, we select t that minimizes the optimization function $P(C)$. In all experiments we used an upper limit of $t = 5$. This technique was able to identify the correct number of subgroups in 77% of the times. In the rest of the cases, the number was different from the correct number by at most 1 except for a single case where it was 2.

4 Data

4.1 Signed Network Extraction

Our data consists of a large amount of discussion threads collected from online discussion forums. We collected around $41,000$ topics (threads) and 1.2M posts from the period between the end of 2008 and the end of 2010. All threads were in English and had 5 posts or more. They covered 11 different domains including: politics, religion, science, etc. The average number of participants per domain is 1320 and per topic is 52. The data was tokenized, sentence-split, and part-of-speech tagged with the OpenNLP toolkit. It was parsed with the Stanford parser (Klein and Manning, 2003).

We randomly selected around 5300 posts (1000 interactions), and asked human annotators to label them. Our annotators were instructed to read all the posts exchanged between two participants and decide whether the interaction between them is positive or negative. We used Amazon Mechanical Turk for annotations. Following previous work (Callison-Burch, 2009; Akkaya et al., 2010), we took several precautions to maintain data integrity. We restricted annotators to those based in the US to maintain an acceptable level of English fluency. We also restricted annotators to those who have more than 95% approval rate for all previous work. Moreover, we asked three different annotators to label every interaction. The label was computed by taking the majority vote among the three annotators. We refer to this data as the *Interactions Dataset*.

We ran a different annotation task where we selected sentences including mentions referring to discussants (names or pronouns) and polarized expressions. Annotators were asked to select sentences where the polarized attribute is referring to the mention and hence show a positive or negative attitude toward other discussion participants. This resulted in a set of 5000 manually annotated sentences. We refer to this data as the *Sentences Dataset*.

We asked three different annotators to label every instance. The kappa measure between the three groups of annotations was 0.62 for the *Interactions Dataset* and 0.64 for the *Sentences Dataset*. To better assess the quality of the annotations, we asked a trained annotator to label 10% of the data. We measured the agreement between the expert annotator

	Class	Pos.	Neg.	Weigh. Avg.
Logistic Reg.	Precision	0.848	0.724	0.809
	Recall	0.884	0.657	0.812
	F-Measure	0.866	0.689	0.81
	Accuracy	-	-	**0.812**
SVM	Precision	0.906	0.71	0.844
	Recall	0.847	0.809	0.835
	F-Measure	0.875	0.756	0.838
	Accuracy	-	-	**0.835**

Table 2: Interaction sign classifier performance.

Classifier	Random	Thresh-Num	Thresh-Perc.	SVM
Accuracy	65%	69%	71%	83.5%

Table 3: A comparison of different sign interaction classifiers.

and the majority label from Mechanical Turk. The kappa measure was 0.69 for the *Interactions Dataset* and 0.67 for the *Sentences Dataset.*

4.2 Sub-group Detection

We used a dataset of more than 42 topics and approximately 9000 posts collected from two political forums (Createdebate[1] and Politicalforum[2]). The forum administrators ran a poll asking participants to select their stance from a set of possible answers and hence the dataset was self-labeled with respect to groups. We also used a set of discussions from the Wikipedia discussion section. When a topic on Wikipedia is disputed, the editors of that topic start a discussion about it. We collected 117 Wikipedia discussion threads. The threads contain a total of 1,867 posts. The discussions were annotated by an expert annotator (a professor in sociolinguistics, not an author of the paper) who was instructed to read each of the Wikipedia discussion threads in its entirety and determine whether the discussants split into subgroups, in which case he was asked to identify the subgroup membership for each discussant. In total, we had 159 topics with an average of approximately 500 posts, 60 participants and 2.7 subgroups per topic. Examples of the topics include: Arizona immigration law, airport security, oil spill, evolution, Ireland partitions, abortion and many others.

5 Results and Discussion

We performed experiments on the data described in the previous section. We trained and tested the sentence with the attitude detection classifiers described in Section 3.1 using the *Sentences Dataset.* We also trained and tested the interaction sign classifier described in Section 3.2 using the *Interactions Dataset.* We built one signed social network for every domain (e.g. politics, economics, etc.). We decided to build a network for every domain as opposed to one single network because the relation between any two individuals may vary across domains (e.g. politics vs. science). In the rest of this section, we will describe the experiments we did to assess the performance of the sentences with attitude detection and interaction sign prediction steps.

In addition to classical evaluation, we evaluate our results using the structural balance theory which has been shown to hold both theoretically (Heider, 1946) and empirically (Leskovec et al., 2010c). We validate our results by showing that the *automatically* extracted networks mostly agree with the theory. We evaluated the approach using the structural balance theory because it presents a global (pertaining to relations between multiple edges) and large-scale (used millions of posts and thousands of users) evaluation of the results as opposed to traditional evaluation which is local in nature (only considers one edge at a time) and smaller in scale (used thousands of posts).

5.1 Identifying Sentences with Attitude

We compare the proposed methods to two baselines. The first baseline is based on the work of (Thomas et al., 2006). We used the speaker agreement component presented in (Thomas et al., 2006) as a baseline. The speaker agreement component is one step in their approach. In this component, they used an SVM classifier trained using a window of text surrounding references to other speakers to predict agreement/disagreement between speakers.

We build an SVM text classifier trained on the sentence at which the mention referring to the other participant occurred. We refer to this baseline as the *T*ext Classification approach. The second baselines adopts the language model approach presented in (Hassan et al., 2010). Two language models are trained using a stream of words, part-of-speech tags, and dependency relations, one for sentences that show an attitude and one for sentences that do not. New sentences are classified based on generation likelihoods. We refer to this baseline as the *L*anguage Models approach.

We tested this component using the *Sentences Dataset* described in Section 4. We compared the performance of the proposed method and the two

[1] www.createdebate.com
[2] www.politicalforum.com

	Extracted Networks				Random Networks			
Domain	(+ + +)	(+ + −)	(+ − −)	(− − −)	(+ + +)	(+ + −)	(+ − −)	(− − −)
abortion	51.67	26.31	18.92	0.48	35.39	43.92	18.16	2.52
current-events	67.36	22.26	8.76	0.23	54.08	36.90	8.39	0.64
off-topic-chat	65.28	23.54	9.45	0.25	58.07	34.59	6.88	0.46
economics	72.68	18.30	7.77	0.00	66.50	29.09	4.22	0.20
political opinions	60.60	24.24	12.81	0.43	45.97	40.79	12.06	1.19
environment	47.46	32.54	17.26	0.30	37.38	43.61	16.89	2.12
latest world news	58.29	22.41	16.33	0.62	42.26	42.20	13.98	1.56
religion	47.17	25.89	22.56	1.42	39.68	42.94	15.51	1.87
science-technology	57.53	26.03	14.33	0.00	50.14	38.93	10.05	0.87
terrorism	64.96	23.36	9.46	0.73	41.54	42.42	14.36	1.68

Table 4: Percentage of different types of triangles in the extracted networks vs. the random networks.

Method	Accuracy	Precision	Recall	F1
Text Classification	60.4	61.1	60.2	60.6
Language Models	80.3	81.0	79.4	80.2
Relation Extraction	82.3	82.3	82.3	82.3

Table 5: Comparison of attitude identification methods.

baselines. Table 5 compares the precision, recall, F1, and accuracy for the three methods. The text classification based approach does much worse than others. The reasons is that it ignores the structure and uses much less information (part-of-speech tags and dependency trees are not used) compared to the other methods. Additionally, the short length of the sentences compared to what is typical in text classification may have had a bad effect on the performance. Both other models try to learn the characteristics of the path connecting the mention and the polarized expression. We notice that optimizing the weights for unigram and bigrams features using SVM results in a better performance compared to language models because it does not have the constraints imposed by the former model on the learned weights.

We evaluated the importance of the feature types (i.e. dependency vs. pos tags vs words) by measuring the chi-squared statistic for every feature with respect to the class. Dependency features were most helpful, but other types of features helped improve the performance as well.

5.2 Interaction Sign Classifier

We used the relation detection classifier described in Section 3.1 to find sentences with positive and negative attitude. The output of this classifier was used to compute the features described in Section 3.2, which were used to train a classifier that predicts the sign of an interaction between any two individuals.

We used both Support Vector Machines (SVM) and logistic regression to train the sign interaction classifier. We report several performance metrics for them in Table 2. We notice that the SVM classifier performs better with an accuracy of 83.5% and an F-measure of 81%. All results were computed using 10 fold cross validation on the labeled data. To better assess the performance of the proposed classifier, we compare it to a baseline that labels the relation as negative if the percentage of negative sentences exceeds a particular threshold, otherwise it is labeled as positive. The thresholds were empirically estimated using a separate development set. The accuracy of this baseline is only 71%.

To better assess the performance of the proposed classifier, we compare it to three baselines. The first is a random baseline that predicts an interaction as positive with probability p that equals the proportion of positive instances to all instances in the training set. The second classifier (Thresh-Num) labels the edge as negative if the number of negative instances exceeds a threshold T_n. The third classifier (Thresh-Perc) labels the edge as negative if the percentage of negative instances to all instances exceeds a threshold T_p. The cutoff thresholds were estimated using a separate development set.

The 3 baselines were tested using the entire labeled dataset. The SVM classifier was tested using 10 fold cross validation. The accuracy of the random classifier, the two based on a cut off number and percentage , and the SVM classifier are shown in Table 3. We notice that the random classifier performs worst, and the classifier based on percentage cutoff outperforms the one based on number cutoff. The SVM classifier significantly outperforms all other classifiers. We tried to train a classifier using both the number and percentage of negative and positive posts. The improvement over using the baseline using the percentage of negative posts was not statistically significant.

We evaluated the importance of the features listed

in Table 1 by measuring the chi-squared statistic for every feature with respect to the class. We found out that the features describing the interaction between the two participants are more informative than the ones describing individuals characteristics. The later features are still helpful though and they improve the performance by a statistically significant amount. We also noticed that all features based on percentages are more informative than those based on counts. The most informative features are: percentage of negative posts per tread, percentage of negative sentences per post, percentage of positive posts per thread, number of negative posts, and discussion domain.

5.3 Structural Balance Theory

The structural balance theory is a psychological theory that tries to explain the dynamics of signed social interactions. It has been shown to hold both theoretically (Heider, 1946) and empirically (Leskovec et al., 2010c). In this section, we study the agreement between the theory and our *automatically* extracted networks. The theory has its origins in the work of Heider (1946). It was then formalized in a graph theoretic form by (Cartwright and Harary, 1956). The theory is based on the principles that "the friend of my friend is my friend", "the enemy of my friend is my enemy", "the friend of my enemy is my enemy", and variations on these. The structural balance theory states that triangles that have an odd number of positive signs (+ + + and + - -) are balanced, while triangles that have an even number of positive signs (- - - and + + -) are not.

In this section, we compare the predictions of edge signs made by our system to the structural balance theory by counting the frequencies of different types of triangles in the predicted network. Table 4 shows the frequency of every type of triangle for 10 different domains. To better understand these numbers, we compare them to the frequencies of triangles in a set of random networks. We shuffle the signs for all edges on every network keeping the fractions of positive and negative edges constant. We repeat shuffling for 1000 times and report the average.

We find that the all-positive triangle $(+\ +\ +)$ is overrepresented in the generated network compared to chance across all domains. We also see that the triangle with two positive edges $(+\ +\ -)$, and the all-negative triangle $(-\ -\ -)$ are underrepresented compared to chance across all domains. The triangle with a single positive edge is slightly overrepresented in most but not all of the topics compared to chance. This shows that the predicted networks mostly agree with the structural balance theory. The slightly non standard behavior of the triangle with one positive edge could be explained in light of the weak balance theory. In this theory, Davis (1967) states that this triangle, which corresponds to the "enemy of enemy is my friend" proposition, holds only if the network can be partitioned into exactly two subsets, but not when there are more than two. In general, the percentage of balanced triangles in the predicted networks is higher than in the shuffled networks, and hence the balanced triangles are significantly overrepresented compared to chance showing that our *automatically* constructed network is similar to explicit signed networks in that they both mostly agree with the balance theory.

5.4 Sub-Group Detection

We compare the performance of the sub-group detection method to three baselines. The first baseline uses graph clustering (GC) to partition a network based on the frequency of interaction between participants. We build a graph where each node represents a participant. Edges link participants if they exchange posts, and edge weights are based on the number of posts exchanged. The second baseline (TC) is based on the premise that participants with similar text are more likely to belong to the same subgroup. We measure text similarity by computing the cosine similarity between the tf-idf representations of the text in a high dimensional vector space. We tried two methods for partitioning those graphs: spectral partitioning (Luxburg, 2007) and a hierarchical agglomeration algorithm which works by greedily optimizing the modularity for graphs (Clauset et al., 2004). The third baseline is based on stance classification approaches (e.g. (Tan et al., 2011)). In this baseline we put all the participants who use more positive text in one subgroup and the participants who use more negative text in another subgroup. Text polarity is identified using the method described in Section 3.1.

Table 6 shows the average purity (*Purity*), entropy (*Entropy*), Normalizes Mutual Information (*NMI*), and Rand Index (*RandIndex*) values of the method based on signed networks and the baselines using different partitioning algorithms. The differences in the results shown in the table are statistically significant at the 0.05 level (as indicated by a 2-tailed

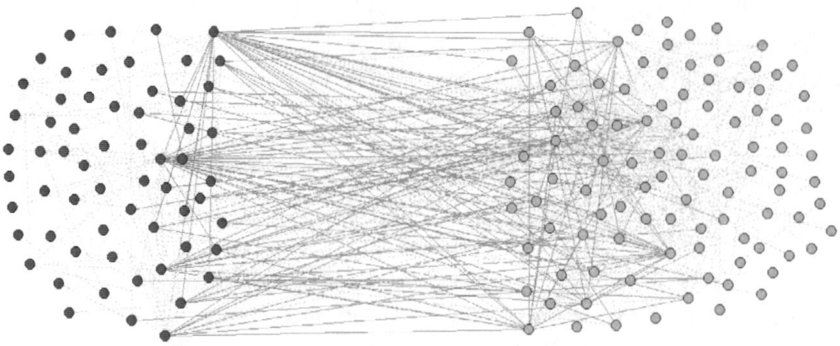

Figure 2: A signed network representing participants in a discussion about the "Health Care Reform Bill". Blue (dark) nodes represent participants with the bill, Yellow (light) nodes represent participants against the bill, red (solid) edges represent negative attitude, while green (dashed) edges represent positive attitude.

	Createdebate				Politicalforum				Wikipedia			
Method	Purity	Entropy	NMI	RandIndex	Purity	Entropy	NMI	RandIndex	Purity	Entropy	NMI	RandIndex
GC - Spectral	0.50	0.85	0.28	0.40	0.50	0.88	0.27	0.39	0.49	0.89	0.33	0.35
GC - Hierarchical	0.48	0.86	0.30	0.41	0.47	0.89	0.31	0.40	0.49	0.87	0.38	0.39
TC - Spectral	0.50	0.85	0.31	0.43	0.48	0.90	0.30	0.45	0.51	0.87	0.40	0.46
TC - Hierarchical	0.49	0.90	0.35	0.46	0.48	0.91	0.33	0.49	0.53	0.80	0.40	0.49
Text Polarity	0.55	0.80	0.38	0.49	0.54	0.91	0.31	0.38	0.34	0.95	0.30	0.40
Signed Networks	**0.64**	**0.74**	**0.46**	**0.59**	**0.58**	**0.80**	**0.43**	**0.55**	**0.65**	**0.54**	**0.51**	**0.60**

Table 6: Comparison of the sub-group detection method to baseline systems

paired t-test).

We notice that partitioning the signed network that was automatically extracted from text results in significantly better partitions on the three datasets as indicated by the higher Purity, NMI, and RandIndex and the lower Entropy values it achieves. We believe that the first two baselines performed poorly because the interaction frequency and the text similarity are not key factors in identifying subgroup structures. Many people would respond to people they disagree with more, while others would mainly respond to people they agree with most of the time. Also, people in opposing subgroups tend to use very similar text when discussing the same topic and hence text clustering does not work as well. The baseline that classifies the stance of discussants based on the polarity of their text performed bad too because it overlooks the fact that most of the discussed topics in our datasets have multiple aspects and a discussant may use both positive and negative text targeting different aspects of the topic. An example of a signed network and the corresponding subgtoups as extracted from real data is showm in Figure 2.

6 Conclusions

In this paper, we have shown that natural language processing techniques can be reliably used to extract signed social networks from text correspondences. We believe that this work brings us closer to understanding the relation between language use and social interactions and opens the door to further research efforts that go beyond standard social network analysis by studying the interplay of positive and negative connections. We rigorously evaluated the proposed methods on labeled data and connected our analysis to social psychology theories to show that our predictions mostly agree with them. Finally, we presented potential applications that benefit from the automatically extracted signed network.

Acknowledgments

This research was funded in part by the Office of the Director of National Intelligence, Intelligence Advanced Research Projects Activity. All statements of fact, opinion or conclusions contained herein are those of the authors and should not be construed as representing the official views or policies of IARPA, the ODNI or the U.S. Government

References

Cem Akkaya, Alexander Conrad, Janyce Wiebe, and Rada Mihalcea. 2010. Amazon mechanical turk for subjectivity word sense disambiguation. In *Proceedings of the NAACL HLT 2010 Workshop on Creating Speech and Language Data with Amazon's Mechanical Turk*, CSLDAMT '10, pages 195–203.

Carmen Banea, Rada Mihalcea, and Janyce Wiebe. 2008. A bootstrapping method for building subjectivity lexicons for languages with scarce resources. In *LREC'08*.

Nikhil Bansal, Avrim Blum, and Shuchi Chawla. 2004. Correlation Clustering. *Machine Learning*, 56(1):89–113.

Mohit Bansal, Claire Cardie, and Lillian Lee. 2008. The power of negative thinking: Exploiting label disagreement in the min-cut classification framework. In *Proceedings of the 23rd International Conference on Computational Linguistics: Posters*.

Philip Bramsen, Martha Escobar-Molano, Ami Patel, and Rafael Alonso. 2011. Extracting social power relationships from natural language. In *Proceedings of the 49th Annual Meeting of the Association for Computational Linguistics: Human Language Technologies - Volume 1*, pages 773–782.

Michael J. Brzozowski, Tad Hogg, and Gabor Szabo. 2008. Friends and foes: ideological social networking. In *Proceeding of the twenty-sixth annual SIGCHI conference on Human factors in computing systems*, pages 817–820, New York, NY, USA.

Razvan C. Bunescu and Raymond J. Mooney. 2005. A shortest path dependency kernel for relation extraction. In *Proceedings of the conference on Human Language Technology and Empirical Methods in Natural Language Processing*, HLT '05, pages 724–731, Stroudsburg, PA, USA. Association for Computational Linguistics.

Chris Callison-Burch. 2009. Fast, cheap, and creative: evaluating translation quality using amazon's mechanical turk. In *Proceedings of the 2009 Conference on Empirical Methods in Natural Language Processing: Volume 1 - Volume 1*, EMNLP '09, pages 286–295.

Dorwin Cartwright and Frank Harary. 1956. Structure balance: A generalization of heiders theory. *Psych. Rev.*, 63.

Aaron Clauset, Mark E. J. Newman, and Cristopher Moore. 2004. Finding community structure in very large networks. *Phys. Rev. E*, 70:066111.

Cristian Danescu-Niculescu-Mizil, Lillian Lee, Bo Pang, and Jon M. Kleinberg. 2011. Echoes of power: Language effects and power differences in social interaction. *CoRR*.

J. A. Davis. 1967. Clustering and structural balance in graphs. *Human Relations*, 20:181–187.

David Elson, Nicholas Dames, and Kathleen McKeown. 2010. Extracting social networks from literary fiction. In *Proceedings of the 48th Annual Meeting of the Association for Computational Linguistics*, pages 138–147, Uppsala, Sweden, July.

Michel Galley, Kathleen McKeown, Julia Hirschberg, and Elizabeth Shriberg. 2004. Identifying agreement and disagreement in conversational speech: use of bayesian networks to model pragmatic dependencies. In *Proceedings of the 42nd Annual Meeting on Association for Computational Linguistics*, ACL '04, Stroudsburg, PA, USA. Association for Computational Linguistics.

Anatoliy Gruzd and Caroline Haythornthwaite. 2008. Automated discovery and analysis of social networks from threaded discussions. In *Proceedings of the International Network of Social Network Analysis (INSNA)*, St. Pete Beach, Florida.

Ahmed Hassan, Vahed Qazvinian, and Dragomir Radev. 2010. What's with the attitude?: identifying sentences with attitude in online discussions. In *Proceedings of the 2010 Conference on Empirical Methods in Natural Language Processing*, pages 1245–1255.

Vasileios Hatzivassiloglou and Kathleen R. McKeown. 1997. Predicting the semantic orientation of adjectives. In *EACL'97*, pages 174–181.

Vasileios Hatzivassiloglou and Janyce Wiebe. 2000. Effects of adjective orientation and gradability on sentence subjectivity. In *COLING*, pages 299–305.

Fritz Heider. 1946. Attitudes and cognitive organization. *Journal of Psychology*, 21:107–112.

Soo-Min Kim and Eduard Hovy. 2004. Determining the sentiment of opinions. In *COLING*, pages 1367–1373.

Dan Klein and Christopher D. Manning. 2003. Accurate unlexicalized parsing. In *ACL'03*, pages 423–430.

Jérôme Kunegis, Andreas Lommatzsch, and Christian Bauckhage. 2009. The slashdot zoo: mining a social network with negative edges. In *Proceedings of the 18th international conference on World wide web*, pages 741–750, New York, NY, USA.

Adrienne Lehrer. 1974. Semantic fields and lezical structure. North Holland, Amsterdam and New York.

Jure Leskovec, Daniel Huttenlocher, and Jon Kleinberg. 2010a. Predicting positive and negative links in online social networks. In *Proceedings of the 19th international conference on World wide web*, pages 641–650, New York, NY, USA.

Jure Leskovec, Daniel Huttenlocher, and Jon Kleinberg. 2010b. Signed networks in social media. In *Proceedings of the 28th international conference on Human factors in computing systems*, pages 1361–1370, New York, NY, USA.

Jure Leskovec, Daniel Huttenlocher, and Jon Kleinberg. 2010c. Signed networks in social media. In *CHI 2010*, pages 1361–1370, New York, NY, USA. ACM.

Chen Lin, Jiang-Ming Yang, Rui Cai, Xin-Jing Wang, and Wei Wang. 2009. Simultaneously modeling semantics and structure of threaded discussions: a sparse coding approach and its applications. In *SIGIR '09*, pages 131–138.

Ulrike Luxburg. 2007. A tutorial on spectral clustering. *Statistics and Computing*, 17:395–416, December.

Andrew McCallum, Xuerui Wang, and Andrés Corrada-Emmanuel. 2007. Topic and role discovery in social networks with experiments on enron and academic email. *J. Artif. Int. Res.*, 30:249–272, October.

Akiko Murakami and Rudy Raymond. 2010. Support or oppose?: classifying positions in online debates from reply activities and opinion expressions. In *Proceedings of the 23rd International Conference on Computational Linguistics: Posters*, pages 869–875.

Souneil Park, KyungSoon Lee, and Junehwa Song. 2011. Contrasting opposing views of news articles on contentious issues. In *Proceedings of the 49th Annual Meeting of the Association for Computational Linguistics: Human Language Technologies - Volume 1*, pages 340–349.

Ellen Riloff and Janyce Wiebe. 2003. Learning extraction patterns for subjective expressions. In *EMNLP'03*, pages 105–112.

Hiroya Takamura, Takashi Inui, and Manabu Okumura. 2005. Extracting semantic orientations of words using spin model. In *ACL'05*, pages 133–140.

Chenhao Tan, Lillian Lee, Jie Tang, Long Jiang, Ming Zhou, and Ping Li. 2011. User-level sentiment analysis incorporating social networks. In *Proceedings of the 17th ACM SIGKDD international conference on Knowledge discovery and data mining*, KDD '11, pages 1397–1405.

Matt Thomas, Bo Pang, and Lillian Lee. 2006. Get out the vote: Determining support or opposition from congressional floor-debate transcripts. In *In Proceedings of EMNLP*, pages 327–335.

Peter Turney and Michael Littman. 2003. Measuring praise and criticism: Inference of semantic orientation from association. *ACM Transactions on Information Systems*, 21:315–346.

Kiri Wagstaff, Claire Cardie, Seth Rogers, and Stefan Schrödl. 2001. Constrained k-means clustering with background knowledge. In *Proceedings of the Eighteenth International Conference on Machine Learning*, pages 577–584.

Janyce Wiebe. 2000. Learning subjective adjectives from corpora. In *Proceedings of the Seventeenth National Conference on Artificial Intelligence and Twelfth Conference on Innovative Applications of Artificial Intelligence*, pages 735–740.

Theresa Wilson, Paul Hoffmann, Swapna Somasundaran, Jason Kessler, Janyce Wiebe, Yejin Choi, Claire Cardie, Ellen Riloff, and Siddharth Patwardhan. 2005a. Opinionfinder: a system for subjectivity analysis. In *Proceedings of HLT/EMNLP on Interactive Demonstrations*, HLT-Demo '05, pages 34–35, Stroudsburg, PA, USA. Association for Computational Linguistics.

Theresa Wilson, Janyce Wiebe, and Paul Hoffmann. 2005b. Recognizing contextual polarity in phrase-level sentiment analysis. In *HLT/EMNLP'05*, Vancouver, Canada.

Bo Yang, William Cheung, and Jiming Liu. 2007. Community mining from signed social networks. *IEEE Trans. on Knowl. and Data Eng.*, 19(10):1333–1348.

Generative Goal-Driven User Simulation for Dialog Management

Aciel Eshky
ILCC
School of Informatics
University of Edinburgh
a.eshky@sms.ed.ac.uk

Ben Allison
ILCC
School of Informatics
University of Edinburgh

Mark Steedman
ILCC
School of Informatics
University of Edinburgh
{ballison, steedman}@inf.ed.ac.uk

Abstract

User simulation is frequently used to train statistical dialog managers for task-oriented domains. At present, goal-driven simulators (those that have a persistent notion of what they wish to achieve in the dialog) require some task-specific engineering, making them impossible to evaluate intrinsically. Instead, they have been evaluated extrinsically by means of the dialog managers they are intended to train, leading to circularity of argument. In this paper, we propose the first fully generative goal-driven simulator that is fully induced from data, without hand-crafting or goal annotation. Our goals are latent, and take the form of topics in a topic model, clustering together semantically equivalent and phonetically confusable strings, implicitly modelling synonymy and speech recognition noise. We evaluate on two standard dialog resources, the Communicator and Let's Go datasets, and demonstrate that our model has substantially better fit to held out data than competing approaches. We also show that features derived from our model allow significantly greater improvement over a baseline at distinguishing real from randomly permuted dialogs.

1 Introduction

Automatically simulating user behaviour in human-machine dialogs has become vital for training statistical dialog managers in task-oriented domains. These managers are often trained with some variant of reinforcement learning (Sutton and Barto, 1998), where optimal behaviour is sought or learnt through the exploration of the space of possible dialogs. Although learning by interacting with human subjects is a possibility (Gašić et al., 2011), it has been argued that user simulation avoids the expensive, labour intensive, and error-prone experience of exposing real humans to fledgling dialog systems (Eckert et al., 1997).

Training effective dialog managers should benefit from exposure to properties exhibited by real users. Table 1 shows an example dialog in a domain such as we consider, where the objective is to simulate at the semantic level. In such task oriented domains, the user has a *goal* (in this case, to book a flight from New York to Osaka), and the machine is tasked with fulfilling it. Notice that the user is consistent with this goal throughout the dialog, in that they do not provide contradictory information (although an ASR error is present), but that every mention of their destination city uses a different string. This motivates our first desideratum: that simulation be consistent over the course of a dialog. Furthermore, one can imagine users not always responding identically in identical situations: we thus additionally require *variability*. In this paper we demonstrate a fully generative, latent variable probability model exhibiting both of these properties.

Thus far, consistent simulators have been partially deterministic and have required some hand-engineering. As a result, it has only been possible to evaluate them extrinsically using dialog managers. This is circular because we need simulators to train managers, but need managers to evaluate simulators. The issue is that judgements of quality of each depend on the specifics of the other and that a proper evaluation of one depends on the correct functioning of the other. Furthermore, there is little reason to assume that because a simulator performs well with a certain dialog manager, it would perform similarly

Speech	Semantic Representation
M: Hello, How Can I help?	M: GREETING M: META_REQUEST_INFO
U: A trip from New York City to Osaka, please.	U: PROVIDE *orig_city* **New York City** U: PROVIDE *dest_city* **Salt Lake City**
M: Leaving from New York City to Salt Lake City. What day would you like to travel?	M: IMPLICIT_CONFIRM *orig_dest_city* M: REQUEST *depart_date*
U: No, no. Leaving from New York to Osaka in Japan.	U: NO_ANSWER *null* **no** U: PROVIDE *orig_city* **New York** U: PROVIDE *dest_city* **Osaka Japan**
M: Leaving from New York to Osaka Japan, correct?	M: EXPLICIT_CONFIRM *orig_city* M: EXPLICIT_CONFIRM *dest_city*
U: Yes.	U: YES_ANSWER *null* **yes**

Table 1: An example of a dialog in speech and its semantic equivalent. M and U denote machine and user utterances respectively. Note how a single speech utterance is split by the semantic parser into multiple logical utterances, each of which is broken down to an ACT, *slot*, and **value**. We consider resources where gold standard transcriptions are not available; thus there will be speech recognition noise, e.g. **Osaka** rendered as **Salt Lake City**, something our model is able to capture.

well with other managers. In contrast, a probabilistic formulation such as we propose allows us to evaluate our models intrinsically using standard machine learning metrics, and without reference to a *specific* manager, thus breaking the circularity, and guarding against such experimental biases.

We demonstrate the efficacy of our model on two tasks, and compare it to two other approaches. Firstly we use a standard bigram model as conceived by Eckert et al. (1997) and Levin and Pieraccini (2000); secondly we compare to a probabilistic goal-based simulator where the goals are string literals, as envisaged by Scheffler and Young (2002) and Schatzmann et al. (2007b). We demonstrate substantial improvement over these models in terms of predicting heldout data on two standard dialog resources: DARPA Communicator (Levin et al., 2000; Georgila et al., 2005b) and Let's Go (Black and Eskenazi, 2009).

2 Related Work

2.1 Related Work on User Simulation

User simulation as a stochastic process was first envisioned by Eckert et al. (1997): their *Bigram* model conditions user utterances exclusively on the preceding machine utterance. This was extended by Levin and Pieraccini (2000), who manually restrict the model to estimating "sensible" pairs of user and machine utterances by assigning all others probability zero.

Bigram models ensure that a locally sensible response to a machine utterance is provided by the simulator; however, they do not ensure that it provides responses consistent with one another throughout the dialog. Several approaches have attempted to overcome this problem. Pietquin (2004), for example, explicitly models a user goal as a set of slot-value pairs randomly generated once per dialog. He then hand selects parameters to ensure that the user's actions are in accordance with their goal.

Jung et al. (2009) use large amounts of dialog state annotations (e.g. what information has been provided so far) to learn Conditional Random Fields over the user utterances, and assume that those features ensure user consistency. Georgila et al. (2005a) instead consider only act-slot pairs, and thus inconsistency is not a factor.

Scheffler and Young (2002) simulate user behaviour by introducing rules for actions that depend on the user goal, and probabilistic modelling for actions that are not goal-dependent. They then map out a decision network that determines user actions at every node prior to the start of the dialog. Agenda-based user simulation, another approach from the literature, assumes a probability distribution over the user goal which is either induced from data (Schatzmann et al., 2007b), or is manually set when no data is available (Schatzmann et al., 2007a). An agenda, which is a stack-like structure of utterances to be produced given the goal, is then devised deterministically. Keizer et al. (2010) combine the decision network with the agenda and goal to allow for some variability for some actions. These models ensure consistency but restrict the variability in user behaviour that can be accommodated. Furthermore, because these approaches do not define a complete probability distribution over user behaviour, they restrict possibilities for their evaluation, a point to which we now turn.

2.2 Related Work on Simulator Evaluation

No standardised metric of evaluation has been established for user simulators largely because they have been so inextricably linked to dialog managers. The most popular method of evaluation relies on generating synthetic dialogs through the interaction of the user simulator with some dialog manager. Schatzmann et al. (2005) hand-craft a simple deterministic dialog manager based on finite automata, and compute similarity measures between these synthetically produced dialogs and real dialogs. Georgila et al. (2006) use a scoring function to evaluate synthetic dialogs using accuracy, precision, recall, and perplexity, while Schatzmann et al. (2007b) rely on dialog completion rates. Williams (2008) use a Cramer–von Mises test, a hypothesis test to determine whether simulated and real dialogs are significantly different, while Janarthanam and Lemon (2009) use Kullback Leibler Divergence between the empirical distributions over acts in real and simulated dialogs. Singh et al. (2000) and Ai and Litman (2008) judge the consistency of human quality ranked synthetic dialogs generated by different simulators interacting with the IT-SPOKE dialog system.

Schatzmann et al. (2007b) use a simulator to train a statistical dialog manager and then evaluate the learned policy. Because this only indirectly evaluates the simulator, it is inappropriate as a sole measure of quality.

There has been far less evaluation of simulators without a dialog manager. The main approach is to compute precision and recall on an utterance basis, which is intended to measure the similarity between real user responses in the corpora and simulated user responses produced under similar circumstances (Schatzmann et al., 2005; Georgila et al., 2006). However, this is a harsh evaluation as it assumes a correct or "best" answer, and penalises valid variability in user behaviour.

3 Dialog as a Statistical Process

We consider a dialog to be a series of *turns*, comprised of multiple *utterances*. Each Utterance consists of an ACT, a *slot*, and a **value**, as shown in Table 1. Dialogs proceed by the user and the machine alternating turns. Because the dialogs are of mixed initiative, there is no restriction on the number of contiguous machine or user utterances.

Our aim is to model the user, and are interested in the conditional distribution of the user utterances given the dialog up to that point. In other words, we are interested in the distribution $p(u_i|d_1 \ldots d_{i-1})$, where d_n is either a machine utterance m_n or a user utterance u_n.

4 Models of Users in Dialogs

This section describes several models of increasing complexity: a Bigram model, which serves as a baseline; an upper-bound on String-Goal models, which we design to mimic the behaviour of previous goal-based approaches, but with a probabilistic formulation; and finally our approach, the Topic-Goal model.

4.1 Bigram Model

The simplest model we define over dialogs is the bigram model of Eckert et al. (1997):

$$p(u_i|\mathbf{m}) = p(u_i|m_{i-1}) \quad (1)$$

$$p(\mathbf{u}|\mathbf{m}) = \prod_i p(u_i|\mathbf{m}) \quad (2)$$

The probability of each user utterance u_i (the complete {ACT, *slot*, **value**} triple) is dependent only on the machine utterance immediately preceding it (the slight abuse of notation m_{i-1} here does not mean the utterance at $i-1$ in the machine utterance list, but the utterance immediately preceding the i-th), and utterances in the dialog are conditionally independent of one another. (Georgila et al. (2006) found no benefit from increasing the Markov horizon). Since each utterance is generated independently of others in the dialog with the same context, there is no enforced consistency between utterances.

Since we require a distribution over all possible utterances, assigning non–zero probability to cases outside of the training data, our bigram model is interpolated with a unigram model, which itself is interpolated with a smoothing model which assumes independence between the act, slot, and value elements of the utterance. Interpolation weights are set to maximise probability of a development set of dialogs. Each sub-model uses the maximum likelihood estimator (the relative frequency of the utterance), and unseen machine utterances place full weight on the unigram/smoothed model (ignoring the bigram probability since it has no meaning if m_{i-1} is unobserved). We label this model the Bigram model in subsequent experiments.

4.2 Goal-Based Models

One way to ensure consistency and more realistic behaviour is to have a *goal* for the user in the dialog, which corresponds to values for slots required in the problem. For instance, they might be the origin and destination cities in a flight booking domain. In standard machine learning terms, the goal becomes a latent variable g in a probability model. We can then define a distribution over utterances as:

$$p(u_i|\mathbf{m}, g) = p(u_i|m_{i-1}, g) \quad (3)$$

$$p(\mathbf{u}|\mathbf{m}) = \sum_g p(g) \prod_i p(u_i|m_{i-1}, g) \quad (4)$$

4.3 An Upper-Bound on String-Goal Models

The simplest variant of g has string values for each of the slots the user is required to provide in order for the dialog to succeed. Thus we may have:

$g =$ [*orig_city*: **New York**; *dest_city*: **Osaka**]

as presented in Schatzmann et al. (2005) and Schatzmann et al. (2007b). However, in these simulators, while the goal is probabilistic, there is no distribution over utterances given the goal because utterances are assembled deterministically from a series of rule applications. There is also no marginalisation over the goal as in (4) above.

The issue with a model of user goals as strings in this fashion is that users describe the same values in multiple ways (**Osaka Japan**, **Osaka**), and speech recognition errors corrupt consistent user input (**Osaka** mis-recognised as **Salt Lake City**). Users also might legitimately switch their goals mid-dialog. Inference in the model would have allow for these possibilities: we would have to marginalise over all possible goal switches.

For the sake of comparison, we compute an upper-bound on string-goal models, which gives a flavour for how such models would perform *optimistically*. The upper-bound assigns probability to dialogs as follows: for each utterance u_i if the corresponding value v_i has been seen before in the dialog, the probability used for that utterance is just $p(a_i, s_i|m_{i-1})$, that is, the probability of the act a_i and slot s_i only; there is no penalty for repetition of the value. If the value is unseen in the dialog, we use the full probability of the utterance from the bigram model as described above. This is optimistic because there is no penalty for repeated goal changes besides that imposed by the bigram model itself, and no penalty is imposed for choosing between previously sampled goals as would be necessary in a probability model.

Any string-based model necessarily assigns lower probabilities to data than the upper bound, because it would penalise goal changes (in a probabilistic sense; that is, there would be a term to reflect the probability of some new goal given the old) to allow for the discrepancy in values present in dialogs. In contrast, our upper bound does not include such a term. Furthermore, once multiple goal values had been uttered in the dialog, we would have to sample one to use for the next utterance, which would again incur some cost: again, we do not have such a cost in our upper bound.

We could in theory use an external model of noise to account for these value discrepancies (and the ASR errors we model in the next section). However, this would further decrease the probability, as some probability mass currently assigned to the heldout data would have to be reserved for the possibility of string renderings other than those we observe.

It bears reiterating that our upper bound on string-goals is not a generative model: however, it allows us to assign probabilities to unseen data (albeit optimistically), and thus provides us with a point of comparison. Although not technically a model, we refer to this as the String-Goal model for the remainder of the paper.

4.4 Topic-Goal Model

To motivate our proposal, consider that over the course of a dialog one could look at the set of all values used for some slot, for example the destination city, as a count vector:

$v_{\text{dest\_city}}$ = **Salt Lake**:1; **Osaka**:2; **Osaka Japan**:1

The above vector may arise because the user actually wants to go to **Osaka**, but the destination is initially mis-recognised as **Salt Lake**, and the user finally disambiguates with the addition of the country. Such situations are common in the noisy dialog resources from which simulators are induced—however, any string-based goal will necessarily consider these different renderings to be different goals, and will require resampling or smoothing terms to deal with them.

Our approach instead treats the count vector as samples from a topic model; that is, a mixture over multinomial distributions. Whilst by far the most popular topic model is LDA (Blei et al., 2003), it provides too flexible a distribution over count vectors to be used with such small samples (we confirmed the poor suitability of this model in preliminary experiments). Instead we use the simpler Mixture-of-Multinomials model, where the latent topic is sampled once per dialog instead of once per value uttered. We describe below how parameters to this model are estimated, and focus for now on how the resulting model assigns probability to dialogs.

In this formulation, the latent goal for each slot, which was previously a string, now becomes an indicator for a topic in a topic model. Each topic can in theory generate any string (so the model is inherently smoothed), but most strings in most topics will have only the smoothing weight and most probability mass will be on a small number of highly correlated strings. We treat the slots as being independent of one another in the goal, and thus:

$$p(g) = \prod_s p(z_s) \tag{5}$$

Where z_s is the topic indicator for some slot s. If slot s has associated with it a count vector of values $\mathbf{v_s}$, each looking like the example above, then the distribution over the values used for each slot becomes:

$$p(v_s) = \sum_{z_s} p(z_s)\, p(v_s|z_s) \tag{6}$$

We then define a bigram-based Act model to describe the probabilities of the {ACT, *slot*} pairs to which these values belong, so that:

$$p(\mathbf{u}|\mathbf{m}) = \prod_s p(z_s) \cdot \prod_i p(a_i, s_i|m_{i-1})\, p(v_i|z_{s_i}) \tag{7}$$

In reality, some slots will not have corresponding values, or will be slots whose values are not appropriate to model in the above way. Dates and times, for example, have ordinal and structural relations between them, and a model which treats them as disconnected entities is inappropriate. For utterances defined over such slots we use a standard bigram model as in (1), and for appropriate utterances we use a topic-goal model as in (7). This constitutes the only domain knowledge necessary to adapt the model for a new resource. We refer to this model as the Topic-Goal model.

4.4.1 Topic Model Parameter Estimation

Our topic model is a Bayesian version of the Mixture-of-Multinomials model. Under this model, each dialog has associated with it a latent variable z_s for each slot s in the goal, which indicates which topic is used to draw the values for that slot. Conditioned on z, independent samples are drawn from the distribution over words to which that value of z corresponds—however, the effect in the marginal distribution over words is to strongly prefer sets which have co-occurred in training as these are assigned to the same topic.

Bayesian inference in mixture models has been described in detail in Neal (1991) and Griffiths and Steyvers (2004), so we give only a brief account here for our particular model. We take r appropriately-spaced samples from a Gibbs' sampler over the posterior mixture parameters θ, ϕ: θ are the word-topic parameters and ϕ are the mixture proportions. We assume a uniform Dirichlet prior on θ and ϕ, leading to Dirichlet posteriors which we integrate out in the predictive distribution over v using the standard Dirichlet integral. For each of our r samples we have components z parameterised by γ_{rz} (the Dirichlet parameter for the z-th mixture component in the r-th sample) and α_{rzj} for each word j in the z-th topic for the r-th sample. The $\bullet$ notation indicates a sum over the corresponding index, i.e. $\gamma_{r\bullet} = \sum_z \gamma_{rz}$. Then:

$$p(v) = \frac{1}{|r|} \sum_r \sum_z \frac{\gamma_{rz}}{\gamma_{r\bullet}} p(v|\alpha_{rz}) \quad (8)$$

$$p(v|\alpha) = \frac{\Gamma(\alpha_\bullet)}{\Gamma(\alpha_\bullet + v_\bullet)} \prod_j \frac{\Gamma(v_j + \alpha_j)}{\Gamma(\alpha_j)} \quad (9)$$

This states that each of the r samples has topics z which are multinomial distributions with posteriors governed by parameters α_{rz}. For any of these topics, the distribution over v is as given in Equation (9) (we suppress the subscripting of α here for the different samples and topics, since this holds whatever its value). The final predictive probability given in Equation (8) averages over the samples r and the topics z (with topics weighted by their parameters γ_{rz}).

5 Experimental Setup

Our experiments use two standard corpora, the first of which is DARPA Communicator (DC), a flight booking domain collected between 2000-2001 through the interaction of real users with 10 different systems (Levin et al., 2000). It was later automatically annotated by Georgila et al. (2005b) to include semantic information. The second corpora is Let's Go (LG), years 2007, 2008, and 2009, distributed as part of the Spoken Dialog Challenge (Black and Eskenazi, 2009). Let's Go is a bus routing domain in Pittsburgh collected by having the general public interact with the CMU dialog system to find their way through the city. The dialogs in both corpora are of mixed-initiative, having a free number of contiguous system and user responses.

We preprocessed the corpora, converting Communicator XML-tagged files and Let's Go system log files into sequences of ACT, *slot*, and **value** utterances. Table 2 gives examples. We then divided the corpora into training, development and test sets as follows: Communicator contains 2285 dialogs in total, and Let's Go contains 17992, and in each case we selected 80% of dialogs at random for training, 10% for development, and 10% for testing.

DC:	PROVIDE_INFO *orig_city* **Boston**
LG:	INFORM *place* [departure_place **CMU**, arrival_place **airport**]

Table 2: Example utterances from the two corpora. Note how in addition to the value, the Let's Go utterances contain properties (departure_place and arrival_place).

Let's Go is a noisy corpus that contains far more speech recognition errors than Communicator. In addition, users tend to be more flexible with their bus routes than they are with their flight destinations, and so values are a lot more varied throughout the course of Let's Go dialogs than Communicator ones. Furthermore, Let's Go semantic parses contain ambiguity not present in Communicator; the parser fails to distinguish departure from arrival places over 90% of the time, and instead assigns them a generic Single_Place property. Our current model assumes the decisions made by the semantic parser are correct. In reality however, a better model would incorporate potential noise in the semantic parse in a joint model. We defer this more complex treatment for future work.

Free model parameters are set by a simple search on the development set, where the objective is likelihood—for the bigram model the parameters are the interpolation weights, and for the topic model we search for the number of topics and smoothing constant for the topic distributions. For Let's Go, since we can have multiple places provided in a single act, we treat each utterance as containing a set of values and build the count vector for the topic model as the union of these sets over the whole dialog. The slots over which the topic model is defined for Communicator are *dest_city* and *orig_city* (this takes into account PROVIDE and REPROVIDE acts). For Let's Go we derive the model over the three properties: single_place, arrival_place and departure_place, as opposed to the less informative slot *place*.

6 Evaluating the Simulators

We evaluate each of the models in terms of the probability they assign to the test data. This metric is more suitable than the precision and recall metrics which have been previously used, because it acknowledges that, rather than each user response being "correct" at the point which it is observed, there

Model	DC(A)	DC(P)	LG(A)	LG(P)
Topic	**252.78**	**860.2**	**113.45**	**1417.06**
String	270.09	1286.03	169.87	4578.23
Bigram	347.88	5979.53	223.23	10125.87
Act	9.56	5.2	2.77	2.34

Table 3: The mean per-utterance perplexity on heldout data. DC-A is all acts for Communicator, while DC-P is the calculated on PROVIDE acts alone (the acts on which our model is designed to improve prediction). LG-A and LG-P have the same meaning for Let's Go.

is a distribution over possible responses. Because the models we define are full probability models, we are able to compute this metric and do not need to use an arbitrarily selected dialog manager for evaluation.

The heldout probability metric should be understood as a means of comparing the relative viability of different models of the same data. Note that we are reporting the probability of unobserved data, rather than data from which the models were induced, and are thus measuring the generalisability of the models (in contrast, maximising the probability of the training data would simply encourage overfitting). The absolute numbers are hard to interpret, as there is no hard upper bound; while it may be appealing to think of an upper bound of 1, this is incorrect as it would imply that there was no variability in the data. However, it should be understood that assigning particular behaviour higher probability means that the model is more likely to exhibit it when run in simulation mode—and since the user behaviour in question has not been seen at training time, this measures the extent to which the models have generalised beyond the training data relative to one another.

We report the mean per-utterance log probability of unseen data, that is, the probability of the whole heldout corpus divided by the number of user utterances.

6.1 Results

Figure 1 shows the results of our evaluation. We see that the Bigram model is weak on both resources. The results of the String Goal model suggest that, even using the generous evaluation we do here, there

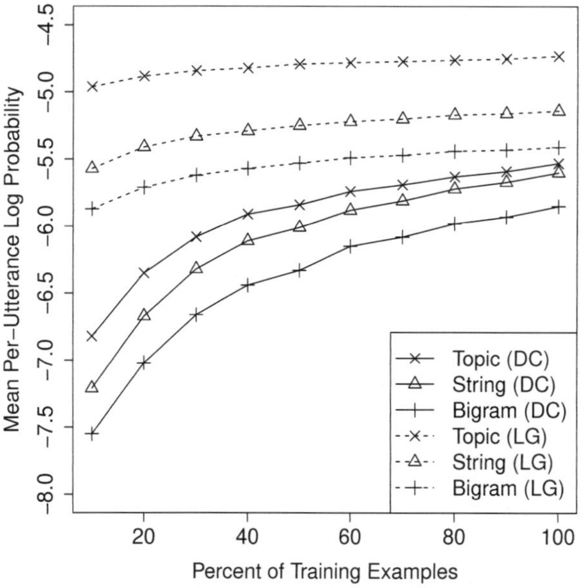

Figure 1: Heldout probability of the two resources for varying percentages of training dialogs. Note that while the percentages match across resources, Let's Go is much larger and thus the absolute numbers of dialogs are different, which explains the better performance on Let's Go.

is much variability due to synonymy and recognition errors which string goals are unable to capture (in contrast to our Topic Goal model). The Topic Goal model explains this much more easily by grouping commonly co–occurring values into the same topic. Table 3 shows the perplexities corresponding to the performances with 100% training data for all acts and just PROVIDE acts (perplexity is 2^{-lp} where lp is the log probability). Improvements are more apparent when we compute the probability over PROVIDE acts alone, which the models are designed to handle. And since perplexity is not on a log scale, the differences are more pronounced. The Act model, which is a bigram model over {ACT, *slot*} pairs alone excluding the values, demonstrates the vast discrepancy in uncertainty between the full problem and the valueless prediction problem. We note that the perplexity of our Act model on Communicator is comparable to that of Georgila et al. (2006).

6.2 Example Simulator Behaviour

In this section we give examples of our Topic Goal model simulator in generation mode, which corresponds to sampling from the induced model.

d	z_{dest_city} [probability]	proportion of samples	user utterance given topic z_{dest_city} and machine utterance REQUEST_INFO *dest_city*
1	**Norfolk Virginia** [0.562]	0.264	PROVIDE_INFO *dest_city* **Norfolk Virginia**
	Norfolk [0.234]	0.111	PROVIDE_INFO *dest_city* **Norfolk**
	Newark Virginia [0.088]	0.039	PROVIDE_INFO *dest_city* **Newark Virginia**
	Virginia Beach [0.0412]	0.028	PROVIDE_INFO *orig_city* **Las Vegas Nevada**
	Newark [0.040]	0.028	NO_ANSWER *null* **no**
		0.025	COMMAND *start_over* **start over**
2	**Chicago** [0.350]	0.164	PROVIDE_INFO *dest_city* **Chicago**
	Chicago Illinois [0.182]	0.082	PROVIDE_INFO *dest_city* **Chicago Illinois**
	Duluth Minnesota [0.124]	0.057	PROVIDE_INFO *dest_city* **New Orleans**
	New Orleans [0.122]	0.055	PROVIDE_INFO *dest_city* **Duluth Minnesota**
	New Orleans Louisiana [0.085]	0.039	PROVIDE_INFO *dest_city* **New Orleans Louisiana**
		0.028	NO_ANSWER *null* **no**
3	**Anchorage** [0.539]	0.252	PROVIDE_INFO *dest_city* **Anchorage**
	Anchorage Alaska [0.148]	0.072	PROVIDE_INFO *dest_city* **Anchorage Alaska**
	Jacksonville Florida [0.124]	0.056	PROVIDE_INFO *dest_city* **Jacksonville Florida**
	Great Anchorage Alaska [0.098]	0.048	PROVIDE_INFO *dest_city* **Great Anchorage Alaska**
	Duluth Minnesota [0.057]	0.047	PROVIDE_INFO *orig_city* **Hartford Connecticut**
		0.026	PROVIDE_INFO *dest_city* **Duluth Minnesota**

Table 4: Examples of sampling from the topic goal model. Left: top 5 strings (with probabilities) sampled from topics for three different dialogs *d*. Right: top 6 utterances (plus fraction of samples in 10,000) generated in response to the machine utterance "REQUEST_INFO *dest_city*" and conditioned on the topic z_{dest_city}.

Our examples are drawn from the model induced for the Communicator data. Sampling from standard distributions can be implemented following the algorithms in Bishop (2006) and other statistical resources. Utterances are sampled by sampling ACT, *slot* pairs from the distribution $p(a_i, s_i|m_{i-1})$ (drawing a value from a multinomial distribution). If we sample a PROVIDE_INFO act, we check whether we have sampled a topic for the corresponding slot thus far in the dialog. If not, we sample one by drawing a topic indicator from $p(z_s) = \frac{\gamma_{rz}}{\gamma_{\bullet\bullet}}$ and then drawing a multinomial distribution over strings from the Dirichlet posterior corresponding to z. Once the topic for the slot is set, we sample **values** as draws from the fixed multinomial and add these to the ACT, *slot* pair.

Table 4 shows some examples drawn from the model. For each row in the table (corresponding to a new dialog *d*), we sample a topic for the *dest_city* and *orig_city* as needed, and sample 10000 utterances given that topic. The left hand side of the table shows the top five strings in the sampled topic, while the right hand side shows the top six utterances in response to REQUEST_INFO *dest_city*. Note that the proportion of utterances on the right does not match the probability of the values on the left because of the presence of other user acts besides PROVIDE *dest_city*.

7 Evaluating Model Consistency

Having shown in the previous section that our Topic Goal model is a much better predictor of heldout data than the String Goal model or Bigram model, we now turn to a demonstration of the model's capturing of consistency.

In the face of value synonymy and ASR errors, we define *inconsistent* dialogs to be ones that are locally coherent but lack the structure of a real dialog from one turn to the next. We then suggest that an appropriate task for consistent models is distinguishing between consistent and inconsistent dialogs.

To test this hypothesis, we devise the following classification problem: can we discriminate between

Baseline	Dialog length (turns)
	Mean, standard deviation, min and max acts per turn
	Presence of special machine acts (flight offer and confirm)
	Presence of user acts (provide a dest city and arrival city)
	Proportion of acts which were provides
String Consistency	Did the user provide inconsistent information about dest city?
	Did the user provide inconsistent information about orig city?
Topic Model	Ranked list of posterior probabilities of top 50 topics
	Normalised probability of dialog for topic model

Table 5: Feature sets for consistency experiments

real dialogs and those generated by randomly sampling turns from different dialogs? In this section we induce classifiers over various feature sets to demonstrate that we can, and that the Topic Goal model contains far more useful information in this regard than string-based consistency features. (The bigram model by definition provides no help here, since the units of which dialogs consist contain the entire window of context used for the bigram model).

We take our training and development data from the Communicator corpus in the previous section, and create a classification problem as follows: real dialogs form positive examples in the classification problem. To create negative examples, we sample {machine, user} turns at random from the appropriate resource. We keep a histogram over real dialog lengths, and sample a number of turns for our "fake" dialogs proportional to this histogram. We then sample this many turns from the frequency distribution over turns in the real data, and create exactly as many dialogs in this fashion as real dialogs in the data. The result is an equal number of dialogs comprised of real turns, of (expected) real length, but where the sequence of turns is highly unlikely to be coherent given the random sampling. The classification problem is thus far from trivial. We do this from our training data to produce data with which to train the classifier, and from our development data to provide test instances. This gives rise to 2500 training instances, and 500 test instances.

We learn linear SVMs with various features described in Table 6. These feature sets are designed to capture different aspects of consistency: the baseline features are intended to capture surface level features of the dialogs, inspired by (Schatzmann et al., 2005) where they provide trivial separation of real from simulated dialogs. However, our setting is different: we do not seek to tell real dialogs from fully simulated ones, but real dialogs from scrambled versions of real dialogs. In addition to length-based features, we add binary presence indicator for several user and machine acts highly correlated with the completion of dialogs, as well as for acts which indicate the provision of information and the proportion of all acts occupied by these. The table gives a complete list of these Baseline (B) features.

We derive a second set of features intended to replicate the utility of string-based goals: we set up binary features to fire if contradictory information is provided for the slots over the course of the dialog. These are our String Consistency (SC) features.

Finally, we use our topic-model simulator to derive consistency features. Our features are the posterior distribution over topics for each slot given that dialog. Our topics are induced from the real training dialogs, and their posterior probabilities computed for all dialogs relative to this model. We take posterior probabilities of the fifty most probable topics for each of the *dest_city* and *orig_city* slots as features, as well as the normalised log probability of the dialog (the log probability divided by the number of user utterances). These form our Topic Model (TM) features.

Our classifiers are linear SVMs, and we use libsvm (Chang and Lin, 2011), scaling features to the range $[0-1]$. All other parameters are left at their defaults.

Feature Set	Accuracy
Baseline (B)	74.34 ±3.77
String Consistency (SC)	63.60 ±4.27
B + SC	77.63 ±3.58
Topic Model (TM)	79.61 ±3.44
B + SC + TM	85.96 ±2.89

Table 6: Performances for the classifiers. Errors are 95% intervals to the accuracies assuming they are parameters to a binomial distribution

7.1 Results

The results of the classifiers are shown in Table 5. Since we have an equally balanced binary classification task, accuracy is the most appropriate metric. Here we see that the baseline and string consistency features have roughly the same discriminatory potential, and their union produces a slight improvement. The topic model features are far superior to this, and the union of all three sets gives a further improvement.

These results demonstrate that our model encodes notions of consistency which go substantially beyond those defined at the level of strings. Features defined over the latent topic goal space substantially improve performance in a difficult discrimination task, demonstrating that our model captures an important notion of how real dialogs appear that is not shared by the other models we consider.

8 Concluding Remarks and Future Work

This paper presents a fully generative goal driven user simulator, the first to merge both consistency and variability within a fully probabilistic framework. We evaluate our model on two task-based dialog domains, Let's Go and Communicator, and find it to outperform both a simple bigram model and an upper bound on probability models where the strings are represented as goals, in terms of the probability the model assigns to heldout dialogs.

We then move on to show that features derived from the model lead to substantial improvement in detecting real dialogs from those where the turns have been selected at random from all turns in the training data: this is a fairly difficult task, but our model allows significant improvement over strong and sensible baselines.

Our model could be extended in a number of ways. It could be improved to incorporate noise resulting from the decisions made by the semantic parser. Another possible improvement is to explore the effects of introducing dependency between the slots in the user goal, which would enforce more plausible values pairings and would potentially improve the simulator's performance. The effects of a dependence assumption between the different utterances occurring in a single user turn under the act model can also be explored. We would also like to use our simulator to train a POMDP-based dialog manager using a form of reinforcement learning.

References

Hua Ai and Diane J. Litman. 2008. Assessing dialog system user simulation evaluation measures using human judges. In *Proceedings of ACL-08: HLT*.

Christopher M. Bishop. 2006. *Pattern Recognition and Machine Learning (Information Science and Statistics)*. Springer-Verlag New York, Inc.

Alan W. Black and Maxine Eskenazi. 2009. The Spoken Dialogue Challenge. In *Proceedings of SIGDIAL 2009*, SIGDIAL '09.

David M. Blei, Andrew Y. Ng, and Michael I. Jordan. 2003. Latent dirichlet allocation. *Journal of Machine Learning Research*, 3:993–1022, March.

Chih-Chung Chang and Chih-Jen Lin. 2011. LIBSVM: A library for support vector machines. *ACM Transactions on Intelligent Systems and Technology*, 2:27:1–27:27.

Wieland Eckert, Esther Levin, and Roberto Pieraccini. 1997. User modeling for spoken dialogue system evaluation. In *Proceedings of IEEE Workshop on Automatic Speech Recognition and Understanding*.

M. Gašić, F. Jurcicek, B. Thomson, K. Yu, and S. Young. 2011. On-line policy optimisation of spoken dialogue systems via live interaction with human subjects. In *Automatic Speech Recognition and Understanding, 2011 IEEE Workshop on*, Hawaii, December.

Kallirroi Georgila, James Henderson, and Oliver Lemon. 2005a. Learning user simulations for information state update dialogue systems. In *Proceedings InterSpeech 2005*.

Kallirroi Georgila, Oliver Lemon, and James Henderson. 2005b. Automatic annotation of communicator dialogue data for learning dialogue strategies and user simulations. In *Proceedings Ninth Workshop on the Semantics and Pragmatics of Dialogue*.

Kallirroi Georgila, James Henderson, and Oliver Lemon. 2006. User Simulation for Spoken Dialogue Systems:

Learning and Evaluation. In *Proceedings InterSpeech 2006*.

Thomas L. Griffiths and Mark Steyvers. 2004. Finding scientific topics. *PNAS*, 101(suppl. 1):5228–5235.

Srinivasan Janarthanam and Oliver Lemon. 2009. A two-tier user simulation model for reinforcement learning of adaptive referring expression generation policies. In *Proceedings of SIGDIAL 2009*, SIGDIAL '09, pages 120–123.

Sangkeun Jung, Cheongjae Lee, Kyungduk Kim, Minwoo Jeong, and Gary Geunbae Lee. 2009. Data-driven user simulation for automated evaluation of spoken dialog systems. *Computer Speech & Language*, 23(4):479–509.

Simon Keizer, Milica Gašić, Filip Jurčíček, François Mairesse, Blaise Thomson, Kai Yu, and Steve Young. 2010. Parameter estimation for agenda-based user simulation. In *Proceedings of SIGDIAL 2010*.

Esther Levin and Roberto Pieraccini. 2000. A stochastic model of human-machine interaction for learning dialog strategies. In *IEEE Transactions on Speech and Audio Processing*.

E. Levin, S. Narayanan, R. Pieraccini, K. Biatov, E. Bocchieri, G. Di Fabbrizio, W. Eckert, S. Lee, A. Pokrovsky, M. Rahim, P. Ruscitti, and M. Walker. 2000. The AT&T-DARPA communicator mixed-initiative spoken dialog system. In *In ICSLP*.

Radford Neal. 1991. Bayesian Mixture Modeling by Monte Carlo Simulation. Technical report, University of Toronto.

Olivier Pietquin. 2004. *A Framework for Unsupervised Learning of Dialogue Strategies*. Ph.D. thesis, Faculté Polytechnique de Mons, TCTS Lab (Belgique), apr.

Jost Schatzmann, Kallirroi Georgila, and Steve Young. 2005. Quantitative evaluation of user simulation techniques for spoken dialogue systems. In *Proceeings of 6th SIGDIAL Workshop*.

Jost Schatzmann, Blaise Thomson, Karl Weilhammer, Hui Ye, and Steve Young. 2007a. Agenda-based user simulation for bootstrapping a POMDP dialogue system. In *HLT-NAACL (Short Papers)*, NAACL-Short '07.

Jost Schatzmann, Blaise Thomson, and Steve Young. 2007b. Statistical User Simulation with a Hidden Agenda. In *Proceedings 8th SIDdial Workshop on Discourse and Dialogue*, September.

Konrad Scheffler and Steve Young. 2002. Automatic learning of dialogue strategy using dialogue simulation and reinforcement learning. In *Proceedings of HLT 2002*.

Satinder P. Singh, Michael J. Kearns, Diane J. Litman, and Marilyn A. Walker. 2000. Empirical evaluation of a reinforcement learning spoken dialogue system. In *Proceedings of the Seventeenth National Conference on Artificial Intelligence and Twelfth Conference on Innovative Applications of Artificial Intelligence*.

Richard S. Sutton and Andrew G. Barto. 1998. *Reinforcement Learning: An Introduction*. MIT Press, Cambridge, MA.

Jason D. Williams. 2008. Evaluating user simulations with the Cramer-von Mises divergence. *Speech Communication*, 50(10):829–846, October.

Optimising Incremental Dialogue Decisions Using Information Density for Interactive Systems

Nina Dethlefs, Helen Hastie, Verena Rieser and Oliver Lemon
School of Mathematical and Computer Sciences
Heriot-Watt University, Edinburgh, Scotland
n.s.dethlefs | h.hastie | v.t.rieser | o.lemon@hw.ac.uk

Abstract

Incremental processing allows system designers to address several discourse phenomena that have previously been somewhat neglected in interactive systems, such as backchannels or barge-ins, but that can enhance the responsiveness and naturalness of systems. Unfortunately, prior work has focused largely on deterministic incremental decision making, rendering system behaviour less flexible and adaptive than is desirable. We present a novel approach to incremental decision making that is based on *Hierarchical Reinforcement Learning* to achieve an interactive optimisation of Information Presentation (IP) strategies, allowing the system to generate and comprehend backchannels and barge-ins, by employing the recent psycholinguistic hypothesis of *information density (ID)* (Jaeger, 2010). Results in terms of average rewards and a human rating study show that our learnt strategy outperforms several baselines that are not sensitive to ID by more than 23%.

1 Introduction

Recent work on incremental systems has shown that adapting a system's turn-taking behaviour to be more human-like can improve the user's experience significantly, based on incremental models of automatic speech recognition (ASR) (Baumann et al., 2011), dialogue management (Buss et al., 2010), and speech generation (Skantze and Hjalmarsson, 2010). All of these approaches are based on the same general abstract architecture of incremental processing (Schlangen and Skantze, 2011). While this architecture offers inherently incremental mechanisms to update and revise input hypotheses, it is affected by a number of drawbacks, shared by deterministic models of decision making in general: they rely on hand-crafted rules which can be time-consuming and expensive to produce, they do not provide a mechanism to deal with uncertainty introduced by varying user behaviour, they are unable to generalise and adapt flexibly to unseen situations, and they do not use automatic optimisation. Statistical approaches to incremental processing that address some of these problems have been suggested by Raux and Eskenazi (2009), who use a cost matrix and decision theoretic principles to optimise turn-taking in a dialogue system under the constraint that users prefer no gaps and no overlap at turn boundaries. Also, DeVault et al. (2009) use maximum entropy classification to support responsive overlap in an incremental system by predicting the completions of user utterances. Selfridge et al. (2011) use logistic regression models to predict the stability and accuracy of incremental speech recognition results to enhance performance without causing delay. For related work on (deterministic) incremental language generation, please see (Kilger and Finkler, 1995; Purver and Otsuka, 2003).

Recent years have seen a number of data-driven approaches to interactive systems that automatically adapt their decisions to the dialogue context using Reinforcement Learning (Levin et al., 2000; Walker, 2000; Young, 2000; Singh et al., 2002; Pietquin and Dutoit, 2006; Henderson et al., 2008; Cuayáhuitl et al., 2010; Thomson, 2009; Young et al., 2010; Lemon, 2011; Janarthanam and Lemon, 2010; Rieser et al., 2010; Cuayáhuitl and Dethlefs,

2011; Dethlefs and Cuayáhuitl, 2011). While these approaches have been shown to enhance the performance and adaptivity of interactive systems, unfortunately none of them has yet been combined with incremental processing.

In this paper, we present a novel approach to incremental decision making for output planning that is based on Hierarchical Reinforcement Learning (HRL). In particular, we address the problem of optimising IP strategies while allowing the system to generate and comprehend backchannels and barge-ins based on a partially data-driven reward function. Generating backchannels can be beneficial for grounding in interaction. Similarly, barge-ins can lead to more efficient interactions, e.g. when a system can clarify a bad recognition result immediately before acting based on a misrecognition.

A central concept to our approach is Information Density (ID) (Jaeger, 2010), a psycholinguistic hypothesis that human utterance production is sensitive to a uniform distribution of information across the utterance. This hypothesis has also been adopted for low level output planning recently, see e.g. Rajkumar and White (2011). Our results in terms of average rewards and a human rating study show that a learning agent that is sensitive to ID can learn when it is most beneficial to generate feedback to a user, and outperforms several other agents that are not sensitive to ID.

2 Incremental Information Presentation

2.1 Information Presentation Strategies

Our example domain of application is the Information Presentation phase in an interactive system for restaurant recommendations, extending previous work by Rieser et al. (2010). This previous work incrementally constructs IP strategies according to the predicted user reaction, whereas our approach focuses on whether and when to generate backchannels and barge-ins and how to react to user barge-ins in the context of dynamically changing input hypotheses. We therefore implement a simplified version of Rieser et al.'s model. Their system distinguished two steps: the selection of an IP strategy and the selection of attributes to present to the user. We assume here that the choice of attributes is determined by matching the types specified in the user input, so that our system only needs to choose a strategy for presenting its results. Attributes include *cuisine, food quality, location, price range* and *service quality* of a restaurant. The system then performs a database lookup and chooses among three main IP strategies *summary, comparison, recommendation* and several ordered combinations of these. Please see Rieser et al. (2010) for details. Table 1 shows examples of the main types of IP strategies that we generate.

2.2 Backchannels and Barge-ins

An important advantage of incremental processing can be the increased reactiveness of systems. In this paper, we focus on the phenomena of backchannels and barge-ins that can act as feedback in an interaction for both user and system. Figure 1 shows some examples. *Backchannels* can often be interpreted as signals of grounding. Coming from the user, the system may infer that the user is following the presentation of information or is confirming a piece of information without trying to take the turn. Similarly, we can allow a system to generate backchannels to the user to confirm that it understands the user's preferences, i.e. receives high confidence scores from the ASR module. An important decision for a dialogue system is then *when to generate a backchannel?*

Barge-ins typically occur in different situations. The user may barge-in on the system to correct an ASR error (such as 'Italian' instead of 'Indian' in Figure 1) or the system may want to barge-in on the user to confirm a low-confidence ASR hypothesis so as to be able to start an immediate database look up for results. In the former case, the user barging-in on the system, we assume that the system has two choices: *yielding the turn* to the user, or *trying to keep* the turn. In the latter case, the system barging-in on the user, the system would have to decide *if and when it would be beneficial to barge-in* on a user utterance. In the following sections, we will develop a model of dialogue optimisation that can address these question based on Hierarchical RL that optimises system behaviour based on trade-offs defined in terms of ID.

Type	Example
Comparison	The restaurant *Roma* is in the medium price range, but does not serve excellent food. The restaurants *Firenze* and *Verona* both have great food but are more expensive. The restaurant *Verona* has good service, too.
Recommendation	Restaurant *Verona* has the best overall match with your query. It is a bit more expensive, but has great food and service.
Summary	I found 24 Italian restaurants in the city centre that match your query. 11 of them are in the medium price range, 5 are cheap and 8 are expensive.

Table 1: Examples of IP as a *comparison, recommendation* and *summary* for a user looking for Italian restaurants in the city centre that have a good price for value.

Backchannel 1 (the system backchannels)

USR I want Italian food [500 ms] in the city centre...
SYS uh-huh
SYS OK. I found 24 Italian restaurants in the city centre. The restaurant *Roma* is in the medium price range, but does not have great food. The restaurants *Firenze* and *Verona* ...

Backchannel 2 (the user backchannels)

USR I want Italian food in the centre of town ...
SYS OK. I found 35 central Italian restaurants ...
USR OK.
SYS The restaurant *Verona* has great food but is also a bit expensive. The *Roma* is cheaper, but not as central as *Verona* ...

Barge-ins 1 (the user barges-in on system)

USR I want Italian food in the centre of town ...
SYS I found 35 Indian ...
USR Not Indian, I want Italian.
SYS OK, Italian ...
SYS I have 24 Italian restaurants ...

Barge-ins 2 (the system barges-in on user)

USR I need an Italian restaurant that is located ...
SYS I'm sorry. Did you say Indian or Italian?
USR I said Italian. And in the centre of town please.
SYS OK, let me see. I have 24 Italian restaurants ...

Figure 1: Example phenomena generated with the learnt policy. The agent has learnt to produce backchannels and barge-ins at the appropriate moment and alternative strategies to deal with user barge-ins.

3 Information Theory

Information Theory as introduced by Shannon (1948) is based on two main concepts: a *communication channel* through which information is transferred in bits and the *information gain*, i.e. the information load that each bit carries. For natural language, the assumption is that people aim to communicate according to the channel's capacity, which corresponds to the hearer's capacity in terms of cognitive load. If they go beyond that, the cognitive load of the listener gets too high. If they stay (far) below, too little information is transferred per bit (i.e., the utterance is inefficient or uninformative). The information gain of each word, which is indicative of how close we are to the channel's capacity, can be computed using entropy measures.

3.1 Information Density

Psycholinguistic research has presented evidence for users distributing information across utterances uniformly, so that each word is carrying roughly the same amount of information. This has been observed for phonetic phenomena based on words (Bell et al., 2003) and syllables (Aylett and Turk, 2004), and for syntactic phenomena (Levy and Jaeger, 2007; Jaeger, 2010). Relating ID to likelihood, we can say that the less frequent a word is, the more information it is likely to carry (Jaeger, 2010). For example the word *'the'* often has a high corpus frequency but a low ID.

The ID is defined as the log-probability of an event (i.e. a word) (Shannon, 1948; Levy and Jaeger, 2007), so that for an utterance u consisting of the word sequence $w_1 \ldots w_{i-1}$, we can compute the ID at each point during the utterance as:

$$log \frac{1}{P(u)} = \sum_{i=1}^{n} log \frac{1}{P(w_i|w_1 \ldots w_{i-1})} \quad (1)$$

While typically the context of a word is given by all preceding words of the utterance, we follow Genzel and Charniak (2002) in restricting our computation to tri-grams for computability reasons. Given a language model of the domain, we can therefore optimise ID in system-generated discourse, where we treat ID as "an optimal solution to the problem of *rapid yet error-free communication* in a noisy environment" (Levy and Jaeger (2007), p.2). We will now transfer the notion of ID to IP and investigate the distribution of information over user restaurant queries.

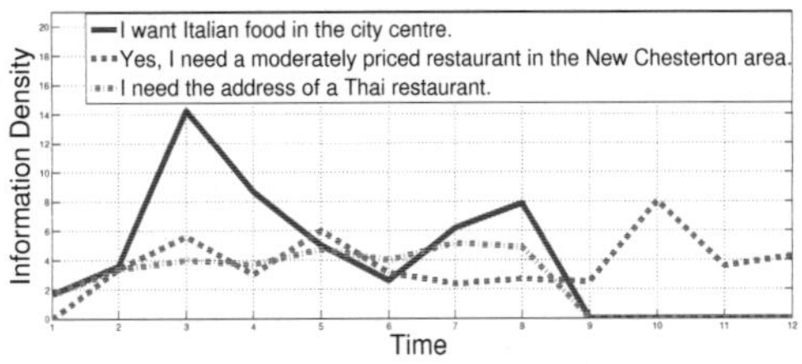

Figure 2: Information Density for example utterances, where peaks indicate places of high density.

3.2 Information Density in User Utterances

We aim to use ID for incremental IP in two ways: (1) to estimate the best moment for generating backchannels or barge-ins to the user, and (2) to decide whether to yield or keep the current system turn in case of a user barge-in. While we do not have specific data on human barge-in behaviour, we know from the work of (Jaeger, 2010), e.g., that ID influences human language production. We therefore hypothesise a relationship between ID and incremental phenomena. A human-human data collection is planned for the near future.

To compute the ID of user and system utterances at each time step, we estimated an $n-$gram language model (using Kneser-Ney smoothing) based on a transcribed corpus of human subjects interacting with a system for restaurant recommendations of Rieser et al. (2011).[1] The corpus contained user utterances as exemplified in Figure 1 and allowed us to compute the ID at any point during a user utterance.[2] In this way, we can estimate points of low density which may be eligible for a barge-in or a backchannel. Figure 2 shows some example utterances drawn from the corpus and their ID including the first sentence from Figure 1. These examples were typical for what could generally be observed from the corpus. We see that while information is transmitted with varying amounts of density, the main bits of information are transmitted at a scale between 2 and 7.

Due to a lack of human data for the system utterances, we use the same corpus data to compute the ID of system utterances.[3] The learning agent can use this information to consider the trade-off of yielding a current turn to the user or trying to keep it, e.g., in case of a user barge-in given the ID of its own turn and of the user's incoming turn. Such decisions will be made incrementally in our domain given dynamically changing hypotheses of user input.

4 Incremental Utterance Optimisation

To optimise incremental decision making for an interactive system given the optimisation measure of ID, we formalise the dialogue module as a Hierarchical Reinforcement Learning agent and learn an optimal action policy by mapping states to actions and optimising a long-term reward signal. The dialogue states can be seen as representing the system's knowledge about the task, the user and the environment. The dialogue actions correspond to the system's capabilities, such as *present the results* or *barge-in on the user*. They also handle incremental updates in the system. In addition, we need a transition function that specifies the way that actions change the environment (as expressed in the state representation) and a reward function which specifies a numeric value for each action taken. In this way, decision making can be seen as a finite sequence of states, actions and rewards $\{s_0, a_0, r_1, s_1, a_1, ..., r_{t-1}, s_t\}$, where the goal is to induce an optimal strategy automatically using Reinforcement Learning (RL) (Sutton and Barto, 1998).

We used Hierarchical RL, rather than flat RL, because the latter is affected by the *curse of dimensionality*, the fact that the state space grows exponentially according to the state variables taken into account. This affects the scalability of flat RL agents

[1] Available at `http://www.macs.hw.ac.uk/ilabarchive/classicproject/data/login.php`.

[2] Note that our model does not currently handle out-of-domain words. In future work, we will learn when to seek clarification.

[3] We plan a data collection of such utterances for the future, but for now make the assumption that using the corpus data is informative since they are from the same domain.

and limits their application to small-scale problems. Since timing is crucial for incremental approaches, where processing needs to be fast, we choose a hierarchical setting for better scalability. We denote the hierarchy of RL agents as M^i_j where the indexes i and j only identify an agent in a unique way, they do not specify the execution sequence of subtasks, which is subject to optimisation. Each agent of the hierarchy is defined as a Semi-Markov Decision Process (SMDP) consisting of a 4-tuple $< S^i_j, A^i_j, T^i_j, R^i_j >$. Here, S^i_j denotes the set of states, A^i_j denotes the set of actions, and T^i_j is a probabilistic state transition function that determines the next state s' from the current state s and the performed action a. $R^i_j(s', \tau | s, a)$ is a reward function that specifies the reward that an agent receives for taking an action a in state s lasting τ time steps (Dietterich, 1999). Since actions in SMDPs may take a variable number of time steps to complete, the variable τ represents this number of time steps. The organisation of the learning process into discrete time steps allows us to define incremental hypothesis updates as state updates and transitions in an SMDP. Whenever conditions in the learning environment change, such as the recogniser's best hypothesis of the user input, we represent them as transitions from one state to another. At each time step, the agent checks for changes in its state representation and takes the currently best action according to the new state. The best action in an incremental framework can also include generating a *backchannel* to the user to indicate the status of grounding or *barging-in* to confirm an uncertain piece of information. Once information has been presented to the user, it is *committed* or *realised*. Realised information is represented in the agent's state, so that it can monitor its own output.

Actions in a Hierarchical Reinforcement learner can be either primitive or composite. The former are single-step actions that yield single rewards, and the latter are multi-step actions that correspond to SMDPs and yield cumulative rewards. Decision making occurs at any time step of an SMDP: after each single-step action, we check for any updates of the environment that require a system reaction or change of strategy. If no system action is required (e.g. because the user is speaking), the system can decide to do nothing. The goal of each SMDP is to find an optimal policy π^* that maximises the reward for each visited state, according to

$$\pi^{*i}_j(s) = \arg\max_{a \in A} Q^{*i}_j(s, a), \qquad (2)$$

where $Q^i_j(s, a)$ specifies the expected cumulative reward for executing action a in state s and then following π^*. We use HSMQ-Learning to induce dialogue policies, see (Cuayáhuitl, 2009), p. 92.

5 Experimental Setting

5.1 Hierarchy of Learning Agents

The HRL agent in Figure 3 shows how the tasks of (1) dealing with incrementally changing input hypotheses, (2) choosing a suitable IP strategy and (3) presenting information, are connected. Note that we focus on a detailed description of models $M^1_{0...3}$ here, which deal with barge-ins and backchannels and are the core of this paper. Please see Dethlefs et al. (2012) for details of an RL model that deals with the remaining decisions.

Briefly, model M^0_0 deals with dynamic input hypotheses. It chooses when to listen to an incoming user utterance (M^1_3) and when and how to present information ($M^1_{0...2}$) by calling and passing control to a child subtask. The variable 'incrementalStatus' characterises situations in which a particular (incremental) action is triggered, such as a floor holder *'let me see'*, a correction or self-correction. The variable 'presStrategy' indicates whether a strategy for IP has been chosen or not, and the variable 'userReaction' shows the user's reaction to an IP episode. The 'userSilence' variable indicates whether the user is speaking or not. The detailed state and action space of the agents is given in Figure 4. We distinguish actions for Information Presentation (IP), actions for attribute presentation and ordering (Slot-ordering), and incremental actions (Incremental).

Models $M^1_{0...2}$ correspond to different ways of presenting information to the user. They perform attribute selection and ordering and then call the child agents $M^2_{0...4}$ for attribute realisation. Whenever a user barges in over the system, these agents will decide to either yield the turn to the user or to try and keep the turn based on information density. The variables representing the status of the cuisine,

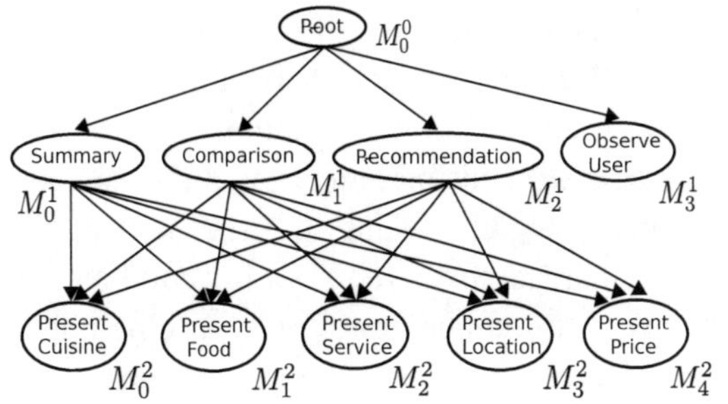

Figure 3: Hierarchy of learning agent for incremental Information Presentation and Slot Ordering.

food, location, price and service of restaurants indicate whether the slot is of interest to the user (we assume that 0 means that the user does not care about this slot), and what input confidence score is currently associated with the value of the slot. For example, if our current best hypothesis is that the user is interested in Indian restaurants, the variable 'statusCuisine' will have a value between 1-3 indicating the strength of this hypothesis. Once slots have been presented to the user, they are *realised* and can only be changed through a correction or self-correction.

Model M_3^1 is called whenever the user is speaking. The system's main choice here is to remain silent and listen to the user or barge-in to request the desired cuisine, location, or price range of a restaurant. This can be beneficial in certain situations, such as when the system is able to increase its confidence for a slot from 'low' to 'high' through barging-in with a direct clarification request, e.g. *'Did you say Indian?'* (and thereby saving several turns that may be based on a wrong hypothesis). This can also be harmful in certain situations, though, assuming that users have a general preference for not being barged-in on. The learning agent will need to learn to distinguish these situations. This agent is also responsible for generating backchannels and will over time learn the best moments to do this.

Models $M_{0...4}^2$ choose surface forms for presentation to the user from hand-crafted templates. They are not the focus of this paper, however, and therefore not presented in detail. The state-action space size of this agent is roughly 1.5 million.[4] The agent reaches its goal state (defined w.r.t. the state vari-

[4]Note that a flat RL agent, in contrast, would need 8×10^{25} million state-actions to represent this problem.

States M_0^0
incrementalStatus {0=none,1=holdFloor,2=correct,3=selfCorrect}
observeUser {0=unfilled,1=filled}
presStrategy {0=unfilled,1=filled}
userReaction {0=none,1=select,2=askMore,3=other}
userSilence={0=false,1=true}
Actions M_0^0
IP: compare M_1^1, recommend M_2^1, summarise M_0^1, summariseCompare, summariseRecommend, summariseCompareRecommend,
Incremental: correct, selfCorrect, holdFloor, observeUser
Goal State M_0^0 0, 1, 1, 0, ?

States $M_{0...2}^1$
IDSystem={0=low,1=medium, 2=high}
statusCuisine {0=unfilled,1=low,2=medium,3=high,4=realised}
statusQuality {0=unfilled,1=low,2=medium,3=high,4=realised}
statusLocation {0=unfilled,1=low,2=medium,3=high,4=realised}
statusPrice {0=unfilled,1=low,2=medium,3=high,4=realised}
statusService {0=unfilled,1=low,2=medium,3=high,4=realised}
turnType {0=holding, 1=resuming, 2=keeping, 3=yielding}
userBargeIn {0=false, 1=true}
Actions $M_{0...2}^1$
Slot-ordering: presentCuisine M_0^2, presentQuality M_1^2, presentLocation M_2^2, presentPrice M_3^2, presentService M_4^2,
Incremental: yieldTurn, keepTurn
Goal State $M_{0...2}^1$?, $\vee$ 4, 0 $\vee$ 4, 0 $\vee$ 4, 0 $\vee$ 4, 0 $\vee$ 4, ?, ?

States M_3^1
bargeInOnUser={0=undecided,1=yes, 2=no}
IDUser={0=low,1=medium, 2=high, 3=falling, 4=rising}
statusCuisine {0=unfilled,1=low,2=medium,3=high,4=realised}
statusLocation {0=unfilled,1=low,2=medium,3=high,4=realised}
statusPrice {0=unfilled,1=low,2=medium,3=high,4=realised}
Actions M_3^1
Incremental: doNotBargeIn, bargeInCuisine, bargeInLocation, bargeInPrice, backchannel
Goal State M_3^1 >0, ?, 0 $\vee$ 4, 0 $\vee$ 4, 0 $\vee$ 4

States $M_{0...4}^2$
IDSystem={0=low,1=medium, 2=high}
IDUser={0=low,1=medium, 2=high, 3=falling, 4=rising}
surfaceForm {0=unrealised,1=realised}
Actions $M_{0...4}^2$
Surface Realisation: [alternative surface realisations]
e.g. '\$number\$ restaurants serve \$cuisine\$ food', '\$number\$ places are located in \$area\$, etc.
Goal State $M_{0...4}^2$?, ?, 1

Figure 4: The state and action space of the HRL agent. The goal state is reached when all items (that the user specified in the search query) have been presented. Question marks mean that a variable does not affect the goal state, which can be reached regardless of the variable's value.

ables in Fig. 4) when an IP strategy has been chosen and all information has been presented.

5.2 The Simulated Environment

For a policy to converge, a learning agent typically needs several thousand interactions in which it is exposed to a multitude of different circumstances. For our domain, we designed a simulated environment with three main components addressing IP, incremental input hypotheses and ID. Using this simulation, we trained the agent for 10 thousand episodes, where one episode corresponds to one recommendation dialogue.

5.2.1 Information Presentation

To learn a good IP strategy, we use a user simulation[5] by Rieser et al. (2010) which was estimated from human data and uses bi-grams of the form $P(a_{u,t}|IP_{s,t})$, where $a_{u,t}$ is the predicted user reaction at time t to the system's IP strategy $IP_{s,t}$ in state s at time t. We distinguish the user reactions of *select* a restaurant, *addMoreInfo* to the current query to constrain the search, and *other*. The last category is usually considered an undesirable user reaction that the system should learn to avoid. The simulation uses linear smoothing to account for unseen situations. In this way, we can predict the most likely user reaction to each system action. Even though previous work has shown that n-gram-based simulations can lead to dialogue inconsistencies, we assume that for the present study this does not present a problem, since we focus on generating single utterances and on obtaining user judgements for single, independent utterances.

5.2.2 Input Hypothesis Updates

While the IP strategies can be used for incremental and non-incremental dialogue, the second part of the simulation deals explicitly with the dynamic environment updates that the system will need to be sensitive to in an incremental setting. We assume that for each restaurant recommendation, the user has the option of filling any or all of the attributes *cuisine, food quality, location, price range* and *service quality*. The possible values of each attribute and possible confidence scores for each value are shown in Table 2. A score of 0 means that the user does not care about the attribute, 1 means that the system's confidence in the attribute's value is low, 2 that the confidence is medium, and 3 means that the confidence is high. A value of 4 means that the attribute has already been *realised*, i.e. communicated to the user. At the beginning of a learning episode, we assign each attribute a possible value and confidence score with equal probability. For food and service quality, we assume that the user is never interested in bad food or service. Subsequently, confidence scores can change at each time step. In future work these transition probabilities will be estimated from a data collection, though the following assumptions are realistic based on our experience. We assume that a confidence score of 0 changes to any other value with a likelihood of 0.05. A confidence score of 1 changes with a probability of 0.3, a confidence score of 2 with a probability of 0.1 and a confidence score of 3 with a probability of 0.03. Once slots have been realised, their value is set to 4. They cannot be changed then without an explicit correction. We also assume that realised slots change with a probability of 0.1. If they change, we assume that half of the time, the user is the origin of the change (because they changed their mind) and half of the time the system is the origin of the change (because of an ASR or interpretation error). Each time a confidence score is changed, it has a probability of 0.5 for also changing its value. The resulting input to the system are data structures of the form *present(cuisine=Indian), confidence=low*. The probability of observing this data structure in our simulation is 0.1 (for Indian) $\times$ 0.2 (for low confidence) $=$ 0.02. Its probability of changing to *present(cuisine=italian), confidence=high* is 0.1 (for changing from low to medium) $\times$ 0.05 (for changing from Indian to Italian) $=$ 0.005.

5.2.3 Information Density Updates

We simulate ID of user utterances based on probabilistic context-free grammars (PCFG) that were automatically induced from the corpus data in Section 3.2 using the ABL algorithm (van Zaanen, 2000). This algorithm takes a set of strings as input and computes a context-free grammar as output by aligning strings based on Minimum Edit Distance. We use the $n-$gram language models trained earlier to

[5]The simulation data are available from `www.classic-project.org`.

Attribute	Values	Confidence
Cuisine	Chinese, French, German, Indian, Italian, Japanese, Mexican, Scottish, Spanish, Thai	0, 1, 2, 3, 4
Quality	bad, adequate, good, very good	0, 1, 2, 3, 4
Location	7 distinct areas of the city	0, 1, 2, 3, 4
Price	cheap, good-price-for-value, expensive, very expensive	0, 1, 2, 3, 4
Service	bad, adequate, good, very good	0, 1, 2, 3, 4

Table 2: User goal slots for restaurant queries with possible values and confidence scores.

add probabilities to grammar rules. We use these PCFGs to simulate user utterances to which the system has to react. They can be meaningful utterances such as *'Show me restaurants nearby'* or less meaningful fragments such as *'um let me see, do you... hm'*. The former type is more frequent in the data, but both types can be simulated along with their ID (clearly, the first type is more dense than the second).

In addition to simulating user utterances, we hand-crafted context-free grammars of system utterances and augmented them with probabilities estimated using the same user corpus data as above (where again, we make the assumption that this is to some extent feasible given the shared domain). We use the simulated system utterances to compute varying degrees of ID for the system.

Both measures, the ID of user and system utterances, can inform the system during learning to balance the trade-off between them for generating and receiving backchannels and barge-ins.

5.3 A Reward Function for Incremental Dialogue Based on Information Density

To train the HRL agent, we use a partially data-driven reward function. For incremental IP, we use rewards that are based on human intuition. The agent receives

$$R = \begin{cases} +100 & \text{if the user selects an item,} \\ 0 & \text{if the user adds further constraints to the search,} \\ -100 & \text{if the user does something else or a self-correction,} \\ -0.5 & \text{for the system holding a turn,} \\ -1 & \text{otherwise.} \end{cases}$$

The agent is encouraged to choose those sequences of actions that lead to the user selecting a restaurant as quickly as possible. If the agent is not sure what to say (because planning has not finished), it can generate a floor holding marker, but should in any case avoid a self-correction due to having started speaking too early.

The remaining rewards are based on ID scores computed incrementally during an interaction. The agent receives the following rewards, where infoDensity(Usr) and infoDensity(Sys) refer to the ID of the current user and system utterance, respectively, as defined in Equation 1.

$$R = \begin{cases} \text{-infoDensity(Usr)} & \text{for keeping a turn, barging-in or a backchannel,} \\ \text{-infoDensity(Sys)} & \text{for yielding a turn.} \end{cases}$$

These two measures encourage the agent to consider the trade-offs between its own ID and the one transmitted by an incoming user utterance. Barging-in on a user utterance at a low ID point then yields a small negative reward, whereas barging-in on a user utterance at a high ID point yields a high negative reward. Both rewards are negative because barging-in on the user always contains some risk. Similarly, keeping a turn over a non-dense user utterance receives a smaller negative reward than keeping it over a dense user utterance. A reward of -2 is assigned for barging-in over a user utterance fragment with a falling ID to reflect results from a qualitative study of our corpus data: humans tend to barge-in *between* information peaks, so that a barge-in to clarify a low-confidence slot appears immediately before the ID is rising again for a new slot. The exact best moment for barge-ins and backchannels to occur will be subject to optimisation.

6 Experimental Results

The agent learns to barge-in or generate backchannels to users at points where the ID is low but rising. In particular, the agent learns to barge-in *right before* information density peaks in an incoming user utterance to clarify or request slots that are still open from the previous information density peak. If a user has specified their desired cuisine type but the system has received a low ASR confidence score for it, it may barge-in to clarify the slot. This case was illustrated in the last example in Figure 1, where the system clarified the previous (cuisine) slot (which is associated with a high ID) just before the user specifies the location slot (which again would have a high ID). The main benefit the system can gain through clarification barge-ins is to avoid self-corrections when having acted based on a low ASR confidence, leading to more efficient interactions.

The system learns to generate backchannels *after* information peaks to confirm newly acquired slots that have a high confidence. An example is shown in the first dialogue fragment in Figure 1.

In addition, the system learns to yield its current turn to a user that is barging-in if its own ID is low, falling or rising, or if the ID of the incoming user utterance is high. If the system's own ID is high, but the user's is not, it will try to keep the turn.[6] This is exemplified in the third dialogue fragment in Figure 1.

We compare our learnt policy against two baselines. **Baseline 1** was designed to always generate barge-ins *after* an information peak in a user utterance, i.e. when ID has just switched from *high* to *falling*. We chose this baseline to confirm that users indeed prefer barge-ins before information peaks rather than at any point of low ID. Baseline 1 yields a turn to a user barge-in if its own ID is low and tries to keep it otherwise. **Baseline 2** generates barge-ins and backchannels randomly and at any point during a user utterance. The decision of yielding or keeping a turn in case of a user barge-in is also random. Both baselines also use HRL to optimise their IP strategy. We do not compare different IP strategies, which has been done in detail by Rieser et al. (2010). All results are summarised in Table 3.

[6]Incidentally, this also helps to prevent the system yielding its turn to a user backchannel; cf. Example 2 in Fig. 1.

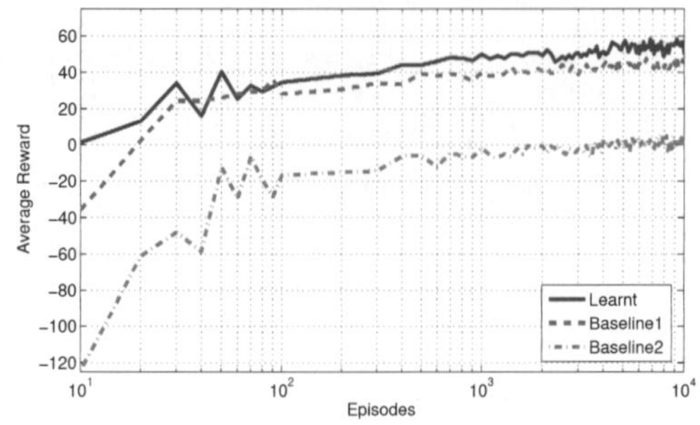

Figure 5: Performance in terms of rewards (averaged over 10 runs) for the HRL agent and its baselines.

6.1 Average Rewards over Time

Figure 5 shows the performance of all systems in terms of average rewards in simulation. The learnt policy outperforms both baselines. While the learnt policy and Baseline 1 appear to achieve similar performance, an absolute comparison of the last 1000 episodes of each behaviour shows that the improvement of the HRL agent over Baseline 1 corresponds to 23.42%. The difference between the learnt policy and its baselines is significant at $p < 0.0001$ according to a paired t-test and has a high effect size of $r = 0.85$.

The main reason for these different performances is the moment each system will barge-in. Since Baseline 1 barges-in on users after an information peak, when ID may still be high, it continuously receives a negative reward reflecting the user preference for late barge-ins. As a result of this continuous negative reward, the agent will then learn to avoid barge-ins altogether, which may in turn lead to less efficient interactions because low confidence ASR scores are clarified only late in the interaction.

The main problem of the random barge-ins of Baseline 2 is that users may often have to restart a turn because the system barged-in too early or in the middle of an information peak. In addition, Baseline 2 needs to occasionally self-correct its own utterances because it started to present information too early, when input hypotheses were not yet stable enough to act upon them.

Policy	Average Reward	User Rating (%)
Learnt	$55.54^{**,*}$	$43\%^{**}$
Baseline 1	45.0^{**}	26%
Baseline 2	1.47	31%

Table 3: Comparison of policies in terms of average rewards and user ratings. * indicates a significant improvement over Baseline 1 and ** over Baseline 2.

6.2 Human Rating Study

To confirm our simulation-based results, we conducted a user rating study on the CrowdFlower crowd sourcing platform.[7] Participants were shown user utterances along with three options of barging-in over them. For example: | `I want [OPTION 1] Italian food [OPTION 2] in the city [OPTION 3] centre`|, where `OPTION 1` corresponds to the learnt policy, `OPTION 2` to Baseline 2 and `OPTION 3` to Baseline 1.

Users were asked to choose one option which they considered the best moment for a barge-in. Participants in the study rated altogether 144 utterances. They preferred the *learnt* system 63 times (43%), Baseline 1 37 times (26%) and Baseline 2 44 times (31%). This is statistically significant at $p < 0.02$ according to a Chi-Square test ($\chi^2 = 7.542$, df = 2). In a separate test, directly comparing the *learnt* policy and Baseline 1, *learnt* was chosen significantly more often than Baseline 1; i.e. 79% of the time (for 127 utterances, using a 1-tailed Sign test, $p < 0.0001$). Finally, *learnt* was directly compared to Baseline 2 and shown to be significantly more often chosen; i.e. 59% of the time (138 utterances, 1-tailed Sign test, $p < 0.025$). These results provide evidence that an optimisation of the timing of generating barge-ins and backchannels in incremental dialogue can be sensitive to fine-grained cues in evolving ID and therefore achieve a high level of adaptivity. Such sensitivity is difficult to hand-craft as can be concluded w.r.t. the performance of Baseline 1, which received similar rewards to *learnt* in simulation, but is surprisingly beaten by the random Baseline 2 here. This indicates a strong human dislike for late barge-ins. The bad performance of Baseline 2 in terms of average rewards was due to the random barge-ins leading to less efficient dialogues.

[7] `www.crowdflower.com`

Regarding user ratings however, Baseline 2 was preferred over Baseline 1. This is most likely due to the timing of barge-ins: since Baseline 2 has a chance of barging-in at earlier occasions than Baseline 1, it may have received better ratings. The evaluation shows that humans care about timing of a barge-in regarding the density of information that is currently conveyed and dislike late barge-ins. ID is then useful in determining when to barge-in. We can therefore further conclude that ID can be a feasible optimisation criterion for incremental decision making.

7 Conclusion and Future Work

We have presented a novel approach to incremental dialogue decision making based on *Hierarchical RL* combined with the notion of *information density*. We presented a learning agent in the domain of IP for restaurant recommendations that was able to generate backchannels and barge-ins for higher responsiveness in interaction. Results in terms of average rewards and a human rating study have shown that a learning agent that is optimised based on a partially *data-driven reward function* that addresses information density can learn to decide when and if it is beneficial to barge-in or backchannel on user utterances and to deal with backchannels and barge-ins from the user. Future work can take several directions. Given that ID is a measure influencing human language production, we could replace our template-based surface realiser by an agent that optimises the information density of its output. Currently we learn the agent's behaviour offline, before the interaction, and then execute it statistically. More adaptivity towards individual users and situations could be achieved if the agent was able to learn from ongoing interactions. Finally, we can confirm the human results obtained from an overhearer-style evaluation in a real interactive setting and explicitly extend our language model to discourse phenomena such as pauses or hesitations to take them into account in measuring ID.

Acknowledgements

The research leading to this work has received funding from EC's FP7 programmes: (FP7/2011-14) under grant agreement no. 287615 (PARLANCE); (FP7/2007-13) under grant agreement no. 216594 (CLASSiC); (FP7/2011-14) under grant agreement no. 270019 (SPACEBOOK);

and (FP7/2011-16) under grant agreement no. 269427 (STAC). Many thanks to Michael White for discussion of the original idea of using information density as an optimisation metric.

References

Matthew Aylett and Alice Turk. 2004. The smooth signal redundancy hypothesis: A functional explanation for the relationships between redundancy, prosodic prominence, and duration in spontaneous speech. *Language and Speech*, 47(1):31–56.

Timo Baumann, Okko Buss, and David Schlangen. 2011. Evaluation and Optimisation of Incremental Processors. *Dialogue and Discourse*, 2(1).

Alan Bell, Dan Jurafsky, Eric Fossler-Lussier, Cynthia Girand, Michelle Gregory, and Daniel Gildea. 2003. Effects of disfluencies, predictability, and utterance position on word form variation in english conversation. *Journal of the Acoustic Society of America*, 113(2):1001–1024.

Okko Buss, Timo Baumann, and David Schlangen. 2010. Collaborating on Utterances with a Spoken Dialogue Systen Using an ISU-based Approach to Incremental Dialogue Management. In *Proceedings of 11th Annual SIGdial Meeting on Discourse and Dialogue*.

Heriberto Cuayáhuitl and Nina Dethlefs. 2011. Spatially-aware Dialogue Control Using Hierarchical Reinforcement Learning. *ACM Transactions on Speech and Language Processing (Special Issue on Machine Learning for Robust and Adaptive Spoken Dialogue System)*, 7(3).

Heriberto Cuayáhuitl, Steve Renals, Oliver Lemon, and Hiroshi Shimodaira. 2010. Evaluation of a hierarchical reinforcement learning spoken dialogue system. *Computer Speech and Language*, 24(2):395–429.

Heriberto Cuayáhuitl. 2009. *Hierarchical Reinforcement Learning for Spoken Dialogue Systems*. PhD Thesis, University of Edinburgh, School of Informatics.

Nina Dethlefs and Heriberto Cuayáhuitl. 2011. Combining Hierarchical Reinforcement Learning and Bayesian Networks for Natural Language Generation in Situated Dialogue. In *Proceedings of the 13th European Workshop on Natural Language Generation (ENLG)*, Nancy, France.

Nina Dethlefs, Helen Hastie, Verena Rieser, and Oliver Lemon. 2012. Optimising Incremental Generation for Spoken Dialogue Systems: Reducing the Need for Fillers. In *Proceedings of the International Conference on Natural Language Generation (INLG)*, Chicago, Illinois, USA.

David DeVault, Kenji Sagae, and David Traum. 2009. Can I finish? Learning when to respond to incremental interpretation result in interactive dialogue. In *Proceedings of the 10th Annual SigDial Meeting on Discourse and Dialogue*, Queen Mary University, UK.

Thomas G. Dietterich. 1999. Hierarchical Reinforcement Learning with the MAXQ Value Function Decomposition. *Journal of Artificial Intelligence Research*, 13:227–303.

Dmitriy Genzel and Eugene Charniak. 2002. Entropy Rate Constancy in Text. In *Proceedings of the 40th Annual Meeting on Association for Computational Linguistics*, pages 199–206.

James Henderson, Oliver Lemon, and Kallirroi Georgila. 2008. Hybrid Reinforcement/Supervised Learning of Dialogue Policies from Fixed Data Sets. *Computational Linguistics*, 34(4):487–511.

T. Florian Jaeger. 2010. Redundancy and reduction: Speakers manage syntactic information density. *Cognitive Psychology*, 61:23–62.

Srini Janarthanam and Oliver Lemon. 2010. Learning to Adapt to Unknown Users: Referring Expression Generation in Spoken Dialogue Systems. In *Proceedings of the 48th Annual Meeting of the Association for Computational Linguistics (ACL)*, pages 69–78, July.

Anne Kilger and Wolfgang Finkler. 1995. Incremental generation for real-time applications. Technical report, DFKI Saarbruecken, Germany.

Oliver Lemon. 2011. Learning What to Say and How to Say It: Joint Optimization of Spoken Dialogue Management and Natural Language Generation.

Esther Levin, Roberto Pieraccini, and Wieland Eckert. 2000. A Stochastic Model of Computer-Human Interaction for Learning Dialogue Strategies. *IEEE Transactions on Speech and Audio Processing*, 8:11–23.

Roger Levy and T. Florian Jaeger. 2007. Speakers optimize information density through syntactic reduction. *Advances in Neural Information Processing Systems*, 19.

Olivier Pietquin and Dutoit. 2006. A Probabilistic Framework for Dialogue Simulation and Optimal Strategy Learning. *IEEE Transactions on Speech and Audio Processing*, 14(2):589–599.

Matthew Purver and Masayuki Otsuka. 2003. Incremental Generation by Incremental Parsing. In *Proceedings of the 6th UK Special-Interesting Group for Computational Linguistics (CLUK) Colloquium*.

Rajakrishnan Rajkumar and Michael White. 2011. Linguistically Motivated Complementizer Choice in Surface Realization. In *Proceedings of the EMNLP-11 Workshop on Using Corpora in NLG*, Edinburgh, Scotland.

Antoine Raux and Maxine Eskenazi. 2009. A Finite-State Turn-Taking Model for Spoken Dialog Systems. In *Proceedings of the 10th Conference of the*

North American Chapter of the Association for Computational Linguistics—Human Language Technologies (NAACL-HLT), Boulder, Colorado.

Verena Rieser, Oliver Lemon, and Xingkun Liu. 2010. Optimising Information Presentation for Spoken Dialogue Systems. In *Proceedings of the 48th Annual Meeting of the Association for Computational Linguistics (ACL)*, Uppsala, Sweden.

Verena Rieser, Simon Keizer, Xingkun Liu, and Oliver Lemon. 2011. Adaptive Information Presentation for Spoken Dialogue Systems: Evaluation with Human Subjects. In *Proceedings of the 13th European Workshop on Natural Language Generation (ENLG)*, Nancy, France.

David Schlangen and Gabriel Skantze. 2011. A General, Abstract Model of Incremental Dialogue Processing. *Dialogue and Discourse*, 2(1).

Ethan Selfridge, Iker Arizmendi, Peter Heeman, and Jason Williams. 2011. Stability and Accuracy in Incremental Speech Recognition. In *Proceedings of the 12th Annual SigDial Meeting on Discourse and Dialogue*, Portland, Oregon.

Claude Shannon. 1948. A Mathematical Theory of Communications. *Bell Systems Technical Journal*, 27(4):623–656.

Satinder Singh, Diane Litman, Michael Kearns, and Marilyn Walker. 2002. Optimizing Dialogue Management with Reinforcement Learning: Experiments with the NJFun System. *Journal of Artificial Intelligence Research*, 16:105–133.

Gabriel Skantze and Anna Hjalmarsson. 2010. Towards Incremental Speech Generation in Dialogue Systems. In *Proceedings of the 11th Annual SigDial Meeting on Discourse and Dialogue*, Tokyo, Japan.

Richard Sutton and Andrew Barto. 1998. *Reinforcement Learning: An Introduction*. MIT Press, Cambridge, MA.

Blaise Thomson. 2009. *Statistical Methods for Spoken Dialogue Management*. Ph.D. thesis, University of Cambridge.

Menno van Zaanen. 2000. Bootstrapping Syntax and Recursion using Alignment-Based Learning. In *Proceedings of the Seventeenth International Conference on Machine Learning*, ICML '00, pages 1063–1070.

Marilyn Walker. 2000. An Application of Reinforcement Learning to Dialogue Strategy Selection in a Spoken Dialogue System for Email. *Journal of Artificial Intelligence Research (JAIR)*, 12:387–416.

Steve Young, Milica Gasic, Simon Keizer, Francois Mairesse, Jost Schatzmann, Blaise Thomson, and Kai Yu. 2010. The Hidden Information State Model: A Practical Framework for POMDP-based Spoken Dialogue Management. *Computer Speech and Language*, 24(2):150–174.

Steve Young. 2000. Probabilistic Methods in Spoken Dialogue Systems. *Philosophical Transactions of the Royal Society (Series A)*, 358(1769):1389–1402.

Mixed Membership Markov Models for Unsupervised Conversation Modeling

Michael J. Paul
Center for Language and Speech Processing
Johns Hopkins University
Baltimore, MD 21218, USA
mpaul@cs.jhu.edu

Abstract

Recent work has explored the use of hidden Markov models for unsupervised discourse and conversation modeling, where each segment or block of text such as a message in a conversation is associated with a hidden state in a sequence. We extend this approach to allow each block of text to be a mixture of multiple classes. Under our model, the probability of a class in a text block is a log-linear function of the classes in the previous block. We show that this model performs well at predictive tasks on two conversation data sets, improving thread reconstruction accuracy by up to 15 percentage points over a standard HMM. Additionally, we show quantitatively that the induced word clusters correspond to speech acts more closely than baseline models.

1 Introduction

The proliferation of social media in recent years has lead to an increased use of informal Web data in the language processing community. With this rising interest in social domains, it is natural to consider models which explicitly incorporate the conversational patterns of social text. Compared to the naive approach of treating conversations as flat documents, models which include conversation structure have been shown to improve tasks such as forum search (Elsas and Carbonell, 2009; Seo et al., 2009), question answering and expert finding (Xu et al., 2008; Wang et al., 2011a), and interpersonal relationship identification (Diehl et al., 2007).

While conversational features may be important, Web-derived corpora are not always annotated with this information, and the nature of conversations on the Web can vary wildly across domains and venues. Addressing these concerns, there has been recent work with *unsupervised* models of Web conversations based on hidden Markov models (Ritter et al., 2010), where each state corresponds to a conversational class or "act." Unlike more traditional uses of HMMs in which a single token is emitted per time step, HMM emissions in conversations correspond to entire blocks of text, such that an entire message is generated at each step. Because each time step is associated with a block of variables, we refer to this type of HMM as a *block HMM* (Fig. 1a).

While block HMMs offer a concise model of inter-message structure, they have the limitation that each text block (message) belongs to exactly one class. Many modern generative models of text, in contrast, allow documents to contain many latent classes. For example, topic models such as Latent Dirichlet Allocation (LDA) (Blei et al., 2003) assume each document has its own distribution over multiple classes (often called "topics"). For many predictive tasks, topic models outperform single-class generative models such as Naive Bayes. These properties could similarly be desirable in conversation modeling. An email might contain a request, a question, and an answer to a previous question – three distinct dialog acts within a single message. This motivates the desire to allow a message to be a *mixture* of classes.

In this paper, we introduce a new type of model which combines the functionality of topic models, which posit latent class assignments to each individual token, with Markovian sequence models, which

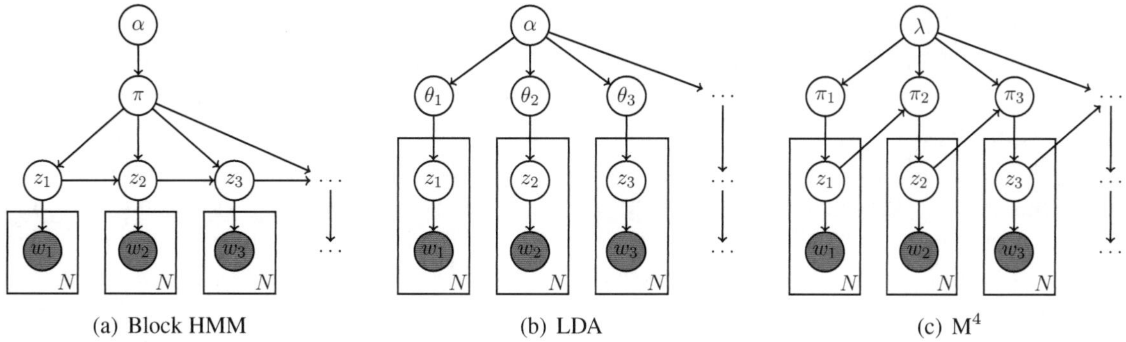

Figure 1: The graphical models for the block HMM (left) where each block of tokens depends on exactly one latent class, LDA (center) where each token individually depends on a latent class, and M^4 (right) where the class distributions are dependent across blocks. Some parameters are omitted for simplicity. This figure depicts the Bayesian variant of the block HMM (Ritter et al., 2010) where the transition distributions π depend on a Dirichlet(α) prior.

govern the transitions between text blocks in a sequence. We generalize the block HMM approach so that there is no longer a one-to-one correspondence between states in the Markov chain and latent discourse classes. Instead, we allow a state in the HMM to correspond to a mixture of many classes: we refer to this family of models as **mixed membership Markov models (M^4)**. Instead of defining explicit transition probabilities from one class to another as in a traditional HMM, we define the distribution over classes as a function of the entire histogram of class assignments of the previous text segment. We define our model using the same number of parameters as a standard HMM (§2), and we present a straightforward approximate inference algorithm (§3).

While we introduce a general model, we will focus on the task of unsupervised conversation modeling. Specifically, we build off the Bayesian block HMMs used by Ritter et al. (2010) for modeling Twitter conversations, which will be our primary baseline. After discussing related work (§4), we present experimental results on a set of Twitter conversations as well as a set of threads from CNET discussion forums (§5). We show that M^4 increases thread reconstruction accuracy by up to 15% compared to the HMM of Ritter et al. (2010), and we reduce variation of information against speech act annotations by an average of 18% from HMM and LDA baselines. To the best of our knowledge, this work is the first attempt to quantitatively compare unsupervised models against gold standard speech act annotations.

2 M^4: Mixed Membership Markov Models

In this section, we extend the block HMM by introducing mixed membership Markov models (M^4).

Under the block HMM, as utilized by Ritter et al. (2010), messages in a conversation flow according to a Markov process, where the words of messages are generated according to language models associated with a state in a hidden Markov model. The intuition is that HMM states should correspond to some notion of a conversation "act" such as QUESTION or ANSWER. The intuition is the same under M^4, but now each token in a message is given its own class assignment, according to a class distribution for that particular message. A message's class distribution depends on the class assignments of the previous message, yielding a model that retains sequential dependencies between messages, while allowing for finer grained class allocation than the block HMM. Modeling messages (or more generally, text blocks) as a mixture of multiple classes rather than a single class gives rise to the "mixed membership" property.

In the subsections below, we formalize and analyze this new model.

2.1 Structure Assumptions

We first define the discourse structure and terminology we will be assuming. The discourse structure is a directed graph, where nodes correspond to segments of a document (which we will refer to as "blocks" of text), and the edges define the dependencies between them.

Thus, a text *block* is a set of tokens, while a *document* consists of the discourse graph and all blocks associated with it. In the context of modeling conversation threads, which will be the focus of our experiments later, we will assume a block corresponds to a single message in a thread. The parent of a message m is the message to which it is a response; if a message is not in response to anything in particular, then it has no parent. Any replies to the message m are the children of m. The thread as a whole is called a document.

The discourse graph should be acyclic. A directed acyclic graph (DAG) offers a flexible representation of discourse (Rosé et al., 1995), but for simplicity, we will restrict this and assume that each subgraph is a tree; i.e. no message has multiple parents. The graph as a whole may be a forest: for example, someone could write a new message in a conversation that is not directly in reply to any previous message, so this message would not have any parents, and would form the root of a new tree in the forest.

2.2 Generative Story

Extending the block HMM, latent classes in M^4 are now associated with each individual token, rather than one class for an entire block. The key difference between the generative process behind M^4 and the block HMM is that the transition distributions are defined with a log-linear model, which uses class assignments in a block as features to define the distribution over classes for the children of that block. Put another way, a state in M^4 corresponds to a class histogram, and transitions between states are functions of the log-linear parameters.

Given a block b, we will use the notation $\mathbf{b}$ to denote the block's feature vector, which consists of the histogram of latent class assignments for the tokens of b.[1] There are K classes. Additionally, we assume each feature vector has an extra cell containing an indicator denoting whether the block has no parent – this allows us to learn transitions from a "start" state. We also include a bias feature that is always 1, to learn a default weight for each class. There are thus $K + 2$ features which are used to predict the probability of each of the K classes. The features are weighted by transition parameters, denoted λ. The random variable z denotes a latent class, and ϕ_z is a discrete distribution over word types – that is, each class is associated with a unigram language model. The transition distribution over classes is denoted π, which is given in terms of λ and the feature vector of the parent block.

Under this model, a corpus $\mathcal{D}$ is generated by:

1. For each (j, k) in the transition matrix $\Lambda_{K \times K+2}$:
   (a) Draw transition weight $\lambda_{jk} \sim \mathcal{N}(0, \sigma^2)$.
2. For each class j:
   (a) Draw word distribution $\phi_j \sim \text{Dirichlet}(\omega)$.
3. For each block b of each document d in $\mathcal{D}$:
   (a) Set class probability $\pi_{bj} = \frac{\exp(\lambda_j^{\mathrm{T}}\mathbf{a})}{\sum_{j'} \exp(\lambda_{j'}^{\mathrm{T}}\mathbf{a})}$ for all classes j, where $\mathbf{a}$ is the feature vector for block a, the parent of b.
   (b) For each token n in block b:
      i. Sample class $z_{(b,n)} \sim \pi_b$.
      ii. Sample word $w_{(b,n)} \sim \phi_z$.

For each block of text in a document (e.g. each message in a conversation), the distribution over classes π is computed as a function of the feature vector of the block's parent and the transition parameters (feature weights) Λ. Each λ_{jk} has an intuitive interpretation: a positive value means that the occurrence of class k in a parent block increases the probability that j will appear in the next block, while a negative value reduces this probability.

The observed words of each block are generated by repeatedly sampling classes from the block's distribution π, and for each sampled class z, a single word is sampled from the class-specific distribution over words ϕ_z. In contrast, under the block HMM, a class z is sampled once from the transition distribution, and words are repeatedly sampled from ϕ_z.

We place a symmetric Dirichlet prior on each ϕ with concentration parameter ω, which smoothes the word distributions, and we place a 0-mean Gaussian prior on each λ parameter, which acts as a regularizer. The graphical diagram is shown in Figure 1 along with the block HMM and LDA. This figure

[1] One could also use other functions of the class histograms rather than the raw counts themselves. For example, we experimented with binary indicator features (i.e. "does class k appear anywhere in block b?"), but this performed consistently worse in early experiments, and we do not consider this further.

shows how M^4 combines the sequential dependencies of the block HMM with the token-specific class assignments of LDA.

2.3 Discussion

Like the block HMM, M^4 is a type of HMM. A latent sequence under M^4 forms a Markov chain in which a state corresponds to a histogram of classes. (For simplicity, we are ignoring the extra features of the start state indicator and bias in this discussion.) If we assume *a priori* that the length of a block is unbounded, then this state space is $\mathbb{N}^K$ where $0 \in \mathbb{N}$. The probability of transitioning from a state $\mathbf{b}$ to another state $\tilde{\mathbf{b}} \in \mathbb{N}^K$ is:

$$P(\mathbf{b} \rightarrow \tilde{\mathbf{b}}) \propto \zeta_N \text{Multinomial}(\tilde{\mathbf{b}} | \pi(\mathbf{b}), N) \quad (1)$$

where $N = \sum_k \tilde{\mathbf{b}}_k$, ζ_N is the probability that a block has N tokens,[2] and $\pi(\mathbf{b})$ is the transition distribution given a vector $\mathbf{b}$. This follows from the generative story defined above, with an additional step of generating the number of tokens N from the distribution ζ.

We currently define a block b's distribution π_b in terms of the discrete feature vector $\mathbf{a}$ given by its parent a. We could have instead made π_b a function of the parent's distribution π_a – this would lead to a model that assumes a dynamical system over a continuous space rather than a Markov chain. However, as a generative story we believe it makes more sense for a block's distribution to depend on the actual class values which are emitted by the parent. Similar arguments are made by Blei and Mcauliffe (2007) when designing supervised topic models.

Under a block HMM with one class per block, there are K states corresponding to the K classes, requiring $K \times K$ parameters to define the transition matrix. Under M^4, there is a countably infinite number of states, but the transitions are still defined by $K \times K$ parameters (ignoring extra features). M^4 thus utilizes a larger state space without increasing the number of free parameters.

3 Inference and Parameter Estimation

We must infer the values of the hidden variables $\mathbf{z}$ as well as the parameters for the word distributions Φ and transition weights Λ. Standard HMM dynamic programming algorithms cannot straightforwardly be used for M^4 because of the unboundedly large state space. We instead turn to Markov chain Monte Carlo (MCMC) methods as a tool for approximate inference. We derive a stochastic EM algorithm in which we alternate between sampling class assignments for the word tokens and optimizing the transition parameters, outlined in the following two subsections.

3.1 Latent Class Sampling

To explore the posterior distribution over latent classes, we use a collapsed Gibbs sampler such that we marginalize out each word multinomial ϕ and only need to sample the token assignments $\mathbf{z}$ conditioned on each other. Given the current state of the sampler, we sample a token's class according to:

$$P(z_{(b,n)} = k | \mathbf{z}_{-(b,n)}, \mathbf{w}, \lambda, \omega) \propto \quad (2)$$

$$\frac{\exp(\lambda_k^{\mathrm{T}} \mathbf{a})}{\sum_{k'} \exp(\lambda_{k'}^{\mathrm{T}} \mathbf{a})} \frac{n_k^w + \omega}{n_k + W\omega} \prod_{c \in \mathcal{C}} \prod_j \left(\frac{\exp(\lambda_j^{\mathrm{T}} \mathbf{b})}{\sum_{j'} \exp(\lambda_{j'}^{\mathrm{T}} \mathbf{b})} \right)^{n_c^j}$$

The notation n_k^w indicates the number of tokens with word type w that have been assigned to topic k. W is the vocabulary size. a is the parent block of b, and $\mathcal{C}$ is the set of b's children. $\mathbf{b}$ is the feature vector corresponding to block b (i.e. the class histogram plus the bias feature), where the histogram includes the incremented count of the candidate class k.

This sampling distribution is very similar to that of LDA (Griffiths and Steyvers, 2004), but the distribution over "topics" is now a function of the previous block, which gives the leftmost term. The rightmost term is a result of the dependency of the child blocks ($\mathcal{C}$) on the class assignments of b.

Due to the rightmost term, the complexity of computing the sampling distribution is quadratic in the number of classes, rather than the linear complexity of a single-class HMM. Our assumption is that the number of sequence-dependent classes (e.g. speech acts or discourse states) will be reasonably small. If it is desired to have a large number of latent topics as is common in LDA, this model could be combined with a standard topic model without sequential dependencies, as explored by Ritter et al. (2010).

[2] The distribution over the number of tokens can be arbitrary, as this is observed and does not affect inference. In topic models, this is sometimes assumed to be Poisson (Blei et al., 2003).

3.2 Transition Parameter Optimization

Differentiating the corpus likelihood with respect to Λ yields the standard equation for log-linear models:

$$\frac{\partial \ell}{\partial \lambda_{zk}} = \sum_b \mathbf{a}_k \left(n_b^z - n_b \frac{\exp(\lambda_z^{\mathrm{T}} \mathbf{a})}{\sum_{z'} \exp(\lambda_{z'}^{\mathrm{T}} \mathbf{a})} \right) - \frac{\lambda_{zk}}{\sigma^2} \tag{3}$$

where a is the parent of block b, $\mathbf{a}$ is the feature vector associated with a, n_b^z is the number of times class z occurs in block b and n_b is the total number of tokens in block b.

Standard optimization methods can be used to learn these parameters. In our experiments, we find that we obtain good results by simply performing a single iteration of gradient ascent after each sampling iteration t,[3] with the following update:

$$\lambda_{zk}^{(t+1)} = \lambda_{zk}^{(t)} + \eta(t) \frac{\partial \ell}{\partial \lambda_{zk}} \tag{4}$$

where η is a step size function.

4 Related Work

Hidden Markov models have a recent history as simple models of document structure. Stolcke et al. (2000) used HMMs as a general model of discourse with an application to speech acts (or dialog acts) in conversations. Barzilay and Lee (2004) applied HMMs as an *unsupervised* model of discourse. This work used HMMs to model the progression of sentences in articles, and was shown to be useful for ordering sentences and generating summaries of news articles. More recently, Wang et al. (2011b) experimented with similar tasks using a related HMM-based model called the Structural Topic Model.

Unsupervised HMMs were applied to conversational data by Ritter et al. (2010) who experimented with Twitter conversations. The authors also experimented with incorporating a topic model on top of the HMM to distinguish speech acts from topical clusters, with mixed results. Joty et al. (2011) extended this work by enriching the emission distributions and using additional features such as speaker and position information. An approach to unsupervised discourse modeling that does not use HMMs is the latent permutation model of Chen et al. (2009). This model assumes each segment (e.g. paragraph) in a document is associated with a latent class or topic, and the ordering of topics within a document is modeled as a deviation from some canonical ordering.

Extensions to the block HMM have incorporated mixed membership properties within blocks, notably the Markov Clustering Topic Model (Hospedales et al., 2009), which allows each HMM state to be associated with its own distribution over topics in a topic model. Like the block HMM, this still assumes a relatively small number of HMM states, but with an extra layer of latent variables before the observations are emitted. This is more restrictive than the unbounded state space of M^4.

Decoupling HMM states from latent classes was considered by Beal et al. (1997) with the Factorial HMM, which uses factorized state representations. The Factorial HMM is most often used to model independent Markov chains, whereas M^4 has a dense graphical model topology: the probability of each of the latent classes depends on the counts of all of the classes in the previous block. The trick in M^4 is to define the transition matrix via a function of a limited number of parameters, allowing tractable inference in a model with arbitrarily many states.

In topic models, log-linear formulations of latent class distributions[4] are utilized in correlated topic models (Blei and Lafferty, 2007) as a means of incorporating covariance structure among topic probabilities. Applying log-linear regression to potentially many features was combined with LDA by Mimno and McCallum (2008), who model the Dirichlet prior over topics as a function of document features. In M^4, such features would correspond to the class histograms of previous blocks, introducing additional dependencies between documents.

One topic model that imposes sequential dependencies between documents is Sequential LDA (Du et al., 2010), which models a document as a sequence of segments (such as paragraphs) governed by a Pitman-Yor process, in which the latent topic distribution of one segment serves as the base distribution for the next segment. This is in the spirit

[3]Incremental updates are justified under the generalized EM algorithm (Dempster et al., 1977). Each gradient step with respect to λ corresponds to a generalized M-step, while each sampling iteration corresponds to a stochastic E-step.

[4]This formulation corresponds to the *natural* parameterization of the multinomial distribution.

of our work, where the latent classes in a segment depend on the class distribution of the previous segment. By using the Pitman-Yor process, however, this work assumes topics are positively correlated, i.e. the occurrence of a topic in one segment makes it likely to appear in the next. In contrast, we wish to learn arbitrary transitions, both positive and negative, between the latent classes.

5 Experiments with Conversation Data

We experiment with two corpora of text-based asynchronous conversations on the Web. One of these is annotated with speech act labels, against which we compare our unsupervised clusters. We measure the predictive capabilities of the model via perplexity experiments and the task of thread reconstruction.

5.1 Data Sets

First, we use a corpus of discussion threads from CNET forums (Kim et al., 2010), which are mostly technical discussion and support. This corpus includes 321 threads and a total of 1309 messages, with an average message length of 78 tokens after preprocessing.[5] Second, we use the Twitter data set created by Ritter et al. (2010). We consider 36K conversation threads for a total of 100K messages with average length 13.4 tokens.

Both data sets are already annotated with the reply structure, so the discourse graph is given. We preprocess the data by treating contiguous blocks of punctuation as tokens, and we remove infrequent words. The Twitter corpus has some additional preprocessing, such as converting URLs to a single word type.

5.2 Baseline Models

Our work is motivated by the Bayesian HMM approach of Ritter et al. (2010) – the model we refer to as the block HMM (BHMM) – and we consider this our primary baseline. (See also (Goldwater and Griffiths, 2007) for more details on Bayesian HMMs with Dirichlet priors.) We also compare against LDA, which makes latent assignments at the token-level, but blocks of text are independent of each other. In other words, BHMM models sequential dependencies but allows only single-class membership, whereas LDA uses no sequence information but has a mixed membership property. M^4 combines these two properties.

We use standard Gibbs samplers for both baseline models, and we optimize the Dirichlet hyperparameters (for the transition and topic distributions) using Minka's fixed-point iterations (2003).

5.3 Incorporating Background Distributions

In our experiments, we find that the intrusion of common stop words can make the results difficult to interpret, but we do not want to perform simple stop word removal because common function words often play important roles in the latent classes (i.e. speech acts) of the conversation data we consider here. We instead handle this by extending our model to include a "background" distribution over words which is independent of the latent classes in a document; this was also done by Wang et al. (2011b).

The idea is to introduce a binary switching variable x into the model which determines whether a word is generated from the general background distribution or from the distribution specific to a latent class z. Loosely, if the marginal probability of a word was given by $p(w) = \sum_z p(w|z)p(z)$, the introduction of a background distribution gives the marginal probability $p(w) = p(x = 0)p(w|B) + p(x = 1)\sum_z p(w|z)$. This is common practice and we will not go into detail; see (Chemudugunta et al., 2006) for a general example on sampling switching variables. We augment all three models with a background distribution in exactly the same way, so that the comparison is fair. We use a $\text{Beta}(10.0, 10.0)$ prior over the switching distribution.

5.4 Experimental Setup

All of our results are averaged across four randomly initialized chains which are run for 5000 iterations, with five samples collected during the final 500 iterations. We take small gradient steps of decreasing size with $\eta(t) = 0.1/(1000 + t)$.

We set $\sigma^2 = 10.0$ as the variance of the λ weights. We use optimized asymmetric priors as described in §5.2, and we use a symmetric Dirichlet for the word distributions, following Wallach et al. (2009). We sample the scaling hyperparameter ω via

[5]Three messages in this corpus have multiple parents. For the sake of conciseness, we simply remove these threads rather than introducing a method to model multiple parents.

	5	10	15	20	25
CNET					
Unigram	63.07	63.07	63.07	63.07	63.07
LDA	57.16	54.35	52.88	51.63	50.50
BHMM	61.26	61.06	60.92	60.86	60.85
M^4	60.38	59.58	59.26	59.21	59.25
Twitter					
Unigram	93.00	93.00	93.00	93.00	93.00
LDA	83.70	78.40	74.01	70.91	70.16
BHMM	90.51	89.94	89.68	89.59	89.38
M^4	88.44	86.17	85.50	85.55	86.31

Table 1: Average perplexity of held-out data for various numbers of latent classes.

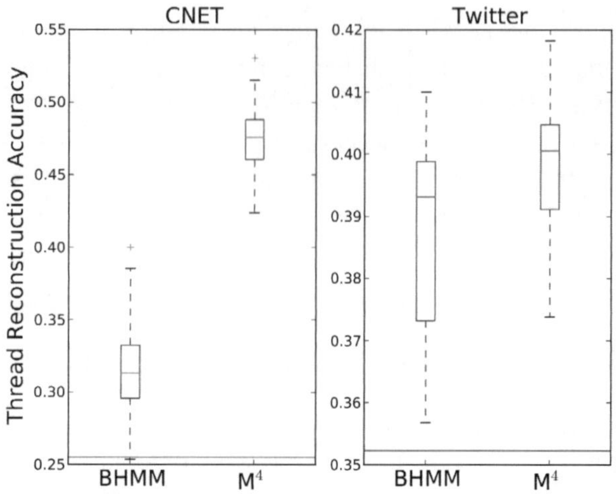

Figure 2: Accuracy at the task of thread reconstruction. The horizontal bar indicates a random baseline.

Metropolis-Hastings proposals: we add Gaussian-distributed noise to the log of the current ω, then exponentiate this to yield the proposed $\omega^{(\text{new})}$. This log-space proposal ensures that ω is always positive.

When computing the transition distributions for M^4, we normalize the class histograms so that the counts to sum to 1. This helps with numeric stability because the input vectors stay within a small bounded range.[6]

5.5 Experimental Results

5.5.1 Perplexity

We begin with standard measures of the perplexity of held-out data. For these experiments, we train on 75% of the data, and test on the remaining 25%. We run the sampler for 500 iterations using the word distributions and transition parameters learned during training; we compute the average perplexity from the final ten sampling iterations.

Results for different numbers of classes are shown in Table 1. These results demonstrate the advantage of models with the mixed membership property. Although LDA outperforms both sequence models, this is be expected. Each block's topic distribution is stochastically generated with LDA, whereas in the two sequence models, the distribution over classes is simply a deterministic function of the previous block. This allows LDA to infer parameters that fit the data more tightly. Comparing only the two sequence models, we find that M^4 does significantly better than BHMM in all cases with $p < 0.05$.

If capturing sequence information is not important, then LDA may provide a better fit to a corpus than sequence models. In the next two subsections, we will consider tasks where the sequential structure is important, thus LDA is not an appropriate choice.

5.5.2 Thread Reconstruction

A natural predictive task of the sequence models is to reconstruct the discourse graph of a document where the structure is unknown. In the conversation domain, this corresponds to the task of *thread reconstruction* (Yeh and Harnly, 2006; Wang et al., 2011c). Given only a flat structure, can we recover the reply structure of messages in the conversation?

Previous work with BHMM found the optimal structure by computing the likelihood of all permutations of a thread or sequence (Ritter et al., 2010; Wang et al., 2011b). We take a more practical approach and find the optimal structure as part of our inference procedure. We do this by treating the parent of each block as a hidden variable to be inferred. The parent of block b is the random variable r_b, and we alternate between sampling values of the latent classes $\mathbf{z}$ and the parents $\mathbf{r}$. The sampling distributions are annealed, as a search technique to find the best configuration of assignments (Finkel et al., 2005). At temperature τ, we sample a block's parent according to:

$$P(r_b = a|\mathbf{z}, \lambda) \propto \prod_j \left(\frac{\exp(\lambda_j^{\mathrm{T}} \mathbf{a})}{\sum_{j'} \exp(\lambda_{j'}^{\mathrm{T}} \mathbf{a})} \right)^{n_b^j/\tau} \quad (5)$$

[6]Implementations of both M^4 and the block HMM will be available at http://cs.jhu.edu/~mpaul

For each conversation thread, any message is a candidate for the parent of block b (except b itself) including the dummy "start" block.

As before, we train on 75% of the data, and run this experiment on the remaining 25%. We run the sampler for 500 iterations, cooling τ by 1% after each iteration, where $\tau^{(0)} = 1$. We measure accuracy as the percentage of blocks whose assignment for r_b matches the true parent. For each fold, we run this estimation procedure from five random initializations and average the results. Like Ritter et al. (2010), we do not enforce temporal constraints in the thread structure for this experiment. We are purely evaluating the predictive abilities of the model rather than its performance in a full-fledged reconstruction setup, which would require richer features beyond the scope of this paper.

Figure 2 shows results comparing M^4 against BHMM. Because all blocks are independent under LDA, it cannot be used in this experiment; using LDA would amount to a random baseline.

We plot the distribution of results from various samples and various numbers of classes in $\{5, \ldots, 25\}$. Most of the variance is across folds and samples; we find that there is not a strong trend in accuracy as a function of the number of classes. This suggests that most of the sequence predictions are carried by a small subset of the classes.

On average, M^4 outperforms BHMM by more than 15 points on the CNET corpus. M^4 is also better on the Twitter corpus, but the difference is not so stark. This seems to confirm our intuition that the advantage of M^4 over BHMM is greater when the blocks are longer; tweets may be short enough that the single-class assumption is not as limiting.

5.5.3 Speech Act Discovery

Thus far, we have investigated the predictive power of the model, but we would also like to determine if the inferred clusters correspond to human-interpretible classes. In the case of conversation data, our hope is that some of the latent classes represent *speech acts* or dialog acts (Searle, 1975). While there is a body of work in supervised speech act classification (Cohen et al., 2004; Bangalore et al., 2006; Surendran and Levow, 2006; Qadir and Riloff, 2011), the variety of conversation domains on the Web motivates the use of unsupervised approaches.

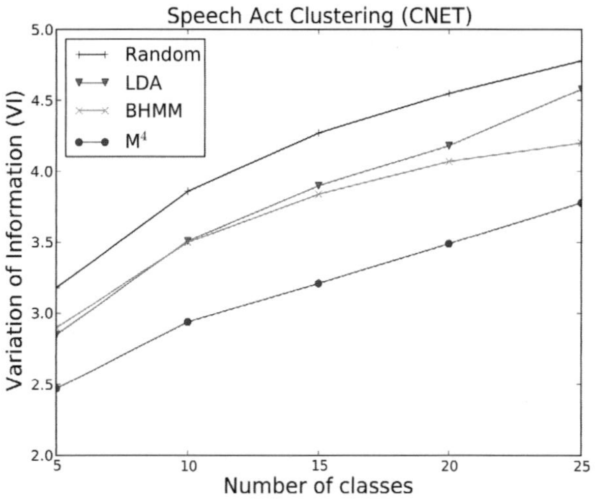

Figure 3: The variation of information between the human-created speech act annotations of the CNET corpus and the latent class assignments by various models.

The CNET corpus is annotated with twelve speech act classes: QUESTION and ANSWER, which are both broken down into multiple sub-classes, as well as RESOLUTION, REPRODUCTION, and OTHER (Kim et al., 2010). We would like to quantitatively measure how closely the latent states induced by our model match these annotations.[7]

We can measure this with *variation of information* (Meila, 2003), which has been used in recent years for unsupervised evaluation, e.g. in part-of-speech clustering (Goldwater and Griffiths, 2007). Given two sets of variable assignments $\mathbf{z}$ and $\mathbf{z}'$, the variation of information is defined as $H(Z|Z') + H(Z'|Z)$. In other words, given one clustering, how much uncertainty do we have about the other? Results are shown in Figure 3: a lower value corresponds to higher similarity.

On the CNET corpus, M^4 outperforms both baselines in all cases by a very significant margin. Qualitatively, we see clusters and transition parameters that make sense. For example, the class with top words $\{i, my, have, computer, am, ?, tried, help\}$ is most likely to begin a thread (with $\lambda = +1.94$) and appears to describe questions or requests for

[7]Some messages have multiple labels. Since messages are not annotated at finer granularities, we handle this by simply duplicating such messages, once per label, and measuring clustering performance on this expanded set of labeled data which now has one label per token.

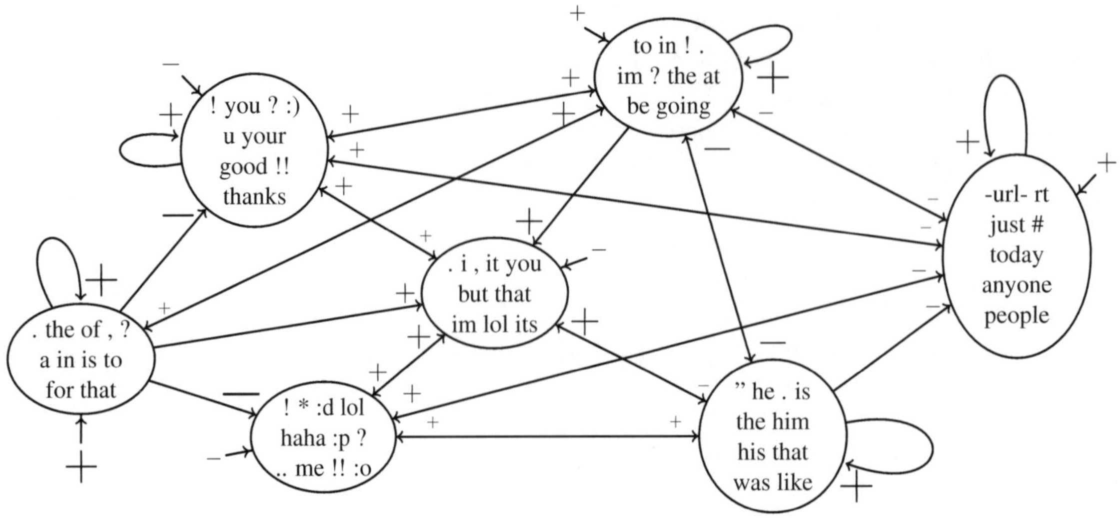

Figure 4: Example output from a model trained on the Twitter corpus with 15 classes (7 shown). Each node corresponds to a class learned by the model, and the most probable words are shown for each class. The symbols + and − on the directed edges denote the sign of the λ associated with transitioning from one class to another, and the size of the symbols is scaled by the magnitude of λ. Non-edge arrows going into a node represent the weight of starting a conversation with that class. Low-magnitude weights are not shown, and some edges are omitted to avoid clutter.

help. The class is not likely to be followed by itself ($\lambda = -0.32$) but is likely to be followed by the class with words $\{you, your, /, com, ., http, windows\}$ (with $\lambda = +1.38$).

The Twitter corpus does not have speech act annotations, so we offer example output in Figure 4. We again see patterns that we might expect to find in social media conversations, and some classes appear to correspond to speech acts such a declarations, personal questions, and replies. For example, the class in the center of the figure has words like *you* and *but* which suggests it is used in reply to other messages, and indeed we see that it has a positive weight of following almost every class, but a negative weight for actually starting a thread. Conversely, the class containing URLs (which corresponds to the act of sharing news or media) is likely to begin a thread, but is not likely to follow other classes except itself.

How well unsupervised models can truly capture speech acts is an open question. Much as LDA "topics" do not always correspond to what humans would judge to be semantic classes (Chang et al., 2009), the conversation classes inferred by unsupervised sequence models are similarly unlikely to be a perfect fit to human-assigned classes. Nevertheless, these results suggest M^4 is a step forward. Our model provides a framework for defining inter-message transitions as functions of multiple classes, which will be a desirable property for many corpora.

6 Conclusion

We have presented mixed membership Markov models (M^4), which extend the simple HMM approach to discourse modeling by positing class assignments at the level of individual tokens. This allows blocks of text to belong to potentially multiple classes, a property that relates M^4 to topic models. This type of model can be viewed as an HMM with an expanded state space, but because the transition probabilities are a function of a small number of parameters, the output remains human-interpretible.

M^4 can be taken as a general family of models and can be readily extended. In this work, we focused on introducing a model of *inter*-message structure, but certainly more sophisticated models of *intra*-message structure beyond unigram language models could be incorporated into M^4. Standard topic model extensions such as n-gram models (Wallach, 2006) can straightforwardly be applied here, and indeed we already applied such an extension by incorporating background distributions in §5.3. For conversational data, it could make sense to segment messages (e.g. into sentences) and constraint each segment to belong to one class or speech act; modifications along these lines have been applied to topic models as well (Gruber et al., 2007). While we have focused on conversation modeling, M^4 is a general probabilistic model that could be applied to other discourse applications, for example modeling sentences or paragraphs in articles rather than messages in conversations; it could also be applied to data beyond text.

Compared to a Bayesian block HMM, M^4 performs much better at a variety of tasks. A drawback is that the time complexity of inference as presented here is quadratic in the number of classes rather than linear. Improving this may be the subject of future research. Another potential avenue of future work is to model transitions such that a Dirichlet prior for the class distribution of a block, rather than the class distribution itself, depends on the previous class assignments. This would yield a model that more closely resembles LDA, but with topic priors that encode sequence information.

Acknowledgements

Thanks to Matt Gormley, Mark Dredze, Jason Eisner, the members of my lab and the anonymous reviewers for helpful feedback and discussions. This material is based upon work supported by a National Science Foundation Graduate Research Fellowship under Grant No. DGE-0707427 and a Dean's Fellowship from the Johns Hopkins University Whiting School of Engineering.

References

Srinivas Bangalore, Giuseppe Di Fabbrizio, and Amanda Stent. 2006. Learning the structure of task-driven human-human dialogs. In *Proceedings of the 21st International Conference on Computational Linguistics and the 44th annual meeting of the Association for Computational Linguistics*, ACL-44, pages 201–208.

Regina Barzilay and Lillian Lee. 2004. Catching the drift: Probabilistic content models, with applications to generation and summarization. In *HLT-NAACL 2004: Main Proceedings*, pages 113–120, Boston, Massachusetts, USA, May 2 - May 7. Association for Computational Linguistics.

M. J. Beal, Z. Ghahramani, and C. E. Rasmussen. 1997. Factorial hidden markov models. In *Machine Learning*, volume 29, pages 29–245.

D. Blei and J. Lafferty. 2007. A correlated topic model of science. *Annals of Applied Statistics*, 1(1):17–35.

David M. Blei and Jon D. Mcauliffe. 2007. Supervised topic models. In *Advances in Neural Information Processing Systems 21*.

David Blei, Andrew Ng, and Michael Jordan. 2003. Latent dirichlet allocation. *Journal of Machine Learning Research*, 3.

Jonathan Chang, Jordan Boyd-Graber, Sean Gerrish, Chong Wang, and David Blei. 2009. Reading Tea Leaves: How Humans Interpret Topic Models. In *Neural Information Processing Systems (NIPS)*.

Chaitanya Chemudugunta, Padhraic Smyth, and Mark Steyvers. 2006. Modeling general and specific aspects of documents with a probabilistic topic model. In *NIPS*, pages 241–248.

Harr Chen, S. R. K. Branavan, Regina Barzilay, and David R. Karger. 2009. Global models of document structure using latent permutations. In *Proceedings of Human Language Technologies: The 2009 Annual Conference of the North American Chapter of the Association for Computational Linguistics*, NAACL '09, pages 371–379.

William W. Cohen, Vitor R. Carvalho, and Tom M. Mitchell. 2004. Learning to classify email into "speech acts". In *Proceedings of EMNLP 2004*, pages 309–316, Barcelona, Spain, July. Association for Computational Linguistics.

A. P. Dempster, N. M. Laird, and D. B. Rubin. 1977. Maximum likelihood from incomplete data via the em algorithm. *Journal of the Royal Statistical Society. Series B (Methodological)*, 39(1):1–38.

Christopher P. Diehl, Galileo Namata, and Lise Getoor. 2007. Relationship identication for social network discovery. In *AAAI'07*.

Lan Du, Wray Buntine, and Huidong Jin. 2010. Sequential latent dirichlet allocation: Discover underlying topic structures within a document. *2010 IEEE International Conference on Data Mining*, pages 148–157.

Jonathan L. Elsas and Jaime Carbonell. 2009. It pays to be picky: An evaluation of thread retrieval in online forums. In *32nd Annual International ACM SIGIR Conference on Research and Development on Information Retrieval(SIGIR 2009)*.

Jenny Rose Finkel, Trond Grenager, and Christopher D. Manning. 2005. Incorporating non-local information into information extraction systems by gibbs sampling. In *ACL*.

Sharon Goldwater and Tom Griffiths. 2007. A fully bayesian approach to unsupervised part-of-speech tagging. In *Proceedings of the 45th Annual Meeting of the Association of Computational Linguistics*, pages 744–751, Prague, Czech Republic, June. Association for Computational Linguistics.

Tom Griffiths and Mark Steyvers. 2004. Finding scientific topics. In *Proceedings of the National Academy of Sciences of the United States of America*.

Amit Gruber, Michal Rosen-Zvi, and Yair Weiss. 2007. Hidden topic markov models. In *Artificial Intelligence and Statistics (AISTATS)*, San Juan, Puerto Rico.

Timothy Hospedales, Shaogang Gong, and Tao Xiang. 2009. A markov clustering topic model for mining behaviour in video. In *International Conference on Computer Vision (ICCV)*.

Shafiq R. Joty, Giuseppe Carenini, and Chin-Yew Lin. 2011. Unsupervised modeling of dialog acts in asynchronous conversations. In *IJCAI*, pages 1807–1813.

Su Nam Kim, Li Wang, and Timothy Baldwin. 2010. Tagging and linking web forum posts. In *Proceedings of the Fourteenth Conference on Computational Natural Language Learning*, CoNLL '10, pages 192–202.

Marina Meila. 2003. Comparing clusterings by the variation of information. *Learning Theory and Kernel Machines*, pages 173–187.

D. Mimno and A. McCallum. 2008. Topic models conditioned on arbitrary features with dirichlet-multinomial regression. In *UAI*.

Tom Minka. 2003. Estimating a dirichlet distribution.

Ashequl Qadir and Ellen Riloff. 2011. Classifying sentences as speech acts in message board posts. In *Proceedings of the 2011 Conference on Empirical Methods in Natural Language Processing*, pages 748–758, Edinburgh, Scotland, UK., July. Association for Computational Linguistics.

Alan Ritter, Colin Cherry, and Bill Dolan. 2010. Unsupervised modeling of twitter conversations. In *Human Language Technologies: The 2010 Annual Conference of the North American Chapter of the Association for Computational Linguistics*, HLT '10, pages 172–180.

Carolyn Penstein Rosé, Barbara Di Eugenio, Lori S. Levin, and Carol Van Ess-Dykema. 1995. Discourse processing of dialogues with multiple threads. In *Proceedings of the 33rd annual meeting on Association for Computational Linguistics*, ACL '95, pages 31–38.

John Searle, 1975. *A taxonomy of illocutionary acts.* University of Minnesota Press, Minneapolis.

Jangwon Seo, W. Bruce Croft, and David A. Smith. 2009. Online community search using thread structure. In *ACM Conference on Information and Knowledge Management (CIKM 2009)*, pages 1907–1910.

Andreas Stolcke, Noah Coccaro, Rebecca Bates, Paul Taylor, Carol Van Ess-Dykema, Klaus Ries, Elizabeth Shriberg, Daniel Jurafsky, Rachel Martin, and Marie Meteer. 2000. Dialogue act modeling for automatic tagging and recognition of conversational speech. *Computational Linguistics*, 26(3):339–373, September.

Dinoj Surendran and Gina-Anne Levow. 2006. Dialog act tagging with support vector machines and hidden markov models. In *Interspeech*.

Hanna M. Wallach, David Mimno, and Andrew McCallum. 2009. Rethinking LDA: Why priors matter. In *NIPS*.

H.M. Wallach. 2006. Topic modeling: beyond bag-of-words. In *ICML '06: Proceedings of the 23rd international conference on Machine learning*, pages 977–984.

Hongning Wang, Chi Wang, ChengXiang Zhai, and Jiawei Han. 2011a. Learning online discussion structures by conditional random fields. In *34th Annual International ACM SIGIR Conference on Research and Development in Information Retrieval (SIGIR'11)*, pages 435–444.

Hongning Wang, Duo Zhang, and ChengXiang Zhai. 2011b. Structural topic model for latent topical structure analysis. In *ACL*, pages 1526–1535. The Association for Computer Linguistics.

Li Wang, Marco Lui, Su Nam Kim, Joakim Nivre, and Timothy Baldwin. 2011c. Predicting thread discourse structure over technical web forums. In *Proceedings of EMNLP 2011*, pages 13–25.

Gu Xu, Hang Li, and Wei-Ying Ma. 2008. Fora: Leveraging the power of internet communities for question answering. In *1st International Workshop on Question Answering on the Web (QAWeb08)*.

Jen-Yuan Yeh and Aaron Harnly. 2006. Email thread reassembly using similarity matching. In *Proceedings of the 3rd Conference on Email and Anti-Spam (CEAS 2006)*, pages 64–71.

An Entity-Topic Model for Entity Linking

Xianpei Han **Le Sun**
Institute of Software, Chinese Academy of Sciences
HaiDian District, Beijing, China.
{xianpei, sunle}@nfs.iscas.ac.cn

Abstract

Entity Linking (*EL*) has received considerable attention in recent years. Given many name mentions in a document, the goal of EL is to predict their referent entities in a knowledge base. Traditionally, there have been two distinct directions of EL research: one focusing on the effects of mention's *context compatibility*, assuming that "*the referent entity of a mention is reflected by its context*"; the other dealing with the effects of document's *topic coherence*, assuming that "*a mention's referent entity should be coherent with the document's main topics*". In this paper, we propose a generative model – called *entity-topic model*, to effectively join the above two complementary directions together. By jointly modeling and exploiting the context compatibility, the topic coherence and the correlation between them, our model can accurately link all mentions in a document using both the local information (including the *words* and the *mentions* in a document) and the global knowledge (including *the topic knowledge*, *the entity context knowledge* and *the entity name knowledge*). Experimental results demonstrate the effectiveness of the proposed model.

1 Introduction

Entity Linking (EL) has received considerable research attention in recent years (McNamee & Dang, 2009; Ji et al., 2010). Given many name mentions in a document, the goal of EL is to predict their referent entities in a given knowledge base (KB), such as the *Wikipedia*[1]. For example, as shown in Figure 1, an EL system should identify the referent entities of the three mentions *WWDC*, *Apple* and *Lion* correspondingly are the entities *Apple Worldwide Developers Conference*, *Apple Inc.* and *Mac OS X Lion* in KB. The EL problem appears in many different guises throughout the areas of natural language processing, information retrieval and text mining. For instance, in many applications we need to collect all appearances of a specific entity in different documents, EL is an effective way to resolve such an information integration problem. Furthermore, EL can bridge the mentions in documents with the semantic information in knowledge bases (e.g., *Wikipedia* and *Freebase* [2]), thus can provide a solid foundation for knowledge-rich methods.

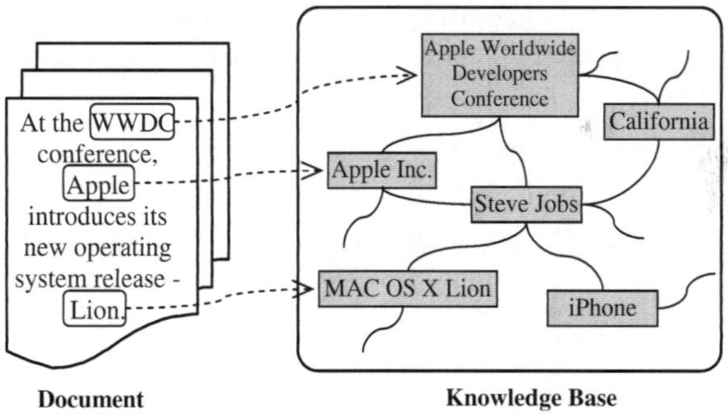

Figure 1. A Demo of Entity Linking

Unfortunately, the accurate EL is often hindered by the *name ambiguity* problem, i.e., a name may refer to different entities in different contexts. For example, the name *Apple* may refer to more than 20 entities in Wikipedia, such as *Apple Inc.*, *Apple (band)* and *Apple Bank*. Traditionally, there have been two distinct directions in EL to resolve the *name ambiguity* problem: one focusing on the effects of mention's *context compatibility* and the other dealing with the effects of document's *topic coherence*. EL methods based on context

[1] www.wikipedia.org

[2] www.freebase.com

compatibility assume that "*the referent entity of a mention is reflected by its context*"(Mihalcea & Cosomai, 2007; Zhang et al., 2010; Zheng et al., 2010; Han & Sun, 2011; Kataria et al., 2011; Sen 2012). For example, the context compatibility based methods will identify the referent entity of the mention *Lion* in Figure 1 is the entity *Mac OS X Lion*, since this entity is more compatible with its context words *operating system* and *release* than other candidates such as *Lion(big cats)* or *Lion(band)*. EL methods based on topic coherence assume that "*a mention's referent entity should be coherent with document's main topics*" (Medelyan et al., 2008; Milne & Witten, 2008; Kulkarni et al., 2009; Han et al., 2011). For example, the topic coherence based methods will link the mention *Apple* in Figure 1 to the entity *Apple Inc.*, since it is more coherent with the document's topic *MAC OS X Lion Release* than other referent candidates such as *Apple (band)* or *Apple Bank*.

In recent years, both of the above two EL directions have shown their effectiveness to some extent, and obviously they are *complementary* to each other. Therefore we believe that bring the above two directions together will enhance the EL performance. Traditionally, the above two directions are usually be brought together using a hybrid method (Zhang and Sim, 2011; Ratinov et al., 2011; Han et al., 2011), i.e., the context compatibility and the topic coherence are first *separately* modeled, then their EL evidence are combined through an additional model. For example, Zhang and Sim (2011) first models the context compatibility as a context similarity and the topic coherence as a similarity between the underlying topics of documents and KB entries, then these two similarities are combined through an additional SVM classifier for the final EL decision.

The main drawback of these hybrid methods, however, is that they model the context compatibility and the topic coherence *separately*, which makes it difficult to capture the *mutual reinforcement* effect between the above two directions. That is, the topic coherence and the context compatibility are highly correlated and their evidence can be used to reinforce each other in EL decisions. For example, in Figure 1, if the context compatibility gives a high likelihood the mention *Apple* refers to the entity *Apple Inc.*, then this likelihood will give more evidence for this document's topic is about *MAC OS X Lion*, and it in turn will reinforce the topic coherence between the entity *MAC OS X Lion* and the document. In reverse, once we known the topic of this document is about *MAC OS X Lion*, the context compatibility between the mention *Apple* and the entity *Apple Inc.* can be improved as the importance of the context words *operating system* and *release* will be increased using the topic knowledge. In this way, we believe that modeling the above two directions *jointly*, rather than *separately*, will further improve the EL performance by capturing the *mutual reinforcement* effect between the context compatibility and the topic coherence.

In this paper, we propose a method to *jointly* model and exploit the context compatibility, the topic coherence and the correlation between them for better EL performance. Specifically, we propose a generative probabilistic model – called *entity-topic model*, which can uniformly model the text compatibility and the topic coherence as the *statistical dependencies* between the *mentions*, the *words*, the underlying *entities* and the underlying *topics* of a document by assuming that each document is generated according to the following two assumptions:

1) **Topic coherence assumption**: *All entities in a document should be centered around the main topics of the document.* For example, the entity *Apple Inc.* tends to occur in documents about *IT*, but the entity *Apple Bank* will more likely to occur in documents about *bank* or *investment*.

2) **Context compatibility assumption**: *The context words of a mention should be centered on its referent entity.* For example, the words *computer*, *phone* and *music* tends to occur in the context of the entity *Apple Inc.*, meanwhile the words *loan*, *invest* and *deposit* will more likely to occur in the context of the entity *Apple Bank*.

In this way, the entity-topic model uniformly models the context compatibility, the topic coherence and the correlation between them as the dependencies between the observed information (the *mentions* and the *words*) in a document and the hidden information we want to know (the underlying *topics* and *entities*) through the global knowledge (including *the topic knowledge*, *the entity name knowledge* and *the entity context knowledge*). And the EL problem can now be decomposed into the following two inference tasks:

1) *Predicting the underlying topics and the underlying entities of a document* based on the observed information and the global knowledge. We call such a task the ***prediction task***;

2) *Estimating the global knowledge from data.* Notice that the topic knowledge, the entity name knowledge and the entity context knowledge are all not previously given, thus we need to estimate them from data. We call such a task the ***knowledge discovery task***.

Because the accurate inference of the above two tasks is intractable in our entity-topic model, this paper also develops an approximate inference algorithm – the Gibbs sampling algorithm to solve them.

Contributions. The main contributions of this paper are summarized below:

- We propose a generative probabilistic model, the *entity-topic model*, which can *jointly* model and exploit the context compatibility, the topic coherence and the correlation between them for better EL performance;
- We develop a *Gibbs sampling algorithm* to solve the two inference tasks of our model: 1) Discovering the global knowledge from data; and 2) Collectively making accurate EL decisions.

This paper is organized as follows. Section 2 describes the proposed entity-topic model. Section 3 demonstrates the Gibbs sampling algorithm. The experimental results are presented and discussed in Section 4. The related work is reviewed in Section 5. Finally we conclude this paper in Section 6.

2 The Entity-Topic Model for Entity Linking

In this section, we describe the proposed entity-topic model. In following we first demonstrate how to capture the context compatibility, the topic coherence and the correlation between them in the document generative process, then we incorporate the global knowledge generation into our model for knowledge estimation from data.

2.1 Document Generative Process

As shown in Section 1, we jointly model the context compatibility and the topic coherence as the statistical dependencies in the entity-topic model by assuming that all documents are generated in a topical coherent and context compatible way. In following we describe the document generative process.

In our model, each document d is assumed composed of two types of information, i.e., the *mentions* and the *words*. Formally, we represent a document as:

*A **document** is a collection of M mentions and N words, denoted as* $\mathbf{d} = \{m_1, ..., m_M; w_1, ..., w_N\}$, *with* m_i *the* i^{th} *mention and* w_j *the* j^{th} *word.*

For example, the document in Figure 1 is represented as $\mathbf{d}$ = {***WWDC***, ***Apple***, ***Lion***; *at*, *the*, *conference*, …}, where *WWDC*, *Apple*, *Lion* are the three mentions and the other are the words.

To generate a document, our model relies on three types of global knowledge, including:

- **Topic Knowledge** ϕ (*The entity distribution of topics*): In our model, all entities in a document are generated based on its underlying topics, with each topic is a group of semantically related entities. Statistically, we model each topic as a multinomial distribution of entities, with the probability indicating the likelihood an entity to be extracted from this topic. For example, we may have a topic $\phi_{Apple\ Inc.}$= {*Steve Jobs*$^{0.12}$, *iPhone*$^{0.07}$, *iPod*$^{0.08}$, ...}, indicating the likelihood of the entity *Steve Jobs* be extracted from this topic is *0.12*, etc.
- **Entity Name Knowledge** ψ (*The name distribution of entities*): In our model, all name mentions are generated using the name knowledge of its referent entity. Specifically, we model the name knowledge of an entity as a multinomial distribution of its names, with the probability indicating the likelihood this entity is mentioned by the name. For example, the name knowledge of the entity *Apple Inc.* may be $\psi_{Apple\ Inc.}$ = {*Apple*$^{0.51}$, *Apple Computer Inc.*$^{0.10}$, *Apple Inc.*$^{0.07}$, ...}, indicating that the entity *Apple Inc.* is mentioned by the name *Apple* with probability *0.51*, etc.
- **Entity Context Knowledge** ξ (*The context word distribution of entities*): In our model, all context words of an entity's mention are generated using its context knowledge. Concretely, we model the context knowledge of an entity as a multinomial distribution of words, with the probability indicating the likelihood a word appearing in this entity's context. For example, we may have $\xi_{Apple\ Inc.}$= {*phone*$^{0.07}$, *computer*$^{0.10}$, *IT*$^{0.06}$, *phone*$^{0.002}$, ...}, indicating that the word *computer* appearing in the context of the entity *Apple Inc.* with probability *0.1*, etc.

Given the topic knowledge ϕ, the entity name knowledge ψ and the entity context knowledge ξ

1. For each doc d in **D,** sample its topic distribution $\theta_d \sim Dir(\alpha)$;
2. For each of the M_d mentions m_i in doc d:
   a) Sample a topic assignment $z_i \sim Mult(\theta_d)$;
   b) Sample an entity assignment $e_i \sim Mult(\phi_{z_i})$;
   c) Sample a mention $m_i \sim Mult(\psi_{e_i})$;
3. For each of the N_d words w_i in doc d:
   a) Sample a target entity it describes from d's referent entities $a_i \sim Unif(e_{m_1}, e_{m_2}, \cdots, e_{m_d})$;
   b) Sample a describing word using a_i's context word distribution $w_i \sim Mult(\xi_{a_i})$.

Figure 2. The document generative process, with $Dir(.)$, $Mult(.)$ and $Unif(.)$ correspondingly *Dirichlet*, *Multinomial* and *Uniform distribution*

Given the entity list **E** = $\{e_1, e_2, ..., e_E\}$ in the knowledge base, the word list **V** = $\{w_1, w_2, ..., w_v\}$, the entity name list **K** = $\{n_1, n_2, ..., n_K\}$ and the global knowledge described in above, the generation process of a document collection (corpus) **D** = $\{d_1, d_2, ..., d_D\}$ is shown in Figure 2. To demonstrate the generation process, we also demonstrate how the document in Figure 1 can be generated using our model in following steps:

Step 1: The model generates the topic distribution of the document as θ_d = {*Apple Inc.*$^{0.45}$, *Operating System(OS)*$^{0.55}$};

Step 2: For the three mentions in the document:

i. According to the topic distribution θ_d, the model generates their topic assignments as z_1=*Apple Inc.*, z_2 = *Apple Inc.*, z_3 = *OS*;

ii. According to the topic knowledge $\phi_{Apple\ Inc.}$, ϕ_{OS} and the topic assignments z_1, z_2, z_3, the model generates their entity assignments as e_1 = *Apple Worldwide Developers Conference*, e_2 = *Apple Inc.*, e_3 = *Mac OS X Lion*;

iii. According to the name knowledge of the entities *Apple Worldwide Developers Conference, Apple Inc.* and *Mac OS X Lion*, our model generates the three mentions as m_1=*WWDC*, m_2 = *Apple*, m_3 = *Lion*;

Step 3: For all words in the document:

i. According to the referent entity set in document $\mathbf{e_d}$ = {*Apple Worldwide Developers Conference*, *Apple Inc.*, *Mac OS X Lion*}, the model generates the target entity they describes as a_3=*Apple Worldwide Developers Conference* and a_4=*Apple Inc.*;

ii. According to their target entity and the context knowledge of these entities, the model generates the context words in the document. For example, according to the context knowledge of the entities *Apple Worldwide Developers Conference*, the model generates its context word w_3 =*conference*, and according to the context knowledge of the entity *Apple Inc.*, the model generates its context word w_4 = *introduces*.

Through the above generative process, we can see that all entities in a document are extracted from the document's underlying topics, ensuring the topic coherence; and all words in a document are extracted from the context word distributions of its referent entities, resulting in the context compatibility. Furthermore, the generation of topics, entities, mentions and words are highly correlated, thus our model can capture the correlation between the topic coherence and the context compatibility.

2.2 Global Knowledge Generative Process

The entity-topic model relies on three types of global knowledge (including the topic knowledge, the entity name knowledge and the entity context knowledge) to generate a document. Unfortunately, all three types of global knowledge are unknown and thus need to be estimated from data. In this paper we estimate the global knowledge through Bayesian inference by also incorporating the knowledge generation process into our model.

Specifically, given the topic number T, the entity number E, the name number K and the word number V, the entity-topic model generates the global knowledge as follows:

1) $\phi|\beta \sim Dir(\beta)$

For each topic z, our model samples its entity distribution ϕ_z from an E-dimensional Dirichlet distribution with hyperparameter β

2) $\psi|\gamma \sim Dir(\gamma)$

For each entity e, our model samples its name distribution ψ_e from a K-dimensional Dirichlet distribution with hyperparameter γ

3) $\xi|\delta \sim Dir(\delta)$

For each entity e, our model samples its context word distribution ξ_e from a V-dimensional Dirichlet distribution with hyperparameter $\delta\delta$

Finally, the full entity-topic model is shown in Figure 3 using the plate representation.

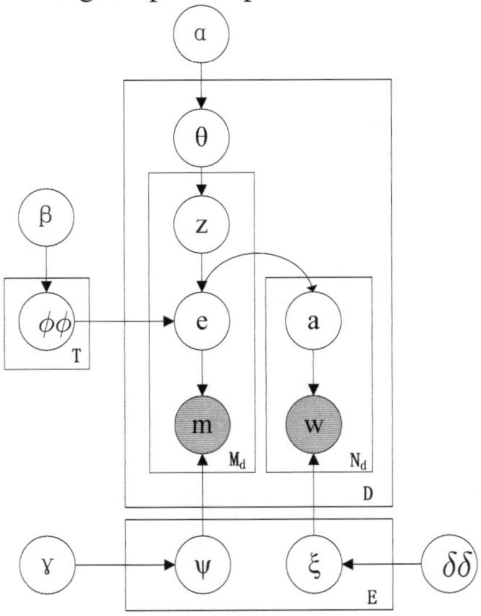

Figure 3. The plate representation of the entity-topic model

2.3 The Probability of a Corpus

Using the entity-topic model, the probability of generating a corpus $\mathbf{D}=\{d_1, d_2, ..., d_D\}$ given hyperparameters $\alpha\alpha\beta\beta\gamma\gamma$and $\delta\delta$can be expressed as:

$$P(\mathbf{D};\alpha,\beta,\gamma,\delta) = \prod_{d} P(\mathbf{m_d},\mathbf{w_d};\alpha,\beta,\gamma,\delta)$$

$$= \prod_{d}\sum_{\mathbf{e_d}} P(\mathbf{e_d}|\alpha,\beta)P(\mathbf{m_d}|\mathbf{e_d},\gamma)P(\mathbf{w_d}|\mathbf{e_d},\delta)$$

$$= \int_{\phi} P(\phi|\beta)\int_{\psi} P(\psi|\gamma)\prod_{d}\sum_{\mathbf{e_d}} P(\mathbf{m_d}|\mathbf{e_d},\psi)$$

$$\times \int_{\xi} P(\xi|\delta)\sum_{\mathbf{a_d}} P(\mathbf{a_d}|\mathbf{e_d})P(\mathbf{w_d}|\mathbf{a_d},\xi)$$

$$\times \int_{\theta} P(\theta|\alpha)P(\mathbf{e_d}|\theta,\phi)d\theta d\xi d\psi d\phi \quad (2.1)$$

where $\mathbf{m_d}$ and $\mathbf{e_d}$ correspondingly the set of mentions and their entity assignments in document d, $\mathbf{w_d}$ and $\mathbf{a_d}$ correspondingly the set of words and their entity assignments in document d.

3 Inference using Gibbs Sampling

In this section, we describe how to resolve the entity linking problem using the entity-topic model. Overall, there were two inference tasks for EL:

1) ***The prediction task***. Given a document d, predicting its *entity assignments* ($\mathbf{e_d}$ for mentions and $\mathbf{a_d}$ for words) and *topic assignments* ($\mathbf{z_d}$). Notice that here the EL decisions are just the prediction of per-mention entity assignments ($\mathbf{e_d}$).

2) ***The knowledge discovery task***. Given a corpus $\mathbf{D}=\{d_1, d_2, ..., d_D\}$, estimating the global knowledge (including *the entity distribution of topics* $\phi\phi$ *the name distribution* $\psi\psi$and *the context word distribution* $\xi\xi$*of entities*) from data.

Unfortunately, due to the heaven correlation between *topics*, *entities*, *mentions* and *words* (the correlation is also demonstrated in Eq. (2.1), where the integral is intractable due to the coupling between $\theta\theta$ $\phi\phi\psi\psi$and $\xi\xi$, the accurate inference of the above two tasks is intractable. For this reason, we propose an approximate inference algorithm – the *Gibbs sampling algorithm* for the entity-topic model by extending the well-known Gibbs sampling algorithm for LDA (Griffiths & Steyvers, 2004). In Gibbs sampling, we first construct the posterior distribution $P(\mathbf{z},\mathbf{e},\mathbf{a}|\mathbf{D})$, then this posterior distribution is used to: 1) estimate $\theta\theta$ $\phi\phi\psi\psi$ and $\xi\xi$ and 2) predict the entities and the topics of all documents in D. Specifically, we first derive the joint posterior distribution from Eq. (2.1) as:

$$P(\mathbf{z},\mathbf{e},\mathbf{a}|\mathbf{D}) \propto P(\mathbf{z})P(\mathbf{e}|\mathbf{z})P(\mathbf{m}|\mathbf{e})P(\mathbf{a}|\mathbf{e})P(\mathbf{w}|\mathbf{a})$$

where

$$P(\mathbf{z}) = (\frac{\Gamma(T\alpha)}{\Gamma(\alpha)^T})^D \prod_{d=1}^{D} \frac{\prod_t \Gamma(\alpha + C_{dt}^{DT})}{\Gamma(T\alpha + C_{d*}^{DT})} \quad (3.1)$$

is the probability of the joint topic assignment $\mathbf{z}$ to all mentions $\mathbf{m}$ in corpus D, and

$$P(\mathbf{e}|\mathbf{z}) = (\frac{\Gamma(E\beta)}{\Gamma(\beta)^E})^T \prod_{t=1}^{T} \frac{\prod_e \Gamma(\beta + C_{te}^{TE})}{\Gamma(E\beta + C_{t*}^{TE})} \quad (3.2)$$

is the conditional probability of the joint entity assignments $\mathbf{e}\mathbf{e}$to all mentions $\mathbf{m}$ in corpus D given all topic assignments $\mathbf{z}\mathbf{z}$and

$$P(\mathbf{m}|\mathbf{e}) = (\frac{\Gamma(K\gamma)}{\Gamma(\gamma)^K})^E \prod_{e=1}^{E} \frac{\prod_m \Gamma(\gamma + C_{em}^{EM})}{\Gamma(K\gamma + C_{e*}^{EM})} \quad (3.3)$$

is the conditional probability of all mentions $\mathbf{m}\mathbf{m}$ given all per-mention entity assignments $\mathbf{e}\mathbf{e}$and

$$P(\mathbf{a}|\mathbf{e}) = \prod_{d=1}^{D} \prod_{e \subset \mathbf{e_d}} (\frac{C_{de}^{DE}}{C_{d*}^{DE}})^{C_{de}^{DA}} \quad (3.4)$$

is the conditional probability of the joint entity assignments $\mathbf{a}\mathbf{a}$to all words $\mathbf{w}$ in corpus D given all per-mention entity assignments $\mathbf{e}\mathbf{e}$and

$$P(\mathbf{w}|\mathbf{a}) = (\frac{\Gamma(V\delta)}{\Gamma(\delta)^V})^E \prod_{e=1}^{E} \frac{\prod_w \Gamma(\delta + C_{ew}^{EW})}{\Gamma(V\delta + C_{e*}^{EW})} \quad (3.5)$$

is the conditional probability of all words $\mathbf{w}$ given all per-word entity assignments $\mathbf{a}$. In all above formulas, $\Gamma(.)$ is the Gamma function, C_{dt}^{DT} is the times topic *t* has been assigned for all mentions in document *d*, $C_{d*}^{DT} = \sum_t C_{dt}^{DT}$ is the topic number in document *d*, and C_{te}^{TE}, C_{em}^{EM}, C_{de}^{DE}, C_{de}^{DA}, C_{ew}^{EW} have similar explanation.

Based on the above joint probability, we construct a Markov chain that converges to the posterior distribution $P(\mathbf{z}, \mathbf{e}, \mathbf{a}|\mathbf{D})$ and then draw samples from this Markov chain for inference. For entity-topic model, each state in the Markov chain is an assignment (including *topic assignment to a mention, entity assignment to a mention* and *entity assignment to a word*). In Gibbs sampling, all assignments are sequentially sampled conditioned on all the current other assignments. So here we only need to derive the following three fully conditional assignment distributions:

1) $P(z_i = t|\mathbf{z}_{-i}, \mathbf{e}, \mathbf{a}, \mathbf{D})$: the topic assignment distribution to a mention given the current other topic assignments $\mathbf{z}_{-i}$, the current entity assignments $\mathbf{e}$ and $\mathbf{a}$;
2) $P(e_i = e|\mathbf{z}, \mathbf{e}_{-i}, \mathbf{a}, \mathbf{D})$: the entity assignment distribution to a mention given the current entity assignments of all other mentions $\mathbf{e}_{-i}$, the current topic assignments $\mathbf{z}$ and the current entity assignments of context words $\mathbf{a}$;
3) $P(a_i = e|\mathbf{z}, \mathbf{e}, \mathbf{a}_{-i}, \mathbf{D})$: the entity assignment distribution to a context word given the current entity assignments of all other context words $\mathbf{a}_{-i}$, the current topic assignments $\mathbf{z}$ and the current entity assignments $\mathbf{e}$ of mentions.

Using the Formula 3.1-3.5, we can derive the above three conditional distributions as (where m_i is contained in doc *d*):

$$P(z_i = t|\mathbf{z}_{-i}, \mathbf{e}, \mathbf{a}, \mathbf{D}) \propto \frac{C_{(-i)dt}^{DT} + \alpha}{C_{(-i)d*}^{DT} + T\alpha} \times \frac{C_{(-i)te}^{TE} + \beta}{C_{(-i)t*}^{TE} + E\beta}$$

where the topic assignment to a mention is determined by the probability this topic appearing in doc *d* (the 1st term) and the probability the referent entity appearing in this topic (the 2nd term);

$$P(e_i = e|\mathbf{z}, \mathbf{e}_{-i}, \mathbf{a}, \mathbf{D}) \propto \frac{C_{(-i)te}^{TE} + \beta}{C_{(-i)t*}^{TE} + E\beta} \times \frac{C_{(-i)em}^{EM} + \gamma}{C_{(-i)e*}^{EM} + K\gamma} \times (\frac{C_{(-i)de}^{DE} + 1}{C_{(-i)de}^{DE}})^{C_{de}^{DA}}$$

where the entity assignment to a mention is determined by the probability this entity extracted from the assigned topic (the 1st term), the probability this entity is referred by the name *m* (the 2nd term) and the contextual words describing this entity in doc *d* (the 3rd term);

$$P(a_i = e|\mathbf{z}, \mathbf{e}, \mathbf{a}_{-i}, \mathbf{D}) \propto \frac{C_{de}^{DE}}{C_{d*}^{DE}} \times \frac{C_{(-i)ew}^{EW} + \delta}{C_{(-i)e*}^{EW} + V\delta}$$

where the entity assignment to a word is determined by the number of times this entity has been assigned to mentions in doc *d* (the 1st term) and the probability the word appearing in the context of this entity (the 2nd term).

Finally, using the above three conditional distributions, we iteratively update all assignments of corpus $\mathbf{D}$ until coverage, then the global knowledge is estimated using the final assignments, and the final entity assignments are used as the referents of their corresponding mentions.

Inference on Unseen Documents. When unseen documents are given, we predict its entities and topics using the incremental Gibbs sampling algorithm described in (Kataria et al., 2011), i.e., we iteratively update the entity assignments and the topic assignments of an unseen document as the same as the above inference process, but with the previously learned global knowledge fixed.

Hyperparameter setting. One still problem here is the setting of the hyperparameters α, β, γ and δ. For α and β, this paper empirically set the value of them to $\alpha = 50/T$ and $\beta = 0.1$ as in Griffiths & Steyvers(2004). For γ, we notice that $K\gamma$ is the number of pseudo names added to each entity, when $\gamma = 0$ our model only mentions an entity using its previously used names. Observed that an entity typically has a fixed set of names, we set γ to a small value by setting $K\gamma = 1.0$. For δ, we notice that $V\delta$ is the number of pseudo words added to each entity, playing the role of smoothing its context word distribution. As there is typically a relatively loose correlation between an entity and its context words, we set δ to a relatively large value by fixing the total smoothing words added to each entity, a typical value is $V\delta = 2000$.

4 Experiments

In this section, we evaluate our method and compare it with the traditional EL methods. We first explain the experimental settings in Section 4.1-4.4, then discuss the results in Section 4.5.

4.1 Knowledge Base

In our experiments, we use the Jan. 30, 2010 English version of Wikipedia as the knowledge base, which contains over 3 million entities. Notice that we also take the general concepts in Wikipedia (such as *Apple*, *Video*, *Computer*, etc.) as entities, so the entity in this paper may not strictly follow its definition.

4.2 Data Sets

There are two standard data sets for EL: IITB[3] and TAC 2009 EL data set (McNamee & Dang, 2009), where IITB focuses on *aggressive recall* EL and TAC 2009 focuses on EL on *salient mentions*. Due to the collective nature of our method, we mainly used the **IITB** as the primary data set as the same as Kulkarni et al.(2009) and Han et al.(2011). But we also give the EL accuracies on the TAC 2009 in Sect. 4.5.4 as auxiliary results.

Overall, the IITB data set contains 107 web documents. For each document, the name mentions' referent entities in Wikipedia are manually annotated to be as exhaustive as possible. In total, 17,200 name mentions are annotated, with 161 name mentions per document on average. In our experiments, we use only the name mentions whose referent entities are contained in Wikipedia.

4.3 Evaluation Criteria

This paper adopted the same performance metrics used in the Kulkarni et al. (2009), which includes ***Recall***, ***Precision*** and ***F1***. Let M^* be the golden standard set of the EL results (each EL result is a pair (*m, e*), with *m* the mention and *e* its referent entity), M be the set of EL results outputted by an EL system, then these metrics are computed as:

$$Precision = \frac{|M \cap M^*|}{|M|}$$

$$Recall = \frac{|M \cap M^*|}{|M^*|}$$

where two EL results are considered equal if and only if both their mentions and referent entities are equal. As the same as Kulkarni et al.(2009), *Precision* and *Recall* are averaged across documents and overall *F1* is used as the primary performance metric by computing from average *Precision* and *Recall*.

4.4 Baselines

We compare our method with five baselines which are described as follows:

Wikify!. This is a context compatibility based EL method using vector space model (Mihalcea & Csomai, 2007). *Wikify!* computes the context compatibility using the word overlap between the mention's context and the entity's Wikipedia entry.

EM-Model. This is a statistical context compatibility based EL method described in Han & Sun(2011), which computes the compatibility by integrating the evidence from the entity popularity, the entity name knowledge and the context word distribution of entities.

M&W. This is a relational topic coherence based EL method described in Milne & Witten(2008). *M&W* measures an entity's topic coherence to a document as its average semantic relatedness to the *unambiguous* entities in the document.

CSAW. This is an EL method which combines context compatibility and topic coherence using a hybrid method (Kulkarni et al., 2009), where context compatibility and topic coherence are first separated modeled as context similarity and the sum of all *pair-wise* semantic relatedness between the entities in the document, then the entities which can maximize the weighted sum of the context compatibility and the topic coherence are identified as the referent entities of the document.

EL-Graph. This is a graph based hybrid EL method described in Han et al. (2011), which first models the context compatibility as text similarity and the topic coherence of an entity as its node importance in a referent graph which captures all mention-entity and entity-entity relations in a document, then a random walk algorithm is used to collectively find all referent entities of a document.

Except for *CSAW* and *EL-Graph*, all other baselines are designed only to link the salient name mentions (i.e., key phrases) in a document. In our experiment, in order to compare the EL performances on also the non-salient name mentions, we push these systems' recall by reducing their respective importance thresholds of linked mentions.

[3] http://www.cse.iitb.ac.in/~soumen/doc/QCQ/

4.5 Experimental Results

4.5.1 *Overall Performance*

We compared our method with all the above five baselines. For our method, we estimate the global knowledge using all the articles in the Jan. 30, 2010 English version of Wikipedia, and totally there were 3,083,158 articles. For each article, the mentions within it are detected using the methods described in Medelyan et al.(2008) and all terms in an article are used as context words, so a term may both be a mention and a context word. The topic number of our model is $T = 300$ (will be empirically set in Sect 4.5.2). To train the entity-topic model, we run 500 iterations of our Gibbs sampling algorithm to converge. The training time of our model is nearly one week on our server using 20 GB RAM and one core of 3.2 GHz CPU. Since the training can be done offline, we believe that the training time is not critical to the real-world usage as the online inference on new document is very quick. Using the above settings, the overall results are shown in Table 1.

	Precision	**Recall**	**F1**
Wikify!	*0.55*	*0.28*	*0.37*
EM-Model	*0.82*	*0.48*	*0.61*
M&W	*0.80*	*0.38*	*0.52*
CSAW	*0.65*	*0.73*	*0.69*
EL-Graph	*0.69*	*0.76*	*0.73*
Our Method	***0.81***	***0.80***	***0.80***

Table 1. The overall results on IITB data set

From the overall results in Table 1, we can see that:

1) By *jointly* modeling and exploiting the context compatibility and the topic coherence, our method can achieve competitive performance: ① compared with the context compatibility baselines *Wikify!* and *EM-Model,* our method correspondingly gets 43% and 19% F1 improvement; ② compared with the topic coherence baselines *M&W*, our method achieves 28% F1 improvement; ③ compared with the hybrid baselines *CSAW* and *EL-Graph*, our method correspondingly achieves 11% and 7% F1 improvement.

2) Compared with the *context compatibility only* and the *topic coherence only* methods, the main advantage of our method is that, rather than only achieved high entity linking precision on *salient* mentions, it can also effectively link the *non-salient* mentions in a document: this is demonstrated in our method's significant *Recall* improvement: a 32~52% Recall improvement over baselines *Wikify!*, *EM-Model* and *M&W*. We believe this is because a document usually contains little evidence for EL decisions on non-salient mentions, so with either only context compatibility or only topic coherence the evidence is not enough for EL decisions on these non-salient mentions, and bring these two directions together is critical for the accurate EL on these mentions.

3) Compared with the *hybrid* methods, the main advantage of our method is the improvement of EL precision (a 11~16% improvement over baselines *CSAW* and *EL-Graph*), we believe this is because: ① Our method can further capture the mutual reinforcement effect between the context compatibility and the topic coherence; ② The traditional hybrid methods usually determine the topic coherence of an entity to a document using *all entities* in the document, in comparison our method uses only *the entities in the same topic*, we believe this is more reasonable for EL decisions.

4.5.2 *Parameter Tuning*

One still parameter of our method is the topic number *T*. An appropriate *T* will distribute entities into well-organized topics, in turn it will capture the co-occurrence information of entities. Figure 4 plots the *F1* at different *T* values. We can see that the *F1* is not very sensitive to the topic number and with $T = 300$ our method achieves its best *F1* performance.

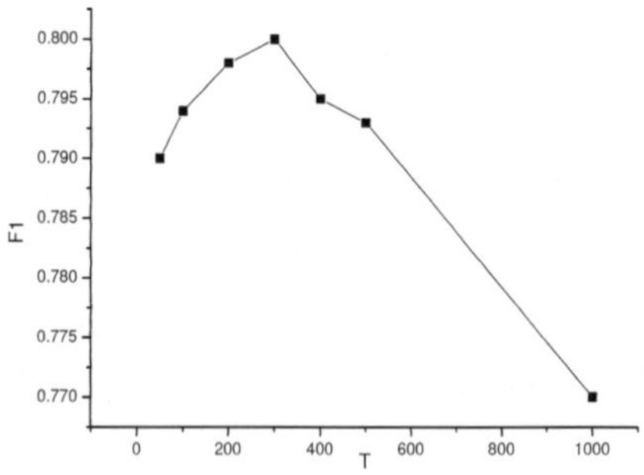

Figure 4. The *F1* vs. the topic number *T*

4.5.3 *Detailed Analysis*

In this section we analyze why and how our method works well in detail. Generally, we believe the main advantages of our method are:

1) **The effects of topic knowledge**. One main advantage of our model is that the topic knowledge

can provide a *document-specific entity prior* for EL. Concretely, using the topic knowledge and the topic distribution of documents, the prior for an entity appearing in a document d is highly related to the document's topics:

$$P(e|d) = \sum_z P(z|d)P(e|z)$$

This prior is obviously more reasonable than the "information less prior" (i.e., all entities have equal prior) or "a global entity popularity prior" (Han & Sun, 2011). To demonstrate, Table 2-3 show the 3 topics where the *Apple Inc.* and the fruit *Apple* have the largest generation probability *P(e|z)* from these topics. We can see that the topic knowledge can provide a reasonable prior for entities appearing in a document: the *Apple Inc.* has a large prior in documents about *Computer*, *Video* and *Software*, and the fruit *Apple* has a large prior in documents about *Wine*, *Food* and *Plant*.

Topic(**Computer**)	Topic(**Video**)	Topic(**Software**)
Computer	*Video*	*Computer software*
CPU	*Mobile phone*	*Microsoft Windows*
Hardware	*Mass media*	*Linux*
Personal computer	*Music*	*Web browser*
Computer memory	*Television*	*Operating system*

Table 2. The 3 topics where the *Apple Inc.* has the largest P(e|z)

Topic(**Wine**)	Topic(**Food**)	Topic(**Plant**)
Wine	*Food*	*Plant*
Grape	*Restaurant*	*Flower*
Vineyard	*Meat*	*Leaf*
Winery	*Cheese*	*Tree*
Apple	*Vegetable*	*Fruit*

Table 3. The 3 topics where the fruit *Apple* has the largest P(e|z)

2) **The effects of a fine-tuned context model**. The second advantage of our model is that it provides a statistical framework for fine-tuning the context model from data. To demonstrate such an effect, Table 4 compares the EL performance of ① the entity-topic model with no context model is used (*No Context*), i.e., we determine the referent entity of a mention by deleting the 3rd term of the formula $P(e_i = e|\mathbf{z}, \mathbf{e}_{-i}, \mathbf{a}, \mathbf{D})$ in Section 3; ② with the context model estimated using the entity's Wikipedia page (*Article Content*), ③ with the context model estimated using the 50 word window of all its mentions in Wikipedia (*Mention Context*) and; ④ with the context model in the original entity-topic model (*Entity-Topic Model*). From Table 4 we can see that a fine-tuned context model will result in a 2~7% F1 improvement.

Context Model	**F1**
No Context	*0.73*
Article Content	*0.75*
Mention Context	*0.78*
Entity-Topic Model	***0.80***

Table 4. The *F1* using different context models

3) **The effects of joint model**. The third advantage of our model is that it *jointly* model the context compatibility and the topic coherence, which bring two benefits: ① the mutual reinforcement between the two directions can be captured in our model; ② the context compatibility and the topic coherence are uniformly modeled and jointly estimated, which makes the model more accurate for EL.

4.5.4 *EL Accuracies on TAC 2009 dataset*

We also compare our method with the top 5 EL systems in TAC 2009 and the two state-of-the-art systems (*EM-Model* and *EL-Graph*) on TAC 2009 data set in Figure 5 (For *EL-Graph* and our method, a NIL threshold is used to detect whether the referent entity is contained in the knowledge base, if the knowledge base not contains the referent entity, we assign the mention to a NIL entity). From Figure 5, we can see that our method is competitive: 1) Our method can achieve a 3.4% accuracy improvement over the best system in TAC 2009; 2) *Our method*, *EM-Model* and *EL-Graph* get very close accuracies (0.854, 0.86 and 0.838 correspondingly), we believe this is because: ① The mentions to be linked in TAC data set are mostly salient mentions; ② The influence of the NIL referent entity problem, i.e., the referent entity is not contained in the given knowledge base: Most referent entities (67.5%) on TAC 2009 are NIL entity and our method has no special handling on this problem, rather than other methods such as the *EM-Model*, which affects the overall performance of our method.

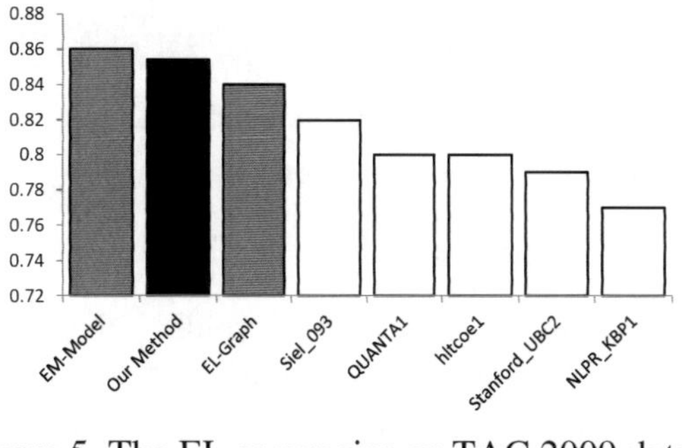

Figure 5. The EL accuracies on TAC 2009 dataset

5 Related Work

In this section, we briefly review the related work of EL. Traditionally, the *context compatibility* based methods link a mention to the entity which has the largest compatibility with it. Cucerzan (2007) modeled the compatibility as the cosine similarity between the vector space representation of mention's context and of entity's Wikipedia entry. Mihalcea & Csomai (2007), Bunescu & Pasca (2006), Fader et al. (2009), Gottipati et al.(2011) and Zhang et al.(2011) extended the vector space model with more information such as the entity category and the acronym expansion, etc. Han & Sun (2011) proposed a generative model which computes the compatibility using the evidences from entity's popularity, name distribution and context word distribution. Kataria et al.(2011) and Sen (2012) used a latent topic model to learn the context model of entities. Zheng et al. (2010), Dredze et al. (2010), Zhang et al. (2010), Zhou et al. (2010) and Ji & Chen(2011) employed the ranking techniques to further take relations between candidate entities into account.

On the other side, the *topic coherence* based methods link a mention to the entity which are most coherent to the document containing it. Medelyan et al. (2008) measured the topic coherence of an entity to a document as the weighted average of its relatedness to the unambiguous entities in the document. Milne and Witten (2008) extended Medelyan et al. (2008)'s coherence by incorporating commonness and context quality. Bhattacharya and Getoor (2006) modeled the topic coherence as the likelihood an entity is generated from the latent topics of a document. Sen (2012) modeled the topic coherence as the groups of co-occurring entities. Kulkarni et al. (2009) modeled the topic coherence as the sum of all pair-wise relatedness between the referent entities of a document. Han et al.(2011) and Hoffart et al.(2011) modeled the topic coherence of an entity as its node importance in a graph which captures all mention-entity and entity-entity relations in a document.

6 Conclusions and Future Work

This paper proposes a generative model, the entity-topic model, for entity linking. By uniformly modeling context compatibility, topic coherence and the correlation between them as statistical dependencies, our model provides an effective way to jointly exploit them for better EL performance.

In this paper, the entity-topic model can only link mentions to the previously given entities in a knowledge base. For future work, we want to overcome this limit by incorporating an *entity discovery* ability into our model, so that it can also discover and learn the knowledge of previously unseen entities from a corpus for linking name mentions to these entities.

Acknowledgments

The work is supported by the National Natural Science Foundation of China under Grants no. 90920010 and 61100152. Moreover, we sincerely thank the reviewers for their valuable comments.

References

Adafre, S. F. & de Rijke, M. 2005. *Discovering missing links in Wikipedia.* In: Proceedings of the 3rd international workshop on Link discovery.

Bhattacharya, I. and L. Getoor. 2006. *A latent dirichlet model for unsupervised entity resolution.* In: Proceedings of SIAM International Conference on Data Mining.

Blei, D. M. and A. Y. Ng, et al. (2003). *Latent dirichlet allocation.* In: The Journal of Machine Learning Research 3: 993--1022.

Bunescu, R. & Pasca, M. 2006. *Using encyclopedic knowledge for named entity disambiguation.* In: Proceedings of EACL, vol. 6.

Brown, P., Pietra, S. D., Pietra, V. D., and Mercer, R. 1993. *The mathematics of statistical machine translation: parameter estimation.* Computational Linguistics, 19(2), 263-31.

Chen, S. F. & Goodman, J. 1999. *An empirical study of smoothing techniques for language modeling.* In Computer Speech and Language, London; Orlando: Academic Press, c1986-, pp. 359-394.

Cucerzan, S. 2007. *Large-scale named entity disambiguation based on Wikipedia data.* In: Proceedings of EMNLP-CoNLL, pp. 708-716.

De Beaugrande, R. A. and W. U. Dressler. 1981. Introduction to text linguistics, Chapter V, Longman London.

Dredze, M., McNamee, P., Rao, D., Gerber, A. & Finin, T. 2010. *Entity Disambiguation for Knowledge Base Population.* In: Proceedings of the 23rd International Conference on Computational Linguistics.

Fader, A., Soderland, S., Etzioni, O. & Center, T. 2009. *Scaling Wikipedia-based named entity disambiguation to arbitrary web text.* In: Proceedings of Wiki-AI Workshop at IJCAI, vol. 9.

Gottipati, S., Jiang, J. 2011. *Linking Entities to a Knowledge Base with Query Expansion.* In: Proceedings of EMNLP.

Griffiths, T. L. and M. Steyvers. 2004. *Finding scientific topics.* In: Proceedings of the National Academy of Sciences of the United States of America.

Han, X., Sun, L. and Zhao J. 2011. *Collective Entity Linking in Web Text: A Graph-Based Method.* In: Proceedings of 34th Annual ACM SIGIR Conference.

Han, X. and Sun, L. 2011. *A Generative Entity-Mention Model for Linking Entities with Knowledge Base.* In: Proceedings of ACL-HLT.

Hoffart, J., Yosef, M. A., et al. 2011. *Robust Disambiguation of Named Entities in Text.* In: Proceedings of EMNLP.

Jelinek, Frederick and Robert L. Mercer. 1980. *Interpolated estimation of Markov source parameters from sparse data.* In: Proceedings of the Workshop on Pattern Recognition in Practice.

Kataria, S. S., Kumar, K. S. and Rastogi, R. 2011. *Entity Disambiguation with Hierarchical Topic Models.* In: Proceedings of KDD.

Kulkarni, S., Singh, A., Ramakrishnan, G. & Chakrabarti, S. 2009. *Collective annotation of Wikipedia entities in web text.* In: Proceedings of the 15th ACM SIGKDD international conference on Knowledge discovery and data mining, pp. 457-466.

Li, X., Morie, P. & Roth, D. 2004. *Identification and tracing of ambiguous names: Discriminative and generative approaches.* In: *Proceedings of the National Conference on Artificial Intelligence*, pp. 419-424.

McNamee, P. & Dang, H. T. 2009. *Overview of the TAC 2009 Knowledge Base Population Track.* In: Proceeding of Text Analysis Conference.

Ji, H., et al. 2010. *Overview of the TAC 2010 knowledge base population track.* In: Proceedings of Text Analysis Conference.

Ji, H. and Chen, Z. 2011. *Collaborative Ranking: A Case Study on Entity Linking.* In: Proceedings of EMNLP.

Milne, D. & Witten, I. H. 2008. *Learning to link with Wikipedia.* In: Proceedings of the 17th ACM conference on Conference on information and knowledge management.

Milne, D., et al. 2006. *Mining Domain-Specific Thesauri from Wikipedia: A case study.* In Proc. of IEEE/WIC/ACM WI.

Medelyan, O., Witten, I. H. & Milne, D. 2008. *Topic indexing with Wikipedia.* In: Proceedings of the AAAI WikiAI workshop.

Mihalcea, R. & Csomai, A. 2007. *Wikify!: linking documents to encyclopedic knowledge.* In: Proceedings of the sixteenth ACM conference on Conference on information and knowledge management, pp. 233-242.

Pedersen, T., Purandare, A. & Kulkarni, A. 2005. *Name discrimination by clustering similar contexts.* Computational Linguistics and Intelligent Text Processing, pp. 226-237.

Ratinov, L. and D. Roth, et al. 2011. *Local and Global Algorithms for Disambiguation to Wikipedia.* In: Proceedings of ACL.

Sen, P. 2012. Collective context-aware topic models for entity disambiguation. In Proceedings of WWW '12, New York, NY, USA, ACM.

Zhang, W., Su, J., Tan, Chew Lim & Wang, W. T. 2010. *Entity Linking Leveraging Automatically Generated Annotation.* In: Proceedings of the 23rd International Conference on Computational Linguistics (Coling 2010).

Zheng, Z., Li, F., Huang, M. & Zhu, X. 2010. *Learning to Link Entities with Knowledge Base.* In: The Proceedings of the Annual Conference of the North American Chapter of the ACL.

Zhou, Y., Nie, L., Rouhani-Kalleh, O., Vasile, F. & Gaffney, S. 2010. *Resolving Surface Forms to Wikipedia Topics.* In: Proceedings of the 23rd International Conference on Computational Linguistics (Coling 2010), pp. 1335-1343.

Zhang, W. and Sim, Y. C., et al. 2011. *Entity Linking with Effective Acronym Expansion, Instance Selection and Topic Modeling.* In: Proceedings of IJCAI.

Linking Named Entities to Any Database

Avirup Sil* Temple University Philadelphia, PA avi@temple.edu

Ernest Cronin* St. Joseph's University Philadelphia, PA ernest.cronin@gmail.com

Penghai Nie St. Joseph's University Philadelphia, PA nph87903@gmail.com

Yinfei Yang St. Joseph's University Philadelphia, PA yangyin7@gmail.com

Ana-Maria Popescu Yahoo! Labs Sunnyvale, CA amp@yahoo-inc.com

Alexander Yates Temple University Philadelphia, PA yates@temple.edu

Abstract

Existing techniques for disambiguating named entities in text mostly focus on Wikipedia as a target catalog of entities. Yet for many types of entities, such as restaurants and cult movies, relational databases exist that contain far more extensive information than Wikipedia. This paper introduces a new task, called Open-Database Named-Entity Disambiguation (Open-DB NED), in which a system must be able to resolve named entities to symbols in an arbitrary database, without requiring labeled data for each new database. We introduce two techniques for Open-DB NED, one based on distant supervision and the other based on domain adaptation. In experiments on two domains, one with poor coverage by Wikipedia and the other with near-perfect coverage, our Open-DB NED strategies outperform a state-of-the-art Wikipedia NED system by over 25% in accuracy.

1 Introduction

Named-entity disambiguation (NED) is the task of linking names mentioned in text with an established catalog of entities (Bunescu and Pasca, 2006; Ratinov et al., 2011). It is a vital first step for semantic understanding of text, such as in grounded semantic parsing (Kwiatkowski et al., 2011), as well as for information retrieval tasks like person name search (Chen and Martin, 2007; Mann and Yarowsky, 2003).

NED requires a catalog of symbols, called referents, to which named-entities will be resolved. Most NED systems today use Wikipedia as the catalog of referents, but exclusive focus on Wikipedia as a target for NED systems has significant drawbacks: despite its breadth, Wikipedia still does not contain all or even most real-world entities mentioned in text. As one example, it has poor coverage of entities that are mostly important in a small geographical region, such as hotels and restaurants, which are widely discussed on the Web. 57% of the named-entities in the Text Analysis Conference's (TAC) 2009 entity linking task refer to an entity that does not appear in Wikipedia (McNamee et al., 2009). Wikipedia is clearly a highly valuable resource, but it should not be thought of as the only one.

Instead of relying solely on Wikipedia, we propose a novel approach to NED, which we refer to as *Open-DB* NED: the task is to resolve an entity to Wikipedia or to *any* relational database that meets mild conditions about the format of the data, described below. Leveraging structured, relational data should allow systems to achieve strong accuracy, as with domain-specific or database-specific NED techniques like Hoffart *et al.*'s NED system for YAGO (Hoffart et al., 2011). And because of the availability of huge numbers of databases on the Web, many for specialized domains, a successful system for this task will cover entities that a Wikipedia NED or database-specific system cannot.

We investigate two complementary learning strategies for Open-DB NED, both of which significantly relax the assumptions of traditional NED systems. The first strategy, a distant supervision approach, uses the relational information in a given database and a large corpus of unlabeled text to learn a database-specific model. The second strategy, a domain adaptation approach, assumes a single source database that has accompanying labeled data. Classifiers in this setting must learn a model that transfers from the source database to any new database, without requiring new training data for the new database. Experiments show that both strategies outperform a state-of-the-art Wikipedia NED system by wide margins without requiring any labeled data from the test domain, highlighting the significant advantage of having domain-specific relational data.

The next section contrasts Open-DB NED with previous work. Section 3 formalizes the task. Sections 4 and 5 present our distant supervision strategy and domain-adaptation strategy, respectively. Section 6 introduces a technique that is a hybrid of the two learning strategies. Section 7 describes our experiments, and Section 8 concludes.

2 Previous Work

As mentioned above, restricting the catalog of referents to Wikipedia, as most recent NED systems do (Bunescu and Pasca, 2006; Mihalcea and Csomai, 2007; Fader et al., 2009; Han and Zhao, 2009; Kulkarni et al., 2009; Ratinov et al., 2011), can restrict the coverage of the system. Zhou *et al.* (2010) estimate that 23% of names in Yahoo! news articles have no referent in Wikipedia, and Cucerzan (2007) estimates the rate at 16% in MSNBC news articles. There is reason to suspect that these estimates are on the low side, however, as news tends to cover popular entities, which are most likely to appear in Wikipedia; the mentions in TAC's 2009 entity linking task are drawn from both newswire and blogs, and have a far higher rate (57%) of missing Wikipedia entries. Lin *et al.* (2012) find that 33% of mentions in a corpus of 500 million Web documents cannot be linked to Wikipedia.

NED systems that are focused on specific domains (or verticals) greatly benefit from repositories of domain-specific knowledge, only a subset of which may be found in Wikipedia. For example, Pantel and Fuxman (2011) use a query-click graph to resolve names in search engine queries to a large product catalog from a commercial search engine, while Dalvi *et al.* (2009; 2012) focus on movie and restaurant databases. Bellare and McCallum (2009) use the sequence information available in citation text to link author, title, and venue names to a publication database. Open-DB NED systems work on any database, so they can serve as baselines for domain-specific NED tasks, as well as provide disambiguation for domains where no domain-specific NED system exists.

Numerous previous studies have considered distant or weak supervision from a single relational database as an alternative to manual supervision for information extraction (Hoffmann et al., 2011; Weld et al., 2009; Bellare and McCallum, 2007; Bunescu and Mooney, 2007; Mintz et al., 2009; Riedel et al., 2010; Yao et al., 2010). In contrast to these systems, our distant supervision NED system provides a meta-algorithm for generating an NED system for *any* database and any entity type.

Existing domain adaptation or transfer learning approaches are inappropriate for the Open-DB NED task, either because they require labeled data in both the source and target domains (Daumé III et al., 2010; Ben-David et al., 2010), or because they leverage some notion of distributional similarity between words in the source and target domains (Blitzer et al., 2006; Huang and Yates, 2009), which does not apply to the database symbols across the two domains. Instead, our domain adaptation technique uses *domain-independent* features of relational data, which apply regardless of the actual contents of the database, as explained further below.

3 The Open-DB NED Problem and Assumptions

3.1 Problem Formulation

A *mention* is an occurrence of a named-entity in a document. Formally, a mention $m = (d, start, end)$ is a triple consisting of a document d, as well as a start and end position for the mention within the document. We say that d is the *context* of m. A *relational database* is a 2-tuple (S, R). Here, S is a set of symbols for constants, attributes, and relations in the database, and $R = \{r_1, \dots, r_n\}$ is a set of relation instances of the form $r_i = \{(c_{1,1}, \dots, c_{1,k_i}), \dots, (c_{n_i,1}, \dots, c_{n_i,k_i})\}$, where each c_j is taken from S, k_i is the *arity* of relation r_i and n_i is the number of known instances of r_i. We will write example database symbols in

movie		
id	title	year
1	Next Door	1975
2	Next Door	2005
3	Next Door	2008
4	Next Door	2008
5	Next Door	2010
...	...	...

actor	
id	name
1	Nicole Kreux
2	Richard Ryan
3	Kristoffer Joner
4	Lee Perkins
5	Carla Valentine
...	...

acted_in		
movie_id	actor_id	role
5	1	Evelyn
5	2	Bruce
2	3	John
1	4	Kid
3	5	Elana
...	...	...

player			
id	name	height	position
1	Carlos Lee	6'2"	LF
2	Rob Bironas	6'0"	K
3	Chris Johnson	6'3"	3B
4	Chris Johnson	5'11"	RB
5	Chris Johnson	6'1"	DB
...	...	...	...

team	
id	name
1	San Diego Padres
2	Houston Texans
3	Tennessee Titans
4	Oakland Raiders
5	Houston Astros
...	...

plays_for	
player_id	team_id
4	3
5	2
3	5
1	5
2	3
...	...

Figure 1: Example movie database (above) and sports database (below) in BCNF.

`teletype`, and mentions in "quotations." For a particular database DB, we refer to its components as $DB.S$ and $DB.R$. For a set of databases D, define the set of referents as $S_D = (\bigcup_{DB \in D} DB.S) \cup \{OOD\}$, where OOD is a special symbol indicating something that is "out of database", or not found in any of the databases in D.

Given a corpus C, a set of mentions M that occur in C, and a set of databases D, the Open-DB NED task is to produce a function $f : M \rightarrow S_D$, which identifies an appropriate target symbol from one of the databases in D, or determines that the mention is OOD. Note that this problem formulation assumes no labeled data. This is significantly more challenging than traditional NED settings, but allows the system to generalize easily to any new database. In the domain adaptation section below, we relax this condition somewhat, to allow labeled data for a small number of initial databases; the system must then transfer what it learns from the labeled domains to any new database. Also note that the focus for this paper is disambiguation; we assume that the set of mentions are correctly demarcated in the input text. Previous systems, such as Lex (Downey et al., 2007), have investigated the task of finding correct named-entity boundaries in text.

3.2 Assumptions

To allow our systems to handle arbitrary databases, we need to make some assumptions about a standard format for the data. We will assume that databases are provided in a particular form, called *Boyce-Codd Normal Form* (BCNF) (Silberschatz et al., 2010). A relational schema is said to be in BCNF when all redundancy based on functional dependency has been removed, although other types of redundancy may still exist. Formally, a schema R is said to be in BCNF with respect to a set of functional dependencies $\mathcal{F}$ if for every one of the dependencies $(X \rightarrow Y) \in \mathcal{F}$, either

1. $Y \subset X$, meaning this is a trivial functional dependency, or

2. X is a *superkey*, meaning that X is a set of attributes that together define a unique ID for the relation.

In practice, this is a relatively safe assumption as database designers often aim for even stricter normal forms. For databases not in BCNF, such as tables extracted from Web pages, standard algorithms exist for converting them into BCNF, given appropriate functional dependencies, although there are sets of functional dependencies for which BCNF is not achievable. Figure 1 shows two example databases in BCNF. We use these tables as examples throughout the paper.

We will additionally assume that all attributes, including names and nicknames, of entities that are covered by the database are treated as functional dependencies of the entity. Again, in practice, this is a fairly safe assumption as this is part of good database design, but if a database does not conform to this, then there will be some entities in the database that our algorithms cannot resolve to. This assumption implies that it is enough to use the set of superkeys for relations as the set of possible referents; our algorithms make use of this fact.

Finally, we will assume the existence of a function $\mu(s, t)$ which indicates whether the text t is a valid surface form of database symbol s. Our experiments in Section 7.3 explore several possible simple definitions for this function.

4 A Distant Supervision Strategy for Open-DB NED

Our first approach to the Open-DB NED problem relies on the fact that, while many mentions are indeed ambiguous and difficult to resolve correctly, most mentions have only a very small number of possible referents in a given database. "Chris Johnson" is the name of doubtless thousands of people, but for articles that are reasonably well-aligned with our sports database, most of the time the name will refer to just three different people. Most sports names are in fact less ambiguous still. Thus, taking a corpus of unlabeled sports articles, we use the information in the database to provide (uncertain) labels, and then train a log-linear model from this probabilistically-labeled data.

This strategy requires a set of features for the model. Traditionally, such features would be hand-crafted for a particular domain and database. As a first step towards our Open-DB system, we present a log-linear model for disambiguation, as well as a simple feature-generation algorithm that produces a large set of useful features from a BCNF database. We then present a distant-supervision learning procedure for this model.

4.1 Disambiguation Model

Let S_D be the set of possible referents. We construct a vector of feature functions $\mathbf{f}(m, s)$ describing the degree to which m and $s \in S_D$ appear to match one another. The feature functions are described below. The model includes a vector of weights $\mathbf{w}$, one weight per feature function, and sets the probability of entity s given m and $\mathbf{w}$ as:

$$P(s|m, \mathbf{w}) = \frac{\exp(\mathbf{w} \cdot \mathbf{f}(m, s))}{\sum_{s' \in S_D} \exp(\mathbf{w} \cdot \mathbf{f}(m, s'))} \qquad (1)$$

4.2 Database-driven Feature Generation

Figure 2 shows our algorithm for automatically generating feature functions $f_i(m, s)$ from a BCNF database. As mentioned above, we only need to consider resolving to database symbols s that are keys, or unique IDs, for some tuple in a database. For an entity in the database with key id, the feature generation algorithm generates two types of feature functions: attribute counts and similar entity counts. Each of these features measures the similarity between the information stored in the database about the entity id, and the information in the text in d surrounding mention m.

An *attribute count* feature function $f_{i,j}^{att}(m, id)$ for the jth attribute of relation r_i counts how many attributes of the entity id appear near m. For example, if id is `5` in the `movie` relation in Figure 1, the feature function for attribute `year` would count how often `2010` matches the text surrounding mention m. Defining precisely whether a database symbol "matches" a word or phrase is a subtle issue; we explore several possibilities in Section 7.3. In addition

Algorithm: Feature Generation

Input: DB, a database in BCNF
Output: $\mathbf{F}$, a set of feature functions
Initialization: $\mathbf{F} \leftarrow \emptyset$

Attribute Count Feature Functions:
For each relation $r_i \in DB.R$
  For each j in $\{1, \ldots, k_i\}$
    Define function $f_{i,j}^{att}(m, id)$:
      $count \leftarrow 0$
      Identify the tuple $t \in r_i$ containing id
      $val \leftarrow t_j$
      $count \leftarrow count + ContextMatches(val, m)$
      return $count$
    $\mathbf{F} \leftarrow \mathbf{F} \cup \{f_{i,j}^{att}\}$

Similar-Entity Count Feature Functions:
For each relation $r_i \in DB.R$
  For each j in $\{1, \ldots, k_i\}$
    Define function $f_{i,j}^{sim}(m, id)$:
      $count \leftarrow 0$
      Identify the tuple $t \in r_i$ containing id
      $val \leftarrow t_j$
      Identify the set of similar tuples T':
        $T' = \{t' | t' \in r_i, t'_j = val\}$
      For each tuple $t' \in T'$
        For each $j' \in \{1, \ldots, k_i\}$
          $val' \leftarrow t'_j$
          $count \leftarrow count + ContextMatches(val', m)$
      return $count$
    $\mathbf{F} \leftarrow \mathbf{F} \cup \{f_{i,j}^{sim}\}$

Figure 2: Feature generation algorithm. The $ContextMatches(s, m)$ function counts how many times a string that matches database symbol s appears in the context of m. In our implementation, we use all of $d(m)$ as the context. Matching between strings and database symbols is discussed in Sec. 7.3.

to attribute counts for attributes within a single relation, we also use attributes from relations that have been inner-joined on primary key and foreign key pairs. For example, for movies, we include attributes such as director name, genre, and actor name. High values for these attribute count features indicate that the text around m closely matches the information in the database about entity id, and therefore id is a strong candidate for the referent of m. We use the whole document as the context for finding matches, although other variants are worth future investigation.

A *similar entity count* feature function $f_{i,j}^{sim}(m, id)$ for the jth attribute in relation r_i counts how many entities similar to id are mentioned in the neighborhood of m. As an example, consider a mention of "Chris Johnson", $id = 3$, and the similar entity feature for the `position` attribute of the `players` relation in the sports database. The feature function would first identify that `3B` is the position of the player with $id = 3$. It would then identify all players that had the same position. Finally, it would count how often any attributes of this set of players appear near "Chris Johnson". Likewise, the similar entity feature for the `team id` attribute would count how many teammates of the player with $id = 3$ appear near "Chris Johnson". A high count for this teammate feature is a strong clue that id is the correct referent for m, while a high count for players of the same position is a weak but still valuable clue.

4.3 Parameter Estimation via Distant Supervision

Using string similarity, we can heuristically determine that three IDs with `name` attribute `Chris Johnson` are highly likely to be the correct target for a mention of "Chris Johnson". Our distant supervision parameter estimation strategy is to move as much probability mass as possible onto the set of realistic referents obtained via string similarity. Since our features rely on finding attributes and similar entities, the side effect of this strategy is that most of the probability mass for a particular mention is moved onto the one target ID with high attribute count and similar entity count features, thus disambiguating the entity. Although the string-similarity heuristic is typically noisy, the strong information in the database and the fact that many entity mentions are typically not ambiguous allows the technique to learn effectively from unlabeled text.

Let $\phi(m, DB)$ be a heuristic string-matching function that returns a set of plausible ID values in database DB for mention m. The objective function for this training procedure is a modified marginal log likelihood (MLL) function that encourages probability mass to be placed on the heuristically-matched targets:

$$MLL(M, \mathbf{w}) = \sum_{m \in M} \log \sum_{id \in \phi(m, DB)} P(id|m, \mathbf{w})$$

This objective is smooth but non-convex. We use a gradient-based optimization procedure that finds a local maximum. Our implementation uses an open-source version of the LBFG-S optimization technique (Liu and Nocedal, 1989). The gradient of our objective is given by

$$\frac{\partial LL(M, \mathbf{w})}{\partial w_i} = \sum_{m \in M} \mathbf{E}_{id \in \phi(m, DB)} \left[f_i(m, id) \right] - \mathbf{E}_{id \in DB.S} \left[f_i(m, id) \right]$$

where the expectations are taken according to $P(id|m, \mathbf{w})$.

5 A Domain-Adaptation Strategy for Open-DB NED

Our domain-adaptation strategy builds an Open-DB NED system by training it on labeled examples from an initial database or small set of initial databases. Unlike traditional NED, however, the purpose in Open-DB NED is to resolve to any database. Thus the strategy must take care to build a model that can transfer what it has learned to a new database, without requiring additional labeled data for the new database.

At first, the problem seems intractable — just because a system can disambiguate between "Next Door", the 2005 Norwegian film, and "Next Door", the 1975 short film by director Andrew Silver, that seems to provide little benefit for disambiguating between different athletes named "Andre Smith." The crux of the problem lies in the fact that database-driven features are domain-specific. Counting how many times the director of a movie appears is highly useful in the movie domain, but worthless in the sports domain.

Our solution works by re-defining the problem in such a way that we can define domain-independent and database-independent features. For example, rather than counting how often the director of a movie appears in the context around a movie mention, we create a domain-independent Count Att(m, s) feature function that counts how often *any* attribute of s appears in the context of m. For movies, Count Att will add together counts for appearances of a movie's production year and IMDB rating, among other attributes. In the sports domain, Count Att will add together counts for appearances of a player's height, position, salary, *etc.*. But in either domain, the feature is well-defined, and in either domain, larger values of the feature indicate a better match between m and s. Thus there is a hope for training a model with domain-independent features like Count Att on labeled data from one domain, say movies, and producing a model that has high accuracy on the sports domain.

We first formalize the notion of a domain adaptation NED model, and then describe our algorithm for producing such a model. We say that a *domain* consists of a database DB as well as a distribution $\mathcal{D}(\mathcal{M})$, where $\mathcal{M}$ is the space of mentions. For instance, the movie domain might consist of the Internet Movie Database (IMDB) and a distribution that places most probability mass on documents about movies and Hollywood stars. In *domain adaptation*, a system observes a set of training examples $(m, s, g(m, s))$, where instances $m \in \mathcal{M}$ are drawn from a *source* domain's distribution $\mathcal{D}_S$ and referents s are drawn from the source domain's database DB_S. The labels $g(m, s)$ are boolean values indicating a correct or incorrect match between the mention and referent. The system must then learn a hypothesis for classifying examples (m, s) drawn from a *target* domain's distribution $\mathcal{D}_T$ and database DB_T. Note that for domain adaptation, we cannot use the more traditional problem formulation in which the referent s is a label (*i.e.*, $s = g(m)$) for the mention, since the set of possible referents changes from domain to domain, and therefore the output of g would be completely different from one domain to the next.

Table 1 lists the domain-independent features used in our domain adaptation model. These features use the attribute counts and similar entity counts from the distant supervision model as subroutines. By aggregating over those domain-dependent feature functions, the domain adaptation system arrives at feature functions that can be defined for *any* database, rather than for a specific database.

Domain-Independent Feature Functions	
Count Att:	$\sum_{i,j} f^{att}_{i,j}(m, s)$
Count Sim:	$\sum_{i,j} f^{sim}_{i,j}(m, s)$
Count All:	Count Att + Count Sim
Count Unique:	$\sum_{i,j} \begin{cases} 0 & \text{if } f^{att}_{i,j}(m, s) = 0, \\ 1 & \text{if } f^{att}_{i,j}(m, s) > 0. \end{cases}$
Count Num:	$\sum_{i,j \mid j \text{ is a numeric att.}} f^{att}_{i,j}(m, s)$

Table 1: Primary feature functions for a domain adaptation approach to NED. These features made the biggest difference in our experiments, but we also tested variations such as counting unique numeric attribute appearances, counting unique similar entities, counting relation name appearances, counting extended attributed appearances, and others.

Note that there is a tradeoff between the domain adaptation technique and the distant supervision technique. The domain adaptation model has access to labeled data, unlike the distant supervision model. In addition, the domain adaptation model requires no text whatsoever from the target domain, not even an unlabeled corpus, to set weights for the target domain. Once trained, it is ready for NED over any database that meets our assumptions, out of the box. However, because the model needs to be able to transfer to arbitrary new domains, the domain adaptation model is restricted to domain-independent features, which are "coarser-grained." That is, the distant supervision model has the ability to place more weight on attributes like director rather than genre, or team rather than position, if those attributes are more discriminative. The domain adaptation model cannot place different weights on the different attributes, since those weights would not transfer across databases.

As with distant supervision, the domain adaptation strategy uses a log-linear model over these feature functions. We use standard techniques for training the model using labeled data from the source domain: conditional log likelihood (CLL) as the objective function, and LBFG-S for convex optimization.

$$CLL(L, \mathbf{w}) = \sum_{(m,id,label) \in L} \log P(label|m, id, \mathbf{w})$$

The training algorithm is guaranteed to converge to the globally optimal parameter setting for this objective function over the training data. The manually annotated data contains only positive examples; to generate negative examples, we use the same name-matching heuristic $\phi(m, DB)$ to identify a set of potentially confusing bad matches. On test data, we use the trained model to choose the id for a given m with the highest probability of being correct.

6 A Hybrid Model

The distant supervision and domain adaptation strategies use two very different sources of evidence for training a disambiguation classifier: the string-matching heuristic and unlabeled text from the target domain for the the distant supervision model, and aggregate features over labeled text from a separate domain for domain adaptation. This begs the question, do these sources of evidence complement one another? To address this question, we design a Hybrid model with features and training strategies from both distant supervision and domain adaptation.

The training data consists of a set L_S of labeled mentions from a source domain, a source database DB_S, a set of unlabeled mentions M_T from the target domain, and the target-domain database DB_T. The full feature set of the Hybrid model is the union of the distant supervision feature functions for the target domain and the domain-independent domain adaptation feature functions. Note that the distant supervision feature functions are domain-specific, so they almost always will be uniformly zero on L_S, but the domain adaptation feature functions will be activated on both L_S and M_T. The combined training objective for the Hybrid model is:

$$LL(L_S, M_T, \mathbf{w}) = CLL(L_S, \mathbf{w}) + MLL(M_T, \mathbf{w})$$

7 Experiments

Our experiments compare our strategies for Open-DB NED against one another, as well as against a Wikipedia NED system from previous work, on two domains: sports and movies.

7.1 Data

For the movie domain, we collected a set of 156 cult movie titles from an online movie site (www.olivefilms.com). For each movie title, we executed a Web search using a commercial search engine, and collected the top five documents for each title from the search engine's results. Nearly all top-five results included at least one mention of an entity not found in Wikipedia; overall, only 16% of the mentions could be linked to Wikipedia. After stripping javascript and html annotations, we removed documents with fewer than 50 words, leaving a total of 770 documents. We select one occurrence of any of the 156 movie titles from each document as our set of mentions. Many titles are ambiguous not just among different movies with the same name, but also among novels, plays, geographical entities, and assorted other types of entities. To provide labels for these mentions, we use both a movie database and Wikipedia. We downloaded the complete data dump from the online Internet Movie Database (IMDB, www.imdb.com). For our set of possible referents, we use the set of all key values in IMDB, and the set of all Wikipedia articles. Annotators manually labeled each mention using this set of referents. Table 2 shows summary statistics about this labeled data.

For the sports domain, we downloaded all player data from Yahoo!, Inc.'s sports database for the years 2011-2012 and two American sports leagues, the National Football League (NFL) and Major League Baseball (MLB). From the database, we extracted ambiguous player names and team names, including names like "Philadelphia" which may refer to `Philadelphia Eagles` in the NFL data, `Philadelphia Phillies` in the MLB data, or the city of `Philadelphia` itself (in both types of data). We then collected 1300 Yahoo! news articles which include a mention that partially matches at least one of these database symbols. We manually labeled a random sample of 564 mentions from this data, including 279 player name mentions and 285 city name mentions. Many player name and place name mentions are ambiguous between the two sports leagues, as well as with teams or players from other leagues. In order to focus on the hardest cases, we specifically exclude mentions like "Philadelphia" from the labeled data if any of their

domain	$\|M\|$	$\mathbf{E}\|\phi(m, DB)\|$	OOD	Wiki
movies	770	2.6	13%	16%
sports	549	4.5	0%	100%

Table 2: Number of mentions, average number of referents per mention, % of mentions that are OOD, and % of mentions that are in Wikipedia in our movie and sports data.

System	Accuracy
No-Wikipedia Domain Adapt.	0.61
DocSim-Wikipedia Domain Adapt.	**0.69**

Table 3: Including a simple document-similarity feature for comparing a mention's context with a Wikipedia page provides an 8% improvement over ignoring Wikipedia information.

unambiguous completions appears in the same article (that is, if either of the team names "Philadelphia Eagles" or "Philadelphia Phillies" appears in the same article, we exclude the "Philadelphia" mention). As before, the set of possible referents includes the symbol OOD, key values from the sports database, and Wikipedia articles, and a given mention may be labeled with both a sports entity and a Wikipedia article, if appropriate. All of our data is available from the last author's website.

7.2 Evaluation Metric

We report on a version of exact-match accuracy. The system chooses the most likely label $\hat{s}$ for each m. This is judged correct if $\hat{s}$ matches the correct label s exactly, or (in cases where both a Wikipedia and a database entity are considered correct) if one of the labels matches $\hat{s}$ exactly. This metric allows systems to resolve against either reference, Wikipedia or another database, without requiring it to match both if the same entity appears in both references.

7.3 Exact or Partial Matching?

One important question in the design of our systems is how to determine the "match" between database symbols and text. This question comes into play in two components of our systems: it affects the computation of feature functions that count how often a match of some attribute is found in text, and it affects which set of heuristically-determined database entities are considered to be possible matches for a given mention.

We experiment with two different matching strategies between a symbol s and text t, exact matching and partial matching. Exact matching $\mu_{exact}(s, t)$ requires the sequence of characters in s to appear exactly (modulo character encoding) in t. For instance, the database value `Chris Johnson` would match "Chris Johnson", but not "C. Johnson" or "Johnson" in text. For partial matching, we used different tests for numeric and textual entities. For numeric entities, $\mu_{partial}$ matched s and t if the numeric value of one was within 10% of the other, so that `5312` would match "5,000." We made no attempt to convert numeric phrases, such as "3.6 million", into numeric values. For textual entities, $\mu_{partial}$ matched s and t if at least one token from each matched exactly. Thus `Chris Johnson` matches both "Chris" and "C. Johnson".

We found $\mu_{partial}$ to be consistently superior for computing $\phi(m, DB)$, since it has much better recall for mentions like "Philadelphia". On the other hand, if we use $\mu_{partial}$ for computing our models' feature functions, like the Count Att(m, s) in the domain adaptation model, counts varied widely across domains. A simple version of the domain adaptation classifier (only the Count All and Count Unique features) trained on sports data and tested on movies achieved an accuracy of 24% using $\mu_{partial}$, compared with 61% using μ_{exact}. For all remaining tests, we used μ_{exact} for computing features, and $\mu_{partial}$ for computing $\phi(m, DB)$.

7.4 Incorporating Wikipedia referents

Thus far, all of our features work on relational data, not Wikipedia. In order to allow our systems to link to Wikipedia, we create a single "document similarity" feature describing the similarity between the text around a mention and the text appearing on a Wikipedia page. We build a vector space model of both the document containing the mention and the Wikipedia page, remove stopwords, and use cosine similarity to compute this feature.

To evaluate the effectiveness of this Wikipedia feature, we tested two versions of our domain adaptation system, both trained on sports data and tested

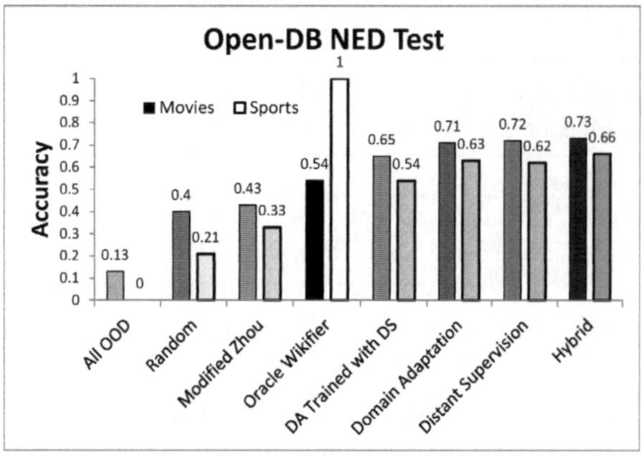

Figure 3: **All three Open-DB NED strategies outperform a state-of-the-art Wikipedia NED system by 25% or more on sports and movies, and outperform a Wikipedia NED system with oracle information by 14% or more on the movie data.** Differences between the Modified Zhou Wikifier and the Open-DB strategies are statistically significant ($p < 0.01$, Fisher's exact test) on both domains.

on the movies domain. The first version involves no Wikipedia information whatsoever, thus it has no reason to select a Wikipedia article over OOD. The second system includes the document similarity feature. Table 3 shows the results of these systems. Encouragingly, our single document similarity feature produces a significant improvement over the model without Wikipedia information, so we use this feature in all of our systems tested below. More sophisticated use of Wikipedia is certainly possible, and an important question for future work is how to combine Open-DB NED more seamlessly with Wikipedia NED.

7.5 Comparing Open-DB NED Strategies

For each domain, we compare our domain-adaptation strategy, distant supervision, and hybrid strategies. The domain-adaptation model is trained on the labeled data for sports when testing on movies, and *vice versa*. We use a movies test set of 180 mentions that is separate from the development data used for the above tests. For the distant supervision strategy, we use the entire collection of texts from each domain as input (1300 articles for sports, 770 articles for movies), with the labels removed during training.

We compare against a state-of-the-art Wikipedia NED system used in production by a major Web company. This system is a modified version of the system described by Zhou et al. (2010), where certain features have been removed for efficiency. We refer to this as the Modified-Zhou Wikifier. This system uses a gradient-boosted decision tree and multiple local and global features for computing the similarity between a mention's context and a Wikipedia article. We also test a hypothetical system, Oracle Wikifier, which is given no information about entities in IMDB, but is assumed to be able to correctly resolve any mention that refers to an entity found in Wikipedia. Thus, this system has perfect accuracy on mentions that can be found in Wikipedia, and accuracy similar to a baseline that predicts randomly on all mentions that fall outside of Wikipedia[1]. Oracle-Wikifier serves as an upper bound on systems that have no access to a domain-specific database. In addition, we compare against two standard baselines: a classifier that always predicts OOD, and a classifier that chooses randomly. Finally, we compare against a system that trains the domain adaptation model using distant supervision ("DA Trained with DS").

Figure 3 shows our results. All three Open-DB approaches outperform the baseline techniques on this test by wide margins, with the Hybrid model increasing by 30% or more over the random baseline. On the movie domain, the Hybrid model outperforms the Oracle Wikifier by nearly 20%. Encouragingly, the Hybrid model consistently outperforms both distant supervision and domain adaptation, suggesting that the two sources of evidence are partially complementary. Distant supervision performs better on the movies test, whereas domain adaptation has the advantage on sports. The differences among all three Open-DB approaches is relatively small, compared with the difference between these approaches and Oracle Wikifier on the movie data.

The domain adaptation system outperforms DA Trained with DS on both domains, suggesting that labeled data from a separate domain is better evidence for parameter estimates than unlabeled data from the same domain. The distant supervision system also outperforms DA Trained with

[1]Alternatively, one could make the oracle system predict OOD on all mentions that fall outside of Wikipedia. Random predictions perform better on our data.

DS on both domains, suggesting that the fine-grained, domain-specific features do in fact provide more helpful information than the coarser-grained, domain-independent features of the domain adaptation model.

All of the Open-DB NED systems outperform the Modified Zhou Wikifier on both data sets by a wide margin. In fact the Modified Zhou Wikifier has similar results on both domains, despite the fact that Wikipedia has far greater coverage on sports than movies. In part, the poor performance of the Modified Zhou Wikifier reflects the difficult nature of the task. In previous experiments on an MSNBC news test set it reached 85% accuracy, but a random classifier there achieved 60% accuracy compared with 21% on our sports data. Another difficulty with the Modified Zhou Wikifier is its strong preference for globally common entities. It consistently classifies mentions that are ambiguous between a city and a team (like "Chicago" in "Chicago sweeps the Red Sox") as cities when they should be resolved to teams, in large part because `Chicago` is a more common referent in general text than either of the baseball teams that play in that city. In sports articles, however, both meanings are common, and only the surrounding context can help determine the correct referent.

Besides wikifiers, NED systems may also be compared with dictionary-based word sense disambiguation techniques like the Lesk algorithm[2] (Lesk, 1986). The Lesk algorithm is "open" in the sense that it works for arbitrary dictionaries, and it defines a vector space model of the dictionary definitions that may be likened to the attribute-value model in our representation of entities in the database. Our approach, however, estimates parameters for a statistical model from data, whereas the Lesk algorithm uses an equal weight for all attributes. To make an empirical comparison, we created a variant of the Lesk algorithm for relational data: we took the disambiguation model from Eqn. 1, supplied all of the features from the distant supervision model, and manually set $\mathbf{w} = \mathbf{1}$. This "relational Lesk" model achieves an accuracy of 0.11 on movies, and 0.15 on sports, significantly below the random baseline. Giving equal weight to noisy attributes like `genre` and more discriminative attributes like `director` significantly hurts the performance.

[2]We thank the reviewers for making this connection.

For both the movie and sports domain, approximately 80% of the Hybrid model's errors are because of predicting database symbols, when the correct referent is a Wikipedia page or OOD. This nearly always occurs because some words in the context of a mention match an attribute of an incorrect database referent. For instance, the `crime` genre is an attribute for several movies, but it also matches in contexts surrounding book titles and numerous other entities. In the movie domain, most of the remaining errors are incorrect OOD predictions for mentions that should resolve to the database, but the article contains no attributes or similar entities to the database entity. In the sports domain, many of the remaining errors were due to predicting incorrect player referents. Quite often, this was because the document discusses a fantasy sports league or team, where players from different professional sports teams are mixed together on a "fantasy team" belonging to a fan of the sport. Since players in the fantasy leagues have different teammates than they do in the database, these articles consistently confuse our methods.

8 Conclusion and Future Work

This paper introduces the task of Open-DB Named Entity Disambiguation, and presents two distinct strategies for solving this task. Experiments indicate that a mixture of the two strategies significantly outperforms a state-of-the-art Wikipedia NED system, on a dataset where Wikipedia has good coverage and on another dataset where Wikipedia has poor coverage. The results indicate that there is a significant benefit to leveraging other sources of knowledge in addition to Wikipedia, and that it is possible to leverage this knowledge without requiring labeled data for each new source. The initial success of these Open-DB NED approaches indicates that this task is a promising area for future research, including exciting extensions that link large numbers of domain-specific databases to text.

Acknowledgments

This work was supported in part by a gift from Yahoo!, Inc.

References

Kedar Bellare and Andrew McCallum. 2007. Learning extractors from unlabeled text using relevant databases. In *Sixth International Workshop on Information Integration on the Web*.

Kedar Bellare and Andrew McCallum. 2009. Generalized Expectation Criteria for Bootstrapping Extractors using Record-Text Alignment. In *Empirical Methods in Natural Language Processing (EMNLP-09)*.

Shai Ben-David, John Blitzer, Koby Crammer, Alex Kulesza, Fernando Pereira, and Jennifer Wortman Vaughan. 2010. A theory of learning from different domains. *Machine Learning*, 79:151–175.

John Blitzer, Ryan McDonald, and Fernando Pereira. 2006. Domain adaptation with structural correspondence learning. In *EMNLP*.

Razvan Bunescu and Raymond Mooney. 2007. Learning to extract relations from the web using minimal supervision. In *Proceedings of the 45th Annual Meeting of the Association for Computational Linguistics (ACL-07)*.

R. Bunescu and M. Pasca. 2006. Using encyclopedic knowledge for named entity disambiguation. In *Proceedings of the 11th Conference of the European Chapter of the Association for Computational Linguistics (EACL-06)*.

Ying Chen and James Martin. 2007. Towards Robust Unsupervised Personal Name Disambiguation. In *EMNLP*, pages 190–198.

Silviu Cucerzan. 2007. Large-scale named entity disambiguation based on wikipedia data. In *Proceedings of the 2007 Joint Conference on Empirical Methods in Natural Language Processing and Computational Natural Language Learning (EMNLP-CoNLL)*, pages 708–716.

Nilesh N. Dalvi, Ravi Kumar, Bo Pang, and Andrew Tomkins. 2009. Matching Reviews to Objects using a Language Model. In *EMNLP*, pages 609–618.

Nilesh N. Dalvi, Ravi Kumar, and Bo Pang. 2012. Object matching in tweets with spatial models. In *WSDM*, pages 43–52.

Hal Daumé III, Abhishek Kumar, and Avishek Saha. 2010. Frustratingly easy semi-supervised domain adaptation. In *Proceedings of the ACL Workshop on Domain Adaptation (DANLP)*.

D. Downey, M. Broadhead, and O. Etzioni. 2007. Locating complex named entities in web text. In *Procs. of the 20th International Joint Conference on Artificial Intelligence (IJCAI 2007)*.

Anthony Fader, Stephen Soderland, and Oren Etzioni. 2009. Scaling wikipedia-based named entity disambiguation to arbitrary web text. In *Proceedings of the WikiAI 09 - IJCAI Workshop: User Contributed Knowledge and Artificial Intelligence: An Evolving Synergy*.

Xianpei Han and Jun Zhao. 2009. Named entity disambiguation by leveraging Wikipedia semantic knowledge. In *Proceeding of the 18th ACM Conference on Information and Knowledge Management (CIKM)*, pages 215–224.

Johannes Hoffart, Mohamed Amir Yosef, Ilaria Bordino, Hagen Furstenau, Manfred Pinkal, Marc Spaniol, Bilyana Taneva, Stefan Thater, and Gerhard Weikum1. 2011. Robust Disambiguation of Named Entities in Text. In *EMNLP*, pages 782–792.

Raphael Hoffmann, Congle Zhang, Xiao Ling, Luke Zettlemoyer, and Daniel S. Weld. 2011. Knowledge-Based Weak Supervision for Information Extraction of Overlapping Relations. In *Proceedings of the Annual Meeting of the Association for Computational Linguistics (ACL)*.

Fei Huang and Alexander Yates. 2009. Distributional representations for handling sparsity in supervised sequence labeling. In *Proceedings of the Annual Meeting of the Association for Computational Linguistics (ACL)*.

Sayali Kulkarni, Amit Singh, Ganesh Ramakrishnan, and Soumen Chakrabarti. 2009. Collective annotation of wikipedia entities in web text. In *Proceedings of the 15th ACM SIGKDD International Conference on Knowledge Discovery and Data Mining (KDD)*, pages 457–466.

Tom Kwiatkowski, Luke Zettlemoyer, Sharon Goldwater, and Mark Steedman. 2011. Lexical Generalization in CCG Grammar Induction for Semantic Parsing. In *Proceedings of the Conference on Empirical Methods in Natural Language Processing (EMNLP)*.

M.E. Lesk. 1986. Automatic sense disambiguation using machine readable dictionaries: How to tell a pine cone from an ice cream cone. In *Proceedings of the SIGDOC Conference*.

Thomas Lin, Mausam, and Oren Etzioni. 2012. Entity linking at web scale. In *Knowledge Extraction Workshop (AKBC-WEKEX), 2012*.

D.C. Liu and J. Nocedal. 1989. On the limited memory method for large scale optimization. *Mathematical Programming B*, 45(3):503–528.

G.S. Mann and D. Yarowsky. 2003. Unsupervised personal name disambiguation. In *CoNLL*.

Paul McNamee, Mark Dredze, Adam Gerber, Nikesh Garera, Tim Finin, James Mayfield, Christine Piatko, Delip Rao, David Yarowsky, and Markus Dreyer. 2009. HLTCOE Approaches to Knowledge Base Population at TAC 2009. In *Text Analysis Conference*.

Rada Mihalcea and Andras Csomai. 2007. Wikify!: Linking documents to encyclopedic knowledge. In

Proceedings of the Sixteenth ACM Conference on Information and Knowledge Management (CIKM), pages 233–242.

Mike Mintz, Steven Bills, Rion Snow, and Daniel Jurafsky. 2009. Distant supervision for relation extraction without labeled data. In *Proceedings of the 47th Annual Meeting of the Association for Computational Linguistics (ACL-2009)*, pages 1003–1011.

Patrick Pantel and Ariel Fuxman. 2011. Jigs and Lures: Associating Web Queries with Structured Entities. In *ACL*.

L. Ratinov, D. Roth, D. Downey, and M. Anderson. 2011. Local and global algorithms for disambiguation to wikipedia. In *Proc. of the Annual Meeting of the Association of Computational Linguistics (ACL)*.

Sebastian Riedel, Limin Yao, and Andrew McCallum. 2010. Modeling relations and their mentions without labeled text. In *Proceedings of the Sixteenth European Conference on Machine Learning (ECML-2010)*, pages 148–163.

Avi Silberschatz, Henry F. Korth, and S. Sudarshan. 2010. *Database System Concepts*. McGraw-Hill, sixth edition.

Daniel S. Weld, Raphael Hoffmann, and Fei Wu. 2009. Using Wikipedia to Bootstrap Open Information Extraction. In *ACM SIGMOD Record*.

Limin Yao, Sebastian Riedel, and Andrew McCallum. 2010. Collective cross-document relation extraction without labelled data. In *Proceedings of the 2010 Conference on Empirical Methods in Natural Language Processing (EMNLP-2010)*, pages 1013–1023.

Yiping Zhou, Lan Nie, Omid Rouhani-Kalleh, Flavian Vasile, and Scott Gaffney. 2010. Resolving surface forms to wikipedia topics. In *Proceedings of the 23rd International Conference on Computational Linguistics (Coling)*, pages 1335–1343.

Towards Efficient Named-Entity Rule Induction for Customizability

Ajay Nagesh[1,2]
[1]IITB-Monash Research Academy
ajaynagesh@cse.iitb.ac.in

Ganesh Ramakrishnan
[2]IIT Bombay
ganesh@cse.iitb.ac.in

Laura Chiticariu
IBM Research - Almaden
chiti@us.ibm.com

Rajasekar Krishnamurthy
IBM Research - Almaden
rajase@us.ibm.com

Ankush Dharkar
SASTRA University
ankushdharkar@cse.sastra.edu

Pushpak Bhattacharyya
IIT Bombay
pb@cse.iitb.ac.in

Abstract

Generic rule-based systems for Information Extraction (IE) have been shown to work reasonably well out-of-the-box, and achieve state-of-the-art accuracy with further domain customization. However, it is generally recognized that manually building and customizing rules is a complex and labor intensive process. In this paper, we discuss an approach that facilitates the process of building customizable rules for Named-Entity Recognition (NER) tasks via rule induction, in the Annotation Query Language (AQL). Given a set of basic features and an annotated document collection, our goal is to generate an initial set of rules with reasonable accuracy, that are interpretable and thus can be easily refined by a human developer. We present an efficient rule induction process, modeled on a four-stage manual rule development process and present initial promising results with our system. We also propose a simple notion of extractor complexity as a first step to quantify the interpretability of an extractor, and study the effect of induction bias and customization of basic features on the accuracy and complexity of induced rules. We demonstrate through experiments that the induced rules have good accuracy and low complexity according to our complexity measure.

1 Introduction

Named-entity recognition (NER) is the task of identifying mentions of rigid designators from text belonging to named-entity types such as persons, organizations and locations (Nadeau and Sekine, 2007). Generic NER rules have been shown to work reasonably well-out-of-the-box, and with further domain customization (Chiticariu et al., 2010b), achieve quality surpassing state-of-the-art results. Table 1

System	Dataset	$F_{\beta=1}$ Generic	$F_{\beta=1}$ Customized
GATE	ACE2002	57.8	82.2
SystemT	ACE 2005	57.32	88.95
	CoNLL 2003	64.15	91.77
	Enron	76.53	85.29

Table 1: Quality of generic vs. customized rules.

summarizes the quality of NER rules out-of-the-box and after domain customization in the GATE (Cunningham et al., 2011) and SystemT (Chiticariu et al., 2010a) systems, as reported in (Maynard et al., 2003) and (Chiticariu et al., 2010b) respectively.

Rule-based systems are widely used in enterprise settings due to their *explainability*. Rules are transparent, which leads to better explainability of errors. One can easily identify the cause of a false positive or negative, and refine the rules without affecting other correct results identified by the system. Furthermore, rules are typically easier to understand by an IE developer and can be customized for a new domain without requiring additional labeled data.

Typically, a rule-based NER system consists of a combination of four categories of rules (Chiticariu et al., 2010b): (1) *Basic Feature (BF)* rules to identify components of an entity such as first name and last name. (2) *Candidate definition (CD)* rules to identify complete occurrences of an entity by combining the output of multiple BF rules, e.g., first name followed by last name is a person candidate. (3) *Candidate refinement (CR)* rules to refine candidates generated by CD rules. E.g., discard candidate persons contained within organizations. (4) *Consolidation rules (CO)* to resolve overlapping candidates generated by multiple CD and CR rules.

A well-known drawback that influences the adoptability of rule-based NER systems is the manual effort required to build the rules. A common approach to address this problem is to build a generic NER extractor and then customize it for specific domains. While this approach partially alleviates the problem, substantial manual effort (in the order of several person weeks) is still required for the two stages as reported in (Maynard et al., 2003; Chiticariu et al., 2010b). In this paper, we present initial work towards facilitating the process of building a generic NER extractor using induction techniques.

Specifically, given as input an annotated document corpus, a set of BF rules, and a default CO rule for each entity type, our goal is to generate a set of CD and CR rules such that the resulting extractor constitutes a good starting point for further refinement by a developer. Since the generic NER extractor has to be manually customized, a major challenge is to ensure that the generated rules have good accuracy, and, at the same time, that they are *not too complex*, and consequently *interpretable*.

The main contributions in this paper are

1. An *efficient* system for NER rule induction, using a highly expressive rule language (AQL) as the target language. The first phase of rule induction uses a combination of *clustering* and *relative least general generalization (RLGG)* techniques to learn CD rules. The second phase identifies CR rules using a propositional rule learner like *JRIP* to learn accurate compositions of CD rules.
2. Usage of induction biases to enhance the interpretability of rules. These biases capture the expertise gleaned from manual rule development and constrain the search space in our induction system.
3. Definition of an initial notion of extractor complexity to quantify the interpretability of an extractor and to guide the process of adding induction biases to favor learning *less complex* extractors. This is to ensure that the rules are easily customizable by the developer.
4. Scalable induction process through usage of SystemT, a state-of-the-art IE system which serves as a highly efficient theorem prover for AQL, and performance optimizations such as clustering of examples and parallelizing various modules (E.g.: propositional rule learning).

Roadmap We first describe preliminaries on SystemT and AQL (Section 3) and define the target language for our induction algorithm and the notion of rule complexity (Section 4). We then present our approach for inducing CD and CR rules, and discuss induction biases that would favor interpretability (Section 5), and discuss the results of an empirical evaluation (Section 6). We conclude with avenues for improvement in the future (Section 7).

2 Related Work

Existing approaches to rule induction for IE focus on rule-based systems based on the cascading grammar formalism exemplified by the Common Pattern Specification Language (CPSL) (Appelt and Onyshkevych, 1998), where rules are specified as a sequence of basic features that describe an entity, with limited predicates in the context of an entity mention. Patel et al. (2009) and Soderland (1999) elaborate on top-down techniques for induction of IE rules, whereas (Califf and Mooney, 1997; Califf and Mooney, 1999) discuss a bottom-up IE rule induction system that uses the *relative least general generalization (RLGG)* of examples[1]. However, in all these systems, the expressivity of the rule-representation language is restricted to that of capturing sequence information. As discussed in Section 3, contextual clues and higher level rule interactions such as *filtering* and *join* are very difficult, if not impossible to express in such representations without resorting to custom code. Learning higher level interactions between rules has received little attention. Our technique for learning higher level interactions is similar to the induction of *ripple down rules* (Gaines and Compton, 1995), which, to the best of our knowledge, has not been previously applied to IE. A framework for refining AQL extractors based on an annotated document corpus described in (Liu et al., 2010). We present complementary techniques for inducing an initial extractor that can be automatically refined in this framework.

3 Preliminaries

SystemT is a declarative IE system based on an algebraic framework. In SystemT, developers write rules in AQL. To represent annotations in a docu-

[1]Our work also makes use of RLGGs but computes these generalizations for clusters of examples, instead of pairs.

```
R1:  create view Caps as
       extract regex /[A-Z](\w|-)+/ on D.text as match from Document D;

R2:  create view First as
       extract dictionary 'FirstNameGazeteer' on D.text as match from Document D;

R3:  create view Last as
       extract dictionary 'LastNameGazeteer' on D.text as match from Document D;

R4:  create view PersonFirst as
       select F.match as match
       from First F, Caps C
       where Equals(F.match, C.match);

R5:  create view PersonFirstLast as
       select CombineSpans(F.match, L.match) as match
       from First F, Last L, Caps C
       where FollowsTok(F.match, L.match, 0, 0) and Equals(L.match, C.match);

R6:  create view PersonCandidate as
       (select R.match from PersonFirst R)
       union all
       (select R.match from PersonFirstLast R);

R7:  create view PersonInvalid as
       select P.match
       from PersonCandidate P, Organization O
       where Overlaps (P.match, O.match);

R8:  create view PersonAll as
       (select R.match from PersonCandidate R)
       minus
       (select R.match from PersonInvalid R);

R9:  create view Person as
       select R.match
       from PersonAll R
       consolidate on R.match using 'ContainedWithin';
```

Complexity of extractor C(E) = 15 + C(Organization)

Figure 1: Example *Person* extractor in AQL

ment, AQL uses a simple relational data model with three types: a *span* is a region of text within a document identified by its "begin" and "end" positions; a *tuple* is a fixed-size list of spans; a *relation*, or *view*, is a multi-set of tuples, where every tuple in the view must be of the same size.

Figure 1 shows a portion of a *Person* extractor written in AQL. The basic building block of AQL is a *view*. A *view* is a logical description of a set of tuples in terms of (i) the document text (denoted as a special view called *Document*), and (ii) the contents of other views, as specified in the *from* clauses of each statement. Figure 1 also illustrates five of the basic constructs that can be used to define a view, and which we explain next. The complete specification can be found in the AQL manual (IBM, 2012). In the paper, we will use 'rules' and 'views' interchangeably.

The *extract* statement specifies basic character-level extraction primitives such as regular expression and dictionary matching over text, creating a tuple for each match. As an example, rule R_1 uses the *extract* statement to identify matches (*Caps* spans) of a regular expression for capitalized words.

The *select* statement is similar to the SQL select statement but it contains an additional *consolidate on* clause (explained further), along with an extensive collection of text-specific predicates. Rule R_5 illustrates a complex example: it selects *First* spans immediately followed within zero tokens by a *Last* span, where the latter is also a *Caps* span. The two conditions are specified using two join predicates: *FollowsTok* and *Equals* respectively. For each triplet of *First*, *Last* and *Caps* spans satisfying the two predicates, the *CombineSpans* built-in scalar function in the select clause constructs larger *PersonFirstLast* spans that begin at the begin position of the *First* span, and end at the end position of the *Last* (also *Caps*) span.

The *union all* statement merges the outputs of two or more statements. For example, rule R_6 unions person candidates identified by rules R_4 and R_5.

The *minus* statement subtracts the output of one statement from the output of another. For example, rule R_8 defines a view *PersonAll* by filtering out *PersonInvalid* tuples from the set of *PersonCandidate* tuples. Notice that rule R_7 used to define the view *PersonInvalid* illustrates another join predicate of AQL called *Overlaps*, which returns true if its two argument spans overlap in the input text. Therefore, at a high level, rule R_8 removes person candidates that overlap with an *Organization* span. (The *Organization* extractor is not depicted in the figure.)

The *consolidate* clause of a *select* statement removes selected overlapping spans from the indicated column of the input tuples, according to the specified policy (for instance, 'ContainedWithin'). For example, rule R_9 retains *PersonAll* spans that are not contained in other *PersonAll* spans.

Internally, SystemT compiles an AQL extractor into an executable plan in the form of a graph of *operators*. The formal definition of these operators takes the form of an algebra (Reiss et al., 2008), similar to relational algebra, but with extensions for text processing. The decoupling between AQL and the operator algebra allows for greater rule expressivity because the rule language is not constrained by the need to compile to a finite state transducer, as in grammar systems based on the CPSL standard. In fact, join predicates such as *Overlaps*, as well as filter operations (*minus*) are extremely difficult to express in CPSL systems such as GATE without an escape to custom code (Chiticariu et al., 2010b). In addition, the decoupling between the AQL specification of *"what"* to extract from *"how"* to extract it, allows greater flexibility in choosing an efficient execution strategy among the many possible operator graphs that may exist for the same AQL extractor. Therefore, extractors written in AQL achieve orders of magnitude higher throughput (Chiticariu et al., 2010a).

4 Induction Target Language

Our goal is to automatically generate NER extractors with good quality, and at the same time, manageable complexity, so that the extractors can be further refined and customized by the developer. To this end, we focus on inducing extractors using the subset of AQL constructs described in Section 3. We note that we have chosen a small subset of AQL constructs that are sufficient to implement several common operations required for NER. However, AQL is a much more expressive language, and incorporating additional constructs is subject to our future work.

In this section we describe the building blocks of our target language, and propose a simple definition for measuring the complexity of an extractor.

Target Language. The components of the target language are as follows, and summarized in Table 2.

Basic features (BF): *BF views* are specified using the *extract* statement, such as rules R_1 to R_3 in Figure 1. In this paper, we assume as input a set of *basic features*, consisting of dictionaries and regular expressions.

Candidate definition (CD): *CD* views are expressed using the *select* statement to combine BF views with join predicates (e.g., *Equals*, *FollowsTok* or *Overlaps*), and the *CombineSpans* scalar function to construct larger candidate spans from input spans. Rules R_4 and R_5 in Figure 1 are example CD rules. In general, a CD view is defined as: *"Select all spans constructed from* $view_1$, $view_2$, ..., $view_n$, *such that all join predicates are satisfied"*.

Candidate refinement (CR): *CR* views are used to discard spans output by the CD views that may be incorrect. In general, a CR view is defined as: *"From the list of spans of* $view_{valid}$ *subtract all those spans that belong to* $view_{invalid}$*"*. $view_{valid}$ is obtained by joining all the positive CD clues on the *Equals* predicate and $view_{invalid}$ is obtained by joining all the negative overlapping clues with the *Overlaps* predicate and subsequently 'union'ing all the negative clues. (*e.g.*, similar in spirit to rules R_6, R_7 and R_8 in Figure 1, except that the subtraction is done from a single view and not the *union* of multiple views).

Consolidation (CO): Finally, a *select* statement with a fixed *consolidate* clause is used for each entity type to remove overlapping spans from CR views. An example CO view is defined by rule R_9 in Figure 1.

Extractor Complexity. Since our goal is to generate extractors with manageable complexity, we must introduce a quantitative measure of extractor complexity, in order to (1) judge the complexity of the extractors generated by our system, and (2) reduce the search space considered by the induction system.

To this end, we define a simple complexity score that is a function of the number of rules, and the number of input views to each rule of the extractor. In particular, we define the *length of rule* R, denoted as $L(R)$, as the number of input views in the *from* clause(s) of the view. For example, in Figure 1, we have $L(R_4) = 2$ and $L(R_5) = 3$, since R_4 and R_5 have two, and respectively three views in the *from* clause. Furthermore, $L(R_8) = 2$ since each of the two inner statements of R_8 has one *from* clause with a single input view. The complexity of BF rules (e.g., R_1 to R_3) and CO rules (e.g., R_9) is always 1, since these types of rules have a single input view. We define the *complexity of extractor* E, denoted as $C(E)$ as the sum of lengths of all rules of E. For example, the complexity of the *Person* extractor from Figure 1 is 15, plus the length of all rules involved in defining *Organization*, which are omitted from the figure.

Our simple notion of rule length is motivated by existing literature in the area of database systems (Abiteboul et al., 1995), where the *size* of a conjunctive query is determined only by the number of atoms in the body of the query (e.g., items in the FROM clause), and it is independent on the number of join variables (i.e., items in the WHERE clause), or the size of the head of the query (e.g., items in the SELECT clause). As such, our notion of complexity is rather coarse, and we shall discuss its shortcomings in detail in Section 6.2. However, we shall show that the complexity score significantly reduces the search space of our induction techniques leading to

Phase name	AQL statements	Prescription	Rule Type
Basic Features	`extract`	Off-the-shelf, Learning using prior work (Riloff, 1993; Li et al., 2008)	Basic Features Definition
Phase 1 (Clustering and RLGG)	`select`	Bottom-up learning (LGG), Top-down refinement	Development of Candidate Rules
Phase 2 (Propositional Rule Learning)	`select, union all, minus`	RIPPER, Lightweight Rule Induction	Candidate Rules Filtering
Consolidation	`consolidate, union all`	Manually identified consolidation rules, based on domain knowledge	Consolidation rules

Table 2: Phases in induction, the language constructs invoked in each phase, the prescriptions for inducing rules in the phase and the corresponding type of rule in manual rule development.

simpler and smaller extractors, and therefore constitutes a good basis for more comprehensive measures of interpretability in the future.

5 Induction of Rules

Since the goal is to generate rules that can be customized by humans, the overall structure of the induced rules must be similar in spirit to what a developer following best practices would write. Hence, the induction process is divided into multiple phases. Figure 2 shows the correspondence between the phases of induction and the types of rules. In Table 2, we summarize the phases of our induction algorithm, along with the subset of AQL constructs that comprise the language of the rules learnt in that phase, the possible methods prescribed for inducing the rules and their correspondence with the stages in the manual rule development.

Our induction system generates rules for two of the four categories, namely CD and CR rules as highlighted in Figure 2. We assume that we are given the BFs in the form of dictionaries and regular expressions. Prior work on learning dictionaries (Riloff, 1993) and regular expressions (Li et al., 2008) could be leveraged to semi-automate the process of defining the basic features.

We represent each example, in conjunction with relevant background knowledge in the form *first order horn clauses*. This background knowledge will serve as input to our induction system. The first phase of induction uses a combination of *clustering* and *relative least general generalization (RLGG)* (Nienhuys-Cheng and Wolf, 1997; Muggleton and Feng, 1992) techniques. At the end of this phase, we have a number of CD rules. In the second phase, we begin by forming a structure called the *span-view table*. Broadly speaking, this is an attribute-value table formed by all the views induced in the first phase along with the textual spans generated by them. The attribute-value table is used as input to a propositional rule learner such as *JRIP* to learn accurate compositions of a useful (as determined by the learning algorithm) subset of the CD rules. This forms the second phase of our system. The rules learnt from this phase are the CR rules. At various phases, several induction biases are introduced to enhance the interpretability of rules. These biases capture the expertise gleaned from manual rule development and constrain the search space in our induction system.

The *hypothesis language* of our induction system is *Annotation Query Language (AQL)* and we use *SystemT* as the *theorem prover*. SystemT provides a very fast rule execution engine and is crucial in our induction system as we test multiple hypotheses in the search for the more promising ones. AQL provides a very expressive rule representation language that is proven to be capable of encoding all the paradigms that any rule-based representation can encode. The dual advantages of *rich rule-representation* and *execution efficiency* are the main motivation behind our choice.

We discuss our induction procedure in detail next.

5.1 Basic Features and Background Knowledge

We assume that we are provided with a set of dictionaries and regular expressions for defining all our basic *create view* statements. R_1, R_2 and R_3 in Figure 1 are such basic view definitions. The basic views are compiled and executed in SystemT over the training document collection and the resulting spans are represented by equivalent predicates in first order logic. Essentially, each training example is represented as a definite clause,

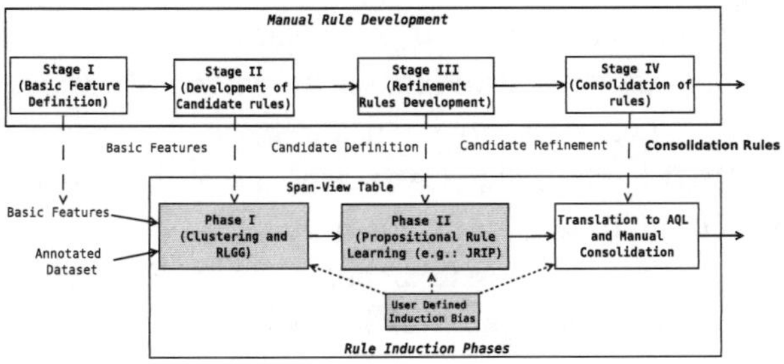

Figure 2: Correspondence between Manual Rule development and Rule Induction.

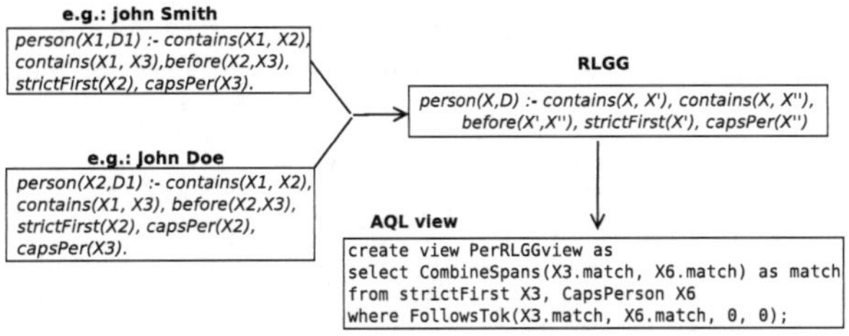

Figure 3: Relative Least General Generalization

that includes in its body, the basic view-types encoded as background knowledge predicates. To establish relationships between different background knowledge predicates for each training example, we define some additional *"glue predicates"* such as `contains` and `before`.

5.2 Induction of Candidate Definition Rules

Clustering Module. We obtain non-overlapping clusters of examples within each type, by computing similarities between their representations as definite clauses. We present the intuition behind this approach in Figure 3 which illustrates the process of taking two examples and finding their generalization. It is worthwhile to look at generalizations of instances that are similar. For instance, two token person names such as *Mark Waugh* and *Mark Twain* are part of a single cluster. However, we would not be able to generalize a two-token name (*e.g., Mark Waugh*) with another name consisting of initials followed by a token (*e.g., M. Waugh*). Using a wrapper around the hierarchical agglomerative clustering implemented in LingPipe[2], we cluster examples and look at generalizations only within each cluster. Clustering also helps improve efficiency by reducing the computational overhead, since otherwise, we would have to consider generalizations of all pairs of examples (Muggleton and Feng, 1992).

RLGG computation. We compute our CD rules as the *relative least general generalization (RLGG)* (Nienhuys-Cheng and Wolf, 1997; Muggleton and Feng, 1992) of examples in each cluster. Given a set of clauses in first order logic, their RLGG is the least generalized clause in the subsumption lattice of the clauses relative to the background knowledge (Nienhuys-Cheng and Wolf, 1997). RLGG is associative, and we use this fact to compute RLGGs of sets of examples in a cluster. The RLGG of two bottom clauses as computed in our system and its translation to an AQL view is illustrated in Figure 3. We filter out noisy RLGGs and convert the selected RLGGs into the equivalent AQL views. Each such AQL view is treated as a CD rule. We next discuss the process of filtering-out noisy RLGGs. We interchangeably refer to the RLGGs and the clusters they represent .

Iterative Clustering and RLGG filtering. Since clustering is sub-optimal, we expected some clusters in a single run of clustering to have poor RLGGs, either in terms of complexity or precision. We therefore use an iterative clustering approach, based on the *separate-and-conquer* (Fürnkranz, 1999) strategy. In each iteration, we pick the clusters with the best RLGGs and remove all examples covered by those RLGGs. The best RLGGs must have precision and number of examples covered above a pre-specified threshold.

5.3 Induction of Candidate Refinement Rules

Span-View Table. The CD views from phase 1 along with the textual spans they generate, yield the *span-view table*. The rows of the table correspond to the *set of spans* returned by all the CD views. The columns correspond to the set of CD view names. Each span either belongs to one of the named entity types (PER, ORG or LOC) or is none of them (NONE); the type information constitutes its class label (see Figure 4 for an illustrated example). The cells in the table correspond to either a match (M) or a no-match (N) or partial/overlapping match (O) of a span generated by a CD view. This attribute-value table is used as input to a propositional rule learner

[2]http://alias-i.com/lingpipe/demos/tutorial/cluster/read-me.html

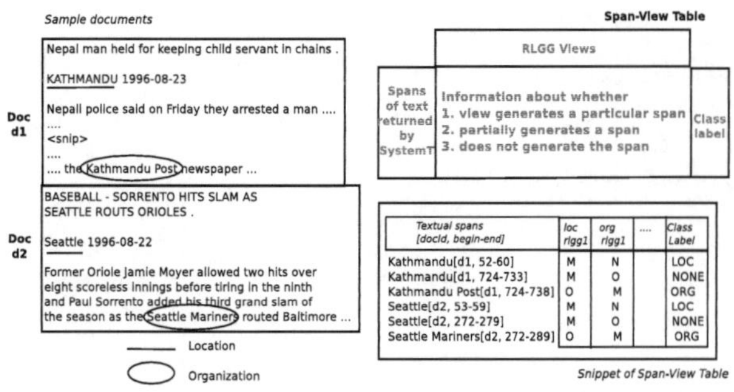

Figure 4: Span-View Table

like *JRIP* to learn compositions of CD views.

Propositional Rule Learning. Based on our study of different propositional rule learners, we decided to use *RIPPER* (Fürnkranz and Widmer, 1994) implemented as the *JRIP* classifier in weka (Witten et al., 2011). Some considerations that favor JRIP are (i) absence of rule ordering, (ii) ease of conversion to AQL and (iii) amenability to add induction biases in the implementation.

A number of syntactic biases were introduced in JRIP to aid in the interpretability of the induced rules. We observed in our manually developed rules that CR rules for a type involve interaction between CDs for the same type and negations (not-overlaps, not matches) of CDs of the other types. This bias was incorporated by constraining a JRIP rule to contain only positive features (CDs) of the same type (say PER) and negative features (CDs) of only other types (ORG and LOC, in this case).

The output of the JRIP algorithm is a set of rules, one set for each of PER, ORG and LOC. Here is an example rule: **`PER-CR-Rule`** $\Leftarrow$ **`(PerCD = m) AND (LocCD != o)`** which is read as : *"If a span matches PerCD and does not overlap with LocCD, then that span denotes a PER named entity"*. Here **`PerCD`** is $\{$**`[FirstName`** $\wedge$ **`CapsPerson][LastName`** $\wedge$ **`CapsPerson]`**$\}$ [3] and **`LocCD`** is $\{$**`[CapsPlace`** $\wedge$ **`CitiesDict]`**$\}$. This rule filters out wrong person annotations like *"Prince William"* in *Prince William Sound*. (This is the name of a location but has overlapped with a person named entity.) In AQL, this effect can be achieved most elegantly by the **`minus`** (filter) construct. Such an AQL rule will filter all those occurrences of *Prince William* from the list of persons that overlap with a city name.

Steps such as clustering, computation of RLGGs, JRIP, and theorem proving using SystemT were parallelized. Once the CR views for each type of named entity are learnt, many forms of consolidations (COs) are possible, both within and across types. A simple consolidation policy that we have incorporated in the system is as follows: union all the rules of a particular type, then perform a *contained within* consolidation, resulting in the final set of consolidated views for each named entity type.

6 Experiments

We evaluate our system on CoNLL03 (Tjong Kim Sang and De Meulder, 2003), a collection of Reuters news stories. We used the CoNLL03 training set for induction and report results on the CoNLL03 test collection.

The basic features (BFs) form the primary input to our induction system. We experimented with three sets of BFs:

*Initial set(**E1**)*: The goal in this setup is to induce an initial set of rules based on a small set of reasonable BFs. We use a conservative initial set consisting of 15 BFs (5 regular expressions and 10 dictionaries).

*Enhanced set (**E2**)*: Based on the results of E1, we identify a set of additional domain independent BFs[4]. Five views were added to the existing set in E1 (1 regular expression and 4 dictionaries). The goal is to observe whether our approach yields reasonable accuracies compared to generic rules developed manually.

*Domain customized set (**E3**)*: Based on the knowledge of the domain of the training dataset (CoNLL03), we introduced a set of features specific to this dataset. These included sports-related person, organization and location dictionaries[5]. These views were added to the existing set in E2. The intended goal is to observe what are the best possible accuracies that could be achieved with BFs customized to a particular domain.

The set of parameters for iterative clustering on which the accuracies reported are : the precision threshold for the RLGGs of the clusters was 70%

[3] Two consecutive spans where the 1st is FirstName and CapsPerson and the 2nd is LastName and CapsPerson.

[4] E.g., the feature *preposition dictionary* was added in E2 to help identify organization names such as *Bank of England*.

[5] Half of the documents in CoNLL03 are sports-related.

	Train			Test			
Type	P	R	F	P	R	F	C(E)
E1 (Initial set)							
PER	88.5	41.4	56.4	92.5	39.4	55.3	144
ORG	89.1	7.3	13.4	85.9	5.2	9.7	22
LOC	91.6	54.5	68.3	87.3	55.3	67.8	105
Overall	90.2	35.3	50.7	89.2	33.3	48.5	234
E2 (Enhanced set)							
PER	84.7	52.9	65.1	87.5	49.9	63.5	233
ORG	88.2	7.8	14.3	85.8	5.9	11.0	99
LOC	92.1	58.6	71.7	88.6	59.1	70.9	257
Overall	88.6	40.7	55.8	88.0	38.2	53.3	457
E3 (Domain customized set)							
PER	89.9	57.3	70.0	91.7	56.0	69.5	430
ORG	86.9	50.9	64.2	86.9	47.5	61.4	348
LOC	90.8	67.0	77.1	84.3	67.3	74.8	356
Overall	89.4	58.7	70.9	87.3	57.0	68.9	844

Table 3: Results on CoNLL03 dataset with different basic feature sets

and the number of examples covered by each RLGG was 5. We selected the top 5 clusters from each iteration whose RLGGs crossed this threshold. If there were no such clusters then we would lower the precision threshold to 35% (half of the threshold). When no new clusters were formed, we ended the iterations.

6.1 Experiments and Results

Effect of Augmenting Basic Features. Table 3 shows the accuracy and complexity of rules induced with the three basic feature sets E1, E2 and E3, respectively [6]. The overall F-measure on the test dataset is 48.5% with E1, it increases to around 53.3% with E2 and is highest at 68.9% with E3. As we increase the number of BFs, the accuracies of the induced extractors increases, at the cost of an increase in complexity. In particular, the recall increases significantly across the board, and is more prominent between E2 and E3, where the additional domain specific features result in recall increase from 5.9% to 47.5% for ORG. The precision increases slightly for PER, but decreases slightly for LOC and ORG with the addition of domain specific features.

Comparison with manually developed rules. We compared the induced extractors with the manually developed extractors of (Chiticariu et al., 2010b), heretofore referred to as *manual extractors*. (For a detailed analysis, we obtained the extractors from the authors). Table 4 shows the accuracy and complexity of the induced rules with E2 and E3 and the manual extractors for the generic domain and, respectively, customized for the CoNLL03 domain. (In the table, ignore the column *Induced (without bias)*, which is discussed later). Our technique compares reasonably with the manually constructed generic extractor for two of the three entity types; and on precision for all entity types, especially since our system generated the rules in 1 hour, whereas the development of manual rules took much longer [7]. Additional work is required to match the manual customized extractor's performance, primarily due to shortcomings in our current target language. Recall that our framework is limited to a small subset of AQL constructs for expressing CD and CR rules, and there is a single consolidation rule. In particular, advanced constructs such as dynamic dictionaries are not supported, and the set of predicates to the Filter construct supported in our system is restricted to predicates over other concepts, which is only a subset of those used in (Chiticariu et al., 2010b). The manual extractors also contain a larger number of rules covering many different cases, improving the accuracy, but also leading to a higher complexity score. To better analyze the complexity, we also computed the average rule length for each extractor by dividing the complexity score by the number of AQL views of the extractor. The average rule length is 1.78 and 1.87 for the induced extractors with E2 and E3, respectively, and 1.9 and 2.1 for the generic and customized extractors of (Chiticariu et al., 2010b), respectively. The average rule length increases from the generic extractor to the customized extractor in both cases. On average, however, an individual induced rule is slightly smaller than a manually developed rule.

Effect of Bias. The goal of this experiment is to demonstrate the importance of biases in the induction process. The biases added to the system are broadly of two types: (i) Partition of basic features based on types (ii) Restriction on the type of CD views that can appear in a CR view. [8] Without

[6]These are the results for the configuration with bias.

[7] (Chiticariu et al., 2010b) mentions that customization for 3 domains required 8 person weeks. It is reasonable to infer that developing the generic rules took comparable effort.

[8]For e.g., person CR view can contain only person CD views as positive clues and CD views of other types as negative clues.

(i) many semantically similar basic features (especially, regular expressions) would match a given token, leading to an increase in the length of a CD a rule. For example, in the CD rule [FirstNameDict][CapsPerson ∧ CapsOrg]} (*"A FirstNameDict span followed by a CapsPerson span that is also a CapsOrg span"*), CapsPerson and CapsOrg are two very similar regular expressions identifying capitalized phrases that look like person, and respectively, organization names, with small variations (e.g., the former may allow special characters such as '-'). Including both BFs in a CD rule leads to a larger rule that is unintuitive for a developer. The former bias excludes such CD rules from consideration.

The latter type of bias prevents CD rules of one type to appear as positive clues for a CR rule of a different type. For instance, without this bias, one of the CR rules obtained was `Per` ⇐ `(OrgCD = m) AND (LocCD != o)` (*"If a span matches OrgCD and does not overlap with LocCD, then that span denotes a PER named entity"*. Here `OrgCD` was {`[CapsOrg][CapsOrg]`} and `LocCD` was {`[CapsLoc` ∧ `CitiesDict]`}. The inclusion of an Organization CD rule as a positive clue for a Person CR rule is unintuitive for a developer.

Table 4, shows the effect (for E2 and E3) on the test dataset of disabling and enabling bias during the induction of CR rules using JRIP. Adding bias improves the precision of the induced rules. Without bias, however, the system is less constrained in its search for high recall rules, leading to slightly higher overall F measure. This comes at the cost of an increase in extractor complexity and average rule length. For example, for E2, the average rule length decreases from 2.17 to 1.78 after adding the bias. Overall, our results show that biases lead to less complex extractors with only a very minor effect on accuracy, thus biases are important factors contributing to inducing rules that are understandable and may be refined by humans.

Comparison with other induction systems. We also experimented with two other induction systems, Aleph[9] and ALP[10], a package that implements one of the reportedly good information extraction algorithms (Ciravegna, 2001). While induction in Aleph was performed with the same target language as in our approach, the target language of ALP is JAPE, which has been shown (Chiticariu et al., 2010b) to lack in some of the constructs (such as minus) that AQL provides and which form a part of our target language (especially the rule refinement phase). However, despite experimenting with all possible parameter configurations for each of these (in each of E1, E2 and E3 settings), the accuracies obtained were substantially (30-50%) worse and the extractor complexity was much (around 60%) higher when compared to our system (with or without bias). Additionally, Aleph takes close to three days for induction, whereas both ALP and our system require less than an hour.

6.2 Discussion

Weak and Strong CDs reflected in CRs. In our experiments, we found that varying the precision and complexity thresholds while inducing the CDs (*c.f* Section 5) affected the F1 of the final extractor only minimally. But reducing the precision threshold generally improved the precision of the final extractor, which seemed counterintuitive at first. We found that CR rules learned by JRIP consist of a strong CD rule (high precision, typically involving a dictionary) and a weak CD rule (low precision, typically involving only regular expressions). The strong CD rule always corresponded to a positive clue (match) and the weak CD rule corresponded to the negative clue (overlaps or not-matches). This is illustrated in the following CR rule: `PER` ⇐ `(PerCD = m) AND (OrgCD != o)` where `(PerCD` is {`[CapsPersonR] [CapsPersonR` ∧ `LastNameDict]`} and `(OrgCD` is {`[CapsOrgR][CapsOrgR][CapsOrgR]`}. This is posited to be the way the CR rule learner operates – it tries to learn conjunctions of weak and strong clues so as to filter one from the other. Therefore, setting a precision threshold too high limited the number of such weak clues and the ability of the CR rule learner to find such rules.

Interpretability. Measuring interpretability of rules is a difficult problem. In this work, we have taken a first step towards measuring interpretability using a coarse grain measure in the form of a simple notion of complexity score. The complexity is very helpful in comparing alternative rule sets based on

[9] A system for inductive logic programming. See http://www.cs.ox.ac.uk/activities/machlearn/Aleph/aleph.html

[10] http://code.google.com/p/alpie/

		Chiticariu et al. 2010b				Induced (With Bias)				Induced (Without Bias)			
		P	R	F	C(E)	P	R	F	C(E)	P	R	F	C(E)
Generic (E2)	*PER*	82.2	60.3	69.5	945	87.5	49.9	63.5	233	85.8	53.7	66.0	476
	ORG	75.7	17.5	28.5	1015	85.8	5.9	11.0	99	74.1	15.7	25.9	327
	LOC	72.2	86.1	78.6	921	88.6	59.1	70.9	257	85.9	61.5	71.7	303
	Overall	75.9	54.6	63.5	1015	88.0	38.2	53.3	457	84.2	43.5	57.4	907
Customised (E3)	*PER*	96.3	92.2	94.2	2154	91.7	56.0	69.5	430	90.7	60.3	72.4	359
	ORG	91.1	85.1	88.0	2154	86.9	47.5	61.4	348	90.4	46.8	61.7	397
	LOC	93.3	91.7	92.5	2154	84.3	67.3	74.8	356	83.9	69.1	75.8	486
	Overall	93.5	89.6	91.5	2160	87.3	57.0	68.9	844	87.8	58.7	70.4	901

Table 4: Comparison of induced rules (with and without bias) and manually developed rules. (CoNLL03 test dataset)

the number of rules, and the size of each rule, but exhibits a number of shortcomings described next. First, it disregards other components of a rule besides its from clause, for example, the number of items in the select clause, or the where clause. Second, rule developers use semantically meaningful view names such as those shown in Figure 1 to help them recall the semantics of a rule at a high-level, an aspect that is not captured by the complexity measure. Automatic generation of meaningful names for induced views is an interesting direction for future work. Finally, the overall structure of an extractors is not considered. In simple terms, an extractor consisting of 5 rules of size 1 is indistinguishable from an extractor consisting of a single rule of size 5, and it is arguable which of these extractors is more interpretable. More generally, the extent of this shortcoming is best explained using an example. When informally examining the rules induced by our system, we found that CD rules are similar in spirit to those written by rule developers. On the other hand, the induced CR rules are too fine-grained. In general, rule developers group CD rules with similar semantics, then write refinement rules at the higher level of the group, as opposed to the lower level of individual CD views. For example, one may write multiple CD rules for candidate person names of the form ⟨*First*⟩⟨*Last*⟩, and multiple CD rules of the form ⟨*Last*⟩, ⟨*First*⟩. One would then union together the candidates from each of the two groups into two different views, e.g., *PerFirstLast* and *PerLastCommaFirst*, and write filter rules at the higher level of these two views, e.g., *"Remove PerLastCommaFirst spans that overlap with a PerFirstLast span"*. In contrast, our induction algorithm considers CR rules consisting of combinations of CD rules directly, leading to many semantically similar CR rules, each operating over small parts of a larger semantic group (see rule in Section 6.1). This results in repetition, and qualitatively less interpretable rules, since humans prefer higher levels of abstraction and generalization. This nuance is not captured by the complexity score which may deem an extractor consisting of many rules, where many of the rules operate at higher levels of groups of candidates to be more complex than a smaller extractor with many fine-grained rules. Indeed, as shown before, the complexity of the induced extractors is much smaller compared to that of manual extractors, although the latter follow the semantic grouping principle and are considered more interpretable.

7 Conclusion

We presented a system for efficiently inducing named entity annotation rules in the AQL language. The design of our approach is aimed at producing accurate rules that can be understood and refined by humans, by placing special emphasis on low complexity and efficient computation of the induced rules, while mimicking a four stage approach used for manually constructing rules. The induced rules have good accuracy and low complexity according to our complexity measure. While our complexity measure informs the biases in our system and leads to simpler, smaller extractors, it captures extractor interpretability only to a certain extent. Therefore, we believe more work is required to devise a more comprehensive quantitative measure for interpretability, and refine our techniques in order to increase the interpretability of induced rules. Other interesting directions for future work are introducing more constructs in our framework, and applying our techniques to other languages.

References

S. Abiteboul, R. Hull, and V. Vianu. 1995. *Foundations of Databases*. Addison Wesley Publishing Co.

Douglas E. Appelt and Boyan Onyshkevych. 1998. The common pattern specification language. In *TIPSTER workshop*.

Mary Elaine Califf and Raymond J. Mooney. 1997. Applying ilp-based techniques to natural language information extraction: An experiment in relational learning. In *IJCAI Workshop on Frontiers of Inductive Logic Programming*.

Mary Elaine Califf and Raymond J. Mooney. 1999. Relational learning of pattern-match rules for information extraction. In *AAAI*.

Laura Chiticariu, Rajasekar Krishnamurthy, Yunyao Li, Sriram Raghavan, Frederick R. Reiss, and Shivakumar Vaithyanathan. 2010a. Systemt: an algebraic approach to declarative information extraction. In *ACL*.

Laura Chiticariu, Rajasekar Krishnamurthy, Yunyao Li, Frederick Reiss, and Shivakumar Vaithyanathan. 2010b. Domain adaptation of rule-based annotators for named-entity recognition tasks. In *EMNLP*.

Fabio Ciravegna. 2001. (lp)2, an adaptive algorithm for information extraction from web-related texts. In *In Proceedings of the IJCAI-2001 Workshop on Adaptive Text Extraction and Mining*.

Hamish Cunningham, Diana Maynard, Kalina Bontcheva, Valentin Tablan, Niraj Aswani, Ian Roberts, Genevieve Gorrell, Adam Funk, Angus Roberts, Danica Damljanovic, Thomas Heitz, Mark A. Greenwood, Horacio Saggion, Johann Petrak, Yaoyong Li, and Wim Peters. 2011. *Text Processing with GATE (Version 6)*.

J. Fürnkranz and G. Widmer. 1994. Incremental reduced error pruning. pages 70–77.

Johannes Fürnkranz. 1999. Separate-and-conquer rule learning. *Artif. Intell. Rev.*, 13(1):3–54, February.

B. R. Gaines and P. Compton. 1995. Induction of ripple-down rules applied to modeling large databases. *J. Intell. Inf. Syst.*, 5:211–228, November.

IBM, 2012. *IBM InfoSphere BigInsights - Annotation Query Language (AQL) reference*. `http://publib.boulder.ibm.com/infocenter/bigins/v1r3/topic/com.ibm.swg.im.infosphere.biginsights.doc/doc/biginsights_aqlref_con_aql-overview.html`.

Yunyao Li, Rajasekar Krishnamurthy, Sriram Raghavan, Shivakumar Vaithyanathan, and H. V. Jagadish. 2008. Regular expression learning for information extraction. In *EMNLP*.

Bin Liu, Laura Chiticariu, Vivian Chu, H. V. Jagadish, and Frederick R. Reiss. 2010. Automatic rule refinement for information extraction. *Proc. VLDB Endow.*, 3:588–597.

Diana Maynard, Kalina Bontcheva, and Hamish Cunningham. 2003. Towards a semantic extraction of named entities. In *In Recent Advances in Natural Language Processing*.

Stephen Muggleton and C. Feng. 1992. Efficient induction in logic programs. In *ILP*.

D. Nadeau and S. Sekine. 2007. A survey of named entity recognition and classification. *Linguisticae Investigationes*, 30:3–26.

Shan-Hwei Nienhuys-Cheng and Ronald de Wolf. 1997. *Foundations of Inductive Logic Programming*.

Anup Patel, Ganesh Ramakrishnan, and Pushpak Bhattacharyya. 2009. Incorporating linguistic expertise using ilp for named entity recognition in data hungry indian languages. In *ILP*.

Frederick Reiss, Sriram Raghavan, Rajasekar Krishnamurthy, Huaiyu Zhu, and Shivakumar Vaithyanathan. 2008. An algebraic approach to rule-based information extraction. In *ICDE*.

Ellen Riloff. 1993. Automatically constructing a dictionary for information extraction tasks. In *AAAI*.

Stephen Soderland. 1999. Learning information extraction rules for semi-structured and free text. *Mach. Learn.*, 34:233–272.

Erik F. Tjong Kim Sang and Fien De Meulder. 2003. Introduction to the conll-2003 shared task: language-independent named entity recognition. In *HLT-NAACL*.

Ian H. Witten, Eibe Frank, and Mark A. Hall. 2011. *Data Mining: Practical Machine Learning Tools and Techniques*. Morgan Kaufmann, Amsterdam, 3rd edition.

Active Learning for Imbalanced Sentiment Classification

Shoushan Li[†]**, Shengfeng Ju**[†]**, Guodong Zhou**[†*]
[†]Natural Language Processing Lab
School of Computer Science and Technology
Soochow University, Suzhou, 215006, China
{shoushan.li, shengfeng.ju}@gmail.com,
gdzhou@suda.edu.cn

Xiaojun Li[‡]
[‡]College of Computer and Information Engineering
Zhejiang Gongshang University
Hangzhou, 310035, China
lixj@mail.zjgsu.edu.cn

Abstract

Active learning is a promising way for sentiment classification to reduce the annotation cost. In this paper, we focus on the imbalanced class distribution scenario for sentiment classification, wherein the number of positive samples is quite different from that of negative samples. This scenario posits new challenges to active learning. To address these challenges, we propose a novel active learning approach, named co-selecting, by taking both the imbalanced class distribution issue and uncertainty into account. Specifically, our co-selecting approach employs two feature subspace classifiers to collectively select most informative minority-class samples for manual annotation by leveraging a certainty measurement and an uncertainty measurement, and in the meanwhile, automatically label most informative majority-class samples, to reduce human-annotation efforts. Extensive experiments across four domains demonstrate great potential and effectiveness of our proposed co-selecting approach to active learning for imbalanced sentiment classification.

1 Introduction

Sentiment classification is the task of identifying the sentiment polarity (e.g., positive or negative) of a natural language text towards a given topic (Pang et al., 2002; Turney, 2002) and has become the core component of many important applications in opinion analysis (Cui et al., 2006; Li et al., 2009; Lloret et al., 2009; Zhang and Ye, 2008).

Most of previous studies in sentiment classification focus on learning models from a large number of labeled data. However, in many real-world applications, manual annotation is expensive and time-consuming. In these situations, active learning approaches could be helpful by actively selecting most informative samples for manual annotation. Compared to traditional active learning for sentiment classification, active learning for imbalanced sentiment classification faces some unique challenges.

As a specific type of sentiment classification, imbalanced sentiment classification deals with the situation in which there are many more samples of one class (called *majority class*) than the other class (called *minority class*), and has attracted much attention due to its high realistic value in real-world applications (Li et al., 2011a). In imbalanced sentiment classification, since the minority-class samples (denoted as *MI* samples) are normally much sparse and thus more precious and informative for learning compared to the majority-class ones (denoted as *MA* samples), it is worthwhile to spend more on manually annotating *MI* samples to guarantee both the quality and quantity of *MI* samples. Traditionally, uncertainty has been popularly used as a basic measurement in active learning (Lewis and Gale, 2004). Therefore, how to select most informative *MI* samples for manual annotation without violating the basic

* Corresponding author

uncertainty requirement in active learning is challenging in imbalanced sentiment classification.

In this paper, we address above challenges in active learning for imbalanced sentiment classification. The basic idea of our active learning approach is to use two complementary classifiers for collectively selecting most informative *MI* samples: one to adopt a certainty measurement for selecting most possible *MI* samples and the other to adopt an uncertainty measurement for selecting most uncertain *MI* samples from the most possible *MI* samples returned from the first classifier. Specifically, the two classifiers are trained with two disjoint feature subspaces to guarantee their complementariness. This also applies to selecting most informative *MA* samples. We call our novel active learning approach co-selecting due to its collectively selecting informative samples through two disjoint feature subspace classifiers. To further reduce the annotation efforts, we only manually annotate those most informative *MI* samples while those most informative *MA* samples are automatically labeled using the predicted labels provided by the first classifier.

In principle, our active learning approach differs from existing ones in two main aspects. First, a certainty measurement and an uncertainty measurement are employed in two complementary subspace classifiers respectively to collectively select most informative *MI* samples for manual annotation. Second, most informative *MA* samples are automatically labeled to further reduce the annotation cost. Evaluation across four domains shows that our active learning approach is effective for imbalanced sentiment classification and significantly outperforms the state-of-the-art active learning alternatives, such as uncertainty sampling (Lewis and Gale, 2004) and co-testing (Muslea et al., 2006).

The remainder of this paper is organized as follows. Section 2 overviews the related work on sentiment classification and active learning. Section 3 proposes our active learning approach for imbalanced sentiment classification. Section 4 reports the experimental results. Finally, Section 5 draws the conclusion and outlines the future work.

2 Related Work

In this section, we give a brief overview on sentiment classification and active learning.

2.1 Sentiment Classification

Sentiment classification has become a hot research topic in NLP community and various kinds of classification methods have been proposed, such as unsupervised learning methods (Turney, 2002), supervised learning methods (Pang et al., 2002), semi-supervised learning methods (Wan, 2009; Li et al., 2010), and cross-domain classification methods (Blitzer et al., 2007; Li and Zong, 2008; He et al., 2011). However, imbalanced sentiment classification is relatively new and there are only a few studies in the literature.

Li et al. (2011a) pioneer the research in imbalanced sentiment classification and propose a co-training algorithm to perform semi-supervised learning for imbalanced sentiment classification with the help of a great amount of unlabeled samples. However, their semi-supervised approach to imbalanced sentiment classification suffers from the problem that their balanced selection strategy in co-training would generate many errors in late iterations due to the imbalanced nature of the unbalanced data. In comparison, our proposed active learning approach can effectively avoid this problem. By the way, it is worth to note that the experiments therein show the superiority of under-sampling over other alternatives such as cost-sensitive and one-class classification for imbalanced sentiment classification.

Li et al. (2011b) focus on supervised learning for imbalanced sentiment classification and propose a clustering-based approach to improve traditional under-sampling approaches. However, the improvement of the proposed clustering-based approach over under-sampling is very limited.

Unlike all the studies mentioned above, our study pioneers active learning on imbalanced sentiment classification.

2.2 Active Learning

Active leaning, as a standard machine learning problem, has been extensively studied in many research communities and several approaches have been proposed to address this problem (Settles, 2009). Based on different sample selection strategies, they can be grouped into two main categories: (1) uncertainty sampling (Lewis and Gale, 2004) where the active learner iteratively select most uncertain unlabeled samples for manual annotation; and (2) committee-based sampling where the active learner selects those unlabeled samples which have the largest disagreement among several committee classifiers. Besides query by committee (QBC) as the first of such type (Freund et al., 1997), co-testing learns a committee of member classifiers from different views and selects those contention points (i.e., unlabeled examples on which the views predict different labels) for manual annotation (Muslea et al., 2006).

However, most previous studies focus on the scenario of balanced class distribution and only a few recent studies address the active learning issue on imbalanced classification problems including Yang and Ma (2010), Zhu and Hovy (2007), Ertekin et al. (2007a) and Ertekin et al. (2007b)[2]. Unfortunately, they straightly adopt the uncertainty sampling as the active selection strategy to address active learning in imbalanced classification, which completely ignores the class imbalance problem in the selected samples.

Attenberg and Provost (2010) highlights the importance of selecting samples by considering the proportion of the classes. Their simulation experiment on text categorization confirms that selecting class-balanced samples is more important than traditional active selection strategies like uncertainty. However, the proposed experiment is simulated and non real strategy is proposed to balance the class distribution of the selected samples.

Doyle et al. (2011) propose a real strategy to select balanced samples. They first select a set of uncertainty samples and then randomly select balanced samples from the uncertainty-sample set. However, the classifier used for selecting balanced samples is the same as the one for supervising uncertainty, which makes the balance control unreliable (the selected uncertainty samples take very low confidences which are unreliable to correctly predict the class label for controlling the balance). Different from their study, our approach possesses two merits: First, two feature subspace classifiers are trained to finely integrate the certainty and uncertainty measurements. Second, the *MA* samples are automatically annotated, which reduces the annotation cost in a further effort.

[2] Ertekin et al. (2007a) and Ertekin et al. (2007b) select samples closest to the hyperplane provided by the SVM classifier (within the margin). Their strategy can be seen as a special case of uncertainty sampling.

3 Active Learning for Imbalanced Sentiment Classification

Generally, active learning can be either stream-based or pool-based (Sassano, 2002). The main difference between the two is that the former scans through the data sequentially and selects informative samples individually, whereas the latter evaluates and ranks the entire collection before selecting most informative samples at batch. As a large collection of samples can easily gathered once in sentiment classification, pool-based active learning is adopted in this study.

Figure 1 illustrates a standard pool-based active learning approach, where the most important issue is the sampling strategy, which evaluates the informativeness of one sample.

Input:

  Labeled data *L*;

  Unlabeled pool *U*;

Output:

  New Labeled data *L*

Procedure:

Loop for *N* iterations:

(1). Learn a classifier using current *L*

(2). Use current classifier to label all unlabeled samples

(3). Use the sampling strategy to select *n* most informative samples for manual annotation

(4). Move newly-labeled samples from *U* to *L*

Figure 1: Pool-based active learning

3.1 Sampling Strategy: Uncertainty vs. Certainty

As one of the most popular selection strategies in active learning, uncertainty sampling depends on an uncertainty measurement to select informative samples. Since sentiment classification is a binary classification problem, the uncertainty measurement of a document d can be simply defined as follows:

$$Uncer(d) = \min_{y \in \{pos, neg\}} P(y \mid d)$$

Where $P(y \mid d)$ denotes the posterior probability of the document d belonging to the class y and {pos, neg} denotes the class labels of positive and negative.

In imbalanced sentiment classification, *MI* samples are much sparse yet precious for learning and thus are believed to be more valuable for manual annotation. The key in active learning for imbalanced sentiment classification is to guarantee both the quality and quantity of newly-added *MI* samples. To guarantee the selection of *MI* samples, a certainty measurement is necessary. In this study, the certainty measurement is defined as follows:

$$Cer(d) = \max_{y \in \{pos, neg\}} P(y \mid d)$$

Meanwhile, in order to balance the samples in the two classes, once an informative *MI* sample is manually annotated, an informative *MA* sample is automatically labeled. In this way, the annotated data become more balanced than a random selection strategy.

However, the two sampling strategies discussed above are apparently contradicted: while the uncertainty measurement is prone to selecting the samples whose posterior probabilities are nearest to 0.5, the certainty measurement is prone to selecting the samples whose posterior probabilities are nearest to 1. Therefore, it is essential to find a solution to balance uncertainty sampling and certainty sampling in imbalanced sentiment classification,

3.2 Co-selecting with Feature Subspace Classifiers

In sentiment classification, a document is represented as a feature vector generated from the feature set $F = \{f_1, ..., f_m\}$. When a feature subset, i.e., $F^S = \{f_1^S, ..., f_r^S\}$ ($r < m$), is used, the original m-dimensional feature space becomes an r-dimensional feature subspace. In this study, we call a classifier trained with a feature subspace a feature subspace classifier.

Our basic idea of balancing both the uncertainty measurement and the certainty measurement is to train two subspace classifiers to adopt them respectively. In our implementation, we randomly select two disjoint feature subspaces, each of which is used to train a subspace classifier. On one side, one subspace classifier is employed to select some certain samples; on the other side, the other classifier is employed to select the most uncertain sample from those certain samples for manual annotation. In this way, the selected samples are certain in terms of one feature subspace for selecting more possible *MI* samples. Meanwhile, the selected sample remains uncertain in terms of the other feature subspace to introduce uncertain knowledge into current learning model. We name this approach as co-selecting because it collectively selects informative samples by two separate classifiers. Figure 2 illustrates the co-selecting algorithm. In our algorithm, we strictly constrain the balance of the samples between the two classes, i.e., positive and negative. Therefore, once two samples are annotated with the same class label, they will not be added to the labeled data, as shown in step (7) in Figure 2.

Input:

Labeled data L with balanced samples over the two classes

Unlabeled pool U

Output:

New Labeled data L

Procedure:

Loop for N iterations:

(1). Randomly select a feature subset F^S with size r (with the proportion $\theta = r / m$) from F

(2). Generate a feature subspace from F^S and train a corresponding feature subspace classifier C_{Cer} with L

(3). Generate another feature subspace from the complement set of F^S, i.e., $F - F^S$ and train a corresponding feature subspace classifier C_{Uncer} with L

(4). Use C_{Cer} to select top certain k positive and k negative samples, denoted as a sample set CER_1

(5). Use C_{Uncer} to select the most uncertain positive sample and negative sample from CER_1

(6). Manually annotate the two selected samples

(7). If the annotated labels of the two selected samples are different from each other:

Add the two newly-annotated samples into L

Figure 2: The co-selecting algorithm

There are two parameters in the algorithm: the size of the feature subspace for training the first subspace classifier, i.e., θ and the number of selected certain samples, i.e., *k*. Both of the two parameters will be empirically studied in our experiments.

3.3 Co-selecting with Selected *MA* Samples Automatically Labeled

---

Input:

Labeled data *L* with balanced samples over the two classes

Unlabeled pool *U*

MA and *MI* Label (positive or negative)

Output:

New Labeled data *L*

Procedure:

Loop for *N* iterations:

(1). Randomly select a proportion of features (with the proportion θ) from F to get a feature subset F^S

(2). Generate a feature subspace from F^S and train a corresponding subspace classifier C_{Cer} with *L*

(3). Generate another feature subspace from the complement set of F^S, i.e., $F - F^S$ and train a corresponding subspace classifier C_{Uncer} with *L*

(4). Use C_{Cer} to select top certain *k* positive and *k* negative samples, denoted as a sample set CER_1

(5). Use C_{Uncer} to select the most uncertain positive sample and negative sample from CER_1

(6). Manually annotate the sample that is predicted as a *MI* sample by C_{Cer} and automatically annotate the sample that is predicted as *majority class*

(7). If the annotated labels of the two selected samples are different from each other:

Add the two newly-annotated samples into *L*

Figure 3: The co-selecting algorithm with selected *MA* samples automatically labeled

To minimize manual annotation, it is a good choice to automatically label those selected *MA* samples. In our co-selecting approach, automatically labeling those selected *MA* samples is easy and straightforward: the subspace classifier for monitoring the certainty measurement provides an ideal solution to annotate the samples that have been predicted as *majority class*. Figure 3 shows the co-selecting algorithm with those selected *MA* samples automatically labeled. The main difference from the original co-selecting is shown in Step (6) in Figure 3. Another difference is the input where a prior knowledge of which class is *majority class* or *minority class* should be known. In real applications, it is not difficult to know this. We first use a classifier trained with the initial labeled data to test all unlabeled data. If the predicted labels in the classification results are greatly imbalanced, we can assume that the unlabeled data is imbalanced, and consider the dominated class as *majority class*.

4 Experimentation

In this section, we will systematically evaluate our active learning approach for imbalanced sentiment classification and compare it with the state-of-the-art active learning alternatives.

4.1 Experimental Setting

Dataset

We use the same data as used by Li et al. (2011a). The data collection consists of four domains: Book, DVD, Electronic, and Kitchen (Blitzer et al., 2007). For each domain, we randomly select an initial balanced labeled data with 50 negative samples and 50 positive samples. For the unlabeled data, we randomly select 2000 negative samples, and 14580/12160/7140/7560 positive samples from the four domains respectively, keeping the same imbalanced ratio as the whole data. For the test data in each domain, we randomly extract 800 negative samples and 800 positive samples.

Classification algorithm

The Maximum Entropy (ME) classifier implemented with the Mallet [3] tool is mainly adopted, except that in the margin-based active learning approach (Ertekin et al., 2007a) where SVM is implemented with light-SVM [4]. The features for classification are unigram words with Boolean weights.

---

[3] http://mallet.cs.umass.edu/

[4] http://www.cs.cornell.edu/people/tj/svm_light/

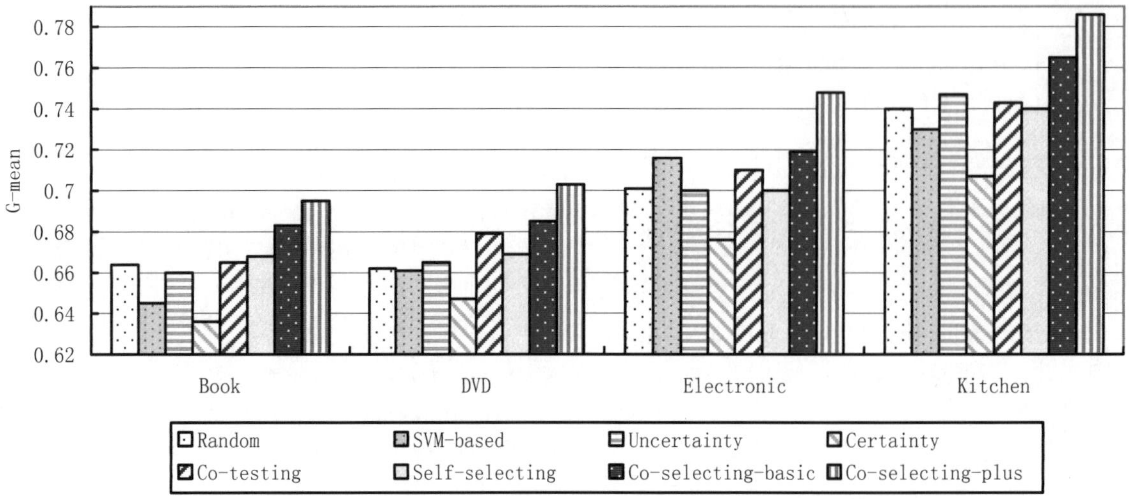

Figure 4: Performance comparison of different active learning approaches on imbalanced sentiment classification

Evaluation metrics

The popular geometric mean $G\text{-}mean=\sqrt{TP_{rate} \times TN_{rate}}$ is adopted, where TP_{rate} is the true positive rate (also called positive recall or sensitivity) and TN_{rate} is the true negative rate (also called negative recall or specificity) (Kubat and Matwin, 1997).

4.2 Experimental Results

For thorough comparison, various kinds of active learning approaches are implemented including:

- **Random**: randomly select the samples from the unlabeled data for manual annotation;
- **Margin-based**: iteratively select samples closest to the hyperplane provided by the SVM classifier, which is suggested by Ertekin et al. (2007a) and Ertekin et al. (2007b). One sample is selected in each iteration;
- **Uncertainty**: iteratively select samples using the uncertainty measurement according to the output of ME classifier. One sample is selected in each iteration;
- **Certainty:** iteratively select class-balanced samples using the certainty measurement according to the output of ME classifier. One positive and negative sample (the positive and negative label is provided by the ME classifier) are selected in each iteration;
- **Co-testing**: first get contention samples (i.e., unlabeled examples on which the member classifiers predict different labels) and then select the least confidence one among the hypotheses of different member classifiers, i.e., the aggressive strategy as described Muslea et al. (2006). Specifically, the member classifiers are two subspace classifiers trained by splitting the whole feature space into two disjoint subspaces of same size;
- **Self-selecting**: first select *k* uncertainty samples and then randomly select a positive and negative sample from the uncertainty-sample set, which is suggested by Doyle et al. (2011). We call it self-selecting since only one classifier is involved to measure uncertainty and predict class labels.

For those approaches involving random selection of features, we run 5 times for them and report the average results. Note that the samples selected by these approaches are imbalanced. To address the problem of classification on imbalanced data, we adopt the under-sampling strategy which has been shown effective for supervised imbalanced sentiment classification (Li et al., 2011a). Our active learning approach includes two versions: the co-selecting algorithm as described in Section 3.2 and the co-selecting with selected *MA* samples automatically labeled as described in Section 3.3. For clarity, we refer the former as **co-selecting-basic** and the latter as **co-selecting-plus** in the following.

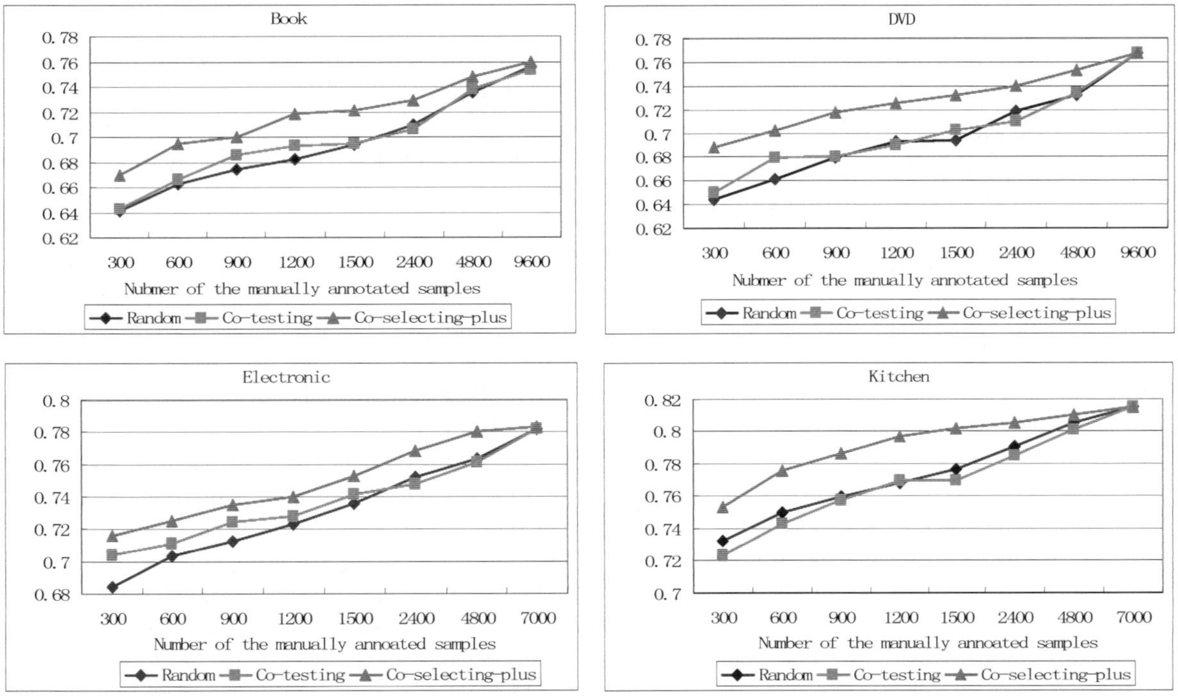

Figure 5: Performance comparison of three active learning approaches: random selection, co-testing and co-selecting-plus, by varying the number of the selected samples for manually annotation

Comparison with other active learning approaches

Figure 4 compares different active learning approaches to imbalanced sentiment classification when 600 unlabeled samples are selected for annotation. Specifically, the parameters θ and k is set to be 1/16 and 50 respectively. Figure 4 justifies that it is challenging to perform active learning in imbalanced sentiment classification: the approaches of **margin-based**, **uncertainty-based** and **self-selecting** perform no better than random selection while **co-testing** only outperforms random selection in two domains: DVD and Electronic with only a small improvement (about 1%). In comparison, our approaches, both **co-selecting-basic** and **co-selecting-plus** significantly outperform the random selection approach on all the four domains. It also shows that **co-selecting-plus** is preferable over **co-selecting-basic**. This verifies the effectiveness of automatically labeling those selected *MA* samples in imbalanced sentiment classification.

Specifically, we notice that only using the certainty measurement (i.e., **certainty**) performs worst, which reflects that only considering sample balance factor in imbalanced sentiment classification is not helpful.

Figure 5 compares our approach to other active learning approaches by varying the number of the selected samples for manually annotation. For clarity, we only include random selection and **co-testing** in comparison and do not show the performances of the other active learning approaches due to their similar behavior to random selection. From this figure, we can see that **co-testing** is effective on Book and Electronic when less than 1500 samples are selected for manual annotation but it fails to outperform random selection in the other two domains. In contract, our **co-selecting-plus** approach is apparently more advantageous and significantly outperforms random selection across all domains (p-value<0.05) when less than 4800 samples are selected for manual annotation.

Sensitiveness of the parameters θ

The size of the feature subspace is an important parameter in our approach. Figure 6 shows the performance of **co-selecting-plus** with varying sizes of the feature subspaces for the first subspace classifier C_{Cer}. From Figure 6, we can see that a choice of the proportion θ between 1/8 and 1/32 is recommended. This result also shows that the size of the feature subspace for selecting certain samples should be much less than that for selecting uncertain samples, which indicates the more important role of the uncertainty measurement in active learning.

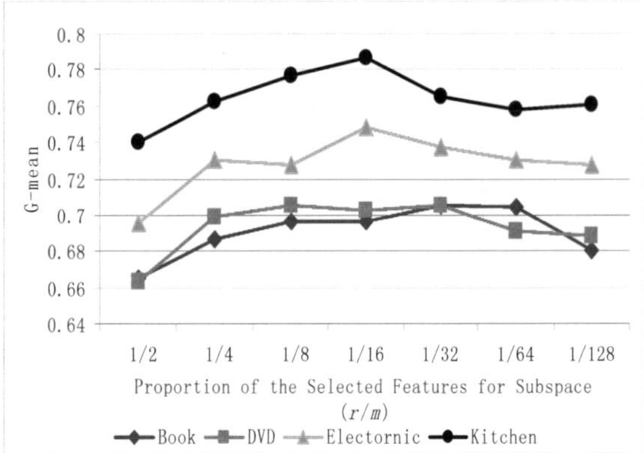

Figure 6: Performance of **co-selecting-plus** over varying sizes of feature subspaces (θ)

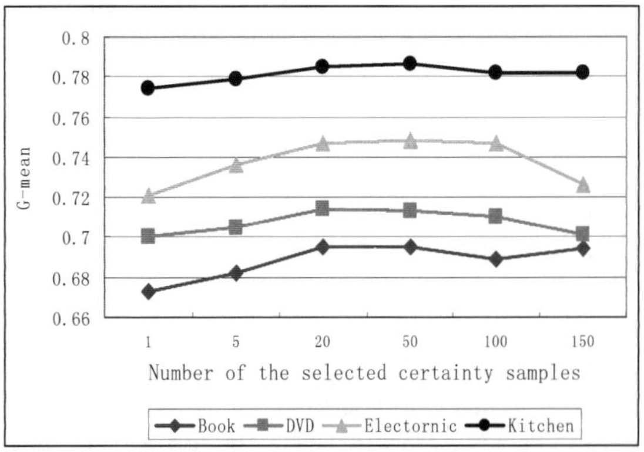

Figure 7: Performance of **co-selecting-plus** over varying numbers of the selected certain samples (k)

Sensitiveness of parameter *k*

Figure 7 presents the performance of **co-selecting-plus** with different numbers of the selected certain samples in each iteration, i.e., parameter k. Empirical studies suggest that setting k between 20 and 100 could get a stable performance. Also, this figure demonstrates that using certainty as the only query strategy is much less effective (see the result when k=1). This once again verifies the importance of the uncertainty strategy in active learning.

Number of *MI* samples selected for manual annotation

In Table 1, we investigate the number of the *MI* samples selected for manual annotation using different active learning approaches when a total of 600 unlabeled samples are selected for annotation. From this table, we can see that almost all the existing active learning approaches can only select a small amount of *MI* samples, taking similar imbalanced ratios as the whole unlabeled data. Although the **certainty** approach could select many *MI* samples for annotation, this approach performs worst due to its totally ignoring the uncertainty factor. When our approach is applied, especially **co-selecting-plus**, more *MI* samples are selected for manual annotation and finally included to learn the models. This greatly improves the effectiveness of our active learning approach.

Table 1: The number of *MI* samples selected for manual annotation when 600 samples are annotated on the whole.

	Book	DVD	Electronic	Kitchen
Random	71	82	131	123
SVM-based	65	72	135	106
Uncertainty	78	93	137	136
Certainty	160	200	236	227
Co-testing	89	84	136	109
Self-selecting	87	95	141	126
Co-selecting-basic	101	112	179	174
Co-selecting-plus	161	156	250	272

Precision of automatically labeled *MA* samples

In **co-selecting-plus**, all the added *MA* samples are automatically labeled by the first subspace classifier. It is encouraging to observe that 92.5%, 91.25%, 92%, and 93.5% of automatically labeled *MA* samples are correctly annotated in Book, DVD, Electronic, and Kitchen respectively. This suggests that the subspace classifiers are able to predict the *MA* samples with a high precision. This indicates the rationality of automatically annotating *MA* samples.

5 Conclusion

In this paper, we propose a novel active learning approach, named co-selecting, to reduce the annotation cost for imbalanced sentiment classification. It first trains two complementary classifiers with two disjoint feature subspaces and then uses them to collectively select most informative *MI* samples for manual annotation, leaving most informative *MA* samples for automatic annotation. Empirical studies show that our co-selecting approach is capable of greatly reducing the annotation cost and in the meanwhile, significantly outperforms several active learning alternatives

For the future work, we are interested in applying our co-selecting approach to active learning for other imbalanced classification tasks, especially those with much higher imbalanced ratio.

Acknowledgments

The research work described in this paper has been partially supported by three NSFC grants, No.61003155, No.60873150 and No.90920004, one National High-tech Research and Development Program of China No.2012AA011102, Open Projects Program of National Laboratory of Pattern Recognition, and the NSF grant of Zhejiang Province No.Z1110551. We also thank the three anonymous reviewers for their helpful comments.

References

Attenberg J. and F. Provost. 2010. Why Label when you can Search? Alternatives to Active Learning for Applying Human Resources to Build Classification Models Under Extreme Class Imbalance. In *Proceeding of KDD-10*, 423-432.

Blitzer J., M. Dredze and F. Pereira. 2007. Biographies, Bollywood, Boom-boxes and Blenders: Domain Adaptation for Sentiment Classification. In *Proceedings of ACL-07*, 440-447.

Cui H., V. Mittal, and M. Datar. 2006. Comparative Experiments on Sentiment Classification for Online Product Reviews. In *Proceedings of AAAI-06*, pp.1265-1270.

Doyle S., J. Monaco, M. Feldman, J. Tomaszewski and A. Madabhushi. 2011. An Active Learning based Classification Strategy for the Minority Class Problem: Application to Histopathology Annotation. *BMC Bioinformatics*, 12: 424, 1471-2105.

Ertekin S., J. Huang, L. Bottou and C. Giles. 2007a. Learning on the Border: Active Learning in Imbalanced Data Classification. In *Proceedings of CIKM-07*, 127-136.

Ertekin S., J. Huang, L. Bottou and C. Giles. 2007b. Active Learning in Class Imbalanced Problem. In *Proceedings of SIGIR-07*, 823-824.

Freund Y., H. Seung, E. Shamir and N. Tishby. 1997. Selective Sampling using the Query by Committee algorithm. *Machine Learning*, 28(2-3), 133-168.

He Y., C. Lin and H. Alani. 2011. Automatically Extracting Polarity-Bearing Topics for Cross-Domain Sentiment Classification. In *Proceeding of ACL-11*, 123-131.

Lewis D. and W. Gale. 1994. Training Text Classifiers by Uncertainty Sampling. In *Proceedings of SIGIR-94*, 3-12.

Li F., Y. Tang, M. Huang and X. Zhu. 2009. Answering Opinion Questions with Random Walks on Graphs. In *Proceedings of ACL-IJCNLP-09*, 737-745.

Li S. and C. Zong. 2008. Multi-domain Sentiment Classification. In *Proceedings of ACL-08*, short paper, pp.257-260.

Li S., C. Huang, G. Zhou and S. Lee. 2010. Employing Personal/Impersonal Views in Supervised and Semi-supervised Sentiment Classification. In *Proceedings of ACL-10*, pp.414-423.

Li S., Z. Wang, G. Zhou and S. Lee. 2011a. Semi-supervised Learning for Imbalanced Sentiment Classification. In *Proceeding of IJCAI-11*, 826-1831.

Li S., G. Zhou, Z. Wang, S. Lee and R. Wang. 2011b. Imbalanced Sentiment Classification. In *Proceedings of CIKM-11*, poster paper, 2469-2472.

Lloret E., A. Balahur, M. Palomar, and A. Montoyo. 2009. Towards Building a Competitive Opinion Summarization System. In *Proceedings of NAACL-09 Student Research Workshop and Doctoral Consortium*, 72-77.

Kubat M. and S. Matwin. 1997. Addressing the Curse of Imbalanced Training Sets: One-Sided Selection. In *Proceedings of ICML-97*, 179–186.

Muslea I., S. Minton and C. Knoblock . 2006. Active Learning with Multiple Views. *Journal of Artificial Intelligence Research*, vol.27, 203-233.

Pang B. and L. Lee. 2008. Opinion Mining and Sentiment Analysis: Foundations and Trends. *Information Retrieval*, vol.2(12), 1-135.

Pang B., L. Lee and S. Vaithyanathan. 2002.Thumbs up? Sentiment Classification using Machine Learning Techniques. In *Proceedings of EMNLP-02*, 79-86.

Settles B. 2009. Active Learning Literature Survey. *Computer Sciences Technical Report 1648*, University of Wisconsin, Madison, 2009.

Turney P. 2002. Thumbs up or Thumbs down? Semantic Orientation Applied to Unsupervised Classification of reviews. In *Proceedings of ACL-02*, 417-424.

Wan X. 2009. Co-Training for Cross-Lingual Sentiment Classification. In *Proceedings of ACL-IJCNLP-09*, 235–243.

Yang Y. and G. Ma. 2010. Ensemble-based Active Learning for Class Imbalance Problem. *J. Biomedical Science and Engineering,* vol.3,1021-1028.

Zhang M. and X. Ye. 2008. A Generation Model to Unify Topic Relevance and Lexicon-based Sentiment for Opinion Retrieval. In *Proceedings of SIGIR-08*, 411-418.

Zhu J. and E. Hovy. 2007. Active Learning for Word Sense Disambiguation with Methods for Addressing the Class Imbalance Problem. In *Proceedings of ACL-07*, 783-793.

A Weakly Supervised Model for Sentence-Level Semantic Orientation Analysis with Multiple Experts

Lizhen Qu and Rainer Gemulla and Gerhard Weikum
Max Planck Institute for Informatics
Saarbrücken, Germany
{lqu,rgemulla,weikum}@mpi-inf.mpg.de

Abstract

We propose the weakly supervised *Multi-Experts Model* (MEM) for analyzing the semantic orientation of opinions expressed in natural language reviews. In contrast to most prior work, MEM predicts both opinion polarity and opinion strength at the level of individual sentences; such fine-grained analysis helps to understand better why users like or dislike the entity under review. A key challenge in this setting is that it is hard to obtain sentence-level training data for both polarity and strength. For this reason, MEM is weakly supervised: It starts with potentially noisy indicators obtained from coarse-grained training data (i.e., document-level ratings), a small set of diverse base predictors, and, if available, small amounts of fine-grained training data. We integrate these noisy indicators into a unified probabilistic framework using ideas from ensemble learning and graph-based semi-supervised learning. Our experiments indicate that MEM outperforms state-of-the-art methods by a significant margin.

1 Introduction

Opinion mining is concerned with analyzing opinions expressed in natural language text. For example, many internet websites allow their users to provide both natural language reviews and numerical ratings to items of interest (such as products or movies). In this context, opinion mining aims to uncover the relationship between users and (features of) items. Preferences of users to items can be well understood by coarse-grained methods of opinion mining, which focus on analyzing the semantic orientation of documents as a whole. To understand *why* users like or dislike certain items, however, we need to perform more fine-grained analysis of the review text itself.

In this paper, we focus on sentence-level analysis of semantic orientation (SO) in online reviews. The SO consists of *polarity* (positive, negative, or other[1]) and *strength* (degree to which a sentence is positive or negative). Both quantities can be analyzed jointly by mapping them to numerical ratings: Large negative/positive ratings indicate a strong negative/positive orientation. A key challenge in fine-grained rating prediction is that fine-grained training data for both polarity and strength is hard to obtain. We thus focus on a weakly supervised setting in which only coarse-level training data (such as document ratings and subjectivity lexicons) and, optionally, a small amount of fine-grained training data (such as sentence polarities) is available.

A number of lexicon-based approaches for phrase-level rating prediction has been proposed in the literature (Taboada et al., 2011; Qu et al., 2010). These methods utilize a subjectivity lexicon of words along with information about their semantic orientation; they focus on phrases that contain words from the lexicon. A key advantage of sentence-level methods is that they are able to cover all sentences in a review and that phrase identification is avoided. To the best of our knowledge, the problem of rating prediction at the sentence level has not been addressed in the literature. A naive approach would be to simply average phrase-level ratings. Such an approach performs

[1] We assign polarity *other* to text fragments that are off-topic or not directly related to the entity under review.

poorly, however, since (1) phrases are analyzed out of context (e.g., modal verbs or conditional clauses), (2) domain-dependent information about semantic orientation is not captured in the lexicons, (3) only phrases that contain lexicon words are covered. Here (1) and (2) lead to low precision, (3) to low recall.

To address the challenges outlined above, we propose the weakly supervised *Multi-Experts Model* (MEM) for sentence-level rating prediction. MEM starts with a set of potentially noisy indicators of SO including phrase-level predictions, language heuristics, and co-occurrence counts. We refer to these indicators as *base predictors*; they constitute the set of experts used in our model. MEM is designed such that new base predictors can be easily integrated. Since the information provided by the base predictors can be contradicting, we use ideas from ensemble learning (Dietterichl, 2002) to learn the most confident indicators and to exploit domain-dependent information revealed by document ratings. Thus, instead of averaging base predictors, MEM integrates their features along with the available coarse-grained training data into a unified probabilistic model.

The integrated model can be regarded as a Gaussian process (GP) model (Rasmussen, 2004) with a novel *multi-expert prior*. The multi-expert prior decomposes into two component distributions. The first component distribution integrates sentence-local information obtained from the base predictors. It forms a special realization of stacking (Dzeroski and Zenko, 2004) but uses the features from the base predictors instead of the actual predictions. The second component distribution propagates SO information across similar sentences using techniques from graph-based semi-supervised learning (GSSL) (Zhu et al., 2003; Belkin et al., 2006). It aims to improve the predictions on sentences that are not covered well enough by our base predictors. Traditional GSSL algorithms support either discrete labels (classification) or numerical labels (regression); we extend these techniques to support both types of labels simultaneously. We use a novel variant of word sequence kernels (Cancedda et al., 2003) to measure sentence similarity. Our kernel takes the relative positions of words but also their SO and synonymity into account.

Our experiments indicate that MEM significantly outperforms prior work in both sentence-level rating prediction and sentence-level polarity classification.

2 Related Work

There exists a large body of work on analyzing the semantic orientation of natural language text. Our approach is unique in that it is weakly supervised, predicts both polarity and strength, and operates on the sentence level.

Supervised approaches for sentiment analysis focus mainly on opinion mining at the document level (Pang and Lee, 2004; Pang et al., 2002; Pang and Lee, 2005; Goldberg and Zhu, 2006), but have also been applied to sentence-level polarity classification in specific domains (Mao and Lebanon, 2006; Pang and Lee, 2004; McDonald et al., 2007). In these settings, a sufficient amount of training data is available. In contrast, we focus on opinion mining tasks with little or no fine-grained training data.

The weakly supervised HCRF model (Täckström and McDonald, 2011b; Täckström and McDonald, 2011a) for sentence-level polarity classification is perhaps closest to our work in spirit. Similar to MEM, HCRF uses coarse-grained training data and, when available, a small amount of fine-grained sentence polarities. In contrast to MEM, HCRF does not predict the strength of semantic orientation and ignores the order of words within sentences.

There exists a large number of lexicon-based methods for polarity classification (Ding et al., 2008; Choi and Cardie, 2009; Hu and Liu, 2004; Zhuang et al., 2006; Fu and Wang, 2010; Ku et al., 2008). The lexicon-based methods of (Taboada et al., 2011; Qu et al., 2010) also predict ratings at the phrase level; these methods are used as experts in our model.

MEM leverages ideas from ensemble learning (Dietterichl, 2002; Bishop, 2006) and GSSL methods (Zhu et al., 2003; Zhu and Ghahramani, 2002; Chapelle et al., 2006; Belkin et al., 2006). We extend GSSL with support for multiple, heterogenous labels. This allows us to integrate our base predictors as well as the available training data into a unified model that exploits that strengths of algorithms from both families.

3 Base Predictors

Each of our *base predictors* predicts the polarity or the rating of a single phrase. As indicated above, we do not use these predictions directly in MEM but instead integrate the features of the base predictors (see Sec. 4.4). MEM is designed such that new base predictors can be integrated easily.

Our base predictors use a diverse set of available web and linguistic resources. The hope is that this diversity increases overall prediction performance (Dietterichl, 2002): The *statistical polarity predictor* focuses on local syntactic patterns; it is based on corpus statistics for SO-carrying words and opinion topic words. The *heuristic polarity predictor* uses manually constructed rules to achieve high precision but low recall. Both the *bag-of-opinions rating predictor* and the *SO-CAL rating predictor* are based on lexicons. The BoO predictor uses a lexicon trained from a large generic-domain corpus and is recall-oriented; the SO-CAL predictor uses a different lexicon with manually assigned weights and is precision-oriented.

3.1 Statistical Polarity Predictor

The polarity of an SO-carrying word strongly depends on its target word. For example, consider the phrase "I began this novel with the *greatest* of *hopes* [...]". Here, "greatest" has a positive semantic orientation in all subjectivity lexicons, but the combination "greatest of hopes" often indicates a negative sentiment. We refer to a pair of SO-carrying word ("greatest") and a target word ("hopes") as an *opinion-target pair*. Our statistical polarity predictor learns the polarity of opinions and targets jointly, which increases the robustness of its predictions.

Syntactic dependency relations of the form $A \xrightarrow{R} B$ are a strong indicator for opinion-target pairs (Qiu et al., 2009; Zhuang et al., 2006); e.g., "great" $\xrightarrow{\text{nmod}}$ "product". To achieve high precision, we only consider pairs connected by the following predefined set of shortest dependency paths: verb $\xleftarrow{\text{subj}}$ noun, verb $\xleftarrow{\text{obj}}$ noun, adj $\xrightarrow{\text{nmod}}$ noun, adj $\xrightarrow{\text{prd}}$ verb $\xleftarrow{\text{subj}}$ noun. We only retain opinion-target pairs that are sufficiently frequent.

For each extracted pair z, we count how often it co-occurs with each document polarity $y \in \mathcal{Y}$, where $\mathcal{Y} = \{\textit{positive}, \textit{negative}, \textit{other}\}$ denotes the set of polarities. If z occurs in a document but is preceded by a negator, we treat it as a co-occurrence of opposite document polarity. If z occurs in a document with polarity *other*, we count the occurrence with only half weight, i.e., we increase both $\#z$ and $\#(\textit{other}, z)$ by 0.5. These documents are typically a mixture of positive and negative opinions so that we want to reduce their impact. The marginal distribution of polarity label y given that z occurs in a sentence is estimated as $P(y \mid z) = \#(y, z)/\#z$. The predictor is trained using the text and ratings of the reviews in the training data, i.e., without relying on fine-grained annotations.

The statistical polarity predictor can be used to predict sentence-level polarities by averaging the phrase-level predictions. As discussed previously, such an approach is problematic; we use it as a baseline approach in our experimental study. We also employ phrase-level averaging to estimate the variance of base predictors; see Sec. 4.3. Denote by $Z(\mathbf{x})$ the set of opinion-target pairs in sentence $\mathbf{x}$. To predict the sentence polarity $y \in \mathcal{Y}$, we take the Bayesian average of the phrase-level predictors: $P(y \mid Z(\mathbf{x})) = \sum_{z \in Z(\mathbf{x})} P(y \mid z) P(z) = \sum_{z \in Z(\mathbf{x})} P(y, z)$. Thus the most likely polarity is the one with the highest co-occurrence count.

3.2 Heuristic Polarity Predictor

Heuristic patterns can also serve as base predictors. In particular, we found that some authors list positive and negative aspects separately after keywords such as "pros" and "cons". A heuristic that exploits such patterns achieved a high precision ($> 90\%$) but low recall ($< 5\%$) in our experiments.

3.3 Bag-of-Opinions Rating Predictor

We leverage the bag-of-opinion (BoO) model of Qu et al. (2010) as a base predictor for phrase-level ratings. The BoO model was trained from a large generic corpus without fine-grained annotations.

In BoO, an opinion consists of three components: an SO-carrying word (e.g., "good"), a set of intensifiers (e.g., "very") and a set of negators (e.g., "not"). Each opinion is scored based on these words (represented as a boolean vector $\mathbf{b}$) and the polarity of the SO-carrying word (represented as $\text{sgn}(r) \in \{-1, 1\}$) as indicated by the MPQA lexicon of Wilson et al. (2005). In particular, the score is computed as $\text{sgn}(r)\boldsymbol{\omega}^{\text{T}}\mathbf{b}$, where $\boldsymbol{\omega}$ is the learned weight vector. The sign function $\text{sgn}(r)$ ensures consistent weight assignment for intensifiers and negators. For example, an intensifier like "very" can obtain a large positive or a large negative weight depending on whether it is used with a positive or negative SO-carrying word, respectively.

3.4 SO-CAL Rating Predictor

The Semantic Orientation Calculator (SO-CAL) of Taboada et al. (2011) also predicts phrase-level ratings via a scoring function similar to the one of BoO. The SO-CAL predictor uses a manually created lexicon, in which each word is classified as either an SO-carrying word (associated with a numerical score), an intensifier (associated with a modifier on the numerical score), or a negator. SO-CAL employs various heuristics to detect irrealis and to correct for the positive bias inherent in most lexicon-based classifiers. Compared to BoO, SO-CAL has lower recall but higher precision.

4 Multi-Experts Model

Our multi-experts model incorporates features from the individual base predictors, coarse-grained labels (i.e., document ratings or polarities), similarities between sentences, and optionally a small amount of sentence polarity labels into an unified probabilistic model. We first give an overview of MEM, and then describe its components in detail.

4.1 Model Overview

Denote by $\mathbf{X} = \{\mathbf{x}_1, \ldots, \mathbf{x}_N\}$ a set of sentences. We associate each sentence $\mathbf{x}_i$ with a set of *initial labels* $\hat{\mathbf{y}}_i$, which are strong indicators of semantic orientation: the coarse-grained rating of the corresponding document, the polarity label of our heuristic polarity predictor, the phrase-level ratings from the SO-CAL predictor, and optionally a manual polarity label. Note that the number of initial labels may vary from sentence to sentence and that initial labels are heterogeneous in that they refer to either polarities or ratings. Let $\hat{\mathbf{Y}} = \{\hat{\mathbf{y}}_1, \ldots, \hat{\mathbf{y}}_N\}$. Our goal is to predict the unobserved ratings $\mathbf{r} = \{r_1, \ldots, r_N\}$ of each sentence.

Our multi-expert model is a probabilistic model for $\mathbf{X}$, $\hat{\mathbf{Y}}$, and $\mathbf{r}$. In particular, we model the rating vector $\mathbf{r}$ via a multi-expert prior $P_{\mathrm{E}}(\mathbf{r} \mid \mathbf{X}, \boldsymbol{\beta})$ with parameter $\boldsymbol{\beta}$ (Sec. 4.2). P_{E} integrates both features from the base predictors and sentence similarities. We correlate ratings to initial labels via a set of conditional distributions $P_b(\hat{\mathbf{y}}^b \mid \mathbf{r})$, where b denotes the type of initial label (Sec. 4.3). The posterior of $\mathbf{r}$ is then given by

$$P(\mathbf{r} \mid \mathbf{X}, \hat{\mathbf{Y}}, \boldsymbol{\beta}) \propto \prod_b P_b(\hat{\mathbf{y}}^b \mid \mathbf{r}) P_{\mathrm{E}}(\mathbf{r} \mid \mathbf{X}, \boldsymbol{\beta}).$$

Note that the posterior is influenced by both the multi-expert prior and the set of initial labels.

We use MAP inference to obtain the most likely rating of each sentence, i.e., we solve

$$\operatorname*{argmin}_{\mathbf{r}, \boldsymbol{\beta}} - \sum_b \log(P_b(\hat{\mathbf{y}}^b \mid \mathbf{r})) - \log(P_{\mathrm{E}}(\mathbf{r} \mid \mathbf{X}, \boldsymbol{\beta})),$$

where as before $\boldsymbol{\beta}$ denotes the model parameters. We solve the above optimization problem using cyclic coordinate descent (Friedman et al., 2008).

4.2 Multi-Expert Prior

The multi-expert prior $P_{\mathrm{E}}(\mathbf{r} \mid \mathbf{X}, \boldsymbol{\beta})$ consists of two component distributions $\mathcal{N}_1$ and $\mathcal{N}_2$. Distribution $\mathcal{N}_1$ integrates features from the base predictors, $\mathcal{N}_2$ incorporates sentence similarities to propagate information across sentences.

In a slight abuse of notation, denote by $\mathbf{x}_i$ the set of features for the i-th sentence. Vector $\mathbf{x}_i$ contains the features of all the base predictors but also includes bigram features for increased coverage of syntactic patterns; see Sec. 4.4 for details about the feature design. Let $m(\mathbf{x}_i) = \boldsymbol{\beta}^{\mathrm{T}}\mathbf{x}_i$ be a linear predictor for r_i, where $\boldsymbol{\beta}$ is a real weight vector. Assuming Gaussian noise, r_i follows a Gaussian distribution $\mathcal{N}_1(r_i \mid m_i, \sigma^2)$ with mean $m_i = m(\mathbf{x}_i)$ and variance σ^2. Note that predictor m can be regarded as a linear combination of base predictors because both m and each of the base predictors are linear functions. By integrating all features into a single function, the base predictors are trained jointly so that weight vector $\boldsymbol{\beta}$ automatically adapts to domain-dependent properties of the data. This integrated approach significantly outperformed the alternative approach of using a weighted vote of the individual predictions made by the base predictors. We regularize the weight vector $\boldsymbol{\beta}$ using a Laplace prior $P(\boldsymbol{\beta} \mid \alpha)$ with parameter α to encourage sparsity.

Note that the bigram features in $\mathbf{x}_i$ partially capture sentence similarity. However, such features cannot be extended to longer subsequences such as trigrams due to data sparsity: useful features become as infrequent as noisy terms. Moreover, we would like to capture sentence similarity using gapped (i.e., non-consecutive) subsequences. For example, the sentences "The book is an easy read." and "It is easy to read." are similar but do not share any consecutive bigrams. They do share the subsequence "easy read", however. To capture this similarity, we make use of a novel sentiment-augmented variant of word sequence kernels (Cancedda et al., 2003). Our kernel is used to construct a similarity matrix $\mathbf{W}$ among sentences and the corresponding regularized Laplacian $\widetilde{\mathbf{L}}$. To capture the intuition that similar sentences should have similar ratings, we introduce a Gaussian prior $\mathcal{N}_2(\mathbf{r} \mid 0, \widetilde{\mathbf{L}}^{-1})$ as a component into our multi-expert prior; see Sec. 4.5 for details and a discussion of why this prior encourages similar ratings for similar sentences.

Since the two component distributions feature different expertise, we take their product and obtain the multi-expert prior

$$P_{\mathrm{E}}(\mathbf{r} \mid \mathbf{X}, \boldsymbol{\beta}) \propto \mathcal{N}_1(\mathbf{r} \mid \mathbf{m}, \mathbf{I}\sigma^2)\mathcal{N}_2(\mathbf{r} \mid 0, \widetilde{\mathbf{L}}^{-1})P(\boldsymbol{\beta} \mid \alpha),$$

where $\mathbf{m} = (m_1, \ldots, m_N)$. Note that the normalizing constant of P_{E} can be ignored during MAP inference since it does not depend on $\boldsymbol{\beta}$.

4.3 Incorporating Initial Labels

Recall that the initial labels $\hat{\mathbf{Y}}$ are strong indicators of semantic orientation associated with each sentence; they correspond to either discrete polarity labels or to continuous rating labels. This heterogeneity constitutes the main difficulty for incorporating the initial labels via the conditional distributions $P_b(\hat{\mathbf{y}}^b \mid \mathbf{r})$. We assume independence throughout so that $P_b(\hat{\mathbf{y}}^b \mid \mathbf{r}) = \prod_i P_b(\hat{y}_i^b \mid r_i)$.

Rating Labels For continuous labels, we assume Gaussian noise and set $P_b(\hat{y}_i^b \mid r_i) = \mathcal{N}(\hat{y}_i^b \mid r_i, \eta_i^b)$, where variance η_i^b is a type- and sentence-dependent.

For SO-CAL labels, we simply set $\eta_i^{\text{SO-CAL}} = \eta^{\text{SO-CAL}}$, where $\eta^{\text{SO-CAL}}$ is a hyperparameter. The SO-CAL scores have limited influence in our overall model; we found that more complex designs lead to little improvement. We proceed differently for document ratings. Our experiment suggests that document ratings constitute the most important indicator of the SO of a sentence. Thus sentence ratings should be close to document ratings unless strong evidence to the contrary exists. In other words, we want variance η_i^{Doc} to be small.

When no manually created sentence-level polarity labels are available, we set the value of η_i^{Doc} depending on the polarity class. In particular, we set $\eta_i^{\text{Doc}} = 1$ for both positive and negative documents, and $\eta_i^{\text{Doc}} = 2$ for neutral documents. The reasoning behind this choice is that sentence ratings in neutral documents express higher variance because these documents often contain a mixture of positive and negative sentences.

When a small set of manually created sentence polarity labels is available, we train a classifier that predicts whether the sentence polarity coincides with the document polarity. If so, we set the corresponding variance η_i^{Doc} to a small value; otherwise, we choose a larger value. In particular, we train a logistic regression classifier (Bishop, 2006) using the following binary features: (1) an indicator variable for each document polarity, and (2) an indicator variable for each triple of base predictor, predicted polarity, and document polarity (set to 1 if the polarities match). We then set $\eta_i^{\text{Doc}} = (\tau p_i)^{-1}$, where p_i is the probability of matching polarities obtained from the classifier and τ is a hyperparameter that ensures correct scaling.

Polarity Labels We now describe how to model the correlation between the polarity of a sentence and its rating. An simple and effective approach is to partition the range of ratings into three consecutive partitions, one for each polarity class. We thus considering the polarity classes {*positive*, *other*, *negative*} as ordered and formulate polarity classification as an ordinal regression problem (Chu and Ghahramani, 2006). We immediately obtain the distribution

$$\begin{aligned}
P_b(\hat{y}_i^b = \text{pos} \mid r_i) &= \Phi\left(\frac{r_i - b^+}{\sqrt{\eta^b}}\right) \\
P_b(\hat{y}_i^b = \text{oth} \mid r_i) &= \Phi\left(\frac{b^+ - r_i}{\sqrt{\eta^b}}\right) - \Phi\left(\frac{b^- - r_i}{\sqrt{\eta^b}}\right) \\
P_b(\hat{y}_i^b = \text{neg} \mid r_i) &= \Phi\left(\frac{b^- - r_i}{\sqrt{\eta^b}}\right),
\end{aligned}$$

where b^+ and b^- are the partition boundaries between *positive/other* and *other/negative*, respectively,[2] $\Phi(x)$ denotes the cumulative distribution function of the

[2] We set $b^+ = 0.3$ and $b^- = -0.3$ to calibrate to SO-CAL, which treats ratings in $[-0.3, 0, 3]$ as polarity *other*.

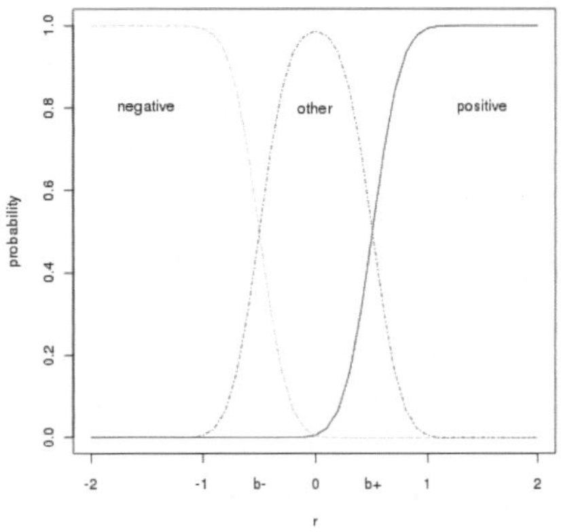

Figure 1: Distribution of polarity given rating.

Gaussian distribution, and variance η^b is a hyper-parameter. It is easy to verify that $\sum_{\hat{y}_i^b \in \mathcal{Y}} p(\hat{y}_i^b \mid r_i) = 1$. The resulting distribution is shown in Fig. 1. We can use the same distribution to use MEM for sentence-level polarity classification; in this case, we pick the polarity with the highest probability.

4.4 Incorporating Base Predictors

Base predictors are integrated into MEM via component $\mathcal{N}_1(r_i \mid m_i, \sigma^2)$ of the multi-expert prior (see Sec. 4.2). Recall that m_i is a linear function of the features $\mathbf{x}_i$ of each sentence. In this section, we discuss how $\mathbf{x}_i$ is constructed from the features of the base predictors. New base predictors can be integrated easily by exposing their features to MEM.

Most base predictors operate on the phrase level; our goal is to construct features for the entire sentence. Denote by n_i^b the number of phrases in the i-th sentence covered by base predictor b, and let $\mathbf{o}_{ij}^b$ denote a set of associated features. Features $\mathbf{o}_{ij}^b$ may or may not correspond directly to the features of base predictor b; see the discussion below. A straightforward strategy is to set $\mathbf{x}_i^b = (n_i^b)^{-1} \sum_j \mathbf{o}_{ij}^b$. We proceed slightly differently and average the features associated with phrases of positive prior polarity separately from those of phrases with negative prior polarity (Taboada et al., 2011). We then concatenate the averaged feature vectors, i.e., we set $\mathbf{x}_i^b = (\bar{\mathbf{o}}_{ij}^{b,pos} \ \bar{\mathbf{o}}_{ij}^{b,neg})$, where $\bar{\mathbf{o}}_{ij}^{b,p}$ denotes the average of the feature vectors $\mathbf{o}_{ij}^b$ associated with phrases of prior polarity p. This procedure allows us to learn a different weight for each feature depending on its context (e.g., the weight of intensifier "very" may differ for positive and negative phrases). We construct $\mathbf{x}_i$ by concatenating the sentence-level features $\mathbf{x}_i^b$ of each base predictor and a feature vector of bigrams.

To integrate a base predictor, we only need to specify the relevant features and, if applicable, prior phrase polarities. For our choice of base predictors, we use the following features:

SO-CAL predictor. The prior polarity of a SO-CAL phrase is given by the polarity of its SO-carrying word in the SO-CAL lexicon. The feature vector $\mathbf{o}_{ij}^{\text{SO-CAL}}$ consists of the weight of the SO-carrying word from the lexicon as well the set of negator words, irrealis marker words, and intensifier words in the phrase. Moreover, we add the first two words preceding the SO-carrying word as context features (skipping nouns, negators, irrealis markers, and intensifiers, and stopping at clause boundaries). All words are encoded as binary indicator features.

BoO predictor. Similar to SO-CAL, we determine the prior polarity of a phrase based on the BoO dictionary. In contrast to SO-CAL, we directly use the BoO score as a feature because the BoO predictor weights have been trained on a very large corpus and are thus reliable. We also add irrealis marker words in the form of indicator features.

Statistical polarity predictor. Recall that the statistical polarity predictor is based on co-occurrence counts of opinion-topic pairs and document polarities. We treat each opinion-topic pair as a phrase and use the most frequently co-occurring polarity as the phrase's prior polarity. We use the logarithm of the co-occurrence counts with positive, negative, and other polarity as features; this set of features performed better than using the co-occurrence counts or estimated class probabilities directly. We also add the same type of context features as for SO-CAL, but rescale each binary feature by the logarithm of the occurrence count $\#z$ of the opinion-topic pair (i.e., the features take values in $\{0, \log \#z\}$).

4.5 Incorporating Sentence Similarities

The component distribution $\mathcal{N}_2(\mathbf{r} \mid 0, \widetilde{\mathbf{L}}^{-1})$ in the multi-expert prior encourages similar sentences to have similar ratings. The main purpose of $\mathcal{N}_2$ is to propagate information from sentences on which the base predictors perform well to sentences for which base prediction is unreliable or unavailable (e.g., because they do not contain SO-carrying words). To obtain this distribution, we first construct an $N \times N$ sentence similarity matrix $\mathbf{W}$ using a sentiment-augmented word sequence kernel (see below). We then compute the regularized graph Laplacian $\widetilde{\mathbf{L}} = \mathbf{L} + \mathbf{I}/\lambda^2$ based on the unnormalized graph Laplacian $\mathbf{L} = \mathbf{D} - \mathbf{W}$ (Chapelle et al., 2006), where $\mathbf{D}$ be a diagonal matrix with $d_{ii} = \sum_j w_{ij}$ and hyperparameter λ^2 controls the scale of sentence ratings.

To gain insight into distribution $\mathcal{N}_2$, observe that

$$\mathcal{N}_2(\mathbf{r} \mid 0, \widetilde{\mathbf{L}}^{-1}) \propto \exp\Big(-\frac{1}{2}\sum_{i,j} w_{ij}(r_i - r_j)^2 - \|\mathbf{r}\|_2^2/\lambda^2\Big).$$

The left term in the exponent forces the ratings of similar sentences to be similar: the larger the sentence similarity w_{ij}, the more penalty is paid for dissimilar ratings. For this reason, $\mathcal{N}_2$ has a smoothing effect. The right term is an L2 regularizer and encourages small ratings; it is controlled by hyperparameter λ^2.

The entries w_{ij} in the sentence similarity matrix determine the degree of smoothing for each pair of sentence ratings. We compute these values by a novel sentiment-augmented word sequence kernel, which extends the well-known word sequence kernel of Cancedda et al. (2003) by (1) BoO weights to strengthen the correlation of sentence similarity and rating similarity and (2) synonym resolution based on WordNet (Miller, 1995).

In general, a word sequence kernel computes a similarity score of two sequences based on their shared subsequences. In more detail, we first define a score function for a pair of shared subsequences, and then sum up these scores to obtain the overall similarity score. Consider for example the two sentences "The book is an easy read." (s_1) and "It is easy to read." (s_2) along with the shared subsequence "is easy read" (u). Observe that the words "an" and "to" serve as gaps as they are not part of the subsequence. We represent subsequence u in sentence s via a real-valued projection function $\phi_u(s)$. In our example, $\phi_u(s_1) = v_{\text{is}} v^g_{\text{an}} v_{\text{easy}} v_{\text{read}}$ and $\phi_u(s_2) = v_{\text{is}} v_{\text{easy}} v^g_{\text{to}} v_{\text{read}}$. The decay factors $v_w \in (0, 1]$ for matching words characterize the importance of a word (large values for significant words). On the contrary, decay factors $v^g_w \in (0, 1]$ for gap words are penalty terms for mismatches (small values for significant words). The score of subsequence u is defined as $\phi_u(s_1)\phi_u(s_2)$. Thus two shared subsequences have high similarity if they share significant words and few gaps. Following Cancedda et al. (2003), we define the similarity between two sequences as

$$k_n(s_i, s_j) = \sum_{u \in \Omega^n} \phi_u(s_i)\phi_u(s_j),$$

where Ω is a finite set of words and n denotes the length of the considered subsequences. This similarity function can be computed efficiently using dynamic programming.

To apply the word sequence kernel, we need to specify the decay factors. A traditional choice is $v_w = \log(\frac{N}{N_w})/\log(N)$, where N_w is the document frequency of the word w and N is the total number of documents. This IDF decay factor is not well-suited to our setting: Important opinion words such as "great" have a low IDF value due to their high document frequency. To overcome this problem, we incorporate additional weights for SO-carrying words using the BoO lexicon. To do so, we first rescale the BoO weights into $[0, 1]$ using the sigmoid $g(w) = (1 + \exp(-a\omega_w + b))^{-1}$, where ω_w denotes the BoO weight of word w.[3] We then set $v_w = \min(\log(\frac{N}{N_w})/\log(N) + g(w), 0.9)$. The decay factor for gaps is given by $v^g_w = 1 - v_w$. Thus we strongly penalize gaps that consist of infrequent words or opinion words.

To address data sparsity, we incorporate synonyms and hypernyms from WordNet into our kernel. In particular, we represent words found in WordNet by their first two synset names (for verbs, adjectives, nouns) and their direct hypernym (nouns only). Two words are considered the same when their synsets overlap. Thus, for example, "writer" has the same representation as "author".

To build the similarity matrix $\mathbf{W}$, we construct a k-nearest-neighbor graph for all sentences.[4] We consider subsequences consisting of three words (i.e., $w_{ij} = k_3(s_i, s_j)$); longer subsequences are overly sparse, shorter subsequences are covered by the bigrams features in $\mathcal{N}_1$.

[3] We set $a = 2$ and $b = 1$ in our experiments.

[4] We use $k = 15$ and only consider neighbors with a similarity above 0.001.

5 Experiments

We evaluated both MEM and a number of alternative approaches for both sentence-level polarity classification and sentence-level strength prediction across a number of domains. We found that MEM outperforms state-of-the-art approaches by a significant margin.

5.1 Experimental Setup

We implemented MEM as well as the HCRF classifier of (Täckström and McDonald, 2011a; Täckström and McDonald, 2011b), which is the best-performing estimator of sentence-level polarity in the weakly-supervised setting reported in the literature. We train both methods using (1) only coarse labels (MEM-Coarse, HCRF-Coarse) and (2) additionally a small number of sentence polarities (MEM-Fine, HCRF-Fine[5]). We also implemented a number of baselines for both polarity classification and strength prediction: a document oracle (DocOracle) that simply uses the document label for each sentence, the BoO rating predictor (Base_{BoO}), and the SO-CAL rating predictor ($\text{Base}_{\text{SO-CAL}}$). For polarity classification, we compare our methods also to the statistical polarity predictor ($\text{Base}_{\text{polarity}}$). To judge on the effectiveness of our multi-export prior for combining base predictors, we take the majority vote of all base predictors and document polarity as an additional baseline (Majority-Vote). Similarly, for strength prediction, we take the arithmetic mean of the document rating and the phrase-level predictions of Base_{BoO} and $\text{Base}_{\text{SO-CAL}}$ as a baseline (Mean-Rating). We use the same hyperparameter setting for MEM across all our experiments.

We evaluated all methods on Amazon reviews from different domains using the corpus of Ding et al. (2008) and the test set of Täckström and McDonald (2011a). For each domain, we constructed a large balanced dataset by randomly sampling 33,000 reviews from the corpus of Ding et al. (2008). We chose the books, electronics, and music domains for our experiments; the dvd domain was used for development. For sentence polarity classification, we use the test set of Täckström and McDonald (2011a), which contains roughly 60 reviews per domain (20 for each polarity). For strength evaluation, we created a test set of 300 pairs of sentences per domain from the polarity test set. Each pair consisted of two sentences of the same polarity; we manually determined which of the sentences is more positive. We chose this pairwise approach because (1) we wanted the evaluation to be invariant to the scale of the predicted ratings, and (2) it much easier for human annotators to rank a pair of sentences than to rank a large collection of sentences.

We followed Täckström and McDonald (2011b) and used 3-fold cross-validation, where each fold consisted of a set of roughly 20 documents from the test set. In each fold, we merged the test set with the reviews from the corresponding domain. For MEM-Fine and HCRF-Fine, we use the data from the other two folds as fine-grained polarity annotations. For our experiments on polarity classification, we converted the predicted ratings of MEM, Base_{BoO}, and $\text{Base}_{\text{SO-CAL}}$ into polarities by the method described in Sec. 4.3. We compare the performance of each method in terms of accuracy, which is defined as the fraction of correct predictions on the test set (correct label for polarity / correct ranking for strength). All reported numbers are averages over the three folds. In our tables, boldface numbers are statistically significant against all other methods (t-test, p-value 0.05).

5.2 Results for Polarity Classification

Table 1 summarizes the results of our experiments for sentence polarity classification. The base predictors perform poorly across all domains, mainly due to the aforementioned problems associated with averaging phrase-level predictions. In fact, DocOracle performs almost always better than any of the base predictors. However, accurracy increases when we combine base predictors and DocOracle using majority voting, which indicates that ensemble methods work well.

When no fine-grained annotations are available (HCRF-Coarse, MEM-Coarse), both MEM-Coarse and Majority-Vote outperformed HCRF-Coarse, which in turn has been shown to outperform a number of lexicon-based methods as well as classifiers trained on document labels (Täckström and McDonald, 2011a). MEM-Coarse also performs better than Majority-Vote. This is because MEM propagates

[5]We used the best-performing model that fuses HCRF-Coarse and the supervised model (McDonald et al., 2007) by interpolation.

	Book	Electronics	Music	Avg
$\text{Base}_{\text{polarity}}$	43.7	40.3	43.8	42.6
Base_{BoO}	50.9	48.9	52.6	50.8
$\text{Base}_{\text{SO-CAL}}$	44.6	50.2	45.0	46.6
DocOracle	51.9	49.6	59.3	53.6
Majority-Vote	53.7	53.4	58.7	55.2
HCRF-Coarse	52.2	53.4	57.2	54.3
MEM-Coarse	54.4	54.9	**64.5**	57.9
HCRF-Fine	55.9	**61.0**	58.7	58.5
MEM-Fine	**59.7**	59.6	63.8	**61.0**

Table 1: Accuracy of polarity classification per domain and averaged across domains.

	Book		Electronics		Music	
	op	fact	op	fact	op	fact
HCRF-Fine	55.7	55.9	**63.3**	54.6	59.0	57.4
MEM-Fine	**58.9**	**62.4**	60.7	**56.7**	**64.5**	**60.8**

Table 2: Accuracy of polarity classification for sentences with opinion words (op) and without opinion words (fact).

evidence across similar sentences, which is especially useful when no explicit SO-carrying words exist. Also, MEM learns weights of features of base predictors, which leads to a more adaptive integration, and our ordinal regression formulation for polarity prediction allows direct competition among positive and negative evidence for improved accuracy.

When we incorporate a small amount of sentence polarity labels (HCRF-Fine, MEM-Fine), the accuracy of all models greatly improves. HCRF-Fine has been shown to outperform the strongest supervised method on the same dataset (McDonald et al., 2007; Täckström and McDonald, 2011b). MEM-Fine falls short of HCRF-Fine only in the electronics domain but performs better on all other domains. In the book and music domains, where MEM-Fine is particularly effective, many sentences feature complex syntactic structure and SO-carrying words are often used without reference to the quality of the product (but to describe contents, e.g., "a love story" or "a horrible accident").

Our models perform especially well when they are applied to sentences containing no or few opinion words from lexicons. Table 2 reports the evaluation results for both sentences containing SO-carrying words from either MPQA or SO-CAL lexicons and for sentences containing no such words. The results explain why our model falls short of HCRF-Fine in the electronics domain: reviews of electronic products contain many SO-carrying words, which almost always express opinions. Nevertheless, MEM-Fine handles sentences without explicit SO-carrying words well across all domains; here the propagation of information across sentences helps to learn the SO of facts (such as "short battery life").

We found that for all methods, most of the errors are caused by misclassifying positive/negative sentences as *other* and vice versa. Moreover, sentences with polarity opposite to the document polarity are hard cases if they do not feature frequent strong patterns. Another difficulty lies in off-topic sentences, which may contain explicit SO-carrying words but are not related to the item under review. This is one of the main reasons for the poor performance of the lexicon-based methods.

Overall, we found that MEM-Fine is the method of choice. Thus our multi-expert model can indeed balance the strength of the individual experts to obtain better estimation accuracy.

5.3 Results for Strength Prediction

Table 3 shows the accuracy results for strength prediction. Here our models outperformed all baselines by a large margin. Although document ratings are strong indicators in the polarity classification task, they lead to worse performance than lexicon-based methods. The main reason for this drop in accuracy is that the document oracle assigns the same rating to all sentences within a review. Thus DocOracle cannot rank sentences from the same review, which is a severe limitation. This shortage can be partly compensated by averaging the base predictions and document rating (Mean-Rating). Note that it is non-trivial to apply existing ensemble methods for the weights of individual base predictors because of the absence of the sentence ratings as training labels. In contrast, our MEM models use indirect supervision to adaptively assign weights to the features from base predictors. Similar to polarity classification, a small amount of sentence polarity labels often improved the performance of MEM.

	Book	Electronics	Music	Avg
Base_{BoO}	58.3	51.6	53.5	54.5
$\text{Base}_{\text{SO-CAL}}$	60.6	57.1	47.6	55.1
DocOracle	45.1	36.2	41.4	40.9
Mean-Rating	70.3	57.0	60.8	62.7
MEM-Coarse	68.7	60.5	**69.5**	66.2
MEM-Fine	**72.4**	**63.3**	67.2	**67.6**

Table 3: Accuracy of strength prediction.

6 Conclusion

We proposed the Multi-Experts Model for analyzing both opinion polarity and opinion strength at the sentence level. MEM is weakly supervised; it can run without any fine-grained annotations but is also able to leverage such annotations when available. MEM is driven by a novel multi-expert prior, which integrates a number of diverse base predictors and propagates information across sentences using a sentiment-augmented word sequence kernel. Our experiments indicate that MEM achieves better overall accuracy than alternative methods.

References

Mikhail Belkin, Partha Niyogi, and Vikas Sindhwani. 2006. Manifold regularization: A geometric framework for learning from labeled and unlabeled examples. *The Journal of Machine Learning Research*, 7:2399–2434.

Christopher M. Bishop. 2006. *Pattern recognition and machine learning*, volume 4. Springer New York.

Nicola Cancedda, Éric Gaussier, Cyril Goutte, and Jean-Michel Renders. 2003. Word-sequence kernels. *Journal of Machine Learning Research*, 3:1059–1082.

Oliver Chapelle, Bernhard Schölkopf, and Alexander Zien. 2006. *Semi-Supervised Learning*. MIT Press.

Yejin Choi and Claire Cardie. 2009. Adapting a polarity lexicon using integer linear programming for domain-specific sentiment classification. In *Proceedings of the Conference on Empirical Methods in Natural Language Processing*, volume 2, pages 590–598.

Wei Chu and Zoubin Ghahramani. 2006. Gaussian processes for ordinal regression. *Journal of Machine Learning Research*, 6(1):1019.

Thomas G. Dietterichl. 2002. Ensemble learning. *The Handbook of Brain Theory and Neural Networks*, pages 405–408.

Xiaowen Ding, Bing Liu, and Philip S. Yu. 2008. A holistic lexicon-based approach to opinion mining. In *Proceedings of the International Conference on Web Search and Data Mining*, pages 231–240.

Saso Dzeroski and Bernard Zenko. 2004. Is combining classifiers with stacking better than selecting the best one? *Machine Learning*, 54(3):255–273.

Jerome H. Friedman, Trevor Hastie, and Rob Tibshirani. 2008. Regularization paths for generalized linear models via coordinate descent. Technical report.

Guohong Fu and Xin Wang. 2010. Chinese sentence-level sentiment classification based on fuzzy sets. In *Proceedings of the International Conference on Computational Linguistics*, pages 312–319. Association for Computational Linguistics.

Andrew B. Goldberg and Xiaojun Zhu. 2006. Seeing stars when there aren't many stars: Graph-based semi-supervised learning for sentiment categorization. In *HLT-NAACL 2006 Workshop on Textgraphs: Graph-based Algorithms for Natural Language Processing*.

Minqing Hu and Bing Liu. 2004. Mining and summarizing customer reviews. In *Proceedings of the ACM SIGKDD Conference on Knowledge Discovery and Data Mining*, pages 168–177.

Lun-Wei Ku, I-Chien Liu, Chia-Ying Lee, Kuan hua Chen, and Hsin-Hsi Chen. 2008. Sentence-level opinion analysis by copeopi in ntcir-7. In *Proceedings of NTCIR-7 Workshop Meeting*.

Yi Mao and Guy Lebanon. 2006. Isotonic Conditional Random Fields and Local Sentiment Flow. *Advances in Neural Information Processing Systems*, pages 961–968.

Ryan T. McDonald, Kerry Hannan, Tyler Neylon, Mike Wells, and Jeffrey C. Reynar. 2007. Structured models for fine-to-coarse sentiment analysis. In *Proceedings of the Annual Meeting on Association for Computational Linguistics*, volume 45, page 432.

George A. Miller. 1995. WordNet: a lexical database for English. *Communications of the ACM*, 38(11):39–41.

Bo Pang and Lillian Lee. 2004. A sentimental education: Sentiment analysis using subjectivity summarization based on minimum cuts. In *Proceedings of the Annual Meeting on Association for Computational Linguistics*, pages 271–278.

Bo Pang and Lillian Lee. 2005. Seeing stars: Exploiting class relationships for sentiment categorization with respect to rating scales. In *Proceedings of the Annual Meeting of the Association for Computational Linguistics*, pages 124–131.

Bo Pang, Lillian Lee, and Shivakumar Vaithyanathan. 2002. Thumbs up?: sentiment classification using machine learning techniques. In *Proceedings of the Conference on Empirical Methods in Natural Language Processing*, pages 79–86.

Guang Qiu, Bing Liu, Jiajun Bu, and Chun Chen. 2009. Expanding Domain Sentiment Lexicon through Double Propagation. In *International Joint Conference on Artificial Intelligence*, pages 1199–1204.

Lizhen Qu, Georgiana Ifrim, and Gerhard Weikum. 2010. The bag-of-opinions method for review rating prediction from sparse text patterns. In *Proceedings of the International Conference on Computational Linguistics*, pages 913–921.

Carl Edward Rasmussen. 2004. *Gaussian processes in machine learning*. Springer.

Maite Taboada, Julian Brooke, Milan Tofiloski, Kimberly D. Voll, and Manfred Stede. 2011. Lexicon-based methods for sentiment analysis. *Computational Linguistics*, 37(2):267–307.

Oscar Täckström and Ryan T. McDonald. 2011a. Discovering Fine-Grained Sentiment with Latent Variable Structured Prediction Models. In *Proceedings of the European Conference on Information Retrieval*, pages 368–374.

Oscar Täckström and Ryan T. McDonald. 2011b. Semi-supervised latent variable models for sentence-level sentiment analysis. *In Proceedings of the Annual Meeting of the Association for Computational Linguistics*, pages 569–574.

Theresa Wilson, Janyce Wiebe, and Paul Hoffmann. 2005. Recognizing contextual polarity in phrase-level sentiment analysis. In *Proceedings of the Human Language Technology Conference and the Conference on Empirical Methods in Natural Language Processing*, pages 347–354.

Xiaojin Zhu and Zoubin Ghahramani. 2002. Learning from labeled and unlabeled data with label propagation. Technical report.

Xiaojin Zhu, Zoubin Ghahramani, and John Lafferty. 2003. Semi-supervised learning using Gaussian fields and harmonic functions. In *Proceedings of the International Conference on Machine Learning*, pages 912–919.

Li Zhuang, Feng Jing, and Xiaoyan Zhu. 2006. Movie review mining and summarization. In *Proceedings of the ACM international conference on Information and knowledge management*, pages 43–50.

Collocation Polarity Disambiguation Using Web-based Pseudo Contexts

Yanyan Zhao, Bing Qin and Ting Liu*
Harbin Institute of Technology, Harbin, China
{yyzhao, bqin, tliu}@ir.hit.edu.cn

Abstract

This paper focuses on the task of collocation polarity disambiguation. The *collocation* refers to a binary tuple of a polarity word and a target (such as ⟨long, battery life⟩ or ⟨long, startup⟩), in which the sentiment orientation of the polarity word ("long") changes along with different targets ("battery life" or "startup"). To disambiguate a collocation's polarity, previous work always turned to investigate the polarities of its surrounding contexts, and then assigned the majority polarity to the collocation. However, these contexts are limited, thus the resulting polarity is insufficient to be reliable. We therefore propose an unsupervised three-component framework to expand some pseudo contexts from web, to help disambiguate a collocation's polarity.Without using any additional labeled data, experiments show that our method is effective.

1 Introduction

In recent years, more attention has been paid to sentiment analysis as it has been widely used in various natural language processing applications, such as question answering (Wiebe et al., 2003; Yu and Hatzivassiloglou, 2003), information extraction (Riloff et al., 2005) and opinion-oriented summarization (Hu and Liu, 2004; Liu et al., 2005). Meanwhile, it also brings us lots of interesting and challenging research topics, such as subjectivity analysis (Riloff and Wiebe, 2003), sentiment classification (Pang et al., 2002; Kim and Hovy, 2005; Wilson et al., 2009; He et al., 2011), opinion retrieval (Zhang et al., 2007; Zhang and Ye, 2008; Li et al., 2010) and so on.

One fundamental task for sentiment analysis is to determine the semantic orientations of words. For example, the word "beautiful" is positive, while "ugly" is negative. Many researchers have developed several algorithms for this purpose and generated large *static* lexicons of words marked with prior polarities (Hatzivassiloglou and McKeown, 1997; Turney et al., 2003; Esuli, 2008; Mohammad et al., 2009; Velikovich et al., 2010). However, there exist some polarity-ambiguous words, which can *dynamically* reflect different polarities along with different contexts. A typical polarity-ambiguous word "长" ("long" in English) is shown with two example sentences as follows.

1. 该相机的[电池寿命]^{t}很[长]^p。(Positive)

   Translated as: The [battery life]^t of this camera is [long]^p. (Positive)

2. 该相机的[启动时间]^{t}很[长]^p。(Negative)

   Translated as: This camera has [long]^p [startup]^t. (Negative)

The phrases marked with *p* superscript are the polarity-ambiguous words, and the phrases marked with *t* superscript are targets modified by the polarity words. In the above two sentences, the sentiment orientation of the polarity word "长" ("long" in English) changes along with different targets. When modifying the target "电池寿命" ("battery life" in English), its polarity is positive; and when modifying "启动时间" ("startup" in English), its polarity is

*Correspondence author: tliu@ir.hit.edu.cn

negative. In this paper, *we especially **define** the **collocation** as a binary tuple of the polarity-ambiguous word and its modified target*, such as ⟨长,电池寿命⟩ (⟨long, battery life⟩ in English) or ⟨长,启动时间⟩ (⟨long, startup⟩ in English). This paper concentrates on the task of **collocation polarity disambiguation**.

This is an important task as the problem of polarity-ambiguity is frequent. We analyze 4,861 common binary tuples of polarity words and their modified targets from 478 reviews[1], and find that over 20% of them are the collocations defined in this paper. Therefore, the task of collocation polarity disambiguation is worthy of study.

For a sentence s containing such a collocation c, since the in-sentence features are always ambiguous, it is difficult to disambiguate the polarity of c by using them. Thus some previous work turned to investigate its surrounding contexts' polarities (such as the sentences before or after s), and then assigned the majority polarity to the collocation c (Hatzivassiloglou and McKeown, 1997; Hu and Liu, 2004; Kanayama and Nasukawa, 2006). However, since the amount of contexts from the original review is very limited, the final resulting polarity for the collocation c is insufficient to be reliable.

Fortunately, most collocations may appear multiple times, in different forms, both within the same review and within topically-related reviews. Thus for a collocation, we can collect large amounts of contexts from other reviews to improve its polarity disambiguation. These expanded contexts are called ***pseudo contexts*** in this paper. Some previous work used the similar methods. For example, Ding (Ding et al., 2008) expanded some pseudo contexts from a topically-related review set. But since the review set is limited, the expanded contexts are still limited and unreliable. In order to overcome this problem, we propose an unsupervised three-component framework to expand more pseudo contexts from web for the collocation polarity disambiguation.

Without using any labeled data, experiments on a Chinese data set from four product domains show that the three-component framework is feasible and the web-based pseudo contexts are useful for the collocation polarity disambiguation. Compared to other previous work, our method achieves an *F1* score of 72.02%, which is about 15% higher.

The remainder of this paper is organized as follows. Section 2 introduces the related work. Section 3 shows the proposed approach including three independent components. Section 4 and 5 presents the experiments and results. Finally we conclude this paper in Section 6.

2 Related Work

The key of the collocation polarity disambiguation task is to recognize the polarity word's sentiment orientation of a collocation. There are basically two types of approaches for word polarity recognition: corpus-based and dictionary-based approaches. Corpus-based approaches find co-occurrence patterns of words in the large corpora to determine the word sentiments, such as the work in (Hatzivassiloglou and McKeown, 1997; Wiebe, 2000; Riloff and Wiebe, 2003; Turney et al., 2003; Kaji and Kitsuregawa, 2007; Velikovich et al., 2010). On the other hand, dictionary-based approaches use synonyms and antonyms in WordNet to determine word sentiments based on a set of seed polarity words. Such approaches are studied in (Kim and Hovy, 2006; Esuli and Sebastiani, 2005; Kamps et al., 2004). Overall, most of the above approaches aim to generate a large *static* polarity word lexicon marked with prior polarities.

However, it is not sensible to predict a word's sentiment orientation without considering its context. In fact, even in the same domain, a word may indicate different polarities depending on what targets it is applied to, especially for the polarity-ambiguous words, such as "长" ("long" in English) shown in Section 1. Based on these, we need to consider both the polarity words and their modified targets, i.e., the collocations mentioned in this paper, rather than only the polarity words.

To date, the task in this paper is similar with much previous work. Some researchers exploited the features of the sentences containing collocations to help disambiguate the polarity of the polarity-ambiguous word. For example, Hatzivassiloglou (Hatzivassiloglou and McKeown, 1997) and Kanayama (Kanayama and Nasukawa, 2006) used conjunction rules to solve this problem from large domain corpora. Suzuki (Suzuki et al., 2006)

[1]The dataset will be introduced in Section 4.1 in detail.

took into account many contextual information of the word within the sentence, such as exclamation words, emoticons and so on. However, the experimental results show that these in-sentence features are not rich enough.

Instead of considering the current sentence alone, some researchers exploited external information and evidences in other sentences or other reviews to infer the collocation's polarity. For a collocation, Hu (Hu and Liu, 2004) analyzed its surrounding sentences' polarities to disambiguate its polarity. Ding (Ding et al., 2008) proposed a holistic lexicon-based approach of using global information to solve this problem. However, the contexts or evidences from these two methods are limited and unreliable. Except for the above unsupervised methods, some researchers (Wilson et al., 2005; Wilson et al., 2009) proposed supervised methods for this task, which need large annotated corpora.

In addition, many related works tried to learn word polarity in a specific domain, but ignored the problem that even the same word in the same domain may indicate different polarities (Jijkoun et al., 2010; Bollegala et al., 2011). And some work (Lu et al., 2011) combined difference sources of information, especially the lexicons and heuristic rules for this task, but ignored the important role of the context. Besides, there exists some research focusing on word sense subjectivity disambiguation, which aims to classify a word sense into subjective or objective (Wiebe and Mihalcea, 2006; Su and Markert, 2009). Obviously, this task is different from ours.

3 The Proposed Approach

3.1 Overview

The motivation of our approach is to make full use of web sources to collect more useful pseudo contexts for a collocation, whose original contexts are limited or unreliable. The framework of our approach is illustrated in Figure 1.

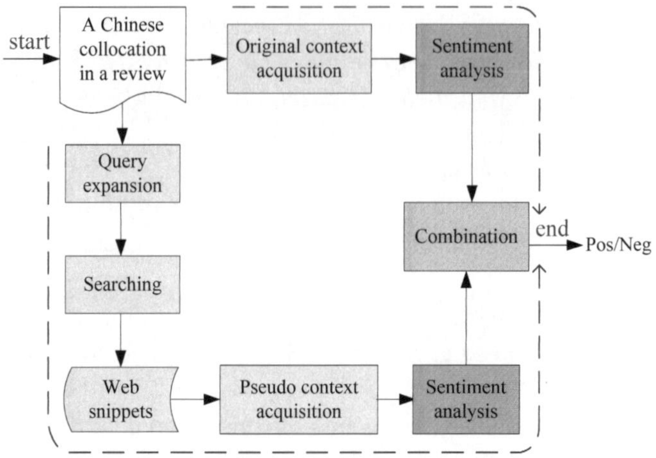

Figure 1: The framework of our approach.

In order to disambiguate a collocation's polarity, three components are carried out:

1. Query Expansion and Pseudo Context Acquisition: This paper uses the collocation as query. For a collocation, three heuristic query expansion strategies are used to generate more flexible queries, which have the same or completely opposite polarity with this collocation. Searching these queries in the domain-related websites, lots of snippets can be acquired. Then we can extract the pseudo contexts from these snippets.

2. Sentiment Analysis: For both original contexts and the expanded pseudo contexts from web, a simple lexicon-based sentiment computing method is used to recognize each context's polarity.

3. Combination: Two strategies are designed to integrate the polarities of the original and pseudo contexts, under the assumption that these two kinds of contexts can be complementary to each other.

It is worth noting that this three-component framework is flexible and we can try to design different strategies for each component. Next sections will give a simple example strategy for each component to show its feasibility and effectiveness.

3.2 Query Expansion and Pseudo Context Acquisition

3.2.1 Why Expanding Queries

For a collocation, such as ⟨长,电池寿命⟩ (⟨long, battery life⟩ in English), the most intuitive query used for searching is constructed by the form of "target + polarity word", i.e., 电池寿命长 (battery life long in English). Even if we search this query alone, a great many web snippets covering the polarity word and target will be retrieved. But why do we still need to expand the queries?

In fact, for a collocation, though the amount of the retrieved snippets is large, lots of them cannot provide accurate pseudo contexts. The reason is that the polarity words in some snippets do not really modify the targets, such as in the sentence "The *battery life* is short, and finds few buyers for a *long* time." There exist no modifying relation between "*battery life*" and "*long*".

In order to filter these meaningless snippets, we can simply search with a new query "电池寿命长" by ***surrounding it with quotes*** (noted as **Strategy0**). However, this can drastically decline the amount of snippets. In addition, as the new query is short, in many retrieved snippets, there also exist no modifying relations between the polarity words and targets. As a result, if we just use this query strategy, the expanded pseudo contexts are limited and cannot yield ideal performance.

Therefore, we need to design some effective query expansion strategies to ensure that (1) the polarity words do modify the targets in the retrieved web snippets, and (2) the snippets are more enough.

3.2.2 Query Expansion Strategy

We first investigate the modifying relations between polarity words and the targets, and then construct effective queries.

Observed from previous work (Bloom et al., 2007; Kobayashi et al., 2004; Popescu and Etzioni, 2005), there are two kinds of common relations between the polarity words and their targets. One is the "subject-copula-predicate" relation, such as the relationship between "long" and "battery life" in the sentence "The *battery life* of this camera is *long*". The other is the "attribute-head" relation, such as the relationship between them in the sentence "This camera has *long battery life*".

As a result, three heuristic query expansion strategies are adopted to construct efficient queries for searching. Take the collocation ⟨长,电池寿命⟩ (⟨long, battery life⟩ in English) as an example, the strategies are described as follows.

Strategy1: target + *modifier* + polarity word: Such as the query "电池寿命很长" or "电池寿命非常长" ("the battery life is *very* long" in English). Different from Strategy0, this strategy adds a *modifier* element. It refers to the words that are used to change the degree of a polarity word, such as "很" or "非常" ("very" in English). Due to the usage of the modifiers, the queries from this strategy can satisfy the "subject-copula-predicate" relation.

Strategy2: *modifier* + polarity word + 的+ target: Such as the query "很长的电池寿命" or "非常长的电池寿命" ("*very* long battery life" in English). This strategy also uses *modifiers* to modify polarity words, and the generated queries can satisfy the "attribute-head" relation.

Strategy3: *negation word* + polarity word + 的+ target: Such as the query "不长的电池寿命" or "没有长的电池寿命" ("*not* long battery life" in English). This strategy uses *negation words* to modify the polarity words. And the queries from this strategy can satisfy the "attribute-head" relation. The only difference is that the polarity of this kind of queries is opposite to that of the collocation.

Similar to the queries from Strategy0, the queries generated by Strategy1∼3 are all searched with quotes. In addition, note that the *modifier* and the *negation word* are taken from *Modifier Lexicon* and *Negation Lexicon* introduced in Table 2.

3.2.3 Pseudo Context Acquisition

For each query from Strategy0∼3, we search it in some websites to acquire the related snippets. If we directly search it using Google without site restrictions, it does return all the snippets containing the query, but lots of them are non-reviews. Further, the pseudo contexts generated by these non-reviews are useless or even harmful. To overcome this problem, the ***advanced search*** of Google is used to search the query within the *forum sites* of the product domain. We can flexibly choose several popular forum sites for each domain. The URLs of the forum sites used in this paper are listed in Table 1.

Formally, given a collocation c, the expanded pseudo contexts *Conx(c)* can be obtained using the following function:

$$\begin{aligned} Conx(c) &= \textstyle\bigcup_{i=0}^{3} f(Query_i) \\ &= \textstyle\bigcup_{i=0}^{3} \bigcup_{j=1}^{n} f(query_{ij}) \end{aligned} \quad (1)$$

Here, $Query_i$ is the query set generated by the ith query expansion strategy; $query_{ij}$ is the jth query generated by the ith strategy. And the parameter n is the total number of queries from the ith query expansion strategy. From this function, we can collect the contexts of c by summing up all the pseudo contexts from every $query_{ij}$.

Domain	URL
Camera	http://www.qqdc.com.cn
	http://forums.nphoto.net
	http://dc.pconline.com.cn
	http://photobbs.it168.com
	http://club.tech.sina.com.cn/dc
Car	http://bbs.chetx.com
	http://bbs.pcauto.com.cn
	http://club.autohome.com.cn
	http://bbs.cheshi.com
	http://www.xcar.com.cn
	http://www.autohome.com.cn
Notebook	http://benyouhui.it168.com/index.php
	http://nbbbs.zol.com.cn
	http://www.ibijiben.com
	http://notebook.pconline.com.cn
	http://nbbbs.enet.com.cn
Phone	http://bbs.imobile.com.cn
	http://sjbbs.zol.com.cn
	http://bbs.shouji.com.cn
	http://bbs.cnmo.com
	http://forum.younet.com

Table 1: The URLs used in context expansion for different domains.

Algorithm: Pseudo Context Expansion Algorithm

Input: A collocation *c* and the URL list
Output: The pseudo context set *Conx*(*c*)

1. Use Strategy0~3 to expand *c* and the expanded queries are saved as a set *Query*(*c*).
2. For any query $q \in$ Query(*c*), acquire its pseudo contexts *Conx*(*q*) as follows:
   (1) search *q* in the domain-related URL list, the top 100 retrieved snippets for each URL are collected as *Snip*(*q*)
   (2) for each snippet $sp \in Snip(q)$
   - find the sentence *s* containing *q*
   - obtain the two sentences before and after *s* as the contexts of *q* in this *sp*, noted as *Conx*(*q, sp*)

   $$Conx(q) = \bigcup_{sp \in Snip(q)} Conx(q, sp)$$
3. $Conx(c) = \bigcup_{q \in Query(c)} Conx(q) = \bigcup_{q \in Query(c)} \bigcup_{sp \in Snip(q)} Conx(q, sp)$

Figure 2: The algorithm for pseudo context acquisition.

Lexicon	Content
Modifier Lexicon	很, 比较, 非常, 十分, 太, 特, 特别, 挺, 相当, 格外, 分外 ("very" or "quite" in English)
Negation Lexicon	没有, 不, 不是 ("no" or "not" in English)
Positive Lexicon	There are 3,730 Chinese words are collected from HOWNET[1]
Negative Lexicon	There are 3,116 Chinese words are collected from HOWNET.

[1] http://www.keenage.com/html/e_index.html.

Table 2: The lexicons used in this paper.

In detail, the pseudo context acquisition algorithm for a collocation *c* is illustrated in Figure 2. Note that, the original context acquisition of *c* can be considered as a simplified version of the pseudo context acquisition. That's because the current review containing *c* can be considered as only one snippet in pseudo context acquisition. Thus, we can just carry out the two steps in (2) of Figure 2 to obtain the original contexts.

Analyzing either the pseudo contexts or the original contexts, we can find that not all of them are useful contexts. Thus we will simply filter the noisy ones by context sentiment computation, and choose the contexts showing sentiment orientations as the useful contexts.

3.3 Sentiment Analysis

For both the original and expanded pseudo contexts, we employ the lexicon-based sentiment computing method (Hu and Liu, 2004) to compute the polarity value for each context. This unsupervised approach is quite straightforward and makes use of the sentiment lexicons in Table 2.

The polarity value *Polarity*(*con*) for a context *con* is computed by summing up the polarity values of all words in *con*, making use of both the word polarity defined in the positive and negative lexicons and the contextual shifters defined in the negation lexicon. The algorithm is illustrated in Figure 3.

In this algorithm, *n* is the parameter controlling the window size within which the negation words have influence on the polarity words, and here *n* is set to 3.

Normally, if the polarity value *Polarity*(*con*) is more than 0, the context *con* is labeled as positive; if less than 0, the context is negative. We also consider the transitional words, such as "但是" ("but" in English). Finally, the contexts with positive/negative polarities are used as the useful contexts.

Domain	# of reviews	# of c (All)	# of single c (Sig)	Sig / All (%)	# of multiple c / kinds of multiple c
Camera	138	295	183	62.03	112 / 35
Car	161	232	131	56.47	101 / 33
Notebook	56	147	94	63.95	53 / 20
Phone	123	327	192	58.72	135 / 35
Total	478	1001	600	59.94	401 / 123 $\approx$ 3.3

Table 3: Statistics for the Chinese collocation corpus.

Algorithm: Sentiment Analysis

Input: a context *con*, and three lexicons: *Positive_Dic*, *Negative_Dic*, *Negation_Dic*
Output: Polarity value *Polarity(con)*
1. Segment *con* into word set *W(con)*
2. For each word $w \in W(con)$, compute its polarity value *Polarity(w)* as follows:
   (1) if $w \in$ *Positive_Dic*, *Polarity(w)* = 1;
   (2) if $w \in$ *Negative_Dic*, *Polarity(w)* = -1;
   (3) otherwise, *Polarity(w)* = 0;
   (4) Within the window of *n* words previous to *w*, if there is a word $w' \in$ *Negation_Dic*, *Polarity(w)* = -*Polarity(w)*
3. $Polarity(con) = \sum_{w \in W(con)} Polarity(w)$

Figure 3: The algorithm for context polarity computation.

3.4 Combination

After the pseudo context acquisition and polarity computation, two kinds of effective contexts: *original contexts* and *pseudo contexts*, and their corresponding polarities can be obtained.

In order to yield a relatively accurate polarity *Polarity(c)* for a collocation *c*, we exploit the following combination methods:

1. **Majority Voting**: Rather than considering the difference between the two kinds of contexts, this combination method relies on the polarity tag of each context. Suppose *c* has *n* effective contexts (including original and pseudo contexts), it can obtain *n* polarity tags based on the individual sentiment analysis algorithm. The polarity tag receiving more votes is chosen as the final polarity of *c*.

2. **Complementation**: For a collocation *c*, we first employ "Majority Voting" method just on the expanded pseudo contexts to obtain the polarity tag. If the polarity of *c* cannot be recognized[2], the majority polarity tag voted on the original contexts is chosen as the final polarity tag.

4 Experimental Setup

4.1 Dataset and Evaluation Metrics

We conduct the experiments on a Chinese collocation corpus of four product domains, which is from the Task3 of the Chinese Opinion Analysis Evaluation (COAE)[3] (Zhao et al., 2008). Table 3 describes the corpus in detail.

From 478 reviews, 1,001 collocations (454 positive and 547 negative) with polarity-ambiguous words are found and manually annotated by two annotators. Cohen's kappa (Cohen, 1960), a measure of inter-annotator agreement ranging from zero to one, is 0.83, indicating a good strength of agreement [4]. In Table 3, *Sig* of the fourth column denotes the collocations that appear once in all the domain-related reviews. And *multiple* in the last column denotes the collocations that appear several times. From Table 3, we can find that among all the reviews, nearly 60% collocations only appear once. Even for the *multiple* collocations, they averagely appear less than 4 times. Therefore, for a collocation, if we only consider its original contexts alone or the expanded pseudo contexts from the domain-related review set alone, the contexts are obviously limited and unreliable.

Instead of using accuracy, we use precision (*P*), recall (*R*) and F-measure (*F1*) to measure the performance of this task. That's because two kinds of collocations' polarities cannot be disambiguated. One

[2]The reason will be explained in the last paragraph of Section 4.1.
[3]http://www.ir-china.org.cn/coae2008.html
[4]A small number of collocations are still difficult to be disambiguated from contexts.

is the sparse collocations, which obtain no effective contexts. The other is the collocations that acquire the same amount of positive and negative contexts. The metrics are defined as follows.

$$P = \frac{correctly\ disambiguated\ collocations}{disambiguated\ collocations} \quad (2)$$

$$R = \frac{correctly\ disambiguated\ collocations}{all\ collocations} \quad (3)$$

$$F1 = \frac{2PR}{P+R} \quad (4)$$

4.2 System Description

In order to compare our method with previous work, we build several systems as follows:

$NoExp$: Following the method proposed by Hu (Hu and Liu, 2004), without using the expanded pseudo contexts, we only consider the two original contexts Sen_{bef} and Sen_{aft} of a collocation *c* in the current review. **If** Sen_{bef} expresses the polarity *polar*, then $Polarity(ac) = polar$. **Else if** Sen_{aft} expresses the polarity $polar'$, then $Polarity(ac) = polar'$. **Else**, this method cannot disambiguate the polarity of *c*. In this method, the transitional words, such as "但是" ("but" in English) are considered.

$Exp_{dataset}$: Following the method proposed by Ding (Ding et al., 2008), we solve this task with the help of the pseudo contexts in the domain-related review dataset. For a collocation *c* appearing in many domain-related reviews, this method refers to the polarities of the same *c* in other reviews. The majority polarity is chosen as final polarity.

$Exp_{web+sig}$: This method is the same as our method in this paper, except for (1) not combining the original contexts, and (2) not using all the three query expansion strategies, but just using the *single* (abbv. *sig*) Strategy0. This method expands the pseudo contexts from the *web*. The majority polarity is chosen as the final polarity.

$Exp_{web+exp}$: This method is the same as our proposed method in this paper, except for not combining the original contexts. It expands the pseudo contexts from the *web*. And the "*exp*" in the subscript means that this method uses all the query expansion strategies. The majority polarity of all the pseudo contexts is chosen as the final polarity.

$Exp^{mv/c}_{web+exp+com}$: This is the method proposed in this paper, which combines the original and expanded pseudo contexts. The superscript "*mv/c*" is short for the two combination methods: **M**ajority **V**oting and **C**omplementation.

5 Results

5.1 Comparisons among All the Systems

In fact, all the systems shown in Section 4.2 can be considered as *context* based methods. The essential difference among them lies in the contexts they used. For a collocation, the contexts for $NoExp$ are two original contexts from the current review. Breaking down the boundary of the current review, $Exp_{dataset}$ explores the pseudo contexts from other domain-related reviews. Further, $Exp_{web+sig}$, $Exp_{web+exp}$ and $Exp^{mv/c}_{web+exp+com}$ expand the pseudo contexts from web, which can be considered as a large corpus and can provide more evidences for the collocation polarity disambiguation.

System	*P*(%)	*R*(%)	*F1*(%)
$NoExp$	67.32	41.16	51.08
$Exp_{dataset}$	68.14	47.85	56.22
$Exp_{web+sig}$	70.00	53.85	60.87
$Exp_{web+exp}$	74.97	63.14	68.55
$Exp^{mv}_{web+exp+com}$	75.53	67.83	71.47
$Exp^{c}_{web+exp+com}$	74.36	69.83	72.02

Table 4: Comparative results for the collocation polarity disambiguation task.

Table 4 illustrates the comparative results of all systems for collocation polarity disambiguation. It can be observed that our system $Exp^{mv}_{web+exp+com}$ and $Exp^{c}_{web+exp+com}$ outperform all the other systems. We discuss the experimental results as follows:

$NoExp$ yields the worst performance, especially on the recall. The reason is that the original contexts used in this system are limited, and some of them are even noisy. In comparison, $Exp_{dataset}$ adds a post-processing step of expanding pseudo contexts from the topically-related review dataset, which achieves a better result with an absolute improvement of 5.14% (*F1*). This suggests that the contexts expanded from other reviews are helpful in disambiguating the collocation's polarity.

However, $Exp_{dataset}$ is just effective in disambiguating the polarity of such a collocation c, which appears many times in the domain-related reviews. From Table 3, we can notice that this kind of collocations only accounts for 40% in all the collocations, and further they appear less than 4 times on average. Thus, for such a collocation c, the pseudo contexts expanded from other reviews that contain the same c are still far from enough, since the review set size in this system is not very large.

In order to avoid the context limitation problem, we expand more pseudo contexts from web for each collocation. We first try to use a simple query form (Strategy0) for web mining. Table 4 illustrates that the corresponding system $Exp_{web+sig}$ outperforms the system $Exp_{dataset}$. It can demonstrate that our web mining based pseudo context expansion is useful for disambiguating the collocation's polarity, since this system can explore more contexts. However, we can find that the performance is not very ideal. This system can generate some harmful contexts for the reason of the wrong modifying relations between polarity words and targets in the retrieved snippets.

Thus this paper adds three query expansion strategies to generate more and accurate pseudo contexts. Table 4 shows that the corresponding system $Exp_{web+exp}$ can achieve a better result with *F1* = 68.55%, which is significantly (χ^2 test with $p < 0.01$) outperforms $Exp_{web+sig}$. It demonstrates that the query expansion strategies are useful.

Finally, Table 4 gives the results of our method in this paper, $Exp^{mv}_{web+exp+com}$ and $Exp^{c}_{web+exp+com}$, which combines the original and expanded pseudo contexts to yield a final polarity. We can observe that both of these systems outperform the system $NoExp$ of just using the original contexts and the system $Exp_{web+exp}$ of just using the expanded pseudo contexts. This can illustrate that the two kinds of contexts are complementary to each other. In addition, we can also find that the two combination methods produce similar results. In detail, $Exp^{mv}_{web+exp+com}$ disambiguates 899 collocations, 679 of them are correct; $Exp^{c}_{web+exp+com}$ disambiguates 940 collocations, 699 of them are correct.

We can further find that, although the amount of original contexts is small, it also plays an important role in disambiguating the polarities of the collocations that cannot be recognized by the expanded pseudo contexts.

5.2 The Contributions of the Query Expansion Strategies

The expanded pseudo contexts from our method can be partly credited to the query expansion strategies. Based on this, this section aims to analyze the different contributions of the query expansion strategies in our method.

Strategy	P(%)	R(%)	F1(%)	Avg(#)
Strategy0	70.00	53.85	60.87	71
Strategy1	74.14	55.84	63.70	112
Strategy2	61.84	37.56	46.74	26
Strategy3	64.34	33.17	43.77	20
$Exp_{web+exp}$	74.97	63.14	**68.55**	229

Table 5: The performance of our method based on each query expansion strategy for collocation polarity disambiguation.

Table 5 provides the performance of our method based on each query expansion strategy for collocation polarity disambiguation. For each strategy, "*Avg*" in Table 5 denotes the average number of the expanded pseudo contexts for each collocation. From this table, we can find that the larger the "*Avg*" is, the better (*F1*) the strategy is. In detail, Strategy1 with the largest "*Avg*" has the best performance; and Strategy3 with the fewest "*Avg*" has the worst performance. This can further demonstrate our idea that more and effective pseudo contexts can improve the performance of the collocation polarity disambiguation task. $Exp_{web+exp}$ integrates all the query expansion strategies and obtains much more "*Avg*". Therefore, this can significantly increase the recall value, and further produce a better result. On the other hand, the results in Table 5 show that these heuristic query expansion strategies are effective.

5.3 Deep Experiments in the Three-Component Framework

In order to do a detailed analysis into our three-component framework, some deep experiments are made:

Query Expansion The aim of query expansion is to retrieve lots of relative snippets, from which we can extract the useful pseudo contexts. For each

	Strategy0 (%)	Strategy1 (%)	Strategy2 (%)	Strategy3 (%)
Query Expansion	76.75	94.50	85.50	85.25
Pseudo Context	71.25	73.50	67.50	74.50
Sentiment Analysis	63.00	68.25	59.00	69.75

Table 6: The accuracies of the query expansion, pseudo context and sentiment analysis for each strategy.

snippet, if the polarity word of the collocation does modify the target, we consider this snippet as a correct query expansion result.

Pseudo Context For each expanded pseudo context from web, if it shows the same sentiment orientation with the collocation (or opposite with the collocation's polarity because of the usage of transitional words), we consider this context as a correct pseudo context.

Sentiment Analysis For each expanded pseudo context, if its polarity can be correctly recognized by the polarity computation method in Figure 3, and meanwhile it shows the same sentiment orientation with the collocation, we consider this context as a correct one.

Table 6 illustrates the accuracy of each experiment for each strategy in detail, where 400 web retrieved snippets for *Query Expansion* and 400 expanded pseudo contexts for *Pseudo Context* and *Sentiment Analysis* are randomly selected and manually evaluated for each strategy.

Seen from Table 6, we can find that:

1. For *Query Expansion*, all strategies yield good accuracies except for Strategy0. This can draw a same conclusion with our analysis in Section 3.2.1. The queries from Strategy0 are short, thus in many retrieved snippets, there exist no modifying relations between the polarity words and targets. Accordingly, the pseudo contexts from these snippets are incorrect. This can result in the low accuracy of Strategy0. On the other hand, we can find that the other three query expansion strategies perform well.

2. Although the final result of our three-component framework is good, the accuracies of *Pseudo Context* and *Sentiment Analysis* for each strategy is not very high. This is perhaps caused by unrefined work on the specific sub-stages. For example, we get all the pseudo contexts using the algorithm in Figure 2. However, in some reviews, the two sentences before and after the target sentence have no polarity relation with the target sentence itself. This can bring in some noises. On the other hand, the context polarity computation algorithm in Figure 3 is just a simple attempt, which is not the best way to compute the context's polarity.

In fact, this paper aims to try some simple algorithms for each component to validate the effectiveness of the three-component framework. We will polish every component of our framework in future.

6 Conclusion and Future Work

This paper proposes a web-based context expansion framework for collocation polarity disambiguation. The basic assumption of this framework is that, if a collocation appears in different forms, both within the same review and within topically-related reviews, then the large amounts of pseudo contexts from these reviews can help to disambiguate such a collocation's polarity. Based on this assumption, this framework includes three independent components. First, the heuristic query expansion strategies are adopted to expand pseudo contexts from web; then a simple but effective polarity computation method is used to recognize the polarities for both the original contexts and the expanded pseudo contexts; and finally, we integrate the polarities from the original and pseudo contexts as the collocation's polarity. Without using any additional labeled data, experiments on a Chinese data set from four product domains show that the proposed framework outperforms other previous work.

This paper can be concluded as follows:

1. A framework including three independent components is proposed for collocation polarity disambiguation. We can try other different algorithms for each component.

2. Web-based pseudo contexts are effective for disambiguating a collocation's polarity.

3. The query expansion strategies are promising, which can generate more useful and correct contexts.

4. The initial contexts from current reviews and the expanded contexts from web are complementary to each other.

The immediate extension of our work is to polish each component of this framework, such as improving the accuracy of query expansion and pseudo context acquisition, using other effective polarity computing methods for each context and so on. In addition, we will explore other query expansion strategies to generate more effective contexts.

Acknowledgments

We thank the anonymous reviewers for their helpful comments. This work was supported by National Natural Science Foundation of China (NSFC) via grant 61133012, the National "863" Leading Technology Research Project via grant 2012AA011102, the Ministry of Education Research of Social Sciences Youth funded projects via grant 12YJCZH304 and the Fundamental Research Funds for the Central Universities via grant No.HIT.NSRIF.2013090.

References

Kenneth Bloom, Navendu Garg, and Shlomo Argamon. 2007. Extracting appraisal expressions. In *HLT-NAACL 2007*, pages 308–315.

D. Bollegala, D. Weir, and J. Carroll. 2011. Using multiple sources to construct a sentiment sensitive thesaurus for cross-domain sentiment classification. In *Proceedings of the 49th Annual Meeting of the Association for Computational Linguistics: Human Language Technologies-Volume 1*, pages 132–141. Association for Computational Linguistics.

Jacob Cohen. 1960. A coefficient of agreement for nominal scales. *Educational and Psychological Measurement*, 20(1):37 - 46.

Xiaowen Ding, Bing Liu, and Philip S. Yu. 2008. A holistic lexicon-based approach to opinion mining. In *Proceedings of the Conference on Web Search and Web Data Mining (WSDM)*, pages 231–240.

A. Esuli and F. Sebastiani. 2005. Determining the semantic orientation of terms through gloss analysis. In *Proceedings of the ACM SIGIR Conference on Information and Knowledge Management (CIKM)*, pages 617–624.

A. Esuli. 2008. Automatic generation of lexical resources for opinion mining: models, algorithms and applications. In *ACM SIGIR Forum*, volume 42, pages 105–106. ACM.

V. Hatzivassiloglou and K.R. McKeown. 1997. Predicting the semantic orientation of adjectives. In *Proceedings of the eighth conference on European chapter of the Association for Computational Linguistics*, pages 174–181. Association for Computational Linguistics.

Yulan He, Chenghua Lin, and Harith Alani. 2011. Automatically extracting polarity-bearing topics for cross-domain sentiment classification. In *Proceedings of the 49th Annual Meeting of the Association for Computational Linguistics: Human Language Technologies*, pages 123–131, Portland, Oregon, USA, June. Association for Computational Linguistics.

M. Hu and B. Liu. 2004. Mining and summarizing customer reviews. In *Proceedings of the tenth ACM SIGKDD international conference on Knowledge discovery and data mining*, pages 168–177. ACM.

V. Jijkoun, M. De Rijke, and W. Weerkamp. 2010. Generating focused topic-specific sentiment lexicons. In *Proceedings of the 48th Annual Meeting of the Association for Computational Linguistics*, pages 585–594. Association for Computational Linguistics.

N. Kaji and M. Kitsuregawa. 2007. Building lexicon for sentiment analysis from massive collection of html documents. In *Proceedings of the Joint Conference on Empirical Methods in Natural Language Processing and Computational Natural Language Learning (EMNLP-CoNLL)*, pages 1075–1083.

Jaap Kamps, Maarten Marx, R. ort. Mokken, and Maarten de Rijke. 2004. Using wordnet to measure semantic orientation of adjectives. In *Proceedings of LREC-2004*, pages 1115–1118.

H. Kanayama and T. Nasukawa. 2006. Fully automatic lexicon expansion for domain-oriented sentiment analysis. In *Proceedings of the 2006 Conference on Empirical Methods in Natural Language Processing*, pages 355–363. Association for Computational Linguistics.

Soo-Min Kim and Eduard Hovy. 2005. Automatic detection of opinion bearing words and sentences. In *Proceedings of IJCNLP-2005*, pages 61–66.

S.-M. Kim and E. Hovy. 2006. Identifying and analyzing judgment opinions. In *Proceedings of the Joint Human Language Technology/North American Chapter of the ACL Conference (HLT-NAACL)*, pages 200–207.

Nozomi Kobayashi, Kentaro Inui, Yuji Matsumoto, Kenji Tateishi, and Toshikazu Fukushima. 2004. Collecting evaluative expressions for opinion extraction. In *Proceedings of the International Joint Conference on Natural Language Processing (IJCNLP)*, pages 584–589.

Binyang Li, Lanjun Zhou, Shi Feng, and Kam-Fai Wong. 2010. A unified graph model for sentence-based opinion retrieval. In *Proceedings of the 48th Annual Meeting of the Association for Computational Linguistics*, page 1367 - 1375.

Bing Liu, Minqing Hu, and Junsheng Cheng. 2005. Opinion observer: analyzing and comparing opinions on the web. In *Proceedings of WWW-2005*, pages 342–351.

Y. Lu, M. Castellanos, U. Dayal, and C.X. Zhai. 2011. Automatic construction of a context-aware sentiment lexicon: an optimization approach. In *Proceedings of the 20th international conference on World wide web*, pages 347–356. ACM.

S. Mohammad, C. Dunne, and B. Dorr. 2009. Generating high-coverage semantic orientation lexicons from overtly marked words and a thesaurus. In *Proceedings of the 2009 Conference on Empirical Methods in Natural Language Processing: Volume 2-Volume 2*, pages 599–608. Association for Computational Linguistics.

Bo Pang, Lillian Lee, and Shivakumar Vaithyanathan. 2002. Thumbs up? sentiment classification using machine learning techniques. In *Proceedings of EMNLP-2002*, pages 79–86.

Ana-Maria Popescu and Oren Etzioni. 2005. Extracting product features and opinions from reviews. In *hltemnlp2005*, pages 339–346.

Ellen Riloff and Janyce Wiebe. 2003. Learning extraction patterns for subjective expressions. In *Proceedings of EMNLP-2003*, pages 105–112.

Ellen Riloff, Janyce Wiebe, and William Phillips. 2005. Exploiting subjectivity classification to improve information extraction. In *Proceedings of AAAI-2005*, pages 1106–1111.

Fangzhong Su and Katja Markert. 2009. Subjectivity recognition on word senses via semi-supervised mincuts. In *Human Language Technologies: The 2009 Annual Conference of the North American Chapter of the ACL*, pages 1–9.

Yasuhiro Suzuki, Hiroya Takamura, and Manabu Okumura. 2006. Application of semi-supervised learning to evaluative expression classification. In *Computational Linguistics and Intelligent Text Processing*, pages 502–513.

P. Turney, M.L. Littman, et al. 2003. Measuring praise and criticism: Inference of semantic orientation from association. *ACM Transactions on Information Systems (TOIS)*, 21(4):315–346.

Leonid Velikovich, Sasha Blair-Goldensohn, Kerry Hannan, and Ryan McDonald. 2010. The viability of web-derived polarity lexicons. In *The 2010 Annual Conference of the North American Chapter of the Association for Computational Linguistics*, pages 777–785.

Jan Wiebe and Rada Mihalcea. 2006. Word sense and subjectivity. In *Proceedings of the Conference on Computational Linguistics / Association for Computational Linguistics (COLING/ACL)*, pages 1065–1072.

Janyce Wiebe, Eric Breck, and Chris Buckley. 2003. Recognizing and Organizing Opinions Expressed in the World Press. In *Papers from the AAAI Spring Symposium on New Directions in Question Answering*, pages 24–26.

Janyce Wiebe. 2000. Learning subjective adjectives from corpora. In *Proceedings of AAAI*, pages 735–740.

Theresa Wilson, Janyce Wiebe, and Paul Hoffmann. 2005. Recognizing contextual polarity in phrase-level sentiment analysis. In *Proceedings of HLT/EMNLP-2005*, pages 347–354.

Theresa Wilson, Janyce Wiebe, and Paul Hoffmann. 2009. Recognizing contextual polarity: an exploration of features for phrase-level sentiment analysis. *Computational Linguistics*, 35(3).

Hong Yu and Vasileios Hatzivassiloglou. 2003. Towards answering opinion questions: separating facts from opinions and identifying the polarity of opinion sentences. In *Proceedings of EMNLP-2003*, pages 129–136.

Min Zhang and Xingyao Ye. 2008. A generation model to unify topic relevance and lexicon-based sentiment for opinion retrieval. In *Proceedings of the ACM Special Interest Group on Information Retrieval (SIGIR)*, pages 411–419.

Wei Zhang, Clement Yu, and Weiyi Meng. 2007. Opinion retrieval from blogs. In *In proceedings of CIKM*, page 831 - 840.

Jun Zhao, Hongbo Xu, Xuanjing Huang, Songbo Tan, Kang Liu, and Qi Zhang. 2008. Overview of chinese opinion analysis evaluation 2008.

Aligning Predicates across Monolingual Comparable Texts using Graph-based Clustering

Michael Roth and **Anette Frank**
Department of Computational Linguistics
Heidelberg University
Germany
{mroth,frank}@cl.uni-heidelberg.de

Abstract

Generating coherent discourse is an important aspect in natural language generation. Our aim is to learn factors that constitute coherent discourse from data, with a focus on how to realize predicate-argument structures in a model that exceeds the sentence level. We present an important subtask for this overall goal, in which we align predicates across comparable texts, admitting partial argument structure correspondence. The contribution of this work is two-fold: We first construct a large corpus resource of comparable texts, including an evaluation set with manual predicate alignments. Secondly, we present a novel approach for aligning predicates across comparable texts using graph-based clustering with Mincuts. Our method significantly outperforms other alignment techniques when applied to this novel alignment task, by a margin of at least 6.5 percentage points in F_1-score.

1 Introduction

Discourse coherence is an important aspect in natural language generation (NLG) applications. A number of theories have investigated coherence inducing factors. A prominent example is *Centering Theory* (Grosz et al., 1995), which models local coherence by relating the choice of referring expressions to the importance of an entity at a certain stage of a discourse. A data-driven model based on this theory is the *entity-based approach* by Barzilay and Lapata (2008), which models coherence phenomena by observing sentence-to-sentence transitions of entity occurrences.

Barzilay and Lapata show that their approach can discriminate between a coherent and a non-coherent set of ordered sentences. However, their model is not able to generate alternative entity realizations by itself. Furthermore, the entity-based approach only investigates realization patterns for individual entities in discourse in terms of core grammatical functions. It does not investigate the interplay between entity transitions and realization patterns for full-fledged semantic structures. This interplay, however, is an important factor for a semantics-based, generative model of discourse coherence.

The main hypothesis of our work is that we can automatically learn context-specific realization patterns for predicate argument structures (PAS) from a semantically parsed corpus of comparable text pairs. Our assumption builds on the success of previous research, where comparable and parallel texts have been exploited for a range of related learning tasks, e.g., unsupervised discourse segmentation (Barzilay and Lee, 2004) and bootstrapping semantic analyzers (Titov and Kozhevnikov, 2010).

For our purposes, we are interested in finding corresponding PAS across comparable texts that are known to talk about the same events, and hence involve the same set of underlying event participants. By aligning predicates in such texts, we can investigate the factors that determine discourse coherence in the realization patterns for the involved arguments. These include the specific forms of argument realization, as a pronoun or a specific type of referential expression, as studied in prior work in NLG (Belz et al., 2009, inter alia). The specific set-up we examine, however, allows us to further investigate the factors that govern the *non-realization* of an argument position, as a special form of coherence inducing element in discourse. Example (1), extracted from our corpus of aligned texts,illustrates this point: Both texts report on the same event of locating victims in an avalanche. While (1.a) explicitly talks about the location of this event, the role remains implicit in the second sentence of (1.b), given that it can be recovered from the preceding sentence. In fact, realization of this argument role would impede the fluency of discourse by being overly repetitive.

(1) a. ...The official said that [no bodies]$_{\text{Arg1}}$ had been recovered [from the avalanches]$_{\text{Arg2}}$ which occurred late Friday in the Central Asian country near the Afghan border some 300 kilometers (185 miles) southeast of the capital Dushanbe.

b. Three other victims were trapped *in an avalanche* in the village of Khichikh. [None of the victims bodies]$_{\text{Arg1}}$ have been found [ ]$_{\text{Argm-loc}}$.

This phenomenon clearly relates to the problem of discourse-linking of implicit roles, a very challenging task in discourse processing.[1] In our work, we consider this problem from a content-based generation perspective, concentrating on the discourse factors that allow for the omission of a role.

Thus, our aim is to identify comparable predications across aligned texts, and to study the discourse coherence factors that determine the realization patterns of arguments in the respective discourses. This can be achieved by considering the full set of arguments that can be recovered from the aligned predications. This paper focuses on the first of these tasks, henceforth called *predicate alignment*.[2]

In line with data-driven approaches in NLP, we automatically align predicates in a suitable corpus of paired texts. The induced alignments will (i) serve to identify events described in both comparable texts, and (ii) provide information about the underlying argument structures and how they are realized in each context to establish a coherent discourse. We investigate a graph-based clustering method for inducing such alignments as clustering provides a suitable framework to implicitly relate alignment decisions to one another, by exploiting global information encoded in a graph.

The remainder of this paper is structured as follows: In Section 2, we discuss previous work in related tasks. Section 3 describes our task and a suitable data set. Section 4 introduces a graph-based clustering model using Mincuts for the alignment of predicates. Section 5 outlines the experiments and presents evaluation results. Finally, we conclude in Section 6 and discuss future work.

2 Related Work

The task of aligning words in general has been studied extensively in previous work, for example as part of research in statistical machine translation (SMT). Typically, alignment models in SMT are trained by observing and (re-)estimating co-occurrence counts of word pairs in parallel sentences (Brown et al., 1993). The same methods have also been applied in monolingual settings, for example to align words in paraphrases (Cohn et al., 2008). In contrast to traditional word alignment tasks, our focus is not on pairs of isolated sentences but on aligning predicates within the discourse contexts in which they are situated. Furthermore, text pairs for our task should not be strictly parallel as we are specifically interested in the impact of different discourse contexts. In Section 5, we will show that this particular setting indeed constitutes a more challenging task compared to traditional word alignment in parallel or paraphrasing sentences.

Another set of related tasks is found in the area of textual inference. Since 2006, there have been regular challenges on the task of Recognizing Textual Entailment (RTE). In the original task description, Dagan et al. (2006) define *textual entailment* "as a directional relationship between pairs of text expressions, denoted by T - the entailing 'Text' -, and H - the entailed 'Hypothesis'. (...) T *entails* H if the meaning of H can be inferred from the meaning of T, as would typically be interpreted by people." Although this relation does not necessarily require the presence of corresponding predicates, previous work by MacCartney et al. (2008) shows that word alignments can serve as a good indicator of entailment.

[1] See the recent SemEval 2010 task: *Linking Events and their Participants in Discourse*, (Ruppenhofer et al., 2010).

[2] Note that we provide details regarding the construction of a suitable data set and further examples involving non-realized arguments in a complementary paper (Roth and Frank, 2012).

As a matter of fact, the same holds true for the task of detecting paraphrases. In contrast to RTE, this latter task requires bi-directional entailments, i.e., each of the two phrases must entail the other. Wan et al. (2006) show that a simple approach solely based on word (and lemmatized n-gram) overlap can already achieve an F_1-score of up to 83% for detecting paraphrases in the Microsoft Research Paraphrase Corpus (Dolan and Brockett, 2005, MSRPC). In fact, this is just 0.6% points below the state-of-the-art results recently reported by Socher et al. (2011).

The MSRPC and data sets from the first RTE challenges only consisted of isolated pairs of sentences. The Fifth PASCAL Recognizing Textual Entailment Challenge (Bentivogli et al., 2009) introduced a "Search Task", where entailing sentences for a hypothesis have to be found in a set of full documents. This new task first opened the doors for assessing the role of discourse (Mirkin et al., 2010a; Mirkin et al., 2010b) in RTE. However, this setting is still limited as discourse contexts are only provided for the entailing part (T) of each text pair but not for the hypothesis H.

A further task related to ours is the detection of event coreference. The goal of this task is to identify all mentions of the same event within a document and, in some settings, also across documents. However, the task setting is typically more restricted than ours in that its focus lies on identical events/references (cf. Walker et al. (2006), Weischedel et al. (2011), inter alia). In particular, verbalizations of different aspects of an event (e.g., 'buy'–'sell', 'kill'–'die', 'recover'–'find') are generally not linked in this paradigm. In contrast to coreference methods that identify chains of events, we are interested in pairs of corresponding predicates (and their argument structure), for which we can observe alternative realizations in discourse.

3 Aligning Predicates Across Texts

This section summarizes how we built a large corpus of comparable texts, as a basis for the *predicate alignment* task. We motivate the choice of the corpus and present a strategy for extracting comparable text pairs. Subsequently, we report on the preparation of an evaluation data set with manual predicate alignments across the paired texts. We conclude this section with an example that showcases the potential of using aligned predicates for the study of coherence phenomena. More detailed information regarding corpus creation, annotation guidelines and additional examples illustrating the potential of this corpus can be found in Roth and Frank (2012).

3.1 Corpus Creation

The goal of our work is to investigate coherence factors for argument structure realization, using comparable texts that describe the same events, but that include variation in textual presentation. This requirement fits well with the news domain, for which we can trace varying textual sources that describe the same underlying events. The English Gigaword Fifth Edition (Parker et al., 2011) corpus (henceforth just *Gigaword*) is one of the largest corpus collections for English. It comprises a total of 9.8 million newswire articles from seven distinct sources.

In previous work (Roth and Frank, 2012), we introduced *GigaPairs*, a sub-corpus extracted from Gigaword that includes over 160,000 pairs of newswire articles from distinct sources. GigaPairs has been derived from Gigaword using the pairwise similarity method on headlines presented by Wubben et al. (2009). In addition to calculating the similarity of news titles, we impose an additional date constraint to further increase the precision of extracted pairs of texts. Random inspection of about 100 documents revealed only two texts describing different events. Overall, we extracted 167,728 document pairs containing a total of 50 million word tokens. Each document in this corpus consists of up to 7.564 words with a mean and median of 301 and 213 words, respectively. All texts have been pre-processed using MATE tools (Björkelund et al., 2010; Bohnet, 2010), a pipeline of NLP modules including a state-of-the-art semantic role labeler that computes PropBank/NomBank annotations (Palmer et al., 2005; Meyers et al., 2008).

3.2 Gold Standard Annotation

We selected 70 text pairs from the GigaPairs corpus for manual predicate alignment. All document pairs were randomly chosen with the constraint that each text consists of 100 to 300 words.[3] Predi-

[3]This constraint is satisfied by 75.3% of all documents in GigaPairs.

cates identified by the semantic parser are provided as pre-labeled annotations for alignment. We asked two students[4] to tag corresponding predicates across each text pair. Following standard practice in word alignment tasks (cf. Cohn et al. (2008)) the annotators were instructed to distinguish between *sure* and *possible* alignments, depending on how certainly, in their opinion, two predicates describe verbalizations of the same event. The following examples show predicate pairings marked as sure (2) and as possible alignments (3).

(2) a. The regulator ruled on September 27 that Nasdaq too was qualified to bid for OMX [...]
   b. The authority [...] had already approved a similar application by Nasdaq.

(3) a. Myanmar's military government said earlier this year it has released some 220 political prisoners [...]
   b. The government has been regularly releasing members of Suu Kyi's National League for Democracy party [...]

In total, the annotators (A/B) aligned 487/451 sure and 221/180 possible alignments with a Kappa score (Cohen, 1960) of 0.86.[5] For the construction of a gold standard, we merged the alignments from both annotators by taking the union of all possible alignments and the intersection of all sure alignments. Cases which involved a sure alignment on which the annotators disagreed were resolved in a group discussion with the first author.

We split the final corpus into a development set of 10 document pairs and a test set of 60 document pairs. The test set contains a total of 3,453 predicates (1,531 nouns and 1,922 verbs). Its gold standard annotation consists of 446 sure and 361 possible alignments, which corresponds to an average of 7.4 sure (6.0 possible) alignments per document pair. Most of the gold alignments (82.4%) are between predicates of the same part-of-speech (242 noun and 423 verb pairs). A total of 383 gold alignments (47.5%) have been annotated between predicates with identical lemma form. Diverging numbers of realized arguments can be observed in 320 pairs (39.7%).

[4]Both annotators are students in computational linguistics, one undergraduate (A) and one postgraduate (B) student.

[5]Following Brockett (2007), we computed agreement on labeled annotations, including unaligned predicate pairs as an additional *null* category.

3.3 Potential for Discourse Coherence

This section presents an example of an aligned predicate pair from our development set that illustrates the potential of aggregating corresponding PAS across comparable texts. The example represents one of eleven cases involving unrealized arguments that can be found in our development set of only ten document pairs.

(4) a. The Chadians said they$_{\text{Arg0}}$ had fled in fear of their lives.
   b. The United Nations says some 20,000 refugees$_{\text{Arg0}}$ have fled into Cameroon$_{\text{Arg1}}$.

In both sentences, the Arg0 role of the predicate flee is filled, but Arg1 (here: the goal) has not been realized in (4.a). However, sentence (4.a) is still part of a coherent discourse, as a role filler for the omitted argument can be inferred from the preceding context. For the goal of our work, we are interested in factors that license such omissions of an argument. Potential factors on the discourse level include the information status of the entity filling an argument position, and its salience at the corresponding point in discourse. Roth and Frank (2012) discuss additional examples that demonstrate the importance of factors on further linguistic levels, e.g., lexical choice of predicates and their syntactic realization.

In the example above, the aggregation of aligned PAS presents an effective means to identify appropriate fillers for unrealized roles. Hence, we can utilize each such pair as one positive and one negative training instance for a model of discourse coherence that controls the omissibility of arguments. In what follows, we introduce an alignment approach that can be used to automatically acquire more training data using the entire GigaPairs corpus.

4 Model

For the automatic induction of predicate alignments across texts, we opt for an unsupervised graph-based clustering method. In this section, we first define a graph representation for pairs of documents. In particular, predicates are represented as nodes in such a graph and similarities between predicates as edges. We then proceed to describe various similarity measures that can be used to identify similar predicate instances. Finally, we introduce the clustering algorithm that we apply to graphs (representing pairs of documents) in order to induce alignments between corresponding predicates.

4.1 Graph representation

We build a bipartite graph representation for each pair of texts, using as vertices the predicate argument structures assigned in pre-processing (cf. Section 3.1). We represent each predicate as a node and integrate information about arguments only implicitly. Given the sets of predicates P_1 and P_2 of two comparable texts T_1 and T_2, respectively, we formally define an undirected graph G_{P_1,P_2} as follows:

$$G_{P_1,P_2} = \langle V, E \rangle \quad \text{where} \quad \begin{array}{c} V = P_1 \cup P_2 \\ E = P_1 \times P_2 \end{array} \tag{1}$$

Edge weights. We specify the edge weight between two nodes representing predicates $p_1 \in P_1$ and $p_2 \in P_2$ as a weighted linear combination of four similarity measures described in the next section: *WordNet* and *VerbNet* similarity, *Distributional* similarity and *Argument* similarity.

$$\begin{aligned} w_{p_1p_2} = & \ \lambda_1 * \text{sim}_{\text{WN}}(p_1, p_2) \\ + & \ \lambda_2 * \text{sim}_{\text{VN}}(p_1, p_2) \\ + & \ \lambda_3 * \text{sim}_{\text{Dist}}(p_1, p_2) \\ + & \ \lambda_4 * \text{sim}_{\text{Arg}}(p_1, p_2) \end{aligned} \tag{2}$$

Initially we set all weighting parameters $\lambda_1 \ldots \lambda_4$ to have uniform weights by default. In Section 5, we define an optimized weighting setting for the individual similarity measures.

4.2 Similarity Measures

We employ a number of similarity measures that make use of complementary information that is type-based ($\text{sim}_{\text{WN/VN/Dist}}$) or token-based ($\text{sim}_{\text{Arg}}$).[6] Given two lemmatized predicates p_1, p_2 and their set of arguments $A_1 = \text{args}(p_1)$, $A_2 = \text{args}(p_2)$, we define the following measures.

WordNet similarity. Given all pairs of synsets s_1, s_2 that contain the predicates p_1, p_2, respectively, we compute the maximal similarity using the information theoretic measure described in Lin (1998). Our implementation exploits the WordNet hierarchy (Fellbaum, 1998) to find the synset of the least common subsumer (lcs) and uses the pre-computed Information Content (IC) files from Pedersen et al. (2004) to compute Lin's measure:

$$\text{sim}_{\text{WN}}(p_1, p_2) = \frac{IC(\text{lcs}(s_1, s_2))}{IC(s_1) * IC(s_2)} \tag{3}$$

In order to compute similarities between verbal and nominal predicates, we further use derivation information from NomBank (Meyers et al., 2008): if a noun represents a nominalization of a verbal predicate, we resort to the corresponding verb synset. If no relation can be found between two predicates, we set a default value of $sim_{\text{WN}} = 0$. This applies in particular to all cases that involve a predicate not present in WordNet.

VerbNet similarity. To overcome systematic problems with the WordNet verb hierarchy (cf. Richens (2008)), we further compute similarity between verbal predicates using VerbNet (Kipper et al., 2008). Verbs in VerbNet are categorized into semantic classes according to their syntactic behavior. A class C can recursively embed sub-classes $C_s \in sub(C)$ that represent finer semantic and syntactic distinctions. We define a simple similarity function that defines fixed similarity scores between 0 and 1 for pairs of predicates p_1, p_2 depending on their relatedness within the VerbNet class hierarchy:

$$\text{sim}_{\text{VN}}(p_1, p_2) = \begin{cases} 1.0 & \text{if } \exists C : p_1, p_2 \in C \\ 0.8 & \text{if } \exists C, C_s : C_s \in sub(C) \\ & \quad \wedge \ p_1, p_2 \in C \cup C_s \\ 0.0 & \text{else} \end{cases} \tag{4}$$

Distributional similarity. As some predicates may not be covered by the WordNet and VerbNet hierarchies, we additionally calculate similarity based on distributional meaning in a semantic space (Landauer and Dumais, 1997). Following the traditional bag-of-words approach that has been applied in related tasks (Guo and Diab, 2011; Mitchell and Lapata, 2010), we consider the 2,000 most frequent context words $c_1, \ldots, c_{2000} \in C$ as dimensions of a vector space and define predicates as vectors using their Pointwise Mutual Information (PMI):

$$\vec{p} = (\text{PMI}(p, c_1), \ldots, \text{PMI}(p, c_{2000})) \tag{5}$$

[6] All token-based frequency counts (i.e., $freq()$ and $idf()$) are computed over all documents from the AFP and APW parts of the English Gigaword Fifth Edition.

$$\text{with} \quad \text{PMI}(x, y) = \frac{\text{freq}(x, y)}{\text{freq}(x) * \text{freq}(y)}$$

Given the vector representations of two predicates, we calculate their similarity as the cosine of the angle between the two vectors:

$$\text{sim}_{\text{Dist}}(p_1, p_2) = \frac{\vec{p_1} \cdot \vec{p_2}}{|\vec{p_1}| * |\vec{p_2}|} \tag{6}$$

Argument similarity. While the previous similarity measures are purely type-based, *argument similarity* integrates token-based, i.e., discourse-specific, similarity information about predications by taking into account the similarity of their arguments. This measure calculates the association between the arguments A_1 of the first and the arguments A_2 of the second predicate by determining the ratio of overlapping words in both argument sets.

$$\text{sim}_{\text{Arg}}(p_1, p_2) = \frac{\sum_{w \in A_1 \cap A_2} \text{idf}(w)}{\sum_{w \in A_1} \text{idf}(w) + \sum_{w \in A_2} \text{idf}(w)} \tag{7}$$

In order to give higher weight to (rare) content words, we weight each word by its Inverse Document Frequency (IDF), which we calculate over all documents d from the AFP and APW sections of the Gigaword corpus:

$$\text{idf}(w) = \log \frac{|D|}{|\{d : w \in D|\}} \tag{8}$$

Normalization. In order to make the outputs of all similarity measures comparable, we normalize their value ranges on the development set to have a mean and standard deviation of 1.0.

4.3 Mincut-based Clustering

Our graph clustering method uses minimum cuts (or *Mincut*) in order to partition the bipartite text graph into clusters of aligned predicates. A Mincut operation divides a given graph into two disjoint subgraphs. Each minimum cut is performed as a cut between some source node s and some target node t, such that (i) each of the two nodes will be in a different sub-graph and (ii) the sum of weights of all removed edges will be as small as possible. Our system determines each Mincut using an implementation of the method by Goldberg and Tarjan (1986).[7]

[7] Basic graph operations are performed using the freely available Java library JGraph, cf. `http://jgrapht.org/`.

```
function CLUSTER(G)
    clusters ← ∅
    E ← GETEDGES(G)                                ▷ Step 1
    e ← GETEDGEWITHLOWESTWEIGHT(E)
    s ← GETSOURCENODE(e)
    t ← GETTARGETNODE(e)
    G' ← MINCUT(G, s, t)                           ▷ Step 2
    C ← GETCONNECTEDCOMPONENTS(G')
    for all G_s ∈ C do                             ▷ Step 3
        if SIZE(G_s) <= 2 then
            clusters ← clusters ∪ G_s
        else
            clusters ← clusters ∪ CLUSTER(G_s)
        end if
    end for
    return clusters;
end function
```

Figure 2: Pseudo code of our clustering algorithm

As our goal is to induce clusters that correspond to pairs of similar predicates, we set a maximum number of two nodes per cluster as stopping criterion. Given an input graph G, our algorithm recursively applies Mincuts in three steps as described in Figure 2. Step 1 identifies the edge e with lowest weight in the given graph G. Step 2 performs the actual Mincut operation on G. Finally, the stopping criterion and recursion are applied in Step 3. An example of a clustered graph is illustrated in Figure 1.

The advantage of our method compared to off-the-shelf clustering techniques is two-fold: On the one hand, the clustering algorithm is free of any parameters, such as the number of clusters or a clustering threshold, that require fine-tuning. On the other hand, the approach makes use of a termination criterion that very well represents the nature of the goal of our task, namely to align pairs of predicates across comparable texts. The next section provides empirical evidence for the advantage of this approach.

5 Experiments

This section evaluates our graph-clustering model on the task of aligning predicates across comparable texts. For comparison to related tasks and methods, we describe different evaluation settings, vari-

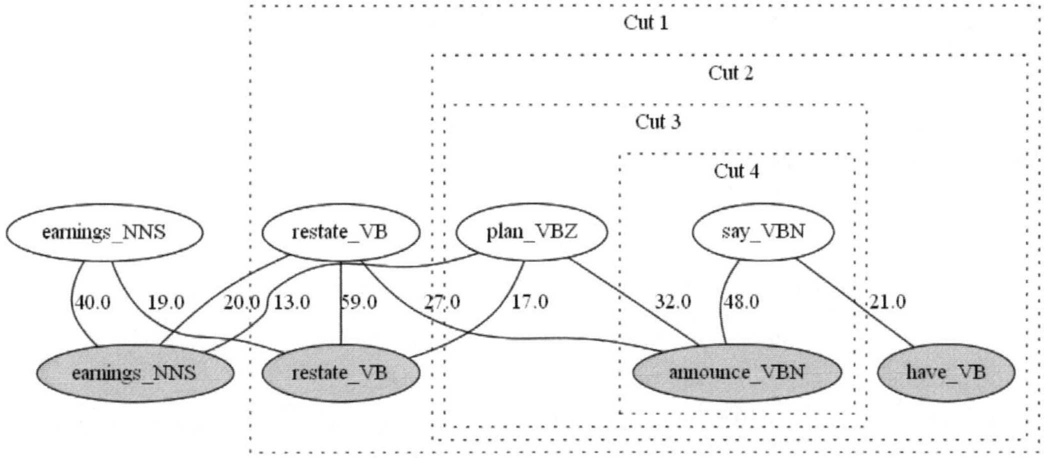

Figure 1: The predicates of two sentences (white: "The company has said it plans to restate its earnings for 2000 through 2002."; grey: "The company had announced in January that it would have to restate earnings (. . .)") from the Microsoft Research Paragraph Corpus are aligned by computing clusters with minimum cuts.

ous baselines, as well as results for these baselines and the model presented above.

5.1 Settings

In order to benchmark our model against traditional methods for word alignment, we first apply our graph-based alignment model (**Full**) on three sentence-based paraphrase corpora. This model uses the similarity measures defined in Section 4.2 and the clustering algorithm introduced in Section 4.3.

In a second experiment, we evaluate **Full** on our novel task of inducing predicate alignments across comparable monolingual texts, using the **GigaPairs** data set described in Section 3. We evaluate against the manually annotated gold alignments in the test data set described in Section 3.2. To gain more insight into the performance of the various similarity measures included in the **Full** model, we evaluate simplified versions that omit individual similarity measures (**Full–[measure name]**).

The relative differences in performance against various baselines will help us quantify the differences and difficulties between a traditional sentence-based word alignment setting and our novel alignment task that operates on full texts.

5.1.1 Sentence-level Alignment Setting

For sentence-based predicate alignment we make use of the following three corpora that are word-aligned subsets of the paraphrase collections described in (Cohn et al., 2008): **MTC** consists of 100 sentence pairs from the Multiple-Translation Chinese Corpus (Huang et al., 2002), **Leagues** contains 100 sentential paraphrases from two translations of Jules Verne's "Twenty Thousand Leagues Under the Sea", and **MSR** is a sub-set of the Microsoft Research Paraphrase Corpus (Dolan and Brockett, 2005), consisting of 130 sentence pairs. All three paraphrase collections are in English.

Results for these experiments are reported in Section 5.3.1. Note that in order to determine alignment candidates, we apply the same pre-processing steps as used for the annotation of our corpus. The semantic parser identified an average number of 3.8, 5.1 and 4.7 predicates per text (i.e., per paraphrase sentence) in **MTC**, **Leagues** and **MSR**, respectively. All models are evaluated against the subset of gold standard alignments (cf. Cohn et al. (2008)) between pairs of words marked as predicates.

5.1.2 Text-level Alignment Setting

Results for our own data set, **GigaPairs**, are reported in Section 5.3.2. In this setting, models are evaluated against the annotated gold standard alignments between predicates as described in Section 3.2. Since all text pairs in **GigaPairs** comprise multiple sentences each, the average number of predicates per text to consider (27.5) is much higher than in the paraphrase settings. As the full graph representation becomes rather inefficient to handle (by default, edges are inserted between all predicate pairs), we use the development set of 10 text pairs to estimate

	MTC			Leagues			MSR		
	Precision	Recall	F1	Precision	Recall	F1	Precision	Recall	F1
LemmaId	25.1**	74.9	37.6**	31.5**	67.2	42.9**	42.3**	90.8	57.7**
Greedy	74.8**	**88.3****	81.0	75.0**	**86.0****	80.1	80.7**	**97.0****	88.1
WordAlign	**99.3**	86.6	**92.5**	**98.7**	78.5	**87.4**	**99.5**	96.0*	**97.7***
Full	92.3	72.2	81.1	92.7	69.4	79.4	94.5	88.3	91.3

Table 1: Results for sentence-based predicte alignment in the three benchmark settings **MTC**, **Leagues** and **MSR** (all numbers in %); results that significantly differ from **Full** are marked with asterisks (* p<0.05; ** p<0.01).

a threshold on predicate similarity for adding edges. We tested all thresholds from 1.5 to 4.0 with a step-size of 0.25 and found 2.5 to perform best. This threshold is applied in the evaluation of all graph-based models.

5.2 Baselines

A simple baseline for both settings is to align all predicates whose lemmas are identical. This baseline, henceforth called **LemmaId**, is computed as a lower bound for all settings. In order to assess the benefits of the clustering step, we propose a second baseline that uses the same similarity measures and thresholds as our **Full** model, but omits the clustering step described in Section 4.3. Instead, it greedily computes as many 1-to-1 alignments as possible, starting from the highest similarity to the learned threshold (**Greedy**).

As a more sophisticated baseline, we make use of alignment tools commonly used in statistical machine translation (SMT). For the three sentence-based paraphrase settings **MTC**, **Leagues** and **MSR**, Cohn et al. (2008) readily provide GIZA++ (Och and Ney, 2003) alignments as part of their word-aligned paraphrase corpus. For the experiments in the **GigaPairs** setting, we train our own word alignment model using the state-of-the-art word alignment tool Berkeley Aligner (Liang et al., 2006). As word alignment tools require pairs of sentences as input, we first extract paraphrases in the latter setting using a re-implementation of the paraphrase detection system by Wan et al. (2006).[8] In the following section, we abbreviate both baselines using SMT alignment tools as **WordAlign**.

[8]Note that the performance of this system lies slightly below the state-of-the-art results reported by Socher et al. (2011) However, we were not able to reproduce the results of Socher et al. using the publicly available release of their software.

5.3 Results

We measure precision as the number of predicted alignments that are annotated in the gold standard divided by the total number of predictions. Recall is measured as the number of correctly predicted *sure* alignments divided by the total number of *sure* alignments in the gold standard. This conforms to evaluation measures used for word alignment models in SMT (Och and Ney, 2003). Following Cohn et al. (2008), we subsequently compute the F_1-score as the harmonic mean between precision and recall.

We compute statistical significance of result differences with a paired t-test (Cohen, 1995) over the affected test set documents and provide corresponding significance levels where appropriate.

5.3.1 Sentence-level Predicate Alignment

The results for **MTC**, **Leagues** and **MSR** are presented in Table 1. The numbers indicate that **WordAlign** consistently outperforms all other models on the three data sets in terms of F_1-score. Statistical significance of result differences between **WordAlign** and **Full** can only be observed for recall and F_1-score on the **MSR** data set ($p<0.05$). Other differences are not significant due to high variance of results compared to data set sizes.

The overall performance of **WordAlign** does not come much as a surprise, seeing that all three data sets consist of highly parallel sentence pairs. In fact, the results for **LemmaId** show that by aligning all predicates with identical lemmas, most of the sure alignments in the three settings are already covered. The reason for the low precision lies in the fact that the same lemma can occur multiple times in the same paraphrase, a phenomenon that is better handled by **WordAlign**, **Greedy** and **Full**. Interestingly, the **Greedy** model achieves the highest recall in all settings but it performs below our **Full** model in terms of precision and F_1-score. The performance differences between **Greedy** and **Full** are statistically significant ($p<0.01$) regarding precision and recall.

5.3.2 Text-level Predicate Alignment

We now turn to the experiments on our own data set, **GigaPairs**, which comprises full documents of unequal lengths instead of pairs of single sentences. Table 2 presents the results for our full model and the three baselines. From all four approaches, **WordAlign** yields lowest performance. We observe two main reasons for this: On the one hand, sentence paraphrase detection does not perform perfectly. Hence, the extracted sentence pairs do not always contain gold alignments. On the other hand, even sentence pairs that contain gold alignments are generally less parallel than in the previous settings, which make them harder to align. The increased difficulty can also be seen in the results for the **Greedy** baseline, which only achieves an F_1-score of 20.1% in this setting. In contrast, we observe that the majority of all sure alignments (60.3%) can be retrieved by applying the **LemmaId** model.

The **Full** model achieves a recall of 46.6%, but it significantly outperforms **LemmaId** ($p<0.01$) in terms of precision (58.7%, +18.4 percentage points). This is an important factor for us, as we plan to use the alignments in subsequent tasks. With 52.0%, **Full** achieves the best overall F_1-score.

Ablating similarity measures. All aforementioned results were conducted in experiments with a uniform weighting scheme of similarity measures as introduced in Section 4.3. Table 3 shows the performance impact of individual similarity measures by removing them completely (i.e., setting their weight to 0.0). The numbers indicate that not all measures contribute positively to the overall performance when using equal weights. However, a significant difference can only be observed when removing the argument similarity measure, which drastically reduces the results. This clearly highlights the importance of incorporating the context of individual predications in this task.

Tuning weights. Subsequently, we tested various combinations of weights on our development set in order to estimate a good overall weighting scheme.

	Precision	Recall	F1
LemmaId	40.3**	**60.3****	48.3
Greedy	19.6**	20.6**	20.1**
WordAlign	19.7**	15.2**	17.2**
Full	**58.7**	46.6	**52.0**

Table 2: Results for **GigaPairs** (all numbers in %); results that significantly differ from **Full** are marked with asterisks (* $p<0.05$; ** $p<0.01$).

	Precision	Recall	F1
Full–WN	58.9	48.0	52.9
Full–VN	57.3	48.7	52.6
Full–Dist	54.3	42.8	47.9
Full–Args	40.1**	24.0**	30.0**
Full	58.7	46.6	52.0
Full+tuned	**59.7****	**50.7****	**54.8****

Table 3: Impact of removing individual measures and using a tuned weighting scheme (all numbers in %); results that significantly differ from **Full** are marked with asterisks (* $p<0.05$; ** $p<0.01$).

This tuning procedure is implemented as a brute-force technique, in which we fix the weight of one similarity measure and allow all other measures to receive a weight assignment between 0.25 to 5.0 times the fixed weight. Finally, the resulting weights are normalized to sum to 1.0. We found the best performing weighting scheme to be 0.09, 0.48, 0.24 and 0.19 for $\lambda_1, \ldots, \lambda_4$, respectively (cf. Eq. (2), Section 4). The performance gains of the resulting model (**Full+tuned**) can be seen in Table 3. Computing statistical significance of the result differences between **Full+tuned** and all baseline models confirmed significant improvements ($p<0.01$) for both precision and F_1-score.

5.4 Error Analysis

We perform an error analysis on the output of **Full+tuned** on the development set of **GigaPairs** in order to determine re-occurring problems. In total, the model missed 13 out of 35 sure alignments (Type I errors) and predicted 23 alignments not annotated in the gold standard (Type II errors).

Six Type I errors (46%) occurred when the lemma of an affected predicate occurred more than once in a text and the model missed a correct link. Vice versa, identical predicates that refer to different events have been the source of 8 Type II errors (35%). We observe that these errors are frequently related to predicates, such as "say" and "appear", that often occur in news texts. Altogether, we find 15 Type II errors (65%) that are due to high predicate similarity despite low argument overlap (cf. Example (5)).

(5) a. The US alert (...) followed intelligence reports that ...
b. The Foreign Ministry announcement called on Japanese citizens to be cautious ...

We observe that argument overlap itself can be low even for correct alignments. This clearly indicates that a better integration of context is needed. Example (6.a) illustrates a case in which the agent of a warning event is not realized. Here, contextual information is required to correctly align it to the first warning event in (6.b). This involves inference beyond the local PAS.

(6) a. The US alert (...) is one step down from a full $[\text{travel}]_{\text{Arg1}}$ warning $[\ ]_{\text{Arg0}}$.
b. Japan has issued a travel alert ...(which) follows similar warnings [from American and British $\text{authorities}]_{\text{Arg0}}$. (...) An official said it was highly unusual for $[\text{Tokyo}]_{\text{Arg0}}$ to issue such a warning ...

6 Conclusion

We presented a novel task for *predicate alignment* across comparable monolingual texts, which we address using graph-based clustering with Mincuts. The motivation for this task is to acquire empirical data for studying discourse coherence factors related to argument structure realization.

As a first step, we constructed a data set of comparable texts that provide full discourse contexts for alternative verbalizations of the same underlying events. The data set is derived from all newswire pairs found in the English Gigaword Fifth Edition and contains a total of more than 160,000 paired documents.

A subset of these pairs forms an evaluation set, annotated with gold alignments that relate predications, which exhibit a (possibly partial) corresponding argument structure. We established that the annotation task, while difficult, can be performed with good inter-annotator agreement (κ at 0.86).

Our main contribution is a novel clustering approach using Mincuts for aligning predications across comparable texts. Our experiments established that recursive clustering improves on greedy selection methods by profiting from global information encoded in the graph representation. While the Mincut-based method is in itself unsupervised, a small amount of development data is needed to tune parameters for the construction of particularly suitable input graphs.

We tested our full model against two additional baselines: simple heuristic alignment based on identical lemma forms and a combination of techniques from SMT and paraphrase detection. The evaluation for our novel task was complemented by a traditional word alignment task using established paraphrase data sets. We determined clear differences in performance for all models for the two types of task settings. While word alignment methods from SMT outperform the competing models in the sentence-based alignment tasks, they perform poorly in the discourse setting.

In future work, we will enhance our model by incorporating more refined similarity measures including discourse-based criteria. We will further explore tuning techniques, e.g., a more suitable preselection method for edges in graph construction, in order to increase either precision or recall. The decision of optimizing towards one measure or another is clearly task-dependent. In our case, high precision is favorable as we plan to learn accurate discourse model parameters from the computed alignments. Even though such an optimization will result in an overall lower recall, application of the alignment model on the entire GigaPairs corpus can still provide us with a large amount of precise predicate alignments. Using this set of alignments, we will then proceed to exploit contextual information in order to learn a semantic model for discourse coherence in argument structure realization.

Acknowledgements

We are grateful to the Landesgraduiertenförderung Baden-Württemberg for funding within the research initiative "Coherence in language processing" at Heidelberg University. We thank Danny Rehl and Lukas Funk for annotation.

References

Eneko Agirre, Daniel Cer, Mona Diab, and Aitor Gonzalez-Agirre. 2012. SemEval-2012 Task 6: A pilot on semantic textual similarity. In *Proceedings of the 6th International Workshop on Semantic Evaluations*, Montreal, Canada, June. to appear.

Regina Barzilay and Mirella Lapata. 2008. Modeling local coherence: An entity-based approach. *Computational Linguistics*, 34(1):1–34.

Regina Barzilay and Lillian Lee. 2004. Catching the drift: Probabilistic content models, with applications to generation and summarization. In *Proceedings of the Human Language Technology Conference of the North American Chapter of the Association for Computational Linguistics,* Boston, Mass., 2–7 May 2004, pages 113–120.

Anja Belz, Eric Kow, Jette Viethen, and Albert Gatt. 2009. The grec main subject reference generation challenge 2009: overview and evaluation results. In *Proceedings of the 2009 Workshop on Language Generation and Summarisation*, pages 79–87.

Luisa Bentivogli, Ido Dagan, Hoa Trang Dang, Danilo Giampiccolo, and Bernardo Magnini. 2009. The fifth pascal recognizing textual entailment challenge. In *Proceedings of TAC.*

Anders Björkelund, Bernd Bohnet, Love Hafdell, and Pierre Nugues. 2010. A high-performance syntactic and semantic dependency parser. In *Coling 2010: Demonstration Volume*, pages 33–36, Beijing, China, August. Coling 2010 Organizing Committee.

Bernd Bohnet. 2010. Top accuracy and fast dependency parsing is not a contradiction. In *Proceedings of the 23rd International Conference on Computational Linguistics (Coling 2010)*, pages 89–97, Beijing, China, August. Coling 2010 Organizing Committee.

Chris Brockett. 2007. *Aligning the RTE 2006 Corpus.* Microsoft Research.

Peter F. Brown, Vincent J. Della Pietra, Stephan A. Della Pietra, and Robert L. Mercer. 1993. The mathematics of statistical machine translation: Parameter estimation. *Computational Linguistics*, 19:263–311.

Jacob Cohen. 1960. A coefficient of agreement for nominal scales. *Educational and Psychological Measurement*, 20:37–46.

Paul R. Cohen. 1995. *Empirical methods for artificial intelligence*. MIT Press, Cambridge, MA, USA.

Trevor Cohn, Chris Callison-Burch, and Mirella Lapata. 2008. Constructing Corpora for Development and Evaluation of Paraphrase Systems. 34(4).

Ido Dagan, Oren Glickman, and Bernardo Magnini. 2006. The PASCAL recognising textual entailment challenge. In J. Quiñonero-Candela, I. Dagan, and B. Magnini, editors, *Machine Learning Challenges*, pages 177–190. Springer, Heidelberg, Germany.

William B. Dolan and Chris Brockett. 2005. Automatically constructing a corpus of sentential paraphrases. In *Proceedings of the Third International Workshop on Paraphrasing*.

Christiane Fellbaum, editor. 1998. *WordNet: An Electronic Lexical Database*. MIT Press, Cambridge, Mass.

Adrew V. Goldberg and Robert E. Tarjan. 1986. A new approach to the maximum flow problem. In *Proceedings of the eighteenth annual ACM symposium on Theory of computing*, pages 136–146, New York, NY, USA.

Barbara J. Grosz, Aravind K. Joshi, and Scott Weinstein. 1995. Centering: A framework for modeling the local coherence of discourse. *Computational Linguistics*, 21(2):203–225.

Weiwei Guo and Mona Diab. 2011. Semantic topic models: Combining word distributional statistics and dictionary definitions. In *Proceedings of the 2011 Conference on Empirical Methods in Natural Language Processing*, pages 552–561, July.

Shudong Huang, David Graff, and George Doddington. 2002. *Multiple-Translation Chinese Corpus*. Linguistic Data Consortium, Philadelphia.

Karin Kipper, Anna Korhonen, Neville Ryant, and Martha Palmer. 2008. A Large-scale Classification of English Verbs. 42(1):21–40.

Thomas K. Landauer and Susan T. Dumais. 1997. A solution to Plato's problem: The Latent Semantic Analysis theory of the acquisition, induction, and representation of knowledge. *Psychological Review*, 104:211–240.

Percy Liang, Benjamin Taskar, and Dan Klein. 2006. Alignment by agreement. In *North American Association for Computational Linguistics (NAACL)*, pages 104–111.

Dekang Lin. 1998. An information-theoretic definition of similarity. In *Proceedings of the 15th International Conference on Machine Learning,* Madison, Wisc., 24–27 July 1998, pages 296–304.

Bill MacCartney, Michael Galley, and Christopher D. Manning. 2008. A phrase-based alignment model for natural language inference. In *Proceedings of the 2008 Conference on Empirical Methods in Natural Language Processing,* Waikiki, Honolulu, Hawaii, 25-27 October 2008.

Adam Meyers, Ruth Reeves, and Catherine Macleod. 2008. *NomBank v1.0*. Linguistic Data Consortium, Philadelphia.

Shachar Mirkin, Jonathan Berant, Ido Dagan, and Eyal Shnarch. 2010a. Recognising entailment within discourse. In *Proceedings of the 23rd International Conference on Computational Linguistics (Coling 2010)*, Beijing, China, August. Coling 2010 Organizing Committee.

Shachar Mirkin, Ido Dagan, and Sebastian Padó. 2010b. Assessing the role of discourse references in entailment inference. In *Proceedings of the 48th Annual Meeting of the Association for Computational Linguistics,* Uppsala, Sweden, 11–16 July 2010.

Jeff Mitchell and Mirella Lapata. 2010. Composition in Distributional Models of Semantics. 34(8):1388–1429.

Franz Josef Och and Hermann Ney. 2003. A Systematic Comparison of Various Statistical Alignment Models. 29(1):19–51.

Martha Palmer, Daniel Gildea, and Paul Kingsbury. 2005. The proposition bank: An annotated corpus of semantic roles. *Computational Linguistics*, 31(1):71–105.

Robert Parker, David Graff, Jumbo Kong, Ke Chen, and Kazuaki Maeda. 2011. *English Gigaword Fifth Edition.* Linguistic Data Consortium, Philadelphia.

Ted Pedersen, Siddharth Patwardhan, and Jason Michelizzi. 2004. WordNet::Similarity – Measuring the relatedness of concepts. In *Companion Volume to the Proceedings of the Human Language Technology Conference of the North American Chapter of the Association for Computational Linguistics,* Boston, Mass., 2–7 May 2004, pages 267–270.

Tom Richens. 2008. Anomalies in the wordnet verb hierarchy. In *Proceedings of the 22nd International Conference on Computational Linguistics (Coling 2008)*, pages 729–736. Association for Computational Linguistics.

Michael Roth and Anette Frank. 2012. Aligning predicate argument structures in monolingual comparable texts: A new corpus for a new task. In *Proceedings of the First Joint Conference on Lexical and Computational Semantics*, Montreal, Canada, June.

Josef Ruppenhofer, Caroline Sporleder, Roser Morante, Collin Baker, and Martha Palmer. 2010. SemEval-2010 Task 10: Linking Events and Their Participants in Discourse. In *Proceedings of the 5th International Workshop on Semantic Evaluations*, pages 45–50, Uppsala, Sweden, July.

Richard Socher, Eric H. Huang, Jeffrey Pennington, Andrew Y. Ng, and Christopher D. Manning. 2011. Dynamic pooling and unfolding recursive autoencoders for paraphrase detection. In *Advances in Neural Information Processing Systems (NIPS 2011)*.

Ivan Titov and Mikhail Kozhevnikov. 2010. Bootstrapping semantic analyzers from non-contradictory texts. In *Proceedings of the 48th Annual Meeting of the Association for Computational Linguistics,* Uppsala, Sweden, 11–16 July 2010, pages 958–967.

Christopher Walker, Stephanie Strassel, Julie Medero, and Kazuaki Maeda. 2006. *ACE 2005 Multilingual Training Corpus.* Linguistic Data Consortium, Philadelphia.

Stephen Wan, Mark Dras, Robert Dale, and Cecile Paris. 2006. Using dependency-based features to take the "Para-farce" out of paraphrase. In *Proceedings of the Australasian Language Technology Workshop*, pages 131–138.

Ralph Weischedel, Martha Palmer, Mitchell Marcus, Eduard Hovy, Sameer Pradhan, Lance Ramshaw, Nianwen Xue, Ann Taylor, Jeff Kaufman, Michelle Franchini, Mohammed El-Bachouti, Robert Belvin, and Ann Houston. 2011. *OntoNotes Release 4.0.* Linguistic Data Consortium, Philadelphia.

Sander Wubben, Antal van den Bosch, Emiel Krahmer, and Erwin Marsi. 2009. Clustering and matching headlines for automatic paraphrase acquisition. In *Proceedings of the 12th European Workshop on Natural Language Generation (ENLG 2009)*, pages 122–125, Athens, Greece, March. Association for Computational Linguistics.

Local and Global Context for Supervised and Unsupervised Metonymy Resolution

Vivi Nastase
HITS gGmbH
Heidelberg, Germany
vivi.nastase@h-its.org

Alex Judea
University of Stuttgart
Stuttgart, Germany
alexander.judea@ims.uni-stuttgart.de

Katja Markert
University of Leeds
Leeds, UK
K.Markert@leeds.ac.uk

Michael Strube
HITS gGmbH
Heidelberg, Germany
michael.strube@h-its.org

Abstract

Computational approaches to metonymy resolution have focused almost exclusively on the local context, especially the constraints placed on a potentially metonymic word by its grammatical collocates. We expand such approaches by taking into account the larger context. Our algorithm is tested on the data from the metonymy resolution task (Task 8) at SemEval 2007. The results show that incorporation of the global context can improve over the use of the local context alone, depending on the types of metonymies addressed. As a second contribution, we move towards unsupervised resolution of metonymies, made feasible by considering ontological relations as possible readings. We show that such an unsupervised approach delivers promising results: it beats the supervised most frequent sense baseline and performs close to a supervised approach using only standard lexico-syntactic features.

1 Introduction

With the exception of explicit tasks in metonymy and metaphor analysis, computational treatment of language relies on the assumption that the texts to be processed have a literal interpretation. This contrasts with the fact that figurative expressions are common in language, as exemplified by the metonymy in the excerpt from a Wikipedia article in Example 1 and another in Example 2 from the SemEval 2007 metonymy resolution task (Markert and Nissim, 2009).

(1) In the gold medal game, *Canada* defeated the American team 2-0 to win their third consecutive gold.

(2) This keyword is only required when your relational database is *Oracle*.

The *defeating* in Example 1 will not be done by the country as such, but by a team representing the country in a sporting event. Hence, in a metonymy a potentially metonymic expression or word (here *Canada*) stands for a conceptually related entity (here, people of Canada). In the second Example, a company name (*Oracle*) stands for a product (database) developed by the company.

Metonymy resolution can be important for a variety of tasks. Textual entailment may need metonymy resolution (Bentivogli et al., 2007): for example, we would like to be able to induce from Example 1 the hypothesis

The Canadian team won ....

Leveling and Hartrumpf (2008) show that metonymy recognition on location proper names helps geographical information retrieval by excluding metonymically used place names from consideration (such as Example 1 or the use of *Vietnam* for the *Vietnam war*). Metonymies also frequently interact with anaphora resolution (Nunberg, 1995; Markert and Hahn, 2002), as in Example 1 where the metonymic use of *Canada* is referred to by a plural pronoun afterward (*their*).

Metonymies can be quite regular: company names can be used for their management or their products, country names can be used for associated sports teams. Following from this, the currently prevalent set-up for metonymy resolution — as in the SemEval 2007 task — provides a manually compiled list of frequent readings or metonymic patterns such as `organization-for-product` for prespecified semantic classes (such as organizations) as well as annotated examples for these patterns so that systems can then treat metonymy resolution as a (supervised) word sense disambiguation task. However, this approach needs novel, manual provision of readings as well as annotated examples for each new semantic class.

In contrast, we will see readings as relations between the potentially metonymic word (PMW) and other concepts in a large concept network, a priori allowing all possible relations as readings. We base this approach on the observation that metonymic words stand in for concepts that they are related with – e.g. the part for the whole, the company for the product. These readings are obtained on the fly and are therefore independent of manually provided, preclassified interpretations or semantic classes, leading eventually to the possibility of unsupervised metonymy resolution. We achieve this by first linking a PMW to an article in Wikipedia. Then we extract from a large concept network derived from Wikipedia the relations surrounding the PMW.

As there will be (many) more than one such relation, these need to be ranked or scored. We achieve this in a probabilistic framework where we condition the probability of a relation on the context of the PMW. This ranking showcases our second major innovation in that the flexibility of our framework allows us to incorporate a wider context than in most prior approaches. Let us consider the indications for metonymic readings and its interpretation in Example 1, on the one hand, and Example 2, on the other hand. In Example 1, the grammatical relation to the verb *defeat* and the verb's selectional preferences indicate the metonymy. We will call all such grammatically related words and the grammatical relations *the local context* of the PMW. Such types of local context have been used by most prior approaches (Pustejovsky, 1991; Hobbs et al., 1993; Fass, 1991; Nastase and Strube, 2009, among others). However, Example 2 shows that the local context can be ambiguous or often weak, such as the verb *to be*. In these examples, the wider context (*database*, *keyword*) is a better indication for a metonymy but has not been satisfactorily integrated in prior approaches (see Section 2). We here call all words surrounding the PMW but not grammatically related to it *the global context*.

In our approach we integrate both the local and the global context in our probabilistic framework. For the local context, we compute the selectional preferences for the words related to the PMW from a corpus of English Wikipedia articles and generalize them in the Wikipedia concept network, thus (automatically) providing a set of *abstractions* – general concepts in the network that capture the semantic classes required by the local context. In the next step we compute probabilities of the global context surrounding the PMWs under each (locally required) abstraction, and combine this with the selectional preferences of the grammatically related words. That we can integrate local and global context in one probabilistic but also knowledge-based framework is possible because we combine two descriptions of meaning – ontological and distributional – by exploiting different sources of information in Wikipedia (category-article hierarchy and article texts).

We compute the probabilities of the relations (= readings) between the concept corresponding to the PMW and its directly related concepts. These can be used either (i) as additional features in a supervised approach or (ii) directly for unsupervised resolution. We do both in this paper and show that (i) the supervised approach using both local and global context can outperform one using just local context, dependent on the semantic class studied and (ii) that an unsupervised approach — although lower than the supervised one — outperforms the supervised most frequent reading baseline and performs close to a standard supervised model with the basic set of lexico-syntactic features (Nissim and Markert, 2005).

2 Related Work

The word sense disambiguation setting for metonymy resolution as developed by Nissim and Markert (2005) and used for the SemEval 2007 task (Markert and Nissim, 2009) uses a small, prespecified number of frequently occurring readings.

The approaches building on this work (Farkas et al., 2007; Nicolae et al., 2007, among others) are supervised, mostly using shallow surface features as well as grammatical relations.[1] Most effective in the SemEval task as summarized in Markert and Nissim (2009) has been the local, grammatical context, with the two systems relying on the global context or the local/global context in a BOW model (Leveling, 2007; Poibeau, 2007) not outperforming the most frequent reading baseline. We believe that might be due to the lack of a link between the local and global context in these approaches — in our work, we condition the global context on the abstractions and selectional preferences yielded by the local context and achieve better results.

Lapata (2003), Shutova (2009) as well as Roberts and Harabagiu (2011) deal with the issue of logical metonymy, where the participant stands in for the full event: e.g. *Mary enjoyed the book.*, where *book* stands in for *reading the book*, and this missing event (*reading*) can be inferred from a corpus. Utiyama et al. (2000), Lapata (2003) propose a probabilistic model for finding the correct interpretation of such metonymies in an unsupervised manner. However, these event type metonymies differ from the problem dealt with in our paper and the SemEval 2007 task in that their recognition (i.e. their distinction from literal occurrences) is achieved simply by grammatical patterns (a noun instead of a gerund or to-infinitive following the verb) and the problem is limited to interpretation.

Our view of relations in a concept network being the interpretations of metonymies is strongly reminiscent of older work in metonymy resolution such as Hobbs et al. (1993), Fass (1991), Markert and Hahn (2002) or the use of a generative lexicon and its relations in Pustejovsky (1991), which also are unsupervised. However, these approaches lacked scalability due to the use of small hand-modeled knowledge bases which our use of a very large Wikipedia-derived ontology overcomes. In addition, most of these approaches (Fass, 1991; Hobbs et al., 1993; Pustejovsky, 1991; Harabagiu, 1998) rely on the view that metonymies violate selectional restrictions in their immediate, local context, usually those imposed by the verbs on their arguments. As can be seen in the Example 2, this misses metonymies which do not violate selectional restrictions. Nastase and Strube (2009) use more flexible probabilistic selectional preferences instead of strict constraint violations as well as WordNet as a larger taxonomy but are also restricted to the local context. Markert and Hahn (2002) do propose a treatment of metonymies that takes into account the larger discourse in the form of anaphoric relations between a metonymy and the prior context. However, they constrain discourse integration to potential PMWs that are definite NPs and the context to few previous noun phrases. In addition, their framework uses a strict rule-based ranking of competing readings that cannot be easily extended.

The work presented here also relies on a concept network, built automatically from Wikipedia. This resource provides us with links between entities in the text, and also a variety of ontological relations for the PMW, that will allow us to identify a wide variety of metonymic interpretations. Our approach combines information from the concept network with automatically acquired selectional preferences as well as a possibility to combine in a probabilistic framework the influence of the local and global context on the interpretation of a potentially metonymic word.

3 The Approach

The approach we present takes into account both the local, grammatical, context and the larger textual context of a potentially metonymic word. Figure 1 presents a graphical representation of our approach.

On the one hand, the word/term to be interpreted (the potentially metonymic word/term – PMW) is mapped onto a concept in the concept network (Section 3.3), which gives us access to the conceptual relations ($\mathcal{R}_i$) between the PMW and other concepts ($c_x \in C_{\mathcal{R}_i}$). On the other hand, any word w grammatically related to the PMW via a grammatical relation r provides us with semantic restrictions on the interpretation of the PMW, namely preferred semantic classes A_j (we call them *abstractions*) and a selectional preference score.[2] These are automatically

[1] Brun et al. (2007) is semi-supervised but again relies on the local grammatical context.

[2] We restrict the grammatical context that provides selectional preferences to verbs or adjectives grammatically related

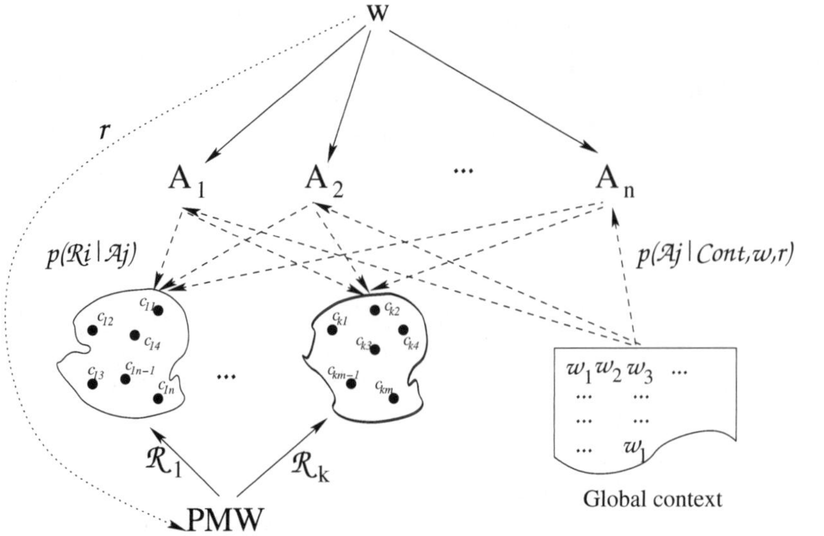

Figure 1: Metonymy resolution using selectional preferences A_j derived from local context w and r, semantic relations $\mathcal{R}_i$ to the PMW from a concept network, and the global context surrounding a term to be interpreted

acquired by using a corpus of Wikipedia articles and a repository of encyclopedic knowledge (presented in Section 3.1), as described in detail in 3.2. Because the abstractions A_j and the PMW's related concepts (c_x) come from the same structured resource, we can compute the probabilities for each $\mathcal{R}_i$ given the grammatically related word w and the grammatical relation r. The global context can also easily be added to the computation, as the probability of each word in the context relative to an abstraction A_j can be computed through the resource's *is_a* hierarchy and its link to Wikipedia articles. This is detailed in Section 3.4.

3.1 A concept network obtained from Wikipedia

We use a Wikipedia article dump (January 2011) which provided over 3.5 million English articles, interconnected through a hierarchy of categories and hyperlinks. This partly structured repository is transformed into a large-scale multilingual concept network, whose nodes are concepts corresponding to articles or categories in Wikipedia (Nastase et al., 2010). Concepts in this network are connected through a variety of semantic relations (e.g. *is a, member of, nationality*) derived from category names and infoboxes. The version of WikiNet used had 3,707,718 nodes and 49,931,266 relation instances of 494 types, and is freely available[3].

WikiNet is used here as a concept inventory, and its links and structure to generalize more specific concepts identified in texts to general concepts. The fact that nodes in WikiNet correspond to articles/categories in Wikipedia is used to link article texts in Wikipedia to general concepts, for the purpose of computing various probability scores (detailed in Section 3.4).

3.2 Selectional preferences and abstractions

To compute selectional preferences we use the set of English Wikipedia articles, which describe specific concepts. Wikipedia contributors are encouraged to insert hyperlinks, which link important terms in an article to the corresponding articles. A hyperlink consists of two parts, the actual link (i.e. a URL) and a phrase to appear in the text. Hyperlinks then constitute a bridge from the textual level to the conceptual level without the need for word sense disambiguation. We exploit these links to gather concept arguments for verbs and adjectives, and generalize these using the concept network built from Wikipedia.

The corpus of Wikipedia articles was first enriched with hyperlinks, making the "one sense per

to the PMW.

[3]`http://www.h-its.org/english/research/nlp/download/wikinet.php`

Algorithm 1 computeSelPrefs(G,WkN)

Input: G – grammatical relation triples
WkN – WikiNet
M – maximum number of generalization steps
Output: Γ

$\Gamma = \{\}$
for all (w, r) such that $(c, r, w) \in G$ **do**
  $\mathcal{S} = \{(c, f)|$f is the frequency of (c, r, w) in $G\}$
  $\Gamma_{w,r} = \mathcal{S}$
  mdl = MDL($\Gamma_{w,r}, \mathcal{S}$)
  for all i = 1,M **do**
    $\Gamma' = abstract(\mathcal{S}, WkN)$
    mdl$_{\Gamma'}$ = MDL($\Gamma', \mathcal{S}$)
    if mdl$_{\Gamma'}$ < mdl **then**
      $\Gamma_{w,r} = \Gamma'$
  $\Gamma = \{\Gamma_{w,r}\} \cup \Gamma$
return Γ

Algorithm 2 MDL($\Gamma, \mathcal{S}$)

Input: $\Gamma = \{(c, f)\}$ – a scored list of concepts
$\mathcal{S}$ – the set of observations (concept collocates)
Output: MDL($\Gamma, \mathcal{S}$)

$\widehat{\theta} = < f_1, ..., f_n >; (c_i, f_i) \in \Gamma$
remove $\{(c, f) \in \Gamma | f = 1\}$ // parameter description length :
$L(\widehat{\theta}|\Gamma) = \frac{|\Gamma|-1}{2} * log(|\mathcal{S}|)$ // data description length :
for all $(c, f) \in \Gamma$ **do**
  $L(\mathcal{S}|\Gamma, \widehat{\theta}) = L(\mathcal{S}|\Gamma, \widehat{\theta}) + f * log(\frac{f}{hyponyms(c)*|\Gamma|})$
return $L(\widehat{\theta}|\Gamma) - L(\mathcal{S}|\Gamma, \widehat{\theta})$

Algorithm 3 abstract($\mathcal{S}$,WkN)

Input: $\mathcal{S} = \{(c, f)|(w, \mathcal{R}, c) \in G\}$
WkN – WikiNet
Output: $\mathcal{S}'$

$\mathcal{S}' = \{\}$
for $c|(c, \_) \in \mathcal{S}$ **do**
  while c has only one *is_a* link **do**
    $c = c', (c, is\_a, c') \in WkN$
  $C = \{(c', c)|(c, is\_a, c') \in WkN\}$
  for $(c', c) \in C$ **do**
    if $(c', f') \in \mathcal{S}'$ **then**
      replace (c', f') with $(c', f' + \frac{f}{|C|}), (c, f) \in \mathcal{S}$ in $\mathcal{S}'$
    else
      $\mathcal{S}' \cup = \{(c', f)\}, (c, f) \in \mathcal{S}$
// Remove hyponyms.
for all $\{(c, c') \in \mathcal{S}'|(c', is\_a, c) \in WkN\}$ **do**
  // update frequency f of c
  $f_c = f_c + f_{c'}, f \in \mathcal{S}$
  delete c'
return $\mathcal{S}'$

discourse" assumption – a phrase that appears associated with a hyperlink once in the article body will be associated with the same hyperlink throughout the article (this applies to the article title as well, which is not hyperlinked in the article itself). This new version of the corpus was then split into sentences, and those without hyperlinks were removed. The remaining 18 million sentences were parsed with a parallelized version of Ensemble[4] (Surdeanu and Manning, 2010), and we extracted G, the set of all grammatical relations of the type *(verb, dependency, hyperlink)* and *(adjective, dependency, hyperlink)*, with the hyperlinks resolved to their corresponding node (concept) in the network ($|G|$ = 1,578,413 triples). For each verb and adjective in the extracted collocations, and for each of their dependency relations, their collocates were generalized in the network defined by the hypernym/hyponym relations in WikiNet following a method similar to the Minimum Description Length principle (Li and Abe, 1998).

Essentially, we aimed to determine a small set of (more general) concepts that describe the set of collocates for a word w and grammatical relation r. Starting from the concept collocates gathered, we go upwards following WikiNet's *is_a* links, and for each node found that covers at least N concept collocates (N is a parameter, N=2 in the experiments presented here), the MDL score of the node is computed (Algorithm 2). We place a limit M on the number of upward steps in the hierarchy (M=3 in our experiments). The disjoint set of nodes that has the lowest overall MDL score is chosen (Γ), and for each node in this cut (which we call *abstraction*), we compute the selectional preference score, based on the number of concepts it dominates.

As an example, for the verb *defeat*, the corpus leads to collocations such as[5]:

defeat
  nsubj
    Earle Page (10357) – 8, Manuela Maleeva (1092361) – 7, New York Yankees (10128601) – 5, Tommy Haas (1118005) – 5, . . .
  obj

[4] `http://www.surdeanu.name/mihai/ensemble/`

[5] The format is:
Article name (Article Id) – frequency.

New York Yankees (10128601) – 9, Oakland Athletics (11641124) – 6, Phoenix Suns (11309373) – 4, Jason Suttie (10080653) – 3, Ravana (100234) – 3, ...

Determining abstractions and selectional preferences leads to the following information[6]:

defeat

nsubj

Martial artists (118977183) – 0.5, Person (219599) – 0.3518, Interest (146738) – 0.037, ...

obj

Video games (9570081) – 0.25, British games (24489088) – 0.25, Person (219599) – 0.1445, Interest (146738) – 0.1341, ...

3.3 Linking the PMW to the concept network

In our environment, linking the PMW to the concept network is equivalent to finding its corresponding concept in our ontology, WikiNet. We see this corresponding concept as the literal reading of the PMW. Doing so is a non-trivial task (see the Cross-Lingual Link Discovery task at NTCIR-9 (Tang et al., 2011) and the Cross-Lingual Entity Linking task – part of the Knowledge Base Population track – at TAC 2011[7]). In our particular setting, where we use the metonymy data from SemEval 2007, the domain of the PMW is well defined: locations and companies, respectively. Using these constraints, finding the corresponding Wikipedia articles is much simplified, by using the category hierarchy and constraining the concepts to fall under the *Geography* and *Companies* categories respectively. When multiple options are present, we find instead a matching disambiguation page. In this case we pick the article that is listed first on this disambiguation page. On a manually checked random sample, the accuracy of the approach was 100% (on a sample of 100 PMWs).

3.4 Scoring conceptual relations with local and global context

We work under the assumption that the concept corresponding to the PMW is related to the possible interpretations through a semantic relation, in particular one that is captured in the concept network. After

[6]The format is:
Concept name (Concept Id) – selectional preference score.

[7]http://nlp.cs.qc.cuny.edu/kbp/2011/

countries	: *Administrator_of, Architect_of, Based_in, Built_in, Continent, ...*
companies	: *Association, Brand, Company, Distributed_by, Executive_of, ...*

Table 1: Example conceptual relations

establishing the connection to the resource by linking the PMW to the concept c_{PMW} corresponding to its literal interpretation (see Section 3.3), we extract the relations in which it is involved ($\mathcal{R}_i, i = 1, k$), and the concepts it is connected to through these relations ($\mathcal{C}_{\mathcal{R}_i} = \{c_x | (c_{PMW}\mathcal{R}_i c_x)\}$). Table 1 shows examples of conceptual relations extracted for companies and countries.

We are interested in computing the likelihood of a conceptual relation being the correct interpretation of a PMW, given its local and global context $p(\mathcal{R}_i|Cont, w, r)$.

3.4.1 The local context

The local context considered in this work are all grammatically related verbs and adjectives w and their associated grammatical relation r. The grammatical analysis (see Section 3.2) provides the set of abstractions corresponding to the grammatically related word w and grammatical relation r: $A_j, j = 1, n$. Remember that these are local context constraints on the interpretation of the PMW.

Through the knowledge resource used we can establish and quantify connections between each c_x and A_j, and thus between each $\mathcal{R}_i$ and A_j:

$$(3) \qquad p(\mathcal{R}_i|A_j) = \sum_{x \in C_{\mathcal{R}_i}} p(c_x|A_j)$$

where $p(c_x|A_j)$ is the probability of concept c_x under abstraction A_j, which is computed based on the semantic relations in WikiNet:

$$p(c_x|A_j) = \sum_{H} \prod_{h_i \in H} p(h_i|h_{i+1})$$

where H is in turn each path from c_x to A_j following *is_a* links in WikiNet, starting with c_x (i.e. $h_0 = c_x$) and ending in A_j. $p(h_i|h_{i+1})$ is the probability of the child node h_i given its ancestor h_{i+1}. Within this work we assume a uniform probability distribution in each node:

$$p(h_i|h_{i+1}) = \frac{1}{|descendants(h_{i+1})|}$$

Through this, it is straightforward that $\sum_{c_x} p(c_x|A_j) = 1$ when c_x ranges over all concepts subsumed by A_j, and is thus a valid probability distribution.

3.4.2 The global context

The abstractions obtained before are concepts. We extract all nodes in the network subsumed by these concepts, and their corresponding articles in Wikipedia (if they have one). This produces "abstraction-specific" article sets, based on which we compute the probability of the global context of a PMW for each abstraction. We are interested in the probability of an abstraction, given the context and the word w and grammatical relation r, which we compute as:

$$p(A_j|Cont, w, r) = \frac{p(Cont|A_j, w, r) * p(A_j, w, r)}{p(Cont, w, r)}$$

which, considering that $p(Cont, w, r)$ is the same for a given context, we approximate as

$$p(A_j|Cont) \approx p(Cont|A_j) * p(A_j, w, r)$$

$p(A_j, w, r) = p(A_j|w, r) * p(w, r)$, and we approximate it through the computed selectional preference $p(A_j|w, r)$, since $p(w, r)$ is constant for a given example to analyze.

$$\begin{aligned} p(Cont|A_j, w, r) &= \sum_{j=1}^{n} p(Cont|A_j)p(A_j|w, r) \\ &= \sum_{j=1}^{n}(\prod_{l=1}^{m} p(w_l|A_j))p(A_j|w, r) \end{aligned}$$

where $Cont$ is the global context consisting of m words $w_l, l = 1, m$.[8]

[8]The global context therefore could be all words in a text or all words in a sentence or any other token-based definition in our framework. As the SemEval 2007 data gives metonymic examples in a three-sentence context we use all the words in the 3 sentences as our global context.

$$p(w_l|A_j) = \frac{count(w_l, \mathcal{A}_j)}{|\mathcal{A}_j|}$$

where $\mathcal{A}_j$ is the set of articles subsumed by abstraction A_j, and $count(w_l, \mathcal{A}_j)$ is the number of times word w_l appears in the article collection $\mathcal{A}_j$.

3.4.3 Putting it all together

This enables us now to compute $p(\mathcal{R}_i|Cont, w, r)$ based on the formulas 3, 4:

$$p(\mathcal{R}_i|Cont, w, r) = \sum_{j=1}^{n}(p(\mathcal{R}_i|A_j) * p(A_j|Cont, w, r))$$

4 Experiments

The computed probabilities for each conceptual relation (= potential readings) of the PMW in the concept network can be used as features in a supervised framework or directly as an unsupervised prediction, returning the most likely conceptual relation given the context as the required reading.

Although the latter is our ultimate goal, to allow comparison with related work from the metonymy resolution task (Task 8) at SemEval 2007, we first investigate the supervised set-up. We then simulate the unsupervised setting in Section 4.3.

4.1 Data

We use the data from the metonymy resolution task (Task 8) at SemEval 2007. It consists of training and test data for country and company names which are potentially metonymic. Table 2 shows the statistics of the data, and the possible interpretations for the PMWs. The training-test division was achieved randomly so that the test data can have metonymic readings for which no training data exists, showing again the limitations of a supervised approach of prespecified readings.

Grammatical features The features used by Nissim and Markert (2005), and commonly used for the supervised classification of metonymy readings (Markert and Nissim, 2009):

- grammatical role of PMW (subj, obj, ...);
- lemmatized head/modifier of PMW (announce, say, ...);

reading	train	test
locations	925	908
literal	737	721
mixed	15	20
othermet	9	11
obj-for-name	0	4
obj-for-representation	0	0
place-for-people	161	141
place-for-event	3	10
place-for-product	0	1
organizations	1090	842
literal	690	520
mixed	59	60
othermet	14	8
obj-for-name	8	6
obj-for-representation	1	0
org-for-members	220	161
org-for-event	2	1
org-for-product	74	67
org-for-facility	15	16
org-for-index	7	3

Table 2: Statistics for the Task 8 data

- determiner of PMW (def, indef, bare, demonst, other, ...);
- grammatical number of PMW (sg, pl);
- number of grammatical roles in which the PMW appears in its current context;
- number of words in PMW.

All these features can be extracted from the grammatically annotated and POS tagged data provided by the organizers.

The annotations provided are dependency relations, many of which contain a preposition as an argument (e.g. (to, *pp*, UK) from the example ... *the visit to the UK of* ...). Such relations are not informative, but together with the head that dominates the prepositional complement (e.g. *visit to*) they may be. Because of this, we process the provided annotations and add wherever possible to the simple prepositions the head of their subsuming constituent. This would change the above mentioned dependency to (visit, *prep-to*, UK).

Semantic relations as features To evaluate the proposed approach we use the PMW's conceptual relations as features. The feature values are the $p(\mathcal{R}_i|Cont, w, r)$ scores.

For the "countries" portion of the data this adds 109 semantic relation features, and for companies 29 features. Table 1 showed examples of these new features.

4.2 Supervised learning

We use the SMO classifier in the WEKA machine learning toolkit (Witten and Frank, 2000) with its standard settings, training on the SemEval 2007 (Task 8) training set.

Table 3 shows the results of various configurations on the test data, in comparison with a most frequent reading baseline (assigning literal to all PMWs) as well as a system M&N that shows the results computed using only the features proposed by Nissim and Markert (2005). In addition, we compare to the best results[9] at SemEval 2007 (SE_{max}) and Nastase and Strube (2009) (N09). Nastase and Strube (2009) added WordNet supersenses as features, and their values are selectional preferences computed with reference to WordNet. These are similar to our abstractions, which in our approach serve to link the local and the global context to the ontological relations, but do not appear as features.

Our system SP shows the results obtained using the M&N features plus the conceptual relation features conditioned on both local and global context whereas SP_{local} and SP_{global} use conceptual relations conditioned on local ($p(A_j|Cont, w, r) \approx p(A_j|w, r)$) or global context ($p(A_j|Cont, w, r) \approx p(A_j|Cont) = \sum_{j=1}^{n}(\prod_{l=1}^{m} p(w_l|A_j))$) only.

While the differences in overall accuracies are small, there are significant differences in classifying individual classes, as shown in Tables 4 – 5[10], where the *distrib.* column shows the class distribution in the test data. It is interesting to note that, in our setting, the global context is more useful than the local

[9]We show the best result for each category, not necessarily from the overall best performing system. This holds for Tables 4 and 5 as well.

[10]The detailed results for previous approaches are reproduced from (Nastase and Strube, 2009). We include only the classes that have a non-zero F-score for at least one of the presented approaches.

task ↓ method →	baseline	SE_{max}	N09	M&N	SP	SP_{local}	SP_{global}	SP_{unsup}
LOCATION-COARSE	79.4	85.2	86.1	83.4	85.8	83.0	85.0	81.6
LOCATION-MEDIUM	79.4	84.8	85.9	82.3	85.7	82.7	84.6	81.5
LOCATION-FINE	79.4	84.4	85.0	81.3	84.7	82.1	83.8	81.0
ORGANIZATION-COARSE	61.8	76.7	74.9	74.0	77.0	76.4	76.8	67.8
ORGANIZATION-MEDIUM	61.8	73.3	72.4	69.4	74.6	74.0	74.4	66.3
ORGANIZATION-FINE	61.8	72.8	71.0	68.5	72.8	71.9	72.7	65.3

Table 3: Accuracy scores

task ↓ method →	distrib.	SE_{max}	N09	SP
LOCATION-COARSE				
literal	79.4	91.2	91.6	91.4
non-literal	20.6	57.6	59.1	58.5
LOCATION-MEDIUM				
literal	79.4	91.2	91.6	91.4
metonymic	18.4	58.0	61.5	61.6
mixed	2.2	8.3	16	9.1
LOCATION-FINE				
literal	79.4	91.2	91.6	91.4
place-for-people	15.5	58.9	61.7	61.1
place-for-event	1.1	16.7	0	0
obj-for-name	0.4	66.7	0	0
mixed	2.2	8.3	16	9.1

Table 4: Fine-grained results for each classification task for countries (F-scores)

task ↓ method →	distrib.	SE_{max}	N09	SP
ORGANIZATION-COARSE				
literal	61.8	82.5	81.4	82.7
non-literal	38.2	65.2	61.6	65.5
ORGANIZATION-MEDIUM				
literal	61.8	82.5	81.4	82.7
metonymic	31.0	60.4	58.7	63.1
mixed	7.2	30.8	26.8	27.4
ORGANIZATION-FINE				
literal	61.8	82.6	81.4	82.7
org-for-members	19.1	63.0	59.7	66.5
org-for-product	8.0	50.0	44.4	35.0
org-for-facility	2.0	22.2	36.3	45.5
org-for-name	0.7	80.0	58.8	44.4
mixed	7.2	34.3	27.1	27.4

Table 5: Fine-grained results for each classification task for companies (F-scores)

one for resolving metonymies. Combining local and global evidence improves over both, indicating that the information they provide is not redundant.

For companies the difference is small in terms of accuracy, but in classification of individual classes the difference in performance is higher, but because of the small data size not statistically significant.

Countries in WikiNet have a high number of surrounding relations, because they are used as categorization criteria for professionals, for example, which generates fine-grained relations such as *Administrator_of, Ambassador_of, Chemist_of ...*. Such a fine grained distinction between different professions for people in a country is not necessary, or indeed, desirable, for the metonymy resolution task. The results show that despite this shortcoming, the results are on par with the state-of-the-art, but in future work we plan to explore the task of relation generalization and its impact on the current task.

4.3 Simulating unsupervised metonymy resolution

In an unsupervised metonymy resolution approach, we would assign as interpretation the conceptual relation whose probability given the PMW, global and local contexts is highest. To simulate then the unsupervised metonymy resolution task, we make the relation features (used in the supervised approach) binary, where for each instance the relation that has highest probability has the value 1, the others 0.

Using only the relation features simulates an unsupervised approach – this set-up learns a mapping between the relations used as features and the metonymy classes in the data used. Column SP_{Unsup} in Table 3 shows the results obtained in this configuration. As expected the results are lower, but still close to the supervised method when using only grammatical features (M&N) for the location setting. The results also significantly beat the baseline (apart from the Location-Fine setting). One feature that contributes greatly to the results, especially for the company semantic class, is the grammatical role of the PMW, but we could not incorporate this in the unsupervised setting.

The results in the simulated unsupervised setting indicate that relations are a viable substitute for manually provided classes in an unsupervised framework, while leaving space for improvement.

5 Conclusion

We have explored the usage of local and global context for the task of metonymy resolution in a probabilistic framework. The global context has been rarely used for the task of determining the intended reading of a potentially metonymic word (PMW) in context. We rely on automatically computed selectional preferences, extracted from a corpus of Wikipedia articles, and generalized based on a concept network also extracted from Wikipedia. Despite relying on automatically derived resources, the presented approach produces results on-a-par with current state-of-the-art systems. The method described here is also a step towards the unsupervised resolution of metonymic words in context, by taking into account knowledge about the concept corresponding to the literal interpretation of the PMW, and its relations to other concepts. This framework would also allow for exploring the metonymy resolution phenomena in various languages (since Wikipedia and WikiNet are multilingual), and investigate whether the same relations apply or different languages have different metonymic patterns.

Acknowledgments

Katja Markert is the recipient of an Alexander-von-Humboldt Fellowship for Experienced Researchers. This work was financially supported by the EC-funded project CoSyne (FP7-ICT-4-24853) and the Klaus Tschirra Foundation. We thank the reviewers for the helpful comments, and Helga Krämer-Houska for additional support for conference participation.

References

Luisa Bentivogli, Elena Cabrio, Ido Dagan, Danilo Giampiccolo, Medea Lo Leggio, and Bernardo Magnini. 2007. Building textual entailment specialized data sets: A methodology for isolating linguistic phenomena relevant to inference. In *Proceedings of the 7th International Conference on Language Resources and Evaluation,* La Valetta, Malta, 17–23 May 2010.

Caroline Brun, Maud Ehrmann, and Guillaume Jacquet. 2007. XRCE-M: A hybrid system for named entity metonymy resolution. In *Proceedings of the 4th International Workshop on Semantic Evaluations (SemEval-1),* Prague, Czech Republic, 23–24 June 2007, pages 488–491.

Richárd Farkas, Eszter Simon, György Szarvas, and Dániel Varga. 2007. GYDER: Maxent metonymy resolution. In *Proceedings of the 4th International Workshop on Semantic Evaluations (SemEval-1),* Prague, Czech Republic, 23–24 June 2007, pages 161–164.

Dan C. Fass. 1991. met*: A method for discriminating metonomy and metaphor by computer. *Computational Linguistics*, 17(1):49–90.

Sanda M. Harabagiu. 1998. Deriving metonymic coercions from WordNet. In *Proceedings of the Workshop on the Usage of WordNet in Natural Language Systems,* Montral, Quebec, Canada, 16 August, 1998, pages 142–148.

Jerry Hobbs, Mark Stickel, Douglas Appelt, and Paul Martin. 1993. Interpretation as abduction. *Artificial Intelligence*, 63(1-2):69–142.

Maria Lapata. 2003. Probabilistic text structuring: Experiments with sentence ordering. In *Proceedings of the 41st Annual Meeting of the Association for Computational Linguistics,* Sapporo, Japan, 7–12 July 2003, pages 545–552.

Johannes Leveling and Sven Hartrumpf. 2008. On metonymy recognition for geographic information retrieval. *International Journal of Geographical Information Science*, 22(3):289–299.

Johannes Leveling. 2007. FUH (FernUniversität in Hagen): Metonymy recognition using different kinds of context for a memory-based learner. In *Proceedings of the 4th International Workshop on Semantic Evaluations (SemEval-1),* Prague, Czech Republic, 23–24 June 2007, pages 153–156.

Hang Li and Naoki Abe. 1998. Generalizing case frames using a thesaurus and the MDL principle. *Computational Linguistics*, 24(2):217–244.

Katja Markert and Udo Hahn. 2002. Metonymies in discourse. *Artificial Intelligence*, 135(1/2):145–198.

Katja Markert and Malvina Nissim. 2009. Data and models for metonymy resolution. *Language Resources and Evaluation*, 43(2):123–138.

Vivi Nastase and Michael Strube. 2009. Combining collocations, lexical and encyclopedic knowledge for metonymy resolution. In *Proceedings of the 2009 Conference on Empirical Methods in Natural Language Processing,* Singapore, 6-7 August 2009, pages 910–918.

Vivi Nastase, Michael Strube, Benjamin Börschinger, Cäcilia Zirn, and Anas Elghafari. 2010. WikiNet: A very large scale multi-lingual concept network. In *Proceedings of the 7th International Conference on Language Resources and Evaluation,* La Valetta, Malta, 17–23 May 2010.

Cristina Nicolae, Gabriel Nicolae, and Sanda Harabagiu. 2007. UTD-HLT-CG: Semantic architecture for metonymy resolution and classification of nominal relations. In *Proceedings of the 4th International Workshop on Semantic Evaluations (SemEval-1),* Prague, Czech Republic, 23–24 June 2007, pages 454–459.

Malvina Nissim and Katja Markert. 2005. Learning to buy a Renault and talk to BMW: A supervised approach to conventional metonymy. In *Proceedings of the 6th International Workshop on Computational Semantics,* Tilburg, Netherlands, January 12-14, 2005.

Geoffrey Nunberg. 1995. Transfers of meaning. *Journal of Semantics*, 12(1):109–132.

Thierry Poibeau. 2007. Up13: Knowledge-poor methods (sometimes) perform poorly. In *Proceedings of the 4th International Workshop on Semantic Evaluations (SemEval-1),* Prague, Czech Republic, 23–24 June 2007, pages 418–421.

James Pustejovsky. 1991. The generative lexicon. *Computational Linguistics*, 17(4):209–241.

Kirk Roberts and Sanda M. Harabagiu. 2011. Unsupervised learning of selectional restrictions and detection of argument coercions. In *Proceedings of the 2011 Conference on Empirical Methods in Natural Language Processing,* Edinburgh, UK, 27-29 July 2011, pages 980–990.

Ekaterina Shutova. 2009. Sense-based interpretation of logical metonymy using a statistical method. In *Proceedings of the Joint Conference of the 47th Annual Meeting of the Association for Computational Linguistics and the 4th International Joint Conference on Natural Language Processing,* Singapore, 2–7 August 2009, pages 1–9.

Mihai Surdeanu and Christopher D. Manning. 2010. Ensemble Models for Dependency Parsing: Cheap and Good? In *Proceedings of Human Language Technologies 2010: The Conference of the North American Chapter of the Association for Computational Linguistics,* Los Angeles, Cal., 2–4 June 2010, pages 649–652.

Ling-Xiang Tang, Shlomo Geva, Andrew Trotman, Yue Xu, and Kelly Y. Itakura. 2011. Overview of the NTCIR-9 crosslink task: Cross-lingual link discovery. In *Proceedings of the 9th NII Test Collection for IR Systems Workshop meeting – NTCIR-9* Tokyo, Japan, 6–9 December 2011.

Masao Utiyama, Masaki Murata, and Hitoshi Isahara. 2000. A statistical approach to the processing of metonymy. In *Proceedings of the 18th International Conference on Computational Linguistics,* Saarbrücken, Germany, 31 July – 4 August 2000, pages 885–891.

Ian H. Witten and Eibe Frank. 2000. *Data Mining: Practical Machine Learning Tools and Techniques with Java Implementations.* Morgan Kaufmann, San Diego, CA.

Learning Verb Inference Rules from Linguistically-Motivated Evidence

Hila Weisman[§], **Jonathan Berant**[†], **Idan Szpektor**[‡], **Ido Dagan**[§]
§ Computer Science Department, Bar-Ilan University
† The Blavatnik School of Computer Science, Tel Aviv University
‡ Yahoo! Research Israel
{weismah1,dagan}@cs.biu.ac.il
{jonatha6}@post.tau.ac.il
{idan}@yahoo-inc.com

Abstract

Learning inference relations between verbs is at the heart of many semantic applications. However, most prior work on learning such rules focused on a rather narrow set of information sources: mainly distributional similarity, and to a lesser extent manually constructed verb co-occurrence patterns. In this paper, we claim that it is imperative to utilize information from various textual scopes: verb co-occurrence within a sentence, verb co-occurrence within a document, as well as overall corpus statistics. To this end, we propose a much richer novel set of linguistically motivated cues for detecting entailment between verbs and combine them as features in a supervised classification framework. We empirically demonstrate that our model significantly outperforms previous methods and that information from each textual scope contributes to the verb entailment learning task.

1 Introduction

Inference rules are an important building block of many semantic applications, such as Question Answering (Ravichandran and Hovy, 2002) and Information Extraction (Shinyama and Sekine, 2006). For example, given the sentence "*Churros are coated with sugar*", one can use the rule 'coat → cover' to answer the question "*What are Churros covered with?*". Inference rules specify a directional inference relation between two text fragments, and we follow the *Textual Entailment* modeling of inference (Dagan et al., 2006), which refers to such rules as *entailment rules*. In this work we focus on one of the most important rule types, namely, lexical entailment rules between verbs (*verb entailment*), *e.g.,* 'whisper → talk', 'win → play' and 'buy → own'. The significance of such rules has led to active research in automatic learning of entailment rules between verbs or verb-like structures (Zanzotto et al., 2006; Abe et al., 2008; Schoenmackers et al., 2010).

Most prior efforts to learn verb entailment rules from large corpora employed distributional similarity methods, assuming that verbs are semantically similar if they occur in similar contexts (Lin, 1998; Berant et al., 2012). This led to the automatic acquisition of large scale knowledge bases, but with limited precision. Fewer works, such as *VerbOcean* (Chklovski and Pantel, 2004), focused on identifying verb entailment through verb instantiation of manually constructed patterns. For example, the sentence "*he scared and even startled me*" implies that 'startle → scare'. This led to more precise rule extraction, but with poor coverage since contrary to nouns, in which patterns are common (Hearst, 1992), verbs do not co-occur often within rigid patterns. However, verbs do tend to co-occur in the same document, and also in different clauses of the same sentence.

In this paper, we claim that on top of standard pattern-based and distributional similarity methods, corpus-based learning of verb entailment can greatly benefit from exploiting additional linguistically-motivated cues that are specific to verbs. For instance, when verbs co-occur in different clauses of the same sentence, the syntactic relation between the clauses can be viewed as a proxy for the semantic relation between the verbs. Moreover, we claim that to improve performance it is crucial to combine information sources from different textual scopes: verb co-occurrence within a sentence and within a document, distributional similarity over the entire corpus, etc.

Our contribution in this paper is two-fold. First, we suggest a novel set of entailment *indicators* that help to detect the likelihood of verb entailment. Our novel indicators are specific to verbs and are linguistically-motivated. Second, we encode our novel indicators as features within a supervised classification framework and integrate them with other standard features adapted from prior work. This results in a supervised corpus-based learning method that combines verb entailment information at the sentence, document and corpus levels.

We test our model on a manually labeled data set, and show that it outperforms the best performing previous work by 24%. In addition, we examine the effectiveness of indicators that operate at the sentence-level, document-level and corpus-level. This analysis reveals that using a rich and diverse set of indicators that capture sentence-level interactions between verbs substantially improves verb entailment detection.

2 Background

The main approach for learning entailment rules between verbs and verb-like structures has employed the *distributional hypothesis*, which assumes that words with similar meanings appear in similar contexts. For example, we expect the words *'buy'* and *'purchase'* to occur with similar subjects and objects in a large corpus. This observation has led to ample work on developing both symmetric and directional similarity measures that attempt to capture semantic relations between lexical items by comparing their neighborhood context (Lin, 1998; Weeds and Weir, 2003; Geffet and Dagan, 2005; Szpektor and Dagan, 2008; Kotlerman et al., 2010).

A far less explored direction for learning verb entailment involves exploiting verb co-occurrence in a sentence or a document. One prominent work is Chklovsky and Pantel's VerbOcean (2004). In VerbOcean, the authors manually constructed 33 patterns and divided them into five pattern groups, where each group signals one of the following five semantic relations: *similarity*, *strength*, *antonymy*, *enablement* and *happens-before*. For example, the pattern *'Xed and later Yed'* signals the *happens-before* relation between the verbs *'X'* and *'Y'*. Starting with candidate verb pairs based on a distributional similarity measure, the patterns are used to choose a semantic relation per verb pair based on the different patterns this pair instantiates. This method is more precise than distributional similarity approaches, but it is highly susceptible to sparseness issues, since verbs do not typically co-occur within rigid patterns. Utilizing verb co-occurrence at the document level, Chambers and Jurafsky (2008) estimate whether a pair of verbs is narratively related by counting the number of times the verbs share an argument in the same document. In a similar manner, Pekar (2008) detects entailment rules between templates from shared arguments within discourse-related clauses in the same document.

Recently, supervised classification has become standard in performing various semantic tasks. Mirkin et al. (2006) introduced a system for learning entailment rules between nouns (*e.g.,* 'novel → book') that combines distributional similarity and Hearst patterns as features in a supervised classifier. Pennacchiotti and Pantel (2009) augment Mirkin et al's features with web-based features for the task of entity extraction. Hagiwara et al. (2009) perform synonym identification based on both distributional and contextual features. Tremper (2010) extract "loose" sentence-level features in order to identify the *presupposition* relation (*e.g.,* , the verb *'win'* presupposes the verb *'play'*). Last, Berant et al. (2012) utilized various distributional similarity features to identify entailment between lexical-syntactic predicates.

In this paper, we follow the supervised approach for semantic relation detection in order to identify verb entailment. While we utilize and adapt useful features from prior work, we introduce a diverse set of novel features for the task, effectively combining verb co-occurrence information at the sentence, document, and corpus levels.

3 Linguistically-Motivated Indicators

As mentioned in Section 1, verbs behave quite differently from nouns in corpora. In this section, we introduce linguistically motivated indicators that are specific to verbs and may signal the semantic relation between verb pairs. Then, in Section 4 we describe how these indicators are exactly encoded as features within a supervised classification framework.

Verb co-occurrence When (non-auxiliary) verbs co-occur in a sentence, they are often the main verbs of different clauses. We thus aim to use information about the relation between clauses to learn about the relation between the clauses' main verbs. *Discourse markers* (Hobbs, 1979; Schiffrin, 1988) are lexical terms such as *'because'* and *'however'* that indicate a semantic relation between discourse fragments (i.e., propositions or speech acts). We suggest that these markers can indicate semantic relations between the main verbs of the connected clauses. For example, in the sentence *"He always snores while he sleeps"*, the marker *'while'* indicates a temporal relation between the clauses, indicating that *'snoring'* occurs while *'sleeping'* (and so *'snore → sleep'*).

Often the relation between clauses is not expressed explicitly with an overt discourse marker, but is still implied by the syntactic structure of the sentence. For example, in dependency parsing the relation can be captured by labeled dependency edges expressing that one clause is an adverbial adjunct of the other, or that two clauses are coordinated. This can indicate the existence (or lack) of entailment between verbs. For instance, in the sentence *"When I walked into the room, he was working out"*, the verb *'walk'* is an adverbial adjunct of the verb *'work out'*. Such co-occurrence structure does not indicate a deep semantic relation, such as entailment, between the two verbs.

Verb classes Verb classes are sets of semantically-related verbs sharing some linguistic properties (Levin, 1993). One of the most general verb classes are stative vs. event verbs (Jackendoff, 1983). Stative verb, such as *'love'* and *'think'*, usually describe a state that lasts some time. On the other hand, event verbs, such as *'run'* and *'kiss'*, describe an action. We hypothesize that verb classes are relevant for determining entailment, for example, that stative verbs are not likely to entail event verbs.

Verb generality Verb-particle constructions are multi-word expressions consisting of a head verb and a particle, *e.g., switch off* (Baldwin and Villavicencio, 2002). We conjecture that the more general a verb is, the more likely it is to appear with many different particles. Detecting verb generality can help us tackle an infamous property of distributional similarity methods, namely, the difficulty in detecting the direction of entailment (Berant et al., 2012). For example, the verb *'cover'* appears with many different particles such as *'up'* and *'for'*, while the verb *'coat'* does not. Thus, assuming we have evidence for an entailment relation between the two verbs, this indicator can help us discern the direction of entailment and determine that 'coat → cover'.

Typed Distributional Similarity As discussed in section 2, distributional similarity is the most common source of information for learning semantic relations between verbs. Yet, we suggest that on top of standard distributional similarity measures, which take several verbal arguments into account (such as subject, object, etc.) simultaneously, we should also focus on each type of argument independently. In particular, we apply this approach to compute similarity between verbs based on the set of adverbs that modify them. Our hypothesis is that adverbs may contain relevant information for capturing the direction of entailment. If a verb appears with a small set of adverbs, it is more likely to be a specific verb that already conveys a specific action or state, making an additional adverb redundant. For example, the verb *'whisper'* conveys a specific manner of talking and will probably not appear with the adverb *'loudly'*, while the verb *'talk'* is more likely to appear with such an adverb. Thus, measuring similarity based solely on adverb modifiers could reveal this phenomenon.

4 Supervised Entailment Detection

In the previous section, we discussed linguistic observations regarding novel indicators that may help in detecting entailment relations between verbs. We next describe how to incorporate these indicators as features within a supervised framework for learning lexical entailment rules between verbs. We follow prior work on supervised lexical semantics (Mirkin et al., 2006; Hagiwara et al., 2009; Tremper, 2010) and address the rule learning task as a classification task. Specifically, given an ordered verb pair (v_1, v_2) as input, we learn a classifier that detects whether the entailment relation '$v_1 \rightarrow v_2$' holds for this pair.

We next detail how our novel indicators, as well as other diverse sources of information found useful in prior work, are encoded as features. Then, we describe the learning model and our feature analysis procedure.

4.1 Entailment features

Most of our features are based on information extracted from the target verb pair co-occurring within varying textual scopes (sentence, document, corpus). Hence, we group the features according to their related scope. Naturally, when the scope is small, *i.e.,* at a sentence level, the semantic relation between the verbs is easier to discern but the information may be sparse. Conversely, when co-occurrence is loose the relation is harder to discern but coverage is increased.

4.1.1 Sentence-level co-occurrence

We next detail features that address co-occurrence of the target verb pair within a sentence. These include our novel linguistically-motivated indicators, as well as features that were adapted from prior work.

Discourse markers As discussed in Section 3, discourse markers may signal relations between the main verbs of adjacent clauses. The literature is abundant with taxonomies that classify markers to various discourse relations (Mann and Thompson, 1988; Hovy and Maier, 1993; Knott and Sanders, 1998). Inspired by Marcu and Echihabi (2002), we employ markers that are mapped to four discourse relations *'Contrast'*, *'Cause'*, *'Condition'* and *'Temporal'*, as specified in Table 1. This definition can be viewed as a relaxed version of VerbOcean's (Chklovski and Pantel, 2004) patterns, although the underlying intuition is different (see Section 3).

For a target verb pair (v_1, v_2) and each discourse relation r, we count the number of times that v_1 is the main verb in the main clause, v_2 is the main verb in the subordinate clause, and the clauses are connected via a marker mapped to r. For example, given the sentence "*You must enroll in the competition before you can participate in it*", the verb pair (*'enroll'*,*'participate'*) appears in the *'Temporal'* relation, indicated by the marker *'before'*, where *'enroll'* is in the main clause. Each count is then normalized by the total number of times (v_1, v_2) appear with any marker. The same procedure is done when v_1 is in the subordinate clause and v_2 in the main clause. We term the features by the relevant discourse relation, *e.g., 'v1-contrast-v2'* refers to v_1 being in the main clause and connected to the subordinate clause via a *contrast* marker.

Dependency relations between clauses As noted in Section 3, the syntactic structure of verb co-occurrence can indicate the existence or lack of entailment. In dependency parsing this may be expressed via the label of the dependency relation connecting the main and subordinate clauses. In our experiments we used the ukWaC corpus[1] (Baroni et al., 2009) which was parsed by the MALT parser (Nivre et al., 2006). Hence, we identified three MALT dependency relations that connect a main clause with its subordinate clause. The first relation is the object complement relation *'obj'*. In this case the subordinate clause is an object complement of the main clause. For example, in "*it surprised me that the lizard could talk*" the verb pair (*'surprise'*,*'talk'*) is connected by the *'obj'* relation. The second relation is the adverbial adjunct relation *'adv'*, in which the subordinate clause is adverbial and describes the time, place, manner, etc. of the main clause, *e.g.,* "*he gave his consent without thinking about the repercussions*". The last relation is the coordination relation *'coord'*, *e.g.,* "*every night my dog Lucky sleeps on the bed* ***and*** *my cat Flippers naps in the bathtub*".

Similar to discourse markers, we compute for each verb pair (v_1,v_2) and each dependency label d the proportion of times that v_1 is the main verb of the main clause, v_2 is the main verb of the subordinate clause, and the clauses are connected by dependency relation d, out of all the times they are connected by any dependency relation. We term the features by the dependency label, *e.g., 'v1-adv-v2'* refers to v_1 being in the main clause and connected to the subordinate clause via an *adverbial* adjunct.

[1] `http://wacky.sslmit.unibo.it/doku.php?id=corpora`

Discourse Rel.	Discourse Markers
Contrast	although , despite , but , whereas , notwithstanding , though
Cause	because , therefore , thus
Condition	if , unless
Temporal	whenever , after , before , until , when , finally , during , afterwards , meanwhile

Table 1: Discourse relations and their mapped markers.

Pattern-based We follow Chklovski and Pantel (2004) and extract occurrences of *VerbOcean* patterns that are instantiated by the target verb pair. As mentioned in Section 2, VerbOcean patterns were originally grouped into five semantic classes. Based on a preliminary study we conducted, we decided to utilize only four *strength*-class patterns as positive indicators for entailment, *e.g.,* "he *scared and even startled* me", and three *antonym*-class patterns as negative indicators for entailment, *e.g.,* "you can *either open or close* the door". We note that these patterns are also commonly used by RTE systems[2].

Since the corpus pattern counts were very sparse, we defined for a target verb pair (v_1, v_2) two binary features: the first denotes whether the verb pair instantiates at least one positive pattern, and the second denotes whether the verb pair instantiates at least one negative pattern. For example, given the aforementioned sentences, the value of the positive feature for the verb pair (*'startle','scare'*) is '1'. Patterns are directional, and so the value of (*'scare','startle'*) is '0'.

Polarity We compute the proportion of times that the two verbs appear in different polarity. For example, in "*he didn't say why he left*", the verb *'say'* appears in negative polarity and the verb *'leave'* in positive polarity. Such change in polarity is usually an indicator of non-entailment between the two verbs.

Tense ordering The temporal relation between verbs may provide information about their semantic relation. For each verb pair co-occurrence, we extract the verbs' tenses and order them as follows: *past* $<$ *present* $<$ *future*. We then add the features *'tense-v1<tense-v2'*, *'tense-v1=tense-v2'*, and *'tense-v1>tense-v2'*, corresponding to the proportion of times the tense of v_1 is smaller, equal to, or bigger than the tense of v_2. This indicates the prevalent temporal relation between the verbs in the corpus and may assist in detecting the direction of entailment. *e.g.,* if tense-v1>tense-v2, the verb pair is less likely to entail.

[2] http://aclweb.org/aclwiki/index.php?title=RTE_Knowledge_Resources#Ablation_Tests

Co-reference Following Tremper (2010), in every co-occurrence of (v_1,v_2) we extract for each verb the set of arguments at either the subject or object positions, denoted A_1 and A_2 (for v_1 and v_2, respectively). We then compute the proportion of co-occurrences in which v_1 and v_2 share an argument, *i.e.,* $A_1 \cap A_2 \neq \phi$, out of all the co-occurrences in which both A_1 and A_2 are non-empty. The intuition, which is similar to distributional similarity, is that semantically related verbs tend to share arguments.

Syntactic and lexical distance Following Tremper (2010) again, we compute the average distance d in dependency edges between the co-occurring verbs. We compute three features corresponding to three bins indicating if $d < 3$, $3 \leq d \leq 7$, or $d > 7$. Similar features are computed for the distance in words (bins are $0 < d < 5$, $5 \leq d \leq 10$, $d > 10$). This feature provides insight into the syntactic relatedness of the verbs.

Sentence-level pmi Pointwise mutual information (pmi) between v_1 and v_2 is computed, where the co-occurrence scope is a sentence. Higher pmi should hint at semantically related verbs.

4.1.2 Document-level co-occurrence

This group of features addresses co-occurrence of a target verb pair within the same document. These features are less sparse, but tend to capture coarser semantic relations between the target verbs.

Narrative score Chambers and Jurafsky (2008) suggested a method for learning sequences of actions or events (expressed by verbs) in which a single entity is involved. They proposed a pmi-like *narrative score* (see Eq. (1) in their paper) that estimates whether a pair consisting of a verb and one of its dependency relations (v_1, r_1) is narratively-related to another such pair (v_2, r_2). Their estimation is based on quantifying the likelihood that two verbs will share an argument that instantiates both the dependency position (v_1, r_1) and (v_2, r_2) within documents in which the two verbs co-occur. For example, given the document "*Lindsay was prosecuted for DUI. Lindsay was convicted of DUI.*" the pairs (*'prosecute'*,*'subj'*) and (*'convict'*,*'subj'*) share the argument *'Lindsay'* and are part of a narrative chain. Such narrative relations may provide cues to the semantic relatedness of the verb pair.

We compute for every target verb pair nine features using their narrative score. In four features, $r_1 = r_2$ and the common dependency is either a subject, an object, a preposition complement (*e.g.,* "we meet at the *station*.), or an adverb (termed *chamb-subj*, *chamb-obj*, and so on). In the next three features, $r_1 \neq r_2$ and r_1, r_2 denote either a subject, object, or preposition complement[3] (termed *chamb-subj-obj* and so on). Last, we add as features the average of the four features where $r_1 = r_2$ (termed *chamb-same*), and the average of the three features where $r_1 \neq r_2$ (termed *chamb-diff*).

Document-level pmi Similar to sentence-level pmi, we compute the pmi between v_1 and v_2, but this time the co-occurrence scope is a document.

4.1.3 Corpus-level statistics

The final group of features ignores sentence or document boundaries and is based on overall corpus statistics.

Distributional similarity Following our hypothesis regarding typed distributional similarity (Section 3), we first compute for each verb and each argument (subject, object, preposition complement and adverb) a separate vector that counts the number of times each word in the corpus instantiates the argument of that verb. In addition, we also compute a vector that is the concatenation of the previous separate vectors, which captures the standard distributional similarity statistics. We then apply three state-of-the-art distributional similarity measures, *Lin* (Lin, 1998), *Weeds precision* (Weeds and Weir, 2003) and *BInc* (Szpektor and Dagan, 2008), to compute for every verb pair a similarity score between each of the five count vectors[4]. We term each feature by the method and argument, *e.g.,* *weeds-prep* and *lin-all* represent the Weeds measure over prepositional complements and the Lin measure over all arguments.

Verb classes Following our discussion in Section 3, we first measure for each target verb v a "stative" feature f by computing the proportion of times it appears in progressive tense, since stative verbs usually do not appear in the progressive tense (*e.g.,* *'knowing'*). Then, given a verb pair (v_1,v_2) and their corresponding stative features f_1 and f_2, we add two features $f_1 \cdot f_2$ and $\frac{f_1}{f_2}$, which capture the interaction between the verb classes of the two verbs.

Verb generality For each verb, we add as a feature the number of different particles it appears with in the corpus, following the hypothesis that this is a cue to its generality. Then, given a verb pair (v_1,v_2) and their corresponding features f_1 and f_2, we add the feature $\frac{f_1}{f_2}$. We expect that when $\frac{f_1}{f_2}$ is high, v_1 is more general than v_2, which is a negative entailment indicator.

4.2 Learning model and feature analysis

The total number of features in our model as described above is 63. We combine the features in a supervised classification framework with a linear SVM. Since our model contains many novel features, it is important to investigate their utility for detecting verb entailment. To that end, we employ feature ranking methods as suggested by Guyon et al. (2003). In feature ranking methods, features are ranked by some score computed for each feature independently. In this paper we use Pearson correlation between the feature values and the corresponding labels as the ranking criterion.

[3] adverbs never instantiate the subject, object or preposition complement positions.

[4] We employ the common practice of using the pmi between a verb and an argument rather than the argument count as the argument's weight.

5 Evaluation and Analysis

5.1 Experimental Setting

To evaluate our proposed supervised model, we constructed a dataset containing labeled verb pairs. We started by randomly sampling 50 verbs out of the common verbs in the RCV1 corpus[5], which we denote here as *seed verbs*. Next, we extracted the 20 most similar verbs to each seed verb according to the Lin similarity measure (Lin, 1998), which was computed on the RCV1 corpus. Then, for each seed verb v_s and one of its extracted similar verbs v_s^i we generated the two directed pairs (v_s, v_s^i) and (v_s^i, v_s), which represent the candidate rules '$v_s \rightarrow v_s^i$' and '$v_s^i \rightarrow v_s$' respectively. To reduce noise, we filtered out verb pairs where one of the verbs is an auxiliary or a light verb such as *'do'*, *'get'* and *'have'*. This step resulted in 812 verb pairs as our dataset[6], which were manually annotated by the authors as representing a valid entailment rule or not. To annotate these pairs, we generally followed the rule-based approach for entailment rule annotation, where a rule '$v_1 \rightarrow v_2$' is considered as correct if the annotator could think of reasonable contexts under which the rule holds (Dekang and Pantel, 2001; Szpektor et al., 2004). In total 225 verb pairs were labeled as entailing (the rule '$v_1 \rightarrow v_2$' was judged as correct) and 587 verb pairs were labeled as non-entailing (the rule '$v_1 \rightarrow v_2$' was judged as incorrect). The Inter-Annotator Agreement (IAA) for a random sample of 100 pairs was moderate (0.47), as expected from the rule-based approach (Szpektor et al., 2007).

For each verb pair, all 63 features within our model (Section 4) were computed using the ukWaC corpus (Baroni et al., 2009), which contains 2 billion words. For classification, we utilized SVM-perf's (Joachims, 2005) linear SVM implementation with default parameters, and evaluated our model by performing 10-fold cross validation (CV) over the labeled dataset.

[5] `http://trec.nist.gov/data/reuters/reuters.html`

[6] The data set is available at `http://www.cs.biu.ac.il/~nlp/downloads/verb-pair-annotation.html`

5.2 Feature selection and analysis

As discussed in Section 4.2, we followed the feature ranking method proposed by Guyon et al. (2003) to investigate the utility of our proposed features. Table 2 depicts the 10 most positively and negatively correlated features with entailment according to the Pearson correlation measure

From Table 2, it is clear that distributional similarity features are amongst the most positively correlated with entailment, which is in line with prior work (Geffet and Dagan, 2005; Kotlerman et al., 2010). Looking more closely, our suggestion for typed distributional similarity proved to be useful, and indeed most of the highly correlated distributional similarity features are typed measures. Standing out are the adverb-typed measures, with two features in the top 10, including the highest, *'Weeds-adverb'*, and *'BInc-adverb'*. We also note that the highly correlated distributional similarity measures are directional, *Weeds* and *BInc*.

The table also indicates that document-level co-occurrence contributes positively to entailment detection. This includes both the Chambers narrative measure, with the typed feature *Chambers-obj*, and document-level PMI, which captures a more loose co-occurrence relationship between verbs. Again, we point at the significant correlation of our novel typed measures with verb entailment, in this case the typed narrative measure.

Last, our feature analysis shows that many of our novel co-occurrence features at the sentence level contribute useful negative information. For example, verbs connected via an adverbial adjunct (*'v2-adverb-v1'*) or an object complement (*'v1-obj-v2'*) are negatively correlated with entailment. In addition, the novel *'verb generality'* feature as well as the tense difference feature (*'tense-v1 > tense-v2'*) are also strong negative indicators. On the other hand, *'v2-coord-v1'* is positively correlated with entailment. This shows that encoding various aspects of verb co-occurrence at the sentence level can lead to better prediction of verb entailment. Finally, we note that PMI at the sentence level is highly correlated with entailment even more than at the document level, since the local textual scope is more indicative, though sparser.

To conclude, our feature analysis shows that fea-

Rank	Top Positive	Top Negative
1	Weeds-adverb	tense-v1 > tense-v2
2	Sentence-level PMI	v2-adverb-v1 co-occurrence
3	Weeds-subj	v2-obj-v1 co-occurrence
4	Weeds-prep	v1-obj-v2 co-occurrence
5	Weeds-all	v1-adverb-v2 co-occurrence
6	Chambers-obj	verb generality $\frac{f_1}{f_2}$
7	v2-coord-v1 co-occurrence	v1-contrast-v2
8	BInc-adverb	tense-v1 < tense-v2
9	Document-level PMI	lexical-distance 0-5
10	Chambers-same	Lin-subj

Table 2: Top 10 positive and negative features according to the Pearson correlation score.

tures at all levels: sentence, document and corpus, contain useful information for entailment detection, both positive and negative, and should be combined together. Moreover, many of our novel features are among the highly correlated features, showing that devising a rich set of verb-specific and linguistically-motivated features provides better discriminative evidence for entailment detection.

5.3 Results and Analysis

We compared our method to the following baselines which were mostly taken from or inspired by prior work:

Random: A simple decision rule: for any pair (v_1, v_2), randomly classify as "yes" with a probability equal to the number of entailing verb pairs out of all verb pairs in the labeled dataset (*i.e.,* $\frac{225}{812} = 0.277$).

VO-KB: A simple unsupervised rule: for any pair (v_1, v_2), classify as "yes" if the pair appears in the *strength* relation (corresponding to entailment) in the VerbOcean knowledge-base, which was computed over Web counts.

VO-ukWaC: A simple unsupervised rule: for any pair (v_1, v_2), classify as "yes" if the value of the positive VerbOcean feature is '1' (Section 4.1, computed over ukWaC).

TDS: Include only the 15 distributional similarity features in our supervised model. This baseline extends Berant et al. (2012), who trained an entailment classifier over several distributional similarity features, and provides an evaluation of the discriminative power of distributional similarity alone, without co-occurrence features.

Method	P%	R%	AUC	F_1
All	**40.2**	**71.0**	**0.65**	**0.51**
TDS+VO	36.8	53.2	0.58	0.41
TDS	34.6	44.8	0.56	0.37
Random	27.9	28.8	0.51	0.28
VO-KB	33.1	14.8	0.53	0.2
VO-ukWaC	23.3	4.7	0.29	0.08

Table 3: Average precision, recall, AUC and F_1 for our method and the baselines.

TDS+VO: Include only the 15 typed distributional similarity features and the two VerbOcean features in our supervised model. This baseline is inspired by Mirkin et al. (2006), who combined distributional similarity features and Hearst patterns (Hearst, 1992) for learning entailment between nouns.

All: Our full-blown model, including all features described in Section 4.1.

For all tested methods, we performed 10-fold cross validation and averaged Precision, Recall, Area under the ROC curve (AUC) and F_1 over the 10 folds. Table 3 presents the results of our full-blown model as well as the baselines.

First, we note that, as expected, the VerbOcean baselines *VO-KB* and *VO-ukWaC* provide low recall,

Method	P%	R%	AUC	F_1
All	40.2	71.0	0.65	0.51
Sent+Corpus-level	39.7	70.4	0.64	0.50
Sent+Doc-level	39.0	70.0	0.63	0.50
Doc+Corpus-level	37.7	64.0	0.62	0.47
Sent-level	35.8	63.8	0.59	0.46
Doc-level	30.0	45.4	0.52	0.35
Corpus-level	35.4	58.1	0.58	0.44

Table 4: Average precision, recall, AUC and F_1 for each subset of the feature groups.

due to the sparseness of rigid pattern instantiation for verbs both in the ukWaC corpus and on the web. Yet, VerbOcean positive and negative patterns do add some discriminative power over only distributional similarity measures, as seen by the improvement of *TDS+VO* over *TDS* in all criteria. But, it is the combination of all types of information sources that yields the best performance. Our complete model, employing the full set of features, outperforms all other models in terms of both precision and recall. Its improvement in terms of F_1 over the second best model (*TDS+VO*), which includes all distributional similarity features as well as pattern-based features, is by 24%. This result shows the benefits of integrating linguistically motivated co-occurrence features with traditional pattern-based and distributional similarity information.

To further investigate the contribution of features at various co-occurrence levels, we trained and tested our model with all possible combinations of feature groups corresponding to a certain co-occurrence scope (sentence, document and corpus). Table 4 presents the results of these tests.

The most notable result of this analysis is that sentence-level features play an important role within our model. Indeed, removing either the document-level features (*Sent+Corpus-level*) or the corpus-level features (*Sent+Doc-level*) results in only a slight decline in performance. Yet, removing the sentence-level features (*Doc+Corpus-level*), ends in a more substantial decline of 8.5% in F_1. In addition, sentence-level features alone (*Sent-level*) provide the best discriminative power for verb entailment, compared to document and corpus levels, which include distributional similarity features. Yet, we note that sentence-level features alone do not capture all the information within our model, and they should be combined with one of the other feature groups to reach performance close to the complete model. This shows again the importance of combining co-occurrence indicators at different levels.

As an additional insight from Table 4, we point out that document-level features are not good entailment indicators by themselves (*Doc-level* in Table 4), and they perform worse than the distributional similarity baseline (*TDS* at Table 3). Still, they do complement each of the other feature groups. In particular, since the *Sent+Doc-level* model performs almost as good as the full model, this subset may be a good substitute to the full model, since its features are easier to extract from large corpora, as they may be extracted in an on-line fashion, processing one document at a time (contrary to corpus-level features).

As a final analysis, we randomly sampled correct entailment rules learned by our model but missed by the typed distributional similarity classifier (TDS). Our overall impression is that employing co-occurrence information helps to better capture entailment relations other than synonymy and troponymy. For example, our model learns that *acquire* → *own*, corresponding to the *cause-effect* entailment relation, and that *patent* → *invent*, corresponding to the *presupposition* entailment relation.

6 Conclusions and Future Work

We presented a supervised classification model for detecting lexical entailment between verbs. At the heart of our model stand novel linguistically motivated indicators that capture positive and negative entailment information. These indicators encompass co-occurrence relationships between verbs at the sentence, document and corpus level, as well as more fine-grained typed distributional similarity measures. Our model incorporates these novel indicators together with useful features from prior work, combining co-occurrence and distributional similarity information about verb pairs.

Our experiment over a manually labeled dataset showed that our model significantly outperforms several state-of-the-art models both in terms of Precision and Recall. Further feature analysis indicated that our novel indicators contribute greatly to the performance of the model, and that co-occurrence at multiple levels, combined with distributional similarity features, is necessary to achieve the model's best performance.

In future work we'd like to investigate which indicators may contribute to learning different fine-grained types of entailment, such as presupposition and cause-effect, and attempt to perform a more fine-grained classification to subtypes of entailment.

Acknowledgments

This work was partially supported by the Israel Science Foundation grant 1112/08, the PASCAL-2 Network of Excellence of the European Community FP7-ICT-2007-1-216886, and the European Community's Seventh Framework Programme (FP7/2007-2013) under grant agreement no. 287923 (EXCITEMENT).

References

Shuya Abe, Kentaro Inui, and Yuji Matsumoto. 2008. Acquiring event relation knowledge by learning cooccurrence patterns and fertilizing cooccurrence samples with verbal nouns. In *Proceedings of IJCNLP*.

Timothy Baldwin and Aline Villavicencio. 2002. Extracting the unextractable: a case study on verb-particles. In *proceedings of COLING*.

Marco Baroni, Silvia Bernardini, Adriano Ferraresi, and Eros Zanchetta. 2009. The wacky wide web: A collection of very large linguistically processed web-crawled corpora. *Language Resources and Evaluation*, 43(3):209–226.

Jonathan Berant, Ido Dagan, and Jacob Goldberger. 2012. Learning entailment relations by global graph structure optimization. *Computational Linguistics*, 38(1):73–111.

Nathanael Chambers and Dan Jurafsky. 2008. Unsupervised learning of narrative event chains. In *Proceedings of ACL*.

Timothy Chklovski and Patrick Pantel. 2004. Verb ocean: Mining the web for fine-grained semantic verb relations. In *Proceedings of EMNLP*.

Ido Dagan, Oren Glickman, and Bernardo Magnini. 2006. The pascal recognising textual entailment challenge. In *Machine Learning Challenges*, volume 3944 of *Lecture Notes in Computer Science*, pages 177–190. Springer.

Lin Dekang and Patrick Pantel. 2001. Dirt - discovery of inference rules from text. In *In Proceedings of the ACM SIGKDD Conference on Knowledge Discovery and Data Mining*.

Maayan Geffet and Ido Dagan. 2005. The distributional inclusion hypotheses and lexical entailment. In *Proceedings of ACL*.

Isabelle Guyon and Andre Elisseeff. 2003. An introduction to variable and feature selection. *Journal of Machine Learning Research*, 3:1157–1182.

Masato Hagiwara, Yasuhiro Ogawa, and Katsuhiko Toyama. 2009. Supervised synonym acquisition using distributional features and syntactic patterns. In *Journal of Natural Language Processing*.

Marti Hearst. 1992. Automatic acquisition of hyponyms from large text corpora. In *Proceedings of COLING*.

Jerry Hobbs. 1979. Coherence and coreference. *Cognitive Science*, 3:67–90.

Eduard Hovy and Elisabeth Maier. 1993. *Organizing Discourse Structure Relations using Metafunctions*. Pinter Publishing.

Ray Jackendoff. 1983. *Semantics and Cognition*. The MIT Press.

T. Joachims. 2005. A support vector method for multivariate performance measures. In *Proceedings of ICML*.

Alistair Knott and Ted Sanders. 1998. The classification of coherence relations and their linguistic markers: An exploration of two languages. In *Journal of Pragmatics*.

Lili Kotlerman, Ido Dagan, Idan Szpektor, and Maayan Zhitomirsky-Geffet. 2010. Directional distributional similarity for lexical inference. *Natural Language Engineering*, 16(4):359–389.

Beth Levin. 1993. *English Verb Classes and Alternations: A Preliminary Investigation*. University Of Chicago Press.

Dekang Lin. 1998. An information-theoretic definition of similarity. In *Proceedings of ICML*.

William Mann and Sandra Thompson. 1988. Rhetorical structure theory: Toward a functional theory of text organization. *Text*, 8(3):243–281.

Daniel Marcu and Abdessamad Echihabi. 2002. An unsupervised approach to recognizing discourse relations. In *Proceedings of ACL*.

Shachar Mirkin, Ido Dagan, and Maayan Geffet. 2006. Integrating pattern-based and distributional similarity methods for lexical entailment acquisition. In *Proceedings of the COLING/ACL*.

Joakim Nivre, Johan Hall, and Jens Nilsson. 2006. Maltparser: A data-driven parser-generator for dependency parsing. In *Proceedings of LREC*.

Viktor Pekar. 2008. Discovery of event entailment knowledge from text corpora. *Comput. Speech Lang.*, 22(1):1–16.

Marco Pennacchiotti and Patrick Pantel. 2009. Entity extraction via ensemble semantics. In *Proceedings of EMNLP*.

Deepak Ravichandran and Eduard Hovy. 2002. Learning surface text patterns for a question answering system. In *Proceedings of ACL*.

Deborah Schiffrin. 1988. *Discourse Markers*. Cambridge University Press.

Stefan Schoenmackers, Jesse Davis, Oren Etzioni, and Daniel S. Weld. 2010. Learning first-order horn clauses from web text. In *Proceedings of EMNLP*.

Yusuke Shinyama and Satoshi Sekine. 2006. Preemptive information extraction using unrestricted relation discovery. In *Proceedings of NAACL-HLT*.

Idan Szpektor and Ido Dagan. 2008. Learning entailment rules for unary templates. In *Proceedings of COLING*.

Idan Szpektor, Hristo Tanev, and Ido Dagan. 2004. Scaling web-based acquisition of entailment relations. In *In Proceedings of EMNLP*.

Idan Szpektor, Eyal Shnarch, and Ido Dagan. 2007. Instance based evaluation of entailment rule acquisition. In *Proceedings of the 45th Annual Meeting of the Association of Computational Linguistics*.

Galina Tremper. 2010. Weakly supervised learning of presupposition relations between verbs. In *Proceedings of ACL student workshop*.

Julie Weeds and David Weir. 2003. A general framework for distributional similarity. In *Proceedings of EMNLP*.

Fabio Massimo Zanzotto, Marco Pennacchiotti, and Maria Teresa Pazienza. 2006. Discovering asymmetric entailment relations between verbs using selectional preferences. In *Proceedings of the COLING/ACL*.

Spectral Dependency Parsing with Latent Variables

Paramveer S. Dhillon[1], Jordan Rodu[2], Michael Collins[3], Dean P. Foster[2] and Lyle H. Ungar[1]
[1]Computer & Information Science/ [2]Statistics, University of Pennsylvania, Philadelphia, PA, U.S.A
[3] Computer Science, Columbia University, New York, NY, U.S.A
{dhillon|ungar@cis.upenn.edu}, {jrodu|foster@wharton.upenn.edu}
mcollins@cs.columbia.edu

Abstract

Recently there has been substantial interest in using spectral methods to learn generative sequence models like HMMs. Spectral methods are attractive as they provide globally consistent estimates of the model parameters and are very fast and scalable, unlike EM methods, which can get stuck in local minima. In this paper, we present a novel extension of this class of spectral methods to learn dependency tree structures. We propose a simple yet powerful latent variable generative model for dependency parsing, and a spectral learning method to efficiently estimate it. As a pilot experimental evaluation, we use the spectral tree probabilities estimated by our model to re-rank the outputs of a near state-of-the-art parser. Our approach gives us a moderate reduction in error of up to 4.6% over the baseline re-ranker.

1 Introduction

Markov models have been for two decades a workhorse of statistical pattern recognition with applications ranging from speech to vision to language. Adding latent variables to these models gives us additional modeling power and have shown success in applications like POS tagging (Merialdo, 1994), speech recognition (Rabiner, 1989) and object recognition (Quattoni et al., 2004). However, this comes at the cost that the resulting parameter estimation problem becomes non-convex and techniques like EM (Dempster et al., 1977) which are used to estimate the parameters can only lead to locally optimal solutions.

Recent work by Hsu et al. (2008) has shown that globally consistent estimates of the parameters of HMMs can be found by using spectral methods, particularly by singular value decomposition (SVD) of appropriately defined linear systems. They avoid the NP Hard problem of the global optimization problem of the HMM parameters (Terwijn, 2002), by putting restrictions on the smallest singular value of the HMM parameters. The main intuition behind the model is that, although the observed data (i.e. words) seem to live in a very high dimensional space, but in reality they live in a very low dimensional space (size $k \sim 30 - 50$) and an appropriate eigen decomposition of the observed data will reveal the underlying low dimensional dynamics and thereby revealing the parameters of the model. Besides ducking the NP hard problem, the spectral methods are very fast and scalable to train compared to EM methods.

In this paper we generalize the approach of Hsu et al. (2008) to learn dependency tree structures with latent variables.[1] Petrov et al. (2006) and Musillo and Merlo (2008) have shown that learning PCFGs and dependency grammars respectively with latent variables can produce parsers with very good generalization performance. However, both these approaches rely on EM for parameter estimation and can benefit from using spectral methods.

We propose a simple yet powerful latent variable generative model for use with dependency pars-

[1]Actually, instead of using the model by Hsu et al. (2008) we work with a related model proposed by Foster et al. (2012) which addresses some of the shortcomings of the earlier model which we detail below.

ing which has one hidden node for each word in the sentence, like the one shown in Figure 1 and work out the details for the parameter estimation of the corresponding spectral learning model. At a very high level, the parameter estimation of our model involves collecting unigram, bigram and trigram counts sensitive to the underlying dependency structure of the given sentence.

Recently, Luque et al. (2012) have also proposed a spectral method for dependency parsing, however they deal with *horizontal markovization* and use hidden states to model sequential dependencies within a word's sequence of children. In contrast with that, in this paper, we propose a spectral learning algorithm where latent states are not restricted to HMM-like distributions of modifier sequences for a particular head, but instead allow information to be propagated through the entire tree.

More recently, Cohen et al. (2012) have proposed a spectral method for learning PCFGs.

Its worth noting that recent work by Parikh et al. (2011) also extends Hsu et al. (2008) to latent variable dependency trees like us but under the restrictive conditions that model parameters are trained for a specified, albeit arbitrary, tree topology.[2] In other words, all training sentences and test sentences must have identical tree topologies. By doing this they allow for node-specific model parameters, but must retrain the model entirely when a different tree topology is encountered. Our model on the other hand allows the flexibility and efficiency of processing sentences with a variety of tree topologies from a single training run.

Most of the current state-of-the-art dependency parsers are discriminative parsers (Koo et al., 2008; McDonald, 2006) due to the flexibility of representations which can be used as features leading to better accuracies and the ease of reproducibility of results. However, unlike discriminative models, generative models can exploit unlabeled data. Also, as is common in statistical parsing, re-ranking the outputs of a parser leads to significant reductions in error (Collins and Koo, 2005).

Since our spectral learning algorithm uses a gen-

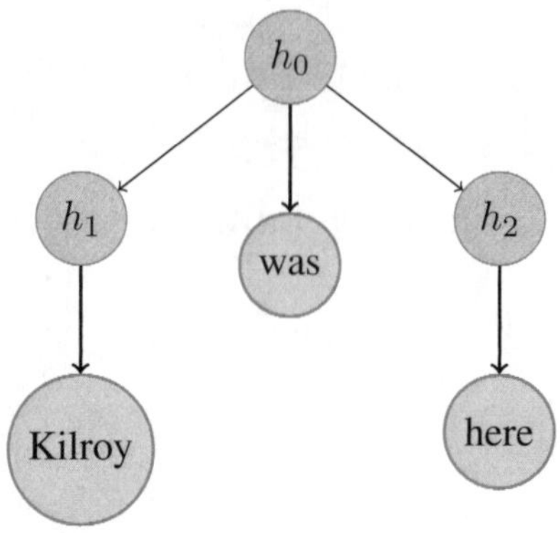

Figure 1: Sample dependency parsing tree for "Kilroy was here"

erative model of words given a tree structure, it can score a tree structure i.e. its probability of generation. Thus, it can be used to re-rank the n-best outputs of a given parser.

The remainder of the paper is organized as follows. In the next section we introduce the notation and give a brief overview of the spectral algorithm for learning HMMs (Hsu et al., 2008; Foster et al., 2012). In Section 3 we describe our proposed model for dependency parsing in detail and work out the theory behind it. Section 4 provides experimental evaluation of our model on Penn Treebank data. We conclude with a brief summary and future avenues for research.

2 Spectral Algorithm For Learning HMMs

In this section we describe the spectral algorithm for learning HMMs.[3]

2.1 Notation

The HMM that we consider in this section is a sequence of hidden states $h \in \{1, \ldots, k\}$ that follow the Markov property:

$$p(h_t | h_1, \ldots, h_{t-1}) = p(h_t | h_{t-1})$$

and a sequence of observations $x \in \{1, \ldots, n\}$ such that

$$p(x_t | x_1, \ldots, x_{t-1}, h_1, \ldots, h_t) = p(x_t | h_t)$$

[2]This can be useful in modeling phylogeny trees for instance, but precludes most NLP applications, since there is a need to model the full set of different tree topologies possible in parsing.

[3]As mentioned earlier, we use the model by Foster et al. (2012) which is conceptually similar to the one by Hsu et al. (2008), but does further dimensionality reduction and thus has lower sample complexity. Also, critically, the fully reduced dimension model that we use generalizes much more cleanly to trees.

The parameters of this HMM are:

- A vector π of length k where $\pi_i = p(h_1 = i)$: The probability of the start state in the sequence being i.
- A matrix T of size $k \times k$ where $T_{i,j} = p(h_{t+1} = i | h_t = j)$: The probability of transitioning to state i, given that the previous state was j.
- A matrix O of size $n \times k$ where $O_{i,j} = p(x = i | h = j)$: The probability of state h emitting observation x.

Define δ_j to be the vector of length n with a 1 in the jth entry and 0 everywhere else, and $\text{diag}(v)$ to be the matrix with the entries of v on the diagonal and 0 everywhere else.

The joint distribution of a sequence of observations $x_1, \ldots, x_m$ and a sequence of hidden states $h_1, \ldots, h_m$ is:

$$p(x_1, \ldots, x_m, h_1, \ldots, h_m) = \pi_{h_1} \prod_{j=2}^{m-1} T_{h_j, h_{j-1}} \prod_{j=1}^{m} O_{x_j, h_j}$$

Now, we can write the marginal probability of a sequence of observations as

$$p(x_1, \ldots x_m) = \sum_{h_1, \ldots, h_m} p(x_1, \ldots, x_m, h_1, \ldots, h_m)$$

which can be expressed in matrix form[4] as:

$$p(x_1, \ldots, x_m) = \mathbf{1}^\top A_{x_m} A_{x_{m-1}} \cdots A_{m_1} \pi$$

where $A_{x_m} \equiv T \text{diag}(O^\top \delta_{x_m})$, and $\mathbf{1}$ is a k-dimensional vector with every entry equal to 1.

A is called an "observation operator", and is effectively a third order tensor, and A_{x_m} which is a matrix, gives the distribution vector over states at time $m+1$ as a function of the state distribution vector at the current time m and the current observation δ_{x_m}. Since A_{x_m} depends on the hidden state, it is not observable, and hence cannot be directly estimated.

[4] This is essentially the matrix form of the standard dynamic program (forward algorithm) used to estimate HMMs.

However, Hsu et al. (2008) and Foster et al. (2012) showed that under certain conditions there exists a fully observable representation of the observable operator model.

2.2 Fully observable representation

Before presenting the model, we need to address a few more points. First, let U be a "representation matrix" (eigenfeature dictionary) which maps each observation to a reduced dimension space ($n \rightarrow k$) that satisfies the conditions:

- $U^\top O$ is invertible
- $|U_{ij}| < 1$.

Hsu et al. (2008); Foster et al. (2012) discuss U in more detail, but U can, for example, be obtained by the SVD of the bigram probability matrix (where $P_{ij} = p(x_{t+1} = i | x_t = j)$) or by doing CCA on neighboring n-grams (Dhillon et al., 2011).

Letting $y_i = U^\top \delta_{x_i}$, we have

$$p(x_1, \ldots, x_m) = c_\infty^\top C(y_m) C(y_{m-1}) \ldots C(y_1) c_1 \quad (1)$$

where

$$\begin{aligned} c_1 &= \mu \\ c_\infty &= \mu^\top \Sigma^{-1} \\ C(y) &= K(y) \Sigma^{-1} \end{aligned}$$

and μ, Σ and K, described in more detail below, are quantities estimated by frequencies of unigrams, bigrams, and trigrams in the observed (training) data.

Under the assumption that data is generated by an HMM, the distribution $\hat{p}$ obtained by substituting the estimated values $\hat{c}_1$, $\hat{c}_\infty$, and $\widehat{C}(y)$ into equation (1) converges to p sufficiently fast as the amount of training data increases, giving us consistent parameter estimates. For details of the convergence proof, please see Hsu et al. (2008) and Foster et al. (2012).

3 Spectral Algorithm For Learning Dependency Trees

In this section, we first describe a simple latent variable generative model for dependency parsing. We then define some extra notation and finally present the details of the corresponding spectral learning algorithm for dependency parsing, and prove that our learning algorithm provides a consistent estimation of the marginal probabilities.

It is worth mentioning that an alternate way of approaching the spectral estimation of latent states for dependency parsing is by converting the dependency trees into linear sequences from root-to-leaf and doing a spectral estimation of latent states using Hsu et al. (2008). However, this approach would not give us the correct probability distribution over trees as the probability calculations for different paths through the trees are not independent. Thus, although one could calculate the probability of a path from the root to a leaf, one cannot generalize from this probability to say anything about the neighboring nodes or words. Put another way, when a parent has more than the one descendant, one has to be careful to take into account that the hidden variables at each child node are all conditioned on the hidden variable of the parent.

3.1 A latent variable generative model for dependency parsing

In the standard setting, we are given training examples where each training example consists of a sequence of words $x_1, \ldots, x_m$ together with a dependency structure over those words, and we want to estimate the probability of the observed structure. This marginal probability estimates can then be used to build an actual generative dependency parser or, since the marginal probability is conditioned on the tree structure, it can be used re-rank the outputs of a parser.

As in the conventional HMM described in the previous section, we can define a simple latent variable first order dependency parsing model by introducing a hidden variable h_i for each word x_i. The joint probability of a sequence of observed nodes $x_1, \ldots, x_m$ together with hidden nodes $h_1, \ldots, h_m$ can be written as

$$p(x_1, \ldots, x_m, h_1, \ldots, h_m) = \pi_{h_1} \prod_{j=2}^{m} t_{d(j)}(h_j | h_{pa(j)}) \prod_{j=1}^{m} o(x_j | h_j) \quad (2)$$

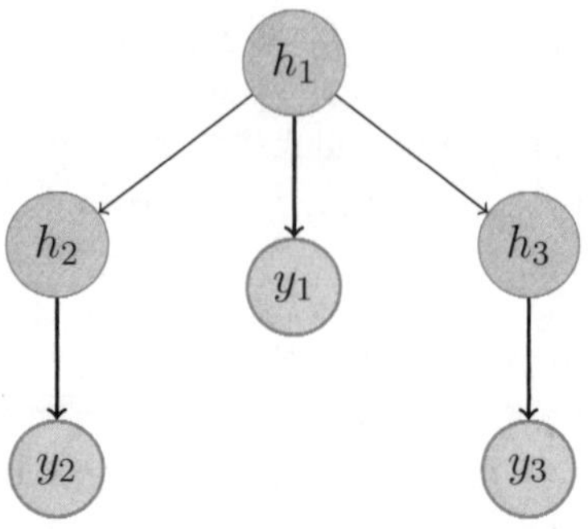

Figure 2: Dependency parsing tree with observed variables y_1, y_2, and y_3.

where $pa(j)$ is the parent of node j and $d(j) \in \{L, R\}$ indicates whether h_j is a left or a right node of $h_{pa(j)}$. For simplicity, the number of hidden and observed nodes in our tree are the same, however they are not required to be so.

As is the case with the conventional HMM, the parameters used to calculate this joint probability are unobservable, but it turns out that under suitable conditions a fully observable model is also possible for the dependency tree case with the parameterization as described below.

3.2 Model parameters

We will define both the theoretical representations of our observable parameters, and the sampling versions of these parameters. Note that in all the cases, the estimated versions are unbiased estimates of the theoretical quantities.

Define T_d and T_d^u where $d \in \{L, R\}$ to be the hidden state transition matrices from parent to left or right child, and from left or right child to parent (hence the u for 'up'), respectively. In other words (referring to Figure 2)

$$\begin{aligned} T_R &= t(h_3 | h_1) \\ T_L &= t(h_2 | h_1) \\ T_R^u &= t(h_1 | h_3) \\ T_L^u &= t(h_1 | h_2) \end{aligned}$$

Let $U_{x(i)}$ be the ith entry of vector $U^\top \delta_x$ and $G = U^\top O$. Further, recall the notation $\text{diag}(v)$, which is a matrix with elements of v on its diagonal, then:

- Define the k-dimensional vector μ (unigram

counts):

$$\mu = G\pi$$
$$[\hat{\mu}]_i = \sum_{u=1}^{n} \bar{c}(u) U_{u(i)}$$

where $\bar{c}(u) = \frac{c(u)}{N_1}$, $c(u)$ is the count of observation u in the training sample, and $N_1 = \sum_{u \in n} c(u)$.

- Define the $k \times k$ matrices Σ_L and Σ_R (*left child-parent* and *right child-parent* bigram counts):

$$[\hat{\Sigma}_L]_{i,j} = \sum_{u=1}^{n} \sum_{v=1}^{n} \bar{c}_L(u,v) U_{u(j)} U_{v(i)}$$
$$\Sigma_L = G T_L^u \mathrm{diag}(\pi) G^\top$$
$$[\hat{\Sigma}_R]_{i,j} = \sum_{u=1}^{n} \sum_{v=1}^{n} \bar{c}_R(u,v) U_{u(j)} U_{v(i)}$$
$$\Sigma_R = G T_R^u \mathrm{diag}(\pi) G^\top$$

where $\bar{c}_L(u,v) = \frac{c_L(u,v)}{N_{2_L}}$, $c_L(u,v)$ is the count of bigram (u,v) where u is the left child and v is the parent in the training sample, and $N_{2_L} = \sum_{(u,v) \in n \times n} c_L(u,v)$. Define $\bar{c}_R(u,v)$ similarly.

- Define $k \times k \times k$ tensor K (*left child-parent-right child* trigram counts):

$$\hat{K}_{i,j,l} = \sum_{u=1}^{n} \sum_{v=1}^{n} \sum_{w=1}^{n} \bar{c}(u,v,w) U_{w(i)} U_{u(j)} U_{v(l)}$$
$$K(y) = G T_L \mathrm{diag}(G^\top y) T_R^u \mathrm{diag}(\pi) G^\top$$

where $\bar{c}(w,u,v) = \frac{c(w,u,v)}{N_3}$, $c(w,u,v)$ is the count of bigram (w,u,v) where w is the left child, u is the parent and v is the right child in the training sample, and $N_3 = \sum_{(w,u,v) \in n \times n \times n} c(w,u,v)$.

- Define $k \times k$ matrices Ω_L and Ω_R (skip-bigram counts (left child-right child) and (right child-left child)) [5]:

$$[\hat{\Omega}_L]_{i,j} = \sum_{u=1}^{n} \sum_{v=1}^{n} \sum_{w=1}^{n} \bar{c}(u,v,w) U_{w(i)} U_{u(j)}$$
$$\Omega_L = G T_L T_R^u \mathrm{diag}(\pi) G^\top$$
$$[\hat{\Omega}_R]_{i,j} = \sum_{u=1}^{n} \sum_{v=1}^{n} \sum_{w=1}^{n} \bar{c}(u,v,w) U_{w(j)} U_{u(i)}$$
$$\Omega_R = G T_R T_L^u \mathrm{diag}(\pi) G^\top$$

3.3 Parameter estimation

Using the above definitions, we can estimate the parameters of the model, namely $\mu, \Sigma_L, \Sigma_R, \Omega_L, \Omega_R$ and K, from the training data and define observables useful for the dependency model as[6]

$$c_1 = \mu$$
$$c_\infty^T = \mu^T \Sigma_R^{-1}$$
$$E_L = \Omega_L \Sigma_R^{-1}$$
$$E_R = \Omega_R \Sigma_L^{-1}$$
$$D(y) = E_L^{-1} K(y) \Sigma_R^{-1}$$

As we will see, these quantities allow us to recursively compute the marginal probability of the dependency tree, $\hat{p}(x_1, \ldots, x_m)$, in a bottom up manner by using belief propagation.

To see this, let $hch(i)$ be the set of hidden children of hidden node i (in Figure 2 for instance, $hch(1) = \{2,3\}$) and let $och(i)$ be the set of observed children of hidden node i (in the same figure $och(i) = \{1\}$). Then compute the marginal probability $p(x_1, \ldots, x_m)$ from Equation 2 as

$$r_i(h) = \prod_{j \in hch(i)} \alpha_j(h) \prod_{j \in och(i)} o(x_j | h) \tag{3}$$

where $\alpha_i(h)$ is defined by summing over all the hidden random variables i.e., $\alpha_i(h) = \sum_{h'} p(h'|h) r_i(h')$.

This can be written in a compact matrix form as

$$\overrightarrow{r_i}^\top = 1^\top \prod_{j \in hch(i)} diag(T_{d_j}^\top \overrightarrow{r_j}) \cdot \prod_{j \in och(i)} diag(O^\top \delta_{x_j}) \tag{4}$$

[5] Note than $\Omega_R = \Omega_L^T$, which is not immediately obvious from the matrix representations.

[6] The details of the derivation follow directly from the matrix versions of the variables.

where $\vec{r_i}$ is a vector of size k (the dimensionality of the hidden space) of values $r_i(h)$. Note that since in Equation 2 we condition on whether x_j is the left or right child of its parent, we have separate transition matrices for left and right transitions from a given hidden node $d_j \in \{L, R\}$.

The recursive computation can be written in terms of observables as:

$$\vec{r_i}^\top = c_\infty^\top \prod_{j \in hch(i)} D(E_{d_j}^\top \vec{r_j}) \cdot \prod_{j \in och(i)} D((U^\top U)^{-1} U^\top \delta_{x_j})$$

The final calculation for the marginal probability of a given sequence is

$$\hat{p}(x_1, \ldots, x_m) = \vec{r_1}^\top c_1 \tag{5}$$

The spectral estimation procedure is described below in Algorithm 1.

Algorithm 1 Spectral dependency parsing (Computing marginal probability of a tree.)

1: **Input:** Training examples- $x^{(i)}$ for $i \in \{1, \ldots, M\}$ along with dependency structures where each sequence $x^{(i)} = x_1^{(i)}, \ldots, x_{m_i}^{(i)}$.
2: Compute the spectral parameters $\hat{\mu}$, $\hat{\Sigma}_R$, $\hat{\Sigma}_L$, $\hat{\Omega}_R$, $\hat{\Omega}_L$, and $\hat{K}$
#Now, for a given sentence, we can recursively compute the following:
3: **for** $x_j^{(i)}$ for $j \in \{m_i, \ldots, 1\}$ **do**
4: Compute:

$$\vec{r_i}^\top = c_\infty^\top \prod_{j \in hch(i)} D(E_{d_j}^\top \vec{r_j}) \cdot \prod_{j \in och(i)} D((U^\top U)^{-1} U^\top \delta_{x_j})$$

5: **end for**
6: Finally compute

$$\hat{p}(x_1, \ldots, x_{m_i}) = \vec{r_1}^\top c_1$$

#The marginal probability of an entire tree.

3.4 Sample complexity

Our main theoretical result states that the above scheme for spectral estimation of marginal probabilities provides a guaranteed consistent estimation scheme for the marginal probabilities:

Theorem 3.1. *Let the sequence $\{x_1, \ldots, x_m\}$ be generated by an $k \geq 2$ state HMM. Suppose we are given a U which has the property that $U^\top O$ is invertible, and $|U_{ij}| \leq 1$. Suppose we use equation (5) to estimate the probability based on N independent triples. Then*

$$N \geq C_m \frac{k^2}{\epsilon^2} \log\left(\frac{k}{\delta}\right) \tag{6}$$

where C_m is specified in the appendix, implies that

$$1 - \epsilon \leq \left|\frac{\widehat{p}(x_1, \ldots, x_m)}{p(x_1, \ldots, x_m)}\right| \leq 1 + \epsilon$$

holds with probability at least $1 - \delta$.

Proof. A sketch of the proof, in the case without directional transition parameters, can be found in the appendix. The proof with directional transition parameters is almost identical. □

4 Experimental Evaluation

Since our algorithm can score any given tree structure by computing its marginal probability, a natural way to benchmark our parser is to generate n-best dependency trees using some standard parser and then use our algorithm to re-rank the candidate dependency trees, e.g. using the log spectral probability as described in Algorithm 1 as a feature in a discriminative re-ranker.

4.1 Experimental Setup

Our base parser was the discriminatively trained MSTParser (McDonald, 2006), which implements both first and second order parsers and is trained using MIRA (Crammer et al., 2006) and used the standard baseline features as described in McDonald (2006).

We tested our methods on the English Penn Treebank (Marcus et al., 1993). We use the standard splits of Penn Treebank; i.e., we used sections 2-21 for training, section 22 for development and section 23 for testing. We used the PennConverter[7] tool to convert Penn Treebank from constituent to dependency format. Following (McDonald, 2006; Koo

[7] `http://nlp.cs.lth.se/software/treebank_converter/`

et al., 2008), we used the POS tagger by Ratnaparkhi (1996) trained on the full training data to provide POS tags for development and test sets and used 10-way jackknifing to generate tags for the training set. As is common practice we stripped our sentences of all the punctuation. We evaluated our approach on sentences of all lengths.

4.2 Details of spectral learning

For the spectral learning phase, we need to just collect word counts from the training data as described above, so there are no tunable parameters as such. However, we need to have access to an attribute dictionary U which contains a k dimensional representation for each word in the corpus. A possible way of generating U as suggested by Hsu et al. (2008) is by performing SVD on bigrams P_{21} and using the left eigenvectors as U. We instead used the eigenfeature dictionary proposed by Dhillon et al. (2011) (LR-MVL) which is obtained by performing CCA on neighboring words and has provably better sample complexity for rare words compared to the SVD alternative.

We induced the LR-MVL embeddings for words using the Reuters RCV1 corpus which contains about 63 million tokens in 3.3 million sentences and used their context oblivious embeddings as our estimate of U. We experimented with different choices of k (the size of the low dimensional projection) on the development set and found $k = 10$ to work reasonably well and fast. Using $k = 10$ we were able to estimate our spectral learning parameters $\mu, \Sigma_{L,R}, \Omega_{L,R}, K$ from the entire training data in under 2 minutes on a 64 bit Intel 2.4 Ghz processor.

4.3 Re-ranking the outputs of MST parser

We could not find any previous work which describes features for discriminative re-ranking for dependency parsing, which is due to the fact that unlike constituency parsing, the base parsers for dependency parsing are discriminative (e.g. MST parser) which obviates the need for re-ranking as one could add a variety of features to the baseline parser itself. However, parse re-ranking is a good testbed for our spectral dependency parser which can score a given tree. So, we came up with a baseline set of features to use in an averaged perceptron re-ranker (Collins, 2002). Our baseline features comprised of two main features which capture information that varies across the different n-best parses and moreover were not used as features by the baseline MST parser, ⟨POS-left-modifier ∧ POS-head ∧ POS-right-modifier⟩ and ⟨POS-left/right-modifier ∧ POS-head ∧ POS-grandparent⟩[8]. In addition to that we used the log of spectral probability ($\hat{p}(x_1, \ldots, x_m)$ - as calculated using Algorithm 1) as a feature.

Method	Accuracy	Complete
I Order		
MST Parser (No RR)	90.8	37.2
RR w. Base. Features	91.3	37.5
RR w. Base. Features +log $\hat{p}$	**91.7**	**37.8**
II Order		
MST Parser (No RR)	91.8	40.6
RR w. Base. Features	92.4	41.0
RR w. Base. Features +log $\hat{p}$	**92.7**	**41.3**

Table 1: (Unlabeled) Dependency Parse re-ranking results for English test set (Section 23). **Note:** 1). RR = Re-ranking 2). *Accuracy* is the number of words which correctly identified their parent and *Complete* is the number of sentences for which the entire dependency tree was correct. 3). Base. Features are the two re-ranking features described in Section 4.3. 4). $\log \hat{p}$ is the spectral log probability feature.

We used the MST parser trained on entire training data to generate a list of n-best parses for the development and test sets. The n-best parses for the training set were generated by 3-fold cross validation, where we train on 2 folds to get the parses for the third fold. In all our experiments we used $n = 50$. The results are shown in Table 1. As can be seen, the best results give up to 4.6% reduction in error over the re-ranker which uses just the baseline set of features.

5 Discussion and Future Work

Spectral learning of structured latent variable models in general is a promising direction as has been shown by the recent interest in this area. It allows us to circumvent the ubiquitous problem of getting stuck in local minima when estimating the latent variable models via EM. In this paper we ex-

[8]One might be able to come up with better features for dependency parse re-ranking. Our goal in this paper was just to get a reasonable baseline.

tended the spectral learning ideas to learn a simple yet powerful dependency parser. As future work, we are working on building an end-to-end parser which would involve coming up with a spectral version of the inside-outside algorithm for our setting. We are also working on extending it to learn more powerful grammars e.g. split head-automata grammars (SHAG) (Eisner and Satta, 1999).

6 Conclusion

In this paper we proposed a novel spectral method for dependency parsing. Unlike EM trained generative latent variable models, our method does not get stuck in local optima, it gives consistent parameter estimates, and it is extremely fast to train. We worked out the theory of a simple yet powerful generative model and showed how it can be learned using a spectral method. As a pilot experimental evaluation we showed the efficacy of our approach by using the spectral probabilities output by our model for re-ranking the outputs of MST parser. Our method reduced the error of the baseline re-ranker by up to a moderate 4.6%.

7 Appendix

This appendix offers a sketch of the proof of Theorem 1. The proof uses the following definitions, which are slightly modified from those of Foster et al. (2012).

Definition 1. *Define* Λ *as the smallest element of* μ, Σ^{-1}, Ω^{-1}, *and* $K()$. *In other words,*

$$\Lambda \equiv \min\{\min_i |\mu_i|, \min_{i,j} |\Sigma_{ij}^{-1}|, \min_{i,j} |\Omega_{ij}^{-1}|, \\ \min_{i,j,k} |K_{ijk}|, \min_{i,j} |\Sigma_{ij}|, \min_{i,j} |\Omega_{ij}|, \}$$

where $K_{ijk} = K(\delta_j)_{ik}$ *are the elements of the tensor* $K()$.

Definition 2. *Define* σ_k *as the smallest singular value of* Σ *and* Ω.

The proof relies on the fact that a row vector multiplied by a series of matrices, and finally multiplied by a column vector amounts to a sum over all possible products of individual entries in the vectors and matrices. With this in mind, if we bound the largest relative error of any particular entry in the matrix by, say, ω, and there are, say, s parameters (vectors and matrices) being multiplied together, then by simple algebra the total relative error of the sum over the products is bounded by ω^s.

The proof then follows from two basic steps. First, one must bound the maximal relative error, ω for any particular entry in the parameters, which can be done using central limit-type theorems and the quantity Λ described above. Then, to calculate the exponent s one simply counts the number of parameters multiplied together when calculating the probability of a particular sequence of observations.

Since each hidden node is associated with exactly one observed node, it follows that $s = 12m + 2L$, where L is the number of levels (for instance in our example "Kilroy was here" there are two levels). s can be easily computed for arbitrary tree topologies.

It follows from Foster et al. (2012) that we achieve a sample complexity

$$N \geq \frac{128k^2s^2}{\epsilon^2\,\Lambda^2\sigma_k^4}\log\left(\frac{2k}{\delta}\right) \cdot \overbrace{\frac{\epsilon^2/s^2}{(\sqrt[s]{1+\epsilon}-1)^2}}^{\approx 1} \quad (7)$$

leading to the theorem stated above.

Lastly, note that in reality one does not see Λ and σ_k but instead estimates of these quantities; Foster et al. (2012) shows how to incorporate the accuracy of the estimates into the sample complexity.

Acknowledgement: We would like to thank Emily Pitler for valuable feedback on the paper.

References

Shay Cohen, Karl Stratos, Michael Collins, Dean Foster, and Lyle Ungar. Spectral learning of latent-variable pcfgs. In *Association of Computational Linguistics (ACL)*, volume 50, 2012.

Michael Collins. Ranking algorithms for named-entity extraction: boosting and the voted perceptron. In *Proceedings of the 40th Annual Meeting on Association for Computational Linguistics*, ACL '02, pages 489–496, Stroudsburg, PA, USA, 2002. Association for Computational Linguistics. URL `http://dx.doi.org/10.3115/1073083.1073165`.

Michael Collins and Terry Koo. Discriminative reranking for natural language parsing. *Comput.*

Linguist., 31(1):25–70, March 2005. ISSN 0891-2017.

Koby Crammer, Ofer Dekel, Joseph Keshet, Shai Shalev-Shwartz, and Yoram Singer. Online passive-aggressive algorithms. *Journal of Machine Learning Research*, 7:551–585, 2006.

A. P. Dempster, N. M. Laird, and D. B. Rubin. Maximum likelihood from incomplete data via the em algorithm. *JRSS, SERIES B*, 39(1):1–38, 1977.

Paramveer S. Dhillon, Dean Foster, and Lyle Ungar. Multi-view learning of word embeddings via cca. In *Advances in Neural Information Processing Systems (NIPS)*, volume 24, 2011.

Jason Eisner and Giorgio Satta. Efficient parsing for bilexical context-free grammars and head-automaton grammars. In *Proceedings of the 37th Annual Meeting of the Association for Computational Linguistics (ACL)*, pages 457–464, University of Maryland, June 1999. URL `http://cs.jhu.edu/~jason/papers/#acl99`.

Dean Foster, Jordan Rodu, and Lyle Ungar. Spectral dimensionality reduction for HMMs. *ArXiV http://arxiv.org/abs/1203.6130*, 2012.

D Hsu, S M. Kakade, and Tong Zhang. A spectral algorithm for learning hidden markov models. *arXiv:0811.4413v2*, 2008.

Terry Koo, Xavier Carreras, and Michael Collins. Simple semi-supervised dependency parsing. In *In Proc. ACL/HLT*, 2008.

F. Luque, A. Quattoni, B. Balle, and X. Carreras. Spectral learning for non-deterministic dependency parsing. In *EACL*, 2012.

Mitchell P. Marcus, Mary Ann Marcinkiewicz, and Beatrice Santorini. Building a large annotated corpus of english: the penn treebank. *Comput. Linguist.*, 19:313–330, June 1993. ISSN 0891-2017.

Ryan McDonald. *Discriminative learning and spanning tree algorithms for dependency parsing*. PhD thesis, University of Pennsylvania, Philadelphia, PA, USA, 2006. AAI3225503.

Bernard Merialdo. Tagging english text with a probabilistic model. *Comput. Linguist.*, 20:155–171, June 1994. ISSN 0891-2017.

Gabriele Antonio Musillo and Paola Merlo. Unlexicalised hidden variable models of split dependency grammars. In *Proceedings of the 46th Annual Meeting of the Association for Computational Linguistics on Human Language Technologies: Short Papers*, HLT-Short '08, pages 213–216, Stroudsburg, PA, USA, 2008. Association for Computational Linguistics.

Ankur P. Parikh, Le Song, and Eric P. Xing. A spectral algorithm for latent tree graphical models. In *ICML*, pages 1065–1072, 2011.

Slav Petrov, Leon Barrett, Romain Thibaux, and Dan Klein. Learning accurate, compact, and interpretable tree annotation. In *Proceedings of the 21st International Conference on Computational Linguistics and the 44th annual meeting of the Association for Computational Linguistics*, ACL-44, pages 433–440, Stroudsburg, PA, USA, 2006. Association for Computational Linguistics.

Ariadna Quattoni, Michael Collins, and Trevor Darrell. Conditional random fields for object recognition. In *In NIPS*, pages 1097–1104. MIT Press, 2004.

Lawrence R. Rabiner. A tutorial on hidden markov models and selected applications in speech recognition. In *Proceedings of the IEEE*, pages 257–286, 1989.

Adwait Ratnaparkhi. A Maximum Entropy Model for Part-Of-Speech Tagging. In Eric Brill and Kenneth Church, editors, *Proceedings of the Empirical Methods in Natural Language Processing*, pages 133–142, 1996.

Sebastiaan Terwijn. On the learnability of hidden markov models. In *Proceedings of the 6th International Colloquium on Grammatical Inference: Algorithms and Applications*, ICGI '02, pages 261–268, London, UK, UK, 2002. Springer-Verlag. ISBN 3-540-44239-1.

A Phrase-Discovering Topic Model Using Hierarchical Pitman-Yor Processes

Robert V. Lindsey
University of Colorado, Boulder
robert.lindsey@colorado.edu

William P. Headden III
Two Cassowaries Inc.
headdenw@twocassowaries.com

Michael J. Stipicevic
Google Inc.
stip@google.com

Abstract

Topic models traditionally rely on the bag-of-words assumption. In data mining applications, this often results in end-users being presented with inscrutable lists of *topical unigrams*, single words inferred as representative of their topics. In this article, we present a hierarchical generative probabilistic model of *topical phrases*. The model simultaneously infers the location, length, and topic of phrases within a corpus and relaxes the bag-of-words assumption within phrases by using a hierarchy of Pitman-Yor processes. We use Markov chain Monte Carlo techniques for approximate inference in the model and perform slice sampling to learn its hyperparameters. We show via an experiment on human subjects that our model finds substantially better, more interpretable topical phrases than do competing models.

1 Introduction

Probabilistic topic models have been the focus of intense study in recent years. The archetypal topic model, Latent Dirichlet Allocation (LDA), posits that words within a document are conditionally independent given their topic (Blei et al., 2003). This "bag-of-words" assumption is a common simplification in which word order is ignored, but one which introduces undesirable properties into a model meant to serve as an unsupervised exploratory tool for data analysis.

When an end-user runs a topic model, the output he or she is often interested in is a list of topical unigrams, words probable in a topic (hence, representative of it). In many situations, such as during the use of the topic model for the analysis of a new or ill-understood corpus, these lists can be insufficiently informative. For instance, if a layperson ran LDA on the NIPS corpus, he would likely get a topic whose most prominent words include *policy*, *value*, and *reward*. Seeing these words isolated from their context in a list would not be particularly insightful to the layperson unfamiliar with computer science research. An alternative to LDA which produced richer output like *policy iteration algorithm*, *value function*, and *model-based reinforcement learning* alongside the unigrams would be much more enlightening. Most situations where a topic model is actually useful for data exploration require a model whose output is rich enough to dispel the need for the user's extensive prior knowledge of the data.

Furthermore, lists of topical unigrams are often made only marginally interpretable by virtue of their non-compositionality, the principle that a collocation's meaning typically is not derivable from its constituent words (Schone and Jurafsky, 2001). For example, the meaning of *compact disc* as a music medium comes from neither the unigram *compact* nor the unigram *disc*, but emerges from the bigram as a whole. Moreover, non-compositionality is topic dependent; *compact disc* should be interpreted as a music medium in a music topic, and as a small region bounded by a circle in a mathematical topic. LDA is prone to decompose collocations into different topics and violate the principle of non-compositionality, and its unigram lists are harder to interpret as a result.

We present an extension of LDA called Phrase-Discovering LDA (PDLDA) that satisfies two desiderata: providing rich, interpretable output and honoring the non-compositionality of collocations. PDLDA is built in the tradition of the "Topical N-Gram" (TNG) model of Wang et al. (2007). TNG is a topic model which satisfies the first desideratum by producing lists of representative, topically cohesive n-grams of the form shown in Figure 1. We diverge from TNG by our addressing the second desideratum, and we do so through a more straightforward and intuitive definition of what constitutes a phrase and its topic. In the furtherance of our goals, we employ a hierarchical method of modeling phrases that uses dependent Pitman-Yor processes to ameliorate overfitting. Pitman-Yor processes have been successfully used in the past in n-gram (Teh, 2006) and LDA-based models (Wallach, 2006) for creating Bayesian language models which exploit word order, and they prove equally useful in this scenario of exploiting both word order and topics.

This article is organized as follows: after describing TNG, we discuss PDLDA and how PDLDA addresses the limitations of TNG. We then provide details of our inference procedures and evaluate our model against competing models on a subset of the TREC AP corpus (Harman, 1992) in an experiment on human subjects which assesses the interpretability of topical n-gram lists. The experiment is premised on the notion that topic models should be evaluated through a real-world task instead of through information-theoretic measures which often negatively correlate with topic quality (Chang et al., 2009).

2 Background: LDA and TNG

LDA represents documents as probabilistic mixtures of latent topics. Each word w in a corpus $\mathbf{w}$ is drawn from a distribution ϕ indexed by a topic z, where z is drawn from a distribution θ indexed by its document d. The formal definition of LDA is

$$\theta_d \sim \text{Dirichlet}(\alpha) \qquad z_i \mid d, \theta \sim \text{Discrete}(\theta_d)$$
$$\phi_z \sim \text{Dirichlet}(\beta) \qquad w_i \mid z_i, \phi \sim \text{Discrete}(\phi_{z_i})$$

where θ_d is document d's topic distribution, ϕ_z is topic z's distribution over words, z_i is the topic assignment of the ith token, and w_i is the ith word. α and β are hyperparameters to the Dirichlet priors. Here and throughout the article, we use a bold font for vector notation: for example, $\mathbf{z}$ is the vector of all topic assignments, and its ith entry, z_i, corresponds to the topic assignment of the ith token in the corpus.

TNG extends LDA to model n-grams of arbitrary length in order to create the kind of rich output for text mining discussed in the introduction. It does this by representing a joint distribution $P(\mathbf{z}, \mathbf{c}|\mathbf{w})$ where each c_i is a Boolean variable that signals the start of a new n-gram beginning at the ith token. $\mathbf{c}$ partitions a corpus into consecutive non-overlapping n-grams of various lengths. Formally, TNG differs from LDA by the distributional assumptions

$$\begin{aligned} w_i \mid w_{i-1}, z_i, c_i = 1, \phi &\sim \text{Discrete}(\phi_{z_i}) \\ w_i \mid w_{i-1}, z_i, c_i = 0, \sigma &\sim \text{Discrete}(\sigma_{z_i w_{i-1}}) \\ c_i \mid w_{i-1}, z_{i-1}, \pi &\sim \text{Bernoulli}(\pi_{z_{i-1} w_{i-1}}) \end{aligned}$$

where the new distributions π_{zw} and σ_{zw} are endowed with conjugate prior distributions: $\pi_{zw} \sim \text{Beta}(\lambda)$ and $\sigma_{zw} \sim \text{Dirichlet}(\delta)$. When $c_i = 0$, word w_i is joined into a topic-specific bigram with w_{i-1}. When $c_i = 1$, w_i is drawn from a topic-specific unigram distribution and is the start of a new n-gram.

An unusual feature of TNG is that words within a *topical n-gram*, a sequence of words delineated by $\mathbf{c}$, do not share the same topic. To compensate for this after running a Gibbs sampler, Wang et al. (2007) analyze each topical n-gram post hoc as if the topic of the final word in the n-gram was the topic assignment of the entire n-gram. Though this design simplifies inference, we perceive it as a shortcoming since the aforementioned principle of non-compositionality supports the intuitive idea that each collocation ought to be drawn from a single topic. Another potential drawback of TNG is that the topic-specific bigram distributions σ_{zw} share no probability mass between each other or with the unigram distributions ϕ_z. Hence, observing a bigram under one topic does not make it more likely under another topic or make its constituent unigrams more probable. To be more concrete, in TNG, observing *space shuttle* under a topic z (or under two topics, one for each word) regrettably does not make *space shuttle* more likely under a topic $z' \neq z$, nor does it make observing *shuttle* more likely under any topic. Smoothing, the sharing of probability mass between

matter	chemical reactions	like charges repel
atoms	atomic number	positively charged nucleus
elements	hydrogen atoms	unlike charges attract
electrons	hydrogen atom	outer energy level
atom	periodic table	reaction takes place
molecules	chemical change	negatively charged electrons
form	physical properties	chemical change takes place
oxygen	chemical reaction	form new substances
hydrogen	water molecules	physical change takes place
particles	sodium chloride	form sodium chloride
element	small amounts	modern atomic theory
solution	positive charge	electrically charged particles
substance	carbon atoms	increasing atomic number
reaction	physical change	second ionization energies
nucleus	chemical properties	higher energy levels

(a) Topic 1

president	supreme court	civil rights act
congress	new york	civil rights movement
vote	democratic party	supreme court ruled
party	vice president	president theodore roosevel
constitution	political parties	second continental congress
state	national government	equal rights amendment
members	executive branch	strong central government
office	civil rights	sherman antitrust act
government	new government	civil rights legislation
states	political party	public opinion polls
elected	andrew jackson	major political parties
representatives	chief justice	congress shall make
senate	federal government	federal district court
house	state legislatures	supreme court decisions
washington	public opinion	american foreign policy

(b) Topic 2

words	main idea	word processing center
word	topic sentence	word processing systems
sentence	english language	word processing equipment
write	following paragraph	speak different languages
writing	words like	use quotation marks
paragraph	quotation marks	single main idea
sentences	direct object	use words like
meaning	word processing	topic sentence states
use	sentence tells	present perfect tense
subject	figurative language	express complete thoughts
language	writing process	word processing software
read	following sentences	use formal english
example	subject matter	standard american english
verb	standard english	collective noun refers
topic	use words	formal standard english

(c) Topic 3

energy	natural resources	nuclear power plants
used	natural gas	nuclear power plant
oil	heat energy	important natural resources
heat	iron ore	electric power plants
coal	carbon dioxide	called fossil fuels
use	potential energy	important natural resource
fuel	solar energy	produce large amounts
produce	light energy	called solar energy
power	fossil fuels	electric light bulb
source	hot water	use electrical energy
light	steam engine	use solar energy
electricity	large amounts	carbon dioxide gas
burn	sun's energy	called potential energy
gas	radiant energy	gas called carbon dioxide
gasoline	nuclear energy	called crude oil

(d) Topic 4

water	water vapor	water vapor condenses
air	air pollution	warm air rises
temperature	air pressure	cold air mass
heat	warm air	called water vapor
liquid	cold water	water vapor changes
gas	earth's surface	process takes place
gases	room temperature	warm air mass
hot	boiling point	clean air act
pressure	drinking water	gas called water vapor
atmosphere	atmospheric pressure	dry spell holds
warm	cold war	air pressure inside
cold	high temperatures	sewage treatment plant
surface	liquid water	air pollution laws
oxygen	cold air	high melting points
clouds	warm water	high melting point

(e) Topic 5

china	middle east	2000 years ago
africa	western europe	east india company
india	north africa	eastern united states
europe	mediterranean sea	4000 years ago
people	years ago	southwestern united states
chinese	roman empire	middle atlantic states
asia	far east	northeastern united states
egypt	southeast asia	western united states
world	west africa	southeastern united states
rome	saudi arabia	200 years ago
land	capital letter	middle atlantic region
east	asia minor	indus river valley
trade	united states	western roman empire
countries	capital city	british north america act
empire	centuries ago	coast guard station

(f) Topic 6

Figure 1: Six out of one hundred topics found by our model, PDLDA, on the Touchstone Applied Science Associates (TASA) corpus (Landauer and Dumais, 1997). Each column within a box shows the top fifteen phrases for a topic and is restricted to phrases of a minimum length of one, two, or three words, respectively. The rows are ordered by likelihood.

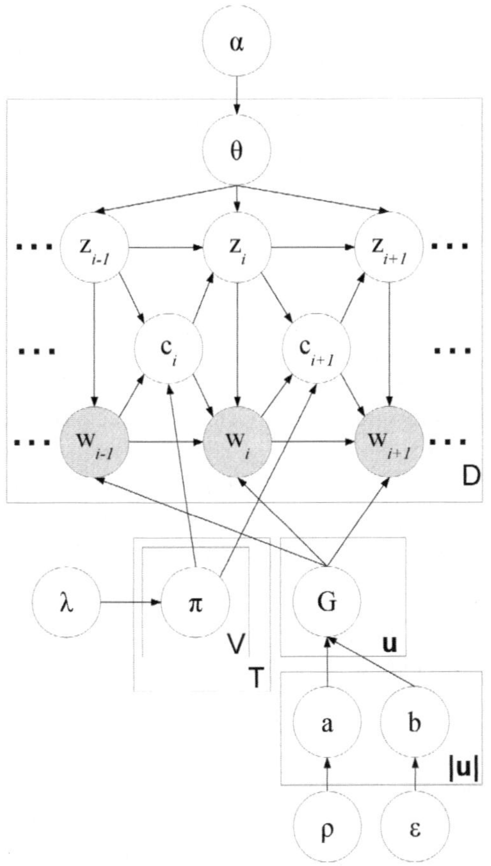

Figure 2: PDLDA drawn in plate notation.

contexts, is desirable so that a model like this does not need to independently infer the probability of every bigram under every topic. The advantages of smoothing are especially pronounced for small corpora or for a large number of topics. In these situations, the observed number of bigrams in a given topic will necessarily be very small and thus not support strong inferences.

3 PDLDA

A more natural definition of a topical phrase, one which meets our second desideratum, is to have each phrase possess a single topic. We adopt this intuitive idea in PDLDA. It can also be understood through the lens of Bayesian changepoint detection. Changepoint detection is used in time series models in which the generative parameters periodically change abruptly (Adams and MacKay, 2007). Viewing a sentence as a time series of words, we posit that the generative parameter, the topic, changes periodically in accordance with the changepoint indicators **c**. Because there is no restriction on the number of words between changepoints, topical phrases can be arbitrarily long but will always have a single topic drawn from θ_d.

The full definition of PDLDA is given by

$$\begin{aligned}
w_i \mid \mathbf{u} &\sim \text{Discrete}(G_{\mathbf{u}}) \\
G_{\mathbf{u}} &\sim \text{PYP}(a_{|\mathbf{u}|}, b_{|\mathbf{u}|}, G_{\pi(\mathbf{u})}) \\
G_{\emptyset} &\sim \text{PYP}(a_0, b_0, H) \\
z_i \mid d, z_{i-1}, \theta_d, c_i &\sim \begin{cases} \delta_{z_{i-1}} & \text{if } c_i = 0 \\ \text{Discrete}\left(\theta_d\right) & \text{if } c_i = 1 \end{cases} \\
c_i \mid w_{i-1}, z_{i-1}, \pi &\sim \text{Bernoulli}\left(\pi_{w_{i-1}z_{i-1}}\right)
\end{aligned}$$

with the prior distriutions over the parameters as

$$\begin{aligned}
\theta_d \sim \text{Dirichlet}\left(\alpha\right) \qquad & \pi_{zw} \sim \text{Beta}\left(\lambda\right) \\
a_{|\mathbf{u}|} \sim \text{Beta}\left(\rho\right) \qquad & b_{|\mathbf{u}|} \sim \text{Gamma}\left(\epsilon\right)
\end{aligned}$$

Like TNG, PDLDA assumes that the probability of a changepoint c_{i+1} after the ith token depends on the current topic z_i and word w_i. This causes the length of a phrase to depend on its topic and constituent words. The changepoints explicitly model which words tend to start and end phrases in each document. Depending on c_i, z_i is either set deterministically to the preceding topic (when $c_i = 0$) or is drawn anew from θ_d (when $c_i = 1$). In this way, each topical phrase has a single topic drawn from its document's topic distribution. As in TNG, the parameters π_{zw} and θ_d are given conjugate priors parameterized by λ and α.

Let **u** be a *context vector* consisting of the phrase topic and the past m words: $\mathbf{u} \triangleq < z_i, w_{i-1}, w_{i-2}, \ldots, w_{i-m} >$. The operator $\pi(\mathbf{u})$ denotes the prefix of **u**, the vector with the rightmost element of **u** removed. $|\mathbf{u}|$ denotes the length of **u**, and $\emptyset$ represents an empty context. For practical reasons, we pad **u** with a special start symbol when the context overlaps a phrase boundary. For example, the first word w_i of a phrase beginning at a position i necessarily has $c_i = 1$; consequently, all the preceding words w_{i-j} in the context vector are treated as start symbols so that w_i is effectively drawn from a topic-specific unigram distribution.

In PDLDA, each token is drawn from a distribution conditioned on its context **u**. When $m = 1$, this conditioning is analogous to TNG's word distribution. However, in contrast with TNG, the word

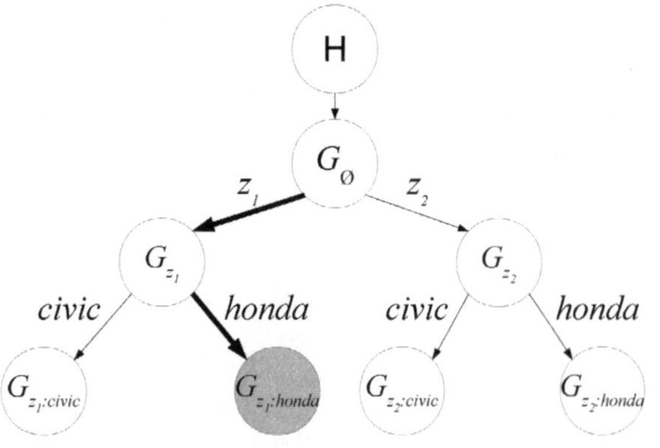

Figure 3: Illustration of the hierarchical Pitman-Yor process for a toy two-word vocabulary $V = \{honda, civic\}$ and two-topic ($T = 2$) model with $m = 1$. Each node G in the tree is a Pitman-Yor process whose base distribution is its parent node, and H is a uniform distribution over V. When, for example, the context is $\mathbf{u} = z_1 : honda$, the darkened path is followed and the probability of the next word is calculated from the shaded node using Equation 1, which combines predictions from all the nodes along the darkened path.

distributions used are Pitman-Yor processes (PYPs) linked together into a tree structure. This hierarchical construction creates the desired smoothing among different contexts. The next section explains this hierarchical distribution in more detail.

3.1 Hierarchical Pitman-Yor process

Words in PDLDA are emitted from $G_{\mathbf{u}}$, which has a PYP prior (Pitman and Yor, 1997). PYPs are a generalization of the Dirichlet Process, with the addition of a discount parameter $0 \leq a \leq 1$. When considering the distribution of a sequence of words $\mathbf{w}$ drawn *iid* from a PYP-distributed G, one can analytically marginalize G and consider the resulting conditional distribution of $\mathbf{w}$ given its parameters a, b, and base distribution ϕ. This marginal can best be understood by considering the distribution of any $w_i|w_1, \ldots, w_{i-1}, a, b, \phi$, which is characterized by a generative process known as the generalized *Chinese Restaurant Process* (CRP) (Pitman, 2002). In the CRP metaphor, one imagines a restaurant with an unbounded number of tables, where each table has one shared dish (a draw from ϕ) and can seat an unlimited number of customers. The CRP specifies a process by which customers entering the restaurant choose a table to sit at and, consequently, the dish they eat. The first customer to arrive always sits at the first table. Subsequent customers sit at an occupied table k with probability proportional to $c_k - a$ and choose a new unoccupied table with probability proportional to $b + ta$, where c_k is the number of customers seated at table k and t is the number of occupied tables in G. For our language modeling purposes, "customers" are word tokens and "dishes" are word types.

The hierarchical PYP (HPYP) is an intuitive recursive formulation of the PYP in which the base distribution ϕ is itself PYP-distributed. Figure 3 demonstrates this principle as applied to PDLDA. The hierarchy forms a tree structure, where leaves are restaurants corresponding to full contexts and internal nodes correspond to partial contexts. An edge between a parent and child node represents a dependency of the child on the parent, where the base distribution of the child node is its parent. This smooths each context's distribution like the Bayesian n-gram model of Teh (2006), which is a Bayesian version of interpolated Kneser-Ney smoothing (Chen and Goodman, 1998). One ramification of this setup is that if a word occurs in a context $\mathbf{u}$, the sharing makes it more likely in other contexts that have something in common with $\mathbf{u}$, such as a shared topic or word.

The HPYP gives the following probability for a word following the context $\mathbf{u}$ being w:

$$P_{\mathbf{u}}(w \mid \tau, \mathbf{a}, \mathbf{b}) = \frac{c_{\mathbf{u}w\cdot} - a_{|\mathbf{u}|}t_{\mathbf{u}w}}{b_{|\mathbf{u}|} + c_{\mathbf{u}\cdot\cdot}} + \frac{b_{|\mathbf{u}|} + a_{|\mathbf{u}|}t_{\mathbf{u}\cdot}}{b_{|\mathbf{u}|} + c_{\mathbf{u}\cdot\cdot}} P_{\pi(\mathbf{u})}(w \mid \tau, \mathbf{a}, \mathbf{b}) \quad (1)$$

where $P_{\pi(\emptyset)}(w|\tau, \mathbf{a}, \mathbf{b}) = G_\emptyset(w)$, $c_{\mathbf{u}w\cdot}$ is the number of customers eating dish w in restaurant $\mathbf{u}$, and $t_{\mathbf{u}w}$ is the number of tables serving w in restaurant $\mathbf{u}$, and τ represents the current seating arrangement. Here and throughout the rest of the paper, we use a dot to indicate marginal counts: e.g., $c_{\mathbf{u}w\cdot} = \sum_k c_{\mathbf{u}wk}$ where $c_{\mathbf{u}wk}$ is the number of customers eating w in $\mathbf{u}$ at table k. The base distribution of $G_\emptyset$ was chosen to be uniform: $H(w) = 1/V$ with V being the vocabulary size. The above equation an interpolation between distributions of context lengths

$|\mathbf{u}|, |\mathbf{u}|-1, \ldots 0$ and realizes the sharing of statistical strength between different contexts.

3.2 Inference

In this section, we describe Markov chain Monte Carlo procedures to sample from $P(\mathbf{z}, \mathbf{c}, \tau | \mathbf{w}, U)$, the posterior distribution over topic assignments $\mathbf{z}$, phrase boundaries $\mathbf{c}$, and seating arrangements τ given an observed corpus $\mathbf{w}$. Let U be shorthand for $\alpha, \lambda, \mathbf{a}, \mathbf{b}$. In order to draw samples from $P(\mathbf{z}, \mathbf{c}, \tau | \mathbf{w}, U)$, we employ a Metropolis-Hastings sampler for approximate inference. The sampler we use is a *collapsed* sampler (Griffiths and Steyvers, 2004), wherein θ, ϕ, and $\mathbf{G}$ are analytically marginalized. Because we marginalize each G, we use the Chinese Restaurant Franchise representation of the hierarchical PYPs (Teh, 2006). However, rather than onerously storing the table assignment of every token in $\mathbf{w}$, we store only the counts of how many tables there are in a restaurant and how many customers are sitting at each table in that restaurant. We refer the inquisitive reader to the appendix of Teh (2006) for further details of this procedure.

Our sampling strategy for a given token i in document d is to jointly propose changes to the changepoint c_i and topic assignment z_i, and then to the seating arrangement τ. Recall that according to the model, if $c_i = 0$, $z_i = z_{i-1}$; otherwise z_i is generated from the topic distribution for document d. Since the topic assignment remains the same until a new changepoint at a position i' is reached, each token w_j for j from position i until $i'-1$ will depend on z_i because for these j, $z_j = z_i$. We call this set of tokens the *phrase suffix* of the ith token and denote it $s(i)$. More formally, let $s(i)$ be the maximal set of continuous indices $j \geq i$ including i such that, if $j \neq i$, $c_j = 0$. That is, $s(i)$ are the indices comprising the remainder of the phrase beginning at position i. In addition, let $x(i)$ indicate the *extended suffix* version of $s(i)$ which includes one additional index: $x(i) \triangleq \{s(i) \cup \{\max(s(i)) + 1\}\}$. In addition to the words in the suffix $s(i)$, the changepoint indicator variables c_j for j in $x(i)$ are also conditioned on z_i. To make these dependencies more explicit, we refer to $\mathbf{z}_{s(i)} \triangleq z_j \; \forall j \in s(i)$, which are constrained by the model to share a topic.

The variables that depend directly on z_i, c_i are $\mathbf{z}_{s(i)}, \mathbf{w}_{s(i)}, \mathbf{c}_{x(i)}$. The proposal distribution first draws from a multinomial over $T+1$ options: one option for $c_i = 0, z_i = z_i - 1$; and one for $c_i = 1$ paired with each possible $z_i = z \in 1 \ldots T$. This is given by

$$P(\mathbf{z}_{s(i)}, c_i \mid \mathbf{z}_{\neg s(i)}, \mathbf{c}_{\neg i}, \tau_{\neg s(i)}, \mathbf{w}, U) \propto$$

$$\prod_{j \in x(i)} \frac{n^{\neg x(j)}_{z_{j-1} w_{j-1} c_j} + \lambda_{c_j}}{n^{\neg x(j)}_{z_{j-1} w_{j-1} \cdot} + \lambda_0 + \lambda_1}$$

$$\prod_{j \in s(i)} P(z_j \mid \mathbf{c}, \mathbf{z}_{\neg s(j)}, U) \quad P_{\mathbf{u}_j}(\mathbf{w}_j \mid \tau_{\neg s(i)}, U)$$

with

$$P(z_j \mid \mathbf{c}, \mathbf{z}_{\neg s(j)}, U) = \begin{cases} \dfrac{n^{\neg s(j)}_{dz_j} + \alpha}{n^{\neg s(j)}_{d\cdot} + T\alpha} & \text{if } c_j = 1 \\ \delta_{z_j, z_{j-1}} & \text{if } c_j = 0 \end{cases}$$

where $P_{\mathbf{u}_j}(\mathbf{w}_j \mid \tau_{\neg s(i)}, U)$ is given by Equation 1, T is the number of topics, $n^{\neg s(j)}_{dz}$ is the number of phrases in document d that have topic z when $s(j)$'s assignment is excluded, and $n^{\neg s(j)}_{zwc}$ is the number of times a changepoint c has followed a word w with topic z when $s(j)$'s assignments are excluded.

After drawing a proposal for $c_i, \mathbf{z}_{s(i)}$ for token i, the sampler adds a customer eating w_i to a table serving w_i in restaurant $\mathbf{u}_i$. An old table k is selected with probability $\propto \max(0, c_{\mathbf{u}wk} - a_{|\mathbf{u}|})$ and a new table is selected with probability $\propto (b_{|\mathbf{u}_i|} + a_{|\mathbf{u}_i|} t_{\mathbf{u}_i \cdot}) P_{\pi(\mathbf{u})}(w_i)$.

Let $\mathbf{z}'_{s(i)}, c'_i, \tau'_{s(i)}$ denote the proposed change to $\mathbf{z}_{s(i)}, c_i, \tau_{s(i)}$. We accept the proposal with probability $\min(A, 1)$ where

$$A = \frac{\hat{P}(\mathbf{z}'_{s(i)}, c'_i, \tau'_{s(i)}) \, Q(\mathbf{z}_{s(i)}, c_i, \tau_{s(i)})}{\hat{P}(\mathbf{z}_{s(i)}, c_i, \tau_{s(i)}) \, Q(\mathbf{z}'_{s(i)}, c'_i, \tau'_{s(i)})}$$

where Q is the proposal distribution and $\hat{P}$ is the true unnormalized distribution. $\hat{P}$ differs from Q in that the probability of each word w_j and the seating arrangement depends only on $\neg s(j)$, as opposed to the simplification of using $\neg s(i)$. Almost all proposals are accepted; hence, this theoretically motivated Metropolis Hastings correction step makes little difference in practice.

Because the parameters $\mathbf{a}$ and $\mathbf{b}$ have no intuitive interpretation and we lack any strong belief about what they should be, we give them vague priors where $\rho_1 = \rho_2 = 1$ and $\epsilon_1 = 10$, $\epsilon_2 = .1$. We then interleave a slice sampling algorithm (Neal, 2000) between sweeps of the Metropolis-Hastings sampler to learn these parameters. We chose not to do inference on α in order to make the tests of our model against TNG more equitable.

4 Related Work

An integral part of modeling topical phrases is the relaxation of the bag-of-words assumption in LDA. There are many models that make this relaxation. Among them, Griffiths and Steyvers (2005) present a model in which words are generated either conditioned on a topic or conditioned on the previous word in a bigram, but not both. They use this to model human performance on a word-association task. Wallach (2006) experiments with incorporating LDA into a bigram language model. Her model uses a hierarchical Dirichlet to share parameters across bigrams in a topic in a manner similar to our use of PYPs, but it lacks a notion of the topic being shared between the words in an n-gram. The Hidden Topic Markov Model (HTMM) (Gruber et al., 2007) assumes that all words in a sentence have the same topic, and consecutive sentences are likely to have the same topic. By dropping the independence assumption among topics, HTMM is able to achieve lower perplexity scores than LDA at minimal additional computational costs. These models are unconcerned with topical n-grams and thus do not model phrases.

Johnson (2010) presents an Adaptor Grammar model of topical phrases. Adaptor Grammars are a framework for specifying nonparametric Bayesian models over context-free grammars in which certain subtrees are "memoized" or remembered for reuse. In Johnson's model, subtrees corresponding to common phrases for a topic are memoized, resulting in a model in which each topic is associated with a distribution over whole phrases. While it is a theoretically elegant method for finding topical phrases, for large corpora we found inference to be impractically slow.

5 Phrase Intrusion Experiment

Perplexity is the typical information theoretic measure of language model quality used in lieu of extrinsic measures, which are more difficult and costly to run. However, it is well known that perplexity

Trial 1 of 80	Trial 3 of 80
countries britain france museum	fda book smoking cigarettes
Trial 2 of 80	**Trial 4 of 80**
air force beverly hills defense minister u.s. troops	roman catholic church air traffic controllers roman catholic priest roman catholic bishop

Figure 4: Experimental setup of the phrase intrusion experiment in which subjects must click on the n-gram that does not belong.

scores may negatively correlate with actual quality as assessed by humans (Chang et al., 2009). With that fact in mind, we expanded the methodology of Chang et al. (2009) to create a "phrase intrusion" task that quantitatively compares the quality of the topical n-gram lists produced by our model against those of other models.

Each of 48 subjects underwent 80 trials of a web-based experiment on Amazon Mechanical Turk, a reliable (Paolacci et al., 2010) and increasingly common venue for conducting online experiments. In each trial, a subject is presented with a randomly ordered list of four n-grams (cf. Figure 4). Each subject's task is to select the *intruder phrase*, a spurious n-gram not belonging with the others in the list. If, other than the intruder, the items in the list are all on the same topic, then subjects can easily identify the intruder because the list is semantically cohesive and makes sense. If the list is incohesive and has no discernible topic, subjects must guess arbitrarily and performance is at random.

To construct each trial's list, we chose two topics z and z' ($z \neq z'$), then selected the three most probable n-grams from z and the intruder phrase, an n-gram probable in z' and improbable in z. This design ensures that the intruder is not identifiable due solely to its being rare. Interspersed among the phrase intrusion trials were several simple screening trials intended to affirm that subjects possessed a minimal level of attentiveness and reading comprehension. For example, one such screening trial presented subjects with the list *banana*, *apple*, *television*, *orange*. Subjects who got any of these trials

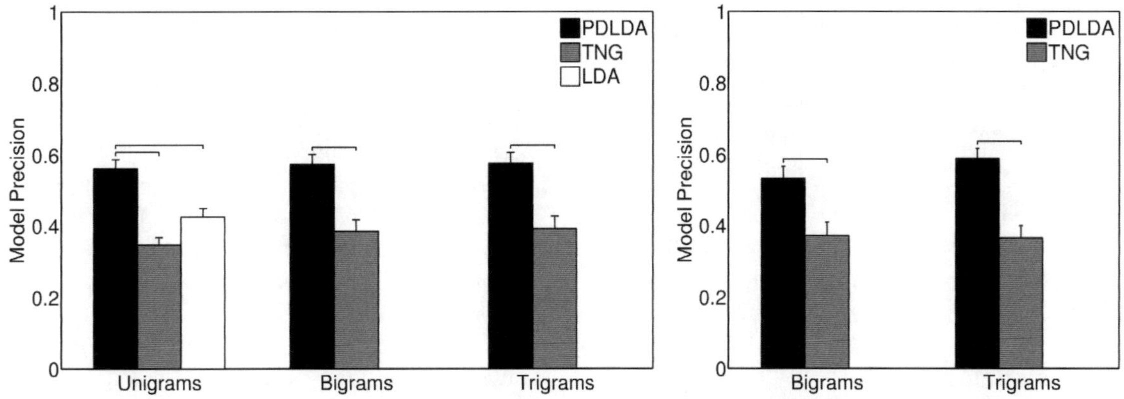

Figure 5: An across-subject measure of the ability to detect intruders as a function of n-gram size and model. Excluding trials with repeated words does not qualitatively affect the results.

wrong were excluded from our analyses.

Each subject was presented with trials constructed from the output of PDLDA and TNG for unigrams, bigrams, and trigrams. For unigrams, we also tested the output of the original smoothed LDA (Blei et al., 2003). The experiment was conducted twice for a 2,246-document subset of the TREC AP corpus (Blei et al., 2003; Harman, 1992): the first time proceeded as described above, but the second time did not allow word repetition within a topic's list. The topical phrases found by TNG and PDLDA often revolve around a central n-gram, with other words pre- or post- appended to it. In this intrusion experiment, any n-gram not containing the central word or phrase may be trivially identifiable, regardless of its relevance to the topic. For example, the intruder in Trial 4 of Figure 4 is easily identifiable even if a subject does not understand English. This second experiment was designed to test whether our conclusions hinge on word repetition.

We used the MALLET toolbox (McCallum, 2002) for the implementations of LDA and TNG. Each model was run with 100 topics for 5,000 iterations. We set $m = 2$, $\alpha = .01$, $\beta = .01$, $\lambda = 1$, $\pi_1 = \pi_2 = 1$, $\rho_1 = 10$, and $\rho_2 = .1$. For all models, we treated certain punctuation as the start of a phrase by setting $c_j = 1$ for all tokens j immediately following periods, commas, semicolons, and exclamation and question marks. To reduce runtime, we removed stopwords occuring in the MALLET toolbox's stopword list. Because TNG and LDA had trouble with single character words not in the stoplist, we manually removed them before the experiment. Any token immediately following a removed word was treated as if it were the start of a phrase.

As in Chang et al. (2009), performance is measured via model precision, the fraction of subjects agreeing with the model. It is defined as $\text{MP}_k^{m,n} = \sum_s \mathbb{1}(i_{k,s}^{m,n} = \omega_{k,s}^{m,n})/S$ where $\omega_{k,s}^{m,n}$ is the index of the intruding n-gram for subject s among the words generated from the kth topic of model m, $i_{k,s}^{m,n}$ is the intruder selected by s, and S is the number of subjects. The model precisions are shown in Figure 5. PDLDA achieves the highest precision in all conditions. Model precision is low in all models, which is a reflection of how challenging the task is on a small corpus laden with proper nouns and low-frequency words. Figure 5b demonstrates that the outcome of the experiment does not depend strongly on whether the topical n-gram lists have repeated words.

6 Conclusion

We presented a topic model which simultaneously segments a corpus into phrases of varying lengths and assigns topics to them. The topical phrases found by PDLDA are much richer sources of information than the topical unigrams typically produced in topic modeling. As evidenced by the phrase-intrusion experiment, the topical n-gram lists that PDLDA finds are much more interpretable than those found by TNG.

The formalism of Bayesian changepoint detection arose naturally from the intuitive assumption that the topic of a sequence of tokens changes periodically, and that the tokens in between changepoints comprise a phrase. This formalism provides a principled way to discover phrases within the LDA framework. We presented a model embodying these principles and showed how to incorporate dependent Pitman-Yor processes into it.

Acknowledgements

The first author is supported by an NSF Graduate Research Fellowship. The first and second authors began this project while working at J.D. Power & Associates. We are indebted to Michael Mozer, Matt Wilder, and Nicolas Nicolov for their advice.

References

Ryan Prescott Adams and David J.C. MacKay. 2007. Bayesian online changepoint detection. Technical report, University of Cambridge, Cambridge, UK.

David M. Blei, Andrew Y. Ng, Michael I. Jordan, and John Lafferty. 2003. Latent dirichlet allocation. *Journal of Machine Learning Research*, 3:993–1022.

Jonathan Chang, Jordan Boyd-Graber, Sean Gerrish, Chong Wang, and David M. Blei. 2009. Reading tea leaves: How humans interpret topic models. In *Neural Information Processing Systems (NIPS)*.

Stanley F. Chen and Joshua Goodman. 1998. An empirical study of smoothing techniques for language modeling. Technical Report TR-10-98, Center for Research in Computing Technology, Harvard University.

T. L. Griffiths and M. Steyvers. 2004. Finding scientific topics. *Proceedings of the National Academy of Sciences*, 101(Suppl. 1):5228–5235, April.

Thomas L. Griffiths, Mark Steyvers, David M. Blei, and Joshua B. Tenenbaum. 2005. Integrating topics and syntax. In *Advances in Neural Information Processing Systems 17*, pages 537–544. MIT Press.

Thomas L. Griffiths, Joshua B. Tenenbaum, and Mark Steyvers. 2007. Topics in semantic representation. *Psychological Review*, 114:211–244.

Amit Gruber, Yair Weiss, and Michal Rosen-Zvi. 2007. Hidden topic Markov models. *Journal of Machine Learning Research - Proceedings Track*, 2:163–170.

Donna Harman. 1992. Overview of the first text retrieval conference (trec–1). In *Proceedings of the first Text REtrieval Conference (TREC–1)*, Washington DC, USA.

Mark Johnson. 2010. PCFGs, Topic Models, Adaptor Grammars and Learning Topical Collocations and the Structure of Proper Names. In *Proceedings of the 48th Annual Meeting of the Association for Computational Linguistics*, pages 1148–1157, Uppsala, Sweden, July. Association for Computational Linguistics.

Thomas K. Landauer and Susan T. Dumais. 1997. A solution to plato's problem: The latent semantic analysis theory of acquisition, induction, and representation of knowledge. *Psychological Review*, 104(2):211 – 240.

Andrew Kachites McCallum. 2002. Mallet: A machine learning for language toolkit. http://mallet.cs.umass.edu.

Radford Neal. 2000. Slice sampling. *Annals of Statistics*, 31:705–767.

Gabriele Paolacci, Jesse Chandler, and Panagiotis G. Ipeirotis. 2010. Running experiments on Amazon Mechanical Turk. *Judgment and Decision Making*, 5(5):411–419.

J. Pitman and M. Yor. 1997. The two-parameter Poisson-Dirichlet distribution derived from a stable subordinator. *Annals of Probability*, 25:855–900.

J. Pitman. 2002. Combinatorial stochastic processes. Technical Report 621, Department of Statistics, University of California at Berkeley.

Patrick Schone and Daniel Jurafsky. 2001. Is knowledge-free induction of multiword unit dictionary headwords a solved problem? In Lillian Lee and Donna Harman, editors, *Proceedings of the 2001 Conference on Empirical Methods in Natural Language Processing*, pages 100–108.

Yee Whye Teh. 2006. A hierarchical Bayesian language model based on Pitman-Yor processes. In *Proceedings of the 21st International Conference on Computational Linguistics and the 44th Annual Meeting of the Association for Computational Linguistics*, ACL-44, pages 985–992, Morristown, NJ, USA. Association for Computational Linguistics.

Hanna M. Wallach. 2006. Topic modeling: beyond bag-of-words. In *Proceedings of the 23rd International Conference on Machine Learning*, pages 977–984.

Xuerui Wang, Andrew McCallum, and Xing Wei. 2007. Topical n-grams: Phrase and topic discovery, with an application to information retrieval. In *Proceedings of the 7th IEEE International Conference on Data Mining*.

A Bayesian Model for Learning SCFGs with Discontiguous Rules

Abby Levenberg
Dept. of Computer Science
University of Oxford
ablev@cs.ox.ac.uk

Chris Dyer
School of Computer Science
Carnegie Mellon Univeristy
cdyer@cs.cmu.edu

Phil Blunsom
Dept. of Computer Science
University of Oxford
pblunsom@cs.ox.ac.uk

Abstract

We describe a nonparametric model and corresponding inference algorithm for learning Synchronous Context Free Grammar derivations for parallel text. The model employs a Pitman-Yor Process prior which uses a novel base distribution over synchronous grammar rules. Through both synthetic grammar induction and statistical machine translation experiments, we show that our model learns complex translational correspondences— including discontiguous, many-to-many alignments—and produces competitive translation results. Further, inference is efficient and we present results on significantly larger corpora than prior work.

1 Introduction

In the twenty years since Brown et al. (1992) pioneered the first word-based statistical machine translation (SMT) models substantially more expressive models of translational equivalence have been developed. The prevalence of complex phrasal, discontiguous, and non-monotonic translation phenomena in real-world applications of machine translation has driven the development of hierarchical and syntactic models based on synchronous context-free grammars (SCFGs). Such models are now widely used in translation and represent the state-of-the-art in most language pairs (Galley et al., 2004; Chiang, 2007). However, while the models used for translation have evolved, the way in which they are learnt has not: naïve word-based models are still used to infer translational correspondences from parallel corpora.

In this work we bring the learning of the minimal units of translation in step with the representational power of modern translation models. We present a nonparametric Bayesian model of translation based on SCFGs, and we use its posterior distribution to infer synchronous derivations for a parallel corpus using a novel Gibbs sampler. Our model is able to: *1*) directly model many-to-many alignments, thereby capturing non-compositional and idiomatic translations; *2*) align discontiguous phrases in both the source and target languages; *3*) have no restrictions on the length of a rule, the number of nonterminal symbols per rule, or their configuration.

Learning synchronous grammars is hard due to the high polynomial complexity of dynamic programming and the exponential space of possible rules. As such most prior work for learning SCFGs has relied on inference algorithms that were heuristically constrained or biased by word-based alignment models and small experiments (Wu, 1997; Zhang et al., 2008; Blunsom et al., 2009; Neubig et al., 2011). In contrast to these previous attempts, our SCFG model scales to large datasets (over 1.3M sentence pairs) without imposing restrictions on the form of the grammar rules or otherwise constraining the set of learnable rules (e.g., with a word alignment).

We validate our sampler by demonstrating its ability to recover grammars used to generate synthetic datasets. We then evaluate our model by inducing word alignments for SMT experiments in several typologically diverse language pairs and across a range of corpora sizes. Our results attest to our model's ability to learn synchronous grammars encoding complex translation phenomena.

2 Prior Work

The goal of directly inducing phrasal translation models from parallel corpora has received a lot of attention in the NLP and SMT literature. Marcu and Wong (2002) presented an ambitious maximum likelihood model and EM inference algorithm for learning phrasal translation representations. The first issue this model faced was a massive parameter space and intractable inference. However a more subtle issue is that likelihood based models of this form suffer from a degenerate solution, resulting in the model learning whole sentences as phrases rather than minimal units of translation. DeNero et al. (2008) recognised this problem and proposed a nonparametric Bayesian prior for contiguous phrases. This had the dual benefits of biasing the model towards learning minimal translation units, and integrating out the parameters such that a much smaller set of statistics would suffice for inference with a Gibbs sampler. However this work fell short by not evaluating the model independently, instead only presenting results in which it was combined with a standard word-alignment initialisation, thus leaving open the question of its efficacy.

The fact that flat phrasal models lack a structured approach to reordering has led many researchers to pursue SCFG induction instead (Wu, 1997; Cherry and Lin, 2007; Zhang et al., 2008; Blunsom et al., 2009). The asymptotic time complexity of the inside algorithm for even the simplest SCFG models is $O(|\mathbf{s}|^3|\mathbf{t}|^3)$, too high to be practical for most real translation data. A popular solution to this problem is to heuristically restrict inference to derivations which agree with an independent alignment model (Cherry and Lin, 2007; Zhang et al., 2008). However this may have the unintended effect of biasing the model back towards the initial alignments that they attempt to improve upon. More recently Neubig et al. (2011) reported a novel Bayesian model for phrasal alignment and extraction that was able to model phrases of multiple granularities via a synchronous Adaptor Grammar. However this model suffered from the common problem of intractable inference and results were presented for a very small number of samples from a heuristically pruned beam, making interpreting the results difficult.

Blunsom et al. (2009) presented an approach similar to ours that implemented a Gibbs sampler for a nonparametric Bayesian model of ITG. While that work managed to scale to a non-trivially sized corpus, like other works it relied on a state-of-the-art word alignment model for initialisation. Our model goes further by allowing discontiguous phrasal translation units. Surprisingly, the freedom that this extra power affords allows the Gibbs sampler we propose to mix more quickly, allowing state-of-the-art results from a simple initialiser.

3 Model

We use a nonparametric generative model based on the 2-parameter Pitman-Yor process (PYP) (Pitman and Yor, 1997), a generalisation of the Dirichlet Process, which has been used for various NLP modeling tasks with state-of-the-art results such as language modeling, word segmentation, text compression and part of speech induction (Teh, 2006; Goldwater et al., 2006; Wood et al., 2011; Blunsom and Cohn, 2011). In this section we first provide a brief definition of the SCFG formalism and then describe our PYP prior for them.

3.1 Synchronous Context-Free Grammar

An synchronous context-free grammar (SCFG) is a 5-tuple $\langle \Sigma, \Delta, V, S, R \rangle$ that generalises context-free grammar to generate strings concurrently in two languages (Lewis and Stearns, 1968). Σ is a finite set of source language terminal symbols, Δ is a finite set of target language terminal symbols, V is a set of nonterminal symbols, with a designated start symbol S, and R is a set of synchronous rewrite rules. A string pair is generated by starting with the pair $\langle S_1 \mid S_1 \rangle$ and recursively applying rewrite rules of the form $X \rightarrow \langle \mathbf{s}, \mathbf{t}, \mathbf{a} \rangle$ where the left hand side (LHS) X is a nonterminal in V, $\mathbf{s}$ is a string in $(\Sigma \cup V)^*$, $\mathbf{t}$ is a string in $(\Delta \cup V)^*$ and $\mathbf{a}$ specifies a one-to-one mapping (bijection) between nonterminal symbols in $\mathbf{s}$ and $\mathbf{t}$. The following are examples:[1]

$$\text{VP} \rightarrow \langle\ \textit{schlage}\ \text{NP}_1\ \text{NP}_2\ \textit{vor} \mid \textit{suggest}\ \text{NP}_2\ \textit{to}\ \text{NP}_1\ \rangle$$
$$\text{NP} \rightarrow \langle\ \textit{die Kommission} \mid \textit{the commission}\ \rangle$$

[1]The nonterminal alignment $\mathbf{a}$ is indicated through subscripts on the nonterminals.

In a probabilistic SCFG, rules are associated with probabilities such that the probabilities of all rewrites of a particular LHS category sum to 1.

Translation with SCFGs is carried out by parsing the source language with the monolingual source language projection of the grammar (using standard monolingual parsing algorithms), which induces a parallel tree structure and translation in the target language (Chiang, 2007). Alignment or synchronous parsing is the process of concurrently parsing both the source and target sentences, uncovering the derivation or derivations that give rise to a string pair (Wu, 1997; Dyer, 2010).

Our goal is to infer the most probable SCFG derivations that explain a corpus of parallel sentences, given a nonparametric prior over probabilistic SCFGs. In this work we will consider grammars with a single nonterminal category X.

3.2 Pitman-Yor Process SCFG

Before training we have no way of knowing how many rules will be needed in our grammar to adequately represent the data. By using the Pitman-Yor process as a prior on the parameters of a synchronous grammar we can formulate a model which prefers smaller numbers of rules that are reused often, thereby avoiding degenerate grammars consisting of large, overly specific rules. However, as the data being fit grows, the model can become more complex. The PYP is parameterised by a *discount* parameter d, a *strength* parameter θ, and the base distribution $\mathcal{G}_0$, which gives the prior probability of an event (in our case, events are rules) before any observations have occurred. The discount is subtracted from each positive rule count and dampens the rich get richer effect where frequent rules are given higher probability compared to infrequent ones. The strength parameter controls the variance, or concentration, about the base distribution.

In our model, a draw from a PYP is a distribution over SCFG rules with a particular LHS (in fact, it is a distribution over all well-formed rules). From this distribution we can in turn draw individual rules:

$$\begin{aligned} \mathcal{G}_X &\sim \text{PY}(d, \theta, \mathcal{G}_0), \\ \text{X} \rightarrow \langle \mathbf{s}, \mathbf{t}, \mathbf{a} \rangle &\sim \mathcal{G}_X. \end{aligned}$$

Although the PYP has no known analytical form, we can marginalise out the $\mathcal{G}_X$'s and reason about individual rules directly using the process described by Teh (2006). In this process, at time n a rule r_n is generated by stochastically deciding whether to make another copy of a previously generated rule or to draw a new one from the base distribution, $\mathcal{G}_0$. Let $\boldsymbol{\varphi} = (\varphi_1, \varphi_2, \ldots)$ be the sequence of draws from $\mathcal{G}_0$; thus $|\boldsymbol{\varphi}|$ is the total number of draws from $\mathcal{G}_0$. A rule r_n corresponds to a selection of a φ_k. Let c_k be a counter indicating the number of times φ_k has been selected. In particular, we set r_n to φ_k with probability

$$\frac{c_k - d}{\theta + n},$$

and increment c_k, or with probability

$$\frac{\theta + d \cdot |\boldsymbol{\varphi}|}{\theta + n},$$

we draw a new rule from $\mathcal{G}_0$, append it to $\boldsymbol{\varphi}$, and use it for r_n.

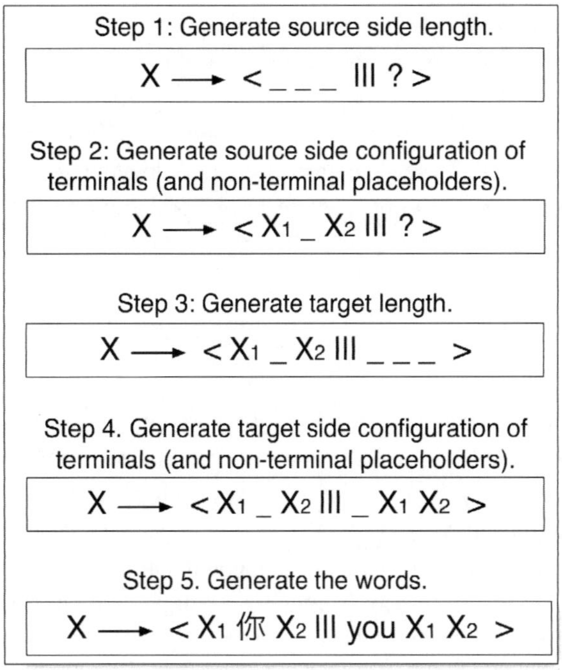

Figure 1: Example generation of a synchronous grammar rule in our $\mathcal{G}_0$.

3.3 Base Distribution

The base distribution $\mathcal{G}_0$ for the PYP assigns probability to a rule based our belief about what constitutes a good rule independent of observing any of the data. We describe a novel generative process for all rules $X \rightarrow \langle \mathbf{s}, \mathbf{t}, \mathbf{a} \rangle$ that encodes these beliefs.

We describe the generative process generally here in text, and readers may refer to the example in Figure 1. The process begins by generating the source length (total number of terminal and nonterminal symbols, written $|\mathbf{s}|$) by drawing from a Poisson distribution with mean 1:

$$|\mathbf{s}| \sim \text{Poisson}(1) \ .$$

This assigns high probability to shorter rules, but arbitrarily long rules are possible with a low probability. Then, for every position in $\mathbf{s}$, we decide whether it will contain a terminal or nonterminal symbol by repeated, independent draws from a Bernoulli distribution. Since we believe that shorter rules should be relatively more likely to contain terminal symbols than longer rules, we define the probability of a terminal symbol to be $\phi^{|\mathbf{s}|}$ where $0 < \phi < 1$ is a hyperparameter.

$$s_i \sim \text{Bernoulli}(\phi^{|\mathbf{s}|}) \quad \forall\, i \in [1, |\mathbf{s}|] \ .$$

We next generate the length of the target side of the rule. Let $\#_{\text{NT}}(\mathbf{s})$ denote the number of nonterminal symbols we generated in $\mathbf{s}$, i.e., the arity of the rule. Our intuition here is that source and target lengths should be similar. However, to ensure that the rule is well-formed, $\mathbf{t}$ must contain exactly as many nonterminal symbols as the source does. We therefore draw the number of target terminal symbols from a Poisson whose mean is the number of terminal symbols in the source, plus a small constant λ_0 to ensure that it is greater than zero:

$$|\mathbf{t}| - \#_{\text{NT}}(\mathbf{s}) \sim \text{Poisson}\left(|\mathbf{s}| - \#_{\text{NT}}(\mathbf{s}) + \lambda_0\right) \ .$$

We then determine whether each position in $\mathbf{t}$ is a terminal or nonterminal symbol by drawing uniformly from the bag of $\#_{\text{NT}}(\mathbf{s})$ source nonterminals and $|\mathbf{t}| - \#_{\text{NT}}(\mathbf{s})$ terminal indicators, without replacement. At this point we have created a rule template which indicates how large the rule is, whether each position contains a terminal or nonterminal symbol, and the reordering of the source nonterminals $\mathbf{a}$. To conclude the process we must select the terminal types from the source and target vocabularies. To do so, we use the following distribution:

$$P_{\text{terminals}}(\mathbf{s}, \mathbf{t}) = \frac{P_{M1\leftarrow}(\mathbf{s}, \mathbf{t}) + P_{M1\rightarrow}(\mathbf{s}, \mathbf{t})}{2}$$

where $P_{M1\leftarrow}(\mathbf{s}, \mathbf{t})$ ($P_{M1\rightarrow}(\mathbf{s}, \mathbf{t})$) first generates the source (target) terminals from uniform draws from the vocabulary, then generates the string in the other language according to IBM MODEL 1, marginalizing over the alignments (Brown et al., 1993).

4 Gibbs Sampler

In this section we introduce a Gibbs sampler that enables us to perform posterior inference given a corpus of sentence pairs. Our innovation is to represent the synchronous derivation of a sentence pair in a hierarchical 4-dimensional binary alignment grid, with elements $z_{[s,t,u,v]} \in \{0, 1\}$.

The settings of the grid variables completely determine the SCFG rules in the current derivation. A setting of a binary variable $z_{[s,t,u,v]} = 1$ represents a constituent linking the source span $[s, t]$ and the target span $[u, v]$ in the current derivation; variables with a value of 0 indicate no link between spans $[s, t]$ and $[u, v]$.[2] This relationship from our grid representation is illustrated in Figure 2a.

Our Gibbs sampler operates over the space of all the random variables $z_{[s,t,u,v]}$, resampling one at a time. Changes to a single variable imply that at most *two* additional rules must be generated, as illustrated in Figure 2b. The probability of choosing a binary setting of 0 or 1 for a variable is proportional to the probability of generating the two derivations under the model described in the previous section. Note that for a given sentence, most of the bispan variables must be set to 0 otherwise they would violate the *strict nesting constraint* required for valid SCFG derivations. We discuss below how to exploit this fact to limit the number of binary variables that must be resampled for each sentence.

To be valid, a Gibbs sampler must be *ergodic* and satisfy *detailed balance*. Ergodicity requires that there is non-zero probability that any state in the sampler be reachable from any other state. Clearly

[2] Our grid representation is the synchronous generalisation of the well-known correspondence between CFG derivations and Boolean matrices; see Lee (2002) for an overview.

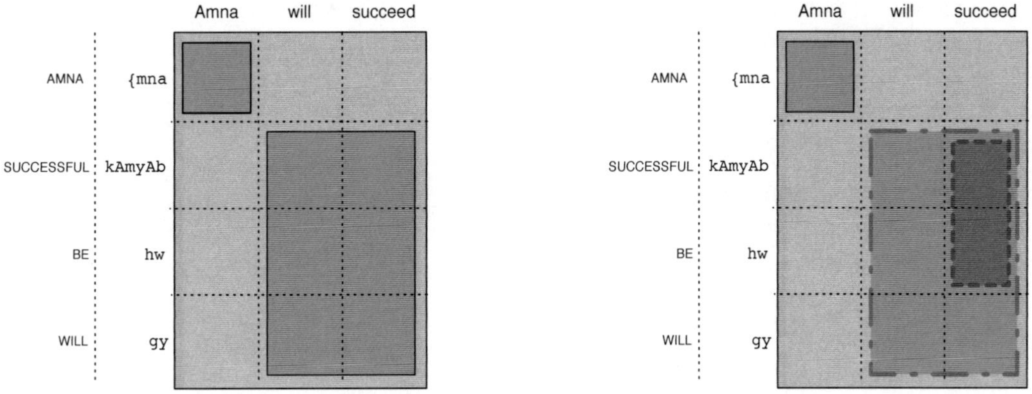

(a) An example grid representation of a synchronous derivation. The SCFG rules (annotated with their bispans) that correspond to this setting of the grid are:

$X_{[0,4,0,3]} \rightarrow$
$\langle X_{[0,1,0,1]}\, X_{[1,4,1,3]} \mid X_{[0,1,0,1]}\, X_{[1,4,1,3]} \rangle$
$X_{[0,1,0,1]} \rightarrow$ ⟨ `{mna` | *Amna* ⟩
$X_{[1,4,1,3]} \rightarrow$ ⟨ `kAmyAb hw gy` | *will succeed* ⟩

(b) The toggle operator resamples a bispan variable (here, $z_{[1,3,2,3]}$, shown in blue) to determine whether it should be subtracted from the immediately dominating rule (bispan in red) and made into a child rule in the derivation. This would require the addition of the following two rules:

$X_{[1,4,1,3]} \rightarrow$ ⟨ $X_{[1,3,2,3]}$ `gy` | *will* $X_{[1,3,2,3]}$ ⟩
$X_{[1,3,2,3]} \rightarrow$ ⟨ `kAmyAb hw` | *succeed* ⟩

Alternatively, the active bispan variable can be set so it is *not* a constituent, which would require the single rule:

$X_{[1,4,1,3]} \rightarrow$ ⟨ `kAmyAb hw gy` | *will succeed* ⟩

Figure 2: A single operation of the Gibbs sampler for a binary alignment grid.

our operator satisfies this since given any configuration of the alignment grid we can use the toggle operator to flatten the derivation to a single rule and then break it back down to reach any derivation.

Detailed balance requires that the probability of transitioning between two possible adjacent sampler states respects their joint probabilities in the stationary distribution. One way to ensure this is to make the order in which bispan variables are visited deterministic and independent of the variables' current settings. Then, the probability of the sampler targeting any bispan in the grid is equal regardless of the current configuration of the alignment grid.

A naive instantiation of this strategy is to visit all $|\mathbf{s}|^2|\mathbf{t}|^2$ bispans in some order. However, since we wish to be able to draw many samples, this is not computationally feasible. A much more efficient approach avoids resampling variables that would result in violations without visiting each of them individually. However, to ensure detailed balanced is maintained, the order that we resample bispans has to match the order we would sample them using any exhaustive approach. We achieve this by always checking a derivation top-down, from largest to smallest bispan. Under this ordering, whether or not a smaller bispan is visited will be independent of how the larger ones were resampled. Furthermore, the set of variables that may be resampled is fixed given this ordering. Therefore, the probability of sampling any possible bispan in the sentence pair is still uniform (ensuring detailed balance), while our sampler remains fast.

5 Evaluation

The preceding sections have introduced a model, and accompanying inference technique, designed to induce a posterior distribution over SCFG derivations containing discontiguous and phrasal translation rules. The evaluation that follows aims to determine our models ability to meet these design goals, and to do so in a range of translation scenarios.

In order to validate both the model and the sampler's ability to learn an SCFG we first conduct a synthetic experiment in which the true grammar is known. Subsequently we conduct a series of experiments on real parallel corpora of increasing sizes to explore the empirical properties of our model.

5.1 Synthetic Data Experiments

Prior work on SCFG induction for SMT has validated modeling claims by reporting BLEU scores on real translation tasks. However, the combination of noisy data and the complexity of SMT pipelines conspire to obscure whether models actually achieve their design goals, normally stated in terms of an ability to induce SCFGs with particular properties.

Here we include a small synthetic data experiment to clearly validate our models ability to learn an SCFG that includes discontiguous and phrasal translation rules with non-monotonic word order.

Using the probabilistic SCFG shown in the top half of Table 1 we stochastically generated three thousand parallel sentence pairs as training data for our model. We then ran the Gibbs sampler for fifty iterations through the data.

The bottom half of Table 1 lists the five rules with the highest marginal probability estimated by the sampler. Encouragingly our model was able to recover a grammar very close to the original. Even for such a small grammar the space of derivations is enormous and the task of recovering it from a data sample is non-trivial. The divergence from the true probabilities is due to the effect of the prior assigning shorter rules higher probability. With a larger data sample we would expect the influence of the prior in the posterior to diminish.

GRAMMAR RULE	TRUE PROBABILITY
$X \rightarrow \langle X_1\, a\, X_2 \mid X_1\, X_2\, 1 \rangle$	0.2
$X \rightarrow \langle b\, c\, d \mid 3\, 2 \rangle$	0.2
$X \rightarrow \langle b\, d \mid 3 \rangle$	0.2
$X \rightarrow \langle d \mid 3 \rangle$	0.2
$X \rightarrow \langle c\, d \mid 3\, 1 \rangle$	0.2
SAMPLED RULE	**SAMPLED PROBABILITY**
$X \rightarrow \langle d \mid 3 \rangle$	0.25
$X \rightarrow \langle b\, d \mid 3 \rangle$	0.24
$X \rightarrow \langle c\, d \mid 3\, 1 \rangle$	0.24
$X \rightarrow \langle b\, c\, d \mid 3\, 2 \rangle$	0.211
$X \rightarrow \langle X_1\, a\, X_2 \mid X_1\, X_2\, 1 \rangle$	0.012

Table 1: Manually created SCFG used to generate synthetic data, and the five most probable inferred rules by our model.

	ZH-EN NIST	UR-EN NIST	DE-EN EUROPARL
TRAIN (SRC)	8.6M	1.2M	34M
TRAIN (TRG)	9.5M	1.0M	36M
DEV (SRC)	22K	18K	26K
DEV (TRG)	27K	16K	28K

Table 2: Corpora statistics (in words).

5.2 Machine Translation Evaluation

Ultimately the efficacy of a model for SCFG induction will be judged on its ability to underpin a state-of-the-art SMT system. Here we evaluate our model by applying it to learning word alignments for parallel corpora from which SMT systems are induced. We train models across a range of corpora sizes and for language pairs that exhibit the type of complex alignment phenomena that we are interested in modeling: Chinese → English (ZH-EN), Urdu → English (UR-EN) and German → English (DE-EN).

Data and Baselines

The UR-EN corpus is the smallest of those used in our experiments and is taken from the NIST 2009 translation evaluation.[3] The ZH-EN data is of a medium scale and comes from the FBIS corpus. The DE-EN pair constitutes the largest corpus and is taken from Europarl, the proceedings of the European Parliament (Koehn, 2003). Statistics for the data are shown in Table 2. We measure translation quality via the BLEU score (Papineni et al., 2001).

All translation systems employ a Hiero translation model during decoding. Baseline word alignments were obtained by running GIZA++ in both directions and symmetrizing using the `grow-diag-final-and` heuristic (Och and Ney, 2003; Koehn et al., 2003). Decoding was performed with the `cdec` decoder (Dyer et al., 2010) with the synchronous grammar extracted using the techniques developed by Lopez (2008). All translation systems include a 5-gram language model built from a five hundred million token subset

[3] `http://www.itl.nist.gov/iad/mig/tests/mt/2009/`

Language Pair	Test Set	Model 4 Baseline	Model 1 Initialisation	PYP-SCFG Weak M1 Init.	PYP-SCFG Strong HMM Init.
UR-EN	MT09	23.1	18.5	23.7	**24.0**
ZH-EN	MT03-08	29.4	19.8	28.3	**29.8**
DE-EN	EuroParl	28.4	25.5	27.8	**29.2**

Table 3: Results for the SMT experiments in BLEU . The baseline is produced using a full GIZA++ run. The MODEL 1 INITIALISATION column is from the initialisation alignments using MODEL 1 and no sampling. The PYP-SCFG columns show results for the 500th sample for both MODEL 1 and HMM initialisations.

of all the English data made available for the NIST 2009 shared task (Graff, 2003).

Experimental Setup

To obtain the PYP-SCFG word alignments we ran the sampler for five hundred iterations for each of the language pairs and experimental conditions described below. We used the approach of Newman et al. (2007) to distribute the sampler across multiple threads. The strength θ and discount d hyperparameters of the Pitman-Yor Processes, and the terminal penalty ϕ (Section 3.3), were inferred using slice sampling (Neal, 2000).

The Gibbs sampler requires an initial set of derivations from which to commence sampling. In our experiments we investigated both *weak* and a *strong* initialisations, the former based on word alignments from IBM Model 1 and the latter on alignments from an HMM model (Vogel et al., 1996). For decoding we used the word alignments implied by the derivations in the final sample to extract a Hiero grammar with the same standard set of relative frequency, length, and language model features used for the baseline.

Weak Initialisation

Our first translation experiments ascertain the degree to which our proposed Gibbs sampling inference algorithm is able to learn good synchronous derivations for the PYP-SCFG model. A number of prior works on alignment with Gibbs samplers have only evaluated models initialised with the more complex GIZA++ alignment models (Blunsom et al., 2009; DeNero et al., 2008), as a result it can be difficult to separate the performance of the sampler from that of the initialisation. In order to do this, we initialise the sampler

Language Pair	PYP-SCFG Model 1 Init.	PYP-SCFG HMM Init.
UR-EN	1.93/2.08	1.45/1.58
ZH-EN	3.47/4.28	1.69/2.37
DE-EN	4.05/4.77	1.50/2.04

Table 4: Average source/target rule lengths in the PYP-SCFG models after the 500th sample for the different initialisations.

using just the MODEL 1 distribution used in the PYP-SCFG model's base distribution. We denote this a weak initialisation as no alignment models outside of those included in the PYP-SCFG model influence the resulting word alignments. The BLEU scores for translation systems built from the five hundredth sample are show in the WEAK M1 INIT. column of Table 3. Additionally we build a translation system from the MODEL 1 alignment used to initialise the sampler without using using our PYP-SCFG model or sampling. BLEU scores are shown in the MODEL 1 INITIALISATION column of Table 3. Firstly it is clear MODEL 1 is indeed a weak initialiser as the resulting translation systems achieve uniformly low BLEU scores. In contrast, the models built from the output of the Gibbs sampler for the PYP-SCFG model achieve BLEU scores comparable to those of the MODEL 4 BASELINE. Thus the sampler has moved a good distance from its initialisation, and done so in a direction that results in better synchronous derivations.

Strong Initialisation

Given we have established that the sampler can produce state-of-the-art translation results from a weak initialisation, it is instructive to investigate whether initialising the model with a strong alignment system, the GIZA++ HMM (Vogel et al., 1996), leads to further improvements. Column HMM INIT. of Table 3 shows the results for initialising with the HMM word alignments and sampling for 500 iterations. Starting with a stronger initial sample results in both quicker mixing and better translation quality for the same number of sampling iterations.

Table 4 compares the average lengths of the rules produced by the sampler with both the strong and weak initialisers. As the size of the training corpora increases (UR-EN → ZH-EN → DE-EN) we see that the average size of the rules produced by the weakly initialised sampler also increases, while that of the strongly initialised model stays relatively uniform. Initially both samplers start out with a large number of long rules and as the sampling progresses the rules are broken down into smaller, more generalisable, pieces. As such we conclude from these metrics that after five hundred samples the strongly initialised model has converged to sampling from a mode of the distribution while the weakly initialised model converges more slowly and on the longer corpora is still travelling towards a mode. This suggests that longer sampling runs, and Gibbs operators that make simultaneous updates to multiple parts of a derivation, would enable the weakly initialised model to obtain better translation results.

Grammar Analysis

The BLEU scores are informative as a measure of translation quality but we also explored some of the differences in the grammars obtained from the PYP-SCFG model compared to the standard approach. In Figures 3 and 4 we show some basic statistics of the grammars our model produces. From Figure 3 we see that the number of unique rules in the PYP-SCFG grammar decreases steadily as the sampler iterates through the data, so the model is finding an increasingly sparser distribution with fewer but better quality rules as sampling progresses. Note that the gradient of the curves appears to be a function of the size of the corpus and suggests that the model built from the large DE-EN corpus would benefit from a longer sampling run. Figure 4 shows the distribution of rules with a given arity as a percentage

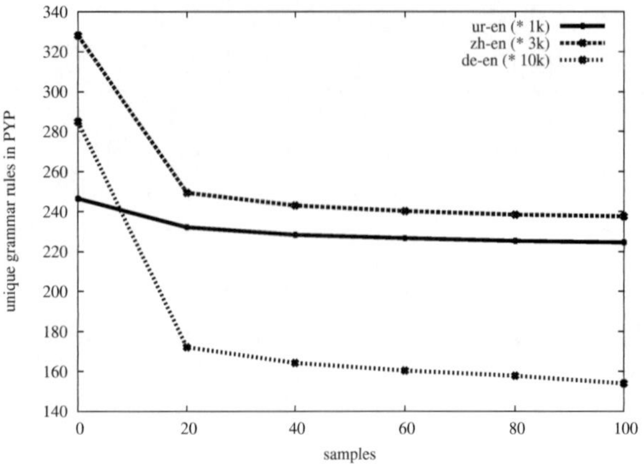

Figure 3: Unique grammar rules for each language pair as a function of the number of samples. The number of rule types decreases monotonically as sampling continues. Rule counts are displayed by normalised corpus size (see Table 2).

X→ ⟨ 底 | end of ⟩
X→ ⟨ 届 全 | ninth ⟩*
X→ ⟨ 运作 X | charter X ⟩
X→ ⟨ 信心 | confidence in ⟩
X→ ⟨ 中国 政府 X | the chinese government X ⟩
X→ ⟨ 都 是 | are ⟩
X→ ⟨ 新华社 北京 X | beijing , X ⟩*
X→ ⟨ 有关 部门 | departments concerned ⟩
X→ ⟨ 新华社 华盛顿 X | washington , X ⟩*
X→ ⟨ 鲍威尔 X_1 了 X_2 , | he X_1 X_2 , ⟩*

Table 5: The five highest ZH-EN probability rules in the Hiero grammar built from the PYP-SCFG that are not in the baseline Hiero grammar (top), and the top five rules in the baseline Hiero grammar that are not in the PYP-SCFG grammar (bottom). An * indicates a bad translation rule.

of the full grammar after the final sampling iteration. The model prior biases the results to shorter rules as the vast majority of the model probability mass is on rules with zero, one or two nonterminals.

Tables 5 and 6 show the most probable rules in the Hiero translation system obtained using the PYP-SCFG alignments that are not present in the TM from the GIZA++ alignments and visa versa. For both language pairs, four of the top five rules in

$X \rightarrow \langle$ yh | it is $\rangle$
$X \rightarrow \langle$ zmyn | the earth $\rangle$
$X \rightarrow \langle$ yhy X | the same X $\rangle$
$X \rightarrow \langle X_1$ nhyN X_2 gy | X_2 not be $X_1 \rangle$
$X \rightarrow \langle X_1$ gY kh X_2 | recommend that X_2 $X_1 \rangle$*

$X \rightarrow \langle$ hwN gY | will $\rangle$
$X \rightarrow \langle$ Gyr mlky | international $\rangle$*
$X \rightarrow \langle X_1$ *rAye kY X_2 | X_2 to X_1 sources $\rangle$*
$X \rightarrow \langle$ nY X_1 nhyN kyA X_2 | did not X_1 $X_2 \rangle$*
$X \rightarrow \langle$ xAtwn X_1 ky X_2 | woman X_2 the $X_1 \rangle$

Table 6: Five of the top scoring rules in the UR-EN Hiero grammar from sampled PYP-SCFG alignments (top) versus the baseline UR-EN Hiero grammar rules not in the sampled grammar (bottom). An * indicates a bad translation rule.

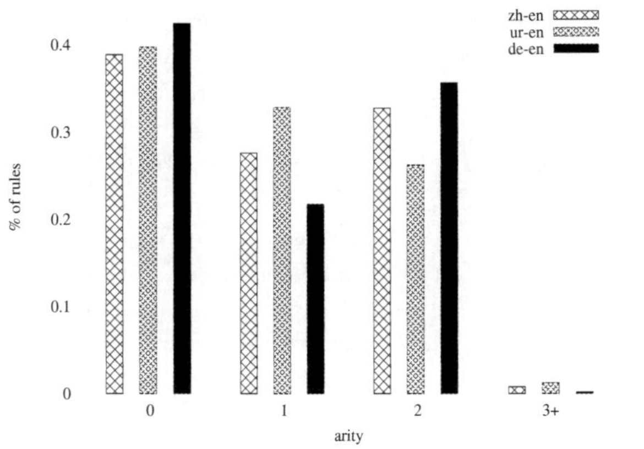

Figure 4: The percentage of rules with a given arity in the final grammar of the PYP-SCFG model.

the PYP-SCFG grammar that are not in the heuristically extracted grammar are correct and minimal phrasal units of translation, whereas only two of the top probability rules in the GIZA++ grammar are of good translation quality.

6 Conclusion and Further Work

In this paper we have presented a nonparametric Bayesian model for learning SCFGs directly from parallel corpora. We have also introduced a novel Gibbs sampller that allows for efficient posterior inference. We show state-of-the-art results and learn complex translation phenomena, including discontiguous and many-to-many phrasal alignments, without applying any heuristic restrictions on the model to make learning tractable. Our evaluation shows that we can use a principled approach to induce SCFGs designed specifically to utilize the full power of grammar based SMT instead of relying on complex word alignment heuristics with inherent bias.

Future work includes the obvious extension to learning SCFGs that contain multiple nonterminals instead of a single nonterminal grammar. We also expect that expanding our sampler beyond strict binary sampling may allow us to explore the space of hierarchical word alignments more quickly allowing for faster mixing. We expect with these extensions our model of grammar induction may further improve translation output.

Acknowledgements

This work was supported by a grant from Google, Inc. and EPRSRC grant no. EP/I010858/1 (Levenberg and Blunsom), the U. S. Army Research Laboratory and U. S. Army Research Office under contract/grant no. W911NF-10-1-0533 (Dyer).

References

P. Blunsom and T. Cohn. 2011. A hierarchical pitman-yor process hmm for unsupervised part of speech induction. In *Proceedings of the 49th Annual Meeting of the Association for Computational Linguistics: Human Language Technologies*, pages 865–874, Portland, Oregon, USA, June. Association for Computational Linguistics.

P. Blunsom, T. Cohn, C. Dyer, and M. Osborne. 2009. A gibbs sampler for phrasal synchronous grammar induction. In *Proceedings of the Joint Conference of the 47th Annual Meeting of the ACL and the 4th International Joint Conference on Natural Language Processing of the AFNLP*, pages 782–790, Suntec, Singapore, August. Association for Computational Linguistics.

P. F. Brown, V. J. D. Pietra, R. L. Mercer, S. A. D. Pietra, and J. C. Lai. 1992. An estimate of an upper bound for the entropy of english. *Computational Linguistics*, 18(1):31–40.

P. F. Brown, V. J. D. Pietra, S. A. D. Pietra, and R. L. Mercer. 1993. The mathematics of statistical machine translation: parameter estimation. *Computational Linguistics*, 19(2):263–311.

C. Cherry and D. Lin. 2007. Inversion transduction grammar for joint phrasal translation modeling.

In *Proceedings of SSST, NAACL-HLT 2007 / AMTA Workshop on Syntax and Structure in Statistical Translation*, pages 17–24, Rochester, New York, April. Association for Computational Linguistics.

D. Chiang. 2007. Hierarchical phrase-based translation. *Computational Linguistics*, 33(2):201–228.

J. DeNero, A. Bouchard-Côté, and D. Klein. 2008. Sampling alignment structure under a Bayesian translation model. In *Proceedings of the 2008 Conference on Empirical Methods in Natural Language Processing*, pages 314–323, Honolulu, Hawaii, October. Association for Computational Linguistics.

C. Dyer, A. Lopez, J. Ganitkevitch, J. Weese, F. Ture, P. Blunsom, H. Setiawan, V. Eidelman, and P. Resnik. 2010. cdec: A decoder, alignment, and learning framework for finite-state and context-free translation models. In *Proceedings of the ACL 2010 System Demonstrations*, ACLDemos '10, pages 7–12.

C. Dyer. 2010. Two monolingual parses are better than one (synchronous parse). In *Proc. of NAACL*.

M. Galley, M. Hopkins, K. Knight, and D. Marcu. 2004. What's in a translation rule? In D. M. Susan Dumais and S. Roukos, editors, *HLT-NAACL 2004: Main Proceedings*, pages 273–280, Boston, Massachusetts, USA, May 2 - May 7. Association for Computational Linguistics.

S. Goldwater, T. L. Griffiths, and M. Johnson. 2006. Contextual dependencies in unsupervised word segmentation. In *Proceedings of the 21st International Conference on Computational Linguistics and 44th Annual Meeting of the Association for Computational Linguistics*, Syndney, Australia.

D. Graff. 2003. English Gigaword. Linguistic Data Consortium (LDC-2003T05).

P. Koehn, F. J. Och, and D. Marcu. 2003. Statistical phrase-based translation. In *NAACL '03: Proceedings of the 2003 Conference of the North American Chapter of the Association for Computational Linguistics on Human Language Technology*, pages 48–54, Morristown, NJ, USA. Association for Computational Linguistics.

P. Koehn. 2003. Europarl: A multilingual corpus for evaluation of machine translation.

L. Lee. 2002. Fast context-free grammar parsing requires fast Boolean matrix multiplication. *Journal of the ACM*, 49(1):1–15.

P. M. Lewis, II and R. E. Stearns. 1968. Syntax-directed transduction. *J. ACM*, 15:465–488, July.

A. Lopez. 2008. *Machine Translation by Pattern Matching*. Ph.D. thesis, University of Maryland.

D. Marcu and D. Wong. 2002. A phrase-based,joint probability model for statistical machine translation. In *Proceedings of the 2002 Conference on Empirical Methods in Natural Language Processing*, pages 133–139. Association for Computational Linguistics, July.

R. Neal. 2000. Slice sampling. *Annals of Statistics*, 31:705–767.

G. Neubig, T. Watanabe, E. Sumita, S. Mori, and T. Kawahara. 2011. An unsupervised model for joint phrase alignment and extraction. In *Proceedings of the 49th Annual Meeting of the Association for Computational Linguistics: Human Language Technologies*, pages 632–641, Portland, Oregon, USA, June. Association for Computational Linguistics.

D. Newman, A. Asuncion, P. Smyth, and M. Welling. 2007. Distributed inference for latent dirichlet allocation. In *NIPS*. MIT Press.

F. J. Och and H. Ney. 2003. A systematic comparison of various statistical alignment models. *Computational Linguistics*, 29(1):19–51, March.

K. Papineni, S. Roukos, T. Ward, and W.-J. Zhu. 2001. Bleu: a method for automatic evaluation of machine translation. In *ACL '02: Proceedings of the 40th Annual Meeting on Association for Computational Linguistics*, pages 311–318, Morristown, NJ, USA. Association for Computational Linguistics.

J. Pitman and M. Yor. 1997. The two-parameter Poisson-Dirichlet distribution derived from a stable subordinator. *Ann. Probab.*, 25:855–900.

Y. W. Teh. 2006. A hierarchical Bayesian language model based on Pitman-Yor processes. In *Proceedings of the 21st International Conference on Computational Linguistics and 44th Annual Meeting of the Association for Computational Linguistics*, pages 985–992.

S. Vogel, H. Ney, and C. Tillmann. 1996. HMM-based word alignment in statistical translation. In *Proceedings of the 16th conference on Computational linguistics*, pages 836–841, Morristown, NJ, USA. Association for Computational Linguistics.

F. Wood, J. Gasthaus, C. Archambeau, L. James, and Y. W. Teh. 2011. The sequence memoizer. *Communications of the Association for Computing Machines*, 54(2):91–98.

D. Wu. 1997. Stochastic inversion transduction grammars and bilingual parsing of parallel corpora. *Computational Linguistics*, 23:377–403, September.

H. Zhang, C. Quirk, R. C. Moore, and D. Gildea. 2008. Bayesian learning of non-compositional phrases with synchronous parsing. In *Proceedings of ACL-08: HLT*, pages 97–105, Columbus, Ohio, June. Association for Computational Linguistics.

Multiple Aspect Summarization Using Integer Linear Programming

Kristian Woodsend and **Mirella Lapata**
Institute for Language, Cognition and Computation
School of Informatics, University of Edinburgh
10 Crichton Street, Edinburgh EH8 9AB
k.woodsend@ed.ac.uk, mlap@inf.ed.ac.uk

Abstract

Multi-document summarization involves many aspects of content selection and surface realization. The summaries must be informative, succinct, grammatical, and obey stylistic writing conventions. We present a method where such individual aspects are learned separately from data (without any hand-engineering) but optimized jointly using an integer linear programme. The ILP framework allows us to combine the decisions of the expert learners and to select and rewrite source content through a mixture of objective setting, soft and hard constraints. Experimental results on the TAC-08 data set show that our model achieves state-of-the-art performance using ROUGE and significantly improves the informativeness of the summaries.

1 Introduction

Automatic summarization has enjoyed wide popularity in natural language processing (see the proceedings of the Document Understanding and Text Analysis conferences) due to its potential for practical applications but also because it incorporates many important aspects of both natural language understanding and generation. Of the many summarization paradigms that have been identified over the years (see Sparck Jones (1999) and Mani (2001) for comprehensive overviews), multi-document summarization — the task of producing summaries from clusters of thematically related documents — has consistently attracted attention.

Despite considerable research effort, the automatic generation of multi-document summaries that resemble those written by humans remains challenging. This is primarily due to the task itself which is complex and subject to several constraints: the summary must be maximally informative and minimally redundant, grammatical, coherent, adhere to a pre-specified length and stylistic conventions. An ideal model would learn to output summaries that simultaneously meet all these constraints from data (i.e., document clusters and their corresponding summaries). This *global inference problem* is, however, hard — the solution space is large and the lack of easily accessible datasets an obstacle to joint learning. It is thus no surprise that previous work has focused on specific aspects of joint learning.

Initial global formulations of the multi-document summarization task focused on extractive summarization and used approximate greedy algorithms for finding the sentences of the summary. Goldstein et al. (2000) search for the set of sentences that are both relevant and non-redundant, whereas Filatova and Hatzivassiloglou (2004) model multi-document summarization as an instance of the maximum coverage set problem.[1] More recent work improves on the search problem by considering exact solutions and permits a limited amount of rewriting. McDonald (2007) proposes an integer linear programming formulation that maximizes the sum of relevance scores of the selected sentences penalized by the

[1] Given C, a finite set of weighted elements, a collection T of subsets of C, and an integer k, find those k sets that maximize the total number of elements in the union of T's members (Hochba, 1997).

sum of redundancy scores of all pairs of selected sentences. Gillick et al. (2008) develop an exact solution for a model similar to Filatova and Hatzivassiloglou (2004) under the assumption that the value of a summary is the sum of values of the unique concepts (approximated by bigrams) it contains. Subsequent work (Gillick et al., 2009; Berg-Kirkpatrick et al., 2011) extends this model to allow sentence compression in the form of word or constituent deletion.

In this paper we propose a model for multi-document summarization that attempts to cover many different aspects of the task such as content selection, surface realization, paraphrasing, and stylistic conventions. These aspects are learned separately using specific "expert" predictors, but are optimized jointly using an integer linear programming model (ILP) to generate the output summary.[2] All experts are learned from data without requiring additional annotation over and above the summaries written for each document cluster. Our predictors include the use of unique bigram information to model content and avoid redundancy, positional information to model important and poor locations of content, and language modeling to capture stylistic conventions. Learning each predictor separately gives better generalization, while the ILP framework allows us to combine the decisions of the expert learners through the use of objectives, hard and soft constraints.

The experts work collaboratively to rewrite the content using rules extracted from document clusters and model summaries. We adopt the synchronous tree substitution grammar (STSG) formalism (Eisner, 2003) which can model non-isomorphic tree structures (the grammar rules can comprise trees of arbitrary depth) and is thus suited to text-rewriting tasks which typically involve a number of local modifications to the input text. Specifically, we propose quasi-synchronous tree substitution grammar (QTSG) as a flexible formalism to learn general tree-edits from *loosely-aligned* phrase structure trees.

We evaluate our model on the 100-word "non-update" summarization task as defined in the the Text Analysis Conference (TAC 2008). Experimental results show that our method obtains performance comparable and in some cases superior to state-of-the-art, in terms of ROUGE and human ratings of summary grammaticality and informativeness. Importantly, there is nothing inherent in our model that is specific to this particular summarization task. As all of the different experts are learned from data, it could easily adapt to other summarization styles or conventions as needed.

2 Related work

Recent years have seen increased interest in global inference methods for summarization. ILP-based models have been developed for several subtasks ranging from sentence compression (Clarke and Lapata, 2008), to single- and multi-document summarization (McDonald, 2007; Martins and Smith, 2009; Gillick and Favre, 2009; Woodsend and Lapata, 2010; Berg-Kirkpatrick et al., 2011), and headline generation (Deshpande et al., 2007; Woodsend et al., 2010). Most of these approaches are either purely extractive or implement a single rewrite operation, namely word deletion. Although it is well-known that hand-written summaries often exhibit additional edits and sentence recombinations (Jing, 2002), the challenges involved in acquiring the rewrite rules, interfacing them with inference, and ensuring grammatical output make the development of abstractive models non-trivial.

Our work is closest to Gillick et al. (2008) who also develop an ILP model for multi-document summarization. A key assumption in their model which we also follow is that input documents contain a variety of concepts, each of which are allocated a value, and the goal of a good summary is to maximize the sum of these values subject to the length constraint. The authors use bigrams as concepts and their frequency in the input documents as a proxy for their value. This model can also perform sentence compression (see also Gillick et al. (2009)), however, the deletion rules are hand-coded. Berg-Kirkpatrick et al. (2011) build on this work by recasting it as a structured prediction problem. They essentially combine the same bigram content scoring system with features relating to the parse tree

[2] Our task is standard multi-document summarization and should not be confused with "guided" summarization where system and human summarizers are given a list of important aspects to cover in the summary. Our usage of the term aspects broadly refers to the different types of constraints (e.g., relating to content or style) a summary must meet, but these are learned rather than specified in advance.

which they learn using a maximum-margin SVM trained on annotated gold-standard compressions.

Our multi-document summarization model jointly optimizes different aspects of the task involving both content selection and surface realization. Each individual aspect has its own dedicated expert, which we argue is advantageous as it renders inference simpler and affords flexibility (e.g., additional aspects can be incorporated into the model or trained separately on different datasets). Our work differs from Gillick et al. (2009) and Berg-Kirkpatrick et al. (2011) in three important respects. Firstly, we develop a genuinely abstractive model that is not limited to deletion. Our rewrite rules are encoded in quasi-synchronous tree substitution grammar and learned automatically from source documents and their summaries. Unlike previous applications of STSG to sentence compression (Cohn and Lapata, 2009; Cohn and Lapata, 2008) our quasi-synchronous TSG does not attempt to learn the complete translation from source to target sentence; it only loosely links the syntactic structure of the two (Smith and Eisner, 2006), and is therefore well suited to describing the relationship between documents and their abstracts. Secondly, our content selection component extends to features beyond the bigram horizon, as we learn to identify important concepts based on syntactic and positional information. We also learn which words are unlikely to appear in a summary. Thirdly, unlike Berg-Kirkpatrick et al. (2011) our model does not try to learn all the parameters (e.g., content, rewrite rules, style) of the summarization problem jointly; although decoupling learning from inference is perhaps less elegant from a modeling perspective, the learning process is more robust and reliable.

3 Modeling

There are many aspects to producing a good summary of multiple documents. The important content needs to be captured, typically key facts in each individual document, and information seen across the cluster. Stylistic features may be different in the summary from original documents. For instance, summaries tend to use more concise language, sources are not attributed as they are in news articles, and relative dates are not included. In addition, the summary must be fluent, coherent, and respect a pre-specified maximum length requirement.

We present an approach where elements of all the above considerations are learned from training data by separate dedicated components, and then combined in an integer linear programme. Content selection is performed partly through identifying the most salient topics (bigrams); an additional component learns to identify which information from the source documents should be in the summary based on positional information. Meanwhile, in terms of surface realization, a language model identifies the words that *should not* be in the output summaries, whereas a separate component learns to exclude sentences that are poor candidates for summaries. QTSG rules, learned from the training corpus, are used to generate alternative compressions and paraphrases of the source sentences, in the style suitable for the summaries. Finally, an ILP model combines the output of these components into a summary, jointly optimizing content selection and surface realization preferences, and providing the flexibility to treat some components as soft while others as hard constraints.

3.1 Document Representation

Given an input sentence, our approach deconstructs it into component phrases and clauses, typical of a phrase structure parser. In our experiments, we obtain this representation from the output of the Stanford parser (Klein and Manning, 2003) but any other broadly similar parser could be used instead. Nodes in the parse tree represent points where QTSG rules can be applied (and paraphrases generated), and they also represent decision points for the ILP. In the following, we will refer to these decision nodes as the set $\mathcal{N}$, and decisions for each node using the binary variable z_i, $i \in \mathcal{N}$.

3.2 Content Selection Using Bigrams

We follow Gillick et al. (2008) in modeling the information content of the summary as the weighted sum of the individual information units it contains. We represent information units as the set of bigrams $\mathcal{B}$ seen in the source documents. The weight w of each bigram is calculated from the number of source documents where the bigram was seen. The summary is thus given the score $f_{\mathcal{B}}(z)$, i.e., the weighted sum of its information units:

$$f_{\mathcal{B}}(z) = \sum_{j \in \mathcal{B}} w_j b_j \quad (1)$$

where w_j is the weight of concept j, b_j a binary variable to indicate if concept j is present in the summary, and $j \in \mathcal{B}$.

Importantly, each information unit is counted only once; this encourages wide coverage of the source documents, and removes any drive towards redundant information without actively discouraging it, contrary to other global formulations where redundancy measures form part of the objective (McDonald, 2007). The counting mechanism is achieved by linking the variables z indicating nodes in the parse tree and b indicating bigrams:

$$b_j \leq \sum_{i \in \mathcal{N}: j \in \mathcal{B}_i} z_i \qquad \forall j \in \mathcal{B} \quad (2)$$

where $\mathcal{B}_i \subset \mathcal{B}$ is the subset of bigrams that are contained in node i. A drawback of the global nature of this counting mechanism, however, is that it cannot be integrated with local features such as those described below; our approach takes local features into account but these are weighted by other components.

3.3 Content Selection Using Salience

The bigram approach is a powerful method for identifying important concepts within the document cluster. It works particularly well in the sentence extraction paradigm. However, additional elements are known to be good predictors of important information. Examples include the position of a sentence in the document (e.g., first sentences often contain salient information), whether it contains proper nouns, numbers, pronouns, mentions of money, and so on. We decided to learn which of these elements (represented as nodes in the parse tree) are informative from training data. Specifically, sentences in the cluster documents were aligned to sentences from corresponding human summaries. Alignment was based rather simply on identifying the sentence pairs with the highest number of overlapping bigrams, without compensating for sentence length, or matching the sequence of information in the summaries and source documents (Nelken and Schieber, 2006). Matched sentences in the source documents were given positive labels, while unaligned sentences were given negative labels. These labels were then propagated to phrase structure nodes.

Weight	Feature
1.21	From first sentence in document
0.73	Contains proper nouns
0.68	Contains nouns
0.57	From first paragraph
0.53	From first three sentences
0.51	Contains numbers
-0.50	Contains pronouns
0.32	Contains money

Table 1: Weights and features of SVM that predicts the salience of summary content. Negative weights indicate information that should not be included in the summary.

We trained an SVM on this data (tree nodes and their labels) using surface features that do not overlap with bigram information: sentence and paragraph position, POS-tag information. Table 1 shows the most important features learned by the model as predictors of salient content.

The summary can be given a salience score $f_S(z)$ using the raw SVM prediction scores of the individual parse tree nodes:

$$f_S(z) = \sum_{i \in \mathcal{N}} (\Phi(i) \cdot \theta)\, z_i \quad (3)$$

where $\Phi(i)$ is the feature vector for node i, and θ the weights learned by the SVM.

3.4 Surface Realization Using Style

Some sentences in the source documents will make poor summary sentences, despite the information they contain, and therefore contrary to the predictions of the content selection indicators described above. This may be because the source sentence is very short, or is expressed as a quotation, or contains many pronouns that will not be resolved when the sentence is extracted.

Our idea is to learn which sentences are poor from a stylistic perspective using again aligned training data. We train a second SVM on the aligned sentences and their labels using surface features at the sentence level, such as sentence length and POS-tag information. The most important features learned by

Weight	Feature
-1.04	Word count less than 10
-0.83	Word count less than 20
-0.30	Question
-0.30	Quotation
-0.14	Personal pronouns

Table 2: Weights and features of SVM that predicts poor candidate sentences.

the model as predictors of poor sentences, and the weights assigned to them, are shown in Table 2.

The predictions of the SVM are incorporated into the ILP as a hard constraint, by forcing all parse tree nodes within those sentences predicted as poor (the set $\mathcal{N}^-$) to be zero:

$$z_i = 0 \quad \forall i \in \mathcal{N}^-. \tag{4}$$

3.5 Surface Realization Using Lexical Preferences

Human-written summaries differ from the source news articles in a number of ways. They delete extraneous information, merge material from several sentences, employ paraphrases and syntactic transformations, change the order of the source sentences and replace phrases or clauses with more general or specific descriptions. We could attempt to learn the "language of summaries" with a language model which we could then use to guide the generation process (e.g., by producing maximally probable output). Aside from the logistics of gathering training data large enough to provide robust estimates, we believe that a more compelling approach is to focus on the words that are *unlikely* to appear in the summary despite appearing in the source documents.

A comparison of the language models generated from the source documents and model summaries, even at the unigram level, is revealing. Table 3 shows lexemes that appear in both source and summary documents, but where the likelihood of the lexeme appearing in the summary is much less than that of it appearing the document, taking into account that the summary is much shorter anyway. The final column shows the $\log_{10}$-ratio ($L(w)$) between the two probabilities. We can see that least probable words are those that correspond to attributing information sources (e.g., *said, told, according to, spokesman*), dates described relatively (e.g., *last Monday*), and events that are in the process of happening (e.g., *coming, going*).

Lexeme w	Source count	Summary count	$L(w)$
say	5670	88	-1.63
go	638	11	-1.52
last	616	9	-1.69
get	543	15	-1.05
tell	512	8	-1.62
come	488	12	-1.17
know	404	9	-1.27
monday	391	8	-1.35
think	382	7	-1.46
next	239	7	-0.99
spokesman	197	4	-1.36

Table 3: Counts of lexemes in the source news articles and summaries, and measure of the ratio of their probabilities (for most common lexemes with ratio < -0.95).

As the amount of training data tends to be limited — there are usually only a few human-written summaries available per document cluster — we use a unigram language model, but conceivably a longer-range n-gram could be employed in the same vein. We incorporate preferences about summary language into the model as a soft constraint. The log-ratio values $f_{\mathcal{LR}}(z)$ are included in the objective and defined at the tree node level:

$$f_{\mathcal{LR}}(z) = \sum_{i \in \mathcal{N}} \sum_{w \in \mathcal{W}_i} L(w) z_i \tag{5}$$

where $L(w)$, $w \in \mathcal{W}_i$ is the log-ratio value for an individual word w:

$$L(w) = \log_{10} \frac{P_{\text{src}}(w)}{P_{\text{sum}}(w)},$$

$P_{\text{src}}(w)$ and $P_{\text{sum}}(w)$ are the probabilities of word w appearing in the source and summary documents respectively, and $\mathcal{W}_i$ is the set of words at parse tree node i. Importantly, we include only those those lexemes with negative $L(w)$ values. This guides the model *away from* the kind of phrases described above, but not towards any particular language preferences.

3.6 Quasi-synchronous Tree Substitution Grammar

Rewrite rules involving substitutions, deletions and reorderings are captured in our model using a quasi-synchronous tree substitution grammar. Given an input (source) sentence S1 or its parse tree T1, the QTSG contains rules for generating possible translation trees T2. A grammar node in the target tree T2 is modeled on a subset of nodes in the source tree, with a rather loose alignment between the trees.

We extract QTSG rules from aligned source and summary sentence pairs represented by their phrase structure trees. Our algorithm builds up a list of leaf node alignments based on lexical identity. Direct parent nodes are aligned where more than one child node aligns. This quasi-synchronous "bottom-up" process gives us better ability to match non-isomorphic structures. We do not assume an alignment between source and target root nodes, nor do we require a surjective alignment of all target nodes to the source tree. QTSG rules are then created from aligned nodes above the leaf node level if all the nodes in the target tree can be explained using nodes from the source. Individual rewrite rules describe the mapping of source tree fragments into target tree fragments, and so the grammar represents the space of valid target trees that can be produced from a given source tree (Eisner, 2003; Cohn and Lapata, 2009).

Examples of the most frequent QTSG rules learned by the above process are shown in Figure 1. Many of the rules relate to the compression of noun phrases through deletion, and examples are shown in the upper box. Others capture the compression of verb phrases (middle box). An important rewrite operation is the abstraction of a sentence from a more complex source sentence, adding final punctuation if necessary (lower box).

At generation, paraphrases are created from source sentence parse trees by identifying and applying QTSG rules with matching structure. The transduction process starts at the root node of the parse tree, applying QTSG rules to sub-trees until leaf nodes are reached. Note that we do not use the Bayesian probability model normally associated with quasi-synchronous grammars (Smith and Eisner, 2006); instead, we ask the QTSG to provide

$\langle \text{NP}, \text{NP} \rangle \rightarrow \langle [\text{NP}_{\boxed{1}}\ \text{PP}], [\text{NP}_{\boxed{1}}] \rangle$
$\langle \text{NP}, \text{NP} \rangle \rightarrow \langle [\text{NP}_{\boxed{1}}\ \text{VP}], [\text{NP}_{\boxed{1}}] \rangle$
$\langle \text{NP}, \text{NP} \rangle \rightarrow \langle [\text{NP}_{\boxed{1}}\ \text{SBAR}], [\text{NP}_{\boxed{1}}] \rangle$
$\langle \text{NP}, \text{NP} \rangle \rightarrow \langle [\text{NP}_{\boxed{1}}\ ,\ \text{NP}\ ,], [\text{NP}_{\boxed{1}}] \rangle$
$\langle \text{NP}, \text{NP} \rangle \rightarrow \langle [\text{NP}_{\boxed{1}}\ \text{CC NP}], [\text{NP}_{\boxed{1}}] \rangle$
$\langle \text{NP}, \text{NP} \rangle \rightarrow \langle [\text{NNP NNP}_{\boxed{1}}], [\text{NNP}_{\boxed{1}}] \rangle$
$\langle \text{NP}, \text{NP} \rangle \rightarrow \langle [\text{DT}_{\boxed{1}}\ \text{JJ NN}_{\boxed{2}}], [\text{DT}_{\boxed{1}}\ \text{NN}_{\boxed{2}}] \rangle$

$\langle \text{VP}, \text{VP} \rangle \rightarrow \langle [\text{VP}_{\boxed{1}}\ \text{CC VP}], [\text{VP}_{\boxed{1}}] \rangle$
$\langle \text{VP}, \text{VP} \rangle \rightarrow \langle [\text{VP CC VP}_{\boxed{1}}], [\text{VP}_{\boxed{1}}] \rangle$
$\langle \text{VP}, \text{VP} \rangle \rightarrow \langle [\text{VP}_{\boxed{1}}\ ,\ \text{CC VP}], [\text{VP}_{\boxed{1}}] \rangle$

$\langle \text{S}, \text{S} \rangle \rightarrow \langle [\text{NP}_{\boxed{1}}\ \text{VP}_{\boxed{2}}], [\text{NP}_{\boxed{1}}\ \text{VP}_{\boxed{2}}\ .] \rangle$
$\langle \text{S}, \text{S} \rangle \rightarrow \langle [\text{ADVP}\ ,\ \text{NP}_{\boxed{1}}\ \text{VP}_{\boxed{2}}\ .], [\text{NP}_{\boxed{1}}\ \text{VP}_{\boxed{2}}\ .] \rangle$

Figure 1: Examples of most frequently learned QTSG rules. Boxed subscripts show aligned nodes.

paraphrases that are *acceptable* rather than *probable*, and generate all paraphrases licensed by the QTSG.

The alternative paraphrases are incorporated into the target phrase structure tree as choices that the ILP can make. We use the set $\mathcal{C} \subset \mathcal{N}$ to be the set of nodes where a choice of paraphrases is available, and $\mathcal{C}_i \subset \mathcal{N}, i \in \mathcal{C}$ to be the actual paraphrases of i. Where there are alternatives, it makes sense of course to select only one, which we implement using the constraint:

$$\sum_{j \in \mathcal{C}_i} z_j = z_i \qquad \forall i \in \mathcal{C}, j \in \mathcal{C}_i \qquad (6)$$

More generally, we need to constrain the output to ensure that a parse tree structure is maintained. For each node $i \in \mathcal{N}$, the set $\mathcal{D}_i \subset \mathcal{N}$ contains the list of dependent nodes (both ancestors and descendants) of node i, so that each set $\mathcal{D}_i$ contains the nodes that depend on the presence of i. We introduce a constraint to force node i to be present if any of its dependent nodes are chosen:

$$z_j \rightarrow z_i \qquad \forall i \in \mathcal{N}, j \in \mathcal{D}_i \qquad (7)$$

3.7 The ILP Objective

The model we propose for generating a multi-document summary is expressed as an integer linear programme and incorporates the content selection and surface realization preferences, as well as the soft and hard constraints described in the preceding sections. The objective of the optimization problem is to maximize the score contributed by the various elements of content selection ($f_{\mathcal{B}}(z)$ and $f_{S}(z)$) and soft surface realization constraints ($f_{\mathcal{LR}}(z)$) :

$$\max_{z} f_{\mathcal{B}}(z) + f_{S}(z) + f_{\mathcal{LR}}(z) \quad (8)$$

This objective is subject to the constraints (2), (4), (6), and (7) that represent hard constraint decisions, or maintain the logical integrity of the model. An overall length constraint completes the model:

$$\sum_{i \in \mathcal{N}} l_i z_i \leq l_{\max} \quad (9)$$

where l_i is the number of words generated by choosing node i, and $l_{\max}$ is the global word length limit.

Note that the scores in the objective are for each tree node and not each sentence. This affords the model flexibility: the content selection elements are generally not competing with each other to give a decision on a sentence (see McDonald (2007)). Instead, components are marking positive and negative nodes. The ILP is implicitly searching the grammar rules for ways to rewrite the sentence, with the aim of including the salient nodes while removing negative-scoring nodes (deleting them increases the score of the node to zero). Figure 2 shows an example of a source sentence where the bigram, salience and language preference components of the ILP work together to score nodes in the parse tree. The nodes $NP_{\boxed{1}}$, $VP_{\boxed{3}}$ and $VP_{\boxed{4}}$ all have positive scores, while "said Tuesday" is negative. As a rewrite possibility, the rewrite rule shown bottom left is available, which will remove the negative node. Further rewrite rules allow $VP_{\boxed{2}}$ to be compressed. The output actually generated by the model used sub-trees (b) and (d) — the final text is included in Table 6.

4 Experimental Set-up

Data Our model was evaluated on the TAC non-update multi-document summarization task which involves generating a 100-word-limited summary from a cluster of 10 related input documents; additionally, TAC provides a set of four model summaries for each cluster, written by human experts. We used the 44 document clusters from TAC-2009 as training data, to learn the different elements of the model. The 48 document clusters of TAC-2008 were reserved for the generation of test summaries.[3]

Training The two components described in Sections 3.3 and 3.4 were trained using binary SVM classifiers, with labels inferred automatically via alignment. The salience classifier was trained on 102,754 node instances (16,042 positive and 86,712 negative). The style classifier was trained on 20,443 sentence instances (2,083 positive and 18,360 negative). We learned the feature weights with a linear SVM, using the software SVM-OOPS (Woodsend and Gondzio, 2009). Because of the high compression rate in this task, sentence alignment leads to an unbalanced data set. We compensated for this by using different SVM hyper-parameters C^+ and C^- as the loss multiplier for misclassification of positive and negative training samples respectively. SVM hyper-parameters were chosen that gave the highest F1 values using 10-fold cross-validation. The salience SVM obtained a precision of 0.28 and recall of 0.43. Precision for the style SVM was 0.20 and recall 0.63, respectively. The classifiers on their own would thus not be great predictors of salience or style, but in practice they were useful for breaking ties in bigram scores.

Aligned sentences from the training data were also used to learn the quasi-synchronous tree substitution grammar, using the process described in Section 3.6. Rules seen fewer than 3 times were removed, resulting in a total of 339 QTSG rules. Two unigram language models (see Section 3.5) were trained on the source articles and summaries, respectively. Their probabilities were compared to give the word list shown in Table 3. We removed words with a source count less than 50, providing a list of 60 lexemes. The resulting integer linear programmes were solved using SCIP,[4] and it took 55 seconds on average to read in and solve a document cluster problem.

Evaluation We compared our model against two systems. As a baseline, we used the ICSI-1 extractive system (Gillick et al., 2008) which is also based on ILP and was highly ranked in the TAC-2008 evaluation. We also compared against the "learned phrase compression" system of Berg-Kirkpatrick et

[3]This split follows Berg-Kirkpatrick et al. (2011).

[4]http://scip.zib.de/

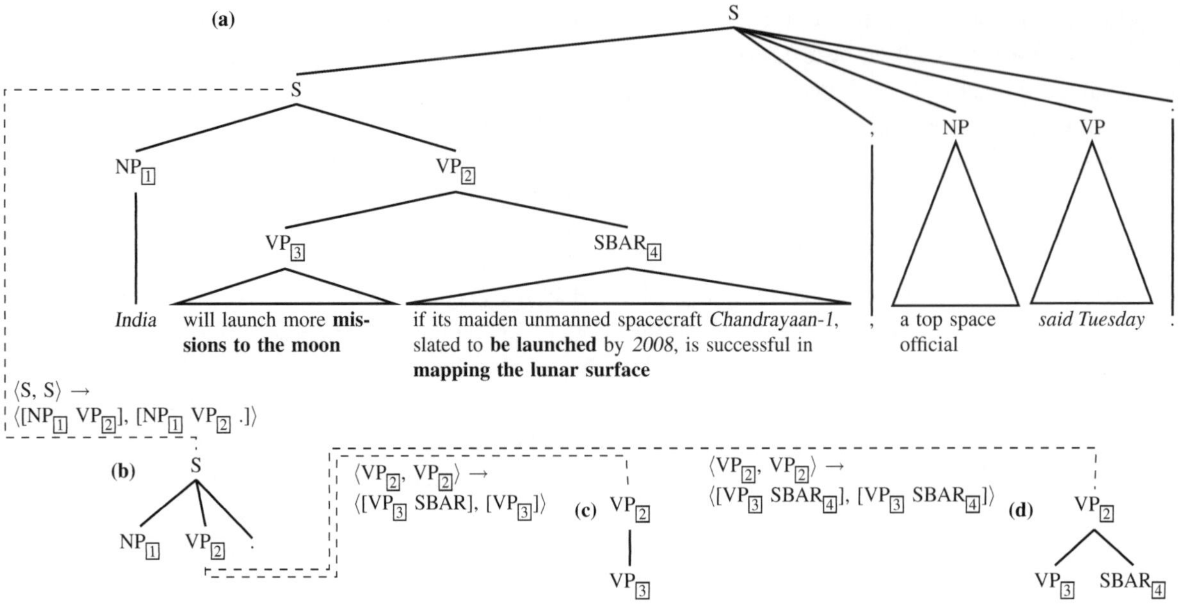

Figure 2: Sentence representation provided to the ILP. (a) The source sentence representation (child nodes condensed for space reasons). **Bigrams** are shown in bold, slanted text indicates *phrases with high salience scores* f_S, while *said Tuesday* is penalized by $f_{\mathcal{LR}}$. Alternative sub-trees (b), (c) and (d) are created using QTSG rules (dashed lines). The output sentence (see Table 6) was generated from sub-trees (b) and (d).

al. (2011) (henceforth B-K), which has the highest reported ROUGE scores that we are aware of.[5] In addition to the full model described in Section 3, we also produced outputs where each of the five components described in Sections 3.2–3.6 were removed, to assess their individual contribution.

We evaluated the output summaries in two ways, using automatic measures and human judgements. Automatic evaluation was performed with ROUGE (Lin and Hovy, 2003) using TAC-2008 parameter settings. We report bigram overlap (ROUGE-2) and skip-bigram (ROUGE-SU4) recall values. We also used Translation Edit Rate (TER, Snover et al. (2006)) to examine the systems' rewrite potential. TER is defined as the minimum number of edits (insertions, deletions, substitutions, and shifts) required to change the system output so that it exactly matches a reference (here, the reference is the most closely aligning source sentence). The perfect TER score is 0, however note that it can be higher than 1 due to insertions.

Our judgement elicitation study was conducted as follows. We randomly selected ten document clusters from the test set and generated summaries with our model (and its lesser variations). We also included the corresponding ICSI-1 and B-K summaries, and one randomly-selected model summary. The study was conducted over the Internet using Mechanical Turk and was completed by 54 volunteers, all self reported native English speakers. Participants were first asked to read the documents in each cluster. Next, they were asked a few comprehension questions to ensure they had understood and processed the documents. Finally, they were presented with a summary and asked to rate it along two dimensions: grammaticality (is the summary fluent and grammatical?), and informativeness (are the main topics captured in the summary?). The subjects used a 1–5 rating scale, with half-points allowed. Participants who declared themselves as non-native English speakers, did not answer the comprehension questions correctly or took only a few minutes to complete the task were eliminated.

5 Results

Our results are summarized in Table 4. Let us first discuss those obtained using ROUGE-2 (2-R) and ROUGE-SU4 (SU4-R) recall values. As can be seen

[5] We are grateful to Taylor Berg-Kirkpatrick for making his system output available to us.

Models	ROUGE		TER (%)				Sentences		
	2-R	SU4-R	Ins	Del	Sub	Shift	Count	CR (%)	Mod (%)
ICSI-1	11.03	13.96	—	—	—	—	200	—	—
B-K	**11.71**	**14.47**	0.2	26.2	2.3	0.4	216	74.0	63.9
MA-ILP	11.37	**14.47**	0.7	11.6	5.3	0.6	191	89.1	61.8
ILP w/o bigrams	9.24	12.66	0.8	15.4	11.8	1.2	205	85.4	80.0
ILP w/o salience	11.38	14.71	1.1	19.1	12.0	1.3	233	82.1	92.3
ILP w/o style	**11.83**	**15.09**	1.4	17.4	18.9	1.7	271	84.1	86.3
ILP w/o log-ratio	11.41	14.70	1.2	16.9	12.5	1.5	223	84.3	90.1
ILP w/o QTSG	10.32	13.68	0	0	0	0	163	100.0	0

Table 4: Performance of the multiple-aspect ILP model against comparison systems using ROUGE and the four components of TER (insertion, deletion, substitution, shifts). In the lower section, performance of our model without (w/o) each component in turn. The final columns show the number of source sentences, the average compression ratio, and the proportion of sentences modified.

from the upper section of Table 4, the systems incorporating some form of rewriting gain slightly higher ROUGE scores than ICSI-1. The multiple aspects ILP system (MA-ILP) yields ROUGE scores similar to B-K, despite performing rewriting operations which increase the scope for error and without requiring any hand-crafted compression rules or manually annotated training data. Indeed, the outputs of the two systems are not significantly different under ROUGE (using a paired t-test, $p > 0.5$).

In the lower section of Table 4, we show the performance of our model when each of the contributing components described in Section 3 are removed. Clearly the bigram content indicators are an important element for the ROUGE scores, as their removal yields a reduction of 2.46 points (see the row ILP w/o bigrams in Table 4). The model without QTSG rules (ILP w/o QTSG) is effectively limited to sentence extraction, and removing rewrite rules also lowers ROUGE scores to levels similar to ICSI-1. ROUGE scores are increased by allowing the model to select "poor quality" sentences (ILP w/o style), higher indeed than those of the B-K system. The inclusion of non-summary language (ILP w/o log-ratio) does not affect ROUGE scores to the same extent that bigrams and QTSG do.

Table 4 includes a break-down of the systems' rewrite operations as measured by TER. We also show the number of source sentences (Count), the average compression ratio (CR %) and the proportion of sentences modified (Mod %) by each system. As can be seen, MA-ILP draws on fewer sentences, performs less deletion and more rewriting than B-K. The number of deletions increases when individual ILP components are removed and so does the number of substitutions. All the subsystems are more aggressive in their rewriting than when used in combination (higher TER, higher compression rate and a larger number of sentences are modified). Expectedly, when removing the QTSG rules, the ILP is limited to a pure extractive system (last row in Table 4).

Models	Grammar	Inform
ICSI-1	**4.68**	2.55
B-K	4.40	2.70
MA-ILP	**4.68**	**3.90**
ILP w/o style	3.30	2.67
Gold	4.90	4.75

Table 5: Mean ratings on system output output.

The results of our human evaluation study are shown in Table 5. We elicited grammaticality and informativeness ratings for a randomly selected model summary, ICSI-1, B-K, the multiple aspect ILP (MA-ILP), and the ILP w/o style which we included in this study as it performed best under ROUGE. ICSI-1, B-K, and MA-ILP are rated highly on the grammaticality dimension. MA-ILP is indistinguishable from the sentence extraction system (ICSI-1). Both systems are significantly more grammatical than B-K ($\alpha < 0.05$, using a Post-hoc Tukey test). Notice that summaries created by the ILP w/o style are rated poorly by humans, contrary to ROUGE. The style component stops very short

Florida's Governor Jeb Bush asked the US Supreme Court to intervene to keep a comatose woman alive, over the wishes of her husband, who wants to disconnect the feeding tube that has sustained her for 14 years. Her husband, Michael Schiavo, and her parents, Robert and Mary Schindler, have conflicts of interest that prevent them from fairly deciding whether to keep her alive. Some doctors have testified that Terri Schiavo is in a persistent vegetative state with no hope for recovery. The state House in Florida passed a bill Thursday to extend life support for a brain-damaged woman.

The space agencies of India and France signed an agreement to cooperate in launching a satellite in four years that will help make climate predictions more accurate. The Indian Space Research Organization (ISRO) has short-listed experiments from five nations including the United States, Britain and Germany, for a slot on India's unmanned moon mission Chandrayaan-1 to be undertaken by 2006-2007, the Press Trust of India (PTI) reported Monday. India will launch more missions to the moon if its maiden unmanned spacecraft Chandrayaan-1, slated to be launched by 2008, is successful in mapping the lunar surface.

Table 6: Example summaries generated by the multiple aspects model (MA-ILP).

sentences and quotations from being included in the summary even if they have quite high bigram or content scores. Without it, the model tends to generate summaries that are fragmentary and lacking proper context, resulting in lower grammaticality (and informativeness) when judged by humans. The MA-ILP system obtains the highest rating with respect to information content. It is significantly better ($\alpha < 0.05$) than ICSI-1 and B-K. This is not entirely surprising as our model includes additional content selection elements over and above the bigram units. There is still a significant gap from all systems to the gold-standard human-authored summaries. Example output summaries of the full ILP model are shown in Table 6.

Overall, we obtain best results when considering the contributions from the individual model experts collectively. This suggests that additional improvements could be obtained with more experts. It is also possible that optimizing the relative weightings of experts in the ILP objective would improve output. The TER analysis shows that the experts have a tempering effect on each other, resulting in less aggressive, but qualitatively better, rewriting than when used individually. Generally, experts work together to shape an output sentence, but they can also compete. In the future, we also plan to test the ability of the model to adapt to other multi-document summarization tasks, where the location of summary information is not as regular as it is in news articles. We would also like interface our model with sentence ordering and more generally with some notion of the coherence of the generated summary.

Acknowledgments We are grateful to Micha Elsner for his input on earlier versions of this work. We would also like to thank members of the ILCC at the School of Informatics for valuable discussions and comments. We acknowledge the support of EPSRC through project grants EP/I032916/1 and EP/I017127/1.

References

Taylor Berg-Kirkpatrick, Dan Gillick, and Dan Klein. 2011. Jointly learning to extract and compress. In *Proceedings of the 49th Annual Meeting of the Association for Computational Linguistics: Human Language Technologies*, pages 481–490, Portland, Oregon.

James Clarke and Mirella Lapata. 2008. Global inference for sentence compression: An integer linear programming approach. *Journal of Artificial Intelligence Research*, 31:273–381.

Trevor Cohn and Mirella Lapata. 2008. Sentence compression beyond word deletion. In *Proceedings of the 22nd International Conference on Computational Linguistics*, pages 137–144, Manchester, UK.

Trevor Cohn and Mirella Lapata. 2009. Sentence compression as tree transduction. *Journal of Artificial Intelligence Research*, 34:637–674.

Pawan Deshpande, Regina Barzilay, and David Karger. 2007. Randomized decoding for selection-and-ordering problems. In *Human Language Technologies 2007: The Conference of the North American Chapter of the Association for Computational Linguistics;*

Proceedings of the Main Conference, pages 444–451, Rochester, New York.

Jason Eisner. 2003. Learning non-isomorphic tree mappings for machine translation. In *Proceedings of the ACL Interactive Poster/Demonstration Sessions*, pages 205–208, Sapporo, Japan.

Elena Filatova and Vasileios Hatzivassiloglou. 2004. A formal model for information selection in multi-sentence text extraction. In *Proceedings of the 20th International Conference on Computational Linguistics*, pages 397–403, Geneva, Switzerland.

Dan Gillick and Benoit Favre. 2009. A scalable global model for summarization. In *Proceedings of the Workshop on Integer Linear Programming for Natural Language Processing*, pages 10–18, Boulder, Colorado.

Dan Gillick, Benoit Favre, and Dilek Hakkani-tür. 2008. The ICSI summarization system at TAC 2008. In *Proceedings of the Text Analysis Conference*.

Dan Gillick, Benoit Favre, Dilek Hakkani-tür, Berndt Bohnet, Yang Liu, and Shasha Xie. 2009. The ICSI/UTD summarization system at TAC 2009. In *Proceedings of the Text Analysis Conference*.

Jade Goldstein, Vibhu Mittal, Jaime Carbonell, and Mark Kantrowitz. 2000. Multi-document summarization by sentence extraction. In *Proceedings of the 2000 NAACL–ANLP Workshop on Automatic Summarization*, pages 40–48, Seattle, Washington.

Dorit S. Hochba. 1997. Approximating covering and packing problems: Set cover, vertex cover, independent set, and related problems. In Dorit S. Hochba, editor, *Approximation Algorithms for NP-Hard Problems*, pages 94–143. PWS Publishing Company, Boston, MA.

Honyang Jing. 2002. Using Hidden Markov modeling to decompose human-written summaries. *Computational Linguistics*, 28(4):527–544.

Dan Klein and Christopher D. Manning. 2003. Accurate unlexicalized parsing. In *Proceedings of the 41st Association for Computational Linguistics*, pages 423–430, Sapporo, Japan.

Chin-Yew Lin and Eduard H. Hovy. 2003. Automatic evaluation of summaries using n-gram co-occurrence statistics. In *Proceedings of HLT–NAACL*, pages 71–78, Edmonton, Canada.

Inderjeet Mani. 2001. *Automatic Summarization*. John Benjamins Pub Co.

André Martins and Noah A. Smith. 2009. Summarization with a joint model for sentence extraction and compression. In *Proceedings of the Workshop on Integer Linear Programming for Natural Language Processing*, pages 1–9, Boulder, Colorado.

Ryan McDonald. 2007. A study of global inference algorithms in multi-document summarization. In *Proceedings of the 29th European conference on IR Research*, pages 557–564, Rome, Italy.

Rani Nelken and Stuart Schieber. 2006. Towards robust context-sensitive sentence alignment for monolingual corpora. In *Proceedings of the 11th Conference of the European Chapter of the Association for Computational Linguistics*, pages 161–168, Trento, Italy.

David Smith and Jason Eisner. 2006. Quasi-synchronous grammars: Alignment by soft projection of syntactic dependencies. In *Proceedings of Workshop on Statistical Machine Translation*, pages 23–30, NYC.

Matthew Snover, Bonnie Dorr, Richard Schwartz, Linnea Micciulla, and John Makhoul. 2006. A study of translation edit rate with targeted human annotation. In *Proceedings of the 7th Conference of the Association for Machine Translation in the Americas*, pages 223–231, Cambridge.

Karen Sparck Jones. 1999. Automatic summarizing: Factors and directions. In Inderjeet Mani and Mark T. Maybury, editors, *Advances in Automatic Text Summarization*, pages 1–33. MIT Press, Cambridge.

Kristian Woodsend and Jacek Gondzio. 2009. Exploiting separability in large-scale linear support vector machine training. *Computational Optimization and Applications*.

Kristian Woodsend and Mirella Lapata. 2010. Automatic generation of story highlights. In *Proceedings of the 48th Annual Meeting of the Association for Computational Linguistics*, pages 565–574, Uppsala, Sweden.

Kristian Woodsend, Yansong Feng, and Mirella Lapata. 2010. Title generation with quasi-synchronous grammar. In *Proceedings of the 2010 Conference on Empirical Methods in Natural Language Processing*, pages 513–523, Cambridge, MA.

Minimal Dependency Length in Realization Ranking

Michael White and **Rajakrishnan Rajkumar**
Department of Linguistics
The Ohio State University
Columbus, OH, USA
{mwhite,raja}@ling.osu.edu

Abstract

Comprehension and corpus studies have found that the tendency to minimize dependency length has a strong influence on constituent ordering choices. In this paper, we investigate dependency length minimization in the context of discriminative realization ranking, focusing on its potential to eliminate egregious ordering errors as well as better match the distributional characteristics of sentence orderings in news text. We find that with a state-of-the-art, comprehensive realization ranking model, dependency length minimization yields statistically significant improvements in BLEU scores and significantly reduces the number of heavy/light ordering errors. Through distributional analyses, we also show that with simpler ranking models, dependency length minimization can go overboard, too often sacrificing canonical word order to shorten dependencies, while richer models manage to better counterbalance the dependency length minimization preference against (sometimes) competing canonical word order preferences.

1 Introduction

In this paper, we show that for the constituent ordering problem in surface realization, incorporating insights from the minimal dependency length theory of language production (Temperley, 2007) into a discriminative realization ranking model yields significant improvements upon a state-of-the-art baseline. We demonstrate empirically using OpenCCG, our CCG-based (Steedman, 2000) surface realization system, the utility of a global feature encoding the total dependency length of a given derivation. Although other works in the realization literature have used phrase length or head-dependent distances in their models (Filippova and Strube, 2009; Velldal and Oepen, 2005; White and Rajkumar, 2009, i.a.), to the best of our knowledge, this paper is the first to use insights from the minimal dependency length theory directly and study their effects, both qualitatively and quantitatively.

The impetus for this paper was the discovery that despite incorporating a sophisticated syntactic model borrowed from the parsing literature—including features with head-dependent distances at various scales—White & Rajkumar's (2009) realization ranking model still often performed poorly on weight-related decisions such as when to employ heavy-NP shift. Table 1 illustrates this point. In wsj_0034.9, the full model (incorporating numerous syntactic features) succeeds in reproducing the reference sentence, which is clearly preferable to the rather awkward variant selected by the baseline model (using various n-gram models). However, in wsj_0013.16, the full model fails to shift the temporal modifier *for now* next to the phrasal verb *turned down*, leaving it at the end of its very long verb phrase where it is highly ambiguous (with multiple intervening attachment sites). Conversely, in wsj_0044.3, the full model shifts *before* next to the verb, despite the NP *cheating* being very light, yielding a very confusing ordering given that *before* is meant to be intransitive.

The syntactic features in White & Rajkumar's (2009) realization ranking model are taken from Clark & Curran's (2007) normal form model

wsj_0034.9	they fell **into oblivion after the 1929 crash** .
FULL	[same]
BASELINE	they fell *after the 1929 crash into oblivion* .
wsj_0013.16	separately , the Federal Energy Regulatory Commission [$_{VP}$ turned down **for now** [$_{NP}$ a request by Northeast [$_{VP}$ seeking approval of [$_{NP}$ its possible purchase of PS of New Hampshire]]]] .
FULL	separately , the Federal Energy Regulatory Commission [$_{VP}$ turned down [$_{NP}$ a request by Northeast [$_{VP}$ seeking approval of [$_{NP}$ its possible purchase of PS of New Hampshire]]] *for now*] .
wsj_0044.3	she had seen **cheating before** , but these notes were uncanny .
FULL	she had seen *before cheating* , but these notes were uncanny .

Table 1: Examples of OpenCCG output with White & Rajkumar's (2009) models—the first represents a successful case, the latter two egregious ordering errors

(Table 3; see Section 3). In this model, head-dependenct distances are considered in conjunction with lexicalized and unlexicalized CCG derivation steps, thereby appearing in numerous features. As such, the model takes into account the interaction of dependency length with derivation steps, but in essence **does not consider the main effect of dependency length** itself. In this light, our investigation of dependency length minimization can be viewed as examining the question of whether realization ranking models can be made more accurate—and in particular, avoid egregious ordering errors—by incorporating a feature to account for the main effect of dependency length.

It is important to observe at this point that dependency length minimization is more of a preference than an optimization objective, which must be balanced against other order preferences at times. A closer reading of Temperley's (2007) study reveals that dependency length can sometimes run counter to many canonical word order choices. A case in point is the class of examples involving pre-modifying adjunct sequences that precede both the subject and the verb. Assuming that their parent head is the main verb of the sentence, a long-short sequence would minimize overall dependency length. However, in 613 examples found in the Penn Treebank, the average length of the first adjunct was 3.15 words while the second adjunct was 3.48 words long, thus reflecting a short-long pattern, as illustrated in the Temperley p.c. example in Table 2. Apart from these, Hawkins (2001) shows that arguments are generally located closer to the verb than adjuncts. Gildea and Temperley (2007) also suggest that adverb placement might involve cases which go against dependency length minimization. An examination of 295 legitimate long-short post-verbal constituent orders (counter to dependency length) from Section 00 of the Penn Treebank revealed that temporal adverb phrases are often involved in long-short orders, as shown in wsj_0075.13 in Table 2. In our setup, the preference to minimize dependency length can be balanced by features capturing preferences for alternate choices (e.g. the argument-adjunct distinction in our dependency ordering model, Table 4). Via distributional analyses, we show that while simpler realization ranking models can go overboard in minimizing dependency length, richer models largely succeed in overcoming this issue, while still taking advantage of dependency length minimization to avoid egregious ordering errors.

2 Background

2.1 Minimal Dependency Length

Comprehension and corpus studies (Gibson, 1998; Gibson, 2000; Temperley, 2007) point to the tendency of production and comprehension systems to adhere to principles of dependency length minimization. The idea of dependency length minimization is based on Gibson's (1998) Dependency Locality Theory (DLT) of comprehension, which predicts that longer dependencies are more difficult to process. DLT predictions have been further validated using comprehension studies involving eye-tracking corpora (Demberg and Keller, 2008). DLT metrics also correlate reasonably well with activation decay over time expressed in computational models of

Temperley (p.c.)	[In 1976], [as a film student at the Purchase campus of the State University of New York], Mr. Lane, shot ...
wsj_0075.13	The Treasury also said it plans to sell [$ 10 billion] [in 36-day cash management bills] [on Thursday].

Table 2: Counter-examples to dependency length minimization

comprehension (Lewis et al., 2006; Lewis and Vasishth, 2005).

Extending these ideas from comprehension, Temperley (2007) poses the question: Does language production reflect a preference for shorter dependencies as well so as to facilitate comprehension? By means of a study of Penn Treebank data, Temperley shows that English sentences do display a tendency to minimize the sum of all their head-dependent distances as illustrated by a variety of constructions. Further, Gildea and Temperley (2007) report that random linearizations have higher dependency lengths compared to actual English, while an "optimal" algorithm (from the perspective of dependency length minimization), which places dependents on either sides of a head in order of increasing length, is closer to actual English. Tily (2010) also applies insights from the above cited papers to show that dependency length constitutes a significant pressure towards language change. For head-final languages (e.g., Japanese), dependency length minimization results in the "long-short" constituent ordering in language production (Yamashita and Chang, 2001). More generally, Hawkins's (1994; 2000) processing domains, dependency length minimization and end-weight effects in constituent ordering (Wasow and Arnold, 2003) are all very closely related. The dependency length hypothesis goes beyond the predictions made by Hawkins' *Minimize Domains* principle in the case of English clauses with three postverbal adjuncts: Gibson's DLT correctly predicts that the first constituent tends to be shorter than the second, while Hawkins' approach does not make predictions about the relative orders of the first two constituents.

However, it would be very reductive to consider dependency length minimization as the sole factor in language production. In fact, a large body of prior work discusses a variety of other factors involved in language production. These other preferences are either correlated with dependency length or can override the minimal dependency length preference. Complexity (Wasow, 2002; Wasow and Arnold, 2003), animacy (Snider and Zaenen, 2006; Branigan et al., 2008), information status considerations (Wasow and Arnold, 2003; Arnold et al., 2000), the argument-adjunct distinction (Hawkins, 2001) and lexical bias (Wasow and Arnold, 2003; Bresnan et al., 2007) are a few prominent factors. More recently, Anttila et al. (2010) argued that the principle of end weight can be revised by calculating weight in prosodic terms to provide more explanatory power. As Temperley (2007) suggests, a satisactory model should combine insights from multiple approaches, a theme which we investigate in this work by means of a rich feature set adapted from the parsing and realization literature. Our feature design has been inspired by the conclusions of the above-cited works pertaining to the role of dependency length minimization in syntactic choice in conjuction with other factors influencing constituent order. However, going beyond Temperley's corpus study, we confirm the utility of incorporating a feature for minimizing dependency length into machine-learned models with hundreds of thousands of features found to be useful in previous parsing and realization work, and investigate the extent to which these features can counterbalance a dependency length minimization preference in cases where canonical word order considerations should prevail.

2.2 Surface Realization with Combinatory Categorial Grammar (CCG)

We provide here a brief overview of CCG and the OpenCCG realizer; for further details, see the works cited below.

CCG (Steedman, 2000) is a unification-based categorial grammar formalism defined almost entirely in terms of lexical entries that encode sub-

Feature Type	Example
LexCat + Word	s/s/np + before
LexCat + POS	s/s/np + IN
Rule	$s_{dcl} \rightarrow$ np $s_{dcl}\backslash$np
Rule + Word	$s_{dcl} \rightarrow$ np $s_{dcl}\backslash$np + bought
Rule + POS	$s_{dcl} \rightarrow$ np $s_{dcl}\backslash$np + VBD
Word-Word	$\langle$company, $s_{dcl} \rightarrow$ np $s_{dcl}\backslash$np, bought$\rangle$
Word-POS	$\langle$company, $s_{dcl} \rightarrow$ np $s_{dcl}\backslash$np, VBD$\rangle$
POS-Word	$\langle$NN, $s_{dcl} \rightarrow$ np $s_{dcl}\backslash$np, bought$\rangle$
Word + Δ_w	$\langle$bought, $s_{dcl} \rightarrow$ np $s_{dcl}\backslash$np$\rangle$ + d_w
POS + Δ_w	$\langle$VBD, $s_{dcl} \rightarrow$ np $s_{dcl}\backslash$np$\rangle$ + d_w
Word + Δ_p	$\langle$bought, $s_{dcl} \rightarrow$ np $s_{dcl}\backslash$np$\rangle$ + d_p
POS + Δ_p	$\langle$VBD, $s_{dcl} \rightarrow$ np $s_{dcl}\backslash$np$\rangle$ + d_p
Word + Δ_v	$\langle$bought, $s_{dcl} \rightarrow$ np $s_{dcl}\backslash$np$\rangle$ + d_v
POS + Δ_v	$\langle$VBD, $s_{dcl} \rightarrow$ np $s_{dcl}\backslash$np$\rangle$ + d_v

Table 3: Basic and dependency features from Clark & Curran's (2007) normal form model; distances are in intervening words, punctuation marks and verbs, and are capped at 3, 3 and 2, respectively

categorization as well as syntactic features (e.g. number and agreement). OpenCCG is a parsing/generation library which includes a hybrid symbolic-statistical chart realizer (White, 2006; White and Rajkumar, 2009). The input to the OpenCCG realizer is a semantic graph, where each node has a lexical predication and a set of semantic features; nodes are connected via dependency relations. Internally, such graphs are represented using Hybrid Logic Dependency Semantics (HLDS), a dependency-based approach to representing linguistic meaning (Baldridge and Kruijff, 2002). Alternative realizations are ranked using integrated n-gram or averaged perceptron scoring models. In the experiments reported below, the inputs are derived from the gold standard derivations in the CCGbank (Hockenmaier and Steedman, 2007), and the outputs are the highest-scoring realizations found during the realizer's chart-based search.[1]

3 Feature Design

In the realm of paraphrasing using tree linearization, Kempen and Harbusch (2004) explore features which have later been appropriated into classification approaches for surface realization (Filippova and Strube, 2007). Prominent features include information status, animacy and phrase length. In the case of ranking models for surface realization, by far the most comprehensive experiments involving linguistically motivated features are reported in work of Cahill for German realization ranking (Cahill et al., 2007; Cahill and Riester, 2009). Apart from language model and Lexical Functional Grammar (LFG) c-structure and f-structure based features, Cahill also designed and incorporated features modeling information status considerations.

The feature sets explored in this paper extend those in previous work on realization ranking with OpenCCG using averaged perceptron models (White and Rajkumar, 2009; Rajkumar et al., 2009; Rajkumar and White, 2010) to include more comprehensive ordering features. The feature classes are listed below, where DEPLEN, HOCKENMAIER and DEPORD are novel, and the rest are as in earlier OpenCCG models. The inclusion of the DEPORD features is intended to yield a model with a similarly rich set of ordering features as Cahill and Forster's (2009) realization ranking model for German. Except where otherwise indicated, features are integer-valued, representing counts of occurrences in a derivation.

DEPLEN The total of the length between all semantic heads and dependents for a realization, where length is in intervening words[2] excluding punctuation. For length purposes, collapsed named entities were counted as a single word in the experiments reported here.

NGRAMS The log probabilities of the word sequence scored using three different n-gram models: a trigram word model, a trigram word model with named entity classes replacing words, and a trigram model over POS tags and supertags.

HOCKENMAIER As an extra component of the generative baseline, the log probability of the derivation according to (a reimplementation

[1]The realizer can also be run using inputs derived from OpenCCG's parser, though informal experiments suggest that parse errors tend to decrease generation quality.

[2]We also experimented with two other definitions of dependency length described in the literature, namely (1) counting only nouns and verbs to approximate counting by discourse referents (Gibson, 1998) and (2) omitting function words to approximate prosodic weight (Anttila et al., 2010); however, realization ranking accuracy was slightly worse than counting all non-punctuation words.

Feature Type	Example
HeadBroadPos + Rel + Precedes + HeadWord + DepWord	⟨VB, Arg0, dep, wants, he⟩
... + HeadWord + DepPOS	⟨VB, Arg0, dep, wants, PRP⟩
... + HeadPOS + DepWord	⟨VB, Arg0, dep, VBZ, he⟩
... + HeadWord + DepPOS	⟨VB, Arg0, dep, VBZ, PRP⟩
HeadBroadPos + Side + DepWord1 + DepWord2	⟨NN, left, an, important⟩
... + DepWord1 + DepPOS2	⟨NN, left, an, JJ⟩
... + DepPOS1 + DepWord2	⟨NN, left, DT, important⟩
... + DepPOS1 + DepPOS2	⟨NN, left, DT, JJ⟩
... + Rel1 + Rel2	⟨NN, left, Det, Mod⟩

Table 4: Basic head-dependent and sibling dependent ordering features

of) Hockenmaier's (2003) generative syntactic model.

DISCRIMINATIVE NGRAMS Sequences from each of the n-gram models in the perceptron model.

AGREEMENT Features for subject-verb and animacy agreement as well as balanced punctuation.

C&C NF BASE The features from Clark & Curran's (2007) normal form model, listed in Table 3, minus the distance features.

C&C NF DISTANCE The distance features from the C&C normal form model, where the distance between a head and its dependent is measured in intervening words, punctuation marks or verbs; caps of 3, 3 and 2 (resp.) on the distances have the effect of binning longer distances.

DEPORD Several classes of features for ordering heads and dependents as well as sibling dependents on the same side of the head. The basic features—using words, POS tags and dependency relations, grouped by the broad POS tag of the head—are shown in Table 4. There are also similar features using words and a word class (instead of words and POS tags), where the class is either the named entity class, COLOR for color words, PRO for pronouns, one of 60-odd suffixes culled from the web, or HYPHEN or CAP for hyphenated or capitalized words. Additionally, there are features for detecting definiteness of an NP or PP (where the definiteness value is used in place of the POS tag).

Model	# Alph Feats	# Model Feats
GLOBAL	4	4
DEPLEN-GLOBAL	5	5
DEPORD-NONF	790,887	269,249
DEPORD-NODIST	1,035,915	365,287
DEPLEN-NODIST	1,035,916	366,094
DEPORD-NF	1,173,815	431,226
DEPLEN	1,173,816	428,775

Table 6: Model sizes—number of features in alphabet for each model (satisfying count cutoff of 5) along with number active in model after 5 training epochs

4 Evaluation

4.1 Experimental Conditions

We followed the averaged perceptron training procedure of White and Rajkumar (2009) with a couple of updates. First, as noted earlier, we used a reimplementation of Hockenmaier's (2003) generative syntactic model as an extra component of our generative baseline; and second, only five epochs of training were used, which was found to work as well as using additional epochs on the development set. As in the earlier work, the models were trained on the standard training sections (02–21) of an enhanced version of the CCGbank, using a lexico-grammar extracted from these sections.

The models tested in the experiments reported below are summarized in Table 5. The three groups of models are designed to test the impact of the dependency length feature when added to feature sets of increasing complexity. In more detail, the GLOBAL and DEPLEN-GLOBAL models contain dense features on entire derivations; their values are the log probabilities of the three n-gram mod-

Model	Dep Len	Ngram Mods	Hocken-maier	Discr Ngrams	Agree-ment	C&C NF Base	C&C NF Dist	Dep Ord
GLOBAL	N	Y	Y	N	N	N	N	N
DEPLEN-GLOBAL	Y	Y	Y	N	N	N	N	N
DEPORD-NONF	N	Y	Y	Y	Y	N	N	Y
DEPORD-NODIST	N	Y	Y	Y	Y	Y	N	Y
DEPLEN-NODIST	Y	Y	Y	Y	Y	Y	N	Y
DEPORD-NF	N	Y	Y	Y	Y	Y	Y	Y
DEPLEN	Y	Y	Y	Y	Y	Y	Y	Y

Table 5: Legend for experimental conditions

els used in the earlier work along with the Hockenmaier model (and the dependency length feature, in DEPLEN-GLOBAL). The second group is centered on DEPORD-NODIST, which contains all features except the dependency length feature and the distance features in Clark & Curran's normal form model, which may indirectly capture some dependency length minimization preferences. In addition to DEPLEN-NODIST—where the dependency length feature is added—this group also contains DEPORD-NONF, which is designed to test (as a side comparison) whether the Clark & Curran normal form base features are still useful even when used in conjunction with the new dependency ordering features. In the final group, DEPORD-NF contains all the features examined in this paper except the dependency length feature, while DEPLEN contains all the features including the dependency length feature. Note that the learned weight of the total dependency length feature was negative in each case, as expected.

Table 6 shows the sizes of the various models. For each model, the alphabet—whose size increases to over a million features—is the set of applicable features found to have discriminative value in at least 5 training examples; from these, a subset are made active (i.e., take on a non-zero weight) through perceptron updates when the feature value differs between the model-best and oracle-best realization.

4.2 BLEU Results

Following the usual practice in the realization ranking, we first evaluate our results quantitatively using exact matches and BLEU (Papineni et al., 2002), a corpus similarity metric developed for MT evaluation. Realization results for the development and test sections appear in Table 7. For all three model groups, the dependency length feature yields significant increases in BLEU scores, even in comparison to the model (DEPORD-NF) containing Clark & Curran's distance features in addition to the new dependency ordering features (as well as all other features but total dependency length). The second group additionally shows that the Clark & Curran normal form base features do indeed have a significant impact on BLEU scores even when used with

Model	% Exact	BLEU	Signif
Sect 00			
GLOBAL	33.03	0.8292	-
DEPLEN-GLOBAL	34.73	**0.8345**	***
DEPORD-NONF	42.33	0.8534	**
DEPORD-NODIST	43.12	0.8560	-
DEPLEN-NODIST	43.87	**0.8587**	***
DEPORD-NF	43.44	0.8590	-
DEPLEN	44.56	**0.8610**	**
Sect 23			
GLOBAL	34.75	0.8302	-
DEPLEN-GLOBAL	34.70	**0.8330**	***
DEPORD-NODIST	41.42	0.8561	-
DEPLEN-NODIST	42.95	**0.8603**	***
DEPORD-NF	41.32	0.8577	-
DEPLEN	42.05	**0.8596**	**

Table 7: Development (Section 00) & test (Section 23) set results—exact match percentage and BLEU scores, along with statistical significance of BLEU compared to the unmarked model in each group (* = $p < 0.1$, ** = $p < 0.05$, *** = $p < 0.01$); significant within-group winners (at $p < 0.05$) are shown in bold

Model	% DL Lower	% DL Greater	DL Mean	Signif
GOLD	n.a.	n.a.	41.02	-
GLOBAL	17.23	21.59	42.40	***
DEPLEN-GLOBAL	24.37	12.81	40.29	***
DEPORD-NONF	15.76	19.34	42.34	***
DEPORD-NODIST	14.58	19.06	42.03	***
DEPLEN-NODIST	17.75	14.82	40.87	n.s.
DEPORD-NF	14.96	17.65	41.58	***
DEPLEN	16.28	14.78	40.97	n.s.

Table 8: Dependency length compared to corpus—percentage of realizations with dependency length less than and greater than gold standard, along with mean dependency length, whose significance is tested against gold; 1671 development set (Section 00) complete realizations analyzed

Model	% Short / Long	% Long / Short	% Eq	% Single Constit
GOLD	25.25	4.87	4.08	65.79
GLOBAL	23.15	7.86	3.94	65.04
DEPLEN-GLOBAL	24.58	5.57	4.09	65.76
DEPORD-NONF	23.13	6.61	4.03	66.23
DEPORD-NODIST	23.38	6.52	3.94	66.15
DEPLEN-NODIST	24.03	5.38	4.01	66.58
DEPORD-NF	23.74	5.92	3.96	66.40
DEPLEN	24.36	5.36	4.07	66.21

Table 9: Distribution of various kinds of post-verbal constituents in the development set (Section 00); 4692 gold cases considered

the new dependency ordering model, as DEPORD-NONF is significantly worse than DEPORD-NODIST (the impact of the distance features is evident in the increases from the second group to the third group). As with the dev set, the dependency length feature yielded a significant increase in BLEU scores for each comparison on the test set also.

For each group, the statistical significance of the difference in BLEU scores between a model and the unmarked model (-) is determined by bootstrap resampling (Koehn, 2004).[3] Note that although the differences in BLEU scores are small, they end up being statistically significant because the models frequently yield the same top scoring realization, and reliably deliver improvements in the cases where they differ. In particular, note that DEPLEN and DEPORD-NF agree on the best realization 81% of the time, while DEPLEN-NODIST and DEPORD-NODIST have 78.1% agreement, and DEPLEN-GLOBAL and GLOBAL show 77.4% agreement; by comparison, DEPORD-NODIST and GLOBAL only agree on the best realization 51.1% of the time.

4.3 Detailed Analyses

The effect of the dependency length feature on the distribution of dependency lengths is illustrated in Table 8. The table shows the mean of the total dependency length of each realized derivation compared to the corresponding gold standard derivation, as well as the number of derivations with greater and lower dependency length. According to paired t-tests, the mean dependency lengths for the DEPLEN-NODIST and DEPLEN models do not differ significantly from the gold standard. In contrast, the mean dependency length of all the models that do not include the dependency length feature does differ significantly ($p < 0.001$) from the gold standard. Additionally, all these models have more realizations with dependency length greater than the gold standard, in comparison to the dependency length minimizing models; this shows the efficacy of the dependency length feature in approximating the gold standard. Interestingly, the DEPLEN-GLOBAL model significantly undershoots the gold standard on mean dependency length, and has the most skewed distribution of sentences with greater vs. lesser dependency length than the gold standard.

Apart from studying dependency length directly, we also looked at one of the attested effects of dependency length minimization, viz. the tendency to prefer short-long post-verbal constituents in production (Temperley, 2007). The relative lengths of adjacent post-verbal constituents were computed and their distribution is shown in Table 9. While calculating length, punctuation marks were excluded. Four kinds of constituents were found in the post-verbal domain. For every verb, apart from single constituents and equal length constituents, short-long and long-short sequences were also observed. Table 9 demonstrates that for both the gold standard corpus as well as the realizer models, short-long constituents were more frequent than long-short or equal length constituents. This follows the trend re-

[3]Kudos to Kevin Gimpel for making his resampling scripts available from http://www.ark.cs.cmu.edu/MT/paired_bootstrap_v13a.tar.gz.

Model	% Light / Heavy	% Heavy / Light	Signif
GOLD	8.60	0.36	-
GLOBAL	7.73	2.02	***
DEPLEN-GLOBAL	8.35	0.75	**
DEPORD-NONF	7.98	1.15	***
DEPORD-NODIST	8.04	1.12	***
DEPLEN-NODIST	8.23	0.45	n.s.
DEPORD-NF	8.26	0.71	**
DEPLEN	8.36	0.51	n.s.

Table 10: Distribution of heavy unequal constituents (length difference > 5) in Section 00; 4692 gold cases considered and significance tested against the gold standard using a χ-square test

ported by previous corpus studies of English (Temperley, 2007; Wasow and Arnold, 2003). The figures reported here show the tendency of the DEPLEN* models to be closer to the gold standard than the other models, especially in the case of short-long constituents.

We also performed an analysis of relative constituent lengths focusing on light-heavy and heavy-light cases; specifically, we examined unequal length constituent sequences where the length difference of the constituents was greater than 5, and the shorter constituent was under 5 words. Table 10 shows the results. Using a χ-square test, the distribution of heavy unequal length constituent counts in the DEPLEN-NODIST and DEPLEN models does not significantly differ from that of the gold standard. In contrast, for all the other models, the counts do differ significantly from the gold standard.

4.4 Examples

Table 11 shows examples of how the dependency length feature (DEPLEN) affects the output even in comparison to a model (DEPORD) with a rich set of discriminative syntactic and dependency ordering features, but no features directly targeting relative weight. In wsj_0015.7, the dependency length model produces an exact match, while the DEPORD model fails to shift the short temporal adverbial *next year* next to the verb, leaving a confusingly repetitive *this year next year* at the end of the sentence. In wsj_0020.1, the dependency length model produces a nearly exact match with just an equally acceptable inversion of *closely watching*. By contrast, the DEPORD model mistakenly shifts the direct object *South Korea, Taiwan and Saudia Arabia* to the end of the sentence where it is difficult to understand following two very long intervening phrases. In wsj_0021.8, both models mysteriously put *not* in front of the auxiliary and leave out the complementizer, but DEPORD also mistakenly leaves *before* at the end of the verb phrase where it is again apt to be interpreted as modifying the preceding verb. In wsj_0075.13, both models put the temporal modifier *on Thursday* in its canonical VP-final position, despite this order running counter to dependency length minimization. Finally, wsj_0014.2 shows a case where DEPORD is nearly an exact match (except for a missing comma), but the dependency length model fronts the PP *on the 12-member board*, where it is grammatical but rather marked (and not motivated in the discourse context).

4.5 Interim Discussion

The experiments show a consistent positive effect of the dependency length feature in improving BLEU scores and achieving a better match with the corpus distributions of dependency length and short/long constituent orders. The results in Table 10 are particulary encouraging, as they show that minimizing dependency length reduces the number of realizations in which a heavy constituent precedes a light one down to essentially the level of the corpus, thereby eliminating many realizations that can be expected to have egregious errors like those shown in Table 11.

Intriguingly, there is some evidence that a negatively weighted total dependency length feature can go too far in minimizing dependency length, in the absence of other informative features to counterbalance it. In particular, the DEPLEN-GLOBAL model in Table 8 has significantly lower dependency length than the corpus, but in the richer models with discriminative synactic and dependency ordering features, there are no significant differences. It may still be though that additional features are necessary to counteract the tendency towards dependency length minimization, for example to ensure that initial constituents play their intended role in establishing and continuing topics in discourse, as also observed in Table 11.

wsj_0015.7	the exact amount of the refund will be determined **next year** based on actual collections made until Dec. 31 of this year .
DEPLEN	[same]
DEPORD	the exact amount of the refund will be determined based on actual collections made until Dec. 31 of this year *next year* .
wsj_0020.1	the U.S. , claiming some success in its trade diplomacy , removed South Korea , Taiwan and Saudi Arabia from a list of countries it is closely watching for allegedly failing to honor U.S. patents , copyrights and other intellectual-property rights .
DEPLEN	the U.S. claiming some success in its trade diplomacy , removed **South Korea , Taiwan and Saudi Arabia** from a list of countries it is *watching closely* for allegedly failing to honor U.S. patents , copyrights and other intellectual-property rights .
DEPORD	the U.S. removed from a list of countries it is *watching closely* for allegedly failing to honor U.S. patents , copyrights and other intellectual-property rights , claiming some success in its trade diplomacy , *South Korea , Taiwan and Saudi Arabia* .
wsj_0021.8	but he has not said before that the country wants half the debt forgiven .
DEPLEN	but he *not* has said **before** ∅ the country wants half the debt forgiven .
DEPORD	but he *not* has said ∅ the country wants half the debt forgiven **before** .
wsj_0075.13	The Treasury also said it plans to sell [$ 10 billion] [in 36-day cash management bills] [on Thursday].
DEPLEN	[same]
DEPORD	[same]
wsj_0014.2	they succeed Daniel M. Rexinger , retired Circuit City executive vice president , and Robert R. Glauber , U.S. Treasury undersecretary , on the 12-member board .
DEPORD	they succeed Daniel M. Rexinger , retired Circuit City executive vice president , and Robert R. Glauber , U.S. Treasury undersecretary ∅ on the 12-member board .
DEPLEN	*on the 12-member board* they succeed Daniel M. Rexinger , retired Circuit City executive vice president , and Robert R. Glauber , U.S. Treasury undersecretary .

Table 11: Examples of realized output for full models with and without the dependency length feature

4.6 Targeted Human Evaluation

To determine whether heavy-light ordering differences often represent ordering errors (including egregious ones), rather than simply representing acceptable variation, we conducted a targeted human evaluation on examples of this kind. Specifically, for each of the DEPLEN* models and their corresponding models without the dependency length feature, we chose the 25 sentences from the development section whose realizations exhibited the greatest difference in dependency length between sibling constituents appearing in opposite orders, and asked two judges (not the authors) to choose which of the two realizations best expressed the meaning of the reference sentence in a grammatical and fluent way, with the choice forced (2AFC). Table 12 shows the results. Agreement between the judges was high,

Model	% Preferred	% Agr	Signif
GLOBAL	22	-	-
DEPLEN-GLOBAL	78	84	***
DEPORD-NODIST	24	-	-
DEPLEN-NODIST	76	92	***
DEPORD-NF	26	-	-
DEPLEN	74	96	***

Table 12: Targeted human evaluation—percentage of realizations preferred by two human judges in a 2AFC test among the 25 development set sentences with the greatest differences in dependency length, with a binomial test for significance

with only one disagreement on the realizations from the DEPLEN and DEPORD-NF models (involving an acceptable paraphrase in our judgment), and only four disagreements on the DEPLEN-GLOBAL and GLOBAL realizations. Pooling the judgments, the preference for the DEPLEN* models was well above the chance level of 50% according to a binomial test ($p < 0.001$ in each case). Inspecting the data ourselves, we found that many of the items did indeed involve egregious ordering errors that the DEPLEN* models managed to avoid.

5 Related Work

As noted in the introduction, to the best of our knowledge this paper is the first to examine the impact of dependency length minimization on realization ranking. While there have been quite a few papers to date reporting results on Penn Treebank data, since the various systems make different assumptions regarding the specificity of their inputs, all but the most broad-brushed comparisons remain impossible at present, and thus detailed studies such as the present one can only be made within the context of different models for the same system. Some progress on this issue has been made in the context of the Generation Challenges Surface Realization Shared Task (Belz et al., 2011), but it remains to be seen to what extent fair cross-system comparisons using common inputs can be achieved.

For (very) rough comparison purposes, Table 13 lists our results in the context of those reported for various other systems on PTB Section 23. As the table shows, the OpenCCG scores are quite competitive, exceeded only by Callaway's (2005) extensively hand-crafted system as well as Bohnet et al.'s (2011) system on shared task shallow inputs (-S), which performs much better than their system on deep inputs (-D) that more closely resemble OpenCCG's.

System	Coverage	BLEU	% Exact
Callaway (05)	98.5%	0.9321	57.5
Bohnet et al.-S (11)	100%	0.8911	-
OpenCCG (12)	97.1%	0.8596	42.1
OpenCCG (09)	97.1%	0.8506	40.5
Ringger et al. (04)	100%	0.836	35.7
Bohnet et al.-D (11)	100%	0.7943	-
Langkilde-Geary (02)	83%	0.757	28.2
Guo et al. (08)	100%	0.7440	19.8
Hogan et al. (07)	≈100%	0.6882	-
OpenCCG (08)	96.0%	0.6701	16.0
Nakanishi et al. (05)	90.8%	0.7733	-

Table 13: PTB Section 23 BLEU scores and exact match percentages in the NLG literature (Nakanishi et al.'s results are for sentences of length 20 or less)

6 Conclusions

In this paper, we have investigated dependency length minimization in the context of realization ranking, focusing on its potential to eliminate egregious ordering errors as well as better match the distributional characteristics of sentence orderings in news text. When added to a state-of-the-art, comprehensive realization ranking model, we showed that including a dense, global feature for minimizing total dependency length yields statistically significant improvements in BLEU scores and significantly reduces the number of heavy-light ordering errors. Going beyond the BLEU metric, we also conducted a targeted human evaluation to confirm the utility of the dependency length feature in models of varying richness. Interestingly, even with the richest model, in some cases we found that the dependency length feature still appears to go too far in minimizing dependency length, suggesting that further counter-balancing features—especially ones for the sentence-initial position (Filippova and Strube, 2009)—warrant investigation in future work.

Acknowledgments

This work was supported in part by NSF grants no. IIS-1143635 and IIS-0812297. We thank the anonymous reviewers for helpful comments and discussion, and Scott Martin and Dennis Mehay for their participation in the targeted human evaluation.

References

Arto Anttila, Matthew Adams, and Mike Speriosu. 2010. The role of prosody in the English dative alternation. *Language and Cognitive Processes*.

Jennifer E. Arnold, Thomas Wasow, Anthony Losongco, and Ryan Ginstrom. 2000. Heaviness vs. newness: The effects of structural complexity and discourse status on constituent ordering. *Language*, 76:28–55.

Jason Baldridge and Geert-Jan Kruijff. 2002. Coupling CCG and Hybrid Logic Dependency Semantics. In *Proc. ACL-02*.

Anja Belz, Mike White, Dominic Espinosa, Eric Kow, Deirdre Hogan, and Amanda Stent. 2011. The first surface realisation shared task: Overview and evaluation results. In *Proceedings of the Generation Challenges Session at the 13th European Workshop on Natural Language Generation*, pages 217–226, Nancy, France, September. Association for Computational Linguistics.

Bernd Bohnet, Simon Mille, Benoît Favre, and Leo Wanner. 2011. <stumaba >: From deep representation to surface. In *Proceedings of the Generation Challenges Session at the 13th European Workshop on Natural Language Generation*, pages 232–235, Nancy, France, September. Association for Computational Linguistics.

H Branigan, M Pickering, and M Tanaka. 2008. Contributions of animacy to grammatical function assignment and word order during production. *Lingua*, 118(2):172–189.

Joan Bresnan, Anna Cueni, Tatiana Nikitina, and R. Harald Baayen. 2007. Predicting the Dative Alternation. *Cognitive Foundations of Interpretation*, pages 69–94.

Aoife Cahill and Arndt Riester. 2009. Incorporating information status into generation ranking. In *Proceedings of,* ACL-IJCNLP '09, pages 817–825, Morristown, NJ, USA. Association for Computational Linguistics.

Aoife Cahill, Martin Forst, and Christian Rohrer. 2007. Designing features for parse disambiguation and realisation ranking. In Miriam Butt and Tracy Holloway King, editors, *Proceedings of the 12th International Lexical Functional Grammar Conference*, pages 128–147. CSLI Publications, Stanford.

Charles Callaway. 2005. The types and distributions of errors in a wide coverage surface realizer evaluation. In *Proceedings of the 10th European Workshop on Natural Language Generation*.

Stephen Clark and James R. Curran. 2007. Wide-Coverage Efficient Statistical Parsing with CCG and Log-Linear Models. *Computational Linguistics*, 33(4):493–552.

Vera Demberg and Frank Keller. 2008. Data from eye-tracking corpora as evidence for theories of syntactic processing complexity. *Cognition*, 109(2):193–210.

Katja Filippova and Michael Strube. 2007. Generating constituent order in German clauses. In *ACL 2007, Proceedings of the 45th Annual Meeting of the Association for Computational Linguistics, June 23-30, 2007, Prague, Czech Republic*. The Association for Computer Linguistics.

Katja Filippova and Michael Strube. 2009. Tree linearization in English: Improving language model based approaches. In *Proceedings of Human Language Technologies: The 2009 Annual Conference of the North American Chapter of the Association for Computational Linguistics, Companion Volume: Short Papers*, pages 225–228, Boulder, Colorado, June. Association for Computational Linguistics.

Edward Gibson. 1998. Linguistic complexity: Locality of syntactic dependencies. *Cognition*, 68:1–76.

Edward Gibson. 2000. Dependency locality theory: A distance-based theory of linguistic complexity. In Alec Marantz, Yasushi Miyashita, and Wayne O'Neil, editors, *Image, Language, brain: Papers from the First Mind Articulation Project Symposium*. MIT Press, Cambridge, MA.

Daniel Gildea and David Temperley. 2007. Optimizing grammars for minimum dependency length. In *Proceedings of the 45th Annual Meeting of the Association of Computational Linguistics*, pages 184–191, Prague, Czech Republic, June. Association for Computational Linguistics.

Yuqing Guo, Josef van Genabith, and Haifeng Wang. 2008. Dependency-based n-gram models for general purpose sentence realisation. In *Proc. COLING-08*.

John A. Hawkins. 1994. *A Performance Theory of Order and Constituency*. Cambridge University Press, New York.

John A. Hawkins. 2000. The relative order of prepositional phrases in English: Going beyond manner-place-time. *Language Variation and Change*, 11(03):231–266.

John A. Hawkins. 2001. Why are categories adjacent? *Journal of Linguistics*, 37:1–34.

Julia Hockenmaier and Mark Steedman. 2007. CCG-bank: A Corpus of CCG Derivations and Dependency Structures Extracted from the Penn Treebank. *Computational Linguistics*, 33(3):355–396.

Julia Hockenmaier. 2003. *Data and models for statistical parsing with Combinatory Categorial Grammar*. Ph.D. thesis, University of Edinburgh.

Deirdre Hogan, Conor Cafferkey, Aoife Cahill, and Josef van Genabith. 2007. Exploiting multi-word units in history-based probabilistic generation. In *Proc. EMNLP-CoNLL*.

Gerard Kempen and Karin Harbusch. 2004. Generating natural word orders in a semi-free word order language: Treebank-based linearization preferences for German. In Alexander F. Gelbukh, editor, *CICLing*, volume 2945 of *Lecture Notes in Computer Science*, pages 350–354. Springer.

Philipp Koehn. 2004. Statistical significance tests for machine translation evaluation. In Dekang Lin and Dekai Wu, editors, *Proceedings of EMNLP 2004*, pages 388–395, Barcelona, Spain, July. Association for Computational Linguistics.

Irene Langkilde-Geary. 2002. An empirical verification of coverage and correctness for a general-purpose sentence generator. In *Proc. INLG-02*.

R. L. Lewis and S. Vasishth. 2005. An activation-based model of sentence processing as skilled memory retrieval. *Cognitive Science*, 29:1–45, May.

Richard L. Lewis, Shravan Vasishth, and Julie Van Dyke. 2006. Computational principles of working memory in sentence comprehension. *Trends in Cognitive Sciences*, 10(10):447–454.

Hiroko Nakanishi, Yusuke Miyao, and Jun'ichi Tsujii. 2005. Probabilistic methods for disambiguation of an HPSG-based chart generator. In *Proc. IWPT-05*.

Kishore Papineni, Salim Roukos, Todd Ward, and Wei-Jing Zhu. 2002. BLEU: a method for automatic evaluation of machine translation. In *Proc. ACL-02*.

Rajakrishnan Rajkumar and Michael White. 2010. Designing agreement features for realization ranking. In *Coling 2010: Posters*, pages 1032–1040, Beijing, China, August. Coling 2010 Organizing Committee.

Rajakrishnan Rajkumar, Michael White, and Dominic Espinosa. 2009. Exploiting named entity classes in CCG surface realization. In *Proceedings of Human Language Technologies: The 2009 Annual Conference of the North American Chapter of the Association for Computational Linguistics, Companion Volume: Short Papers*, pages 161–164, Boulder, Colorado, June. Association for Computational Linguistics.

Eric Ringger, Michael Gamon, Robert C. Moore, David Rojas, Martine Smets, and Simon Corston-Oliver. 2004. Linguistically informed statistical models of constituent structure for ordering in sentence realization. In *Proc. COLING-04*.

Neal Snider and Annie Zaenen. 2006. Animacy and syntactic structure: Fronted NPs in English. In M. Butt, M. Dalrymple, and T.H. King, editors, *Intelligent Linguistic Architectures: Variations on Themes by Ronald M. Kaplan*. CSLI Publications, Stanford.

Mark Steedman. 2000. *The Syntactic Process*. MIT Press.

David Temperley. 2007. Minimization of dependency length in written English. *Cognition*, 105(2):300 – 333.

Harry Tily. 2010. *The Role of Processing Complexity in Word Order Variation and Change*. Ph.D. thesis, Stanford University.

Erik Velldal and Stefan Oepen. 2005. Maximum entropy models for realization ranking. In *Proc. MT-Summit X*.

Thomas Wasow and Jennifer Arnold. 2003. *Post-verbal Constituent Ordering in English*. Mouton.

Tom Wasow. 2002. *Postverbal Behavior*. CSLI Publications, Stanford.

Michael White and Rajakrishnan Rajkumar. 2009. Perceptron reranking for CCG realization. In *Proceedings of the 2009 Conference on Empirical Methods in Natural Language Processing*, pages 410–419, Singapore, August. Association for Computational Linguistics.

Michael White. 2006. Efficient Realization of Coordinate Structures in Combinatory Categorial Grammar. *Research on Language & Computation*, 4(1):39–75.

Hiroko Yamashita and Franklin Chang. 2001. "Long before short" preference in the production of a head-final language. *Cognition*, 81.

Framework of Automatic Text Summarization Using Reinforcement Learning

Seonggi Ryang
Graduate School of Information Science and Technology
University of Tokyo
sryang@is.s.u-tokyo.ac.jp

Takeshi Abekawa
National Institute of Informatics
abekawa@nii.ac.jp

Abstract

We present a new approach to the problem of automatic text summarization called Automatic Summarization using Reinforcement Learning (ASRL) in this paper, which models the process of constructing a summary within the framework of reinforcement learning and attempts to optimize the given score function with the given feature representation of a summary. We demonstrate that the method of reinforcement learning can be adapted to automatic summarization problems naturally and simply, and other summarizing techniques, such as sentence compression, can be easily adapted as actions of the framework.

The experimental results indicated ASRL was superior to the best performing method in DUC2004 and comparable to the state of the art ILP-style method, in terms of ROUGE scores. The results also revealed ASRL can search for sub-optimal solutions efficiently under conditions for effectively selecting features and the score function.

1 Introduction

Automatic text summarization aims to automatically produce a short and well-organized summary of single or multiple documents (Mani, 2001). Automatic summarization, especially multi-document summarization, has been an increasingly important task in recent years, because of the exponential explosion of available information. The brief summary that the summarization system produces allows readers to quickly and easily understand the content of original documents without having to read each individual document, and it should be helpful for dealing with enormous amounts of information.

The extractive approach to automatic summarization is a popular and well-known approach in this field, which creates a summary by directly selecting some textual units (e.g., words and sentences) from the original documents, because it is difficult to genuinely evaluate and guarantee the linguistic quality of the produced summary.

One of the most well-known extractive approaches is maximal marginal relevance (MMR), which scores each textual unit and extracts the unit that has the highest score in terms of the MMR criteria (Goldstein et al., 2000). Greedy MMR-style algorithms are widely used; however, they cannot take into account the whole quality of the summary due to their greediness, although a summary should convey all the information in given documents. Global inference algorithms for the extractive approach have been researched widely in recent years (Filatova and Hatzivassiloglou, 2004; McDonald, 2007; Takamura and Okumura, 2009) to consider whether the summary is "good" as a whole. These algorithms formulate the problem as integer linear programming (ILP) to optimize the score: however, as ILP is non-deterministic polynomial-time hard (NP-hard), the time complexity is very large. Consequently, we need some more efficient algorithm for calculations.

We present a new approach to the problem of automatic text summarization called Automatic Summarization using Reinforcement Learning (ASRL), which models the process of construction of a summary within the framework of reinforcement learning and attempts to optimize the given score function with the given feature representation of a summary. We demonstrate that the method of reinforcement learning can be adapted to problems with automatic summarization naturally and simply, and other summarizing techniques, such as sentence compression, can be easily adapted as actions of the framework, which should be helpful to enhance the quality of the summary that is produced. This is the first paper utilizing reinforcement learning for problems with automatic summarization of text.

We evaluated ASRL with the DUC2004 summarization task 2, and the experimental results revealed ASRL is superior to the best method of performance in DUC2004 and comparable with the state of the art ILP-style method, based on maximum coverage with the knapsack constraint problem, in terms of ROUGE scores with experimental settings. We also evaluated ASRL in terms of optimality and execution time. The experimental results indicated ASRL can search the state space efficiently for some sub-optimal solutions under the condition of effectively selecting features and the score function, and produce a summary whose score denotes the expectation of the score of the same features' states. The evaluation of the quality of a produced summary only depends on the given score function, and therefore it is easy to adapt the new method of evaluation without having to modify the structure of the framework.

2 Formulation of Extractive Approach

We first focus on the extractive approach, which is directly used to produce a summary by extracting some textual units, by avoiding the difficulty of having to consider the genuine linguistic quality of a summary.

The given document (or documents) in extractive summarization approaches is reduced to the set of textual units: $D = \{x_1, x_2, \cdots, x_n\}$, where n is the size of the set, and x_i denotes individual textual units. Note that any textual unit is permitted, such as *character*, *word*, *sentence*, *phrase*, and *conceptual unit*. If we determine a *sentence* is a textual unit to be extracted, the formulated problem is a problem of extracting sentences from the source document, which is one of the most popular settings for summarization tasks.

Next, we define the score function, $score(S)$, for any subset of the document: $S \subset D$. Subset S is one of the summaries of the given document. The aim of this summarization problem is to find the summary that maximizes this function when the score function is given. The score function is typically defined by taking into consideration the tradeoff between relevance and redundancy.

Then, we define length function $L(S)$, which indicates the length of summary S. The length is also arbitrary, which can be based on the *character*, *word*, and *sentence*. We assume the limitation of summary length K is given in summarization tasks.

Finally, we define the extractive approach of the automatic summarization problem as:

$$\begin{aligned} S^* &= \arg\max_{S \subset D} score(S) \qquad (1) \\ \text{s.t.} &\quad L(S) \leq K. \end{aligned}$$

3 Motivation

We can regard the extractive approach as a search problem. It is extremely difficult to solve this search problem because the final result of evaluation given by the given score function is not available until it finishes, and we therefore need to try all combinations of textual units. Consequently, the score function, which denotes some criterion for the quality of a summary, tends to be determined so that the function can be decomposed to components and it is solved with global inference algorithms, such as ILP. However, both decomposing the score function properly and utilizing the evaluation of half-way process of searches are generally difficult. For example, let us assume that we design the score function by using some complex semantic considerations to take into account the readability of a summary, and the score is efficiently calculated if the whole summary is given. Then, formulating the problem as a global inference problem and solving it with methods of integer linear programming might generally be difficult, because of the complex composition of the score function, despite the ease with which the whole summary is evaluated. The readability score might be based on extremely complex calculations of dependency relations, or a great deal of external knowledge the summarizer cannot know merely from the source documents. In fact, it is ideal that we can only directly utilize the score function, in the sense that we do not have to consider the decomposed form of the given score function.

We need to consider the problem with automatic summarization to be the same as that with reinforcement learning to handle these problems. Reinforcement learning is one of the solutions to three problems.

- The learning of the agent only depends on the reward provided by the environment.
- Furthermore, the reward is delayed, in the sense that the agent cannot immediately know the actual evaluation of the executed action.
- The agent only estimates the value of the state with the information on rewards, without knowledge of the actual form of the score function, to maximize future rewards.

We suggest the formulation of the problem as we have just described will enable us to freely design the score function without limitations and expand the capabilities of automatic summarization.

4 Models of Extractive Approach for Reinforcement Learning

4.1 Reinforcement Learning

Reinforcement learning is a powerful method of solving planning problems, especially problems formulated as Markov decision processes (MDPs) (Sutton and Barto, 1998). The agent of reinforcement learning repeats three steps until terminated at each episode in the learning process.

1. The agent observes current *state* s from the *environment*, contained in state space $\mathcal{S}$.
2. Next, it determines and executes next *action* a according to current policy π. Action a is contained in the action space limited by the current state: $\mathcal{A}(s)$, which is a subset of whole action space $\mathcal{A} = \bigcup_{s \in S} \mathcal{A}(s)$. Policy π is the strategy for selecting action, represented as a conditional distribution of actions: $p(a|s)$.
3. It then observes next state s' and receives *reward* r from the environment.

The aim of reinforcement learning is to find optimal policy π^* only with information on sample trajectories and to reward the experienced agent.

We describe how to adapt the extractive approach to the problem of reinforcement learning in the sections that follow.

4.2 State

A state denotes a summary. We represent state s as a tuple of summary S (a set of textual units) and additional state variables: $s = (S, A, f)$. We assume s has the history of actions A that the agent executed to achieve this state. Additionally, s has the binary state variable, $f \in \{0, 1\}$, which denotes whether s is a terminal state or not. Initial state s_0 is $(\emptyset, \emptyset, 0)$.

We assume the d-dimensional feature representation of state s: $\phi(s) \in \mathbb{R}^d$, which only depends on the feature of summary $\phi'(S) \in \mathbb{R}^{d-1}$. Given $\phi'(S)$, we define the features as:

$$\phi(s) = \begin{cases} (\phi'(S), 0)^{\mathrm{T}} & (L(S) \leq K) \\ (\mathbf{0}, 1)^{\mathrm{T}} & (K < L(S)) \end{cases}. \tag{2}$$

This definition denotes that summaries that violate the length limitation are shrunk to a single feature, $(\mathbf{0}, 1)^{\mathrm{T}}$, which means it is not a summary.

Note the features of the state only depend on the features of the summary, not on the executed actions to achieve the state. Unlike naive search methods, this property has the potential for different states to be represented as the same vector, which has the same features. The agent, however, should search as many possible states as it can. Therefore, the generalization function of the feature representation is of utmost importance. The accurate selection of features contributes to reducing the search space and provides efficient learning as will be discussed later.

4.3 Action

An action denotes a transition operation that produces a new state from a current state. We assumed all actions were deterministic in this study. We define $\mathbf{insert}_i (1 \leq i \leq n)$ actions, each of which inserts textual unit x_i to the current state unless the state is terminated, as described in the following diagram:

$$\begin{matrix} s_t & a_t & s_{t+1} \\ \begin{pmatrix} S_t \\ A_t \\ 0 \end{pmatrix} & \xrightarrow{\textbf{insert}_i} & \begin{pmatrix} S_t \cup \{x_i\} \\ A_t \cup \{\textbf{insert}_i\} \\ 0 \end{pmatrix} \end{matrix}. \quad (3)$$

In addition to insertion actions, we define **finish** that terminates the current episode in reinforcement learning:

$$\begin{matrix} s_t & a_t & s_{t+1} \\ \begin{pmatrix} S_t \\ A_t \\ 0 \end{pmatrix} & \xrightarrow{\textbf{finish}} & \begin{pmatrix} S_t \\ A_t \cup \{\textbf{finish}\} \\ 1 \end{pmatrix} \end{matrix} \quad (4)$$

Note that $f_t = 1$ means state s_t is a terminal state.

Then, the whole action set, $\mathcal{A}$, is defined by $\textbf{insert}_i$ and **finish**:

$$\mathcal{A} = \{\textbf{insert}_1, \textbf{insert}_2, \cdots, \textbf{insert}_n, \textbf{finish}\}. \quad (5)$$

We can calculate the available actions limited by state s_t:

$$\mathcal{A}(s_t) = \begin{cases} \mathcal{A} \backslash A_t & (L(S_t) \leq K) \\ \{\textbf{finish}\} & (K < L(S_t)) \end{cases}. \quad (6)$$

This definition means that the agent may execute one of the actions that have not yet been executed in this episode, and it has no choice but to finish if the summary of the current state already violates length limitations.

4.4 Reward

The agent receives a reward from the environment as some kind of criterion of how good the action the agent executed was. If the current state is s_t, the agent executes a_t, and the state makes a transition into s_{t+1}; then, the agent receives the reward, r_{t+1}:

$$r_{t+1} = \begin{cases} score(S_t) & (a_t = \textbf{finish}, L(S_t) \leq K) \\ -R_{penalty} & (a_t = \textbf{finish}, K < L(S_t)) \\ 0 & \text{(otherwise)} \end{cases}, \quad (7)$$

where $R_{penalty} > 0$.

The agent can receive the score awarded by the given score function if and only if the executed action is **finish** and the summary length is appropriate. If the summary length is inappropriate but the executed action is **finish**, the environment awards a penalty to the agent. The most important point of this definition is that the agent receives nothing under the condition where the next state is not terminated. In this sense, the reward is delayed. Due to this definition, maximizing the expectation of future rewards is equivalent to maximizing the given score function, and we do not need to consider the decomposed form of the score function, i.e., we only need to consider the final score of the whole summary.

4.5 Value Function Approximation

Our aim is to find the optimal policy. This is achieved by obtaining the optimal *state value function*, $V^*(s)$, because if we obtain this, the greedy policy is optimal, which determines the action so as to maximize the state value after the transition occurred. Therefore, our aim is equivalent to finding $V^*(s)$. Let us try to estimate the *state value function* with parameter $\theta \in \mathbb{R}^d$:

$$V(s) = \theta^{\mathrm{T}} \phi(s). \quad (8)$$

We can also represent and estimate the *action value function*, $Q(s, a)$, by using $V(s)$:

$$Q(s, a) = r + \gamma V(s'), \quad (9)$$

where the execution of a causes the state transition from s to s' and the agent receives reward r, and $\gamma (0 \leq \gamma \leq 1)$ is the discount rate. Note that all actions are deterministic in this study.

By using these value functions, we define the policy as the conditional distribution, $p(a|s; \theta, \tau)$, which is parameterized by θ and a temperature parameter τ:

$$p(a|s; \theta, \tau) = \frac{e^{Q(s,a)/\tau}}{\sum_{a'} e^{Q(s,a')/\tau}}. \quad (10)$$

Temperature τ decreases as learning progresses, which causes the policy to be greedier. This softmax selection strategy is called Boltzmann selection.

4.6 Learning Algorithm

The goal of learning is to estimate θ. We use the TD (λ) algorithm with function approximation (Sutton and Barto, 1998). Algorithm 1 represents the whole system of our method, called Automatic Summarization using Reinforcement Learning (ASRL)

Algorithm 1 ASRL

Input: document $D = \{x_1, x_2, \cdots, x_n\}$,
score function $score(S)$

1: initialize $\theta = \mathbf{0}$
2: **for** $k = 1$ **to** N **do**
3: $s \leftarrow (\emptyset, \emptyset, 0)$
// initial state
4: $e = \mathbf{0}$
5: **while** s is not terminated **do**
6: $a \sim p(a|s; \theta, \tau_k)$
// selects action with current policy
7: $(s', r) \leftarrow \text{execute}(s, a)$
// observes next state and receive reward
8: $\delta \leftarrow r + \gamma\theta^{\mathrm{T}}\phi(s') - \theta^{\mathrm{T}}\phi(s)$
// calculates TD-error
9: $e \leftarrow \gamma\lambda e + \phi(s)$
// updates the eligibility trace
10: $\theta \leftarrow \theta + \alpha_k \delta e$
// learning with current learning rate
11: $s \leftarrow s'$
12: **end while**
13: **end for**
14: $s \leftarrow (\emptyset, \emptyset, 0)$
15: **while** s is not terminated **do**
16: $a \leftarrow \max_a Q(s, a)$
// selects action greedily
with the learned policy
17: $(s', r) \leftarrow \text{execute}(s, a)$
18: $s \leftarrow s'$
19: **end while**
20: **return** the summary of s

in this paper. N is the number of learning episodes, and $e(\in \mathbb{R}^d)$ and $\lambda(0 \leq \lambda \leq 1)$ correspond to the eligibility trace and the trace decay parameter. The eligibility trace, e, conveys all information on the features of states that the agent previously experienced, with previously decaying influences of features due to decay parameter λ and discount rate γ (Line 9).

Line 1 initializes parameter θ to start up its learning. The following procedures from Lines 2 to 13 learn θ with the TD (λ) algorithm, by using information on actual interactions with the environment. Learning rate α_k and temperature parameter τ_k decay as the learning episode progresses. The best summary with the obtained policy is calculated in steps from Lines 14 to 19. If the agent can estimate θ properly, greedy output is the optimal solution.

5 Models of Combined Approach for Reinforcement Learning

We formulated the extractive approach as a problem with reinforcement learning in the previous section. In fact, we can also formulate a more general model of summarization, since evaluation only depends on the final state and it is not actually very important to regard the given documents as a set of textual units contained in the original documents.

We explain how to take into account other methods within the ASRL framework by modifying the models in this section, with an example of sentence compression. We assume that we have a method of sentence compression, $comp(x)$, and that a textual unit to be extracted is a sentence. What we have to do is to only simply modify the definitions of the state and action. Note that this is just one example of the combined method. Even other summarization systems can be similarly adapted to ASRL.

5.1 State

We do not want to execute sentence compression twice, so we have to modify the state variables to convey the information: $s = (S, A, c, f)$, where $c \in \{0, 1\}$, and S, A, and f are the same definitions as previously described.

5.2 Action

We add deterministic action **comp** to $\mathcal{A}$, which produces the new summary constructed by compressing the last inserted sentence of the current summary:

$$\overset{s_t}{\begin{pmatrix} S_t \\ A_t \\ 0 \\ 0 \end{pmatrix}} \xrightarrow[]{\textbf{comp}} \overset{s_{t+1}}{\begin{pmatrix} S_t \backslash \{x_c\} \cup \{comp(x_c)\} \\ A_t \cup \{\textbf{comp}\} \\ 1 \\ 0 \end{pmatrix}}, \tag{11}$$

where x_c is the last sentence that is inserted into S_t. Next, we modify $\textbf{insert}_i$ and **finish**:

$$\overset{s_t}{\begin{pmatrix} S_t \\ A_t \\ c_t \\ 0 \end{pmatrix}} \xrightarrow[]{\textbf{insert}_i} \overset{s_{t+1}}{\begin{pmatrix} S_t \cup \{x_i\} \\ A_t \cup \{\textbf{insert}_i\} \\ 0 \\ 0 \end{pmatrix}}, \tag{12}$$

$$\begin{pmatrix} S_t \\ A_t \\ c_t \\ 0 \end{pmatrix}_{s_t} \xrightarrow[a_t]{\textbf{finish}} \begin{pmatrix} S_t \\ A_t \cup \{\textbf{finish}\} \\ c_t \\ 1 \end{pmatrix}_{s_{t+1}}. \quad (13)$$

Note $\mathbf{comp} \in A(s_t)$ may be executed if and only if $c_t = 0$. $\mathbf{insert}_i$ resets c to 0.

6 Experiments

We conducted three experiments in this study. First, we evaluated our method with ROUGE metrics (Lin, 2004), in terms of ROUGE-1, ROUGE-2, and ROUGE-L. Second, we conducted an experiment on measuring the optimization capabilities of ASRL, with the scores we obtained and the execution time. Third, we evaluated ASRL taking into consideration sentence compression by using a very naive method, in terms of ROUGE-1, ROUGE-2, and ROUGE-3.

6.1 Experimental Settings

We used sentences as textual units for the extractive approach in this research. Each sentence and document were represented as a bag-of-words vector with *tf*idf* values, with stopwords removed. All tokens were stemmed by using Porter's stemmer (Porter, 1980).

We experimented with our proposed method on the dataset of DUC2004 task2. This is a multi-document summarization task that contains 50 document clusters, each of which has 10 documents. We set up the length limitation to 665 bytes, used in the evaluation of DUC2004.

We set up the parameters of ASRL where the number of episodes $N = 300$, the training rate $\alpha_k = 0.001 \cdot 101/(100 + k^{1.1})$, and the temperature $\tau_k = 1.0 \cdot 0.987^{k-1}$ where k was the number of episodes that decayed as learning progressed. Both discount rate γ and trace decay parameter λ were fixed to 1 for episodic tasks. The penalty, $R_{penalty}$, was fixed to 1.

We used the following score function in this study:

$$score(S) = \sum_{x_i \in S} \lambda_s Rel(x_i) - \sum_{x_i, x_j \in S, i<j} (1 - \lambda_s) Red(x_i, x_j), \quad (14)$$

where

$$Rel(x_i) = Sim(x_i, D) + Pos(x_i)^{-1} \quad (15)$$
$$Red(x_i, x_j) = Sim(x_i, x_j). \quad (16)$$

λ_s is the parameter for the trade-off between relevance and redundancy, $Sim(x_i, D)$ and $Sim(x_i, x_j)$ correspond to the cosine similarities between sentence x_i and the sentence set of the given original documents D, and between sentence x_i and sentence x_j. $Pos(x_i)$ is the position of the occurrence of x_i when we index sentences in each document from top to bottom with one origin. This score function was determined by reference to McDonald (2007). We set $\lambda_s = 0.9$ in this experiment.

We designed $\phi'(S)$, i.e., the vector representation of a summary, to adapt it to the summarization problem as follows.

- **Coverage of important words**: The elements are the top 100 words in terms of the *tf*idf* of the given document with binary representation.
- **Coverage ratio**: This is calculated by counting up the number of top 100 elements included in the summary.
- **Redundancy ratio**: This is calculated by counting up the number of elements that excessively cover the top 100 elements.
- **Length ratio**: This is the ratio between the length of the summary and length limitation K.
- **Position**: This feature takes into consideration the position of sentence occurrences. It is calculated with $\sum_{x \in S} Pos(x)^{-1}$.

Consequently, $\phi'(S)$ is a 104-dimensional vector.

We executed ASRL 10 times with the settings previously described and used all the results for evaluation.

We used the dataset of DUC2003, which is a similar task that contains 30 document clusters and each cluster had 10 documents, to determine τ_k and λ_s. We determined the parameters so that they would converge properly and become close to the optimal solutions calculated by ILP, under the conditions that the described feature representation and the score function were given.

	ROUGE-1	ROUGE-2	ROUGE-L
ASRL	0.39013	0.09479	0.33769
MCKP	0.39033	0.09613	0.34225
PEER65	0.38279	0.09217	0.33099
ILP	0.34712	0.07528	0.31241
GREEDY	0.30618	0.06400	0.27507

Table 1: Results of ROUGE evaluation compared with other peers in DUC2004. Scores for ILP and GREEDY have statistically significant differences from scores of ASRL.

6.2 Evaluation

We compared ASRL with four other conventional methods.

- **GREEDY**: This method is a simple greedy algorithm, which repeats the selection of the sentence with the highest score of the remaining sentences by using an MMR-like method of scoring as follows:

$$x = \arg\max_{x \in D \setminus S}[\lambda_s Rel(x) - (1-\lambda_s)\max_{x_i \in S} Red(x, x_i)], \quad (17)$$

  where S is the current summary.

- **ILP**: This indicates the method proposed by McDonald (2007) for maximizing the score function (14) with integer linear programming.

- **PEER65**: This is the best performing system in task 2 of the DUC2004 competition in terms of ROUGE-1 proposed by Conroy et al. (2004).

- **MCKP**: This method was proposed by Takamura and Okamura (2009). MCKP defines an automatic summarization problem as a maximum coverage problem with a knapsack constraint, which uses *conceptual units* (Filatova and Hatzivassiloglou, 2004), and composes the meaning of sentences, as textual units and attempts to cover as many units as possible under the knapsack constraint.

7 Results

7.1 Evaluation with ROUGE

We evaluated our method of ASRL with ROUGE, in terms of ROUGE-1, ROUGE-2, and ROUGE-L.

	ROUGE-1	ROUGE-2	ROUGE-L
ASRL.0	0.39274	0.09537	0.34010
ASRL.1	0.39243	0.09683	0.33855
ASRL.2	0.39241	0.09597	0.34070
ASRL.3	0.39190	0.09580	0.33898
ASRL.4	0.39054	0.09579	0.33663
ASRL.5	0.38911	0.09395	0.33551
ASRL.6	0.38866	0.09392	0.33701
ASRL.7	0.38854	0.09338	0.33661
ASRL.8	0.38821	0.09363	0.33833
ASRL.9	0.38532	0.09281	0.33321

Table 2: Results of ROGUE evaluation for each ASRL peer of 10 results in DUC2004. ASRL did not converge with stable solution with these experimental settings because of property of randomness.

The experimental results are summarized in Tables 1 and 2. Table 1 lists the results for the comparison and Table 2 lists all the results for ASRL peers.

The results imply ASRL is superior to PEER65, ILP, and GREEDY, and comparable to MCKP with these experimental settings in terms of ROUGE metrics. Note that ASRL is a kind of approximate method, because actions are selected probabilistically and the method of reinforcement learning occasionally converges with some sub-optimal solution. This can be expected from Table 2, which indicates the results vary although each ASRL solution converged with some solution. However, in this experiment, ASRL achieved higher ROUGE scores than ILP, which achieved optimal solutions. This seems to have been caused by the properties of the features, which we will discuss later. It seems this feature representation is useful for efficiently searching the feature space. The method of mapping a state to features is, however, approximate in the sense that some states will shrink to the same feature vector, and ASRL therefore has no tendency to converge with some stable solution.

7.2 Evaluation of Optimization Capabilities

Since we proposed our method as an approach to approximate optimization, there was the possibility of convergence with some sub-optimal solution as previously discussed. We also evaluated our approach from the point of view of the obtained scores and the execution time to confirm whether our method had

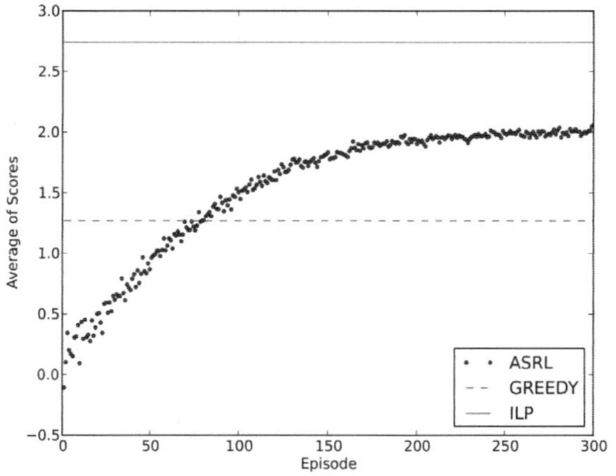

Figure 1: Average score for each episode in ASRL in DUC2004. Horizontal lines indicate scores of summaries obtained with ILP and GREEDY.

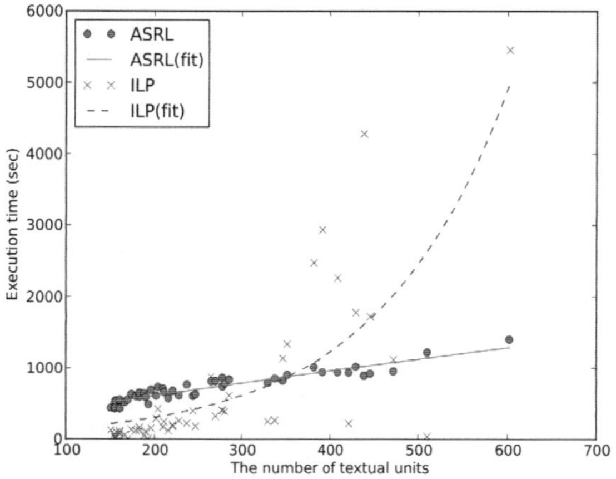

Figure 2: Execution time on number of textual units for each problem in DUC2004. Plot of ASRL is fitted to linear function and that of ILP is fitted to exponential function.

optimization capabilities.

The experimental results are plotted in Figures 1 and 2. Figure 1 plots the average for the rewards (i.e., scores) that the agent obtained for each episode. The horizontal line for ILP is the average for the optimal scores of (14). The score in ASRL increases as the number of episodes increases, and overtakes the score of GREEDY at some episode. The agent attempts to come close to the optimal score line of ILP but seems to fail, and finally converges to some local optimal solution. We should increase the number of episodes, adjust parameters α and τ, and select more appropriate features for the state to improve the optimization capabilities of ASRL.

Figure 2 plots the execution time for each peer. The horizontal axis is the number of textual units, i.e., the number of sentences in this experiment. The vertical axis is the execution time taken by the task. The plots of ASRL and ILP fit a linear function for the former and an exponential function for the latter. The experimental results indicate that while the execution time for ILP tends to increase exponentially, that for ASRL increases linearly. The time complexity of ASRL is linear with respect to the number of actions because the agent has to select the next action from the available actions for each episode, whose time complexity is naively $O(|\mathcal{A}|)$. As $\mathbf{insert}_i$ actions are dominant in the extractive approach, the execution time increases linearly with respect to the number of textual units. However, ILP has to take into account the combinations of textual units, whose number increases exponentially.

In conclusion, both the experimental results indicate that ASRL efficiently calculated a summary that was sub-optimal, but that was of relatively high-quality in terms of ROUGE metrics, with the experimental settings we used.

7.3 Evaluation of Effects of Sentence Compression

We also evaluated the combined approach with sentence compression. We evaluated the method described in Section 5 called ASRLC in this experiment for the sake of convenience. We used a very naive method of sentence compression for this experiment, which compressed a sentence to only important words, i.e., selecting word order by using the *tf*idf* score to compress the length to about half. This method of compression did not take into consideration either readability or linguistic quality. Note we wanted to confirm what effect the other methods would have, and we expected this to improve the ROUGE-1 score. We used the ROUGE-3 score in this evaluation instead of ROUGE-L, to confirm whether naive sentence compression occurred.

The experimental results are summarized in Ta-

	ROUGE-1	ROUGE-2	ROUGE-3
ASRL	0.39013	0.09479	0.03435
ASRLC	0.39141	0.09259	0.03239

Table 3: Evaluation of combined methods.

ble 3, which indicates ROUGE-1 increases but ROUGE-2 and ROUGE-3 decrease as expected. The variations, however, are small. This phenomenon was reported by Lin (2003) in that the effectiveness of sentence compression by local optimization at the sentence level was insufficient. Therefore, we would have to consider the range of applications with the combined method.

8 Discussion

8.1 Local Optimality of ASRL

We will discuss why ASRL seems to converge with some "good" local optimum with the described experimental settings in this section.

Since our model of the state value function was simply linear and our parameter estimation was implemented by TD (λ), which is a simple method in RL, it seems simply employing more efficient or state-of-the-art reinforcement learning methods may improve the performance of ASRL, such as GTD and GTD2 (Sutton et al., 2009b; Sutton et al., 2009a). These methods basically only contribute to faster convergence, and the score that they will converge to might not differ significantly. As a result, it would not matter much which method was used for optimization.

The main point of this problem is modeling the feature representation of states, and this causes sub-optimality. The vector representation of states shrinks the different states to a single representation, i.e., the agent regards states whose features are similar to be similar states. Due to this property, the policy of reinforcement learning is learned to maximize *the expected score* of each feature vector, which includes many states. Such sub-optimality *averagely balanced* by the feature representation raises the possibility of achieving states that have a high-quality summary with a low score, since we do not have a genuine score function.

Thus, the most important thing in our method is to intentionally design the features of states and the score function, so that the agent can generalize states, while taking into consideration truly-essential features for the required summarization. It would be useful if the forms of features and the score function could be arbitrarily designed by the user because there is the capability of obtaining a high-quality summaries.

8.2 Potential of Combined Method

Other useful methods, even other summarization systems, can easily be adapted to ASRL as was described in Section 5. The experimental results revealed that sentence compression has some effect. In fact, all operations that produce a new summary from an old summary can be used, i.e., even other summarizing methods can be employed for an action. We assumed a general combined method may have a great deal of potential to enhance the quality of summaries.

8.3 Can We Obtain "a Global Policy"?

We formulated each summarization task as a reinforcement learning task in this paper, i.e., where each learned policy differs. As this may be a little unnatural, we wanted to obtain a single learned policy, i.e., a global policy.

However, we assessed that we cannot achieve a global policy with these feature and score function settings because the best vector, which is the feature representation of the summary that achieves an optimal score under the current settings, seems to vary for each cluster, even if the domain of the clusters is the same (e.g., a news domain). Having said that, we simultaneously surmised that we could obtain a global policy if we could obtain a highly general, crucial, and efficient feature representation of a summary. We also think a global policy is essential in terms of reinforcement learning and we intend to attempt to achieve this in future work.

9 Conclusion

We presented a new approach to the problem of automatic text summarization called ASRL in this paper, which models the process of constructing a summary with the framework of reinforcement learning and attempts to optimize the given score function with the given feature representation.

The experimental results demonstrated ASRL tends to converge sub-optimally, and excessively depends on the formulation of features and the score function. Although it is difficult, we believe this formulation would enable us to improve the quality of summaries by designing them freely.

We intend to employ the ROUGE score as the score function in future work, and obtain the parameters of the state value function. Using these results, we will attempt to obtain a single learned policy by employing the ROUGE score or human evaluations as rewards. We also intend to consider efficient features and a score to achieve stable convergence. In addition, we plan to use other methods of function approximation, such as RBF networks.

References

J.M. Conroy, J.D. Schlesinger, J. Goldstein, and D.P. O ′ leary. 2004. Left-brain/right-brain multi-document summarization. In *Proceedings of the Document Understanding Conference (DUC 2004)*.

E. Filatova and V. Hatzivassiloglou. 2004. A formal model for information selection in multi-sentence text extraction. In *Proceedings of the 20th international conference on Computational Linguistics*, page 397. Association for Computational Linguistics.

J. Goldstein, V. Mittal, J. Carbonell, and M. Kantrowitz. 2000. Multi-document summarization by sentence extraction. In *Proceedings of the 2000 NAACL-ANLPWorkshop on Automatic summarization-Volume 4*, pages 40–48. Association for Computational Linguistics.

C.Y. Lin. 2003. Improving summarization performance by sentence compression: a pilot study. In *Proceedings of the sixth international workshop on Information retrieval with Asian languages-Volume 11*, pages 1–8. Association for Computational Linguistics.

C.Y. Lin. 2004. Rouge: A package for automatic evaluation of summaries. In *Proceedings of the workshop on text summarization branches out (WAS 2004)*, volume 16.

I. Mani. 2001. *Automatic summarization*, volume 3. John Benjamins Pub Co.

R. McDonald. 2007. A study of global inference algorithms in multi-document summarization. *Advances in Information Retrieval*, pages 557–564.

MF Porter. 1980. An algorithm for suffix stripping. *Program: electronic library and information systems*, 14(3):130–137.

R.S. Sutton and A.G. Barto. 1998. *Reinforcement learning: An introduction*, volume 1. Cambridge Univ Press.

R.S. Sutton, H.R. Maei, D. Precup, S. Bhatnagar, D. Silver, C. Szepesvári, and E. Wiewiora. 2009a. Fast gradient-descent methods for temporal-difference learning with linear function approximation. In *Proceedings of the 26th Annual International Conference on Machine Learning*, pages 993–1000. ACM.

R.S. Sutton, C. Szepesvári, and H.R. Maei. 2009b. A convergent o (n) algorithm for off-policy temporal-difference learning with linear function approximation.

H. Takamura and M. Okumura. 2009. Text summarization model based on maximum coverage problem and its variant. In *Proceedings of the 12th Conference of the European Chapter of the Association for Computational Linguistics*, pages 781–789. Association for Computational Linguistics.

Large Scale Decipherment for Out-of-Domain Machine Translation

Qing Dou and Kevin Knight
Information Sciences Institute
Department of Computer Science
University of Southern California
{qdou,knight}@isi.edu

Abstract

We apply slice sampling to Bayesian decipherment and use our new decipherment framework to improve out-of-domain machine translation. Compared with the state of the art algorithm, our approach is highly scalable and produces better results, which allows us to decipher ciphertext with billions of tokens and hundreds of thousands of word types with high accuracy. We decipher a large amount of monolingual data to improve out-of-domain translation and achieve significant gains of up to 3.8 BLEU points.

1 Introduction

Nowadays, state of the art statistical machine translation (SMT) systems are built using large amounts of bilingual parallel corpora. Those corpora are used to estimate probabilities of word-to-word translation, word sequences rearrangement, and even syntactic transformation. Unfortunately, as parallel corpora are expensive and not available for every domain, performance of SMT systems drops significantly when translating out-of-domain texts (Callison-Burch et al., 2008).

In general, it is easier to obtain in-domain monolingual corpora. Is it possible to use domain specific monolingual data to improve an MT system trained on parallel texts from a different domain? Some researchers have attempted to do this by adding a domain specific dictionary (Wu et al., 2008), or mining unseen words (Daumé and Jagarlamudi, 2011) using one of several translation lexicon induction techniques (Haghighi et al., 2008; Koehn and Knight, 2002; Rapp, 1995). However, a dictionary is not always available, and it is difficult to assign probabilities to a translation lexicon.

(Ravi and Knight, 2011b) have shown that one can use decipherment to learn a full translation model from non-parallel data. Their approach is able to find translations, and assign probabilities to them. But their work also has certain limitations. First of all, the corpus they use to build the translation system has a very small vocabulary. Secondly, although their algorithm is able to handle word substitution ciphers with limited vocabulary, its deciphering accuracy is low.

The contributions of this work are:

- We improve previous decipherment work by introducing a more efficient sampling algorithm. In experiments, our new method improves deciphering accuracy from 82.5% to 88.1% on (Ravi and Knight, 2011b)'s domain specific data set. Furthermore, we also solve a very large word substitution cipher built from the English Gigaword corpus and achieve 92.2% deciphering accuracy on news text.

- With the ability to handle a much larger vocabulary, we learn a domain specific translation table from a large amount of monolingual data and use the translation table to improve out-of-domain machine translation. In experiments, we observe significant gains of up to 3.8 BLEU points. Unlike previous works, the translation table we build from monolingual data do not only contain unseen words but also words seen in parallel data.

2 Word Substitution Ciphers

Before we present our new decipherment framework, we quickly review word substitution decipherment.

Recently, there has been an increasing interest in decipherment work (Ravi and Knight, 2011a; Ravi and Knight, 2008). While letter substitution ciphers can be solved easily, nobody has been able to solve a word substitution cipher with high accuracy.

As shown in Figure 1, a word substitution cipher is generated by replacing each word in a natural language (plaintext) sequence with a cipher token according to a substitution table. The mapping in the table is deterministic – each plaintext word type is only encoded with one unique cipher token. Solving a word substitution cipher means recovering the original plaintext from the ciphertext without knowing the substitution table. The only thing we rely on is knowledge about the underlying language.

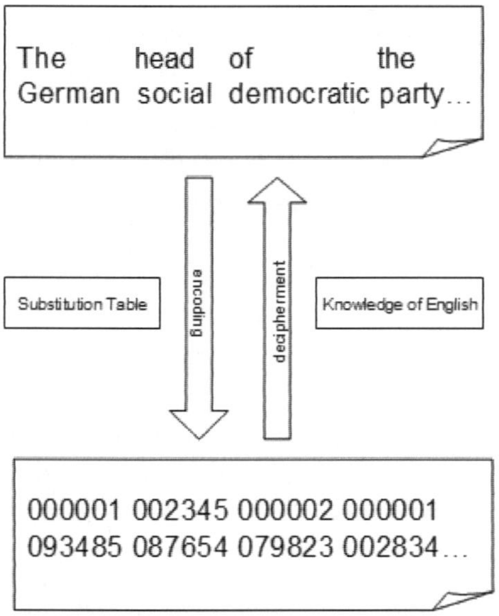

Figure 1: Encoding and Decipherment of a Word Substitution Cipher

How can we solve a word substitution cipher? The approach is similar to those taken by cryptanalysts who try to recover keys that convert encrypted texts to readable texts. Suppose we observe a large cipher string f and want to decipher it into English e. We can follow the work in (Ravi and Knight, 2011b) and assume that the cipher string f is generated in the following way:

- Generate English plaintext sequence $e = e_1, e_2 ... e_n$ with probability P(e).
- Replace each English plaintext token e_i with a cipher token f_i with probability $P(f_i|e_i)$.

Based on the above generative story, we write the probability of the cipher string f as:

$$P(f)_\theta = \sum_e P(e) \cdot \prod_i^n P_\theta(f_i|e_i) \qquad (1)$$

We use this equation as an objective function for maximum likelihood training. In the equation, $P(e)$ is given by an ngram language model, which is trained using a large amount of monolingual texts. The rest of the task is to manipulate channel probabilities $P_\theta(f_i|e_i)$ so that the probability of the observed texts $P(f)_\theta$ is maximized.

Theoretically, we can directly apply EM, as proposed in (Knight et al., 2006), or Bayesian decipherment (Ravi and Knight, 2011a) to solve the problem. However, unlike letter substitution ciphers, word substitution ciphers pose much greater challenges to algorithm scalability. To solve a word substitution cipher, the EM algorithm has a computational complexity of $O(N \cdot V^2 \cdot R)$ and the complexity of Bayesian method is $O(N \cdot V \cdot R)$, where V is the size of plaintext vocabulary, N is the length of ciphertext, and R is the number of iterations. In the world of word substitution ciphers, both V and N are very large, making these approaches impractical. (Ravi and Knight, 2011b) propose several modifications to the existing algorithms. However, the modified algorithms are only an approximation of the original algorithms and produce poor deciphering accuracy, and they are still unable to handle very large scale ciphers.

To address the above problems, we propose the following two new improvements to previous decipherment methods.

- We apply slice sampling (Neal, 2000) to scale up to ciphers with a very large vocabulary.
- Instead of deciphering using the original ciphertext, we break the ciphertext into bigrams, collect their counts, and use the bigrams with their counts for decipherment.

The new improvements allow us to solve a word substitution cipher with billions of tokens and hundreds of thousands of word types. Through better approximation, we achieve a significant increase in deciphering accuracy. In the following section, we present details of our new approach.

3 Slice Sampling for Bayesian Decipherment

In this section, we first give an introduction to Bayesian decipherment and then describe how to use slice sampling for it.

3.1 Bayesian Decipherment

Bayesian inference has been widely used in natural language processing (Goldwater and Griffiths, 2007; Blunsom et al., 2009; Ravi and Knight, 2011b). It is very attractive for problems like word substitution ciphers for the following reasons. First, there are no memory bottlenecks as compared to EM, which has an $O(N \cdot V^2)$ space complexity. Second, priors encourage the model to learn a sparse distribution.

The inference is usually performed using Gibbs sampling. For decipherment, a Gibbs sampler keeps drawing samples from plaintext sequences according to derivation probability $P(d)$:

$$P(d) = P(e) \cdot \prod_{i}^{n} P(c_i|e_i) \quad (2)$$

In Bayesian inference, $P(e)$ is still given by an ngram language model, while the channel probability is modeled by the Chinese Restaurant Process (CRP):

$$P(c_i|e_i) = \frac{\alpha \cdot prior + count(c_i, e_i)}{\alpha + count(e_i)} \quad (3)$$

Where $prior$ is the base distribution (we set prior to $\frac{1}{C}$ in all our experiments, where C is the number of word types in ciphertext), and count, also called "cache", records events that occurred in the history. Each sampling operation involves changing a plaintext token e_i, which has V possible choices, where V is the plaintext vocabulary size, and the final sample is chosen with probability $\frac{P(d)}{\sum_{n=1}^{V} P(d)}$.

3.2 Slice Sampling

With Gibbs sampling, one has to evaluate all possible plaintext word types (10k—1M) for each sample decision. This become intractable when the vocabulary is large and the ciphertext is long. Slice sampling (Neal, 2000) can solve this problem by automatically adjusting the number of samples to be considered for each sampling operation.

Suppose the derivation probability for current sample is $P(current\_s)$. Then slice sampling draws a sample in two steps:

- Select a threshold T uniformly from the range $\{0, P(current\_s)\}$.
- Draw a new sample new_s uniformly from a pool of candidates: $\{new\_s|P(new\_s) > T\}$.

From the above two steps, we can see that given a threshold T, we only need to consider those samples whose probability is higher than the threshold. This will lead to a significant reduction on the number of samples to be considered, if probabilities of the most samples are below T. In practice, the first step is easy to implement, while it is difficult to make the second step efficient. An obvious way to collect candidate samples is to go over all possible samples and record those with probabilities higher than T. However, doing this will not save any time. Fortunately, for Bayesian decipherment, we are able to complete the second step efficiently.

According to Equation 1, the probability of the current sample is given by a language model $P(e)$ and a channel model $P(c|e)$. The language model is usually an ngram language model. Suppose our current sample $current\_s$ contains English tokens X, Y, and Z at position $i-1$, i, and $i+1$ respectively. Let c_i be the cipher token at position i. To obtain a new sample, we just need to change token Y to Y'. Since the rest of the sample stays the same, we only need to calculate the probability of any trigram [1]: $P(XY'Z)$ and the channel model probability: $P(c_i|Y')$, and multiply them together as shown in Equation 4.

$$P(XY'Z) \cdot P(c_i|Y') \quad (4)$$

[1]The probability is given by a bigram language model.

In slice sampling, each sampling operation has two steps. For the first step, we choose a threshold T uniformly between 0 and $P(XYZ) \cdot P(c_i|Y)$. For the second step, there are two cases.

First, we notice that two types of Y' are more likely to pass the threshold T: (1) Those that have a very high trigram probability , and (2) those that have high channel model probability. To find candidates that have high trigram probability, we build sorted lists ranked by $P(XY'Z)$, which can be precomputed off-line. We only keep the top K English words for each of the sorted list. When the last item Y_K in the list satisfies $P(XY_kZ) \cdot prior < T$, We draw a sample in the following way: set $A = \{Y'|P(XY'Z) \cdot prior > T\}$ and set $B = \{Y'|count(c_i, Y') > 0\}$, then we only need to sample Y' uniformly from $A \cup B$ until Equation 4 is greater than T. [2]

Second, what happens when the last item Y_K in the list does not satisfy $P(XY_kZ) \cdot prior < T$? Then we always choose a word Y' randomly and accept it as a new sample if Equation 4 is greater than T.

Our algorithm alternates between the two cases. The actual number of choices the algorithm looks at depends on the K and the total number of possible choices. In different experiments, we find that when $K = 500$, the algorithm only looks at 0.06% of all possible choices. When $K = 2000$, this further reduces to 0.007%.

3.3 Deciphering with Bigrams

Since we can decipher with a bigram language model, we posit that a frequency list of ciphertext bigrams may contain enough information for decipherment. In our letter substitution experiments, we find that breaking ciphertext into bigrams doesn't hurt decipherment accuracy. Table 1 shows how full English sentences in the original data are broken into bigrams and their counts.

man they took our land .	took	our	2
they took our arable land .	they	took	2
	land	.	2
	man	they	1
	arable	land	1

Table 1: Converting full sentences to bigrams

Instead of doing sampling on full sentences, we treat each bigram as a full "sentence". There are two advantages to use bigrams and their counts for decipherment.

First of all, the bigrams and counts are a much more compact representation of the original ciphertext with full sentences. For instance, after breaking a billion tokens from the English Gigaword corpus, we find only 29m bigrams and 58m tokens, which is only 1/17 of the original text. In practice, we further discard all bigrams with low frequency, which makes the ciphertext even shorter.

Secondly, using bigrams significantly reduces the number of sorted lists (from $|V|^2$ to $2|V|$) mentioned in the previous section. The number of lists reduces from $|V|^2$ to $2|V|$ because words in a bigram only have one neighbor. Therefore, for any word W in a bigram, we need only $2|V|$ lists ("words to the right of W" and "words to the left of W") instead of $|V|^2$ lists ("pairs of words that surround W").

3.4 Iterative Sampling

Although we can directly apply slice sampling on a large number of bigrams, we find that gradually including less frequent bigrams into a sampling process saves deciphering time – we call this iterative sampling:

- Break the ciphertext into bigrams and collect their counts
- Keep bigrams whose counts are greater than a threshold α. Then initialize the first sample randomly and use slice sampling to perform maximum likelihood training. In the end, extract a translation table T according to the final sample.
- Lower the threshold α to include more bigrams into the sampling process. Initialize the first sample using the translation table obtained from the previous sampling run (for each ci-

[2] It is easy to prove that all other candidates that are not in the sorted list and with $count(c_i, Y') = 0$ have a upper bound probability: $P(XY_kZ) \cdot prior$. Therefore, they are ignored when $P(XY_kZ) \cdot prior < T$.

pher token f, choose a plaintext token e whose $P(c|f)$ is the largest). Perform sampling again.

- Repeat until $\alpha = 1$.

3.5 Parallel Sampling

Inspired by (Newman et al., 2009), our parallel sampling procedure is described below:

- Collect bigrams and their counts from ciphertext and split the bigrams into N parts.
- Run slice sampling on each part for 5 iterations independently.
- Combine counts from each part to form a new count table and run sampling again on each part using the new table.[3]

4 Decipherment Experiments

In this section, we evaluate our new sampling algorithm in two different experiments. In the first experiment, we compare our method with (Ravi and Knight, 2011b) on their data set to prove correctness of our approach. In the second experiment, we scale up to the whole English Gigaword corpus and achieve a much higher deciphering accuracy.

4.1 Deciphering Transtac Corpus

4.1.1 Data

We split the Transtac corpus the same way it was split in (Ravi and Knight, 2011b). The data used to create ciphertext consists of 1 million tokens, and 3397 word types. The data for language model training contains 2.7 million tokens and 25761 word types.[4] The ciphertext is created by replacing each English word with a cipher word.

We use a bigram language model for decipherment training. When the training terminates, a translation table with probability $P(c|e)$ is built based on the counts collected from the final sample. For decoding, we employ a trigram language model using full sentences. We use Moses (Koehn et al., 2007) to perform the decoding. We set the distortion limit to 0 and cube the translation probabilities. Essentially, Moses tries to find an English sequence e that maximizes $P(e) \cdot P(c|e)^3$

Method	Deciphering Accuracy
Ravi and Knight	80.0 (with bigram LM)
	82.5 (with trigram LM)
Slice Sampling	88.1 (with bigram LM)

Table 2: Decipherment Accuracy on Transtac Corpus from (Ravi and Knight, 2011b)

Gold	Decoded
man i've come to file a complaint against some people .	man i've come to hand a telephone lines some people .
man they took our land .	man they took our farm .
they took our arable land .	they took our slide door .
okay man .	okay man .
eighty donums .	miflih donums .

Table 3: Sample Decoding Results on Transtac Corpus from (Ravi and Knight, 2011b)

4.1.2 Results

We evaluate the performance of our algorithm by decipherment accuracy, which measures the percentage of correctly deciphered cipher tokens. Table 2 compares the deciphering accuracy with the state of the art algorithm.

Results show that our algorithm improves the deciphering accuracy to 88.1%, which amounts to 33% reduction in error rate. This justifies our claim: doing better approximation using slice sampling improves decipherment accuracy.

Table 3 shows the first 5 decoding results and compares them with the gold plaintext. From the table we can see that the algorithm recovered the majority of the plaintext correctly.

4.2 Deciphering Gigaword Corpus

To prove the scalability of our new approach, we apply it to solve a much larger word substitution cipher built from English Gigaword corpus. The corpus contains news articles from different news agencies

[3]Except for combining the counts to form a new count table, other parameters remain the same. For instance, each part i has its own prior set to $\frac{1}{C_i}$, where C_i is the number of word types in that part of ciphertext.

[4]In practice, we replaced singletons with a "UNK" symbol, leaving around 16904 word types.

and has a much larger vocabulary compared with the Transtac corpus.

4.2.1 Data

We split the corpus into two parts chronologically. Each part contains approximately 1.2 billion tokens. We uses the first part to build a word substitution cipher, which is 10k times longer than the one in the previous experiment, and the second part to build a bigram language model. [5]

4.2.2 Results

We first use a single machine and apply iterative sampling to solve a 68 million token cipher. Then we use the result from the first step to initialize our parallel sampling process, which uses as many as 100 machines. For evaluation, we calculate deciphering accuracy over the first 1000 sentences (33k tokens).

After 2000 iterations of the parallel sampling process, the deciphering accuracy reaches 92.2%. Figure 2 shows the learning curve of the algorithm. It can be seen from the graph that both token and type accuracy increase as more and more data becomes available.

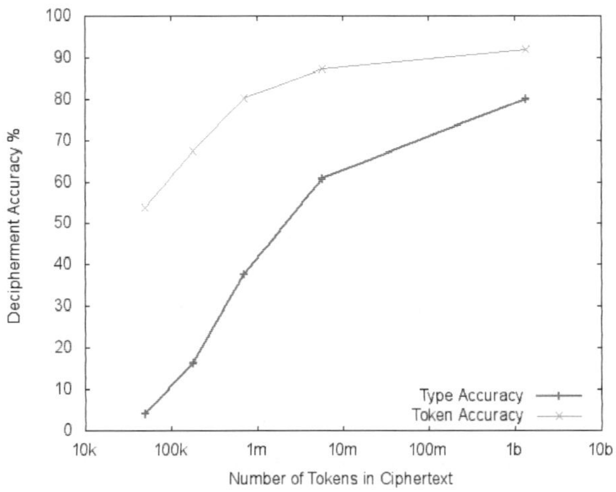

Figure 2: Learning curve for a very large word substitution cipher: Both token and type accuracy rise as more and more ciphertext becomes available.

[5]Before building the language model, we replace low frequency word types with an "UNK" symbol, leaving 129k unique word types.

5 Improving Out-of-Domain Machine Translation

Domain specific machine translation (MT) is a challenge for statistical machine translation (SMT) systems trained on parallel corpora. It is common to see a significant drop in translation quality when translating out-of-domain texts. Although it is hard to find parallel corpora for any specific domain, it is relatively easy to find domain specific monolingual corpora. In this section, we show how to use our new decipherment framework to learn a domain specific translation table and use it to improve out-of-domain translations.

5.1 Baseline SMT System

We build a state of the art phrase-based SMT system using Moses (Koehn et al., 2007). The baseline system has 3 models: a translation model, a reordering model, and a language model. The language model can be trained on monolingual data, and the rest are trained on parallel data. By default, Moses uses the following 8 features to score a candidate translation:

- direct and inverse translation probabilities
- direct and inverse lexical weighting
- phrase penalty
- a language model
- a re-ordering model
- word penalty

Each of the 8 features has its own weight, which can be tuned on a held-out set using minimum error rate training. (Och, 2003). In the following sections, we describe how to use decipherment to learn domain specific translation probabilities, and use the new features to improve the baseline.

5.2 Learning a New Translation Table with Decipherment

From a decipherment perspective, machine translation is a much more complex task than solving a word substitution cipher and poses three major challenges:

- Mappings between languages are nondeterministic, as words can have multiple translations

- Re-ordering of words
- Insertion and deletion of words

Fortunately, our decipherment model does not assume deterministic mapping and is able to discover multiple translations. For the reordering problem, we treat Spanish as a simple word substitution for French. Despite the simplification in the assumption, we still expect to learn a useful word-to-word lexicon via decipherment and use the lexicon to improve our baseline.

Problem formulation: By ignoring word reorderings, we can formulate MT decipherment problem as word substitution decipherment. We view source language f as ciphertext and target language e as plaintext. Our goal is to decipher f into e and estimate translation probabilities based on the decipherment.

Probabilistic decipherment: Similar to solving a word substitution cipher, all we have to do here is to estimate the translation model parameters $P_\theta(f|e)$ using a large amount of monolingual data in f and e respectively. According to Equation 5, our objective is to estimate the model parameters so that the probability of source text P(f) is maximized.

$$\arg\max_{\theta} \sum_{e} P(e) \cdot \prod_{i}^{n} P_\theta(f_i|e_i) \tag{5}$$

Building a translation table: Once the sampling process completes, we estimate translation probability $P(f|e)$ from the final sample using maximum likelihood estimation. We also decipher from the reverse direction to estimate $P(e|f)$. Finally, we build a phrase table by taking translation pairs seen in both decipherments.

5.3 Combining Phrase Tables

We now have two phrase tables: one learnt from parallel corpus and one learnt from non-parallel monolingual corpus through decipherment. The phrase table learnt through decipherment only contains word to word translations, and each translation option only has two scores. Moses has a function to decode with multiple phrase tables, so we just need to add the newly learnt phrase table and specify two more weights for the scores in it. During decoding, if a source word only appears in the decipherment table, that table's translation will be used. If a source word exists in both tables, Moses will create two separate decoding paths and choose the best one after taking other features into account. If a word is not seen in either of the tables, it is copied literally to the output.

Train	French: 28.5 million tokens Spanish: 26.6 million tokens
Tune	French: 28k tokens Spanish: 26k tokens
Test	French: 30k tokens Spanish: 28k tokens

Table 4: Europarl Training, Tuning, and Testing Data

6 MT Experiments and Results

6.1 Data

In our MT experiments, we translate French into Spanish and use the following corpora to learn our translation systems:

- Europarl Corpus (Koehn, 2005): The Europarl parallel corpus is extracted from the proceedings of the European Parliament and includes versions in 11 European languages. The corpus contains articles from the political domain and is used to train our baseline system. We use the 6th version of the corpus. After cleaning, there are 1.3 million lines left for training. We use the last 2k lines for tuning and testing (1k for each), and the rest for training. Details of training, tuning, and testing data are listed in Table 4.

- EMEA Corpus (Tiedemann, 2009): EMEA is a parallel corpus made out of PDF documents from the European Medicines Agency. It contains articles from the medical domain, which is a good test bed for out-of-domain tasks. We use the first 2k pairs of sentences for tuning and testing (1k for each), and use the rest (1.1 million lines) for decipherment training. We split the training corpus in ways that no parallel sentences are included in the training set. The splitting methods are listed in Table 5.

For decipherment training, we use lexical translation tables learned from the Europarl corpus to ini-

Comparable EMEA :
French: Every odd line, 8.7 million tokens
Spanish: Every even line, 8.1 million tokens
Non-parallel EMEA:
French: First 550k sentences, 9.1 million tokens
Spanish: Last 550k sentences, 7.7 million tokens

Table 5: EMEA Decipherment Training Data

French	Spanish	$P(fr\|es)$	$P(es\|fr)$
<	<	0.32	1.00
hépatique	hepático	0.88	0.08
	hepática	0.76	0.85
injectable	inyectable	0.91	0.92
dl	dl	1.00	0.70
>	>	0.32	1.00
ribavirine	ribavirina	0.40	1.00
olanzapine	olanzapina	0.57	1.00
clairance	aclaramiento	0.99	0.64
pelliculéss	recubiertos	1.00	1.00
pharmaco-cinétique	farmaco-cinético	1.00	1.00

Table 7: 10 most frequent OOV words in the table learnt from non-parallel EMEA corpus

tialize our sampling process.

6.2 Results

BLEU (Papineni et al., 2002) is used as a standard evaluation metric. We compare the following 3 systems in our experiments, and present the results in Table 6.

- **Baseline:** Trained on Europarl
- **Decipher-CP:** Trained on Europarl + Comparable EMEA
- **Decipher-NP:** Trained on Europarl + Non-Parallel EMEA

Our baseline system achieves 38.2 BLEU score on Europarl test set. In the second row of Table 6, the test set changes to EMEA, and the baseline BLEU score drops to 24.9. In the third row, the baseline score rises to 30.5 with a language model built from EMEA corpus. Although it is much higher than the previous baseline, we further improve it by including a new phrase table learnt from domain specific monolingual data. In a real out-of-domain task, we are unlikely to have any parallel data to tune weights for the new phrase table. Therefore, we can only set it manually. In experiments, each score in the new phrase table has a weight of 5, and the BLEU score rises up to 33.2. In the fourth row of the table, we assume that there is a small amount of domain specific parallel data for tuning. With better weights, our baseline BLEU score increases to 37.3, and our combined systems increase to 41.1 and 39.7 respectively. In the last row of the table, we compare the combined systems with an even better baseline. This time, the baseline is given half of the EMEA tuning set for training and uses the other half for weight tuning. Results show that our combined systems still outperform the baseline.

The phrase table learnt from monolingual data consists of both observed and unknown words. Table 7 shows the top 10 most frequent OOV words in the table learnt from non-parallel EMEA corpus. Among the 10 words, 9 have correct translations. It is interesting to see that our algorithm finds multiple correct translations for the word "hépatique". The only mistake in the table is sensible as French word "pelliculés" is translated into "recubiertos con película" in Spanish.

7 Conclusion and Future Work

We apply slice sampling to Bayesian Decipherment and show significant improvement in deciphering accuracy compared with the state of the art algorithm. Our method is not only accurate but also highly scalable. In experiments, we decipher at the scale of the English Gigaword corpus, which contains over billions of tokens and hundreds of thousands word types. We further show the value of our new decipherment algorithm by using it to improve out-of-domain translation. In the future, we will work with more language pairs, especially those with significant word re-orderings. Moreover, the monolingual corpora used in the experiments are far smaller than what our algorithm can handle. We will continue to work in scenarios where large amount of monolingual data is readily available.

Train Data	Tune Data	Tune LM	Test Data	Test LM	Baseline	Decipher-CP	Decipher-NP
Europarl	Europarl	Europarl	Europarl	Europarl	38.2		
Europarl	Europarl	Europarl	EMEA	Europarl	24.9		
Europarl	Europarl	Europarl	EMEA	EMEA	30.5	33.2 (+2.7)	32.4 (+1.9)
Europarl	EMEA	EMEA	EMEA	EMEA	37.3	41.1 (+3.8)	39.7 (+2.4)
Europarl + EMEA	EMEA	EMEA	EMEA	EMEA	67.4	68.7 (+1.3)	68.7 (+1.3)

Table 6: MT experiment results: The table shows how much the combined systems outperform the baseline system in different experiments. Each row has a different set of training, tuning, and testing data. Baseline is trained on parallel data only. Tune LM and Test LM specify language models used for tuning and testing respectively. Decipher-CP and Decipher-NP use a phrase table learnt from comparable and non-parallel EMEA corpus respectively.

8 Acknowledgments

This work was supported by NSF Grant 0904684. The authors would like to thank Philip Koehen, David Chiang, Jason Riesa, Ashish Vaswani, and Hui Zhang for their comments and suggestions.

References

Phil Blunsom, Trevor Cohn, Chris Dyer, and Miles Osborne. 2009. A Gibbs sampler for phrasal synchronous grammar induction. In *Proceedings of the Joint Conference of the 47th Annual Meeting of the ACL and the 4th International Joint Conference on Natural Language Processing of the AFNLP*. Association for Computational Linguistics.

Chris Callison-Burch, Cameron Fordyce, Philipp Koehn, Christof Monz, and Josh Schroeder. 2008. Further meta-evaluation of machine translation. In *Proceedings of the Third Workshop on Statistical Machine Translation*. Association for Computational Linguistics.

Hal Daumé, III and Jagadeesh Jagarlamudi. 2011. Domain adaptation for machine translation by mining unseen words. In *Proceedings of the 49th Annual Meeting of the Association for Computational Linguistics: Human Language Technologies*. Association for Computational Linguistics.

Sharon Goldwater and Tom Griffiths. 2007. A fully Bayesian approach to unsupervised part-of-speech tagging. In *Proceedings of the 45th Annual Meeting of the Association of Computational Linguistics*. Association for Computational Linguistics.

Aria Haghighi, Percy Liang, Taylor Berg-Kirkpatrick, and Dan Klein. 2008. Learning bilingual lexicons from monolingual corpora. In *Proceedings of ACL-08: HLT*. Association for Computational Linguistics.

Kevin Knight, Anish Nair, Nishit Rathod, and Kenji Yamada. 2006. Unsupervised analysis for decipherment problems. In *Proceedings of the COLING/ACL 2006 Main Conference Poster Sessions*. Association for Computational Linguistics.

Philipp Koehn and Kevin Knight. 2002. Learning a translation lexicon from monolingual corpora. In *Proceedings of the ACL-02 Workshop on Unsupervised Lexical Acquisition*. Association for Computational Linguistics.

Philipp Koehn, Hieu Hoang, Alexandra Birch, Chris Callison-Burch, Marcello Federico, Nicola Bertoldi, Brooke Cowan, Wade Shen, Christine Moran, Richard Zens, Chris Dyer, Ondřej Bojar, Alexandra Constantin, and Evan Herbst. 2007. Moses: open source toolkit for statistical machine translation. In *Proceedings of the 45th Annual Meeting of the ACL on Interactive Poster and Demonstration Sessions*. Association for Computational Linguistics.

Philipp Koehn. 2005. Europarl: A parallel corpus for statistical machine translation. In *In Proceedings of the Tenth Machine Translation Summit*, Phuket, Thailand. Asia-Pacific Association for Machine Translation.

Radford Neal. 2000. Slice sampling. *Annals of Statistics*, 31.

David Newman, Arthur Asuncion, Padhrai Smyth, and Max Welling. 2009. Distributed algorithms for topic models. *Journal of Machine Learning Research*, 10.

Franz Josef Och. 2003. Minimum error rate training in statistical machine translation. In *Proceedings of the 41st Annual Meeting on Association for Computational Linguistics*. Association for Computational Linguistics.

Kishore Papineni, Salim Roukos, Todd Ward, and Wei-Jing Zhu. 2002. Bleu: a method for automatic evaluation of machine translation. In *Proceedings of the 40th Annual Meeting on Association for Computational Linguistics*. Association for Computational Linguistics.

Reinhard Rapp. 1995. Identifying word translations in non-parallel texts. In *Proceedings of the 33rd annual meeting on Association for Computational Linguistics*. Association for Computational Linguistics.

Sujith Ravi and Kevin Knight. 2008. Attacking decipherment problems optimally with low-order n-gram models. In *Proceedings of the Conference on Empirical Methods in Natural Language Processing*. Association for Computational Linguistics.

Sujith Ravi and Kevin Knight. 2011a. Bayesian inference for Zodiac and other homophonic ciphers. In *Proceedings of the 49th Annual Meeting of the Association for Computational Linguistics: Human Language Technologies*. Association for Computational Linguistics.

Sujith Ravi and Kevin Knight. 2011b. Deciphering foreign language. In *Proceedings of the 49th Annual Meeting of the Association for Computational Linguistics: Human Language Technologies*. Association for Computational Linguistics.

Jörg Tiedemann. 2009. News from OPUS – a collection of multilingual parallel corpora with tools and interfaces. In *Recent Advances in Natural Language Processing V*, volume 309 of *Current Issues in Linguistic Theory*. John Benjamins.

Hua Wu, Haifeng Wang, and Chengqing Zong. 2008. Domain adaptation for statistical machine translation with domain dictionary and monolingual corpora. In *Proceedings of the 22nd International Conference on Computational Linguistics*. Association for Computational Linguistics.

N-gram-based Tense Models for Statistical Machine Translation

Zhengxian Gong[1] **Min Zhang**[2] **Chewlim Tan**[3] **Guodong Zhou**[1*]
[1] School of Computer Science and Technology, Soochow University, Suzhou, China 215006
[2] Human Language Technology, Institute for Infocomm Research, Singapore 138632
[3] School of Computing, National University of Singapore, Singapore 117417
{zhxgong, gdzhou}@suda.edu.cn mzhang@i2r.a-star.edu.sg tancl@comp.nus.edu.sg

Abstract

Tense is a small element to a sentence, however, error tense can raise odd grammars and result in misunderstanding. Recently, tense has drawn attention in many natural language processing applications. However, most of current Statistical Machine Translation (SMT) systems mainly depend on translation model and language model. They never consider and make full use of tense information. In this paper, we propose n-gram-based tense models for SMT and successfully integrate them into a state-of-the-art phrase-based SMT system via two additional features. Experimental results on the NIST Chinese-English translation task show that our proposed tense models are very effective, contributing performance improvement by 0.62 BLUE points over a strong baseline.

1 Introduction

For many NLP applications, such as event extraction and summarization, tense has been regarded as a key factor in providing temporal order. However, tense information has been largely overlooked by current SMT research. Consider the following example:

SRC: 这 项 禁运 是 冷战 的 结果 , 不 能 反映 现在 的 情势 , 更 未 反映 中国 与 欧盟 间 的 伙伴 关系 。

REF:The embargo **is** a result of the Cold War and **does** not reflect the present situation nor the partnership between China and the EU.

MOSES: the embargo **is** the result of the cold war, not reflect the present situation, it **did** not reflect the partnership with the european union.

Although the translated text produced by Moses[1] is understandable, it has very odd tense combination from the grammatical aspect, i.e. with tense inconsistency (*is/does* in REF vs. *is/did* in Moses). Obviously, slight modification, such as changing "is" into "was", can much improve the readability of the translated text. It is also interesting to note that such modification can much affect the evaluation. If we change "did" to "does", the BLEU-4 score increases from 22.65 to 27.86 (as matching the 4-gram "does not reflect the" in REF). However, if we change "is" to "was", the BLEU score decreases from 22.65 to 21.44.

The above example seems special. To testify its impact on SMT in wider range, we design a special experiment based on the 2005 NIST MT data (see section 6.1). This data has 4 references. We choose one reference and modify its sentences with error tense[2]. After that, we use other 3 references to measure this reference. The modified reference leads to a sharp drop in BLEU-4 score, from 52.46 to 50.27 in all. So it is not a random phenomenon that tense can affect translation results.

The key is how to detect tense errors and choose correct tenses during the translation procedure. By carefully comparing the references with Moses output, we obtain the following useful observations,

Observation(1): to most simple sentences, coordinate verbs should be translated with the same tense while they have different tense in Moses output;

Observation(2): to some compound sentences,

*Corresponding author.

[1] http://www.statmt.org/moses/

[2] Such changes are small by mainly modifying one auxiliary verb for a sentence, such as "$is \rightarrow was$", "$has \rightarrow had$".

the subordinate clause should have the consistent tense with its main clause while Moses fails;

Observation(3): the diversity of tense usage in a document is common. However, in most cases, the neighbored sentences tends to share the same main tense. In some extreme examples, one tense (past or present), even dominates the whole document.

One possible solution to model above observations is using rules. Dorr (2002) refers to six basic English tense structures and defines the possible paired combinations of "present, past, future". But the practical cases are very complicated, especially in news domain. There are a lot of complicated sentences in news articles. Our preliminary investigation shows that such six paired combinations can only cover limited real cases in Chinese-English SMT.

This paper proposes a simple yet effective method to model above observations. For each target sentence in the training corpus, we first parse it and extract its tense sequence. Then, a target-side tense n-gram model is constructed. Such model can be used to estimate the rationality of tense combination in a sentence and thus supervise SMT to reduce tense inconsistency errors against **Observations (1)** and **(2)** in the sentence-level. In comparison, **Observation (3)** actually reflects the tense distributions among one document. After extracting each main tense for each sentence, we build another tense n-gram model in the document-level. For clarity, this paper denotes document-level tense as "inter-tense" and sentence-level tense as "intra-tense".

After that, we propose to integrate such tense models into SMT systems in a dynamic way. It is well known there are many errors in the current MT output (David et al., 2006). Unlike previously making trouble with reference texts, the BLEU-4 score cannot be influenced obviously by modifying a small part of abnormal sentences in a static way. In our system, both inter-tense and intra-tense model are integrated into a SMT system via additional features and thus can supervise the decoding procedure. During decoding, once some words with correct tense can be determined, with the help of language model and other related features, the small component–"tense"–can affect surrounding words and improve the performance of the whole sentence. Our experimental results (see the examples in Section 6.4) show the effectiveness of this way.

Rather than the rule-based model, our models are fully statistical-based. So they can be easily scaled up and integrated into either phrase-based or syntax-based SMT systems. In this paper, we employ a strong phrase-based SMT baseline system, as proposed in Gong et al. (2011), which uses document as translation unit, for better incorporating document-level information.

The rest of this paper is organized as follows: Section 2 reviews the related work. Section 3 and 4 are related to tense models. Section 3 describes the preprocessing work for building tense models. Section 4 presents how to build target-side tense models and discuss their characteristics. Section 5 shows our way of integrating such tense models into a SMT system. Session 6 gives the experimental results. Finally, we conclude this paper in Section 7.

2 Related Work

In this section, we focus on related work on integrating the tense information into SMT. Since both inter- and intra-tense models need to analyze and extract tense information, we also give a brief overview on tense prediction (or tagging).

2.1 Tense Prediction

The tense prediction task often needs to build a model based on a large corpus annotated with temporal relations and thus its focus is on how to recognize, interpret and normalize time expressions. As a representative, Lapata and Lascarides (2006) proposed a simple yet effective data-intensive approach. In particular, they trained models on main and subordinate clauses connected with some special temporal marker words, such as "after" and "before", and employed them in temporal inference.

Another typical task is cross-lingual tense predication. Some languages, such as English, are inflectional, whose verbs can express tense via certain stems or suffix, while others, such as Chinese often lack inflectional forms. Take Chinese to English translation as example, if Chinese text contains particle word "了(Le)", the nearest Chinese verb prefers to be translated into English verb with the past tense. Ye and Zhang (2005), Ye et al. (2007) and Liu et al. (2011) focus on labeling the tenses for keywords in source-side language.

Ye and Zhang (2005) first built a small amount of manually-labeled data, which provide the tense mapping from Chinese text to English text. Then, they trained a CRF-based tense classifier to label tense on Chinese documents. Ye et al. (2007) further reported that syntactic features contribute most to the marking of aspectual information. Liu et al. (2011) proposed a parallel mapping method to automatically generate annotated data. In particular, they used English verbs to label tense information for Chinese verbs via a parallel Chinese-English corpus.

It is reasonable to label such source-side verb to supervise the translation process since the tense of English sentence is often determined by verbs. The problem is that due to the diversity of English verb inflection, it is difficult to map such Chinese tense information into the English text. To our best knowledge, although above works attempt to serve for SMT, all of them fail to address how to integrate them into a SMT system.

2.2 Machine Translation with Tense

Dorr (1992) described a two-level knowledge representation model based on Lexical Conceptual Structures (LCS) for machine translation which integrates the aspectual information and the lexical-semantic information. Her system is based on an inter-lingual model and does not belong to a SMT system.

Olsen et al. (2001) relied on LCS to generate appropriately-tensed English translations for Chinese. In particular, they addressed tense reconstruction on a binary taxonomy (present and past) for Chinese text and reported that incorporating lexical aspect features of telicity can obtain a 20% to 35% boost in accuracy on tense realization.

Ye et al. (2006) showed that incorporating latent features into tense classifiers can boost the performance. They reported the tense resolution results based on the best-ranked translation text produced by a SMT system. However, they did not report the variation of translation performance after introducing tense information.

3 Preprocessing for Tense Modeling

In this paper, tense modeling is done on the target-side language. Since our experiments are done on Chinese to English SMT, our tense models are learned only from the English text. In the literature, the taxonomy of English tenses typically includes three basic tenses (i.e. present, past and future) plus their combination with the progressive and perfective aspects. Here, we consider four basic tenses: present, past, future and UNK (unknown) and ignore the aspectual information. Furthermore, we assume that one sentence has only one main tense but maybe has many subordinate tenses.

This section describes the preprocessing work of building tense models, which mainly involves how to extract tense sequence via tense verbs.

3.1 Tense Verbs

Lapata et al.(2006) used syntactic parse trees to find clauses connected with special aspect markers and collected them to train some special classifiers for temporal inference. Inspired by their work, we use the Stanford parser[3] to parse tense sequence for each sentence.

Take the following three typical sentences as examples, (a) is a simple sentence which contains two coordinate verbs, while (b) and (c) are compound sentences and (b) contains a quoted text.

(a) Japan's constitution renounces the right to go to war and prohibits the nation from having military forces except for self-defense.

(b) "We also hope Hong Kong will not be affected by diseases like the severe acute respiratory syndrome again!" , added Ms. Yang.

(c) Cheng said he felt at home in Hong Kong and he sincerely wished Hong Kong more peaceful and more prosperous.

Figure 1 shows the parse tree with Penn Treebank style for each sentence, which has strict level structures and POS tags for all the terminal words. Here, the level structures mainly contribute to extract main tense for each sentence (to be described in Section 3.2) and POS tags are utilized to detect *tense verbs*, i.e. verbs with tense information.

Normally, POS tags in the parse tree can distinguish five different forms of verbs: the base form (tagged as VB), and forms with overt endings D for

[3] http://nlp.stanford.edu/software/lex-parser.shtml

```
(ROOT
 (S
  (NP
   (NP (NNP Japan) (POS 's))
   (NN constitution))
  (VP
   (VP (VBZ renounces)
    (NP (DT the) (NN right)
     (S
      (VP (TO to)
       (VP (VB go)
        (PP (TO to)
         (NP (NN war)))))))))
   (CC and)
   (VP (VBZ prohibits)
    (NP (DT the) (NN nation))
    (PP (IN from)
     (S
      (VP (VBG having)
       (NP (JJ military) (NNS forces))
       (PP (IN except)
        (PP (IN for)
         (NP (NN self-defense)))))))))))
```

(a)

```
(ROOT
 (SINV (`` ``)
  (S
   (NP (PRP We))
   (ADVP (RB also))
   (VP (VBP hope)
    (SBAR
     (S
      (NP (NNP Hong) (NNP Kong))
      (VP (MD will) (RB not)
       (VP (VB be)
        (VP (VBN affected)
         (PP (IN by)
          (NP
           (NP (NNS diseases))
           (PP (IN like)
            (NP (DT the) (JJ severe) (JJ acute) (NN
respiratory) (NN syndrome)))))
         (ADVP (RB again)))))))))
  (. !) ('' '')
  (VP (VBD added))
  (NP (NNP Ms.) (NNP Yang))
   (. .)))
```

(b)

```
(ROOT
 (S
  (S
   (NP (NNP Cheng))
   (VP (VBD said)
    (SBAR
     (S
      (NP (PRP he))
      (VP (VBD felt)
       (PP (IN at) (NP (NN home)))
       (PP (IN in) (NP (NNP Hong) (NNP Kong)))))))))
  (CC and)
  (S
   (NP (PRP he))
   (ADVP (RB sincerely))
   (VP (VBD wished)
    (S
     (S
      (NP (NNP Hong) (NNP Kong))
      (ADJP
       (ADJP (RBR more) (JJ peaceful))
       (CC and)
       (ADJP (RBR more) (JJ prosperous)))))))
  (. .)))
```

(c)

Figure 1: The Stanford parse trees with Penn Treebank style

past tense, G for present participle, N for past participle, and Z for third person singular present. It is worth noting that VB, VBG and VBN cannot determine the specific tenses by themselves. In addition, the verbs with POS tag "MD" need to be specially considered to distinguish future tense from other tenses.

Algorithm 1 illustrates how to determine what tense a node has. If the return value is not "UNK", the node belongs to a *tense verb*.

Algorithm 1 Determine the tense of a node.

Input:
The TreeNode of one parse tree, $leafnode$;
Output:
The tense, $tense$;

$tense = \text{``}UNK''$
Obtaining the POS tag $lpostag$ from $leafnode$;
Obtaining the word $lword$ from $leafnode$;
if ($lpostag$ in [$\text{``}VBP''$, $\text{``}VBZ''$]) **then**
  $tense = \text{``}present''$
else if ($lpostag == \text{``}VBD''$]) **then**
  $tense = \text{``}past''$
else if ($lpostag == \text{``}MD''$]) **then**
  if ($lword$ in [$\text{``}will''$, $\text{``}ll''$, $\text{``}shall''$]) **then**
    $tense = \text{``}future''$
  else if ($lword$ in [$\text{``}would''$, $\text{``}could''$]) **then**
    $tense = \text{``}past''$
  else
    $tense = \text{``}present''$
  end if
end if
return $tense$;

3.2 Tense Extraction Based on Tense Verbs

As described in Section 1, the inter-tense (document-level) refers to the main tense of one sentence and the intra-tense (sentence-level) corresponds to all tense sequence of one sentence. This section introduces how to recognize the main tense and extract all useful tense sequence for each sentence.

The idea of determining the main tense is to find the *tense verb* located in the top level of a parse tree. According to the Penn Treebank style, the method to determine the main tense can be described as follows:

(1) Traverse the parse tree top-down until a tree node containing more than one child is identified, denoted as S_m .

(2) Consider each child of S_m with tag "VP", recursively traverse such "VP" node to find a tense verb. If found, use it as the main tense and return the tense; if not, go to step (3).

(3) Consider each child of S_m with tag "S", which actually corresponds to subordinate clause of this sentence. Starting from the first subordinate clause, apply the similar policy of step (2) to find the tense verb. If not found, search remaining subordinate clauses.

(4) If no tense verb found, return "UNK" as the main tense.

Here, "VP" nodes dominated by S_m **directly** are preferred over those located in subordinate clauses. This is to ensure that the main tense is decided by the top-level tense verb.

Take Figure 1 as an example, the main tense of sentence (a) and (b) can be determined only by step (2). The tense verb of "(VBZ renounces)" dominated in the "VP" tag determines that (a) is in present tense. Similarly the node "(VBD added)" indicates that (b) is in past tense. Sentence (c) needs to be further treated by step (3) since there is no "VP" nodes dominated by S_m directly. The node "(VBD said)" located in the first subordinate clause shows its main tense is "past".

The next task is to extract the tense sequence for each sentence. They are determined by all tense verbs in this sentence according to the strict top-down order. For example, the tense sequence of sentence (a), (b) and (c) are {present, present}, {present, future, past} and {past, past, past}. In order to explore whether the main tense of intra-tense model has an impact on SMT or not, we introduce a special marker "*" to denote the main tense. So the tense sequence marked with main tense of (a), (b) and (c) are {present*, present},{present, future, past*} and {past*, past, past}. It is worth noting, the intra-tense model (see Section 4) based on the latter tense sequence is different to the former.

4 N-gram-based Tense Models

4.1 Tense N-gram Estimation

After applying the previous method to extract tense for an English text corpus, we can obtain a big tense corpus.

Given the current tense is indexed as t_i, we call the previous $n-1$ tenses plus the current tense as tense n-gram.

Based on the tense corpus, tense n-gram statistics can be done according to the Formula 1.

$$P(t_i|t_{(i-(n-1))}, ..., t_{(i-1)}) = \frac{count(t_{(i-(n-1))}, \ldots, t_{(i-1)}, t_i)}{count(t_{(i-(n-1))}, ..., t_{(i-1)})} \quad (1)$$

Here, the function of "count" return the tense n-gram frequency. In order to avoid doing specific smoothing work, we estimate tense n-gram probability using SRI language modeling (SRILM) tool (Stolcke, 2002).

To compute the probability of intra-tense n-gram, we first extract all tense sequence for each sentence and put them into a new file. Based on this new file, we can get the intra-tense n-gram model via SRILM tool.

To compute the probability of inter-tense n-gram, we need to extract the main tense for each sentence at first. Then, for each document, we re-organized the main tenses of all sentences into a special line. After putting all these special lines into a new file, we can use SRILM to obtain the inter-tense n-gram model.

4.2 Characteristic of Tense N-gram Models

We construct n-gram-based tense models on English Gigaword corpus (LDC2003T05). This corpus is used to build language model for most SMT systems. It includes 30221 documents (we remove such files: file size is less than 1K or the number of continuous "UNK" tenses is greater than 5).

Figure 2 shows the unigram and bigram probabilities (**Log10-style**) for intra-tense and inter-tense.

The part (a) and (c) in Figure 2 refer to unigram. The horizontal axis indicts tense type, and the vertical axis shows its probabilities. The parts (a) and (c) also indicate "present" and "past" are two main tense types in news domain.

The part (b) and (d) refer to bigram. The horizontal axis indicts history tense. Each different colorful bar indicts one current tense. The vertical axis shows the transfer possibilities from a history tense to a current tense.

The part (b)[4] reflects transfer possibilities of tense types in one sentence. It also slightly reflects some linguistic information. For example, in one sentence, the probability of co-occurrence of "present → present", "past → past" and "future → present" is more than other combinations, which can be against tense inconsistency errors described in Observation (1) and (2) (see Section 1). However, it seems strange that "present → past" exceeds "present → future". We checked our corpus and found a lot of sentences like this–"the bill has been . . . , he said. ".

The part (d) shows tense type can be switched between two neighbored sentences. However, it shows the strong tendency to use the same tense type for

[4]The co-occurrence of the "UNK" tense and other tense types in one sentence cannot happen, so the "UNK" tense is omitted.

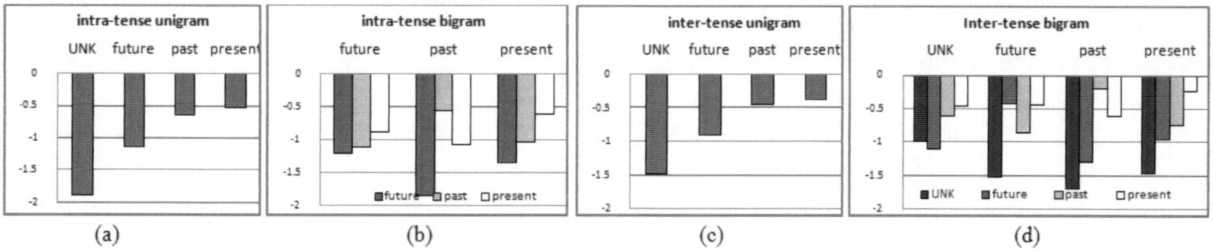

Figure 2: statistics of intra-tense and inter-tense N-gram

neighbored sentences. This statistics conform to the previous **observation (3)** very much.

5 Integrating N-gram-based Tense Models into SMT

In this section, we discuss how to integrate the previous tense models into a SMT system.

5.1 Basic phrase-based SMT system

It is well known that the translation process of SMT can be modeled as obtaining the best translation **e** of the source sentence **f** by maximizing following posterior probability(Brown et al., 1993):

$$\begin{aligned} e_{best} &= \arg\max_{e} P(e|f) \\ &= \arg\max_{e} P(f|e)P_{lm}(e) \end{aligned} \quad (2)$$

where $P(e|f)$ is a translation model and P_{lm} is a language model.

Our baseline is a modified Moses, which follows Koehn et al. (2003) and adopts similar six groups of features. Besides, the log-linear model (Och and Ney, 2000) is employed to linearly interpolate these features for obtaining the best translation according to the formula 3:

$$e_{best} = \arg\max_{e} \sum_{m=1}^{M} \lambda_m h_m(e,f) \quad (3)$$

where $h_m(e,f)$ is a feature function, and λ_m is the weight of $h_m(e,f)$ optimized by a discriminative training method on a held-out development data(Och, 2003).

5.2 The Workflow of Our System

Our system works as follows:

When a hypothesis has covered all source-side words during the decoding procedure, the decoder first obtains tense sequence for such hypothesis and computes intra-tense feature F_s(see Section 5.3). At the same time, it recognizes the main tense of this hypothesis and associate the main tense of previous sentence to compute inter-tense feature F_m (see Section 5.3).

Next, the decoder uses such two additional feature values to re-score this hypothesis automatically and choose one hypothesis with highest score as the final translation.

After translating one sentence, the decoder caches its main tense and pass it to the next sentence. When one document has been processed, the decoder cleans this cache.

In order to successfully implement above workflow, we should firstly design some related features, then resolve another key problem of determining tense (especially main tense) for SMT output. They are described in Section 5.3 and 5.4 respectively.

5.3 Two Additional Features

Although the previous tense models show strong tendency to use the consistent tenses for one sentence or one document, other tense combinations also can be permitted. So we should use such models in a soft and dynamic way. We design two features: inter-tense feature and intra-tense feature. And the weight of each feature is tuned by the MERT script in Moses packages.

Given main tense sequence of one document $t_1, \ldots, t_m$, the inter-tense feature F_m is calculated according to the following formula:

$$F_m = \prod_{i=2}^{m} P(t_i | t_{i-(n-1)}, \ldots, t_{(i-1)}) \quad (4)$$

The $P(\cdot)$ of formula 4 can be estimated by the formula 1. It is worth noting the first sentence of one document often scares tense information since it corresponds to the title at most cases. To the first sentence, the $P(\cdot)$ value is set to $\frac{1}{4}$ (4 tense types).

Given tense sequence of one sentence $s_1, \ldots, s_e$ $(e > 1)$, the intra-tense feature F_s is calculated as follows:

$$F_s = \sqrt[e-1]{\prod_{i=2}^{e} P(s_i | s_{i-(n-1)}, \ldots, s_{(i-1)})} \quad (5)$$

Here the square-root operator is used to avoid punishing translations with long tense sequence. It is worth noting if the sentence only contains one tense, the $P(\cdot)$ value of formula 5 is also set to $\frac{1}{4}$.

Since the average length of intra-tense sequence is about 2.5, we mainly consider intra-tense bigram model and thus n equals to 2. [5]

5.4 Determining Tense For SMT Output

The current SMT systems often produce odd translations partly because of abnormal word ordering and uncompleted text etc. For these abnormal translated texts, the syntactic parser cannot work well in our initial experiments, so the previous method to parse main tense and tense sequence of regular texts cannot be applied here too.

Fortunately, the solely utilization of Stanford POS tagger for our SMT output is not bad although it has the same issues described in Och et al. (2002). The reason may be that phrase-based SMT contains short contexts that POS tagger can utilize while the syntax parser fails.

Once obtaining a completed hypothesis, the decoder will pass it to the Stanford POS tagger and according to *tense verbs* to get all tense sequence for this hypothesis. However, since the POS tagger can not return the information about level structures, the decoder cannot recognize the main tense from such tense sequence.

Liu et al. (2011) once used target-side verbs to label tense of source-side verbs. It is natural to consider whether Chinese verbs can provide similar clues in an opposite direction.

Since Chinese verbs have good correlation with English verbs (described in section 6.2), we obtain

```
(IP
 (NP (NR 中国))
 (VP
 (VP (NP (NT 今天))
   (VP (VV 公布) (AS 了)
    (NP (CP (IP (VP
         (NP (NT 去年))
         (VP (VV 打击)
          (NP (NN 走私)))))
      (DEC 的))
     (NP (NN 成果)))))
 (PU 。))
```

Source-side parse tree

```
(ROOT
 (S
  (NP (NNP Today) (NNP China))
  (VP
   (VP (VBD announced)
    (NP
     (NP
      (NP (JJ last) (NN year) (POS 's))
      (NNS results))
     (PP (IN of)
      (NP
       (NP (DT the) (NN crackdown))
       (PP (IN on)
        (NP (NN smuggling)))))))
  (. .)))
```

Target-side parse tree

Figure 3: trees for parallel sentences

main tense for SMT output according to such *tense verb*, which corresponds to the "VV"(Chinese POS labels are different to English ones, "VV" refers to Chinese verb) node in the top level of the source-side parse tree. Take Figure 3 as an example, the English node "(VBD announced)" is a *tense verb* which can tell the main tense for this English sentence. The Chinese verb "(VV公布)" in the top-level of the Chinese parse tree is just the corresponding part for this English verb.

So, before translating one sentence, the decoder first parses it and records the location of one Chinese "VV" node which located in the top-level, denotes this location as S_{area}.

Once a completed hypothesis is generated, according to the phrase alignment information, the decoder can map S_{area} into the English location T_{area} and obtain the main tense according to the POS tags in T_{area} .

If T_{area} does not contain *tense verb*, such as the verb POS tags in the list of {VB, VBN, VBG}, which cannot tell tense type by themselves, our system permits to find main tense in the left/right 3 words neighbored to T_{area}. And the proportion that the top-level verb of Chinese has a verb correspondence in English can reach to 83% in this way.

6 Experimentation

6.1 Experimental Setting for SMT

In our experiment, SRI language modeling toolkit was used to train a 5-Gram general language model on the Xinhua portion of the Gigaword corpus. Word alignment was performed on the training parallel corpus using GIZA++ (Och and Ney, 2000) in two directions. For evaluation, the NIST

[5] In our experiment, the intra-tense bigram model can obtain the comparable performance to the trigram model. And the inter-tense trigram model can not exceed the bigram one.

BLEU script (version 13) with the default setting is used to calculate the BLEU score (Papineni et al., 2002), which measures case-insensitive matching of 4-grams. To see whether an improvement is statistically significant, we also conduct significance tests using the paired bootstrap approach (Koehn, 2004). In this paper, "***" and "**" denote p-values equal to 0.05, and bigger than 0.05, which mean significantly better, moderately better respectively.

Corpus		Sentences	Documents
Role	Name		
Train	FBIS	228455	10000
Dev	NIST2003	919	100
Test	NIST2005	1082	100

Table 1: Corpus statistics

We use FBIS as the training data, the 2003 NIST MT evaluation test data as the development data, and the 2005 NIST MT test data as the test data. Table 1 shows the statistics of these data sets (with document boundaries annotated).

6.2 The Correlation of Chinese Verbs and English Verbs

In this section, an additional experiment is designed to show English Verbs have close correspondence with Chinese Verbs.

We use the Stanford POS tagger to tag the Chinese and English sentences in our training corpus respectively at first. Then we utilize Giza++ to build alignment for these special Word-POS pairs. According to the alignment results, we find the corresponding relation for some special POS tags in two languages.

Chinese Verb POS	English POS		Number
VV	Verb POS	VBD	89830
		VBP	27276
		VBZ	32588
		MD	40378
		VBG	86025
		VBN	75019
		VB	153596
		In sum:	504712
	Other Non-Verb		149318
Verb Corresponding Ratio			0.77169

Table 2: The Chinese and English Verb Pos Alignment

The "Number" column of Table 2 shows the numbers of Chinese words with "VV" tag corresponding to English words with different verb POS tags. We found Chinese verbs have more than 77% possibilities to align to English verbs in total. However, our method will fail when some special Chinese sentences only contain noun predicates.

6.3 Experimental Results

All the experiment results are showed on the table 3. Our Baseline is a modified Moses. The major modification is input and output module in order to translate using document as unit. The performance of our baseline exceeds the baseline reported by Gong et al. (2011) about 2 percent based on the similar training and test corpus.

System	BLEU Dev(%)	BLEU on Test(%) BLEU	NIST
Moses_Md(Baseline)	29.21	28.30	8.4528
Baseline+F_m	30.56	28.87(***)	8.7935
Baseline+F_s	31.28	28.61(**)	8.5645
Baseline+$F_s(*)$	31.04	28.74(**)	8.6271
Baseline+F_m+F_s	31.75	28.88(***)	8.7987
Baseline+F_m+F_s(*)	31.42	28.92(***)	8.8201

Table 3: The performance of using different feature combinations

The system denoted as "Baseline+F_m" integrates the inter-tense feature. The performance boosts 0.57(***) in BLEU score.

The system denoted as "Baseline+F_s" integrates the intra-tense feature into the baseline. The improvement is less than the inter-tense model, only 0.31(**). It seems the tenses in one sentence has more flexible formats than the document-level ones. It is worth noting, this method can gain higher performance on the develop data than the one of "Baseline+F_m" while fail to improve the test data. Maybe the related weight is tuned over-fit.

The system denoted as "Baseline+F_s(*)" is slightly different from "Baseline+F_s". This experiment is to check whether the main tense has an impact on intra-tense model or not (see Section 3.2). Here, the intra-tense model based on the tense sequence with main tense marker is slightly different to the model showed in Figure 2. The results are slightly better than the previous system by 0.13.

Finally, we use the two features together (Baseline+F_m+F_s). The best way improved the performance by 0.62(***) in BLEU score over our baseline.

6.4 Discussion

Table 4 shows special examples whose intra-tenses are changed in our proposed system. The example 1 and 2 show such modification can improve the BLEU score but the example 3 obtains negative impact. From these examples, we can see not only tense verbs have changed but also their surrounding words have subtle variation.

No.	BLEU	Translation sentence
1	8.64	Baseline: the gulf countries , the bahraini royal family members by the military career of part of the banned to their marriage stories like children , **have** become the theme of television films .
	19.71	Ours: the gulf country **is** a member of the bahraini royal family , a risk by military career **risks** part of the banned to their marriage like children , **has** become a story of the television and film industry .
2	17.16	Baseline:economists **said** that the sharp appreciation of the euro , in the recent investigation **continues** to have an impact on economic confidence , it **is** estimated that the economy is expected to rebound to pick up .
	24.25	Ours: economists **said** that the sharp appreciation of the euro , in the recent investigation **continued** to have an impact on economic confidence and therefore no reason to predict the economy expected to pick up a rebound .
3	73.03	Baseline: the middle east news agency **said** that , after the concerns of all parties concerned in the middle east peace process , israel and palestine , egypt , the united states , russia and several european countries **will** hold a meeting in washington .
	72.95	Ours: the middle east news agency **said** that after the concerns of all parties in the middle east peace process , israel and palestine , egypt , the united states , russia and several european countries **held** a meeting in washington .

Table 4: Examples with tense variation using intra-tense model

From the results showed on Table 3, the document-level tense model seems more effective than the sentence-level one. We manually choose and analyzed 5 documents with significant improvement in the test data. The part (a) of Figure 4 shows the main tense distributions of one reference. The main tense distributions for the baseline and our proposed system are showed in the part (b) and (c) respectively. These documents have different numbers of sentences but all less than 10. The vertical axis indicates different tense: 1 to "past", 2 to "present", 3 to "future" and 4 to "UNK". It is obvious that our system has closer distributions to the ones of this reference.

The examples in Table 5 indicate the joint impact of inter-tense and intra-tense model on SMT. Sentence 1) and 2) are two neighbored sentences in one document. Both the reference and our output tend to use the same main tense type, but the former is in "past" tense and the latter is in "present" tense. The baseline cannot show such tendency. Although our main tense is different to the reference one, the consistent tenses in document level bring better translation results than the baseline. And the tenses in sentence level also show better consistency than the baseline.

Src:
1)以色列 屯民 则 封锁 一 条 主要 道路 , 抗议 屯垦区 遭 迫击炮 攻击 。
2)巴勒斯坦 解放 组织 领袖 阿巴斯 也 获准 前往 约旦河 西岸 城镇 伯利恒 , 这 是 过去 四 年 来 以色列 当局 首 次 准许 巴勒斯坦 重要 领导 人物 参加 耶诞节 庆典 。
Ref:
1)Israeli settlers **blockaded** a major road to protest a mortar attack on the settlement area.
2)PLO leader Abbas **had** also been allowed to go to the West Bank town of Bethlehem , which **is** the first time in the past four years Israeli authorities **have** allowed a senior Palestinian leader to attend Christmas celebrations.
Baseline:
1)israel **has** imposed a main road to protest by mortars attack .
2)the palestinian leader also **visited** the west bank cities and towns to bethlehem , which in the past four years , the israeli authorities **allowed** the palestinian leading figures attended the ceremony .
Ours:
1)israel **has** imposed a main road to protest against the mortars attack .
2)leader of the palestinian liberation organization **have** also been allowed to go to the west bank towns , bethlehem in the past four years . this **is** the first time the israeli authorities **allow** palestinian leading figures attended the ceremony .

Table 5: the joint impact of inter- tense and intra-tense models on SMT

7 Conclusion

This paper explores document-level SMT from the tense perspective. In particular, we focus on how to build document-level and sentence-level tense models and how to integrate such models into a popular SMT system.

Compared with the inter-tense model which greatly improves the performance of SMT, the intra-tense model needs to be further explored. The reasons are many folds, e.g. the failure to exclude quoted texts when modeling intra-tense, since tenses in quoted texts behave much diversely from normal texts. In the future work, we will focus on modeling intra-tense variation according to specific sentence types and using more features to improve it.

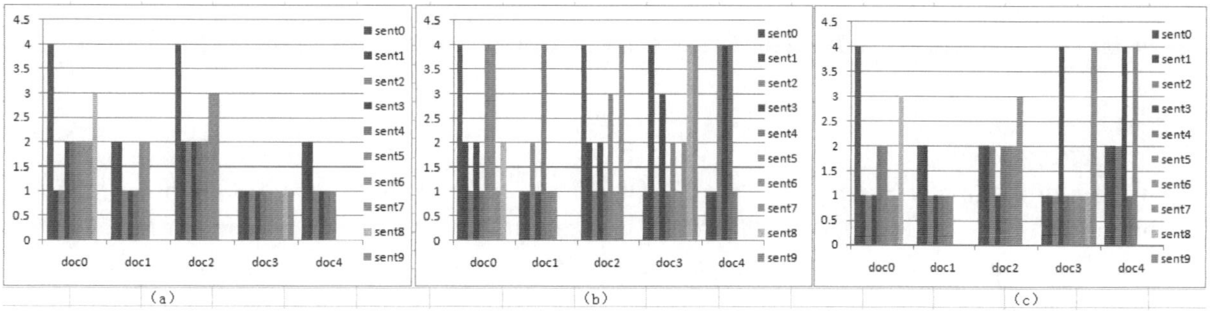

Figure 4: the comparison of the inter-tense distributions for reference, baseline and our proposed system

Acknowledgments

This research is supported by part by NUS FRC Grant R252-000-452-112, the National Natural Science Foundation of China under grant No.90920004 and 61003155, the National High Technology Research and Development Program of China (863 Program) under grant No.2012AA011102.

References

P.F. Brown, S.A. Della Pietra, V.J. Della Pietra and R.L. Mercer. 1992. The Mathematics of Statistical Machine Translation: Parameter Estimation. *Computational Linguistics*, 19(2):263-311.

Vilar David, Jia Xu, DȞaro L. F., and Hermann Ney. 2006. Error Analysis of Machine Translation Output. In *Proceedings of the 5th International Conference on Language Resources and Evaluation*, pages 697-702, Genoa, Italy.

Bonnie J. Dorr. 1992. A parameterized approach to integrating aspect with lexical-semantics for machine translation. In *Proceedings of of ACL-2002*, pages 257-264.

Bonnie J. Dorr and Terry Gaasterland. 2002. Constraints on the Generation of Tense, Aspect, and Connecting Words from Temporal Expressions. Technical Reports from UMIACS.

Zhengxian Gong, Min Zhang and Guodong Zhou. 2011. Cached-based Document-level Statistical Machine Translation. In *Proceedings of the 2011 Conference on Empirical Methods in Natural Language Processing*, pages 909-919.

Philipp Koehn, Franz Josef Och ,and DanielMarcu. 2003. Statistical Phrase-Based Translation. In *Proceedings of NAACL-2003*, pages 48-54.

Philipp Koehn. 2004. Statistical Significance Tests for Machine Translation Evaluation. In *Proceedings of the 2004 Conference on Empirical Methods in Natural Language Processing*, pages 388-395.

Mirella Lapata, Alex Lascarides. 2006. Learning Sentence-internal Temporal Relations. *Journal of Artificial Intelligence Research*, 27:85-117.

Feifan Liu, Fei Liu and Yang Liu. 2011. Learning from Chinese-English Parallel Data for Chinese Tense Prediction. In *Proceedings of IJCNLP-2011*, pages 1116-1124,Chiang Mai, Thailand.

Franz Josef Och and Hermann Ney. 2000. Improved Statistical Alignment Models. In *Proceedings of of ACL-2000*, pages 440-447.

Franz Josef Och, Daniel Gildea, Sanjeev Khudanpur, et.al. 2002. A smorgasbord of Features for Statistical Machine Translation. In *Proceedings of NAACL-2004*, pages 440-447.

Franz Josef Och. 2003. Minimum Error Rate Training in Statistical Machine Translation. In *Proceedings of ACL-2003*,pages 160-167, Sapporo, Japan,July.

Mari Olsen, David Traum,Carol Van Ess-Dykema and Amy Weinberg. 2001. Implicit Cues for Explicit Generation: Using Telicity as a Cue for Tense Structure in a Chinese to English MT System. In *Proceedings of MT Summit VIII*, Santiago de Compostella, Spain.

Kishore Papineni, Salim Roukos, Todd Ward, and Weijing Zhu. 2002. BLEU: A Method for Automatic Evaluation of Machine Translation. In *Proceedings of ACL-2002*, pages 311-318.

Andreas Stolcke. 2002. SRILM-an extensible language modeling toolkit. In *Proceedings of the International Conference on Spoken Language Processing*,pages 901-904.

Yang Ye and Zhu Zhang. 2005. Tense tagging for verbs in cross-lingual context: A case study. In *Proceedings of IJCNLP-2005*, pages 885-895.

Yang Ye, V.li Fossum, Steven Abney. 2006. Latent features in Temporal Reference Translation. *Fifth SIGHAN Workshop on Chinese Language Processing*, pages 48-55.

Yang Ye, Karl-Michael Schnelder, Steven Abney. 2007. Aspect Marker Generation in English-to-Chinese Machine Translation. *Proceedings of MT Summit XI*, pages 521-527,Copenhagen, Denmark.

Source Language Adaptation for Resource-Poor Machine Translation

Pidong Wang
Department of Computer Science
National University of Singapore
13 Computing Drive
Singapore 117417
wangpd@comp.nus.edu.sg

Preslav Nakov
QCRI
Qatar Foundation
Tornado Tower, P.O. 5825
Doha, Qatar
pnakov@qf.org.qa

Hwee Tou Ng
Department of Computer Science
National University of Singapore
13 Computing Drive
Singapore 117417
nght@comp.nus.edu.sg

Abstract

We propose a novel, language-independent approach for improving machine translation from a resource-poor language to X by *adapting* a large bi-text for a related resource-rich language and X (the same target language). We assume a small bi-text for the resource-poor language to X pair, which we use to learn word-level and phrase-level paraphrases and cross-lingual morphological variants between the resource-rich and the resource-poor language; we then adapt the former to get closer to the latter. Our experiments for Indonesian/Malay–English translation show that using the large adapted resource-rich bi-text yields 6.7 BLEU points of improvement over the unadapted one and 2.6 BLEU points over the original small bi-text. Moreover, combining the small bi-text with the adapted bi-text outperforms the corresponding combinations with the unadapted bi-text by 1.5–3 BLEU points. We also demonstrate applicability to other languages and domains.

1 Introduction

Statistical machine translation (SMT) systems learn how to translate from large sentence-aligned bilingual corpora of human-generated translations, called *bi-texts*. Unfortunately, collecting sufficiently large, high-quality bi-texts is hard, and thus most of the 6,500+ world languages remain resource-poor. Fortunately, many of these resource-poor languages are related to some resource-rich language, with whom they overlap in vocabulary and share cognates, which offers opportunities for bi-text reuse.

Example pairs of such resource rich–poor languages include Spanish–Catalan, Finnish–Estonian, Swedish–Norwegian, Russian–Ukrainian, Irish–Gaelic Scottish, Standard German–Swiss German, Modern Standard Arabic–Dialectical Arabic (e.g., Gulf, Egyptian), Turkish–Azerbaijani, etc.

Previous work has already demonstrated the benefits of using a bi-text for a related resource-rich language to X (e.g., X=English) to improve machine translation from a resource-poor language to X (Nakov and Ng, 2009; Nakov and Ng, 2012). Here we take a different, orthogonal approach: we *adapt* the resource-rich language to get closer to the resource-poor one.

We assume a small bi-text for the resource-poor language, which we use to learn word-level and phrase-level paraphrases and cross-lingual morphological variants between the two languages. Assuming translation into the same target language X, we adapt (the source side of) a large training bi-text for a related resource-rich language and X.

Training on the adapted large bi-text yields very significant improvements in translation quality compared to both (a) training on the unadapted version, and (b) training on the small bi-text for the resource-poor language. We further achieve very sizable improvements when combining the small bi-text with the large adapted bi-text, compared to combining the former with the unadapted bi-text.

While we focus on adapting Malay to look like Indonesian in our experiments, we also demonstrate the applicability of our approach to another language pair, Bulgarian–Macedonian, which is also from a different domain.

2 Related Work

One relevant line of research is on machine translation between closely related languages, which is arguably simpler than general SMT, and thus can be handled using word-for-word translation, manual language-specific rules that take care of the necessary morphological and syntactic transformations, or character-level translation/transliteration. This has been tried for a number of language pairs including Czech–Slovak (Hajič et al., 2000), Turkish–Crimean Tatar (Altintas and Cicekli, 2002), Irish–Scottish Gaelic (Scannell, 2006), and Bulgarian–Macedonian (Nakov and Tiedemann, 2012). In contrast, we have a different objective – we do not carry out full translation but rather adaptation since our ultimate goal is to translate into a third language X.

A special case of this same line of research is the translation between dialects of the same language, e.g., between Cantonese and Mandarin (Zhang, 1998), or between a dialect of a language and a standard version of that language, e.g., between some Arabic dialect (e.g., Egyptian) and Modern Standard Arabic (Bakr et al., 2008; Sawaf, 2010; Salloum and Habash, 2011). Here again, manual rules and/or language-specific tools are typically used. In the case of Arabic dialects, a further complication arises by the informal status of the dialects, which are not standardized and not used in formal contexts but rather only in informal online communities[1] such as social networks, chats, Twitter and SMS messages. This causes further mismatch in domain and genre.

Thus, translating from Arabic dialects to Modern Standard Arabic requires, among other things, normalizing informal text to a formal form. In fact, this is a more general problem, which arises with informal sources like SMS messages and Tweets for just any language (Aw et al., 2006; Han and Baldwin, 2011). Here the main focus is on coping with spelling errors, abbreviations, and slang, which are typically addressed using string edit distance, while also taking pronunciation into account. This is different from our task, where we try to adapt good, formal text from one language into another.

A second relevant line of research is on language adaptation and normalization, when done specifically for improving SMT into another language.

For example, Marujo et al. (2011) described a rule-based system for adapting Brazilian Portuguese (BP) to European Portuguese (EP), which they used to adapt BP–English bi-texts to EP–English. They report small improvements in BLEU for EP–English translation when training on the adapted "EP"–En bi-text compared to using the unadapted BP–En (38.55 vs. 38.29), or when an EP–English bi-text is used in addition to the adapted/unadapted one (41.07 vs. 40.91 BLEU). Unlike this work, which heavily relied on language-specific rules, our approach is statistical, and largely language-independent; moreover, our improvements are much more sizable.

A third relevant line of research is on reusing bi-texts between related languages without or with very little adaptation, which works well for very closely related languages. For example, our previous work (Nakov and Ng, 2009; Nakov and Ng, 2012) experimented with various techniques for combining a small bi-text for a resource-poor language (Indonesian or Spanish, pretending that Spanish is resource-poor) with a much larger bi-text for a related resource-rich language (Malay or Portuguese); the target language of all bi-texts was English. However, our previous work did not attempt language adaptation, except for very simple transliteration for Portuguese–Spanish that ignored context entirely; since it could not substitute one word for a completely different word, it did not help much for Malay–Indonesian, which use unified spelling. Still, once we have language-adapted the large bi-text, it makes sense to try to combine it further with the small bi-text; thus, below we will directly compare and combine these two approaches.

Another alternative, which we do not explore in this work, is to use cascaded translation using a pivot language (Utiyama and Isahara, 2007; Cohn and Lapata, 2007; Wu and Wang, 2009). Unfortunately, using the resource-rich language as a pivot (poor→rich→X) would require an additional parallel poor–rich bi-text, which we do not have. Pivoting over the target X (rich→X→poor) for the purpose of language adaptation, on the other hand, would miss the opportunity to exploit the relationship between the resource-poor and the resource-rich language; this would also be circular since the first step would ask an SMT system to translate its own training data (we only have one rich–X bi-text).

[1] The Egyptian Wikipedia is one notable exception.

3 Malay and Indonesian

Malay and Indonesian are closely related, mutually intelligible Austronesian languages with 180 million speakers combined. They have a unified spelling, with occasional differences, e.g., *kerana* vs. *karena* ('because'), *Inggeris* vs. *Inggris* ('English'), and *wang* vs. *uang* ('money').

They differ more substantially in vocabulary, mostly because of loan words, where Malay typically follows the English pronunciation, while Indonesian tends to follow Dutch, e.g., *televisyen* vs. *televisi*, *Julai* vs. *Juli*, and *Jordan* vs. *Yordania*.

While there are many cognates between the two languages, there are also a lot of false friends, e.g., *polisi* means *policy* in Malay but *police* in Indonesian. There are also many partial cognates, e.g., *nanti* means both *will* (future tense marker) and *later* in Malay but only *later* in Indonesian.

Thus, fluent Malay and fluent Indonesian can differ substantially. Consider, for example, Article 1 of the *Universal Declaration of Human Rights*:[2]

- *Semua manusia dilahirkan bebas dan samarata dari segi kemuliaan dan hak-hak. Mereka mempunyai pemikiran dan perasaan hati dan hendaklah bertindak di antara satu sama lain dengan semangat persaudaraan.* (**Malay**)
- *Semua orang dilahirkan merdeka dan mempunyai martabat dan hak-hak yang sama. Mereka dikaruniai akal dan hati nurani dan hendaknya bergaul satu sama lain dalam semangat persaudaraan.* (**Indonesian**)

There is only 50% overlap at the word level, but the actual vocabulary overlap is much higher, e.g., there is only one word in the Malay text that does not exist in Indonesian: *samarata* ('equal'). Other differences are due to the use of different morphological forms, e.g., *hendaklah* vs. *hendaknya* ('conscience'), derivational variants of *hendak* ('want').

Of course, word choice in translation is often a matter of taste. Thus, we asked a native speaker of Indonesian to adapt the Malay version to Indonesian while preserving as many words as possible:

- *Semua manusia dilahirkan bebas dan mempunyai martabat dan hak-hak yang sama. Mereka mempunyai pemikiran dan perasaan dan hendaklah bergaul satu sama lain dalam semangat persaudaraan.* (**Indonesian**)

Obtaining this latter version from the original Malay text requires three word-level operations: (1) deletion of *dari*, *segi*, (2) insertion of *yang*, *sama*, and (3) substitution of *samarata* with *mempunyai*.

Unfortunately, we do not have parallel Malay-Indonesian text, which complicates the process of learning when to apply these operations. Thus, below we restrict our attention to the simplest and most common operation of word substitution only, leaving the other two[3] operations for future work.

Note that word substitution is enough in many cases, e.g., it is all that is needed for the following Malay-Indonesian sentence pair:[4]

- *KDNK Malaysia dijangka cecah 8 peratus pada tahun 2010.*
- *PDB Malaysia akan mencapai 8 persen pada tahun 2010.*

4 Method

We improve machine translation from a resource-poor language (Indonesian) to English by *adapting* a bi-text for a related resource-rich language (Malay) and English, using *word-level* and *phrase-level* paraphrases and cross-lingual morphological variants.

4.1 Word-Level Paraphrasing

Given a Malay sentence, we generate a confusion network containing multiple Indonesian word-level paraphrase options for each Malay word. Each such Indonesian option is associated with a corresponding weight in the network, which is defined as the probability of this option being a translation of the original Malay word (see Eq. 1 below). We decode this confusion network using a large Indonesian language model, thus generating a ranked list of n corresponding adapted "Indonesian" sentences.

Then, we pair each such adapted "Indonesian" sentence with the English counter-part for the Malay sentence it was derived from, thus obtaining a synthetic "Indonesian"–English bi-text. Finally, we combine this synthetic bi-text with the original Indonesian–English one to train the final Indonesian–English SMT system.

Below we first describe how we generate word-level Indonesian options and corresponding weights for the Malay words. Then, we explain how we build, decode, and improve the confusion network.

[2]English: *All human beings are born free and equal in dignity and rights. They are endowed with reason and conscience and should act towards one another in a spirit of brotherhood.*

[3]There are other potentially useful operations, e.g., a correct translation for the Malay *samarata* can be obtained by splitting it into the Indonesian sequence *sama rata*.

[4]*Malaysia's GDP is expected to reach 8 percent in 2010.*

4.1.1 Inducing Word-Level Paraphrases

We use pivoting over English to induce potential Indonesian translations for a given Malay word.

First, we generate separate word-level alignments for the Indonesian–English and the Malay–English bi-texts. Then, we induce Indonesian-Malay word translation pairs assuming that if an Indonesian word i and a Malay word m are aligned to the same English word e, they could be mutual translations. Each translation pair is associated with a conditional probability, estimated by pivoting over English:

$$\Pr(i|m) = \sum_e \Pr(i|e)\Pr(e|m) \quad (1)$$

$\Pr(i|e)$ and $\Pr(e|m)$ are estimated using maximum likelihood from the word alignments. Following (Callison-Burch et al., 2006), we further assume that i is conditionally independent of m given e.

4.1.2 Confusion Network Construction

Given a Malay sentence, we construct an Indonesian confusion network, where each Malay word is augmented with a set of network transitions: possible Indonesian word translations. The weight of such a transition is the conditional Indonesian-Malay translation probability as calculated by Eq. 1; the original Malay word is assigned a weight of 1.

Note that we paraphrase *each* word in the input Malay sentence as opposed to only those Malay words that we believe not to exist in Indonesian, e.g., because they do not appear in our Indonesian monolingual text. This is necessary because of the large number of false friends and partial cognates between Malay and Indonesian (see Section 3).

Finally, we decode the confusion network for a Malay sentence using a large Indonesian language model, and we extract an n-best list.[5] Table 1 shows the 10-best adapted "Indonesian" sentences[6] we generated for the confusion network in Figure 1.

4.1.3 Further Refinements

Many of our paraphrases are bad: some have very low probabilities, while others involve rare words for which the probability estimates are unreliable.

Moreover, the options we propose for a Malay word are inherently restricted to the small Indonesian vocabulary of the Indonesian–English bi-text. Below we describe how we address these issues.

Score-based filtering. We filter out translation pairs whose probabilities (Eq. 1) are lower than some threshold (tuned on the dev dataset), e.g., 0.01.

Improved estimations for $\Pr(i|e)$. We concatenate k copies of the Indonesian–English bi-text and one copy of the Malay–English bi-text, where the value of k is selected so that we have roughly the same number of Indonesian and Malay sentences. Then, we generate word-level alignments for the resulting bi-text. Finally, we truncate these alignments keeping them for one copy of the original Indonesian–English bi-text only. Thus, we end up with improved word alignments for the Indonesian–English bi-text, and with better estimations for Eq. 1. Since Malay and Indonesian share many cognates, this improves word alignments for Indonesian words that occur rarely in the small Indonesian–English bi-text but are relatively frequent in the larger Malay–English one; it also helps for some frequent words.

Cross-lingual morphological variants. We increase the Indonesian options for a Malay word using morphology. Since the set of Indonesian options for a Malay word in pivoting is restricted to the Indonesian vocabulary of the small Indonesian–English bi-text, this is a severe limitation of pivoting. Thus, assuming a large monolingual Indonesian text, we first build a lexicon of the words in the text. Then, we lemmatize these words using two different lemmatizers: the Malay lemmatizer of Baldwin and Awab (2006), and a similar Indonesian lemmatizer. Since these two analyzers have different strengths and weaknesses, we combine their outputs to increase recall. Next, we group all Indonesian words that share the same lemma, e.g., for *minum*, we obtain {*diminum, diminumkan, diminumnya, makan-minum, makananminuman, meminum, meminumkan, meminumnya, meminum-minuman, minum, minum-minum, minum-minuman, minuman, minumanku, minumannya, peminum, peminumnya, perminum, terminum*}. Since Malay and Indonesian are subject to the same morphological processes and share many lemmata, we use such groups to propose Indonesian translation options for a Malay word. We first lemmatize the target Malay word, and then we find all groups of Indonesian words the Malay lemmata belong to.

[5] For balance, in case of less than n adaptations for a Malay sentence, we randomly repeat some of the available ones.

[6] According to a native Indonesian speaker, options 1 and 3 in Table 1 are perfect adaptations, options 2 and 5 have a wrong word order, and the rest are grammatical though not perfect.

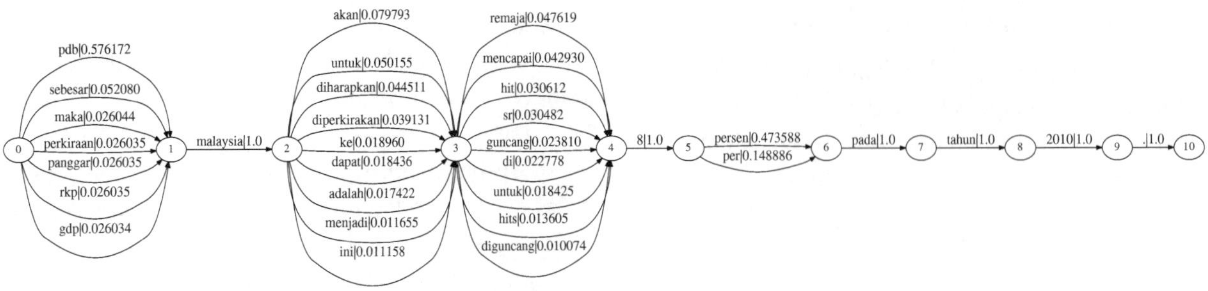

Figure 1: Indonesian confusion network for the Malay sentence "*KDNK Malaysia dijangka cecah 8 peratus pada tahun 2010.*" Arcs with scores below 0.01 are omitted, and words that exist in Indonesian are not paraphrased (for better readability).

Rank	"Indonesian" Sentence			
1	pdb	malaysia	akan	mencapai 8 persen pada tahun 2010 .
2	pdb	malaysia	untuk	mencapai 8 persen pada tahun 2010 .
3	pdb	malaysia	diperkirakan	mencapai 8 persen pada tahun 2010 .
4	maka	malaysia	akan	mencapai 8 persen pada tahun 2010 .
5	maka	malaysia	untuk	mencapai 8 persen pada tahun 2010 .
6	pdb	malaysia	dapat	mencapai 8 persen pada tahun 2010 .
7	maka	malaysia	diperkirakan	mencapai 8 persen pada tahun 2010 .
8	sebesar	malaysia	akan	mencapai 8 persen pada tahun 2010 .
9	pdb	malaysia	diharapkan	mencapai 8 persen pada tahun 2010 .
10	pdb	malaysia	ini	mencapai 8 persen pada tahun 2010 .

Table 1: The 10-best "Indonesian" sentences extracted from the confusion network in Figure 1.

The union of these groups is the set of morphological variants that we will add to the confusion network as additional options for the Malay word.[7] For example, given *seperminuman* ('drinking') in the Malay input, we first find its stem *minum*, and then we get the above example set of Indonesian words, which contains some reasonable substitutes such as *minuman* ('drink'). In the confusion network, the weight of the original Malay word is set to 1, while the weight of a morphological option is one minus the minimum edit distance ratio (Ristad and Yianilos, 1998) between it and the Malay word, multiplied by the highest probability for all pivoting variants for the Malay word.

4.2 Phrase-Level Paraphrasing

Word-level paraphrasing ignores context when generating Indonesian variants, relying on the Indonesian language model to make the right contextual choice. We also try to model context more directly by generating adaptation options at the *phrase level.*

[7]While the different morphological forms typically have different meanings, e.g., *minum* ('drink') vs. *peminum* ('drinker'), in some cases the forms could have the same translation in English, e.g., *minum* ('drink', verb) vs. *minuman* ('drink', noun). This is our motivation for trying morphological variants, even though they are almost exclusively derivational, and thus quite risky as translational variants; see also (Nakov and Ng, 2011).

Phrase-level paraphrase induction. We use standard phrase-based SMT techniques to build separate phrase tables for the Indonesian–English and the Malay–English bi-texts, where we have four conditional probabilities: forward/reverse phrase translation probability, and forward/reverse lexicalized phrase translation probability. We pivot over English to generate Indonesian-Malay phrase pairs, whose probabilities are derived from the corresponding ones in the two phrase tables using Eq. 1.

Cross-lingual morphological variants. While phrase-level paraphrasing models context better, it remains limited in the size of its Indonesian vocabulary by the small Indonesian–English bi-text, just like word-level paraphrasing was. We address this by transforming the sentences in the *development* and the *test* Indonesian–English bi-texts into confusion networks, where we add Malay morphological variants for the Indonesian words, weighting them as before. Note that we do not alter the training bi-text.

4.3 Combining Bi-texts

We combine the Indonesian–English and the synthetic "Indonesian"–English bi-texts as follows:

Simple concatenation. Assuming the two bi-texts are of comparable quality, we simply train an SMT system on their concatenation.

Balanced concatenation with repetitions. However, the two bi-texts are not directly comparable and are clearly not equally good as a source of training data for an Indonesian-English SMT system. For one thing, the "Indonesian"–English bi-text is obtained from n-best lists, i.e., it has exactly n very similar variants for each Malay sentence. Moreover, the original Malay–English bi-text is much larger in size than the Indonesian–English one, and now it has been further expanded n times in order to become an "Indonesian"–English bi-text, which means that it will dominate the concatenation due to its size. In order to counter-balance this, we repeat the smaller Indonesian–English bi-text enough times so that we can make the number of sentences it contains roughly the same as for the "Indonesian"–English bi-text; then we concatenate the two bi-texts and we train an SMT system on the resulting bi-text.

Sophisticated phrase table combination. Finally, we experiment with a method for combining phrase tables proposed in (Nakov and Ng, 2009; Nakov and Ng, 2012). The first phrase table is extracted from word alignments for the balanced concatenation with repetitions, which are then truncated so that they are kept for only one copy of the Indonesian–English bi-text. The second table is built from the simple concatenation. The two tables are then merged as follows: all phrase pairs from the first one are retained, and to them are added those phrase pairs from the second one that are not present in the first one. Each phrase pair retains its original scores, which are further augmented with 1–3 additional feature scores indicating its origin: the first/second/third feature is 1 if the pair came from the first/second/both table(s), and 0 otherwise. We experiment using all three, the first two, or the first feature only; we also try setting the features to 0.5 instead of 0. This makes the following six combinations (0, 00, 000, .5, .5.5, .5.5.5); on testing, we use the one that achieves the highest BLEU score on the development set.

Other possibilities for combining the phrase tables include using alternative decoding paths (Birch et al., 2007), simple linear interpolation, and direct phrase table merging with extra features (Callison-Burch et al., 2006); they were previously found inferior to the last two approaches above (Nakov and Ng, 2009; Nakov and Ng, 2012).

5 Experiments

We run two kinds of experiments: (a) *isolated*, where we train on the synthetic "Indonesian"–English bi-text only, and (b) *combined*, where we combine it with the Indonesian–English bi-text.

5.1 Datasets

In our experiments, we use the following datasets, normally required for Indonesian–English SMT:

- **Indonesian–English train bi-text (*IN2EN*):** 28,383 sentence pairs; 915,192 English tokens; 796,787 Indonesian tokens;
- **Indon.–English dev bi-text (*IN2EN-dev*):** 2,000 sentence pairs; 36,584 English tokens; 35,708 Indonesian tokens;
- **Indon.–English test bi-text (*IN2EN-test*):** 2,018 sentence pairs; 37,101 English tokens; 35,509 Indonesian tokens;
- **Monolingual English text (*EN-LM*):** 174,443 sentences; 5,071,988 English tokens.

We also use a Malay–English set (to be turned into "Indonesian"–English), and monolingual Indonesian text (for decoding the confusion network):

- **Malay–English train bi-text (*ML2EN*):** 290,000 sentence pairs; 8,638,780 English tokens; 8,061,729 Malay tokens;
- **Monolingual Indonesian text (*IN-LM*):** 1,132,082 sentences; 20,452,064 Indonesian tokens.

5.2 Baseline Systems

We build five baseline systems – two using a single bi-text, *ML2EN* or *IN2EN*, and three combining *ML2EN* and *IN2EN*, using simple concatenation, balanced concatenation, and sophisticated phrase table combination. The last combination is a very strong baseline and the most relevant one we need to improve upon.

5.3 Isolated Experiments

The isolated experiments only use the adapted "Indonesian"–English bi-text, which allows for a direct comparison to using *ML2EN* / *IN2EN* only.

5.3.1 Word-Level Paraphrasing

In our word-level paraphrasing experiments, we adapt Malay to Indonesian using three kinds of confusion networks (see Section 4.1.3 for details):

- ***CN:pivot*** – using word-level pivoting only;
- ***CN:pivot′*** – using word-level pivoting, with probabilities from word alignments for *IN2EN* that were improved using *ML2EN*;
- ***CN:pivot′+morph*** – *CN:pivot′* augmented with cross-lingual morphological variants.

There are two parameter values to be tuned on *IN2EN-dev* for the above confusion networks: (1) the minimum pivoting probability threshold for the Malay-Indonesian word-level paraphrases, and (2) the number of n-best Indonesian-adapted sentences that are to be generated for each input Malay sentence. We try $\{0.001, 0.005, 0.01, 0.05\}$ for the threshold and $\{1, 5, 10\}$ for n.

5.3.2 Phrase-Level Paraphrasing

In our phrase-level paraphrasing experiments, we use pivoted phrase tables (PPT) with the following features for each phrase table entry (in addition to the phrase penalty; see Section 4.2 for more details):

- ***PPT:1*** – only uses the forward conditional translation probability;
- ***PPT:4*** – uses all four conditional probabilities;
- ***PPT:4::CN:morph*** – *PPT:4* but used with a cross-lingual morphological confusion network for the dev/test Indonesian sentences.

Here we tune one parameter only: the number of n-best Indonesian-adapted sentences to be generated for each input Malay sentence; we try $\{1, 5, 10\}$.

5.4 Combined Experiments

These experiments assess the impact of our adaptation approach when combined with the original Indonesian–English bi-text *IN2EN* as opposed to combining *ML2EN* with *IN2EN* (as was in the last three baselines). We experiment with the same three combinations: simple concatenation, balanced concatenation, and sophisticated phrase table combination. We tune the parameters as before; for the last combination, we further tune the six extra feature combinations (see Section 4.3 for details).

6 Results and Discussion

For all tables, statistically significant improvements ($p < 0.01$), according to Collins et al. (2005)'s sign test, over the baseline are in **bold**; in case of two baselines, underline is used for the second baseline.

System	BLEU
ML2EN	14.50
IN2EN	18.67
Simple concatenation	**18.49**
Balanced concatenation	**19.79**
Sophisticated phrase table combination	**20.10**$_{(.5.5)}$

Table 2: **The five baselines.** The subscript indicates the parameters found on *IN2EN-dev* and used for *IN2EN-test*. The scores that are statistically significantly better than *ML2EN* and *IN2EN* ($p < 0.01$, Collins' sign test) are shown in **bold** and are underlined, respectively.

6.1 Baseline Experiments

The results for the baseline systems are shown in Table 2. We can see that training on *ML2EN* instead of *IN2EN* yields over 4 points absolute drop in BLEU (Papineni et al., 2002) score, even though *ML2EN* is about 10 times larger than *IN2EN* and both bi-texts are from the same domain. This confirms the existence of important differences between Malay and Indonesian. While simple concatenation does not help, balanced concatenation with repetitions improves by 1.12 BLEU points over *IN2EN*, which shows the importance of giving *IN2EN* a proper weight in the combined bi-text. This is further reconfirmed by the sophisticated phrase table combination, which yields an additional absolute gain of 0.31 BLEU points.

6.2 Isolated Experiments

Table 3 shows the results for the isolated experiments. We can see that word-level paraphrasing improves by up to 5.56 and 1.39 BLEU points over the two baselines (both statistically significant). Compared to *ML2EN*, *CN:pivot* yields an absolute improvement of 4.41 BLEU points, *CN:pivot′* adds another 0.59, and *CN:pivot′+morph* adds 0.56 more. The scores for TER (v. 0.7.25) and METEOR (v. 1.3) are on par with those for BLEU (NIST v. 13).

Table 3 further shows that the optimal parameters for the word-level SMT systems (*CN:**) involve a very low probability cutoff, and a high number of n-best sentences. This shows that they are robust to noise, probably because bad source-side phrases are unlikely to match the test-time input. Note also the effect of repetitions: good word choices are shared by many n-best sentences, and thus they would have higher probabilities compared to bad word choices.

	System	n-gram precision 1-gr.	2-gr.	3-gr.	4-gr.	BLEU	TER	METEOR
	ML2EN (baseline)	48.34	19.22	9.54	4.98	14.50	67.14	43.28
	IN2EN (baseline)	55.04	23.90	12.87	7.18	18.67	61.99	54.34
	CN:pivot	54.50	24.41	13.09	7.35	**18.91**$^{(+4.41,+0.24)}_{(0.005,10best)}$	61.94	51.07
	CN:pivot′	55.05	25.09	13.60	7.69	<u>**19.50**</u>$^{(+5.00,+0.83)}_{(0.001,10best)}$	61.25	51.97
(i)	*CN:pivot′+morph*	55.97	25.73	14.06	7.99	<u>**20.06**</u>$^{(+5.56,+1.39)}_{(0.005,10best)}$	60.31	55.65
	PPT:1	55.11	25.04	13.66	7.80	<u>**19.58**</u>$^{(+5.08,+0.91)}_{(10best)}$	60.92	51.93
	PPT:4	56.64	26.20	14.53	8.40	<u>**20.63**</u>$^{(+6.13,+1.96)}_{(10best)}$	59.33	54.23
(ii)	*PPT:4::CN:morph*	56.91	26.53	14.76	8.55	<u>**20.89**</u>$^{(+6.39,+2.22)}_{(10best)}$	59.30	57.19
	System combination: (i) + (ii)	57.73	27.00	15.03	8.71	<u>**21.24**</u>$^{(+6.74,+2.57)}$	58.19	54.63

Table 3: **Isolated experiments.** The subscript shows the best tuning parameters, and the superscript shows the absolute test improvement over the *ML2EN* and the *IN2EN* baselines. The last line shows system combination results.

	Combination with	Combining *IN2EN* with an adapted version of *ML2EN*: Simple Concatenation	Balanced Concatenation	Sophisticated Combination
(i)	+ *ML2EN* (unadapted; baseline)	18.49	19.79	20.10$_{(.5.5)}$
	+ *CN:pivot*	**19.99**$^{(+1.50)}_{(0.001,1best)}$	20.16$^{(+0.37)}_{(0.001,10best)}$	20.32$^{(+0.22)}_{(0.01,10best,.5.5)}$
	+ *CN:pivot′*	**20.03**$^{(+1.54)}_{(0.05,1best)}$	**20.80**$^{(+1.01)}_{(0.05,10best)}$	**20.55**$^{(+0.45)}_{(0.05,10best,.5.5)}$
(ii)	+ *CN:pivot′+morph*	**20.60**$^{(+2.11)}_{(0.01,10best)}$	**21.15**$^{(+1.36)}_{(0.01,10best)}$	**21.05**$^{(+0.95)}_{(0.01,5best,00)}$
	+ *PPT:1*	**20.61**$^{(+2.12)}_{(1best)}$	**20.71**$^{(+0.92)}_{(10best)}$	20.32$^{(+0.22)}_{(1best,000)}$
	+ *PPT:4*	**20.75**$^{(+2.26)}_{(1best)}$	**21.08**$^{(+1.29)}_{(5best)}$	**20.76**$^{(+0.66)}_{(10best,.5.5.5)}$
(iii)	+ *PPT:4::CN:morph*	**21.01**$^{(+2.52)}_{(1best)}$	**21.31**$^{(+1.52)}_{(5best)}$	**20.98**$^{(+0.88)}_{(10best,.5)}$
	System combination: (i) + (ii) + (iii)	**21.55**$^{(+3.06)}$	**21.64**$^{(+1.85)}$	**21.62**$^{(+1.52)}$

Table 4: **Combined experiments: BLEU.** The best tuning parameter values are in subscript, and the absolute test improvement over the corresponding baseline (on top of each column) is in superscript.

The gap between *ML2EN* and *IN2EN* for unigram precision could be explained by vocabulary differences between Malay and Indonesian. Compared to *IN2EN*, all *CN:** models have higher 2/3/4-gram precision. However, *CN:pivot* has lower unigram precision, which could be due to bad word alignments, as the results for *CN:pivot′* show.

When morphological variants are further added, the unigram precision improves by almost 1% absolute over *CN:pivot′*. This shows the importance of morphology for overcoming the limitations of the small Indonesian vocabulary of the *IN2EN* bi-text.

The lower part of Table 3 shows that phrase-level paraphrasing performs a bit better. This confirms the importance of modeling context for closely-related languages like Malay and Indonesian, which are rich in false friends and partial cognates. We further see that using more scores in the phrase table is better. Extending the Indonesian vocabulary with cross-lingual morphological variants is still helpful, though not as much as at the word-level.

Finally, the combination of the output of the best PPT and the best CN systems using MEMT (Heafield and Lavie, 2010) yields even further improvements, which shows that the two kinds of paraphrases are complementary. The best overall BLEU score for our isolated experiments is 21.24, which is better than the results for all five baselines in Table 2, including the three bi-text combination baselines, which only achieve up to 20.10 BLEU.

6.3 Combined Experiments

Table 4 shows the performance of the three bi-text combination strategies (see Section 4.3 for additional details) when applied to combine *IN2EN* (1) with the original *ML2EN* and (2) with various adapted versions of it.

We can see that for the word-level paraphrasing experiments (*CN:**), all combinations except for *CN:pivot* perform significantly better than their corresponding baselines, but the improvements are most sizeable for the simple concatenation.

Note that while there is a difference of 0.31 BLEU points between the balanced concatenation and the sophisticated combination for the original *ML2EN*, they differ little for the adapted versions. This is probably due to the sophisticated combination assuming that the second bi-text is worse than the first one, which is not really the case for the adapted versions: as Table 3 shows, they all outperform *IN2EN*.

Overall, phrase-level paraphrasing performs a bit better than word-level paraphrasing, and system combination with MEMT improves even further. This is consistent with the isolated experiments.

7 Further Analysis

Paraphrasing non-Indonesian words only. In *CN:** above, we paraphrased *each* word in the Malay input, because of false friends like *polisi* and partial cognates like *nanti*. This risks proposing worse alternatives, e.g., changing *beliau* ('he', respectful) to *ia* ('he', casual), which confusion network weights and LM would not always handle. Thus, we tried paraphrasing non-Indonesian words only, i.e., those not in *IN-LM*. Since *IN-LM* occasionally contains some Malay-specific words, we also tried paraphrasing words that occur at most t times in *IN-LM*. Table 5 shows that this hurts by up to 1 BLEU point for $t = 0; 10$, and a bit less for $t = 20; 40$.

System	BLEU
CN:pivot, $t = 0$	$17.88_{(0.01,5best)}$
CN:pivot, $t = 10$	$17.88_{(0.05,10best)}$
CN:pivot, $t = 20$	$18.14_{(0.01,5best)}$
CN:pivot, $t = 40$	$18.34_{(0.01,5best)}$
CN:pivot (i.e., paraphrase all)	$18.91_{(0.005,10best)}$

Table 5: **Paraphrasing non-Indonesian words only:** those appearing at most t times in *IN-LM*.

Manual evaluation. We asked a native Indonesian speaker who does not speak Malay to judge whether our "Indonesian" adaptations are more understandable to him than the original Malay input for 100 random sentences. We presented him with two extreme systems: (a) the conservative *CN:pivot,t*=0 vs. (b) *CN:pivot'+morph*. Since the latter is noisy, the top 3 choices were judged for it. Table 6 shows that *CN:pivot,t*=0 is better/equal to the original 53%/31% of the time. In contrast, *CN:pivot'+morph* is typically worse than the original; even compared to the best in top 3, the better:worse ratio is 45%:43%.

Still, this latter model works better, which means that phrase-based SMT systems are robust to noise and prefer more variety. Note also that the judgments were at the sentence level, while phrases are sub-sentential, i.e., there can be many good phrases in a "bad" sentence.

System	Better	Equal	Worse
CN:pivot, $t = 0_{(Rank1)}$	53%	31%	16%
CN:pivot'+morph$_{(Rank1)}$	38%	8%	54%
CN:pivot'+morph$_{(Rank2)}$	41%	9%	50%
CN:pivot'+morph$_{(Rank3)}$	32%	11%	57%
CN:pivot'+morph$_{(Ranks:1-3)}$	45%	12%	43%

Table 6: **Human judgments: Malay vs. "Indonesian".** The parameter values are those from Tables 3 and 5.

Reversed Adaptation. In all experiments above, we were adapting the Malay sentences to look like Indonesian. Here we try to reverse the direction of adaptation, i.e., to adapt Indonesian to Malay: we thus build a "Malay" confusion network for each dev/test Indonesian sentence to be used as an input to a Malay–English SMT system trained on the *ML2EN* dataset. We tried two variations of this idea:

- ***lattice***: Use Indonesian-to-Malay confusion networks directly as input to the *ML2EN* SMT system, i.e., tune a log-linear model using confusion networks for the source side of the *IN2EN-dev* dataset, and then evaluate the tuned system using confusion networks for the source side of the *IN2EN-test* dataset.
- ***1-best***: Use the 1-best output from the Indonesian-to-Malay confusion network for each sentence of *IN2EN-dev* and *IN2EN-test*. Then pair each 1-best output with the corresponding English sentence. Finally, get an adapted "Malay"–English development set and an adapted "Malay"–English test set, and use them to tune and evaluate the *ML2EN* SMT system.

Table 7 shows that both variations perform worse than *CN:pivot*. We believe this is because *lattice* encodes many options, but does not use a Malay LM, while *1-best* uses a Malay LM, but has to commit to 1-best. In contrast, *CN:pivot* uses both n-best outputs and an Indonesian LM; designing a similar setup for reversed adaptation is a research direction we would like to pursue in future work.

System	BLEU
CN:pivot (Malay→Indonesian)	$18.91_{(0.005,10best)}$
CN:pivot (Indonesian→Malay) – lattice	$17.22_{(0.05)}$
CN:pivot (Indonesian→Malay) – 1-best	$17.77_{(0.001)}$

Table 7: **Reversed adaptation: Indonesian to Malay.**

Adapting Macedonian to Bulgarian. We experimented with another pair of closely-related languages,[8] Macedonian (*MK*) and Bulgarian (*BG*), using data from a different, non-newswire domain: the OPUS corpus of movie subtitles (Tiedemann, 2009). We used datasets of sizes that are comparable to those in the previous experiments: 160K *MK2EN* and 1.5M *BG2EN* sentence pairs (1.2M and 11.5M *EN* words). Since the sentences were short, we used 10K *MK2EN* sentence pairs for tuning and testing (77K and 72K English words). For the LM, we used 9.2M Macedonian and 433M English words.

Table 8 shows that both *CN:** and *PPT:** yield statistically significant improvements over balanced concatenation with unadapted *BG2EN*; system combination with MEMT improves even further. This indicates that our approach can work for other pairs of related languages and even for other domains.

We should note though that the improvements here are less sizeable than for Indonesian/Malay. This may be due to our monolingual *MK* dataset being smaller (10M *MK* vs. 20M *IN* words), and too noisy, containing many OCR errors, typos, concatenated words, and even some Bulgarian text. Moreover, Macedonian and Bulgarian are arguably somewhat more dissimilar than Malay and Indonesian.

System	BLEU	TER	METEOR
BG2EN (baseline)	24.57	57.64	41.60
MK2EN (baseline)	26.46	54.55	46.15
Balanced concatenation of *MK2EN* with an adapted *BG2EN*			
+ *BG2EN* (unadapted)	**27.33**	54.61	48.16
+ *CN:pivot′ +morph*	**27.97**$^{(+0.64,+1.51)}$	54.08	49.65
+ *PPT:4::CN:morph*	**28.38**$^{(+1.05,+1.92)}$	53.35	48.21
Combining last three	**29.05**$^{(+1.72,+2.59)}$	52.31	50.96

Table 8: **Improving Macedonian–English SMT by adapting Bulgarian to Macedonian.**

[8]There is a heated political and linguistic debate about whether Macedonian represents a separate language or is a regional literary form of Bulgarian. Since there are no clear criteria for distinguishing a dialect from a language, linguists are divided on this issue. Politically, the Macedonian remains unrecognized as a language by Bulgaria and Greece.

8 Conclusion and Future Work

We have presented a novel approach for improving machine translation for a resource-poor language by *adapting* a bi-text for a related resource-rich language, using confusion networks, word/phrase-level paraphrasing, and morphological analysis.

We have achieved very significant improvements over several baselines (6.7 BLEU points over an unadapted version of *ML2EN*, 2.6 BLEU points over *IN2EN*, and 1.5–3 BLEU points over three bi-text combinations of *ML2EN* and *IN2EN*), thus proving the potential of the idea. We have further demonstrated the applicability of the general approach to other languages and domains.

In future work, we would like to add word deletion, insertion, splitting, and concatenation as allowed editing operations. We further want to explore tighter integration of word-based and phrase-based paraphrasing. Finally, we plan experiments with other language pairs and application to other linguistic problems.

Acknowledgments

We would like to give special thanks to Harta Wijaya and Aldrian Obaja Muis, native speakers of Indonesian, for their help in the linguistic analysis of the input and output of our system. We would also like to thank the anonymous reviewers for their constructive comments and suggestions, which have helped us improve the quality of this paper.

This research is supported by the Singapore National Research Foundation under its International Research Centre @ Singapore Funding Initiative and administered by the IDM Programme Office.

References

Kemal Altintas and Ilyas Cicekli. 2002. A machine translation system between a pair of closely related languages. In *Proceedings of the 17th International Symposium on Computer and Information Sciences*, ISCIS '02, pages 192–196.

AiTi Aw, Min Zhang, Juan Xiao, and Jian Su. 2006. A phrase-based statistical model for SMS text normalization. In *Proceedings of the 21st International Conference on Computational Linguistics and 44th Annual Meeting of the Association for Computational Linguistics*, ACL-COLING '06.

Hitham Abo Bakr, Khaled Shaalan, and Ibrahim Ziedan. 2008. A hybrid approach for converting written Egyptian colloquial dialect into diacritized Arabic. In *Proceedings of the 6th International Conference on Informatics and Systems*, INFOS '08.

Timothy Baldwin and Su'ad Awab. 2006. Open source corpus analysis tools for Malay. In *Proceedings of the 5th International Conference on Language Resources and Evaluation*, LREC '06, pages 2212–2215.

Alexandra Birch, Miles Osborne, and Philipp Koehn. 2007. CCG supertags in factored statistical machine translation. In *Proceedings of the Second Workshop on Statistical Machine Translation*, WMT '07, pages 9–16.

Chris Callison-Burch, Philipp Koehn, and Miles Osborne. 2006. Improved statistical machine translation using paraphrases. In *Proceedings of the Human Language Technology Conference of NAACL*, HLT-NAACL '06, pages 17–24.

Trevor Cohn and Mirella Lapata. 2007. Machine translation by triangulation: Making effective use of multi-parallel corpora. In *Proceedings of the 45th Annual Meeting of the Association for Computational Linguistics*, ACL '07, pages 728–735.

Michael Collins, Philipp Koehn, and Ivona Kučerová. 2005. Clause restructuring for statistical machine translation. In *Proceedings of the 43rd Annual Meeting of the Association for Computational Linguistics*, ACL '05, pages 531–540.

Jan Hajič, Jan Hric, and Vladislav Kuboň. 2000. Machine translation of very close languages. In *Proceedings of the Sixth Conference on Applied Natural Language Processing*, ANLP '00, pages 7–12.

Bo Han and Timothy Baldwin. 2011. Lexical normalisation of short text messages: Makn sens a #twitter. In *Proceedings of the 49th Annual Meeting of the Association for Computational Linguistics: Human Language Technologies*, ACL-HLT '11, pages 368–378.

Kenneth Heafield and Alon Lavie. 2010. Combining machine translation output with open source: The Carnegie Mellon multi-engine machine translation scheme. *The Prague Bulletin of Mathematical Linguistics*, 93(1):27–36.

Luís Marujo, Nuno Grazina, Tiago Luís, Wang Ling, Luísa Coheur, and Isabel Trancoso. 2011. BP2EP - adaptation of Brazilian Portuguese texts to European Portuguese. In *Proceedings of the 15th Conference of the European Association for Machine Translation*, EAMT '11, pages 129–136.

Preslav Nakov and Hwee Tou Ng. 2009. Improved statistical machine translation for resource-poor languages using related resource-rich languages. In *Proceedings of the Conference on Empirical Methods in Natural Language Processing*, EMNLP '09, pages 1358–1367.

Preslav Nakov and Hwee Tou Ng. 2011. Translating from morphologically complex languages: A paraphrase-based approach. In *Proceedings of the 49th Annual Meeting of the Association for Computational Linguistics: Human Language Technologies*, ACL-HLT '11, pages 1298–1307.

Preslav Nakov and Hwee Tou Ng. 2012. Improving statistical machine translation for a resource-poor language using related resource-rich languages. *Journal of Artificial Intelligence Research*, 44:179–222.

Preslav Nakov and Jörg Tiedemann. 2012. Combining word-level and character-level models for machine translation between closely-related languages. In *Proceedings of the 50th Annual Meeting of the Association for Computational Linguistics*, ACL-Short '12.

Kishore Papineni, Salim Roukos, Todd Ward, and Wei-Jing Zhu. 2002. BLEU: a method for automatic evaluation of machine translation. In *Proceedings of the 40th Annual Meeting of the Association for Computational Linguistics*, ACL '02, pages 311–318.

Eric Ristad and Peter Yianilos. 1998. Learning string-edit distance. *IEEE Transactions on Pattern Analysis and Machine Intelligence*, 20(5):522–532.

Wael Salloum and Nizar Habash. 2011. Dialectal to Standard Arabic paraphrasing to improve Arabic-English statistical machine translation. In *Proc. of the Workshop on Algorithms and Resources for Modelling of Dialects and Language Varieties*, pages 10–21.

Hassan Sawaf. 2010. Arabic dialect handling in hybrid machine translation. In *Proceedings of the 9th Conference of the Association for Machine Translation in the Americas*, AMTA '09.

Kevin P. Scannell. 2006. Machine translation for closely related language pairs. In *Proceedings of the LREC 2006 Workshop on Strategies for Developing Machine Translation for Minority Languages*.

Jörg Tiedemann. 2009. News from OPUS - a collection of multilingual parallel corpora with tools and interfaces. In *Recent Advances in Natural Language Processing*, volume V, pages 237–248.

Masao Utiyama and Hitoshi Isahara. 2007. A comparison of pivot methods for phrase-based statistical machine translation. In *Proceedings of the Human Language Technology Conference of NAACL*, HLT-NAACL '07, pages 484–491.

Hua Wu and Haifeng Wang. 2009. Revisiting pivot language approach for machine translation. In *Proceedings of the Joint Conference of the 47th Annual Meeting of the ACL*, ACL '09, pages 154–162.

Xiaoheng Zhang. 1998. Dialect MT: a case study between Cantonese and Mandarin. In *Proceedings of the 17th International Conference on Computational Linguistics*, COLING '98, pages 1460–1464.

Exploiting Reducibility in Unsupervised Dependency Parsing

David Mareček and **Zdeněk Žabokrtský**
Charles University in Prague, Faculty of Mathematics and Physics
Institute of Formal and Applied Linguistics
Malostranské náměstí 25, 11800 Prague, Czech Republic
{marecek,zabokrtsky}@ufal.mff.cuni.cz

Abstract

The possibility of deleting a word from a sentence without violating its syntactic correctness belongs to traditionally known manifestations of syntactic dependency. We introduce a novel unsupervised parsing approach that is based on a new n-gram reducibility measure. We perform experiments across 18 languages available in CoNLL data and we show that our approach achieves better accuracy for the majority of the languages then previously reported results.

1 Introduction

The true nature of the notion of dependency (after removing sedimentary deposits of rules imposed only by more or less arbitrary conventions) remains still somewhat vague and elusive. This holds in spite of a seemingly strong background intuition and even after a decade of formalized large-scale dependency-based resources being available to the research community. It is undeniable that a huge progress has been reached in the field of supervised dependency parsing, especially due to the CoNLL shared task series. However, when it comes to unsupervised parsing, there are surprisingly few clues we could rely on.

As mentioned e.g. by Kübler et al. (2009), one of the traditional linguistic criteria for recognizing dependency relations (including their head-dependent orientation) is that a head H of a construction C determines the syntactic category of C and can often replace C. Or, in words of Dependency Analysis by Reduction (Lopatková et al., 2005), stepwise deletion of dependent elements within a sentence preserves its syntactic correctness. A similar idea of dependency analysis by splitting a sentence into all possible acceptable fragments is used by Gerdes and Kahane (2011).

Of course, all the above works had to respond to the notorious fact that there are many language phenomena precluding the ideal (word by word) sentence reducibility (e.g. in the case of prepositional groups, or in the case of subjects in English finite clauses). However, we disregard their solutions tentatively and borrow only the very core of the reducibility idea: if a word can be removed from a sentence without damaging it, then it is likely to be dependent on some other (still present) word.

As it is usual with dichotomies in natural languages, it seems more adequate to use a continuous scale instead of the reducible-irreducible opposition. That is why we introduce a simple reducibility measure based on n-gram corpus statistics. We employ this reducibility measure as the main feature in our unsupervised parsing procedure.

The procedure is based on a commonly used Bayesian inference technique called Gibbs sampling (Gilks et al., 1996). In our sampler, the more reducible a given token is, the more likely it is to be sampled as a dependant and not as a head. After certain number of sampling iterations, for each sentence a final dependency tree is created (one token per node, including punctuation) that maximizes the product of edge probabilities gathered along the sampling history.

Our approach allows to utilize information from

very large corpora. While the computationally demanding sampling procedure can be applied only on limited data, the unrepeated precomputation of statistics for reducibility estimates can easily exploit much larger data.

We are not aware of any other published work on unsupervised parsing employing reducibility or a similar idea. Dominating approaches in unsupervised parsing are typically based on repeated patterns, and not on the possibility of a deletion inside a pattern. It seems that the two views of dependency (frequent co-occurrence of head-dependant pair, versus reducibility of the dependant) are rather complementary, so fruitful combinations can be hopefully expected in future.

The remainder of this paper is structured as follows. Section 2 briefly outlines the state of the art in unsupervised dependency parsing. Our measure of reducibility based on a large monolingual corpus is presented in Section 3. Section 4 shows our models which serve for generating probability estimates for edge sampling described in Section 5. Experimental parsing results for languages included in CoNLL shared task treebanks are summarized in Section 6. Section 7 concludes this article.

2 Related Work

The most popular approach in unsupervised dependency parsing of the recent years is to employ Dependency Model with Valence (DMV), which was introduced by Klein and Manning (2004). The inference algorithm was further improved by Smith (2007) and Cohen et al. (2008). Headden, Johnson and McClosky (2009) introduced the Extended Valence Grammar (EVG) and added lexicalization and smoothing. Blunsom and Cohn (2010) use tree substitution grammars, which allow learning larger dependency fragments.

Unfortunately, many of these works show results only for English.[1] However, the main feature of unsupervised methods should be their applicability across a wide range of languages. Such experiments were done by Spitkovsky (2011b; 2011c), where the parsing algorithm was evaluated on all 19 languages included in CoNLL 2006 (Buchholz and Marsi, 2006) and 2007 (Nivre et al., 2007) shared tasks.

The fully unsupervised linguistic analysis (Spitkovsky et al., 2011a) shows that the unsupervised part-of-speech tags may be more useful for this task than the supervised ones.

Another possibility for obtaining dependency structures for languages without any linguistically annotated resources can be the projection using a parallel treebank with a resource-rich language (typically English). McDonald et al. (2011) showed that such projection produce better structures than the current unsupervised parsers do. However, our task is different. We would like to produce structures that are not burdened by any linguistic conventions.

In this paper, we describe a novel approach to unsupervised dependency parsing. Our model differs from DMV, since we employ the *reducibility* feature and use *fertility* of nodes instead of generating *STOP* signs.

We use Gibbs sampling procedure for inference instead of Variational Bayes, which has been more common for induction of linguistic strucures. Gibbs sampling algorithm for grammar induction was used also by Mareček and Žabokrtský (2011). However, their sampling algorithm produces generally non-projective trees. Our sampler, which is described in Section 5, introduces a completely different small-change operator that guarantees projective edges.

3 Computing Reducibility scores

We call a word (or a sequence of words) in a sentence *reducible*, if the sentence after removing the word remains grammatically correct. Although we cannot automatically recognize grammaticality of such newly created sentence, we can search for it in a large corpus. If we find it, we assume the word was reducible in the original sentence.

Since the number of such reducible word sequences found in any corpus will be low, we determine the reducibility scores from their individual types (part-of-speech tags). This then implicitly allows some sharing of the scores between different word sequences.

The necessity to search for the whole sentences in the corpus and not only for some smaller context (considering, for example, just left and right neigh-

[1]The state-of-the-art unsupervised parsers achieve more than 50% of attachment score measured on the Penn Treebank.

bor), which would lead to lower sparsity, is rationalized by the following example:

Their children went to school.
I took their children to school.

The verb *'went'* would be reducible in the context *'their children went to school'*, because the sequence *'their children to school'* occurs in the second sentence. One could find such examples frequently even for large contexts. For instance, verbs in free word-order languages can be placed almost at any position in a sentence; therefore, without the full sentence context, they would have to be considered as reducible. To prevent this, we decided to work exclusively with the full sentence context instead of shorter contexts.

Other way that would lead to lower sparsity would be searching for sequences of part-of-speech tags instead of sequences of word forms. However, this also does not bring desired results. For instance, the two following sentence patterns

DT NNS VBD IN DT NN .
DT NNS VBD DT NN .

are quite frequent in English and we can deduce from them that the preposition IN is reducible. But this is of course a wrong deduction, since the preposition cannot be removed from the prepositional phrase. Using part-of-speech tags instead of word forms is thus not suitable for computing reducibility scores.

Although we search for reducible sequences of word forms in the corpus, we compute reducibility scores for sequences of part-of-speech tags. This requires to have the corpus morphologically disambiguated. A sequences of part-of-speech tags will be denoted as "PoS n-gram" in the following text.

Assume a PoS n-gram $g = [t_1, \ldots, t_n]$. We go through the corpus and search for all its occurrences. For each such occurrence, we remove the respective words from the current sentence and check in the corpus whether the rest of the sentence occurs at least once elsewhere in the corpus.[2] If so, then such occurrence of PoS n-gram is reducible, otherwise it is not. We denote the number of such reducible occurrences of PoS n-gram g by $r(g)$. The number of all its occurrences is $c(g)$.

[2]We do not take into account sentences with less then 10 words, because they could be nominal (without any verb) and might influence the reducibility scores of verbs.

unigrams	R	bigrams	R	trigrams	R
VB	0.04	VBN IN	0.00	IN DT JJ	0.00
TO	0.07	IN DT	0.02	JJ NN IN	0.00
IN	0.11	NN IN	0.04	NN IN NNP	0.00
VBD	0.12	NNS IN	0.05	VBN IN DT	0.00
CC	0.13	JJ NNS	0.07	JJ NN .	0.00
VBZ	0.16	NN .	0.08	DT JJ NN	0.04
NN	0.22	DT NNP	0.09	DT NNP NNP	0.05
VBN	0.24	DT NN	0.09	NNS IN DT	0.14
.	0.32	NN ,	0.11	NNP NNP .	0.15
NNS	0.38	DT JJ	0.13	NN IN DT	0.23
DT	0.43	JJ NN	0.14	NNP NNP ,	0.46
NNP	0.78	NNP .	0.15	IN DT NNP	0.55
JJ	0.84	NN NN	0.22	DT NN IN	0.59
RB	2.07	IN NN	0.67	NNP NNP NNP	0.64
,	3.77	NNP NNP	0.76	IN DT NN	0.80
CD	55.6	IN NNP	1.81	IN NNP NNP	4.27

Table 1: Reducibility scores of the most frequent English n-grams. (*V** are verbs, *N** are nouns, *DET* are determiners, *IN* are prepositions, *JJ* are adjectives, *RB* are adverbs, *CD* are numerals, and *CC* are coordinating conjunctions)

The relative reducibility $R(g)$ of a PoS n-gram g is then computed as

$$R(g) = \frac{1}{N}\frac{r(g) + \sigma_1}{c(g) + \sigma_2}, \quad (1)$$

where the normalization constant N, which expresses relative reducibility over all the PoS n-grams (denoted by G), causes the scores are concentrated around the value 1.

$$N = \frac{\sum_{g \in G}(r(g) + \sigma_1)}{\sum_{g \in G}(c(g) + \sigma_2)} \quad (2)$$

Smoothing constants σ_1 and σ_2, which prevent reducibility scores from being equal to zero, are set to

$$\sigma_1 = \frac{\sum_{g \in G} r(g)}{\sum_{g \in G} c(g)}, \qquad \sigma_2 = 1 \quad (3)$$

This setting causes that even if a given PoS n-gram is not reducible anywhere in the corpus, its reducibility score is $1/(c(g) + 1)$.

Tables 1, 2, and 3 show reducibility scores of the most frequent PoS n-grams of three selected languages: English, German, and Czech. If we consider only unigrams, we can see that the scores for verbs are often among the lowest. Verbs are followed by prepositions and nouns, and the scores for adjectives

unigrams	R	bigrams	R	trigrams	R
VVPP	0.00	NN APPR	0.00	NN APPR NN	0.01
APPR	0.27	APPR ART	0.00	ADJA NN APPR	0.01
VVFIN	0.28	ART ADJA	0.00	APPR ART ADJA	0.01
APPRART	0.32	NN VVPP	0.00	NN KON NN	0.01
VAFIN	0.37	NN $(	0.01	ADJA NN $.	0.01
KON	0.37	NN NN	0.01	NN ART NN	0.32
NN	0.43	NN ART	0.21	ART NN ART	0.49
ART	0.49	ADJA NN	0.28	NN ART ADJA	0.90
$(	0.57	NN $,	0.67	ADJA NN ART	0.95
$.	1.01	NN VAFIN	0.85	NN APPR ART	0.95
NE	1.14	NN VVFIN	0.89	NN VVPP $.	1.01
CARD	1.38	NN $.	0.95	ART NN APPR	1.35
ADJA	2.38	ART NN	1.07	ART ADJA NN	1.58
$,	2.94	NN KON	2.41	APPR ART NN	2.60
ADJD	3.54	APPR NN	2.65	APPR ADJA NN	2.65
ADV	7.69	APPRART NN	3.06	ART NN VVFIN	9.51

Table 2: Reducibility scores of the most frequent German n-grams. (*V** are verbs, *N** are nouns, *ART* are articles, *APPR** are prepositions, *ADJ** are adjectives, *ADV* are adverbs, *CARD* are numerals, and *KON* are conjunctions)

unigrams	R	bigrams	R	trigrams	R
P4	0.00	RR AA	0.00	RR NN Z:	0.00
RV	0.00	Z: J,	0.00	NN RR AA	0.00
Vp	0.06	Vp NN	0.00	NN AA NN	0.16
Vf	0.06	VB NN	0.12	AA NN RR	0.23
P7	0.16	NN Vp	0.13	NN RR NN	0.46
J,	0.24	NN VB	0.18	NN J^ NN	0.46
RR	0.28	NN RR	0.22	AA NN NN	0.47
VB	0.33	NN AA	0.23	NN Z: Z:	0.48
NN	0.72	NN J^	0.62	NN Z: NN	0.52
J^	1.72	AA NN	0.62	NN NN NN	0.70
C=	1.85	NN NN	0.70	AA AA NN	0.72
PD	2.06	NN Z:	0.97	AA NN Z:	0.86
AA	2.22	Z: NN	1.72	NN NN Z:	1.38
Dg	3.21	Z: Z:	1.97	RR NN NN	2.26
Z:	4.01	J^ NN	2.05	RR AA NN	2.65
Db	4.62	RR NN	2.20	Z: NN Z:	8.32

Table 3: Reducibility scores of the most frequent Czech n-grams. (*V** are verbs, *N** are nouns, *P** are pronouns, *R** are prepositions, *A** are adjectives, *D** are adverbs, *C** are numerals, *J** are conjunctions, and *Z** is punctuation)

and adverbs are very high for all three examined languages. That is desired, because the reducible unigrams will more likely become leaves in dependency trees. Considering bigrams, the couples [*determiner – noun*], [*adjective – noun*], and [*preposition – noun*] obtained reasonably high scores. However, there are also n-grams such as the German trigram [*determiner – noun – preposition*] (ART-NN-APPR) whose reducibility score is undesirably high.[3]

4 Models

We introduce a new generative model that is different from the widely used Dependency Model with Valence (DMV). In DMV (Klein and Manning, 2004) and in the extended model EVG (Headden III et al., 2009), there is a *STOP* sign indicating that no more dependents in a given direction will be generated. Given a certain head, all its dependents in left direction are generated first, then the *STOP* sign in that direction, then all its right dependents and then *STOP* in the other direction. This process continues recursively for all generated dependents.

Our model introduces *fertility* of a node, which substitutes the *STOP* sign. For a given head, we first generate the number of its left and right children (*fertility model*) and then we fill these positions by generating its individual dependents (*edge model*). If a zero fertility is generated in both the directions, the head becomes a leaf.

Besides the fertility model and the edge model, we use two more models (*subtree model* and *distance model*), which force the generated trees to have more desired shape.[4]

4.1 Fertility Model

We express a fertility of a node by a pair of numbers: the number of its left dependents and the number of its right dependents. For example, fertility “1-3” means that the node has one left and three right dependents, fertility “0-0” indicates that it is a leaf. Fertility is conditioned by part-of-speech tag of the node and it is computed following the Chinese restaurant process. This means that if a specific fertility has been frequent for a given PoS tag in the past, it is more likely to be generated again. The formula for computing probability of fertility f_i of a word on the position i in the corpus is as follows:

$$P_f(f_i|t_i) = \frac{c^{-i}(\text{“}t_i, f_i\text{”}) + \alpha P_0(f_i)}{c^{-i}(\text{“}t_i\text{”}) + \alpha}, \quad (4)$$

[3]The high reducibility score of ART-NN-APPR was probably caused by German particles, which have the same PoS tag as prepositions.

[4]In fact, the *subtree model* and the *distance model* disrupt a bit the generative story, because the probabilites do not sum up to one when they are used. However, they proved to help with inducing better linguistic structures.

where t_i is part-of-speech tag of the word on the position i, $c^{-i}(\text{“}t_i, f_i\text{”})$ stands for the count of words with PoS tag t_i and fertility f_i in the history, and P_0 is a prior probability for the given fertility which depends on the total number of node dependents denoted by $|f_i|$ (the sum of numbers of left and right dependents):

$$P_0(f_i) = \frac{1}{2^{|f_i|+1}} \quad (5)$$

This prior probability has a nice property: for a given number of nodes, the product of fertility probabilities over all the nodes is equal for all possible dependency trees. This ensures the stability of this model during the inference.

Besides the basic fertility model, we introduce also an extended fertility model, which uses frequency of a given word form for generating number of children. We assume that the most frequent words are mostly function words (e.g. determiners, prepositions, auxiliary verbs, conjunctions). Such words tend to have a stable number of children, for example (i) some function words are exclusively leaves, (ii) prepositions have just one child, and (iii) attachment of auxiliary verbs depends on the annotation style, but number of their children is also not very variable. The higher the frequency of a word form, the higher probability mass is concentrated on one specific number of children and the lower Dirichlet hyperparameter α in Equation 4 is needed. The extended fertility is described by equation

$$P'_f(f_i|t_i, w_i) = \frac{c^{-i}(\text{“}t_i, f_i\text{”}) + \frac{\alpha_e}{F(w_i)} P_0(f_i)}{c^{-i}(\text{“}t_i\text{”}) + \frac{\alpha_e}{F(w_i)}}, \quad (6)$$

where $F(w_i)$ is a frequency of the word w_i, which is computed as a number of words w_i in our corpus divided by number of all words.

4.2 Edge Model

After the fertility (number of left and right dependents) is generated, the individual slots are filled using the *edge model*. A part-of-speech tag of each dependent is conditioned by part-of-speech tag of the head and the edge direction (position of the dependent related to the head).[5]

Similarly as for the fertility model, we employ Chinese restaurant process to assign probabilities of individual dependent.

$$P_e(t_j|t_i, d_j) = \frac{c^{-i}(\text{“}t_i, t_j, d_j\text{”}) + \beta}{c^{-i}(\text{“}t_i, d_j\text{”}) + \beta|T|}, \quad (7)$$

where t_i and t_j are the part-of-speech tags of the head and the generated dependent respectively; d_j is a direction of edge between the words i and j, which can have two values: *left* and *right*. $c^{-i}(\text{“}t_i, t_j, d_j\text{”})$ stands for the count of edges $t_i \leftarrow t_j$ with the direction d_j in the history, $|T|$ is a number of unique tags in the corpus and β is a Dirichlet hyperparameter.

4.3 Distance Model

Distance model is an auxiliary model that prevents the resulting trees from being too flat. Ideally, it would not be needed, but experiments showed that it helps to infer better trees. This simple model says that shorter edges are more probable than longer ones. We define probability of a distance between a word and its parent as its inverse value,[6] which is then normalized by the normalization constant ϵ_d.

$$P_d(i, j) = \frac{1}{\epsilon_d}\left(\frac{1}{|i-j|}\right)^{\gamma} \quad (8)$$

The hyperparameter γ determines the weight of this model.

4.4 Subtree Model

The subtree model uses the reducibility measure. It plays an important role since it forces the reducible words to be leaves and reducible n-grams to be subtrees. Words with low reducibility are forced towards the root of the tree. We define $desc(i)$ as a sequence of tags $[t_l, \ldots, t_r]$ that corresponds to all the descendants of the word w_i including w_i, i.e. the whole subtree of w_i. The probability of such subtree is proportional to its reducibility $R(desc(i))$. The hyperparameter δ determines the weight of the model; ϵ_s is a normalization constant.

$$P_s(i) = \frac{1}{\epsilon_s} R(desc(i))^{\delta} \quad (9)$$

[5]For the edge model purposes, the PoS tag of the technical root is set to '<root>' and it is in the zero-th position in the sentence, so the head word of the sentence is always its right dependent.

[6]Distance between any word and the technical root of the dependency tree was set to 10. Since each technical root has only one dependent, this value does not affect the model.

4.5 Probability of the Whole Treebank

We want to maximize the probability of the whole generated treebank, which is computed as follows:

$$P_{treebank} = \prod_{i=1}^{n} (P'_f(f_i|t_i, w_i) \quad (10)$$
$$P_e(t_i|t_{\pi(i)}, d_i) \quad (11)$$
$$P_d(i, \pi(i)) \quad (12)$$
$$P_s(i)), \quad (13)$$

where $\pi(i)$ denotes the parent of the word on the position i. We multiply the probabilities of fertility, edge, distance from parent, and subtree over all words (nodes) in the corpus. The extended fertility model P'_f can be substituted by its basic variant P_f.

5 Sampling Algorithm

For stochastic searching for the most probable dependency trees, we employ Gibbs sampling, a standard Markov Chain Monte Carlo technique (Gilks et al., 1996). In each iteration, we loop over all words in the corpus in a random order and change the dependencies in their neighborhood (a small change described in Section 5.2). In the end, "average" trees based on the whole sampling are built.

5.1 Initialization

Before the sampling starts, we initialize the projective trees randomly. For doing so, we tried the following two initializers:

- For each sentence, we choose randomly one word as the head and attach all other words to it.
- We are picking one word after another in a random order and we attach it to the nearest left (or right) neighbor that has not been attached yet. The left-right choice is made by a coin flip. If it is not possible to attach a word to one side, we attach it to the other side. The last unattached word becomes the head of the sentence.

While the first method generates only flat trees, the second one can generate all possible projective trees. However, the sampler converges to similar results for both the initializations. Therefore we conclude that the choice of the initialization mechanism is not so important here and we choose the first one due to its simplicity.

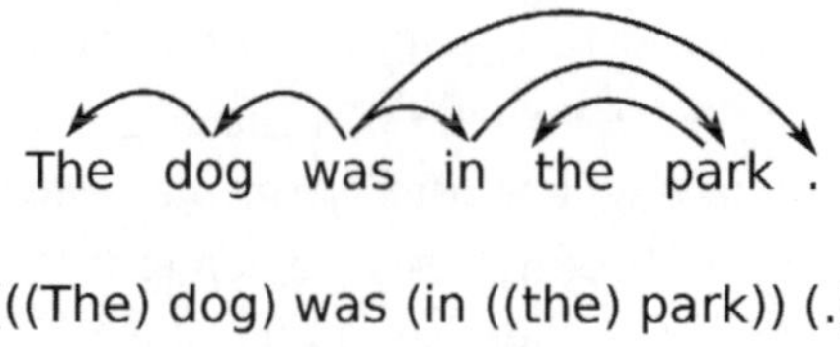

Figure 1: Arrow and bracketing notation of a projective dependency tree.

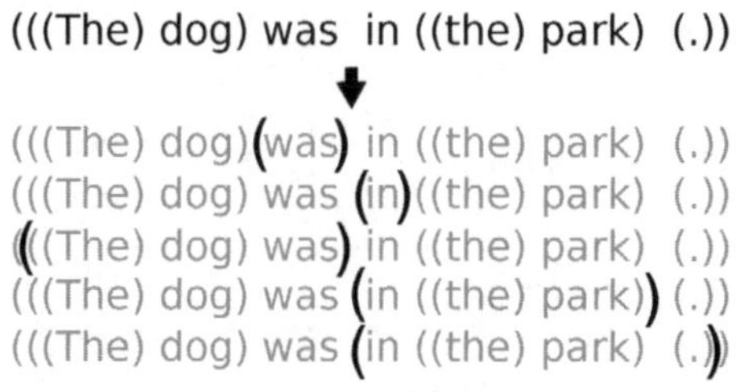

Figure 2: An example of small change in a projective tree. The bracket (in the park) is removed and there are five possibilities how to replace it.

5.2 Small Change Operator

We use the bracketing notation for illustrating the small change operator. Each projective dependency tree consisting of n words can be expressed by n pairs of brackets. Each bracket pair belongs to one node and delimits its descendants from the rest of the sentence. Furthermore, each bracketed segment contains just one word that is not embedded deeper; this node is the segment head. An example of this notation is in Figure 1.

The small change is then very simple. We remove one pair of brackets and add another, so that the conditions defined above are not violated. An example of such change is in Figure 2.

From the perspective of dependency structures, the small change can be described as follows:

1. Pick a random non-root word w (the word *in* in our example) and find its parent p (the word *was*).
2. Find all other children of w and p (the words *dog*, *park*, and .) and denote this set by C.
3. Choose the new head out of w and p. Mark the new head as g and the second candidate as d. Attach d to g.

4. Select a neighborhood D adjacent to the word d as a continuous subset of C and attach all words from D to d. D may be also empty.

5. Attach the remaining words from C that were not in D to the new head g.

5.3 Building "Average" Trees

The "burn-in" period is set to 10 iterations. After this period, we begin to count how many times an edge occurs at a particular location in the corpus. These counts are collected over the whole corpus with the collection-rate 0.01.[7]

When the samling is finished, we build final dependency trees based on the edge counts obtained during the sampling. We employ the maximum spanning tree (MST) algorithm (Chu and Liu, 1965) to find them; the weights of edges for computing MST correspond to the number of times they were present during the sampling. This averaging method was used also by Mareček and Žabokrtský (2011).

Other possibilities for obtaining final dependency trees would be using Eisner's projective algorithm (Eisner, 1996) or using annealing method (favoring more likely changes) at the end of the sampling. However, the general non-projective MST algorithm enable non-projective edges, which are by no means negligible in treebanks (Havelka, 2007).

6 Experiments and Evaluation

We evaluate our parser on 20 treebanks (18 languages) included in CoNLL shared tasks 2006 (Buchholz and Marsi, 2006) and 2007 (Nivre et al., 2007).

Similarly to some previous papers on unsupervised parsing (Gillenwater et al., 2011; Spitkovsky et al., 2011b), the tuning experiments were performed on English only. We used English for checking functionality of the individual models and for optimizing hyperparameter values. The best configuration of the parser achieved on English development data was then used for parsing all other languages. This simulates the situation in which we have only one treebank (English) on which we can tune our parser and we want to parse other languages for which we have no manually annotated treebanks.

[7] After each small change is made, the edges from the whole corpus are collected with a probability 0.01.

language	tokens (mil.)	language	tokens (mil.)
Arabic	19.7	Greek	20.9
Basque	14.1	Hungarian	26.3
Bulgarian	18.8	Italian	39.7
Catalan	27.0	Japanese	2.6
Czech	20.3	Portuguese	31.7
Danish	15.9	Slovenian	13.7
Dutch	27.1	Spanish	53.4
English	85.0	Swedish	19.2
German	56.9	Turkish	16.5

Table 4: Wikipedia texts statistics

6.1 Data

We need two kinds of data for our experiments: a smaller treebank, which is used for sampling and for evaluation, and a large corpus, from which we compute n-gram reducibility scores.

The treebanks are taken from the CoNLL shared task 2006 and 2007. The experiments are performed for all languages except for Chinese.[8] We use only the testing parts of the treebanks (the files `test.conll`) for the dependency tree induction. As a source of the part-of-speech tags, we use the fine-grained gold PoS tags, which are in the fifth column in the CoNLL format.

For obtaining reducibility scores, we used the W2C corpus[9] of Wikipedia articles, which was downloaded by Majliš and Žabokrtský (2012). Their statistics across languages are shown in Table 4. To make them useful, the necessary preprocessing steps must have been done. The texts were first automatically segmented and tokenized[10] and then they were part-of-speech tagged by TnT tagger (Brants, 2000), which was trained on the respective CoNLL training data (the files `train.conll`). The quality of such tagging is not very high, since we do not use any lexicons[11] or pretrained models. However, it is sufficient for obtaining good reducibility scores.

[8] We do not have appropriate Chinese segmenter that would segment Chinese texts in the same way as in CoNLL.

[9] `http://ufal.mff.cuni.cz/~majlis/w2c/`

[10] The segmentation to sentences and tokenization was performed using the TectoMT framework (Popel and Žabokrtský, 2010).

[11] Using lexicons or another pretrained models for tagging means using other sources of human annotated data, which is not allowed if we want to compare our results with others.

6.2 Setting the Hyperparameters

The applicability of individual models and their parameters were tested on development data set of English (the file `en/dtest.conll` in CoNLL shared task 2007).

After several experiments, we have observed that the extended fertility model provides better results than the basic fertility model; the parser using the basic fertility model achieved 44.1% attachment score for English, whereas the extended fertility model increased the score to 46.8%. The four hyperparameters α_e (extended fertility model), β (edge model), γ (distance model), and δ (subtree model), were set by a grid search algorithm,[12] which found the following optimal values:

$$\alpha_e = 0.01, \quad \beta = 1, \quad \gamma = 1.5, \quad \delta = 1$$

In informal experiments, parameters were tuned also for other treebanks and we found out that they vary across languages. Therefore, adjusting the hyperparameters on another language would probably change the scores significantly.

6.3 Evaluation

The best setting from the experiments on English is now used for evaluating our parser on all CoNLL languages. To be able to compare our parser attachment score to previously published results, the following steps must be done:

- We take the testing part of each treebank (the file `test.conll`) and remove all the punctuation marks. If the punctuation node is not a leaf, its children are attached to the parent of the removed node.

- Some previous papers report results on up-to-10-words sentences only. Therefore we extract such sentences from the test data and evaluate on this subsets as well.

[12]Here we make use of manually annotated trees. However, we use only English treebank an we are setting only four numbers out of several previously given values (e.g α_e out of 0.01, 0.1, 1, 10). These numbers could be tuned also by inspecting the outputs. So we believe this method can be treated as unsupervised.

CoNLL		≤ 10 tokens		all sentences	
language	year	gil11	our	spi11	our
Arabic	06	–	40.5	16.6	**26.5**
Arabic	07	–	48.0	**49.5**	27.9
Basque	07	–	30.8	24.0	**26.8**
Bulgarian	06	**58.3**	53.2	43.9	**46.0**
Catalan	07	–	63.5	**59.8**	47.0
Czech	06	53.2	**58.9**	27.7	**49.5**
Czech	07	–	63.7	28.4	**48.0**
Danish	06	45.9	**49.5**	38.3	**38.6**
Dutch	06	33.5	**48.8**	27.8	**44.2**
English	07	–	64.1	45.2	**49.2**
German	06	46.7	**60.8**	30.4	**44.8**
Greek	07	–	30.2	13.2	**20.2**
Hungarian	07	–	61.8	34.7	**51.8**
Italian	07	–	50.5	**52.3**	43.3
Japanese	06	57.7	**65.4**	50.2	**50.8**
Portuguese	06	54.0	**62.3**	36.7	**50.6**
Slovenian	06	**50.9**	21.0	**32.2**	18.1
Spanish	06	57.9	**67.3**	50.6	**51.9**
Swedish	06	45.0	**60.5**	**50.0**	48.2
Turkish	07	–	13.0	**35.9**	15.7
	Average:	50.3*	**54.7***	37.4	**40.0**

Table 5: Comparison of directed attachment scores with previously reported results on CoNLL treebanks. The column "gil11" contains results reported by Gillenwater et al (2011) (see the best configuration in Table 7 in their paper). They provided only results on sentences of up to 10 tokens from CoNLL 2006 treebanks. Results in the column "spi11" are taken from Spitkovsky et al (2011b), best configuration in Table 6 in their paper. The average score in the last line is computed across all comparable results, i.e. for comparison with "gil11" only the CoNLL'06 results are averaged (*). Our parser was not evaluated on Turkish CoNLL'06 data and Chinese data, because we have not them available.

The resulting scores are given in Table 5. We compare our results with results previously reported by Gillenwater (2011) and Spitkovsky (2011b), who used the CoNLL data for evaluation too. Since they provide results for several configurations of their parsers, we choose only the best one from each the paper. We define the best configuration as the one with the highest average attachment score across all the tested languages.

We can see that our parser outperforms the previously published ones. In one case, it is better for 8 out of 10 data sets, in the other case, it is better for 14 out of 20 data sets. The average attachment scores, which are computed only from the results present for both compared parsers, also confirm the improvement.

However, it is important to note that we used an additional source of information, namely large unannotated corpora for computing reducibility scores, while the others used only the CoNLL data.

6.4 Error Analysis

Our main motivation for developing an unsupervised dependency parser was that we wanted to be able to parse any language. However, the experiments show that our parser fails for some languages. In this section, we try to analyze and explain some of the most substantial types of errors.

Auxiliary verbs in Slovenian – In the Slovenian treebank, many verbs are composed of two words: main verb (marked as `Verb-main`) and auxiliary verb (`Verb-copula`). Our parser choose the auxiliary verb as the head and the main verb and all its dependants become its children. That is why the attachment score is so poor (only 18.1%). In fact, the induced structure is not so bad. The main verb is switched with the auxiliary one which causes also the wrong attachment of all its dependants.

Articles in German – Attachment of about one half of German articles is wrong. Instead of the article being attached below the appropriate noun, the noun is attached below the article. It is a similar problem as the aforementioned Slovenian auxiliary verbs. The dependency between content and function word is switched and the dependants of the content word are attached to the function word. Klein and Manning (2004) observed a similar behavior in their experiments with DMV.

Noun phrases in English – The structure of phrases that consist of more nouns are often induced badly. This is caused probably by ignoring word forms. For example, the structure of the sequence '*NN NN NN*' can be hardly recognized by our parser.

fert.	edge	dist.	subtr.	en	de	cs
			(random baseline)	19.8	18.4	26.7
✓				8.71	13.7	14.9
	✓			18.9	20.2	26.5
		✓		23.6	19.5	25.3
			✓	28.2	23.7	33.5
✓	✓			21.2	22.9	23.5
✓		✓		19.9	19.7	25.5
✓			✓	7.8	17.5	22.7
	✓	✓		24.1	19.5	27.1
	✓		✓	25.5	27.5	40.7
		✓	✓	31.2	25.2	33.1
✓	✓	✓		30.7	26.2	22.0
✓	✓		✓	14.1	18.1	34.6
✓		✓	✓	36.1	32.2	38.9
	✓	✓	✓	34.8	26.7	42.4
✓	✓	✓	✓	**46.8**	**36.5**	**47.2**

Table 6: Ablation analysis. Unlabeled attachment scores for different combinations of model components (fertility model, edge model, distance model and subtree model). The scores are computed on all sentences of the development data. Punctuation is included into the evaluation.

6.5 Ablation Analysis

To investigate the impact of individual components of the model, we run the parser for all possible component combinations. We choose three languages along the scale of word order freedom: English (very rigid word order), Czech (relatively free word order), and German (somewhere in the middle). The attachment scores are shown in Table 6. If no model is used for the inference and the sampling algorithm samples completely random trees, we get the *random baseline* score, which is 19.8% for English[13]. From the perspective of the *subtree model*, which implements the reducibility feature, we can see that it is the most useful model here. Alone, it improves the score for English to 28.2%. If we do not use it, the score decreases from 46.8% (when all models are used) to 30.7%. Very important is also the distance model which eliminates the possibility of attaching all words to one head word. If we omit

[13]This relatively high baseline scores are caused by the MST algorithm, which chooses the most frequent edges from random trees i.e. the shortest ones.

it, the score for English falls drastically to 14.1%. Some combinations of models have their scores far below the baseline. This is caused by the fact that some regularities have been found but the structures are induced differently and thus all attachments are wrong.

6.6 Induction without Wikipedia Corpus

We have performed also experiments using exclusively the CoNLL data. However, the numbers of reducible words in CoNLL training set were very low (50 words at maximum in CoNLL 2006 training data and 10 words at maximum in CoNLL 2007 training data). This led to completely unreliable reducibility scores and the consequent poor results.

7 Conclusions and Future Work

We have shown that employing the reducibility feature is useful in unsupervised dependency parsing task. We extracted the n-gram reducibility scores from a large corpus, and then made the computationally demanding inference on smaller data using only these scores. We evaluated our parser on 18 languages included in CoNLL and for 14 of them, we achieved higher attachment scores than previously published results.

The most errors were caused by function words, which sometimes take over the dependents of adjacent content words. This can be caused by the fact that the reducibility cannot handle function words correctly, because they must be reduced together with a content word, not one after another.

In future work, we would like to estimate the hyperparameters automatically. Furthermore, we would like to get rid of manually designed PoS tags and use some kind of unsupervised clusters in order to have all the annotation process completely unsupervised. We would also like to employ lexicalized models that should help in situations in which the PoS tags are too coarse.

Finally, we would like to move towards deeper syntactic structures, where the tree would be formed only by content words and the function words would be treated in a different way.

Software

The source code of our unsupervised dependency parser including the script for computing reducibility scores from large corpora is available at `http://ufal.mff.cuni.cz/~marecek/udp`.

Acknowledgement

This research was supported by the grants GAUK 116310, GA201/09/H057 (Res Informatica), LM2010013, MSM0021620838, and by the European Commission's 7th Framework Program (FP7) under grant agreement n° 247762 (FAUST). We thank anonymous reviewers for their valuable comments and suggestions.

References

Phil Blunsom and Trevor Cohn. 2010. Unsupervised induction of tree substitution grammars for dependency parsing. In *Proceedings of the 2010 Conference on Empirical Methods in Natural Language Processing*, EMNLP '10, pages 1204–1213, Stroudsburg, PA, USA. Association for Computational Linguistics.

Thorsten Brants. 2000. TnT - A Statistical Part-of-Speech Tagger. *Proceedings of the sixth conference on Applied natural language processing*, page 8.

Sabine Buchholz and Erwin Marsi. 2006. CoNLL-X shared task on multilingual dependency parsing. In *Proceedings of the Tenth Conference on Computational Natural Language Learning*, CoNLL-X '06, pages 149–164, Stroudsburg, PA, USA. Association for Computational Linguistics.

Y. J. Chu and T. H. Liu. 1965. On the Shortest Arborescence of a Directed Graph. *Science Sinica*, 14:1396–1400.

Shay B. Cohen, Kevin Gimpel, and Noah A. Smith. 2008. Logistic normal priors for unsupervised probabilistic grammar induction. In *Neural Information Processing Systems*, pages 321–328.

Jason Eisner. 1996. Three New Probabilistic Models for Dependency Parsing: An Exploration. In *Proceedings of the 16th International Conference on Computational Linguistics (COLING-96)*, pages 340–345, Copenhagen, August.

Kim Gerdes and Sylvain Kahane. 2011. Defining dependencies (and constituents). In *Proceedings of Dependency Linguistics 2011*, Barcelona.

Walter R. Gilks, S. Richardson, and David J. Spiegelhalter. 1996. *Markov chain Monte Carlo in practice*. Interdisciplinary statistics. Chapman & Hall.

Jennifer Gillenwater, Kuzman Ganchev, João Graça, Fernando Pereira, and Ben Taskar. 2011. Posterior Sparsity in Unsupervised Dependency Parsing. *The Journal of Machine Learning Research*, 12:455–490, February.

Jiří Havelka. 2007. Beyond Projectivity: Multilingual Evaluation of Constraints and Measures on Non-Projective Structures. In *Proceedings of the 45th Annual Meeting of the Association for Computational Linguistics*, pages 608–615.

William P. Headden III, Mark Johnson, and David McClosky. 2009. Improving unsupervised dependency parsing with richer contexts and smoothing. In *Proceedings of Human Language Technologies: The 2009 Annual Conference of the North American Chapter of the Association for Computational Linguistics*, NAACL '09, pages 101–109, Stroudsburg, PA, USA. Association for Computational Linguistics.

Dan Klein and Christopher D. Manning. 2004. Corpus-based induction of syntactic structure: models of dependency and constituency. In *Proceedings of the 42nd Annual Meeting on Association for Computational Linguistics*, ACL '04, Stroudsburg, PA, USA. Association for Computational Linguistics.

Sandra Kübler, Ryan T. McDonald, and Joakim Nivre. 2009. *Dependency Parsing*. Synthesis Lectures on Human Language Technologies. Morgan & Claypool Publishers.

Markéta Lopatková, Martin Plátek, and Vladislav Kuboň. 2005. Modeling syntax of free word-order languages: Dependency analysis by reduction. In Václav Matoušek, Pavel Mautner, and Tomáš Pavelka, editors, *Lecture Notes in Artificial Intelligence, Proceedings of the 8th International Conference, TSD 2005*, volume 3658 of *Lecture Notes in Computer Science*, pages 140–147, Berlin / Heidelberg. Springer.

Martin Majliš and Zdeněk Žabokrtský. 2012. Language richness of the web. In *Proceedings of the Eight International Conference on Language Resources and Evaluation (LREC 2012)*, Istanbul, Turkey, May. European Language Resources Association (ELRA).

David Mareček and Zdeněk Žabokrtský. 2011. Gibbs Sampling with Treeness constraint in Unsupervised Dependency Parsing. In *Proceedings of RANLP Workshop on Robust Unsupervised and Semisupervised Methods in Natural Language Processing*, pages 1–8, Hissar, Bulgaria.

Ryan McDonald, Slav Petrov, and Keith Hall. 2011. Multi-source transfer of delexicalized dependency parsers. In *Proceedings of the 2011 Conference on Empirical Methods in Natural Language Processing*, pages 62–72, Edinburgh, Scotland, UK., July. Association for Computational Linguistics.

Joakim Nivre, Johan Hall, Sandra Kübler, Ryan McDonald, Jens Nilsson, Sebastian Riedel, and Deniz Yuret. 2007. The CoNLL 2007 Shared Task on Dependency Parsing. In *Proceedings of the CoNLL Shared Task Session of EMNLP-CoNLL 2007*, pages 915–932, Prague, Czech Republic, June. Association for Computational Linguistics.

Martin Popel and Zdeněk Žabokrtský. 2010. TectoMT: modular NLP framework. In *Proceedings of the 7th international conference on Advances in natural language processing*, IceTAL'10, pages 293–304, Berlin, Heidelberg. Springer-Verlag.

Noah Ashton Smith. 2007. *Novel estimation methods for unsupervised discovery of latent structure in natural language text*. Ph.D. thesis, Baltimore, MD, USA. AAI3240799.

Valentin I. Spitkovsky, Hiyan Alshawi, Angel X. Chang, and Daniel Jurafsky. 2011a. Unsupervised dependency parsing without gold part-of-speech tags. In *Proceedings of the 2011 Conference on Empirical Methods in Natural Language Processing (EMNLP 2011)*.

Valentin I. Spitkovsky, Hiyan Alshawi, and Daniel Jurafsky. 2011b. Lateen EM: Unsupervised training with multiple objectives, applied to dependency grammar induction. In *Proceedings of the 2011 Conference on Empirical Methods in Natural Language Processing (EMNLP 2011)*.

Valentin I. Spitkovsky, Hiyan Alshawi, and Daniel Jurafsky. 2011c. Punctuation: Making a point in unsupervised dependency parsing. In *Proceedings of the Fifteenth Conference on Computational Natural Language Learning (CoNLL-2011)*.

Improving Transition-Based Dependency Parsing with Buffer Transitions

Daniel Fernández-González
Departamento de Informática
Universidade de Vigo
Campus As Lagoas, 32004
Ourense, Spain
danifg@uvigo.es

Carlos Gómez-Rodríguez
Departamento de Computación
Universidade da Coruña
Campus de Elviña, 15071
A Coruña, Spain
carlos.gomez@udc.es

Abstract

In this paper, we show that significant improvements in the accuracy of well-known transition-based parsers can be obtained, without sacrificing efficiency, by enriching the parsers with simple transitions that act on buffer nodes.

First, we show how adding a specific transition to create either a left or right arc of length one between the first two buffer nodes produces improvements in the accuracy of Nivre's arc-eager projective parser on a number of datasets from the CoNLL-X shared task. Then, we show that accuracy can also be improved by adding transitions involving the topmost stack node and the second buffer node (allowing a limited form of non-projectivity).

None of these transitions has a negative impact on the computational complexity of the algorithm. Although the experiments in this paper use the arc-eager parser, the approach is generic enough to be applicable to any stack-based dependency parser.

1 Introduction

Dependency parsing has become a very active research area in natural language processing in recent years. The dependency representation of syntax simplifies the syntactic parsing task, since no non-lexical nodes need to be postulated by the parsers; while being convenient in practice, since dependency representations directly show the head-modifier and head-complement relationships which form the basis of predicate-argument structure. This has led to the development of various data-driven dependency parsers, such as those by Yamada and Matsumoto (2003), Nivre et al. (2004), McDonald et al. (2005), Martins et al. (2009), Huang and Sagae (2010) or Tratz and Hovy (2011), which can be trained directly from annotated data and produce accurate analyses very efficiently.

Most current data-driven dependency parsers can be classified into two families, commonly called **graph-based** and **transition-based** parsers (McDonald and Nivre, 2011). Graph-based parsers (Eisner, 1996; McDonald et al., 2005) are based on global optimization of models that work by scoring subtrees. On the other hand, transition-based parsers (Yamada and Matsumoto, 2003; Nivre et al., 2004), which are the focus of this work, use local training to make greedy decisions that deterministically select the next parser state. Among the advantages of transition-based parsers are the linear time complexity of many of them and the possibility of using rich feature models (Zhang and Nivre, 2011).

In particular, many transition-based parsers (Nivre et al., 2004; Attardi, 2006; Sagae and Tsujii, 2008; Nivre, 2009; Huang and Sagae, 2010; Gómez-Rodríguez and Nivre, 2010) are **stack-based** (Nivre, 2008), meaning that they keep a stack of partially processed tokens and an input buffer of unread tokens. In this paper, we show how the accuracy of this kind of parsers can be improved, without compromising efficiency, by extending their set of available transitions with **buffer transitions**. These are transitions that create a dependency arc involving some node in the buffer, which would typically be considered unavailable for linking by these algorithms. The rationale is that buffer transitions construct some "easy" dependency arcs in advance, before the involved nodes reach the stack, so that the classifier's job when choosing among standard transitions is simplified.

To test the approach, we use the well-known arc-eager parser by (Nivre, 2003; Nivre et al., 2004) as a baseline, showing improvements in accuracy on most datasets of the CoNLL-X shared task (Buchholz and Marsi, 2006). However, the techniques discussed in this paper are generic and can also be applied to other stack-based dependency parsers.

The rest of this paper is structured as follows: Section 2 is an introduction to transition-based parsers and the arc-eager parsing algorithm. Section 3 presents the first novel contribution of this paper, **projective buffer transitions**, and discusses their empirical results on CoNLL-X datasets. Section 4 does the same for a more complex set of transitions, **non-projective buffer transitions**. Finally, Section 5 discusses related work and Section 6 sums up the conclusions and points out avenues for future work.

2 Preliminaries

We now briefly present some basic definitions for transition-based dependency parsing; a more thorough explanation can be found in (Nivre, 2008).

2.1 Dependency graphs

Let $w = w_1 \dots w_n$ be an input string. A **dependency graph** for w is a directed graph $G = (V_w, A)$; where $V_w = \{0, 1, \dots, n\}$ is a set of nodes, and $A \subseteq V_w \times L \times V_w$ is a set of labelled arcs. Each node in V_w encodes the position of a token in w, where 0 is a dummy node used as artificial root. An arc (i, l, j) will also be called a **dependency link** labelled l from i to j. We say that i is the syntactic **head** of j and, conversely, that j is a **dependent** of i. The **length** of the arc (i, l, j) is the value $|j - i|$.

Most dependency representations of syntax do not allow arbitrary dependency graphs. Instead, they require dependency graphs to be **forests**, i.e., acyclic graphs where each node has at most one head. In this paper, we will work with parsers that assume dependency graphs $G = (V_w, A)$ to satisfy the following properties:

- Single-head: every node has at most one incoming arc (if $(i, l, j) \in A$, then for every $k \neq i$, $(k, l', j) \notin A$).
- Acyclicity: there are no directed cycles in G.
- Node 0 is a root, i.e., there are no arcs of the form $(i, l, 0)$ in A.

A dependency forest with a single root (i.e., where all the nodes but one have at least one incoming arc) is called a **tree**. Every dependency forest can trivially be represented as a tree by adding arcs from the dummy root node 0 to every other root node.

For reasons of computational efficiency, many dependency parsers are restricted to work with forests satisfying an additional restriction called projectivity. A dependency forest is said to be **projective** if the set of nodes reachable by traversing zero or more arcs from any given node k corresponds to a continuous substring of the input (i.e., is an interval $\{x \in V_w \mid i \leq x \leq j\}$). For trees with a dummy root node at position 0, this is equivalent to not allowing dependency links to cross when drawn above the nodes (planarity).

2.2 Transition systems

A **transition system** is a nondeterministic state machine that maps input strings to dependency graphs. In this paper, we will focus on **stack-based transition systems**. A stack-based transition system is a quadruple $S = (C, T, c_s, C_t)$ where

- C is a set of parser **configurations**. Each configuration is of the form $c = (\sigma, \beta, A)$ where σ is a list of nodes of V_w called the **stack**, β is a list of nodes of V_w called the **buffer**, and A is a set of dependency arcs,
- T is a finite set of **transitions**, each of which is a partial function $t : C \to C$,
- c_s is an initialization function, mapping a sentence $w_1 \dots w_n$ to an **initial configuration** $c_s = ([0], [1, \dots, n], \emptyset)$,
- C_t is the set of **terminal configurations** $C_t = (\sigma, [], A) \in C$.

Transition systems are nondeterministic devices, since several transitions may be applicable to the same configuration. To obtain a deterministic parser from a transition system, a classifier is trained to greedily select the best transition at each state. This training is typically done by using an **oracle**, which is a function $o : C \rightarrow T$ that selects a single transition at each configuration, given a tree in the training set. The classifier is then trained to approximate this oracle when the target tree is unknown.

2.3 The arc-eager parser

Nivre's arc-eager dependency parser (Nivre, 2003; Nivre et al., 2004) is one of the most widely known and used transition-based parsers (see for example (Zhang and Clark, 2008; Zhang and Nivre, 2011)). This parser works by reading the input sentence from left to right and creating dependency links as soon as possible. This means that links are created in a strict left-to-right order, and implies that while leftward links are built in a bottom-up fashion, a rightward link $a \rightarrow b$ will be created before the node b has collected its right dependents.

The arc-eager transition system has the following four transitions (note that, for convenience, we write a stack with node i on top as $\sigma|i$, and a buffer whose first node is i as $i|\beta$):

- SHIFT : $(\sigma, i|\beta, A) \Rightarrow (\sigma|i, \beta, A)$.
- REDUCE : $(\sigma|i, \beta, A) \Rightarrow (\sigma, \beta, A)$. Precondition: $\exists k, l' \mid (k, l', i) \in A$.
- LEFT-ARC$_l$: $(\sigma|i, j|\beta, A) \Rightarrow (\sigma, j|\beta, A \cup \{(j, l, i)\})$. Preconditions: $i \neq 0$ and $\nexists k, l' \mid (k, l', i) \in A$ (single-head)
- RIGHT-ARC$_l$:
$(\sigma|i, j|\beta, A) \Rightarrow (\sigma|i|j, \beta, A \cup \{(i, l, j)\})$.

The SHIFT transition reads an input word by removing the first node from the buffer and placing it on top of the stack. The REDUCE transition pops the stack, and it can only be executed if the topmost stack node has already been assigned a head. The LEFT-ARC transition creates an arc from the first node in the buffer to the node on top of the stack, and then pops the stack. It can only be executed if the node on top of the stack does not already have a head. Finally, the RIGHT-ARC transition creates an arc from the top of the stack to the first buffer node, and then removes the latter from the buffer and moves it to the stack.

The arc-eager parser has linear time complexity. In principle, it is restricted to projective dependency forests, but it can be used in conjunction with the pseudo-projective transformation (Nivre et al., 2006) in order to capture a restricted subset of non-projective forests. Using this setup, it scored as one of the top two systems in the CoNLL-X shared task.

3 Projective buffer transitions

In this section, we show that the accuracy of stack-based transition systems can benefit from adding one of a pair of new transitions, which we call **projective buffer transitions**, to their transition sets.

3.1 The transitions

The two projective buffer transitions are defined as follows:

- LEFT-BUFFER-ARC$_l$:
$(\sigma, i|j|\beta, A) \Rightarrow (\sigma, j|\beta, A \cup \{(j, l, i)\})$.
- RIGHT-BUFFER-ARC$_l$:
$(\sigma, i|j|\beta, A) \Rightarrow (\sigma, i|\beta, A \cup \{(i, l, j)\})$.

The LEFT-BUFFER-ARC transition creates a leftward dependency link from the second node to the first node in the buffer, and then removes the first node from the buffer. Conversely, the RIGHT-BUFFER-ARC transition creates a rightward dependency link from the first node to the second node in the buffer, and then removes the second node. We call these transitions projective buffer transitions because, since they act on contiguous buffer nodes, they can only create projective arcs.

Adding one (or both) of these transitions to a projective or non-projective stack-based transition system does not affect its correctness, as long as this starting system cannot generate configurations (σ, β, A) where a buffer node has a head in A[1]: it cannot affect completeness because we are not removing existing transitions, and therefore any dependency graph that the original system could build

[1]Most stack-based transition systems in the literature disallow such configurations. However, in parsers that allow them (such as those defined by Gómez-Rodríguez and Nivre (2010)), projective buffer transitions can still be added without affecting correctness if we impose explicit single-head and acyclicity preconditions on them. We have not included these preconditions by default for simplicity of presentation.

will still be obtainable by the augmented one; and it cannot affect soundness (be it for projective dependency forests or for any superset of them) because the new transitions can only create projective arcs and cannot violate the single-head or acyclicity constraints, given that a buffer node cannot have a head.

The idea behind projective buffer transitions is to create dependency arcs of length one (i.e., arcs involving contiguous nodes) *in advance* of the standard arc-building transitions that need at least one of the nodes to get to the stack (LEFT-ARC and RIGHT-ARC in the case of the arc-eager transition system).

Our hypothesis is that, as it is known that short-distance dependencies are easier to learn for transition-based parsers than long-distance ones (McDonald and Nivre, 2007), handling these short arcs in advance and removing their dependent nodes will make it easier for the classifier to learn how to make decisions involving the standard arc transitions.

Note that the fact that projective buffer transitions create arcs of length 1 is not explicit in the definition of the transitions. For instance, if we add the LEFT-BUFFER-ARC$_l$ transition only to the arc-eager transition system, LEFT-BUFFER-ARC$_l$ will only be able to create arcs of length 1, since it is easy to see that the first two buffer nodes are contiguous in all the accessible configurations. However, if we add RIGHT-BUFFER-ARC$_l$, this transition will have the potential to create arcs of length greater than 1: for example, if two consecutive RIGHT-BUFFER-ARC$_l$ transitions are applied starting from a configuration $(\sigma, i|i+1|i+2|\beta, A)$, the second application will create an arc $i \rightarrow i+2$ of length 2.

Although we could have added the length-1 restriction to the transition definitions, we have chosen the more generic approach of leaving it to the oracle instead. While the oracle typically used for the arc-eager system follows the simple principle of executing transitions that create an arc as soon as it has the chance to, adding projective buffer transitions opens up new possibilities: we may now have several ways of creating an arc, and we have to decide in which cases we train the parser to use one of the buffer transitions and in which cases we prefer to train it to ignore the buffer transitions and delegate to the standard ones. Following the hypothesis explained above, our policy has been to train the parser to use buffer transitions whenever possible for arcs of length one, and to not use them for arcs of length larger than one. To test this idea, we also conducted experiments with the alternative policy "use buffer transitions whenever possible, regardless of arc length": as expected, the obtained accuracies were (slightly) worse.

The chosen oracle policy is generic and can be plugged into any stack-based parser: for a given transition, first check whether it is possible to build a gold-standard arc of length 1 with a projective buffer transition.[2] If so, choose that transition, and if not, just delegate to the original parser's oracle.

3.2 Experiments

To empirically evaluate the effect of projective buffer transitions on parsing accuracy, we have conducted experiments on eight datasets of the CoNLL-X shared task (Buchholz and Marsi, 2006): Arabic (Hajič et al., 2004), Chinese (Chen et al., 2003), Czech (Hajič et al., 2006), Danish (Kromann, 2003), German (Brants et al., 2002), Portuguese (Afonso et al., 2002), Swedish (Nilsson et al., 2005) and Turkish (Oflazer et al., 2003; Atalay et al., 2003).

As our baseline parser, we use the arc-eager projective transition system by Nivre (2003). Table 1 compares the accuracy obtained by this system alone with that obtained when the LEFT-BUFFER-ARC and RIGHT-BUFFER-ARC transitions are added to it as explained in Section 3.1.

Accuracy is reported in terms of labelled (LAS) and unlabelled (UAS) attachment score. We used SVM classifiers from the LIBSVM package (Chang and Lin, 2001) for all languages except for Chinese, Czech and German. In these, we used the LIBLINEAR package (Fan et al., 2008) for classification, since it reduces training time in these larger datasets. Feature models for all parsers were specifically tuned for each language.[3]

[2] In this context, "possible" means that we can create the arc without losing the possibility of creating other gold-standard arcs. In the case of RIGHT-BUFFER-ARC, this involves checking that the candidate dependent node has no dependents in the gold-standard tree (if it has any, we cannot remove it from the stack or it would not be able to collect its dependents, so we do not use the buffer transition).

[3] All the experimental settings and feature models used are included in the supplementary material and also available at `http://www.grupolys.org/~cgomezr/exp/`.

Language	NE		NE+LBA		NE+RBA	
	LAS	UAS	LAS	UAS	LAS	UAS
Arabic	66.43	77.19	**67.78**	**78.26**	63.87	74.63
Chinese	86.46	90.18	82.47	86.14	**86.62**	**90.64**
Czech	77.24	83.40	**78.70**	**84.24**	78.28	83.94
Danish	84.91	89.80	**85.21**	**90.20**	82.53	87.35
German	86.18	88.60	84.31	86.50	**86.48**	**88.90**
Portug.	86.60	90.20	**86.92**	**90.58**	85.55	89.28
Swedish	**83.33**	**88.83**	82.81	88.03	81.66	88.03
Turkish	63.77	74.35	57.42	66.24	**64.33**	**74.73**

Table 1: Parsing accuracy (LAS and UAS, excluding punctuation) of Nivre's arc-eager parser without modification (NE), with the LEFT-BUFFER-ARC transition added (NE+LBA) and with the RIGHT-BUFFER-ARC transition added (NE+RBA). Best results for each language are shown in boldface.

As can be seen in Table 1, adding a projective buffer transition improves the performance of the parser in seven out of the eight tested languages. The improvements in LAS are statistically significant at the .01 level[4] in the Arabic and Czech treebanks.

Note that the decision of *which* buffer transition to add strongly depends on the dataset. In the majority of the treebanks, we can see that when the LEFT-BUFFER-ARC transition improves performance the RIGHT-BUFFER-ARC transition harms it, and vice versa. The exceptions are Czech, where both transitions are beneficial, and Swedish, where both are harmful. Therefore, when using projective buffer transitions in practice, the language and annotation scheme should be taken into account (or tests should be made) to decide which one to use.

Table 2 hints at the reason for this treebank-sensitiveness. By analyzing the relative frequency of leftward and rightward dependency links (and, in particular, of leftward and rightward links of length 1) in the different treebanks, we see a reasonably clear tendency: the LEFT-BUFFER-ARC transition works better in treebanks that contain a large proportion of *rightward* arcs of length 1, and the RIGHT-BUFFER-ARC transition works better in treebanks with a large proportion of *leftward* arcs of length 1. Note that, while this might seem counterintuitive at a first glance, it is coherent with the hypothesis that we formulated in Section 3.1: the advantage of projective buffer transitions is not that they build arcs more accurately than standard arc-building transitions (in fact the opposite might be expected, since they work on nodes while they are still on the buffer and we have less information about their surrounding nodes in our feature models), but that they make it easier for the classifier to decide among standard transitions. The analysis on Table 2 agrees with that explanation: LEFT-BUFFER-ARC improves performance in treebanks where it is not used too often but it can filter out leftward arcs of length 1, making it easier for the parser to be accurate on rightward arcs of length 1; and the converse happens for RIGHT-BUFFER-ARC.

Language	L%	R%	L1%	R1%	Best PBT
Arabic	12.3	87.7	6.5	55.1	LBA
Chinese	58.4	41.6	35.8	15.1	RBA
Czech	41.4	58.6	22.1	24.9	LBA*
Danish	17.1	82.9	10.9	43.0	LBA
German	39.8	60.2	20.3	19.9	RBA
Portug.	32.6	67.4	22.5	26.9	LBA
Swedish	38.2	61.8	24.1	21.8	LBA*
Turkish	77.8	22.2	47.2	10.4	RBA

Table 2: Analysis of the datasets used in the experiments in terms of: percentage of leftward and rightward links (L%, R%), percentage of leftward and rightward links of length 1 (L1%, R1%), and which projective buffer transition works better for each dataset according to the results in Table 1 (LBA = LEFT-BUFFER-ARC, RBA = RIGHT-BUFFER-ARC). Languages where both transitions are beneficial (Czech) or harmful (Swedish) are marked with an asterisk.

[4] Statistical significance was assessed using Dan Bikel's randomized parsing evaluation comparator: http://www.cis.upenn.edu/~dbikel/software.html#comparator

Language	NE		NE+LBA			NE+RBA			NE+LBA+RBA			
	LA	RA	LA*	RA	LBA	LA	RA*	RBA	LA*	RA*	LBA	RBA
Arabic	**58.28**	67.77	42.61	**68.65**	**77.46**	55.88	60.63	**79.70**	37.40	62.28	66.78	75.94
Chinese	85.69	**85.79**	80.92	84.19	**89.00**	**85.96**	84.77	**88.01**	81.08	79.46	87.72	86.33
Czech	85.73	76.44	80.79	**78.34**	**91.07**	**86.25**	76.62	**82.58**	79.49	75.98	90.26	81.97
Danish	89.47	83.92	88.65	**84.16**	**91.72**	86.27	78.04	**92.30**	**90.23**	77.52	88.79	92.10
German	89.15	87.11	83.75	**87.23**	**94.30**	**89.55**	84.38	**95.98**	79.26	81.60	91.66	90.73
Portuguese	**94.77**	84.91	90.83	**85.11**	**97.07**	93.84	81.86	**92.29**	88.72	79.86	96.02	89.26
Swedish	**87.75**	80.74	84.62	**81.30**	**92.83**	87.12	74.77	**90.73**	78.10	72.50	90.86	89.89
Turkish	59.68	**74.21**	53.02	74.01	**72.78**	**60.23**	69.23	**73.91**	49.34	48.48	65.57	41.94

Table 3: Labelled precision of the arcs built by each transition of Nivre's arc-eager parser without modification (NE), with a projective buffer transition added (NE+LBA, NE+RBA) and with both projective buffer transitions added (NE+LBA+RBA). We mark a standard LEFT-ARC (LA) or RIGHT-ARC (LA) transition with an asterisk (LA*, RA*) when it is acting only on a "hard" subset of leftward (rightward) arcs, and thus its precision is not directly comparable to that of (LA, RA). Best results for each language and transition are shown in boldface.

To further test this idea, we computed the labelled precision of each individual transition of the parsers with and without projective buffer transitions, as shown in Table 3. As we can see, projective buffer transitions achieve better precision than standard transitions, but this is not surprising since they act only on "easy" arcs of length 1. Therefore, this high precision does not mean that they actually build arcs more accurately than the standard transitions, since it is not measured on the same set of arcs. Similarly, adding a projective buffer transition decreases the precision of its corresponding standard transition, but this is because the standard transition is then dealing only with "harder" arcs of length greather than 1, not because it is making more errors. A more interesting insight comes from comparing transitions that are acting on the same target set of arcs: we see that, in the languages where LEFT-BUFFER-ARC is beneficial, the addition of this transition always improves the precision of the standard RIGHT-ARC transition; and the converse happens with RIGHT-BUFFER-ARC with respect to LEFT-ARC. This further backs the hypothesis that the filtering of "easy" links achieved by projective buffer transitions makes it easier for the classifier to decide among standard transitions.

We also conducted experiments adding both transitions at the same time (NE+LBA+RBA), but the results were worse than adding the suitable transition for each dataset. Table 3 hints at the reason: the precision of buffer transitions noticeably decreases when both of them are added at the same time, presumably because it is difficult for the classifier to decide between both with the restricted feature information available for buffer nodes.

Language	NE+LBA/RBA		NE+PP (CoNLL X)	
	LAS	UAS	LAS	UAS
Arabic	**67.78**	**78.26**	66.71	77.52
Chinese	86.62	**90.64**	**86.92**	90.54
Czech	**78.70**	84.24	78.42	**84.80**
Danish	**85.21**	**90.20**	84.77	89.80
German	**86.48**	**88.90**	85.82	88.76
Portug.	86.92	90.58	**87.60**	**91.22**
Swedish	82.81	88.03	**84.58**	**89.50**
Turkish	64.33	74.73	**65.68**	**75.82**

Table 4: Comparison of the parsing accuracy (LAS and UAS, excluding punctuation) of Nivre's arc-eager parser with projective buffer transitions (NE+LBA/RBA) and the parser with the pseudo-projective transformation (Nivre et al., 2006)

To further put the obtained results into context, Table 4 compares the performance of the arc-eager parser with the projective buffer transition most suitable for each dataset with the results obtained by the parser with the pseudo-projective transformation by Nivre et al. (2006) in the CoNLL-X shared task, one of the top two performing systems in that event. The reader should be aware that the purpose of this table is only to provide a broad idea of how our approach performs with respect to a well-known reference point, and not to make a detailed comparison, since the two parsers have not been tuned in homogeneous conditions: on the one hand, we had access to the CoNLL-X test sets which were unavailable

System	Arabic	Danish
Nivre et al. (2006)	66.71	84.77
McDonald et al. (2006)	66.91	84.79
Nivre (2009)	67.3	84.7
Gómez-Rodríguez and Nivre (2010)	N/A	83.81
NE+LBA/RBA	**67.78**	**85.21**

Table 5: Comparison of the Arabic and Danish LAS obtained by the arc-eager parser with projective buffer transitions in comparison to other parsers in the literature that report results on these datasets.

for the participants in the shared task; on the other hand, we did not fine-tune the classifier parameters for each dataset like Nivre et al. (2006), but used default values for all languages.

As can be seen in the table, even though the pseudo-projective parser is able to capture non-projective syntactic phenomena, the algorithm with projective buffer transitions (which is strictly projective) outperforms it in four of the eight treebanks, including non-projective treebanks such as the German one.

Furthermore, to our knowledge, our LAS results for Arabic and Danish are currently the best published results for a single-parser system on these datasets, not only outperforming the systems participating in CoNLL-X but also other parsers tested on these treebanks in more recent years (see Table 5).

Finally, it is worth noting that adding projective buffer transitions has no negative impact on efficiency, either in terms of computational complexity or of empirical runtime. Since each projective buffer transition removes a node from the buffer, no more than n such transitions can be executed for a sentence of length n, so adding these transitions cannot increase the complexity of a transition-based parser. In the particular case of the arc-eager parser, using projective buffer transitions reduces the average number of transitions needed to obtain a given dependency forest, as some nodes can be dispatched by a single transition rather than being shifted and later popped from the stack. In practice, we observed that the training and parsing times of the arc-eager parser with projective buffer transitions were slightly faster than without them on the Arabic, Chinese, Swedish and Turkish treebanks, and slightly slower than without them on the other four treebanks, so adding these transitions does not seem to noticeably degrade (or improve) practical efficiency.

4 Non-projective buffer transitions

We now present a second set of transitions that still follow the idea of early processing of some dependency arcs, as in Section 3; but which are able to create arcs skipping over a buffer node, so that they can create some non-projective arcs. For this reason, we call them **non-projective buffer transitions**.

4.1 The transitions

The two non-projective buffer transitions are defined as follows:

- LEFT-NONPROJ-BUFFER-ARC$_l$: $(\sigma|i, j|k|\beta, A) \Rightarrow (\sigma, j|k|\beta, A \cup \{(k, l, i)\})$. Preconditions: $i \neq 0$ and $\nexists m, l' \mid (m, l', i) \in A$ (single-head)
- RIGHT-NONPROJ-BUFFER-ARC$_l$: $(\sigma|i, j|k|\beta, A) \Rightarrow (\sigma|i, j|\beta, A \cup \{(i, l, k)\})$.

The LEFT-NONPROJ-BUFFER-ARC transition creates a leftward arc from the second buffer node to the node on top of the stack, and then pops the stack. It can only be executed if the node on top of the stack does not already have a head. The RIGHT-NONPROJ-BUFFER-ARC transition creates an arc from the top of the stack to the second node in the buffer, and then removes the latter from the buffer. Note that these transitions are analogous to projective buffer transitions, and they use the second node in the buffer in the same way, but they create arcs involving the node on top of the stack rather than the first buffer node. This change makes the precondition that checks for a head necessary for the transition LEFT-NONPROJ-BUFFER-ARC to respect the single-head constraint, since many stack-based parsers can generate configurations where the node on top of the stack has a head.

We call these transitions non-projective buffer transitions because, as they act on non-contiguous nodes in the stack and buffer, they allow the creation of a limited set of non-projective dependency arcs. This means that, when added to a projective parser, they will increase its coverage.[5] On the other hand,

[5]They may also increase the coverage of parsers allowing restricted forms of non-projectivity, but that depends on the par-

Language	NE		NE+LNBA		NE+RNBA	
	LAS	UAS	LAS	UAS	LAS	UAS
Arabic	66.43	77.19	67.13	77.90	**67.21**	**77.92**
Chinese	86.46	90.18	**87.71**	**91.39**	86.98	90.76
Czech	77.24	83.40	**78.88**	**84.72**	78.12	83.78
Danish	84.91	89.80	**85.17**	**90.10**	84.25	88.92
German	86.18	88.60	**86.96**	**88.98**	85.56	88.30
Portug.	86.60	90.20	**86.78**	**90.34**	86.07	89.92
Swedish	83.33	88.83	**83.55**	**89.30**	83.17	88.59
Turkish	63.77	74.35	63.04	73.99	**65.01**	**75.70**

Table 6: Parsing accuracy (LAS and UAS, excluding punctuation) of Nivre's arc-eager parser without modification (NE), with the LEFT-NONPROJ-BUFFER-ARC transition added (NE+LNBA) and with the RIGHT-NONPROJ-BUFFER-ARC transition added (NE+RNBA). Best results for each language are shown in boldface.

adding these transitions to a stack-based transition system does not affect soundness under the same conditions and for the same reasons explained for projective buffer transitions in Section 3.1.

Note that the fact that non-projective buffer transitions are able to create non-projective dependency arcs does not mean that *all* the arcs that they build are non-projective, since an arc on non-contiguous nodes in the stack and buffer may or may not cross other arcs. This means that non-projective buffer transitions serve a dual purpose: not only they increase coverage, but they also can create some "easy" dependency links in advance of standard transitions, just like projective buffer transitions.

Contrary to projective buffer transitions, we do not impose any arc length restrictions on non-projective buffer transitions (either as a hard constraint in the transitions themselves or as a policy in the training oracle), since we would like the increase in coverage to be as large as possible. We wish to allow the parsers to create non-projective arcs in a straightforward way and without compromising efficiency. Therefore, to train the parser with these transitions, we use an oracle that employs them whenever possible, and delegates to the original parser's oracle otherwise.

4.2 Experiments

We evaluate the impact of non-projective buffer transitions on parsing accuracy by using the same baseline parser, datasets and experimental settings as for projective buffer transitions in Section 3.2. As can be seen in Table 6, adding a non-projective buffer transition to the arc-eager parser improves its performance on all eight datasets. The improvements in LAS are statistically significant at the .01 level (Dan Bikel's comparator) for Chinese, Czech and Turkish. Note that the Chinese treebank is fully projective, this means that non-projective buffer transitions are also beneficial when creating projective arcs.

While with projective buffer transitions we observed that each of them was beneficial for about half of the treebanks, and we related this to the amount of leftward and rightward links of length 1 in each; in the case of non-projective buffer transitions we do not observe this tendency. In this case, LEFT-NONPROJ-BUFFER-ARC works better than RIGHT-NONPROJ-BUFFER-ARC in all datasets except for Turkish and Arabic.

As with the projective transitions, we gathered data about the individual precision of each of the transitions. The results were similar to those for the projective transitions, and show that adding a non-projective buffer transition improves the precision of the standard transitions. We also experimentally checked that adding both non-projective buffer transitions at the same time (NE+LNBA+RNBA) achieved worse performance than adding only the most suitable transition for each dataset.

Table 7 compares the performance of the arc-eager parser with the best non-projective buffer transition for each dataset with the results obtained by

ticular subset of non-projective structures captured by each such parser.

	NE+LNBA/RNBA		NE+PP (CoNLL X)	
Language	LAS	UAS	LAS	UAS
Arabic	**67.21**	**77.92**	66.71	77.52
Chinese	**87.71**	**91.39**	86.92	90.54
Czech	**78.88**	84.72	78.42	**84.80**
Danish	**85.09**	**89.98**	84.77	89.80
German	**86.96**	**88.98**	85.82	88.76
Portug.	86.78	90.34	**87.60**	**91.22**
Swedish	83.55	89.30	**84.58**	**89.50**
Turkish	65.01	75.70	**65.68**	**75.82**

Table 7: Comparison of the parsing accuracy (LAS and UAS, excluding punctuation) of Nivre's arc-eager parser with non-projective buffer transitions (NE+LNBA/RNBA) and the parser with the pseudo-projective transformation (Nivre et al., 2006).

System	PP	PR	NP	NR
NE	80.40	80.76	-	-
NE+LNBA/RNBA	**80.96**	**81.33**	**58.87**	15.66
NE+PP (CoNLL-X)	80.71	81.00	50.72	**29.57**

Table 8: Comparison of the precision and recall for projective (PP, PR) and non-projective (NP, NR) arcs, averaged over all datasets, obtained by Nivre's arc-eager parser with and without non-projective buffer transitions (NE+LNBA/RNBA, NE) and the parser with the pseudo-projective transformation (Nivre et al., 2006).

the parser with the pseudo-projective transformation by Nivre et al. (2006) in the CoNLL-X shared task. Note that, like the one in Table 4, this should not be interpreted as a homogeneous comparison. We can see that the algorithm with non-projective buffer transitions obtains better LAS in five out of the eight treebanks. Precision and recall data on projective and non-projective arcs (Table 8) show that, while our parser does not capture as many non-projective arcs as the pseudo-projective transformation (unsurprisingly, as it can only build non-projective arcs in one direction: that of the particular non-projective buffer transition used for each dataset); it does so with greater precision and is more accurate than that algorithm in projective arcs.

Like projective buffer transitions, non-projective transitions do not increase the computational complexity of stack-based parsers. The observed training and parsing times for the arc-eager parser with non-projective buffer transitions showed a small overhead with respect to the original arc-eager (7.1% average increase in training time, 17.0% in parsing time). For comparison, running the arc-eager parser with the pseudo-projective transformation (Nivre et al., 2006) on the same machine produced a 23.5% increase in training time and a 87.5% increase in parsing time.

5 Related work

The approach of adding an extra transition to a parser to improve its accuracy has been applied in the past by Choi and Palmer (2011). In that paper, the LEFT-ARC transition from Nivre's arc-eager transition system is added to a list-based parser. However, the goal of that transition is different from ours (selecting between projective and non-projective parsing, rather than building some arcs in advance) and the approach is specific to one algorithm while ours is generic – for example, the LEFT-ARC transition cannot be added to the arc-standard and arc-eager parsers, or to extensions of those like the ones by Attardi (2006) or Nivre (2009), because these already have it.

The idea of creating dependency arcs of length 1 in advance to help the classifier has been used by Cheng et al. (2006). However, their system creates such arcs in a separate preprocessing step rather than dynamically by adding a transition to the parser, and our approach obtains better LAS and UAS results on all the tested datasets.

The projective buffer transitions presented here bear some resemblance to the easy-first parser by Goldberg and Elhadad (2010), which allows creation of dependency arcs between any pair of contiguous nodes and is based on the idea of "easy" dependency links being created first. However, while the easy-first parser is an entirely new $O(n \log(n))$ algorithm, our approach is a generic extension for stack-based parsers that does not increase their complexity (so, for example, applying it to the arc-eager system as in the experiments in this paper yields $O(n)$ complexity).

Non-projective transitions that create dependency arcs between non-contiguous nodes have been used in the transition-based parser by Attardi (2006). However, the transitions in that parser do not use the second buffer node, since they are not intended to create some arcs in advance. The non-projective buffer transitions presented in this paper can also be added to Attardi's parser.

6 Discussion

We have presented a set of two transitions, called *projective buffer transitions*, and showed that adding one of them to Nivre's arc-eager parser improves its accuracy in seven out of eight tested datasets from the CoNLL-X shared task. Furthermore, adding one of a set of *non-projective buffer transitions* achieves accuracy improvements in all of the eight datasets. The obtained improvements are statistically significant for several of the treebanks, and the parser with projective buffer transitions surpassed the best published single-parser LAS results on two of them. This comes at no cost either on computational complexity or (in the case of projective transitions) on empirical training and parsing times with respect to the original parser.

While we have chosen Nivre's well-known arc-eager parser as our baseline, we have shown that these transitions can be added to any stack-based dependency parser, and we are not aware of any specific property of arc-eager that would make them work better in practice on this parser than on others. Therefore, future work will include an evaluation of the impact of buffer transitions on more transition-based parsers. Other research directions involve investigating the set of non-projective arcs allowed by non-projective buffer transitions, defining different variants of buffer transitions (such as non-projective buffer transitions that work with nodes located deeper in the buffer) or using projective and non-projective buffer transitions at the same time.

Acknowledgments

This research has been partially funded by the Spanish Ministry of Economy and Competitiveness and FEDER (projects TIN2010-18552-C03-01 and TIN2010-18552-C03-02), Ministry of Education (FPU Grant Program) and Xunta de Galicia (Rede Galega de Recursos Lingüísticos para unha Sociedade do Coñecemento).

References

Susana Afonso, Eckhard Bick, Renato Haber, and Diana Santos. 2002. "Floresta sintá(c)tica": a treebank for Portuguese. In *Proceedings of the 3rd International Conference on Language Resources and Evaluation (LREC 2002)*, pages 1968–1703, Paris, France. ELRA.

Nart B. Atalay, Kemal Oflazer, and Bilge Say. 2003. The annotation process in the Turkish treebank. In *Proceedings of EACL Workshop on Linguistically Interpreted Corpora (LINC-03)*, pages 243–246, Morristown, NJ, USA. Association for Computational Linguistics.

Giuseppe Attardi. 2006. Experiments with a multilanguage non-projective dependency parser. In *Proceedings of the 10th Conference on Computational Natural Language Learning (CoNLL)*, pages 166–170.

Sabine Brants, Stefanie Dipper, Silvia Hansen, Wolfgang Lezius, and George Smith. 2002. The tiger treebank. In *Proceedings of the Workshop on Treebanks and Linguistic Theories, September 20-21*, Sozopol, Bulgaria.

Sabine Buchholz and Erwin Marsi. 2006. CoNLL-X shared task on multilingual dependency parsing. In *Proceedings of the 10th Conference on Computational Natural Language Learning (CoNLL)*, pages 149–164.

Chih-Chung Chang and Chih-Jen Lin, 2001. *LIBSVM: A Library for Support Vector Machines*. Software available at http://www.csie.ntu.edu.tw/∼cjlin/libsvm.

K. Chen, C. Luo, M. Chang, F. Chen, C. Chen, C. Huang, and Z. Gao. 2003. Sinica treebank: Design criteria, representational issues and implementation. In Anne Abeillé, editor, *Treebanks: Building and Using Parsed Corpora*, chapter 13, pages 231–248. Kluwer.

Yuchang Cheng, Masayuki Asahara, and Yuji Matsumoto. 2006. Multi-lingual dependency parsing at NAIST. In *Proceedings of the Tenth Conference on Computational Natural Language Learning*, CoNLL-X '06, pages 191–195, Stroudsburg, PA, USA. Association for Computational Linguistics.

Jinho D. Choi and Martha Palmer. 2011. Getting the most out of transition-based dependency parsing. In *Proceedings of the 49th Annual Meeting of the Association for Computational Linguistics: Human Language Technologies: short papers - Volume 2*, HLT '11, pages 687–692, Stroudsburg, PA, USA. Association for Computational Linguistics.

Jason M. Eisner. 1996. Three new probabilistic models for dependency parsing: An exploration. In *Proceedings of the 16th International Conference on Computational Linguistics (COLING)*, pages 340–345.

R.-E. Fan, K.-W. Chang, C.-J. Hsieh, X.-R. Wang, and C.-J. Lin. 2008. LIBLINEAR: A library for large linear classification. *Journal of Machine Learning Research*, 9:1871–1874.

Yoav Goldberg and Michael Elhadad. 2010. An efficient algorithm for easy-first non-directional dependency parsing. In *Human Language Technologies: The 2010 Annual Conference of the North American Chapter of the Association for Computational Linguistics (NAACL HLT)*, pages 742–750.

Carlos Gómez-Rodríguez and Joakim Nivre. 2010. A transition-based parser for 2-planar dependency structures. In *Proceedings of the 48th Annual Meeting of the Association for Computational Linguistics*, ACL '10, pages 1492–1501, Stroudsburg, PA, USA. Association for Computational Linguistics.

Jan Hajič, Otakar Smrž, Petr Zemánek, Jan Šnaidauf, and Emanuel Beška. 2004. Prague Arabic Dependency Treebank: Development in data and tools. In *Proceedings of the NEMLAR International Conference on Arabic Language Resources and Tools.*

Jan Hajič, Jarmila Panevová, Eva Hajičová, Jarmila Panevová, Petr Sgall, Petr Pajas, Jan Štěpánek, Jiří Havelka, and Marie Mikulová. 2006. Prague Dependency Treebank 2.0. CDROM CAT: LDC2006T01, ISBN 1-58563-370-4. Linguistic Data Consortium.

Liang Huang and Kenji Sagae. 2010. Dynamic programming for linear-time incremental parsing. In *Proceedings of the 48th Annual Meeting of the Association for Computational Linguistics*, ACL '10, pages 1077–1086, Stroudsburg, PA, USA. Association for Computational Linguistics.

Matthias T. Kromann. 2003. The Danish dependency treebank and the underlying linguistic theory. In *Proceedings of the 2nd Workshop on Treebanks and Linguistic Theories (TLT)*, pages 217–220, Växjö, Sweden. Växjö University Press.

Andre Martins, Noah Smith, and Eric Xing. 2009. Concise integer linear programming formulations for dependency parsing. In *Proceedings of the Joint Conference of the 47th Annual Meeting of the ACL and the 4th International Joint Conference on Natural Language Processing of the AFNLP (ACL-IJCNLP)*, pages 342–350.

Ryan McDonald and Joakim Nivre. 2007. Characterizing the errors of data-driven dependency parsing models. In *Proceedings of the 2007 Joint Conference on Empirical Methods in Natural Language Processing and Computational Natural Language Learning (EMNLP-CoNLL)*, pages 122–131.

Ryan McDonald and Joakim Nivre. 2011. Analyzing and integrating dependency parsers. *Comput. Linguist.*, 37:197–230.

Ryan McDonald, Fernando Pereira, Kiril Ribarov, and Jan Hajič. 2005. Non-projective dependency parsing using spanning tree algorithms. In *Proceedings of the Human Language Technology Conference and the Conference on Empirical Methods in Natural Language Processing (HLT/EMNLP)*, pages 523–530.

Ryan McDonald, Kevin Lerman, and Fernando Pereira. 2006. Multilingual dependency analysis with a two-stage discriminative parser. In *Proceedings of the 10th Conference on Computational Natural Language Learning (CoNLL)*, pages 216–220.

Jens Nilsson, Johan Hall, and Joakim Nivre. 2005. MAMBA meets TIGER: Reconstructing a Swedish treebank from Antiquity. In Peter Juel Henrichsen, editor, *Proceedings of the NODALIDA Special Session on Treebanks.*

Joakim Nivre, Johan Hall, and Jens Nilsson. 2004. Memory-based dependency parsing. In *Proceedings of the 8th Conference on Computational Natural Language Learning (CoNLL-2004)*, pages 49–56, Morristown, NJ, USA. Association for Computational Linguistics.

Joakim Nivre, Johan Hall, Jens Nilsson, Gülsen Eryiğit, and Svetoslav Marinov. 2006. Labeled pseudo-projective dependency parsing with support vector machines. In *Proceedings of the 10th Conference on Computational Natural Language Learning (CoNLL)*, pages 221–225.

Joakim Nivre. 2003. An efficient algorithm for projective dependency parsing. In *Proceedings of the 8th International Workshop on Parsing Technologies (IWPT 03)*, pages 149–160. ACL/SIGPARSE.

Joakim Nivre. 2008. Algorithms for Deterministic Incremental Dependency Parsing. *Computational Linguistics*, 34(4):513–553.

Joakim Nivre. 2009. Non-projective dependency parsing in expected linear time. In *Proceedings of the Joint Conference of the 47th Annual Meeting of the ACL and the 4th International Joint Conference on Natural Language Processing of the AFNLP (ACL-IJCNLP)*, pages 351–359.

Kemal Oflazer, Bilge Say, Dilek Zeynep Hakkani-Tür, and Gökhan Tür. 2003. Building a Turkish treebank. In Anne Abeillé, editor, *Treebanks: Building and Using Parsed Corpora*, pages 261–277. Kluwer.

Kenji Sagae and Jun'ichi Tsujii. 2008. Shift-reduce dependency DAG parsing. In *Proceedings of the 22nd International Conference on Computational Linguistics (COLING)*, pages 753–760.

Stephen Tratz and Eduard Hovy. 2011. A fast, accurate, non-projective, semantically-enriched parser. In *Proceedings of the 2011 Conference on Empirical Methods in Natural Language Processing*, pages 1257–1268, Edinburgh, Scotland, UK., July. Association for Computational Linguistics.

Hiroyasu Yamada and Yuji Matsumoto. 2003. Statistical dependency analysis with support vector machines.

In *Proceedings of the 8th International Workshop on Parsing Technologies (IWPT)*, pages 195–206.

Yue Zhang and Stephen Clark. 2008. A tale of two parsers: Investigating and combining graph-based and transition-based dependency parsing. In *Proceedings of the Conference on Empirical Methods in Natural Language Processing (EMNLP)*, pages 562–571.

Yue Zhang and Joakim Nivre. 2011. Transition-based dependency parsing with rich non-local features. In *Proceedings of the 49th Annual Meeting of the Association for Computational Linguistics: Human Language Technologies: short papers - Volume 2*, HLT '11, pages 188–193, Stroudsburg, PA, USA. Association for Computational Linguistics.

Generalized Higher-Order Dependency Parsing with Cube Pruning

Hao Zhang   Ryan McDonald
Google, Inc.
{haozhang,ryanmcd}@google.com

Abstract

State-of-the-art graph-based parsers use features over higher-order dependencies that rely on decoding algorithms that are slow and difficult to generalize. On the other hand, transition-based dependency parsers can easily utilize such features without increasing the linear complexity of the shift-reduce system beyond a constant. In this paper, we attempt to address this imbalance for graph-based parsing by generalizing the Eisner (1996) algorithm to handle arbitrary features over higher-order dependencies. The generalization is at the cost of asymptotic efficiency. To account for this, cube pruning for decoding is utilized (Chiang, 2007). For the first time, label tuple and structural features such as valencies can be scored efficiently with third-order features in a graph-based parser. Our parser achieves the state-of-art unlabeled accuracy of 93.06% and labeled accuracy of 91.86% on the standard test set for English, at a faster speed than a reimplementation of the third-order model of Koo et al. (2010).

1 Introduction

The trade-off between rich features and exact decoding in dependency parsing has been well documented (McDonald and Nivre, 2007; Nivre and McDonald, 2008). Graph-based parsers typically trade-off rich feature scope for exact (or near exact) decoding, whereas transition-based parsers make the opposite trade-off. Recent research on both parsing paradigms has attempted to address this.

In the transition-based parsing literature, the focus has been on increasing the search space of the system at decoding time, as expanding the feature scope is often trivial and in most cases only leads to a constant-time increase in parser complexity. The most common approach is to use beam search (Duan et al., 2007; Johansson and Nugues, 2007; Titov and Henderson, 2007; Zhang and Clark, 2008; Zhang and Nivre, 2011), but more principled dynamic programming solutions have been proposed (Huang and Sagae, 2010). In all cases inference remains approximate, though a larger search space is explored.

In the graph-based parsing literature, the main thrust of research has been on extending the Eisner chart-parsing algorithm (Eisner, 1996) to incorporate higher-order features (McDonald and Pereira, 2006; Carreras, 2007; Koo and Collins, 2010). A similar line of research investigated the use of integer linear programming (ILP) formulations of parsing (Riedel and Clarke, 2006; Martins et al., 2009; Martins et al., 2010). Both solutions allow for exact inference with higher-order features, but typically at a high cost in terms of efficiency. Furthermore, specialized algorithms are required that deeply exploit the structural properties of the given model. Upgrading a parser to score new types of higher-order dependencies thus requires significant changes to the underlying decoding algorithm. This is in stark contrast to transition-based systems, which simply require the definition of new feature extractors.

In this paper, we abandon exact search in graph-based parsing in favor of freedom in feature scope. We propose a parsing algorithm that keeps the backbone Eisner chart-parsing algorithm for first-order parsing unchanged. Incorporating higher-order features only involves changing the scoring function of potential parses in each chart cell by expanding the signature of each chart item to include all the non-local context required to compute features. The core chart-parsing algorithm remains the same regardless of which features are incorporated. To control complexity we use cube pruning (Chiang, 2007) with the beam size k in each cell. Furthermore, dynamic programming in the style of Huang and Sagae (2010) can be done by merging k-best items that are equivalent in scoring. Thus, our method is an application of integrated decoding with a language model in MT (Chiang, 2007) to dependency parsing, which has previously been applied to constituent parsing (Huang, 2008). However, unlike Huang, we only have one decoding pass and a single trained model, while Huang's constituent parser maintains a separate generative base model from a following discriminative re-ranking model. We draw connections to related work in Section 6.

Our chart-based approximate search algorithm allows for features on dependencies of an arbitrary order — as well as over non-local structural properties of the parse trees — to be scored at will. In this paper, we use first to third-order features of greater varieties than Koo and Collins (2010). Additionally, we look at higher-order dependency arc-label features, which is novel to graph-based parsing, though commonly exploited in transition-based parsing (Zhang and Nivre, 2011). This is because adding label tuple features would introduce a large constant factor of $O(|L|^3)$, where $|L|$ is the size of the label set L, into the complexity for exact third-order parsing. In our formulation, only the top-ranked labelled arcs would survive in each cell. As a result, label features can be scored without combinatorial explosion. In addition, we explore the use of valency features counting how many modifiers a word can have on its left and right side. In the past, only re-rankers on k-best lists of parses produced by a simpler model use such features due to the difficulty of incorporating them into search (Hall, 2007).

The final parser with all these features is both accurate and fast. In standard experiments for English, the unlabeled attachment score (UAS) is 93.06%, and the labeled attachment score (LAS) is 91.86%. The UAS score is state-of-art. The speed of our parser is 220 tokens per second, which is over 4 times faster than an exact third-order parser that attains UAS of 92.81% and comparable to the state-of-the-art transition-based system of Zhang and Nivre (2011) that employs beam search.

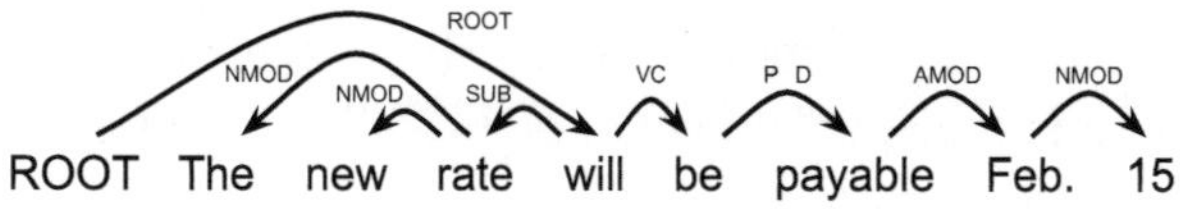

Figure 1: Example Sentence.

2 Graph-based Dependency Parsing

Dependency parsers produce directed relationships between *head* words and their syntactic *modifiers*. Each word modifies exactly one head, but can have any number of modifiers itself. The *root* of a sentence is a designated special symbol which all words in the sentence directly or indirectly modify. Thus, the dependency graph for a sentence is constrained to be a directed tree. The directed syntactic relationships, aka dependency arcs or dependencies for short, can often be labeled to indicate their syntactic role. Figure 1 gives an example dependency tree.

For a sentence $x = x_1 \ldots x_n$, dependency parsing is the search for the set of head-modifier dependency arcs y^* such that $y^* = \text{argmax}_{y \in \mathcal{Y}(x)} f(x, y)$, where f is a scoring function. As mentioned before, y^* must represent a directed tree. $|\mathcal{Y}(x)|$ is then the set of valid dependency trees for x and grows exponentially with respect to its length $|x|$. We further define L as the set of possible arc labels and use the notation $(i \xrightarrow{l} j) \in y$ to indicate that there is a dependency from head word x_i to modifier x_j with label l in dependency tree y.

In practice, $f(x, y)$ is factorized into scoring functions on parts of (x, y). For example, in first-order dependency parsing (McDonald et al., 2005), $f(x, y)$ is factored by the individual arcs:

$$y^* = \underset{y \in \mathcal{Y}(x)}{\text{argmax}}\, f(x, y) = \underset{y \in \mathcal{Y}(x)}{\text{argmax}} \sum_{(i \xrightarrow{l} j) \in y} f(i \xrightarrow{l} j)$$

The factorization of dependency structures into arcs enables an efficient dynamic programming algorithm with running time $O(|x|^3)$ (Eisner, 1996), for the large family of projective dependency structures.

Figure 2 shows the parsing logic for the Eisner algorithm. It has two types of dynamic programming states: *complete items* and *incomplete items*.

Complete items correspond to half-constituents, and are represented as triangles graphically. Incomplete items correspond to dependency arcs, and are represented as trapezoids. The Eisner algorithm is the basis for the more specialized variants of higher-order projective dependency parsing.

Second-order sibling models (McDonald and Pereira, 2006) score adjacent arcs with a common head. In order to score them efficiently, a new state corresponding to modifier pairs was introduced to the chart-parsing algorithm. Due to the careful factorization, the asymptotic complexity of the revised algorithm remains $O(|x|^3)$. The resulting scoring function is:

$$y^* = \operatorname*{argmax}_{y \in \mathcal{Y}(x)} \sum_{(i \xrightarrow{l} j, i \xrightarrow{l'} k) \in y} f(i \xrightarrow{l} j, i \xrightarrow{l'} k)$$

where $(i \xrightarrow{l} j, i \xrightarrow{l'} k) \in y$ indicates two adjacent head-modifier relationships in dependency tree y, one from x_i to x_j with label l and another from x_i to x_k with label l'. Words x_j and x_k are commonly referred to as *siblings*. In order to maintain cubic parsing complexity, adjacent dependencies are scored only if the modifiers occur on the same side in the sentence relative to the head.

Second-order grandchild models (Carreras, 2007) score adjacent arcs in length-two head-modifier chains. For example, if word x_i modifies word x_j with label l, but itself has a dependency to modifier x_k with label l', then we would add a scoring function $f(j \xrightarrow{l} i \xrightarrow{l'} k)$. These are called *grandchild* models as they can score dependencies between a word and its modifier's modifiers, i.e., x_k is the grandchild of x_j in the above example. The states in the Eisner algorithm need to be augmented with the indices to the outermost modifiers in order to score the outermost grandchildren. The resulting algorithm becomes $O(|x|^4)$.

Finally, third-order models (Koo and Collins, 2010) score arc triples such as three adjacent sibling modifiers, called *tri-siblings*, or structures looking at both horizontal contexts and vertical contexts, e.g., *grand-siblings* that score a word, its modifier and its adjacent grandchildren. To accommodate the scorers for these sub-graphs, even more specialized dynamic programming states were introduced. The Koo and Collins (2010) factorization enables

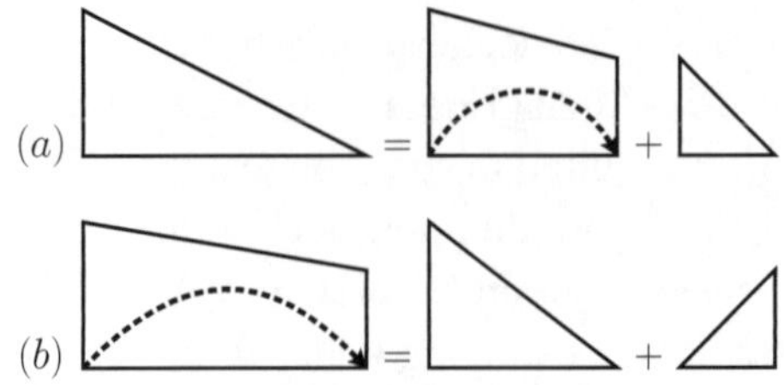

Figure 2: Structures and rules for parsing first-order models with the (Eisner, 1996) algorithm. This shows only the construction of right-pointing dependencies and not the symmetric case of left-pointing dependencies.

the scoring of certain types of third-order dependencies with $O(|x|^4)$ decoder run-time complexity.

Each of these higher-order parsing algorithms makes a clever factorization for the specific model in consideration to keep complexity as low as possible. However, this results in a loss of generality.

3 Generalizing Eisner's Algorithm

In this section, we generalize the Eisner algorithm without introducing new parsing rules. The generalization is straight-forward: expand the dynamic programming state to incorporate feature histories. This is done on top of the two distinct chart items in the $O(|x|^3)$ Eisner chart-parsing algorithm (Figure 2). The advantage of this approach is that it maintains the simplicity of the original Eisner algorithm. Unfortunately, it can increase the run-time complexity of the algorithm substantially, but we will employ cube pruning to regain tractability. Because our higher-order dependency parsing algorithm is based the Eisner algorithm, it is currently limited to produce projective trees only.

3.1 Arbitrary n-th-order dependency parsing

We start with the simplest case of sibling models. If we want to score sibling arcs, at rule (b) in Figure 2, we can see that the complete item lying between the head and the modifier (the middle of the three items) does not contain information about the outermost modifier of the head, which is the previous dependency constructed and the sibling to the modifier of the dependency currently being constructed. This fact suggests that, in order to score modifier bigrams, the complete item states should be augmented by the outermost modifier. We can augment the chart items with such information, which

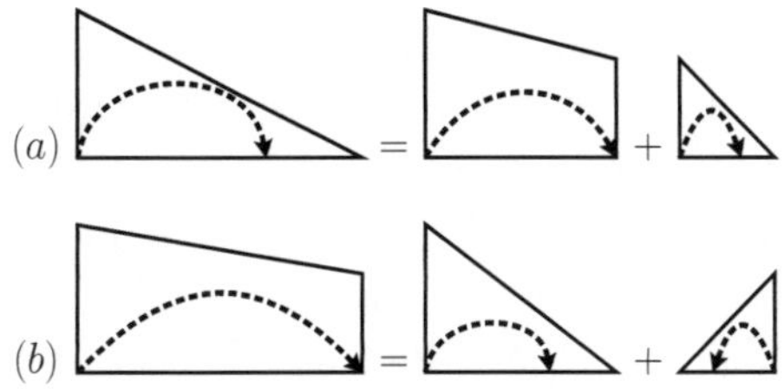

Figure 3: Structures and rules for parsing models based on modifier bigrams, with a generalized (Eisner, 1996) algorithm. Here the dashed arrows indicate additional information stored in each chart-cell. Specifically the previous modifier in complete chart items.

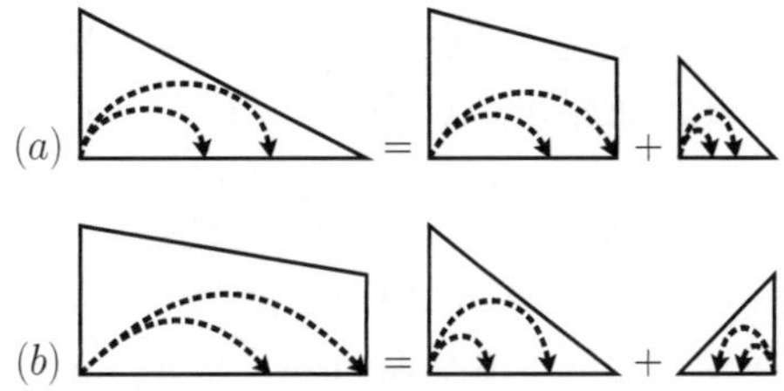

Figure 4: Structures and rules for parsing models based on modifier trigrams in horizontal contexts, with a generalized (Eisner, 1996) algorithm. Here the dashed arrows indicate the previous two modifiers to the head in each chart item.

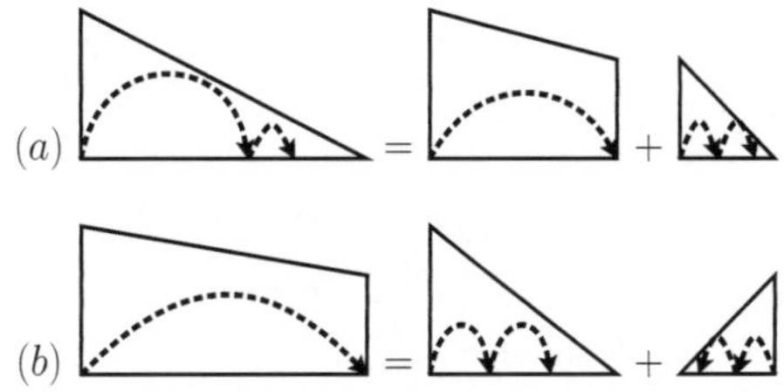

Figure 5: Structures and rules for parsing models based on modifier trigrams in vertical contexts, with a generalized (Eisner, 1996) algorithm. Here the dashed arrows indicate the modifier to the head and the modifier's modifier, forming a modifier chain of length two.

is shown in Figure 3. It refines the complete items by storing the previously constructed dependency to the outermost modifiers. Note that now the signature of the complete items is not simply the end-point indexes, but contains the index of the outer modifier.

Using this chart item augmentation it is now possible to score both first-order arcs as well as second-order sibling arcs. In fact, by symmetry, the new dynamic program can also score the leftmost and rightmost grandchildren of a head-modifier pair, in rule (a) and rule (b) respectively. By counting the number of free variables in each parsing rule, we see that the parsing complexity is $O(|x|^5)$, which is higher than both McDonald and Pereira (2006) and Carreras (2007). The added complexity comes from the fact that it is now possible to score a third-order dependency consisting of the head, the modifier, the sibling, and the outermost grandchild jointly.

We can go further to augment the complete and incomplete states with more parsing history. Figure 4 shows one possible next step of generalization. We generalize the states to keep track of the latest two modifiers of the head. As a result, it becomes possible to score tri-siblings involving three adjacent modifiers and grand-siblings involving two outermost grandchildren – both of which comprise the third-order Model 2 of Koo and Collins (2010) – plus potentially any additional interactions of these roles. Figure 5 shows another possible generalization. We keep modifier chains up to length two in the complete states. The added history enables the computation of features for great-grandchildren relationships: $(h \xrightarrow{l} m \xrightarrow{l'} gc \xrightarrow{l''} ggc)$.

In general, we can augment the complete and incomplete states with n variables representing the possible parsing histories and loop over the cross product of the histories in the innermost loop of Eisner algorithm. The cardinality of the cross product is $|x|^n \cdot |x|^n$. Thus, the complexity of the algorithm augmented by n variables is $O(|x|^3 \cdot |x|^{2n}) = O(|x|^{3+2n})$, where $n \geq 0$. Note that this complexity is for unlabeled parsing. A factor of $|L|$ for all or a subset of the encoded arcs must be multiplied in when predicting labeled parse structures.

3.2 History-based dependency parsing

The previous n modifiers, either horizontal or vertical, is a potential signature of parsing history. We can put arbitrary signatures of parsing history into the chart items so that when we score a new item, we can draw the distinguishing power of features based on an arbitrarily deep history. For example, consider the *position* of a modifier, which is the position in which it occurs amongst its siblings relative to the location of the head. We can store the position of the last modifier into both chart states. In complete states, this signature tells us the position of the outermost modifier, which is the valency of the head in the left or right half-constituent.

In the extreme case, we can use full subtrees as histories, although the cardinality of the set of histories would quickly become exponential, especially when one considers label ambiguity. Regardless, the high complexity associated with this generalization, even for second or third-order models, requires us to appeal to approximate search algorithms.

3.3 Advantage of the generalization

The complexity analysis earlier in this section reveals the advantage of such a generalization scheme. It factorizes a dynamic programming state for dependency parsing into two parts: 1) the structural state, which consists of the boundaries of incomplete and complete chart items, and accounts for the $O(|x|^3)$ term in the analysis, and 2) the feature history, which is a signature of the internal content of a sub-parse and accounts for the $O(|x|^{2n})$ term. The rules of the deductive parsing system – the Eisner algorithm – stay the same as long as the structural representation is unchanged. To generalize the parser to handle richer features, one can simply enrich the feature signature and the scoring function without changing the structural state. A natural grouping of states follows where all sub-parses sharing the same chart boundaries are grouped together. This grouping will enable the cube pruning in Section 4 for approximate search.

There is another advantage of keeping the Eisner parsing logic unchanged: derivations one-to-one correspond to dependency parse trees. Augmenting the complete and incomplete states does not introduce spurious ambiguity. This grouping view is useful for proving this point. Introducing higher order features in each chart item will cause sub-derivations to be re-ranked only. As a result, the final Viterbi parse can differ from the one from the standard Eisners algorithm. But the one-to-one correspondence still holds.

4 Approximate Search with Cube Pruning

In machine translation decoding, an n-gram language model can be incorporated into a translation model by augmenting the dynamic programming states for the translation model with the boundary $n-1$ words on the target side. The complexity for exact search involves a factor of $|x|^{4n-4}$ in the hierarchical phrase-based model of Chiang (2007), where $|x|$ is the input sentence length. The standard technique is to force a beam size k on each translation state so that the possible combinations of language model histories is bounded by k^2. Furthermore, if the list of k language model states are sorted from the lowest cost to the highest cost, we can assume the best combinations will still be among the combinations of the top items from each list, although the incorporation of n-gram features breaks the monotonic property of the underlying semi-ring.

Cube pruning is based on this approximation (Chiang, 2007). It starts with the combination of the top items in the lists to be combined. At each step, it puts the neighbors of the current best combination, which consists of going one position down in one of the k-best lists, into a priority queue. The algorithm stops when k items have been popped off from the queue. At the final step, it sorts the popped items since they can be out-of-order. It reduces the combination complexity from $O(k^2)$ to $O(k \cdot \log(k))$.

Our history-augmented parsing is analogous to MT decoding. The possible higher-order histories can similarly be limited to at most k in each complete or incomplete item. The core loop of the generalized algorithm which has a complexity of $O(|x|^{2n})$ can similarly be reduced to $O(k \cdot \log(k))$. Therefore, the whole parsing algorithm remains $O(|x|^3)$ regardless how deep we look into parsing history. Figure 6 illustrates the computation. We apply rule (b) to combine two lists of augmented complete items and keep the combinations with the highest model scores. With cube pruning, we only explore cells at $(0,0)$, $(0,1)$, $(1,0)$, $(2,0)$, and $(1,1)$, without the need to evaluate scoring functions for the remaining cells in the table. Similar computation happens with rule (a).

In this example cube pruning does find the highest scoring combination, i.e., cell $(1,1)$. However, note that the scores are not monotonic in the order in which we search these cells as non-local features are used to score the combinations. Thus, cube pruning may not find the highest scoring combination. This approximation is at the heart of cube pruning.

4.1 Recombination

The significance of using feature signatures is that when two combinations result in a state with the identical feature signature the one with the highest score survives. This is the core principle of dynamic programming. We call it *recombination*. It denotes the same meaning as *state-merging* in Huang and Sagae (2010) for transition-based parsers.

In cube pruning, with recombination, the k-best items in each chart cell are locally optimal (in the pruned search space) over all sub-trees with an equivalent state for future combinations. The cube pruning algorithm without recombination degenerates to a recursive k-best re-scoring algorithm since each of the k-best items would be unique by itself as a sub-tree. It should be noted that by working on a chart (or a forest, equivalently) the algorithm is already applying recombination at a coarser level.

In machine translation, due to its large search space and the abstract nature of an n-gram language model, it is more common to see many sub-trees with the same language model feature signature, making recombination crucial (Chiang, 2007). In constituent parser reranking (Huang, 2008), recombination is less likely to happen since the reranking features capture peculiarities of local tree structures. For dependency parsing, we hypothesize that the higher-order features are more similar to the n-gram language model features in MT as they tend to be common features among many sub-trees. But as the feature set becomes richer, recombination tends to have a smaller effect. We will discuss the empirical results on recombination in Section 5.4.

5 Experiments

We define the scoring function $f(x, y)$ as a linear classifier between a vector of features and a corresponding weight vector, i.e., $f(x, y) = w \cdot \phi(x, y)$. The feature function ϕ decomposes with respect to scoring function f. We train the weights to optimize the first-best structure. We use the max-loss variant of the margin infused relaxed algorithm (MIRA) (Crammer et al., 2006) with a hamming-loss margin as is common in the dependency parsing literature (Martins et al., 2009; Martins et al., 2010). MIRA only requires a first-best decoding algorithm, which in our case is the approximate chart-based parsing algorithms defined in Sections 3 and 4. Because our decoding algorithm is approximate, this may lead to invalid updates given to the optimizer (Huang and

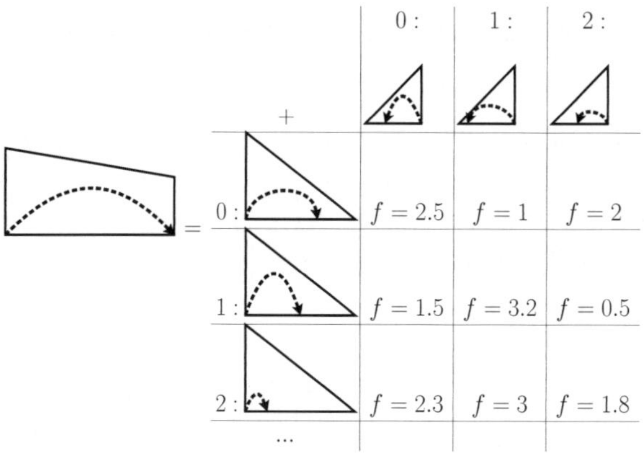

Figure 6: Combining two lists of complete items with cube pruning.

Fayong, 2012). However, we found that ignoring or modifying such updates led to negligible differences in practice. In all our experiments, we train MIRA for 8 epochs and use a beam of $k = 5$ during decoding. Both these values were determined on the English development data.

5.1 Features

The feature templates we use are drawn from the past work on graph-based parsing and transition-based parsing. The base templates for the higher-order dependencies are close to Koo and Collins (2010), with the major exception that our features include label-tuple information. The basic features include identities, part of speech tags, and labels of the words in dependency structures. These atomic features are conjoined with the directions of arcs to create composite n-gram features. The higher-order dependency features can be categorized into the following sub-groups, where we use h to indicate the head, m the modifier, s the modifier's sibling and gc a grandchild word in a dependency part.

- (labeled) modifier features: $(h \xrightarrow{l} m)$
- (labeled) sibling features: $(h \xrightarrow{l} m, h \xrightarrow{l'} s)$
- (labeled) outermost grandchild features:
  $(h \xrightarrow{l} m \xrightarrow{l'} gc)$
- (labeled) tri-sibling features:
  $(h \xrightarrow{l} m, h \xrightarrow{l'} s, h \xrightarrow{l''} s_2)$
- (labeled) grand-sibling features:
  $(h \xrightarrow{l} m \xrightarrow{l'} gc, h \xrightarrow{l} m \xrightarrow{l''} gc_2)$,

- (labeled) sibling and grandchild conjoined features: $(h \xrightarrow{l} m, h \xrightarrow{l'} s, m \xrightarrow{l''} gc)$

The general history features include valencies of words conjoined with the directions of the dominating arcs. The positions of the modifiers are also conjoined with the higher-order dependency features in the previous list.

The features that are new compared to Koo and Collins (2010) are the label tuple features, the sibling and grandchild conjoined features, and the valency features. We determine this feature set based on experiments on the development data for English. In Section 5.3 we examine the impact of these new features on parser performance.

Parser	*UAS*	*LAS*	*Toks/Sec*
Huang and Sagae (2010)	92.1-	-	-
Zhang and Nivre (2011)	92.9-	91.8-	-
Zhang and Nivre (reimpl.) (beam=64)	92.73	91.67	760
Zhang and Nivre (reimpl.) (beam=256)	92.75	91.71	190
Koo and Collins (2010)	93.04	-	-
1st-order exact (reimpl.)	91.80	90.50	2070
2nd-order exact (reimpl.)	92.40	91.12	1110
3rd-order exact (reimpl.)	92.81	-†	50
this paper	93.06	91.86	220

Table 1: Comparing this work in terms of parsing accuracy compared to state-of-the-art baselines on the English test data. We also report results for a re-implementation of exact first to third-order graph-based parsing and a re-implementation of Zhang and Nivre (2011) in order to compare parser speed. †Our exact third-order implementation currently only supports unlabeled parsing.

5.2 Main Results

Our first set of results are on English dependencies. We used the Penn WSJ Treebank converted to dependencies with Penn2Malt[1] conversion software specifying Yamada and Matsumoto head rules and Malt label set. We used the standard splits of this data: sections 2-21 for training; section 22 for validation; and section 23 for evaluation. We evaluated our parsers using standard labeled accuracy scores (LAS) and unlabeled accuracy scores (UAS) excluding punctuation. We report run-times in tokens per second. Part-of-speech tags are predicted as input using a linear-chain CRF.

Results are given in Table 1. We compare our method to a state-of-the-art graph-based parser (Koo and Collins, 2010) as well as a state-of-the-art transition-based parser that uses a beam (Zhang and Nivre, 2011) and the dynamic programming transition-based parser of Huang and Sagae (2010). Additionally, we compare to our own implementation of exact first to third-order graph-based parsing and the transition-based system of Zhang and Nivre (2011) with varying beam sizes.

There are a number of points to make. First, approximate decoding with rich features and cube pruning gives state-of-the-art labeled and unlabeled parsing accuracies relative to previously reported results. This includes the best graph-based parsing results of Koo and Collins (2010), which has near identical performance, as well as the best beam-based and dynamic-programming-based transition parsers (Huang and Sagae, 2010; Zhang and Nivre, 2011). Second, at a similar toks/sec parser speed, our method achieves better performance than the transition-based model of Zhang and Nivre (2011) with a beam of 256. Finally, compared to an implementation of an exact third-order parser – which provides us with an apples-to-apples comparison in terms of features and runtime – approximate decoding with cube pruning is both more accurate and while being 4-5 times as fast. It is more accurate as it can easily incorporate more complex features and it is faster since its asymptotic complexity is lower. We should point out that our third-order reimplementation is a purely unlabeled parser as we do not have an implementation of an exact labeled third-order parser. This likely under estimates its accuracy, but also significantly overestimates its speed.

Next, we looked at the impact of our system on non-English treebanks. Specifically we focused on two sets of data. The first is the Chinese Treebank converted to dependencies. Here we use the identical training/validation/evaluation splits and experimental set-up as Zhang and Nivre (2011). Additionally, we evaluate our system on eight other languages from the CoNLL 2006/2007 shared-task (Buchholz and Marsi, 2006; Nivre et al., 2007). We selected the following four data sets since they are primarily projective treebanks (<1.0% non-projective arcs): Bulgarian and Spanish from CoNLL 2006 as well as Catalan and Italian from CoNLL 2007. Currently our method is restricted to predicting strictly projective trees as it

[1] http://w3.msi.vxu.se/~nivre/research/Penn2Malt.html

uses the Eisner chart parsing algorithm as its backbone. We also report results from four additional CoNLL data sets reported in Rush and Petrov (2012) in order to directly compare accuracy. These are German, Japanese, Portuguese and Swedish. For all data sets we measure UAS and LAS excluding punctuation and use gold tags as input to the parser as is standard for these data sets.

Results are given in Table 2. Here we compare to our re-implementations of Zhang and Nivre (2011), exact first to third-order parsing and Rush and Petrov (2012) for the data sets in which they reported results. We again see that approximate decoding with rich features and cube pruning has higher accuracy than transition-based parsing with a large beam. In particular, for the ZH-CTB data set, our system is currently the best reported result. Furthermore, our system returns comparable accuracy with exact third-order parsing, while being significantly faster and more flexible.

5.3 Ablation studies

In this section, we analyze the contributions from each of the feature groups. Each row in Table 3 uses a super set of features than the previous row. All systems use our proposed generalized higher-order parser with cube-pruning. I.e., they are all using the Eisner chart-parsing algorithm with expanded feature signatures. The only difference between systems is the set of features used. This allows us to see the improvement from additional features.

The first row uses no higher-order features. It is equivalent to the first-order model from Table 1. The only difference is that it uses the k-best algorithm to find the first-best, so it has additional overhead compared to the standard Viterbi algorithm. Each of the following rows gets a higher accuracy than its previous row by adding more higher order features. Putting in the sibling and grandchild conjoined features and the valency features yields a further improvement over the approximation of Koo and Collins (2010). Thus, the addition of new higher-order features, including valency, extra third-order, and label tuple features, results in increased accuracy. However, this is not without cost as the run-time in terms of tokens/sec decreases (300 to 220). But this decrease is not asymptotic, as it would be if one were to exactly search over our final model with these additional features, e.g., valency would at least multiply an additional $O(n)$ factor.

Higher-order Features	*UAS*	*LAS*	*Toks/Sec*
none	91.74	90.46	1510
McDonald (2006) features + labels	92.48	91.25	860
Carreras (2007) features + labels	92.85	91.66	540
Koo (2010) features + labels	92.92	91.75	300
all features	93.06	91.86	220

Table 3: Generalized higher-order parsing with cube pruning using different feature sets.

Beam	*Recombination*	*UAS*	*LAS*	*Toks/Sec*
2	no	92.86	91.63	280
2	yes	92.89	91.65	260
5	no	93.05	91.85	240
5	yes	93.06	91.86	230
10	yes	93.05	91.85	140

Table 4: Showing the effect of better search on accuracy and speed on the English test data with a fixed model.

5.4 Impact of Search Errors

Since our decoding algorithm is not exact, it could return sub-optimal outputs under the current model. We analyze the effect of search errors on accuracies in Table 4. We vary the beam size at each cell and switch the option for signature-based recombination to make search better or worse to see how much impact it has on the final accuracy.

The results indicate that a relatively small per-cell beam is good enough. Going from a beam of 2 to 5 increases accuracy notably, but going to a larger beam size has little effect but at a cost in terms of efficiency. This suggests that most of the parser ambiguity is represented in the top-5 feature signatures at each chart cell. Furthermore, recombination does help slightly, but more so at smaller beam sizes.

If we keep the beam size constant but enlarge the feature scope from second-order to third-order, one would expect more search errors to occur. We measured this empirically by computing the number of sentences where the gold tree had a higher model score than the predicted tree in the English evaluation data. Indeed, larger feature scopes do lead to more search errors, but the absolute number of search errors is usually quite small – there are only 19 search errors using second-order features and 32 search errors using third-order plus valency features out of 2416 English test sentences. Part of the reason for this is that there are only 12 la-

Language	Zhang and Nivre (reimpl.) (beam=64)	Zhang and Nivre (reimpl.) (beam=256)	Rush and Petrov‡	1st-order exact (reimpl.)	2nd-order exact (reimpl.)	3rd-order exact (reimpl.)	this paper
BG-CONLL	92.22 / 87.87	92.28 / 87.91	91.9- / -	91.98 / 87.13	93.02 / 88.13	92.96 / -	**93.08 / 88.23**
CA-CONLL	93.76 / 87.74	93.83 / 87.85		92.83 / 86.22	93.45 / 87.19	**94.07** / -	94.00 / **88.08**
DE-CONLL	89.18 / 86.50	88.94 / 86.58	90.8- / -	89.28 / 86.06	90.87 / 87.72	91.29 / -	**91.35 / 88.42**
ES-CONLL	86.64 / 83.25	86.62 / 83.11		85.35 / 81.53	86.80 / 82.91	87.26 / -	**87.48 / 84.05**
IT-CONLL	85.51 / 81.12	85.45 / 81.10		84.98 / 80.23	85.46 / 80.66	86.49 / -	**86.54 / 82.15**
JA-CONLL	92.70 / 91.03	92.76 / 91.09	92.3- / -	93.00 / 91.03	93.20 / 91.25	**93.36** / -	93.24 / **91.45**
PT-CONLL	91.32 / 86.98	91.28 / 86.88	91.5- / -	90.36 / 85.77	91.36 / 87.22	91.66 / -	**91.69 / 87.70**
SV-CONLL	90.84 / 85.30	91.00 / **85.42**	90.1- / -	89.32 / 82.06	90.50 / 83.01	90.32 / -	**91.44** / 84.58
ZH-CTB	86.04 / 84.48†	86.14 / 84.57		84.38 / 82.62	86.63 / 84.95	86.77 / -	**86.87 / 85.19**
AVG	89.80 / 86.03	89.81 / 86.06		89.05 / 84.74	90.14 / 85.89	90.46 / -	**90.63 / 86.65**

Table 2: UAS/LAS for experiments on non-English treebanks. Numbers in bold are the highest scoring system. Zhang and Nivre is a reimplementation of Zhang and Nivre (2011) with beams of size 64 and 256. Rush and Petrov are the UAS results reported in Rush and Petrov (2012). N^{th}-order exact are implementations of exact 1st-3rd order dependency parsing. †For reference, Zhang and Nivre (2011) report 86.0/84.4, which is previously the best result reported on this data set. ‡It should be noted that Rush and Petrov (2012) do not jointly optimize labeled and unlabeled dependency structure, which we found to often help. This, plus extra features, accounts for the differences in UAS.

bels in the Penn2Malt label set, which results in little non-structural ambiguity. In contrast, Stanford-style dependencies contain a much larger set of labels (50) with more fine-grained syntactic distinctions (De Marneffe et al., 2006). Training and testing a model using this dependency representation[2] increases the number of search errors of the full model to 126 out 2416 sentences. But that is still only 5% of all sentences and significantly smaller when measured per dependency.

6 Related Work

As mentioned in the introduction, there has been numerous studies on trying to reconcile the rich-features versus exact decoding trade-off in dependency parsing. In the transition-based parsing literature this has included the use of beam search to increase the search space (Duan et al., 2007; Johansson and Nugues, 2007; Titov and Henderson, 2007; Zhang and Clark, 2008; Zhang and Nivre, 2011). Huang and Sagae (2010) took a more principled approach proposing a method combining shift-reduce parsing with dynamic programming. They showed how feature signatures can be compiled into dynamic programming states and how best-first search can be used to find the optimal transition sequence. However, when the feature scope becomes large, then the state-space and resulting search space can be either intractable or simply non-practical to explore. Thus, they resort to an approximate beam search that still exploring an exponentially-larger space than greedy or beam-search transition-based systems. One can view the contribution in this paper as being the complement of the work of Huang and Sagae (2010) for graph-based systems. Our approach also uses approximate decoding in order to exploit arbitrary feature scope, while still exploring an exponentially-large search space. The primary difference is how the system is parameterized, over dependency sub-graphs or transitions. Another critical difference is that a chart-based algorithm, though still subject to search errors, is less likely to be hindered by an error made at one word position because it searches over many parallel alternatives in a bottom-up search as opposed to a left-to-right pass.

In the graph-based parsing literature, exact parsing algorithms for higher-order features have been studied extensively (McDonald and Pereira, 2006; Carreras, 2007; Koo and Collins, 2010), but at a high computational cost as increasing the order of a model typically results in an asymptotic increase in

[2]This model gets 90.4/92.8 LAS/UAS which is comparable to the UAS of 92.7 reported by Rush and Petrov (2012).

running time. ILP formulations of parsing (Riedel and Clarke, 2006; Martins et al., 2009; Martins et al., 2010) also allow for exact inference with higher-order features, but again at a high computational cost as ILP's have, in the worst-case, exponential run-time with respect to the sentence length. Studies that have abandoned exact inference have focused on sampling (Nakagawa, 2007), belief propagation (Smith and Eisner, 2008), Lagrangian relaxation (Koo et al., 2010; Martins et al., 2011), and more recently structured prediction cascades (Weiss and Taskar, 2010; Rush and Petrov, 2012). However, these approximations themselves are often computationally expensive, requiring multiple decoding/sampling stages in order to produce an output. All the methods above, both exact and approximate, require specialized algorithms for every new feature that is beyond the scope of the previous factorization. In our method, the same parsing algorithm can be utilized (Eisner's + cube pruning) just with slight different feature signatures.

Our proposed parsing model draws heavily on the work of Huang (2008). Huang introduced the idea of "forest rescoring", which uses cube pruning to enable the incorporation of non-local features into a constituency parsing model providing state-of-the art performance. This paper is the extension of such ideas to dependency parsing, also giving state-of-the-art results. An important difference between our formulation and forest rescoring is that we only have one decoding pass and a single trained model, while forest rescoring, as formulated by Huang (2008), separates a generative base model from a following discriminative re-ranking model. Hence, our formulation is more akin to the one pass decoding algorithm of Chiang (2007) for integrated decoding with a language model in machine translation. This also distinguishes it from previous work on dependency parse re-ranking (Hall, 2007) as we are not re-ranking/re-scoring the output of a base model but using a single decoding algorithm and learned model at training and testing.

This work is largely orthogonal to other attempts to speed up chart parsing algorithms. This includes work on coarse-to-fine parsing (Charniak and Johnson, 2005; Petrov and Klein, 2007; Rush and Petrov, 2012), chart-cell closing and pruning (Roark and Hollingshead, 2008; Roark and Hollingshead, 2009), and dynamic beam-width prediction (Bodenstab et al., 2011). Of particular note, Rush and Petrov (2012) report run-times far better than our cube pruning system. At the heart of their system is a linear time vine-parsing stage that prunes most of the search space before higher-order parsing. This effectively makes their final system linear time in practice as the higher order models have far fewer parts to consider. One could easily use the same first-pass pruner in our cube-pruning framework.

In our study we use cube pruning only for decoding and rely on inference-based learning algorithms to train model parameters. Gimpel and Smith (2009) extended cube pruning concepts to partition-function and marginal calculations, which would enable the training of probabilistic graphical models.

Finally, due to its use of the Eisner chart-parsing algorithm as a backbone, our model is fundamentally limited to predicting projective dependency structures. Investigating extensions of this work to the non-projective case is an area of future study. Work on defining bottom-up chart-parsing algorithms for non-projective dependency trees could potentially serve as a mechanism to solving this problem (Gómez-Rodríguez et al., 2009; Kuhlmann and Satta, 2009; Gómez-Rodríguez et al., 2010).

7 Conclusion

In this paper we presented a method for generalized higher-order dependency parsing. The method works by augmenting the dynamic programming signatures of the Eisner chart-parsing algorithm and then controlling complexity via cube pruning. The resulting system has the flexibility to incorporate arbitrary feature history while still exploring an exponential search space efficiently. Empirical results show that the system gives state-of-the-art accuracies across numerous data sets while still maintaining practical parsing speeds – as much as 4-5 times faster than exact third-order decoding.

Acknowledgments: We would like to thank Sasha Rush and Slav Petrov for help modifying their hypergraph parsing code. We would also like to thank the parsing team at Google for providing interesting discussions and new ideas while we conducted this work, as well as comments on earlier drafts of the paper.

References

N. Bodenstab, A. Dunlop, K. Hall, and B. Roark. 2011. Beam-width prediction for efficient context-free parsing. In *Proc. ACL*.

S. Buchholz and E. Marsi. 2006. CoNLL-X shared task on multilingual dependency parsing. In *Proc. of CoNLL*.

X. Carreras. 2007. Experiments with a higher-order projective dependency parser. In *Proc. of the CoNLL Shared Task Session of EMNLP-CoNLL*.

E. Charniak and M. Johnson. 2005. Coarse-to-fine n-best parsing and maxent discriminative reranking. In *Proc. ACL*.

D. Chiang. 2007. Hierarchical phrase-based translation. *Computational Linguistics*, 33(2).

K. Crammer, O. Dekel, J. Keshet, S. Shalev-Shwartz, and Y. Singer. 2006. Online passive-aggressive algorithms. *Journal of Machine Learning Research*.

M. De Marneffe, B. MacCartney, and C.D. Manning. 2006. Generating typed dependency parses from phrase structure parses. In *Proc. of LREC*.

X. Duan, J. Zhao, and B. Xu. 2007. Probabilistic parsing action models for multi-lingual dependency parsing. In *Proc. of EMNLP-CoNLL*.

J. Eisner. 1996. Three new probabilistic models for dependency parsing: an exploration. In *Proc. of COLING*.

K. Gimpel and N.A. Smith. 2009. Cube summing, approximate inference with non-local features, and dynamic programming without semirings. In *Proc. EACL*.

C. Gómez-Rodríguez, M. Kuhlmann, G. Satta, and D. Weir. 2009. Optimal reduction of rule length in linear context-free rewriting systems. In *Proc. NAACL*.

C. Gómez-Rodríguez, M. Kuhlmann, and G. Satta. 2010. Efficient parsing of well-nested linear context-free rewriting systems. In *Proc. NAACL*.

K. Hall. 2007. K-best spanning tree parsing. In *Proc. of ACL*.

L. Huang and S. Fayong. 2012. Structured perceptron with inexact search. In *Proc. of NAACL*.

L. Huang and K. Sagae. 2010. Dynamic programming for linear-time incremental parsing. In *Proc. of ACL*.

L. Huang. 2008. Forest reranking: Discriminative parsing with non-local features. In *Proc. of ACL*.

R. Johansson and P. Nugues. 2007. Incremental dependency parsing using online learning. In *Proc. of EMNLP-CoNLL*.

T. Koo and M. Collins. 2010. Efficient third-order dependency parsers. In *Proc. of ACL*.

T. Koo, A. Rush, M. Collins, T. Jaakkola, and D. Sontag. 2010. Dual decomposition for parsing with non-projective head automata. In *Proc. of EMNLP*.

M. Kuhlmann and G. Satta. 2009. Treebank grammar techniques for non-projective dependency parsing. In *Proc. EACL*.

A. F. T. Martins, N. Smith, and E. P. Xing. 2009. Concise integer linear programming formulations for dependency parsing. In *Proc. of ACL*.

A. F. T. Martins, N. Smith, E. P. Xing, P. M. Q. Aguiar, and M. A. T. Figueiredo. 2010. Turbo parsers: Dependency parsing by approximate variational inference. In *Proc. of EMNLP*.

A. F. T. Martins, N. Smith, M. A. T. Figueiredo, and P. M. Q. Aguiar. 2011. Dual decomposition with many overlapping components. In *Proc of EMNLP*.

R. McDonald and J. Nivre. 2007. Characterizing the errors of data-driven dependency parsing models. In *Proc. of EMNLP-CoNLL*.

R. McDonald and F. Pereira. 2006. Online learning of approximate dependency parsing algorithms. In *Proc. of EACL*.

R. McDonald, K. Crammer, and F. Pereira. 2005. Online large-margin training of dependency parsers. In *Proc. of ACL*.

T. Nakagawa. 2007. Multilingual dependency parsing using global features. In *Proc. of EMNLP-CoNLL*.

J. Nivre and R. McDonald. 2008. Integrating graph-based and transition-based dependency parsers. In *Proc. of ACL*.

J. Nivre, J. Hall, S. Kübler, R. McDonald, J. Nilsson, S. Riedel, and D. Yuret. 2007. The CoNLL 2007 shared task on dependency parsing. In *Proc. of EMNLP-CoNLL*.

S. Petrov and D. Klein. 2007. Improved inference for unlexicalized parsing. In *Proc. NAACL*.

S. Riedel and J. Clarke. 2006. Incremental integer linear programming for non-projective dependency parsing. In *Proc. of EMNLP*.

B. Roark and K. Hollingshead. 2008. Classifying chart cells for quadratic complexity context-free inference. In *Proc. COLING*.

B. Roark and K. Hollingshead. 2009. Linear complexity context-free parsing pipelines via chart constraints. In *Proce. NAACL*.

A. Rush and S. Petrov. 2012. Efficient multi-pass dependency pruning with vine parsing. In *Proc. of NAACL*.

D. Smith and J. Eisner. 2008. Dependency parsing by belief propagation. In *Proc. of EMNLP*.

I. Titov and J. Henderson. 2007. Fast and robust multilingual dependency parsing with a generative latent variable model. In *Proc. of EMNLP-CoNLL*.

D. Weiss and B. Taskar. 2010. Structured prediction cascades. In *Proc. of AISTATS*.

Y. Zhang and S. Clark. 2008. A Tale of Two Parsers: Investigating and Combining Graph-based and Transition-based Dependency Parsing. In *Proc. of EMNLP*.

Y. Zhang and J. Nivre. 2011. Transition-based dependency parsing with rich non-local features. In *Proc. of ACL-HLT*, volume 2.

Universal Grapheme-to-Phoneme Prediction Over Latin Alphabets

Young-Bum Kim and Benjamin Snyder
University of Wisconsin-Madison
{ybkim,bsnyder}@cs.wisc.edu

Abstract

We consider the problem of inducing grapheme-to-phoneme mappings for unknown languages written in a Latin alphabet. First, we collect a data-set of 107 languages with known grapheme-phoneme relationships, along with a short text in each language. We then cast our task in the framework of supervised learning, where each known language serves as a training example, and predictions are made on unknown languages. We induce an undirected graphical model that learns phonotactic regularities, thus relating textual patterns to plausible phonemic interpretations across the entire range of languages. Our model correctly predicts grapheme-phoneme pairs with over 88% F1-measure.

1 Introduction

Written language is one of the defining technologies of human civilization, and has been independently invented at least three times through the course of history (Daniels and Bright, 1996). In many ways written language reflects its more primary spoken counterpart. Both are subject to some of the same forces of change, including human migration, cultural influence, and imposition by empire. In other ways, written language harkens further to the past, reflecting aspects of languages long since gone from their spoken forms. In this paper, we argue that this imperfect relationship between written symbol and spoken sound can be automatically inferred from textual patterns. By examining data for over 100 languages, we train a statistical model to automatically relate graphemic patterns in text to phonemic sequences for never-before-seen languages.

We focus here on the the alphabet, a writing system that has come down to us from the Sumerians. In an idealized alphabetic system, each phoneme in the language is unambiguously represented by a single grapheme. In practice of course, this ideal is never achieved. When existing alphabets are melded onto new languages, they must be imperfectly adapted to a new sound system. In this paper, we exploit the fact that a single alphabet, that of the Romans, has been adapted to a very large variety of languages.

Recent research has demonstrated the effectiveness of cross-lingual analysis. The joint analysis of several languages can increase model accuracy, and enable the development of computational tools for languages with minimal linguistic resources. Previous work has focused on settings where just a handful of languages are available. We treat the task of grapheme-to-phoneme analysis as a test case for larger scale multilingual learning, harnessing information from dozens of languages.

On a more practical note, accurately relating graphemes and phonemes to one another is crucial for tasks such as automatic speech recognition and text-to-speech generation. While pronunciation dictionaries and transcribed audio are available for some languages, these resources are entirely lacking for the vast majority of the world's languages. Thus, automatic and generic methods for determining sound-symbol relationships are needed.

Our paper is based on the following line of reasoning: that character-level textual patterns mirror phonotactic regularities; that phonotactic regularities are shared across related languages and universally constrained; and that textual patterns for a newly observed language may thus reveal its underlying phonemics. Our task can be viewed as an easy case of lost language decipherment – one where the underlying alphabetic system is widely known.

Nevertheless, the task of grapheme-to-phoneme prediction is challenging. Characters in the Roman alphabet can take a wide range of phonemic values across the world's languages. For example, depending on the language, the grapheme "c" can represent the following phonemes:[1]

- /k/ (unvoiced velar plosive)
- /c/ (unvoiced palatal plosive)
- /s/ (unvoiced alveolar fricative)
- /ǀ/ (dental click)
- /d͡ʒ/ (affricated voiced postalveolar fricative)
- /t͡ʃ/ (affricated unvoiced postalveolar fricative)
- /t͡s/ (affricated unvoiced alveolar fricative)

To make matters worse, the same language may use a single grapheme to ambiguously represent *multiple* phonemes. For example, English orthography uses "c" to represent both /k/ and /s/. Our task is thus to select a *subset* of phonemes for each language's graphemes. We cast the subset selection problem as a set of related binary prediction problems, one for each possible grapheme-phoneme pair. Taken together, these predictions yield the grapheme-phoneme mapping for that language.

We develop a probabilistic undirected graphical model for this prediction problem, where a large set of languages serve as training data and a single held-out language serves as test data. Each training and test language yields an instance of the graph, bound together through a shared set of features and parameter values to allow cross-lingual learning and generalization.

In the graph corresponding to a given language, each node represents a grapheme-phoneme pair $(g : p)$. The node is labeled with a binary value to indicate whether grapheme g can represent phoneme p in the language. In order to allow coupled labelings across the various grapheme-phoneme pairs of the language, we employ a connected graph structure, with an automatically learned topology shared across the languages. The node and edge features are derived from textual co-occurrence statistics for the graphemes of each language, as well as general information about the language's family and region. Parameters are jointly optimized over the training languages to maximize the likelihood of the node labelings given the observed feature values. See Figure 1 for a snippet of the model.

We apply our model to a novel data-set consisting of grapheme-phoneme mappings for 107 languages with Roman alphabets and short texts. In this setting, we consider each language in turn as the test language, and train our model on the remaining 106 languages. Our highest performing model achieves an F1-measure of 88%, yielding perfect predictions for over 21% of languages. These results compare quite favorably to several baselines.

Our experiments lead to several conclusions. (i) Character co-occurence features alone are not sufficient for cross-lingual predictive accuracy in this task. Instead, we map raw contextual counts to more linguistically meaningful generalizations to learn effective cross-lingual patterns. (ii) A connected graph topology is crucial for learning linguistically coherent grapheme-to-phoneme mappings. Without any edges, our model yields perfect mappings for only 10% of test languages. By employing structure learning and including the induced edges, we more than double the number of test languages with perfect predictions. (iii) Finally, an analysis of our grapheme-phoneme predictions shows that they do not achieve certain global characteristics observed across true phoneme inventories. In particular, the level of "feature economy" in our predictions is too low, suggesting an avenue for future research.

[1] For some brief background on phonetics, see Section 2. Note that we use the term "phoneme" throughout the paper, though we also refer to "phonetic" properties. As we are dealing with texts (written in a roughly phonemic writing system), we have no access to the true contextual phonetic realizations, and even using IPA symbols to relate symbols across languages is somewhat theoretically suspect.

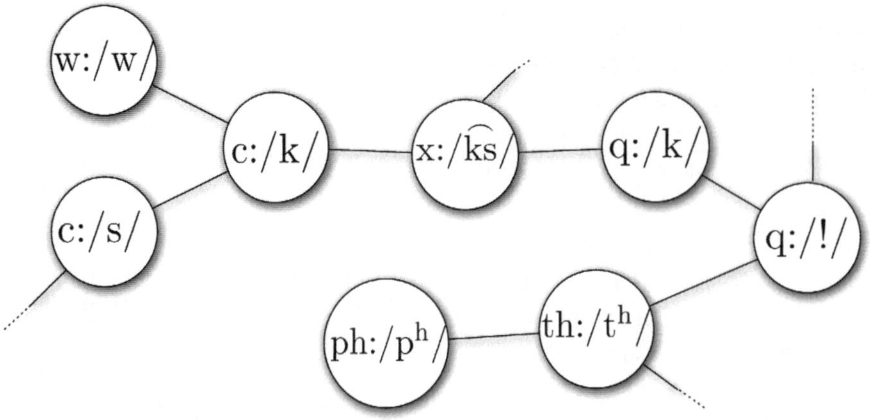

Figure 1: **A snippet of our undirected graphical model.** The binary-valued nodes represent whether a particular grapheme-phoneme pair is allowed by the language. Sparse edges are automatically induced to allow joint training and prediction over related inventory decisions.

2 Background and Related Work

In this section, we provide some background on phonetics and phoneme inventories. We also review prior work on grapheme-to-phoneme prediction and multilingual modeling.

2.1 Phoneme Inventories

The sounds of the world's languages are produced through a wide variety of articulatory mechanisms. Consonants are sounds produced through a partial or complete stricture of the vocal tract, and can be roughly categorized along three independent dimensions: *(i) Voicing:* whether or not oscillation of the vocal folds accompanies the sound. For example, /t/ and /d/ differ only in that the latter is voiced. *(ii) Place of Articulation:* where in the anatomy of the vocal tract the stricture is made. For example, /p/ is a bilabial (the lips touching one another) while /k/ is a velar (tongue touching touching the soft palate). *(iii) Manner of Articulation*: the manner in which the airflow is regulated. For example, /m/ is a nasal (air flowing through the nostrils), while /p/ is a plosive (obstructed air suddenly released through the mouth).

In contrast, vowels are voiced sounds produced with an open vocal tract. They are categorized primarily based on the position of the tongue and lips, along three dimensions: *(i) Roundedness:* whether or not the lips are rounded during production of the sound; *(ii) Height:* the vertical position of the tongue; *(iii) Backness:* how far forward the tongue lies.

Linguists have noted several statistical regularities found in phoneme inventories throughout the world. *Feature economy* refers to the idea that languages tend to minimize the number of differentiating characteristics (e.g. different kinds of voicing, manner, and place) that are used to distinguish consonant phonemes from one another (Clements, 2003). In other words, once an articulatory feature is used to mark off one phoneme from another, it will likely be used again to differentiate other phoneme pairs in the same language. The principle of *Maximal perceptual contrast* refers to the idea that the set of vowels employed by a language will be located in phonetic space to maximize their perceptual distances from one another, thus relieving the perceptual burden of the listener (Liljencrants and Lindblom, 1972). In an analysis of our results, we will observe that our model's predictions do not always follow these principles.

Finally, researchers have noted that languages exhibit set patterns in how they sequence their phonemes (Kenstowicz and Kisseberth, 1979). Certain sequences are forbidden outright by languages, while others are avoided or favored. While many of these patterns are language-specific, others seem more general, either reflecting anatomical constraints, common language ancestry, or universal aspects of the human language system. These phonotactic regularities and constraints are mirrored in graphemic patterns, and as our experiments show, can be explicitly modeled to achieve high accuracy in our task.

2.2 Grapheme-to-Phoneme Prediction

Much prior work has gone into developing methods for accurate grapheme-to-phoneme prediction. The common assumption underlying this research has been that some sort of knowledge, usually in the form of a pronunciation dictionary or phonemically annotated text, is available for the language at hand. The focus has been on developing techniques for dealing with the phonemic ambiguity present both in annotated and unseen words. For example, Jiampojamarn and Kondrak (Jiampojamarn and Kondrak, 2010) develop a method for aligning pairs of written and phonemically transcribed strings; Dwyer and Kondrak (Dwyer and Kondrak, 2009) develop a method for accurate letter-to-phoneme conversion while minimizing the number of training examples; Reddy and Goldsmith (Reddy and Goldsmith, 2010) develop an MDL-based approach to finding subword units that align well to phonemes.

A related line of work has grown around the task of machine transliteration. In this task, the goal is to automatically transliterate a name in one language into the written form of another language. Often this involves some level of phonetic analysis in one or both languages. Notable recent work in this vein includes research by Sproat et al (Sproat et al., 2006) on transliteration between Chinese and English using comparable corpora, and Ravi and Knight (Ravi and Knight, 2009) who take a decipherment approach to this problem.

Our work differs from all previous work on grapheme-to-phoneme prediction in that (i) we assume no knowledge for our target language beyond a small unannotated text (and possibly some region or language family information), and (ii) our goal is to construct the inventory of mappings between the language's letters and its phonemes (the latter of which we do not know ahead of time). When a grapheme maps to more than one phoneme, we do not attempt to disambiguate particular instances of that grapheme in words.

A final thread of related work is the task of quantitatively categorizing writing systems according to their levels of phonography and logography (Sproat, 2000; Penn and Choma, 2006). As our data-set consists entirely of Latin-based writing systems, our work can be viewed as a more fine-grained computational exploration of the space of writing systems, with a focus on phonographic systems with the Latin pedigree.

2.3 Multilingual Analysis

An influential thread of previous multilingual work starts with the observation that rich linguistic resources exist for some languages but not others. The idea then is to *project* linguistic information from one language onto others via parallel data. Yarowsky and his collaborators first developed this idea and applied it to the problems of part-of-speech tagging, noun-phrase bracketing, and morphology induction (Yarowsky and Wicentowski, 2000; Yarowsky et al., 2000; Yarowsky and Ngai, 2001), and other researchers have applied the idea to syntactic and semantic analysis (Hwa et al., 2005; Padó and Lapata, 2006) In these cases, the existence of a bilingual parallel text along with highly accurate predictions for one of the languages was assumed.

Another line of work assumes the existence of bilingual parallel texts without the use of any supervision (Dagan et al., 1991; Resnik and Yarowsky, 1997). This idea has been developed and applied to a wide variety tasks, including morphological analysis (Snyder and Barzilay, 2008a; Snyder and Barzilay, 2008b), part-of-speech induction (Snyder et al., 2008; Snyder et al., 2009a; Naseem et al., 2009), and grammar induction (Snyder et al., 2009b; Blunsom et al., 2009; Burkett et al., 2010). An even more recent line of work does away with the assumption of parallel texts and performs joint unsupervised induction for various languages through the use of coupled priors in the context of grammar induction (Cohen and Smith, 2009; Berg-Kirkpatrick and Klein, 2010).

In contrast to these previous approaches, the method we propose does not assume the existence of any parallel text, but instead assumes that labeled data exists for a wide variety of languages. In this regard, our work most closely resembles recent work which trains a universal morphological analyzer us-

	phonemes	#lang	ent
a	/a/ /ɐ/ /ɑ/ /ə/ /ʌ/	106	1.25
c	/c/ /d͡ʒ/ /k/ /s/ /t͡s/ /t͡ʃ/ /ǀ/	62	2.33
ch	/k/ /t͡ʃ/ /x/ /ʃ/	39	1.35
e	/e/ /i/ /æ/ /ə/ /ɛ/	106	1.82
h	/-/ /h/ /x/ /ø/ /ɦ/	85	1.24
i	/i/ /j/ /ɪ/	106	0.92
j	/d͡ʒ/ /h/ /j/ /t͡ʃ/ /x/ /ɟ/ /ʒ/	79	2.05
o	/o/ /u/ /ɒ/ /ʉ/	103	1.47
ph	/f/ /pʰ/	15	0.64
q	/k/ /q/ /!/	32	1.04
r	/r/ /ɽ/ /ɾ/ /ʀ/ /ʁ/	95	1.50
th	/tʰ/ /θ/	15	0.64
u	/u/ /w/ /y/ /ɨ/ /ʊ/ /ʏ/	104	0.96
v	/b/ /f/ /v/ /w/ /β/	70	1.18
w	/u/ /v/ /w/	74	0.89
x	/k͡s/ /x/ /ǁ/ /ʃ/	44	1.31
z	/d͡z/ /s/ /t͡s/ /z/ /θ/	72	0.93

Table 1: Ambiguous graphemes and the set of phonemes that they may represent among our set of 107 languages.

ing a structured nearest neighbor approach for 8 languages (Kim et al., 2011). Our work extends this idea to a new task and also considers a much larger set of languages. As our results will indicate, we found that a nearest neighbor approach was not as effective as our proposed model-based approach.

3 Data and Features

In this section we discuss the data and features used in our experiments.

3.1 Data

The data for our experiments comes from three sources: (i) grapheme-phoneme mappings from an online encyclopedia, (ii) translations of the Universal Declaration of Human Rights (UDHR)[2], and *(iii)* entries from the World Atlas of Language Structures (WALS) (Haspelmath and Bibiko, 2005).

To start, we downloaded and transcribed image files containing grapheme-phoneme mappings for several hundred languages from an online encyclopedia of writing systems[3]. We then cross-referenced the languages with the World Atlas of Language Structures (WALS) database (Haspelmath and Bibiko, 2005) as well as the translations available for the Universal Declaration of Human Rights (UDHR). Our final set of 107 languages includes those which appeared consistently in all three sources and that employ a Latin alphabet. See Figure 2 for a world map annotated with the locations listed in the WALS database for these languages, as well as their language families. As seen from the figure, these languages cover a wide array of language families and regions.

We then analyzed the phoneme inventories for the 107 languages. We decided to focus our attention on graphemes which are widely used across these languages with a diverse set of phonemic values. We measured the ambiguity of each grapheme by calculating the entropy of its phoneme sets across the languages, and found that 17 graphemes had entropy > 0.5 and appeared in at least 15 languages. Table 1 lists these graphemes, the set of phonemes that they can represent, the number of languages in our data-set which employ them, and the entropy of their phoneme-sets across these languages. The data, along with the feature vectors discussed below, are published as part of this paper.

3.2 Features

The key intuition underlying this work is that graphemic patterns in text can reveal the phonemes which they represent. A crucial step in operationalizing this intuition lies in defining input features that have cross-lingual predictive value. We divide our feature set into three categories.

Text Context Features: These features represent the textual environment of each grapheme in a language. For each grapheme g, we consider counts of graphemes to the immediate left and right of g in the UDHR text. We define five feature templates, including counts of (1) single graphemes to the left of g, (2) single graphemes to the right of g, (3) pairs of graphemes to the left of g, (4) pairs of graphemes to the right of g, and (5) pairs of graphemes surrounding g. As our experiments below show, this set of features on its own performs poorly. It seems that

[2]http://www.ohchr.org/en/udhr/pages/introduction.aspx

[3]http://www.omniglot.com/writing/langalph.htm#latin

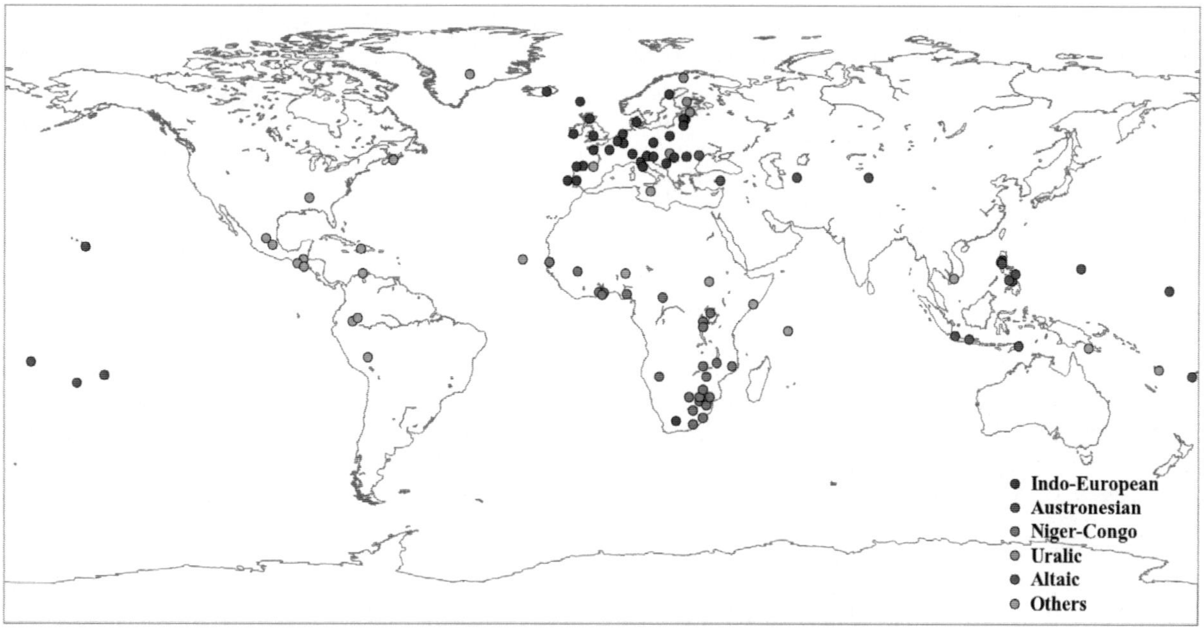

Figure 2: Map and language families of languages in our data-set

these features are too language specific and not abstract enough to yield effective cross-lingual generalization. Our next set of features was designed to alleviate this problem.

Phonemic Context Features: A perfect feature-set would depend on the entire set of grapheme-to-phoneme predictions for a language. In other words, we would ideally map *all* the graphemes in our text to phonemes, and then consider the plausibility of the resulting phoneme sequences. In practice, of course, this is impossible, as the set of possible grapheme-to-phoneme mappings is exponentially large. As an imperfect proxy for this idea, we made the following observation: for most Latin graphemes, the most common phonemic value across languages is the identical IPA symbol of that grapheme (e.g. the most common phoneme for *g* is /g/, the most common phoneme for *t* is /t/, etc). Using this observation, we again consider all contexts in which a grapheme appears, but this time map the surrounding graphemes to their IPA phoneme equivalents. We then consider various linguistic properties of these surrounding "phonemes" – whether they are vowels or consonants, whether they are voiced or not, their manner and places of articulation – and create phonetic context features. The process is illustrated in Figure 3. The intuition here is that these features can (noisily) capture the *phonotactic context* of a grapheme, allowing our model to learn general phonotactic constraints. As our experiments below demonstrate, these features proved to be quite powerful.

Language Family Features: Finally, we consider features drawn from the WALS database which capture general information about the language – specifically, its region (e.g. Europe), its small language family (e.g. Germanic), and its large language family (e.g. Indo-European). These features allow our model to capture family and region specific phonetic biases. For example, African languages are more likely to use *c* and *q* to represents clicks than are European languages. As we mention below, we also consider conjunctions of all features. Thus, a language family feature can combine with a phonetic context feature to represent a family specific phonotactic constraint. Interestingly, our experiments below show that these features are not needed for highly accurate prediction.

3.3 Feature Discretization and Filtering

It is well known that many learning techniques perform best when continuous features are binned and

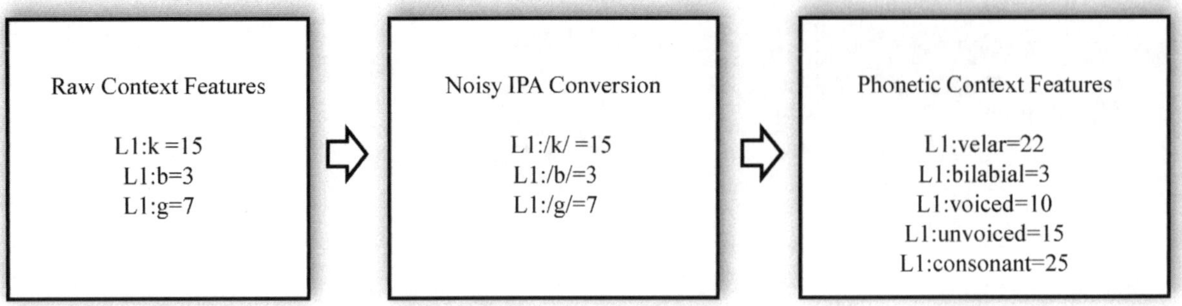

Figure 3: **Generating phonetic context features.** First, character context features are extracted for each grapheme. The features drawn here give the counts of the character to the immediate left of the grapheme. Next, the contextual characters are noisily converted to phones using their IPA notation. Finally, phonetic context features are extracted. In this case, phones /k/ and /g/ combine to give a "velar" count of 22, while /g/ and /b/ combine to give a "voiced" count of 10.

converted to binary values (Dougherty et al., 1995). As a preprocessing step, we therefore discretize and filter the count-based features outlined above. We adopt the technique of Recursive Minimal Entropy Partitioning (Fayyad and Irani, 1993). This technique recursively partitions feature values so as to minimize the conditional entropy of the labels. Partitioning stops when the gain in label entropy falls below the number of additional bits in overhead needed to describe the new feature split. This leads to a (local) minimum description length discretization.

We noticed that most of our raw features (especially the text features) could not achieve even a single split point without increasing description length, as they were not well correlated with the labels. We decided to use this heuristic as a feature selection technique, discarding such features. After this discretization and filtering, we took the resulting binary features and added their pairwise conjunctions to the set. This process was conducted separately for each leave-one-out scenario, without observation of the test language labels. Table 2 shows the total number of features before the discretization/filtering as well as the typical numbers of features obtained after filtering (the exact numbers depend on the training/test split).

	Raw	Filtered
# Text Features	28,474	1,848
# Phonemic Features	28,948	7,799
# Family Features	66	32
Total	57,488	9,679

Table 2: **Number of features** in each category before and after discretization/filtering. Note that the pair-wise conjunction features are not included in these counts.

4 Model

Using the features described above, we develop an undirected graphical model approach to our prediction task. Corresponding to each training language is an instance of our undirected graph, labeled with its true grapheme-phoneme mapping. We learn weights over our features which optimally relate the input features of the training languages to their observed labels. At test-time, the learned weights are used to predict the labeling of the held-out test language.

More formally, we assume a set of graph nodes $1, ..., m$ with edges between some pairs of nodes (i, j). Each node corresponds to a grapheme-phoneme pair $(g : p)$ and can be labeled with a binary value. For each training language ℓ, we observe a text $\mathbf{x}^{(\ell)}$ and a binary labeling of the graph nodes $\mathbf{y}^{(\ell)}$. For each node i, we also obtain a feature vector $f_i(\mathbf{x}^{(\ell)})$, by examining the language's text and extracting textual and noisy phonetic patterns (as detailed in the previous section). We obtain similar feature vectors for edges (i, j): $g_{jk}(\mathbf{x}^{(\ell)})$. We then parameterize the probability of each labeling using a log-linear form over node and edge factors:[4]

[4]The delta function $\delta(p)$ evaluates to 1 when predicate p is

$$\log P(\mathbf{y}^{(\ell)}|\mathbf{x}^{(\ell)}) = \sum_i \lambda_i \cdot [f_i(\mathbf{x}^{(\ell)})\ \delta(y_i^{(\ell)} = 1)]$$
$$+ \sum_{j,k} \lambda_{jk1} \cdot [g_{jk}(\mathbf{x}^{(\ell)})\ \delta(y_j^{(\ell)} = 1 \wedge y_k^{(\ell)} = 1)]$$
$$+ \sum_{j,k} \lambda_{jk2} \cdot [g_{jk}(\mathbf{x}^{(\ell)})\ \delta(y_j^{(\ell)} = 1 \wedge y_k^{(\ell)} = 0)]$$
$$+ \sum_{j,k} \lambda_{jk3} \cdot [g_{jk}(\mathbf{x}^{(\ell)})\ \delta(y_j^{(\ell)} = 0 \wedge y_k^{(\ell)} = 1)]$$
$$- \log Z(\mathbf{x}^{(\ell)}, \lambda)$$

The first term sums over nodes i in the graph. For each i, we extract a feature vector $f_i(\mathbf{x}^{(\ell)})$. If the label of node i is 1, we take the dot product of the feature vector and corresponding parameters, otherwise the term is zeroed out. Likewise for the graph edges j, k: we extract a feature vector, and depending on the labels of the two vertices y_j and y_k, take a dot product with the relevant parameters. The final term is a normalization constant to ensure that the probabilities sum to one over all possible labelings of the graph.

Before learning our parameters, we first automatically induce the set of edges in our graph, using the PC graph structure learning algorithm (Spirtes et al., 2000). This procedure starts with a fully connected undirected graph structure, and iteratively removes edges between nodes that are conditionally independent given other neighboring nodes in the graph according to a statistical independence test over all training languages. In our graphs we have 75 nodes, and thus 2,775 potential edges. Running the structure learning algorithm on our data yields sparse graphs, typically consisting of about 50 edges. In each leave-one-out scenario, a single structure is learned for all languages.

Once the graph structure has been induced, we learn parameter values by maximizing the L2-penalized conditional log-likelihood over all training languages:[5]

$$L(\lambda) = \sum_\ell \log P(\mathbf{y}^{(\ell)}|\mathbf{x}^{(\ell)}) - C||\lambda||^2$$

true, and to 0 when p is false.

[5] In our experiments, we used an L2 penalty weight of .5 for node features and .1 for edge features. Similar results are observed for a wide range of values.

The gradient takes the standard form of a difference between expected and observed feature counts (Lafferty et al., 2001). Expected counts, as well as predicted assignments at test-time, are computed using loopy belief propagation (Murphy et al., 1999). Numerical optimization is performed using L-BFGS (Liu and Nocedal, 1989).

5 Experiments

In this section, we describe the set of experiments performed to evaluate the performance of our model. Besides our primary undirected graphical model, we also consider several baselines and variants, in order to assess the contribution of our model's graph structure as well as the features used. In all cases, we perform leave-one-out cross-validation over the 107 languages in our data-set.

5.1 Baselines

Our baselines include:

1. A majority baseline, where the most common binary value is chosen for each grapheme-phoneme pair,
2. two linear SVM's, one trained using the discretized and filtered features described in Section 3.2, and the other using the raw continuous features,
3. a Nearest Neighbor classifier, which chooses the closest training language for each grapheme-phoneme pair in the discretized feature space, and predicts its label, and
4. a variant of our model with no edges between nodes (essentially reducing to a set of independent log-linear classifiers).

5.2 Evaluation

We report our results using three evaluation metrics of increasing coarseness.

1. **Phoneme-level**: For individual grapheme-phoneme pairs (e.g. a:/ɐ/, a:/ʌ/, c:/k/, c:/tʃ/) our task consists of a set of binary predictions, and can thus be evaluated in terms of precision, recall, and F1-measure. We report micro-averages of these quantities across all

	Phoneme			Grapheme	Language
	Precision	Recall	F1	Accuracy	Accuracy
MAJORITY	80.47	57.47	67.06	55.54	2.8
SVM CONTINUOUS	79.87	64.48	79.87	59.07	3.74
SVM DISCRETE	90.55	78.27	83.97	70.78	8.41
NEAREST NEIGHBOR	85.35	79.43	82.28	67.97	2.8
MODEL: NO EDGES	89.35	82.05	85.54	73.96	10.28
FULL MODEL	91.06	83.98	87.37	78.58	**21.5**
MODEL: NO FAMILY	**92.43**	**84.67**	**88.38**	**80.04**	19.63
MODEL: NO TEXT	89.58	81.43	85.31	75.86	15.89
MODEL: NO PHONETIC	86.52	74.19	79.88	69.6	9.35

Table 3: The performance of baselines and variants of our model, evaluated at the phoneme-level (binary predictions), whole-grapheme accuracy, and whole-language accuracy.

grapheme-phoneme pairs in all leave-one-out test languages.

2. **Grapheme-level**: We also report grapheme-level accuracy. For this metric, we consider each grapheme g and examine its predicted labels over all its possible phonemes: $(g : p_1), (g : p_2), ..., (g : p_k)$. If all k binary predictions are correct, then the grapheme's phoneme-set has been correctly predicted. We report the percentage of all graphemes with such correct predictions (micro-averaged over all graphemes in all test language scenarios).

3. **Language-level**: Finally, we assess language-wide performance. For this metric, we report the percentage of test languages for which our model achieves perfect predictions on all grapheme-phoneme pairs, yielding a perfect mapping.

5.3 Results

The results for the baselines and our model are shown in Table 3. The majority baseline yields 67% F1-measure on the phoneme-level binary prediction task, with 56% grapheme accuracy, and about 3% language accuracy.

Using undiscretized raw count features, the SVM improves phoneme-level performance to about 80% F1, but fails to provide any improvement on grapheme or language performance. In contrast, the SVM using discretized and filtered features achieves performance gains in all three categories, achieving 71% grapheme accuracy and 8% language accuracy. The nearest neighbor baseline achieves performance somewhere in between the two SVM variants.

The unconnected version of our model achieves similar, though slightly improved performance over the discretized SVM. Adding the automatically induced edges into our model leads to significant gains across all three categories. Phoneme-level F1 reaches 87%, grapheme accuracy hits 79%, and language accuracy more than doubles, achieving 22%. It is perhaps not surprising that the biggest relative gains are seen at the language level: by jointly learning and predicting an entire language's grapheme-phoneme inventory, our model ensures that language-level coherence is maintained.

Recall that three sets of features are used by our models. (1) language family and region features, (2) textual context features, and (3) phonetic context features. We now assess the relative merits of each set by considering our model's performance when the set has been removed. Table 3 shows several striking results from this experiment. First, it appears that dropping the region and language family features actually improves performance. This result is somewhat surprising, as we expected these features to be quite informative. However, it appears that whatever information they convey is redundant when considering the text-based feature sets. We next observe that dropping the textual context features leads to a small drop in performance. Finally, we see that dropping the phonetic context features seriously degrades our model's accuracy. Achieving robust cross-linguistic generalization apparently requires a level of feature abstraction not achieved by character-level context features alone.

6 Global Inventory Analysis

In the previous section we saw that our model achieves relatively high performance in predicting grapheme-phoneme relationships for never-before-seen languages. In this section we analyze the predicted phoneme inventories and ask whether they display the statistical properties observed in the gold-standard mappings.

As outlined in Section 2, consonant phonemes can be represented by the three articulatory features of voicing, manner, and place. The principle of feature economy states that phoneme inventories will be organized to minimize the number of distinct articulatory features used in the language, while maximizing the number of resulting phonemes. This principle has several implications. First, we can measure the *economy index* of a consonant system by computing the ratio of the number of consonantal phonemes to the number of articulatory features used in their production: $\frac{\#\text{consonants}}{\#\text{features}}$ (Clements, 2003). The higher this value, the more economical the sound system.

Secondly, for each articulatory dimension we can calculate the empirical distribution over values observed across the consonants of the language. Since consonants are produced as combinations of the three articulatory dimensions, the greatest number of consonants (for a given set of utilized feature values) will be produced when the distributions are close to uniform. Thus, we can measure how economical each feature dimension is by computing the entropy of its distribution over consonants. For example, in an economical system, we would expect roughly half the consonants to be voiced, and half to be unvoiced.

Table 4 shows the results of this analysis. First, we notice that the average entropy of voiced vs. unvoiced consonants is nearly identical in both cases, close to the optimal value. However, when we examine the dimensions of place and manner, we notice that the entropy induced by our model is not as high as that of the true consonant inventories, implying a suboptimal allocation of consonants. In fact, when we examine the economy index (ratio of consonants to features), we indeed find that – on average – our model's predictions are not as economical as the gold standard. This analysis suggests that we might obtain a more powerful predictive model by taking the principle of feature economy into account.

	H(voice)	H(place)	H(manner)	Economy Index
True	0.9739	2.7355	2.4725	1.6536
Predicted	0.9733	2.6715	2.4163	1.6337

Table 4: Measures of feature economy applied to the predicted and true consonant inventories (averaged over all 107 languages).

7 Conclusions

In this paper, we considered a novel problem: that of automatically relating written symbols to spoken sounds for an unknown language using a known writing system – the Latin alphabet. We constructed a data-set consisting of grapheme-phoneme mappings and a short text for over 100 languages. This data allows us to cast our problem in the supervised learning framework, where each observed language serves as a training example, and predictions are made on a new language. Our model automatically learns how to relate textual patterns of the unknown language to plausible phonemic interpretations using induced phonotactic regularities.

Acknowledgments

This work is supported by the NSF under grant IIS-1116676. Any opinions, findings, or conclusions are those of the authors, and do not necessarily reflect the views of the NSF.

References

Taylor Berg-Kirkpatrick and Dan Klein. 2010. Phylogenetic grammar induction. In *Proceedings of the ACL*, pages 1288–1297, Uppsala, Sweden, July. Association for Computational Linguistics.

P. Blunsom, T. Cohn, C. Dyer, and M. Osborne. 2009. A gibbs sampler for phrasal synchronous grammar induction. In *Proceedings of the Joint Conference of the*

47th Annual Meeting of the ACL and the 4th International Joint Conference on Natural Language Processing of the AFNLP: Volume 2-Volume 2, pages 782–790. Association for Computational Linguistics.

David Burkett, Slav Petrov, John Blitzer, and Dan Klein. 2010. Learning better monolingual models with unannotated bilingual text. In *Proceedings of CoNLL*.

G.N. Clements. 2003. Feature economy in sound systems. *Phonology*, 20(3):287–333.

Shay B. Cohen and Noah A. Smith. 2009. Shared logistic normal distributions for soft parameter tying in unsupervised grammar induction. In *Proceedings of the NAACL/HLT*.

Ido Dagan, Alon Itai, and Ulrike Schwall. 1991. Two languages are more informative than one. In *Proceedings of the ACL*, pages 130–137.

P.T. Daniels and W. Bright. 1996. *The world's writing systems*, volume 198. Oxford University Press New York, NY.

James Dougherty, Ron Kohavi, and Mehran Sahami. 1995. Supervised and unsupervised discretization of continuous features. In *ICML*, pages 194–202.

K. Dwyer and G. Kondrak. 2009. Reducing the annotation effort for letter-to-phoneme conversion. In *Proceedings of the Joint Conference of the 47th Annual Meeting of the ACL and the 4th International Joint Conference on Natural Language Processing of the AFNLP: Volume 1-Volume 1*, pages 127–135. Association for Computational Linguistics.

Usama M Fayyad and Keki B Irani. 1993. Multi-interval discretization of continuous-valued attributes for classification learning. In *Proceedings of the International Joint Conference on Uncertainty in AI*, pages 1022–1027.

M. Haspelmath and H.J. Bibiko. 2005. *The world atlas of language structures*, volume 1. Oxford University Press, USA.

R. Hwa, P. Resnik, A. Weinberg, C. Cabezas, and O. Kolak. 2005. Bootstrapping parsers via syntactic projection across parallel texts. *Journal of Natural Language Engineering*, 11(3):311–325.

S. Jiampojamarn and G. Kondrak. 2010. Letter-phoneme alignment: An exploration. In *Proceedings of the 48th Annual Meeting of the Association for Computational Linguistics*, pages 780–788. Association for Computational Linguistics.

M.J. Kenstowicz and C.W. Kisseberth. 1979. *Generative phonology*. Academic Press San Diego, CA.

Young-Bum Kim, João Graça, and Benjamin Snyder. 2011. Universal morphological analysis using structured nearest neighbor prediction. In *Proceedings of the 2011 Conference on Empirical Methods in Natural Language Processing*, pages 322–332, Edinburgh, Scotland, UK., July. Association for Computational Linguistics.

John D. Lafferty, Andrew McCallum, and Fernando C. N. Pereira. 2001. Conditional random fields: Probabilistic models for segmenting and labeling sequence data. In *Proceedings of the Eighteenth International Conference on Machine Learning*, pages 282–289.

J. Liljencrants and B. Lindblom. 1972. Numerical simulation of vowel quality systems: the role of perceptual contrast. *Language*, pages 839–862.

D.C. Liu and J. Nocedal. 1989. On the limited memory bfgs method for large scale optimization. *Mathematical programming*, 45(1):503–528.

K.P. Murphy, Y. Weiss, and M.I. Jordan. 1999. Loopy belief propagation for approximate inference: An empirical study. In *Proceedings of the Fifteenth conference on Uncertainty in artificial intelligence*, pages 467–475. Morgan Kaufmann Publishers Inc.

Tahira Naseem, Benjamin Snyder, Jacob Eisenstein, and Regina Barzilay. 2009. Multilingual part-of-speech tagging: two unsupervised approaches. *Journal of Artificial Intelligence Research*, 36(1):341–385.

Sebastian Padó and Mirella Lapata. 2006. Optimal constituent alignment with edge covers for semantic projection. In *Proceedings of ACL*, pages 1161 1168.

G. Penn and T. Choma. 2006. Quantitative methods for classifying writing systems. In *Proceedings of the Human Language Technology Conference of the NAACL, Companion Volume: Short Papers*, pages 117–120. Association for Computational Linguistics.

S. Ravi and K. Knight. 2009. Learning phoneme mappings for transliteration without parallel data. In *Proceedings of Human Language Technologies: The 2009 Annual Conference of the North American Chapter of the Association for Computational Linguistics*, pages 37–45. Association for Computational Linguistics.

S. Reddy and J. Goldsmith. 2010. An mdl-based approach to extracting subword units for grapheme-to-phoneme conversion. In *Human Language Technologies: The 2010 Annual Conference of the North American Chapter of the Association for Computational Linguistics*, pages 713–716. Association for Computational Linguistics.

Philip Resnik and David Yarowsky. 1997. A perspective on word sense disambiguation methods and their evaluation. In *Proceedings of the ACL SIGLEX Workshop on Tagging Text with Lexical Semantics: Why, What, and How?*, pages 79–86.

B. Snyder and R. Barzilay. 2008a. Unsupervised multilingual learning for morphological segmentation. *Proceedings of ACL-08: HLT*, pages 737–745.

Benjamin Snyder and Regina Barzilay. 2008b. Crosslingual propagation for morphological analysis. In *Proceedings of the AAAI*, pages 848–854.

Benjamin Snyder, Tahira Naseem, Jacob Eisenstein, and Regina Barzilay. 2008. Unsupervised multilingual learning for POS tagging. In *Proceedings of EMNLP*, pages 1041–1050.

B. Snyder, T. Naseem, J. Eisenstein, and R. Barzilay. 2009a. Adding more languages improves unsupervised multilingual part-of-speech tagging: A bayesian non-parametric approach. In *Proceedings of Human Language Technologies: The 2009 Annual Conference of the North American Chapter of the Association for Computational Linguistics*, pages 83–91. Association for Computational Linguistics.

Benjamin Snyder, Tahira Naseem, and Regina Barzilay. 2009b. Unsupervised multilingual grammar induction. In *Proceedings of the ACL*, pages 73–81.

P. Spirtes, C.N. Glymour, and R. Scheines. 2000. *Causation, prediction, and search*, volume 81. The MIT Press.

R. Sproat, T. Tao, and C.X. Zhai. 2006. Named entity transliteration with comparable corpora. In *Proceedings of the 21st International Conference on Computational Linguistics and the 44th annual meeting of the Association for Computational Linguistics*, pages 73–80. Association for Computational Linguistics.

R.W. Sproat. 2000. *A computational theory of writing systems*. Cambridge Univ Pr.

David Yarowsky and Grace Ngai. 2001. Inducing multilingual pos taggers and np bracketers via robust projection across aligned corpora. In *Proceedings of the NAACL*, pages 1–8.

David Yarowsky and Richard Wicentowski. 2000. Minimally supervised morphological analysis by multimodal alignment. In *ACL '00: Proceedings of the 38th Annual Meeting on Association for Computational Linguistics*, pages 207–216, Morristown, NJ, USA. Association for Computational Linguistics.

David Yarowsky, Grace Ngai, and Richard Wicentowski. 2000. Inducing multilingual text analysis tools via robust projection across aligned corpora. In *Proceedings of HLT*, pages 161–168.

Name Phylogeny: A Generative Model of String Variation

Nicholas Andrews and **Jason Eisner** and **Mark Dredze**
Department of Computer Science and Human Language Technology Center of Excellence
Johns Hopkins University
3400 N. Charles St., Baltimore, MD 21218 USA
{noa,eisner,mdredze}@jhu.edu

Abstract

Many linguistic and textual processes involve transduction of strings. We show how to learn a stochastic transducer from an unorganized collection of strings (rather than string pairs). The role of the transducer is to organize the collection. Our generative model explains similarities among the strings by supposing that some strings in the collection were not generated *ab initio*, but were instead derived by transduction from other, "similar" strings in the collection. Our variational EM learning algorithm alternately reestimates this phylogeny and the transducer parameters. The final learned transducer can quickly link any test name into the final phylogeny, thereby locating variants of the test name. We find that our method can effectively find name variants in a corpus of web strings used to refer to persons in Wikipedia, improving over standard untrained distances such as Jaro-Winkler and Levenshtein distance.

1 Introduction

Systematic relationships between pairs of strings are at the core of problems such as transliteration (Knight and Graehl, 1998), morphology (Dreyer and Eisner, 2011), cross-document coreference resolution (Bagga and Baldwin, 1998), canonicalization (Culotta et al., 2007), and paraphrasing (Barzilay and Lee, 2003). Stochastic transducers such as probabilistic finite-state transducers are often used to capture such relationships. They model a conditional distribution $p(y \mid x)$, and are ordinarily trained on input-output *pairs* of strings (Dreyer et al., 2008).

In this paper, we are interested in learning from an *unorganized* collection of strings, some of which might have been derived from others by *transformative linguistic processes* such as abbreviation, morphological derivation, historical sound or spelling change, loanword formation, translation, transliteration, editing, or transcription error. We assume that each string was derived from at most one parent, but may give rise to any number of children.

The difficulty is that most or all of these parent-child relationships are unobserved. We must reconstruct this evolutionary phylogeny. At the same time, we must fit the parameters of a model of the relevant linguistic process $p(y \mid x)$, which says what sort of children y might plausibly be derived from parent x. Learning this model of $p(y \mid x)$ helps us organize the training collection by reconstructing its phylogeny, and also permits us to generalize to new forms.

We will focus on the problem of name variation. We observe a collection of person names—full names, nicknames, abbreviated or misspelled names, etc. Some of these names can refer to the same person; we hope to detect this. It would be an unlikely coincidence if two mentions of John Jacob Jingleheimer Schmidt referred to different people, since this is a long and unusual name. Similarly, John Jacob Jingelhimer Smith and Dr. J. J. Jingleheimer may also be related names for this person. That is, these names may be derived from one another, via unseen relationships, although we cannot be sure.

Readers may be reminded of unsupervised clustering, in which "suspiciously similar" points can be explained as having been generated by the same cluster. Since each name is linked to at most one parent, our setting resembles single-link clustering—with a learned, asymmetric distance measure $p(y \mid x)$.

We will propose a generative process that makes explicit assumptions about how strings are copied with mutation. It is assumed to have generated all the names in the collection, in an unknown order. Given learned parameters, we can ask the model whether a name Dr. J. J. Jingelheimer in the collection is more likely to have been generated from scratch, or derived from some previous name.

1.1 Related Work

Several previous papers have also considered learning transducers or other models of word pairs when the pairing between inputs and outputs is not given. Most commonly, one observes parallel or comparable corpora in two languages, and must reconstruct a matching from one language's words to the other's before training on the resulting pairs (Schafer, 2006b; Klementiev and Roth, 2006; Haghighi et al., 2008; Snyder et al., 2010; Sajjad et al., 2011).

Hall and Klein (2010) extend this setting to more than two languages, where the phylogenetic tree is known. A given lexeme (abstract word) can be realized in each language by at most one word (string type), derived from the parent language's realization of the same lexeme. The system must match words that share an underlying lexeme (i.e., cognates), creating a matching of each language's vocabulary to its parent language's vocabulary. A further challenge is that the parent words are *unobserved* ancestral forms.

Similarly, Dreyer and Eisner (2011) organize words into morphological paradigms of a given structure. Again words with the same underlying lexeme (i.e., morphemes) must be identified. A lexeme can be realized in each grammatical inflection (such as "first person plural present") by exactly one word type, related to other inflected forms of the same lexeme, which as above may be unobserved. Their inference setting is closer to ours because the input is an unorganized collection of words—input words are not tagged with their grammatical inflections. This contrasts with the usual multilingual setting where each word is tagged with its true language.

In one way, our problem differs significantly from the above problems. We are interested in random variation that may occur *within* a language as well as across languages. A person name may have *unboundedly* many different variants. This is unlike the above problems, in which a lexeme has at most K realizations, where K is the (small) number of languages or inflections.[1] We cannot assign the observed strings to positions in an existing structure that is shared across all lexemes, such as a given phylogenetic tree whose K nodes represent languages, or a given inflectional grid whose K cells represent grammatical inflections. Rather, we must organize them into a idiosyncratic phylogenetic tree whose nodes are the string types or tokens themselves.

Names and words are not the only non-biological objects that are copied with mutation. Documents, database records, bibliographic entries, code, and images can evolve in the same way. Reconstructing these relationships has been considered by a number of papers on authorship attribution, near-duplicate detection, deduplication, record linkage, and plagiarism detection. A few such papers reconstruct a phylogeny, as in the case of chain letters (Bennett et al., 2003), malware (Karim et al., 2005), or images (Dias et al., 2012). In fact, the last of these uses the same minimum spanning tree method that we apply in §5.3. However, these papers do not *train* a similarity measure as we do. To our knowledge, these two techniques have not been combined outside biology.

In molecular evolutionary analysis, phylogenetic techniques *have* often been combined with estimation of some parametric model of mutation (Tamura et al., 2011). However, names mutate differently from biological sequences, and our mutation model for names (§4, §8) reflects that. We also posit a specific process (§3) that generates the name phylogeny.

2 An Example

A fragment of a phylogeny for person names is shown in Figure 1. Our procedure learned this automatically from a collection of name tokens, without observing any input/output pairs. The nodes of the phylogeny are the observed name types,[2] each one associated with a count of observed tokens.

Each arrow corresponds to a hypothesized mutation. These mutations reflect linguistic processes such as misspelling, initialism, nicknaming, transliteration, etc. As an exception, however, each arrow from the distinguished root node $\diamondsuit$ generates an initial name for a new entity. The descendants of this initial name are other names that subsequently evolved for that entity. Thus, the child subtrees of $\diamondsuit$ give a partition of the name types into entities.

Thanks to the phylogeny, the seemingly disparate names Ghareeb Nawaz and Muinuddin Chishti are seen to refer to the same entity. They may be traced back to their common ancestor Khawaja Gharib-

[1] In the above problems, one learns a set of $O(K)$ or $O(K^2)$ specialized transducers that relate Latin to Italian, singular to plural, etc. We instead use one global mutation model that applies to all names—but see footnote 14 on incorporating specialized transductions (Latin to Italian) within our mutation model.

[2] We cannot currently hypothesize unobserved intermediate forms, e.g., common ancestors of similar strings. See §6.2.

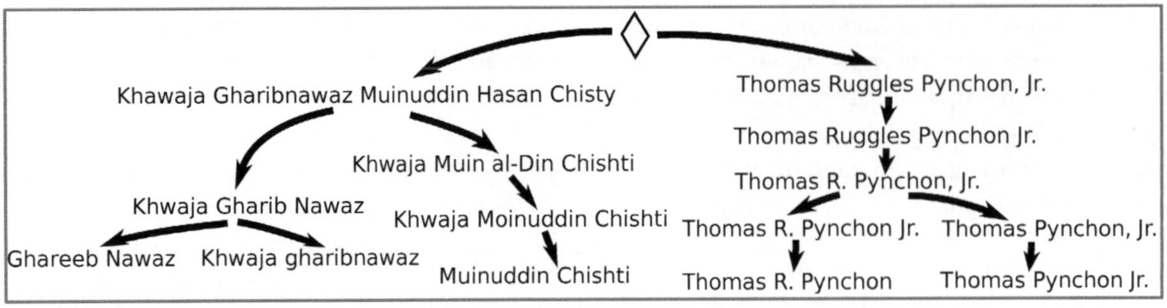

Figure 1: A portion of a spanning tree found by our model.

nawaz Muinuddin Hasan Chisty, from which both were derived via successive mutations.

Not shown in Figure 1 is our learned family p of conditional probability distributions, which models the likely mutations in this corpus. Our EM learning procedure found p jointly with the phylogeny. Specifically, it alternated between improving p and improving the distribution over phylogenies. At the end, we extracted the single best phylogeny.

Together, the learned p and the phylogeny in Figure 1 form an *explanation* of the observed collection of names. What makes it more probable than other explanations? Informally, two properties:

- Each node in the tree is plausibly derived from its parent. More precisely, the product of the edge probabilities under p is comparatively high. A different p would have reduced the probability of the events in this phylogeny. A different phylogeny would have involved a more improbable collection of events, such as replacing Chishti with Pynchon, or generating many unrelated copies of Pynchon directly from $\diamondsuit$.

- In the phylogeny, the parent names tend to be used often enough that it is plausible for variants of these names to have emerged. Our model says that new tokens are derived from previously generated tokens. Thus—other things equal—Barack Obama is more plausibly a variant of Barack Obama, Jr. than of Barack Obama, Sr. (which has fewer tokens).

3 A Generative Model of Tokens

Our model should reflect the *reasons* that name variation exists. A named entity has the form $y = (e, w)$ where w is a string being used to refer to entity e. A single entity e may be referred to on different occasions by different name strings w. We suppose that this is the result of *copying* the entity with occasional *mutation* of its name (as in asexual reproduction).

Thus, we assume the following simple generative process that produces an *ordered sequence* of tokens $y_1, y_2, \ldots$, where $y_i = (e_i, w_i)$.

• After the first k tokens $y_1, \ldots y_k$ have been generated, the author responsible for generating y_{k+1} must choose whom to talk about next. She is likely to think of someone she has heard about often in the past. So to make this choice, she selects one of the previous tokens y_i uniformly at random, each having probability $1/(k + \alpha)$; or else she selects $\diamondsuit$, with probability $\alpha/(k + \alpha)$.

• If the author selected a previous token y_i, then with probability $1 - \mu$ she copies it faithfully, so $y_{k+1} = y_i$. But with probability μ, she instead draws a mutated token $y_{k+1} = (e_{k+1}, w_{k+1})$ from the mutation model $p(\cdot \mid y_i)$. This preserves the entity ($e_{k+1} = e_i$ with probability 1), but the new name w_{k+1} is a stochastic transduction of w_i drawn from $p(\cdot \mid w_i)$.[3] For example, in referring to e_i, the author may shorten and respell w_i = Khwaja Gharib Nawaz into w_{k+1} = Ghareeb Nawaz (Figure 1).

• If the author selected $\diamondsuit$, she must choose a fresh entity $y_{k+1} = (e_{k+1}, w_{k+1})$ to talk about. So she sets e_{k+1} to a newly created entity, sampling its name w_{k+1} from the distribution $p(\cdot \mid \diamondsuit)$. For example, w_{k+1} = Thomas Ruggles Pynchon, Jr. (Figure 1). Nothing prevents w_{k+1} from being a name that is already in use for another entity (i.e., w_{k+1} may equal w_j for some $j \leq k$).

[3] Straightforward extensions are to allow a variable mutation rate $\mu(y_i)$ that depends on properties of y_i, and to allow w_{k+1} to depend on known properties of e_i. See footnote 14 for further discussion of enriched tokens.

3.1 Relationship to other models

If we ignore the name strings, we can see that the sequence of entities $e_1, e_2, \ldots e_N$ is being generated from a Chinese restaurant process (CRP) with concentration parameter α. To the extent that α is low (so that $\diamond$ is rarely used), a few randomly chosen entities will dominate the corpus.

The CRP is equivalent to sampling $e_1, e_2, \ldots$ IID from an unknown distribution that was itself drawn from a Dirichlet process with concentration α. This is indeed a standard model of a distribution over entities. For example, Hall et al. (2008) use it to model venues in bibliographic entries.

From this characterization of the CRP, one can see that any permutation of this entity sequence would have the same probability. That is, our distribution over sequences of *entities* e is **exchangeable**.

However, our distribution over sequences of *named entities* $y = (e, w)$ is **non-exchangeable**. It assigns different probabilities to different orderings of the same tokens. This is because our model posits that later authors are influenced by earlier authors, copying entity names from them with mutation. So ordering is important. The mutation process is not symmetric—for example, Figure 1 reflects a tendency to shorten rather than lengthen names.

Non-exchangeability is one way that our present model differs from (parametric) transformation models (Eisner, 2002) and (non-parametric) transformation processes (Andrews and Eisner, 2011). These too are defined using mutation of strings or other types. From a transformation process, one can draw a distribution over types, from which the tokens are then sampled IID. This results in an *exchangeable* sequence of tokens, just as in the Dirichlet process.

We avoid transformation models here for three reasons. (1) Inference is more expensive. (2) A transformation process seems less realistic as a model of authorship. It constructs a distribution over derivational *paths*, similar to the paths in Figure 1. It effectively says that each token is generated by recapitulating some previously used path from $\diamondsuit$, but with some chance of deviating *at each step*. For an author to generate a name token this way, she would have to know the whole derivational history of the previous name she was adapting. Our present model instead allows an author simply to select a name she previously saw and copy or mutate its surface form. (3) One should presumably prefer to explain a novel name y as a mutation of a *frequent* name x, other things equal (§2). But surprisingly, inference under the transformation process does not prefer this.[4]

Another view of our present model comes from the literature on random graphs (e.g., for modeling social networks or the link structure of the web). In a *preferential attachment* model, a graph's vertices are added one by one, and each vertex selects some previous vertices as its neighbors. Our phylogeny is a *preferential attachment tree*, a random *directed* graph in which each vertex selects a *single* previous vertex as its parent. Specifically, it is a *random recursive tree* (Smythe and Mahmoud, 1995) whose vertices are the tokens.[5] To this simple random topology we have added a random labeling process with mutation. The first α vertices are labeled with $\diamondsuit$.

4 A Mutation Model for Strings

Our model in §3 samples the next token y, when it is not simply a faithful copy, from $p(y \mid x)$ or $p(y \mid \diamondsuit)$. The key step there is to sample the name string w_y from $p(w_y \mid w_x)$ or $p(w_y \mid \diamondsuit)$.

Our model of these distributions could easily incorporate detailed linguistic knowledge of the mutation process (see §8). Here we describe the specific model that we use in our experiments. Like many such models, it can be regarded as a stochastic finite-state string-to-string transducer parameterized by θ.

There is much prior work on stochastic models of edit distance (Ristad and Yianilos, 1998; Bilenko and Mooney, 2003; Oncina and Sebban, 2006; Schafer, 2006a; Bouchard-Côté et al., 2008; Dreyer et al., 2008, among others). For the present experiments, we designed a moderately simple one that employs (1) conditioning on one character of right context, (2) latent "edit" and "no-edit" regions to capture the fact that groups of edits are often made in close proximity, and (3) some simple special handling for the distribution conditioned on the root $p(w_y \mid \diamondsuit)$.

We assume a stochastic mutation process which, when given an input string w_x, edits it from left to

[4] The very fact that x has been frequently observed demonstrates that it has often chosen to stop mutating. This implies that it is likely to choose stop again rather than mutate into y.

[5] This is not the tree shown in Figure 1, whose vertices are types rather than tokens.

right into an output string w_y. Then $p(w_y \mid w_x)$ is the total probability of all operation sequences on w_x that would produce w_y. This total can be computed in time $O(|w_x| \cdot |w_y|)$ by dynamic programming.

Our process has four character-level edit operations: copy, substitute, insert, delete. It also has a distinguished no-edit operation that behaves exactly like copy. At each step, the process first randomly chooses whether to edit or no-edit, conditioned only on whether the previous operation was an edit. If it chooses to edit, it chooses a random edit type with some probability conditioned on the next input character. In the case of insert or substitute, it then randomly chooses an output character, conditioned on the type of edit *and* the next input character.

It is common to mutate a name by editing contiguous substrings (e.g., words). Contiguous regions of copying versus editing can be modeled by a low probability of transitioning between no-edit and edit regions.[6] Note that an edit region may include some copy edits (or substitute edits that replace a character with itself) without leaving the edit region. This is why we distinguish copy from no-edit.

Input and output strings are augmented with a trailing EOS ("end-of-string") symbol that is seen by the single-character lookahead. If the next character is EOS, the only available edit is insert. Alternatively, if the process selects no-edit, then EOS is copied to the output string and the process terminates.

In the case of $p(w_y \mid \diamondsuit)$, the input string is empty, and both input and output are augmented with a trailing EOS$'$ character that behaves like EOS. Then w_y is generated by a sequence of insertions followed by a copy. These are conditioned as usual on the next character, here EOS$'$, so the model can learn to insert more or different characters when the input is $\diamondsuit$.

The parameters θ determining the conditional probabilities of the different operations and characters are estimated with backoff smoothing.

5 Inference

The input to inference is a collection of named entity tokens y. Most are *untagged tokens* of the form $y = (?, w)$. In a semi-supervised setting, however, some of the tokens may be *tagged tokens* of the form $y = (e, w)$, whose true entity is known. The entity tags place a constraint on the phylogeny, since each child subtree of $\diamondsuit$ must correspond to exactly one entity.

5.1 An unrealistically supervised setting

Suppose we were lucky enough to fully observe the *sequence* of named entity tokens $y_i = (e_i, w_i)$ produced by our generative model. That is, suppose all tokens were tagged *and we knew their ordering.*

Yet there would still be something to infer: which tokens were derived from which previous tokens. This phylogeny is described by a spanning tree over the tokens. Let us see how to infer it.

For each potential edge $x \rightarrow y$ between named entity tokens, define $\delta(y \mid x)$ to be the probability of choosing x and copying it (possibly with mutation) to obtain y. So

$$\delta(y_j \mid \diamondsuit) = \alpha\, p(y_j \mid \diamondsuit) \quad (1)$$

$$\delta(y_j \mid y_i) = \mu\, p(y_j \mid y_i) + (1-\mu)\mathbb{1}(y_j = y_i) \quad (2)$$

except that if $i \geq j$ or if $e_i \neq e_j$, then $\delta(y_j \mid y_i) = 0$ (since y_j can only be derived from an *earlier* token y_i with the *same entity*).

Now the prior probability of generating $y_1, \ldots y_N$ with a given phylogenetic tree is easily seen to be a product over all tree edges, $\prod_j \delta(y_j \mid \text{pa}(y_j))$ where $\text{pa}(y_j)$ is the parent of y_j. As a result, it is known that the following are *efficient to compute* from the $(N+1) \times (N+1)$ matrix of δ values (see §5.3):

(a) the max-probability spanning tree

(b) the total probability of all spanning trees

(c) the marginal probability of each edge, under the posterior distribution on spanning trees

(a) is our single best guess of the phylogeny. We use this during evaluation. (b) gives the model likelihood, i.e., the total probability of the observed data $y_1, \ldots y_N$. To locally maximize the model likelihood, (c) can serve as the E step of our EM algorithm (§6) for tuning our mutation model. The M step then retrains the mutation model's parameters θ on input-output pairs $w_i \rightarrow w_j$, weighting each pair by its edge's posterior marginal probability (c), since that is the expected count of a $w_i \rightarrow w_j$ mutation. This computation is iterated.

[6] This somewhat resembles the traditional affine gap penalty in computational biology (Gusfield, 1997), which makes deletions or insertions cheaper if they are consecutive. We instead make consecutive edits cheaper regardless of the edit type.

5.2 The unsupervised setting

Now we turn to a real setting—fully unsupervised data. Two issues will force us to use an approximate inference algorithm. First, we have an *untagged* corpus: a token's entity tag e is never observed. Second, the *order* of the tokens is not observed, so we do not know which other tokens are candidate parents.

Our first approximation is to consider only phylogenies over *types* rather than tokens.[7] The type phylogeny in Figure 1 represents a set of possible token phylogenies. Each node of Figure 1 represents an untagged name type $y = (?, w)$. By grouping all n_y tokens of this type into a single node, we mean that the *first* token of y was derived by mutation from the parent node, while each *later* token of y was derived by copying an (unspecified) earlier token of y.

A token phylogeny *cannot* be represented in this way if two or more tokens of y were created by mutations. In that case, their name strings are equal only *by coincidence*. They may have different parents (perhaps of different entities), whereas the y node in a type phylogeny can have only one parent.

We argue, however, that these unrepresentable token phylogenies are comparatively unlikely *a posteriori* and can be reasonably ignored during inference. The first token of y is necessarily a mutation, but later tokens are much more likely to be copies. The probability of generating a later token y by copying some previous token is *at least*

$$(1 - \mu)/(N + \alpha),$$

while the probability of generating it in some other way is *at most*

$$\max(\alpha\, p(y \mid \diamondsuit),\ \ \mu \max_{x \in \mathcal{Y}} p(y \mid x))$$

where $\mathcal{Y}$ is the set of observed types. The second probability is typically much smaller: an author is unlikely to invent exactly the observed string y, certainly from $\diamondsuit$ but even by mutating a similar string x (especially when the mutation rate μ is small).

How do we evaluate a type phylogeny? Consider the probability of generating untagged tokens $y_1, \ldots y_N$ in that order and respecting the phylogeny:

$$\left(\prod_{k=1}^{N} \frac{1}{k + \alpha}\right) \prod_{y \in \mathcal{Y}} g(y \mid \mathrm{pa}(y)) \left(\prod_{i=1}^{n_y - 1} i\,(1 - \mu)\right) \tag{3}$$

where $g(y \mid \mathrm{pa}(y))$ is a factor for generating the *first* token of y from its parent $\mathrm{pa}(y)$, defined by

$$\begin{aligned} g(y \mid \diamondsuit) &= \alpha \cdot p(y \mid \diamondsuit) & (4)\\ g(y \mid x) &= \mu \cdot (\text{\# tokens of } x \text{ preceding} \\ &\qquad \text{first token of } y) \cdot p(y \mid x) & (5) \end{aligned}$$

But we do not actually know the token order: by assumption, our input corpus is only an *unordered* bag of tokens. So we must treat the hidden ordering like any other hidden variable and maximize the *marginal* likelihood, which sums (3) over all *possible* orderings (permutations). This sum can be regarded as the number of permutations $N!$ (which is fixed given the corpus) times the expectation of (3) for a permutation chosen uniformly at random.

This leads to our second approximation. We approximate this expectation of the product (3) with a product of expectations of its individual factors.[8] To find the expectation of (5), observe that the *expected* number of tokens of x that precede the first token of y is $n_x/(n_y+1)$, since each of the n_x tokens of x has a $1/(n_y + 1)$ chance of falling before all n_y tokens of y. It follows that the approximated probability of generating all tokens in *some* order, with our given type parentage, is *proportional to*

$$\prod_{y \in \mathcal{Y}} \delta(y \mid \mathrm{pa}(y)) \tag{6}$$

where

$$\begin{aligned} \delta(y \mid \diamondsuit) &= \alpha \cdot p(y \mid \diamondsuit) & (7)\\ \delta(y \mid x) &= \mu \cdot p(y \mid x) \cdot n_x/(n_y + 1) & (8) \end{aligned}$$

and the constant of proportionality depends on the corpus.

The above equations are analogous to those in §5.1. Again, the approximate posterior probability of a given type parentage tree is *edge-factored*—it is the product of individual edge weights defined by δ. Thus, we are again eligible to use the spanning tree algorithms in §5.3 below.

[7] Working over types improves the quality of our second approximation, and also speeds up the spanning tree algorithms. §6 explains how to regard this approximation as variational EM.

[8] In general this is an overestimate for each phylogeny.

Notice that the ratio α/μ controls the preference for an entity to descend from $\diamondsuit$ versus an existing entity. Thus, by tuning this ratio, we can control the number of entities inferred by our method, where each entity corresponds to one of the child subtrees of $\diamondsuit$.

Also note that n_x in the numerator of (8) means that y's parent is more likely to be frequent. Also, $n_y + 1$ in the denominator means that a frequent y is not as likely to have any parent $x \neq \diamondsuit$, because its first token probably falls early in the sequence where there are fewer available parents $x \neq \diamondsuit$.

5.3 Spanning tree algorithms

Define a complete directed graph G over the vertices $\mathcal{Y} \cup \{\diamondsuit\}$. The weight of an edge $x \rightarrow y$ is defined by $\delta(y \mid x)$. The (approximate) posterior probability of a given phylogeny given our evidence, is proportional to the product of the δ values of its edges.

Formally, let $\mathcal{T}_\diamondsuit(G)$ denote the set of spanning trees of G rooted at $\diamondsuit$, and define the weight of a particular spanning tree $T \in \mathcal{T}_\diamondsuit(G)$ to be the product of the weights of its edges:

$$w(T) = \prod_{(x \rightarrow y) \in T} \delta(y \mid x) \tag{9}$$

Then the posterior probability of spanning tree T is

$$p_\theta(T) = \frac{w(T)}{Z(G)} \tag{10}$$

where $Z(G) = \sum_{T \in \mathcal{T}_\diamondsuit(G)} w(T)$ is the partition function, i.e. the total probability of generating the data G via any spanning tree of the form we consider. This distribution is determined by the parameters θ of the transducer p_θ, along with the ratio α/μ.

There exist several algorithms to find the single maximum-probability spanning tree, notably Tarjan's implementation of the Chu-Liu-Edmonds algorithm, which runs in $O(m \log n)$ for a sparse graph or $O(n^2)$ for a dense graph (Tarjan, 1977). Figure 1 shows a spanning tree found by our model using Tarjan's algorithm. Here n is the number of vertices (in our case, types and $\diamond$), while m is the number of edges (which we can keep small by pruning, §6.1).

6 Training the Transducer with EM

Our inference algorithm assumes that we know the transducer parameters θ. We now explain how to optimize θ to maximize the marginal likelihood of the training data. This marginal likelihood sums over all the other latent variables in the model—the spanning tree, the alignments between strings, and the hidden token ordering.

The EM procedure repeats the following until convergence:

E-step: Given θ, compute the posterior marginal probabilities c_{xy} of all possible phylogeny edges.

M-step Given all c_{xy}, retrain θ to assign a high conditional probability to the mutations on the probable edges.

We actually use a variational EM algorithm: our E step approximates the true distribution q over all phylogenies with the closest distribution p that assigns positive probability only to type-based phylogenies. This distribution is given by (10) and minimizes KL($p \parallel q$). We argued in section §5.2 that it should be a good approximation. The posterior marginal probability of a directed edge from vertex x to vertex y, according to (10), is

$$c_{xy} = \sum_{T \in \mathcal{T}_\diamondsuit(G):(x \rightarrow y) \in T} p_\theta(T) \tag{11}$$

The probability c_{xy} is a "pseudocount" for the expected number of mutations from x to y. This is at most 1 under our assumptions.

Calculating c_{xy} requires summing over all spanning trees of G, of which there are n^{n-2} for a fully connected graph with n vertices. Fortunately, Tutte (1984) shows how to compute this sum by the following method, which extends Kirchhoff's classical matrix-tree theorem to weighted directed graphs. This result has previously been employed in non-projective dependency parsing (Koo et al., 2007; Smith and Smith, 2007).

Let $\mathbf{L} \in \mathbb{R}^{n \times n}$ denote the Laplacian of G, namely

$$\mathbf{L} = \begin{cases} \sum_{x'} \delta(y \mid x') & \text{if } x = y \\ -\delta(y \mid x) & \text{if } x \neq y \end{cases} \tag{12}$$

Tutte's theorem relates the determinant of the Laplacian to the spanning trees in graph G. In particular, the cofactor $\mathbf{L}^{0,0}$ is equal to the sum of the weights of all directed spanning trees rooted at 0, which (supposing $\diamondsuit$ is indexed at 0) yields the partition function $Z(G)$.

The edge marginals of interest are related to the log partition function by

$$c_{xy} = \frac{\partial Z(G)}{\partial \delta(y \mid x)} \tag{13}$$

which has the closed-form solution

$$c_{xy} = \begin{cases} \delta(y \mid \diamondsuit)\mathbf{L}^{-1}_{yy} & \text{if } x = y \\ \delta(y \mid x)(\mathbf{L}^{-1}_{xx} - \mathbf{L}^{-1}_{xy}) & \text{if } x \neq y \end{cases} \tag{14}$$

Thus, the problem of computing edge marginals reduces to that of computing a matrix inverse, which may be done in $O(n^3)$ time.

At the M step, we retrain the mutation model parameters θ to maximize $\sum_{xy} c_{xy} \log p(w_y \mid w_x)$. This is tantamount to maximum conditional likelihood training on a supervised collection of (w_x, w_y) pairs that are respectively weighted by c_{xy}.

The M step is nontrivial because the term $p(w_y \mid w_x)$ sums over a hidden alignment between two strings. It may be performed by an inner loop of EM, where the E step uses dynamic programming to efficiently consider all possible alignments, as in (Ristad and Yianilos, 1996). In practice, we have found it effective to take only a single step of this inner loop. Such a Generalized EM procedure enjoys the same convergence properties as EM, but may reach a local optimum faster (Dempster et al., 1977).

6.1 Pruning the graph

For large graphs, it is essential to prune the number of edges to avoid considering all $n(n-1)$ input-output pairs. To prune the graph, we eliminate all edges between strings that do not share any common trigrams (case- and diacritic-insensitive), by setting their matrix entries to 0. As a result, the graph Laplacian is a sparse matrix, which often allows faster matrix inversion using preconditioned iterative algorithms. Furthermore, pruned edges do not appear in any spanning tree, so the E step will find that their posterior marginal probabilities are 0. This means that the input-output pairs corresponding to these edges can be ignored when re-estimating the transducer parameters in the M step. We found that pruning significantly improves training time with no appreciable loss in performance.[9]

6.2 Training with unobserved tokens?

A deficiency of our method is that it assumes that authors of our corpus have *only* been exposed to previous tokens in our corpus. In principle, one could also train with U additional tokens (e, w) where we observe neither e nor w, for very large U. This is the "universe of discourse" in which our authors operate.[10] In this case, we would need (expensive) new algorithms to reconstruct the strings w. However, this model could infer a more realistic phylogeny by positing unobserved ancestral or intermediate forms that relate the observed tokens, as in transformation models (Eisner, 2002; Andrews and Eisner, 2011).

7 Experimental Evaluation

7.1 Data preparation

Scraping Wikipedia. Wikipedia documents many variant names for entities. As a result, it has frequently been used as a source for mining name variations, both within and across languages (Parton et al., 2008; Cucerzan, 2007). We used Wikipedia to create a list of name aliases for different entities. Specifically, we mined English Wikipedia[11] for all redirects: page names that lead directly to another page. Redirects are created by Wikipedia users for resolving common name variants to the correct page. For example, the pages titled Barack Obama Junior and Barack Hussein Obama automatically redirect to the page titled Barack Obama. This redirection implies that the first two are name variants of the third. Collecting all such links within English Wikipedia yields a large number of aliases for each page. However, many redirects are for topics other than individual people, and these would be poor examples of name variation. In addition, some phrases

[9] For instance, on a dataset of approximately 6000 distinct names, pruning reduced the number of outgoing edges at each vertex to fewer than 100 per vertex.

[10] Notice that the N observed tokens would be approximately exchangeable in this setting: they are unlikely to depend on one another when $N \ll U$, and hence their order no longer matters much. In effect, generating the U hidden tokens constructs a rich distribution (analogous to a sample from the Dirichlet process) from which the N observed tokens are then sampled IID.

[11] Using a Wikipedia dump from February 2, 2011.

Ho Chi Minh, Ho chi mihn, Ho-Chi Minh, Ho Chih-minh
Guy Fawkes, Guy fawkes, Guy faux, Guy Falks, Guy Faukes, Guy Fawks, Guy foxe, Guy Falkes
Nicholas II of Russia, Nikolai Aleksandrovich Romanov, Nicholas Alexandrovich of Russia, Nicolas II
Bill Gates, Lord Billy, Bill Gates, BillGates, Billy Gates, William Gates III, William H. Gates
William Shakespeare, William shekspere, William shakspeare, Bill Shakespear
Bill Clinton, Billll Clinton, William Jefferson Blythe IV, Bill J. Clinton, William J Clinton

Figure 2: Sample alias lists scraped from Wikipedia. Note that only partial alias lists are shown for space reasons.

that redirect to an entity are descriptions rather than names. For example, 44th President of the United States also links to Barack Obama, but it is not a name variant.

Freebase filtering. To improve data quality we used Freebase, a structured knowledge base that incorporates information from Wikipedia. Among its structured information are entity types, including the type "person." We filtered the Wikipedia redirect collection to remove pairs where the target page was not listed as a person in Freebase. Additionally, to remove redirects that were not proper names (44th President of the United States), we applied a series of rule based filters to remove bad aliases: removing numerical names, parentheticals after names, quotation marks, and names longer than 5 tokens, since we found that these long names were rarely person names (e.g. United States Ambassador to the European Union, Success Through a Positive Mental Attitude which links to the author Napoleon Hill.) While not perfect, these modifications dramatically improved quality. The result was a list of 78,079 different person entities, each with one or more known names or aliases. Some typical names are shown in Figure 2.

Estimating empirical type counts. Our method is really intended to be run on a corpus of string tokens. However, for experimental purposes, we instead use the above dataset of string *types* because this allows us to use the "ground truth" given by the Wikipedia redirects. To synthesize token counts, empirical token frequencies for each type were estimated from the LDC Gigaword corpus,[12] which is a corpus of newswire text spanning several years. Wikipedia name types that did not appear in Gigaword were assigned a "backoff count" of one. Note that by virtue of the domain, many misspellings will not appear; however, edges "popular" names (which may be canonical names) will be assigned higher weight.

7.2 Experiments

We begin by evaluating the generalization ability of a transducer trained using a transformation model. To do so, we measure log-likelihood on held-out entity title and alias pairs. We then verify that the generalization ability according to log-likelihood translates into gains for a name matching task. For the experiments in this section, we use $\alpha = 0.9$ and $\mu = 0.1$.[13]

Held-out log-likelihood. We construct pairs of entity title (input) and alias (output) names from the Wikipedia data. For different amounts of supervised data, we trained the transformation model on the training set, and plotted the log-likelihood of held-out test data for the transducer parameters at each iteration of EM. The held-out test set is constructed from a disjoint set of Wikipedia entities, the same number of entities as in the training set. We used different corpora of 1000 and 1500 entities for train and test.

Name matching. For each alias a in a test set (not seen at training time), we produce a ranking of test entity titles t according to transducer probabilities $p_\theta(a \mid t)$. A good transducer should assign high probability to transformations from the correct title for the alias. Mean reciprocal rank (MRR) is a commonly used metric to estimate the quality of a ranking, which we report in Figure 4. The reported mean is over all aliases in the test data. In addition to evaluating the ranking for different initializations of our transducer, we compare to two baselines: Levenshtein distance and Jaro-Winkler similarity. Jaro-Winkler is a measure on strings that was specifically designed for record linkage (Winkler, 1999). The

[12]LDC Catalog No. LDC2003T05.

[13]We did not find these parameters to be sensitive.

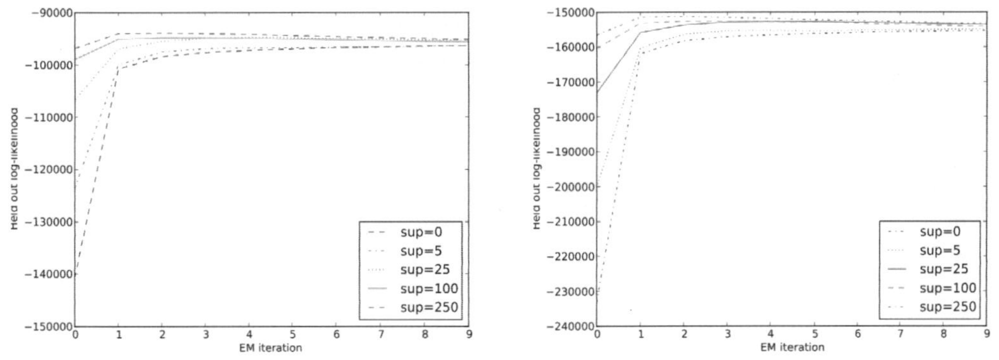

(a) 1000 entities.

(b) 1500 entities.

Figure 3: Learning curves for different initializations of the transducer parameters. Above, "sup=100" (for instance) means that 100 entities were used as training data to initialize the transducer parameters (constructing pairs between all title-alias pairs for those Wikpedia entities).

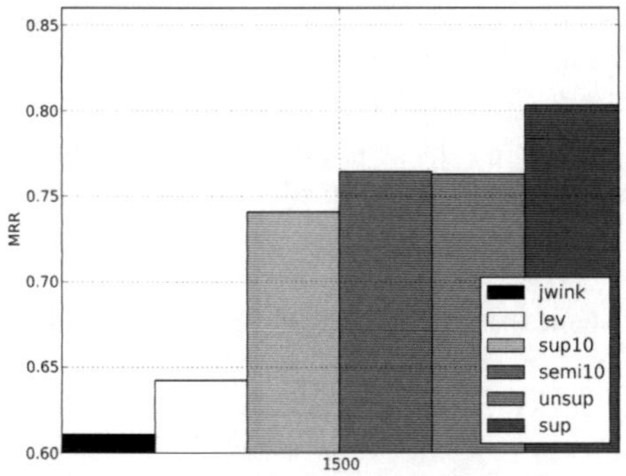

Figure 4: Mean reciprocal rank (MRR) results for different training conditions: "sup10" means that 10 entities (roughly 40 name pairs) were used as training data for the transducer; "semi10" means that the "sup10" model was used as initialization before re-estimating the parameters using our model; "unsup" is the transducer trained using our model without any initial supervision; "sup" is trained on all 1500 entities in the training set (an upper bound on performance); "jwink" and "lev" correspond to Jaro-Winkler and Levenshtein distance baselines.

matching experiments were performed on a corpus of 1500 entities (with separate corpora of the same size for training and test).

8 Conclusions and Future Work

We have presented a new unsupervised method for learning string-to-string transducers. It learns from a collection of related strings whose relationships are unknown. The key idea is that some strings are mutations of common strings that occurred earlier. We compute a distribution over the unknown phylogenetic tree that relates these strings, and use it to reestimate the transducer parameters via EM.

One direction for future work would be more sophisticated transduction models than the one we developed in §4. For names, this could include learning common nicknames (nonparametrically); explicitly modeling abbreviation processes such as initials; conditioning on name components such as title and middle name; and transliterating across languages.[14] In other domains, one could model bibliographic entry propagation, derivational morphology, or historical sound change (again using language tags).

Another future direction would be to incorporate the context of tokens in order to help reconstruct which tokens are coreferent. For example, we might extend the generative story to generate a context for token (e, w) conditioned on e. Combining contextual similarity with string similarity has previously proved very useful for identifying cognates (Schafer and Yarowsky, 2002; Schafer, 2006b; Bergsma and Van Durme, 2011). In our setting it would help to distinguish people with identical names, as well as determining whether two people with similar names are really the same.

[14]These last two points suggest that the mutation model should operate not on simple (entity, string) pairs, but on richer representations in which the name has been parsed into its components (Eisenstein et al., 2011), labeled with a language ID, and perhaps labeled with a phonological pronunciation. These additional properties of a named entity may be either observed or latent in training data. For example, if w_y and ℓ_y denote the string and language of name y, then define $p(y \mid x) = p(\ell_y \mid \ell_x) \cdot p(w_y \mid \ell_y, \ell_x, w_x)$. The second factor captures transliteration from language ℓ_x to language ℓ_y, e.g., by using §4's model with an (ℓ_x, ℓ_y)-specific parameter setting.

References

Nicholas Andrews and Jason Eisner. 2011. Transformation process priors. In *NIPS 2011 Workshop on Bayesian Nonparametrics: Hope or Hype?*, Sierra Nevada, Spain, December. Extended abstract (3 pages).

A. Bagga and B. Baldwin. 1998. Algorithms for scoring coreference chains. In *LREC*.

Regina Barzilay and Lillian Lee. 2003. Learning to paraphrase: an unsupervised approach using multiple-sequence alignment. In *Proc. of NAACL-HLT*, pages 16–23, Stroudsburg, PA, USA.

C. H. Bennett, M. Li, , and B. Ma. 2003. Chain letters and evolutionary histories. *Scientific American*, 288(3):76–81, June. More mathematical version available at `http://www.cs.uwaterloo.ca/~mli/chain.html`.

Shane Bergsma and Benjamin Van Durme. 2011. Learning bilingual lexicons using the visual similarity of labeled web images. In *Proc. of IJCAI*, pages 1764–1769, Barcelona, Spain.

Mikhail Bilenko and Raymond J. Mooney. 2003. Adaptive duplicate detection using learnable string similarity measures. In *Proc. of ACM SIGKDD International Conference on Knowledge Discovery and Data Mining*, KDD '03, pages 39–48, New York, NY, USA. ACM.

Alexandre Bouchard-Côté, Percy Liang, Thomas Griffiths, and Dan Klein. 2008. A probabilistic approach to language change. In *Proc. of NIPS*, pages 169–176.

S. Cucerzan. 2007. Large-scale named entity disambiguation based on Wikipedia data. In *Proc. of EMNLP*.

Aron Culotta, Michael Wick, Robert Hall, Matthew Marzilli, and Andrew McCallum. 2007. Canonicalization of database records using adaptive similarity measures. In *Proc. of ACM SIGKDD International Conference on Knowledge Discovery and Data Mining*, KDD '07, pages 201–209.

A. P. Dempster, N. M. Laird, and D. B. Rubin. 1977. Maximum likelihood from incomplete data via the EM algorithm. *Journal of the Royal Statistical Society. Series B (Methodological)*, 39(1):1–38.

Z. Dias, A. Rocha, and S. Goldenstein. 2012. Image phylogeny by minimal spanning trees. *IEEE Trans. on Information Forensics and Security*, 7(2):774–788, April.

Markus Dreyer and Jason Eisner. 2011. Discovering morphological paradigms from plain text using a Dirichlet process mixture model. In *Proc. of EMNLP*, pages 616–627. Supplementary material (9 pages) also available.

Markus Dreyer, Jason Smith, and Jason Eisner. 2008. Latent-variable modeling of string transductions with finite-state methods. In *Proc. of EMNLP*, pages 1080–1089, Honolulu, Hawaii, October. Association for Computational Linguistics.

Jacob Eisenstein, Tae Yano, William Cohen, Noah Smith, and Eric Xing. 2011. Structured databases of named entities from Bayesian nonparametrics. In *Proc. of the First workshop on Unsupervised Learning in NLP*, pages 2–12, Edinburgh, Scotland, July. Association for Computational Linguistics.

Jason Eisner. 2002. Transformational priors over grammars. In *Proceedings of the Conference on Empirical Methods in Natural Language Processing (EMNLP)*, Philadelphia, July.

Dan Gusfield. 1997. *Algorithms on Strings, Trees, and Sequences—Computer Science and Computational Biology*. Cambridge University Press.

Aria Haghighi, Percy Liang, Taylor Berg-Kirkpatrick, and Dan Klein. 2008. Learning bilingual lexicons from monolingual corpora. In *Proc. of ACL-08: HLT*, pages 771–779.

David Hall and Dan Klein. 2010. Finding cognates using phylogenies. In *Association for Computational Linguistics (ACL)*.

Rob Hall, Charles Sutton, and Andrew McCallum. 2008. Unsupervised deduplication using cross-field dependencies. In *Proc. of the ACM SIGKDD International Conference On Knowledge Discovery and Data Mining*, KDD '08, pages 310–317.

Md. Enamul. Karim, Andrew Walenstein, Arun Lakhotia, and Laxmi Parida. 2005. Malware phylogeny generation using permutations of code. *Journal in Computer Virology*, 1(1–2):13–23.

Alexandre Klementiev and Dan Roth. 2006. Weakly supervised named entity transliteration and discovery from multilingual comparable corpora. In *Proc. of COLING-ACL*, pages 817–824.

K. Knight and J. Graehl. 1998. Machine transliteration. *Computational Linguistics*, 24:599–612.

Terry Koo, Amir Globerson, Xavier Carreras, and Michael Collins. 2007. Structured prediction models via the matrix-tree theorem. In *Proc. of EMNLP-CoNLL*, pages 141–150.

Jose Oncina and Marc Sebban. 2006. Using learned conditional distributions as edit distance. In *Proc. of the 2006 Joint IAPR international Conference on Structural, Syntactic, and Statistical Pattern Recognition*, SSPR'06/SPR'06, pages 403–411.

Kristen Parton, Kathleen R. McKeown, James Allan, and Enrique Henestroza. 2008. Simultaneous multilingual search for translingual information retrieval. In *Proceeding of the ACM conference on Information and Knowledge Management*, CIKM '08, pages 719–728.

Eric Sven Ristad and Peter N. Yianilos. 1996. Learning string edit distance. Technical Report CS-TR-532-96, Princeton University, Department of Computer Science.

Eric Sven Ristad and Peter N. Yianilos. 1998. Learning string edit distance. *IEEE Transactions on Pattern Recognition and Machine Intelligence*, 20(5):522–532, May.

Hassan Sajjad, Alexander Fraser, and Helmut Schmid. 2011. An algorithm for unsupervised transliteration mining with an application to word alignment. In *Proc. of ACL*, pages 430–439.

Charles Schafer and David Yarowsky. 2002. Inducing translation lexicons via diverse similarity measures and bridge languages. In *Proc. of CONLL*, pages 146–152.

Charles Schafer. 2006a. Novel probabilistic finite-state transducers for cognate and transliteration modeling. In *7th Biennial Conference of the Association for Machine Translation in the Americas (AMTA)*.

Charles Schafer. 2006b. *Translation Discovery Using Diverse Smilarity Measures*. Ph.D. thesis, Johns Hopkins University.

David A. Smith and Noah A. Smith. 2007. Probabilistic models of nonprojective dependency trees. In *Proc. of EMNLP-CoNLL*, pages 132–140.

R. T. Smythe and H. M. Mahmoud. 1995. A survey of recursive trees. *Theory of Probability and Mathematical Statistics*, 51(1–27).

Benjamin Snyder, Regina Barzilay, and Kevin Knight. 2010. A statistical model for lost language decipherment. In *Proc. of ACL*, pages 1048–1057.

Koichiro Tamura, Daniel Peterson, Nicholas Peterson, Glen Stecher, Masatoshi Nei, and Sudhir Kumar. 2011. Mega5: Molecular evolutionary genetics analysis using maximum likelihood, evolutionary distance, and maximum parsimony methods. *Molecular Biology and Evolution*, 28(10):2731–2739.

R E Tarjan. 1977. Finding optimum branchings. *Networks*, 7(1):25–35.

W. Tutte. 1984. *Graph Theory*. Addison-Wesley.

William E. Winkler. 1999. The state of record linkage and current research problems. Technical report, Statistical Research Division, U.S. Census Bureau.

Syntactic surprisal affects spoken word duration in conversational contexts

Vera Demberg, Asad B. Sayeed, Philip J. Gorinski, and Nikolaos Engonopoulos
M2CI Cluster of Excellence and
Department of Computational Linguistics and Phonetics
Saarland University
66143 Saarbrücken, Germany
{vera,asayeed,philipg,nikolaos}@coli.uni-saarland.de

Abstract

We present results of a novel experiment to investigate speech production in conversational data that links speech rate to information density. We provide the first evidence for an association between syntactic surprisal and word duration in recorded speech. Using the AMI corpus which contains transcriptions of focus group meetings with precise word durations, we show that word durations correlate with syntactic surprisal estimated from the incremental Roark parser over and above simpler measures, such as word duration estimated from a state-of-the-art text-to-speech system and word frequencies, and that the syntactic surprisal estimates are better predictors of word durations than a simpler version of surprisal based on trigram probabilities. This result supports the uniform information density (UID) hypothesis and points a way to more realistic artificial speech generation.

1 Introduction

The uniform information density (UID) hypothesis suggests that speakers try to distribute information uniformly across their utterances (Frank and Jaeger, 2008). Information density can be measured in terms of the surprisal incurred at each word, where surprisal is defined as the negative log-probability of an event. This paper sets out to test whether UID holds across different linguistic levels, i.e. whether speakers adapt word duration during production to syntactic surprisal, such that words with higher surprisal have longer durations than words with lower surprisal. We investigate this question in a corpus of transcribed speech from a mix of native and non-native English speakers, a population that is a non-trivial component of the user base for language technologies developed for English. This data reflects a casual, uncontrolled conversational environment.

Using linear mixed-effects modeling, we found that syntactic surprisal as calculated from a top-down incremental PCFG parser accounts for a significant amount of variation in spoken word duration, using an HMM-trained text-to-speech system as a baseline. The findings of this paper provide additional support the uniform information density hypothesis and furthermore have implications for the design of text-to-speech systems, which currently do not take into account higher-level linguistic information such as syntactic surprisal (or even word frequencies) for their word duration models.

1.1 Related work

The use of word-level surprisal as a predictor of processing difficulty is based on the notion that processing difficulty results when a word is encountered that is unexpected given its preceding context. The amount of surprisal on a word w_i can be formalized as the log of the inverse conditional probability of w_i given the preceding words in the sentence $w_1 \dots w_{i-1}$, or $-\log P(w_i|w_{1\dots i-1})$. If this probability is low, then the word is unexpected, and surprisal is high. Surprisal can be estimated in different ways, e.g. from word sequences (n-grams) or with respect to the possible syntactic structures covering a sentence prefix (see Section 4).

Hale (2001) showed that surprisal calculated from a probabilistic Earley parser correctly predicts well-known processing phenomena that were believed to emerge from structural ambiguities (e.g., garden paths) and Levy (2008) further demonstrated the relevance of surprisal to human sentence processing difficulty on a range of syntactic processing difficulty phenomena.

There is existing work in correlating information-theoretic measures of linguistic redundancy to the observed duration of speech units. Aylett and Turk (2006) demonstrate that the contextual predictability of a syllable (n-gram log probability) has an inverse relationship to syllable duration in speech. Their experiments were performed using a carefully articulated speech synthesis training corpus.

This type of work fits into a larger programme of understanding how speakers schedule utterances to avoid high variation in the transmission of linguistic information over time, also known as the Uniform Information Density (UID) hypothesis (Florian Jaeger, 2010). Levy and Jaeger (2007) show that the reduction of optional *that*-complementizers in English is related to trigram surprisal; low surprisal predicts a high likelihood of reduction. Florian Jaeger (2010) shows the same result of increased reduction when the complementizer is more predictable according to information density calculated in terms of the main verb's subcategorization frequency.

Frank and Jaeger (2008) provide evidence that a UID account can predict the use of reduced forms of "be", "have", and "not" in English. They use the surprisal of the candidate word itself as well as surprisals of the word before and after, computing bigram and trigram estimates directly from the corpus without smoothing or backoff.

Jurafsky et al. (2001) report a corpus study similar to ours, showing that words that are more predictable from context are reduced. As measures of word predictability, they use bigram and trigram models, as well as joint probabilities, but not syntactic surprisal.

Within the same theme of utterance duration vs. information content, Piantadosi et al. (2011) performed a study using Google-derived n-gram datasets on the lexica of multiple languages, including English, Portuguese, and Czech. For every word in a given language's lexicon, they calculated 2-, 3-, and 4-gram surprisal values using the Google dataset for every occurrence of the word, and then they took the mean surprisal for that word over all occurrences. The 3-gram surprisal values in particular were a better predictor of orthographic length than unigram frequency, providing evidence for the use of information content and contextual predictability as improvement over a Zipf's Law view of communicative efficiency. This is an n-gram approach to supporting the UID hypothesis.

However, there is some counter-evidence for the UID-based view. Kuperman et al. (2007) analyzed the relationship between linguistic unit predictability and syllable duration in read-aloud speech in Dutch. Dutch makes use of interfix morphemes *-s-* and *-e(n)-* in certain contexts to make compound nouns, preferring a null interfix in most cases. For example, the Dutch noun *kandidaatsexamen* ("Bachelor's examination") is composed of *kandidaat-*, *-s-*, and *-examen*.

Kuperman et al. find that the greater the predictability of the interfix from the morphological context (i.e., the surrounding members of the compound), the *longer* the duration of the pronunciation of the interfix. To illustrate, if *-s-* is more expected after *kandidaat* or if *kandidaatsexamen* is a frequent compound, we would therefore expect the *-s-* to be pronounced longer, given the correlations they found. Their finding runs counter to a strong view of UID's fine-grained control over speech rate, but it is focused on the morphological level. They hypothesize that this counter-intuitive result may be driven by complex paradigmatic constraints in the choice of morpheme.

Our work, however, focuses on the syntactic level rather than the paradigmatic. What we seek to answer in our work is the extent to which an information density-based analysis can not only be applied to real speech data in context but also be derived from higher-level syntactic analyses, a combination hitherto little explored. Existing broad-coverage work on syntactic surprisal has largely focused on comprehension phenomena, such as Demberg and Keller (2008), Roark et al. (2009), and Frank (2010). We provide a production study in a vein similar to that of Kuperman et al., but show that frequency effects work in the expected direction at the syntactic level. This in turn expands upon the view supported by n-gram-based work such as that of Piantadosi et al. (2011); Levy and Jaeger (2007); Jurafsky et al. (2001), showing that information content above the n-gram level is important in guiding spoken language production in humans.

1.2 Implications for Potential Applications

Spoken dialogue systems are of increasing economic and technological importance in recent times, particularly as it is now feasible to include this technology in everything from small consumer devices to industrial equipment. With this increase in importance, there is also unsurprisingly growing scientific emphasis in understanding its usability and safety characteristics. Recent work (Fang et al., 2009; Taube-Schiff and Segalowitz, 2005) has shown that linguistic information presentation has an effect on user behaviour, but the overall granularity of this behaviour is still not well-understood.

Other potential applications exist in any place where text-to-speech technologies can be applied, such as in real-time spoken machine translation and communications systems for the disabled.

In demonstrating that we can observe speakers behaving in the manner predicted by the UID hypothesis in conversational contexts, we provide evidence for a finer-level of granularity necessary for controlling the rate of information presentation in artificial systems.

1.3 AMI corpus

The Augmented Multi-Party Interaction (AMI) corpus is a collection of recorded, transcribed conversations spanning 100 hours of simulated meetings. The corpus contains a number of data streams including speech, video, and whiteboard writing. Transcription of the meetings was performed manually, and the transcripts contain word-level time bounds that were produced by an automatic speech recognition system.

The freely-available AMI corpus is one of a very small number of efforts that contain orthographic transcriptions that are time-aligned at a word level. We chose it for the realism of the setting in which it was recorded; the physical presence of multiple speakers in an unstructured discussion reflects a potentially high level of noise in which we would be looking for surprisal correspondences, potentially increasing the application value of the correspondences we find.

1.4 Organization

The remainder of this paper proceeds as follows. In section 2, we describe at a high level the procedure we used to test our hypothesis that parser-derived surprisal values can partly account for utterance-duration variation. Then (section 3.2) we discuss the MARY text-to-speech system, from which we derive "canonical" word utterance durations. We describe the way we process and filter the AMI meeting corpus in section 3.1. In section 4, we describe in detail our predictors, frequency counts, trigram surprisal, and Roark parser surprisal. Sections 5 and 6 describe how we use linear mixed effects modeling to find significant correlations between our predictors and the response variable, and we finally make some concluding remarks in section 7.

2 Design

The overall design of our experiment is schematically depicted in Figure 1. We extract the words and the word-by-word timings from the AMI corpus, keeping track of each word's position in the corpus by conversation ID, speaker turn, and chronological order. As we describe in the next section, we filter the words for anomalies.

After pre-processing, for each word in the corpus, we extract the following predictors: canonical speech durations from the MARY text-to-speech system, logarithmic word frequencies, n-gram surprisal, and surprisal values produced by the Roark (2001a); Roark et al. (2009) parser (see Section 4). The next sections describe how and from where these values are obtained[1].

Finally, we run mixed effects regression model analyses (Baayen et al., 2008) with the observed durations as a response variable and the predictors mentioned above in order to detect whether syntactic surprisal is a significant positive predictor of spoken word durations above and beyond the more basic effects of canonical word duration and word frequency.

[1] We will make this data widely available upon publication.

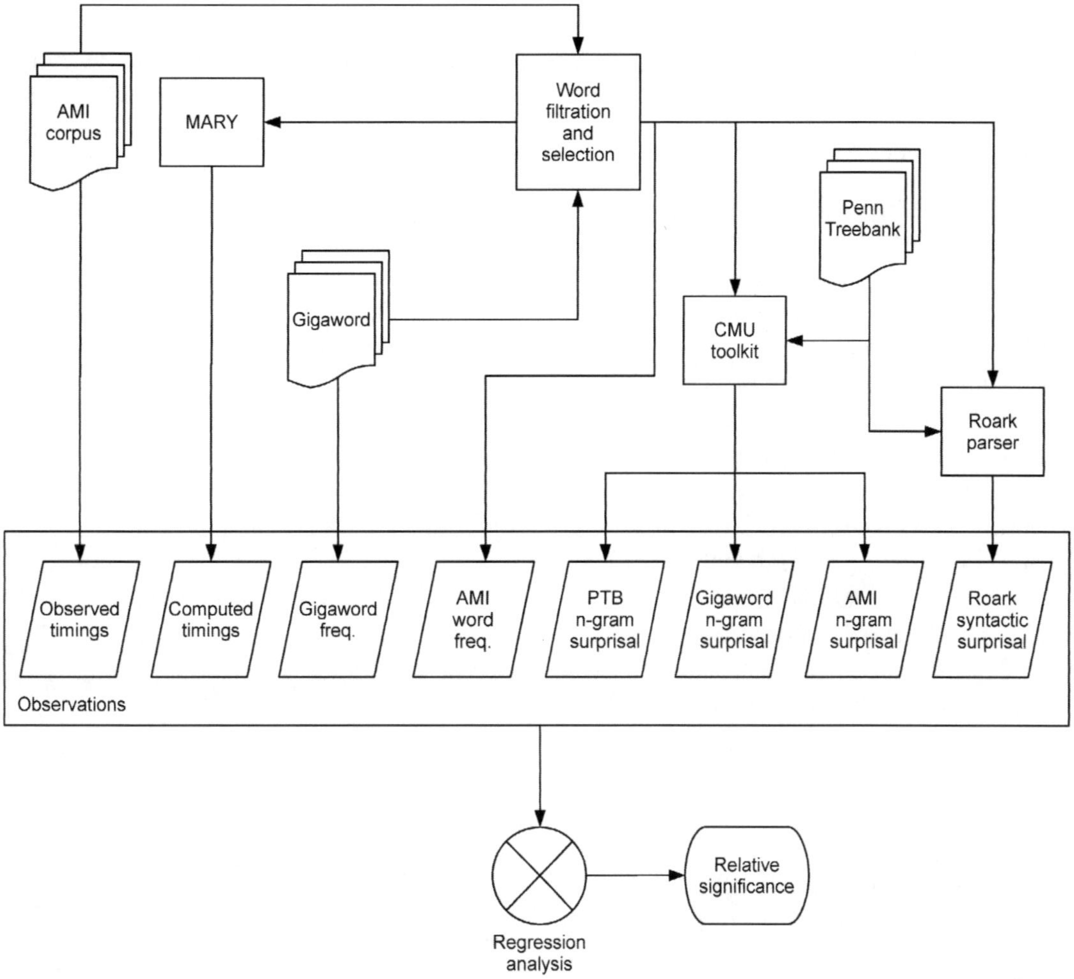

Figure 1: Schematic overview of experiment.

3 Experimental materials

3.1 Corpus preparation

The AMI corpus is provided in the NITE XML Toolkit (NXT) format. We developed a custom interpreter to assemble the relevant data streams: words, meeting IDs, speaker IDs, speaker turns, and observed word durations.

In addition to grouping and re-ordering the information found in the original XML corpus, two more steps were taken to eliminate confounding noise from the data. Non-words (e.g. "uhm", "uh-hmm", etc.) were filtered out, as were incomplete words or incorrectly transcribed words (e.g. "recogn", "somethi", etc); the criterion for rejection was presence in the English Gigaword corpus with subsequent minor corrections by hand, e.g., mapping unseen verbs back into the corpus and correcting obvious common misspellings.[2]

Finally, turns that did not make for complete sentences, e.g., utterances that were interrupted in mid-

[2] A reviewer asks about the extent to which our Gigaword filtering process may remove words we might want to keep but admit words we want to reject. As Gigaword is mostly newswire text, we do not expect the latter case to hold often. AMI is hand-transcribed and uses consistent spellings for non-word interjections (easy to remove), and any spelling mistakes would have to coincide exactly with a Gigaword mistake.

The other way around (rejecting what should be allowed) is easier to check, and we find that of 13K word types in AMI, about 7.2% are rejected for non-appearance in Gigaword, after filtering for interjections like "mm-hmm". However, we manually checked them and returned all but 2.9% of word types to the corpus. These tend to be very low-frequency types. The manual check suggests that ultimately there would be few false rejections.

sentence, were filtered out in order to maximize the proportion of complete parses in surprisal calculation.

3.2 Word duration model

In order to investigate whether there is an association between high/low surprisal and increased/decreased word duration, one needs to have a baseline measure of what constitutes the "canonical" duration of each word—in other words, to account for the fact that some words have longer pronunciations than others. As one reviewer notes, one way of estimating word durations would be to calculate the average duration of each word in the corpus. However, this approach would be insensitive to the phonological, syllabic and phrasal context that a word occurs in, which can have a large effect on word duration. Therefore, we use word duration estimates from the state-of-the-art open-source text-to-speech system MARY (Schröder et al., 2008, version 4.3.1), with the default voice package included in this version (`cmu-slt-hsmm`).

The `cmu-slt-hsmm` voice package uses a Hidden Markov model, trained on the female US English section of the CMU ARCTIC database (Kominek and Black, 2003), to predict prosodic attributes of each individual synthesized phone, including duration. Training was carried out using a version of the HTS system (Zen et al., 2007), modified for using the MARY context features (Schröder et al., 2008) for estimating the parameters of the model and for decoding. Those features include[3]:

- phonological features of the current and neighboring phonemes
- syllabic and lexical features (e.g. syllable stress, (estimated) part-of-speech, position of syllable in word)
- phrasal / sentential features (e.g. sentence/phrase boundaries, neighboring pauses and punctuation)

For each word in the AMI corpus, we obtained two alternative estimates of word duration: one version which is independent of a word's sentential context, and a second version which does take into account the sentential context (such as phrasal/sentential and across-word-boundaries phonological features) the word occurs in. In other words, we obtain MARY word duration estimates in the second version by running individual whole sentences through MARY, segmented by standard punctuation marks used in the AMI corpus transcriptions. For each version, we obtained phone durations using MARY and calculate the total duration of a word as the sum of the estimated phone durations for that word. These durations serve as the "canonical" baselines to which the observed durations of the words in the AMI corpus are compared.

3.3 Word frequency baselines

In order to account for the effects of simple word frequency on utterance duration, we extracted two types of frequency counts. One was taken directly from the AMI corpus alone. The other was taken from a 151 million word (4.3 million full-paragraph) sample of the English Gigaword corpus. These came from the following newswire sources: Agence France Press, Associated Press Worldstream, New York Times Newswire, and the Xinhua News Agency English Service. These sources are organized by month-of-year. We selected the subset of Gigaword by randomly selecting month-of-year files from those sources with uniform probability. Punctuation was stripped from the beginnings and ends of words before taking the frequency counts.

4 Surprisal models

For predicting the surprisal of utterances in context, two different types of models were used— n-gram probabilities models, as well as Roark's 2001 incremental top-down parser capable of calculating prefix probabilities. We also estimated word frequencies to account for words being spoken more quickly due to their higher frequency which is independent of structural surprisal.

The n-gram probabilities models, while being fast in both training and application, inherently capture very limited contextual influences on surprisal. The full-fledged parser, on the other hand, quantifies sur-

[3] For further information about how HMM-based voices for MARY TTS are trained, see `http://mary.opendfki.de/wiki/HMMVoiceCreation`

prisal based in the prefix probability of the complete sentence prefix and captures long-distance effects by conditioning on c-commanding lexical items as well as non-local node labels such as parents, grandparents and siblings from the left context.

CMU n-grams We used the CMU Statistical Natural Language Modeling Toolkit to provide a convenient way to calculate n-grams probabilities. For the prediction of surprisal, we calculated 3-gram models, 4-gram models and 5-gram models with Witten-Bell smoothing. Different n-gram models were trained on the full Gigaword corpus, as well as the AMI corpus.

To avoid overfitting, the AMI text corpus was split into 10 sub-corpora of equal word counts, preserving coherence of meetings. N-gram probabilities were then calculated for each of the sub-corpora using models trained on the 9 others.

We also produced a trigram model using the text of chapter 2–21 of the Penn Treebank's (PTB) underlying Wall Street Journal corpus. This consists of approximately one million tokens. We generated this model because it is the underlying training data for the Roark parser, described below.

Syntactic Surprisal from Roark parser In order to capture the effect of syntactically expected vs. unexpected events, we can calculate the syntactic surprisal of each word in a sentence. The syntactic surprisal at word S_{w_i} is defined as the difference between the prefix probability at word w_i and the prefix probability at word w_{i-1}. The prefix probability at word w_i is the sum of the probabilities of all trees T spanning words $w_1 \ldots w_i$; see also (Levy, 2008; Demberg and Keller, 2008).

$$S_{w_i} = \log \sum_T P(T, w_1..w_{i-1}) - \log \sum_T P(T, w_1..w_i)$$

The top-down incremental Roark parser (Roark, 2001a) has the characteristic that all partial left-to-right parses are *rooted*: they form a single tree with one root. A set of heuristics ensures that rule application occurs only through node expansion within the connected structure.[4] The grammar-derived prefix probabilities of a given sentence prefix can there-

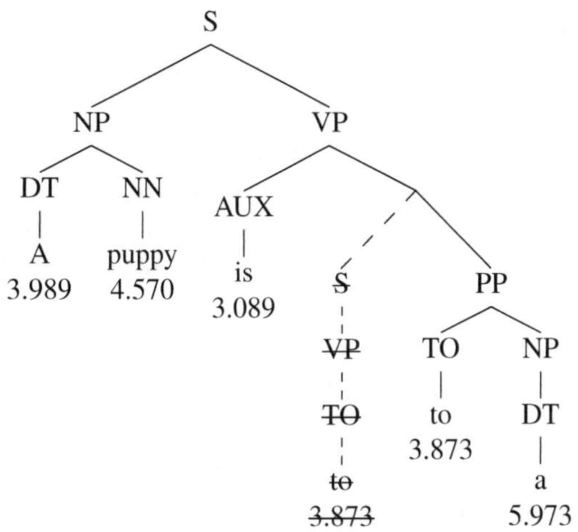

Figure 2: Top-ranked partial parse of *A puppy is to a dog what a kitten is to a cat.*, stopping at the second *a* and providing the Roark parser surprisal values by word. The branch with dashed lines and struck-out symbols represents an analysis abandoned at the appearance of the *a*.

fore be calculated directly by multiplying the probabilities of all rules used to generate the prefix tree. The Roark parser shares this characteristic of generating fully connected structures with Earley parsers (Earley, 1970) and left corner parsers (Rosenkrantz and II, 1970).

The Roark parser uses a beam search. As the amount of probability mass lost has been shown to be small (Roark, 2001b), the surprisal estimates can be assumed to be a good approximation. The beam width of the parser search is controlled by a "base parsing threshold", which defines the distance in terms of natural log-probability between the most probable parse and the least probable parse within the beam. For the experiments reported here, the parsing beam was set to 21 (default setting is 12). A wider beam also reduces the effects of pruning.

The parser was trained on Wall Street Journal sections 2–21 and applied to parse the full sentences of the AMI corpus, collecting predicted surprisal at each word (see Figure 2 for an example).

The syntactic surprisal can be furthermore be decomposed into a structural and a lexical part: sometimes, high surprisal might be due to a word being incompatible with the high-probability syntactic structures, other times high surprisal might just be due to a lexical item being unexpected. It is inter-

[4]The formulae for the calculation of the prefix probabilities from the PCFG rules can be found in Roark et al. (2009).

esting to evaluate these two aspects of syntactic surprisal separately, and the Roark parser conveniently outputs both surprisal estimates. Structural surprisal is estimated from the occurrence counts of the application of syntactic rules during the parse discounting the effect of lexical probabilities, while lexical surprisal is calculated from the probabilities of the derivational step from the POS-tag to lexical item.

5 Linear mixed effects modelling

In order to test whether surprisal estimates correlate with speech durations, we use linear mixed effects models (LME, Pinheiro and Bates (2000)). This type of model can be thought of as a generalization of linear regression that allows the inclusion of random factors as well as fixed factors.We treat speakers as a random factor, which means that our models contain an intercept term for each speaker, representing the individual differences in speech rates. Furthermore, we include a random slope for the predictors (e.g. frequency, canonical duration, surprisal), essentially accounting for idiosyncrasies of a participant with respect to the predictor, such that only the part of the variance that is common to all participants and is attributed to that predictor.

In a first step, we fit a baseline model with all predictors related to a word's canonical duration and its frequency as well as their random slopes to the observed word durations. Models with more than two random slopes generally did not converge. We therefore included in the baseline model only the two best random slopes (in terms of model fit). We then calculated the residuals of that model, the part of the observed word durations that cannot be accounted for through canonical word durations or word frequency.

For each of our predictors of interest (n-gram surprisal, syntactic surprisal), we then fit another linear mixed-effects model with random slopes to the residuals of the baseline model. This two-step procedure allows us to make sure to avoid problems of collinearity between e.g. surprisal and word frequency or canonical duration. A simpler (but less conservative) method is to directly add the predictors of interest to the baseline model. Results for both modelling variants lead to the same conclusions for our model, so we here report the more conservative two-step model. We compare models based on the Akaike Information Criterion (AIC).

6 Results

Our baseline model uses speech durations from the AMI corpus as the response variable and canonical duration estimates from the MARY TTS system and log word frequencies as predictors. We exclude from the analysis all data points with zero duration (effectively, punctuation) or a real duration longer than 2 seconds. Furthermore, we exclude all words which were never seen in Gigaword and any words for which syntactic surprisal couldn't be estimated. This leaves us with 771,234 out of the 799,997 data points with positive duration.

MARY duration models As mentioned in the earlier sections, we have calculated different versions of the MARY estimated word durations: one model without the sentential context and one model with the sentential context. In our regression analyses, we find, as expected, that the model which includes sentential context achieves a much better fit with the actually measured word durations from the AMI corpus (AIC = 32167) than the model without context (AIC = 70917).

Word frequency estimates We estimated word frequencies from several different resources, from the AMI corpus to have a spoken domain frequency and from Gigaword as a very large resource. We find that both frequency estimates significantly improve model fit over a model that does not contain frequency estimates. Including both frequency estimates improves model fit with respect to a model that includes just one of the predictors (all $p < 0.0001$).

Furthermore, including into the regression an interaction of estimated word duration and word frequency also significantly increases model fit ($p < 0.0001$). This means that words which are short and frequent have longer duration than would be estimated by adding up their length and frequency effects.

Baseline model Fixed effects of the fitted model are shown in Table 2. We see a highly significant effect in the expected direction for both the canonical duration estimate and word frequency. The positive coefficient for MARY_CONTEXT means that TTS duration estimates are positively correlated with the measured word durations. The negative coefficient for WORDFREQUENCY means that more frequent words are spoken faster than less frequent words. Finally, the negative coefficient for the interaction between word durations and frequencies means that the duration estimate for short frequent and long infrequent words is less extreme than otherwise predicted by the main effects of duration and frequency.

	Ami Dur	Mary Word	Mary Cntxt	Giga Freq	PTB Freq	AMI Freq	AMI 3grm	Giga 4grm
Mary_Word	.36	1						
Mary_Cntxt	.42	.72	1					
GigaFreq	-.35	-.52	-.65	1				
PTBFreq	-.33	-.48	-.62	.98	1			
AMIFreq	-.33	-.61	-.57	.65	.62	1		
AMI3gram	.21	.40	.41	-.41	-.39	-.68	1	
Giga4gram	.24	.33	.44	-.59	-.59	-.44	.61	1
Srprsl	.29	.40	.48	-.71	-.73	-.50	.50	.73

Table 1: Correlations (pearson) of model predictors.

Note though that the predictors are also correlated (for correlations of the main predictors used in these analyses, see Table 1), so there is some collinearity in the below model. Since we are less interested in the exact coefficients and significance sizes for these baseline predictors, this does not have to bother us too much. What is more important, is that we remove any collinearity between the baseline predictors and our predictors of interest, i.e. the surprisal estimates from the ngram models and parser. Therefore, we run separate regression models for these predictors on the residuals of the baseline model.

N-gram estimates We estimated 3-gram, 4-gram and 5-gram models on the AMI corpus (9-fold-cross), the Penn Treebank and the Gigaword Corpus. We found that coefficient estimates and significance levels of the resulting models were comparable. This is not surprising, given that 4-gram and 5-gram models were backing of to 3-grams or smaller contexts for more than 95% of cases on the AMI and PTB corpora (both ca. 1m words), and thus were correlated at $p > .98$. On the Gigaword Corpus, the larger contexts were seen more often (5-grams: 11%, 4-grams: 36%), but still correlation with 3-grams were high at ($p > .96$).

Predictor	Coef	t-value	Sig
INTERCEPT	0.3098	212.11	***
MARY_CONTEXT	0.4987	95.48	***
AMIWORDFREQUENCY	-0.0282	-32.28	***
GIGAWORDFREQUENCY	-0.0275	-62.44	***
MARY_CNTXT:GIGAFREQ	-0.0922	-45.41	***

Table 2: Baseline linear mixed effects model of speech durations on the AMI corpus data for MARY_CONTEXT (including the sentential context), WORDFREQUENCY under speaker with random intercept for speaker and random slopes under speaker. Predictors are centered.

Predictor	Coef	t-value	Sig
INTERCEPT	0.3099	212.94	***
MARY_CONTEXT	0.4970	94.60	***
AMIWORDFREQUENCY	-0.0279	-31.98	***
GIGAWORDFREQUENCY	-0.0254	-53.68	***
GIGA4GRAMSURPRISAL	0.0027	11.81	***
MARY_CNTXT:GIGAFREQ	-0.0912	-44.87	***

Table 3: Linear mixed effects model of speech durations including 4-gram surprisal trained on gigaword as a predictor.

N-gram model surprisal estimated on newspaper texts from PTB or Gigaword were statistically significant positive predictors of spoken word durations beyond simple word frequencies (but PTB ngram surprisal did not improve fit over models containing Gigaword frequency estimates). Counter-intuitively however, ngram models estimated based on the AMI corpus have a small *negative* coefficient in models that already include word frequency as a predictor – residuals of an AMI-estimated ngram model with respect to word frequency are very noisy and do not show a clear correlation anymore with word durations.

Surprisal Surprisal effects were found to have a robust significant positive coefficient, meaning that words with higher surprisal are spoken more slowly / clearly than expected when taking into account only canonical word duration and word frequency. Surprisal achieves a better model fit than any of the n-gram models, based on a comparsion of AICs, and Surprisal significantly improved model fit over a model including frequencies and ngram models based on AMI and Gigaword. Table 4 shows the estimate for SURPRISAL on the residuals of the model in Table 2.

Predictor	Coef	t-value	Sig
INTERCEPT	-0.0154	-23.45	***
SURPRISAL	0.0024	26.09	***

Table 4: Linear mixed effects model of surprisal (based on Roark parser) with random intercept for speaker and random slope. The response variable is residual word durations from the model shown in Table 3.

Surprisal estimated from the Roark parser also remains a significant positive predictor when regressed against the residuals of a baseline model including both 3-gram surprisal from the AMI corpus and 4-gram surprisal from the Gigaword corpus. In order to make really sure that the observed surprisal effect has indeed to do with syntax and can not be explained away as a frequency effect, we also calculated frequency estimates for the corpus based on the Penn Treebank. The significant positive surprisal effect remains stable, also when run on the residuals of a model which includes PTB trigrams and PTB frequencies.

It is difficult from these regression models to intuitively grasp the size of the effect of a particular predictor on reading times, since one would have to know the exact range and distribution of each predictor. To provide some intuition, we calculate the estimated effect size of Roark surprisal on speech durations. Per Roark surprisal "unit", the model estimates a 7 msec difference[5]. The range of Roark surprisal in our data set is roughly from 0 to 25, with most values between 2 and 15. For a word like "thing" which in one instance in the AMI corpus was estimated with a surprisal of 2.179 and in another instance as 16.277, the estimated difference in duration between these instances would thus be 104msec, which is certainly an audible difference. (Full range for Roark surprisal: 174msec, whereas full range for gigaword 4gram surprisal is 35 msec.)

When analysing the surprisal effect in more detail, we find that both the syntactic component of surprisal and its lexical component are significant positive predictors of word durations, as well as the interaction between them, which has a negative slope. A model with the separate components and their interaction achieves a better model fit (in AIC and BIC scores) than a model with only the full surprisal effect. The detailed model is shown in Table 5.

[5]2.4msec for a unit of residualized Roark surprisal, but it is even less intuitive what that means, hence we calculate with non-residualized surprisal here.

Predictor	Coef	t-value	Sig
INTERCEPT	-0.0219	-18.77	***
STRUCTSURPRISAL	0.0009	2.71	**
LEXICALSURPRISAL	0.0044	24.00	***
STRUCT:LEXICAL	-0.0004	- 6.83	***

Table 5: Linear mixed effects model of residual speech durations wrt. baseline model from Table 3, with random intercept for speaker and random slope for structural and lexical component of surprisal, estimated using the Roark parser.

To summarize, the positive coefficient of surprisal means that words which carry a lot of information from a structural point of view are spoken more slowly than words that carry less such information. These results thus provide good evidence for our hypothesis that the predictability of syntactic structure affects phonetic realization and that speakers use speech rate to achieve more uniform information density.

Native vs. non-native speakers Finally, we also compared effects in our native vs. non-native speaker populations, see Table 6. Both populations show the same effects and tell the same story (note that significance values can't be compared as the sample sizes are different). It might be possible to interpret the findings in the sense that native speakers are more proficient at adapting their speech rate to (syntactic) complexity to achieve more uniform information density, given the slightly higher coefficient and significance for Surprisal for native speakers. Since the effects are statistically significant for both groups, we don't want to make too strong claims about differences between the groups.

7 Conclusions and future work

We have shown evidence in this work that syntactic surprisal effects in transcribed speech data can be detected through word utterance duration in both native and non-native speech, and we did so using a meeting corpus not specifically designed to isolate these effects. This result is the potential foundation for futher work in applied, experimental, and

Predictor	Native English Coef	t-value	Sig	Non-native Coef	t-value	Sig
INTERCEPT	0.2947	149.74	***	0.3221	175.38	***
MARY_CONTEXT	0.5304	69.27	***	0.4699	67.77	***
AMIWORDFREQUENCY	-0.0226	-18.10	***	-0.0321	-28.00	***
GIGAWORDFREQUENCY	-0.0264	-41.19	***	-0.0248	-39.58	***
GIGAWORD4-GRAMS	0.0018	5.36	***	0.0033	10.85	***
MARY_CONTEXT:GIGAFREQ	-0.0810	-27.20	***	-0.0993	-35.71	***
SURPRISAL	0.0033	24.21	***	0.0018	15.09	***
no of data points	320,592			391,106		

$*p < 0.05$, $**p < 0.01$, $***p < 0.001$

Table 6: Native speakers are possibly slightly better at adapting their speech rate to syntactic surprisal than non-native speakers. Surprisal value is for model with residuals of other predictors as dependent variable.

theoretical psycholinguistics. It provides additional direct support for approaches based on the UID hypothesis.

From an applied perspective, the fact that frequency and syntactic surprisal have a significant effect beyond what a HMM-trained TTS model would predict for individual words is a case for further research into incorporating syntactic models into speech production systems. Our methodology immediately provides a framework for estimating the word-by-word effect on duration for increased naturalness in TTS output. This is relevant to spoken dialogue systems because it appears that synthesized speech requires a greater level of attention from the dialogue system users when compared to the same words delivered in natural speech (Delogu et al., 1998). Some of this effect may be attributable to peaks in information density which are caused by current generation systems not compensating for areas of high information density through speech rate, lexical and structural choice.

Furthermore, syntax and semantics have been observed to interact with the mode of speech delivery. Eye-tracking experiments by Swift et al. (2002) showed that there was a synthetic vs. natural speech difference in the time required to pay attention to an object referred to using definite articles, but not indefinite articles. Our result points a way towards a direction for explaining of this phenomenon by demonstrating that the differences between current-technology artificial speech and natural speech can be partially explained through higher-level syntactic features.

However, further experimentation is required on other measures of syntactic complexity (e.g. DLT, Gibson (2000)) as well as other levels of representation such as the semantic level. From a theoretical and neuroanatomical perspective, the finding that a measure of syntactic ambiguity reduction has an effect on the phonological layer of production has additional implications for the organization of the human language production system.

References

Aylett, M. and Turk, A. (2006). Language redundancy predicts syllabic duration and the spectral characteristics of vocalic syllable nuclei. *Journal of the acoustical society of America*, 119(5):3048–3059.

Baayen, R., Davidson, D., and Bates, D. (2008). Mixed-effects modeling with crossed random effects for subjects and items. *Journal of memory and language*, 59(4):390–412.

Delogu, C., Conte, S., and Sementina, C. (1998). Cognitive factors in the evaluation of synthetic speech. *Speech Communication*, 24(2):153–168.

Demberg, V. and Keller, F. (2008). Data from eye-tracking corpora as evidence for theories of syntactic processing complexity. *Cognition*, 109:193–210.

Earley, J. (1970). An efficient context-free parsing algorithm. *Commun. ACM*, 13(2):94–102.

Fang, R., Chai, J. Y., and Ferreira, F. (2009). Between linguistic attention and gaze fixations in multimodal conversational interfaces. In *International Conference on Multimodal Interfaces*, pages 143–150.

Florian Jaeger, T. (2010). Redundancy and reduction: Speakers manage syntactic information density. *Cognitive Psychology*, 61(1):23–62.

Frank, A. and Jaeger, T. F. (2008). Speaking rationally: uniform information density as an optimal strategy for language production. In *The 30th annual meeting of the Cognitive Science Society*, pages 939—944.

Frank, S. (2010). Uncertainty reduction as a measure of cognitive processing effort. In *Proceedings of the 2010 Workshop on Cognitive Modeling and Computational Linguistics*, pages 81–89, Uppsala, Sweden.

Gibson, E. (2000). Dependency locality theory: A distance-dased theory of linguistic complexity. In Marantz, A., Miyashita, Y., and O'Neil, W., editors, *Image, Language, Brain: Papers from the First Mind Articulation Project Symposium*, pages 95–126. MIT Press, Cambridge, MA.

Hale, J. (2001). A probabilistic Earley parser as a psycholinguistic model. In *Proceedings of the 2nd Conference of the North American Chapter of the Association for Computational Linguistics*, volume 2, pages 159–166, Pittsburgh, PA.

Jurafsky, D., Bell, A., Gregory, M., and Raymond, W. (2001). Evidence from reduction in lexical production. *Frequency and the emergence of linguistic structure*, 45:229.

Kominek, J. and Black, A. (2003). The cmu arctic speech databases for speech synthesis research. *Language Technologies Institute, Carnegie Mellon University, Pittsburgh, PA, Tech. Rep. CMULTI-03-177 http://festvox. org/cmu arctic*.

Kuperman, V., Pluymaekers, M., Ernestus, M., and Baayen, H. (2007). Morphological predictability and acoustic duration of interfixes in dutch compounds. *The Journal of the Acoustical Society of America*, 121(4):2261–2271.

Levy, R. (2008). Expectation-based syntactic comprehension. *Cognition*, 106(3):1126–1177.

Levy, R. and Jaeger, T. F. (2007). Speakers optimize information density through syntactic reduction. In *Advances in Neural Information Processing Systems*.

Piantadosi, S., Tily, H., and Gibson, E. (2011). Word lengths are optimized for efficient communication. *Proceedings of the National Academy of Sciences*, 108(9).

Pinheiro, J. C. and Bates, D. M. (2000). *Mixed-effects models in S and S-PLUS*. Statistics and computing series. Springer-Verlag.

Roark, B. (2001a). Probabilistic top-down parsing and language modeling. *Computational linguistics*, 27(2):249–276.

Roark, B. (2001b). *Robust probabilistic predictive syntactic processing: motivations, models, and applications*. PhD thesis, Brown University.

Roark, B., Bachrach, A., Cardenas, C., and Pallier, C. (2009). Deriving lexical and syntactic expectation-based measures for psycholinguistic modeling via incremental top-down parsing. In *Proceedings of the 2009 Conference on Empirical Methods in Natural Language Processing*, pages 324–333, Singapore. Association for Computational Linguistics.

Rosenkrantz, D. J. and II, P. M. L. (1970). Deterministic left corner parsing (extended abstract). In *SWAT (FOCS)*, pages 139—152.

Schröder, M., Charfuelan, M., Pammi, S., and Türk, O. (2008). The MARY TTS entry in the Blizzard Challenge 2008. In *Proc. Blizzard Challenge*. Citeseer.

Swift, M. D., Campana, E., Allen, J. F., and Tanenhaus, M. K. (2002). Monitoring eye movements as an evaluation of synthesized speech. In *Proceedings of the IEEE 2002 Workshop on Speech Synthesis*.

Taube-Schiff, M. and Segalowitz, N. (2005). Linguistic attention control: attention shifting governed by grammaticized elements of language. *Journal of experimental psychology Learning memory and cognition*, 31(3):508–519.

Zen, H., Nose, T., Yamagishi, J., Sako, S., Masuko, T., Black, A., and Tokuda, K. (2007). The HMM-based speech synthesis system (HTS) version 2.0.

In *Proc. of Sixth ISCA Workshop on Speech Synthesis*, pages 294–299.

Why Question Answering using Sentiment Analysis and Word Classes

Jong-Hoon Oh[*] **Kentaro Torisawa**[†] **Chikara Hashimoto** [‡]
Takuya Kawada[§] **Stijn De Saeger**[¶] **Jun'ichi Kazama**[‖] **Yiou Wang**[**]
Information Analysis Laboratory
Universal Communication Research Institute
National Institute of Information and Communications Technology (NICT)
{[*]rovellia,[†]torisawa,[‡]ch,[§]tkawada,[¶]stijn,[‖]kazama,[**]wangyiou}@nict.go.jp

Abstract

In this paper we explore the utility of sentiment analysis and semantic word classes for improving why-question answering on a large-scale web corpus. Our work is motivated by the observation that a why-question and its answer often follow the pattern that *if something undesirable happens, the reason is also often something undesirable*, and *if something desirable happens, the reason is also often something desirable*. To the best of our knowledge, this is the first work that introduces sentiment analysis to non-factoid question answering. We combine this simple idea with semantic word classes for ranking answers to why-questions and show that on a set of 850 why-questions our method gains 15.2% improvement in precision at the top-1 answer over a baseline state-of-the-art QA system that achieved the best performance in a shared task of Japanese non-factoid QA in NTCIR-6.

1 Introduction

Question Answering (QA) research for factoid questions has recently achieved great success as demonstrated by IBM's Watson at Jeopardy: its accuracy has been reported to be around 85% on factoid questions (Ferrucci et al., 2010). Although recent shared QA tasks (Voorhees, 2004; Peñas et al., 2011; Fukumoto et al., 2007) have stimulated the research community to move beyond factoid QA, comparatively little attention has been paid to QA for non-factoid questions such as *why* questions and *how to* questions, and the performance of the state-of-art non-factoid QA systems reported in the literature (Murata et al., 2007; Surdeanu et al., 2011; Verberne et al., 2010) remains considerably lower than that of factoid QA (i.e., 34% in MRR at top-150 results on why-questions (Verberne et al., 2010)).

In this paper we explore the utility of sentiment analysis (Pang et al., 2002; Turney, 2002; Nakagawa et al., 2010) and semantic word classes for improving why-question answering (why-QA) on a large-scale web corpus. The inspiration behind this work is the observation that why-questions and their answers often have the following tendency:

- *if something undesirable happens, the reason is often also something undesirable*, and
- *if something desirable happens, its reason is often also desirable*.

Consider the following question **Q1**, and its answer candidates **A1-1** and **A1-2**.

- **Q1**: Why does cancer occur?
- **A1-1**: Carcinogens such as nitrosamine and benzopyrene *may increase the risk of* cancer by altering DNA in cells.
- **A1-2**: Maintaining a healthy weight *may lower the risk of* various types of cancer.

Here **A1-1** describes an undesirable event related to cancer, while **A1-2** suggests a desirable action for its prevention. Our hypothesis suggests that **A1-1** is more appropriate for answering **Q1**. If this hypothesis holds, we can obtain a significant improvement in performance on why-QA tasks by exploiting the sentiment orientation[1] of expressions obtainable

[1] In this paper we denote the *desirable/undesirable* polarity of an expression by the term "sentiment orientation" instead of "semantic orientation" to avoid confusion with our different notion of "semantic word classes."

by automatic sentiment analysis of questions and answers.

A second observation motivating this work is that there are often significant associations between the lexico-semantic classes of words in a question and those in its answer sentence. For instance, questions concerning diseases like **Q1** often have answers that include references to specific semantic word classes such as chemicals (like **A1-1**), viruses, body parts, and so on. Capturing such statistical correlations between diseases and harmful substances may lead to higher why-QA performance. For this purpose we use classes of semantically similar words that were automatically acquired from a large web corpus using an EM-based clustering method (Kazama and Torisawa, 2008).

Another issue is that simply introducing the sentiment orientation of words or phrases in question and answer sentences in a naive way is insufficient, since answer candidate sentences may contain multiple sentiment expressions with different polarities in answer candidates (i.e., about 33% of correct answers had such multiple sentiment expressions with different polarities in our test set). For example, if **A1-2** contained a second sentiment expression with negative polarity like the example below,

> "Trusting a specific food *is not effective for* preventing cancer, but maintaining a healthy weight *may help lower the risk of* various types of cancer."

both **A1-1** and **A1-2** would contain sentiment expressions with the same polarity as that of **Q1**. Thus, it is difficult to expect that the sentiment orientation alone will work well for recognizing **A1-1** as a correct answer to **Q1**. To address this problem, we consider the combination of sentiment polarity and the contents of sentiment expressions associated with the polarity in questions and their answer candidates as well. To deal with the data sparseness problem arising in using the content of sentiment expressions, we developed a feature set that combines the polarity and the semantic word classes effectively.

We exploit these two main ideas (concerned with the sentiment orientation and the semantic classes described so far) for training a supervised classifier to rank answer candidates to why-questions. Through a series of experiments on 850 Japanese why-questions, we showed that the proposed semantic features were effective in identifying correct answers, and our proposed method obtained more than 15% improvement in precision of its top answer (P@1) over our baseline, which achieved the best performance in the non-factoid QA task in NTCIR-6 (Murata et al., 2007). We also show that our method can potentially perform with high precision (64.8% in P@1) when answer candidates containing at least one correct answer are given to our re-ranker.

2 Approach

Our proposed method is composed of *answer retrieval* and *answer re-ranking*. The first step, answer retrieval, extracts a set of answer candidates to a why-question from 600 million Japanese Web corpus. The answer retrieval is our implementation of the state-of-art method that has shown the best performance in the shared task of Japanese non-factoid QA in NTCIR-6 (Murata et al., 2007; Fukumoto et al., 2007). The second step, answer re-ranking, is the focus of this work.

2.1 Answer Retrieval

We use Solr[2] to retrieve documents from a 600 million Japanese Web page corpus[3]for a given why-question. Let a set of content words in a why-question be $T = \{t_1, \cdots, t_n\}$. Two boolean queries for a why-question, "t_1 AND $\cdots$ AND t_n" and "t_1 OR $\cdots$ OR t_n," are given to Solr and top-300 documents for each query are retrieved. Note that retrieved documents by each query have different coverage and relevance to a given why-question. To keep balance between the coverage and relevance of retrieved documents, we use a set of retrieved documents by these two queries for obtaining answer candidates. Each document in the result of document retrieval is split into a set of answer candidates consisting of five subsequent sentences[4]. Subsequent answer candidates can share up to two sentences to avoid errors due to wrong document segmentation.

[2] http://lucene.apache.org/solr

[3] To the best of our knowledge, few Japanese non-factoid QA systems in the literature have used such a large-scale corpus.

[4] The length of acceptable answer candidates for why-QA in the literature ranges from one sentence to two paragraphs (Fukumoto et al., 2007; Murata et al., 2007; Higashinaka and Isozaki, 2008; Verberne et al., 2007; Verberne et al., 2010).

Answer candidate ac for question q is ranked according to scoring function $S(q, ac)$ given in Eq. (1) (Murata et al., 2007). Murata et al. (2007)'s method uses text search to look for answer candidates containing terms from the question with additional clue terms referring to "reason" or "cause." Following the original method we used *riyuu* (*reason*), *genin* (*cause*) and *youin* (*cause*) as clue terms. The top-20 answer candidates for each question are passed on to the next step, which is answer re-ranking. $S(q, ac)$ assigns a score to answer candidates like tf-idf, where $1/dist(t_1, t_2)$ functions like tf and $1/df(t_2)$ is idf for given terms t_1 and t_2 that are shared by q and ac.

$$S(q, ac) = max_{t_1 \in T} \sum_{t_2 \in T} \phi \times log(ts(t_1, t_2)) \quad (1)$$

$$ts(t_1, t_2) = \frac{N}{2 \times dist(t_1, t_2) \times df(t_2)}$$

Here T is a set of terms including nouns, verbs, and adjectives in question q that appear in answer candidate ac. Note that the clue terms are added to T if they exist in ac. N is the total number of documents (600 million), $dist(t_1, t_2)$ represents the distance (the number of characters) between t_1 and t_2 in answer candidate ac, $df(t)$ is the document frequency of term t, and $\phi \in \{0, 1\}$ is an indicator, where $\phi = 1$ if $ts(t_1, t_2) > 1$, $\phi = 0$ otherwise.

2.2 Answer Re-ranking

Our re-ranker is a supervised classifier (SVMs) (Vapnik, 1995) that uses three types of feature sets: features expressing morphological and syntactic analysis of questions and answer candidates, features representing semantic word classes appearing in questions and answer candidates, and features from sentiment analysis. All answer candidates of a question are ranked in a descending order of their score given by SVMs. We trained and tested the re-ranker using 10-fold cross validation on a corpus composed of 850 why-questions and their top-20 answer candidates provided by the answer retrieval procedure in Section 2.1. The answer candidates were manually annotated by three human annotators (not by the authors). Our corpus construction method is described in more detail in Section 4.

3 Features for Answer Re-ranking

This section describes our feature sets for answer re-ranking: features expressing morphological and syntactic analysis (MSA), features representing semantic word class (SWC), and features indicating sentiment analysis (SA). MSA, which has been widely used for re-ranking answers in the literature, is used to identify associations between questions and answers at the morpheme, word phrase, and syntactic dependency levels. The other two feature sets are proposed in this paper. SWC is devised for identifying semantic word class associations between questions and answers. SA is used for identifying sentiment orientation associations between questions and answers as well as expressing the combination of each sentiment expression and its polarity. Table 1 summarizes the respective feature sets, each of which is described in detail below.

3.1 Morphological and Syntactic Analysis

MSA including n-grams of morphemes, words, and syntactic dependencies has been widely used for re-ranking answers in non-factoid QA (Higashinaka and Isozaki, 2008; Surdeanu et al., 2011; Verberne et al., 2007; Verberne et al., 2010). We use MSA as a baseline feature set in this work.

We represent all sentences in a question and its answer candidate in three ways: morphemes, word phrases (*bunsetsu*[5]) and syntactic dependency chains. These are obtained using a morphological analyzer[6] and a dependency parser[7]. From each question and answer candidate we extract n-grams of morphemes, word phrases, and syntactic dependencies, where n ranges from 1 to 3. Syntactic dependency n-grams are defined as a syntactic dependency chain containing n word phrases. Syntactic dependency 1-grams coincide with word phrase 1-grams, so they are ignored.

Table 1 defines four types of MSA (MSA1 to MSA4). MSA1 is n-gram features from all sentences in a question and its answer candidates and distinguishes an n-gram feature found in a question from that same feature found in answer candidates. MSA2 contains n-grams found in the answer

[5] A *bunsetsu* is a syntactic constituent composed of a content word and several function words such as post-positions and case markers. It is the smallest unit of syntactic analysis in Japanese.

[6] http://nlp.ist.i.kyoto-u.ac.jp/EN/index.php?JUMAN

[7] http://nlp.ist.i.kyoto-u.ac.jp/EN/index.php?KNP

MSA1	Morpheme n-grams, word phrase n-grams, and syntactic dependency n-grams in a question and its answer candidate, where n ranges from 1 to 3. n-grams in a question and those in an answer candidate are distinguished.
MSA2	**MSA1**'s n-grams in an answer candidate that contain a question term.
MSA3	**MSA1**'s n-grams that contain a clue term including *riyuu* (reason), *genin* (cause) and *youin* (cause). These n-grams in a question and those in an answer candidate are distinguished.
MSA4	The ratio of the number of question terms in an answer candidate to the total number of question terms.
SWC1	Word class n-grams in a question and its answer candidate. These n-grams in a question and those in an answer candidate are distinguished.
SWC2	**SWC1**'s n-grams in an answer candidate whose original **MSA1**'s n-grams contain any question term.
SA@W1	Word polarity n-grams in a question and its answer candidate. These n-grams in a question and those in an answer candidate are distinguished.
SA@W2	**SA@W1**'s n-grams in an answer candidate whose original **MSA1** n-grams contain any question term.
SA@W3	Joint class-polarity n-grams in a question and its answer candidate. These n-grams in a question and those in an answer candidate are distinguished.
SA@W4	**SA@W3**'s n-grams in an answer candidates whose original **MSA1** n-grams contain any question term.
SA@P1	The indicator for polarity agreement between sentiment phrases, one in a question and the other in an answer candidate: 1 if any pair of such sentiment phrases has polarity in agreement, 0 otherwise.
SA@P2	The phrase-polarity, positive or negative, of a pair of sentiment phrases for which the indicator in SA@P1 is 1.
SA@P3	Morpheme n-grams, word phrase n-grams, and syntactic dependency n-grams in sentiment phrases are coupled with their phrase-polarity, where n ranges from 1 to 3. These n-grams in a question and those in an answer candidate are distinguished.
SA@P4	**SA@P3**'s n-grams in an answer candidates that contain a question term.
SA@P5	The ratio of the number of question terms in sentences that have sentiment phrases in answer candidates to the total number of question terms.
SA@P6	Word class n-grams in sentiment phrases are coupled with phrase-polarity. These n-grams in a question and those in an answer candidate are distinguished.
SA@P7	**SA@P6**'s n-grams in an answer candidates, whose original **MSA1**'s n-grams include any question term.
SA@P8	Joint class-polarity n-grams in sentiment phrases of a question and its answer candidate are coupled with phrase-polarity of the sentiment phrases. These n-grams in a question and those in an answer candidate are distinguished.
SA@P9	**SA@P8**'s n-grams in an answer candidates, whose original **MSA1**'s n-grams include any question term.
SA@P10	A pair of **SA@P6**'s n-grams, one from sentiment phrases in a question and the other from those in an answer candidate, where the two sentiment phrases should have the same sentiment orientation.

Table 1: Features used in training our re-ranker

candidates that themselves contain a term from the question (e.g., "*types of cancer*" in example **A1-2**). MSA3 is the n-gram feature that contains one of the clue terms used for answer retrieval (*riyuu* (reason), *genin* (cause) or *youin* (cause)). Here too, n-grams obtained from the questions and answer candidates are distinguished. Finally, MSA4 is the percentage of the question terms found in an answer candidate.

3.2 Semantic Word Class

Semantic word classes are sets of semantically similar words. We construct these semantic word classes by using the noun clustering algorithm proposed in Kazama and Torisawa (2008). The algorithm follows the distributional hypothesis, which states that semantically similar words tend to appear in similar contexts (Harris, 1954). By treating syntactic dependency relations between words as "contexts," the clustering method defines a probabilistic model of noun-verb dependencies with hidden classes as:

$$p(n, v, r) = \sum_c p(n|c)p(\langle v, r\rangle|c)p(c) \qquad (2)$$

Here, n is a noun, v is a verb or noun on which n depends via a grammatical relation r (post-positions in Japanese), and c is a hidden class. Dependency relation frequencies were obtained from our 600-million page web corpus, and model parameters $p(n|c)$, $p(\langle v, r\rangle|c)$ and $p(c)$ were estimated using the EM algorithm (Hofmann, 1999). We successfully clustered 5.5 million nouns into 500 classes. For each noun n, EM clustering estimates a probability distribution over hidden variables representing semantic classes. From this distribution we obtained discrete semantic word classes by assigning each noun n to semantic class $c = argmax_{c^*}\ p(c^*|n)$. The resulting classes actually form clean semantic categories such as *chemicals*, *nutrients*, *diseases* and *conditions*, in our examples of Q1 and Q2. The following are the top-10 words (English translation) according to $p(c|n)$ for these classes.

chemicals: acetylene, hydrogenation product, phosphoric monoester, methacrylate, levoglucosan, ammonium salt, halogenated organic compound, benzonitrile, alkyne, nitrosamine

nutrients: glucide, carbonhydrate, mineral, salt, sugar, water, fat, vitamin, nutrients, protein

diseases: pneumonia, neuritis, cancer, oral leukoplakia, pachymeningitis, acidosis, encephalitis, abdominal injury, valvulitis, gingivitis

conditions: proficiency, decrepitude, deficiency, impurity, abnormalities, floated, crisis, displacement, condition, shortage

Semantic word class (SWC) features are used to capture associations between semantic classes of words in the question and those in the answer candidates. For example:

- **Q2**: Why does rickets ($W_{disease}$) occur in children?
- **A2**: Deficiency ($W_{condition}$) of vitamin D ($W_{nutrients}$) can cause rickets ($W_{disease}$).

$W_{condition}$, $W_{disease}$ and $W_{nutrients}$ represent semantic word classes of *conditions*, *diseases* and *nutrients*, respectively. If this question-answer pair is given to the classifier as a positive training sample, we expect it to learn that if a disease name appears in a question then, everything else being equal, answers including nutrient names are more likely to be correct. Note that in principle the same association could be learned between word pairs, i.e., *rickets* and *vitamin D*. However, we found that word level associations are often too specific, and because of data sparseness this knowledge cannot easily be generalized to unseen questions. This is our main motivation for introducing broad coverage semantic word classes into the feature set.

We call the feature set with the word classes SWC and use two types of SWC, as shown in Table 1. To obtain the first type (SWC1), we convert all nouns in the MSA1 n-grams into their respective word classes, and keep all n-grams that contain at least one word class. We call these features *word class n-grams*. Again, word class n-grams obtained from questions are distinguished from the ones in answer candidates. For example, we extract "$W_{disease}$ occur" as a word class 2-gram from **Q2**.

The second type of SWC, SWC2, represents word class n-grams in an answer candidate, in which question terms are replaced by their respective semantic word classes. For example, $W_{disease}$ in word class 2-gram "cause $W_{disease}$" from **A2** is the semantic word class of *rickets*, one of the question terms. These features capture the correspondence between semantic word classes in the question and answer candidates.

3.3 Sentiment Analysis

Sentiment analysis (SA) features are classified into word-polarity and phrase-polarity features. We use *opinion extraction tool*[8] and sentiment orientation lexicon in the tool for these features.

3.3.1 Opinion Extraction Tool

Opinion extraction tool is a software, the implementation of Nakagawa et al. (2010). It extracts linguistic expressions representing opinions (henceforth, we call them sentiment phrases) from a Japanese sentence and then identifies the polarity of these sentiment phrases using machine learning techniques. For example, *rickets occur* in **Q2** and *Deficiency of vitamin D can cause rickets* in **A2** can be identified as sentiment phrases with a negative polarity. The tool identifies sentiment phrases and their polarity by using polarities of words and dependency subtrees as evidence, where these polari ties are given in a word polarity dictionary.

In this paper, we use a trained model and a word polarity dictionary (containing about 35,000 entries) distributed via the ALAGIN forum[9] for our sentiment analysis. Table 2 shows the performance of *opinion extraction tool*, precision (P), recall (R) and F-value (F), in this setting (reported in the Japanese homepage of this tool). In the evaluation of sentiment-phrase extraction, an extracted sentiment phrase is determined as correct if its head word is the same as one in the gold standard. Polarity classification is evaluated under the condition that all of the sentiment phrases are correctly extracted.

	P	R	F
Sentiment-phrase extraction	0.602	0.408	0.486
Polarity classification (pos.)	0.873	0.893	0.883
Polarity classification (neg.)	0.866	0.842	0.854

Table 2: The performance of *opinion extraction tool*

3.3.2 Word Polarity (SA@W)

Polarities of words are identified by simply looking up the word polarity dictionary of *opinion ex-*

[8] Available at http://alaginrc.nict.go.jp/opinion/index_e.html

[9] http://www.alagin.jp/index-e.html. Only the members of the ALAGIN forum can access these resources.

traction tool. Word polarity features are used for identifying associations between the polarity of words in a question and that in a correct answer. For example:

- **Q2**: Why does rickets (W^-) occur in children?
- **A2**: Deficiency (W^-) of vitamin D can cause rickets (W^-).

Here, W^- represents negative word polarities. We expect our classifier to learn from this question and answer pair that if a word with negative polarity appears in a question then its correct answer is likely to contain a negative polarity word as well.

SA@W1 and SA@W2 in Table 1 are sentiment analysis features from *word polarity n-grams*, which contain at least one word that has word polarities. We obtain these n-grams by converting all nouns in MSA1 n-grams into their word polarities through dictionary lookup. For example, from Q2 in the above example we extract "W^- occur" as a word polarity 2-gram. SA@W1 is concerned with *all* word polarity n-grams in questions and answer candidates. For SA@W2, we restrict word polarity n-grams from SA@W1 to those whose original n-gram include a question term.

Furthermore, word polarities are coupled with semantic word classes so that our classifier can identify meaningful combinations of both. For example, *deficiency* in **A2** can be represented as $W^-_{condition}$ by its respective semantic word class and word polarity, which allows for the representation of *undesirable conditions*. This in turn lets our system learn meaningful correlations between words expressing these kind of negative conditions and their connection to questions asking about diseases. SA@W3 and SA@W4 are features from this combination. They are defined in the same way as SA@W1 and SA@W2 except that word polarities are replaced with the combination of semantic word classes and word polarities. We call n-grams in SA@W3 and SA@W4 *joint (word) class-polarity n-grams*.

3.3.3 Phrase Polarity (SA@P)

Opinion extraction tool is applied to question and its answer candidate to identify sentiment phrases and their phrase-polarities. In preliminary tests we found that sentiment phrases do not help to identify correct answers if answer sentences including the sentiment phrases do not have any term from the question. So we restrict the target sentiment phrases to those acquired from sentences containing at least one question term. From these sentiment phrases we extract three categories of features.

First, SA@P1 and SA@P2 are features concerned with phrase-polarity agreement between sentiment phrases in a question and its answer candidate. We consider all possible pairs of sentiment phrases from the question and answer. If any such pair agrees in phrase-polarity, an indicator for the agreement and its polarity in the agreement become features SA@P1 and SA@P2, respectively.

Secondly, following the original hypothesis underlying this paper, we assume that sentiment phrases often represent the core part of the correct answer (e.g., A2 above) and it is important to express the content of the sentiment phrases in features. SA@P3 and SA@P4 were devised for this purpose. SA@P3 represents this sentiment phrase contents as n-grams of morphemes, words, and syntactic dependencies of sentiment phrases, together with their phrase-polarity. Furthermore, SA@P4 is the subset of SA@P3 n-grams restricted to those that include terms found in the question, and SA@P5 indicates the percentage of sentiment n-grams from the question that are found in a given answer candidate.

Finally, features SA@P6 through SA@P9 use semantic word classes to generalize the content features mentioned above. These features consist of word class n-grams and joint class-polarity n-grams taken from sentiment phrases, together with their phrase polarity. Similar to the definition of SA@P4, for SA@P7 and SA@P9 we restrict ourselves to n-grams containing a question term. SA@P10 represents the semantic content of two sentiment phrases with the same sentiment orientation (one from a question and the other from an answer candidate) using word class n-grams, together with the phrase-polarity in agreement.

4 Test Set

We prepared three sets of why-questions (QS1, QS2 and QS3) and used these questions to build two test sets for our experiments.

Why-questions in **QS1** are taken from the Japanese version of *Yahoo! Answers* (called *Yahoo! Chiebukuro*)[10]. We automatically extracted

[10] We used "Yahoo! Chiebukuro Data (2nd edition)" which is

questions consisting of a single sentence and containing the interrogative *naze* (*why*), and our annotators verified that these questions are meaningful without further context. For example, they discarded questions like "Why doesn't the WBC (world boxing council) make an objection to the WBC (World baseball classic)?" (the object of the objection is unclear) and "Why do minors trade at the auction even though it is disallowed by the rules" (information about which auction is not provided).

Because questions in *Yahoo! Answers* are aimed at human readers, users often "set the stage" by giving lots of background information about their question. This often leads to large stylistic differences between the questions in *Yahoo! Answers* and those typically posed to a QA system. We therefore created a second set of why-questions, **QS2**, whose style should be more appropriate for a QA system (examples showing these differences are given in the supplementary materials of this paper). Six human annotators (not the authors) were asked to create why-questions in their own words, keeping in mind that the questions they create are for a QA system. In addition, the annotators were asked to verify on the Web that the questions they created ask about some real event or phenomena. For example, a question like "Why does Mars appear blue?" is disallowed in QS2 because "Mars appears blue" is false. Note that the correct answer to these questions does not have to be either in our target corpus or in real-world Web texts. These two sets of why-questions, QS1 and QS2, are used to build a test set for evaluating our proposed method.

Finally, **QS3** contains why-questions that have at least one answer in our target corpus (600 million Japanese Web page corpus). For creating such why-questions, four human annotators (not the authors) were given a text passage composed of three continuous sentences and asked to locate the reasons for some event as described in this passage. Then they created a why-question for which the description is a correct answer. Because randomly selected passages from our target corpus have little chance of generating good why-questions we extracted passages from our target corpus that include at least one of the clue terms used in our answer retrieval step (i.e. *riyuu* (*reason*), *genin* (*cause*), or *youin* (*cause*)). This setting may not necessarily reflect a "real world" distribution of why-questions, in which ideally a wide range of people ask questions that may or may not have an answer in our corpus. However, QS3 allows us to evaluate our method under the *idealized* conditions where we have a perfect answer retrieval module whose answer candidates always contain at least one correct answer (the source passage used for creating the why-question). This setting allows us to estimate the *ideal-case* performance of our method. Under these circumstances we found that our method achieves almost 65% precision in P@1, which suggests that it can potentially perform with high precision if the answer candidates given by the answer retrieval module contain at least one correct answer. This is the main purpose of QS3. Additionally, we use QS3 for building training data, to check whether questions that do not reflect the real-world distribution of why-questions are useful for improving the system's performance on "real-world" questions (see Section 5.1).

In addition, we checked QS1, QS2 and QS3 for questions having the same topic, to avoid the possibility that the distribution of questions is biased towards certain topics. We manually extracted the questions' topic words and randomly selected a single representative question from all questions with the same topic. For example, "Why does Twitter only allow 140 characters?" and "Why is Twitter so popular?" both have as topic *Twitter*. In the end we obtained 250 questions in QS1, 250 questions in QS2 and 350 questions in QS3.

For evaluation we prepared two test sets, Set1 and Set2. *Set1* contains question-answer pairs whose questions are taken from QS1 and QS2. In our experiment, we evaluate systems with 10-fold cross validation on Set1. *Set2* has question-answer pairs whose questions are from QS3. Set2 is mainly used for estimating estimate the ideal-case performance of our method with a perfect answer retrieval module. Furthermore Set2 is used as additional training data in evaluating systems with 10-fold cross validation on Set1. We used our answer retrieval system to obtain the top-20 answer candidates for each question, and all question-answer (candidate) pairs were checked by three annotators, where their inter-rater agreement (Fleiss' kappa) was 0.634, indicating substantial agreement. Finally, correct answers to each question were determined by majority vote.

provided by Yahoo Japan Corporation and contains 16 million questions asked from April, 2004 to April 2009.

Q1:二酸化炭素などの温室効果ガスが増えると海面水位が上昇するといわれているのはなぜですか？ (Why does the increase of greenhouse gases such as carbon dioxide in the atmosphere lead to a rise of ocean level?)
A1: .. 化石燃料等の使用が増えるにつれて、温室効果ガスが大 気中に大量に放出され、その濃度が増加し、大気中に吸収される 熱が増えたことにより、地球規模での気温上昇が進行しています。 これが地球温暖化です。 ... 温暖化による海水膨張と両極の氷解で、海面が平均９～８８ｃｍ上昇すると警告しています。 (The burning of fossil fuels contributes to the increase of atmospheric concentrations of greenhouse gases and this makes the atmosphere absorb more thermal radiation. As a result, Earth's average surface temperature increases. This is global warming. ... There are warnings that the increase of sea water and melting of polar ice due to the global warming may cause sea-surface height to rise by 9–88 cm on average.
Q2:ヘモグロビンが不足すると体が酸素不足になるのはなぜですか？ (Why does hemoglobin deficiency cause lack of oxygen in the human body?)
A2:... ヘモグロビンは酸素を体の中に運び、いらなくなった二酸化炭素を持ち帰り、肺から外に出すなど重要な働きをしています。もし鉄分が不足してヘモグロビンが少ししか作られないと、全身に運ばれる酸素の量が減少し、カラダが酸素不足になります。.. (... Hemoglobin has an important role in the human body of carrying oxygen to the organs and transferring carbon dioxide back to the lungs, to be dispensed from the organism. If the amount of hemoglobin produced by the body is insufficient due to iron deficiency, the amount of oxygen delivered throughout the body decreases, causing oxygen deficiency. ...)

Table 3: Correct question-answer pairs in our test set

Table 3 shows a sample of correct question-answer pairs in our test set. Please see the supplementary materials of this paper for more examples.

Note that word and phrase polarities are not considered by the annotators in building our test sets and these polarities are automatically identified using a word polarity dictionary and *opinion extraction tool*. We confirmed that about 35% of questions and 40% of answer candidates had at least one sentiment phrase by *opinion extraction tool*, and about 45% of questions and 85% of answer candidates contained at least one word having polarity by a word polarity dictionary.

5 Experiments

We use TinySVM[11] with a linear kernel for training our re-ranker. Evaluation was done by P@1 (Precision of the top answer) and MAP (Mean Average Precision). P@1 measures how many questions have a correct top answer candidate. MAP, widely used in evaluation of IR systems, measures the overall quality of the top-n answer candidates (n=20 in this experiment) using the formula:

$$MAP = \frac{1}{|Q|} \sum_{q \in Q} \frac{\sum_{k=1}^{n} (Prec(k) \times rel(k))}{|A_q|} \quad (3)$$

Here Q is a set of why-questions, A_q is a set of correct answers to why-question $q \in Q$, $Prec(k)$ is the precision at cut-off k in the top-n answer candidates, $rel(k)$ is an indicator, 1 if the item at rank k is a correct answer in A_q, 0 otherwise.

We evaluated all systems using 10-fold cross validation in two ways. In the first setting we performed 10-fold cross validation on Set1. Set1 consists of 10,000 question-answer pairs (500 questions with their 20 answer candidates), and was partitioned into 10 subsamples such that the questions in one subsample do not overlap with those of the other subsamples. 9 subsamples (9,000 question-answer pairs) were used as training data and the remaining subsample (1,000 question-answer pairs) was retained as test data. This experiment is called **CV(Set1)**. It shows the effect of answer re-ranking when evaluating our proposed method with training data built with real world why-questions alone. In the second setting, we used the same 10 subsamples of Set1 as in CV(Set1) and exploited Set2 (composed of 7,000 question-answer pairs) as additional training data for 10-fold cross validation. As a result, in each fold 16,000 question-answer pairs (9,000 from Set1 and 7,000 from Set2) were used as training data for re-rankers, and all systems were evaluated on the remaining 1,000 question-answer pair subsample from Set1. We call this setting **CV(Set1+Set2)**. It verifies whether training data that does not necessarily reflect a real-world distribution of why-questions can improve why-QA performance on real-world questions.

5.1 Results

Table 4 shows the evaluation results of six different systems. For each system, we represent the performance in P@1 and MAP. B-QA is a system of our answer retrieval and the other five re-rank top-20 answer candidates using their own re-ranker.

B-QA: our answer retrieval system, our implementation of Murata et al. (2007).

B-Ranker: a system that has a re-ranker trained with morphological and syntactic analysis (MSA) features alone.

[11] http://chasen.org/~taku/software/TinySVM/

System	CV(Set1)		CV(Set1+Set2)	
	P@1	MAP	P@1	MAP
B-QA	0.222 (0.368)	0.270 (0.447)	0.222 (0.368)	0.270 (0.447)
B-Ranker	0.256 (0.424)	0.319 (0.528)	0.274 (0.454)	0.323 (0.535)
B-Ranker+CR	0.262 (0.434)	0.319 (0.528)	0.278 (0.460)	0.325 (0.538)
B-Ranker+WN	0.257 (0.425)	0.320 (0.530)	0.275 (0.455)	0.325 (0.538)
Proposed	**0.336 (0.56)**	**0.377 (0.624)**	**0.374 (0.619)**	**0.391 (0.647)**
UpperBound	0.604 (1)	0.604 (1)	0.604 (1)	0.604 (1)

Table 4: Comparison of systems

B-Ranker+CR: a system has a re-ranker trained with our MSA features and the causal relation (CR) features used in Higashinaka and Isozaki (2008). The CR features include binary features indicating whether an answer candidate contains a causal relation pattern, which causal relation pattern the answer candidate has, and whether the question-answer pair contains a causal relation instance — cause in the answer, effect in the question). We acquired causal relation instances from our target corpus using the method from (De Saeger et al., 2009), and exploited the *top*-100,000 causal relation instances and the patterns that extracted them for CR features. Note that these CR features are introduced only for comparing our semantic features with ones in Higashinaka and Isozaki (2008) and they are not a part of our method.

B-Ranker+WN: its re-ranker is trained with our MSA features and the WordNet features in Verberne et al. (2010). The WordNet features include the percentage of the question terms and their synonyms in WordNet synsets found in an answer candidate and the semantic relatedness score between a question and its answer candidate, the average of the concept similarity between each question term and all of the answer terms by *WordNet::Similarity* (Pedersen et al., 2004). We used the Japanese WordNet 1.1 (Bond et al., 2009) for these WordNet features. Note that the Japanese WordNet 1.1 has 93,834 Japanese words linked to 57,238 WordNet synsets, while the English WordNet 3.0 covers 155,287 words linked to 117,659 synsets. Due to this lower coverage, the WordNet features in Japanese may have a less power for finding a correct answer than those in English used in Verberne et al. (2010).

Proposed: our proposed method. All of the MSA, SWC and SA features are used for training our re-ranker.

UpperBound: a system that ranks all n correct answers as the top n results of the 20 answer candidates if there are any. This indicates the performance upperbound in this experiment. The relative performance of each system compared to *UpperBound* is shown in parentheses.

The proposed method achieved the best performance both in CV(Set1) and CV(Set1+Set2). Our method shows a significant improvement (11.4–15.2% in P@1 and 10.7–12.1% in MAP) over our answer retrieval method, B-QA. Its improvement over B-Ranker, B-Ranker+CR and B-Ranker+WN (7.6–10% in P@1 and 5.7–6.6% in MAP) shows the effectiveness of our proposed feature set over the features used in previous works. Both B-Ranker+CR and B-Ranker+WN did not show significant performance improvement over B-Ranker. At least in our setting, the causal relation and WordNet features did not prove effective. The performance gap between B-Ranker and B-QA (3.4–5.2% in P@1 and 4.9–5.3% in MAP) suggests the effectiveness of re-ranking. All systems consistently show better performance in CV(Set1+Set2) than CV(Set1). This suggests that training data built with why-questions that does not reflect real-world distribution of why-questions is useful in training re-rankers.

We investigate the contribution of each type of features to the performance by removing one feature set from the all feature sets in training our re-ranker. In this experiment, we split SA into $SA@W$ (features expressing words and their polarity) and $SA@P$ (features expressing phrases and their polarity) to investigate their contribution either. The results are summarized in Table 5.

In Table 5, **MSA+SWC+SA** represents our proposed method using all feature sets. The performance gap between **MSA+SWC+SA** and the others confirms that all the features contributed to a higher

System	CV(Set1)		CV(Set1+Set2)	
	P@1	MAP	P@1	MAP
SWC+SA	0.302	0.324	0.314	0.332
MSA+SWC	0.308	0.349	0.318	0.358
MSA+SA	0.300	0.352	0.314	0.364
MSA+SWC+SA@W	0.312	0.358	0.325	0.365
MSA+SWC+SA@P	0.323	0.369	0.358	0.384
MSA+SWC+SA	**0.336**	**0.377**	**0.374**	**0.391**
UpperBound	0.604	0.604	0.604	0.604

Table 5: Evaluation with different combination of feature sets used in training our re-ranker

performance. The significant performance improvement by SA (features from sentiment analysis) and SWC (features from semantic word classes) (The gap between **MSA+SWC+SA** and **MSA+SWC** was 2.8–6% and that between **MSA+SWC+SA** and **MSA+SA** was 3.6%–6% in P@1) supports the hypothesis for sentiment analysis and semantic word classes in this paper.

Though the performance gap between **MSA+SWC+SA** and **MSA+SWC+SA@P** (1.3%–1.6% in P@1) shows that SA@W is useful in training our re-ranker, we found that **MSA+SWC+SA@W** made only 0.4–0.7% improvement over **MSA+SWC**. We believe that this is mainly because SA@W and SWC are based on semantic and sentiment information at the word level, and these often capture a similar type of information. For instance, disease names that are grouped together into one class in SWC are typically classified as negative in SA@W. Therefore the similarity in the information provided by SA@W and SWC causes a classifier trained with both of these features to obtain only a minor improvement over a classifier using only one of the features.

To estimate the *ideal-case* performance of our proposed method, we made another experiment by using Set1 as training data for our re-ranker and Set2 as test data for evaluating our proposed method. Here, we assume a perfect answer retrieval module that adds the source passage that was used for generating the original why-question in Set2 as a correct answer to the set of existing answer candidates, giving 21 answer candidates. The performance of our method in this setting was 64.8% in P@1 and 66.6% in MAP. This evaluation result suggests that our re-ranker can potentially perform with high precision when at least one correct answer in answer candidates is given by the answer retrieval module.

6 Related Work

In the QA literature, Higashinaka and Isozaki (2008), Verberne et al. (2010), and Surdeanu et al. (2011) are closest to our work. The first two deal with why-questions, the last with how-questions. Similar to our method, they use machine learning techniques to re-rank answer candidates to non-factoid questions based on various combinations of syntactic, semantic and other statistical features such as the density and frequency of question terms in the answer candidates and patterns for causal relations in the answer candidates. Especially for why-QA, Higashinaka and Isozaki (2008) used causal relation features and Verberne et al. (2010) exploited WordNet features as a kind of semantic features for training their re-ranker, where we used these features, respectively, for B-Ranker+CR and B-Ranker+WN in our experiment.

Our work differs from the above approaches in that we propose semantic word classes and sentiment analysis as a new type of semantic features, and show their usefulness in why-QA. Sentiment analysis has been used before on the slightly unusual task of opinion question answering, where the system is asked to answer subjective opinion questions (Stoyanov et al., 2005; Dang, 2008; Li et al., 2009). To the best of our knowledge though, no previous work has systematically explored the use of sentiment analysis in a general QA setting beyond opinion questions.

7 Conclusion

In this paper, we have explored the utility of sentiment analysis and semantic word classes for ranking answer candidates to why-questions. We proposed a set of semantic features that exploit sentiment analysis and semantic word classes obtained from large-scale noun clustering, and used them to train an answer candidate re-ranker. Through a series of experiments on 850 why-questions, we showed that the proposed semantic features were effective in identifying correct answers, and our proposed method obtained more than 15% improvement in precision of its top answer (P@1) over our baseline, a state-of-the-art IR based QA system. We plan to use new semantic knowledge such as semantic orientation, excitatory or inhibitory, proposed in Hashimoto et al. (2012) for improving why-QA.

References

Francis Bond, Hitoshi Isahara, Sanae Fujita, Kiyotaka Uchimoto, Takayuki Kuribayashi, and Kyoko Kanzaki. 2009. Enhancing the japanese wordnet. In *Proceedings of the 7th Workshop on Asian Language Resources*, pages 1–8.

Hoa Tran Dang. 2008. Overview of the TAC 2008 opinion question answering and summarization tasks. In *Proc. TAC 2008*.

Stijn De Saeger, Kentaro Torisawa, Jun'ichi Kazama, Kow Kuroda, and Masaki Murata. 2009. Large scale relation acquisition using class dependent patterns. In *Proc. of ICDM 2009*, pages 764–769.

David A. Ferrucci, Eric W. Brown, Jennifer Chu-Carroll, James Fan, David Gondek, Aditya Kalyanpur, Adam Lally, J. William Murdock, Eric Nyberg, John M. Prager, Nico Schlaefer, and Christopher A. Welty. 2010. Building Watson: An overview of the DeepQA project. *AI Magazine*, 31(3):59–79.

Junichi Fukumoto, Tsuneaki Kato, Fumito Masui, and Tsunenori Mori. 2007. An overview of the 4th question answering challenge (QAC-4) at NTCIR workshop 6. In *Proc. of NTCIR-6*.

Zellig Harris. 1954. Distributional structure. *Word*, 10(23):146–162.

Chikara Hashimoto, Kentaro Torisawa, Stijn De Saeger, Jong-Hoon Oh, and Jun'ichi Kazama. 2012. Excitatory or inhibitory: A new semantic orientation extracts contradiction and causality from the web. In *Proceedings of EMNLP-CoNLL 2012*.

Ryuichiro Higashinaka and Hideki Isozaki. 2008. Corpus-based question answering for why-questions. In *Proc. of IJCNLP*, pages 418–425.

Thomas Hofmann. 1999. Probabilistic latent semantic indexing. In *Proc. of the 22nd annual international ACM SIGIR conference on Research and development in information retrieval*, SIGIR '99, pages 50–57.

Jun'ichi Kazama and Kentaro Torisawa. 2008. Inducing gazetteers for named entity recognition by large-scale clustering of dependency relations. In *Proc. of ACL-08: HLT*, pages 407–415.

Fangtao Li, Yang Tang, Minlie Huang, and Xiaoyan Zhu. 2009. Answering opinion questions with random walks on graphs. In *Proc. of the Joint Conference of the 47th Annual Meeting of the ACL and the 4th International Joint Conference on Natural Language Processing of the AFNLP: Volume 2 - Volume 2*, pages 737–745.

Masaki Murata, Sachiyo Tsukawaki, Toshiyuki Kanamaru, Qing Ma, and Hitoshi Isahara. 2007. A system for answering non-factoid Japanese questions by using passage retrieval weighted based on type of answer. In *Proc. of NTCIR-6*.

Tetsuji Nakagawa, Kentaro Inui, and Sadao Kurohashi. 2010. Dependency tree-based sentiment classification using CRFs with hidden variables. In *Human Language Technologies: The 2010 Annual Conference of the North American Chapter of the Association for Computational Linguistics*, pages 786–794, Los Angeles, California, June. Association for Computational Linguistics.

Bo Pang, Lillian Lee, and Shivakumar Vaithyanathan. 2002. Thumbs up? Sentiment classification using machine learning techniques. In *Proc. of the 2002 Conference on Empirical Methods in Natural Language Processing (EMNLP)*, pages 79–86.

Ted Pedersen, Siddharth Patwardhan, and Jason Michelizzi. 2004. WordNet::Similarity: measuring the relatedness of concepts. In *Demonstration Papers at HLT-NAACL 2004*, HLT-NAACL–Demonstrations '04, pages 38–41.

Anselmo Peñas, Eduard H. Hovy, Pamela Forner, Álvaro Rodrigo, Richard F. E. Sutcliffe, Corina Forascu, and Caroline Sporleder. 2011. Overview of QA4MRE at CLEF 2011: Question answering for machine reading evaluation. In *CLEF*.

Veselin Stoyanov, Claire Cardie, and Janyce Wiebe. 2005. Multi-perspective question answering using the opqa corpus. In *Proceedings of the conference on Human Language Technology and Empirical Methods in Natural Language Processing*, HLT '05, pages 923–930.

Mihai Surdeanu, Massimiliano Ciaramita, and Hugo Zaragoza. 2011. Learning to rank answers to non-factoid questions from web collections. *Computational Linguistics*, 37(2):351–383.

Peter D. Turney. 2002. Thumbs up or thumbs down?: semantic orientation applied to unsupervised classification of reviews. In *Proc. of the 40th Annual Meeting on Association for Computational Linguistics*, ACL '02, pages 417–424.

Vladimir N. Vapnik. 1995. *The nature of statistical learning theory*. Springer-Verlag New York, Inc., New York, NY, USA.

Suzan Verberne, Lou Boves, Nelleke Oostdijk, and Peter-Arno Coppen. 2007. Evaluating discourse-based answer extraction for *why*-question answering. In *SIGIR*, pages 735–736.

Suzan Verberne, Lou Boves, Nelleke Oostdijk, and Peter-Arno Coppen. 2010. What is not in the bag of words for why-QA? *Computational Linguistics*, 36:229–245.

Ellen M. Voorhees. 2004. Overview of the TREC 2004 question answering track. In *TREC*.

Natural Language Questions for the Web of Data

Mohamed Yahya[1], Klaus Berberich[1], Shady Elbassuoni[2]
Maya Ramanath[3], Volker Tresp[4], Gerhard Weikum[1]
[1] Max Planck Institute for Informatics, Germany
[2] Qatar Computing Research Institute
[3] Dept. of CSE, IIT-Delhi, India [4] Siemens AG, Corporate Technology, Munich, Germany
{myahya,kberberi,weikum}@mpi-inf.mpg.de
selbassuoni@qf.org.qa
ramanath@cse.iitd.ac.in volker.tresp@siemens.com

Abstract

The Linked Data initiative comprises structured databases in the Semantic-Web data model RDF. Exploring this heterogeneous data by structured query languages is tedious and error-prone even for skilled users. To ease the task, this paper presents a methodology for translating natural language questions into structured SPARQL queries over linked-data sources.

Our method is based on an integer linear program to solve several disambiguation tasks jointly: the segmentation of questions into phrases; the mapping of phrases to semantic entities, classes, and relations; and the construction of SPARQL triple patterns. Our solution harnesses the rich type system provided by knowledge bases in the web of linked data, to constrain our semantic-coherence objective function. We present experiments on both the question translation and the resulting query answering.

1 Introduction

1.1 Motivation

Recently, very large, structured, and semantically rich knowledge bases have become available. Examples are Yago (Suchanek et al., 2007), DBpedia (Auer et al., 2007), and Freebase (Bollacker et al., 2008). DBpedia forms the nucleus of the Web of Linked Data (Heath and Bizer, 2011), which interconnects hundreds of RDF data sources with a total of 30 billion subject-property-object (SPO) triples.

The diversity of linked-data sources and their high heterogeneity make it difficult for humans to search and discover relevant information. As linked data is in RDF format, the standard approach would be to run structured queries in triple-pattern-based languages like SPARQL, but only expert programmers are able to precisely specify their information needs and cope with the high heterogeneity of the data (and absence or very high complexity of schema information). For less initiated users the only option to query this rich data is by keyword search (e.g., via services like sig.ma (Tummarello et al., 2010)). None of these approaches is satisfactory. Instead, the by far most convenient approach would be to search in knowledge bases and the Web of linked data by means of natural-language questions.

As an example, consider a quiz question like "Which female actor played in Casablanca and is married to a writer who was born in Rome?". The answer could be found by querying several linked data sources together, like the IMDB-style LinkedMDB movie database and the DBpedia knowledge base, exploiting that there are entity-level `sameAs` links between these collections. One can think of different formulations of the example question, such as "Which actress from Casablanca is married to a writer from Rome?". A possible SPARQL formulation, assuming a user familiar with the schema of the underlying knowledge base(s), could consist of the following six triple patterns (joined by shared-variable bindings): `?x hasGender female`, `?x isa actor`, `?x actedIn Casablanca_(film)`, `?x marriedTo ?w`, `?w isa writer`, `?w bornIn Rome`. This complex query, which involves multiple joins, would yield good results, but it is difficult for the user to come up with the precise choices for relations, classes, and entities. This would require familiarity with the contents of the knowledge base, which no average user is expected to have. Our goal is to automatically create such structured queries by mapping the user's question into this representation. Keyword search is usually not a viable alternative when the information need involves joining multiple triples to construct the final result, notwithstanding good attempts like that of Pound et al. (2010). In the example, the obvious keyword query "female actress Casablanca married writer born Rome" lacks a clear specification of the relations among the different entities.

1.2 Problem

Given a natural language question q_{NL} and a knowledge base KB, our goal is to translate q_{NL} into a formal query q_{FL} that captures the information need expressed by q_{NL}.

We focus on input questions that put the emphasis on entities, classes, and relations between them. We do not consider aggregations (counting, max/min, etc.) and negations. As a result, we generate structured queries of the form known as conjunctive queries or select-project-join queries in database terminology. Our target language is SPARQL 1.0, where the above focus leads to queries that consist of multiple triple patterns, that is, conjunctions of SPO search conditions. We do not use any pre-existing query templates, but generate queries from scratch as they involve a variable number of joins with a-priori unknown join structure.

A major challenge is in the ambiguity of the phrases occurring in a natural-language question. Phrases can denote entities (e.g., the city of Casablanca or the movie Casablanca), classes (e.g., actresses, movies, married people), or relations/properties (e.g., `marriedTo` between people, `played` between people and movies). A priori, we do not know if a phrase should be mapped to an entity, a class, or a relation. In fact, some phrases may denote any of these three kinds of targets. For example, a phrase like "wrote score for" in a question about film music composers, could map to the composer-film relation `wroteSoundtrackForFilm`, to the class of `movieSoundtracks` (a subclass of music pieces), or to an entity like the movie "The Score". Depending on the choice, we may arrive at a structurally good query (with triple patterns that can actually be joined) or at a meaningless and non-executable query (with disconnected triple patterns). This generalized disambiguation problem is much more challenging than the more focused task of named entity disambiguation (NED). It is also different from general word sense disambiguation (WSD), which focuses on the meaning of individual words (e.g., mapping them to WordNet synsets).

1.3 Contribution

In our approach, we introduce new elements towards making translation of questions into SPARQL triple patterns more expressive and robust. Most importantly, we solve the disambiguation and mapping tasks jointly, by encoding them into a comprehensive integer linear program (ILP): the segmentation of questions into meaningful phrases, the mapping of phrases to semantic entities, classes, and relations, and the construction of SPARQL triple patterns. The ILP harnesses the richness of large knowledge bases like Yago2 (Hoffart et al., 2011b), which has information not only about entities and relations, but also about surface names and textual patterns by which web sources refer to them. For example, Yago2 knows that "Casablanca" can refer to the city or the film, and "played in" is a pattern that can denote the `actedIn` relation. In addition, we can leverage the rich type system of semantic classes. For example, knowing that Casablanca is a film, for translating "played in" we can focus on relations with a type signature whose range includes films, as opposed to sports teams, for example. Such information is encoded in judiciously designed constraints for the ILP. Although we intensively harness Yago2, our approach does not depend on a specific choice of knowledge base or language resource for type information and phrase/name dictionaries. Other knowledge bases such as DBpedia can be easily plugged in.

Based on these ideas, we have developed a framework and system, called DEANNA (DEep Answers for maNy Naturally Asked questions), that comprises a full suite of components for question decomposition, mapping constituents into the semantic concept space, generating alternative candidate mappings, and computing a coherent mapping of all constituents into a set of SPARQL triple patterns that can be directly executed on one or more linked data sources.

2 Background

We use the Yago2 knowledge base, with its rich type system, as a semantic backbone. Yago2 is composed of instances of binary relations derived from Wikipedia and WordNet. The instances, called *facts*, provide both ontological information and instance data. Figure 1 shows sample facts from Yago2. Each fact is composed of *semantic items* that can be divided into relations, entities, and classes. Entities and classes together are referred to as *concepts*.

Subject	Predicate	Object
film	subclassOf	production
Casablanca_(film)	type	film
"Casablanca"	means	Casablanca_(film)
"Casablanca"	means	Casablanca,_Morocco
Ingrid_Bergman	actedIn	Casablanca_(film)

Figure 1: Sample knowledge base

Examples of relations are type, subclassOf, and actedIn. Each relation has a type signature: classes for the relation's domain and range. Classes, such as person and film group entities. Entities are represented in canonical form such as Ingrid_Bergman and Casablanca_(film). A special type of entities are literals, such as strings, numbers, and dates.

3 Framework

Given a natural language question, Figure 2 shows the tasks DEANNA performs to translate a question into a structured query. The first three steps prepare the input for constructing a disambiguation graph for mapping the phrases in a question onto entities, classes, and relations, in a coherent manner. The fourth step formulates this generalized disambiguation problem as an ILP with complex constraints and computes the best solution using an ILP solver. Finally, the fifth and sixth step together use the disambiguated mapping to construct an executable SPARQL query.

A question sentence is a sequence of tokens, $q_{NL} = (t_0, t_1, ..., t_n)$. A phrase is a contiguous subsequence of tokens $(t_i, t_{i+1}, ..., t_{i+l}) \subseteq q_{NL}, 0 \leq i, 0 \leq l \leq n$. The input question is fed into the following pipeline of six steps:

1. **Phrase detection**. Phrases are detected that potentially correspond to semantic items such as 'Who', 'played in', 'movie' and 'Casablanca'.
2. **Phrase mapping** to semantic items. This includes finding that the phrase 'played in' can either refer to the semantic relation actedIn or to playedForTeam and that the phrase 'Casablanca' can potentially refer to Casablanca_(film) or Casablanca,_Morocco. This step merely constructs a candidate space for the mapping. The actual disambiguation is addressed by step 4, discussed below.
3. **Q-unit generation**. Intuitively, a *q-unit* is a triple composed of phrases. Their generation and role will be discussed in detail in the next section.
4. **Joint disambiguation**, where the ambiguities in the phrase-to-semantic-item mapping are resolved. This entails resolving the ambiguity in phrase borders, and above all, choosing the best fitting candidates from the semantic space of entities, classes, and relations. Here, we determine for our running example that 'played in' refers to the semantic relation actedIn and not to playedForTeam and the phrase 'Casablanca' refers to Casablanca_(film) and not Casablanca,_Morocco.
5. **Semantic items grouping** to form semantic triples. For example, we determine that the relation marriedTo connects person referred to by 'Who' and writer to form the semantic triple person marriedTo writer. This is done via q-units.
6. **Query generation**. For SPARQL queries, semantic triples such as person marriedTo writer have to be mapped to suitable triple patterns with appropriate join conditions expressed through common variables: ?x type person, ?x marriedTo ?w, and ?w type writer for the example.

3.1 Phrase Detection

A *detected phrase* p is a pair $< Toks, l >$ where $Toks$ is a phrase and l is a label, $l \in \{concept, relation\}$, indicating whether a phrase is a relation phrase or a concept phrase. P_r is the set of all detected relation phrases and P_c is the set of all detected concept phrases.

One special type of detected relation phrase is the *null phrase*, where no relation is explicitly mentioned, but can be induced. The most prominent example of this is the case of adjectives, such as 'Australian movie', where we know there is a relation being expressed between 'Australia' and 'movie'.

We use multiple detectors for detecting phrases of

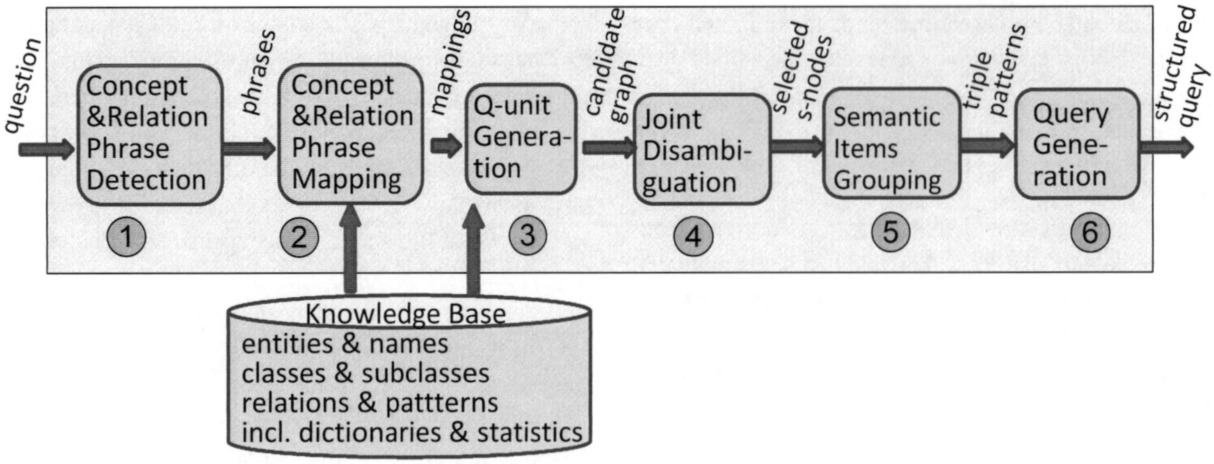

Figure 2: Architecture of DEANNA.

different types. For concept detection, we use a detector that works against a phrase-concept dictionary which looks as follows:

{'Rome','eternal city'} → `Rome`
{'Casablanca'} → `Casablanca_(film)`

We experimented with using third-party named entity recognizers but the results were not satisfactory. This dictionary was mostly constructed as part of the knowledge base, independently of the question-to-query translation task in the form of instances of the `means` relation in Yago2, an example of which is shown in Figure 1

For relation detection, we experimented with various approaches. We mainly rely on a relation detector based on ReVerb (Fader et al., 2011) with additional POS tag patterns, in addition to our own which looks for patterns in dependency parses.

3.2 Phrase Mapping

After phrases are detected, each phrase is mapped to a set of semantic items. The mapping of concept phrases also relies on the phrase-concept dictionary.

To map relation phrases, we rely on a corpus of textual patterns to relation mappings of the form:

{'play','star in','act','leading role'} → `actedIn`
{'married', 'spouse','wife'} → `marriedTo`

Distinct phrase occurrences will map to different semantic item instances. We discuss why this is important when we discuss the construction of the disambiguation graph and variable assignment in the structured query.

3.3 Dependency Parsing & Q-Unit Generation

Dependency parsing identifies triples of tokens, or *triploids*, $\langle t_{rel}, t_{arg1}, t_{arg2} \rangle$, where $t_{rel}, t_{arg1}, t_{arg2} \in q_{NL}$ are seeds for phrases, with the triploid acting as a seed for a potential SPARQL triple pattern. Here, t_{rel} is the seed for the relation phrase, while t_{arg1} and t_{arg2} are seeds for the two arguments. At this point, there is no attempt to assign subject/object roles to the arguments.

Triploids are collected by looking for specific dependency patterns in dependency graphs (de Marneffe et al., 2006). The most prominent pattern we look for is a verb and its arguments. Other patterns include adjectives and their arguments, prepositionally modified tokens and objects of prepositions.

By combining triploids with detected phrases, we obtain *q-units*. A q-unit is a triple of sets of phrases, $\langle \{p_{rel} \in P_r\}, \{p_{arg1} \in P_c\}, \{p_{arg2} \in P_c\} \rangle$, where $t_{rel} \in p_{rel}$ and similarly for arg_1 and arg_2. Conceptually, one can view a q-unit as a placeholder node with three sets of edges, each connecting the same q-node to a phrase that corresponds to a relation or concept phrase in the same q-unit. This notion of nodes and edges will be made more concrete when we present our disambiguation graph construction.

3.4 Disambiguation of Phrase Mappings

The core contribution of this paper is a framework for disambiguating phrases into semantic items – covering relations, classes, and entities in a unified manner. This can be seen as a joint task combining named entity disambiguation for entities, word sense disambiguation for classes (common nouns), and relation extraction. The next section presents the disambiguation framework in detail.

3.5 Query Generation

Once phrases are mapped to unique semantic items, we proceed to generate queries in two steps. First, semantic items are grouped into triples. This is done using the triploids generated earlier. The power of using a knowledge base is that we have a rich type system that allows us to tell if two semantic items are compatible or not. Each relation has a type signature and we check whether the candidate items are compatible with the signature.

We did not assign subject/object roles in triploids and q-units because a natural language relation phrase might express the inverse of a semantic relation, e.g., the natural language expression 'directed by' and the relation `isDirectorOf` with respect to the movies domain are inverses of each other. Therefore, we check which assignment of $arg1$ and $arg2$ is compatible with the semantic relation. If both arrangements are compatible, then we give preference to the assignment given by the dependency parsers.

Once semantic items are grouped into triples, it is an easy task to expand them to SPARQL triple patterns. This is done by replacing each semantic class with a distinct type-constrained variable. Note that this is the reason why each distinct phrase maps to a distinct instance of a semantic class, to ensure correct variable assignment. This becomes clear when we consider the question "Which singer is married to a singer?", which requires two distinct variables each constrained to bind to an entity of type `singer`.

4 Joint Disambiguation

The goal of the disambiguation step is to compute a partial mapping of phrases onto semantic items, such that each phrase is assigned to at most one semantic item. This step also resolves the phrase-boundary ambiguity, by enforcing that only non-overlapping phrases are mapped. As the result of disambiguating one phrase can influence the mapping of other phrases, we consider all phrases jointly in one big disambiguation task.

In the following, we construct a disambiguation graph that encodes all possible mappings. We impose a variety of complex constraints (mutual exclusion among overlapping phrases, type constraints among the selected semantic items, etc.), and define an objective function that aims to maximize the joint quality of the mapping. The graph construction itself may resemble similar models used in NED (e.g., (Milne and Witten, 2008; Kulkarni et al., 2009; Hoffart et al., 2011a)). Recall, however, that our task is more complex because we jointly consider entities, classes, and relations in the candidate space of possible mappings. Because of this complication and to capture our complex constraints, we do not employ graph algorithms, but model the general disambiguation problem as an ILP.

4.1 Disambiguation Graph

Joint disambiguation takes place over a disambiguation graph $DG = (V, E)$, where $V = V_s \cup V_p \cup V_q$ and $E = E_{sim} \cup E_{coh} \cup E_q$, where:

- V_s is the set of semantic items, $v_s \in V_s$ is an *s-node*.
- V_p is the set of phrases, $v_p \in V_p$ is called a *p-node*. We denote the set of p-nodes corresponding to relation phrases by V_{r_p} and the set of p-nodes corresponding to concept phrases by V_{r_c}.
- V_q is a set of placeholder nodes for q–units, called *q-nodes*. They represent phrase triples.
- $E_{sim} \subseteq V_p \times V_s$ is a set of weighted *similarity edges* that capture the strength of the mapping of a phrase to a semantic item.
- $E_{coh} \subseteq V_s \times V_s$ is a set of weighted *coherence edges* that capture the semantic coherence between two semantic items. Semantic coherence is discussed in more detail later in this section.
- $E_q \subseteq V_q \times V_p \times d$, where $d \in \{rel, arg_1, arg_2\}$ is a *q-edge*. Each such edge connects a placeholder q-node to a p-node with a specific role as a relation, or one of the two arguments. A q-unit, as presented earlier, can be seen as a q-node along with its outgoing q-edges.

Figure 3 shows the disambiguation graph for our running example (excluding coherence edges between s-nodes).

4.2 Edge Weights

We next describe how the weights on similarity edges and semantic coherence edges are defined.

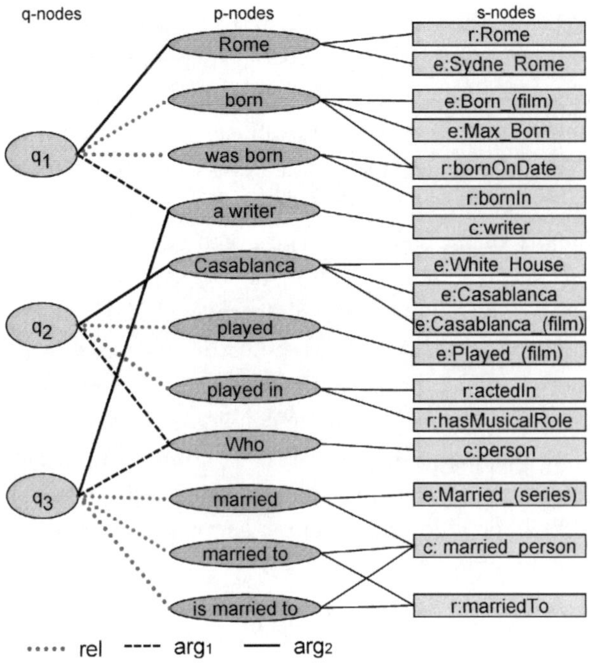

Figure 3: Disambiguation graph for the running example.

4.2.1 Semantic Coherence

Semantic coherence, Coh_{sem}, captures to what extent two semantic items occur in the same context. This is different from semantic similarity (Sim_{sem}), which is usually evaluated using the distance between nodes in a taxonomy (Resnik, 1995). While we expect Sim_{sem}(George_Bush, Woody_Allen) to be higher than Sim_{sem}(Woody_Allen, Terminator) we would like Coh_{sem}(Woody_Allen, Terminator), both of which are from the entertainment domain, to be higher than Coh_{sem}(George_Bush, Woody_Allen).

For Yago2, we characterize an entity e by its *inlinks* $InLinks(e)$: the set of Yago2 entities whose corresponding Wikipedia pages link to the entity.

To be able to compare semantic items of different semantic types (entities, relations, and classes), we need to extend this to classes and relations. For class c with entities e, its inlinks are defined as follows:

$$InLinks(c) = \bigcup_{e \in c} Inlinks(e)$$

For relations, we only consider those that map entities to entities (e.g. actedIn, produced), for which we define the set of inlinks as follows:

$$InLinks(r) = \bigcup_{(e_1,e_2) \in r} (InLinks(e_1) \cap InLinks(e_2))$$

The intuition behind this is that when the two arguments of an instance of the relation co-occur, then the relation is being expressed.

We define the semantic coherence (Coh_{sem}) between two semantic items s_1 and s_2 as the Jaccard coefficient of their sets of inlinks.

4.2.2 Similarity Weights

Similarity weights are computed differently for entities, classes, and relations. For entities, we use a normalized prior score based on how often a phrase refers to a certain entity in Wikipedia. For classes, we use a normalized prior that reflects the number of members in a class. Finally, for relations, similarity reflects the maximum n-gram similarity between the phrase and any of the relation's surface forms. We use Lucene for indexing and searching the relation surface forms.

4.3 Disambiguation Graph Processing

The result of disambiguation is a subgraph of the disambiguation graph, yielding the most coherent mappings. We employ an ILP to this end. Before describing our ILP, we state some necessary definitions:

- Triple dimensions: $d \in \{rel, arg_1, arg_2\}$
- Tokens: $T = \{t_0, t_1, ..., t_n\}$.
- Phrases: $P = \{p_0, p_1, ..., p_k\}$.
- Semantic items: $S = \{s_0, s_1, ..., s_l\}$.
- Token occurrences: $\mathcal{P}(t) = \{p \in P \mid t \in p\}$.
- $X_i \in \{0, 1\}$ indicates if p-node i is selected.
- $Y_{ij} \in \{0, 1\}$ indicates if p-node i maps to s-node j.
- $Z_{kl} \in \{0, 1\}$ indicates if s-nodes k, l are *both* selected so that their coherence edge matters.
- $Q_{mnd} \in \{0, 1\}$ indicates if the q-edge between q-node m and p-node n for d is selected.
- C_j, E_j and R_j are $\{0, 1\}$ constants indicating if s-node j is a class, entity, or relation, resp.
- w_{ij} is the weight for a p–s similarity edge.
- v_{kl} is the weight for an s–s semantic coherence edge.
- $t_{rc} \in \{0, 1\}$ indicates if the relation s-node r is type-compatible with the concept s-node c.

Given the above definitions, our objective function is

$$maximize \quad \alpha \sum_{i,j} w_{ij} Y_{ij} + \beta \sum_{k,l} v_{kl} Z_{kl} + \gamma \sum_{m,n,d} Q_{mnd}$$

subject to the following constraints:

1. A p-node can be assigned to one s-node *at most*:

$$\sum_j Y_{ij} \leq 1, \ \forall i$$

2. If a p-s similarity edge is chosen, then the respective p-node must be chosen:

$$Y_{ij} \leq X_i, \ \forall j$$

3. If s-nodes k and l are chosen ($Z_{kl} = 1$), then there are p-nodes mapping to each of the s-nodes k and l ($Y_{ik} = 1$ for some i *and* $Y_{jl} = 1$ for some j):

$$Z_{kl} \leq \sum_i Y_{ik} \text{ and } Z_{kl} \leq \sum_j Y_{jl}$$

4. No token can appear as part of two phrases:

$$\sum_{i \in \mathcal{P}(t)} X_i \leq 1, \forall t \in T$$

5. At most one q-edge is selected for a dimension:

$$\sum_n Q_{mnd} \leq 1, \ \forall m, d$$

6. If the q-edge mnd is chosen ($Q_{mnd} = 1$) then p-node n must be selected:

$$Q_{mnd} \leq X_n, \ \forall m, d$$

7. Each semantic triple should include a relation:

$$E_r \geq Q_{mn'd} + X_{n'} + Y_{n'r} - 2 \ \forall m, n', r, d = rel$$

8. Each triple should have at least one class:

$$\begin{aligned} C_{c_1} + C_{c_2} \geq \ & Q_{mn''d_1} + X_{n''} + Y_{n'''c_1} + \\ & Q_{mn'''d_2} + X_{n'''} + Y_{n'''c_2} - 5, \\ \forall m, n'', n''', r, c_1, c_2, & d_1 = arg1, d_2 = arg2 \end{aligned}$$

This is not invoked for existential questions that return Boolean answers and are translated to `ASK` queries in SPARQL. An example is the question "Did Tom Cruise act in Top Gun?", which can be translated to `ASK {Tom_Cruise actedIn Top_Gun}`.

9. Type constraints are respected (through q-edges):

$$\begin{aligned} t_{rc_1} + t_{rc_2} \geq \ & Q_{mn'd_1} + X_{n'} + Y_{n'r} + \\ & Q_{mn''d_2} + X_{n''} + Y_{n'''c_1} + \\ & Q_{mn'''d_3} + X_{n'''} + Y_{n'''c_2} - 7 \\ \forall m, n', n'', n''', r, c_1, c_2, & \\ d_1 = rel, d_2 = arg1, d3 = arg2 & \end{aligned}$$

The above is a sophisticated ILP, and most likely NP-hard. However, even with ten thousands of variables it is within the regime of modern ILP solvers. In our experiments, we used Gurobi (Gur, 2011), and achieved run-times – typically of a few seconds.

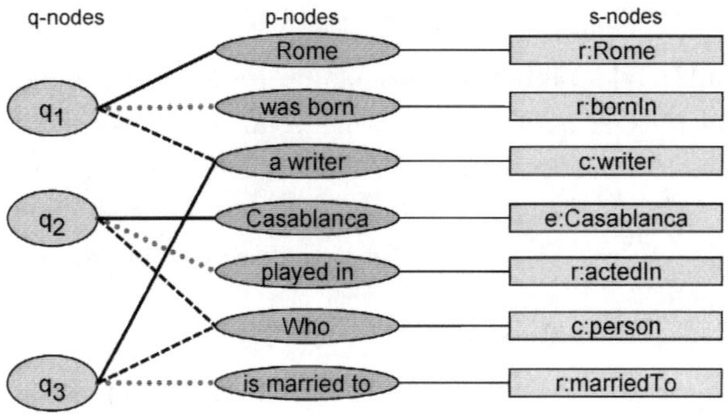

Figure 4: Computed subgraph for the running example.

Figure 4 shows the resulting subgraph for the disambiguation graph of Figure 3. Note how common p-nodes between q-units capture joins.

5 Evaluation

5.1 Datasets

Our experiments are based on two collections of questions: the QALD-1 task for question answering over linked data (QAL, 2011) and a collection of questions used in (Elbassuoni et al., 2011; Elbassuoni et al., 2009) in the context of the NAGA project, for informative ranking of SPARQL query answers (Elbassuoni et al. (2009) evaluated the SPARQL queries, but the underlying questions are formulated in natural language.) The NAGA collection is based on linking data from IMDB with the Yago2 knowledge base. This is an interesting linked-data case: IMDB provides data about movies, actors, directors, and movie plots (in the form of descriptive keywords and phrases); Yago2 adds semantic types and relational facts for the participating entities. Yago2 provides nearly 3 million concepts and 100 relations, of which 41 lie within the scope of our framework.

Typical example questions for these two collections are: "Which software has been published by Mean Hamster Software?" for QALD-1, and "Which director has won the Academy Award for Best director and is married to an actress that has won the Academy Award for Best Actress?" for NAGA. For both collections, some questions are out-of-scope for our setting, because they mention entities or relations that are not available in the underlying datasets, contain date or time comparisons, or involve aggregation such as counting. After removing these questions, our test set consists of 27 QALD-1 training questions out of a total of 50 and 44 NAGA questions, out of a total of 87. We used the 19 questions from the QALD-1 test set that are within the scope of our method for tuning the hyper-parameters (α, β, γ) in the ILP objective function.

5.2 Evaluation Metrics

We evaluated the output of DEANNA at three stages in the processing pipeline: a) after the disambiguation of phrases, b) after the generation of the SPARQL query, and c) after obtaining answers from the underlying linked-data sources. This way, we could obtain insights into our building blocks, in addition to assessing the end-to-end performance. In particular, we could assess the goodness of the question-to-query translation *independently* of the actual answer quality which may depend on particularities of the underlying datasets (e.g., slight mismatches between query terminology and the names in the data.)

At each of the three stages, the output was shown to two human assessors who judged whether an output item was good or not. If the two were in disagreement, then a third person resolved the judgment.

For the *disambiguation* stage, the judges looked at each q-node/s-node pair, in the context of the question and the underlying data schemas, and determined whether the mapping was correct or not and whether any expected mappings were missing. For the *query-generation* stage, the judges looked at each triple pattern and determined whether the pattern was meaningful for the question or not and whether any expected triple pattern was missing. Note that, because our approach does not use any query templates, the same question may generate semantically equivalent queries that differ widely in terms of their structure. Hence, we rely on our evaluation metrics that are based on triple patterns, as there is no gold-standard query for a given question. For the *query-answering* stage, the judges were asked to identify if the result sets for the generated queries are satisfactory.

With these assessments, we computed overall quality measures by both micro-averaging and macro-averaging. Micro-averaging aggregates over all assessed items (e.g., q-node/s-node pairs or triple patterns) regardless of the questions to which they belong. Macro-averaging first aggregates the items for the same question, and then averages the quality measure over all questions.

For a question q and item set s in one of the stages of evaluation, let $correct(q, s)$ be the number of correct items in s, $ideal(q)$ be the size of the ideal item set and $retrieved(q, s)$ be the number of retrieved items, we define coverage and precision as follows:

$$cov(q, s) = correct(q, s)/ideal(q)$$

$$prec(q, s) = correct(q, s)/retrieved(q, s).$$

5.3 Results & Discussion

5.3.1 Disambiguation

Table 1 shows the results for disambiguation in terms of macro and micro coverage and precision. For both datasets, coverage is high as few mappings are missing. We obtain perfect precision for QALD-1 as no mapping that we generate is incorrect, while for NAGA we generate few incorrect mappings.

5.3.2 Query Generation

Table 2 shows the same metrics for the generated triple patterns. The results are similar to those for disambiguation. Missing or incorrect triple patterns can be attributed to (i) incorrect mappings in the disambiguation stage or (ii) incorrect detection of dependencies between phrases despite having the correct mappings.

5.3.3 Question Answering

Table 3 shows the results for query answering. Here, we attempt to generate answers to questions by executing the generated queries over the datasets. The table shows the number of questions for which the system successfully generated SPARQL queries (#queries), and among those, how many resulted in satisfactory answers as judged by our evaluators (#satisfactory). Answers were considered unsatisfactory when: 1) the generated SPARQL query was wrong, 2) the result set was empty due to the incompleteness of the underlying knowledge base, or 3) a small fraction of the result set was relevant to the question. For both sets of questions, most of the queries that were perceived unsatisfactory were ones that returned no answers. Table 4 shows a set of example QALD questions, the corresponding SPARQL queries and sample answers.

Benchmark	QALD-1	NAGA
cov_{macro}	0.973	0.934
$prec_{macro}$	1.000	0.934
cov_{micro}	0.963	0.945
$prec_{micro}$	1.000	0.941

Table 1: Disambiguation

Benchmark	QALD-1	NAGA
cov_{macro}	0.975	0.894
$prec_{macro}$	1.000	0.941
cov_{micro}	0.956	0.847
$prec_{micro}$	1.000	0.906

Table 2: Query generation

Benchmark	QALD-1	NAGA
#questions	27	44
#queries	20	41
#satisfactory	10	15
#relaxed	+3	+3

Table 3: Query answering

Question	Generated Query	Sample Answers
1. Who was the wife of President Lincoln?	`?x marriedTo Abraham_Lincoln . ?x type person`	`Mary_Todd_Lincoln`
2. In which films did Julia Roberts as well as Richard Gere play?	`?x type movie . Richard_Gere actedIn ?x . Julia_Roberts actedIn ?x`	`Runaway_Bride` `Pretty_Woman`
3. Which actors were born in Germany?	`?x type actor . ?x bornIn Germany`	NONE

Table 4: Example questions, the generated SPARQL queries and their answers

Queries that produced *no* answers, such as the third query in Table 4 were further relaxed using an incarnation of the techniques described in (Elbassuoni et al., 2009), by retaining the triple patterns expressing type constraints and relaxing all other triple patterns. Relaxing a triple pattern was done by replacing all entities with variables and casting entity mentions into keywords that are attached to the relaxed triple pattern. For example, the QALD question "Which actors were born in Germany?" was translated into the following SPARQL query: `?x type actor . ?x bornIn Germany` which produced no answers when run over the Yago2 knowledge base since the relation `bornIn` relates people to cities and not countries in Yago2. The query was then relaxed into: `?x type actor . ?x bornIn ?z[Germany]`. This relaxed (and keyword-augmented) triple-pattern query was then processed the same way as triple-pattern queries without any keywords. The results of such query were then ranked based on how well they match the keyword conditions specified in the relaxed query using the ranking model in (Elbassuoni et al., 2009). Using this technique, the top ranked results for the relaxed query were all actors born in German cities as shown in Table 5.

After relaxation, the judges again assessed the results of the relaxed queries and determined whether they were satisfactory or not. The number of additional queries that obtained satisfactory answers after relaxation are shown under #relaxed in Table 3.

The evaluation data, in addition to a demonstration of our system (Yahya et al., 2012), can be found at `http://mpi-inf.mpg.de/yago-naga/deanna/`.

6 Related Work

Question answering has a long history in NLP and IR research. The Web and Wikipedia have proved to be a valuable resource for answering fact-oriented questions. State-of-the-art methods (Hirschman and Gaizauskas, 2001; Kwok et al., 2001; Zheng, 2002; Katz et al., 2007; Dang et al., 2007; Voorhees, 2003) cast the user's question into a keyword query to a Web search engine (perhaps with phrases for location and person names or other proper nouns). Key to finding good results is to retrieve and rank sentences or short passages that contain all or most keywords and are likely to yield good answers. Together with trained classifiers for the question type (and thus the desired answer type), this methodology performs fairly well for both factoid and list questions.

IBM's Watson project (Ferrucci et al., 2010) demonstrated a new kind of *deep QA*. A key element in Watson's approach is to decompose complex questions into several cues and sub-cues, with the aim of generating answers from matches for the various cues (tapping into the Web and Wikipedia). Knowledge bases like DBpedia (Auer et al., 2007), Freebase (Bollacker et al., 2008), and Yago (Suchanek et al., 2007)) are used for both answering parts of questions that can be translated to structured form (Chu-Carroll et al., 2012) and type-checking possible answer candidates and thus filtering out spurious results (Kalyanpur et al., 2011).

The recent QALD-1 initiative (QAL, 2011) proposed a benchmark task to translate questions into SPARQL queries over linked-data sources like DBpedia and MusicBrainz. FREyA (Damljanovic et al., 2011), the best performing system, relies on

Q: ?x type actor.?x wasBornIn ?z[Germany]
Martin_Lawrence type actor. Martin_Lawrence wasBornIn Frankfurt_am_Main
Robert_Schwentke type actor.Robert_Schwentke wasBornIn Stuttgart
Willy_Millowitsch type actor.Willy_Millowitsch wasBornIn Cologne
Jerry_Zaks type actor.Jerry_Zaks wasBornIn Stuttgart

Table 5: Top-4 results for the QALD question "Which actors were born in Germany?" after relaxation

interaction with the user to interpret the question. Earlier work on mapping questions into structured queries includes the work by Frank et al. (2007) and Unger and Cimiano (2011). Frank et al. (2007) used lexical-conceptual templates for query generation. However, this work did not address the crucial issue of disambiguating the constituents of the question. In Pythia, Unger and Cimiano (2011) relied on an ontology-driven grammar for the question language so that questions could be directly mapped onto the vocabulary of the underlying ontology. Such grammars are obviously hard to craft for very large, complex, and evolving knowledge bases. Nalix is an attempt to bring question answering to XML data (Li, Yang, and Jagadish, 2007) by mapping questions to XQuery expressions, relying on human interaction to resolve possible ambiguity.

Very recently, Unger et al. (2012) developed a template-based approach based on Pythia, where questions are automatically mapped to structured queries in a two step process. First, a set of query templates are generated for a question, independent of the knowledge base, determining the structure of the query. After that, each template is instantiated with semantic items from the knowledge base. This performs reasonably well for the QALD-1 benchmark: out of 50 test questions, 34 could be mapped, and 19 were correctly answered.

Efforts on user-friendly exploration of structured data include keyword search over relational databases (Bhalotia et al., 2002) and structured keyword search (Pound et al., 2010). The latter is a compromise between full natural language and structured queries, where the user provides the structure and the system takes care of the disambiguation of keyword phrases.

Our joint disambiguation method was inspired by recent work on NED (Milne and Witten, 2008; Kulkarni et al., 2009; Hoffart et al., 2011a) and WSD (Navigli, 2009). In contrast to this prior work on related problems, our graph construction and constraints are more complex, as we address the joint mapping of arbitrary phrases onto entities, classes, or relations. Moreover, instead of graph algorithms or factor-graph learning, we use an ILP for solving the ambiguity problem. This way, we can accommodate expressive constraints, while being able to disambiguate all phrases in a few seconds.

DEANNA uses dictionaries of names and phrases for entities, classes, and relations. Spitkovsky and Chang (2012) recently released a huge dictionary of pairs of phrases and Wikipedia links, derived from Google's Web index. For relations, Nakashole et al. (2012) released PATTY, a large taxonomy of patterns with semantic types.

7 Conclusions and Future Work

We presented a method for translating natural-language questions into structured queries. The novelty of this method lies in modeling several mapping stages as a joint ILP problem. We harness type signatures and other information from large-scale knowledge bases. Although our model, in principle, leads to high combinatorial complexity, we observed that the Gurobi solver could handle our judiciously designed ILP very efficiently. Our experimental studies showed very high precision and good coverage of the query translation, and good results in the actual question answers.

Future work includes relaxing some of the limitations that our current approach still has. First, questions with aggregations cannot be handled at this point. Second, queries sometimes return empty answers although they perfectly capture the original question, but the underlying data sources are incomplete or represent the relevant information in an unexpected manner. We plan to extend our approach of combining structured data with textual descriptions, and generate queries that combine structured search predicates with keyword or phrase matching.

References

Auer, S.; Bizer, C.; Kobilarov, G.; Lehmann, J.; Cyganiak, R.; and Ives, Z. G. 2007. DBpedia: A Nucleus for a Web of Open Data. In *ISWC/ASWC*.

Bhalotia, G.; Hulgeri, A.; Nakhe, C.; Chakrabarti, S.; and Sudarshan, S. 2002. Keyword Searching and Browsing in Databases using BANKS. In *ICDE*.

Bollacker, K. D.; Evans, C.; Paritosh, P.; Sturge, T.; and Taylor, J. 2008. Freebase: a Collaboratively Created Graph Database for Structuring Human Knowledge. In *SIGMOD*.

Chu-Carroll, J.; Fan, J.; Boguraev, B. K.; Carmel, D.; and Sheinwald, D.; Welty, C. 2012. Finding needles in the haystack: Search and candidate generation. In *IBM J. Res. & Dev., vol 56, no.3/4*.

Damljanovic, D.; Agatonovic, M.; and Cunningham, H. 2011. *FREyA: an Interactive Way of Querying Linked Data using Natural Language*.

Dang, H. T.; Kelly, D.; and Lin, J. J. 2007. Overview of the trec 2007 question answering track. In *TREC*.

de Marneffe, M. C.; Maccartney, B.; and Manning, C. D. 2006. Generating typed dependency parses from phrase structure parses. In *LREC*.

Elbassuoni, S.; Ramanath, M.; Schenkel, R.; Sydow, M.; and Weikum, G. 2009. Language-model-based ranking for queries on rdf-graphs. In *CIKM*.

Elbassuoni, S.; Ramanath, M.; and Weikum, G. 2011. Query relaxation for entity-relationship search. In *ESWC*.

Fader, A.; Soderland, S.; and Etzioni, O. 2011. Identifying relations for open information extraction. In *EMNLP*.

Ferrucci, D. A.; Brown, E. W.; Chu-Carroll, J.; Fan, J.; Gondek, D.; Kalyanpur, A.; Lally, A.; Murdock, J. W.; Nyberg, E.; Prager, J. M.; Schlaefer, N.; and Welty, C. A. 2010. Building Watson: An Overview of the DeepQA Project. *AI Magazine* 31(3).

Frank, A.; Krieger, H.-U.; Xu, F.; Uszkoreit, H.; Crysmann, B.; Jörg, B.; and Schäfer, U. 2007. Question Answering from Structured Knowledge Sources. *J. Applied Logic* 5(1).

Gurobi Optimization, Inc. 2012. Gurobi Optimizer Reference Manual. http://www.gurobi.com/.

Heath, T., and Bizer, C. 2011. *Linked Data: Evolving the Web into a Global Data Space*. San Rafael, CA: Morgan & Claypool, 1 edition.

Hirschman, L., and Gaizauskas, R. 2001. Natural Language Question Answering: The View from Here. *Nat. Lang. Eng.* 7.

Hoffart, J.; Mohamed, A. Y.; Bordino, I.; Fürstenau, H.; Pinkal, M.; Spaniol, M.; Taneva, B.; Thaterm S.; and Weikum, G. 2011. Robust Disambiguation of Named Entities in Text. In *EMNLP*.

Hoffart, J.; Suchanek, F. M.; Berberich, K.; Lewis-Kelham, E.; de Melo, G.; and Weikum, G. 2011. Yago2: exploring and querying world knowledge in time, space, context, and many languages. In *WWW (Companion Volume)*.

Kalyanpur, A.; Murdock, J. W.; Fan, J.; and Welty, C. A. 2011. Leveraging community-built knowledge for type coercion in question answering. In *International Semantic Web Conference*.

Katz, B.; Felshin, S.; Marton, G.; Mora, F.; Shen, Y. K.; Zaccak, G.; Ammar, A.; Eisner, E.; Turgut, A.; and Westrick, L. B. 2007. CSAIL at TREC 2007 Question Answering. In *TREC*.

Kulkarni, S.; Singh, A.; Ramakrishnan, G.; and Chakrabarti, S. 2009. Collective annotation of wikipedia entities in web text. In *KDD*.

Kwok, C. C. T.; Etzioni, O.; and Weld, D. S. 2001. Scaling Question Answering to the Web. In *WWW*.

Li, Y.; Yang, H.; and Jagadish, H. V. 2007. NaLIX: A Generic Natural Language Search Environment for XML Data. *ACM Trans. Database Syst.* 32(4).

Milne, D. N., and Witten, I. H. 2008. Learning to link with wikipedia. In *CIKM*.

Ndapandula Nakashole, Gerhard Weikum and Fabian Suchanek 2012. PATTY: A Taxonomy of Relational Patterns with Semantic Types. In *EMNLP*.

Navigli, R. 2009. Word sense disambiguation: A survey. *ACM Comput. Surv.* 41(2).

Pound, J.; Ilyas, I. F.; and Weddell, G. E. 2010. Expressive and Flexible Access to Web-extracted Data: A Keyword-based Structured Query Language. In *SIGMOD*.

2011. 1st Workshop on Question Answering over Linked Data (QALD-1). http://www.sc.cit-ec.uni-bielefeld.de/qald-1.

Resnik, P. 1995. Using Information Content to Evaluate Semantic Similarity in a Taxonomy. In *IJCAI*.

Spitkovsky, V. I. Spitkovsky; Chang, A. X. ; 2012. A Cross-Lingual Dictionary for English Wikipedia Concepts. In *LREC*.

Suchanek, F. M.; Kasneci, G.; and Weikum, G. 2007. Yago: a core of semantic knowledge. In *WWW*.

Tummarello, G.; Cyganiak, R.; Catasta, M.; Danielczyk, S.; Delbru, R.; and Decker, S. 2010. Sig.ma: Live views on the web of data. *J. Web Sem.* 8(4).

Unger, C.; and Cimiano, P. 2011. Pythia: Compositional Meaning Construction for Ontology-Based Question Answering on the Semantic Web. In *NLDB*.

Unger, C.; Bühmann, L.; Lehmann, J.; Ngonga Ngomo, A.-C.; Gerber, D.; and Cimiano, P. 2012. Template-based question answering over RDF data. In *WWW*.

Voorhees, E. M. 2003. Overview of the trec 2003 question answering track. In *TREC*.

Yahya, M.; Berberich, K.; Elbassuoni, S.; Ramanath, M.; Tresp, V.; and Weikum, G. 2012. Deep answers for naturally asked questions on the web of data. In *WWW*.

Zheng, Z. 2002. AnswerBus Question Answering System. In *HLT*.

Answering Opinion Questions on Products by Exploiting Hierarchical Organization of Consumer Reviews

Jianxing Yu, Zheng-Jun Zha, Tat-Seng Chua
School of Computing
National University of Singapore
{jianxing, zhazj, chuats}@comp.nus.edu.sg

Abstract

This paper proposes to generate appropriate answers for opinion questions about products by exploiting the hierarchical organization of consumer reviews. The hierarchy organizes product aspects as nodes following their parent-child relations. For each aspect, the reviews and corresponding opinions on this aspect are stored. We develop a new framework for opinion Questions Answering, which enables accurate question analysis and effective answer generation by making use the hierarchy. In particular, we first identify the (explicit/implicit) product aspects asked in the questions and their sub-aspects by referring to the hierarchy. We then retrieve the corresponding review fragments relevant to the aspects from the hierarchy. In order to generate appropriate answers from the review fragments, we develop a multi-criteria optimization approach for answer generation by simultaneously taking into account review salience, coherence, diversity, and parent-child relations among the aspects. We conduct evaluations on 11 popular products in four domains. The evaluated corpus contains 70,359 consumer reviews and 220 questions on these products. Experimental results demonstrate the effectiveness of our approach.

1 Introduction

With the rapid development of E-commerce, most retail websites encourage consumers to post reviews to express their opinions on the products. For example, the review "*The battery of Nokia N95 is amazing.*" reveals positive opinion on the aspect "*battery*" of product *Nokia N95*. An *aspect* here refers to a component or an attribute of a certain product. Numerous consumer reviews are now available online, and these reviews contain rich opinionated information on various aspects of products. They are naturally a valuable resource for answering opinion questions about products, such as "*How do people think about the battery of Nokia N95?*" Opinion Question Answering (opinion-QA) on products seeks to uncover consumers' thinking and feeling about the products or aspects of products. It is different from traditional factual QA, where the questions ask for the fact, such as "*Where is the capital of United States?*" and the answer is "*Washington, D.C.*"

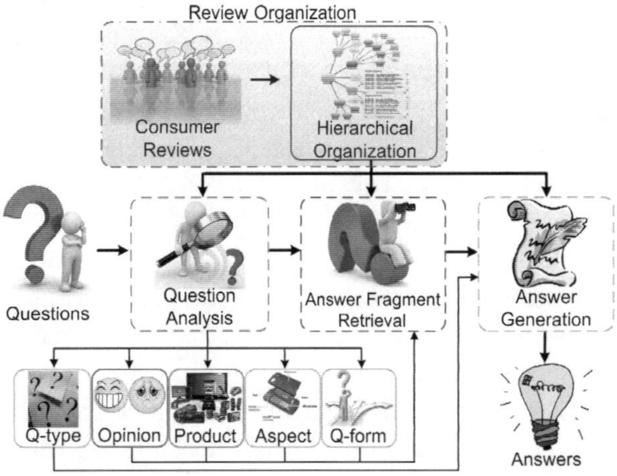

Figure 1: Overview of product opinion-QA framework

For a product opinionated question, the answer should not be just a best answer. It should reflect the opinions of various segments of users, and incorporate both positive and negative viewpoints. Hence the answer should be a summarization of public opinions and comments on the product or specific aspect asked in the question (Jiang et al., 2010). In addition, it should also include public opinions and comments on the sub-aspects. Such answers would help users to understand the inherent reasons of the opinions on the asked aspect. For example, the question "*What do people think the camera of Nokia 5800?*" asks for public positive and negative opinions on the aspect "*camera*" of product "*Nokia 5800.*" The summarization of opinions on the sub-aspects such as "*lens*" and "*resolution*" would help users better understand that the public complaints on the aspect "*camera*" are due to the poor "*lens*" and/or low "*resolution.*" Moreover, the answer should be presented following the general-to-specific logic, i.e., from general aspects to specific sub-aspects. This makes the answer easier to understand by the users (Ouyang et al., 2009).

Current Opinion-QA methods mainly include three components, including question analysis that identifies aspects and opinions asked in the questions, answer fragment retrieval, and answer generation which summarizes the retrieved fragments (Lloret et al., 2011). Although existing methods show encouraging performance, they are usually not able to generate satisfactory answers due to the following drawbacks. First, current methods often identify aspects as the noun phrases in the questions. However, noun phrases contain noises that are not aspects. This gives rise to imprecise aspect identification. For example, in the question "*What reasons can I persuade my wife that people prefer the battery of Nokia N95?*" noun phrases "*wife*" and "*people*" are not aspects. Moreover, current methods relied on noun phrases are not able to reveal the implicit aspects, which are not explicitly asked in the questions. For example, the question "*Is iPhone 4 expensive?*" asks about the aspect "*price*", but the term "*price*" does not appear in the question. Second, current methods cannot discover sub-aspects of the asked aspect due to its ignorance of parent-child relations among aspects. Third, the answers generated by the existing methods do not follow the general-to-specific logic, leading to difficulty in understanding the answers.

To overcome these problems, we can resort to the hierarchical organization of consumer reviews on products. As illustrated in Figure 2, the hierarchy organizes product aspects as nodes, following their parent-child relations. For each aspect, the reviews and corresponding opinions on this aspect are stored. Such hierarchy can naturally facilitate to identify aspects asked in questions. While explicit aspects can be recognized by referring to the hierarchy, implicit aspects can be inferred based on the associations between sentiment terms and aspects in the hierarchy (Yu et al., 2011). The sentiment terms are discovered from the reviews on corresponding aspects. Moreover, by following the parent-child relations in the hierarchy, sub-aspects of the asked aspect can be directly acquired, and the answers can present aspects from general to specific.

Motivated by the above observations, we propose to exploit the hierarchical organization of consumer reviews for product opinion-QA. As illustrated in Figure 1, our framework first organizes consumer reviews of a certain product into a hierarchical organization. The resulting hierarchy is in turn used to help question analysis and relevant review fragments retrieval. In order to generate appropriate answers from the retrieved fragments, we develop a multi-criteria optimization approach by simultaneously taking into account review salience, coherence, and diversity. The parent-child relations among aspects are also incorporated into the approach to ensure the answers be general-to-specific. We conduct evaluations on 11 popular products in four domains. The evaluated corpus contains 70,359 consumer reviews and 220 questions on these products. More details of the dataset are discussed in Section 4. Experimental results to demonstrate the effectiveness of our approach.

The main contributions of this paper include,

- We propose to exploit the hierarchical organization of consumer reviews for answering opinion questions on products.
- With the help of the hierarchy, our proposed framework can accurately identify (explicit/implicit) aspects asked in the questions, and the corresponding sub-aspects.
- We develop a multi-criteria optimization approach to generate informative, coherent, diverse and general-to-specific answers.

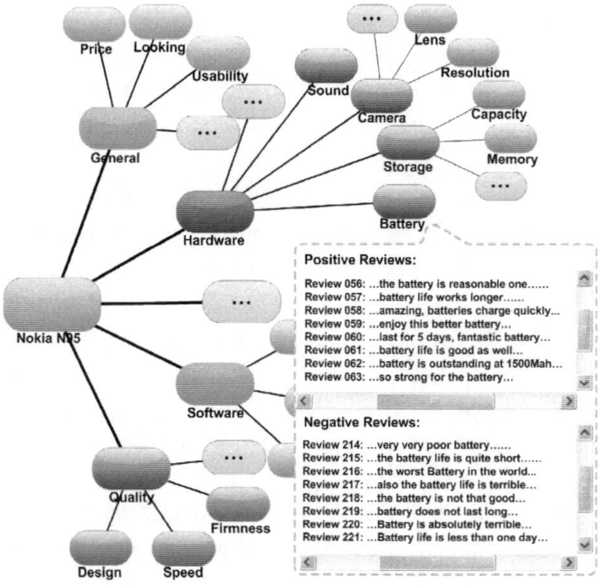

Figure 2: Hierarchical organization for *Nokia N95*

The rest of this paper is organized as follows. Section 2 introduces the components of hierarchical organization of reviews, question analysis, and answer fragment retrieval. Section 3 elaborates the multi-criteria optimization approach for answer generation . Section 4 presents experimental details, while Section 5 reviews related works. Finally, Section 6 concludes this paper with future works.

2 Hierarchical Organization, Question Analysis, and Answer Fragment Retrieval

Let $\mathcal{R} = \{r_1, \cdots, r_{|\mathcal{R}|}\}$ denote a collection of consumer reviews of a certain product. Each review reflects consumer opinions on the product and/or product aspects. Let q denote an opinion question, which asks for public opinions on a product or some aspects of the product. The task is to retrieve the opinionated review fragments relevant to the asked product/product aspects, and summarize these fragments to form an appropriate answer to question q.

Next, we introduce the components of hierarchical organization that organizes consumer reviews into a hierarchy, question analysis which identifies the products/aspects and opinions asked in the questions, and answer fragment retrieval that retrieves review fragments relevant to the questions.

2.1 Hierarchical Organization of Reviews

We employ the method proposed by Yu et al. (2011) to organize consumer reviews of a product into a hierarchical organization. As shown in Figure 2, the hierarchy organizes product aspects as nodes, following their parent-child relations. In particular, this method first automatically acquires an initial aspect hierarchy from the domain knowledge and identifies aspects commented in the reviews. It then incrementally inserts the identified aspects into appropriate positions in the initial hierarchy, and finally obtains an aspect hierarchy that allocates all the newly identified aspects. The consumer reviews are then organized to their corresponding aspect nodes in the hierarchy. Sentiment classification is then performed to determine consumer opinions on the reviews.

The reported performance of Yu et al. (2011) on aspect identification, aspect hierarchy generation and sentiment classification are 0.731, 0.705, 0.787 in terms of average F_1-measure, respectively.

2.2 Question Analysis and Answer Fragment Retrieval

Question analysis consists of five sub-tasks: recognizing product asked in the question; identifying aspects in the question; classifying opinions that the question asks for (the asked opinion could be positive, negative or both); identifying the question type (e.g. asking for public opinions, or the reason of the opinions, etc.); and identifying the question form (i.e. comparative question or single form question).

Recognizing the product: A name entity recognizer [1] is trained to recognize the product name. In particular, we collect 420 auxiliary questions from Yahoo!Answer [2], and manually annotate the product names (submitted as supplementary material in Appendix A). A name entity recognizer for product is learned on these data, with unigrams and POS tags as features. Given a testing question, the recognizer predicts each word as *B*, *I*, *E* or *O*, where *B*, *I*, *E* denote the begin, internal, and end of a product name respectively, and *O* corresponds to other words.

Identifying aspects: As aforementioned, simply extracting the noun phrases as aspects would import noises. Also, some "implicit" aspects do not ex-

[1] http://nlp.stanford.edu/software/CRF-NER.shtml

[2] http://answers.yahoo.com

plicitly appear in the reviews. One simple solution for these problems can resort to the review hierarchy. The hierarchy has organized product aspects, which can be used to filter the noise noun phrases for accurately identifying the explicit aspects. For the implicit aspects, we observe they are usually modified by some peculiar sentiment terms (Su et al., 2008). For example, the aspect "*size*" is often modified by the sentiment terms such as "*large*", but seldom by the terms such as "*expensive*." Thus, there are some associations between the aspects and sentiment terms. Such associations can be learned from the hierarchy and leveraged to infer the implicit aspects (Yu et al., 2011). In order to simultaneously identify the (explicit/implicit) aspects, we adopt a hierarchical classification technique. The technique simultaneously learns to identify explicit aspects, and discovers the associations between aspects and sentiment terms by multiple classifiers. In particular, given a testing question, we identify its aspect by hierarchically classify (Silla et al., 2011) it into the appropriate aspect node of a particular product hierarchy. The classification greedily searches a path in the hierarchy from top to down. The search begins at the root node, and stops at the leaf node or a specific node where the relevance score is lower than a pre-defined threshold. The relevance score on each node is determined by a SVM classifier. Multiple SVM classifiers are learned on the hierarchy, one distinct classifier for a node. The reviews that are stored in the node and its child-nodes are used as training samples. We employ the features of noun terms, and sentiment terms in the sentiment lexicon provided by *MPQA* project (Wilson et al., 2005).

Classifying the opinions: Given a set of testing questions, we first distinguish the opinion questions from the factual ones (Yu et al., 2003). Since the opinion questions often contain one or more sentiment terms, we classify them by employing the sentiment terms in the sentiment lexicon provided from MPQA project (Wilson et al., 2005). Subsequently, we learn a SVM sentiment classifier to determine the opinion polarity of the opinion questions. In particular, the reviews and corresponding opinions stored in the hierarchy are used as training samples, which are represented by the unigram features.

Identifying the question type: Opinion questions are often categorized into four types (Ku et al., 2007),

- **Attitude** question, asking for public opinion on a product or product aspect, such as "*What do people think iPhone 3gs?*"
- **Reason** question, asking for the reason of public opinion on a product or product aspect, such as "*Why do people like iPhone 3gs?*"
- **Target** question, asking for the object in the public opinion, such as "*Which phone is better than Nokia N95?*"
- **Yes/No** question, asking for whether a statement is correct, such as "*Is Nokia N95 bad?*"

We formulate the question type identification as a multi-class classification problem. A multi-class SVM classifier [3] is learned for the classification. We collect 420 auxiliary questions from Yahoo!Answer and manually annotate their types (submitted as supplementary material in Appendix B). These questions are used for training, with POS tags and question words (i.e. why, what, how, do, is) as features.

Identifying the question form: Question form includes single and comparative. A question is viewed as comparative if it contains comparative adjectives and adverbs (e.g. cheaper, etc.), otherwise as the single form (Moghaddam et al., 2011). The POS tags are exploited to detect comparative adjectives (i.e. tag "*JJR*") and adverbs (i.e. tag "*RBR*").

After analyzing the question, we retrieve all review sentences on the asked aspect and all its subaspects from a certain product hierarchy, and choose the ones relevant to the opinion asked in the question. For the single form question, we view the retrieved sentences as the answer fragments. For the comparative questions, we select comparative sentences on the compared products from the retrieved sentences, and treat them as the answer fragments. Subsequently, question type is used to define the template for the answers. In particular, for the questions asking for reason and attitude, we generate the answers by summarizing corresponding answer fragments. For questions seeking for a target as the answer, we output the product names based on the majority voting of the opinions in the retrieved answer fragments. For the yes/no questions, we first generate the "yes/no" answer based on the

[3] http://svmlight.joachims.org/svm_multiclass.html

consistency between the asked opinions and the major opinions in the answer fragments, and then summarize these fragments to form the answers.

3 Answer Generation

Answer generation aims to generate an appropriate answer for a given opinion question based on the retrieved answer fragments, i.e., review sentences. An answer is essentially a sequence of sentences. Hence, the task of answer generation is to select sentences from the retrieved answer fragments and order them appropriately. We formulate this task into a multi-criteria optimization problem. We incorporate multiple criteria in the answer generation process, including answer salience, coherence, and diversity. The parent-child relations between aspects is also incorporated to ensure the answer follow the general-to-specific logic. In the next subsections, we will introduce details of the proposed multi-criteria optimization approach.

3.1 Formulation

We first introduce the multiple criteria and then present the optimization problem.

Salience is used to measure the representativeness of the answer. A good answer should consist of salient review sentences. Let $\mathcal{S}$ denote the set of retrieved sentences. We define a binary variable $s_i \in \{0, 1\}$ to indicate the selection of sentence i for the answer, i.e. $s_i = 1$ (or 0) indicates that s_i is selected (or not). Let ω_i denote the salience of sentence i. The estimation of ω_i will be described in Section 3.2. The salience score of the answer (i.e., a set of sentences) is computed by summing up the scores of all its constituent sentences, as $\sum_{i\in\mathcal{S}} \omega_i s_i$.

Coherence is used to quantify the readability of an answer. To make the answer readable, the constituent sentences in the answer should be ordered properly. That is, the adjacent sentences should be coherent. We define $e_{i,j} \in \{0, 1\}$ to indicate whether the sentences i and j are adjacent in the answer; where $e_{i,j} = 1$ (or 0) means they are (or not) adjacent. The coherence between two adjacent sentences is measured by c_{ij}. The estimation of c_{ij} will be described in Section 3.3. As aforementioned, the answer is expected to be presented in a general-to-specific manner, i.e. from general aspects to specific sub-aspects. We define $h_{i,j}$ in Eq.1 to measure the general-to-specific coherence of sentences i and j.

$$h_{i,j} = \begin{cases} e^{-\frac{1}{level_i - level_j}}; & \text{if } level_i \neq level_j; \\ 1; & \text{otherwise}, \end{cases} \quad (1)$$

where $level_i$ denotes level position of the aspect commented in sentence i by referring to the hierarchy, with the root level being 0. The coherence score of the answer is computed by summing up the scores of all its adjacent sentences as, $\sum_{j\in\mathcal{S}} \sum_{i\in\mathcal{S}} h_{i,j} c_{i,j} e_{i,j}$.

Diversity. A good answer should diversely cover all the important information. We introduce a matrix $\mathcal{M}$ in Eq.2 to measure the pairwise diversities among sentences. $\mathcal{M}_{ij}$ corresponds to the diversity between sentences i and j. When sentences i and j comment on the same aspects, $\mathcal{M}_{ij}$ will favor to select the pair of sentences that discusses on diverse content (i.e. low similarity). Otherwise, the pair of sentences commented on different aspects is viewed to be diverse, and $\mathcal{M}_{ij}$ is set as a constant bigger than one.

$$\mathcal{M}_{ij} = \begin{cases} 1 - similar(i, j) & if\ i, j\ commented\ on\ same\ aspect \\ \varphi & otherwise, \end{cases} \quad (2)$$

where φ is a constant [4].

Multi-Criteria Optimization We integrate the above criteria into the multi-criteria optimization formulation,

$$\begin{aligned} \max\{&\lambda_1 \cdot \textstyle\sum_{i\in\mathcal{S}} \omega_i s_i + \lambda_2 \cdot \sum_{j\in\mathcal{S}} \sum_{i\in\mathcal{S}} h_{i,j} c_{i,j} e_{i,j} \\ &+ \lambda_3 \cdot \textstyle\sum_{j\in\mathcal{S}} \sum_{i\in\mathcal{S}} s_i \mathcal{M}_{ij}; \end{aligned}$$
$$\begin{cases} s_i, e_{i,j} \in \{0, 1\}, \forall i, j; \\ \lambda_1 + \lambda_2 + \lambda_3 = 1,\ 0 \le \lambda_1, \lambda_2, \lambda_3 \le 1, \end{cases} \quad (3)$$

where λ_1, λ_2, λ_3 are the trade-off parameters.

We further incorporate the following constrains into the optimization framework, so as to derive appropriate answers.

- The length of the answer is up to K,

$$\sum_{i\in\mathcal{S}} l_i s_i \le K, \quad (4)$$

  where l_i is the length of sentence i.
- When sentence i is not selected (i.e. $s_i = 0$), the adjacency between any sentence to i is set

[4] Empirically set to 10 in the experiment.

to zero (i.e. $\sum_{i \in \mathcal{S}} e_{i,j} = \sum_{i \in \mathcal{S}} e_{j,i} = 0$). When sentence i is selected, there are two sentences adjacent to sentence i in the answer, one before i and another after i. (i.e. $\sum_{i \in \mathcal{S}} e_{i,j} = \sum_{i \in \mathcal{S}} e_{j,i} = 1$).

$$\sum_{i \in \mathcal{S}} e_{i,j} = \sum_{i \in \mathcal{S}} e_{j,i} = s_j, \ \forall j. \quad (5)$$

- In order to avoid falling into a cycle in sentence selection, we employ the following constraints (Deshpande et al., 2009).

$$\begin{array}{l} \sum_{i \in \mathcal{S}} f_{0,i} = n+1; \\ \sum_{i \in \mathcal{S}} f_{i,n+1} \geq 1; \\ \sum_{i \in \mathcal{S}} f_{i,j} - \sum_{i \in \mathcal{S}} f_{j,i} = s_j, \ \forall j; \\ 0 \leq f_{i,j} \leq (n+1) \cdot e_{i,j}, \ \forall i,j, \end{array} \quad (6)$$

where the variable $f_{i,j}$ is an integer to number the selected adjacent sentences from 1 to n+1, and the first selected sentence is numbered $f_{0,i}$ = n + 1. If the last selected sentence obtains a number $f_{i,n+1}$ which is bigger then 1, then the selection has no cycle.

Solution

Given the salience weights $\omega_i|_{i=1}^{\mathcal{S}}$, and coherence weights $c_{i,j}|_{i,j=1}^{\mathcal{S}}$, the above multi-criteria optimization problem can be solved by *Integer Linear Programming* (Schrijver et al., 1998). The optimal solutions $s_i|_{i=1}^{\mathcal{S}}$ and $e_{i,j}|_{i,j=1}^{\mathcal{S}}$ indicate the selected sentences and the order of them. In the next subsections, we will introduce the estimations of $\omega_i|_{i=1}^{\mathcal{S}}$ and $c_{i,j}|_{i,j=1}^{\mathcal{S}}$.

3.2 Salience Weight Estimation

The salience weight of sentence i is formulated as $\omega_i = \sum_{g=1}^{G} \varphi_g(i)/G$, where $\varphi(i)$ denotes the measurement for the importance of sentence i. We define seven measurements (i.e. $G = 7$) below.

Helpfulness: Many forum websites provide a helpfulness score, which is used to rate the quality of a review. The sentences that come from helpful reviews are often representative (Mizil et al., 2009). We compute $\varphi(i)$ of sentence i by using helpfulness score from its host review.

Timeliness: The new coming sentence often contains more updated and useful information (Liu et al., 2008). $\varphi(i)$ is the post time of sentence i. We normalize it to $[0,1]$.

Grammaticality: The grammatical sentence is often more readable. We employ the method in Agichtein et al. (2008) to calculate the grammar score. In particular, $\varphi(i)$ is calculated by the KL-divergence between language models of sentence i to Wikipedia articles.

Position: The first sentence in a review is usually informative (He et al., 2011). $\varphi(i)$ is computed based on the position of the sentence in the review, i.e. $\varphi(i) = 1/position_i$.

Aspect Frequency: The sentence that contains the frequent aspects is often salient (Nishikawa et al., 2010). Hence, $\varphi(i)$ is computed as the sum of the frequency for aspects in sentence i.

Centroid Distance: As aforementioned, review sentences are stored in the corresponding aspect nodes in the hierarchy. The sentence that is close to the centroid of the reviews stored in an aspect node is more likely to be salient (Erkan et al., 2004). $\varphi(i)$ is computed as the Cosine similarity between sentence i to the corresponding review cluster centroid based on the unigram features.

Local Density: The sentence would be informative when it is in the dense part of the aspect node in the feature space (Scott et al., 1992). We employ *Multivariate Kernel Density Estimation* to estimate the density. We first represent all the sentences stored in each node into feature vectors, with unigram as features. The density of a sentence is then calculated as $\varphi(\boldsymbol{x}) = \sum_{i=1}^{n} K_H(\boldsymbol{x} - \boldsymbol{x_i})/n$, where $\boldsymbol{x}$ denotes the feature vector of sentence i, n is the size of sentences stored in the node, and $K_H(\boldsymbol{x}) = (2\pi)^{-1/2} \exp(-1/2(\boldsymbol{x}^T \boldsymbol{x}))$ represents the *Gaussian* kernel.

3.3 Coherence Weight Estimation

The coherence $c_{i,j}$ between sentences i and j is formulated as $c_{i,j} = \boldsymbol{\mu} \cdot \boldsymbol{\psi}(\boldsymbol{i}, \boldsymbol{j})$, where $\boldsymbol{\mu}$ is a weight vector, and $\boldsymbol{\psi}(\boldsymbol{i}, \boldsymbol{j})$ denotes the feature function. $\boldsymbol{\psi}(\boldsymbol{i}, \boldsymbol{j})$ takes two sentences i and j as input, and outputs a vector with each dimension indicating the present/absent of a feature. In order to capture the sequential relations among sentences, we utilize features as the *Cartesian* product over the terms of N-gram (N=1,2) and POS tags generated from sentences i and j (Lapata et al., 2003).

To learn the weight vector $\boldsymbol{\mu}$, we employ the *Passive-Aggressive* algorithm (Crammer et al.,

2006). It is an online learning algorithm, so that we can update the weight when more consumer reviews are available. The algorithm takes up one training sample and outputs the solution that has the highest score under the current weight. If the output differs from training samples, the weight vector is updated according to Eq.7. Since the consumer reviews often include multiple sentences, we can directly use the adjacency of these sentences as training samples. In particular, we treat the adjacent sentence pairs in the reviews as training samples (i.e. $c_{i,j} = 1$).

$$\min \|\boldsymbol{\mu}^{i+1} - \boldsymbol{\mu}^{i}\| \\ \begin{cases} \boldsymbol{\mu}^{i+1} \cdot \boldsymbol{\Psi}(\mathbf{p}, \mathbf{q}^*) - \boldsymbol{\mu}^{i+1} \cdot \boldsymbol{\Psi}(\mathbf{p}, \hat{\mathbf{q}}) \geq \tau(\hat{\mathbf{q}}, \mathbf{q}^*); \\ \tau(\hat{\mathbf{q}}, \mathbf{q}^*) = \frac{2 \cdot T(\hat{\mathbf{q}}, \mathbf{q}^*)}{m(m-1)/2}, \end{cases} \tag{7}$$

where $\boldsymbol{\mu}^i$ is the current weight vector and $\boldsymbol{\mu}^{i+1}$ is the updated vector, $\mathbf{q}^*$ and $\hat{\mathbf{q}}$ are the gold standard and predicted sequence of sentences, respectively, $\mathbf{p}$ denotes a set of sentences, $\boldsymbol{\Psi}(\cdot)$ is the feature function on the whole feature space (i.e. $\sum \boldsymbol{\psi}(\cdot)$), $\tau(\cdot,\cdot)$ is a *Kendall's tau* lost function (Lapata et al., 2006), $T(\cdot,\cdot)$ represents the number of inversion operations that needs to bring $\hat{\mathbf{q}}$ to $\mathbf{q}^*$, and m denotes the number of sentences.

4 Evaluations

In this section, we evaluate the effectiveness of the proposed approach, in terms of question analysis and answer generation.

4.1 Data Set and Experimental Settings

We employed the product review dataset used in Yu et al. (2011) as corpus. As illustrated in Table 1, the dataset contained 70,359 reviews about 11 popular products in four domains. In addition, we created 220 questions for these products by referring to real questions in Yahoo!Anwser service. We corrected the typos and grammar errors for these real questions. Each product contains 15 opinion questions and 5 factual questions, respectively. All questions were shown in Appendix C in supplementary material. Three annotators were invited to generate the gold standard. Each question was labeled by two annotators. The labels include product name, product aspect, opinion, question type and question form. The average inter-rater agreement in terms of Kappa statistics is 89%. These annotators were then invited to read the reviews, and create the ground truth answers by selecting and ordering some review sentences. Such process is time consuming and labor-intensive. We speed up the annotation process as follows. We first collected all the review sentences in the answers generated by three evaluated methods to be discussed in Section 4.3.1. In addition, we sampled the top-N (N=20) sentences on each asked aspect and its sub-aspects respectively, where the sentences were ranked based on their salient weights in Section 3.2. We then provided such subset of review sentences to the three annotators, and let them individually create an answer of up to 100 words (i.e. K=100) for each question.

Product Name	*Domain*	*Review#*	*Sentence#*
Canon EOS 450D (Canon EOS)	camera	440	628
Fujifilm Finepix AX245W (Fujifilm)	camera	541	839
Panasonic Lumix DMC-TZ7 (Panasonic)	camera	650	1,546
Apple MacBook Pro (MacBook)	laptop	552	4,221
Samsung NC10 (Samsung)	laptop	2,712	4,946
Apple iPod Touch 2nd (iPod Touch)	MP3	4,567	10,846
Sony NWZ-S639 16GB (Sony NWZ)	MP3	341	773
BlackBerry Bold 9700 (BlackBerry)	phone	4,070	11,008
iPhone 3GS 16GB (iPhone 3GS)	phone	12,418	43,527
Nokia 5800 XpressMusic (Nokia 5800)	phone	28,129	75,001
Nokia N95	phone	15,939	44,379

Table 1: Statistics of the product review dataset, # denotes the number of the reviews/sentences.

We employed *precision* (P), *recall* (R) and F_1-measure (F_1) as the evaluation metric for question analysis, and utilized *ROUGE* (Lin et al., 2003) as the metric to evaluate the quality of answer generation. *ROUGE* is a widely accepted standard for summarization, which measures the quality of the summarized answers by counting the overlapping N-grams between the answers generated by machine and human, respectively. In the experiment, we reported the F_1-measure of *ROUGE-1*, *ROUGE-2* and *ROUGE-SU4*, which count the overlapping unigrams, bigrams and skip-4 bigrams respectively. *ROUGE-1* can measure informativeness of the answers, while higher order *ROUGE-N* (*N=2,4*) captures the matching of subsequences, which can measure the fluency and readability of the answers. For the trade-off parameters, we empirically set $\lambda_1 = 0.4$, $\lambda_2 = 0.3$ and $\lambda_3 = 0.3$.

4.2 Evaluations on Question Analysis

We first evaluated the performance of product recognition, opinion/factual question classification, opinion classification, question type and question form identification. The experimental results are shown in Table 2. The results show that traditional methods achieve encouraging performance on the aforementioned tasks.

Evaluated Topics	*P*	*R*	F_1
Product recognition	0.755	0.618	0.680
Opinion/factual	0.897	0.895	0.893
Opinion classification	0.755	0.745	0.748
Question type	0.800	0.775	0.783
Question form	0.910	0.903	0.905

Table 2: Performance of question analysis.

Methods	*P*	*R*	F_1
Our method	**0.851***$*$	**0.763***$*$	**0.805***$*$
Balahur's method	0.825	0.400	0.538

Table 3: Performance of aspect identification for question analysis. $*$ denotes the results (i.e. P, R, F_1) are tested for statistical significance using T-Test, p-values$<$0.05.

Methods	*P*	*R*	F_1
Our method	**0.726***$*$	**0.643***$*$	**0.682***$*$
Su's method	0.689	0.571	0.625

Table 4: Performance of implicit aspect identification for question analysis. T-Test, p-values$<$0.05

We next examined the performance of our approach on aspect identification. The method proposed by Balahur et al. (2008) was reimplemented as the baseline, which identifies aspects based on noun phrase extraction. This method achieved good performance on the opinion QA task in TAC 2008 and was employed in subsequent works. As demonstrated in Table 3, our approach significantly outperforms Balahur's method by over 49.4% in terms of average F_1-measure. A probable reason is that Balahur's method relies on noun phrases, which may mis-identify some noise noun phrases as aspects, while our approach performs hierarchical classification based on the hierarchy, which can leverage the prior knowledge encoded in the hierarchy to filter out the noise and obtain accurate aspects.

Moreover, we evaluated the effectiveness of our approach on implicit aspect identification. The 70 implicit aspect questions in our question corpus were used here. The method proposed by Su et al. (2008) was reimplemented as the baseline. It identifies implicit aspects by mutual clustering, and it was evaluated in Yu et al. (2011). As shown in Table 4, our approach significantly outperforms Su's method by over 9.1% in terms of average F_1-measure. The results show that the hierarchy can help to identify implicit aspects by exploiting the underlying associations among sentiment terms and aspects.

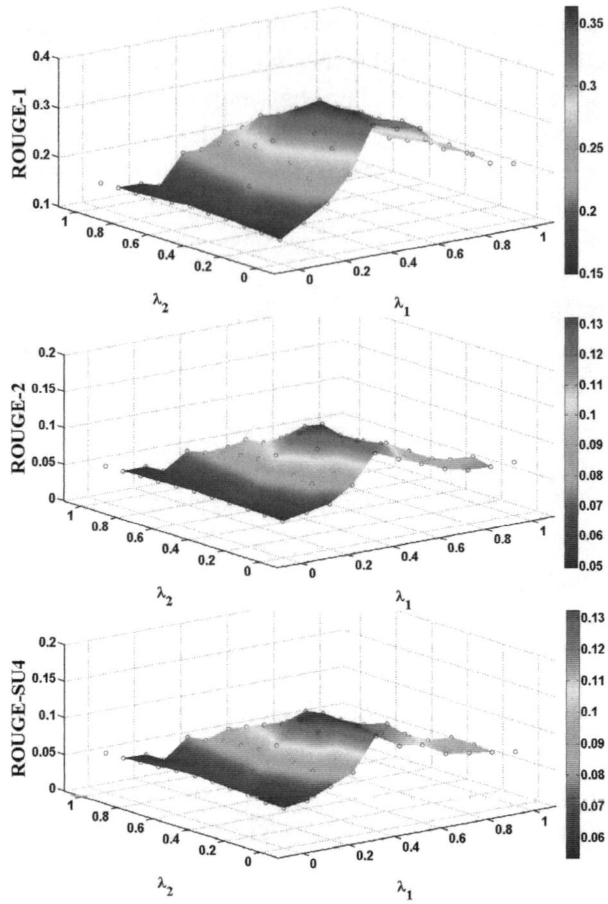

Figure 3: Evaluations on multiple optimization criteria in terms of *ROUGE-1*, *ROUGE-2*, and *ROUGE-SU4*, respectively.

Methods	ROUGE1	ROUGE2	ROUGE-SU4
Our method	**0.364***$*$	**0.137***$*$	**0.138***$*$
Li's method	0.127	0.043	0.049
Lloret's method	0.149	0.058	0.065

Table 5: Performance of answer generation. T-Test, p-values$<$0.05.

4.3 Evaluations on Answer Generation

4.3.1 Comparisons to the State-of-the-Arts

We compared our multi-criteria optimization approach against two state-of-the-arts methods: a) the method presented in Li et al. (2009), which selects some retrieved sentences to generate the answers based on a graph-based algorithm; b) the method proposed by Lloret et al. (2011) that forms the answers by re-ranking the retrieved sentences.

As shown in Table 5, our approach outperforms Li's method and Lloret's method by the significant absolute gains of over 23.7%, and 21.5% respectively, in terms of average *ROUGE-1*. It improves the performance over these two methods in terms of average *ROUGE-2* by the absolute gains of over 9.41% and 7.87%, respectively; and in terms of *ROUGE-SU4* by the absolute gains of over 8.86% and 7.31%, respectively. By analyzing the results, we find that the improvements come from the use of the hierarchical organization and the answer generation algorithm which exploits multiple criteria, especially the parent-child relation among aspects. In addition, our approach can generate the answers by following the general-to-specific logic, while Li's and Lloret's methods fail to do so due to their ignorance of parent-child relations among aspects.

4.3.2 Evaluations on the Effectiveness of Multiple Criteria

We further evaluated the effectiveness of each optimization criterion by tuning the trade-off parameters (i.e. λ_1, λ_2, and λ_3). We fixed λ_1 as a constant in $[0, 1]$ with 0.1 as an interval, and updated λ_2 from 0 to $1 - \lambda_1$, $\lambda_3 = 1 - \lambda_1 - \lambda_2$, correspondingly. The performance change is shown in Figure 3 in terms of *ROUGE-1*, *ROUGE-2*, and *ROUGE-SU4*, respectively. The best performance is achieved at $\lambda_1 = 0.4$, $\lambda_2 = 0.3$, $\lambda_3 = 0.3$. We observe the performance drops dramatically when any parameter (i.e. λ_1, λ_2, λ_3) is close to 0 (i.e. remove any of the corresponding criterion). Thus, we can conclude that all the criteria are useful in answer generation. We also find that the performance change is sharp when λ_1 changes. This indicates that the salience criterion is crucial for answer generation.

Table 6 shows the exemplar answers generated by our approach. Each answer first gives the statistic of positive and negative reviews. This helps user to quickly get an overview of public opinions. The summary of relevant review sentences is then presented in the answer. The answer diversely comments the asked aspect and all its available sub-aspects following the general-to-specific logic. Moreover, we feel that the answers are informative and readable.

5 Related Works

In this section, we review existing works related to the four components of our approach, including organization of reviews, question analysis, answer fragment retrieval, and answer generation.

For organization of reviews, Carenini et al. (2006) proposed to organize the reviews by a hand-crafted taxonomy, which was not scalable. Yu et al. (2011) exploited the domain knowledge and consumer reviews to automatically generate a hierarchy for organizing consumer reviews.

Question analysis often has to distinguish the opinion question from the factual one, and find the key points asked in the questions, such as the product aspect and product name. For example, Yu et al. (2003) proposed to separate opinions from facts at both document and sentence level, and determine the polarity on the opinionated sentences in the answer documents. Similarly, Somasundaran et al. (2007) utilized a SVM classifier to recognize opinionated sentences. The paper argued that the subjective types (i.e. sentiment and arguing) can improve the performance of opinion-QA. Later, Ku et al. (2007) proposed a two-layered classifier for question analysis, and retrieved the answer-fragments by keyword matching. In particular, they first identified the opinion questions, and classified them into six predefined question types, including holder, target, attitude, reason, majority, and yes/no. These question types and corresponding polarity on the questions were used to filter non-relevant sentences in the answer fragments. F_1-measure was employed as the evaluation metric.

For the topic of answer generation in opinion-QA, Li et al. (2009) formulated it as a sentence ranking task. They argued that the answers should be simultaneously relevant to topics and opinions asked in the questions. They thus designed the graph-based methods (i.e. PageRank and HITS) to select some high-ranked sentences to form answers. They first built a graph on the retrieved sentences, with each sentence as the node, and the similarity (i.e. Cosine similarity) between each sentences pair as the

Question 1: What reasons do people give for preferring iPhone 3gs?
There are 9,928 opinionated reviews about product "iphone 3gs", with 5,717 positive and 4,221 negative reviews. This phone is amazing and I would recommend it to anyone. It looks funky and cool. It is worth the money. It's great organiser, simple easy to use software. It is super fast, excellent connection via wifi or 3G. It is able to instantly access email. It's amazing and has so many free apps. The design is so simple and global. The hardware is good and reliable. The camera is a good and colors are vibrant. The touch screen is user friendly and the aesthetics are top notch. Battery is charged quickly, and power save right after stop using.
Question 2: Does anyone think it is expensive to get a iPhone 3GS?
Yes. There are 2,645 opinionated reviews on aspect "price" about product "iphone 3gs", with 889 positive and 1,756 negative reviews. Throw the costly phone, apple only knows to sell stupid stuff expensively. Don't fool yourself with iPhone 3gs, believing that it costs much by Apple luxurious advertising. Apple is so greedy and it just wants to earn easy & fast money by selling its techless product expensively. The phone will charge once you insert any sim card. iPhone 3gs is high-priced due to the capacitive and Apple license. You need to pay every application at the end it costs too much. The network provider will make up some of the cost of the phone on your call charges.

Table 6: Sample answers of our approach.

weight of the corresponding edge. Given a question, its similarity to each sentence in the graph was computed. Such similarity was viewed as the relevant score to the corresponding sentence. The sentences then were ranked based on three metric, i.e. relevant score to the query, similarity score obtained from the graph algorithm over sentences, and degree of opinion matching to the query. Respectively, Lloret et al. (2011) proposed to form answers by re-ranking the retrieved sentences based on the metric of word frequency, non-redundancy and the number of noun phrases. Their method includes three components, including information retrieval, opinion mining and text summarization. Evaluations were conducted on the TAC 2008 Opinion Summarization track. Afterwards, Moghaddam et al. (2011) developed a system called *AQA* to generate answers for questions about products (i.e. opinion QA on products). It classifies the questions into five types, including target, attitude, reason, majority and yes/no. As compared to Ku et al. (2007), the question types of holder and majority are not included. They argued that product questions were seldom asked for the holders, since the holders (i.e. reviewers) were commonly shown in the reviews. Also, product questions mainly asked for majority opinions, and majority type was thus not considered. The *AQA* system includes five components, including question analysis, question expansion, high quality review retrieval, subjective sentence extraction, and answer grouping. The answers are generated by aggregating opinions in the retrieved fragments.

6 Conclusions and Future Works

In this paper, we have developed a new product opinion-QA framework, which exploits the hierarchical organization of consumer reviews on products. With the help of the hierarchical organization, our framework can accurately identify the aspects asked in the questions and also discover their sub-aspects. We have further formulated the answer generation from retrieved review sentences as a multi-criteria optimization problem. The multiple criteria used include answer salience, diversity, and coherence. The parent-child relations between the aspects are incorporated into the approach to ensure that the answers follow the general-to-specific logic. The proposed framework has been evaluated on 11 popular products in four domains using 220 questions on the products. Significant performance improvements were obtained. In the future, we will explore the more sophisticated NLP features to improve the proposed framework. This will be done by incorporating more NLP features in salience and coherence weights estimation.

Acknowledgments

This work is supported in part by NUS-Tsinghua Extreme Search (NExT) project under the grant number: R-252-300-001-490. We give warm thanks to the project and anonymous reviewers for their comments.

References

E. Agichtein, C. Castillo, and D. Donato. Finding High-Quality Content in Social Media. *WSDM*, 2008.

A. Balahur, E. Boldrini, O. Ferrandez, A. Montoyo, M. Palomar, and R. Munoz. The DLSIUAES Team's Participation in the TAC 2008 Tracks. *TAC*, 2008.

C. Cardie, J. Wiebe, T. Wilson, and D. Litman. Combining Low-level and Summary Representations of Opinions for Multi-Perspective Question Answering. *AAAI*, 2003.

G. Carenini, R. Ng, and E. Zwart. Multi-document Summarization of Evaluative Text. *ACL*, 2006.

P. Cimiano. Ontology Learning and Population from Text: Algorithms, Evaluation and Applications. *Springer-Verlag New York, Inc. Secaucus, NJ, USA*, 2006.

K. Crammer, O. Dekel, J. Keshet, S.S. Shwartz, and Y. Singer. Online Passive Aggressive Algorithms. *Journal of Machine Learning Research*, 2006.

P. Deshpande, R. Barzilay, and D.R. Karger. Randomized Decoding for Selection-and-Ordering Problems. *NAACL*, 2007.

G. Erkan and D.R. Radev. LexRank: Graph-based lexical centrality as salience in text summarization. *AAAI*, 2004.

T. Givon. Syntax: A functional-typological Introduction. *Benjamins Pub*, 1990.

J. He and D. Dai. Summarization of Yes/No Questions Using a Feature Function Model. *JMLR*, 2011.

P. Jiang, H. Fu, C. Zhang, and Z. Niu. A Framework for Opinion Question Answering. *IMS*, 2010.

H.D. Kim, D.H. Park, V.G.V. Vydiswaran, and C.X. Zhai. Opinion Summarization using Entity Features and Probabilistic Sentence Coherence Optimization: UIUC at TAC 2008 Opinion Summarization Pilot. *TAC*, 2008.

D. Koller and M. Sahami. Hierarchically Classifying Documents Using Very Few Words. *ICML*, 1997.

L.W. Ku, Y.T. Liang, and H.H. Chen. Question Analysis and Answer Passage Retrieval for Opinion Question Answering Systems. *International Journal of Computational Linguistics & Chinese Language Processing*, 2007.

M. Lapata. Probabilistic Text Structuring: Experiments with Sentence Ordering. *ACL*, 2003.

M. Lapata. Automatic Evaluation of Information Ordering: Kendallś Tau. *Computational Linguistics*, 2006.

F. Li, Y. Tang, M. Huang, and X. Zhu. Answering Opinion Questions with Random Walks on Graphs. *ACL/AFNLP*, 2009.

C.Y. Lin and E.Hovy. Automatic Evaluation of Summaries Using N-gram Co-Occurrence Statistics. *HLT-NAACL*, 2003.

Y. Liu, X. Huang, A. An, and X. Yu. Modeling and Predicting the Helpfulness of Online Reviews. *ICDM*, 2008.

E. Lloret, A. Balahur, M. Palomar, and A. Montoyo. Towards a Unified Approach for Opinion Question Answering and Summarization. *ACL-HLT*, 2011.

H. Nishikawa, T. Hasegawa, Y. Matsuo, and G. Kikui. Opinion Summarization with Integer Linear Programming Formulation for Sentence Extraction and Ordering. *COLING*, 2010.

C.D. Mizil and G. Kossinets and J. Kleinberg and L. Lee. How Opinions are Received by Online Communities: A Case Study on Amazon.com Helpfulness Votes. *WWW*, 2009.

S. Moghaddam and M. Ester. AQA: Aspect-based Opinion Question Answering. *IEEE-ICDMW*, 2011.

Y. Ouyang, W. Li, and Q. Lu. An Integrated Multi-document Summarization Approach based on Word Hierarchical Representation. *ACL-IJCNLP*, 2009.

A. Schrijver. Theory of Linear and Integer Programming. *John Wiley & Sons*, 1998.

D.W. Scott. Multivariate Density Estimation: Theory, Practice, and Visualization. *John Wiley & Sons, Inc.*, 1992.

C. Silla and A. Freitas. A Survey of Hierarchical Classification Across Different Application Domains. *Data Mining and Knowledge Discovery*, 2011.

S. Somasundaran, T. Wilson, J. Wiebe and V. Stoyanov. QA with Attitude: Exploiting Opinion Type Analysis for Improving Question Answering in Online Discussions and the News. *ICWSM*, 2007.

V. Stoyanov, C. Cardie and J. Wiebe. Multi-Perspective Question Answering Using the OpQA Corpus. *EMNLP*, 2005.

Q. Su, X. Xu, H. Guo, X. Wu, X. Zhang, B. Swen, and Z. Su. Hidden Sentiment Association in Chinese Web Opinion Mining. *WWW*, 2008.

T. Wilson, J. Wiebe, and P. Hoffmann. Recognizing Contextual Polarity in Phrase-level Sentiment Analysis. *HLT/EMNLP*, 2005.

J. Yu, Z.J. Zha, M. Wang, K. Wang and T.S. Chua. Domain-Assisted Product Aspect Hierarchy Generation: Towards Hierarchical Organization of Unstructured Consumer Reviews. *EMNLP*, 2011.

J. Yu, Z.J. Zha, M. Wang, and T.S. Chua. Hierarchical Organization of Unstructured Consumer Reviews. *WWW*, 2011.

J. Yu, Z.J. Zha, M. Wang and T.S. Chua. Aspect Ranking: Identifying Important Product Aspects from Online Consumer Reviews. *ACL*, 2011.

H. Yu and V. Hatzivassiloglou. Towards Answering Opinion Questions: Separating Facts from Opinions and Identifying the Polarity of Opinion Sentences. *EMNLP*, 2003.

Locally Training the Log-Linear Model for SMT

Lemao Liu[1], **Hailong Cao**[1], **Taro Watanabe**[2], **Tiejun Zhao**[1], **Mo Yu**[1], **CongHui Zhu**[1]
[1]School of Computer Science and Technology
Harbin Institute of Technology, Harbin, China
[2]National Institute of Information and Communication Technology
3-5 Hikari-dai, Seika-cho, Soraku-gun, Kyoto, Japan
{lmliu,hailong,tjzhao,yumo,chzhu}@mtlab.hit.edu.cn
taro.watanabe@nict.go.jp

Abstract

In statistical machine translation, minimum error rate training (MERT) is a standard method for tuning a single weight with regard to a given development data. However, due to the diversity and uneven distribution of source sentences, there are two problems suffered by this method. First, its performance is highly dependent on the choice of a development set, which may lead to an unstable performance for testing. Second, translations become inconsistent at the sentence level since tuning is performed globally on a document level. In this paper, we propose a novel local training method to address these two problems. Unlike a global training method, such as MERT, in which a single weight is learned and used for all the input sentences, we perform training and testing in one step by learning a sentence-wise weight for each input sentence. We propose efficient incremental training methods to put the local training into practice. In NIST Chinese-to-English translation tasks, our local training method significantly outperforms MERT with the maximal improvements up to 2.0 BLEU points, meanwhile its efficiency is comparable to that of the global method.

1 Introduction

Och and Ney (2002) introduced the log-linear model for statistical machine translation (SMT), in which translation is considered as the following optimization problem:

$$\begin{aligned}\hat{e}(f;W) &= \arg\max_{e} \mathbf{P}(e|f;W) \\ &= \arg\max_{e} \frac{\exp\{W \cdot h(f,e)\}}{\sum_{e'} \exp\{W \cdot h(f,e')\}} \\ &= \arg\max_{e} \{W \cdot h(f,e)\}, \qquad (1)\end{aligned}$$

where f and e (e') are source and target sentences, respectively. h is a feature vector which is scaled by a weight W. Parameter estimation is one of the most important components in SMT, and various training methods have been proposed to tune W. Some methods are based on likelihood (Och and Ney, 2002; Blunsom et al., 2008), error rate (Och, 2003; Zhao and Chen, 2009; Pauls et al., 2009; Galley and Quirk, 2011), margin (Watanabe et al., 2007; Chiang et al., 2008) and ranking (Hopkins and May, 2011), and among which minimum error rate training (MERT) (Och, 2003) is the most popular one.

All these training methods follow the same pipeline: they train only a single weight on a given development set, and then use it to translate all the sentences in a test set. We call them a global training method. One of its advantages is that it allows us to train a single weight offline and thereby it is efficient. However, due to the diversity and uneven distribution of source sentences(Li et al., 2010), there are some shortcomings in this pipeline.

Firstly, on the document level, the performance of these methods is dependent on the choice of a development set, which may potentially lead to an unstable translation performance for testing. As referred in our experiment, the BLEU points on NIST08 are

Source		Candidate Translation			
i	f_i	j	e_{ij}	h	*score*
1	我 是 学生 。	1	I am students .	<2, 1>	0.5
		2	I was students .	<1,1>	0.2
2	今天 星期 几 ?	1	week several today ?	<1,2>	0.3
		2	today several weeks .	<3,2>	0.1

(a)

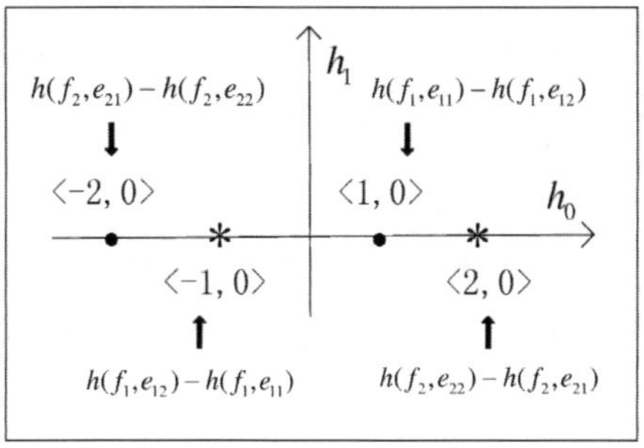

(b)

Figure 1: (a). An Example candidate space of dimensionality two. *score* is a evaluation metric of e. (b). The non-linearly separable classification problem transformed from (a) via tuning as ranking (Hopkins and May, 2011). Since score of e_{11} is greater than that of e_{12}, $\langle 1, 0\rangle$ corresponds to a possitive example denoted as "•", and $\langle -1, 0\rangle$ corresponds to a negative example denoted as "*". Since the transformed classification problem is not linearly separable, there does not exist a single weight which can obtain e_{11} and e_{21} as translation results meanwhile. However, one can obtain e_{11} and e_{21} with weights: $\langle 1, 1\rangle$ and $\langle -1, 1\rangle$, respectively.

19.04 when the Moses system is tuned on NIST02 by MERT. However, its performance is improved to 21.28 points when tuned on NIST06. The automatic selection of a development set may partially address the problem. However it is inefficient since tuning requires iteratively decoding an entire development set, which is impractical for an online service.

Secondly, translation becomes inconsistent on the sentence level (Ma et al., 2011). Global training method such as MERT tries to optimize the weight towards the best performance for the whole set, and it can not necessarily always obtain good translation for every sentence in the development set. The reason is that different sentences may need different optimal weights, and MERT can not find a single weight to satisfy all of the sentences. **Figure** 1(a) shows such an example, in which a development set contains two sentences f_1 and f_2 with translations e and feature vectors h. When we tune examples in **Figure** 1(a) by MERT, it can be regarded as a non-linearly separable classification problem illustrated in **Figure** 1(b). Therefore, there exists no single weight W which simultaneously obtains e_{11} and e_{21} as translation for f_1 and f_2 via Equation (1). However, we can achieve this with two weights: $\langle 1, 1\rangle$ for f_1 and $\langle -1, 1\rangle$ for f_2.

In this paper, inspired by KNN-SVM (Zhang et al., 2006), we propose a local training method, which trains sentence-wise weights instead of a single weight, to address the above two problems. Compared with global training methods, such as MERT, in which training and testing are separated, our method works in an online fashion, in which training is performed during testing. This online fashion has an advantage in that it can adapt the weights for each of the test sentences, by dynamically tuning the weights on translation examples which are similar to these test sentences. Similar to the method of development set automatical selection, the local training method may also suffer the problem of efficiency. To put it into practice, we propose incremental training methods which avoid retraining and iterative decoding on a development set.

Our local training method has two advantages: firstly, it significantly outperforms MERT, especially when test set is different from the development set; secondly, it improves the translation consistency. Experiments on NIST Chinese-to-English translation tasks show that our local training method significantly gains over MERT, with the maximum improvements up to 2.0 BLEU, and its efficiency is comparable to that of the global training method.

2 Local Training and Testing

The local training method (Bottou and Vapnik, 1992) is widely employed in computer vision (Zhang et al., 2006; Cheng et al., 2010). Compared with the global training method which tries to fit a single weight on the training data, the local one learns weights based on the local neighborhood information for each test example. It is superior to the global one when the data sets are not evenly distributed (Bottou and Vapnik, 1992; Zhang et al., 2006).

Algorithm 1 Naive Local Training Method

Input: $T = \{t_i\}_{i=1}^{N}$(test set), K (retrieval size), Dev(development set), D(retrieval data)
Output: Translation results of T
1: **for all** sentence t_i such that $1 \leq i \leq N$ **do**
2: Retrieve the training examples D^i with size K for t_i from D according to a similarity;
3: Train a local weight W^i based on Dev and D^i;
4: Decode t_i with W^i;
5: **end for**

Suppose T be a test set, Dev a development set, and D a retrieval data. The local training in SMT is described in the **Algorithm** 1. For each sentence t_i in test set, training examples D^i is retrieved from D using a similarity measure (line 2), a weight W^i is optimized on Dev and D^i (line 3)[1], and, finally, t_i is decoded with W^i for testing (line 4). At the end of this algorithm, it returns the translation results for T. Note that weights are adapted for each test sentence t_i in line 3 by utilizing the translation examples D^i which are similar to t_i. Thus, our local training method can be considered as an adaptation of translation weights.

Algorithm 1 suffers a problem of training efficiency in line 3. It is impractical to train a weight W^i on Dev and D^i from scratch for every sentence, since iteratively decoding Dev and D^i is time consuming when we apply MERT. To address this problem, we propose a novel incremental approach which is based on a two-phase training.

On the first phase, we use a global training method, like MERT, to tune a baseline weight on the development set Dev in an offline manner. On the second phase, we utilize the retrieved examples to incrementally tune sentence-wise local weights based on the baseline weight. This method can not only consider the common characteristics learnt from the Dev, but also take into account the knowledge for each individual sentence learnt from similar examples during testing. On the phase of incremental training, we perform decoding only once for retrieved examples D^i, though several rounds of decoding are possible and potentially better if one does not seriously care about training speed. Furthermore, instead of on-the-fly decoding, we decode the retrieval data D offline using the parameter from our baseline weight and its nbest translation candidates are saved with training examples to increase the training efficiency.

Algorithm 2 Local Training Method Based on Incremental Training

Input: $T = \{t_i\}_{i=1}^{N}$ (test set), K (retrieval size), Dev (development set), $D = \{\langle f_s, \mathbf{r}_s \rangle\}_{s=1}^{s=S}$ (retrieval data),
Output: Translation results of T
1: Run global Training (such as MERT) on Dev to get a baseline weight W_b; **// Phase 1**
2: Decode each sentence in D to get $D = \{\langle f_s, \mathbf{c}_s, \mathbf{r}_s \rangle\}_{s=1}^{s=S}$;
3: **for all** sentence t_i such that $1 \leq i \leq N$ **do**
4: Retrieve K training examples $D^i = \{\langle f_j^i, \mathbf{c}_j^i, \mathbf{r}_j^i \rangle\}_{j=1}^{j=K}$ for t_i from D according to a similarity;
5: Incrementally train a local weight W^i based on W_b and D^i; **// Phase 2**
6: Decode t_i with W^i;
7: **end for**

The two-phase local training algorithm is described in **Algorithm** 2, where $\mathbf{c}_s$ and $\mathbf{r}_s$ denote the translation candidate set and reference set for each sentence f_s in retrieval data, respectively, and K is the retrieval size. It globally trains a baseline weight W_b (line 1), and decodes each sentence in retrieval data D with the weight W_b (line 2). For each sentence t_i in test set T, it first retrieves training examples D^i from D (line 4), and then it runs local training to tune a local weight W^i (line 5) and performs testing with W^i for t_i (line 6). Please note that the two-phase training contains global training in line 1 and local training in line 5.

From Algorithm 2, one can see that our method is effective even if the test set is unknow, for example, in the scenario of online translation services, since the global training on development set and decoding

[1] Usually, the quality of development set Dev is high, since it is manually produced with multiple references. This is the main reason why Dev is used as a part of new development set to train W^i.

on retrieval data can be performed offline.

In the next two sections, we will discuss the details about the similarity metric in line 4 and the incremental training in line 5 of Algorithm 2.

3 Acquiring Training Examples

In line 4 of Algorithm 2, to retrieve training examples for the sentence t_i , we first need a metric to retrieve similar translation examples. We assume that the metric satisfy the property: more similar the test sentence and translation examples are, the better translation result one obtains when decoding the test sentence with the weight trained on the translation examples.

The metric we consider here is derived from an example-based machine translation. To retrieve translation examples for a test sentence, (Watanabe and Sumita, 2003) defined a metric based on the combination of edit distance and TF-IDF (Manning and Schütze, 1999) as follows:

$$\begin{aligned}\text{dist}(f_1, f_2) &= \theta \times \text{edit-dist}(f_1, f_2) + \\ &(1 - \theta) \times \text{tf-idf}(f_1, f_2),\end{aligned} \quad (2)$$

where $\theta (0 \leq \theta \leq 1)$ is an interpolation weight, $f_i (i = 1, 2)$ is a word sequence and can be also considered as a document. In this paper, we extract similar examples from training data. Like example-based translation in which similar source sentences have similar translations, we assume that the optimal translation weights of the similar source sentences are closer.

4 Incremental Training Based on Ultraconservative Update

Compared with retraining mode, incremental training can improve the training efficiency. In the field of machine learning research, incremental training has been employed in the work (Cauwenberghs and Poggio, 2001; Shilton et al., 2005), but there is little work for tuning parameters of statistical machine translation. The biggest difficulty lies in that the feature vector of a given training example, i.e. translation example, is unavailable until actually decoding the example, since the derivation is a latent variable. In this section, we will investigate the incremental training methods in SMT scenario.

Following the notations in Algorithm 2, W_b is the baseline weight, $D^i = \{\langle f_j^i, \mathbf{c}_j^i, \mathbf{r}_j^i \rangle\}_{j=1}^K$ denotes training examples for t_i. For the sake of brevity, we will drop the index i, $D^i = \{\langle f_j, \mathbf{c}_j, \mathbf{r}_j \rangle\}_{j=1}^K$, in the rest of this paper. Our goal is to find an optimal weight, denoted by W^i, which is a local weight and used for decoding the sentence t_i. Unlike the global method which performs tuning on the whole development set $Dev + D^i$ as in Algorithm 1, W^i can be incrementally learned by optimizing on D^i based on W_b. We employ the idea of ultraconservative update (Crammer and Singer, 2003; Crammer et al., 2006) to propose two incremental methods for local training in Algorithm 2 as follows.

Ultraconservative update is an efficient way to consider the trade-off between the progress made on development set Dev and the progress made on D^i. It desires that the optimal weight W^i is not only close to the baseline weight W_b, but also achieves the low loss over the retrieved examples D^i. The idea of ultraconservative update can be formalized as follows:

$$\min_W \left\{ \mathbf{d}(W, W_b) + \lambda \cdot \mathbf{Loss}(D^i, W) \right\}, \quad (3)$$

where $\mathbf{d}(W, W_b)$ is a distance metric over a pair of weights W and W_b. It penalizes the weights far away from W_b and it is L_2 norm in this paper. $\mathbf{Loss}(D^i, W)$ is a loss function of W defined on D^i and it evaluates the performance of W over D^i. λ is a positive hyperparameter. If D^i is more similar to the test sentence t_i, the better performance will be achieved for the larger λ. In particular, if D^i consists of only a single sentence t_i, the best performance will be obtained when λ goes to infinity.

4.1 Margin Based Ultraconservative Update

MIRA(Crammer and Singer, 2003; Crammer et al., 2006) is a form of ultraconservative update in (3) whose **Loss** is defined as hinge loss based on margin over the pairwise translation candiates in D^i. It tries to minimize the following quadratic program:

$$\frac{1}{2} ||W - W_b||^2 + \frac{\lambda}{K} \sum_{j=1}^{K} \max_{1 \leq n \leq |\mathbf{c}_j|} \left(\ell_{jn} - W \cdot \Delta h(f_j, e_{jn}) \right)$$

with

$$\Delta h(f_j, e_{jn}) = h(f_j, e_{j\cdot}) - h(f_j, e_{jn}), \quad (4)$$

where $h(f_j, e)$ is the feature vector of candidate e, e_{jn} is a translation member of f_j in $\mathbf{c}_j$, $e_{j\cdot}$ is the oracle one in $\mathbf{c}_j$, ℓ_{jn} is a loss between $e_{j\cdot}$ and e_{jn} and it is the same as referred in (Chiang et al., 2008), and $|\mathbf{c}_j|$ denotes the number of members in $\mathbf{c}_j$.

Different from (Watanabe et al., 2007; Chiang et al., 2008) employing the MIRA to globally train SMT, in this paper, we apply MIRA as one of local training method for SMT and we call it as margin based ultraconservative update (MBUU for shortly) to highlight its advantage of incremental training in line 5 of Algorithm 2.

Further, there is another difference between MBUU and MIRA in (Watanabe et al., 2007; Chiang et al., 2008). MBUU is a batch update mode which updates the weight with all training examples, but MIRA is an online one which updates with each example (Watanabe et al., 2007) or part of examples (Chiang et al., 2008). Therefore, MBUU is more ultraconservative.

4.2 Error Rate Based Ultraconservative Update

Instead of taking into account the margin-based hinge loss between a pair of translations as the $\mathbf{L}oss$ in (3), we directly optimize the error rate of translation candidates with respect to their references in D^i. Formally, the objective function of error rate based ultraconservative update (EBUU) is as follows:

$$\frac{1}{2}\|W - W_b\|^2 + \frac{\lambda}{K}\sum_{j=1}^{K}\mathbf{Error}(\mathbf{r}_j; \hat{e}(f_j; W)), \quad (5)$$

where $\hat{e}(f_j; W)$ is defined in Equation (1), and $\mathbf{Error}(\mathbf{r}_j, e)$ is the sentence-wise minus BLEU (Papineni et al., 2002) of a candidate e with respect to $\mathbf{r}_j$.

Due to the existence of L_2 norm in objective function (5), the optimization algorithm MERT can not be applied for this question since the exact line search routine does not hold here. Motivated by (Och, 2003; Smith and Eisner, 2006), we approximate the $\mathbf{Error}$ in (5) by the expected loss, and then derive the following function:

$$\frac{1}{2}\|W - W_b\|^2 + \frac{\lambda}{K}\sum_{j=1}^{K}\sum_{e}\mathbf{Error}(\mathbf{r}_j; e)\mathbf{P}_\alpha(e|f_j; W), \quad (6)$$

Systems	NIST02	NIST05	NIST06	NIST08
Moses	30.39	26.31	25.34	19.07
Moses_hier	33.68	26.94	26.28	18.65
In-Hiero	31.24	27.07	26.32	19.03

Table 1: The performance comparison of the baseline In-Hiero VS Moses and Moses_hier.

with

$$\mathbf{P}_\alpha(e|f_j; W) = \frac{\exp[\alpha W \cdot h(f_j, e)]}{\sum_{e' \in \mathbf{c}_j}\exp[\alpha W \cdot h(f_j, e')]}, \quad (7)$$

where $\alpha > 0$ is a real number valued smoother. One can see that, in the extreme case, for $\alpha \to \infty$, (6) converges to (5).

We apply the gradient decent method to minimize the function (6), as it is smooth with respect to λ. Since the function (6) is non-convex, the solution obtained by gradient descent method may depend on the initial point. In this paper, we set the initial point as W_b in order to achieve a desirable solution.

5 Experiments and Results

5.1 Setting

We conduct our experiments on the Chinese-to-English translation task. The training data is FBIS corpus consisting of about 240k sentence pairs. The development set is NIST02 evaluation data, and the test datasets are NIST05, NIST06,and NIST08.

We run GIZA++ (Och and Ney, 2000) on the training corpus in both directions (Koehn et al., 2003) to obtain the word alignment for each sentence pair. We train a 4-gram language model on the Xinhua portion of the English Gigaword corpus using the SRILM Toolkits (Stolcke, 2002) with modified Kneser-Ney smoothing (Chen and Goodman, 1998). In our experiments the translation performances are measured by case-insensitive BLEU4 metric (Papineni et al., 2002) and we use mteval-v13a.pl as the evaluation tool. The significance testing is performed by paired bootstrap re-sampling (Koehn, 2004).

We use an in-house developed hierarchical phrase-based translation (Chiang, 2005) as our baseline system, and we denote it as **In-Hiero**. To obtain satisfactory baseline performance, we tune In-Hiero system for 5 times using MERT, and then se-

Methods	Steps	Seconds
Global method	Decoding	2.0
Local method	Retrieval	+0.6
	Local training	+0.3

Table 2: The efficiency of the local training and testing measured by sentence averaged runtime.

Methods		NIST05	NIST06	NIST08
Global	MERT	27.07	26.32	19.03
Local	MBUU	27.75^{+}	27.88^{+}	20.84^{+}
	EBUU	27.85^{+}	27.99^{+}	21.08^{+}

Table 3: The performance comparison of local training methods (MBUU and EBUU) and a global method (MERT). NIST05 is the set used to tune λ for MBUU and EBUU, and NIST06 and NIST08 are test sets. + means the local method is significantly better than MERT with $p < 0.05$.

lect the best-performing one as our baseline for the following experiments. As Table 1 indicates, our baseline In-Hiero is comparable to the phrase-based MT (Moses) and the hierarchical phrase-based MT (Moses_hier) implemented in Moses, an open source MT toolkit[2] (Koehn et al., 2007). Both of these systems are with default setting. All three systems are trained by MERT with 100 best candidates.

To compare the local training method in Algorithm 2, we use a standard global training method, MERT, as the baseline training method. We do not compare with Algorithm 1, in which retraining is performed for each input sentence, since retraining for the whole test set is impractical given that each sentence-wise retraining may take some hours or even days. Therefore, we just compare Algorithm 2 with MERT.

5.2 Runtime Results

To run the Algorithm 2, we tune the baseline weight W_b on NIST02 by MERT[3]. The retrieval data is set as the training data, i.e. FBIS corpus, and the retrieval size is 100. We translate retrieval data with W_b to obtain their 100 best translation candidates. We use the simple linear interpolated TF-IDF metric with $\theta = 0.1$ in Section 3 as the retrieval metric.

[2]See web: http://www.statmt.org

[3]W_b is exactly the weight of **In-Hiero** in Table 1.

	NIST05	NIST06	NIST08
NIST02	0.665	0.571	0.506

Table 4: The similarity of development and three test datasets.

For an efficient tuning, the retrieval process is parallelized as follows: the examples are assigned to 4 CPUs so that each CPU accepts a query and returns its top-100 results, then all these top-100 results are merged into the final top-100 retrieved examples together with their translation candidates. In our experiments, we employ the two incremental training methods, i.e. MBUU and EBUU. Both of the hyper-parameters λ are tuned on NIST05 and set as 0.018 and 0.06 for MBUU and EBUU, respectively. In the incremental training step, only one CPU is employed.

Table 2 depicts that testing each sentence with local training method takes 2.9 seconds, which is comparable to the testing time 2.0 seconds with global training method[4]. This shows that the local method is efficient. Further, compared to the retrieval, the local training is not the bottleneck. Actually, if we use LSH technique (Andoni and Indyk, 2008) in retrieval process, the local method can be easily scaled to a larger training data.

5.3 Results and Analysis

Table 3 shows the main results of our local training methods. The EBUU training method significantly outperforms the MERT baseline, and the improvement even achieves up to 2.0 BLEU points on NIST08. We can also see that EBUU and MBUU are comparable on these three test sets. Both of these two local training methods achieve significant improvements over the MERT baseline, which proves the effectiveness of our local training method over global training method.

Although both local methods MBUU and EBUU achieved improvements on all the datasets, their gains on NIST06 and NIST08 are significantly higher than those achieved on NIST05 test dataset. We conjecture that, the more different a test set and a development set are, the more potential improvem-

[4]The runtime excludes the time of tuning and decoding on D in Algorithm 2, since both of them can be performanced offline.

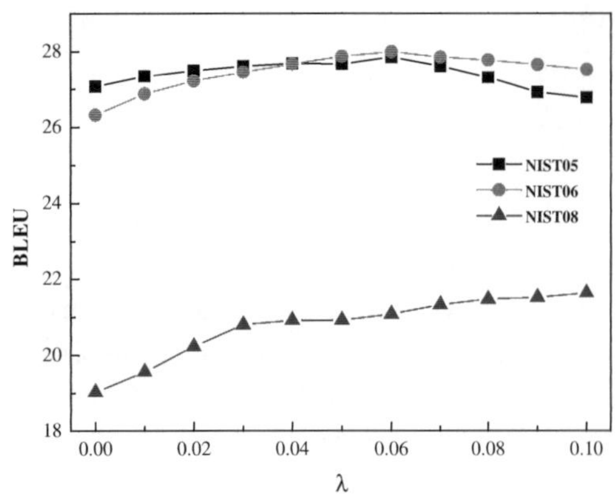

Figure 2: The peformance of EBUU for different λ over all the test datasets. The horizontal axis denotes the values of λ in function (6), and the vertical one denotes the BLEU points.

Metthods	Dev	NIST08
MERT	NIST02	19.03
	NIST05	20.06
	NIST06	21.28
EBUU	NIST02	21.08

Table 5: The comparison of MERT with different development datasets and local training method based on EBUU.

nts local training has for the sentences in this test set. To test our hypothesis, we measured the similarity between the development set and a test set by the average value[5] of accumulated TF-IDF scores of development dataset and each sentence in test datasets. Table 4 shows that NIST06 and NIST08 are more different from NIS02 than NIST05, thus, this is potentially the reason why local training is more effective on NIST06 and NIST08.

As mentioned in Section 1, the global training methods such as MERT are highly dependent on development sets, which can be seen in Table 5. Therefore, the translation performance will be degraded if one chooses a development data which is not close

[5]Instead of using the similarity between two documents development and test datasets, we define the similarity as the average similarity of the development set and the sentences in test set. The reason is that it reduces its dependency on the number of sentences in test dataset, which may cause a bias.

Methods	Number	Percents
MERT	1735	42.3%
EBUU	1606	39.1%

Table 6: The statistics of sentences with 0.0 sentence-level BLEU points over three test datasets.

to the test data. We can see that, with the help of the local training, we still gain much even if we selected an unsatisfactory development data.

As also mentioned in Section 1, the global methods do not care about the sentence level performance. Table 6 depicts that there are 1735 sentences with zero BLEU points in all the three test datasets for MERT. Besides obtaining improvements on document level as referred in Table 3, the local training methods can also achieve consistent improvements on sentence level and thus can improve the users' experiences.

The hyperparameters λ in both MBUU (4) and EBUU (6) has an important influence on translation performance. Figure 2 shows such influence for EBUU on the test datasets. We can see that, the performances on all these datasets improve as λ becomes closer to 0.06 from 0, and the performance continues improving when λ passes over 0.06 on NIST08 test set, where the performance constantly improves up to 2.6 BLEU points over baseline. As mentioned in Section 4, if the retrieved examples are very similar to the test sentence, the better performance will be achieved with the larger λ. Therefore, it is reasonable that the performances improved when λ increased from 0 to 0.06. Further, the turning point appearing at 0.06 proves that the ultraconservative update is necessary. We can also see that the performance on NIST08 consistently improves and achieves the maximum gain when λ arrives at 0.1, but those on both NIST05 and NIST06 achieves the best when it arrives at 0.06. This phenomenon can also be interpreted in Table 4 as the lowest similarity between the development and NIST08 datasets.

Generally, the better performance may be achieved when more examples are retrieved. Actually, in Table 7 there seems to be little dependency between the numbers of examples retrieved and the translation qualities, although they are positively re-

Retrieval Size	NIST05	NIST06	NIST08
40	27.66	27.81	20.87
70	27.77	27.93	21.08
100	27.85	27.99	21.08

Table 7: The performance comparison by varying retrieval size in Algorithm 2 based on EBUU.

Methods	NIST05	NIST06	NIST08
MERT	27.07	26.32	19.03
EBUU	27.85	27.99	21.08
Oracle	29.46	29.35	22.09

Table 8: The performance of Oracle of 2-best results which consist of 1-best resluts of MERT and 1-best resluts of EBUU.

lated approximately.

Table 8 presents the performance of the oracle translations selected from the 1-best translation results of MERT and EBUU. Clearly, there exists more potential improvement for local training method.

6 Related Work

Several works have proposed discriminative techniques to train log-linear model for SMT. (Och and Ney, 2002; Blunsom et al., 2008) used maximum likelihood estimation to learn weights for MT. (Och, 2003; Moore and Quirk, 2008; Zhao and Chen, 2009; Galley and Quirk, 2011) employed an evaluation metric as a loss function and directly optimized it. (Watanabe et al., 2007; Chiang et al., 2008; Hopkins and May, 2011) proposed other optimization objectives by introducing a margin-based and ranking-based indirect loss functions.

All the methods mentioned above train a single weight for the whole development set, whereas our local training method learns a weight for each sentence. Further, our translation framework integrates the training and testing into one unit, instead of treating them separately. One of the advantages is that it can adapt the weights for each of the test sentences.

Our method resorts to some translation examples, which is similar as example-based translation or translation memory (Watanabe and Sumita, 2003; He et al., 2010; Ma et al., 2011). Instead of using translation examples to construct translation rules for enlarging the decoding space, we employed them to discriminatively learn local weights.

Similar to (Hildebrand et al., 2005; Lü et al., 2007), our method also employes IR methods to retrieve examples for a given test set. Their methods utilize the retrieved examples to acquire translation model and can be seen as the adaptation of translation model. However, ours uses the retrieved examples to tune the weights and thus can be considered as the adaptation of tuning. Furthermore, since ours does not change the translation model which needs to run GIZA++ and it incrementally trains local weights, our method can be applied for online translation service.

7 Conclusion and Future Work

This paper proposes a novel local training framework for SMT. It has two characteristics, which are different from global training methods such as MERT. First, instead of training only one weight for document level, it trains a single weight for sentence level. Second, instead of considering the training and testing as two separate units, we unify the training and testing into one unit, which can employ the information of test sentences and perform sentence-wise local adaptation of weights.

Local training can not only alleviate the problem of the development data selection, but also reduce the risk of sentence-wise bad translation results, thus consistently improve the translation performance. Experiments show gains up to 2.0 BLEU points compared with a MERT baseline. With the help of incremental training methods, the time incurred by local training was negligible and the local training and testing totally took 2.9 seconds for each sentence.

In the future work, we will further investigate the local training method, since there are more room for improvements as observed in our experiments. We will test our method on other translation models and larger training data[6].

Acknowledgments

We would like to thank Hongfei Jiang and Shujie Liu for many valuable discussions and thank three

[6]Intuitionally, when the corpus of translation examples is larger, the retrieval results in Algorithm 2 are much similar as the test sentence. Therefore our method may favor this.

anonymous reviewers for many valuable comments and helpful suggestions. This work was supported by National Natural Science Foundation of China (61173073,61100093), and the Key Project of the National High Technology Research and Development Program of China (2011AA01A207), and the Fundamental Research Funds for Central Universites (HIT.NSRIF.2013065).

References

Alexandr Andoni and Piotr Indyk. 2008. Near-optimal hashing algorithms for approximate nearest neighbor in high dimensions. *Commun. ACM*, 51(1):117–122, January.

Phil Blunsom, Trevor Cohn, and Miles Osborne. 2008. A discriminative latent variable model for statistical machine translation. In *Proceedings of ACL*, pages 200–208, Columbus, Ohio, June. Association for Computational Linguistics.

Léon Bottou and Vladimir Vapnik. 1992. Local learning algorithms. *Neural Comput.*, 4:888–900, November.

G. Cauwenberghs and T. Poggio. 2001. Incremental and decremental support vector machine learning. In *Advances in Neural Information Processing Systems (NIPS*2000)*, volume 13.

Stanley F Chen and Joshua Goodman. 1998. An empirical study of smoothing techniques for language modeling. In *Technical Report TR-10-98*. Harvard University.

Haibin Cheng, Pang-Ning Tan, and Rong Jin. 2010. Efficient algorithm for localized support vector machine. *IEEE Trans. on Knowl. and Data Eng.*, 22:537–549, April.

David Chiang, Yuval Marton, and Philip Resnik. 2008. Online large-margin training of syntactic and structural translation features. In *Proceedings of the Conference on Empirical Methods in Natural Language Processing*, EMNLP '08, pages 224–233, Stroudsburg, PA, USA. Association for Computational Linguistics.

David Chiang. 2005. A hierarchical phrase-based model for statistical machine translation. In *Proceedings of the 43rd Annual Meeting on Association for Computational Linguistics*, ACL '05, pages 263–270, Stroudsburg, PA, USA. Association for Computational Linguistics.

Koby Crammer and Yoram Singer. 2003. Ultraconservative online algorithms for multiclass problems. *J. Mach. Learn. Res.*, 3:951–991, March.

Koby Crammer, Ofer Dekel, Joseph Keshet, Shai Shalev-Shwartz, and Yoram Singer. 2006. Online passive-aggressive algorithms. *J. Mach. Learn. Res.*, 7:551–585, December.

Michel Galley and Chris Quirk. 2011. Optimal search for minimum error rate training. In *Proceedings of the 2011 Conference on Empirical Methods in Natural Language Processing*, pages 38–49, Edinburgh, Scotland, UK., July. Association for Computational Linguistics.

Yifan He, Yanjun Ma, Josef van Genabith, and Andy Way. 2010. Bridging smt and tm with translation recommendation. In *Proceedings of the 48th Annual Meeting of the Association for Computational Linguistics*, pages 622–630, Uppsala, Sweden, July. Association for Computational Linguistics.

S. Hildebrand, M. Eck, S. Vogel, and Alex Waibel. 2005. Adaptation of the translation model for statistical machine translation based on information retrieval. In *Proceedings of EAMT*. Association for Computational Linguistics.

Mark Hopkins and Jonathan May. 2011. Tuning as ranking. In *Proceedings of the 2011 Conference on Empirical Methods in Natural Language Processing*, pages 1352–1362, Edinburgh, Scotland, UK., July. Association for Computational Linguistics.

Philipp Koehn, Franz Josef Och, and Daniel Marcu. 2003. Statistical phrase-based translation. In *Proc. of HLT-NAACL*. ACL.

Philipp Koehn, Hieu Hoang, Alexandra Birch, Chris Callison-Burch, Marcello Federico, Nicola Bertoldi, Brooke Cowan, Wade Shen, Christine Moran, Richard Zens, Chris Dyer, Ondřej Bojar, Alexandra Constantin, and Evan Herbst. 2007. Moses: open source toolkit for statistical machine translation. In *Proceedings of the 45th Annual Meeting of the ACL on Interactive Poster and Demonstration Sessions*, ACL '07, pages 177–180, Stroudsburg, PA, USA. Association for Computational Linguistics.

Philipp Koehn. 2004. Statistical significance tests for machine translation evaluation. In *Proc. of EMNLP*. ACL.

Mu Li, Yinggong Zhao, Dongdong Zhang, and Ming Zhou. 2010. Adaptive development data selection for log-linear model in statistical machine translation. In *Proceedings of the 23rd International Conference on Computational Linguistics*, COLING '10, pages 662–670, Stroudsburg, PA, USA. Association for Computational Linguistics.

Yajuan Lü, Jin Huang, and Qun Liu. 2007. Improving statistical machine translation performance by training data selection and optimization. In *Proceedings of the 2007 Joint Conference on Empirical Methods in Natural Language Processing and Computational Natural Language Learning (EMNLP-CoNLL)*, pages

343–350, Prague, Czech Republic, June. Association for Computational Linguistics.

Yanjun Ma, Yifan He, Andy Way, and Josef van Genabith. 2011. Consistent translation using discriminative learning - a translation memory-inspired approach. In *Proceedings of the 49th Annual Meeting of the Association for Computational Linguistics: Human Language Technologies*, pages 1239–1248, Portland, Oregon, USA, June. Association for Computational Linguistics.

Christopher D. Manning and Hinrich Schütze. 1999. *Foundations of statistical natural language processing*. MIT Press, Cambridge, MA, USA.

Robert C. Moore and Chris Quirk. 2008. Random restarts in minimum error rate training for statistical machine translation. In *Proceedings of the 22nd International Conference on Computational Linguistics - Volume 1*, COLING '08, pages 585–592, Stroudsburg, PA, USA. Association for Computational Linguistics.

Franz Josef Och and Hermann Ney. 2000. Improved statistical alignment models. In *Proceedings of the 38th Annual Meeting on Association for Computational Linguistics*, ACL '00, pages 440–447, Stroudsburg, PA, USA. Association for Computational Linguistics.

Franz Josef Och and Hermann Ney. 2002. Discriminative training and maximum entropy models for statistical machine translation. In *Proceedings of the 40th Annual Meeting on Association for Computational Linguistics*, ACL '02, pages 295–302, Stroudsburg, PA, USA. Association for Computational Linguistics.

Franz Josef Och. 2003. Minimum error rate training in statistical machine translation. In *Proceedings of the 41st Annual Meeting of the Association for Computational Linguistics*, pages 160–167, Sapporo, Japan, July. Association for Computational Linguistics.

Kishore Papineni, Salim Roukos, Todd Ward, and Wei-Jing Zhu. 2002. Bleu: a method for automatic evaluation of machine translation. In *Proceedings of 40th Annual Meeting of the Association for Computational Linguistics*, pages 311–318, Philadelphia, Pennsylvania, USA, July. Association for Computational Linguistics.

Adam Pauls, John Denero, and Dan Klein. 2009. Consensus training for consensus decoding in machine translation. In *Proceedings of the 2009 Conference on Empirical Methods in Natural Language Processing*, pages 1418–1427, Singapore, August. Association for Computational Linguistics.

Alistair Shilton, Marimuthu Palaniswami, Daniel Ralph, and Ah Chung Tsoi. 2005. Incremental training of support vector machines. *IEEE Transactions on Neural Networks*, 16(1):114–131.

Andreas Stolcke. 2002. Srilm - an extensible language modeling toolkit. In *Proc. of ICSLP*.

Taro Watanabe and Eiichiro Sumita. 2003. Example-based decoding for statistical machine translation. In *Proc. of MT Summit IX*, pages 410–417.

Taro Watanabe, Jun Suzuki, Hajime Tsukada, and Hideki Isozaki. 2007. Online large-margin training for statistical machine translation. In *Proceedings of the 2007 Joint Conference on Empirical Methods in Natural Language Processing and Computational Natural Language Learning (EMNLP-CoNLL)*, pages 764–773, Prague, Czech Republic, June. Association for Computational Linguistics.

Hao Zhang, Alexander C. Berg, Michael Maire, and Jitendra Malik. 2006. Svm-knn: Discriminative nearest neighbor classification for visual category recognition. In *Proceedings of the 2006 IEEE Computer Society Conference on Computer Vision and Pattern Recognition - Volume 2*, CVPR '06, pages 2126–2136, Washington, DC, USA. IEEE Computer Society.

Bing Zhao and Shengyuan Chen. 2009. A simplex armijo downhill algorithm for optimizing statistical machine translation decoding parameters. In *Proceedings of Human Language Technologies: The 2009 Annual Conference of the North American Chapter of the Association for Computational Linguistics, Companion Volume: Short Papers*, NAACL-Short '09, pages 21–24, Stroudsburg, PA, USA. Association for Computational Linguistics.

Iterative Annotation Transformation with Predict-Self Reestimation for Chinese Word Segmentation

Wenbin Jiang and **Fandong Meng** and **Qun Liu** and **Yajuan Lü**

Key Laboratory of Intelligent Information Processing
Institute of Computing Technology
Chinese Academy of Sciences
{jiangwenbin, mengfandong, liuqun, lvyajuan}@ict.ac.cn

Abstract

In this paper we first describe the technology of automatic annotation transformation, which is based on the annotation adaptation algorithm (Jiang et al., 2009). It can automatically transform a human-annotated corpus from one annotation guideline to another. We then propose two optimization strategies, iterative training and predict-self reestimation, to further improve the accuracy of annotation guideline transformation. Experiments on Chinese word segmentation show that, the iterative training strategy together with predict-self reestimation brings significant improvement over the simple annotation transformation baseline, and leads to classifiers with significantly higher accuracy and several times faster processing than annotation adaptation does. On the Penn Chinese Treebank 5.0, it achieves an F-measure of 98.43%, significantly outperforms previous works although using a single classifier with only local features.

1 Introduction

Annotation guideline adaptation depicts a general pipeline to integrate the knowledge of corpora with different underling annotation guidelines (Jiang et al., 2009). In annotation adaptation two classifiers are cascaded together, where the classification results of the lower classifier are used as guiding features of the upper classifier, in order to achieve more accurate classification. This method can automatically adapt the divergence between different annotation guidelines and bring improvement to Chinese word segmentation. However, the need of cascaded classification decisions makes it less practical for tasks of high computational complexity such as parsing, and less efficient to incorporate more than two annotated corpora.

In this paper, we first describe the algorithm of automatic annotation transformation. It is based on the annotation adaptation algorithm, and it focuses on the automatic transformation (rather than adaptation) of a human-annotated corpus from one annotation guideline to another. First, a classifier is trained on the corpus with an annotation guideline not desired, it is used to classify the corpus with the annotation guideline we want, so as to obtain a corpus with parallel annotation guidelines. Then a second classifier is trained on the parallelly annotated corpus to learn the statistical regularity of annotation transformation, and it is used to process the previous corpus to transform its annotation guideline to that of the target corpus. Instead of the online knowledge integration methodology of annotation adaptation, annotation transformation can lead to improved classification accuracy in an offline manner by using the transformed corpora as additional training data for the classifier. This method leads to an enhanced classifier with much faster processing than the cascaded classifiers in annotation adaptation.

We then propose two optimization strategies, iterative training and predict-self reestimation, to further improve the accuracy of annotation transformation. Although the transformation classifiers can only be trained on corpora with autogenerated (rather than gold) parallel annotations, an iterative training procedure can gradually improve the transformation accuracy by iteratively optimizing the parallelly annotated corpora. Both source-to-target and target-to-source annotation transformations are performed in each training iteration, and the transformed corpora are used to provide better annotations for the parallelly annotated corpora of the next iteration; then the better parallelly annotated corpora will result in more accurate transformation classifiers, which will generate better transformed corpora in the new iteration. The predict-self reestimation is based on the following hypothesis, a better transformation result should be easier to be transformed back to the original form. The predict-self heuristic is also validated by Daumé III (2009) in unsupervised dependency parsing.

Experiments in Chinese word segmentation show that, the iterative training strategy together with predict-self reestimation brings significant improvement over the simple annotation transformation baseline. We perform optimized annotation transformation from the People's Daily (Yu et al., 2001) to the Penn Chinese Treebank 5.0 (CTB) (Xue et al., 2005), in order to improve the word segmenter with CTB annotation guideline. Compared to annotation adaptation, the optimized annotation transformation strategy leads to classifiers with significantly higher accuracy and several times faster processing on the same data sets. On CTB 5.0, it achieves an F-measure of 98.43%, significantly outperforms previous works although using a single classifier with only local features.

The rest of the paper is organized as follows. Section 2 describes the classification-based Chinese word segmentation method. Section 3 details the simple annotation transformation algorithm and the two optimization methods. After the introduction of related works in section 4, we give the experimental results on Chinese word segmentation in section 5.

2 Classification-Based Chinese Word Segmentation

Chinese word segmentation can be formalized as the problem of sequence labeling (Xue and Shen, 2003), where each character in the sentence is given a boundary tag denoting its position in a word. Following Ng and Low (2004), joint word segmentation and part-of-speech (POS) tagging can also be solved in a character classification approach by extending the boundary tags to include POS information. For word segmentation we adopt the 4 boundary tags of Ng and Low (2004), b, m, e and s, where b, m and e mean the beginning, the middle and the end of a word, and s indicates a single-character word. The word segmentation result can be generated by splitting the labeled character sequence into subsequences of pattern s or bm^*e, indicating single-character words or multi-character words, respectively.

Algorithm 1 Perceptron training algorithm.

Input: Training examples (x_i, y_i)
$\vec{\alpha} \leftarrow \mathbf{0}$
for $t \leftarrow 1 \,..\, T$ **do**
  for $i \leftarrow 1 \,..\, N$ **do**
    $z_i \leftarrow \text{argmax}_{z \in \mathbf{GEN}(x_i)} \mathbf{\Phi}(x_i, z) \cdot \vec{\alpha}$
    if $z_i \neq y_i$ **then**
      $\vec{\alpha} \leftarrow \vec{\alpha} + \mathbf{\Phi}(x_i, y_i) - \mathbf{\Phi}(x_i, z_i)$
Output: Parameters $\vec{\alpha}$

We choose the perceptron algorithm (Collins, 2002) to train the character classifier. It is an online training algorithm and has been successfully used in many NLP tasks, including POS tagging (Collins, 2002), parsing (Collins and Roark, 2004) and word segmentation (Zhang and Clark, 2007; Jiang et al., 2008; Zhang and Clark, 2010).

The training procedure learns a discriminative model mapping from the inputs $x \in X$ to the outputs $y \in Y$, where X is the set of sentences in the training corpus and Y is the set of corresponding labeled results. We use the function $\mathbf{GEN}(x)$ to enumerate the candidate results of an input x, and the function $\mathbf{\Phi}$ to map a training example $(x, y) \in X \times Y$ to a feature vector $\mathbf{\Phi}(x, y) \in R^d$. Given the character sequence x, the decoder finds the output $F(x)$ that maximizes the score function:

$$\begin{aligned} F(x) &= \underset{y \in \mathbf{GEN}(x)}{\text{argmax}} \ \mathbf{S}(y|\vec{\alpha}, \mathbf{\Phi}, x) \\ &= \underset{y \in \mathbf{GEN}(x)}{\text{argmax}} \ \mathbf{\Phi}(x, y) \cdot \vec{\alpha} \end{aligned} \quad (1)$$

Where $\vec{\alpha} \in R^d$ is the parameter vector (that is, the discriminative model) and $\mathbf{\Phi}(x, y) \cdot \vec{\alpha}$ is the inner product of $\mathbf{\Phi}(x, y)$ and $\vec{\alpha}$.

Algorithm 1 shows the perceptron algorithm for tuning the parameter $\vec{\alpha}$. The "averaged parameters"

Type	Feature Templates		
Unigram	C_{-2}	C_{-1}	C_0
	C_1	C_2	
Bigram	$C_{-2}C_{-1}$	$C_{-1}C_0$	C_0C_1
	C_1C_2	$C_{-1}C_1$	
Property	$Pu(C_0)$		
	$T(C_{-2})T(C_{-1})T(C_0)T(C_1)T(C_2)$		

Table 1: Feature templates for classification-based Chinese segmentation model.

technology (Collins, 2002) is used for better performance. The feature templates for the classifier is shown in Table 1. C_0 denotes the current character, while C_{-i}/C_i denote the ith character to the left/right of C_0. The function $Pu(\cdot)$ returns *true* for a punctuation character and *false* for others, the function $T(\cdot)$ classifies a character into four types: number, date, English letter and others.

3 Iterative and Predict-Self Annotation Transformation

This section first describes the technology of automatic annotation transformation, then introduces the two optimization strategies, iterative training and predict-self reestimation. Iterative training takes a global view, it conducts several rounds of bidirectional annotation transformations, and improve the transformation performance round by round. Predict-self reestimation takes a local view instead, it considers each training sentence, and improves the transformation performance by taking into account the predication result of the reverse transformation. The two strategies can be adopted jointly to obtain better transformation performance.

3.1 Automatic Annotation Transformation

Annotation adaptation can integrate the knowledge from two corpora with different underling annotation guidelines. First, a classifier (source classifier) is trained on the corpus (source corpus) with an annotation standard (source annotation) not desired, it is then used to classify the corpus (target corpus) with the annotation standard (target annotation) we want. Then a second classifier (transformation classifier [1]) is trained on the target corpus with

Type	Feature Templates		
Baseline	C_{-2}	C_{-1}	C_0
	C_1	C_2	
	$C_{-2}C_{-1}$	$C_{-1}C_0$	C_0C_1
	C_1C_2	$C_{-1}C_1$	
	$Pu(C_0)$		
	$T(C_{-2})T(C_{-1})T(C_0)T(C_1)T(C_2)$		
Guiding	α		
	$C_{-2}\circ\alpha$	$C_{-1}\circ\alpha$	$C_0\circ\alpha$
	$C_1\circ\alpha$	$C_2\circ\alpha$	
	$C_{-2}C_{-1}\circ\alpha$	$C_{-1}C_0\circ\alpha$	$C_0C_1\circ\alpha$
	$C_1C_2\circ\alpha$	$C_{-1}C_1\circ\alpha$	
	$Pu(C_0)\circ\alpha$		
	$T(C_{-2})T(C_{-1})T(C_0)T(C_1)T(C_2)\circ\alpha$		

Table 2: Feature templates for annotation transformation, where α is short for $\alpha(C_0)$, representing the source annotation of C_0.

the source classifier's classification result as guiding features. In decoding, a raw sentence is first decoded by the source classifier, and then inputted into the transformation classifier together with the annotations given by the source classifier, so as to obtain an improved classification result.

However, annotation adaptation has a drawback, it has to cascade two classifiers in decoding to integrate the knowledge in two corpora, thus seriously degrades the processing speed. This paper describes a variant of annotation adaptation, name annotation transformation, aiming at automatic transformation (rather than adaptation) between annotation standards of human-annotated corpora. In annotation transformation, a source classifier and a transformation classifier are trained in the same way as in annotation adaptation. The transformation classifier is used to process the source corpus, with the classification label derived from the segmented sentences as the guiding features, so as to relabel the source corpus with the target annotation guideline. By integrating the target corpus and the transformed source corpus for the training of the character classifier, improved classification accuracy can be achieved.

Both the source classifier and the transformation classifier are trained with the perceptron algorithm. The feature templates used for the source classifier are the same with those for the baseline

[1]It is called *target classifier* in (Jiang et al., 2009). We think that *transformation classifier* better reflects its role, the renaming also avoids name confusion in the optimized annotation transformation.

Algorithm 2 Baseline annotation transformation.

function ANNOTRANS($\mathcal{C}_s, \mathcal{C}_t$)
  $\mathcal{M}_s \leftarrow$ TRAIN($\mathcal{C}_s$)
  $\mathcal{C}_t^s \leftarrow$ ANNOTATE($\mathcal{M}_s, \mathcal{C}_t$)
  $\mathcal{M}_{s\rightarrow t} \leftarrow$ TRANSTRAIN($\mathcal{C}_t^s, \mathcal{C}_t$)
  $\mathcal{C}_s^t \leftarrow$ TRANSANNOTATE($\mathcal{M}_{s\rightarrow t}, \mathcal{C}_s$)
  $\mathcal{C}_*^t \leftarrow \mathcal{C}_s^t \cup \mathcal{C}_t$
  return $\mathcal{C}_*^t$
function DECODE($\mathcal{M}$, $\mathbf{\Phi}$, x)
  return $\text{argmax}_{y\in\mathbf{GEN}(x)}\ \mathbf{S}(y|\mathcal{M}, \mathbf{\Phi}, x)$

character classifier. The feature templates for the transformation classifier are the same with those in annotation adaptation, as listed in Table 2. Algorithm 2 shows the overall training algorithm for annotation transformation. $\mathcal{C}_s$ and $\mathcal{C}_t$ denote the source corpus and the target corpus; $\mathcal{M}_s$ and $\mathcal{M}_{s\rightarrow t}$ denote the source classifier and the transformation classifier; $\mathcal{C}_p^q$ denotes the p corpus relabeled in q annotation guideline, for example $\mathcal{C}_s^t$ is the source corpus transformed to target annotation guideline; Functions TRAIN and TRANSTRAIN both invoke the perceptron algorithm, yet with different feature sets; Functions ANNOTATE and TRANSANNOTATE call the function DECODE with different models (source/transformation classifiers), feature functions (without/with guiding features), and inputs (raw/source-annotated sentences).

The best training iterations for the functions TRAIN and TRANSTRAIN are determined on the developing sets of the source corpus and the target corpus, respectively. In the algorithm the parameters corresponding to developing sets are omitted for simplicity. Compared to the online knowledge integration methodology of annotation adaptation, annotation transformation leads to improved performance in an offline manner by integrating corpora before the training procedure. This manner could achieve processing several times as fast as the cascaded classifiers in annotation adaptation. In the following we will describe the two optimization strategies in details.

3.2 Iterative Training for Annotation Transformation

The training of annotation transformation is based on an auto-generated (rather than gold) parallelly annotated corpus, where the source annotation is provided by the source classifier. Therefore, the performance of transformation training is correspondingly determined by the accuracy of the source classifier.

Algorithm 3 Iterative annotation transformation.

1: **function** ITERANNOTRANS($\mathcal{C}_s, \mathcal{C}_t$)
2:   $\mathcal{M}_s \leftarrow$ TRAIN($\mathcal{C}_s$)
3:   $\mathcal{C}_t^s \leftarrow$ ANNOTATE($\mathcal{M}_s, \mathcal{C}_t$)
4:   $\mathcal{M}_t \leftarrow$ TRAIN($\mathcal{C}_t$)
5:   $\mathcal{C}_s^t \leftarrow$ ANNOTATE($\mathcal{M}_t, \mathcal{C}_s$)
6:   **repeat**
7:     $\mathcal{M}_{s\rightarrow t} \leftarrow$ TRANSTRAIN($\mathcal{C}_t^s, \mathcal{C}_t$)
8:     $\mathcal{M}_{t\rightarrow s} \leftarrow$ TRANSTRAIN($\mathcal{C}_s^t, \mathcal{C}_s$)
9:     $\mathcal{C}_s^t \leftarrow$ TRANSANNOTATE($\mathcal{M}_{s\rightarrow t}, \mathcal{C}_s$)
10:     $\mathcal{C}_t^s \leftarrow$ TRANSANNOTATE($\mathcal{M}_{t\rightarrow s}, \mathcal{C}_t$)
11:     $\mathcal{C}_*^t \leftarrow \mathcal{C}_s^t \cup \mathcal{C}_t$
12:     $\mathcal{M}_* \leftarrow$ TRAIN($\mathcal{C}_*^t$)
13:   **until** EVAL($\mathcal{M}_*$) converges
14:   **return** $\mathcal{C}_*^t$
15: **function** DECODE($\mathcal{M}$, $\mathbf{\Phi}$, x)
16:   **return** $\text{argmax}_{y\in\mathbf{GEN}(x)}\ \mathbf{S}(y|\mathcal{M}, \mathbf{\Phi}, x)$

We propose an iterative training procedure to gradually improve the transformation accuracy by iteratively optimizing the parallelly annotated corpora. In each training iteration, both source-to-target and target-to-source annotation transformations are performed, and the transformed corpora are used to provide better annotations for the parallelly annotated corpora of the next iteration. Then in the new iteration, the better parallelly annotated corpora will result in more accurate transformation classifiers, so as to generate better transformed corpora.

Algorithm 3 shows the overall procedure of the iterative training method. The loop of lines 6-13 iteratively performs source-to-target and target-to-source annotation transformations. The source annotations of the parallelly annotated corpora, $\mathcal{C}_t^s$ and $\mathcal{C}_s^t$, are initialized by applying the source and target classifiers respectively on the target and source corpora (lines 2-5). In each training iteration, the transformation classifiers are trained on the current parallelly annotated corpora (lines 7-8), they are used to produce the transformed corpora (lines 9-10) which provide better annotations for the parallelly annotated corpora of the next iteration. The iterative training terminates when the performance of the classifier trained on the merged corpus $\mathcal{C}_s^t \cup \mathcal{C}_t$ converges.

The discriminative training of TRANSTRAIN predicts the target annotations with the guidance of source annotations. In the first iteration, the transformed corpora generated by the transformation classifiers are better than the initialized ones generated by the source and target classifiers, due to the assistance of the guiding features. In the following iterations, the transformed corpora provide better annotations for the parallelly annotated corpora of the subsequent iteration, the transformation accuracy will improve gradually along with optimization of the parallelly annotated corpora until convergence.

3.3 Predict-Self Reestimation for Annotation Transformation

The predict-self hypothesis is implicit in many unsupervised learning approaches, such as Markov random field. This methodology has also been successfully used by Daumé III (2009) in unsupervised dependency parsing. The basic idea of predict-self is that, if a prediction is a better candidate for an input, it can be easier converted back to the original input by a reverse procedure. If applied to the task of annotation transformation, predict-self indicates that a better transformation candidate following the target annotation guideline can be easier transformed back to the original form following the source annotation guideline.

The most intuitionistic strategy to introduce the predict-self methodology into annotation transformation is using a reversed annotation transformation procedure to filter out unreliable predictions of the previous transformation. In detail, a source-to-target annotation transformation is performed on the source annotated sentence to obtain a prediction that follows the target annotation guideline, then a second, target-to-source transformation is performed on this prediction result to check whether it can be transformed back to the previous source annotation. Transformation results failing in this reversal verification are discarded, so this strategy is named predict-self filtration.

A more precious strategy can be called predict-self reestimation. Instead of using the reversed transformation procedure for filtration, the reestimation strategy integrates the scores given by the source-to-target and target-to-source annotation transformation models when evaluating the transformation candidates. By properly tuning the relative weights of the two transformation directions, better transformation performance would be achieved. The scores of the two transformation models are weighted integrated in a log-linear manner:

$$\begin{aligned} &\mathbf{S}^{+}(y|\mathcal{M}_{s\to t}, \mathcal{M}_{t\to s}, \mathbf{\Phi}, x) \\ &\quad = (1-\lambda) \times \mathbf{S}(y|\mathcal{M}_{s\to t}, \mathbf{\Phi}, x) \\ &\qquad + \lambda \times \mathbf{S}(x|\mathcal{M}_{t\to s}, \mathbf{\Phi}, y) \end{aligned} \tag{2}$$

The weight parameter λ is tuned on the developing set. To integrating the predict-self reestimation into the iterative transformation training, a reversed transformation model is introduced and the enhanced scoring function above is used when the function TRANSANNOTATE invokes the function DECODE.

4 Related Works

Researches focused on the automatic adaptation between different corpora can be roughly classified into two kinds, adaptation between different domains (with different statistical distribution) (Blitzer et al., 2006; Daumé III, 2007), and adaptation between different annotation guidelines (Jiang et al., 2009; Zhu et al., 2011). There are also some efforts that totally or partially resort to manual transformation rules, to conduct treebank conversion (Cahill and Mccarthy, 2002; Hockenmaier and Steedman, 2007; Clark and Curran, 2009), and word segmentation guideline transformation (Gao et al., 2004; Mi et al., 2008). This work focuses on the automatic transformation between annotation guidelines, and proposes better annotation transformation technologies to improve the transformation accuracy and the utilization rate of human-annotated knowledge.

The iterative training procedure proposed in this work shares some similarity with the co-training algorithm in parsing (Sarkar, 2001), where the training procedure lets two different models learn from each other during parsing the raw text. The key idea of co-training is utilize the complementarity of different parsing models to mine additional training data from raw text, while iterative training for annotation transformation emphasizes the iterative optimization of the parellelly annotated corpora used

Partition	Sections	# of word
CTB		
Training	$1-270$ $400-931$ $1001-1151$	0.47M
Developing	$301-325$	6.66K
Test	$271-300$	7.82K
PD		
Training	$02-06$	5.86M
Test	01	1.07M

Table 3: Data partitioning for CTB and PD.

to train the transformation models. The predict-self methodology is implicit in many unsupervised learning approaches, it has been successfully used by (Daumé III, 2009) in unsupervised dependency parsing. We adapt this idea to the scenario of annotation transformation to improve transformation accuracy.

In recent years many works have been devoted to the word segmentation task. For example, the introduction of global training or complicated features (Zhang and Clark, 2007; Zhang and Clark, 2010); the investigation of word structures (Li, 2011); the strategies of hybrid, joint or stacked modeling (Nakagawa and Uchimoto, 2007; Kruengkrai et al., 2009; Wang et al., 2010; Sun, 2011), and the semi-supervised and unsupervised technologies utilizing raw text (Zhao and Kit, 2008; Johnson and Goldwater, 2009; Mochihashi et al., 2009; Hewlett and Cohen, 2011). We estimate that the annotation transformation technologies can be adopted jointly with complicated features, system combination and semi-supervised/unsupervised technologies to further improve segmentation performance.

5 Experiments and Analysis

We perform annotation transformation from People's Daily (PD) (Yu et al., 2001) to Penn Chinese Treebank 5.0 (CTB) (Xue et al., 2005), following the same experimental setting as the annotation adaptation work (Jiang et al., 2009) for convenience of comparison. The two corpora are segmented following different segmentation guidelines and differ largely in quantity of data. CTB is smaller in size with about 0.5M words, while PD is much larger, containing nearly 6M words.

	Test on (F_1%)	
Train on	CTB	SPD
CTB	97.35	86.65($\downarrow$ 10.70)
SPD	91.23($\downarrow$ 3.02)	94.25

Table 4: Performance of the perceptron classifiers for Chinese word segmentation.

Model	**Time** (s)	**Accuracy** (F_1%)
Merging	**1.33**	93.79
Anno. Adapt.	4.39	97.67
Anno. Trans.	**1.33**	**97.69**
Baseline	1.21	97.35

Table 5: Comparison of the baseline annotation transformation, annotation adaptation and a simple corpus merging strategy.

To approximate more general scenarios of annotation adaptation problems, we extract from PD a subset which is comparable to CTB in size. We randomly select $20,000$ sentences (0.45M words) from the PD training data as the new training set, and 1000/1000 sentences from the PD test data as the new test/developing set. [2] We name the smaller version of PD as SPD. The balanced source corpus and target corpus also facilitate the investigation of annotation transformation.

5.1 Baseline Classifiers for Word Segmentation

We train the baseline perceptron classifiers described in section 2 on the training sets of SPD and CTB, using the developing sets to determine the best training iterations. The performance measurement indicators for word segmentation is balanced F-measure, $F = 2PR/(P + R)$, a function of Precision P and Recall R. where P is the percentage of words in segmentation result that are segmented correctly, and R is the percentage of correctly segmented words in the gold standard words.

Accuracies of the baseline classifiers are listed in Table 4. We also report the performance of the classifiers on the test sets of the opposite corpora. Experimental results are in line with our expectations. A classifier performs better in its corresponding test set, and performs significantly worse on a test set following a different annotation guideline.

[2] There are many extremely long sentences in original PD corpus, we split them into normal sentences according to period punctuations.

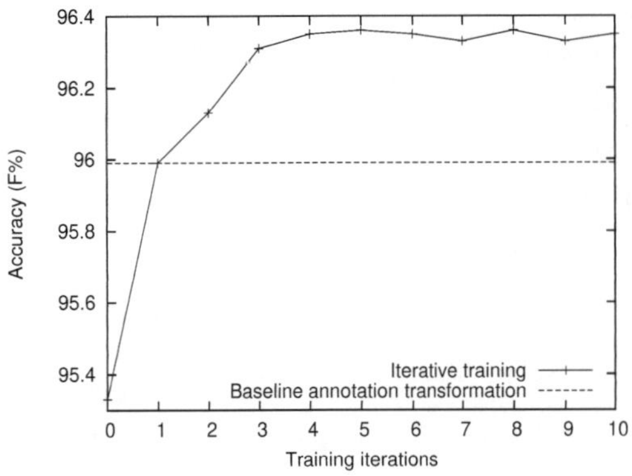

Figure 1: Learning curve of iterative training for annotation transformation.

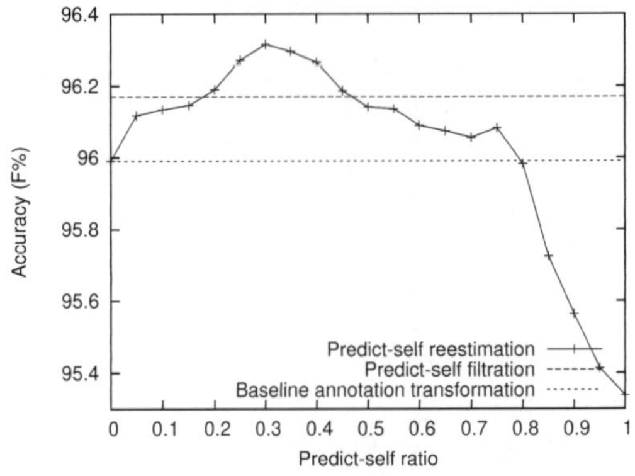

Figure 2: Performance of predict-self filtration and predict-self reestimation.

5.2 Annotation Transformation vs. Annotation Adaptation

Experiments of annotation transformation are conducted on the direction of SPD-to-CTB. The transformed corpus can be merged into the regular corpus, so as to train an enhanced classifier. As comparison, the cascaded model of annotation adaptation (Jiang et al., 2009) is faithfully implemented (yet using our feature representation) and tested on the same adaptation direction.

Table 5 shows the performances of the classifiers resulted by the baseline annotation transformation and annotation adaptation, as well as the classifier trained on the directly merged corpus. The time costs for decoding are also listed to facilitate the comparison of practicality. We find that the simple corpus merging strategy leads to dramatic decrease in accuracy, due to the different and incompatible annotation guidelines. The baseline annotation transformation method leads to a classifier with accuracy increment comparable to that of the annotation adaptation strategy, while consuming only one third of the decoding time.

5.3 Iterative Training with Predict-Self Reestimation

We adopt the iterative training strategy to the baseline annotation transformation model. The CTB developing set is used to determine the best training iteration for annotation transformation from SPD to CTB. After each iteration, we test the performance of the classifier trained on the merged corpus. Figure 1 shows the performance curve, with iterations ranging from 1 to 10. The performance of the baseline annotation transformation model is naturally included in the curve (located at iteration 1). The curve shows that the performance of the classifier trained on the merged corpus consistently improves from iteration 2 to iteration 5.

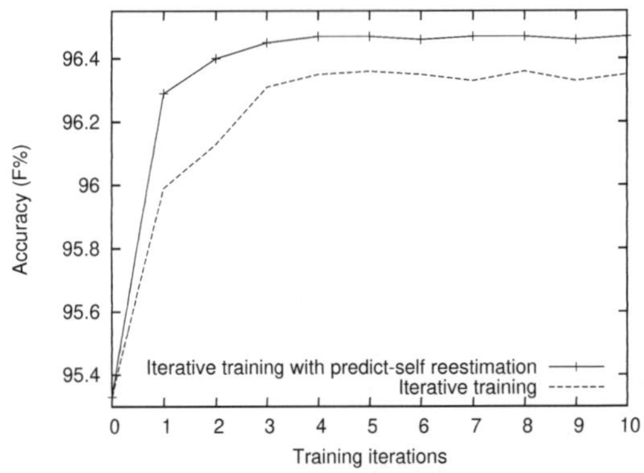

Figure 3: Learning curve of iterative training with predict-self reestimation for annotation transformation.

Experimental results of predict-self filtration and predict-self reestimation are shown in Figure 2. The curve shows the performance of the predict-self reestimation according to a series of weight parameters, ranging from 0 to 1 with step 0.05. The point at $\lambda = 0$ shows the performance of the baseline annotation transformation strategy. The upper horizontal line shows the performance of predict-self filtration. We find that predict-self filtration brings slight improvement over the baseline, and predict-self reestimation outperforms the filtration strategy when λ falls in a proper range. An initial analysis on the experimental results of predict-self filtration

Model	Time (s)	Accuracy (F_1%)
SPD → CTB		
Anno. Adapt.	4.39	97.67
Opt. Trans.	**1.33**	**97.97**
PD → CTB		
Anno. Adapt.	4.76	98.15
Opt. Trans.	**1.37**	**98.43**
Previous Works		
(Jiang et al., 2008)		97.85
(Kruengkrai et al., 2009)		97.87
(Zhang and Clark, 2010)		97.79
(Sun, 2011)		98.17

Table 6: The performance of the iterative annotation transformation with predict-self reestimation compared with annotation adaptation.

shows that, the filtration discards 5% of the training sentences and these discarded sentences contain nearly 10% of training words. It can be confirmed that the sentences discarded by predict-self filtration are much longer and more complicated. With a properly tuned weight, predict-self reestimation can make better use of the training data. The best F-measure improvement achieved over the annotation transformation baseline is 0.3 points, a little worse than that brought by iterative training.

Figure 3 shows the performance curve of iterative annotation transformation with predict-self reestimation. We find that the predict-self reestimation brings improvement to the iterative training at each iteration. The maximum performance is achieved at iteration 4. The corresponding model is evaluated on the test set of CTB, table 6 shows the experimental results. Compared to annotation adaptation, the optimized annotation transformation strategy leads to a classifier with significantly higher accuracy and several times faster processing. When using the whole PD as the source corpus, the final classifier [3] achieves an F-measure of 98.43%, significantly outperforms previous works although using a single classifier with only local features. Of course, the comparison between our system and previous works without using additional training data is unfair. This work aim to find another way to improve Chinese word segmentation, which focuses on the collection of more training data instead of making full use of a certain corpus. We believe that the performance can be further improved by adopting the advanced technologies of previous works, such as complicated features and model combination.

Considering the fact that today some corpora for word segmentation are really large (usually tens of thousands of sentences), it is necessary to obtain the latest CTB and investigate whether and how much does annotation transformation bring improvement to a much higher baseline. On the other hand, it is valuable to conduct experiments with more source-annotated training data, such as the SIGHAN dataset, to investigate the trend of improvement along with the increment of the additional annotated sentences. It is also valuable to evaluate the improved word segmenter on the out-of-domain datasets. However, currently most corpora for Chinese word segmentation do not explicitly distinguish the domains of their data sections, it makes such evaluations difficult to conduct.

6 Conclusion and Future Works

In this paper, we first describe an annotation transformation algorithm to automatically transform a human-annotated corpus from one annotation guideline to another. Then we propose two optimization strategies, iterative training and predict-self reestimation, to further improve the accuracy of annotation guideline transformation. On Chinese word segmentation, the optimized annotation transformation strategy leads to classifiers with obviously better performance and several times faster processing on the same datasets, compared to annotation adaptation. When adopting the whole PD as the source corpus, the final classifier significantly outperforms previous works on CTB 5.0, although using a single classifier with only local features.

As future works, we will investigate the acceleration of the iterative training and the weight parameter tuning, and extend the optimized annotation transformation strategy to joint Chinese word segmentation and POS tagging, parsing and other NLP tasks.

Acknowledgments

The authors were supported by National Natural Science Foundation of China, Contracts 90920004

[3]The predict-self reestimation ratio λ is fixed after the first training iteration for efficiency.

and 61100082, and 863 State Key Project No. 2011AA01A207. We are grateful to the anonymous reviewers for their thorough reviewing and valuable suggestions.

References

John Blitzer, Ryan McDonald, and Fernando Pereira. 2006. Domain adaptation with structural correspondence learning. In *Proceedings of EMNLP*.

Aoife Cahill and Mairead Mccarthy. 2002. Automatic annotation of the penn treebank with lfg f-structure information. In *in Proceedings of the LREC Workshop*.

Stephen Clark and James R. Curran. 2009. Comparing the accuracy of ccg and penn treebank parsers. In *Proceedings of ACL-IJCNLP*.

Michael Collins and Brian Roark. 2004. Incremental parsing with the perceptron algorithm. In *Proceedings of ACL 2004*.

Michael Collins. 2002. Discriminative training methods for hidden markov models: Theory and experiments with perceptron algorithms. In *Proceedings of EMNLP*, pages 1–8, Philadelphia, USA.

Hal Daumé III. 2007. Frustratingly easy domain adaptation. In *Proceedings of ACL*.

Hal Daumé III. 2009. Unsupervised search-based structured prediction. In *Proceedings of ICML*.

Jianfeng Gao, Andi Wu, Mu Li, Chang-Ning Huang, Hongqiao Li, Xinsong Xia, and Haowei Qin. 2004. Adaptive chinese word segmentation. In *Proceedings of ACL*.

Daniel Hewlett and Paul Cohen. 2011. Fully unsupervised word segmentation with bve and mdl. In *Proceedings of ACL*.

Julia Hockenmaier and Mark Steedman. 2007. Ccgbank: a corpus of ccg derivations and dependency structures extracted from the penn treebank. In *Computational Linguistics*, volume 33(3), pages 355–396.

Wenbin Jiang, Liang Huang, Yajuan Lv, and Qun Liu. 2008. A cascaded linear model for joint chinese word segmentation and part-of-speech tagging. In *Proceedings of ACL*.

Wenbin Jiang, Liang Huang, and Qun Liu. 2009. Automatic adaptation of annotation standards: Chinese word segmentation and pos tagging–a case study. In *Proceedings of the 47th ACL*.

Mark Johnson and Sharon Goldwater. 2009. Improving nonparameteric bayesian inference: experiments on unsupervised word segmentation with adaptor grammars. In *Proceedings of NAACL*.

Canasai Kruengkrai, Kiyotaka Uchimoto, Junichi Kazama, Yiou Wang, Kentaro Torisawa, and Hitoshi Isahara. 2009. An error-driven word-character hybrid model for joint chinese word segmentation and pos tagging. In *Proceedings of ACL-IJCNLP*.

Zhongguo Li. 2011. Parsing the internal structure of words: A new paradigm for chineseword segmentation. In *Proceedings of ACL*.

Haitao Mi, Deyi Xiong, and Qun Liu. 2008. Research on strategy of integrating chinese lexical analysis and parser. *In Journal of Chinese Information Processing*.

Daichi Mochihashi, Takeshi Yamada, and Naonori Ueda. 2009. Bayesian unsupervised word segmentation with nested pitman-yor language modeling. In *Proceedings of ACL-IJCNLP*.

Tetsuji Nakagawa and Kiyotaka Uchimoto. 2007. A hybrid approach to word segmentation and pos tagging. In *Proceedings of ACL*.

Hwee Tou Ng and Jin Kiat Low. 2004. Chinese part-of-speech tagging: One-at-a-time or all-at-once? word-based or character-based? In *Proceedings of EMNLP*.

Anoop Sarkar. 2001. Applying co-training methods to statistical parsing. In *Proceedings of NAACL*.

Weiwei Sun. 2011. A stacked sub-word model for joint chinese word segmentation and part-of-speech tagging. In *Proceedings of ACL*.

Kun Wang, Chengqing Zong, and Keh-Yih Su. 2010. A character-based joint model for chinese word segmentation. In *Proceedings of COLING*.

Nianwen Xue and Libin Shen. 2003. Chinese word segmentation as lmr tagging. In *Proceedings of SIGHAN Workshop*.

Nianwen Xue, Fei Xia, Fu-Dong Chiou, and Martha Palmer. 2005. The penn chinese treebank: Phrase structure annotation of a large corpus. In *Natural Language Engineering*.

Shiwen Yu, Jianming Lu, Xuefeng Zhu, Huiming Duan, Shiyong Kang, Honglin Sun, Hui Wang, Qiang Zhao, and Weidong Zhan. 2001. Processing norms of modern chinese corpus. Technical report.

Yue Zhang and Stephen Clark. 2007. Chinese segmentation with a word-based perceptron algorithm. In *Proceedings of ACL 2007*.

Yue Zhang and Stephen Clark. 2010. A fast decoder for joint word segmentation and pos-tagging using a single discriminative model. In *Proceedings of EMNLP*.

Hai Zhao and Chunyu Kit. 2008. Unsupervised segmentation helps supervised learning of character tagging for word segmentation and named entity recognition. In *Proceedings of SIGHAN Workshop*.

Muhua Zhu, Jingbo Zhu, and Minghan Hu. 2011. Better automatic treebank conversion using a feature-based approach. In *Proceedings of ACL*.

Automatically Constructing a Normalisation Dictionary for Microblogs

Bo Han,[♠♡] **Paul Cook,**[♡] and **Timothy Baldwin**[♠♡]
♠ NICTA Victoria Research Laboratory
♡ Department of Computing and Information Systems, The University of Melbourne
hanb@student.unimelb.edu.au, paulcook@unimelb.edu.au,
tb@ldwin.net

Abstract

Microblog normalisation methods often utilise complex models and struggle to differentiate between correctly-spelled unknown words and lexical variants of known words. In this paper, we propose a method for constructing a dictionary of lexical variants of known words that facilitates lexical normalisation via simple string substitution (e.g. *tomorrow* for *tmrw*). We use context information to generate possible variant and normalisation pairs and then rank these by string similarity. Highly-ranked pairs are selected to populate the dictionary. We show that a dictionary-based approach achieves state-of-the-art performance for both F-score and word error rate on a standard dataset. Compared with other methods, this approach offers a fast, lightweight and easy-to-use solution, and is thus suitable for high-volume microblog pre-processing.

1 Lexical Normalisation

A staggering number of short text "microblog" messages are produced every day through social media such as Twitter (Twitter, 2011). The immense volume of real-time, user-generated microblogs that flows through sites has been shown to have utility in applications such as disaster detection (Sakaki et al., 2010), sentiment analysis (Jiang et al., 2011; González-Ibáñez et al., 2011), and event discovery (Weng and Lee, 2011; Benson et al., 2011). However, due to the spontaneous nature of the posts, microblogs are notoriously noisy, containing many non-standard forms — e.g., *tmrw* "tomorrow" and *2day* "today" — which degrade the performance of natural language processing (NLP) tools (Ritter et al., 2010; Han and Baldwin, 2011). To reduce this effect, attempts have been made to adapt NLP tools to microblog data (Gimpel et al., 2011; Foster et al., 2011; Liu et al., 2011b; Ritter et al., 2011). An alternative approach is to pre-normalise non-standard lexical variants to their standard orthography (Liu et al., 2011a; Han and Baldwin, 2011; Xue et al., 2011; Gouws et al., 2011). For example, *se u 2morw!!!* would be normalised to *see you tomorrow!* The normalisation approach is especially attractive as a preprocessing step for applications which rely on keyword match or word frequency statistics. For example, *earthqu*, *eathquake*, and *earthquakeee* — all attested in a Twitter corpus — have the standard form *earthquake*; by normalising these types to their standard form, better coverage can be achieved for keyword-based methods, and better word frequency estimates can be obtained.

In this paper, we focus on the task of lexical normalisation of English Twitter messages, in which out-of-vocabulary (OOV) tokens are normalised to their in-vocabulary (IV) standard form, i.e., a standard form that is in a dictionary. Following other recent work on lexical normalisation (Liu et al., 2011a; Han and Baldwin, 2011; Gouws et al., 2011; Liu et al., 2012), we specifically focus on one-to-one normalisation in which one OOV token is normalised to one IV word.

Naturally, not all OOV words in microblogs are lexical variants of IV words: named entities, e.g., are prevalent in microblogs, but not all named entities are included in our dictionary. One challenge for lexical normalisation is therefore to distinguish those OOV tokens that require normalisation from those that are well-formed. Recent unsupervised approaches have not attempted to distinguish such tokens from other types of OOV tokens (Cook and Stevenson, 2009; Liu et al., 2011a), limiting their applicability to real-world normalisation tasks. Other approaches (Han and Baldwin, 2011; Gouws et al., 2011) have followed a cascaded approach in which lexical variants are first identified, and then normalised. However, such two-step approaches suffer from poor lexical variant identification performance, which is propagated to the normalisation step. Motivated by the observation that most lexical variants have an unambiguous standard form (especially for longer tokens), and that a lexical variant and its standard form typically occur in similar contexts, in this paper we propose methods for automatically constructing a lexical normalisation dictionary — a dictionary whose entries consist of (lexical variant, standard form) pairs — that enables type-based normalisation.

Despite the simplicity of this dictionary-based normalisation method, we show it to outperform previously-proposed approaches. This very fast, lightweight solution is suitable for real-time processing of the large volume of streaming microblog data available from Twitter, and offers a simple solution to the lexical variant detection problem that hinders other normalisation methods. Furthermore, this dictionary-based method can be easily integrated with other more-complex normalisation approaches (Liu et al., 2011a; Han and Baldwin, 2011; Gouws et al., 2011) to produce hybrid systems.

After discussing related work in Section 2, we present an overview of our dictionary-based approach to normalisation in Section 3. In Sections 4 and 5 we experimentally select the optimised context similarity parameters and string similarity reranking method. We present experimental results on the unseen test data in Section 6, and offer some concluding remarks in Section 7.

2 Related Work

Given a token t, lexical normalisation is the task of finding $\arg\max P(s|t) \propto \arg\max P(t|s)P(s)$, where s is the standard form, i.e., an IV word. Standardly in lexical normalisation, t is assumed to be an OOV token, relative to a fixed dictionary. In practice, not all OOV tokens should be normalised; i.e., only lexical variants (e.g., *tmrw* "tomorrow") should be normalised and tokens that are OOV but otherwise not lexical variants (e.g., *iPad* "iPad") should be unchanged. Most work in this area focuses only on the normalisation task itself, oftentimes assuming that the task of lexical variant detection has already been completed.

Various approaches have been proposed to estimate the error model, $P(t|s)$. For example, in work on spell-checking, Brill and Moore (2000) improve on a standard edit-distance approach by considering multi-character edit operations; Toutanova and Moore (2002) build on this by incorporating phonological information. Li et al. (2006) utilise distributional similarity (Lin, 1998) to correct misspelled search queries.

In text message normalisation, Choudhury et al. (2007) model the letter transformations and emissions using a hidden Markov model (Rabiner, 1989). Cook and Stevenson (2009) and Xue et al. (2011) propose multiple simple error models, each of which captures a particular way in which lexical variants are formed, such as phonetic spelling (e.g., *epik* "epic") or clipping (e.g., *walkin* "walking"). Nevertheless, optimally weighting the various error models in these approaches is challenging.

Without pre-categorising lexical variants into different types, Liu et al. (2011a) collect Google search snippets from carefully-designed queries from which they then extract noisy lexical variant–standard form pairs. These pairs are used to train a conditional random field (Lafferty et al., 2001) to estimate $P(t|s)$ at the character level. One shortcoming of querying a search engine to obtain training pairs is it tends to be costly in terms of time and bandwidth. Here we exploit microblog data directly to derive (lexical variant, standard form) pairs, instead of relying on external resources. In more-recent work, Liu et al. (2012) endeavour to improve the accuracy of top-*n* normalisation candidates by integrating human cognitive inference, character-level transformations and spell checking in their normalisation model. The encouraging results shift the focus to reranking and promoting the correct normalisation to the top-*1* position. However, like much previous work on lexical normalisation, this work assumes perfect lexical variant detection.

Aw et al. (2006) and Kaufmann and Kalita (2010) consider normalisation as a machine translation task from lexical variants to standard forms using off-the-shelf tools. These methods do not assume that lexical variants have been pre-identified; however, these methods do rely on large quantities of labelled training data, which is not available for microblogs.

Recently, Han and Baldwin (2011) and Gouws et al. (2011) propose two-step unsupervised approaches to normalisation, in which lexical variants are first identified, and then normalised. They approach lexical variant detection by using a context fitness classifier (Han and Baldwin, 2011) or through dictionary lookup (Gouws et al., 2011). However, the lexical variant detection of both methods is rather unreliable, indicating the challenge of this aspect of normalisation. Both of these approaches incorporate a relatively small normalisation dictionary to capture frequent lexical variants with high precision. In particular, Gouws et al. (2011) produce a small normalisation lexicon based on distributional similarity and string similarity (Lodhi et al., 2002). Our method adopts a similar strategy using distributional/string similarity, but instead of constructing a small lexicon for preprocessing, we build a much wider-coverage normalisation dictionary and opt for a fully lexicon-based end-to-end normalisation approach. In contrast to the normalisation dictionaries of Han and Baldwin (2011) and Gouws et al. (2011) which focus on very frequent lexical variants, we focus on moderate frequency lexical variants of a minimum character length, which tend to have unambiguous standard forms; our intention is to produce normalisation lexicons that are complementary to those currently available. Furthermore, we investigate the impact of a variety of contextual and string similarity measures on the quality of the resulting lexicons. In summary, our dictionary-based normalisation approach is a lightweight end-to-end method which performs both lexical variant detection and normalisation, and thus is suitable for practical online preprocessing, despite its simplicity.

3 A Lexical Normalisation Dictionary

Before discussing our method for creating a normalisation dictionary, we first discuss the feasibility of such an approach.

3.1 Feasibility

Dictionary lookup approaches to normalisation have been shown to have high precision but low recall (Han and Baldwin, 2011; Gouws et al., 2011). Frequent (lexical variant, standard form) pairs such as (u, you) are typically included in the dictionaries used by such methods, while less-frequent items such as $(g0tta, gotta)$ are generally omitted. Because of the degree of lexical creativity and large number of non-standard forms observed on Twitter, a wide-coverage normalisation dictionary would be expensive to construct manually. Based on the assumption that lexical variants occur in similar contexts to their standard forms, however, it should be possible to automatically construct a normalisation dictionary with wider coverage than is currently available.

Dictionary lookup is a type-based approach to normalisation, i.e., every token instance of a given type will always be normalised in the same way. However, lexical variants can be ambiguous, e.g., *y* corresponds to "you" in *yeah, y r right! LOL* but "why" in *AM CONFUSED!!! y you did that?* Nevertheless, the relative occurrence of ambiguous lexical variants is small (Liu et al., 2011a), and it has been observed that while shorter variants such as *y* are often ambiguous, longer variants tend to be unambiguous. For example *bthday* and *4eva* are unlikely to have standard forms other than "birthday" and "forever", respectively. Therefore, the normalisation lexicons we produce will only contain entries for OOVs with character length greater than a specified threshold, which are likely to have an unambiguous standard form.

3.2 Overview of approach

Our method for constructing a normalisation dictionary is as follows:

Input: Tokenised English tweets

1. Extract (OOV, IV) pairs based on distributional similarity.

2. Re-rank the extracted pairs by string similarity.

Output: A list of (OOV, IV) pairs ordered by string similarity; select the top-n pairs for inclusion in the normalisation lexicon.

In Step 1, we leverage large volumes of Twitter data to identify the most distributionally-similar IV type for each OOV type. The result of this process is a set of (OOV, IV) pairs, ranked by distributional similarity. The extracted pairs will include (lexical variant, standard form) pairs, such as (*tmrw*, *tomorrow*), but will also contain false positives such as (*Tusday*, *Sunday*) — *Tusday* is a lexical variant, but its standard form is not "Sunday" — and (*Youtube*, *web*) — *Youtube* is an OOV named entity, not a lexical variant. Nevertheless, lexical variants are typically formed from their standard forms through regular processes (Thurlow, 2003) — e.g., the omission of characters — and from this perspective *Sunday* and *web* are not plausible standard forms for *Tusday* and *Youtube*, respectively. In Step 2, we therefore capture this intuition to re-rank the extracted pairs by string similarity. The top-n items in this re-ranked list then form the normalisation lexicon, which is based only on development data.

Although computationally-expensive to build, this dictionary can be created offline. Once built, it then offers a very fast approach to normalisation.

We can only reliably compute distributional similarity for types that are moderately frequent in a corpus. Nevertheless, many lexical variants are sufficiently frequent to be able to compute distributional similarity, and can potentially make their way into our normalisation lexicon. This approach is not suitable for normalising low-frequency lexical variants, nor is it suitable for shorter lexical variant types which — as discussed in Section 3.1 — are more likely to have an ambiguous standard form. Nevertheless, previously-proposed normalisation methods that can handle such phenomena also rely in part on a normalisation lexicon. The normalisation lexicons we create can therefore be easily integrated with previous approaches to form hybrid normalisation systems.

4 Contextually-similar Pair Generation

Our objective is to extract contextually-similar (OOV, IV) pairs from a large-scale collection of microblog data. Fundamentally, the surrounding words define the primary context, but there are different ways of representing context and different similarity measures we can use, which may influence the quality of generated normalisation pairs.

In representing the context, we experimentally explore the following factors: (1) context window size (from 1 to 3 tokens on both sides); (2) n-gram order of the context tokens (unigram, bigram, trigram); (3) whether context words are indexed for relative position or not; and (4) whether we use all context tokens, or only IV words. Because high-accuracy linguistic processing tools for Twitter are still under exploration (Liu et al., 2011b; Gimpel et al., 2011; Ritter et al., 2011; Foster et al., 2011), we do not consider richer representations of context, for example, incorporating information about part-of-speech tags or syntax. We also experiment with a number of simple but widely-used geometric and information theoretic distance/similarity measures. In particular, we use Kullback–Leibler (KL) divergence (Kullback and Leibler, 1951), Jensen–Shannon (JS) divergence (Lin, 1991), Euclidean distance and Cosine distance.

We use a corpus of 10 million English tweets to do parameter tuning over, and a larger corpus of tweets in the final candidate ranking. All tweets were collected from September 2010 to January 2011 via the Twitter API.[1] From the raw data we extract English tweets using a language identification tool (Lui and Baldwin, 2011), and then apply a simplified Twitter tokeniser (adapted from O'Connor et al. (2010)). We use the Aspell dictionary (v6.06)[2] to determine whether a word is IV, and only include in our normalisation dictionary OOV tokens with at least 64 occurrences in the corpus and character length ≥ 4, both of which were determined through empirical observation. For each OOV word type in the corpus, we select the most similar IV type to form (OOV, IV) pairs. To further narrow the search space, we only consider IV words which are morphophonemically similar to the OOV type, following settings in Han and Baldwin (2011).[3]

[1] `https://dev.twitter.com/docs/streaming-api/methods`

[2] `http://aspell.net/`

[3] We only consider IV words within an edit distance of 2 or a phonemic edit distance of 1 from the OOV type, and we further

In order to evaluate the generated pairs, we randomly selected 1000 OOV words from the 10 million tweet corpus. We set up an annotation task on Amazon Mechanical Turk,[4] presenting five independent annotators with each word type (with no context) and asking for corrections where appropriate. For instance, given *tmrw*, the annotators would likely identify it as a non-standard variant of "tomorrow". For correct OOV words like *iPad*, on the other hand, we would expect them to leave the word unchanged. If 3 or more of the 5 annotators make the same suggestion (in the form of either a canonical spelling or leaving the word unchanged), we include this in our gold standard for evaluation. In total, this resulted in 351 lexical variants and 282 correct OOV words, accounting for 63.3% of the 1000 OOV words. These 633 OOV words were used as (OOV, IV) pairs for parameter tuning. The remainder of the 1000 OOV words were ignored on the grounds that there was not sufficient consensus amongst the annotators.[5]

Contextually-similar pair generation aims to include as many correct normalisation pairs as possible. We evaluate the quality of the normalisation pairs using "Cumulative Gain" (CG):

$$\text{CG} = \sum_{i=1}^{N'} rel'_i$$

Suppose there are N' correct generated pairs (oov_i, iv_i), each of which is weighted by rel'_i, the frequency of oov_i to indicate its relative importance; for example, $(\textit{thinkin}, \textit{thinking})$ has a higher weight than $(\textit{g0tta}, \textit{gotta})$ because *thinkin* is more frequent than *g0tta* in our corpus. In this evaluation we don't consider the position of normalisation pairs, and nor do we penalise incorrect pairs. Instead, we push distinguishing between correct and incorrect pairs into the downstream re-ranking step in which we incorporate string similarity information.

Given the development data and CG, we run an exhaustive search of parameter combinations over our development corpus. The five best parameter combinations are shown in Table 1. We notice the CG is almost identical for the top combinations. As a context window size of 3 incurs a heavy processing and memory overhead over a size of 2, we use the 3rd-best parameter combination for subsequent experiments, namely: context window of ± 2 tokens, token bigrams, positional index, and KL divergence as our distance measure.

To better understand the sensitivity of the method to each parameter, we perform a post-hoc parameter analysis relative to a default setting (as underlined in Table 2), altering one parameter at a time. The results in Table 2 show that bigrams outperform other n-gram orders by a large margin (note that the evaluation is based on a log scale), and information-theoretic measures are superior to the geometric measures. Furthermore, it also indicates using the positional indexing better captures context. However, there is little to distinguish context modelling with just IV words or all tokens. Similarly, the context window size has relatively little impact on the overall performance, supporting our earlier observation from Table 1.

5 Pair Re-ranking by String Similarity

Once the contextually-similar (OOV, IV) pairs are generated using the selected parameters in Section 4, we further re-rank this set of pairs in an attempt to boost morphophonemically-similar pairs like $(\textit{bananaz}, \textit{bananas})$, and penalise noisy pairs like $(\textit{paninis}, \textit{beans})$.

Instead of using the small 10 million tweet corpus, from this step onwards, we use a larger corpus of 80 million English tweets (collected over the same period as the development corpus) to develop a larger-scale normalisation dictionary. This is because once pairs are generated, re-ranking based on string comparison is much faster. We only include in the dictionary OOV words with a token frequency > 15 to include more OOV types than in Section 4, and again apply a minimum length cutoff of 4 characters.

To measure how well our re-ranking method promotes correct pairs and demotes incorrect pairs (including both OOV words that should not be normalised, e.g. $(\textit{Youtube}, \textit{web})$, and incorrect normal-

only consider the top 30% most-frequent of these IV words.

[4]https://www.mturk.com/mturk/welcome

[5]Note that the objective of this annotation task is to identify lexical variants that have agreed-upon standard forms irrespective of context, as a special case of the more general task of lexical normalisation (where context may or may not play a significant role in the determination of the normalisation).

Rank	Window size	n-gram	Positional index?	Lex. choice	Sim/distance measure	log(CG)
1	±3	2	Yes	All	KL divergence	19.571
2	±3	2	No	All	KL divergence	19.562
3	±2	2	Yes	All	KL divergence	19.562
4	±3	2	Yes	IVs	KL divergence	19.561
5	±2	2	Yes	IVs	JS divergence	19.554

Table 1: The five best parameter combinations in the exhaustive search of parameter combinations

Window size		n-gram		Positional index?		Lexical choice		Similarity/distance measure	
±1	19.325	1	19.328	Yes	**19.328**	IVs	**19.335**	KL divergence	**19.328**
±2	19.327	2	**19.571**	No	19.263	All	19.328	Euclidean	19.227
±3	**19.328**	3	19.324					JS divergence	19.311
								Cosine	19.170

Table 2: Parameter sensitivity analysis measured as log(CG) for correctly-generated pairs. We tune one parameter at a time, using the default (underlined) setting for other parameters; the non-exhaustive best-performing setting in each case is indicated in **bold**.

isations for lexical variants, e.g. (*bcuz*, *cause*)), we modify our evaluation metric from Section 4 to evaluate the *ranking* at different points, using Discounted Cumulative Gain (DCG@N: Jarvelin and Kekalainen (2002)):

$$\text{DCG}@N = rel_1 + \sum_{i=2}^{N} \frac{rel_i}{\log_2(i)}$$

where rel_i again represents the frequency of the OOV, but it can be gain (a positive number) or loss (a negative number), depending on whether the ith pair is correct or incorrect. Because we also expect correct pairs to be ranked higher than incorrect pairs, DCG@N takes both factors into account.

Given the generated pairs and the evaluation metric, we first consider three baselines: no re-ranking (i.e., the final ranking is that of the contextual similarity scores), and re-rankings of the pairs based on the frequencies of the OOVs in the Twitter corpus, and the IV unigram frequencies in the Google Web 1T corpus (Brants and Franz, 2006) to get less-noisy frequency estimates. We also compared a variety of re-rankings based on a number of string similarity measures that have been previously considered in normalisation work (reviewed in Section 2). We experiment with standard edit distance (Levenshtein, 1966), edit distance over double metaphone codes (phonetic edit distance: (Philips, 2000)), longest common subsequence ratio over the consonant edit distance of the paired words (hereafter, denoted as consonant edit distance: (Contractor et al., 2010)), and a string subsequence kernel (Lodhi et al., 2002).

In Figure 1, we present the DCG@N results for each of our ranking methods at different rank cut-offs. Ranking by OOV frequency is motivated by the assumption that lexical variants are frequently used by social media users. This is confirmed by our findings that lexical pairs like (*goin*, *going*) and (*nite*, *night*) are at the top of the ranking. However, many proper nouns and named entities are also used frequently and ranked at the top, mixed with lexical variants like (*Facebook*, *speech*) and (*Youtube*, *web*). In ranking by IV word frequency, we assume the lexical variants are usually derived from frequently-used IV equivalents, e.g. (*abou*, *about*). However, many less-frequent lexical variant types have high-frequency (IV) normalisations. For instance, the highest-frequency IV word *the* has more than 40 OOV lexical variants, such as *tthe* and *thhe*. These less-frequent types occupy the top positions, reducing the cumulative gain. Compared with these two baselines, ranking by default contextual similarity scores delivers promising results. It successfully ranks many more intuitive normalisation pairs at the top, such as (*2day*, *today*) and (*wknd*, *weekend*), but also ranks some incorrect pairs highly, such as (*needa*, *gotta*).

The string similarity-based methods perform better than our baselines in general. Through manual analysis, we found that standard edit distance ranking is fairly accurate for lexical variants with low edit distance to their standard forms, but fails to identify heavily-altered variants like (*tmrw*, *tomorrow*). Consonant edit distance is similar to standard edit distance, but places many longer words at the top of the ranking. Edit distance over double metaphone codes (phonetic edit distance) performs particularly well for lexical variants that include character repetitions — commonly used for emphasis on Twitter — because such repetitions do not typically alter the phonetic codes. Compared with the other methods, the string subsequence kernel delivers encouraging results. It measures common character subsequences of length n between (OOV, IV) pairs. Because it is computationally expensive to calculate similarity for larger n, we choose n=2, following Gouws et al. (2011). As N (the lexicon size cut-off) increases, the performance drops more slowly than the other methods. Although this method fails to rank heavily-altered variants such as (*4get*, *forget*) highly, it typically works well for longer words. Given that we focus on longer OOVs (specifically those longer than 4 characters), this ultimately isn't a great handicap.

6 Evaluation

Given the re-ranked pairs from Section 5, here we apply them to a token-level normalisation task using the normalisation dataset of Han and Baldwin (2011).

6.1 Metrics

We evaluate using the standard evaluation metrics of precision (P), recall (R) and F-score (F) as detailed below. We also consider the false alarm rate (FA) and word error rate (WER), also as shown below. FA measures the negative effects of applying normalisation; a good approach to normalisation should not (incorrectly) normalise tokens that are already in their standard form and do not require normalisation.[6] WER, like F-score, shows the overall benefits of normalisation, but unlike F-score, measures how many token-level edits are required for the output to be the same as the ground truth data. In general, dictionaries with a high F-score/low WER and low FA are preferable.

$$P = \frac{\text{\# correctly normalised tokens}}{\text{\# normalised tokens}}$$

$$R = \frac{\text{\# correctly normalised tokens}}{\text{\# tokens requiring normalisation}}$$

$$F = \frac{2PR}{P+R}$$

$$FA = \frac{\text{\# incorrectly normalised tokens}}{\text{\# normalised tokens}}$$

$$WER = \frac{\text{\# token edits needed after normalisation}}{\text{\# all tokens}}$$

6.2 Results

We select the three best re-ranking methods, and best cut-off N for each method, based on the highest DCG@N value for a given method over the development data, as presented in Figure 1. Namely, they are string subsequence kernel (S-dict, N=40,000), double metaphone edit distance (DM-dict, N=10,000) and default contextual similarity without re-ranking (C-dict, N=10,000).[7]

We evaluate each of the learned dictionaries in Table 3. We also compare each dictionary with the performance of the manually-constructed Internet slang dictionary (HB-dict) used by Han and Baldwin (2011), the small automatically-derived dictionary of Gouws et al. (2011) (GHM-dict), and combinations of the different dictionaries. In addition, the contribution of these dictionaries in hybrid normalisation approaches is also presented, in which we first normalise OOVs using a given dictionary (combined or otherwise), and then apply the normalisation method of Gouws et al. (2011) based on consonant edit distance (GHM-norm), or the approach of Han and Baldwin (2011) based on the summation of many unsupervised approaches (HB-norm), to the remaining OOVs. Results are shown in Table 3, and discussed below.

6.2.1 Individual Dictionaries

Overall, the individual dictionaries derived by the re-ranking methods (DM-dict, S-dict) perform bet-

[6] FA + P $\leq$ 1 because some lexical variants might be incorrectly normalised.

[7] We also experimented with combining ranks using Mean Reciprocal Rank. However, the combined rank didn't improve performance on the development data. We plan to explore other ranking aggregation methods in future work.

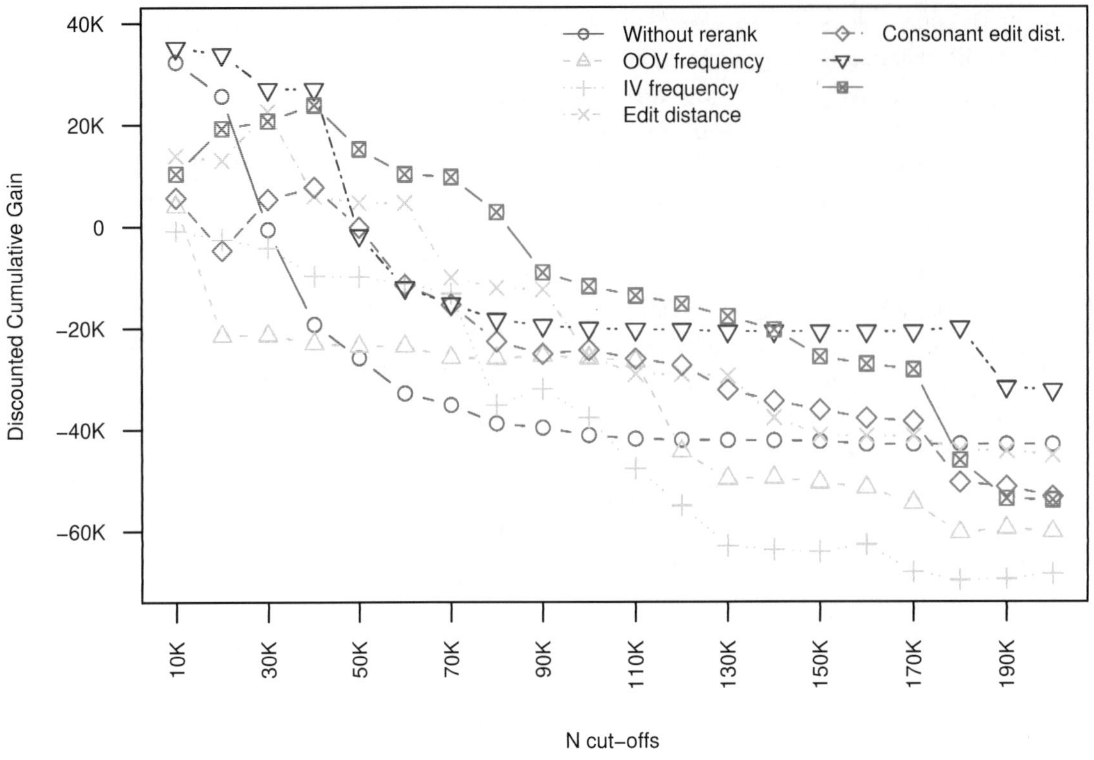

Figure 1: Re-ranking based on different string similarity methods.

ter than that based on contextual similarity (C-dict) in terms of precision and false alarm rate, indicating the importance of re-ranking. Even though C-dict delivers higher recall — indicating that many lexical variants are correctly normalised — this is offset by its high false alarm rate, which is particularly undesirable in normalisation. Because S-dict has better performance than DM-dict in terms of both F-score and WER, and a much lower false alarm rate than C-dict, subsequent results are presented using S-dict only.

Both HB-dict and GHM-dict achieve better than 90% precision with moderate recall. Compared to these methods, S-dict is not competitive in terms of either precision or recall. This result seems rather discouraging. However, considering that S-dict is an automatically-constructed dictionary targeting lexical variants of varying frequency, it is not surprising that the precision is worse than that of HB-dict — which is manually-constructed — and GHM-dict — which includes entries only for more-frequent OOVs for which distributional similarity is more accurate. Additionally, the recall of S-dict is hampered by the restriction on lexical variant token length of 4 characters.

6.2.2 Combined Dictionaries

Next we look to combining HB-dict, GHM-dict and S-dict. In combining the dictionaries, a given OOV word can be listed with different standard forms in different dictionaries. In such cases we use the following preferences for dictionaries — motivated by our confidence in the normalisation pairs of the dictionaries — to resolve conflicts: HB-dict > GHM-dict > S-dict.

When we combine dictionaries in the second section of Table 3, we find that they contain complementary information: in each case the recall and F-score are higher for the combined dictionary than any of the individual dictionaries. The combination of HB-dict+GHM-dict produces only a small improvement in terms of F-score over HB-dict (the better-performing dictionary) suggesting that, as claimed, HB-dict and GHM-dict share many frequent normalisation pairs. HB-dict+S-dict and GHM-dict+S-dict, on the other hand, improve sub-

Method	Precision	Recall	F-Score	False Alarm	Word Error Rate
C-dict	0.474	0.218	0.299	0.298	0.103
DM-dict	0.727	0.106	0.185	0.145	0.102
S-dict	0.700	0.179	0.285	0.162	0.097
HB-dict	0.915	0.435	0.590	0.048	0.066
GHM-dict	**0.982**	0.319	0.482	**0.000**	0.076
HB-dict+S-dict	0.840	0.601	0.701	0.090	0.052
GHM-dict+S-dict	0.863	0.498	0.632	0.072	0.061
HB-dict+GHM-dict	0.920	0.465	0.618	0.045	0.063
HB-dict+GHM-dict+S-dict	0.847	0.630	**0.723**	0.086	**0.049**
GHM-dict+GHM-norm	0.338	0.578	0.427	0.458	0.135
HB-dict+GHM-dict+S-dict+GHM-norm	0.406	0.715	0.518	0.468	0.124
HB-dict+HB-norm	0.515	0.771	0.618	0.332	0.081
HB-dict+GHM-dict+S-dict+HB-norm	0.527	**0.789**	0.632	0.332	0.079

Table 3: Normalisation results using our derived dictionaries (contextual similarity (C-dict); double metaphone rendering (DM-dict); string subsequence kernel scores (S-dict)), the dictionary of Gouws et al. (2011) (GHM-dict), the Internet slang dictionary (HB-dict) from Han and Baldwin (2011), and combinations of these dictionaries. In addition, we combine the dictionaries with the normalisation method of Gouws et al. (2011) (GHM-norm) and the combined unsupervised approach of Han and Baldwin (2011) (HB-norm).

stantially over HB-dict and GHM-dict, respectively, indicating that S-dict contains markedly different entries to both HB-dict and GHM-dict. The best F-score and WER are obtained using the combination of all three dictionaries, HB-dict+GHM-dict+S-dict. Furthermore, the difference between the results using HB-dict+GHM-dict+S-dict and HB-dict+GHM-dict is statistically significant ($p < 0.01$), based on the computationally-intensive Monte Carlo method of Yeh (2000), demonstrating the contribution of S-dict.

6.2.3 Hybrid Approaches

The methods of Gouws et al. (2011) (i.e. GHM-dict+GHM-norm) and Han and Baldwin (2011) (i.e. HB-dict+HB-norm) have lower precision and higher false alarm rates than the dictionary-based approaches; this is largely caused by lexical variant detection errors.[8] Using all dictionaries in combination with these methods — HB-dict+GHM-dict+S-dict+GHM-norm and HB-dict+GHM-dict+S-dict+HB-norm — gives some improvements, but the false alarm rates remain high. Despite the limitations of a pure dictionary-based approach to normalisation — discussed in Section 3.1 — the current best practical approach to normalisation is to use a lexicon, combining hand-built and automatically-learned normalisation dictionaries.

[8]Here we report results that do not assume perfect detection of lexical variants, unlike the original published results in each case.

Error type	OOV	Standard form	
		Dict.	Gold
(a) plurals	*playe*	*players*	*player*
(b) negation	*unlike*	*like*	*dislike*
(c) possessives	*anyones*	*anyone*	*anyone's*
(d) correct OOVs	*iphone*	*phone*	*iphone*
(e) test data errors	*durin*	*during*	*durin*
(f) ambiguity	*siging*	*signing*	*singing*

Table 4: Error types in the combined dictionary (HB-dict+GHM-dict+S-dict)

6.3 Discussion and Error Analysis

We first manually analyse the errors in the combined dictionary (HB-dict+GHM-dict+S-dict) and give examples of each error type in Table 4. The most frequent word errors are caused by slight morphological variations, including plural forms (a), negations (b), possessive cases (c), and OOVs that are correct and do not require normalisation (d). In addition, we also notice some missing annotations where lexical variants are skipped by human annotations but captured by our method (e). Ambiguity (f) definitely exists in longer OOVs, however, these cases do not appear to have a strong negative impact on the normalisation performance. An example of a remain-

Length cut-off (N)	#Variants	Precision	Recall ($\geq N$)	Recall (all)	False Alarm
$\geq$4	556	0.700	0.381	0.179	0.162
$\geq$5	382	0.814	0.471	0.152	0.122
$\geq$6	254	0.804	0.484	0.104	0.131
$\geq$7	138	0.793	0.471	0.055	0.122

Table 5: S-dict normalisation results broken down according to OOV token length. Recall is presented both over the subset of instances of length $\geq N$ in the data ("Recall ($\geq N$)"), and over the entirety of the dataset ("Recall (all)"); "#Variants" is the number of token instances of the indicated length in the test dataset.

ing miscellaneous error is *bday* "birthday", which is mis-normalised as *day*.

To further study the influence of OOV word length relative to the normalisation performance, we conduct a fine-grained analysis of the performance of the derived dictionary (S-dict) in Table 5, broken down across different OOV word lengths. The results generally support our hypothesis that our method works better for longer OOV words. The derived dictionary is much more reliable for longer tokens (length 5, 6, and 7 characters) in terms of precision and false alarm. Although the recall is relatively modest, in the future we intend to improve recall by mining more normalisation pairs from larger collections of microblog data.

7 Conclusions and Future Work

In this paper, we describe a method for automatically constructing a normalisation dictionary that supports normalisation of microblog text through direct substitution of lexical variants with their standard forms. After investigating the impact of different distributional and string similarity methods on the quality of the dictionary, we present experimental results on a standard dataset showing that our proposed methods acquire high quality (lexical variant, standard form) pairs, with reasonable coverage, and achieve state-of-the-art end-to-end lexical normalisation performance on a real-world token-level task. Furthermore, this dictionary-lookup method combines the detection and normalisation of lexical variants into a simple, lightweight solution which is suitable for processing of high-volume microblog feeds.

In the future, we intend to improve our dictionary by leveraging the constantly-growing volume of microblog data, and considering alternative ways to combine distributional and string similarity. In addition to direct evaluation, we also want to explore the benefits of applying normalisation for downstream social media text processing applications, e.g. event detection.

Acknowledgements

We would like to thank the three anonymous reviewers for their insightful comments, and Stephan Gouws for kindly sharing his data and discussing his work.

NICTA is funded by the Australian government as represented by Department of Broadband, Communication and Digital Economy, and the Australian Research Council through the ICT centre of Excellence programme.

References

AiTi Aw, Min Zhang, Juan Xiao, and Jian Su. 2006. A phrase-based statistical model for SMS text normalization. In *Proceedings of COLING/ACL 2006*, pages 33–40, Sydney, Australia.

Edward Benson, Aria Haghighi, and Regina Barzilay. 2011. Event discovery in social media feeds. In *Proceedings of the 49th Annual Meeting of the Association for Computational Linguistics: Human Language Technologies (ACL-HLT 2011)*, pages 389–398, Portland, Oregon, USA.

Thorsten Brants and Alex Franz. 2006. Web 1T 5-gram Version 1.

Eric Brill and Robert C. Moore. 2000. An improved error model for noisy channel spelling correction. In *Proceedings of the 38th Annual Meeting of the Association for Computational Linguistics*, pages 286–293, Hong Kong.

Monojit Choudhury, Rahul Saraf, Vijit Jain, Animesh Mukherjee, Sudeshna Sarkar, and Anupam Basu. 2007. Investigation and modeling of the structure of texting language. *International Journal on Document Analysis and Recognition*, 10:157–174.

Danish Contractor, Tanveer A. Faruquie, and L. Venkata Subramaniam. 2010. Unsupervised cleansing of noisy text. In *Proceedings of the 23rd International Conference on Computational Linguistics (COLING 2010)*, pages 189–196, Beijing, China.

Paul Cook and Suzanne Stevenson. 2009. An unsupervised model for text message normalization. In *CALC '09: Proceedings of the Workshop on Computational Approaches to Linguistic Creativity*, pages 71–78, Boulder, USA.

Jennifer Foster, Özlem Çetinoglu, Joachim Wagner, Joseph L. Roux, Stephen Hogan, Joakim Nivre, Deirdre Hogan, and Josef van Genabith. 2011. #hardtoparse: POS Tagging and Parsing the Twitterverse. In *Analyzing Microtext: Papers from the 2011 AAAI Workshop*, volume WS-11-05 of *AAAI Workshops*, pages 20–25, San Francisco, CA, USA.

Kevin Gimpel, Nathan Schneider, Brendan O'Connor, Dipanjan Das, Daniel Mills, Jacob Eisenstein, Michael Heilman, Dani Yogatama, Jeffrey Flanigan, and Noah A. Smith. 2011. Part-of-speech tagging for Twitter: Annotation, features, and experiments. In *Proceedings of the 49th Annual Meeting of the Association for Computational Linguistics: Human Language Technologies (ACL-HLT 2011)*, pages 42–47, Portland, Oregon, USA.

Roberto González-Ibáñez, Smaranda Muresan, and Nina Wacholder. 2011. Identifying sarcasm in Twitter: a closer look. In *Proceedings of the 49th Annual Meeting of the Association for Computational Linguistics: Human Language Technologies (ACL-HLT 2011)*, pages 581–586, Portland, Oregon, USA.

Stephan Gouws, Dirk Hovy, and Donald Metzler. 2011. Unsupervised mining of lexical variants from noisy text. In *Proceedings of the First workshop on Unsupervised Learning in NLP*, pages 82–90, Edinburgh, Scotland, UK.

Bo Han and Timothy Baldwin. 2011. Lexical normalisation of short text messages: Makn sens a #twitter. In *Proceedings of the 49th Annual Meeting of the Association for Computational Linguistics: Human Language Technologies (ACL-HLT 2011)*, pages 368–378, Portland, Oregon, USA.

K. Jarvelin and J. Kekalainen. 2002. Cumulated gain-based evaluation of IR techniques. *ACM Transactions on Information Systems*, 20(4).

Long Jiang, Mo Yu, Ming Zhou, Xiaohua Liu, and Tiejun Zhao. 2011. Target-dependent Twitter sentiment classification. In *Proceedings of the 49th Annual Meeting of the Association for Computational Linguistics: Human Language Technologies (ACL-HLT 2011)*, pages 151–160, Portland, Oregon, USA.

Joseph Kaufmann and Jugal Kalita. 2010. Syntactic normalization of Twitter messages. In *International Conference on Natural Language Processing*, Kharagpur, India.

S. Kullback and R. A. Leibler. 1951. On information and sufficiency. *Annals of Mathematical Statistics*, 22:49–86.

John D. Lafferty, Andrew McCallum, and Fernando C. N. Pereira. 2001. Conditional random fields: Probabilistic models for segmenting and labeling sequence data. In *Proceedings of the Eighteenth International Conference on Machine Learning*, pages 282–289, San Francisco, CA, USA.

Vladimir I. Levenshtein. 1966. Binary codes capable of correcting deletions, insertions, and reversals. *Soviet Physics Doklady*, 10:707–710.

Mu Li, Yang Zhang, Muhua Zhu, and Ming Zhou. 2006. Exploring distributional similarity based models for query spelling correction. In *Proceedings of COLING/ACL 2006*, pages 1025–1032, Sydney, Australia.

Jianhua Lin. 1991. Divergence measures based on the shannon entropy. *IEEE Transactions on Information Theory*, 37(1):145–151.

Dekang Lin. 1998. Automatic retrieval and clustering of similar words. In *Proceedings of the 36th Annual Meeting of the ACL and 17th International Conference on Computational Linguistics (COLING/ACL-98)*, pages 768–774, Montreal, Quebec, Canada.

Fei Liu, Fuliang Weng, Bingqing Wang, and Yang Liu. 2011a. Insertion, deletion, or substitution? normalizing text messages without pre-categorization nor supervision. In *Proceedings of the 49th Annual Meeting of the Association for Computational Linguistics: Human Language Technologies (ACL-HLT 2011)*, pages 71–76, Portland, Oregon, USA.

Xiaohua Liu, Shaodian Zhang, Furu Wei, and Ming Zhou. 2011b. Recognizing named entities in tweets. In *Proceedings of the 49th Annual Meeting of the Association for Computational Linguistics: Human Language Technologies (ACL-HLT 2011)*, pages 359–367, Portland, Oregon, USA.

Fei Liu, Fuliang Weng, and Xiao Jiang. 2012. A broad-coverage normalization system for social media language. In *Proceedings of the 50th Annual Meeting of the Association for Computational Linguistics (ACL 2012)*, Jeju, Republic of Korea.

Huma Lodhi, Craig Saunders, John Shawe-Taylor, Nello Cristianini, and Chris Watkins. 2002. Text classification using string kernels. *J. Mach. Learn. Res.*, 2:419–444.

Marco Lui and Timothy Baldwin. 2011. Cross-domain feature selection for language identification. In *Proceedings of the 5th International Joint Conference on Natural Language Processing (IJCNLP 2011)*, pages 553–561, Chiang Mai, Thailand.

Brendan O'Connor, Michel Krieger, and David Ahn. 2010. TweetMotif: Exploratory search and topic summarization for Twitter. In *Proceedings of the 4th International Conference on Weblogs and Social Media (ICWSM 2010)*, pages 384–385, Washington, USA.

Lawrence Philips. 2000. The double metaphone search algorithm. *C/C++ Users Journal*, 18:38–43.

Lawrence R. Rabiner. 1989. A tutorial on hidden Markov models and selected applications in speech recognition. *Proceedings of the IEEE*, 77(2):257–286.

Alan Ritter, Colin Cherry, and Bill Dolan. 2010. Unsupervised modeling of Twitter conversations. In *Proceedings of Human Language Technologies: The 11th Annual Conference of the North American Chapter of the Association for Computational Linguistics (NAACL-HLT 2010)*, pages 172–180, Los Angeles, USA.

Alan Ritter, Sam Clark, Mausam, and Oren Etzioni. 2011. Named entity recognition in tweets: An experimental study. In *Proceedings of the 2011 Conference on Empirical Methods in Natural Language Processing (EMNLP 2011)*, pages 1524–1534, Edinburgh, Scotland, UK.

Takeshi Sakaki, Makoto Okazaki, and Yutaka Matsuo. 2010. Earthquake shakes Twitter users: real-time event detection by social sensors. In *Proceedings of the 19th International Conference on the World Wide Web (WWW 2010)*, pages 851–860, Raleigh, North Carolina, USA.

Crispin Thurlow. 2003. Generation txt? The sociolinguistics of young people's text-messaging. *Discourse Analysis Online*, 1(1).

Kristina Toutanova and Robert C. Moore. 2002. Pronunciation modeling for improved spelling correction. In *Proceedings of the 40th Annual Meeting of the ACL and 3rd Annual Meeting of the NAACL (ACL-02)*, pages 144–151, Philadelphia, USA.

Official Blog Twitter. 2011. 200 million tweets per day. Retrived at August 17th, 2011.

Jianshu Weng and Bu-Sung Lee. 2011. Event detection in Twitter. In *Proceedings of the 5th International Conference on Weblogs and Social Media (ICWSM 2011)*, Barcelona, Spain.

Zhenzhen Xue, Dawei Yin, and Brian D. Davison. 2011. Normalizing microtext. In *Proceedings of the AAAI-11 Workshop on Analyzing Microtext*, pages 74–79, San Francisco, USA.

Alexander Yeh. 2000. More accurate tests for the statistical significance of result differences. In *Proceedings of the 23rd International Conference on Computational Linguistics (COLING 2010)*, pages 947–953, Saarbrücken, Germany.

Unsupervised PCFG Induction for Grounded Language Learning with Highly Ambiguous Supervision

Joohyun Kim **Raymond J. Mooney**
Department of Computer Science
The University of Texas at Austin
1616 Guadalupe, Suite 2.408
Austin, TX 78701, USA
{scimitar,mooney}@cs.utexas.edu

Abstract

"Grounded" language learning employs training data in the form of sentences paired with relevant but ambiguous perceptual contexts. Börschinger et al. (2011) introduced an approach to grounded language learning based on unsupervised PCFG induction. Their approach works well when each sentence potentially refers to one of a small set of possible meanings, such as in the sportscasting task. However, it does not scale to problems with a large set of potential meanings for each sentence, such as the navigation instruction following task studied by Chen and Mooney (2011). This paper presents an enhancement of the PCFG approach that scales to such problems with highly-ambiguous supervision. Experimental results on the navigation task demonstrates the effectiveness of our approach.

1 Introduction

The ultimate goal of "grounded" language learning is to develop computational systems that can acquire language more like a human child. Given only supervision in the form of sentences paired with relevant but ambiguous perceptual contexts, a system should learn to interpret and/or generate language describing situations and events in the world. For example, systems have learned to commentate simulated robot soccer games by learning from sample sportscasts (Chen and Mooney, 2008; Liang et al., 2009; Börschinger et al., 2011), or understand navigation instructions by learning from action traces produced when following the directions (Chen and Mooney, 2011; Tellex et al., 2011).

Börschinger et al. (2011) recently introduced an approach to grounded language learning using unsupervised induction of *probabilistic context free grammars* (PCFGs) to learn from ambiguous contextual supervision. Their approach first constructs a large set of production rules from sentences paired with descriptions of their ambiguous context, and then trains the parameters of this grammar using EM. Parsing a novel sentence with this grammar gives a parse tree which contains the formal *meaning representation* (MR) for this sentence. This approach works quite well on the sportscasting task originally introduced by Chen and Mooney (2008). In this task, each sentence in a natural-language commentary describing activity in a simulated robot soccer game is paired with the small set of actions observed within the past 5 seconds, one of which is usually described by the sentence. Even with this low level of ambiguity in a constrained domain, their method constructs a PCFG with about 33,000 productions. More fundamentally, their approach is restricted to a finite set of potential meaning representations, and the grammar size grows at least linearly with the number of possible MRs, which in turn is inevitably exponential in the number of objects and actions in the domain.

The navigation task studied by Chen and Mooney (2011) provides much more ambiguous supervision. In this task, each instructional sentence is paired with a formal *landmarks plan* (represented as a large graph) that includes a full description of the observed actions and world-states that result when someone follows this instruction. An instruction generally refers to a subgraph of this large graph. Therefore, there are a combinatorial number of possible meanings to which a given sentence can refer.

Chen and Mooney (2011) circumvent this combinatorial problem by never explicitly enumerating the exponential number of potential meanings for each sentence. Their system first induces a semantic lexicon that maps words and short phrases to formal representations of actions and objects in the world. This lexicon is learned by finding words and phrases whose occurrence highly correlates with specific observed actions and objects in the simulated environment when executing the corresponding instruction. This learned lexicon is then used to directly infer a formal MR for observed instructional sentences using a greedy covering algorithm. These inferred MRs are then used to train a supervised semantic parser capable of mapping novel sentences to their formal meanings.

We present a novel enhancement of Börschinger et al.'s PCFG approach that uses Chen and Mooney's lexicon learner to avoid a combinatorial explosion in the number of productions. The learned lexicon is first used to build a hierarchy of semantic *lexemes* (i.e. lexicon entries) called the *Lexeme Hierarchy Graph* (LHG) for each ambiguous landmarks plan in the training data. The intuition behind utilizing an LHG is that the MR for each lexeme constitutes a semantic concept that corresponds to some natural-language (NL) word or phrase. Therefore, the LHG represents how complex semantic concepts are composed of simpler semantic concepts and ultimately connected to NL words and phrases. Börschinger et al.'s approach instead produces NL groundings at the level of atomic MR constituents, which causes an explosion in the number of PCFG productions for complex MR languages. We estimated that Börschinger et al.'s approach would require more than 20! ($> 10^{18}$) productions for our navigation problem.[1] On the other hand, our method, which uses correspondences from the LHG at the semantic concept level, constructs a more focused PCFG of tractable size. It then extracts the MR for a novel sentence from the most-probable parse tree for the resulting PCFG. Our approach can produce a large, combinatorial number of different MRs for a wide range of novel sentences by composing relevant MR components from the resulting parse tree, whereas Börschinger et al.'s approach is only able to output MRs that are explicitly included as a nonterminals in the original learned PCFG.

The remainder of the paper is organized as follows. Section 2 reviews Börschinger et al.'s PCFG approach as well as the navigation task and data. Section 3 describes our enhanced PCFG approach and Section 4 presents an experimental evaluation of it. Then, Section 5 discusses the unique aspects of our approach and Section 6 describes additional related work. Finally, Section 7 presents future research directions and Section 8 gives our conclusions.

2 Background

2.1 Existing PCFG Approach

Our approach extends that of Börschinger et al. (2011), which in turn was inspired by a series of previous techniques (Lu et al., 2008; Liang et al., 2009; Kim and Mooney, 2010) following the idea of constructing correspondences between NL and MR in a single probabilistic generative framework. Particularly, their approach automatically constructs a PCFG that generates NL sentences from MRs, which indicates how atomic MR constituents are probabilistically related to NL words. The nonterminals in the grammar correspond to complete MRs, MR constituents, and NL phrases. The nonterminal for a composite MR generates each of its MR constituents, and each atomic MR, x, generates an NL phrase, $Phrase_x$. Each $Phrase_x$ then generates a sequence of $Word_x$'s for describing x, and each $Word_x$ can generate each possible word in the natural language. This allows the system to learn the words and phrases used to describe each atomic MR by properly weighting these rules. Figure 1 shows one possible derivation tree for a sample NL-MR pair and the PCFG rules that are constructed for it. Once a set of productions are assembled, their probabilities are learned using the Inside-Outside algorithm. Computing the most probable parse for a novel sentence with the trained PCFG provides its

[1] The corpus contains quite a few examples with landmarks plans containing more than 20 actions. This results in at least 20! permutations representing possible alignments between actions and NL words.

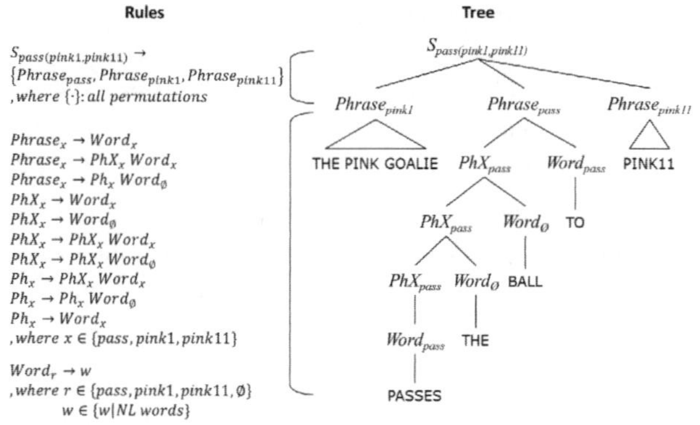

Figure 1: Derivation tree for the NL/MR pair: THE PINK GOALIE PASSES THE BALL TO PINK11 / $pass(pink1, pink11)$. Left side shows PCFG rules that are added for each stage (full MR to atomic MRs, and atomic MRs to NL words).

preferred MR interpretation in the topmost nonterminal.

Unfortunately, as discussed earlier, this approach only works for finite MR languages, and the grammar becomes intractably large even for finite but complex MRs. It effectively assumes that MRs are fairly small and includes every possible MR constituent as a nonterminal in the PCFG. This is not tractable for more complex MRs. Therefore, our extension incorporates a learned lexicon to constrain the space of productions, thereby making the size of the PCFG tractable for complex MRs, and even giving it the ability to handle infinite MR languages. Moreover, when processing novel sentences, our approach can produce a large space of novel MRs that were not anticipated during training, which is not the case for Börschinger et al.'s approach.

2.2 Navigation Task and Dataset

We employ the task and data introduced by Chen and Mooney (2011) whose goal is to interpret and follow NL navigation instructions in a virtual world. Figure 2 shows a sample execution path in a particular virtual world. The challenge is learning to perform this task by simply observing humans following instructions. Formally, given training data of the form $\{(e_1, a_1, w_1), \ldots, (e_n, a_n, w_n)\}$, where e_i is an NL instruction, a_i is an observed action sequence, and w_i is the current world state (patterns of floors and walls, positions of any objects, etc.), we want to produce the correct actions a_j for a novel (e_j, w_j).

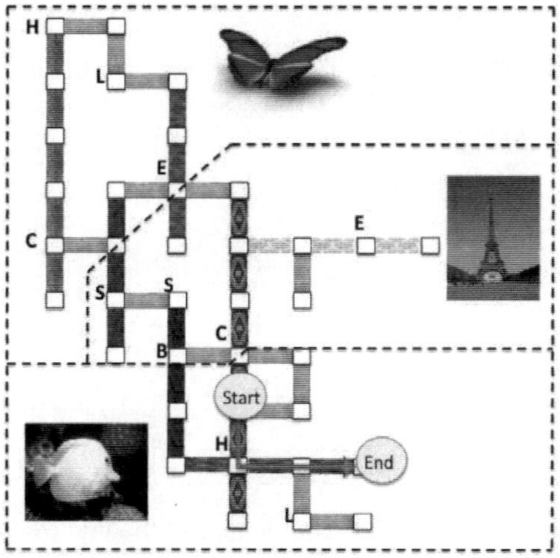

Figure 2: Sample virtual world from Chen and Mooney (2011) of interconnecting hallways with different floor and wall patterns and objects indicated by letters (e.g. "H" for hatrack).

Instruction:	"at the easel, go left and then take a right onto the blue path at the corner"
Landmarks plan:	**Travel** (steps: 1) , **Verify (at: EASEL** , side: CONCRETE HALLWAY) , **Turn (LEFT)** , Verify (front: CONCRETE HALLWAY) , **Travel** (steps: 1) , **Verify** (side: BLUE HALLWAY , **front: WALL**) , **Turn (RIGHT)** , **Verify** (back: WALL , **front: BLUE HALLWAY** , front: CHAIR , front: HATRACK , left: WALL , right: EASEL)

Figure 3: Sample instruction with its constructed landmarks plan, components in bold compose the correct plan.

In order to learn, their system infers the intended formal plan p_i (the MR for a sentence) which produced the action sequence a_i from the instruction e_i. However, there is a large space of possible plans for any given action sequence. Chen and Mooney first construct a formal *landmarks plan*, c_i, for each a_i, which is a graph representing the context of every action and the world-state encountered during the execution of the sequence. The correct plan MR, p_i, is assumed to be a subgraph of c_i, and this causes a combinatorial matching problem between e_i and c_i in order to learn the correct meaning of e_i among all the possible subgraphs of c_i. The landmarks and correct plans for a sample instruction are shown in Figure 3, illustrating the complexity of the MRs.

Instead of directly solving the combinatorial correspondence problem, they first learn a semantic lex-

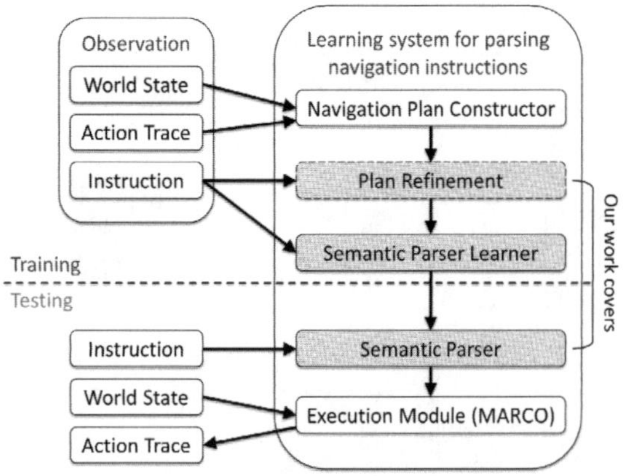

Figure 4: An overview of Chen and Mooney (2011)'s system. Our method replaces the plan refinement and semantic parser parts.

icon that maps words and short phrases to small subgraphs representing their inferred meanings from the (e_i, c_i) pairs. The lexicon is learned by evaluating pairs of n-grams, w_j, and MR graphs, m_j, and scoring them based on how much more likely m_j is a subgraph of the context c_i when w occurs in the corresponding instruction e_i. This process is similar to other "cross-situational" approaches to learning word meanings (Siskind, 1996; Thompson and Mooney, 2003). Then, a *plan refinement* step estimates p_i from c_i by greedily selecting high-scoring lexemes of the form (w_j, m_j) whose words and phrases (w_j) cover the instruction e_i and introduce components (m_j) from the landmarks plan c_i. The refined plans are used to construct supervised training data (e_i, p_i) for a supervised semantic-parser learner. The trained semantic parser can parse a novel instruction into a formal plan, which is finally executed for end-to-end evaluation. Figure 4 illustrates the overall system.

As this figure indicates, our new PCFG method replaces the plan refinement and semantic parser components in their system with a unified model that both disambiguates the training data and learns a semantic parser. We use the landmarks plans and the learned lexicon produced by Chen and Mooney (2011) as inputs to our system.[2]

[2]In our experiments, we used the top 1,000 lexemes learned by Chen and Mooney (2011).

3 Our PCFG Approach

Like Börschinger et al. (2011), our approach learns a semantic parser directly from ambiguous supervision, specifically NL instructions paired with their complete landmarks plans as context. Our method incorporates the semantic lexemes as building blocks to find correspondences between NL words and semantic concepts represented by the lexeme MRs, instead of building connections between NL words and every possible MR constituent as in Börschinger et al.'s approach. Particularly, we utilize the hierarchical subgraph relationships between the MRs in the learned semantic lexicon to produce a smaller, more focused set of PCFG rules.[3] The intuition behind our approach is analogous to the hierarchical relations between nonterminals in syntactic parsing, where higher-level categories such as S, VP, or NP are further divided into smaller categories such as V, N, or Det, thereby forming a hierarchical structure. Inspired by this idea, we introduce a directed acyclic graph called the Lexeme Hierarchy Graph (LHG) which represents the hierarchical relationships between lexeme MRs. Since complex lexeme MRs represent complicated semantic concepts while simple MRs represent simple concepts, it is natural to construct a hierarchy amongst them. The LHGs for all of the training examples are used to construct production rules for the PCFG, which are then parametrized using EM. Finally, a novel sentence is semantically parsed by computing its most-probable parse using the trained PCFG, and then its MR is extracted from the resulting parse tree.

3.1 Constructing a Lexeme Hierarchy Graph

An LHG represents the hierarchy of lexical meanings relevant to a particular training instance by encoding the subgraph relations between the MRs of relevant lexemes. Algorithm 1 describes how an LHG is constructed for an ambiguous training pair of a sentence and its corresponding context, (e_i, c_i). First, we obtain all relevant lexemes (w_j^i, m_j^i) in the lexicon L, where the MR m_j^i is a subgraph of the context c_i (denoted as $m_j^i \subset c_i$). These lexemes are

[3]The total number of PCFG rules constructed for our navigation training sets is about 18,000, while Börschinger et al.'s method produces 33,000 rules for the much simpler sportscasting domain.

Algorithm 1 LEXEME HIERARCHY GRAPH (LHG)

Input: Training instance (e_i, c_i), Lexicon L
Output: Lexeme hierarchy graph for (e_i, c_i)

Find relevant lexemes $(w_1^i, m_1^i), \ldots, (w_n^i, m_n^i)$
  s.t. $m_j^i \subset c_i$
Create a starting node T; $MR(T) \leftarrow c_i$
for all m_j^i in the descending order of size **do**
  Create a node T_j^i; $MR(T_j^i) \leftarrow m_j^i$
  PLACELEXEME(T_j^i,T)
end for

procedure PLACELEXEME(T',T)
  for all children T_j of T **do**
    if $MR(T') \subset MR(T_j)$ **then**
      PLACELEXEME(T',T_j)
    end if
  end for
  if T' was not placed under any child T_j **then**
    Add T' as child of T
  end if
end procedure

sorted in descending order based on the number of nodes in their MRs m_j^i. Then, after setting the context c_i as the MR of the root node ($MR(T) \leftarrow c_i$), lexemes are inserted, in order, into the graph to create a hierarchy of MRs, where each child's MR is a subgraph of the MR of each of its parents. Figure 5 illustrates a sample construction of an LHG for the following landmarks plan (c_i):

```
Turn(RIGHT),
Verify(side:HATRACK, front:SOFA),
Travel(steps:3),
Verify(at:EASEL)
```

The initial LHG may contain nodes with too many children. This is a problem, because when we subsequently extract PCFG rules, we need to add a production for every k-permutation of the children of each node (see Section 3.2). To reduce the branching factor in the LHG, we introduce *pseudo-lexeme* nodes by repeatedly combining the two most similar children of each node. Pseudocode for the process is shown in Algorithm 2. The MR for a pseudo-lexeme is the minimal graph, m', that is a supergraph of both of the lexeme MRs that it combines. The pair of

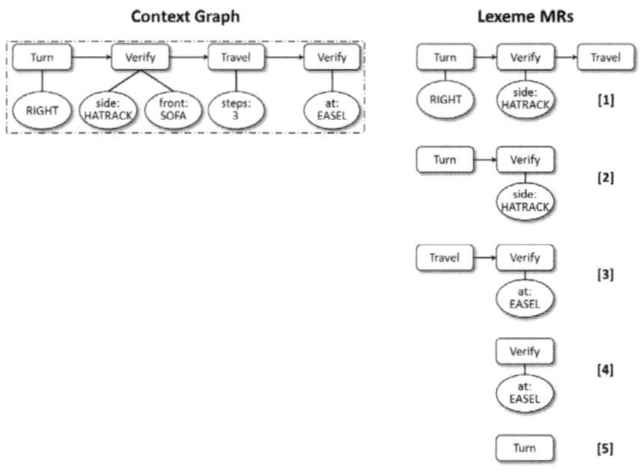

(a) All relevant lexemes are obtained for the training example and ordered by the number of nodes in their MR.

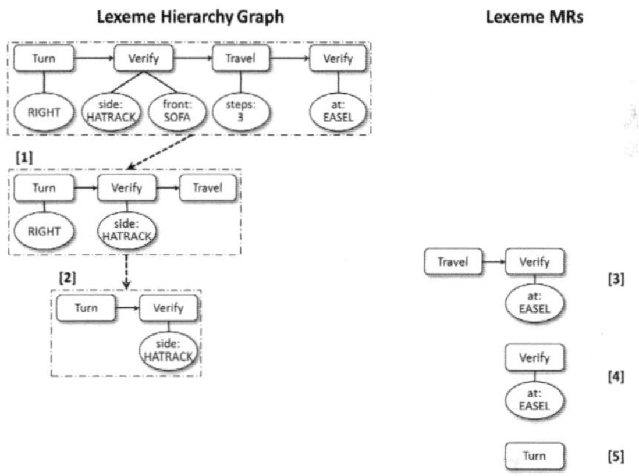

(b) Lexeme MR [1] is added as a child of the top node. MR [2] is a subgraph of [1], so it is added as its child.

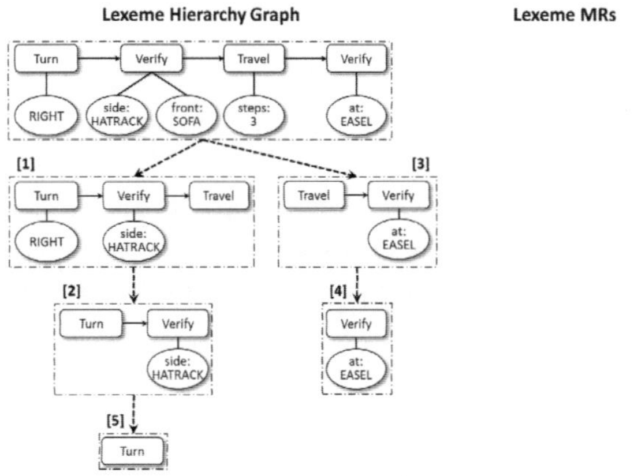

(c) MR [3] is not a subgraph of [1] or [2], so it is added as a child of the root. MR [4] is added under [3], and MR [5] is recursively filtered down and added under [2].

Figure 5: Sample LHG construction.

Algorithm 2 ADDING PSEUDO LEXEMES TO LHG

Input: LHG with root T
Output: LHG with pseudo lexemes added
procedure RECONSTRUCTLHG(T)
  repeat
    $((T_i, T_j), m') \leftarrow$ pick the most similar pair (T_i, T_j) of children of T and the minimal extension m' s.t. $MR(T_i) \subset m'$, $MR(T_j) \subset m'$, $m' \subset MR(T)$
    Add child T' of T; $MR(T') \leftarrow m'$
    Move T_i and T_j to be children of T'
  until There are no more pairs to combine
  for all non-leaf children T_k of T **do**
    RECONSTRUCTLHG(T_k)
  end for
end procedure

most similar children, (m_i, m_j), is determined by measuring the fraction of the nodes in m_i and m_j that overlap with their minimum extension m' and is calculated as follows:

$$Sim(m_i, m_j, m') = \frac{|m_i| + |m_j|}{2\,|m'|}$$

where $|m|$ is the number of nodes in the MR m. Adding pseudo-lexemes also has another advantage. They can be considered to be higher-level semantic concepts composed of two or more sub-concepts. These higher-level concepts will likely occur in other training examples as well, which allows for more flexible interpretations. For example, assuming the rule $A \rightarrow BCD$ is constructed from an LHG, we will introduce a pseudo lexeme E and build two rules $A \rightarrow BE$ and $E \rightarrow CD$. It is likely that E also occurs in another rule constructed from other training examples such as $E \rightarrow FG$. This increases the model's expressive power by supporting additional derivations such as $A \rightarrow^* BFG$, providing more flexibility when parsing novel NL sentences.

3.2 Composing PCFG Rules

The next step composes PCFG rules from the LHGs and is summarized in Figure 6. We basically follow the scheme of Börschinger et al. (2011), but instead of generating NL words from each atomic MR, words are generated from each lexeme MR, and smaller lexeme MRs are generated from more complex ones as given by the LHGs. A nonterminal S_m is generated for the MR, m, of each LHG node. Then, for every LHG node, T, with MR, m, we add rules of the form $S_m \rightarrow S_{m_i} ... S_{m_j}$, where the RHS is some k-permutation of the nonterminals for the MRs of the children of node T. Börschinger et al. assume that every atomic MR generates at least one NL word. However, since we do not know which subgraph of the overall context (i.e. c_i, the MR of the root node) conveys the intended plan and is therefore expressed in the NL instruction, we must allow each ordered subset of the children of a node (i.e. each k-permutation) to be a possible generation.

$Root \rightarrow S_c, \quad \forall c \in contexts$

$\forall$*non-leaf node and its MR* m
$S_m \rightarrow \{S_{m_1}, \ldots, S_{m_n}\},$
  where $m_1, \ldots, m_n$: *children lexeme MR of* m,
    $\{\cdot\}$: *all* k-*permutations for* $k = 1, \ldots, n$

$\forall$*lexeme MR* m
$S_m \rightarrow Phrase_m$
$Phrase_m \rightarrow Word_m$
$Phrase_m \rightarrow PhX_m\ Word_m$
$Phrase_m \rightarrow Ph_m\ Word_\emptyset$
$PhX_m \rightarrow Word_m$
$PhX_m \rightarrow Word_\emptyset$
$PhX_m \rightarrow PhX_m\ Word_m$
$PhX_m \rightarrow PhX_m\ Word_\emptyset$
$Ph_m \rightarrow PhX_m\ Word_m$
$Ph_m \rightarrow Ph_m\ Word_\emptyset$
$Ph_m \rightarrow Word_m$
$Word_m \rightarrow s, \quad \forall s \text{ s.t. } (s, m) \in lexicon\ L$
$Word_m \rightarrow w, \quad \forall word\ w \in s \text{ s.t. } (s, m) \in lexicon\ L$

$Word_\emptyset \rightarrow w, \quad \forall word\ w \in NLs$

Figure 6: Summary of the rule generation process. *NLs* refer to the set of NL words in the corpus. Lexeme rules come from the schemata of Börschinger et al. (2011), and allow every lexeme MR to generate one or more NL words. Note that pseudo-lexeme nodes do not produce NL words.

The rest of the process more closely follows Börschinger et al.'s. Every MR, m, of a lexeme node[4] generates a rule $S_m \rightarrow Phrase_m$, and every $Phrase_m$ generates a sequence of NL words, including one or more "content words" ($Word_m$) for expressing m and zero or more "extraneous" words ($Word_\emptyset$). While Börschinger et al. have $Word_m$ generate all possible NL words (each of which are

[4]We exclude pseudo-lexeme nodes in this process, because they should only generate words through generating lexemes.

subsequently weighted by EM training), in our approach, each $Word_m$ only produces the NL phrase associated with m in the lexicon, or individual words that appear in this phrase. The words not covered by $Word_m$ also can be generated by $Word_\emptyset$ which has rules for every word. Ph_m and PhX_m ensure that $Phrase_m$ produces at least one $Word_m$, where PhX_m indicates that one or more $Word_m$'s have already been generated, and Ph_m indicates that no $Word_m$ has yet been generated.

3.3 Parsing Novel NL Sentences

To learn the parameters of the resulting PCFG, we use the Inside-Outside algorithm.[5] Then, the standard probabilistic CKY algorithm is used to produce the most probable parse for novel NL sentences (Jurafsky and Martin, 2000).

Börschinger et al. (2011) simply read the MR, m, for a sentence off the top S_m nonterminal of the most probable parse tree. However, in our approach, the correct MR is constructed by properly composing the appropriate subset of lexeme MRs from the most-probable parse tree. This allows the system to produce a wide variety of novel MRs for novel sentences, as long as the correct MR is a subgraph of the complete context (c_i) for at least one of the training sentences.

First, the parse tree is pruned to remove all subtrees starting with $Phrase_x$ nodes. This leaves a tree consisting of the $Root$ and a set of S_m nodes. The pruned subtrees only concern generating NL words and phrases from the selected MRs. The remaining tree shows which MR constituents were selected from the available context, from which the sentence is then generated. Each leaf in the pruned tree represents an MR constituent that was used to generate a phrase in the sentence. These are the constituents we want to assemble and compose into a final MR for the sentence.

Algorithm 3 describes the procedure for extracting the final MR from the pruned parse tree. Figure 7 graphically depicts a sample trace of this algorithm. The algorithm recursively traverses the parse tree. When a leaf-node is reached, it marks all of the nodes in its MR. After traversing all of its children,

Algorithm 3 CONSTRUCT PARSED MR RESULT

```
Input: Parse tree T for input NL, e, with all
  Phrase_x subtrees removed.
Output: Semantic parse MR, m, for e
procedure OBTAINPARSEDOUTPUT(T)
  if T is a leaf then
    return MR(T) with all its nodes marked
  end if
  for all children T_i of T do
    m_i ← OBTAINPARSEDOUTPUT(T_i)
    Mark the nodes in MR(T) corresponding
      to the marked nodes in m_i
  end for
  if T is not the root then
    return MR(T)
  end if
  return MR(T) with unmarked nodes removed
end procedure
```

a node in the MR for the current parse-tree node is marked iff its corresponding node in any of the children's MRs were marked. The final output is the MR constructed by removing all of the unmarked nodes from the MR for the root node.

4 Experimental Evaluation

For evaluation, we used the same data and methodology as Chen and Mooney (2011). Please see their paper for more details.

4.1 Data

We used the English instructions and follower data collected by MacMahon et al. (2006).[6] This data contains 706 route instructions for three virtual worlds. The instructions were produced by six instructors for 126 unique starting and ending location pairs spread evenly across the three worlds, and there were 1 to 15 human followers for each instruction who executed an average of 10.4 actions per instruction. Each instruction is a paragraph consisting of an average of 5.0 sentences, each containing an average of 7.8 words. Chen and Mooney constructed the additional single-sentence corpus by matching each sentence with the majority of human

[5]We used the implementation available at http://web.science.mq.edu.au/~mjohnson/Software.htm which was also used by Börschinger et al. (2011).

[6]Available at http://www.cs.utexas.edu/users/ml/clamp/navigation/

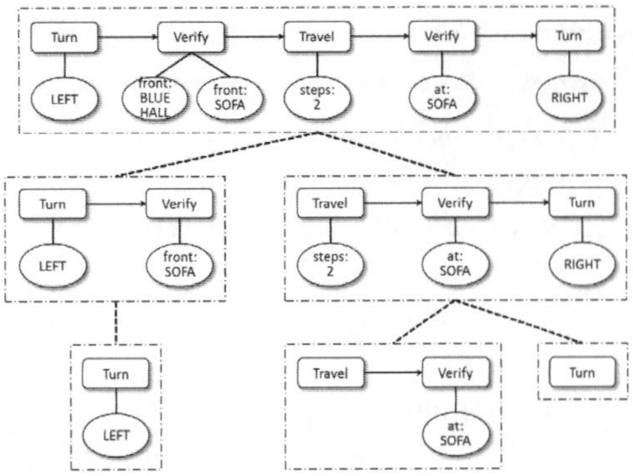

(a) Pruned parse tree showing only MRs for S_m nodes

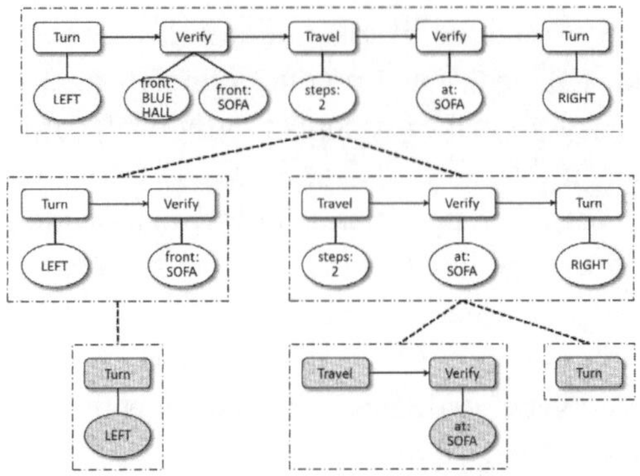

(b) Leaf nodes have all their elements marked

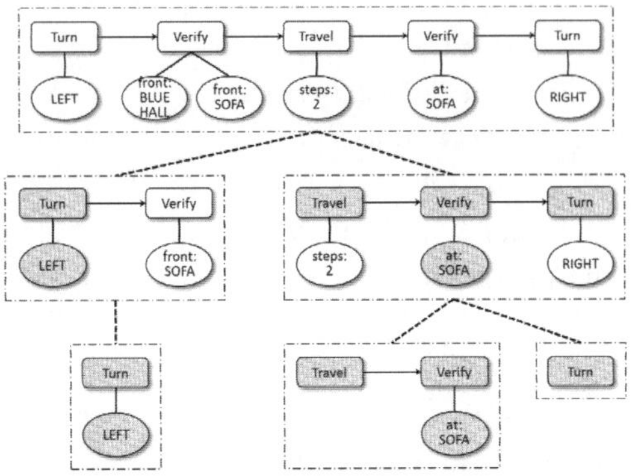

(c) Upper level nodes are marked according to leaf-node markings

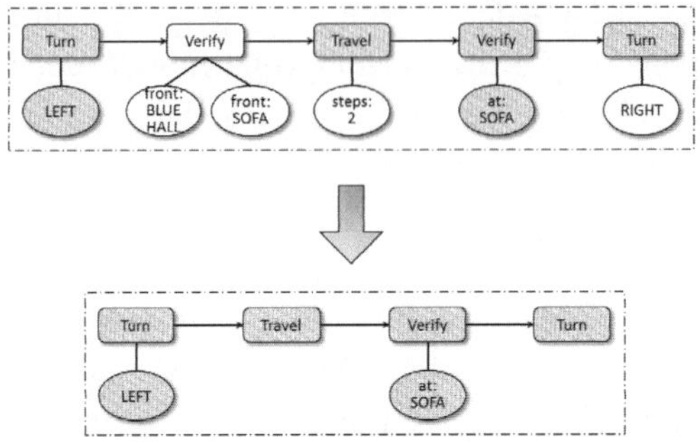

(d) Removing all unmarked elements for the root node leads to the final MR output

Figure 7: Sample construction of MR output from pruned parse tree.

followers' actions. We use this single-sentence version for training, but use both the single-sentence and the original paragraph version for testing. Each sentence was manually annotated with a "gold standard" execution plan, which is used for evaluation but not for training.

4.2 Methodology and Results

Experiments were conducted using "leave one environment out" cross-validation, training on two environments and testing on the third, averaging over all three test environments. We perform direct comparison to the best results of Chen and Mooney (2011) (referred to as CM). A Wilcoxon signed-rank test is performed for statistical significance, and '$*$' denotes significant differences ($p < .01$) in the tables.

Semantic Parsing Results

We first evaluated how well our system learns to map novel NL sentences for new test environments into their correct MRs. Partial semantic-parsing accuracy (Chen and Mooney, 2011) is calculated by comparing the system's MR output to the hand-annotated gold standard. Accuracy is measured in terms of precision, recall, and F1 for individual MR constituents (thereby awarding partial credit for approximately correct MRs).

	Precision	Recall	F1
Our system	87.58	$*$65.41	$*$**74.81**
CM	$*$90.22	55.10	68.37

Table 1: Test accuracy for semantic parsing. '$*$' denotes difference is statistically significant.

Table 1 demonstrates that our method outperforms CM by 6 points in F1. Our PCFG-based approach is able to probabilistically disambiguate the training data as well as simultaneously learn a statistical semantic parser within a single framework. This results in better overall performance compared to CM, since they lose potentially useful information, particularly during the refinement stage, due to the separate disjoint components of the system.

	Single-sentence	Paragraph
Our system	***57.22%**	***20.17%**
CM	54.40%	16.18%

Table 2: Successful plan execution rates for novel test data. '$*$' means statistical significance.

Navigation Plan Execution Results

Next, we test the end-to-end system by executing the parsed navigation plans for test instructions in novel environments to see if they reach the exact desired destinations in the environment. Table 2 shows the successful end-to-end navigation-task completion rate for both single-sentences and complete paragraph instructions.

Again, our system outperforms CM's best results since more accurate semantic parsing produces more successful plans. However, the difference in performance is smaller than that observed for semantic parsing. This is because the redundancy in the human generated instructions allows an incorrect semantic parse to be successful, as long as the errors do not affect its ability to guide the system to the correct destination.

5 Discussion

Our approach improves on Börschinger et al. (2011)'s method in the following ways:

• The building blocks for associating NL and MR are semantic lexemes instead of atomic MR constituents. This prevents the number of constructed PCFG rules from becoming intractably large as happens with Börschinger et al.'s approach. As previously mentioned, lexeme MRs are intuitively analogous to syntactic categories in that complex lexeme MRs represent complicated semantic concepts whereas higher-level syntactic categories such as S, VP, or NP represent complex syntactic structures.

• Our approach has the ability to produce previously unseen MRs, whereas Börschinger et al. can only generate an MR if it is explicitly included in the PCFG rules constructed from the training data. Even though our MR parse is restricted to be a subgraph of some training context, c_i, our model allows for exponentially many combinations.

In addition, our approach can produce a wider range of MR outputs than Chen and Mooney (2011)'s even though we use their semantic lexicon as input. Their system deterministically builds a supervised training set by greedily selecting high-scoring lexemes, thus implicitly including only high-scoring lexemes during training. On the other hand, our probabilistic approach also considers relatively low-scoring but useful lexemes, thereby utilizing more semantic concepts in the lexicon. In particular, this explains why our approach obtains higher *recall* in the evaluation of semantic parsing.

Even though we have demonstrated our approach on the specific task of following navigation instructions, it is straightforward to apply it to other language-grounding tasks where NL sentences potentially refer to some subset of states, events, or actions in the world, as long as this overall context can be represented as a semantic graph or logical form. Since the semantic lexicon is an input to our system, other approaches to lexicon learning are also easily incorporated.

6 Related Work

Most work on learning semantic parsers that map natural-language sentences to formal representations of their meaning have relied upon totally supervised training data consisting of NL/MR pairs (Zelle and Mooney, 1996; Zettlemoyer and Collins, 2005; Kate and Mooney, 2006; Wong and Mooney, 2007; Zettlemoyer and Collins, 2007; Lu et al., 2008; Zettlemoyer and Collins, 2009). Several recent approaches have investigated grounded learning from ambiguous supervision extracted from perceptual context. A number of approaches (Kate and Mooney, 2007; Chen and Mooney, 2008; Chen et al., 2010; Kim and Mooney, 2010; Börschinger et al., 2011) assume training data consisting of a set of sentences each associated with a small set of MRs, one of which is usually the correct meaning of the sentence. Many of these approaches (Kate and Mooney, 2007; Chen and Mooney, 2008; Chen et al., 2010) disambiguate the data and match NL sentences to their correct MR by iteratively retraining a supervised semantic parser. Kim and Mooney (2010) proposed a generative semantic parsing model that first chooses which MRs to describe and then generates a hybrid tree structure (Lu et al., 2008) containing both the MR and NL sentence. They train this model on ambiguous data using EM. As previously discussed, Börschinger et al. (2011) use a PCFG generative model and also train it on ambiguous data using EM. Liang et al. (2009) assume each sentence maps to one *or more* semantic *records* (i.e. MRs) and trains a hierarchical semi-Markov generative model using EM, and then finds a Viterbi alignment between NL words and records and their constituents. Several recent projects (Branavan et al., 2009; Vogel and Jurafsky, 2010) use NL instructions to guide *reinforcement learning* from independent exploration with delayed rewards. These systems do not even need the ambiguous supervision obtained from observing humans follow instructions; however, they do not learn semantic parsers that map sentences to complex, structural representations of their meaning.

Interpreting and executing NL navigation instructions is our primary task, and several other recent projects have studied related problems. Shimizu and Haas (2009) present a system that parses natural language instructions into actions. However, they limit the number of possible actions to only 15 and treat the problem as a sequence labeling problem that is solved using a CRF with supervised training. Matuszek et al. (2010) developed a system that learns to map NL instructions to executable commands for a robot navigating in an environment constructed by a laser range finder. However, their approach has limitations of ignoring any objects or other landmarks in the environment to which the instructions can refer. There are several recent projects (Vogel and Jurafsky, 2010; Kollar et al., 2010; Tellex et al., 2011) which learn to follow instructions in more linguistically complex environments. However, they assume predefined spatial words, direct matching between NL words and the names of objects and other landmarks in the MR, and/or an existing syntactic parser. By contrast, our work does not assume any prior linguistic knowledge, syntactic, lexical, or semantic, and must *learn* the mapping between NL words and phrases and the MR terms describing landmarks.

7 Future Work

In the future, we would like to develop a better lexicon learner since our PCFG approach critically relies on the quality of the learned lexicon. Particularly, we would like to investigate how syntactic information (such as part-of-speech tags induced using unsupervised learning) could be used to improve semantic-lexicon learning. For example, some of the current lexicon entries violate the general constraint that nouns usually refer to objects and verbs to actions. Ideally, the lexicon learner would be able to induce and then utilize this sort of relationship between syntax and semantics.

In addition, we want to investigate the use of *discriminative reranking* (Collins, 2000), which has proven effective in various other NLP tasks. We would expect the final MR output to improve if a discriminative model, which uses additional global features, is used to rerank the top-k parses produced by our generative PCFG model.

8 Conclusions

We have presented a novel method for learning a semantic parser given only highly ambiguous supervision. Our model enhances Börschinger et al. (2011)'s approach to reducing the problem of grounded learning of semantic parsers to PCFG induction. We use a learned semantic lexicon to aid the construction of a smaller and more focused set of PCFG productions. This allows the approach to scale to complex MR languages that define a large (potentially infinite) space of representations for capturing the meaning of sentences. By contrast, the previous PCFG approach requires a finite MR language and its grammar grows intractably large for even moderately complex MR languages. In addition, our algorithm for composing MRs from the final parse tree provides the flexibility to produce a wide range of novel MRs that were not seen during training. Evaluations on a previous corpus of navigational instructions for virtual environments has demonstrated the effectiveness of our method compared to a recent competing system.

Acknowledgments

We thank the anonymous reviewers and David Chen for useful comments that helped improve this paper. This work was funded by NSF grants IIS-0712907 and IIS-1016312. Experiments were performed on the Mastodon Cluster, provided by NSF grant EIA-0303609.

References

Benjamin Börschinger, Bevan K. Jones, and Mark Johnson. 2011. Reducing grounded learning tasks to grammatical inference. In *Proceedings of the Conference on Empirical Methods in Natural Language Processing (EMNLP-11)*, pages 1416–1425, Stroudsburg, PA, USA. Association for Computational Linguistics.

S.R.K. Branavan, Harr Chen, Luke S. Zettlemoyer, and Regina Barzilay. 2009. Reinforcement learning for mapping instructions to actions. In *Joint Conference of the 47th Annual Meeting of the Association for Computational Linguistics and the 4th International Joint Conference on Natural Language Processing of the Asian Federation of Natural Language Processing (ACL-IJCNLP)*, Singapore.

David L. Chen and Raymond J. Mooney. 2008. Learning to sportscast: A test of grounded language acquisition. In *Proceedings of 25th International Conference on Machine Learning (ICML-2008)*, Helsinki, Finland, July.

David L. Chen and Raymond J. Mooney. 2011. Learning to interpret natural language navigation instructions from observations. In *Proceedings of the 25th AAAI Conference on Artificial Intelligence (AAAI-11)*, San Francisco, CA, USA, August.

David L. Chen, Joohyun Kim, and Raymond J. Mooney. 2010. Training a multilingual sportscaster: Using perceptual context to learn language. *Journal of Artificial Intelligence Research*, 37:397–435.

Michael Collins. 2000. Discriminative reranking for natural language parsing. In *Proceedings of the Seventeenth International Conference on Machine Learning (ICML-2000)*, pages 175–182, Stanford, CA, June.

Daniel Jurafsky and James H. Martin. 2000. *Speech and Language Processing: An Introduction to Natural Language Processing, Computational Linguistics, and Speech Recognition*. Prentice Hall, Upper Saddle River, NJ.

R. J. Kate and R. J. Mooney. 2006. Using string-kernels for learning semantic parsers. In *Proceedings of the 21st International Conference on Computational Linguistics and 44th Annual Meeting of the Association for Computational Linguistics (COLING/ACL-06)*, pages 913–920, Sydney, Australia, July.

Rohit J. Kate and Raymond J. Mooney. 2007. Learning language semantics from ambiguous supervision. In *Proceedings of the Twenty-Second Conference on Artificial Intelligence (AAAI-07)*, pages 895–900, Vancouver, Canada, July.

Joohyun Kim and Raymond. J. Mooney. 2010. Generative alignment and semantic parsing for learning from ambiguous supervision. In *Proceedings of the 23rd International Conference on Computational Linguistics (COLING-10)*, pages 543–551. Association for Computational Linguistics.

Thomas Kollar, Stefanie Tellex, Deb Roy, and Nicholas Roy. 2010. Toward understanding natural language directions. In *Proceedings of Human Robot Interaction Conference (HRI-2010)*.

P. Liang, M. I. Jordan, and D. Klein. 2009. Learning semantic correspondences with less supervision. In *Joint Conference of the 47th Annual Meeting of the Association for Computational Linguistics and the 4th International Joint Conference on Natural Language Processing of the Asian Federation of Natural Language Processing (ACL-IJCNLP)*, Singapore.

Wei Lu, Hwee Tou Ng, Wee Sun Lee, and Luke S. Zettlemoyer. 2008. A generative model for parsing natural language to meaning representations. In *Proceedings of the Conference on Empirical Methods in Natural Language Processing (EMNLP-08)*, pages 783–792, Morristown, NJ, USA. Association for Computational Linguistics.

M. MacMahon, B. Stankiewicz, and B. Kuipers. 2006. Walk the talk: Connecting language, knowledge, and action in route instructions. In *Proceedings of the Twenty-First National Conference on Artificial Intelligence (AAAI-06)*, Boston, MA, July.

Cynthia Matuszek, Dieter Fox, and Karl Koscher. 2010. Following directions using statistical machine translation. In *Proceedings of the 5th ACM/IEEE international conference on Human-robot interaction (HRI-10)*, pages 251–258, New York, NY, USA. ACM.

Nobuyuki Shimizu and Andrew Haas. 2009. Learning to follow navigational route instructions. In *Proceedings of the Twenty First International Joint Conference on Artificial Intelligence (IJCAI-2009)*.

Jeffrey M. Siskind. 1996. A computational study of cross-situational techniques for learning word-to-meaning mappings. *Cognition*, 61(1):39–91, October.

Stefanie Tellex, Thomas Kolla, Steven Dickerson, Matthew R. Walter, Ashis G. Banerjee, Seth Teller, and Nicholas Roy. 2011. Understanding natural language commands for robotic navigation and mobile manipulation. In *Proceedings of the National Conference on Artificial Intelligence (AAAI-11)*, August.

Cynthia A. Thompson and Raymond J. Mooney. 2003. Acquiring word-meaning mappings for natural language interfaces. *Journal of Artificial Intelligence Research*, 18:1–44.

Adam Vogel and Dan Jurafsky. 2010. Learning to follow navigational directions. In *Proceedings of the 48th Annual Meeting of the Association for Computational Linguistics (ACL-10)*.

Yuk Wah Wong and Raymond J. Mooney. 2007. Learning synchronous grammars for semantic parsing with lambda calculus. In *Proceedings of the 45th Annual Meeting of the Association for Computational Linguistics (ACL-07)*, pages 960–967, Prague, Czech Republic, June.

John M. Zelle and Raymond J. Mooney. 1996. Learning to parse database queries using inductive logic programming. In *Proceedings of the Thirteenth National Conference on Artificial Intelligence (AAAI-96)*, pages 1050–1055, Portland, OR, August.

Luke S. Zettlemoyer and Michael Collins. 2005. Learning to map sentences to logical form: Structured classification with probabilistic categorial grammars. In *Proceedings of 21st Conference on Uncertainty in Artificial Intelligence (UAI-2005)*, Edinburgh, Scotland, July.

Luke S. Zettlemoyer and Michael Collins. 2007. Online learning of relaxed CCG grammars for parsing to logical form. In *Proceedings of the 2007 Joint Conference on Empirical Methods in Natural Language Processing and Computational Natural Language Learning (EMNLP-CoNLL-07)*, pages 678–687, Prague, Czech Republic, June.

Luke .S. Zettlemoyer and Micheal Collins. 2009. Learning context-dependent mappings from sentences to logical form. In *Proceedings of the Joint Conference of the 47th Annual Meeting of the ACL and the 4th International Joint Conference on Natural Language Processing of the AFNLP (ACL-IJCNLP-09)*, pages 976–984. Association for Computational Linguistics.

Forced Derivation Tree based Model Training to Statistical Machine Translation

Nan Duan
Microsoft Research Asia
nanduan@microsoft.com

Mu Li
Microsoft Research Asia
muli@microsoft.com

Ming Zhou
Microsoft Research Asia
mingzhou@microsoft.com

Abstract

A *forced derivation tree* (**FDT**) of a sentence pair $\{f, e\}$ denotes a derivation tree that can translate f into its accurate target translation e. In this paper, we present an approach that leverages structured knowledge contained in FDTs to train component models for statistical machine translation (SMT) systems. We first describe how to generate different FDTs for each sentence pair in training corpus, and then present how to infer the optimal FDTs based on their derivation and alignment qualities. As the first step in this line of research, we verify the effectiveness of our approach in a BTG-based phrasal system, and propose four FDT-based component models. Experiments are carried out on large scale English-to-Japanese and Chinese-to-English translation tasks, and significant improvements are reported on both translation quality and alignment quality.

1 Introduction

Most of today's SMT systems depends heavily on parallel corpora aligned at the word-level to train their different component models. However, such annotations do have their drawbacks in training.

On one hand, word links predicted by automatic aligners such as GIZA++ (Och and Ney, 2004) often contain errors. This problem gets even worse on language pairs that differ substantially in word orders, such as English and Japanese/Korean/German. The descent of the word alignment quality will lead to inaccurate component models straightforwardly.

On the other hand, several component models are designed to supervise the decoding procedures, which usually rely on training examples extracted from word-aligned sentence pairs, such as distortion models (Tillman, 2004; Xiong et al., 2006; Galley and Manning, 2008) and sequence models (Banchs et al., 2005; Quirk and Menezes, 2006; Vaswani et al., 2011). Ideally, training examples of models are expected to match most of the situations that could be met in decoding procedures. But actually, plain structures of word alignments are too coarse to provide enough knowledge to ensure this expectation.

This paper presents an FDT-based model training approach to SMT systems by leveraging structured knowledge contained in FDTs. An FDT of a sentence pair $\{f, e\}$ denotes a derivation tree that can translate f into its accurate target translation e. The principle advantage of this work is two-fold. First, using alignments induced from the 1-best FDTs of all sentence pairs, the overall alignment quality of training corpus can be improved. Second, comparing to word alignments, FDTs can provide richer structured knowledge for various component models to extract training instances. Our FDT-based model training approach performs via three steps: (1) **generation**, where an *FDT space* composed of different FDTs is generated for each sentence pair in training corpus by the *forced decoding* technique; (2) **inference**, where the optimal FDTs are extracted from the FDT space of each sentence pair based on both derivation and alignment qualities measured by a *memory-based re-ranking model*; (3) **training**, where various component models are trained based on the optimal FDTs extracted in the inference step.

Our FDT-based model training approach can be adapted to SMT systems with arbitrary paradigms.

As the first step in this line of research, our approach is verified in a phrase-based SMT system on both English-to-Japanese and Chinese-to-English translation tasks . Significant improvements are reported on both translation quality (up to 1.31 BLEU) and word alignment quality (up to 3.15 F-score).

2 Forced Derivation Tree for SMT

A forced derivation tree (**FDT**) of a sentence pair $\{f, e\}$ can be defined as a pair $\mathcal{G} =< \mathcal{D}, \mathcal{A} >$:

- $\mathcal{D}$ denotes a derivation that can translate f into e accurately, using a set of translation rules.
- $\mathcal{A}$ denotes a set of word links (i, j) indicating that $e_i \in e$ aligns to $f_j \in f$.

In this section, we first describe how to generate FDTs for each sentence pair in training corpus, which is denoted as the *generation* step, and then present how to select the optimal FDT for each sentence pair, which is denoted as the *inference* step. We leave a real application of FDTs to the model training in a phrase-based SMT system in Section 3.

2.1 Generation

We first describe how to generate multiple FDTs for each sentence pair in training corpus $\mathcal{C}$ based on the forced decoding (**FD**) technique, which performs via the following four steps:

1. Train component models needed for a specific SMT paradigm $\mathcal{M}$ based on training corpus $\mathcal{C}$;
2. Perform MERT on the development data set to obtain a set of optimized feature weights;
3. For each $\{f, e\} \in \mathcal{C}$, translate f into accurate e based on $\mathcal{M}$, component models trained in step 1, and feature weights optimized in step 2;
4. For each $\{f, e\} \in \mathcal{C}$, output the hypergraph (Huang and Chiang, 2005) $\mathcal{H}(f, e)$ generated in step 3 as its *FDT space*.

In step 3: (1) all partial hypotheses that do not match any sequence in e will be discarded; (2) derivations covering identical source and target words but with different alignments will be kept as different partial candidates, as they can produce different FDTs for the same sentence pair. For each $\{f, e\}$, the probability of each $\mathcal{G} \in \mathcal{H}(f, e)$ is computed as:

$$p(\mathcal{G}|\mathcal{H}(f,e)) = \frac{exp\{\psi(\mathcal{G})\}}{\sum_{\mathcal{G}' \in \mathcal{H}(f,e)} exp\{\psi(\mathcal{G}')\}} \quad (1)$$

where $\psi(\mathcal{G})$ is the FD model score assigned to $\mathcal{G}$.

For each sentence pair, different alignment candidates can be induced from its different forced derivation trees generated in the generation step, because FD can use phrase pairs with different internal word links extracted from other sentence pairs to reconstruct the given sentence pair, which could lead to better word alignment candidates.

2.2 Inference

Given an FDT space $\mathcal{H}(f, e)$, we propose a memory-based re-ranking model (**MRM**), which selects the best FDT $\hat{\mathcal{G}}$ as follows:

$$\begin{aligned} \hat{\mathcal{G}} &= \underset{\mathcal{G} \in \mathcal{H}(f,e)}{argmax} \frac{exp\{\sum_i \lambda_i h_i(\mathcal{G})\}}{\sum_{\mathcal{G}' \in \mathcal{H}(f,e)} exp\{\sum_i \lambda_i h_i(\mathcal{G}')\}} \\ &= \underset{\mathcal{G} \in \mathcal{H}(f,e)}{argmax} \sum_i \lambda_i h_i(\mathcal{G}) \end{aligned} \quad (2)$$

where $h_i(\mathcal{G})$ is feature function and λ_i is its feature weight. Here, *memory* means the whole translation history that happened in the generation step will be used as the evidence to help us compute features.

From the definition we can see that the quality of an FDT directly relates to two aspects: its derivation $\mathcal{D}$ and alignments $\mathcal{A}$. So two kinds of features are used to measure the overall quality of each FDT.

(I) The features in the first category measure the derivation quality of each FDT, including:

- $h(\bar{e}|\bar{f})$, source-to-target translation probability of a translation rule $r = \{\bar{f}, \bar{e}\}$.

$$h(\bar{e}|\bar{f}) = \frac{\sum_{\{f,e\} \in \mathcal{C}} frac_{\mathcal{H}(f,e)}(\bar{f}, \bar{e})}{\sum_{\{f,e\} \in \mathcal{C}} \sum_{\bar{e}'} frac_{\mathcal{H}(f,e)}(\bar{f}, \bar{e}')} \quad (3)$$

$frac_{\mathcal{H}(f,e)}(\bar{f}, \bar{e})$ denotes the fractional count of r used in generating $\mathcal{H}(f, e)$:

$$frac_{\mathcal{H}(f,e)}(\bar{f}, \bar{e}) = \sum_{\mathcal{G} \in \mathcal{H}(f,e)} 1_r(\mathcal{G}) p(\mathcal{G}|\mathcal{H}(f,e))$$

$1_r(\mathcal{G})$ is an indicator function that equals 1 when r is used in $\mathcal{G}$ and 0 otherwise. In practice, we use $p_{\mathcal{H}(f,e)}(r)$ of r to approximate

$frac_{\mathcal{H}(f,e)}(\bar{f},\bar{e})$ when the size of $\mathcal{H}(f,e)$ is too large to enumerate all FDTs:

$$p_{\mathcal{H}(f,e)}(r) = \frac{\omega(r)\mathcal{O}(head(r))\prod_{v\in tail(r)}\mathcal{I}(v)}{\mathcal{Z}(f)}$$

where $\omega(r)$ is the weight of translation rule r in the FDT space $\mathcal{H}(f,e)$, $\mathcal{Z}$ is a normalization factor that equals to the inside probability of the root node in $\mathcal{H}(f,e)$, $\mathcal{I}(v)$ and $\mathcal{O}(v)$ are the standard inside and outside probabilities of a node v in $\mathcal{H}(f,e)$, $head(r)$ and $tail(r)$ are the head node and a set of tail nodes of a translation rule r in $\mathcal{H}(f,e)$ respectively.

- $h(\bar{f}|\bar{e})$, target-to-source translation probability of a translation rule $r = \{\bar{f},\bar{e}\}$.

$$h(\bar{f}|\bar{e}) = \frac{\sum_{\{f,e\}\in C} frac_{\mathcal{H}(f,e)}(\bar{f},\bar{e})}{\sum_{\{f,e\}\in C}\sum_{\bar{f}'} frac_{\mathcal{H}(f,e)}(\bar{f}',\bar{e})} \quad (4)$$

- $h_{\#}(r)$, smoothed usage count for translation rule $r = \{\bar{f},\bar{e}\}$ in the whole generation step.

$$h_{\#}(r) = \frac{1}{1+e^{\{-\sum_{\{f,e\}\in C} frac_{\mathcal{H}(f,e)}(\bar{f},\bar{e})\}}} \quad (5)$$

  In this paper, the sigmoid function is used to make sure that the feature values of different translation rules are in a proper value range.

- $h_r(\mathcal{G})$, number of translation rules used in $\mathcal{G}$.

- $h_d(\mathcal{G})$, structure-based score of $\mathcal{G}$. For FDTs generated by phrase-based paradigms, it can be computed by distortion models; while for FDTs generated by syntax-based paradigms, it can be computed by either parsing models or syntactic LMs (Charniak et al., 2003).

The overfitting issue in the generation step can be alleviated by leveraging memory-based features in the inference step. $h_{\#}(r)$ is used to penalize those long translation rules which tend to occur in only a few training sentences and are used few times in FD, $h_r(\mathcal{G})$ adjust our MRM to prefer FDTs consisting of more translation rules, $h_d(\mathcal{G})$ is used to select FDTs with better parse tree-like structures, which can be induced from their derivations directly.

(II) The features in the second category measure the alignment quality of each FDT, including:

- word pair translation probabilities trained from IBM models (Brown et al., 1993);
- log-likelihood ratio (Moore, 2005);
- conditional link probability (Moore, 2005);
- count of unlinked words;
- counts of inversion and concatenation.

Many alignment-inspired features can be used in MRM. This paper only uses those commonly-used ones that have already been proved useful in many previous work (Moore, 2005; Moore et al., 2006; Fraser and Marcu, 2006; Liu et al., 2010).

Following the common practice in SMT research, the MERT algorithm (Och, 2003) is used to tune feature weights in MRM. Due to the fact that all FDTs of each sentence pair share identical translation, we cannot use BLEU as the error criterion any more. Instead, alignment F-score is used as the alternative. We will show in Section 5 that after the inference step, alignment quality can be improved by replacing original alignments of each sentence pair with alignments induced from its 1-best FDT. Future work could experiment with other error criterions, such as reordering-based loss functions (Birch et al., 2010; Talbot et al., 2011; Birch and Osborne, 2011) or span F1 (DeNero and Uszkoreit, 2011).

3 Training in Phrase-based SMT

As the first step in this line of research, we explore the usage of FDT-based model training method in a phrase-based SMT system (Xiong et al., 2006), which employs Bracketing Transduction Grammar (BTG) (Wu, 1997) to parse parallel sentences. The reason of choosing this system is due to the prominent advantages of BTG, such as the simplicity of the grammar and the good coverage of syntactic diversities between different language pairs. We first describe more details of FDTs under BTG. Then, four FDT-based component models are presented.

3.1 BTG-based FDT

Given a sentence pair $f = \{f_0, ..., f_J\}$ and $e = \{e_0, ..., e_I\}$ in training corpus, its FDT $\mathcal{G}$ generated based on BTG is a binary tree, which is presented by a set of terminal translation states $\mathcal{T}$ and a set of non-terminal translation states $\mathcal{N}$, where:

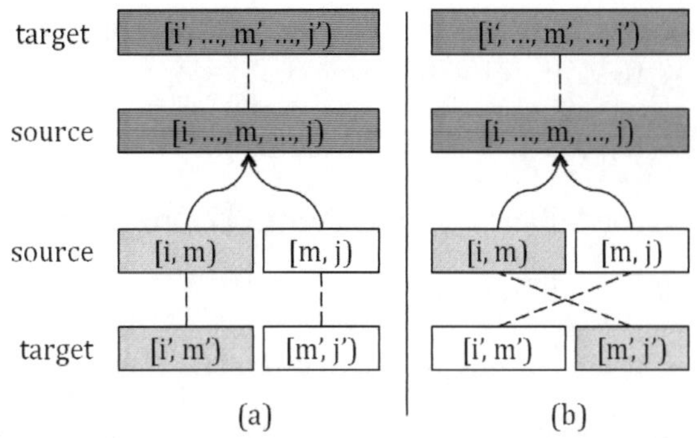

Figure 1: $\mathcal{S} = \{\bar{f}_{[i,j)}, \bar{e}_{[i',j')}, \bar{\mathcal{A}}, m, m', \mathcal{R}\}$ is denoted by the dark-shaded rectangle pair. It can be split into two child translation states, $\mathcal{S}_l$, which is denoted by the light-shaded rectangle pair, and $\mathcal{S}_r$, which is denoted by the white rectangle pair. Dash lines within rectangle pairs denote their internal alignments and solid lines with rows denote BTG rules. (a) uses $[\cdot]$ to combine two translation states, while (b) uses $\langle\cdot\rangle$. Both $\mathcal{S}_l$ and $\mathcal{S}_r$ belong to $\mathcal{T} \cup \mathcal{N}$.

- each *terminal translation state* $\mathcal{S} \in \mathcal{T}$ is a 3-tuple $\{\bar{f}_{[i,j)}, \bar{e}_{[i',j')}, \bar{\mathcal{A}}\}$, in which $\bar{f}_{[i,j)}$ denotes the word sequence that covers the source span $[i, j)$ of f, $\bar{e}_{[i',j')}$ denotes the target translation of $\bar{f}_{[i,j)}$, which is the word sequence that covers the target span $[i', j')$ of e at the same time, $\bar{\mathcal{A}}$ is a set of word links that aligns $\bar{f}_{[i,j)}$ and $\bar{e}_{[i',j')}$.
- each *non-terminal translation state* $\mathcal{S} \in \mathcal{N}$ is a 5-tuple $\{\bar{f}_{[i,j)}, \bar{e}_{[i',j')}, \bar{\mathcal{A}}, m, m', \mathcal{R}\}$[1]. The first 3 elements have the same meanings as in $\mathcal{T}$, while m and m' denote two split points that divide $\mathcal{S}$ into two child translation states, $\mathcal{S}_l$ and $\mathcal{S}_r$, $\mathcal{R}$ denotes a BTG rule, which is either a $[\cdot]$ operation or a $\langle\cdot\rangle$ operation[2]. The relationship between $\mathcal{S}_l$, $\mathcal{S}_r$ and S is illustrated in Figure 1.

All terminal translation states of the sentence pair $\{f, e\}$ are disjoint but cover $f_{[0,J+1)}$ and $e_{[0,I+1)}$ at the same time, where $J = |f|$ and $I = |e|$, and all non-terminal translation states correspond to the partial decoding states generated during decoding.

3.2 FDT-based Translation Model

First, an FDT-based translation model (**FDT-TM**) is presented for our BTG-based system.

[1]We sometimes omit m, m' and $\mathcal{R}$ for a simplicity reason.

[2]A $[\cdot]$ operation combines the translations of two consecutive source spans $[i, m)$ and $[m, j)$ in a monotonic way; while a $\langle\cdot\rangle$ operation combines them in an inverted way.

Given sentence pairs in training corpus with their corresponding FDT spaces, we train FDT-TM in two different ways: (1) The first only uses the 1-best FDT of each sentence pair. Based on each alignment $\mathcal{A}$ induced from each 1-best FDT $\mathcal{G}$, all possible bilingual phrases are extracted. Then, the maximum likelihood estimation (MLE) is used to compute probabilities and generate an FDT-TM. (2) The second uses the n-best FDTs of each sentence pair, which is motivated by several studies (Venugopal et al., 2008; Liu et al., 2009). For each sentence pair $\{f, e\}$, we first induce n alignments $\{\mathcal{A}_1, ..., \mathcal{A}_n\}$ from the top n FDTs $\Omega = \{\mathcal{G}_1, ..., \mathcal{G}_n\} \subset \mathcal{H}(f, e)$. Each $\mathcal{A}_k$ is annotated with the posterior probability of its corresponding FDT $\mathcal{G}_k$ as follows:

$$p(\mathcal{A}_k|\mathcal{G}_k) = \frac{exp\{\sum_i \lambda_i h_i(\mathcal{G}_k)\}}{\sum_{\mathcal{G}_{k'} \in \Omega} exp\{\sum_i \lambda_i h_i(\mathcal{G}_{k'})\}} \tag{6}$$

where $\sum_i \lambda_i h_i(\mathcal{G}_k)$ is the model score assigned to $\mathcal{G}_k$ by MRM. Then, all possible bilingual phrases are extracted from the expanded training corpus built using n-best alignments for each sentence pair. The count of each phrase pair is now computed as the sum of posterior probabilities, instead of the sum of absolute frequencies. Last, MLE is used to compute probabilities and generate an FDT-TM.

3.3 FDT-based Distortion Model

In Xiong's BTG system, training instances of the distortion model (DM) are pruned based on heuristic rules, aiming to keep the training size acceptable. But this will cause the examples remained cannot cover all reordering cases that could be met in real decoding procedures. To overcome this drawback, we propose an FDT-based DM (**FDT-DM**).

Given the 1-best FDT $\mathcal{G}$ of a sentence pair $\{f, e\}$, all non-terminal translation states $\{\mathcal{S}_1, ..., \mathcal{S}_K\}$ are first extracted. For each $\mathcal{S}_k$, we split it into two child translation states $\mathcal{S}_{kl}$ and $\mathcal{S}_{kr}$. A training instance can be then obtained, using the BTG operation $\mathcal{R} \in \mathcal{S}_k$ as its class label and boundary words of two translation blocks $(\bar{f}_{\mathcal{S}_{kl}}, \bar{e}_{\mathcal{S}_{kl}})$ and $(\bar{f}_{\mathcal{S}_{kr}}, \bar{e}_{\mathcal{S}_{kr}})$ contained in $\mathcal{S}_{kl}$ and $\mathcal{S}_{kr}$ as its features. Last, the FDT-DM is trained based on all training instances by a MaxEnt toolkit, which can cover both local and global reordering situations due to its training instance extraction mechanism. Figure 2 shows an example of extracting training instances from an FDT.

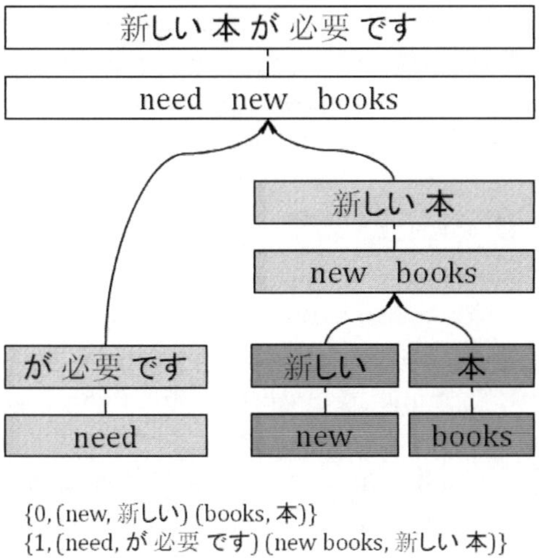

Figure 2: An example of extracting training instances from an FDT, where solid lines with rows denote BTG operations and dash lines denote alignments. Two instances can be extracted from this FDT, where 0 and 1 denote a $[\cdot]$ operation and a $\langle\cdot\rangle$ operation respectively. In DM training, the number (0 or 1) in each instance is used as a label, while boundary words are extracted from each instance's two phrase pairs and used as lexical features.

3.4 FDT-based Source Language Model

We next propose an FDT-based source language model (**FDT-SLM**).

Given the 1-best FDT $\mathcal{G}$ of a sentence pair $\{f, e\}$, we first extract a reordered source word sequence $f' = \{f'_0, ..., f'_J\}$ from $\mathcal{G}$, based on the order of terminal translation states in $\mathcal{G}$ which covers the target translation e from left to right. This procedure can be illustrated by Algorithm 1. Then, all reordered source sentences of training corpus are used to train a source LM. During decoding, each time when a new hypothesis is generated, we obtain its reordered source word sequence as well, compute a LM score based on FDT-SLM and use it as a new feature:

$$h_{SLM}(f') = \prod_{k=1}^{J} p(f'_k | f'_{k-n+1}, ..., f'_{k-1}) \quad (7)$$

3.5 FDT-based Rule Sequence Model

The last contribution in this section is an FDT-based rule sequence model (**FDT-RSM**).

Given the 1-best FDT $\mathcal{G}$ of a sentence pair $\{f, e\}$, we first extract a sequence of translation rule applications $\{r_1, ..., r_K\}$ based on Algorithm 2, where $r_k = (\bar{f}_{[i,j)}, \bar{e}_{[i',j')})$ denotes the kth phrase pair. Figure 3 gives an example of extracting a rule sequence from an FDT. An FDT-RSM is trained based on all rule sequences extracted from training corpus. During decoding, each time when a new hypothesis is generated, we compute an FDT-RSM score based on its rule sequence and use it as a new feature:

$$h_{RSM}(f, e) = \prod_{k=1}^{K} p(r_k | r_{k-n+1}, ..., r_{k-1}) \quad (8)$$

Algorithm 1: Sequence Extraction in FDT-SLM

let $f' = \emptyset$;
let $\bar{\mathcal{S}} = \{\mathcal{S}_{1'}, ..., \mathcal{S}_{K'}\}$ represents an ordered sequence of terminal translation states whose target phrases cover e from left to right orderly;
foreach $\mathcal{S} \in \bar{\mathcal{S}}$ *in the left-to-right order* **do**
    extract $\bar{f}_{[i,j)}$ from $\mathcal{S}$;
    append $\bar{f}_{[i,j)}$ to f';
    append a blank space to f';
end
return f' as a reordered source word sequence.

Algorithm 2: Sequence Extraction in FDT-RSM

let $r' = \emptyset$;
let $\bar{\mathcal{S}} = \{\mathcal{S}_{1'}, ..., \mathcal{S}_{K'}\}$ represents an ordered sequence of terminal translation states whose target phrases cover e from left to right orderly;
foreach $\mathcal{S} \in \bar{\mathcal{S}}$ *in the left-to-right order* **do**
    extract a phrase pair $(\bar{f}_{[i,j)}, \bar{e}_{[i',j')})$ from $\mathcal{S}$;
    add $r_k = (\bar{f}_{[i,j)}, \bar{e}_{[i',j')})$ to r';
end
return r' as a rule sequence.

The main difference between FDT-SLM and FDT-RSM is that the former is trained based on monolingual n-grams; while the latter is trained based on bilingual phrases. Although these two models are trained and computed in an LM style, they are used as reordering features, because they help SMT decoder find better decoding sequences.

Of course, the usage of FDTs need not be limited to the BTG-based system, and we consider using FDTs generated by SCFG-based systems or traditional left-to-right phrase-based systems in future.

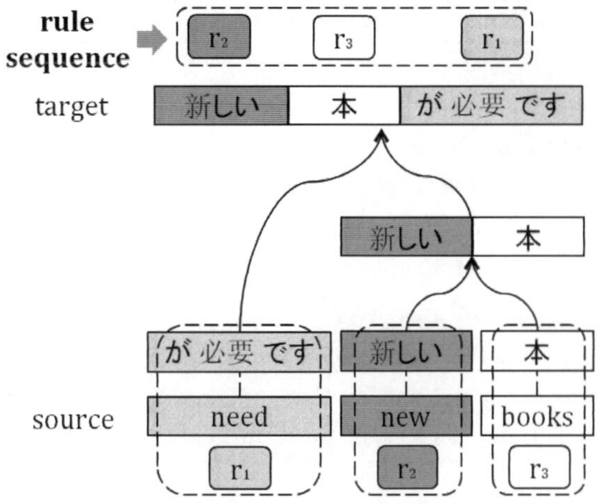

Figure 3: An example of extracting a rule sequence from an FDT. In order to generate the correct target translation, the desired rule sequence should be $r_2 \Rightarrow r_3 \Rightarrow r_1$.

4 Related Work

4.1 Forced Decoding/Alignment

Schwartz (2008) used forced decoding to leverage multilingual corpus to improve translation quality; Shen et al. (2008) used forced alignment to train a better phrase segmentation model; Wuebker et al. (2010) used forced alignment to re-estimate translation probabilities using a leaving-one-out strategy. We consider the usage of FD in Section 2.1 to be a direct extension of these approaches, but one that generates FDTs for parallel data rather than focusing on phrase segmentation or probability estimation.

4.2 Pre-reordering

Pre-reordering (PRO) techniques (Collins et al., 2005; Xu et al., 2009; Genzel et al., 2010; Lee et al., 2010) used features from syntactic parse trees to reorder source sentences at training and translation time. A parser is often indispensable to provide syntactic information for such methods. Recently, DeNero and Uszkoreit (2011) proposed an approach that induced parse trees automatically from word-aligned training corpus to perform PRO for a phrase-based SMT system, instead of relying on treebanks. First, binary parse trees are induced from word-aligned training corpus. Based on them, a monolingual parsing model and a tree reordering model are trained to pre-reorder source words into the target-language-like order. Their work is distinct from ours because it focused on inducing sentence structures for the PRO task, but mirrors ours in demonstrating that there is a potential role for structure-based training corpus in SMT model training.

4.3 Distortion Models

Lexicalized distortion models (Tillman, 2004; Zens and Ney, 2006; Xiong et al., 2006; Galley and Manning, 2008;) are widely used in phrase-based SMT systems. Training instances of these models are extracted from word-aligned sentence pairs. Due to efficiency reasons, only parts of all instances are kept and used in DM training, which cannot cover all possible reordering situations that could be met in decoding. In FDT-DM, by contrast, training instances are extracted from FDTs. Such instances take both local and global reordering cases into consideration.

4.4 Sequence Models

Feng et al. (2010) proposed an SLM in a phrase-based SMT system. They used it as a reordering feature in the sense that it helped the decoder to find correct decoding sequences. The difference between their model and our FDT-SLM is that, in their work, the reordered source sequences are extracted based on word alignments only; while in our FDT-SLM, such sequences are obtained based on FDTs.

Quirk and Menezes (2006) proposed a Minimal Translation Unit (MTU) -based sequence model and used it in their treelet system; Vaswani et al. (2011) proposed a rule Markov model to capture dependencies between minimal rules for a top-down tree-to-string system. The key difference between FDT-RSM and previous work is that the rule sequences are extracted from FDTs, and no parser is needed.

5 Experiments

5.1 Data and Metric

Experiments are carried out on English-to-Japanese (E-J) and Chinese-to-English (C-E) MT tasks.

For *E-J task*, bilingual data used contains 13.3M sentence pairs after pre-processing. The Japanese side of bilingual data is used to train a 4-gram LM. The development set (*dev*) which contains 2,000 sentences is used to optimize the log-linear SMT model. Two test sets are used for evaluation, which contain 5,000 sentences (*test-1*) and 999 sentences (*test-2*) respectively. In all evaluation data sets, each source sentence has only one reference translation.

For *C-E task*, bilingual data used contains 0.5M sentence pairs with high translation quality, including LDC2003E07, LDC2003E14, LDC2005T06, LDC2005T10, LDC2005E83, LDC2006E26, LDC2006E34, LDC2006E85 and LDC2006E92. A 5-gram LM is trained on the Xinhua portion of LDC English Gigaword Version 3.0. NIST 2004 (*MT04*) data set is used as dev set, and evaluation results are measured on NIST 2005 (*MT05*) and NIST 2008 (*MT08*) data sets. In all evaluation data sets, each source sentence has four reference translations.

Default word alignments for both SMT tasks are performed by GIZA++ with the *intersect-diag-grow* refinement. Translation quality is measured in terms of *case-insensitive BLEU* (Papineni et al., 2002) and reported in percentage numbers.

5.2 Baseline System

The phrase-based SMT system proposed by Xiong et al. (2006) is used as the baseline system, with a MaxEnt principle-based lexicalized reordering model integrated, which is used to handle reorderings in decoding. The maximum lengths for the source and target phrases are 5 and 7 on E-J task, and 3 and 5 on C-E task. The beam size is set to 20.

5.3 Translation Quality on E-J Task

We first evaluate the effectiveness of our FDT-based model training approach on E-J translation task, and present evaluation results in Table 1, in which *BTG* denotes the performance of the baseline system.

FDT-TM denotes the improved system that uses FDT-TM proposed in Section 3.2 instead of original phrase table. As described in Section 3.2, we tried different sizes of n-best FDTs to induce alignments for phrase extraction and found the optimal choice is 5. Besides, in order to make full use of the training corpus, for those sentence pairs that are failed in FD, we just use their original word alignments to extract bilingual phrases. We can see from Table 1 that FDT-TM outperforms the BTG system significantly.

FDT-DM denotes the improved system that uses FDT-DM proposed in Section 3.3 instead of original distortion model. Comparing to baseline DM which has length limitation on training instances, training examples of FDT-DM are extracted from 1-best FDTs without any restriction. This makes our new DM can cover both local and global reordering situations that might be met in decoding procedures. We can see from Table 1 that using FDT-DM, significant improvements can be achieved.

FDT-SLM denotes the improved system that uses FDT-SLM proposed in Section 3.4 as an additional feature, in which the maximum n-gram order is 4. However, from Table 1 we notice that with FDT-SLM integrated, only 0.2 BLEU improvements can be obtained. We analyze decoding-logs and find that the reordered source sequences of n-best translations are very similar, which, we think, can explain why improvements of using this model are so limited.

FDT-RSM denotes the improved system that uses FDT-RSM proposed in Section 3.5 as an additional feature. The maximum order of this model is 3. From Table 1 we can see that FDT-RSM outperforms BTG significantly, with up to 0.48 BLEU improvements. Comparing to FDT-SLM, FDT-RSM performs slightly better as well. We think it is due to the fact that bilingual phrases can provide more discriminative power than monolingual n-grams do.

Last, all these four FDT-based models (FDT-TM, FDT-DM, FDT-SLM and FDT-RSM) are put together to form an improved system that is denoted as *FDT-ALL*. It can provide an averaged 1.2 BLEU improvements on these three evaluation data sets.

BLEU	dev	test-1	test-2
BTG	20.60	20.27	13.15
FDT-TM	21.21	20.71(+0.44)	13.98(+0.83)
FDT-DM	21.13	20.79(+0.52)	14.25(+1.10)
FDT-SLM	20.84	20.50(+0.23)	13.36(+0.21)
FDT-RSM	21.07	20.75(+0.48)	13.59(+0.44)
FDT-ALL	**21.83**	**21.34(+1.07)**	**14.46(+1.31)**
PRO	21.89	21.81	14.69

Table 1: FDT-based model training on E-J task.

Pre-reordering (*PRO*) is often used on language pairs, e.g. English and Japanese, with very different word orders. So we compare our method with PRO as well. We re-implement the PRO method proposed by Genzel (2010) and show its results in Table 1. On dev and test-2, FDT-ALL performs comparable to PRO, with no syntactic information needed at all.

5.4 Translation Quality on C-E Task

We then evaluate the effectiveness of our FDT-based model training approach on C-E translation task, and present evaluation results in Table 2, from which we can see significant improvements as well.

BLEU	MT03	MT05	MT08
BTG	38.73	38.01	23.78
FDT-TM	39.14	38.31(+0.30)	24.30(+0.52)
FDT-DM	39.27	38.56(+0.55)	24.50(+0.72)
FDT-SLM	38.97	38.22(+0.21)	24.04(+0.26)
FDT-RSM	39.06	38.33(+0.32)	24.13(+0.35)
FDT-ALL	**39.59**	**38.72(+0.71)**	**24.67(+0.89)**

Table 2: FDT-based model training on C-E task

Comparing to numbers in Table 1, the gains coming from the first two FDT-based models become small on C-E task. This might be due to the fact that the word alignment quality in C-E task is more reliable than that in E-J task for TM and DM training.

5.5 Effect on Alignment Quality

We compare the qualities of alignments predicted by GIZA++ and alignments induced from 1-best FDTs.

For E-J task, 575 English-Japanese sentence pairs are manually annotated with word alignments. 382 sentence pairs are used as the dev set, and the other 193 sentence pairs are used as the test set. For C-E task, 491 Chinese-English sentence pairs are manually annotated with word alignments. 250 sentence pairs are used as the dev set, and the other 241 sentence pairs are used as the test set. Both Japanese and Chinese sentences are adapted to our own word segmentation standards respectively. Table 3 shows the comparison results. Comparing to C-E language pair (S-V-O), E-J language pair (S-O-V) has much lower F-scores, due to its very different word order.

F-score	from GIZA++	from 1-best FDTs
dev_{EJ}	54.75%	57.93%(+3.18%)
$test_{EJ}$	55.32%	58.47%(+3.15%)
dev_{CE}	81.32%	83.37%(+2.05%)
$test_{CE}$	80.61%	82.51%(+1.90%)

Table 3: Comparison of alignment qualities predicted by GIZA++ and induced from 1-best FDTs.

From Table 3 we can see that the F-score improves on all language pairs when using alignments induced from 1-best FDTs, rather than GIZA++.

5.6 Effect on Classification Accuracy

In the BTG system, the MaxEnt model is used as a binary classifier to predict reordering operations of neighbor translation blocks. As the baseline DM and our FDT-DM have different mechanisms on training instance extraction procedures, we compare the classification accuracies of these two DMs in Table 4 to show the effect of different training instances. The MaxEnt toolkit (Zhang, 2004) is used to optimize feature weights using the l-BFGS method (Byrd et al., 1995). We set the iteration number to 200 and Gaussian prior to 1 for avoiding overfitting. Table 4 shows that when using training instances extracted from FDTs, classification accuracy of reorderings improves on both E-J and C-E tasks. This is because FDTs can provide more deterministic and structured knowledge for training instance extraction, which can cover both local and global reordering cases.

	baseline DM	FDT-based DM
E-J	93.67%	95.60%(+1.93%)
C-E	95.85%	97.52%(+1.67%)

Table 4: Comparison of classification accuracies of DMs based on instances extracted by different mechanisms.

6 Conclusions

In this paper, we have presented an FDT-based model training approach to SMT. As the first step in this research direction, we have verified our method on a phrase-based SMT system, and proposed four FDT-based component models. Experiments on both E-J and C-E tasks have demonstrated the effectiveness of our approach. Summing up, comparing to plain word alignments, FDTs provide richer structured knowledge for more accurate SMT model training. Several potential research topics can be explored in future. For example, FDTs can be used in a pre-reordering framework. This is feasible in the sense that FDTs can provide both tree-like structures and reordering information. We also plan to adapt our FDT-based model training approach to SCFG-based and traditional left-to-right phrase-based systems.

References

Peter Brown, Stephen Pietra, Vincent Pietra, and Robert Mercer. 1993. *The Mathematics of Statistical Machine Translation: Parameter Estimation*, Computational Linguistics.

Rafael Banchs, Josep Crego, Adri'a Gispert, Patrik Lambert, and Jos Mario. 2005. *Statistical Machine Translation of Euparl Data by using Bilingual N-grams*, In Proceedings of the ACL Workshop on Building and Using Parallel Texts.

Alexandra Birch, Phil Blunsom, and Miles Osborne. 2010. *Metrics for MT evaluation: Evaluating reordering*, Machine Translation.

Alexandra Birch and Miles Osborne. 2011. *Reordering metrics for MT*, In Proceedings of the Association for Computational Linguistics.

Richard Byrd, Peihuang Lu, Jorge Nocedal, and Ciyou Zhu. 1995. *A limited memory algorithm for bound constrained optimization*, SIAM Journal of Science and Statistical Computing.

Eugene Charniak, Kevin Knight, and Kenji Yamada. 2003. *Syntax-based Language Models for Statistical Machine Translation*, MT Summit.

Michael Collins, Philipp Koehn, and Ivona Kucerova. 2005. *Clause Restructuring for Statistical Machine Translation*, In Proceedings of the Association for Computational Linguistics.

John DeNero and Jakob Uszkoreit. 2011. *Inducing Sentence Structure from Parallel Corpora for Reordering*, In Proceedings of the Conference on Empirical Methods in Natural Language Processing.

Minwei Feng, Arne Mauser, and Hermann Ney. 2010. *A Source-side Decoding Sequence Model for Statistical Machine Translation*, In Proceedings of the Conference of the Association for Machine Translation.

Alexander Fraser and Daniel Marcu. 2006. *Semi-Supervised Training for Statistical Word Alignment*, In Proceedings of the International Conference on Computational Linguistics and Annual Meeting of the Association for Computational Linguistics.

Dmitriy Genzel. 2010. *Automatically learning source-side reordering rules for large scale machine translation*, In Proceedings of the Conference on Computational Linguistics.

Liang Huang and David Chiang. 2005. *Better k-best Parsing*, In Proceedings of International Conference on Parsing Technologies,.

Young-Suk Lee, Bing Zhao, and Xiaoqiang Luo. 2010. *Constituent Reordering and Syntax Models for English-to-Japanese Statistical Machine Translation*, In Proceedings of the Conference on Computational Linguistics.

Yang Liu, Tian Xia, Xinyan Xiao, and Qun Liu. 2009. *Weighted Alignment Matrices for Statistical Ma-chine Translation*, In Proceedings of the Conference on Empirical Methods in Natural Language Processing.

Yang Liu, Qun Liu, and Shouxun Lin. 2010. *Discriminative Word Alignment by Linear Modeling*, Computational Linguistics.

Robert Moore. 2005. *A Discriminative Framework for Bilingual Word Alignment*, In Proceedings of Human Language Technology Conference and Conference on Empirical Methods in Natural Language Processing.

Robert Moore, Wen-tau Yih, and Andreas Bode. 2006. *Improved Discriminative Bilingual Word Alignment*, In Proceedings of the International Conference on Computational Linguistics and Annual Meeting of the Association for Computational Linguistics.

Haitao Mi, Liang Huang, and Qun Liu. 2008. *Forest-based Translation*, In Proceedings of the Association for Computational Linguistics.

Galley Michel and Christopher D. Manning. 2008. *A Simple and Effective Hierarchical Phrase Reordering Model*, In Proceedings of the Conference on Empirical Methods in Natural Language Processing.

Franz Och. 2003. *Minimum Error Rate Training in Statistical Machine Translation*, In Proceedings of the Association for Computational Linguistics.

Franz Och and Hermann Ney. 2004. *The Alignment Template Approach to Statistical Machine Translation*, Computational Linguistics.

Kishore Papineni, Salim Roukos, Todd Ward, and Weijing Zhu. 2002. *BLEU: a method for automatic evaluation of machine translation*, In Proceedings of the Association for Computational Linguistics.

Chris Quirk and Arul Menezes. 2006. *Do we need phrases? Challenging the conventional wisdom in Statistical Machine Translation*, In Proceedings of the North American Chapter of the Association for Computational Linguistics.

Lane Schwartz. 2008. *Multi-Source Translation Methods*, In Proceedings of the Conference of the Association for Machine Translation.

Wade Shen, Brian Delaney, Tim Anderson, and Ray Slyh. 2008. *The MIT-LL/AFRL IWSLT-2008 MT System*, International Workshop on Spoken Language Translation.

David Talbot, Hideto Kazawa, Hiroshi Ichikawa, Jason Katz-Brown, Masakazu Seno, and Franz Och. 2011. *A lightweight evaluation framework for machine translation reordering*, In Proceedings of the Sixth Workshop on Statistical Machine Translation.

Ashish Vaswani, Haitao Mi, Liang Huang, and David Chiang. 2011. *Rule Markov Models for Fast Tree-to-String Translation*, In Proceedings of the Association for Computational Linguistics.

Ashish Venugopal, Andreas Zollmann, Noah Smith, and Stephan Vogel. 2008. *Wider Pipelines: N-best Alignments and Parses in MT Training*, In Proceedings of the Conference of the Association for Machine Translation.

Joern Wuebker, Arne Mauser, and Hermann Ney. 2010. *Training Phrase Translation Models with Leaving-One-Out*, In Proceedings of the Association for Computational Linguistics.

Dekai Wu. 1997. *Stochastic Inversion Transduction Grammars and Bilingual Parsing of Parallel Corpora*, Computational Linguistics.

Deyi Xiong, Qun Liu, and Shouxun Lin. 2006. *Maximum entropy based phrase reordering model for statistical machine translation*, In Proceedings of the Association for Computational Linguistics.

Peng Xu, Jaeho Kang, Michael Ringgaard, and Franz Och. 2009. *Using a Dependency Parser to Improve SMT for Subject-Object-Verb Languages*, In Proceedings of the North American Chapter of the Association for Computational Linguistics.

Richard Zens and Hermann Ney. 2006. *Discriminative Reordering Models for Statistical Machine Translation*, In Proceedings of the Workshop on Statistical Machine Translation.

Le Zhang. 2004. *Maximum Entropy Modeling Toolkit for Python and C++*.

Multi-instance Multi-label Learning for Relation Extraction

Mihai Surdeanu[†], Julie Tibshirani[†], Ramesh Nallapati[⋆], Christopher D. Manning[†]
[†] Stanford University, Stanford, CA 94305
{mihais, jtibs, manning}@stanford.edu
[⋆] Artificial Intelligence Center, SRI International
nallapat@ai.sri.com

Abstract

Distant supervision for relation extraction (RE) – gathering training data by aligning a database of facts with text – is an efficient approach to scale RE to thousands of different relations. However, this introduces a challenging learning scenario where the relation expressed by a pair of entities found in a sentence is unknown. For example, a sentence containing *Balzac* and *France* may express *BornIn* or *Died*, an unknown relation, or no relation at all. Because of this, traditional supervised learning, which assumes that each example is explicitly mapped to a label, is not appropriate. We propose a novel approach to multi-instance multi-label learning for RE, which jointly models all the instances of a pair of entities in text and all their labels using a graphical model with latent variables. Our model performs competitively on two difficult domains.

1 Introduction

Information extraction (IE), defined as the task of extracting structured information (e.g., events, binary relations, etc.) from free text, has received renewed interest in the "big data" era, when petabytes of natural-language text containing thousands of different structure types are readily available. However, traditional supervised methods are unlikely to scale in this context, as training data is either limited or nonexistent for most of these structures. One of the most promising approaches to IE that addresses this limitation is *distant supervision*, which generates training data automatically by aligning a database of facts with text (Craven and Kumlien, 1999; Bunescu and Mooney, 2007).

$$\text{DB} = \begin{pmatrix} \textit{BornIn}(\text{Barack Obama, United States}) \\ \textit{EmployedBy}(\text{Barack Obama, United States}) \end{pmatrix}$$

Sentence	Latent Label
Barack Obama is the 44th and current President of the United States.	*EmployedBy*
Obama was born in the United States just as he has always said.	*BornIn*
United States President Barack Obama meets with Chinese Vice President Xi Jinping today.	*EmployedBy*
Obama ran for the United States Senate in 2004.	–

Figure 1: Training sentences generated through distant supervision for a database containing two facts.

In this paper we focus on distant supervision for relation extraction (RE), a subproblem of IE that addresses the extraction of labeled relations between two named entities. Figure 1 shows a simple example for a RE domain with two labels. Distant supervision introduces two modeling challenges, which we highlight in the table. The first challenge is that some training examples obtained through this heuristic are not valid, e.g., the last sentence in Figure 1 is not a correct example for any of the known labels for the tuple. The percentage of such false positives can be quite high. For example, Riedel et al. (2010) report up to 31% of false positives in a corpus that matches Freebase relations with New York Times articles. The second challenge is that the same pair of entities may have multiple labels and it is unclear which label is instantiated by any textual mention of the given tuple. For example, in Figure 1, the tuple (*Barack Obama*, *United States*) has two valid labels: *BornIn* and *EmployedBy*, each (latently) instantiated in different sentences. In the

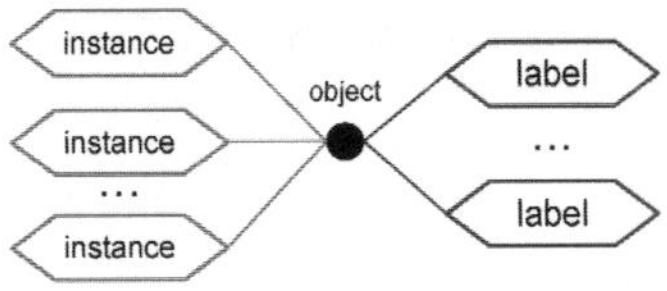

Figure 2: Overview of multi-instance multi-label learning. To contrast, in traditional supervised learning there is one instance and one label per object. For relation extraction the object is a tuple of two named entities. Each mention of this tuple in text generates a different instance.

Riedel corpus, 7.5% of the entity tuples in the training partition have more than one label.

We summarize this multi-instance multi-label (MIML) learning problem in Figure 2. In this paper we propose a novel graphical model, which we called `MIML-RE`, that targets MIML learning for relation extraction. Our work makes the following contributions:

(a) To our knowledge, `MIML-RE` is the first RE approach that jointly models both multiple instances (by modeling the latent labels assigned to instances) and multiple labels (by providing a simple method to capture dependencies between labels). For example, our model learns that certain labels tend to be generated jointly while others cannot be jointly assigned to the same tuple.

(b) We show that `MIML-RE` performs competitively on two difficult domains.

2 Related Work

Distant supervision for IE was introduced by Craven and Kumlien (1999), who focused on the extraction of binary relations between proteins and cells/tissues/diseases/drugs using the Yeast Protein Database as a source of distant supervision. Since then, the approach grew in popularity (Bunescu and Mooney, 2007; Bellare and McCallum, 2007; Wu and Weld, 2007; Mintz et al., 2009; Riedel et al., 2010; Hoffmann et al., 2011; Nguyen and Moschitti, 2011; Sun et al., 2011; Surdeanu et al., 2011a). However, most of these approaches make one or more approximations in learning. For example, most proposals heuristically transform distant supervision to traditional supervised learning (i.e., single-instance single-label) (Bellare and McCallum, 2007; Wu and Weld, 2007; Mintz et al., 2009; Nguyen and Moschitti, 2011; Sun et al., 2011; Surdeanu et al., 2011a). Bunescu and Mooney (2007) and Riedel et al. (2010) model distant supervision for relation extraction as a multi-instance single-label problem, which allows multiple mentions for the same tuple but disallows more than one label per object. Our work is closest to Hoffmann et al. (2011). They address the same problem we do (binary relation extraction) with a MIML model, but they make two approximations. First, they use a deterministic model that aggregates latent instance labels into a set of labels for the corresponding tuple by OR-ing the classification results. We use instead an object-level classifier that is trained jointly with the classifier that assigns latent labels to instances and can capture dependencies between labels. Second, they use a Perceptron-style additive parameter update approach, whereas we train in a Bayesian framework. We show in Section 5 that these approximations generally have a negative impact on performance.

MIML learning has been used in fields other than natural language processing. For example, Zhou and Zhang (2007) use MIML for scene classification. In this problem, each image may be assigned multiple labels corresponding to the different scenes captured. Furthermore, each image contains a set of patches, which forms the bag of instances assigned to the given object (image). Zhou and Zhang propose two algorithms that reduce the MIML problem to a more traditional supervised learning task. In one algorithm, for example, they convert the task to a multi-instance single-label problem by creating a separate bag for each label. Due to this, the proposed approach cannot model inter-label dependencies. Moreover, the authors make a series of approximations, e.g., they assume that each instance in a bag shares the bag's overall label. We instead model all these issues explicitly in our approach.

In general, our approach belongs to the category of models that learn in the presence of incomplete or incorrect labels. There has been interest among machine learning researchers in the general problem of noisy data, especially in the area of instance-based learning. Brodley and Friedl (1999) summarize past approaches and present a simple, all-purpose method to filter out incorrect data before training. While potentially applicable to our problem, this approach is completely general and cannot incorporate our domain-specific knowledge about how the noisy data is generated.

3 Distant Supervision for Relation Extraction

Here we focus on distant supervision for the extraction of *relations between two entities*. We define a *relation* as the construct $r(e_1, e_2)$, where r is the relation name, e.g., *BornIn* in Figure 1, and e_1 and e_2 are two entity names, e.g., *Barack Obama* and *United States*. Note that there are entity tuples (e_1, e_2) that participate in multiple relations, $r_1, \ldots, r_i$. In other words, the tuple (e_1, e_2) is the object illustrated in Figure 2 and the different relation names are the labels. We define an *entity mention* as a sequence of text tokens that matches the corresponding entity name in some text, and *relation mention* (for a given relation $r(e_1, e_2)$) as a pair of entity mentions of e_1 and e_2 in the same sentence. Relation mentions thus correspond to the instances in Figure 2.[1] As the latter definition indicates, we focus on the extraction of relations expressed in a single sentence. Furthermore, we assume that entity mentions are extracted by a different process, such as a named entity recognizer.

We define the task of *relation extraction* as a function that takes as input a document collection ($\mathcal{C}$), a set of entity mentions extracted from $\mathcal{C}$ ($\mathcal{E}$), a set of known relation labels ($\mathcal{L}$) and an extraction model, and outputs a set of relations ($\mathcal{R}$) such that any of the relations extracted is supported by at least one sentence in $\mathcal{C}$. To train the extraction model, we use a database of relations ($\mathcal{D}$) that are instantiated at least once in $\mathcal{C}$. Using distant supervision, $\mathcal{D}$ is aligned with sentences in $\mathcal{C}$, producing relation mentions for all relations in $\mathcal{D}$.

4 Model

Our model assumes that each relation mention involving an entity pair has exactly one label, but allows the pair to exhibit multiple labels across different mentions. Since we do not know the actual relation label of a mention in the distantly supervised setting, we model it using a latent variable z that can take one of the k pre-specified relation labels as well as an additional *NIL* label, if no relation is expressed by the corresponding mention. We model the multiple relation labels an entity pair can assume

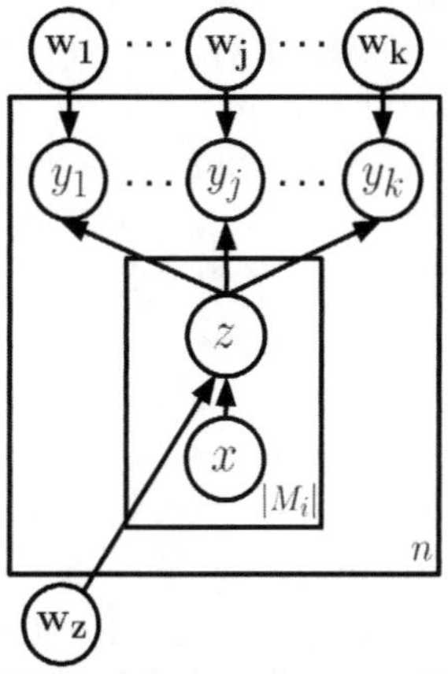

Figure 3: MIML model plate diagram. We unrolled the y plate to emphasize that it is a collection of binary classifiers (one per relation label), whereas the z classifier is multi-class. Each z and y_j classifier has an additional prior parameter, which is omitted here for clarity.

using a multi-label classifier that takes as input the latent relation types of the all the mentions involving that pair. The two-layer hierarchical model is shown graphically in Figure 3, and is described more formally below. The model includes one multi-class classifier (for z) and a set of binary classifiers (for each y_j). The z classifier assigns latent labels from $\mathcal{L}$ to individual relation mentions or *NIL* if no relation is expressed by the mention. Each y_j classifier decides if relation j holds for the given entity tuple, using the mention-level classifications as input. Specifically, in the figure:

- n is the number of distinct entity tuples in $\mathcal{D}$;
- M_i is the set of mentions for the ith entity pair;
- x is a sentence and z is the latent relation classification for that sentence;
- $\mathbf{w_z}$ is the weight vector for the multi-class mention-level classifier;
- k is the number of known relation labels in $\mathcal{L}$;
- y_j is the top-level classification decision for the entity pair as to whether the jth relation holds;
- $\mathbf{w_j}$ is the weight vector for the binary top-level classifier for the jth relation.

Additionally, we define P_i (N_i) as the set of all known positive (negative) relation labels for the ith entity tuple. In this paper, we construct N_i as $\mathcal{L} \setminus P_i$, but, in general, other scenarios are possible. For example, both Sun et al. (2011) and Surdeanu et

[1]For this reason, we use relation mention and relation instance interchangeably in this paper.

al. (2011a) proposed models where N_i for the ith tuple (e_1, e_2) is defined as: $\{r_j \mid r_j(e_1, e_k) \in \mathcal{D}, e_k \neq e_2, r_j \notin P_i\}$, which is a subset of $\mathcal{L} \setminus P_i$. That is, entity e_2 is considered a negative example for relation r_j (in the context of entity e_1) only if r_j exists in the training data with a different value.

The addition of the object-level layer (for $\mathbf{y}$) is an important contribution of this work. This layer can capture information that cannot be modeled by the mention-level classifier. For example, it can learn that two relation labels (e.g., *BornIn* and *SpouseOf*) cannot be generated jointly for the same entity tuple. So, if the z classifier outputs both these labels for different mentions of the same tuple, the $\mathbf{y}$ layer can cancel one of them. Furthermore, the $\mathbf{y}$ classifiers can learn when two labels tend to appear jointly, e.g., *CapitalOf* and *Contained* between two locations, and use this occurrence as positive reinforcement for these labels. We discuss the features that implement these ideas in Section 5.

4.1 Training

We train the proposed model using hard discriminative Expectation Maximization (EM). In the Expectation (E) step we assign latent mention labels using the current model (i.e., the mention and relation level classifiers). In the Maximization (M) step we retrain the model to maximize the log likelihood of the data using the current latent assignments.

In the equations that follow, we refer to $\mathbf{w_1}, \ldots, \mathbf{w_k}$ collectively as $\mathbf{w_y}$ for compactness. The vector $\mathbf{z_i}$ contains the latent mention-level classifications for the ith entity pair, while $\mathbf{y_i}$ represents the corresponding set of gold-standard labels (that is, $y_i^{(r)} = 1$ if $r \in P_i$, and $y_i^{(r)} = 0$ for $r \in N_i$.) Using these notations, the log-likelihood of the data is given by:

$$LL(\mathbf{w_y}, \mathbf{w_z}) = \sum_{i=1}^{n} \log p(\mathbf{y_i}|\mathbf{x_i}, \mathbf{w_y}, \mathbf{w_z}) = \sum_{i=1}^{n} \log \sum_{\mathbf{z_i}} p(\mathbf{y_i}, \mathbf{z_i}|\mathbf{x_i}, \mathbf{w_y}, \mathbf{w_z})$$

The joint probability in the inner summation can be broken up into simpler parts:

$$\begin{aligned} p(&\mathbf{y_i}, \mathbf{z_i}|\mathbf{x_i}, \mathbf{w_y}, \mathbf{w_z}) \\ &= p(\mathbf{z_i}|\mathbf{x_i}, \mathbf{w_z}) p(\mathbf{y_i}|\mathbf{z_i}, \mathbf{w_y}) \\ &= \prod_{m \in M_i} p(z_i^{(m)}|x_i^{(m)}, \mathbf{w_z}) \prod_{r \in P_i \cup N_i} p(y_i^{(r)}|\mathbf{z_i}, \mathbf{w_y^{(r)}}) \end{aligned}$$

where the last step follows from conditional independence. Thus the log-likelihood for this problem is not convex (it includes a sum of products). However, we can still use EM, but the optimization focuses on maximizing the lower bound of the log-likelihood, i.e., we maximize the above joint probability for each entity pair in the database. Rewriting this probability in log space, we obtain:

$$\begin{aligned} \log p(&\mathbf{y_i}, \mathbf{z_i}|\mathbf{x_i}, \mathbf{w_y}, \mathbf{w_z}) \\ &= \sum_{m \in M_i} \log p(z_i^{(m)}|x_i^{(m)}, \mathbf{w_z}) + \\ &\sum_{r \in P_i \cup N_i} \log p(y_i^{(r)}|\mathbf{z_i}, \mathbf{w_y^{(r)}}) \end{aligned} \tag{1}$$

The algorithm proceeds as follows.

E-step: In this step we infer the mention-level classifications $\mathbf{z_i}$ for each entity tuple, given all its mentions, the gold labels $\mathbf{y_i}$, and current model, i.e., $\mathbf{w_z}$ and $\mathbf{w_y}$ weights. Formally, we seek to find:

$$\mathbf{z_i}^* = \arg\max_{\mathbf{z}} p(\mathbf{z}|\mathbf{y_i}, \mathbf{x_i}, \mathbf{w_y}, \mathbf{w_z})$$

However it is computationally intractable to consider all vectors $\mathbf{z}$ as there is an exponential number of possible assignments, so we approximate and consider each mention separately. Concretely,

$$\begin{aligned} p(&z_i^{(m)}|\mathbf{y_i}, \mathbf{x_i}, \mathbf{w_y}, \mathbf{w_z}) \\ &\propto p(\mathbf{y_i}, z_i^{(m)}|\mathbf{x_i}, \mathbf{w_y}, \mathbf{w_z}) \\ &\approx p(z_i^{(m)}|x_i^{(m)}, \mathbf{w_z}) p(\mathbf{y_i}|\mathbf{z'_i}, \mathbf{w_y}) \\ &= p(z_i^{(m)}|x_i^{(m)}, \mathbf{w_z}) \prod_{r \in P_i \cup N_i} p(y_i^{(r)}|\mathbf{z'_i}, \mathbf{w_y^{(r)}}) \end{aligned}$$

where $\mathbf{z'_i}$ contains the previously inferred mention labels for group i, with the exception of component m whose label is replaced by $z_i^{(m)}$. So for $i = 1, \ldots, n$, and for each $m \in M_i$ we calculate:

$$z_i^{(m)*} = \arg\max_{z} p(z|x_i^{(m)}, \mathbf{w_z}) \times \prod_{r \in P_i \cup N_i} p(y_i^{(r)}|\mathbf{z'_i}, \mathbf{w_y^{(r)}}) \tag{2}$$

Intuitively, the above equation indicates that mention labels are chosen to maximize: (a) the probabilities assigned by the mention-level model; (b) the probability that the correct relation labels are assigned to the corresponding tuple; and (c) the probability that the labels known to be incorrect are *not* assigned to the tuple. For example, if a particular mention label receives a high mention-level probability but it is known to be a negative label for that tuple, it will receive a low overall score.

M-step: In this step we find $\mathbf{w_y}, \mathbf{w_z}$ that maximize the lower bound of the log-likelihood, i.e., the probability in equation (1), given the current assignments for $\mathbf{z_i}$. From equation (1) it is clear that this can be maximized separately with respect to $\mathbf{w_y}$ and $\mathbf{w_z}$. Intuitively, this step amounts to learning the weights for the mention-level classifier ($\mathbf{w_z}$) and the weights for each of the k top-level classifiers ($\mathbf{w_y}$). The updates are given by:

$$\mathbf{w_z^*} = \arg\max_{\mathbf{w}} \sum_{i=1}^{n} \sum_{m \in M_i} \log p(z_i^{(m)*} | x_i^{(m)}, \mathbf{w}) \quad (3)$$

$$\mathbf{w_y^{(r)*}} = \arg\max_{\mathbf{w}} \sum_{1 \leq i \leq n \ s.t. \ r \in P_i \cup N_i} \log p(y_i^{(r)} | \mathbf{z_i^*}, \mathbf{w}) \quad (4)$$

Note that these are standard updates for logistic regression. We obtained these weights using $k+1$ logistic classifiers: one multi-class classifier for $\mathbf{w_z}$ and k binary classifiers for each relation label $r \in \mathcal{L}$. We implemented all using the L2-regularized logistic regression from the publicly-downloadable Stanford CoreNLP package.[2] The main difference between the classifiers is how features are generated: the mention-level classifier computes its features based on x_i, whereas the relation-level classifiers generate features based on the current assignments for $\mathbf{z_i}$ and the corresponding relation label r. We discuss the actual features used in our experiments in Section 5.

4.2 Inference

Given an entity tuple, we obtain its relation labels as follows. We first classify its mentions:

$$z_i^{(m)*} = \arg\max_{z} p(z | x_i^{(m)}, \mathbf{w_z}) \quad (5)$$

then decide on the final relation labels using the top-level classifiers:

$$y_i^{(r)*} = \arg\max_{y \in \{0,1\}} p(y | \mathbf{z_i^*}, \mathbf{w_y^{(r)}}) \quad (6)$$

4.3 Implementation Details

We discuss next several details that are crucial for the correct implementation of the above model.

Initialization: Since EM is not guaranteed to converge at the global maximum of the observed data likelihood, it is important to provide it with good starting values. In our context, the initial values are labels assigned to $\mathbf{z_i}$, which are required to compute equation (2) in the first iteration ($\mathbf{z_i'}$). We generate these values using a local logistic regression classifier that uses the same features as the mention-level classifier in the joint model but treats each relation mention independently. We train this classifier using "traditional" distant supervision: for each relation in the database $\mathcal{D}$ we assume that all the corresponding mentions are positive examples for the corresponding label (Mintz et al., 2009). Note that this heuristic repeats relation mentions with different labels for the tuples that participate in multiple relations. For example, all the relation mentions in Figure 1 will yield datums with both the *EmployedBy* and *BornIn* labels. Despite this limitation, we found that this is a better initialization heuristic than random assignment.

For the second part of equation (2), we initialize the relation-level classifier with a model that replicates the *at least one* heuristic of Hoffmann et al. (2011). Each $\mathbf{w_y^{(r)}}$ model has a single feature with a high positive weight that is triggered when label r is assigned to any of the mentions in $\mathbf{z_i^*}$.

Avoiding overfitting: A naïve implementation of our approach leads to an unrealistic training scenario where the z classifier generates predictions (in equation (2)) for the same datums it has seen in training in the previous iteration. To avoid this overfitting problem we used cross validation: we divided the training tuples in K distinct folds and trained K different mention-level classifiers. Each classifier outputs $p(z|x_i^{(m)}, \mathbf{w_z})$ for tuples in a given fold during the E-step (equation (2)) and is trained (equation (3)) using tuples from all other folds.

[2] nlp.stanford.edu/software/corenlp.shtml

At testing time, we compute $p(z|x_i^{(m)}, \mathbf{w_z})$ in equation (5) as the average of the probabilities of the above set of mention classifiers:

$$p(z|x_i^{(m)}, \mathbf{w_z}) = \frac{\sum_{j=1}^{K} p(z|x_i^{(m)}, \mathbf{w_z^j})}{K}$$

where $\mathbf{w_z^j}$ are the weights of the mention classifier responsible for fold j. We found that this simple bagging model performs slightly better in practice (a couple of tenths of a percent) than training a single mention classifier on the latent mention labels generated in the last training iteration.

Inference during training: During the inference process in the E-step, the algorithm incrementally "flips" mention labels based on equation (2), for each group of mentions M_i. Thus, $\mathbf{z_i'}$ changes as the algorithm progresses, which may impact the label assigned to the remaining mentions in that group. To avoid any potential bias introduced by the arbitrary order of mentions as seen in the data, we randomize each group M_i before we inspect its mentions.

5 Experimental Results

5.1 Data

We evaluate our algorithm on two corpora. The first was developed by Riedel et al. (2010) by aligning Freebase[3] relations with the New York Times (NYT) corpus. They used the Stanford named entity recognizer (Finkel et al., 2005) to find entity mentions in text and constructed relation mentions only between entity mentions in the same sentence.

Riedel et al. (2010) observes that evaluating on this corpus underestimates true extraction accuracy because Freebase is incomplete. Thus, some relations extracted during testing will be incorrectly marked as wrong, simply because Freebase has no information on them. To mitigate this issue, Riedel et al. (2010) and Hoffman et al. (2011) perform a second evaluation where they compute the accuracy of labels assigned to a set of relation mentions that they manually annotated. To avoid any potential annotation biases, we instead evaluate on a second corpus that has comprehensive annotations generated by experts for all test relations.

We constructed this second dataset using mainly resources distributed for the 2010 and 2011 KBP shared tasks (Ji et al., 2010; Ji et al., 2011). We generated training relations from the knowledge base provided by the task organizers, which is a subset of the English Wikipedia infoboxes from a 2008 snapshot. Similarly to the corpus of Riedel et al., these infoboxes contain open-domain relations between named entities, but with a different focus. For example, more than half of the relations in the evaluation data are alternate names of organizations or persons (e.g., *org:alternate_names*) or relations associated with employment and membership (e.g., *per:employee_of*) (Ji et al., 2011). We aligned these relations against a document collection that merges two distinct sources: (a) the collection provided by the shared task, which contains approximately 1.5 million documents from a variety of sources, including newswire, blogs and telephone conversation transcripts; and (b) a complete snapshot of the English Wikipedia from June 2010. During training, for each entity tuple (e_1, e_2), we retrieved up to 50 sentences that contain both entity mentions.[4] We used Stanford's CoreNLP package to find entity mentions in text and, similarly to Riedel et al. (2010), we construct relation mention candidates only between entity mentions in the same sentence. We analyzed a set of over 2,000 relation mentions and we found that 39% of the mentions where e_1 is an organization name and 36% of mentions where e_1 is a person name do not express the corresponding relation.

At evaluation time, the KBP shared task requires the extraction of all relations $r(e_1, e_2)$ given a query that contains only the first entity e_1. To accommodate this setup, we adjusted our sentence extraction component to use just e_1 as the retrieval query and we kept up to 50 sentences that contain a mention of the input entity for each evaluation query. For tuning and testing we used the 200 queries from the 2010 and 2011 evaluations. We randomly selected 40 queries for development and used the remaining 160 for the formal evaluation.

To address the large number of negative examples in training, Riedel et al. subsampled them randomly with a retention probability of 10%. For the KBP corpus, we followed the same strategy, but we used

[3] freebase.com

[4] Sentences were ranked using the similarity between their parent document and the query that concatenates the two entity names. We used the default Lucene similarity measure.

	# of gold relations in training	# of gold relations in testing	% of gold entity tuples with more than one label in training	% of gold entity tuples with multiple mentions in text in training	% of mentions that do not express their relation	# of relation labels
Riedel	4,700	1,950	7.5%	46.4%	up to 31%	51
KBP	183,062	3,334	2.8%	65.1%	up to 39%	41

Table 1: Statistics about the two corpora used in this paper. Some of the numbers for the Riedel dataset is from (Riedel et al., 2010; Hoffmann et al., 2011).

a subsampling probability of 5% because this led to the best results in development for all models.

Table 1 provides additional statistics about the two corpora. The table indicates that having multiple mentions for an entity tuple is a very common phenomenon in both corpora, and that having multiple labels per tuple is more common in the Riedel dataset than KBP (7.5% vs. 2.8%).

5.2 Features

Our model requires two sets of features: one for the mention classifier (z) and one for the relation classifier (y). In the Riedel dataset, we used the same features as Riedel et al. (2010) and Hoffmann et al. (2011) for the mention classifier. In the KBP dataset, we used a feature set that was developed in our previous work (Surdeanu et al., 2011b). These features can be grouped in three classes: (a) features that model the two entities, such as their head words; (b) features that model the syntactic context of the relation mention, such as the dependency path between the two entity mentions; and (c) features that model the surface context, such as the sequence of part of speech tags between the two entity mentions. We used these features for all the models evaluated on the KBP dataset.[5]

For the relation-level classifier, we developed two feature groups. The first models Hoffmann et al.'s *at least one* heuristic using a single feature, which is set to true if at least one mention in $\mathbf{z_i}$ has the label r, which is modeled by the current relation classifier. The second group models the dependencies between relation labels. This is implemented by a set of $|\mathcal{L}| - 1$ features, where feature j is instantiated whenever the label modeled (r) is predicted jointly with another label r_j ($r_j \in \mathcal{L}, r_j \neq r$) in $\mathbf{z_i}$. These features learn both positive and negative reinforcements between labels. For example, if labels r_1 and r_2 tend to be generated jointly, the feature for the corresponding dependency will receive a positive weight in the models for r_1 and r_2. Similarly, if r_1 and r_2 cannot be generated jointly, the model will assign a negative weight to feature 2 in r_1's classifier and to feature 1 in r_2's classifier. Note that this feature is asymmetric, i.e., feature 1 in r_2's classifier may have a different value than feature 2 in r_1's classifier, depending on the accuracy of the individual predictions for r_1 and r_2.

5.3 Baselines

We compare our approach against three models:

Mintz++ – This is the model used to initialize the mention-level classifier in our model. As discussed in Section 4.3, this model follows the "traditional" distant supervision heuristic, similarly to (Mintz et al., 2009). However, our implementation has several advantages over the original model: (a) we model each relation mention independently, whereas Mintz et al. collapsed all the mentions of the same entity tuple into a single datum; (b) we allow multi-label outputs for a given entity tuple at prediction time by OR-ing the predictions for the individual relation mentions corresponding to the tuple (similarly to (Hoffmann et al., 2011))[6]; and (c) we use the simple bagging strategy described in Section 4.3 to combine multiple models. Empirically, we observed that these changes yield a significant improvement over the original proposal. For this reason, we consider this model a strong baseline on its own.

Riedel – This is the "at-least-once" model reported in (Riedel et al., 2010), which had the best performance in that work. This approach models the task as a multi-instance single-label problem. Note that this is the only model shown here that does not allow multi-label outputs for an entity tuple.

[5]To avoid an excessive number of features in the KBP experiments, we removed features seen less than five times in training.

[6]We also allow multiple labels per tuple at training time, in which case we replicate the corresponding datum for each label. However, this did not improve performance significantly compared to selecting a single label per datum during training.

Hoffmann – This is the "MultiR" model, which performed the best in (Hoffmann et al., 2011). This models RE as a MIML problem, but learns using a Perceptron algorithm and uses a deterministic "at least one" decision instead of a relation classifier. We used Hoffman's publicly released code[7] for the experiments on the Riedel dataset and our own implementation for the KBP experiments.[8]

5.4 Results

We tuned all models using three-fold cross validation for the Riedel dataset and using the development queries for the KBP dataset. `MIML-RE` has two parameters that require tuning: the number of EM epochs (T) and the number of folds for the mention classifiers (K).[9] The values obtained after tuning are $T = 15, K = 5$ for the Riedel dataset and $T = 8, K = 3$ for KBP. Similarly, we tuned the number of epochs for the Hoffmann model on the KBP dataset, obtaining an optimal value of 20.

On the Riedel dataset we evaluate all models using standard precision and recall measures. For the KBP evaluation we used the official KBP scorer,[10] with two changes: (a) we score with the parameter `anydoc` set to true, which configures the scorer to accept relation mentions as correct regardless of their supporting document; and (b) we score only on the subset of gold relations that have at least one mention in our sentences. The first decision is necessary because the gold KBP answers contain supporting documents only from the corpus provided by the organizers but we retrieve candidate answers from multiple collections. The second is required because the focus of this work is not on sentence retrieval but on RE, which should be evaluated in isolation.[11]

Similarly to previous work, we report precision/recall curves in Figure 4. We evaluate two variants of `MIML-RE`: one that includes all the features for the y model, and another (`MIML-RE At-Least-One`) which has only the *at least one* feature. For all the Bayesian models implemented here, we sorted the predicted relations by the noisy-or score of the top predictions for their mentions. Formally, we rank a relation r predicted for group i, i.e., $r \in \mathbf{y}_i^*$, using:

$$\text{noisyOr}_i(r) = 1 - \prod_{m \in M_i} (1 - s_i^{(m)}(r))$$

where $s_i^{(m)}(r) = p(r|x_i^{(m)}, \mathbf{w_z})$ if $r = z_i^{(m)*}$ or 0 otherwise. The noisy-or formula performs well for ranking because it integrates model confidence (the higher the probabilities, the higher the score) and redundancy (the more mentions are predicted with a label, the higher that label's score). Note that the above ranking score does not include the probability of the relation classifier (equation (6)) for `MIML-RE`. While we use equation (6) to generate $\mathbf{y}_i^*$, we found that the corresponding probabilities are too coarse to provide a good ranking score. This is caused by the fact that our relation-level classifier works with a small number of (noisy) features. Lastly, for our implementation of the Hoffmann et al. model, we used their ranking heuristic (sorting predictions by the maximum extraction score for that relation).

6 Discussion

Figure 4 indicates that `MIML-RE` generally outperforms the current state of the art. In the Riedel dataset, `MIML-RE` has higher overall recall than the Riedel et al. model, and, for the same recall point, `MIML-RE`'s precision is between 2 and 15 points higher. For most of the curve, our model obtains better precision for the same recall point than the Hoffmann model, which currently has the best reported results on this dataset. The difference is as high as 5 precision points around the middle of the curve. The Hoffmann model performs better close to the extremities of the curve (low/high recall). Nevertheless, we argue that our model is more stable than Hoffmann's: `MIML-RE` yields a smoother precision/recall curve, without most of the depressions seen in the Hoffmann results. In the KBP dataset, `MIML-RE` performs consistently better than our implementation of Hoffmann's model, with higher precision values for the same recall point, and much higher overall recall. We believe that these differences are caused by our Bayesian framework,

[7] `cs.washington.edu/homes/raphaelh/mr/`

[8] The decision to reimplement the Hoffmann model was a practical one, driven by incompatibilities between their implementation and our KBP framework.

[9] We could also tune the prior parameters for both our model and Mintz++, but we found in early experiments that the default value of 1 yields the best scores for all priors.

[10] `nlp.cs.qc.cuny.edu/kbp/2011/scoring.html`

[11] Due to these changes, the scores reported in this paper are not directly comparable with the shared task scores.

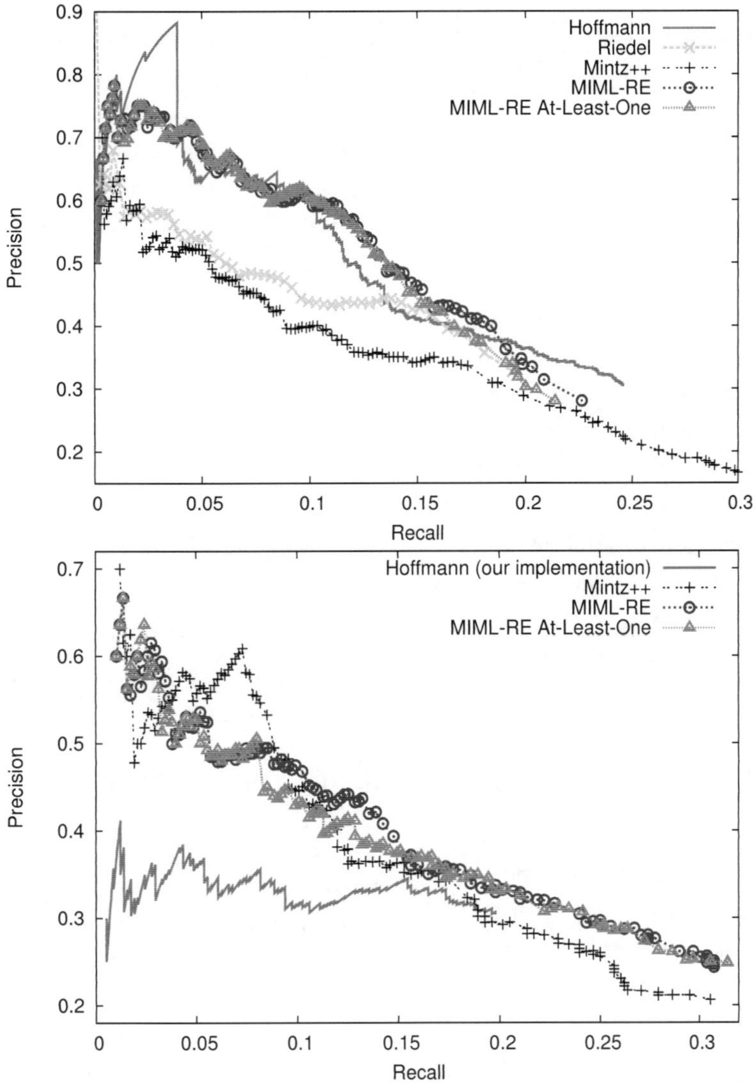

Figure 4: Results in the Riedel dataset (top) and the KBP dataset (bottom). The Hoffmann scores in the KBP dataset were generated using our implementation. The other Hoffmann and Riedel results were taken from their papers.

which provides a more formal implementation of the MIML problem.

Figure 4 also indicates that `MIML-RE` yields a consistent improvement over Mintz++ (with the exception of a few points in the low-recall portion of the KBP curves). The difference in precision for the same recall point is as high as 25 precision points in the Riedel dataset and up to 5 points in KBP. Overall, the best F1 score of `MIML-RE` is slightly over 1 point higher than the best F1 score of Mintz++ in the Riedel dataset and 3 points higher in KBP. Considering that Mintz++ is a strong baseline and we evaluate on two challenging domains, we consider these results proof that the correct modeling of the MIML scenario is beneficial.

Lastly, Figure 4 shows that `MIML-RE` outperforms its variant without label-dependency features (`MIML-RE At-Least-One`) in the higher-recall part of the curve in the Riedel dataset. The improvement is approximately 1 F1 point throughout the last segment of the curve. The overall increase in F1 was found to be significant ($p = 0.0296$) in a one-sided, paired t-test over randomly sampled test data. We see a smaller improvement in KBP (concentrated around the middle of the curve), likely because the number of entity tuples with multiple labels in training is small (see Table 1). Nevertheless, this exercise shows that, when dependencies between labels exist in a dataset, modeling them, which can be trivially done in `MIML-RE`, is useful.

	P	R	F1
Hoffmann (our implementation)	48.6	29.8	37.0
Mintz++	43.8	**36.8**	40.0
MIML-RE	**64.8**	31.6	**42.6**
MIML-RE At-Least-One	56.1	32.5	41.1

Table 2: Results at the highest F1 point in the precision/recall curve on the dataset that contains groups with at least 10 mentions.

In a similar vein, we tested the models previously described on a subset of the Riedel evaluation dataset that only includes groups with at least 10 mentions. This corpus contains approximately 2% of the groups from the original testing partition, out of which 90 tuples have at least one known label and 1410 groups serve as negative examples.

For conciseness, we do not include the entire precision/recall curves for this experiment, but summarize them in Table 2, which lists the performance peak (highest F1 score) for each of the models investigated. The table shows that `MIML-RE` obtains the highest F1 score overall, 1.5 points higher than `MIML-RE At-Least-One` and 2.6 points higher than Mintz++. More importantly, for approximately the same recall point, `MIML-RE` obtains a precision that is over 8 percentage points higher than that of `MIML-RE At-Least-One`. A post-hoc inspection of the results indicates that, indeed, `MIML-RE` successfully eliminates undesired labels when two (or more) incompatible labels are jointly assigned to the same tuple. Take for example the tuple (*Mexico City*, *Mexico*), for which the correct relation is */location/administrative_division/country*. `MIML-RE At-Least-One` incorrectly predicts the additional */location/location/contains* relation, while `MIML-RE` does not make this prediction because it recognizes that these two labels are incompatible in general: one location cannot both be within another location and contain it. Indeed, examining the weights assigned to label-dependency features in `MIML-RE`, we see that the model has assigned a large negative weight to the dependency feature between */location/location/contains* and */location/administrative_division/country* for the */location/location/contains* class. We also observe positive dependencies between labels. For example, `MIML-RE` learns that the relations */people/person/place_lived* and */people/person/place_of_birth* tend to co-occur and assigns a positive weight to this dependency feature for the corresponding classes.

These results strongly suggest that when all aspects of the MIML scenario are present, our model can successfully capture them and make use of the additional structure to improve performance.

7 Conclusion

In this paper we showed that distant supervision for RE, which generates training data by aligning a database of facts with text, poses a distinct multi-instance multi-label learning scenario. In this setting, each entity pair to be modeled typically has multiple instances in the text and may have multiple labels in the database. This is considerably different from traditional supervised learning, where each instance has a single, explicit label.

We argued that this MIML scenario should be formally addressed. We proposed, to our knowledge, the first approach that models all aspects of the MIML setting, i.e., the latent assignment of labels to instances and dependencies between labels assigned to the same entity pair.

We evaluated our model on two challenging domains and obtained state-of-the-art results on both. Our model performs well even when not all aspects of the MIML scenario are common, and as seen in the discussion, shows significant improvement when evaluated on entity pairs with many labels or mentions. When all aspects of the MIML scenario are present, our model is well-equipped to handle them.

The code and data used in the experiments reported in this paper are available at: `http://nlp.stanford.edu/software/mimlre.shtml`.

Acknowledgments

We gratefully acknowledge the support of Defense Advanced Research Projects Agency (DARPA) Machine Reading Program under Air Force Research Laboratory (AFRL) prime contract no. FA8750-09-C-0181. Any opinions, findings, and conclusion or recommendations expressed in this material are those of the author(s) and do not necessarily reflect the view of the DARPA, AFRL, or the US government. We gratefully thank Raphael Hoffmann and Sebastian Riedel for sharing their code and data and for the many useful discussions.

References

Kedar Bellare and Andrew McCallum. 2007. Learning extractors from unlabeled text using relevant databases. In *Proceedings of the Sixth International Workshop on Information Extraction on the Web*.

Carla Brodley and Mark Friedl. 1999. Identifying mislabeled training data. *Journal of Artificial Intelligence Research (JAIR)*.

Razvan Bunescu and Raymond Mooney. 2007. Learning to extract relations from the web using minimal supervision. In *Proceedings of the 45th Annual Meeting of the Association for Computational Linguistics*.

Mark Craven and Johan Kumlien. 1999. Constructing biological knowledge bases by extracting information from text sources. In *Proceedings of the Seventh International Conference on Intelligent Systems for Molecular Biology*.

Jenny Rose Finkel, Trond Grenager, and Christopher D. Manning. 2005. Incorporating non-local information into information extraction systems by gibbs sampling. In *Proceedings of the 43nd Annual Meeting of the Association for Computational Linguistics*.

Raphael Hoffmann, Congle Zhang, Xiao Ling, Luke Zettlemoyer, and Daniel S. Weld. 2011. Knowledge-based weak supervision for information extraction of overlapping relations. In *Proceedings of the Annual Meeting of the Association for Computational Linguistics (ACL)*.

Heng Ji, Ralph Grishman, Hoa T. Dang, Kira Griffitt, and Joe Ellis. 2010. Overview of the TAC 2010 knowledge base population track. In *Proceedings of the Text Analytics Conference*.

Heng Ji, Ralph Grishman, and Hoa T. Dang. 2011. Overview of the TAC 2011 knowledge base population track. In *Proceedings of the Text Analytics Conference*.

Mike Mintz, Steven Bills, Rion Snow, and Daniel Jurafsky. 2009. Distant supervision for relation extraction without labeled data. In *Proceedings of the 47th Annual Meeting of the Association for Computational Linguistics*.

Truc Vien T. Nguyen and Alessandro Moschitti. 2011. End-to-end relation extraction using distant supervision from external semantic repositories. In *Proceedings of the 49th Annual Meeting of the Association for Computational Linguistics: Human Language Technologies*.

Sebastian Riedel, Limin Yao, and Andrew McCallum. 2010. Modeling relations and their mentions without labeled text. In *Proceedings of the European Conference on Machine Learning and Knowledge Discovery in Databases (ECML PKDD '10)*.

Ang Sun, Ralph Grishman, Wei Xu, and Bonan Min. 2011. New York University 2011 system for KBP slot filling. In *Proceedings of the Text Analytics Conference*.

Mihai Surdeanu, Sonal Gupta, John Bauer, David McClosky, Angel X. Chang, Valentin I. Spitkovsky, and Christopher D. Manning. 2011a. Stanford's distantly-supervised slot-filling system. In *Proceedings of the Text Analytics Conference*.

Mihai Surdeanu, David McClosky, Mason R. Smith, Andrey Gusev, and Christopher D. Manning. 2011b. Customizing an information extraction system to a new domain. In *Proceedings of the Workshop on Relational Models of Semantics*, Portland, Oregon, June.

Fei Wu and Dan Weld. 2007. Autonomously semantifying Wikipedia. In *Proceedings of the International Conference on Information and Knowledge Management (CIKM)*.

Z.H. Zhou and M.L. Zhang. 2007. Multi-instance multi-label learning with application to scene classification. In *Advances in Neural Information Processing Systems (NIPS)*.

An "AI readability" formula for French as a foreign language

Thomas François
IRCS, University of Pennsylvania
3401 Walnut Street Suite 400A Room 423
Philadelphia, PA 19104, USA
frthomas@sas.upenn.edu

Cédrick Fairon
CENTAL, UCLouvain
Place Blaise Pascal, 1
1348 Louvain-la-Neuve, Belgium
Cedrick.Fairon@uclouvain.be

Abstract

This paper present a new readability formula for French as a foreign language (FFL), which relies on 46 textual features representative of the lexical, syntactic, and semantic levels as well as some of the specificities of the FFL context. We report comparisons between several techniques for feature selection and various learning algorithms. Our best model, based on support vector machines (SVM), significantly outperforms previous FFL formulas. We also found that semantic features behave poorly in our case, in contrast with some previous readability studies on English as a first language.

1 Introduction

Whether in a first language (L1) or a second and foreign language (L2), learning to read has been and remains one of the major concerns of education. When a teacher wants to improve his/her students' reading skills, he/she uses reading exercises, whether there are guided or independent. For this practice to be efficient, it is necessary that the texts suit the level of students (O'Connor et al., 2002). This condition is sometimes difficult to meet for teachers wishing to get off the beaten tracks by not using texts from levelled textbooks or readers.

In this context, readability formulas have long been used to help teachers faster select texts for their students. These formulas are reproducible methods that aim at matching readers and texts relative to their reading difficulty level. The Flesch (1948) and Dale and Chall (1948) formulas are probably the best-known examples of those. They are typical of classic formulas, the first major methodological paradigm developed in the field during the 40's and 50's. They were kept as parsimonious as possible, using linear regression to combined two, or sometimes, three surface features, such as word mean length, sentence mean length, or proportion of out-of-simple-vocabulary words.

Later, some scholars (Kintsch and Vipond, 1979; Redish and Selzer, 1985) argued that the classic formulas suffer from several shortcomings. These formulas only take into account superficial features, ignoring other important aspects contributing to text difficulty, such as coherence, content density, inference load, etc. They also omit the interactive aspect of the reading process. In the 80's, a second paradigm, inspired by structuro-cognitivist theories, intended to overcome these issues. It focused on higher textual dimensions, such as inference load (Kintsch and Vipond, 1979; Kemper, 1983), density of concepts (Kintsch and Vipond, 1979), or macrostructure (Meyer, 1982). However, these attempts did not achieve better results than the classic approach, even though they used more principled and more complex features.

Recently, a third paradigm, referred to as the "AI readability" by François (2011a), has emerged in the field. Studies that are part of this current share three key features: the use of a large number of texts assessed by experts (coming from textbooks, simplified newspapers or web resources) as training data ; the use of NPL-enable features able to capture a wider range of readability factors, and the combination of those features through a machine learning algorithm. Since the work of Si and Callan (2001), this paradigm have spawn several studies for English (Collins-Thompson and Callan, 2005; Heilman et al., 2008; Schwarm and Ostendorf, 2005; Feng et al., 2010).

However, for French, the field is far from being so thriving. To our knowledge, only two "AI readability" have been designed so far for French L1 and only one for French as a foreign language (FFL) (see Section 2). This paper reports some experiments aimed at designing a more efficient readability model for FFL. In Section 2, it is further argue why a new formula was necessary for FFL. Section 3 covers the various methodological steps required to devise the model, whose results are reported in Section 4. Finally, Section 5 discusses some interesting insights gained by this work.

2 Readability models for French

Readability of French never enjoyed a large success: while readability studies on English dates back to the 20's, it is only in 1957 that the French-speaking world discovered it through the work of Conquet (1957). Since then, only a few studies focused on the topic.

The two first French L1 formulas were adaptations of the Flesch formula (Kandel and Moles, 1958; de Landsheere, 1963). It is only with Henry (1975) that French got a model fitting the particularities of the language. Henry used cloze tests to assess the level of 60 texts from primary and secondary school textbooks and trained three formulas on this corpus. It is worth mentioning that Henry's formulas have been applied to FFL by Cornaire (1988). During the same time, Richaudeau explored a different path, as a representative of the structuro-cognitivist paradigm. He used the number of words recalled by a subject after he/she has just read a sentence as a device to measure understanding and provided an "efficiency formula" of texts (Richaudeau, 1979). Although more modern in its conception, Richaudeau's hard-to-implement formula did not achieve the same recognition in the French speaking world as Henry's.

After those two major efforts, few works followed. It is worth mentioning two more authors: Mesnager (1989), who designed a classic formula for children that draw inspiration from the Dale and Chall (1948) formula and Daoust et al. (1996), who developed SATO-CALIBRAGE, a program assessing text difficulty from the first to the eleventh grade. It can be considered as the first "AI formula" for French L1, since it made use of NLP-enabled features. It is also the last formula published for French L1, if we except the adaptation of the model by Collins-Thompson and Callan (2004) to French.

As regards to French L2, the literature is even sparser. Tharp (1939) published a first formula taking into account one particularity of the L2 context: the cognates. Those are words sharing a similar form and meaning across two languages and having a facilitating effect in reading. This idea was recently replicated by Uitdenbogerd (2005), who combined a syntactic feature, the mean number of words per sentence, with the number of cognates per 100 words in her formula. Although taking into account this effect of the L1 on L2 reading is very interesting, these two studies are confined to a limited audience: English speakers learning French. As regards a more generic approach, François (2009) recently published an "AI formula" for FFL, based on logistic regression and ten features. Among those, he stressed the use of verbal tense information as a way to improve performance. However, the set of features he experimented remains limited (about 20).

From all this, it seems clear that FFL readability needs to be addressed more thoroughly, especially if we are willing to get a generic model, able to make predictions for L2 readers with any L1 background. The rest of this paper describes one such attempt.

3 Design of the formula

The design of an "AI readability" formula involves the same three steps as a classification problem. First, one need to gather a gold-standard corpus large enough to reliably train the parameters of a learning algorithm, as described in Section 3.1. The next step, covered in Section 3.2, consists in defining a set of predictors, that is to say, linguistic characteristics of the texts that will be used to predict the difficulty level of new texts. Finally, the best subset of these predictors is combined within a learning algorithm to obtain the best model possible. Experiments at this level are reported in Section 3.3.

3.1 The corpus

A gold-standard for readability consists in texts labelled according to their difficulty. For this, it is first necessary to choose a difficulty scale used for the labels (for English L1, it is usually the 12 grade levels scale), that also constrains the output of the formula. Then, each text have to be assessed with a method able to measure the reading comprehension level of the target population.

Regarding the scale, an obvious choice for the foreign language context was the beginner/intermediate/advanced continuum, recently redefined in the Common European Framework of Reference for Languages (CEFR) (Council of Europe, 2001) as the six following levels: A1 (Breakthrough); A2 (Waystage); B1 (Threshold); B2 (Vantage); C1 (Effective Operational Proficiency) and C2 (Mastery). This scale has now become the reference for foreign language education, at least in Europe.

Assessing the reading difficulty of texts with respect to a target population of readers was a more challenging issue. Several techniques have been used in the literature, the most important of which are comprehension tests, cloze tests and expert judgements. They all postulate a given population of readers, although relying on expert judgements save the need for a sample of subjects to take a test. In this case, texts comes from textbooks whose content difficulty have been assessed by the publishers.

This last criterion is now mainstream in "AI readability", since it is very practical and facilitates the creation of a large corpus, but it has its own shortcomings. Studies such as van Oosten et al. (2011) found that expert agreement on a same corpus of texts might be insufficient for a classification task.

For this study, we nevertheless relied on expert judgements, since we needed a large amount of labelled texts to ensure a robust statistical learning. We selected 28 FFL textbooks, published after 2001 and designed for adults or adolescents learning FFL for general purposes. From those, we extracted 2,160 texts related to a reading comprehension task and assigned to each of them the same level as the textbook it came from.

As it was expected from van Oosten et al. (2011)'s study, differences in the publishers' conception of difficulty led to an heterogeneous labelling between textbooks. This heterogeneity was detected in three of the six levels (A1, A2, and B1) using ANOVA based on two classic readability features as independent variables: the mean number of words per sentence and the mean number of letters per word. A subsequent qualitative analysis revealed that most of the heterogeneity was coming from textbooks following the new didactic approach recommended by the CEFR: the task-oriented approach, which focuses more on the task than the text when labelling the overall reading activity. Therefore, we decided to remove those type of textbooks from our corpus, which amounted to 5 books and 249 texts. The remaining 1,852 excerpts were kept for our experiments. Their distribution is displayed in Table 1 as regard to the number of texts and tokens.

3.2 The predictors

In a second step, every text of the corpus was represented as a numeric vector of 406 features, each of them representing a linguistic dimension of the text as a single number. Their implementation drew on two different sources of inspiration: the existing predictors in the English and French literature and the psycholinguistic literature on the reading process. The complete set was classified in four families, depending on the kind of information each one is supposed to represent. These families were: "lexical", "syntactic", "semantic", and "specific to FFL context". Each of them was further divided in subfamilies, described in the rest of the section [1].

3.2.1 Lexical Features

Lexical features have been shown to be the most important level of information in many readability studies (Chall and Dale, 1995; Lorge, 1944). It is then not surprising that a wide range of lexical predictors have been developed in the literature. Our own set comprised the following subfamilies:

Statistics of lexical frequencies: frequencies of words in a text are a good indicator of the text's overall difficulty (Stenner, 1996). They are usually summarized via the mean, but we also tested the median, the interquartile range, as well as the 75th and 90th percentiles.

[1]Space restrictions did not enable us to formally defined each variable used in this study. The reader may consult François (2011b) for a more comprehensive description.

A1	A2	B1	B2	C1	C2	Total
$430(58.561)$	$380(75.779)$	$552(176.973)$	$198(71.701)$	$184(92.327)$	$108(35.202)$	$1,852(510;543)$

Table 1: Distribution of the number of texts and tokens per level in our corpus.

We used *Lexique3* (New et al., 2007) as our frequency database. It is a lexicon including about 50,000 lemmas and 125,000 inflected forms whose frequencies were obtained from movie subtitles. Since French has a rich morphology, we considered the probabilities of both lemma and inflected forms. Moreover, following an idea from Elley (1969), we also computed the above mentioned statistics for given POS words, such as content word, nouns, verbs, etc.

Percentage of words not in a reference list: part of the Dale and Chall (1948)'s formula, this feature is one of the most famous in readability. For our experiments, two word lists for FFL were used: the well-known – but already dated – Gougenheim et al. (1964)'s list and a second one that was found at the end of one FFL textbook: *Alter Ego* (Berthet et al., 2006). Different sizes were also experimented for both lists.

Word length: mean word length is another classic feature in readability (Flesch, 1948; Smith, 1961). We used various statistics based on the number of letters per word (mean, median, percentiles, etc.).

N-grams models: Si and Callan (2001) shown that n-grams models can successfully be applied to readability. We then used both a simple unigram approach based on the frequencies from *Lexique3*, and a more complex bigram model trained on two different corpora: the Google n-grams (Michel et al., 2011) and a corpus of newspaper articles from *Le Soir* amounting to $5,000,000$ words [2]. Both were normalized according the length n of the text as follows:

$$P(text) = \frac{1}{n} \sum_{i=1}^{n} \log P(w_i|h) \qquad (1)$$

where w_i is the ith word and h a limited history of length 0 (unigram) or 1 (bigram).

[2]Smoothing algorithms used were respectively the simple Good-Turing algorithm (Gale and Sampson, 1995) for unigrams and linear interpolation (Chen and Goodman, 1999) for the bigrams.

Lexical diversity: the repetition effect is another factor known to affect the reading process (Bowers, 2000). It has been mainly implemented through the classic type-token ratio (TTR) that suffers from being dependent on the text length. This is why we defined a normalized TTR, which is the mean score of several TTRs, computed on text's fragments of equal length. This way, long texts were made comparable with short ones.

Orthographic neighborhood: we finally suggested a new lexical variable, based on the fact that some characteristics of the orthographic neighbors [3] of a word are known to impact the reading of this word (Andrews, 1997). Thirteen predictors were implemented to account for the number or the frequency of the orthographic neighbors of all words in a text.

3.2.2 Syntactic features

The syntactic level of information is another traditional area of investigation in readability. Although most of the scholars in the field agree that it does not lead to such efficient predictors as the lexical level, they have noticed it can be combined with the latter to improve performance of readability formulas. We therefore investigated the following subfamilies:

Sentence length: the traditional approach to syntactic difficulty relied on the number of words per sentence. We have approached it through various statistics such as the mean, the median, or several percentiles.

Part of speech ratios: Bormuth (1966) demonstrated the good predictive power of some POS ratios in a text. We computed 156 ratios based on TreeTagger's POS (Schmid, 1994). They operated as proxies for the syntactic complexity of sentences, since we did not use features based on a parser [4].

[3]The orthographic neighbors of a word X have been defined by Coltheart (1978) as all the words of the same length as X and varying from it only by one letter (eg. FIST and GIST).

[4]This choice was motivated as follows. Bormuth (1966), who performed a manual annotation of the syntactic structures

Verbs: although the tense and moods found in a text have been hardly considered in the field, Carreiras et al. (1997) suggested that verbal aspects are important while building a mental representation of a text and therefore impact its understanding. They help the reader to distinguish between major and minor elements associated with events described by these verbs. We therefore replicated and enhanced the feature set proposed by François (2009), considering either binary indicators or proportions of the use of tenses or moods in a text.

3.2.3 Semantic features

The importance of semantic and cognitive factors have been particularly stressed by the structuro-cognitivist paradigm, although Miller and Kintsch (1980), as well as Kemper (1983), eventually admitted not being able to demonstrate the superiority of those new predictors over traditional ones. More recent work also reported limited evidence of this alleged superiority (Pitler and Nenkova, 2008; Feng et al., 2010). In order to clarify as much as possible the situation for FFL, we implemented the following features:

Personnalization level: Dale and Tyler (1934) suggested that informal texts should be easier to read and that informality might be assessed through the type of personal pronouns found in a text. On this assumption, 13 variables were defined to take into account various personal pronouns proportions in the text.

Conceptual density: Kintsch et al. (1975) showed that the number of propositions as well as the number of different arguments in a sentence influence its reading time. Following Kintsch's propositional model, we used *Densidées* (Lee et al., 2010) to capture conceptual complexity. It is a program able to estimate the mean number of propositions per word in a text using 35 rules relying on lexical and POS clues.

in its corpus, noticed that features based on parse trees were less efficient than classic ones, such as sentence length or part of speech ratios. Therefore, it seemed unlikely that the information collected by means of syntactic parsers, which are still committing a significant number of errors, at least for French, would belie these findings.

Lexical cohesion : the level of cohesion in a text was measured as the average cosine of all pair of adjacent sentences in the text. Each sentence was represented by a numeric weighted vector (based on words) and projected in a vector space. As suggested by Foltz and al. (1998), two methods were used to define the vector space and weight every word: the *tf-idf* (term frequency-inverse document frequency) and the latent semantic analysis (LSA). The first approach, called "word overlap", corresponds to the "noun overlap" defined by Graesser et al. (2004, 199), except that all type of POS are taken into account. For LSA, we applied a singular value decomposition (SVD), and after comparing various sizes with a cross-validation procedure, we retained a small 15-dimensional space.

3.2.4 Features specific to FFL

Apart from the effect of cognates (Uitdenbogerd, 2005; Tharp, 1939), few features specific to the L2 context were previously investigated. It is probably because such an approach requires to train a model for each pair of language of interest and gather suitable data for evaluation. Since our study intended to design a generic model, we focused on specific predictors affecting L2 reading, whatever the learner's mother tongue is:

Multi-word expressions (MWE): MWEs are acknowledged to cause problems to L2 learners for production (Bahns and Eldaw, 1993). However, the effect of MWE on the reception side remains unclear, especially for beginners. Ozasa et al. (2007) tested the mean of the absolute frequency of all MWEs in a text as an indication of its difficulty, but it appeared non significant. In a latter experiment involving a larger set of MWE-based predictors, François and Watrin (2011) detected a significant, but limited effect. We therefore replicated this set, which includes variables based on the frequencies of MWE, their syntactic structure, their number or their length. Frequencies were estimated on the same corpora as the bigram model described above (Google and *Le Soir*).

Type of text: Finally, we defined five simple variables aiming at identifying dialogues, such as presence of commas, ratio of punctuation, etc. as suggested by Henry (1975). This focus on dialogue was

Level of information	Tag	Description of the variable	ρ
Lexical	PA-Alterego	Proportion of absent words from a list of easy words	0.65^3
	X90FFFC	90th percentile of inflected forms for content words only	-0.64^3
	ML3	Unigram model based on lemmas	-0.55^3
	NLM	Mean number of letters per word	0.48^3
	TTR	Type-token ratio based on lemma	0.28^3
	MedNeigh+Freq	Median number of more frequent neighbor for words	-0.23^3
Syntactic	NMP	Mean number of words per sentence	0.62^3
	NWS90	Length (in words) of the 90th percentile sentence	0.61^3
	LSDaoust	Percentage of sentences longer than 30 words (Daoust et al., 1996)	0.56^3
	PPres	Presence of at least one present participle in the text	0.44^3
	PRO.PRE	Ratio of pronouns on prepositions	-0.35^3
	PPres-C	Proportion of present participle among verbs	0.41^3
	PPasse	Presence of at least one past participle	0.39^3
	Impf	Presence of at least one imperfect	0.27^3
	Subp	Presence of at least one subjunctive present	0.27^3
	Cond	Presence of at least one conditional	0.23^3
	Imperatif	Presence of at least one imperative	0.02
	Subi	Presence of at least one subjunctive imperfect	0.05
Semantic	avLocalLsa-Lem	Average intersentential cohesion measured via LSA	0.63^3
	PP1P2	Percentage of P1 and P2 personal pronouns	-0.33^3
Specific	NACoII	Proportion of MWE having the structure NOUN ADJ	0.29^3
	BINGUI	Presence of commas	0.46^3

Table 2: Spearman correlation for some predictors in our set with difficulty. A positive correlation means that the difficulty of texts increases with the value of the predictor. Signification levels are the following $^1 : < 0.05$; $^2 : < 0.01$; and $^3 : < 0.001$.

explained by their extensive use in foreign language teaching, especially in the first levels. Furthermore, even for L1, various scholars stressed the fact that dialogues are often written in a simpler style and have a more mundane content (Dolch, 1948; Flesch, 1948).

3.3 The algorithms

The last step in the development of our formula was to select the most informative subset of features and combine them in a state-of-the-art machine learning algorithm. The algorithms originally considered were six: multinomial and ordinal logistic regression (respectively MLR and OLR), classification trees, bagging, boosting (both based on decision trees) and support vector machine (SVM). However, since the logistic models and the SVM clearly outperformed the others three, we will reported only about those in the next section.

4 Results

The experiments based on this methodology were twofold. First, we assessed the predictive power of each of the 406 features, considered in a bivariate relationship with difficulty. Second, we selected various subsets of features for training models and compared their performance. The two next sections summarize the main findings obtained during these two steps.

4.1 The efficiency of predictors

Spearman correlation was used to assess the efficiency of each predictor, to better account for nonlinear relationships with the criterion. Values for some variables among the four families are reported in Table 2. In accordance with the literature, it appeared that the best family of predictors were the lexical one, followed by the syntactic one. On the contrary, semantic and specific to FFL features did not perform so well, with the exception of the LSA-based feature (*avLocalLsa-Lem*).

Of all predictors, the best was surprisingly *PA-Alterego*, a list-based variable inspired by Dale and Chall (1948), but adapted to the FFL context, since the list of easy words used came from a FFL textbook (*Alter Ego 1*). This suggests that, although the predictive power of "specific to FFL" features was low, specialization to the FFL context was beneficial at other levels.

4.2 The models

Once the best single predictors were identified, it was possible to combine several of them in a readability model for comparison. This required some corpus preparation. Since preliminary experiments showed that the equal prior probabilities are required to ensure a unbiased training, the whole corpus was resampled to get the same number of texts per level (108), which amounted to a total of 648 texts. We then split this smaller corpus into two sets. 240 texts were kept for development purposes, mainly feature selection and estimation of the meta-parameters γ and C for the SVM. The remaining 408 texts were used for evaluating performance of our readability models.

4.2.1 Selection of the features

Several ways of selecting the smallest "best" subset of features were compared, given that some variables are partly redundant when combined together. The first method was based on the structuro-cognitivist assumption that readability formulas should include other features than just lexico-syntactical ones, in order to maximize variety of information. Therefore, we tried an "expert" selection, keeping either the best feature among each of the four families (set **Exp1**), or the two best features (set **Exp2**) [5].

These "expert" approaches were compared to an automatic selection, using either a stepwise procedure [6] for logistic regression (OLR and MLR) or a built-in regularization (Bishop, 2006, 10) for the SVM, based on the 46 best predictors inside each subfamily.

For the sake of comparison, we also defined two other sets: one that corresponds to a random classification (the empty subset), and a baseline, based on two classics predictors (number of letters per word and number of words per sentence), which aimed to mimic classic formulas such as those of Flesch (1948) or Dale and Chall (1948). A summary of the features included in each subset is available in Table 3.

4.2.2 Evaluation of the models

The next step then consisted in training logistic and SVM models for each of the above subsets. Their performances, reported in Table 4, were assessed using five measures: the multiple correlation ratio (R), the accuracy (acc), the adjacent accuracy [7] ($adjacc$), the root mean square error ($rmse$) and the mean absolute error (mae). It should be noted that each of these measures was estimated through a ten-fold cross-validation procedure, which allowed us to compare performances of different models with a T-test.

The comparison between the models was performed in two steps. First, we computed T-tests based on $adjacc$ to compare the models based on a same set of features (either **Exp1**, **Exp2**, or **Auto**). This allowed us to pick up the best classifier for each set. In a second step, these three best models were compared the same way, which resulted in the selection of the very best classifier. The decision of adopting the adjacent accuracy as a criterion instead of the accuracy was motivated by our conviction that our system should rather avoid serious errors (i.e. larger than one level) than be more accurate, while sometimes generating terrible mistakes. However, it appeared that both metrics were mostly consistent.

The performance of the different models are displayed in Table 4. It is first interesting to note that the baseline (based on SVM) already gives interesting results. It reaches a classification accuracy of 34%, which is about twice the random. As regards the first model (**Exp1**), based on RLM and including four predictors, it outperforms the baseline by 5%, a difference close to significance ($t(9) = 1.77; p = 0.055$). Therefore, combining variables from several families seems to improve performance over the "classic" baseline, limited to lexico-syntactic features.

This finding is reinforced by the SVM model from **Exp2**, which includes eight features. It performs significantly better than the baseline ($t(9) =$

[5] For the syntactic level, since the two best variables belonged to the same subfamily (see Section 3.2) and were too highly intercorrelated, the 90th percentile of the sentence length (*NWS90*) was replaced by the best feature from another subfamily: the presence of at least one present participle (*PPres*).

[6] In order to suppress as much random effects as possible, the selection process was repeated 100 times via a bootstrapping .632 procedure (Tufféry, 2007, 396-371) and only the features selected at least 50 times out of 100 were kept.

[7] Heilman et al. (2008) defined it as "the proportion of predictions that were within one level of the human assigned label for the given text".

Model name	Classifieur	Set of features
Exp1	OLR, MLR and SVM	PA-Alterego + NMP + avLocalLsa-Lem + BINGUI
Exp2	OLR, MLR and SVM	PA-Alterego + X90FFFC + NMP + PPres + avLocalLsa-Lem + PP1P2 + BINGUI + NACoII
Auto-OLR	OLR	PA-Alterego + NMP + PPres + ML3
Auto-MLR	MLR	PA-Alterego + Cond + Imperatif + Impf + PPasse + PPres + Subi + Subp + BINGUI + TTR + NWS90 + LSDaoust + MedNeigh+Freq
Auto-SVM	SVM	all the 46 variables

Table 3: Results from the two selection process: expert and automatic. Description of the features can be found in Table 2.

Model	Classifier	Parameters	R	acc	adjacc	rmse	mae
Random	/	/	/	16.6	44.4	/	/
Baseline	SVM	$\gamma = 0.05; C = 25$	0.62	34.0	68.2	1.51	1.06
Exp1	RLM	/	0.70	39.4	74.2	1.34	0.97
Exp2	SVM	$\gamma = 0.002; C = 75$	0.73	40.8	77.9	1.28	0.94
Auto-OLR	OLR	/	0.71	39.6	76.1	1.33	0.96
Auto	SVM	$\gamma = 0.004; C = 5$	0.73	49.1	79.6	1.27	0.90

Table 4: Evaluation measures for the best difficulty model from each feature set (**Exp1**, **Exp2** and **Auto**), along with values for a random classification, and the "classic" baseline.

$2.36; p = 0.02$), with an accuracy gain of 7%. However, to that point, it was not clear whether this superiority was indeed a consequence of maximizing the kind of information brought to the model or merely the result of the increased number of predictor.

We thus performed another experiment to address this issue. The model **Exp1** was compared with **Auto-OLR**, the best ordinal logistic model obtained through the stepwise selection (see Tables 4 and 3), and previously discarded as a result of the T-test comparisons. Like **Exp1**, it also contains four predictors, but they are all lexical or syntactic features. Therefore, this model does not maximize the type of information. Surprisingly, we observed that **Auto-OLR** obtained similar and even slightly better performance than **Exp1** (+2% for both acc and $adjacc$). Thus, the claim that maximizing the source of information should yield better models did not stand on our data.

Finally, our best performing model was based on the **Auto** feature set and SVM. Its accuracy was increased by 8% in comparison with the **Exp2** model, which is clearly a significant improvement ($t(9) = 2.61; p = 0.01$), and outperformed the baseline by 15%. As mentioned previously, this model includes 46 features coming from our four families. It is worth mentioning that the quality of the predictions is not the same across the levels, as shown in Table 5. They are more accurate for classes situated at both ends of the difficulty scale, namely A1, C1 and C2. For A1, this is explained because texts for beginners are more typical, having very short sentences and simple words. However, the case of C1 and C2 classes is more surprising and might be due to some specificities of the learning algorithm.

	A1	A2	B1	B2	C1	C2
Adj. acc.	100%	71%	67%	71%	86%	83%

Table 5: Adjacent accuracy per level, computed on one of the 10 folds. Its adjacent accuracy was 79%, which is very similar to the average value of the model.

We also assessed the specific contribution of each family of features in two ways: on one hand, we trained a model including only the features from this family; on the other hand, we trained a model including all features except those from this family. Results for the four families are displayed at Table 6.

It appeared that the lexical family was the most accurate set of predictors (40.5%) and yielded the highest loss in performance when set aside, especially for adjacent accuracy. In fact, this was the only set whose absence significantly impacted adjacent accuracy, suggesting that the other type of predictors can only improve the accuracy of predictions, but are not able to reduce the amount of critical mistakes. The second best family was, expectedly, the syntactic one. Its accuracy closely match that of the lexical set, although more severe mistakes were made, as shown by the drop in adjacent accuracy. Finally, our two other families was clearly inferior, but they still improved slightly the accuracy of our model, although not the adjacent accuracy.

	Family only		**All except family**	
	Acc.	Adj. acc.	Acc.	Adj. acc.
Lexical	40.5	75.6	41.1	73.5
Syntactic	39.3	69.5	43.2	78.4
Semantic	28.8	61.5	47.8	79.2
FFL	24.9	58.5	47.8	79.6

Table 6: Accuracy and adjacent accuracy (in percentage) for models either using only one family of predictors, or including all 46 features except those of one family.

4.2.3 Comparaison with previous work

Comparisons with other FFL models are difficult to provide: not only there are few formulas available for FFL, but some of these focus on a different audience, making comparability low. This is why we were able to compare our results with only two previous models.

The first of them is a classic readability formula by Kandel and Moles (1958), which is an adaptation of the Flesch (1948) formula for French:

$$Y = 207 - 1.015lp - 0.736lm \quad (2)$$

where Y is a readability score ranging from 100 (easiest) to 0 (harder); lp is the average number of words per sentence and lm is the average number of syllables per 100 words. Although it was not designed for FFL, we considered it, since it is one of the most well-known formula for French and the two features combined are very general. Their predictive power should not vary much in both contexts, as shown by Greenfield (2004) for English. We evaluated it on the same test corpus as our SVM model and obtained really lower values : a R of 0.55 and an accuracy of 33%.

The second model was that of François (2009), which is based on a multinomial logistic regression including ten features: a unigram model similar to *ML3*, the number of letters per word, the number of words per sentence, and binary variables indicating the presence of a past participle, present participle, imperfect, infinitive, conditional, future and present subjunctive tenses in the text. To our knowledge, this model is the best current generic model available for FFL. On our data, it yielded an accuracy of 41% and an adjacent accuracy of 72.7%, both estimated through a 10-fold cross-validation procedure. Therefore, our new approach achieved an accuracy gain of 8% over this state-of-the-art model, which was considered as a significant difference ($t(9) = 3.72; p = 0.002$).

Apart of those two studies, Uitdenbogerd (2005) also developed recently a FFL formula. However, as explained previously, this work focused on a specific category of L2 readers, the English-speakers learning FFL, which resulted in a different problem. She reported a higher R than us (0.87 against 0.73). However, this value might be the training one and was estimated on a small amount of novel beginnings. It is therefore likely that our model generalize better, especially across genres and L2 readers with different L1 backgrounds.

5 Discussion and conclusion

In this paper, we introduced a new "AI readability" formula for FFL, able to predict the level of texts according to the largely-spread CEFR scale. Our model is based on a SVM classifier and combines 46 features corresponding to several levels of linguistic information. Among those, we suggested some new features: the normalized TTR and the set of variables based on several characteristics of words' neighbors. Comparing our approach with two previously published formulas, our model significantly outperformed both these works. Therefore, it represent a robust generic solution for FFL readers willing to find various kind of texts that suit their linguistic abilities.

Besides the creation of a new FFL readability formula, this study produced two valuable insights. First, we showed that maximizing the type of linguistic information might not be the best path to go, since a model based on four lexico-syntactic features yielded predictions as accurate as those of a model relying on our *Exp1* set of variables. However, this finding might be partly accounted by the lower predictive power of the features from the semantic and specific-to-FFL family, with the notable exception of the LSA-based predictor (*avLocalLsa-Lem*), which is the third best predictor when considered alone.

This leads us to our second finding, relative to the

set of semantic features. Yet their importance was largely praised in the structuro-cognitivist paradigm and in most of the recent works, our experiments cast serious doubts about their efficiency, at least in a L2 context. Not only the expert models, to which we imposed the presence of one or two semantic predictors, did not perform the best, but none of the features from our semantic set was retained during the automatic selection of the variables for the logistic models. On the contrary, in some subsets, the LSA-based feature was sometimes considered as collinear with the other variables. Finally and foremost, we showed that dropping the semantic features did not impact significantly the performance of our best model.

With reservations one may have because of the limited number of semantic predictors in our set, these results however raise some concerns about whether the information coming from semantic variables is really different from that carried by lexico-syntactic features. Our results clearly show that this may not be the case. This conclusion contradicts the assumptions of the structuro-cognitivist paradigm, but corroborates Chall and Dale (1995)'s view that the information carried by semantic predictors is largely correlated with that of lexico-syntactical ones.

Further investigation on this issue would definitely be worthwhile, since several facts could explain these contradictory findings. First, it might be that semantic and lexical predictors are correlated because the methods used for the parameterization of the semantic factors heavily relie on lexical information. This is the case for the LSA, as well as for the propositional approach of the content density.

Alternatively, this difference with other work in L1 could be due to the L2 context. Chall and Dale (1995) explained that the lexicon and the syntax are more important for children learning to read than for more advanced readers, who then become more sensitive to organisationnal aspects. From the threshold hypothesis (Alderson, 1984), we know that before reaching a sufficient level of proficiency, L2 learners struggle mostly with the lexicon and the syntactic structures. This might explain why lexico-syntactic predictors were so predominant in our experiments. Some further experiments are thus needed to investigate which of these facts better account for our findings on the semantic features.

A last avenue of research worth mentioning would be to develop the family of specific-to-FFL predictors, to determine whether taking into account the impact of a given L1 language on the readability of L2 texts would increase performance over a generic model enough so that tuning efforts are worthwhile.

Acknowledgments

Thomas François was an Aspirant F.N.R.S. when this work was performed. The writing of this paper was done while being a recipient of a Fellowship of the Belgian American Educational Foundation. We thank both for their support. We would also like to acknowledge the invaluable help of Bernadette Dehottay for the collection of the corpus used in that study.

References

J.C. Alderson. 1984. Reading in a foreign language : a reading problem or a language problem ? In J.C. Alderson and A.H Urquhart, editors, *Reading in a Foreign Language*, pages 1–24. Longman, New York.

S. Andrews. 1997. The effect of orthographic similarity on lexical retrieval: Resolving neighborhood conflicts. *Psychonomic Bulletin & Review*, 4(4):439–461.

J. Bahns and M. Eldaw. 1993. Should We Teach EFL Students Collocations? *System*, 21(1):101–14.

A. Berthet, C. Hugot, V. Kizirian, B. Sampsonis, and M. Waendendries. 2006. *Alter Ego 1*. Hachette, Paris.

C.M. Bishop. 2006. *Pattern recognition and machine learning*. Springer, New York.

J.R. Bormuth. 1966. Readability: A new approach. *Reading research quarterly*, 1(3):79–132.

J.S. Bowers. 2000. In defense of abstractionist theories of repetition priming and word identification. *Psychonomic bulletin and review*, 7(1):83–99.

M. Carreiras, N. Carriedo, M.A. Alonso, and A. Fernández. 1997. The role of verb tense and verb aspect in the foregrounding of information during reading. *Memory & Cognition*, 25(4):438–446.

J.S. Chall and E. Dale. 1995. *Readability Revisited: The New Dale-Chall Readability Formula*. Brookline Books, Cambridge.

S. Chen and J. Goodman. 1999. An empirical study of smoothing techniques for language modeling. *Computer Speech and Language*, 13(4):359–393.

K. Collins-Thompson and J. Callan. 2004. A language modeling approach to predicting reading difficulty. In

Proceedings of HLT/NAACL 2004, pages 193–200, Boston, USA.

K. Collins-Thompson and J. Callan. 2005. Predicting reading difficulty with statistical language models. *Journal of the American Society for Information Science and Technology*, 56(13):1448–1462.

M. Coltheart. 1978. Lexical access in simple reading tasks. In G. Underwood, editor, *Strategies of information processing*, pages 151–216. Academic Press, London.

A. Conquet. 1957. *La lisibilité*. Assemblée Permanente des CCI de Paris, Paris.

C.M. Cornaire. 1988. La lisibilité : essai d'application de la formule courte d'Henry au français langue étrangère. *Canadian Modern Language Review*, 44(2):261–273.

Council of Europe. 2001. *Common European Framework of Reference for Languages: Learning, Teaching, Assessment*. Press Syndicate of the University of Cambridge.

E. Dale and J.S. Chall. 1948. A formula for predicting readability. *Educational research bulletin*, 27(1):11–28.

E. Dale and R.W. Tyler. 1934. A study of the factors influencing the difficulty of reading materials for adults of limited reading ability. *The Library Quarterly*, 4:384–412.

F. Daoust, L. Laroche, and L. Ouellet. 1996. SATO-CALIBRAGE: Présentation d'un outil d'assistance au choix et à la rédaction de textes pour l'enseignement. *Revue québécoise de linguistique*, 25(1):205–234.

G. de Landsheere. 1963. Pour une application des tests de lisibilité de Flesch à la langue française. *Le Travail Humain*, 26:141–154.

E.W. Dolch. 1948. *Problems in reading*. The Garrard Press, Champaign : Illinois.

W.B. Elley. 1969. The assessment of readability by noun frequency counts. *Reading Research Quarterly*, 4(3):411–427.

L. Feng, M. Jansche, M. Huenerfauth, and N. Elhadad. 2010. A Comparison of Features for Automatic Readability Assessment. In *COLING 2010: Poster Volume*, pages 276–284.

R. Flesch. 1948. A new readability yardstick. *Journal of Applied Psychology*, 32(3):221–233.

P.W. Foltz, W. Kintsch, and T.K. Landauer. 1998. The measurement of textual coherence with latent semantic analysis. *Discourse processes*, 25(2):285–307.

T. François and P. Watrin. 2011. On the contribution of MWE-based features to a readability formula for French as a foreign language. In *Proceedings of the International Conference RANLP 2011*.

T. François. 2009. Combining a statistical language model with logistic regression to predict the lexical and syntactic difficulty of texts for FFL. In *Proceedings of the 12th Conference of the EACL : Student Research Workshop*, pages 19–27.

T. François. 2011a. La lisibilité computationnelle : un renouveau pour la lisibilité du français langue première et seconde ? *International Journal of Applied Linguistics (ITL)*, 160:75–99.

T. François. 2011b. *Les apports du traitement automatique du langage à la lisibilité du français langue étrangère*. Ph.D. thesis, Université Catholique de Louvain. Thesis Supervisors : Cédrick Fairon and Anne Catherine Simon.

W.A. Gale and G. Sampson. 1995. Good-Turing frequency estimation without tears. *Journal of Quantitative Linguistics*, 2(3):217–237.

G. Gougenheim, R. Michéa, P. Rivenc, and A. Sauvageot. 1964. *L'élaboration du français fondamental (1er degré)*. Didier, Paris.

A.C. Graesser, D.S. McNamara, M.M. Louwerse, and Z. Cai. 2004. Coh-Metrix: Analysis of text on cohesion and language. *Behavior Research Methods, Instruments, & Computers*, 36(2):193–202.

J. Greenfield. 2004. Readability formulas for EFL. *Japan Association for Language Teaching*, 26(1):5–24.

M. Heilman, K. Collins-Thompson, and M. Eskenazi. 2008. An analysis of statistical models and features for reading difficulty prediction. In *Proceedings of the Third Workshop on Innovative Use of NLP for Building Educational Applications*, pages 1–8.

G. Henry. 1975. *Comment mesurer la lisibilité*. Labor, Bruxelles.

L. Kandel and A. Moles. 1958. Application de l'indice de Flesch à la langue française. *Cahiers Études de Radio-Télévision*, 19:253–274.

S. Kemper. 1983. Measuring the inference load of a text. *Journal of Educational Psychology*, 75(3):391–401.

W. Kintsch and D. Vipond. 1979. Reading comprehension and readability in educational practice and psychological theory. In L.G. Nilsson, editor, *Perspectives on Memory Research*, pages 329–365. Lawrence Erlbaum, Hillsdale, NJ.

W. Kintsch, E. Kozminsky, W.J. Streby, G. McKoon, and J.M. Keenan. 1975. Comprehension and recall of text as a function of content variables1. *Journal of Verbal Learning and Verbal Behavior*, 14(2):196–214.

H. Lee, P. Gambette, E. Maillé, and C. Thuillier. 2010. Densidées: calcul automatique de la densité des idées dans un corpus oral. In *Actes de la douxime Rencontre des tudiants Chercheurs en Informatique pour le Traitement Automatique des langues (RECITAL)*.

I. Lorge. 1944. Predicting readability. *the Teachers College Record*, 45(6):404–419.

J. Mesnager. 1989. Lisibilité des textes pour enfants: un nouvel outil? *Communication et Langages*, 79:18–38.

B.J.F. Meyer. 1982. Reading research and the composition teacher: The importance of plans. *College composition and communication*, 33(1):37–49.

J.B. Michel, Y.K. Shen, A.P. Aiden, A. Veres, M.K. Gray, The Google Books Team, J.P. Pickett, D. Hoiberg, D. Clancy, P. Norvig, J. Orwant, S. Pinker, M.A. Nowak, and E.L. Aiden. 2011. Quantitative analysis of culture using millions of digitized books. *Science*, 331(6014):176–182.

J.R. Miller and W. Kintsch. 1980. Readability and recall of short prose passages: A theoretical analysis. *Journal of Experimental Psychology: Human Learning and Memory*, 6(4):335–354.

B. New, M. Brysbaert, J. Veronis, and C. Pallier. 2007. The use of film subtitles to estimate word frequencies. *Applied Psycholinguistics*, 28(04):661–677.

R.E. O'Connor, K.M. Bell, K.R. Harty, L.K. Larkin, S.M. Sackor, and N. Zigmond. 2002. Teaching reading to poor readers in the intermediate grades: A comparison of text difficulty. *Journal of Educational Psychology*, 94(3):474–485.

T. Ozasa, G. Weir, and M. Fukui. 2007. Measuring readability for Japanese learners of English. In *Proceedings of the 12th Conference of Pan-Pacific Association of Applied Linguistics*.

E. Pitler and A. Nenkova. 2008. Revisiting readability: A unified framework for predicting text quality. In *Proceedings of the Conference on Empirical Methods in Natural Language Processing*, pages 186–195.

J.C. Redish and J. Selzer. 1985. The place of readability formulas in technical communication. *Technical communication*, 32(4):46–52.

F. Richaudeau. 1979. Une nouvelle formule de lisibilité. *Communication et Langages*, 44:5–26.

H. Schmid. 1994. Probabilistic part-of-speech tagging using decision trees. In *Proceedings of International Conference on New Methods in Language Processing*, volume 12. Manchester, UK.

S.E. Schwarm and M. Ostendorf. 2005. Reading level assessment using support vector machines and statistical language models. *Proceedings of the 43rd Annual Meeting on Association for Computational Linguistics*, pages 523–530.

L. Si and J. Callan. 2001. A statistical model for scientific readability. In *Proceedings of the Tenth International Conference on Information and Knowledge Management*, pages 574–576. ACM New York, NY, USA.

E.A. Smith. 1961. Devereaux readability index. *The Journal of Educational Research*, 54(8):289–303.

A.J. Stenner. 1996. Measuring reading comprehension with the lexile framework. In *Fourth North American Conference on Adolescent/Adult Literacy*.

J.B. Tharp. 1939. The Measurement of Vocabulary Difficulty. *Modern Language Journal*, pages 169–178.

S. Tufféry. 2007. *Data mining et statistique décisionnelle l'intelligence des données*. Éd. Technip, Paris.

S. Uitdenbogerd. 2005. Readability of French as a foreign language and its uses. In *Proceedings of the Australian Document Computing Symposium*, pages 19–25.

P. van Oosten, V. Hoste, and D. Tanghe. 2011. A posteriori agreement as a quality measure for readability prediction systems. In A. Gelbukh, editor, *Computational Linguistics and Intelligent Text Processing*, volume 6609 of *Lecture Notes in Computer Science*, pages 424–435. Springer, Berlin / Heidelberg.

Dynamic Programming for Higher Order Parsing of Gap-Minding Trees

Emily Pitler, Sampath Kannan, Mitchell Marcus
Computer and Information Science
University of Pennsylvania
Philadelphia, PA 19104
epitler,kannan,mitch@seas.upenn.edu

Abstract

We introduce *gap inheritance*, a new structural property on trees, which provides a way to quantify the degree to which intervals of descendants can be nested. Based on this property, two new classes of trees are derived that provide a closer approximation to the set of plausible natural language dependency trees than some alternative classes of trees: unlike projective trees, a word can have descendants in more than one interval; unlike spanning trees, these intervals cannot be nested in arbitrary ways. The *1-Inherit* class of trees has *exactly* the same empirical coverage of natural language sentences as the class of mildly non-projective trees, yet the optimal scoring tree can be found in an order of magnitude less time. *Gap-minding trees* (the second class) have the property that all edges into an interval of descendants come from the same node, and thus an algorithm which uses only single intervals can produce trees in which a node has descendants in multiple intervals.

1 Introduction

Dependency parsers vary in what *space of possible tree structures* they search over when parsing a sentence. One commonly used space is the set of *projective* trees, in which every node's descendants form a contiguous interval in the input sentence. Finding the optimal tree in the set of projective trees can be done efficiently (Eisner, 2000), even when the score of a tree depends on higher order factors (McDonald and Pereira, 2006; Carreras, 2007; Koo and Collins, 2010). However, the projectivity assumption is too strict for all natural language dependency trees; for example, only 63.6% of Dutch sentences from the CoNLL-X training set are projective (Table 1).

At the other end of the spectrum, some parsers search over all *spanning trees*, a class of structures much larger than the set of plausible linguistic structures. The maximum scoring directed spanning tree can be found efficiently when the score of a tree depends only on edge-based factors (McDonald et al., 2005b). However, it is NP-hard to extend MST to include sibling or grandparent factors (McDonald and Pereira, 2006; McDonald and Satta, 2007). MST-based non-projective parsers that use higher order factors (Martins et al., 2009; Koo et al., 2010), utilize different techniques than the basic MST algorithm. In addition, learning is done over a relaxation of the problem, so the inference procedures at training and at test time are not identical.

We propose two new classes of trees between projective trees and the set of all spanning trees. These two classes provide a closer approximation to the set of plausible natural language dependency trees: unlike projective trees, a word can have descendants in more than one interval; unlike spanning trees, these intervals cannot be nested in arbitrary ways. We introduce *gap inheritance*, a new structural property on trees, which provides a way to quantify the degree to which these intervals can be nested. Different levels of gap inheritance define each of these two classes (Section 3).

The *1-Inherit* class of trees (Section 4) has *exactly* the same empirical coverage (Table 1) of natural language sentences as the class of *mildly non-projective trees* (Bodirsky et al., 2005), yet the optimal scoring tree can be found in an order of magnitude less time (Section 4.1).

Gap-minding trees (the second class) have the

property that all edges into an interval of descendants come from the same node. Non-contiguous intervals are therefore *decoupled* given this single node, and thus an algorithm which uses only single intervals (as in projective parsing) can produce trees in which a node has descendants in multiple intervals (as in mildly non-projective parsing (Gómez-Rodríguez et al., 2011)). A procedure for finding the optimal scoring tree in this space is given in Section 5, which can be searched in yet another order of magnitude faster than the *1-Inherit* class.

Unlike the class of spanning trees, it is still tractable to find the optimal tree in these new spaces when higher order factors are included. An extension which finds the optimal scoring gap-minding tree with scores over pairs of adjacent edges (grandparent scoring) is given in Section 6. These gap-minding algorithms have been implemented in practice and empirical results are presented in Section 7.

2 Preliminaries

In this section, we review some relevant definitions from previous work that characterize degrees of non-projectivity. We also review how well these definitions cover empirical data from six languages: Arabic, Czech, Danish, Dutch, Portuguese, and Swedish. These are the six languages whose CoNLL-X shared task data are either available open source[1] or from the LDC[2].

A *dependency tree* is a rooted, directed spanning tree that represents a set of dependencies between words in a sentence.[3] The tree has one artificial root node and vertices that correspond to the words in an input sentence w_1, w_2,...,w_n. There is an edge from h to m if m depends on (or modifies) h.

Definition 1. *The* projection *of a node is the set of words in the subtree rooted at it (including itself).*

A tree is *projective* if, for every node in the tree, that node's projection forms a contiguous interval in the input sentence order.

A tree is *non-projective* if the above does not hold, i.e., there exists at least one word whose descendants do not form a contiguous interval.

Definition 2. *A* gap *of a node v is a non-empty, maximal interval that does not contain any words in the projection of v but lies between words that are in the projection of v. The* gap degree of a node *is the number of gaps it has. The* gap degree of a tree *is the maximum of the gap degrees of its vertices. (Bodirsky et al., 2005)*

Note that a projective tree will have gap degree 0.

Two subtrees *interleave* if there are vertices l_1, r_1 from one subtree and l_2, r_2 from the other such that $l_1 < l_2 < r_1 < r_2$.

Definition 3. *A tree is* well-nested *if no two* disjoint *subtrees interleave (Bodirsky et al., 2005).*

Definition 4. *A* mildly non-projective *tree has gap degree at most one and is well-nested.*

Mildly non-projective trees are of both theoretical and practical interest, as they correspond to derivations in Lexicalized Tree Adjoining Grammar (Bodirsky et al., 2005) and cover the overwhelming majority of sentences found in treebanks for Czech and Danish (Kuhlmann and Nivre, 2006).

Table 1 shows the proportion of mildly non-projective sentences for Arabic, Czech, Danish, Dutch, Portuguese, and Swedish, ranging from 95.4% of Portuguese sentences to 99.9% of Arabic sentences.[4] This definition covers a substantially larger set of sentences than projectivity does — an assumption of projectivity covers only 63.6% (Dutch) to 90.2% (Swedish) of examples (Table 1).

3 Gap Inheritance

Empirically, natural language sentences seem to be mostly mildly non-projective trees, but mildly non-projective trees are quite expensive to parse ($O(n^7)$ (Gómez-Rodríguez et al., 2011)). The parsing complexity comes from the fact that the definition allows two non-contiguous intervals of a projection to be tightly coupled, with an unbounded number of edges passing back and forth between the two intervals; however, this type of structure seems unusual

[1] http://ilk.uvt.nl/conll/free_data.html

[2] LDC catalogue numbers LDC2006E01 and LDC2006E02

[3] Trees are a reasonable assumption for most, but not all, linguistic structures. Parasitic gaps are an example in which a word perhaps should have multiple parents.

[4] While some of the treebank structures are ill-nested or have a larger gap degree because of annotation decisions, some linguistic constructions in German and Czech are ill-nested or require at least two gaps under any reasonable representation (Chen-Main and Joshi, 2010; Chen-Main and Joshi, 2012).

	Arabic		Czech		Danish		Dutch		Portuguese		Swedish		Parsing
Mildly non-proj	1458	(99.9)	72321	(99.5)	5175	(99.7)	12896	(96.6)	8650	(95.4)	10955	(99.2)	$O(n^7)$
Mild+1-Inherit	1458	(99.9)	72321	(99.5)	5175	(99.7)	12896	(96.6)	8650	(95.4)	10955	(99.2)	$O(n^6)$
Mild+0-Inherit	1394	(95.5)	70695	(97.2)	4985	(96.1)	12068	(90.4)	8481	(93.5)	10787	(97.7)	$O(n^5)$
Projective	1297	(88.8)	55872	(76.8)	4379	(84.4)	8484	(63.6)	7353	(81.1)	9963	(90.2)	$O(n^3)$
# Sentences	1460		72703		5190		13349		9071		11042		

Table 1: The number of sentences from the CoNLL-X training sets whose parse trees fall into each of the above classes. The two new classes of structures, *Mild+0-Inherit* and *Mild+1-Inherit*, have more coverage of empirical data than projective structures, yet can be parsed faster than mildly non-projective structures. Parsing times assume an edge-based factorization with no pruning of edges. The corresponding algorithms for Mild+1-Inherit and Mild+0-Inherit are in Sections 4 and 5.

for natural language. We therefore investigate if we can define further structural properties that are both appropriate for describing natural language trees and which admit more efficient parsing algorithms.

Let us first consider an example of a tree which both has gap degree at most one and satisfies well-nestedness, yet appears to be an unrealistic structure for a natural language syntactic tree. Consider a tree which is rooted at node x_{n+2}, which has one child, node x_{n+1}, whose projection is $[x_1, x_{n+1}] \cup [x_{n+3}, x_{2n+2}]$, with n children (x_1, ..., x_n), and each child x_i has a child at x_{2n-i+3}. This tree is well-nested, has gap degree 1, but all n of x_{n+1}'s children have edges into the other projection interval.

We introduce a further structural restriction in this section, and show that trees satisfying our new property can be parsed more efficiently with no drop in empirical coverage.

Definition 5. *A child is* gap inheriting *if its parent has gap degree 1 and it has descendants on both sides of its parent's gap. The* inheritance degree *of a node is the number of its children which inherit its gap. The* inheritance degree of a tree *is the maximum inheritance degree over all its nodes.*

Figure 1 gives examples of trees with varying degrees of gap inheritance. Each projection of a node with a gap is shown with two matching rectangles. If a child has a projection rectangle nested inside each of the parent's projection rectangles, then that child inherits the parent's gap. Figure 1(a) shows a mildly projective tree (with inheritance degree 2), with both node 2 and node 11 inheriting their parent (node 3)'s gap (note that both the dashed and dotted rectangles each show up inside both of the solid rectangles). Figure 1(b) shows a tree with inheritance degree 1: there is now only one pair of rectangles (the dotted ones) which show up in both of the solid ones. Figure 1(c) shows a tree with inheritance degree 0: while there are gaps, each set of matching rectangles is contained within a single rectangle (projection interval) of its parent, i.e., the two dashed rectangles of node 2's projection are contained within the left interval of node 3; the two dotted rectangles of node 12's projection are contained within the right interval of node 3, etc.

We now ask:

1. How often does gap inheritance occur in the parses of natural language sentences found in treebanks?

2. Furthermore, how often are there *multiple* gap inheriting children of the same node (inheritance degree at least two)?

Table 1 shows what proportion of mildly non-projective trees have the added property of gap inheritance degree 0 (Mild+0-Inherit) or have gap inheritance degree 1 (Mild+1-Inherit). Over all six languages, there are *no* examples of multiple gap inheritance — Mild+1-Inherit has exactly the same empirical coverage as the unrestricted set of mildly non-projective trees.

4 Mild+1-Inherit Trees

There are some reasons from syntactic theory why we might expect at most one child to inherit its parent's gap. Traditional Government and Binding theories of syntax (Chomsky, 1981) assume that there is an underlying projective (phrase structure) tree, and that gaps primarily arise through movement of

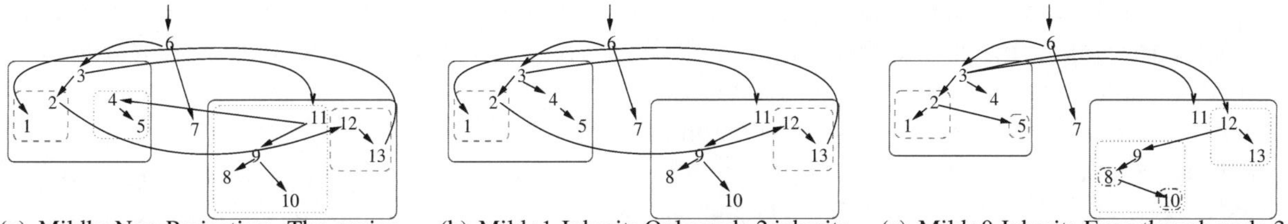

(a) Mildly Non-Projective: The projections (set of descendants) of both node 2 (the dashed red rectangles) and node 11 (dotted magenta) appear in both of node 3's intervals (the solid blue rectangles).

(b) Mild+1-Inherit: Only node 2 inherits node 3's gap: the dashed red rectangles appear in each of the two solid blue rectangles.

(c) Mild+0-Inherit: Even though node 3 has children with gaps (node 2 and node 12), neither of them inherit node 3's gap. There are several nodes with gaps, but every node with a gap is properly contained within just one of its parent's intervals.

Figure 1: Rectangles that match in color and style indicate the two projection intervals of a node, separated by a gap. In all three trees, node 3's two projection intervals are shown in the two solid blue rectangles. The number of children which inherit its gap vary, however; in 1(a), two children have descendants within both sides; in 1(b) only one child has descendants on both sides; in 1(c), none of its children do.

subtrees (constituents). One of the fundamental assumptions of syntactic theory is that movement is upward in the phrase structure tree.[5]

Consider one movement operation and its effect on the gap degree of all other nodes in the tree: (a) it should have no effect on the gap degree of the nodes in the subtree itself, (b) it can create a gap for an ancestor node if it moves *out* of its projection interval, and (c) it can create a gap for a non-ancestor node if it moves *in* to its projection interval. Now consider which cases can lead to gap inheritance: in case (b), there is a single path from the ancestor to the root of the subtree, so the parent of the subtree will have no gap inheritance and any higher ancestors will have a single child inherit the gap created by this movement. In case (c), it is possible for there to be multiple children that inherit this newly created gap if multiple children had descendents on both sides. However, the assumption of upward movement in the phrase structure tree should rule out movement into the projection interval of a non-ancestor. Therefore, under these syntactic assumptions, we would expect at most one child to inherit a parent's gap.

[5]The Proper Binding Condition (Fiengo, 1977) asserts that a moved element leaves behind a *trace* (unpronounced element), which must be *c-commanded* (Reinhart, 1976) by the corresponding pronounced material in its final location. Informally, c-commanded means that the first node is descended from the lowest ancestor of the other that has more than one child.

4.1 Parsing Mild+1-Inherit Trees

Finding the optimal Mild+1-Inherit tree can be done by bottom-up constructing the tree for each node and its descendants. We can maintain subtrees with two intervals (two endpoints each) and one root ($O(n^5)$ space). Consider the most complicated possible case: a parent that has a gap, a (single) child which inherits the gap, and additional children. An example of this is seen with the parent node 3 in Figure 1(b).

This subtree can be constructed by first starting with the child spanning the gap, updating its root index to be the parent, and then expanding the interval indices to the left and right to include the other children. In each case, only one index needs to be updated at a time, so the optimal tree can be found in $O(n^6)$ time. In the Figure 1(b) example, the subtree rooted at 3 would be built by starting with the intervals $[1, 2] \cup [12, 13]$ rooted at 2, first adding the edge from 2 to 3 (so the root is updated to 3), then adding an edge from 3 to 4 to extend the left interval to $[1, 5]$, and then adding an edge from 3 to 11 to extend the right interval to $[8, 13]$. The subtree corresponds to the completed item $[1, 5] \cup [8, 13]$ rooted at 3.

This procedure corresponds to Gómez-Rodríguez et al. (2011)'s $O(n^7)$ algorithm for parsing mildly non-projective structures if the most expensive step (*Combine Shrinking Gap Centre*) is dropped; this step would only ever be needed if a parent node has more than one child inheriting its gap.

This is also similar in spirit to the algorithm described in Satta and Schuler (1998) for parsing a restricted version of TAG, in which there are some limitations on adjunction operations into the spines of trees.[6] That algorithm has similar steps and items, with the root portion of the item replaced with a node in a phrase structure tree (which may be a non-terminal).

5 Gap-minding Trees

The algorithm in the previous section used $O(n^5)$ space and $O(n^6)$ time. While more efficient than parsing in the space of mildly projective trees, this is still probably not practically implementable. Part of the difficulty lies in the fact that gap inheritance causes the two non-contiguous projection intervals to be coupled.

Definition 6. *A tree is called* gap-minding[7] *if it has gap degree at most one, is well-nested, and has gap inheritance degree 0.*

Gap-minding trees still have good empirical coverage (between 90.4% for Dutch and 97.7% for Swedish). We now turn to the parsing of gap-minding trees and show how a few consequences of its definition allow us to use items ranging over only *one* interval.

In Figure 1(c), notice how each rectangle has edges incoming from *exactly one* node. This is not unique to this example; all projection intervals in a gap-minding tree have incoming edges from exactly one node outside the interval.

Claim 1. *Within a gap-minding tree, consider any node n with a gap (i.e., n's projection forms two non-contiguous intervals $[x_i, x_j] \cup [x_k, x_l]$). Let p be the parent of n.*

1. *For each of the intervals of n's projection:*
   - *(a) If the interval contains n, the only edge incoming to that interval is from p to n.*
   - *(b) If the interval does not contain n, all edges incoming to that interval come from n.*
2. *For the gap interval ($[x_{j+1}, x_{k-1}]$):*
   - *(a) If the interval contains p, then the only edge incoming is from p's parent to p*
   - *(b) If the interval does not contain p, then all edges incoming to that interval come from p.*

As a consequence of the above, $[x_i, x_j] \cup \{n\}$ forms a gap-minding tree rooted at n, $[x_k, x_l] \cup \{n\}$ also forms a gap-minding tree rooted at n, and $[x_{j+1}, x_{k-1}] \cup \{p\}$ forms a gap-minding tree rooted at p.

Proof. (Part 1): Assume there was a directed edge (x, y) such that y is inside a projection interval of n and x is not inside the same interval, and $x \neq y \neq n$. y is a descendant of n since it is contained in n's projection. Since there is a directed edge from x to y, x is y's parent, and thus x must also be a descendant of n and therefore in another of n's projection intervals. Since x and y are in different intervals, then whichever child of n that x and y are descended from would have inherited n's gap, leading to a contradiction.

(Part 2): First, suppose there existed a set of nodes in n's gap which were not descended from p. Then p has a gap over these nodes. (p clearly has descendants on each side of the gap, because all descendants of n are also descendants of p). n, p's child, would then have descendants on both sides of p's gap, which would violate the property of no gap inheritance. It is also not possible for there to be edges incoming from other descendants of p outside the gap, as that would imply another child of p being ill-nested with respect to n. □

From the above, we can build gap-minding trees using only single intervals, potentially with a single node outside of the interval. Our objective is to find the maximum scoring gap-minding tree, in which the score of a tree is the sum of the scores of its edges. Let $\mathbf{Score(p, x)}$ indicate the score of the directed edge from p to x.

Therefore, the main type of sub-problems we will use are:

[6] That algorithm has a running time of $O(Gn^5)$, where as written G would likely add a factor of n^2 with bilexical selectional preferences; this can be lowered to n using the same technique as in Eisner and Satta (2000) for non-restricted TAG.

[7] The terminology is a nod to the London Underground but imagines parents admonishing children to mind the gap.

1. $\mathbf{C[i, j, p]}$: The maximum score of any gap-minding tree, rooted at p, with vertices $[i, j] \cup \{p\}$ (p may or may not be within $[i, j]$).

This improves our space requirement, but not necessarily the time requirement. For example, if we built up the subtree in Figure 1(c) by concatenating the three intervals $[1, 5]$ rooted at 3, $[6, 7]$ rooted at 6, and $[8, 13]$ rooted at 3, and add the edge $6 \rightarrow 3$, we would still need 6 indices to describe this operation (the four interval endpoints and the two roots), and so we have not yet improved the running time over the *Inherit-1* case.

By part 2, we can concatenate one interval of a child with its gap, knowing that the gap is entirely descended from the child's parent, and forget the concatenation split point between the parent's other descendants and this side of the child. This allows us to substitute all operations involving 6 indices with two operations involving just 5 indices. For example, in Figure 1(c), we could first merge $[6, 7]$ rooted at 6 with $[8, 13]$ rooted at 3 to create an interval $[6, 13]$ and say that it is descended from 6, with the rightmost side descended from its child 3. That step required 5 indices. The following step would merge this concatenated interval ($[6, 13]$ rooted at 6 and 3) with $[1, 5]$ rooted at 3. This step also requires only 5 indices.

Our helper subtype we make use of is then:

2. $\mathbf{D[i, j, p, x, b]}$: The maximum score of any set of two gap-minding trees, one rooted at p, one rooted at x, with vertices $[i, j] \cup \{p, x\}$ ($x \notin [i, j]$, p may or may not be in $[i, j]$), such that for some k, vertices $[i, k]$ are in the tree rooted at p if $b = \mathit{true}$ (and at x if $b = \mathit{false}$), and vertices $[k + 1, j]$ are in the tree rooted at x (p).

Consider an optimum scoring gap-minding tree T rooted at p with vertices $V = [i, j] \cup \{p\}$ and edges E, where $E \neq \emptyset$. The form of the dynamic program may depend on whether:

- p is within (i, j) **(I)** or external to $[i, j]$ **(E)**[8]

[8]In the discussion we will assume that $p \neq i$ and $p \neq j$, since any optimum solution with $V = [i, j] \cup \{i\}$ and a root at i will be equivalent to $V = [i + 1, j] \cup \{i\}$ rooted at i (and similarly for $p = j$).

We can exhaustively enumerate all possibilities for T by considering all valid combinations of the following binary cases:

- p has a single child **(S)** or multiple children **(M)**
- i and j are descended from the same child of p **(C)** or different children of p **(D)**

Note that case **(S/D)** is not possible: i and j cannot be descended from different children of p if p has only a single child. We therefore need to find the maximum scoring tree over the three cases of **S/C**, **M/C**, and **M/D**.

Claim 2. *Let T be the optimum scoring gap-minding tree rooted at p with vertices $V = [i, j] \cup \{p\}$. Then T and its score are derived from one of the following:*

S/C *If p has a single child x in T, then if $p \in (i, j)$* **(I)**, *T's score is* $\mathbf{Score(p, x) + C[i, p-1, x] + C[p + 1, j, x]}$; *if $p \notin [i, j]$* **(E)**, *T's score is* $\mathbf{Score(p, x) + C[i, j, x]}$.

M/C *If p has multiple children in T and i and j are descended from the same child x in T, then there is a split point k such that T's score is:* $\mathbf{Score(p, x) + C[i, k, x] + D[k + 1, j, p, x, T]}$ *if x is on the left side of its own gap, and T's score is:* $\mathbf{Score(p, x) + C[k, j, x] + D[i, k - 1, p, x, F]}$ *if x is on the right side.*

M/D *If p has multiple children in T and i and j are descended from different children in T, then there is a split point k such that T's score is* $\mathbf{C[i, k, p] + C[k + 1, j, p]}$.

T has the maximum score over each of the above cases, for all valid choices of x and k.

Proof. **Case S/C**: If p has exactly one child x, then the tree can be decomposed into the edge from p to x and the subtree rooted at x. If p is outside the interval, then the maximum scoring such tree is clearly $\mathbf{Score(p, x) + C[i, j, x]}$. If p is inside, then x has a gap across p, and so using Claim 1, the maximum scoring tree rooted at p with a single child x has score of $\mathbf{Score(p, x) + C[i, p - 1, x] + C[p + 1, j, x]}$.

Case M/C: If there are multiple children and the endpoints are descended from the same child x, then the child x has to have gap degree 1. x itself is on either the left or right side of its gap. For the moment, assume x is in the left interval. By Claim 1, we can split up the score of the tree as the score of the edge from p to x ($\mathbf{Score(p, x)}$), the score of the subtree corresponding to the projection of x to the left of its gap ($\mathbf{C[i, k, x]}$), and the score of the subtrees rooted at p with its remaining children and the subtree rooted at x corresponding to the right side of x's projection ($\mathbf{D[k + 1, j, p, x, T]}$). The case in which x is on the right side of its gap is symmetric.

Case M/D: If there are multiple children and the endpoints are descended from different children of p, then there must exist a split point k that partitions the children of p into two non-empty sets, such that each child's projection is either entirely on the left or entirely on the right of the split point. We show one such split point to demonstrate that there always exists at least one. Let x be the child of p that i is descended from, and let x_l and x_r be x's leftmost and right descendants, respectively.[9] Consider all the children of p (whose projections taken together partition $[i, j] - \{p\}$). No child can have descendants both to the left of x_r and to the right of x_r, because otherwise that child and x would be *ill-nested*. Therefore we can split up the interval at x_r to have two gap-minding trees, both rooted at p. The score of T is then the sum of the scores of the best subtree rooted at p over $[i, k]$ ($\mathbf{C[i, k, p]}$) and the score of the best subtree rooted at p over $[k+1, j]$ ($\mathbf{C[k + 1, j, p]}$).

The above cases cover all non-empty gap-minding trees, so the maximum will be found. □

Using Claim 2 to Devise an Algorithm The above claim showed that any problem of type $\mathbf{C}$ can be decomposed into subproblems of types $\mathbf{C}$ and $\mathbf{D}$. From the definition of $\mathbf{D}$, any problem of type $\mathbf{D}$ can clearly be decomposed into two problems of type $\mathbf{C}$ — simply split the interval at the split point known to exist and assign p or x as the roots for each side of the interval, as prescribed by the boolean b:

$$\mathbf{D(i, j, p, x, T) = max_k C[i, k, p] + C[k + 1, j, x]}$$
$$\mathbf{D(i, j, p, x, F) = max_k C[i, k, x] + C[k + 1, j, p]}$$

[9] Note that $x_l = i$ by construction, and $x_r \neq j$ (because the endpoints are descended from different children).

Algorithm 1 makes direct use of the above claims. Note that in every gap-minding tree referred to in the cases above, all vertices that were not the root formed a single interval. Algorithm 1 builds up trees in increasing sizes of $[i, j] \cup \{p\}$. The tree in $\mathbf{C[i, j, p]}$ corresponds to the maximum of four subroutines: SingleChild (**S/C**), EndpointsDiff (**M/D**), EndsFromLeftChild (**M/C**), and EndsFromRightChild (**M/C**). The $\mathbf{D}$ subproblems are filled in with the subroutine Max2Subtrees, which uses the above discussion. The maximum score of any gap-minding tree is then found in $\mathbf{C[1, n, 0]}$, and the tree itself can be found using backpointers.

5.1 Runtime analysis

If the input is assumed to be the complete graph (any word can have any other word as its parent), then the above algorithm takes $O(n^5)$ time. The most expensive steps are **M/C**, which take $O(n^2)$ time to fill in each of the $O(n^3)$ $\mathbf{C}$ cells. and solving a $\mathbf{D}$ subproblem, which takes $O(n)$ time on each of the $O(n^4)$ possible such problems.

Pruning: In practice, the set of edges considered (m) is not necessarily $O(n^2)$. Many edges can be ruled out beforehand, either based on the distance in the sentence between the two words (Eisner and Smith, 2010), the predictions of a local ranker (Martins et al., 2009), or the marginals computed from a simpler parsing model (Carreras et al., 2008).

If we choose a pruning strategy such that each word has at most k potential parents (incoming edges), then the running time drops to $O(kn^4)$. The five indices in an **M/C** step were: i, j, k, p, and x. As there must be an edge from p to x, and x only has k possible parents, there are now only $O(kn^4)$ valid such combinations. Similarly, each $\mathbf{D}$ subproblem (which ranges over i, j, k, p, x) may only come into existence because of an edge from p to x, so again the runtime of these such steps drops to $O(kn^4)$.

6 Extension to Grandparent Factorizations

The ability to define slightly non-local features has been shown to improve parsing performance. In this section, we assume a *grandparent-factored* model, where the score of a tree is now the sum over scores of (g, p, c) triples, where (g, p) and (p, c) are both directed edges in the tree. Let $\mathbf{Score(g, p, c)}$ indicate the score of this grandparent-parent-child triple. We now show how to extend the above algorithm to find the maximum scoring gap-minding tree with grandparent scoring.

Our two subproblems are now $\mathbf{C[i, j, p, g]}$ and $\mathbf{D[i, j, p, x, b, g]}$; each subproblem has been augmented with an additional grandparent index g, which has the meaning that g is p's parent. Note that g must be outside of the interval $[i, j]$ (if it were not, a cycle would be introduced). Edge scores are now computed over (g, p, x) triples. In particular, claim 2 is modified:

Claim 3. *Let T be the optimum scoring gap-minding tree rooted at p with vertices $V = [i, j] \cup \{p\}$, where $p \in (i, j)$* **(I)**, *with a grandparent index g ($g \notin V$). Then T and its score are derived from one of the following:*

S/C *If p has a single child x in T, then if $p \in (i, j)$* **(I)**, *T's score is* $\mathbf{Score(g, p, x)} + \mathbf{C[i, p-1, x, p]} + \mathbf{C[p+1, j, x, p]}$; *if $p \notin [i, j]$* **(E)**, *T's score is* $\mathbf{Score(g, p, x)} + \mathbf{C[i, j, x, p]}$.

M/C *If p has multiple children in T and i and j are descended from the same child x in T, then there is a split point k such that T's score is:* $\mathbf{Score(g, p, x)} + \mathbf{C[i, k, x, p]} + \mathbf{D[k+1, j, p, x, T, g]}$ *if x is on the left side of its own gap, and T's score is:* $\mathbf{Score(g, p, x)} + \mathbf{C[k, j, x, p]} + \mathbf{D[i, k-1, p, x, F, g]}$ *if x is on the right side.*

M/D *If p has multiple children in T and i and j are descended from different children in T, then there is a split point k such that T's score is* $\mathbf{C[i, k, p, g]} + \mathbf{C[k+1, j, p, g]}$.

T has the maximum score over each of the above cases, for all valid choices of x and k.

Note that for subproblems rooted at p, g is the grandparent index, while for subproblems rooted at x, p is the updated grandparent index. The $\mathbf{D}$ subproblems with the grandparent index are shown below:

$$\mathbf{D(i, j, p, x, T, g)} = \mathbf{max_k C[i, k, p, g]} + \mathbf{C[k+1, j, x, p]}$$
$$\mathbf{D(i, j, p, x, F, g)} = \mathbf{max_k C[i, k, x, p]} + \mathbf{C[k+1, j, p, g]}$$

We have added another index which ranges over n, so without pruning, we have now increased the running time to $O(n^6)$. However, every step now includes both a g and a p (and often an x), so there is at least one implied edge in every step. If pruning is done in such a way that each word has at most k parents, then each word's set of grandparent and parent possibilities is at most k^2. To run all of the **S/C** steps, we therefore need $O(k^2 n^3)$ time; for all of the **M/C** steps, $O(k^2 n^4)$ time; for all of the **M/D** steps, $O(kn^4)$; for all of the **D** subproblems, $O(k^2 n^4)$. The overall running time is therefore $O(k^2 n^4)$, and we have shown that when edges are sufficiently pruned, grandparent factors add only an extra factor of k, and not a full extra factor of n.

7 Experiments

The space of projective trees is strictly contained within the space of gap-minding trees which is strictly contained within spanning trees. Which space is most appropriate for natural language parsing may depend on the particular language and the type and frequencies of non-projective structures found in it. In this section we compare the parsing accuracy across languages for a parser which uses either the Eisner algorithm (projective), MST (spanning trees), or MaxGapMindingTree (gap-minding trees) as its decoder for both training and inference.

We implemented both the basic gap-minding algorithm and the gap-minding algorithm with grandparent scoring as extensions to MSTParser[10]. MSTParser (McDonald et al., 2005b; McDonald et al., 2005a) uses the Margin Infused Relaxed Algorithm (Crammer and Singer, 2003) for discriminative training. Training requires a decoder which produces the highest scoring tree (in the space of valid trees) under the current model weights. This same decoder is then used to produce parses at test time. MSTParser comes packaged with the Eisner algorithm (for projective trees) and MST (for spanning trees). MSTParser also includes two second order models: one of which is a projective decoder that also scores siblings (Proj+Sib) and the other of which produces non-projective trees by rearranging edges after producing a projective tree (Proj+Sib+Rearr). We add a further decoder with

[10]http://sourceforge.net/projects/mstparser/

the algorithm presented here for gap minding trees, and plan to make the extension publicly available. The gap-minding decoder has both an edge-factored implementation and a version which scores grandparents as well.[11]

The gap-minding algorithm is much more efficient when edges have been pruned so that each word has at most k potential parents. We use the weights from the trained MST models combined with the Matrix Tree Theorem (Smith and Smith, 2007; Koo et al., 2007; McDonald and Satta, 2007) to produce marginal probabilities of each edge. We wanted to be able to both achieve the running time bound and yet take advantage of the fact that the size of the set of reasonable parent choices is variable. We therefore use a hybrid pruning strategy: each word's set of potential parents is the *smaller* of a) the top k parents (we chose $k = 10$) or b) the set of parents whose probabilities are above a threshold (we chose $th = .001$). The running time for the gap-minding algorithm is then $O(kn^4)$; with the grandparent features the gap-minding running time is $O(k^2n^4)$.

The training and test sets for the six languages come from the CoNLL-X shared task.[12] We train the gap-minding algorithm on sentences of length at most 100[13] (the vast majority of sentences). The projective and MST models are trained on all sentences and are run without any pruning. The Czech training set is much larger than the others and so for Czech only the first 10,000 training sentences were used. Testing is on the full test set, with no length restrictions.

The results are shown in Table 2. The first three lines show the first order gap-minding decoder compared with the first order projective and MST de-

	Ar	Cz	Da	Du	Pt	Sw
Proj.	78.0	80.0	88.2	79.8	87.4	86.9
MST	78.0	80.4	88.1	84.6	86.7	86.2
Gap-Mind	77.6	80.8	88.6	83.9	86.8	86.0
Proj+Sib	78.2	80.0	88.9	81.1	87.5	88.1
+Rearr	78.5	81.3	89.3	85.4	88.2	87.7
GM+Grand	78.3	82.1	89.1	84.6	87.7	88.5

Table 2: Unlabeled Attachment Scores on the CoNLL-X shared task test set.

coders. The gap-minding decoder does better than the projective decoder on Czech, Danish, and Dutch, the three languages with the most non-projectivity, even though it was at a competitive disadvantage in terms of both pruning and (on languages with very long sentences) training data. The gap-minding decoder with grandparent features is better than the projective decoder with sibling features on all six of the languages. On some languages, the local search decoder with siblings has the absolute highest accuracy in Table 2; on other languages (Czech and Swedish) the gap-minding+grandparents has the highest accuracy. While not directly comparable because of the difference in features, the promising performance of the gap-minding+grandparents decoder shows that the space of gap-minding trees is larger than the space of projective trees, yet unlike spanning trees, it is tractable to find the best tree with higher order features. It would be interesting to extend the gap-minding algorithm to include siblings as well.

8 Conclusion

Gap inheritance, a structural property on trees, has implications both for natural language syntax and for natural language parsing. We have shown that the mildly non-projective trees present in natural language treebanks *all* have zero or one children inherit each parent's gap. We also showed that the assumption of 1 gap inheritance removes a factor of n from parsing time, and the further assumption of 0 gap inheritance removes yet another factor of n. The space of gap-minding trees provides a closer fit to naturally occurring linguistic structures than the space of projective trees, and unlike spanning trees, the inclusion of higher order factors does not substantially increase the difficulty of finding the maximum scoring tree in that space.

[11]The grandparent features used were identical to the features provided within MSTParser for the second-order sibling parsers, with one exception — many features are conjoined with a direction indicator, which in the projective case has only two possibilities. We replaced this two-way distinction with a six-way distinction of the six possible orders of the grandparent, parent, and child.

[12]MSTParser produces labeled dependencies on CoNLL formatted input. We replace all labels in the training set with a single dummy label to produce unlabeled dependency trees.

[13]Because of long training times, the gap-minding with grandparent models for Portuguese and Swedish were trained on only sentences up to 50 words.

Acknowledgments

We would like to thank Aravind Joshi for comments on an earlier draft. This material is based upon work supported under a National Science Foundation Graduate Research Fellowship.

Algorithm 1: MaxGapMindingTree

```
Init: ∀_{i∈[1,n]} C[i,i,i] = 0
for size = 0 to n − 1 do
  for i = 1 to n − size do
    j = i + size
    /* Endpoint parents                      */
    if size > 0 then
      C[i,j,i] = C[i+1,j,i]
      C[i,j,j] = C[i,j−1,j]
    /* Interior parents                      */
    for p = i+1 to j−1 do
      C[i,j,p] = max (SingleChild(i,j,p),
      EndpointsDiff(i,j,p),
      EndsFromLeftChild(i,j,p),
      EndsFromRightChild(i,j,p))
    /* Exterior parents                      */
    forall the p ∈ [0,i−1] ∪ [j+1,n] do
      C[i,j,p] = max (SingleChild(i,j,p),
      EndpointsDiff(i,j,p),
      EndsFromLeftChild(i,j,p),
      EndsFromRightChild(i,j,p))
    /* Helper subproblems                    */
    for p ∈ [0,n] do
      forall the x ∈ PosChild[p] ∧ x ∉ [i,j] do
        if p ≠ j then
          D[i,j,p,x,T] = Max2Subtrees(i,j,p,x,T)
        if p ≠ i then
          D[i,j,p,x,F] = Max2Subtrees(i,j,p,x,F)
Final answer: C[1,n,0]
```

Function SingleChild(i,j,p)

```
X = PosChild[p] ∩ [i,j]
/* Interior p                                */
if p > i ∧ p < j then
  return max_{x∈X} C[i,p−1,x]
         +C[p+1,j,x] + Score(p,x)
/* Exterior p                                */
else
  return max_{x∈X} C[i,j,x] + Score(p,x)
```

Function EndpointsDiff(i,j,p)

```
return max_{k∈[i,j−1]} C[i,k,p] + C[k+1,j,p]
```

Function EndsFromLeftChild(i,j,p)

```
/* Interior p                                */
if p > i ∧ p < j then
  X = PosChild[p] ∩ [i,p−1]
  forall the x ∈ X ∧ x < p do
    K[x] = [x,p−1]
/* Exterior p                                */
else
  X = PosChild[p] ∩ [i,j]
  forall the x ∈ X do
    K = [x,j−2]
return max_{x∈X,k∈K[x]} C[i,k,x]
       +Score(p,x) + D[k+1,j,p,x,T]
```

Function EndsFromRightChild(i,j,p)

```
/* Interior p                                */
if p > i ∧ p < j then
  X = PosChild[p] ∩ [p+1,j]
  forall the x ∈ X ∧ x > p do
    K[x] = [p+1,x]
/* Exterior p                                */
else
  X = PosChild[p] ∩ [i,j]
  forall the x ∈ X do
    K[x] = [i+2,x]
return max_{x∈X,k∈K[x]} C[k,j,x]
       +Score(p,x) + D[i,k−1,p,x,F]
```

Function Max2Subtrees(i,j,p,x,pOnLeft)

```
/* Interior p                                */
if p ≥ i ∧ p ≤ j then
  if pOnLeft then
    K = [p,j−1]
    return max_{k∈K} C[i,k,p] + C[k+1,j,x]
  else
    K = [i,p−1]
    return max_{k∈K} C[i,k,x] + C[k+1,j,p]
/* Exterior p                                */
else
  K = [i,j−1]}
  if pOnLeft then
    return max_{k∈K} C[i,k,p] + C[k+1,j,x]
  else
    return max_{k∈K} C[i,k,x] + C[k+1,j,p]
```

References

M. Bodirsky, M. Kuhlmann, and M. Möhl. 2005. Well-nested drawings as models of syntactic structure. In *In Tenth Conference on Formal Grammar and Ninth Meeting on Mathematics of Language*, pages 88–1. University Press.

X. Carreras, M. Collins, and T. Koo. 2008. Tag, dynamic programming, and the perceptron for efficient, feature-rich parsing. In *Proceedings of CoNLL*, pages 9–16. Association for Computational Linguistics.

X. Carreras. 2007. Experiments with a higher-order projective dependency parser. In *Proceedings of the CoNLL Shared Task Session of EMNLP-CoNLL*, volume 7, pages 957–961.

J. Chen-Main and A. Joshi. 2010. Unavoidable ill-nestedness in natural language and the adequacy of tree local-mctag induced dependency structures. In *Proceedings of the Tenth International Workshop on Tree Adjoining Grammar and Related Formalisms (TAG+ 10)*.

J. Chen-Main and A.K. Joshi. 2012. A dependency perspective on the adequacy of tree local multi-component tree adjoining grammar. In *Jóurnal of Logic and Computation*. (to appear).

N. Chomsky. 1981. *Lectures on Government and Binding*. Dordrecht: Foris.

K. Crammer and Y. Singer. 2003. Ultraconservative online algorithms for multiclass problems. *Journal of Machine Learning Research*, 3:951–991, March.

J. Eisner and G. Satta. 2000. A faster parsing algorithm for lexicalized tree-adjoining grammars. In *Proceedings of the 5th Workshop on Tree-Adjoining Grammars and Related Formalisms (TAG+5)*, pages 14–19.

J. Eisner and N.A. Smith. 2010. Favor short dependencies: Parsing with soft and hard constraints on dependency length. In Harry Bunt, Paola Merlo, and Joakim Nivre, editors, *Trends in Parsing Technology: Dependency Parsing, Domain Adaptation, and Deep Parsing*, chapter 8, pages 121–150. Springer.

J. Eisner. 2000. Bilexical grammars and their cubic-time parsing algorithms. In Harry Bunt and Anton Nijholt, editors, *Advances in Probabilistic and Other Parsing Technologies*, pages 29–62. Kluwer Academic Publishers, October.

R. Fiengo. 1977. On trace theory. *Linguistic Inquiry*, 8(1):35–61.

C. Gómez-Rodríguez, J. Carroll, and D. Weir. 2011. Dependency parsing schemata and mildly non-projective dependency parsing. *Computational Linguistics*, 37(3):541–586.

T. Koo and M. Collins. 2010. Efficient third-order dependency parsers. In *Proceedings of ACL*, pages 1–11.

T. Koo, A. Globerson, X. Carreras, and M. Collins. 2007. Structured prediction models via the matrix-tree theorem. In *Proceedings of EMNLP-CoNLL*.

T. Koo, A.M. Rush, M. Collins, T. Jaakkola, and D. Sontag. 2010. Dual decomposition for parsing with non-projective head automata. In *Proceedings of EMNLP*, pages 1288–1298.

M. Kuhlmann and J. Nivre. 2006. Mildly non-projective dependency structures. In *Proceedings of COLING/ACL*, pages 507–514.

A.F.T. Martins, N.A. Smith, and E.P. Xing. 2009. Concise integer linear programming formulations for dependency parsing. In *Proceedings of ACL*, pages 342–350.

R. McDonald and F. Pereira. 2006. Online learning of approximate dependency parsing algorithms. In *Proceedings of EACL*, pages 81–88.

R. McDonald and G. Satta. 2007. On the complexity of non-projective data-driven dependency parsing. In *Proceedings of the 10th International Conference on Parsing Technologies*, pages 121–132.

R. McDonald, K. Crammer, and F. Pereira. 2005a. Online large-margin training of dependency parsers. In *Proceedings of ACL*, pages 91–98.

R. McDonald, F. Pereira, K. Ribarov, and J. Hajič. 2005b. Non-projective dependency parsing using spanning tree algorithms. In *Proceedings of HLT-EMNLP*, pages 523–530.

T. Reinhart. 1976. *The Syntactic Domain of Anaphora*. Ph.D. thesis, Massachusetts Institute of Technology.

G. Satta and W. Schuler. 1998. Restrictions on tree adjoining languages. In *Proceedings of COLING-ACL*, pages 1176–1182.

D.A. Smith and N.A. Smith. 2007. Probabilistic models of nonprojective dependency trees. In *Proceedings of EMNLP-CoNLL*.

Joint Entity and Event Coreference Resolution across Documents

Heeyoung Lee, Marta Recasens, Angel Chang, Mihai Surdeanu, Dan Jurafsky
Stanford University, Stanford, CA 94305
{heeyoung,recasens,angelx,mihais,jurafsky}@stanford.edu

Abstract

We introduce a novel coreference resolution system that models entities and events jointly. Our iterative method cautiously constructs clusters of entity and event mentions using linear regression to model cluster merge operations. As clusters are built, information flows between entity and event clusters through features that model semantic role dependencies. Our system handles nominal and verbal events as well as entities, and our joint formulation allows information from event coreference to help entity coreference, and vice versa. In a cross-document domain with comparable documents, joint coreference resolution performs significantly better (over 3 CoNLL F1 points) than two strong baselines that resolve entities and events separately.

1 Introduction

Most coreference resolution systems focus on entities and tacitly assume a correspondence between entities and noun phrases (NPs). Focusing on NPs is a way to restrict the challenging problem of coreference resolution, but misses coreference relations like the one between *hanged* and *his suicide* in (1), and between *placed* and *put* in (2).

1. (a) **One of the key suspected Mafia bosses arrested yesterday** has hanged himself.
   (b) Police said **Lo Presti** had hanged himself.
   (c) His suicide appeared to be related to clan feuds.
2. (a) **The New Orleans Saints** placed **Reggie Bush** on the injured list on Wednesday.
   (b) **Saints** put **Bush** on I.R.

As (1c) shows, NPs can also refer to events, and so corefer with phrases other than NPs (Webber, 1988). By being anchored in spatio-temporal dimensions, events represent the most frequent referent of verbal elements. In addition to time and location, events are characterized by their participants or arguments, which often correspond with discourse entities. This two-way feedback between events and their arguments (or entities) is the core of our approach. Since arguments play a key role in describing an event, knowing that two arguments corefer is useful for finding coreference relations between events, and knowing that two events corefer is useful for finding coreference relations between entities. In (1), the coreference relation between *One of the key suspected Mafia bosses arrested yesterday* and *Lo Presti* can be found by knowing that their predicates (i.e., *has hanged* and *had hanged*) corefer. On the other hand, the coreference relations between the arguments *Saints* and *Bush* in (2) helps to determine the coreference relation between their predicates *placed* and *put*.

In this paper, we take a holistic approach to coreference. We annotate a corpus with cross-document coreference relations for nominal and verbal mentions. We focus on both intra and inter-document coreference because this scenario is at the same time more challenging and more relevant to real-world applications such as news aggregation. We use this corpus to train a model that jointly addresses references to both entities and events across documents. The contributions of this work are the following:

- We introduce a novel approach for entity and event coreference resolution. At the core of our approach is an iterative algorithm that cautiously constructs clusters of entity and event mentions using linear regression to model cluster merge operations. Importantly, our model allows information to flow between clusters of both types through features that model context using semantic role dependencies.

- We annotate and release a new corpus with coreference relations between both entities and events across documents. The relations annotated are both intra and inter-document, which more accurately models real-world scenarios.
- We evaluate our cross-document coreference resolution system on this corpus and show that our joint approach significantly outperforms two strong baselines that resolve entities and events separately.

2 Related Work

Entity coreference resolution is a well studied problem with many successful techniques for identifying mention clusters (Ponzetto and Strube, 2006; Haghighi and Klein, 2009; Stoyanov et al., 2009; Haghighi and Klein, 2010; Raghunathan et al., 2010; Rahman and Ng, 2011, inter alia). Most of these techniques focus on matching compatible noun pairs using various syntactic and semantic features, with efforts targeted toward improving features and clustering models.

Prior work showed that models that jointly resolve mentions across multiple entities result in better performance than simply resolving mentions in a pairwise fashion (Denis and Baldridge, 2007; Poon and Domingos, 2008; Wick et al., 2008; Lee et al., 2011, inter alia). A natural extension is to perform coreference jointly across both entities and events. Yet there has been little attempt in this direction.

We know of only limited work that incorporates event-related information in entity coreference, typically by incorporating the verbs in context as features. For instance, Haghighi and Klein (2010) include the governor of the head of nominal mentions as features in their model. Rahman and Ng (2011) also used event-related information by looking at which semantic role the entity mentions can have and the verb pairs of their predicates. We confirm that such features are useful but also show that the complementary features for verbal mentions lead to even better performance, especially when event and entity clusters are jointly modeled.

Compared to the extensive work on entity coreference, the related problem of event coreference remains relatively under-explored, with minimal work on how entity and event coreference can be considered jointly on an open domain. Early work on event coreference for MUC (Humphreys et al., 1997; Bagga and Baldwin, 1999) focused on scenario-specific events. More recently, there have been approaches that looked at event coreference for wider domains. Chen and Ji (2009) proposed using spectral graph clustering to cluster events. Bejan and Harabagiu (2010) proposed a nonparametric Bayesian model for open-domain event resolution. However, most of this prior work focused only on event coreference, whereas we address both entities and events with a single model. Humphreys et al. (1997) considered entities as well as events, but due to the lack of a corpus annotated with event coreference, their approach was only evaluated implicitly in the MUC-6 template filling task. To our knowledge, the only previous work that considered entity and event coreference resolution jointly is He (2007), but limited to the medical domain and focused on just five semantic categories.

3 Architecture

Following the intuition introduced in Section 1, our approach iteratively builds clusters of event and entity mentions jointly. As more information becomes available (e.g., finding out that two verbal mentions have arguments that belong to the same entity cluster), the features of both entity and event mentions are re-generated, which prompts future clustering operations. Our model follows a cautious (or "baby steps") approach, which we previously showed to be successful for entity coreference resolution (Raghunathan et al., 2010; Lee et al., 2011). However, unlike our previous work, which used deterministic rules, in this paper we learn a coreference resolution model using linear regression. Algorithm 1 summarizes the flow of the proposed algorithm. We detail its steps next. We describe the training procedure in Section 4 and the features used in Section 5.

Algorithm 1: Joint Coreference Resolution

```
   input  : set of documents 𝒟
   input  : coreference model Θ
   // clusters of mentions:
1  ℰ = {}
   // clusters of documents:
2  𝒞 = clusterDocuments(𝒟)
3  foreach document cluster c in 𝒞 do
       // all mentions in one doc cluster:
4      ℳ = extractMentions(c)
       // singleton mention clusters:
5      ℰ' = buildSingletonClusters(ℳ)
       // high-precision deterministic sieves:
6      ℰ' = applyHighPrecisionSieves(ℰ')
       // iterative event/entity coreference:
7      while ∃ e1, e2 ∈ ℰ' s.t. score(e1, e2, Θ) > 0.5 do
8          (e1, e2) = arg max_{e1,e2∈ℰ'} score(e1, e2, Θ)
9          ℰ' = merge(e1, e2, ℰ')
       // pronoun sieve:
10     ℰ' = applyPronounSieve(ℰ')
       // append to global output:
11     ℰ = ℰ + ℰ'
   output : ℰ
```

3.1 Document Clustering

Our approach starts with several steps that reduce the search space for the actual coreference resolution task. The first is document clustering, which clusters the set of input documents ($\mathcal{D}$) into a set of document clusters ($\mathcal{C}$). In the subsequent steps we only cluster mentions that appear in the same document cluster. We found this to be very useful in practice because, in addition to reducing the search space, it provides a word sense disambiguation mechanism based on corpus-wide topics. For example, without document clustering, our algorithm may decide to cluster two mentions of the verb *hit*, but knowing that one belongs to a cluster containing earthquake reports and the other to a cluster with reports on criminal activities, this decision can be avoided.[1]

Any non-parametric clustering algorithm can be used in this step. In this paper, we used the algorithm proposed by Surdeanu et al. (2005). This algorithm is an Expectation Maximization (EM) variant where the initial points (and the number of clusters) are selected from the clusters generated by a hierarchical agglomerative clustering algorithm using geometric heuristics. This algorithm performs well on our data. For example, in the training dataset, only two topics (handling different earthquake events) are incorrectly merged into the same cluster.

3.2 Mention Extraction

In this step (4 in Algorithm 1) we extract nominal, pronominal, and verbal mentions. We extract nominal and pronominal mentions using the mention identification component in the publicly downloadable Stanford coreference resolution system (Raghunathan et al., 2010; Lee et al., 2011). We consider as verbal mentions all words whose part of speech starts with `VB`, with the exception of some auxiliary/copulative verbs (*have*, *be* and *seem*). For each of the identified mentions we build a singleton cluster (step 5 in Algorithm 1).

Crucially, we do not make a formal distinction between entity and event mentions. This distinction is not trivial to implement (e.g., is the noun *earthquake* an entity or an event mention?) and an imperfect classification would negatively affect the following coreference resolution. Instead, we simply classify mentions into verbal or nominal, and use this distinction later during feature generation (Section 5). To compare event nouns (e.g., *development*) with verbal mentions, the "derivationally related form" relation in WordNet is used.

3.3 High-precision Entity Resolution Sieves

To further reduce the problem's search space, in step 6 of Algorithm 1 we apply a set of high-precision filters from the Stanford coreference resolution system. This system is a collection of deterministic models (or "sieves") for entity coreference resolution that incorporate lexical, syntactic, semantic, and discourse information. These sieves are applied from higher to lower precision. As clusters are built, information such as mention gender and number is propagated across mentions in the same cluster, which helps subsequent decisions. The Stanford system obtained the highest score at the CoNLL-2011 shared task on English coreference resolution.

For this step, we selected all the sieves from the Stanford system with the exception of the pronoun resolution sieve. All the remaining sieves (listed in Table 1) have high precision because they employ linguistic heuristics with little ambiguity, e.g.,

[1] Since different mentions of the verb *say* in the same topic might refer to different events, they are only merged if they have coreferent arguments.

High-precision sieves
Discourse processing sieve
Exact string match sieve
Relaxed string match sieve
Precise constructs sieve (e.g., appositives)
Strict head match sieves
Proper head noun match sieve
Relaxed head matching sieve

Table 1: Deterministic sieves in step 6 of Algorithm 1.

one sieve clusters together two entity mentions only when they have the same head word. Note that all these heuristics were designed for within-document coreference. They work well in our context because we apply them in individual document clusters, where the one-sense-per-discourse principle still holds (Yarowsky, 1995).

Importantly, these sieves do not address verbal mentions. That is, all verbal mentions are still in singleton clusters after this step. Furthermore, none of these sieves use features that facilitate the joint resolution of nominal and verbal mentions (e.g., features from semantic role frames). All these limitations are addressed next.

3.4 Iterative Entity/Event Resolution

In this stage (steps 7 – 9 in Algorithm 1), we construct entity and event clusters using a cautious or "baby steps" approach. We use a single linear regressor (Θ) to model cluster merge operations between both verbal and nominal clusters. Intuitively, the linear regressor models the quality of the merge operation, i.e., a score larger than 0.5 indicates that more than half of the mention pairs introduced by this merge are correct. We discuss the training procedure that yields this scoring function in Section 4. In each iteration, we perform the merge operation that has the highest score. Once two clusters are merged (step 9) we regenerate all the mention features to reflect the current clusters. We stop when no merging operation with an overall benefit is found.

This iterative procedure is the core of our joint coreference resolution approach. This algorithm transparently merges both entity and event mentions and, importantly, allows information to flow between clusters of both types as merge operations take place. For example, assume that during iteration i we merge the two *hanged* verbs in the first example in Section 1 (because they have the same lemma). Because of this merge, in iteration $i+1$ the nominal mentions *Lo Presti* and *One of the key suspected Mafia bosses* have the same semantic role for verbs assigned to the same cluster. This is a strong hint that these two nominal mentions belong to the same cluster. Indeed, the feature that models this structure received one of the highest weights in our linear regression model (see Section 7).

3.5 Pronoun Sieve

Our approach concludes with the pronominal coreference resolution sieve from the Stanford system. This sieve is necessary because our current resolution algorithm ignores mention ordering and distance (i.e., in step 7 we compare all clusters regardless of where their mentions appear in the text). As previous work has proved, the structure of the text is crucial for pronominal coreference (Hobbs, 1978). For this reason, we handle pronouns outside of the main algorithm block.

4 Training the Cluster Merging Model

Two observations drove our choice of model and training algorithm. First, modeling the merge operation as a classification task is not ideal, because only a few of the resulting clusters are entirely correct or incorrect. In practice, most of the clusters will contain some mention pairs that are correct and some that are not. Second, generating training data for the merging model is not trivial: a brute force approach that looks at all the possible combinations is exponential in the number of mentions. This is both impractical and unnecessary, as some of these combinations are unlikely to be seen in practice.

We address these observations with Algorithm 2. The algorithm uses gold coreference labels to train a linear regressor that models the quality of the clusters produced by merge operations. We define the quality score q of a new cluster as the percentage of new mention pairs (i.e., not present in either one of the clusters to be merged) that are correct:

$$q = \frac{links_{correct}}{links_{correct} + links_{incorrect}} \tag{1}$$

where $links_{(in)correct}$ is the number of newly introduced (in)correct pairwise mention links when two clusters are merged.

Algorithm 2: Training Procedure

input : set of documents $\mathcal{D}$
input : correct mention clusters $\mathcal{G}$
1 $\mathcal{C}$ = clusterDocuments($\mathcal{D}$)
// linear regression coreference model:
2 Θ = assignInitialWeights($\mathcal{C}, \mathcal{G}$)
// repeat for T epochs:
3 **for** $t = 1$ **to** T **do**
// training data for linear regressor:
4 $\Gamma = \{\}$
5 **foreach** document cluster c **in** $\mathcal{C}$ **do**
6 $\mathcal{M}$ = extractMentions(c)
7 $\mathcal{E}$ = buildSingletonClusters($\mathcal{M}$)
8 $\mathcal{E}$ = applyHighPrecisionSieves($\mathcal{E}$)
// gather training examples
// as clusters are built:
9 **while** $\exists\, e_1, e_2 \in \mathcal{E} s.t.\ sco(e_1, e_2, \Theta) > 0.5$ **do**
10 **forall** $e'_1, e'_2 \in \mathcal{E}$ **do**
11 q = qualityOfMerge($e'_1, e'_2, \mathcal{G}$)
12 Γ = append(e'_1, e'_2, q, Γ)
13 $(e_1, e_2) = \arg\max_{e_1, e_2 \in \mathcal{E}} \text{sco}(e_1, e_2, \Theta)$
14 $\mathcal{E}$ = merge($e_1, e_2, \mathcal{E}$)
// train using data from last epoch:
15 Θ' = trainLinearRegressor(Γ)
// interpolate with older model:
16 $\Theta = \lambda\Theta + (1 - \lambda)\Theta'$
output : Θ

We address the potential explosion in training data size by considering only merge operations that are likely to be inspected by the algorithm as it runs. To achieve this, Algorithm 2 repeatedly runs the actual clustering algorithm (as given by the current model Θ) over the training dataset (steps 5 – 14).[2] When the algorithm iteratively constructs its clusters (steps 9 – 14), we generate training data from all possible cluster pairs available during a particular iteration (steps 10 – 12). For each pair, we compute its score using Equation 1 (step 11) and add it to the training corpus Γ (step 12). Note that this avoids inspecting many of the possible cluster combinations: once a cluster is built (e.g., during the previous iterations or by the deterministic sieves in step 8), we do not generate training data from its members, but rather treat it as an atomic unit. On the other hand, our approach generates more training data than online learning, which trains using only the actual decisions taken during inference in each iteration (i.e., the pair (e_1, e_2) in step 13).

After each epoch we have a new training corpus Γ, which we use to train the new linear regression model Θ' (step 15), which is then interpolated with the old one (step 16).

Our training procedure is similar in spirit to transformation based learning (TBL) (Brill, 1995). Similarly to TBL, our approach repeatedly applies the model over the training data and attempts to minimize the error rate of the current model. However, while TBL learns rules that directly minimize the current error rate, our approach achieves this indirectly, by incorporating the reduction in error rate in the score of the generated datums. This allows us to fit a linear regression to this task, which, as discussed before, is a better model for this task.

Just like any hill-climbing algorithm, our approach has the risk of converging to a local maximum. To mitigate this risk, we do not initialize our model Θ with random weights, but rather use hints from the deterministic sieves. This procedure (listed in step 2) runs the high-precision sieves introduced in Section 3.3 and, just like the data generation loop in Algorithm 2, creates training examples from the clusters available after every merge operation. Since these deterministic models address only nominal clusters, at the end we generate training data for events by inspecting all the pairs of singleton verbal clusters. Using this data, we train the initial linear regression model.

We trained our model using L2 regularized linear regression with a regularization coefficient of 1.0. We did not tune the regularization coefficient. We ran the training algorithm for 10 epochs, although we observed minimal changes after three epochs. We tuned the interpolation weight (λ) to a value of 0.7 using our development corpus.

5 Features

We list in Table 2 the features used by the linear regression model. As the table indicates, our feature set relies heavily on semantic roles, which were extracted using the SwiRL semantic role labeling (SRL) system (Surdeanu et al., 2007).[3] Because SwiRL addresses only verbal predicates, we extended it to handle nominal predicates. In this

[2]We skip the pronoun sieve here because it does not affect the decisions taken during the iterative resolution steps.

[3]http://www.surdeanu.name/mihai/swirl/

Feature Name	Applies to Entities (E) or Events (V)	Description and Example
Entity Heads	E	Cosine similarity of the head-word vectors of two clusters. The head-word vector stores the head words of all mentions in a cluster and their frequencies. For example, the vector for the three-mention cluster {*Barack Obama*, *President Obama*, *US president*}, is {*Obama*:2, *president*:1}.
Event Lemmas	V	Cosine similarity of the lemma vectors of two clusters. For example, the lemma vector for the cluster {*murdered*, *murders*, *hitting*} is {*murder*:2, *hit*:1}.
Links between Synonyms	E, V	The percentage of newly-introduced mention links after the merge that are WordNet synonyms (Fellbaum, 1998). For example, when merging the following two clusters, {*hit*, *strike*} and {*strike*, *join*, *say*}, two out of the six new links are between words that belong to the same WordNet synset: (*hit* – *strike*) and (*strike* – *strike*).
Number of Coreferent Arguments or Predicates	E, V	The total number of shared arguments and predicates between mentions in the two clusters. We use the cluster IDs of the corresponding arguments/predicates to check for identity. For example, when comparing the event clusters {*bought*} and {*acquired*}, extracted from the sentences $[AMD]_{\texttt{Arg0}}$ *bought* $[ATI]_{\texttt{Arg1}}$ and $[AMD]_{\texttt{Arg0}}$ *acquired* $[ATI]_{\texttt{Arg1}}$, the value of this feature is 2 because the two mentions share one `Arg0` and one `Arg1` argument (assuming that the clusters {*AMD*, *AMD*} and {*ATI*, *ATI*} were previously created). For entity clusters, this feature counts the number of coreferent predicates. In addition to PropBank-style roles, for event mentions we also include the closest left and right entity mentions in order to capture any arguments missed by the SRL system.
Coreferent Arguments in a Specific Role?	E, V	Indicator feature set to 1 if the two clusters have at least one coreferent argument in a given role. We generate one variant of this feature for each argument label, e.g., `Arg0`, `Arg1`, etc. For example, the value of this feature for `Arg0` for the clusters {*bought*} and {*acquired*} in the above example is 1.
Coreferent Predicate in a Specific Role?	E	Indicator feature set to 1 if the two clusters have at least one coreferent predicate for a given role. For example, for the clusters {*the man*} and {*the person*}, extracted from the sentences *helped* $[the\ man]_{\texttt{Arg1}}$ and *helped* $[the\ person]_{\texttt{Arg1}}$, the value of this feature is 1 if the two *helped* verbs were previously clustered together.
2nd Order Similarity of Mention Words	E	Cosine similarity of vectors containing words that are distributionally similar to words in the cluster mentions. We built these vectors by extracting the top-ten most-similar words in Dekang Lin's similarity thesaurus (Lin, 1998) for all the nouns/adjectives/verbs in a cluster. For example, for the singleton cluster {*a new home*}, we construct this vector by expanding *new* and *home* to: {*new:1*, *original:1*, *old:1*, *existing:1*, *current:1*, *unique:1*, *modern:1*, *different:1*, *special:1*, *major:1*, *small:1*, *home:1*, *house:1*, *apartment:1*, *building:1*, *hotel:1*, *residence:1*, *office:1*, *mansion:1*, *school:1*, *restaurant:1*, *hospital:1* }.
Number; Animacy; Gender; NE Label	E	Cosine similarity of number, gender, animacy, and NE label vectors. For example, the number and gender vectors for the two-mention cluster {*systems*, *a pen*} are Number = {singular:1, plural:1}, Gender = {neutral:2}.

Table 2: List of features used when comparing two clusters. If any of the two clusters contains a verbal mention we consider the merge an operation between event (V) clusters; otherwise it is a merge between entity (E) clusters. We append to all entity features the suffix `Proper` or `Common` based on the type of the head word of the first mention in each of the two clusters. We use the suffix `Proper` only if both head words are proper nouns.

paper we used a single heuristic: the possessor of a nominal event's predicate is marked as its `Arg0`, e.g., *Logan* is the `Arg0` to *run* in *Logan's run*.[4]

[4]A principled solution to this problem is to use an SRL system for nominal predicates trained using NomBank (Meyers et al., 2004). We will address this in future work.

We extracted named entity labels using the named entity recognizer from the Stanford CoreNLP suite.

6 Evaluation

6.1 Corpus

The training and test data sets were derived from the EventCorefBank (ECB) corpus[5] created by Bejan and Harabagiu (2010) to study event coreference since standard corpora such as OntoNotes (Pradhan et al., 2007) contain a small number of annotated event clusters. The ECB corpus consists of 482 documents from Google News clustered into 43 topics, where a topic is described as a seminal event. The reason for including comparable documents was to increase the number of cross-document coreference relations. Bejan and Harabagiu (2010) only annotated a selection of events.

For the purpose of our study, we extended the original corpus in two directions: (i) fully annotated sentences, and (ii) entity coreference relations. In addition, we removed relations other than coreference (e.g., subevent, purpose, related, etc.) that had been originally annotated. We revised and completed the original annotation by annotating every entity and event in the sentences that were (partially) annotated. The annotation was performed by four experts, using the Callisto annotation tool.[6] The annotation guidelines and the generated corpus are available here.[7]

Our annotation of the ECB corpus followed the OntoNotes (Pradhan et al., 2007) standard for coreference annotation, with a few extensions to handle events. For nouns, we annotated full NPs (with all modifiers), excluding appositive phrases and nominal predicates. Only premodifiers that were proper nouns or possessive phrases were annotated. For events, we annotated the semantic head of the verb phrase. We extended the OntoNotes guidelines by also annotating singletons (but we do not score them; see below), and by including all events mentions (not only those mentioned at least once with an NP). This required us to be specific with respect to:

[5] `http://faculty.washington.edu/bejan/data/ECB1.0.tar.gz`

[6] `http://callisto.mitre.org`

[7] `http://nlp.stanford.edu/pubs/jcoref-corpus.zip`

	Training	Dev	Test	Total
# Topics	12	3	28	43
# Documents	112	39	331	482
# Entities	459	46	563	1068
# Entity Mentions	1723	259	3465	5447
# Events	300	30	444	774
# Event Mentions	751	140	1642	2533

Table 3: Corpus statistics.

⟨ENTITY COREFID="26"⟩ A publicist ⟨/ENTITY⟩ ⟨EVENT COREFID="4"⟩ says ⟨/EVENT⟩ ⟨ENTITY COREFID="23"⟩ Tara Reid ⟨/ENTITY⟩ has ⟨EVENT COREFID="3"⟩ checked ⟨/EVENT⟩ ⟨ENTITY COREFID="23"⟩ herself ⟨/ENTITY⟩ ⟨EVENT COREFID="3*"⟩ into ⟨/EVENT⟩ ⟨ENTITY COREFID="28"⟩ rehab ⟨/ENTITY⟩.

Figure 1: Annotation example.

Light verbs Verbs such as *give* and *make* followed by a noun (e.g., *make an offer*) were not annotated, but the noun was.

Phrasal verbs We annotated the verb together with the preposition or adverb (e.g., *check in*).

Idioms They were annotated with all their elements (e.g., *booze it up*).

The first topic was annotated by all four annotators as burn-in. Afterwards, annotation disagreements were resolved between all annotators and the next three topics were annotated again by all four annotators to measure agreement. Following Passonneau (2004), we computed an inter-annotator agreement of $\alpha = 0.55$ (Krippendorff, 2004) on these three topics, indicating moderate agreement among the annotators. Given the complexity of the task, we consider this to be a good score. For example, the average of the CoNLL F1 between any two annotators is 73.58, which is much higher than the system scores reported in the literature.

After annotating the four topics, disagreements were resolved again and all the documents in the four topics were corrected to match the consensus. The rest of the corpus was split between the four annotators, and each document was annotated by a single annotator. Figure 1 shows an example. Table 3 shows the corpus statistics, including the training, development (dev) and test set splits. The dev topics were used for tuning the interpolation parameter λ from Section 4.

System		MUC R	MUC P	MUC F1	B^3 R	B^3 P	B^3 F1	CEAF-ϕ_4 R	CEAF-ϕ_4 P	CEAF-ϕ_4 F1	BLANC R	BLANC P	BLANC F1	CoNLL F1
Baseline 1 Wo/ SRL	Entity	47.4	72.3	57.2	44.1	**82.7**	57.5	**42.5**	21.9	28.9	60.1	78.3	64.8	47.9
	Event	56.0	56.8	56.4	59.8	71.9	65.3	32.2	31.6	31.9	63.5	68.8	65.7	51.2
	Both	49.9	75.4	60.0	44.9	**83.9**	58.5	46.2	23.3	31.0	60.9	81.2	66.1	49.8
Baseline 2 With SRL	Entity	52.7	**73.0**	61.2	48.6	80.8	60.7	41.8	24.1	30.6	63.4	78.4	68.2	50.8
	Event	59.2	57.0	58.1	62.3	70.8	66.3	31.5	33.2	32.3	65.4	68.0	66.6	52.2
	Both	54.5	**76.4**	63.7	48.7	82.6	61.3	**46.3**	25.5	32.9	63.9	81.1	69.2	52.6
This paper	Entity	**60.7**	70.6	**65.2**	**55.5**	74.9	**63.7**	39.3	**29.5**	**33.7**	**66.9**	**79.6**	**71.5**	**54.2**
	Event	**62.7**	**62.8**	**62.7**	**62.5**	**73.9**	**67.7**	**34.0**	**33.9**	**33.9**	**67.6**	**78.5**	**71.7**	**54.8**
	Both	**61.2**	75.9	**67.8**	**53.9**	79.0	**64.1**	45.2	**30.0**	**35.8**	**67.1**	**82.2**	**72.3**	**55.9**

Table 4: Performance of the two baselines and our model. We report scores for entity clusters, event clusters and the complete task using five metrics.

6.2 Evaluation

We use five coreference evaluation metrics widely used in the literature:

MUC (Vilain et al., 1995) Link-based metric which measures how many predicted and gold clusters need to be merged to cover the gold and predicted clusters, respectively.

B^3 (Bagga and Baldwin, 1998) Mention-based metric which measures the proportion of overlap between predicted and gold clusters for a given mention.

CEAF (Luo, 2005) Entity-based metric that, unlike B^3, enforces a one-to-one alignment between gold and predicted clusters. We employ the entity-based version of CEAF.

BLANC (Recasens and Hovy, 2011) Metric based on the Rand index (Rand, 1971) that considers both coreference and non-coreference links to address the imbalance between singleton and coreferent mentions.

CoNLL F1 Average of MUC, B^3, and CEAF-ϕ_4. This was the official metric in the CoNLL-2011 shared task (Pradhan et al., 2011).

We followed the CoNLL-2011 evaluation methodology, that is, we removed all singleton clusters, and apposition/copular relations before scoring.

We evaluated the systems on three different settings: only on entity clusters, only on event clusters, and on the complete task, i.e., both entities and events. Note that the gold corpus separates clusters into entity and event clusters (see Table 3), but our system does not make this distinction at runtime. In order to compute the entity-only and event-only scores in Table 4, we implemented the following procedure: (a) when scoring entity clusters, we removed all mentions that were found to be coreferent with at least one gold event mention and not coreferent with any gold entity mentions; and (b) we performed the opposite action when scoring event clusters. This procedure is necessary because our mention identification component is not perfect, i.e., it generates mentions that do not exist in the gold annotation. Furthermore, this procedure is conservative with respect to the clustering errors of our system, e.g., all spurious mentions that our system includes in a cluster with a gold entity mention are considered for the entity score, regardless of their gold type (event or entity).

6.3 Results

Table 4 compares the performance of our system against two strong baselines that resolve entities and events separately. Baseline 1 uses a modified Stanford coreference resolution system after our document clustering and mention identification steps. Because the original Stanford system implements only entity coreference, we extended it with an extra sieve that implements lemma matching for events. This additional sieve merges two verbal clusters (i.e., clusters that contain at least one verbal mention) or a verbal and a nominal cluster when at least two lemmas of mention head words are the same between clusters, e.g., *helped* and *the help*.

The second baseline adds two more sieves to Baseline 1. Both these sieves model entity and event contextual information using semantic roles. The first sieve merges two nominal clusters when two mentions in the respective clusters have the same head words and two mentions (possibly with different heads) modify with the same role label two predicates that have the same lemma. For example, this sieve merges the clusters {*Obama, the president*} (seen in the text [*Obama*]$_{\texttt{Arg0}}$ *attended* and [*the president*]$_{\texttt{Arg1}}$ *was elected*) and {*Obama*} (seen in the text [*Obama*]$_{\texttt{Arg1}}$ *was elected*), because they share a mention with the same head word (*Obama*) and two mentions modify with the same role (`Arg1`) predicates with the same lemma (*elect*). The second sieve implements the complementary action for event clusters. That is, it merges two verbal clusters when at least two mentions have the same lemma and at least two mentions have semantic arguments with the same role label and the same lemma.

7 Discussion

The first block in Table 4 indicates that lemma matching is a strong baseline for event resolution. Most of the event scores for Baseline 1 are actually higher than the corresponding entity scores, which were obtained using the highest ranked system at the CoNLL-2011 shared task (Lee et al., 2011). Adding contextual information using semantic roles (Baseline 2) helps both entities and events. The CoNLL F1 for Baseline 2 increases almost 3 points for entities and 1 point for events. This demonstrates that local syntactico-semantic context is important for coreference resolution even in a cross-document setting and that the current state-of-the-art in SRL can model this context accurately.

The best scores (almost unanimously) are obtained by the model proposed in this paper, which scores 3.4 CoNLL F1 points higher than Baseline 2 for entities, and 2.6 points higher for events. For the complete task, our approach scores 3.3 CoNLL F1 points higher than Baseline 2, and 6.1 points higher than Baseline 1. This demonstrates that a holistic approach to coreference resolution improves the resolution of both entities and events more than models that address aspects of the task separately. To further understand our experiments, we listed the top five entity/event features with the highest weights in our model in Table 5. The table indicates that six out of the ten features serve the purpose of passing information between entity and event clusters. For example, the "Coreferent Argument for `Arg1`" feature is triggered when two event clusters have `Arg1` arguments that already belong to the same entity cluster. This allows information from previous entity coreference operations to impact future merges of event clusters. This is the crux of our iterative approach to joint coreference resolution.

Entity Feature	Weight
Entity Heads – Proper	1.10
Coreferent Predicate for `ArgM-LOC` – Common	0.45
Entity Heads – Common	0.36
Coreferent Predicate for `Arg0` – Proper	0.29
Coreferent Predicate for `Arg2` – Common	0.28

Event Feature	Weight
Event Lemmas	0.45
Coreferent Argument for `Arg1`	0.19
Links between Synonym	0.16
Coreferent Argument for `Arg2`	0.13
Number of Coreferent Arguments	0.07

Table 5: Top five features with the highest weights.

Finally, we performed an error analysis by manually evaluating 100 errors. We distinguished nine major types of errors. Their ratios together with a description and an example are given in Table 6.

This work demonstrates that an approach that jointly models entities and events is better for cross-document coreference resolution. However, our model can be improved. For example, document clustering and coreference resolution can be solved jointly, which we expect would improve both tasks. Furthermore, our iterative coreference resolution procedure (Algorithm 1) could be modified to account for mention ordering and distance, which would allow us to include pronominal resolution in our joint model, rather than addressing it with a separate deterministic sieve.

8 Conclusion

We have presented a holistic model for cross-document coreference resolution that jointly solves references to events and entities by handling both nominal and verbal mentions. Our joint resolution algorithm allows event coreference to help improve entity coreference, and vice versa. In addition, our iterative procedure, based on a linear regressor that models the quality of cluster merges, allows each

Error Type (Ratio)	Description	Example
Pronoun resolution (36%)	The pronoun is incorrectly resolved by the pronominal sieve of the Stanford deterministic entity system. These errors include (only a small number of) event pronouns.	He said *Timmons* aimed and missed **his** target.
Semantics beyond role frames (20%)	The semantics of the coreference relation cannot be captured by role frames or WordNet.	Israeli forces on Tuesday killed *at least 40 people* ... The Israeli army said the UN school in the Jabaliya refugee camp was hit ... and that **the dead** included a number of Hamas militants.
Arguments of nominal events (17%)	The arguments of two nominal events are not detected and thus not coreferred.	The attack on *the school* has caused widespread shock across Israel ... while Israeli forces on Tuesday killed at least 40 people during an attack on **a United Nations-run school in Gaza**.
Cascaded errors (7%)	Entities or events are not coreferred due to errors in a previous merge iteration in the same semantic frame. In the example below, we failed to link the two *die* verbs, which leads to the listed entity error.	An Australian climber who survived two nights stuck on Mount Cook after seeing *his brother* die ... **Dr Mark Vinar, 43**, is presumed dead ...
Initial high-precision sieves (6%)	An error made by the initial high-precision entity resolution sieves is propagated to our model.	Timmons told police he fired when he thought he saw someone in the other group reach for a gun ... 15-year-old Timmons was at the scene of the shooting and had **a gun**.
Phrasal verbs (6%)	The meaning of a phrasal verb is not captured.	A relative unknown will *take over* the title role of Doctor Who ... But **the casting of Smith** is a stroke of genius.
Linear regression (4%)	Recall error made by the regression model when the features are otherwise correct.	The Interior Department on Thursday *issued* "revised" regulations ... Interior Secretary Dirk Kempthorne **announced** major changes ...
Mention detection (3%)	The mention detection module detects a spurious mention.	Police have arrested a man ... in the parking lot crosswalk at Sam's Club in Bloomington.
SRL (1%)	The SRL system fails to label the semantic role. In this example, *jail* is detected as the ArgM-MNR of *hanged* instead of ArgM-LOC.	A Mafia boss in Palermo hanged himself in **jail**.

Table 6: Error analysis. Mentions to be resolved are in **bold face**, correct antecedents are in *italics*, and our system's predictions are underlined.

merging state to benefit from the previous merged entity and event mentions. This approach allows us to start with a set of high-precision coreference relations and gradually add new ones to increase recall.

The experimental evaluation shows that our coreference algorithm gives markedly better F1 for both entities and events, outperforming two strong baselines that handle entities and events separately, measured by all the standard measures: MUC, B^3, CEAF-ϕ_4, BLANC and the official CoNLL-2011 metric. This is noteworthy since each measure has been shown to place primary emphasis in evaluating a different aspect of the coreference resolution task.

Our system is tailored for cross-document coreference resolution on a corpus that contains news articles that repeatedly report on a smaller number of topics. This makes it particularly suitable for real-world applications such as multi-document summarization and cross-document information extraction. We also release our labeled corpus to facilitate extensions and comparisons to our work.

Acknowledgements

We acknowledge the support of Defense Advanced Research Projects Agency (DARPA) Machine Reading Program under Air Force Research Laboratory (AFRL) prime contract no. FA8750-09-C-0181. Any opinions, findings, and conclusion or recommendations expressed in this material are those of the author(s) and do not necessarily reflect the view of the DARPA, AFRL, or the US government. MR is supported by a Beatriu de Pinós postdoctoral scholarship (2010 BP-A 00149) from Generalitat de Catalunya. AC is supported by a SAP Stanford Graduate Fellowship. We also gratefully thank Cosmin Bejan for sharing his code and the useful discussions.

References

Amit Bagga and Breck Baldwin. 1998. Algorithms for scoring coreference chains. In *Proceedings of the LREC 1998 Workshop on Linguistic Coreference*, pages 563–566.

Amit Bagga and Breck Baldwin. 1999. Cross-document event coreference: Annotations, experiments, and observations. In *Proceedings of the ACL 1999 Workshop on Coreference and Its Applications*, pages 1–8.

Cosmin Bejan and Sanda Harabagiu. 2010. Unsupervised Event Coreference Resolution with Rich Linguistic Features. In *Proceedings of ACL 2010*, pages 1412–1422.

Eric Brill. 1995. Transformation-based error-driven learning and natural language processing: a case study in part of speech tagging. *Computational Linguistics*, 21(4):543–565.

Zheng Chen and Heng Ji. 2009. Graph-based event coreference resolution. In *Proceedings of the ACL-IJCNLP 2009 Workshop on Graph-based Methods for Natural Language Processing*, pages 54–57.

Pascal Denis and Jason Baldridge. 2007. Joint determination of anaphoricity and coreference resolution using integer programming. In *Proceedings of NAACL-HLT 2007*.

Christiane Fellbaum. 1998. *WordNet: An Electronic Lexical Database*. MIT Press, Cambridge.

Aria Haghighi and Dan Klein. 2009. Simple coreference resolution with rich syntactic and semantic features. In *Proceedings of EMNLP 2009*, pages 1152–1161.

Aria Haghighi and Dan Klein. 2010. Coreference resolution in a modular, entity-centered model. In *Proceedings of HLT-NAACL 2010*, pages 385–393.

Tian He. 2007. *Coreference Resolution on Entities and Events for Hospital Discharge Summaries*. Thesis, Massachusetts Institute of Technology.

Jerry R. Hobbs. 1978. Resolving pronoun references. *Lingua*, 44(4):311–338.

Kevin Humphreys, Robert Gaizauskas, and Saliha Azzam. 1997. Event coreference for information extraction. In *Proceedings of the Workshop On Operational Factors In Practical Robust Anaphora Resolution For Unrestricted Texts*, pages 75–81.

Klaus Krippendorff. 2004. *Content Analysis: An Introduction to its Methodology*. Sage, Thousand Oaks, CA, second edition.

Heeyoung Lee, Yves Peirsman, Angel Chang, Nathanael Chambers, Mihai Surdeanu, and Dan Jurafsky. 2011. Stanford's multi-pass sieve coreference resolution system at the CoNLL-2011 shared task. In *Proceedings of CoNLL 2011: Shared Task*, pages 28–34.

Dekang Lin. 1998. Automatic retrieval and clustering of similar words. In *Proceedings of COLING-ACL 1998*, pages 768–774.

Xiaoqiang Luo. 2005. On coreference resolution performance metrics. In *Proceedings of HLT-EMNLP 2005*, pages 25–32.

A. Meyers, R. Reeves, C. Macleod, R. Szekely, V. Zielinska, B. Young, and R. Grishman. 2004. The NomBank project: an interim report. In *Proceedings of the HLT-NAACL 2004 Workshop on Frontiers in Corpus Annotation*, pages 24–31.

Rebecca Passonneau. 2004. Computing reliability for coreference annotation. In *Proceedings of LREC 2004*, pages 1503–1506.

Simone Paolo Ponzetto and Michael Strube. 2006. Exploiting semantic role labeling, WordNet and Wikipedia for coreference resolution. In *Proceedings of HLT-NAACL 2006*, pages 192–199.

Hoifung Poon and Pedro Domingos. 2008. Joint unsupervised coreference resolution with Markov logic. In *Proceedings of EMNLP 2008*, pages 650–659.

Sameer S. Pradhan, Lance Ramshaw, Ralph Weischedel, Jessica MacBride, and Linnea Micciulla. 2007. Unrestricted coreference: Identifying entities and events in OntoNotes. In *Proceedings of ICSC 2007*, pages 446–453.

Sameer Pradhan, Lance Ramshaw, Mitchell Marcus, Martha Palmer, Ralph Weischedel, and Nianwen Xue. 2011. CoNLL-2011 shared task: Modeling unrestricted coreference in OntoNotes. In *Proceedings of CoNLL 2011: Shared Task*, pages 1–27.

Karthik Raghunathan, Heeyoung Lee, Sudarshan Rangarajan, Nathanael Chambers, Mihai Surdeanu, Dan Jurafsky, and Chris Manning. 2010. A multi-pass sieve for coreference resolution. In *Proceedings of EMNLP 2010*, pages 492–501.

Altaf Rahman and Vincent Ng. 2011. Coreference resolution with world knowledge. In *Proceedings of ACL 2011*, pages 814–824.

William M. Rand. 1971. Objective criteria for the evaluation of clustering methods. *Journal of the American Statistical Association*, 66(336):846–850.

Marta Recasens and Eduard Hovy. 2011. BLANC: Implementing the Rand index for coreference evaluation. *Natural Language Engineering*, 17(4):485–510.

Veselin Stoyanov, Nathan Gilbert, Claire Cardie, and Ellen Riloff. 2009. Conundrums in noun phrase coreference resolution: Making sense of the state-of-the-art. In *Proceedings of ACL-IJCNLP 2009*, pages 656–664.

Mihai Surdeanu, Jordi Turmo, and Alicia Ageno. 2005. A hybrid unsupervised approach for document clustering. In *Proceedings of KDD 2005*, pages 685–690.

Mihai Surdeanu, Lluís Màrquez, Xavier Carreras, and Pere R. Comas. 2007. Combination strategies for semantic role labeling. *Journal of Artificial Intelligence Research*, 29:105–151.

Marc Vilain, John Burger, John Aberdeen, Dennis Connolly, and Lynette Hirschman. 1995. A model-theoretic coreference scoring scheme. In *Proceedings of MUC-6*, pages 45–52.

Bonnie Lynn Webber. 1988. Discourse deixis: reference to discourse segments. In *Proceedings of ACL 1988*, pages 113–122.

Michael L. Wick, Khashayar Rohanimanesh, Karl Schultz, and Andrew McCallum. 2008. A unified approach for schema matching, coreference and canonicalization. In *Proceedings of KDD 2008*, pages 722–730.

David Yarowsky. 1995. Unsupervised word sense disambiguation rivaling supervised methods. In *Proceedings of ACL 1995*, pages 189–196.

Joint Chinese Word Segmentation, POS Tagging and Parsing

Xian Qian **Yang Liu**
Computer Science Department
The University of Texas at Dallas
qx,yangl@hlt.utdallas.edu

Abstract

In this paper, we propose a novel decoding algorithm for discriminative joint Chinese word segmentation, part-of-speech (POS) tagging, and parsing. Previous work often used a pipeline method – Chinese word segmentation followed by POS tagging and parsing, which suffers from error propagation and is unable to leverage information in later modules for earlier components. In our approach, we train the three individual models separately during training, and incorporate them together in a unified framework during decoding. We extend the CYK parsing algorithm so that it can deal with word segmentation and POS tagging features. As far as we know, this is the first work on joint Chinese word segmentation, POS tagging and parsing. Our experimental results on Chinese Tree Bank 5 corpus show that our approach outperforms the state-of-the-art pipeline system.

1 Introduction

For Asian languages such as Japanese and Chinese that do not contain explicitly marked word boundaries, word segmentation is an important first step for many subsequent language processing tasks, such as POS tagging, parsing, semantic role labeling, and various applications. Previous studies for POS tagging and syntax parsing on these languages sometimes assume that gold standard word segmentation information is provided, which is not the real scenario. In a fully automatic system, a pipeline approach is often adopted, where raw sentences are first segmented into word sequences, then POS tagging and parsing are performed. This kind of approach suffers from error propagation. For example, word segmentation errors will result in tagging and parsing errors. Additionally, early modules cannot use information from subsequent modules. Intuitively a joint model that performs the three tasks together should help the system make the best decisions.

In this paper, we propose a unified model for joint Chinese word segmentation, POS tagging, and parsing. Three sub-models are independently trained using the state-of-the-art methods. We do not use the joint inference algorithm for training because of the high complexity caused by the large amount of parameters. We use linear chain Conditional Random Fields (CRFs) (Lafferty et al., 2001) to train the word segmentation model and POS tagging model, and averaged perceptron (Collins, 2002) to learn the parsing model. During decoding, parameters of each sub-model are scaled to represent its importance in the joint model. Our decoding algorithm is an extension of CYK parsing. Initially, weights of all possible words together with their POS tags are calculated. When searching the parse tree, the word and POS tagging features are dynamically generated and the transition information of POS tagging is considered in the span merge operation.

Experiments are conducted on Chinese Tree Bank (CTB) 5 dataset, which is widely used for Chinese word segmentation, POS tagging and parsing. We compare our proposed joint model with the pipeline system, both built using the state-of-the-art sub-models. We also propose an evaluation metric to calculate the bracket scores for parsing in the face of word segmentation errors. Our experimental results show that the joint model significantly outperforms the pipeline method based on the state-of-the-art sub-models.

2 Related Work

There is very limited previous work on joint Chinese word segmentation, POS tagging, and parsing. Previous joint models mainly focus on word segmentation and POS tagging task, such as the virtual nodes method (Qian et al., 2010), cascaded linear model (Jiang et al., 2008a), perceptron (Zhang and Clark, 2008), sub-word based stacked learning (Sun, 2011), reranking (Jiang et al., 2008b). These joint models showed about $0.2 - 1\%$ F-score improvement over the pipeline method. Recently, joint tagging and dependency parsing has been studied as well (Li et al., 2011; Lee et al., 2011).

Previous research has showed that word segmentation has a great impact on parsing accuracy in the pipeline method (Harper and Huang, 2009). In (Jiang et al., 2009), additional data was used to improve Chinese word segmentation, which resulted in significant improvement on the parsing task using the pipeline framework. Joint segmentation and parsing was also investigated for Arabic (Green and Manning, 2010). A study that is closely related to ours is (Goldberg and Tsarfaty, 2008), where a single generative model was proposed for joint morphological segmentation and syntactic parsing for Hebrew. Different from that work, we use a discriminative model, which benefits from large amounts of features and is easier to deal with unknown words. Another main difference is that, besides segmentation and parsing, we also incorporate the POS tagging model into the CYK parsing framework.

3 Methods

For a given Chinese sentence, our task is to generate the word sequence, its POS tag sequence, and the parse tree (constituent parsing). A joint model is expected to make more optimal decisions than a pipeline approach; however, such a model will be too complex and it is difficult to estimate model parameters. Therefore we do not perform joint inference for training. Instead, we develop three individual models independently during training and perform joint decoding using them. In this section, we first describe the three sub-models and then the joint decoding algorithm.

3.1 Word Segmentation Model

Methods for Chinese word segmentation can be broadly categorized into character based and word based models. Previous studies showed that character-based models are more effective to detect out-of-vocabulary words while word-based models are more accurate to predict in-vocabulary words (Zhang et al., 2006). Here, we use order-0 semi-Markov model (Sarawagi and Cohen, 2004) to take advantages of both approaches.

More specifically, given a sentence $\mathbf{x} = c_1, c_2, \ldots, c_l$ (where c_i is the ith Chinese character, l is the sentence length), the character-based model assigns each character with a word boundary tag. Here we use the *BCDIES* tag set, which achieved the best official performance (Zhao and Kit, 2008): *B*, *C*, *D*, *E* denote the first, second, third, and last character of a multi-character word respectively, *I* denotes the other characters, and *S* denotes the single character word. We use the same character-based feature templates as in the best official system, shown in Table 1 (1.1-1.3), including character unigram and bigram features, and transition features. Linear chain CRFs are used for training.

Feature templates in the word-based model are shown in Table 1 (1.4-1.6), including word features, sub-word features, and character bigrams within words. The word feature is activated if a predicted word w is in the vocabulary (i.e., appears in training data). Subword(w) is the longest in-vocabulary word within w. To use word features, we adopt a K-best reranking approach. The top K candidate segmentation results for each training sample are generated using the character-based model, and the gold segmentation is added if it is not in the candidate set. We use the Maximum Entropy (ME) model to learn the weights of word features such that the probability of the gold candidate is maximal.

A problem arises when combining the two models and using it in joint segmentation and parsing, since the linear chain used in the character-based model is incompatible with CYK parsing model and the word-based model due to the transition informa-

Character Level Feature Templates	
(1.1)	$c_{i-2}y_i, c_{i-1}y_i, c_iy_i, c_{i+1}y_i, c_{i+2}y_i$
(1.2)	$c_{i-1}c_iy_i, c_ic_{i+1}y_i, c_{i-1}c_{i+1}y_i$
(1.3)	$y_{i-1}y_i$
Word Level Feature Templates	
(1.4)	word w
(1.5)	subword(w)
(1.6)	character bigrams within w

Table 1: Feature templates for word segmentation. c_i is the ith character in the sentence, y_i is its label, w is a predicted word.

tion. Thus, we slightly modify the linear chain CRF-s by fixing the weights of transition features during training and testing. That is, weights of impossible transition features (e.g., *B*→*B*) are set to $-\infty$, and weights of the other transition features (e.g., *E*→*B*) are set to 0. In this way, the transition feature could be neglected in testing for two reasons. First, all illegal label assignments are prohibited in prediction, since their weights are $-\infty$; second, because weights of legal transition features are 0, they do not affect the prediction at all. In the following, transition features are excluded.

Now we can use order-0 semi Markov model as the hybrid model. We define the score of a word as the sum of the weights of all the features within the word. Formally, the score of a multi-character word $w = c_i, \ldots, c_j$ is defined as:

$$\begin{aligned} &score_{seg}(\mathbf{x}, i, j) = \theta_{CRF} \cdot \mathbf{f}_{CRF}(\mathbf{x}, y_i = B) + \ldots \\ &+\theta_{CRF} \cdot \mathbf{f}_{CRF}(\mathbf{x}, y_j = E) + \theta_{ME} \cdot \mathbf{f}_{ME}(\mathbf{x}, i, j) \\ &\equiv \theta_{seg}\mathbf{f}_{seg}(\mathbf{x}, i, j) \end{aligned} \quad (1)$$

where $\mathbf{f}_{CRF}$ and $\mathbf{f}_{ME}$ are the feature vectors in the character and word based models respectively, and $\theta_{CRF}, \theta_{ME}$ are their corresponding weight vectors. For simplicity, we denote $\theta_{seg} = \theta_{CRF \oplus ME}$, $\mathbf{f}_{seg} = \mathbf{f}_{CRF \oplus ME}$, where $\theta_{CRF \oplus ME}$ means the concatenation of θ_{CRF} and θ_{ME}. Scores for single character words are defined similarly. These word scores will be used in the joint segmentation and parsing task Section 3.4.

3.2 POS Tagging Model

Though syntax parsing model can directly predict the POS tag itself, we choose not to use this, but use an independent POS tagger for two reasons. First, there is a large amount of data with labeled POS tags but no syntax annotations, such as the People's Daily corpus and SIGHAN bakeoff corpora (Jin and Chen, 2008). Such data can only be used to train POS taggers, but not for training the parsing model. Often using a larger training set will result in a better POS tagger. Second, the state-of-the-art POS tagging systems are often trained by sequence labeling models, not parsing models.

(2.1)	$w_{i-2}t_i, w_{i-1}t_i, w_it_i, w_{i+1}t_i, w_{i+2}t_i$
(2.2)	$w_{i-2}w_{i-1}t_i, \quad w_{i-1}w_it_i, \quad w_iw_{i+1}t_i,$ $w_{i+1}w_{i+2}t_i \; w_{i-1}w_{i+1}t_i$
(2.3)	$c_1(w_i)t_i, \quad c_2(w_i)t_i, \quad c_3(w_i)t_i, \quad c_{-2}(w_i)t_i$ $c_{-1}(w_i)t_i$
(2.4)	$c_1(w_i)c_2(w_i)t_i, c_{-2}(w_i)c_{-1}(w_i)t_i$
(2.5)	$l(w_i)t_i$
(2.5)	$t_{i-1}t_i$

Table 2: Feature templates for POS tagging. w_i is the ith word in the sentence, t_i is its POS tag. For a word w, $c_j(w)$ is its jth character, $c_{-j}(w)$ is the last j^{th} character, and $l(w)$ is its length.

The POS tagging problem is to assign a POS tag $t \in \mathcal{T}$ to each word in a sentence. We also use linear chain CRFs for POS tagging. Feature templates shown in Table 2 are the same as those in (Qian et al., 2010), which have been shown effective on CTB corpus. Three feature sets are considered: (i) word level features, including surrounding word unigrams, bigrams, and word length; (ii) character level features, such as the first and last characters in the words; (iii) transition features.

3.3 Parsing Model

We choose discriminative models for parsing since it is easy to handle unknown words by simply adding character level features. Online structured learning algorithms were demonstrated to be effective for training, such as stochastic optimization (Finkel et al., 2008). In this study, we use averaged perceptron algorithm for parameter estimation since it is easier to implement and has competitive performance.

A Context Free Grammar (CFG) consists of (i) a set of terminals; (ii) a set of nonterminals $\{N^k\}$; (iii) a designated start symbol ROOT; and (iv) a set of rules, $\{r = N^i \rightarrow \zeta^j\}$, where ζ^j is a sequence of terminals and nonterminals. In the parsing task, ter-

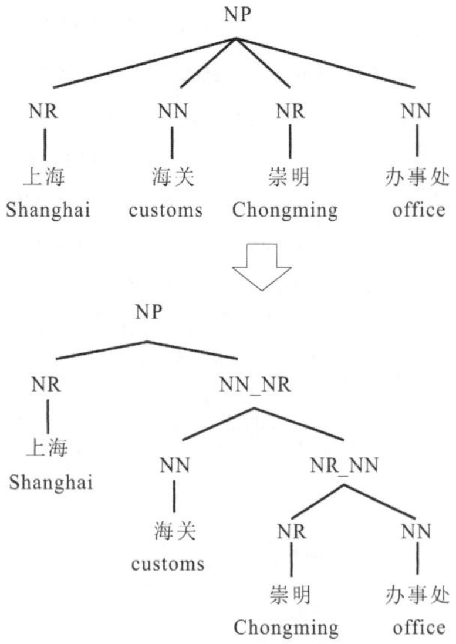

Figure 1: Parse tree binarization

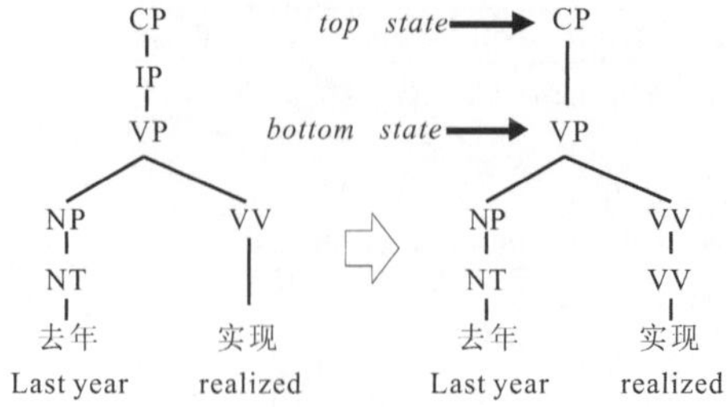

Figure 2: Unary rule normalization. Nonterminal-yield unary chains are collapsed to single unary rules. Identity unary rules are added to spans that have no unary rule.

minals are the words, and nonterminals are the POS tags and phrase types. In this paper, nonterminal is named **state** for short. A parse tree T of sentence $\mathbf{x}$ can be factorized into several one-level subtrees, each corresponding to a rule r.

In practice, binarization of rules is necessary to obtain cubic parsing time. That is, the right hand side of each rule should contain no more than 2 states. We used right branching binarization, as illustrated in Figure 1. We did not use parent annotation, since we found it degraded the performance in our experiments (shown in Section 4). We used the same preprocessing step as (Harper and Huang, 2009), collapsing all the allowed nonterminal-yield unary chains to single unary rules. Therefore, all spans in the binarized trees contain no more than one unary rules. To facilitate decoding, we unify the form of spans so that each span contains exactly one unary rule. This is done by adding identity unary rules ($N \rightarrow N$) to spans that have no unary rule. These identity unary rules will be removed in evaluation. Hence, there are two states of a span: the top state $\overline{N}$ and the bottom state $\underline{N}$ that correspond to the left and right hand of the unary rule $r^{unary} = \overline{N} \rightarrow \underline{N}$ respectively, as shown in Figure 2.

Table 3 lists the feature templates we use for parsing. There are 4 feature sets: (i) bottom state features $\mathbf{f}_{bottom}(i, j, \mathbf{x}, \underline{N}_{i,j})$, which depend on the bottom states; (ii) top state features $\mathbf{f}_{top}(i, j, \mathbf{x}, \overline{N}_{i,j})$; (iii) unary rule features $\mathbf{f}_{unary}(i, j, \mathbf{x}, r_{i,j}^{unary})$, which extract the transition information from bottom states to top states; (iv) binary rule features $\mathbf{f}_{binary}(i, j, k, \mathbf{x}, r_{i,j,k}^{binary} = \underline{N}_{i,j} \rightarrow \overline{N}_{i,k-1} + \overline{N}_{k,r})$, where $\overline{N}_{i,k-1}, \overline{N}_{k,r}$ are the top states of the left and right children.

The score function for a sentence $\mathbf{x}$ with parse tree T is defined as:

$$
\begin{aligned}
& score(\mathbf{x}, T) = \\
& \sum_{\underline{N}_{i,j} \in T} \theta_{bottom} \cdot \mathbf{f}_{bottom}(i, j, \mathbf{x}, \underline{N}_{i,j}) \\
& + \sum_{\overline{N}_{i,j} \in T} \theta_{top} \cdot \mathbf{f}_{top}(i, j, \mathbf{x}, \overline{N}_{i,j}) \\
& + \sum_{r_{i,j}^{unary} \in T} \theta_{unary} \cdot \mathbf{f}_{unary}(i, j, \mathbf{x}, r_{i,j}^{unary}) \\
& + \sum_{r_{i,j,k}^{binary} \in T} \theta_{binary} \cdot \mathbf{f}_{binary}(i, j, \mathbf{x}, r_{i,j,k}^{binary})
\end{aligned}
$$

where $\theta_{bottom}, \theta_{top}, \theta_{unary}, \theta_{binary}$ are the weight vectors of the four feature sets.

Given the training corpus $\{(\mathbf{x}_i, \tilde{T}_i)\}$, the learning task is to estimate the weight vectors so that for each sentence $\mathbf{x}_i$, the gold standard tree $\tilde{T}_i$ achieves the maximal score among all the possible trees. The perceptron algorithm is guaranteed to find the solution if it exists.

3.4 Joint Decoding

The three models described above are separately trained to make parameter estimation feasible as well as optimize each individual component. In test-

(3.1)	**Binary rule templates**			
	$\underline{N} \rightarrow \overline{N}_l + \overline{N}_r$			
	$X_l\ X_{m-1}X_r\ len_l len_r$		$X_l\ X_m\ X_r\ len_l\ len_r$	
	$X_l\ X_{m-1}\ X_r\ word_{m-1}$(ROOT)		$X_l + X_m\ X_r\ word_m$(ROOT)	
(3.2)	**Unary rule templates**			
	$\overline{N} \rightarrow \underline{N}$			
(3.3)	**Bottom state templates**			
	$X_l len$	$X_r len$		
	$X_{l-2}X_{l-1}\ X_{r+1} len$		$X_{l-1}\ X_{r+1}\ X_{r+2} len$	
	$wl_l wl_r X_l len$	$wl_l wl_r X_r len$	$X_l X_r wl_l len$	$X_l X_r wl_r len$
	$word_l word_r X_l X_r len$	$word_l word_r X_l X_r$		
	$X_{l-1}X_l$(LEAF)	$X_{l+1}X_l$(LEAF)	$X_l word_l$(LEAF)	$X_l wl_l$(LEAF)
	$X_{l+a}X_{r+b} len$	$word_{l+a} word_{r+b}$	$-1 \leq a, b \leq 1$	
(3.3)	**Top state templates**			
	$X_{l-1}X_l$(LEAF)	$X_{l+1}X_l$(LEAF)	$X_l word_l$(LEAF)	$X_l wl_l$(LEAF)
	$X_{l+a}X_{r+b} len$	$word_{l+a} word_{r+b}$	$-1 \leq a, b \leq 1$	

Table 3: Feature templates for parsing, where X can be word, first and last character of word, first and last character bigram of word, POS tag. X_{l+a}/X_{r-a} denotes the first/last a^{th} X in the span, while X_{l-a}/X_{r+a} denotes the ath X left/right to span. X_m is the first X of right child, and X_{m-1} is the last X of the left child. *len*, *len$_l$*, *len$_r$* denote the length of the span, left child and right child respectively. *wl* is the length of word. ROOT/LEAF means the template can only generate the features for the root/initial span.

ing, we perform joint decoding to combine information from the three models. Parameters of word segmentation (θ_{seg}), POS tagging (θ_{pos}), and parsing models ($\theta_{parse} = \theta_{bottom \oplus top \oplus\ unary \oplus bianry}$) are scaled by three positive hyper-parameters α, β, and γ respectively, which control their contribution in the joint model. If $\alpha >> \beta >> \gamma$, then the joint model is equivalent to a pipeline model, in which there is no feedback from downstream models to upstream ones. For well tuned hyper-parameters, we expect that segmentation and POS tagging results can be improved by parsing information. The hyper-parameters are tuned on development data. In the following sections, for simplicity we drop α, β, γ, and just use $\theta_{seg}, \theta_{pos}, \theta_{parse}$ to represent the scaled parameters.

The basic idea of our decoding algorithm is to extend the CYK parsing algorithm so that it can deal with transition features in POS tagging and segmentation scores in word segmentation.

3.4.1 Algorithm

The joint decoding algorithm is shown in Algorithm 1. Given a sentence $\mathbf{x} = c_1, \ldots, c_l$, Line 0 calculates the scores of all possible words in the sentence using Eq(1). There are $l(l+1)/2$ word candidates in total.

Surrounding words are important features for POS tagging and parsing; however, they are unavailable because segmentation is incomplete before parsing. Therefore, we adopt pseudo surrounding features by simply fixing the context words as the single most likely ones. Given a word candidate $w_{i,j}$ from c_i to c_j, its previous word s' is the rightmost one in the best word sequence of $c_1, \ldots, c_{i-1}$, which can be obtained by dynamic programming. Recursively, the second word left to $w_{i,j}$ is the previous word of s'. The next word of $w_{i,j}$ is defined similarly. In Line 1, we use bidirectional Viterbi decoding to obtain all the surrounding words. In the forward direction, the algorithm starts from the first character boundary to the last, and finds the best previous word for the ith character boundary b_i. In the backward direction, the algorithm starts from right to left, and finds the best next word of each b_i.

In Line 2, for each word candidate, we can calculate the score of each POS tag using state features in the POS tagging model, since the context words are available now. The score function of word $w_{i,j}$ with POS tag t is:

$$score_{seg \oplus pos}(\mathbf{x}, i, j, t) = score_{seg}(\mathbf{x}, i, j) + \theta_{pos} \cdot \mathbf{f}_{pos}(\mathbf{x}, w_{i,j}, t) \quad (2)$$

In Line 3, POS tags of surrounding words can be obtained similarly using bidirectional decoding.

Algorithm 1 Joint Word Segmentation, POS tagging, and Parsing Algorithm

Input: Sentence $\mathbf{x} = c_1, \ldots, c_l$, beam size B, scaled word segmentation model, POS tagging model and parsing model.

Output: Word sequence, POS tag sequence, and parse tree

0: $\forall 0 \leq i \leq j \leq l-1$, calculate $score_{seg}(\mathbf{x}, i, j)$ using Equation (1)

1: For each character boundary $b_i, 0 \leq i \leq l$, get the best previous and next words of b_i using bidirectional Viterbi decoding

2: $\forall 0 \leq i \leq j \leq l-1, t \in \mathcal{T}$, calculate $score_{seg \oplus pos}(\mathbf{x}, i, j, t)$ using Equation (2)

3: $\forall b_i, 0 \leq i \leq l, t \in \mathcal{T}$, get the best POS tags of words left/right to b_i using bidirectional viterbi decoding.

4: For each word candidate $w_{i,j}, 0 \leq i \leq j \leq l-1$

5: For each bottom state $\underline{N}$, POS tag $t \in \mathcal{T}$ ◁ step 1 (Line 5-7): get bottom states

6: $score_{bottom}(\mathbf{x}, i, j, w_{i,j}, t, \underline{N}) = score_{seg \oplus pos}(\mathbf{x}, i, j, t) + \theta_{bottom} \cdot \mathbf{f}_{bottom}(\mathbf{x}, i, j, w_{i,j}, t, \underline{N})$

7: Keep B best $score_{bottom}$.

8: For each top state $\overline{N}$ ◁ step 2 (Line 8-9): get top states

9: $score_{top}(\mathbf{x}, i, j, w_{i,j}, t, \overline{N}) = \max_{\underline{N}} \{score_{bottom}(\mathbf{x}, i, j, w_{i,j}, t, \underline{N}) + \theta_{top} \cdot \mathbf{f}_{top}(\mathbf{x}, i, j, w_{i,j}, t, \underline{N})$ $+\theta_{unary} \cdot \mathbf{f}_{unary}(\mathbf{x}, i, j, w_{i,j}, t, \overline{N} \rightarrow \underline{N})\}$

10: **for** $i = 0, \ldots, l-1$ **do**

11: **for** $width = 1, \ldots, l-1$ **do**

12: $j = i + width$

13: **for** $k = i+1, \ldots, j$ **do**

14: $score_{bottom}(\mathbf{x}, i, j, \mathbf{w}, \mathbf{t}, \underline{N}) = \max_{l,r} \{score_{top}(\mathbf{x}, i, k-1, \mathbf{w}_l, \mathbf{t}_l, \overline{N}_l) + score_{top}(\mathbf{x}, k, j, \mathbf{w}_r, \mathbf{t}_r, \overline{N}_r)$ $+\theta_{binary} \cdot \mathbf{f}_{binary}(\mathbf{x}, i, j, k, \mathbf{w}, \mathbf{t}, \underline{N} \rightarrow \overline{N}_r + \overline{N}_r) + \theta_{pos} \cdot \mathbf{f}_{pos}(t_l^{last} \rightarrow t_r^{first})$ $+\theta_{bottom}\mathbf{f}_{bottom}(\mathbf{x}, i, j, \mathbf{w}, \mathbf{t}, \underline{N})\}$

15: Keep B best $score_{bottom}$ ◁ step 1 (Line 14-15): get bottom states

16: For each top state $\overline{N}$ ◁ step 2 (Line 16-17): get top states

17: $score_{top}(\mathbf{x}, i, j, \mathbf{w}, \mathbf{t}, \overline{N}) = \max_{\underline{N}} \{score_{bottom}(\mathbf{x}, i, j, \mathbf{w}, \mathbf{t}, \underline{N})$ $+\theta_{unary} \cdot \mathbf{f}_{unary}(\mathbf{x}, i, j, \mathbf{w}, \mathbf{t}, \overline{N} \rightarrow \underline{N})\}$

18: **end for**

19: **end for**

20: **end for**

Line	0	1	2	3	6	9	14	15	Total Bound(w.r.t. l)
Complexity	l^2	l^2	$\|\mathcal{T}\|l^2$	$\|\mathcal{T}\|^2 l^2$	$\|\mathcal{T}\|Ml^2$	BMl^2	l^3MB^2	BMl^2	l^3MB^2

Table 4: Complexity Analysis of Algorithm 1.

That is, for $w_{i,j}$ with POS tag t, we use Viterbi algorithm to search the optimal POS tags of its left and right words.

In Lines 4-9, each word was initialized as a basic span. A span structure in the joint model is a 6-tuple: $S(i, j, \mathbf{w}, \mathbf{t}, \underline{N}, \overline{N})$, where i, j are the boundary indices, $\mathbf{w}, \mathbf{t}$ are the word sequence and POS sequence within the span respectively, and $\underline{N}, \overline{N}$ are the bottom and top states. There are two types of surrounding n-grams: one is inside the span, for example, the first word of a span, which can be obtained from $\mathbf{w}$; the other is outside the span, for example, the previous word of a span, which is obtained from the pseudo context information. The score of a basic span depends on its corresponding word and POS pair score, and the weights of the active state and unary features.

To avoid enumerating the combination of the bottom and top states, initialization for each span is divided into 2 steps. In the first step, the score of every bottom state is calculated using bottom state features, and only the B best states are maintained (see Line 6-7). In the second step, top state features and unary rule features are used to get the score of each top state (Line 9), and only the top B states are preserved.

Similarly, there are two steps in the merge operation: $S(i, j, \mathbf{w}, \mathbf{t}, \underline{N}, \overline{N}) = S_l(i, k, \mathbf{w}_l, \mathbf{t}_l, \underline{N_l}, \overline{N_l}) + S_r(k+1, j, \mathbf{w}_r, \mathbf{t}_r, \underline{N_r}, \overline{N_r})$. The score of the bottom state $\underline{N}$ is calculated using binary features $\mathbf{f}_{binary}(\mathbf{x}, i, j, k, \mathbf{w}, \mathbf{t}, \underline{N} \rightarrow \overline{N}_r + \overline{N}_r)$, bottom state features $\mathbf{f}_{bottom}(\mathbf{x}, i, j, \mathbf{w}, \mathbf{t}, \underline{N})$, and POS tag transition features that depend on the boundary POS tags of S_l and S_r. See Line 14 of Algorithm 1, where t_l^{last} and t_r^{first} are the POS tags of the last word in the left child span and the first word in the right child span respectively.

3.4.2 Complexity analysis

Given a sentence of length l, the complexity for each line of Algorithm 1 is listed in Table 4, where $|\mathcal{T}|$ is the size of POS tag set, M is the number of states, and B is the beam size.

4 Experiments

4.1 Data

For comparison with other systems, we use the CT-B5 corpus, which has been studied for Chinese word segmentation, POS tagging and parsing. We use the standard train/develop/test split of the data. Details are shown in Table 5.

	CTB files	# sent.	# words
Training	1-270 400-1151	18089	493,939
Develop	301-325	350	6,821
Test	271-300	348	8,008

Table 5: Training, development, and test data of CTB 5.

4.2 Evaluation Metric

We evaluate system performance on the individual tasks, as well as the joint tasks.[1] For word segmentation, three metrics are used for evaluation: precision (P), recall (R), and F-score (F) defined by 2PR/(P+R). Precision is the percentage of correct words in the system output. Recall is the percentage of words in gold standard annotations that are correctly predicted. For parsing, we use the standard parseval evaluation metrics: bracketing precision, recall and F-score.

[1]Note that the joint task refers to automatic segmentation and tagging/parsing. It can be achieved using a pipeline system or our joint decoding method.

For joint word segmentation and POS tagging, a word is correctly predicted if both the boundaries and the POS tag are correctly identified. For joint segmentation, POS tagging, and parsing task, when calculating the bracket scores using existing parseval tools, we need to consider possible word segmentation errors. To do this, we add the word boundary information in states – a bracket is correct only if its boundaries, label and word segmentation are all correct. One example is shown in Figure 3. Notice that identity unary rules are removed during evaluation. The basic spans are characters, not words, because the number of words in reference and prediction may be different. POS tags are removed since they do not affect the bracket scores. If the segmentation is perfect, then the bracket scores of the modified tree are exactly the same as the original tree. This is similar to evaluating parsing performance on speech transcripts with automatic sentence segmentation (Roark et al., 2006).

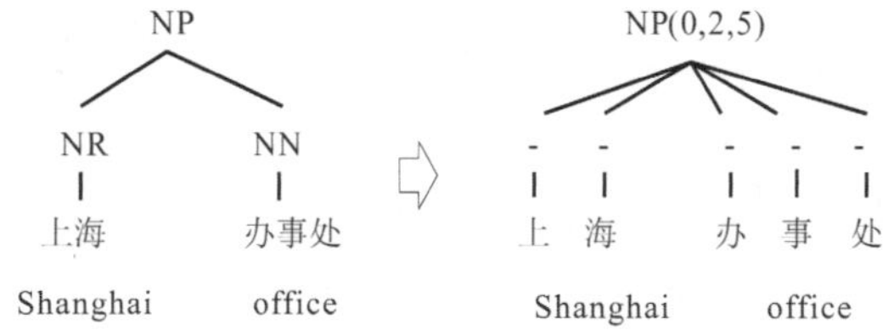

Figure 3: Boundary information is added to states to calculate the bracket scores in the face of word segmentation errors. Left: the original parse tree, Right: the converted parse tree. The numbers in the brackets are the indices of the character boundaries based on word segmentation.

4.3 Parameter Estimation

We train three submodels using the gold features, that is, POS tagger is trained using the perfect segmentation, and parser is trained using perfect segmentation and POS tags. Some studies reported that better performance may be achieved by training subsequent models using representative output of the preceding models (Che et al., 2009). Hence for comparison we trained another parser using automatically generated POS tags obtained from 10-fold cross validation, but did not find significant difference between these two parsers when testing on the perfectly segmented development dataset. Therefore we use the parser trained with perfect POS tags for the joint task.

Three hyper-parameters, α, β, and γ, are tuned on development data using a heuristic search. Parameters that achieved the best joint parsing result are selected. In the search, we fixed $\gamma = 1$ and varied α, β. First, we set $\beta = 1$, and enumerate $\alpha = \frac{1}{4}, \frac{1}{2}, 1, 2, \ldots$, and choose the best α^*. Then, we set $\alpha = \alpha^*$ and vary $\beta = \frac{1}{4}, \frac{1}{2}, 1, 2, \ldots$, and select the best β^*.

Table 6 lists the parameters we used for training the submodels, as well as the hyper-parameters for joint decoding.

Model	Parameter	Value
Character based word segmentor	Gaussian prior	0.01
	# Feature	3,875,802
Word based word segmentor	Gaussian prior	0.01
	# Feature	312,533
POS tagger	Gaussian prior	0.1
	# Feature	48,608,802
Parser	Iteration Number	10
	# Feature	49,369,843
Joint	Hyper-parameter α	4
	Hyper-parameter β	0.5
	Hyper-parameter γ	1
	Beam Size B	20

Table 6: Parameters used in our system.

4.4 Experimental Results

In this section we first show that our sub-models are better than or comparable to state-of-the-art systems, and then the joint model is superior to the pipeline approach.

4.4.1 Evaluating Sub-models

Table 7 shows word segmentation results using our word segmentation submodel, in comparison to a few state-of-the-art systems. For our segmentor, we show results for two variants: one removes transition features as described in Section 3.1, the other uses CRFs to learn the weights of transition features. We can see that our system is competitive with all the others except Sun's that used additional idiom resources. Our two word segmentors have similar performance. Since the one without transition features can be naturally integrated into the joint system, we use it in the following joint tasks.

System	P	R	F
(Jiang et al., 2008b)	-	-	97.74
(Jiang et al., 2008a)	-	-	97.85
(Kruengkrai et al., 2009)	97.46	98.29	97.87
(Zhang and Clark, 2010)	-	-	97.78
(Zhang and Clark, 2011)	-	-	97.78
(Sun, 2011)	-	-	98.17
Ours (w/o transition features)	97.45	98.24	97.85
Ours (with transition features)	97.44	98.23	97.84

Table 7: Word segmentation results.

For the POS tagging only task that takes gold standard word segmentation as input, we have two systems. One uses the linear chain CRFs as described in Section 3.2, the other is obtained using the parser described in Section 3.3 – the parser generates POS tag hypotheses when POS tag features are not used. The POS tagging accuracy is 95.53% and 95.10% using these two methods respectively. The better performance from the former system may be because the local label dependency is more helpful for POS tagging than the long distance dependencies that might be noisy. This result also confirms our choice of using an independent POS tagger for the sub-model, rather than relying on a parser for POS tagging. However, since there are no reported results for this setup, we demonstrate the competence of our POS tagger using the joint word segmentation and POS tagging task. Table 8 shows the performance of a few systems along with ours, all using the pipeline approach where automatic segmentation is followed by POS tagging. We can see that our POS tagger is comparable to the others.

System	P	R	F
(Jiang et al., 2008b)	-	-	93.37
(Jiang et al., 2008a)	-	-	93.41
(Kruengkrai et al., 2009)	93.28	94.07	93.67
(Zhang and Clark, 2010)	-	-	93.67
(Zhang and Clark, 2011)	-	-	93.67
(Sun, 2011)	-	-	94.02
Ours (pipeline)	93.10	93.96	93.53

Table 8: Results for the joint word segmentation and POS tagging task.

For parsing, Table 9 presents the parsing result on gold standard segmented sentence. Notice that the result of (Harper and Huang, 2009; Zhang and

Clark, 2011) are not directly comparable to ours, as they used a different data split. The best published system result on CTB5 is Petrov and Klein's, which used PCFG with latent Variables. Our system performs better mainly because it benefits from a large amount of features.

System	LP	LR	F
(Petrov and Klein, 2007)	84.8	81.9	83.3
(Jiang et al., 2009)	-	-	82.35
(Harper and Huang, 2009)*	83.22	82.84	83.03
(Zhang and Clark, 2011)*	78.6	78.0	78.3
Ours	84.57	83.68	**84.13**
Ours (w/ parent annotation)	83.35	82.73	83.04
Ours (no POS tag feature)	83.49	82.97	83.23

Table 9: Parsing results using gold standard word segmentation.

For our parser, besides the model described in Section 3.3, we tried two variations: one does not use the automatic POS tag features, the other one is learned on the parent annotated training data. The results in Table 9 show that there is a performance degradation when using parent annotation. This may be due to the introduction of a large number of states, resulting in sparse features. We also notice that with the help of the POS tag information, even automatically generated, the parser gained 0.9% improvement in F-score. This demonstrates the advantage of using a better independent POS tagger and incorporating it in parsing.

Finally Table 10 shows the results for the three tasks using our joint decoding method in comparison to the pipeline method. We can see that the joint model outperforms the pipeline one. This is mainly because of a better parsing module as well as joint decoding. In the table we also include results of (Jiang et al., 2009), which is the only reported joint parsing result we found using the same data split on CTB5. They achieved 80.28% parsing F-score using automatic word segmentation. Their adapted system Jiang09^{+} leveraged additional corpus to improve Chinese word segmentation, resulting in an F-score of 81.07%. Our system has better performance than these.

System	Task	P	R	F
Jiang09	Parse	-	-	80.28
Jiang09^{+}	Parse	-	-	81.07
Ours Pipeline	Seg.	97.45	98.24	97.85
	POS	93.10	93.96	93.53
	Parse	81.87	81.65	81.76
Ours Joint	Seg.	97.56	98.36	97.96
	POS	93.43	94.20	93.81
	Parse	83.03	82.66	**82.85**

Table 10: Results for the joint segmentation, tagging, and parsing task using pipeline and joint models.

4.5 Error Analysis

We compared the results from the pipeline and our joint decoding systems in order to understand the impact of the joint model on word segmentation and POS tagging. We notice that the joint model tend to generate more words than the pipeline model. For example, "巴尔一行" is one word in the pipeline model, but correctly segmented as two words "巴尔/一行" in the joint model. This tendency of segmentation also makes it fail to recognize some long words, especially OOV words. For example, "事实上" is segmented as "事实/上". In the data set, we find that, the joint model corrected 10 missing boundaries over the pipeline method, and introduced 3 false positive segmentation errors.

For the analysis of POS tags, we only examined the words that are correctly segmented by both the pipeline and the joint models. Table 11 shows the increase and decrease of error patterns of the joint model over the pipeline POS tagger. An error pattern "X → Y" means that the word whose true tag is 'X' is assigned a tag 'Y'. All the patterns are ranked in descending order of the reduction/increase of the error number. We can see that the joint model has a clear advantage in the disambiguation of {VV, NN} and {DEG, DEC}, which results in the overall improved performance. In contrast, the joint method performs worse on ambiguous POS pairs such as $\{NN, NR\}$. This observation is similar to those reported by (Li et al., 2011; Hatori et al., 2011).

5 Conclusion

In this paper, we proposed a new algorithm for joint Chinese word segmentation, POS tagging, and parsing. Our algorithm is an extension of the CYK

error pattern	#	↓	error pattern	#	↑
NN→ VV	47	19	NN→ NR	15	12
VV→ NN	42	13	NR→ NN	7	5
DEG→ DEC	23	10	JJ→ P	1	4
NN→ JJ	29	8	NN→ DT	2	4
DEC→ DEG	11	4	P→ VV	3	2
JJ→ NN	12	4	AD→ NN	1	2

Table 11: POS tagging error patterns. # means the error number of the corresponding pattern made by the pipeline tagging model. ↓ and ↑ mean the error number reduced or increased by the joint model.

parsing method. The sub-models are independently trained for the three tasks to reduce model complexity and optimize individual sub-models. Our experiments demonstrate the advantage of the joint models. In the future work, we will compare this joint model to the pipeline approach that uses multiple candidates or soft decisions in the early modules. We will also investigate methods for joint learning as well as ways to speed up the joint decoding algorithm.

Acknowledgments The authors thank Zhongqiang Huang for his help with experiments. This work is partly supported by DARPA under Contract No. HR0011-12-C-0016. Any opinions expressed in this material are those of the authors and do not necessarily reflect the views of DARPA.

References

Wanxiang Che, Zhenghua Li, Yongqiang Li, Yuhang Guo, Bing Qin, and Ting Liu. 2009. Multilingual dependency-based syntactic and semantic parsing. In *Proceedings of CoNLL 09*, pages 49–54.

Michael Collins. 2002. Discriminative training methods for hidden markov models: Theory and experiments with perceptron algorithms. In *Proceedings of EMNLP 2002*, pages 1–8.

Jenny Rose Finkel, Alex Kleeman, and Christopher D. Manning. 2008. Efficient, feature-based, conditional random field parsing. In *Proceedings of ACL-08: HLT*, pages 959–967.

Yoav Goldberg and Reut Tsarfaty. 2008. A single generative model for joint morphological segmentation and syntactic parsing. In *Proceedings of ACL 2008: HLT*, pages 371–379.

Spence Green and Christopher D. Manning. 2010. Better arbic parsing: Baselines, evaluations, and analysis. In *Proceedings of Coling 2010*, pages 394–402.

Mary Harper and Zhongqiang Huang. 2009. Chinese statistical parsing. In *Gale Book*.

Jun Hatori, Takuya Matsuzaki, Yusuke Miyao, and Jun'ichi Tsujii. 2011. Incremental joint pos tagging and dependency parsing in chinese. In *Proceedings of IJCNLP 2011*, pages 1216–1224.

Wenbin Jiang, Liang Huang, Qun Liu, and Yajuan Lü. 2008a. A cascaded linear model for joint chinese word segmentation and part-of-speech tagging. In *Proceedings of ACL 2008: HLT*, pages 897–904.

Wenbin Jiang, Haitao Mi, and Qun Liu. 2008b. Word lattice reranking for chinese word segmentation and part-of-speech tagging. In *Proceedings of Coling 2008*, pages 385–392.

Wenbin Jiang, Liang Huang, and Qun Liu. 2009. Automatic adaptation of annotation standards: Chinese word segmentation and pos tagging – a case study. In *Proceedings of ACL-IJCNLP 2009*, pages 522–530.

Guangjin Jin and Xiao Chen. 2008. The fourth international chinese language processing bakeoff: Chinese word segmentation, named entity recognition and chinese pos tagging. In *Proceedings of Sixth SIGHAN Workshop on Chinese Language Processing*.

Canasai Kruengkrai, Kiyotaka Uchimoto, Jun'ichi Kazama, Yiou Wang, Kentaro Torisawa, and Hitoshi Isahara. 2009. An error-driven word-character hybrid model for joint chinese word segmentation and pos tagging. In *Proceedings of ACL 2009*, pages 513–521.

John Lafferty, Andrew McCallum, and Fernando Pereira. 2001. Conditional random fields: Probabilistic models for segmenting and labeling sequence data. In *Proceedings of ICML 2001*, pages 282–289.

John Lee, Jason Naradowsky, and David A. Smith. 2011. A discriminative model for joint morphological disambiguation and dependency parsing. In *Proceedings A-CL 2011: HLT*, pages 885–894.

Zhenghua Li, Min Zhang, Wanxiang Che, Ting Liu, Wenliang Chen, and Haizhou Li. 2011. Joint models for chinese pos tagging and dependency parsing. In *Proceedings of EMNLP 2011*, pages 1180–1191.

Slav Petrov and Dan Klein. 2007. Improved inference for unlexicalized parsing. In *Proceedings of NAACL 2007*, pages 404–411.

Xian Qian, Qi Zhang, Yaqian Zhou, Xuanjing Huang, and Lide Wu. 2010. Joint training and decoding using virtual nodes for cascaded segmentation and tagging tasks. In *Proceedings of EMNLP 2010*, pages 187–195.

Brian Roark, Mary Harper, Eugene Charniak, Bonnie Dorr, Mark Johnson, Jeremy G. Kahn, Yang Liu, Mari Ostendorf, John Hale, Anna Krasnyanskaya, Matthew Lease, Izhak Shafran, Matthew Snover, Robin Stewart, Lisa Yung, and Lisa Yung. 2006. Sparseval: Evaluation metrics for parsing speech. In *Proceedings Language Resources and Evaluation (LREC)*.

Sunita Sarawagi and William W. Cohen. 2004. Semi-markov conditional random fields for information extraction. In *Proceedings of NIPS 2004*.

Weiwei Sun. 2011. A stacked sub-word model for joint chinese word segmentation and part-of-speech tagging. In *Proceedings of ACL 2011*, pages 1385–1394.

Yue Zhang and Stephen Clark. 2008. Joint word segmentation and POS tagging using a single perceptron. In *Proceedings of ACL 2008: HLT*, pages 888–896.

Yue Zhang and Stephen Clark. 2010. A fast decoder for joint word segmentation and POS-tagging using a single discriminative model. In *Proceedings of EMNLP 2010*, pages 843–852.

Yue Zhang and Stephen Clark. 2011. Syntactic processing using the generalized perceptron and beam search. *Comput. Linguist.*, 37(1):105–151.

Ruiqiang Zhang, Genichiro Kikui, and Eiichiro Sumita. 2006. Subword-based tagging for confidence-dependent chinese word segmentation. In *Proceedings of the COLING/ACL 2006*, pages 961–968.

Hai Zhao and Chunyu Kit. 2008. Unsupervised segmentation helps supervised learning of character tagging forword segmentation and named entity recognition. In *Proceedings of Sixth SIGHAN Workshop on Chinese Language Processing*, pages 106–111.

Translation Model Based Cross-Lingual Language Model Adaptation: from Word Models to Phrase Models

Shixiang Lu, Wei Wei, Xiaoyin Fu, and Bo Xu
Interactive Digital Media Technology Research Center
Institute of Automation, Chinese Academy of Sciences
95 Zhongguancun East Road, Haidian District, Beijing 100190, China
{shixiang.lu,wei.wei.media,xiaoyin.fu,xubo}@ia.ac.cn

Abstract

In this paper, we propose a novel translation model (TM) based cross-lingual data selection model for language model (LM) adaptation in statistical machine translation (SMT), from word models to phrase models. Given a source sentence in the translation task, this model directly estimates the probability that a sentence in the target LM training corpus is similar. Compared with the traditional approaches which utilize the first pass translation hypotheses, cross-lingual data selection model avoids the problem of noisy proliferation. Furthermore, phrase TM based cross-lingual data selection model is more effective than the traditional approaches based on bag-of-words models and word-based TM, because it captures contextual information in modeling the selection of phrase as a whole. Experiments conducted on large-scale data sets demonstrate that our approach significantly outperforms the state-of-the-art approaches on both LM perplexity and SMT performance.

1 Introduction

Language model (LM) plays a critical role in statistical machine translation (SMT). It seems to be a universal truth that LM performance can always be improved by using more training data (Brants et al., 2007), but only if the training data is reasonably well-matched with the desired output (Moore and Lewis, 2010). It is also obvious that among the large training data the topics or domains of discussion will change (Eck et al., 2004), which causes the mismatch problems with the translation task. For this reason, most researchers preferred to select similar training data from the large training corpus in the past few years (Eck et al., 2004; Zhao et al., 2004; Kim, 2005; Masskey and Sethy, 2010; Axelrod et al., 2011). This would empirically provide more accurate lexical probabilities, and thus better match the translation task at hand (Axelrod et al., 2011).

Many previous data selection approaches for LM adaptation in SMT depend on the first pass translation hypotheses (Eck et al., 2004; Zhao et al., 2004; Kim, 2005; Masskey and Sethy, 2010), they select the sentences which are similar to the translation hypotheses. These schemes are overall limited by the quality of the translation hypotheses (Tam et al., 2007 and 2008), and better initial translation hypotheses lead to better selected sentences (Zhao et al., 2004). However, while SMT has achieved a great deal of development in recent years, the translation hypotheses are still far from perfect (Wei and Pal, 2010), which have many noisy data. The noisy translation hypotheses mislead data selection process (Xu et al., 2001; Tam et al., 2006 and 2007; Wei and Pal, 2010), and thus take noisy data into the selected training data, which causes *noisy proliferation* and degrades the performance of adapted LM.

Furthermore, traditional approaches for LM adaptation are based on bag-of-words models and considered to be *context independent*, despite of their state-of-the-art performance, such as TF-IDF (Eck et al., 2004; Zhao et al., 2004; Hildebrand et al., 2005; Kim, 2005; Foster and Kuhn, 2007), centroid similarity (Masskey and Sethy, 2010), and cross-lingual similarity (CLS) (Ananthakrishnan et al., 2011a). They all perform at the word level, exact only term matching schemes, and do not take into account any contextual information when modeling the selection by single words in isolation, which degrade the quality of selected sentences.

In this paper, we argue that it is beneficial to model the data selection based on the source translation task directly and capture the contextual information for LM adaptation. To this end, we propose a more principled translation model (TM) based cross-lingual data selection model for LM adaptation, from word models to phrase models. We assume that the data selection should be performed by the cross-lingual model and at the phrase level. Given a source sentence in the translation task, this model directly estimates the probability before translation that a sentence in the target LM training corpus is similar. Therefore, it does not require the translation task to be pre-translation as in monolingual adaptation, and can address the problem of noisy proliferation.

To the best of our knowledge, this is the first extensive and empirical study of using phrase TM based cross-lingual data selection for LM adaptation. This model learns the transform probability of a multi-term phrase in a source sentence given a phrase in the target sentence of LM training corpus. Compared with bag-of-words models and word-based TM that account for selecting single words in isolation, this model performs at the phrase level and captures some *contextual information* in modeling the selection of phrase as a whole, thus it is potentially more effective. More precise data selection can be determined for phrases than for words. In this model, we propose a linear ranking model framework to further improve the performance, referred to the linear discriminant function (Duda et al., 2001; Collins, 2002; Gao et al., 2005) in pattern classification and information retrieval (IR), where different models are incorporated as features, as we will show in our experiments.

Unlike the general TM in SMT, we explore the use of TextRank algorithm (Mihalcea et al., 2004) to identify and eliminate unimportant words (e.g., non-topical words, common words) for corpus preprocessing, and construct TM by *important words*. This reduces the average number of words in cross-lingual data selection model, thus improving the efficiency. Moreover, TextRank utilizes the context information of words to assign term weights (Lee et al., 2008), which makes phrase TM based cross-lingual data selection model play its advantage of capturing the contextual information, thus further improving the performance.

The remainder of this paper is organized as follows. Section 2 introduces the related work of LM adaptation. Section 3 presents the framework of cross-lingual data selection for LM adaptation. Section 4 describes our proposed TM based cross-lingual data selection model: from word models to phrase models. In section 5 we present large-scale experiments and analyses, and followed by conclusions and future work in section 6.

2 Related Work

TF-IDF and cosine similarity have been widely used for LM adaptation (Eck et al., 2004; Zhao et al., 2004; Hildebrand et al., 2005; Kim, 2005; Foster and Kuhn, 2007). Masskey and Sethy (2010) selected the auxiliary data by computing centroid similarity score to the centroid of the in-domain data. The main idea of these methods is to select the sentences which are similar to the first pass translation hypotheses or in-domain corpus from the large LM training corpus, and estimate the bias LM for SMT system to improve the translation quality.

Tam et al. (2007 and 2008) proposed a bilingual-LSA model for LM adaptation. They integrated the LSA marginal into the target generic LM using marginal adaptation which minimizes the Kullback-Leibler divergence between the adapted LM and the generic LM. Ananthakrishnan et al. (2011a) proposed CLS to bias the count and probability of corresponding n-gram through weighting the LM training corpus. However, these two cross-lingual approaches focus on modify LM itself, which are different from data selection method for LM adaptation. In our comparable experiments, we apply CLS for the first time to the task of cross-lingual data selection for LM adaptation. Due to lack of smoothing measure for sparse vector representation in CLS, the similarity computation is not accurate which degrades the performance of adapted LM. To avoid this, we add smoothing measure like TF-IDF, called CLS_s, as we will discuss in the experiments.

Snover et al. (2008) used a word TM based CLIR

system (Xu et al., 2001) to select a subset of target documents comparable to the source document for adapting LM. Because of the data sparseness in the document state and it operated at the document level, this model selected large quantities of irrelevant text, which may degrade the adapted LM (Eck et al., 2004; Ananthakrishnan et al., 2011b). In our word TM based cross-lingual data selection model, we operate at the sentence level and add the smoothing mechanism by integrating with the background word frequency model, and these can significantly improve the performance. Axelrod et al. (2011) proposed a bilingual cross-entropy difference to select data from parallel corpus for domain adaptation which captures the contextual information slightly, and outperformed monolingual cross-entropy difference (Moore and Lewis, 2010), which first shows the advantage of bilingual data selection. However, its performance depends on the parallel in-domain corpus which is usually hard to find, and its application is assumed to be limited.

3 Cross-Lingual Data Selection for Language Model Adaptation

Our LM adaptation is an unsupervised similar training data selection guided by TM based cross-lingual data selection model. For the source sentences in the translation task, we estimate a new LM, the bias LM, from the corresponding target LM training sentences which are selected as the similar sentences. Since the size of the selected sentences is small, the corresponding bias LM is specific and more effective, giving high probabilities to those phrases that occur in the desired output translations.

Following the work of (Zhao et al., 2004; Snover et al., 2008), the generic LM $P_g(w_i|h)$ and the bias LM $P_b(w_i|h)$ are combined using linear interpolation as the adapted LM $P_a(w_i|h)$, which is shown to improve the performance over individual model,

$$P_a(w_i|h) = \mu P_g(w_i|h) + (1-\mu)P_b(w_i|h) \quad (1)$$

where the interpolation factor μ can be simply estimated using the Powell Search algorithm (Press et al., 1992) via cross-validation.

Our work focuses on TM based cross-lingual data selection model, from word model to phrase models, and the quality of this model is crucial to the performance of adapted LM.

4 Translation Model for Cross-Lingual Data Selection (CLTM)

Let $Q = \mathbf{q}_1, \ldots, \mathbf{q}_j$ be a source sentence in the translation task and $S = \mathbf{w}_1, \ldots, \mathbf{w}_i$ be a sentence in the general target LM training corpus, thus cross-lingual data selection model can be framed probabilistically as maximizing the $P(S|Q)$. By Bayes' rule,

$$P(S|Q) = \frac{P(S)P(Q|S)}{P(Q)} \quad (2)$$

where the prior probability $P(S)$ can be viewed as uniform, and the $P(Q)$ is constant across all sentences. Therefore, selecting a sentence to maximize $P(S|Q)$ is equivalent to selecting a sentence that maximizes $P(Q|S)$.

4.1 Word-Based Translation Model for Cross-Lingual Data Selection (CLWTM)

4.1.1 Cross-Lingual Sentence Selection Model

Following the work of (Xu et al., 2001; Snover et al., 2008), CLWTM can be described as

$$P(Q|S) = \prod_{q \in Q} P(q|S) \quad (3)$$

$$P(q|S) = \alpha P(q|C_q) + (1-\alpha) \sum_{w \in S} P(q|w)P(w|S) \quad (4)$$

where α is the interpolation weight empirically set as a constant[1], $P(q|w)$ is the word-based TM which is estimated by IBM Model 1 (Brown et al., 1993) from the parallel corpus, $P(q|C_q)$ and $P(w|S)$ are the un-smoothed background and sentence model, respectively, estimated using maximum likelihood estimation (MLE) as

$$P(q|C_q) = \frac{freq(q, C_q)}{|C_q|} \quad (5)$$

$$P(w|S) = \frac{freq(w, S)}{|S|} \quad (6)$$

where C_q refers to the translation task, $freq(q, C_q)$ refers to the number of times q occurs in C_q, $freq(w, S)$ refers to the number of times w occurs in S, and $|C_q|$ and $|S|$ are the sizes of the translation task and the current target sentence, respectively.

[1]As in Xu et al. (2001), a value of 0.3 was used for α.

4.1.2 Ranking Candidate Sentences

Because of the data sparseness in the sentence state which degrades the model, Equation (6) does not perform well in our data selection experiments. Inspired by the work of (Berger et al., 1999) in IR, we make the following smoothing mechanism:

$$P(q|S) = \alpha P(q|C_q) + (1-\alpha) \sum_{w \in S} P(q|w) P_s(w|S) \quad (7)$$

$$P_s(w|S) = \beta P(w|C_s) + (1-\beta) P(w|S) \quad (8)$$

$$P(w|C_s) = \frac{freq(w, C_s)}{|C_s|} \quad (9)$$

where $P(w|C_s)$ is the un-smoothed background model, estimated using MLE as Equation (5), C_s refers to the LM training corpus and $|C_s|$ refers to its size. Here, β is interpolation weight; notice that letting $\beta = 0$ in Equation (8) reduces the model to the un-smoothed model in Equation (4).

4.2 Phrase-Based Translation Model for Cross-Lingual Data Selection (CLPTM)

4.2.1 Cross-Lingual Sentence Selection Model

The phrase-based TM (Koehn et al., 2003; Och and Ney, 2004) has shown superior performance compared to the word-based TM. In this paper, the goal of phrase-based TM is to transfer S into Q. Rather than transferring single words in isolation, the phrase model transfers one sequence of words into another sequence of words, thus incorporating contextual information. Inspired by the work of web search (Gao et al., 2010) and question retrieval in community question answer (Q&A) (Zhou et al., 2011), we assume the following generative process: first the sentence S is broken into K non-empty word sequences $\mathbf{w}_1, \ldots, \mathbf{w}_k$, then each is transferred into a new non-empty word sequences $\mathbf{q}_1, \ldots, \mathbf{q}_k$, and finally these phrases are permutated and concatenated to form the sentence Q, where q and w denote the phrases or consecutive sequence of words.

To formulate this generative process, let U denote the segmentation of S into K phrases $\mathbf{w}_1, \ldots, \mathbf{w}_k$, and let V denote the K phrases $\mathbf{q}_1, \ldots, \mathbf{q}_k$, we refer to these $(\mathbf{w}_i, \mathbf{q}_i)$ pairs as bi-phrases. Finally, let M denote a permutation of K elements representing the final ranking step.

Next we place a probability distribution over rewrite pairs. Let $B(S, Q)$ denote the set of U, V, M triples that transfer S into Q. Here we assume a uniform probability over segmentations, so the phrase-based selection probability can be formulated as

$$P(Q|S) \propto \sum_{\substack{(U,V,M) \in \\ B(S,Q)}} P(V|S,U) \cdot P(M|S,U,V) \quad (10)$$

Then, we use the maximum approximation to the sum:

$$P(Q|S) \approx \max_{\substack{(U,V,M) \in \\ B(S,Q)}} P(V|S,U) \cdot P(M|S,U,V) \quad (11)$$

Although we have defined a generative model for transferring S into Q, our goal is to calculate the ranking score function over existing Q and S. However, this model can not be used directly for sentence ranking because Q and S are often of different lengths, the length of S is almost 1.5 times to that of Q in our corpus, leaving many words in S unaligned to any word in Q. This is another key difference between our task and SMT. As pointed out by the previous work (Berger and Lafferty, 1999; Gao et al., 2010; Zhou et al., 2011), sentence-query selection requires a distillation of the sentence, while selection of natural language tolerates little being thrown away. Thus we restrict our attention to those *key sentence words* that form the distillation of S, do not consider the unaligned words in S, and assume that Q is transfered only from the key sentence words.

In this paper, the key sentence words are identified via word alignment. Let $A = a_1 \ldots a_J$ be the "hidden" word alignment, which describes a mapping from a term position j in Q to a word position a_j in S. We assume that the positions of the key sentence words are determined by the Viterbi alignment $\hat{A}$, which can be obtained using IBM Model 1 (Brown et al., 1993) as follows:

$$\begin{aligned} \hat{A} &= \arg\max_A P(Q, A|S) \\ &= \arg\max_A \Big\{ P(J|I) \prod_{j=1}^{J} P(q_j|w_{a_j}) \Big\} \\ &= \Big[\arg\max_{a_j} P(q_j|w_{a_j}) \Big]_{j=1}^{J} \end{aligned} \quad (12)$$

Given $\hat{A}$, when scoring a given Q/S pair, we restrict our attention to those U, V, M triples that are consistent with $\hat{A}$, which we denote as $B(S, Q, \hat{A})$. Here, consistency requires that if two words are aligned in $\hat{A}$, then they must appear in the same biphrase $(\mathbf{w}_i, \mathbf{q}_i)$. Once the word alignment is fixed, the final permutation is uniquely determined, so we can safely discard that factor. Then Equation (11) can be written as

$$P(Q|S) \approx \max_{\substack{(U,V,M)\in \\ B(S,Q,\hat{A})}} P(V|S, U) \quad (13)$$

For the sole remaining factor $P(V|S, U)$, we assume that a segmented queried question $V = \mathbf{q}_1, \ldots, \mathbf{q}_k$ is generated from left to right by transferring each phrase $\mathbf{w}_1, \ldots, \mathbf{w}_k$ independently, as follows:

$$P(V|S, U) = \prod_{k=1}^{K} P(\mathbf{q}_k|\mathbf{w}_k) \quad (14)$$

where $P(\mathbf{q}_k|\mathbf{w}_k)$ is a phrase translation probability computed from the parallel corpus, which can be estimated in two ways (Koehn et al., 2003; Och and Ney, 2004): relative frequency and lexical weighting, and has two format: phrase translation probability and lexical weight probability.

In order to find the maximum probability assignment $P(Q|S)$ efficiently, we use a dynamic programming approach, somewhat similar to the monotone decoding algorithm described in the work (Och, 2002). We consider quantity a_j as the maximal probability of the most likely sequence of phrases in S covering the first j words in Q, therefore the probability can be calculated using the following recursion:

step (1). Initialization:

$$\alpha_0 = 1 \quad (15)$$

step (2). Induction:

$$\alpha_j = \sum_{j'<j, \mathbf{q}=q_{j'+1} \cdots q_j} \left\{\alpha_{j'} P(\mathbf{q}|\mathbf{w}_\mathbf{q})\right\} \quad (16)$$

step (3). Total:

$$P(Q|S) = \alpha_J \quad (17)$$

4.2.2 Ranking Candidate Sentences

However, directly using the phrase-based TM, computed in Equations (15) to (17), to rank the candidate sentences does not perform well. Inspired by the linear discriminant function (Duda et al., 2001; Collins, 2002; Gao et al., 2005) in pattern classification and IR, we therefore propose a linear ranking model framework for cross-lingual data selection model in which different models are incorporated as features.

We consider the linear ranking model as follows:

$$\begin{aligned} Score(Q, S) &= \lambda^T \cdot H(Q, S) \\ &= \sum_{n=1}^{N} \lambda_n h_n(Q, S) \end{aligned} \quad (18)$$

where the model has a set of N features, and each feature is an arbitrary function that maps $(Q|S)$ to a real value, i.e., $H(Q, S) \in \mathbf{R}$. λ_n for $n = 1 \ldots N$ is the corresponding parameters of each feature, and we optimize these parameters using the Powell Search algorithm (Press et al., 1992) via cross-validation.

The used features in the linear ranking model are as follows:

- Phrase translation feature (PT): $h_{PT}(Q, S, A) = \log P(Q|S)$, where $P(Q|S)$ is computed using Equations (15) to (17), and $P(\mathbf{q}_k|\mathbf{w}_k)$ is phrase translation probability.
- Inverted phrase translation feature (IPT): $h_{IPT}(S, Q, A) = \log P(S|Q)$, where $P(S|Q)$ is computed using Equations (15) to (17), and $P(\mathbf{w}_k|\mathbf{q}_k)$ is inverted phrase translation probability.
- Lexical weight feature (LW): $h_{LW}(Q, S, A) = \log P(Q|S)$, where $P(Q|S)$ is computed using Equations (15) to (17), and $P(\mathbf{q}_k|\mathbf{w}_k)$ is lexical weight probability.
- Inverted lexical weight feature (ILW): $h_{ILW}(S, Q, A) = \log P(S|Q)$, where $P(S|Q)$ is computed using Equations (15) to (17), and $P(\mathbf{w}_k|\mathbf{q}_k)$ is inverted lexical weight probability.
- Unaligned word penalty feature (UWP): $h_{UWP}(Q, S, A)$, which is defined as the ratio between the number of unaligned terms and the total number of terms in Q.

- Word-based translation feature (WT): $h_{WT}(Q, S, A) = \log P(Q|S)$, where $P(Q|S)$ is the word-based TM defined by Equations (3) and (7).

4.3 Eliminating Unimportant Words (EUW)

To improve the efficiency of cross-lingual data selection process, we consider the translation task, the LM training corpus and the parallel corpus in our task are constructed by the key words or important words, and thus construct TM by the key words or important words, which is another key difference between our task and SMT. We identify and eliminate unimportant words, somewhat similar to Q&A retrieval (Lee et al., 2008; Zhou et al., 2011). Thus, the average number of words (the total word number in Q and S) in cross-lingual sentence selection model would be minimized naturally, and the efficiency of cross-lingual data selection would be improved.

In this paper, we adopt a variant of TextRank algorithm (Mihalcea and Tarau, 2004), a graph-based ranking model for key word extraction which achieves state-of-the-art accuracy. It identifies and eliminates unimportant words from the corpus, and assumes that a word is unimportant if it holds a relatively low significance in the corpus. Compared with the traditional approaches, such as TF-IDF, TextRank utilizes the context information of words to assign term weights (Lee et al., 2008), so it further improves the performance of CLPTM, as we will show in the experiments.

Following the work of (Lee et al., 2008), the ranking algorithm proceeds as follows. First, all the words in a given document are added as vertices in a graph. Then edges are added between words (vertices) if the words co-occur in a fixed-sized window. The number of co-occurrences becomes the weight of an edge. When the graph is constructed, the score of each vertex is initialized as 1, and the PageRank based ranking algorithm is run on the graph iteratively until convergence. The TextRank score $R^k_{w_i,D}$ of a word w_i in document D at kth iteration is defined as follows:

$$R^k_{w_i,D} = (1-d) + d \cdot \sum_{\forall j:(i,j)\in G} \frac{e_{i,j}}{\sum_{\forall l:(j,l)\in G} e_{j,l}} R^{k-1}_{w_j,D} \quad (19)$$

where d is a damping factor usually set as a constant[2], and $e_{i,j}$ is an edge weight between w_i and w_j.

In our experiments, we manually set the proportion to be removed as 25%, that is to say, 75% of total words in the documents would be remained as the important words.

5 Experiments

We measure the utility of our proposed LM adaptation approach in two ways: (a) comparing reference translations based perplexity of adapted LMs with the generic LM, and (b) comparing SMT performance of adapted LMs with the generic LM.

5.1 Corpus and Tasks

We conduct experiments on two Chinese-to-English translation tasks: IWSLT-07 (dialogue domain) and NIST-06 (news domain).

IWSLT-07. The bilingual training corpus comes from BTEC[3] and CJK[4] corpus, which contains 3.82K sentence pairs with 3.0M/3.1M Chinese/English words. The LM training corpus is from the English side of the parallel data (BTEC, CJK, and CWMT2008[5]), which consists of 1.34M sentences and 15.2M English words. The test set is IWSLT-07 test set which consists of 489 sentences, and the development set is IWSLT-05 test set which consists of 506 sentences.

NIST-06. The bilingual training corpus comes from Linguistic Data Consortium (LDC)[6], which consists of 3.4M sentence pairs with 64M/70M Chinese/English words. The LM training corpus is from the English side of the parallel data as well as the English Gigaword corpus[7], which consists of 11.3M sentences. The test set is 2006 NIST MT Evaluation test set which consists of 1664 sentences, and the development set is 2005 NIST MT Evaluation test set which consists of 1084 sentences.

[2] As in Lee et al. (2008), a value of 0.85 was used for d.

[3] Basic Traveling Expression Corpus

[4] China-Japan-Korea

[5] The 4th China Workshop on Machine Translation

[6] LDC2002E18, LDC2002T01, LDC2003E07, LDC2003E14, LDC2003T17, LDC2004T07, LDC2004T08, LDC2005T06, LDC2005T10, LDC2005T34, LDC2006T04, LDC2007T09

[7] LDC2007T07

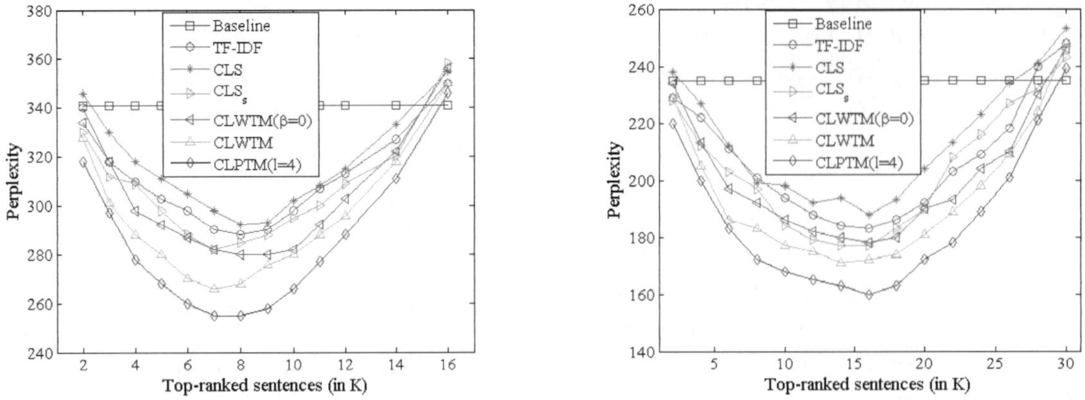

(a)IWSLT-07 (b)NIST-06

Figure 1: English reference translations based perplexity of adapted LMs vs. the size of selected training data with different approaches on two development sets.

5.2 Perplexity Analysis

We randomly divide the development set into five subsets and conduct 5-fold cross-validation experiments. In each trial, we tune the parameter μ in Equation (1) and parameter λ in Equation (18) with four of five subsets and then apply it to one remaining subset. The experiments reported below are those averaged over the five trials.

We estimate the generic 4-gram LM with the entire LM training corpus as the baseline. Then, we select the top-N sentences which are similar to the development set, estimate the bias 4-gram LMs (with n-gram cutoffs tuned as above) with these selected sentences, and interpolate with the generic 4-gram LM as the adapted LMs. All the LMs are estimated by the SRILM toolkit (Stolcke, 2002). Perplexity is a metric of LM performance, and the lower perplexity value indicates the better performance. Therefore, we estimate the perplexity of adapted LMs according to English reference translations.

Figure 1 shows the perplexity of adapted LMs vs. the size of selected data. In this paper, we choose TF-IDF as the foundation of our solution since TF-IDF has gained the state-of-the-art performance for LM adaptation (Eck et al., 2004; Hildebrand et al., 2005; Kim, 2005; Foster and Kuhn, 2007). CLS refers to the cross-lingual similarity of (Ananthakrishnan et al., 2011a), and CLS_s is our proposed improved algorithm on CLS with optimization measure like TF-IDF. CLWTM($\beta = 0$) refers to Snover et al. (2008), which is the un-smooth version of our proposed CLWTM in the document state. CLPTM($l = 4$) is our proposed CLPTM with a maximum phrase length of four, and we score the target sentences by the highest scoring Q/S pair.

Task	Method	Perplexity	Reduction
IWSLT-07	Baseline	524.1	–
	TF-IDF	471.4	10.06%
	CLS	475.7	9.23%
	CLS_s	468.9	10.53%
	CLWTM($\beta = 0$)	463.5	11.56%
	CLWTM	**451.5**	**13.85%**
	CLPTM($l = 4$)	**435.3**	**16.94%**
NIST-06	Baseline	398.3	–
	TF-IDF	346.2	13.08%
	CLS	351.6	11.72%
	CLS_s	340.9	14.41%
	CLWTM($\beta = 0$)	341.1	14.36%
	CLWTM	**332.7**	**16.47%**
	CLPTM($l = 4$)	**319.2**	**19.86%**

Table 1: English reference translations based perplexity of adapted LMs with different approaches on two test sets, with the top 8K sentences on IWSLT-07 and top 16K sentences on NIST-06, respectively.

The results in Figure 1 indicate that English reference translations based perplexity of adapted LMs decreases consistently with increase of the size of selected top-N sentences, and increases consistently after a certain size in all approaches. Therefore, proper size of similar sentences with the translation task makes the adapted LM perform well, but if too many noisy data are taken into the selected sentences, the performance becomes worse. Similar observations have been done by (Eck et al., 2004;

Task	#	Method	BLEU
IWSLT-07	1	Baseline	33.60
	2	TF-IDF	34.14
	3	CLS	34.08
	4	CLS_s	34.18
	5	CLWTM($\beta = 0$)	34.22
	6	**CLWTM**	**34.30**
	7	**CLPTM($l = 4$)**	**34.49**
NIST-06	8	Baseline	29.15
	9	TF-IDF	29.78
	10	CLS	29.73
	11	CLS_s	29.84
	12	CLWTM($\beta = 0$)	29.87
	13	**CLWTM**	**29.93**
	14	**CLPTM($l = 4$)**	**30.17**

Table 2: Comparison of SMT performance ($p < 0.05$) with different approaches for LM adaptation on two test sets.

Axelrod et al., 2011). Furthermore, it is comforting that our approaches (CLWTM and CLPTM($l = 4$)) performs better and are more stable than other approaches.

According to the perplexity results in Figure 1, we select the top 8K sentences on IWSLT-07 and top 16K sentences on NIST-06 which are similar to the test set for adapting LM, respectively. Table 1 shows English reference translations based perplexity of adapted LMs on two test sets. Our approaches have significantly reduction in perplexity compared with other approaches, and the results indicate that adapted LMs are significantly better predictors of the corresponding translation task at hand than the generic LM. We use these adapted LMs for next translation experiments to show the detailed performance of selected training data for LM adaptation.

5.3 Translation Experiments

We carry out translation experiments on the test set by hierarchical phrase-based (HPB) SMT (Chiang, 2005 and 2007) system to demonstrate the utility of LM adaptation on improving SMT performance by BLEU score (Papineni et al., 2002). The generic LM and adapted LMs are estimated as above in perplexity analysis experiments. We use minimum error rate training (Och, 2003) to tune the feature weights of HPB for maximum BLEU score on the development set with serval groups of different start weights.

Table 2 shows the main translation results on two test sets, and the improvements are statistically significant at the 95% confidence interval with respect to the baseline. From the comparison results, we get some clear trends:

(1) Cross-lingual data selection model outperforms the traditional approaches which utilize the first pass translation hypotheses (row 4 vs. row2; row 11 vs. row 9), but the detailed impact of noisy data in the translation hypotheses on data selection will be shown in the next section (section 5.4).

(2) CLWTM significantly outperforms CLS_s (row 6 vs. row 4; row 13 vs. row 11), we suspect that word-based TM makes more accurate cross-lingual data selection model than single cross-lingual projection (Ananthakrishnan et al., 2011a).

(3) Compared with (Snover et al., 2008), adding the smoothing mechanism in the sentence state for CLWTM significantly improves the performance (row 6 vs. row 5; row 13 vs. row 12).

(4) Phrase-based TM (CLPTM) significantly outperforms the state-of-the-art approaches based on bag-of-words models and word-based TM (row 7 vs. row 2, row 4, row 5 and row 6; row 14 vs. row 9, row 11, row 12 and row 13).

Task	Translation Hypotheses	BLEU
IWSLT-07	First Pass	34.14
	Second Pass	34.31
NIST-06	First Pass	29.78
	Second Pass	29.91

Table 3: The impact of noisy data in the translation hypotheses on the performance of LM adaptation.

5.4 Impact of Noisy Data in the Translation Hypotheses

The experiment results in Table 2 indicate the second pass translation hypotheses (row 2 and row 9) made by TF-IDF are better than the first pass translation hypotheses (row 1 and row 8), so we consider that these translations have less noisy data. Thus, they were considered as the new translation hypotheses (the second pass) to select the similar sentences for LM adaptation by TF-IDF.

Table 3 shows the impact of noisy data in the translation hypotheses on the performance of adapted LMs. The observed improvement suggests that better initial translations which have less noisy data

Task	Phrase Length	BLEU
IWSLT-07	$l = 1$	34.33
	$l = 2$	34.44
	$l = 3$	34.49
	$l = 4$	34.49
NIST-06	$l = 1$	29.97
	$l = 2$	30.07
	$l = 3$	30.14
	$l = 4$	30.17

Table 4: The impact of phrase length in CLPTM on the performance of LM adaptation, and the maximum phrase length is four.

lead to better adapted LMs, and thereby better second iteration translations. Therefore, it is advisable to use cross-lingual data selection for LM adaptation in SMT, which can address the problem of noisy proliferation.

5.5 Impact of Phrase Length

The results in Table 4 show that longer phrases do yield some visible improvement up to the maximum length of four. This may suggest that some properties captured by longer phrases are also captured by other features. The performances when the phrase length is 1 are better than that of single word-based TM (row 6 and row 13 in Table 2), this suspect that the features in our linear ranking model are useful. However, it will be instructive to explore the methods of preserving the improvement generated by longer phrase when more features are incorporated in the future work.

5.6 Impact of Eliminating Unimportant Words

Table 5 shows the results of EUW by TextRank algorithm on the performance of CLTM for LM adaptation. Initial represents that we do not eliminate unimportant words. Average number represents the average number of words (the total word number in Q and S) in cross-lingual data selection model. The average number is reduced when unimportant words are eliminated, from 19 to 12 on IWSLT-07 and from 37 to 24 on NIST-06, respectively. This makes the cross-lingual data selection process become more efficient. In CLWTM, the performance with EUW is basically the same with that of the initial state; but in CLPTM, EUW outperforms the initial state because TextRank algorithm utilizes the context information of words when assigning term weights, thus makeing CLPTM play its advantage of capturing the contextual information.

Task	Method	Average Number	BLEU	
			CLWTM	CLPTM ($l = 4$)
IWSLT-07	Initial	19	34.31	34.47
	EUW	12	34.30	34.49
NIST-06	Initial	37	29.91	30.12
	EUW	24	29.93	30.17

Table 5: The impact of eliminating unimportant words by TextRank algorithm on the performance of CLTM for LM adaptation.

6 Conclusions and Future Work

In this paper, we propose a novel TM based cross-lingual data selection model for LM adaptation in SMT, from word models to phrase models, and aims to find the LM training corpus which are similar to the translation task at hand. Unlike the general TM in SMT, we explore the use of TextRank algorithm to identify and eliminate unimportant words for corpus preprocessing, and construct TM by important words. Compared with the traditional approaches which utilize the first pass translation hypotheses, cross-lingual data selection avoids the problem of noisy proliferation. Furthermore, phrase TM based cross-lingual data selection is more effective than the traditional approaches based on bag-of-words models and word-based TM, because it captures contextual information in modeling the selection of phrase as a whole. Large-scale experiments are conducted on LM perplexity and SMT performance, and the results demonstrate that our approach solves the two aforementioned disadvantages and significantly outperforms the state-of-the-art methods for LM adaptation.

There are some ways in which this research could be continued in the future. First, we will utilize our approach to mine large-scale corpora by distributed infrastructure system, and investigate the use of our approach for other domains, such as speech translation system. Second, the significant improvement of LM adaptation based on cross-lingual data selection is exciting, so it will be instructive to explore other knowledge based cross-lingual data selection for LM adaptation, such as latent semantic model.

Acknowledgments

This work was supported by 863 program in China (No. 2011AA01A207). We thank Guangyou Zhou for his helpful discussions and suggestions. We also thank the anonymous reviewers for their insightful comments.

References

Sankaranarayanan Ananthakrishnan, Rohit Prasad, and Prem Natarajan. 2011a. On-line language model biasing for statistical machine translation. In *Proceedings of ACL*, pages 445-449.

Sankaranarayanan Ananthakrishnan, Stavros Tsakalidis, Rohit Prasad, and Prem Natarajan. 2011b. Online language model biasing for multi-pass automatic speech recognition. In *Proceedings of INTERSPEECH*, pages 621-624.

Amittai Axelrod, Xiaodong He, and Jianfeng Gao. 2011. Domain adaptation via pseudo in-domain data selection. In *Proceedings of EMNLP*, pages 355-362.

Adam Berger and John Lafferty. 1999. Information retrieval as statistical translation. In *Proceedings of SIGIR*, pages 222-229.

Thorsten Brants, Ashok C. Popat, Peng Xu, Franz J. Och, and Jeffrey Dean. 2007. Large language models in machine translation. In *Proceedings of EMNLP*, pages 858-867.

Peter F. Brown, Vincent J. Della Pietra, Stephen A. Della Pietra, and Robert L. Mercer. 1993. The mathematics of statistical machine translation: parameter estimation. *Computational Linguistics*, 19(2):263-311.

David Chiang. 2005. A hierarchical phrase-based model for statistical machine translation. In *Proceedings of ACL*, pages 263-270.

David Chiang. 2007. Hierarchical phrase-based translation. *Computational Linguistics*, 33(2):201-228.

Michael Collins. 2002. Discriminative training methods for hidden markov models: theory and experiments with the perceptron algorithm. In *Proceedings of EMNLP*, pages 1-8.

Richard O. Duda, Peter E. Hart, and David G. Stork. 2001. Pattern classification. John Wiley & Sons, Inc.

Matthias Eck, Stephan Vogel, and Alex Waibel. 2004. Language model adaptation for statistical machine translation based on information retrieval. In *Proceedings of LREC*, pages 327-330.

George Foster and Roland Kuhn. 2007. Mixture-model adaptation for SMT. In *Proceedings of ACL*, pages 128-135.

Jianfeng Gao, Haoliang Qi, Xinsong Xia, and Jian-Yun Nie. 2005. Linear discriminative model for information retrieval. In *Proceedings of SIGIR*, pages 290-297.

Jianfeng Gao, Xiaodong He, and Jian-Yun Nie. 2010. Clickthrough-based translation models for web search: from word models to phrase models. In *Proceedings of CIKM*, pages 1139-1148.

Almut Silja Hildebrand, Matthias Eck, Stephan Vogel, and Alex Waibel. 2005. Adaptation of the translation model for statistical machine translation based information retrieval. In *Proceedings of EAMT*, pages 133-142.

Woosung Kim. 2005. Language model adaptation for automatic speech recognition and statistical machine translation. *Ph.D. thesis*, The Johns Hopkins University.

Philipp Koehn, Franz Josef Och, and Daniel Marcu. 2003. Statistical phrase-based translation. In *Proceedings of NAACL*, pages 48-54.

Jung-Tae Lee, Sang-Bum Kim, Young-In Song, and Hae-Chang Rim. 2008. Bridging lexical gaps between queries and questions on large online Q&A collections with compact translation models. In *Proceedings of EMNLP*, pages 410-418.

Sameer Masskey and Abhinav Sethy. 2010. Resampling auxiliary data for language model adaptation in machine translation for speech. In *Proceedings of ICASSP*, pages 4817-4820.

Rada Mihalcea and Paul Tarau. 2004. TextRank: Bringing order into text. In *Proceedings of EMNLP*, pages 404-411.

Robert C. Moore and William Lewis. 2010. Intelligent selection of language model training data. In *Proceedings of ACL*, pages 220-224.

Franz Josef Och. 2002. Statistical mahcine translation: from single word models to alignment templates. *Ph.D thesis*, RWTH Aachen.

Franz Josef Och. 2003. Minimum error rate training in statistical machine translation. In *Proceedings of ACL*, pages 160-167.

Franz Josef Och and Hermann Ney. 2004. The alignment template approach to statistical machine translation. *Computational Linguistics*, 30(4):417-449.

Kishore Papineni, Salim Roukos, Todd Ward, and Wei-jing Zhu. 2002. BLEU: A method for automatic evaluation of machine translation. In *Proceedings of ACL*, pages 311-318.

William H. Press, Saul A. Teukolsky, William T. Vetterling, and Brian P. Flannery. 1992. *Numerical Recipes in C*. Cambridge University Press.

Matthew Snover, Bonnie Dorr, and Richard Marcu. 2008. Language and translation model adaptation using comparable corpora. In *Proceedings of EMNLP*, pages 857-866.

Andreas Stolcke. 2002. SRILM - An extensible language modeling toolkit. In *Proceedings of ICSLP*, pages 901-904.

Yik-Cheung Tam and Tanja Schultz. 2006. Unsupervised language model adaptation using latent semantic marginals. In *Proceedings of ICSLP*, pages 2206-2209.

Yik-Cheung Tam, Ian Lane, and Tanja Schultz. 2007. Bilingual-LSA based LM adaptation for spoken language translation. In *Proceedings of ACL*, pages 520-527.

Yik-Cheung Tam, Ian Lane, and Tanja Schultz. 2008. Bilingual-LSA based adaptation for statistical machine translation. *Machine Translation*, 21:187-207.

Bin Wei and Christopher Pal. 2010. Cross lingual adaptation: an experiment on sentiment classifications. In *Proceedings of ACL*, pages 258-262.

Jinxi Xu, Ralpha Weischedel, and Chanh Nguyen. 2001. Evaluating a probabilistic model for cross-lingual information retrieval. In *Proceedings of SIGIR*, pages 105-110.

Xiaobing Xue, Jiwoon Jeon, and W. Bruce Croft. 2008. Retrieval models for question and answer archives. In *Proceedings of SIGIR*, pages 475-482.

Bing Zhao, Matthias Eck, and Stephan Vogel. 2004. Language model adaptation for statistical machine translation with structured query models. In *Proceedings of COLING*, pages 411-417.

Guangyou Zhou, Li Cai, Jun Zhao, and Kang Liu. 2011. Phrase-based translation model for question retrieval in community question answer archives. In *Proceedings of ACL*, pages 653-662.

Open Language Learning for Information Extraction

Mausam, Michael Schmitz, Robert Bart, Stephen Soderland, and Oren Etzioni
Turing Center
Department of Computer Science and Engineering
University of Washington, Seattle
{mausam,schmmd,rbart,soderlan,etzioni}@cs.washington.edu

Abstract

Open Information Extraction (IE) systems extract relational tuples from text, without requiring a pre-specified vocabulary, by identifying relation phrases and associated arguments in arbitrary sentences. However, state-of-the-art Open IE systems such as REVERB and WOE share two important weaknesses – (1) they extract only relations that are mediated by verbs, and (2) they ignore *context*, thus extracting tuples that are not asserted as factual. This paper presents OLLIE, a substantially improved Open IE system that addresses both these limitations. First, OLLIE achieves high yield by extracting relations mediated by nouns, adjectives, and more. Second, a context-analysis step increases precision by including contextual information from the sentence in the extractions. OLLIE obtains 2.7 times the area under precision-yield curve (AUC) compared to REVERB and 1.9 times the AUC of WOE^{parse}.

1. "After winning the Superbowl, the Saints are now the top dogs of the NFL."
   O: (the Saints; win; the Superbowl)
2. "There are plenty of taxis available at Bali airport."
   O: (taxis; be available at; Bali airport)
3. "Microsoft co-founder Bill Gates spoke at ..."
   O: (Bill Gates; be co-founder of; Microsoft)
4. "Early astronomers believed that the earth is the center of the universe."
   R: (the earth; be the center of; the universe)
   W: (the earth; be; the center of the universe)
   O: ((the earth; be the center of; the universe) *AttributedTo* believe; Early astronomers)
5. "If he wins five key states, Romney will be elected President."
   R,W: (Romney; will be elected; President)
   O: ((Romney; will be elected; President) *ClausalModifier* if; he wins five key states)

Figure 1: OLLIE (O) has a wider syntactic range and finds extractions for the first three sentences where REVERB (R) and WOE^{parse} (W) find none. For sentences #4,5, REVERB and WOE^{parse} have an incorrect extraction by ignoring the context that OLLIE explicitly represents.

1 Introduction

While traditional Information Extraction (IE) (ARPA, 1991; ARPA, 1998) focused on identifying and extracting specific relations of interest, there has been great interest in scaling IE to a broader set of relations and to far larger corpora (Banko et al., 2007; Hoffmann et al., 2010; Mintz et al., 2009; Carlson et al., 2010; Fader et al., 2011). However, the requirement of having pre-specified relations of interest is a significant obstacle. Imagine an intelligence analyst who recently acquired a terrorist's laptop or a news reader who wishes to keep abreast of important events. The substantial endeavor in analyzing their corpus is the *discovery* of important relations, which are likely not pre-specified. Open IE (Banko et al., 2007) is the state-of-the-art approach for such scenarios.

However, the state-of-the-art Open IE systems, REVERB (Fader et al., 2011; Etzioni et al., 2011) and WOE^{parse} (Wu and Weld, 2010) suffer from two key drawbacks. Firstly, they handle a limited subset of sentence constructions for expressing relationships. Both extract only relations that are mediated by verbs, and REVERB further restricts this to a subset of verbal patterns. This misses important information mediated via other syntactic entities such as nouns and adjectives, as well as a wider range of verbal structures (examples #1-3 in Figure 1).

Secondly, REVERB and WOE^{parse} perform only a local analysis of a sentence, so they often extract relations that are not asserted as factual in the sentence (examples #4,5). This often occurs when the relation is within a belief, attribution, hypothetical or other conditional context.

In this paper we present OLLIE (**O**pen **L**anguage **L**earning for **I**nformation **E**xtraction), [1] our novel Open IE system that overcomes the limitations of previous Open IE by (1) expanding the syntactic scope of relation phrases to cover a much larger number of relation expressions, and (2) expanding the Open IE representation to allow additional context information such as attribution and clausal modifiers. OLLIE extractions obtain a dramatically higher yield at higher or comparable precision relative to existing systems.

The outline of the paper is as follows. First, we provide background on Open IE and how it relates to Semantic Role Labeling (SRL). Section 3 describes the syntactic scope expansion component, which is based on a novel approach that learns *open pattern templates*. These are relation-independent dependency parse-tree patterns that are automatically learned using a novel bootstrapped training set. Section 4 discusses the *context analysis* component, which is based on supervised training with linguistic and lexical features.

Section 5 compares OLLIE with REVERB and WOE^{parse} on a dataset from three domains: News, Wikipedia, and a Biology textbook. We find that OLLIE obtains 2.7 times the area in precision-yield curves (AUC) as REVERB and 1.9 times the AUC as WOE^{parse}. Moreover, for specific relations commonly mediated by nouns (*e.g.*, 'is the president of') OLLIE obtains two order of magnitude higher yield. We also compare OLLIE to a state-of-the-art SRL system (Johansson and Nugues, 2008) on an IE-related end task and find that they both have comparable performance at argument identification and have complimentary strengths in sentence analysis. In Section 6 we discuss related work on pattern-based relation extraction.

2 Background

Open IE systems extract tuples consisting of argument phrases from the input sentence and a phrase from the sentence that expresses a relation between the arguments, in the format (arg1; rel; arg2). This is done without a pre-specified set of relations and with no domain-specific knowledge engineering. We compare OLLIE to two state-of-the-art Open IE systems: (1) REVERB (Fader et al., 2011), which uses shallow syntactic processing to identify relation phrases that begin with a verb and occur between the argument phrases;[2] (2) WOE^{parse} (Wu and Weld, 2010), which uses bootstrapping from entries in Wikipedia info-boxes to learn extraction patterns in dependency parses. Like REVERB, the relation phrases begin with verbs, but can handle long-range dependencies and relation phrases that do not come between the arguments. Unlike REVERB, WOE does not include nouns within the relation phrases (*e.g.*, cannot represent 'is the president of' relation phrase). Both systems ignore context around the extracted relations that may indicate whether it is a supposition or conditionally true rather than asserted as factual (see #4-5 in Figure 1).

The task of *Semantic role labeling* is to identify arguments of verbs in a sentence, and then to classify the arguments by mapping the verb to a semantic frame and mapping the argument phrases to roles in that frame, such as agent, patient, instrument, or benefactive. SRL systems can also identify and classify arguments of relations that are mediated by nouns when trained on NomBank annotations. Where SRL begins with a verb or noun and then looks for arguments that play roles with respect to that verb or noun, Open IE looks for a phrase that expresses a relation between a pair of arguments. That phrase is often more than simply a single verb, such as the phrase 'plays a role in', or 'is the CEO of'.

3 Relational Extraction in OLLIE

Figure 2 illustrates OLLIE's architecture for learning and applying binary extraction patterns. First, it uses a set of high precision seed tuples from REVERB to bootstrap a large training set. Second, it learns *open pattern templates* over this training set. Next, OLLIE applies these pattern templates at extraction time. This section describes these three steps in detail. Finally, OLLIE analyzes the context around the tuple (Section 4) to add information (attribution, clausal modifiers) and a confidence function.

[1] Available for download at http://openie.cs.washington.edu

[2] Available for download at http://reverb.cs.washington.edu/

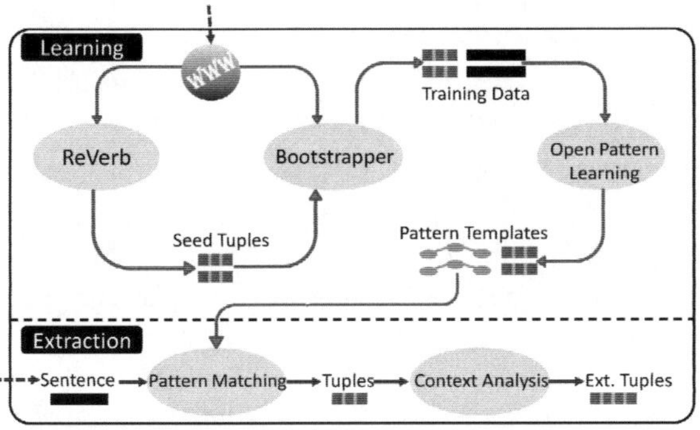

Figure 2: System architecture: OLLIE begins with seed tuples from REVERB, uses them to build a bootstrap training set, and learns open pattern templates. These are applied to individual sentences at extraction time.

3.1 Constructing a Bootstrapping Set

Our goal is to automatically create a large training set, which encapsulates the multitudes of ways in which information is expressed in text. The key observation is that almost every relation can also be expressed via a REVERB-style verb-based expression. So, bootstrapping sentences based on REVERB's tuples will likely capture all relation expressions.

We start with over 110,000 seed tuples – these are high confidence REVERB extractions from a large Web corpus (ClueWeb)[3] that are asserted at least twice and contain only proper nouns in the arguments. These restrictions reduce ambiguity while still covering a broad range of relations. For example, a seed tuple may be (Paul Annacone; is the coach of; Federer) that REVERB extracts from the sentence "Paul Annacone is the coach of Federer."

For each seed tuple, we retrieve all sentences in a Web corpus that contains all content words in the tuple. We obtain a total of 18 million sentences. For our example, we will retrieve all sentences that contain 'Federer', 'Paul', 'Annacone' and some syntactic variation of 'coach'. We may find sentences like "Now coached by Annacone, Federer is winning more titles than ever."

Our bootstrapping hypothesis assumes that all these sentences express the information of the original seed tuple. This hypothesis is not always true. As an example, for a seed tuple (Boyle; is born in; Ireland) we may retrieve a sentence "Felix G. Wharton was born in Donegal, in the northwest of Ireland, a county where the Boyles did their schooling."

[3]http://lemurproject.org/clueweb09.php/

To reduce bootstrapping errors we enforce additional dependency restrictions on the sentences. We only allow sentences where the content words from arguments and relation can be linked to each other via a linear path of size four in the dependency parse. To implement this restriction, we only use the subset of content words that are headwords in the parse tree. In the above sentence 'Ireland', 'Boyle' and 'born' connect via a dependency path of length six, and hence this sentence is rejected from the training set. This reduces our set to 4 million (seed tuple, sentence) pairs.

In our implementation, we use Malt Dependency Parser (Nivre and Nilsson, 2004) for dependency parsing, since it is fast and hence, easily applicable to a large corpus of sentences. We post-process the parses using Stanford's CCprocessed algorithm, which compacts the parse structure for easier extraction (de Marneffe et al., 2006).

We randomly sampled 100 sentences from our bootstrapping set and found that 90 of them satisfy our bootstrapping hypothesis (64 without dependency constraints). We find this quality to be satisfactory for our needs of learning general patterns.

Bootstrapped data has been previously used to generate positive training data for IE (Hoffmann et al., 2010; Mintz et al., 2009). However, previous systems retrieved sentences that only matched the two arguments, which is error-prone, since multiple relations can hold between a pair of entities (*e.g.*, Bill Gates is the CEO of, a co-founder of, and has a high stake in Microsoft).

Alternatively, researchers have developed sophisticated probabilistic models to alleviate the effect of noisy data (Riedel et al., 2010; Hoffmann et al., 2011). In our case, by enforcing that a sentence additionally contains some syntactic form of the relation content words, our bootstrapping set is naturally much cleaner.

Moreover, this form of bootstrapping is better suited for Open IE's needs, as we will use this data to generalize to other unseen relations. Since the relation words in the sentence and seed match, we can learn general pattern templates that may apply to other relations too. We discuss this process next.

3.2 Open Pattern Learning

OLLIE's next step is to learn general patterns that encode various ways of expressing relations. OL-

Extraction Template	Open Pattern
1. (arg1; be {rel} {prep}; arg2)	{arg1} ↑nsubjpass↑ {rel:postag=VBN} ↓{prep_∗}↓ {arg2}
2. (arg1; {rel}; arg2)	{arg1} ↑nsubj↑ {rel:postag=VBD} ↓dobj↓ {arg2}
3. (arg1; be {rel} by; arg2)	{arg1} ↑nsubjpass↑ {rel:postag=VBN} ↓agent↓ {arg2}
4. (arg1; be {rel} of; arg2)	{rel:postag=NN;**type=Person**} ↑nn↑ {arg1} ↓nn↓ {arg2}
5. (arg1; be {rel} {prep}; arg2)	{arg1} ↑nsubjpass↑ {slot:postag=VBN;**lex** ∈**announce**|**name**|**choose...**} ↓dobj↓ {rel:postag=NN} ↓{prep_∗}↓ {arg2}

Figure 3: Sample open pattern templates. Notice that some patterns (1-3) are purely syntactic, and others are semantic/lexically constrained (in bold font). A dependency parse that matches pattern #1 is shown in Figure 4.

LIE learns *open pattern templates* – a mapping from a dependency path to an open extraction, *i.e.*, one that identifies both the arguments and the exact (REVERB-style) relation phrase. Figure 3 gives examples of high-frequency pattern templates learned by OLLIE. Note that some of the dependency paths are completely unlexicalized (#1-3), whereas in other cases some nodes have lexical or semantic restrictions (#4, 5).

Open pattern templates encode the ways in which a relation (in the first column) may be expressed in a sentence (second column). For example, a relation (Godse; kill; Gandhi) may be expressed with a dependency path (#2) {Godse}↑nsubj↑{kill:postag=VBD}↓dobj↓{Gandhi}.

To learn the pattern templates, we first extract the dependency path connecting the arguments and relation words for each seed tuple and the associated sentence. We annotate the relation node in the path with the exact relation word (as a lexical constraint) and the POS (postag constraint). We create a relation template from the seed tuple by normalizing 'is'/'was'/'will be' to 'be', and replacing the relation content word with {rel}.[4]

If the dependency path has a node that is not part of the seed tuple, we call it a *slot* node. Intuitively, if slot words do not negate the tuple they can be skipped over. As an example, 'hired' is a slot word for the tuple (Annacone; is the coach of; Federer) in the sentence "Federer hired Annacone as a coach". We associate postag and lexical constraints with the slot node as well. (see #5 in Figure 3).

Next, we perform several syntactic checks on each candidate pattern. These checks are the constraints that we found to hold in very general patterns, which we can safely generalize to other unseen relations. The checks are: (1) There are no slot nodes in the path. (2) The relation node is in the middle of arg1 and arg2. (3) The preposition edge (if any) in the pattern matches the preposition in the relation. (4) The path has no *nn* or *amod* edges.

If the checks hold true we accept it as a purely *syntactic pattern* with no lexical constraints. Others are *semantic/lexical patterns* and require further constraints to be reliable as extraction patterns.

3.2.1 Purely Syntactic Patterns

For syntactic patterns, we aggressively generalize to unseen relations and prepositions. We remove all lexical restrictions from the relation nodes. We convert all preposition edges to an abstract {prep_∗} edge. We also replace the specific prepositions in extraction templates with {prep}.

As an example, consider the sentences, "Michael Webb appeared on Oprah..." and "...when Alexander the Great advanced to Babylon." and associated seed tuples (Michael Webb; appear on; Oprah) and (Alexander; advance to; Babylon). Both these data points return the same open pattern after generalization: "{arg1} ↑nsubj↑ {rel:postag=VBD} ↓{prep_∗}↓ {arg2}" with the extraction template (arg1, {rel} {prep}, arg2). Other examples of syntactic pattern templates are #1-3 in Figure 3.

3.2.2 Semantic/Lexical Patterns

Patterns that do not satisfy the checks are not as general as those that do, but are still important. Constructions like "Microsoft co-founder Bill Gates..." work for some relation words (*e.g.*, founder, CEO, director, president, *etc.*) but would not work for other nouns; for instance, from "Chicago Symphony Orchestra" we should not conclude that (Orchestra; is the Symphony of; Chicago).

Similarly, we may conclude (Annacone; is the coach of; Federer) from the sentence "Federer hired Annacone as a coach.", but this depends on the semantics of the slot word, 'hired'. If we replaced

[4]Our current implementation only allows a single relation content word; extending to multiple words is straightforward – the templates will require rel1, rel2,. . .

'hired' by 'fired' or 'considered' then the extraction would be false.

To enable such patterns we retain the lexical constraints on the relation words and slot words.[5] We collect all patterns together based only on the syntactic restrictions and convert the lexical constraint into a list of words with which the pattern was seen. Example #5 in Figure 3 shows one such lexical list.

Can we generalize these lexically-annotated patterns further? Our insight is that we can generalize a list of lexical items to other similar words. For example, if we see a list like {CEO, director, president, founder}, then we should be able to generalize to 'chairman' or 'minister'.

Several ways to compute semantically similar words have been suggested in the literature like Wordnet-based, distributional similarity, *etc.* (*e.g.*, (Resnik, 1996; Dagan et al., 1999; Ritter et al., 2010)). For our proof of concept, we use a simple overlap metric with two important Wordnet classes – Person and Location. We generalize to these types when our list has a high overlap ($> 75\%$) with hyponyms of these classes. If not, we simply retain the original lexical list without generalization. Example #4 in Figure 3 is a type-generalized pattern.

We combine all syntactic and semantic patterns and sort in descending order based on frequency of occurrence in the training set. This imposes a natural ranking on the patterns – more frequent patterns are likely to give higher precision extractions.

3.3 Pattern Matching for Extraction

We now describe how these open patterns are used to extract binary relations from a new sentence. We first match the open patterns with the dependency parse of the sentence and identify the base nodes for arguments and relations. We then expand these to convey all the information relevant to the extraction.

As an example, consider the sentence: "I learned that the 2012 Sasquatch music festival is scheduled for May 25th until May 28th." Figure 4 illustrates the dependency parse. To apply pattern #1 from Figure 3 we first match arg1 to 'festival', rel to 'scheduled' and arg2 to '25th' with prep 'for'. However, (festival, be scheduled for, 25th) is not a very meaningful extraction. We need to expand this further.

[5] For highest precision extractions, we may also need semantic constraints on the arguments. In this work, we increase our yield by ignoring the argument-type constraints.

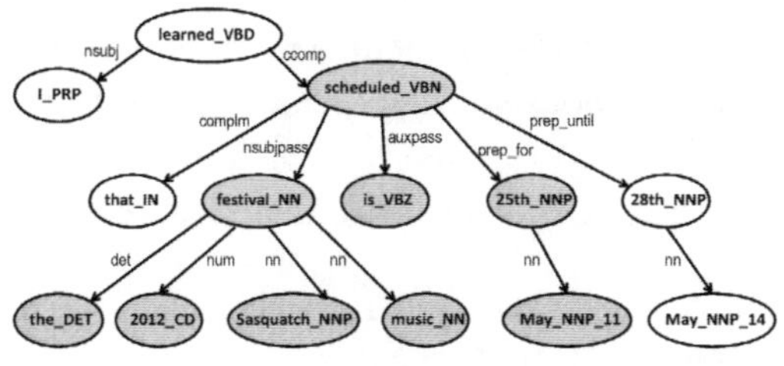

Figure 4: A sample dependency parse. The colored/greyed nodes represent all words that are extracted from the pattern {arg1} ↑nsubjpass↑ {rel:postag=VBN} ↓{prep_∗}↓ {arg2}. The extraction is (the 2012 Sasquatch Music Festival; is scheduled for; May 25th).

For the arguments we expand on *amod, nn, det, neg, prep_of, num, quantmod* edges to build the noun-phrase. When the base noun is not a proper noun, we also expand on *rcmod, infmod, partmod, ref, prepc_of* edges, since these are relative clauses that convey important information. For relation phrases, we expand on *advmod, mod, aux, auxpass, cop, prt* edges. We also include *dobj* and *iobj* in the case that they are not in an argument. After identifying the words in arg/relation we choose their order as in the original sentence. For example, these rules will result in the extraction (the Sasquatch music festival; be scheduled for; May 25th).

3.4 Comparison with WOE^{parse}

OLLIE's algorithm is similar to that of WOE^{parse} – both systems follow the basic structure of bootstrap learning of patterns based on dependency parse paths. However, there are three significant differences. WOE uses Wikipedia-based bootstrapping, finding a sentence in a Wikipedia article that contains the infobox values. Since WOE does not have access to a seed relation phrase, it heuristically assigns all intervening words between the arguments in the parse as the relation phrase. This often results in under-specified or nonsensical relation phrases. For example, from the sentence "David Miscavige learned that after Tom Cruise divorced Mimi Rogers, he was pursuing Nicole Kidman." WOE's heuristics will extract the relation *divorced was pursuing* between 'Tom Cruise' and 'Nicole Kidman'. OLLIE, in contrast, produces well-formed relation phrases by basing its templates on REVERB relation phrases.

Secondly, WOE does not assign semantic/lexical restrictions to its patterns, and thus, has lower precision due to aggressive syntactic generalization. Finally, WOE is designed to have verb-mediated relation phrases that do not include nouns, thus missing important relations such as 'is the president of'. In our experiments (see Figure 5) we find WOE^{parse} to have lower precision and yield than OLLIE.

4 Context Analysis in OLLIE

We now turn to the context analysis component, which handles the problem of extractions that are not asserted as factual in the text. In some cases, OLLIE can handle this by extending the tuple representation with an extra field that turns an otherwise incorrect tuple into a correct one. In other cases, there is no reliable way to salvage the extraction, and OLLIE can avoid an error by giving the tuple a low confidence.

Cases where OLLIE extends the tuple representation include conditional truth and attribution. Consider sentence #4 in Figure 1. It is not asserting that the earth is the center of the universe. OLLIE adds an *AttributedTo* field, which makes the final extraction valid (see OLLIE extraction in Figure 1). This field indicates who said, suggested, believes, hopes, or doubts the information in the main extraction.

Another case is when the extraction is only conditionally true. Sentence #5 in Figure 1 does not assert as factual that (Romney; will be elected; President), so it is an incorrect extraction. However, adding a condition ("if he wins five states") can turn this into a correct extraction. We extend OLLIE to have a *ClausalModifier* field when there is a dependent clause that modifies the main extraction.

Our approach for extracting these additional fields makes use of the dependency parse structure. We find that attributions are marked by a *ccomp* (clausal complement) edge. For example, in the parse of sentence #4 there is a ccomp edge between 'believe' and 'center'. Our algorithm first checks for the presence of a ccomp edge to the relation node. However, not all ccomp edges are attributions. We match the context verb (*e.g.*, 'believe') with a list of communication and cognition verbs from VerbNet (Schuler, 2006) to detect attributions. The context verb and its subject then populate the *AttributedTo* field.

Similarly, the clausal modifiers are marked by *advcl* (adverbial clause) edge. We filter these lexically, and add a ClausalModifier field when the first word of the clause matches a list of 16 terms created using a training set: {if, when, although, because, ...}.

OLLIE has high precision for AttributedTo and ClausalModifier fields, nearly 98% on a development set, however, these two fields do not cover all the cases where an extraction is not asserted as factual. To handle others, we train OLLIE's confidence function to reduce the confidence of an extraction if its context indicates it is likely to be non-factual.

We use a supervised logistic regression classifier for the confidence function. Features include the frequency of the extraction pattern, the presence of AttributedTo or ClausalModifier fields, and the position of certain words in the extraction's context, such as function words or the communication and cognition verbs used for the AttributedTo field. For example, one highly predictive feature tests whether or not the word 'if' comes before the extraction when no ClausalModifier fields are attached. Our training set was 1000 extractions drawn evenly from Wikipedia, News, and Biology sentences.

5 Experiments

Our experiments evaluate three main questions. (1) How does OLLIE's performance compare with existing state-of-the-art open extractors? (2) What are the contributions of the different sub-components within OLLIE? (3) How do OLLIE's extractions compare with semantic role labeling argument identification?

5.1 Comparison of Open IE Systems

Since Open IE is designed to handle a variety of domains, we create a dataset of 300 random sentences from three sources: News, Wikipedia and Biology textbook. The News and Wikipedia test sets are a random subset of Wu and Weld's test set for WOE^{parse}. We ran three systems, OLLIE, REVERB and WOE^{parse} on this dataset resulting in a total of 1,945 extractions from all three systems. Two annotators tagged the extractions as correct if the sentence asserted or implied that the relation was true. Inter-annotator agreement was 0.96, and we retained the subset of extractions on which the two annotators agree for further analysis.

All systems associate a confidence value with an extraction – ranking with these confidence values generates a precision-yield curve for this dataset. Figure 5 reports the curves for the three systems.

We find that OLLIE has a higher performance, owing primarily to its higher yield at comparable preci-

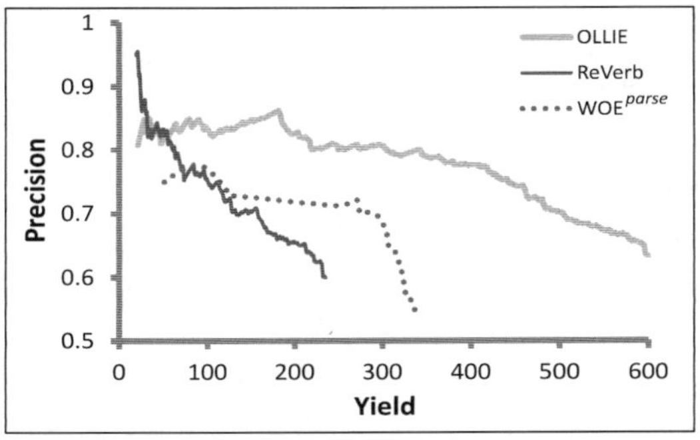

Figure 5: Comparison of different Open IE systems. OLLIE achieves substantially larger area under the curve than other Open IE systems.

sion. OLLIE finds 4.4 times more correct extractions than REVERB and 4.8 times more than WOE^{parse} at a precision of about 0.75. Overall, OLLIE has 2.7 times larger area under the curve than REVERB and 1.9 times larger than WOE^{parse}.[6] We use the Bootstrap test (Cohen, 1995) to find that OLLIE's better performance compared to the two systems is highly statistically significant.

We perform further analysis to understand the reasons behind the high yield from OLLIE. We find that 40% of the OLLIE extractions that REVERB misses are due to OLLIE's use of parsers – REVERB misses those because its shallow syntactic analysis cannot skip over the intervening clauses or prepositional phrases between the relation phrase and the arguments. About 30% of the additional yield is those extractions where the relation is not between its arguments (see instance #1 in Figure 1). The rest are due to other causes such as OLLIE's ability to handle relationships mediated by nouns and adjectives, or REVERB's shallow syntactic analysis, *etc.* In contrast, OLLIE misses very few extractions returned by REVERB, mostly due to parser errors.

We find that WOE^{parse} misses extractions found by OLLIE for a variety of reasons. The primary cause is that WOE^{parse} does not include nouns in relation phrases. It also misses some verb-based patterns, probably due to training noise. In other cases, WOE^{parse} misses extractions due to ill-formed relation phrases (as in the example of Section 3.4: 'divorced was pursuing' instead of the correct relation 'was pursuing').

While the bulk of OLLIE's extractions in our test set were verb-mediated, our intuition suggests that there exist many relationships that are most naturally expressed via noun phrases. To demonstrate this effect, we chose four such relations – *is capital of, is president of, is professor at,* and *is scientist of.* We ran our systems on 100 million random sentences from the ClueWeb corpus. Figure 6 reports the yields of these four relations.[7]

Relation	OLLIE	REVERB	incr.
is capital of	8,566	146	59x
is president of	21,306	1,970	11x
is professor at	8,334	400	21x
is scientist of	730	5	146x

Figure 6: OLLIE finds many more correct extractions for relations that are typically expressed by noun phrases – up to 146 times that of REVERB. WOE^{parse} outputs no instances of these, because it does not allow nouns in the relation. These results are at point of maximum yield (with comparable precisions around 0.66).

OLLIE found up to 146 times as many extractions for these relations than REVERB. Because WOE^{parse} does not include nouns in relation phrases, it is unable to extract any instance of these relations. We examine a sample of the extractions to verify that noun-mediated extractions are the main reason for this large yield boost over REVERB (73% of OLLIE extractions were noun-mediated). High-frequency noun patterns like "Obama, the president of the US", "Obama, the US president", "US President Obama" far outnumber sentences of the form "Obama is the president of the US". These relations are seldom the primary information in a sentence, and are typically mentioned in passing in noun phrases that express the relation.

For some applications, noun-mediated relations are important, as they associate people with work places and job titles. Overall, we think of the results in Figure 6 as a "best case analysis" that illustrates the dramatic increase in yield for certain relations, due to syntactic scope expansion in Open IE.

5.2 Analysis of OLLIE

We perform two control experiments to understand the value of semantic/lexical restrictions in pattern learning and precision boost due to context analysis component.

[6]Evaluating recall is difficult at this scale – however, since yield is proportional to recall, the area differences also hold for the equivalent precision-recall curves.

[7]We multiply the total number of extractions with precision on a sample for that relation to estimate the yield.

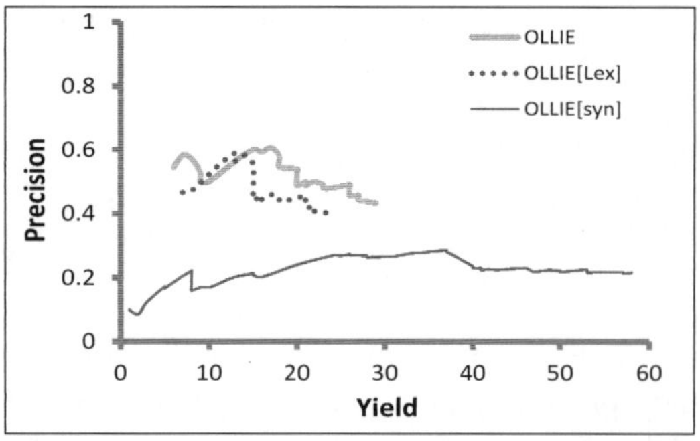

Figure 7: Results on the subset of extractions from patterns with semantic/lexical restrictions. Ablation study on patterns with semantic/lexical restrictions. These patterns without restrictions (OLLIE[syn]) result in low precision. Type generalization improves yield compared to patterns with only lexical constraints (OLLIE[lex]).

Are semantic restrictions important for open pattern learning? How much does type generalization help? To answer these questions we compare three systems – OLLIE without semantic or lexical restrictions (OLLIE[syn]), OLLIE with lexical restrictions but no type generalization (OLLIE[lex]) and the full system (OLLIE). We restrict this experiment to the patterns where OLLIE adds semantic/lexical restrictions, rather than dilute the result with patterns that would be unchanged by these variants.

Figure 7 shows the results of this experiment on our dataset from three domains. As the curves show, OLLIE was correct to add lexical/semantic constraints to these patterns – precision is quite low without the restrictions. This matches our intuition, since these are not completely general patterns and generalizing to all unseen relations results in a large number of errors. OLLIE[lex] performs well though at lower yield. The type generalization helps the yield somewhat, without hurting the precision. We believe that a more data-driven type generalization that uses distributional similarity (*e.g.*, (Ritter et al., 2010)) may help much more. Also, notice that overall precision numbers are lower, since these are the more difficult relations to extract reliably. We conclude that lexical/semantic restrictions are valuable for good performance of OLLIE.

We also compare our full system to a version that does not use the context analysis of Section 4. Figure 8 compares OLLIE to a version (OLLIE[pat]) that does not add the AttributedTo and ClausalModifier fields, and, instead of context-sensitive confidence function, uses the pattern frequency in the training set as a ranking function. 10% of the sentences have an OLLIE extraction with ClausalModifier and 6% have AttributedTo fields. Adding ClausalModifier corrects errors for 21% of extractions that have a ClausalModifier and does not introduce any new errors. Adding AttributedTo corrects errors for 55% of the extractions with AttributedTo and introduces an error for 3% of the extractions. Overall, we find that OLLIE gives a significant boost to precision over OLLIE[pat] and obtains 19% additional AUC.

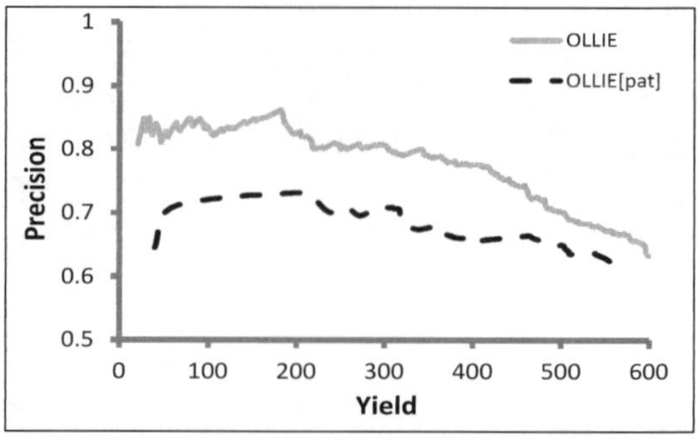

Figure 8: Context analysis increases precision, raising the area under the curve by 19%.

Finally, we analyze the errors made by OLLIE. Unsurprisingly, because of OLLIE's heavy reliance on the parsers, parser errors account for a large part of OLLIE's errors (32%). 18% of the errors are due to aggressive generalization of a pattern to all unseen relations and 12% due to incorrect application of lexically annotated patterns. About 14% of the errors are due to important context missed by OLLIE. Another 12% of the errors are because of the limitations of binary representation, which misses important information that can only be expressed in n-ary tuples.

We believe that as parsers become more robust OLLIE's performance will improve even further. The presence of context-related errors suggests that there is more to investigate in context analysis. Finally, in the future we wish to extend the representation to include n-ary extractions.

5.3 Comparison with SRL

Our final evaluation suggests answers to two important questions. First, how does a state-of-the-art Open IE system do in terms of absolute recall? Second, how do Open IE systems compare against state-of-the-art SRL systems?

SRL, as discussed in Section 2, has a very different goal – analyzing verbs and nouns to identify their arguments, then mapping the verb or noun to a semantic frame and determining the role that each argument plays in that frame. These verbs and nouns need not make the full relation phrase, although, recent work has shown that they may be converted to Open IE style extractions with additional post-processing (Christensen et al., 2011).

While a direct comparison between OLLIE and a full SRL system is problematic, we can compare performance of OLLIE and the argument identification step of an SRL system. We set each system the following task – "based on a sentence, find all noun-pairs that have an asserted relationship." This task is permissive for both systems, as it does not require finding an exact relation phrase or argument boundary, or determining the argument roles in a relation.

We create a gold standard by tagging a random 50 sentences of our test set to identify all pairs of NPs that have an asserted relation. We only counted relation expressed by a verb or noun in the text, and did not include relations expressed simply with "of" or apostrophe-s. Where a verb mediates between an argument and multiple NPs, we represent this as a binary relation for all pairs of NPs.

For example the sentence, "Macromolecules translocated through the phloem include proteins and various types of RNA that enter the sieve tubes through plasmodesmata." has five binary relations.

arg1:	arg2:	relation term
Macromolecules	phloem	translocated
Macromolecules	proteins	include
Macromolecules	types of RNA	include
types of RNA	sieve tubes	enter
types of RNA	plasmodesmata	enter

We find an average of 4.0 verb-mediated relations and 0.3 noun-mediated relations per sentence. Evaluating OLLIE against this gold standard helps to answer the question of absolute recall: what percentage of binary relations expressed in a sentence can our systems identify.

For comparison, we use a state-of-the-art SRL system from Lund University (Johansson and Nugues, 2008), which is trained on PropBank (Martha and Palmer, 2002) for its verb-frames and NomBank (Meyers et al., 2004) for noun-frames. The PropBank version of the system won the very competitive 2008 CONLL SRL evaluation.

We conduct this experiment by manually comparing the outputs of LUND and OLLIE against the gold standard. For each pair of NPs in the gold standard we determine whether the systems find a relation with that pair of NPs as arguments. Recall is based on the percentage of NP pairs where the head nouns matches head nouns of two different arguments in an extraction or semantic frame. If the argument value is conjunctive, we count a match against the head noun of each item in the list. We also count cases where system output would match the gold standard, given perfect co-reference.

	LUND	OLLIE	union
Verb relations	0.58 (0.69)	0.49 (0.55)	0.71 (0.83)
Noun relations	0.07 (0.33)	0.13 (0.13)	0.20 (0.33)
All relations	0.54 (0.67)	0.47 (0.52)	0.67 (0.80)

Figure 9: Recall of LUND and OLLIE on binary relations. In parentheses is recall with oracle co-reference. Both systems identify approximately half of all argument pairs, but have lower recall on noun-mediated relations.

Figure 9 shows the recall for OLLIE and LUND, with recall based on oracle co-referential matches in parentheses. Our analysis shows strong recall for both systems for verb-mediated relations: LUND finding about two thirds of the argument pairs and OLLIE finding over half. Both systems have low recall for noun-mediated relations, with most of LUND's recall requiring co-reference. We observe that a union of the two systems raises recall to 0.71 for verb-mediated relations and 0.83 with co-reference, demonstrating that each system is identifying argument pairs that the other missed.

It is not surprising that OLLIE has recall of approximately 0.5, since it is tuned for high precision extraction, and avoids less reliable extractions from constructions such as reduced relative clauses and gerunds, or from noun-mediated relations with long-range dependencies. In contrast, SRL is tuned to identify the argument structure for nearly all verbs and nouns in a sentence. The missing recall from SRL is primarily where it does not identify both arguments of a binary relation, or where the correct argument is buried in a long argument phrase, but is not its head noun.

It is surprising that LUND, trained on NomBank, identifies so few noun-mediated argument pairs without co-reference. An example will make this clear. For the sentence, "Clarcor, a maker of packaging and filtration products, said ...", the target relation is between Clarcor and the products it makes. LUND identifies a frame *maker.01* in which argument A0 has head noun 'maker' and A1 is a PP headed by 'products', missing the actual name of the maker without co-reference post-processing. OLLIE finds the extraction (Clarcor; be a maker of; packaging and filtration products) where the heads of both arguments matched those of the target. In another example, LUND identifies "his" and "brother" as the arguments of the frame *brother.01*, rather than the actual names of the two brothers.

We can draw several conclusions from this experiment. First, nouns, although less frequently mediating relations, are much harder and both systems are failing significantly on those – OLLIE is somewhat better. Two, neither systems dominates the other; in fact, recall is increased significantly by a union of the two. Three, and probably most importantly, significant information is still being missed by both systems, and more research is warranted.

6 Related Work

There is a long history of bootstrapping and pattern learning approaches in traditional information extraction, *e.g.*, DIPRE (Brin, 1998), SnowBall (Agichtein and Gravano, 2000), Espresso (Pantel and Pennacchiotti, 2006), PORE (Wang et al., 2007), SOFIE (Suchanek et al., 2009), NELL (Carlson et al., 2010), and PROSPERA (Nakashole et al., 2011). All these approaches first bootstrap data based on seed instances of a relation (or seed data from existing resources such as Wikipedia) and then learn lexical or lexico-POS patterns to create an extractor. Other approaches have extended these to learning patterns based on full syntactic analysis of a sentence (Bunescu and Mooney, 2005; Suchanek et al., 2006; Zhao and Grishman, 2005).

OLLIE has significant differences from the previous work in pattern learning. First, and most importantly, these previous systems learn an extractor for each relation of interest, whereas OLLIE is an open extractor. OLLIE's strength is its ability to generalize from one relation to many other relations that are expressed in similar forms. This happens both via syntactic generalization and type generalization of relation words (sections 3.2.1 and 3.2.2). This capability is essential as many relations in the test set are not even seen in the training set – in early experiments we found that non-generalized pattern learning (equivalent to traditional IE) had significantly less yield at a slightly higher precision.

Secondly, previous systems begin with seeds that consist of a pair of entities, whereas we also include the content words from REVERB relations in our training seeds. This results in a much higher precision bootstrapping set and high rule precision while still allowing morphological variants that cover noun-mediated relations. A third difference is in the scale of the training – REVERB yields millions of training seeds, where previous systems had orders of magnitude less. This enables OLLIE to learn patterns with greater coverage.

The closest to our work is the pattern learning based open extractor WOE^{parse}. Section 3.4 details the differences between the two extractors. Another extractor, StatSnowBall (Zhu et al., 2009), has an Open IE version, which learns general but shallow patterns. Preemptive IE (Shinyama and Sekine, 2006) is a paradigm related to Open IE that first groups documents based on pairwise vector clustering, then applies additional clustering to group entities based on document clusters. The clustering steps make it difficult for it to scale to large corpora.

7 Conclusions

Our work describes OLLIE, a novel Open IE extractor that makes two significant advances over the existing Open IE systems. First, it expands the syntactic scope of Open IE systems by identifying relationships mediated by nouns and adjectives. Our experiments found that for some relations this increases the number of correct extractions by two orders of magnitude. Second, by analyzing the context around an extraction, OLLIE is able to identify cases where the relation is not asserted as factual, but is hypothetical or conditionally true. OLLIE increases precision by reducing confidence in those extractions or by associating additional context in the extractions, in the form of attribution and clausal modifiers. Overall, OLLIE obtains 1.9 to 2.7 times more area under precision-yield curves compared to existing state-of-the-art open extractors. OLLIE is available for download at http://openie.cs.washington.edu.

Acknowledgments

This research was supported in part by NSF grant IIS-0803481, ONR grant N00014-08-1-0431, DARPA contract FA8750-09-C-0179 and the Intelligence Advanced Research Projects Activity (IARPA) via Air Force Research Laboratory (AFRL) contract number FA8650-10-C-7058. The U.S. Government is authorized to reproduce and distribute reprints for Governmental purposes notwithstanding any copyright annotation thereon. The views and conclusions contained herein are those of the authors and should not be interpreted as necessarily representing the official policies or endorsements, either expressed or implied, of IARPA, AFRL, or the U.S. Government. This research is carried out at the University of Washington's Turing Center.

We thank Fei Wu and Dan Weld for providing WOE's code and Anthony Fader for releasing REVERB's code. Peter Clark, Alan Ritter, and Luke Zettlemoyer provided valuable feedback on the research and Dipanjan Das helped us with state-of-the-art SRL systems. We also thank the anonymous reviewers for their comments on an earlier draft.

References

E. Agichtein and L. Gravano. 2000. Snowball: Extracting relations from large plain-text collections. In *Procs. of the Fifth ACM International Conference on Digital Libraries*.

ARPA. 1991. *Proc. 3rd Message Understanding Conf.* Morgan Kaufmann.

ARPA. 1998. *Proc. 7th Message Understanding Conf.* Morgan Kaufmann.

M. Banko, M. Cafarella, S. Soderland, M. Broadhead, and O. Etzioni. 2007. Open information extraction from the Web. In *Procs. of IJCAI*.

S. Brin. 1998. Extracting Patterns and Relations from the World Wide Web. In *WebDB Workshop at 6th International Conference on Extending Database Technology, EDBT'98*, pages 172–183, Valencia, Spain.

Razvan C. Bunescu and Raymond J. Mooney. 2005. A shortest path dependency kernel for relation extraction. In *Proc. of HLT/EMNLP*.

Andrew Carlson, Justin Betteridge, Bryan Kisiel, Burr Settles, Estevam R. Hruschka Jr., and Tom M. Mitchell. 2010. Toward an architecture for never-ending language learning. In *Procs. of AAAI*.

Janara Christensen, Mausam, Stephen Soderland, and Oren Etzioni. 2011. An analysis of open information extraction based on semantic role labeling. In *Proceedings of the 6th International Conference on Knowledge Capture (K-CAP '11)*.

Paul R. Cohen. 1995. *Empirical Methods for Artificial Intelligence*. MIT Press.

Ido Dagan, Lillian Lee, and Fernando C. N. Pereira. 1999. Similarity-based models of word cooccurrence probabilities. *Machine Learning*, 34(1-3):43–69.

Marie-Catherine de Marneffe, Bill MacCartney, and Christopher D. Manning. 2006. Generating typed dependency parses from phrase structure parses. In *Language Resources and Evaluation (LREC 2006)*.

Oren Etzioni, Anthony Fader, Janara Christensen, Stephen Soderland, and Mausam. 2011. Open information extraction: the second generation. In *Proceedings of the International Joint Conference on Artificial Intelligence (IJCAI '11)*.

Anthony Fader, Stephen Soderland, and Oren Etzioni. 2011. Identifying relations for open information extraction. In *Proceedings of EMNLP*.

Raphael Hoffmann, Congle Zhang, and Daniel S. Weld. 2010. Learning 5000 relational extractors. In *Proceedings of the 48th Annual Meeting of the Association for Computational Linguistics*, ACL '10, pages 286–295.

Raphael Hoffmann, Congle Zhang, Xiao Ling, Luke S. Zettlemoyer, and Daniel S. Weld. 2011. Knowledge-based weak supervision for information extraction of overlapping relations. In *ACL*, pages 541–550.

Richard Johansson and Pierre Nugues. 2008. The effect of syntactic representation on semantic role labeling. In *Proceedings of the 22nd International Conference on Computational Linguistics (COLING 08)*, pages 393–400.

Paul Kingsbury Martha and Martha Palmer. 2002. From treebank to propbank. In *Proceedings of the Third International Conference on Language Resources and Evaluation (LREC 02)*.

A. Meyers, R. Reeves, C. Macleod, R. Szekely, V. Zielinska, B. Young, and R. Grishman. 2004. Annotating Noun Argument Structure for NomBank. In *Proceedings of LREC-2004*, Lisbon, Portugal.

Mike Mintz, Steven Bills, Rion Snow, and Dan Jurafsky. 2009. Distant supervision for relation extraction without labeled data. In *ACL-IJCNLP '09: Proceedings of the Joint Conference of the 47th Annual Meeting of the ACL and the 4th International Joint Conference on Natural Language Processing of the AFNLP: Volume 2*, pages 1003–1011.

Ndapandula Nakashole, Martin Theobald, and Gerhard Weikum. 2011. Scalable knowledge harvesting with high precision and high recall. In *Proceedings of the Fourth International Conference on Web Search and Web Data Mining (WSDM 2011)*, pages 227–236.

Joakim Nivre and Jens Nilsson. 2004. Memory-based dependency parsing. In *Proceedings of the Conference on Natural Language Learning (CoNLL-04)*, pages 49–56.

Patrick Pantel and Marco Pennacchiotti. 2006. Espresso: Leveraging generic patterns for automatically harvesting semantic relations. In *Proceedings of 21st International Conference on Computational Linguistics and*

44th Annual Meeting of the Association for Computational Linguistics (ACL'06).

P. Resnik. 1996. Selectional constraints: an information-theoretic model and its computational realization. *Cognition.*

Sebastian Riedel, Limin Yao, and Andrew McCallum. 2010. Modeling relations and their mentions without labeled text. In *ECML/PKDD (3)*, pages 148–163.

Alan Ritter, Mausam, and Oren Etzioni. 2010. A latent dirichlet allocation method for selectional preferences. In *Proceedings of the 48th Annual Meeting of the Association for Computational Linguistics (ACL '10).*

Karin Kipper Schuler. 2006. *VerbNet: A Broad-Coverage, Comprehensive Verb Lexicon.* Ph.D. thesis, University of Pennsylvania.

Y. Shinyama and S. Sekine. 2006. Preemptive information extraction using unrestricted relation discovery. In *Procs. of HLT/NAACL.*

Fabian M. Suchanek, Georgiana Ifrim, and Gerhard Weikum. 2006. Combining linguistic and statistical analysis to extract relations from web documents. In *Procs. of KDD*, pages 712–717.

Fabian M. Suchanek, Mauro Sozio, and Gerhard Weikum. 2009. Sofie: a self-organizing framework for information extraction. In *Proceedings of WWW*, pages 631–640.

Gang Wang, Yong Yu, and Haiping Zhu. 2007. Pore: Positive-only relation extraction from wikipedia text. In *Proceedings of 6th International Semantic Web Conference and 2nd Asian Semantic Web Conference (ISWC/ASWC'07)*, pages 580–594.

Fei Wu and Daniel S. Weld. 2010. Open information extraction using Wikipedia. In *Proceedings of the 48th Annual Meeting of the Association for Computational Linguistics (ACL '10).*

Shubin Zhao and Ralph Grishman. 2005. Extracting relations with integrated information using kernel methods. In *Procs. of ACL.*

Jun Zhu, Zaiqing Nie, Xiaojiang Liu, Bo Zhang, and Ji-Rong Wen. 2009. StatSnowball: a statistical approach to extracting entity relationships. In *WWW '09: Proceedings of the 18th international conference on World Wide Web*, pages 101–110, New York, NY, USA. ACM.

Modelling Sequential Text with an Adaptive Topic Model

Lan Du*
Department of Computing
Macquarie University
Sydney, Australia
lan.du@mq.edu.au

Wray Buntine*
Canberra Research Lab
National ICT Australia
Canberra, Australia
wray.buntine@nicta.com.au

Huidong Jin*
CSIRO Mathematics, Informatics
and Statistics,
Canberra, Australia
warren.jin@csiro.au

Abstract

Topic models are increasingly being used for text analysis tasks, often times replacing earlier semantic techniques such as latent semantic analysis. In this paper, we develop a novel adaptive topic model with the ability to adapt topics from both the previous segment and the parent document. For this proposed model, a Gibbs sampler is developed for doing posterior inference. Experimental results show that with topic adaptation, our model significantly improves over existing approaches in terms of perplexity, and is able to uncover clear sequential structure on, for example, Herman Melville's book "Moby Dick".

1 Introduction

Natural language text usually consists of topically structured and coherent components, such as groups of sentences that form paragraphs and groups of paragraphs that form sections. Topical coherence in documents facilitates readers' comprehension, and reflects the author's intended structure. Capturing this structural topical dependency should lead to improved topic modelling. It also seems reasonable to propose that text analysis tasks that involve the structure of a document, for instance, summarisation and segmentation, should also be improved by topic models that better model that structure.

Recently, topic models are increasingly being used for text analysis tasks such as summarisation (Arora and Ravindran, 2008) and segmentation (Misra et al., 2011; Eisenstein and Barzilay, 2008), often times replacing earlier semantic techniques such as latent semantic analysis (Deerwester et al., 1990). Topic models can be improved by better modelling the semantic aspects of text, for instance integrating collocations into the model (Johnson, 2010; Hardisty et al., 2010) or encouraging topics to be more semantically coherent (Newman et al., 2011) based on lexical coherence models (Newman et al., 2010), modelling the structural aspects of documents, for instance modelling a document as a set of segments (Du et al., 2010; Wang et al., 2011; Chen et al., 2009), or improving the underlying statistical methods (Teh et al., 2006; Wallach et al., 2009). Topic models, like statistical parsing methods, are using more sophisticated latent variable methods in order to model different aspects of these problems.

In this paper, we are interested in developing a new topic model which can take into account the structural topic dependency by following the higher level document subject structure, but we hope to retain the general flavour of topic models, where components (*e.g.*, sentences) can be a mixture of topics. Thus we need to depart from the earlier HMM style models, see, *e.g.*, (Blei and Moreno, 2001; Gruber et al., 2007). Inspired by the idea that documents usually exhibits internal structure (*e.g.*, (Wang et al., 2011)), in which semantically related units are clustered together to form semantically structural segments, we treat documents as sequences of segments (*e.g.*, sentences, paragraphs, sections, or chapters). In this way, we can model the topic correlation be-

*This work was partially done when Du was at College of Engineering & Computer Science, the Australian National University when working together with Buntine and Jin there.

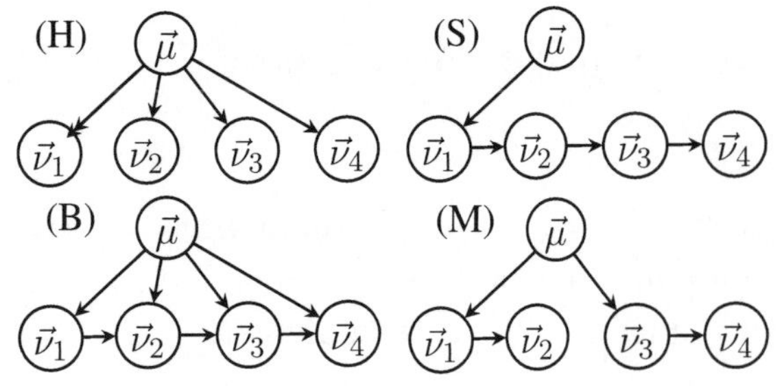

Figure 1: Different structural relationships for topics of sections in a 4-part document, hierarchical (H), sequential (S), both (B) or mixed (M).

tween the segments in a "bag of segments" fashion, *i.e.*, beyond the "bag of words" assumption, and reveal how topics evolve among segments.

Indeed, we were impressed by the improvement in perplexity obtained by the *segmented topic model* (STM) (Du et al., 2010), so we considered the problem of whether one can add sequence information into a structured topic model as well. Figure 1 illustrates the type of structural information being considered, where the vectors are some representation of the content. STM is represented by the hierarchical model. A strictly sequential model would seem unrealistic for some documents, for instance books. A topic model using the strictly sequential model was developed (Du et al., 2012) but it reportedly performs halfway between STM and LDA. In this paper, we develop an adaptive topic model to go beyond a strictly sequential model while allow some hierarchical influence. There are two possible hybrids, one called "mixed" has distinct breaks in the sequence, while the other called "both" overlays both sequence and hierarchy and there could be relative strengths associated with the arrows. We employ the "both" hybrid but use the relative strengths to adaptively allow it to approximate the "mixed" hybrid.

Research in Machine Learning and Natural Language Processing has attempted to model various topical dependencies. Some work considers structure within the sentence level by mixing hidden Markov models (HMMs) and topics on a word by word basis: the aspect HMM (Blei and Moreno, 2001) and the HMM-LDA model (Griffiths et al., 2005) that models both short-range syntactic dependencies and longer semantic dependencies. These models operate at a finer level than we are considering at a segment (like paragraph or section) level. To make a tool like the HMM work at higher levels, one needs to make stronger assumptions, for instance assigning each sentence a single topic and then topic specific word models can be used: the hidden topic Markov model (Gruber et al., 2007) that models the transitional topic structure; a global model based on the generalised Mallows model (Chen et al., 2009), and a HMM based content model (Barzilay and Lee, 2004). Researchers have also considered time-series of topics: various kinds of dynamic topic models, following early work of (Blei and Lafferty, 2006), represent a collection as a sequence of sub-collections in epochs. Here, one is modelling the collections over broad epochs, not the structure of a single document that our model considers.

This paper is organised as follows. We first present background theory in Section 2. Then the new model is presented in Section 3, followed by Gibbs sampling theory and algorithm in Sections 4 and 5 respectively. Experiments are reported in Section 6 with a conclusion in Section 7.

2 Background

The basic topic model is first presented in Section 2.1, as a point of departure. In seeking to develop a general sequential topic model, we hope to go beyond a strictly sequential model and allow some hierarchical influence. This, however, presents two challenges: modelling and statistical inference. Hierarchical inference (and thus sequential inference) over probability vectors can be handled using the theory of hierarchical Poisson-Dirichlet processes (PDPs). This is presented in Section 2.2.

2.1 The LDA model

The benchmark model for topic modelling is latent Dirichlet allocation (LDA) (Blei et al., 2003), a latent variable model of documents. Documents are indexed by i, and words $\vec{w}$ are observed data. The latent variables are $\vec{\mu}_i$ (*the topic distribution* for a document) and $\vec{z}$ (the *topic assignments* for observed words), and the model parameter of $\vec{\phi}_k$'s (*word distributions*). These notation are later extended in Table 1. The generative model is as follows:

$$\begin{aligned} \vec{\phi}_k &\sim \text{Dirichlet}_W(\vec{\gamma}) && \forall\, k \\ \vec{\mu}_i &\sim \text{Dirichlet}_K(\vec{\alpha}) && \forall\, i \\ z_{i,l} &\sim \text{Discrete}_K(\vec{\mu}_i) && \forall\, i,l \\ w_{i,l} &\sim \text{Discrete}_K\left(\vec{\phi}_{z_{i,l}}\right) && \forall\, i,l\,. \end{aligned}$$

$\text{Dirichlet}_K(\cdot)$ is a K-dimensional Dirichlet distribution. The hyper-parameter $\vec{\gamma}$ is a Dirichlet prior on *word distributions* (*i.e.*, a Dirichlet smoothing on the multinomial parameter $\vec{\phi}_k$ (Blei et al., 2003)) and the Dirichlet prior $\vec{\alpha}$ on topic distributions.

2.2 Hierarchical PDPs

A discrete probability vector $\vec{\mu}$ of finite dimension K is sampled from some distribution $F_\tau(\vec{\mu}_0)$ with a parameter set, say τ, and is also dependent on a parent probability vector $\vec{\mu}_0$ also of finite dimension K. Then a sample of size N is taken according to the probability vector $\vec{\mu}$, represented as $\vec{z} \in \{1,...,K\}^N$. This data is collected into counts $\vec{n} = (n_1,...,n_K)$ where n_k is the number of data in $\vec{z}$ with value k and $\sum_k n_k = N$. This situation is represented as follows:

$$\vec{\mu} \sim F_\tau(\vec{\mu}_0); \quad \vec{z}_i \sim \text{Discrete}_K(\vec{\mu}) \text{ for } i = 1,...,N\,.$$

Commonly in topic modelling, the Dirichlet distribution is used for discrete probability vectors. In this case $F_\tau(\vec{\mu}_0) \equiv \text{Dirichlet}_K(b\vec{\mu}_0)$, $\tau \equiv (K,b)$ where b is the concentration parameter. Bayesian analysis yields a marginalised likelihood, after integrating out $\vec{\mu}$, of

$$p\left(\vec{z}\,\middle|\,\tau,\vec{\mu}_0,\text{Dirichlet}\right) = \frac{\text{Beta}\left(\vec{n}+b\vec{\mu}_0\right)}{\text{Beta}\left(b\vec{\mu}_0\right)}\,, \quad (1)$$

where $\text{Beta}(\cdot)$ is the vector valued function normalising the Dirichlet distribution. A problem here is that $p(\vec{z}|b,\vec{\mu}_0)$ is an intractable function of $\vec{\mu}_0$.

Dirichlet processes and Poisson-Dirichlet processes alleviate this problem by using an auxiliary variable trick (Robert and Casella, 2004). That is, we introduce an *auxiliary variable* over which we also sample but do not need to record. The auxiliary variable is the *table count*[1] which is a t_k for each n_k and it represents the number of "tables" over which the n_k "customers" are spread out. Thus the following constraints hold:

$$0 \le t_k \le n_k \quad \text{and} \quad t_k = 0 \text{ iff } n_k = 0\,. \quad (2)$$

When the distribution over probability vectors follows a Poisson-Dirichlet process which has two parameters $\tau \equiv (a,b)$ and the parent distribution $\vec{\mu}_0$, then $F_\tau(\vec{\mu}_0) \equiv \text{PDP}(a,b,\vec{\mu}_0)$. Here a is the *discount parameter*, b the *concentration parameter* and $\vec{\mu}_0$ the base measure. In this case Bayesian analysis yields an augmented marginalised likelihood (Buntine and Hutter, 2012), after integrating out $\vec{\mu}$, of

$$p\left(\vec{z},\vec{t}\,\middle|\,\tau,\vec{\mu}_0,\text{PDP}\right) = \frac{(b|a)_T}{(b)_N}\prod_k S^{n_k}_{t_k,a}\left(\mu_{0,k}\right)^{t_k} \quad (3)$$

where $T = \sum_k t_k$, $(x|y)_N = \prod_{n=0}^{N-1}(x+ny)$ denotes the Pochhammer symbol, $(x)_N = (x|1)_N$, and $S^N_{M,a}$ is a generalized Stirling number that is readily tabulated (Buntine and Hutter, 2012).

There are two fundamental things to notice about Equation (3). Positively, the term in $\vec{\mu}_0$ takes the form of a multinomial likelihood, so we can propagate it up and perform inference on $\vec{\mu}_0$ unencumbered by the functional mess of Equation (1). Thus Poisson-Dirichlet processes allow one to do Bayesian reasoning on hierarchies of probability vectors (Teh, 2006; Teh et al., 2006). Negatively, however, one needs to sample the auxiliary variables $\vec{t}$ leading to some problems: The range of t_k, $\{0,...,n_k\}$, is broad. Also, contributions from individual data z_i have been lost so the mixing of the MCMC can sometimes be slow. We confirmed these problems on our first implementation of the Adaptive Topic Model presented next in Section 3.

A further improvement on PDP sampling is achieved in (Chen et al., 2011), where another auxiliary variable is introduced, a so-called *table indicator*, that for each datum z_i indicates whether it is the "head of its table" (recall the n_k data are spread over t_k tables, each table has one and only one "head"). Let $r_i = 1$ if z_i is the "head of its table," and zero otherwise. According to this "table" logic, the number of tables for n_k must be the number of data z_i that are also head of table, so $t_k = \sum_{i=1}^N 1_{z_i=k}1_{r_i=1}$. Moreover, given this definition, the first constraint of Equation (2) on t_k is

[1] Based on the Chinese Restaurant analogy (Teh et al., 2006), each table has a dish, a data value, while data, the customer, is assigned to tables, and multiple tables can serve the same dish.

automatically satisfied. Finally, with t_k tables then there must be exactly t_k heads of table, and we are indifferent about which data are heads of table, thus

$$p\left(\vec{z}, \vec{r} \middle| \tau, \vec{\mu}_0, \text{PDP}\right) = p\left(\vec{z}, \vec{t} \middle| \tau, \vec{\mu}_0, \text{PDP}\right) \prod_k \binom{n_k}{t_k}^{-1}. \tag{4}$$

When using this marginalised likelihood in a Gibbs sampler, the z_i themselves are usually latent so also sampled, and we develop a blocked Gibbs sampler for (z_i, r_i). Since $\vec{r}$ only appears indirectly through the table counts $\vec{t}$, one does not need to store the $\vec{r}$, instead just resamples an r_i when needed according to the proportion t_w/n_w where $z_i = w$.

3 The proposed Adaptive Topic Model

In this section an adaptive topic model (AdaTM) is developed, a fully structured topic model, by using a PDP to simultaneously model the hierarchical and the sequential topic structures. Documents are assumed to be broken into a sequence of segments. Topic distributions are used to mimic the subjects of documents and subtopics of their segments. The notations and terminologies used in the following sections are given in Table 1.

In AdaTM, the two topic structures are captured by drawing topic distributions from the PDPs with two base distributions as follows. The document topic distribution $\vec{\mu}_i$ and the jth segment topic distribution $\vec{\nu}_{i,j}$ are linearly combined to give a base distribution for the $(j+1)^{th}$ segment's topic distribution $\vec{\nu}_{i,j+1}$. The topic distribution of the first segment, *i.e.*, $\vec{\nu}_{i,1}$, is drawn directly with the base distribution $\vec{\mu}_i$. Call this generative process *topic adaptation*. The graphical representation of AdaTM is shown in Figure 2, and clearly shows the combination of sequence and hierarchy for the topic probabilities. Note the linear combination at each node $\vec{\nu}_{i,j}$ is weighted with latent proportions $\rho_{i,j}$.

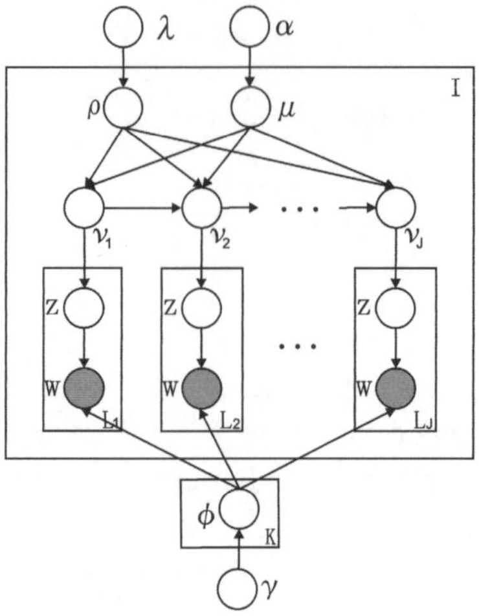

Figure 2: The adaptive topic model: $\vec{\mu}$ is the document topic distribution, $\vec{\nu}_1, \vec{\nu}_2, \ldots, \vec{\nu}_J$ are the segment topic distributions, and $\vec{\rho}$ is a set of the mixture weights.

Table 1: List of notation for AdaTM

K	number of topics
I	number of documents
J_i	number of segments in document i
$L_{i,j}$	number of words in document i, segment j
W	number of words in dictionary
$\vec{\mu}_i$	document topic probabilities for document i
$\vec{\alpha}$	K-dimensional prior for each $\vec{\mu}_i$
$\vec{\nu}_{i,j}$	segment topic probabilities for document i and segment j
$\rho_{i,j}$	mixture weight associating with the link between $\vec{\nu}_{i.j}$ and $\vec{\nu}_{i,j-1}$
$\vec{\Phi}$	word probability vectors as a $K \times W$ matrix
$\vec{\phi}_k$	word probability vector for topic k, entries in Φ
$\vec{\gamma}$	W-dimensional prior for each $\vec{\phi}_k$
$w_{i,j,l}$	word in document i, segment j, position l
$z_{i,j,l}$	topic for word $w_{i,j,l}$

The resultant model for AdaTM is:

$$\begin{aligned}
\vec{\phi}_k &\sim \text{Dirichlet}_W(\vec{\gamma}) && \forall\, k \\
\vec{\mu}_i &\sim \text{Dirichlet}_K(\vec{\alpha}) && \forall\, i \\
\rho_{i,j} &\sim \text{Beta}(\lambda_S, \lambda_T) && \forall\, i,j \\
\vec{\nu}_{i,j} &\sim \text{PDP}\left(\rho_{i,j}\vec{\nu}_{i,j-1} + (1-\rho_{i,j})\vec{\mu}_i, a, b\right) && \\
z_{i,j,l} &\sim \text{Discrete}_K(\vec{\nu}_{i,j}) && \forall\, i,j,l \\
w_{i,j,l} &\sim \text{Discrete}_K\left(\vec{\phi}_{z_{i,j,l}}\right) && \forall\, i,j,l\,.
\end{aligned}$$

For notational convenience, let $\vec{\nu}_{i,0} = \vec{\mu}_i$. Assume the dimensionality of the Dirichlet distribution (*i.e.*, the number of topics) is known and fixed, and word probabilities are parameterised with a $K \times W$ matrix $\vec{\Phi} = (\vec{\phi}_1, ..., \vec{\phi}_K)$.

4 Gibbs Sampling Formulation

Given observations and model parameters, computing the posterior distribution of latent variables is infeasible for AdaTM due to the intractable computa-

Table 2: List of statistics for AdaTM

$M_{i,k,w}$	the total number of words in document i with dictionary index w and being assigned to topic k
$M_{k,w}$	total $M_{i,k,w}$ for document i, *i.e.*, $\sum_i M_{i,k,w}$
$\vec{M}_k$	vector of W values $M_{k,w}$
$n_{i,j,k}$	topic count in document i segment j for topic k
$N_{i,j}$	topic total in document i segment j, *i.e.*, $\sum_{k=1}^{K} n_{i,j,k}$
$t_{i,j,k}$	table count in the CPR for document i and paragraph j, for topic k that is inherited back to paragraph $j-1$ and $\vec{\mu}_{i,j-1}$.
$s_{i,j,k}$	table count in the CPR for document i and paragraph j, for topic k that is inherited back to the document and $\vec{\mu}_i$.
$T_{i,j}$	total table count in the CRP for document i and segment j, equal to $\sum_{k=1}^{K} t_{i,j,k}$.
$S_{i,j}$	total table count in the CRP for document i and segment j, equal to $\sum_{k=1}^{K} s_{i,j,k}$.
$\vec{t}_{i,j}$	table count vector of $t_{i,j,k}$'s for segment j.
$\vec{s}_{i,j}$	table count vector of $s_{i,j,k}$'s for segment j.

tion of marginal probabilities. Therefore, we have to use approximate inference techniques. This section proposes a blocked Gibbs sampling algorithm based on methods from Chen et al. (2011). Table 2 lists all statistics needed in the algorithm. Note for easier understanding, terminologies of the Chinese Restaurant Process (Teh et al., 2006) will be used, *i.e.*, customers, dishes and restaurants, correspond to words, topics and segments respectively.

The first major complication, over the use of the hierarchical PDP and Equation (3) and the table indicator trick of Equation (4), is handling the linear combination of $\rho_{i,j}\vec{\nu}_{i,j-1} + (1-\rho_{i,j})\vec{\mu}_i$ used in the PDPs. We manage this as follows: First, Equation (3) shows that a contribution of the form $(\mu_{0,k})^{t_k}$ results. In our case, this becomes

$$\prod_k \left(\rho_{i,j}\nu_{i,j-1,k} + (1-\rho_{i,j})\mu_{i,k}\right)^{t'_{i,j,k}}$$

where $t'_{i,j,k}$ is the corresponding introduced auxiliary variable the table count which is involved with constraints on $n_{i,j,k}+t_{i,j+1,k}$, from Equation (2). To deal with this power of a sum, we break the counts $t'_{i,j,k}$ into two parts, those that contribute to $\vec{\nu}_{i,j-1}$ and those that contribute to $\vec{\mu}_i$. We call these parts $t_{i,j,k}$ and $s_{i,j,k}$ respectively. The product can then be expanded and $\rho_{i,j}$ integrated out. This yields:

$$\text{Beta}\left(S_{i,j}+\lambda_S, T_{i,j}+\lambda_T\right)\prod_k \nu_{i,j-1,k}^{t_{i,j,k}}\mu_{i,k}^{s_{i,j,k}} .$$

The powers $\nu_{i,j-1,k}^{t_{i,j,k}}$ and $\mu_{i,k}^{s_{i,j,k}}$ can then be pushed up to the next nodes in the PDP/Dirichlet hierarchy. Note the standard constraints and table indicators are also needed here.

The precise form of the table indicators needs to be considered as well since there is a hierarchy for them, and this is the second major complication in the model. As discussed in Chen et al. (2011), table indicators are not required to be recorded, instead, randomly sampled in Gibbs cycles. The table indicators when known can be used to reconstruct the table counts $t_{i,j,k}$ and $s_{i,j,k}$, and are reconstructed by sampling from them. For now, denote the table indicators as $u_{i,j,l}$ for word $w_{i,j,l}$.

To complete a formulation suitable for Gibbs sampling, we first compute the marginal distribution of the observations $\vec{w}_{1:I,1:J}$ (words), the topic assignments $\vec{z}_{1:I,1:J}$ and the table indicators $\vec{u}_{1:I,1:J}$. The Dirichlet integral is used to integrate out the document topic distributions $\vec{\mu}_{1:I}$ and the topic-by-words matrix $\vec{\Phi}$, and the joint posterior distribution computed for a PDP is used to recursively marginalise out the segment topic distributions $\vec{\nu}_{1:I,1:J}$. With these variables marginalised out, we derive the following marginal distribution

$$\begin{aligned}
&p(\vec{z}_{1:I,1:J}, \vec{w}_{1:I,1:J}, \vec{u}_{1:I,1:J} \,|\, \vec{\alpha}, \vec{\gamma}, a, b) = \qquad (5)\\
&\prod_{i=1}^{I} \frac{\text{Beta}_K\left(\vec{\alpha}+\sum_{j=1}^{J_i}\vec{s}_{i,j}\right)}{\text{Beta}_K\left(\vec{\alpha}\right)} \prod_{k=1}^{K} \frac{\text{Beta}_W\left(\vec{\gamma}+\vec{M}_k\right)}{\text{Beta}_W\left(\vec{\gamma}\right)}\\
&\prod_{i=1}^{I}\prod_{j=1}^{J_i} \text{Beta}\left(S_{i,j}+\lambda_S, T_{i,j}+\lambda_T\right) \frac{(b|a)_{T_{i,j}+S_{i,j}}}{(b)_{N_{i,j}+T_{i,j+1}}}\\
&\prod_{i=1}^{I}\prod_{j=1}^{J_i}\prod_{k=1}^{K} \binom{n_{i,j,k}+t_{i,j+1,k}}{t_{i,j,k}+s_{i,j,k}}^{-1} S^{n_{i,j,k}+t_{i,j+1,k}}_{t_{i,j,k}+s_{i,j,k},a} .
\end{aligned}$$

And the following constraints apply:

$$t_{i,j,k}+s_{i,j,k} \le n_{i,j,k}+t_{i,j+1,k}, \qquad (6)$$
$$t_{i,j,k}+s_{i,j,k} = 0 \text{ iff } n_{i,j,k}+t_{i,j+1,k} = 0 . \qquad (7)$$

The first constraint falls out naturally when table indicators are used. For convenience of the formulas, set $t_{i,J_i+1,k} = 0$ (there is no $J_i + 1$ segment) and $t_{i,1,k} = 0$ (the first segment only uses $\vec{\mu}_i$).

Now let us consider again the table indicators $u_{i,j,l}$ for word $w_{i,j,l}$. If this word is in topic k at document i and segment j, then it contributes a count to $n_{i,j,k}$. It also indicates if it contributes a new table, or a count to $t'_{i,j,k}$ for the PDP at this node. However, as we discussed above, this then contributes to either $t_{i,j,k}$ or $s_{i,j,k}$. If it contributes to $t_{i,j,k}$, then it recurses up to contribute a data count to the PDP for document i segment $j-1$. Thus it also needs a table indicator at that node. Consequently, the table indicator $u_{i,j,l}$ for word $w_{i,j,l}$ must specify whether it contributes a table to all PDP nodes reachable by it in the graph.

We define $u_{i,j,l}$ specifically as $u_{i,j,l} = (u_1, u_2)$ such that $u_1 \in [-1, 0, 1]$ and $u_2 \in [1, \cdots, j]$, where u_2 indicates segment denoted by node ν_j up to which $w_{i,j,l}$ contributes a table. Given u_2, $u_1 = -1$ denotes $w_{i,j,l}$ contributes a table count to $s_{i,u_2,k}$ and $t_{i,j',k}$ for $u_2 < j' \leq j$; $u_1 = 0$ denotes $w_{i,j,l}$ does not contribute a table to node u_2, but contributes a table count to $t_{i,j',k}$ for $u_2 < j' \leq j$; and $u_1 = 1$ denotes $w_{i,j,l}$ contributes a table count to each $t_{i,j',k}$ for $u_2 \leq j' \leq j$.

Now, we are ready to compute the conditional probabilities for jointly sampling topics and table indicators from the model posterior of Equation (5).

5 Gibbs Sampling Algorithm

The Gibbs sampler iterates over words, doing a blocked sample of $(z_{i,j,l}, u_{i,j,l})$. The first task is to reconstruct $u_{i,j,l}$ since it is not stored. Since the posterior of Equation (5) does not explicitly mention the $u_{i,j,l}$'s, they occur indirectly through the table counts, and we can randomly reconstruct them by sampling them uniformly from the space of possibilities. Following this, we then remove the values $(z_{i,j,l}, u_{i,j,l})$ from the full set of statistics. Finally, we block sample new values for $(z_{i,j,l}, u_{i,j,l})$ and add them to the statistics. The new $u_{i,j,l}$ is subsequently forgotten and the $z_{i,j,l}$ recorded.

Reconstructing table indicator $u_{i,j,l}$: We start at the node indexed i, j. If $s_{i,j,k}+t_{i,j,k} = 1$ and $n_{i,j,k}+t_{i,j+1,k} > 1$ then no tables can be removed since there is only one table but several customers at the table. Thus $u_{i,j,l} = (u_1, u_2) = (0, j)$ and there is no sampling. Otherwise, by symmetry arguments, we sample u_1 via

$$p(u_1 = -1, 0, 1 | u_2 = j, z_{i,j,l} = k) \propto \left(s_{i,j,k}, t_{i,j,k}, n_{i,j,k} + t_{i,j+1,k} - s_{i,j,k} - t_{i,j,k}\right),$$

since there are $n_{i,j,k}+t_{i,j+1,k}$ data distributed across the three possibilities. If after sampling $u_1 = -1$, the data contributes a table count up to $\vec{\mu}_i$ and so $u_{i,j,l} = (u_1, u_2) = (-1, j)$. If $u_1 = 0$, the $u_{i,j,l} = (u_1, u_2) = (0, j)$. Otherwise, the data contributes a table count up to the parent PDP for $\vec{\nu}_{i,j-1}$ and we recurse, repeating the sampling process at the parent node. Note, however, that the table indicator $(0, j')$ for $j' < j$ is equivalent to the table indicator $(1, j'+1)$ as far as statistics is concerned.

Block sampling $(z_{i,j,l}, u_{i,j,l})$: The full set of possibilities are, for each possible topic $z_{i,j,l} = k$:

- no tables are created, so $u_{i,j,l} = (0, j)$,
- tables are created contributing a table count all the way up to node j' $(\leq j)$ but stop at j' and do not subsequently contribute a count to $\vec{\mu}_i$, so $u_{i,j,l} = (1, j')$,
- tables are created contributing a table count all the way up to node $j' \leq j$ but stop at j' and also subsequently contribute a count to $\vec{\mu}_i$, so $u_{i,j,l} = (-1, j')$.

These three possibilities lead to detailed but fairly straight forward changes to the posterior of Equation (5). Thus a full blocked sampler for $(z_{i,j,l}, u_{i,j,l})$ can be constructed.

Estimates: learnt values of $\vec{\mu}_i$, $\vec{\nu}_{i,j}$, $\vec{\phi}_k$ are needed for evaluation, perplexity calculations, *etc.* These are estimated by taking averages after the Gibbs sampler has burnt in, using the standard posterior means for Dirichlets and Poisson-Dirichlets.

6 Experiments

In the experimental work, we have three objectives: (1) to explore the setting of hyper-parameters, (2) to compare the model with the earlier sequential LDA (SeqLDA) of (Du et al., 2012), STM of (Du et al., 2010) and standard LDA, and (3) to view the results in detail on a number of characteristic problems.

Table 3: Datasets

	#docs	#segs	#words	vocab
Pat-A	500	51,748	2,146,464	16,573
Pat-B	397	9,123	417,631	7,663
Pat-G06	500	11,938	655,694	6,844
Pat-H	500	11,662	562,439	10,114
Pat-F	140	3,181	166,091	4,674
Prince-C	1	26	10,588	3,292
Prince-P	1	192	10.588	3,292
Moby Dick	1	135	88,802	16,223

6.1 Datasets

For general testing, five patent datasets are randomly selected from U.S. patents granted in 2009 and 2010. Patents in Pat-A are selected from international patent class (IPC) "A", which is about "HUMAN NECESSITIES"; those in Pat-B are selected from class "B60" about "VEHICLES IN GENERAL"; those in Pat-H are selected from class "H" about "ELECTRICITY"; those in Pat-F are selected from class "F" about "MECHANICAL ENGINEERING; LIGHTING; HEATING; WEAPONS; BLASTING"; and those in Pat-G are selected from class "G06" about "COMPUTING; CALCULATING; COUNTING". All the patents in these five datasets are split into paragraphs that are taken as segments, and the sequence of paragraphs in each patent is reserved in order to maintain the original layout. All the stop words, the top 10 common words, the uncommon words (i.e., words in less than five patents) and numbers have been removed.

Two books used for more detailed investigation are "The Prince" by Niccolò Machiavelli and "Moby Dick" by Herman Melville. They are split into chapters and/or paragraphs which are treated as segments, and only stop-words are removed. Table 3 shows in detail the statistics of these datasets after preprocessing.

6.2 Design

Perplexity, a standard measure of dictionary-based compressibility, is used for comparison. When reporting test perplexities, the held-out perplexity measure (Rosen-Zvi et al., 2004) is used to evaluate the generalisation capability to the unseen data. This is known to be unbiased. To compute the held-out perplexity, 20% of patents in each data set was randomly held out from training to be used for testing. For this, 1000 Gibbs cycles were done for burn-in followed by 500 cycles with a lag for 100 for parameter estimation.

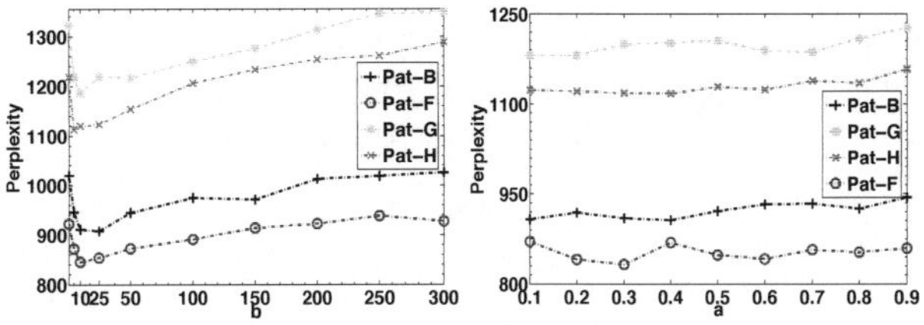

(a) fix $a = 0$ (b) fix $b = 10$

Figure 3: Analysis of parameters of Poisson-Dirichlet process. (a) shows how perplexity changes with b; (b) shows how it changes with a.

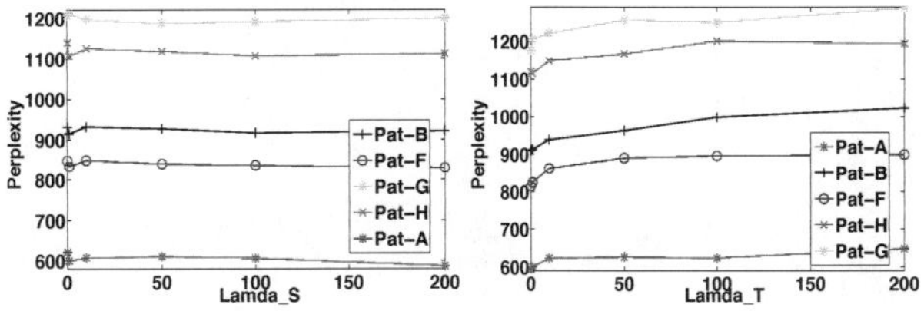

(a) fix $\lambda_T = 1$ (b) fix $\lambda_S = 1$

Figure 4: Analysis of the two parameters for Beta distribution. (a) how perplexity changes with λ_S; (b) how it changes with λ_T.

We implemented all the four models, *e.g.*, LDA, STM, SeqTM and AdaTM in C, and ran them on a desktop with Intel Core i5 CPU (2.8GHz×4), even though our code is not multi-threaded. Perplexity calculations, data input and handling, *etc.*, were the same for all algorithms. We note that the current AdaTM implementation is an order of magnitude slower than regular LDA per major Gibbs cycle.

6.3 Hyper-parameters in AdaTM

Experiments on the impact of the hyper-parameters on the patent data sets were as follows: First, fixing $K = 50$, the Beta parameters $\lambda_T = 1$ and $\lambda_S = 1$, optimise symmetric α, and do two variations *fix-a:* $a = 0.0$, trying $b = 1, 5, 10, 25, ..., 300$, and *fix-b:* $b = 10$, trying $a = 0.1, 0.2, ..., 0.9$. Second, *fix-*λ_T *(fix-*λ_S*)*: fix $a = 0.2$ and $\lambda_T(\lambda_S) = 1$, optimise b and α, change $\lambda_S(\lambda_T) = 0.1, 1, 10, 50, 100, 200$. Figures 3 and 4 show the corresponding plots. Figure 3(b) and Figure 4(a) show that varying the values of a and λ_S does not significantly change the

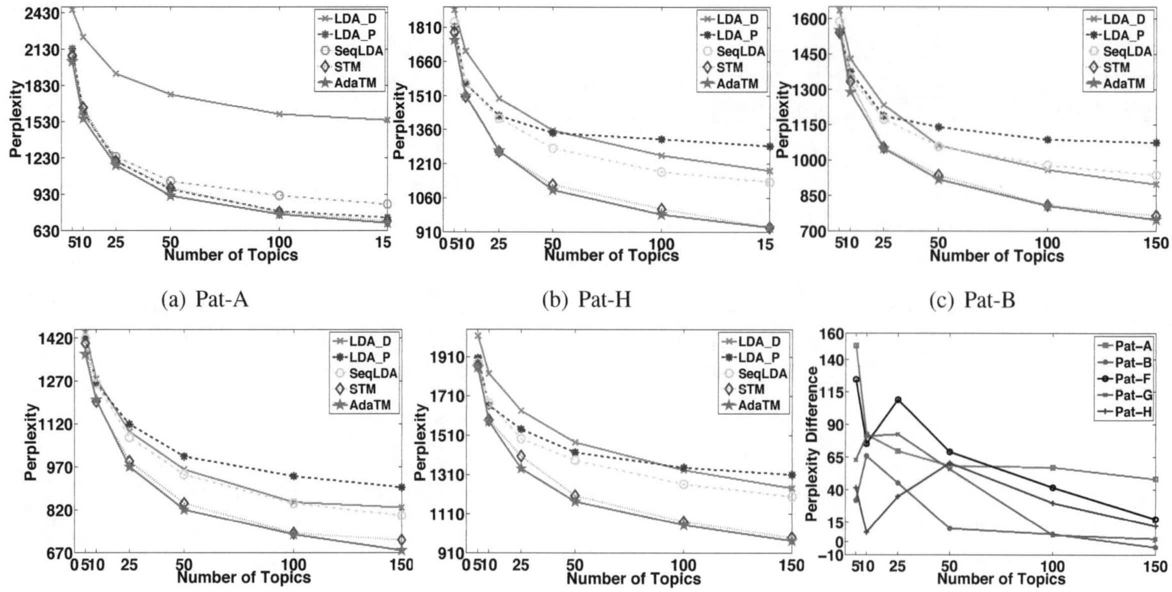

(a) Pat-A (b) Pat-H (c) Pat-B

(d) Pat-F (e) Pat-G (f) Shuffle

Figure 5: Perplexity comparisons.

perplexity. In contrast, Figure 3(a) shows different b values significantly change perplexity. Therefore, we sought to optimise b. The experiment of fixing $\lambda_S = 1$ and changing λ_T shows a small λ_T is preferred.

6.4 Perplexity Comparison

Perplexity comparisons were done with the default settings $a = 0.2$, $\alpha = 0.1$, $\gamma = 0.01$, $\lambda_S = 1$, $\lambda_T = 1$ and b optimised automatically using the scheme from (Du et al., 2012). Figure 5 shows the results on these five patent datasets for different numbers of topics. LDA_D is LDA run on whole patents, and LDA_P is LDA run on the paragraphs within patents. Table 4 gives the p-values of a one-tail paired t-test for AdaTM versus the others, where lower p-value indicates AdaTM has statistically significant lower perplexity. From this we can see that AdaTM is statistically significantly better than SeqLDA and LDA, and somewhat better than STM.

In addition, we ran another set of experiments by randomly shuffling the order of paragraphs in each patent several times before running AdaTM. Then, we calculate the difference between perplexities with and without random shuffle. Figure 5(f) shows the plot of differences in each data sets. The positive difference means randomly shuffling the order of paragraphs indeed increases the perplexity. It can further prove that there does exist sequential topic structure in patents, which confirms the finding in (Du et al., 2012).

6.5 Topic Evolution Comparisons

All the comparison experiments reported in this section are run with 20 topics, the upper limit for easy visualisation, and without optimising any parameters. The Dirichlet Priors are fixed as $\alpha_k = 0.1$ and $\gamma_w = 0.01$. For AdaTM, SeqLDA, and STM, $a = 0.0$ and $b = 100$ for "The Prince" and $b = 200$ for "Moby Dick". These settings have proven robust in experiments. To align the topics so visualisations match, the sequential models are initialised using an LDA model built at the chapter level. Moreover, all the models are run at both the chapter and the paragraph level. With the common initialisation, both paragraph level and chapter level models can

Table 4: P-values for one-tail paired t-test on the five patent datasets.

	AdaTM				
	Pat-G	Pat-A	Pat-F	Pat-H	Pat-B
LDA_D	.0001	.0001	.0002	.0001	.0001
LDA_P	.0041	.0030	.0022	.0071	.0096
SeqLDA	.0029	.0047	.0003	.0012	.0023
STM	.0220	.0066	.0210	.0629	.0853

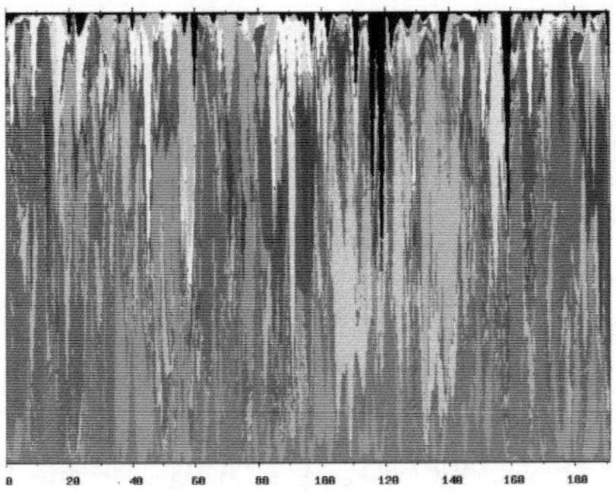

(a) Evolution of paragraph topics for LDA

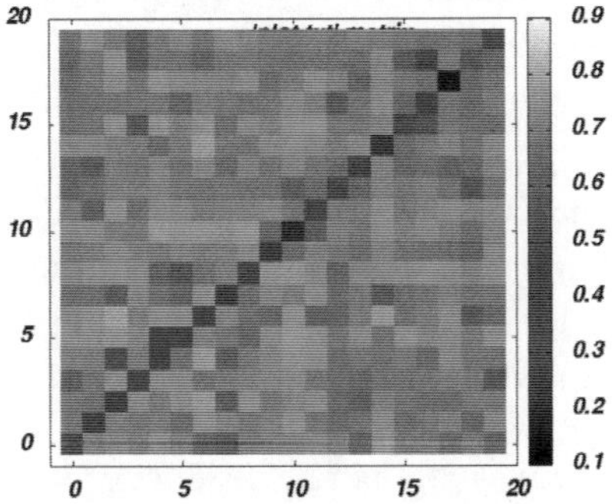

(b) Topic alignment of LDA versus AdaTM topics for chapters

Figure 6: Analysis on "The Prince".

be aligned.

To visualise topic evolution, we use a plot with one colour per topic displayed over the sequence. Figure 6(a) shows this for LDA run on paragraphs of "The Prince". The proportion of 20 topics is the Y-axis, spread across the unit interval. The paragraphs run along the X-axis, so the topic evolution is clearly displayed. One can see there is no sequential structure in this derived by the LDA model, and similar plots result from "Moby Dick" for LDA. Figure 6(b) shows the alignment of topics between the initialising model (LDA+chapters) and AdaTM run on chapters. Each point in the matrix gives the Hellinger distance between the corresponding topics, color coded. The plots for the other models, chapters or paragraphs, are similar so plots like Figure 6(a) for the other models can be meaningfully compared.

Figure 7 then shows the corresponding evolution plots for AdaTM and SeqLDA on chapters and paragraphs. The contrast of these with LDA is stark. The large improvement in perplexity for AdaTM (see Section 6.4) along with no change in lexical coherence (see Section 6.2) means that the sequential information is actually beneficial statistically. Note that SeqLDA, while exhibiting slightly stronger sequential structure than AdaTM in these

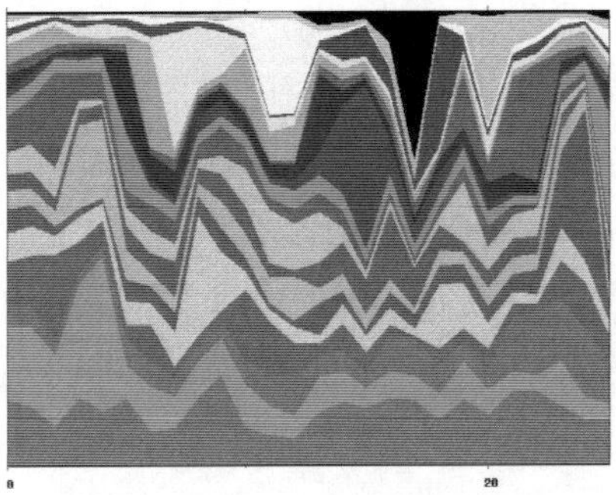

(a) AdaTM on chapters

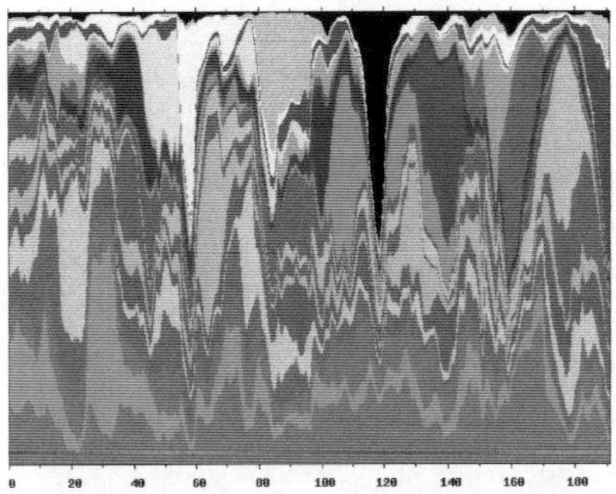

(b) AdaTM on paragraphs

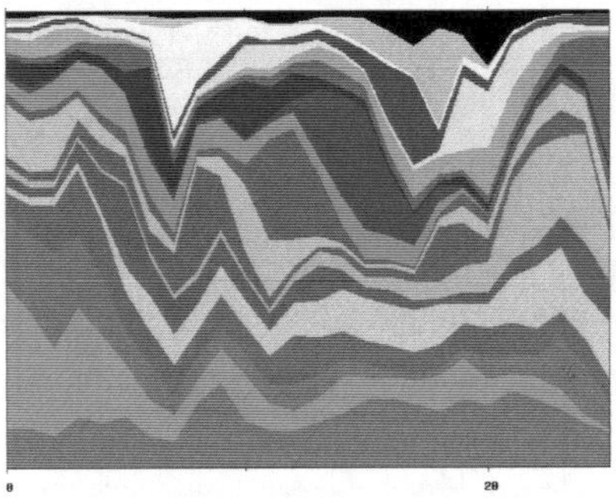

(c) SeqLDA on chapters

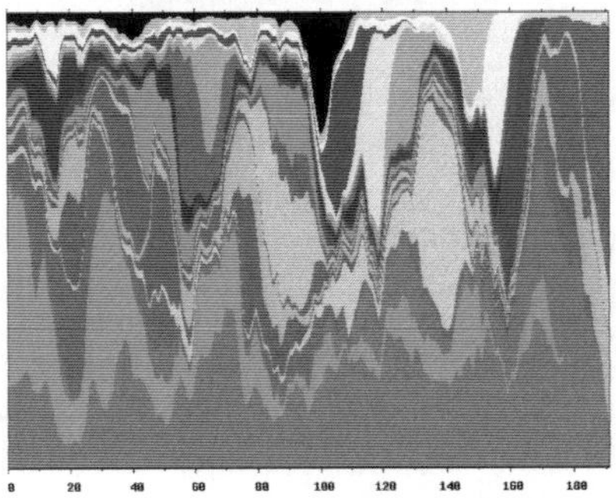

(d) SeqLDA on paragraphs

Figure 7: Topic Evolution on "The Prince".

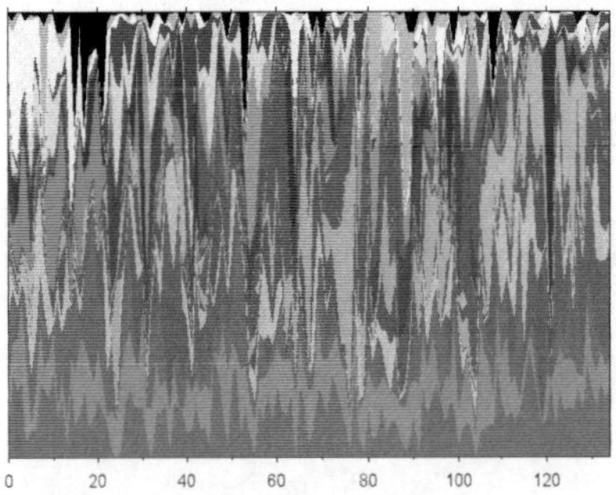

(a) LDA on chapters

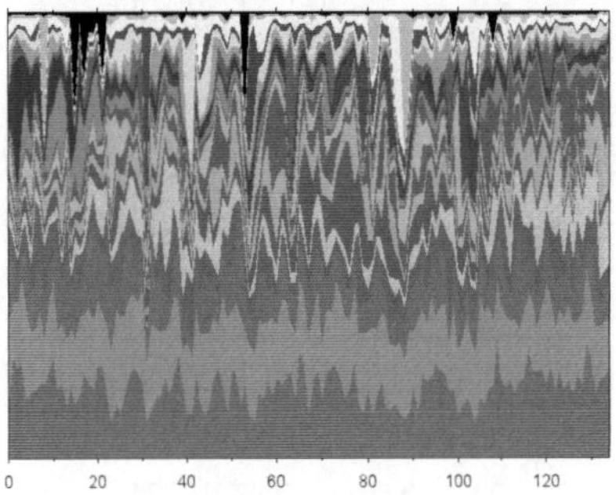

(b) STM on Chapters

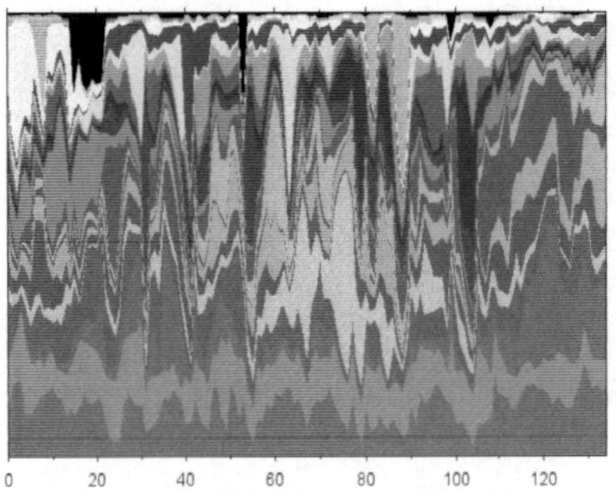

(c) AdaTM on Chapters

Figure 8: Topic Evolution on "Moby Dick".

figures has significantly worse test perplexity, so its sequential affect is too strong and harming results. Also, note that some topics have different time sequence profiles between AdaTM and SeqLDA. Indeed, inspection of the top words for each show these topics differ somewhat. So while the LDA to AdaTM/SeqLDA topic correspondences are quite good due to the use of LDA initialisation, the correspondences between AdaTM and SeqLDA have degraded. We see that AdaTM has nearly as good sequential characteristics as SeqLDA. Furthermore, segment topic distribution $\nu_{i,j}$ of SeqLDA are gradually deviating from the document topic distribution μ_i, which is not the case for AdaTM.

Results for "Moby Dick" on chapters are comparable. Figure 8 shows similar topic evolution plots for LDA, STM and AdaTM. In contrast, the AdaTM topic evolutions are much clearer for the less frequent topics, as shown in Figure 8(c). Various parts of this are readily interpreted from the storyline. Here we briefly discuss topics by their colour: *black:* Captain Peleg and the business of signing on; *yellow:* inns, housing, bed; *mauve:* Queequeg; *azure:* (around chapters 60-80) details of whales *aqua:* (peaks at 8, 82, 88) pulpit, schools and mythology of whaling.

We see that AdaTM can be used to understand the topics with regards to the sequential structure of a book. In contrast, the sequential nature for LDA and STM is lost in the noise. It can be very interesting to apply the proposed topic models to some text analysis tasks, such as topic segmentation, summarisation, and semantic title evaluation, which are subject to our future work.

7 Conclusion

A model for adaptive sequential topic modelling has been developed to improve over a simple exchangeable segments model STM (Du et al., 2010) and a naive sequential model SeqLDA (Du et al., 2012) in terms of perplexity and its confirmed ability to uncover sequential structure in the topics. One could extract meaningful topics from a book like Herman Melville's "Moby Dick" and concurrently gain their sequential profile. The current Gibbs sampler is slower than regular LDA, so future work is to speed up the algorithm.

Acknowledgments

The authors would like to thank all the anonymous reviewers for their valuable comments. Lan Du was supported under the Australian Research Council's Discovery Projects funding scheme (project numbers DP110102506 and DP110102593). Dr. Huidong Jin was partly supported by CSIRO Mathematics, Informatics and Statistics for this work. NICTA is funded by the Australian Government as represented by the Department of Broadband, Communications and the Digital Economy and the Australian Research Council through the ICT Center of Excellence program.

References

R. Arora and B. Ravindran. 2008. Latent Dirichlet allocation and singular value decomposition based multi-document summarization. In *ICDM '08: Proc. of 2008 Eighth IEEE Inter. Conf. on Data Mining*, pages 713–718.

R. Barzilay and L. Lee. 2004. Catching the drift: Probabilistic content models, with applications to generation and summarization. In *HLT-NAACL 2004: Main Proceedings*, pages 113–120. Association for Computational Linguistics.

D.M. Blei and J.D. Lafferty. 2006. Dynamic topic models. In *ICML '06: Proc. of 23rd international conference on Machine learning*, pages 113–120.

D.M. Blei and P.J. Moreno. 2001. Topic segmentation with an aspect hidden Markov model. In *Proc. of 24th annual international ACM SIGIR conference on Research and development in information retrieval*, pages 343–348.

D.M. Blei, A.Y. Ng, and M.I. Jordan. 2003. Latent Dirichlet allocation. *Journal of Machine Learning Research*, 3:993–1022.

W. Buntine and M. Hutter. 2012. A Bayesian view of the Poisson-Dirichlet process. Technical Report arXiv:1007.0296v2, *ArXiv*, Cornell, February.

H. Chen, S.R.K. Branavan, R. Barzilay, and D.R. Karger. 2009. Global models of document structure using latent permutations. In *Proceedings of Human Language Technologies: The 2009 Annual Conf. of the North American Chapter of the Association for Computational Linguistics*, pages 371–379, Stroudsburg, PA, USA. Association for Computational Linguistics.

C. Chen, L. Du, and W. Buntine. 2011. Sampling for the Poisson-Dirichlet process. In *European Conf. on Machine Learning and Principles and Practice of Knowledge Discovery in Database*, pages 296–311.

S.C. Deerwester, S.T. Dumais, T.K. Landauer, G.W. Furnas, and R.A. Harshman. 1990. Indexing by latent semantic analysis. *Journal of the American Society of Information Science*, 41(6):391–407.

L. Du, W. Buntine, and H. Jin. 2010. A segmented topic model based on the two-parameter Poisson-Dirichlet process. *Machine Learning*, 81:5–19.

L. Du, W. Buntine, H. Jin, and C. Chen. 2012. Sequential latent dirichlet allocation. *Knowledge and Information Systems*, 31(3):475–503.

J. Eisenstein and R. Barzilay. 2008. Bayesian unsupervised topic segmentation. In *Proc. of Conf. on Empirical Methods in Natural Language Processing*, pages 334–343. Association for Computational Linguistics.

T.L. Griffiths, M. Steyvers, D.M. Blei, and J.B. Tenenbaum. 2005. Integrating topics and syntax. In *Advances in Neural Information Processing Systems 17*, pages 537–544.

A. Gruber, Y. Weiss, and M. Rosen-Zvi. 2007. Hidden topic markov models. *Journal of Machine Learning Research - Proceedings Track*, 2:163–170.

E.A. Hardisty, J. Boyd-Graber, and P. Resnik. 2010. Modeling perspective using adaptor grammars. In *Proc. of the 2010 Conf. on Empirical Methods in Natural Language Processing*, pages 284–292, Stroudsburg, PA, USA. Association for Computational Linguistics.

M. Johnson. 2010. PCFGs, topic models, adaptor grammars and learning topical collocations and the structure of proper names. In *Proc. of 48th Annual Meeting of the ACL*, pages 1148–1157, Uppsala, Sweden, July. Association for Computational Linguistics.

H. Misra, F. Yvon, O. Capp, and J. Jose. 2011. Text segmentation: A topic modeling perspective. *Information Processing & Management*, 47(4):528–544.

D. Newman, J.H. Lau, K. Grieser, and T. Baldwin. 2010. Automatic evaluation of topic coherence. In *North American Chapter of the Association for Computational Linguistics - Human Language Technologies*, pages 100–108.

D. Newman, E.V. Bonilla, and W. Buntine. 2011. Improving topic coherence with regularized topic models. In J. Shawe-Taylor, R.S. Zemel, P. Bartlett, F.C.N. Pereira, and K.Q. Weinberger, editors, *Advances in Neural Information Processing Systems 24*, pages 496–504.

C.P. Robert and G. Casella. 2004. *Monte Carlo statistical methods*. Springer. second edition.

M. Rosen-Zvi, T. Griffiths, M. Steyvers, and P. Smyth. 2004. The author-topic model for authors and documents. In *Proc. of 20th conference on Uncertainty in Artificial Intelligence*, pages 487–494.

Y. W. Teh, M. I. Jordan, M. J. Beal, and D. M. Blei. 2006. Hierarchical Dirichlet processes. *Journal of the American Statistical Association*, 101:1566–1581.

Y. W. Teh. 2006. A hierarchical Bayesian language model based on Pitman-Yor processes. In *Proc. of 21st Inter. Conf. on Computational Linguistics and the 44th annual meeting of the Association for Computational Linguistics*, pages 985–992.

H. Wallach, D. Mimno, and A. McCallum. 2009. Rethinking LDA: Why priors matter. In *Advances in Neural Information Processing Systems 19*.

H. Wang, D. Zhang, and C. Zhai. 2011. Structural topic model for latent topical structure analysis. In *Proc. of 49th Annual Meeting of the Association for Computational Linguistics: Human Language Technologies - Volume 1*, pages 1526–1535, Stroudsburg, PA, USA. Association for Computational Linguistics.

A Comparison of Vector-based Representations for Semantic Composition

William Blacoe and **Mirella Lapata**
Institute for Language, Cognition and Computation
School of Informatics, University of Edinburgh
10 Crichton Street, Edinburgh EH8 9AB
w.b.blacoe@sms.ed.ac.uk, mlap@inf.ed.ac.uk

Abstract

In this paper we address the problem of modeling compositional meaning for phrases and sentences using distributional methods. We experiment with several possible combinations of representation and composition, exhibiting varying degrees of sophistication. Some are shallow while others operate over syntactic structure, rely on parameter learning, or require access to very large corpora. We find that shallow approaches are as good as more computationally intensive alternatives with regards to two particular tests: (1) phrase similarity and (2) paraphrase detection. The sizes of the involved training corpora and the generated vectors are not as important as the fit between the meaning representation and compositional method.

1 Introduction

Distributional models of semantics have seen considerable success at simulating a wide range of behavioral data in tasks involving semantic cognition and also in practical applications. For example, they have been used to model judgments of semantic similarity (McDonald, 2000) and association (Denhire and Lemaire, 2004; Griffiths et al., 2007) and have been shown to achieve human level performance on synonymy tests (Landauer and Dumais, 1997; Griffiths et al., 2007) such as those included in the Test of English as a Foreign Language (TOEFL). This ability has been put to practical use in numerous natural language processing tasks such as automatic thesaurus extraction (Grefenstette, 1994), word sense discrimination (Schütze, 1998), language modeling (Bellegarda, 2000), and the identification of analogical relations (Turney, 2006).

While much research has been directed at the most effective ways of constructing representations for individual words, there has been far less consensus regarding the representation of larger constructions such as phrases and sentences. The problem has received some attention in the connectionist literature, particularly in response to criticisms of the ability of connectionist representations to handle complex structures (Smolensky, 1990; Plate, 1995). More recently, several proposals have been put forward for computing the meaning of word combinations in vector spaces. This renewed interest is partly due to the popularity of distributional methods and their application potential to tasks that require an understanding of larger phrases or complete sentences.

For example, Mitchell and Lapata (2010) introduce a general framework for studying vector *composition*, which they formulate as a function f of two vectors $\mathbf{u}$ and $\mathbf{v}$. Different composition models arise, depending on how f is chosen. Assuming that composition is a linear function of the Cartesian product of $\mathbf{u}$ and $\mathbf{v}$ allows to specify *additive* models which are by far the most common method of vector combination in the literature (Landauer and Dumais, 1997; Foltz et al., 1998; Kintsch, 2001). Alternatively, assuming that composition is a linear function of the tensor product of $\mathbf{u}$ and $\mathbf{v}$, gives rise to models based on *multiplication*.

One of the most sophisticated proposals for semantic composition is that of Clark et al. (2008) and the more recent implementation of Grefenstette and

Sadrzadeh (2011a). Using techniques from logic, category theory, and quantum information they develop a compositional distributional semantics that brings type-logical and distributional vector space models together. In their framework, words belong to different type-based categories and different categories exist in different dimensional spaces. The category of a word is decided by the number and type of adjoints (arguments) it can take and the composition of a sentence results in a vector which exists in sentential space. Verbs, adjectives and adverbs act as relational functions, are represented by matrices, and modify the properties of nouns, that are represented by vectors (see also Baroni and Zamparelli (2010) for a proposal similar in spirit). Clarke (2012) introduces context-theoretic semantics, a general framework for combining vector representations, based on a mathematical theory of meaning as context, and shows that it can be used to describe a variety of models including that of Clark et al. (2008).

Socher et al. (2011a) and Socher et al. (2011b) present a framework based on recursive neural networks that learns vector space representations for multi-word phrases and sentences. The network is given a list of word vectors as input and a binary tree representing their syntactic structure. Then, it computes an n-dimensional representation p of two n-dimensional children and the process is repeated at every parent node until a representation for a full tree is constructed. Parent representations are computed essentially by concatenating the representations of their children. During training, the model tries to minimize the reconstruction errors between the n-dimensional parent vectors and those representing their children. This model can also compute compositional representations when the tree structure is not given, e.g., by greedily inferring a binary tree.

Although the type of function used for vector composition has attracted much attention, relatively less emphasis has been placed on the basic distributional representations on which the composition functions operate. In this paper, we examine three types of distributional representation of increasing sophistication and their effect on semantic composition. These include a simple semantic space, where a word's vector represents its co-occurrence with neighboring words (Mitchell and Lapata, 2010), a syntax-aware space based on weighted distributional tuples that encode typed co-occurrence relations among words (Baroni and Lenci, 2010), and word embeddings computed with a neural language model (Bengio, 2001; Collobert and Weston, 2008). Word embeddings are distributed representations, low-dimensional and real-valued. Each dimension of the embedding represents a latent feature of the word, hopefully capturing useful syntactic and semantic properties.

Using these representations, we construct several compositional models, based on addition, multiplication, and recursive neural networks. We assess the effectiveness of these models using two evaluation protocols. The first one involves modeling similarity judgments for short phrases gathered in human experiments (Mitchell and Lapata, 2010). The second one is paraphrase detection, i.e., the task of examining two sentences and determining whether they have the same meaning (Socher et al., 2011a). We find that shallow approaches are as good as more computationally intensive alternatives. They achieve considerable semantic expressivity without any learning, sophisticated linguistic processing, or access to very large corpora.

Our contributions in this work are three-fold: an empirical comparison of a broad range of compositional models, some of which are introduced here for the first time; the use of an evaluation methodology that takes into account the full spectrum of compositionality from phrases to sentences; and the empirical finding that relatively simple compositional models can be used to perform competitively on the paraphrase detection and phrase similarity tasks.

2 Modeling

The elementary objects that we operate on are vectors associated with words. We instantiate these word representations following three distinct semantic space models which we describe in Section 2.1 below. Analogously, in Section 2.2 we consider three methods of vector composition, i.e., how a phrase or a sentence can be represented as a vector using the vectors of its constituent words. Combining different vector representations and composition methods gives rise to several compositional models whose performance we evaluate in Sections 3 and 4.

2.1 Word Representations

For all of our experiments we employ column vectors from a Cartesian, finitely-dimensional space. The dimensionality will depend on the source of the vectors involved. Similarly, the component values inside each source's vectors are not to be interpreted in the same manner. Nonetheless, they have in common that they originate from distributive corpus statistics.

Co-occurence-based Semantic Space Word meaning is commonly represented in a high-dimensional space, where each component corresponds to some contextual element in which the word is found. The contextual elements can be words themselves, or larger linguistic units such as sentences or documents, or even more complex linguistic representations such as the argument slots of predicates. A semantic space that is often employed in studying compositionality across a variety of tasks (Mitchell and Lapata, 2010; Grefenstette and Sadrzadeh, 2011a) uses a context window of five words on either side of the target word, and 2,000 vector dimensions. These are the common context words in the British National Corpus (BNC), a corpus of about 100 million tokens. Their values are set to the ratio of the probability of the context word given the target word to the probability of the context word overall.

More formally, let us consider the BNC as a set of sentences:

$$BNC = \{Sen_1^{(BNC)}, ..., Sen_{n_{BNC}}^{(BNC)}\} \tag{1}$$

where the i-th sentence is a sequence of words $Sen_i = (w_1^{(i)}, ..., w_{n_i}^{(i)})$ from the BNC's vocabulary Voc_{BNC}. Then $freq_w$ is the amount of times that each word $w \in Voc_{BNC}$ appears in the BNC. Mitchell and Lapata (2010) collect the M most frequent non-stoplist words in the set $ctxt_{top} = \{w_1^{(top)}, ..., w_M^{(top)}\}$ and let them consitute the word vectors' dimensions. Each dimension's value is obtained from a co-occurrence count:

$$coCount_w[j] = \sum_{i=1}^{n_{BNC}} \sum_{t=1}^{n_i} \tag{2}$$

$$|\{k \in [t-5; t+5] \mid w_t^{(i)} = w,\ w_k^{(i)} = w_j^{(top)}\}|$$

for $w \in Voc_{BNC}$ and $j = 1, ..., M$. Using these counts, they define word vectors component-wise.

$$wdVec_w^{(rp)}[j] = \frac{p(w_j^{(top)}|w)}{p(w_j^{(top)})} = \tag{3}$$

$$\frac{coCount_w[j]}{freq_w} \times \frac{totalCount}{freq_{w_j^{(top)}}}$$

for $j = 1, ..., M$, where $totalCount$ is the total number of words in the BNC.

This space is relatively simple, it has few parameters, requires no preprocessing other than tokenization and involves no syntactic information or parameter learning. Despite its simplicity, it is a good starting point for studying representations for compositional models as a baseline against which to evaluate more elaborate models.

Neural Language Model Another perhaps less well-known approach to meaning representation is to represent words as continuous vectors of parameters. Such word vectors can be obtained with an unsupervised *neural language model* (NLM, Bengio (2001); Collobert and Weston (2008)) which jointly learns an embedding of words into a vector space and uses these vectors to predict how likely a word is, given its context.

We induced word embeddings with Collobert and Weston (2008)'s neural language model. The model is discriminative and non-probabilistic. Each word $i \in \mathcal{D}$ (the vocabulary) is embedded into a d-dimensional space using a lookup table $LT_W(\cdot)$:

$$LT_W(i) = W_i \tag{4}$$

where $W \in \mathbb{R}^{d \times |\mathcal{D}|}$ is a matrix of parameters to be learned. $W_i \in \mathbb{R}^d$ is the i-th column of W and d is the word vector size to be chosen by the user. The parameters W are automatically trained during the learning process using backpropagation.

Specifically, at each training update, the model reads an n-gram $x = (w_1, \ldots, w_n)$ from the corpus. The n-gram is paired with a *corrupted* n-gram $\tilde{x} = (w_1, \ldots, \tilde{w_n})$ where $\tilde{w_n} \neq w_n$ is chosen uniformly from the vocabulary. The model concatenates the learned embeddings of the n words and predicts a score for the n-gram sequence using the learned embeddings as features. The training criterion is that

n-grams that are present in the training corpus must have a score at least some margin higher than the corrupted n-grams. The model learns via gradient descent over the neural network parameters and the embedding lookup table. Word vectors are stored in a word embedding matrix which captures syntactic and semantic information from co-occurrence statistics. As these representations are learned, albeit in an unsupervised manner, one would hope that they capture word meanings more succinctly, compared to the simpler distributional representations that are merely based on co-occurrence.

We trained the neural language model on the BNC. We optimized the model's parameters on a word similarity task using 4% of the BNC as development data. Specifically, we used WordSim353, a benchmark dataset (Finkelstein et al., 2001), consisting of relatedness judgments (on a scale of 0 to 10) for 353 word pairs. We experimented with vectors of varying dimensionality (ranging from 50 to 200, with a step size of 50). The size of the target word's context window was 2, 3 and 4 in turn. The rate at which embeddings were learned ranged from 3.4×10^{-10} to 6.7×10^{-10} to 10^{-9}. We ran each training process for 1.1×10^8 to 2.7×10^8 iterations (ca. 2 days). We obtained the best results with 50 dimensions, a context window of size 4, and a embedding learning rate of 10^{-9}. The NLM with these parameters was then trained for 1.51×10^9 iterations (ca. 2 weeks).

Figure 1 illustrates a two-dimensional projection of the embeddings for the 500 most common words in the BNC. We only show two out of the actual 50 dimensions involved, but one can already begin to see clusterings of a syntactic and semantic nature. In one corner, for example, we encounter a grouping of possessive pronouns together with the possessive clitic *'s*. The singular ones *my*, *her* and *his* are closely positioned, as are the plural ones *our*, *your* and *their*. Also, there is a clustering of sociopolitical terms, such as *international*, *country*, *national*, *government*, and *council*.

Distributional Memory Tensor Baroni and Lenci (2010) present Distributional Memory, a generalized framework for distributional semantics from which several special-purpose models can be derived. In their framework distributional information is extracted from the corpus once, in the form of a set of weighted word-link-word tuples arranged into a third-order tensor. Different matrices are then generated from the tensor, and their rows and columns give rise to different semantic spaces appropriate for capturing different semantic problems. In this way, the same distributional information can be shared across tasks such as word similarity or analogical learning.

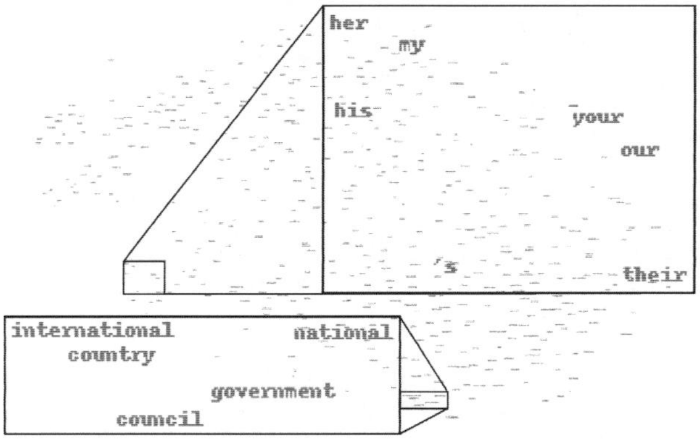

Figure 1: A two-dimensional projection of the word embeddings we trained on the BNC using Turian et al.'s (2010) implementation of the NLM. Two small sections have been blown up to a legible scale. They show examples of syntactic and semantic clustering, respectively.

word w	link l	co-word v	value c
1950s-n	of	essence-n	2.4880
1950s-n	during	bring-v	16.4636
Anyone-n	nmod	reaction-n	1.2161
American-n	coord-1	athlete-n	5.6485
American-j	nmod	wasp-n	3.4945
American-n	such_as-1	country-n	14.4269
American-n	sbj_tr	build-v	23.1014

Table 1: Example entries in Baroni and Lenci (2010)'s tensor

More formally, Baroni and Lenci (2010) construct a 3-dimensional tensor T assigning a value c to instances of word pairs w, v and a connecting link-word l. This representation operates over a dependency-parsed corpus and the scores c are obtained via counting the occurrences of tuples, and weighting the raw counts by mutual information. Table 1 presents examples of tensor entries. These were taken from a distributional memory tensor[1]

[1] Available at http://clic.cimec.unitn.it/dm/.

frequency	link l	co-word v
17059	obj	include-v
16713	obj	use-v
16573	obj	call-v
16475	obj	see-v
15962	obj	make-v
15707	nmod-1	other-j
15554	nmod-1	new-j
15224	obj	find-v
15221	nmod-1	more-j
14715	nmod-1	first-j
14348	obj	give-v

Table 2: The 11 most frequent contexts in Baroni and Lenci (2010)'s tensor (v and j represent verbs and adjectives, respectively).

that Baroni and Lenci obtained via preprocessing several corpora: the web-derived ukWac corpus of about 1.915 billion words, a mid-2009 dump of the English Wikipedia containing about 820 million words, and the BNC.

Extracting a 3-dimensional tensor from the BNC alone would create very sparse representations. We therefore extract so-called word-fibres, essentially projections onto a lower-dimensional subspace, from the same tensor Baroni and Lenci (2010) collectively derived from the 3 billion word corpus just described (henceforth 3-BWC). We view the 3-dimensional tensor

$$T = \{(w_1^{(T)}, l_1^{(T)}, v_1^{(T)}, c_1^{(T)}), \ldots\} \quad (5)$$

as a mapping which assigns each target word w a non-zero value c, given the context (l, v). All word-context combinations not listed in T are implicitly assigned a zero value.

Now we consider two possible approaches for obtaining vectors, depending on their application. First, we let the D most frequent contexts

$$ctxt_D = \{(l_1, v_1), \ldots, (l_D, v_D)\} \quad (6)$$

constitute the D dimensions that each word vector will have. Table 2 shows the 11 contexts (l, v) that appear most frequently in T. Thus, each target word's vector is defined component-wise as:

$$wdVec_w[j] = \begin{cases} c, & \text{if } (w, l_j, v_j, c) \in T \\ 0, & \text{otherwise} \end{cases} \quad (7)$$

for $j = 1, \ldots, D$. This approach is used when a fixed vector dimensionality is necessary.

A more dynamic approach is possible when very few words $w_1, \ldots, w_n$ are involved in a test. Their representations can then have a denser format, that is, with no zero-valued components. For this we identify the set of contexts common to the words involved,

$$\begin{aligned} ctxt_{dyn} &= \{(l_1^{(dyn)}, v_1^{(dyn)}), (l_2^{(dyn)}, v_2^{(dyn)}), \ldots\} \quad (8) \\ &= \{(l, v) \mid (w_i, l, v, c) \in T, c \in \mathbb{R}, i = 1, \ldots, n\} \end{aligned}$$

Each context (l, v) again constitutes a vector dimension. The dimensionality varies strongly depending on the selection of words, but if n does not exceed 4, the dimensionality $|ctxt_{dyn}|$ will typically be substantial enough. In this approach, each word's vector consists of the values c found along with that word and its context in the tensor.

$$wdVec_{w_i}[j] = c, \quad (9)$$

where $(w_i, l_j^{(dyn)}, v_j^{(dyn)}, c) \in T$, for $j = 1, \ldots, |ctxt_{dyn}|$.

2.2 Composition Methods

In our experiments we compose word vectors to create representations for phrase vectors and sentence vectors. The phrases we are interested in consist of two words each: an adjective and a noun like *black hair*, a compound noun made up of two nouns such as *oil industry*, or a verbal phrase with a transitive verb and an object noun, e.g., *pour tea*.

Conceiving of a phrase $phr = (w_1, w_2)$ as a binary tuple of words, we obtain its vector from its words' vectors either by addition:

$$phrVec_{(w_1,w_2)} = wdVec_{w_1} + wdVec_{w_2} \quad (10)$$

or by point-wise multiplication:

$$phrVec_{(w_1,w_2)} = wdVec_{w_1} \odot wdVec_{w_2} \quad (11)$$

In the same way we acquire a vector $senVec_i$ representing a sentence $Sen_i = (w_1^{(i)}, \ldots, w_{n_i}^{(i)})$ from the vectors for $w_1, \ldots, w_{n_i}$. We simply sum the existing word vectors, that is, vectors obtained via the respective corpus for words that are not on our stoplist:

$$senVec_i^{(+)}[j] = \sum_{\substack{k=1,\ldots,n_i \\ wdVec_{w_k} \text{exists}}} wdVec_{w_k}[j] \quad (12)$$

And do the same with point-wise multiplication:

$$senVec_i^{(\odot)}[j] = \prod_{\substack{k=1,\dots,n_i \\ wdVec_{w_k}\text{exists}}} wdVec_{w_k}[j] \qquad (13)$$

The multiplication model in (13) can be seen as an instantiation of the categorical compositional framework put forward by Clark et al. (2008). In fact, a variety of multiplication-based models can be derived from this framework; and comparisons against component-wise multiplication on phrase similarity tasks yield comparable results (Grefenstette and Sadrzadeh, 2011a; Grefenstette and Sadrzadeh, 2011b). We thus opt for the model (13) as an example of compositional models based on multiplication due to its good performance across a variety of tasks, including language modeling and prediction of reading difficulty (Mitchell, 2011).

Our third method, for creating phrase and sentence vectors alike, is the application of Socher et al. (2011a)'s model. They use the Stanford parser (Klein and Manning, 2003) to create a binary parse tree for each input phrase or sentence. This tree is then used as the basis for a deep recursive autoencoder (RAE). The aim is to construct a vector representation for the tree's root bottom-up where the leaves contain word vectors. The latter can in theory be provided by any type of semantic space, however Socher et al. use word embeddings provided by the neural language model (Collobert and Weston, 2008).

Given the binary tree input structure, the model computes parent representations p from their children (c_1, c_2) using a standard neural network layer:

$$p = f(W^{(1)}[c_1; c_2] + b^{(1)}), \qquad (14)$$

where $[c_1; c_2]$ is the concatenation of the two children, f is an element-wise activation function such as tanh, b is a bias term, and $W \in \mathbb{R}^{n \times 2n}$ is an encoding matrix that we want to learn during training. One way of assessing how well p represents its direct children is to decode their vectors in a reconstruction layer:

$$[c'_1; c'_2] = f(W^{(2)}p + b^{(2)}) \qquad (15)$$

During training, the goal is to minimize the reconstruction errors of all input pairs at nonterminal nodes p in a given parse tree by computing the square of the Euclidean distance between the original input and its reconstruction:

$$E_{rec}([c_1; c_2]) = \frac{1}{2}||[c_1; c_2] - [c'_1; c'_2]||^2 \qquad (16)$$

Socher et al. (2011a) extend the standard recursive autoencoder sketched above in two ways. Firstly, they present an unfolding autoencoder that tries to reconstruct all leaf nodes underneath each node rather than only its direct children. And secondly, instead of transforming the two children directly into a parent p, they introduce another hidden layer inbetween.

We obtained three compositional models per representation resulting in nine compositional models overall. Plugging different representations into the additive and multiplicative models is relatively straightforward. The RAE can also be used with arbitrary word vectors. Socher et al. (2011a) obtain best results with 100-dimensional vectors which we also used in our experiments. NLM vectors were trained with this dimensionality on the BNC for 7.9×10^8 iterations (with window size 4 and an embedding learning rate of 10^{-9}). We constructed a simple distributional space with $M = 100$ dimensions, i.e., those connected to the 100 most frequent co-occurrence words. In the case of vectors obtained from Baroni and Lenci (2010)'s DM tensor, we differentiated between phrases and sentences, due to the disparate amount of words contained in them (see Section 2.1). To represent phrases, we used vectors of dynamic dimensionality, since these form a richer and denser representation. The sentences considered in Section 4 are too large for this approach and all word vectors must be members of the same vector space. Hence, these sentence vectors have fixed dimensionality $D = 100$, consisting of the "most significant" 100 dimensions, i.e., those reflecting the 100 most frequent contexts.

3 Experiment 1: Phrase Similarity

Our first experiment focused on modeling similarity judgments for short phrases gathered in human experiments. Distributional representations of individual words are commonly evaluated on tasks based on their ability to model semantic similarity relations, e.g., synonymy or priming. Thus, it seems appropriate to evaluate phrase representations in a

	dim.	c.m.	Adj-N	N-N	V-Obj
SDS (BNC)	2000	+	0.37	0.38	0.28
	2000	⊙	**0.48**	**0.50**	**0.35**
	100	RAE	0.31	0.30	0.28
DM (3-BWC)	vary	+	0.37	0.30	0.29
	vary	⊙	0.21	0.37	0.33
	100	RAE	0.25	0.26	0.09
NLM (BNC)	50	+	0.28	0.26	0.24
	50	⊙	0.26	0.22	0.18
	100	RAE	0.19	0.24	0.28

Table 3: Correlation coefficients of model predictions with subject similarity ratings (Spearman's ρ); columns show dimensionality: fixed or varying (see Section 2.1), composition method: + is additive vector composition, ⊙ is component-wise multiplicative vector composition, RAE is Socher et al. (2011a)'s recursive auto-encoder.

similar manner. Specifically, we used the dataset from Mitchell and Lapata (2010) which contains similarity judgments for adjective-noun, noun-noun and verb-object phrases, respectively.[2] Each item is a phrase pair phr_1, phr_2 which has a human rating from 1 (very low similarity) to 7 (very high similarity).

Using the composition models described above, we compute the cosine similarity of phr_1 and phr_2:

$$phrSim_{phr_1,phr_2} = \frac{phrVec_{phr_1} \cdot phrVec_{phr_2}}{|phrVec_{phr_1}| \times |phrVec_{phr_2}|} \quad (17)$$

Model similarities were evaluated against the human similarity ratings using Spearman's ρ correlation coefficient.

Table 3 summarizes the performance of the various models on the phrase similarity dataset. Rows in the table correspond to different vector representations: the simple distributional semantic space (SDS) from Mitchell and Lapata (2010), Baroni and Lenci's (2010) distributional memory tensor (DM) and the neural language model (NLM), for each phrase combination: adjective noun (Adj-N), noun-noun (N-N) and verb object (V-Obj). For each phrase type we report results for each compositional model, namely additive (+), multiplicative (⊙) and recursive autoencoder (RAE). The table also shows the dimensionality of the input vectors next to the vector representation.

As can be seen, for SDS the best performing model is multiplication, as it is mostly for DM. With regard to NLM, vector addition yields overall better results. In general, neither DM or NLM in any compositional configuration are able to outperform SDS with multiplication. All models in Table 3 are significantly correlated with the human similarity judgments ($p < 0.01$). Spearman's ρ differences of 0.3 or more are significant at the 0.01 level, using a t-test (Cohen and Cohen, 1983).

4 Experiment 2: Paraphrase Detection

Although the phrase similarity task gives a fairly direct insight into semantic similarity and compositional representations, it is somewhat limited in scope as it only considers two-word constructions rather than naturally occurring sentences. Ideally, we would like to augment our evaluation with a task which is based on large quantities of natural data and for which vector composition has practical consequences. For these reasons, we used the Microsoft Research Paraphrase Corpus (MSRPC) introduced by Dolan et al. (2004). The corpus consists of sentence pairs Sen_{i_1}, Sen_{i_2} and labels indicating whether they are in a paraphrase relationship or not. The vector representations obtained from our various compositional models were used as features for the paraphrase classification task.

The MSRPC dataset contains 5,801 sentence pairs, we used the standard split of 4,076 training pairs (67.5% of which are paraphrases) and 1,725 test pairs (66.5% of which are paraphrases). In order to judge whether two sentences have the same meaning we employ Fan et al. (2008)'s liblinear classifier. For each of our three vector sources and three different compositional methods, we create the following features: (a) a vector representing the pair of input sentences either via concatenation ("con") or subtraction ("sub"); (b) a vector encoding which words appear therein ("enc"); and (c) a vector made up of the following four other pieces of information: the cosine similarity of the sentence vectors, the length of Sen_{i_1}, the length of Sen_{i_2}, and the unigram overlap among the two sentences.

In order to encode which words appear in

[2] The dataset is publicly available from http://homepages.inf.ed.ac.uk/s0453356/share

	NLM (BNC)	DM (3-BWC)	SDS (BNC)
+	69.04 (con, other)	**73.51** (other)	72.93 (other)
⊙	67.83 (sub, other)	67.54 (other)	**73.04** (other)
RAE	**70.26** (con, other)	68.29 (sub, other)	69.10 (con, other)

Table 4: Paraphrase classification accuracy in %. Included features are in parentheses: "con" is sentence vector concatenation, "sub" is sentence vector subtraction, "other" stands for 4 other features (see Section 4)

	NLM (BNC)	DM (3-BWC)	SDS (BNC)
+	81.00 (con, other)	**82.16** (other)	80.76 (other)
⊙	80.41 (sub, other)	80.18 (other)	**82.33** (other)
RAE	**81.28** (con, other)	80.43 (sub, other)	80.68 (con, other)

Table 5: Paraphrase classification F1-score in %. The involved features are exactly the same as in Table 4.

each sentence and how often, we define a vector $wdCount_i$ for sentence Sen_i and enumerate all words occuring in the MSRPC:

$$Voc_{MSRPC} = \{w_1^{(MSRPC)}, ..., w_{n_{MSRPC}}^{(MSRPC)}\} \quad (18)$$

giving the word count vectors n_{MSRPC} dimensions. Thus the k-th component of $wdCount_i$ is the frequency with which the word $w_k^{(MSRPC)}$ appears in $Sen_i = (w_1^{(i)}, ..., w_{n_i}^{(i)})$:

$$wdCount_i[k] = |\{j \in [1;n_i] \,|\, w_k^{(MSRPC)} = w_j^{(i)}\}| \quad (19)$$

for $k = 1, ..., n_{MSRPC}$. Even though n_{MSRPC} may be large, the computer files storing our feature vectors do not explode in size because *wdCount* contains many zeros and the classifier allows a sparse notation of (non-zero) feature values.

Regarding the last four features, we measured the similarity between sentences the same way as we did with phrases in section 3.

$$senSim_{i_1,i_2} = \frac{senVec_{i_1} \cdot senVec_{i_2}}{|senVec_{i_1}| \times |senVec_{i_2}|} \quad (20)$$

Note that this is the cosine of the angle between $senVec_{i_1}$ and $senVec_{i_2}$. This enables us to observe the similarity or dissimilarity of two sentences independent of their sentence length. Even though each contained word increases or decreases the norm of the resulting sentence vector, this does not distort the overall similarity value, due to normalization.

The lengths of Sen_{i_1} and Sen_{i_2} are simply the number of words they contain. The unigram overlap feature value may be viewed as the cardinality of the intersection of each sentence's multiset-bag-of-words. The latter is encoded in the already-introduced *wdCount* vectors. Therefore,

$$uniOverlap_{i_1,i_2} = \sum_{k=1}^{n_{MSRPC}} \min_{s=1,2} \{wdCount_{i_s}[k]\} \quad (21)$$

In order to establish which features work best for each representation and composition method, we exhaustively explored all combinations on a development set (20% of the original MSRPC training set). Tables 4 (accuracy) and 5 (F1) show our results on the test set with the best feature combinations for each model (shown in parentheses). Each row corresponds to a different type of composition and each column to a different word representation model.

As can be seen, the distributional memory (DM) is the best performing representation for the additive composition model. The neural language model (NLM) gives best results for the recursive autoencoder (RAE), although the other two representations come close. And finally the simple distributional semantic space (SDS) works best with multiplication. Also note that the best performing models, namely DM with addition and SDS with multiplication, use a basic feature space consisting only of the cosine similarity of the composed sentence vectors, the length of the two sentences involved, and their unigram word overlap.

Although our intention was to use the paraphrase detection task as a test-bed for evaluating compositional models rather than achieving state-of-the-art results, Table 6 compares our approach against previous work on the same task and dataset. Initial research concentrated on individual words rather than sentential representations. Several approaches used

Model	Acc.	F1
Baseline	66.5	79.9
Mihalcea et al. (2006)	70.3	81.3
Rus et al. (2008)	70.6	80.5
Qiu et al. (2006)	72.0	81.6
Islam and Inkpen (2007)	72.6	81.3
Mitchell and Lapata (2010) ($\odot$)	**73.0**	**82.3**
Baroni and Lenci (2010) ($+$)	**73.5**	**82.2**
Fernando and Stevenson (2008)	74.1	82.4
Wan et al. (2006)	75.6	83.0
Das and Smith (2009)	76.1	82.7
Socher et al. (2011a)	76.8	83.6

Table 6: Overview of results on the MSRCP (test corpus). Accuracy differences of 3.3 or more are significant at the 0.01 level (using the χ^2 statistic).

WordNet in conjunction with distributional similarity in an attempt to detect meaning conveyed by synonymous words (Islam and Inkpen, 2007; Mihalcea et al., 2006; Fernando and Stevenson, 2008). More recently, the addition of syntactic features based on dependency parse trees (Wan et al., 2006; Das and Smith, 2009) has been shown to substantially boost performance. The model of Das and Smith (2009), for example, uses quasi-synchronous dependency grammar to model the structure of the sentences involved in the comparison and their correspondences. Socher et al. (2011a) obtain an accuracy that is higher than previously published results. This model is more sophisticated than the one we used in our experiments (see Table 4 and 5). Rather than using the output of the RAE as features for the classifier, it applies dynamic pooling, a procedure that takes a similarity matrix as input (e.g., created by sentences with differing lengths) and maps it to a matrix of fixed size that represents more faithfully the global similarity structure.[3]

Overall, we observe that our own models do as well as some of the models that employ WordNet and more sophisticated syntactic features. With regard to F1, we are comparable with Das and Smith (2009) and Socher et al. (2011a) without using elaborate features, or any additional manipulations over and above the output of the composition functions which if added could increase performance.

[3]Without dynamic pooling, their model yields an accuracy of 74.2.

5 Discussion

In this paper we systematically compared three types of distributional representation and their effect on semantic composition. Our comparisons involved a simple distributional semantic space (Mitchell and Lapata, 2010), word embeddings computed with a neural language model (Collobert and Weston, 2008) and a representation based on weighted word-link-word tuples arranged into a third-order tensor (Baroni and Lenci, 2010). These representations vary in many respects: the amount of preprocessing and linguistic information involved (the third-order tensor computes semantic representations over parsed corpora), whether the semantic space is the by-product of a learning process (in the neural language model the parameters of the lookup table must be learned), and data requirements (the third-order tensor involves processing billions of words). These representations served as input to three composition methods involving addition, multiplication and a deep recursive autoencoder. Again these methods differ in terms of how they implement compositionality: addition and multiplication are commutative and associative operations and thus ignore word order and, more generally, syntactic structure. In contrast, the recursive autoencoder is syntax-aware as it operates over a parse tree. However, the composed representations must be learned with a neural network.

We evaluated nine models on the complementary tasks of phrase similarity and paraphrase detection. The former task simplifies the challenge of finding an adequate method of composition and places more emphasis on the representation, whereas the latter poses, in a sense, the ultimate challenge for composition models. It involves entire sentences exhibiting varied syntactic constructions and in the limit involves genuine natural language undertanding. Across both tasks our results deliver a consistent message: simple is best. Despite being in theory more expressive, the representations obtained by the neural language model and the third-order tensor cannot match the simple semantic space on the phrase similarity task. In this task syntax-oblivious composition models are superior to the more sophisticated recursive autoencoder. The latter performs better on the paraphrase detection task when its output is fed to a classifier. The simple semantic space may not take word order or sentence structure into account, but nevertheless achieves considerable semantic expressivity: it is on par with the third-order tensor without having access to as much data (3 billion words) or a syntactically parsed corpus.

What do these findings tell us about the future of compositional models for distributional semantics? The problem of finding the right methods of vector composition cannot be pursued independent of the choice of lexical representation. Having tested many model combinations, we argue that in a good model of distributive semantics representation and composition must go hand in hand, i.e., they must be mutually learned.

Acknowledgments We are grateful to Jeff Mitchell for his help with the re-implementation of his models. Thanks to Frank Keller and Micha Elsner for their input on earlier versions of this work and to Richard Socher for technical assistance. We acknowledge the support of EPSRC through project grant EP/I032916/1.

References

Marco Baroni and Alessandro Lenci. 2010. Distributional memory: A general framework for corpus-based semantics. *Computational Linguistics*, 36(4):673–721.

Marco Baroni and Roberto Zamparelli. 2010. Nouns are vectors, adjectives are matrices: Representing adjective-noun constructions in semantic space. In *Proceedings of the 2010 Conference on Empirical Methods in Natural Language Processing*, pages 1183–1193, Cambridge, MA.

Jerome R. Bellegarda. 2000. Exploiting latent semantic information in statistical language modeling. *Proceedings of the Institute of of Electrical and Electronics Engineers*, 88(8):1279–1296.

Yoshua Bengio. 2001. Neural net language models. *Scholarpedia*, 3(1):3881.

Stephen Clark, Bob Coecke, and Mehrnoosh Sadrzadeh. 2008. A compositional distributional model of meaning. In *Proceedings of the 2nd Quantum Interaction Symposium*, pages 133–140, Oxford, UK.

Daoud Clarke. 2012. A context-theoretic framework for compositionality in distributional semantics. *Computational Linguistics*, 38(1):41–71.

J Cohen and P Cohen. 1983. *Applied Multiple Regression/Correlation Analysis for the Behavioral Sciences*. Hillsdale, NJ: Erlbaum.

Ronan Collobert and Jason Weston. 2008. A unified architecture for natural language processing: deep neural networks with multitask learning. In *Proceedings of the 25th International Conference on Machine Learning*, pages 160–167, New York, NY. ACM.

Dipanjan Das and Noah A. Smith. 2009. Paraphrase identification as probabilistic quasi-synchronous recognition. In *Proceedings of the Joint Conference of the 47th Annual Meeting of the ACL and the 4th International Joint Conference on Natural Language Processing of the AFNLP*, pages 468–476, Suntec, Singapore.

G. Denhire and B. Lemaire. 2004. A computational model of children's semantic memory. In *Proceedings of the 26th Annual Meeting of the Cognitive Science Society*, pages 297–302, Mahwah, NJ. Lawrence Erlbaum Associates.

Bill Dolan, Chris Quirk, and Chris Brockett. 2004. Unsupervised construction of large paraphrase corpora: Exploiting massively parallel news sources. In *Proceedings of the 20th International Conference on Computational Linguistics*, pages 350–356, Geneva, Switzerland. COLING.

Rong-En Fan, Kai-Wei Chang, Cho-Jui Hsieh, Xiang-Rui Wang, and Chih-Jen Lin. 2008. Liblinear: A library for large linear classification. *Journal of Machine Learning Research*, 9:1871–1874.

Samuel Fernando and Mark Stevenson. 2008. A semantic similarity approach to paraphrase detection. *Technology*.

Lev Finkelstein, Evgeniy Gabrilovich, Yossi Matias, Ehud Rivlin, Zach Solan, Gadi Wolfman, and Eytan Ruppin. 2001. Placing search in context: the concept revisited. In *WWW*, pages 406–414.

Peter Foltz, Walter Kintsch, and Thomas Landauer. 1998. The measurement of textual coherence with latent semantic analysis. *Discourse Process*, 15:285–307.

Edward Grefenstette and Mehrnoosh Sadrzadeh. 2011a. Experimental support for a categorical compositional distributional model of meaning. In *Proceedings of the 2011 Conference on Empirical Methods in Natural Language Processing*, pages 1394–1404, Edinburgh, Scotland.

Edward Grefenstette and Mehrnoosh Sadrzadeh. 2011b. Experimenting with transitive verbs in a DisCoCat. In *Proceedings of the GEMS 2011 Workshop on GEometrical Models of Natural Language Semantics*, pages 62–66, Edinburgh, UK.

Gregory Grefenstette. 1994. *Explorations in Automatic Thesaurus Discovery*. Kluwer Academic Publishers, Norwell, MA.

Thomas L. Griffiths, Mark Steyvers, and Joshua B. Tenenbaum. 2007. Topics in semantic representation. *Psychological Review*, 114(2):211–244.

Aminul Islam and Diana Inkpen. 2007. Semantic similarity of short texts. In *Proceedings of the International Conference on Recent Advances in Natural Language Processing*, Borovets, Bulgaria.

Walter Kintsch. 2001. Predication. *Cognitive Science*, 25(2):173–202.

Dan Klein and Christopher D. Manning. 2003. Accurate unlexicalized parsing. In *Proceedings of the 41st Annual Meeting of the Association for Computational Linguistics*, pages 423–430, Sapporo, Japan.

T. K. Landauer and S. T. Dumais. 1997. A solution to Plato's problem: the latent semantic analysis theory of acquisition, induction and representation of knowledge. *Psychological Review*, 104(2):211–240.

Scott McDonald. 2000. *Environmental Determinants of Lexical Processing Effort*. Ph.D. thesis, University of Edinburgh.

Rada Mihalcea, Courtney Corley, and Carlo Strapparava, 2006. *Corpus-based and knowledge-based measures of text semantic similarity*, pages 775–780. AAAI Press.

Jeff Mitchell and Mirella Lapata. 2010. Composition in distributional models of semantics. *Cognitive Science*, 38(8):1388–1429.

Jeff Mitchell. 2011. *Composition in distributional models of semantics*. Ph.D. thesis, University of Edinburgh.

Tony A. Plate. 1995. Holographic reduced representations. *IEEE Transactions on Neural Networks*, 6(3):623–641.

Long Qiu, Min-Yen Kan, and Tat-Seng Chua. 2006. Paraphrase recognition via dissimilarity significance classification. In *Proceedings of the 2006 Conference on Empirical Methods in Natural Language Processing*, pages 18–26, Sydney, Australia.

Vasile Rus, Philip M. McCarthy, Mihai C. Lintean, Danielle S. McNamara, and Arthur C. Graesser. 2008. Paraphrase identification with lexico-syntactic graph subsumption. In David Wilson and H. Chad Lane, editors, *Florida Artificial Intelligence Research Society Conference*, pages 201–206. AAAI Press.

Hinrich Schütze. 1998. Automatic word sense discrimination. *Computational Linguistics*, 24(1):97–124.

Paul Smolensky. 1990. Tensor product variable binding and the representation of symbolic structures in connectionist systems. *Artificial Intelligence*, 46:159–216.

Richard Socher, Eric H. Huang, Jeffrey Pennin, Andrew Y. Ng, and Christopher D. Manning. 2011a. Dynamic Pooling and Unfolding Recursive Autoencoders for Paraphrase Detection. In *Advances in Neural Information Processing Systems 24*, pages 801–809. Granada, Spain.

Richard Socher, Jeffrey Pennington, Eric H. Huang, Andrew Y. Ng, and Christopher D. Manning. 2011b. Semi-supervised recursive autoencoders for predicting sentiment distributions. In *Proceedings of the 2011 Conference on Empirical Methods in Natural Language Processing*, pages 151–161, Edinburgh, Scotland.

Joseph Turian, Lev Ratinov, and Yoshua Bengio. 2010. Word representations: a simple and general method for semi-supervised learning. In *Proceedings of the 48th Annual Meeting of the Association for Computational Linguistics*, pages 384–394, Uppsala, Sweden.

Peter D. Turney. 2006. Similarity of semantic relations. *Computational Linguistics*, 32(3):379–416.

Stephen Wan, Mark Dras, Robert Dale, and Cecile Paris. 2006. Using dependency-based features to take the "para-farce" out of paraphrase. In *Proceedings of the Australasian Language Technology Workshop 2006*, pages 131–138, Sydney, Australia.

Exploiting Chunk-level Features to Improve Phrase Chunking

Junsheng Zhou Weiguang Qu Fen Zhang
Jiangsu Research Center of Information Security & Privacy Technology
School of Computer Science and Technology
Nanjing Normal University. Nanjing, China, 210046
Email:{zhoujs,wgqu}@njnu.edu.cn zf9646@126.com

Abstract

Most existing systems solved the phrase chunking task with the sequence labeling approaches, in which the chunk candidates cannot be treated as a whole during parsing process so that the chunk-level features cannot be exploited in a natural way. In this paper, we formulate phrase chunking as a joint segmentation and labeling task. We propose an efficient dynamic programming algorithm with pruning for decoding, which allows the direct use of the features describing the internal characteristics of chunk and the features capturing the correlations between adjacent chunks. A relaxed, online maximum margin training algorithm is used for learning. Within this framework, we explored a variety of effective feature representations for Chinese phrase chunking. The experimental results show that the use of chunk-level features can lead to significant performance improvement, and that our approach achieves state-of-the-art performance. In particular, our approach is much better at recognizing long and complicated phrases.

1 Introduction

Phrase chunking is a Natural Language Processing task that consists in dividing a text into syntactically correlated parts of words. Theses phrases are non-overlapping, i.e., a word can only be a member of one chunk (Abney, 1991). Generally speaking, there are two phrase chunking tasks, including text chunking (shallow parsing), and noun phrase (NP) chunking. Phrase chunking provides a key feature that helps on more elaborated NLP tasks such as parsing, semantic role tagging and information extraction.

There is a wide range of research work on phrase chunking based on machine learning approaches. However, most of the previous work reduced phrase chunking to sequence labeling problems either by using the classification models, such as SVM (Kudo and Matsumoto, 2001), Winnow and voted-perceptrons (Zhang et al., 2002; Collins, 2002), or by using the sequence labeling models, such as Hidden Markov Models (HMMs) (Molina and Pla, 2002) and Conditional Random Fields (CRFs) (Sha and Pereira, 2003). When applying the sequence labeling approaches to phrase chunking, there exist two major problems. Firstly, these models cannot treat globally a sequence of continuous words as a chunk candidate, and thus cannot inspect the internal structure of the candidate, which is an important aspect of information in modeling phrase chunking. In particular, it makes impossible the use of local indicator function features of the type "the chunk consists of POS tag sequence $p_1 ... ,p_k$". For example, the Chinese NP "农业/NN(agriculture) 生产/NN(production) 和/CC(and) 农村/NN(rural) 经济/NN(economic) 发展/NN(development)" seems relatively difficult to be correctly recognized by a sequence labeling approach due to its length. But if we can treat the sequence of words as a whole and describe the formation pattern of POS tags of this chunk with a regular expression-like form "[NN]+[CC][NN]+", then it is more likely to be correctly recognized, since this pattern might better express the characteristics of its constituents. As another example, consider the recognition of special terms. In Chinese corpus, there exists a kind of NPs called special terms, such as "『生命

(Life) 禁区(Forbidden Zone) 』", which are bracketed with the particular punctuations like "『, 』, 「, 」, 《, 》". When recognizing the special terms, it is difficult for the sequence labeling approaches to guarantee the matching of particular punctuations appearing at the starting and ending positions of a chunk. For instance, the chunk candidate "『 生命(Life) 禁区(Forbidden Zone)" is considered to be an invalid chunk. But it is easy to check this kind of punctuation matching in a single chunk by introducing a chunk-level feature.

Secondly, the sequence labeling models cannot capture the correlations between adjacent chunks, which should be informative for the identification of chunk boundaries and types. In particular, we find that some headwords in the sentence are expected to have a stronger dependency relation with their preceding headwords in preceding chunks than with their immediately preceding words within the same chunk. For example, in the following sentence:

" [双方/PN(Bilateral)]_NP [经贸/NN(economic and trade) 关系/NN(relations)]_NP [正/AD(just) 稳步/AD(steadily) 发展/VV(develop)]_VP "

if we can find the three headwords "双方", "关系" and "发展" located in the three adjacent chunks with some head-finding rules, then the headword dependency expressed by headword bigrams or trigrams should be helpful to recognize these chunks in this sentence.

In summary, the inherent deficiency in applying the sequence labeling approaches to phrase chunking is that the chunk-level features one would expect to be very informative cannot be exploited in a natural way.

In this paper, we formulate phrase chunking as a joint segmentation and labeling problem, which offers advantages over previous learning methods by providing a natural formulation to exploit the features describing the internal structure of a chunk and the features capturing the correlations between the adjacent chunks.

Within this framework, we explored a variety of effective feature representations for Chinese phrase chunking. The experimental results on Chinese chunking corpus as well as English chunking corpus show that the use of chunk-level features can lead to significant performance improvement, and that our approach performs better than other approaches based on the sequence labeling models.

2 Related Work

In recent years, many chunking systems based on machine learning approaches have been presented. Some approaches rely on *k*-order generative probabilistic models, such as HMMs (Molina and Pla, 2002). However, HMMs learn a generative model over input sequence and labeled sequence pairs. It has difficulties in modeling multiple non-independent features of the observation sequence. To accommodate multiple overlapping features on observations, some other approaches view the phrase chunking as a sequence of classification problems, including support vector machines (SVMs) (Kudo and Matsumoto 2001) and a variety of other classifiers (Zhang et al., 2002). Since these classifiers cannot trade off decisions at different positions against each other, the best classifier based shallow parsers are forced to resort to heuristic combinations of multiple classifiers. Recently, CRFs were widely employed for phrase chunking, and presented comparable or better performance than other state-of-the-art models (Sha and Pereira 2003; McDonald et al. 2005). Further, Sun et al. (2008) used the latent-dynamic conditional random fields (LDCRF) to explicitly learn the hidden substructure of shallow phrases, achieving state-of-the-art performance over the NP-chunking task on the CoNLL data.

Some similar approaches based on classifiers or sequence labeling models were also used for Chinese chunking (Li et al., 2003; Tan et al., 2004; Tan et al., 2005). Chen et al. (2006) conducted an empirical study of Chinese chunking on a corpus, which was extracted from UPENN Chinese Treebank-4 (CTB4). They compared the performances of the state-of-the-art machine learning models for Chinese chunking, and proposed some Tag-Extension and novel voting methods to improve performance.

In this paper, we model phrase chunking with a joint segmentation and labeling approach, which offer advantages over previous learning methods by explicitly incorporating the internal structural feature and the correlations between the adjacent chunks. To some extent, our model is similar to Semi-Markov Conditional Random Fields (called a Semi-CRF), in which the segmentation and labeling can also be done directly (Sarawagi and Cohen, 2004). However, Semi-CRF just models label dependency, and it cannot capture more correlations between adjacent chunks, as is done in our approach. The limitation of Semi-CRF leads to its relatively low performance.

3 Problem Formulation

3.1 Chunk Types

Unlike English chunking, there is not a benchmarking corpus for Chinese chunking. We follow the studies in (Chen et al. 2006) so that a more direct comparison with state-of-the-art systems for Chinese chunking would be possible. There are 12 types of chunks: ADJP, ADVP, CLP, DNP, DP, DVP, LCP, LST, NP, PP, QP and VP in the chunking corpus (Xue et al., 2000). The training and test corpus can be extracted from CTB4 with a public tool, as depicted in (Chen et al. 2006).

3.2 Sequence Labeling Approaches to Phrase Chunking

The standard approach to phrase chunking is to use tagging techniques with a BIO tag set. Words in the input text are tagged with one of B for the beginning of a contiguous segment, I for the inside of a contiguous segment, or O for outside a segment. For instance, the sentence (word segmented and POS tagged) "他/NR(He) 到达/VV(reached) 北京/NR(Beijing) 机场/NN(airport) 。/PU" will be tagged as follows:

Example 1:

S1: [NP 他][VP 到达][NP 北京/机场][O 。]

S2: 他/B-NP 到达/B-VP 北京/B-NP 机场/I-NP 。/O

Here S1 denotes that the sentence is tagged with chunk types, and S2 denotes that the sentence is tagged with chunk tags based on the BIO-based model. With the data representation like the S2, the problem of phrase chunking can be reduced to a sequence labeling task.

3.3 Phrase Chunking via a Joint Segmentation and Labeling Approach

To tackle the problems with the sequence labeling approaches to phrase chunking, we formulate it as a joint problem, which maps a Chinese sentence x with segmented words and POS tags to an output y with tagged chunk types, like the S1 in Example 1. The joint model considers all possible chunk boundaries and corresponding chunk types in the sentence, and chooses the overall best output. This kind of parser reads the input sentences from left to right, predicts whether current segment of continuous words is some type of chunk. After one chunk is found, parser move on and search for next possible chunk.

Given a sentence x, let y denote an output tagged with chunk types, and GEN a function that enumerates a set of segmentation and labeling candidates GEN(x) for x. A parser is to solve the following "argmax" problem:

$$\begin{aligned}\hat{y} &= \arg\max_{y \in GEN(x)} w^T \cdot \Phi(y) \\ &= \arg\max_{y \in GEN(x)} w^T \cdot \sum_{i=1}^{|y|} \phi(y_{[1..i]})\end{aligned} \tag{1}$$

where Φ and ϕ are global and local feature maps and w is the parameter vector to learn. The inner product $w^T \cdot \phi(y_{[1..i]})$ can be seen as the confidence score of whether y_i is a chunk. The parser takes into account confidence score of each chunk, by using the sum of local scores as its criteria. Markov assumption is necessary for computation, so ϕ is usually defined on a limited history.

The main advantage of the joint segmentation and labeling approach to phrase chunking is to allow for integrating both the internal structural features and the correlations between the adjacent chunks for prediction. The two basic components of our model are decoding and learning algorithms, which are described in the following sections.

4 Decoding

The inference technique is one of the most important components for a joint segmentation and labeling model. In this section, we propose a dynamic programming algorithm with pruning to efficiently produce the optimal output.

4.1 Algorithm Description

Given an input sentence x, the decoding algorithm searches for the highest-scored output with recognized chunks. The search space of combined candidates in the joint segmentation and labeling task is very large, which is an exponential growth in the number of possible candidates with increasing sentence size. The rate of growth is $O(2^n T^n)$ for the joint system, where n is the length of the sentence and T is the number of chunk types. It is natural to use some greedy heuristic search algorithms for inference in some similar joint problems (Zhang and Clark, 2008; Zhang and Clark, 2010). However, the greedy heuristic search algorithms only explore a fraction of the whole space (even with beam search) as opposed to dynamic programming. Additionally, a specific advantage of the dynamic programming algorithm is that constraints required in a valid prediction sequence can be handled in a principled way. We show that dynamic programming is in fact possible for this joint problem, by introducing some effective pruning schemes.

To make the inference tractable, we first make a first-order Markov assumption on the features used in our model. In other words, we assume that the chunk c_i and the corresponding label t_i are only associated with the preceding chunk c_{i-1} and the label t_{i-1}. Suppose that the input sentence has n words and the constant M is the maximum chunk length in the training corpus. Let $V(b,e,t)$ denote the highest-scored segmentation and labeling with the last chunk starting at word index b, ending at word index e and the last chunk type being t. One way to find the highest-scored segmentation and labeling for the input sentence is to first calculate the $V(b,n\text{-}1,t)$ for all possible start position $b \in (n\text{-}M)..n\text{-}1$, and all possible chunk type t, respectively, and then pick the highest-scored one from these candidates. In order to compute $V(b,n\text{-}1,t)$, the last chunk needs to be combined with all possible different segmentations of words $(b\text{-}M)..b\text{-}1$ and all possible different chunk types so that the highest-scored can be selected. According to the principle of optimality, the highest-scored among the segmentations of words $(b\text{-}M)..b\text{-}1$ and all possible chunk types with the last chunk being word $b'..b\text{-}1$ and the last chunk type being t' will also give the highest score when combined with the word $b..n\text{-}1$ and tag t. In this way, the search task is reduced recursively into smaller subproblems, where in the base case the subproblems $V(0,e,t)$ for $e \in 0..M\text{-}1$, and each possible chunk type t, are solved in straightforward manner. And the final highest-scored segmentation and labeling can be found by solving all subproblems in a bottom-up fashion.

The pseudo code for this algorithm is shown in Figure 1. It works by filling an n by n by T table *chart*, where n is the number of words in the input sentence *sent*, and T is the number of chunk types. *chart*[b,e,t] records the value of subproblem $V(b,e,t)$. *chart*[0, e, t] can be computed directly for e = 0..M-1 and for chunk type t=1..T. The final output is the best among *chart*[b,n-1,t], with b= n-M..n-1, and t=1..T.

Inputs: sentence *sent* (word segmented and POS tagged)
Variables:
word index b for the start of chunk;
word index e for the end of chunk;
word index p for the start of the previous chunk.
chunk type index t for the current chunk;
chunk type index t' for the previous chunk;
Initialization:
for e = 0.. M-1:
  for t =1..T:
    chart[0,e,t] ←single chunk *sent*[0,e] and type t
Algorithm:
for e = 0..n-1:
  for b = (e-M)..e:
    for t =1..T:
      chart[b,e,t]←the highest scored segmentation and labeling among those derived by combining *chart*[p,b-1,t'] with *sent*[b,e] and chunk type t, for p = (b-M)..b-1, t' =1..T.
Outputs: the highest scored segmentation and labeling among *chart*[b,n-1,t], for b=n-M..n-1, t =1..T.

Figure 1: A dynamic-programming algorithm for phrase chunking.

4.2 Pruning

The time complexity of the above algorithm is $O(M^2T^2n)$, where M is the maximum chunk size. It is linear in the length of sentence. However, the constant in the O is relatively large. In practice, the search space contains a large number of invalid partial candidates, which make the algorithm slow. In this section we describe three partial output pruning schemes which are helpful in speeding up the algorithm.

Firstly, we collect chunk type transition information between chunk types by observing every pair of adjacent chunks in the training corpus, and record a chunk type transition matrix. For example, from the Chinese Treebank that we used for our experiments, a transition from chunk type ADJP to ADVP does not occur in the training corpus, the corresponding matrix element is set to *false*, *true* otherwise. During decoding, the chunk type transition information is used to prune unlikely combinations between current chunk and the preceding chunk by their chunk types.

Secondly, a POS tag dictionary is used to record POS tags associated with each chunk type. Specifically, for each chunk type, we record all POS tags appearing in this type of chunk in the training corpus. During decoding, a segment of continuous words that contains only allowed POS tags according to the POS tag dictionary will be considered to be a valid chunk candidate.

Finally, the system records the maximum number of words for each type of chunk in the training corpus. For example, in the Chinese Treebank, most types of chunks have one to three words. The few chunk types that are seen with length bigger than ten are NP, QP and ADJP. During decoding, the chunk candidate whose length is greater than the maximum chunk length associated with its chunk type will be discarded.

For the above pruning schemes, development tests show that it improves the speed significantly, while having a very small negative influence on the accuracy.

5 Learning

5.1 Discriminative Online Training

By defining features, a candidate output y is mapped into a global feature vector, in which each dimension represents the count of a particular feature in the sentence. The learning task is to set the parameter values w using the training examples as evidence.

Online learning is an attractive method for the joint model since it quickly converges within a few iterations (McDonald, 2006). We focus on an online learning algorithm called MIRA, which is a relaxed, online maximum margin training algorithm with the desired accuracy and scalability properties (Crammer, 2004). Furthermore, MIRA is very flexible with respect to the loss function. Any loss function on the output is compatible with MIRA since it does not require the loss to factor according to the output, which enables our model to be optimized with respect to evaluation metrics directly. Figure 2 outlines the generic online learning algorithm (McDonald, 2006) used in our framework.

MIRA updates the parameter vector w with two constraints: (1) the positive example must have a higher score by a given margin, and (2) the change to w should be minimal. This second constraint is to reduce fluctuations in w. In particular, we use a generalized version of MIRA (Crammer et al., 2005; McDonald, 2006) that can incorporate *k-best* decoding in the update procedure.

Input: Training set $S = \{(x_t, y_t)\}_{t=1}^{T}$
1: $w^{(0)} = 0$; $v = 0$; $i = 0$
2: for $iter = 1$ to N do
3: for $t = 1$ to T do
4: $w^{(i+1)}$ = update $w^{(i)}$ according to (x_t, y_t)
5: $v = v + w^{(i+1)}$
6: $i = i + 1$
7: end for
8: end for
9: $w = v/(N \times T)$
Output: weight vector w

Figure 2: Generic Online Learning Algorithm

In each iteration, MIRA updates the weight vector w by keeping the norm of the change in the weight vector as small as possible. Within this framework, we can formulate the optimization problem as follows (McDonald, 2006):

$$w^{(i+1)} = \arg\min_w \left\| w - w^{(i)} \right\|$$
$$s.t.\ \forall y' \in best_k(x_t; w^{(i)}): \qquad (2)$$
$$w^T \cdot \Phi(y_t) - w^T \cdot \Phi(y') \geq L(y_t, y')$$

where $best_k(x_t; w^{(i)})$ represents a set of top *k-best* outputs for x_t given the weight vector $w^{(i)}$. In our implementation, the top *k-best* outputs are obtained with a straightforward *k-best* extension to the decoding algorithm in section 4.1. The above quadratic programming (QP) problem can be solved using Hildreth's algorithm (Yair Censor, 1997). Replacing Eq. (2) into line 4 of the algorithm in Figure 2, we obtain *k-best* MIRA.

As shown in (McDonald, 2006), parameter averaging can effectively avoid overfitting. The final weight vector w is the average of the weight vectors after each iteration.

5.2 Loss Function

For the joint segmentation and labeling task, there are two alternative loss functions: 0-1 loss and F1 loss. 0-1 loss gives credit only when the entire output sequence is correct: there is no notion of partially correct solutions. The most common loss function for joint segmentation and labeling problems is F_1 measure over chunks. This is the geometric mean of precision and recall over the (properly-labeled) chunk identification task, defined as follows.

$$L^F(y,\hat{y}) \triangleq 1 - \frac{2|y \cap y'|}{|y| + |y'|} \quad (3)$$

where the cardinality of y is simply the number of chunks identified. The cardinality of the intersection is the number of chunks in common. As can be seen in the definition, one is penalized both for identifying too many chunks (penalty in the denominator) and for identifying too few (penalty in the numerator).

In our experiments, we will compare the performance of the systems with different loss functions.

5.3 Features

Table 1 shows the feature templates for the joint segmentation and labeling model. In the row for feature templates, c, t, w and p are used to represent a chunk, a chunk type, a word and a POS tag, respectively. And c_0 and c_{-1} represent the current chunk and the previous chunk respectively. Similarly, w_{-1}, w_0 and w_1 represent the previous word, the current word and the next word, respectively.

Although it is slightly less natural to do so, part of the features used in the sequence labeling models can also be represented in our approach. Therefore the features employed in our model can be divided into three types: the features similar to those used in the sequence labeling models (called SL-type features), the features describing internal structure of a chunk (called Internal-type features), and the features capturing the correlations between the adjacent chunks (called Correlation-type features).

Firstly, some features associated with a single label (here refers to label "B" and "I") used in the sequence labeling models are also represented in our model. In Table 1, templates 1-4 are SL-type features, where *label*(w) denotes the label indicating the position of the word w in the current chunk; *len*(c) denotes the length of chunk c. For example, given an NP chunk "北京(Beijing) 机场(Airport)", which includes two words, the value of *label*("北京") is "B" and the value of *label*("机场") is "I". *Bigram*(w) denotes the word bigrams formed by combining the word to the left of w and the one to the right of w. And the same meaning is for *biPOS*(w). Template *specitermMatch*(c) is used to check the punctuation matching within chunk c for the special terms, as illustrated in *section* 1.

Secondly, in our model, we have a chance to treat the chunk candidate as a whole during decoding, which means that we can employ more expressive features in our model than in the sequence labeling models. In Table 1, templates 5-13 concern the Internal-type features, where *start_word*(c) and *end_word*(c) represent the first word and the last word of chunk c, respectively. Similarly, *start_POS*(c) and *end_POS*(c) represent the POS tags associated with the first word and the last word of chunk c, respectively. These features aim at expressing the formation patterns of the current chunk with respect to words and POS tags. Template *internalWords*(c) denotes the concatenation of words in chunk c, while *internalPOSs*(c) denotes the sequence of POS tags in chunk c using regular expression-like form, as illustrated in *section* 1.

Finally, in Table 1, templates 14-28 concern the Correlation-type features, where *head*(c) denotes the headword extracted from chunk c, and *headPOS*(c) denotes the POS tag associated with the headword in chunk c. These features take into account various aspects of correlations between adjacent chunks. For example, we extracted the headwords located in adjacent chunks to form headword bigrams to express semantic dependency between adjacent chunks. To find the headword within every chunk, we referred to the head-finding rules from (Bikel, 2004), and made a simple modification to them. For instance, the head-finding rule for NP in (Bikel, 2004) is as follows:

(NP (r NP NN NT NR QP) (r))

Since the phrases are non-overlapping in our task, we simply remove the overlapping phrase tags NP and QP from the rule, and then the rule is modified as follows:

(NP (r NN NT NR) (r))

Additionally, the different bigrams formed by combining the first word (or POS) and last word (or POS) located in two adjacent chunks can also capture some correlations between adjacent chunks, and templates 17-22 are designed to express this kind of bigram information.

ID	*Feature template*
1	$wlabel(w)\ t_0$ for all w in c_0
2	$bigram\ (w)\ label(w)t_0$ for all w in c_0
3	$biPOS(w)\ label(w)t_0$ for all w in c_0
4	$w_{-1}w_1 label(w_0)\ t_0$, where $len(c_0)$=1
5	$start\_word(c_0)t_0$
6	$start\_POS(c_0)t_0$
7	$end\_word(c_0)t_0$
8	$end\_POS(c_0)t_0$
9	$wend\_word\ (c_0)\ t_0$ where $w \in c_0$ $and\ w \neq end\_word(c_0)$
10	$pend\_POS\ (c_0)\ t_0$ where $p \in c_0$ $and\ p \neq end\_POS(c_0)$
11	$internalPOSs(c_0)\ t_0$
12	$internalWords(c_0)\ t_0$
13	$specitermMatch(c_0)$
14	$t_{-1}t_0$
15	$head(c_{-1})t_{-1}head(c_0)t_0$
16	$headPOS(c_{-1})t_{-1}headPOS(c_0)t_0$
17	$end\_word(c_{-1})t_{-1}start\_word(c_0)t_0$
18	$end\_POS(c_{-1})t_{-1}start\_POS(c_0)t_0$
19	$end\_word(c_{-1})t_{-1}end\_word(c_0)t_0$
20	$end\_POS(c_{-1})t_{-1}end\_POS(c_0)t_0$
21	$start\_word(c_{-1})t_{-1}start\_word(c_0)t_0$
22	$start\_POS(c_{-1})t_{-1}start\_POS(c_0)t_0$
23	$end\_word(c_{-1})t_0$
24	$end\_POS(c_{-1})t_0$
25	$t_{-1}t_0 start\_word(c_0)$
26	$t_{-1}t_0 start\_POS(c_0)$
27	$internalWords(c_{-1})\ t_{-1}\ internalWords(c_0)\ t_0$
28	$internalPOSs(c_{-1})\ t_{-1}\ internalPOSs(c_0)\ t_0$

Table 1: Feature templates.

6 Experiments

6.1 Data Sets and Evaluation

Following previous studies on Chinese chunking in (Chen et al., 2006), our experiments were performed on the CTB4 dataset. The dataset consists of 838 files. In the experiments, we used the first 728 files (FID from chtb 001.fid to chtb 899.fid) as training data, and the other 110 files (FID from chtb 900.fid to chtb 1078.fid) as testing data. The training set consists of 9878 sentences, and the test set consists of 5920 sentences. The standard evaluation metrics for this task are precision p (the fraction of output chunks matching the reference chunks), recall r (the fraction of reference chunks returned), and the F-measure given by $F = 2pr/(p + r)$.

Our model has two tunable parameters: the number of training iterations N; the number of top *k-best* outputs. Since we were interested in finding an effective feature representation at chunk-level for phrase chunking, we fixed $N = 10$ and $k = 5$ for all experiments. In the following experiments, our model has roughly comparable training time to the sequence labeling approach based on CRFs.

6.2 Chinese NP chunking

NP is the most important phrase in Chinese chunking and about 47% phrases in the CTB4 Corpus are NPs. In this section, we present the results of our approach to NP recognition.

Table 2 shows the results of the two systems using the same feature representations as defined in Table 1, but using different loss functions for learning. As shown, learning with F1 loss can improve the F-score by 0.34% over learning with 0-1 loss. It is reasonable that the model optimized with respect to evaluation metrics directly can achieve higher performance.

Loss Function	Precision	Recall	F1
0-1 loss	91.39	90.93	91.16
F1 loss	**92.03**	**90.98**	**91.50**

Table 2: Experimental results on Chinese NP chunking.

6.3 Chinese Text Chunking

There are 12 different types of phrases in the chunking corpus. Table 3 shows the results from two different systems with different loss functions for learning. Observing the results in Table 3, we can see that learning with F1 loss can improve the F-score by 0.36% over learning with 0-1 loss, similar to the case in NP recognition. More specifically, learning with F1 loss provides much better results for ADJP, ADVP, DVP, NP and VP, respectively. And it yields equivalent or comparable results to 0-1 loss in other categories.

	F1 loss			0-1 loss		
	precision	recall	*F1*	precision	recall	*F1*
ADJP	87.86	87.09	87.47	86.74	86.55	86.64
ADVP	90.66	78.73	84.27	91.91	76.68	83.61
CLP	0.00	0.00	0.00	1.32	5.88	2.15
DNP	99.42	99.93	99.68	99.42	99.95	99.69
DP	99.46	99.76	99.61	99.46	99.76	99.61
DVP	99.61	99.61	99.61	99.22	99.61	99.42
LCP	99.74	99.96	99.85	99.74	99.93	99.84
LST	87.50	52.50	65.63	87.50	52.50	65.63
NP	91.87	91.01	91.44	91.34	90.52	90.93
PP	99.57	99.77	99.67	99.57	99.77	99.67
QP	96.45	96.64	96.55	96.45	97.07	96.76
VP	90.14	90.39	90.26	89.92	89.79	89.85
ALL	**92.54**	**91.68**	**92.11**	92.30	91.20	91.75

Table 3: Experimental results on Chinese text chunking.

6.4 Comparison with Other Models

Chen et al. (2006) compared the performance of the state-of-the-art machine learning models for Chinese chunking, and found that the SVMs approach yields higher accuracy than respective CRFs, Transformation-based Learning (TBL) (Megyesi, 2002), and Memory-based Learning (MBL) (Sang, 2002) approaches.

In this section, we give a comparison and analysis between our model and other state-of-the-art machine learning models for Chinese NP chunking and text chunking tasks. Performance of our model and some of the best results from the state-of-the-art systems are summarized in Table 4. Row "Voting" refers to the phrase-based voting methods based on four basic systems, which are respectively SVMs, CRFs, TBL and MBL, as depicted in (Chen et al., 2006). Observing the results in Table 4, we can see that for both NP chunking and text chunking tasks, our model achieves significant performance improvement over those state-of-the-art systems in terms of the F1-score, even for the voting methods. For text chunking task, our approach improves performance by 0.65% over SVMs, and 0.43% over the voting method, respectively.

	Method	*F1*
NP chunking	CRFs	89.72
	SVMs	90.62
	Voting	91.13
	Ours	**91.50**
Text chunking	CRFs	90.74
	SVMs	91.46
	Voting	91.68
	Ours	**92.11**

Table 4: Comparisons of chunking performance for Chinese NP chunking and text chunking.

In particular, for NP chunking task, the F1-score of our approach is improved by 0.88% in comparison with SVMs, the best single system. Further, we investigated the likely cause for performance improvement by comparing the recognized results from our system and SVMs respectively. We first sorted NPs by their length, and then calculated the F1-scores associated with different lengths for the two systems respectively. Figure 3 shows the comparison of F1-scores of the two systems by the chunk length. In the Chinese chunking corpus, the max NP length is 27, and the mean NP length is 1.5. Among all NPs, the NPs with the length 1 account for 81.22%. For the NPs with the length 1, our system gives slight improvement by 0.28% over SVMs. From the figure, we can see that the performance gap grows rapidly with the increase of the chunk length. In particular, the gap between the two systems is 27.73% when the length hits 4. But the gap begins to become smaller with further growth of the chunk length. The reasons may include the following two aspects. First, the number of NPs with the greater length is relatively small in the corpus. Second, the NPs with greater length in Chinese corpus often exhibit some typical rules. For example, an NP with length 8 is given as follows.

"棉花/NN(cotton) 、/PU 油料/NN(oil) 、/PU 药材/NN(drug) 、/PU 蔬菜/NN(vegetable) 等/ETC (et al)".

The NP consists of a sequence of nouns simply separated by a punctuation "、". So it is also easy to be recognized by the sequence labeling approach based on SVMs. In summary, the above investigation indicates that our system is better at recognizing the long and complicated phrases compared with the sequence labeling approaches.

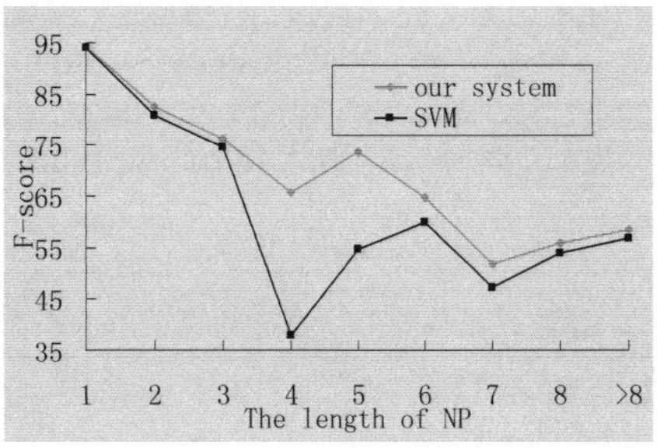

Figure 3: Comparison of F1-scores of NP recognition on Chinese corpus by the chunk length.

6.5 Impact of Different Types of Features

Our phrase chunking model is highly dependent upon chunk-level information. To establish the impact of each type of feature (SL-type, Internal-type, Correlation-type), we look at the improvement in F1-score brought about by adding each type of features. Table 5 shows the accuracy with various features added to the model.

First consider the effect of the SL-type features. If we use only the SL-type features, the system achieves slightly lower performance than CRFs or SVMs, as shown in Table 4. Since the SL-type features consist of the features associated with single label, not including the features associated with label bigrams. Then, adding the Internal-type features to the system results in significant performance improvement on NP chunking and on text chunking, achieving 2.53% and 1.37%, respectively. Further, if Correlation-type features are used, the F1-scores on NP chunking and on text chunking are improved by 1.01% and 0.66%, respectively. The results show a significant impact due to the use of Internal-type features and Correlation-type features for both NP chunking and text chunking.

Task Type	Feature Type	F1
NP chunking	SL-type	87.96
	+Internal-type	90.49
	+Correlation-type	91.50
Text chunking	SL-type	90.08
	+Internal-type	91.45
	+Correlation-type	92.11

Table 5: Test F1-scores for different types of features on Chinese corpus.

6.6 Performance on Other Languages

We mainly focused on Chinese chunking in this paper. However, our approach is generally applicable to other languages including English, except that the definition of feature templates may be language-specific. To validate this point, we evaluated our system on the CoNLL 2000 data set, a public benchmarking corpus for English chunking (Sang and Buchholz 2000). The training set consists of 8936 sentences, and the test set consists of 2012 sentences.

We conducted both the NP-chunking and text chunking experiments on this data set with our approach, using the same feature templates as in Chinese chunking task excluding template 13. To find the headword within every chunk, we referred to the head-finding rules from (Collins, 1999), and made a simple modification to them in a similar way as in Chinese. As we can see from Table 6, our model is able to achieve better performance compared with state-of-the-art systems. Table 6 also shows state-of-the-art performance for both NP-chunking and text chunking tasks. LDCRF's results presented in (Sun et al., 2008) are the state-of-the-art for the NP chunking task, and SVM's results presented in (Wu et al., 2006) are the state-of-the-art for the text chunking task.

Moreover, the performance should be further improved if some additional features tailored for English chunking are employed in our model. For example, we can introduce an orthographic feature type called Token feature and the affix feature into the model, as used in (Wu et al., 2006).

	Method	Precision	Recall	F1
NP chunking	Ours	94.79	94.65	**94.72**
	LDCRF	94.65	94.03	94.34
Text chunking	Ours	94.31	94.12	**94.22**
	SVMs	94.12	94.13	94.12

Table 6: Performance on English corpus.

7 Conclusions and Future Work

In this paper we have presented a novel approach to phrase chunking by formulating it as a joint segmentation and labeling problem. One important advantage of our approach is that it provides a natural formulation to exploit chunk-level features. The experimental results on both Chinese chunking and English chunking tasks show that the use of chunk-level features can lead to significant performance improvement and that our approach outperforms the best in the literature.

Future work mainly includes the following two aspects. Firstly, we will explore applying external information, such as semantic knowledge, to represent the chunk-level features, and then incorporate them into our model to improve the performance. Secondly, we plan to apply our approach to other joint segmentation and labeling tasks, such as clause identification and named entity recognition.

Acknowledgments

This research is supported by Projects 61073119, 60773173 under the National Natural Science Foundation of China, and project BK2010547 under the Jiangsu Natural Science Foundation of China. We would also like to thank the excellent and insightful comments from the three anonymous reviewers.

References

Steven P. Abney. 1991. Parsing by chunks. In Robert C. Berwick, Steven P. Abney, and Carol Tenny, editors, Principle-Based Parsing , pages 257-278. Kluwer Academic Publishers.

Daniel M, Bikel. 2004. On the Parameter Space of Generative Lexicalized Statistical Parsing Models. Ph.D. thesis, University of Pennsylvania.

Wenliang Chen, Yujie Zhang, and Hitoshi Isahara. 2006. An empirical study of Chinese chunking. In Proceedings of the COLING/ACL 2006 Main Conference Poster Sessions, pages 97-104.

Michael Collins. 2002. Discriminative training methods for hidden Markov models: Theory and experiments with perceptron algorithms. In Proc. EMNLP-02.

Michael Collins. 1999. Head-Driven Statistical Models for Natural Language Parsing. Ph.D. thesis, University of Pennsylvania.

Koby Crammer. 2004. Online Learning of Complex Categorial Problems. Hebrew University of Jerusalem, PhD Thesis.

Taku Kudo and Yuji Matsumoto. 2001. Chunking with support vector machines. In Proceedings of NAACL01.

Koby Crammer, Ryan McDonald, and Fernando Pereira. 2005. Scalable large-margin online learning for structured classification. In NIPS Workshop on Learning With Structured Outputs.

Heng Li, Jonathan J. Webster, Chunyu Kit, and Tianshun Yao. 2003. Transductive hmm based chinese text chunking. In Proceedings of IEEE NLPKE2003, pages 257-262, Beijing, China.

Ryan McDonald, Femando Pereira, Kiril Ribarow, and Jan Hajic. 2005. Non-projective dependency parsing using spanning tree algorithms. In Proceedings of HLT/EMNLP, pages 523-530.

Ryan. McDonald, K. Crammer, and F. Pereira, 2005. Flexible Text Segmentation with Structured Multilabel Classification. In Proceedings HLT/EMNLP, pages 987- 994.

Ryan McDonald. 2006. Discriminative Training and Spanning Tree Algorithms for Dependency Parsing. University of Pennsylvania, PhD Thesis.

Beata Megyesi. 2002. Shallow parsing with pos taggers and linguistic features. Journal of Machine Learning Research, 2:639-668.

Antonio Molina and Ferran Pla. 2002. Shallow parsing using specialized hmms. Journal of Machine Learning Research., 2:595- 613.

E.F.T.K Sang and S. Buchholz. 2000. Introduction to the CoNLL-2000 shared task: Chunking. In Proceedings CoNLL-00, pages 127-132.

Sunita Sarawagi and W. Cohen. 2004. Semi-markov conditional random fields for information extraction. In Proceedings of NIPS 17, pages 1185–1192.

Fei Sha and Fernando Pereira. 2003. Shallow parsing with conditional random fields. In Proceedings of HLT-NAACL03.

Xu Sun, Louis-Philippe Morency, Daisuke Okanohara, and Jun'ichi Tsujii. 2008. Modeling Latent-Dynamic in Shallow Parsing: A Latent Conditional Model with Improved Inference. In Proceedings of the 22nd International Conference on Computational Linguistics, pages 841–848.

Yongmei Tan, Tianshun Yao, Qing Chen, and Jingbo Zhu. 2004. Chinese chunk identification using svms plus sigmoid. In IJCNLP, pages 527-536.

Yongmei Tan, Tianshun Yao, Qing Chen, and Jingbo Zhu. 2005. Applying conditional random fields to chinese shallow parsing. In Proceedings of CICLing-2005, pages 167-176.

Erik F. Tjong Kim Sang. 2002. Memory-based shallow parsing. JMLR, 2(3):559-594.

Yu-Chieh Wu, Chia-Hui Chang, and Yue-Shi Lee. 2006. A general and multi-lingual phrase chunking model based on masking method. In Proceedings of 7th International Conference on Intelligent Text Processing and Computational Linguistics, pages 144-155.

Nianwen Xue, Fei Xia, Shizhe Huang, and Anthony Kroch. 2000. The bracketing guidelines for the penn chinese treebank. Technical report, University of Pennsylvania.

Stavros A. Zenios Yair Censor. 1997. Parallel Optimization: Theory, Algorithms, and Applications. Oxford University Press.

Tong Zhang, F. Damerau, and D. Johnson. 2002. Text chunking based on a generalization of winnow. Journal of Machine Learning Research, 2:615-637.

Yue Zhang and Stephen Clark. 2008. Joint word segmentation and POS tagging using a single perceptron. In Proceedings of ACL/HLT, pages 888-896.

Yue Zhang and Stephen Clark. 2010. A fast decoder for joint word segmentation and POS-tagging using a single discriminative model. In Proceedings of EMNLP, pages 843-852.

A Beam-Search Decoder for Grammatical Error Correction

Daniel Dahlmeier[1] and **Hwee Tou Ng**[1,2]
[1]NUS Graduate School for Integrative Sciences and Engineering
[2]Department of Computer Science, National University of Singapore
{danielhe,nght}@comp.nus.edu.sg

Abstract

We present a novel beam-search decoder for grammatical error correction. The decoder iteratively generates new hypothesis corrections from current hypotheses and scores them based on features of grammatical correctness and fluency. These features include scores from discriminative classifiers for specific error categories, such as articles and prepositions. Unlike all previous approaches, our method is able to perform correction of whole sentences with multiple and interacting errors while still taking advantage of powerful existing classifier approaches. Our decoder achieves an F_1 correction score significantly higher than all previous published scores on the Helping Our Own (HOO) shared task data set.

1 Introduction

Grammatical error correction is an important problem in natural language processing (NLP) that has attracted an increasing amount of interest over the last few years. Grammatical error correction promises to provide instantaneous accurate feedback to language learners, e.g., learners of English as a Second Language (ESL).

The dominant paradigm that underlies most error correction systems to date is multi-class classification. A classifier is trained to predict a word from a *confusion set* of possible correction choices, given some feature representation of the surrounding sentence context. During testing, the classifier predicts the most likely correction for each test instance. If the prediction differs from the observed word used by the writer and the classifier is sufficiently confident in its prediction, the observed word is replaced by the prediction. Although considerable progress has been made, the classification approach suffers from some serious shortcomings. Each classifier corrects a single word for a specific error category individually. This ignores dependencies between the words in a sentence. Also, by conditioning on the surrounding context, the classifier implicitly assumes that the surrounding context is free of grammatical errors, which is often not the case. Finally, the classifier typically has to commit to a single one-best prediction and is not able to change its decision later or explore multiple corrections. Instead of correcting each word individually, we would like to perform global inference over corrections of whole sentences which can contain multiple and interacting errors.

An alternative paradigm is to view error correction as a statistical machine translation (SMT) problem from "bad" to "good" English. While this approach can naturally correct whole sentences, a standard SMT system cannot easily incorporate models for specific grammatical errors. It also suffers from the paucity of error-annotated training data for grammar correction. As a result, applying a standard SMT system to error correction does not produce good results, as we show in this work.

In this work, we present a novel beam-search decoder for grammatical error correction that combines the advantages of the classification approach and the SMT approach. Starting from the original input sentence, the decoder performs an iterative search over possible sentence-level hypotheses to find the best sentence-level correction. In each iteration, a set of *proposers* generates new hypotheses by making incremental changes to the hypotheses found so far. A set of *experts* scores the new hypotheses on criteria of grammatical correctness. These experts include discriminative classifiers for specific error categories, such as articles and prepositions. The decoder model calculates the overall hypothesis score for each hypothesis as a linear combination of the expert scores. The weights of the decoder model are discriminatively trained on a development set of error-annotated sentences. The highest scoring hypotheses are kept in the search beam for the next iteration. This search procedure continues until the beam is empty or the maximum number of iterations has been reached. The highest scoring hypothesis is returned as the sentence-level correction. We evaluate our proposed decoder in the context of the Helping Our Own (HOO) shared task on grammatical error correction (Dale and Kilgarriff, 2011). Our decoder achieves an F_1 score of 25.48% which improves upon the current state of the art.

The remainder of this paper is organized as follows. The next section gives an overview of related work. Section 3 describes the proposed beam-search decoder. Sections 4 and 5 describe the experimental setup and results, respectively. Section 6 provides further discussion. Section 7 concludes the paper.

2 Related Work

In this section, we summarize related work in grammatical error correction. For a more detailed review, the readers can refer to (Leacock et al., 2010).

The classification approach to error correction has mainly focused on correcting article and preposition errors (Knight and Chander, 1994; Han et al., 2006; Chodorow et al., 2007; Tetreault and Chodorow, 2008; Gamon, 2010; Dahlmeier and Ng, 2011b; Rozovskaya and Roth, 2011). The advantage of the classification approach is that it can make use of powerful machine learning algorithms in connection with arbitrary features from the sentence context. Typical features include surrounding N-grams, part-of-speech (POS) tags, chunks, etc. In fact, a considerable amount of research effort has been invested in finding better features.

The SMT approach to error corrections has received comparatively less attention. Brockett *et al.* (2006) use an SMT system to correct errors involving mass noun errors. Because no large annotated learner corpus was available, the training data was created artificially from non-learner text. Lee and Seneff (2006) describe a lattice-based correction system with a domain-specific grammar for spoken utterances from the flight domain. The work in (Désilets and Hermet, 2009) uses simple round-trip translation with a standard SMT system to correct grammatical errors. Dahlmeier and Ng (2011a) correct collocation errors using phrase-based SMT and paraphrases induced from the writer's native language. Park and Levy (2011) propose a noisy channel model for error correction. While their motivation to correct whole sentences is similar to ours, their proposed generative method differs substantially from our discriminative decoder. Park and Levy's model does not allow the use of discriminative expert classifiers as our decoder does, but instead relies on a bigram language model to find grammatical corrections. Indeed, they point out that the language model often fails to distinguish grammatical and ungrammatical sentences.

To the best of our knowledge, our work is the first discriminatively trained decoder for whole-sentence grammatical error correction.

3 Decoder

In this section, we describe the proposed beam-search decoder and its components.

The task of the decoder is to find the best hypothesis (i.e., the best corrected sentence) for a given input sentence. To accomplish this, the decoder needs to be able to perform two tasks: generating new hypotheses from current ones, and discriminating good hypotheses from bad ones. This is achieved by two groups of modules which we call *proposers* and *experts*, respectively. Proposers take a hypothesis and generate a set of new hypotheses, where each new hypothesis is the result of making an incremental change to the current hypothesis. Experts score hypotheses on particular aspects of grammaticality. This can be a general language model score, or the output of classifiers for particular error categories, for example for article and preposition usage. The overall score for a hypothesis is a linear combination of the expert scores. Note that in our decoder, each hypothesis corresponds to a complete sentence. This makes it easy to apply syntactic processing, like POS tagging, chunking, and dependency parsing, which provides necessary features for the expert models. The highest scoring hypotheses are kept in the search beam for the next iteration. The search ends when the beam is empty or the maximum number of iterations has been reached. The highest scoring hypothesis found during the search is returned as the sentence-level correction. The modular design of the decoder makes it easy to extend the model to new error categories by adding specific proposers and experts without having to change the decoding algorithm.

3.1 Proposers

The proposers generate new hypotheses, given a hypothesis. Because the number of possible hypotheses grows exponentially with the sentence length, enumerating all possible hypotheses is infeasible. Instead, each proposer only makes a small incremental change to the hypothesis in each iteration. A change corresponds to a correction of a single word or phrase. We experiment with the following proposers in this work. Additional proposers for other error categories can easily be added to the decoder.

- **Spelling** Generate a set of new hypotheses, by replacing a misspelled word with each correction proposed by a spellchecker.
- **Articles** For each noun phrase (NP), generate two new hypotheses by changing the observed article. Possible article choices are *a/an*, *the*, and the empty article ϵ.
- **Prepositions** For each prepositional phrase (PP), generate a set of new hypotheses by changing the observed preposition. For each preposition, we define a confusion set of possible corrections.
- **Punctuation insertion** Insert commas, periods, and hyphens based on a set of simple rules.
- **Noun number** For each noun, change its number from singular to plural or vice versa.

3.2 Experts

The experts score hypotheses on particular aspects of grammaticality to help the decoder to discriminate grammatical hypotheses from ungrammatical ones. We employ two types of expert models. The first type of expert model is a standard N-gram language model. The language model expert is not specialized for any particular type of error. The second type of experts is based on linear classifiers and is specialized for particular error categories. We use the following classifier experts in our work. The features for the classifier expert models include features from N-grams, part-of-speech (POS) tags, chunks, web-scale N-gram counts, and dependency parse trees. Additional experts can easily be added to the decoder.

- **Article expert** Predict the correct article for a noun phrase.
- **Preposition expert** Predict the correct preposition for a prepositional phrase.
- **Noun number expert** Predict whether a noun should be in the singular or plural form.

The outputs of the experts are used as hypothesis features in the decoder, as described in the next section.

3.3 Hypothesis Features

Each hypothesis is associated with a vector of real-valued features which are indicators of grammaticality and are computed from the output of the expert models. We call these features *hypothesis features* to distinguish them from the features of the expert classifiers. The simplest hypothesis feature is the log probability of the hypothesis under the N-gram language model expert. To avoid a bias towards shorter hypotheses, we normalize the probability by the length of the hypothesis:

$$score_{lm} = \frac{1}{|\mathbf{h}|} \log Pr(\mathbf{h}), \qquad (1)$$

where $\mathbf{h}$ is a hypothesis sentence and $|\mathbf{h}|$ is the hypothesis length in tokens.

For the classifier-based experts, we define two types of features. The first is the *average score* of the hypothesis under the expert model:

$$score_{avg} = \frac{1}{n}\sum_{i=1}^{n}\left(\mathbf{u}^T f(\mathbf{x}_\mathbf{i}^\mathbf{h}, y_i^\mathbf{h})\right), \quad (2)$$

where $\mathbf{u}$ is the expert classifier weight vector, $\mathbf{x}_\mathbf{i}^\mathbf{h}$ and $y_i^\mathbf{h}$ are the feature vector and the observed class, respectively, for the i-th instance extracted from the hypothesis $\mathbf{h}$ (e.g., the i-th NP in the hypothesis for the article expert), and f is a feature map that computes the expert classifier features. The average score reflects how much the expert model "likes" the hypothesis. The second expert score, which we call *delta score*, is the maximum difference between the highest scoring class and the observed class in any instance from the hypothesis:

$$score_{delta} = \max_{i,y}\left(\mathbf{u}^T f(\mathbf{x}_\mathbf{i}^\mathbf{h}, y) - \mathbf{u}^T f(\mathbf{x}_\mathbf{i}^\mathbf{h}, y_i^\mathbf{h})\right). \quad (3)$$

Generally speaking, the delta score measures how much the model "disagrees" with the hypothesis.

Finally, each hypothesis has a number of *correction count features* that keep track of how many corrections have been made to the hypothesis so far. For example, there is a feature that counts how often the article correction $\epsilon \rightarrow the$ has been applied. We also add aggregated correction count features for each error category, e.g., how many article corrections have been applied in total. The correction count features allow the decoder to learn a bias against overcorrecting sentences and to learn which types of corrections are more likely and which are less likely.

3.4 Decoder Model

The hypothesis features described in the previous subsection are combined to compute the score of a hypothesis according to the following linear model:

$$s = \mathbf{w}^T f_E(\mathbf{h}), \quad (4)$$

where $\mathbf{w}$ is the decoder model weight vector and f_E is a feature map that computes the hypothesis features described above, given a set of experts E. The weight vector $\mathbf{w}$ is tuned on a development set of error-annotated sentences using the PRO ranking optimization algorithm (Hopkins and May, 2011).[1]

[1] We also experimented with the MERT algorithm (Och, 2003) but found that PRO achieved better results.

PRO performs decoder parameter tuning through a pair-wise ranking approach. The algorithm starts by sampling hypothesis pairs from the N-best list of the decoder. The metric score for each hypothesis induces a ranking of the two hypotheses in each pair. The task of finding a weight vector that correctly ranks hypotheses can then be reduced to a simple binary classification task. In this work, we use PRO to optimize the F_1 correction score, which is defined in Section 4.2. PRO requires a sentence-level score for each hypothesis. As F_1 score is not decomposable, we optimize sentence-level F_1 score which serves as an approximation of the corpus-level F_1 score. Similarly, Hopkins and May optimize a sentence-level BLEU approximation (Lin and Och, 2004) instead of the corpus-level BLEU score (Papineni et al., 2002). We observed that optimizing sentence-level F_1 score worked well in practice in our experiments.

3.5 Decoder Search

Given a set of proposers, experts, and a tuned decoder model, the decoder can be used to correct new unseen sentences. This is done by performing a search over possible hypothesis candidates. The decoder starts with the input sentence as the initial hypothesis, i.e., assuming that all words are correct. It then performs a beam search over the space of possible hypotheses to find the best hypothesis correction $\hat{\mathbf{h}}$ for an input sentence $\mathbf{e}$. The search proceeds in iterations until the beam is empty or the maximum number of iterations has been reached. In each iteration, the decoder takes each hypothesis in the beam and generates new hypothesis candidates using all the available proposers. The hypotheses are evaluated by the expert models that compute the hypothesis features and finally scored using the decoder model. As the search space grows exponentially, it is infeasible to perform exhaustive search. Therefore, we prune the search space by only accepting the most promising hypotheses to the pool of hypotheses for future consideration. If a hypothesis has a higher score than the best hypothesis found in previous iterations, it is definitely added to the pool. Otherwise, we use a simulated annealing strategy where hypotheses with a lower score can still be accepted with a certain probability which depends on the difference between the hypothesis score and

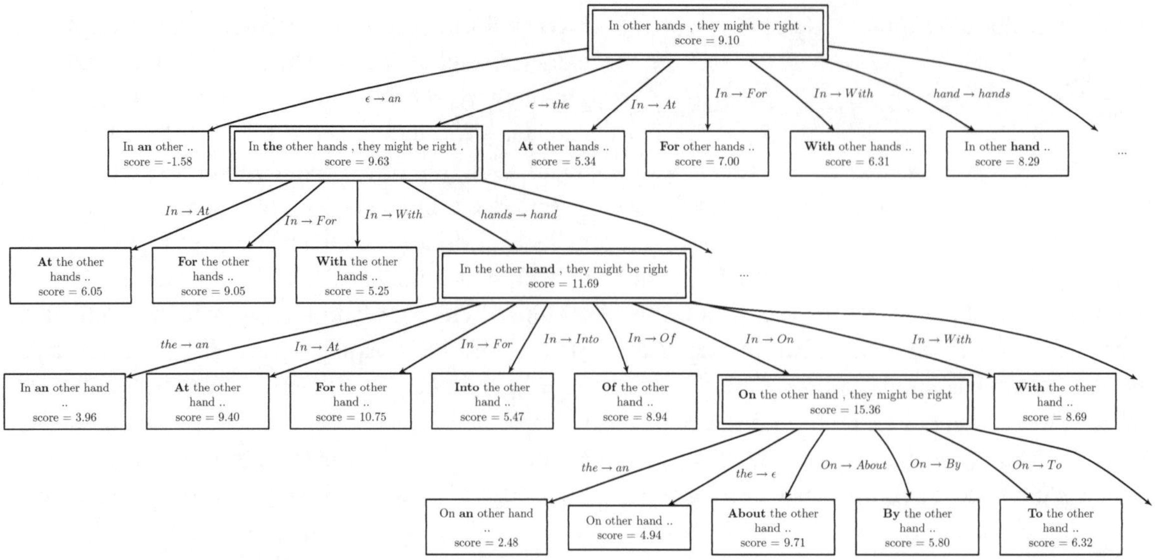

Figure 1: Example of a search tree produced by the beam-search decoder for the input *In other hands, they might be right.* The highest scoring hypothesis found is *On the other hand, they might be right.* Some hypotheses are omitted due to space constraints.

the score of the best hypothesis and the "temperature" of the system. We lower the temperature after each iteration according to an exponential cooling schedule. Hypotheses that have been explored before are not considered again to avoid cycles in the search. From all hypotheses in the pool, we select the top k hypotheses and add them to the beam for the next search iteration. The decoding algorithm is shown in Algorithm 1. The decoder can be considered an *anytime algorithm* (Russell and Norvig, 2010), as it has a current best hypothesis correction available at any point of the search, while gradually improving the result by searching for better hypotheses. An example of a search tree produced by our decoder is shown in Figure 1.

The decoding algorithm shares some similarities with the beam-search algorithm frequently used in SMT. There is however a difference between SMT decoding and grammar correction decoding that is worth pointing out. In SMT decoding, every input word needs to be translated exactly once. In contrast, in grammar correction decoding, the majority of the words typically do *not* need any correction (in the HOO data, for example, there are on average 6 errors per 100 words). On the other hand, some words might require *multiple* corrections, for example spelling correction followed by noun number correction. Errors can also be inter-dependent, where correcting one word makes it necessary to change another word, for example to preserve agreement. Our decoding algorithm has the option to correct some words multiple times, while leaving other words unchanged.

4 Experiments

We evaluate our decoder in the context of the HOO shared task on grammatical error correction. The goal of the task is to automatically correct errors in academic papers from NLP. The readers can refer to the overview paper (Dale and Kilgarriff, 2011) for details. We compare our proposed method with two baselines: a phrase-based SMT system (described in Section 4.3) and a pipeline of classifiers (described in Section 4.4).

4.1 Data

We split the HOO development data into an equal sized training (HOO-TRAIN) and tuning (HOO-TUNE) set. The official HOO test data (HOO-TEST) is used for evaluation. In the HOO shared task, participants were allowed to raise objections regarding the gold-standard annotations (corrections) of the test data after the test data was released. As a result, the gold-standard annotations could be biased in fa-

Algorithm 1 The beam-search decoding algorithm. $\mathbf{e}$: original sentence, $\mathbf{w}$: decoder weight vector, P: set of proposers, E: set of experts, k: beam width, M: maximum number of iterations, T, c: initial temperature and cooling schedule for simulated annealing ($0 < c < 1$).

```
procedure decode(e, w, P, E, k, M)
  beam ← {e}
  previous ← {e}
  h_best ← e
  s_best ← w^T f_E(h_best)
  i ← 0
  while beam ≠ ∅ ∧ i < M do
      pool ← {}
      for all h ∈ beam do
          for all p ∈ P do
              for all h' ∈ p.propose(h) do
                  if h' ∈ previous then
                      continue
                  previous ← previous ∪ {h'}
                  s_h' ← w^T f_E(h')
                  if accept(s_h', s_best, T) then
                      pool ← pool ∪ {(h', s_h')}
      beam ← ∅
      for all (h, s_h) ∈ nbest(pool, k) do
          beam ← beam ∪ {h}
          if s_h > s_best then
              h_best ← h
              s_best ← s_h
      T ← T × c
      i ← i + 1
  return h_best

procedure accept(s_h, s_best, T)
  δ ← s_h − s_best
  if δ > 0 then
      return true
  if exp(δ/T) > random() then
      return true else return false
```

vor of specific systems participating in the shared task. We obtain both the original and the final official gold-standard annotations and report evaluation results on both annotations.

We use the ACL Anthology[2] as training data for the expert models. We crawl all non-OCR documents from the anthology, except those documents that overlap with the HOO data. Section headers, references, etc. are automatically removed. The Web 1T 5-gram corpus (Brants and Franz, 2006) is used for language modeling and collecting web N-gram counts. Table 1 gives an overview of the data sets.

[2]http://www.aclweb.org/anthology-new/

Data Set	Sentences	Tokens
HOO-TRAIN	467	11,373
HOO-TUNE	472	11,435
HOO-TEST	722	18,790
ACL-ANTHOLOGY	943,965	22,465,690

Table 1: Overview of the data sets.

4.2 Evaluation

We evaluate performance by computing precision, recall, and F_1 correction score without bonus as defined in the official HOO report (Dale and Kilgarriff, 2011)[3]. F_1 correction score is simply the F_1 measure (van Rijsbergen, 1979) between the corrections (called *edits* in HOO) proposed by a system and the gold-standard corrections. Let $\{\mathbf{e}_1, \ldots, \mathbf{e}_n\}$ be a set of test sentences and let $\{\mathbf{g}_1, \ldots, \mathbf{g}_n\}$ be the set of gold-standard edits for the sentences. Let $\{\mathbf{h}_1, \ldots, \mathbf{h}_n\}$ be the set of corrected sentences output by a system. One difficulty in the evaluation is that the set of system edits $\{\mathbf{d}_1, \ldots, \mathbf{d}_n\}$ between the test sentences and the system outputs is ambiguous. For example, assume that the original test sentence is *The data is similar with test set.*, the system output is *The data is similar to the test set.*, and the gold-standard edits are two corrections $with \rightarrow to$, $\epsilon \rightarrow the$ that change *with* to *to* and insert *the* before *test set*. The official HOO scorer however extracts a single system edit $with \rightarrow to\ the$ for this instance. As the extracted system edit is different from the gold-standard edits, the system would be considered wrong, although it proposes the *exact same* corrected sentence as the gold standard edits. This problem has also been recognized by the HOO shared task organizers (see (Dale and Kilgarriff, 2011), Section 5).

Our *MaxMatch* (M^2) scorer (Dahlmeier and Ng, 2012) overcomes this problem through an efficient algorithm that computes the set of system edits which has the maximum overlap with the gold-standard edits. We use the M^2 scorer as the main evaluation metric in our experiments. Additionally, we also report results with the official HOO scorer. Once the set of system edits is extracted, precision, recall, and F_1 measure are computed as follows.

[3]"Without bonus" means that a system does not receive extra credit for not making corrections that are considered optional in the gold standard.

$$P = \frac{\sum_{i=1}^{n} |\mathbf{d}_i \cap \mathbf{g}_i|}{\sum_{i=1}^{n} |\mathbf{d}_i|} \quad (5)$$

$$R = \frac{\sum_{i=1}^{n} |\mathbf{d}_i \cap \mathbf{g}_i|}{\sum_{i=1}^{n} |\mathbf{g}_i|} \quad (6)$$

$$F_1 = 2 \times \frac{P \times R}{P + R} \quad (7)$$

We note that the M^2 scorer and the HOO scorer adhere to the same score definition and only differ in the way the system edits are computed. For statistical significance testing, we use sign-test with bootstrap re-sampling (Koehn, 2004) with 1,000 samples.

4.3 SMT Baseline

We build a baseline error correction system, using the MOSES SMT system (Koehn et al., 2007). Word alignments are created automatically on "good-bad" parallel text from HOO-TRAIN using GIZA++ (Och and Ney, 2003), followed by phrase extraction using the standard heuristic (Koehn et al., 2003). The maximum phrase length is 5. Parameter tuning is done on the HOO-TUNE data with the PRO algorithm (Hopkins and May, 2011) implemented in MOSES. The optimization objective is sentence-level BLEU (Lin and Och, 2004). We note that the objective function is not the same as the final evaluation F_1 score. Also, the training and tuning data are small by SMT standards. The aim for the SMT baseline is not to achieve a state-of-the-art system, but to serve as the simplest possible baseline that uses only off-the-shelf software.

4.4 Pipeline Baseline

The second baseline system is a pipeline of classifier-based and rule-based correction steps. Each step takes sentence segmented plain text as input, corrects one particular error category, and feeds the corrected text into the next step. No search or global inference is applied. The correction steps are:

1. Spelling errors
2. Article errors
3. Preposition errors
4. Punctuation errors
5. Noun number errors

We use the following tools for syntactic processing: OpenNLP[4] for POS tagging, YamCha (Kudo and Matsumoto, 2003) for constituent chunking, and the MALT parser (Nivre et al., 2007) for dependency parsing. For language modeling, we use RandLM (Talbot and Osborne, 2007).

For spelling correction, we use GNU Aspell[5]. Words that contain upper-case characters inside the word or are shorter than four characters are excluded from spell checking. The spelling dictionary is augmented with all words that appear at least 10 times in the ACL-ANTHOLOGY data set.

Article correction is cast as a multi-class classification problem. As the learning algorithm, we choose multi-class confidence-weighted (CW) learning (Crammer et al., 2009) which has been shown to perform well for NLP problems with high dimensional and sparse feature spaces. The possible classes are the articles *a*, *the*, and the empty article ϵ. The article *an* is normalized as *a* and restored later using a rule-based heuristic. We consider all NPs that are not pronouns and do not have a non-article determiner, e.g., *this, that*. The classifier is trained on over 5 million instances from ACL-ANTHOLOGY. We use a combination of features proposed by (Rozovskaya et al., 2011) (which include lexical and POS N-grams, lexical head words, etc.), web-scale N-gram count features from the Web 1T 5-gram corpus following (Bergsma et al., 2009), and dependency head and child features. During testing, a correction is proposed if the predicted article is different from the observed article used by the writer, and the difference between the confidence score for the predicted article and the confidence score for the observed article is larger than a threshold. Threshold parameters are tuned via a grid-search on the HOO-TUNE data. We tune a separate threshold value for each class.

Preposition correction and noun number correction are analogous to article correction. They differ only in terms of the classes and the features. For preposition correction, the classes are 36 frequent English prepositions[6]. The features are surrounding

[4] `http://opennlp.sourceforge.net`

[5] `http://aspell.net`

[6] *about, along, among, around, as, at, beside, besides, between, by, down, during, except, for, from, in, inside, into, of, off, on, onto, outside, over, through, to, toward, towards, under,*

lexical N-grams, web-scale N-gram counts, and dependency features following (Tetreault et al., 2010). The preposition classifier is trained on 1 million training examples from the ACL-ANTHOLOGY. For noun number correction, the classes are *singular* and *plural*. The features are lexical N-grams, web-scale N-gram counts, dependency features, the noun lemma, and a binary countability feature. The noun number classifier is trained on over 5 million examples from ACL-ANTHOLOGY. During testing, the singular or plural word surface form is generated using WordNet (Fellbaum, 1998) and simple heuristics. Punctuation correction is done using a set of simple rules developed on the HOO development data.

At the end of every correction step, all proposed corrections are filtered using a 5-gram language model from the Web 1T 5-gram corpus and only corrections that strictly increase the normalized language model score of the sentence are applied.

4.5 Decoder

We experiment with different decoder configurations with different proposers and expert models. In the simplest configuration, the decoder only has the spelling proposer and the language model expert. We then add the article proposer and expert, the preposition proposer and expert, the punctuation proposer, and finally the noun number proposer and expert. We refer to the final configuration with all proposers and experts as the *full decoder model*. Note that error categories are corrected jointly and not in sequential steps as in the pipeline.

To make the results directly comparable to the pipeline, the decoder uses the same resources as the pipeline. As the expert models, we use a 5-gram language model from the Web 1T 5-gram corpus with the Berkeley LM (Pauls and Klein, 2011)[7] in the decoder and the CW-classifiers described in the last section. The spelling proposer uses the same spellchecker as the pipeline, and the punctuation proposer uses the same rules as the pipeline. The beam width and the maximum number of iterations are set to 10. In earlier experiments, we found that larger values had no effect on the result. The simulated annealing temperature T is initialized to 10 and the exponential cooling schedule c is set to 0.9. The decoder weight vector is initialized as follows. The weight for the language model score and the weights for the classifier expert average scores are initialized to 1.0, and the weights for the classifier expert delta scores are initialized to -1.0. The weights for the correction count features are initialized to zero. For PRO optimization, we use the HOO-TUNE data and the default PRO parameters from (Hopkins and May, 2011): we sample 5,000 hypothesis pairs from the N-best list (N = 100) for every input sentence and keep the top 50 sample pairs with the highest difference in F_1 measure. The weights are optimized using MegaM (Daumé III, 2004) and interpolated with the previous weight vector with an interpolation parameter of 0.1. We normalize feature values to avoid having features on a larger scale dominate features on a smaller scale. We linearly scale all hypothesis features to a unit interval $[0, 1]$. The minimum and maximum values for each feature are estimated from the development data. We use an early stopping criterion that terminates PRO if the objective function on the tuning data drops. To balance the skewed data where samples without errors greatly outnumber samples with errors, we give a higher weight to sample pairs where the decoder proposed a valid correction. We found a weight of 20 to work well, based on initial experiments on the HOO-TUNE data. We keep all these parameters fixed for all experiments.

5 Results

The complete results of our experiments are shown in Table 2. Each row contains the results for one error correction system. Each system is scored on the original and official gold-standard annotations, both with the M^2 scorer and the official HOO scorer. This results in four sets of precision, recall, and F_1 scores for each system. The best published result to date on this data set is the UI Run1 system from the HOO shared task. We include their system as a reference point.

We make the following observations. First, the scores on the official gold-standard annotations are higher compared to the original gold-standard annotations. We note that the gap between the two

underneath, until, up, upon, with, within, without

[7]Berkeley LM is written in Java and was easier to integrate into our Java-based decoder than RandLM.

System	Original gold-standard						Official gold-standard					
	M^2 scorer			HOO scorer			M^2 scorer			HOO scorer		
	P	R	F_1	P	R	F_1	P	R	F_1	P	R	F_1
UI Run1	40.86	11.21	**17.59**	38.13	10.42	**16.37**	54.61	14.57	**23.00**	50.72	13.34	**21.12**
	P	R	F_1	P	R	F_1	P	R	F_1	P	R	F_1
SMT	9.84	7.77	**8.68**	15.25	5.31	**7.87**	23.35	7.38	**11.21**	15.82	5.30	**7.93**
Pipeline	P	R	F_1	P	R	F_1	P	R	F_1	P	R	F_1
Spelling	50.00	0.79	1.55	40.00	0.64	1.25	50.00	0.76	1.49	40.00	0.61	1.20
+ Articles	30.86	10.23	15.36	28.04	9.55	14.25	34.42	10.97	16.64	31.78	10.41	15.68
+ Prepositions	27.44	11.90	16.60	24.82	11.15	15.38	30.54	12.77	18.01	27.90	12.04	16.82
+ Punctuation	28.91	14.55	19.36 †	26.57	13.91	**18.25** †	32.88	15.99	21.51	30.63	15.41	**20.50**
+ Noun number	28.77	16.13	**20.67** †	24.68	14.22	18.04 †	32.34	17.50	**22.71**	28.36	15.71	20.22
Decoder	P	R	F_1	P	R	F_1	P	R	F_1	P	R	F_1
Spelling	36.84	0.69	1.35	22.22	0.41	0.80	36.84	0.66	1.30	22.22	0.42	0.83
+ Articles	19.84	12.59	15.40	17.99	12.00	14.39	22.45	13.72	17.03 ∗	20.70	13.27	16.16
+ Prepositions	22.62	14.26	17.49 ∗	19.30	12.95	15.50	24.84	15.14	18.81 ∗	21.36	13.78	16.74
+ Punctuation	24.27	18.09	20.73 ∗†	20.40	16.24	18.08	27.13	19.58	22.75 ∗	23.07	17.65	19.99
+ Noun number	30.28	19.17	**23.48** ∗†	24.29	16.24	**19.46** ∗†	33.59	20.53	**25.48** ∗†	27.30	17.55	**21.36** ∗

Table 2: Experimental results on HOO-TEST. Precision, recall, and F_1 score are shown in percent. The best F_1 score for each system is highlighted in bold. Statistically significant improvements ($p < 0.01$) over the pipeline baseline are marked with an asterisk (∗). Statistically significant improvements over the UI Run1 system are marked with a dagger (†). All improvements of the pipeline and the decoder over the SMT baseline are statistically significant.

annotations is the largest for the UI Run1 system which confirms the suspected bias of the official gold-standard annotations in favor of participating systems. Second, the scores computed with the M^2 scorer are higher than the scores computed with the official HOO scorer. With more error categories and more ambiguity in the edits segmentation, the gap between the scorers widens. In the case of the full pipeline and decoder model, the HOO scorer even shows a *decrease* in F_1 score when the score actually goes up as shown by the M^2 scorer. We therefore focus on the scores of the M^2 scorer from now on. The SMT baseline achieves 8.68% and 11.21% F_1 on the original and official gold standard, respectively. Although the worst system in our experiments, it would still have claimed the third place in the HOO shared task. One problem is certainly the small amount of training data. Another reason is that the phrase-based model is unaware of syntactic structure and cannot express correction rules of the form $NP \rightarrow the\ NP$. Instead, it has to have seen the exact correction rule, e.g., $house \rightarrow the\ house$, in the training data. As a result, the model does not generalize well. The pipeline achieves state-of-the-art results. Each additional correction step improves the score. Our proposed decoder achieves the best result. When only a few error categories are corrected, the pipeline and the decoder are close to each other. When more error categories are added, the gap between the pipeline and the decoder becomes larger. The full decoder model achieves an F_1 score of 23.48% and 25.48% on the original and official gold standard, respectively, which is statistically significantly better than both the pipeline system and the UI Run1 system.

6 Discussion

As pointed out in Section 3.5, the majority of sentences require zero or few corrections. Therefore, the depth of the search tree is typically small. In our experiments, the average depth of the search tree is only 1.9 (i.e., 0.9 corrections per sentence) on the test set. Usually, the search depth will be one larger than the number of corrections made, since the decoder will explore the next level of the search tree before deciding that none of the new hypotheses are better than the current best one. On the other hand, there are many possible hypotheses that can be proposed for any sentence. The breadth of the search tree is therefore quite large. In our experiments, the decoder explored on average 99 hypotheses per sentence on the test set.

PRO iteration	P	R	F_1
1	14.13	20.17	16.62
2	19.71	20.85	20.27
3	23.12	21.03	22.02
4	24.35	20.85	22.47
5	25.53	20.51	22.75
6	26.27	20.34	22.93
7	27.25	20.68	**23.52**
8	26.73	19.83	22.77

Table 3: PRO tuning of the full decoder model on HOO-TUNE

Feature	Weight
$a \rightarrow the$	-1.3660
$a \rightarrow \epsilon$	0.5253
$the \rightarrow a$	-0.9997
$the \rightarrow \epsilon$	0.0532
$\epsilon \rightarrow a$	0.0694
$\epsilon \rightarrow the$	-0.0529

Table 4: Example of PRO-tuned weights for article correction count features for the full decoder model.

We found that PRO tuning is very important to achieve good performance for our decoder. Most importantly, PRO tunes the correction count features that bias the decoder against over-correcting sentences thus improving precision. But PRO is also able to improve recall during tuning. Table 3 shows the trajectory of the performance for the full decoder model during PRO tuning on HOO-TUNE. After PRO tuning has converged, we inspect the learned weight vector and observe some interpretable patterns learned by PRO. First, the language model score and all classifier expert average scores receive positive weights, while all classifier expert delta scores receive negative weights, in line with our initial intuition described in Section 3.3. Second, most correction count features receive negative weights, thus acting as a bias against correction if it is not necessary. Finally, the correction count features reveal which corrections are more likely and which are less likely. For example, article replacement errors are less common in the HOO-TUNE data than article insertions or deletions. The weights learned for the article correction count features shown in Table 4 reflect this.

Although our decoder achieves state-of-the-art results, there remain many error categories which the decoder currently cannot correct. This includes, for example, verb form errors (*Much research (have → has) been put into ...*) and lexical choice errors (*The (concerned → relevant) relation ...*). We believe that our decoder provides a promising framework to build grammatical error correction systems that include these types of errors in the future.

7 Conclusion

We have presented a novel beam-search decoder for grammatical error correction. The model performs end-to-end correction of whole sentences with multiple, interacting errors, is discriminatively trained, and incorporates existing classifier-based models for error correction. Our decoder achieves an F_1 correction score of 25.48% on the HOO shared task which outperforms the current state of the art on this data set.

Acknowledgments

This research is supported by the Singapore National Research Foundation under its International Research Centre @ Singapore Funding Initiative and administered by the IDM Programme Office.

References

S. Bergsma, D. Lin, and R. Goebel. 2009. Web-scale N-gram models for lexical disambiguation. In *Proceedings of IJCAI.*

T. Brants and A. Franz. 2006. Web 1T 5-gram corpus version 1.1. Technical report, Google Research.

C. Brockett, W. B. Dolan, and M. Gamon. 2006. Correcting ESL errors using phrasal SMT techniques. In *Proceedings of COLING-ACL.*

M. Chodorow, J. Tetreault, and N.R. Han. 2007. Detection of grammatical errors involving prepositions. In *Proceedings of the 4th ACL-SIGSEM Workshop on Prepositions.*

K. Crammer, M. Dredze, and A. Kulesza. 2009. Multi-class confidence weighted algorithms. In *Proceedings of EMNLP.*

D. Dahlmeier and H.T. Ng. 2011a. Correcting semantic collocation errors with L1-induced paraphrases. In *Proceedings of EMNLP.*

D. Dahlmeier and H.T. Ng. 2011b. Grammatical error correction with alternating structure optimization. In *Proceedings of ACL.*

D. Dahlmeier and H.T. Ng. 2012. Better evaluation for grammatical error correction. In *Proceedings of HLT-NAACL.*

R. Dale and A. Kilgarriff. 2011. Helping Our Own: The HOO 2011 pilot shared task. In *Proceedings of the 2011 European Workshop on Natural Language Generation*.

H. Daumé III. 2004. Notes on CG and LM-BFGS optimization of logistic regression. Paper available at `http://pub.hal3.name#daume04cg-bfgs`, implementation available at `http://hal3.name/megam/`.

A. Désilets and M. Hermet. 2009. Using automatic roundtrip translation to repair general errors in second language writing. In *Proceedings of MT-Summit XII*.

C. Fellbaum, editor. 1998. *WordNet: An electronic lexical database*. MIT Press, Cambridge,MA.

M. Gamon. 2010. Using mostly native data to correct errors in learners' writing: A meta-classifier approach. In *Proceedings of HLT-NAACL*.

N.R. Han, M. Chodorow, and C. Leacock. 2006. Detecting errors in English article usage by non-native speakers. *Natural Language Engineering*, 12(02).

M. Hopkins and J. May. 2011. Tuning as ranking. In *Proceedings of EMNLP*.

K. Knight and I. Chander. 1994. Automated postediting of documents. In *Proceedings of AAAI*.

P. Koehn, F.J. Och, and D. Marcu. 2003. Statistical phrase-based translation. In *Proceedings of HLT-NAACL*.

P. Koehn, H. Hoang, A. Birch, C. Callison-Burch, M. Federico, N. Bertoldi, B. Cowan, W. Shen, C. Moran, R. Zens, C. Dyer, O. Bojar, A. Constantin, and E. Herbst. 2007. Moses: Open source toolkit for statistical machine translation. In *Proceedings of ACL Demonstration Session*.

P. Koehn. 2004. Statistical significance tests for machine translation evaluation. In *Proceedings of EMNLP*.

T Kudo and Y. Matsumoto. 2003. Fast methods for kernel-based text analysis. In *Proceedings of ACL*.

C. Leacock, M. Chodorow, M. Gamon, and J. Tetreault. 2010. *Automated Grammatical Error Detection for Language Learners*. Morgan & Claypool Publishers.

J. Lee and S. Seneff. 2006. Automatic grammar correction for second-language learners. In *Proceedings of Interspeech*.

C.-Y. Lin and F.J. Och. 2004. ORANGE: a method for evaluating automatic evaluation metrics for machine translation. In *Proceedings of COLING*.

J. Nivre, J. Hall, J. Nilsson, A. Chanev, G. Eryigit, S. Kübler, S. Marinov, and M. Marsi. 2007. MaltParser: A language-independent system for data-driven dependency parsing. *Natural Language Engineering*, 13.

F.J. Och and H. Ney. 2003. A systematic comparison of various statistical alignment models. *Computational Linguistics*, 29(1).

F.J. Och. 2003. Minimum error rate training in statistical machine translation. In *Proceedings of ACL*.

K. Papineni, S. Roukos, T. Ward, and W.-J. Zhu. 2002. BLEU: A method for automatic evaluation of machine translation. In *Proceedings of ACL*.

Y. A. Park and R. Levy. 2011. Automated whole sentence grammar correction using a noisy channel model. In *Proceedings of ACL*.

A. Pauls and D. Klein. 2011. Faster and smaller N-gram language models. In *Proceedings of ACL-HLT*.

A. Rozovskaya and D. Roth. 2011. Algorithm selection and model adaptation for ESL correction tasks. In *Proceedings of ACL-HLT*.

A. Rozovskaya, M. Sammons, J. Gioja, and D. Roth. 2011. University of Illinois system in HOO text correction shared task. In *Proceedings of the Generation Challenges Session at the 13th European Workshop on Natural Language Generation*.

S. Russell and P. Norvig, 2010. *Artificial Intelligence: A Modern Approach*, chapter 27. Prentice Hall.

D. Talbot and M. Osborne. 2007. Randomised language modelling for statistical machine translation. In *Proceedings of ACL*.

J. Tetreault and M. Chodorow. 2008. The ups and downs of preposition error detection in ESL writing. In *Proceedings of COLING*.

J. Tetreault, J. Foster, and M. Chodorow. 2010. Using parse features for preposition selection and error detection. In *Proceedings of ACL*.

C. J. van Rijsbergen. 1979. *Information Retrieval*. Butterworth, 2nd edition.

A Statistical Relational Learning Approach to Identifying Evidence Based Medicine Categories

Mathias Verbeke[◇] **Vincent Van Asch**[♣] **Roser Morante**[♣]

Paolo Frasconi[♠] **Walter Daelemans**[♣] **Luc De Raedt**[◇]

[◇] Department of Computer Science, Katholieke Universiteit Leuven, Belgium
{mathias.verbeke, luc.deraedt}@cs.kuleuven.be
[♣] Department of Linguistics, Universiteit Antwerpen, Belgium
{roser.morante, vincent.vanasch, walter.daelemans}@ua.ac.be
[♠] Dipartimento di Sistemi e Informatica, Università degli Studi di Firenze, Italy
p-f@dsi.unifi.it

Abstract

Evidence-based medicine is an approach whereby clinical decisions are supported by the best available findings gained from scientific research. This requires efficient access to such evidence. To this end, abstracts in evidence-based medicine can be labeled using a set of predefined medical categories, the so-called *PICO* criteria. This paper presents an approach to automatically annotate sentences in medical abstracts with these labels. Since both structural and sequential information are important for this classification task, we use *kLog*, a new language for statistical relational learning with kernels. Our results show a clear improvement with respect to state-of-the-art systems.

1 Introduction

Evidence-based medicine (EBM) or *evidence-based practice (EBP)* combines clinical expertise, the preferences and values of the patient and the best available evidence to make good patient care decisions. Clinical research findings are systematically reviewed, appraised and used to improve the patient care, for which efficient access to such evidence is required. In order to facilitate the search process, medical documents are labeled using a set of predefined medical categories, the *PICO criteria.* PICO is an acronym for the mnemonic concepts that are used to construct queries when searching for scientific evidence in the EBM process. The need to automatize the annotation process has initiated research into automatic approaches to annotate sentences in medical documents with the PICO labels.

As indicated by Kim et al. (2011), both the structural information of the words in the sentence, and that of the sentences in the document are important features for this task. Furthermore, sequential information can leverage the dependencies between different sentences in the text. Therefore we propose an approach using *kLog* (Frasconi et al., 2012) to tackle this problem. kLog is a new language for statistical relational learning with kernels, that is embedded in Prolog, and builds upon and links together concepts from database theory, logic programming and learning from interpretations. Learning from interpretations is a logical and relational learning setting (De Raedt et al., 2008) in which the examples are interpretations, that is, sets of tuples that are true in the examples. In a sense, each example can be viewed as a small relational database. kLog is able to transform relational into graph-based representations and apply kernel methods to extract an extended high-dimensional feature space.

The choice for kLog was motivated by previous results (Verbeke et al., 2012), where we showed that a statistical relational learning approach using kLog is able to process the contextual aspects of language improving on state-of-the-art results for hedge cue detection. However, the current task adds two levels of complexity. First, next to the relations between the words in the sentence, now also the relations between the sentences in the document become important. In the proposed approach, we first generate a feature space with kLog that captures the intrasentential properties and relations. Hereafter, these features serve as input for a structured output support vector machine that can handle sequence tagging

(Tsochantaridis et al., 2004), in order to take the intersentential features into account. Second, since there are more than two categories, and each sentence can have multiple labels, the problem is now a multiclass multilabel classification task.

The main contribution of this paper is that we show that kLog's relational nature and its ability to declaratively specify and use background knowledge is beneficial for natural language learning problems. This is shown on the NICTA-PIBOSO corpus, for which we present results that indicate a clear improvement on the state-of-the-art.

The remainder of this paper is organized as follows. In Section 2, we outline earlier work that is related to the research presented here. Section 3 describes the methodology of our method. We present a thorough evaluation of our method in Section 4. The last section draws conclusions and presents some ideas for future work.

2 Related Work

EBM is an approach to clinical problem-solving based on "systematically finding, appraising, and using contemporaneous research findings as the basis for clinical decisions" (Rosenberg and Donald, 1995). The evidence-based process consists of four steps: (1) Formulating a question from a patient's problem; (2) Searching the literature for relevant clinical articles; (3) Evaluating the evidence; And (4) implementing useful findings in clinical practice. Given the amounts of medical publications available in databases such as PubMed, automating step 2 is crucial to help doctors in their practice. Efforts in this direction from the NLP community have so far focused on corpus annotation (Demner-Fushman and Lin, 2007; Kim et al., 2011), text categorization (Davis-Desmond and Mollá, 2012), summarization (Mollá and Santiago-Martínez, 2011), and question-anwering (Niuet al., 2003; Demner-Fushman and Lin, 2007).

The existing corpora are usually annotated with the PICO mnemonic (Armstrong, 1999) concepts, that are used to build queries when searching for literature for EBM purposes. The PICO concepts are: primary Problem (P) or population, main Intervention (I), main intervention Comparison (C), and Outcome of intervention (O). PICO helps determining what terms are important in a query and therefore it helps building the query, which is sent to the search repositories. Once the documents are found, they need to be read by a person who eliminates irrelevant documents.

The first attempt to classify PICO concepts is presented in Demner-Fushman and Lin (2007), who apply a rule-based approach to identify sentences where PICO concepts occur and a supervised approach to classify sentences that contain an *Outcome*. The features used by this classifier are n-grams, position, and semantic information from the parser used to process the data. The system is trained on 275 abstracts manually annotated. The accuracies reported range from 80% for *Population*, 86% for *Problem*, 80% for *Intervention*, and, from 64% to 95% for *Outcome* depending on the test set of abstracts.

Kim et al. (2011) perform a similar classification task in two steps. First a classifier identifies the sentences that contain PICO concepts, and then another classifier assigns PICO tags to the sentences found to be relevant by the previous classifier. The system is based on a CRF algorithm and is trained on the NICTA-PIBOSO corpus. This dataset contains 1,000 medical abstracts manually annotated with an extension of the PICO tagset, for which the definitions are listed in Table 1. The annotation is performed at sentence level and one sentence may have more than one tag. An example of an annotated abstract from the corpus can be found in the supplementary material. The features used by the algorithm include features derived from the context, semantic relations, structure and sequencing of the text. The system is evaluated for 5-way and 6-way classification and results are provided apart from structured and unstructured abstracts. The F-scores for structured abstracts is 89.32% for 5-way classification and 80.88% for 6-way classification, whereas for unstructured abstracts it is 71.54% for 5-way classification and 64.66% for 6-way classification.

Chung (2009) uses CRF to classify PICO concepts by combining them with general categories associated with rhetorical roles: *Aim*, *Method*, *Results* and *Conclusion*. Her system is tested on corpora of abstracts of randomized control trials. First structured abstracts with headings labeled with PICO

Background	Material that informs and may place the current study in perspective, e.g. work that preceded the current; information about disease prevalence; etc.
Population	The group of individual persons, objects or items comprising the study's sample, or from which the sample was taken for statistical measurement
Intervention	The act of interfering with a condition to modify it or with a process to change its course (includes prevention)
Outcome	The sentence(s) that best summarizes the consequences of an intervention
Study Design	The type of study that is described in the abstract
Other	Any sentence not falling into one of the other categories and presumed to provide little help with clinical decision making, i.e. non-key or irrelevant sentences

Table 1: Definitions of the semantic tags used as annotation categories (taken from Kim et al. (2011)).

concepts are used. A sentence level classification task is performed, assigning only one rhetorical role per sentence. The F-scores obtained range from 0.93 to 0.98. Then another sentence level classification task is performed to automatically assign the labels *Intervention*, *Participant* and *Outcome Measures* to sentences in unstructured and structured abstracts without headings. F-scores of up to 0.83 and 0.84 are obtained for *Intervention* and *Outcome Measure* sentences.

Other work aimed at identifying rhetorical zones in biomedical articles. In this case areas of text are classified in terms of the rhetorical categories *Introduction*, *Methods*, *Results* and *Discussion* (IMRAD) (Agarwal and Yu, 2009) or richer categories, such as problem-setting or insight (Mizuta et al., 2006).

There exists a wide range of statistical relational learning systems (Getoor and Taskar, 2007; De Raedt et al., 2008), and many of these systems are in principle useful for natural language processing. The most popular formalism today is Markov Logic, which has already been used for natural language processing tasks such as semantic role labeling (Riedel and Meza-Ruiz, 2008) and coreference resolution (Poon and Domingos, 2008). With respect to Markov Logic, two distinguishing features of kLog are that 1) it employs kernel based methods grounded in statistical learning theory, and 2) it employs a Prolog like language for defining and using background knowledge. As Prolog is a programming language, this is more flexible that the formalism used by Markov Logic.

3 Methodology

In learning from examples, or *interpretations* (De Raedt et al., 2008), the instances are sampled identically and independently from some unknown but fixed distribution. They can be represented as pairs $z = (x, y)$, in which x represents the inputs and y the outputs. An example interpretation can be found in Figure 3, where the hasCategory relation represents y in this case, since it is the target relation we want to predict. The inputs x are formed by all other facts. The task is now to learn a function $h : X \rightarrow Y$ that maps the inputs to the outputs. Sentences may have multiple labels. Hence this is a structured output task where the output is a sequence of sets of labels attached to the sentences in a given document.

kLog is the new statistical relational language for learning with kernels that we use to tackle the PICO categories classification task. The novelty of kLog is that, based on the regular, linguistic features, it allows to define an extended high-dimensional feature space that is also able to take relational features into account in a principled manner. Furthermore, its declarative approach offers a flexible and interpretable way to construct features.

The choice of kLog is motivated by our previous results (Verbeke et al., 2012), where we showed that the relational representation of the domain as used by kLog is able to take the contextual aspects of language into account. Whereas there we only used the relations at the sentence level, the current task adds a new level of complexity, since the identification of PICO categories in abstracts also requires to take into account various relations between the sentences of an abstract. The general workflow of our approach is depicted in Figure 1, which will be de-

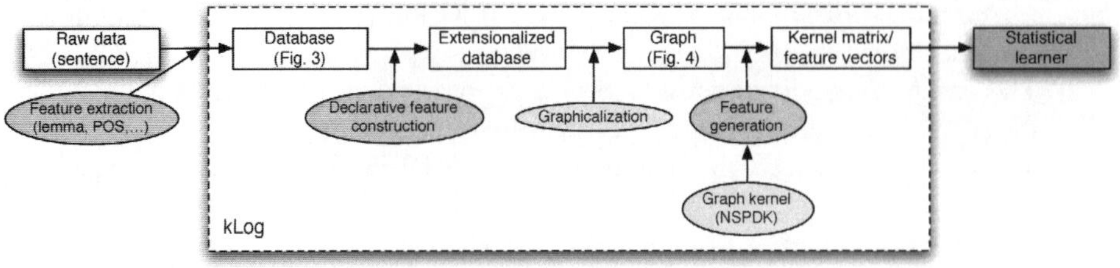

Figure 1: General kLog workflow.

scribed step by step in the following paragraphs.

Preprocessing The sentences have been preprocessed with a named entity tagger and a dependency parser.

Named entity tagging has been performed with the BiogaphTA named entity module, which matches token sequences with entries in the UMLS database[1]. UMLS integrates over 2 million names for some 900,000 concepts from more than 60 families of biomedical vocabularies (Bodenreider, 2004). The tagger matches sequences with a length of maximum 4 tokens. This covers 66.2% of the UMLS entries. By using UMLS, different token sequences referring to the same concept can be mapped to the same concept identifier (CID). The BiographTA named entity tagger has been evaluated on the BioInfer corpus (Pyysalo et al., 2007) obtaining a 72.02 F1 score.

Dependency parsing has been performed with the GENIA dependency parser GDep (Sagae and Tsujii, 2007), which uses a best-first probabilistic shift-reduce algorithm based on the LR algorithm (Knuth, 1965) and extended by the pseudo-projective parsing technique. This parser is a version of the KSDep dependency parser trained on the GENIA Treebank for parsing biomedical text. KSDep was evaluated in the CoNLL Shared Task 2007 obtaining a Labeled Attachment Score of 89.01% for the English dataset. GDEP outputs the lemmas, chunks, Genia named entities and dependency relations of the tokens in a sentence.

This information can be represented as an Entity/Relationship (E/R) diagram, a modeling paradigm that is frequently used in database theory (Garcia-Molina et al., 2008). The E/R-model for the problem under consideration is shown in Figure 2, which provides an abstract representation of the examples, i.e. medical abstracts in this case. We will show later how this abstract representation can be unrolled for each example, resulting in a graph; cf. also Figure 4 for our example sentence. This relational database representation will serve as the input for kLog.

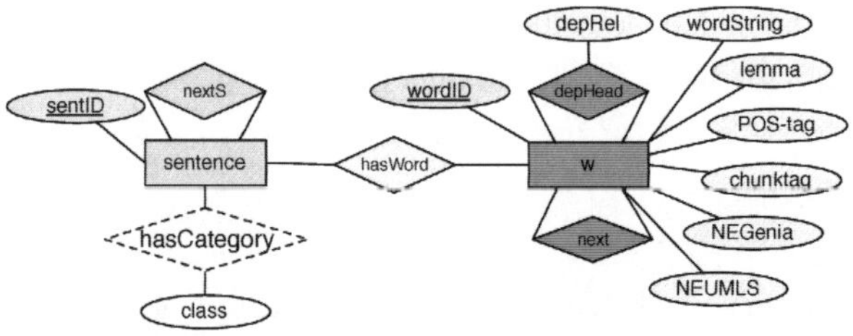

Figure 2: E/R-diagram modeling the sentence identification task.

The *entities* are the words and sentences in the abstract. They are represented by the rectangles in the E/R-model. Each entity can have a number of properties attached to it, depicted by the ovals and has a unique identifier (underlined properties). As in database theory, each entity corresponds with a tuple, or *fact*, in the database.

Figure 3 shows a part of an example interpretation z. For example, w(w4_1,'Surgical','Surgical',b-np,jj,'O','O') specifies a word entity, with w4_1 as identifier and the other arguments as properties. As indicated before, as lexical information we take the token string itself, its lemma, the part-of-speech tag and the chunk tag into account. We also include some semantic information, namely two binary values indicating if the word is a (biological) named entity. sentence(s4,4) represents a sentence entity, with its index in the abstract as a property.

Furthermore, the E/R-diagram also contains a number of *relationships*, which are represented by

[1]From UMLS only the MRCONSO.RRF and MRSTY.RRF files are used.

```
sentence(s4,4)
hasCategory(s4,'background')
w(w4_1,'Surgical','Surgical',b-np,
jj,'O','O') hasWord(s4,w4_1)
dh(w4_1,w4_2,nmod)
nextW(w4_2,w4_1)
w(w4_2,'excision','excision',i-np,
nn,'O','O') hasWord(s4,w4_2)
dh(w4_2,w4_5,sub)
nextW(w4_3,w4_2)
w(w4_3,'of','of',b-pp,in,'O','O')
hasWord(s4,w4_3)
dh(w4_3,w4_2,nmod)
nextW(w4_4,w4_3)
w(w4_4,'CNV','CNV',b-np,nn,
'B-protein','O') hasWord(s4,w4_4)
dh(w4_4,w4_3,pmod)
nextW(w4_5,w4_4)
...
```

Figure 3: Part of an example interpretation z, representing the example sentence in Figure 4.

the diamonds. They are linked to the entities that participate in the relationship, or stand alone if they characterize general properties of the interpretation. An example relation is nextW(w4_2,w4_1), which indicates the sequence of the words in the sentence. dh(w4_1,w4_2,nmod) specifies that word w4_1 is a noun modifier of word w4_2, and thus serves to incorporate the dependency relationships between the words. hasCategory(s4,'background') signifies that sentence s4 is a sentence describing background information. This relation is the target relation that we want to predict for this task and will not be taken into account as a feature, but is listed in the database and only used during the training of the model.

Since the previously described entities and relationships are listed explicitly in the database, these are called *extensional relations*, in contrast to the *intensional relations*, as we will describe next.

Declarative feature construction A strength of kLog is that it is also capable of constructing features *declaratively*, by using intensional relations. This enables one to encode additional background knowledge based on a small set of preprocessed features, which renders experimentation very flexible and makes the results more interpretable. It furthermore allows one to limit the required features to the core discriminative ones. These intensional features are defined through definite clauses, and is done using an extension of the declarative programming language Prolog. The following features were used. We make a distinction between the features used for structured and unstructured abstracts.

For structured abstracts, four intensional relations were defined. The relation lemmaRoot(S,L) is specified as:

```
lemmaRoot(S,L) ←
   hasWord(S, I),
   w(I,_,L,_,_,_,_),
   dh(I,_,root).
```

For each sentence, it only selects the lemmas of the root word in the dependency tree, which markedly limits the number of word features used. The following relations are related to, and try to capture the document structure imposed by the section headers present in the structured abstracts. hasHeaderWord(S,X) identifies whether a sentence is a header of a section. In order to realize this, it selects the words of a sentence that count more than four characters (to discard short names of biological entities), which all need to be uppercase.

```
hasHeaderWord(S,X) ←
   w(W,X,_,_,_,_,_),
   hasWord(S,W),
   (atom(X) -> name(X,C) ; C = X),
   length(C,Len),
   Len > 4,
   all_upper(C).
```

Also the sentences below a certain section header need to be marked as belonging to this section, which is done by the relation hasSectionHeader(S,X).

```
hasSectionHeader(S,X) ←
   nextS(S1,S),
   hasHeaderWord(S1,X).
hasSectionHeader(S,X) ←
   nextS(S1,S),
   not isHeaderSentence(S),
   once(hasSectionHeader(S1,X)).
```

For the unstructured abstracts, also the lemmaRoot relation is used, but next to the lemma, now also the part-of-speech tag of the root word is taken into account. Since the unstructured abstracts lack section headers, other features were needed to distinguish between the different sections, for which the relation prevLemmaRoot proved to be very informative. It adds the lemma of the root word in the previous sentence as a property to the current sentence under consideration.

```
prevLemmaRoot(S,L) ←
    nextS(S1,S),
    lemmaRoot(S1,L,_).
```

The intensional predicates are grounded. This is a proces similar to materialization in databases, that is, the atoms implied by the background knowledge and the facts in the example are all computed using Prolog's deduction mechanism. This leads to the *extensionalized database*, in which both the extensional as well as the grounded intensional predicates are listed.

Graphicalization and feature generation In the third step, the interpretations are *graphicalized*, i.e. transformed into graphs. Since the facts that form the interpretation still conform to the E/R-diagram, this can be interpreted as unfolding the E/R-diagram over the data. An example illustrating this process is given in Figure 4. Each interpretation is converted into a bipartite graph, for which there is a vertex for every ground atom of every E-relation, one for every ground atom of every R-relation, and an undirected edge $\{e, r\}$ if an entity e participates in relationship r.

The obtained graphs can then be used in the next step for *feature generation*. This is done by means of a graph kernel κ, which calculates the similarity between two graphicalized interpretations. Any graph kernel that allows fast computations on large graphs and has a flexible bias to enable heterogeneous features can in theory be applied. In the current implementation, an extension of the Neighborhood Subgraph Pairwise Distance Kernel (NSPDK) (Costa and De Grave, 2010) is used.

NSPDK is a decomposition kernel (Haussler, 1999), in which pairs of subgraphs are compared

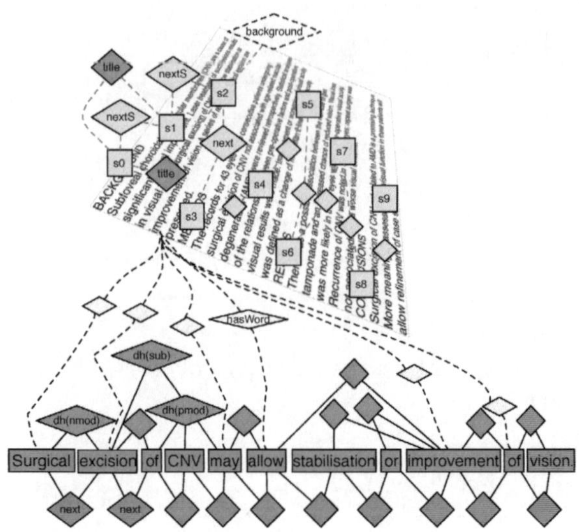

Figure 4: Graphicalization G_z of interpretation z.

to each other in order to calculate the similarity between two graphs. These subgraphs can be seen as circles in the graph, and are defined by three hyperparameters. First of all, there is the center of the subgraph, the *kernel point*, which can be any entity or relation in the graph. The entities and relations to be taken into account as kernel points are marked beforehand as a subset of the intensional and extensional domain relations. The *radius* r determines the size of the subgraphs and defines which entities or relations around the kernel point are taken into account. Each entity or relation that is within a number of r edges away from the kernel point is considered to be part of the subgraph. The third hyperparameter, the *distance* d, determines how far apart from each other the kernel points can be. Each subgraph around a kernel point that is within a distance d or less from the current kernel point will be considered. This is captured by the relation $R_{r,d}(A_v, B_u, G)$ between two rooted subgraphs A_v, B_u and a graph G, which selects all pairs of neighborhood graphs of radius r whose roots are at distance d in a given graph G.

The kernel $\kappa_{r,d}(G, G')$ between graphs G and G' on the relation $R_{r,d}$ is then defined as:

$$\kappa_{r,d}(G, G') = \sum_{\substack{A_v, B_u \in R^{-1}_{r,d}(G) \\ A'_{v'}, B'_{u'} \in R^{-1}_{r,d}(G')}} \delta(A_v, A'_{v'})\delta(B_u, B'_{u'}) \quad (1)$$

For efficiency reasons, an upper bound is imposed on the radius and distance parameters, which leads to the following kernel definition:

$$K_{r^*,d^*}(G, G') = \sum_{r=0}^{r^*} \sum_{d=0}^{d^*} \kappa_{r,d}(G, G') \quad (2)$$

We hereby limit the sum of the $\kappa_{r,d}$ kernels for all increasing values of the radius and distance parameter up to a maximum given value of r^*, respectively d^*.

The result of this graphicalization and feature generation process is an extended, high-dimensional feature space, which serves as input for the statistical learner in the next step.

Learning The constructed feature space contains one feature vector per sentence. This implies that the sequence information of the sentences at the document level is not taken into account yet. Since the order of the sentences in the abstract is a valuable feature for this prediction problem, a learner that reflects this in the learning process is needed, although in principle any statistical learner can be used on the feature space constructed by kLog. Therefore we opted for SVM-HMM[2] (Tsochantaridis et al., 2004), which is an implementation of structural support vector machines for sequence tagging. In contrast to a conventional Hidden Markov Model, SVM-HMM is able to take these entire feature vectors as observations, and not just atomic tokens.

In our case, the instances to be tagged are formed by the sentences for which feature vectors were created in the previous step. The *qid* is a special feature that is used in the structured SVM to restrict the generation of constraints. Since every document needs to be represented as a sequence of sentences, in SVM-HMM, the qid's are used to obtain the document structure. The order of the HMM was set to 2, which means that the two previous sentences were considered for collective classification. The cost value was set to 500, and was determined via cross-validation. For epsilon, the default value, 0.5, was kept, since this mainly only influences the running time and memory consumption during training.

[2]`http://www.cs.cornell.edu/people/tj/svm_light/svm_hmm.html`

	All	S	U
Nb. Abstracts	1000	376	624
Nb. Sentences	10379	4774	5605
- Background	2557	669	1888
- Intervention	690	313	377
- Outcome	4523	2240	2283
- Population	812	369	443
- Study Design	233	149	84
- Other	1564	1034	530

Table 2: Number of abstracts and sentences for Structured (S) and Unstructured (U) abstract sets, including number of sentences per class (taken from (Kim et al., 2011)).

4 Evaluation

We evaluate the performance of kLog against a baseline system and a memory-based tagger (Daelemans and van den Bosch, 2005). The results are also compared against those from Kim et al. (2011), which is the state-of-the-art system for this task.

4.1 Datasets

We perform our experiments on the NICTA-PIBOSO dataset from Kim et al. (2011) (kindly provided by the authors). It contains 1,000 abstracts of which 500 were retrieved from MEDLINE by querying for diverse aspects in the traumatic brain injury and spinal cord injury domain. The dataset consists of two types of abstracts. If the abstract contains section headings (e.g. *Background*, *Methodology*, *Results*, etc.), it is considered to be *structured*. This information can be used as a feature in the model. The other abstracts are regarded *unstructured*.

The definitions of the semantic tags used as annotations categories are a variation on the PICO tag set, with the addition of two additional categories (see Table 1 in Section 2). Each sentence can be annotated with multiple classes. This renders the task a multiclass multilabel classification problem. The statistics on this dataset can be found in Table 2.

In order to apply the same evaluation setting as Kim et al. (2011), we used the dataset from Demner-Fushman et al. (2005) as external dataset. It consists of 100 sentences of which 51 are structured. Because the semantic tag set used for annotation slightly differs from the one presented in Table 1, and to make our results comparable, we will use the same mapping as used in Kim et al. (2011).

4.2 Baseline and benchmarks

We compare the kLog system to three other systems: a baseline system, a memory-based system, and the scores reported by Kim et al. (2011).

The memory-based system that we use is based on the memory-based tagger MBT[3] (Daelemans and van den Bosch, 2005). This machine learner is originally designed for part-of-speech tagging. It processes data on a sentence basis by carrying out sequential tagging, *viz.* the class label or other features from previously tagged tokens can be used when classifying a new token. In our setup, the sentences of an abstract are taken as the processing unit and the collection of all sentences in an abstract is taken as one sequence.

The features that are used to label a sentence are the class labels of four previous sentences, the ambitags of the following two sentences, the lemma of the dependency root of the sentence, the position of the sentence in the abstract, the lemma of the root of the previous sentence, and section information. For each root lemma, all possible class labels, as observed in the training data, are concatenated into one ambitag. These tags are stored in a list. An ambitag for a sentence is retrieved by looking up the root lemma in this list. The position of the sentence is expressed by a number. Section information is obtained by looking for a previous sentence that consists of only one token in uppercase. Finally, basic lemmatization is carried out by removing a final *S*. All other settings of MBT are the default settings and no feature optimization nor feature selection has been carried out to prevent overfitting.

When a class label contains multiple labels, like e.g. *population* and *study design*, these labels are concatenated in an alphabetically sorted manner. This method of working reduces the multilabel problem to a problem with many different labels, i.e. the label powerset method of Tsoumakas et al. (2010).

The baseline system is exactly the same as the memory-based system except that no machine learner is included. The most frequent class label in the training data, i.e. *Outcome*, is assigned to each instance. The memory-based system enables us to compare kLog against a basic machine learning approach, using few features. The majority baseline system enables us to compare the memory-based system and kLog against a baseline in which no information about the observations is used.

[3]http://ilk.uvt.nl/mbt [16 March 2012]

4.3 Parametrization

From the kernel definition it might be clear that the kLog hyperparameters, namely the distance d and radius r, can have a strong influence on the results. This requires a deliberate choice during parametrization. From a linguistic perspective, the use of unigrams and bigrams is justifiable, since most phrases that reveal clues on the structure of the abstract (e.g. *evaluation measures*, *methodolody*, *future work*) can be expressed with single or pairs of words. This is reflected by a distance and radius both set to 1, which enables to take all possible combinations of consecutive words into account and captures the relational information attached to the word in focus, i.e. the current kernel point. This is confirmed by cross-validation on other settings for the hyperparameters.

Since kLog generates a feature vector, only the sequence information at word level is taken into account by kLog. Since we use a sequence labeling approach as statistical learner, i.e. SVM-HMM, at the level of the abstract this information is however implicitly taken into account during learning. For SVM-HMM, only the cost parameter C, which regulates the trade-off between the slack and the magnitude of the weight-vector, and ϵ, that specifies the precision to which constraints are required to be satisfied by the solution, were optimized by means of cross-validation. For the other parameters, the default values were used.

4.4 Results

Experiments are run on structured and unstructured abstracts separately. On the NICTA-PIBOSO corpus, we performed 10-fold cross-validation. Over all folds, all labels, i.e. the parts of the multilabels, are compared in a binary way between gold standard and prediction. Summing all true positives, false positives, and false negatives over all folds leads to micro-averaged F-scores. This was done for two different settings. In one setting, *CV/6-way*, we combined the labeling of the sentences with the identification of irrelevant information, by adding the *Other* label as an extra class in the classification. The results are listed in Table 3.

CV/6-way	MBT		Kim et al.		kLog	
Label	S	U	S	U	S	U
Background	71.0	61.3	81.84	68.46	86.19	76.90
Intervention	24.3	6.4	20.25	12.68	26.05	16.14
Outcome	87.9	70.4	92.32	72.94	92.99	77.69
Population	50.6	15.9	56.25	39.80	35.62	21.58
Study Design	45.9	13.10	43.95	4.40	45.5	6.67
Other	86.1	20.9	69.98	24.28	87.98	24.42

Table 3: F-scores per class for structured (S) and unstructured (U) abstracts.

For this setting, kLog is able to outperform both MBT and the system of Kim et al. (2011), for both structured and unstructured abstracts on all classes except *Population*. From Table 4, where the micro-average F-scores over all classes and for all settings are listed, it can be observed that kLog performs up to 3.73% better than MBT over structured abstracts, and 9.67% better over unstructured ones.

Although to a lesser extent for the structured abstracts, the same pattern can be observed for the *CV/5-way* setting, where we tried to classify the sentences only, without considering the irrelevant ones. The per-class results for this setting are shown in Table 5. Now the scores for *Population* are comparable to the other systems, due to which we assume these sentences are similar in structure to the ones labeled with *Other*.

For the external corpus, the results are listed in Table 6. Although kLog performs comparably for the individual classes *Background* and *Intervention*, its overall performance is worse on the structured abstracts. In case of the unstructured abstracts, kLog performs better on the majority of the individual classes and in overall performance for the 5-way setting, and comparable for the 4-way setting.

	Baseline		MBT		kLog	
Method	S	U	S	U	S	U
CV/6-way	43.90	41.87	80.56	57.47	84.29	67.14
CV/5-way	61.79	46.66	86.96	64.37	87.67	72.95
Ext/5-way	66.18	6.76	36.34	11.56	20.50	14.00
Ext/4-way	30.11	27.23	67.29	55.96	50.40	50.50

Table 4: Micro-averaged F1-score obtained for structured (S) and unstructured (U) abstracts, both for 10-fold cross-validation (CV) and on the external corpus (Ext).

CV/5-way	MBT		Kim et al.		kLog	
Label	S	U	S	U	S	U
Background	87.1	64.9	87.92	70.67	91.45	80.06
Intervention	48.0	6.9	48.08	21.39	45.58	22.65
Outcome	95.8	75.9	96.03	80.51	96.21	83.04
Population	70.9	21.4	63.88	43.15	63.96	23.32
Study Design	50.0	7.4	47.44	8.6	48.08	4.50

Table 5: F-scores per class for 5-way classification over structured (S) and unstructured (U) abstracts.

	MBT		Kim et al.		kLog	
Label	S	U	S	U	S	U
			Ext/5-way			
Background	58.9	15.7	56.18	15.67	58.30	29.10
Intervention	21.5	13.8	15.38	28.57	40.00	34.30
Outcome	29.3	17.8	81.34	60.45	27.80	24.10
Population	10.7	17.8	35.62	28.07	5.60	28.60
Other	40.7	3.5	46.32	15.77	11.40	8.50
			Ext/4-way			
Background	90.4	67.5	77.27	37.5	65	68.6
Intervention	29	23.1	28.17	8.33	28.1	32.3
Outcome	74.1	74.6	90.5	78.77	72.4	72.7
Population	48.7	23.8	42.86	28.57	11.8	15.4

Table 6: F-scores per class for 5-way and 4-way classification over structured (S) and unstructured (U) abstracts on the external corpus.

As a general observation, it is important to note that there is a high variability between the different labels. Due to kLog's ability to take the structured input into account, we assume a correlation between the sentence structure of the label and the prediction quality. We intend to perform an extensive error analysis, in order to detect patterns which may allow us to incorporate additional declarative background knowledge into our model.

5 Conclusions

We presented a statistical relational learning approach for the automatic identification of PICO categories in medical abstracts. To this extent, we used kLog, a new framework for logical and relational learning with kernels. Due to its graphical approach, it is able to exploit the full relational representation, that is often inherent in language structure. Since contextual features are often essential and relations are prevalent, the aim of this paper was to show that statistical relational learning in general, and the graph kernel-based approach of kLog in particular, is specifically suited for problems in natural language learning.

In future work, we intend to explore additional ways to incorporate background knowledge in a declarative way, since it renders the language learning problem more intuitive and gives a better understanding of feature contribution. Furthermore, we also want to investigate the use of SRL approaches for high-relational domains, and make a clear comparison with related techniques.

6 Acknowledgements

This research is funded by the Research Foundation Flanders (FWO project G.0478.10 - Statistical Relational Learning of Natural Language), and made possible through financial support from the KU Leuven Research Fund (GOA project 2008/08 Probabilistic Logic Learning), the University of Antwerp (GOA project BIOGRAPH) and the Italian Ministry of Education, University, and Research (PRIN project 2009LNP494 - Statistical Relational Learning: Algorithms and Applications). The authors would like to thank Fabrizio Costa, Kurt De Grave and the anonymous reviewers for their valuable feedback.

References

Shashank Agarwal and Hong Yu. 2009. Automatically Classifying Sentences in Full-text Biomedical Articles into Introduction, Methods, Results and Discussion. *Bioinformatics*, 25(23):3174–3180.

E. C. Armstrong. 1999. The Well-built Clinical Question: the Key to Finding the Best Evidence Efficiently. *WMJ*, 98(2):25–28.

Olivier Bodenreider. 2004. The Unified Medical Language System (UMLS): Integrating Biomedical Terminology. *Nucleic Acids Research*, 32(Suppl.1):D267–D270.

Grace Y Chung. 2009. Sentence Retrieval for Abstracts of Randomized Controlled Trials. *BMC Medical Informatics and Decision Making*, 9(10).

Fabrizio Costa and Kurt De Grave. 2010. Fast Neighborhood Subgraph Pairwise Distance Kernel. *Proceedings of the 26th International Conference on Machine Learning*, 255–262, Haifa, Israel. Omnipress.

Walter Daelemans and Antal van den Bosch. 2005. *Memory-Based Language Processing.*. Studies in Natural Language Processing. Cambridge University Press, Cambridge, UK.

P. Davis-Desmond and Diego Mollá. 2012. Detection of Evidence in Clinical Research Papers. *Proceedings of the Australasian Workshop On Health Informatics and Knowledge Management (HIKM 2012)*, Melbourne, Australia, 129:13–20. Australian Computer Society, Inc.

Dina Demner-Fushman, Barbara Few, Susan E. Hauser, and George Thoma. 2005. Automatically Identifying Health Outcome Information in MEDLINE Records. *Journal of the American Medical Informatics Association (JAMIA)*, 13:52–60.

Dina Demner-Fushman and Jimmy Lin. 2007. Answering Clinical Questions with Knowledge Based and Statistical Techniques. *Computational Linguistics*, 33(1):63–103.

Luc De Raedt, Paolo Frasconi, Kristian Kersting, and Stephen Muggleton, editors. 2008. *Probabilistic Inductive Logic Programming*. In: Lecture Notes in Computer Science (LNCS), 4911. Springer-Verlag, Heidelberg, Germany.

Paolo Frasconi, Fabrizio Costa, Luc De Raedt, and Kurt De Grave. 2012. kLog - a Language for Logical and Relational Learning with Kernels. *arXiv:1205.3981v2*.

Hector Garcia-Molina, Jeff Ullman, and Jennifer Widom. 2008. *Database Systems: The Complete Book*. Prentice Hall Press, Englewood Cliffs, NJ, USA.

Lise Getoor and Ben Taskar. 2007. *Introduction to Statistical Relational Learning (Adaptive Computation and Machine Learning)*. The MIT Press, Cambridge, MA, USA.

David Haussler. 1999. Convolution kernels on discrete structures. *Technical report (UCSC-CRL-99-10), University of California at Santa Cruz*.

Su Nam Kim, David Martinez, Lawrence Cavedon, and Lars Yencken. 2011. Automatic Classification of Sentences to Support Evidence Based Medicine. *BMC Bioinformatics*, 12(2):S5.

Donald E. Knuth. 1965. On the Translation of Languages from Left to Right. *Information and Control*, 8: 607–639.

Y. Mizuta, A. Korhonen, T. Mullen, and N. Collier. 2006. Zone Analysis in Biology Articles as a Basis for Information Extraction. *International Journal of Medical Informatics*, 75(6):468–487.

Diego Mollá and Mara Elena Santiago-Martínez. 2011. Development of a Corpus for Evidence Medicine Summarisation. *Proceedings of the 2011 Australasian Language Technology Workshop (ALTA 2011)*, Canberra, Australia, 86–94. Association for Computational Linguistics.

Yun Niu, Graeme Hirst, Gregory McArthur, and Patricia Rodriguez-Gianolli. 2003. Answering Clinical

Questions with Role Identification. *Proceedings of the ACL, Workshop on Natural Language Processing in Biomedicine*. Sapporo, Japan, 73–80. Association for Computational Linguistics.

Hoifung Poon and Pedro Domingos. 2008. Joint unsupervised coreference resolution with Markov logic. *Proceedings of the Conference on Empirical Methods in Natural Language Processing (EMNLP 2008*. Honolulu, Hawaii, 650–659. Association for Computational Linguistics.

Sampo Pyysalo, Filip Ginter, Juho Heimonen, Jari Björne, Jorma Boberg, Jouni Järvinen, and Tapio Salakoski. 2007. BioInfer: a Corpus for Information Extraction in the Biomedical Domain. *BMC Bioinformatics*, 8:50.

Sebastian Riedel and Ivan Meza-Ruiz. 2008. Collective semantic role labelling with Markov logic. *Proceedings of the Twelfth Conference on Computational Natural Language Learning (CoNLL 2008*. Manchester, United Kingdom, 193–197. Association for Computational Linguistics.

William Rosenberg and Anna Donald. 1995. Evidence Based Medicine: an Approach to Clinical Problem Solving. *British Medical Journal*, 310(6987):1122–1126.

Kenji Sagae and Jun'ichi Tsujii. 2007. Dependency Parsing and Domain Adaptation with LR Models and Parser Ensembles. *Proceedings of the CoNLL Shared Task Session of EMNLP-CoNLL 2007*, Prague, Czech Republic, 1044–1050. Association for Computational Linguistics.

Ioannis Tsochantaridis, Thomas Hofmann, Thorsten Joachims, and Yasemin Altun. 2004. Support Vector Machine Learning for Interdependent and Structured Output Spaces. *Proceedings of the twenty-first international conference on Machine learning (ICML)*, Alberta, Canada, 104–111. ACM.

Grigorios Tsoumakas and Ioannis Katakis and Ioannis P. Vlahavas. Oded Maimon and Lior Rokach, editors. 2010. Mining Multi-label Data. In: *Data Mining and Knowledge Discovery Handbook*, 2nd ed., 667–685. Springer-Verlag, Heidelberg, Germany.

Mathias Verbeke, Paolo Frasconi, Vincent Van Asch, Roser Morante, Walter Daelemans, and Luc De Raedt. 2012. Kernel-based Logical and Relational Learning with kLog for Hedge Cue Detection. *Proceedings of the 21th International Conference on Inductive Logic Programming*, in press.

Lyrics, Music, and Emotions

Rada Mihalcea
University of North Texas
rada@cs.unt.edu

Carlo Strapparava
FBK-irst
strappa@fbk.eu

Abstract

In this paper, we explore the classification of emotions in songs, using the music and the lyrics representation of the songs. We introduce a novel corpus of music and lyrics, consisting of 100 songs annotated for emotions. We show that textual and musical features can both be successfully used for emotion recognition in songs. Moreover, through comparative experiments, we show that the joint use of lyrics and music brings significant improvements over each of the individual textual and musical classifiers, with error rate reductions of up to 31%.

1 Introduction

Language and music are peculiar characteristics of human beings. The capability of producing and enjoying language and music appears in every human society, regardless of the richness of its culture (Nettl, 2000).

Importantly, language and music complement each other in many different ways. For instance, looking at music and language in terms of features, we can observe that music organizes pitch and rhythm in ways that language does not, and it lacks the specificity of language in terms of semantic meaning. On the other hand, language is built from categories that are absent in music (e.g., nouns and verbs), whereas music seems to have a deeper power over our emotions than does ordinary speech.

Composers, musicians, and researchers in poetry and literature alike have been long fascinated by the combination of language and music, even since the time of the earliest written records of music encountered in musical settings for poetry. Despite this interest, and despite the long history of the interaction between music and lyrics, there is only little work that explicitly focuses on the connection between music and lyrics.

In this paper, we focus on the connection between the musical and linguistic representations in popular songs, and their role in the expression of *affect*. We introduce a novel corpus of lyrics and music, annotated for emotions at line level, and explore the automatic recognition of emotions using both textual and musical features. Through comparative experiments, we show that emotion recognition can be performed using either textual or musical features, and that the joint use of lyrics and music can improve significantly over classifiers that use only one dimension at a time. We believe our results demonstrate the promise of using joint music-lyric models for song processing.

2 Related Work

The literature on music analysis is noticeably large, and there are several studies concerning the music's power over emotions (Juslin and Sloboda, 2001), thinking (Rauscher et al., 1993), or physical effort (Karageorghis and Priest, 2008).

In particular, there has been significant research in music and psychology focusing on the idea of a parallel between affective cues in music and speech (Sundberg, 1982; Scherer, 1995). For instance, (Scherer, 2004) investigated the types of emotions that can be induced by music, their mechanisms, and how they can be empirically measured. (Juslin and

Laukka, 2003) conducted a comprehensive review of vocal expressions and music performance, finding substantial overlap in the cues used to convey basic emotions in speech and music.

The work most closely related to ours is the combination of audio and lyrics for emotion classification in songs, as thoroughly surveyed in (Kim et al., 2010). Although several methods have been proposed, including a combination of textual features and beats per minute and MPEG descriptors (Yang and Lee, 2004); individual audio and text classifiers for arousal and valence, followed by a combination through meta-learning (Yang et al., 2008); and the use of crowdsourcing labeling from Last.fm to collect large datasets of songs annotated for emotions (Laurier et al., 2008; Hu et al., 2009), all this previous work was done at song level, and most of it focused on valence-arousal classifications. None of the previous methods considered the fine-grained classification of emotions at line level, as we do, and none of them considered the six Ekman emotions used in our work.

Other related work consists of the development of tools for music accessing, filtering, classification, and retrieval, focusing primarily on music in digital format such as MIDI. For instance, the task of music retrieval and music recommendation has received a lot of attention from both the arts and the computer science communities (see for instance (Orio, 2006) for an introduction to this task). There are also several works on MIDI analysis. Among them, particularly relevant to our research is the work by (Das et al., 2000), who described an analysis of predominant up-down motion types within music, through extraction of the kinematic variables of music velocity and acceleration from MIDI data streams. (Cataltepe et al., 2007) addressed music genre classification (e.g., classic, jazz, pop) using MIDI and audio features, while (Wang et al., 2004) automatically aligned acoustic musical signals with their corresponding textual lyrics. MIDI files are typically organized into one or more parallel "tracks" for independent recording and editing. A reliable system to identify the MIDI track containing the *melody*[1] is very relevant for music information retrieval, and there are several approaches that have been proposed to address this issue (Rizo et al., 2006; Velusamy et al., 2007).

Another related study concerned with the interaction of lyrics and music using an annotated corpus is found in (O'Hara, 2011), who presented preliminary research that checks whether the expressive meaning of a particular harmony or harmonic sequence could be deduced from the lyrics it accompanies, by using harmonically annotated chords from the Usenet group alt.guitar.tab.

Finally, in natural language processing, there are a few studies that mainly exploited the lyrics component of the songs, while generally ignoring the musical component. For instance, (Mahedero et al., 2005) dealt with language identification, structure extraction, and thematic categorization for lyrics. (Xia et al., 2008) addressed the task of sentiment classification in lyrics, recognizing positive and negative moods in a large dataset of Chinese pop songs, while (Yang and Lee, 2009) approached the problem of emotion identification in lyrics, classifying songs from allmusic.com using a set of 23 emotions.

3 A Corpus of Music and Lyrics Annotated for Emotions

To enable our exploration of emotions in songs, we compiled a corpus of 100 popular songs (e.g., *Dancing Queen* by ABBA, *Hotel California* by Eagles, *Let it Be* by The Beatles). Popular songs exert a lot of power on people, both at an individual level as well as on groups, mainly because of the message and emotions they convey. Songs can lift our moods, make us dance, or move us to tears. Songs are able to embody deep feelings, usually through a combined effect of both music and lyrics.

The corpus is built starting with the MIDI tracks of each song, by extracting the parallel alignment of melody and lyrics. Given the non-homogeneous quality of the MIDI files available on the Web, we asked a professional MIDI provider for high quality MIDI files produced for singers and musicians. The MIDI files, which were purchased from the provider, contain also lyrics that are synchronized with the notes. In these MIDI files, the melody channel is unequivocally decided by the provider, making it easier to extract the music and the corresponding lyrics.

[1]A melody can be defined as a "cantabile" sequence of notes, usually the sequence that a listener can remember after hearing a song.

MIDI format. MIDI is an industry-standard protocol that enables electronic musical instruments, computers, and other electronic equipment to communicate and synchronize with each other. Unlike analog devices, MIDI does not transmit an audio signal: it sends event messages about musical notation, pitch, and intensity, control signals for parameters such as volume, vibrato, and panning, and cues and clock signals to set the tempo. As an electronic protocol, it is notable for its widespread adoption throughout the music industry.

MIDI files are typically created using computer-based sequencing software that organizes MIDI messages into one or more parallel "tracks" for independent recording, editing, and playback. In most sequencers, each track is assigned to a specific MIDI channel, which can be then associated to specific instrument patches. MIDI files can also contain lyrics, which can be displayed in synchrony with the music.

Starting with the MIDI tracks of a song, we extract and explicitly encode the following features. At the song level, the key of the song (e.g., G major, C minor). At the line level, we represent the raising, which is the musical interval (in half-steps) between the first note in the line and the most important note (i.e., the note in the line with the longest duration). Finally, at the note level, we encode the time code of the note with respect to the beginning of the song; the note aligned with the corresponding syllable; the degree of the note with relation to the key of the song; and the duration of the note.

Table 1 shows statistics on the corpus. An example from the corpus, consisting of the first two lines from the Beatles' song *A hard day's night*, is illustrated in Figure 3.

SONGS	100
SONGS IN "MAJOR" KEY	59
SONGS IN "MINOR" KEY	41
LINES	4,976
ALIGNED SYLLABLES / NOTES	34,045

Table 1: Some statistics of the corpus

Emotion Annotations with Mechanical Turk. In order to explore the classification of emotions in songs, we needed a gold standard consisting of manual emotion annotations of the songs. Following previous work on emotion annotation of text (Alm et al., 2005; Strapparava and Mihalcea, 2007), to annotate the emotions in songs we use the six basic emotions proposed by (Ekman, 1993): ANGER, DISGUST, FEAR, JOY, SADNESS, SURPRISE. To collect the annotations, we use the Amazon Mechanical Turk service, which was previously found to produce reliable annotations with a quality comparable to those generated by experts (Snow et al., 2008).

The annotations are collected at line level, with a separate annotation for each of the six emotions. We collect numerical annotations using a scale between 0 and 10, with 0 corresponding to the absence of an emotion, and 10 corresponding to the highest intensity. Each HIT (i.e., annotation session) contains an entire song, with a number of lines ranging from 14 to 110, for an average of 50 lines per song.

The annotators were instructed to: (1) Score the emotions from the writer perspective, not their own perspective; (2) Read and interpret each line in context; i.e., they were asked to read and understand the entire song before producing any annotations; (3) Produce the six emotion annotations independent from each other, accounting for the fact that a line could contain none, one, or multiple emotions. In addition to the lyrics, the song was also available online, so they could listen to it in case they were not familiar with it. The annotators were also given three different examples to illustrate the annotation.

While the use of crowdsourcing for data annotation can result in a large number of annotations in a very short amount of time, it also has the drawback of potential spamming that can interfere with the quality of the annotations. To address this aspect, we used two different techniques to prevent spam. First, in each song we inserted a "checkpoint" at a random position in the song – a fake line that reads "Please enter 7 for each of the six emotions." Those annotators who did not follow this concrete instruction were deemed as spammers who produce annotations without reading the content of the song, and thus removed. Second, for each remaining annotator, we calculated the Pearson correlation between her emotion scores and the average emotion scores of all the other annotators. Those annotators with a correlation with the average of the other annotators below 0.4 were also removed, thus leaving only the reliable annotators in the pool.

```
<song filename=AHARDDAY.m2a>
<key time=0>G major</key>
<line pvers=1 raising=3 anger=1.5 disgust=0.7 sadness=2.5 surprise=0.8 >
<token time=5040 orig–note=B degree=3 duration=210>IT</token>
<token time=5050 orig–note=B degree=3 duration=210>'S </token>
<token time=5280 orig–note=C' degree=4 duration=210>BEEN </token>
<token time=5520 orig–note=B degree=3 duration=210>A </token>
<token time=5760 orig–note=D' degree=5 duration=810>HARD </token>
<token time=6720 orig–note=D' degree=5 duration=570>DAY</token>
<token time=6730 orig–note=D' degree=5 duration=570>'S </token>
<token time=7440 orig–note=D' degree=5 duration=690>NIGHT</token>
</line>
<line pvers=2 raising=5 anger=3.5 disgust=2 sadness=1.2 surprise=0.2 >
<token time=8880 orig–note=C' degree=4 duration=212>AND </token>
<token time=9120 orig–note=D' degree=5 duration=210>I</token>
<token time=9130 orig–note=D' degree=5 duration=210>'VE </token>
<token time=9360 orig–note=C' degree=4 duration=210>BEEN </token>
<token time=9600 orig–note=D' degree=5 duration=210>WOR</token>
<token time=9840 orig–note=F' degree=7– duration=930>KING </token>
<token time=10800 orig–note=D' degree=5 duration=210>LI</token>
<token time=11040 orig–note=C' degree=4 duration=210>KE </token>
<token time=11050 orig–note=C' degree=4 duration=210>A </token>
<token time=11280 orig–note=D' degree=5 duration=330>D</token>
<token time=11640 orig–note=C' degree=4 duration=90>O</token>
<token time=11760 orig–note=B degree=3 duration=330>G</token>
</line>
```

Figure 1: Two lines of a song in the corpus: *It-'s been a hard day-'s night, And I-'ve been wor-king li-ke a d-o-g*

For each song, we start by asking for ten annotations. After spam removal, we were left with about two-five annotations per song. The final annotations are produced by averaging the emotions scores produced by the reliable annotators. Figure 3 shows an example of the emotion scores produced for two lines. The overall correlation between the remaining reliable annotators was calculated as 0.73, which represents a strong correlation.

For each of the six emotions, Table 2 shows the number of lines that had that emotion present (i.e., the score of the emotion was different from 0), as well as the average score for that emotion over all 4,976 lines in the corpus. Perhaps not surprisingly, the emotions that are dominant in the corpus are JOY and SADNESS – which are the emotions that are often invoked by people as the reason behind a song.

Note that the emotions do not exclude each other: i.e., a line that is labeled as containing JOY may also contain a certain amount of SADNESS, which is the reason for the high percentage of songs containing both JOY and SADNESS. The emotional load for the overlapping emotions is however very different. For instance, the lines that have a JOY score of 5 or higher have an average SADNESS score of 0.34. Conversely, the lines with a SADNESS score of 5 or higher have a JOY score of 0.22.

Emotion	Number lines	Average
ANGER	2,516	0.95
DISGUST	2,461	0.71
FEAR	2,719	0.77
JOY	3,890	3.24
SADNESS	3,840	2.27
SURPRISE	2,982	0.83

Table 2: Emotions in the corpus of 100 songs: number of lines including a certain emotion, and average emotion score computed over all the 4,976 lines.

4 Experiments and Evaluations

Through our experiments, we seek to determine the extent to which we can automatically determine the emotional load of each line in a song, for each of the six emotion dimensions.

We use two main classes of features: textual features, which build upon the textual representation of the lyrics; and musical features, which rely on the musical notation associated with the songs. We run three sets of experiments. The first one is intended to determine the usefulness of the textual features for emotion classification. The second set specifically focuses on the musical features. Finally, the last set of experiments makes joint use of textual and musical features.

The experiments are run using linear regression,[2] and the results are evaluated by measuring the Pearson correlation between the classifier predictions and the gold standard. For each experiment, a tenfold cross validation is run on the entire dataset.[3]

4.1 Textual Features

First, we attempt to identify the emotions in a line by relying exclusively on the features that can be derived from the lyrics of the song. We decided to focus on those features that were successfully used in the past for emotion classification (Strapparava and Mihalcea, 2008). Specifically, we use: (1) unigram features obtained from a bag-of-words representation, which are the features typically used by corpus-based methods; and (2) lexicon features, indicating the appartenance of a word to a semantic class defined in manually crafted lexicons, which are often used by knowledge-based methods.

Unigrams. We use a bag-of-words representation of the lyrics to derive unigram counts, which are then used as input features. First, we build a vocabulary consisting of all the words, including stopwords, occurring in the lyrics of the training set. We then remove those words that have a frequency below 10 (value determined empirically on a small development set). The remaining words represent the unigram features, which are then associated with a value corresponding to the frequency of the unigram inside each line. Note that we also attempted to use higher order n-grams (bigrams and trigrams), but evaluations on a small development dataset did not show any improvements over the unigram model, and thus all the experiments are run using unigrams.

Semantic Classes. We also derive and use coarse textual features, by using mappings between words and semantic classes. Specifically, we use the Linguistic Inquiry and Word Count (LIWC) and WordNet Affect (WA) to derive coarse textual features. LIWC was developed as a resource for psycholinguistic analysis (Pennebaker and Francis, 1999; Pennebaker and King, 1999). The 2001 version of LIWC includes about 2,200 words and word stems grouped into about 70 broad categories relevant to psychological processes (e.g., emotion, cognition). WA (Strapparava and Valitutti, 2004) is a resource that was created starting with WordNet, by annotating synsets with several emotions. It uses several resources for affective information, including the emotion classification of Ortony (Ortony et al., 1987). From WA, we extract the words corresponding to the six basic emotions used in our experiments. For each semantic class, we infer a feature indicating the number of words in a line belonging to that class.

Table 3 shows the Pearson correlations obtained for each of the six emotions, when using only unigrams, only semantic classes, or both.

Emotion	Unigrams	Semantic Classes	All Textual
ANGER	0.5525	0.3044	0.5658
DISGUST	0.4246	0.2394	0.4322
FEAR	0.3744	0.2443	0.4041
JOY	0.5636	0.3659	0.5769
SADNESS	0.5291	0.3006	0.5418
SURPRISE	0.3214	0.2153	0.3392
AVERAGE	0.4609	0.2783	0.4766

Table 3: Evaluations using textual features: unigrams, semantic classes, and all the textual features.

4.2 Musical Features.

In a second set of experiments, we explore the role played by the musical features. While the musical notation of a song offers several characteristics that could be potentially useful for our classification experiments (e.g., notes, measures, dynamics, tempo), in these initial experiments we decided to focus on two main features, namely the notes and the key.

Notes. A note is a sign used in the musical notation associated with a song, to represent the relative duration and pitch of a sound. In traditional music theory, the notes are represented using the first seven letters of the alphabet (C-D-E-F-G-A-B), al-

[2] We use the Weka machine learning toolkit.

[3] There is no clear way to determine a baseline for these experiments. A simple baseline that we calculated, which assumed by default an emotional score equal to the average of the scores on the training data, and measured the correlation between these default scores and the gold standard, consistently led to correlations close to 0 (0.0081-0.0221).

though other notations can also be used. Notes can be modified by "accidentals" – a sharp or a flat symbol that can change the note by half a tone. A written note can also have associated a value, which refers to its duration (e.g., whole note; eighth note). Similar to the unigram features, for each note, we record a feature indicating the frequency of that note inside a line.

Key. The key of a song refers to the harmony or "pitch class" used for a song, e.g., *C major*, or *F#*. Sometime the term *minor* or *major* can be appended to a key, to indicate a minor or a major scale. For instance, a song in "the key of C minor" means that the song is harmonically centered on the note C, and it makes use of the minor scale whose first note is C. The key system is the structural foundation of most of the Western music. We use a simple feature that reflects the key of the song. Note that with a few exceptions, when more than one key is used in a song, all the lines in a song will have the same key.

Table 4 shows the results obtained in these classification experiments, when using only the notes as features, only the key, or both.

Emotion	Notes	Key	All Musical
ANGER	0.2453	0.4083	0.4405
DISGUST	0.1485	0.2922	0.3199
FEAR	0.1361	0.2203	0.2450
JOY	0.1533	0.3835	0.4001
SADNESS	0.1738	0.3502	0.3762
SURPRISE	0.0983	0.2241	0.2412
AVERAGE	0.1592	0.3131	0.3371

Table 4: Evaluations using musical features: notes, key, and all the musical features.

4.3 Joint Textual and Musical Features.

To explore the usefulness of the joint lyrics and music representation, we also run a set of experiments that use all the textual and musical features. Table 5 shows the Pearson correlations obtained when using all the features. To facilitate the comparison, the table also includes the results obtained with the textual-only and musical-only features (reported in Tables 3 and 4).

Emotion	All Textual	All Musical	Textual & Musical
ANGER	0.5658	0.4405	0.6679
DISGUST	0.4322	0.3199	0.5068
FEAR	0.4041	0.2450	0.4384
JOY	0.5769	0.4001	0.6456
SADNESS	0.5418	0.3762	0.6193
SURPRISE	0.3392	0.2412	0.3855
AVERAGE	0.4766	0.3371	0.5439

Table 5: Evaluations using both textual and musical features.

5 Discussion

One clear conclusion can be drawn from these experiments: the textual and musical features are both useful for the classification of emotions in songs, and, more importantly, their joint use leads to the highest classification results. Specifically, the joint model gives an error rate reduction of 12.9% with respect to the classifier that uses only textual features, and 31.2% with respect to the classifier that uses only musical features. This supports the idea that lyrics and music represent orthogonal dimensions for the classification of emotions in songs.

Among the six emotions considered, the largest improvements are observed for JOY, SADNESS, and ANGER. This was somehow expected for the first two emotions, since they appear to be dominant in the corpus (see Table 2), but comes as a surprise for ANGER, which is less dominant. Further explorations are needed to determine the reason for this effect.

Looking at the features considered, textual features appear to be the most useful. Nonetheless, the addition of the musical features brings clear improvements, as shown in the last column from the same table.

Additionally, we made several further analyses of the results, as described below.

Feature ablation. To determine the role played by each of the feature groups we consider, we run an ablation study where we remove one feature group at a time from the complete set of features and measure the accuracy of the resulting classifier. Table 6 shows the feature ablation results. Note that feature ablation can also be done in the reverse direction, by

Emotion	All Features	All features, excluding				
		Unigrams	Semantic Classes	Notes	Key	Semantic Classes and Notes
ANGER	0.6679	0.4996	0.5525	0.6573	0.6068	0.6542
DISGUST	0.5068	0.3831	0.4246	0.5013	0.4439	0.4814
FEAR	0.4384	0.3130	0.3744	0.4313	0.4150	0.4114
JOY	0.6456	0.5141	0.5636	0.6432	0.5829	0.6274
SADNESS	0.6193	0.4586	0.5291	0.6176	0.5540	0.6029
SURPRISE	0.3855	0.3083	0.3214	0.3824	0.3421	0.3721
AVERAGE	0.5439	0.4127	0.4609	0.5388	0.4908	0.5249

Table 6: Ablation studies excluding one feature group at a time.

Emotion	Baseline	Textual	Musical	Textual and Musical
ANGER	89.27%	91.14%	89.63%	92.40%
DISGUST	93.85%	94.67%	93.85%	94.77%
FEAR	93.58%	93.87%	93.58%	93.87%
JOY	50.26%	70.92%	61.95%	75.64%
SADNESS	67.40%	75.84%	70.65%	79.42%
SURPRISE	94.83%	94.83%	94.83%	94.83%
AVERAGE	81.53%	86.87%	84.08%	88.49%

Table 7: Evaluations using a coarse-grained binary classification.

keeping only one group of features at a time; the results obtained with the individual feature groups are already reported in Tables 3 and 4.

The ablation studies confirm the findings from our earlier experiments: while the unigrams and the keys are the most predictive features, the semantic classes and the notes are also contributing to the final classification even if to a lesser extent. To measure the effect of these groups of somehow weaker features (semantic classes and notes), we also perform an ablation experiment where we remove both these feature groups from the feature set. The results are reported in the last column of Table 6.

Coarse-grained classification. As an additional evaluation, we transform the task into a binary classification by using a threshold empirically set at 3. Thus, to generate the coarse binary annotations, if the score of an emotion is below 3, we record it as "negative" (i.e., the emotion is absent), whereas if the score is equal to or above 3, we record it as "positive" (i.e., the emotion is present).

For the classification, we use Support Vector Machines (SVM), which are binary classifiers that seek to find the hyperplane that best separates a set of positive examples from a set of negative examples, with maximum margin (Vapnik, 1995). Applications of SVM classifiers to text categorization led to some of the best results reported in the literature (Joachims, 1998).

Table 7 shows the results obtained for each of the six emotions, and for the three major settings that we considered: textual features only, musical features only, and a classifier that jointly uses the textual and the musical features. As before, the classification accuracy for each experiment is reported as the average of the accuracies obtained during a tenfold cross-validation on the corpus. The table also shows a baseline, computed as the average of the accuracies obtained when using the most frequent class observed on the training data for each fold.

As seen from the table, on average, the joint use of textual and musical features is also beneficial for this binary coarser-grained classification. Perhaps not surprisingly, the effect of the classifier is stronger for

Emotion	1,000 news headlines: Best result SEMEVAL'07	1,000 news headlines: (Strapparava and Mihalcea, 08)	4,976 song lines: Joint Text and Music
ANGER	0.3233	0.1978	0.6679
DISGUST	0.1855	0.1354	0.5068
FEAR	0.4492	0.2956	0.4384
JOY	0.2611	0.1381	0.6456
SADNESS	0.4098	0.1601	0.6193
SURPRISE	0.1671	0.1235	0.3855
AVERAGE	0.2993	0.1750	0.5439

Table 8: Results obtained in previous work on emotion classification.

those emotions that are dominant in the corpus, i.e., JOY and SADNESS (see Table 2). The improvement obtained with the classifiers is much smaller for the other emotions (or even absent, e.g., for SURPRISE), which is also explained by their high baseline of over 90%.

Comparison to previous work. There is no previous research that has considered the joint use of lyrics and songs representations for emotion classification at line level, and thus we cannot draw a direct comparison with other work on emotion classification in songs.

Nonetheless, as a point of reference, we consider the previous work done on emotion classification of texts. Table 8 shows the results obtained in previous work for the recognition of emotions in a corpus consisting of 1,000 news headlines (Strapparava and Mihalcea, 2007) annotated for the same six emotions. Specifically, the table shows the best overall correlation results obtained by the three emotion recognition systems in the SEMEVAL task on Affective Text (Strapparava and Mihalcea, 2007): (Chaumartin, 2007; Kozareva et al., 2007; Katz et al., 2007). The table also shows the best results obtained in follow up work carried out on the same dataset (Strapparava and Mihalcea, 2008).

Except for one emotion (FEAR), the correlation figures we obtain are significantly higher than those reported in previous work. As mentioned before, however, a direct comparison cannot be made, since the earlier work used a different, smaller dataset. Moreover, our corpus of songs is likely to be more emotionally loaded than the news titles used in previous work.

6 Conclusions

Popular songs express universally understood meanings and embody experiences and feelings shared by many, usually through a combined effect of both music and lyrics. In this paper, we introduced a novel corpus of music and lyrics, annotated for emotions at line level, and we used this corpus to explore the automatic recognition of emotions in songs. Through experiments carried out on the dataset of 100 songs, we showed that emotion recognition can be performed using either textual or musical features, and that the joint use of lyrics and music can improve significantly over classifiers that use only one dimension at a time.

The dataset introduced in this paper is available by request from the authors of the paper.

Acknowledgments

The authors are grateful to Rajitha Schellenberg for her help with collecting the emotion annotations. Carlo Strapparava was partially supported by a Google Research Award. Rada Mihalcea's work was in part supported by the National Science Foundation award #0917170. Any opinions, findings, and conclusions or recommendations expressed in this material are those of the authors and do not necessarily reflect the views of the National Science Foundation.

References

C. Alm, D. Roth, and R. Sproat. 2005. Emotions from text: Machine learning for text-based emotion prediction. In *Proceedings of the Conference on Empirical*

Methods in Natural Language Processing, pages 347–354, Vancouver, Canada.

Z. Cataltepe, Y. Yaslan, and A. Sonmez. 2007. Music genre classification using MIDI and audio features. *Journal on Advances in Signal Processing*.

F.R. Chaumartin. 2007. Upar7: A knowledge-based system for headline sentiment tagging. In *Proceedings of the Fourth International Workshop on Semantic Evaluations (SemEval-2007)*, Prague, Czech Republic, June.

M. Das, D. Howard, and S. Smith. 2000. The kinematic analysis of motion curves through MIDI data analysis. *Organised Sound*, 5(1):137–145.

P. Ekman. 1993. Facial expression of emotion. *American Psychologist*, 48:384–392.

X. Hu, J. S. Downie, and A. F. Ehmann. 2009. Lyric text mining in music mood classification. In *Proceedings of the International Society for Music Information Retrieval Conference*, Kobe, Japan.

T. Joachims. 1998. Text categorization with Support Vector Machines: learning with mny relevant features. In *Proceedings of the European Conference on Machine Learning*, pages 137–142, Chemnitz, Germany.

P. Juslin and P. Laukka. 2003. Communication of emotion in vocal expression and music performance: Different channels, same code? *Psychological Bulletin*, 129:770–814.

P. N. Juslin and J. A. Sloboda, editors. 2001. *Music and Emotion: Theory and Research*. Oxford University Press.

C. Karageorghis and D. Priest. 2008. Music in sport and exercise : An update on research and application. *The Sport Journal*, 11(3).

P. Katz, M. Singleton, and R. Wicentowski. 2007. Swat-mp:the semeval-2007 systems for task 5 and task 14. In *Proceedings of the Fourth International Workshop on Semantic Evaluations (SemEval-2007)*, Prague, Czech Republic, June.

Y. Kim, E. Schmidt, R. Migneco, B. Morton, P. Richardson, J. Scott, J. Speck, and D. Turnbull. 2010. Music emotion recognition: A state of the art review. In *International Symposium on Music Information Retrieval*.

Z. Kozareva, B. Navarro, S. Vazquez, and A. Montoyo. 2007. Ua-zbsa: A headline emotion classification through web information. In *Proceedings of the Fourth International Workshop on Semantic Evaluations (SemEval-2007)*, Prague, Czech Republic, June.

C. Laurier, J. Grivolla, and P. Herrera. 2008. Multimodal music mood classification using audio and lyrics. In *Proceedings of the International Conference on Machine Learning and Applications*, Barcelona, Spain.

J. Mahedero, A. Martinez, and P. Cano. 2005. Natural language processing of lyrics. In *Proceedings of MM'05*, Singapore, November.

B. Nettl. 2000. An ethnomusicologist contemplates universals in musical sound and musical culture. In N. Wallin, B. Merker, and S. Brown, editors, *The origins of music*, pages 463—472. MIT Press, Cambridge, MA.

T. O'Hara. 2011. Inferring the meaning of chord sequences via lyrics. In *Proceedings of 2nd Workshop on Music Recommendation and Discovery (WOMRAD 2011)*, Chicago, IL, October.

N. Orio. 2006. Music retrieval: A tutorial and review. *Foundations and Trends in Information Retrieval*, 1(1):1–90, November.

A. Ortony, G. L. Clore, and M. A. Foss. 1987. The referential structure of the affective lexicon. *Cognitive Science*, (11).

J. Pennebaker and M. Francis. 1999. Linguistic inquiry and word count: LIWC. Erlbaum Publishers.

J. Pennebaker and L. King. 1999. Linguistic styles: Language use as an individual difference. *Journal of Personality and Social Psychology*, (77).

F. Rauscher, G. Shaw, and K. Ky. 1993. Music and spatial task performance. *Nature*, 365.

D. Rizo, P. Ponce de Leon, C. Perez-Sancho, A. Pertusa, and J. Inesta. 2006. A pattern recognition approach for melody track selection in MIDI files. In *Proceedings of 7th International Symposyum on Music Information Retrieval (ISMIR-06)*, pages 61–66, Victoria, Canada, October.

K. Scherer. 1995. Expression of emotion in voice and music. *Journal of Voice*, 9:235–248.

K. Scherer. 2004. Which emotions can be induced by music? what are the underlying mechanisms? and how can we measure them ? *Journal of New Music Research*, 33:239–251.

R. Snow, B. O'Connor, D. Jurafsky, and A. Ng. 2008. Cheap and fast – but is it good? evaluating non-expert annotations for natural language tasks. In *Proceedings of the Conference on Empirical Methods in Natural Language Processing*, Honolulu, Hawaii.

C. Strapparava and R. Mihalcea. 2007. Semeval-2007 task 14: Affective text. In *Proceedings of the 4th International Workshop on the Semantic Evaluations (SemEval 2007)*, Prague, Czech Republic.

C. Strapparava and R. Mihalcea. 2008. Learning to identify emotions in text. In *Proceedings of the ACM Conference on Applied Computing ACM-SAC 2008*, Fortaleza, Brazile.

C. Strapparava and A. Valitutti. 2004. Wordnet-affect: an affective extension of wordnet. In *Proceedings of the 4th International Conference on Language Resources and Evaluation*, Lisbon.

J. Sundberg. 1982. Speech, song, and emotions. In M. Clynes, editor, *Music, Mind and Brain: The Neuropsychology of Music*. Plenum Press, New York.

V. Vapnik. 1995. *The Nature of Statistical Learning Theory*. Springer, New York.

S. Velusamy, B. Thoshkahna, and K. Ramakrishnan. 2007. Novel melody line identification algorithm for polyphonic MIDI music. In *Proceedings of 13th International Multimedia Modeling Conference (MMM 2007)*, Singapore, January.

Y. Wang, M. Kan, T. Nwe, A. Shenoy, and J. Yin. 2004. LyricAlly: Automatic synchronization of acoustic musical signals and textual lyrics. In *Proceedings of MM'04*, New York, October.

Y. Xia, L. Wang, K.F. Wong, and M. Xu. 2008. Lyric-based song sentiment classification with sentiment vector space model. In *Proceedings of the Association for Computational Linguistics*, Columbus, Ohio.

D. Yang and W. Lee. 2004. Disambiguating music emotion using software agents. In *Proceedings of the International Conference on Music Information Retrieval*, Barcelona, Spain.

D. Yang and W. Lee. 2009. Music emotion identification from lyrics. In *Proceedings of 11th IEEE Symposium on Multimedia*.

Y.-H. Yang, Y.-C. Lin, H.-T. Cheng, I.-B. Liao, Y.-C. Ho, and H. Chen. 2008. Toward multi-modal music emotion classification. In *Proceedings of the 9th Pacific Rim Conference on Multimedia: Advances in Multimedia Information Processing*.

Assessment of ESL Learners' Syntactic Competence Based on Similarity Measures

Su-Youn Yoon
Educational Testing Service
Princeton, NJ 08541
syoon@ets.org

Suma Bhat
Beckman Institute,
Urbana, IL 61801
spbhat2@illinois.edu

Abstract

This study presents a novel method that measures English language learners' syntactic competence towards improving automated speech scoring systems. In contrast to most previous studies which focus on the length of production units such as the mean length of clauses, we focused on capturing the differences in the distribution of morpho-syntactic features or grammatical expressions across proficiency. We estimated the syntactic competence through the use of corpus-based NLP techniques. Assuming that the range and sophistication of grammatical expressions can be captured by the distribution of Part-of-Speech (POS) tags, vector space models of POS tags were constructed. We use a large corpus of English learners' responses that are classified into four proficiency levels by human raters. Our proposed feature measures the similarity of a given response with the most proficient group and is then estimates the learner's syntactic competence level.

Widely *outperforming* the state-of-the-art measures of syntactic complexity, our method attained a significant correlation with human-rated scores. The correlation between human-rated scores and features based on manual transcription was 0.43 and the same based on ASR-hypothesis was slightly lower, 0.42. An important advantage of our method is its robustness against speech recognition errors not to mention the simplicity of feature generation that captures a reasonable set of learner-specific syntactic errors.

1 Introduction

This study provides a novel method that measures ESL (English as a second language) learners' competence in grammar usage (syntactic competence). Being interdisciplinary in nature, it shows how to combine the core findings in the ESL literature with various empirical NLP techniques for the purpose of automated scoring.

Grammar usage is one of the dimensions of language ability that is assessed during non-native proficiency level testing in a foreign language. Overall proficiency in the target language can be assessed by testing the abilities in various areas including fluency, pronunciation, and intonation; grammar and vocabulary; and discourse structure. Testing rubrics for human raters contain descriptors used for the subjective assessment of several of these features. With the recent move towards the objective assessment of language ability (spoken and written), it is imperative that we develop methods for quantifying these abilities and measuring them automatically.

Ortega (2003) indicated that "the *range* of forms that surface in language production and the degree of *sophistication* of such forms" were two important areas in grammar usage and called the combination of these two areas "syntactic complexity." Features that measure syntactic complexity have been frequently studied in ESL literature and have been found to be highly correlated with students' proficiency levels in writing.

Studies in automated speech scoring have focused on fluency (Cucchiarini et al., 2000; Cucchiarini et al., 2002), pronunciation (Witt and Young, 1997;

Witt, 1999; Franco et al., 1997; Neumeyer et al., 2000), and intonation (Zechner et al., 2009), and relatively fewer studies have been conducted on grammar usage. More recently, Lu (2010), Chen and Yoon (2011) and Chen and Zechner (2011) have measured syntactic competence in speech scoring. Chen and Yoon (2011) estimated the complexity of sentences based on the average length of the clauses or sentences. In addition to these length measures, Lu (2010) and Chen and Zechner (2011) measured the parse-tree based features such as the mean depth of parsing tree levels. However, these studies found that these measures did not show satisfactory empirical performance in automatic speech scoring (Chen and Yoon, 2011; Chen and Zechner, 2011) when the features were calculated from the output of a speech recognition engine.

This study considers new features that measure syntactic complexity and is novel in two important ways. First, in contrast to most features that infer syntactic complexity based upon the length of the unit, we directly measure students' sophistication and range in grammar usage. Second, instead of rating a student's response using a scale based on native speech production, our experiments compare it with a similar body of learners' speech. Eliciting native speakers' data and rating it for grammar usage (supervised approach) can be arbitrary, since there can be a very wide range of possible grammatical structures that native speakers utilize. Instead, we proceed in a semi-supervised fashion. A large amount of learners' spoken responses were collected and classified into four groups according to their proficiency level. We then sought to find how distinct the proficiency classes were based on the distribution of POS tags. Given a student's response, we calculated the similarity with a sample of responses for each score level based on the proportion and distribution of Part-of-Speech using NLP techniques.

POS tag distribution has been used in various tasks such as text genre classification (Feldman et al., 2009); in a language testing context, it has been used in grammatical error detection (Chodorow and Leacock, 2000; Tetreault and Chodorow, 2008) and essay scoring. Recently, Roark et al. (2011) explored POS tag distribution to capture the differences in syntactic complexity between healthy subjects and subjects with mild cognitive impairment, but no other research has used POS tag distribution in measuring syntactic complexity, to the best of authors' knowledge.

An assessment of ESL learners' syntactic competence should consider the structure of sentences as a whole - a task which may not be captured by the simplistic POS tag distribution. However, studies of Lu (2010) and Chen and Zechner (2011) showed that more complex syntactic features are unreliable in ASR-based scoring system. Furthermore, we show that POS unigrams or bigrams indeed capture a reasonable portion of learners' range and sophistication of grammar usage in our discussion in Section 7.

This paper will proceed as follows: we will review related work in Section 2 and present the method to calculate syntactic complexity in Section 3. Data and experiment setup will be explained in Section 4 and Section 5. The results will be presented in Section 6. Finally, in Section 7, we discuss the levels of syntactic competence that are captured using our proposed measure.

2 Related Work

Second Language Acquisition (SLA) researchers have developed many quantitative measures to estimate the level of acquisition of syntactic competence. Bardovi-Harlig and Bofman (1989) classified these measures into two groups. The first group is related to the acquisition of specific morphosyntactic features or grammatical expressions. Tests of negations or relative clauses - whether these expressions occurred in the test responses without errors - fell into this group (hereafter, the expression-based group). The second group is related to the length of the clause or the relationship between clauses and hence not tied to particular structures (hereafter, the length-based group). Examples of the second group measures include the average length of clause unit and dependent clauses per sentence unit.

These syntactic measures have been extensively studied in ESL writing. Ortega (2003) synthesized 25 research studies which employed syntactic measures on ESL writing and reported a significant relationship between the proposed features and writing proficiency. He reported that a subset of features such as the mean length of the clause unit increased with students' proficiency. More recently, Lu (2010) has conducted a more systematic study using an automated system. He applied 14 syntactic measures to a large database of Chinese learners' writing samples and found that syntactic measures were strong predictors of students' writing proficiency.

Studies in the area of automated speech scoring have only recently begun to actively investigate the usefulness of syntactic measures for scoring spontaneous speech (Chen et al., 2010; Bernstein et al., 2010). These have identified clause boundaries (identified from manual annotations and automatically) and obtained length-based features. In addition to these conventional syntactic complexity features, Lu (2009) implemented an automated system that calculates the revised Developmental Level (D-Level) Scale (Covington et al., 2006) using natural language processing (NLP) techniques. The original D-Level Scale was proposed by Rosenberg and Abbeduto (1987) based primarily on observations of child language acquisition. They classified children's grammatical acquisition into 7 different groups according to the presence of certain types of complex sentences. The revised D-Level Scale classified sentences into the eight levels according to the presence of particular grammatical expressions. For instance, level 0 is comprised of simple sentences, while level 5 is comprised of sentences joined by subordinating conjunction or nonfinite clauses in an adjunct position. The D-Level Scale has been less studied in the speech scoring. To our knowledge, Chen and Zechner (2011) is the only study that applied the D-Level analyzer to ESL learners' spoken responses.

In contrast to ESL writing, applying syntactic complexity features, both conventional length-based features and D-Level features, presents serious obstacles for speaking. First, the length of the spoken responses are typically shorter than written responses. Most measures are based on sentence or sentence-like units, and in speaking tests that elicit only a few sentences the measures are less reliable. Chen and Yoon (2011) observed a marked decrease in correlation between syntactic measures and proficiency as response length decreased. In addition, speech recognition errors only worsen the situation. Chen and Zechner (2011) showed that the significant correlation between syntactic measures and speech proficiency (correlation coefficient = 0.49) became insignificant when they were applied to the speech recognition word hypotheses. Errors in speech recognition seriously influenced the measures and decreased the performance. Due to these problems, the existing syntactic measures do not seem reliable enough for being used in automated speech proficiency scoring.

In this study, we propose novel syntactic measures which are relatively robust against speech recognition errors and are reliable in short responses. In contrast to recent studies focusing on length-based features, we focus on capturing differences in the distribution of morphosyntactic features or grammatical expressions across proficiency levels. We investigate the distribution of a broader class of grammatical forms through the use of corpus-based NLP techniques.

3 Method

Many previous studies, that assess syntactic complexity based on the distribution of morphosyntactic features and grammatical expressions, limited their experiments to a few grammatical expressions. Covington et al. (2006) and Lu (2009) covered all sentence types, but their approaches were based on expert observation (supervised rubrics), and descriptions of each level were brief and abstract. It is important to develop a more detailed and refined scale, but developing scales in a supervised way is difficult due to the subjectivity and the complexity of structures involved.

In order to overcome this problem, we employed NLP technology and a corpus-based approach. We hypothesize that the level of acquired grammatical forms is signaled by the distribution of the POS tags, and the differences in grammatical proficiency result in differences in POS tag distribution. Based on this assumption, we collected large amount of ESL learners' spoken responses and classified them into four groups according to their proficiency levels. The syntactic competence was estimated based on the similarity between the test responses and learners' corpus.

A POS-based vector space model (VSM), in which the response belonging to separate proficiency levels were converted to vectors and the similarity between vectors were calculated using cosine similarity measure and tf-idf weighting, was employed. Such a score-category-based VSM has been used in automated essay scoring. Attali and Burstein (2006) to assess the lexical content of an essay by comparing the words in the test essay with the words in a sample essays from each score category. We extend this to assessment of grammar usage using vectors of POS tags.

Proficient speakers use complicated grammatical expressions, while beginners use simple expressions and sentences with frequent grammatical errors. POS tags (or sequences) capturing these expressions may be seen in corresponding proportions in each score group. These distributional differences are captured by inverse-document frequency.

In addition, we identify frequent POS tag sequences as those having high mutual information and include them in our experiments. Temple (2000) pointed out that the proficient learners are characterized by increased automaticity in speech production. These speakers tend to memorize frequently used multi-word sequences as a chunk and retrieve the whole chunk as a single unit. The degree of automaticity can be captured by the frequent occurrence of POS sequences with high mutual information.

We quantify the usefulness of the generated features for the purpose of automatic scoring by first considering its correlation with the human scores. We then compare the performance of our features with those in Lu (2011), where the features are a collection of measures of syntactic complexity that have shown promising directions in previous studies.

4 Data

Two different sets of data were used in this study: the AEST 48K dataset and AEST balanced dataset. Both were collections of responses from the AEST, a high-stakes test of English proficiency and had no overlaps. The AEST assessment consists of 6 items in which speakers are prompted to provide responses lasting between 45 and 60 seconds per item. In summary, approximately 3 minutes of speech is collected per speaker.

Among the 6 items, two items are tasks that ask examinees to provide information or opinions on familiar topics based on their personal experience or background knowledge. The four remaining items are integrated tasks that include other language skills such as listening and reading. All items extract spontaneous, unconstrained natural speech. The size, purpose, and speakers' native language information for each dataset is summarized in Table 1.

Each response was rated by trained human raters using a 4-point scoring scale, where 1 indicates a low speaking proficiency and 4 indicates a high speaking proficiency. In order to evaluate the reliability of the human ratings, the data should be scored by two raters. Since none of the AEST balanced data was double scored the inter-rater agreement ratio was estimated using a large (41K) double-scored dataset using the same scoring guidelines and scoring process. The Pearson correlation coefficient was 0.63 suggesting a reasonable inter-rater agreement. The distribution of the scores for this data can be found in Table 2.

We used the AEST 48K dataset as the training data and the AEST balanced dataset as the evaluation data.

5 Experiments

5.1 Overview

Our experimental procedure is as follows. All transcriptions were tagged using the POS tagger described in Section 5.3 and POS tag sequences were extracted. Next, the POS-based VSMs (one for each score class) were created using the AEST 48K dataset. Finally, for a given test response in the AEST balanced dataset, similarity features were generated.

A score-class-specific POS-based VSM was created using POS tags generated from the manual transcriptions. For evaluation, two different types of transcriptions (manual transcription and word hypotheses from the speech recognizer described in Section 5.2) were used in order to investigate the influence of speech recognition errors in the feature performance.

5.2 Speech recognition

An HMM recognizer was trained on AEST 48K dataset - approximately 733 hours of non-native speech collected from 7872 speakers. A gender independent triphone acoustic model and combination

Corpus name	Purpose	Number of speakers	Number of responses	Native languages	Size (Hrs)
AEST 48K data	ASR training and POS model training	7872	47227	China (20%), Korea (19%), Japanese (7%), India (7%), others (46%)	733
AEST balanced data	Feature development and evaluation	480	2880	Korean (15%), Chinese (14%), Japanese (7%), Spanish (9%), Others (55%)	44

Table 1: Data size and speakers native languages

Corpus name	Size	Score1	Score2	Score3	Score4
AEST 48K data	Number of files	1953	16834	23106	5334
	(%)	4	36	49	11
AEST balanced data	Number of files	141	1133	1266	340
	(%)	5	40	45	12

Table 2: Proficiency scores and data sizes

of bigram, trigram, and four-gram language models were used. The word error rate (WER) on the held-out test dataset was 27%.

5.3 POS tagger

POS tags were generated using the POS tagger implemented in the OpenNLP toolkit. It was trained on the Switchboard (SWBD) corpus. This POS tagger was trained on about 528K word/tag pairs and achieved a tagging accuracy of 96.3% on a test set of 379K words. The Penn POS tag set was used in the tagger.

5.4 Unit generation using mutual information

POS bigrams with high mutual information were selected and used as a single unit. First, all POS bigrams which occurred less than 50 times were filtered out. Next, the remaining POS tag bigrams were sorted by their mutual information scores, and two different sets (top50 and top110) were selected. The selected POS pairs were transformed into compound tags. As a result, we generated three sets of POS units by this process: the original POS set without the compound unit (Base), the original set and an additional 50 compound units (Base+mi50), and the original set and an additional 110 units (Base+mi110).

Finally, unigram, bigram and trigram were generated for each set separately. The size of total terms in each condition was presented in table 3.

	Base	Base+mi50	Base+mi110
Unigram	42	93	151
Bigram	1366	4284	9691
Trigram	21918	54856	135430

Table 3: Number of terms used in VSMs

5.5 Building VSMs

For each ngram, three sets of VSMs were built using three sets of tags as terms, yielding a total of nine VSMs. The results were based on the individual model and we did not combine any models.

5.6 Cosine similarity-based features

The cosine similarity has been frequently used in the information retrieval field to identify the relevant documents for the given query. This measures the similarity between a given query and a document by measuring the cosine of the angle between vectors in a high-dimensional space, whereby each term in the query and documents corresponding to a unique dimension. If a document is relevant to the query, then it shares many terms resulting in a small angle. In this study, the term was a single or compound POS tag (unigram,bigram or trigram) weighted by its tf-idf, and the document was the response.

First, the inverse document frequency was calculated from the training data, and each response was treated as a document. Next, responses in the same

	Unigram			Bigram			Trigram		
	Base	Base +mi50	Base +mi110	Base	Base +mi50	Base +mi110	Base	Base +mi50	Base +mi110
Trans-cription	0.301**	0.297**	0.329**	0.427**	0.361**	0.366**	0.402**	0.322**	0.295**
ASR	0.246**	0.272**	0.304**	0.415**	0.348**	0.347**	0.373**	0.311**	0.282**

Table 4: Pearson correlation coefficients between ngram-based features and expert proficiency scores
** Correlation is significant at the 0.01 level

score group were concatenated, and a single vector was generated for each score group. A total of 4 vectors were generated using training data. For each test response, a similarity score was calculated as follows:

$$\cos(\vec{q}, \vec{d_j}) = \frac{\sum_{i=1}^{n} q_i d_{ji}}{\sum_{i=1}^{n} {q_i}^2 \sum_{i=1}^{n} {d_i}^2}$$

$$q_i \equiv tf(t_i, \vec{q}) \times \log\left(\frac{N}{df(t_i)}\right)$$

$$d_{ji} \equiv tf(t_i, \vec{d_j}) \times \log\left(\frac{N}{df(t_i)}\right)$$

where $\vec{q}$ is a vector of the test response,
$\vec{d_j}$ is a vector of the $scoreGroup_j$,
n is the total number of POS tags,
$tf(t_i, \vec{q})$ is the term frequency of POS tag t_i in the test response,
$tf(t_i, \vec{d_j})$ is the term frequency of POS tag t_i in the $scoreGroup_j$,
N is the total number of training responses,
$df(t_i)$ is the document frequency of POS tag t_i in the total training responses

Finally, a total of 4 cos scores (one per score group) were generated. Among these four values, the $cos4$, the similarity score to the responses in the score group 4, was selected as a feature with the following intuition. $cos4$ measures the similarity of a given test response to the representative vector of score class 4; the larger the value, the closer it would be to score class 4.

6 Results

6.1 Correlation

Table 4 shows correlations between cosine similarity features and proficiency scores rated by experts.

The bigram-based features outperformed both unigram-based and trigram-based features. In particular, the similarities using the *base* tag set with bigrams achieved the best performance. By adding the mutual information-based compound units to the original POS tag sets, the performance of features improved in the unigram models. However, there was no performance gain in either bigram or trigram models; on the contrary, there was a large drop in performance. Unigrams have good coverage but limited power in distinguishing different score levels. On the other hand, trigrams have opposite characteristics. Bigrams seem to strike a balance in both coverage and complexity (from among the three considered here) and may thus have resulted in the best performace.

The performance of ASR-based features were comparable to that of transcription-based features. The best performing feature among ASR-based-features were from the bigram and *base* set, with correlations nearly the same as the best performing one among the transcription-based-features. Seeing how close the correlations were in the case of transcription-based and ASR-hypothesis based feature extraction, we conclude that the proposed measure is robust to ASR errors.

6.2 Comparison with other Measures of Syntactic Complexity

We compared the performance of our features with the features of syntactic complexity proposed in (Lu, 2011). Towards this, the clause boundaries of the ASR hypotheses, were automatically detected using the automated clause boundary detection method[1].

[1]The automated clause boundary detection method in this study was a Maximum Entropy Model based on word bigrams, POS tag bigrams, and pause features. The method achieved an

The utterances were then parsed using the Stanford Parser, and a total of 22 features including both length-related features and parse-tree based features were generated using (Lu, 2011). Finally, we calculated Pearson correlation coefficients between these features and human proficiency scores.

Study	Feature	Correlation
Current study	bigram based cos4	0.41**
(Lu, 2011)	DCC	0.14**

Table 5: Comparison between (Lu, 2011) and this study
** Correlation is significant at the 0.01 level

As indicated in Table 5, the best performing feature was mean number of dependent clauses per clause (DCC) and the correlation r was 0.14. No features other than DCC achieved statistically significant correlation. Our best performing feature (bigram based cos4) *widely outperformed* the best of Lu (2011)'s features (correlations approximately 0.3 apart).

A logical explanation for the poor performance of Lu (2011)'s features is that the features are generated using multi-stage automated process, and the errors in each process contributes the low feature performance. For instance, the errors in the automated clause boundary detection may result in a serious drop in the performance. With the spoken responses being particularly short (a typical response in the data set had 10 clauses on average), even one error in clause boundary detection can seriously affect the reliability of features.

7 Discussion

While the measure of syntactic competence that we study here is an abstraction of the overall syntactic competence, without consideration of specific constructions, we analyzed the results further with the intention of casting light on the level of details of syntactic competence that can be explained using our measure. Furthermore, this section will show that bigram POS sequences can yield significant information on the range and sophistication of grammar usage in the specific assessment context (spontaneous speech comprised of only declarative sentences).

ESL speakers with high proficiency scores are expected to use more complicated grammatical expressions that result in a high proportion of POS tags related to these expressions in that score group. The distribution of POS tags was analyzed in detail in order to investigate whether there were systematic distributional changes according to proficiency levels. Owing to space constraints, we restrict our discussion to the analysis using unigrams (base and compound). For each score group, the POS tags were sorted based on the frequencies in training data, and the rank orders were calculated. The more frequent the POS tag, the higher its rank.

A total of 150 POS tags, including the original POS tag set and top 110 compound tags, were classified into 5 classes:

- Absence-of-low-proficiency (ABS): Group of POS tags that appear in all score groups except the lowest proficiency group;
- Increase (INC): Group of POS tags whose ranks increase consistently as proficiency increases;
- Decrease (DEC): Group of POS tags whose ranks decrease consistently as proficiency increases;
- Constant (CON): Group of POS tags whose ranks remain same despite change in proficiency;
- Mix: Group of POS tags of with no consistent pattern in the ranks.

Table 6 presents the number of POS tags in each class.

ABS	INC	DEC	CON	Mix
14	37	33	18	48

Table 6: Tag distribution and proficiency scores

The 'ABS' class mostly consists of 'WP' and 'WDT'; more than 50% of tags in this class are related to these two tags. 'WP' is a Wh-pronoun while 'WDT' is a Wh-determiner. Since most sentences in

F-score of 0.60 on the non-native speakers' ASR hypotheses. A detailed description of the method is presented in (Chen and Zechner, 2011)

our data are declarative sentences, 'Wh' phrase signals the use of relative clause. Therefore, the lack of these tags strongly support the hypothesis that the speakers in score group 1 showed incompetence in the use of relative clauses or their use in limited situations.

The 'INC' class can be sub-classified into three groups: verb, comparative, and relative clause. Verb group is includes the infinitive (TO_VB), passive (VB_VBN, VBD_VBN, VBN, VBN_IN, VBN_RP), and gerund forms (VBG, VBG_RP, VBG_TO). Next, the comparative group encompasses comparative constructions. Finally, the relative clause group signals the presence of relative clauses. The increased proportion of these tags reflects the use of more complicated tense forms and modal forms as well as more frequent use of relative clauses. It supports the hypothesis that speakers with higher proficiency scores tend to use more complicated grammatical expressions.

The 'DEC' class can be sub-classified into five groups: noun, simple tense verb, GW and UH, non-compound, and comparative. The noun group is comprised of many noun or proper noun-related expressions, and their high proportions are consistent with the tendency that less proficient speakers use nouns more frequently. Secondly, the simple tense verb group is comprised of the base form (VB) and simple present and past forms(PRP_VBD, VB, VBD_TO, VBP_TO, VBZ). The expressions in these groups are simpler than those in 'Increase' group.

The 'UH' tag is for interjection and filler words such as 'uh' and 'um', while the 'GW' tag is for word-fragments. These two spontaneous speech phenomena are strongly related to fluency, and it signals problems in speech production. Frequent occurrences of these two tags are evidence of frequent planning problems and their inclusion in the 'DEC' class suggests that instances of speech planning problems decrease with increased proficiency.

Tags in the non-compound group, such as 'DT', 'MD', 'RBS', and 'TO', have related compound tags. The non-compound tags are associated with the expressions that do not co-occur with strongly related words, and they tend to be related to errors. For instance, the non-compound 'MD' tag signals that there is an expression that a modal verb is not followed by 'VB' (base form) and as seen in the examples, 'the project may can change' and 'the others must can not be good', they are related to grammatical errors.

Finally, the comparative group includes 'RBR_JJR'. The decrease of 'RBR_JJR' is related to the correct acquisition of the comparative form. 'RBR' is for comparative adverbs and 'JJR' is for comparative adjectives, and the combination of two tags is strongly related to double-marked errors such as 'more easier'. In the intermediate stage in the acquisition of comparative form, learners tend to use the double-marked form. The compound tags correctly capture this erroneous stage.

The 'Decrease' class also includes three Wh-related tags (WDT_NN, WDT_VBP, WRB), but the proportion is much smaller than the 'Increase' class.

The above analysis shows that the combination of original and compound POS tags correctly capture systematic changes in the grammatical expressions according to changes in proficiency levels.

The robust performance of our proposed measure to speech recognition errors may be better appreciated in the context of similar studies. Compared with the state-of-the art measures of syntactic complexity proposed in Lu (2011) our features achieve significantly better performance especially when generated from ASR hypotheses. It is to be noted that the performance drop between the transcription-based feature and the ASR hypothesis-based feature was marginal.

8 Conclusions

In this paper, we presented features that measure syntactic competence for the automated speech scoring. The features measured the range and sophistication of grammatical expressions based on POS tag distributions. A corpus with a large number of learners' responses was collected and classified into four groups according to proficiency levels. The syntactic competence of the test response was estimated by identifying the most similar group from the learners' corpus. Furthermore, speech recognition errors only resulted in a minor performance drop. The robustness against speech recognition errors is an important advantage of our method.

Acknowledgments

The authors would like to thank Shasha Xie, Klaus Zechner, and Keelan Evanini for their valuable comments, help with data preparation and experiments.

References

Yigal Attali and Jill Burstein. 2006. Automated essay scoring with e–rater R v.2. *The Journal of Technology, Learning, and Assessment*, 4(3).

Kathleen Bardovi-Harlig and Theodora Bofman. 1989. Attainment of syntactic and morphological accuracy by advanced language learners. *Studies in Second Language Acquisition*, 11:17–34.

Jared Bernstein, Jian Cheng, and Masanori Suzuki. 2010. Fluency and structural complexity as predictors of L2 oral proficiency. In *Proceedings of InterSpeech 2010, Tokyo, Japan, September*.

Lei Chen and Su-Youn Yoon. 2011. Detecting structural events for assessing non-native speech. In *Proceedings of the 6th Workshop on Innovative Use of NLP for Building Educational Applications*, pages 38–45.

Miao Chen and Klaus Zechner. 2011. Computing and evaluating syntactic complexity features for automated scoring of spontaneous non-native speech. In *Proceedings of the 49th Annual Meeting of the Association for Computational Linguistics 2011*, pages 722–731.

Lei Chen, Joel Tetreault, and Xiaoming Xi. 2010. Towards using structural events to assess non-native speech. In *Proceedings of the NAACL HLT 2010 Fifth Workshop on Innovative Use of NLP for Building Educational Applications*, pages 74–79.

Martin Chodorow and Claudia Leacock. 2000. An unsupervised method for detecting grammatical errors. In *In Proceedings of NAACL00*, pages 140–147.

Michael A. Covington, Congzhou He, Cati Brown, Lorina Naci, and John Brown. 2006. How complex is that sentence? A proposed revision of the Rosenberg and Abbeduto D-Level Scale. Technical report, CASPR Research Report 2006-01, Athens, GA: The University of Georgia, Artificial Intelligence Center.

Catia Cucchiarini, Helmer Strik, and Lou Boves. 2000. Quantitative assessment of second language learners' fluency: Comparisons between read and spontaneous speech. *The Journal of the Acoustical Society of America*, 107(2):989–999.

Catia Cucchiarini, Helmer Strik, and Lou Boves. 2002. Quantitative assessment of second language learners' fluency: Comparisons between read and spontaneous speech. *The Journal of the Acoustical Society of America*, 111(6):2862–2873.

Sergey Feldman, M.A. Marin, Maria Ostendorf, and Maya R. Gupta. 2009. Part-of-speech histograms for genre classification of text. In *Acoustics, Speech and Signal Processing, 2009. ICASSP 2009. IEEE International Conference on*, pages 4781 –4784, april.

Horacio Franco, Leonardo Neumeyer, Yoon Kim, and Orith Ronen. 1997. Automatic pronunciation scoring for language instruction. In *Proceedings of ICASSP 97*, pages 1471–1474.

Xiaofei Lu. 2009. Automatic measurement of syntactic complexity in child language acquisition. *International Journal of Corpus Linguistics*, 14(1):3–28.

Xiaofei Lu. 2010. Automatic analysis of syntactic complexity in second language writing. *International Journal of Corpus Linguistics*, 15(4):474–496.

Xiaofei Lu. 2011. L2 syntactic complexity analyze. Retrieved March 17, 2012 from `http://www.personal.psu.edu/xxl13/downloads/l2sca.html/`.

Leonardo Neumeyer, Horacio Franco, Vassilios Digalakis, and Mitchel Weintraub. 2000. Automatic scoring of pronunciation quality. *Speech Communication*, pages 88–93.

Lourdes Ortega. 2003. Syntactic complexity measures and their relationship to L2 proficiency: A research synthesis of college–level L2 writing. *Applied Linguistics*, 24(4):492–518.

Brian. Roark, Margaret Mitchell, John-Paul. Hosom, Kristy Hollingshead, and Jeffrey Kaye. 2011. Spoken language derived measures for detecting mild cognitive impairment. *Audio, Speech, and Language Processing, IEEE Transactions on*, 19(7):2081 –2090, sept.

Sheldon Rosenberg and Leonard Abbeduto. 1987. Indicators of linguistic competence in the peer group conversational behavior of mildly retarded adults. *Applied Psycholinguistics*, 8:19–32.

Liz Temple. 2000. Second language learner speech production. *Studia Linguistica*, pages 288–297.

Joel R. Tetreault and Martin Chodorow. 2008. The ups and downs of preposition error detection in esl writing. In *In Proceedings of COLING*.

Silke Witt and Steve Young. 1997. Performance measures for phone-level pronunciation teaching in CALL. In *Proceedings of the Workshop on Speech Technology in Language Learning*, pages 99–102.

Silke Witt. 1999. *Use of the speech recognition in computer-assisted language learning*. Unpublished dissertation, Cambridge University Engineering department, Cambridge, U.K.

Klaus Zechner, Derrick Higgins, Xiaoming Xi, and David M. Williamson. 2009. Automatic scoring of non-native spontaneous speech in tests of spoken english. *Speech Communication*, 51:883–895, October.

A Unified Approach to Transliteration-based Text Input with Online Spelling Correction

Hisami Suzuki **Jianfeng Gao**
Microsoft Research
One Microsoft Way, Redmond WA 98052 USA
{hisamis,jfgao}@microsoft.com

Abstract

This paper presents an integrated, end-to-end approach to online spelling correction for text input. Online spelling correction refers to the spelling correction as you type, as opposed to post-editing. The online scenario is particularly important for languages that routinely use transliteration-based text input methods, such as Chinese and Japanese, because the desired target characters cannot be input at all unless they are in the list of candidates provided by an input method, and spelling errors prevent them from appearing in the list. For example, a user might type *suesheng* by mistake to mean *xuesheng* 学生 'student' in Chinese; existing input methods fail to convert this misspelled input to the desired target Chinese characters. In this paper, we propose a unified approach to the problem of spelling correction and transliteration-based character conversion using an approach inspired by the phrase-based statistical machine translation framework. At the phrase (substring) level, *k* most probable pinyin (Romanized Chinese) corrections are generated using a monotone decoder; at the sentence level, input pinyin strings are directly transliterated into target Chinese characters by a decoder using a log-linear model that refer to the features of both levels. A new method of automatically deriving parallel training data from user keystroke logs is also presented. Experiments on Chinese pinyin conversion show that our integrated method reduces the character error rate by 20% (from 8.9% to 7.12%) over the previous state-of-the art based on a noisy channel model.

1 Introduction

This paper addresses the problem of online spelling correction, which tries to correct users' misspellings as they type, rather than post-editing them after they have already been input. This online scenario is particularly important for languages that routinely use transliteration-based text input methods, including Chinese and Japanese: in these languages, characters (called *hanzi* in Chinese and *kanji/kana* in Japanese) are typically input by typing how they are pronounced in Roman alphabet (called *pinyin* in Chinese, *romaji* in Japanese), and selecting a conversion candidate among those that are offered by an input method system, often referred to as IMEs or input method editors. One big challenge posed by spelling mistakes is that they prevent the desired candidates from appearing as conversion candidates, as in Figure 1: *suesheng* is likely to be a spelling error of *xuesheng* 学生 'student', but it is not included as one of the candidates.

Figure 1: Spelling mistake prevents the desired output (学生) from appearing in the list of candidates

This severely limits the utility of an IME, as spelling errors are extremely common. Speakers of a non-standard dialect and non-native speakers have a particularly hard time, because they may not know the standard pronunciation of the word to begin with, preventing them from inputting the word altogether. Error-tolerant word completion and next word prediction are also highly desirable features for text input on software (onscreen) keyboards for any language, making the current work relevant beyond Chinese and Japanese.

In this paper, we propose a novel, unified system of text input with spelling correction, using

Chinese pinyin-to-hanzi conversion as an example. We first formulate the task of pinyin spelling correction as a substring-based monotone translation problem, inspired by phrase-based statistical machine translation (SMT) systems (Koehn et al., 2003; Och and Ney, 2004): we consider the pinyin input (potentially with errors) as the source language and the error-corrected pinyin as the target, and build a log-linear model for spelling correction. In doing so, we also propose a novel, unsupervised method of collecting parallel training data from user input logs. We then build an integrated end-to-end text input system that directly converts a potentially erroneous input pinyin sequence into a desired hanzi sequence, also formulated as a monotone phrase-based SMT problem, in which the feature functions of the substring-based error correction component are integrated and jointly optimized with the sentence-level feature functions for character conversion

Our method generalizes and improves over the previous state-of-the-art methods for the task of error correction and text input in several crucial respects. First, our error correction model is designed and implemented as a substring-based, fully trainable system based on a log-linear model, which has been shown effective for related tasks such as transliteration and letter-to-phone conversion, but has not been attempted for the task of spelling correction. Second, we build an end-to-end pinyin-to-hanzi conversion system by combining all the feature functions used in the error correction and character conversion components in an SMT-style log-linear model, where the feature weights are trained discriminatively for the end-to-end task. This integration method generalizes the previous approach based on a noisy channel model (Chen and Lee, 2000; Zheng et al. 2011b), in which only the error model and the conversion model probabilities are used and combined with equal weights. Finally, like other statistical systems, the amount and quality of training data control the quality of the outcome; we thus propose a new, language-independent method of deriving parallel data for spelling correction from user keystroke logs.

We performed experiments on various methods of integrating the error correction and character conversion sub-components. Our best system, a fully integrated SMT-based approach, reduces the character error rate by 35% on test data that is completely independent of the creation of error correction and character conversion models.

In what follows, we first give the background of this research in Section 2. We then describe our approach to the spelling correction task (Section 3) and the end-to-end conversion task (Section 4). We summarize our contribution and conclude with remarks for future directions in Section 5.

2 Related Work

The current work builds on many previous works on the task of monotone substring-based transduction, including spelling correction, letter-to-phone conversion and transliteration between different scripts. In particular, our substring-based approach to spelling correction is motivated by the success on transliteration (e.g., Sherif and Kondrak, 2007; Cherry and Suzuki, 2009) and letter-to-phoneme conversion (e.g., Jiampojamarn et al., 2007; Rama et al., 2009). One big challenge of the spelling correction research is the general lack of naturally occurring paired data of contextual spelling errors and their correction. Previous work has therefore either focused on the task of correcting out-of-vocabulary words out of context (e.g., Brill and Moore, 2000; Toutanova and Moore, 2002), or has resorted to innovative methods of data collection. For example, Banko and Brill (2001) generate data artificially by substituting words from a confusion word set in text for building a contextual speller; Whitelaw et al. (2009) use word frequency and edit distance information to harvest error pairs from a web corpus in an unsupervised manner; Bertoldi et al. (2010) intentionally corrupt clean text by adding noise to the data. Another approach to spelling error data collection uses web search query logs, available in large quantity (albeit to limited institutions), and limit its focus on the task of correcting misspelled queries (e.g., Cucerzan and Brill, 2004; Gao et al., 2010; Sun et al., 2010; Duan and Hsu, 2011). The problem of data collection is particularly difficult for pinyin error correction, as pinyin is not a final form of text in Chinese, so it is not recorded in final text. Zheng et al. (2011a) study a log of pinyin input method and use the backspace key to learn the user mistyping behavior, but they do so only for the purpose of data analysis, and do not build a statistical model from this data.

Text input methods have been commercially available for decades for inputting Chinese and Japanese, but have also recently become available for other non-Roman script languages including Arabic and the languages of India.[1] Early research work on text input methods includes e.g., Mori et al. (1998), Chen and Lee (2000) and Gao et al. (2002), all of which approach the problem using a noisy channel model. Discriminative approaches have also been proposed, e.g., Suzuki and Gao (2005); Tokunaga et al. (2011). There is only a very limited amount of work that deals with spelling correction in the context of text input: Zheng et al. (2011b) represents a recent work based on a noisy channel model, which defines our baseline. Their work is strictly word-based and only handles the correction of out-of-vocabulary pinyin words into in-vocabulary pinyin words, while our substring-based model is not limited by these constraints.

The current work also has an affinity to the task of speech translation in that the parallel data between the input (speech signal) and the output (text in foreign language) is not directly available, but is mediated by a corrected (transcribed) form of input. Zhang et al. (2011) is thus relevant to our study, though their approach differs from ours in that we build an integrated system that include the feature functions of both error correction and character conversion sub-systems.

3 Substring-based Spelling Correction using a Log-linear Model

In this section, we describe our approach to pinyin error correction within a log-linear framework. Though our current target is pinyin error correction, the method described in this section is applicable to any language of interest.

The spelling correction problem has been standardly formulated within the framework of noisy channel model (e.g., Kernighan et al., 1990). Let A be the input phonetic string in pinyin. The task of spelling correction is to search for the best correction candidate in pinyin C^* among all possible corrections for each potentially misspelled pinyin A:

$$C^* = \underset{C \in \mathrm{GEN}(A)}{\operatorname{argmax}} P(C|A) \quad \text{... (1)}$$

Applying Bayes' Rule and dropping the constant denominator, we have

$$C^* = \underset{C \in \mathrm{GEN}(A)}{\operatorname{argmax}} P(A|C)P(C) \quad \text{... (2)}$$

where the error model $P(A|C)$ models the translation probability from C to A, and the language model $P(C)$ models how likely the output C is a correctly spelled pinyin sequence. Many variations on the error model have been proposed, including substring-based (Brill and Moore, 2000) and pronunciation-based (Toutanova and Moore, 2002) models.

Our model is inspired by the SMT framework, in which the error correction probability $P(C|A)$ of Equation (1) is directly modeled using a log-linear model of the following form:

$$P(C|A) = \frac{1}{Z(A)} exp \sum_i \lambda_i h_i(A, C) \quad \text{... (3)}$$

where $Z(A)$ is the normalization factor, h_i is a feature function and λ_i is the feature weight. Similarly to phrase-based SMT, many feature functions are derived from the translation and language models, where the translation model-derived features are trained using a parallel corpus of original pinyin and correction pairs. The argmax of Equation (1) defines the search operation: we use a left-to-right beam search decoder to seek for each input pinyin the best correction according to Equation (3).

We first describe how the paired data for deriving the error model probabilities is generated from user logs in Section 3.1, and then how the models are trained and the model weights are learned in Section 3.2. We discuss the results of pinyin error correction as an independent task in Section 3.3.

3.1 Generating error correction pairs from keystroke logs

Unlike English text, which includes instances of misspelled words explicitly, pinyin spelling errors are not found in a corpus, because pinyin is used as a means of inputting text, and is not part of the

[1] A few examples include Google Transliterate (http://www.google.com/transliterate/) and Microsoft Maren (http://www.microsoft.com/middleeast/egypt/cmic/maren/) / ILIT (http://specials.msn.co.in/ilit/Hindi.aspx). Quillpad (http://quillpad.in/) is also popularly used in India.

final written form of the language. Therefore, pinyin error correction pairs must be created intentionally. We chose the method of implementing a version of an input method which records the keystrokes of users while they are asked to type a particular Chinese text in hanzi; in doing so, we captured each keystroke issued by the user behind the scene. Such keystroke logs include the use of the backspace key, from which we compute the pinyin strings after the usage of the backspace keys as well as the putative pinyin string had the user not corrected it using the backspace key.[2] Table 1 shows a few examples of the entries in the keystroke log, along with the computed pinyin strings before and after correction. Each entry (or phrase) in the log represents the unit that corresponds to the sequence the user input at once, at the end of which the user committed to a conversion candidate, which typically consists of one or more words. While the post-correction string can be straightforwardly derived by deleting the same number of characters preceding the backspaces, the computation of the pre-correction string is trickier and ambiguous, because the backspace key is used for the purpose of both deletion and substitution (delete and replace) operations. In Table 1, a backspace usage is indicated by _ in the original keystroke sequence that is logged. In the second example, a deletion interpretation will generate `zhonguo` as a pre-correction string, while substitution interpretation will generate `zhonguoo`. In order to recover the desired pre-correcting string, we compared the prefix of the backspace usage (`zhonguo`) with the substrings after error correction (`zhong`, `zhongg`, `zhonggu...`). We considered that the prefix was spell-corrected into the substring which is the longest and with the smallest edit distance: in this case, `zhonguo` is considered an error for `zhongguo`, therefore recovering the pre-correction string of the whole sequence as `zhonguo`. Note that this method of error data extraction is general and is language-independent. Since paired error correction data do not exist naturally and is expensive to collect for any language, we believe that the proposed method is useful beyond the case of Chinese text input and applicable to the data collection of the spelling correction task in general. In a related work (Baba and Suzuki, 2012), we collected such keystroke data using Amazon's Mechanical Turk for English and Japanese, and released the error-correction pairs for research purposes.[3]

keystroke	pre-correction	post-correction
n a n s _ r e n	nansen	nanren
z h o n g u o _ _ g u o	zhonguo (*zhonguoo)	zhongguo

Table 1: Computation of pre- and post-correction strings from keystroke log

The extracted pairs are still quite noisy, because one error correction behavior might not completely eliminate the errors in typing a word. For example, in trying to type *women* 我们 'we', a user might first type *wmen*, hit the backspaces key four times, retype *womeen*, and commit to a conversion candidate by mistake. We extract the pair (*wmen*, *womeen*) from this log incorrectly, which is one of the causes of the noise in the data. Despite these remaining errors, we use the data without further cleaning, as we expect our approach to be robust against a certain amount of noise.

Keystroke data was collected for three text domains (chat, blog and online forum) from 60 users, resulting in 86,783 pairs after removing duplicates. The data includes the pairs with the same source and target, with about 41% representing the case of correction. We used 5,000 pairs for testing, 1,000 pairs for tuning the log-linear model weights (see the next subsection), and the remaining portion for training the error correction component.

3.2 Training the log-linear model

The translation model captures substring-based spelling error patterns and their transformation probabilities. The model is learned from large amounts of pinyin-correction pairs mined from user keystroke logs discussed above. Take the

[2] Zheng et al. (2011a) also uses the backspace key in the IME log to generate error-correction pairs, but they focus on the usage of a backspace after the desired hanzi characters have been input, i.e., the backspace key is used to delete one or more hanzi characters. In contrast, our method focuses on the use of backspace to delete one or more pinyin characters before conversion. This simulates the scenario of online error correction more truthfully, and can collect paired data in large quantity faster.

[3] Available at http://research.microsoft.com/en-us/downloads/4eb8d4a0-9c4e-4891-8846-7437d9dbd869/default.aspx.

following pinyin-correction pair as an example, where the input pinyin and its correction are aligned at the character level: given a pair (A,C), we align the letters in A with those in C so as to minimize the edit distance between A and C based on single character insertions, deletions and substitutions.

From this pair, we learn a set of error patterns that are consistent with the character alignment,[4] each of which is a pair of substrings indicating how the spelling is transformed from one to another. Some examples of extracted phrases are (`wanmian`, `waimian`) and (`andshi`, `andeshi`). In our implementation, we extract all patterns with a substring length of up to 9 characters. We then learn the translation probabilities for each pair using maximum likelihood estimation (MLE). Let (a,c) denote a pair. For each pair, we learn the translation probabilities $P(c|a)$ and $P(a|c)$, estimated using MLE, as well as lexical weights in two directions following Koehn et al. (2003). Our error correction model is completely substring-based and does not use a word-based lexicon, which gives us the flexibility of generating unseen correction targets as well as supporting pinyin input consisting of multiple words at a time. For the language model, we use a character 9-gram model to capture the knowledge of correctly spelled pinyin words and phrases. We trained the language model using the target portion of the parallel data described in Section 3.1, though it is possible to train it with an arbitrary text in pinyin when such data is available.

In addition to the feature functions derived from the error and language models, we also use word and phrase penalties as feature functions, which are commonly used in SMT. These features also make sense in the current context, as using fewer phrase means encouraging longer ones with more context, and the target character length can capture tendencies to delete or insert words in errors. Overall, the log-linear model uses 7 feature functions: 4 derived from the translation models, word and phrase penalties, and the language model. The model weights were trained using the minimum error rate training algorithm (MERT, Och, 2003). We tried MERT with two objective functions: one that uses the 4-gram BLEU score as straightforwardly adapted from SMT, and the other that minimizes the character error rate (CER). CER is based on the edit distance between the reference and system output, which is used for evaluating the IME accuracy (Section 4.3). It is more directly related with the word/phrase-level accuracy, which we used to evaluate the error correction module in isolation, than the BLEU metric. As we will show below, however, using different objective functions turned out to have only a minimal impact on the spelling correction accuracy.

3.3 Experiments and results

The performance of pinyin error correction was evaluated on two data sets: (1) *log-test*: the test set of the data in Section 3.1, which is derived in the same way as the training data but is noisy, consisting of 5,000 phrases of which 2,020 are misspelled; (2) *CHIME*: the gold standard from the CHIME data set made available by Zheng et al. (2011b),[5] which is also used in the end-to-end evaluation in Section 4. This data set consists of 2,000 sentence pairs of pinyin input with errors and the target hanzi characters, constructed by collecting actual user typing logs of the Lancaster corpus (McEnery and Xiao, 2004), which includes text from newspaper, fiction, and essays.[6] The CHIME data set does not include the corrected pinyin string; we therefore generated this by running a text-to-pinyin utility,[7] and created the pairs before and after error correction for evaluating our pinyin spelling correction module. The set contains 11,968 words of which 908 are misspelled.

The results of the evaluation are given in Table 2. They are for phrase/word-level accuracy, as the log-derived data set is for each phrase (a user-

[4] Consistency here implies two things. First, there must be at least one aligned character pair in the aligned phrase. Second, there must not be any alignments from characters inside the aligned phrase to characters outside the phrase. That is, we do not extract a phrase pair if there is an alignment from within the phrase pair to outside the phrase pair.

[5] Available from http://chime.ics.uci.edu/

[6] Details on the Lancaster corpus are found at http://www.lancs.ac.uk/fass/projects/corpus/LCMC/.

[7] We used an in-house tool, but many tools are available online. Unlike pinyin-to-hanzi, hanzi-to-pinyin is relatively straightforward as most characters have a unique pronunciation.

	1-best	3-best	20-best
log-test: No correction	59.6		
log-test: Noisy Channel	49.5	67.86	84.8
log-test: Proposed (BLEU)	62.46	74.58	86.66
log-test: Proposed (CER)	62.82	75.06	86.8
CHIME: No correction	92.41		
CHIME: Noisy Channel	91.29	95.75	98.82
CHIME: Proposed (BLEU)	93.51	97.38	99.06
CHIME: Proposed (CER)	93.49	97.29	99.08

Table 2: Pinyin error correction accuracy (in %)

defined unit of conversion, consisting of one to a few words), while the CHIME data set is word-segmented. The baseline accuracy is the accuracy of not correcting any error, which is very strong in this task: 59.6% and 92.41% for the two data sets, respectively. The accuracy on the log-test data is generally much lower than the CHIME data, presumably because the latter is cleaner, contains less errors to begin with, and the unit of evaluation is smaller (word) than the log-test (phrase). Though CHIME is an out-of-domain data set, the proposed model works very well on this set, achieving more than 93% accuracy with the best output, significantly (at $p<0.001$ using McNemar's test) improving on the strong baseline of not correcting any error. The proposed log-linear approach is also compared against the noisy channel model baseline, which is simulated by only using one error model-derived feature function $P(A|C)$ and the language model, weighted equally, using the same beam search decoder. Somewhat surprisingly, the noisy channel model results fall below the baseline in both data sets, while the log-linear model improves over the baseline, especially on the 1-best accuracy: all differences between the noisy channel model and the log-linear model outputs are significant. Finally, regarding the effect of using the CER as the objective function of MERT, we only observe minimal impact: none of the differences in accuracy between the BLEU and CER objectives is statistically significant on either data set. For a monotone decoding task such as spelling correction, using either objective function therefore seems to suffice, even though BLEU is more indirect and redundant in capturing the phrase-level accuracy.

4 A Unified Model of Character Conversion with Spelling Correction

In this section we describe our unified model of spelling correction and transliteration-based character conversion. Analogous to the spelling correction task, the character conversion problem can also be considered as a substring-based translation problem. The novelty of our approach lies in the fact that we take advantage of the parallelism between these tasks, and build an integrated model that performs spelling correction and character conversion at the same time, within the log-linear framework. This allows us to optimize the feature weights directly for the end goal, from which from we can expect a better overall conversion accuracy.

4.1 Noisy channel model approach to incorporating error correction in character conversion

The task of pinyin-to-hanzi conversion consists of converting the input phonetic strings provided by the user into the appropriate word string using ideographic characters. This has been formulated within the noisy channel model (Chen and Lee, 2000), in exactly the same manner as the spelling correction, as describe in Equations (1) and (2) in Section 3. Given the pinyin input A, the task is to find the best output hanzi sequence W^*:

$$W^* = \underset{W \in \mathrm{GEN}(A)}{\operatorname{argmax}} P(W|A) = \underset{W \in \mathrm{GEN}(A)}{\operatorname{argmax}} \mathrm{P}(W)P(A|W) \quad \dots(4)$$

In traditional conversion systems which do not consider spelling errors, $P(A|W)$ is usually set to 1 if the word is found in a dictionary of word-pronunciation pairs, which also defines **GEN**(A). Therefore, the ranking of the candidates relies exclusively on the language model probability $P(W)$.

An extension of this formulation to handle spelling errors can be achieved by incorporating an actual error model $P(A|W)$. Assuming a conditional independence of A and W given the error-corrected pinyin sequence C, Equation (4) can be re-written as:

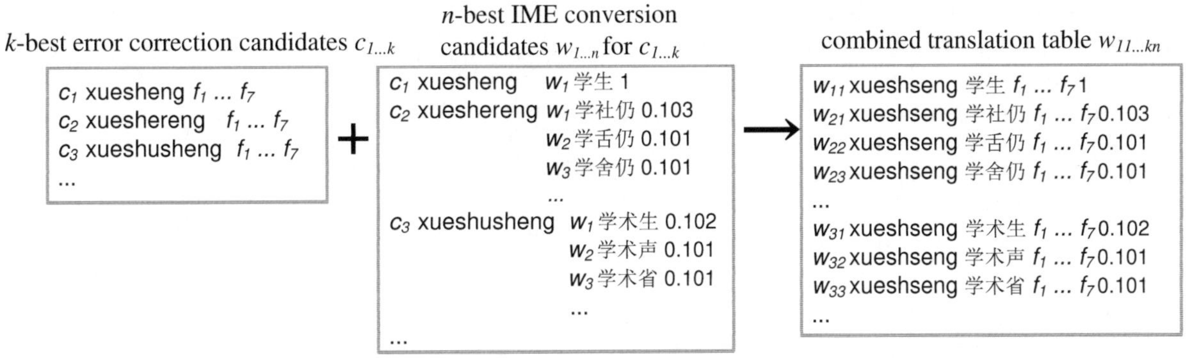

Figure 2: Generation of integrated translation table for the pinyin input a = *xueshseng*

$$
\begin{aligned}
W^* &= \underset{W}{\operatorname{argmax}} P(W|A) \\
&= \underset{W}{\operatorname{argmax}} \sum_C P(W|C)P(C|A) \\
&= \underset{W}{\operatorname{argmax}} \sum_C P(C|W)P(W)P(C|A)
\end{aligned}
$$

Here, $P(C|W)$ corresponds to the channel model of traditional input methods, $P(W)$ the language model, and $P(C|A)$ the pinyin error correction model. There have been attempts to use this formulation in text input: for example, Chen and Lee (2000) trained a syllable-based model for $P(C|A)$ with user keystroke data,[8] and Zheng et al. (2011b) used a model based on a weighted character edit distance whose weights are manually assigned. This noisy channel integration of error correction and character conversion is the state-of-the-art in the task of error-correcting text input, and will serve as our baseline.

4.2 Log-linear model for error-correcting character conversion

Similar to the formulation of our error correction model in Section 3, we adopt the log-linear model for modeling the character conversion probability in (4):

$$P(W|A) = \frac{1}{Z(A)} exp \sum_i \lambda_i h_i(A, W)$$

where $A = a_1,\dots,a_n$ is a sequence of phrases in pinyin, and $W = w_1,\dots,w_n$ is the corresponding sequence in hanzi. A unique challenge of the current task is that the parallel data for A and W do not exist directly. Therefore, we generated the translation phrase table offline by merging the substring-based phrase table generated for the pinyin error correction task in Section 3 with the results of character conversion. This process is described in detail in Figure 2: k-best candidates for each input pinyin phrase a are generated by the error model in Section 3, which are then submitted offline to an IME system to obtain n-best conversion candidates with probabilities. For the IME system, we used an in-house conversion system, which only uses a word trigram language model for ranking. In the resulting translation table, defined for each (a, w) pair, the feature functions and their values are inherited from the pinyin error correction translation table mediated by the correction candidates $c_{1\dots k}$ for a, plus the function that defines the IME conversion probability for (c_j, w). Note that in this final phrase table, the correction candidates for a are latent, only affecting the values of the feature functions.[9] The final end-to-end system uses the following 11 features:

- 7 error correction model features at the phrase level
- IME conversion probability at the phrase level
- language model probability at the sentence level
- word/phrase penalty features at the sentence level

The language model at the sentence level is trained on a large monolingual corpus of Chinese in hanzi, consisting of about 13 million sentences (176 million words). The IME conversion probability

[8] No detail of this data is available in Chen and Lee (2000).

[9] The final phrase table needs to be unique for each phrase pair (a, w), though the process described here results in multiple entries with the same pair having different feature values, because the generation of (a, w) is mediated by multiple correction candidates $c_{1\dots k}$. These entries need to be added up to remove duplicates; we used a heuristic approximation of taking the pair where a equals c_j (i.e., no spelling correction) when multiple entries are found.

also uses a word trigram model, but it is trained on a different data set which we did not have access to; we therefore used both of these models. The values for *k* and *n* can be determined empirically; we used 20 for both of them.[10] This generates maximally 400 conversion candidates for each input pinyin.

The feature weights of the log-linear model are tuned using MERT. As running MERT on a CER-based target criterion on the similar, monotone translation task of spelling correction did not lead to a significant improvement (Section 3.3), we simply report the results of using the 4-gram BLEU as the training criterion in this task.

4.3 Experiments and results

For the evaluation of the end-to-end conversion task, we used the CHIME corpus mentioned above. In order to use the word trigram language model that is built in-house, we re-segmented the CHIME corpus using our word-breaker, resulting in 12,102 words in 2,000 sentences. We then divided the sentences in the corpus randomly into two halves, and performed a two-fold cross validation evaluation. The development portion of the data is used to tune the weights of the feature functions in MERT-style training. We measured our results using character error rate (CER), which is based on the longest common subsequence match in characters between the reference and the best system output. This is a standard metric used in evaluating IME systems (e.g., Mori et al., 1998; Gao et al., 2002). Let N_{REF} be the number of characters in a reference sentence, N_{SYS} be the character length of a system output, and N_{LCS} be the length of the longest common subsequence between them. Then the character-level recall is defined as N_{LCS}/N_{REF}, and the precision as N_{LCS}/N_{SYS}. The CER based on recall and on precision are then defined as 1 – recall and 1 – precision, respectively. We report the harmonic mean of these values, similarly to the widely used F1-measure.

As our goal is to show the effectiveness of the unified approach, we used simpler methods of integrating pinyin error correction with character conversion to create baselines. The simplest baseline is a pre-processing approach: we use the pinyin error correction model to convert *A* into a single best candidate *C*, and run an IME system on *C*. Another more realistic baseline is the noisy channel integration discussed in Section 4.1. We approximated this integration method by re-ranking all the candidates generated by the proposed log-linear model with only the channel and language model probabilities, equally weighted.

	CER on 1-best	CER on 5-best
Baseline: No correction	10.91	7.76
Baseline: Pre-processing	9.93	6.75
Baseline: Zheng et al. (2011b)	8.90	
Baseline: Noisy channel	7.92	3.93
Proposed: SMT model	7.12	3.63
Oracle	4.08	1.51

Table 3: CER results for the conversion task (%)

The results are shown Table 3. 5-best results as well as the 1-best results are shown, because in an IME application, providing the correct candidate in the candidate list is particularly important even if it is not the best candidate. Let us first discuss the 1-best results. The CER of this test corpus using the in-house IME system without correcting any errors is 10.91. The oracle CER, which is the result of applying the IME on the gold standard pinyin input derived from the reference text using a hanzi-to-pinyin converter (as mentioned in Section 3.3), is 4.08, which is the upper-bound imposed by the IME conversion accuracy. The simple pipeline approach of concatenating the pinyin correction component with the character conversion component improves the CER by 1% to 9.93. Assuming that there are on average 20 words in a sentence, and each word consists of 2 characters, 1% CER reduction means one improvement every 2.5 sentences. Noisy channel integration improves over this quite substantially, achieving a CER of 7.92, demonstrating the power of the word language model in character conversion. Incidentally, the CER of the output by Zheng et al. (2011b)'s model is 8.90.[11] Their results are not as good as our noisy channel integration, as their system uses a manually defined error model and a word bigram language model. With the use of additional feature functions weighted discriminatively for the final conversion task, the

[10] From Table 2, we observe that the accuracy of the 20-best output of the spelling correction component is over 99%. An offline run with the IME system on an independent data set also showed that the accuracy of the 20-best IME output is over 99%.

[11] Available at http://chime.ics.uci.edu/.

Overall errors (words)	1,074 / 12,102
Conversion	646 (60.14%)
Over-corrections	155 (14.43%)
Under-correction	161 (14.99%)
Wrong correction	112 (10.42%)

Table 4: Classification of errors

proposed method outperforms all these baselines to reduce the CER to 7.12, a 35% relative error rate reduction compared with the no correction baseline, a 20% reduction against Zheng et al (2011b) and a 10% reduction from our noisy channel baseline. The 5-best results follow the same trend of steady improvement as we use a more integrated system.

In order to understand the characteristics of the errors and remaining issues, we ran an error analysis on the 1-best results of the proposed system. For each word in the test data (all 2,000 sentences) for which the system output had an error, we classified the reasons of failure into one of the four categories: (1) **character conversion error**: correct pinyin was input to the IME but the conversion failed; (2) **over-correction of pinyin input**: the system corrected the pinyin input when it should not have; (3) **under-correction of pinyin input**: the system did not correct an error in the input pinyin when it should have; (4) **wrong correction**: input pinyin string had a spelling error but it was corrected incorrectly.

Table 4 shows the results of the error analysis. We find that somewhat contrary to our expectation, over-correction of the spelling mistakes was not a conspicuous problem, even though the pinyin correction rate of the training data is much higher than that of the test data. We therefore conclude that the error correction model adapts very well to the characteristics of the test data in our integrated SMT-based approach, which trains the unified feature weights to optimize the end goal.

5 Conclusion and Future Work

In this paper we have presented a unified approach to error-tolerant text input, inspired by the phrase-based SMT framework, and demonstrated its effectiveness over the traditional method based on the noisy channel model. We have also presented a new method of automatically collecting parallel data for spelling correction from user keystroke logs, and showed that the log-linear model works well on the task of spelling correction in isolation as well.

In this study, we isolated the problem of spelling errors and studied the effectiveness of error correction over a basic IME system that does not include advanced features such as abbreviated input (e.g., typing only "py" for 朋友 *pengyou* 'friend' or 拼音 *pinyin* in Chinese) and auto-completion (e.g., typing only "ari" for ありがとう *arigatou* 'thank you' in Japanese). Integrating data-driven error correction feature with these advanced features for the benefit of users is the challenge we face in the next step.

Acknowledgements

We are indebted to many colleagues at Microsoft and MSR for their help in conducting this research, particularly to Xi Chen, Pallavi Choudhury, Chris Quirk, Mei-Yuh Hwang and Kristina Toutanova. We are also grateful for the comments we received from the reviewers of this paper.

References

Baba, Y. and H. Suzuki. 2012. How are spelling errors generated and corrected? A study of corrected and uncorrected spelling errors using keystroke logs. In *Proceedings of ACL*.

Banko, M. and E. Brill. 2001. Scaling to very very large corpora for natural language disambiguation. In *Proceedings of ACL*.

Bertoldi, N., M. Cettolo, and M. Federico. 2010. Statistical machine translation of texts with misspelled words. In *Proceedings of HLT-NAACL*.

Brill, E., and R. C. Moore. 2000. An improved error model for noisy channel spelling correction. In *Proceedings of ACL*.

Chen, Z., and K. F. Lee. 2000. A new statistical approach to Chinese Pinyin input. In *Proceedings of ACL*.

Cherry, C., and H. Suzuki. 2009. Discriminative substring decoding for transliteration. In *Proceedings of EMNLP*.

Cucerzan, S., and E. Brill. 2004. Spelling correction as an iterative process that exploits the collective knowledge of web users. In *Proceedings of EMNLP*.

Duan, H., and P. Hsu. 2011. Online spelling correction for query completion. In *Proceedings of WWW*.

Gao, J., J. Goodman, M. Li and K.-F. Lee. 2002. Toward a unified approach to statistical language modeling for Chinese. In *ACM Transactions on*

Asian Language Information Processing, Vol. 1, No. 1, pp 3-33.

Gao, J., X. Li, D. Micol, C. Quirk and X. Sun. 2010. A large scale ranker-based system for search query spelling correction. In *Proceedings of COLING.*

Jiampojamarn, S., G. Kondrak and T. Sherif, 2007. Applying many-to-many alignments and hidden markov models to letter-to-phoneme conversion. In *Proceedings of HLT/NAACL.*

Kernighan, M., K. Church, and W. Gale. 1990. A spelling correction program based on a noisy channel model. In *Proceedings of COLING.*

Koehn, P., F. Och and D. Marcu. 2003. Statistical phrase-based translation. In *Proceedings of HLT-NAACL.*

McEnery, A. and Xiao, Z. 2004. The Lancaster Corpus of Mandarin Chinese: A Corpus for Monolingual and Contrastive Language Study. In *Proceedings of LREC.*

Mori, S., M. Tsuchiya, O. Yamaji and M. Nagao. 1998. *Kana-kanji conversion by a stochastic model. In Proceedings of Information Processing Society of Japan*, SIG-NL-125-10 (in Japanese).

Och, F. J. 2003. Minimum error rate training in statistical machine translation. In *Proceedings of ACL.*

Och, F., and Ney, H. 2004. The alignment template approach to statistical machine translation. *Computational Linguistics*, 30(4): 417-449.

Rama, T., A. K. Singh and S. Kolachina. 2009. Modeling letter-to-phoneme conversion as a phrase based statistical machine translation problem with minimum error rate training. In *Proceedings of the NAACL HLT Student Research Workshop and Doctoral Consortium.*

Sherif, T. and G. Kondrak. 2007. Substring-based transliteration. In *Proceedings of ACL.*

Sun, X., J. Gao, D. Micol and C. Quirk. 2010. Learning phrase-based spelling error models from clickthrough data. In *Proceedings of ACL.*

Suzuki, H. and J. Gao. 2005. A comparative study on language model adaptation using new evaluation metrics. In *Proceedings of EMNLP.*

Toutanova, K., and R. C. Moore. 2002. Pronunciation modeling for improved spelling correction. In *Proceedings of ACL.*

Tokunaga, H., D. Okanohara and S. Mori. 2011. Discriminative method for Japanese kana-kanji input method. In *Proceedings of the Workshop on Advances in Text Input Methods* (WTIM 2011).

Whitelaw, C., B. Hutchinson, G. Y. Chung, and G. Ellis. 2009. Using the web for language independent spellchecking and autocorrection. In *Proceedings of ACL.*

Zhang, Y., L. Deng, X. He and A. Acero. 2011. A novel decision function and the associated decision-feedback learning for speech translation. In *Proceedings of ICASSP.*

Zheng, Y., L. Xie, Z. Liu, M. Sun. Y. Zhang and L. Ru. 2011a. Why press backspace? Understanding user input behaviors in Chinese pinyin input method. In *Proceedings of ACL.*

Zheng, Y., C. Li and M. Sun. 2011b. CHIME: An efficient error-tolerant Chinese pinyin input method. In *Proceedings of IJCAI.*

Excitatory or Inhibitory: A New Semantic Orientation Extracts Contradiction and Causality from the Web

Chikara Hashimoto* **Kentaro Torisawa**† **Stijn De Saeger**‡
Jong-Hoon Oh§ **Jun'ichi Kazama**¶
National Institute of Information and Communications Technology
Kyoto, 619-0289, JAPAN
{*ch, †torisawa, ‡stijn, §rovellia, ¶kazama}@nict.go.jp

Abstract

We propose a new semantic orientation, Excitation, and its automatic acquisition method. Excitation is a semantic property of predicates that classifies them into excitatory, inhibitory and neutral. We show that Excitation is useful for extracting contradiction pairs (e.g., *destroy cancer* $\perp$ *develop cancer*) and causality pairs (e.g., *increase in crime* $\Rightarrow$ *heighten anxiety*). Our experiments show that with automatically acquired Excitation knowledge we can extract one million contradiction pairs and 500,000 causality pairs with about 70% precision from a 600 million page Web corpus. Furthermore, by combining these extracted causality and contradiction pairs, we can generate one million plausible causality hypotheses that are not written in any single sentence in our corpus with reasonable precision.

1 Introduction

Recognizing semantic relations between events in texts is crucial for such NLP tasks as question answering (QA). For example, to answer the question *"What ruined the crops in Japan?"* a QA system must recognize that the sentence *"the Fukushima nuclear power plant caused radioactive pollution and contaminated the crops in Japan"* contains a causal relation and that *contaminate crops* entails *ruin crops* but contradicts *preserve crops*.

To facilitate the acquisition of causality, contradiction, paraphrase and entailment relations between events we propose a new semantic orientation, Excitation, that classifies unary predicates (templates, hereafter) into excitatory, inhibitory and neutral. An excitatory template entails that the main function or effect of the referent of its argument is activated or enhanced (e.g., *cause X*, *preserve X*), while an inhibitory template entails that it is deactivated or suppressed (e.g., *ruin X*, *contaminate X*, *prevent X*).

Excitation is useful for extracting contradiction; if two templates with similar distributional profiles have opposite Excitation polarities, they tend to be contradictions (e.g., *contaminate crops* and *preserve crops*). With extracted contradictions we can distinguish paraphrases from contradictions among distributionally similar phrases. Furthermore, contradiction in itself is important knowledge for Recognizing Textual Entailment (RTE) (Voorhees, 2008).

Excitation is also a powerful indicator of causality. In the physical world, the activation or deactivation of one thing often causes the activation or deactivation of another. Two excitatory or inhibitory templates that co-occur in some temporal or logical order in the same narrative often describe a causal chain of events, like *"the Fukushima nuclear power plant caused radioactive pollution and contaminated crops in Japan"*.

In this paper we propose both the concept of Excitation and an automatic method for its acquisition. Our method acquires Excitation templates based on certain natural, language independent constraints on narrative structures found in text. We also propose acquisition methods for contradiction and causality relations based on Excitation. Our methods extract one million contradiction pairs with over 70% precision, and 500,000 causality pairs with about 70% precision from a 600 million page Web corpus. Moreover, by combining these extracted causality pairs and contradiction pairs, we generated one million plausible causality hypotheses that were not written in any single sentence in our corpus with reasonable precision. For example, a causality hypothesis *prevent radioactive pollution* $\Rightarrow$ *preserve crops* can be generated from an extracted causality *cause radioactive pollution* $\Rightarrow$ *contaminate crops*.

We target the Japanese language in this paper.

2 What is Excitation?

Excitation classifies templates into excitatory, inhibitory, and neutral, as explained below.

excitatory templates entail that the function, effect, purpose or role of their argument's referent is activated or enhanced. (e.g., *cause X*, *buy X*, *produce X*, *import X*, *increase X*, *enable X*)

inhibitory templates entail that the function, effect, purpose or role of their argument's referent is deactivated or suppressed. (e.g., *prevent X*, *discard X*, *remedy X*, *decrease X*, *disable X*)

neutral templates are neither excitatory nor inhibitory. (e.g., *consider X*, *proportional to X*, *related to X*, *evaluate X*, *close to X*)

For example, when *fire* fills the *X* slot of *cause X*, it suggests that the effect of *fire* is activated. If *prevent X*'s slot is filled with *flu*, the effect of *flu* is suppressed. In this study, we aim to acquire excitatory and inhibitory templates that are useful for extracting contradiction and causality, though neutral templates are the most frequent in our data (See Section 5.1). Collectively we call excitatory and inhibitory templates *Excitation templates*, and excitatory and inhibitory two opposite *polarities*.

Excitation is independent of the good/bad semantic orientation. (Hatzivassiloglou and McKeown, 1997; Turney, 2002; Rao and Ravichandran, 2009). For example, *sophisticate X* and *complicate X* are both excitatory, but only the former has a positive connotation. Similarly, *remedy X* and *degrade X* are both inhibitory but only the latter is negative.

General Inquirer (Stone et al., 1966) deals with semantic factors some of which were proposed by Osgood et al. (1957). Their 'activity' factor involves binary opposition between 'active' and 'passive.' Notice that activity and Excitation are independent. In General Inquirer, both *accelerate X* and *abolish X* are active, but only the former is excitatory. Both *accept X* and *abate X* are passive, but only the latter is inhibitory. Pustejovsky (1995) proposed telic and agentive roles, which inspired our excitatory notion, but they have no corresponding notion of inhibitory. Andreevskaia and Bergler (2006) acquired the increase/decrease semantic orientation, which is a subclass of Excitation.

Excitation is inverted if a template's predicate is negated. For example, *preserve X* is excitatory, while *don't preserve X* is inhibitory. We acknowledge that this may seem somewhat counter-intuitive and will address this issue in future work.

3 Excitation Template Acquisition

This section presents our acquisition method of Excitation templates. We introduce constraints in the co-occurrence of templates in text that seem both robust and language independent in Section 3.1. Our method exploits these constraints for the acquisition of Excitation templates. First we construct a template network where nodes are templates and links represent that two connected templates have either SAME or OPPOSITE polarities. Given 46 manually prepared seed templates we calculate the *Excitation value* of each template, a value in range $[-1, 1]$ that is positive if the template is excitatory and negative if it is inhibitory. Technically, our method treats all templates as excitatory or inhibitory, and, upon completion, regards templates with small absolute Excitation values as neutral.

The whole method is a bootstrapping process. Each iteration expands the network and the Excitation value of each template is (re-)calculated.

3.1 Characteristics of Excitation Templates

Our method exploits natural discourse constraints on the possible combinations of (a) the polarity of co-occurring templates, (b) the nouns that fill their argument slots and (c) the connectives that link the templates in a given sentence. Table 1 shows the constraints and Figure 1 shows examples that will be explained shortly. Though our target is Japanese we believe these constraints are universal discourse principles, and as such not language dependent. Examples are given in English for ease of explanation.

We first identify two categories of connectives in our target sentences: AND/THUS-type (e.g., *and*, *thus* and *since*) and BUT-type (e.g., *but* and *though*). Both types suggest a sort of *consistency* or *inconsistency* between predicates. We manually classified 169 frequently used connectives into AND/THUS-

(1) He smoked cigarettes, AND/THUS he suffered lung cancer. (Both *smoke X* and *suffer X* are excitatory.)
(2) He quit cigarettes, AND/THUS was immune from lung cancer. (*quit X* and *immune from X* are inhibitory.)
(3) He smoked cigarettes, BUT didn't suffer lung cancer. (*smoke X* is excitatory, *not suffer X* is inhibitory.)
(4) He quit cigarettes, BUT he suffered lung cancer. (*quit X* is inhibitory, but *suffer X* is excitatory.)
(5) He underwent cancer treatment, AND/THUS he could cure the cancer. (*undergo X* is excitatory, *cure X* is inhibitory.)
(6) He underwent cancer treatment, BUT still had cancer. (Both *undergo X* and *have X* are excitatory.)
(7) **Unnatural:** He smoked cigarettes, BUT he suffered lung cancer. (*smoke X* and *suffer X* are excitatory.)

Figure 1: Examples of constraints: (*cigarettes, lung cancer*) is PNP and (*cancer treatment, cancer*) is NNP.

	PNPs	NNPs	others
AND/THUS	SAME	OPPOSITE	N/A
BUT	OPPOSITE	SAME	N/A

Table 1: Constraint matrix.

and BUT-type (See supplementary materials).

Next we extract sentences from the Web in which two templates co-occur and are joined by one of these connectives, and then classify the noun pairs filling the templates' argument slots into "positively-associated" and "negatively-associated" noun pairs (PNPs and NNPs). Mirroring our definition of Excitation, PNPs are noun pairs in which the referent of the first noun facilitates the emergence of the referent of the second noun. PNPs can range from causally related noun pairs like (*cigarettes, lung cancer*) to "material-product" relation pairs like (*semiconductor, electronic circuit*). We found that PNPs only fill the argument slots of (a) same Excitation polarity templates connected by AND/THUS-type connectives (examples 1 and 2 in Figure 1), or (b) opposite Excitation polarity templates connected by a BUT-type connectives (examples 3 and 4). Violating such constraints (example 7) seems unnatural. Similarly, NNPs are noun pairs in which the referent of one noun suppresses the emergence of the referent of the other noun. Examples include such "inverse causality" pairs as (*cancer treatment, cancer*). NNPs only fill the argument slots of (a) opposite Excitation polarity templates connected by AND/THUS-type connectives (example 5), or (b) same polarity templates connected by a BUT-type connective (example 6).

All these constraints are summarized in Table 1, which we will call the constraint matrix. According to the constraint matrix, we can know whether two templates' polarities are the same or opposite if we know whether a noun pair filling the two templates' slots is PNP or NNP. Conversely, we can know whether a noun pair is PNP or NNP if we know whether two templates whose slots are filled with the noun pair have the same or opposite polarities. We believe these constraints capture certain universal principles of discourse, since it is difficult in any language to produce natural sounding sentences that violate these constraints. We empirically confirm their validity for Japanese in Section 5.1.

3.2 Bootstrapping Approach to Excitation Template Acquisition

To calculate the Excitation values for the templates, we construct a template network where templates are connected by links indicating polarity agreement between two connected templates (either SAME or OPPOSITE polarity), as determined by the constraint matrix. Excitation values are determined by spreading activation applied to the network, given a small number of manually prepared seed templates.

However, we cannot construct the network unless we know whether each noun pair is PNP or NNP, due to the configuration of the constraint matrix, and currently we have no feasible method to classify all of them into PNPs and NNPs in advance. We therefore adopt a bootstrapping method (Figure 2) that starts from manually prepared excitatory and inhibitory seed templates (Step 1 in Figure 2). Our method begins by extracting noun pairs from the Web that co-occur with two seed templates connected by a AND/THUS- or BUT-type connective, and classifies these noun pairs into PNPs and NNPs based on the constraint matrix (Steps 2 and 3). Next, we automatically extract additional (non-seed) template pairs from the Web that co-occur with these PNPs and NNPs. Links (either SAME or OPPOSITE) between all template pairs are determined by the constraint matrix (Step 4), and we construct a template network from both seed and non-seed template pairs (Step 5).

Our method calculates the Excitation values for all the templates in the network by first assigning Excitation values $+1$ and -1 to the excitatory and inhibitory seed templates, and applies a spreading activation method proposed by Takamura et al. (2005) (Step 6) to the network. This method calcu-

1. Prepare initial seed templates with fixed excitation values (either $+1$ or -1).
2. Make seed template pairs that are combinations of two seed templates and a connective (either AND/THUS-type or BUT-type).
3. Extract noun pairs that co-occur with one of the seed template pairs from the Web. Classify the noun pairs into PNPs and NNPs based on the constraints matrix. Filter out those noun pairs that appear as both PNP and NNP on the Web or those whose occurrence frequency is less than or equal to F, which is set to 5.
4. Extract additional (non-seed) template pairs that are filled by one of the PNPs or NNPs from the Web. Determine the link type (SAME or OPPOSITE) for each template pair based on the constraint matrix. If a template pair appears on the Web as having both link types, we determine its link type by majority vote.
5. Construct the template network from all the template pairs. Remove from the network those templates whose number of linked templates is less than D, which is set to 5.
6. Apply Takamura et al.'s method to the network and fix the Excitation value of each template.
7. Extract the top- and bottom-ranked $N \times i$ templates from the result of Takamura et al.'s method. N is a constant, which is set to 30. i is the iteration number. They are used as additional seed templates for the next iteration. The top-ranked templates are given Excitation value $+1$ and the bottom-ranked templates are assigned -1. Go to Step 2.

Figure 2: Bootstrapping for template acquisition.

lates all templates' excitation values by solving the network constraints imposed by the SAME and OPPOSITE links, and the Excitation values of the seed templates (This method is detailed in Section 3.3). In each iteration i, our method selects the $N \times i$ top-ranked and bottom-ranked templates as additional seed templates for the next iteration (N is set to 30) (Step 7). Our method then constructs a new template network using the augmented seed templates and restarts the calculation process. Figure 2 summarizes our bootstrapping process.

Bootstrapping stops after M iterations, with M set to 7 based on our preliminary experiments.

To prepare the initial seed templates we constructed a *maximal* template network that could in theory be created by our bootstrapping method. This maximal network consists of any two templates that co-occur in a sentence with any connective, regardless of their arguments. We manually selected 36 excitatory and 10 inhibitory seed templates from among 114 templates with the most links in the network (See supplementary materials).

3.3 Determining Excitation in the Network

This section details Step 6 of our bootstrapping method, i.e., how Takamura et al.'s method calculates the Excitation value of each template. Their method is based on the spin model in physics, where each electron has a spin of either *up* or *down*. We chose this method due to the straightforward parallel between the spin model and our Excitation template model. Both models capture the spreading of activation (either spin direction or excitation polarity) between neighboring objects in a network. Determining the optimal algorithm for this task is beyond our current scope, but for the purpose of our experiments we found that Takamura et al.'s method gave satisfactory results.

The spin model defines an energy function on a spin network, and each electron's spin can be estimated by minimizing this function:

$$E(\mathbf{x}, W) = -1/2 \times \Sigma_{ij} w_{ij} x_i x_j$$

Here, $x_i, x_j \in \mathbf{x}$ are spins of electrons i and j, and matrix $W = \{w_{ij}\}$ assigns weights to links between electrons. We regard templates as electrons and Excitation polarities as their spins (*up* and *down* correspond to excitatory and inhibitory). We define the weight w_{ij} of the link between templates i and j as:

$$w_{ij} = \begin{cases} 1/\sqrt{d(i)d(j)} & \text{if SAME}(i,j) \\ -1/\sqrt{d(i)d(j)} & \text{if OPPOSITE}(i,j) \end{cases}$$

Here, $d(i)$ denotes the number of templates linked to i. SAME(i,j) (OPPOSITE(i,j)) indicates a SAME (OPPOSITE) link exists between i and j. We obtain excitation values by minimizing the above energy function. Note that after minimizing E, x_i and x_j tend to get the same polarity when w_{ij} is positive. When w_{ij} is negative, x_i and x_j tend to have opposite polarities. Initially seed templates are given values $+1$ or -1 depending on whether they are excitatory or inhibitory, and others are given 0.

We used SUPPIN (`http://www.lr.pi.titech.ac.jp/~takamura/pubs/SUPPIN-0.01.tar.gz`), an implementation of Takamura et al.'s method. Its parameter β is set to the default value (0.75).

4 Knowledge Acquisition by Excitation

This section shows how the concept of Excitation can be used for automatic knowledge acquisition.

4.1 Contradiction Extraction

Our first knowledge acquisition method extracts contradiction pairs like *destroy cancer* $\perp$ *develop cancer*, based on our assumption that they often consist of distributionally similar templates that have a sharp contrast in Excitation value. Concretely, we extract two phrases as a contradiction pair if (a) their templates have opposite Excitation polarities, (b) they share the same argument noun, and (c) the part-of-speech of their predicates is the same. Then the contradiction pairs are ranked by Ct:

$$Ct(p_1, p_2) = |s_1| \times |s_2| \times sim(t_1, t_2)$$

Here p_1 and p_2 are two phrases that satisfy conditions (a), (b) and (c) above, t_1 and t_2 are their respective templates, and $|s_1|$ and $|s_2|$ are the absolute values of t_1 and t_2's excitation values. $sim(t_1, t_2)$ is the distributional similarity proposed by Lin (1998).

Note that "contradiction" here includes what we call "quasi-contradiction." This consists of two phrases such that, if the tendencies of the events they describe get stronger, they eventually become contradictions. For example, the pair *emit smells* $\perp$ *reduce smells* is not logically contradictory since the two events can happen at the same time. However, they become almost contradictory when their tendencies get stronger (i.e., *emit smells more strongly* $\perp$ *thoroughly reduce smells*). We believe quasi-contradictions are useful for NLP tasks.

4.2 Causality Extraction

Our second knowledge acquisition method extracts causality pairs like *increase in crime* $\Rightarrow$ *heighten anxiety* that co-occur with AND/THUS-type connectives in a sentence. The assumption is that if two templates (t_1 and t_2) with a strong Excitation tendency are connected by an AND/THUS-type connective in a sentence, the event described by t_1 and its argument n_1 tends to be a cause of the event described by t_2 and its argument n_2. Here, Excitation strength is expressed by absolute Excitation values. The intuition is that, if the referent of n_1 is strongly activated or suppressed, it tends to have some causal effect on the referent of n_2 in the same sentence.

We focus on extracting causality pairs that co-occur with only "non-causal connectives" like *and*, which are AND/THUS-type connectives that do NOT explicitly signal causality, since causal connectives like *thus* can mask the effectiveness of Excitation. We prepared 139 non-causal connectives (See supplementary materials). We extract two templates such as *increase in X* and *heighten Y* co-occurring with only non-causal connectives, as well as the noun pair that fills the two templates' slots (e.g., (*crime*, *anxiety*)) to obtain causal phrase pairs. In Japanese, the temporal order between events is usually determined by precedence in the sentence. Cs ranks the obtained causality pairs:

$$Cs(p_1, p_2) = |s_1| \times |s_2|$$

Here p_1 and p_2 are the phrases of causality pair, and $|s_1|$ and $|s_2|$ are absolute Excitation values of p_1's and p_2's templates. As is common in the literature, this notion of causality should be interpreted probabilistically rather than logically, i.e., we interpret causality $A \Rightarrow B$ as "*if A happens, the probability of B increases*". This interpretation is often more useful for NLP tasks than a strict logical interpretation.

4.3 Causality Hypothesis Generation

Our third knowledge acquisition method generates plausible causality hypotheses that are not written in any single sentence using the previously extracted contradiction and causality pairs. We assume that if a causal relation (e.g., *increase in crime* $\Rightarrow$ *heighten anxiety*) is valid, its inverse (e.g., *decrease in crime* $\Rightarrow$ *diminish anxiety*) is often valid as well. From a *logical* definition of causation, taking the inverse of an implication obviously does not preserve validity. However, at least under our probabilistic interpretation, taking the inverse of a given causality pair using the extracted contradiction pairs proves to be a viable strategy for generating non-trivial causality hypotheses, as our experiments in Section 5.4 show.

For an extracted causality pair, we generate its inverse as a causality hypothesis by replacing both phrases in the original pair with their contradiction counterparts. For instance, a causality hypothesis *decrease in crime* $\Rightarrow$ *diminish anxiety* is generated from a causality *increase in crime* $\Rightarrow$ *heighten anxiety* by two contradictions, *decrease in crime* $\perp$ *increase in crime* and *diminish anxiety* $\perp$ *heighten anxiety*. Since we are interested in finding *new* causal hypotheses, we filter out hypotheses whose phrase pair co-occurs in a sentence in our corpus. Remaining causality hypotheses are ranked by Hp.

$$Hp(q_1, q_2) = Ct(p_1, q_1) \times Ct(p_2, q_2) \times Cs'(p_1, p_2)$$

Here, q_1 and q_2 are two phrases of a causality hypothesis. p_1 and p_2 are two phrases of a hypothesis's original causality. That is, $p_1 \perp q_1$ and $p_2 \perp q_2$ are contradiction pairs, and $Ct(p_1, q_1)$ and $Ct(p_2, q_2)$ are their contradiction scores. $Cs'(p_1, p_2)$ is the original causality's causality score. Cs' can be Cs

from Section 4.2, but based on preliminary experiments we found the following score works better:

$$Cs'(p_1, p_2) = |s_1| \times |s_2| \times npfreq(n_1, n_2)$$

$|s_1|$ and $|s_2|$ are absolute Excitation values of p_1's and p_2's templates, whose slots are filled with n_1 and n_2. $npfreq(n_1, n_2)$ is the co-occurrence frequency of (n_1, n_2) with polarity-identical template pairs (if (n_1, n_2) is PNP) or with polarity-opposite template pairs (if (n_1, n_2) is NNP). Thus, $npfreq$ indicates a sort of association strength between two nouns.

5 Experiments

This section shows that our template acquisition method acquired many Excitation templates. Moreover, using only the acquired templates we extracted one million contradiction pairs with more than 70% precision, and 500,000 causality pairs with about 70% precision. Further, using only these extracted contradiction and causality pairs we generated one million causality hypotheses with 57% precision.

In our experiments we removed evaluation samples containing the initial seed templates and examples used for annotation instruction from the evaluation data. Three annotators (not the authors) marked all evaluation samples, which were randomly shuffled so that they could not identify which sample was produced by which method. Information about the predicted labels or ranks was also removed from the evaluation data. Final judgments were made by majority vote between the annotators. They were non-experts without formal training in linguistics or semantics. See supplementary materials for our annotation manuals (translated into English).

We used 600 million Japanese Web pages (Akamine et al., 2010) parsed by KNP (Kawahara and Kurohashi, 2006) as a corpus. We restricted the argument positions of templates to *ha* (topic), *ga* (nominative), *wo* (accusative), *ni* (dative), and *de* (instrumental). We discarded templates appearing fewer than 20 times in compound sentences (regardless of connectives) in our corpus.

5.1 Excitation Template Acquisition

We show that our proposed method for template extraction (PROP$_{tmp}$) successfully acquired many Excitation templates from which we obtained a huge number of contradiction and causality pairs, and that Excitation is a reasonably comprehensible notion even for non-experts. We also show that PROP$_{tmp}$ outperformed two baselines by a large margin.

The template network constructed by PROP$_{tmp}$ contained 10,825 templates. Among these, the bootstrapping process classified 8,685 templates as excitatory and 2,140 as inhibitory. Note that these candidates in fact also contain neutral templates, as explained at the beginning of Section 3.

Baselines The baseline methods are ALLEXC and SIM. ALLEXC regards all templates that are randomly extracted from the Web as excitatory, since in our data excitatory templates outnumber inhibitory ones. Actually, in our data neutral templates represent the most frequent class, but since our objective is to acquire excitatory and inhibitory templates, a baseline marking all templates as neutral would make little sense. SIM is a distributional similarity baseline that takes as input the same 10,825 templates of PROP$_{tmp}$ above, constructs a network by connecting two templates whose distributional similarity is greater than zero, and regards two connected templates as having the same polarity. The weight of the links between templates is set to their distributional similarity based on Lin (1998). Then SIM is given the same initial seed templates as PROP$_{tmp}$, by which it calculates the Excitation values of templates using Takamura et al.'s method. As a result, SIM assigned positive Excitation values to all templates, and except for the 10 inhibitory initial seed templates no templates were regarded inhibitory.

Evaluation scheme We randomly sampled 100 templates each from PROP$_{tmp}$'s 8,685 excitatory candidates, PROP$_{tmp}$'s 2,140 inhibitory candidates, all the ALLEXC's templates, and all the SIM's templates, i.e., 400 templates in total. To make the annotators' judgements easier, we randomly filled the argument slot of each template with a noun filling its argument slot in our Web corpus. Three annotators labeled each sample (a combination of a template and a noun) as 'excitatory,' 'inhibitory,' 'neutral,' or 'undecided' if they were not sure about its label.

Results for excitatory In the top graph in Figure 3, 'Proposed' shows PROP$_{tmp}$'s precision curve. The curve is drawn from its 100 samples whose X-axis positions represent their ranks. We plot a dot for every 5 samples. Among the 100 samples, 37 were judged as excitatory, 6 as inhibitory, 45 as neutral, and 6 as 'undecided'. For the remaining 6 samples,

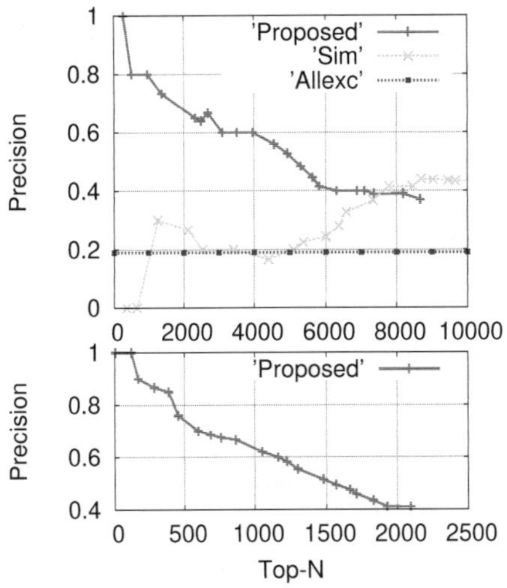

Figure 3: Precision of template acquisition: excitatory (top) and inhibitory (bottom).

the three annotators gave three different labels and the label was not fixed ('split-votes' hereafter). For calculating precision, only the 37 samples labeled excitatory were regarded as correct. PROP_{tmp} outperformed all baselines by a large margin, with an estimated 70% precision for the top 2,000 templates. 'Allexc' and 'Sim' in Figure 3 denote ALLEXC and SIM. Among ALLEXC's 100 samples, 19 were judged as excitatory, 5 as inhibitory, 74 as neutral, and 2 as 'undecided'. SIM's low performance reflects the fact that templates with opposite polarities are sometimes distributionally similar, and as a result get connected by SAME links.

Results for inhibitory 'Proposed' in the bottom graph in Figure 3 shows the precision curve drawn from the 100 samples of PROP_{tmp}'s inhibitory candidates. Among the 100 samples, 41 were judged as inhibitory, 15 as excitatory, 32 as neutral, 4 as 'undecided', and 8 as 'split-votes'. Only the 41 inhibitory samples were regarded as correct. From the curve we estimate that PROP_{tmp} achieved about 70% precision for the top 500. Note that SIM could not acquire any inhibitory templates, yet we can think of no other reasonable baseline for this task.

Inter-annotator agreement The Fleiss' kappa (Fleiss, 1971) of annotator judgements was 0.48 (moderate agreement (Landis and Koch, 1977)). For training, the annotators were given a one-page annotation manual (see supplementary materials), which basically described the same contents in Section 2, in addition to 14 examples of excitatory, 14 examples of inhibitory, and 6 examples of neutral templates that were manually prepared by the authors. Using the manual and the examples, we instructed all the annotators face-to-face for a few hours. We also made sure the evaluation data did not contain any examples used during instruction.

Observations about argument positions Among the 200 evaluation samples of PROP_{tmp} (for both excitatory and inhibitory evaluations), 52 were judged as excitatory, 47 as inhibitory, and 77 as neutral. For the excitatory templates, the numbers of nominative, topic, accusative, dative, and instrumental argument positions are 15, 11, 10, 8, and 8, respectively. For the inhibitory templates, the numbers are 17, 11, 16, 3, and 0. For the neutral templates, the numbers are 8, 23, 17, 21, and 8. Accordingly, we found no noticeable bias with regard to their numbers. Likewise, we found no noticeable bias regarding their usefulness for contradiction and causality acquisition reported shortly, too.

Summary PROP_{tmp} works well, as it outperforms the baselines. Its performance demonstrates the validity of our constraint matrix in Table 1. Besides, since our annotators were non-experts but showed moderate agreement, we conclude that Excitation is a reasonably comprehensible notion.

5.2 Contradiction Extraction

This section shows that our proposed method for contradiction extraction (PROP_{cont}) extracted one million contradiction pairs with more than 70% precision, and that Excitation values are useful for contradiction ranking. As input for PROP_{cont} we took the top 2,000 excitatory and the top 500 inhibitory templates from the previous experiment (i.e., the other templates were regarded as neutral).

Baselines Our baseline methods are RAND_{cont} and PROP_{cont}-NE. RAND_{cont} randomly combines two phrases, each consisting of a template and a noun that they share. It does not rank its output. PROP_{cont}-NE is the same as PROP_{cont} except that it does not use Excitation values; ranking is based only on $sim(t_1, t_2)$. PROP_{cont}-NE does combine phrases with opposite template polarities, just like PROP_{cont}.

Evaluation scheme We randomly sampled 200 phrase pairs from the top one million results of each

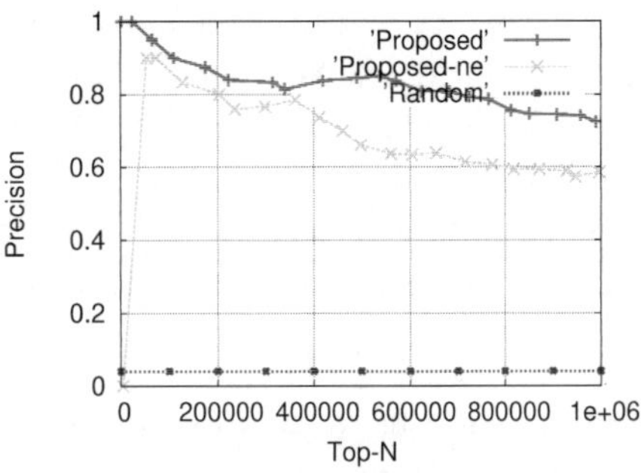

Figure 4: Precision of contradiction extraction.

PROP_{cont} and PROP_{cont}-NE, and 100 samples from the output of RAND_{cont}'s output, giving 500 samples. Three annotators labeled whether the samples are contradictions. Fleiss' kappa was 0.78 (substantial agreement).

Results 'Proposed' in Figure 4 shows the precision curve of PROP_{cont}. PROP_{cont} achieved an estimated 70% precision for its top one million results. Readers might wonder whether PROP_{cont}'s output consists of a small number of template pairs that are filled with many different nouns. If this were the case, PROP_{cont}'s performance would be somewhat misleading. However, we found that PROP_{cont}'s 200 samples contained 194 different template pairs, suggesting that our method can acquire a large variety of contradiction phrases. 'Proposed-ne' is the precision curve for PROP_{cont}-NE. Its precision is more than 10% lower than PROP_{cont} at the top one million results. 'Random' shows that RAND_{cont}'s precision is only 4%. Table 2 shows examples of PROP_{cont}'s outputs and their English translation. The labels 'Cont,' 'Quasi' and '✖' denote whether a pair is contradictory, quasi-contradictory, or not contradictory. Among PROP_{cont}'s 145 samples judged by the annotators as contradiction, 46 were judged as quasi-contradictory by one of the authors. The first ✖ case in Table 2 was caused by the template, X を改善する (*improve X*). It is tricky since it is excitatory when taking arguments like *function*, while it is inhibitory when taking arguments like *disorder*. However, PROP_{tmp} currently cannot distinguish these usages and judged it as inhibitory in our experiments in Section 5.1, though it must be interpreted as excitatory for the ✖ case. The second ✖ case was due to PROP_{tmp}'s error; it incorrectly judged the neutral template, X が関係する (*related to X*), as inhibitory.

Rank	Contradiction Pairs	Label
8,767	アンバランスを是正する ⊥ アンバランスを生じさせる *repair imbalance ⊥ become imbalanced*	Cont
103,581	運転を助ける ⊥ 運転を妨げる *assist the driver ⊥ disturb the driver*	Cont
151,338	緊張感が緩和される ⊥ 緊張を伴う *calm tension ⊥ feel tension*	Quasi
184,014	機能を改善する ⊥ 機能を高める *improve function ⊥ boost function*	✖
316,881	円安が止まる ⊥ 円安が進行する *yen depreciation stops ⊥ yen depreciation develops*	Cont
317,028	騒音がひどくなる ⊥ 騒音は減少する *noise gets worse ⊥ noise abates*	Cont
334,642	酸味がます ⊥ 酸味が消える *a sour taste is augmented ⊥ a sour taste is lost*	Cont
487,496	痛みが発症する ⊥ 痛みを減らす *feel pain ⊥ reduce pain*	Quasi
529,173	アクセスが生ずる ⊥ アクセスを抑制する *access occurs ⊥ curb access*	Cont
555,049	原発をなくす ⊥ 原発を増やす *lose nuclear plants ⊥ augment nuclear plants*	Cont
608,895	放射能が放出される ⊥ 放射能が減る *radioactivity is released ⊥ radioactivity is reduced*	Quasi
638,092	ユーロが下落する ⊥ ユーロが強くなる *Euro falls ⊥ Euro gets strong*	Cont
757,423	シェアを有する ⊥ シェアが低下する *have share (in market) ⊥ share decreases*	Quasi
833,941	活性酸素が放出される ⊥ 活性酸素が関係する *generate active oxygen ⊥ related to active oxygen*	✖
848,331	ガンを破壊する ⊥ ガンを進行させる *destroy cancer ⊥ develop cancer*	Cont
982,980	ウイルスが死滅する ⊥ ウイルスが活性化する *virus becomes extinct ⊥ virus is activated*	Cont

Table 2: Examples of PROP_{cont}'s outputs.

Summary PROP_{cont} is a low cost but high performance method, since it acquired one million contradiction pairs with over 70% precision from only the 46 initial seed templates. Besides, Excitation contributes to contradiction ranking since PROP_{cont} outperformed PROP_{cont}-NE by a 10% margin for the top one million results. Thus we conclude that our assumption on contradiction extraction is valid.

5.3 Causality Extraction

We show that our method for causality extraction (PROP_{caus}) extracted 500,000 causality pairs with about 70% precision, and that Excitation values contribute to the ranking of causal pairs. PROP_{caus} took as input all 10,825 templates classified by PROP_{tmp}.

Baselines RAND_{caus} randomly extracts two phrases that co-occur in a sentence with one of the AND/THUS-type connectives, i.e., it uses not only non-causal connectives but also causal ones like *thus*. FREQ is the same as PROP_{caus} except that it ranks its output by the phrase pair co-occurrence frequency rather than Excitation values.

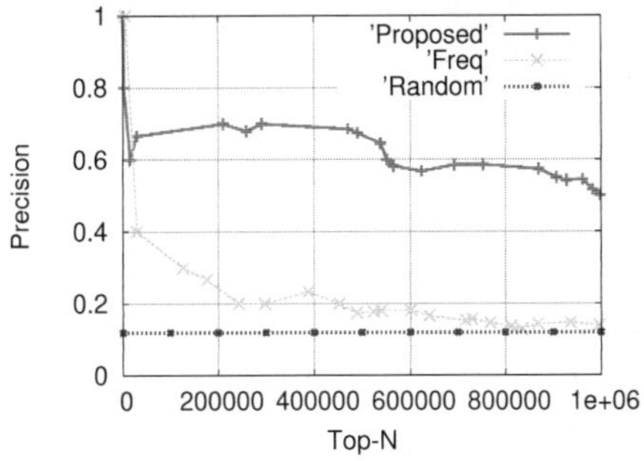

Figure 5: Precision of causality extraction.

Evaluation scheme We randomly sampled 100 pairs each from the top one million results of PROP_{caus} and FREQ, and all RAND_{caus}'s output. The annotators were shown the original sentences from which the samples were extracted. Fleiss' kappa was 0.68 (substantial agreement).

Results 'Proposed' in Figure 5 is the precision curve for PROP_{caus}. From this curve the estimated precision of PROP_{caus} is about 70% around the top 500,000. Note that PROP_{caus} outperformed FREQ by a large margin, and extracted a large variety of causal pairs since its 100 samples contained 91 different template pairs. Table 3 shows examples of PROP_{caus}'s output along with English translations. The labels '✔' and '✖' denote whether a pair is causality or not. The ✖ cases in Table 3 were exceptions to our assumption described in Section 4.2; even if two Excitation templates co-occur in a sentence with an AND/THUS-type connective, they sometimes do not constitute causality. Actually, the first ✖ case consists of two phrases that co-occurred in a sentence with a (non-causal) AND/THUS-type connective but described two events that happen as the effects of introducing the RAID storage system; both are caused by the third event. In the second ✖ case, the two phrases co-occurred in a sentence with a (non-causal) AND/THUS-type connective but just described two opposing events.

Summary PROP_{caus} performs well since it extracted 500,000 causality pairs with about 70% precision. Moreover, Excitation values contribute to causality ranking since PROP_{caus} outperformed FREQ by a large margin. Then we conclude that our assumption on causality extraction is confirmed.

Rank	Causality Pairs	Label
1,036	基礎代謝を高める ⇒ 脂肪燃焼力を高める *increase basal metabolism ⇒ enhance fat-burning ability*	✔
2,128	学習意欲を高める ⇒ 自己学習を促進する *increase desire to learn ⇒ facilitate self-learning*	✔
6,471	信頼性を高める ⇒ 容量を増やす *improve reliability ⇒ increase capacity*	✖
29,638	血中甲状腺ホルモン濃度が高まる ⇒ 新陳代謝が高まる *circulating thyroid hormone level increases ⇒ improves metabolism*	✔
56,868	輸出が増える ⇒ ＧＤＰが増加する *exports increase ⇒ GDP grows*	✔
267,364	血行を促進する ⇒ 新陳代謝を助ける *promote blood circulation ⇒ improve metabolism*	✔
268,670	ＢＳＥが発生する ⇒ 輸入禁止になる *BSE outbreak occurs ⇒ import ban (on beef) is issued*	✔
290,846	視界が良くなる ⇒ 作業効率が向上する *improve the view ⇒ improve the efficiency of work*	✔
322,121	大地震が発生する ⇒ メルトダウンを起こす *giant earthquake occurs ⇒ meltdown is triggered*	✔
532,106	熱効率が良い ⇒ 暖房効果を高める *good at thermal efficiency ⇒ enhance heating efficiency*	✔
563,462	インフレを起こす ⇒ 円安が進行する *promote inflation (in Japan) ⇒ yen depreciation develops*	✔
591,175	利益をもたらす ⇒ 不利益をもたらす *bring profit ⇒ bring detriment*	✖
657,676	体力が落ちる ⇒ 免疫力が下がる *physical strength declines ⇒ immune system weakens*	✔
676,902	国債先物急落を受ける ⇒ 金利が上昇する *sharp fall in government bond futures occurs ⇒ interest rates increase*	✔
914,101	誤差が出る ⇒ めいわくをかける *have a margin of error ⇒ cause trouble*	✔

Table 3: Examples of PROP_{caus}'s outputs.

5.4 Causality Hypothesis Generation

Here we show that our causality hypothesis generation method in Section 4.3 (PROP_{hyp}) extracted one million hypotheses with about 57% precision.

This experiment took the top 100,000 results of PROP_{caus} as input, generated hypotheses from them, and randomly selected 100 samples from the top one million hypotheses. We evaluated only PROP_{caus}, since we could not think of any reasonable baseline for this task. Randomly coupling two phrases might be a baseline, but it would perform so poorly that it could not be a reasonable baseline.

The annotators judged each sample in the same way as Section 5.3, except that we presented them with source causality pairs from which hypotheses were generated, as well as the original sentences of these source pairs. Fleiss' kappa was 0.51 (moderate agreement).

As a result, PROP_{hyp} generated one million hypotheses with 57% precision. It generated various kinds of hypotheses, since these 100 samples contained 99 different template pairs. Table 4 shows some causal hypotheses generated by PROP_{hyp}. The source causal pair is shown in parentheses. The labels '✔' and '✖' denote whether a pair is causality or not. The first ✖ case was due to an error made by

Rank	Causality Hypotheses (and their Origin)	Label
18,886	ストレスが減少する ⇒ 不眠が改善される	✔
	(ストレスが増加する ⇒ 不眠が続く)	✔
	alleviate stress ⇒ remedy insomnia	
	(*increase stress ⇒ continue to have insomnia*)	
93,781	デフレを阻止する ⇒ 税収が増加する	✔
	(デフレが進む ⇒ 税収が減る)	✔
	halt deflation ⇒ tax revenue increases	
	(*deflation is promoted ⇒ tax revenes declines*)	
121,163	楽しみが増大する ⇒ ストレスが減少する	✔
	(楽しみが減る ⇒ ストレスが高まる)	✔
	enjoyment increases ⇒ stress decreases	
	(*enjoyment decreases ⇒ stress grows*)	
205,486	犯罪を減らす ⇒ 不安が無くなる	✔
	(犯罪が増加する ⇒ 不安が高まる)	✔
	decrease in crime ⇒ diminish anxiety	
	(*increase in crime ⇒ heighten anxiety*)	
253,531	塩素を減らす ⇒ バクテリアは増殖する	✔
	(塩素を発生させる ⇒ バクテリアを死滅させる)	✔
	reduce chlorine ⇒ bacteria grow	
	(*generate chlorine ⇒ bacteria extinct*)	
450,353	需要が拡大する ⇒ 失業を減少させる	✔
	(需要が減る ⇒ 失業が増える)	✔
	expand demand ⇒ decrease unemployment rate	
	(*decrease demand ⇒ increase unemployment rate*)	
464,546	消化が悪くなる ⇒ コレステロールを増やす	✖
	(消化を助ける ⇒ コレステロールを減らす)	✖
	(ability of) digestion deteriorates ⇒ cholesterol increases	
	(*aid digestion ⇒ decrease cholesterol*)	
538,310	疲れを軽減する ⇒ 免疫を増強する	✔
	(疲れがたまる ⇒ 免疫が弱まる)	✔
	relieve fatigue ⇒ improve immunity	
	(*feel fatigued ⇒ immunity is weakened*)	
789,481	調子があがる ⇒ トラブルを防げる	✔
	(調子が悪くなる ⇒ トラブルが起きる)	✔
	conditions improve ⇒ prevent troubles	
	(*conditions become bad ⇒ cause troubles*)	
837,850	景気をコントロールする ⇒ 問題を伴う	✖
	(景気が良くなる ⇒ 問題が解消される)	✔
	control economic conditions ⇒ accompany problems	
	(*economic conditions improve ⇒ problems are solved*)	

Table 4: Examples of causality hypotheses.

our causality extraction method PROP_{caus}; the case was erroneous since its original causality was erroneous. The second ✖ case was due to the fact that one of the contradiction phrase pairs used to generate the hypothesis was in fact not contradictory (景気をコントロールする $\not\perp$ 景気が良くなる '*control economic conditions* $\not\perp$ *economic conditions improve*').

From these results, we conclude that our assumption on causality hypothesis generation is valid.

6 Related Work

While the semantic orientation involving good/bad (or desirable/undesirable) has been extensively studied (Hatzivassiloglou and McKeown, 1997; Turney, 2002; Rao and Ravichandran, 2009; Velikovich et al., 2010), we believe Excitation represents a genuinely new semantic orientation.

Most previous methods of contradiction extraction require either thesauri like Roget's or WordNet (Harabagiu et al., 2006; Mohammad et al., 2008; de Marneffe et al., 2008) or large training data for supervision (Turney, 2008). In contrast, our method requires only a few seed templates. Lin et al. (2003) used a few "incompatibility" patterns to acquire antonyms, but they did not report their method's performance on the incompatibility identification task.

Many methods for extracting causality or script-like knowledge between events exist (Girju, 2003; Torisawa, 2005; Torisawa, 2006; Abe et al., 2008; Chambers and Jurafsky, 2009; Do et al., 2011; Shibata and Kurohashi, 2011), but none uses a notion similar to Excitation. As we have shown, we expect that Excitation will improve their performance.

Regarding the acquisition of semantic knowledge that is not explicitly written in corpora, Tsuchida et al. (2011) proposed a novel method to generate semantic relation instances as hypotheses using automatically discovered inference rules. We think that automatically generating plausible semantic knowledge that is not written (explicitly) in corpora as hypotheses and augmenting semantic knowledge base is important for the discovery of so-called "unknown unknowns" (Torisawa et al., 2010), among others.

7 Conclusion

We proposed a new semantic orientation, Excitation, and its acquisition method. Our experiments showed that Excitation allows to acquire one million contradiction pairs with over 70% precision, as well as causality pairs and causality hypotheses of the same volume with reasonable precision from the Web. We plan to make all our acquired knowledge resources available to the research community soon (Visit `http://www.alagin.jp/index-e.html`).

We will investigate additional applications of Excitation in future work. For instance, we expect that Excitation and its related semantic knowledge acquired in this study will improve the performance of Why-QA system like the one proposed by Oh et al. (2012).

References

Shuya Abe, Kentaro Inui, and Yuji Matsumoto. 2008. Two-phrased event relation acquisition: Coupling the relation-oriented and argument-oriented approaches. In *Proceedings of the 22nd International Conference on Computational Linguistics (COLING 2008)*, pages 1–8.

Susumu Akamine, Daisuke Kawahara, Yoshikiyo Kato, Tetsuji Nakagawa, Yutaka I. Leon-Suematsu, Takuya Kawada, Kentaro Inui, Sadao Kurohashi, and Yutaka Kidawara. 2010. Organizing information on the web to support user judgments on information credibility. In *Proceedings of 2010 4th International Universal Communication Symposium Proceedings (IUCS 2010)*, pages 122–129.

Alina Andreevskaia and Sabine Bergler. 2006. Semantic tag extraction from wordnet glosses. In *Proceedings of the 5th International Conference on Language Resources and Evaluation (LREC 2006)*.

Nathanael Chambers and Dan Jurafsky. 2009. Unsupervised learning of narrative schemas and their participants. In *Proceedings of the 47th Annual Meeting of the ACL and the 4th IJCNLP of the AFNLP (ACL-IJCNLP 2009)*, pages 602–610.

Marie-Catherine de Marneffe, Anna Rafferty, and Christopher D. Manning. 2008. Finding contradiction in text. In *Proceedings of the 48th Annual Meeting of the Association of Computational Linguistics: Human Language Technologies (ACL-08: HLT)*, pages 1039–1047.

Quang Xuan Do, Yee Seng Chan, and Dan Roth. 2011. Minimally supervised event causality identification. In *Proceedings of the 2011 Conference on Empirical Methods in Natural Language Processing (EMNLP 2011)*, pages 294–303.

Joseph L. Fleiss. 1971. Measuring nominal scale agreement among many raters. *Psychological Bulletin*, 76(5):378–382.

Roxana Girju. 2003. Automatic detection of causal relations for question answering. In *Proceedings of the 41st Annual Meeting of the Association for Computational Linguistics (ACL 2003), Workshop on Multilingual Summarization and Question Answering - Machine Learning and Beyond*, pages 76–83.

Sanda Harabagiu, Andrew Hickl, and Finley Lacatusu. 2006. Negation, contrast and contradiction in text processing. In *Proceedings of the 21st National Conference on Artificial Intelligence (AAAI-06)*, pages 755–762.

Vasileios Hatzivassiloglou and Kathleen R. McKeown. 1997. Predicting the semantic orientation of adjectives. In *Proceedings of the 35 Annual Meeting of the Association for Computational Linguistics and the 8the Conference of the European Chapter of the Association of Computational Linguistics*, pages 174–181.

Daisuke Kawahara and Sadao Kurohashi. 2006. A fully-lexicalized probabilistic model for Japanese syntactic and case structure analysis. In *Proceedings of the Human Language Technology Conference of the North American Chapter of the ACL (HLT-NAACL2006)*, pages 176–183.

J. Richard Landis and Gary G. Koch. 1977. The measurement of observer agreement for categorical data. *Biometrics*, 33(1):159–174.

Dekang Lin, Shaojun Zhao Lijuan Qin, and Ming Zhou. 2003. Identifying synonyms among distributionally similar words. In *Proceedings of the 18th International Joint Conference on Artificial Intelligence (IJCAI-03)*, pages 1492–1493.

Dekang Lin. 1998. Automatic retrieval and clustering of similar words. In *Proceedings of the 36th Annual Meeting of the Association for Computational Linguistics and 17th International Conference on Computational Linguistics (COLING-ACL1998)*, pages 768–774.

Saif Mohammad, Bonnie Dorr, and Greame Hirst. 2008. Computing word-pair antonymy. In *Proceedings of the 2008 Conference on Empirical Methods in Natural Language Processing*, pages 982–991.

Jong-Hoon Oh, Kentaro Torisawa, Chikara Hashimoto, Takuya Kawada, Stijn De Saeger, Junichi Kazama, and Yiou Wang. 2012. Why question answering using sentiment analysis and word classes. In *Proceedings of EMNLP-CoNLL 2012: Conference on Empirical Methods in Natural Language Processing and Natural Language Learning*.

Charles E. Osgood, George J. Suci, and Percy H. Tannenbaum. 1957. *The measurement of meaning*. University of Illinois Press.

James Pustejovsky. 1995. *The Generative Lexicon*. MIT Press.

Delip Rao and Deepak Ravichandran. 2009. Semi-supervised polarity lexicon induction. In *Proceedings of the 12th Conference of the European Chapter of the ACL*, pages 675–682.

Tomohide Shibata and Sadao Kurohashi. 2011. Acquiring strongly-related events using predicate-argument co-occurring statistics and case frames. In *Proceedings of the 5th International Joint Conference on Natural Language Processing (IJCNLP 2011)*, pages 1028–1036.

Philip J. Stone, Dexter C. Dunphy, Marshall S. Smith, and Daniel M. Ogilvie. 1966. *The General Inquirer: A Computer Approach to Content Analysis*. MIT Press.

Hiroya Takamura, Takashi Inui, and Manabu Okumura. 2005. Extracting semantic orientation of words using spin model. In *Proceedings of the 43rd Annual Meeting of the ACL*, pages 133–140.

Kentaro Torisawa, Stijn De Saeger, Jun'ichi Kazama, Asuka Sumida, Daisuke Noguchi, Yasunari Kakizawa, Masaki Murata, Kow Kuroda, and Ichiro Yamada. 2010. Organizing the web's information explosion to discover unknown unknowns. *New Generation Computing (Special Issue on Information Explosion)*, 28(3):217–236.

Kentaro Torisawa. 2005. Automatic acquisition of expressions representing preparation and utilization of an object. In *Proceedings of the Recent Advances in Natural Language Processing (RANLP05)*, pages 556–560.

Kentaro Torisawa. 2006. Acquiring inference rules with temporal constraints by using japanese coordinated sentences and noun-verb co-occurrences. In *Proceedings of the Human Language Technology Conference of the North American Chapter of the ACL (HLT-NAACL2006)*, pages 57–64.

Masaaki Tsuchida, Kentaro Torisawa, Stijn De Saeger, Jong-Hoon Oh, Jun'ichi Kazama, Chikara Hashimoto, and Hayato Ohwada. 2011. Toward finding semantic relations not written in a single sentence: An inference method using auto-discovered rules. In *Proceedings of the 5th International Joint Conference on Natural Language Processing (IJCNLP 2011)*, pages 902–910.

Peter D. Turney. 2002. Thumbs up or thumbs down? semantic orientation applied to unsupervised classification of reviews. In *Proceedings of the 40th Annual Meeting of the Association for Computational Linguistics (ACL 2002)*, pages 417–424.

Peter Turney. 2008. A uniform approach to analogies, synonyms, antonyms, and associations. In *Proceedings of the 22nd International Conference on Computational Linguistics (COLING 2008)*, pages 905–912.

Leonid Velikovich, Sasha Blair-Goldensohn, Kerry Hannan, and Ryan McDonald. 2010. The viability of web-derived polarity lexicons. In *Human Language Technologies: The 2010 Annual Conference of the North American Chapter of the ACL*, pages 777–785.

Ellen M. Voorhees. 2008. Contradictions and justifications: Extensions to the textual entailment task. In *Proceedings of the 48th Annual Meeting of the Association of Computational Linguistics: Human Language Technologies (ACL-08: HLT)*, pages 63–71.

Enlarging Paraphrase Collections through Generalization and Instantiation

Atsushi Fujita
Future University Hakodate
116-2 Kameda-nakano-cho,
Hakodate, Hokkaido, 041-8655, Japan
fujita@fun.ac.jp

Pierre Isabelle **Roland Kuhn**
National Research Council Canada
283 Alexandre-Taché Boulevard,
Gatineau, QC, J8X 3X7, Canada
{Pierre.Isabelle, Roland.Kuhn}@nrc.ca

Abstract

This paper presents a paraphrase acquisition method that uncovers and exploits generalities underlying paraphrases: paraphrase patterns are first induced and then used to collect novel instances. Unlike existing methods, ours uses both bilingual parallel and monolingual corpora. While the former are regarded as a source of high-quality seed paraphrases, the latter are searched for paraphrases that match patterns learned from the seed paraphrases. We show how one can use monolingual corpora, which are far more numerous and larger than bilingual corpora, to obtain paraphrases that rival in quality those derived directly from bilingual corpora. In our experiments, the number of paraphrase pairs obtained in this way from monolingual corpora was a large multiple of the number of seed paraphrases. Human evaluation through a paraphrase substitution test demonstrated that the newly acquired paraphrase pairs are of reasonable quality. Remaining noise can be further reduced by filtering seed paraphrases.

1 Introduction

Paraphrases are semantically equivalent expressions in the same language. Because "equivalence" is the most fundamental semantic relationship, techniques for generating and recognizing paraphrases play an important role in a wide range of natural language processing tasks (Madnani and Dorr, 2010).

In the last decade, automatic acquisition of knowledge about paraphrases from corpora has been drawing the attention of many researchers. Typically, the acquired knowledge is simply represented as pairs of semantically equivalent sub-sentential expressions as in (1).

(1) a. look like ⇔ resemble
b. control system ⇔ controller

The challenge in acquiring paraphrases is to ensure good coverage of the targeted classes of paraphrases along with a low proportion of incorrect pairs. However, no matter what type of resource has been used, it has proven difficult to acquire paraphrase pairs with both high recall and high precision.

Among various types of corpora, monolingual corpora can be considered the best source for high-coverage paraphrase acquisition, because there is far more monolingual than bilingual text available. Most methods that exploit monolingual corpora rely on the Distributional Hypothesis (Harris, 1968): expressions that appear in similar contexts are expected to have similar meaning. However, if one uses purely distributional criteria, it is difficult to distinguish real paraphrases from pairs of expressions that are related in other ways, such as antonyms and cousin words.

In contrast, since the work in (Bannard and Callison-Burch, 2005), bilingual parallel corpora have been acknowledged as a good source of high-quality paraphrases: paraphrases are obtained by putting together expressions that receive the same translation in the other language (pivot language). Because translation expresses a specific meaning more directly than context in the aforementioned approach, pairs of expressions acquired in this manner tend to be correct paraphrases. However, the coverage problem remains: there is much less bilingual parallel than monolingual text available.

Our objective in this paper is to obtain paraphrases that have high **quality** (like those extracted from bilingual parallel corpora via pivoting) but can be generated in large **quantity** (like those extracted from monolingual corpora via contextual similarity). To achieve this, we propose a method that exploits general patterns underlying paraphrases and uses both bilingual parallel and monolingual sources of information. Given a relatively high-quality set of paraphrases obtained from a bilingual parallel corpus, a set of paraphrase patterns is first induced. Then, appropriate instances of such patterns, i.e., potential paraphrases, are harvested from a monolingual corpus.

After reviewing existing methods in Section 2, our method is presented in Section 3. Section 4 describes our experiments in acquiring paraphrases and presents statistics summarizing the coverage of our method. Section 5 describes a human evaluation of the quality of the acquired paraphrases. Finally, Section 6 concludes this paper.

2 Literature on Paraphrase Acquisition

This section summarizes existing corpus-based methods for paraphrase acquisition, following the classification in (Hashimoto et al., 2011): similarity-based and alignment-based methods.

2.1 Similarity-based Methods

Techniques that use monolingual (non-parallel) corpora mostly rely on the Distributional Hypothesis (Harris, 1968). Because a large quantity of monolingual data is available for many languages, a large number of paraphrase candidates can be acquired (Lin and Pantel, 2001; Paşca and Dienes, 2005; Bhagat and Ravichandran, 2008, etc.). The recipes proposed so far are based on three main ingredients, i.e., features used for representing context of target expression (contextual features), criteria for weighting and filtering features, and aggregation functions.

A drawback of relying only on contextual similarity is that it tends to give high scores to semantically related but non-equivalent expressions, such as antonyms and cousin words. To enhance the precision of the results, filtering mechanisms need to be introduced (Marton et al., 2011).

2.2 Alignment-based Methods

Pairs of expressions that get translated to the same expression in a different language can be regarded as paraphrases. On the basis of this hypothesis, Barzilay and McKeown (2001) and Pang et al. (2003) created monolingual parallel corpora from multiple human translations of the same source. Then, they extracted corresponding parts of such parallel sentences as sub-sentential paraphrases.

Leveraging recent advances in statistical machine translation (SMT), Bannard and Callison-Burch (2005) proposed a method for acquiring sub-sentential paraphrases from bilingual parallel corpora. As in SMT, a translation table is first built on the basis of alignments between expressions, such as words, phrases, and subtrees, across a parallel sentence pair. Then, pairs of expressions (e_1, e_2) in the same language that are aligned with the same expressions in the other language (pivot language) are extracted as paraphrases. The likelihood of e_2 being a paraphrase of e_1 is given by

$$p(e_2|e_1) = \sum_{f \in Tr(e_1,e_2)} p(e_2|f)p(f|e_1), \quad (1)$$

where $Tr(e_1, e_2)$ stands for the set of shared translations of e_1 and e_2. Each factor $p(e|f)$ and $p(f|e)$ is estimated from the number of times e and f are aligned and the number of occurrences of each expression in each language. Kok and Brockett (2010) showed how one can discover paraphrases that do not share any translation in one language by traversing a graph created from multiple translation tables, each corresponding to a bilingual parallel corpus.

This approach, however, suffers from a coverage problem, because both monolingual parallel and bilingual parallel corpora tend to be significantly smaller than monolingual non-parallel corpora. The acquired pairs of expressions include some non-paraphrases as well. Many of these come from erroneous alignments, which are particularly frequent when the given corpus is small.

Monolingual comparable corpora have also been exploited as sources of paraphrases using alignment-based methods. For instance, multiple news articles covering the same event (Shinyama et al., 2002; Barzilay and Lee, 2003; Dolan et al., 2004; Wubben et al., 2009) have been used. Such corpora have also been created manually through crowdsourcing (Chen and Dolan, 2011). However, the availability of monolingual comparable corpora is very limited for most languages; thus, approaches relying on these corpora have typically produced only very small collections of paraphrases. Hashimoto et al. (2011) found a way around this limitation by collecting sentences that constitute explicit definitions of particular words or phrases from monolingual non-parallel Web documents, pairing sentences that define the same noun phrase, and then finding corresponding phrases in each sentence pair. One limitation of this approach is that it requires a considerable amount of labeled data for both the corpus construction and the paraphrase extraction steps.

2.3 Summary

Existing methods have investigated one of the following four types of corpora as their principal resource[1]: monolingual non-parallel corpora, monolingual parallel corpora, monolingual comparable corpora, and bilingual parallel corpora. No matter what type of resource has been used, however, it has proven difficult to acquire paraphrases with both high recall and precision, with the possible exception of the method in (Hashimoto et al., 2011) which requires large amounts of labeled data.

3 Proposed Method

While most existing methods deal with expressions only at the surface level, ours exploits generalities underlying paraphrases to achieve better coverage while retaining high precision. Furthermore, unlike existing methods, ours uses both bilingual parallel and monolingual non-parallel corpora as sources for acquiring paraphrases.

The process is illustrated in Figure 1. First, a set of high-quality seed paraphrases, P_{Seed}, is acquired from bilingual parallel corpora by using an alignment-based method. Then, our method collects further paraphrases through the following two steps.

Generalization (Step 2): Paraphrase patterns are learned from the seed paraphrases, P_{Seed}.

Instantiation (Step 3): A novel set of paraphrase pairs, P_{Hvst}, is finally harvested from monolingual non-parallel corpora using the learned patterns; each newly acquired paraphrase pair is assessed by contextual similarity.

[1]Chan et al. (2011) used monolingual corpora only for re-ranking paraphrases obtained from bilingual parallel corpora. To the best of our knowledge, bilingual comparable corpora have never been used as sources for acquiring paraphrases.

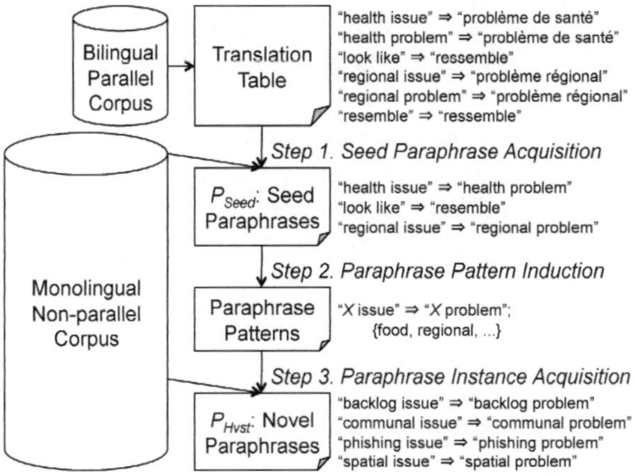

Figure 1: Process of paraphrase acquisition.

The set P_{Seed} acquired early in the process can be pooled with the set P_{Hvst} harvested in the last stage of the process.

3.1 Step 1. Seed Paraphrase Acquisition

The goal of the first step is to obtain a set of high-quality paraphrase pairs, P_{Seed}.

For this purpose, alignment-based methods with bilingual or monolingual parallel corpora are preferable to similarity-based methods applied to non-parallel corpora. Among various options, in this paper, we start from the standard technique proposed by Bannard and Callison-Burch (2005) with bilingual parallel corpora (see also Section 2.2). In particular, we assume the phrase-based SMT framework (Koehn et al., 2003). Then, we purify the results with several filtering methods.

The phrase pair extraction process of phrase-based SMT systems aims at high recall for increased robustness of the translation process. As a result, a naive application of the paraphrase acquisition method produces pairs of expressions that are not exact paraphrases. For instance, the algorithm explained in Koehn (2009, p.134) extracts both "dass" and ", dass" as counterparts of "that" from the sentence pair. To reduce that kind of noise, we apply some filtering techniques to the candidate translation pairs. First, statistically unreliable translation pairs (Johnson et al., 2007) are filtered out. Then, we also filter out phrases made up entirely of stop words (including punctuation marks), both in the language of interest and in the pivot language.

Let P_{Raw} be the initial set of paraphrase pairs extracted from the sanitized translation table. We first

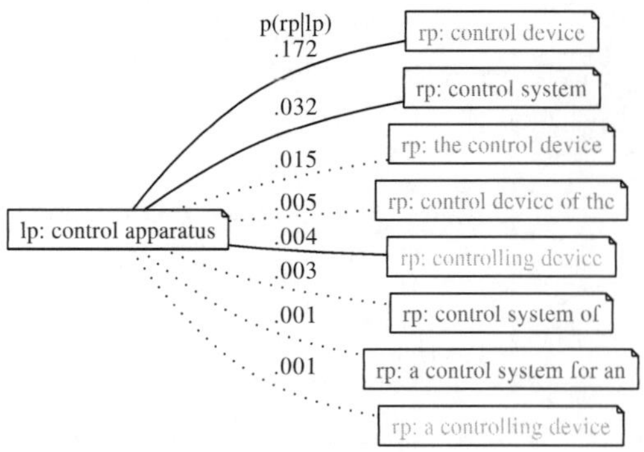

Figure 2: RHS-filtering for "control apparatus".

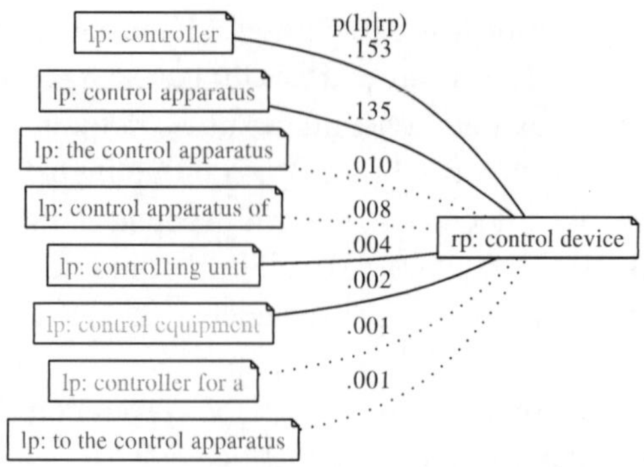

Figure 3: LHS-filtering for "control device".

discard pairs whose difference comprises only stop words, such as "the schools" ⇒ "schools and". We also remove pairs containing only singular-plural differences, such as "family unit" ⇒ "family units". Depending on the language of interest, other types of morphological variants, such as those shown in (2), may also be ignored.

(2) a. "européenne" ⇒ "européen"
(Gender in French)
b. "guten Lösungen" ⇒ "gute Lösungen"
(Case in German)

We further filter out less reliable pairs, such as those shown with dotted lines in Figures 2 and 3. This is carried out by comparing the right-hand side (RHS) phrases of each left-hand side (LHS) phrase, and vice versa[2]. Given a set of paraphrase pairs, RHS phrases corresponding to the same LHS phrase lp are compared. A RHS phrase rp is not licensed iff lp has another RHS phrase rp' ($\neq rp$) which satisfies the following two conditions (see also Figure 2).

- rp' is a word sub-sequence of rp
- rp' is a more likely paraphrase than rp, i.e., $p(rp'|lp) > p(rp|lp)$

LHS phrases for each RHS phrase rp are also compared in a similar manner, i.e., a LHS phrase lp is not qualified as a legitimate source of rp iff rp has another LHS phrase lp' ($\neq lp$) which satisfies the following conditions (see also Figure 3).

- lp' is a word sub-sequence of lp
- lp' is a more likely source than lp, i.e., $p(lp'|rp) > p(lp|rp)$

The two directions of filtering are separately applied and the intersection of their results is retained.

[2]cf. Denkowski and Lavie (2011); they only compared each RHS phrase to its corresponding LHS phrase.

Candidate pairs are finally filtered on the basis of their reliability score. Traditionally, a threshold (th_p) on the conditional probability given by Eq. (1) is used (Du et al., 2010; Max, 2010; Denkowski and Lavie, 2011, etc.). Furthermore, we also require that LHS and RHS phrases exceed a threshold (th_s) on their contextual similarity in a monolingual corpus. This paper neither proposes a specific recipe nor makes a comprehensive comparison of existing recipes for computing contextual similarity, although one particular recipe is used in our experiments (see Section 4.1).

3.2 Step 2. Paraphrase Pattern Induction

From a set of seed paraphrases, P_{Seed}, paraphrase patterns are induced. For instance, from paraphrases in (3), we induce paraphrase patterns in (4).

(3) a. "restraint system" ⇒ "restraint apparatus"
b. "movement against racism"
⇒ "anti-racism movement"
c. "middle eastern countries"
⇒ "countries in the middle east"

(4) a. "X system" ⇒ "X apparatus"
b. "X against Y" ⇒ "anti-Y X"
c. "X eastern Y" ⇒ "Y in the X east"

Word pairs of LHS and RHS phrases will be replaced with variable slots iff they are fully identical or singular-plural variants. Note that stop words are retained. While a deeper level of lexical correspondences, such as "eastern" and "east" in (3c) and "system" and "apparatus" in (3a), could be captured, this would require the use of rich language resources, thereby making the method less portable to resource-poor languages.

Note that our aim is to automatically capture general paraphrase patterns of the kind that have sometimes been manually described (Jacquemin, 1999; Fujita et al., 2007). This is different from approaches that attach variable slots to paraphrases for calculating their similarity (Lin and Pantel, 2001; Szpektor and Dagan, 2008) or for constraining the context in which they are regarded legitimate (Callison-Burch, 2008; Zhao et al., 2009).

3.3 Step 3. Paraphrase Instance Acquisition

Given a set of paraphrase patterns, such as those shown in (4), a set of novel instances, i.e., novel paraphrases, P_{Hvst}, will now be harvested from monolingual non-parallel corpora. In other words, a set of appropriate slot-fillers will be extracted.

First, expressions that match both elements of the pattern, except stop words, are collected from a given monolingual corpus. Pattern matching alone may generate inappropriate pairs, so we then assess the legitimacy of each collected slot-filler.

Let $LHS(\mathbf{w})$ and $RHS(\mathbf{w})$ be the expressions generated by instantiating the k variable slots in LHS and RHS phrases of the pattern with a k-tuple of slot-fillers $\mathbf{w}$ $(= w_1, \ldots, w_k)$, respectively. We estimate how likely $RHS(\mathbf{w})$ is to be a paraphrase of $LHS(\mathbf{w})$ based on the contextual similarity between them using a monolingual corpus; a pair of phrases is discarded if they are used in substantially dissimilar contexts. We use the same recipe and threshold value for th_s with Step 1 in our experiments.

Contextual similarity of antonyms and cousin words can also be high, as they are often used in similar contexts. However, this is not a problem in our framework, because semantic equivalence between $LHS(\mathbf{w})$ and $RHS(\mathbf{w})$ is almost entirely guaranteed as a result of the way the corresponding patterns were learned from a bilingual parallel corpus.

3.4 Characteristics

In terms of coverage, P_{Hvst} is expected to be greatly larger than P_{Seed}, although it will not cover totally different pairs of paraphrases, such as those shown in (1). On the other hand, the quality of P_{Hvst} depends on that of P_{Seed}. Unlike in the pure similarity-based method, P_{Hvst} is constrained by the paraphrase patterns derived from the set of high-quality paraphrases, P_{Seed}, and will therefore generally exclude the kind of semantically similar but non-equivalent pairs that contextual similarity alone tends to extract alongside real paraphrases.

As mentioned in Section 3.1, other types of methods can be used for obtaining high-quality seed paraphrases, P_{Seed}. For instance, the supervised method proposed by Hashimoto et al. (2011) uses the existence of shared words as a feature to determine whether the given pair of expressions are paraphrases, and thereby extracts many pairs sharing the same words. Thus, their output has a high potential to be used as an alternative seed for our method.

Another advantage of our method is that it does not require any labeled data, unlike the supervised methods proposed by Zhao et al. (2009) and Hashimoto et al. (2011).

4 Quantitative Impact

4.1 Experimental Settings

Two different sets of corpora were used as data sources; in both settings, we acquired English paraphrases.

Europarl: The English-French version of the Europarl Parallel Corpus[3] consisting of 1.8M sentence pairs (51M words in English and 56M words in French) was used as a bilingual parallel corpus, while its English side and the English side of the 10^9 French-English corpus[4] consisting of 23.8M sentences (649M words) were used as monolingual data.

Patent: The Japanese-English Patent Translation data (Fujii et al., 2010) consisting of 3.2M sentence pairs (122M morphemes in Japanese and 106M words in English) was used as a bilingual parallel corpus, while its English side and the 30.0M sentences (626M words) from the 2007 chapter of NTCIR unaligned patent documents were used as monolingual data.

To study the behavior of our method for different amounts of bilingual parallel data, we carried out learning curve experiments.

We used our in-house tokenizer for segmentation of English and French sentences and MeCab[5] for Japanese sentences.

[3]http://statmt.org/europarl/, release 6

[4]http://statmt.org/wmt10/training-giga-fren.tar

[5]http://mecab.sourceforge.net/, version 0.98

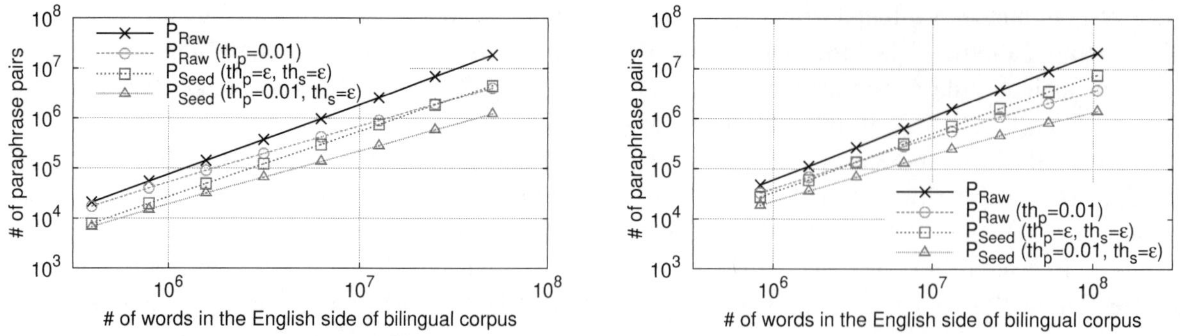

Figure 4: # of paraphrase pairs in P_{Seed} (left: Europarl, right: Patent).

Stop word lists for sanitizing translation pairs and paraphrase pairs were manually compiled: we enumerated 442 English words, 193 French words, and 149 Japanese morphemes, respectively.

From a bilingual parallel corpus, a translation table was created by our in-house phrase-based SMT system, PORTAGE (Sadat et al., 2005). Phrase alignments of each sentence pair were identified by the heuristic "grow-diag-final"[6] with a maximum phrase length 8. The resulting translation pairs were then filtered with the significance pruning technique of (Johnson et al., 2007), using $\alpha + \epsilon$ as threshold.

As contextual features for computing similarity of each paraphrase pair, all of the 1- to 4-grams of words adjacent to each occurrence of a phrase were counted. This is a compromise between less expensive but noisier approaches, such as bag-of-words, and more accurate but more expensive approaches that incorporate syntactic features (Lin and Pantel, 2001; Shinyama et al., 2002; Pang et al., 2003; Szpektor and Dagan, 2008). Contextual similarity is finally measured by taking cosine between two feature vectors.

4.2 Statistics on Acquired Paraphrases

Seed Paraphrases (P_{Seed})

Figure 4 shows the number of paraphrase pairs P_{Seed} obtained from the bilingual parallel corpora. The general trend is simply that the larger the corpus is, the more paraphrases are acquired.

Given the initial set of paraphrases, P_{Raw} ("×"), our filtering techniques ("□") discarded a large portion (63-75% in Europarl and 43-64% in Patent) of them. Pairs with zero similarity were also filtered out, i.e., $th_s = \epsilon$. This suggests that many incorrect and/or relatively useless pairs, such as those shown in Figures 2 and 3, had originally been acquired.

Lines with "○" show the results based on a widely-used threshold value on the conditional probability in Eq. (1), i.e., $th_p = 0.01$ (Du et al., 2010; Max, 2010; Denkowski and Lavie, 2011, etc.). The percentage of paraphrase pairs thereby discarded varied greatly depending on the corpus size (17-78% in Europarl and 31-82% in Patent), suggesting that the threshold value should be determined depending on the given corpus. In the following experiment, however, we conform to the convention $th_p = 0.01$ ("△") to ensure the quality of P_{Seed} that we will be using for inducing paraphrase patterns, even though this results in discarding some less frequent but correct paraphrase pairs, such as "control apparatus" ⇒ "controlling device" in Figure 2.

Paraphrase Patterns

Figures 5 and 6 show the number of paraphrase patterns that our method induced and their coverage against P_{Seed}, respectively. Due to their rather rigid form, the patterns covered no more than 15% of P_{Seed} in Europarl. In contrast, a higher proportion of P_{Seed} in Patent was generalized into patterns. We speculate it is because the patent domain contains many expressions, including technical terms, that have similar variations of constructions.

The acquired patterns were mostly one-variable patterns: 88-93% and 80-91% of total patterns for different variants of the Europarl and Patent settings, respectively. Given that there are far more one-variable patterns than other types, and that one-variable patterns are the simplest type, we henceforth focus on them. More complex patterns, including two-variable patterns (7-11% and 8-17% in each setting), will be investigated in our future work.

[6]http://statmt.org/moses/?n=FactoredTraining.AlignWords

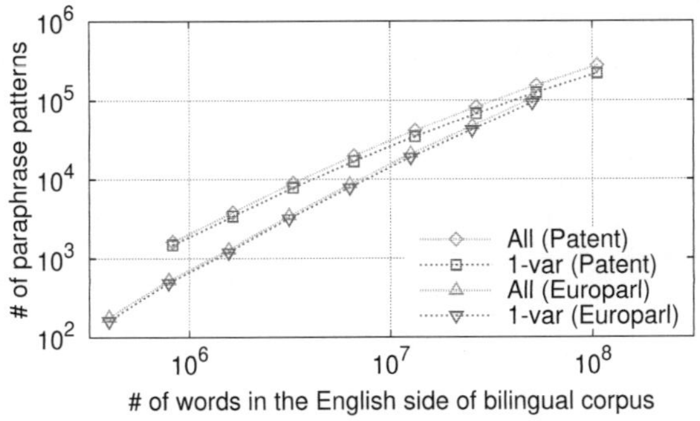

Figure 5: # of paraphrase patterns.

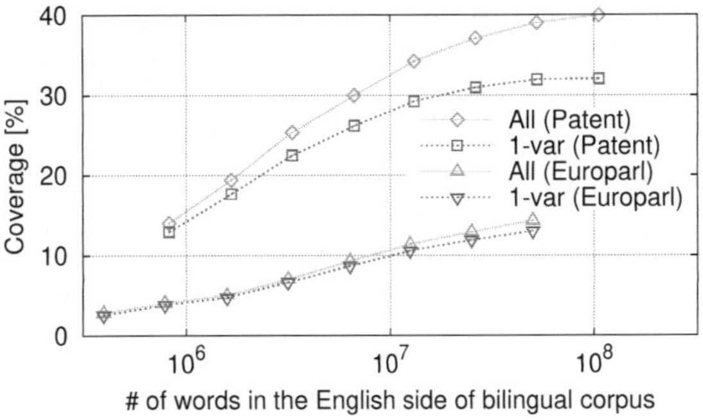

Figure 6: Coverage of the paraphrase patterns.

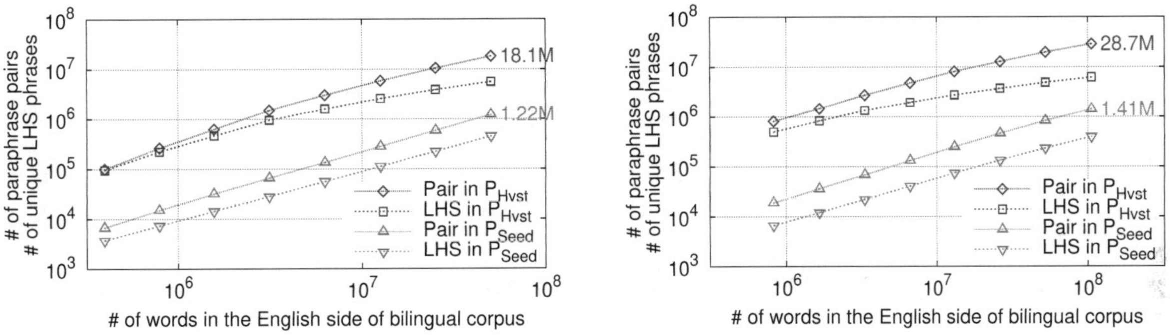

Figure 7: # of paraphrase pairs and unique LHS phrases in P_{Seed} and P_{Hvst} (left: Europarl, right: Patent).

Novel Paraphrases (P_{Hvst})

Using the paraphrase patterns, novel paraphrase pairs, P_{Hvst}, were harvested from the monolingual non-parallel corpora. In this experiment, we only retained one-variable patterns and regarded only single words as slot-fillers for them. Nevertheless, we managed to acquire a large number of paraphrase pairs as depicted in Figure 7, where pairs having zero similarity were excluded. For instance, when the full size of bilingual parallel corpus in Patent was used, we acquired 1.41M pairs of seed paraphrases, P_{Seed}, and 28.7M pairs of novel paraphrases, P_{Hvst}. In other words, our method expanded P_{Seed} by about 21 times. The number of unique LHS phrases that P_{Hvst} covers was also significantly larger than that of P_{Seed}.

Figure 8 highlights the remarkably large ratio of P_{Hvst} to P_{Seed} in terms of the number of paraphrase pairs and the number of unique LHS phrases. The smaller the bilingual corpus is, the higher the ratio is, except when there is only a very small amount of Europarl data. This demonstrates that our method is quite powerful, given a minimum amount of data.

Another striking difference between P_{Seed} and P_{Hvst} is the average number of RHS phrases per unique LHS phrase, i.e., their relative yield. As displayed in Figure 9, the yield for P_{Hvst} increased rapidly with the scaling up of the bilingual corpus, while that of P_{Seed} only grew slowly. The alignment-based method with bilingual corpora cannot produce very many RHS phrases per unique LHS phrase due to its reliance on conditional probability and the surface level processing. In contrast, our method does not limit the number of RHS phrases: each RHS phrase is separately assessed by its similarity to the corresponding LHS phrase. One limitation of our method is that it cannot achieve high yield for P_{Hvst} whenever only a small number of paraphrase patterns can be extracted from the bilingual corpus (see also Figure 5).

Both the ratio of P_{Hvst} to P_{Seed} and the relative yield could probably be increased by scaling up the monolingual corpus. For instance, in the patent domain, monolingual documents 10 times larger than the one used in the above experiments are available at the NTCIR project[7]. It would be interesting to compare the relative gains brought by in-domain versus general-purpose corpora.

[7]http://ntcir.nii.ac.jp/PatentMT-2/

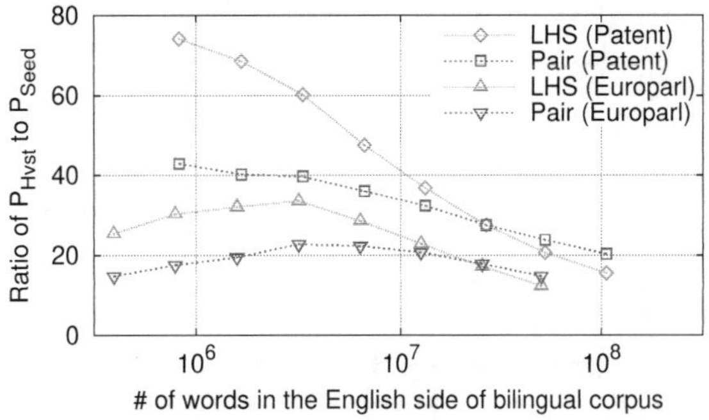

Figure 8: Ratio of P_{Hvst} to P_{Seed}.

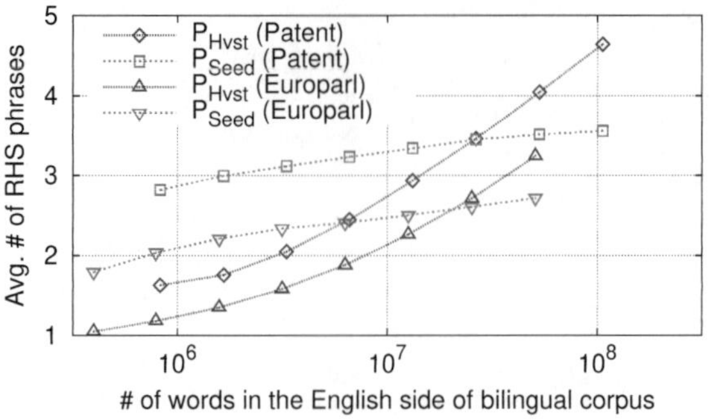

Figure 9: Average # of RHS phrases per LHS phrase.

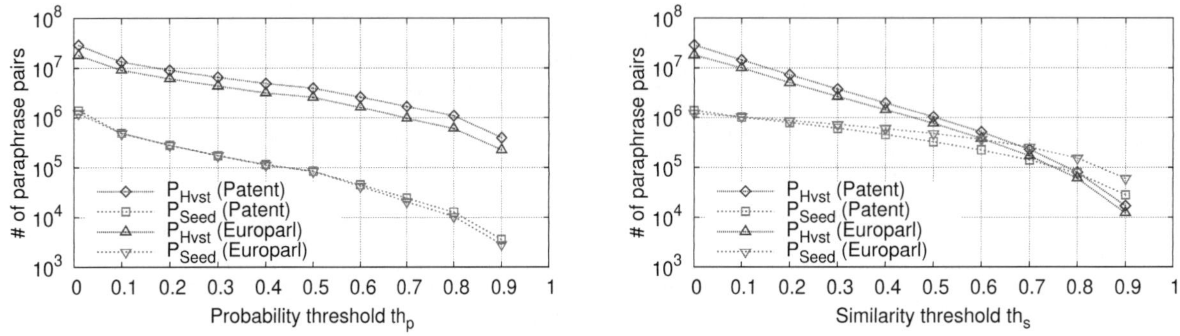

Figure 10: # of acquired paraphrase pairs against threshold values.
(left: probability-based ($0.01 \leq th_p \leq 0.9, th_s = \epsilon$), right: similarity-based ($\epsilon \leq th_s \leq 0.9, th_p = 0.01$))

Finally, we investigated how the number of paraphrase pairs varies depending on the values for the two thresholds, i.e., th_p on the conditional probability and th_s on the contextual similarity, respectively. Figure 10 shows the results when the full sizes of bilingual corpora are used. When the pairs were filtered only with th_p, the number of paraphrase pairs in P_{Hvst} decreased more slowly than that of P_{Seed} according to the increase of the threshold value. This is a benefit from our generalization and instantiation method. The same paraphrase pattern is often induced from more than one paraphrase pair in P_{Seed}. Thus, as long as at least one of them has a probability higher than the given threshold value, corresponding novel paraphrases can be harvested.

On the other hand, as a results of assessing each individual paraphrase pair by the contextual similarity, many pairs in P_{Hvst}, which are supposed to be incorrect instances of their corresponding pattern, are filtered out by a larger threshold value for th_s. In contrast, many pairs in P_{Seed} have a relatively high similarity, e.g., 40% of all pairs have similarity higher than 0.4. This indicates the quality of P_{Seed} is highly guaranteed by the shared translations.

5 Human Evaluation of Quality

To confirm that the quality of P_{Hvst} is sufficiently high, we carried out a substitution test.

First, by substituting sub-sentential paraphrases to existing sentences in a given test corpus, pairs of slightly different sentences were automatically generated. For instance, by applying "looks like" ⇒ "resembles" to (5), (6) was generated.

(5) The roof *looks like* a prehistoric lizard's spine.

(6) The roof *resembles* a prehistoric lizard's spine.

Human evaluators were then asked to score each pair of an original sentence and a paraphrased sentence with the following two 5-point scale grades proposed by Callison-Burch (2008):

Grammaticality: whether the paraphrased sentence is grammatical (1: horrible, 5: perfect)

Meaning: whether the meaning of the original sentence is properly retained by the paraphrased sentence (1: totally different, 5: equivalent)

To make results more consistent and reduce the human labor, evaluators were asked to rate at the same time several paraphrases for the same source phrase. For instance, given a source sentence (5), the evaluators might be given the following sentences in addition to a paraphrased sentence (6).

(7) The roof *seems like* a prehistoric lizard's spine.

(8) The roof *would look like* a prehistoric lizard's spine.

In this experiment, we showed five paraphrases per source phrase, assuming that evaluators would get confused if too large a number of paraphrase candidates were presented at the same time.

5.1 Data for Evaluation

As in previous work (Callison-Burch, 2008; Chan et al., 2011), we evaluated paraphrases acquired from the Europarl corpus on news sentences. Paraphrase examples were automatically generated from the English part of WMT 2008-2011 "newstest" data (10,050 unique sentences) by applying the union of P_{Seed} and P_{Hvst} of the Europarl setting (19.3M paraphrases for 5.95M phrases).

On the other hand, paraphrases acquired from patent documents are much more difficult to evaluate due to the following reasons. First, they may be too domain-specific to be of any use in general areas such as news sentences. However, conducting an in-domain evaluation would be difficult without enrolling domain experts. We expect that paraphrases from a domain can be used safely in that domain. Nevertheless, deciding under what circumstances they can be used safely in another domain is an interesting research question.

To reduce the human labor for the evaluation, sentences were restricted to those with moderate length: 10-30 words, which are expected to provide sufficient but succinct context. To propose multiple paraphrase candidates at the same time, we also restricted phrases to be paraphrased (LHS phrases) to those having at least five paraphrases including ones from P_{Hvst}. This resulted in 60,421 paraphrases for 988 phrase tokens (353 unique phrases).

Finally, we randomly sampled 80 unique phrase tokens and five unique paraphrases for each phrase token (400 examples in total), and asked six people having a high level of English proficiency to evaluate them. Inter-evaluator agreement was calculated from five different pairs of evaluators, each judging the same 10 examples. The remaining 350 examples were divided into six chunks of slightly unequal length, with each chunk being judged by one of the six evaluators.

		5-point		Binary		
	n	G	M	G	M	Both
P_{Seed}	55	4.60	4.35	0.85	0.93	0.78
P_{Hvst}	295	4.22	3.35	0.74	0.67	0.55
Total	350	4.28	3.50	0.76	0.71	0.58

Table 1: Avg. score and precision of binary classification.

5.2 Results

Table 1 shows the average of the original 5-point scale scores and the percentage of examples that are judged correct based on a binary judgment (Callison-Burch, 2008): an example is considered to be correct iff the grammaticality score is 4 or above and/or the meaning score is 3 or above. Paraphrases based on P_{Seed} achieved a quite high performance in both grammaticality ("G") and meaning ("M") in part because of the effectiveness of our filtering techniques. The performance of paraphrases drawn from P_{Hvst} was reasonably high and similar to the scores 0.68 for grammaticality, 0.61 for meaning, and 0.55 for both, of the best model reported in (Callison-Burch, 2008), although it was inferior to P_{Seed}.

Despite the fact that all of our evaluators had a high-level command of English, the agreement was not very high. This was true even when the collected scores were mapped into binary classes. In this case, the κ values (Cohen, 1960) for each criterion were 0.45 and 0.45, respectively, which indicate the agreement was "fair". To obtain a better κ value, the criteria for grading will need to be improved. However, we think that was not too low either[8].

The most promising way for improving the quality of P_{Hvst} is to ensure that paraphrase patterns cover only legitimate paraphrases. We investigated this by filtering the manually scored paraphrase examples with two thresholds for cleaning seed paraphrases P_{Seed}: th_p on the conditional probability estimated using the bilingual parallel corpus and th_s on the contextual similarity in the monolingual non-parallel corpus. Figure 11 shows the average score of the examples whose corresponding paraphrase is obtainable with the given threshold values. Note that the points in the figure with higher threshold values are less reliable than the others, because filtering reduces the number of the manually scored examples

[8]Note that Callison-Burch (2008) might possibly underestimate the chance agreement and overestimate the κ values, because the distribution of human scores would not be uniform.

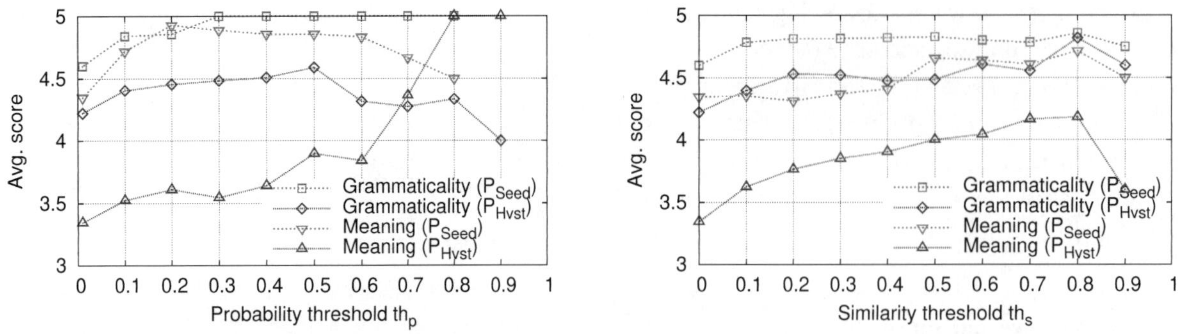

Figure 11: Average score of paraphrase examples against threshold values.
(left: probability-based ($0.01 \leq th_p \leq 0.9, th_s = \epsilon$), right: similarity-based ($\epsilon \leq th_s \leq 0.9, th_p = 0.01$))
The points with higher threshold values are less reliable than the others,
because filtering reduces the number of the manually scored examples used to calculate scores.

used to calculate scores. Nevertheless, it indicates that better filtering of P_{Seed} with higher threshold values is likely to produce a better-quality set of paraphrases P_{Hvst}. For instance, an inappropriate paraphrase pattern (9a) was excluded with $th_p = 0.1$ or $th_s = 0.1$, while correct ones (9b) and (9c) remained even when a large threshold value is used.

(9) a. "X years" $\Rightarrow$ "turn X"
b. "X supplied" $\Rightarrow$ "X provided"
c. "main X" $\Rightarrow$ "most significant X"

Kendall's correlation coefficient τ_B (Kendall, 1938) between the contextual similarity and each of the human scores were 0.24 for grammaticality and 0.21 for meaning, respectively. Although they are rivaling the best results reported in (Chan et al., 2011), i.e., 0.24 and 0.21, similarity metrics should be further investigated to realize a more accurate filtering.

6 Conclusion

In this paper, we exploited general patterns underlying paraphrases to acquire automatically a large number of high-quality paraphrase pairs using both bilingual parallel and monolingual non-parallel corpora. Experiments using two sets of corpora demonstrated that our method is able to leverage information in a relatively small bilingual parallel corpus to exploit large amounts of information in a relatively large monolingual non-parallel corpus. Human evaluation through a paraphrase substitution test revealed that the acquired paraphrases are generally of reasonable quality. Our original objective was to extract from monolingual corpora a large **quantity** of paraphrases whose **quality** is as high as that of paraphrases from bilingual parallel corpora. We have met the quantity part of the objective, and have come close to meeting the quality part.

There are three main directions for our future work. First, we intend to carry out in-depth analyses of the proposed method. For instance, while we showed that the performance of phrase substitution could be improved by removing noisy seed paraphrases, this also strongly affected the quantity. We will therefore investigate similarity metrics in our future work. Other interesting questions related to the work presented here are, as mentioned in Section 4.2, exploitation of patterns with more than one variable, learning curve experiments with different amounts of monolingual data, and comparison of in-domain and general-purpose monolingual corpora. Second, we have an interest in exploiting sophisticated paraphrase patterns; for instance, by inducing patterns hierarchically (recursively) and incorporating lexical resources such as those exemplified in (4). Finally, the developed paraphrase collection will be attested through applications, such as sentence compression (Cohn and Lapata, 2008; Ganitkevitch et al., 2011) and machine translation (Callison-Burch et al., 2006; Marton et al., 2009).

Acknowledgments

We are deeply grateful to our colleagues at National Research Council Canada, especially George Foster, Eric Joanis, and Samuel Larkin, for their technical support. The first author is currently a JSPS (the Japan Society for the Promotion of Science) Post-doctoral Fellow for Research Abroad.

References

Colin Bannard and Chris Callison-Burch. 2005. Paraphrasing with bilingual parallel corpora. In *Proceedings of the 43rd Annual Meeting of the Association for Computational Linguistics (ACL)*, pages 597–604.

Regina Barzilay and Kathleen R. McKeown. 2001. Extracting paraphrases from a parallel corpus. In *Proceedings of the 39th Annual Meeting of the Association for Computational Linguistics (ACL)*, pages 50–57.

Regina Barzilay and Lillian Lee. 2003. Learning to paraphrase: An unsupervised approach using multiple-sequence alignment. In *Proceedings of the 2003 Human Language Technology Conference and the North American Chapter of the Association for Computational Linguistics (HLT-NAACL)*, pages 16–23.

Rahul Bhagat and Deepak Ravichandran. 2008. Large scale acquisition of paraphrases for learning surface patterns. In *Proceedings of the 46th Annual Meeting of the Association for Computational Linguistics (ACL)*, pages 161–170.

Chris Callison-Burch, Philipp Koehn, and Miles Osborne. 2006. Improved statistical machine translation using paraphrases. In *Proceedings of the Human Language Technology Conference of the North American Chapter of the Association for Computational Linguistics (HLT-NAACL)*, pages 17–24.

Chris Callison-Burch. 2008. Syntactic constraints on paraphrases extracted from parallel corpora. In *Proceedings of the 2008 Conference on Empirical Methods in Natural Language Processing (EMNLP)*, pages 196–205.

Tsz Ping Chan, Chris Callison-Burch, and Benjamin Van-Durme. 2011. Reranking bilingually extracted paraphrases using monolingual distributional similarity. In *Proceedings of the Workshop on Geometrical Models of Natual Language Semantics (GEMS)*, pages 33–42.

David L. Chen and William B. Dolan. 2011. Collecting highly parallel data for paraphrase evaluation. In *Proceedings of the 49th Annual Meeting of the Association for Computational Linguistics (ACL)*, pages 190–200.

Jacob Cohen. 1960. A coefficient of agreement for nominal scales. *Educational and Psychological Measurement*, 20(1):37–46.

Trevor Cohn and Mirella Lapata. 2008. Sentence compression beyond word deletion. In *Proceedings of the 22nd International Conference on Computational Linguistics (COLING)*, pages 137–144.

Michael Denkowski and Alon Lavie. 2011. Meteor 1.3: Automatic metric for reliable optimization and evaluation of machine translation systems. In *Proceedings of the 6th Workshop on Statistical Machine Translation (WMT)*, pages 85–91.

Bill Dolan, Chris Quirk, and Chris Brockett. 2004. Unsupervised construction of large paraphrase corpora: Exploiting massively parallel news sources. In *Proceedings of the 20th International Conference on Computational Linguistics (COLING)*, pages 350–356.

Jinhua Du, Jie Jiang, and Andy Way. 2010. Facilitating translation using source language paraphrase lattices. In *Proceedings of the 2010 Conference on Empirical Methods in Natural Language Processing (EMNLP)*, pages 420–429.

Atsushi Fujii, Masao Utiyama, Mikio Yamamoto, Takehito Utsuro, Terumasa Ehara, Hiroshi Echizen-ya, and Sayori Shimohata. 2010. Overview of the patent translation task at the NTCIR-8 workshop. In *Proceedings of NTCIR-8 Workshop Meeting*, pages 371–376.

Atsushi Fujita, Shuhei Kato, Naoki Kato, and Satoshi Sato. 2007. A compositional approach toward dynamic phrasal thesaurus. In *Proceedings of the ACL-PASCAL Workshop on Textual Entailment and Paraphrasing (WTEP)*, pages 151–158.

Juri Ganitkevitch, Chris Callison-Burch, Courtney Napoles, and Benjamin Van Durme. 2011. Learning sentential paraphrases from bilingual parallel corpora for text-to-text generation. In *Proceedings of the 2011 Conference on Empirical Methods in Natural Language Processing (EMNLP)*, pages 1168–1179.

Zellig Harris. 1968. *Mathematical Structures of Language*. John Wiley & Sons.

Chikara Hashimoto, Kentaro Torisawa, Stijn De Saeger, Jun'ichi Kazama, and Sadao Kurohashi. 2011. Extracting paraphrases from definition sentences on the Web. In *Proceedings of the 49th Annual Meeting of the Association for Computational Linguistics (ACL)*, pages 1087–1097.

Christian Jacquemin. 1999. Syntagmatic and paradigmatic representations of term variation. In *Proceedings of the 37th Annual Meeting of the Association for Computational Linguistics (ACL)*, pages 341–348.

Howard Johnson, Joel Martin, George Foster, and Roland Kuhn. 2007. Improving translation quality by discarding most of the phrasetable. In *Proceedings of the 2007 Conference on Empirical Methods in Natural Language Processing and Computational Natural Language Learning (EMNLP-CoNLL)*, pages 967–975.

Maurice Kendall. 1938. A new measure of rank correlation. *Biometrika*, 30(1-2):81–93.

Philipp Koehn, Franz Josef Och, and Daniel Marcu. 2003. Statistical phrase-based translation. In *Proceedings of the 2003 Human Language Technology Conference and the North American Chapter of the Asso-*

ciation for Computational Linguistics (*HLT-NAACL*), pages 48–54.

Philipp Koehn. 2009. *Statistical Machine Translation*. Cambridge University Press.

Stanley Kok and Chris Brockett. 2010. Hitting the right paraphrases in good time. In *Proceedings of Human Language Technologies: The 2010 Annual Conference of the North American Chapter of the Association for Computational Linguistics* (*NAACL-HLT*), pages 145–153.

Dekang Lin and Patrick Pantel. 2001. Discovery of inference rules for question answering. *Natural Language Engineering*, 7(4):343–360.

Nitin Madnani and Bonnie J. Dorr. 2010. Generating phrasal and sentential paraphrases: A survey of data-driven methods. *Computational Linguistics*, 36(3):341–387.

Yuval Marton, Chris Callison-Burch, and Philip Resnik. 2009. Improved statistical machine translation using monolingually-derived paraphrases. In *Proceedings of the 2009 Conference on Empirical Methods in Natural Language Processing* (*EMNLP*), pages 381–390.

Yuval Marton, Ahmed El Kholy, and Nizar Habash. 2011. Filtering antonymous, trend-contrasting, and polarity-dissimilar distributional paraphrases for improving statistical machine translation. In *Proceedings of the 6th Workshop on Statistical Machine Translation* (*WMT*), pages 237–249.

Aurélien Max. 2010. Example-based paraphrasing for improved phrase-based statistical machine translation. In *Proceedings of the 2010 Conference on Empirical Methods in Natural Language Processing* (*EMNLP*), pages 656–666.

Marius Paşca and Péter Dienes. 2005. Aligning needles in a haystack: Paraphrase acquisition across the Web. In *Proceedings of the 2nd International Joint Conference on Natural Language Processing* (*IJCNLP*), pages 119–130.

Bo Pang, Kevin Knight, and Daniel Marcu. 2003. Syntax-based alignment of multiple translations: Extracting paraphrases and generating new sentences. In *Proceedings of the 2003 Human Language Technology Conference and the North American Chapter of the Association for Computational Linguistics* (*HLT-NAACL*), pages 102–109.

Fatiha Sadat, Howard Johnson, Akakpo Agbago, George Foster, Roland Kuhn, Joel Martin, and Aaron Tikuisis. 2005. PORTAGE: A phrase-based machine translation system. In *Proceedings of the ACL Workshop on Building and Using Parallel Texts*, pages 129–132.

Yusuke Shinyama, Satoshi Sekine, Kiyoshi Sudo, and Ralph Grishman. 2002. Automatic paraphrase acquisition from news articles. In *Proceedings of the 2002 Human Language Technology Conference* (*HLT*).

Idan Szpektor and Ido Dagan. 2008. Learning entailment rules for unary templates. In *Proceedings of the 22nd International Conference on Computational Linguistics* (*COLING*). 849-856.

Sander Wubben, Antal van den Bosch, Emiel Krahmer, and Erwin Marsi. 2009. Clustering and matching headlines for automatic paraphrase acquisition. In *Proceedings of the 12th European Workshop on Natural Language Generation*, pages 122–125.

Shiqi Zhao, Haifeng Wang, Ting Liu, and Sheng Li. 2009. Extracting paraphrase patterns from bilingual parallel corpora. *Natural Language Engineering*, 15(4):503–526.

Concurrent Acquisition of Word Meaning and Lexical Categories

Afra Alishahi
a.alishahi@uvt.nl
Communication and Information Sciences
Tilburg University, The Netherlands

Grzegorz Chrupała
gchrupala@lsv.uni-saarland.de
Spoken Language Systems
Saarland University, Germany

Abstract

Learning the meaning of words from ambiguous and noisy context is a challenging task for language learners. It has been suggested that children draw on syntactic cues such as lexical categories of words to constrain potential referents of words in a complex scene. Although the acquisition of lexical categories should be interleaved with learning word meanings, it has not previously been modeled in that fashion. In this paper, we investigate the interplay of word learning and category induction by integrating an LDA-based word class learning module with a probabilistic word learning model. Our results show that the incrementally induced word classes significantly improve word learning, and their contribution is comparable to that of manually assigned part of speech categories.

1 Learning the Meaning of Words

For young learners of a natural language, mapping each word to its correct meaning is a challenging task. Words are often used as part of an utterance rather than in isolation. The meaning of an utterance must be inferred from among numerous possible interpretations that the (usually complex) surrounding scene offers. In addition, the linguistic and visual context in which words are heard and used is often noisy and highly ambiguous. Particularly, many words in a language are polysemous and have different meanings.

Various learning mechanisms have been proposed for word learning. One well-studied mechanism is *cross-situational learning*, a bottom-up strategy based on statistical co-occurrence of words and referents across situations (Quine 1960, Pinker 1989). Several experimental studies have shown that adults and children are sensitive to cross-situational evidence and use this information for mapping words to objects, actions and properties (Smith and Yu 2007, Monaghan and Mattock 2009). A number of computational models have been developed based on this principle, demonstrating that cross-situational learning is a powerful and efficient mechanism for learning the correct mappings between words and meanings from noisy input (e.g. Siskind 1996, Yu 2005, Fazly et al. 2010).

Another potential source of information that can help the learner to constrain the relevant aspects of a scene is the sentential context of a word. It has been suggested that children draw on syntactic cues provided by the linguistic context in order to guide word learning, a hypothesis known as *syntactic bootstrapping* (Gleitman 1990). There is substantial evidence that children are sensitive to the structural regularities of language from a very young age, and that they use these structural cues to find the referent of a novel word (e.g. Naigles and Hoff-Ginsberg 1995, Gertner et al. 2006). In particular, young children have robust knowledge of some of the abstract lexical categories such as nouns and verbs (e.g. Gelman and Taylor 1984, Kemp et al. 2005).

Recent studies have examined the interplay of cross-situational learning and sentence-level learning mechanisms, showing that adult learners of an artificial language can successfully and simultaneously apply cues and constraints from both sources of information when mapping words to their referents (Gillette et al. 1999, Lidz et al. 2010, Koehne and Crocker 2010; 2011). Several computational models have also investigated this interaction by adding manually annotated part-of-speech tags as input to word learning algorithms, and suggesting that integration of lexical categories can boost the performance of a cross-situational model (Yu 2006, Alishahi and Fazly 2010).

However, none of the existing experimental or computational studies have examined the acquisition of word meanings and lexical categories in parallel. They all make the simplifying assumption that *prior* to the onset of word learning, the categorization module has already formed a relatively robust set of lexical categories. This assumption can be justified in the case of adult learners of a second or artificial language. But children's acquisition of categories is most probably interleaved with the acquisition of word meaning, and these two processes must ultimately be studied simultaneously.

In this paper, we investigate concurrent acquisition of word meanings and lexical categories. We use an online version of the LDA algorithm to induce a set of word classes from child-directed speech, and integrate them into an existing probabilistic model of word learning which combines cross-situational evidence with cues from lexical categories. Through a number of simulations of a word learning scenario, we show that our automatically and incrementally induced categories significantly improve the performance of the word learning model, and are closely comparable to a set of gold-standard, manually-annotated part of speech tags.

2 A Word Learning Model

We want to investigate whether lexical categories (i.e. word classes) that are incrementally induced from child-directed speech can improve the performance of a cross-situational word learning model. For this purpose, we use the model of Alishahi and Fazly (2010). This model uses a probabilistic learning algorithm for combining evidence from word–referent co-occurrence statistics and the meanings associated with a set of pre-defined categories. They use child-directed utterances, manually annotated with a small set of part of speech tags, from the Manchester corpus (Theakston et al. 2001) in the CHILDES database (MacWhinney 1995). Their experimental results show that integrating these gold-standard categories into the algorithm boosts its performance over a pure cross-situational version.

The model of Alishahi and Fazly (2010) has the suitable architecture for our goal: it provides an integrated learning mechanism which combines evidence from word-referent co-occurrence with cues from the meaning representation associated with word categories. However, the model has two major shortcomings. First, it assumes that lexical categories are formed and finalized prior to the onset of word learning and that a correct and unique category for a target word can be identified at each point in time, assumptions that are highly unlikely. Second, it does not handle any ambiguity in the meaning of a word. Instead, each word is assumed to have only one correct meaning. Considering the high level of lexical ambiguity in most natural languages, this assumption unreasonably simplifies the word learning problem.

To investigate the plausibility of integrating word and category learning, we use an online algorithm for automatically and incrementally inducing a set of lexical categories. Moreover, we use each word in its original form instead of lemmatizing them, which implies that categories contain different morphological forms of the same word. By applying these changes, we are able to study the contribution of lexical categories to word learning in a more realistic scenario.

Representation of input. The input to the model consists of a sequence of utterances, each paired with a representation of an observed scene. We represent an utterance as a set of words, $U = \{w\}$ (e.g. $\{$*she, went, home, ...*$\}$), and the corresponding scene as a set of semantic features, $S = \{f\}$ (e.g. $\{$ANIMATE, HUMAN, FEMALE, ...$\}$).

Word and category meaning. We represent the meaning of a word as a time-dependent probability distribution $p^{(t)}(\cdot|w)$ over all the semantic features, where $p^{(t)}(f|w)$ is the probability of feature f being associated with word w at time t. In the absence of any prior knowledge, the model assumes a uniform distribution over all features as the meaning of a novel word. Also, a function $\mathrm{cat}^{(t)}(w)$ gives us the category to which a word w in utterance $U^{(t)}$ belongs.

At each point in time, a category c contains a set of word tokens. We assign a meaning to each category as a weighted sum of the meaning learned so far for each of its members, or $p^{(t)}(f|c) = (1/|c|)\sum_{w \in c} p^{(t)}(f|w)$, where $|c|$ is the number of word tokens in c at the current moment.

Learning algorithm. Given an utterance-scene pair $(U^{(t)}, S^{(t)})$ received at time t, the model first calculates an alignment score a for each word $w \in U^{(t)}$ and each semantic feature $f \in S^{(t)}$. A semantic feature can be aligned to a word according to the meaning acquired for that word from previous observations (word-based alignment, or a_w). Alternatively, distributional clues of the word can be used to determine its category, and the semantic features can be aligned to the word according to the meaning associated to its category (category-based alignment, or a_c). We combine these two sources of evidence when estimating an alignment score:

$$a(w|f, U^{(t)}, S^{(t)}) = \lambda(w) \times a_w(w|f, U^{(t)}, S^{(t)}) + (1 - \lambda(w)) \times a_c(w|f, U^{(t)}, S^{(t)}) \quad (1)$$

where the word-based and category-based alignment scores are estimated based on the acquired meanings of the word and its category, respectively:

$$a_w(w|f, U^{(t)}, S^{(t)}) = \frac{p^{(t-1)}(f|w)}{\sum_{w_k \in \mathrm{U}^{(t)}} p^{(t-1)}(f|w_k)}$$

$$a_c(w|f, U^{(t)}, S^{(t)}) = \frac{p^{(t-1)}(f|\mathrm{cat}(w))}{\sum_{w_k \in \mathrm{U}^{(t)}} p^{(t-1)}(f|\mathrm{cat}(w_k))}$$

The relative contribution of the word-based versus the category-based alignment is determined by the weight function $\lambda(w)$. Cross-situational evidence is a reliable cue for frequent words; on the other hand, the category-based score is most informative when the model encounters a low-frequency word (See Alishahi and Fazly (2010) for a full analysis of the frequency effect). Therefore, we define $\lambda(w)$ as a function of the frequency of the word $n(w)$:

$$\lambda(w) = n(w)/(n(w) + 1)$$

Once an alignment score is calculated for each word $w \in U^{(t)}$ and each feature $f \in S^{(t)}$, the model revises the meanings of all the words in $U^{(t)}$ and their corresponding categories as follows:

$$\mathrm{assoc}^{(t)}(w, f) = \mathrm{assoc}^{(t-1)}(w, f) + a(w|f, \mathrm{U}^{(t)}, \mathrm{S}^{(t)})$$

where $\mathrm{assoc}^{(t-1)}(w, f)$ is zero if w and f have not co-occurred before. These association scores are then used to update the meaning of the words in the current input:

$$p^{(t)}(f|w) = \frac{\mathrm{assoc}^{(t)}(f, w)}{\sum_{f_j \in \mathcal{F}} \mathrm{assoc}^{(t)}(f_j, w)} \quad (2)$$

where $\mathcal{F}$ is the set of all features seen so far. We use a smoothed version of this formula to accommodate noisy or rare input. This process is repeated for all the input pairs, one at a time.

Uniform categories. Adding the category-based alignment as a new factor to Eqn. (1) might imply that the role of categories in this model is nothing more than smoothing the cross-situational-based alignment of words and referents. In order to investigate this issue, we use the following alignment formula as an informed baseline in our experiments, where we replace $a_c(\cdot|f, U^{(t)}, S^{(t)})$ with a uniform distribution:[1]

$$a(w|f, U^{(t)}, S^{(t)}) = \lambda(w) \times a_w(w|f, U^{(t)}, S^{(t)}) + (1 - \lambda(w)) \times \frac{1}{|U^{(t)}|} \quad (3)$$

where $a_w(w|f, U^{(t)}, S^{(t)})$ and $\lambda(w)$ are estimated as before. In our experiments in Section 4, we refer to this baseline as the 'uniform' condition.

3 Online induction of word classes with LDA

Empirical findings suggest that young children form their knowledge of abstract categories, such as verbs, nouns, and adjectives, gradually (e.g. Gelman and Taylor 1984, Kemp et al. 2005). In addition, several unsupervised computational models have been proposed for inducing categories of words which resemble part-of-speech categories, by

[1]We thank an anonymous reviewers for suggesting this condition as an informed baseline.

drawing on distributional properties of their context (see for example Redington et al. 1998, Clark 2000, Mintz 2003, Parisien et al. 2008, Chrupała and Alishahi 2010). However, explicit accounts of how such categories can be integrated in a cross-situational model of word learning have been rare. Here we adopt an online version of the model proposed in Chrupała (2011), a method of soft word class learning using Latent Dirichlet Allocation. The approach is much more efficient than the commonly used alternative (Brown clustering, (Brown et al. 1992)) while at the same time matching or outperforming it when the word classes are used as automatically learned features for supervised learning of various language understanding tasks. Here we adopt this model as our approach to learning lexical categories.

In Section 3.1 we describe the LDA model for word classes; in Section 3.2 we discuss the online Gibbs sampler we use for inference.

3.1 Word class learning with LDA

Latent Dirichlet Allocation (LDA) was introduced by Blei et al. (2003) and is most commonly used for modeling the topic structure in document collections. It is a generative, probabilistic hierarchical Bayesian model that induces a set of latent variables, which correspond to the topics. The topics themselves are multinomial distributions over words.

The generative structure of the LDA model is the following:

$$\begin{aligned} \phi_k &\sim \text{Dirichlet}(\beta), & k &\in [1, K] \\ \theta_d &\sim \text{Dirichlet}(\alpha), & d &\in [1, D] \\ z_{n_d} &\sim \text{Categorical}(\theta_d), & n_d &\in [1, N_d] \\ w_{n_d} &\sim \text{Categorical}(\phi_{z_{n_d}}), & n_d &\in [1, N_d] \end{aligned} \quad (4)$$

Chrupała (2011) reinterprets the LDA model in terms of word classes as follows: K is the number of classes, D is the number of unique word types, N_d is the number of context features (such as right or left neighbor) associated with word type d, z_{n_d} is the class of word type d in the n_d^{th} context, and w_{n_d} is the n_d^{th} context feature of word type d. Hyperparameters α and β control the sparseness of the vectors θ_d and ϕ_k.

Wordtype	Features		
How	do_R		
do	How_L	you_R	you_L
you	do_L	do_R	

Table 1: Matrix of context features

1.8M words (CHILDES)		100M words (BNC)	
train	car	can	will
give	bring	June	March
shoes	clothes	man	woman
book	hole	black	white
monkey	rabbit	business	language

Table 2: Most similar word pairs

As an example consider the small corpus consisting of the single sentence *How do you do*. The rows in Table 1 show the features $w_1 \dots w_{N_d}$ for each word type d if we use each word's left and right neighbors as features, and subscript words with $_L$ and $_R$ to indicate left and right.

After inference, the θ_d parameters correspond to word class probability distributions given a word type while the ϕ_k correspond to feature distributions given a word class: the model provides a probabilistic representation for word types independently of their context, and also for contexts independently of the word type.

Probabilistic, *soft* word classes are more expressive than hard categories. First, they make it easy and efficient to express shared ambiguities: Chrupała (2011) gives an example of words used as either first names or surnames, and this shared ambiguity is reflected in the similarity of their word class distributions. Second, with soft word classes it becomes easy to express graded similarity between words: as an example, Table 2 shows a random selection out of the 100 most similar word pairs according to the Jensen-Shannon divergence between their word class distributions, according to a word class model with 25 classes induced from (i) 1.8 million words of the CHILDES corpus or (ii) 100 million word of the BNC corpus. The similarities were measured between each of the 1000 most frequent CHILDES or BNC words.

3.2 Online Gibbs sampling for LDA

There have been a number of attempts to develop online inference algorithms for topic modeling with LDA. A simple modification of the standard Gibbs sampler (**o-LDA**) was proposed by Song et al. (2005) and Banerjee and Basu (2007).

Canini et al. (2009) experiment with three sampling algorithms for online topic inference: (i) **o-LDA**, (ii) incremental Gibbs sampler, and (iii) a particle filter. Only **o-LDA** is truly online in the sense that it does not revisit previously seen documents. The other two, the incremental Gibbs sampler and the particle filter, keep seen documents and periodically resample them. In Canini et al.'s experiments all of the online algorithms perform worse than the standard batch Gibbs sampler on a document clustering task.

Hoffman et al. (2010) develop an online version of the variational Bayes (VB) optimization method for inference for topic modeling with LDA. Their method achieves good empirical results compared to batch VB as measured by perplexity on held-out data, especially when used with large minibatch sizes.

Online VB for LDA is appropriate when streaming documents: with online VB documents are represented as word count tables. In our scenario where we apply LDA to modeling word classes we need to process context features from sentences arriving in a stream: i.e. we need to sample entries from a table like Table 1 in order of arrival rather than row by row. This means that online VB is not directly applicable to online word-class induction.

However it also means that one issue with **o-LDA** identified by Canini et al. (2009) is ameliorated. When sampling in a topic modeling setting, documents are unique and are never seen again. Thus, the topics associated with old documents get *stale* and need to be periodically *rejuvenated* (i.e. resampled). This is the reason why the incremental Gibbs sampler and the particle filter algorithms in Canini et al. (2009) need to keep old documents around and cannot run in a true online fashion. Since for word class modeling we stream context features as they arrive, we will continue to see features associated with the seen word types, and will automatically resample their class assignments. In exploratory experiments we have seen that this narrows the performance gap between the **o-LDA** sampler and the batch collapsed Gibbs sampler.

We present our version of the **o-LDA** sampler in Algorithm 1. For each incoming sentence t we run J passes of sampling, updating the counts tables after each sampling step. We sample the class assignment z_{t_i} for feature w_{t_i} according to:

$$P(z_t|\mathbf{z}_{t-1}, \mathbf{w}_t, \mathbf{d}_t) \propto \frac{(n_{t-1}^{z_t,d_t} + \alpha) \times (n_{t-1}^{z_t,w_t} + \beta)}{\sum_{j=1}^{V_{t-1}} n_{t-1}^{z_t,w_j} + \beta}, \tag{5}$$

where $n_t^{z,d}$ stands for the number of times class z co-occurred with word type d up to step t, and similarly $n_t^{z,w}$ is the number of times feature w was assigned to class z. V_t is the number of unique features seen up to step t, while α and β are the LDA hyperparameters. There are two differences between the original **o-LDA** and our version: we do not initialize the algorithm with a batch run over a prefix of the data, and we allow more than one sampling pass per sentence.[2] Exploratory experiments have shown that batch initialization is unnecessary, and that multiple passes typically improve the quality of the induced word classes.

Algorithm 1 Online Gibbs sampler for word class induction with LDA

```
for t = 1 → ∞ do
    for j = 1 → J do
        for i = 1 → I_t do
            sample z_{t_i} ~ P(z_{t_i} | z_{t_i−1}, w_{t_i}, d_{t_i})
            increment n_t^{z_{t_i},w_{t_i}} and n_t^{z_{t_i},d_{t_i}}
```

Figure 1 shows the top 10 words for each of the 10 word classes induced with our online Gibbs sampler from 1.8 million words of CHILDES. Similarly, Figure 2 shows the top 10 words for 5 randomly chosen topics out of 50, learned online from 100 million words of the BNC.

The topics are relatively coherent and at these levels of granularity express mostly part of speech and subcategorization frame information.

Note that for each word class we show the words most frequently assigned to it while Gibbs sampling.

[2] Note that we do not allow multiple passes over the stream of sentences. Rather, while processing the current sentence, we allow the words in this sentence to be sampled more than once.

do are have can not go put did get play
is that it what not there he was where put
you not I the we what it they your a
to you we and I will not can it on
it a that the not he this right got she
are do is have on in can want did going
one I not shall there then you are we it
is in are on oh with and of have do
the a your of that it this some not very
going want bit go have look got will at little

Figure 1: Top 10 words for 10 classes learned from CHILDES

I you he it they we she , You He
a the more some all no The other I two
as if when that where how because If before what
was is 's had , has are would did said
the his her their this an that its your my

Figure 2: Top 10 words of 5 randomly chosen classes learned from BNC

Since we are dealing with soft classes, most word-types have non-zero assignment probabilities for many classes. Thus frequently occurring words such as *not* will typically be listed for several classes.

4 Evaluation

4.1 Experimental setup

As training data, we extract utterances from the Manchester corpus (Theakston et al. 2001) in the CHILDES database (MacWhinney 1995), a corpus that contains transcripts of conversations with children between the ages of 1 year, 8 months and 3 years. We use the mother's speech from transcripts of 12 children (henceforth referred to by children's names).

We run word class induction while simultaneously outputting the highest scoring word-class label for each word: for a new sentence, we sample class assignments for each feature (doing J passes), update the counts, and then for each word d_{t_i} output the highest scoring class label according to $\operatorname{argmax}_z n_t^{z,d_{t_i}}$ (where $n_t^{z,d_{t_i}}$ stands for the number of times class z co-occurred with word type d_{t_i} up to step t).

During development we ran the online word class induction module on data for Aran, Becky, Carl and Anne and then started the word learning module for the Anne portion while continuing inducing categories. We then evaluated word learning on Anne. We chose the parameters of the word class induction module based on those development results: $\sum_{1=1}^{K} \alpha = 10$, $\beta = 0.1$, $K = 10$ and $J = 20$.

We used cross-validation for the final evaluation. For each of six data files (Anne, Aran, Becky, Carl, Dominic and Gail), we ran word-class induction on the whole corpus with the chosen file last, and then started applying the word-learning algorithm on this last chosen file (while continuing with category induction). We evaluated how well word meanings were learned in those six cases.

We follow Alishahi and Fazly (2010) in the construction of the input. We need a semantic representation paired with each utterance. Such a representation is not available from the corpus and has to be constructed. We automatically construct a gold lexicon for all nouns and verbs in this corpus as follows. For each word, we extract all hypernyms for its first sense in the appropriate (verb or noun) hierarchy in WordNet (Fellbaum 1998), and add the first word in the synset of each hypernym to the set of semantic features for the target word. For verbs, we also extract features from VerbNet (Kipper et al. 2006). A small subset of words (pronouns and frequent quantifiers) are also manually added. This lexicon represents the *true* meaning of each word, and is used in generating the scene representations in the input and in evaluation.

For each utterance in the input corpus, we form the union of the feature representations of all its words. Words not found in the lexicon (i.e. for which we could not extract a semantic representation from WordNet and VerbNet) are removed from the utterance (only for the word learning module).

In order to simulate the high level of noise that children receive from their environment, we follow Alishahi and Fazly (2010) and pair each utterance with a combination of its own scene representation and the scene representation for the following utterance. This decision was based on the intuition that consequent utterances are more likely to be about re-

Utterance:	{	*mommy, ate, broccoli* }
Scene:	{	ANIMATE, HUMAN, ...,
		CONSUMPTION, ACTION, ...
		BROCCOLI, VEGETABLE, ...
		PLATE, OBJECT, ... }

Figure 3: A sample input item to the word learning model

Category	Avg. MAP	Std. Dev.
None	0.626	0.032
Uniform	0.633	0.032
LDA	0.659	0.029
POS	0.672	0.030

Table 3: Final Mean Average Precision scores

lated topics and scenes. This results in a (roughly) 200% ambiguity. In addition, we remove the meaning of one random word from the scene representation of every second utterance in an attempt to simulate cases where the referent of an uttered word is not within the perception field (such as 'daddy is not home yet'). A sample utterance and its corresponding scene are shown in Figure 3.

As mentioned before, many words in our input corpus are polysemous. For such words, we extract different sets of features depending on their manually tagged part of speech and keep them in the lexicon (e.g. the lexicon contains two different entries for *set:N* and *set:V*). When constructing a scene representation for an utterance which contains an ambiguous word, we choose the correct sense from our lexicon according to the word's part of speech tag in Manchester corpus.

In the experiments reported in the next section, we assess the performance of our model on learning words at each point in time: for each target word, we compare its set of features in the lexicon with its probability distribution over the semantic features that the model has learned. We use mean average precision (MAP) to measure how well $p^{(t)}(\cdot|w)$ ranks the features of w.

4.2 Learning curves

To understand whether our categories contribute to learning of word–meaning mappings, we compare the pattern of word learning over time in four conditions. The first condition represents our baseline, in which we do not use category-based alignment in the word learning model by setting $\lambda(w) = 1$ in Eqn. (1). In the second condition we use a set of uniformly distributed categories for alignment, as estimated by Eqn. (3) on page 3 (this condition is introduced to examine whether categories act as more than a simple smoothing factor in the alignment process.) In the third condition we use the categories induced by online LDA in the word learning model. The fourth condition represents the performance ceiling, in which we use the pre-defined and manually annotated part of speech categories from the Manchester corpus.

Table 3 shows the average and the standard deviation of the *final* MAP scores across the six datasets, for the four conditions (no categories, uniform categories, LDA categories and gold part-of-speech tags). The differences between LDA and None, and between LDA and Uniform are statistically significant according to the paired t test ($p < 0.01$), while the difference between LDA and POS is not ($p = 0.16$).

Figure 4 shows the learning curves in each condition, averaged over the six splits explained in the previous section. The top panel shows the average learning curve over the minimum number of sentences across the six sub-corpora (8800 sentences). The curves show that our LDA categories significantly improve the performance of the model over both baselines. That means that using these categories can improve word learning compared to not using them and relying on cross-situational evidence alone. Moreover, LDA-induced categories are not merely acting as a smoothing function the way the 'uniform' categories are. Our results show that they are bringing relevant information to the task at hand, that is, improving word learning by using the sentential context. In fact, this improvement is comparable to the improvement achieved by integrating the 'gold-standard' POS categories.

The middle and bottom panels of Figure 4 zoom in on shorter time spans (5000 and 1000 sentences, respectively). These diagrams suggest that the pattern of improvement over baseline is relatively constant, even at very early stages of learning. In fact, once the model receives enough input data, cross-situational evidence becomes stronger (since fewer words in the input are encountered for the first time) and the contribution of the categories becomes less significant.

4.3 Class granularity

In Figure 5 we show the influence of the number of word classes used on the performance in word learning. It is evident that in the range between 5 to 20 classes the performance of the word learning module is quite stable and insensitive to the exact class granularity. Even with only 5 classes the model can still roughly distinguish noun-like words from verb-like words from pronoun-like words, and this will help learn the meaning elements derived from the higher levels of WordNet hierarchy. Notwithstanding that, ideally we would like to avoid having to pre-specify the number of classes for the word class induction module: we thus plan to investigate non-parametric models such as Hierarchical Dirichlet Process for this purpose.

5 Related Work

This paper investigates the interplay between two language learning tasks which have so far been studied in isolation: the acquisition of lexical categories from distributional clues, and learning the mapping between words and meanings. Previous models have shown that lexical categories can be learned from unannotated text, mainly drawing on distributional properties of words (e.g. Redington et al. 1998, Clark 2000, Mintz 2003, Parisien et al. 2008, Chrupała and Alishahi 2010).

Independently, several computational models have exploited cross-situational evidence in learning the correct mappings between words and meanings, using rule-based inference (Siskind 1996), neural networks (Li et al. 2004, Regier 2005), hierarchical Bayesian models (Frank et al. 2007) and probabilistic alignment inspired by machine translation models (Yu 2005, Fazly et al. 2010).

There are only a few existing computational models that explore the role of syntax in word learning. Maurits et al. (2009) investigates the joint acquisition of word meaning and word order using a batch model. This model is tested on an artificial language with a simple first order predicate representation of meaning, and limited built-in possibilities for word

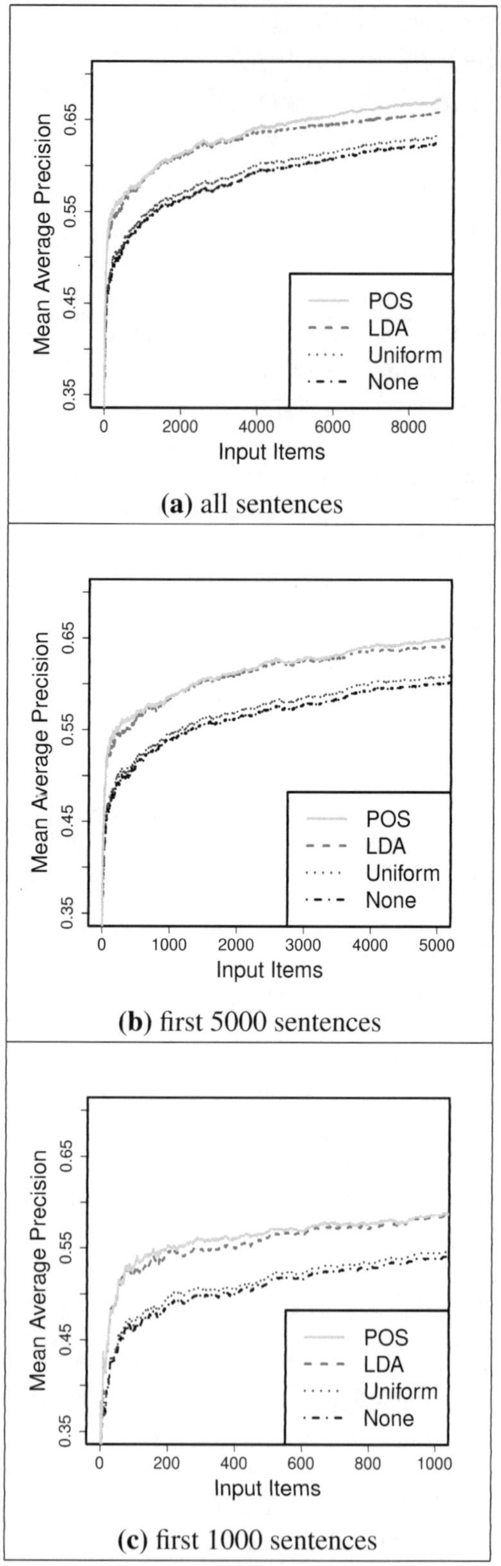

Figure 4: Mean average precision for all observed words at each point in time for four conditions: with gold POS categories, with LDA categories, with uniform categories, and without using categories. Each panel displays a different time span.

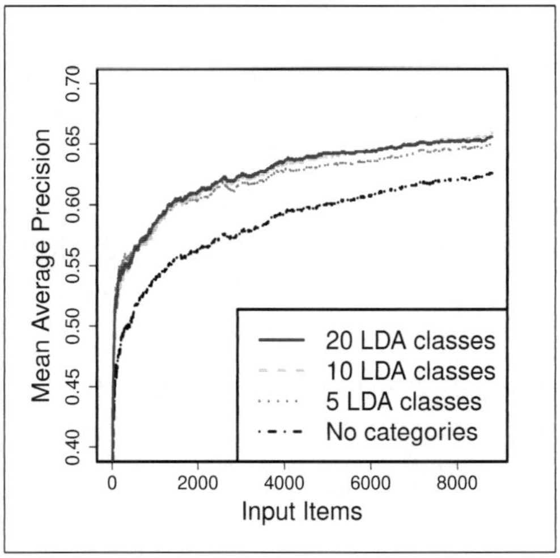

Figure 5: Mean average precision for all observed words at each point in time in four conditions: using online LDA categories of varying numbers of 20, 10 and 5, and without using categories.

order. The model of Niyogi (2002) simulates the mutual bootstrapping effects of syntactic and semantic knowledge in verb learning, that is the use of syntax to aid in inducing the semantics of a verb, and the use of semantics to narrow down possible syntactic frames in which a verb can participate. However, this model relies on manually assigned priors for associations between syntactic and semantic features, and is tested on a toy language with very limited vocabulary and a constrained syntax.

Yu (2006) integrates automatically induced syntactic word categories into his model of cross-situational word learning, showing that they can improve the model's performance. Yu's model also processes input utterances in a batch mode, and its evaluation is limited to situations in which only a coarse distinction between referring words (words that could potentially refer to objects in a scene, e.g. concrete nouns) and non-referring words (words that cannot possibly refer to objects, e.g. function words) is sufficient. It is thus not clear whether information about finer-grained categories (e.g. verbs and nouns) can indeed help word learning in a more naturalistic incremental setting.

On the other hand, the model of Alishahi and Fazly (2010) integrates manually annotated part-of-speech tags into an incremental word learning algorithm, and shows that these tags boost the overall word learning performance, especially for infrequent words.

In a different line of research, a number of models have been proposed which study the acquisition of the link between syntax and semantics within the Combinatory Categorial Grammar (CCG) framework (Briscoe 1997, Villavicencio 2002, Buttery 2006, Kwiatkowski et al. 2012). These approaches set the parameters of a semantic parser on a corpus of utterances paired with a logical form as their meaning.

These models bring in extensive and detailed prior assumptions about the nature of the syntactic representation (i.e. atomic categories such as S and NP, and built-in rules which govern their combination), as well as about the representation of meaning via the formalism of lambda calculus.

This is fundamentally different than the approach taken in this paper, which in comparison only assumes very simple syntactic and semantic representations of syntax. We view word and category learning as stand-alone cognitive tasks with independent representations (word meanings as probabilistic collections of properties or features as opposed to single symbols; categories as sets of word tokens with similar context distribution) and we do not bring in any prior knowledge of specific atomic categories.

6 Conclusion

In this paper, we show the plausibility of using automatically and incrementally induced categories while learning word meanings. Our results suggest that the sentential context that a word appears in across its different uses can be used as a complementary source of guidance for mapping it to its featural meaning representation.

In Section 4 we show that the improvement achieved by our categories is comparable to that gained by integrating gold POS categories. This result is very encouraging, since manually assigned POS tags are typically believed to set the upper bound on the usefulness of category information.

We believe that it automatically induced categories have the potential to do even better: Chrupała and Alishahi (2010) have shown that categories induced from usage data in an unsupervised fashion can be used more effectively than POS categories in a number of tasks. In our experiments here on the development data we observed some improvements over POS categories. This advantage can result from the fact that our categories are more fine-grained (if also more noisy) than POS categories, which sometimes yields more accurate predictions.

One important characteristic of the category induction algorithm we have used in this paper is that it provides a *soft* categorization scheme, where each word is associated with a probability distribution over all categories. In future, we plan to exploit this feature: when estimating the category-based alignment, we can interpolate predictions of multiple categories to which a word belongs, weighted by its probabilities associated with membership in each category.

Acknowledgements

Grzegorz Chrupała was funded by the German Federal Ministry of Education and Research (BMBF) under grant number 01IC10S01O as part of the Software-Cluster project EMERGENT (www.software-cluster.org).

References

Alishahi, A. and Fazly, A. (2010). Integrating Syntactic Knowledge into a Model of Cross-situational Word Learning. In *Proceedings of the 32nd Annual Conference of the Cognitive Science Society*.

Banerjee, A. and Basu, S. (2007). Topic models over text streams: A study of batch and online unsupervised learning. In *SIAM Data Mining*.

Blei, D., Ng, A., and Jordan, M. (2003). Latent dirichlet allocation. *The Journal of Machine Learning Research*, 3:993–1022.

Briscoe, T. (1997). Co-evolution of language and of the language acquisition device. In *Proceedings of the eighth conference on European chapter of the Association for Computational Linguistics*, pages 418–427. Association for Computational Linguistics.

Brown, P. F., Mercer, R. L., Della Pietra, V. J., and Lai, J. C. (1992). Class-based n-gram models of natural language. *Computational Linguistics*, 18(4):467–479.

Buttery, P. (2006). Computational models for first language acquisition. *Computer Laboratory, University of Cambridge, Tech. Rep. UCAM-CLTR-675*.

Canini, K., Shi, L., and Griffiths, T. (2009). Online inference of topics with latent dirichlet allocation. In *Proceedings of the International Conference on Artificial Intelligence and Statistics*.

Chrupała, G. (2011). Efficient induction of probabilistic word classes with LDA. In *International Joint Conference on Natural Language Processing*.

Chrupała, G. and Alishahi, A. (2010). Online Entropy-based Model of Lexical Category Acquisition. In *CoNLL 2010*.

Clark, A. (2000). Inducing syntactic categories by context distribution clustering. In *Proceedings of the 2nd workshop on Learning Language in Logic and the 4th conference on Computational Natural Language Learning*, pages 91–94. Association for Computational Linguistics Morristown, NJ, USA.

Fazly, A., Alishahi, A., and Stevenson, S. (2010). A Probabilistic Computational Model of Cross-Situational Word Learning. *Cognitive Science*, 34(6):1017–1063.

Fellbaum, C., editor (1998). *WordNet, An Electronic Lexical Database*. MIT Press.

Frank, M. C., Goodman, N. D., and Tenenbaum, J. B. (2007). A Bayesian framework for cross-situational word-learning. In *Advances in Neural Information Processing Systems*, volume 20.

Gelman, S. and Taylor, M. (1984). How two-year-old children interpret proper and common names for unfamiliar objects. *Child Development*, pages 1535–1540.

Gertner, Y., Fisher, C., and Eisengart, J. (2006). Learning words and rules: Abstract knowledge of word order in early sentence comprehension. *Psychological Science*, 17(8):684–691.

Gillette, J., Gleitman, H., Gleitman, L., and Lederer, A. (1999). Human simulations of vocabulary learning. *Cognition*, 73(2):135–76.

Gleitman, L. (1990). The structural sources of verb meanings. *Language Acquisition*, 1:135–176.

Hoffman, M., Blei, D., and Bach, F. (2010). Online learning for latent dirichlet allocation. In *Advances in Neural Information Processing Systems*.

Kemp, N., Lieven, E., and Tomasello, M. (2005). Young Children's Knowledge of the" Determiner" and" Adjective" Categories. *Journal of Speech, Language and Hearing Research*, 48(3):592–609.

Kipper, K., Korhonen, A., Ryant, N., and Palmer, M. (2006). Extensive classifications of english verbs. In *Proceedings of the 12th EURALEX International Congress*.

Koehne, J. and Crocker, M. W. (2010). Sentence processing mechanisms influence cross-situational word learning. In *Proceedings of the Annual Conference of the Cognitive Science Society*.

Koehne, J. and Crocker, M. W. (2011). The interplay of multiple mechanisms in word learning. In *Proceedings of the Annual Conference of the Cognitive Science Society*.

Kwiatkowski, T., Goldwater, S., Zettelmoyer, L., and Steedman, M. (2012). A probabilistic model of syntactic and semantic acquisition from child-directed utterances and their meanings. In *Proceedings of the 13th Conference of the European Chapter of the Association for Computational Linguistics*.

Li, P., Farkas, I., and MacWhinney, B. (2004). Early lexical development in a self-organizing neural network. *Neural Networks*, 17:1345–1362.

Lidz, J., Bunger, A., Leddon, E., Baier, R., and Waxman, S. R. (2010). When one cue is better than two: lexical vs . syntactic cues to verb learning. Unpublished manuscript.

MacWhinney, B. (1995). *The CHILDES Project: Tools for Analyzing Talk*. Hillsdale, NJ: Lawrence Erlbaum Associates, second edition.

Maurits, L., Perfors, A. F., and Navarro, D. J. (2009). Joint acquisition of word order and word reference. In *Proceedings of the 31st Annual Conference of the Cognitive Science Society*.

Mintz, T. (2003). Frequent frames as a cue for grammatical categories in child directed speech. *Cognition*, 90(1):91–117.

Monaghan, P. and Mattock, K. (2009). Cross-situational language learning: The effects of grammatical categories as constraints on referential labeling. In *Proceedings of the 31st Annual Conference of the Cognitive Science Society*.

Naigles, L. and Hoff-Ginsberg, E. (1995). Input to Verb Learning: Evidence for the Plausibility of Syntactic Bootstrapping. *Developmental Psychology*, 31(5):827–37.

Niyogi, S. (2002). Bayesian learning at the syntax-semantics interface. In *Proceedings of the 24th annual conference of the Cognitive Science Society*, pages 697–702.

Parisien, C., Fazly, A., and Stevenson, S. (2008). An incremental bayesian model for learning syntactic categories. In *Proceedings of the Twelfth Conference on Computational Natural Language Learning*.

Pinker, S. (1989). *Learnability and Cognition: The Acquisition of Argument Structure*. Cambridge, MA: MIT Press.

Quine, W. (1960). *Word and Object*. Cambridge University Press, Cambridge, MA.

Redington, M., Crater, N., and Finch, S. (1998). Distributional information: A powerful cue for acquiring syntactic categories. *Cognitive Science: A Multidisciplinary Journal*, 22(4):425–469.

Regier, T. (2005). The emergence of words: Attentional learning in form and meaning. *Cognitive Science*, 29:819–865.

Siskind, J. M. (1996). A computational study of cross-situational techniques for learning word-to-meaning mappings. *Cognition*, 61:39–91.

Smith, L. and Yu, C. (2007). Infants rapidly learn words from noisy data via cross-situational statistics. In *Proceedings of the 29th Annual Conference of the Cognitive Science Society*.

Song, X., Lin, C., Tseng, B., and Sun, M. (2005). Modeling and predicting personal information dissemination behavior. In *Proceedings of the eleventh ACM SIGKDD international conference on Knowledge discovery in data mining*, pages 479–488. ACM.

Theakston, A. L., Lieven, E. V., Pine, J. M., and Rowland, C. F. (2001). The role of performance limitations in the acquisition of verb-argument structure: An alternative account. *Journal of Child Language*, 28:127–152.

Villavicencio, A. (2002). The acquisition of a unification-based generalised categorial grammar. In *Proceedings of the Third CLUK Colloquium*, pages 59–66.

Yu, C. (2005). The emergence of links between lexical acquisition and object categorization: A computational study. *Connection Science*, 17(3–4):381–397.

Yu, C. (2006). Learning syntax–semantics mappings to bootstrap word learning. In *Proceedings of the 28th Annual Conference of the Cognitive Science Society*.

Do Neighbours Help? An Exploration of Graph-based Algorithms for Cross-domain Sentiment Classification

Natalia Ponomareva
Statistical Cybermetrics Research group,
University of Wolverhampton, UK
nata.ponomareva@wlv.ac.uk

Mike Thelwall
Statistical Cybermetrics Research group,
University of Wolverhampton, UK
m.thelwall@wlv.ac.uk

Abstract

This paper presents a comparative study of graph-based approaches for cross-domain sentiment classification. In particular, the paper analyses two existing methods: an optimisation problem and a ranking algorithm. We compare these graph-based methods with each other and with the other state-of-the-art approaches and conclude that graph domain representations offer a competitive solution to the domain adaptation problem. Analysis of the best parameters for graph-based algorithms reveals that there are no optimal values valid for all domain pairs and that these values are dependent on the characteristics of corresponding domains.

1 Introduction

The sentiment classification (SC) is an active area of research concerned automatic identification of sentiment strength or valence of texts. SC of product reviews is commercially important and widely researched but it typically needs to be optimised separately for each type of product (i.e. domain). When domain-specific data are absent or insufficient the researchers usually seek solution in semi-supervised, unsupervised or cross-domain approaches. In this paper, we focus on cross-domain methods in order to take advantage of the huge amount of annotated sentiment data available on the Internet. Our aim is to find out to what extent it is possible to learn sentiment phenomena from these data and transfer them to new domains rather than induce them from scratch for each new domain. Previous research has shown that models trained on one data usually give much worse results on another, especially when both data sets belong to completely different domains. This is largely because the sentiment words and their valences depend a lot on the domain where they are expressed. The first problem concerns the words that can convey opposite sentiments with respect to the context or domain. For example, a word "ridiculous" in book reviews may express a negative meaning when talking about a book content, however for reviews on electronics this word can bear a positive meaning when talking about prices. Another and more common problem is related to sentiment words that are specific for each domain. For instance, words like "boring", "inspiring", "engaging" are very common in book reviews but it is almost impossible to find them in reviews on electronics. At the same time, the electronics domain can contain words like "defective", "refund", "return", "customer service", which are very unusual for book reviews.

Several cross-domain approaches have been suggested recently to solve the problem of accuracy loss in cross-domain sentiment classification, namely Structural Correspondence Learning (SCL) (Blitzer et al., 2007), the graph-based approach (Wu et al., 2009) and Spectral Feature Alignment (SFA) (Pan et al., 2010). In this paper, we explore graph-based algorithms which refer to a group of techniques that model data as a graph of documents. This data representation takes into account not only document contents but also document connectivity which is modeled as document sentiment similarity rather than content similarity. Our interest in graph algorithms is two-fold. First, graph-based domain representations can benefit from two independent sources of information: scores given by a machine learning technique which indicate the probability of a document to belong to a sentiment class and similarity relations between documents. Second, unlike other suggested methods, this approach can be easily adapted to multiple classes, which makes it possible to classify documents using finer-grained sentiment scales.

Different graph-based algorithms have been applied to several SA tasks (Pang and Lee, 2005; Goldberg and Zhu, 2006; Wu et al., 2009), but no comparison has been made to find the most appropriate one for SC. Moreover, in the framework of the domain adaption task, we come across the problem of choosing the best set of parameters, which, as we further demonstrate, depends on the characteristics of a corresponding domain pair. Unfortunately, no study has investigated this problem. (Pang and Lee, 2005; Goldberg and Zhu, 2006) exploited the graph-based approach for a semi-supervised task and experimented with data belonging to one domain and, therefore did not come across this issue. The work of (Wu et al., 2009) lacks any discussion about the choice of the parameter values; the authors set some values equal for all domains without mentioning how they obtained these numbers.

The present research brings several contributions. First, we compare two graph-based algorithms in cross-domain SC settings: the algorithm exploited in (Goldberg and Zhu, 2006), which seeks document sentiments as an output of an optimisation problem (OPTIM) and the algorithm adopted by (Wu et al., 2009), that uses ranking to assign sentiment scores (RANK). Second, as document similarity is a crucial factor for satisfactory performance of graph-based algorithms, we suggest and evaluate various sentiment similarity measures. Sentiment similarity is different from topic similarity as it compares documents with respect to the sentiment they convey rather than their topic. Finally, we discover the dependency of algorithm parameter values on domain properties and, subsequently, the impossibility to find universal parameter values suitable for all domain pairs. We discuss a possible strategy for choosing the best set of parameters based on our previous study (Ponomareva and Thelwall, 2012), where we introduced two domain characteristics: domain similarity and domain complexity and demonstrated their strong correlation with cross-domain accuracy loss.

The rest of the paper is structured as follows. In Section 2 we give a short overview of related works on cross-domain SC. Section 3 describes and compares the OPTIM and RANK algorithms. In Section 4 we discuss an issue of document similarity and select document representation that correlates best with document sentiments. Experimental results are described in Section 5 followed by a discussion on the strategy for choosing the best parameter values of the algorithms (Section 6). Finally, in Section 7 we summarise our contributions and discuss further research.

2 Related work

Cross-domain sentiment analysis has received considerable attention during the last five years and, since then, several approaches to tackle this problem have emerged. The most straightforward approach is to use an ensemble of classifiers as tested in several works (Aue and Gamon, 2005; Li and Zong, 2008). It is a well-explored technique in machine learning concerned with training classifiers on domains where annotated data are available and then, combining them in ensembles for the classification of target data. Aue and Gamon (2005) studied several possibilities to combine data from domains with known annotations and came up with the conclusion that an ensemble of classifiers in a meta-classifier gives higher performance than a simple merge of all features.

Structural Correspondence Learning (SCL) (Blitzer et al., 2007) is another domain transfer approach, which was also tested on parts of speech (PoS) tagging (Blitzer et al., 2006). Its underlying idea is to find correspondences between features from source and target domains through modeling their correlations with pivot features. Pivot features are features occurring frequently in both domains, which, at the same time, serve as good predictors of document classes, like the general sentiment words "excellent" and "awful". The extraction of pivot features was made on the basis of their frequency in source and target corpora and their mutual information with positive and negative source labels. The correlations between the pivot features and all other features were modeled using a supervised learning of linear pivot predictors to predict occurrences of each pivot in both domains. The proposed approach was tested on review data from 4 domains (books, DVDs, kitchen appliances and electronics) and demonstrated a significant gain of accuracy for most domain pairs compared to the baseline. However, for a few domains the performance degraded due to feature misalignment: the narrowness of the source domain and diversity of the target domain created false projections of features in the target domain. The authors proposed to correct this misalignment with a small amount of annotated in-domain data.

Spectral Feature Alignment (SFA), introduced by Pan et al. (2010), holds the same idea as SCL, i.e., an alignment of source and target features through their co-occurrences with general sentiment words. But instead of learning representations of pivots in source and target domains the authors used spectral clustering to align domain-specific and domain-independent words into a set of feature-clusters. The constructed clusters were then used for the representation of all data examples and training the sentiment classifier. This new solution yields a significant improvement on cross-domain accuracy compared with SCL for almost all domain pairs.

The method suggested by Bollegala et al. (2011) also relies on word co-occurrences. In particular, the authors presented a method for automatic construction of a sentiment-sensitive thesaurus where each lexical element (either unigram or bigram) is connected to a list of related lexical elements which most frequently appear in the context expressing the same sentiment. This thesaurus is then used on the training step to expand feature vectors with related elements to overcome the feature mismatch problem. The method was tested on the same data set as SCL and SFA but unlike previous works the authors used a combination of domains to create sentiment-sensitive thesauri and to train the cross-domain classifier. They compare the accuracy of their approach with an average accuracy over the results with the same target domain given by SCL and SFA, and concluded that their method surpasses all existing approaches. However, we think that such a comparison is not optimal. Indeed, using the approach described in (Ponomareva and Thelwall, 2012) we can choose the most appropriate data for training our classifier rather than averaging the results given by all data sets. Therefore, instead of average accuracies, the best accuracies with respect to the same target domain should be compared. This comparison leads to opposite conclusions, namely that SCL and SFA significantly outperform the sentiment-sensitive thesaurus-based method.

Unlike the approaches mentioned above, graph-based algorithms exploit relations between documents for finding the correct document scores. We describe them in more details in the next section.

3 Graph-based algorithms

In this section we present and compare 2 graph-based algorithms which use similar graph structures but completely different methods to infer node scores. The RANK algorithm (Wu et al., 2009) is based on node ranking, while OPTIM (Goldberg and Zhu, 2006) determines solution of graph optimisation problem. Initially OPTIM was applied for the rating-inference problem in a semi-supervised setting. This study, for the first time, analyses its behaviour for cross-domain SC and compares its performance with a similar approach.

3.1 OPTIM algorithm

The OPTIM algorithm represents graph-based learning as described in (Zhu et al., 2003). Let us introduce the following notation:

- $G = (V, E)$ is an undirected graph with $2n$ nodes V and weighted edges E.
- L stands for labeled data (source domain data) and U for unlabeled data (target domain data).
- x_i is a graph node which refers to a document, $f(x_i)$ is a true label of a document which is supposed to be unknown even for annotated documents, allowing for noisy labels. Each $x_i \in L$ is connected to y_i which represents a given rating of a document. The edge weight between $x - i$ and y_i is a large number

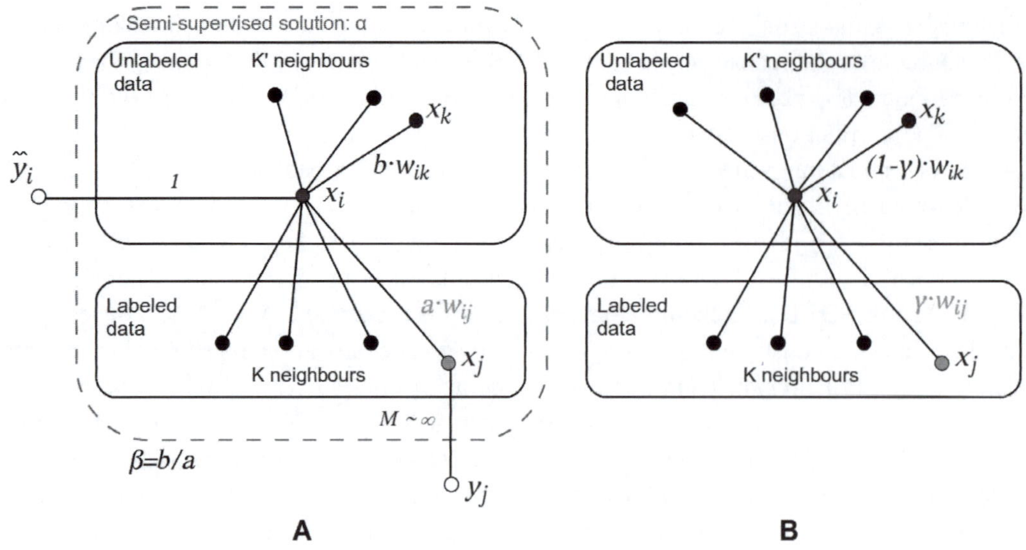

Figure 1: Graph models for the OPTIM (A) and RANK (B) algorithms

M introducing the hard constraints between labeled documents and their ratings. Each $x_i \in U$ is connected to $\hat{y}_i$ that stands for predicted rating of a document. The edge weight between x_i and $\hat{y}_i$ is equal to 1.

- Each unlabeled document x_i is connected to its k nearest labeled documents $kNN_L(i)$ (source domain neighbours). The weight between x_i and $x_j \in kNN_L(i)$ is measured by a given similarity w and denoted $a \cdot w_{ij}$.

- Each unlabeled document x_i is connected to its k' nearest unlabeled documents $k'NN_U(i)$ (target domain neighbours). The weight between x_i and $x_j \in k'NN_U(i)$ is denoted by $b \cdot w_{ij}$.

Figure 1A illustrates the graph structure described. The algorithm is based on the assumption that the rating function $f(x)$ is smooth with respect to the graph, so there are no harsh jumps of sentiment between nearest neighbours. To satisfy the smoothness condition sentiment variability between the closest nodes should be minimised. Another requirement is to minimise the difference between each initial node rating and its final value, although in the case of unlabeled nodes this is optional. Taking into consideration the conditions mentioned the sentiment-inference problem can be formulated as an optimisation problem:

$$\mathcal{L}(f) = \sum_{i \in L} M(f(x_i) - y_i)^2 + \sum_{i \in U} (f(x_i) - \hat{y}_i)^2 + \sum_{i \in U} \sum_{j \in kNN_L(i)} a w_{ij} (f(x_i) - f(x_j))^2 + \sum_{i \in U} \sum_{j \in k'NN_U(i)} b w_{ij} (f(x_i) - f(x_j))^2 \rightarrow min \quad (1)$$

After the substitutions $\alpha = ak + bk'$ and $\beta = \frac{b}{a}$ the final optimisation problem can be written as:

$$\mathcal{L}(f) = \sum_{i \in L} M(f(x_i) - y_i)^2 + \sum_{i \in U} [(f(x_i) - \hat{y}_i)^2 + \frac{\alpha}{k + \beta k'} (\sum_{j \in kNN_L(i)} w_{ij} (f(x_i) - f(x_j))^2 + \sum_{j \in k'NN_U(i)} \beta w_{ij} (f(x_i) - f(x_j))^2)] \rightarrow min \quad (2)$$

where β defines the relative weight between labeled and unlabeled neighbours, while α controls the weight of the graph-based solution with respect to the primarily obtained supervised sentiment scores.

The minimum-loss function which gives the solution of the optimisation problem can be found by setting the gradient to zero. For more details on the problem solution see (Goldberg and Zhu, 2006).

3.2 RANK algorithm

The RANK algorithm has a similar graph structure (Figure 1B): nodes represent labeled and unlabeled documents and there is a parameter (in this case γ) that controls the relative importance of labeled data over unlabeled data and is an analogue of β in OPTIM. The weight of edges between different nodes is also measured by document similarity. However, there are no edges between nodes and their initial sentiments because RANK is an iterative algorithm and each iteration gives new scores to unlabeled nodes while labeled nodes remain constant. More precisely, on each iteration sentiment scores of unlabeled documents are updated on the basis of the weighted sum of sentiment scores of the nearest labeled neighbours and the nearest unlabeled neighbours. The process stops when convergence is achieved, i.e. the difference in sentiment scores is less than a predefined tolerance.

Using the same notation as for OPTIM we can formulate the iterative procedure in the following way:

$$f_k(x_i) = \sum_{j \in kNN_L(i)} \gamma w_{ij} f(x_j) + \sum_{j \in k'NN_U(i)} (1-\gamma) w_{ij} f_{k-1} x_j) \quad (3)$$

where $f_k(x_i)$ is the node sentiment score on the k-th iteration. Document scores are normalised after each iteration to ensure convergence (Wu et al., 2009). It is worth noting that initially the authors did not consider having a different number of neighbours for the source and target domains.

Analysing differences in the graph structures and assumptions of both models we can say that they are almost identical. Even the smoothness condition holds for the RANK algorithm as the score of a node is an averaged sum of the neighbours. The only principal difference concerns the requirement of closeness of initial and final sentiment scores for OPTIM. This condition gives more control on the stability of the algorithm performance.

4 Measure of document similarity

A good measure of document similarity is a key factor for the successful performance of graph-based algorithms. In this section we propose and evaluate several measures of document similarity based on different vector representations and the cosine of document vectors.

Following (Goldberg and Zhu, 2006) and (Pang and Lee, 2005) we consider 2 types of document representations:

- **feature-based**: this involves weighted document features. The question here concerns the features to be selected. When machine learning is employed the answer is straightforward: the most discriminative features are the best ones for our task. However, we assume that we do not know anything about the domain when measuring sentiment similarity and, thus, we should establish the appropriate set of features only relying on our prior knowledge about sentiment words. According to previous studies, adjectives, verbs and adverbs are good indicators of sentiment (Pang and Lee, 2008), therefore, we keep only unigrams and bigrams that contain these PoS. We test two feature weights - tfidf and idf (F_{tfidf} and F_{idf} in Table1 respectively). The evident drawback of such a vector representation concerns the discarding of nouns, which in many cases also bear sentiments. To overcome this issue we introduce a new measure that uses sentiment dictionaries to add nouns expressing sentiments ($F_{idf+SOCAL}$).

- **lexicon-based**: uses sentiment dictionaries to assign scores to lexical elements of two types: words or sentences. The dimension of the corresponding document vector representation conforms with the granularity of the sentiment scale. For example, in case of binary sentiment scales, a document vector consists of two dimensions, where first component corresponds to the percentage of positive words (sentences) and the second component - to the percentage of negative words (sentences). To assign sentiment scores to lexical elements we exploit different sentiment resources, namely

domain	F_{tfidf}	F_{idf}	$F_{idf+SOCAL}$	W_2	W_{10}	S_2
BO	0.61	0.62	0.64	0.49	0.50	0.44
DV	0.61	0.61	0.64	0.56	0.56	0.51
EL	0.62	0.66	0.68	0.47	0.49	0.46
KI	0.65	0.67	0.68	0.51	0.54	0.53

Table 1: Correlation for various similarity measures with sentiment scores of documents across different domains.

SentiWordNet (Esuli and Sebastiani, 2006), SO-CAL (Taboada et al., 2010) and SentiStrength (Thelwall et al., 2012). The scores of sentences are averaged by the number of their positive and negative words. Preliminary experiments show a big advantage of SO-CAL-dictionaries comparing with other resources. SentiWordNet demonstrates quite an unsatisfactory performance, while SentiStrength, being very precise, has an insufficient scope and, therefore, finds no sentiment in a substantial number of documents.

The best document representation is selected on the basis of its correlation with the sentiment scores of documents. To compute correlations for feature-based measures, we take 1000 features with highest average tfidf weights. Table 1 gives the results of a comparison for two document representations and their different settings. Here W_2 and S_2 stand for word-based and sentence-based representations of dimension 2 and W_{10} - for word-based representation of dimension 10. All use SO-CAL-dictionaries to assign scores to words or sentences. Feature-based representations demonstrate significantly better correlations with document sentiments although for some domains, like DV, the lexical element-based representation produces a similar result. Integration of SO-CAL-dictionaries gives insignificant contribution into the overall correlation, which maybe due to the limited number of features participated in the analysis. In our further experiments we use both F_{idf} and $F_{idf+SOCAL}$ document representations.

5 Experimental results

Our data comprises Amazon product reviews on 4 topics: books (BO), electronics (EL), kitchen (KI) and DVDs (DV), initially collected and described by Blitzer et al. (2007). Reviews are rated using a binary scale, 1-2 star reviews are considered as negative and 4-5 star reviews as positive. The data within each domain are balanced: they contain 1000 positive and 1000 negative reviews.

First, we compute a baseline for each domain pair by training a Support Vector Machines (SVMs) classifier using one domain as training data and another as test data. We choose SVMs as our main learning technique because they have proved to be the best supervised algorithm for SC (Pang and Lee, 2008). In particular, we use the LIBSVM library (Chang and Lin, 2011) and a linear kernel function to train the classifier. For the feature set we experiment with different features and feature weights and conclude that unigrams and bigrams weighted with binary values yield the best performance.

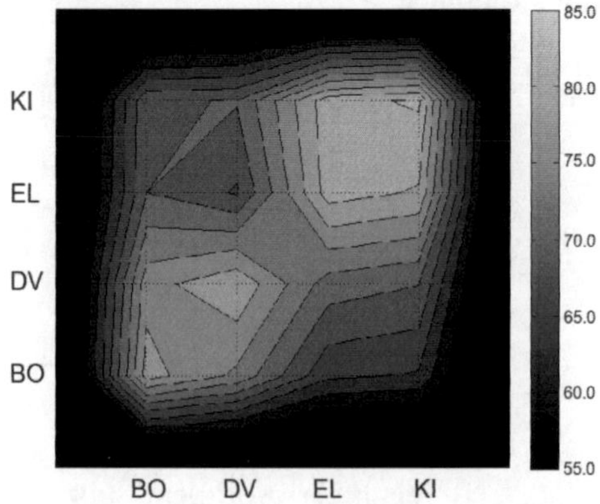

Figure 2: Baseline accuracy for cross-domain SC. (x-axis - source domains, y-axis - target domains).

Figure 2 presents an isoline image of cross-domain accuracies for all domain pairs.[1] Products on the x-axis represent source domains and products

[1]We should point out that in the images the shading between points is not intended to suggest interpolation but is used to highlight the overall pattern. Of course the pattern depends on a domain order on the axes, therefore, similar domains are placed together to make the regions with high and low accuracies evident.

on the y-axis represent target domains. The isolines image of the baseline accuracy delivers a good representation of domain relations. In particular, we can observe two regions with the highest accuracy (EL-KI, KI-EL) and (BO-DV, DV-BO) and two regions with a big performance drop (EL-BO, EL-DV, KI-BO, KI-DV) and (BO-EL, BO-KI, DV-EL, DV-KI). As shown in our previous study (Ponomareva and Thelwall, 2012) the first two regions conform with the most similar domain pairs BO, DV and EL, KI.

OPTIM and RANK require the setting of several parameters: (k, k', α, β) for OPTIM and (k, k', γ) for RANK. As it is computationally expensive to iterate over all possible values of parameters we first run the algorithms on a small matrix of parameters and then apply the gradient descent method which takes the values with highest accuracy as its starting points. We execute both algorithms with different similarity measures, F_{idf} and $F_{idf+SOCAL}$. In Table 2 OPTIM and RANK run with F_{idf}, while OPTIM+SOCAL and RANK+SOCAL run with $F_{idf+SOCAL}$. We give the best accuracies achieved by these algorithms for each domain pair. Unlike the correlations, the accuracies increase significantly with the integration of SO-CAL-dictionaries, the average improvement is about 3% for RANK and 1.5% for OPTIM. In general, RANK consistently outperforms OPTIM for all domain pairs, OPTIM shows competitive performance only for the pairs of similar domains BO-DV, KI-EL and EL-KI. We should also point out that OPTIM is more time-consuming as it requires expensive matrix operations. Due to these advantages of the RANK algorithm, we mostly focus on its analysis in the rest of the paper.

It is interesting to examine the performance of RANK on the basis of the 3D isolines image (Figure 3B). The isolines stretch from left to right indicating that accuracy is almost independent of the source domain. Such behaviour for RANK suggests a positive answer to our question stated in the title: even if domains are quite different, neighbours from the same domain will fix these discrepancies. This property is definitely a big advantage of the RANK algorithm in the context of the cross-domain task as it minimises the importance of the source domain. Obviously more experiments with different data must be accomplished to prove this conclusion with a higher level of confidence.

We also compare graph-based algorithms with other state-of-the-art approaches, such as SCL and SFA (Table 2, Figure 3). The best results in Table 2 are highlighted and if the difference is statistically significant with $\alpha = 0.05$ the corresponding accuracy is underlined. Note that we compare graph-based approaches against the others but not each other, therefore, if the result given by RANK is underlined it means that it is statistically significant only in comparison with SCL and SFA and not with OPTIM. According to Table 2, RANK surpasses SCL for almost all domain pairs with an average difference equal to 2%. Interestingly, without using SO-CAL-dictionaries RANK loses to both SCL and SFA for almost all domain pairs. The advantage of RANK over SFA is disputable as there is not much consistency about when one algorithm outperforms another, except that SFA is better overall for close domains. However Figure 3 suggests an interesting finding: that for domains with different complexities swapping source and target also changes the method that produces the best performance. A comparison of RANK and SCL on the Chinese texts given by (Wu et al., 2009) shows the same phenomenon. It seems that RANK works better when the target domain is simpler, maybe because it can benefit more from in-domain neighbours of the less rich and ambiguous domain. In the future, we plan to increase the impact of lexically different but reliably labeled source data by implementing the SFA algorithm and measuring document similarity between feature clusters rather than separate features.

6 Strategy for choosing optimal parameters

The results of the RANK and OPTIM algorithms presented in the previous section represent the highest accuracies obtained after running gradient descent method. Table 3 lists the best parameter values of the RANK algorithm over several domain pairs. Our attempt to establish some universal values valid for all domain pairs was not successful as the choice of the parameters depends upon the domain properties. Of course, in real life situations we do

source-target	baseline	OPTIM	RANK	OPTIM+ SOCAL	RANK+ SOCAL	SCL	SFA
BO-EL	70.0	74.0	77.2	74.4	**79.8**	77.5	72.5
BO-DV	76.5	78.6	77.4	79.9	79.8	75.8	**81.4**
BO-KI	69.5	74.6	78.6	77.3	**82.8**	78.9	78.8
DV-BO	74.4	78.8	78.9	80.5	**82.1**	79.7	77.5
DV-EL	67.2	73.6	78.8	74.4	**80.9**	74.1	76.7
DV-KI	70.2	75.6	80.4	77.3	**83.2**	81.4	80.8
EL-BO	65.5	67.8	69.9	69.5	73.6	75.4	**75.7**
EL-DV	71.3	74.2	72.6	75.6	77.0	76.2	**77.2**
EL-KI	81.6	83.6	83.2	85.7	85.3	85.9	**86.8**
KI-BO	64.7	68.4	70.9	69.7	**74.8**	68.6	**74.8**
KI-DV	70.1	72.3	72.4	73.4	**78.4**	76.9	77.0
KI-EL	79.7	82.6	81.9	83.7	83.7	**86.8**	85.1
average	71.7	75.3	76.9	76.8	**80.1**	78.1	78.7

Table 2: Comparison of different cross-domain algorithms

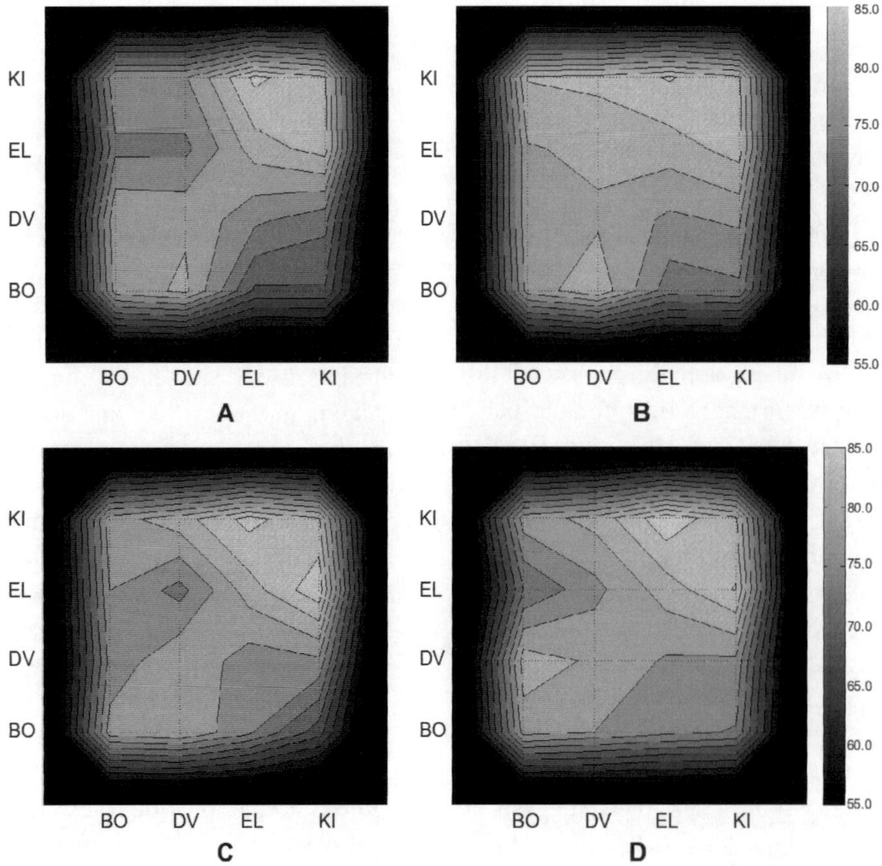

Figure 3: Accuracy obtained with different cross-domain algorithms over various domains: A) OPTIM, B) RANK, C) SCL, D) SFA. (x-axis - source domains, y-axis - target domains).

parameter	BO-EL	BO-DV	BO-KI	EL-BO	EL-DV	EL-KI
γ	0.34	0.78	0.30	0.50	0.55	0.9
k	50	100	25	75	50	200
k'	220	50	40	100	150	10

Table 3: Best number of labeled and unlabeled neighbours for the RANK algorithm over various domain pairs

source-target	similarity	complexity variance	γ
BO-EL	1.23	-1.93	0.34
BO-DV	1.75	0.06	0.76
BO-KI	1.17	-1.26	0.48
DV-BO	1.75	-0.06	0.75
DV-EL	1.22	-1.99	0.52
DV-KI	1.18	-1.32	0.44
EL-BO	1.23	1.93	0.62
EL-DV	1.22	1.99	0.68
EL-KI	1.87	0.67	0.75
KI-BO	1.17	1.26	0.64
KI-DV	1.18	1.32	0.54
KI-EL	1.87	-0.67	0.76

Table 4: Similarity, complexity variance and γ averaged over the best results (confidence level of 95%) of the RANK algorithm. The values are given on various domain pairs

not have a knowledge of the parameter values which produce the best performance and, therefore, it would be useful to elaborate a strategy for choosing the optimal values with respect to a corresponding domain pair. In our previous work (Ponomareva and Thelwall, 2012) we introduced two domain characteristics: domain similarity and domain complexity variance and proved their impact into the cross-domain accuracy loss. Domain similarity and complexity are independent properties of a domain pair as the former measures similarity of data distributions for frequent words, while the latter compares the tails of distributions. In Ponomareva and Thelwall (2012), we tested various metrics to estimate these domain characteristics. As a result, inversed χ^2 was proved to be the best measure of domain similarity as it gave the highest correlation with the cross-domain accuracy drop. The percentage of rare words (words that occur less than 3 times) was found to be the closest approximation to domain complexity as it showed the highest correlation with the in-domain accuracy drop.

It is naturally to assume that if domain similarity and complexity are responsible for the cross-domain accuracy loss, they might influence on the parameter values of domain adaptation algorithms. This is proved to be true for the γ parameter, whose values averaged over the top results of the RANK algorithm are listed in Table 4. We use the confidence interval of 95% to select the top values of γ. Table 4 shows that γ is the lowest for dissimilar domains with a simpler target (negative values of domain complexity variance), which means that the RANK algorithm benefits the most from unlabeled but simpler data. γ grows to values close to 0.6 for dissimilar domains with more complex target (positive values of domain complexity variance), which shows that the impact of simpler source data, though different from target, increases. Finally γ reaches its maximum for similar domains with the same level of complexity. Unfortunately, due to comparable amount of data for each domain, no cases of similar domains with different complexity are observed. We plan to study these particular cases in the future.

High dependency of γ on both domain characteristics is proved numerically. The correlation between γ and domain similarity and complexity reaches 0.91, and decreases drastically when one of these characteristics is ignored.

Concerning the optimal number of labeled and unlabeled neighbours, no regularity is evident (Table 3). In our opinion, that is an effect of choosing the neighbours on the basis of the quantitative threshold. Nevertheless, different domains have distinct pairwise document similarity distributions. Figure 4 demonstrates similarity distributions for BO, EL and DV inside and across domains. Therefore, taking into account only the quantitative threshold we ignore discrepancies

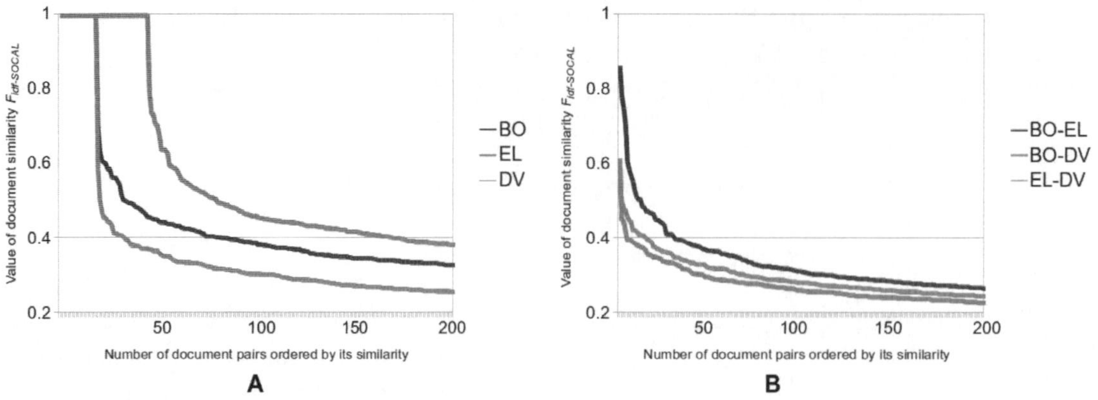

Figure 4: Pairwise document similarity distributions inside domains (A) and across domains (B)

in graph connectivities inside and across domains and may bring "bad" neighbours to participate in decision-making. In our further research we plan to explore the idea of a qualitative threshold, which chooses neighbours according to their similarity and uses the same similarity levels for in-domain and cross-domain graphs.

7 Conclusions and future work

This paper has studied the performance of two graph-based algorithms, OPTIM and RANK when applied to cross-domain sentiment classification. Comparison on their performance on the same data has revealed that, in spite of the similar graph structures, RANK consistently produces better results than OPTIM. We also have compared the graph-based algorithms with other cross-domain methods, including SCL and SFA, and concluded that RANK considerably outperforms SCL and obtains better results than SFA for half of the cases. Given that we consider only the best accuracies obtained with RANK, such comparison is not completely fair but it shows the potential of the RANK algorithm once the strategy for choosing its optimal parameters is established. In this paper, we also discuss some ideas about how to infer optimal parameter values for the algorithms on the basis of domain characteristics. In particular, the strong correlation for γ with domain similarity and complexity has been observed. Unfortunately we are not able to find any regularity in the number of source and target domain neighbours, which we think is the result of the qualitative approach to selecting the closest neighbours.

As a result of this research we have identified the following future directions. First, we plan to improve the RANK performance by choosing the number of neighbours on the basis of the document similarity threshold which we set equal for both in-domain and cross-domain neighbours. We expect that this modification will diminish the number of "bad" neighbours and allow us to reveal a dependency of similarity threshold on some domain properties. Another research direction will focus on the integration of SFA into the similarity measure to overcome the problem of lexical discrepancy in the source and target domains. Finally, as all our conclusions have been drawn on a data set of 12 domain pairs, we plan to increase a number of domains to verify our findings on larger data sets.

Acknowledgments

This work was supported by a European Union grant by the 7th Framework Programme, Theme 3: Science of complex systems for socially intelligent ICT. It is part of the CyberEmotions project (contract 231323).

References

Anthony Aue and Michael Gamon. 2005. Customizing sentiment classifiers to new domains: A case study. In *Proceedings of Recent Advances in Natural Language Processing (RANLP '05)*.

John Blitzer, Ryan McDonald, and Fernando Pereira. 2006. Domain adaptation with structural correspondence learning. In *Proceedings of the 2006 Conference on Empirical Methods in Natural Language Processing (EMNLP '06)*, pages 120–128.

John Blitzer, Mark Dredze, and Fernando Pereira. 2007. Biographies, bollywood, boom-boxes and blenders: Domain adaptation for sentiment classification. In *Proceedings of the 45th Annual Meeting of the Association of Computational Linguistics (ACL '07)*, pages 440–447.

Danushka Bollegala, David Weir, and John Carroll. 2011. Using multiple sources to construct a sentiment sensitive thesaurus for cross-domain sentiment classification. In *Proceedings of the 49th Annual Meeting of the Association for Computational Linguistics (ACL '11)*, pages 132–141.

Chih-Chung Chang and Chih-Jen Lin. 2011. LIBSVM: A library for support vector machines. *ACM Transactions on Intelligent Systems and Technology*, 2:27:1–27:27. Software available at `http://www.csie.ntu.edu.tw/~cjlin/libsvm`.

Andrea Esuli and Fabrizio Sebastiani. 2006. Sentiwordnet: A publicly available lexical resource for opinion mining. In *Proceedings of the 5th Conference on Language Resources and Evaluation (LREC 06)*, pages 417–422.

Andrew B. Goldberg and Xiaojin Zhu. 2006. Seeing stars when there aren't many stars: graph-based semi-supervised learning for sentiment categorization. In *Proceedings of the First Workshop on Graph Based Methods for Natural Language Processing (TextGraphs '06)*, pages 45–52.

Shoushan Li and Chengqing Zong. 2008. Multi-domain sentiment classification. In *Proceedings of ACL-08: HLT, Short Papers*, pages 257–260.

Sinno Jialin Pan, Xiaochuan Niz, Jian-Tao Sunz, Qiang Yangy, and Zheng Chen. 2010. Cross-domain sentiment classification via spectral feature alignment. In *Proceedings of International World Wide Web Conference (WWW '10)*.

Bo Pang and Lillian Lee. 2005. Seeing stars: exploiting class relationships for sentiment categorization with respect to rating scales. In *Proceedings of the 43rd Annual Meeting on Association for Computational Linguistics (ACL '05)*, pages 115–124.

Bo Pang and Lillian Lee. 2008. Opinion mining and sentiment analysis. *Foundations and Trends in Information Retrieval*, 2(1-2):1–135.

Natalia Ponomareva and Mike Thelwall. 2012. Bibliographies or blenders: Which resource is best for cross-domain sentiment analysis? In *Proceedings of the 13th Conference on Intelligent Text Processing and Computational Linguistics (CICLing '12)*.

M. Taboada, J. Brooke, M. Tofiloski, K. Voll, and M. Stede. 2010. Lexicon-based methods for sentiment analysis. *Computational Linguistics*, 37(2):267–307.

M. Thelwall, K. Buckley, and G. Paltoglou. 2012. Sentiment strength detection for the social web. *Journal of the American Society for Information Science and Technology*, 63(1):163–173.

Qiong Wu, Songbo Tan, and Xueqi Cheng. 2009. Graph ranking for sentiment transfer. In *Proceedings of the ACL-IJCNLP 2009 Conference Short Papers*, pages 317–320.

Xiaojin Zhu, Zoubin Ghahramani, and John Lafferty. 2003. Semi-supervised learning using gaussian fields and harmonic functions. In *Proceedings of the 20th International Conference on Machine Learning (ICML '03)*, pages 912–919.

Learning Lexicon Models from Search Logs for Query Expansion

Jianfeng Gao
Microsoft Research, Redmond
Washington 98052, USA
jfgao@microsoft.com

Shasha Xie
Educational Testing Service, Princeton
New Jersey 08540, USA
sxie@ets.org

Xiaodong He
Microsoft Research, Redmond
Washington 98052, USA
xiaohe@microsoft.com

Alnur Ali
Microsoft Bing, Bellevue
Washington 98004, USA
alnurali@microsoft.com

Abstract

This paper explores log-based query expansion (QE) models for Web search. Three lexicon models are proposed to bridge the lexical gap between Web documents and user queries. These models are trained on pairs of user queries and titles of clicked documents. Evaluations on a real world data set show that the lexicon models, integrated into a ranker-based QE system, not only significantly improve the document retrieval performance but also outperform two state-of-the-art log-based QE methods.

1 Introduction

Term mismatch is a fundamental problem in Web search, where queries and documents are composed using different vocabularies and language styles. Query expansion (QE) is an effective strategy to address the problem. It expands a query issued by a user with additional related terms, called *expansion terms*, so that more relevant documents can be retrieved.

In this paper we explore the use of clickthrough data and translation models for QE. We select expansion terms for a query according to how likely it is that the expansion terms occur in the title of a document that is relevant to the query. Assuming that a query is parallel to the titles of documents clicked for that query (Gao et al. 2010a), three lexicon models are trained on query-title pairs extracted from clickthrough data. The first is a word model that learns the translation probability between single words. The second model uses lexicalized triplets to incorporate word dependencies for translation. The third is a bilingual topic model, which represents a query as a distribution of hidden topics and learns the translation between a query and a title term at the semantic level. We will show that the word model provides a rich set of expansion candidates while the triplet and topic models can effectively select good expansion terms, and that a ranker-based QE system which incorporates all three of these models not only significantly improves Web search result but outperforms other log-based QE methods that are state-of-the-art.

There is growing interest in applying user logs to improve QE. A recent survey is due to Baeze-Yates and Ribeiro-Neto (2011). Below, we briefly discuss two log-based QE methods that are closest to ours and are re-implemented in this study for comparison. Both systems use the same type of log data that we used to train the lexicon models. The term correlation model of Cui et al. (2002; 2003) is to our knowledge the first to explore query-document relations for direct extraction of expansion terms for Web search. The method outperforms traditional QE methods that do not use log data e.g. the local analysis model of Xu and Croft (1996). In addition, as pointed out by Cui et al. (2003) there are three important advantages that make log-based QE a promising technology to improve the performance of commercial search engines. First, unlike traditional QE methods that are based on relevance feedback, log-based QE derives expansion terms from search logs, allowing term correlations to be pre-computed offline. Compared to methods that are based on thesauri either compiled manually (Prager et al. 2001) or derived automatically from document collections (Jing and Croft 1994), the log-based method is superior in that it explicitly captures the correlation between query terms and document terms, and thus can bridge the lexical gap between them more effectively. Second, since search logs retrain query-document pairs clicked by millions of users, the term correlations reflect the preference of the majority of users. Third, the term correlations evolve along with the accumulation of user logs, thus can reflect updated user interests at a specific time.

However, as pointed out by Riezler et al. (2008), Cui et al.'s correlation-based method suffers low precision of QE partly because the correlation model does not explicitly capture context information and is susceptible to noise. Riezler et al. developed a QE system by retraining a standard phrase-based statistical machine translation (SMT) system using query-snippet pairs extracted from clickthrough data (Riezler et al. 2008; Riezler and Liu 2010). The SMT-based system can produce cleaner, more relevant expansion terms because rich context information useful for filtering noisy expansions is captured by combining language model and phrase translation model in its decoder. Furthermore, in the SMT system all component models are properly smoothed using sophisticated techniques to avoid sparse data problems while the correlation model relies on pure counts of term frequencies. However, the SMT system is used as a black box in their experiments. So the relative contribution of different SMT components is not verified empirically. In this study we break this black box in order to build a better, simpler QE system. We will show that the proposed lexicon models outperform significantly the term correlation model, and that a simpler QE system that incorporates the lexicon models can beat the sophisticated, black-box SMT system.

2 Lexicon Models

We view search queries and Web documents as two different languages, and cast QE as a means to bridge the language gap by translating queries to documents, represented by their titles. In this section, we will describe three translation models that are based on terms, triplets, and topics, respectively, and the way these models are learned from query-title pairs extracted from clickthrough data.

2.1 Word Model

The word model takes the form of IBM Model 1 (Brown et al. 1993; Berger and Lafferty 1999). Let $Q = (q_1, \dots, q_J)$ be a query, e be an expansion term candidate, the translation probability from Q to e is defined as

$$P(e|Q)_{wm} = \sum_{j=1}^{J} P(e|q_j)P(q_j|Q) \qquad (1)$$

where $P(q|Q)$ is the unsmoothed unigram probability of word q in query Q. The word translation probabilities $P(e|q)$ are estimated on the query-title pairs derived from the clickthrough data by assuming that the title terms are likely to be the desired expansions of the paired query. Our training method follows the standard procedure of training statistical word alignment models proposed by Brown et al. (1993). Formally, we optimize the model parameters θ by maximizing the probability of generating document titles from queries over the entire training corpus:

$$\theta^* = \text{argmax}_\theta \prod_{i=1}^{H} P(D_i|Q_i, \theta) \qquad (2)$$

where both the titles D and the paired queries Q are viewed as bag of words. The translation probability $P(D_i|Q_i, \theta)$ takes the form of IBM Model 1 as

$$P(D|Q, \theta) = \frac{\varepsilon}{(J+1)^I} \prod_{i=1}^{I} \sum_{j=1}^{J} P(w_i|q_j, \theta) \qquad (3)$$

where ε is a constant, I is the length of D, and J is the length of Q. To find the optimal word translation probabilities of IBM Model 1, we used the EM algorithm, where the number of iterations is determined empirically on held-out data.

2.2 Triplet Model

The word model is context independent. The triplet model, which is originally proposed for SMT (Hasan et al. 2008), is intended to capture inter-term dependencies for selecting expansion terms. The model is based on lexicalized triplets (e, q, q') which can be understood as two query terms triggering one expansion term. The translation probability of e given Q for the triplet model is parameterized as

$$P(e|Q)_{tm} = \frac{1}{Z}\sum_{j=1}^{J-1}\sum_{k=j+1}^{J} P(e|q_j, q_k) \quad (4)$$

where Z is a normalization factor based on the corresponding query length, i.e., $Z = \frac{J(J-1)}{2}$, and $P(e_i|q_j, q_k)$ is the probability of translating q_j into e_i given another query word q_k. Since q_k can be any word in Q that is not necessary to be adjacent to q_j, the triple model is able to combine local (i.e. word and phrase level) and global (i.e. query level) contextual information useful for word translation.

Similar to the case of word model, we used the EM algorithm to estimate the translation probabilities $P(e|q, q')$ on the query-title pairs. Since the number of all possible triplets (e, q, q') is large and as a consequence the model training could suffer the data sparseness problem, in our experiments count-based cutoff is applied to prune the model to a manageable size.

2.3 Bilingual Topic Model (BLTM)

The BLTM was originally proposed for Web document ranking by Gao et al. (2011). The idea underlying the model is that a search query and its relevant Web documents share a common distribution of (hidden) topics, but use different (probably overlapping) vocabularies to express these topics. Intuitively, BLTM-based QE works as follows. First, a query is represented as a vector of topics. Then, all the candidate expansion terms, which are selected from document, are ranked by how likely it is that these document terms are selected to best describe those topics. In a sense, BLTM is similar to the word model and the triplet model since they all map a query to a document word. BLTM differs in that the mapping is performed at the topic level (via a language independent semantic representation) rather than at the word level. In our experiments BLTM is found to often select a different set of expansion terms and is complementary to the word model and the triplet model.

Formally, BLTM-based QE assumes the following story of generating e from Q:

1. First, for each topic z, a pair of different word distributions (ϕ_z^Q, ϕ_z^D) are selected from a Dirichlet prior with concentration parameter β, where ϕ_z^Q is a topic-specific query term distribution, and ϕ_z^D a topic-specific document term distribution. Assuming there are T topics, we have two sets of distributions $\mathbf{\Phi}^Q = (\phi_1^Q, \ldots, \phi_T^Q)$ and $\mathbf{\Phi}^D = (\phi_1^D, \ldots, \phi_T^D)$.
2. Given Q, a topic distribution $\boldsymbol{\theta}^Q$ is drawn from a Dirichlet prior with concentration parameter α.
3. Then a document term (i.e., expansion term candidate) e is generated by first selecting a topic z according to the topic distribution $\boldsymbol{\theta}^Q$, and then drawing a word from ϕ_z^D.

Original query	jaguar locator
Ranked expansion candidates (altered words are in italic)	jaguar *finder* *car* locator jaguar *location* jaguar *directory* ... jaguar *list*
Expanded query (selected expansion terms are in italic)	OR (jaguar, *car*) OR (locator, *finder*, *location*, *directory*)

Figure 1. An example of an original query, its expansion candidates and the expanded query generated by the ranker-based QE system.

By summing over all possible topics, we end up with the following model form

$$P_{bltm}(e|Q) = \sum_z P(e|\phi_z^D)P(z|\boldsymbol{\theta}^Q) \quad (5)$$

The BLTM training follows the method described in Gao et al. (2011). We used the EM algorithm to estimate the parameters $(\boldsymbol{\theta}, \mathbf{\Phi}^Q, \mathbf{\Phi}^D)$ of BLTM by maximizing the joint log-likelihood of the query-title pairs and the parameters. In training, we also constrain that the paired query and title have similar fractions of tokens assigned to each topic. The constraint is enforced on expectation using posterior regularization (Ganchev et al. 2010).

3 A Ranker-Based QE System

This section describes a ranker-based QE system in which the three lexicon models described above are incorporated. The system expands an input query in two distinct stages, candidate generation and ranking, as illustrated by an example in Figure 1.

In candidate generation, an input query Q is first tokenized into a sequence of terms. For each term q that is not a stop word, we consult a word model described in Section 2.1 to identify the best M altered words according to their word translation probabilities from q. Then, we form a list of expansion candidates, each of which contains all the original words in Q except for the word that is substituted by one of its altered words. So, for a query with J terms, there are at most $M \times J$ candidates.

In the second stage, all the expansion candidates are ranked using a ranker that is based on the Markov Random Field (MRF) model in which the three lexicon models are incorporated as features. Expansion terms of a query are taken from those terms in the N-best ($N = 10$ in our experiments) expansion candidates of the query that have not been seen in the original query string.

In the remainder of this section we will describe in turn the MRF-based ranker, the ranking features, and the way the ranker parameters are estimated.

3.1 MRF-Based Ranker

The ranker is based on the MRF model that models the joint distribution of $P_\Lambda(E, Q)$ over a set of expansion term random variables $E = \{e_1, \dots, e_I\}$ and a query random variable Q. It is constructed from a graph G consisting of a query node and nodes for each expansion term. Nodes in the graph represent random variables and edges define the independence semantics between the variables. An MRF satisfies the Markov property (Bishop 2006), which states that a node is independent of all of its non-neighboring nodes given observed values of its neighbors, defined by the clique configurations of G. The joint distribution over the random variables in G is defined as

$$P_\Lambda(E, Q) = \frac{1}{Z_\Lambda} \prod_{c \in C(G)} \varphi(c; \Lambda) \qquad (6)$$

where $C(G)$ is the set of cliques in G, and each $\varphi(c; \Lambda)$ is a non-negative potential function defined over a clique configuration c that measures the *compatibility* of the configuration, Λ is a set of parameters that are used within the potential function, and Z_Λ normalizes the distribution. For ranking expansion candidates, we can drop the expensive computation of Z_Λ since it is independent of E, and simply rank each expansion candidate E by its unnormalized joint probability with Q under the MRF. It is common to define MRF potential functions of the exponential form as $\varphi(c; \Lambda) = \exp(\lambda_c f(c))$, where $f(c)$ is a real-valued feature function over clique values and λ_c is the weight of the feature function. Then, we can compute the posterior $P_\Lambda(E|Q)$ as

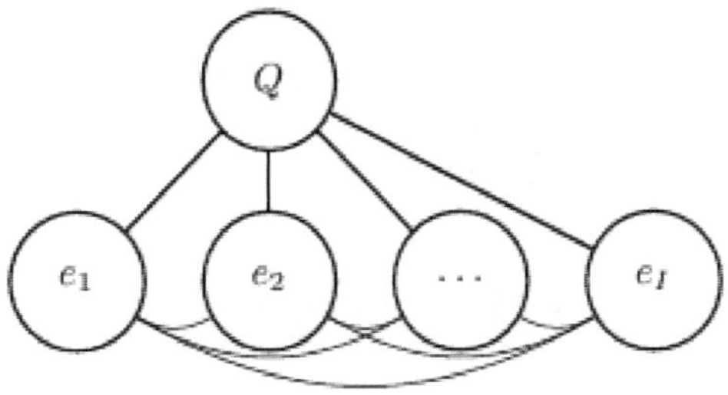

Figure 2: The structure of the Markov random field for representing the term dependency among the query Q and the expansion terms $e_1, \dots, e_I$.

$$P_\Lambda(E|Q) = \frac{P_\Lambda(E, Q)}{P_\Lambda(Q)} \qquad (7)$$

$$\overset{rank}{\Longrightarrow} \sum_{c \in C(G)} \log \varphi(c; \Lambda) = \sum_{c \in C(G)} \lambda_c f(c),$$

which is essentially a weighted linear combination of a set of features.

Therefore, to instantiate the MRF model, one needs to define a graph structure and a set of potential functions. In this paper, the graphical model representation we propose for QE is a fully connected graph shown in Figure 2, where all expansion terms and the original query are assumed dependent with each other. In what follows, we will define six types of cliques that we are interested in defining features (i.e., potential functions) over.

3.2 Features

The cliques and features are inspired by the component models used in SMT systems. The cliques defined in G for MRF can be grouped into two categories. The first includes three types of cliques involving both the query node and one or more expansion terms. The potential functions defined over these cliques attempt to abstract the idea behind the query to title translation models. The other three types, belonging to the second category, involve only expansion terms. Their potential functions attempt to abstract the idea behind the target language models.

The first type of cliques involves a single expansion term and the query node. The potentials functions for these cliques are defined as

$$\varphi_T(e_i, Q; \Lambda) = \exp[\lambda_{wm} f_{wm}(e_i, Q) + \lambda_{tm} f_{tm}(e_i, Q) + \lambda_{bltm} f_{bltm}(e_i, Q)] \quad (6)$$

where the three feature functions of the form $f(e, Q)$ are defined as the log probabilities of translating Q to e according to the word, triplet and topic models defined in Equations (1), (4) and (5), respectively.

$$f_{wm}(e_i, Q) = \log P_{wm}(e_i|Q)$$

$$f_{tm}(e_i, Q) = \log P_{tm}(e_i|Q)$$

$$f_{bltm}(e_i, Q) = \log P_{bltm}(e_i|Q)$$

The second type of cliques contains the query node and two expansion terms, e_i and e_{i+1}, which appear in consecutive order in the expansion. The potential functions over these cliques are defined as

$$\varphi_{ob}(e_i, e_{i+1}, Q; \Lambda) = \exp[\lambda_{ob} f_{ob}(e_i, e_{i+1}, Q)] \quad (7)$$

where the feature $f_{ob}(.)$ is defined as the log probability of generating an expansion bigram given Q

$$f_{ob}(e_i, e_{i+1}|Q) = \log P(e_i, e_{i+1}|Q)$$

Unlike the language models used for document ranking (e.g., Zhai and Lafferty 2001), we cannot compute the bigram probability by simply counting the relative frequency of (e_i, e_{i+1}) in Q because the query is usually very short and the bigram is unlikely to occur. Thus, we approximate the bigram probability by assuming that the words in Q are independent with each other. We thus have

$$P(e_i, e_{i+1}|Q) = \frac{P(e_i, e_{i+1}, Q)}{P(Q)} = \frac{P(e_i)P(e_{i+1}|e_i)\prod_{j=1}^{J} P(q_j|e_i, e_{i+1})}{\prod_{j=1}^{J} P(q_j)},$$

where $P(q_j|e_i, e_{i+1})$ is the translation probability computed using a variant of the triplet model described in Section 2.2. The model variation differs from the one of Equation (4) in two respects. First, it models the translation in a different direction i.e., from expansion to query. Second, we add a constraint to the triplets such that (e_i, e_{i+1}) must be an ordered, contiguous bigram. The model variation is also trained using EM on query-title pairs. $P(e_i)$ and $P(e_{i+1}|e_i)$ are assigned respectively by the unigram and bigram language models, estimated from the collection of document titles of the clickthrough data, and $P(q_j)$ is the unigram probability of the query term, estimated from the collection of queries of the clickthrough data.

The third type of cliques contains the query node and two expansion terms, e_i and e_k, which occur unordered within the expansion. The potential functions over these cliques are defined as

$$\varphi_{ub}(e_i, e_k, Q; \Lambda) = \exp[\lambda_{ub} f_{ub}(e_i, e_k, Q)] \quad (8)$$

where the feature $f_{ub}(.)$ is defined as the log probability of generating a pair of expansion terms (e_i, e_k) given Q

$$f_{ub}(e_i, e_k|Q) = \log P(e_i, e_k|Q).$$

Unlike $f_{ob}(e_i, e_{i+1}|Q)$ defined in Equation (7), this class of features captures long-span term dependency in the expansion candidate. Similar to the computation of $P(e_i, e_{i+1}|Q)$ in Equation (7), we approximate $P(e_i, e_k|Q)$ as

$$P(e_i, e_k|Q) = \frac{P(e_i, e_k, Q)}{P(Q)} = \frac{P(e_i)P(e_k|e_i)\prod_{j=1}^{J} P(q_j|e_i, e_k)}{\prod_{j=1}^{J} P(q_j)},$$

where $P(q_j|e_i, e_k)$ is the translation probability computed using the triplet model described in Section 2.2, but in the expansion-to-query direction. $P(e_i)$ is assigned by a unigram language model estimated from the collection of document titles of the clickthrough data. $P(e_k|e_i)$ is assigned by a co-occurrence model, estimated as

$$P(e_k|e_i) = \frac{N(e_i, e_k)}{\sum_e N(e_i, e)}$$

where $N(e_i, e_k)$ is the number of times that the two terms occur in the same title in clickthrough data.

We now turn to the other three types of cliques that do not contain the query node. The fourth type of cliques contains only one expansion term. The potential functions are defined as

$$\varphi_{um}(e_i; \Lambda) = \exp[\lambda_{um} f_{um}(e_i)] \quad (9)$$
$$f_{um}(e_i) = \log P(e_i)$$

where $P(e_i)$ is the unigram probability computed using a unigram language model trained on the collection of document titles.

The fifth type of cliques contains a pair of terms appearing in consecutive order in the expansion. The potential functions are defined as

$$\varphi_{bm}(e_i, e_{i+1}; \Lambda) = \exp[\lambda_{bm} f_{bm}(e_i, e_{i+1})] \quad (10)$$
$$f_{bm}(e_i, e_{i+1}) = \log P(e_{i+1} | e_i)$$

where $P(e_{i+1}|e_i)$ is the bigram probability computed using a bigram language model trained on the collection of document titles.

The sixth type of cliques contains a pair of terms appearing unordered within the expansion. The potential functions are defined as

$$\varphi_{cm}(e_i, e_k; \Lambda) = \exp[\lambda_{cm} f_{cm}(e_i, e_k)] \quad (11)$$
$$f_{cm}(e_i, e_k) = \log P(e_k | e_i)$$

where $P(e_k|e_i)$ is the assigned by a co-occurrence model trained on the collection of document titles.

3.3 Parameter Estimation

The MRF model uses 8 classes of features defined on 6 types of cliques, as in Equations (6) to (11). Following previous work (e.g., Metzler and Croft 2005; Bendersky et al. 2010), we assume that all features within the same feature class are weighted by the same tied parameter λ. Thus, the number of free parameters of the MRF model is significantly reduced. This not only makes the model training easier but also improves the robustness of the model. After tying the parameters and using the exponential potential function form, the MRF-based ranker can be parameterized as

$$P_\Lambda(E|Q) \overset{rank}{\Longrightarrow} \lambda_{wm} \sum_{i=1}^{I} f_{wm}(e_i, Q) + \quad (12)$$
$$\lambda_{tm} \sum_{i=1}^{I} f_{tm}(e_i, Q) +$$
$$\lambda_{bltm} \sum_{i=1}^{I} f_{bltm}(e_i, Q) +$$
$$\lambda_{ob} \sum_{i=1}^{I-1} f_{ob}(e_i, e_{i+1}, Q) +$$
$$\lambda_{ub} \sum_{i=1}^{I-1} \sum_{k=i+1}^{I} f_{ob}(e_i, e_k, Q) +$$
$$\lambda_{um} \sum_{i=1}^{I} f_{um}(e_i) +$$
$$\lambda_{bm} \sum_{i=1}^{I-1} f_{bm}(e_i, e_{i+1}) +$$
$$\lambda_{cm} \sum_{i=1}^{I-1} \sum_{k=i+1}^{I} f_{cm}(e_i, e_k)$$

where there are in total 8 λ's to be estimated.

Although the MRF is by nature a generative model, it is not always appropriate to train the parameters using conventional likelihood based approaches due to the metric divergence problem (Morgan et al. 2004): i.e., the maximum likelihood estimate is unlikely to be the one that optimizes the evaluation metric. In this study the effectiveness of a QE method is evaluated by first issuing a set of queries which are expanded using the method to a search engine and then measuring the Web search performance. Better QE methods are supposed to lead to better Web search results using the correspondingly expanded query set.

For this reason, the parameters of the MRF-based ranker are optimized directly for Web search. In our experiments, the objective in training is *Normalized Discounted Cumulative Gain* (NDCG, Jarvelin and Kekalainen 2000), which is widely used as quality measure for Web search. Formally, we view parameter training as a multi-dimensional optimization problem, with each feature class as one dimension. Since NDCG is not differentiable, we tried in our experiments numerical algorithms that do not require the computation of gradient. Among the best performers was the Powell Search algorithm (Press et al., 1992). It first constructs a set of N virtual directions that are conjugate (i.e., independent with each other), then it uses *line search* N times ($N = 8$ in our case), each on one virtual direction, to find the optimum. Line search is a one-dimensional optimization algorithm. Our implementation follows the one described in Gao et al. (2005), which is used to optimize averaged precision.

4 Experiments

We evaluate the performance of a QE method by first issuing a set of queries which are expanded using the method to a search engine and then measuring the Web search performance. Better QE methods are supposed to lead to better Web search results using the correspondingly expanded query set.

Due to the characteristics of our QE methods, we cannot conduct experiments on standard test collections such as the TREC data because they do not contain related user logs we need. Therefore, following previous studies of log-based QE (e.g., Cui et al. 2003; Riezler et al. 2008), we use the proprietary datasets that have been developed for building a commercial search engine, and demonstrate the effectiveness of our methods by comparing them against previous state-of-the-art log-based QE methods.

The relevance judgment set consists of 4,000 multi-term English queries. On average, each query is associated with 197 Web documents (URLs). Each query-URL pair has a relevance label. The label is human generated and is on a 5-level relevance scale, 0 to 4, with 4 meaning document D is the most relevant to query Q and 0 meaning D is not relevant to Q.

The relevance judgment set is constructed as follows. First, the queries are sampled from a year of search engine logs. Adult, spam, and bot queries are all removed. Queries are "de-duped" so that only unique queries remain. To reflect a natural query distribution, we do not try to control the quality of these queries. For example, in our query sets, there are roughly 20% misspelled queries, 20% navigational queries, and 10% transactional queries. Second, for each query, we collect Web documents to be judged by issuing the query to several popular search engines (e.g., Google, Bing) and fetching retrieval results from each. Finally, the query-document pairs are judged by a group of well-trained assessors. In this study all the queries are preprocessed as follows. The text is white-space tokenized and lowercased, numbers are retained, and no stemming/inflection treatment is performed. We split the judgment set into two non-overlapping datasets, namely training and test sets, respectively. Each dataset contains 2,000 queries.

The query-title pairs used for model training are extracted from one year of query log files using a procedure similar to Gao et al. (2009). In our experiments we used a randomly sampled subset of 20,692,219 pairs that do not overlap the queries and documents in the test set.

#	QE methods	NDCG@1	NDCG@3	NDCG@10
1	**NoQE**	34.70	36.50	41.54
2	**TC**	33.78	36.57	42.33^{α}
3	**SMT**	34.79^{β}	$36.98^{\alpha\beta}$	$42.84^{\alpha\beta}$
4	**MRF**	$\mathbf{36.10}^{\alpha\beta\gamma}$	$\mathbf{38.06}^{\alpha\beta\gamma}$	$\mathbf{43.71}^{\alpha\beta\gamma}$
5	**MRF**$_{um+bm+cm}$	33.31	36.12	42.26^{α}
6	**MRF**$_{tc}$	34.50^{β}	36.59	42.33^{α}
7	**MRF**$_{wm}$	34.73^{β}	36.62	$42.73^{\alpha\beta}$
8	**MRF**$_{tm}$	$35.13^{\alpha\beta}$	$37.46^{\alpha\beta\gamma}$	$42.82^{\alpha\beta}$
9	**MRF**$_{bltm}$	34.34^{β}	36.19	41.98^{α}
10	**MRF**$_{wm+tm}$	$35.21^{\alpha\beta\gamma}$	$37.46^{\alpha\beta\gamma}$	$42.83^{\alpha\beta}$
11	**MRF**$_{wm+tm+bltm}$	$35.84^{\alpha\beta\gamma}$	$37.70^{\alpha\beta\gamma}$	$43.14^{\alpha\beta\gamma}$

Table 1: Ranking results using BM25 with different query expansion systems. The superscripts α, β, and γ indicate statistically significant improvements ($p < 0.05$) over **NoQE**, **TC**, and **SMT**, respectively. Rows 5 to 11 are different versions of **MRF** in Row 5, They use the same candidate generator but use in the ranker different feature classes, as specified by the subscript. **tc** specifies the feature class defined as the scoring function in Equation (13). Refer to Equation (12) for the names of other feature classes.

Our Web document collection consists of approximately 2.5 billion Web pages. In the retrieval experiments we use the index based on the content fields (i.e., body and title text) of each Web page.

The Web search performance is evaluated by mean NDCG. We report NDCG scores at truncation levels of 1, 3, and 10. We also perform a significance test using the paired t-test. Differences are considered statistically significant when p-value is less than 0.05.

4.1 Comparing Systems

Table 1 shows the main document ranking results using different QE systems, developed and evaluated using the datasets described above.

NoQE (Row 1) is the baseline retrieval system that uses the raw input queries and the BM25 document ranking model. Rows 2 to 4 are different QE systems. Their results are obtained by first expanding a query, then using BM25 to rank the documents with respect to the expanded query.

TC (Row 2) is our implementation of the correlation-based QE system (Cui et al. 2002; 2003). It takes the following steps to expand an input query Q:

1. Extract all query terms q (eliminating stopwords) from Q.
2. Find all documents that have clicks on a query that contains one or more of these query terms.
3. For each title term w in these documents, calculate its evidence of being selected as an expansion term according to the whole query via a scoring function $Score(w|\ Q)$.
4. Select n title terms with the highest score (where the value of n is optimized on training data) and formulate the expanded query by adding these terms into Q.
5. Use the expanded query to rank documents.

The scoring function is based on the term correlation model, and is defined as

$$Score(w|Q) = \ln\left(\prod_{q \in Q} P(w|q) + 1\right) \quad (13)$$

$$P(w|q) = \sum_{D \in \mathbf{D}_q} P(w|D)P(D|q)$$

where $\mathbf{D}_q$ is the set of documents clicked for the queries containing the term q and is collected from search logs, $P(w|D)$ is a normalized *tf-idf* weight of the document term in D, and $P(D|q)$ is the relative occurrence of D among all the documents clicked for the queries containing q. Table 1 shows that **TC** leads to significant improvement over **NoQE** in NDCG@10, but not in NDCG@1 and NDCG@3 (Row 2 vs. Row 1). The result is not entirely consistent with what reported in Cui et al. (2003). A possible reason is that Cui et al. performed the evaluation using documents and search logs collected from the Encarta website, which is much cleaner and more homogenous than the data sets we used. The result suggests that although QE improves the recall of relevant documents, it is also likely to introduce noise that hurts the precision of document retrieval.

SMT (Row 3) is a SMT-based QE system. Following Riezler et al. (2008), the system is an implementation of a phrase-based SMT system with a standard set of features for translation model and language model, combined under a log linear model framework (Koehn et al. 2003). Different from Riezler et al.'s system where the translation model is trained on query-snippet pairs and the language model on queries, in our implementation the translation model is trained on query-title pairs and the language model on titles. To apply the system to QE, expansion terms of a query are taken from those terms in the 10-best translations of the query that have not been seen in the original query string. We see that **SMT** significantly outperforms **TC** in NDCG at all levels. The result confirms the conclusion of Riezler et al., demonstrating that context information is crucial for improving retrieval precision by filtering noisy expansions.

Both **TC** and **SMT**, considered as state-of-the-art QE methods, have been frequently used for comparison in related studies. Thus, we also used them as baselines in our experiments.

MRF (Row 4) is the ranker-based QE system described in Section 3, which uses a MRF-based ranker to incorporate all 8 classes of features derived from a variety of lexicon translation models and language models as in Equation (12). Results show that the ranker-based QE system significantly outperforms both **NoQE** and the two state-of-the-art QE methods. The fact that **MRF** beats **SMT** with a statistically significant margin although the former is a much simpler system indicates that text translation and QE are different tasks and some SMT components, designed for the task of regular text translation, are not as effective in selecting expansion terms. We will explore this in more detail in the next section.

4.2 Comparing Models

The experiments presented in this section investigate in detail the effectiveness of different models, e.g., the lexicon models and the language models described in Sections 2 and 3, in ranking expansion candidates for QE. The results are summarized in Rows 5 to 11 in Table 1, where a number of different versions of the ranker-based QE system are compared. These versions, labeled as $\mathbf{MRF}_f$, use the same candidate generator, and differ in the feature classes (which are specified by the subscript f) incorporated in the MRF-based ranker. In what follows, we focus our discussion on the results of the three lexicon models.

$\mathbf{MRF}_{wm}$ (Row 7) uses the word translation model described in Section 2.1. Both the word model and term correlation model used in $\mathbf{MRF}_{tm}$ (Row 6) are context independent. They differ mainly in the training methods. For the sake of comparison, in our experiment the word model is

EM-trained with the correlation model as initial point. Rezler et al. (2008) hypothesize that statistical translation model is superior to correlation model because the EM training captures the hidden alignment information when mapping document terms to query terms, leading to a better smoothed probability distribution. Our result (Row 7 vs. Row 6) verifies the hypothesis. Notice that $\mathbf{MRF}_{tc}$ outperforms **TC** in NDCG@1 (Row 6 vs. Row 2) mainly because in the former the expansion candidates are generated by a word translation model and are less noisy.

It is encouraging to observe that the rankers using the triplet model features achieve the QE performance either in par with or better than that of **SMT** (Rows 8, 10 and 11 vs. Row 3), although the latter is a much more sophisticated system. The result suggests that not all SMT components are useful for QE. For example, language models are indispensable for translation but are less effective than word models for QE (Row 5 vs. Rows 6 and 7). We also observe that the triplet model not only outperforms significantly the word model due to the use of contextual information (Row 8 vs. Row 7), but also seems to subsume the latter in that combining the features derived from both models in the ranker leads to little improvement over the ranker that uses only the triplet model features (Row 10 vs. Row 8).

The bilingual topic model underperforms the word model and the triplet model (Row 9 vs. Rows 7 and 8). However, we found that the bilingual topic model often selects a different set of expansion terms and is complementary to the other two lexicon models. As a result, unlike the case of combining the word model and triplet model features, incorporating the bilingual topic model features in the ranker leads to some visible improvement in NDCG at all positions (Row 11 vs. Row 10).

To better understand empirically how the MRF-based QE system achieves the improvement, we analyzed the expansions generated by our system in detail and obtained several interesting findings. First, as expected, in comparison with the word model, the triplet translation model is more effective in benefitting long queries, e.g., notably queries containing questions and queries containing song lyrics. Second, unlike the two lexicon models, the bilingual topic model tends to generate expansions that are more likely to relate to an entire query rather than individual query terms. Third, the features involving the order of the expansion terms benefitted queries containing named entities.

5 Related Work

In comparison with log-based methods studied in this paper, the QE methods based on automatic relevance feedback have been studied much more extensively in the information retrieval (IR) community, and have been proved useful for improving IR performance on benchmark datasets such as TREC (e.g., Rocchio 1971; Xu and Croft 1996; Lavrenko 2001; Zhai and Lafferty 2001). However, these methods cannot be applied directly to a commercial Web search engine because the relevant documents are not always available and generating pseudo-relevant documents requires multi-phase retrieval, which is prohibitively expensive. Although automatic relevance feedback is not the focus of this study, our method shares a lot of similarities with some of them. For example, similar to the way the parameters of our QE ranker are estimated, Cao et al. (2008) propose a method of selecting expansion terms to directly optimize average precision. The MRF model has been previously used for QE, in the form of relevance feedback and pseudo-relevance feedback (Metzler et al. 2007; Lang et al. 2010). While their MRF models use the features derived from IR systems such as Indri, we use the SMT-inspired features.

Using statistical translation models for IR is not new (e.g., Berger and Lafferty 1999; Jin et al. 2002; Xue et al. 2008). The effectiveness of the statistical translation-based approach to Web search has been demonstrated empirically in recent studies where word-based and phrase-based translation models are trained on large amounts of clickthrough data (e.g., Gao et al. 2010a; 2011). Our work extends these studies and constructs QE-oriented translation models that capture more flexible dependencies.

In addition to QE, search logs have also been used for other Web search tasks, such as document ranking (Joachims 2002; Agichtein et al. 2006), search query processing and spelling correction (Huang et al. 2010; Gao et al. 2010b) image retrieval (Craswell and Szummer 2007), and user query clustering (Baeza-Yates and Tiberi 2007; Wen et al. 2002).

6 Conclusions

In this paper we extend the previous log-based QE methods in two directions. First, we formulate QE as the problem of translating a source language of queries into a target language of documents, represented as titles. This allows us to adapt the established techniques developed for SMT to QE. Specially, we propose three lexicon models based on terms, lexicalized triplets, and topics, respectively. These models are trained on pairs of user queries and the titles of clicked documents using EM. Second, we present a ranker-based QE system, the heart of which is a MRF-based ranker in which the lexicon models are incorporated as features. We perform experiments on the Web search task using a real world data set. Results show that the proposed system outperforms significantly other state-of-the-art QE systems.

This study is part of a bigger, ongoing project, aiming to develop a real-time QE system for Web search, where simplicity is the key to the success. Thus, what we learned from this study is particularly encouraging. We demonstrate that with large amounts of clickthrough data for model training, simple lexicon models can achieve state-of-the-art QE performance, and that the MRF-based ranker provides a simple and flexible framework to incorporate a variety of features capturing different types of term dependencies in such an effective way that the Web search performance can be directly optimized.

References

Agichtein, E., Brill, E., and Dumais, S. 2006. Improving web search ranking by incorporating user behavior information. In *SIGIR*, pp. 19-26.

Baeze-Yates, R., and Ribeiro-Neto, B. 2011. *Modern Information Retrieval.* Addison-Wesley.

Baeza-Yates, R. and Tiberi, A. 2007. Extracting semantic relations from query logs. In *SIGKDD*, pp. 76-85.

Bai, J., Song, D., Bruza, P., Nie, J-Y., and Cao, G. 2005. Query expansion using term relationships in language models for information retrieval. In *CIKM*, pp. 688-695.

Bendersky, M., Metzler, D., and Croft, B. 2010. Learning concept importance using a weighted dependence model. In *WSDM*, pp. 31-40.

Berger, A., and Lafferty, J. 1999. Information retrieval as statistical translation. In *SIGIR*, pp. 222-229.

Bishop, C. M. 2006. *Patten recognition and machine learning.* Springer.

Blei, D. M., Ng, A. Y., and Jordan, M. J. 2003. Latent Dirichlet allocation. *Journal of Machine Learning Research*, 3: 993-1022.

Brown, P. F., Della Pietra, S. A., Della Pietra, V. J., and Mercer, R. L. 1993. The mathematics of statistical machine translation: parameter estimation. *Computational Linguistics*, 19(2): 263-311.

Cao, G., Nie, J-Y., Gao, J., and Robertson, S. 2008. Selecting good expansion terms for pseudo-relevance feedback. In *SIGIR*, pp. 289-305.

Craswell, N. and Szummer, M. 2007. Random walk on the click graph. In *SIGIR*. pp. 239-246.

Cui, H., Wen, J-R., Nie, J-Y. and Ma, W-Y. 2002. Probabilistic query expansion using query logs. In *WWW*, pp. 325-332.

Cui, H., Wen, J-R., Nie, J-Y. and Ma, W-Y. 2003. Query expansion by mining user log. *IEEE Trans on Knowledge and Data Engineering.* Vol. 15, No. 4. pp. 1-11.

Dempster, A., Laird, N., and Rubin, D. 1977. Maximum likelihood from incomplete data via the EM algorithm. *Journal of the Royal Statistical Society*, 39: 1-38.

Ganchev, K., Graca, J., Gillenwater, J., and Taskar, B. 2010. Posterior regularization for structured latent variable models. *Journal of Machine Learning Research,* 11 (2010): 2001-2049.

Gao, J., Toutanova, K., Yih., W-T. 2011. Clickthrough-based latent semantic models for web search. In *SIGIR*, pp. 675-684.

Gao, J., He, X., and Nie, J-Y. 2010a. Clickthrough-based translation models for web search: from word models to phrase models. In *CIKM,* pp. 1139-1148.

Gao, J., Li, X., Micol, D., Quirk, C., and Sun, X. 2010b. A large scale ranker-based system for query spelling correction. In *COLING*, pp. 358-366.

Gao, J., Yuan, W., Li, X., Deng, K., and Nie, J-Y. 2009. Smoothing clickthrough data for web search ranking. In *SIGIR*, pp. 355-362.

Gao, J., Qi, H., Xia, X., and Nie, J-Y. 2005. Linear discriminant model for information retrieval. In *SIGIR*, pp. 290-297.

Hasan, S., Ganitkevitch, J., Ney, H., and Andres-Fnerre, J. 2008. Triplet lexicon models for statistical machine translation. In *EMNLP*, pp. 372-381.

Huang, J., Gao, J., Miao, J., Li, X., Wang, K., and Behr, F. 2010. Exploring web scale language models for search query processing. In *WWW,* pp. 451-460.

Jarvelin, K. and Kekalainen, J. 2000. IR evaluation methods for retrieving highly relevant documents. In *SIGIR*, pp. 41-48

Jin, R., Hauptmann, A. G., and Zhai, C. 2002. Title language model for information retrieval. In *SIGIR*, pp. 42-48.

Jing, Y., and Croft., B. 1994. An association thesaurus for information retrieval. In *RIAO*, pp. 146-160.

Joachims, T. 2002. Optimizing search engines using clickthrough data. In *SIGKDD*, pp. 133-142.

Koehn, P., Och, F., and Marcu, D. 2003. Statistical phrase-based translation. In *HLT/NAACL*, pp. 127-133.

Lang, H., Metzler, D., Wang, B., and Li, J-T. 2010. Improving latent concept expansion using markov random fields. In *CIKM*, pp. 249-258.

Lavrenko, V., and Croft, B. 2001. Relevance-based language models. In *SIGIR*, pp. 120-128.

Lease, M. 2009. An improved markov random field model for supporting verbose queries. In *SIGIR*, pp. 476-483

Metzler, D., and Croft, B. 2005. A markov random field model for term dependencies. In *SIGIR*, pp. 472-479.

Metzler, D., and Croft, B. 2007. Latent concept expansion using markov random fields. In *SIGIR*, pp. 311-318.

Morgan, W., Greiff, W., and Henderson, J. 2004. *Direct maximization of average precision by hill-climbing with a comparison to a maximum entropy approach.* Technical report. MITRE.

Och, F. 2002. *Statistical machine translation: from single-word models to alignment templates.* PhD thesis, RWTH Aachen.

Prager, J., Chu-Carroll, J., and Czuba, K. 2001. Use of Wordnet hypernyms for answering what is questions. In *TREC 10*.

Press, W. H., Teukolsky, S. A., Vetterling, W. T., and Flannery, B. P. 1992. *Numerical Recipes in C*. Cambridge Univ. Press.

Rocchio, J. 1971. Relevance feedback in information retrieval. In *The SMART retrieval system: experiments in automatic document processing*, pp. 313-323, Prentice-Hall Inc.

Riezler, S., Liu, Y. and Vasserman, A. 2008. Translating queries into snippets for improving query expansion. In *COLING 2008*. 737-744.

Riezler, S., and Liu, Y. 2010. Query rewriting using monolingual statistical machine translation. *Computational Linguistics*, 36(3): 569-582.

Wen, J., Nie, J-Y., and Zhang, H. 2002. Query clustering using user logs. *ACM TOIS*, 20(1): 59-81.

Xu, J., and Croft, B. 1996. Query expansion using local and global document analysis. In *SIGIR*.

Xue, X., Jeon, J., Croft, W. B. 2008. Retrieval models for Question and answer archives. In *SIGIR*, pp. 475-482.

Zhai, C., and Lafferty, J. 2001a. Model-based feedback in the kl-divergence retrieval model. In *CIKM*, pp. 403-410.

Zhai, C., and Lafferty, J. 2001b. A study of smoothing methods for language models applied to ad hoc information retrieval. In *SIGIR*, pp. 334-342.

Joint Inference for Event Timeline Construction

Quang Xuan Do **Wei Lu** **Dan Roth**
Department of Computer Science
University of Illinois at Urbana-Champaign
Urbana, IL 61801, USA
{quangdo2,luwei,danr}@illinois.edu

Abstract

This paper addresses the task of constructing a timeline of events mentioned in a given text. To accomplish that, we present a novel representation of the temporal structure of a news article based on time intervals. We then present an algorithmic approach that jointly optimizes the temporal structure by coupling local classifiers that predict associations and temporal relations between pairs of temporal entities with global constraints. Moreover, we present ways to leverage knowledge provided by event coreference to further improve the system performance. Overall, our experiments show that the joint inference model significantly outperformed the local classifiers by 9.2% of relative improvement in F_1. The experiments also suggest that good event coreference could make remarkable contribution to a robust event timeline construction system.

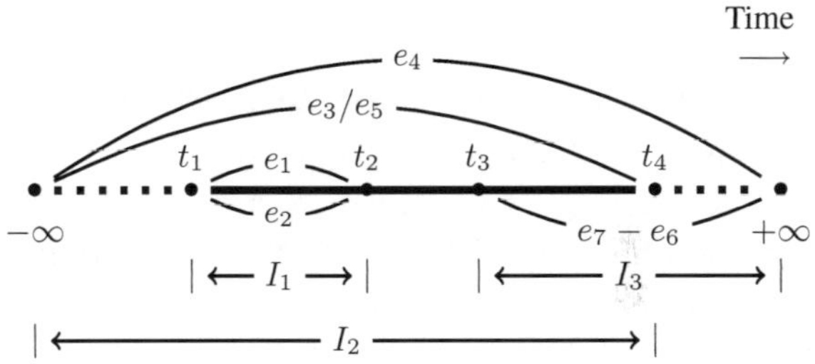

Figure 1: A graphical illustration of our timeline representation. The e's, t's and I's are events, time points and time intervals, respectively.

1 Introduction

Inferring temporal relations amongst a collection of events in a text is a significant step towards various important tasks such as automatic information extraction and document comprehension. Over the past few years, with the development of the TimeBank corpus (Pustejovsky et al., 2003) , there have been several works on building automatic systems for such a task (Mani et al., 2006; Chambers and Jurafsky, 2008; Yoshikawa et al., 2009; Denis and Muller, 2011).

Most previous works devoted much efforts to the task of identifying relative temporal relations (such as *before*, or *overlap*) amongst events (Chambers and Jurafsky, 2008; Denis and Muller, 2011), without addressing the task of identifying correct associations between events and their absolute time of occurrence. Even if this issue is addressed, certain restrictions are often imposed for efficiency reasons (Yoshikawa et al., 2009; Verhagen et al., 2010). In practice, however, being able to automatically infer the correct time of occurrence associated with each event is crucial. Such information not only leads to better text comprehension, but also enables fusion of event structures extracted from multiple articles or domains.

In this work, we are specifically interested in mapping events into an universal *timeline* representation. Besides inferring the relative temporal relations amongst the events, we would also like to automatically infer a specific absolute time of occurrence for each event mentioned in the text. Unlike previous work, we associate each event with a specific absolute time interval inferred from the text. An example timeline representation is illustrated in Fig.

1. Further details of our timeline representation are given in Sec. 2.3.

We perform global inference by combining a collection of local pairwise classifiers through the use of an Integer Linear Programming (ILP) formulation that promotes global coherence among local decisions. The formulation allows our model to predict both event-event relations and event-time interval associations simultaneously. We show that, with the use of time intervals instead of time points, our approach leads to a more concise ILP formulation with reduced number of variables and constraints.

Moreover, we observed that event coreference can reveal important information for such a task. We propose that different event mentions that refer to the same event can be grouped together before classification and performing global inference. This can reduce the amount of efforts in both classification and inference stages and can potentially eliminate mistakes that would be made otherwise without such coreference information. To the best of our knowledge, our proposal of leveraging event coreference to support event timeline construction is novel.

Our experiments on a collection of annotated news articles from the standard ACE dataset demonstrate that our approach produces robust timelines of events. We show that our algorithmic approach is able to combine various local evidences to produce a global coherent temporal structure, with improved overall performance. Furthermore, the experiments show that the overall performance can be further improved by exploiting knowledge from event coreference.

2 Background

We focus on the task of mapping event mentions in a news article to a timeline. We first briefly describe and define several basic concepts.

2.1 Events

Following the annotation guidelines of the ACE project, we define an event as an action or occurrence that happens with associated participants or arguments. We also distinguish between events and event mentions, where a unique event can be coreferred to by a set of explicit event mentions in an article. Formally, an event E^i is co-referred to by a set of event mentions $(e^i_1, e^i_2, \ldots, e^i_k)$. Each event mention e can be written as $p(a_1, a_2, \ldots, a_l)$, where the predicate p is the word that triggers the presence of e in text, and $a_1, a_2, \ldots a_l$ are the arguments associated with e. In this work we focus on four temporal relations between two event mentions including *before*, *after*, *overlap* and *no relation*.

2.2 Time Intervals

Similar to Denis and Muller (2011), we define time intervals as pairs of time endpoints. Each time interval I is denoted by $[t^-, t^+]$, where t^- and t^+ are two time endpoints representing the lower and upper bound of the interval I, respectively, with $t^- \le t^+$. The general form of a time endpoint is written as "*YYYY-MM-DD hh:mm:ss*". An endpoint can be undefined, in which case it is set to an infinity value: $-\infty$, or $+\infty$. There are two types of time intervals:

Explicit intervals are time intervals that can be extracted directly from a given text. For example, consider the following snippet of an article in our data set: *The litigation covers buyers in auctions outside the United States between January 1, 1993 and February 7, 2000.* In this example, we can extract and normalize two time intervals which are explicitly written, including *January 1, 1993* $\rightarrow$ [1993-01-01 00:00:00, 1993-01-01 23:59:59] and *February 7, 2000* $\rightarrow$ [2000-02-07 00:00:00, 2000-02-07 23:59:59]. Moreover, an explicit interval can also be formed by one or more separate explicit temporal expressions. In the example above, the connective term *between* relates the two expressions to form a single time interval: *between January 1, 1993 and February 7, 2000* $\rightarrow$ [1993-01-01 00:00:00, 2000-02-07 23:59:59]. To extract explicit time intervals from text, we use the time interval extractor described in Zhao et al. (2012).

Implicit intervals are time intervals that are not explicitly mentioned in the text. We observed that there are events that cannot be assigned to any precise time interval but are roughly known to occur in the past or in the future relative to the Document Creation Time (DCT) of the article. We introduce two implicit time intervals to represent the past and the future events as $(-\infty, t^-_{DCT}]$ and $[t^+_{DCT}, +\infty)$, respectively. In addition, we also allow an event mention to be assigned into the entire timeline, which is denoted by $(-\infty, +\infty)$ if we cannot identify its time of occurrence. We also consider DCT as an implicit interval.

We say that the time interval I_i precedes the time interval I_j on a timeline if and only if $t_i^+ \leq t_j^-$, which also implies that I_i succeeds I_j if and only if $t_i^- \geq t_j^+$. The two intervals overlap, otherwise.

2.3 Timeline

We define a timeline as a partially ordered set of time intervals. Fig. 1 gives a graphical illustration of an example timeline, where events are annotated and associated with time intervals. Relations amongst events can be properly reflected in the timeline representation. For example, in the figure, the events e_1 and e_2 are both associated with the interval I_1. The relation between them is *no relation*, since it is unclear which occurs first. On the other hand, e_5 and e_3 both happen in the interval I_2 but they form an *overlap* relation. The events e_6 and e_7 occur within the same interval I_3, but e_7 precedes (i.e. *before*) e_6 on the timeline. The event e_4 is associated with the interval $(-\infty, +\infty)$, indicating there is no knowledge about its time of occurrence.

We believe that such a timeline representation for temporally ordering events has several advantages over the temporal graph representations used in previous works (Chambers and Jurafsky, 2008; Yoshikawa et al., 2009; Denis and Muller, 2011). Unlike previous works, in our model the events are partially ordered in a single timeline, where each event is associated with a precise time interval. This improves human interpretability of the temporal relations amongst events and time. This property of our timeline representation, thus, facilitates merging multiple timelines induced from different articles. Furthermore, as we will show later, the use of time intervals within the timeline representation simplifies the global inference formulation and thus the inference process.

3 A Joint Timeline Model

Our task is to induce a globally coherent timeline for a given article. We thus adopt a global inference model for performing the task. The model consists of two components: (1) two local pairwise classifiers, one between event mentions and time intervals (the E–T classifier) and one between event mentions themselves (the E–E classifier), and (2) a joint inference module that enforces global coherency constraints on the final outputs of the two local classifiers. Fig. 2 shows a simplified temporal structure of event mentions and time intervals of an article in our model.

Our E–T classifier is different from previous work (Chambers and Jurafsky, 2008; Yoshikawa et al., 2009; Denis and Muller, 2011), where such classifiers were trained to identify temporal relations between event mentions and a temporal *expression*. In our work, in order to construct absolute timeline of event mentions, temporal expressions are captured and normalized as absolute time intervals. The E–T classifiers are then used to assign event mentions to their contextually corresponding time intervals.

We also lifted several restrictions imposed in previous work (Bethard et al., 2007; Yoshikawa et al., 2009; Verhagen et al., 2010). Specifically, we do not require that event mentions and time expressions have to appear in the same sentence, and we do not require two event mentions have to appear very close to each other (e.g., main event mentions in adjacent sentences) in order to be considered as candidate pairs for classification. Instead, we performed classifications over all pairs of event mentions and time intervals as well as over all pairs of event mentions. We show through experiments that lifting these restrictions is indeed important (see Sec. 5).

Another important improvement over previous work is our global inference model We would like to highlight that our work is also distinct from most previous works in the global inference component. Specifically, our global inference model jointly optimizes the *E-E* relations amongst event mentions and their associations, *E-T*, with temporal information (intervals in our case). Previous work (Chambers and Jurafsky, 2008; Denis and Muller, 2011), on the other hand, assumed that the *E-T* information is given and only tried to improve *E-E*.

3.1 The Pairwise Classifiers

We first describe our local classifiers that associate event mention with time interval and classify temporal relations between event mentions, respectively.

C_{E-T}: is the E–T classifier that associates an event mention with a time interval. Given an event mention and a time interval, the classifier predicts

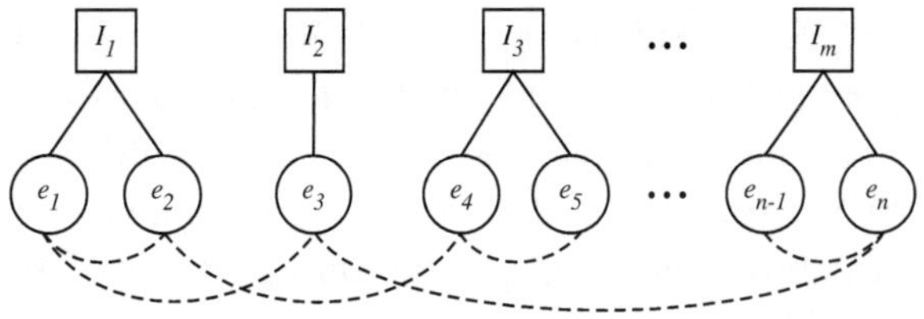

Figure 2: A simplified temporal structure of an article. There are m time intervals $I_1 \cdots I_m$ and n event mentions $e_1 \cdots e_n$. A solid edge indicates an association between an interval and an event mention, whereas a dash edge illustrates a temporal relation between two event mentions.

whether the former associates with the latter.

$$C_{E-T}(e_i, I_j) \rightarrow \{0, 1\}, \\ \forall i, j, 1 \leq i \leq n, 1 \leq j \leq m, \quad (1)$$

where n and m are the number of event mentions and time intervals in an article, respectively.

C_{E-E}: is the E–E classifier that identifies the temporal relation between two event mentions. Given a pair of event mentions, the classifier predicts one of the four temporal relations between them: $\bar{b}$*efore*, $\bar{a}$*fter*, $\bar{o}$*verlap* and $\bar{n}$*o relation*. Specifically:

$$C_{E-E}(e_i, e_j) \rightarrow \{\bar{b}, \bar{a}, \bar{o}, \bar{n}\}, \\ \forall i, j, 1 \leq i, j \leq n, i \neq j, \quad (2)$$

For training of the classifiers, we define a set of features following some previous work (Bethard et al., 2007; Chambers and Jurafsky, 2008; Yoshikawa et al., 2009), together with some additional features that we believe to be helpful for the interval-based representation. We describe the base features below and use † and ‡ to denote the features used for C_{E-T} and C_{E-E}, respectively. We use the term *temporal entity* (or *entity*, for short) to refer to either an event mention or a time interval.

Lexical Features: A set of lexical features related to the temporal entities: (i)†‡ the word, lemma and part-of-speech of the input event mentions and the context surrounding them, where the context is defined as a window of 2 words before and after the mention; (ii)† the modal verbs to the left and to the right of the event mention; (iii)‡ the temporal connectives between the event mentions[1].

[1]We define a list of temporal connectives including *before*, *after*, *since*, *when*, *meanwhile*, *lately*, etc.

Syntactic Features: (i)†‡ which entity appears first in the text; (ii)†‡ whether the two entities appear in the same sentence; (iii)†‡ the quantized number of sentences between the two entities[2]; (iv)†‡ whether the input event mentions are covered by prepositional phrases and what are the heads of the phrases; (v)†‡ if the entities are in the same sentence, what is their least common constituent on the syntactic parse tree; (vi)† whether there is any other temporal entity that is closer to one of the two entities.

Semantic Features‡: A set of semantic features, mostly related to the input event mentions: (i) whether the input event mentions have a common synonym from their synsets in WordNet (Fellbaum, 1998); (ii) whether the input event mentions have a common derivational form derived from WordNet.

Linguistic Features†‡: The tense and the aspect of the input event mentions. We use an in-house rule-based recognizer to extract these features.

Time Interval Features†: A set of features related to the input time interval: (i) whether the interval is implicit; (ii) if it is implicit, identify its interval type: "dct" = $[t^-_{DCT}, t^+_{DCT}]$, "past" = $(-\infty, t^-_{DCT}]$, "feature" = $[t^+_{DCT}, +\infty)$, and "entire" = $(-\infty, +\infty)$; (iii) the interval is before, after or overlapping with the DCT.

We note that unlike many previous work (Mani et al., 2006; Chambers and Jurafsky, 2008; Denis and Muller, 2011), our classifiers do not use any gold annotations of event attributes (event class, tense, aspect, modal and polarity) provided in the TimeBank corpus as features.

In our work, we use a regularized averaged Perceptron (Freund and Schapire, 1999) as our classification algorithm[3]. We used the one-vs.-all scheme to transform a set of binary classifiers into a multiclass classifier (for C_{E-E}). The raw prediction scores were converted into probability distribution using the Softmax function (Bishop 1996). If there are n classes and the raw score of class i is act_i, the posterior estimation for class i is:

$$\tilde{P}(i) = \frac{e^{act_i}}{\sum_{1 \leq j \leq n} e^{act_j}}$$

[2]We quantize the number of sentences between two entities to 0, 1, 2, less than 5 and greater than or equal to 5

[3]Other algorithm (e.g. SVM) gave comparable or worse results, so we only show the results from Averaged Perceptron.

3.2 Joint Inference for Event Timeline

To exploit the interaction among the temporal entities in an article, we optimize the predicted temporal structure, formed by predictions from C_{E-T} and C_{E-E}, w.r.t. a set of global constraints that enforce coherency on the final structure. We perform exact inference using Integer Linear Programming (ILP) as in (Roth and Yih, 2007; Clarke and Lapata, 2008). We use the Gurobi Optimizer[4] as a solver.

Let $\mathcal{I} = \{I_1, I_2, \ldots, I_m\}$ denote the set of time intervals extracted from an article, and let $\mathcal{E} = \{e_1, e_2, \ldots, e_n\}$ denote all event mentions in the same article. Let $\mathcal{EI} = \{(e_i, I_j) \in \mathcal{E} \times \mathcal{I} | e_i \in \mathcal{E}, I_j \in \mathcal{I}\}$ denote the set of all pairs of event mentions and time intervals. We also denote the set of event mention pairs by $\mathcal{EE} = \{(e_i, e_j) \in \mathcal{E} \times \mathcal{E} | e_i \in \mathcal{E}, e_j \in \mathcal{E}, i \neq j\}$. The prediction probability of an association of a pair $eI \in \mathcal{EI}$, given by classifier C_{E-T}, is denoted by $p_{\langle eI,1 \rangle}$[5]. Now, let $\mathcal{R} = \{\bar{b}, \bar{a}, \bar{o}, \bar{n}\}$ be the set of temporal relations between two event mentions. The prediction probability of an event mention pair $ee \in \mathcal{EE}$ that takes temporal relation r, given by C_{E-E}, is denoted by $p_{\langle ee,r \rangle}$. Furthermore, we define $x_{\langle eI,1 \rangle}$ to be a binary indicator variable that takes on the value 1 iff an association is predicted between e and I. Similarly, we define a binary indicator variable $y_{\langle ee,r \rangle}$ of a pair of event mentions ee that takes on the value 1 iff ee is predicted to hold the relation r.

The objective function is then defined as a linear combination of the prediction probabilities from the two local classifiers as follows:

$$\arg\max_{x,y} \Big[\lambda \sum_{eI \in \mathcal{EI}} p_{\langle eI,1 \rangle} \cdot x_{\langle eI,1 \rangle} + (1-\lambda) \sum_{ee \in \mathcal{EE}} \sum_{r \in \mathcal{R}} p_{\langle ee,r \rangle} \cdot y_{\langle ee,r \rangle}\Big] \quad (3)$$

subject to the following constraints:

$$x_{\langle eI,1 \rangle} \in \{0,1\}, \quad \forall eI \in \mathcal{EI} \quad (4)$$

$$y_{\langle ee,r \rangle} \in \{0,1\}, \quad \forall ee \in \mathcal{EE}, r \in \mathcal{R} \quad (5)$$

$$\sum_{r \in \mathcal{R}} y_{\langle ee,r \rangle} = 1, \quad \forall ee \in \mathcal{EE} \quad (6)$$

[4] http://gurobi.com/

[5] This value is complementary to the non-association probability, denoted by $p_{\langle eI,0 \rangle} = 1 - p_{\langle eI,1 \rangle}$

We use the single parameter λ to balance the overall contribution of two components E-T and E-E. λ is determined through cross validation tuning on a development set. We use (4) and (5) to make sure $x_{\langle eI,1 \rangle}$ and $y_{\langle ee,r \rangle}$ are binary values. The equality constraint (6) ensures that exactly one particular relation can be assigned to each event mention pair.

In addition, we also require that each event is associated with only one time interval. These constraints are encoded as follows:

$$\sum_{I \in \mathcal{I}} x_{\langle eI,1 \rangle} = 1, \quad \forall e \in \mathcal{E} \quad (7)$$

Our model also enforces reflexivity and transitivity constraints on the relations among event mentions as follows:

$$y_{\langle e_ie_j,r \rangle} - y_{\langle e_je_i,\hat{r} \rangle} = 0, \quad \forall e_ie_j = (e_i, e_j) \in \mathcal{EE}, i \neq j \quad (8)$$

$$y_{\langle e_ie_j,r_1 \rangle} + y_{\langle e_je_k,r_2 \rangle} - y_{\langle e_ie_k,r_3 \rangle} \leq 1, \quad \forall e_ie_j, e_je_k, e_ie_k \in \mathcal{EE}, i \neq j \neq k \quad (9)$$

The equality constraints in (8) encode reflexive property of event-event relations, where the relation $\hat{r}$ denotes the inversion of the relation r. The set of possible $(r, \hat{r})$ pairs is defined as follows: $\{(\bar{b}, \bar{a}), (\bar{a}, \bar{b}), (\bar{o}, \bar{o}), (\bar{n}, \bar{n})\}$. Following the work of (Bramsen et al., 2006; Chambers and Jurafsky, 2008), we encode transitive closure of relations between event mentions with inequality constraints in (9), which states that if the pair (e_i, e_j) has a certain relation r_1, and the pair (e_j, e_k) has the relation r_2, then the relation r_3 must be satisfied between e_i and e_k. Examples of such triple (r_1, r_2, r_3) include ($\bar{b}$, $\bar{b}$, $\bar{b}$) and ($\bar{a}$, $\bar{a}$, $\bar{a}$).

Finally, to capture the interactions between our local pairwise classifiers we add the following constraints:

$$x_{\langle e_iI_k,1 \rangle} + x_{\langle e_jI_l,1 \rangle} - y_{\langle e_ie_j,\bar{b} \rangle} \leq 1, \quad \forall e_iI_k, e_jI_l \in \mathcal{EI}, \forall e_ie_j \in \mathcal{EE}, \; I_k \text{ precedes } I_l, i \neq j, k \neq l \quad (10)$$

Intuitively, the inequality constraints in (10) specify that a temporal relation between two event mentions can be inferred from their respective associated time intervals. Specifically, if two event mentions e_i and e_j are associated with two time intervals I_k and I_l respectively, and I_k precedes I_l in the timeline, then e_i must happen before e_j.

It is important to note that our interval-based formulation is more concise in terms of the number of variables and constraints needed in the ILP relative to time expression-based (or timepoint-based) formulations used in previous work (Chambers and Jurafsky, 2008). Specifically, in such timepoint-based formulations, the relation between each event mention and each time expression needs to be inferred, resulting in $|\mathcal{E}||\mathcal{T}||\mathcal{R}_{\mathcal{T}}|$ variables, where $|\mathcal{E}|$, $|\mathcal{T}|$, and $|\mathcal{R}_{\mathcal{T}}|$ are the numbers of event mentions, time points, and temporal relations respectively. In contrast, only $|\mathcal{E}||\mathcal{I}|$ variables are required in our formulation, where $|\mathcal{I}|$ is the number of intervals (since we extract intervals explicitly, $|\mathcal{I}|$ is roughly equal to $|\mathcal{T}|$). Furthermore, performing inference with the timepoint-based formulation would require $|\mathcal{E}||\mathcal{T}|$ equality constraints to enforce that each event mention can take only one relation in $\mathcal{R}_I$ for a particular time point, whereas our interval-based model only requires $|\mathcal{E}|$ constraints, since each event is strictly associated with one interval (see Eqn. (7)). We justify the benefits of our formulation later in Sec. 5.4.

4 Incorporating Knowledge from Event Coreference

One of the key contributions of our work is using event coreference information to enhance the timeline construction performance. This is motivated by the following two principles:

(P1) *All mentions of a unique event are associated with the same time interval, and overlap with each other.*

(P2) *All mentions of an event have the same temporal relation with all mentions of another event.*

The example below, extracted from an article published on 03/11/2003 in the Automatic Content Extraction (ACE), 2005, corpus[6] serves to illustrate the significance of event coreference to our task.

The world's most powerful fine art auction houses, Sotheby's and Christie's, have agreed to [e_1^1 = **pay**] *40 million dollars to settle an international price-fixing scam, Sotheby's said. The* [e_2^1 = **payment**], *if approved by the courts, would settle a slew of* [e_1^2 = **suits**] *by clients over auctions held* <u>*between 1993 and 2000*</u> *outside the US. ... Sotheby's and Christie's will each* [e_3^1 = **pay**] *20 million dollars," said Sotheby's, which operates in 34 countries.*

In this example, there are 4 event mentions, whose trigger words are highlighted in bold face. The underlined text gives an explicit time interval: I_1 = [1993-01-01 00:00:00, 2000-12-31 23:59:59] (we ignore 2 other intervals given by *1993* and *2000* to simplify the illustration). Now if we consider the event mention e_2^1, it actually belongs to the implicit future interval I_2 = [2003-03-11 23:59:59, $+\infty$). Nevertheless, there is a reasonable chance that C_{E-T} associates it with I_1, given that they both appear in the same sentence, and there is no direct evident feature indicating the event will actually happen in the future. In such a situation, using a local classifier to identify the correct temporal association could be challenging.

Fortunately, precise knowledge from event coreference may help alleviate such a problem. The knowledge reveals that the 4 event mentions can be grouped into 2 distinct events: $E^1 = \{e_1^1, e_2^1, e_3^1\}$, $E^2 = \{e_1^2\}$. If C_{E-T} can make a strong prediction in associating the event mention e_1^1 (or e_3^1) to I_2, instead of I_1, the system will have a high chance to re-assign e_2^1 to I_2 based on principle (P1). Similarly, if C_{E-E} is effective in figuring out that some mention of event E^1 occurs *after* some mention of E^2, then all the mentions of E^1 would be predicted to occur *after* all mentions in E^2 according to (P2).

To incorporate knowledge from event coreference into our classifiers and the joint inference model, we use the following procedure: (1) performing classification with C_{E-T} and C_{E-E} on the data, (2) using the knowledge from event coreference to overwrite the prediction probabilities obtained by the two local classifiers in step (1), and (3) applying the joint inference model on the new prediction probabilities obtained from (2). We note that if we stop at step (2), we get the outputs of the local classifiers enhanced by event coreference knowledge.

To overwrite the classification probabilities using

[6] http://www.itl.nist.gov/iad/mig/tests/ace/2005/

event coreference knowledge, we propose two approaches as follows:

MaxScore: We define the probability between any mention $e \in E^i$ and an interval I as follows:

$$p_{\langle eI,1\rangle} = \max_{e' \in E^i} \tilde{P}(e', I) \quad (11)$$

where $\tilde{P}(e', I)$ is the classifier (C_{E-T}) probability for associating event mention e' to the time interval.

On the other hand, the probabilities for associating the set of temporal relations, $\mathcal{R}$, to each pair of mentions in $E^i \times E^j$, is given by the following pair:

$$\begin{aligned} (e^i, e^j)^* &= \operatorname*{arg\,max}_{(e^{i'}, e^{j'}) \in E^i \times E^j, r \in \mathcal{R}} \tilde{P}\big((e^{i'}, e^{j'}), r\big) \\ p_{\langle ee,r\rangle} &= \tilde{P}\big((e^i, e^j)^*, r\big), \forall r \in \mathcal{R} \end{aligned} \quad (12)$$

In other words, over all possible event mention pairs and relations, we first pick the pair who globally obtains the highest probability for some relation. Next, we simply take the probability distribution of that event mention pair as the distribution over the relations, for the event pair.

SumScore: The probability between any mention $e \in E^i$ and an interval I is obtained by:

$$p_{\langle eI,1\rangle} = \frac{1}{|E^i|} \sum_{e' \in E^i} \tilde{P}(e', I) \quad (13)$$

To obtain the probability distribution over the set of temporal relations, $\mathcal{R}$, for any pair of mentions in $E^i \times E^j$, we used the following procedure:

$$\begin{aligned} r^* &= \operatorname*{arg\,max}_{r \in \mathcal{R}} \sum_{e^i \in E^i} \sum_{e^j \in E^j} \tilde{P}\big((e^i, e^j), r\big) \\ (e^i, e^j)^* &= \operatorname*{arg\,max}_{(e^{i'}, e^{j'}) \in E^i \times E^j} \tilde{P}\big((e^{i'}, e^{j'}), r^*\big) \\ p_{\langle ee,r\rangle} &= \tilde{P}\big((e^i, e^j)^*, r\big), \forall r \in \mathcal{R} \end{aligned} \quad (14)$$

In other words, given two groups of event mentions, we first compute the total score of each relation, and select the relation which has the highest score. Next from the list of pairs of event mentions from the two groups, we select the pair which has the relation r* with highest score compared to all other pairs. The probability distribution of this pair will be used as the probability distribution of all event mention pairs between the two events.

In both approaches, we assign the *overlap* relations to all pairs of event mentions in the same event with probability 1.0.

5 Experimental Study

We first describe the experimental data and then present and discuss the experimental results.

5.1 Data and Setup

Most previous works in temporal reasoning used the TimeBank corpus as a benchmark. The corpus contains a fairly diverse collection of annotated event mentions, without any specific focus on certain event types. According to the annotation guideline of the corpus, most of verbs, nominalizations, adjectives, predicative clauses and prepositional phrases can be tagged as events. However, in practice, when performing temporal reasoning about events in a given text, one is typically interested in significant and typed events, such as *Killing*, *Legislation*, *Election*. Furthermore, event mentions in TimeBank are annotated with neither event arguments nor event coreference information.

We noticed that the ACE 2005 corpus contains the annotation that we are interested in. The corpus consists of articles annotated with event mentions (with event triggers and arguments) and event coreference information. To create an experimental data set for our work, we selected from the corpus 20 newswire articles published in March 2003. To extract time intervals from the articles, we used the time interval extractor described in (Zhao et al., 2012) with minimal post-processing. Implicit intervals are also added according to Sec. 2.2. We then hired an annotator with expertise in the field to annotate the data with the following information: (i) event mention and time interval association, and (ii) the temporal relations between event mentions, including $\{\bar{b}, \bar{a}, \bar{o}\}$. The annotator was not required to annotate all pairs of event mentions, but as many as possible. Next, we saturated the relations based on the initial annotations as follows: (i) event mentions that had not been associated with any time intervals were assigned to the entire timeline interval $(-\infty, +\infty)$, and (ii) added inferred temporal relations between event mentions with reflectivity and transitivity. Table 1 shows the data statistics before and after saturation. There are totally 8312 event pairs from 20 documents, including *no relation* pairs. We note that in a separate experiment, we still evaluated C_{E-E} on the TimeBank corpus and got better performance

Data	#Intervals	#E-mentions	#E-T	#E-E
Initial	232	324	305	376
Saturated	232	324	324	5940

Table 1: The statistics of our experimental data set.

than a corresponding classifier in an existing work (see Sec. 5.4).

We conducted all experiments with 5-fold cross validation at the instance level on our data set after saturation. The global inference model was applied on a whole document. The results of the systems are reported in averaged precision, recall and F_1 score on the association performance, for C_{E-T}, and the temporal relations (we excluded the $\bar{n}$ relation, for C_{E-E}). We also measured the overall performance of the systems by computing the average of the performance of the classifiers.

5.2 A Baseline

We developed a baseline system that works as follows. It associates an event mention with the closest time interval found in the same sentence. If such an interval is not found, the baseline associates the mention with the closest time interval to the left. If the interval is again not found, the mention will be associated with the DCT interval. The baseline is based on the intuition of natural reading order: events that are mentioned earlier are likely to precede those mentioned later. For the temporal relation between a pair of event mentions, the baseline treats the event mention that appears earlier in the text as temporally happening before the other mention. The baseline performance is shown in the first group of results in Table 2.

5.3 Our Systems

For our systems, we first evaluated the performance of our local pairwise classifiers and the global inference model. The second group of results in Table 2 shows the systems' performance. Overall, the results show that our global inference model relatively outperformed the baseline and the local classifiers by 57.8% and 9.2% in F_1, respectively. We perform a bootstrap resampling significance test (Koehn, 2004) on the output predictions of the local classifiers with and without the inference model. The test shows that the overall improvement with the inference model is statistically significant ($p < 0.01$). This indicates the effectiveness of our joint inference model with global coherence constraints.

Next, we integrated event coreference knowledge into our systems (as described in Sec. 4) and evaluated their performance. Our experiments showed that the *SumScore* approach works better for C_{E-T}, while *MaxScore* is more suitable for C_{E-E}. Our observations showed that event mentions of an event may appear in close proximity with multiple time intervals in the text, making C_{E-T} produce high prediction scores for many event mention-interval pairs. This, consequently, confuses *MaxScore* on the best association of the event and the time intervals, whereas *SumScore* overcomes the problem by averaging out the association scores. On the other hand, C_{E-E} gets more benefit from *MaxScore* because C_{E-E} works better on pairs of event mentions that appear closely in the text, which activate more valuable learning features. We will report the results using the best approach of each classifier.

To evaluate our systems with event coreference knowledge, we first experimented our systems with gold event coreference as given by the ACE 2005 corpus. Table 2 shows the contribution of event coreference to our systems in the third group of the results. The results show that injecting knowledge from event coreference remarkably improved both the local classifiers and the joint inference model. Overall, the system that combined event coreference and the global inference model achieved the best performance, which significantly overtook all other compared systems. Specifically, it outperformed the baseline system, the local classifiers, and the joint inference model without event coreference with 80%, 25%, and 14% of relative improvement in F_1, respectively. It also consistently outperformed the local classifiers enhanced with event coreference. We note that the precision and recall of C_{E-T} in the joint inference model are the same because the inference model enforced each event mention to be associated with exactly one time interval. This is also true for the systems integrated with event coreference because our integration approaches assign only one time interval to an event mention.

We next move to experimenting with automatically learned event coreference systems. In this ex-

	Model	C_{E-T}			C_{E-E}			**Overall**		
		Prec.	*Rec.*	F_1	*Prec.*	*Rec.*	F_1	*Prec.*	*Rec.*	F_1
1	**Baseline**	33.29	33.29	33.29	20.86	32.81	25.03	27.06	33.05	29.16
	No Event Coref.									
2	Local classifiers	62.70	34.50	43.29	40.46	42.42	40.96	51.58	38.46	42.13
	Global inference	47.88	47.88	47.88	41.42	48.04	44.14	44.65	47.96	46.01
	With Gold Event Coref.									
3	Local classifiers	50.88	50.88	50.88	43.86	52.65	47.46	47.37	51.77	49.17
	Global inference	50.88	50.88	50.88	48.04	62.45	54.05	49.46	56.67	52.47
	With Learned Event Coref.									
4	Local classifiers	46.37	46.37	46.37	40.83	45.28	42.60	43.60	45.83	44.49
	Global inference	46.37	46.37	46.37	42.09	52.50	46.47	44.23	49.44	46.42

Table 2: Performance under various evaluation settings. All figures are averaged scores from 5-fold cross-validation experiments.

periment, we re-trained the event coreference system described in Chen et al. (2009) on all articles in the ACE 2005 corpus, excluding the 20 articles used in our data set. The performance of these systems are shown in the fourth group of the results in Table 2. The results show that by using a learned event coreference system, we achieved the same improvement trends as with gold event coreference. However, we did not obtain significant improvement when comparing with global inference without event coreference information. This result shows that the performance of an event coreference system can have a significant impact on the overall performance. While this suggests that a better event coreference system could potentially help the task more, it also opens the question whether event coreference can be benefited from our local classifiers through the use of a joint inference framework. We would like to leave this for future investigations.

5.4 Previous Work-Related Experiments

We also performed experiments using the same setting as in (Yoshikawa et al., 2009), which followed the guidelines of the TempEval challenges (Verhagen et al., 2007; Verhagen et al., 2010), on our saturated data. Several assumptions were made to simplify the task. For example, only main events in adjacent sentences are considered when identifying event-event relations. See (Yoshikawa et al., 2009) for more details. We performed 5-fold cross validation without event coreference. Overall, the system achieved 29.99 F_1 for the local classifiers and 34.69 when the global inference is used. These results are better than the baseline but underperform our full models where those simplification assumptions are not imposed, as shown in Table 2, indicating the importance of relaxing their assumptions in practice.

We also evaluated our C_{E-E} on the TimeBank corpus. We followed the settings of Chambers and Jurafsky (2008) to extract all event mention pairs that were annotated with *before* (or *ibefore*, "immediately before") and *after* (or *iafter*) relations in 183 news articles in the corpus. We trained and evaluated our C_{E-E} on these examples with the same feature set that we evaluated in our experiments above, with gold tense and aspect features but without event type. Following their work, we performed 10-fold cross validation. Our classifier achieved a micro-averaged accuracy of 73.45%, whereas Chambers and Jurafsky (2008) reported 66.8%. We next injected the knowledge of an event coreference system trained on the ACE2005 corpus into our C_{E-E}, and obtained a micro-averaged accuracy of 73.39%. It was not surprising that event coreference did not help in this dataset because: (i) different domains – the event coreference was trained on ACE 05 but applied on TimeBank, and (ii) different annotation guidelines on events in ACE 2005 and TimeBank.

Finally, we conducted an experiment that justifies the advantages of our interval-based inference model over a time point-based inference. To do this, we first converted our data in Table 1 from intervals to time points and infer the temporal relations between the annotated event mentions and the time points: *before*, *after*, *overlap*, and *unknown*. We modified the first component in the objective function in (3) to accommodate these temporal relations. We also made several changes to the constraints, including removing those in (7) since they are no longer required, and adding constraints that ensure the relation between a time point and an event mention takes exactly one value. Proper changes were also made to other constraints in (10) to reflect the fact that time points are considered rather than intervals. We observed that experiment with such a formulation was unable to finish within 5 hours (we terminated the ILP inference after waiting for 5 hours), whereas our interval-based model finished the experiment with an average of 21 seconds per article.

6 Related Work

Research in temporal reasoning recently received much attention. Allen (1983) introduced an interval based temporal logic which has been used widely in the field. Recent efforts in building an annotated temporal corpus (Pustejovsky et al., 2003) has popularized the use of machine learning techniques for the task (Mani et al., 2006; Bethard et al., 2007). This corpus was later used (with simplifications) in two TempEval challenges (Verhagen et al., 2007; Verhagen et al., 2010). In these challenges, several temporal-related tasks were defined including the tasks of identifying the temporal relation between an event mention and a temporal expression in the same sentence, and recognizing temporal relations of pairs of event mentions in adjacent sentences. However, with several restrictions imposed to these tasks, the developed systems were not practical.

Recently, there has been much work attempting to leverage Allen's interval algebra of temporal relations to enforce global constraints on local predictions. The work of Tatu and Srikanth (2008) used global relational constraints to not only expand the training data but also identifies temporal inconsistencies to improve local classifiers. They used greedy search to select the most appropriate configuration of temporal relations among events and temporal expressions. For exact inferences, Bramsen et al. (2006), Chambers and Jurafsky (2008), Denis and Muller (2011), and Talukdar et al. (2012) formulated the temporal reasoning problem in an ILP. However, the inference models in their work were not a joint model involving multiple local classifiers but only one local classifier was involved in their objective functions.

The work of Yoshikawa et al. (2009) did formulate a joint inference model with Markov Logic Network (MLN). They, however, used the same setting as the TempEval challenges, thus only pairs of temporal entities in the same or adjacent sentences are considered. Our work, on the other hand, focuses on constructing an event timeline with time intervals, taking multiple local pairwise predictions into a joint inference model and removing the restrictions on the positions of the temporal entities. Furthermore, we propose for the first time to use event coreference and evaluate the importance of its role in the task of event timeline construction.

7 Conclusions and Future Work

We proposed an interval-based representation of the timeline of event mentions in an article. Our representation allowed us to formalize the joint inference model that can be solved efficiently, compared to a time point-based inference model, thus opening up the possibility of building more practical event temporal inference systems. Our inference model achieved significant improvement over the local classifiers. We also showed that event coreference can naturally support timeline construction, and good event coreference led to significant improvement in the system performance. Specifically, when such gold event coreference knowledge was injected into the model, a significant improvement in the overall performance could be obtained. While our experiments suggest that the temporal classifiers can potentially help enhance the performance of event coreference, in future work we would like to investigate into coupling event coreference with other components in a global inference framework.

Acknowledgments

The authors gratefully acknowledge the support of Defense Advanced Research Projects Agency (DARPA) Machine Reading Program under Air Force Research Laboratory (AFRL) prime contract No. FA8750-09-C-0181, and the Army Research Laboratory (ARL) under agreement W911NF-09-2-0053. The first author also thanks the Vietnam Education Foundation (VEF) for its sponsorship. Any opinions, findings, and conclusion or recommendations expressed in this material are those of the authors and do not necessarily reflect the view of the VEF, DARPA, AFRL, ARL, or the US government.

References

James F. Allen. 1983. Maintaining knowledge about temporal intervals. *Communications of the ACM*.

Steven Bethard, James H. Martin, and Sara Klingenstein. 2007. Timelines from text: Identification of syntactic temporal relations. In *ICSC*.

P. Bramsen, P. Deshpande, Y. K. Lee, and R. Barzilay. 2006. Inducing temporal graphs. In *EMNLP*.

N. Chambers and D. Jurafsky. 2008. Jointly combining implicit constraints improves temporal ordering. In *EMNLP*.

Zheng Chen, Heng Ji, and Robert Haralick. 2009. A pairwise event coreference model, feature impact and evaluation for event coreference resolution. In *Workshop on Events in Emerging Text Types*.

J. Clarke and M. Lapata. 2008. Global inference for sentence compression: An integer linear programming approach. *Journal of Artificial Intelligence Research*.

Pascal Denis and Philippe Muller. 2011. Predicting globally-coherent temporal structures from texts via endpoint inference and graph decomposition. In *IJCAI*.

C. Fellbaum. 1998. *WordNet: An Electronic Lexical Database*. MIT Press.

Yoav Freund and Robert E. Schapire. 1999. Large margin classification using the perceptron algorithm. *Machine Learning*.

Philipp Koehn. 2004. Statistical significance tests for machine translation evaluation. In *EMNLP*.

Inderjeet Mani, Marc Verhagen, Ben Wellner, Chong Min Lee, and James Pustejovsky. 2006. Machine learning of temporal relations. In *ACL*.

J. Pustejovsky, P. Hanks, R. Sauri, A. See, R. Gaizauskas, A. Setzer, D. Radev, B. Sundheim, D. Day, L. Ferro, and M. Lazo. 2003. The TIMEBANK corpus. In *Corpus Linguistics*.

D. Roth and W. Yih. 2007. Global inference for entity and relation identification via a linear programming formulation. In *Introduction to Statistical Relational Learning*.

Partha Pratim Talukdar, Derry Wijaya, and Tom Mitchell. 2012. Coupled temporal scoping of relational facts. In *WSDM*.

Marta Tatu and Munirathnam Srikanth. 2008. Experiments with reasoning for temporal relations between events. In *COLING*.

Marc Verhagen, Robert Gaizauskas, Frank Schilder, Mark Hepple, Graham Katz, and James Pustejovsky. 2007. Semeval-2007 task 15: Tempeval temporal relation identification. In *SemEval-2007*.

Marc Verhagen, Roser Sauri, Tommaso Caselli, and James Pustejovsky. 2010. Semeval-2010 task 13: Tempeval-2. In *SemEval-2010*.

Katsumasa Yoshikawa, Sebastian Riedel, Masayuki Asahara, and Yuji Matsumoto. 2009. Jointly identifying temporal relations with markov logic. In *ACL-IJCNLP*.

Ran Zhao, Quang Do, and Dan Roth. 2012. A robust shallow temporal reasoning system. In *NAACL-HLT Demo*.

Three Dependency-and-Boundary Models for Grammar Induction

Valentin I. Spitkovsky
Stanford University and Google Inc.
valentin@cs.stanford.edu

Hiyan Alshawi
Google Inc., Mountain View, CA, 94043
hiyan@google.com

Daniel Jurafsky
Stanford University, Stanford, CA, 94305
jurafsky@stanford.edu

Abstract

We present a new family of models for unsupervised parsing, *Dependency and Boundary* models, that use cues at constituent boundaries to inform head-outward dependency tree generation. We build on three intuitions that are explicit in phrase-structure grammars but only implicit in standard dependency formulations: (i) Distributions of words that occur at sentence boundaries — such as English determiners — resemble constituent edges. (ii) Punctuation at sentence boundaries further helps distinguish full sentences from fragments like headlines and titles, allowing us to model grammatical differences between complete and incomplete sentences. (iii) Sentence-internal punctuation boundaries help with longer-distance dependencies, since punctuation correlates with constituent edges. Our models induce state-of-the-art dependency grammars for many languages without special knowledge of optimal input sentence lengths or biased, manually-tuned initializers.

1 Introduction

Natural language is ripe with all manner of boundaries at the surface level that align with hierarchical syntactic structure. From the significance of function words (Berant et al., 2006) and punctuation marks (Seginer, 2007; Ponvert et al., 2010) as separators between constituents in longer sentences — to the importance of isolated words in children's early vocabulary acquisition (Brent and Siskind, 2001) — word boundaries play a crucial role in language learning. We will show that boundary information can also be useful in dependency grammar induction models, which traditionally focus on head rather than fringe words (Carroll and Charniak, 1992).

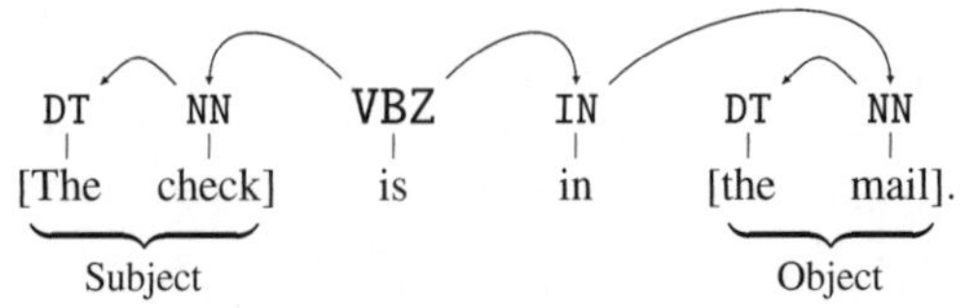

Figure 1: A partial analysis of our running example.

Consider the example in Figure 1. Because the determiner (DT) appears at the left edge of the sentence, it should be possible to learn that determiners may generally be present at left edges of phrases. This information could then be used to correctly parse the sentence-internal determiner in *the mail*. Similarly, the fact that the noun head (NN) of the object *the mail* appears at the right edge of the sentence could help identify the noun *check* as the right edge of the subject NP. As with jigsaw puzzles, working inwards from boundaries helps determine sentence-internal structures of both noun phrases, neither of which would be quite so clear if viewed separately.

Furthermore, properties of noun-phrase edges are partially shared with prepositional- and verb-phrase units that contain these nouns. Because typical head-driven grammars model valence separately for each class of head, however, they cannot see that the left fringe boundary, *The check*, of the verb-phrase is shared with its daughter's, *check*. Neither of these insights is available to traditional dependency formulations, which could learn from the boundaries of this sentence only that determiners might have no left- and that nouns might have no right-dependents.

We propose a family of dependency parsing models that are capable of inducing longer-range implications from sentence edges than just fertilities of their fringe words. Our ideas conveniently lend themselves to implementations that can reuse much of the standard grammar induction machinery, including efficient dynamic programming routines for the relevant expectation-maximization algorithms.

2 The Dependency and Boundary Models

Our models follow a standard generative story for head-outward automata (Alshawi, 1996a), restricted to the split-head case (see below),[1] over lexical word classes $\{c_w\}$: first, a sentence root c_r is chosen, with probability $\mathbb{P}_{\text{ATTACH}}(c_r \mid \diamond;\ \texttt{L})$; $\diamond$ is a special start symbol that, by convention (Klein and Manning, 2004; Eisner, 1996), produces exactly one child, to its left. Next, the process recurses. Each (head) word c_h generates a left-dependent with probability $1 - \mathbb{P}_{\text{STOP}}(\,\cdot \mid \texttt{L};\ \cdots)$, where dots represent additional parameterization on which it may be conditioned. If the child is indeed generated, its identity c_d is chosen with probability $\mathbb{P}_{\text{ATTACH}}(c_d \mid c_h;\ \cdots)$, influenced by the identity of the parent c_h and possibly other parameters (again represented by dots). The child then generates its own subtree recursively and the whole process continues, moving away from the head, until c_h fails to generate a left-dependent. At that point, an analogous procedure is repeated to c_h's right, this time using stopping factors $\mathbb{P}_{\text{STOP}}(\,\cdot \mid \texttt{R};\ \cdots)$. All parse trees derived in this way are guaranteed to be projective and can be described by split-head grammars.

Instances of these split-head automata have been heavily used in grammar induction (Paskin, 2001b; Klein and Manning, 2004; Headden et al., 2009, *inter alia*), in part because they allow for efficient implementations (Eisner and Satta, 1999, §8) of the inside-outside re-estimation algorithm (Baker, 1979). The basic tenet of split-head grammars is that every head word generates its left-dependents independently of its right-dependents. This assumption implies, for instance, that words' left- and right-valences — their numbers of children to each side — are also independent. But it does *not* imply that descendants that are closer to the head cannot influence the generation of farther dependents on the same side. Nevertheless, many popular grammars for unsupervised parsing behave as if a word had to generate all of its children (to one side) — or at least their count — *before* allowing any of these children themselves to recurse.

For example, Klein and Manning's (2004) dependency model with valence (DMV) could be implemented as both head-outward and head-inward automata. (In fact, arbitrary permutations of siblings to a given side of their parent would not affect the likelihood of the modified tree, with the DMV.) We propose to make fuller use of split-head automata's head-outward nature by drawing on information in partially-generated parses, which contain useful predictors that, until now, had not been exploited even in featurized systems for grammar induction (Cohen and Smith, 2009; Berg-Kirkpatrick et al., 2010).

Some of these predictors, including the identity — or even number (McClosky, 2008) — of already-generated siblings, can be prohibitively expensive in sentences above a short length k. For example, they break certain modularity constraints imposed by the charts used in $O(k^3)$-optimized algorithms (Paskin, 2001a; Eisner, 2000). However, in bottom-up parsing and training from text, everything about the yield — i.e., the ordered sequence of all already-generated descendants, on the side of the head that is in the process of spawning off an additional child — is not only known but also readily accessible. Taking advantage of this availability, we designed three new models for dependency grammar induction.

2.1 Dependency and Boundary Model One

DBM-1 conditions all stopping decisions on adjacency and the identity of the fringe word c_e — the currently-farthest descendant (edge) derived by head c_h in the given head-outward direction ($dir \in \{\texttt{L}, \texttt{R}\}$):

$$\mathbb{P}_{\text{STOP}}(\,\cdot \mid dir;\ adj, c_e).$$

In the adjacent case ($adj = \texttt{T}$), c_h is deciding whether to have any children on a given side: a first child's subtree would be right next to the head, so the head and the fringe words coincide ($c_h = c_e$). In the non-adjacent case ($adj = \texttt{F}$), these will be different words and their classes will, in general, not be the same.[2] Thus, non-adjacent stopping decisions will be made independently of a head word's identity. Therefore, all word classes will be equally likely to continue to grow or not, for a specific proposed fringe boundary.

For example, production of *The check is* involves two non-adjacent stopping decisions on the left: one by the noun *check* and one by the verb *is*, both of which stop after generating a first child. In DBM-1,

[1] Unrestricted head-outward automata are strictly more powerful (e.g., they recognize the language $a^n b^n$ in finite state) than the split-head variants, which process one side before the other.

[2] Fringe words differ also from other standard dependency features (Eisner, 1996, §2.3): parse siblings and adjacent words.

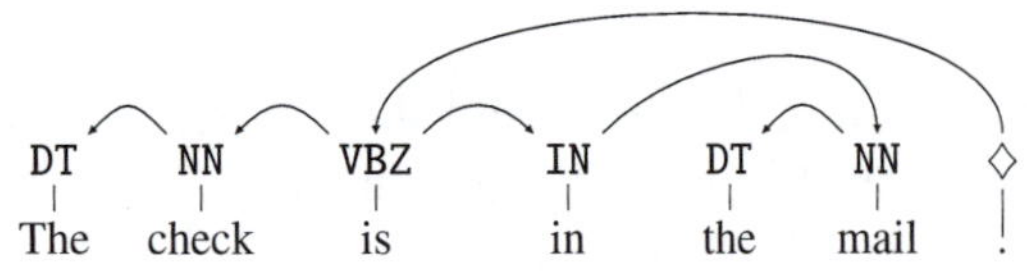

$$\begin{array}{ll}
\mathbb{P} = (1 - \overbrace{\mathbb{P}_{\text{STOP}}(\diamond \mid \texttt{L};\ \texttt{T})}^{0}) & \times\ \mathbb{P}_{\text{ATTACH}}(\texttt{VBZ} \mid \diamond;\ \texttt{L}) \\
\quad \times\ (1 - \mathbb{P}_{\text{STOP}}(\,\cdot \mid \texttt{L};\ \texttt{T},\texttt{VBZ})) & \times\ \mathbb{P}_{\text{ATTACH}}(\texttt{NN} \mid \texttt{VBZ};\ \texttt{L}) \\
\quad \times\ (1 - \mathbb{P}_{\text{STOP}}(\,\cdot \mid \texttt{R};\ \texttt{T},\texttt{VBZ})) & \times\ \mathbb{P}_{\text{ATTACH}}(\texttt{IN} \mid \texttt{VBZ};\ \texttt{R}) \\
\quad \times\ \mathbb{P}_{\text{STOP}}(\,\cdot \mid \texttt{L};\ \texttt{F},\texttt{DT}) \quad \text{// VBZ} & \times\ \mathbb{P}_{\text{STOP}}(\,\cdot \mid \texttt{R};\ \texttt{F},\texttt{NN}) \quad \text{// VBZ} \\
\quad \times\ (1 - \mathbb{P}_{\text{STOP}}(\,\cdot \mid \texttt{L};\ \texttt{T},\texttt{NN}))^2 & \times\ \mathbb{P}^2_{\text{ATTACH}}(\texttt{DT} \mid \texttt{NN};\ \texttt{L}) \\
\quad \times\ (1 - \mathbb{P}_{\text{STOP}}(\,\cdot \mid \texttt{R};\ \texttt{T},\texttt{IN})) & \times\ \mathbb{P}_{\text{ATTACH}}(\texttt{NN} \mid \texttt{IN};\ \texttt{R}) \\
\quad \times\ \mathbb{P}^2_{\text{STOP}}(\,\cdot \mid \texttt{R};\ \texttt{T},\texttt{NN}) & \times\ \mathbb{P}^2_{\text{STOP}}(\,\cdot \mid \texttt{L};\ \texttt{F},\texttt{DT}) \quad \text{// NN} \\
\quad \times\ \mathbb{P}_{\text{STOP}}(\,\cdot \mid \texttt{L};\ \texttt{T},\texttt{IN}) & \times\ \mathbb{P}_{\text{STOP}}(\,\cdot \mid \texttt{R};\ \texttt{F},\texttt{NN}) \quad \text{// IN} \\
\quad \times\ \mathbb{P}^2_{\text{STOP}}(\,\cdot \mid \texttt{L};\ \texttt{T},\texttt{DT}) & \times\ \mathbb{P}^2_{\text{STOP}}(\,\cdot \mid \texttt{R};\ \texttt{T},\texttt{DT}) \\
\quad \times\ \underbrace{\mathbb{P}_{\text{STOP}}(\diamond \mid \texttt{L};\ \texttt{F})}_{1} & \times\ \underbrace{\mathbb{P}_{\text{STOP}}(\diamond \mid \texttt{R};\ \texttt{T})}_{1}.
\end{array}$$

Figure 2: Our running example — a simple sentence and its unlabeled dependency parse structure's probability, as factored by DBM-1; highlighted comments specify heads associated to non-adjacent stopping probability factors.

this outcome is captured by squaring a shared parameter belonging to the left-fringe determiner *The*: $\mathbb{P}_{\text{STOP}}(\,\cdot \mid \texttt{L};\ \texttt{F},\texttt{DT})^2$ — instead of by a product of two factors, such as $\mathbb{P}_{\text{STOP}}(\,\cdot \mid \texttt{L};\ \texttt{F},\texttt{NN}) \cdot \mathbb{P}_{\text{STOP}}(\,\cdot \mid \texttt{L};\ \texttt{F},\texttt{VBZ})$.

In these grammars, dependents' attachment probabilities, given heads, are additionally conditioned only on their relative positions — as in traditional models (Klein and Manning, 2004; Paskin, 2001b):

$$\mathbb{P}_{\text{ATTACH}}(c_d \mid c_h;\ dir).$$

Figure 2 shows a completely factored example.

2.2 Dependency and Boundary Model Two

DBM-2 allows different but related grammars to coexist in a single model. Specifically, we presuppose that all sentences are assigned to one of two classes: complete and incomplete ($comp \in \{\texttt{T},\texttt{F}\}$, for now taken as exogenous). This model assumes that word-word (i.e., head-dependent) interactions in the two domains are the same. However, sentence lengths — for which stopping probabilities are responsible — and distributions of root words may be different.

Consequently, an additional $comp$ parameter is added to the context of two relevant types of factors:

$$\mathbb{P}_{\text{STOP}}(\,\cdot \mid dir;\ adj, c_e, comp);$$
$$\text{and } \mathbb{P}_{\text{ATTACH}}(c_r \mid \diamond;\ \texttt{L}, comp).$$

For example, the new stopping factors could capture the fact that incomplete fragments — such as the noun-phrases *George Morton*, headlines *Energy* and *Odds and Ends*, a line item *c - Domestic car*, dollar quantity *Revenue: $3.57 billion*, the time *1:11am*, and the like — tend to be much shorter than complete sentences. The new root-attachment factors could further track that incomplete sentences generally lack verbs, in contrast to other short sentences, e.g., *Excerpts follow:*, *Are you kidding?*, *Yes, he did.*, *It's huge.*, *Indeed it is.*, *I said, 'NOW?'*, *"Absolutely," he said.*, *I am waiting.*, *Mrs. Yeargin declined.*, *McGraw-Hill was outraged.*, *"It happens."*, *I'm OK, Jack.*, *Who cares?*, *Never mind.* and so on.

All other attachment probabilities $\mathbb{P}_{\text{ATTACH}}(c_d \mid c_h;\ dir)$ remain unchanged, as in DBM-1. In practice, $comp$ can indicate presence of sentence-final punctuation.

2.3 Dependency and Boundary Model Three

DBM-3 adds further conditioning on punctuation context. We introduce another boolean parameter, $cross$, which indicates the presence of intervening punctuation between a proposed head word c_h and its dependent c_d. Using this information, longer-distance punctuation-crossing arcs can be modeled separately from other, lower-level dependencies, via

$$\mathbb{P}_{\text{ATTACH}}(c_d \mid c_h;\ dir, cross).$$

For instance, in *Continentals believe that the strongest growth area will be southern Europe.*, four words appear between *that* and *will*. Conditioning on (the absence of) intervening punctuation could help tell true long-distance relations from impostors. All other probabilities, $\mathbb{P}_{\text{STOP}}(\,\cdot \mid dir;\ adj, c_e, comp)$ and $\mathbb{P}_{\text{ATTACH}}(c_r \mid \diamond;\ \texttt{L}, comp)$, remain the same as in DBM-2.

2.4 Summary of DBMs and Related Models

Head-outward automata (Alshawi, 1996a; Alshawi, 1996b; Alshawi et al., 2000) played a central part as generative models for probabilistic grammars, starting with their early adoption in supervised split-head constituent parsers (Collins, 1997; Collins, 2003). Table 1 lists some parameterizations that have since been used by unsupervised dependency grammar inducers sharing their backbone split-head process.

3 Experimental Set-Up and Methodology

We first motivate each model by analyzing the Wall Street Journal (WSJ) portion of the Penn English Treebank (Marcus et al., 1993),[3] before delving into

[3]We converted labeled constituents into unlabeled dependencies using deterministic "head-percolation" rules (Collins,

Split-Head Dependency Grammar		$\mathbb{P}_{\text{ATTACH}}$ *(head-root)*	$\mathbb{P}_{\text{ATTACH}}$ *(dependent-head)*	$\mathbb{P}_{\text{STOP}}$ *(adjacent and not)*
GB	(Paskin, 2001b)	$1 / \|\{w\}\|$	$d \mid h;\ dir$	$1 / 2$
DMV	(Klein and Manning, 2004)	$c_r \mid \diamond;\ \mathtt{L}$	$c_d \mid c_h;\ dir$	$\cdot \mid dir;\ adj,\ c_h$
EVG	(Headden et al., 2009)	$c_r \mid \diamond;\ \mathtt{L}$	$c_d \mid c_h;\ dir,\ adj$	$\cdot \mid dir;\ adj,\ c_h$
DBM-1	(§2.1)	$c_r \mid \diamond;\ \mathtt{L}$	$c_d \mid c_h;\ dir$	$\cdot \mid dir;\ adj,\ c_e$
DBM-2	(§2.2)	$c_r \mid \diamond;\ \mathtt{L},\ comp$	$c_d \mid c_h;\ dir$	$\cdot \mid dir;\ adj,\ c_e,\ comp$
DBM-3	(§2.3)	$c_r \mid \diamond;\ \mathtt{L},\ comp$	$c_d \mid c_h;\ dir,\ cross$	$\cdot \mid dir;\ adj,\ c_e,\ comp$

Table 1: Parameterizations of the split-head-outward generative process used by DBMs and in previous models.

grammar induction experiments. Although motivating solely from this treebank biases our discussion towards a very specific genre of just one language, it has the advantage of allowing us to make concrete claims that are backed up by significant statistics.

In the grammar induction experiments that follow, we will test each model's incremental contribution to accuracies empirically, across many disparate languages. We worked with all 23 (disjoint) train/test splits from the 2006/7 CoNLL shared tasks (Buchholz and Marsi, 2006; Nivre et al., 2007), spanning 19 languages.[4] For each data set, we induced a baseline grammar using the DMV. We excluded all training sentences with more than 15 tokens to create a conservative bias, because in this set-up the baseline is known to excel (Spitkovsky et al., 2009). Grammar inducers were initialized using (the same) uniformly-at-random chosen parse trees of training sentences (Cohen and Smith, 2010); thereafter, we applied "add one" smoothing at every training step.

To fairly compare the models under consideration — which could have quite different starting perplexities and ensuing consecutive relative likelihoods — we experimented with two termination strategies. In one case, we blindly ran each learner through 40 steps of inside-outside re-estimation, ignoring any convergence criteria; in the other case, we ran until numerical convergence of soft EM's objective function or until the likelihood of resulting Viterbi parse trees suffered — an "early-stopping lateen EM" strategy (Spitkovsky et al., 2011a, §2.3). We evaluated against all sentences of the blind test sets (except one 145-token item in Arabic '07 data).

Table 2 shows experimental results, averaged over all 19 languages, for the DMV baselines and DBM-1 and 2. We did not test DBM-3 in this set-up because most sentence-internal punctuation occurs in longer sentences; instead, DBM-3 will be tested later (see §7), using most sentences,[5] in the final training step of a curriculum strategy (Bengio et al., 2009) that we will propose for DBMs. For the three models tested on shorter inputs (up to 15 tokens) both terminating criteria exhibited the same trend; lateen EM consistently scored slightly higher than 40 EM iterations.

Termination Criterion	DMV	DBM-1	DBM-2
40 steps of EM	33.5	38.8	40.7
early-stopping lateen EM	34.0	39.0	**40.9**

Table 2: Directed dependency accuracies, averaged over all 2006/7 CoNLL evaluation sets (all sentences), for the DMV and two new dependency-and-boundary grammar inducers (DBM-1,2) — using two termination strategies.[6]

4 Dependency and Boundary Model One

The primary difference between DBM-1 and traditional models, such as the DMV, is that DBM-1 conditions non-adjacent stopping decisions on the identities of fringe words in partial yields (see §2.1).

4.1 Analytical Motivation

Treebank data suggests that the class of the fringe word — its part-of-speech, c_e — is a better predictor of (non-adjacent) stopping decisions, in a given direction dir, than the head's own class c_h. A statistical analysis of logistic regressions fitted to the data shows that the (c_h, dir) predictor explains only about 7% of the total variation (see Table 3). This seems low, although it is much better compared to direction alone (which explains less than 2%) and slightly better than using the (current) number of the head's de-

1999), discarding any empty nodes, etc., as is standard practice.

[4]We did not test on WSJ data because such evaluation would not be blind, as parse trees from the PTB are our motivating examples; instead, performance on WSJ serves as a strong baseline in a separate study (Spitkovsky et al., 2012a): bootstrapping of DBMs from mostly incomplete inter-punctuation fragments.

[5]Results for DBM-3 — given only standard input sentences, up to length fifteen — would be nearly identical to DBM-2's.

[6]We down-weighed the four languages appearing in both CoNLL years (see Table 8) by 50% in all reported averages.

Non-Adjacent Stop Predictor	R^2_{adj}	AIC_c
(dir)	0.0149	1,120,200
(n, dir)	0.0726	1,049,175
(c_h, dir)	0.0728	1,047,157
(c_e, dir)	0.2361	904,102.4
(c_h, c_e, dir)	0.3320	789,594.3

Table 3: Coefficients of determination (R^2) and Akaike information criteria (AIC), both adjusted for the number of parameters, for several single-predictor logistic models of non-adjacent stops, given direction dir; c_h is the class of the head, n is its number of descendants (so far) to that side, and c_e represents the farthest descendant (the edge).

scendants on that side, n, instead of the head's class. In contrast, using c_e in place of c_h boosts explanatory power to 24%, keeping the number of parameters the same. If one were willing to roughly square the size of the model, explanatory power could be improved further, to 33% (see Table 3), using both c_e and c_h.

Fringe boundaries thus appear to be informative even in the supervised case, which is not surprising, since using just one probability factor (and its complement) to generate very short (geometric coin-flip) sequences is a recipe for high entropy. But as suggested earlier, fringes should be extra attractive in unsupervised settings because yields are observable, whereas heads almost always remain hidden. Moreover, every sentence exposes two true edges (Hänig, 2010): integrated over many sample sentence beginnings and ends, cumulative knowledge about such markers can guide a grammar inducer inside long inputs, where structure is murky. Table 4 shows distributions of all part-of-speech (POS) tags in the treebank versus in sentence-initial, sentence-final and sentence-root positions. WSJ often leads with determiners, proper nouns, prepositions and pronouns — all good candidates for starting English phrases; and its sentences usually end with various noun types, again consistent with our running example.

4.2 Experimental Results

Table 2 shows DBM-1 to be substantially more accurate than the DMV, on average: 38.8 versus 33.5% after 40 steps of EM.[7] Lateen termination improved both models' accuracies slightly, to 39.0 and 34.0%, respectively, with DBM-1 scoring five points higher.

[7] DBM-1's 39% average accuracy with uniform-at-random initialization is two points above DMV's scores with the "ad-hoc harmonic" strategy, 37% (Spitkovsky et al., 2011a, Table 5).

POS	*% of All Tokens*	*First Tokens*	*Last Tokens*	*Sent. Roots*	*Frag. Roots*
NN	15.94	4.31	36.67	0.10	23.40
IN	11.85	13.54	0.57	0.24	4.33
NNP	11.09	20.49	12.85	0.02	32.02
DT	9.84	23.34	0.34	0.00	0.04
JJ	7.32	4.33	3.74	0.01	1.15
NNS	7.19	4.49	20.64	0.15	17.12
CD	4.37	1.29	6.92	0.00	3.27
RB	3.71	5.96	3.88	0.00	1.50
VBD	3.65	0.09	3.52	46.65	0.93
VB	3.17	0.44	1.67	0.48	6.81
CC	2.86	5.93	0.00	0.00	0.00
TO	2.67	0.37	0.05	0.02	0.44
VBZ	2.57	0.17	1.65	28.31	0.93
VBN	2.42	0.61	2.57	0.65	1.28
PRP	2.08	9.04	1.34	0.00	0.00
VBG	1.77	1.26	0.64	0.10	0.97
VBP	1.50	0.05	0.61	14.33	0.71
MD	1.17	0.07	0.05	8.88	0.57
POS	1.05	0.00	0.11	0.01	0.04
PRP$	1.00	0.90	0.00	0.00	0.00
WDT	0.52	0.08	0.00	0.01	0.13
JJR	0.39	0.18	0.43	0.00	0.09
RP	0.32	0.00	0.42	0.00	0.00
NNPS	0.30	0.20	0.56	0.00	2.96
WP	0.28	0.42	0.01	0.01	0.04
WRB	0.26	0.78	0.02	0.01	0.31
JJS	0.23	0.27	0.06	0.00	0.00
RBR	0.21	0.20	0.54	0.00	0.04
EX	0.10	0.75	0.00	0.00	0.00
RBS	0.05	0.06	0.01	0.00	0.00
PDT	0.04	0.08	0.00	0.00	0.00
FW	0.03	0.01	0.05	0.00	0.09
WP$	0.02	0.00	0.00	0.00	0.00
UH	0.01	0.08	0.05	0.00	0.62
SYM	0.01	0.11	0.01	0.00	0.18
LS	0.01	0.09	0.00	0.00	0.00

Table 4: Empirical distributions for non-punctuation part-of-speech tags in WSJ, ordered by overall frequency, as well as distributions for sentence boundaries and for the roots of complete and incomplete sentences. (A uniform distribution would have $1/36 = 2.\overline{7}\%$ for all POS-tags.)

$\sqrt{1 - \sum_x \sqrt{p_x q_x}}$	*All*	*First*	*Last*	*Sent.*	*Frag.*
Uniform	0.48	0.58	0.64	0.79	0.65
All		0.35	0.40	0.79	0.42
First			0.59	**0.94**	0.57
Last				**0.83**	0.29
Sent.					**0.86**

Table 5: A distance matrix for all pairs of probability distributions over POS-tags shown in Table 4 and the uniform distribution; the BC- (or Hellinger) distance (Bhattacharyya, 1943; Nikulin, 2002) between discrete distributions p and q (over $x \in \mathcal{X}$) ranges from zero (iff $p = q$) to one (iff $p \cdot q = 0$, i.e., when they do not overlap at all).

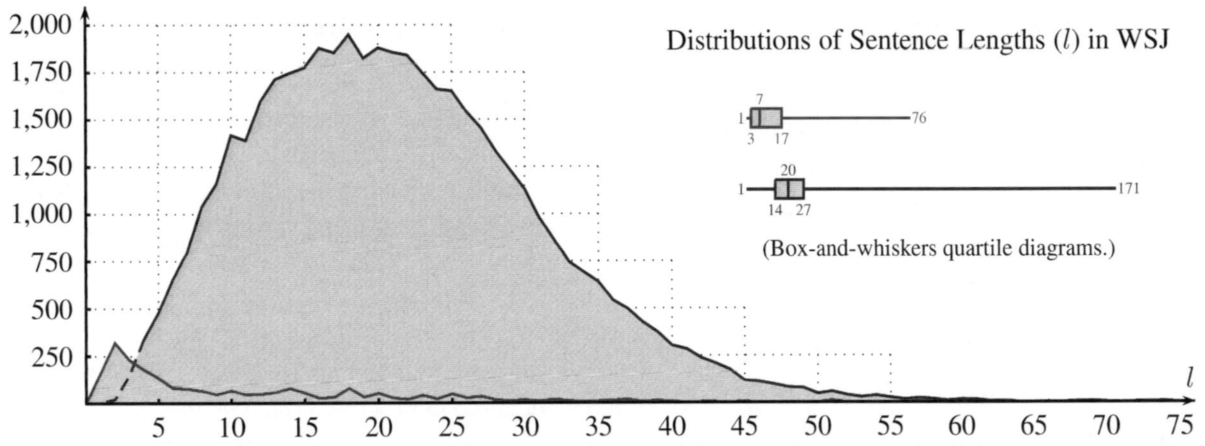

Figure 3: Histograms of lengths (in tokens) for 2,261 non-clausal fragments (red) and other sentences (blue) in WSJ.

5 Dependency and Boundary Model Two

DBM-2 adapts DBM-1 grammars to two classes of inputs (complete sentences and incomplete fragments) by forking off new, separate multinomials for stopping decisions and root-distributions (see §2.2).

5.1 Analytical Motivation

Unrepresentative short sentences — such as headlines and titles — are common in news-style data and pose a known nuisance to grammar inducers. Previous research sometimes took radical measures to combat the problem: for example, Gillenwater et al. (2009) excluded all sentences with three or fewer tokens from their experiments; and Mareček and Zabokrtský (2011) enforced an "anti-noun-root" policy to steer their Gibbs sampler away from the undercurrents caused by the many short noun-phrase fragments (among sentences up to length 15, in Czech data). We refer to such snippets of text as "incomplete sentences" and focus our study of WSJ on non-clausal data (as signaled by top-level constituent annotations whose first character is not S).[8]

Table 4 shows that roots of incomplete sentences, which are dominated by nouns, barely resemble the other roots, drawn from more traditional verb and modal types. In fact, these two empirical root distributions are more distant from one another than either is from the uniform distribution, in the space of discrete probability distributions over POS-tags (see Table 5). Of the distributions we considered, only sentence boundaries are as or more different from (complete) roots, suggesting that heads of fragments too may warrant their own multinomial in the model.

Further, incomplete sentences are uncharacteristically short (see Figure 3). It is this property that makes them particularly treacherous to grammar inducers, since by offering few options of root positions they increase the chances that a learner will incorrectly induce nouns to be heads. Given that expected lengths are directly related to stopping decisions, it could make sense to also model the stopping probabilities of incomplete sentences separately.

5.2 Experimental Results

Since it is not possible to consult parse trees during grammar induction (to check whether an input sentence is clausal), we opted for a proxy: presence of sentence-final punctuation. Using punctuation to divide input sentences into two groups, DBM-2 scored higher: 40.9, up from 39.0% accuracy (see Table 2).

After evaluating these multi-lingual experiments, we checked how well our proxy corresponds to actual clausal sentences in WSJ. Table 6 shows the binary confusion matrix having a fairly low (but positive) Pearson correlation coefficient. False positives

$r_\phi \approx 0.31$	*Clausal*	*non-Clausal*	*Total*
Punctuation	46,829	1,936	48,765
no Punctuation	118	325	443
Total	46,947	2,261	49,208

Table 6: A contingency table for clausal sentences and trailing punctuation in WSJ; the mean square contingency coefficient r_ϕ signifies a low degree of correlation. (For two binary variables, r_ϕ is equivalent to Karl Pearson's better-known product-moment correlation coefficient, ρ.)

[8] I.e., separating top-level types {`S`, `SINV`, `SBARQ`, `SQ`, `SBAR`} from the rest (ordered by frequency): {`NP`, `FRAG`, `X`, `PP`, ...}.

include parenthesized expressions that are marked as noun-phrases, such as *(See related story: "Fed Ready to Inject Big Funds": WSJ Oct. 16, 1989)*; false negatives can be headlines having a main verb, e.g., *Population Drain Ends For Midwestern States*. Thus, our proxy is not perfect but seems to be tolerable in practice. We suspect that identities of punctuation marks (Collins, 2003, Footnote 13) — both sentence-final and sentence-initial — could be of extra assistance in grammar induction, specifically for grouping imperatives, questions, and so forth.

6 Dependency and Boundary Model Three

DBM-3 exploits sentence-internal punctuation contexts by modeling punctuation-crossing dependency arcs separately from other attachments (see §2.3).

6.1 Analytical Motivation

Many common syntactic relations, such as between a determiner and a noun, are unlikely to hold over long distances. (In fact, 45% of all head-percolated dependencies in WSJ are between adjacent words.) However, some common constructions are more remote: e.g., subordinating conjunctions are, on average, 4.8 tokens away from their dependent modal verbs. Sometimes longer-distance dependencies can be vetted using sentence-internal punctuation marks.

It happens that the presence of punctuation between such conjunction (IN) and verb (MD) types serves as a clue that they are not connected (see Table 7*a*); by contrast, a simpler cue — whether these words are adjacent — is, in this case, hardly of any use (see Table 7*b*). Conditioning on crossing punctuation could be of help then, playing a role similar to that of comma-counting (Collins, 1997, §2.1) — and "verb intervening" (Bikel, 2004, §5.1) — in early head-outward models for supervised parsing.

a) $r_\phi \approx -0.40$	*Attached*	*not Attached*	*Total*
Punctuation	337	7,645	7,982
no Punctuation	2,144	4,040	6,184
Total	2,481	11,685	14,166
non-Adjacent	2,478	11,673	14,151
Adjacent	3	12	15
b) $r_\phi \approx +0.00$	*Attached*	*not Attached*	*Total*

Table 7: Contingency tables for IN right-attaching MD, among closest ordered pairs of these tokens in WSJ sentences with punctuation, versus: (a) presence of intervening punctuation; and (b) presence of intermediate words.

6.2 Experimental Results Postponed

As we mentioned earlier (see §3), there is little point in testing DBM-3 with shorter sentences, since most sentence-internal punctuation occurs in longer inputs. Instead, we will test this model in a final step of a staged training strategy, with more data (see §7.3).

7 A Curriculum Strategy for DBMs

We propose to train up to DBM-3 iteratively — by beginning with DBM-1 and gradually increasing model complexity through DBM-2, drawing on the intuitions of IBM translation models 1–4 (Brown et al., 1993). Instead of using sentences of up to 15 tokens, as in all previous experiments (§4–5), we will now make use of nearly all available training data: up to length 45 (out of concern for efficiency), during later stages. In the first stage, however, we will use only a subset of the data with DBM-1, in a process sometimes called *curriculum learning* (Bengio et al., 2009; Krueger and Dayan, 2009, *inter alia*). Our grammar inducers will thus be "starting small" in both senses suggested by Elman (1993): simultaneously scaffolding on model- *and* data-complexity.

7.1 Scaffolding Stage #1: DBM-1

We begin by training DBM-1 on sentences without sentence-internal punctuation but with at least one trailing punctuation mark. Our goal is to avoid, when possible, overly specific arbitrary parameters like the "15 tokens or less" threshold used to select training sentences. Unlike DBM-2 and 3, DBM-1 does not model punctuation or sentence fragments, so we instead explicitly restrict its attention to this cleaner subset of the training data, which takes advantage of the fact that punctuation may generally correlate with sentence complexity (Frank, 2000).[9]

Aside from input sentence selection, our experimental set-up here remained identical to previous training of DBMs (§4–5). Using this new input data, DBM-1 averaged 40.7% accuracy (see Table 8). This is slightly higher than the 39.0% when using sentences up to length 15, suggesting that our heuristic for clean, simple sentences may be a useful one.

[9]More incremental training strategies are the subject of an unpublished companion manuscript (Spitkovsky et al., 2012a).

CoNLL Year & Language		DMV	DBM-1	DBM-2	DBM-3	+*inference* (@10)	(i) Agnostic	(ii) Identified	(iii) Transfer
			Directed Dependency Accuracies for: this Work				*Best of State-of-the-Art Systems* — *Monolingual; POS-*		*Cross-Lingual*
Arabic	2006	12.9	10.6	11.0	11.1	10.9 (34.5)	**33.4** SCAJ$_6$	—	**50.2** S$_{bg}$
	'7	36.6	43.9	44.0	44.4	44.9 (48.8)	**55.6** RF	*54.6* RF$_{H1}$	—
Basque	'7	32.7	34.1	33.0	32.7	33.3 (36.5)	**43.6** SCAJ$_5$	*34.7* MZ$_{NR}$	—
Bulgarian	'7	24.7	59.4	63.6	64.6	**65.2** (70.4)	44.3 SCAJ$_5$	*53.9* RF$_{H1\&2}$	**70.3** S$_{pt}$
Catalan	'7	41.1	61.3	61.1	61.1	62.1 (78.1)	**63.8** SCAJ$_5$	*56.3* MZ$_{NR}$	—
Chinese	'6	50.4	63.1	63.0	63.2	63.2 (65.7)	**63.6** SCAJ$_6$	—	—
	'7	55.3	56.8	57.0	57.1	57.0 (59.8)	**58.5** SCAJ$_6$	*34.6* MZ$_{NR}$	—
Czech	'6	31.5	51.3	52.8	53.0	**55.1** (61.8)	50.5 SCAJ$_5$	—	—
	'7	34.5	50.5	51.2	53.3	**54.2** (67.3)	49.8 SCAJ$_5$	*42.4* RF$_{H1\&2}$	—
Danish	'6	22.4	21.3	19.9	21.8	22.2 (27.4)	**46.0** RF	**53.1** RF$_{H1\&2}$	**56.5** S$_{ar}$
Dutch	'6	44.9	45.9	46.5	46.0	**46.6** (48.6)	32.5 SCAJ$_5$	**48.8** RF$_{H1\&2}$	**65.7** MPH$_{m:p}$
English	'7	32.3	29.2	28.6	29.0	29.6 (51.4)	**50.3** SAJ	*23.8* MZ$_{NR}$	*45.7* MPH$_{el}$
German	'6	27.7	36.3	37.9	38.4	**39.1** (52.1)	33.5 SCAJ$_5$	*21.8* MZ$_{NR}$	**56.7** MPH$_{m:d}$
Greek	'6	36.3	28.1	26.1	26.1	26.9 (36.8)	**39.0** MZ	*33.4* MZ$_{NR}$	**65.1** MPH$_{m:p}$
Hungarian	'7	23.6	43.2	52.1	57.4	**58.2** (68.4)	48.0 MZ	*48.1* MZ$_{NR}$	—
Italian	'7	25.5	41.7	39.8	39.9	40.7 (41.8)	**57.5** MZ	**60.6** MZ$_{NR}$	**69.1** MPH$_{pt}$
Japanese	'6	42.2	22.8	22.7	22.7	22.7 (32.5)	**56.6** SCAJ$_5$	*53.5* MZ$_{NR}$	—
Portuguese	'6	37.1	68.9	72.3	71.1	**72.4** (80.6)	43.2 MZ	*55.8* RF$_{H1\&2}$	**76.9** S$_{bg}$
Slovenian	'6	33.4	30.4	33.0	34.1	**35.2** (36.8)	33.6 SCAJ$_5$	*34.6* MZ$_{NR}$	—
Spanish	'6	22.0	25.0	26.7	27.1	28.2 (51.8)	**53.0** MZ	**54.6** MZ$_{NR}$	**68.4** MPH$_{it}$
Swedish	'6	30.7	48.6	50.3	50.0	**50.7** (63.2)	50.0 SCAJ$_6$	*34.3* RF$_{H1\&2}$	**68.0** MPH$_{m:p}$
Turkish	'6	**43.4**	32.9	33.7	33.4	34.4 (38.1)	40.9 SAJ	**61.3** RF$_{H1}$	—
	'7	**58.5**	44.6	44.2	43.7	44.8 (44.4)	48.8 SCAJ$_6$	—	—
Average:		33.6	40.7	41.7	42.2	**42.9** (51.9)	38.2 SCAJ$_6$	(*best average*, **not** an average of bests)	

Table 8: Average accuracies over CoNLL evaluation sets (all sentences), for the DMV baseline and DBM1–3 trained with a curriculum strategy, and state-of-the-art results for systems that: (i) are also POS-agnostic and monolingual, including SCAJ (Spitkovsky et al., 2011a, Tables 5–6) and SAJ (Spitkovsky et al., 2011b); (ii) rely on gold POS-tag identities to discourage noun roots (Mareček and Zabokrtský, 2011, MZ) or to encourage verbs (Rasooli and Faili, 2012, RF); and (iii) transfer delexicalized parsers (Søgaard, 2011a, S) from resource-rich languages with translations (McDonald et al., 2011, MPH). DMV and DBM-1 trained on simple sentences, from uniform; DBM-2 and 3 trained on most sentences, from DBM-1 and 2, respectively; +*inference* is DBM-3 with punctuation constraints.

7.2 Scaffolding Stage #2: DBM-2 ← DBM-1

Next, we trained on all sentences up to length 45. Since these inputs are punctuation-rich, in both remaining stages we used the constrained Viterbi EM set-up suggested by Spitkovsky et al. (2011b) instead of plain soft EM; we employ an early termination strategy, quitting hard EM as soon as soft EM's objective suffers (Spitkovsky et al., 2011a). Punctuation was converted into Viterbi-decoding constraints during training using the so-called *loose* method, which stipulates that all words in an inter-punctuation fragment must be dominated by a single (head) word, also from that fragment — with only these head words allowed to attach the head words of other fragments, across punctuation boundaries.

To adapt to full data, we initialized DBM-2 using Viterbi parses from the previous stage (§7.1), plus uniformly-at-random chosen dependency trees for the new complex and incomplete sentences, subject to punctuation-induced constraints. This approach improved parsing accuracies to 41.7% (see Table 8).

7.3 Scaffolding Stage #3: DBM-3 ← DBM-2

Next, we repeated the training process of the previous stage (§7.2) using DBM-3. To initialize this model, we combined the final instance of DBM-2 with uniform multinomials for punctuation-crossing attachment probabilities (see §2.3). As a result, average performance improved to 42.2% (see Table 8).

Lastly, we applied punctuation constraints also in inference. Here we used the *sprawl* method — a more relaxed approach than in training, allowing arbitrary words to attach inter-punctuation fragments (provided that each entire fragment still be derived by one of its words) — as suggested by Spitkovsky et al. (2011b). This technique increased DBM-3's average accuracy to 42.9% (see Table 8). Our final result substantially improves over the baseline's 33.6% and compares favorably to previous work.[10]

8 Discussion and the State-of-the-Art

DBMs come from a long line of head-outward models for dependency grammar induction yet their generative processes feature important novelties. One is conditioning on more observable state — specifically, the left and right end words of a phrase being constructed — than in previous work. Another is allowing multiple grammars — e.g., of complete and incomplete sentences — to coexist in a single model. These improvements could make DBMs quick-and-easy to bootstrap directly from any available partial bracketings (Pereira and Schabes, 1992), for example capitalized phrases (Spitkovsky et al., 2012b).

The second part of our work — the use of a curriculum strategy to train DBM-1 through 3 — eliminates having to know tuned cut-offs, such as sentences with up to a predetermined number of tokens. Although this approach adds some complexity, we chose conservatively, to avoid overfitting settings of sentence length, convergence criteria, etc.: stage one's data is dictated by DBM-1 (which ignores punctuation); subsequent stages initialize additional pieces uniformly: uniform-at-random parses for new data and uniform multinomials for new parameters.

Even without curriculum learning — trained with vanilla EM — DBM-2 and 1 are already strong. Further boosts to accuracy could come from employing more sophisticated optimization algorithms, e.g., better EM (Samdani et al., 2012), constrained Gibbs sampling (Mareček and Zabokrtský, 2011) or locally-normalized features (Berg-Kirkpatrick et al., 2010). Other orthogonal dependency grammar induction techniques — including ones based on universal rules (Naseem et al., 2010) — may also benefit in combination with DBMs. Direct comparisons to previous work require some care, however, as there are several classes of systems that make different assumptions about training data (see Table 8).

[10]Note that DBM-1's 39% average accuracy with standard training (see Table 2) was already nearly a full point higher than that of any single previous best system ($SCAJ_6$ — see Table 8).

8.1 Monolingual POS-Agnostic Inducers

The first type of grammar inducers, including our own approach, uses standard training and test data sets for each language, with gold part-of-speech tags as anonymized word classes. For the purposes of this discussion, we also include in this group transductive learners that may train on data from the test sets. Our DBM-3 (decoded with punctuation constraints) does well among such systems — for which accuracies on *all* sentence lengths of the evaluation sets are reported — attaining highest scores for 8 of 19 languages; the DMV baseline is still state-of-the-art for one language; and the remaining 10 bests are split among five other recent systems (see Table 8).[11] Half of the five came from various lateen EM strategies (Spitkovsky et al., 2011a) for escaping and/or avoiding local optima. These heuristics are compatible with how we trained our DBMs and could potentially provide further improvement to accuracies.

Overall, the final scores of DBM-3 were better, on average, than those of any other single system: 42.9 versus 38.2% (Spitkovsky et al., 2011a, Table 6). The progression of scores for DBM-1 through 3 without using punctuation constraints in inference — 40.7, 41.7 and 42.2% — fell entirely above this previous state-of-the-art result as well; the DMV baseline — also trained on sentences without internal but with final punctuation — averaged 33.6%.

8.2 Monolingual POS-Identified Inducers

The second class of techniques assumes knowledge about identities of part-of-speech tags (Naseem et al., 2010), i.e., which word tokens are verbs, which ones are nouns, etc. Such grammar inducers generally do better than the first kind — e.g., by encouraging verbocentricity (Gimpel and Smith, 2011) — though even here our results appear to be competitive. In fact, to our surprise, only in 5 of 19 languages a "POS-identified" system performed better than all of the "POS-agnostic" ones (see Table 8).

8.3 Multi-Lingual Semi-Supervised Parsers

The final broad class of related algorithms we considered extends beyond monolingual data and uses

[11]For Turkish '06, the "right-attach" baseline outperforms even the DMV, at 65.4% (Rasooli and Faili, 2012, Table 1); an important difference between 2006 and 2007 CoNLL data sets has to do with segmentation of morphologically-rich languages.

both identities of POS-tags and/or parallel bitexts to transfer (supervised) delexicalized parsers across languages. Parser projection is by far the most successful approach to date and we hope that it too may stand to gain from our modeling improvements. Of the 10 languages for which we found results in the literature, transferred parsers underperformed the grammar inducers in only one case: on English (see Table 8). The unsupervised system that performed better used a special "weighted" initializer (Spitkovsky et al., 2011b, §3.1) that worked well for English (but less so for many other languages).

DBMs may be able to improve initialization. For example, modeling of incomplete sentences could help in incremental initialization strategies like *baby steps* (Spitkovsky et al., 2009), which are likely sensitive to the proverbial "bum steer" from unrepresentative short fragments, *pace* Tu and Honavar (2011).

8.4 Miscellaneous Systems on Short Sentences

Several recent systems (Cohen et al., 2011; Søgaard, 2011b; Naseem et al., 2010; Gillenwater et al., 2010; Berg-Kirkpatrick and Klein, 2010, *inter alia*) are absent from Table 8 because they do not report performance for all sentence lengths. To facilitate comparison with this body of important previous work, we also tabulated final accuracies for the "up-to-ten words" task under heading @*10*: 51.9%, on average.

9 Conclusion

Although a dependency parse for a sentence can be mapped to a constituency parse (Xia and Palmer, 2001), the probabilistic models generating them use different conditioning: dependency grammars focus on the relationship between arguments and heads, constituency grammars on the coherence of chunks covered by non-terminals. Since redundant views of data can make learning easier (Blum and Mitchell, 1998), integrating aspects of both constituency and dependency ought to be able to help grammar induction. We have shown that this insight is correct: dependency grammar inducers can gain from modeling boundary information that is fundamental to constituency (i.e., phrase-structure) formalisms.

DBMs are a step in the direction towards modeling constituent boundaries jointly with head dependencies. Further steps must involve more tightly coupling the two frameworks, as well as showing ways to incorporate both kinds of information in other state-of-the art grammar induction paradigms.

Acknowledgments

We thank Roi Reichart and Marta Recasens, for many helpful comments on draft versions of this paper, and Marie-Catherine de Marneffe, Roy Schwartz, Mengqiu Wang and the anonymous reviewers, for their apt recommendations. Funded, in part, by Defense Advanced Research Projects Agency (DARPA) Machine Reading Program, under Air Force Research Laboratory (AFRL) prime contract no. FA8750-09-C-0181. Any opinions, findings, and conclusion or recommendations expressed in this material are those of the authors and do not necessarily reflect the view of the DARPA, AFRL, or the US government. First author is grateful to Cindy Chan for her friendship and support over many long months leading up to this publication.

References

H. Alshawi, S. Bangalore, and S. Douglas. 2000. Learning dependency translation models as collections of finite-state head transducers. *Computational Linguistics*, 26.

H. Alshawi. 1996a. Head automata for speech translation. In *ICSLP*.

H. Alshawi. 1996b. Method and apparatus for an improved language recognition system. US Patent 1999/5870706.

J. K. Baker. 1979. Trainable grammars for speech recognition. In *Speech Communication Papers for the 97th Meeting of the Acoustical Society of America*.

Y. Bengio, J. Louradour, R. Collobert, and J. Weston. 2009. Curriculum learning. In *ICML*.

J. Berant, Y. Gross, M. Mussel, B. Sandbank, E. Ruppin, and S. Edelman. 2006. Boosting unsupervised grammar induction by splitting complex sentences on function words. In *BUCLD*.

T. Berg-Kirkpatrick and D. Klein. 2010. Phylogenetic grammar induction. In *ACL*.

T. Berg-Kirkpatrick, A. Bouchard-Côté, J. DeNero, and D. Klein. 2010. Painless unsupervised learning with features. In *NAACL-HLT*.

A. Bhattacharyya. 1943. On a measure of divergence between two statistical populations defined by their probability distributions. *BCMS*, 35.

D. M. Bikel. 2004. Intricacies of Collins' parsing model. *Computational Linguistics*, 30.

A. Blum and T. Mitchell. 1998. Combining labeled and unlabeled data with co-training. In *COLT*.

M. R. Brent and J. M. Siskind. 2001. The role of exposure to isolated words in early vocabulary development. *Cognition*, 81.

P. F. Brown, V. J. Della Pietra, S. A. Della Pietra, and R. L. Mercer. 1993. The mathematics of statistical machine translation: Parameter estimation. *Computational Linguistics*, 19.

S. Buchholz and E. Marsi. 2006. CoNLL-X shared task on multilingual dependency parsing. In *CoNLL*.

G. Carroll and E. Charniak. 1992. Two experiments on learning probabilistic dependency grammars from corpora. Technical report, Brown University.

S. B. Cohen and N. A. Smith. 2009. Shared logistic normal distributions for soft parameter tying in unsupervised grammar induction. In *NAACL-HLT*.

S. B. Cohen and N. A. Smith. 2010. Viterbi training for PCFGs: Hardness results and competitiveness of uniform initialization. In *ACL*.

S. B. Cohen, D. Das, and N. A. Smith. 2011. Unsupervised structure prediction with non-parallel multilingual guidance. In *EMNLP*.

M. Collins. 1997. Three generative, lexicalised models for statistical parsing. In *ACL*.

M. Collins. 1999. *Head-Driven Statistical Models for Natural Language Parsing*. Ph.D. thesis, University of Pennsylvania.

M. Collins. 2003. Head-driven statistical models for natural language parsing. *Computational Linguistics*, 29.

J. Eisner and G. Satta. 1999. Efficient parsing for bilexical context-free grammars and head-automaton grammars. In *ACL*.

J. M. Eisner. 1996. An empirical comparison of probability models for dependency grammar. Technical report, IRCS.

J. Eisner. 2000. Bilexical grammars and their cubic-time parsing algorithms. In H. C. Bunt and A. Nijholt, editors, *Advances in Probabilistic and Other Parsing Technologies*. Kluwer Academic Publishers.

J. L. Elman. 1993. Learning and development in neural networks: The importance of starting small. *Cognition*, 48.

R. Frank. 2000. From regular to context-free to mildly context-sensitive tree rewriting systems: The path of child language acquisition. In A. Abeillé and O. Rambow, editors, *Tree Adjoining Grammars: Formalisms, Linguistic Analysis and Processing*. CSLI Publications.

J. Gillenwater, K. Ganchev, J. Graça, B. Taskar, and F. Pereira. 2009. Sparsity in grammar induction. In *NIPS: Grammar Induction, Representation of Language and Language Learning*.

J. Gillenwater, K. Ganchev, J. Graça, F. Pereira, and B. Taskar. 2010. Posterior sparsity in unsupervised dependency parsing. Technical report, University of Pennsylvania.

K. Gimpel and N. A. Smith. 2011. Concavity and initialization for unsupervised dependency grammar induction. Technical report, CMU.

C. Hänig. 2010. Improvements in unsupervised co-occurrence based parsing. In *CoNLL*.

W. P. Headden, III, M. Johnson, and D. McClosky. 2009. Improving unsupervised dependency parsing with richer contexts and smoothing. In *NAACL-HLT*.

D. Klein and C. D. Manning. 2004. Corpus-based induction of syntactic structure: Models of dependency and constituency. In *ACL*.

K. A. Krueger and P. Dayan. 2009. Flexible shaping: How learning in small steps helps. *Cognition*, 110.

M. P. Marcus, B. Santorini, and M. A. Marcinkiewicz. 1993. Building a large annotated corpus of English: The Penn Treebank. *Computational Linguistics*, 19.

D. Mareček and Z. Zabokrtský. 2011. Gibbs sampling with treeness constraint in unsupervised dependency parsing. In *ROBUS*.

D. McClosky. 2008. Modeling valence effects in unsupervised grammar induction. Technical report, Brown University.

R. McDonald, S. Petrov, and K. Hall. 2011. Multi-source transfer of delexicalized dependency parsers. In *EMNLP*.

T. Naseem, H. Chen, R. Barzilay, and M. Johnson. 2010. Using universal linguistic knowledge to guide grammar induction. In *EMNLP*.

M. S. Nikulin. 2002. Hellinger distance. In M. Hazewinkel, editor, *Encyclopaedia of Mathematics*. Kluwer Academic Publishers.

J. Nivre, J. Hall, S. Kübler, R. McDonald, J. Nilsson, S. Riedel, and D. Yuret. 2007. The CoNLL 2007 shared task on dependency parsing. In *EMNLP-CoNLL*.

M. A. Paskin. 2001a. Cubic-time parsing and learning algorithms for grammatical bigram models. Technical report, UCB.

M. A. Paskin. 2001b. Grammatical bigrams. In *NIPS*.

F. Pereira and Y. Schabes. 1992. Inside-outside reestimation from partially bracketed corpora. In *ACL*.

E. Ponvert, J. Baldridge, and K. Erk. 2010. Simple unsupervised identification of low-level constituents. In *ICSC*.

M. S. Rasooli and H. Faili. 2012. Fast unsupervised dependency parsing with arc-standard transitions. In *ROBUS-UNSUP*.

R. Samdani, M.-W. Chang, and D. Roth. 2012. Unified expectation maximization. In *NAACL-HLT*.

Y. Seginer. 2007. *Learning Syntactic Structure*. Ph.D. thesis, University of Amsterdam.

A. Søgaard. 2011a. Data point selection for cross-language adaptation of dependency parsers. In *ACL*.

A. Søgaard. 2011b. From ranked words to dependency trees: two-stage unsupervised non-projective dependency parsing. In *TextGraphs*.

V. I. Spitkovsky, H. Alshawi, and D. Jurafsky. 2009. Baby Steps: How "Less is More" in unsupervised dependency parsing. In *NIPS: Grammar Induction, Representation of Language and Language Learning*.

V. I. Spitkovsky, H. Alshawi, and D. Jurafsky. 2011a. Lateen EM: Unsupervised training with multiple objectives, applied to dependency grammar induction. In *EMNLP*.

V. I. Spitkovsky, H. Alshawi, and D. Jurafsky. 2011b. Punctuation: Making a point in unsupervised dependency parsing. In *CoNLL*.

V. I. Spitkovsky, H. Alshawi, and D. Jurafsky. 2012a. Bootstrapping dependency grammar inducers from incomplete sentence fragments via austere models – the "wabi-sabi" of unsupervised parsing. In submission.

V. I. Spitkovsky, H. Alshawi, and D. Jurafsky. 2012b. Capitalization cues improve dependency grammar induction. In *WILS*.

K. Tu and V. Honavar. 2011. On the utility of curricula in unsupervised learning of probabilistic grammars. In *IJCAI*.

F. Xia and M. Palmer. 2001. Converting dependency structures to phrase structures. In *HLT*.

Exploring Adaptor Grammars for Native Language Identification

Sze-Meng Jojo Wong **Mark Dras** **Mark Johnson**
Centre for Language Technology
Macquarie University
Sydney, NSW, Australia
{sze.wong,mark.dras,mark.johnson}@mq.edu.au

Abstract

The task of inferring the native language of an author based on texts written in a second language has generally been tackled as a classification problem, typically using as features a mix of n-grams over characters and part of speech tags (for small and fixed n) and unigram function words. To capture arbitrarily long n-grams that syntax-based approaches have suggested are useful, adaptor grammars have some promise. In this work we investigate their extension to identifying n-gram collocations of arbitrary length over a mix of PoS tags and words, using both maxent and induced syntactic language model approaches to classification. After presenting a new, simple baseline, we show that learned collocations used as features in a maxent model perform better still, but that the story is more mixed for the syntactic language model.

1 Introduction

The task of inferring the native language of an author based on texts written in a second language — *native language identification* (NLI) — has, since the seminal work of Koppel et al. (2005), been primarily tackled as a text classification task using supervised machine learning techniques. Lexical features, such as function words, character n-grams, and part-of-speech (PoS) n-grams, have been proven to be useful in NLI (Koppel et al., 2005; Tsur and Rappoport, 2007; Estival et al., 2007). The recent work of Wong and Dras (2011), motivated by ideas from Second Language Acquisition (SLA), has shown that syntactic features — potentially capturing syntactic errors characteristic of a particular native language — improve performance over purely lexical ones.

PoS n-grams can be leveraged to characterise surface syntactic structures: in Koppel et al. (2005), for example, ungrammatical structures were approximated by rare PoS bigrams. For the purpose of NLI, small n-gram sizes like bigram or trigram might not suffice to capture sequences that are characteristic of a particular native language. On the other hand, an attempt to represent these with larger n-grams would not just lead to feature sparsity problems, but also computational efficiency issues. Some form of feature selection should then come into play.

Adaptor grammars (Johnson, 2010), a hierarchical non-parametric extension of PCFGs (and also interpretable as an extension of LDA-based topic models), hold out some promise here. In that initial work, Johnson's model learnt collocations of arbitrary length such as *gradient descent* and *cost function*, under a topic associated with machine learning. Hardisty et al. (2010) applied this idea to perspective classification, learning collocations such as *palestinian violence* and *palestinian freedom*, the use of which as features was demonstrated to help the classification of texts from the Bitter Lemons corpus as either Palestinian or Israeli perspective.

Typically in NLI and other authorship attribution tasks, the feature sets exclude content words, to avoid unfair cues due to potentially different domains of discourse. In our context, then, what we are interested in are 'quasi-syntactic collocations' of either pure PoS (e.g. `NN IN NN`) or a mixture of PoS with function words (e.g. `NN of NN`). The particular question of interest for this paper, then, is to investigate whether the power of adaptor grammars to discover collocations — specifically, ones of arbitrary length that are useful for classification — extends to features beyond the purely lexical.

We examine two different approaches in this paper. We first utilise adaptor grammars for discovery of high performing 'quasi-syntactic collocations' of arbitrary length as mentioned above and use them as classification features in a conventional maximum entropy (maxent) model for identifying the author's native language. In the second approach, we adopt a grammar induction technique to learn a grammar-based language model in a Bayesian setting. The grammar learned can then be used to infer the most probable native language that a given text written in a second language is associated with. The latter approach is actually closer to the work of Hardisty et al. (2010) using adaptor grammars for perspective modeling, which inspired our general approach. This alternative approach is also similar in nature to the work of Börschinger et al. (2011) in which grounded learning of semantic parsers was reduced to a grammatical inference task.

The structure of the paper is as follows. In Section 2, we review the existing work of NLI as well as the mechanics of adaptor grammars along with their applications to classification. Section 3 details the supervised maxent classification of NLI with collocation (n-gram) features discovered by adaptor grammars. The language model-based classifier is described in Section 4. Finally, we present a discussion in Section 5 and follow with concluding remarks.

2 Related Work

2.1 Native Language Identification

Most of the existing research treats the task of native language identification as a form of text classification deploying supervised machine learning approaches.

The earliest notable work in this classification paradigm is that of Koppel et al. (2005) using as features function words, character n-grams, and PoS bigrams, together with some spelling errors. Their experiments were conducted on English essays written by authors whose native language one of Bulgarian, Czech, French, Russian, or Spanish. The corpus used is the first version of *International Corpus of Learner English* (ICLE). Apart from investigating lexical features, syntactic features (errors in particular) were highlighted by Koppel et al. (2005) as potentially useful features, but they only explored this by characterising ungrammatical structures with rare PoS bigrams: they chose 250 rare bigrams from the Brown corpus.

Features for this task can include content words or not: Koppel et al. (2009), in reviewing work in the general area of authorship attribution (including NLI), discuss the (perhaps unreasonable) advantage that content word features can provide, and comment that consequently they "are careful … to distinguish results that exploit content-based features from those that do not". We will not be using content words as features; we therefore note only approaches to NLI that similarly do not use them.

Following Koppel et al. (2005), Tsur and Rappoport (2007) replicated their work and hypothesised that word choices in second language writing is highly influenced by the frequency of native language syllables. They investigated this through measuring classification performance with only character bigrams as features.

Estival et al. (2007) tackled the broader task of developing profiles of authors, including native language and various other demographic and psychometric author traits, across a smaller set of languages (English, Spanish and Arabic). To this end, they deployed various lexical and document structure features.

Wong and Dras (2011), starting from the Koppel et al. (2005) approach, explored the usefulness of syntactic features in a broader sense in which they characterised syntactic errors with cross sections of parse trees obtained from statistical parsers, both horizontal slices of the parse trees in the form of CFG production rules, and the feature schemata used in discriminative parse reranking (Charniak and Johnson, 2005); they also found that using the top 200 PoS bigrams helped. Their results on the second version of the ICLE corpus, across seven languages (those of Koppel et al., plus two Oriental languages, Chinese and Japanese) demonstrated that syntactic features of these kinds lead to significantly better performance than the Koppel et al. features alone, with a top accuracy (on 5-fold cross-validation) of 77.75%.

Subsequently, Wong et al. (2011) explored Bayesian *topic modeling* (Blei et al., 2003; Griffiths and Steyvers, 2004) as a form of feature dimensionality reduction technique to discover coherent latent factors ('topics') that might capture predictive features for individual native languages. Their topics, rather than the typical word n-grams, consisted of bigrams over (only) PoS. However, while there was some evidence of topic cluster coherence, this did not improve classification performance.

The work of the present paper differs in that it uses Bayesian techniques to discover collocations of arbitrary length for use in classification, over a mix of both PoS and function words, rather than for use as feature dimensionality reduction.

2.2 Adaptor Grammars

Adaptor Grammars are a non-parametric extension to PCFGs that are associated with a Bayesian inference procedure. Here we provide an informal introduction to Adaptor Grammars; Johnson et al. (2007) provide a definition of Adaptor Grammars as a hierarchy of mixtures of Dirichlet (or 2-parameter Poisson-Dirichlet) Processes to which the reader should turn for further details.

Adaptor Grammars can be viewed as extending PCFGs by permitting the grammar to contain an unbounded number of productions; they are non-parametric in the sense that the particular productions used to analyse a corpus depends on the corpus itself. Because the set of possible productions is unbounded, they cannot be specified by simply enumerating them, as is standard with PCFGs. Instead, the productions used in an adaptor grammar are specified indirectly using a *base grammar*: the subtrees of the base grammar's "adapted non-terminals" serve as the possible productions of the adaptor grammar (Johnson et al., 2007), much in the way that subtrees function as productions in Tree Substitution Grammars .[1]

Another way to view Adaptor Grammars is that they relax the independence assumptions associated with PCFGs. In a PCFG productions are generated independently conditioned on the parent non-terminal, while in an Adaptor Grammar the probability of generating a subtree rooted in an adapted non-terminal is roughly proportional to the number of times it has been previously generated (a certain amount of mass is reserved to generate "new" subtrees). This means that the distribution generated by an Adaptor Grammar "adapts" based on the corpus being generated.

2.2.1 Mechanics of adaptor grammars

Adaptor Grammars are specified by a PCFG G, plus a subset of G's non-terminals that are called the *adapted non-terminals*, as well as a *discount parameter* a_A, where $0 \leq a_A < 1$ and a *concentration parameter* b_A, where $b > -a$, for each adapted non-terminal A. An adaptor grammar defines a two-parameter Poisson-Dirichlet Process for each adapted non-terminal A governed by the parameters a_A and b_A. For computational purposes it is convenient to integrate out the Poisson-Dirichlet Process, resulting in a predictive distribution specified by a Pitman-Yor Process (PYP). A PYP can be understood in terms of a "Chinese Restaurant" metaphor in which "customers" (observations) are seated at "tables", each of which is labelled with a sample from a "base distribution" (Pitman and Yor, 1997).

In an Adaptor Grammar, unadapted non-terminals expand just as they do in a PCFG; a production r expanding the non-terminal is selected according to the multinomial distribution θ_r over productions specified in the grammar. Each adapted non-terminal A is associated with its own Chinese Restaurant, where the tables are labelled with subtrees generated by the grammar rooted in A. In the Chinese Restaurant metaphor, the customers are expansions of A, each table corresponds to a particular subtree expanding A, and the PCFG specifies the base distribution for each of the adapted non-terminals. An adapted non-terminal A expands as follows. A expands to a subtree t with probability proportional to n_t, where n_t is the number of times t has been previously generated. In addition, A expands using a PCFG rule r expanding A with probability proportional to $(m_A\, a_A + b_A)\, \theta_r$, where m_A is the number of subtrees expanding A (i.e., the number of tables in A's restaurant). Because the underlying Pitman-Yor Processes have a "rich get richer" property, they generate power-law distributions over the subtrees for adapted non-terminals.

[1] For computational efficiency reasons Adaptor Grammars require the subtrees to completely expand to terminals. The *Fragment Grammars* of O'Donnell (2011) lift this restriction.

2.2.2 Adaptor grammars as LDA extension

With the ability to rewrite non-terminals to entire subtrees, adaptor grammars have been used to extend unigram-based LDA topic models (Johnson, 2010). This allows topic models to capture sequences of words with abitrary length rather than just unigrams of word. It has also been shown that it is crucial to go beyond the bag-of-words assumption as topical collocations capture more meaning information and represent more interpretable topics (Wang et al., 2007).

Taking the PCFG formulation for the LDA topic models, it can be modified such that each topic $Topic_i$ generates sequences of words by adapting each of the $Topic_i$ non-terminals (usually indicated with an *underline* in an adaptor grammar). The overall schema for capturing topical collocations with an adaptor grammar is as follows:

$$
\begin{array}{ll}
Sentence \rightarrow Doc_j & j \in 1, \ldots, m \\
Doc_j \rightarrow \_j & j \in 1, \ldots, m \\
Doc_j \rightarrow Doc_j \; Topic_i & i \in 1, \ldots, t; \\
 & j \in 1, \ldots, m \\
\underline{Topic_i} \rightarrow Words & i \in 1, \ldots, t \\
\underline{Words} \rightarrow Word & \\
Words \rightarrow Words \; Word & \\
Word \rightarrow w & w \in V
\end{array}
$$

There is a non-grammar-based approach to finding topical collocations as demonstrated by Wang et al. (2007). Both of these approaches learned useful collocations: for instance, as mentioned in Section 1, Johnson (2010) found collocations such *gradient descent* and *cost function* associated with the topic of machine learning; Wang et al. (2007) found the topic of human receptive system comprises of collocations such as *visual cortext* and *motion detector*.

Adaptor grammars have also been deployed as a form of feature selection in discovering useful collocations for perspective classification. Hardisty et al. (2010) argued that indicators of perspectives are often beyond the length of bigrams and demonstrated that the use of the adaptor grammar inferred n-grams of arbitrary length as features establishes the start-of-the-art performance for perspective classification on the Bitter Lemons corpus, depicting two different perspectives of Israeli and Pelestinian. We are adopting a similar approach in this paper for classifying texts with respect to the author's native language; but the key difference with Hardisty et al. (2010)'s approach is that our focus is on collocations that mix PoS and lexical elements, rather than being purely lexical.

3 Maxent Classification

In this section, we first explain the procedures taken to set up the conventional supervised classification task for NLI through the deployment of adaptor grammars for discovery of 'quasi-syntactic collocations' of arbitrary length. We then present the classification results attained based on these selected sets of n-gram features. In all of our experiments, we investigate two sets of collocations: pure PoS and a mixture of PoS and function words. The idea of examining the latter set is motivated by the results of Wong and Dras (2011) where inclusion of parse production rules lexicalised with function words as features had shown to improve the classification performance relative to unlexicalised ones.

3.1 Experimental Setup

3.1.1 Data and evaluation

The classification experiments are conducted on the second version of ICLE (Granger et al., 2009).[2] Following our earlier NLI work in Wong and Dras (2011), our data set consists of 490 texts written in English by authors of seven different native language groups: Bulgarian, Czech, French, Russian, Spanish, Chinese, and Japanese. Each native language contributes 70 out of the 490 texts. As we are using a relative small data set, we perform k-fold cross-validation, choosing $k = 5$.

3.1.2 Adaptor grammars for supervised classification

We derive two adaptor grammars for the maxent classification setting, where each is associated with a different set of vocabulary (i.e. either pure PoS or the mixture of PoS and function words). We use

[2]Joel Tetreault and Daniel Blanchard from ETS have pointed out (personal communication) that there is a subtle issue with ICLE that could have an impact on the classification performance of NLI tasks; in particular, when character n-grams are used as features, some special characters used in some ICLE texts might affect performance. For our case, this should not be of much issue since they will not appear in our collocations.

the grammar of Johnson (2010) as presented in Section 2.2.2, except that the vocabulary differs: either $w \in V_{pos}$ or $w \in V_{pos+fw}$. For V_{pos}, there are 119 distinct PoS tags based on the Brown tagset. V_{pos+fw} is extended with 398 function words as per Wong and Dras (2011). $m = 490$ is the number of documents, and $t = 25$ the number of topics (chosen as the best performing one from Wong et al. (2011)).

Rules of the form $\texttt{Doc}_j \rightarrow \texttt{Doc}_j\ \texttt{Topic}_i$ that encode the possible topics that are associated with a document j are given similar $\boldsymbol{\alpha}$ priors as used in LDA ($\boldsymbol{\alpha} = 5/t$ where $t = 25$ in our experiments). Likewise, similar $\boldsymbol{\beta}$ priors from LDA are placed on the adapted rules expanding from $\underline{\texttt{Topic}_i} \rightarrow \texttt{Words}$, representing the possible sequences of words that each topic comprises ($\boldsymbol{\beta} = 0.01$).[3] The inference algorithm for the adaptor grammars are based on the Markov Chain Monte Carlo technique made available online by Johnson (2010).[4]

3.1.3 Classification models with n-gram features

Based on the two adaptor grammars inferred, the resulting collocations (n-grams) are extracted as features for the classification task of identifying authors' native language. These n-grams found by the adaptor grammars are only a (not necessarily proper) subset of those n-grams that are strongly characteristic of a particular native language. In principle, one could find all strongly characteristic n-grams by enumerating all the possible instances of n-grams up to a given length if the vocabulary is of a small enough closed set, such as for PoS tags, but this is infeasible when the set is extended to PoS plus function words. The use of adaptor grammars here can be viewed as a form of feature selection, as in Hardisty et al. (2010).

Baseline models To serve as a baseline, we take the commonly used PoS bigrams as per the previous work of NLI (Koppel et al., 2005). A set of 200 PoS bigrams is selected in two ways: the 200 most frequent in the training data (as in Wong and Dras (2011)) and the 200 with the highest information gain (IG) values in the training data (not evaluated in other work).

Enumerated n-gram models Here, we enumerate all the possible n-grams up to a fixed length and select the best of these according to IG, as a generalisation of the baseline. The first motivation for this feature set is that, in a sense, this should give a rough upper bound for the adaptor grammar's PoS-alone n-grams, as these latter should most often be a subset of the former. The second motivation is that it gives a robust comparison for the mixed PoS and function word n-grams, where it is infeasible to enumerate all of them.

ENUM-POS We enumerate all possible n-grams up to the length of 5, and select those that actually occur (i.e. of the $\sum_{i=1}^{5} 119^i$ possible n-grams, this is 218,042 based on the average of 5 folds). We look at the top n-grams up to length 5 selected by IG: the top 2,800 and the top 6,500 (for comparability with adaptor grammar feature sets, below), as well as the top 10,000 and the top 20,000 (to study the effect of larger feature space).

Adaptor grammar n-gram models The classification features are the two sets of selected collocations inferred by the adaptor grammars which are the main interest of this paper.

AG-POS This first set of the adaptor grammar-inferred features comprise of pure PoS n-grams (i.e. V_{pos}). The largest length of n-gram found is 17, but about 97% of the collocations are of length between 2 to 5. We investigate three variants of this feature set: top 200 n-grams of all lengths (based on IG), all n-grams of all lengths ($n = 2,795$ on average), and all n-grams up to the length of 5 ($n = 2,710$ on average).

AG-POS+FW This second set of the adaptor grammar-inferred features are mixtures of PoS and function words (i.e. V_{pos+fw}). The largest length of n-gram found for this set is 19 and the total number of different collocations found is much higher. For the purpose of comparability with the first set of adaptor grammar features, we investigate the following five variants for this feature set: top 200 n-grams of all lengths, all n-grams of all lengths ($n = 6,490$ on average), all n-grams up to the length of 5 ($n = 6,417$ on average), top 2,800 n-grams of all different lengths,

[3] The values of $\boldsymbol{\alpha}$ and $\boldsymbol{\beta}$ are also based on the established values presented in Wong et al. (2011).

[4] Adaptor grammar software is available on `http://web.science.mq.edu.au/~mjohnson/Software.htm`.

Features (n-grams)	Accuracy
BASELINE-POS [top200 MOST-FREQ]	53.87
BASELINE-POS [top200 IG]	56.12
AG-POS [top200 IG]	61.02
AG-POS [all $\leq$17-gram] ($n \approx 2800$)	68.37
AG-POS [all $\leq$ 5-gram] ($n \approx 2700$)	68.57
AG-POS+FW [top200 IG]	58.16
AG-POS+FW [all $\leq$19-gram] ($n \approx 6500$)	**74.49**
AG-POS+FW [all $\leq$5-gram] ($n \approx 6400$)	**74.49**
AG-POS+FW [top2800 IG $\leq$ 19-gram]	71.84
AG-POS+FW [top2800 IG $\leq$ 5-gram]	71.84
ENUM-POS [top2800 IG $\leq$ 5-gram]	69.79
ENUM-POS [top6500 IG $\leq$ 5-gram]	72.44
ENUM-POS [top10K IG $\leq$ 5-gram]	71.02
ENUM-POS [top20K IG $\leq$ 5-gram]	71.43

Table 1: Maxent classification results for individual feature sets (with 5-fold cross validation).

and top 2,800 n-grams up to the length of 5. (All the selections are based on IG).

In our models, all feature values are of binary type. For the classifier, we employ a maximum entropy (MaxEnt) machine learner — MegaM (fifth release) by Hal Daumé III.[5]

3.2 Classification results

Table 1 presents all the classification results for the individual feature sets, along with the baselines. On the whole, both sets of the collocations inferred by the adaptor grammars perform better than the two baselines. We make the following observations:

- Regarding ENUM-POS as a (rough) upper bound, the adaptor grammar AG-POS with a comparable number of features performs almost as well. However, because it is possible to enumerate many more n-grams than are found during the sampling process, ENUM-POS opens up a gap over AG-POS of around 4%.

- Collocations with a mix of PoS and function words do in fact lead to higher accuracy as compared to those of pure PoS (except for the top 200 n-grams); for instance, compare the 2,800 n-grams up to length 5 from the two corresponding sets (71.84 vs. 68.57).

- Furthermore, the adaptor grammar-inferred collocations with mixtures of PoS and function words (AG-POS+FW) in general perform better than our rough upper bound of PoS collocations, i.e. the enumerated PoS n-grams (ENUM-POS): the overall best results of the two feature sets are 74.49 and 72.44 respectively.

[5]MegaM software is available on http://www.cs.utah.edu/~hal/megam/.

Features (n-grams)	Accuracy
AG-POS [all $\leq$ 5-gram] & FW	72.04
ENUM-POS [top2800 $\leq$ 5-gram] & FW	73.67
AG-POS+FW & AG-POS ^{a}	**75.71**
AG-POS+FW & AG-POS ^{b}	74.90
AG-POS+FW & ENUM-POS [top2800] ^{a}	73.88
AG-POS+FW & ENUM-POS [top2800] ^{b}	74.69
AG-POS+FW & ENUM-POS [top10K] ^{b}	74.90
AG-POS+FW & ENUM-POS [top20K] ^{b}	75.10

Table 2: Maxent classification results for combined feature sets (with 5-fold cross validation). ^{a}Features from the two sets are selected based on the overall top 3700 with highest IG; ^{b}features from the two sets are just linearly concatenated.

Given that the AG-POS+FW n-grams are capturing different sorts of document characteristics, they could potentially usefully be combined with the PoS-alone features. We thus combined them with both AG-POS and ENUM-POS feature sets, and the classification results are presented in Table 2. We tried two ways of integrating the feature sets: one way is to take the overall top 2,800 of the two sets based on IG; the other way is to just combine the two sets of features by concatenation of feature vectors (as indicated by *a* and *b* respectively in the result table). For comparability purposes, we considered only n-grams up to the length of 5. A baseline approach to this is just to add in function words as unigram features by feature vector concatenation, giving two further models, AG-POS [all $\leq$ 5-gram] & FW and ENUM-POS [top2800 $\leq$ 5-gram] & FW.

Overall, the classification accuracies attained by the combined feature sets are higher than the individual feature sets. The best performing of all the models is achieved by combining the mixed PoS and function word collocations with the adaptor grammar-inferred PoS, producing the best accuracy thus far of 75.71. This demonstrates that features inferred by adaptor grammars do capture some useful information and function words are playing a role. The way of integrating the two feature sets has different effects on the types of combination. As seen in Table 2, method *a* works better for the combination of the two adaptor grammar feature sets; whereas method *b* works better for combining adaptor grammar features with enumerated n-gram features.

Using adaptor grammar collocations also outperforms the alternative baseline of adding in function words as unigrams. For instance, the best performing combined feature set of both AG-POS and AG-POS+FW does result in higher accuracy as compared to the two alternative baseline models, comparing 75.71 with 72.04 (and 75.71 with 73.67). This demonstrates that our more general PoS plus function word collocations derived from adaptor grammars are indeed useful, and supports the argument of Wang et al. (2007) that they are a useful technique for looking into features beyond just the bag of words.

4 Language Model-based Classification

In this section, we take a language modeling approach to native language identification; the idea here is to adopt grammatical inference to learn a grammar-based language model to represent the texts written by non-English native users. The grammar learned is then used to predict the most probable native language that a document (a sentence) is associated with.

In a sense, we are using a parser-based language model to rank the documents with respect to native language. We draw on the work of Börschinger et al. (2011) for this section. In that work, the task was grounded learning of a semantic parser. Training examples there consisted of natural language strings (descriptions of a robot soccer game) and a set of candidate meanings (actions in the robot soccer game world) for the string; each was tagged with a context identifier reflecting the actual action of the game. A grammar was then induced that would parse the examples, and was used on test data (where the context identifier was absent) to predict the context. We take a similar approach to developing an grammatical induction technique, although where they used a standard LDA topic model-based PCFG, we use an adaptor grammar. We expect that the results will likely to be lower than for the discriminative approach of Section 3. However, the approach is of interest for a few reasons: because, whereas the adaptor grammar plays an ancillary, feature selection role in Section 3, here the feature selection is an organic part of the approach as per the actual implementation of Hardisty et al. (2010); because adaptor grammars can potentially be extended in a natural way with unlabelled data; and because, for the purposes of this paper, it constitutes a second, quite different way to evaluate the use of n-gram collocations.

4.1 Language Models

We derive two adaptor grammar-based language models. One consists of only unigrams and bigrams, and the other finds n-gram collocations, in both cases over either PoS or the mix of PoS and function words. The assumption that we make is that each document (each sentence) is a mixture of two sets of topics: one is the native language-specific topic (i.e. characteristic of the native language) and the other is the generic topic (i.e. characteristic of the second language — English in our case). The generic topic is thus shared across all languages, and will behave quite differently from a language-specific topic, which is not shared. In other words, there are eight topics, representing seven native language groups that are of interest (Bulgarian, Czech, French, Russian, Spanish, Chinese, and Japanese) and the second language English itself.[6]

Bigram models The following rule schema is applicable to both vocabulary types of PoS and the mixture of PoS and function words.

$$
\begin{array}{ll}
Root \rightarrow \_lang\ langTopics & \\
langTopics \rightarrow langTopics\ langTopic & \\
langTopics \rightarrow langTopics\ nullTopic & \\
langTopics \rightarrow langTopic & \\
langTopics \rightarrow nullTopic & \\
\underline{langTopic} \rightarrow Words & \\
\underline{nullTopic} \rightarrow Words & \\
\underline{Words} \rightarrow Word\ Word & \\
Words \rightarrow Word & \\
Word \rightarrow w & w \in V_{pos};\ w \in V_{pos+fw}
\end{array}
$$

N-gram models The grammar is the same as the above with the exception that the non-terminal $Words$ is now rewritten as follows in order to

[6]We could just induce a regular PCFG here, rather than an adaptor grammar, by taking as terminals all pairs of PoS tags. We use the adaptor grammar formulation for comparability.

capture n-gram collocations of arbitrary length.

$Words \rightarrow Words\ Word$
$Words \rightarrow Word$

It should be noted that the two grammars above can in theory be applied to an entire document or on individual sentences. For this present work, we work on the sentence level as the run-time of the current implementation of the adaptor grammars grows proportional to the cube of the sentence length. For each grammar we try both sparse and uniform Dirichlet priors ($\alpha = \{0.01, 0.1, 1.0\}$). The sparse priors encourage only a minority of the rules to be associated with high probabilities.

4.2 Training and Evaluation

As we are using the same data set as per the previous approach, we perform 5-fold cross validation as well. However, the training for each fold is conducted with a different grammar consisting of only the vocabulary that occur in each training fold. The reason is that we are now having a form of *supervised* topic models where the learning process is guided by the native languages. Hence, each of the training sentences are prefixed with the (native) language identifiers $\_lang$, as seen in the *Root* rules of the grammar presented above.

To evaluate the grammars learned, as in Börschinger et al. (2011) we need to slightly modify the grammars above by removing the language identifiers ($\_lang$) from the *Root* rules and then parse the *unlabeled* sentences using a publicly available CKY parser.[7] The predicted native language is inferred from the parse output by reading off the $langTopics$ that the *Root* is rewritten to. We take that as the most probable native language for a particular test sentence. At the document level, we select as the class the language predicted for the largest number of sentences in that document.

4.3 Parsing Results

Tables 3 and 4 present the parsing results at the sentence level and the document level, respectively. On the whole, the results at the sentence level are much poorer as compared to those at the document level. In light of the results of Section 3.2, it is surprising

[7]CKY parser by Mark Johnson is available on `http://web.science.mq.edu.au/~mjohnson/Software.htm`.

Features (n-grams)	Accuracy ($\alpha = 0.01$)	($\alpha = 0.1$)	($\alpha = 1.0$)
AG-POS [bigrams]	26.84	27.03	26.77
AG-POS [n-grams]	25.85	25.78	25.62
AG-POS+FW [bigrams]	28.58	28.40	27.43
AG-POS+FW [n-grams]	26.64	27.64	28.75

Table 3: Language modeling-based classification results based on parsing (at the sentence level).

Features (n-grams)	Accuracy ($\alpha = 0.01$)	($\alpha = 0.1$)	($\alpha = 1.0$)
AG-POS [bigrams]	41.22	38.88	39.69
AG-POS [n-grams]	36.12	34.90	35.20
AG-POS+FW [bigrams]	47.45	46.94	44.64
AG-POS+FW [n-grams]	43.97	49.39	**50.15**

Table 4: Language modeling-based classification results based on parsing (at the document level).

that bigram models appear to perform better than n-gram models for both types of vocabulary, with the exception of AG-POS+FW at the document level. In fact, one would expect n-gram models to perform better in general as it is a generalisation that would contain all the potential bigrams. Nonetheless, the language models over the mixture of PoS and function words appear to be a more suitable representative of our learner corpus as compared to those over purely PoS, confirming the usefulness of integrated function words for the NLI classification task.

It should also be noted that sparse priors generally appear to be more appriopriate; except that for AG-POS+FW n-grams, uniform priors are indeed better and resulted in the highest parsing result of 50.15. (Although all the parsing results are much weaker as compared to the results presented in Section 3.2, they are all higher than the majority baseline of 14.29% i.e. $70/490$).

5 Discussion

Here we take a closer look at how well each approach does in identifying the individual native languages. The confusion matrix for the best model of two approaches are presented in Table 5 and Table 6. Both approaches perform reasonably well for the two Oriental languages (Chinese in particular); this is not a major surprise, as the two languages are not part of the language family that the rest of the languages come from (i.e. Indo-European). Under the supervised maxent classification, misclassifications largely are observed in the Romance ones (French and Spanish) as well as Russian; for the language model-based approach, Bulgarian is identi-

	BL	CZ	RU	FR	SP	CN	JP
BL	[52]	5	7	4	2	-	-
CZ	5	[50]	5	3	4	-	3
RU	6	8	[46]	5	1	-	4
FR	7	3	5	[43]	8	-	4
SP	7	2	4	9	[47]	-	1
CN	-	-	-	-	-	[70]	-
JP	-	-	2	2	1	2	[63]

Table 5: Confusion matrix based on the best performing model under maxent setting (BL:Bulgarian, CZ:Czech, RU:Russian, FR:French, SP:Spanish, CN:Chinese, JP:Japanese).

	BL	CZ	RU	FR	SP	CN	JP
BL	[20]	32	9	6	-	1	2
CZ	2	[59]	3	1	-	-	5
RU	3	41	[19]	2	1	-	4
FR	8	20	4	[31]	4	-	3
SP	7	27	11	12	[9]	-	4
CN	-	2	-	2	-	[62]	4
JP	-	19	1	2	-	1	[47]

Table 6: Confusion matrix based on the best performing model under language modeling setting (BL:Bulgarian, CZ:Czech, RU:Russian, FR:French, SP:Spanish, CN:Chinese, JP:Japanese).

fied poorly, and Spanish moreso. However, the latter approach appears to be better in identifying Czech. On the whole, the maxent approach results in much fewer misclassifications compared to its counterpart.

In fact, there is a subtle difference in the experimental setting of the models derived from the two approaches with respect to the adaptor grammar: the number of topics. Under the maxent setting, the number of topics t was set to 25, while we restricted the models with the language modeling approach to only eight topics (seven for the individual native languages and one for the common second language, English). Looking more deeply into the topics themselves reveals that there appears to be at least two out of the 25 topics (from the supervised models) associated with n-grams that are indicative of the native languages, taking Chinese and Japanese as examples (see the associated topics in Table 7).[8] Perhaps associating each native language with only one generalised topic is not sufficient.

Furthermore, the distribution of n-grams among the topics (i.e. subtrees of collocations derived from the adaptor grammars) are quite different between the two approaches although the total num-

Top 10 Mixture N-grams			
Japanese		**Chinese**	
topic$_2$	**topic$_{23}$**	**topic$_9$**	**topic$_{17}$**
.	.	NN	.
we VB	PPSS VB	a NN	NN NN
our NNS	my NN	NN NN	NNS
our NN	CC	VBN by	NN
NN	VBG	NP .	RB ,
PPSS VB	PPSS think	NP	of NN
about	NN	:	JJ NN
because	PPSS VBD	(	NN .
it .	RB	as	VBG NN
we are	PPSS ' NN	NN NN NN	NN NN NN

Table 7: Top mixture n-grams (collocations) for 4 out of the 25 topics representative of Japanese and Chinese (under maxent setting). N-grams of pronoun with verb are found at the upper end of $Topic_2$ and $Topic_{23}$ reflecting the frequent usage of Japanese; n-grams of noun are top n-grams under $Topic_9$ and $Topic_{17}$ indicating Chinese's common error of determiner-noun disagreement.

ber of n-grams inferred by each approach is about the same. For the language modeling ones, a high number of n-grams were associated with the generic topic $nullTopic$[9] and each language-specific topic $langTopic$ has a lower number of n-grams relative to bi-grams (Table 8) associated with it. For the maxent models, in contrast, the majority of the topics were associated with a higher number of n-grams (Table 9). The smaller number of n-grams to be used as features — and the fact that their extra length means that they will occur more sparsely in the documents — seems to be the core of the problem.

Nonetheless, the language models inferred discover relevant n-grams that are representative of individual native languages. For instance, the bigram `NN NN`, which Wong and Dras (2011) claim may reflect the error of determiner-noun disagreement commonly found amongst Chinese learners, was found under the Chinese topic at the top-2 position with a probability of 0.052 as compared to the other languages at the probability range of 0.0005-0.003. Similarly, one example for Japanese, the mixture bigram `PPSS think`, indicating frequent usage of pronouns within Japanese was seen under the Japanese topic at the top-9 position with a probability of 0.025 in relation to other languages within the range of 0.0002-0.006: this phenomenon as char-

[8]Taking the examples from Wong et al. (2011) as reference, we found similar n-grams that are indicative of Japanese and Chinese.

[9]This is quite plausible as there should be quite a number of structures that are representative of native English speakers that are shared by non-native speakers.

Model Types	N-gram Frequency															
	BGTopic		CZTopic		FRTopic		RUTopic		SPTopic		CNTopic		JPTopic		NullTopic	
	(a)	(b)	(a)	(b)	(a)	(b)	(a)	(b)	(a)	(b)	(a)	(b)	(a)	(b)	(a)	(b)
Bigrams	374	187	352	219	426	165	350	211	351	156	397	351	394	194	867	6169
N-grams	177	159	226	217	151	152	148	202	128	147	357	255	209	226	3089	7794

Table 8: Distribution of n-grams (collocations) for each topic under language modeling setting. (a) subcolumns are for n-grams of pure PoS and (b) subcolumns are for n-grams of mixtures of PoS and function words.

N-gram Frequency																			
Topic$_1$		Topic$_2$		Topic$_3$		Topic$_4$		Topic$_5$		Topic$_6$		Topic$_7$		Topic$_8$		Topic$_9$		Topic$_{10}$	
(a)	(b)	(a)	(b)	(a)	(b)	(a)	(b)	(a)	(b)	(a)	(b)	(a)	(b)	(a)	(b)	(a)	(b)	(a)	(b)
174	443	145	441	136	245	141	341	236	519	169	748	127	340	182	473	109	339	190	236
Topic$_{11}$		Topic$_{12}$		Topic$_{13}$		Topic$_{14}$		Topic$_{15}$		Topic$_{16}$		Topic$_{17}$		Topic$_{18}$		Topic$_{19}$		Topic$_{20}$	
(a)	(b)	(a)	(b)	(a)	(b)	(a)	(b)	(a)	(b)	(a)	(b)	(a)	(b)	(a)	(b)	(a)	(b)	(a)	(b)
57	259	126	455	103	543	211	225	170	459	81	309	238	207	152	475	119	452	333	423
Topic$_{21}$				Topic$_{22}$				Topic$_{23}$				Topic$_{24}$				Topic$_{25}$			
(a)		(b)		(a)		(b)		(a)		(b)		(a)		(b)		(a)		(b)	
245		341		168		492		194		472		201		366		195		190	

Table 9: Distribution of n-grams (collocations) for each topic under maxent setting. (a) subcolumns are for n-grams of pure PoS and (b) subcolumns are for n-grams of mixtures of PoS and function words.

Languages	Excerpts from ICLE
Chinese	... the overpopulation problem in urban area ...
	... The development of country park can directly ...
	... when it comes to urban renewal project ...
	... As developing new town in ...
	... and reserve some country park as ...
Japanese	... I think many people will ...
	... I think governments should not ...
	... I think culture is the most significant ...
	... I think the state should not ...
	... I really think we must live ...

Table 10: Excerpts from ICLE illustrating the common phenomena observed amongst Chinese and Japanese.

acteristic of Japanese speakers has also been noted for different corpora by Ishikawa (2011). (Note that this collocation as well as its pure PoS counterpart `PPSS VB` are amongst the top n-grams discovered under the maxent setting as seen in Table 7.) Table 10 presents some excerpts extracted from the corpus that illustrate these two common phenomena.

To investigate further the issue associated with the number of topics under the language modeling setting, we attempted to extend the adaptor grammar with three additional topics that represent the language family of the seven native languages of interest: Slavic, Romance, and Oriental. (The resulting grammar is presented as below.) However, the parsing result does not improve over the initial setting with eight topics in total.

$$Root \rightarrow \_lang\ langTopics$$
$$langTopics \rightarrow langTopics\ langTopic$$
$$langTopics \rightarrow langTopics\ familyTopic$$
$$langTopics \rightarrow langTopics\ nullTopic$$
$$langTopics \rightarrow langTopic$$
$$langTopics \rightarrow familyTopic$$
$$langTopics \rightarrow nullTopic$$
$$\underline{langTopic} \rightarrow Words$$
$$\underline{familyTopic} \rightarrow Words$$
$$\underline{nullTopic} \rightarrow Words$$
$$Words \rightarrow Words\ Word$$
$$Words \rightarrow Word$$
$$Word \rightarrow w \qquad w \in V_{pos};\ w \in V_{pos+fw}$$

6 Conclusion and Future Work

This paper has shown that the extension of adaptor grammars to discovering collocations beyond the lexical, in particular a mix of PoS tags and function words, can produce features useful in the NLI classification problem. More specifically, when added to a new baseline presented in this paper, the combined feature set of both types of adaptor grammar inferred collocations produces the best result in the context of using n-grams for NLI. The usefulness of the collocations does vary, however, with the technique used for classification.

Future work will involve a broader exploration of the parameter space of the adaptor grammars, in particular the number of topics and the value of α; a look at other non-parametric extensions of PCFGs, such as infinite PCFGs (Liang et al., 2007) for finding a set of non-terminals permitting more fine-grained topics; and an investigation of how the approach can be extended to semi-supervised learning to take advantage of the vast quantity of texts with errors available on the Web.

Acknowledgments

We would like to acknowledge the support of ARC Linkage Grant LP0776267. We also thank the anonymous reviewers for useful feedback. Much gratitude is due to Benjamin Börschinger for his help with the language modeling implementation.

References

David M. Blei, Andrew Ng, and Michael Jordan. 2003. Latent Dirichlet allocation. *Journal of Machine Learning Research*, 3:993–1022.

Benjamin Börschinger, Bevan K. Jones, and Mark Johnson. 2011. Reducing grounded learning tasks to grammatical inference. In *Proceedings of the 2011 Conference on Empirical Methods in Natural Language Processing*, pages 1416–1425, Edinburgh, Scotland, July.

Eugene Charniak and Mark Johnson. 2005. Coarse-to-fine n-best parsing and MaxEnt discriminative reranking. In *Proceedings of the 43rd Annual Meeting on Association for Computational Linguistics*, pages 173–180, Ann Arbor, Michigan, June.

Dominique Estival, Tanja Gaustad, Son-Bao Pham, Will Radford, and Ben Hutchinson. 2007. Author profiling for English emails. In *Proceedings of the 10th Conference of the Pacific Association for Computational Linguistics (PACLING)*, pages 263–272.

Sylviane Granger, Estelle Dagneaux, Fanny Meunier, and Magali Paquot. 2009. *International Corpus of Learner English (Version 2)*. Presses Universitaires de Louvain, Louvian-la-Neuve.

Thomas L. Griffiths and Mark Steyvers. 2004. Finding scientific topics. *Proceedings of the National Academy of Sciences*, 101(suppl. 1):5228–5235.

Eric A. Hardisty, Jordan Boyd-Graber, and Philip Resnik. 2010. Modeling perspective using adaptor grammars. In *Proceedings of the 2010 Conference on Empirical Methods in Natural Language Processing*, EMNLP '10, pages 284–292.

Shun'ichiro Ishikawa. 2011. A New Horizon in Learner Corpus Studies: The Aim of the ICNALE Project. In G. Weir, S. Ishikawa, and K. Poonpon, editors, *Corpora and Language Technologies in Teaching, Learning and Research*, pages 3–11. University of Strathclyde Press, Glasgow, UK.

Mark Johnson, Thomas L. Griffiths, and Sharon Goldwater. 2007. Adaptor grammars: A framework for specifying compositional nonparametric bayesian models. In *Advances in Neural Information Processing Systems 19: Proceedings of the Twentieth Annual Conference on Neural Information Processing Systems*, pages 641–648.

Mark Johnson. 2010. PCFGs, Topic Models, Adaptor Grammars and Learning Topical Collocations and the Structure of Proper Names. In *Proceedings of the 48th Annual Meeting of the Association for Computational Linguistics*, pages 1148–1157, Uppsala, Sweden, July.

Moshe Koppel, Jonathan Schler, and Kfir Zigdon. 2005. Automatically determining an anonymous author's native language. In *Intelligence and Security Informatics*, volume 3495 of *Lecture Notes in Computer Science*, pages 209–217. Springer-Verlag.

Moshe Koppel, Jonathan Schler, and Shlomo Argamon. 2009. Computational Methods in Authorship Attribution. *Journal of the American Society for Information Science and Technology*, 60(1):9–26.

Percy Liang, Slav Petrov, Michael I. Jordan, and Dan Klein. 2007. The infinite pcfg using hierarchical dirichlet processes. In *Proceedings of the 2007 Joint Conference on Empirical Methods in Natural Language Processing and Computational Natural Language Learning*, pages 688–697, Prague, Czech Republic, June.

Timothy O'Donnell. 2011. *Productivity and reuse in language*. Ph.D. thesis, Harvard University.

Jim Pitman and Marc Yor. 1997. The two-parameter Poisson-Dirichlet distribution derived from a stable subordinator. *Annals of Probability*, 25(2):855–900.

Oren Tsur and Ari Rappoport. 2007. Using classifier features for studying the effect of native language on the choice of written second language words. In *Proceedings of the Workshop on Cognitive Aspects of Computational Language Acquisition*, pages 9–16.

Hans van Halteren. 2008. Source language markers in EUROPARL translations. In *Proceedings of the 22nd International Conference on Computational Linguistics (COLING)*, pages 937–944.

Xuerui Wang, Andrew McCallum, and Xing Wei. 2007. Topical n-grams: Phrase and topic discovery, with an application to information retrieval. In *Proceedings of the 2007 Seventh IEEE International Conference on Data Mining*, ICDM '07, pages 697–702.

Sze-Meng Jojo Wong and Mark Dras. 2011. Exploiting parse structures for native language identification. In *Proceedings of the 2011 Conference on Empirical Methods in Natural Language Processing*, pages 1600–1610, Edinburgh, Scotland, July.

Sze-Meng Jojo Wong, Mark Dras, and Mark Johnson. 2011. Topic modeling for native language identification. In *Proceedings of the Australasian Language Technology Association Workshop 2011*, pages 115–124, Canberra, Australia, December.

Discovering Diverse and Salient Threads in Document Collections

Jennifer Gillenwater **Alex Kulesza** **Ben Taskar**
Department of Computer and Information Science
University of Pennsylvania
Philadelphia, PA 19104
{jengi,kulesza,taskar}@cis.upenn.edu

Abstract

We propose a novel probabilistic technique for modeling and extracting salient structure from large document collections. As in clustering and topic modeling, our goal is to provide an organizing perspective into otherwise overwhelming amounts of information. We are particularly interested in revealing and exploiting *relationships* between documents. To this end, we focus on extracting diverse sets of *threads*—singly-linked, coherent chains of important documents. To illustrate, we extract research threads from citation graphs and construct timelines from news articles. Our method is highly scalable, running on a corpus of over 30 million words in about four minutes, more than 75 times faster than a dynamic topic model. Finally, the results from our model more closely resemble human news summaries according to several metrics and are also preferred by human judges.

1 Introduction

The increasing availability of large document collections has the potential to revolutionize our ability to understand the world. However, the scale and complexity of such collections frequently make it difficult to quickly grasp the important details and the relationships between them. As a result, automatic interfaces for data navigation, exploration, aggregation, and analysis are becoming increasingly valuable.

In this work we propose a novel approach: *threading* structured document collections. Consider a large graph, with documents as nodes and edges indicating relationships, as in Figure 1. Our goal is to find a diverse set of paths (or threads) through the collection that are individually coherent and together cover the most salient parts. For example, given a collection of academic papers, we might want to identify the most significant lines of research, threading the citation graph to produce chains of important papers. Or, given news articles connected chronologically, we might want to extract threads of articles to form timelines describing the major events from the most significant news stories. Top-tier news organizations like The New York Times and The Guardian regularly publish such timelines, but have so far been limited to creating them by hand. Other possibile applications might include discovering trends on social media sites, or perhaps mining blog entries for important conversations through trackback links. We show how these kinds of threading tasks can be done efficiently, providing a simple, practical tool for representing graph-based data that offers new possibilities compared with existing models.

The Topic Detection and Tracking (TDT) program (Wayne, 2000) has recently led to some research in this direction. Several of TDT's core tasks, like link detection, topic detection, and topic tracking, can be seen as subroutines for the threading problem. Our work, however, addresses these tasks *jointly*, using a global probabilistic model with a tractable inference algorithm. To achieve this, we employ structured determinantal point processes (SDPPs) (Kulesza

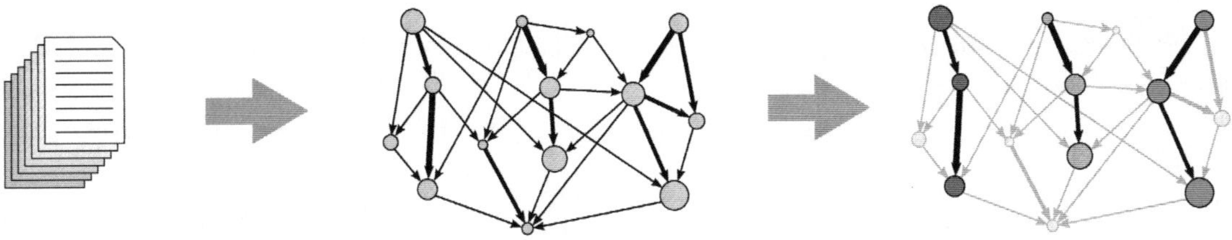

Figure 1: An illustration of document collection threading. We first build a graph from the collection, using measures of importance and relatedness to weight nodes (documents) and build edges (relationships). Then, from this graph, we extract a diverse, salient set of threads to represent the collection. The supplement contains a version of this figure for our real-world news dataset.

and Taskar, 2010), which offer a natural probabilistic model over sets of structures (such as threads) where diversity is desired, and we incorporate k-DPP extensions to control the number of threads (Kulesza and Taskar, 2011).

We apply our model to two real-world datasets, extracting threads of research papers and timelines of news articles. An example of news threads extracted using our model is shown in Figure 2. Quantitative evaluation shows that our model significantly outperforms multiple baselines, including dynamic topic models, in comparisons with human-produced news summaries. It also outperforms baseline methods in a user evaluation of thread coherence, and runs 75 times faster than a dynamic topic model.

The primary contributions of this paper are: (1) proposing a novel framework for finding diverse and salient *sets* of document threads; (2) combining SDPPs and k-DPPs to implement the proposed model; (3) introducing random projections to improve efficiency with only bounded deviation; and (4) demonstrating the model on large-scale, real-world datasets.

2 Related Work

A variety of papers from the topic tracking literature are broadly related to our work (Mei and Zhai, 2005; Blei and Lafferty, 2006; Leskovec et al., 2009; Ahmed and Xing, 2010). Blei and Lafferty (2006) recently introduced dynamic topic models (DTMs). Assuming a division of documents into time slices, a DTM draws in each slice a set of topics from a Gaussian distribution whose mean is determined by the topics from the previous slice. In this way, a DTM generates *topic* threads. In this work we are interested in the related but not identical task of generating *document* threads. We engineer a baseline for constructing document threads from DTM topic threads (see Section 6.2.2), but the topic-centric nature of DTMs means they are not ideal for this task. Figure 2 illustrates some of the issues.

The work of Ahmed and Xing (2010) generalizes DTMs to iDTMs (infinite DTMs) by allowing topics to span only a subset of time slices, and allowing an arbitrary number of topics. However, iDTMs still require placing documents into discrete epochs, and the issue of generating *topic* rather than *document* threads remains. In Section 6 we compare to DTMs but not iDTMs because an implementation of iDTMs was not readily available.

In the information retrieval community there has also been work on extracting temporal information from document collections. Swan and Jensen (2000) proposed a system for finding temporally clustered named entities in news text and presenting them on a timeline. Allan, Gupta, and Khandelwal (2001) introduced the task of *temporal summarization*, which takes a stream of news articles on a particular topic and tries to extract sentences describing important events as they occur. Yan et al (2011) evaluated methods for choosing sentences from temporally clustered documents that are relevant to a query. Here, we are interested not in extracting topically grouped entities or sentences, but instead in organizing a subset of the articles themselves into timelines, with topic identification as a side effect.

There has also been some prior work focusing more directly on threading. Shahaf and

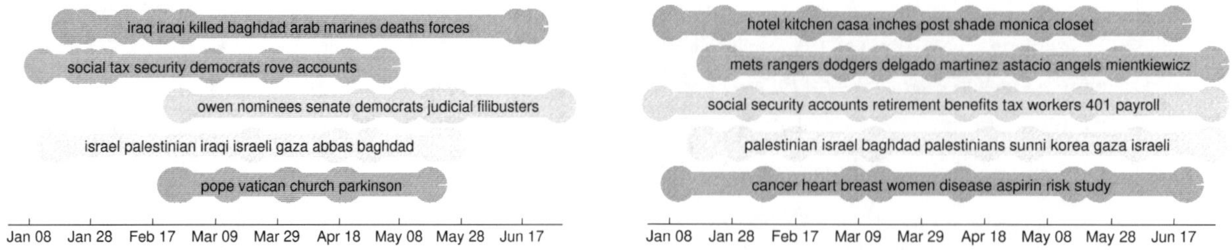

Feb 24: Parkinson's Disease Increases Risks to Pope
Feb 26: Pope's Health Raises Questions About His Ability to Lead
Mar 13: Pope Returns Home After 18 Days at Hospital
Apr 01: Pope's Condition Worsens as World Prepares for End of Papacy
Apr 02: Pope, Though Gravely Ill, Utters Thanks for Prayers
Apr 18: Europeans Fast Falling Away from Church
Apr 20: In Developing World, Choice [of Pope] Met with Skepticism
May 18: Pope Sends Message with Choice of Name

Jan 11: Study Backs Meat, Colon Tumor Link
Feb 07: Patients—and Many Doctors—Still Don't Know How Often Women Get Heart Disease
Mar 07: Aspirin Therapy Benefits Women, but Not in the Way It Aids Men
Mar 16: Study Shows Radiation Therapy Doesn't Increase Heart Disease Risk for Breast Cancer Patients
Apr 11: Personal Health: Women Struggle for Parity of the Heart
May 16: Black Women More Likely to Die from Breast Cancer
May 24: Studies Bolster Diet, Exercise for Breast Cancer Patients
Jun 21: Another Reason Fish is Good for You

Figure 2: A set of five news threads generated by our method (left) and a dynamic topic model (right) for the first half of 2005. Above, the threads are shown on a timeline with the most salient words superimposed; below, the dates and headlines from the threads appearing at the bottom are listed. Topic models are not designed for threading and often link together topically similar documents that do not constitute a coherent news story, as on the right.

Guestrin (2010) and Chieu and Lee (2004) proposed selecting a *single* thread, whereas we seek a *set* of threads, which is a more general task. Shahaf, Guestrin, and Horvitz (2012) recently proposed *metro maps* as alternative structured representations of related news stories. Metro maps are effectively sets of non-chronological threads that are encouraged to intersect and thus create a "map" of events and topics. However, these approaches assume some prior knowledge about content. Shahaf and Guestrin (2010), for example, assume the thread endpoints are specified, and Chieu and Lee (2004) require a set of query words. These inputs make it possible to quickly pare down the document graph. In constrast, we work with very large graphs and consider all possible threads. Furthermore, while some prior work has relied on heuristics and approximate optimization, we can efficiently sample a joint probabilistic model with approximation guarantees.

In previous work on SDPPs (structured DPPs), which we use here to model threads, Kulesza and Taskar (2010) derived exact polynomial-time algorithms for sampling and other inference. However, their experiments involved feature vectors of only 32 dimensions. For text, natural features like word occurrences typically yield dimensionality in the tens of thousands, making SDPP inference prohibitively expensive. We solve this problem by reducing the feature space using random projections (see Section 5). We prove that even a logarithmic number of projections is sufficient to yield a close approximation to the original SDPP distribution.

3 Framework

Before presenting our probabilistic model, we describe a natural framework for representing document collections. We assume that the collection has been transformed into a directed graph $G = (V, E)$ on n vertices, where each node corresponds to a document and each edge represents a relationship between documents whose semantics depend on the task. We also assume the existence of a weight function w on nodes and edges, which measures the importance or salience of documents and the relative strength of the relationships between them. Formally, we define the weight of a path (or thread) $y = (y^{(1)}, y^{(2)}, \ldots, y^{(T)}), (y^{(t)}, y^{(t+1)}) \in E$ by:

$$w(y) = \sum_{t=1}^{T} w\left(y^{(t)}\right) + \sum_{t=1}^{T-1} w\left(y^{(t)}, y^{(t+1)}\right) . \quad (1)$$

Lastly, we also assume the existence of node features. Specifically, let ϕ represent a feature mapping from nodes to $\mathbb{R}^D$ (for example, tf-idf word vectors). The feature map on a thread is then just a sum over the nodes in the thread:

$$\phi(y) = \sum_{t=1}^{T} \phi\left(y^{(t)}\right) . \quad (2)$$

(If it is convenient to have features on edges as well as on nodes, it is possible to accommodate them without affecting asymptotic performance.) Given this framework, our goal is to develop a probabilistic model over sets of k threads of length T, favoring sets whose threads have large weight but are also distinct from one another with respect to ϕ. In other words, a high-probability set under the model should include threads that are both salient and diverse.

This is a daunting problem, given that the number of possible sets of threads is $O(n^{kT})$. For the datasets we use later, the actual number is around 2^{1000}. However, we will show how to construct the desired model in a way that allows efficient inference, even for large datasets, using determinantal point processes (DPPs). We begin with some background.

4 Determinantal point processes

A DPP is a type of distribution over subsets. Formally, a DPP $\mathcal{P}$ on a set of items $\mathcal{Y} = \{y_1, \ldots, y_N\}$ is a probability measure on $2^{\mathcal{Y}}$, the set of all subsets of $\mathcal{Y}$. (In our setting, $\mathcal{Y}$ will be the set of all possible threads.) For every $Y \subseteq \mathcal{Y}$ we have:

$$\mathcal{P}(Y) = \frac{\det(L_Y)}{\sum_{Y \subseteq \mathcal{Y}} \det(L_Y)} = \frac{\det(L_Y)}{\det(L+I)} , \quad (3)$$

where L is a positive semidefinite matrix and I is the $N \times N$ identity matrix. $L_Y \equiv [L_{ij}]_{y_i y_j \in Y}$ denotes the restriction of L to the entries indexed by elements of Y, and $\det(L_\emptyset) = 1$. We can define the entries of L as follows:

$$L_{ij} = q(y_i)\phi(y_i)^\top \phi(y_j) q(y_j) , \quad (4)$$

where we can think of $q(y_i) \in \mathbb{R}^+$ as the "quality" of an item y_i, and $\phi(y_i) \in \mathbb{R}^D$, $\|\phi(y_i)\|_2 = 1$ as a normalized D-dimensional feature vector such that $\phi(y_i)^\top \phi(y_j) \in [-1, 1]$ is a measure of similarity between items y_i and y_j. This simple definition gives rise to a distribution that places most of its weight on sets that are both high quality and diverse. To understand why this is the case, note that determinants are closely related to volumes; in particular, $\det(L_Y)$ is proportional to the volume spanned by the vectors $q(y_i)\phi(y_i)$ for $y_i \in Y$. Thus, sets with high-quality, diverse items have the highest probability; see Figure 3 for an illustration.

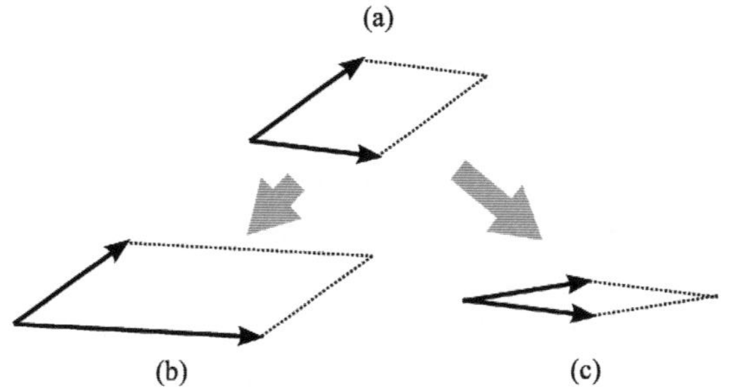

Figure 3: (a) The DPP probability of a set Y depends on the volume spanned by vectors $q(y_i)\phi(y_i)$ for $i \in Y$. (b) As quality (length) increases, so does volume. (c) As similarity increases, volume decreases.

4.1 Structured DPPs

Kulesza and Taskar (2010) introduced *structured* DPPs (SDPPs) to efficiently handle $\mathcal{Y}$ containing exponentially many structures. In our setting, $\mathcal{Y}$ contains all threads of length T, so each $y_i \in \mathcal{Y}$ is a sequence $(y_i^{(1)}, \ldots, y_i^{(T)})$, where $y_i^{(t)}$ is the document included in the thread at position t. When G is a complete graph, there are n^T possible sequences, so $|\mathcal{Y}| = N = n^T$.

In order to allow for efficient normalization and sampling, SDPPs assume a factorization of the quality score $q(y_i)$ and similarity score $\phi(y_i)^\top \phi(y_j)$ into parts, decomposing quality multiplicatively and similarity additively:

$$q(y_i) = \prod_{t=1}^{T} q\left(y_i^{(t)}\right) \quad \phi(y_i) = \sum_{t=1}^{T} \phi\left(y_i^{(t)}\right) \quad (5)$$

For threading, the definition of ϕ is just as given in Equation (2). However, in order to convert the weight function defined in Equation (1) to the appropriate multiplicative form, we use a simple log-linear model, setting $q(y_i) = \exp(\lambda w(y_i))$, where λ is a hyperparameter that effectively governs the balance between quality and diversity by adjusting the dynamic range of the quality function.

An efficient algorithm for sampling structures (in this case, sets of threads) from an SDPP is derived in Kulesza and Taskar (2010). While the details are beyond the scope of this paper, we note that the sampling algorithm requires $O(Tn^2D^2)$ time. If the node degrees are bounded by r then the time is reduced to $O(TrnD^2)$. This is not quite efficient enough when the number of features, D, is large, as it often is for textual tasks, but we will show in Section 5 how to overcome this last hurdle.

Note that, in our later experiments, we fix T to moderate values ($T = 5, 8$) for ease of analysis and display. However, it is possible (and efficient, due to the linear scaling) to allow longer threads, as well as threads of variable length. The latter effect can be achieved by adding a single "dummy" node to the document graph, with incoming edges from all other documents and a single outgoing self-loop edge. Shorter threads will simply transition to this dummy node when they are complete.

4.2 k-DPPs

SDPPs allow us to efficiently model all sets of threads; however, for practical reasons we would prefer to focus only on sets of exactly k threads. To do so we exploit recently developed methods for working with DPPs of fixed size (Kulesza and Taskar, 2011). A k-DPP $\mathcal{P}^k$ is a DPP conditioned on the event that the subset $Y \in \mathcal{Y}$ has cardinality k; formally, whenever $|Y| = k$:

$$\mathcal{P}^k(Y) = \frac{\det(L_Y)}{\sum_{|Y'|=k} \det(L_{Y'})} . \quad (6)$$

In this work we combine k-DPPs with SDPPs, referring to the result as a k-SDPP. We note that using k-SDPPs instead of SDPPs does not affect efficiency of sampling; it merely affords a mechanism for controlling the number of threads.

5 Random projections

As described above, the time complexity for sampling sets from SDPPs is $O(TrnD^2)$. Although this is polynomial, for practical problems nD^2 is prohibitively large. While previous work has dealt only with small datasets, in our experiments we typically have $n, D > 30{,}000$; storing a single message for the message-passing routine involved in SDPP sampling would require over 200 terabytes of memory. To make the model practical, therefore, we turn to techniques for dimensionality reduction.

Standard PCA requires $O(D^3)$ time and would be much too slow. But a classic result of Johnson and Lindenstrauss (1984) shows that high-dimensional points can be *randomly* projected onto a logarithmic number of dimensions while approximately preserving the distances between them. More recently, Magen and Zouzias (2008) extended this idea to the preservation of volumes spanned by sets of points. Here, we use a relationship between determinants and volumes to adapt the latter result. We will prove the following bound on the variational distance between the original k-SDPP and a randomly projected version.

Theorem 1. *Fix* $\epsilon, \delta < 1/2$, *and set* $d =$

$$\max\left\{\frac{2k}{\epsilon}, \frac{24}{\epsilon^2}\left(\frac{\log(3/\delta)}{\log N} + 1\right)\log 2N + k - 1\right\} . \quad (7)$$

Let $\mathcal{P}^k$ *be the* k*-SDPP distribution in Equation (6), let* G *be a* $d \times D$ *random matrix whose entries are independently sampled from* $\mathcal{N}(0, 1/d)$*, and let* $\tilde{\mathcal{P}}^k(Y)$ *be the* k*-SDPP distribution after projecting* ϕ *by* G*—that is, replacing* ϕ *with* $G\phi$*. Then with probability at least* $1 - \delta$,

$$\|\mathcal{P}^k - \tilde{\mathcal{P}}^k\|_1 = \sum_{|Y|=k} |\mathcal{P}^k(Y) - \tilde{\mathcal{P}}^k(Y)| \leq e^{6k\epsilon} - 1 . \quad (8)$$

Note that $e^{6k\epsilon} - 1 \approx 6k\epsilon$ *when* $k\epsilon$ *is small, and* $d = O(\max\{k/\epsilon, (\log(1/\delta) + T\log n)/\epsilon^2\})$.

Practically, Theorem 1 says that if we project ϕ down to dimension d logarithmic in the number of documents and linear in thread length, the L_1 variational distance between the true model and the projected model is bounded.

To prove Theorem 1, we will first state a variant of Magen and Zouzias' result, which bounds the ratio of volumes before and after projection from D down to d dimensions.

Lemma 1. *Let X be a $D \times N$ matrix. Fix $k < N$ and $\epsilon, \delta < 1/2$, and set d and G as in Theorem 1. Then with probability at least $1-\delta$ we have, for all $D \times k$ matrices Y formed by a subset of k columns from X:*

$$(1-\epsilon)^k \le \frac{\mathrm{Vol}(GY)}{\mathrm{Vol}(Y)} \le (1+\epsilon)^k ,$$

where $\mathrm{Vol}(Y)$ *is the k-dimensional volume spanned by the columns of Y and the origin.*

We can make use of the following fact to convert this bound on volumes to a bound on determinants:

$$\mathrm{Vol}(Y) = \frac{1}{k!}\sqrt{\det(Y^\top Y)} . \tag{9}$$

In order to handle the k-SDPP normalization constant

$$\sum_{|Y|=k} \left(\prod_{y_i \in Y} q^2(y_i) \right) \det(\phi(Y)^\top \phi(Y)) , \tag{10}$$

we also must adapt Lemma 1 to *sums* of determinants. The following lemma gives the details.

Lemma 2. *Under the same conditions as Lemma 1, with probability at least $1-\delta$,*

$$(1+2\epsilon)^{-2k} \le \frac{\sum_{|Y|=k} \det((GY)^\top (GY))}{\sum_{|Y|=k} \det(Y^\top Y)} \le (1+\epsilon)^{2k} .$$

Proof.

$$\begin{aligned}
\sum_{|Y|=k} \det((GY)^\top (GY)) & \\
&= \sum_{|Y|=k} (k!\mathrm{Vol}(GY))^2 \\
&\ge \sum_{|Y|=k} \left(k!\mathrm{Vol}(Y)(1-\epsilon)^k \right)^2 \\
&\ge (1+2\epsilon)^{-2k} \sum_{|Y|=k} \det(Y^\top Y) ,
\end{aligned}$$

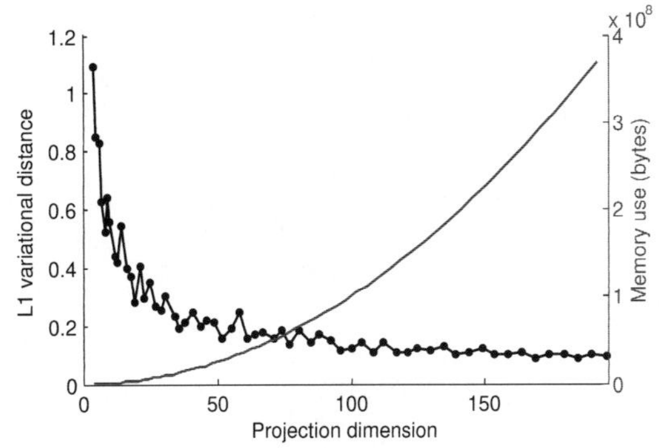

Figure 4: The effect of random projections. In black, on the left, we estimate the L_1 variational distance between the true and projected models. In blue, on the right, we plot the memory required for sampling. Running time is proportional to memory use.

where the first inequality holds with probability at least $1-\delta$ by Lemma 1, and the second follows from the fact that $(1-\epsilon)(1+2\epsilon) \ge 1$ (since $\epsilon < 1/2$), thus $(1-\epsilon)^{2k} \ge (1+2\epsilon)^{-2k}$. A symmetric argument gives the upper bound. □

Proof (of Theorem 1). Let B be the matrix whose columns are given by $B_i = q(y_i)\phi(y_i)$. We have

$$\begin{aligned}
\|\mathcal{P}^k - \tilde{\mathcal{P}}^k\|_1 &= \sum_{|Y|=k} |\mathcal{P}^k(Y) - \tilde{\mathcal{P}}^k(Y)| \\
&= \sum_{|Y|=k} \mathcal{P}^k(Y) \left| 1 - \frac{\tilde{\mathcal{P}}^k(Y)}{\mathcal{P}^k(Y)} \right| \\
&= \sum_{|Y|=k} \mathcal{P}^k(Y) \left| 1 - \frac{\det([GB_Y^\top][GB_Y])}{\det(B_Y^\top B_Y)} \right. \\
&\qquad \left. \cdot \frac{\sum_{|Y'|=k} \det(B_{Y'}^\top B_{Y'})}{\sum_{|Y'|=k} \det([GB_{Y'}^\top][GB_{Y'}])} \right| \\
&\le \left| 1 - (1+\epsilon)^{2k}(1+2\epsilon)^{2k} \right| \sum_{|Y|=k} \mathcal{P}^k(Y) \\
&\le e^{6k\epsilon} - 1 ,
\end{aligned}$$

where the first inequality follows from Lemma 1 and Lemma 2, which hold simultaneously with probability at least $1-\delta$, and the second follows from $(1+a)^b \le e^{ab}$ for $a, b \ge 0$. □

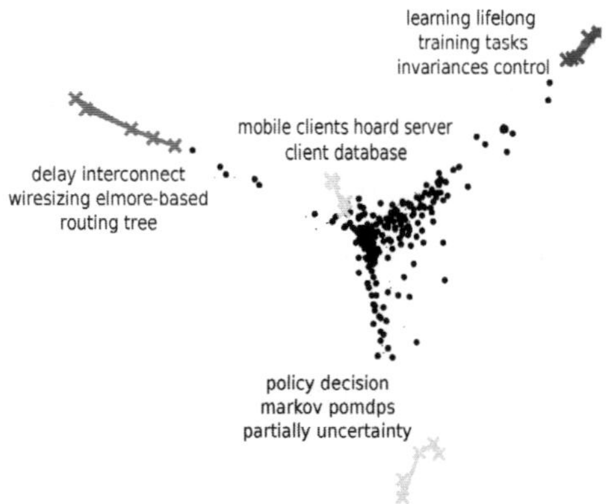

learning lifelong training tasks invariances control

- Locally Weighted Learning for Control
- Discovering Structure in Multiple Learning Tasks: The TC Algorithm
- Learning One More Thing
- Explanation Based Learning for Mobile Robot Perception
- Learning Analytically and Inductively

mobile clients hoard server client database

- A Database Architecture for Handling Mobile Clients
- An Architecture for Mobile Databases
- Database Server Organization for Handling Mobile Clients
- Mobile Wireless Computing: Solutions and Challenges in Data Management
- Energy Efficient Query Optimization

Figure 5: Example threads sampled from a 4-SDPP with thread length $T = 5$ on the Cora dataset. We project from word-space to two dimensions by running PCA on the centroids of the threads. The nodes not on the thread paths form a representative subset of the other documents from Cora. Displayed beside each thread are a few of its maximum-tfidf words. Paper titles from two of the threads are shown to the right.

6 Experiments

We begin by showing the performance of random projections on a small, synthetic threading task where the exact model is tractable, with $n = 600$ and $D = 150$. Figure 4 shows the L_1 variational distance (estimated by sampling) as well as the actual memory required for a variety of projection dimensions d. Note that, as predicted by Theorem 1, fidelity to the true model increases rapidly with d.

6.1 Cora citation graph

To qualitatively illustrate our model, we apply it to Cora (McCallum et al., 2000). Cora is a large collection of academic papers on computer science topics, plus citations between them. We construct a directed graph with papers as nodes and citations as edges; after removing papers with missing metadata or zero outgoing citations, our graph contains $n = 28{,}155$ papers.

To obtain useful threads, we set edge weights to reflect the degree of textual similarity between the citing and cited papers, and set node weights to reflect paper "importance". Edge weights are given by normalized cosine similarity (NCS), which for two documents i and j is the dot product of their normalized tfidf vectors:

$$\frac{\sum_{w\in W} \mathrm{tfidf}_i(w)\mathrm{tfidf}_j(w)}{\sqrt{\sum_{w\in W} \mathrm{tfidf}_i(w)^2}\sqrt{\sum_{w\in W} \mathrm{tfidf}_j(w)^2}},$$

where W is a subset of the words found in the documents. We select W by filtering according to document frequency; that is, we remove words that are too common or too rare. After filtering, there are 50,912 unique words. The node weights are given by LexRank scores (Erkan and Radev, 2004), which are similar to node degrees.

Finally, we build a similarity feature map ϕ to encourage diversity. We represent each document by the 1000 documents to which it is most similar according to NCS; this results in binary ϕ of dimension $m = n$ with exactly 1000 non-zeros. The dot product between the similarity features of two documents is thus proportional to the fraction of top-1000 similar documents they have in common. As described in Section 5, we then randomly project this large feature set from $D \approx 28{,}000$ to $d = 50$ dimensions.

We illustrate the behavior of the resulting model in Figure 5. The discovered threads occupy distinct regions of word-space, standing apart visually, and contain diverse salient terms.

6.2 News articles

For quantitative evaluation, we use newswire data. Our dataset comprises over 200,000 articles from the New York Times, collected from 2005-2007 as part of the English Gigaword corpus (Graff and Cieri, 2009). We split the articles into six-month time periods, with an average of

n = 34,504 articles per period. After filtering, there are a total of 36,356 unique words.

For each time period, we generate a graph with articles as nodes. We use NCS for edge weights, and throw away edges with weight < 0.1. We also require that edges go forward in time; this enforces the chronological ordering of our threads. The supplement contains illustrations of one of the resulting graphs. We use LexRank for node weights and the top-1000 similar documents as similarity features ϕ, projecting to $d = 50$, as before (Section 6.1). We also add a constant feature ρ to ϕ, which controls the overall degree of repulsion; large values of ρ make all documents more similar. This makes the k-SDPP distribution more peaked around diverse sets. For all of the following results, we use $T = 8$ and $k = 10$ so that the resulting timelines are of a manageable size for analysis. However, we tried several values of k and T in our experiments, and did not see significant differences in relative performance. We report all metrics averaged over 100 random samples from the model for each six-month period.

6.2.1 Graph visualizations

The (very large) news graph for the first half of 2005 can be viewed interactively at http://zoom.it/jOKV. In this graph each node (dark circle) represents a news article, and is annotated with its headline. Node size corresponds to weight (LexRank score). Nodes are laid out chronologically, left-to-right, from January to June of 2005. The five colored paths indicate a set of threads sampled from the k-SDPP. Headlines of the articles in each thread are colored to match the thread. Edges are included as described in the paper, but due to the scale of this dataset, only 1% of the edges are shown. Edge thickness corresponds to weight (NCS).

We provide a view of a small subgraph for illustration purposes in Figure 6, which shows the incoming and outgoing edges for a single node. A zoomable version of this subgraph is available at http://zoom.it/GUCR.

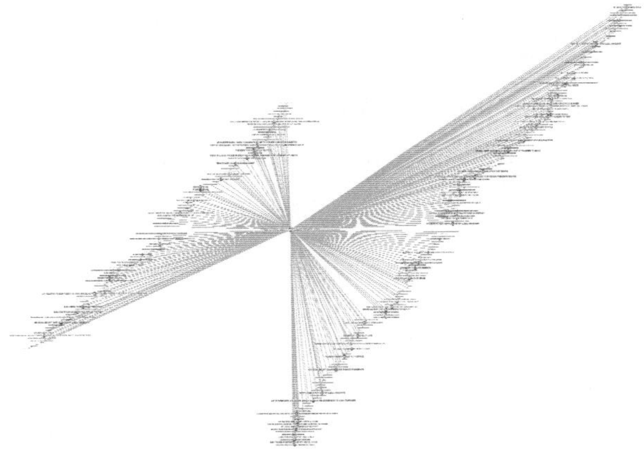

Figure 6: Snapshot of a single article node and all of its neghboring article nodes. See http://zoom.it/GUCR for the zoomable image.

6.2.2 Baselines

k-means baseline: A simple baseline is to split each six-month period of articles into T equal time slices, then apply k-means clustering to each slice, using NCS to measure distance. We then select the most central article from each cluster, and finally match the k articles from time slice i one-to-one with those from slice $i + 1$ by computing the pairing that maximizes the average NCS of the pairs, i.e., the coherence of the threads. The result is a set of k threads of length T, where no two threads contain the same article. In its use of clustering, this baseline is somewhat similar to the "event threading" baseline of Shahaf and Guestrin (2010).

DTM baseline: A more sophisticated baseline is the dynamic topic model (Blei and Lafferty, 2006), which explicitly attempts to find topics that are smooth through time. We use code provided by the authors to fit DTMs with the number of topics set to k and with the data split into T equal slices, as before. We then choose, for each topic at each time step, the document with the highest per-word probability of being generated by that topic. Documents from the same topic form a single thread.

	CosSim	ROUGE-1		ROUGE-2		ROUGE-SU4	
		F	Prec / Rec	F	Prec / Rec	F	Prec / Rec
k-means	29.9	16.5	17.3 / 15.8	0.695	0.725 / 0.669	3.76	3.94 / 3.60
DTM	27.0	14.7	15.5 / 14.0	0.750	0.813 / 0.698	3.44	3.63 / 3.28
k-SDPP	**33.2**	**17.2**	**17.7/16.7**	**0.892**	**0.917/0.870**	**3.98**	**4.11/3.87**

Table 1: Similarity of automatically generated timelines to human summaries. Bold entries are significantly higher than others in the column at 99% confidence, computed using bootstrapping (Hesterberg et al., 2003).

6.2.3 Comparison to human summaries

We compare the threads generated by our baselines and sampled from the k-SDPP to a set of human-generated news summaries. The human summaries are not threaded; they are flat, roughly daily news summaries published by Agence France-Presse and found in the Gigaword corpus, distinguished by their "multi" type tag. A sample summary is included in the supplement. These summaries tend to focus on world news, which is only a subset of the contents of our dataset. However, they allow us to provide an extrinsic evaluation of our method without gold standard timelines. We compute four statistics:

- **Cosine similarity**: NCS (in percent) between the concatenated threads and concatenated human summaries. The hyperparameters for all methods—such as the constant feature magnitude ρ for k-SDPPs and the parameter governing topic proportions for DTMs—were tuned to optimize cosine similarity on a development set from January-June 2005.
- **ROUGE-1**, **2**, and **SU4**: Standard ROUGE scores for summarization evaluation (Lin, 2004).

Table 1 shows the results of these comparisons, averaged across all six half-year intervals. Under each measure, the k-SDPP threads more closely resemble human summaries.

6.2.4 Mechanical Turk evaluation

An important distinction between the baselines and the k-SDPP is that the former are *topic*-oriented, choosing articles that relate to broad subject areas, while our approach is *story*-oriented, chaining together articles with direct individual relationships. An example of this distinction can be seen in Figure 2.

	Rating	Interlopers
k-means	2.73	0.71
DTM	3.19	1.10
k-SDPP	**3.31**	1.15

Table 2: Rating: average coherence score from 1 (worst) to 5 (best). Interlopers: average number of interloper articles identified (out of 2). Bold entries are significantly higher with 95% confidence.

To obtain a large-scale evaluation of thread coherence, we turn to Mechanical Turk. We asked Turkers to read the headlines and first few sentences of each article in a timeline and then rate the overall narrative coherence of the timeline on a scale of 1 ("the articles are totally unrelated") to 5 ("the articles tell a single clear story"). Five separate Turkers rated each timeline; the average ratings are shown in Table 2. Note that k-means does particularly poorly in terms of coherence since it has no way to ensure that clusters are similar between time slices.

We also had Turkers evaluate threads implicitly by performing a simple task. We showed them timelines into which two additional "interloper" articles selected at random had been inserted, and asked them to remove the two articles that they thought should be removed to "improve the flow of the timeline". A screenshot of the task is provided in the supplement. Intuitively, the interlopers should be selected more often when the original timeline is coherent. The average number of interloper articles correctly identified is shown in Table 2.

	Runtime
k-means	625.63
DTM	19,433.80
k-SDPP	**252.38**

Table 3: Time (in seconds) required to produce a complete set of threads. The test machine has eight Intel Xeon E5450 cores and 32GB of memory.

6.2.5 Runtimes

Finally, we report in Table 3 the time required to produce a complete set of threads for each method. This time includes clustering for k-means, model fitting for DTM and random projections, computation of the covariance matrix, and sampling for k-SDPP. We view the graph as an input (much like tfidf vectors for the baselines), and so do not include its computation in the runtime for the k-SDPP. Constructing the graph only requires an additional 160 seconds though.

6.3 Analysis

Below we briefly summarize the main differences between the k-SDPP and the baselines, and discuss their significance.

- Neither baseline *directly* models the document threads themselves. In contrast, the k-SDPP defines a probability distribution over all possible sets of document threads. This makes the k-SDPP a better choice for applications where, for instance, the coherence of individual threads is important.

- While the baselines seek threads that cover or explain as much of the dataset as possible, k-SDPPs are better suited for tasks where a balance between quality and diversity is key, since its hyperparameters correspond to weights on these quantities. With news timelines, for example, we want not just topical diversity but also a focus on the most important stories.

- Both baselines require input to be split into time slices, whereas the k-SDPP does not; this flexibility allows the k-SDPP to put multiple articles from a single time slice in a thread, or to build threads that span only part of the input period.

- While clustering and topic models rely on EM to approximately optimize their objectives, the k-SDPP comes with an exact, polynomial-time sampling algorithm.

Revisiting Figure 2, we can see all of these advantages in action. The k-SDPP produces more consistent threads due to its use of graph information, while the DTM threads, though topic-focused, are less coherent as a story. Furthermore, DTM threads span the entire time period, while our method selects threads covering only relevant spans. The quantitative results in this section underscore the empirical value of these characteristics.

7 Conclusion

We introduced the novel problem of finding diverse and salient threads in graphs of large document collections. We developed a probabilistic approach, combining SDPPs and k-SDPPs, and showed how random projections make inference efficient and yield an approximate model with bounded variational distance to the original. We then demonstrated that the method produces qualitatively reasonable results, and, relative to several baslines, reproduces human news summaries more faithfully, builds more coherent story threads, and is significantly faster. It would be interesting to extend our model to structures beyond linear chains to trees and other structures.

8 Acknowledgements

This material is based upon work supported under a National Science Foundation Graduate Research Fellowship and NSF award 0803256.

References

[Ahmed and Xing2010] A. Ahmed and E. Xing. 2010. Timeline: A Dynamic Hierarchical Dirichlet Process Model for Recovering Birth/Death and Evolution of Topics in Text Stream. In *Proc. UAI.*

[Allan et al.2001] J. Allan, R. Gupta, and V. Khandelwal. 2001. Temporal Summaries of New Topics. In *Proc. SIGIR.*

[Blei and Lafferty2006] D. Blei and J. Lafferty. 2006. Dynamic Topic Models. In *Proc. ICML.*

[Chieu and Lee2004] H. Chieu and Y. Lee. 2004. Query Based Event Extraction along a Timeline. In *Proc. SIGIR.*

[Erkan and Radev2004] G. Erkan and D.R. Radev. 2004. LexRank: Graph-Based Lexical Centrality as Salience in Text Summarization. *Journal of Artificial Intelligence Research*, 22(1):457–479.

[Graff and Cieri2009] D. Graff and C. Cieri. 2009. English Gigaword.

[Hesterberg et al.2003] T. Hesterberg, S. Monaghan, D. Moore, A. Clipson, and R. Epstein. 2003. *Bootstrap Methods and Permutation Tests.*

[Johnson and Lindenstrauss1984] W. B. Johnson and J. Lindenstrauss. 1984. Extensions of Lipschitz Mappings into a Hilbert Space. *Contemporary Mathematics*, 26:189–206.

[Kulesza and Taskar2010] A. Kulesza and B. Taskar. 2010. Structured Determinantal Point Processes. In *Proc. NIPS.*

[Kulesza and Taskar2011] A. Kulesza and B. Taskar. 2011. k-DPPs: Fixed-Size Determinantal Point Processes. In *Proc. ICML.*

[Leskovec et al.2009] J. Leskovec, L. Backstrom, and J. Kleinberg. 2009. Meme-tracking and the Dynamics of the News Cycle. In *Proc. KDD.*

[Lin2004] C.Y. Lin. 2004. Rouge: A package for automatic evaluation of summaries. In *Proc. WAS.*

[Magen and Zouzias2008] A. Magen and A. Zouzias. 2008. Near Optimal Dimensionality Reductions that Preserve Volumes. *Approximation, Randomization and Combinatorial Optimization. Algorithms and Techniques*, pages 523–534.

[McCallum et al.2000] A. McCallum, K. Nigam, J. Rennie, and K. Seymore. 2000. Automating the Construction of Internet Portals with Machine Learning. *Information Retrieval Journal*, 3:127–163.

[Mei and Zhai2005] W. Mei and C. Zhai. 2005. Discovering Evolutionary Theme Patterns From Text: An Exploration of Temporal Text Mining. In *Proc. KDD.*

[Shahaf and Guestrin2010] D. Shahaf and C. Guestrin. 2010. Connecting the Dots Between News Articles. In *Proc. KDD.*

[Shahaf et al.2012] D. Shahaf, C. Guestrin, and E. Horvitz. 2012. Trains of Thought: Generating Information Maps. In *Proc. WWW.*

[Swan and Jensen2000] R. Swan and D. Jensen. 2000. TimeMines: Constructing Timelines with Statistical Models of Word Usage. In *Proc. KDD.*

[Wayne2000] C. Wayne. 2000. Multilingual Topic Detection and Tracking: Successful Research Enabled by Corpora and Evaluation. In *Proc. LREC.*

[Yan et al.2011] R. Yan, X. Wan, J. Otterbacher, L. Kong, X. Li, and Y. Zhang. 2011. Evolutionary Timeline Summarization: A Balanced Optimization Framework via Iterative Substitution. In *Proc. SIGIR.*

Generalizing Sub-sentential Paraphrase Acquisition across Original Signal Type of Text Pairs

Aurélien Max **Houda Bouamor** **Anne Vilnat**

LIMSI-CNRS & Univ. Paris Sud
Orsay, France
firstname.lastname@limsi.fr

Abstract

This paper describes a study on the impact of the original signal (text, speech, visual scene, event) of a text pair on the task of both manual and automatic sub-sentential paraphrase acquisition. A corpus of 2,500 annotated sentences in English and French is described, and performance on this corpus is reported for an efficient system combination exploiting a large set of features for paraphrase recognition. A detailed quantified typology of sub-sentential paraphrases found in our corpus types is given.

1 Introduction

Sub-sentential paraphrases can be acquired from text pairs expressing the same meaning (Madnani and Dorr, 2010). If the semantic similarity of a text pair has a direct impact on the quality of the acquired paraphrases, it has, to our knowledge, never been shown what impact the type of original signal has on paraphrase acquisition. In this work, we consider four types of corpora, which we think are representative of the main types of original semantic signals: text pairs (roughly, sentences) originating *a*) from independent translations of a text (TEXT), *b*) from independent translations of a speech (SPEECH), *c*) from independent descriptions of a visual scene (SCENE), and *d*) from independent descriptions of some event (EVENT). We will report the results of experiments on sub-sentential paraphrase acquisition on all these corpus types in two languages, English and French, and provide some answers to the following questions: What types of paraphrases can be found by human annotators, with what confidence and in which quantities? How well can representative paraphrase acquisition systems perform on each corpus type, and how performance can be improved through combination? On what corpus types can performance be improved by using training material from other corpus types? Our experimental results will provide several indications of the differences and complementarities of the corpus types under study, and will notably show that performance on the most readily available corpus type can be improved by using training data from the set of all other corpus types.

We will first describe the building procedures and characteristics of our corpora (section 2), and then describe our experimental settings for evaluating paraphrase acquisition (section 3.1). Our experiments will first consist of the description (section 3.2) and evaluation (section 3.3) of a system combination on each corpus type and then of our system provided with additional training data from the other corpus types (section 3.4). We will finally briefly review related work (section 4) and discuss our main findings and future work (section 5).

2 Collection of sentence pair corpora

In this study, we will focus on paraphrase acquisition from related sentence pairs characteristic of 4 corpus types, which correspond to different original signal types of text pairs illustrated by the word alignment matrices on Figure 1. A corpus for each type has been collected for 2 languages, English and French, and comprises 625 sentence pairs per language. We now briefly describe how each corpus was built.

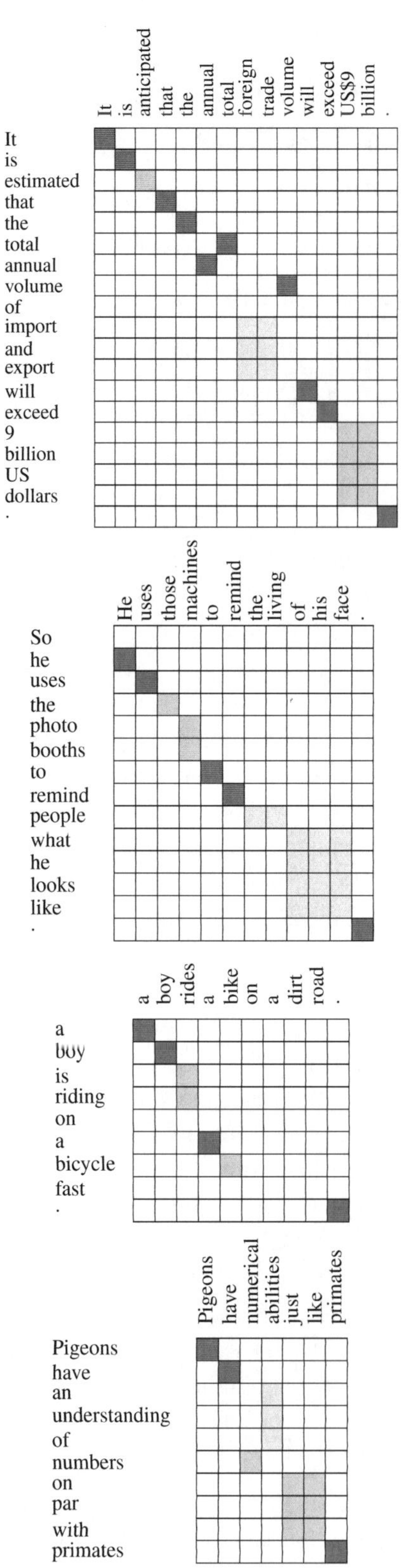

Figure 1: Example reference alignment matrices for (from top to bottom) TEXT, SPEECH, SCENE and EVENT. *Sure* alignments appear in green or gray (identities) and *possible* alignments in yellow.

TEXT For English, we used the MTC corpus[1] (described in (Cohn et al., 2008)) consisting of sets of news article translations from Chinese, and for French the CESTA corpus[2] consisting of sets of news article translations from English. For each sentence cluster, we selected sentence pairs with minimal edit distance above an empirically-selected threshold, covering all clusters first and then selecting from already used clusters to reach the target number of sentence pairs.

e.g. *It is estimated that the total annual volume of import and export will exceed 9 billion US dollars.* ↔ *It is anticipated that the annual total foreign trade volume will exceed US$9 billion.*

SPEECH For English, we used two freely available subtitle files[3] of the French movies *Le Fabuleux Destin d'Amélie Poulain* and *Les Choristes*, and for French we used two subtitle files from the *Desperate Housewives* TV series. We first aligned each parallel corpus using the algorithm described in (Tiedemann, 2007), based on time frames and developed for bilingual subtitles, we then filtered out sentence pairs below a minimal edit distance threshold, and manually removed obvious errors made by the algorithm.

e.g. *So he uses the photo booths to remind people what he looks like.* ↔ *He uses those machines to remind the living of his face.*

SCENE We used the Multiple Video Description Corpus (Chen and Dolan, 2011) obtained from multiple descriptions of short videos. Similarly to what we did for TEXT, we selected sentence pairs from clusters by minimal edit distance above a threshold. An important fact is that for English we were able to use what is described as "verified" descriptions. There were, however, far fewer descriptions available for French, and none had the "verified" status. We decided to use this corpus nonetheless, but with the knowledge that this source for French is of a substantially lower quality (this corpus type will therefore appear as "(SCENE)" in all tables to reflect this).

e.g. *a boy is riding on a bicycle fast.* ↔ *a boy rides a bike on a dirt road.*

[1] http://www.ldc.upenn.edu/Catalog/CatalogEntry.jsp?catalogId=LDC2002T01

[2] http://www.elda.org/article125.html

[3] http://www.opensubtitles.org

	Corpus statistics 500 sentence pairs		Annotator agreements 50 sentence pairs		Tokens in paraphrase statistics not considering identity paraphrases			
					sure para.		possible para.	
	# tokens	# tokens per sent.	sure para.	possible para.	% tokens	# tokens	% tokens	# tokens
ENGLISH								
TEXT	21,473	21.0	66.1	20.4	18.6	4004	12.3	2651
SPEECH	11,049	10.5	79.1	10.9	17.5	1942	31.6	3500
SCENE	7,783	7.5	80.5	35.2	10.9	851	14.0	1094
EVENT	8,609	8.0	65.3	20.5	17.5	1506	14.5	1251
FRENCH								
TEXT	24,641	24.0	64.6	16.6	29.2	7218	6.2	1527
SPEECH	11,850	11.5	82.7	20.8	22.5	2667	16.7	1981
(SCENE)	7,012	6.5	42.8	9.3	3.9	275	9.4	664
EVENT	9,121	9.1	67.8	3.8	19.6	1793	9.6	876

Table 1: Description of all corpora and paraphrase reference sets for English (top) and French (bottom). Note that SCENE for French appears within parentheses as we do not consider it of the same quality as the other corpora.

EVENT We used titles of news article clusters from the Google News[4] news aggregation service. We further refined the clustering algorithm by filtering out article pairs whose publication dates differed from more than one day. We repeated the same selection procedure as for TEXT and SCENE to have a maximal cluster coverage and select more similar pairs first.
e.g. *Pigeons Have an Understanding of Numbers on Par With Primates* ↔ *Pigeons Have Numerical Abilities Just Like Primates*

Table 1 provides various statistics for these corpora. The first observation is that TEXT contains significantly larger sentences than the other types, more than twice as long as those of SPEECH. Annotation was performed following the guidelines proposed by Cohn *et al.* (2008)[5] using the YAWAT tool (Germann, 2008), except that alignments where not initially obtained automatically so as not to bias our annotators' work (there were two annotators per language). The main guidelines that they had to follow were that *sure* and *possible* paraphrases must be distinguished, smaller alignments were to be prefered but any-to-any alignments may be used, and sentences should be aligned as much as possible. Henceforth, we will only consider for all reported statistics and experiments those paraphrases that are not identity pairs (e.g. (*a nice day* ↔ *a nice day*)), as they are considered trivial as far as acquisition is concerned.

Table 1 also reports inter-annotator agreement[6] values computed on sets of 50 sentence pairs. We find that acceptable values are obtained for sure paraphrases, but that low values are obtained for possible paraphrases. This was somehow expected, given the many possible interpretations of possible paraphrases, but was not a problem for our experiments: as we will describe in section 3.1, the evaluation metrics we use will not count them as expected solutions, but will simply not count them as false when proposed as candidates.

Table 1 finally shows proportions and absolute numbers of paraphrases of each type for all corpora. We find that there are approximately the same total number of paraphrases for English (16,799) and French (17,001), but that English corpora collectively have an equivalent number of sure and possible paraphrases (8,303 vs. 8,496) and French have more sure paraphrases (11,953 vs. 5,048). This may be explained by the fact that our annotators worked independently and that the corpora used have differences by nature, as our experiments will show. Other salient results include the fact that TEXT contains more sure paraphrases in number than the other corpora, that SPEECH contains relatively more possible paraphrases than the other corpora, and that SCENE has significantly fewer paraphrases, both in proportion and number. In Figure 2 various mea-

[4] `http://news.google.com`

[5] See `http://staffwww.dcs.shef.ac.uk/people/T.Cohn/paraphrase_guidelines.pdf`

[6] For each paraphrase type, we used the average of recall values obtained for each annotator set as the reference .

	synonymy	typography	tense	inclusion	pragmatics	syntax	morphology	number
				ENGLISH				
TEXT	51.2	7.6	5.1	12.1	0.6	4.4	12.1	6.4
SPEECH	39.8	25.6	3.5	12.3	1.7	3.5	3.5	9.7
SCENE	50.0	1.3	13.5	21.6	0.0	1.3	5.4	6.7
EVENT	36.9	15.0	8.2	19.1	1.3	6.8	6.8	5.4
				FRENCH				
TEXT	46.9	9.0	8.7	2.1	3.6	6.6	3.0	19.8
SPEECH	45.5	14.2	8.0	8.0	2.6	11.6	3.5	6.2
(SCENE)	46.4	5.3	3.5	8.9	0.0	5.3	0.0	30.3
EVENT	28.3	19.7	6.1	16.0	7.4	8.6	7.4	6.1

Table 2: Percentages of paraphrase classes in 50 randomly selected sentence pairs for reference paraphrases for English (top) and French (bottom). Classes are illustrated by the following examples: (*mutual understanding* ↔ *consensus*) (**synonymy**), (*California* ↔ *CA*) (**typography**), (*letting* ↔ *having let*) (**tense**), (*Asian Development Bank* ↔ *Asian Bank*) (**inclusion**), (*police dispatcher* ↔ *woman*) (**pragmatics**), (*grief-stricken* ↔ *struck with grief*) (**syntactic**), (*Vietname* ↔ *Vietnam*) (**morphology**), (*mortgage* ↔ *mortgages*) (**number**).

sures of sentence pair similarities are given. TEXT contains the most similar sentence pairs according to all metrics, with EVENT at a similar level on French. SCENE has sentence pairs that are more similar than those in SPEECH for English, but this is not the case for French. While the metrics used can only provide a crude account of semantic equivalence at the sentence level, these results clearly indicate that translating from text yields more similar sentences than translating from speech.

Table 2 provides a typology of paraphrases found in all our corpora and two languages, where each class has been quantified with respect to the reference alignments.[7] The main observation here is that phrasal **synonymy** (e.g. *mutual understanding* ↔ *consensus*) is the most present phenomenon. It is also interesting to note that the EVENT corpus type, which is easy to collect on a daily basis, contains reference paraphrases spread over all classes. Lastly, it is expected that paraphrases in the **pragmatics** class (e.g. *police dispatcher* ↔ *woman*) would be difficult to acquire, as this would often rely on document context and costly world knowledge.[8]

[7]Note that typologies of paraphrases have already been proposed in the literature (e.g. (Culicover, 1968; Vila et al., 2011)), but that the choice of our classes has been primarily motivated by potential subsequent uses of the acquired paraphrases (paraphrases could be annotated as belonging to more than one class). Note also that our experiments will also include results focused on the **synonymy** class only (cf. Table 5).

[8]Reusing such types of paraphrases into applications would however often be too strongly context-dependent.

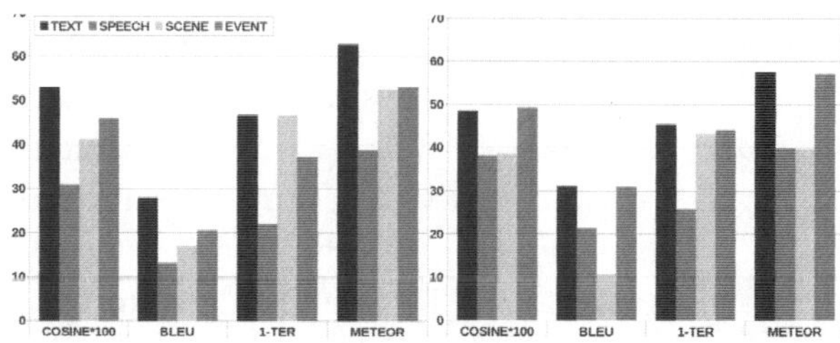

Figure 2: Sentence pair average similarities for all corpora for English (left) and French (right) using the cosine of token vectors, BLEU (Papineni et al., 2002), TER (Snover et al., 2006) and METEOR (Lavie and Agarwal, 2007).

3 Bilingual experiments across corpus types

3.1 Evaluation of paraphrase acquisition

We followed the PARAMETRIC methodology described in (Callison-Burch et al., 2008) for assessing the performance of systems on the task of sub-sentential paraphrase acquisition. In this methodology, a set of paraphrase candidates extracted from a sentence pair is compared with a set of reference paraphrases, obtained through human annotation, by computing usual measures of *precision* (P) and *recall* (R). The first value corresponds to the proportion of paraphrase candidates, denoted $\mathcal{H}$, produced by a system and that are correct relative to the reference set containing *sure* and *possible* paraphrases, denoted $\mathcal{R}_{\text{all}}$. Recall is obtained by measuring the proportion of the reference set of *sure* paraphrases,

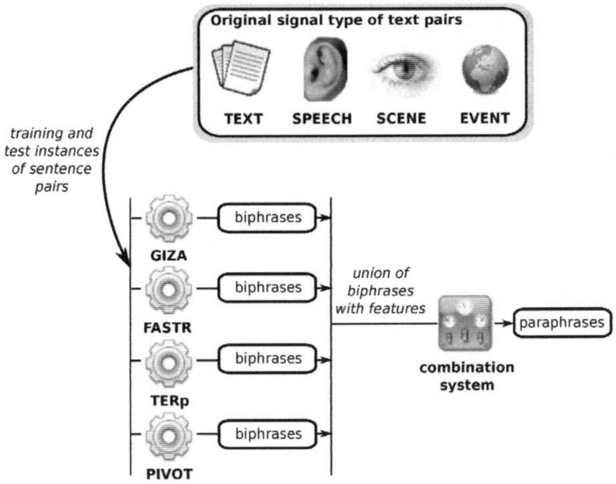

Figure 3: Architecture of our combination system for paraphrase identification.

denoted $\mathcal{R}_{\text{sure}}$, that are found by a system. We also computed an F-measure value (F_1), which considers recall and precision as equally important. These values are thus given by the following formulae:

$$P = \frac{|\mathcal{H} \cap \mathcal{R}_{\text{all}}|}{|\mathcal{H}|} \quad R = \frac{|\mathcal{H} \cap \mathcal{R}_{\text{sure}}|}{|\mathcal{R}_{\text{sure}}|} \quad F_1 = \frac{2PR}{P+R}$$

Note that the way the sets $\mathcal{R}_{\text{all}}$ and $\mathcal{R}_{\text{sure}}$ of reference paraphrase pairs are defined ensures that paraphrase pair candidates that include possible reference paraphrases will not penalize precision while not increasing recall.

All performance values reported in the following sections will be obtained using 10-fold cross-validation and averaging the results on each sub-test. All data sets of cross-validation contain 500 sentence pairs per corpus type, and 125 pairs are kept for development.

3.2 A framework for sub-sentential paraphrase identification

We now describe the systems that will be tested on the various corpora described in section 2 using the methodology described in section 3.1. Following (Bouamor et al., 2012), a combination system is used to automatically weight paraphrase pair candidates produced by individual systems using a set of features aiming at recognizing paraphrases, as illustrated on Figure 3. Four individual systems have been used and are described below: the reasons for considering those systems include their free availability, the possibility of using comparable resources when relevant for our two languages, and the specific characteristics of the techniques used.

Statistical learning of word alignments (GIZA) The GIZA++ tool (Och and Ney, 2004) computes statistical word alignment models of increasing complexity from parallel corpora. It was run on each monolingual corpus of sentence pairs in both directions, symmetrized alignments were kept and classical phrase extraction heuristics were applied (Koehn et al., 2003), without growing phrases with unaligned tokens.

Linguistic knowledge on term variation (FASTR) The FASTR tool (Jacquemin, 1999) spots term variants in large corpora, where variants are described through metarules expressing how the morphosyntactic structure of a term variant can be derived from a given term by means of regular expressions on morphosyntactic categories. Paradigmatic variation can also be expressed with constraints between words, imposing that they be of the same morphological or semantic family using existing resources available in our two languages. Variants for all phrases from one sentence of a pair are extracted from the other sentence, and the intersection of the sets for both directions is kept.

Edit rate on word sequences (TER_p) The TER_p tool (Snover et al., 2010) can be used to compute an optimal set of word and phrase edits that can transform one sentence into another one.[9] Edit types are parameterized by one or more weights which were optimized towards F-measure by hill climbing with 100 random restarts using the held-out data set consisting of 125 sentence pairs for each corpus type.

Translational equivalence (PIVOT) We exploited the paraphrase probability defined by Bannard and Callison-Burch (2005) on bilingual parallel corpora. We used the Europarl corpus[10] of parliamentary debates in English and French, consisting of approximately 1.7 million parallel sentences, using each language as source and pivot in turn. GIZA++

[9]Note that contrarily to what TER_p allows, we did not used the possibility of using word or phrase equivalents as those are only made available for English. This type of knowledge is however captured in part by the FASTR and PIVOT systems.

[10]`http://statmt.org/europarl`

Phrase pair features – edit distance between paraphrases, stem identity, bag-of-tokens similarity, phrase length ratio
Sentence pair features – sentence pair similarity (cosine, BLEU, TER, METEOR), relative position of paraphrases, presence of common tokens at paraphrase boundaries, presence of another paraphrase pair from each system at paraphrase boundaries, presence of a paraphrase at a different position in the other sentence
Distributional features – similarity of token context vectors for each phrase of a paraphrase (derived from counts in the large English-French parallel corpus from WMT'11 (`http://www.statmt.org/wmt11/translation-task.html`) (approx. 30 million parallel sentences)
System features – combination of the individual systems that proposed the paraphrase pair

Table 3: Features used by our classifiers. Discretized intervals based on median values are used for real values, and binarized values are used for combinations.

was used for word alignment and phrase translation probabilities were estimated from them by the MOSES system (Koehn et al., 2007). For each phrase of a sentence pair, we built its set of paraphrases, and extracted its paraphrase from the other sentence with highest probability. We repeated this process in both directions, and finally kept for each phrase its paraphrase pair from any direction with highest probability.

Automatic validation of candidate paraphrases Taking the union of all paraphrase pair candidates from all the above systems for each sentence pair, we perform a Maximum Entropy two-class classification[11], which allows us to include features that were not necessarily exploited or straightforward to exploit by individual systems to determine the probability that each candidate is a good paraphrase. More generally, this allows us to attempt to learn a more generic characterization of paraphrases, which could trivially accept any number of systems as inputs. Positive examples for the classifier are those from the union of candidates that are also in the reference set $\mathcal{R}_{\text{sure}}$, while negative examples are the remaining ones from the union. The features that we used are summarized in Table 3.

3.3 Experimental results

Results for individual systems, their union and our validation system trained on each corpus type are given on Table 4. First, we find that all individual systems fare better on TEXT, for which more training data were available and where semantic equivalence of sentence pairs is most likely. EVENT appears to be the most difficult corpus type, whereas one could say that being the most readily data source this is a disapointing result: we will return to this in section 3.4. In terms of performance on F-measure per corpus type, GIZA performs best for TEXT and SPEECH, containing long sentences with possible repetitions, while TER_p performs on par with GIZA for SCENE and best for EVENT, where equivalences that are rare at the corpus level are more present. FASTR achieves a very low recall, showing that the encoded definitions of term variants do not cover all types of paraphrases, and also possibly that the lexical resource that it uses has incomplete coverage. It nonetheless obtains high precision values, most notably on TEXT. One last comment regarding individual systems is that PIVOT is by far the most precise of all the techniques used, but with a recall much lower than those of GIZA and TER_p: as is the case for FASTR, which makes use of manually-encoded lexical resources, PIVOT encodes in some sense some kind of semantic knowledge.[12]

In all cases, our combination system manages to increase F-measure substantially over the best individual system for a corpus type and the simple union. Improvements are strong on TEXT (resp. +12.5 and +11.6 on English and French) and on SPEECH (+11.7 and +11.1) and quite good on SCENE (+3.2 and +6.4) and on EVENT (+5.4

[11]Using the implementation at: `http://homepages.inf.ed.ac.uk/lzhang10/maxent_toolkit.html`

[12]Note that the fact that English and French were used as the pivot for one another may have had some positive effect here, but, incidentally, the two corpora obtained by translating from the other language (TEXT and SPEECH) are not those where PIVOT fares better. The difference observed may however lie in the higher complexity of the sentences in these corpus types.

	Individual systems												Combination systems					
	GIZA			FASTR			$\text{TER}_{p \to F}$			PIVOT			union			validation		
	P	R	F_1	P	R	F_1	P	R	F_1	P	R	F_1	P	R	F_1	P	R	F_1
ENGLISH																		
TEXT	48.2	58.9	53.0	63.1	5.9	10.7	41.2	66.4	50.9	**73.4**	25.8	38.2	20.8	**80.8**	33.1	68.4	62.8	**65.5**
SPEECH	39.7	44.2	41.8	27.1	3.5	6.3	25.0	50.3	33.4	**79.2**	15.3	25.7	25.5	**71.4**	37.6	51.0	56.3	**53.5**
SCENE	44.8	57.7	50.5	47.4	5.2	9.5	40.1	67.9	50.4	**84.6**	14.6	25.0	36.2	**83.4**	50.5	44.9	66.8	**53.7**
EVENT	19.0	33.9	24.3	62.9	3.1	6.0	28.8	68.7	40.6	**97.4**	11.2	20.1	20.8	**75.5**	32.7	35.0	67.1	**46.0**
FRENCH																		
TEXT	52.5	58.9	55.5	56.9	4.9	9.1	46.4	61.4	52.8	64.5	30.3	41.2	41.5	**77.9**	54.1	**74.7**	61.0	**67.1**
SPEECH	44.0	54.9	48.9	30.7	4.3	7.6	34.8	60.2	44.1	**75.5**	19.0	30.4	31.4	**76.2**	44.5	60.2	59.7	**60.0**
(SCENE)	14.4	43.6	21.7	53.0	4.0	7.4	13.8	75.3	23.4	**94.6**	5.21	9.8	12.7	**86.4**	22.2	19.9	59.8	**29.8**
EVENT	28.7	44.2	34.8	34.4	2.3	4.3	29.9	58.9	39.7	**79.5**	15.0	25.2	25.2	**72.5**	37.4	40.0	56.3	**46.8**

Table 4: Evaluation results for individual systems (left) and combination systems (right) on all corpus types for English (top) and French (bottom). Values in bold are for highest values for a given metric for each corpus type and language.

and +6.1). Recall from Table 1 that TEXT and SPEECH were the two corpus types with the highest number of sure paraphrase examples for both languages: results show that our classifier was able to efficiently use them.

Recall values for the union are quite strong for all corpus types, ranging from 71.4 (SPEECH in English) to 83.4 (SCENE in English). There is, however, a substantial decrease between the unions and the results of our combination systems, although recall values for our systems are roughly between 56 and 67, which may be considered an acceptable range on such a task. Further study of false negatives should help with engineering new features to improve paraphrase recognition. Lastly, we note that precision is in general highest for a specific system (PIVOT), and reaches high values for our validation system on TEXT, where we have the most examples (resp. 68.4 and 74.7 for English and French).

As seen in Table 2, synonymy is the most present phenomenon in all our corpora; it is also probably one of the most useful type of knowledge for many applications. We now therefore focus on this class, for which all the sure paraphrases in our corpora falling in this class have been annotated. Table 5 shows F-measure values for the individual techniques and our combination systems on all corpus types. We first observe that our combination system also always improves here over the best individual system, albeit not by a large margin on EVENT.

	GIZA	FASTR	TER_p	PIVOT	validation
ENGLISH					
TEXT	52.2	6.1	47.3	47.1	68.1
SPEECH	42.6	5.0	30.3	39.5	54.9
SCENE	51.8	6.0	48.0	26.0	56.3
EVENT	22.5	2.1	34.8	24.7	35.5
FRENCH					
TEXT	55.3	3.9	50.7	50.5	70.3
SPEECH	49.8	1.6	40.9	36.2	57.2
(SCENE)	19.6	4.2	23.1	0.0	24.7
EVENT	36.8	3.5	35.3	25.6	39.9

Table 5: F-measure values for test instances in the **synonymy** class (see Table 2) for all individual systems and our validation system for English (top) and French (bottom).

Also, we find that PIVOT performs relatively closer to GIZA and TER_p on TEXT and SPEECH than for the full set of classes, confirming the intuition that translational equivalence may be appropriate to recognize synonymy.

3.4 Experiments across corpus types

To test how different the corpora under study are as regards paraphrase identification, we now consider using as additional training data for our classifiers corpora of the other types, both individually and collectively. Results are given on Table 6.[13]

[13]Note that our results are still given by performing cross-validation averaging over 10 test sets for each tested corpus type.

	+TEXT	+SPEECH	+SCENE	+EVENT	+All
			ENGLISH		
# ex+	7,342	2,296	1,784	1,171	12,593
TEXT	65.5	**66.2**	65.1	**66.2**	65.1
SPEECH	56.0	53.5	52.8	54.8	**56.6**
SCENE	49.7	**54.3**	53.7	53.8	42.7
EVENT	51.1	45.3	42.5	46.0	**56.2**
			FRENCH		
# ex+	12,961	3,340	966	2,160	19,427
TEXT	**67.1**	**67.2**	66.7	67.0	66.6
SPEECH	57.6	**60.0**	56.4	59.6	57.9
(SCENE)	23.7	22.0	**29.8**	23.9	21.1
EVENT	45.2	45.6	44.3	46.8	**49.3**

Table 6: Evaluation results (F_1 scores) for all corpus types for English (top) and French (bottom) when adding training material from other corpus types (values with gray background on the diagonal are when no additional training data are used). "*#ex+*" rows indicate numbers of positive paraphrase examples for each additional corpus type.

The most notable observation is that EVENT is substantially improved by using all available additional training data for English (+10.2), and to a lesser extent for French (+2.5) . It should be noted that no individual corpus type, save TEXT, individually improves results on EVENT, and that results are yet substantially improved over the use of training data from TEXT when using all available data, revealing a collective contribution of all corpus types. The second major observation is that all other corpus types seem to be quite specific in nature, as no addition of training data from other types yields any improvement (with the exception of SPEECH on English), but they often in fact decrease performance. For instance, SCENE in English is substantially negatively impacted by the use of the numerous examples of TEXT (-4 in F-measure) and even more when using all other training data (-9). This underlines the specific nature of this corpus type: independent descriptions of the same scene in a video may be worded with much variation that mostly differ from that present in other corpus types.

Our main conclusion here is therefore that all our corpora under study are quite specific in nature, but that EVENT can benefit from all training data from the other corpus types. We can further note that the fact that TEXT is almost not impacted by additional data may also be explained by the fact that this corpus type contains more than half of the total number of examples for the two languages. Finally, there are substantially more positive paraphrase examples for French (19,427) than for English (12,593).

4 Related work

Over the years, paraphrase acquisition and generation have attracted a wealth of research works that are too many to adequatly summarize here: (Madnani and Dorr, 2010) presents a complete and up-to-date review of the main approaches. Sentential paraphrase collection has been tackled from specific resources increasing the probability of sentences being paraphrases (Dolan et al., 2004; Bernhard and Gurevych, 2008; Wubben et al., 2009), from comparable monolingual corpora (Barzilay and Elhadad, 2003; Fung and Cheung, 2004; Nelken and Shieber, 2006), and even at web scale (Paşca and Dienes, 2005; Bhagat and Ravichandran, 2008).

Various techniques have been proposed for paraphrase acquisition from related sentence pairs (Barzilay and McKeown, 2001; Pang et al., 2003) and from bilingual parallel corpora (Bannard and Callison-Burch, 2005; Kok and Brockett, 2010). The issue of corpus construction for developing and evaluating paraphrase acquisition techniques are addressed in (Cohn et al., 2008; Callison-Burch et al., 2008). To the best of our knowledge, this is the first time that a study in paraphrase acquisition is conducted on several corpus types and for 2 languages. Faruqui and Padó (2011) study the acquisition of *entailment pairs* (premise and hypothesis), with experiments in 3 languages and various domains of newspaper corpora for one language. Although their work is not directly comparable to ours, they report that robustness across domains is difficult to achieve.

Laslty, the evaluation of automatically generated paraphrases has recently received some attention (Liu et al., 2010; Chen and Dolan, 2011; Metzler et al., 2011) although it remains a difficult issue. Application-driven paraphrase generation provides indirect means of evaluating paraphrase generation (Zhao et al., 2009). For instance, the field of Statistical Machine Translation has produced works showing both the usefulness of human-produced

(Schroeder et al., 2009; Resnik et al., 2010) and automatically produced paraphrases (Madnani et al., 2008; Marton et al., 2009; Max, 2010; He et al., 2011) for improving translation performance.

5 Discussion and future work

This work has addressed the issue of sub-sentential paraphrase acquisition from text pairs. Analoguously to bilingual parallel corpora, which are still to date the most reliable resources for automatic acquisition of sub-sentential translations, monolingual parallel corpora are generally regarded as very appropriate for paraphrase acquisition. However, their low availability makes searching for *less parallel* corpora a necessity. In this study, we have attempted to identify corpora of various degrees of semantic textual similarity by considering text pairs originating from various signal types. These signal types allow various degrees of freedom as to how to formulate a text: a text is read and translated into a different language (TEXT); some speech is listened to in the context of a visual story and translated into a different language (SPEECH); some action is looked at and described (SCENE); and some event that took place is concisely reported (EVENT).

The results presented in this paper have shown how these corpora differed in various aspects. First, they contain varying quantities of paraphrases that are differently distributed into paraphrase classes. Individual acquisition techniques, based on statistical learning of word alignments (GIZA), linguistic knowledge on term variation (FASTR), edit rate on word sequence (TER_p), and translational equivalence (PIVOT), for which different performances were observed among them on the same corpus type, were shown to achieve different performances across corpus types. An efficient combination of candidate paraphrases from these individual techniques exploiting additional features to characterize paraphrases has yielded substantial increases in performance on all corpus types; however, it is interesting to note that the highest amplitude in performance across corpus types was not so much on *recall* (amplitude of 10.5 on English and 4.7 on French) than on *precision* (amplitude of 33.4 on English and 34.7[14] on French). This, some other factors aside, emphasizes the fact that the correct idenfication of paraphrases is facilitated when equivalence of semantic content is more probable. Many works have accordingly attempted to identify text units that are *as parallel as possible* from large corpora, and the task of measuring semantic textual similarity, which can find many uses, has received some attention lately (Agirre et al., 2012). However, it itself relies on some knowledge on paraphrasing.

Our avenues for future work lie in three main areas. The first one is to continue our current line of work and study the impact of additional individual acquisition techniques and better characterizations of paraphrases in context, in tandem with working on identifying parallel text pairs in large corpora. Another avenue is to start from the output of high recall techniques and to attempt to characterize the contexts of possible substitution for candidate paraphrases from large corpora as a means to acquire precise paraphrases. As the examples from Table 7 show, some classes of paraphrases, and in particular in the continuum from our **synonymy** to **pragmatics** classes, require the joint acquisition of contextual information that license substitution. Lastly, we plan to apply such knowledge in text-to-text applications.

	synonymy
TEXT	*take part in ↔ participate in*
	great assistance ↔ enormous help
SPEECH	*make a deal ↔ come to an agreement*
	I don't care ↔ I don't give a damn
SCENE	*riding a bicycle ↔ cycling*
	lady ↔ woman
EVENT	*jail escapee ↔ prison fugitive*
	apologizes ↔ expresses regret
	pragmatics
TEXT	*flew in ↔ arrived in*
	flood-control materials ↔ needed supplies
SPEECH	*face ↔ picture*
	want to sleep ↔ dream about sleeping
SCENE	*a man ↔ someone*
	bento ↔ food
EVENT	*violence ↔ bloodshed*
	anger ↔ emotion

Table 7: Examples in English for the **synonymy** and **pragmatics** classes.

[14]Not considering (SCENE) for French.

Acknowledgements

The authors would like to thank the reviewers for their comments and suggestions. This work was partly funded by ANR project Edylex (ANR-09-CORD-008).

References

Eneko Agirre, Daniel Cer, Mona Diab, and Aitor Gonzalez-Agirre. 2012. SemEval-2012 Task 6: A Pilot on Semantic Textual Similarity. In *Proceedings of SemEval*, Montréal, Canada.

Colin Bannard and Chris Callison-Burch. 2005. Paraphrasing with Bilingual Parallel Corpora. In *Proceedings of ACL*, Ann Arbor, USA.

Regina Barzilay and Noemie Elhadad. 2003. Sentence alignment for monolingual comparable corpora. In *Proceedings of EMNLP*, Sapporo, Japan.

Regina Barzilay and Kathleen R. McKeown. 2001. Extracting paraphrases from a parallel corpus. In *Proceedings of ACL*, Toulouse, France.

Delphine Bernhard and Iryna Gurevych. 2008. Answering Learners' Questions by Retrieving Question Paraphrases from Social Q&A Sites. In *Proceedings of the Workshop on Innovative Use of NLP for Building Educational Applications*, Columbus, USA.

Rahul Bhagat and Deepak Ravichandran. 2008. Large scale acquisition of paraphrases for learning surface patterns. In *Proceedings of ACL-HLT*, Columbus, USA.

Houda Bouamor, Aurélien Max, and Anne Vilnat. 2012. Validation of sub-sentential paraphrases acquired from parallel monolingual corpora. In *EACL*, Avignon, France.

Chris Callison-Burch, Trevor Cohn, and Mirella Lapata. 2008. Parametric: An automatic evaluation metric for paraphrasing. In *Proceedings of COLING*, Manchester, UK.

David Chen and William Dolan. 2011. Collecting highly parallel data for paraphrase evaluation. In *Proceedings of ACL*, Portland, USA.

Trevor Cohn, Chris Callison-Burch, and Mirella Lapata. 2008. Constructing corpora for the development and evaluation of paraphrase systems. *Computational Linguistics*, 34(4).

P. W. Culicover. 1968. Paraphrase Generation and Information Retrieval from Stored Text. *Mechanical Translation and Computational Linguistics*, 11:78–88.

Bill Dolan, Chris Quirk, and Chris Brockett. 2004. Unsupervised construction of large paraphrase corpora: Exploiting massively parallel news sources. In *Proceedings of COLING*, Geneva, Switzerland.

Manaal Faruqui and Sebastian Padó. 2011. Acquiring entailment pairs across languages and domains: A data analysis. In *Proceedings of the International Conference on Computational Semantics (IWCS)*, Oxford, UK.

Pascale Fung and Percy Cheung. 2004. Multi-level bootstrapping for extracting parallel sentences from a quasi-comparable corpus. In *Proceedings of COLING*, Geneva, Switzerland.

Ulrich Germann. 2008. Yawat : Yet Another Word Alignment Tool. In *Proceedings of the ACL-HLT, demo session*, Columbus, USA.

Wei He, Shiqi Zhao, Haifeng Wang, and Ting Liu. 2011. Enriching SMT Training Data via Paraphrasing. In *Proceedings of IJCNLP*, Chiang Mai, Thailand.

Christian Jacquemin. 1999. Syntagmatic and paradigmatic representations of term variation. In *Proceedings of ACL*, College Park, USA.

Philipp Koehn, Franz Josef Och, and Daniel Marcu. 2003. Statistical Phrase-Based Translation. In *Proceedings of NAACL-HLT*, Edmonton, Canada.

Philipp Koehn, Hieu Hoang, Alexandra Birch, Chris Callison-Burch, Marcello Federico, Nicola Bertoldi, Brooke Cowan, Wade Shen, Christine Moran, Richard Zens, Chris Dyer, Ondrej Bojar, Alexandra Constantin, and Evan Herbst. 2007. Moses: Open Source Toolkit for Statistical Machine Translation. In *Proceedings of ACL, demo session*, Prague, Czech Republic.

Stanley Kok and Chris Brockett. 2010. Hitting the Right Paraphrases in Good Time. In *Proceedings of NAACL*, Los Angeles, USA.

Alon Lavie and Abhaya Agarwal. 2007. METEOR: An automatic metric for MT evaluation with high levels of correlation with human judgments. In *Proceedings of the ACL Workshop on Statistical Machine Translation*, Prague, Czech Republic.

Chang Liu, Daniel Dahlmeier, and Hwee Tou Ng. 2010. PEM: A paraphrase evaluation metric exploiting parallel texts. In *Proceedings of EMNLP*, Cambridge, USA.

Nitin Madnani and Bonnie J. Dorr. 2010. Generating Phrasal and Sentential Paraphrases: A Survey of Data-Driven Methods . *Computational Linguistics*, 36(3).

Nitin Madnani, Philip Resnik, Bonnie J. Dorr, and Richard Schwartz. 2008. Are multiple reference translations necessary? investigating the value of paraphrased reference translations in parameter optimization. In *Proceedings of AMTA*, Waikiki, USA.

Yuval Marton, Chris Callison-Burch, and Philip Resnik. 2009. Improved Statistical Machine Translation Using Monolingually-derived Paraphrases. In *Proceedings of EMNLP*, Singapore.

Aurélien Max. 2010. Example-Based Paraphrasing for Improved Phrase-Based Statistical Machine Translation. In *Proceedings of EMNLP*, Cambridge, USA.

Donald Metzler, Eduard Hovy, and Chunliang Zhang. 2011. An empirical evaluation of data-driven paraphrase generation techniques. In *Proceedings of ACL-HLT*, Portland, USA.

Rani Nelken and Stuart M. Shieber. 2006. Towards robust context-sensitive sentence alignment for monolingual corpora. In *Proceedings of EACL*, Trento, Italy.

Franz Josef Och and Herman Ney. 2004. The alignment template approach to statistical machine translation. *Computational Linguistics*, 30(4).

Bo Pang, Kevin Knight, and Daniel Marcu. 2003. Syntax-based alignement of multiple translations: Extracting paraphrases and generating new sentences. In *Proceedings of NAACL-HLT*, Edmonton, Canada.

Kishore Papineni, Salim Roukos, Todd Ward, and Wei-Jing Zhu. 2002. Bleu: a method for automatic evaluation of machine translation. In *Proceedings of ACL*, Philadelphia, USA.

Marius Paşca and Peter Dienes. 2005. Aligning Needles in a Haystack: Paraphrase Acquisition Across the Web. In *Proceedings of IJCNLP*, Jeju Island, South Korea.

Philip Resnik, Olivia Buzek, Chang Hu, Yakov Kronrod, Alex Quinn, and Benjamin B. Bederson. 2010. Improving translation via targeted paraphrasing. In *Proceedings of EMNLP*, Cambridge, USA.

Josh Schroeder, Trevor Cohn, and Philipp Koehn. 2009. Word Lattices for Multi-Source Translation. In *Proceedings of EACL*, Athens, Greece.

Matthew Snover, Bonnie J. Dorr, Richard Schwartz, Linnea Micciulla, and John Makhoul. 2006. A Study of Translation Edit Rate with Targeted Human Annotation. In *Proceedings of AMTA*, Boston, USA.

Matthew Snover, Nitin Madnani, Bonnie J. Dorr, and Richard Schwartz. 2010. TER-Plus: paraphrase, semantic, and alignment enhancements to Translation Edit Rate. *Machine Translation*, 23(2-3).

Jörg Tiedemann. 2007. Building a Multilingual Parallel Subtitle Corpus. In *Proceedings of the Conference on Computational Linguistics in the Netherlands*, Leuven, Belgium.

Marta Vila, M. Antònia Martí, and Horacio Rodríguez. 2011. Paraphrase Concept and Typology. A Linguistically Based and Computationally Oriented Approach. *Procesamiento del Lenguaje Natural*, (462-3).

Sander Wubben, Antal van den Bosch, Emiel Krahmer, and Erwin Marsi. 2009. Clustering and maching headlines for automatic paraphrase acquisition. In *Proceedings of the European Workshop on Natural Language Generation*, Athens, Greece.

Shiqi Zhao, Xiang Lan, Ting Liu, and Sheng Li. 2009. Application-driven Statistical Paraphrase Generation. In *Proceedings of ACL-IJCNLP*, Singapore.

Parse, Price and Cut—Delayed Column and Row Generation for Graph Based Parsers

Sebastian Riedel **David Smith** **Andrew McCallum**
Department of Computer Science
University of Massachusetts, Amherst
{riedel,dasmith,mccallum}@cs.umass.edu

Abstract

Graph-based dependency parsers suffer from the sheer number of higher order edges they need to (a) score and (b) consider during optimization. Here we show that when working with LP relaxations, large fractions of these edges can be pruned before they are fully scored—without any loss of optimality guarantees and, hence, accuracy. This is achieved by iteratively parsing with a subset of higher-order edges, adding higher-order edges that may improve the score of the current solution, and adding higher-order edges that are implied by the current best first order edges. This amounts to delayed column and row generation in the LP relaxation and is guaranteed to provide the optimal LP solution. For second order grandparent models, our method considers, or scores, no more than 6–13% of the second order edges of the full model. This yields up to an eightfold parsing speedup, while providing the same empirical accuracy and certificates of optimality as working with the full LP relaxation. We also provide a tighter LP formulation for grandparent models that leads to a smaller integrality gap and higher speed.

1 Introduction

Many problems in NLP, and structured prediction in general, can be cast as finding high-scoring structures based on a large set of candidate parts. For example, in second order graph-based dependency parsing (Kübler et al., 2009) we have to choose a quadratic number of first order and a cubic number of second order edges such that the graph is both high-scoring and a tree. In coreference, we have to select high-scoring clusters of mentions from an exponential number of candidate clusters, such that each mention is in exactly one cluster (Culotta et al., 2007). In segmentation of citation strings, we need to consider a quadratic number of possible segments such that every token is part of exactly one segment (Poon and Domingos, 2007).

What makes such problems challenging is the large number of possible parts to consider. This number not only affects the cost of search or optimization but also slows down the process of scoring parts before they enter the optimization problem. For example, the cubic grandparent edges in second-order dependency parsing slow down dynamic programs (McDonald and Pereira, 2006), belief propagation (Smith and Eisner, 2008) and LP solvers (Martins et al., 2009), since there are more value functions to evaluate, more messages to pass, or more variables to consider. But to even calculate the score for each part we need a cubic number of operations that usually involve expensive feature extraction. This step often becomes a major bottleneck in parsing, and structured prediction in general.

Candidate parts can often be heuristically pruned. In the case of dependency parsing, previous work has used coarse-to-fine strategies where simpler first order models are used to prune unlikely first order edges, and hence all corresponding higher order edges (Koo and Collins, 2010; Martins et al., 2009; Riedel and Clarke, 2006). While such methods can be effective, they are more convoluted, often require training of addition models as well as tuning of thresholding hyper-parameters, and usually provide no guarantees of optimality.

We present an approach that can solve problems with large sets of candidate parts without considering all of these parts in either optimization or scoring. And in contrast to most pruning heuristics, our algorithm can give certificates of optimality before having optimized over, or even scored, all parts. It does so without the need of auxiliary models or tuning of threshold parameters. This is achieved by a delayed column and row generation algorithm that iteratively solves an LP relaxation over a small subset of current candidate parts, and then finds new candidates that score highly and can be inserted into the current optimal solution without removing high scoring existing structure. The latter step subtracts from the cost of a part the price of resources the part requires, and is often referred as *pricing*. Sometimes parts may score highly after pricing, but are necessary in order to make the current solution feasible. We add such parts in a step that roughly amounts to violated *cuts* to the LP.

We illustrate our approach in terms of a second-order grandparent model for dependency parsing. We solve these models by iteratively parsing, pricing, and cutting. To this end we use a variant of the LP relaxation formulated by Martins et al. (2009). Our variant of this LP is designed to be amenable to column generation. It also turns out to be a tighter outer bound that leads to fewer fractional solutions and faster runtimes. To find high scoring grandparent edges without explicitly enumerating all of them, we prune out a large fraction using factorized upper bounds on grandparent scores.

Our parse, price and cut algorithm is evaluated using a non-projective grandparent model on three languages. Compared to a brute force approach of solving the full LP, we only score about 10% of the grandparent edges, consider only 8% in optimization, and so observe an increase in parsing speed of up to 750%. This is possible without loss of optimality, and hence accuracy. We also find that our extended LP formulation leads to a 15% reduction of fractional solutions, up to 12 times higher speed, and generally higher accuracy when compared to the grandparent formulation of Martins et al. (2009).

2 Graph-Based Dependency Parsing

Dependency trees are representations of the syntactic structure of a sentence (Nivre et al., 2007). They determine, for each token of a sentence, the syntactic head the token is modifying. As a lightweight alternative to phrase-based constituency trees, dependency representations have by now seen widespread use in the community in various domains such as question answering, machine translation, and information extraction.

To simplify further exposition, we now formalize the task, and mostly follow the notation of Martins et al. (2009). Consider a sentence $\mathbf{x} = \langle t_0, t_1, \ldots, t_n \rangle$ where $t_1, \ldots, t_n$ correspond to the n tokens of the sentence, and t_0 is an artificial root token. Let $V \triangleq \{0, \ldots, n\}$ be a set of vertices corresponding to the tokens in $\mathbf{x}$, and $\mathcal{C} \subseteq V \times V$ a set of candidate directed edges. Then a directed graph $y \subseteq \mathcal{C}$ is a *legal dependency parse* if and only if it is a tree over V rooted at vertex 0. Given a sentence $\mathbf{x}$, we use $\mathcal{Y}$ to denote the set of its legal parses. Note that all of the above definitions depend on $\mathbf{x}$, but for simplicity we omit this dependency in our notation.

2.1 Arc-Factored Models

Graph-based models define parametrized scoring functions that are trained to discriminate between correct and incorrect parse trees. So called *arc-factored* or *first order* models are the most basic variant of such functions: they assess the quality of a tree by scoring each edge in isolation (McDonald et al., 2005b; McDonald et al., 2005a). Formally, arc-factored models are scoring functions of the form

$$s(y; \mathbf{x}, \mathbf{w}) = \sum_{\langle h,m \rangle \in y} s_{\langle h,m \rangle}(\mathbf{x}, \mathbf{w}) \qquad (1)$$

where $\mathbf{w}$ is a weight vector and $s_{\langle h,m \rangle}(\mathbf{x}, \mathbf{w})$ scores the edge $\langle h, m \rangle$ with respect to sentence $\mathbf{x}$ and weights $\mathbf{w}$. From here on we will omit both $\mathbf{x}$ and $\mathbf{w}$ from our notation if they are clear from the context.

Given such a scoring function, parsing amounts to solving:

$$\begin{aligned} \underset{y}{\text{maximize}} \quad & \sum_{\langle h,m \rangle \in y} s_{\langle h,m \rangle} \\ \text{subject to} \quad & y \in \mathcal{Y}. \end{aligned} \qquad (2)$$

2.2 Higher Order Models

Arc-factored models cannot capture higher order dependencies between two or more edges. Higher order models remedy this by introducing scores for larger configurations of edges appearing in the tree (McDonald and Pereira, 2006). For example, in *grandparent* models, the score of a tree also includes a score $s^{\text{gp}}_{\langle g,p,c\rangle}$ for each grandparent-parent-child triple $\langle g,p,c\rangle$:

$$s(y) = \sum_{\langle h,m\rangle \in y} s_{\langle h,m\rangle} + \sum_{\langle g,p\rangle \in y, \langle p,c\rangle \in y} s^{\text{gp}}_{\langle g,p,c\rangle} \quad (3)$$

There are other variants of higher order models that include, in addition to grandparent triples, pairs of siblings (adjacent or not) or third order edges. However, to illustrate our approach we will focus on grandparent models and note that most of what we present can be generalized to other higher order models.

2.3 Feature Templates

For our later exposition the factored and parametrized nature of the scoring functions will be crucial. In the following we therefore illustrate this property in more detail.

The scoring functions for arcs or higher order edges usually decompose into a sum of feature *template* scores. For example, the grandparent edge score $s^{\text{gp}}_{\langle g,p,c\rangle}$ is defined as

$$s^{\text{gp}}_{\langle g,p,c\rangle} \triangleq \sum_{t \in \mathcal{T}^{\text{gp}}} s^{\text{gp},t}_{\langle g,p,c\rangle} \quad (4)$$

where $\mathcal{T}^{\text{gp}}$ is the set of grandparent templates, and each template $t \in \mathcal{T}^{\text{gp}}$ defines a scoring function $s^{\text{gp},t}_{\langle g,p,c\rangle}$ to assess a specific property of the grandparent-parent-child edge $\langle g,p,c\rangle$.

The template scores again decompose. Considering grandparent scores, we get

$$s^{t}_{\langle g,p,c\rangle} \triangleq \mathbf{w}_t^{\top} \mathbf{f}^t \left(h^t_g, h^t_p, h^t_c, d^t_{g,p,c}\right) \quad (5)$$

where h^t_i is an attribute of token t_i, say h^{101}_i = Part-of-Speech (t_i). The term $d^t_{g,p,c}$ corresponds to a representation of the relation between tokens corresponding to g, p and g. For example, for template 101 it could return their relative positions to each other:

$$d^{101}_{g,p,c} \triangleq \langle \mathbb{I}[g > p], \mathbb{I}[g > c], \mathbb{I}[p > c] \rangle . \quad (6)$$

The feature function $\mathbf{f}^t$ maps the representations of g, p and c into a vector space. For the purposes of our work this mapping is not important, and hence we omit details.

2.4 Learning

The scoring functions we consider are parametrized by a family of per-template weight vectors $\mathbf{w} = \langle \mathbf{w}_t \rangle_{t \in \mathcal{T}}$. During learning we need to estimate $\mathbf{w}$ such that our scoring functions learns to differentiate between correct and incorrect parse trees. This can be achieved in many ways: large margin training, maximizing conditional likelihood, or variants in between. In this work we follow Smith and Eisner (2008) and train the models with stochastic gradient descent on the conditional log-likelihood of the training data, using belief propagation in order to calculate approximate gradients.

3 LP and ILP Formulations

Riedel and Clarke (2006) showed that dependency parsing can be framed as Integer Linear Program (ILP), and efficiently solved using an off-the-shelf optimizer if a cutting plane approach is used.[1] Compared to tailor made dynamic programs, such generic solvers give the practitioner more modeling flexibility (Martins et al., 2009), albeit at the cost of efficiency. Likewise, compared to approximate solvers, ILP and Linear Program (LP) formulations can give strong guarantees of optimality. The study of Linear LP relaxations of dependency parsing has also lead to effective alternative methods for parsing, such as dual decomposition (Koo et al., 2010; Rush et al., 2010). As we see later, the capability of LP solvers to calculate dual solutions is also crucial for efficient and exact pruning. Note, however, that dynamic programs provide dual solutions as well (see section 4.5 for more details).

3.1 Arc-Factored Models

To represent a parse $y \in \mathcal{Y}$ we first introduce an vector of variables $\mathbf{z} \triangleq \langle z_a \rangle_a$ where z_a is 1 if $a \in y$ and 0 otherwise. With this representation parsing amounts to finding a vector $\mathbf{z}$ that corresponds to a legal parse tree and that maximizes $\sum_a z_a s_a$. One way to achieve this is to search through the *convex hull* of all legal incidence vectors, knowing that any linear objectives would take on its maximum on one of the hull's vertices. We will use $\mathcal{Z}$ to denote this convex hull of incidence vectors of legal parse trees,

[1] Such as the highly efficient and free-for-academic-use Gurobi solver.

and call $\mathcal{Z}$ the *arborescence polytope* (Martins et al., 2009). The Minkowski-Weyl theorem tells us that $\mathcal{Z}$ can be represented as an intersection of halfspaces, or constraints, $\mathcal{Z} = \{\mathbf{z}|\mathbf{A}\mathbf{z} \leq \mathbf{b}\}$. Hence optimal dependency parsing, in theory, can be addressed using LPs.

However, it is difficult to describe $\mathcal{Z}$ with a *compact* number of constraints and variables that lend themselves to efficient optimization. In general we therefore work with *relaxations*, or outer bounds, on $\mathcal{Z}$. Such outer bounds are designed to cut off all illegal *integer* solutions of the problem, but still allow for *fractional* solutions. In case the optimum is achieved at an integer vertex of the outer bound, it is clear that we have found the optimal solution to the original problem. In case we find a fractional point, we need to map it onto $\mathcal{Z}$ (e.g., by projection or rounding). Alternatively, we can use the outer bound together with 0/1 constraints on $\mathbf{z}$, and then employ an ILP solver (say, branch-and-bound) to find the true optimum. Given the NP-hardness of ILP, this will generally be slow.

In the following we will present the outer bound $\bar{\mathcal{Z}} \supseteq \mathcal{Z}$ proposed by Martins et al. (2009). Compared to the representation Riedel and Clarke (2006), this bound has the benefit a small polynomial number of constraints. Note, however, that often exponentially many constraints can be efficiently handled if polynomial separation algorithms exists, and that such representations can lead to tighter outer bounds.

The constraints we employ are:

No Head For Root In a dependency tree the root node never has a head. While this could be captured through linear constraints, it is easier to simply restrict the candidate set $\mathcal{C}$ to never contain edges of the form $\langle \cdot, 0 \rangle$.

Exactly One Head for Non-Roots Any non-root token has to have exactly one head token. We can enforce this property through the set of constraints:

$$m > 0 : \sum_{h} z_{\langle h,m \rangle} = 1. \quad \text{(OneHead)}$$

No Cycles A parse tree cannot have cycles. This is equivalent, together with the head constraints above, to enforcing that the tree be fully connected. Martins et al. (2009) capture this connectivity constraint using a *single commodity flow formulation*. This requires the introduction of flow variables $\boldsymbol{\phi} \triangleq \langle \phi_a \rangle_{a \in \mathcal{C}}$. By enforcing that token 0 has n outgoing flow,

$$\sum_{m>0} \phi_{\langle 0,m \rangle} = n, \quad \text{(Source)}$$

that any other token *consumes one unit of flow*,

$$t > 0 : \sum_{h} \phi_{\langle h,t \rangle} - \sum_{m>0} \phi_{\langle t,m \rangle} = 1 \quad \text{(Consume)}$$

and that *flow is zero on disabled arcs*

$$\phi_{\langle h,m \rangle} \leq n z_{\langle h,m \rangle}, \quad \text{(NoFlow)}$$

connectivity can be ensured.

Assuming we have such a representation, parsing with an LP relaxation amounts to solving

$$\begin{array}{ll} \underset{\mathbf{z} \geq \mathbf{0}}{\text{maximize}} & \sum_{a \in A} z_a s_a \\ \text{subject to} & \mathbf{A} \begin{bmatrix} \mathbf{z} \\ \boldsymbol{\phi} \end{bmatrix} \leq \mathbf{b}. \end{array} \quad (7)$$

3.2 Higher Order Models

The 1st-Order LP can be easily extended to capture second (or higher) order models. For for the case of grandparent models, this amounts to introducing another class of variables, $z^{\text{gp}}_{g,p,c}$, that indicate if the parse contains both the edge $\langle g, p \rangle$ and the edge $\langle p, c \rangle$. With the help of the indicators $\mathbf{z}^{\text{gp}}$ we can represent the second order objective as a linear function. We now need an outer bound on the convex hull of vectors $\langle \mathbf{z}, \mathbf{z}^{\text{gp}} \rangle$ where $\mathbf{z}$ is a legal parse tree and $\mathbf{z}^{\text{gp}}$ is a consistent set of grandparent indicators. We will refer to this convex hull as the *grandparent polytope* $\mathcal{Z}^{\text{gp}}$.

We can re-use the constraints $\mathbf{A}$ of section 3.1 to ensure that $\mathbf{z}$ is in $\mathcal{Z}$. To make sure $\mathbf{z}^{\text{gp}}$ is consistent with $\mathbf{z}$, Martins et al. (2009) linearize the equivalence $z^{gp}_{g,p,c} \Leftrightarrow z_{g,p} \wedge z_{p,c}$ we know to hold for legal incidence vectors, yielding

$$g,p,c : z_{\langle g,p \rangle} + z_{\langle p,c \rangle} - z^{\text{gp}}_{\langle g,p,c \rangle} \leq 1 \quad \text{(ArcGP)}$$

and

$$g,p,c : z_{\langle g,p \rangle} \geq z^{\text{gp}}_{\langle g,p,c \rangle}, z_{\langle p,c \rangle} \geq z^{\text{gp}}_{\langle g,p,c \rangle} \quad \text{(GPArc)}$$

There are additional constraints we know to hold in $\mathcal{Z}^{\text{gp}}$. First, we know that for any active edge $\langle p, c \rangle \in$

y with $p > 0$ there is exactly one grandparent edge $\langle g, p, c\rangle$. Likewise, for an inactive edge $\langle p, c\rangle \notin y$ there must be no grandparent edge $\langle g, p, c\rangle$. This can be captured through the constraint:

$$p > 0, c : \sum_g z^{\text{gp}}_{\langle g,p,c\rangle} = z_{\langle p,c\rangle}. \qquad \text{(OneGP)}$$

We also know that if an edge $\langle g, p\rangle$ in inactive, there must not be any grandparent edge $\langle g, p, c\rangle$ that goes through $\langle g, p\rangle$:

$$g, p : \sum_c z^{\text{gp}}_{\langle g,p,c\rangle} \leq n z_{\langle g,p\rangle}. \qquad \text{(NoGP)}$$

It can be easily shown that for *integer* solutions the constraints ArcGP and GPArc of Martins et al. (2009) are sufficient conditions for consistency between $\mathbf{z}$ and $\mathbf{z}^{\text{gp}}$. It can equally be shown that the same holds for the constraints OneGP and NoGP. However, when working with LP relaxations, the two polytopes have different fractional vertices. Hence, by combining both constraint sets, we can get a tighter outer bound on the grandparent polytope $\mathcal{Z}^{\text{gp}}$. In section 6 we show empirically that this combined polytope in fact leads to fewer fractional solutions. Note that when using the union of all four types of constraints, the NoGP constraint is implied by the constraint GPArc (left) by summing over c on both sides, and can hence be omitted.

4 Parse, Price and Cut

We now introduce our parsing algorithm. To this end, we first give a general description of column and row generation for LPs; then, we illustrate how these techniques can be applied to dependency parsing.

4.1 Column and Row Generation

LPs often have too many variables and constraints to be efficiently solved. In such cases delayed column and row generation can substantially reduce runtime by lazily adding variables only when needed (Gilmore and Gomory, 1961; Lübbecke and Desrosiers, 2004).

To illustrate column and row generation let us consider the following general primal LP and its corresponding dual problem:

Primal		*Dual*	
$\underset{\mathbf{z}\geq\mathbf{0}}{\text{maximize}}$	$\mathbf{s}^\intercal\mathbf{z}$	$\underset{\boldsymbol{\lambda}\geq\mathbf{0}}{\text{minimize}}$	$\boldsymbol{\lambda}^\intercal\mathbf{b}$
subject to	$\mathbf{A}\mathbf{z} \leq \mathbf{b}$	subject to	$\mathbf{A}^\intercal\boldsymbol{\lambda} \geq \mathbf{s}.$

Say you are given a primal feasible $\mathbf{z}'$ and a dual feasible $\boldsymbol{\lambda}'$ for which *complementary slackness* holds: for all variables i we have $z'_i > 0 \Rightarrow s_i = \sum_j \lambda'_j a_{i,j}$ and for all constraints j we have $\lambda'_j > 0 \Rightarrow b_j = \sum_i z'_i a_{i,j}$. In this case it is easy to show that $\mathbf{z}'$ is an optimal primal solution, $\boldsymbol{\lambda}'$ and optimal dual solution, and that both objectives meet at these values (Bertsekas, 1999).

The idea behind delayed column and row generation is to only consider a small subset of variables (or *columns*) I and subset of constraints (or *rows*) J. Optimizing over this restricted problem, either with an off-the-shelf solver or a more specialized method, yields the pair $\left(\mathbf{z}'_I, \boldsymbol{\lambda}'_J\right)$ of partial primal and dual solutions. This pair is feasible and complementary with respect to variables I and constraints J. We can extend it to a solution $(\mathbf{z}', \mathbf{y}')$ over all variables and constraints by heuristically setting the remaining primal and dual variables. If it so happens that $(\mathbf{z}', \mathbf{y}')$ is feasible and complementary for all variables and constraints, we have found the optimal solution. If not, we add the constraints and variables for which feasibility and slackness are violated, and resolve the new partial problem.

In practice, the uninstantiated primal and dual variables are often set to 0. In this case complementary slackness holds trivially, and we only need to find violated primal and dual constraints. For primal constraints, $\sum_i z_i a_{i,j} \leq b_i$, searching for violating constraints j is the well-known *separation* step in cutting plane algorithms. For the dual constraints, $\sum_j \lambda_j a_{i,j} \geq s_i$, the same problem is referred to as *pricing*. Pricing is often framed as searching for all, or some, variables i with positive *reduced cost* $r_i \triangleq s_i - \sum_j \lambda_j a_{i,j}$. Note that while these problems are, naturally, dual to each other, they can have very different flavors. When we assess dual constraints we need to calculate a cost s_i for variable i, and usually this cost would be different for different i. For primal constraints the corresponding right-hand-sides are usually much more homogenous.

Algorithm 1 Parse, Price and Cut.

Require: Initial candidate edges and hyperedges P.
Ensure: The optimal $\mathbf{z}$.

1: **repeat**
2: $\quad \mathbf{z}, \boldsymbol{\lambda} \leftarrow \text{parse}(P)$
3: $\quad N \leftarrow \text{price}(\boldsymbol{\lambda})$
4: $\quad M \leftarrow \text{cut}(\mathbf{z})$
5: $\quad P \leftarrow P \cup N \cup M$
6: **until** $N = \emptyset \wedge M = \emptyset$
7: **return** $\mathbf{z}$

The reduced cost $r_i = s_i - \sum_j \lambda_j a_{i,j}$ has several interesting interpretations. First, intuitively it measures the score we could gain by setting $z_i = 1$, and subtracts an estimate of what we would loose because $z_i = 1$ may compete with other variables for shared resources (constraints). Second, it corresponds to the coefficient of z_i in the Lagrangian $L(\boldsymbol{\lambda}, \mathbf{z}) \triangleq \mathbf{s}^{\intercal}\mathbf{z} + \boldsymbol{\lambda}[\mathbf{b} - \mathbf{A}\mathbf{z}]$. For any $\boldsymbol{\lambda}$, $U_{z_i=k} = \max_{\mathbf{z}\geq 0, z_i=k} L(\boldsymbol{\lambda}, \mathbf{z})$ is an upper bound on the best possible primal objective with $z_i = k$. This means that $r_i = U_{z_i=1} - U_{z_i=0}$ is the difference between an upper bound that considers $z_i = 1$, and one that considers $z_i = 0$. The tighter the bound $U_{z_i=0}$ is, the closer r_i is to an upper bound on the maximal increase we can get for setting z_i to 1. At convergence of column generation, complementary slackness guarantees that $U_{z_i=0}$ is tight for all $z'_i = 0$, and hence r_i is a true an upper bound.

4.2 Application to Dependency Parsing

The grandparent formulation in section 3.2 has a cubic number of variables $z_{\langle g,p,c\rangle}$ as well as a cubic number of constraints. For longer sentences this number can slow us down in two ways. First, the optimizer works with a large search space, and will naturally become slower. Second, for every grandparent edge we need to calculate the score $s_{\langle g,p,c\rangle}$, and this calculation can often be a major bottleneck, in particular when using complex feature functions. To overcome this bottleneck, our parse, price and cut algorithm, as shown in algorithm 1, uses column and row generation. In particular, it lazily instantiates the grandparent edge variables $z^{\text{gp}}_{\langle g,p,c\rangle}$, and the corresponding cubic number of constraints. All uninstantiated variables are implicitly set to 0.

The algorithm requires some initial set of variables to start with. In our case this set P contains all first-order edges $\langle h, m\rangle$ in the candidate set $\mathcal{C}$, and for each of these one grandparent edge $\langle 0, h, m\rangle$. The primary purpose of these grandparent edges is to ensure feasibility of the OneGP constraints.

In step 2, the algorithm parses with the current set of candidates P by solving the corresponding LP relaxation. The LP contains all columns and constraints that involve the edges and grandparent edges of P. The solver returns both the best primal solution $\mathbf{z}$ (for both edges and grandparents), and a complementary dual solution $\boldsymbol{\lambda}$.

In step 3 the dual variables $\boldsymbol{\lambda}$ are used to find uninstantiated grandparent edges $\langle g, p, c\rangle$ with positive reduced cost. The price routine returns such edges in N. In step 4 the primal solution is inspected for violations of constraint ArcGP. The cut routine performs this operation, and returns M, the set of edges $\langle g, p, c\rangle$ that violate ArcGP.

In step 5 the algorithm converges if no more constraint violations, or promising new columns, can be found. If there have been violations ($M \neq \emptyset$) or promising columns ($N \neq \emptyset$), steps 2 to 4 are repeated, with the newly found parts added to the problem. Note that LP solvers can be efficiently *warm-started* after columns and rows have been added, and hence the cost of calls to the solver in step 2 is substantially reduced after the first iteration.

4.3 Pricing

In the pricing step we need to efficiently find a set of grandparent edge variables $z^{\text{gp}}_{\langle g,p,c\rangle}$ with positive reduced cost, or the empty set if no such variables exist. Let $\lambda^{\text{OneGP}}_{\langle p,c\rangle}$ be the dual variables for the OneGP constraints and $\lambda^{\text{NoGP}}_{\langle g,p\rangle}$ the duals for constraints NoGP. Then for the reduced cost of $z^{\text{gp}}_{\langle g,p,c\rangle}$ we know that:

$$r_{\langle g,p,c\rangle} = s_{\langle g,p,c\rangle} - \lambda^{\text{OneGP}}_{\langle p,c\rangle} - \lambda^{\text{NoGP}}_{\langle g,p\rangle}. \quad (8)$$

Notice that the duals for the remaining two constraints ArcGP and GPArc do not appear in this equation. This is valid because we can safely set their duals to zero without violating dual feasibility or complementary slackness of the solution returned by the solver.

4.3.1 Upper Bounds for Efficient Pricing

A naive pricing implementation would exhaustively iterate over all $\langle g, p, c\rangle$ and evaluate $r_{\langle g,p,c\rangle}$ for each. In this case we can still substantially reduce the number of grandparent variables that enter the LP, provided many of these variables have non-positive reduced cost. However, we still need to calculate the score $s_{\langle g,p,c\rangle}$ for each $\langle g, p, c\rangle$, an expensive operation we hope to avoid. In the following we present an upper bound on the reduced cost, $\bar{r}^{\text{gp}}_{\langle g,p,c\rangle} \geq r^{\text{gp}}_{\langle g,p,c\rangle}$, which decomposes in a way that allows for more efficient search. Using this bound, we find all new grandparent edges $\bar{N}$ for which this upper bound is positive:

$$\bar{N} \leftarrow \left\{ \langle g, p, c\rangle \,|\, \bar{r}^{\text{gp}}_{\langle g,p,c\rangle} > 0 \right\}. \tag{9}$$

Next we prune away all but the grandparent edges for which the exact reduced cost is positive:

$$N \leftarrow \bar{N} \setminus \{ e : r^{\text{gp}}_e > 0 \}. \tag{10}$$

Our bound $\bar{r}^{\text{gp}}_{\langle g,p,c\rangle}$ on the reduced cost of $\langle g, p, c\rangle$ is based on an upper bound $\bar{s}^{\text{gp}}_{\langle g,p,\cdot\rangle} \geq \max_c s^{\text{gp}}_{\langle g,p,c\rangle}$ on the grandparent score involving $\langle g, p\rangle$ as grandparent and parent, and the bound $\bar{s}^{\text{gp}}_{\langle \cdot,p,c\rangle} \geq \max_g s^{\text{gp}}_{\langle g,p,c\rangle}$ on the grandparent score involving $\langle p, c\rangle$ as parent and child. Concretely, we have

$$\bar{r}^{\text{gp}}_{\langle g,p,c\rangle} \triangleq \min\left(\bar{s}^{\text{gp}}_{\langle g,p,\cdot\rangle}, \bar{s}^{\text{gp}}_{\langle \cdot,p,c\rangle} \right) - \lambda^{\text{OneGP}}_{\langle p,c\rangle} - \lambda^{\text{NoGP}}_{\langle g,p\rangle}. \tag{11}$$

To find edges $\langle g, p, c\rangle$ for which this bound is positive, we can filter out all edges $\langle p, c\rangle$ such that $s^{\text{gp}}_{\langle \cdot,p,c\rangle} - \lambda^{\text{OneGP}}_{\langle p,c\rangle}$ is non-positive. This is possible because NoGP is a $\leq$ constraint and therefore $\lambda^{\text{NoGP}}_{\langle g,p\rangle} \geq 0$.[2] Hence $\bar{r}^{\text{gp}}_{\langle g,p,c\rangle}$ is at most $\bar{s}^{\text{gp}}_{\langle \cdot,p,c\rangle} - \lambda^{\text{OneGP}}_{\langle p,c\rangle}$. This filtering step cuts off a substantial number of edges, and is the main reason why can avoid scoring all edges.

Next we filter, for each remaining $\langle p, c\rangle$, all possible grandparents g according to the definition of $\bar{r}^{\text{gp}}_{\langle g,p,c\rangle}$. This again allows us to avoid calling the grandparent scoring function on $\langle g, p, c\rangle$, and yields the candidate set $\bar{N}$. Only if $\bar{r}^{\text{gp}}_{\langle g,p,c\rangle}$ is positive do we have to evaluate the exact reduced cost and score.

[2]Notice that in section 4.1 we discussed the LP dual in case were all constraints are inequalities. When equality constraints are used, the corresponding dual variables have no sign constraints. Hence we could not make the same argument for $\lambda^{\text{OneGP}}_{\langle p,c\rangle}$.

4.3.2 Upper Bounds on Scores

What remains to be done is the calculation of upper bounds $\bar{s}^{\text{gp}}_{\langle g,p,\cdot\rangle}$ and $\bar{s}^{\text{gp}}_{\langle \cdot,p,c\rangle}$. Our bounds factor into per-template bounds according to the definitions in section 2.3. In particular, we have

$$\bar{s}^{\text{gp}}_{\langle \cdot,p,c\rangle} \triangleq \sum_{t \in \mathcal{T}^{\text{gp}}} \bar{s}^{\text{gp},t}_{\langle \cdot,p,c\rangle} \tag{12}$$

where $\bar{s}^{t}_{\langle \cdot,p,c\rangle}$ is a per-template upper bound defined as

$$\bar{s}^{\text{gp},t}_{\langle \cdot,p,c\rangle} \triangleq \max_{\substack{v \in \text{range}(h^t) \\ e \in \text{range}(d^t)}} \mathbf{w}_t^\top \mathbf{f}^t \left(v, h^t_p, h^t_c, e \right). \tag{13}$$

That is, we maximize over all possible attribute values v any token g could have, and any possible relation e a token g can have to p and c.

Notice that these bounds can be calculated offline, and hence amortize after deployment of the parser.

4.3.3 Tightening Duals

To price variables, we use the duals returned by the solver. This is a valid default strategy, but may lead to $\boldsymbol{\lambda}$ with overcautious reduced costs. Note, however, that we can arbitrary alter $\boldsymbol{\lambda}$ to minimize reduced costs of uninstantiated variables, as long as we ensure that feasibility and complementary slackness are maintained for the instantiated problem.

We use this flexibility for increasing $\lambda^{\text{OneGP}}_{\langle p,c\rangle}$, and hence lowering reduced costs $z^{\text{gp}}_{\langle g,p,c\rangle}$ for all tokens c. Assume that $z_{\langle p,c\rangle} = 0$ and let $r_{\langle p,c\rangle} = \lambda^{\text{OneGP}}_{\langle p,c\rangle} + K$ be the current reduced cost for $z_{\langle p,c\rangle}$ in the instantiated problem. Here K is a value depending on $s_{\langle p,c\rangle}$ and the remaining constraints $z_{\langle p,c\rangle}$ is involved in.

We know that $r_{\langle p,c\rangle} \leq 0$ due to dual feasibility and hence $r_{\langle p,c\rangle}$ may be 0, but note that $r_{\langle p,c\rangle} < 0$ in many cases. In such cases we can increase $\lambda^{\text{OneGP}}_{\langle p,c\rangle}$ to $-K$ and get $r_{\langle p,c\rangle} = 0$. With respect to $z_{\langle p,c\rangle}$ this maintains dual feasibility (because $r_{\langle p,c\rangle} \leq 0$) and complementary slackness (because $z_{\langle p,c\rangle} = 0$). Furthermore, with respect to the $z^{\text{gp}}_{\langle g,p,c\rangle}$ for all tokens c this also maintains feasibility (because the increased $\lambda^{\text{OneGP}}_{\langle p,c\rangle}$ appears with negative sign in 8) and complementary slackness (because $z^{\text{gp}}_{\langle g,p,c\rangle} = 0$ due to $z_{\langle p,c\rangle} = 0$).

4.4 Separation

What happens if both $z_{\langle g,p\rangle}$ and $z_{\langle p,c\rangle}$ are active while $z^{\text{gp}}_{\langle g,p,c\rangle}$ is still implicitly set to 0? In this case we violate constraint ArcGP. We could remedy this by adding the cut $z_{\langle g,p\rangle} + z_{\langle p,c\rangle} \leq 1$, resolve the LP, and then use the dual variable corresponding to this constraint to get an updated reduced cost $r_{\langle g,p,c\rangle}$. However, in practice we found this does not happen as often, and when it does, it is cheaper for us to add the corresponding column $r_{\langle g,p,c\rangle}$ right away instead of waiting to the next iteration to price it.

To find all pairs of variables for $z_{\langle g,p\rangle} + z_{\langle p,c\rangle} \leq 1$ is violated, we first filter out all edges $\langle h, m\rangle$ for which $z_{\langle h,m\rangle} = 0$ as these automatically satisfy any ArcGP constraint they appear in. Now for each $z_{\langle g,p\rangle} > 0$ all $z_{\langle p,c\rangle} > 0$ are found, and if their sum is larger than 1, the corresponding grandparent edge $\langle g, p, c\rangle$ is returned in the result set.

4.5 Column Generation in Dynamic Programs

Column and Row Generation can substantially reduce the runtime of an off-the-shelf LP solver, as we will find in section 6. Perhaps somewhat surprisingly, it can also be applied in the context of dynamic programs. It is well known that for each dynamic program there is an equivalent polynomial LP formulation (Martin et al., 1990). Roughly speaking, in this formulation primal variables correspond to state transitions, and dual variables to value functions (e.g., the forward scores in the Viterbi algorithm).

In pilot studies we have already used DCG to speed up (exact) Viterbi on linear chains (Belanger et al., 2012). We believe it could be equally applied to dynamic programs for higher order dependency parsing.

5 Related Work

Our work is most similar in spirit to the relaxation method presented by Riedel and Smith (2010) that incrementally adds second order edges to a graphical model based on a gain measure—the analog of our reduced cost. However, they always score every higher order edge, and also provide no certificates of optimality.

Several works in parsing, and in MAP inference in general, perform some variant of row generation (Riedel and Clarke, 2006; Tromble and Eisner, 2006; Sontag and Jaakkola, 2007; Sontag et al., 2008). However, none of the corresponding methods lazily add columns, too. The cutting plane method of Riedel (2008) can omit columns, but only if their coefficient is negative. By using the notion of reduced costs we can also omit columns with positive coefficient. Niepert (2010) applies column generation, but his method is limited to the case of k-Bounded MAP Inference.

Several ILP and LP formulations of dependency parsing have been proposed. Our formulation is inspired by Martins et al. (2009), and hence uses fewer constraints than Riedel and Clarke (2006). For the case of grandparent edges, our formulation also improves upon the outer bound of Martins et al. (2009) in terms of speed, tightness, and utility for column generation. Other recent LP relaxations are based on dual decomposition (Rush et al., 2010; Koo et al., 2010; Martins et al., 2011). These relaxations allow the practitioner to utilize tailor-made dynamic programs for tractable substructure, but still every edge needs to be scored. Given that column generation can also be applied in dynamic programs (see section 4.5), our algorithm could in fact accelerate dual decomposition parsing as well.

Pruning methods are a major part of many structured prediction algorithms in general, and of parsing algorithms in particular (Charniak and Johnson, 2005; Martins et al., 2009; Koo and Collins, 2010; Rush and Petrov, 2012). Generally these methods follow a coarse-to-fine scheme in which simpler models filter out large fractions of edges. Such methods are effective, but require tuning of threshold parameters, training of additional models, and generally lead to more complex pipelines that are harder to analyze and have fewer theoretical guarantees.

A* search (Ahuja et al., 1993) has been used to search for optimal parse trees, for example by Klein and Manning (2003) or, for dependency parsing, by Dienes et al. (2003). There is a direct relation between both A* and Column Generation based on an LP formulation of the shortest path problem. Roughly speaking, in this formulation any feasible dual assignments correspond to a consistent (and thus admissible) heuristic, and the corresponding reduced costs can be used as edge weights. Running Dijkstra's algorithm with these weights then amounts to A*. Column generation for the shortest path problem can then be understood as a method to lazily construct a consistent heuristic. In every step this method finds edges for which consistency is violated, and updates the heuristic such that all these edges are consistent.

6 Experiments

We claim that LP relaxations for higher order parsing can be solved without considering, and scoring, all candidate higher order edges. In practice, how many grandparent edges do we need to score, and how many do we need to add to the optimization problem? And what kind of reduction in runtime does this reduction in edges lead to?

We have also pointed out that our outer bound on the grandparent polytope of legal edge and grandparent vectors is tighter than the one presented by Martins et al. (2009). What effect does this bound have on the number of fractional solutions and the overall accuracy?

To answer these questions we will focus on a set of non-projective grandparent models, but point out that our method and formulation can be easily extended to projective parsing as well as other types of higher order edges. We use the Danish test data of Buchholz and Marsi (2006) and the Italian and Hungarian test datasets of Nivre et al. (2007).

6.1 Impact of Price and Cut

Table 1 compares brute force optimization (BF) with the full model, in spirit of Martins et al. (2009), to running parse, price and cut (PPC) on the same model. This model contains all constraints presented in 3.2. The table shows the average number of parsed sentences per second, the average objective, number of grandparent edges scored and added, all relative to the brute force approach. We also present the average unlabeled accuracy, and the percentage of sentences with integer solutions. This number shows us how often we not only found the optimal solution to the LP relaxation, but also the optimal solution to the full ILP.

We first note that both systems achieve the same objective, and therefore, also the same accuracy. This is expected, given that column and row generation are known to yield optimal solutions. Next we see that the number of grandparent edges scored and added to the problem is reduced to 5–13% of the full model. This leads to up to 760% improvement in speed. This improvement comes for free, without any sacrifice in optimality or guarantees. We also notice that in all cases at least 97% of the sentences have no fractional solutions, and are therefore optimal even with respect to the ILP. Table 1 also shows that our bounds on reduced costs are relatively tight. For example, in the case of Italian we score only one percent more grandparent edges than we actually need to add.

Our fastest PCC parser processes about one sentence per second. This speed falls below the reported numbers of Martins et al. (2009) of about 0.6 seconds per sentence. Crucially, however, in contrast to their work, our speed is achieved without any first-order pruning. In addition, we expect further improvements in runtime by optimizing the implementation of our pricing algorithm.

6.2 Tighter Grandparent Polytope

To investigate how the additional grandparent constraints in section 3.2 help, we compare three models, this time without PPC. The first model follows Martins et al. (2009) and uses constraints ArcGP and GPArc only. The second model uses only constraints OneGP and NoGP. The final model incorporates all four constraints.

Table 2 shows speed relative to the baseline model with constraints ArcGP and GPArc, as well as the percentage of integer solutions and the average unlabeled accuracy—all for the Italian and Hungarian datasets. We notice that the full model has less fractional solutions than the partial models, and either substantially (Italian) or slightly (Hungarian) faster runtimes than ArcGP+GPArc. Interestingly, both sets of constraints in isolation perform worse, in particular the OneGP and NoGP model.

7 Conclusion

We have presented a novel method for parsing in second order grandparent models, and a general blueprint for more efficient and optimal structured prediction. Our method lazily instantiates candidate parts based on their reduced cost, and on constraint

	Italian		Hungarian		Danish	
	BF	PPC	BF	PPC	BF	PPC
Sent./sec. relative to BF	100%	**760%**	100%	**380%**	100%	**390%**
GPs Scored relative to BF	100%	**6%**	100%	**12%**	100%	**13%**
GPs Added relative to BF	100%	**5%**	100%	**7%**	100%	**7%**
Objective rel. to BF	100%	100%	100%	100%	100%	100%
% of Integer Solutions	98%	98%	97%	97%	97%	97%
Unlabeled Acc.	88%	88%	81%	81%	88%	88%

Table 1: Parse, Price and Cut (PPC) vs Brute Force (BF). Speed is the number of sentences per second, relative to the speed of BF. Objective, GPs scored and added are also relative to BF.

Constraints	GPArc+ ArcGP	OneGP+ NoGP	All
Sent./sec.	100%	1000%	1200%
% Integer	77%	9%	98%
Unlabeled Acc.	87%	85%	88%

(a) Italian

Constraints	GPArc+ ArcGP	OneGP+ NoGP	All
Sent./sec.	100%	162%	105%
% Integer	71%	3%	97%
Unlabeled Acc.	80%	77%	81%

(b) Hungarian

Table 2: Different outer bounds on the grandparent polytope, for nonprojective parsing of Italian and Danish.

violations. This allows us to discard a large fraction of parts during both scoring and optimization, leading to nearly 800% speed-ups without loss of accuracy and certificates. We also present a tighter bound on the grandparent polytope that is useful in its own right.

Delayed column and row generation is very useful when solving large LPs with off-the-shelf solvers. Given the multitude of work in NLP that uses LPs and ILPs in this way (Roth and Yih, 2004; Clarke and Lapata, 2007), we hope that our approach will prove itself useful for other applications. We stress that this approach can also be used when working with dynamic programs, as pointed out in section 4.5, and therefore also in the context of dual decomposition. This suggests even wider applicability, and usefulness in various structured prediction problems.

The underlying paradigm could also be useful for more approximate methods. In this paradigm, algorithms maintain an estimate of the cost of certain resources (duals), and use these estimates to guide search and the propose new structures. For example, a local-search based dependency parser could estimate how contested certain tokens, or edges, are, and then use these estimates to choose better next proposals. The notion of reduced cost can give guidance on what such estimates should look like.

Acknowledgements

This work was supported in part by the Center for Intelligent Information Retrieval and the University of Massachusetts and in part by UPenn NSF medium IIS-0803847. We gratefully acknowledge the support of Defense Advanced Research Projects Agency (DARPA) Machine Reading Program under Air Force Research Laboratory (AFRL) prime contract no. FA8750-09-C-0181. Any opinions, findings, and conclusion or recommendations expressed in this material are those of the authors and do not necessarily reflect the view of DARPA, AFRL, or the US government.

References

Ravindra K. Ahuja, Thomas L. Magnanti, and James B. Orlin. 1993. *Network Flows: Theory, Algorithms, and Applications*. Prentice Hall, 1 edition, February.

David Belanger, Alexandre Passos, Sebastian Riedel, and Andrew McCallum. 2012. A column generation approach to connecting regularization and map inference. In *Inferning: Interactions between Inference and Learning, ICML 2012 Workshop*.

Dimitri P. Bertsekas. 1999. *Nonlinear Programming*. Athena Scientific, 2nd edition, September.

Sabine Buchholz and Erwin Marsi. 2006. Conll-x shared task on multilingual dependency parsing. In *Proceedings of the 10th Conference on Computational Natural Language Learning (CoNLL' 06)*, CoNLL-X '06, pages 149–164, Stroudsburg, PA, USA. Association for Computational Linguistics.

Eugene Charniak and Mark Johnson. 2005. Coarse-to-fine n-best parsing and maxent discriminative reranking. In *Proceedings of the 43rd Annual Meeting of the Association for Computational Linguistics (ACL '05)*, pages 173–180.

James Clarke and Mirella Lapata. 2007. Modelling compression with discourse constraints. In *Proceedings of the 2007 Joint Conference on Empirical Methods in Natural Language Processing and Computational Natural Language Learning (EMNLP-CoNLL '07)*, pages 1–11.

A. Culotta, M. Wick, R. Hall, and A. McCallum. 2007. First-order probabilistic models for coreference resolution. In *Joint Human Language Technology Conference/Annual Meeting of the North American Chapter of the Association for Computational Linguistics (HLT-NAACL '07)*, pages 81–88.

Peter Dienes, Alexander Koller, and Marco Kuhlmann. 2003. Statistical a-star dependency parsing. In *Proceedings of the workshop on Prospects and Advances of the Syntax/Semantics Interface, Nancy, 2003, pp.85-89.*

P.C. Gilmore and R.E. Gomory. 1961. A linear programming approach to the cutting-stock problem. *Operations research*, pages 849–859.

Dan Klein and Christopher D. Manning. 2003. A* parsing: Fast exact viterbi parse selection. In *Proceedings of the 41st Annual Meeting of the Association for Computational Linguistics (ACL '03)*, pages 119–126.

Terry Koo and Michael Collins. 2010. Efficient third-order dependency parsers. In *Proceedings of the 48th Annual Meeting of the Association for Computational Linguistics (ACL '11)*.

Terry Koo, Alexander M. Rush, Michael Collins, Tommi Jaakkola, and David Sontag. 2010. Dual decomposition for parsing with nonprojective head automata. In *Proceedings of the Conference on Empirical methods in natural language processing (EMNLP '10)*.

Sandra Kübler, Ryan T. McDonald, and Joakim Nivre. 2009. *Dependency Parsing*. Synthesis Lectures on Human Language Technologies. Morgan & Claypool Publishers.

Marco Lübbecke and Jacques Desrosiers. 2004. Selected topics in column generation. *Operations Research*, 53:1007–1023.

R. Kipp Martin, Ronald L. Rardin, and Brian A. Campbell. 1990. Polyhedral characterization of discrete dynamic programming. *Oper. Res.*, 38(1):127–138, February.

André F. T. Martins, Noah A. Smith, and Eric P. Xing. 2009. Concise integer linear programming formulations for dependency parsing. In *Proceedings of the Joint Conference of the 47th Annual Meeting of the ACL and the 4th International Joint Conference on Natural Language Processing of the AFNLP (ACL '09)*, pages 342–350, Morristown, NJ, USA. Association for Computational Linguistics.

André F. T. Martins, Noah A. Smith, Pedro M. Q. Aguiar, and Mário A. T. Figueiredo. 2011. Dual decomposition with many overlapping components. In *Proceedings of the Conference on Empirical methods in natural language processing (EMNLP '11)*, EMNLP '11, pages 238–249, Stroudsburg, PA, USA. Association for Computational Linguistics.

R. McDonald and F. Pereira. 2006. Online learning of approximate dependency parsing algorithms. In *Proceedings of the 11th Conference of the European Chapter of the ACL (EACL '06)*, pages 81–88.

R. McDonald, K. Crammer, and F. Pereira. 2005a. Online large-margin training of dependency parsers. In *Proceedings of the 43rd Annual Meeting of the Association for Computational Linguistics (ACL '05)*, pages 91–98.

R. McDonald, F. Pereira, K. Ribarov, and J. Hajic. 2005b. Non-projective dependency parsing using spanning tree algorithms. In *HLT-EMNLP, 2005*.

Mathias Niepert. 2010. A delayed column generation strategy for exact k-bounded map inference in markov logic networks. In *Proceedings of the 26th Annual Conference on Uncertainty in AI (UAI '10)*, pages 384–391, Corvallis, Oregon. AUAI Press.

J. Nivre, J. Hall, S. Kubler, R. McDonald, J. Nilsson, S. Riedel, and D. Yuret. 2007. The conll 2007 shared task on dependency parsing. In *Conference on Empirical Methods in Natural Language Processing and Natural Language Learning*, pages 915—932.

Hoifung Poon and Pedro Domingos. 2007. Joint inference in information extraction. In *Proceedings of the 22nd AAAI Conference on Artificial Intelligence (AAAI '07)*, pages 913–918.

Sebastian Riedel and James Clarke. 2006. Incremental integer linear programming for non-projective dependency parsing. In *Proceedings of the Conference on Empirical methods in natural language processing (EMNLP '06)*, pages 129–137.

Sebastian Riedel and David A. Smith. 2010. Relaxed marginal inference and its application to dependency parsing. In *Joint Human Language Technology Conference/Annual Meeting of the North American Chapter of the Association for Computational Linguistics (HLT-NAACL '10)*, pages 760–768, Los Angeles, California, June. Association for Computational Linguistics.

Sebastian Riedel. 2008. Improving the accuracy and efficiency of MAP inference for markov logic. In *Proceedings of the 24th Annual Conference on Uncertainty in AI (UAI '08)*, pages 468–475.

D. Roth and W. Yih. 2004. A linear programming formulation for global inference in natural language tasks. In *Proceedings of the 8th Conference on Computational Natural Language Learning (CoNLL' 04)*, pages 1–8.

Alexander Rush and Slav Petrov. 2012. Vine pruning for efficient multi-pass dependency parsing. In *Joint Human Language Technology Conference/Annual Meeting of the North American Chapter of the Association for Computational Linguistics (HLT-NAACL '12)*.

Alexander M. Rush, David Sontag, Michael Collins, and Tommi Jaakkola. 2010. On dual decomposition and linear programming relaxations for natural language processing. In *Proceedings of the Conference on Empirical methods in natural language processing (EMNLP '10)*.

David A. Smith and Jason Eisner. 2008. Dependency parsing by belief propagation. In *Proceedings of the Conference on Empirical Methods in Natural Language Processing (EMNLP)*, pages 145–156, Honolulu, October.

D. Sontag and T. Jaakkola. 2007. New outer bounds on the marginal polytope. In *Advances in Neural Information Processing Systems (NIPS '07)*, pages 1393–1400.

David Sontag, T. Meltzer, A. Globerson, T. Jaakkola, and Y. Weiss. 2008. Tightening LP relaxations for MAP using message passing. In *Proceedings of the 24th Annual Conference on Uncertainty in AI (UAI '08)*.

Roy W. Tromble and Jason Eisner. 2006. A fast finite-state relaxation method for enforcing global constraints on sequence decoding. In *Joint Human Language Technology Conference/Annual Meeting of the North American Chapter of the Association for Computational Linguistics (HLT-NAACL '06)*, pages 423–430.

Domain Adaptation for Coreference Resolution: An Adaptive Ensemble Approach

Jian Bo Yang[†‡*], **Qi Mao**[†], **Qiao Liang Xiang**[†], **Ivor W. Tsang**[†],
Kian Ming A. Chai[§], **Hai Leong Chieu**[§]

[†] School of Computer Engineering, Nanyang Technological University, Singapore
[‡] Electrical and Computer Engineering Department, Duke University, USA
[§] DSO National Laboratories, Singapore

jianbo.yang@duke.edu, {qmao1,qlxiang,ivortsang}@ntu.edu.sg,
{ckianmin,chaileon}@dso.org.sg

Abstract

We propose an adaptive ensemble method to adapt coreference resolution across domains. This method has three features: (1) it can optimize for any user-specified objective measure; (2) it can make document-specific prediction rather than rely on a fixed base model or a fixed set of base models; (3) it can automatically adjust the active ensemble members during prediction. With simplification, this method can be used in the traditional within-domain case, while still retaining the above features. To the best of our knowledge, this work is the first to both (i) develop a domain adaptation algorithm for the coreference resolution problem and (ii) have the above features as an ensemble method. Empirically, we show the benefits of (i) on the six domains of the ACE 2005 data set in domain adaptation setting, and of (ii) on both the MUC-6 and the ACE 2005 data sets in within-domain setting.

1 Introduction

Coreference resolution is a fundamental component of natural language processing (NLP) and has been widely applied in other NLP tasks (Stoyanov et al., 2010). It gathers together noun phrases (mentions) that refer to the same real-world entity (Ng and Cardie, 2002). In the past decade, several coreference resolution systems have been proposed, e.g., (Ng and Cardie, 2002), (Denis and Baldridge, 2007) and (Stoyanov et al., 2010). All of these focus on the within-domain case — to use the labeled documents from a domain to predict on the unlabeled documents in the same domain. However, in practice, there is usually limited labeled data in a specific domain of interest, while there may be plenty of labeled data in other related domains. Effective use of data from the other domains for predicting in the domain of interest is therefore an important strategy in NLP. This is called domain adaptation, and, in this context, the former domains is called the *source domains*, while the latter domain is called the *target domain* (Blitzer et al., 2006; Jiang and Zhai, 2007).

Based on the type of the knowledge to be transferred to the target domain, domain adaptation learning can be categorized as instance-based method, feature-based method, parameter-based method or relational-knowledge-based method (Pan and Yang, 2010). Previously, domain adaptation learning has been successfully used in other NLP tasks such as relation extraction (Jiang, 2009) and POS tagging (Jiang and Zhai, 2007), semantic detection (Tan et al., 2008), name entity recognition (Guo et al., 2009) and entity type classification (Jiang and Zhai, 2007). However, to the best of our knowledge, it has yet to be explored for coreference resolution.

In this paper, we propose an adaptive ensemble method to adapt coreference resolution across domains. This proposed method can be categorized as both feature-based and parameter-based domain adaptation learning methods. It has three main steps: *ensemble creation*, *cross-domain knowledge learning* and *decision inference*. The first step creates the ensemble by collecting a set of base models, which can be any individual methods with various features/instances/parameters settings. The second step analyzes the collected base models from vari-

[*] The work is done during postdoc in NTU, Singapore.

ous domains and learns the cross-domain knowledge between each target domain and the source domain. The third step infers the final decision in the target domain based on all ensemble results.

In addition to domain adaptation, the proposed adaptive ensemble method has the following features that are absent in the other ensemble methods. First, it can optimize any *user-specified objective measure* without using a separate development set. Second, it can provide *document-specific prediction* instead of relying on a fixed base model or a fixed set of base models for all documents. Third, it can automatically *adjust the active ensemble members* in decision inference so that underperforming base models are filtered out. The proposed method can also be used in the traditional within-domain problem with some simplifications.

We conduct experiments for coreference resolution under both the within-domain setting and the domain-adaptation setting. In the within-domain setting, we compare the proposed adaptive ensemble method with the mention-pair methods and other ensemble methods on the MUC-6 and ACE 2005 corpora. The results show that the proposed adaptive ensemble method consistently outperforms these baselines. In the domain adaptation setting, we use the ACE 2005 corpora to create six domain adaptation tasks to evaluate the effectiveness of our domain adaptation learning. The results show that our method outperforms baselines that do not use domain adaptation.

The paper is organized as follows. Section 2 reviews some existing ensemble methods for coreference resolution. Section 3 presents the proposed adaptive ensemble method for domain adaptation problems. Section 4 presents a special case of the proposed method for the within-domain setting. Section 5 presents the experiments under both the within-domain and the domain adaptation settings. We conclude and discuss future work in Section 6.

2 Existing Ensemble Methods

Many ensemble methods have been proposed in the machine learning literature, e.g., bagging (Breiman, 1996), boosting (Freund and Schapire, 1996), random forest (Breiman, 2001) and mixture models (Bishop, 2007). Some of them have been successfully used in coreference resolution (Pang and Fan, 2009; Munson et al., 2005; Rahman and Ng, 2011a). However, these methods only focus on the within-domain setting.

All these methods comprise of two steps: ensemble creation and decision inference. Ng and Cardie (2003) and Vemulapalli et al. (2009) applied the bagging and boosting techniques on the documents to create the ensemble. Recently, Rahman and Ng (2011a) further enriched the ensemble by considering various feature sets and learning models. Specifically, three types of feature sets (conventional, lexical and combined) and three learning algorithms (mention-pair model, mention-ranking model and the clustering-ranking model) are employed. In decision inference, these methods used voting or averaging to get the final prediction. Rahman and Ng (2011a) proposed four voting strategies for prediction: applying best Per-NP-Type model, antecedent-based voting, cluster-based voting and weighted clustering-based voting. Although their approaches achieved promising results in their end-to-end systems, these do not consider the user-specific performance measure during the ensemble learning.

Another branch of ensemble methods uses model selection (Munson et al., 2005; Ng, 2005), similar to the conventional model selection method for generic parameter-tuning. The method of (Munson et al., 2005) first collects a large family of base models. Then, a separate tuning set with ground truth is used to evaluate each base model's performance. Finally, an iterative approach is used to select the best performed base models to form the ensemble. Like other methods, this method uses the average strategy in decision inference. Similarly, the method of (Ng, 2005) ranks base models according to their performance on separate tuning set, and then uses the highest-ranked base model for predicting on test documents. These methods require a separate set of labeled documents to assess the generalization performance.

3 Adaptive Ensemble Method

In this section, we give our adaptive ensemble method for domain adaptation for coreference resolution. We first introduce some notations.

For a corpus of N documents, document $\mathcal{D}_i$

is the ith document, and it contains n_i mentions $\mathbf{m}_i = (m_i^1, \ldots, m_i^{n_i})$ with the ordering of each mention as they appear in the document. The index set of all mention pairs in $\mathcal{D}_i$ is $\mathcal{E}_i = \{(a,b) \mid 1 \leq a < b \leq n_i\}$. The transpose of vector x is x'. The performance measure function for document $\mathcal{D}$ is $\Lambda(g(\mathcal{D}); f(\mathcal{D}))$, where $g(\mathcal{D})$ and $f(\mathcal{D})$ represent the coreference ground-truth and prediction by model f on document $\mathcal{D}$ respectively. In coreference resolution, typical performance measure functions include MUC (Vilain et al., 1995), Rand index (Rand, 1971), B-CUBED (Bagga and Baldwin, 1998) and CEAF (Luo, 2005). In this paper, Λ can either be used as part of an objective function in learning or as an evaluation measure for assessing the performance of a coreference system.

We consider the typical domain adaptation problem, which has one target domain t and p ($p \geq 1$) source domains $s_1, \ldots, s_p$. The target domain contains $N^{(t)}$ labeled documents and M unlabeled documents, while source domains contain $N^{(s_1)}, \ldots, N^{(s_p)}$ labeled documents. Unlabeled data in the source domains are not used. We use $\mathcal{D}_i^{(v)}$ for the ith document in domain v.

3.1 Ensemble Creation

Mention-pair methods have been widely-used for coreference resolution due to their efficiency and effectiveness, and they have often been taken as base models in ensemble learning (Rahman and Ng, 2011a; Munson et al., 2005). We adopt a similar approach by using the standard mention-pair method (Soon et al., 2001; Ng and Cardie, 2002) with various parameters to form the ensemble, though our framework can incorporate other coreference methods in the ensemble. Mention-pair methods usually comprise of two steps. The first step classifies every mention pair into either coreference or non-coreference with a confidence between 0 and 1. The second step partitions the set of mentions into clusters based on the confidence values, where mentions in each cluster are presumed to be the same underlying entity.

Classification We use Soon's approach (Soon et al., 2001) to select a portion of mention pairs to train a binary classifier because this has better generalization (Soon et al., 2001). The positive mention pairs are the anaphoric mention m_i^b ($b = 2, \ldots, n_i$) paired with its closest antecedent mention m_i^a ($a < b$), while the negative mention pairs are the mention m_i^b paired with each of the intervening mentions $m_i^{a+1}, m_i^{a+2}, \ldots, m_i^{b-1}$. Following (Rahman and Ng, 2011a), our binary classifier is SVM with the regularization parameter C. The classifier is trained with the software Liblinear (Fan et al., 2008), which is also used to give probabilistic binary predictions.

Clustering We adopt closest-first clustering (Soon et al., 2001) and best-first clustering (Ng and Cardie, 2002) to determine whether a mention pair is coreferent. For each mention, the closest-first method (or best-first method) links it to the the closest (or the best) preceding mention if the confidence value (obtained from the first step) of this mention pair is above a specified threshold t.

Features For each mention pair, we use the $d = 39$ features proposed by Rahman and Ng (2011b) to represent it. These features can be extracted using the Reconcile software (Stoyanov et al., 2010). We use $\hat{\phi}_{a,b} \in R^d$ to represent the features of a mention pair (m^a, m^b). With this feature set, we found that the linear kernel is insufficient to fit the training data. However, using an rbf kernel would be too computationally expensive. Hence, we augment $\hat{\phi}_{a,b}$ with a $\hat{d}$-dimensional feature vector $[\psi^1 \ \cdots \ \psi^{\hat{d}}]$ to give a new feature vector

$$\phi_{a,b} = [\hat{\phi}_{a,b} \ \psi^1 \ \cdots \ \psi^{\hat{d}}], \tag{1}$$

where the $\hat{d}$ augmented features $[\psi^1 \ \cdots \ \psi^{\hat{d}}]$ are determined by

$$\psi^j = \exp(-\frac{\|\hat{\phi}_{a,b} - c^j\|^2}{d}), \forall j = 1, \ldots, \hat{d}. \tag{2}$$

Herein, $c^1, \ldots, c^{\hat{d}}$ are the $\hat{d}$ centroids of the randomly-selected subset $\mathcal{C}$ from all labeled mention pairs $\{\hat{\phi}_{a,b} \mid (a,b) \in \mathcal{E}_1, \ldots, \mathcal{E}_N\}$. In our experiments, we use the k-means algorithm to obtain the centroids of $\mathcal{C}$.

Ensemble For domain v, we create a domain-specified ensemble $\mathcal{F}^{(v)} = \{f^1, \ldots, f^\ell\}$ of ℓ base models by including the closest-first and best-first mention-pair methods with the different C and t values. If multiple domains are provided, we gather all the domain-specific ensembles into a grand ensemble $\mathcal{F} = \mathcal{F}^{(s_1)} \cup \cdots \mathcal{F}^{(s_p)} \cup \mathcal{F}^{(t)}$.

3.2 Cross-domain Knowledge Learning

Generally, the feature distributions are different in different domains. Therefore, effective domain adaptation requires using some knowledge of cross-domain similarity. We now propose an approach to learn the parametric-distances between the documents in source and target domains to characterize this cross-domain knowledge.

Distances between documents A document $\mathcal{D}_i$ is represented by the sum of its new mention-pair features (Yu and Joachims, 2009; Finley and Joachims, 2005):

$$\Phi(\mathcal{D}_i) = \sum_{(a,b)\in\mathcal{E}_i} \phi_{a,b}. \tag{3}$$

The distance between a source labeled document $\mathcal{D}_i^{(s_u)}$ in domain s_u and a target labeled document $\mathcal{D}_j^{(t)}$ is parameterized as

$$\text{Dist}(\mathcal{D}_i^{(s_u)}, \mathcal{D}_j^{(t)}; \boldsymbol{\mu}) = \boldsymbol{\mu}'\Delta(\mathcal{D}_i^{(s_u)}, \mathcal{D}_j^{(t)}), \tag{4}$$

where vector $\boldsymbol{\mu} \in \mathbb{R}^{d+\hat{d}}$ is to be learned, and vector function $\Delta(\mathcal{D}_i^{(s_u)}, \mathcal{D}_j^{(t)}) \in \mathbb{R}^{d+\hat{d}}$ is the Euclidean distance vector between two documents given by

$$\Delta(\mathcal{D}_i^{(s_u)}, \mathcal{D}_j^{(t)}) = (\Phi(\mathcal{D}_i^{(s_u)}) - \Phi(\mathcal{D}_j^{(t)})) \odot (\Phi(\mathcal{D}_i^{(s_u)}) - \Phi(\mathcal{D}_j^{(t)})). \tag{5}$$

The operator $\odot$ is the element-wise product. Distance (4) is actually the Mahanalobis distance (Yang and Jin, 2006) with the scaling of features:

$$(\Phi(\mathcal{D}_i^{(s_u)}) - \Phi(\mathcal{D}_j^{(t)}))'W(\Phi(\mathcal{D}_i^{(s_u)}) - \Phi(\mathcal{D}_j^{(t)})),$$

where W is a diagonal matrix with diagonal entries $\boldsymbol{\mu}$. Matrix W is diagonal to reduce computation cost and to increase statistical confidence in estimation when there is limited target labeled data (as is typically the case in domain adaptation).

That $\boldsymbol{\mu}$ is the vector of diagonal entries in W requires that each entry in $\boldsymbol{\mu}$ is non-negative. If the lth entry of $\boldsymbol{\mu}$ is non-zero, then the lth feature in $\phi_{a,b}$ contribute towards (4). To ensure that at least B features are used, we also constrain that each entry in $\boldsymbol{\mu}$ is not more than unity and that $\mathbf{1}'\boldsymbol{\mu} \geq B$.

Matching best base models For each labeled document $\mathcal{D}_j^{(v)}$ in domain v, we identify the best performing base model $f_j^{(v)^*}$ in $\mathcal{F}^{(v)}$ with

$$f_j^{(v)^*} = \arg\max_{f\in\mathcal{F}^{(v)}} \Lambda(g(\mathcal{D}_j^{(v)}); f(\mathcal{D}_j^{(v)})), \tag{6}$$

where $\Lambda(\cdot\,;\,\cdot)$ is the the performance objective function to be instantiated in Section 3.3.

Then, for each source domain s_u and document $\mathcal{D}_j^{(t)}$ in the target domain, we find the set $\mathcal{I}(\mathcal{D}_j^{(t)}; s_u)$ of the documents in domain s_u that have the same best performing base model as that for $\mathcal{D}_j^{(t)}$:

$$\mathcal{I}(\mathcal{D}_j^{(t)}; s_u) = \{\mathcal{D}_i^{(s_u)} \mid f_i^{(s_u)^*} = f_j^{(t)^*}, \; i = 1, \ldots, N^{(s_u)}\}. \tag{7}$$

The key idea in $\mathcal{I}(\mathcal{D}_j^{(t)}; s_u)$ is to select documents in a source domain s_u that are similar to document $D_j^{(t)}$ in the sense that they have the same best performing base model under a specific Λ. This ensures that optimization step (to be described next) is targeted towards Λ and not confounded by document pairs that should be disimilar anyway.

Optimization We determine the vector $\boldsymbol{\mu}$ by minimizing the parametric distance (4) between all target labeled documents and their corresponding source labeled document identified in the previous step. That is,

$$\min_{\boldsymbol{\mu}} \boldsymbol{\mu}' \sum_{j=1}^{N^{(t)}} \sum_{\mathcal{D}_i^{(s_u)}\in\mathcal{I}(\mathcal{D}_j^{(t)};s_u)} \Delta(\mathcal{D}_i^{(s_u)}, \mathcal{D}_j^{(t)}). \tag{8}$$

The solution $\boldsymbol{\mu}$ to this linear programming problem can be regarded as the cross-domain knowledge between source domain s_u and the target domain t. Repeating for every source domain s_u, $u = 1, \ldots, p$, gives the cross-domain knowledge between every source domain and the target domain.

The above three-steps procedure selects the effective features for each pair of source and target domains. Generally, the results of feature selection vary for different pairs of source and target domains, due to the diversities of the feature distributions in different domains.

3.3 Decision Inference

After ensemble creation and cross-domain knowledge learning, we need to provide the coreference result on an unseen document in the target domain based on the results of all the members in $\mathcal{F}$. Unlike the previous methods using the voting/average or their variants (Pang and Fan, 2009; Munson et al., 2005; Rahman and Ng, 2011a), we propose the following nearest neighbor based approach.

Given the grand ensemble $\mathcal{F}$ and all labeled documents, the task is to predict on the target unlabeled document $\mathcal{D}_j^{(t)}, j = 1, \ldots, M$. The idea of the proposed method is to first find the k most similar documents $\mathcal{N}(\mathcal{D}_j^{(t)})$ from all labeled documents for document $\mathcal{D}_j^{(t)}$. Then, we choose the base model that performs best on the documents in $\mathcal{N}(\mathcal{D}_j^{(t)})$ as the method $f_j^{(t)^*}$ for document $\mathcal{D}_j^{(t)}$.

Firstly, we employ the parametric-distance (4) to measure the similarity between any labeled document $\mathcal{D}_i^{(v)}, \forall v, i$, from all source and target domains, and the target unlabeled document $\mathcal{D}_j^{(t)}$. Here, the cross-domain knowledge $\boldsymbol{\mu}$ in (4) has already been determined by the optimization (8) in Section 3.2.

Secondly, based on the computed distance values, we select k nearest neighbor documents for the target unlabeled document $\mathcal{D}_j^{(t)}$ from all labeled documents $\mathcal{D}_i^{(v)}, \forall v, i$. These k nearest neighbor documents for document $\mathcal{D}_j^{(t)}$ make up the set $\mathcal{N}(\mathcal{D}_j^{(t)})$.

Thirdly, the optimal base model for the unlabeled document $\mathcal{D}_j^{(t)}$ prediction is chosen by

$$f_j^{(t)^*} = \arg \max_{\mathcal{D}_p \in \mathcal{N}(\mathcal{D}_j^{(t)}),\, f \in \mathcal{F}} \Lambda(g(\mathcal{D}_p); f(\mathcal{D}_p)). \quad (9)$$

We can instantiate the performance objective function $\Lambda(g(\cdot); f(\cdot))$ in expressions (6) and (9) to be any coreference resolution measures, such as MUC, Rand index, B-CUBED and CEAF. We have not known of other (ensemble) coreference resolution methods that optimize for these measures. This absence is possibly due to their complex discrete and non-convex properties.

3.4 Discussion

The above proposed adaptive ensemble approach incorporates the domain adaptation knowledge during (a) the identification of similar documents between different domains and (b) the determination of active ensemble members. Beside these, it has the following features over other (ensemble) coreference methods: (i) It can optimize any user-specified objective measure via (6) and (9). An intuitive recommendation is to directly optimize for an objective function that matches the evaluation measure. (ii) It can make document-specific decisions, as expressions (4) and (9) deal with each testing document separately. (iii) The prediction on the testing document $\mathcal{D}_j^{(t)}$ is not based on all members in $\mathcal{F}$ but only on the active ensemble members $\mathcal{N}(\mathcal{D}_j^{(t)})$. This can filter out some potentially unsuitable base models for document $\mathcal{D}_j^{(t)}$. Moreover, the active ensemble members $\mathcal{N}(\mathcal{D}_j^{(t)})$ is dynamically adjusted for each test document.

For computational cost, the majority is by ensemble creation, since a large number of base models are usually used. This is common among all ensemble methods. In contrast, the costs in (4) and (9) are trivial as both are at the document level. The cost of generating centroids in (2) can also be high if the size of $\mathcal{C}$ is more than ten thousand, but this is still negligible compared to the cost of ensemble creation.

4 Special Case: Within-domain Setting

The adaptive ensemble method presented in Section 3 is for the domain adaptation setting. However, it is possible to simplify it for the special case of within-domain setting. In the within-domain setting, the adaptive ensemble method only has ensemble creation and decision inference steps.

In the ensemble creation step, we still use the closest-first and best-first mention-pair methods with various parameters to create the ensemble. Unlike the domain adaptation setting, here we can only use the labeled documents in the target domain to create the ensemble $\mathcal{F}^{(t)}$. Therefore, the size of ensemble here is reduced by p times compared to the domain adaptation setting.

In the decision inference step, we directly use the Euclidean distance $\Delta(\mathcal{D}_i^{(t)}, \mathcal{D}_j^{(t)})$ in (5) for the labeled document $\mathcal{D}_i^{(t)}, i = 1, \ldots, N^{(t)}$ and unlabeled document $\mathcal{D}_j^{(t)}, j = 1, \ldots, M$. Based on these distance values, we similarly select k nearest neighbor documents $\mathcal{N}(\mathcal{D}_j^{(t)})$ for document $\mathcal{D}_j^{(t)}$, and then determine the final method $f_j^{(t)*}$ for document $\mathcal{D}_j^{(t)}$ by (9) but with $\mathcal{F}$ replaced by $\mathcal{F}^{(t)}$.

5 Experiments

We test the proposed adaptive method and several baselines under both the within-domain and the domain adaptation settings on the MUC-6 and ACE 2005 corpora. MUC-6 contains 60 documents. ACE 2005 contains 599 documents from six different domains: Newswire (NW), Broadcast News (BN), Broadcast Conversations (BC), Webblog (WL), Usenet (UN), and Conversational Telephone Speech (CTS). In all our experiments, we use two popular performance measures, B-CUBED F-measure (Bagga and Baldwin, 1998) and CEAF F-measure (Luo, 2005) [1], to evaluate the coreference resolution result. Since the focus of the paper is to investigate the effectiveness of coreference resolution methods, we use the *gold standard mentions* in all experiments.

For the proposed method, the ensemble $\mathcal{F}^{(v)}$ in every domain v has 208 members totally. They are created by the closest-first and the best-first mention-pair methods using SVM trained with parameter C taking values

$$C \in [0.001, 0.01, 0.1, 1, 10, 100, 1000, 1000] \quad (10)$$

and using clustering with the threshold parameters t taking values

$$t \in [0.2, 0.25, 0.3, 0.34, 0.38, 0.4, 0.42, 0.44, 0.46, 0.48, 0.5, 0.6, 0.7]. \quad (11)$$

The size of the selected subset $\mathcal{C}$ is fixed to 2000, and the number of centroids is determined by the validation procedure from four possible values $[10, 20, 30, 40]$. We use k-means algorithm to compute the centroids. Due to the randomness of subset $\mathcal{C}$ and k-means algorithm, we run the proposed method 5 times and report the average results. For the number of nearest neighbor k, we report three results, each for $k \in \{1, 3, 5\}$.

[1] More exactly, we use the widely used ϕ_3-CEAF F-measure.

Table 1: The settings in the experiments under within-domain setting on MUC-6 and ACE 2005 corpora. $N^{(t)}$ and $M^{(t)}$ and Total are the numbers of training, testing and all documents respectively.

Domain	$N^{(t)}$	$M^{(t)}$	Total
MUC-6	30	30	60
BC	48	12	60
BN	181	45	226
CTS	31	8	39
NW	85	21	106
UN	39	10	49
WL	95	24	119

5.1 Within-domain Setting

We conduct the experiment under the within-domain setting on seven tasks, with the per-domain setting shown in Table 1. The validation set is created by further splitting training data into validation training and validation testing sets with the ratio of $\frac{N^{(t)}}{M^{(t)}}$, where $N^{(t)}$ and $M^{(t)}$ are given in Table 1. In this experiment, we attempt to study the following three things. First, we investigate whether the proposed ensemble method is better than the tuned mention-pair methods and other ensemble methods. Second, we investigate the optimal number of active ensemble members. Third, we investigate the impact to the performance of the coreference system, when different objective measures are used with different evaluation measures.

For the proposed ensemble method, we experimented with nearest neighbor set of sizes $k = 1, 3, 5$ paired with objective function Λ in (9) set to Rand Index, CEAF or B-CUBED. For baselines, the following four are used:

- Two mention-pair baselines. Two baselines are the closest-first and the best-first mention-pair methods with the tuned parameters C and t. In the tuning process, the ranges of C and t are specified in (10) and (11) respectively. These two mention-pair methods are named as S_c and S_b for short.

- Two existing ensemble baselines. The other two baselines are the ensemble methods using the voting procedure in decision inference.

Table 2: B-CUBED F-measure results by all methods under within-domain setting on MUC-6 and ACE 2005 corpora.

	Baselines				Λ = Rand			Λ = CEAF			Λ = B-CUBED		
	S_c	S_b	E_m	E_c	k=1	3	5	k=1	3	5	k=1	3	5
MUC-6	66.1	66.1	61.9	57.1	67.6	67.3	68.5	65.2	64.1	65.5	**68.7**	66.7	67.5
BC	64.1	65.1	34.2	24.8	65.5	65.4	65.7	65.9	65.5	62.9	**66.5**	66.1	66.0
BN	75.9	74.8	57.7	48.0	75.7	75.1	74.9	76.3	75.9	75.3	76.4	76.3	**76.7**
CTS	71.0	65.1	39.6	31.5	70.6	69.3	68.3	71.3	69.9	70.4	**71.7**	70.6	69.1
NW	74.6	74.4	45.6	34.1	74.3	74.8	72.9	73.2	71.4	70.1	**75.0**	74.6	73.7
UN	69.5	70.2	44.1	27.4	70.4	69.9	69.3	69.6	67.6	66.0	70.3	**71.4**	70.3
WL	73.8	75.4	69.8	58.5	75.5	74.6	73.9	75.5	73.0	73.4	**76.2**	75.5	75.6
Average	70.7	70.2	50.4	40.2	71.4	70.9	70.5	71.0	69.6	69.1	**72.1**	71.6	71.3

These two baselines use the same ensemble as the proposed method for fair comparison. In decision inference, these two baselines use the mention-based voting and cluster-based voting respectively, as proposed in (Rahman and Ng, 2011a). In these two baselines, all members in the ensemble participate the voting process. These two ensemble baselines are named as E_m and E_c for short.

Tables 2 and 3 show the experiment results using B-CUBED and CEAF as the evaluation measures respectively. The best result for each of the seven tasks is highlighted in bold. The last rows of the tables show the average performance value among all seven tasks.

From the results, we observe that the proposed ensemble method with objective function matching the evaluation measure and with $k = 1$ generally performs best among all methods and all tasks. Surprisingly, the common ensemble method with mention-based voting E_m and cluster-based voting E_c strategies do not perform well. The plausible reason is the current ensemble may incorporate some bad base models due to inappropriate C and t values, which would undermine the voting result. Nevertheless, it is difficult to judge the quality of the ensemble members in advance. Therefore, this validates the importance of choosing an active set of ensemble members in decision inference. The better performance of the proposed method over the mention-pair baselines S_c and S_b is probably because of the document-specific decision. This is reasonable, as different base models in the ensemble would be good at predicting the different documents. For the proposed ensemble method with various configurations, we observe using an objective function that matches the evaluation measures is generally better. An exception is the MUC-6 and BN tasks in CEAF F-measure. We also observe that the ensemble method with $k = 1$ is generally better than that with the larger k, except the BN and UN tasks in B-CUBED F-measure. This suggests that the fewer the active ensemble members the better the generalization performance. Following (Rahman and Ng, 2011a), we also conduct the Student's t-test, and the results show that the proposed method with the objective function matching the evaluation measure and with $k = 1$ is significantly better than the best baseline. In contrast, the two baseline ensemble methods that use voting are significantly worse than the best baseline. The significance level 0.05.

5.2 Domain-adaptation Setting

We employ ACE 2005 corpora to simulate the domain adaptation settings in experiments. Specifically, we create six domain adaptation tasks, BC, BN, CTS, NW, UN, WL in total. Each task has one target domain and five source domains. For example, in the task UN, the target domain is UN while the other five source domains are BC, BN, CTS, NW and WL. The number of labeled documents in each domain is as the same as in Table 1, except when that domain is the target domain, in which case we use only five labeled documents. The number of test

Table 3: CEAF F-measure results by all methods under within-domain setting on MUC-6 and ACE 2005 corpora.

	Baselines				Λ = Rand			Λ = B-CUBED			Λ = CEAF		
	S_c	S_b	E_m	E_c	k=1	3	5	k=1	3	5	k=1	3	5
MUC-6	62.6	62.5	62.7	57.5	62.0	60.6	61.0	**64.5**	62.7	63.8	63.1	58.7	59.2
BC	58.8	56.5	36.6	26.6	56.7	57.1	57.0	58.3	58.8	57.2	**59.3**	59.2	58.4
BN	67.9	66.5	55.1	44.7	69.4	69.4	69.9	69.8	**70.2**	69.6	69.5	69.0	68.7
CTS	61.0	60.7	38.6	31.5	67.1	66.9	63.6	68.1	68.4	68.2	**68.5**	67.6	67.7
NW	66.9	66.4	41.1	31.2	68.4	68.0	64.6	69.2	68.4	66.4	**69.3**	66.1	66.7
UN	62.5	63.5	46.2	28.9	62.9	61.8	60.9	62.2	63.7	62.9	**63.9**	61.5	60.4
WL	69.7	70.3	63.5	54.3	70.7	70.2	72.5	71.5	71.4	72.3	**72.4**	69.4	70.0
Average	64.2	63.8	49.1	39.2	65.3	64.9	64.2	66.2	66.2	65.8	**66.6**	64.5	64.5

(or unlabeled) documents in the target document is also the same as in Table 1. The validation set is created similarly as in the experiment under within-domain setting.

For the proposed ensemble method, we heuristically determine the parameter B in $\boldsymbol{\mu}$ to be the number of non-zero elements in Γ, where

$$\Gamma = \sum_{j=1}^{N^{(t)}} \sum_{\mathcal{D}_i^{(s_u)} \in \mathcal{I}(\mathcal{D}_j^{(t)};s_u)} \Delta(\mathcal{D}_i^{(s_u)}, \mathcal{D}_j^{(t)}).$$

Making use of the conclusion in the experiments for the within-domain setting, we fix the optimized measure to be the final performance measure in (9). We compare with the following five baselines.

- Two mention-pair baselines in within-domain setting. Two baselines are same as S_c and S_b in the experiments under within-domain settings, except that the labeled training documents are reduced to 5.

- Three proposed adaptive ensemble methods without cross-domain knowledge learning. These three baselines uses neighborhood sizes $k = 1, 3, 5$ with the grand ensemble $\mathcal{F}$ rather than the target domain ensemble $\mathcal{F}^{(t)}$. In another words, these three baselines are the same as the proposed method, but with $\boldsymbol{\mu} = \mathbf{1}$.

Tables 4 and 5 show the experimental results in the domain adaptation settings using B-CUBED and CEAF as the final performance measures respectively. From the results, we can see that the proposed method with cross-domain knowledge generally outperforms all the five baselines. Among them, the best proposed domain adaptation method on average outperforms the best of S_c, S_b by 7.2% for B-CUBED F-measure and 3% for CEAF F-measure. The grand-ensemble baselines are also significantly better than the within-domain baselines. These results clearly illustrate the usefulness of making use of the labeled documents in the source domains. For the comparison between the proposed method with and without cross-domain knowledge learning, all tasks, except UN task in CEAF F-measure, show the superiority of the proposed method with cross-domain knowledge learning. Among them, except tasks BN and CTS in B-CUBED F-measure, the performance gains are among 1%—3% for all tasks in both measures. These results verify the necessity of cross-domain knowledge learning. For the comparison of the proposed method with different k, unlike the results in the within-domain setting, the results here show that choosing optimal k is task-dependent. The reason of this observation is not clear yet. It is plausible due to the increased uncertainties from multiple domains.

6 Conclusions and Future Work

In this paper, we proposed an adaptive ensemble method for coreference resolution under both within-domain and domain adaptation settings. The key advantage of the proposed method is incor-

Table 4: B-CUBED F-measure results by all methods under domain adaptation setting on ACE 2005 corpora, with Λ set to B-CUBED. The *within-domain* and *grand ensemble* methods are the baselines.

	Within-domain		Grand ensemble			Domain-adaptation		
	S_c	S_b	k=1	3	5	k=1	3	5
BC	58.0	65.1	65.0	67.1	67.0	67.5	**68.2**	67.7
BN	72.7	73.8	75.0	75.3	75.0	75.3	**75.4**	74.3
CTS	63.2	62.1	65.7	64.8	64.0	64.1	**65.8**	**65.8**
NW	54.9	54.6	73.6	73.1	74.2	73.0	74.4	**74.7**
UN	66.5	42.7	67.2	68.2	68.9	**69.7**	68.7	68.2
WL	68.6	73.2	73.0	72.6	73.4	**74.8**	74.5	73.6
Average	64.0	61.9	69.9	70.2	70.4	70.7	**71.2**	70.7

Table 5: CEAF F-measure results by all methods under domain adaptation setting on ACE 2005 corpora, with Λ set to CEAF. The *within-domain* and *grand ensemble* methods are the baselines.

	Within-domain		Grand ensemble			Domain-adaptation		
	S_c	S_b	k=1	3	5	k=1	3	5
BC	55.7	43.7	56.9	57.6	57.3	58.5	**58.8**	57.2
BN	65.8	67.2	65.9	64.1	65.8	63.9	62.7	**67.2**
CTS	56.0	51.0	56.6	54.6	53.7	**58.6**	57.4	55.3
NW	52.7	55.0	66.4	64.1	63.8	**69.4**	66.7	66.8
UN	64.0	39.1	63.6	63.7	**64.4**	64.3	62.9	62.7
WL	70.3	64.2	68.1	67.8	70.2	67.3	69.6	**72.0**
Average	60.7	53.4	62.9	62.0	62.5	**63.7**	63.0	63.5

porating the cross-domain knowledge to aid coreference resolution learning. This is useful when the labeled coreference labels are scarce. We also demonstrate that the proposed adaptive ensemble method can be readily applied to conventional coreference tasks without cross-domain knowledge learning. Compared with existing ensemble methods, the proposed method is simultaneously endowed with the following three distinctive features: optimizing any user-specified performance measure, making the document-specific prediction and automatically adjusting the active ensemble members. In the experiments under both within-domain settings and domain adaptation settings, the results evidence the effectiveness of the proposed cross-domain knowledge learning method, and also demonstrate the superiority of the proposed adaptive ensemble method over other baselines.

Currently, the proposed method relies on some limited target annotations. It would be interesting to consider the pure unsupervised tasks that have no any target annotations. Besides, to develop some better ways for document-level representation, e.g., incorporating the domain knowledge, also deserves our attentions. Similarly, to extend the diagonal Mahalanobis matrix to the general covariance matrix is also desirable. Last but not least, to find a more systematical way to determine the optimal k in the proposed method is also our possible future work.

Acknowledgments

This work is supported by DSO grant DSOCL10021.

References

Amit Bagga and Breck Baldwin. 1998. Entity-based cross-document coreferencing using the vector space model. In *Proceedings of the 36th Annual Meeting of the Association for Computational Linguistics and 17th International Conference on Computational Linguistics - Volume 1*, ACL'98, pages 79–85.

Christopher M. Bishop. 2007. *Pattern Recognition and Machine Learning (Information Science and Statistics)*. Springer, 1st ed. 2006. corr. 2nd printing edition, October.

John Blitzer, Ryan McDonald, and Fernando Pereira. 2006. Domain adaptation with structural correspondence learning. In *Proceedings of EMNLP*, pages 120–128.

Leo Breiman. 1996. Bagging predictors. *Machine Learning*, 24(2):123–140, August.

Leo Breiman. 2001. Random forests. *Machine Learning*, 45(1):5–32, October.

Pascal Denis and Jason Baldridge. 2007. Joint determination of anaphoricity and coreference resolution using integer programming. In *Proc HLT*, pages 236–243, Rochester, New York, April.

Rong-En Fan, Kai-Wei Chang, Cho-Jui Hsieh, Xiang-Rui Wang, and Chih-Jen Lin. 2008. LIBLINEAR: A library for large linear classification. *Journal of Machine Learning Research*, 9:1871–1874.

Thomas Finley and Thorsten Joachims. 2005. Supervised clustering with support vector machines. In *Proc. ICML*.

Yoav Freund and Robert E. Schapire. 1996. Experiments with a New Boosting Algorithm. In *Proc. ICML*, pages 148–156.

Honglei Guo, Huijia Zhu, Zhili Guo, Xiaoxun Zhang, Xian Wu, and Zhong Su. 2009. Domain adaptation with latent semantic association for named entity recognition. NAACL '09, pages 281–289.

Jing Jiang and ChengXiang Zhai. 2007. Instance weighting for domain adaptation in NLP. In *Proc. ACL*, pages 264–271, Prague, Czech Republic, June.

Jing Jiang. 2009. Multi-task transfer learning for weakly-supervised relation extraction. In *Proceedings of the Joint Conference of the 47th Annual Meeting of the ACL and the 4th International Joint Conference on Natural Language Processing of the AFNLP*, pages 1012–1020, Suntec, Singapore, August. Association for Computational Linguistics.

Xiaoqiang Luo. 2005. On coreference resolution performance metrics. In *Proceedings of the conference on Human Language Technology and Empirical Methods in Natural Language Processing*, HLT '05, pages 25–32.

Art Munson, Claire Cardie, and Rich Caruana. 2005. Optimizing to arbitrary NLP metrics using ensemble selection. In *Proc HLT and EMNLP*, pages 539–546.

Vincent Ng and Claire Cardie. 2002. Improving machine learning approaches to coreference resolution. In *Proc. ACL*, pages 104–111.

Vincent Ng and Claire Cardie. 2003. Weakly supervised natural language learning without redundant views. In *Proc. HLT-NAACL*.

Vincent Ng. 2005. Machine learning for coreference resolution: From local classification to global ranking. In *Proceedings of the ACL*, pages 157–164.

Sinno Jialin Pan and Qiang Yang. 2010. A survey on transfer learning. *IEEE Transactions on Knowledge and Data Engineering*, 22(10):1345–1359, October.

Wenbo Pang and Xiaozhong Fan. 2009. Chinese coreference resolution with ensemble learning. In *Proc. PACIIA*, pages 236–243.

Altaf Rahman and Vincent Ng. 2011a. Ensemble-based coreference resolution. In *Proceedings of IJCAI*, pages 1884–1889.

Altaf Rahman and Vincent Ng. 2011b. Narrowing the modeling gap: A cluster-ranking approach to coreference resolution. *JAIR*, 1:469–52.

William M. Rand. 1971. Objective criteria for the evaluation of clustering methods. *Journal of the American Statistical Association*, 66(336):pp. 846–850.

W. M. Soon, H. T. Ng, and D. C. Y. Lim. 2001. A machine learning approach to coreference resolution of noun phrases. *Computational Linguistics,*, pages 521–544.

Veselin Stoyanov, Claire Cardie, Nathan Gilbert, Ellen Riloff, David Buttler, and David Hysom. 2010. Coreference resolution with reconcile. In *Proc. ACL*, pages 156–161.

Songbo Tan, Yuefen Wang, Gaowei Wu, and Xueqi Cheng. 2008. Using unlabeled data to handle domain-transfer problem of semantic detection. In *Proceedings of the 2008 ACM symposium on Applied computing*, SAC '08, pages 896–903.

S. Vemulapalli, X. Luo, J.F.Pitrelli, and I. Zitouni. 2009. classifier combination applied to coreference resolution. In *NAACL HLT Student Rsearch Workshop*.

Marc Vilain, John Burger, John Aberdeen, Dennis Connolly, and Lynette Hirschman. 1995. A model-theoretic coreference scoring scheme. In *Proceedings of the 6th conference on Message understanding*, MUC6 '95, pages 45–52.

Liu Yang and Rong Jin. 2006. Distance Metric Learning: A Comprehensive Survey. Technical report, Department of Computer Science and Engineering, Michigan State University.

Chun-Nam John Yu and Thorsten Joachims. 2009. Learning structural SVMs with latent variables. In *Proc. ICML*, pages 1169–1176, New York, NY, USA.

Weakly Supervised Training of Semantic Parsers

Jayant Krishnamurthy
Carnegie Mellon University
5000 Forbes Avenue
Pittsburgh, PA 15213
jayantk@cs.cmu.edu

Tom M. Mitchell
Carnegie Mellon University
5000 Forbes Avenue
Pittsburgh, PA 15213
tom.mitchell@cmu.edu

Abstract

We present a method for training a semantic parser using only a knowledge base and an unlabeled text corpus, without any individually annotated sentences. Our key observation is that multiple forms of weak supervision can be combined to train an accurate semantic parser: *semantic supervision* from a knowledge base, and *syntactic supervision* from dependency-parsed sentences. We apply our approach to train a semantic parser that uses 77 relations from Freebase in its knowledge representation. This semantic parser extracts instances of binary relations with state-of-the-art accuracy, while simultaneously recovering much richer semantic structures, such as conjunctions of multiple relations with partially shared arguments. We demonstrate recovery of this richer structure by extracting logical forms from natural language queries against Freebase. On this task, the trained semantic parser achieves 80% precision and 56% recall, despite never having seen an annotated logical form.

1 Introduction

Semantic parsing converts natural language statements into logical forms in a meaning representation language. For example, the phrase "town in California" might be represented as $\lambda x.\textsc{city}(x) \wedge \textsc{locatedIn}(x, \textsc{California})$, where $\textsc{city}, \textsc{locatedIn}$ and $\textsc{California}$ are predicates and entities from a knowledge base. The expressivity and utility of semantic parsing is derived from this meaning representation, which is essentially a program that is directly executable by a computer. In this sense, broad coverage semantic parsing is the goal of natural language understanding.

Unfortunately, due to data annotation constraints, modern semantic parsers only operate in narrow domains. The best performing semantic parsers are trained using extensive manual annotation: typically, a number of sentences must be annotated with their desired logical form. Although other forms of supervision exist (Clarke et al., 2010; Liang et al., 2011), these methods similarly require annotations for individual sentences. More automated training methods are required to produce semantic parsers with richer meaning representations.

This paper presents an algorithm for training a semantic parser without per-sentence annotations. Instead, our approach exploits two easily-obtainable sources of supervision: a large knowledge base and (automatically) dependency-parsed sentences. The semantic parser is trained to identify relation instances from the knowledge base while simultaneously producing parses that syntactically agree with the dependency parses. Combining these two sources of supervision allows us to train an accurate semantic parser *for any knowledge base* without annotated training data.

We demonstrate our approach by training a Combinatory Categorial Grammar (CCG) (Steedman, 1996) that parses sentences into logical forms containing any of 77 relations from Freebase. Our training data consists of relation instances from Freebase and automatically dependency-parsed sentences from a web corpus. The trained semantic parser extracts binary relations with state-of-the-art performance, while recovering considerably richer semantic structure. We demonstrate recovery of this semantic structure using natural language queries

$$\dfrac{\text{town}}{N : \lambda x.\text{CITY}(x)}\text{Lex} \quad \dfrac{\text{in}}{(N\backslash N)/N : \lambda f.\lambda g.\lambda x.\exists y.f(y) \wedge g(x) \wedge \text{LOCATEDIN}(x,y)}\text{Lex} \quad \dfrac{\text{California}}{N : \lambda x.x = \text{CALIFORNIA}}\text{Lex}$$

$$N\backslash N : \lambda g.\lambda x.\exists y.y = \text{CALIFORNIA} \wedge g(x) \wedge \text{LOCATEDIN}(x,y) \quad (>)$$

$$N : \lambda x.\exists y.y = \text{CALIFORNIA} \wedge \text{CITY}(x) \wedge \text{LOCATEDIN}(x,y) \quad (<)$$

Figure 1: An example parse of "town in California" using the example CCG lexicon. The first stage in parsing retrieves a category from each word from the lexicon, represented by the "Lex" entries. The second stage applies CCG combination rules, in this case both forms of function application, to combine these categories into a semantic parse.

against Freebase. Our weakly-supervised semantic parser predicts the correct logical form for 56% of queries, despite never seeing a labeled logical form.

This paper is structured as follows. We first provide some background information on CCG and the structure of a knowledge base in Section 2. Section 3 formulates the weakly supervised training problem for semantic parsers and presents our algorithm. Section 4 describes how we applied our algorithm to construct a semantic parser for Freebase, and Section 5 presents our results. We conclude with related work and discussion.

2 Background

2.1 Combinatory Categorial Grammar

Combinatory Categorial grammar (CCG) is a linguistic formalism that represents both the syntax and semantics of language (Steedman, 1996). CCG is a lexicalized formalism that encodes all grammatical information in a lexicon Λ. This lexicon contains syntactic and semantic categories for each word. A lexicon may include entries such as:

$$\begin{aligned} \text{town} &:= N : \lambda x.\text{CITY}(x) \\ \text{California} &:= N : \lambda x.x = \text{CALIFORNIA} \\ \text{in} &:= (N\backslash N)/N : \lambda f.\lambda g.\lambda x. \\ &\quad \exists y.f(y) \wedge g(x) \wedge \text{LOCATEDIN}(x,y) \end{aligned}$$

Each entry of the lexicon $w := s : l$ maps a word or short phrase w to a syntactic category s and a logical form l. Syntactic categories s may be atomic (N) or complex ($N\backslash N$). Logical forms l are lambda calculus expressions constructed using predicates from a knowledge base. These logical forms combine during parsing to form a complete logical form for the parsed text.

Parses are constructed by combining adjacent categories using several combination rules, such as forward (>) and backward (<) application:

$$\begin{aligned} X/Y : f \quad Y : g &\implies X : f(g) \quad (>) \\ Y : g \quad X\backslash Y : f &\implies X : f(g) \quad (<) \end{aligned}$$

These rules mean that the complex category X/Y ($X\backslash Y$) behaves like a function which accepts an argument of type Y on its right (left) and returns a value of type X. Parsing amounts to sequentially applying these two rules, as shown in Figure 1. The result of parsing is an ordered pair, containing both a syntactic parse tree and an associated logical form. We refer to such an ordered pair as a semantic parse, or by using the letter ℓ.

Given a lexicon, there may be multiple semantic parses ℓ for a given phrase **w**. Like context-free grammars (CFGs), CCGs can be extended to represent a probability distribution over parses $P(\ell|\mathbf{w};\theta)$ where θ is a parameter vector.

2.2 Knowledge Base

The main input to our system is a propositional knowledge base $K = (E, R, C, \Delta)$, containing entities E, categories C, relations R and relation instances Δ. Categories and relations are predicates which operate on entities and return truth values; categories $c \in C$ are one-place predicates ($\text{CITY}(e)$) and relations $r \in R$ are two-place predicates ($\text{LOCATEDIN}(e_1, e_2)$). Entities $e \in E$ represent real-world entities and have a set of known text names. For example, CALIFORNIA is an entity whose text names include "California" and "CA." Relation instances $r(e_1, e_2) \in \Delta$ are facts asserted by the knowledge base, such as $\text{LOCATEDIN}(\text{SACRAMENTO}, \text{CALIFORNIA})$. Examples of such knowledge bases include Freebase (Bollacker et al., 2008), NELL (Carlson et al., 2010), and YAGO (Suchanek et al., 2007).

The knowledge base influences the semantic parser in two ways. First, CCG logical forms are constructed by combining categories, relations and entities from the knowledge base with logical connectives; hence, the predicates in the knowledge base determine the expressivity of the parser's semantic representation. Second, the known relation instances $r(e_1, e_2) \in \Delta$ are used as weak supervision to train the semantic parser.

3 Weakly Supervised Semantic Parsing

We define *weakly supervised semantic parsing* as the following learning problem.

Input:

1. A knowledge base $K = (E, R, C, \Delta)$, as defined above.
2. A corpus of dependency-parsed sentences S.
3. A CCG lexicon Λ that produces logical forms containing predicates from K. Section 4.1 describes an approach to generate this lexicon.
4. A procedure for identifying mentions of entities from K in sentences from S. (e.g., simple string matching).

Output:

1. Parameters θ for the CCG that produce correct semantic parses ℓ for sentences $s \in S$.

This problem is ill-posed without additional assumptions: since the correct logical form for a sentence is never observed, there is no *a priori* reason to prefer one semantic parse to another. Our training algorithm makes two assumptions about correct semantic parses, which are encoded as weak supervision constraints. These constraints make learning possible by adding an inductive bias:

1. Every relation instance $r(e_1, e_2) \in \Delta$ is expressed by at least one sentence in S (Riedel et al., 2010; Hoffmann et al., 2011).
2. The correct semantic parse of a sentence s contains a subset of the syntactic dependencies contained in a dependency parse of s.

Our weakly supervised training uses these constraints as a proxy for labeled semantic parses. The training algorithm has two steps. First, the algorithm constructs a graphical model that contains both the semantic parser and constant factors encoding the above two constraints. This graphical model is then used to estimate parameters θ for the semantic parser, essentially optimizing θ to produce parses that satisfy the weak supervision constraints. If our assumptions are correct and sufficiently constrain the parameter space, then this procedure will identify parameters for an accurate semantic parser.

3.1 Encoding the Weak Supervision Constraints

The first step of training constructs a graphical model containing the semantic parser and two weak supervision constraints. However, the first weak supervision constraint couples the semantic parses for *every* sentence $s \in S$. Such coupling would result in an undesirably large graphical model. We therefore modify this constraint to enforce that every relation $r(e_1, e_2)$ is expressed at least once in $S_{(e_1,e_2)} \subseteq S$, the subset of sentences which mention both e_1 and e_2. These mentions are detected using the provided mention-identification procedure.

Figure 2 depicts the graphical model constructed for training. The semantic constraint couples the extractions for all sentences $S_{(e_1,e_2)}$, so the graphical model is instantiated once per (e_1, e_2) tuple. The model has 4 types of random variables and values: $S_i = s_i$ represents a sentence, $L_i = \ell_i$ represents a semantic parse, $Z_i = z_i$ represents the satisfaction of the syntactic constraint and $Y_r = y_r$ represents the truth value of relation r. S_i, L_i and Z_i are replicated once for each sentence $s \in S_{(e_1,e_2)}$, while Y_r is replicated once for each relation type r in the knowledge base (all $r \in R$).

For each entity pair (e_1, e_2), this graphical model defines a conditional distribution over $\mathbf{L}, \mathbf{Y}, \mathbf{Z}$ given $\mathbf{S}$. This distribution factorizes as:

$$p(\mathbf{Y} = \mathbf{y}, \mathbf{Z} = \mathbf{z}, \mathbf{L} = \boldsymbol{\ell} | \mathbf{S} = \mathbf{s}; \theta) = \frac{1}{Z_{\mathbf{s}}} \prod_r \Psi(y_r, \boldsymbol{\ell}) \prod_i \Phi(z_i, \ell_i, s_i) \Gamma(s_i, \ell_i; \theta)$$

The factorization contains three replicated factors. Γ represents the semantic parser, which is parametrized by θ and produces a semantic parse ℓ_i for each sentence s_i. Ψ and Φ are deterministic factors representing the two weak supervision constraints. We now describe each factor in more detail.

Semantic Parser

The factor Γ represents the semantic parser, which is a log-linear probabilistic CCG using the input lexicon Λ. Given a sentence s and parameters θ, the parser defines an unnormalized probability distribution over semantic parses ℓ, each of which includes both a syntactic CCG parse tree and logical form.

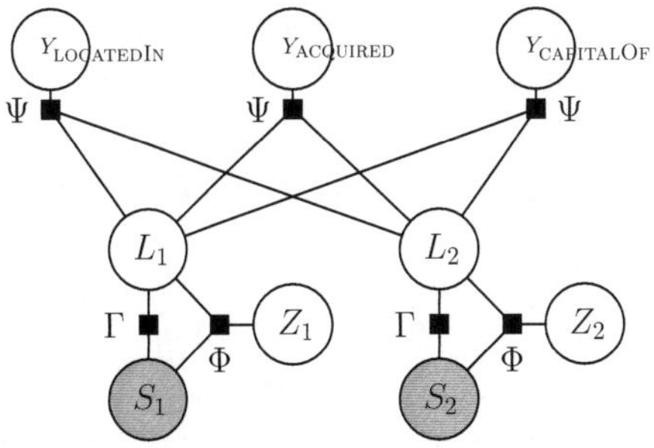

Figure 2: Factor graph containing the semantic parser Γ and weak supervision constraints Ψ and Φ, instantiated for an (e_1, e_2) tuple occurring in 2 sentences S_1 and S_2, with corresponding semantic parses L_1 and L_2. The knowledge base contains 3 relations, represented by the Y variables.

Let $f(\ell, s)$ represent a feature function mapping semantic parses to vectors of feature values[1]. The factor Γ is then defined as:

$$\Gamma(s, \ell; \theta) = \exp\{\theta^T f(\ell, s)\}$$

If the features $f(\ell, s)$ factorize according to the structure of the CCG parse tree, it is possible to perform exact inference using a CKY-style dynamic programming algorithm. However, other aspects of the graphical model preclude exact inference, so we perform approximate inference using beam search. Inference is explained in more detail in Section 3.2.

Semantic Constraint

The semantic constraint states that, given an entity tuple (e_1, e_2), every relation instance $r(e_1, e_2) \in \Delta$ must be expressed somewhere in $S_{(e_1,e_2)}$. Furthermore, no semantic parse can express a relation instance which is not in the knowledge base. This constraint is identical to the multiple deterministic-OR constraint used by Hoffmann et al. (2011) to train a sentential relation extractor.

The graphical model contains a semantic constraint factor Ψ and one binary variable Y_r for each relation r in the knowledge base. Y_r represents whether $r(e_1, e_2)$ is expressed by any sentence in $S_{(e_1,e_2)}$. The Ψ factor determines whether each semantic parse in $\boldsymbol{\ell}$ extracts a relation between e_1 and e_2. It then aggregates these sentence-level extractions using a deterministic OR: if any sentence extracts $r(e_1, e_2)$ then $Y_r = 1$. Otherwise, $Y_r = 0$.

[1]Section 4.3 describes the features used by our semantic parser for Freebase.

$$\begin{aligned}
&\Psi(Y_r, \boldsymbol{\ell}) = \\
&\quad 1 \text{ if } Y_r = 1 \wedge \exists i.\text{EXTRACTS}(\ell_i, r, e_1, e_2) \\
&\quad 1 \text{ if } Y_r = 0 \wedge \nexists i.\text{EXTRACTS}(\ell_i, r, e_1, e_2) \\
&\quad 0 \text{ otherwise}
\end{aligned}$$

The EXTRACTS function determines the relation instances that are asserted by a semantic parse ℓ. $\text{EXTRACTS}(\ell, r, e_1, e_2)$ is true if ℓ asserts the relation $r(e_1, e_2)$ and false otherwise. This function essentially converts the semantic parser into a sentential relation extractor, and its implementation may depend on the types of logical connectives included in the lexicon Λ. Logical forms in our Freebase semantic parser consist of conjunctions of predicates from the knowledge base; we therefore define $\text{EXTRACTS}(\ell, r, e_1, e_2)$ as true if ℓ's logical form contains the clauses $r(x, y)$, $x = e_1$ and $y = e_2$.

Syntactic Constraint

A problem with the semantic constraint is that it admits a large number of ungrammatical parses. The syntactic constraint penalizes ungrammatical parses by encouraging the semantic parser to produce parse trees that agree with a dependency parse of the same sentence. Specifically, the syntactic constraint requires the predicate-argument structure of the CCG parse to agree with the predicate-argument structure of the dependency parse.

Agreement is defined as a function of each CCG rule application in ℓ. In the parse tree ℓ, each rule application combines two subtrees, ℓ_h and ℓ_c, into a single tree spanning a larger portion of the sentence. A rule application is consistent with a dependency parse t if the head words of ℓ_h and ℓ_c have a dependency edge between them in t. $\text{AGREE}(\ell, t)$ is true if and only if every rule application in ℓ is consistent with t. This syntactic constraint is encoded in the graphical model by the Φ factors and **Z** variables:

$$\begin{aligned}
\Phi(z, \ell, s) \;=\; & 1 \text{ if } z = \text{AGREE}(\ell, \text{DEPPARSE}(s)) \\
& 0 \text{ otherwise}
\end{aligned}$$

3.2 Parameter Estimation

To train the model, a single training example is constructed for every tuple of entities (e_1, e_2). The input to the model is $\mathbf{s} = S_{(e_1,e_2)}$, the set of sentences containing e_1 and e_2. The weak supervision variables, $\mathbf{y}, \mathbf{z}$, are the output of the model. $\mathbf{y}$ is constructed by setting $y_r = 1$ if $r(e_1, e_2) \in \Delta$, and 0 otherwise. This setting trains the semantic parser to extract every true relation instance between (e_1, e_2) from some sentence in $S_{(e_1,e_2)}$, while simultaneously avoiding incorrect instances. Finally, $\mathbf{z} = \mathbf{1}$, to encourage agreement between the semantic and dependency parses. The training data for the model is therefore a collection, $\{(\mathbf{s}^j, \mathbf{y}^j, \mathbf{z}^j)\}_{j=1}^n$, where j indexes entity tuples (e_1, e_2).

Training optimizes the semantic parser parameters θ to predict $\mathbf{Y} = \mathbf{y}^j, \mathbf{Z} = \mathbf{z}^j$ given $\mathbf{S} = \mathbf{s}^j$. The parameters θ are estimated by running the structured perceptron algorithm (Collins, 2002) on the training data defined above. The structured perceptron algorithm iteratively applies a simple update rule for each example $(\mathbf{s}^j, \mathbf{y}^j, \mathbf{z}^j)$ in the training data:

$$\begin{aligned} \boldsymbol{\ell}^{predicted} &\leftarrow \arg\max_{\boldsymbol{\ell}} \max_{\mathbf{y},\mathbf{z}} p(\boldsymbol{\ell}, \mathbf{y}, \mathbf{z}|\mathbf{s}^j; \theta^t) \\ \boldsymbol{\ell}^{actual} &\leftarrow \arg\max_{\boldsymbol{\ell}} p(\boldsymbol{\ell}|\mathbf{y}^j, \mathbf{z}^j, \mathbf{s}^j; \theta^t) \\ \theta^{t+1} &\leftarrow \theta^t + \sum_i f(\ell_i^{actual}, s_i) \\ &\quad - \sum_i f(\ell_i^{predicted}, s_i) \end{aligned}$$

Each iteration of training requires solving two maximization problems. The first maximization, $\max_{\boldsymbol{\ell},\mathbf{y},\mathbf{z}} p(\boldsymbol{\ell}, \mathbf{y}, \mathbf{z}|\mathbf{s}; \theta^t)$, is straightforward because $\mathbf{y}$ and $\mathbf{z}$ are deterministic functions of $\boldsymbol{\ell}$. Therefore, it is solved by finding the maximum probability assignment $\boldsymbol{\ell}$, then choosing values for $\mathbf{y}$ and $\mathbf{z}$ that satisfy the weak supervision constraints.

The second maximization, $\max_{\boldsymbol{\ell}} p(\boldsymbol{\ell}|\mathbf{y}, \mathbf{z}, \mathbf{s}; \theta^t)$, is more challenging. When $\mathbf{y}$ and $\mathbf{z}$ are given, the inference procedure must restrict its search to the parses $\boldsymbol{\ell}$ which satisfy these weak supervision constraints. The original formulation of the Ψ factors permitted tractable inference (Hoffmann et al., 2011), but the EXTRACTS function and the Φ factors preclude efficient inference. We approximate this maximization using beam search over CCG parses ℓ. For each sentence s, we perform a beam search to produce $k = 300$ possible semantic parses. We then check the value of Φ for each generated parse and eliminate parses which do not satisfy this syntactic constraint. Finally, we apply EXTRACTS to each parse, then use the greedy approximate inference procedure from Hoffmann et al. (2011) for the Ψ factors.

4 Building a Grammar for Freebase

We apply the training algorithm from the previous section to produce a semantic parser for a subset of Freebase. This section describes details of the grammar we construct for this task, including the construction of the lexicon Λ, some extensions to the CCG parser, and the features used during training. In this section, we assume access to a knowledge base $K = (E, C, R, \Delta)$, a corpus of dependency-parsed sentences S and a procedure for identifying mentions of entities in sentences.

4.1 Constructing the Lexicon Λ

The first step in constructing the semantic parser is defining a lexicon Λ. We construct Λ by applying simple dependency-parse-based heuristics to sentences in the training corpus. The resulting lexicon Λ captures a variety of linguistic phenomena, including verbs, common nouns ("city"), noun compounds ("California city") and prepositional modifiers ("city in California").

The first step in lexicon construction is to use the mention identification procedure to identify all mentions of entities in the sentences S. This process results in (e_1, e_2, s) triples, consisting of sentences with two entity mentions. The dependency path between e_1 and e_2 in s is then matched against the dependency parse patterns in Table 1. Each matched pattern adds one or more lexical entries to Λ

Each pattern in Table 1 has a corresponding lexical category template, which is a CCG lexical category containing parameters e, c and r that are chosen at initialization time. Given the triple (e_1, e_2, s), relations r are chosen such that $r(e_1, e_2) \in \Delta$, and categories c are chosen such that $c(e_1) \in \Delta$ or $c(e_2) \in \Delta$. The template is then instantiated with every combination of these e, c and r values.

After instantiating lexical categories for each sentence in S, we prune infrequent lexical categories to improve parser efficiency. This pruning step is required because the common noun pattern generates a large number of lexical categories, the majority of which are incorrect. Therefore, we eliminate all common noun categories instantiated by fewer than

Part of Speech	Dependency Parse Pattern	Lexical Category Template
Proper Noun	(name of entity e) Sacramento	w $:= N : \lambda x.x = e$ Sacramento $:= N : \lambda x.x =$ SACRAMENTO
Common Noun	$e_1 \xrightarrow{SBJ}$ [is, are, was, ...] $\xleftarrow{OBJ}$ w Sacramento is the capital	w $:= N : \lambda x.c(x)$ capital $:= N : \lambda x.\text{CITY}(x)$
Noun Modifier	$e_1 \xleftarrow{NMOD} e_2$ Sacramento, California	Type change $N : \lambda x.c(x)$ to $N\|N : \lambda f.\lambda x.\exists y.c(x) \wedge f(y) \wedge r(x,y)$ $N : \lambda x.\text{CITY}(x)$ to $N\|N : \lambda f.\lambda x.\exists y.\text{CITY}(x) \wedge f(y) \wedge \text{LOCATEDIN}(x,y)$
Preposition	$e_1 \xleftarrow{NMOD}$ w $\xleftarrow{PMOD} e_2$ Sacramento in California $e_1 \xrightarrow{SBJ}$ VB* $\xleftarrow{ADV}$ w $\xleftarrow{PMOD} e_2$ Sacramento is located in California	w $:= (N\backslash N)/N : \lambda f.\lambda g.\lambda x.\exists y.f(y) \wedge g(x) \wedge r(x,y)$ in $:= (N\backslash N)/N : \lambda f.\lambda g.\lambda x.\exists y.f(y) \wedge g(x) \wedge \text{LOCATEDIN}(x,y)$ w $:= PP/N : \lambda f.\lambda x.f(x)$ in $:= PP/N : \lambda f.\lambda x.f(x)$
Verb	$e_1 \xrightarrow{SBJ}$ w* $\xleftarrow{OBJ} e_2$ Sacramento governs California $e_1 \xrightarrow{SBJ}$ w* $\xleftarrow{ADV}$ [IN,TO] $\xleftarrow{PMOD} e_2$ Sacramento is located in California $e_1 \xleftarrow{NMOD}$ w* $\xleftarrow{ADV}$ [IN,TO] $\xleftarrow{PMOD} e_2$ Sacramento located in California	w* $:= (S\backslash N)/N : \lambda f.\lambda g.\exists x,y.f(y) \wedge g(x) \wedge r(x,y)$ governs $:= (S\backslash N)/N : \lambda f.\lambda g.\exists x,y.f(y) \wedge g(x) \wedge \text{LOCATEDIN}(x,y)$ w* $:= (S\backslash N)/PP : \lambda f.\lambda g.\exists x,y.f(y) \wedge g(x) \wedge r(x,y)$ is located $:= (S\backslash N)/PP : \lambda f.\lambda g.\exists x,y.f(y) \wedge g(x) \wedge \text{LOCATEDIN}(x,y)$ w* $:= (N\backslash N)/PP : \lambda f.\lambda g.\lambda y.f(y) \wedge g(x) \wedge r(x,y)$ located $:= (N\backslash N)/PP : \lambda f.\lambda g.\lambda y.f(y) \wedge g(x) \wedge \text{LOCATEDIN}(x,y)$
Forms of "to be"	(none)	w* $:= (S\backslash N)/N : \lambda f.\lambda g.\exists x.g(x) \wedge f(x)$

Table 1: Dependency parse patterns used to instantiate lexical categories for the semantic parser lexicon Λ. Each pattern is followed by an example phrase that instantiates it. An * indicates a position that may be filled by multiple consecutive words in the sentence. e_1 and e_2 are the entities identified in the sentence, r represents a relation where $r(e_1, e_2)$, and c represents a category where $c(e_1)$. Each template may be instantiated with multiple values for the variables e, c, r.

5 sentences in S. The other rules are less fertile, so we do not need to prune their output.

In addition to these categories, the grammar includes type-changing rules from N to $N|N$. These rules capture noun compounds by allowing nouns to become functions from nouns to nouns. There are several such type-changing rules since the resulting category includes a hidden relation r between the noun and its modifier (see Table 1). As with lexical categories, the set of type changing rules included in the grammar is determined by matching dependency parse patterns to the training data. Similar rules for noun compounds are used in other CCG parsers (Clark and Curran, 2007).

The instantiated lexicon represents the semantics of words and phrases as conjunctions of predicates from the knowledge base, possibly including existentially quantified variables and λ expressions. The syntactic types N and PP are semantically represented as functions from entities to truth values (e.g., $\lambda x.\text{CITY}(x)$), while sentences S are statements with no λ terms, such as $\exists x, y.x = \text{CALIFORNIA} \wedge \text{CITY}(y) \wedge \text{LOCATEDIN}(x, y)$. Variables in the semantic representation (x, y) range over entities from the knowledge base. Intuitively, the N and PP categories represent sets of entities, while sentences represent assertions about the world.

4.2 Extensions to CCG

The semantic parser is trained using sentences from a web corpus, which contains many out-of-domain words. As a consequence, many of the words encountered during training cannot be represented using the vocabulary of predicates from the knowledge base. To handle these extraneous words, we allow the CCG parser to skip words while parsing a sentence. During parsing, the parser first decides whether to retrieve a lexical category for each word in the sentence. The sentence is then parsed as if only the retrieved lexical categories existed.

4.3 Features

The features $f(\ell, s)$ for our probabilistic CCG contain two sets of features. The first set contains lexical features, which count the number of times each lexical entry is used in ℓ. The second set contains rule application features, which count the number of times each combination rule is applied to each possible set of arguments. An argument is defined by its syntactic and semantic category, and in some cases by the lexical entry which created it. We lexicalize arguments for prepositional phrases PP and common nouns (initialized by the second rule in Table 1). This lexicalization allows the parser to distinguish between prepositional phrases headed by different prepositions, as well as between different common nouns. All other types are distinguished solely by syntactic and semantic category.

5 Evaluation

In this section, we evaluate the performance of a semantic parser for Freebase, trained using our weakly-supervised algorithm. Empirical comparison is somewhat difficult because the most comparable previous work – weakly-supervised relation extraction – uses a shallower semantic representation. Our evaluation therefore has two components: (1) a binary relation extraction task, to demonstrate that the trained semantic parser extracts instances of binary relations with performance comparable to other state-of-the-art systems, and (2) a natural language database query task, to demonstrate the parser's ability to extract more complex logical forms than binary relation instances, such as logical expressions involving conjunctions of multiple categories and relations with partially shared arguments.

5.1 Corpus Construction

Our experiments use a subset of 77 relations[2] from Freebase[3] as the knowledge base and a corpus of web sentences. We constructed the sentence corpus by first sampling sentences from a web crawl and parsing them with MaltParser (Nivre et al., 2006). Long sentences tended to have noisy parses while also rarely expressing relations, so we discarded sentences longer than 10 words. Entities were identified by performing a simple string match between canonical entity names in Freebase and proper noun phrases identified by the parser. In cases where a single noun phrase matched multiple entities, we selected the entity participating in the most relations. The resulting corpus contains 2.5 million (e_1, e_2, s) triples, from which we reserved 10% for validation and 10% for testing. The validation set was used to estimate performance during algorithm development, while the test set was used to generate the final experimental results. All triples for each (e_1, e_2) tuple were placed in the same set.

Relation Name	Relation Instances	Sentences
CITYLOCATEDINSTATE	2951	13422
CITYLOCATEDINCOUNTRY	1696	7904
CITYOFPERSONBIRTH	397	440
COMPANIESHEADQUARTEREDHERE	326	432
MUSICARTISTMUSICIAN	251	291
CITYUNIVERSITIES	239	338
CITYCAPITALOFCOUNTRY	123	2529
HASHUSBAND	103	367
PARENTOFPERSON	85	356
HASSPOUSE	81	461

Table 2: Occurrence statistics for the 10 most frequent relations in the training data. "Relation Instances" shows the number of entity tuples (e_1, e_2) that appear as positive examples for each relation, and "Sentences" shows the total number of sentences in which these tuples appear.

Approximately 1% of the resulting (e_1, e_2, s) triples are positive examples, meaning there exists some relation r where $r(e_1, e_2) \in \Delta$[4]. To improve training efficiency and prediction performance, we subsample 5% of the negative examples for training, producing a training set of 125k sentences with 27k positive examples. The validation and test sets retain the original positive/negative ratio. Table 2 shows some statistics of the most frequent relations in the test set.

5.2 Relation Extraction

The first experiment measures the semantic parser's ability to extract relations from sentences in our web corpus. We compare our semantic parser to MULTIR (Hoffmann et al., 2011), which is a state-of-the-art weakly supervised relation extractor. This method uses the same weak supervision constraint and parameter estimation procedure, but replaces the semantic parser by a linear classifier. The features for this classifier include the dependency path between the entity mentions, the type of each mention, and the intervening context (Mintz et al., 2009).

Both the semantic parser and MULTIR were trained by running 5 iterations of the structured per-

[2]These relations are defined by a set of MQL queries and potentially traverse multiple relation links.

[3]http://www.freebase.com

[4]Note that the positive/negative ratio was much lower without the length filter or entity disambiguation, which is partly why filtering was performed.

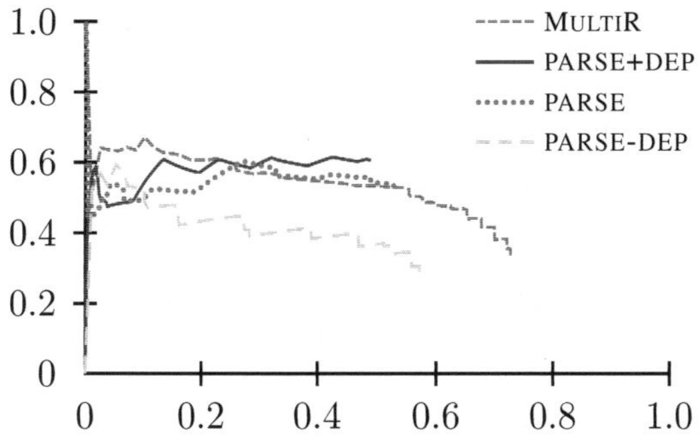

Figure 3: Aggregate precision as a function of recall, for MULTIR (Hoffman et al., 2011) and our three semantic parser variants.

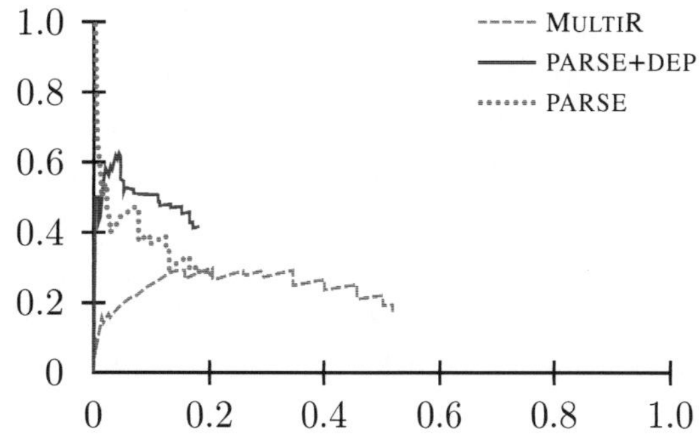

Figure 5: Aggregate precision as a function of recall, ignoring the two most frequent relations, CITYLOCATEDINSTATE and CITYLOCATEDINCOUNTRY.

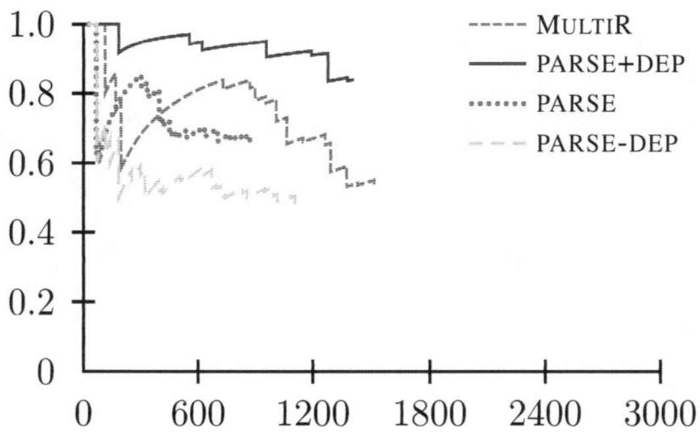

Figure 4: Sentential precision as a function of the expected number of correct extractions for MULTIR (Hoffman et al., 2011) and our three semantic parser variants.

ceptron algorithm[5]. At test time, both models predicted a relation $r \in R$ or NONE for each (e_1, e_2, s) triple in the test set. The parser parses the sentence without considering the entities marked in the sentence, then applies the EXTRACTS function defined in Section 3.1 to identify a relation between e_1 and e_2. We compare three versions of the semantic parser: PARSE, which is the basic semantic parser, PARSE+DEP which additionally observes the correct dependency parse at test time, and PARSE-DEP which is trained without the syntactic constraint. Note that MULTIR uses the sentence's dependency parse to construct its feature vector.

Our evaluation considers two performance measures: aggregate and sentential precision/recall. Aggregate precision takes the union of all extracted relation instances $r(e_1, e_2)$ from the test corpus and compares these instances to Freebase. To produce a precision/recall curve, each extracted instance $r(e_1, e_2)$ is assigned the maximum score over all sentences which extracted it. This metric is easy to compute, but may be inaccurate due to inaccuracies and missing relations in Freebase.

Sentential precision computes the precision of extractions on individual (e_1, e_2, s) tuples. This metric is evaluated by manually sampling and evaluating 100 test sentences from which a relation was extracted per model. Unfortunately, it is difficult to compute recall for this metric, since the true number of sentences expressing relations is unknown. We instead report precision as a function of the expected number of correct extractions, which is directly proportional to recall.

Figure 3 displays aggregate precision/recall and Figure 4 displays sentential precision/recall for all 4 models. Generally, PARSE behaves like MULTIR with somewhat lower recall. In the sentential evaluation, PARSE+DEP outperforms both PARSE and MULTIR. The difference between PARSE+DEP's aggregate and sentential precision stems from the fact that PARSE+DEP extracts each relation instance from more sentences than either MULTIR or PARSE. PARSE-DEP has the worst performance in both evaluations, suggesting the importance of syntactic supervision. Precision in the aggregate experiment is low partially due to examples with incorrect entity disambiguation.

We found that the skewed distribution of relation types hides interesting differences between the models. Therefore, we include Figure 5 comparing our syntactically-supervised parsers to MULTIR, ignoring the two most frequent relations (which together

[5]The structured perceptron algorithm does not converge to a parameter estimate, and we empirically found that performance did not improve beyond 5 iterations.

make up over half of all relation instances). Both PARSE and PARSE+DEP are considerably more precise than MULTIR on these less frequent relations because their compositional meaning representation shares parameter strength between relations. For example, the semantic parsers learn that "in" often combines with a city to form a prepositional phrase; the parsers can apply this knowledge to identify city arguments of any relation. However, MULTIR is capable of higher recall, since its dependency parse features can represent syntactic dependencies that cannot be represented by our semantic parsers. This limitation is a consequence of our heuristic lexicon initialization procedure, and could be rectified by a more flexible initialization procedure.

5.3 Natural Language Database Queries

The second experiment measures our trained parser's ability to correctly translate natural language queries into logical queries against Freebase.

To avoid biasing the evaluation, we constructed a test corpus of natural language queries in a data-driven fashion. We searched the test data for sentences with two related entities separated by an "is a" expression. The portion of the sentence before the "is a" expression was discarded and the remainder retained as a candidate query. For example "Jesse is an author from Austin, Texas," was converted into the candidate query "author from Austin, Texas." Each candidate query was then annotated with a logical form using categories and relations from the knowledge base; candidate queries without satisfactory logical forms were discarded. We annotated 50 validation and 50 test queries in this fashion. The validation set was used to estimate performance during algorithm development and the test set was used to generate the final results. Example queries with their annotated logical forms are shown in Table 3.

Table 4 displays the results of the query evaluation. For this evaluation, we forced the parser to include every word of the query in the parse. Precision is the percentage of successfully parsed queries for which the correct logical form was predicted. Recall is the percentage of all queries for which the correct logical form was predicted. This evaluation demonstrates that the semantic parser successfully interprets common nouns and identifies multiple relations with shared arguments. The performance difference between PARSE and PARSE-DEP also demonstrates the benefit of including syntactic supervision.

Example Query	Logical Form
capital of Russia	$\lambda x.$CITYCAPITALOFCOUNTRY(x, RUSSIA)
wife of Abraham	$\lambda x.$HASHUSBAND(x, ABRAHAM)
vocalist from London, England	$\lambda x.$MUSICIAN(x)$\wedge$ PERSONBORNIN(x, LONDON)$\wedge$ CITYINCOUNTRY(LONDON, ENGLAND)
home of ConocoPhillips in Canada	$\lambda x.$HEADQUARTERS(CONOCOPHILLIPS, x) $\wedge$CITYINCOUNTRY(x, CANADA)

Table 3: Example natural language queries and their correct annotated logical form.

	Precision	Recall
PARSE	0.80	0.56
PARSE-DEP	0.45	0.32

Table 4: Precision and recall for predicting logical forms of natural language queries against Freebase. The table compares PARSE, trained with syntactic supervision to PARSE-DEP, trained without syntactic supervision.

Examining the system output, we find two major sources of error. The first is missing lexical categories for uncommon words (e.g., "ex-guitarist"), which negatively impact recall by making some queries unparsable. The second is difficulty distinguishing between relations with similar type signatures, such as CITYLOCATEDINCOUNTRY and CITYCAPITALOFCOUNTRY.

6 Related Work

There are many approaches to supervised semantic parsing, including inductive logic programming (Zelle and Mooney, 1996), probabilistic and synchronous grammars (Ge and Mooney, 2005; Wong and Mooney, 2006; Wong and Mooney, 2007; Lu et al., 2008), and automatically learned transformation rules (Kate et al., 2005). This work most closely follows the work on semantic parsing using CCG (Zettlemoyer and Collins, 2005; Zettlemoyer and Collins, 2007; Kwiatkowski et al., 2010). These supervised systems are all trained with annotated sentence/logical form pairs; hence these approaches are labor intensive and do not scale to broad domains with large numbers of predicates.

Several recent papers have attempted to reduce the amount of human supervision required to train a semantic parser. One line of work eliminates the need for an annotated logical form, instead using only the correct answer for a database query (Liang et al., 2011) or even a binary correct/incorrect signal (Clarke et al., 2010). This type of feedback may be easier to obtain than full logical forms, but still requires individually annotated sentences. Other approaches are completely unsupervised, but do not tie the language to an existing meaning representation (Poon and Domingos, 2009). It is also possible to self-train a semantic parser without any labeled data (Goldwasser et al., 2011). However, this approach does not perform as well as more supervised approaches, since the parser's self-training predictions are not constrained by the correct logical form.

Recent research has produced several weakly supervised relation extractors (Craven and Kumlien, 1999; Mintz et al., 2009; Wu and Weld, 2010; Riedel et al., 2010; Hoffmann et al., 2011). These systems scale up to hundreds of predicates, but have much shallower semantic representations than semantic parsers. For example, these systems cannot be directly used to respond to natural language queries. This work extends weakly supervised relation extraction to produce richer semantic structure, using only slightly more supervision in the form of dependency parses.

7 Discussion

This paper presents a method for training a semantic parser using only a knowledge base and a corpus of unlabeled sentences. Our key observation is that multiple forms of weak supervision can be combined to train an accurate semantic parser: *semantic supervision* from a knowledge base of facts, and *syntactic supervision* in the form of a standard dependency parser. We presented an algorithm for training a semantic parser in the form of a probabilistic Combinatory Categorial Grammar, using these two types of weak supervision. We used this algorithm to train a semantic parser for an ontology of 77 Freebase predicates, using Freebase itself as the weak semantic supervision.

Experimental results show that our trained semantic parser extracts binary relations as well as a state-of-the-art weakly supervised relation extractor (Hoffmann et al., 2011). Further experiments tested our trained parser's ability to extract more complex meanings from sentences, including logical forms involving conjunctions of multiple relation and category predicates with shared arguments (e.g., $\lambda x.\textsc{musician}(x) \wedge \textsc{personBornIn}(x, \textsc{London}) \wedge \textsc{cityInCountry}(\textsc{London}, \textsc{England})$). To test this capability, we applied the trained parser to natural language queries against Freebase. The semantic parser correctly interpreted 56% of these queries, despite the broad domain and never having seen an annotated logical form. Together, these two experimental analyses suggest that the combination of syntactic and semantic weak supervision is indeed a sufficient basis for training semantic parsers for a diverse range of corpora and predicate ontologies.

One limitation of our method is the reliance on hand-built dependency parse patterns for lexicon initialization. Although these patterns capture a variety of linguistic phenomena, they require manual engineering and may miss important relations. An area for future work is developing an automated way to produce this lexicon, perhaps by extending the recent work on automatic lexicon generation (Kwiatkowski et al., 2010) to the weakly supervised setting. Such an algorithm seems especially important if one wishes to model phenomena such as adjectives, which are difficult to initialize heuristically without generating large numbers of lexical entries.

An elegant aspect of semantic parsing is that it is easily extensible to include more complex linguistic phenomena, such as quantification and events (multi-argument relations). In the future, we plan to increase the expressivity of our parser's meaning representation to capture more linguistic and semantic phenomena. In this fashion, we can make progress toward broad coverage semantic parsing, and thus natural language understanding.

Acknowledgments

This research has been supported in part by DARPA under contract number FA8750-09-C-0179, and by a grant from Google. Additionally, we thank Yahoo! for use of their M45 cluster. We also gratefully acknowledge the contributions of our colleagues on the NELL project, Justin Betteridge for collecting the Freebase relations, Jamie Callan and colleagues for the web crawl, and Thomas Kollar and Matt Gardner for helpful comments on earlier drafts of this paper.

References

Kurt Bollacker, Colin Evans, Praveen Paritosh, Tim Sturge, and Jamie Taylor. 2008. Freebase: a collaboratively created graph database for structuring human knowledge. In *Proceedings of the 2008 ACM SIGMOD International Conference on Management of Data*, pages 1247–1250.

Andrew Carlson, Justin Betteridge, Bryan Kisiel, Burr Settles, Estevam R. Hruschka Jr., and Tom M. Mitchell. 2010. Toward an architecture for never-ending language learning. In *Proceedings of the Twenty-Fourth AAAI Conference on Artificial Intelligence*.

Stephen Clark and James R. Curran. 2007. Wide-coverage efficient statistical parsing with CCG and log-linear models. *Computational Linguistics*, 33(4):493–552.

James Clarke, Dan Goldwasser, Ming-Wei Chang, and Dan Roth. 2010. Driving semantic parsing from the world's response. In *Proceedings of the Fourteenth Conference on Computational Natural Language Learning*.

Michael Collins. 2002. Discriminative training methods for hidden markov models: theory and experiments with perceptron algorithms. In *Proceedings of the Conference on Empirical Methods in Natural Language Processing*.

Mark Craven and Johan Kumlien. 1999. Constructing biological knowledge bases by extracting information from text sources. In *Proceedings of the Seventh International Conference on Intelligent Systems for Molecular Biology*.

Ruifang Ge and Raymond J. Mooney. 2005. A statistical semantic parser that integrates syntax and semantics. In *Proceedings of the Ninth Conference on Computational Natural Language Learning*.

Dan Goldwasser, Roi Reichart, James Clarke, and Dan Roth. 2011. Confidence driven unsupervised semantic parsing. Proceedings of the 49th Annual Meeting of the Association for Computational Linguistics.

Raphael Hoffmann, Congle Zhang, Xiao Ling, Luke S. Zettlemoyer, and Daniel S. Weld. 2011. Knowledge-based weak supervision for information extraction of overlapping relations. In *The 49th Annual Meeting of the Association for Computational Linguistics: Human Language Technologies*.

Rohit J. Kate, Yuk Wah Wong, and Raymond J. Mooney. 2005. Learning to transform natural to formal languages. In *Proceedings, The Twentieth National Conference on Artificial Intelligence and the Seventeenth Innovative Applications of Artificial Intelligence Conference*.

Tom Kwiatkowski, Luke Zettlemoyer, Sharon Goldwater, and Mark Steedman. 2010. Inducing probabilistic CCG grammars from logical form with higher-order unification. In *Proceedings of the 2010 Conference on Empirical Methods in Natural Language Processing*.

Percy Liang, Michael I. Jordan, and Dan Klein. 2011. Learning dependency-based compositional semantics. In *Proceedings of the Association for Computational Linguistics*, Portland, Oregon. Association for Computational Linguistics.

Wei Lu, Hwee Tou Ng, Wee Sun Lee, and Luke S. Zettlemoyer. 2008. A generative model for parsing natural language to meaning representations. In *Proceedings of the Conference on Empirical Methods in Natural Language Processing*.

Mike Mintz, Steven Bills, Rion Snow, and Dan Jurafsky. 2009. Distant supervision for relation extraction without labeled data. In *Proceedings of the Joint Conference of the 47th Annual Meeting of the ACL and the 4th International Joint Conference on Natural Language Processing of the AFNLP*.

Joakim Nivre, Johan Hall, and Jens Nilsson. 2006. Maltparser: A data-driven parser-generator for dependency parsing. In *Proceedings of the 21st International Conference on Computational Linguistics and 44th Annual Meeting of the Association for Computational Linguistics*.

Hoifung Poon and Pedro Domingos. 2009. Unsupervised semantic parsing. In *Proceedings of the 2009 Conference on Empirical Methods in Natural Language Processing*.

Sebastian Riedel, Limin Yao, and Andrew McCallum. 2010. Modeling relations and their mentions without labeled text. In *Proceedings of the 2010 European conference on Machine learning and Knowledge Discovery in Databases*.

Mark Steedman. 1996. *Surface Structure and Interpretation*. The MIT Press.

Fabian M. Suchanek, Gjergji Kasneci, and Gerhard Weikum. 2007. Yago: a core of semantic knowledge. In *Proceedings of the 16th international conference on World Wide Web*, WWW '07, pages 697–706, New York, NY, USA. ACM.

Yuk Wah Wong and Raymond J. Mooney. 2006. Learning for semantic parsing with statistical machine translation. In *Proceedings of the Human Language Technology Conference of the NAACL*.

Yuk Wah Wong and Raymond J. Mooney. 2007. Learning synchronous grammars for semantic parsing with lambda calculus. In *Proceedings of the 45th Annual Meeting of the Association for Computational Linguistics*.

Fei Wu and Daniel S. Weld. 2010. Open information extraction using Wikipedia. In *Proceedings of the 48th*

Annual Meeting of the Association for Computational Linguistics.

John M. Zelle and Raymond J. Mooney. 1996. Learning to parse database queries using inductive logic programming. In *Proceedings of the thirteenth national conference on Artificial Intelligence*.

Luke S. Zettlemoyer and Michael Collins. 2005. Learning to map sentences to logical form: structured classification with probabilistic categorial grammars. In *UAI '05, Proceedings of the 21st Conference in Uncertainty in Artificial Intelligence*.

Luke S. Zettlemoyer and Michael Collins. 2007. Online learning of relaxed ccg grammars for parsing to logical form. In *Proceedings of the 2007 Joint Conference on Empirical Methods in Natural Language Processing and Computational Natural Language Learning*.

Author Index

Joint Conference on Empirical Methods in Natural Language Processing and Computational Natural Language Learning 2012

(EMNLP 2012)

Jeju Island, Korea
12 – 14 July 2012

Volume 2 of 2

ISBN: 978-1-62276-503-4

Printed from e-media with permission by:

Curran Associates, Inc.
57 Morehouse Lane
Red Hook, NY 12571

CURRAN ASSOCIATES INC. proceedings.com

Some format issues inherent in the e-media version may also appear in this print version.

Printed by Curran Associates, Inc. (2013)

Association for Computational Linguistics
209 N. Eighth Street
Stroudsburg, Pennsylvania 18360

Phone: 1-570-476-8006
Fax: 1-570-476-0860

acl@aclweb.org

Additional copies of this publication are available from:

Curran Associates, Inc.
57 Morehouse Lane
Red Hook, NY 12571 USA
Phone: 845-758-0400
Fax: 845-758-2634
Email: curran@proceedings.com
Web: www.proceedings.com

Preface by General and Program Chairs

It is our pleasure to welcome you to the EMNLP-CoNLL 2012 conference, a joint meeting of the Conference on Empirical Methods in Natural Language Learning (EMNLP) and the Conference on Computational Natural Language Learning (CoNLL). After the successful first collaboration in 2007, EMNLP-CoNLL 2012 is being jointly organized by the SIGDAT and SIGNLL special interest groups of the Association of Computational Linguistics.

This time, EMNLP-CoNLL is co-located with, and immediately after ACL's 50th anniversary conference. The choice of the location is an opportunity for the ACL community to return to the beautiful Jeju Island, Korea, following a seven-year hiatus since the Second International Joint Conference on Natural Language Processing (IJCNLP 2005) was held here.

Out of 606 submissions received by EMNLP-CoNLL this year, a total of 36 submissions were eventually withdrawn or rejected without review. From the remaining submissions, 99 were accepted for oral presentation and 40 for poster presentation, for a combined acceptance rate of 24.8%. As in recent editions of EMNLP, authors were given the opportunity to provide supplementary material in conjunction with their submissions, which the program committee could but was not required to take into account during reviewing. Also as in recent editions, authors of accepted papers were offered an additional page in the camera-ready version of their submissions, so that comments received from reviewers could be more easily addressed.

The papers submitted to the conference were subject to a rigorous reviewing process, made possible by efforts of a team of 525 primary and 66 secondary reviewers, acting under the guidance of 22 area chairs. Presence of unsupported claims, or failure to properly compare with previous work, were likely serious obstacles, on the path from initial submission to acceptance and then publication in our proceedings. Luckily, our preface has a guaranteed placement in the proceedings. Therefore, without access to insider data and impressions from previous editions of the conference, we will still go on a limb here, and make the unsupported claim that our team of area chairs has been the greatest. That their expertise, dedication and willingness to go beyond the call of duty had a positive impact on a timely reviewing process and a high-quality conference program, would be an understatement. It has been a pleasure to interact and work with our area chairs.

The schedule of our conference is strengthened by two invited speakers, Eric Xing and Patrick Pantel, who we were very happy to have accept our invitation; and by the CoNLL Shared Task, an annual tradition for the CoNLL conferences. This year's CoNLL Shared Task is Modeling Multilingual Unrestricted Coreference in OntoNotes, and its proceedings and detailed schedule are available separately.

We would like to thank all authors who submitted to our conference, for their willingness to share their knowledge with the rest of us. It may take a few weeks or many years, for the knowledge distilled into the present proceedings to have a measurable impact on our field and beyond. An impact that would not be possible without countless hours spent by authors, from developing ideas to running experiments to building usable systems - steps that often fail, and sometimes succeed.

We would also like to thank all members of the program committee, for their willingness to offer feedback that sometimes reaches extraordinary levels of detail and value to authors. To recognise some of the most dedicated reviewers, we include the Best Reviewer awards a little later in these proceedings.

Naoaki Okazaki, Publications Chair, deserves our special thanks. He brought in a healthy dose of rigor to the planning and preparation of not only this proceedings but also conference materials, matched only by his dedication to deliver under tight scheduling constraints.

If the combination of oral presentations, posters and invited talks that make up EMNLP-CoNLL 2012 is considered a success, it is because it benefited from the touch of many people. Francesco Figari easily kept tabs on our salvos of large and small requests for updates to our conference website. Rich Gerber, Paolo Gai and the larger team managing the conference submission system were quick to offer answers to all our questions. The publication chairs and local arrangements committee of ACL 2012, including Michael White, Maggie Li, Jong Park and especially Gary Geunbae Lee, covered significant tasks on behalf of EMNLP-CoNLL, all with a smile. Chin-Yew Lin, Miles Osborne, Eric Fosler-Lussier, Dekang Lin, Rada Mihalcea, Regina Barzilay, Ulrich Germann and David Yarowsky offered high-level advice or answered detailed questions, drawing upon their experience as organizers of previous ACL-sponsored conferences.

We are grateful to our sponsors (Baidu, Google and Microsoft), for their support of best paper awards and support of student travel in particular, and the financial well-being of the conference in general. It has been an honor to be of service to the conference, for which we would like to thank the community and those who offered us this opportunity. We hope that you enjoy the conference, and have a productive and pleasant stay in South Korea!

Jun'ichi Tsujii, General Chair
James Henderson and Marius Paşca, Program Chairs

General Chair:

Jun'ichi Tsujii, Microsoft Research Asia

Program Chairs:

James Henderson, Xerox Research Centre Europe
Marius Paşca, Google

Area Chairs:

Eugene Agichtein, Emory University
Yejin Choi, Stony Brook University
Hal Daumé III, University of Maryland
Doug Downey, Northwestern University
Chris Dyer, Carnegie Mellon University
Adrià de Gispert, University of Cambridge
Julia Hirschberg, Columbia University
Anna Korhonen, University of Cambridge
Bing Liu, University of Illinois at Chicago
Hwee Tou Ng, National University of Singapore
Patrick Pantel, Microsoft Research
Marco Pennacchiotti, Yahoo! Labs
Slav Petrov, Google
Simone Paolo Ponzetto, Sapienza University of Rome
John Prager, IBM Research
Chris Quirk, Microsoft Research
Sebastian Riedel, University of Massachusetts at Amherst
Hiroya Takamura, Tokyo Institute of Technology
Partha Talukdar, Carnegie Mellon University
Kristina Toutanova, Microsoft Research
Reut Tsarfaty, Uppsala University
Marilyn Walker, University of California at Santa Cruz

Publication Chair:

Naoaki Okazaki, Tohoku University

Program Committee: Reviewers:

Ahmed Abbasi, Robert Abbott, Omri Abend, Meni Adler, Mikhail Ageev, Lars Ahrenberg, Hua Ai, Cem Akkaya, Pranav Anand, Alina Andreevskaia, Ion Androutsopoulos, Eiji Aramaki, Yoav Artzi, Abhishek Arun, Nicholas Asher, Giuseppe Attardi, Necip Fazil Ayan,

Anton Bakalov, Alexandra Balahur, Niranjan Balasubramanian, Timothy Baldwin, Carmen Banea, Ritwik Banerjee, Mohit Bansal, Roy Bar-Haim, Kedar Belare, Anja Belz, Paul Bennett, Stefan Benus, Taylor Berg-Kirkpatrick, Nicola Bertoldi, Justin Betteridge, Chandra Sekhar Bhagavatula, Aditya Bhargava, Jiang Bian, Chris Biemann, Dan Bikel, Alexandra Birch, Arianna Bisazza, Graeme Blackwood, Sasha Blair-Goldensohn, Jim Blevins, Michael Bloodgood, Phil Blunsom, Bernd Bohnet, Ester Boldrini, Antal van den Bosch, Elizabeth Boschee, Jan Botha, Alexandre Bouchard-Côté, Jordan Boyd-Graber, Thorsten Brants, Ulf Brefeld, Chris Brew, Ted Briscoe, Razvan Bunescu, David Burkett, Bill Byrne, Donna Byron,

Chris Callison-Burch, Nicola Cancedda, Marie Candito, Yunbo Cao, Giuseppe Carenini, Michael Carl, Andrew Carlson, Marine Carpuat, Xavier Carreras, Francisco Casacuberta, Dan Cer, Ozlem Cetinoglu, Mauro Cettolo, Joyce Chai, Soumen Chakrabarti, Jason Chang, Ming-Wei Chang, Ciprian Chelba, Hsin-Hsi Chen, Stanley Chen, Colin Cherry, Jackie Cheung, David Chiang, Munmun De Choudhury, Grzegorz Chrupala, Philipp Cimiano, Alex Clark, Steve Clark, Shay Cohen, Trevor Cohn, Bonaventura Coppola, Marta Ruiz Costa-Jussa, Danilo Croce, Tim Van de Cruys, Silviu Cucerzan, Aron Culotta,

Walter Daelemans, Daniel Dahlmeier, Bhavana Dalvi, Dana Dannells, Dipanjan Das, Steve DeNeefe, John DeNero, Vera Demberg, Michael Denkowski, Tejaswini Deoskar, Barry Devereux, Ann Devitt, Mona Diab, Laura Dietz, Mike Dillinger, Nikhil Dinesh, Xiaowen Ding, Bill Dolan, Mark Dras, Mark Dredze, Markus Dreyer, Greg Druck, Kevin Duh, Benjamin van Durme, Marc Dymetman,

Koji Eguchi, Andreas Eisele, Jacob Eisenstein, Jason Eisner, Micha Eisner, Michael Elhadad, Charles Elkan, David Elson, Katrin Erk, Oren Etzioni,

Anthony Fader, Katja Filippova, Radu Florian, George Foster, Jennifer Foster, Anette Frank, Marjorie Freedman, Dayne Freitag, Atsushi Fujita, Sadaoki Furui,

Michael Gamon, Kuzman Ganchev, Juri Ganitkevitch, Jianfeng Gao, Claire Gardent, Matt Gardner, Milica Gasic, Josef van Genabith, Matthew Gerber, Daniel Gildea, Daniel Gillick, Kevin Gimpel, Roxana Girju, Amir Globerson, Yoav Goldberg, Dan Goldwasser, Cyril Goutte, Amit Goyal, João Graça, Spence Green, Ralph Grishman, Joakim Gustafson,

Ryuichiro HIgashinaka, Viet Ha-Thuc, Barry Haddow, Gholamreza Haffari, Patrick Haffner, Jan Hajic, Dilek Hakkani-Tur, David Hall, Keith Hall, Greg Hanneman, Christian Hardmeier, Saša Hasan, Helen Hastie, Jun Hatori, Zhongjun He, Kenneth Heafield, John Henderson, Tsutomu Hirao, Graeme Hirst, Anna Hjalmarsson, Hieu Hoang, Julia Hockenmaier, Liangjie Hong, Mark Hopkins, Veronique Hoste, Edward Hovy, Estevam Hruschka, Yunhua Hu, Fei Huang, Liang Huang, Minlie Huang, Samar Husain,

Francisco Iacobelli, Gonzalo Iglesias, Diana Inkpen, Ann Irvine, Tatsuya Izuha,

Jagadeesh Jagarlamud, Heng Ji, Jing Jiang, Wen Bin Jiang, Richard Johansson, Howard Johnson,

Nobuhiro Kaji, Pallika Kanani, Hiroshi Kanayama, Rohit Kate, Junichi Kazama, Shahram Khadivi, Jin Dong Kim, Irwin King, Tracy King, Brian Kingsbury, Katrin Kirchhoff, Kevin Knight, Philipp

Koehn, Mamoru Komachi, Greg Kondrak, Christian Konig, Terry Koo, Moshe Koppel, Alexander Kotov, Zornitsa Kozareva, Jayant Krishnamurthy, Lun-Wei Ku, Marco Kuhlmann, Roland Kuhn, Seth Kulick, Shankar Kumar, Oren Kurland,

Oier Lopez de Lacalle, Philippe Langlais, Mirella Lapata, Claudia Leacock, John Lee, Yoong Keok Lee, Alessandro Lenci, Gregor Leusch, Abby Levenberg, Chi-Ho Li, Fangtao Li, Mu Li, Shoushan Li, Hui Lin, Thomas Lin, Xiao Ling, Jing Liu, Qun Liu, Yang Liu, Zhanyi Liu, Andrej Ljoje, Adam Lopez, Annie Louis, Bin Lu, Wei Lu, Yue Lu, Michael Lucas, Stephanie Lukin, Yajuan Lv,

Yanjun Ma, Klaus Macherey, Wolfgang Macherey, Nitin Madnani, Wolfgang Maier, Suresh Manandhar, Daniel Marcu, Anna Margolis, Katja Markert, Marie-Catherine de Marneffe, Craig Martell, Andre Martins, Yuval Marton, Spyros Matsoukas, Takuya Matsuzaki, Evgeny Matusov, Mausam, Arne Mauser, Jon May, Andrew McCallum, Diana McCarthy, David McClosky, Ryan McDonald, Kathleen McKeown, Beata Megyesi, Gerard De Melo, Paola Merlo, Haitao Mi, Rada Mihalcea, David Mimno, Yasuhiro Minami, Teru Misu, Yusuke Miyao, Saif Mohammad, Behrang Mohit, Karo Moilanen, Dan Moldovan, Martin Molina, Robert Moore, Paul Morarescu, Pedro Moreno, Shinsuke Mori, Hajime Morita, Alessandro Moschitti, Dana Movshovitz-Attias, Arjun Mukherjee, Vanessa Murdock, Markos Mylonakis, Lluís Mŕrquez,

Tetsuji Nakagawa, Mikio Nakano, Toshiaki Nakazawa, Preslav Nakov, Jason Naradowsky, Vivi Nastase, Roberto Navigli, Mark-Jan Nederhof, Ani Nenkova, Graham Neubig, Alena Neviarouskaya, Vincent Ng, Jian-Yun Nie, John Niekrasz, Hitoshi Nishikawa, Joakim Nivre, Tadashi Nomoto, Scott Nowson,

Brendan O'Connor, Stephan Oepen, Kemal Oflazer, Naoaki Okazaki, Manabu Okumura, Constantin Orasan, Myle Ott,

Sebastian Pado, Shimei Pan, Sinno Jialin Pan, Soo-Min Pantel, Becky Passonneau, Alexandre Passos, Siddharth Patwardhan, Michael Paul, Matthias Paulik, Adam Pauls, Gerald Penn, Sasa Petrovic, Elias Ponvert, Hoifung Poon, Ana-Maria Popescu, Andrei Popescu-Belis, Maja Popovic, Fred Popowich, Matt Post, Peter Prettenhofer, Emily Mower Provost, Sampo Pyysalo,

Yanjun Qi, Silvia Quarteroni,

Dragomir Radev, Altaf Rahman, Bhuvana Ramabhadran, Maya Ramanath, Owen Rambow, Ari Rappoport, Sujith Ravi, Deepak Ravichandran, Emmanuel Rayner, Sravana Reddy, Ines Rehbein, Roi Reichart, Joseph Reisinger, David Reitter, Jason Riesa, Verena Rieser, Stefan Riezler, German Rigau, Ellen Riloff, Laura Rimell, Eric Ringger, Alan Ritter, Brian Roark, Andrew Rosenberg, Paolo Rosso, Dan Roth, Wang Rui, Josef Ruppenhofer, Alexander Rush, Graham Russell,

Stijn De Saeger, Kenji Sagae, Mark Sammons, Sunita Sarawagi, Anoop Sarkar, Christina Sauper, Hassan Sawaf, Frank Schilder, Hinrich Schuetze, Bjoern Schuller, Holger Schwenk, Djamé Seddah, Satoshi Sekine, Hendra Setiawan, Burr Settles, Fei Sha, Libin Shen, Shuming Shi, Ekaterina Shutova, Mário J. Silva, Fabrizio Silvestri, Michel Simard, Sameer Singh, Kairit Sirts, Gabriel Skantze, Jason Smith, Noah Smith, Ronnie Smith, Ben Snyder, Stephen Soderland, Radu Soricut, Lucia Specia, Valentin Spitkovsky, Caroline Sporleder, Vivek Srikumar, Mark Steedman, Benno Stein, Amanda Stent, Svetlana Stoyanchev, Veselin Stoyanov, Carlo Strapparava, Michael Strube, Keh-Yih Su, Michael Subotin, Fabian Suchanek, Katsuhito Sudoh, Ang Sun, Mihai Surdeanu, Idan Szpektor, Diarmuid Ó Séaghdha,

David Talbot, Songbo Tan, Joseph Tepperman, Joel Tetreault, Blaise Thomson, Joerg Tiedemann,

Christoph Tillmann, Ivan Titov, Cigdem Toprak, Kentaro Torisawa, Roy Tromble, Oren Tsur, Yoshimasa Tsuruoka, Peter Turney, Oscar Täckström,

Raghavendra Udupa, Jakob Uszkoreit, Masao Utiyama,

Lucy Vanderwende, Tony Veale, Paola Velardi, Rossano Venturini, Yannick Versley, Jette Viethen, David Vilar, Aline Villavicencio, Andreas Vlachos, Martin Volk,

Sabine Schulte im Walde, Stephen Wan, Xiaojun Wan, Haifeng Wang, Taro Watanabe, Furu Wei, Gerhard Weikum, Ralph Weischedel, Ji-Rong Wen, Chris Wendt, Dominic Widdows, Janyce Wiebe, Derry Wijaya, Shuly Wintner, Kamfai Wong, Frank Wood, Fei Wu, Joern Wuebker,

Yunqing Xia, Deyi Xiong, Peng Xu, Nianwen Xue,

Grace Yang, Muyun Yang, Yi Yang, Alexander Yates, Mark Yatskar, Ainur Yessenalina, Elad Yom-Tov, Jianxing Yu, Yisong Yue,

Wlodek Zadrozny, Fabio Massimo Zanzotto, Richard Zens, Torsten Zesch, Luke Zettlemoyer, Bing Zhang, Congle Zhang, Hao Zhang, Hui Zhang, Joy Zhang, Lei Zhang, Min Zhang, Qi Zhang, Yue Zhang, Bing Zhao, Shiqi Zhao, Tiejun Zhao, Wayne Xin Zhao, Jing Zheng, Liu Zhiyuan, Bowen Zhou, Guodong Zhou, Ming Zhou, Jing-Bo Zhu, Xiaodan Zhu, Chengqing Zong, Geoff Zweig

Program Committee: Secondary Reviewers:

Gabor Angeli, Gerlof Bouma, Steven Burrows, Paula Carvalho, Diego Ceccarelli, Janara Christensen, Eric Corlett, Bart Desmet, Frank Ferraro, Tiziano Flati, Francisco Guzman, Yifan He, Dirk Hovy, Rubén Izquierdo, Jiarong Jiang, Tetsuo Kiso, Effi Levi, Baichuan Li, Nedim Lipka, Lemao Liu, Jeff Lund, Pierre Magistry, Thang Luong Minh, Makoto Miwa, Abdelrahman Mohamed, Taesun Moon, Tanmoy Mukherjee, Ryo Nagata, Franco Maria Nardini, Viet-An Nguyen, Gozde Ozbal, Wang Pidong, Barbara Plank, Quentin Pleple, Natalia Ponomareva, Vladimir Popescu, Daniel Preotiuc, Ju Qi, Kyle Rawlins, Majid Razmara, Nils Reiter, Joseph Le Roux, Benoît Sagot, Mohammad Salameh, Baskaran Sankaran, Uma Sawant, Roy Schwartz, Aliaksei Severyn, Kathrin Spreyer, Gabriele Tolomei, Olga Uryopina, Rakesh Varna, Zhiyang Wang, Zhuoran Wang, Jonny Weese, Michael Wick, Wei Xu, Haiqin Yang, Xuchen Yao, Mo Yu, Yintao Yu, Jiajun Zhang, Bo Zhao, Shanheng Zhao, Tu Zhaopeng, Chao Zhou

Invited Talks:

"On Learning Sparse Structured Input-Output Models"

Eric Xing, Carnegie Mellon University

In many modern problems across areas such as natural language processing, computer vision, and social media inference, one is often interested in learning a Sparse Structured Input-Output Model (SIOM), in which the input variables of the model such as lexicons in a document bear rich structures due to the syntactic and semantic dependences between them in the text; and the output variables such as the elements in a multi-way classification, a parse, or a topic representation are also structured because of their interrelatedness. A SIOM can nicely capture rich structural properties in the data and in the problem, but it also raises severe computational and theoretical challenge on sparse, consistent, and tractable model identification and inference.

In this talk, I will present models, algorithms, and theories that learn Sparse SIOMs of various kinds in very high dimensional input/output space, with fast and highly scalable optimization procedures, and strong statistical guarantees. I will demonstrate application of our approach to problems in large-scale text classification, topic modeling, and dependency parsing.

"The Appification of the Web and the Renaissance of Conversational User Interfaces"

Patrick Pantel, Microsoft Research

The appification of the Web is triggering a fundamental shift in how users access information. We are moving from centralized access points, such as search engines, towards highly specialized, and yet fragmented, functionalities in disconnected apps. This talk explores an entity-centric conversational interface as a mechanism to overcome this fragmentation, highlighting the numerous associated NLP challenges and opportunities that lie ahead.

Consider mobile scenarios, where the traditional search engine paradigm is being cannibalized by search and browse functionalities built directly into specialized apps. For example, while users can search for restaurants and products using their mobile browser, they are increasingly turning directly to applications such as Yelp, Urbanspoon and Amazon. However, interoperability between applications and lacking generalized interfaces to their functionalities pose serious scalability challenges. In this talk, we argue for an entity-centric conversational interface in which natural user interactions with entities are paired with actions that can be performed on the entities, thus enabling the brokering of web pages and applications that can satisfy the intended action. In this vision, the broker is aware of all entities and actions of interest to its users, understands the intent of the user, and provides direct actionable results through APIs with external providers satisfying the intent. The user saves clicks and time to accomplish her intended action and can discover related actions. New revenue streams open up from paid action placement and lead generation opportunities. At the forefront of this direction are a number of NLP challenges in the areas of entity recognition, entity linking, knowledge extraction, intent recognition, and dialog modeling, to name a few.

We end by proposing one particular technique for learning and mapping user intents in a search interface. In an annotation study conducted over a traffic sample of web usage logs, we found that a large proportion of user queries involve actions on entities, calling for an automatic approach to identifying relevant actions for entity-bearing queries. We pose the problem of finding actions that can be performed on entities as the problem of doing probabilistic inference in a graphical model that captures how entity-bearing information requests are generated. Given a large collection of real-world queries and clicks from a commercial search engine, the models are learned efficiently through maximum likelihood estimation using an EM algorithm. Given a new query, inference enables the recommendation of a set of pertinent actions and providers. We propose an evaluation methodology for measuring the relevance of our recommended actions, and show empirical evidence of the quality and the diversity of the discovered actions.

Best Reviewer Awards:

Hua Ai
Ion Androutsopoulos
Yoav Artzi
Mohit Bansal
Aditya Bhargava
Graeme Blackwood
Sasha Blair-Goldensohn
David Burkett
Marie Candito
Marine Carpuat
Xavier Carreras
Soumen Chakrabarti
Colin Cherry
Mark Dredze
Kevin Duh
David Elson
Katja Filippova
Matthew Gerber
Kevin Gimpel
Yoav Goldberg
Spence Green
Greg Hanneman
Saša Hasan
Alexander Kotov
Jayant Krishnamurthy
Marco Kuhlmann
Roland Kuhn
Mirella Lapata
Annie Louis
Andre Martins
Ryan McDonald
Robert Moore
Arjun Mukherjee
Vanessa Murdock
Jason Naradowsky
Roberto Navigli
Vincent Ng
John Niekrasz
Joakim Nivre
Becky Passonneau
Hoifung Poon
Andrei Popescu-Belis
Owen Rambow
Ines Rehbein
Alan Ritter
Alexander Rush
Noah Smith
Oren Tsur
Oscar Täckström
Lucy Vanderwende
Jette Viethen
Gerhard Weikum
Janyce Wiebe
Joern Wuebker
Yue Zhang

Table of Contents

Conference Program

Thursday, July 12, 2012

Session 1-AM-0P: Opening

09:00-09:15 Opening Remarks

Session 1-AM-1P: Plenary Session: Invited Talk
Session Chair: James Henderson

09:15-10:30 Invited Talk: On Learning Sparse Structured Input-Output Models (Eric Xing, Carnegie Mellon University)

10:30-11:00 Coffee Break

Session 1-AM-2A: Machine Translation: Bilingual Lexicons and Alignment
Session Chair: David Chiang

11:00-11:30 *Syntactic Transfer Using a Bilingual Lexicon*
Greg Durrett, Adam Pauls and Dan Klein

11:30-12:00 *Regularized Interlingual Projections: Evaluation on Multilingual Transliteration*
Jagadeesh Jagarlamudi and Hal Daume III

12:00-12:30 *Bilingual Lexicon Extraction from Comparable Corpora Using Label Propagation*
Akihiro Tamura, Taro Watanabe and Eiichiro Sumita

Session 1-AM-2B: Social Media: Author Style and Attribution
Session Chair: Janyce Wiebe

11:00-11:30 *Lexical Differences in Autobiographical Narratives from Schizophrenic Patients and Healthy Controls*
Kai Hong, Christian G. Kohler, Mary E. March, Amber A. Parker and Ani Nenkova

11:30-12:00 *Streaming Analysis of Discourse Participants*
Benjamin Van Durme

12:00-12:30 *Detecting Subgroups in Online Discussions by Modeling Positive and Negative Relations among Participants*
Ahmed Hassan, Amjad Abu-Jbara and Dragomir Radev

Thursday, July 12, 2012 (continued)

Session 1-AM-2C: Dialogue and Interactive Systems
Session Chair: Michael White

11:00-11:30 *Generative Goal-Driven User Simulation for Dialog Management*
Aciel Eshky, Ben Allison and Mark Steedman

11:30-12:00 *Optimising Incremental Dialogue Decisions Using Information Density for Interactive Systems*
Nina Dethlefs, Helen Hastie, Verena Rieser and Oliver Lemon

12:00-12:30 *Mixed Membership Markov Models for Unsupervised Conversation Modeling*
Michael J. Paul

Session 1-AM-2D: Information Extraction: Entity Disambiguation
Session Chair: Raymond Mooney

11:00-11:30 *An Entity-Topic Model for Entity Linking*
Xianpei Han and Le Sun

11:30-12:00 *Linking Named Entities to Any Database*
Avirup Sil, Ernest Cronin, Penghai Nie, Yinfei Yang, Ana-Maria Popescu and Alexander Yates

12:00-12:30 *Towards Efficient Named-Entity Rule Induction for Customizability*
Ajay Nagesh, Ganesh Ramakrishnan, Laura Chiticariu, Rajasekar Krishnamurthy, Ankush Dharkar and Pushpak Bhattacharyya

12:30-14:00 Lunch

Session 1-PM-1A: Sentiment Analysis
Session Chair: Bing Liu

14:00-14:30 *Active Learning for Imbalanced Sentiment Classification*
Shoushan Li, Shengfeng Ju, Guodong Zhou and Xiaojun Li

14:30-15:00 *A Weakly Supervised Model for Sentence-Level Semantic Orientation Analysis with Multiple Experts*
Lizhen Qu, Rainer Gemulla and Gerhard Weikum

15:00-15:30 *Collocation Polarity Disambiguation Using Web-based Pseudo Contexts*
Yanyan Zhao, Bing Qin and Ting Liu

Thursday, July 12, 2012 (continued)

Session 1-PM-1B: Semantics: Nouns, Verbs and Predicates
Session Chair: Rada Mihalcea

14:00-14:30 *Aligning Predicates across Monolingual Comparable Texts using Graph-based Clustering*
Michael Roth and Anette Frank

14:30-15:00 *Local and Global Context for Supervised and Unsupervised Metonymy Resolution*
Vivi Nastase, Alex Judea, Katja Markert and Michael Strube

15:00-15:30 *Learning Verb Inference Rules from Linguistically-Motivated Evidence*
Hila Weisman, Jonathan Berant, Idan Szpektor and Ido Dagan

Session 1-PM-1C: Machine Learning: Latent Models
Session Chair: Alexandre Klementiev

14:00-14:30 *Spectral Dependency Parsing with Latent Variables*
Paramveer Dhillon, Jordan Rodu, Michael Collins, Dean Foster and Lyle Ungar

14:30-15:00 *A Phrase-Discovering Topic Model Using Hierarchical Pitman-Yor Processes*
Robert Lindsey, William Headden and Michael Stipicevic

15:00-15:30 *A Bayesian Model for Learning SCFGs with Discontiguous Rules*
Abby Levenberg, Chris Dyer and Phil Blunsom

Session 1-PM-1D: Summarization
Session Chair: Dragomir Radev

14:00-14:30 *Multiple Aspect Summarization Using Integer Linear Programming*
Kristian Woodsend and Mirella Lapata

14:30-15:00 *Minimal Dependency Length in Realization Ranking*
Michael White and Rajakrishnan Rajkumar

15:00-15:30 *Framework of Automatic Text Summarization Using Reinforcement Learning*
Seonggi Ryang and Takeshi Abekawa

15:30-16:00 Coffee Break

Thursday, July 12, 2012 (continued)

Session 1-PM-2A: Machine Translation
Session Chair: Xiong Deyi

16:00-16:30 *Large Scale Decipherment for Out-of-Domain Machine Translation*
Qing Dou and Kevin Knight

16:30-17:00 *N-gram-based Tense Models for Statistical Machine Translation*
Zhengxian Gong, Min Zhang, Chew Lim Tan and Guodong Zhou

17:00-17:30 *Source Language Adaptation for Resource-Poor Machine Translation*
Pidong Wang, Preslav Nakov and Hwee Tou Ng

Session 1-PM-2B: Dependency Parsing
Session Chair: Emily Pitler

16:00-16:30 *Exploiting Reducibility in Unsupervised Dependency Parsing*
David Mareček and Zdeněk Žabokrtský

16:30-17:00 *Improving Transition-Based Dependency Parsing with Buffer Transitions*
Daniel Fernández-González and Carlos Gómez-Rodríguez

17:00-17:30 *Generalized Higher-Order Dependency Parsing with Cube Pruning*
Hao Zhang and Ryan McDonald

Session 1-PM-2C: Phonemes, Words and Speech
Session Chair: Pascale Fung

16:00-16:30 *Universal Grapheme-to-Phoneme Prediction Over Latin Alphabets*
Young-Bum Kim and Benjamin Snyder

16:30-17:00 *Name Phylogeny: A Generative Model of String Variation*
Nicholas Andrews, Jason Eisner and Mark Dredze

17:00-17:30 *Syntactic Surprisal Affects Spoken Word Duration in Conversational Contexts*
Vera Demberg, Asad Sayeed, Philip Gorinski and Nikolaos Engonopoulos

Thursday, July 12, 2012 (continued)

Session 1-PM-2D: Question Answering
Session Chair: Alessandro Moschitti

Session 1-PM-3P: Poster Session and Reception (18:00-22:00)

Thursday, July 12, 2012 (continued)

Dynamic Programming for Higher Order Parsing of Gap-Minding Trees
Emily Pitler, Sampath Kannan and Mitchell Marcus

Joint Entity and Event Coreference Resolution across Documents
Heeyoung Lee, Marta Recasens, Angel Chang, Mihai Surdeanu and Dan Jurafsky

Joint Chinese Word Segmentation, POS Tagging and Parsing
Xian Qian and Yang Liu

Translation Model Based Cross-Lingual Language Model Adaptation: from Word Models to Phrase Models
Shixiang Lu, Wei Wei, Xiaoyin Fu and Bo Xu

Open Language Learning for Information Extraction
Mausam, Michael Schmitz, Stephen Soderland, Robert Bart and Oren Etzioni

Modelling Sequential Text with an Adaptive Topic Model
Lan Du, Wray Buntine and Huidong Jin

A Comparison of Vector-based Representations for Semantic Composition
William Blacoe and Mirella Lapata

Exploiting Chunk-level Features to Improve Phrase Chunking
Junsheng Zhou, Weiguang Qu and Fen Zhang

A Beam-Search Decoder for Grammatical Error Correction
Daniel Dahlmeier and Hwee Tou Ng

A Statistical Relational Learning Approach to Identifying Evidence Based Medicine Categories
Mathias Verbeke, Vincent Van Asch, Roser Morante, Paolo Frasconi, Walter Daelemans and Luc De Raedt

Lyrics, Music, and Emotions
Rada Mihalcea and Carlo Strapparava

Assessment of ESL Learners' Syntactic Competence Based on Similarity Measures
Su-Youn Yoon and Suma Bhat

Thursday, July 12, 2012 (continued)

Thursday, July 12, 2012 (continued)

Friday, July 13, 2012

Session 2-AM-1P: Plenary Session: Invited Talk
Session Chair: Marius Pasca

09:15-10:30 Invited Talk: The Appification of the Web and the Renaissance of Conversational User Interfaces (Patrick Pantel, Microsoft Research)

10:30-11:00 Coffee Break

Session 2-AM-2A: Machine Translation: Role of Syntax
Session Chair: Qun Liu

Session 2-AM-2B: Information Extraction: Temporally-Aware Extraction
Session Chair: Jong-Hoon Oh

Friday, July 13, 2012 (continued)

Session 2-AM-2C: Discourse and Generation
Session Chair: Anette Frank

11:00-11:30 *A Novel Discriminative Framework for Sentence-Level Discourse Analysis*
Shafiq Joty, Giuseppe Carenini and Raymond Ng

11:30-12:00 *Using Discourse Information for Paraphrase Extraction*
Michaela Regneri and Rui Wang

12:00-12:30 *Generating Non-Projective Word Order in Statistical Linearization*
Bernd Bohnet, Anders Björkelund, Jonas Kuhn, Wolfgang Seeker and Sina Zarriess

Session 2-AM-2D: CoNLL Shared Task
Session Chair: Sameer Pradhan

11:00-12:30 CoNLL Shared Task Session

12:30-13:45 Lunch

13:45-14:30 SIGDAT and SIGNLL Business Meetings

Session 2-PM-1A: Semantics: Words and Topics
Session Chair: Roi Reichart

14:30-15:00 *Learning Syntactic Categories Using Paradigmatic Representations of Word Context*
Mehmet Ali Yatbaz, Enis Sert and Deniz Yuret

15:00-15:30 *Exploring Topic Coherence over Many Models and Many Topics*
Keith Stevens, Philip Kegelmeyer, David Andrzejewski and David Buttler

Friday, July 13, 2012 (continued)

Session 2-PM-1B: Machine Translation: Pruning
Session Chair: Kevin Knight

14:30-15:00 *Entropy-based Pruning for Phrase-based Machine Translation*
Wang Ling, João Graça, Isabel Trancoso and Alan Black

15:00-15:30 *A Systematic Comparison of Phrase Table Pruning Techniques*
Richard Zens, Daisy Stanton and Peng Xu

Session 2-PM-1C: Evaluation
Session Chair: Billy Tak-Ming Wong

14:30-15:00 *Probabilistic Finite State Machines for Regression-based MT Evaluation*
Mengqiu Wang and Christopher D. Manning

15:00-15:30 *An Empirical Investigation of Statistical Significance in NLP*
Taylor Berg-Kirkpatrick, David Burkett and Dan Klein

Session 2-PM-1D: CoNLL Shared Task
Session Chair: Alessandro Moschitti

14:30-15:30 CoNLL Shared Task Session

15:30-16:00 Coffee Break

Session 2-PM-2A: Information Extraction: Relation and Event Extraction
Session Chair: Mausam

16:00-16:30 *Employing Compositional Semantics and Discourse Consistency in Chinese Event Extraction*
Peifeng Li, Guodong Zhou, Qiaoming Zhu and Libin Hou

16:30-17:00 *Reading The Web with Learned Syntactic-Semantic Inference Rules*
Ni Lao, Amarnag Subramanya, Fernando Pereira and William W. Cohen

17:00-17:30 *Ensemble Semantics for Large-scale Unsupervised Relation Extraction*
Bonan Min, Shuming Shi, Ralph Grishman and Chin-Yew Lin

Friday, July 13, 2012 (continued)

Session 2-PM-2B: Parsing Models and Evaluation
Session Chair: Ivan Titov

16:00-16:30 *Forest Reranking through Subtree Ranking*
Richard Farkas and Helmut Schmid

16:30-17:00 *Parser Showdown at the Wall Street Corral: An Empirical Investigation of Error Types in Parser Output*
Jonathan K. Kummerfeld, David Hall, James R. Curran and Dan Klein

17:00-17:30 *Extending Machine Translation Evaluation Metrics with Lexical Cohesion to Document Level*
Billy T. M. Wong and Chunyu Kit

Session 2-PM-2C: Large-Scale NLP Algorithms
Session Chair: Benjamin van Durme

16:00-16:30 *Fast Large-Scale Approximate Graph Construction for NLP*
Amit Goyal, Hal Daume III and Raul Guerra

16:30-17:00 *Building a Lightweight Semantic Model for Unsupervised Information Extraction on Short Listings*
Doo Soon Kim, Kunal Verma and Peter Yeh

17:00-17:30 *Sketch Algorithms for Estimating Point Queries in NLP*
Amit Goyal, Hal Daume III and Graham Cormode

Session 2-PM-2D: Machine Learning: Inference
Session Chair: Jennifer Gillenwater

16:00-16:30 *Monte Carlo MCMC: Efficient Inference by Approximate Sampling*
Sameer Singh, Michael Wick and Andrew McCallum

16:30-17:00 *On Amortizing Inference Cost for Structured Prediction*
Vivek Srikumar, Gourab Kundu and Dan Roth

17:00-17:30 *Exact Sampling and Decoding in High-Order Hidden Markov Models*
Simon Carter, Marc Dymetman and Guillaume Bouchard

Saturday, July 14, 2012

Session 3-AM-1P: Plenary Session
Session Chair: Jun'ichi Tsujii

09:00-09:30 *PATTY: A Taxonomy of Relational Patterns with Semantic Types*
Ndapandula Nakashole, Gerhard Weikum and Fabian Suchanek

09:30-10:00 *Training Factored PCFGs with Expectation Propagation*
David Hall and Dan Klein

10:00-10:30 *A Coherence Model Based on Syntactic Patterns*
Annie Louis and Ani Nenkova

10:30-11:00 Coffee Break

Session 3-AM-2A: Machine Translation: Decoding
Session Chair: Preslav Nakov

11:00-11:30 *Language Model Rest Costs and Space-Efficient Storage*
Kenneth Heafield, Philipp Koehn and Alon Lavie

11:30-12:00 *Document-Wide Decoding for Phrase-Based Statistical Machine Translation*
Christian Hardmeier, Joakim Nivre and Jörg Tiedemann

12:00-12:30 *Left-to-Right Tree-to-String Decoding with Prediction*
Yang Feng, Yang Liu, Qun Liu and Trevor Cohn

Saturday, July 14, 2012 (continued)

Session 3-AM-2B: Distributional and Compositional Semantics
Session Chair: Bo Pang

11:00-11:30 *Semantic Compositionality through Recursive Matrix-Vector Spaces*
Richard Socher, Brody Huval, Christopher D. Manning and Andrew Y. Ng

11:30-12:00 *Polarity Inducing Latent Semantic Analysis*
Wen-tau Yih, Geoffrey Zweig and John Platt

12:00-12:30 *First Order vs. Higher Order Modification in Distributional Semantics*
Gemma Boleda, Eva Maria Vecchi, Miquel Cornudella and Louise McNally

Session 3-AM-2C: Discourse: Coreference Resolution
Session Chair: Mihai Surdeanu

11:00-11:30 *Learning-based Multi-Sieve Co-reference Resolution with Knowledge*
Lev Ratinov and Dan Roth

11:30-12:00 *Joint Learning for Coreference Resolution with Markov Logic*
Yang Song, Jing Jiang, Wayne Xin Zhao, Sujian Li and Houfeng Wang

12:00-12:30 *Resolving "This-issue" Anaphora*
Varada Kolhatkar and Graeme Hirst

Session 3-AM-2D: Information Retrieval
Session Chair: Jianfeng Gao

11:00-11:30 *Entity based Q&A Retrieval*
Amit Singh

11:30-12:00 *Constructing Task-Specific Taxonomies for Document Collection Browsing*
Hui Yang

12:00-12:30 *Besting the Quiz Master: Crowdsourcing Incremental Classification Games*
Jordan Boyd-Graber, Brianna Satinoff, He He and Hal Daume III

12:30-14:00 Lunch

Saturday, July 14, 2012 (continued)

Saturday, July 14, 2012 (continued)

Session 3-PM-1D: Word Sense Disambiguation
Session Chair: Marc Dymetman

14:00-14:30 *Joining Forces Pays Off: Multilingual Joint Word Sense Disambiguation*
Roberto Navigli and Simone Paolo Ponzetto

14:30-15:00 *A New Minimally-Supervised Framework for Domain Word Sense Disambiguation*
Stefano Faralli and Roberto Navigli

15:00-15:30 *Grounded Models of Semantic Representation*
Carina Silberer and Mirella Lapata

15:30-16:00 Coffee Break

Session 3-PM-2A: Syntax and Parsing: Joint Parsing Models
Session Chair: Jason Eisner

16:00-16:30 *Improved Parsing and POS Tagging Using Inter-Sentence Consistency Constraints*
Alexander Rush, Roi Reichart, Michael Collins and Amir Globerson

16:30-17:00 *Unified Dependency Parsing of Chinese Morphological and Syntactic Structures*
Zhongguo Li and Guodong Zhou

17:00-17:30 *A Transition-Based System for Joint Part-of-Speech Tagging and Labeled Non-Projective Dependency Parsing*
Bernd Bohnet and Joakim Nivre

Session 3-PM-2B: Social Media
Session Chair: Alan Ritter

16:00-16:30 *Identifying Event-related Bursts via Social Media Activities*
Xin Zhao, Baihan Shu, Jing Jiang, Yang Song, Hongfei Yan and Xiaoming Li

16:30-17:00 *User Demographics and Language in an Implicit Social Network*
Katja Filippova

17:00-17:30 *Revisiting the Predictability of Language: Response Completion in Social Media*
Bo Pang and Sujith Ravi

Saturday, July 14, 2012 (continued)

Session 3-PM-2C: NLP Applications
Session Chair: Chikara Hashimoto

16:00-16:30 *Supervised Text-based Geolocation Using Language Models on an Adaptive Grid*
Stephen Roller, Michael Speriosu, Sarat Rallapalli, Benjamin Wing and Jason Baldridge

16:30-17:00 *A Discriminative Model for Query Spelling Correction with Latent Structural SVM*
Huizhong Duan, Yanen Li, ChengXiang Zhai and Dan Roth

17:00-17:30 *Characterizing Stylistic Elements in Syntactic Structure*
Song Feng, Ritwik Banerjee and Yejin Choi

Session 3-PM-3P: Closing

17:30-17:45 Closing: Closing Remarks

Cross-Lingual Language Modeling with Syntactic Reordering for Low-Resource Speech Recognition

Ping Xu and Pascale Fung
Human Language Technology Center
Department of Electronic and Computer Engineering
The Hong Kong University of Science and Technology, Clear Water Bay, Hong Kong
xuping@ust.hk, pascale@ece.ust.hk

Abstract

This paper proposes cross-lingual language modeling for transcribing source resource-poor languages and translating them into target resource-rich languages if necessary. Our focus is to improve the speech recognition performance of low-resource languages by leveraging the language model statistics from resource-rich languages. The most challenging work of cross-lingual language modeling is to solve the syntactic discrepancies between the source and target languages. We therefore propose syntactic reordering for cross-lingual language modeling, and present a first result that compares inversion transduction grammar (ITG) reordering constraints to IBM and local constraints in an integrated speech transcription and translation system. Evaluations on resource-poor Cantonese speech transcription and Cantonese to resource-rich Mandarin translation tasks show that our proposed approach improves the system performance significantly, up to 3.4% relative WER reduction in Cantonese transcription and 13.3% relative bilingual evaluation understudy (BLEU) score improvement in Mandarin transcription compared with the system without reordering.

1 Introduction

Statistical language modeling techniques have achieved remarkable success in speech and language processing (Clarkson and Rosenfeld, 1997; Stolcke, 2002). However, this success largely depends on the availability of a large amount of suitable text data in a language. Without sufficient text data for training, it is very difficult to build a practical and usable statistical language model. Therefore, most of the advances have been reported in so called *resource-rich* language such as English, Mandarin and Japanese, after creating linguistic resources of these languages at considerable cost. Today there are more than 6000 living languages spoken in the world (Gordon et al., 2005), and most of them have little transcribed texts and are considered as *resource-poor* languages (Nakov and Ng, 2009). Many of these languages are actually spoken by a huge number of speakers (e.g. some Chinese and Indian languages), and thus there is still a great demand to build speech and language processing systems for these languages.

Owing to data scarcity, most often an interpolation (Bellegarda, 2004) of language models between a resource-poor language and a resource-rich language is used in most low-resource ASR systems. Some researchers have proposed transforming resource-rich language models to resource-poor language models by word-level transduction, either in a context-independent or context-dependent manner (Hori et al., 2003; Akita and Kawahara, 2006; Jensson et al., 2009; Neubig et al., 2010). In (Jensson et al., 2009), a simple dictionary based context-independent transduction from a resource-rich language to a resource-poor language is exploited to improve speech recognition of the resource-poor language. In (Hori et al., 2003; Akita and Kawahara, 2006; Neubig et al., 2010), context-dependent transduction is exploited. In their case, the resource-poor language is a spoken language, and the resource-rich language is a written language. They carried out language model transformation since the input speech is in speaking-style and the output text is in written-style.

Others have investigated cross-lingual information between a resource-poor language and a resource-rich language. In (Khudanpur and Kim, 2002), cross-language cues are used to improve a language model of a resource-poor language. They used cross-lingual unigram probabilities trained from a story-specific parallel corpus of the resource-poor and resource-rich languages. They interpolate the language model of the resource-poor language with those unigram probabilities. In (Kim and Khudanpur, 2003), an n-gram language model in a resource-poor language is interpolated with cross-lingual unigram trigger probabilities. These triggers are word pairs of the resource-poor and resource-rich languages with the highest mutual information across these two languages. Another way of estimating those unigram probabilities is using latent semantic analysis by measuring cosine similarities from a document-aligned corpus for any given word pair (Kim and Khudanpur, 2004).

Both interpolation and word-level transduction approaches fail to meet the challenge of syntactic discrepancies between the resource-poor and resource-rich languages. This syntactic discrepancies exist, for example, even between the Sinitic languages and Indian languages[1] of the same family. Sinitic languages such as Cantonese/Yue, Shanghai/Wu, etc. are officially considered as "dialects" of the standard Chinese Mandarin (or Putonghua)[2]. However, they differ greatly from Mandarin in all aspects and are not mutually comprehensible. For instance, in addition to lexical and pronunciation differences, Cantonese Chinese (Lee, 2011) differs syntactically from Mandarin as well - we found that there are approximately 10% syntactic inversions between sentences of the two forms of Chinese.

We suggest that a better approach than interpolation and word-level transduction is to use *cross-lingual language modeling* with syntactic reordering. A reordering model with reordering constraints, such as ITG constraints (Wu, 1997), IBM constraints (Berger et al., 1996), and local constraints (Kumar and Byrne, 2005) can account for the syntactic differences. It has been shown in (Zens and Ney, 2003; Kanthak et al., 2005; Dreyer et al., 2007) that ITG constraints perform better than other constraints when tackling the reordering between many language pairs. Previous work on weighted finite-state transducer (WFST) based speech translation such as (Casacuberta et al., 2004; Zhou et al., 2005; Zhou et al., 2006; Mathias and Byrne, 2006; Matusov et al., 2006; Saon and Picheny, 2007) only train the reordering model using IBM constraints, local constraints or ad hoc rules. We will use ITG constraints, which have only been applied to text translation tasks before, to model the syntactic differences in cross-lingual language modeling for speech recognition.

We will implement a *cross-lingual language model* using WFSTs, and integrate it into a WFST-based speech recognition search space to give both resource-poor language and resource-rich language transcriptions. This creates an integrated speech transcription and translation framework.

This paper is organized as follows: Section 2 presents our proposed cross-lingual language modeling with syntactic reordering. In Section 3, we discuss speech recognition with cross-lingual language models. Section 4 and 5 give the experimental setup and results. We conclude our work at the end of this paper.

2 Cross-lingual Language Modeling with Syntactic Reordering

In automatic speech recognition (ASR), given an observed source speech vector X, the decoding process searches the best word sequence $\hat{v}_1^I$ (consists of words $v_1, v_2, ..., v_I$) by maximizing the posterior probability $P(v_1^I|X)$, where v_1^I is the source transcript representing the transcription of the source speech (see Eq. (1)). According to Bayes' law, we can decompose $P(v_1^I|X)$ into an acoustic model $P(X|v_1^I)$ and a language model $P(v_1^I)$. If a source language L_v is a resource-rich language, then the language model $P(v_1^I)$ can be well estimated from sufficient training texts. However, if the source lan-

[1]For example, Hindi and Malayalam (Geethakumary, 2002).

[2]Since Cantonese does not have an official written form, there are very few written texts available for training language models. In this paper, we treat Cantonese as a typical resource-poor language and Mandarin as a typical resource-rich language. This language pair will be used for illustration purposes throughout this paper.

guage L_v is a resource-poor language, then the language model $P(v_1^I)$ cannot be reliably or robustly estimated due to lack of training texts.

$$\begin{aligned}\hat{v}_1^I &= \arg\max_{v_1^I} P(v_1^I|X) \qquad (1)\\ &= \arg\max_{v_1^I} P(X|v_1^I)P(v_1^I)\\ &= \arg\max_{v_1^I} P(X|v_1^I)\sum_{w_1^J} P(v_1^I|w_1^J)P(w_1^J)\\ &\approx \arg\max_{v_1^I} P(X|v_1^I)\max_{w_1^J} P(v_1^I|w_1^J)P(w_1^J)\end{aligned}$$

Since this paper tackles the language modeling challenge for low-resource speech recognition, here we just assume that the source language L_v is a resource-poor language. We further assume that there is a target language L_w, which is a resource-rich language closely related to the language L_v. In order to improve the language model $P(v_1^I)$ of the resource-poor language L_v, we introduce *cross-lingual language modeling* by decomposing the language model $P(v_1^I)$ into a translation model $P(v_1^I|w_1^J)$ and a language model $P(w_1^J)$ of the resource-rich language L_w (see Eq. (1)). w_1^J is the target resource-rich language transcript that consists of words $w_1, w_2, ..., w_J$. $P(v_1^I|w_1^J)P(w_1^J)$ is defined as a *cross-lingual language model*. It leverages the abundant statistics from the language model $P(w_1^J)$ to improve the language model $P(v_1^I)$ of the resource-poor language.

The translation model $P(v_1^I|w_1^J)$ can be estimated by addressing the discrepancies between the resource-poor language L_v and the resource-rich language L_w, which can be modeled from a parallel corpus of the L_v transcript v_1^I and the L_w transcript w_1^J. For the syntactic inversions, we reorder the word or phrase positions of the L_w language model into those of the L_v language model. We have observed that most of the words are aligned monotonically between L_v and L_w within a phrase. This paper, therefore only considers phrase-level reordering, which effectively preserves the monotonic word sequences within phrases, and significantly reduces the number of reordering paths compared with word-level reordering.

2.1 Preprocessing: Phrase Extraction and Segmentation

Our discussion starts with phrase extraction from the parallel corpus. We define a phrase sequence $\tilde{v}_1^K$ (consists of phrases $\tilde{v}_1, \tilde{v}_2, ..., \tilde{v}_K$) segmented from the word-level L_v transcript v_1^I and $\tilde{w}_1^K$ (consists of phrases $\tilde{w}_1, \tilde{w}_2, ..., \tilde{w}_K$) segmented from the word-level L_w transcript w_1^J. Furthermore, we define a reordering sequence r_1^K, of which the detail can be found in Section 2.2.

The phrase-level translation model $P(v_1^I|w_1^J)$ is decomposed into four components (see Eq. (2)): *segmentation model* $P(\tilde{w}_1^K|w_1^J)$, *phrasal reordering model* $P(r_1^K|\tilde{w}_1^K, w_1^J)$, *phrase-to-phrase transduction model* $P(\tilde{v}_1^K|r_1^K, \tilde{w}_1^K, w_1^J)$ and *reconstruction model* $P(v_1^I|\tilde{v}_1^K, r_1^K, \tilde{w}_1^K, w_1^J)$. Before presenting each component model, we need to extract two phrase tables for the L_v transcript and the L_w transcript, respectively.

$$\begin{aligned}P(v_1^I|w_1^J) \approx \max_{\tilde{v}_1^K, r_1^K, \tilde{w}_1^K} & P(\tilde{w}_1^K|w_1^J)\cdot\\ & P(r_1^K|\tilde{w}_1^K, w_1^J)\cdot\\ & P(\tilde{v}_1^K|r_1^K, \tilde{w}_1^K, w_1^J)\cdot\\ & P(v_1^I|\tilde{v}_1^K, r_1^K, \tilde{w}_1^K, w_1^J) \qquad (2)\end{aligned}$$

The phrase extraction is based on word-to-word alignments of the parallel corpus. We train word alignments in both directions with GIZA++, and then symmetrize the two alignments using the *refined method* (Och and Ney, 2003). Figure 1 shows an example of word-to-word alignment results between an L_v transcript (Cantonese) and an L_w transcript (Mandarin), from which phrase-to-phrase alignments are derived by identifying deletion, substitution, insertion and inversion.

Prior to phrasal reordering, the segmentation model $P(\tilde{w}_1^K|w_1^J)$ implemented by a segmentation WFST S_w is applied to segment a word sequence w_1^J in the L_w language model into a phrase sequence $\{\tilde{w}_1, \tilde{w}_2, ..., \tilde{w}_K\}$. The maximum number of words that can be segmented into one phrase is controlled by a *segmentation order* s. An example of S_w is shown in Figure 3(a1). It segments a word sequence $\{w_1, w_2, w_3\}$ into a phrase sequence $\{w_1, w_2\_w_3\}$ after performing *composition* (Mohri, 2009) with the target L_w language model (see Figure 3(b1 & b2))[3].

[3]The "_" symbol is used to indicate the concatenation of con-

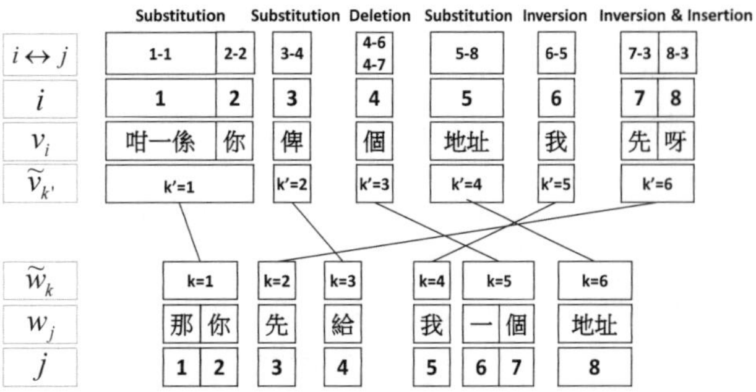

Figure 1: An example (in English: Please give me an address first) of phrase extraction from word-to-word alignments. i and j are word indexes. k' and k are phrase indexes. $i \leftrightarrow j$ represents the word-to-word alignment. $k \leftrightarrow k'$ represents the indentified phrase-to-phrase alignment.

2.2 Phrasal Reordering Model

Given a phrase sequence $\{\tilde{w}_1, \tilde{w}_2, ..., \tilde{w}_K\}$ of the L_w transcript, the role of the reordering model $P(r_1^K | \tilde{w}_1^K, w_1^J)$ is to reorder phrase positions of the L_w transcript into those of the L_v transcript by permutation of $\tilde{w}_1^K$ according to a reordering sequence $\{r_1^K : r_k \in \{1, 2, ..., K\}, r_k \neq r_{k' \neq k}\}$. The phrase sequence $\{\tilde{w}_1, \tilde{w}_2, ..., \tilde{w}_K\}$ is therefore reordered into $\{\tilde{w}_{r_1}, \tilde{w}_{r_2}, ..., \tilde{w}_{r_K}\}$ consequently (see Figure 2 where $K = 3$). Since arbitrary permutations of K phrases are NP-hard (Knight, 1999), reordering constraints have to be set over r_1^K to reduce the number of permutations.

There are three reordering constraints widely used in statistical machine translation, namely local constraints, IBM constraints and ITG constraints. Here we would like to point out that this is the first time that reordering constraints have been incorporated into a cross-lingual language model for speech recognition.

Reordering Constraints

Local constraints make the restriction that one phrase can jump at most $L-1$ phrases either forward or backward, where L is the reordering distance (or window size of permutation)[4]. The generation of r_1^K under local constraints can be viewed as solving of the following problem (Kløve, 2009):

How many permutations of $\{1, 2, \ldots k \ldots, K\}$ satisfy $|r_k - k| < L$ for all k?

IBM constraints, a superset of local constraints (Dreyer et al., 2007), generate permutations r_1^K deviate from the monotonic phrase order $\{r_1^K : r_k = k\}$. More specifically, any phrase position r_k can be selected from the positions of the first m yet uncovered phrases (see Eq. (3)). A typical value of m is 4 (Zens and Ney, 2003), and we write IBM constraints with $m = 4$ as IBM(4).

$$r_k \in \begin{cases} \{1, 2, ..., k-1+m; r_k \neq r_{k' \neq k}\} \\ \text{if } k \leq K+1-m, \\ \{1, 2, ..., K; r_k \neq r_{k' \neq k}\} \\ \text{if } K+1-m < k \leq K. \end{cases} \quad (3)$$

ITG constraints provide a more faithful coverage of syntactic reordering in the parallel data than local constraints and IBM constraints. Our presentation of ITG constraints starts with defining of some permutation sets. Let S_K be the set of permutations on {1,2,...,K}. A permutation $r_1^K \in S_K$, where $r_1^K = r_1 r_2 \ldots r_K$, contains a subsequence of type $\tau \in S_M$ if and only if a sequence of indices $1 \leq i_1 < i_2 < \ldots < i_M \leq K$ exists such that $r_{i_1} r_{i_2} \ldots r_{i_M}$ has all the same pairwise comparisons as τ. We denote the set of permutations of S_K not containing subsequences of type τ by $S_K(\tau)$. If we have sets $S_K(\tau_1), \ldots, S_K(\tau_p)$, we denote the set $S_K(\tau_1) \cap \ldots \cap S_K(\tau_p)$ by $S_K(\tau_1, \ldots, \tau_p)$ (Barcucci et al., 2000). ITG constraints allow the permutation set $S_K(3142, 2413)$, which forbids subsequence of type $(3, 1, 4, 2)$ and its dual $(2, 4, 1, 3)$. Explicitly, ITG constraints avoid any permutation r_1^K satisfying either $r_{i_2} < r_{i_4} < r_{i_1} < r_{i_3}$ or $r_{i_3} < r_{i_1} < r_{i_4} < r_{i_2}$, where $1 \leq i_1 < i_2 < i_3 < i_4 \leq K$. In (Wu, 1997), these forbidden subsequences are called "inside-out" transpositions. They are fairly distorted matchings, and hardly observed in real parallel data.

In order to get an intuitive sense of the reordering capability of those three constraints, we list the number of permutations under local constraints, IBM constraints as well as ITG constraints[5] in Table 1.

secutive words forming a phrase.

[4]The concept of reordering distance also applies to other constraints.

[5]Interestingly, when $K = L$, the number of permutations under ITG constraints $N_{ITG} = |S_K(3142, 2413)|$, and $|S_K(3142, 2413)|$ equals the $K-1$-th Schröder numbers s_{K-1} (Ehrenfeucht et al., 1998)

Table 1: Comparison of permutation number under local constraints (N_{Local}), IBM constraints ($N_{IBM(4)}$) and ITG constraints (N_{ITG}). The comparison is constrained by the phrase number K and the reordering distance L.

		K=2	K=3	K=4	K=5	K=6	K=7	K=8	K=9	K=10
L=2	N_{Local}	2	3	5	8	13	21	34	55	89
	$N_{IBM(4)}$	2	3	5	8	13	21	34	55	89
	N_{ITG}	2	3	5	8	13	21	34	55	89
L=3	N_{Local}	2	6	14	31	73	172	400	932	2177
	$N_{IBM(4)}$	2	6	14	31	73	172	400	932	2177
	N_{ITG}	2	6	12	25	57	124	268	588	1285
L=4	N_{Local}	2	6	24	78	230	675	2069	6404	19708
	$N_{IBM(4)}$	2	6	24	78	230	675	2069	6404	19708
	N_{ITG}	2	6	22	52	122	321	885	2304	5880
L=5	N_{Local}	2	6	24	120	504	1902	6902	25231	95401
	$N_{IBM(4)}$	2	6	24	96	330	1066	3451	11581	39264
	N_{ITG}	2	6	22	90	236	602	1714	5269	16385
L=6	N_{Local}	2	6	24	120	720	3720	17304	76110	329462
	$N_{IBM(4)}$	2	6	24	96	384	1374	4718	16275	57749
	N_{ITG}	2	6	22	90	394	1108	3014	9038	29618

We can see that given the same K ($K \leq 10$) and L ($L \leq 6$), IBM constraints have less permutations than local constraints, and ITG constraints have less permutations than IBM constraints in general (only one exception when $K = L = 6$). These observations indicate that ITG constraints can filter out more unlikely permutations for a fixed reordering distance, resulting in longer distance reordering capability.

Table 1 also tells us that the phrase number K and the reordering distance L for any of the constraints cannot be too large for practical implementation. For instance, if $L = 6$ and K goes from 6 to 7, the order of magnitude of N_{Local}, $N_{IBM(4)}$ and N_{ITG} increases from 2 to 3. Hence, phrases for permutation should be selective to cover the most possible re-orderings. If long reordering distances are allowed, unlikely permutations should be pruned so that the memory consumption becomes manageable.

Reordering Sequence Distribution

So far we have discussed the issue that how to generate permutations for the reordering model using reordering constraints. Another issue is how to parameterize the reordering sequence distribution. Both ITG constraints and other constraints assume that all permutations are equally probable. However, it makes sense to restrict those non-monotonic reorderings when performing the translation. This not only helps the search of the most likely permutation, but also guides the pruning of unlikely permutations.

$$\begin{aligned} P(r_1^K|\tilde{w}_1^K, w_1^J) &= P(r_1)\prod_{k=2}^{K} P(r_k|r_{k-1}, \tilde{w}_1^K) \\ &= P(r_1)\prod_{k=2}^{K} P(r_k|r_{k-1}) \end{aligned} \quad (4)$$

We make a first order Markov assumption over the phrasal reordering model $P(r_1^K|\tilde{w}_1^K, w_1^J)$ (see Eq. (4)). The reordering sequence distribution is parameterized to assign decreasing likelihood to phrase reorderings $\{\tilde{w}_{r_1}, \tilde{w}_{r_2}, \ldots, \tilde{w}_{r_K}\}$ that diverge from the original word order (Och et al., 1999; Kumar et al., 2005). Suppose $\tilde{w}_{r_k} = w_l^{l'}$ and $\tilde{w}_{r_{k-1}} = w_q^{q'}$, the reordering sequence distribution is set as Eq. (5), where p_0 is a tuning factor. We normalize the probabilities $P(r_k|r_{k-1})$ such that $\sum_{k'=1,k'\neq r_{k-1}}^{K} P(r_k = k'|r_{k-1}) = 1$.

$$\begin{aligned} P(r_k|r_{k-1}) &= p_0^{|l-q'-1|} \\ P(r_1 = k) &= \frac{1}{K}; k \in \{1, 2, ..., K\} \end{aligned} \quad (5)$$

Assume that we have a phrase sequence $\{\tilde{w}_1, \tilde{w}_2, \tilde{w}_3\}$, Figure 2 shows the phrasal reordering model implemented by a reordering WFST Ω_r under the first order Markov assumption for this phrase sequence.

Figure 3(a2) gives one more example of Ω_r, which reorders the phrase sequence $\{w_1, w_2\_w_3\}$ into $\{w_2\_w_3, w_1\}$[6]. Within the WFST paradigm, reordering models under any of those constraints can be integrated into the cross-lingual language model.

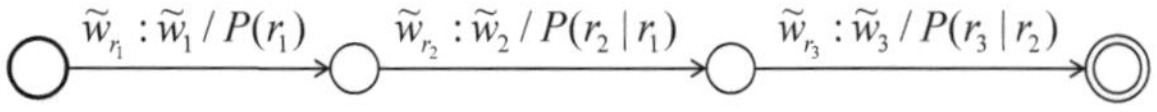

Figure 2: An example of reordering WFST Ω_r implementing the phrasal reordering model under the first order Markov assumption.

2.3 Phrase-to-Phrase Transduction Model

Once the phrase sequence of the L_w transcript is reordered into the L_v transcript order, we use the phrase-to-phrase transduction model specified in Eq. (6) to perform the cross-language transduction. Given sufficient parallel training data, the context-dependent phrase-to-phrase transduction model can be estimated using the GIATI method (Casacuberta and Vidal, 2004). However, for the translation task with scarce training data, the context-dependent transduction probabilities may not be reliably estimated. Therefore, we assume that a phrase $\tilde{v}_k$ is generated independently by each phrase $\tilde{w}_{r_k}$. $C(\tilde{v}_k, \tilde{w}_{r_k})$ is the number of times that phrase $\tilde{v}_k$ is aligned to $\tilde{w}_{r_k}$ in the parallel corpus. This model can be implemented by a WFST T_{vw} which transduces $\tilde{v}_k$ to $\tilde{w}_{r_k}$. Figure 3(a3) shows an example of T_{vw} transducing $v_2\_v_3$ to $w_2\_w_3$.

$$\begin{aligned} P(\tilde{v}_1^K | r_1^K, \tilde{w}_1^K, w_1^J) &= P(\tilde{v}_1^K | r_1^K, \tilde{w}_1^K) \\ &= \prod_{k=1}^{K} P_k(\tilde{v}_k | \tilde{w}_{r_k}) \\ &= \prod_{k=1}^{K} \frac{C(\tilde{v}_k, \tilde{w}_{r_k})}{\sum_{\tilde{v}_k} C(\tilde{v}_k, \tilde{w}_{r_k})} \end{aligned} \tag{6}$$

2.4 Reconstruction Model

Reconstruction model $P(v_1^I | \tilde{v}_1^K, r_1^K, \tilde{w}_1^K, w_1^J)$ operates in the opposite direction as the segmentation model. It generates a word sequence v_1^I from a phrase sequence $\tilde{v}_1^K$. The reconstruction model can be implemented by a WFST R_v. An example of R_v is shown in Figure 3(a4), which reconstructs a phrase $v_2\_v_3$ into a word sequence $\{v_2, v_3\}$.

[6]For simplicity, reordering sequence distributions are not shown there.

3 Speech Recognition with Cross-Lingual Language Models

The translation model $P(v_1^I | w_1^J)$ can be constructed via WFST *composition* (denoted by $\circ$) (Mohri, 2009) of all the component models as shown in Eq. (7) and Figure 3, where $\mathcal{T}$ is the final composed WFST that transduces v_1^I to w_1^J.

$$\mathcal{T} = R_v \circ T_{vw} \circ \Omega_r \circ S_w \tag{7}$$

The cross-lingual language model G_{cl} is constructed through composition (see Eq. (8)) of the translation model and a resource-rich language model G.

$$G_{cl} = \mathcal{T} \circ G = R_v \circ T_{vw} \circ \Omega_r \circ S_w \circ G \tag{8}$$

As the way of integrating a resource-rich language model G into ASR search space (Mohri et al., 2008), we can integrate the cross-lingual language model G_{cl} into ASR search space in a globally optimized way as well. The search space can be implemented using a transducer ASR, which is formulated with a unified WFST approach as shown in Eq. (9). Here H transduces HMM states to context-dependent phones. C represents a transduction from context-dependent phones to context-independent phones. L is a lexicon transducer which maps context-independent phone sequences to word strings restricted to the input symbols of the cross-lingual language model transducer G_{cl}.

$$ASR = H \circ C \circ L \circ G_{cl} \tag{9}$$

Eq. (9) outputs the recognition result in a resource-rich language. If recognition system requires recognition outputs in a resource-poor language, then the search space should be constructed as Eq. (10), where π is a *projection* (Mohri, 2009) operator which projects the input label to the output label. Before decoding, the recognition transducer ASR can be optimized by a determinization operation right after each composition.

$$ASR = H \circ C \circ L \circ \pi(G_{cl}) \tag{10}$$

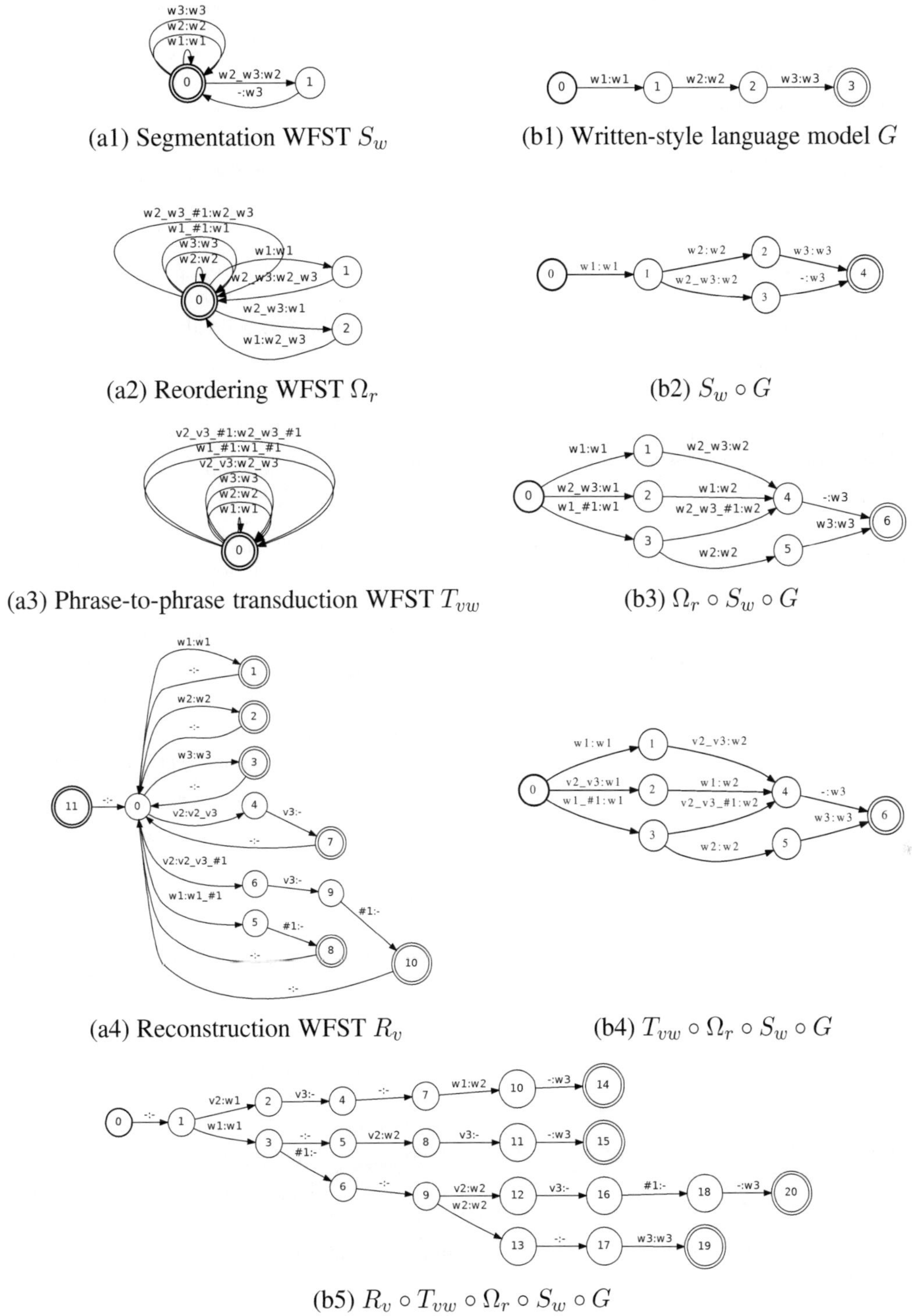

(a1) Segmentation WFST S_w

(b1) Written-style language model G

(a2) Reordering WFST Ω_r

(b2) $S_w \circ G$

(a3) Phrase-to-phrase transduction WFST T_{vw}

(b3) $\Omega_r \circ S_w \circ G$

(a4) Reconstruction WFST R_v

(b4) $T_{vw} \circ \Omega_r \circ S_w \circ G$

(b5) $R_v \circ T_{vw} \circ \Omega_r \circ S_w \circ G$

Figure 3: Illustration of constructing a cross-lingual language model via WFSTs: a word sequence $\{w_1, w_2, w_3\}$ represented by the L_w language model G (b1) is segmented into a phrase sequence $\{w_1, w_2\_w_3\}$ (b2); $\{w_1, w_2\_w_3\}$ is reordered into $\{w_2\_w_3, w_1\}$ (b3); phrase $w_2\_w_3$ is transduced to $v_2\_v_3$ (b4); phrase $v_2\_v_3$ is reconstructed into a word sequence $\{v_2, v_3\}$ (b5). wk and vk represent w_k and v_k, respectively. "-" refers to ϵ or null symbol. Auxiliary symbols $\#1, \#2, \cdots$ are used to make the WFST *determinizable* (Mohri, 2009) such that the transducer can be optimized by a *determinization* (Mohri, 2009) operation which significantly reduces the search network size.

4 Experimental Setup

4.1 Corpus and Model Training

To investigate the performance of our proposed cross-lingual language models, we have chosen Cantonese as a resource-poor language and Mandarin as a resource-rich language. We have collected Cantonese parliamentary speech from the Hong Kong Legislative Council. Currently we only have 4152 parallel transcribed sentences containing 19.4 hours of speech. It is separated into three sets, a training set (11.9 hours, 2700 sentences), a development set (3.7 hours, 788 sentences), and an evaluation set (3.8 hours, 664 sentences). The sentences in the evaluation set are a bit longer than those in the development set. The parallel transcriptions of the training set constitute a parallel corpus, which includes Cantonese transcription (manual transcription) of 106k words and Mandarin transcription (Hansard[7] transcription) of 80k words. The statistics of substitutions, insertions, deletions and inversions identified in the parallel corpus are shown in Table 2. Besides the parallel corpus, we have a set of additional Mandarin transcriptions, which has 31M words.

Table 2: No. of substitutions, insertions, deletions and inversions identified in the parallel corpus with different segmentation order s.

Segmentation Order	$s=2$	$s=3$	$s=4$	$s=5$
Substitutions	30921	22723	19011	17106
Insertions	4657	3820	3641	3295
Deletions	1365	1158	1066	1030
Inversions	3000	2876	2814	2779
Total	39943	30577	26532	24210

The training set is used for training an acoustic model (including H and C) using a Maximum Likelihood criterion. It adopts 13 MFCC coefficients, together with 13 delta coefficients and 13 acceleration coefficients as the acoustic features. The acoustic model comprises 73 Hidden Markov Models (HMMs) to represent 70 Cantonese phonemes as well as silence, short pause, and noise. During the acoustic model training, tied-state cross-word triphones are constructed by decision tree clustering.

[7]Hansard is a name of the printed transcripts of parliamentary debates.

The parallel corpus is used for training the translation model T. Together with the parallel corpus, the additional Mandarin transcriptions are used for training an interpolated word-level trigram language model G, where the lexicon size is about 28K. A modified scheme of Kneser-Ney discounting is applied for the language model G with a back-off threshold of 1 for unigram and 2 for bigram. The cross-lingual language model G_{cl} can be obtained by composition of T and G.

4.2 Decoding and Evaluation Method

Decoding of the speech recognition search space ASR is performed by T^3 Decoder (Dixon et al., 2009), which is a state-of-the-art WFST-based LVCSR speech decoder. Decoding of ASR in Eq. (9) gives Mandarin outputs. Decoding of ASR in Eq. (10) gives Cantonese outputs.

In our experiments, we use the following evaluation criteria:

WER (word error rate). The WER is computed as the minimum number of substitution, insertion and deletion operations that have to be performed to convert the generated sentence into the reference sentence (Zens et al., 2004). The WER relates the speech recognition accuracy. The lower WER, the better.

BLEU (bilingual evaluation understudy) score. The BLEU score measures the precision of n-grams (unigrams, bigrams, trigrams and fourgrams) with respect to a reference translation with a penalty for too short sentences (Papineni et al., 2002). The BLEU score reflects the translation accuracy. The larger BLEU score, the better.

We perform WER evaluation of decoding outputs of Eq. (10) and BLEU score evaluation of decoding outputs of Eq. (9) using the evaluation set. The WER evaluation is on the Cantonese output against the Cantonese reference transcription (manual transcription). The BLEU score evaluation is on the Mandarin output against the Mandarin reference transcription (Hansard transcription).

4.3 Parameter Settings

The performance of our proposed cross-lingual language models is sensitive to many parameters. Firstly, segmentation order s affects phrase extraction. The optimal value depends on the language

Table 3: WER and BLEU score for decoding results of $H \circ C \circ L \circ G$, $H \circ C \circ L \circ \pi(G_{cl})$ without reordering, and $H \circ C \circ L \circ \pi(G_{cl})$ with reordering under various constraints.

Models	$H \circ C \circ L \circ G$	$H \circ C \circ L \circ \pi(G_{cl})$ $G_{cl} = \mathcal{T}_3 \circ G$ $\mathcal{T}_3 = R_v \circ T_{vw} \circ S_w$	$H \circ C \circ L \circ \pi(G_{cl})$ $G_{cl} = \mathcal{T}_3 \circ G, \mathcal{T}_3 = R_v \circ T_{vw} \circ \Omega_r \circ S_w$		
			Local Constraints	IBM Constraints	ITG Constraints
WER(%)	29.85	27.05	26.35	26.20	26.13
BLEU	N/A	29.23	32.29	32.81	33.12

pair and the size of corpus. Secondly, p_0 in the first order Markov assumption affects the decoding results. Thirdly, the number of reordering permutations or paths are formidable when the reordering distance L is long as suggested by Table 1. Therefore, we apply histogram pruning to reordering paths, which only maintains top N most likely ones. The development set is used for tuning parameters p_0 and N.

5 Experimental Results

The evaluation results of the proposed cross-lingual language models G_{cl} with reordering under various constraints are presented in Table 3, where $G_{cl} = \mathcal{T}_s \circ G = \mathcal{T}_3 \circ G$.[8] In general, reordering has a significant effect on enhancing the performance of recognition and translation in the sense of WER reduction and BLEU improvement. Compared with the cross-lingual language model without reordering, the cross-lingual language model with reordering under local constraints gives 0.70% absolute WER reduction and 3.06 absolute BLEU improvement. The cross-lingual language model with reordering under IBM constraints gives 0.85% absolute WER reduction and 3.58 absolute BLEU improvement. The cross-lingual language model with reordering under ITG constraints yields the best performance, with 0.92% absolute WER reduction and 3.89 absolute BLEU improvement. All WER improvements pointed out here are statistically significant at 99% confidence according to a two-proportional z-test, and all BLEU improvements are statistically significant at 95% confidence according to a paired student t-test using bootstrap resampling.

[8] We have chosen segmentation order $s = 3$ because it works the best in our system.

6 Conclusions

We have proposed cross-lingual language modeling with phrase-level syntactic reordering for low-resource speech recognition. The cross-lingual language modeling enriches a resource-poor language model by leveraging the language model from a closely related resource-rich language. It provides an effective method to solve the low-resource language modeling challenge by using a large amount of resource-rich language (e.g. Mandarin) data and a small amount of resource-poor language (e.g. Cantonese) data, as well as some parallel data of resource-poor and resource-rich languages. With a cross-lingual language model, our ASR system can decode speech into transcriptions, either in a resource-poor language or a resource-rich language, using a single WFST-based speech decoder.

We have presented a first end-to-end WFST source to target language transcription and translation system with syntactic reordering and global optimization. Our work is the first to use ITG constraints for the syntactic reordering in such an integrated system. We also did comparative study of ITG constraints, IBM constraints and local constraints in the reordering model, for completeness. We have also presented the determinizable design of each transducer for composing a cross-lingual language model such that we can optimize the search network by determinization. This is crucially important to successfully build a practical integrated system, and, of course, the work is extremely challenging.

Experiments on Cantonese recognition and Cantonese to Mandarin translation tasks have shown that our proposed cross-lingual language model substantially improves the performance of the recognition and translation. The best system gives 12.5% relative WER reduction in Cantonese (resource-poor language) transcriptions over the system using interpolation. The best reordering model gives 3.4% relative WER reduction and 13.3% relative BLEU score improvement in Mandarin (resource-rich language) transcriptions over the system without reordering. The improvements have been found to be statistically significant.

Even though the objective of our work is for speech recognition, our proposed cross-lingual language modeling can be easily applied to speech translation of other language pairs for efficient direct decoding from source speech to target text.

7 Acknowledgments

This work is partially supported by ITS/189/09 and CERG#612211. The authors would like to thank Dr. Tasuku Oonishi for providing access to the T^3 decoder, and thank Prof. Sadaoki Furui and his team for useful discussions. Thanks should go to Yue Yu and Percy Cheung for collecting the Cantonese and Mandarin parallel data. Thanks also go to Ricky Chan for training the Cantonese acoustic model and Dr. Markus Saers for helping on training the GIZA word-to-word alignment models.

References

Y. Akita and T. Kawahara. 2006. Efficient estimation of language model statistics of spontaneous speech via statistical transformation model. In *Proceedings of the IEEE International Conference on Acoustics, Speech and Signal Processing*, volume 1, pages 1049–1052.

E. Barcucci, A. Del Lungo, E. Pergola, and R. Pinzani. 2000. Permutations avoiding an increasing number of length-increasing forbidden subsequences. *Discrete Mathematics and Theoretical Computer Science*, 4(1):31–44.

J.R. Bellegarda. 2004. Statistical language model adaptation: review and perspectives. *Speech communication*, 42(1):93–108.

A.L. Berger, P.F. Brown, S.A. Della Pietra, V.J. Della Pietra, A.S. Kehler, and R.L. Mercer. 1996. Language translation apparatus and method using context-based translation models. US Patent 5,510,981.

F. Casacuberta and E. Vidal. 2004. Machine translation with inferred stochastic finite-state transducers. *Computational Linguistics*, 30(2):205–225.

F. Casacuberta, H. Ney, F.J. Och, et al. 2004. Some approaches to statistical and finite-state speech-to-speech translation. *Computer Speech & Language*, 18(1):25–47.

P. Clarkson and R. Rosenfeld. 1997. Statistical language modeling using the cmu-cambridge toolkit. In *5th European Conference on Speech Communication and Technology*.

P.R. Dixon, T. Oonishi, K. Iwano, and S. Furui. 2009. Recent development of wfst-based speech recognition decoder. In *Proceedings of 2009 APSIPA Annual Summit and Conference*, pages 138–147, Sapporo, Japan.

M. Dreyer, K. Hall, and S. Khudanpur. 2007. Comparing reordering constraints for smt using efficient bleu oracle computation. In *Proceedings of SSST, NAACL-HLT 2007 / AMTA Workshop on Syntax and Structure in Statistical Translation*, pages 103–110, Rochester, New York.

A. Ehrenfeucht, T. Harju, P. Ten Pas, and G. Rozenberg. 1998. Permutations, parenthesis words, and schröder numbers. *Discrete mathematics*, 190(1):259–264.

V. Geethakumary. 2002. A contrastive analysis of hindi and malayalam. *Language in India*.

R.G. Gordon, B.F. Grimes, and Summer Institute of Linguistics. 2005. *Ethnologue: Languages of the world*, volume 15. SIL International, Dallas TX, USA.

T. Hori, D. Willett, and Y. Minami. 2003. Language model adaptation using wfst-based speaking-style translation. In *Proceedings of the IEEE International Conference on Acoustics, Speech and Signal Processing*, volume 1, pages 228–231.

A.T. Jensson, T. Oonishi, K. Iwano, and S. Furui. 2009. Development of a wfst based speech recognition system for a resource deficient language using machine translation. In *Proceedings of APSIPA ASC 2009: Asia-Pacific Signal and Information Processing Association, 2009 Annual Summit and Conference*, pages 50–56.

S. Kanthak, D. Vilar, E. Matusov, R. Zens, and H. Ney. 2005. Novel reordering approaches in phrase-based statistical machine translation. In *Proceedings of the ACL Workshop on Building and Using Parallel Texts*, pages 167–174. Association for Computational Linguistics.

S. Khudanpur and W. Kim. 2002. Using cross-language cues for story-specific language modeling. In *7th International Conference on Spoken Language Processing*.

W. Kim and S. Khudanpur. 2003. Cross-lingual lexical triggers in statistical language modeling. In *Proceedings of the 2003 conference on Empirical methods in natural language processing*, pages 17–24. Association for Computational Linguistics.

W. Kim and S. Khudanpur. 2004. Cross-lingual latent semantic analysis for language modeling. In *Proceed-*

ings of the IEEE International Conference on Acoustics, Speech and Signal Processing, volume 1, pages I257–I260. IEEE.

T. Kløve. 2009. Generating functions for the number of permutations with limited displacement. *The Electronic Journal of Combinatorics*, 16(R104).

K. Knight. 1999. Decoding complexity in word-replacement translation models. *Computational Linguistics*, 25(4):607–615.

S. Kumar and W. Byrne. 2005. Local phrase reordering models for statistical machine translation. In *Proceedings of Human Language Technology Conference / Conference on Empirical Methods in Natural Language Processing (HLT/EMNLP)*, pages 161–168, Vancouver, Canada.

S. Kumar, Y. Deng, and W. Byrne. 2005. A weighted finite state transducer translation template model for statistical machine translation. *Natural Language Engineering*, 12(1):35–75.

J. Lee. 2011. Toward a parallel corpus of spoken cantonese and written chinese. In *Proceedings of the 5th International Joint Conference on Natural Language Processing*, pages 1462–1466, Chiang Mai, Thailand.

L. Mathias and W. Byrne. 2006. Statistical phrase-based speech translation. In *Proceedings of the IEEE International Conference on Acoustics, Speech and Signal Processing*, volume 1, pages 561–564.

E. Matusov, S. Kanthak, and H. Ney. 2006. Integrating speech recognition and machine translation: Where do we stand? In *Proceedings of the IEEE International Conference on Acoustics, Speech and Signal Processing*, volume 5, pages V1217–V1220. IEEE.

M. Mohri, F. C. N. Pereira, and M. Riley. 2008. Speech recognition with weighted finite-state transducers. *Handbook on Speech Processing and Speech Communication, Part E: Speech Recognition*.

M. Mohri. 2009. Weighted automata algorithms. *Handbook of Weighted Automata*, pages 213–254.

P. Nakov and H.T. Ng. 2009. Improved statistical machine translation for resource-poor languages using related resource-rich languages. In *Proceedings of the 2009 Conference on Empirical Methods in Natural Language Processing*, volume 3, pages 1358–1367. Association for Computational Linguistics.

G. Neubig, Y. Akita, S. Mori, and T. Kawahara. 2010. Improved statistical models for smt-based speaking style transformation. In *Proceedings of the IEEE International Conference on Acoustics, Speech and Signal Processing*, pages 5206–5209.

F.J. Och and H. Ney. 2003. A systematic comparison of various statistical alignment models. *Computational Linguistics*, 29(1):19–51.

F.J. Och, C. Tillmann, and H. Ney. 1999. Improved alignment models for statistical machine translation. In *Proceedings of the Joint SIGDAT Conf. on EMNLP and VLC*, pages 20–28, College Park, MD, USA.

K. Papineni, S. Roukos, T. Ward, and W.J. Zhu. 2002. Bleu: a method for automatic evaluation of machine translation. In *Proceedings of the 40th annual meeting on association for computational linguistics*, pages 311–318. Association for Computational Linguistics.

G. Saon and M. Picheny. 2007. Lattice-based viterbi decoding techniques for speech translation. In *Automatic Speech Recognition & Understanding, 2007. ASRU. IEEE Workshop on*, pages 386–389. IEEE.

A. Stolcke. 2002. Srilm-an extensible language modeling toolkit. In *7th International Conference on Spoken Language Processing*.

D. Wu. 1997. Stochastic inversion transduction grammars and bilingual parsing of parallel corpora. *Computational Linguistics*, 23(3):377–403.

R. Zens and H. Ney. 2003. A comparative study on reordering constraints in statistical machine translation. In *Proceedings of the 41st Annual Meeting on Association for Computational Linguistics*, pages 144–151, Sapporo, Japan. Association for Computational Linguistics.

R. Zens, H. Ney, T. Watanabe, and E. Sumita. 2004. Reordering constraints for phrase-based statistical machine translation. In *Proceedings of the 20th international conference on Computational Linguistics*, pages 205–211, Geneva, Switzerland. Association for Computational Linguistics.

B. Zhou, S.F. Chen, and Y. Gao. 2005. Constrained phrase-based translation using weighted finite-state transducers. In *Proceedings of the IEEE International Conference on Acoustics, Speech and Signal Processing*, volume 1, pages 1017–1020.

B. Zhou, S. F. Chen, and Y. Gao. 2006. Folsom: A fast and memory-efficient phrase-based approach to statistical machine translation. In *Spoken Language Technology Workshop*, pages 226–229. IEEE.

Resolving Complex Cases of Definite Pronouns: The Winograd Schema Challenge

Altaf Rahman and **Vincent Ng**
Human Language Technology Research Institute
University of Texas at Dallas
Richardson, TX 75083-0688
{altaf,vince}@hlt.utdallas.edu

Abstract

We examine the task of resolving complex cases of definite pronouns, specifically those for which traditional linguistic constraints on coreference (e.g., Binding Constraints, gender and number agreement) as well as commonly-used resolution heuristics (e.g., string-matching facilities, syntactic salience) are not useful. Being able to solve this task has broader implications in artificial intelligence: a restricted version of it, sometimes referred to as the Winograd Schema Challenge, has been suggested as a conceptually and practically appealing alternative to the Turing Test. We employ a knowledge-rich approach to this task, which yields a pronoun resolver that outperforms state-of-the-art resolvers by nearly 18 points in accuracy on our dataset.

1 Introduction

Despite the significant amount of work on pronoun resolution in the natural language processing community in the past forty years, the problem is still far from being solved. Its difficulty stems in part from its reliance on sophisticated knowledge sources and inference mechanisms. The sentence pair below, which we will subsequently refer to as the *shout* example, illustrates how difficult the problem can be:

(1a) Ed shouted at Tim because he crashed the car.
(1b) Ed shouted at Tim because he was angry.

The pronoun *he* refers to *Tim* in 1a and *Ed* in 1b. Humans can resolve the pronoun easily, but state-of-the-art coreference resolvers cannot. The reason is that humans have the kind of *world knowledge* needed to resolve the pronouns that machines do not. Our world knowledge tells us that if someone is angry, he may shout at other people. Since *Ed* shouted, he should be the one who was angry. Our world knowledge also tells us that we may shout at someone who made a mistake and that crashing a car is a mistake. Combining these two pieces of evidence, we can easily infer that *Tim* crashed the car.

Our goal in this paper is to examine the resolution of *complex* cases of definite pronouns that appear in sentences exemplified by the *shout* example. Specifically, each sentence (1) has two clauses separated by a discourse connective (i.e., the connective appears *between* the two clauses, just like *because* in the *shout* example), where the first clause contains two or more candidate antecedents (e.g., *Ed* and *Tim*), and the second clause contains the target pronoun (e.g., *he*); and (2) the target pronoun agrees in gender, number, and semantic class with each candidate antecedent, but does not have any overlap in content words with any of them. For convenience, we will refer to the target pronoun that appears in this kind of sentences as a *difficult* pronoun.

Note that many traditional linguistic constraints on coreference are no longer useful for resolving difficult pronouns. For instance, syntactic constraints such as the Binding Constraints will not be useful, since the pronoun and the candidate antecedents appear in different clauses separated by a discourse connective; and constraints concerning agreement in gender, number, and semantic class will not be useful, since the pronoun and the candidate antecedents are compatible with respect to all these attributes. Traditionally important clues provided by various

I(a)	**The city councilmen** refused the demonstrators a permit because *they* feared violence.
I(b)	The city councilmen refused **the demonstrators** a permit because *they* advocated violence.
II(a)	James asked **Robert** for a favor, but *he* refused.
II(b)	**James** asked Robert for a favor, but *he* was refused.
III(a)	**Keith** fired Blaine but *he* did not regret.
III(b)	Keith fired **Blaine** although *he* is diligent.
IV(a)	Emma did not pass the ball to **Janie**, although *she* was open.
IV(b)	**Emma** did not pass the ball to Janie, although *she* should have.
V(a)	Medvedev will cede the presidency to **Putin** because *he* is more popular.
V(b)	**Medvedev** will cede the presidency to Putin because *he* is less popular.

Table 1: Sample twin sentences. The target pronoun in each sentence is italicized, and its antecedent is boldfaced.

string-matching facilities will not be useful either, since the pronoun and its candidate antecedents do not have any words in common.

As in the *shout* example, we ensure that each sentence has a *twin*. Twin sentences were used extensively by researchers in the 1970s to illustrate the difficulty of pronoun resolution (Hirst, 1981). We consider two sentences as twins if (1) they are identical up to and possibly including the discourse connective; and (2) the difficult pronouns in them are lexically identical but have different antecedents. The presence of twins implies that syntactic salience, a commonly-used heuristic in pronoun resolution that prefers the selection of syntactically salient candidate antecedents, may no longer be useful, since the candidate in the subject position is not more likely to be the correct antecedent than the other candidates.

To enable the reader to get a sense of how hard it is to resolve difficult pronouns, Table 1 shows sample twin sentences from our dataset. Note that state-of-the-art pronoun resolvers (e.g., JavaRAP (Qiu et al., 2004), GuiTaR (Poesio and Kabadjov, 2004), as well as those designed by Mitkov (2002) and Charniak and Elsner (2009)) and coreference resolvers (e.g., BART (Versley et al., 2008), CherryPicker (Rahman and Ng, 2009), Reconcile (Stoyanov et al., 2010), the Stanford resolver (Raghunathan et al., 2010; Lee et al., 2011)) cannot accurately resolve the difficult pronouns in these structurally simple sentences, as they do not have the mechanism to capture the fine distinctions between twin sentences. In other words, when given these sentences, the best that the existing resolvers can do to resolve the pronouns is guessing. This could be surprising to a non-coreference researcher, but it is indeed the state of the art.

A natural question is: why do existing resolvers not attempt to handle difficult pronouns? One reason could be that these difficult pronouns do not appear frequently in standard evaluation corpora such as MUC, ACE, and OntoNotes (Bagga, 1998; Haghighi and Klein, 2009). In fact, the Stanford coreference resolver (Lee et al., 2011), which won the CoNLL-2011 shared task on coreference resolution, adopts the once-popular rule-based approach, resolving pronouns simply with rules that encode the aforementioned traditional linguistic constraints on coreference, such as the Binding constraints and gender and number agreement.

The infrequency of occurrences of difficult pronouns in these standard evaluation corpora by no means undermines their significance, however. In fact, being able to automatically resolve difficult pronouns has broader implications in artificial intelligence. Recently, Levesque (2011) has argued that the problem of resolving the difficult pronouns in a carefully chosen set of twin sentences, which he refers to as the Winograd Schema Challenge[1], could serve as a conceptually and practically appealing alternative to the well-known Turing Test (Turing,

[1]Levesque (2011) defines a Winograd Schema as a small reading comprehension test involving the question of which of the two candidate antecedents for the definite pronoun in a given sentence is its correct antecedent. Levesque names this challenge after Winograd because of his pioneering attempt to use a well-known pair of twin sentences — specifically the first pair in Table 1 — to illustrate the difficulty of natural language understanding (Winograd, 1972). Strictly speaking, we are addressing a relaxed version of the Challenge: while Levesque focuses solely on definite pronouns whose resolution requires background knowledge *not* expressed in the words of a sentence, we do not impose such a condition on a sentence.

1950). The reason should perhaps be clear given the above discussion: this is an easy task for a subject who can "understand" natural language but a challenging task for one who can only make intelligent guesses. Levesque believes that "with a very high probability", anything that can resolve correctly a series of difficult pronouns "is thinking in the full-bodied sense we usually reserve for people". Hence, being able to make progress on this task enables us to move one step closer to building an intelligent machine that can truly understand natural language.

To sum up, an important contribution of our work is that it opens up a new line of research involving a problem whose solution requires a deeper understanding of a text. With recent advances in knowledge extraction from text, we believe that time is ripe to tackle this problem. It is worth noting that some researchers have focused on other kinds of anaphors that are hard to resolve, including bridging anaphors (e.g., Poesio et al. (2004)) and anaphors referring to abstract entities, such as those realized by verb phrases in dialogs (e.g., Byron (2002), Strube and Müller (2003), Müller (2007)). Nevertheless, to our knowledge, there has been little work that specifically targets difficult pronouns.

Given the complexity of our task, we investigate a variety of sophisticated knowledge sources for resolving difficult pronouns, and combine them via a machine learning approach. Note that there has been a recent surge of interest in extracting world knowledge from online encyclopedias such as Wikipedia (e.g., Ponzetto and Strube (2006, 2007), Poesio et al. (2007)), YAGO (e.g., Bryl et al. (2010), Rahman and Ng (2011), Uryupina et al. (2011)), and Freebase (e.g., Lee et al. (2011)). However, the resulting extractions are primarily IS-A relations (e.g., *Barack Obama* IS-A *U. S. president*), which would not be useful for resolving definite pronouns.

2 Dataset Creation

We asked 30 undergraduate students who are not affiliated with this research to compose sentence pairs (i.e., twin sentences) that conform to the constraints specified in the introduction. Each student was also asked to annotate the candidate antecedents, the target pronoun, and the correct antecedent for each sentence she composed. Note that a sentence may contain multiple pronouns, but exactly one of them — the one explicitly annotated by its author — is the target pronoun. Each sentence pair was cross-checked by one other student to ensure that it (1) conforms to the desired constraints and (2) does not contain pronouns with ambiguous antecedents (in other words, a human should not be confused as to which candidate antecedent is the correct one). At the end of the process, 941 sentence pairs were considered acceptable, and they formed our dataset. These sentences cover a variety of topics, ranging from real events (e.g., Iran's plan to attack the Saudi ambassador to the U.S.), to events and characters in movies (e.g., Batman and Robin), to purely imaginary situations (e.g., the *shout* example). We partition these sentence pairs into a training set and a test set following a 70/30 ratio.

While not requested by us, the students annotated exactly two candidate antecedents for each sentence. For ease of exposition, we will assume below that there are two candidate antecedents per sentence.

3 Machine Learning Framework

Since our goal is to determine which of the two candidate antecedents is the correct antecedent for the target pronoun in each sentence, our system assumes as input the sentence, the target pronoun, and the two candidate antecedents.

We employ machine learning to combine the features derived from different knowledge sources. Specifically, we employ a *ranking-based* approach. Ranking-based approaches have been shown to outperform their classification-based counterparts (Denis and Baldridge, 2007, 2008; Iida et al., 2003; Yang et al., 2003). Given a pronoun and two candidate antecedents, we aim to train a ranking model that *ranks* the two candidates such that the correct antecedent is assigned a higher rank.

More formally, given training sentence S_k containing target pronoun A_k, correct antecedent C_k and incorrect antecedent I_k, we create two feature vectors, $\mathbf{x}_{CA_k}$ and $\mathbf{x}_{IA_k}$, where $\mathbf{x}_{CA_k}$ is generated from A_k and C_k, and $\mathbf{x}_{IA_k}$ is generated from A_k and I_k. The training set consists of ordered pairs of feature vectors ($\mathbf{x}_{CA_k}$, $\mathbf{x}_{IA_k}$), and the goal of the training procedure is to acquire a ranker that minimizes the number of violations of pairwise rankings provided in the training set. We train this ranker using Joachims' (2002) SVM^{light} package. It is worth noting that we do *not* exploit the fact that each sentence has a twin in training or testing.

After training, the ranker can be applied to the test instances, which are created in the same way as the training instances. For each test instance, the target pronoun is resolved to the higher-ranked candidate antecedent.

Component	# Features	Features
Narrative Chains	1	NC
Google	4	G1, G2, G3, G4
FrameNet	4	FN1, FN2, FN3, FN4
Heuristic Polarity	3	HPOL1, HPOL2, HPOL3
Learned Polarity	3	LPOL1, LPOL2, LPOL3
Connective-Based Relation	1	CBR
Semantic Compat.	3	SC1, SC2, SC3
Lexical Features	68,331	antecedent- independent and dependent features

Table 2: Summary of the features described in Section 4.

4 Linguistic Features

We derive linguistic features for resolving difficult pronouns from eight components, as described below. To enable the reader to keep track of these features more easily, we summarize them in Table 2.

4.1 Narrative Chains

Consider the following sentence:

(2) Ed punished Tim because he tried to escape.

Humans resolve *he* to *Tim* by exploiting the world knowledge that someone who tried to escape is bad and therefore should be punished. Such kind of knowledge can be extracted from *narrative chains*.

Narrative chains are partially ordered sets of events centered around a common *protagonist*, aiming to encode the kind of knowledge provided by *scripts* (Schank and Abelson, 1977). While scripts are hand-written, narrative chains can be learned from unannotated text. Below is a chain learned by Chambers and Jurafsky (2008):

borrow-s invest-s spend-s pay-s raise-s lend-s

As we can see, a narrative chain is composed of a sequence of events (verbs) together with the roles of the protagonist. Here, "s" denotes the subject role, even though a chain can contain a mix of "s" and "o" (the object role). From this chain, we know that the person who borrows something (probably money) may invest, spend, pay, or lend it.

We employ narrative chains to heuristically predict the antecedent for the target pronoun, and encode the prediction as a feature. The heuristic decision procedure operates as follows. Given a sentence, we first determine the event the target pronoun participates in *and* its role in the event. As an example, we determine that in sentence (2) *he* participates in the *try* event and the *escape* event as a *subject*.[2] Second, we determine the event(s) that the candidate antecedents participate in. In (2), both candidate antecedents participate in the *punish* event. Third, we pair each event participated by each candidate antecedent with each event participated by the pronoun. In our example, we would create two pairs, (*punish*, *try-s*) and (*punish*, *escape-s*). Note that *try* and *escape* are associated with the role of the pronoun that we extracted in the first step. Fourth, for each such pair, we extract all the narrative chains containing both elements in the pair from Chambers and Jurafsky's output.[3] This step results in one chain being extracted, which contains punish-o and escape-s. In other words, the protagonist in this chain is the subject of an *escape* event and the object of a *punish* event. Fifth, from the extracted chain, we obtain the role played by the pronoun (i.e., the protagonist) in the event in which the candidate antecedents participate. In our example, the pronoun plays an object role in the *punish* event. Finally, we extract the candidate antecedent that plays the extracted role, which in our example is the second antecedent, *Tim*.[4]

We create a binary feature, NC, which encodes this heuristic decision, and compute its value as follows. Assume in the rest of the paper that i_1 and i_2 are the feature vectors corresponding to the first candidate antecedent and the second candidate an-

[2]Throughout the paper, the subject/object of an event refers to its *deep* rather than *surface* subject/object. We determine the grammatical role of an NP using the Stanford dependency parser (de Marneffe et al., 2006) and a set of simple heuristics.

[3]We employ narrative chains of length 12, which are available from `http://cs.stanford.edu/people/nc/schemas/schemas-size12`.

[4]For an alternative way of using narrative chains for coreference resolution, see Irwin et al. (2011).

tecedent, respectively.[5] For our running example, since *Tim* is predicted to be the antecedent of *he*, the value of NC in i_2 is 1, and its value in i_1 is 0. For notational convenience, we write NC(i_1)=0 and NC(i_2)=1, and will follow this convention when describing the features in the rest of the paper.

Finally, we note that NC(i_1) and NC(i_2) will both be set to zero if (1) the pronoun and the antecedents do not participate in events, or (2) no narrative chains can be extracted in step 4 above, or (3) step 4 enables us to extract more than one chain and these chains indicate that the candidate antecedent can have both a subject role and an object role.

4.2 Google

Consider the following sentences:

(3a) Lions eat zebras because they are predators.
(3b) The knife sliced through the flesh because it was sharp.

Humans resolve *they* to *Lions* in (3a) by exploiting the world knowledge that predators attack and eat other animals. Similarly, humans resolve *it* to *the knife* in (3b) by exploiting the world knowledge that the word *sharp* can be used to describe a knife but not flesh. To acquire this kind of world knowledge, we learn patterns of word usage from the Web by issuing search queries. To facilitate our discussion, let us first introduce some notation. Let a sentence S be denoted by a triple (Z_1, $Conn$, Z_2), where Z_1 and Z_2 are the clauses preceding and following the discourse connective $Conn$, respectively; $A \in Z_2$ be the pronoun governed by the verb V; W be the sequence of words following V in S; and $C_1, C_2 \in Z_1$ be the candidate antecedents.

Given a sentence, we generate four queries: (Q1) C_1V; (Q2) C_2V; (Q3) C_1VW; and (Q4) C_2VW. If v is a verb-to-be followed by an adjective J, we generate two more queries: (Q5) JC_1 and (Q6) JC_2. To exemplify, six queries are generated for (3b): (Q1) "knife was"; (Q2) "flesh was"; (Q3) "knife was sharp"; (Q4) "flesh was sharp"; (Q5) "sharp knife"; and (Q6) "sharp flesh". On the other hand, only four queries are generated for (3a): (Q1) "lions are"; (Q2) "zebras are"; (Q3) "lions are predators"; and (Q4) "zebras are predators".

Using the counts returned by Google for these queries, we create four features, G1, G2, G3, and G4, whose values are determined by Rules 1, 2, 3, and 4, respectively, as described below.

Rule 1: **if** count(Q1) $>$ count(Q2) by at least $x\%$ **then** G1(i_1)=1 and G1(i_2)=0; **else if** count(Q2) $>$ count(Q1) by at least $x\%$ **then** G1(i_2)=1 and G1(i_1)=0; **else** G1(i_1)=G1(i_2)=0.

Rule 2: **if** count(Q3) $>$ count(Q4) by at least $x\%$ **then** G2(i_1)=1 and G2(i_2)=0; **else if** count(Q4) $>$ count(Q3) by at least $x\%$ **then** G2(i_2)=1 and G2(i_1)=0; **else** G2(i_1)=G2(i_2)=0.

Rule 3: **if** count(Q5) $>$ count(Q6) by at least $x\%$ **then** G3(i_1)=1 and G3(i_2)=0; **else if** count(Q6) $>$ count(Q5) by at least $x\%$ **then** G3(i_2)=1 and G3(i_1)=0; **else** G3(i_1)=G3(i_2)=0.

Rule 4: **if** one of G1(i_1) and G1(i_2) is 1, **then** G4(i_1)=G1(i_1) and G4(i_2)=G1(i_2); **else if** one of G2(i_1) and G2(i_2) is 1, **then** G4(i_1)=G2(i_1) and G4(i_2)=G2(i_2); **else if** one of G3(i_1) and G3(i_2) is 1, **then** G4(i_1)=G3(i_1) and G4(i_2)=G3(i_2); **else** G4(i_1)=G4(i_2)=0.

The role of the threshold x should be obvious: it ensures that a heuristic decision is made only if the difference between the counts for the two queries are sufficiently large, because otherwise there is no reason for us to prefer one candidate antecedent to the other. In all of our experiments, we set x to 20.

Note that other researchers have also used lexico-syntactic patterns to generate search queries for bridging anaphora resolution (e.g., Poesio et al. (2004)), other-anaphora resolution (e.g., Modjeska et al. (2003)), and learning selectional preferences for pronoun resolution (e.g., Yang et al. (2005)). However, in each of these three cases, the target *relations* (e.g., the part-whole relation in the case of bridging anaphora resolution, and the subject-verb and verb-object relations in the case of selectional preferences) are specific enough that they can be effectively captured by specific patterns. For example,

[5]The nth candidate antecedent in a sentence is the nth annotated NP encountered when processing the sentence in a left-to-right manner. In sentence (2), *Ed* is the first candidate antecedent and *Tim* is the second.

to determine whether *the wheel* is part of *the car* in bridging anaphora resolution, Poesio et al. employ queries of the form "X of Y", where X and Y would be replaced with *the wheel* and *the car*, respectively. On the other hand, we are not targeting a particular type of relation. Rather, we intend to capture world knowledge like *lions rather than zebras are predators*. Such knowledge may not be expressed as a relation and hence may not be easily captured using specific patterns. For this reason, we need to employ patterns as general as those such as Q3 and Q4.

4.3 FrameNet

If we generate search queries as described in the previous subsection for the *shout* example, it is unlikely that Google will return meaningful counts to us. The reason is that both candidate antecedents in the sentence are proper names belonging to the same type (which in this case is PERSON).

However, in some cases, we may be able to generate more meaningful queries from such kind of sentences. Consider the following sentence:

(4) John killed Jim, so he was arrested.

To generate meaningful queries, we make one observation: *John* and *Jim* played different roles in a *kill* event. Hence, we can replace these proper names with their roles. We propose to obtain these roles from FrameNet (Baker et al., 1998). More generally, for each proper name e in a given sentence, we (1) determine the event in which e is involved (using the Stanford dependency parser); (2) search for the FrameNet frame corresponding to the event as well as e's role in the event; and (3) replace the name with its FrameNet role. In our example, since both names are involved in the *kill* event, we retrieve the FrameNet frame for *kill*. Given that *John* and *Jim* are the subject and object of *kill*, we can extract their semantic roles directly from the frame, which are *killer* and *victim*, respectively.[6] Consequently, we replace the two names with their extracted semantic roles, and generate the search queries from the resulting sentence in the same way as before.

Note that if no frames can be found for the verb in the first clause, no search queries will be generated. After obtaining the query counts, we generate four binary features, FN1, FN2, FN3, FN4, whose values are computed based on the same four heuristic rules that were discussed in the previous subsection.

4.4 Heuristic Polarity

Some sentences involve comparing the two candidate antecedents. Consider the following sentences:

(5a) John was defeated by Jim in the election even though he is more popular.

(5b) John was defeated by Jim in the election because he is more popular.

The pronoun *he* refers to *John* in (5a) and *Jim* in (5b). To see how we can design an algorithm for resolving these pronouns, it would be useful to understand how humans resolve them. The phrase *more popular* has a positive sentiment. In (5a), the use of *even though* yields a clause of concession, which flips the polarity of *more popular* (from positive to negative), whereas in (5b), the use of *because* yields a clause of cause, which does not change the polarity of *more popular* (i.e., *more popular* remains positive). Since *more popular* is used to describe *he*, *he* is "better" in (5b) but "worse" in (5a). Now, the word *defeat* has a positive sentiment, and since *Jim* is the *deep subject* of *defeat*, *Jim* is "better" and *John* is "worse". Finally, in (5b), *he* and *Jim* are "better", so *he* is resolved to *Jim*; on the other hand, in (5a), *he* and *John* are "worse", so *he* is resolved to *John*.

We automate this (human) method for resolving pronouns as follows. We begin by determining whether we can assign a *rank value* (i.e., "better" or "worse") to the pronoun and the two candidate antecedents. For instance, to determine the rank value of the pronoun A, we first determine the polarity value p_A of its *anchor* word w_A, which is either the verb v for which A serves as the deep subject, or the adjective modifying A if v does not exist,[7] using Wilson et al.'s (2005b) subjectivity lexicon.[8] If p_A is not NEUTRAL, we check whether it can be flipped by the context of w_A. We consider three kinds of polarity-reversing context: negation, comparative adverb, and discourse connective. Specifically, we determine whether w_A is negated using the Stanford dependency parser, which explic-

[6] We heuristically map grammatical roles to semantic roles.

[7] In the sentiment analysis and opinion mining literature, (w_A, p_A) is known as an opinion-target pair.

[8] The lexicon contains 8221 words, each of which is hand labeled with a polarity of POSITIVE, NEGATIVE, or NEUTRAL.

itly annotates instances of negation; we determine the existence of a comparative adverb (e.g., "more", "less") using the POS tag "RBR"; and we determine whether A exists in a clause headed by a polarity-reversing connective, such as *although*. After flipping p_A by context, we can infer A's rank value from it. Specifically, A's rank value is "better" if p_A is positive; "worse" if p_A is negative; and "cannot be determined" if p_A is neutral. The polarity values of the two candidate antecedents can be determined in a similar fashion. Note that sometimes we may need to infer rank values. For example, given the sentence "Jane is prettier than Jill", *prettier* has a positive polarity, so its modifying NP, *Jane*, has a "better" rank, and we can infer that *Jill*'s rank is "worse".

We create three features, HPOL1, HPOL2, and HPOL3, based on our heuristic polarity determination component. Specifically, if the rank value of the pronoun or the rank value of one or both of the candidate antecedents cannot be determined, the values of all three binary features will be set to zero for both i_1 and i_2. Otherwise, we compute the values of the three features as follows. To compute HPOL1, which is a binary feature, we (1) employ a heuristic resolution procedure, which resolves the pronoun to the candidate antecedent with the same rank value, and then (2) encode the outcome of this heuristic procedure as the value of HPOL1. For example, since the first candidate antecedent, *John*, is predicted to be the antecedent in (5a), HPOL1(i_1)=1 and HPOL1(i_2)=0. The value of HPOL2 is the concatenation of the polarity values determined for the pronoun and the candidate antecedent. Referring again to (5a), HPOL2(i_1)=positive-positive and HPOL2(i_2)=positive-negative. To compute HPOL3 for a given instance, we simply take its HPOL2 value and append the connective to it. Using (5a) as an example, HPOL3(i_1)=positive-positive-even-though and HPOL3(i_1)=positive-negative-even-though.

4.5 Machine-Learned Polarity

In the previous subsection, we compute the polarity of a word by updating its prior polarity heuristically with contextual information. We hypothesized that polarity could be computed more accurately by employing a sentiment analyzer that can capture richer contextual information. For this reason, we employ OpinionFinder (Wilson et al., 2005a), which has a pre-trained classifier for annotating the phrases in a sentence with their contextual polarity values.

Given a sentence and the polarity values of the phrases annotated by OpinionFinder, we determine the rank values of the pronoun and the two candidate antecedents by mapping them to the polarized phrases using the dependency relations provided by the Stanford dependency parser. We create three binary features, LPOL1, LPOL2, and LPOL3, whose values are computed in the same way as HPOL1, HPOL2, and HPOL3, respectively, except that the computation here is based on the machine-learned polarity values rather than the heuristically determined polarity values.

4.6 Connective-Based Relations

Consider the following sentences:

(6a) Google bought Motorola because they want its customer base.

(6b) Google bought Motorola because they are rich.

Humans resolve *they* to *Google* in (6a) by exploiting the world knowledge that there is a causal relation (signaled by the discourse connective *because*) between the *want* event and the *buy* event. A similar mechanism is used to resolve *they* to *Google* in (6b): from world knowledge we know that there is a causal relation between *rich* and *buy*.

We automate this (human) method for resolving pronouns as follows. First, we gather connective-based relations of this kind from a large, unannotated corpus. In our experiments, we use as our unannotated corpus the documents in three text corpora (namely, BLLIP, Reuters, and English Gigaword), but retain only those sentences that contain a single discourse connective and do not begin with the connective. From these sentences, we collect triples and their frequencies of occurrences in the corpus. Each triple is of the form (V,$Conn$,X), where $Conn$ is a discourse connective, V is a stemmed verb in the clause preceding $Conn$, and X is a stemmed verb or an adjective in the clause following $Conn$. Each triple essentially denotes a relation between V and X expressed by $Conn$. Conceivably, the strength of the relation in a triple increases with its frequency count.

We use the frequency counts of these triples to heuristically predict the correct antecedent for a target pronoun. Given a sentence where $Conn$ is the discourse connective, X is the stemmed verb governing the target pronoun A or the adjective modifying A (if X is a *to be* verb), and V is the stemmed verb governing the candidate antecedents, we retrieve the frequency count of the triple (V,$Conn$,X). If the count is at least 100, we employ a procedure for heuristically selecting the antecedent for the target anaphor. Specifically, if X is a verb, then it resolves the target pronoun to the candidate antecedent that has the same grammatical role as the pronoun. However, if X is an adjective and the sentence does not involve comparison, then it resolves the target pronoun to the candidate antecedent serving as the subject of V.

We create a binary feature, CBR, that encodes this heuristic decision. In our running example, the triple (*buy*, *because*, *want*) occurs 860 times in our corpus, so the pronoun *they* is resolved to the candidate antecedent that occurs as the subject of *buy*. Hence, CBR(i_1)=1 and CBR(i_2)=0. However, had the triple occurred less than 100 times, both of these features would have been set to zero.

4.7 Semantic Compatibility

Some of the queries generated by the Google component, such as Q1 and Q2, aim to capture the semantic compatibility between a candidate antecedent, C, and the verb governing the target pronoun, V. However, using web search queries to estimate semantic compatibility has potential problems, including (1) a *precision* problem: the fact that C and V appear next to each other in a query does not necessarily imply that a subject-verb relation exists between them; and (2) a *recall* problem: these queries fail to capture subject-verb relations where C and V are not immediately adjacent to each other.

To address these potential problems, we compute knowledge of selectional preferences from a large, unannotated corpus. As before, we create our unannotated corpus using the documents in BLLIP, Reuters, and English Gigaword. Specifically, we first parse each sentence in the corpus using the Stanford dependency parser. Then, for each stemmed verb v and each stemmed noun n in the corpus, we collect the following statistics: (1) the number of times n is the subject of v; (2) the number of times n is the direct object of v; (3) the mutual information (MI) of v and n (with n as the subject of v); and (4) the MI of v and n (with n as the direct object of v).[9]

To understand how we use these statistics to generate features for resolving pronouns, consider the following sentence:

(7) The man stole the neighbor's bike because he needed one.

Assuming that the target pronoun and its governing verb V has grammatical relation GR, we create three features, SC1, SC2, and SC3, based on our semantic compatibility component. SC1 encodes the MI value of the head noun of a candidate antecedent and V (and GR). SC2 is a binary feature whose value indicates which of the candidate antecedents has a larger MI value with V (and GR). SC3 is the same as SC2, except that MI is replaced with corpus frequency. In other words, SC2 and SC3 employ different measures to heuristically predict the correct antecedent for the target pronoun. If the target pronoun is governed by a *to be* verb, the values of these three features will all be set to zero.

Given our running example, we first retrieve the following corpus-based statistics: MI(*need*:subj, *man*)=0.6322; MI(*need*:subj, *neighbor*)=0.3975; count(*need*:subj, *man*)=474; and count(*need*:subj, *neighbor*)=68. Using these statistics, we can then compute the aforementioned features for our example. Specifically, SC1(i_1)=0.6322, SC1(i_2)=0.3975, SC2(i_1)=1, SC2(i_2)=0, SC3(i_1)=1, and SC3(i_2)=0.

4.8 Lexical Features

We exploit the coreference-annotated training documents by creating *lexical* features from them. These lexical features can be divided into two categories, depending on whether they are computed based on the candidate antecedents.

Let us begin with the *antecedent-independent* features. Assuming that W is an arbitrary word in a sentence S that is not part of a candidate antecedent and $Conn$ is the connective in S, we create three types of binary-valued antecedent-independent features, namely (1) *unigrams*, where we create one

[9]We use the same formula as described in Section 4.2 of Bergsma and Lin (2006) to compute MI values.

feature for each W; (2) *word pairs*, where we create features by pairing each W appearing before $Conn$ with each W appearing after $Conn$, excluding adjective-noun and noun-adjective pairs[10]; and (3) *word triples*, where we augment each word pair in (2) with $Conn$. The value of each feature f indicates the presence or absence of f in S.

Next, we compute the *antecedent-dependent* features. Let (1) H_{C_1} and H_{C_2} be the head words of candidate antecedents C_1 and C_2, respectively; (2) V_{C_1}, V_{C_2}, and V_A be the verbs governing C_1, C_2, and the target pronoun A, respectively; and (3) J_{C_1}, J_{C_2}, and J_A be the adjectives modifying C_1, C_2, and A, respectively.[11] We create from each candidate antecedent four features, each of which is a word pair. From C_1, we create (H_{C_1}, V_{C_1}), (H_{C_1}, J_{C_1}), (H_{C_1}, V_A), and (H_{C_1}, J_A), all of which will appear in the feature vector corresponding to C_1. A similar set of four features are created from C_2. These antecedent-dependent features are all binary-valued.

It is worth mentioning that while we also considered word triples in the connective-based relations component and word pairs in the semantic compatibility component, in those components we determine their usefulness in an unsupervised manner, whereas by employing them as lexical features we determine their usefulness in a supervised manner.

5 Evaluation

5.1 Experimental Setup

Dataset. We report results on the test set, which comprises 30% of our hand-annotated sentence pairs (see Section 2 for details).

Evaluation metrics. Results are expressed in terms of accuracy, which is the percentage of correctly resolved target pronouns. We also report the percentages of these pronouns that are (1) not resolved and (2) incorrectly resolved.

5.2 Results and Discussion

The Random baseline. Our first baseline is a resolver that randomly guesses the antecedent for the target pronoun in each sentence. Since there are two candidate antecedents per sentence, the Random baseline should achieve an accuracy of 50%.

The Stanford resolver. Our second baseline is the Stanford resolver (Lee et al., 2011), which achieves the best performance in the CoNLL 2011 shared task (Pradhan et al., 2011). As a rule-based resolver, it does not exploit any coreference-annotated data.

Recall from Section 3 that our system assumes as input not only a sentence containing a target pronoun but also the two candidate antecedents. To ensure a fair comparison, the same input is provided to this and other baselines. Hence, if the Stanford resolver decides to resolve the target pronoun, it will resolve it to one of the two candidate antecedents. However, if it does not have enough confidence about resolving it, it will leave it unresolved. Its performance on the test set is shown in the "Unadjusted Scores" column in row 1 of Table 3. As we can see, it correctly resolves 40.1% of the pronouns, incorrectly resolves 29.8% of them, and does not make any decision on the remaining 30.1%.

Given that the Random baseline correctly resolves 50% of pronouns and the Stanford resolver correctly resolves only 40.1% of the pronouns, it is tempting to conclude that Stanford does not perform as well as Random. However, recall that Stanford leaves 30.1% of the pronouns unresolved. Hence, to ensure a fairer comparison, we produce "adjusted" scores for the Stanford resolver, where we "force" it to resolve all of the unresolved target pronouns by assuming that probabilistically half of them will be resolved correctly. This adjusted score is shown in the "Adjusted Scores" column in row 1 of Table 3. As we can see, Stanford achieves an accuracy of 55.1%, which is 5.1 points higher than that of Random.

The Baseline Ranker. To understand whether the somewhat unsatisfactory Stanford results can be attributed to its inability to exploit the training data, we employ as our third baseline a mention ranker that is trained in the same way as our system (see Section 3), except that it employs 39 commonly-used linguistic features for learning-based coreference resolution (see Table 1 of Rahman and Ng (2009) for a description of these features). Hence, the performance difference between this Baseline Ranker and our system can be attributed entirely

[10]Pairing an adjective A in one clause with a noun N in another clause may mislead the learner into thinking that N is modified by A, and hence we do not create such pairs.

[11]If C_1, C_2, and A are not modified by adjectives, no adjective-based features will be created.

		Unadjusted Scores			Adjusted Scores		
	Coreference System	Correct	Wrong	No Decision	Correct	Wrong	No Decision
1	Stanford	40.07%	29.79%	30.14%	55.14%	44.86%	0.00%
2	Baseline Ranker	47.70%	47.16%	5.14%	50.27%	49.73%	0.00%
3	Stanford+Baseline Ranker	53.49%	43.12%	3.39%	55.19%	44.77%	0.00%
4	Our system	**73.05%**	26.95%	0.00%	**73.05%**	26.95%	0.00%

Table 3: Results of the Stanford resolver, the Baseline Ranker, the Combined resolver, and our system.

to the difference between the two linguistic feature sets. Results of the Baseline Ranker are shown in row 2 of Table 3. Before score adjustment, it correctly resolves 47.7% of the target pronouns, incorrectly resolves 47.2% of them, and leaves the remaining 5.1% unresolved. (Note that we output "no decision" if the ranker assigns the same rank value to both candidate antecedents.) After score adjustment, its accuracy is 50.3%, which is 0.3 points higher than that of Random but statistically indistinguishable from it.[12] On the other hand, its accuracy is 4.9 points lower than that of Stanford, and the difference between their performance is significant. While it seems somewhat surprising that a supervised resolver does not perform as well as a rule-based resolver, neither of them employs knowledge sources that are particularly useful for our dataset. In other words, despite given access to annotated data, the Baseline Ranker may not be able to make effective use of it due to the lack of useful features.

The Combined resolver. We create a fourth baseline by combining the Stanford resolver and the Baseline Ranker. The motivation is that the former can provide better precision and the latter can provide better recall by handling "no decision" cases not covered by the former. Note that the Baseline Ranker will be applied to resolve only those pronouns that are left unresolved by Stanford. Results in row 3 of Table 3 show that the adjusted accuracy of this Combined resolver is 55.2%, which is statistically indistinguishable from Stanford's adjusted accuracy. Hence, these results show that the addition of the Baseline Ranker does not help improve Stanford's resolution accuracy.

Our system. Results of our system, which is trained using the features described in Section 4 in combination with a ranking model, are shown in row 4 of Table 3. As we can see, our system achieves an accuracy of 73.1%, significantly outperforming the Combined resolver by 17.9 points in accuracy. These results suggest that our features are more useful for resolving difficult pronouns than those commonly used for coreference resolution.

[12]All statistical significance test results in this paper are obtained using the paired t-test, with $p < 0.05$.

Feature Type	Correct	Wrong	No Decision
All features	73.05%	26.95%	0.00%
−Narrative Chains	68.97%	31.03%	0.00%
−Google	65.96%	34.04%	0.00%
−FrameNet	72.16%	27.84%	0.00%
−Heuristic Polarity	71.45%	28.55%	0.00%
−Learned Polarity	72.70%	27.30%	0.00%
−Connective-Based Rel.	71.28%	28.72%	0.00%
−Semantic Compat.	71.81%	28.19%	0.00%
−Lexical Features	60.11%	25.35%	14.54%

Table 4: Results of feature ablation experiments.

5.3 Feature Analysis

In an attempt to gain additional insight into the performance contribution of each of the eight types of features used in our system, we conduct feature ablation experiments. The unadjusted scores of these experiments are shown in Table 4, where each row shows the performance of the model trained on all types of features except for the one shown in that row. For easy reference, the performance of the model trained on all types of features is shown in row 1 of the table.

A few points deserve mention. First, performance drops significantly whichever feature type is removed. This suggests that all eight feature types are contributing positively to overall accuracy. Second, the *Google*-based features and the *Lexical Features* are the most useful, and those generated via *FrameNet* and *Learned Polarity* are the least useful *in the presence of* other feature types. While it is somewhat surprising that *Learned Polarity* is not more useful than *Heuristic Polarity*, we speculate the reason can be attributed to the fact that the corpus on which OpinionFinder was trained was quite different from ours. Finally, even without using the

Feature Type	Correct	Wrong	No Decision
Narrative Chains	30.67%	24.47%	44.86%
Google	33.16%	7.09%	59.75%
FrameNet	7.27%	4.08%	88.65%
Learned Polarity	4.79%	2.66%	92.55%
Heuristic Polarity	7.27%	1.77%	90.96%
Connective-Based Rel.	14.01%	8.69%	77.30%
Semantic Compat.	23.58%	13.12%	63.30%
Lexical Features	56.91%	43.09%	0.00%

Table 5: Results of single-feature coreference models.

Lexical Features, our system still outperforms all the baseline resolvers: as can been implied from the last row of Table 4, in the absence of the *Lexical Features*, our resolver achieves an adjusted accuracy of 67.4%, which is only 5.7 points less than that obtained when the full feature set is employed. Hence, while the *Lexical Features* are useful, their importance should not be over-emphasized.

To get a better idea of the utility of each feature type, we conduct another experiment in which we train eight models, each of which employs exactly one type of features. Their unadjusted scores are shown in Table 5. As we can see, *Learned Polarity* has the smallest contribution, whereas the *Lexical Features* have the largest contribution.

5.4 Error Analysis

While our resolver significantly outperforms state-of-the-art resolvers, there is a lot of room for improvement. To help direct future research on the resolution of difficult pronouns, we analyze the major sources of errors made by our resolver.

Our analysis reveals that many of the errors correspond to cases that cannot be handled by any of the eight components of our resolver. To understand these cases, consider first the strengths and weaknesses of *Narrative Chains* and *Google*, the two components that contribute the most to overall performance after *Lexical Features*.

Google is especially good at capturing facts, such as *lions are predators* and *zebras are not predators*, helping us correctly resolve sentences such as (5a) and (5b), as well as those in sentence pair (I) in Table 1. However, it may not be good at handling pronouns whose resolution requires an understanding of the connection between the facts or events described in the two clauses of a sentence. The reason is that establishing such a connection requires that we construct a search query composed of information extracted from both clauses, and the resulting, possibly long, query is likely to receive no hit count due to data sparseness. Investigating how to construct such queries while avoiding data sparseness would be an interesting line of future work.

Narrative chains, on the other hand, are useful for capturing the relationship between the events described in the two clauses. However, they are computed over verbs, and therefore cannot capture such a relationship when one or both of the events involved are not described by verbs. For example, narrative chains fail to capture the causal relation between the event expressed by *angry* and *shout* in sentence (1b). It is also worth mentioning that some pronouns that could have been resolved using narrative chains are not owing to the *coverage* and *accuracy* of Chambers and Jurafsky's (2008) chains, but we believe that these recall and precision problems could be addressed by (1) inducing chains from a larger corpus and (2) using semantic roles rather than grammatical roles in the induction process.

Some resolution errors arise from errors in polarity analysis. This can be attributed to the simplicity of our *Heuristic Polarity* component: determining the polarity of a word based on its prior polarity is too naïve. Fine-grained polarity analysis would be a promising solution to this problem (see Pang and Lee (2008) and Liu (2012) for related work).

6 Conclusions

We investigated the resolution of complex cases of definite pronouns, a problem that was under extensive discussion by coreference researchers in the 1970s but has received revived interest owing in part to its relevance to the Turing Test. Our experimental results indicate that it is a challenge for state-of-the-art resolvers, and while we proposed new knowledge sources for addressing this challenge, our resolver still has a lot of room for improvement. In particular, our error analysis indicates that further gains could be achieved via more accurate sentiment analysis and induction of world knowledge from corpora or the Web. In addition, we plan to integrate our resolver into a general-purpose coreference system and evaluate the resulting resolver on standard evaluation corpora such as MUC, ACE, and OntoNotes.

Acknowledgments

We thank the three anonymous reviewers for their detailed and insightful comments on an earlier draft of the paper. This work was supported in part by NSF Grants IIS-0812261 and IIS-1147644.

References

Amit Bagga. 1998. *Coreference, Cross-Document Coreference, and Information Extraction Methodologies*. Ph.D. thesis, Duke University.

Collin F. Baker, Charles J. Fillmore, and John B. Lowe. 1998. The Berkeley FrameNet project. In *Proceedings of the 36th Annual Meeting of the Association for Computational Linguistics and the 17th International Conference on Computational Linguistics*, pages 86–90.

Shane Bergsma and Dekang Lin. 2006. Bootstrapping path-based pronoun resolution. In *Proceedings of the 21st International Conference on Computational Linguistics and 44th Annual Meeting of the Association for Computational Linguistics*, pages 33–40.

Volha Bryl, Claudio Guiliano, Luciano Serafini, and Kateryna Tymoshenko. 2010. Using background knowledge to support coreference resolution. In *Proceedings of the 19th European Conference on Artificial Intelligence*, pages 759–764.

Donna K. Byron. 2002. Resolving pronominal reference to abstract entities. In *Proceedings of the 40th Annual Meeting of the Association for Computational Linguistics*, pages 80–87.

Nathanael Chambers and Dan Jurafsky. 2008. Unsupervised learning of narrative event chains. In *Proceedings of the 46th Annual Meeting of the Association for Computational Linguistics: Human Language Technologies*, pages 787–797.

Eugene Charniak and Micha Elsner. 2009. EM works for pronoun anaphora resolution. In *Proceedings of the 12th Conference of the European Chapter of the Association for Computational Linguistics*, pages 148–156.

Marie-Catherine de Marneffe, Bill MacCartney, and Christopher D. Manning. 2006. Generating typed dependency parses from phrase structure parses. In *Proceedings of the 5th International Conference on Language Resources and Evaluation*, pages 449–454.

Pascal Denis and Jason Baldridge. 2007. A ranking approach to pronoun resolution. In *Proceedings of the Twentieth International Conference on Artificial Intelligence*, pages 1588–1593.

Pascal Denis and Jason Baldridge. 2008. Specialized models and ranking for coreference resolution. In *Proceedings of the 2008 Conference on Empirical Methods in Natural Language Processing*, pages 660–669.

Aria Haghighi and Dan Klein. 2009. Simple coreference resolution with rich syntactic and semantic features. In *Proceedings of the 2009 Conference on Empirical Methods in Natural Language Processing*, pages 1152–1161.

Graeme Hirst. 1981. *Anaphora in Natural Language Understanding*. Springer Verlag.

Ryu Iida, Kentaro Inui, Hiroya Takamura, and Yuji Matsumoto. 2003. Incorporating contextual cues in trainable models for coreference resolution. In *Proceedings of the EACL Workshop on The Computational Treatment of Anaphora*.

Joseph Irwin, Mamoru Komachi, and Yuji Matsumoto. 2011. Narrative schema as world knowledge for coreference resolution. In *Proceedings of the Fifteenth Conference on Computational Natural Language Learning: Shared Task*, pages 86–92.

Thorsten Joachims. 2002. Optimizing search engines using clickthrough data. In *Proceedings of the Eighth ACM SIGKDD International Conference on Knowledge Discovery and Data Mining*, pages 133–142.

Heeyoung Lee, Yves Peirsman, Angel Chang, Nathanael Chambers, Mihai Surdeanu, and Dan Jurafsky. 2011. Stanford's multi-pass sieve coreference resolution system at the CoNLL-2011 shared task. In *Proceedings of the Fifteenth Conference on Computational Natural Language Learning: Shared Task*, pages 28–34.

Hector J. Levesque. 2011. The Winograd Schema Challenge. In *AAAI Spring Symposium: Logical Formalizations of Commonsense Reasoning*.

Bing Liu. 2012. *Sentiment Analysis and Opinion Mining*. Morgan & Claypool Publishers.

Ruslan Mitkov, Richard Evans, and Constantin Orasan. 2002. A new, fully automatic version of Mitkov's knowledge-poor pronoun resolution method. In Al. Gelbukh, editor, *Computational Linguistics and Intelligent Text Processing*, pages 169–187. Springer.

Natalia N. Modjeska, Katja Markert, and Malvina Nissim. 2003. Using the web in machine learning for other-anaphora resolution. In *Proceedings of the 2003 Conference on Empirical Methods in Natural Language Processing*, pages 176–183.

Christoph Müller. 2007. Resolving it, this, and that in unrestricted multi-party dialog. In *Proceedings of the 45th Annual Meeting of the Association of Computational Linguistics*, pages 816–823.

Bo Pang and Lillian Lee. 2008. Opinion mining and sentiment analysis. *Foundations and Trends in Information Retrieval* 2(1–2):1–135.

Massimo Poesio and Mijail A. Kabadjov. 2004. A general-purpose, off-the-shelf anaphora resolution module: Implementation and preliminary evaluation. In *Proceedings of the 4th International Conference on Language Resources and Evaluation*, pages 663–666.

Massimo Poesio, Rahul Mehta, Axel Maroudas, and Janet Hitzeman. 2004. Learning to resolve bridging references. In *Proceedings of the 42nd Annual Meeting of the Association for Computational Linguistics*, pages 143–150.

Massimo Poesio, David Day, Ron Artstein, Jason Duncan, Vladimir Eidelman, Claudio Giuliano, Rob Hall, Janet Hitzeman, Alan Jern, Mijail Kabadjov, Stanley Yong Wai Keong, Gideon Mann, Alessandro Moschitti, Simone Ponzetto, Jason Smith, Josef Steinberger, Michael Strube, Jian Su, Yannick Versley, Xiaofeng Yang, and Michael Wick. 2007. ELERFED: Final report of the research group on Exploiting Lexical and Encyclopedic Resources For Entity Disambiguation. Technical report, Summer Workshop on Language Engineering, Center for Language and Speech Processing, Johns Hopkins University, Baltimore, MD.

Simone Paolo Ponzetto and Michael Strube. 2006. Exploiting semantic role labeling, WordNet and Wikipedia for coreference resolution. In *Proceedings of the Human Language Technology Conference and Conference of the North American Chapter of the Association for Computational Linguistics*, pages 192–199.

Simone Paolo Ponzetto and Michael Strube. 2007. Knowledge derived from Wikipedia for computing semantic relatedness. *Journal of Artificial Intelligence Research*, 30:181–212.

Sameer Pradhan, Lance Ramshaw, Mitchell Marcus, Martha Palmer, Ralph Weischedel, and Nianwen Xue. 2011. CoNLL-2011 Shared Task: Modeling unrestricted coreference in OntoNotes. In *Proceedings of the Fifteenth Conference on Computational Natural Language Learning: Shared Task*, pages 1–27.

Long Qiu, Min-Yen Kan, and Tat-Seng Chua. 2004. A public reference implementation of the RAP anaphora resolution algorithm. In *Proceedings of the 4th International Conference on Language Resources and Evaluation*, pages 291–294.

Karthik Raghunathan, Heeyoung Lee, Sudarshan Rangarajan, Nate Chambers, Mihai Surdeanu, Dan Jurafsky, and Christopher Manning. 2010. A multi-pass sieve for coreference resolution. In *Proceedings of the 2010 Conference on Empirical Methods in Natural Language Processing*, pages 492–501.

Altaf Rahman and Vincent Ng. 2009. Supervised models for coreference resolution. In *Proceedings of the 2009 Conference on Empirical Methods in Natural Language Processing*, pages 968–977.

Altaf Rahman and Vincent Ng. 2011. Coreference resolution with world knowledge. In *Proceedings of the 49th Annual Meeting of the Association for Computational Linguistics: Human Language Technologies*, pages 814–824.

Roger C. Schank and Robert P. Abelson. 1977. *Scripts, Plans, Goals, and Understanding*. Lawrence Erlbaum.

Veselin Stoyanov, Claire Cardie, Nathan Gilbert, Ellen Riloff, David Buttler, and David Hysom. 2010. RECONCILE: A coreference resolution research platform. In *Proceedings of the ACL 2010 Conference Short Papers*, pages 156–161.

Michael Strube and Christoph Müller. 2003. A machine learning approach to pronoun resolution in spoken dialogue. In *Proceedings of the 41st Annual Meeting of the Association for Computational Linguistics*, pages 168–175.

Alan M. Turing. 1950. Computing machinery and intelligence. *Mind*, 59:433–460.

Olga Uryupina, Massimo Poesio, Claudio Giuliano, and Kateryna Tymoshenko. 2011. Disambiguation and filtering methods in using Web knowledge for coreference resolution. In *Proceedings of the 24th International Florida Artificial Intelligence Research Society Conference*, pages 317–322.

Yannick Versley, Simone Paolo Ponzetto, Massimo Poesio, Vladimir Eidelman, Alan Jern, Jason Smith, Xiaofeng Yang, and Alessandro Moschitti. 2008. BART: A modular toolkit for coreference resolution. In *Proceedings of the ACL-08: HLT Demo Session*, pages 9–12.

Theresa Wilson, Paul Hoffmann, Swapna Somasundaran, Jason Kessler, Janyce Wiebe, Yejin Choi, Claire Cardie, Ellen Riloff, and Siddharth Patwardhan. 2005a. Opinionfinder: A system for subjectivity analysis. In *Proceedings of HLT/EMNLP 2005 Interactive Demonstrations*, pages 34–35.

Theresa Wilson, Janyce M. Wiebe, and Paul Hoffmann. 2005b. Recognizing contextual polarity in phrase-level sentiment analysis. In *Proceedings of the Joint Human Language Technology Conference and Conference on Empirical Methods in Natural Language Processing*, pages 347–354.

Terry Winograd. 1972. *Understanding Natural Language*. Academic Press, Inc., New York.

Xiaofeng Yang, Guodong Zhou, Jian Su, and Chew Lim Tan. 2003. Coreference resolution using competitive learning approach. In *Proceedings of the 41st Annual Meeting of the Association for Computational Linguistics*, pages 176–183.

Xiaofeng Yang, Jian Su, and Chew Lim Tan. 2005. Improving pronoun resolution using statistics-based semantic compatibility information. In *Proceedings of the 43rd Annual Meeting of the Association for Computational Linguistics*, pages 165–172.

A Sequence Labelling Approach to Quote Attribution

Tim O'Keefe[†] **Silvia Pareti**[◇] **James R. Curran**[†] **Irena Koprinska**[†] **Matthew Honnibal**[‡]

[†]ə-lab, School of IT
University of Sydney
NSW 2006, Australia
{tokeefe,james,irena}@it.usyd.edu.au

[◇]School of Informatics
University of Edinburgh
United Kingdom
S.Pareti@sms.ed.ac.uk

[‡]Centre for Language Technology
Macquarie University
NSW 2109, Australia
matthew.honnibal@mq.edu.au

Abstract

Quote extraction and attribution is the task of automatically extracting quotes from text and attributing each quote to its correct speaker. The present state-of-the-art system uses gold standard information from previous decisions in its features, which, when removed, results in a large drop in performance. We treat the problem as a sequence labelling task, which allows us to incorporate sequence features without using gold standard information. We present results on two new corpora and an augmented version of a third, achieving a new state-of-the-art for systems using only realistic features.

1 Introduction

News stories are often driven by the quotes made by politicians, sports stars, musicians, and celebrities. When these stories exit the news cycle, the quotes they contain are often forgotten by both readers and journalists. A system that automatically extracts quotes and attributes those quotes to the correct speaker would enable readers and journalists to place news in the context of all comments made by a person on a given topic.

Though quote attribution may appear to be a straightforward task, the simple rule-based approaches proposed thus far have produced disappointing results. Going beyond these to machine learning approaches presents several problems that make quote attribution surprisingly difficult. The main challenge is that while a large portion of quotes can be attributed to a speaker based on simple rules, the remainder have few or no contextual clues as to who the correct speaker is. Additionally, many quote sequences, such as dialogues, rely on the reader understanding that there is an alternating sequence of speakers, which creates dependencies between attribution decisions made by a classifier.

Elson and McKeown (2010) is the only study that directly uses machine learning in quote attribution, treating the task as a classification task, where each quote is attributed independently of other quotes. To handle conversations and similar constructs they use gold standard information about speakers of previous quotes as features for their model. This is an unrealistic assumption, since gold standard information is not available in practice.

The primary contribution of this paper is that we reformulate quote attribution as a sequence labelling task. This allows us to use sequence features without having to use the unrealistic gold standard features that were used in Elson and McKeown (2010). We experiment with three sequence decoding models including greedy, Viterbi and a linear chain Conditional Random Field (CRF).

Furthermore we present results on two new corpora and an augmented version of a third. The two new corpora are from news articles from the Wall Street Journal and the Sydney Morning Herald respectively, while the third corpus is an extension to the classic literature corpus from Elson and McKeown (2010). Our results show that a quote attribution system using only realistic features is highly feasible for the news domain, with accuracies of 92.4% on the SMH corpus and 84.1% on the WSJ corpus.

2 Background

Early work into quote attribution by Zhang et al. (2003) focused on identifying when different characters were talking in children's stories, so that a speech synthesis system could read the quoted parts in different voices. While they were able to extract quotes with high precision and recall, their attribution accuracy was highly dependent on the document in question, ranging from 47.6% to 86.7%. Mamede and Chaleira (2004) conducted similar research on children's stories written in Portuguese. Their system proved to be very good at extracting quotes through simple rules, but when using a hand-crafted decision tree to attribute those quotes to a speaker, they achieved an accuracy of only 65.7%.

In the news domain, both Pouliquen et al. (2007) and Sarmento and Nunes (2009) proposed rule-based systems that work over large volumes of text. Both systems aimed for high precision at the expense of low recall, as their data contained many redundant quotes. More recently, SAPIENS, a French-language quote extraction and attribution system, was developed by de La Clergerie et al. (2011). It conducts a full parse of the text, which allows it to use patterns to extract direct and indirect quotes, as well as the speaker of each quote. Their evaluation found that 19 out of 40 quotes (47.5%) had a correct span and author, while a further 19 had an incorrect author, and 4 had an incorrect span. In related work, Sagot et al. (2010) built a lexicon of French reported speech verbs, and conducted some analysis of different types of quotes.

Glass and Bangay (2007) approached the task with a three stage method. For each quote they first find the nearest speech verb, they then find the grammatical actor of that speech verb, and finally they select the appropriate speaker for that actor. To achieve each of these subtasks they built a model with several manually weighted features that good candidates should possess. For each subtask they then choose the candidate with the largest weighted sum of features. Their full approach yields an accuracy of 79.4% on a corpus of manually annotated fiction books.

Schneider et al. (2010) describe PICTOR, which is principally a quote visualisation tool. Their task was to find direct and indirect quotes, which they attribute to a text span representing the speaker. To do this they constructed a specialised grammar, which was built with reference to a small development corpus. With a permissive evaluation metric their grammar-based approach yielded 86% recall and 75% precision, however this dropped to 52% recall and 56% precision when measured in terms of completely correct quote-speaker pairs.

The work most similar to ours is the work by Elson and McKeown (2010). Their aim was to automatically identify both quotes and speakers, and then to attribute each quote to a speaker, in a corpus of classic literature that they compiled themselves. To identify potential speakers they used the Stanford NER tagger (Finkel et al., 2005) and a method outlined in Davis et al. (2003) that allowed them to find nominal character references. They then grouped name variants and pronominal mentions into a coreference chain.

To attribute a quote to a speaker they first classified the quotes into categories. Several of the categories have a speaker explicit in their structure, so they attribute quotes to those speakers with no further processing. For the remaining categories, they cast the attribution problem as a binary classification task, where each quote-speaker pair has a "speaker" or "not speaker" label predicted by the classifier. They then reconciled these independent decisions using various techniques to produce a single speaker prediction for each quote. For the simple category predictions they achieved 93-99% accuracy, while for the more complicated categories they achieved 63-64%, with an overall result of 83% accuracy. This compares favourably with their rule-based baseline, which achieved an accuracy of 52%.

While the results of Elson and McKeown (2010) appear encouraging, they are misleading for two reasons. First their corpus does not include quotes where all three annotators chose different speakers. While these quotes include some cases where the annotators chose coreferent spans, it also includes cases of legitimate disagreement about the speaker. An automated system would likely find these cases challenging. Second both their category predictions and machine learning predictions rely on gold standard information from previous quotes, which is not available in practice. In our study we address both these issues.

	Proportion (%)			Accuracy (%)		
	LIT	WSJ	SMH	LIT	WSJ	SMH
Quote-Said-Person	17.9	20.2	3.1	98.9	99.8	99.1
Quote-Person-Said	2.8	6.1	16.6	97.7	97.0	98.5
Other Trigram	0.1	2.3	0.3	66.7	56.2	54.5
Quote-Said-Pronoun	1.9	0.1	0.0	38.6	100.0	0.0
Quote-Pronoun-Said	5.9	8.8	13.5	36.5	92.2	93.9
Other Anaphors	0.1	0.1	0.2	0.0	100.0	62.5
Added*	24.6	28.3	23.9	89.7	76.3	97.5
Backoff	11.0	33.9	32.3	-	-	-
Alone	18.0	0.2	9.7	-	-	-
Conversation*	17.7	0.2	0.3	85.2	0.0	8.3
Total	100.0	100.0	100.0	60.5	57.2	55.8

Table 1: The proportion of quotes in each category and the accuracy of the speaker prediction based on the category. The two categories marked with an asterisk (*) depend on previous decisions.

3 Corpora

We evaluate our methods on two new corpora coming from the news domain, and an augmented version of an existing corpus, which covers classic literature. They are described below.

3.1 Columbia Quoted Speech Attribution Corpus (LIT)

The first corpus we use was originally created by Elson and McKeown (2010). It is a set of excerpts from 11 fictional 19th century works by six well-known authors, split into 18 documents. In total it contains 3,126 quotes annotated with their speakers.

Elson and McKeown used an automated system to find named entity spans and nominal mentions in the text, with the named entities being linked to form a coreference chain (they did not link nominal mentions). The corpus was built using Amazon's Mechanical Turk, with three annotations per quote. To ensure quality, all annotations from poorly performing annotators were removed, as were quotes where each annotator chose a different speaker. Though excluding some quotes ensures quality annotations, it causes gaps in the quote chains, which is a problem for sequence labelling. Furthermore, the cases where annotators disagreed are likely to be challenging, so removing them from the corpus could make results appear better than they would be in practice.

To rectify this, we conducted additional annotation of the quotes that were excluded by the original authors. Two postgraduates annotated 654 additional quotes, with a raw agreement of 79% over 48 double-annotated quotes. Our annotators reported seeing some errors in existing annotations, so we had one annotator check 400 existing annotations for correctness. This additional check found that 92.5% of the quotes were correctly annotated.

3.2 PDTB Attribution Corpus Extension (WSJ)

Our next corpus is an extension to the attribution annotations found in the Penn Discourse TreeBank (PDTB). The original PDTB contains several forms of discourse, including assertions, beliefs, facts, and eventualities. These can be attributed to named entities or to unnamed, pronominal, or implicit sources. Recent work by Pareti (2012) conducted further annotation of this corpus, including reconstructing attributions that were only partially annotated, and introducing additional information. From this corpus we use only direct quotes and the directly quoted portions of mixed quotes, giving us 4,923 quotes.

For the set of potential speakers we use the BBN pronoun coreference and entity type corpus (Weischedel and Brunstein, 2005), with automatically coreferred pronouns. We automatically matched BBN entities to PDTB extension speakers, and included the PDTB speaker where no matching BBN entity could be found. This means an automatic system has an opportunity to find the correct speaker for all quotes in the corpus.

3.3 Sydney Morning Herald Corpus (SMH)

We compiled the final corpus from a set of news documents taken from the Sydney Morning Herald website[1]. We randomly selected 965 documents published in 2009 that were not obituaries, opinion pages, advertisements or other non-news stories. To conduct the annotation we employed 11 non-expert annotators via the outsourcing site Freelancer[2], as well as five expert annotators from our research group. A total of 400 news stories were double-annotated, with at least 33 double-annotated stories per annotator. Raw agreement on the speaker of each quote was high at 98.3%. These documents had already been annotated with named entities as part of a separate research project (Hachey et al., 2012), which includes manually constructed coreference chains. The resulting corpus contains 965 documents, with 3,535 quotes.

3.4 Corpus Comparisons

In order to compare the corpora we categorise the quotes into the categories defined by Elson and McKeown (2010), as shown in Table 1. We assigned quotes to these categories by testing (after text preprocessing) whether the quote belonged to each category, in the order shown below:

1. *Trigram* – the quote appears consecutively with a mention of an entity, and a reported speech verb, in any order;

2. *Anaphors* – same as above, except that the mention is a pronoun;

3. *Added* – the quote is in the same paragraph as another quote that precedes it;

4. *Conversation* – the quote appears in a paragraph on its own, and the two paragraphs preceding the current paragraph each contain a single quote, with alternating speakers;

5. *Alone* – the quote is in a paragraph on its own;

6. *Miscellaneous* – the quote matches none of the preceding categories. This category is called "Backoff" in Elson and McKeown (2010).

[1] http://www.smh.com.au

[2] http://www.freelancer.com

Unsurprisingly, the two corpora from the news domain share similar proportions of quotes in each category. The main differences are that the SMH uses a larger number of pronouns compared to the WSJ, which tends to use explicit attribution more frequently. The SMH also has a significant proportion of quotes that appear alone in a paragraph, while the WSJ has almost none. Finally, when attributing a quote using a trigram pattern, the SMH mostly uses the Quote-Person-Said pattern, while the WSJ mostly uses the Quote-Said-Person pattern. These differences probably reflect the editorial guidelines of the two newspapers.

The differences between the news corpora and the literature corpus are more substantial. Most notably the LIT corpus has a much higher proportion of quotes that fall into the *Conversation* and *Alone* categories. This is unsurprising as both monologues and dialogues are common in fiction, but are rare in newswire. The two news corpora have more quotes in the *Trigram* and *Backoff* categories.

4 Quote Extraction

Quote extraction is the task of finding the spans that represent quotes within a document. There are three types of quotes that can appear:

1. *Direct quotes* appear entirely between quotation marks, and are used to indicate that the speaker said precisely what is written;

2. *Indirect quotes* do not appear between or contain quotation marks, and are used to get the speaker's point across without implying that the speaker used the exact words of the quote;

3. *Mixed quotes* are indirect quotes that contain a directly quoted portion.

In this work, we limit ourselves to detecting direct quotes and the direct portions of mixed quotes.

To extract quotes we use a regular expression that searches for text between quotation marks. We also deal with the special case of multi-paragraph quotes where one quotation mark opens the quote and every new paragraph that forms part of the quote, with a final quotation mark only at the very end of the quote. This straightforward approach yields over 99% accuracy on all three corpora.

5 Quote Attribution

Given a document with a set of quotes and a set of entities, quote attribution is the task of finding the entity that represents the speaker of each quote, based on the context provided by the document. Identifying the correct entity can involve choosing either an entire coreference chain representing an entity, or identifying a specific span of text that represents the entity.

In practice, most applications only need to know which coreference chain represents the speaker, not which particular span in the text. Despite this, the best evidence about which chain is the speaker is found in the context of the individual text spans, and most existing systems aim to get the particular entity span correct. This presents a problem for evaluation, as an incorrect entity span may be identified, but it might still be part of the correct coreference chain. We chose to count attributions as correct if they attributed the quote to the correct coreference chain for both the LIT and SMH corpora, while for the WSJ corpus, where the full coreference chains do not exist, we evaluated an attribution as correct if it was to the correct entity span in the text.

5.1 Rule-based Baseline

To establish the effectiveness of our method we built a rule-based baseline system. For each quote it proceeds with the following steps:

1. Search backwards in the text from the end of the sentence the quote appears in for a reported speech verb
2. If the verb is found return the entity mention nearest the verb (ignoring mentions in quotes), in the current sentence or any sentence preceding it
3. If not, return the mention of an entity nearest the end of the quote (ignoring mentions in quotes), in the current sentence or any sentence preceding it

This forms a reasonable baseline as it is able to pick up the quotes that fall into the more simple categories, such as the *Trigram* category and the *Added* category. It is also able to make a guess at the more complicated categories, without using gold standard information as the category predictions do.

6 Experimental Setup

We use two classifiers: a logistic regression implementation available in LIBLINEAR (Fan et al., 2008), and a Conditional Random Field (CRF) from CRF-Suite (Okazaki, 2007). Both packages use maximum likelihood estimation with L2 regularisation. We experimented with several values for the coefficient on a development set, but found that it had little impact, so stuck with the default value. All of our machine learning experiments use the same text encoding, which is explained below, and all use the category predictions when they are available.

6.1 Text Encoding

We encode our text similarly to Elson and McKeown (2010). The major steps are:

1. Replace all quotes and speakers with special symbols;
2. Replace all reported speech verbs with a symbol. Elson and McKeown (2010) provided us with their list of reported speech verbs;
3. Part-of-Speech (POS) tag the text and remove adjectives, adverbs, and other parts of speech that do not contribute useful information. We used the POS tagger from Curran and Clark (2003);
4. Remove any paragraphs or sentences where no quotes, pronouns or names occur.

All features that will be discussed are calculated with respect to this encoding (e.g. word distance would be the number of words in the encoded text, rather than the number of words in the original text).

6.2 Features

In our experiments we use the feature set from Elson and McKeown (2010). The features for a particular pair of target quote (q) and target speaker (s) are summarised below.

Distance features including number of words between q and s, number of paragraphs between q and s, number of quotes between q and s, and number of entity mentions between q and s

Corpus	Sequence Features		
	Gold	Pred	None
LIT	74.7	49.0	49.6
WSJ	87.3	74.1	82.9
SMH	95.0	85.6	92.4

Table 2: Accuracy results comparing the E&M approach with gold standard, predicted or no sequence features.

Paragraph features derived from the 10 paragraphs preceding the quote (including the paragraph the quote is in), includes number of mentions of s, number of mentions of other speakers, number of words in each paragraph, and number of quotes in each paragraph

Nearby features relating to the two tokens either side of q and s, includes binary features for each position indicating whether the position is punctuation, s, q, a different speaker, a different quote, or a reported speech verb

Quote features about q itself, including whether s is mentioned within it, whether other speakers are mentioned within it, how far the quote is from the start of its paragraph and the length in words of q

Sequence features that depend on the speakers chosen for the previous quotes, includes number of quotes in the 10 paragraphs preceding and including the paragraph where q appears that were attributed to s, and the number that were attributed to other speakers

6.3 Elson and McKeown Reimplementation

As part of our study we reproduce the core results of Elson and McKeown (2010) (E&M), as we believe it is a state-of-the-art system. This allows us to determine the effectiveness of our approach when compared to a state-of-the-art approach, and it also allows us to determine how well the E&M approach performs on other corpora. In this section we will briefly summarise the key elements needed to reproduce their work.

The E&M approach makes a binary classification between "speaker" and 'not speaker" for up to 15 candidate speakers for each quote. They then reconcile these 15 classifications into one speaker prediction for the quote. While E&M experimented with several different reconciliation methods, we simply chose the speaker with the highest probability attached to its "speaker" label.

We conducted an experiment using our implementation of the E&M method on the original, unaugmented E&M corpus, to see how our result compared with E&M 's 83%. On our test set we achieved 78.2%, however this rose to 82.3% when performing 10-fold cross validation across the whole corpus. Though this is a large difference, it is not necessarily that surprising, as our test set contains documents by authors which are unseen, whereas both the original E&M test set and all the cross validation test sets contain documents by authors that the learner has seen before.

In their work, E&M make a simplifying assumption that all previous attribution decisions were correct. Due to this, their sequence features use gold standard labels from previous quotes, which makes their results unrealistic. In Table 2 we show the effect of replacing the gold standard sequence features with features based on the predicted labels, or with no sequence features at all. All three corpora show a significant drop in accuracy, with the LIT corpus in particular suffering a drop of more than 25%. This motivates our study into including sequence information without using gold standard labels.

7 Class Models

We consider two class models for our experiments, which are described in detail below. The binary model is able to take advantage of more data but has less competition between decisions, while the n-way model has more competition with less data. Both models are used with all the decoding methods, with the exception that the binary model is unsuitable for the CRF experiments.

7.1 Binary

When working with n previous speakers, a binary class model works by predicting n independent "speaker" versus "not speaker" labels, one for each quote-speaker pair. As the classifications are independent the n decisions need to be reconciled, as more than one speaker might be predicted. We reconcile the n decisions by attributing the quote to the speaker with the highest "speaker" probability. Using a binary class with reconciliation in a greedy decoding model is equivalent to the method in Elson and McKeown (2010), except that the gold standard sequence features are replaced with predicted sequence features.

7.2 n-way

A key advantage of the binary class model is that when predicting "speaker" versus "not speaker" the classifier only needs to predict one probability, and thus can take into account the evidence of all other quote-speaker pairs. The drawback to the binary model is that the probabilities assigned to the candidate speakers do not need to directly compete against each other. In other words when assigning a binary probability to a candidate speaker, the classifier does not take into account how good the other candidate speakers are.

To rectify these issues we experiment with a single classification for each quote, where the classifier directly decides between up to n candidate speakers per quote. As speaker-specific evidence is far too sparse, we encode the speakers with their ordinal position backwards from the quote. In other words, the candidate speaker immediately preceding the quote would be labelled "speaker1", the speaker preceding it would be "speaker2" and so on. The classifier then directly predicts these labels. This representation means that candidate speakers need to directly compete for probability mass, although it has the drawback that the evidence for the higher-numbered speakers is quite sparse.

The features we use for this representation are similar to the features used in the E&M binary model. The key difference is that where there were individual features that were calculated with respect to the speaker, there are now n features, one for each of the speaker candidates. This allows the model to account for the strength of other candidates when assigning a speaker label.

8 Sequence Decoding

We noted in the previous section that the E&M results are based on the unrealistic assumption that all previous quotes were attributed correctly. In this section we outline three sequence decoding approaches that remove this unrealistic assumption, without removing all of the transition information that it provides. We believe the transition information is important as many quotes have no explicit attribution in the text, and instead rely on the reader understanding something about the sequence of speakers.

For these experiments we regard the set of speaker attributions in a document as the sequence that we want to decode. Each individual state therefore represents a sequence of w previous attribution decisions, and a decision for the current quote. Obtaining a probability for this state can be done in one of two ways. Either the transition probabilities from state to state can be learned explicitly, or the w previous attribution decisions can be used to build the sequence features for the current state, which implicitly encodes the transition probabilities.

8.1 Greedy Decoding

In sequence decoding the greedy algorithm calculates the probability of each label at a decision point based on the predictions it has already made for previous decisions. More concretely this means we apply a standard classifier at each step, with the sequence features being calculated from the predictions made in previous steps. Greedy decoding is efficient in that it only considers one possible history at each decision point, but it is consequently unable to make trade-offs between good previous choices and good current choices, which means that in general it will not return the optimum sequence of labels. As greedy decoding is an efficient algorithm we do not restrict w, the number of previous decisions, beyond the 10 paragraph restriction that is already in place.

8.2 Viterbi Decoding

Viterbi decoding finds the most probable path through a sequence of decisions. It does this by determining the probabilities of each of the labels at the current decision point, with each of the possible histories of decisions within a given window w. These probabilities can be multiplied together with the previous decisions to retrieve a joint probability for the entire sequence. The final decision for each quote is then just the speaker which is predicted by the sequence with the largest joint probability.

Although they do not come with probabilities, we chose to include the category predictions in our Viterbi model. As we already know that they are accurate indicators of the speaker we assign them a probability of 100%, which effectively forces the Viterbi decoder to choose the category predictions when they are available. It is worth noting that quotes are only assigned to the *Conversation* category if the two prior quotes had alternating speakers. As such, during the Viterbi decoding the categorisation of the quote actually needs to be recalculated with regard to the two previous attribution decisions. By forcing the Viterbi decoder to choose category predictions when they are available, we get the advantage that quote sequences with no intervening text may be forced into the *Conversation* category, which is typically under-represented otherwise.

Both the sequences using the binary class and the n-way class can be decoded using the Viterbi algorithm, so we experiment with both class models. We also experiment with varying window sizes (w), in order to gain insight into how many previous decisions impact the current decision. Though the Viterbi algorithm is able to find the best sequence of probabilities without the need for an exhaustive search, it can still take an impractical amount of time to run. As such we ignore all but the 10 most promising sequences at each decision point.

8.3 Conditional Random Field (CRF) Decoding

The key drawback with the logistic regression experiments described thus far is that the sequence features are trained with gold standard information. This means that during the training phase the sequence features have perfect information about previous speakers and are thus unrealistically good predictors of the final outcome. When the resulting model is used with the less accurate predicted sequence features, it is overconfident about the information those features provide.

We account for this by using a first-order linear chain CRF model, which learns the probabilities of progressing from speaker to speaker more directly. During training the CRF is able to learn the association between features and labels, as well as the chance of transitioning from one label to the next. It also has the advantage of avoiding the label bias problem that would be present in the equivalent Hidden Markov Model (Lafferty et al., 2001).

Though the n-way class model can be used directly in a CRF, the binary class model is more challenging. The main problem is that the "speaker" versus "not speaker" output of the binary classifier does not directly form a meaningful sequence that the CRF can learn over. If the reconciliation step is included it effectively adds an extra layer to the linear chain, making learning more difficult. Due to these difficulties we only use the n-way class model in our CRF experiments.

9 Results

The main result of our experiments with the E&M method is the large drop in accuracy that occurs when the gold standard sequence features are removed, which can be seen in Table 3. When using the binary class model this results in a drop of 25.1% for the LIT corpus, while for the WSJ and SMH corpora the drop is less substantial at 4.4% and 2.6%, respectively. For the LIT corpus the drop is so severe that it actually performs worse than the simple rule-based system. Even more surprisingly, when the predictions from previous decisions are used with a simple greedy decoder, the accuracy drops even further for all three corpora. This indicates that the classifier is putting too much weight on the gold standard sequence features during training, and is misled into making poor decisions when the predicted features are used during test time.

Table 4 shows the results for the n-way class model. Compared to the binary model, the n-way class model generally produced lower results, although the results were more stable to changes in parameters and decoders. The only corpus that produced better results with the n-way class model was the WSJ corpus, which does not have full entity coreference information. This indicates that the n-way model may be helpful when there is more variety in the choice of entities.

The final results we would like to discuss here are the CRF results. On all three corpora the CRF results are underwhelming. The major issue that we can see when applying a CRF model to this task is that the sequences that it needs to learn over are entire documents. This means that for the LIT corpus the training set consisted of only 12 sequences, while

Corpus	E&M	Rule	No seq.	Greedy	Viterbi		
					$w = 1$	$w = 2$	$w = 5$
LIT	*74.7*	**53.3**	49.6	49.0	46.0	49.8	45.9
WSJ	*87.3*	77.9	82.9	74.1	82.3	**83.1**	**83.1**
SMH	*95.0*	91.2	**92.4**	85.6	91.7	90.5	84.1

Table 3: Accuracy on test set with the binary class model. Italicised results indicate gold standard information is used. Bold results show the best realistic result for each corpus.

Corpus	Gold seq.	Rule	No seq.	Greedy	Viterbi			CRF
					$w = 1$	$w = 2$	$w = 5$	
LIT	*68.6*	**53.3**	47.1	46.7	42.5	46.5	44.4	48.6
WSJ	*88.9*	77.9	83.6	77.0	**84.1**	83.7	83.3	79.6
SMH	*94.4*	**91.2**	90.0	89.6	89.5	90.1	90.4	91.0

Table 4: Accuracy on test set with the n-way class model. Italicised results indicate gold standard information is used. Bold results show the best realistic result for each corpus.

the test set consisted of 6 sequences. With so few sequences it is unsurprising that the CRF model did not perform well. The limited range of the first order linear chain model could also have played a part in the poor performance of the CRF models. However, moving to a higher-order model is problematic as the number of transition probabilities that need to be calculated increases exponentially with the order of the model.

10 Conclusion

In this paper, we present the first large-scale evaluation of a quote attribution system on newswire from the 1989 Wall Street Journal (WSJ) and the 2009 Sydney Morning Herald (SMH), as well as comparing against previous work (Elson and McKeown, 2010) on 19th-century literature.

We show that when Elson and McKeown's unrealistic use of gold-standard history information is removed, accuracy on all three corpora drops substantially. We demonstrate that by treating quote attribution as a sequence labelling task, we can achieve results that are very close to their results on newswire, though not for literature.

In future work, we intend to further explore the sequence features that have a large impact on accuracy, and to find similar features or proxies for the sequence features that would be beneficial. We will also explore other approaches to representing quote attribution with a CRF. For the task more broadly, it would be beneficial to compare methods of finding indirect and mixed quotes, and to evaluate how well quote attribution performs on those quotes as opposed to just direct quotes.

Our newswire results, 92.4% for the SMH and 84.1% for the WSJ corpus, demonstrate it is possible to develop an accurate and practical quote extraction system. On the LIT corpus our best result was from the simple rule-based system, which yielded 53.3%. It is clear that literature poses an ongoing research challenge.

Acknowledgements

We would like to thank David Elson for helping us to reimplement his method and Bonnie Webber for her feedback and assistance. O'Keefe has been supported by a University of Sydney Merit scholarship and a Capital Markets CRC top-up scholarship; Pareti has been supported by a Scottish Informatics and Computer Science Alliance (SICSA) studentship. This work has been supported by ARC Discovery grant DP1097291 and the Capital Markets CRC Computable News project.

References

James R. Curran and Stephen Clark. 2003. Investigating GIS and smoothing for maximum entropy taggers. In *Proceedings of the tenth conference on*

European chapter of the Association for Computational Linguistics, pages 91–98.

Peter T. Davis, David K. Elson, and Judith L. Klavans. 2003. Methods for precise named entity matching in digital collections. In *Proceedings of the 3rd ACM/IEEE-CS Joint Conference on Digital libraries*, pages 125–127.

Eric de La Clergerie, Benoit Sagot, Rosa Stern, Pascal Denis, Gaelle Recource, and Victor Mignot. 2011. Extracting and visualizing quotations from news wires. *Human Language Technology. Challenges for Computer Science and Linguistics*, pages 522–532.

David. K Elson and Kathleen. R McKeown. 2010. Automatic attribution of quoted speech in literary narrative. In *Proceedings of AAAI*, pages 1013–1019.

Rong-En Fan, Kai-Wei Chang, Cho-Jui Hsieh, Xiang-Rui Wang, and Chih-Jen Lin. 2008. LIBLINEAR: A library for large linear classification. *Journal of Machine Learning Research*, 9:1871–1874.

Jenny Rose Finkel, Trond Grenager, and Christopher Manning. 2005. Incorporating non-local information into information extraction systems by gibbs sampling. In *Proceedings of the 43rd Annual Meeting on Association for Computational Linguistics*, pages 363–370.

Kevin Glass and Shaun Bangay. 2007. A naive salience-based method for speaker identification in fiction books. In *Proceedings of the 18th Annual Symposium of the Pattern Recognition Association of South Africa (PRASA07)*, pages 1–6.

Ben Hachey, Will Radford, Joel Nothman, Matthew Honnibal, and James R. Curran. 2012. Evaluating entity linking with Wikipedia. *Artificial Intelligence*. (in press).

John Lafferty, Andrew McCallum, and Fernando C.N. Pereira. 2001. Conditional random fields: Probabilistic models for segmenting and labeling sequence data. *International Conference on Machine Learning*, pages 282–289.

Nuno Mamede and Pedro Chaleira. 2004. Character identification in children stories. *Advances in Natural Language Processing*, pages 82–90.

Naoaki Okazaki. 2007. CRFsuite: a fast implementation of Conditional Random Fields (CRFs). URL `http://www.chokkan.org/software/crfsuite/`.

Silvia Pareti. 2012. A database of attribution relations. In *Proceedings of the Eight International Conference on Language Resources and Evaluation (LREC'12)*, pages 3213–3217.

Bruno Pouliquen, Ralf Steinberger, and Clive Best. 2007. Automatic detection of quotations in multilingual news. In *Proceedings of Recent Advances in Natural Language Processing*, pages 487–492.

Benoît Sagot, Laurence Danlos, and Rosa Stern. 2010. A lexicon of french quotation verbs for automatic quotation extraction. In *7th international conference on Language Resources and Evaluation - LREC 2010*.

Luis Sarmento and Sergio Nunes. 2009. Automatic extraction of quotes and topics from news feeds. In *4th Doctoral Symposium on Informatics Engineering*.

Nathan Schneider, Rebecca Hwa, Philip Gianfortoni, Dipanjan Das, Michael Heilman, Alan W. Black, Frederik L. Crabbe, and Noah A. Smith. 2010. Visualizing topical quotations over time to understand news discourse. Technical Report CMU-LTI-01-013, Carnegie Mellon University.

Ralph Weischedel and Ada Brunstein. 2005. BBN pronoun coreference and entity type corpus. *Linguistic Data Consortium, Philadelphia*.

Jason Zhang, Alan Black, and Richard Sproat. 2003. Identifying speakers in children's stories for speech synthesis. In *Proceedings of EUROSPEECH*, pages 2041–2044.

SSHLDA: A Semi-Supervised Hierarchical Topic Model

Xian-Ling Mao♠*, Zhao-Yan Ming♡, Tat-Seng Chua♡, Si Li♣, Hongfei Yan♠†, Xiaoming Li♠
♠Department of Computer Science and Technology, Peking University, China
♡School of Computing, National University of Singapore, Singapore
♣School of ICE, Beijing University of Posts and Telecommunications, China
{xianlingmao,lxm}@pku.edu.cn, yhf@net.pku.edu.cn
{chuats,mingzhaoyan}@nus.edu.sg, lisi@bupt.edu.cn

Abstract

Supervised hierarchical topic modeling and unsupervised hierarchical topic modeling are usually used to obtain hierarchical topics, such as hLLDA and hLDA. Supervised hierarchical topic modeling makes heavy use of the information from observed hierarchical labels, but cannot explore new topics; while unsupervised hierarchical topic modeling is able to detect automatically new topics in the data space, but does not make use of any information from hierarchical labels. In this paper, we propose a semi-supervised hierarchical topic model which aims to explore new topics automatically in the data space while incorporating the information from observed hierarchical labels into the modeling process, called *Semi-Supervised Hierarchical Latent Dirichlet Allocation (SSHLDA)*. We also prove that hLDA and hLLDA are special cases of SSHLDA. We conduct experiments on Yahoo! Answers and ODP datasets, and assess the performance in terms of perplexity and clustering. The experimental results show that predictive ability of SSHLDA is better than that of baselines, and SSHLDA can also achieve significant improvement over baselines for clustering on the FScore measure.

1 Introduction

Topic models, such as latent Dirichlet allocation (LDA), are useful NLP tools for the statistical analysis of document collections and other discrete data. Furthermore, hierarchical topic modeling is able to obtain the relations between topics — parent-child and sibling relations. Unsupervised hierarchical topic modeling is able to detect automatically new topics in the data space, such as hierarchical Latent Dirichlet Allocation (hLDA) (Blei et al., 2004). hLDA makes use of nested Dirichlet Process to automatically obtain a L-level hierarchy of topics. Modern Web documents, however, are not merely collections of words. They are usually documents with hierarchical labels – such as Web pages and their placement in hierarchical directories (Ming et al., 2010). Unsupervised hierarchical topic modeling cannot make use of any information from hierarchical labels, thus supervised hierarchical topic models, such as *hierarchical Labeled Latent Dirichlet Allocation* (hLLDA) (Petinot et al., 2011), are proposed to tackle this problem. hLLDA uses hierarchical labels to automatically build corresponding topic for each label, but it cannot find new latent topics in the data space, only depending on hierarchy of labels.

As we know that only about 10% of an iceberg's mass is seen outside while about 90% of it is unseen, deep down in water. We think that a corpus with hierarchical labels should include not only observed topics of labels, but also there are more latent topics, just like icebergs. hLLDA can make use of the information from labels; while hLDA can explore latent topics. How can we combine the merits of the two types of models into one model?

An intuitive and simple combinational method is like this: first, we use hierarchy of labels as basic hierarchy, called Base Tree (BT); then we use hLDA to build automatically topic hierarchy for each leaf

*This work was done in National University of Singapore.
†Corresponding author.

node in BT, called Leaf Topic Hierarchy (LTH); finally, we add each LTH to corresponding leaf in the BT and obtain a hierarchy for the entire dataset. We refer the method as Simp-hLDA. The performance of the Simp-hLDA is not so good, as can be seen from the example in Figure 3 (b). The drawbacks are: (i) the leaves in BT do not obtain reasonable and right words distribution, such as "Computers & Internet" node in Figure 3 (b), its topical words, "the to you and a", is not about "Computers & Internet"; (ii) the non-leaf nodes in BT cannot obtain words distribution, such as "Health" node in Figure 3 (b); (iii) it is a heuristic method, and thus Simp-hLDA has no solid theoretical basis.

To tackle the above drawbacks, we explore the use of probabilistic models for such a task where the hierarchical labels are merely viewed as a part of a hierarchy of topics, and the topics of a path in the whole hierarchy generate a corresponding document. Our proposed generative model learns both the latent topics of the underlying data and the labeling strategies in a joint model, by leveraging on the hierarchical structure of labels and Hierarchical Dirichlet Process.

We demonstrate the effectiveness of the proposed model on large, real-world datasets in the question answering and website category domains on two tasks: the topic modeling of documents, and the use of the generated topics for document clustering. Our results show that our joint, semi-hierarchical model outperforms the state-of-the-art supervised and unsupervised hierarchical algorithms. The contributions of this paper are threefold: (1) We propose a joint, generative semi-supervised hierarchical topic model, i.e. Semi-Supervised Hierarchical Latent Dirichlet Allocation (SSHLDA), to overcome the defects of hLDA and hLLDA while combining the their merits. SSHLDA is able to not only explore new latent topics in the data space, but also makes use of the information from the hierarchy of observed labels; (2) We prove that hLDA and hLLDA are special cases of SSHLDA; (3) We develop a gibbs sampling inference algorithm for the proposed model.

The remainder of this paper is organized as follows. We review related work in Section 2. In Section 3, we introduce some preliminaries; while we introduce *SSHLDA* in Section 4. Section 5 details a gibbs sampling inference algorithm for SSHLDA; while Section 6 presents the experimental results. Finally, we conclude the paper and suggest directions for future research in Section 7.

2 Related Work

There have been many variations of topic models. The existing topic models can be divided into four categories: *Unsupervised non-hierarchical topic models, Unsupervised hierarchical topic models*, and their corresponding supervised counterparts.

Unsupervised non-hierarchical topic models are widely studied, such as LSA (Deerwester et al., 1990), pLSA (Hofmann, 1999), LDA (Blei et al., 2003), Hierarchical-concept TM (Chemudugunta et al., 2008c; Chemudugunta et al., 2008b), Correlated TM (Blei and Lafferty, 2006) and Concept TM (Chemudugunta et al., 2008a; Chemudugunta et al., 2008b) etc. The most famous one is Latent Dirichlet Allocation (LDA). LDA is similar to pLSA, except that in LDA the topic distribution is assumed to have a Dirichlet prior. LDA is a completely unsupervised algorithm that models each document as a mixture of topics. Another famous model that not only represents topic correlations, but also learns them, is the Correlated Topic Model (CTM). Topics in CTM are not independent; however it is noted that only pairwise correlations are modeled, and the number of parameters in the covariance matrix grows as the square of the number of topics.

However, the above models cannot capture the relation between super and sub topics. To address this problem, many models have been proposed to model the relations, such as Hierarchical LDA (HLDA) (Blei et al., 2004), Hierarchical Dirichlet processes (HDP) (Teh et al., 2006), Pachinko Allocation Model (PAM) (Li and McCallum, 2006) and Hierarchical PAM (HPAM) (Mimno et al., 2007) etc. The relations are usually in the form of a hierarchy, such as the tree or Directed Acyclic Graph (DAG). Blei et al. (2004) proposed the hLDA model that simultaneously learns the structure of a topic hierarchy and the topics that are contained within that hierarchy. This algorithm can be used to extract topic hierarchies from large document collections.

Although unsupervised topic models are sufficiently expressive to model multiple topics per document, they are inappropriate for labeled corpora because they are unable to incorporate the observed labels into their learning procedure. Several modifications of LDA to incorporate supervision have been proposed in the literature. Two such models, Supervised LDA (Blei and McAuliffe, 2007; Blei and McAuliffe, 2010) and DiscLDA (Lacoste-Julien et al., 2008) are first proposed to model documents associated only with a single label. Another category of models, such as the MM-LDA (Ramage et al., 2009b), Author TM (Rosen-Zvi et al., 2004), Flat-LDA (Rubin et al., 2011), Prior-LDA (Rubin et al., 2011), Dependency-LDA (Rubin et al., 2011) and Partially LDA (PLDA) (Ramage et al., 2011) etc., are not constrained to one label per document because they model each document as a bag of words with a bag of labels. However, these models obtain topics that do not correspond directly with the labels. Labeled LDA (LLDA) (Ramage et al., 2009a) can be used to solve this problem.

None of these non-hierarchical supervised models, however, leverage on dependency structure, such as parent-child relation, in the label space. For hierarchical labeled data, there are also few models that are able to handle the label relations in data. To the best of our knowledge, only hLLDA (Petinot et al., 2011) and HSLDA (Perotte et al., 2011) are proposed for this kind of data. HSLDA cannot obtain a probability distribution for a label. Although hLLDA can obtain a distribution over words for each label, hLLDA is unable to capture the relations between parent and child node using parameters, and it also cannot detect automatically latent topics in the data space. In this paper, we will propose a generative topic model to tackle these problems of hLLDA.

3 Preliminaries

The nested Chinese restaurant process (nCRP) is a distribution over hierarchical partitions (Blei et al., 2004). It generalizes the Chinese restaurant process (CRP), which is a distribution over partitions. The CRP can be described by the following metaphor. Imagine a restaurant with an infinite number of tables, and imagine customers entering the restaurant in sequence. The dth customer sits at a table accord-

Table 1: Notations used in the paper.

Sym	Description
V	Vocabulary (word set), w is a word in V
D	Document collection
T_j	The set of paths in the sub-tree whose root is the jth leaf node in the hierarchy of observed topics
m	A document m that consists of words and labels
$\mathbf{w}_m$	The text of document m, w_i is i^{th} words in **w**
$\mathbf{c}_m$	The topic set of document m
$\mathbf{c}_{o_m}$	The set of topics with observed labels for document m
$\mathbf{c}_{e_m}$	The set of topics without labels for document m
$\boldsymbol{c}_{e_{-m}}$	The set of latent topics for all documents other than m
$\boldsymbol{z}_{e_m}$	The assignment of the words in the mth document to one of the latent topics
$\boldsymbol{w}_{e_m}$	The set of the words belonging to one of the latent topics in the the mth document
$z_{m,n}$	The assignment of the nth word in the mth document to one of the L available topics
$\mathbf{z}$	The set of $z_{m,n}$ for all words in all documents
c_i	A topic in the ith level in the hierarchy
θ	The word distribution set for Z, i.e., $\{\theta\}_{z\in\mathbf{c}}$
α	Dirichlet prior of θ
δ_{c_i}	The multinomial distribution over the sub-topics of c_{i-1}
μ_{c_i}	Dirichlet prior of δ_{c_i}
η	Dirichlet prior of β
β	The multinomial distribution of words
θ_m	The distributions over topics for document m
$\boldsymbol{\theta}$	The set for θ_m, $m \in \{1, ..., D\}$

ing to the following distribution,

$$p(c_d = k|c_{1:(d-1)}) \propto \begin{cases} m_k & \text{if } k \text{ is previous occupied} \\ \gamma & \text{if } k \text{ is a new tabel,} \end{cases} \quad (1)$$

where m_k is the number of previous customers sitting at table k and γ is a positive scalar. After D customers have sat down, their seating plan describes a partition of D items.

In the nested CRP, imagine now that tables are organized in a hierarchy: there is one table at the first level; it is associated with an infinite number of tables at the second level; each second-level table is associated with an infinite number of tables at the third level; and so on until the Lth level. Each customer enters at the first level and comes out at the Lth level, generating a path with L tables as she sits in each restaurant. Moving from a table at level l to one of its subtables at level $l+1$, the customer draws following the CRP using Formula (1). In this paper, we will make use of nested CRP to explore latent topics in data space.

To elaborate our model, we first define two concepts. If a model can learn a distribution over words for a label, we refer the topic with a corresponding label as a **labeled topic**. If a model can learn an unseen and latent topic without a label, we refer the

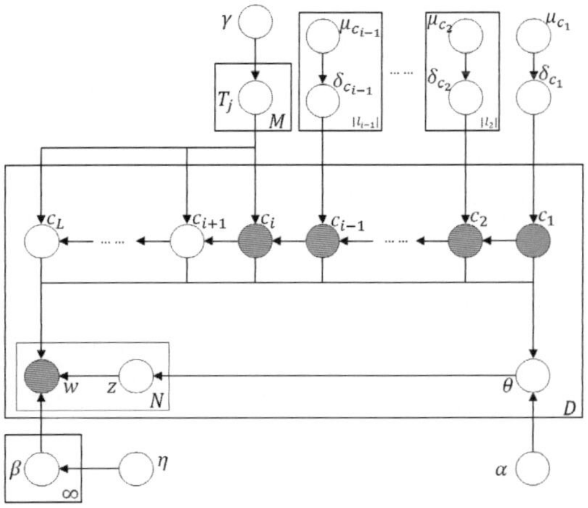

Figure 1: The graphical model of SSHLDA.

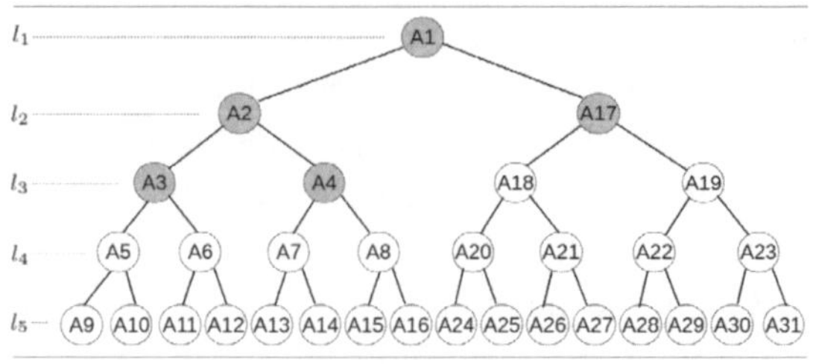

Figure 2: One illustration of SSHLDA. The tree has 5 levels. The shaded nodes are observed topics, and circled nodes are latent topics. The latent topics are generated automatically by SSHLDA model. After learning, each node in this tree will obtain a corresponding probability distribution over words, i.e. a topic.

topic as a **latent topic**.

4 The Semi-Supervised Hierarchical Topic Model

In this section, we will introduce a semi-supervised hierarchical topic model, i.e., the *Semi-Supervised Hierarchical Latent Dirichlet Allocation* (SSHLDA). SSHLDA is a probabilistic graphical model that describes a process for generating a hierarchical labeled document collection. Like hierarchical Labeled LDA (hLLDA) (Petinot et al., 2011), SSHLDA can incorporate labeled topics into the generative process of documents. On the other hand, like hierarchical Latent Dirichlet Allocation (hLDA) (Blei et al., 2004), SSHLDA can automatically explore latent topic in data space, and extend the existing hierarchy of observed topics. SSHLDA makes use of not only observed topics, but also latent topics.

The graphical model of SSHLDA is illustrated in Figure 1. In the model, N is the number of words in a document, D is the total number of documents in a collection, M is the number of leaf nodes in hierarchical observed nodes, c_i is a node in the ith level in the hierarchical tree, η, α and μ_{c_i} are dirichlet prior parameters, β_k is a distribution over words, θ is a document-specific distribution over topics, δ_{c_i} is a multinomial distribution over observed sub-topics of topic c_i, w is an observed word, z is the topic assigned to w, $Dir_k(.)$ is a k-dimensional Dirichlet distribution, T_j is a set of paths in the hierarchy of latent topics for j^{th} leaf node in the hierarchy of observed topics, γ is a Multi-nomial distribution over paths in the tree. All notations used in this paper are listed in Table 1.

SSHLDA, as shown in Figure 1, assumes the following generative process:

(1) For each table $k \in T$ in the infinite tree,
 - (a) Draw a topic $\beta_k \sim Dir(\eta)$.

(2) For each document, $m \in \{1, 2, ..., D\}$
 - (a) Let c_1 be the root node.
 - (b) For each level $l \in \{2, ..., L\}$:
   - (i) If nodes in this level have been observed, draw a node c_l from $Mult(\delta_{c_{l-1}}|\mu_{c_{l-1}})$.
   - (ii) Otherwise, draw a table c_l from restaurant c_{l-1} using Formula (1).
 - (c) Draw an L-dimensional topic proportion vector θ_m from $Dir(\alpha)$.
 - (d) For each word $n \in \{1, ..., N\}$:
   - (i) Draw $z \in \{1, ..., L\}$ from $Mult(\theta)$.
   - (ii) Draw w_n from the topic associated with restaurant c_z.

As the example showed in Figure 2, we assume that we have known a hierarchy of observed topics: {A1,A2,A17,A3,A4}, and assume the height of the desired topical tree is $L = 5$. All circled nodes are latent topics, and shaded nodes are observed topics. A possible generative process for a document *m* can be: It starts from A1, and chooses node A17 at level 2, and then chooses A18, A20 and A25 in the following levels. Thus we obtain a path: $\boldsymbol{c}_m = \{A1, A17, A18, A20, A25\}$. After getting the path for m, SSHLDA generates each word from one of topics in this set of topics $\boldsymbol{c}_m$.

5 Probabilistic Inference

In this section, we describe a Gibbs sampling algorithm for sampling from the posterior and corresponding topics in the SSHLDA model. The Gibbs sampler provides a method for simultaneously exploring the model parameter space (the latent topics of the whole corpus) and the model structure space (L-level trees).

In SSHLDA, we sample the paths $\boldsymbol{c}_m$ for document m and the per-word level allocations to topics in those paths $z_{m,n}$. Thus, we approximate the posterior $p(\boldsymbol{c}_m, \boldsymbol{z}_m|\gamma, \eta, \boldsymbol{w}, \boldsymbol{\mu})$. The hyper-parameter γ reflects the tendency of the customers in each restaurant to share tables, η denotes the expected variance of the underlying topics (e.g., $\eta \ll 1$ will tend to choose topics with fewer high-probability words), μ_{c_i} is the dirichlet prior of δ_{c_i}, and $\boldsymbol{\mu}$ is the set of μ_{c_i}. $w_{m,n}$ denotes the nth word in the mth document; and $c_{m,l}$ represents the restaurant corresponding to the lth-level topic in document m; and $z_{m,n}$, the assignment of the nth word in the mth document to one of the L available topics. All other variables in the model, θ and β, are integrated out. The Gibbs sampler thus assesses the values of $z_{m,n}$ and $c_{m,l}$.

The Gibbs sampler can be divided into two main steps: the sampling of level allocations and the sampling of path assignments.

First, given the values of the SSHLDA hidden variables, we sample the $c_{m,l}$ variables which are associated with the CRP prior. Noting that $\boldsymbol{c}_m$ is composed of $\boldsymbol{c}_{o_m}$ and $\boldsymbol{c}_{e_m}$, $\boldsymbol{c}_{o_m}$ is the set of observed topics for document m, and $\boldsymbol{c}_{e_m}$ is the set of latent topics for document m. The conditional distribution for $\boldsymbol{c}_m$, the L topics associated with document m, is:

$$\begin{aligned} &p(\boldsymbol{c}_m|\boldsymbol{z}, \boldsymbol{w}, \boldsymbol{c}_{-m}, \boldsymbol{\mu}) \\ &=p(\boldsymbol{c}_{o_m}|\boldsymbol{\mu})p(\boldsymbol{c}_{e_m}|\boldsymbol{z}_{e_m}, \boldsymbol{w}_{e_m}, \boldsymbol{c}_{e-m}) \\ &\propto p(\boldsymbol{c}_{o_m}|\boldsymbol{\mu})p(\boldsymbol{w}_{e_m}|\boldsymbol{c}_{e_m}, \boldsymbol{w}_{e-m}, \boldsymbol{z}_{e_m}) \\ &\quad p(\boldsymbol{c}_{e_m}|\boldsymbol{c}_{e-m}) \end{aligned} \tag{2}$$

where

$$p(\boldsymbol{c}_{o_m}|\boldsymbol{\mu}) = \prod_{i=0}^{|\boldsymbol{c}_{o_m}|-1} p(c_{i,m}|\mu_{c_i}) \tag{3}$$

and

$$\begin{aligned} &p(\boldsymbol{w}_{e_m}|\boldsymbol{c}_{e_m}, \boldsymbol{w}_{e-m}, \boldsymbol{z}_{e_m}) \\ &= \prod_{l=1}^{|c_{e_m}|} \left(\frac{\Gamma(n^{\cdot}_{c_{e_m,l},-m} + |V|\eta)}{\prod_w \Gamma(n^w_{c_{e_m,l},-m} + \eta)} \times \right. \\ &\left. \frac{\prod_w \Gamma(n^w_{c_{e_m,l},-m} + n^w_{c_{e_m,l},m} + \eta)}{\Gamma(n^{\cdot}_{c_{e_m,l},-m} + n^{\cdot}_{c_{e_m,l},m} + |V|\eta)} \right) \end{aligned} \tag{4}$$

$\boldsymbol{c}_{e-m}$ is the set of latent topics for all documents other than m, $\boldsymbol{z}_{e_m}$ is the assignment of the words in the mth document to one of the latent topics, and $\boldsymbol{w}_{e_m}$ is the set of the words belonging to one of the latent topics in the the mth document. $n^w_{c_{e_m,l},-m}$ is the number of instances of word w that have been assigned to the topic indexed by $c_{e_m,l}$, not including those in the document m.

Second, given the current state of the SSHLDA, we sample the $z_{m,n}$ variables of the underlying SSHLDA model as follows:

$$\begin{aligned} &p(z_{m,n} = j|\boldsymbol{z}_{-(m,n)}, \boldsymbol{w}, \boldsymbol{c}_m, \boldsymbol{\mu}) \\ &\quad\propto \frac{n^m_{-n,j} + \alpha}{n^m_{-n,\cdot} + |\boldsymbol{c}_m|} \cdot \frac{n^{w_{m,n}}_{-n,j} + \eta_{w_{m,n}}}{n^{\cdot}_{-(m,n)} + |V|} \end{aligned} \tag{5}$$

Having obtained the full conditional distribution, the Gibbs sampling algorithm is then straightforward. The $z_{m,n}$ variables are initialized to determine the initial state of the Markov chain. The chain is then run for a number of iterations, each time finding a new state by sampling each $z_{m,n}$ from the distribution specified by Equation (5). After obtaining individual word assignments $\mathbf{z}$, we can estimate the topic multinomials and the per-document mixing proportions. Specifically, the topic multinomials are estimated as:

$$\beta_{\mathbf{c}_{\mathbf{m},\mathbf{j}},i} = p(w_i|z_{\mathbf{c}_{\mathbf{m},\mathbf{j}}}) = \frac{\eta + n_{z_{\mathbf{c}_{\mathbf{m},\mathbf{j}}}}^{w_i}}{|V|\eta + \sum n^{\cdot}_{z_{\mathbf{c}_{\mathbf{m},\mathbf{j}}}}} \tag{6}$$

while the per-document mixing proportions fixed can be estimated as:

$$\theta_{m,j} = \frac{\alpha + n^m_{\cdot,j}}{|\mathbf{c}_\mathbf{m}|\alpha + n^m_{\cdot,\cdot}}, j \in 1, ..., |\mathbf{c}_\mathbf{m}| \tag{7}$$

5.1 Relation to Existing Models

In this section, we draw comparisons with the current state-of-the-art models for hierarchical topic modeling (Blei et al., 2004; Petinot et al., 2011) and show that at certain choices of the parameters of our model, these methods fall out as special cases.

Our method generalises not only *hierarchical Latent Dirichlet Allocation* (hLDA), but also *Hierarchical Labeled Latent Dirichlet Allocation* (hLLDA). Our proposed model provides a unified framework allowing us to model hierarchical labels while to explore new latent topics.

Equivalence to hLDA As introduced in Section 2, hLDA is a unsupervised hierarchical topic model. In this case, there are no observed nodes, that is, the corpus has no hierarchical labels. This means $\boldsymbol{c}_m$ is equal to $\boldsymbol{c}_{e_m,m}$; meanwhile the factor $p(\boldsymbol{c}_{o_m,m}|\boldsymbol{\mu})$ is always equal to one because each document has root node, and this allows us to rewrite Formula (2) as:

$$p(\boldsymbol{c}_m|\boldsymbol{z}, \boldsymbol{w}, \boldsymbol{c}_{-m}, \boldsymbol{\mu}) \\ \propto p(\boldsymbol{w}_{\boldsymbol{c}_m}|\boldsymbol{c}, \boldsymbol{w}_{-m}, \boldsymbol{z})p(\boldsymbol{c}_m|\boldsymbol{c}_{-m}) \quad (8)$$

which is exactly the same as the conditional distribution for $\boldsymbol{c}_m$, the L topics associated with document m in hLDA model. In this case, our model becomes equivalent to the hLDA model.

Equivalence to hLLDA hLLDA is a supervised hierarchical topic model, which means all nodes in hierarchy are observed. In this case, $\boldsymbol{c}_m$ is equal to $\boldsymbol{c}_{o_m,m}$, and this allows us to rewrite Formula (2) as:

$$p(\boldsymbol{c}_m|\boldsymbol{z}, \boldsymbol{w}, \boldsymbol{c}_{-m}, \boldsymbol{\mu}) = p(\boldsymbol{c}_m|\boldsymbol{\mu}) \propto p(\boldsymbol{c}_{o_m}|\boldsymbol{\mu}) \quad (9)$$

which is exactly the same as the step " Draw a random path assignment c_m" in the generative process for hLLDA. Consequentially, in this sense our model is equivalent to hLLDA.

6 Experiments

We demonstrate the effectiveness of the proposed model on large, real-world datasets in the question answering and website category domains on two tasks: the topic modeling of documents, and the use of the generated topics for document clustering.

6.1 Datasets

To construct comprehensive datasets for our experiments, we crawled data from two websites. First, we crawled nearly all the questions and associated answer pairs (QA pairs) of two top categories of Yahoo! Answers: *Computers & Internet* and *Health*. This produced forty-three subcategories from 2005.11 to 2008.11, and an archive of 6,345,786 QA documents. We refer the Yahoo! Answer data as *Y_Ans*.

Table 2: The statistics of the datasets.

Datasets	#labels	#paths	Max level	#docs
Y_Ans	46	35	4	6,345,786
O_Hlth	6695	6505	10	54939
O_Home	2432	2364	9	24254

In addition, we first crawled two categories of Open Directory Project (ODP)*: *Home* and *Health*. Then, we removed all categories whose number of Web sites is less than 3. Finally, for each of Web sites in categories, we submited the url of each Web site to Google and used the words in the snippet and title of the first returned result to extend the summary of the Web site. We denote the data from the category *Home* as *O_Home*, and the data from the category *Health* as *O_Hlth*.

The statistics of all datasets are summarized in Table 2. From this table, we can see that these datasets are very diverse: *Y_Ans* has much fewer labels than *O_Hlth* and *O_Home*, but have much more documents for each label; meanwhile the depth of hierarchical tree for *O_Hlth* and *O_Home* can reach level 9 or above.

All experiments are based on the results of models with a burn-in of 10000 Gibbs sampling iterations, symmetric priors $\alpha = 0.1$ and free parameter $\eta = 1.0$; and for $\boldsymbol{\mu}$, we can obtain the estimation of μ_{c_i} by fixed-point iteration (Minka, 2003).

6.2 Case Study

With topic modeling, the top associated words of topics can be used as good descriptors for topics in a hierarchy (Blei et al., 2003; Blei and McAuliffe, 2010). We show in Figure 3 a pair of comparative example of the proposed model and a baseline model over *Y_Ans* dataset. The tree-based topic visualizations of Figure 3 (a) and (b) are the results of SSHLDA and Simp-hLDA.

We have three major observations from the example: (i) SSHLDA is a unified and generative model, after learning, it can obtain a hierarchy of topics;

*http://dmoz.org/

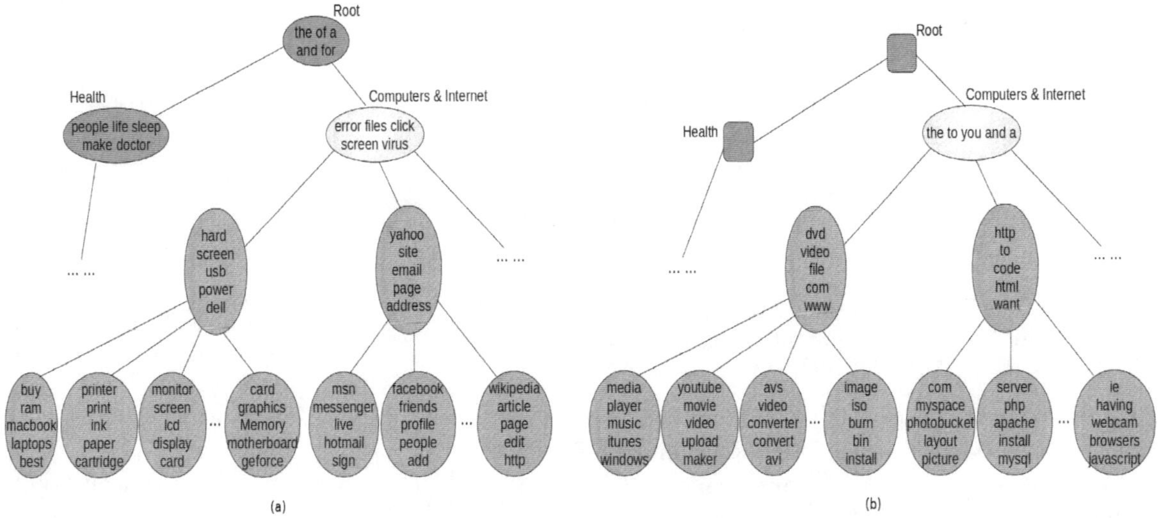

Figure 3: (a) A sub network discovered on *Y_Ans* dataset using SSHLDA, and the whole tree has 74 nodes; (b) A sub network discovered on *Y_Ans* dataset using Simp-hLDA algorithm, and the whole tree has 89 nodes. In both figures, the shaded and squared nodes are observed labels, not topics; the shaded and round nodes are topics with observed labels; blue nodes are topics but without labels and the yellow node is one of leaves in hierarchy of labels. Each topic represented by top 5 terms.

while Simp-hLDA is a heuristic method, and its result is a mixture of label nodes and topical nodes. For example, Figure 3 (b) shows that the hierarchy includes label nodes and topic nodes, and each of labeled nodes just has a label, but label nodes in Figure 3 (a) have their corresponding topics. (ii) During obtaining a hierarchy, SSHLDA makes use of the information from observed labels, thus it can generate a logical, structual hierarchy with parent-child relations; while Simp-hLDA does not incorporate prior information of labels into its generation process, thus although it can obtain a hierarchy, many parent-child pairs have not parent-child relation. For example, in Figure 3 (b), although label "root" is a parent of label "Computers & Internet", the topical words of label "Computers & Internet" show the topical node is not a child of label "root". However, in Figure 3 (a), label "root" and "Computers & Internet" has corresponding parent-child relation between their topical words. (iii) In a hierarchy of topics, if a topical node has corresponding label, the label can help people understand descendant topical nodes. For example, when we know node "error files click screen virus" in Figure 3 (a) has its label "Computers & Internet", we can understand the child topic "hard screen usb power dell" is about "computer hardware". However, in Figure 3 (b), the labels in parent nodes cannot provide much information to understand descendant topical nodes because many label nodes have not corresponding right topical words, such as label "Computers & Internet", its topical words, "the to you and a", do not reflect the connotation of the label.

These observations further confirm that SSHLDA is better than the baseline model.

6.3 Perplexity Comparison

A good topic model should be able to generalize to unseen data. To measure the prediction ability of our model and baselines, we compute the perplexity for each document d in the test sets. *Perplexity*, which is widely used in the language modeling and topic modeling community, is equivalent algebraically to the inverse of the geometric mean per-word likelihood (Blei et al., 2003). Lower perplexity scores mean better. Our model, SSHLDA, will compare with three state-of-the-art models, i.e. Simp-hLDA, hLDA and hLLDA. Simp-hLDA has been introduced in Section 1, and hLDA and hLLDA has been reviewed in Section 2. We keep 80% of the data collection as the training set and use the remaining collection as the held-out test set. We build the models based on the train set and compute the preplexity of the test set to evaluate the models. Thus, our goal is to achieve lower perplexity score on a held-out test set. The perplexity of M test documents is calculated as:

$$perplexity(D_{test}) = exp\left\{ -\frac{\sum_{d=1}^{M}\sum_{m=1}^{N_d}\log p(w_{dm})}{\sum_{d=1}^{M} N_d} \right\} \quad (10)$$

where D_{test} is the test collection of M documents, N_d is document length of document d and w_{dm} is m^{th} word in document d.

We present the results over the *O_Hlth* dataset in Figure 4. We choose top 3-level labels as observed, and assume other labels are not observed, i.e. $l = 3$. From the figure, we can see that the perplexities of SSHLDA, are lower than that of Simp-hLDA, hLDA and hLLDA at different value of the tree height parameter, i.e. $L \in \{5, 6, 7, 8\}$. It shows that the performance of SSHLDA is always better than the state-of-the-art baselines, and means that our proposed model can model the hierarchical labeled data better than the state-of-the-art models. We can also obtain similar experimental results over *Y_Ans* and *O_Home* datasets, and their detailed description is not included in this paper due to the limitation of space.

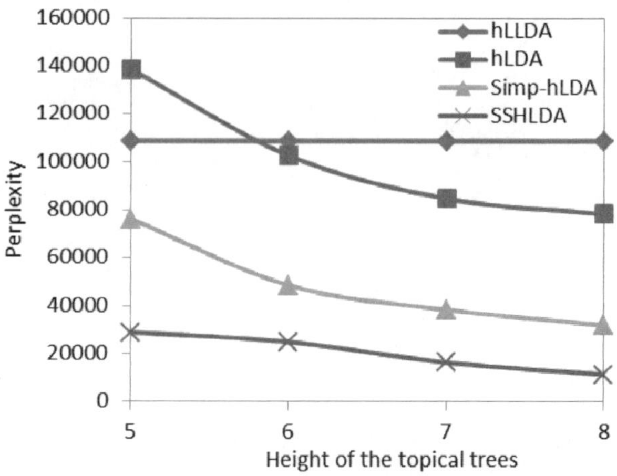

Figure 4: Perplexities of hLLDA, hLDA, Simp-hLDA and SSHLDA. The results are run over the O_Hlth dataset, with the height of the hierarchy of observed labels $l = 3$. The X-axis is the height of the whole topical tree (L), and Y-axis is the perplexity.

6.4 Clustering performance

To evaluate indirectly the performance of the proposed model, we compare the clustering performance of following systems: 1) the proposed model; 2) Simp-hLDA; 3) hLDA; 4) agglomerative clustering algorithm. There are many agglomerative clustering algorithms, and in this paper, we make use of the single-linkage method in a software package called CLUTO (Karypis, 2005) to obtain hierarchies of clusters over our datasets, with words as features. We refer the method as *h-clustering*.

Given a document collection *DS* with a *H-level* hierarchy of labels, each label in the hierarchy and corresponding documents will be taken as the ground truth of clustering algorithms. The hierarchy of labels denoted as *GT-tree*. The process of evaluation is as follows. First, we choose top l*-level* labels in GT-tree as an observed hierarchy, i.e. Base Tree (BT), and we need to construct a L*-level* hierarchy ($l < L <= H$) over the documents DS using a model. The remaining labels in GT-tree and corresponding documents are the ground truth classes, each class denoted as C_i. Then, (i) for h-clustering, we run single-linkage method over the documents DS. (ii) for Simp-hLDA, hLDA runs on the documents in each leaf-node in BT, and the height parameter is $(L - l)$ for each hLDA. After training, each document is assigned to top-1 topic according to the distribution over topics for the document. Each topic and corresponding documents forms a new cluster. (iii) for hLDA, hLDA runs on all documents in DS, and the height parameter is L. Similar to Simp-hLDA, each document is assigned to top-1 topic. Each topic and corresponding documents forms a new cluster. (iv) for SSHLDA, we set height parameter as L. After training, each document is also assigned to top-1 topic. Topics and their corresponding documents form a hierarchy of clusters.

6.4.1 Evaluation Metrics

For each dataset we obtain corresponding clusters using the various models described in previous sections. Thus we can use clustering metrics to measure the quality of various algorithms by using a measure that takes into account the overall set of clusters that are represented in the new generated part of a hierarchical tree.

One such measure is the FScore measure, introduced by (Manning et al., 2008). Given a particular class C_r of size n_r and a particular cluster S_i of size n_i, suppose n_{ri} documents in the cluster S_i belong to C_r, then the FScore of this class and cluster is defined to be

$$F(C_r, S_i) = \frac{2 \times R(C_r, S_i) \times P(C_r, S_i)}{R(C_r, S_i) + P(C_r, S_i)} \quad (11)$$

where $R(C_r, S_i)$ is the recall value defined as n_{ri}/n_r, and $P(C_r, S_i)$ is the precision value defined as n_{ri}/n_i for the class C_r and the cluster S_i. The FScore of the class C_r, is the maximum FScore value attained at any node in the hierarchical clustering tree T. That is,

$$F(C_r) = \max_{S_i \in T} F(C_r, S_i). \quad (12)$$

The FScore of the entire clustering solution is then defined to be the sum of the individual class FScore weighted according to the class size.

$$FScore = \sum_{r=1}^{c} \frac{n_r}{n} F(C_r), \quad (13)$$

where c is the total number of classes. In general, the higher the FScore values, the better the clustering solution is.

6.4.2 Experimental Results

Each of hLDA, Simp-hLDA and SSHLDA needs a parameter—the height of the topical tree, i.e. L; and for Simp-hLDA and SSHLDA, they need another parameter—the height of the hierarchical observed labels, i.e l. The h-clustering does not have any height parameters, thus its FScore will keep the same values at different height of the topical tree. With choosing the height of hierarchical labels for *O_Home* as 4, i.e. $l = 4$, the results of our model and baselines with respect to the height of a hierarchy are shown in Figure 5.

From the figure, we can see that our proposed model can achieve consistent improvement over the baseline models at different height, i.e. $L \in \{5, 6, 7, 8\}$. For example, the performance of SSHLDA can reach 0.396 at height 5 while the h-clustering, hLDA and hLLDA only achieve 0.295, 0.328 and 0.349 at the same height. The result shows that our model can achieve about 34.2%, 20.7% and 13.5% improvements over h-clustering, hLDA and hLLDA at height 5. The improvements are significant by t-test at the 95% significance level. We can also obtain similar experimental results over *Y_Ans* and *O_Hlth*. However, for the same reason of limitation of space, their detailed descriptions are skipped in this paper.

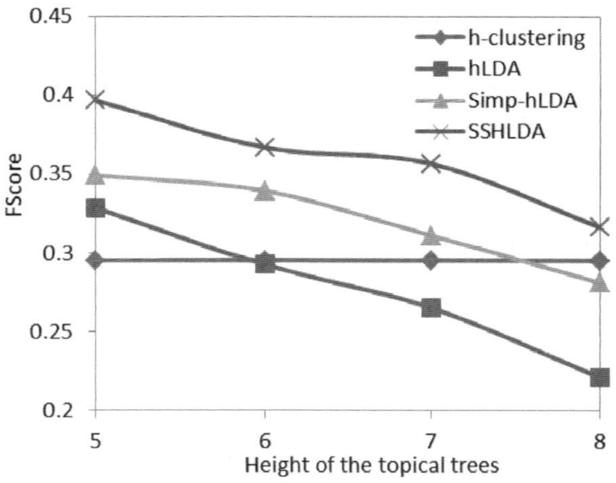

Figure 5: FScore measures of h-clustering, hLDA, Simp-hLDA and SSHLDA. The results are run over the O_Home dataset, with the height of the hierarchy of observed labels $l = 3$. The X-axis is the height of the whole topical tree (L), and Y-axis is the FScore measure.

7 Conclusion and Future work

In this paper, we have proposed a semi-supervised hierarchical topic models, i.e. SSHLDA, which aims to solve the drawbacks of hLDA and hLLDA while combine their merits. Specially, SSHLDA incorporates the information of labels into generative process of topic modeling while exploring latent topics in data space. In addition, we have also proved that hLDA and hLLDA are special cases of SSHLDA. We have conducted experiments on the Yahoo! Answers and ODP datasets, and assessed the performance in terms of Perplexity and FScore measure. The experimental results show that the prediction ability of SSHLDA is the best, and SSHLDA can also achieve significant improvement over the baselines on Fscore measure.

In the future, we will continue to explore novel topic models for hierarchical labeled data to further improve the effectiveness; meanwhile we will also apply SSHLDA to other media forms, such as image, to solve related problems in these areas.

Acknowledgments

This work was partially supported by NSFC with Grant No.61073082, 60933004, 70903008 and NExT Search Centre, which is supported by the Singapore National Research Foundation & Interactive Digital Media R&D Program Office, MDA under research grant (WBS:R-252-300-001-490).

References

D. Blei and J. Lafferty. 2006. Correlated topic models. *Advances in neural information processing systems*, 18:147.

D.M. Blei and J.D. McAuliffe. 2007. Supervised topic models. In *Proceeding of the Neural Information Processing Systems(nips)*.

D.M. Blei and J.D. McAuliffe. 2010. Supervised topic models. *Arxiv preprint arXiv:1003.0783*.

D.M. Blei, A.Y. Ng, and M.I. Jordan. 2003. Latent dirichlet allocation. *The Journal of Machine Learning Research*, 3:993–1022.

D. Blei, T.L. Griffiths, M.I. Jordan, and J.B. Tenenbaum. 2004. Hierarchical topic models and the nested chinese restaurant process. *Advances in neural information processing systems*, 16:106.

C. Chemudugunta, A. Holloway, P. Smyth, and M. Steyvers. 2008a. Modeling documents by combining semantic concepts with unsupervised statistical learning. *The Semantic Web-ISWC 2008*, pages 229–244.

C. Chemudugunta, P. Smyth, and M. Steyvers. 2008b. Combining concept hierarchies and statistical topic models. In *Proceeding of the 17th ACM conference on Information and knowledge management*, pages 1469–1470. ACM.

C. Chemudugunta, P. Smyth, and M. Steyvers. 2008c. Text modeling using unsupervised topic models and concept hierarchies. *Arxiv preprint arXiv:0808.0973*.

S. Deerwester, S.T. Dumais, G.W. Furnas, T.K. Landauer, and R. Harshman. 1990. Indexing by latent semantic analysis. *Journal of the American society for information science*, 41(6):391–407.

T. Hofmann. 1999. Probabilistic latent semantic analysis. In *Proc. of Uncertainty in Artificial Intelligence, UAI'99*, page 21. Citeseer.

G. Karypis. 2005. Cluto: Software for clustering high dimensional datasets. *Internet Website (last accessed, June 2008), http://glaros.dtc.umn.edu/gkhome/cluto/cluto/overview*.

S. Lacoste-Julien, F. Sha, and M.I. Jordan. 2008. ndisclda: Discriminative learning for dimensionality reduction and classification. *Advances in Neural Information Processing Systems*, 21.

W. Li and A. McCallum. 2006. Pachinko allocation: Dag-structured mixture models of topic correlations. In *Proceedings of the 23rd international conference on Machine learning*, pages 577–584. ACM.

C.D. Manning, P. Raghavan, and H. Schutze. 2008. *Introduction to information retrieval*, volume 1. Cambridge University Press Cambridge.

D. Mimno, W. Li, and A. McCallum. 2007. Mixtures of hierarchical topics with pachinko allocation. In *Proceedings of the 24th international conference on Machine learning*, pages 633–640. ACM.

Z.Y. Ming, K. Wang, and T.S. Chua. 2010. Prototype hierarchy based clustering for the categorization and navigation of web collections. In *Proceeding of the 33rd international ACM SIGIR*, pages 2–9. ACM.

T.P. Minka. 2003. Estimating a dirichlet distribution. *Annals of Physics*, 2000(8):1–13.

A. Perotte, N. Bartlett, N. Elhadad, and F. Wood. 2011. Hierarchically supervised latent dirichlet allocation. *Neural Information Processing Systems (to appear)*.

Y. Petinot, K. McKeown, and K. Thadani. 2011. A hierarchical model of web summaries. In *Proceedings of the 49th Annual Meeting of the ACL: Human Language Technologies: short papers-Volume 2*, pages 670–675. ACL.

D. Ramage, D. Hall, R. Nallapati, and C.D. Manning. 2009a. Labeled lda: A supervised topic model for credit attribution in multi-labeled corpora. In *Proceedings of the 2009 Conference on Empirical Methods in Natural Language Processing: Volume 1-Volume 1*, pages 248–256. Association for Computational Linguistics.

D. Ramage, P. Heymann, C.D. Manning, and H. Garcia-Molina. 2009b. Clustering the tagged web. In *Proceedings of the Second ACM International Conference on Web Search and Data Mining*, pages 54–63. ACM.

D. Ramage, C.D. Manning, and S. Dumais. 2011. Partially labeled topic models for interpretable text mining. In *Proceedings of the 17th ACM SIGKDD international conference on Knowledge discovery and data mining*, pages 457–465. ACM.

M. Rosen-Zvi, T. Griffiths, M. Steyvers, and P. Smyth. 2004. The author-topic model for authors and documents. In *Proceedings of the 20th conference on Uncertainty in artificial intelligence*, pages 487–494. AUAI Press.

T.N. Rubin, A. Chambers, P. Smyth, and M. Steyvers. 2011. Statistical topic models for multi-label document classification. *Arxiv preprint arXiv:1107.2462*.

Y.W. Teh, M.I. Jordan, M.J. Beal, and D.M. Blei. 2006. Hierarchical dirichlet processes. *Journal of the American Statistical Association*, 101(476):1566–1581.

Improving NLP through Marginalization of Hidden Syntactic Structure

Jason Naradowsky, Sebastian Riedel, and **David A. Smith**
Department of Computer Science
University of Massachusetts Amherst
Amherst, MA, 01003, U.S.A.
{narad, riedel, dasmith}@cs.umass.edu

Abstract

Many NLP tasks make predictions that are inherently coupled to syntactic relations, but for many languages the resources required to provide such syntactic annotations are unavailable. For others it is unclear exactly how much of the syntactic annotations can be effectively leveraged with current models, and what structures in the syntactic trees are most relevant to the current task.

We propose a novel method which avoids the need for any syntactically annotated data when predicting a related NLP task. Our method couples latent syntactic representations, constrained to form valid dependency graphs or constituency parses, with the prediction task via specialized factors in a Markov random field. At both training and test time we marginalize over this hidden structure, learning the optimal latent representations for the problem. Results show that this approach provides significant gains over a syntactically uninformed baseline, outperforming models that observe syntax on an English relation extraction task, and performing comparably to them in semantic role labeling.

1 Introduction

Many NLP tasks are inherently tied to syntax, and state-of-the-art solutions to these tasks often rely on syntactic annotations as either a source for useful features (Zhang et al., 2006, path features in relation extraction) or as a scaffolding upon which a more narrow, specialized classification can occur (as often done in semantic role labeling). This decoupling of the end task from its intermediate representation is sometimes known as the **two-stage** approach (Chang et al., 2010) and comes with several drawbacks. Most notably this decomposition prohibits the learning method from utilizing the labels from the end task when predicting the intermediate representation, a structure which must have some correlation to the end task to provide any benefit.

Relying on intermediate representations that are specifically syntactic in nature introduces its own unique set of problems. Large amounts of syntactically annotated data is difficult to obtain, costly to produce, and often tied to a particular domain that may vary greatly from that of the desired end task. Additionally, current systems often utilize only a small amount of the annotation for any particular task. For instance, performing named entity recognition (NER) jointly with constituent parsing has been shown to improve performance on both tasks, but the only aspect of the syntax which is leveraged by the NER component is the location of noun phrases (Finkel and Manning, 2009). By instead discovering a latent representation jointly with the end task we address all of these concerns, alleviating the need for any syntactic annotations, while simultaneously attempting to learn a latent syntax relevant to both the particular domain and structure of the end task.

We phrase the joint model as factor graph and marginalize over the hidden structure of the intermediate representation at both training and test time, to optimize performance on the end task. Inference is done via loopy belief propagation, making this framework trivially extensible to most graph structures. Computation over latent syntactic representations is made tractable with the use of special combinatorial factors which implement unlabeled variants of common dynamic-programming parsing algorithms, constraining the hidden representation to realize valid dependency graphs or constituency trees.

We apply this strategy to two common NLP tasks, coupling a model for the end task prediction with latent and general syntactic representations via specialized logical factors which learn associations between latent and observed structure. In comparisons with identical models which observe "gold" syntactic annotations, derived from off-the-shelf parsers or provided with the corpora, we find that our hidden marginalization method is comparable in both tasks and almost every language tested, sometimes significantly outperforming models which observe the true syntax.

The following sections serves as a preliminary, introducing an inventory of factors and variables for constructing factor graph representations of syntactically-coupled NLP tasks. Section 3 explores the benefits of this method on relation extraction (RE), where we compare the use dependency and constituency structure as latent representations. We then turn to a more established semantic role labeling (SRL) task (§4) where we evaluate across a wide range of languages.

2 Latent Pseudo-Syntactic Structure

The models presented in this paper are phrased in terms of variables in an undirected graphical model, Markov random field. More specifically, we implement the model as a factor graph, a bipartite graph composed of factors and variables in which we can efficiently compute the marginal beliefs of any variable set with the sum-product algorithm for cyclic graphs, *loopy belief propagation*,. We now introduce the basic variable and factor components used throughout the paper.

2.1 Latent Dependency Structure

Dependency grammar is a lexically-oriented syntactic formalism in which syntactic relationships are expressed as dependencies between individual words. Each non-root word specifies another as its head, provided that the resulting structure forms a valid directed graph, ie. there are no cycles in the graph. Due to the flexibility of this representation it is often used to describe free-word-order languages, and increasingly preferred in NLP for more language-in-use scenarios. A dependency graph can be modeled with the following nodes, as first proposed by Smith and Eisner (2008):

- Let $\{Link(i,j) : 0 \leq i \leq j \leq n, n \neq j\}$ be $O(n^2)$ boolean variables corresponding to the possible links in a dependency parse. $L_{i,j}$ = true implies that there is a dependency from parent i to child j.

- Let $\{LINK(i,j) : 0 \leq i \leq j \leq n, n \neq j\}$ be $O(n^2)$ unary factors, each paired with a corresponding $Link(i,j)$ variable and expressing the independent belief that $Link(i,j)$ = true.

2.2 Latent Constituency Structure

Alternatively we can describe the more structured constituency formalism by setting up a representation over span variables:

- Let $\{Span(i,j) : 0 \leq i < j \leq n\}$ be $O(n^2)$ boolean variables such that $Span(i,j) =$ true iff there is a bracket spanning i to j [1].

- Let $\{\text{SPAN}(i,j) : 0 \leq i < j \leq n\}$ be $O(n^2)$ unary factors, each attached to the corresponding $Span(i,j)$ variable. These factors score the independent suitability of each span to appear in an unlabeled constituency tree.

All boolean variables presented in this paper will be paired to unary factors in this manner, which we will omit in future descriptions. This encompasses the necessary *representational* structure for both syntactic formalisms, but nothing introduced up to this point guarantees that either of these representations will form a valid tree or DAG.

2.3 Combinatorial Factors

Naively constraining these latent representations through the introduction of many interconnected ternary factors is possible, but would likely be computationally intractable. However, as observed in

[1] In practice, we do not need to include variables for spans of width 1 or n, since they will always be true.

Smith and Eisner (2008), we can encapsulating common dynamic programming algorithms within special-purpose factors to efficiently globally constrain variable configurations . Since the outgoing messages from such factors to a variable can be computed from the factor's posterior beliefs about that variable, there is no difficulty in exchanging beliefs between these special-purpose factors and the rest of the graph, and inference can proceed using the standard sum-product or max-product belief propagation. Here we present two combinatorial factors that provide efficient ways of constraining the model to fit common syntactic frameworks.

- Let CKYTREE be a global combinatorial factor, as used in previous work in efficient parsing (Naradowsky and Smith, 2012), attached to all the $Span(i, j)$ variables. This factor contributes a factor of 1 to the model's score iff the span variables collectively form a legal, binary bracketing and a factor of 0 otherwise. It enforces, therefore, a hard constraint on the variables, computing beliefs via an unlabeled variant of the inside-outside algorithm.

- Let DEP-TREE be a global combinatorial factor, as presented in Smith and Eisner (2008), which attaches to all $Link(i, j)$ variables and similarly contributes a factor of 1 iff the configuration of $Link$ variables forms a valid projective dependency graph. A graph is projective if its edges do not cross.

2.4 Marginal MAP Inference

It is straightforward to train these latent variable models to maximize the marginal probability of their outputs, conditioning on their inputs, and marginalizing out the latent syntactic variables. To compute feature expectations, we can use marginal inference techniques such as sampling and sum-product belief propagation to compute marginal probabilities.

A knottier problem arises when we want to find the best assignment to the variables of interest while marginalizing out "nuisance" latent variables. This is the problem of **marginal MAP** inference—sometimes known as consensus decoding—which has been shown to be NP-hard and without a polynomial time approximation scheme (Sima'an, 1996; Casacuberta and Higuera, 2000). In the NLP community, these inference problems often arise when dealing with *spurious ambiguity* where multiple derivations can lead to the same derived structure. In tree substitution grammars, for instance, there may be many ways of combining elementary trees to produce the same output tree; in machine translation, many different elementary phrases or elementary tree pairs might produce the same output string. For syntactic parsing, Goodman (1996) proposed a variational method for summing out spurious ambiguity that was equivalent to minimum Bayes risk decoding (Goel and Byrne, 2000; Kumar and Byrne, 2004) with a constituent-recall loss function. For MT, May and Knight (2006) proposed methods for determinizing tree automata to reduce ambiguity, and Li et al. (2009) proposed a variational method based on n-gram loss functions. More recently, Liu and Ihler (2011) analyzed message-passing algorithms for marginal MAP.

In this paper, we adopt a simple minimum Bayes risk decoding scheme. First, we perform sum-product belief propagation on the full factor graph. Then, we maximize the expected accuracy of the variables of interest, subject to any hard constraints on them (such as mutual exclusion among labels). In some cases with complex combinatorial constraints, this simple MBR scheme has proved more effective than exact decoding over all variables (Auli and Lopez, 2011).

3 Relation Extraction

Performing a syntax-based NLP task in most real-world scenarios requires that the incoming data first be parsed using a pre-trained parsing model. For some tasks, like relation extraction, many data sets lack syntactic annotation and these circumstances persist even into the training phase. In this section we explore such scenarios and contrast the use of parser-provided syntactic annotation to marginalizing over latent representations of constituency or dependency syntax. We show the hidden syntactic models are not just competitive with these "oracle" models, but in some configurations can actually outperform them.

Relation extraction is the task of identifying semantic relations between sets of entities in text (as illustrated in Fig. 1b), and a good proving ground for latent syntactic methods for two reasons. First, because entities share a semantic relationship, under most linguistic analyses these entities will also share some syntactic relation. Indeed, syntactic features have long been an extremely useful source of information for relation extraction systems (Culotta and Sorensen, 2004; Mintz et al., 2009). Secondly, relation extraction has been a common task for pioneering efforts in processing data mined from the internet, and otherwise noisy or out-of-domain data. In particular, large noisily-annotated data sets have been generated by leveraging freely available knowledge bases such as Freebase (Bollacker et al., 2008; Mintz et al., 2009). Such data sets have been utilized successfully for relation extraction from the web (Bunescu and Mooney, 2007).

3.1 Model

We present a simple model for representing relational structure, with the only variables present being a set of boolean-valued variables representing an undirected dependency between two entities, and an additional set of boolean label variables representing the type label of the relation.

- Let $\{Rel(i,j : 0 \le i < j \le n\}$ be $O(n^2)$ boolean variables such that $Rel(i,j) = \textsf{true}$ iff there is a relation spanning i to j.
- Let $\{Rel\text{-}Label(i,j,\lambda) : \lambda \in L, \text{and } 0 \le i < j \le n\}$ be $O(|L|n^2)$ boolean variables such that $Rel\text{-}Label(i,j,\lambda) = \textsf{true}$ iff there is a relation spanning i to j with relation type λ.
- Let $\{\text{ATMOST1}(i,j) : 0 \le i < j \le n\}$ be $O(n^2)$ factors, each coordinating the set L of possible nonterminal variables to the Rel variable at each i,j tuple, allowing a $Rel\text{-}Label$ variable to be $\textsf{true}$ iff all other label variables are $\textsf{false}$ and $Rel(i,j) = \textsf{true}$.

Here the $Rel(i,j)$ and $Rel\text{-}Label(i,j)$ variables simply express the representation of the problem, while the ATMOST1 factors are logical constraints ensuring that only one label will apply to a particular relation.

3.2 Coordination Factors

An important contribution of this work is the introduction of a flexible, general framework for connecting the latent and observable partitions of the model. We accomplish this through the use of two additional factors, each expressing the same basic logic, which learn when to coordinate and when to ignore correlations between the latent syntax and the end task. While here we specify binary and ternary versions of these factors, they also generalize to higher dimensions.

- Let $\{\text{D-CONNECT}(i,j,k) : 0 \le i < j \le n; 0 \le k \le n\}$ be $O(n^3)$ factors coordinating any number of dependency syntax $Link(i,j)$ variables with representational variables on the end task, multiplying in 1 to the model score unless all variables are on, in which case it multiplies a connective potential ϕ derived from its features. Thus it functions logically as a soft NAND factor. In this ternary formulation k represents a hidden dependency head or pivot which is shared between two syntactic dependencies anchored at the indices of the entities in the relation (as illustrated in Fig. 1).
- Let $\{\text{C-CONNECT}(i,j) : 0 \le i < j \le n\}$ be $O(n^2)$ factors coordinating syntactic $Span(i,j)$ and relation arc $Rel(i,j)$, identically to D-CONNECT but with a 1-to-1 mapping. Intuitively the joint model might learn $\phi > 1$, i.e., constituency spans and task prediction relations are more likely to be coterminous.

The difficulty in working with latent dependency syntax is that we posit that the RE variables do not share a 1-to-1 mapping with variables in the hidden representation. We expect instead, according to linguistic intuition, that a relation between entities at position i and j in the sentence should have corresponding syntactic dependencies but that they are likely to realize this by sharing the same head word (as depicted in Fig.1), a word whose identity should help label the relation. Therefore we introduce a special coordination factor, D-CONNECT as a ternary factor to capture the relationship between pairs of latent syntactic variables and a single relation variable, pivoting on the same unknown head word.

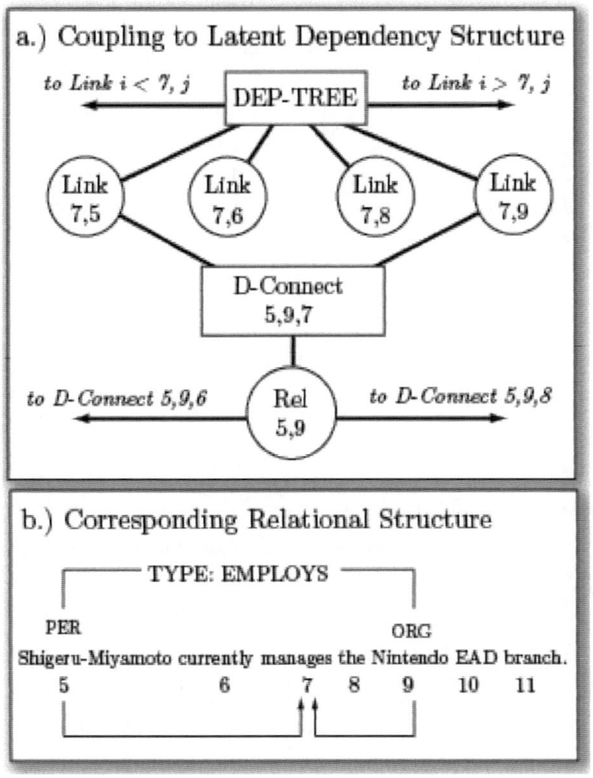

Figure 1: Latent Dependency coupling for the RE task. The D-CONNECT factor expresses ternary connection relations because the shared head word of the proposed relation is unknown. As is convention, variables are represented by circles, factors by rectangles.

We introduce six model scenarios.

- **Baseline**, simply the arc-factored model consisting only of *Rel* and corresponding *Label* variables for each entity. Features on the relation factors, which are common to all model configurations, are combinations of lexical information (i.e., the words that form the entity, the pos-tags of the entities, etc.) as well as the distance between the relation. This is a lightweight model and generally does not attempt to exhaustively leverage all possible proven sources of useful features (Zhou et al., 2005) towards a higher absolute score, but rather to serve as a point of comparison to the models which rely on syntactic information.

- **Baseline-Ent**, a variant of **Baseline** with additional features which include combinations of mention type, entity type, and entity sub-type.

- **Oracle D-Parse**, in which we also instantiate a full set of latent dependency syntax variables, and connect them to the baseline model using D-CONNECT factors. Syntax variables are clamped to their true values.

- **Oracle C-Parse**, the constituency syntax analogue of **Oracle D-Parse**.

- **Hidden D-Parse**, which is an extension of **Oracle D-Parse** in which we connect all syntax variables to a DEP-TREE factor, syntax variables are unobserved, and are learned jointly with the end task. The features for latent syntax are a subset of those used in dependency parsing (McDonald et al., 2005).

- **Hidden C-Parse**, the constituency syntax analogue of **Hidden D-Parse**. The feature set is similar but bigrams are taken over the words defining the constituent span, rather than the words defining the head/modifier relation.

Coordination factor features for the syntactically-informed models are particularly important. This became evident in initial experiments where the baseline was often able to outperform the hidden syntactic model. However, inclusion of entity and mention label features into the connection factors provides the model with greater reasoning over when to coordinate or ignore the relation predictions with the underlying syntax. These are a proper subset of the **Baseline-Ent** features.

3.3 Data

We evaluate these models using the 2005 Automatic Content Extraction (ACE) data set (Walker, 2006), using the English (dual-annotated) and Chinese (solely annotator #1 data set) sections. Each corpus is annotated with entity mentions—tagged as PER, ORG, LOC, or MISC—and, where applicable, what type of relation exists between them (e.g., coarse: PHYS; fine: Located). But like most corpora available for the task, the burden of acquiring corresponding syntactic annotation is left to the researcher. In this situation it is common to turn to existing pre-trained parsing models.

We generate our data by first splitting the raw text paragraphs into sentences. Chinese sentences

ACE Results												
	English						Chinese					
	Unlabeled			Labeled			Unlabeled			Labeled		
Model	P	R	F1	P	R	F1	P	R	F1	P	R	F1
Baseline	85.4	57.0	68.4	83.0	55.3	66.4	42.9	26.8	33.0	42.6	21.3	28.4
Baseline-Ent	87.2	65.4	74.8	85.8	64.4	73.6	55.2	31.1	39.8	51.2	29.4	37.4
Oracle D-Parse	89.3	67.4	76.8	89.3	66.2	75.4	60.0	32.6	42.2	58.1	31.3	40.7
Hidden D-Parse	87.8	69.8	77.7	85.3	67.8	75.6	48.0	32.0	38.4	47.2	30.0	36.7
Oracle C-Parse	89.1	68.7	77.6	87.5	67.5	76.2	66.8	37.8	**48.3**	63.8	37.0	**46.8**
Hidden C-Parse	90.5	69.9	**78.9**	88.8	68.6	**77.4**	56.3	32.3	41.0	53.4	31.6	39.7

Table 1: Relation Extraction Results. Models using hidden constituency syntax provide significant gains over the syntactically-uniformed baseline model in both languages, but the advantages of the latent syntax were mitigated on the smaller Chinese data set.

are also tokenized according to Penn Chinese Treebank standards (Xue et al., 2005). The sentences are then tagged and parsed using the Stanford CoreNLP tools, using the standard pre-trained models for tagging (Toutanvoa and Manning, 2000), and the factored parsing model of Klein and Manning (2002). The distributed grammar is trained on a variety of sources, including the standard Wallstreet Journal corpus, but also biomedical, translation, and questions. We then apply entity and relation annotations noisily to the data, collapsing multi-word entities into one term. We filter out sentences with fewer than two entities (and are thus incapable of containing relations) and sentences with more than 40 words (to keep the parses more reliable). This yields 6966 sentences for English data, but unfortunately only 747 sentences for the Chinese. Nine of every ten sentences comprise the training set, with every tenth sentence reserved for test.

3.4 Results

We train all models using 20 iterations of stochastic gradient descent, each with a maximum of 10 BP iterations (though in practice we find convergence to often occur much earlier). The results are presented in Table 1, showing precision, recall, and F-measure for both labeled and unlabeled prediction. For English, not only is the hidden marginalization method a suitable replacement for the syntactic trees provided by pre-trained, state-of-the-art models, but in both configurations we find that inducing an optimal hidden structure is preferable to the parser-produced annotations. On Chinese, where the data set is atypically small, we still observe improved performance over the baseline in the constituency-based model though it is not able to match the observed syntax model.

Despite the intuition that both entities occupy roles as modifiers of the same verb, we find that the **Hidden D-Parse** model often fails to recover the correct latent structure, and that even when successful dependency parses are observed, the head word is often not uniquely indicative of the relation type (as *known* is not strongly correlated with the relation type EMPLOYS in the phrase: *Shigeru Miyamoto, best known for his work at the video game company Nintendo*). Hence when it comes to relation extraction, at least on our relatively small data sets, we find the simplest approach to latent syntactic structure is the best.

We now turn to the task of semantic role labeling to evaluate this method on a more established hand-annotated data set, and a more varied set of languages.

4 Semantic Role Labeling

The task of semantic role labeling (SRL) aims to detect and label the semantic relationships between particular words, most commonly verbs (referred to in the domain as *predicates*), and their *arguments* (Meza-Ruiz and Riedel, 2009).

In a manner similar to RE, there is a strong correlation between the presence of an SRL relation and there existing an underlying syntactic dependency, though this is not always expressed as directly as a 1-to-1 correspondence. This has historically motivated a reliance on syntactic annotation, and some of the most successful methods have simply applied

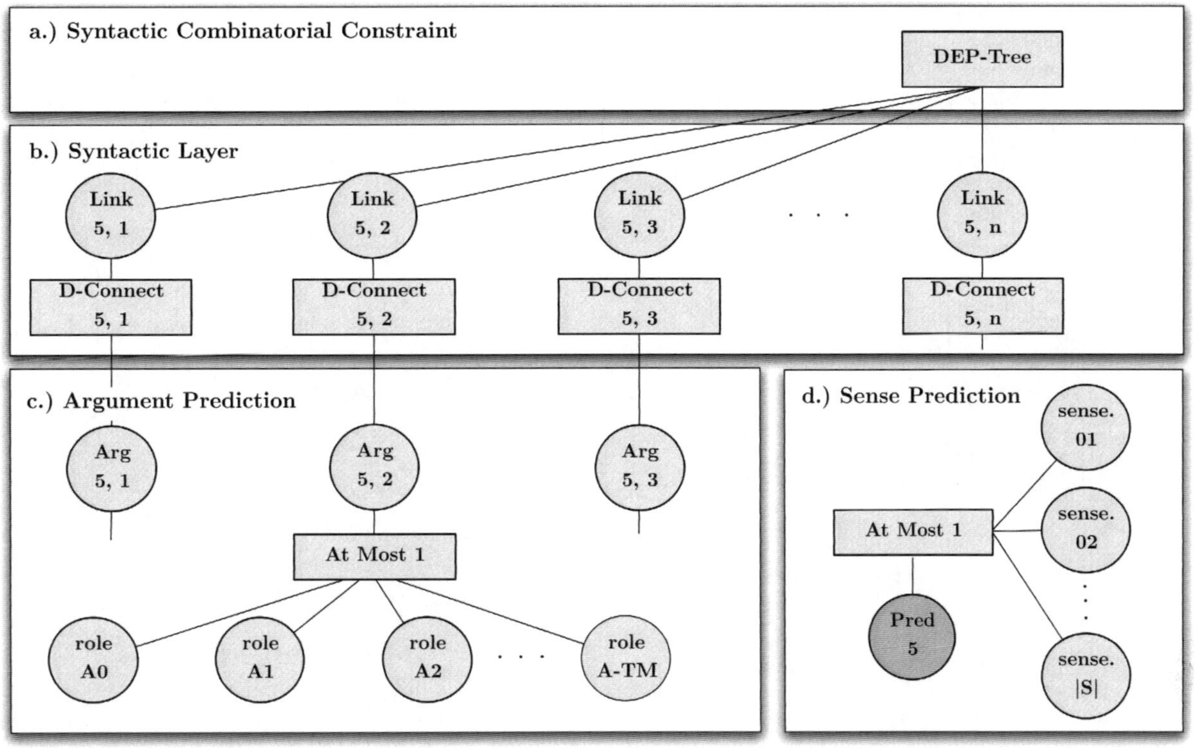

Figure 2: A tiered graphic representing the three different SRL model configurations. The baseline system is described in the bottom (c & d), the separate panels highlighting the independent predictions of this model: sense labels are assigned in an entirely separate process from argument prediction. Pruning in the model takes place primarily in this tier, since we observe true predicates we only instantiate over these indices. The middle tier (b.) illustrates the syntactic representation layer, and the connective factors between syntax and SRL. In the observed syntax model the $Link$ variables are clamped to their correct values, with no need for a factor to coordinate them to form a valid tree. Finally, the hidden model comprises all layers, including a combinatorial syntactic constraint (a.) over syntactic variables. In this scenario all labels in (b.) are hidden at both training and test time.

feature-rich classifiers to the parsed trees. Related work has recognized the large annotation burden the task demands, but aimed to keep the syntactic annotations and induce semantic roles (Lang and Lapata, 2010). In this section we will take the opposite approach, disregarding the syntactic annotations which we argue are more costly to acquire, as they require more formal linguistic training to produce.

4.1 Model

We present a simple, flexible model for SRL in which sense predictions are made independently of the rest of the model, and argument predictions are made independently of each other. The model structure is composed as depicted in Fig. 2.

- Let $\{Arg(i,j) : 0 \leq i < j \leq n\}$ be $O(n^2)$ boolean variables such that $Arg(i,j) = \textsf{true}$ iff predicate i takes token j as an argument.
- Let $\{Role(i,j,\lambda) : \lambda \in L, \text{ and } 0 \leq i < j \leq n\}$ be $O(|L|n^2)$ boolean variables such that $Role(i,j,\lambda) = \textsf{true}$ iff $Arg(i,j)$ is $\textsf{true}$ and takes the role label λ.
- Let $\{Sense(i,\sigma) : \sigma \in S, \text{ and } 0 \leq i \leq n\}$ be $O(|S|n)$ boolean variables such that $Sense(i,\sigma) = \textsf{true}$ iff predicate i has sense σ.

4.1.1 Features

At the coarsest level both the SRL and RE models are specifying binary predictions between a pair of indices in the sentence, and a set of labels for each dependency that happens to be $\textsf{true}$. Similarly we use almost identical features in SRL as we did in

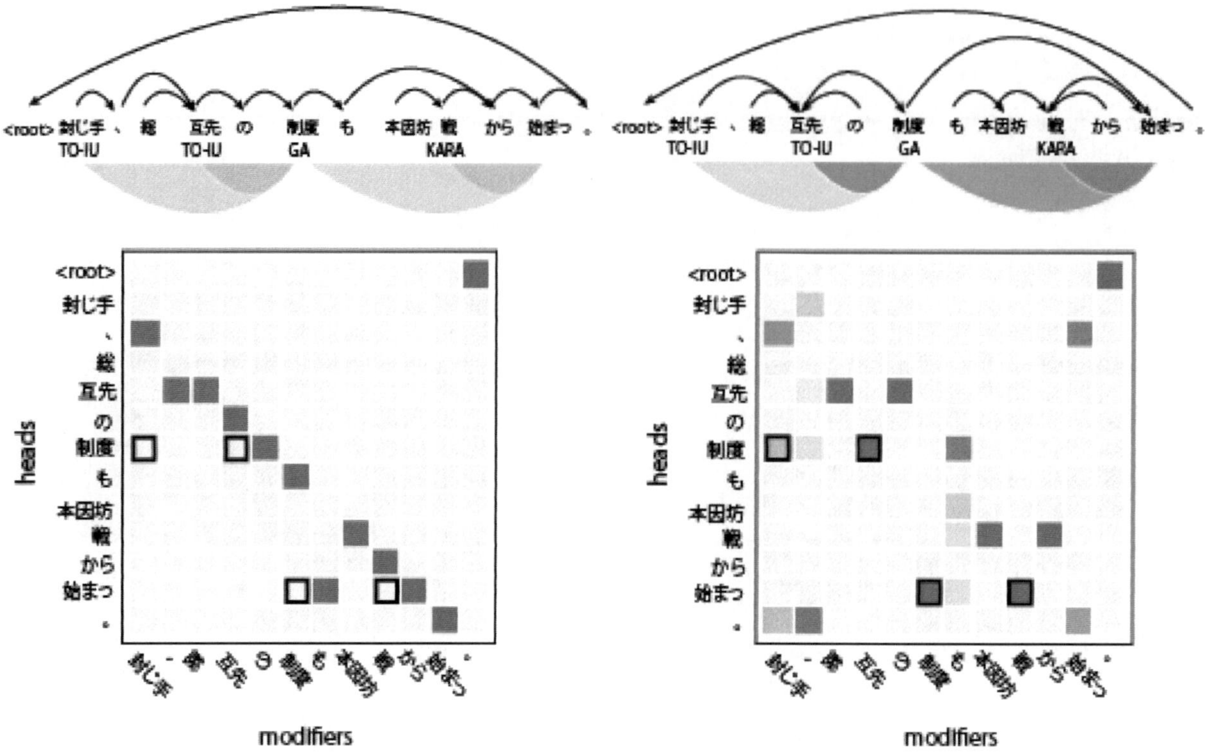

Figure 3: Examining the learned hidden representation for SRL. In this example the syntactic dependency arcs derived from gold standard syntactic annotations (*left*) are entirely disjoint from the correct predicate/arguments pairs (shown in the heatmaps by the squares outlined in black), and the observed syntax model fails to recover any of the correct predictions. In contrast, the hidden model structure (*right*) learns a representation that closely parallels the desired end task predictions, helping it recover three of the four correct SRL predictions (shaded arcs: red corresponds to a correct prediction, with true labels GA, KARA, etc.), and providing some evidence towards the fourth. The dependency tree corresponding to the hidden structure is derived by edge-factored decoding: dependency variables whose beliefs > 0.5 are classified as true (though some arcs not relevant to the SRL predictions are omitted for clarity).

RE, with the sole exception that we incorporate the observable lemma and morphological features into bigrams on predicate/argument pairs. For sense prediction we rely only on unigram features taken in a close ($w = 2$) window of the target predicate.

For the coordinating factors we use subsets of combinations of word, part-of-speech, and capitalization features taken between head and argument, and concatenate these with the distance and direction between the predicate and argument. We do not find the performance of the system to be as sensitive to which features are present in the coordinating factors as we did in the RE task.

4.2 Data

We evaluate our SRL model using the data set developed for the CoNLL 2009 shared task competition (Hajič et al., 2009), which features seven languages and provides an ideal opportunity to measure the ability of the hidden structure to generalize across languages of disparate origin and varied characteristics. It also provides the opportunity to observe a variety of different annotation styles and biases, some of which our model was able to uncover as ill-suited to common models for the task. The data itself provides word, lemma, part-of-speech, and morphological feature information, along with gold dependency parses. Words which denote predicates are identified, and their (train time) arguments are provided. They are also annotated with a sense label for each predicate, which is scored as an additional SRL dependency. Thus the task involves predicting for each predicate a set of argument dependencies and the sense label associated with that predicate.

Data	Model	Unlabeled			Labeled			CoNLL 2009 F1		
		P	R	F1	P	R	F1	MAX.	MEAN	MED.
Catalan	Baseline	92.20	62.43	74.48	73.80	58.76	65.43			
	Oracle Syn.	98.48	96.17	**97.31**	70.42	68.78	**69.59**	80.3	71.0	74.1
	Hidden Syn.	95.21	92.84	94.01	68.86	67.15	67.99			
Chinese	Baseline	72.48	64.82	68.44	65.97	59.00	62.29			
	Oracle Syn.	98.57	78.98	**87.69**	87.64	70.22	**77.97**	78.6	72.2	70.4
	Hidden Syn.	90.79	79.09	84.53	81.97	71.40	76.32			
Czech	Baseline	97.73	56.50	71.61	84.80	48.80	61.84			
	Oracle Syn.	98.62	81.25	89.09	92.94	68.25	**74.84**	85.4	72.4	71.7
	Hidden Syn.	92.39	89.35	**90.85**	74.41	71.96	73.16			
English	Baseline	92.46	71.56	80.68	84.56	65.45	73.78			
	Oracle Syn.	96.75	82.25	**88.91**	85.48	72.67	**78.55**	85.6	75.6	72.1
	Hidden Syn.	95.06	79.06	86.32	83.82	69.72	76.12			
German	Baseline	93.49	44.24	60.06	75.00	35.49	48.18			
	Oracle Syn.	95.18	79.11	86.41	73.24	60.87	66.49	79.7	68.1	67.8
	Hidden Syn.	91.92	86.26	**89.00**	69.47	65.19	**67.26**			
Japanese	Baseline	91.64	43.36	58.87	80.41	38.05	51.66			
	Oracle Syn.	93.84	48.15	63.64	90.06	46.21	61.08	78.2	62.7	72.0
	Hidden Syn.	90.88	73.47	**81.25**	73.42	59.36	**65.65**			
Spanish	Baseline	82.90	39.47	53.48	67.64	32.21	43.64			
	Oracle Syn.	98.96	94.19	**96.52**	70.68	67.27	**68.93**	80.5	70.4	73.4
	Hidden Syn.	96.15	90.53	93.25	68.81	64.79	66.74			

Table 2: SRL Results. The hidden model excels on the unlabeled prediction results, often besting the scores obtained using the parses distributed with the CoNLL data sets. These gains did not always translate to the labeled task where poor sense prediction hindered absolute performance.

4.3 Results

We evaluate across a set of model configurations analogous to before. All experiments used 30 iterations of SGD with a Gaussian prior, and a max 10 iterations of BP to compute the marginals for each example. In comparison to the CoNLL competition entries (Table 2, rightmost columns) our syntactically-informed models generally fall in the middle of the rankings. This is not surprising given the independent predictions of the model and the very general, language universal assumptions we have made in the model structure and feature sets. However, in terms of gauging the usefulness of the hidden syntactic marginalization method the results are extremely compelling, with only marginal differences between the performance of the observed-syntax model, especially relative to the baseline.

And despite the simplicity of the model, we still manage to perform at state-of-the-art levels in a few instances, sometimes outperforming most of the competition entries without observing any syntax. The performance on Chinese is an example of this, with our system outperforming all but the best system, and the hidden syntactic model only slightly behind.

Abstracting away from the performance comparisons against other systems, the unlabeled results are the more revealing evidence for the use of hidden syntactic structure. Here the average hidden model score (88.89) almost outperforms the observed syntax model (90.22, and vs. 66.80 baseline), mostly due to the large margins on the unlabeled Japanese scores. The strong independence between sense prediction and argument prediction hinders performance on the labeled task, but on all languages we find an extremely significant improvement exploiting hidden syntactic structure in comparison to the baseline system—the hidden model recovers more than 92% of the gap between the baseline and the observed syntax model. It is also interesting to note that in the shared task competition the two languages which systems lost the most performance between their parsing F1 and their SRL F1 were Japanese and German. As illustrated in Fig. 3, the correspondence between syntax and SRL are extremely, and systematically, poor. In this example our hidden structure model was able to assign strong beliefs to the latent syntactic variables which correspond to the correct predicate/argument pairs, allowing it to correctly identify three of the four SRL arguments when the joint model failed to recover one.

5 Related Work

This work is perhaps mostly closely related to the Learning over Constrained Latent Representations (LCLR) framework of Chang et al. (2010). Their abstract problem formulation is identical: both paradigms seek to couple the end task to an intermediate representation which is not accessible to the learning algorithm. However much of the intent, scale, and methodology is different. LCLR aims to provide a flexible latent structure for increasing the representational power of the model in a useful way, and is demonstrated on tasks and domains where data availability is not a key concern. In contrast, while our hidden structure models may outperform their observed syntax counterparts, our focus is as much on alleviating the burden of procuring large amounts of syntactic annotation as it is about increasing the expressiveness of the model. To that end we constrain a more sophisticated latent representation and couple it to highly structured output predictions, opposed to binary classification problems. In methodology, we perform the more computationally intensive marginalization operation instead of maximizing.

Marginalization of hidden structure is also fundamental to other work, and featured most prominently in generative Bayesian latent variable models (Teh et al., 2006). Our approach is trained discriminatively, affording the use of very rich feature sets and the prediction of partial structures without needing to specify a full derivation. Similar approaches have been used in more linear latent variable CRF-based models (McCallum et al., 2005), but these must only marginalize only over hidden states of a much more compact representation. Naively extending this to tree-based constraints would often be computationally inefficient, and we avoid intractability through the encapsulation of much of the dynamic programming machinery into specialized factors. Moreover, using loopy belief propagation means that the inference method is not closely coupled to the task structure, and need not change when applying this method to other types of graphs.

6 Conclusion

We have presented a novel method of coupling syntactically-oriented NLP tasks to combinatorially-constrained hidden syntactic representations, and have shown that marginalizing over this latent representation not only provides significant improvements over syntactically-uninformed baselines, but occasionally improves performance when compared to systems which observe syntax. On the task of relation extraction we find that a constituency representation provides the most improvement over the baseline, while in the SRL domain our model is extremely competitive with the best reported results on Chinese, and outperforms the model using the provided parses on German and Japanese.

We believe this method delivers very promising results in our presented tasks, opening the door to new lines of research examining what types of constraints and what configurations of hidden structure are most beneficial for particular tasks and languages. Moreover, we present one type of coordinating factor, as both D-CONNECT and C-CONNECT logically express a soft NAND function, but more sophisticated coupling schemes are another natural direction to pursue. Finally, we use sum-product variant of belief propagation inference, but more specialized inference schemes may show additional benefits.

Acknowledgements

We would like to thank Andrea Gesmundo for help in procuring sections of the CoNLL 2009 shared task data. This work was supported in part by the Center for Intelligent Information Retrieval and in part by Army prime contract number W911NF-07-1-0216 and University of Pennsylvania subaward number 103-548106. The University of Massachusetts also gratefully acknowledges the support of Defense Advanced Research Projects Agency (DARPA) Machine Reading Program under Air Force Research Laboratory (AFRL) prime contract no. FA8750-09-C-0181. Any opinions, findings, and conclusion or recommendations expressed in this material are those of the authors and do not necessarily reflect the view of the DARPA, AFRL, or the US government.

References

Michael Auli and Adam Lopez. 2011. A comparison of loopy belief propagation and dual decomposition for integrated CCG supertagging and parsing. In *ACL*, pages 470–480.

Kurt Bollacker, Colin Evans, Praveen Paritosh, Tim Sturge, and Jamie Taylor. 2008. Freebase: a collaboratively created graph database for structuring human knowledge. In *SIGMOD*, pages 1247–1250, New York, NY, USA. ACM.

Razvan C. Bunescu and Raymond J. Mooney. 2007. Learning to extract relations from the web using minimal supervision. In *ACL*.

Francisco Casacuberta and Colin De La Higuera. 2000. Computational complexity of problems on probabilistic grammars and transducers. In *ICGI*, pages 15–24.

M. Chang, D. Goldwasser, D. Roth, and V. Srikumar. 2010. Discriminative learning over constrained latent representations. In *NAACL*.

Aron Culotta and Jeffery Sorensen. 2004. Dependency tree kernels for relation extraction. In *ACL*, Barcelona, Spain.

Jenny Rose Finkel and Christopher D. Manning. 2009. Joint parsing and named entity recognition. In *NAACL*, pages 326–334.

Vaibbhava Goel and William J. Byrne. 2000. Minimum Bayes risk automatic speech recognition. *Computer Speech and Language*, 14(2):115–135.

Joshua T. Goodman. 1996. Parsing algorithms and metrics. In *ACL*, pages 177–183.

Jan Hajič, Massimiliano Ciaramita, Richard Johansson, Daisuke Kawahara, Maria Antònia Martí, Lluís Màrquez, Adam Meyers, Joakim Nivre, Sebastian Padó, Jan Štěpánek, Pavel Straňák, Mihai Surdeanu, Nianwen Xue, and Yi Zhang. 2009. The CoNLL-2009 shared task: Syntactic and semantic dependencies in multiple languages. In *CoNLL: Shared Task*, pages 1–18.

Dan Klein and Chris Manning. 2002. Fast exact inference with a factored model for natural language processing. In *NIPS*.

Shankar Kumar and William Byrne. 2004. Minimum Bayes-risk decoding for statistical machine translation. In *HLT-NAACL*, pages 169–176.

Joel Lang and Mirella Lapata. 2010. Unsupervised induction of semantic roles. In *HLT-NAACL*, pages 939–947.

Zhifei Li, Jason Eisner, and Sanjeev Khudanpur. 2009. Variational decoding for statistical machine translation. In *ACL*, pages 593–601.

Qiang Liu and Alexander Ihler. 2011. Variational algorithms for marginal MAP. In *UAI*, pages 453–462.

Jonathan May and Kevin Knight. 2006. A better n-best list: Practical determinization of weighted finite tree automata. In *HLT-NAACL*, pages 351–358.

Andrew McCallum, Kedar Bellare, and Fernando C. N. Pereira. 2005. A conditional random field for discriminatively-trained finite-state string edit distance. In *UAI*, pages 388–395.

Ryan McDonald, Fernando Pereira, Kiril Ribarov, and Jan Hajic. 2005. Non-projective dependency parsing using spanning tree algorithms. In *HLT-EMNLP*, pages 523–530.

Ivan Meza-Ruiz and Sebastian Riedel. 2009. Jointly identifying predicates, arguments and senses using Markov logic. In *NAACL*.

Mike Mintz, Steven Bills, Rion Snow, and Daniel Jurafsky. 2009. Distant supervision for relation extraction without labeled data. In *ACL*, pages 1003–1011.

Jason Naradowsky and David A. Smith. 2012. Combinatorial constraints for constituency parsing in graphical novels. Technical report, University of Massachusetts Amherst.

Khalil Sima'an. 1996. Computational complexity of probabilistic disambiguation by means of tree-grammars. In *COLING*, pages 1175–1180.

David A. Smith and Jason Eisner. 2008. Dependency parsing by belief propagation. In *EMNLP*, pages 145–156.

Y. W. Teh, M. I. Jordan, M. J. Beal, and D. M. Blei. 2006. Hierarchical Dirichlet processes. *Journal of the American Statistical Association*, 101(476):1566–1581.

Kristina Toutanvoa and Christopher D. Manning. 2000. Enriching the knowledge sources used in a maximum entropy part-of-speech tagger. In *EMNLP*, pages 63–70.

Christopher Walker. 2006. Ace 2005 multilingual training corpus. number ldc2006t06. In *Linguistic Data Consortium*.

Nianwen Xue, Fei Xia, Fu-Dong Chiou, and Martha Palmer. 2005. The penn chinese treebank: Phrase structure annotation of a large corpus. In *Natural Language Engineering*, pages 207–238.

Min Zhang, Jie Zhang, and Jian Su. 2006. Exploring syntactic features for relation extraction using a convolution tree kernel. In *NAACL*, pages 288–295.

GuoDong Zhou, Jian Su, Jie Zhang, and Min Zhang. 2005. Exploring various knowledge in relation extraction. In *ACL*, pages 427–434.

Type-Supervised Hidden Markov Models for Part-of-Speech Tagging with Incomplete Tag Dictionaries

Dan Garrette
Department of Computer Science
The University of Texas at Austin
dhg@cs.utexas.edu

Jason Baldridge
Department of Linguistics
The University of Texas at Austin
jbaldrid@utexas.edu

Abstract

Past work on learning part-of-speech taggers from tag dictionaries and raw data has reported good results, but the assumptions made about those dictionaries are often unrealistic: due to historical precedents, they assume access to information about labels in the raw and test sets. Here, we demonstrate ways to learn hidden Markov model taggers from incomplete tag dictionaries. Taking the MIN-GREEDY algorithm (Ravi et al., 2010) as a starting point, we improve it with several intuitive heuristics. We also define a simple HMM emission initialization that takes advantage of the tag dictionary and raw data to capture both the openness of a given tag and its estimated prevalence in the raw data. Altogether, our augmentations produce improvements to performance over the original MIN-GREEDY algorithm for both English and Italian data.

1 Introduction

Learning accurate part-of-speech (POS) taggers based on plentiful labeled training material is generally considered a solved problem. The best taggers obtain accuracies of over 97% for English newswire text in the Penn Treebank, which can be considered as an upper-bound that matches human performance on the same task (Manning, 2011). However, as Manning notes, this story changes as soon as one is working with different assumptions and data, including having less training data, different kinds of training data, other languages, and other domains. Such POS tagging work has been plentiful and includes efforts to induce POS tags without labels (Christodoulopoulos et al., 2010); learn from POS-tag dictionaries (Ravi et al., 2010), incomplete dictionaries (Hasan and Ng, 2009) and human-constructed dictionaries (Goldberg et al., 2008); bootstrap taggers for a language based on knowledge about other languages (Das and Petrov, 2011), and creating supervised taggers for new, challenging domains such as Twitter (Gimpel et al., 2011).

Here, we focus on learning from tag dictionaries. This is often characterized as unsupervised or weakly supervised training. We adopt the terminology *type-supervised* training to distinguish it from unsupervised training from raw text and supervised training from word tokens labeled with their parts-of-speech. Work on type-supervision goes back to (Merialdo, 1994), who introduced the still standard procedure of using a bigram Hidden Markov Model (HMM) trained via Expectation Maximization.

Early research appeared to show that learning from types works nearly as well as learning from tokens, with researchers in the 1990s obtaining accuracies up to 96% on English (e.g. Kupiec (1992)). However, the tag dictionaries in these cases were obtained from labeled tokens. While replicating earlier experiments, Banko and Moore (2004) discovered that performance was highly dependent on cleaning tag dictionaries using statistics gleaned from the *tokens*. This greatly simplifies the job of a type-supervised HMM: it no longer must entertain entries for uncommon word-tag pairs (or mistaken pairs due to annotation errors), which otherwise stand on equal footing with the common ones. When the full, noisy tag dictionary was employed, Banko and Moore found accuracies dropped from 96% to 77%.

Banko and Moore's observations spurred a new line of research that sought to improve performance in the face of full, noisy dictionaries; see Ravi and

Knight (2009) for an overview. The highest accuracy achieved to date under these assumptions is 91.6% (Ravi et al., 2010). However, as is often noted (including by the authors themselves), many papers that work on learning taggers from tag dictionaries make unrealistic assumptions about the tag dictionaries they use as input (Toutanova and Johnson, 2008; Ravi and Knight, 2009; Hasan and Ng, 2009). For example, tag dictionaries are typically constructed with every token-tag pair in the data, including those that appear only in the test set. This means that the evaluation of these taggers does not measure how they perform on sentences that contain unseen words or unseen word-tag pairs, a likely occurrence in real use of a trained tagger.

We show that it is possible to achieve good tagging accuracy using a noisy and incomplete tag dictionary that has no access to the tags of the raw and test data and no access to the tag frequency information of the labeled training data from which the dictionary is drawn. We build on Ravi et al.'s (2010) model minimization approach, which reduces dictionary noise by greedily approximating the minimum set of tag bigrams needed to cover the raw data and exploits that information as a constraint on the initialization of the model before running EM. We extend their method in four distinct ways.

1. Enable the algorithm to be used with incomplete dictionaries by exploiting the type-based information provided by the tag dictionary and raw text to initialize EM, and by training a standard supervised HMM on the output of EM.
2. Improve the greedy procedure to find a better minimized set of tag-tag bigrams.
3. Modify the method to return only the set of bigrams required to tag sentences instead of keeping all bigrams chosen by minimization.
4. Exploit the paths found during minimization as a direct initialization for EM.

Together, these improvements make it possible to use model minimization in a realistic context, and obtain higher performance: on English, results go from 63.5% for a vanilla HMM to 82.1% for an HMM that uses strategies to deal with unknowns, then to 85.0% with Ravi and Knight's minimization and finally to 88.5% with our enhancements.

2 Supervision for HMMs

Hidden Markov Models (HMMs) are well-known generative probabilistic sequence models commonly used for POS-tagging. The probability of a tag sequence given a word sequence is determined from the product of emission and transition probabilities:

$$P(t|w) \propto \prod_{i=1}^{N} P(w_i|t_i) \cdot P(t_i|t_{i-1})$$

HMMs can be trained directly from labeled data by calculating maximum likelihood estimates or from incomplete data using Expectation Maximization (EM) (Dempster et al., 1977). We use both strategies in this work: EM is used to estimate models that can automatically label raw tokens, and then a new HMM is estimated from that auto-labeled data.

2.1 Token-supervised training

We use a simple but effective smoothing regime to account for unknown words and unseen tag-tag transitions. For emissions:

$$P(w_i|t_i) = \frac{C(t_i, w_i) + \alpha(t_i)P_{uni}(w_i)}{C(t_i) + \alpha(t_i)}$$

where $P_{uni}(w_i)$ is the unigram probability of w_i, and $\alpha(t_i)$ is a tag specific amount of mass for smoothing. We use one-count smoothing (Chen and Goodman, 1996), where $\alpha(t_i)$ is based on the number of words that occur with t_i once:

$$\alpha(t_i) = |w_i : C(t_i, w_i) = 1|$$

Since open-class tags occur more frequently with words that appear once, they will reserve more mass for unknown words than closed-class tags will. The transition distributions are smoothed in a similar fashion:

$$P(t_i|t_{i-1}) = \frac{C(t_{i-1}, t_i) + \lambda(t_{i-1})P_{uni}(t_i)}{C(t_{i-1}) + \lambda(t_{i-1})}$$

$$\lambda(t_{i-1}) = |t_i : C(t_{i-1}, t_i) = 1|$$

This simple scheme is quite effective: an HMM trained on the Penn Treebank sections 0-18 and evaluated on sections 19-21 and smoothed in this way obtains 96.5% accuracy. We do not use gold standard labels elsewhere for this paper, but do use this model on the output of type-supervised HMMs.

2.2 Type-supervised training

We are primarily interested in learning taggers from tag dictionaries combined with unlabeled text. As is standard, we use EM to iteratively estimate the transition and emission probability parameters to maximize the likelihood of unlabeled data. It is known, however, that EM has particular problems learning a good HMM for POS tagging (Johnson, 2007; Ravi and Knight, 2009). One reason is that EM generally tries to learn probability distributions that are fairly uniform while POS tag frequencies are quite skewed. For example, "a" appears in the training data with seven different tags, but 99.9% of "a" tokens are determiners. Thus, the accuracy of anything approaching a uniform distribution for "a" tags will suffer greatly. In the context of unsupervised POS tagging models, modeling this distinction greatly improves results (Moon et al., 2010). Here, we can simply exploit the tag dictionary and raw data.

An initial set of parameters for the transitions and emissions must be supplied as the input to EM. Given just a tag dictionary, the simplest initialization is to set all tag transitions to be uniform, ranging over all tag continuations, while for emissions, a uniform distribution over all words that occur with the tag is assigned. This may be appropriate when a complete tag dictionary is available, including complete information for words that appear only in the test data. This is because there will never be any unknown words during model estimation or inference. Likewise, there will never be a situation where the tag dictionary rules out all possible tag transitions between two adjacent tokens in training or testing. As a result, no smoothing is needed in this scenario.

The problem with this is that estimating a model based on type-supervision requires raw text, and if we have an incomplete tag dictionary, some of the words in that text will be missing from the tag dictionary. In a Bayesian setting, priors provide mass for such tokens; models are estimated using either Gibbs sampling or variational inference (Johnson, 2007). However, we use vanilla EM here; as a consequence, once a parameter is zero, it is always zero. We thus need to ensure that mass is reserved for words outside the tag dictionary at the start of EM. (For transitions, uniform distributions are sufficient since the set of tags is closed.)

2.3 Emission probability initialization

The simplest way to initialize the emission distributions is to assign a count of one to every entry in the tag dictionary, and one count for unknowns. Then, during each iteration of EM, the expectation step is able to estimate new non-zero counts for all possible emissions encountered in the raw corpus. This basic strategy allows one to train an HMM with EM using only an incomplete tag dictionary and raw text. However, this basic approach for emission probabilities produces bad unknown-word probabilities. Specifically, if for each tag we simply assume one count for each entry in the tag dictionary and one count for unknowns and then normalize, the probability of an unknown word having a specific tag is inversely correlated with the number of word types associated with the tag in the tag dictionary. In other words, a tag that appears with a smaller number of distinct words will be seen by the HMM as being a better candidate tag for an unknown word. Unfortunately this is the opposite behavior we want since closed-class tags like *determiner* and *preposition* are bad candidates for tagging novel words.

For type-supervised training, we can do much better. Note that $C(w,t)$ comes in two varieties: w is either found in the tag dictionary (known word types), or it is not (unknown word types). We refer to the later as td-unknown: these are words that occur in the raw word sequence used for EM but which do not occur in the tag dictionary. These are thus different unknowns from words have not been observed in the dictionary or in the raw set but which may be encountered at test time. Computing the full $C(w,t)$ is necessary since we want $P(w|t)$ to cover known and td-unknown words. We must thus determine both $C_{known}(w,t)$ and $C_{unk_{td}}(w,t)$.

First, we focus on calculating $C_{known}(w,t)$. If a word w appears $C(w)$ times in the raw corpus, and is seen with $|TD(w)|$ tags in the tag dictionary, then assume for each t in $TD(w)$:

$$C_{known}(w,t) = C(w) \;/\; |TD(w)|$$

and $C_{known}(w,t) = 0$ for all other t. In other words, we split $C(w)$, the count of w tokens in the corpus, evenly among each of w's possible tags. This provides us with an estimate of the true $C(w,t)$ by approximating the portion of the counts of each word type that may be associated with that tag. Note that while this will give us zeros for any words that don't appear in the raw corpus, this is not a problem because EM training is based only on that corpus.

Second, we look at td-unknown word types: those in the raw data that are *not* found in the tag dictionary. Given the value $P(unk_{td}|t)$ for the likelihood of an unknown word given a tag t, we can compute estimated counts $C_{unk_{td}}(w, t)$ for a td-unknown word w using

$$C_{unk_{td}}(w, t) = C(w) \cdot P(unk_{td}|t)$$

where $C(w)$, again, comes from the raw corpus. This has the effect of spreading $C(w)$, the count of tokens of that unknown word w, across all of the possible tags, with each tag receiving a proportion of the total count as determined by $P(unk_{td}|t)$.

The challenge, then, is to compute $P(unk_{td}|t)$. For this, we have two potential sources of knowledge, the tag dictionary and the raw token sequence, each telling us complementary information.

First, the tag dictionary tells us about the openness of a tag—the likelihood that an unseen word will have that label—based on our previously-discussed intuition that we are more likely to see a new word with a tag that is known to be associated with many words already. Thus, we can estimate $P_{td}(unk_{td}|t)$ by simply normalizing the $|TD(t)|$ values:

$$P_{td}(unk_{td}|t) = \frac{|TD(t)|^2}{\sum_{t' \in Tags} |TD(t')|^2}$$

We exaggerate the differences between tags by squaring the $|TD(t)|$ terms to draw an even larger distinction between open and closed class types.

Unfortunately, if we calculate an estimated word count directly from this using $C_{unk_{td}}(w, t) = C(w) \cdot P_{td}(unk_{td}|t)$, the $C_{unk_{td}}(w, t)$ values would be taken without any regard to the overall likelihood of tag t. Since $C_{known}(NN)$ is very high, $C_{unk_{td}}(NN)$ will seem very low by comparison. Likewise, since $C_{known}(RB)$ is much lower, $C_{unk_{td}}(RB)$ will seem very high by comparison.

$P(unk_{td}|t)$ must account for the overall likelihood of t so that the $C_{unk_{td}}(w, t)$ values will be scaled appropriately according to the overall likelihood of t. For this, we use our second knowledge source: the raw data. Based on the $C_{known}(w, t)$ values as given above, the raw data tells us about the overall expectation of a word having a particular tag. From this, we can estimate the tag distribution for known words: $C_{known}(t) = \sum_{w' \in V} C_{known}(w', t)$ and then normalize to get $P_{known}(t)$.

Finally, we need to combine $P_{td}(unk_{td}|t)$ and $P_{known}(t)$ into a single $P(unk_{td}|t)$ that accounts for both the openness of a tag and its overall prevalence. We would like this combination to use the high $P_{known}(NN)$ to boost $P(unk_{td}|NN)$ and the low $P_{known}(RB)$ to dampen $P(unk_{td}|RB)$. So, we compute and normalize:

$$P(unk_{td}|t) \propto \frac{|TD(t)|^2}{\sum_{t' \in Tags} |TD(t')|^2} \cdot P_{known}(t)$$

2.4 Auto-supervised post-EM smoothing

The initialization accounting for td-unknown words given above allows EM to be run on the raw token sequence, but it provides no probability for words that are truly unseen (in either the tag dictionary or the raw data). Consequently, any novel words in the test set will have zero emission probabilities, leading to extremely low unknown-word accuracies.

To overcome this problem, we perform a simple post-processing step after EM, which we refer to as **auto-supervised** training. We take the HMM trained by EM and use it to label the raw corpus. This gives us an automatically-labeled corpus that can be used for standard *supervised* training (without EM) to produce a new HMM. The effect of this post-processing step is to smooth the counts learned from EM onto any new words encountered during testing. This procedure significantly improves the ability of the HMM to label unknown words.

As a final note, it would of course be possible to use other models at this stage, such as a Conditional Random Field (Lafferty et al., 2001).

3 Enhancing MIN-GREEDY

As was discussed above, one of the major problems for type-supervised POS-tagger training with EM is a tag dictionary with low-frequency entries such as the word "a" being associated with the *foreign word* tag when nearly all of its instances are as a determiner. To avoid the need for manually pruning the tag dictionary, Ravi and Knight (2009)

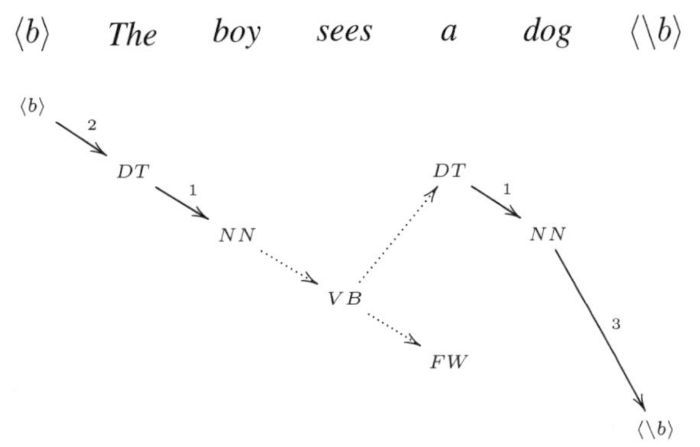

Figure 1: MIN-GREEDY graph showing a state in the first phase. Numbered, solid arrows: order of chosen bigrams; dotted: potential choices.

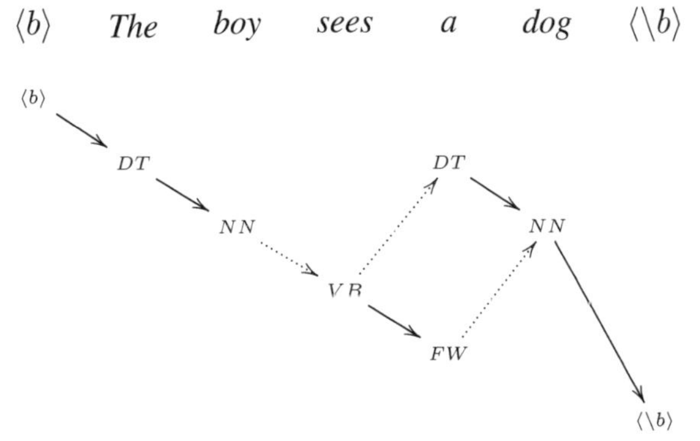

Figure 2: Start of the second MIN-GREEDY phase.

proposed that low-probability tags might be automatically filtered from the tag dictionary through a model minimization procedure applied to the raw text and constrained by the full tag dictionary. Ravi et al. (2010) develop a faster approach for model minimization using a greedy algorithm that they call MIN-GREEDY. It is this algorithm that we extend.

3.1 The original MIN-GREEDY algorithm

The MIN-GREEDY algorithm starts by initializing a graph with a vertex for each possible tag of each token in the raw data. The set of possible tags for each token is the set of tags associated with that word in the tag dictionary.Special *sentence start* and *sentence end* vertices are added to the graph for each sentence to mark its beginning and end. Unlike Ravi et al. (2010), we allow for an incomplete tag dictionary, meaning that our scenario has the additional complication that the tag set for some raw-corpus

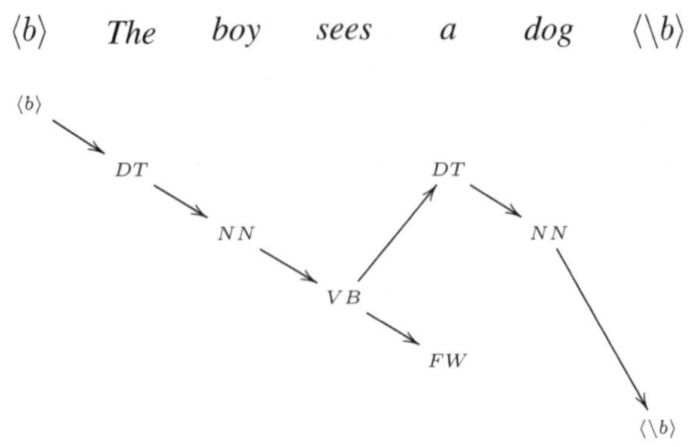

Figure 3: Potential MIN-GREEDY conclusion.

words will not be known. For these words, the full set of tags is used. Note that this increases the ambiguity and overall number of edges in the graph.

The MIN-GREEDY algorithm works in three phases: Greedy Set Cover, Greedy Path Completion, and Iterative Model-Fitting. In the first two phases, the algorithm chooses tag bigrams that form the edges of the graph. The goal of these phases is to select a set of edges that is sufficient to allow a path through every sentence in the raw corpus. The algorithm greedily selects these edges in an attempt to quickly approximate the minimal set of tag bigrams needed to accomplish this goal. In the final phase, the algorithm runs several iterations of EM in order to fit the bigram set to the raw data.

In the first phase, Greedy Set Cover, the algorithm selects tag bigrams in an effort to *cover* all of the word tokens. A word token is considered *covered* if there is at least one tag bigram edge connected to at least one of its vertices. At each iteration, the algorithm examines the entire graph, across all sentences, to find the tag bigram that, if added, would maximize the number of newly covered words.

Consider the graph in Figure 1. Assume, for the example, that this sentence comprises the entire raw corpus. At the start of the first phase, no tag bigrams are selected. On the first iteration, the algorithm chooses the tag bigram DT→NN because this tag bigram describes two edges for a total of four words newly covered: *The*, *boy*, *a*, and *dog*. On the second iteration, there are only three word tokens left uncovered: the start symbol, *sees*, and the end symbol. At this point, as the figure shows, there are five tag bigrams that would each result in covering one additional token. Since there are no tag bigrams whose choosing would result in covering more than one additional token, the algorithm randomly chooses one of these five. The algorithm iterates like this until all words are covered, as in, for example, Figure 2.

The second phase of the MIN-GREEDY algorithm, Greedy Path Completion, seeks to fill *holes* in the tag paths found in the graph. A *hole* is a potential edge that, if added, would connect two existing edges. At each iteration, the algorithm finds the tag bigram that, if selected, would maximize the number of holes that would be filled across all raw sentences.

The example graph in Figure 2 shows a potential start of the second phase. At this point, there are three tag bigrams that each fill one hole if selected, and the algorithm randomly selects one. Iteration continues until there is a complete tag path through each sentence in the raw corpus. One potential resolution for the example is given in Figure 3.

Once a set of tag bigrams has been generated that allows for a complete tag path through every sentence of the raw corpus, MIN-GREEDY begins its final phase: Iterative Model-Fitting. In this phase, the algorithm trains a succession of type-supervised HMM models. Each iteration trains an HMM and then uses it to tag the raw corpus, the result of which is used to prepare inputs for the next iteration.

Iterative Model-Fitting begins with the minimized set of bigrams returned from the second phase of MIN-GREEDY. This set is used as a hard constraint on the allowable tag bigrams during type-supervised HMM training. While EM is running, the only tag transitions that are counted are those that fall into the minimized tag bigram set; all other transition counts are ignored. Once an HMM has been trained, it is immediately used to tag the raw corpus, producing a set of auto-labeled sentences. For the second iteration of the phase, we extract a constrained tag dictionary from the auto-labeled corpus by simply taking every word/tag pair appearing in the data. This new tag dictionary is a subset of the original, full, tag dictionary, and hopefully has fewer low-frequency entries that would cause problems for EM.

We use this constrained tag dictionary to again perform type-supervised HMM training, but without any constraints on the allowable tag bigrams. This produces our third HMM. Using this HMM, we can, again, tag the raw corpus, producing another set of auto-labeled sentences. We can then extract the set of tag bigrams appearing in this data to produce a new set of tag transition constraints, similar to what was returned by the second phase. With this set of tag transition constraints, and the full tag dictionary, we can perform another round of type-supervised HMM training, and repeat the entire process.

The third MIN-GREEDY phase continues iterating, alternating between training an HMM using a constrained set of tag transitions and training one using a constrained tag dictionary. The size of the set of constrained tag bigrams produced is tracked on each iteration, and the algorithm is considered to have converged when this value changes by less than five percent. The final result of the MIN-GREEDY algorithm is a trained HMM.

The evaluation of the MIN-GREEDY algorithm, as described in Ravi et al. (2010), was performed only for scenarios with a complete tag dictionary (including all raw and test word types). As such, no techniques were described for handling unknown words. Because we are interested in the more realistic scenario of an incomplete tag dictionary, we augment the original MIN-GREEDY setup with the smoothing techniques described above.

3.2 Improving tag bigram selection

One of the major problems with the MIN-GREEDY algorithm is that its heuristics for choosing the next tag bigram frequently result in many-way ties. In the first two phases of MIN-GREEDY, the greedy procedure looks for the tag bigram that will have the most positive impact. In the Greedy Set Cover phase this means choosing the tag bigram that would cover the most new tokens, and in the Greedy Path Completion phase this means choosing the tag bigram that would fill the most holes. However, it is frequently the case that there are many distinct tag bigrams that would cover the most new tokens or fill the most holes, leaving the MIN-GREEDY algorithm with no choice but to randomly select from these options. Since there are frequently cases of having many dozens of options, it is clear that some of those choices *must* be better than others, even though MIN-GREEDY does not make a distinction and considers them all to be equally good choices.

Consider the example in Figure 1 representing a possible state of the minimization graph. To have reached this stage, tag bigram DT→NN would have been chosen since it covered the highest number of tokens: four. Additionally, $\langle b \rangle$→DT and NN→$\langle \backslash b \rangle$ could have been chosen as the second and third tag bigrams since they tied for the most new tokens covered: one. For the state shown in this figure, there is only one uncovered token, *sees*, but three tag bigrams that cover it. Since each of these tag bigrams covers exactly one new word, they are all considered by MIN-GREEDY to be equally good choices as the next tag bigram for inclusion, and the algorithm will choose one at random. However, it should be clear that the VB→FW tag bigram is wrong while the other two would lead to a correct answer. As such, we would like for the algorithm to avoid choosing VB→FW, and to pick one of the others.

In order to push the algorithm into choosing the right tag bigrams in these otherwise ambiguous situations, we have added an additional criterion to the bigram-choosing heuristic: after narrowing down the set of tag bigrams to those that cover the most new tokens, we further narrow the choice of bigrams by minimizing the number of new word-type/tag pairs that would be added to the result. Consider our example. If we choose the tag bigram NN→VB or VB→DT, then exactly one new word-type/tag pair would be added to our result: *sees*/VB (since *boy*/NN and *a*/DT would already have been added by the incorporation of previous selected tag bigrams). By contrast if we choose the tag bigram VB→FW then *two* new word-type/tag pairs would be added: *sees*/VB and *a*/FW.

Minimizing the number of new word/tag pairs added by the algorithm has two main advantages. First, it keeps the selected bigrams focused on the same vertices, which results in fewer holes that the Greedy Path Completion phase must deal with. Secondly, it keeps the selected bigrams focused on more common tags for each word type, such as *a*/DT, and keeps it away from rare tags, such as *a*/FW.

3.3 Only tag bigrams on minimization paths

As was described above, the output of MIN-GREEDY's second stage is a minimized set of tag bigrams which is used as a constraint on the first iteration of the third stage, Iterative Model-Fitting. However, in order to determine when to stop adding new bigrams during the first two phases, the MIN-GREEDY algorithm must try to find complete tag paths through each sentence in the raw corpus, stopping once a tag path has been found for each one. While the algorithm is trying to select only the tag bigrams that are necessary for a complete tagging, it happens frequently that bigrams are selected that are not actually used on any tag path.

Consider the example shown in Figure 3. The graph has a complete path through the sentence, but also contains an extraneous edge, VB→FW, that is not used on the path. Assuming that this tag bigram is not used on the tag path of any other sentence, it can safely be removed from the resultant set to produce a smaller set of tag bigrams, getting us even closer to the minimized set that we desire.

To find the set of tag bigrams excluding these extraneous edges, we modify the MIN-GREEDY algorithm. During the first and second phases of the algorithm, we check all raw data sentences for a completed path after each tag bigram is selected. If a completed path is found for a sentence, we store that path immediately. Once a path is found for every sentence, we extract the set of bigrams used on these paths, and pass that set, instead of the full set of selected bigrams, to the third phase of the algorithm.

Note that it is important that we store the completed paths as soon as they are completed. Since sentences are completed at different stages, and more tag bigrams are selected after some of these sentences are complete, it is inevitable that some sentences will end up with multiple complete tag paths by the end of the second phase. However, we seek only the *first* such path. Tag bigrams are selected in order of their impact, so bigrams selected earlier are better and should be preferred. Considering again the example in Figure 3, based on the frequency of the tags, it is likely that, given the presence of other sentences in the raw corpus, the tag path including bigrams VB→DT and DT→NN would be found before the one including VB→FW and FW→NN. Since they are more frequent bigrams, we would want to keep the first path even if the second is completed at a later time.

The result of this improvement is a smaller, cleaner minimized tag bigram set to be delivered to the third phase of MIN-GREEDY.

Scenario	Total	Known	Unk.
0. Random baseline (choose tag randomly from tag dictionary)	63.53	65.49	2.38
1. HMM baseline (simple EM with tag dictionary and raw text)	69.20	71.42	0.27
2. HMM baseline + auto-supervised training	82.33	83.67	40.46
3. HMM baseline + auto-supervised training + emission initialization	82.05	83.27	44.31
4. MIN-GREEDY (Ravi et al., 2010) with add-one smoothing	74.79	77.17	0.45
5. MIN-GREEDY with add-one smoothing + auto-supervised	86.10	87.59	39.74
6. MIN-GREEDY with add-one smoothing + auto-supervised + emission init	85.02	86.33	44.28
7. 6 + enhanced tag bigram choice heuristic	86.71	88.08	43.93
8. 6 + restrict tag bigrams to tag paths of minimization-tagged output	87.01	88.40	43.74
9. 6 + HMM initialization from minimization-tagged output	**88.52**	**89.92**	**44.80**
10. 6 + 7 + 8 + 9	**88.51**	**89.92**	**44.80**

Table 1: English tagging accuracy using PTB sections 00-15 to build the tag dictionary. *Known* word types are those appearing in the tag dictionary.

3.4 EM initialization with minimization output

As a final improvement to MIN-GREEDY, we took the set of completed tag paths returned from the second phase of the algorithm, as described in the previous section, and used them as labeled data to initialize an HMM for EM training.

Since we modified MIN-GREEDY to produce a set of completed tag paths for sentences, we can take this to be a complete set of labels for the raw corpus. Furthermore, since we were careful about storing paths as soon as they become completed by the minimization process, and the tag bigrams are chosen in order of frequency, there will be more high-frequency bigrams than low-frequency. As a result, this labeling will contain good tag transitions and token labelings. As such, the labeled data produced by the second phase provides useful information beyond a simple set of sufficient bigrams: it contains legitimate frequency information that can be used to initialize the HMM. We, therefore, initialize an HMM directly from this data to start EM.

4 Evaluation[1]

English data. We evaluate on the Penn Treebank (Marcus et al., 1993). In all cases we use the first 47,996 tokens of section 16 as our raw data, sections 19–21 as our development set, and perform the final evaluation on sections 22–24.

[1]Source code, scripts, and data to reproduce the results presented here can be found at `github.com/dhgarrette/type-supervised-tagging-2012emnlp`

We evaluate two differently sized tag dictionaries. The first is extracted directly from sections 00–15 (751,059 tokens) and the second from sections 00–07 (379,908 tokens). The former contains 39,087 word types, 45,331 word/tag entries, a per-type ambiguity of 1.16 and yields a per-token ambiguity of 2.21 on the raw corpus (treating unknown words as having all 45 possible tags). The latter contains 26,652 word types, 30,662 word/tag entries, a per-type ambiguity of 1.15 and yields a per-token ambiguity of 2.03 on the raw corpus. In both cases, every word/tag pair found in the relevant sections was used in the tag dictionary: no pruning was performed.

Italian data. As a second evaluation, we use the TUT corpus (Bosco et al., 2000). To verify that our approach is language-independent without the need for specific tuning, we executed our tests on the Italian data without any trial runs, parameter modifications, or other changes. We divided the TUT data, taking the first half of each of the five sections as input to the tag dictionary, the next quarter as raw data, and the last quarter as test data. All together, the tag dictionary was constructed from 41,000 tokens consisting of 7,814 word types, 8,370 word/tag pairs, per-type ambiguity of 1.07 and a per-token ambiguity of 1.41 on the raw data. The raw data consisted of 18,574 tokens and the test contained 18,763 tokens.

Results We ran eleven experiments for each data set with results shown in Tables 1 and 2. All scores are reported as the percentage of tokens for which the correct tag was assigned. Accuracy is shown as

Scenario	PTB (00-07) Total	Known	Unk.	TUT Total	Known	Unk.
0. Random	64.98	68.04	2.81	62.81	76.10	1.58
1. HMM basic	69.32	72.70	0.56	60.70	73.77	0.51
2. HMM + auto-super	81.50	83.67	37.46	70.03	80.64	21.12
3. HMM + auto-super + init	81.71	83.62	42.89	70.89	80.91	24.74
4. MIN-GREEDY + add-1	68.86	72.20	0.92	53.96	65.49	0.84
5. MIN-GREEDY + add-1 + auto-super	80.78	82.88	38.02	70.85	82.41	17.60
6. MIN-GREEDY + add-1 + auto-super + init	80.92	82.80	42.64	71.52	81.56	**25.28**
7. 6 + enhanced bigram choice heuristic	86.69	88.83	43.07	71.48	81.57	24.98
8. 6 + restrict tag bigrams to tag paths	80.86	82.73	42.84	**72.86**	**83.45**	24.08
9. 6 + HMM init from minimization output	87.61	89.74	**44.18**	72.00	82.28	24.65
10. 6 + 7 + 8 + 9	**87.95**	**90.12**	43.74	71.99	82.50	23.57

Table 2: Tagging accuracy using PTB sections 00-07 and TUT to build the tag dictionary. *Known* word types are those appearing in the tag dictionary. Scenario numbers correspond to Table 1.

the Total (all word types), Known (word types found in the tag dictionary), and Unknown (word types not found in the tag dictionary).

Experiments 1–3 evaluate our smoothing techniques applied directly to the task of type-supervised HMM training with EM, without MIN-GREEDY. The basic HMM consistently beats the baseline random tagger, the auto-supervision technique makes an enormous improvement for both known and unknown words, and the the emission initialization yields a sizable improvement for unknown words.

Experiments 4–6 evaluated our reimplementation of MIN-GREEDY. We start with the most basic level of smoothing needed to work in a type-supervised scenario. For the smaller PTB tag dictionary and the TUT data, MIN-GREEDY actually has lower performance than the HMM alone. This indicates that if the tag dictionary has a low degree of ambiguity, then MIN-GREEDY can make the situation worse. However, with our smoothing techniques, we regain similar improvements as with the HMM.

Finally we performed experiments evaluating combinations of our improvements to MIN-GREEDY. Scenarios 7–9 show each improvement taken in turn. Scenario 10 shows the results for using all three improvements. For the English data, the best results are found when all the improvements are used. When taken individually, the bigram choice heuristic and HMM initialization from minimization output each consistently outperform the improved-MIN-GREEDY baseline on English. However, restricting the tag bigrams to that in the minimization-tagged output causes problems in the smaller PTB scenario, presumably falling to a local maximum like MIN-GREEDY that the other improvements are able to help the algorithm avoid.

Though the accuracy improvements are less than for English, the Italian results show that our MIN-GREEDY enhancements make an appreciable difference for a language and dataset for which the approaches considered were run sight unseen.

Error analysis One of the primary goals of model minimization is to automatically eliminate low-probability entries from the tag dictionary that might confuse the EM algorithm (Ravi et al., 2010). In order to see how well our techniques are able to identify and eliminate these unlikely word/tag pairs, we analyzed the tagging errors from each experiment. In doing so, we discovered that the two of the most problematic words for the EM algorithm are "a" and "in". We ran further experiments explore what was happening with those words. The results, using PTB sections 00–07 are shown in Table 3.

In PTB sections 00-07 the word "a" appears 7630 times and with 7 different tags. This includes 7621 occurrences with tag DT, 3 with tag SYM (symbol), and 1 time with LS (list item marker). As such, we would want the HMM to lean heavily toward tag DT when tagging the token "a". Unfortunately, the rare tags confuse the EM procedure and end up with dis-

tok	model output	tokens tagged by scenario 3	6	7	8	9	10
a	DT	32	4	4	4	2424	2425
	LS	1531	0	0	0	0	0
	SYM	731	2356	2305	2356	0	0
in	IN	12	15	2024	4	2042	2047
	FW	1922	1910	0	0	0	0
	RP	20	27	0	2037	0	0

Table 3: Number of times, for the words "a" and "in", the tagger trained by the particular scenario selected the given tag. Experiments used PTB sections 00-07 for the initial tag dictionary. Scenario numbers correspond to Table 1.

proportionately high probabilities. Our experiment training an HMM without minimization (scenario 3) resulted in 1531 "a" tokens being tagged LS, 731 as SYM, and only 32 tagged as DT.

The situation is similar with the word "in", which appears 6155 times with 5 different tags in the 8 sections. Of these, 6073 occurrences are tagged IN (preposition), 63 are RP (particle), and 1 is FW (foreign word). Again, EM without minimization is confused by the rare tokens, assigning FW 1922 times and IN 12 times.

The minimization procedure attempts to overcome this problem by removing unlikely tags from the tag dictionary automatically. As is show in Table 3, MIN-GREEDY without our enhancements is able to reject the problematic LS as a tag for "a", but unable to do so for SYM, resulting in 2356 tokens tagged SYM and only 4 tagged DT. Similarly, MIN-GREEDY is unable to reject FW as a tag for "in".

Our enhancements to MIN-GREEDY improve the situation. More careful choosing of bigrams during minimization results in the avoidance of LS and FW (but not SYM) for "a" as well as FW and RP for "in". Restricting the tag bigrams output from MIN-GREEDY to just those on tag paths avoids LS and FW for "a" and FW for "in". Finally, using the tagged sentences from MIN-GREEDY as noisy supervision for EM initialization eliminates all rare tags, as does the use of all three enhancements together.

5 Conclusion

Our results show it is possible to create accurate POS-taggers using type-supervision with incomplete tag dictionaries by extending the MIN-GREEDY algorithm of Ravi et al. (2010). The most useful change we made to the MIN-GREEDY procedure was the implementation of a better heuristic for picking tag bigrams. An intuitive and straightforward emission initialization provides the necessary basis to run EM on a given raw token sequence. Using EM output on this raw sequence as auto-labeled material to a supervised HMM then proves highly effective for generalization to new texts containing previously unseen word types.

Vaswani et al (2010) explore the use of minimum description length principles in a Bayesian model as a way of capturing model minimization, inspired by the MIN-GREEDY algorithm. The advantage there is that only a single objective function needs to be optimized, rather than having initialization followed by an iterative back and forth with pruning of tag-tag pairs. Our own next steps are to move in a similar direction to explore the possibilities for encoding the intuitions we developed for initialization and minimization as a single generative model.

Goldberg et al. (2008) note that fixing noisy dictionaries by hand is actually quite feasible, and suggest that effort should focus on exploiting human knowledge rather than just algorithmic improvements. We agree; however, our ultimate motivation is to use this work to tackle bootstrapping from very small tag dictionaries or dictionaries obtained from linguists or resources other than a corpus, and for tag sets that are more ambiguous (e.g., supertagging for CCGbank (Hockenmaier and Steedman, 2007)). Such efforts require automatic *expansion* of tag dictionaries, which then need be constrained based on available raw token sequences using methods such as those explored here. In this respect, the somewhat idiosyncratic noise in the corpus-derived dictionaries used here make a good test.

Acknowledgements

We thank Yoav Goldberg, Sujith Ravi, and the reviewers for their feedback. This work was supported by the U.S. Department of Defense through the U.S. Army Research Office (grant number W911NF-10-1-0533) and via a National Defense Science and Engineering Graduate Fellowship for the first author.

References

Michele Banko and Robert C. Moore. 2004. Part-of-speech tagging in context. In *Proceedings of COLING*, pages 556–561, Geneva, Switzerland.

Cristina Bosco, Vincenzo Lombardo, Daniela Vassallo, , and Leonardo Lesmo. 2000. Building a treebank for Italian: a data-driven annotation schema. In *Proceedings of LREC*.

Stanley F. Chen and Joshua Goodman. 1996. An empirical study of smoothing techniques for language modeling. In *Proceedings of ACL*, pages 310–318, Santa Cruz, California, USA.

Christos Christodoulopoulos, Sharon Goldwater, and Mark Steedman. 2010. Two decades of unsupervised pos induction: How far have we come? In *Proceedings of EMNLP*.

Dipanjan Das and Slav Petrov. 2011. Unsupervised part-of-speech tagging with bilingual graph-based projections. In *Proceedings of ACL-HLT*, pages 600–609, Portland, Oregon, USA.

Arthur P. Dempster, Nan M. Laird, and Donald. B. Rubin. 1977. Maximum likelihood from incomplete data via the EM algorithm. *Journal of the Royal Statistical Society: Series B (Statistical Methodology)*, 39:1–22.

Kevin Gimpel, Nathan Schneider, Brendan O'Connor, Dipanjan Das, Daniel Mills, Jacob Eisenstein, Michael Heilman, Dani Yogatama, Jeffrey Flanigan, and Noah A. Smith. 2011. Part-of-speech tagging for twitter: Annotation, features, and experiments. In *Proceedings of ACL-HLT*, pages 42–47, Portland, Oregon, USA.

Yoav Goldberg, Meni Adler, and Michael Elhadad. 2008. EM can find pretty good HMM POS-taggers (when given a good start). In *Proceedings ACL*, pages 746–754.

Kazi Saidul Hasan and Vincent Ng. 2009. Weakly supervised part-of-speech tagging for morphologically-rich, resource-scarce languages. In *Proceedings of EACL*, pages 363–371, Athens, Greece.

Julia Hockenmaier and Mark Steedman. 2007. Ccgbank: A corpus of ccg derivations and dependency structures extracted from the penn treebank. *Computational Linguistics*, 33(3):355–396.

Mark Johnson. 2007. Why doesn't EM find good HMM POS-taggers? In *Proceedings EMNLP-CoNLL*, pages 296–305.

Julian Kupiec. 1992. Robust part-of-speech tagging using a hidden markov model. *Computer Speech & Language*, 6(3):225–242.

John Lafferty, Andrew McCallum, and Fernando Pereira. 2001. Conditional random fields: Probabilistic models for segmenting and labeling sequence data. In *Proceedings of ICML*, pages 282–289. Morgan Kaufmann.

Christopher D. Manning. 2011. Part-of-speech tagging from 97% to 100%: Is it time for some linguistics? In Alexander Gelbukh, editor, *Proceedings of CICLing*, volume 6608 of *Lecture Notes in Computer Science*, pages 171–189.

Mitchell P. Marcus, Beatrice Santorini, and Mary Ann Marcinkiewicz. 1993. Building a large annotated corpus of English: The Penn Treebank. *Computational Linguistics*, 19(2):313–330.

Bernard Merialdo. 1994. Tagging English text with a probabilistic model. *Computational Linguistics*, 20(2):155–171.

Taesun Moon, Katrin Erk, and Jason Baldridge. 2010. Crouching dirichlet, hidden markov model: Unsupervised POS tagging with context local tag generation. In *Proceedings of EMNLP*, pages 196–206, Cambridge, MA.

Sujith Ravi and Kevin Knight. 2009. Minimized models for unsupervised part-of-speech tagging. In *Proceedings of ACL-AFNLP*.

Sujith Ravi, Ashish Vaswani, Kevin Knight, and David Chiang. 2010. Fast, greedy model minimization for unsupervised tagging. In *Proceedings of COLING*, pages 940–948.

Kristina Toutanova and Mark Johnson. 2008. A bayesian lda-based model for semi-supervised part-of-speech tagging. In *Proceedings of NIPS*.

Ashish Vaswani, Adam Pauls, and David Chiang. 2010. Efficient optimization of an mdl-inspired objective function for unsupervised part-of-speech tagging. In *Proceedings of the ACL 2010 Conference Short Papers*, pages 209–214, Uppsala, Sweden.

Explore Person Specific Evidence in Web Person Name Disambiguation

Liwei Chen, Yansong Feng, Lei Zou, Dongyan Zhao
Institute of Computer Science and Technology
Peking University
Beijing
{clwclw88,fengyansong,zoulei,zhaodongyan}@pku.edu.cn

Abstract

In this paper, we investigate different usages of feature representations in the web person name disambiguation task which has been suffering from the mismatch of vocabulary and lack of clues in web environments. In literature, the latter receives less attention and remains more challenging. We explore the feature space in this task and argue that collecting person specific evidences from a corpus level can provide a more reasonable and robust estimation for evaluating a feature's importance in a given web page. This can alleviate the *lack of clues* where discriminative features can be reasonably weighted by taking their corpus level importance into account, not just relying on the current local context. We therefore propose a topic-based model to exploit the person specific global importance and embed it into the person name similarity. The experimental results show that the corpus level topic information provides more stable evidences for discriminative features and our method outperforms the state-of-the-art systems on three WePS datasets.

1 Introduction

Resolving ambiguity associated with person names found on the Web is a key challenge in many Internet applications, such as information retrieval, question answering, open information extraction, automatic knowledge acquisition(Wu and Weld, 2008) and so on. For example, if you want to know more about a guy named *George Foster* and feed Yahoo! with his name, the results are not satisfactory where you get more than 40 different persons named *George Foster* scattering in the top 100 returned pages. None of the dominant search engines currently helps users group those returned pages into clusters according to whether they refer to the same person. Users thus have to either read those pages carefully or adjust their queries by adding extra modifiers. This motivates an intensive study in automatically resolving person name ambiguity in various web applications.

However, resolving web person name ambiguity is not a trivial task. Due to the difficulties in figuring out or predicting the number of namesakes in the returned pages, the task has been investigated in an unsupervised learning fashion in the literature, which is apparently different from the traditional word sense disambiguation or entity linking/disambiguation tasks, where the inventories of candidate word senses or entities are usually known given the target word or entity mention.

A general framework for this task can be formulated as first extracting various features from the web pages, and then grouping these pages into several clusters each of which is assumed to represent one specific person. Despite of the inevitably noisy nature of web data, a key challenge is how to handle the data sparsity problem which we mean as: **mismatch of vocabulary** and **lack of clues**. The former refers to the case that two web pages may describe the same person but use different words thus the word overlap between them are small. Various features, including entities, biographical information, URL, etc., have been introduced to bridge the gap(Mann and Yarowsky, 2003; Kalashnikov et al., 2008a; Ikeda et al., 2009; Jiang et al., 2009), and external knowledge resources are also employed to capture the semantic relationship between entities(Han and Zhao, 2009, 2010). However, a more challenging scenario is that there are few clues available in the web pages. For example, there is a page mentioning a nutritionist *Emily Bender* in WePS2 dataset(Javier et al., 2009). Throughout the whole page we can find only one word, *nutrition*, related to her identification, while other pages about the nutritionist in the dataset contain substantial materials about her profession and job. In this case, current efforts, focusing on either feature engineering or background knowledge, are incapable to exploiting these limited clues from the current page to the whole *Emily Bender* document set, where *nutrition*, as an important feature for recognizing a nutritionist, should be paid more attention.

As far as we know, there is less work focusing on exploring person specific information to relieve the *lack of clues* problem. Traditional vector space model (VSM) is most widely used to accommodate various features, but it ignores any relations between them(Mann and Yarowsky, 2003; Ikeda et al., 2009). Beyond bag-of-features, two kinds of features are explored, co-occurrences of entities and Wikipedia based semantic relationship between entities, both of which provide a reasonable relatedness for entity pairs. More recent works adopt one of these relationships(Jiang et al., 2009; Kalashnikov et al., 2008a; Han and Zhao, 2009). Han and Zhao try to model both aspects, but their co-occurrence estimation, estimated from held-out resources, fails to capture the person specific importance for a feature, which is crucial to enhance limited clues in a corpus level, e.g., the significance of *nutrition* for *Emily Bender* in WePS1 dataset.

In this paper, we explore different usages of features and propose an approach which mines cross document information to capture the person specific importance for a feature. Specifically, we construct a semantic graph from Wikipedia concepts appearing in all documents that contain the target name (which we refer to *name observation set*), then group them into several topics and further weight each feature by considering both the relatedness of the feature to its corresponding topic and the importance of this topic in the current name observation set. By incorporating both the Wikipedia and topic information into our person name similarity, our model exploits both Wikipedia based background knowledge and person specific importance. We argue that the corpus level importance provides more stable evidences for discriminative features in various scenarios, especially the tough case. We compared our model with the state of the arts on three WePS datasets (from the First and Second Web People Search Clustering Task), and our experiments show that our model consistently outperforms other competitive models on all three datasets.

In the rest of this paper, we first review related work, and in Section 3, show how we exploit the person specific importance in our disambiguation model. Experiment results are discussed in Section 4. We conclude this paper in Section 5.

2 Related Work

Web person name ambiguity resolution can be formally defined as follows: Given a set of web pages $\{d_1, d_2, ..., d_n\}$, where each page d_i $(i = 1, ..., n)$ contains an ambiguous name N which may correspond to several persons holding this name among these pages. The disambiguation system should group these name observations into j cluster $\{c_1, c_2, ..., c_j\}$ each of which is expected to contain web pages about the same person.

As mentioned before, the task is usually formulated in a unsupervised fashion, including two steps: feature extraction and person clustering. Most research efforts so far have been made to the former, exploring various features according to specific applications, while the second step is currently dominated by hierarchical agglomerative clustering (HAC). According to the reliance of extra knowledge resources, existing works can be categorized into non-resource methods and resource-based methods. Non-resource methods extract various local features from the context of ambiguous names, and compute the similarity between feature vectors. These features include plain words(Bagga and Baldwin, 1998), biographical information(Mann and Yarowsky, 2003; Niu et al., 2004), named entities, compound key phrases, hyperlinks(Ikeda et al., 2009), etc. The similarity between namesakes are usually measured by the cosine similarity(Bagga and Baldwin, 1998), or other graph based metrics(Iria et al., 2007; Kalashnikov et al., 2008a; Jiang et al., 2009). Those methods pay more attention to extracting informative features and their co-occurrences, but they usually treat the features locally, and ignore the semantic relatedness of features beyond the current document.

Resource-based approaches, on the other hand, can leverage external resources to benefit from rich background knowledge, which is crucial to remedy the data sparsity problem. The employed resources include raw texts available on the web and online encyclopedias. Kalashnikov et al. and Yiming et al. use extra web corpora to obtain co-occurrences between named entities. Rao et al. use Google Snippets to provide more contexts. By employing Wikipedia, the largest online encyclopedia, rich background knowledge about the semantic relatedness between entities can be leveraged to improve the disambiguation performance, and relieve the coverage problem, to some extent. Bunescu and Pasca and Cucerzan utilize Wikipedia's category hierarchy to disambiguate entities, while Pilz uses Wikipedia's link information. Han and Zhao adopt Wikipedia semantic relatedness to compute the similarity between name observations. They also combine multiple knowledge sources and capture explicit semantic relatedness between concepts and implicit semantic relationship embedded in a semantic graph simultaneously(Han and Zhao, 2010).

Most approaches discussed above explore various features in the current page or rely on external knowledge resources to bridge the vocabulary gap, but pay less attention to the *lack of clues* since they ignore the person specific evidence in the current corpus level. Our model focuses on solving the data sparsity problem by utilizing other web pages in the same name observation set to provide a robust but person specific weighting for discriminative features beyond the current document alone. In terms of extra resources, the Wikipedia based model (WS) by Han and Zhao (2009) is close to our model. The WS model uses Wikipedia to capture the relationship between entities in the local context to bridge the vocabulary gap, but it is incapable to evaluate the importance of a feature with regarding to the target name, hence is unable to make use of limited clues in the current web page. Our method captures person specific evidences by generating topics from all concepts in the current name observation set and weighting a feature accordingly. In this case, discriminative features that are sparse in the current page can be globally weighted so as to provide a more accurate and stable person name similarity.

3 The Model

Our model consists of three steps: feature extraction, topic generation and name disambiguation. For an ambiguous name, we first extract three types of features and construct a semantic graph from all Wikipedia concepts extracted from the current name observation set. We then collect global person specific evidences by clustering these concepts on the graph into different topics, which in turn are used to weight each concept by considering the importance of its corresponding topic in the current name observation set and its highly related neighbors in both the topic and its local context. At last, we incorporate the proposed topic representation into the person name similarity functionand adopt the hierarchical agglomerative clustering (HAC) algorithm to group these web pages.

3.1 Feature Extraction

We extract features from the contexts of ambiguous names, including Wikipedia concepts, named entities and biographical information, such as email addresses, phone numbers and birth years.

Wikipedia Concept Extraction Each concept in Wikipedia is described by an article containing hyperlinks to other concepts which are supposed to related to the current one. All the linking relations in Wikipedia construct a huge semantic graph, where we can mine rich semantic relationship between concepts(David and Ian, 2008). We collect Wikipedia concepts from all web pages in the dataset by comparing all n-grams (up to 8) from the dataset to Wikipedia anchor text dictionary and checking whether it is a Wikipedia concept surface form. We further prune the extracted concepts according to their keyphraseness(Mihalcea and Csomai, 2007). Initially, each concept is weighted according to its average semantic relateness(David and Ian, 2008) with other concepts in the current page.

Named Entity and Biographical Information Extraction Although Wikipedia concepts can provide rich background knowledge, they suffer from the limited coverage. It is common that some discriminative features are not likely to be found in Wikipedia, such as names of infamous people or organizations, email addresses, phone numbers, etc. We therefore extract two extra kinds of features, named entities that do not appear in the Wikipedia anchor text dictionary, and biographical information. We use Stanford Named Entity Recognizer(Finkel et al., 2005) to collect named entities which are not in the Wikipedia list. We use regular expressions to extract email address, phone numbers and birth years. For convenience, we will also call concept features for Wikipedia concept features and non-concept features for the other two in the rest of this paper.

3.2 Topic Generation and Weighting Scheme

Now we proceed to describe the key step of our model, topic generation and weighting strategy. The purpose of introducing topics into our model is to exploit the corpus level importance of a feature for a given name so that we will not miss any discriminative features which are few in the current name observation but have shown significant importance over the whole name observation set.

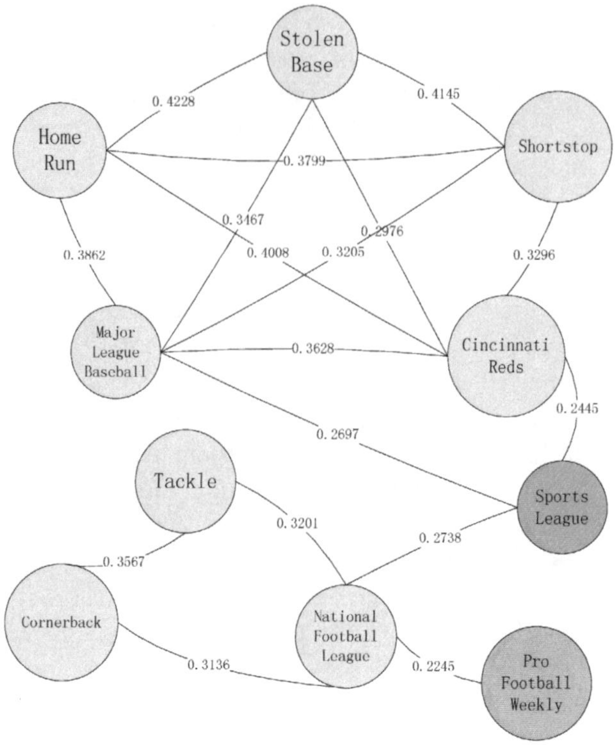

Figure 1: An abridged example of the semantic graph for *George Foster*. The green node *Sports League* is a hub node, and the yellow node *Pro Football Weekly* is an outlier.

Graph Construction In our model, we capture the topic structure through a semantic graph. Specifically, for each name observation set, we connect all Wikipedia concepts appearing in the current observation set by their pairwise semantic relatedness-David and Ian (2008)to form a semantic graph.

The constructed graph is usually very dense since any pair of unrelated concepts would be connected by a small semantic relatedness resulting in many light-weighted or even meaningless edges. We therefore propose to prune some light-weighted edges to make the graph stable and easier to harvest reasonable topics. We use the following strategies to prune the graph:

- If an edge's weight is lower than a predefined threshold, it will be pruned.
- If two vertices of an edge do not co-occur in any web page of the current observation set, then this edge will be pruned.

The second rule is set to be strict and is proposed to handle the following circumstance. Some general concepts, such as swimming, football, basketball and golf, will be measured highly related with each other by Wikipedia semantic relatedness and thus are very likely to be grouped into one topic, however, they are discriminative on their own when disambiguating different persons. For example, the concept *swimming* is discriminative enough to distinguish Russian swimmer Popov from basketball player Popov. So it is not a good idea to group these concepts into one topic. The proposed co-occurrence rule is based on the above observation that it is rare that such kind of general concepts, e.g., swim and basketball, often co-occur with each other when talking about one specific person. After the pruning step, for each ambiguous name, we get a semantic graph from all Wikipedia concepts extracted in this name observation set. Figure 1 illustrates an abridged version of a semantic graph for *George Foster*.

Graph Clustering Considering the graph construction strategy we use, it is more suitable for us to group the concepts on the graph into several topics using a density-based clustering model.

We choose SCAN algorithm Xu et al. (2007) to perform the clustering step. The SCAN algorithm utilizes a neighborhood structure to measure the similarity between two vertices. If a vertex has a minimal of μ neighbors with a similarity larger than ε, it is called a *core*. The algorithm[1] starts from a random vertex in a graph, examining whether it is a core or not. If yes, the algorithm will expand a cluster from this vertex recursively, otherwise the vertex will be assigned either a hub node or an outlier depending on the number of its neighboring clusters. A hub node connects to more than one cluster, while an outlier connects to one or no cluster. Take the semantic graph in Figure 1 for example, the node *Sports League* is a hub node, while the node *Pro Football Weekly* is an outlier. Finally, all concepts in the graph are grouped into $K + 2$ parts (K is the number of the clusters, and is determined automatically), including K clusters, the set of hub nodes and the set of outliers.

One problem of applying SCAN in our work is that it is originally designed for unweighted graphs. We have to adapt it to our weighted graph by modifying the similarity function between two nodes as follows:

$$sim(c_1, c_2) = \alpha \times \frac{sim_{nb}(c_1, c_2)}{1+\alpha} + \frac{sr(c_1, c_2)}{1+\alpha} \quad (1)$$

and $sim_{nb}(c_1, c_2)$ is defined as:

$$sim_{nb}(c_1, c_2) = \frac{\sum\limits_{c \in N(c_1) \cap N(c_2)} \frac{sr(c_1,c)+sr(c_2,c)}{2}}{|N(c_1) \cup N(c_2)|}$$

where $N(c)$ is the neighbor set of concept c. This new similarity function contains two parts: the neighborhood similarity and the semantic relatedness between two concepts. We combine them using a linear combination, where α is a weight tuned during training.

Topic Generation Now we will map the clustering results into different topics. Intuitively, each cluster will be treated as a topic. However, we found that hub nodes usually correspond to general concepts which may be related to many topics, but with a loose relatedness. We thus *distribute* each general concept into its every related topic, but with a lower weight to distinguish from ordinary concepts in this topic.

Outliers may be concepts which are far away from main themes of the corpus, or noise concepts. We calculate the average semantic relatedness of an outlier with its neighbor concepts that belong to one topic. If the result is lower than a threshold, this outlier will be discarded, otherwise it will be treated as a non-concept feature.

Now we are able to map the clustering results into different topics. Intuitively, each cluster will be treated as a topic. However, we found that hub nodes usually correspond to general concepts, e.g., *education* or *public*, which may be related to many topics, but with a loose relatedness. We thus *distribute* each general concept into its every related topic, but with a lower weight to distinguish from ordinary concepts in this topic. Outliers are found to contain concepts which are far away from main topics of the document set and look like noise concepts. We therefore calculate the average semantic relatedness of an outlier node with its neighboring concepts which belong to some topics. If the average relatedness is lower than a threshold, this node will be discarded, otherwise it will be treated as a non-concept feature.

Weighting Topics After generating all topics, we should weight each topic according to its importance in the current name observation set as well as the quality of the topic (cluster). Intuitively, if most concepts in the topic are considered to be discriminative in the current name set and they are closely related to each other, this topic should be weighted as important. By properly weighting the generated topics, we can capture the importance of a concept reliably in the corpus level (in the current name observation set) rather than in the current page solely.

Before we weight a topic, we first explain how we re-weight a hub concept in a topic since our initial feature weighting scheme(Han and Zhao, 2009) works on individual web page, lacks cross document information and is likely to over-estimate the impor-

[1]We omit the details of SCAN for brevity, and refer interested reader to Xu et al. (2007) for more details.

tance of a hub node (general concept) by by assigning a higher weight. Suppose a hub node h connects to a topic t with n neighbors, namely $c_1, c_2, \cdots, c_n$. The similarity between this hub node and the topic is computed by averaging the semantic relatedness between this hub node and these n neighbors:

$$sim(h,t) = \frac{1}{n}\sum_{i=1}^{n} sr(h, c_i). \quad (2)$$

We then update the weight of this hub node by considering its similarity with this topic: $w_t(h) = w(h) \times sim(h,t)$ from which we can see that the hub node receives a lower weight than before indicating that it is not as important as ordinary concepts in a topic.

Now we proceed to weight the topic t by taking into account the frequencies of its concepts and the coherence between the concepts and their neighborhood in topic t:

$$w(t) = \frac{\sum_{i=1}^{n} f(c_i)}{n} \times \frac{\sum_{i=1}^{n} n\_coh(c_i, t)}{n} \quad (3)$$

where topic t contains n concepts $\{c_1, c_2, ..., c_n\}$, $f(c)$ is the frequency of concept c over current name observation set, specially, when c is a hub node concept, we will distribute its frequency according to equation (2), having $f_t(c) = f(c)sim(c,t)$. And $n\_coh(c,t)$ is the neighborhood coherence of concept c with topic t, defined as:

$$n\_coh(c,t) = \frac{\sum_{q \in N(c) \cap t} sr(q,c)}{|N(c) \cap t|} \quad (4)$$

where $N(c)$ is the neighboring node set of concept c.

By incorporating corpus level concept frequencies into topic weighting, discriminative concepts that are sparse in one document and suppressed by conventional models can benefit from their corpus level importance as well as their coherence in related topics.

3.3 Clustering Person Name Observations

Now the remaining key step is to compute the similarity between two name observations. The similarity proposed in GRAPE(Jiang et al., 2009) measures two documents by bridge tags (common features) shared by two document graphs. Specifically, Jiang et al. utilize *cohesion* to weight a bridge tag in a document. The more bridge tags two documents share, the stronger the cohesion of each bridge tag is, and in turn the more similar the two documents are.

However, this similarity bears a shortcoming that the bridge tags shared by the two documents require an exact match of features, which does not take any semantic relatedness into consideration. If two web pages mentioning the same person but have few features in common, the GRAPE similarity may not work properly. We, therefore, propose a new similarity measure combining topic similarity, topic based connectivity strength and GRAPE's connectivity strength.

Matching Topics to Person Name Observations We first describe how to match the generated topics to different name observations. In order to avoid unreliable estimation, we only match a topic to a name observation when they share at least one concept. To measure the relatedness between a topic and a name observation, we formulate this similarity as the weighted average of semantic relatedness between each concept from one side and its closely related counterpart from the other side,defined as:

$$sim(A \to B) = \frac{\sum_{a \in A} w_A(a) \times w_B(b_a) \times sr(a, b_a)}{\sum_{a \in A} w_A(a) \times w_B(b_a)} \quad (5)$$

$$sim(A,B) = (sim(A \to B) + sim(B \to A))/2,$$

where A can be a topic and B a name observation or vice versa, b_a is a concept in B that is most related to concept a, $w_A(a)$ represents the weight of concept a estimated by the averaged relatedness between a and other concepts in A.

Person Name Similarity Now we describe the first component in our proposed measure: topic similarity, which is calculated through the common topics shared by the two name observations, o_1 and o_2:

$$TSm(o_1, o_2) = \sum_{t \in T(o_1,o_2)} sim(o_1, t) \times sim(o_2, t) \times sim(o_1 \cap t, o_2 \cap t) \times w(t) \quad (6)$$

where $T(o_1, o_2)$ contains all common topics of o_1 and o_2, $w(t)$ is the weight of topic t estimated using equation (3), both $sim(o_i, t)$ and $sim(o_1 \cap t, o_2 \cap t)$ measure the similarity between two concept sets and can be estimated using equation (5). The underlying idea of the equation is, if two name observations share more and closer common topics, and also these topics receive higher weights according to the current name observation set, then the two observations should be more related to each other.

Specifically, the factor $sim(o_1 \cap t, o_2 \cap t)$ is designed to measure the fine relatedness between o_1 and o_2 given the topic t. Sometimes, both o_1 and o_2 are mapped to t and both close to this topic, but in fact they depict different aspects of t since some of our topics are more general thus include several aspects. The comparison of their intersections will provide a more detailed view for their similarity.

Inspired by the use of bridge tags in GRAPE(Jiang et al., 2009), we propose to capture the connection strength between concept sets by the means of our topics. We consider common topics as the bridge tags and define our topic based connectivity strength between two name observations as:

$$TCS(o_1, o_2) = \frac{1}{2} \sum_{t \in T(o_1, o_2)} sim(o_1 \cap t, o_2 \cap t) \times (Cohs(o_1, t) + Cohs(o_2, t)) \quad (7)$$

Note that we still need $sim(o_1 \cap t, o_2 \cap t)$ to capture the fine differences inside a topic. $Cohs(o, t)$ is a cohesion measure to capture the relatedness between non-concept features in o and concept features in t, defined as:

$$Cohs(o, t) = \sum_{c \in o \cap t} w(t) \times \sum_{q \in EB(o)} occ(c, q) f_o(c) f_o(q) \quad (8)$$

where $EB(o)$ contains all non-concept features in o (e.g., non-Wikipedia entities and biographical information), $occ(c, q)$ is the co-occurring number of concept c and feature q, $f_o(q)$ is the relative frequency of q in observation o. It is easy to find that a higher cohesion can be achieved by larger overlap between o and t, higher topic weight and more co-occurrences of concept features in t and other features in o.

The third part is the original connectivity strength defined in GRAPE(Jiang et al., 2009): $CS(o_1, o_2)$, calculated using plain features without topics (we omit the details for brevity). Finally, we linearly combine equation (6), (7) and $CS(o_1, o_2)$ into the person name similarity function as:

$$S(o_1, o_2) = \alpha_1 \times TSm(o_1, o_2) + \alpha_2 \times TCS(o_1, o_2) + (1 - \alpha_1 - \alpha_2) \times CS(o_1, o_2) \quad (9)$$

where α_1 and α_2 are optimized during training.

This final similarity function will then be embedded into a normal HAC algorithm to group the web pages into different namesakes where we compute the centroid-based distance between clusters(Mann and Yarowsky, 2003).

4 Experiments

We compare our model with competitive baselines on three WePS datasets. In the following, we first describe the experimental setup, and then discuss the their performances.

4.1 Data

Wikipedia Data Wikipedia offers free copies of all available data to interested users in their website. We used the one released in March 6th, 2009 in our experiments. We identified over 4,000,000 highly connected concepts in this dump; each concept links to 10 other concepts in average.

WePS Datasets We used three datasets in our experiments, WePS1 Training and Testing (Artiles et al., 2007), WePS2 Testing (Javier et al., 2009). These datasets collected names from three different resources including Wikipedia names, program committee of a computer science conference and US census. Each name were queried in Yahoo! Search and top N result pages (100 pages in WePS1 and 150 pages in WePS2) were obtained and manually labeled.

4.2 Baselines

We compare our model TM with four baseline methods: (1)VSM: traditional vector space model with cosine similarity. We use features extracted in Section 3.1 and weight them using TFIDF. The documents are grouped using standard HAC algorithm. (2)GRAPE(Jiang et al., 2009): we re-implement the state-of-the-art system which outperforms any models that do not use extra knowledge resources reported in WePS1 and WePS2. (3)WS: the Wikipedia

Semantic method(Han and Zhao, 2009). This system uses Wikipedia to enhance the results of name disambiguation. (4)SSR: the Structural Semantic relatedness model(Han and Zhao, 2010) creates a semantic graph to re-calculate the semantic relatedness between features, and captures both explicit semantic relations and implicit structural semantic knowledge. We also build two variants of TM: TM-nTW which removes topic weighting to examine what effect the topic weighting strategy can make and whether it can provide a person specific evidence and TM-nCP which does not use co-occurring information to prune the semantic graph to examine whether the pruning is effective.

4.3 Parameters

There are several parameters to be tuned in our model. In the SCAN algorithm, we use default parameters according to (Xu et al., 2007) with an exception: the weight α is tuned exhaustively to be 0.2. Note that the number of topics are automatically decided by SCAN. The semantic graph pruning threshold is set to 0.27 tuned on a held out set. The smoothing parameters in equation (9) are: $\alpha_1 = 0.3$, $\alpha_2 = 0.2$ which are tuned using cross validation. Optimization of some parameters will be addressed in detail in the following subsection. In HAC, all optimal merging thresholds are selected by applying leave-one-out cross validation.

4.4 Results and Discussion

We adopt the same evaluation process as (Han and Zhao, 2009), and evaluating these models using Purity, Inverse Purity and the F-measure (also used in WePS Task Artiles et al. (2007)). The overall performance is shown in Table 1, and the best scores are in boldface.

Let us first look at our model and its variants, TM-nTW and TM-nCP. By introducing the corpus level topic weighting scheme, our model improves in average 1.6% consistently over all datasets. Recall that our topic weightings are obtained over the whole name observation set beyond local context, this improvement indicates that this corpus level person specific evidences render the person similarity more reasonably than that of single document. On the other hand, by pruning the semantic graph, our model improves averagely 1.3% over TM-nCP. This shows that our co-occurrence based pruning strategy can help render the semantic graph with less noisy edges, thus generate more reasonable topics.

Table 1: Web person name disambiguation results on all three WePS datasets

WePS1 Training			
Method	**P**	**IP**	**FMeasure**
VSM	0.86	0.86	0.85
GRAPE	**0.93**	0.90	**0.91**
WS	0.88	0.89	0.87
SSR	0.82	**0.92**	0.85
TM-nTW	0.91	0.89	0.90
TM-nCP	0.92	0.90	**0.91**
TM	**0.93**	0.91	**0.91**
WePS1 Testing			
Method	**P**	**IP**	**FMeasure**
VSM	0.79	0.85	0.81
GRAPE	0.93	0.83	0.87
WS	0.88	**0.90**	0.88
SSR	0.85	0.83	0.84
TM-nTW	0.93	0.85	0.88
TM-nCP	0.92	0.86	0.88
TM	**0.94**	0.86	**0.90**
WePS2 Testing			
Method	**P**	**IP**	**FMeasure**
VSM	0.82	0.87	0.83
GRAPE	0.88	**0.90**	0.89
WS	0.85	0.89	0.86
SSR	0.89	0.84	0.86
TM-nTW	0.92	0.87	0.89
TM-nCP	**0.93**	0.88	0.90
TM	**0.93**	0.89	**0.91**

Generally, our proposed model works best consistently over all three datasets. Our method gains 9.3% improvement on average in three datasets compared with VSM, 1.7% improvement compared to GRAPE, 3.8% over WS and 6.7% over SSR. We also performed significance testing on F-measures: the differences between our model and other models are significant. We notice there are many noisy or short web pages which lead to inaccurate concept extraction, but this cross document evidences, to some extent, can remedy this. In the *Emily Bender* example, our system correctly groups the odd page, which contains limited clues, into the *nutritionist* cluster, while the rest, excluding WS and SSR, failed. Surprisingly, SSR combines both kinds of relations and implicit structural knowledge, but performs in the same bulk with VSM in WePS1 training set. We think the reason may be that some name observation sets are too small to estimate non-concept relatedness via random walk. In WePS1 training set, many names in this dataset contains several namesakes, each of which corresponds to a few web pages. In this case, our corpus level weighting scheme and WS show no advantage over GRAPE which considers word co-occurrences solely. From the results, we can also find that there is no clear winner between GRAPE and WS. The former does not use Wikipedia relatedness but only includes local relationship, and performs even slightly better than WS in WePS2, which indicates that non-Wikipedia concepts are important disambiguation features as well.

4.5 Parameter Optimization

In this subsection, we discuss the optimization of several parameters in the proposed method. In total we need to set four parameters. The first one is the edge pruning threshold during graph construction; the second one is the weight α in SCAN algorithm; the third one and the forth one are the combination parameters in the final similarity function. We will address the first two in the following. The last two combination parameters are tuned by exhaustively searching the space and omitted here for brevity

First, we configure the pruning threshold. Intuitively, larger threshold can prune more unimportant edges and improve the disambiguation performance. However, if the threshold is too large, we may prune important edges and harm the results. The F-measure of our method with respect to the pruning threshold is plotted in Figure 2.

From Figure 2, we can know that in all three data sets, a pruning threshold of 0.27 will lead to the best performance. Both increasing and decreasing of this pruning threshold will cause a decline of the F-Measure, because they will either leave more noisy light-weighted edges or prune some important edges.

Secondly, we configure the neighborhood similarity weight. The larger this weight is, the more neighborhood information can influence the similarity between two nodes in the semantic graph. We plot the

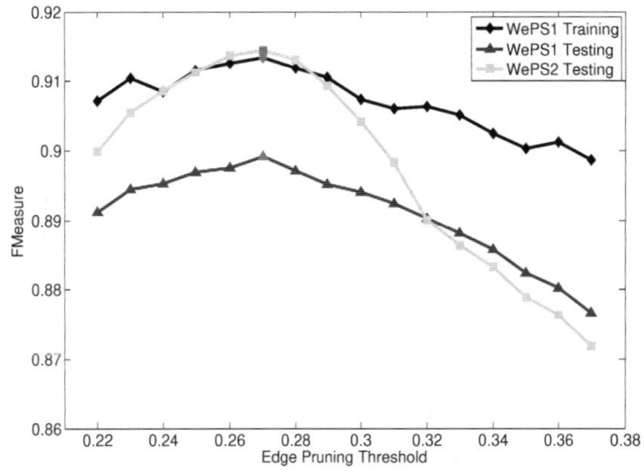

Figure 2: The F-Measure v.s. the edge pruning threshold on three data sets.

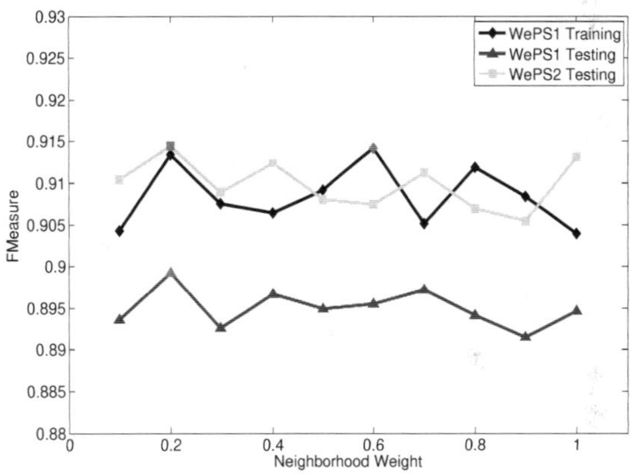

Figure 3: The F-Measure v.s. the neighborhood similarity weight on three data sets.

performance of our method regarding to the neighborhood similarity weight in Figure 3.

From Figure 3, we know that for the WePS 1 Testing and WePS2 Testing data sets, a neighborhood similarity weight of 0.2 can result in the best performance, but for WePS 1 Training set, the weight for the best performance is 0.6. In fact, when the neighborhood similarity weight varies from 0 to 1, the difference between the best and worst performance are less than 0.01, which indicates that neighborhood similarity is as considerable as semantic relatedness.

5 Conclusion and Future Work

In this paper, we explore the feature space in the web person name disambiguation task and propose a topic-based model which exploits corpus level person specific evidences to handle the data sparsity challenges, especially the case that limited evidences can be collected from the local context. In particular, we harvest topics from wikipedia concepts appearing in the name observation set, and weight a concept based on both the relatedness of the concept to its corresponding topic and the importance of this topic in the current name observation set, so that some discriminative but sparse features can obtain more reliable weights. Experimental results show that our weighting strategy does its job and the proposed model outperforms the-state-of-the-art systems. Our current work utilizes the topic information shared in one name observation set but is incapable to handle sparse name set, which needs more accurate relation extraction inside the name observations. Jointly modeling entity linking and person (entity) disambiguation tasks will be an interesting direction where the two tasks are closely related and usually need to be considered at the same time. Investigating the person name disambiguation task in different web applications will also be of great importance, e.g., disambiguating a name in streaming data or during knowledge base construction. In addition, graphical model, which has been studied in academic author disambiguation, may be a good choice to cope with the noises and non-standard forms in web data.

Acknowledgments

We would like to thank Yidong Chen, Wei Wang and Tinghua Wang for their useful discussions and the anonymous reviewers for their helpful comments which greatly improved the work and the presentation. This work was supported by the National High Technology Research and Development Program of China (Grant No. 2012AA011101), National Natural Science Foundation of China (Grant No.61003009) and Research Fund for the Doctoral Program of Higher Education of China (Grant No.20100001120029).

References

Artiles, J., Gonzalo, J., and Sekine, S. (2007). The semeval-2007 weps evaluation: establishing a benchmark for the web people search task. In *SemEval*, SemEval '07, pages 64–69, Stroudsburg, PA, USA. Association for Computational Linguistics.

Bagga, A. and Baldwin, B. (1998). Entity-based cross-document coreferencing using the vector space model. In *ACL*, pages 79–85, Stroudsburg, PA, USA. Association for Computational Linguistics.

Bunescu, R. C. and Pasca, M. (2006). Using encyclopedic knowledge for named entity disambiguation. In *EACL*. The Association for Computer Linguistics.

Cucerzan, S. (2007). Large-scale named entity disambiguation based on wikipedia data. In *EMNLP-CoNLL*, pages 708–716. ACL.

David, M. and Ian, H. (2008). An effective, low-cost measure of semantic relatedness obtained from wikipedia links. In *AAAI*, AAAI '08.

Finkel, J. R., Grenager, T., and Manning, C. (2005). Incorporating non-local information into information extraction systems by gibbs sampling. In *ACL*, pages 363–370, Ann Arbor, Michigan. Association for Computational Linguistics.

Han, X. and Zhao, J. (2009). Named entity disambiguation by leveraging wikipedia semantic knowledge. In *CIKM*, CIKM '09, pages 215–224, New York, NY, USA. ACM.

Han, X. and Zhao, J. (2010). Structural semantic relatedness: a knowledge-based method to named entity disambiguation. In *ACL*, ACL '10, pages 50–59, Stroudsburg, PA, USA. Association for Computational Linguistics.

Ikeda, M., Ono, S., Sato, I., Yoshida, M., and Nakagawa, H. (2009). Person name disambiguation on the web by two-stage clustering. In *WWW*.

Iria, J., Xia, L., and Zhang, Z. (2007). Wit: web people search disambiguation using random walks. In *SemEval*, SemEval '07, pages 480–483, Stroudsburg, PA, USA. Association for Computational Linguistics.

Javier, A., Julio, G., and Satoshi, S. (2009). Weps 2 evaluation campaign: Overview of the web people search clustering task. In *WWW 2009*.

Jiang, L., Wang, J., An, N., Wang, S., Zhan, J., and Li, L. (2009). Grape: A graph-based framework for disambiguating people appearances in web search. In *ICDM*, ICDM '09, pages 199–208, Washington, DC, USA. IEEE Computer Society.

Kalashnikov, D. V., Chen, Z., Mehrotra, S., and Nuray-Turan, R. (2008a). Web people search via connection analysis. *IEEE Trans. on Knowl. and Data Eng.*, 20:1550–1565.

Kalashnikov, D. V., Nuray-Turan, R., and Mehrotra, S. (2008b). Towards breaking the quality curse.: a web-querying approach to web people search. In *SIGIR*, SIGIR '08, pages 27–34, New York, NY, USA. ACM.

Mann, G. S. and Yarowsky, D. (2003). Unsupervised personal name disambiguation. In *CONLL*, CONLL '03, pages 33–40, Stroudsburg, PA, USA. Association for Computational Linguistics.

Mihalcea, R. and Csomai, A. (2007). Wikify!: linking documents to encyclopedic knowledge. In *Proceedings of CIKM'07*, pages 233–242.

Niu, C., Li, W., and Srihari, R. K. (2004). Weakly supervised learning for cross-document person name disambiguation supported by information extraction. In *ACL*, ACL '04, Stroudsburg, PA, USA. Association for Computational Linguistics.

Pilz, A. (2010). Entity disambiguation using link based relations extracted from wikipedia. In *ICML*.

Rao, D., Garera, N., and Yarowsky, D. (2007). Jhu1: an unsupervised approach to person name disambiguation using web snippets. In *SemEval*, SemEval '07, pages 199–202, Stroudsburg, PA, USA. Association for Computational Linguistics.

Wu, F. and Weld, D. S. (2008). Automatically refining the wikipedia infobox ontology. In *WWW*, WWW '08, pages 635–644, New York, NY, USA. ACM.

Xu, X., Yuruk, N., Feng, Z., and Schweiger, T. A. J. (2007). Scan: a structural clustering algorithm for networks. In *Proceedings of KDD*, KDD '07, pages 824–833, New York, NY, USA. ACM.

Yiming, L., Zaiqing, N., Taoyuan, C., Ying, G., and Ji-Rong, W. (2007). Name disambiguation using web connection. In *AAAI*.

Inducing a Discriminative Parser to Optimize Machine Translation Reordering

Graham Neubig[1,2], Taro Watanabe[2], Shinsuke Mori[1]
[1]Graduate School of Informatics, Kyoto University
Yoshida Honmachi, Sakyo-ku, Kyoto, Japan
[2]National Institute of Information and Communication Technology
3-5 Hikari-dai, Seika-cho, Soraku-gun, Kyoto, Japan

Abstract

This paper proposes a method for learning a discriminative parser for machine translation reordering using only aligned parallel text. This is done by treating the parser's derivation tree as a latent variable in a model that is trained to maximize reordering accuracy. We demonstrate that efficient large-margin training is possible by showing that two measures of reordering accuracy can be factored over the parse tree. Using this model in the pre-ordering framework results in significant gains in translation accuracy over standard phrase-based SMT and previously proposed unsupervised syntax induction methods.

1 Introduction

Finding the appropriate word ordering in the target language is one of the most difficult problems for statistical machine translation (SMT), particularly for language pairs with widely divergent syntax. As a result, there is a large amount of previous research that handles the problem of reordering through the use of improved reordering models for phrase-based SMT (Koehn et al., 2005), hierarchical phrase-based translation (Chiang, 2007), syntax-based translation (Yamada and Knight, 2001), or pre-ordering (Xia and McCord, 2004).

In particular, systems that use source-language syntax allow for the handling of long-distance reordering without large increases in decoding time. However, these require a good syntactic parser, which is not available for many languages. In recent work, DeNero and Uszkoreit (2011) suggest that unsupervised grammar induction can be used to create source-sentence parse structure for use in translation as a part of a pre-ordering based translation system.

In this work, we present a method for inducing a parser for SMT by training a discriminative model to maximize reordering accuracy while treating the parse tree as a latent variable. As a learning framework, we use online large-margin methods to train the model to directly minimize two measures of reordering accuracy. We propose a variety of features, and demonstrate that learning can succeed when no linguistic information (POS tags or parse structure) is available in the source language, but also show that this linguistic information can be simply incorporated when it is available. Experiments find that the proposed model improves both reordering and translation accuracy, leading to average gains of 1.2 BLEU points on English-Japanese and Japanese-English translation without linguistic analysis tools, or up to 1.5 BLEU points when these tools are incorporated. In addition, we show that our model is able to effectively maximize various measures of reordering accuracy, and that the reordering measure that we choose has a direct effect on translation results.

2 Preordering for SMT

Machine translation is defined as transformation of source sentence $F = f_1 \dots f_J$ to target sentence $E = e_1 \dots e_I$. In this paper, we take

The first author is now affiliated with the Nara Institute of Science and Technology.

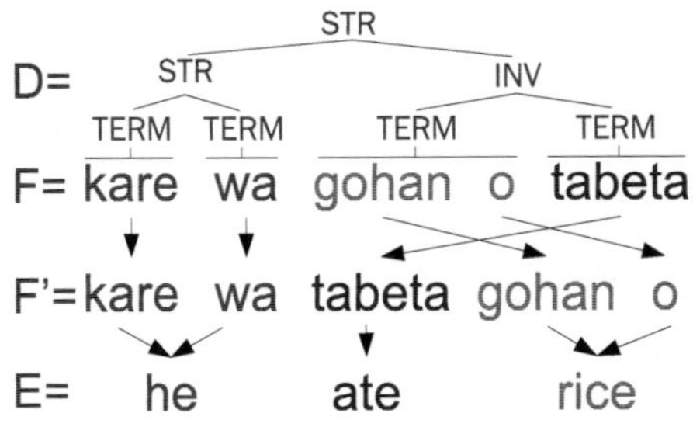

Figure 1: An example with a source sentence F reordered into target order F', and its corresponding target sentence E. D is one of the BTG derivations that can produce this ordering.

the pre-ordering approach to machine translation (Xia and McCord, 2004), which performs translation as a two step process of reordering and translation (Figure 1). Reordering first deterministically transforms F into F', which contains the same words as F but is in the order of E. Translation then transforms F' into E using a method such as phrase-based SMT (Koehn et al., 2003), which can produce accurate translations when only local reordering is required.

This general framework has been widely studied, with the majority of works relying on a syntactic parser being available in the source language. Reordering rules are defined over this parse either through machine learning techniques (Xia and McCord, 2004; Zhang et al., 2007; Li et al., 2007; Genzel, 2010; Dyer and Resnik, 2010; Khalilov and Sima'an, 2011) or linguistically motivated manual rules (Collins et al., 2005; Xu et al., 2009; Carpuat et al., 2010; Isozaki et al., 2010b). However, as building a parser for each source language is a resource-intensive undertaking, there has also been some interest in developing reordering rules without the use of a parser (Rottmann and Vogel, 2007; Tromble and Eisner, 2009; DeNero and Uszkoreit, 2011; Visweswariah et al., 2011), and we will follow this thread of research in this paper.

In particular, two methods deserve mention for being similar to our approach. First, DeNero and Uszkoreit (2011) learn a reordering model through a three-step process of bilingual grammar induction, training a monolingual parser to reproduce the induced trees, and training a reordering model that selects a reordering based on this parse structure. In contrast, our method trains the model in a single step, treating the parse structure as a latent variable in a discriminative reordering model. In addition Tromble and Eisner (2009) and Visweswariah et al. (2011) present models that use binary classification to decide whether each pair of words should be placed in forward or reverse order. In contrast, our method uses traditional context-free-grammar models, which allows for simple parsing and flexible parameterization, including features such as those that utilize the existence of a span in the phrase table. Our work is also unique in that we show that it is possible to directly optimize several measures of reordering accuracy, which proves important for achieving good translations.[1]

3 Training a Reordering Model with Latent Derivations

In this section, we provide a basic overview of the proposed method for learning a reordering model with latent derivations using online discriminative learning.

3.1 Space of Reorderings

The model we present here is based on the bracketing transduction grammar (BTG, Wu (1997)) framework. BTGs represent a binary tree derivation D over the source sentence F as shown in Figure 1. Each non-terminal node can either be a straight (STR) or inverted (INV) production, and terminals (TERM) span a non-empty substring $\boldsymbol{f}$.[2]

The ordering of the sentence is determined by the tree structure and the non-terminal labels STR and INV, and can be built bottom-up. Each subtree represents a source substring $\boldsymbol{f}$ and its reordered counterpart $\boldsymbol{f}'$. For each terminal node, no reordering occurs and $\boldsymbol{f}$ is equal to $\boldsymbol{f}'$.

[1]The semi-supervised method of Katz-Brown et al. (2011) also optimizes reordering accuracy, but requires manually annotated parses as seed data.

[2]In the original BTG framework used in translation, terminals produce a bilingual substring pair $\boldsymbol{f}/\boldsymbol{e}$, but as we are only interested in reordering the source F, we simplify the model by removing the target substring $\boldsymbol{e}$.

For each non-terminal node spanning $\boldsymbol{f}$ with its left child spanning $\boldsymbol{f}_1$ and its right child spanning $\boldsymbol{f}_2$, if the non-terminal symbol is STR, the reordered strings will be concatenated in order as $\boldsymbol{f}' = \boldsymbol{f}'_1\boldsymbol{f}'_2$, and if the non-terminal symbol is INV, the reordered strings will be concatenated in inverted order as $\boldsymbol{f}' = \boldsymbol{f}'_2\boldsymbol{f}'_1$.

We define the space of all reorderings that can be produced by the BTG as $\mathcal{F}'$, and attempt to find the best reordering $\hat{F}'$ within this space.[3]

3.2 Reorderings with Latent Derivations

In order to find the best reordering $\hat{F}'$ given only the information in the source side sentence F, we define a scoring function $S(F'|F)$, and choose the ordering of maximal score:

$$\dot{F}' = \arg\max_{F'} S(F'|F).$$

As our model is based on reorderings licensed by BTG derivations, we also assume that there is an underlying derivation D that produced F'. As we can uniquely determine F' given F and D, we can define a scoring function $S(D|F)$ over derivations, find the derivation of maximal score

$$\dot{D} = \arg\max_{D} S(D|F)$$

and use $\dot{D}$ to transform F into F'.

Furthermore, we assume that the score $S(D|F)$ is the weighted sum of a number of feature functions defined over D and F

$$S(D|F, \boldsymbol{w}) = \sum_i w_i \phi_i(D, F)$$

where ϕ_i is the ith feature function, and w_i is its corresponding weight in weight vector $\boldsymbol{w}$.

Given this model, we must next consider how to learn the weights $\boldsymbol{w}$. As the final goal of our model is to produce good reorderings F', it is natural to attempt to learn weights that will allow us to produce these high-quality reorderings.

[3]BTGs cannot reproduce all possible reorderings, but can handle most reorderings occurring in natural translated text (Haghighi et al., 2009).

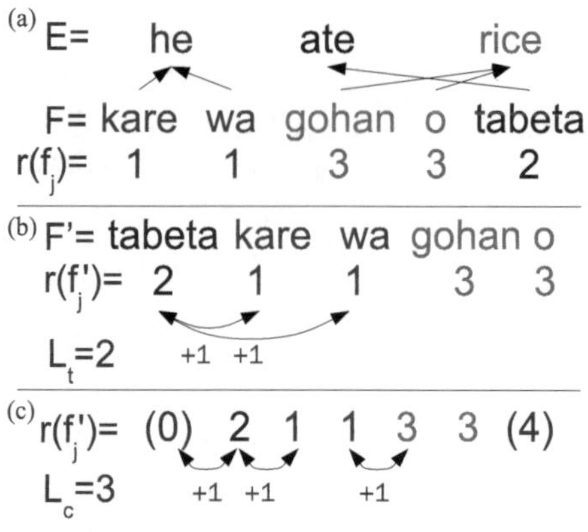

Figure 2: An example of (a) the ranking function $r(f_j)$, (b) loss according to Kendall's τ, (c) loss according to chunk fragmentation.

4 Evaluating Reorderings

Before we explain the learning algorithm, we must know how to distinguish whether the F' produced by the model is good or bad. This section explains how to calculate oracle reorderings, and assign each F' a *loss* and an *accuracy* according to how well it reproduces the oracle.

4.1 Calculating Oracle Orderings

In order to calculate reordering quality, we first define a ranking function $r(f_j|F, A)$, which indicates the relative position of source word f_j in the proper target order (Figure 2 (a)). In order to calculate this ranking function, we define $A = \boldsymbol{a}_1, \ldots, \boldsymbol{a}_J$, where each $\boldsymbol{a}_j$ is a set of the indices of the words in E to which f_j is aligned.[4] Given these alignments, we define an ordering function $\boldsymbol{a}_{j_1} < \boldsymbol{a}_{j_2}$ that indicates that the indices in $\boldsymbol{a}_{j_1}$ come before the indices in $\boldsymbol{a}_{j_2}$. Formally, we define this function as "the first index in $\boldsymbol{a}_{j_1}$ is at most the first index in $\boldsymbol{a}_{j_2}$, similarly for the last index, and either the first or last index in $\boldsymbol{a}_{j_1}$ is less than that of $\boldsymbol{a}_{j_2}$."

Given this ordering, we can sort every alignment $\boldsymbol{a}_j$, and use its relative position in the sentence to assign a rank to its word $r(f_j)$. In

[4]Null alignments require special treatment. To do so, we can place unaligned brackets and quotes directly before and after the spans they surround, and attach all other unaligned words to the word directly to the right for head-initial languages (e.g. English), or left for head-final languages (e.g. Japanese).

the case of ties, where neither $\boldsymbol{a}_{j_1} < \boldsymbol{a}_{j_2}$ nor $\boldsymbol{a}_{j_2} < \boldsymbol{a}_{j_1}$, both f_{j_1} and f_{j_2} are assigned the same rank. We can now define measures of reordering accuracy for F' by how well it arranges the words in order of ascending rank. It should be noted that as we allow ties in rank, there are multiple possible F' where all words are in strictly ascending order, which we will call *oracle* orderings.

4.2 Kendall's τ

The first measure of reordering accuracy that we will consider is Kendall's τ (Kendall, 1938), a measure of pairwise rank correlation which has been proposed for evaluating translation reordering accuracy (Isozaki et al., 2010a; Birch et al., 2010) and pre-ordering accuracy (Talbot et al., 2011). The fundamental idea behind the measure lies in comparisons between each pair of elements f'_{j_1} and f'_{j_2} of the reordered sentence, where $j_1 < j_2$. Because $j_1 < j_2$, f'_{j_1} comes before f'_{j_2} in the reordered sentence, the ranks should be $r(f'_{j_1}) \le r(f'_{j_2})$ in order to produce the correct ordering.

Based on this criterion, we first define a loss $L_t(F')$ that will be higher for orderings that are further from the oracle. Specifically, we take the sum of all pairwise orderings that do not follow the expected order

$$L_t(F') = \sum_{j_1=1}^{J-1} \sum_{j_2=j_1+1}^{J} \delta(r(f'_{j_1}) > r(f'_{j_2}))$$

where $\delta(\cdot)$ is an indicator function that is 1 when its condition is true, and 0 otherwise. An example of this is given in Figure 2 (b).

To calculate an accuracy measure for ordering F', we first calculate the maximum loss for the sentence, which is equal to the total number of non-equal rank comparisons in the sentence[5]

$$\max_{\tilde{F}'} L_t(F') = \sum_{j_1=1}^{J-1} \sum_{j_2=j_1+1}^{J} \delta(r(f'_{j_1}) \ne r(f'_{j_2})). \quad (1)$$

[5]The traditional formulation of Kendall's τ assumes no ties in rank, and thus the maximum loss can be calculated as $J(J-1)/2$.

Finally, we use this maximum loss to normalize the actual loss to get an accuracy

$$A_t(F') = 1 - \frac{L_t(F')}{\max_{\tilde{F}'} L_t(\tilde{F}')},$$

which will take a value between 0 (when F' has maximal loss), and 1 (when F' matches one of the oracle orderings). In Figure 2 (b), $L_t(F') = 2$ and $\max_{\tilde{F}'} L_t(\tilde{F}') = 8$, so $A_t(F') = 0.75$.

4.3 Chunk Fragmentation

Another measure that has been used in evaluation of translation accuracy (Banerjee and Lavie, 2005) and pre-ordering accuracy (Talbot et al., 2011) is chunk fragmentation. This measure is based on the number of chunks that the sentence needs to be broken into to reproduce the correct ordering, with a motivation that the number of continuous chunks is equal to the number of times the reader will have to jump to a different position in the reordered sentence to read it in the target order. One way to measure the number of continuous chunks is considering whether each word pair f'_j and f'_{j+1} is discontinuous (the rank of f'_{j+1} is not equal to or one greater than f'_j)

$$\text{DISCONT}(f'_j, f'_{j+1}) = \delta(r(f'_j) \ne r(f'_{j+1}) \wedge r(f'_j) + 1 \ne r(f'_{j+1}))$$

and sum over all word pairs in the sentence to create a sentence-based loss

$$L_c(F') = \sum_{j=1}^{J-1} \text{DISCONT}(f'_j, f'_{j+1}) \quad (2)$$

While this is the formulation taken by previous work, we found that this under-penalizes bad reorderings of the first and last words of the sentence, which can contribute to the loss only once, as opposed to other words which can contribute to the loss twice. To account for this, when calculating the chunk fragmentation score, we additionally add two sentence boundary words f_0 and f_{J+1} with ranks $r(f_0) = 0$ and $r(f_{J+1}) = 1 + \max_{f'_j \in F'} r(f'_j)$ and redefine the summation in Equation (2) to consider these words (e.g. Figure 2 (c)).

procedure WEIGHTUPDATE(F, A, $\boldsymbol{w}$)
  $\mathcal{D} \leftarrow \text{parse}(F, \boldsymbol{w})$ ▷ Create parse forest
  $\dot{D} \leftarrow \underset{D \in \mathcal{D}}{\text{argmax}}\ S(D|F, \boldsymbol{w}) + L(D|F, A)$
    ▷ Find the model parse
  $\hat{D} \leftarrow \underset{D \in \mathcal{D}}{\text{argmin}}\ L(D|F, A) - \alpha S(D|F, \boldsymbol{w})$
    ▷ Find the oracle parse
  if $L(\hat{D}|F, A) \neq L(\dot{D}|F, A)$ **then**
    $\boldsymbol{w} \leftarrow \beta(\boldsymbol{w} + \gamma(\phi(\hat{D}, F) - \phi(\dot{D}, F)))$
      ▷ Perform weight update
  end if
end procedure

Figure 3: An online update for sentence F, alignment A, and weight vector $\boldsymbol{w}$. α is a very small constant, and β and γ are defined by the update strategy.

Similarly to Kendall's τ, we can also define an accuracy measure between 0 and 1 using the maximum loss, which will be at most $J + 1$, which corresponds to the total number of comparisons made in calculating the loss[6]

$$A_c(F') = 1 - \frac{L_c(F')}{J+1}.$$

In Figure 2 (c), $L_c(F') = 3$ and $J + 1 = 6$, so $A_c(F') = 0.5$.

5 Learning a BTG Parser for Reordering

Now that we have a definition of loss over reorderings produced by the model, we have a clear learning objective: we would like to find reorderings F' with low loss. The learning algorithm we use to achieve this goal is motivated by discriminative training for machine translation systems (Liang et al., 2006), and extended to use large-margin training in an online framework (Watanabe et al., 2007).

5.1 Learning Algorithm

Learning uses the general framework of large-margin online structured prediction (Crammer et al., 2006), which makes several passes through the data, finding a derivation with high model score (the *model* parse) and a derivation with minimal loss (the *oracle* parse), and updating $\boldsymbol{w}$ if these two parses diverge (Figure 3).

In order to create both of these parses efficiently, we first create a parse forest encoding a large number of derivations $\mathcal{D}_i$ according to the model scores. Next, we find the model parse $\dot{D}_i$, which is the parse in the forest $\mathcal{D}_i$ that maximizes the sum of the model score and the loss $S(D_k|F_k, \boldsymbol{w}) + L(D_k|F_k, A_k)$. It should be noted that here we are considering not only the model score, but also the derivation's loss. This is necessary for loss-driven large-margin training (Crammer et al., 2006), and follows the basic intuition that during training, we would like to make it easier to select negative examples with large loss, causing these examples to be penalized more often and more heavily.

We also find an oracle parse $\hat{D}_i$, which is selected solely to minimize the loss $L(D_k|F_k, A_k)$. One important difference between the model we describe here and traditional parsing models is that the target derivation $\hat{D}_k$ is a latent variable. Because many D_k achieve a particular reordering F', many reorderings F' are able to minimize the loss $L(F'_k|F_k, A_k)$. Thus it is necessary to choose a single oracle derivation to treat as the target out of many equally good reorderings. DeNero and Uszkoreit (2011) resolve this ambiguity with four features with empirically tuned scores before training a monolingual parser and reordering model. In contrast, we follow previous work on discriminative learning with latent variables (Yu and Joachims, 2009), and break ties within the pool of oracle derivations by selecting the derivation with the largest model score. From an implementation point of view, this can be done by finding the derivation that minimizes $L(D_k|F_k, A_k) - \alpha S(D_k|F_k, \boldsymbol{w})$, where α is a constant small enough to ensure that the effect of the loss will always be greater than the effect of the score.

Finally, if the model parse $\dot{D}_k$ has a loss that is greater than that of the oracle parse $\hat{D}_k$, we update the weights to increase the score of the oracle parse and decrease the score of the model parse. Any criterion for weight updates may be used, such as the averaged perceptron (Collins, 2002) and MIRA (Crammer et al., 2006), but

[6]It should be noted that for sentences of length one or sentences with tied ranks, the maximum loss may be less than $J+1$, but for simplicity we use this approximation.

we opted to use Pegasos (Shalev-Shwartz et al., 2007) as it allows for the introduction of regularization and relatively stable learning.

To perform this full process, given a source sentence F_k, alignment A_k, and model weights $\boldsymbol{w}$ we need to be able to efficiently calculate scores, calculate losses, and create parse forests for derivations D_k, the details of which will be explained in the following sections.

5.2 Scoring Derivation Trees

First, we must consider how to efficiently assign scores $S(D|F,\boldsymbol{w})$ to a derivation or forest during parsing. The most standard and efficient way to do so is to create local features that can be calculated based only on the information included in a single node d in the derivation tree. The score of the whole tree can then be expressed as the sum of the scores from each node:

$$\begin{aligned} S(D|F,\boldsymbol{w}) &= \sum_{d \in D} S(d|F,\boldsymbol{w}) \\ &= \sum_{d \in D} \sum_{i} w_i \phi_i(d,F). \end{aligned}$$

Based on this restriction, we define a number of features that can be used to score the parse tree. To ease explanation, we represent each node in the derivation as $d = \langle s, l, c, c+1, r \rangle$, where s is the node's symbol (STR, INV, or TERM), while l and r are the leftmost and rightmost indices of the span that d covers. c and $c+1$ are the rightmost index of the left child and leftmost index of the right child for non-terminal nodes.

All features are intersected with the node label s, so each feature described below corresponds to three different features (or two for features applicable to only non-terminal nodes).

- ϕ_{lex}: Identities of words in positions f_l, f_r, f_c, f_{c+1}, f_{l-1}, f_{r+1}, $f_l f_r$, and $f_c f_{c+1}$.

- ϕ_{class}: Same as ϕ_{lex}, but with words abstracted to classes. We use the 50 classes automatically generated by Och (1999)'s method that are calculated during alignment in standard SMT systems.

- $\phi_{balance}$: For non-terminals, features indicating whether the length of the left span $(c-l+1)$ is lesser than, equal to, or greater than the length of the right span $(r-c)$.

- ϕ_{table}: Features, bucketed by length, that indicate whether "$f_l \ldots f_r$" appears as a contiguous phrase in the SMT training data, as well as the log frequency of the number of times the phrase appears total and the number of times it appears as a contiguous phrase (DeNero and Uszkoreit, 2011). Phrase length is limited to 8, and phrases of frequency one are removed.

- ϕ_{pos}: Same as ϕ_{lex}, but with words abstracted to language-dependent POS tags.

- ϕ_{cfg}: Features indicating the label of the spans $f_l \ldots f_r$, $f_l \ldots f_c$, and $f_{c+1} \ldots f_r$ in a supervised parse tree, and the intersection of the three labels. When spans do not correspond to a span in the supervised parse tree, we indicate "no span" with the label "X" (Zollmann and Venugopal, 2006).

Most of these features can be calculated from only a parallel corpus, but ϕ_{pos} requires a POS tagger and ϕ_{cfg} requires a full syntactic parser in the source language. As it is preferable to have a method that is applicable in languages where these tools are not available, we perform experiments both with and without the features that require linguistic analysis tools.

5.3 Finding Losses for Derivation Trees

The above features ϕ and their corresponding weights $\boldsymbol{w}$ are all that are needed to calculate scores of derivation trees at test time. However, during training, it is also necessary to find model parses according to the loss-augmented scoring function $S(D|F,\boldsymbol{w}) + L(D|F,A)$ or oracle parses according to the loss $L(D|F,A)$. As noted by Taskar et al. (2003), this is possible if our losses can be factored in the same way as the feature space. In this section, we demonstrate that the loss $L(d|F,A)$ for the evaluation measures we defined in Section 4 can (mostly) be factored over nodes in a fashion similar to features.

5.3.1 Factoring Kendall's τ

For Kendall's τ, in the case of terminal nodes, $L_t(d = \langle \text{TERM}, l, r \rangle | F, A)$ can be calculated by performing the summation in Equation (1). We can further define this sum recursively and use memoization for improved efficiency

$$L_t(d|F, A) = L_t(\langle \text{TERM}, l, r-1 \rangle | F, A) + \sum_{j=l}^{r-1} \delta(r(f_j) > r(f_r)). \quad (3)$$

For non-terminal nodes, we first focus on straight non-terminals with parent node $d = \langle \text{STR}, l, c, c+1, r \rangle$, and left and right child nodes $d_l = \langle s_l, l, lc, lc+1, c \rangle$ and $d_r = \langle s_r, c+1, rc, rc+1, r \rangle$. First, we note that the loss for the subtree rooted at d can be expressed as

$$L_t(d|F, A) = L_t(d_l|F, A) + L_t(d_r|F, A) + \sum_{j_1=l}^{c} \sum_{j_2=c+1}^{r} \delta(r(f_{j_1}) > r(f_{j_2})).$$

In other words, the subtree's total loss can be factored into the loss of its left subtree, the loss of its right subtree, and the additional loss contributed by comparisons between the words spanning both subtrees. In the case of inverted terminals, we must simply reverse the comparison in the final sum to be $\delta(r(f_{j_1}) < r(f_{j_2}))$.

5.3.2 Factoring Chunk Fragmentation

Chunk fragmentation loss can be factored in a similar fashion. First, it is clear that the loss for the terminal nodes can be calculated efficiently in a fashion similar to Equation (3). In order to calculate the loss for non-terminals d, we note that the summation in Equation (2) can be divided into the sum over the internal bi-grams in the left and right subtrees, and the bi-gram spanning the reordered trees

$$L_c(d|F, A) = L_c(d_l|F, A) + L_c(d_r|F, A) + \text{DISCONT}(f'_c, f'_{c+1}).$$

However, unlike Kendall's τ, this equation relies not on the ranks of f_c and f_{c+1} in the original sentence, but on the ranks of f'_c and f'_{c+1} in the reordered sentence. In order to keep track of these values, it is necessary to augment each node in the tree to be $d = \langle s, l, c, c+1, r, tl, tr \rangle$ with two additional values tl and tr that indicate the position of the leftmost and rightmost words after reordering. Thus, a straight non-terminal parent d with children $d_l = \langle s_l, l, lc, lc+1, c, tl, tlr \rangle$ and $d_r = \langle s_r, c+1, rc, rc+1, r, trl, tr \rangle$ will have loss as follows

$$L_c(d|F, A) = L_c(d_l|F, A) + L_c(d_r|F, A) + \text{DISCONT}(f_{tlr}, f_{trl})$$

with a similar calculation being possible for inverted non-terminals.

5.4 Parsing Derivation Trees

Finally, we must be able to create a parse forest from which we select model and oracle parses. As all feature functions factor over single nodes, it is possible to find the parse tree with the highest score in $O(J^3)$ time using the CKY algorithm. However, when keeping track of target positions for calculation of chunk fragmentation loss, there are a total of $O(J^5)$ nodes, an unreasonable burden in terms of time and memory. To overcome this problem, we note that this setting is nearly identical to translation using synchronous CFGs with an integrated bigram LM, and thus we can employ cube-pruning to reduce our search space (Chiang, 2007).

6 Experiments

Our experiments test the reordering and translation accuracy of translation systems using the proposed method. As reordering metrics, we use Kendall's τ and chunk fragmentation (Talbot et al., 2011) comparing the system F' and oracle F' calculated with manually created alignments. As translation metrics, we use BLEU (Papineni et al., 2002), as well as RIBES (Isozaki et al., 2010a), which is similar to Kendall's τ, but evaluated on the target sentence E instead of the reordered sentence F'. All scores are the average of three training runs to control for randomness in training (Clark et al., 2011).

For translation, we use Moses (Koehn et al., 2007) with lexicalized reordering (Koehn et al., 2005) in all experiments. We test three types

	en-ja				ja-en			
	Chunk	τ	BLEU	RIBES	Chunk	τ	BLEU	RIBES
ORIG	61.22	73.46	21.87	68.25	66.42	72.99	18.34	65.36
3-STEP	63.51	72.55	21.45	67.66	67.17	73.01	17.78	64.42
3-STEP+ϕ_{pos}	64.28	72.11	21.45	67.44	67.56	74.21	18.18	64.65
3-STEP+ϕ_{cfg}	65.76	75.32	21.67	68.47	67.23	74.06	18.18	64.93
LADER	73.19	78.44	**23.11**	69.86	**75.14**	**79.14**	**19.54**	**66.93**
LADER+ϕ_{pos}	73.97	79.24	**23.32**	69.78	**75.49**	**78.79**	**19.89**	**67.24**
LADER+ϕ_{cfg}	**75.06**	**80.53**	**23.36**	**70.89**	**75.14**	77.80	19.35	66.12

Table 2: Reordering (chunk, τ) and translation (BLEU, RIBES) results for each system. Bold numbers indicate no significant difference from the best system (bootstrap resampling with $p > 0.05$) (Koehn, 2004).

	sent.	word (ja)	word (en)
RM-train	602	14.5k	14.3k
RM-test	555	11.2k	10.4k
TM/LM	329k	6.08M	5.91M
Tune	1166	26.8k	24.3k
Test	1160	28.5k	26.7k

Table 1: The number of sentences and words for training and testing the reordering model (RM), translation model (TM), and language model (LM).

of pre-ordering: original order with $F' \leftarrow F$ (ORIG), pre-orderings learned using the 3-step process of DeNero and Uszkoreit (2011) (3-STEP), and the proposed model with latent derivations (LADER).[7] Except when stated otherwise, LADER was trained to minimize chunk fragmentation loss with a cube pruning stack pop limit of 50, and the regularization constant of 10^{-3} (chosen through cross-validation).

We test our systems on Japanese-English and English-Japanese translation using data from the Kyoto Free Translation Task (Neubig, 2011). We use the training set for training translation and language models, the development set for weight tuning, and the test set for testing (Table 1). We use the designated development and test sets of manually created alignments as training data for the reordering models, removing sentences of more than 60 words.

As default features for LADER and the monolingual parsing and reordering models in 3-STEP, we use all the features described in Section 5.2 except ϕ_{pos} and ϕ_{cfg}. In addition, we test systems with ϕ_{pos} and ϕ_{cfg} added. For English, we use the Stanford parser (Klein and Manning, 2003) for both POS tagging and CFG parsing. For Japanese, we use the KyTea tagger (Neubig et al., 2011) for POS tagging,[8] and the EDA word-based dependency parser (Flannery et al., 2011) with simple manual head-rules to convert a dependency parse to a CFG parse.

6.1 Effect of Pre-ordering

Table 2 shows reordering and translation results for ORIG, 3-STEP, and LADER. It can be seen that the proposed LADER outperforms the baselines in both reordering and translation.[9] There are a number of reasons why LADER outperforms 3-STEP. First, the pipeline of 3-STEP suffers from error propogation, with errors in monolingual parsing and reordering resulting in low overall accuracy.[10] Second, as Section 5.1 describes, LADER breaks ties between oracle parses based on model score, allowing easy-to-reproduce model parses to be chosen during training. In fact, LADER generally found trees that followed from syntactic constituency, while 3-STEP more often used terminal nodes

[7] Available open-source: `http://phontron.com/lader`

[8] In addition, following the example of Sudoh et al. (2011a)'s reordering rules, we lexicalize all particles.

[9] It should be noted that our results for 3-STEP are significantly worse than those of DeNero and Uszkoreit (2011). Likely reasons include a 20x difference in training data size, the fact that we are using naturally translated text as opposed to text translated specifically to create word alignments, or differences in implementation.

[10] When using oracle parses, chunk accuracy was up to 81%, showing that parsing errors are highly detrimental.

	en-ja				ja-en			
	Chunk	τ	BLEU	RIBES	Chunk	τ	BLEU	RIBES
L_c	**73.19**	78.44	**23.11**	69.86	**75.14**	**79.14**	**19.54**	**66.93**
L_t	70.37	79.57	22.57	69.47	72.51	78.93	18.52	66.26
$L_c + L_t$	72.55	**80.58**	**22.89**	**70.34**	74.44	**79.82**	19.21	**66.48**

Table 3: Results for systems trained to optimize chunk fragmentation (L_c) or Kendall's τ (L_t).

that spanned constituent boundaries (as long as the phrase frequency was high). Finally, as Section 6.2 shows in detail, the ability of LADER to maximize reordering accuracy directly allows for improved reordering and translation results.

It can also be seen that incorporating POS tags or parse trees improves accuracy of both LADER and 3-STEP, particularly for English-Japanese, where syntax has proven useful for pre-ordering, and less so for Japanese-English, where syntactic pre-ordering has been less successful (Sudoh et al., 2011b).

We also tested Moses's implementation of hierarchical phrase-based SMT (Chiang, 2007), which achieved BLEU scores of 23.21 and 19.30 for English-Japanese and Japanese-English respectively, approximately matching LADER in accuracy, but with a significant decrease in decoding speed. Further, when pre-ordering with LADER and hierarchical phrase-based SMT were combined, BLEU scores rose to 23.29 and 19.69, indicating that the two techniques can be combined for further accuracy improvements.

6.2 Effect of Training Loss

Table 3 shows results when one of three losses is optimized during training: chunk fragmentation (L_c), Kendall's τ (L_t), or the linear interpolation of the two with weights chosen so that both losses contribute equally ($L_t + L_c$). In general, training successfully maximizes the criterion it is trained on, and $L_t + L_c$ achieves good results on both measures. We also find that L_c and $L_c + L_t$ achieve the best translation results, which is in concert with Talbot et al. (2011), who find chunk fragmentation is better correlated with translation accuracy than Kendall's τ. This is an important result, as methods such as that of Tromble and Eisner (2009) optimize pairwise word comparisons equivalent to L_t, which may not be optimal for translation.

	en-ja BLEU/RIBES		ja-en BLEU/RIBES	
ORIG	21.87	68.25	18.34	65.36
MAN-602	**23.11**	**69.86**	**19.54**	**66.93**
AUTO-602	22.39	69.19	18.58	66.07
AUTO-10K	22.53	**69.68**	18.79	**66.89**

Table 4: Results based on data size, and whether manual or automatic alignments are used in training.

6.3 Effect of Automatic Alignments

Table 4 shows the difference between using manual and automatic alignments in the training of LADER. LADER is able to improve over the ORIG baseline in all cases, but when equal numbers of manual and automatic alignments are used, the reorderer trained on manual alignments is significantly better. However, as the number of automatic alignments is increased, accuracy improves, approaching that of the system trained on a smaller number of manual alignments.

7 Conclusion

We presented a method for learning a discriminative parser to maximize reordering accuracy for machine translation. Future work includes application to other language pairs, development of more sophisticated features, investigation of probabilistic approaches to inference, and incorporation of the learned trees directly in tree-to-string translation.

Acknowledgments

We thank Isao Goto, Tetsuo Kiso, and anonymous reviewers for their helpful comments, and Daniel Flannery for helping to run his parser.

References

Satanjeev Banerjee and Alon Lavie. 2005. METEOR: An automatic metric for MT evaluation with improved correlation with human judgments. In *Proc. ACL Workshop*.

Alexandra Birch, Miles Osborne, and Phil Blunsom. 2010. Metrics for MT evaluation: evaluating reordering. *Machine Translation*, 24(1):15–26.

Marine Carpuat, Yuval Marton, and Nizar Habash. 2010. Improving arabic-to-english statistical machine translation by reordering post-verbal subjects for alignment. In *Proc. ACL*.

David Chiang. 2007. Hierarchical phrase-based translation. *Computational Linguistics*, 33(2).

Jonathan H. Clark, Chris Dyer, Alon Lavie, and Noah A. Smith. 2011. Better hypothesis testing for statistical machine translation: Controlling for optimizer instability. In *Proc. ACL*, pages 176–181.

Michael Collins, Philipp Koehn, and Ivona Kucerova. 2005. Clause restructuring for statistical machine translation. In *Proc. ACL*.

Michael Collins. 2002. Discriminative training methods for hidden markov models: Theory and experiments with perceptron algorithms. In *Proc. EMNLP*, pages 1–8.

Koby Crammer, Ofer Dekel, Joseph Keshet, Shai Shalev-Shwartz, and Yoram Singer. 2006. Online passive-aggressive algorithms. *Journal of Machine Learning Research*, 7:551–585.

John DeNero and Jakob Uszkoreit. 2011. Inducing sentence structure from parallel corpora for reordering. In *Proc. EMNLP*.

Chris Dyer and Philip Resnik. 2010. Context-free reordering, finite-state translation. In *Proc. HLT-NAACL*.

Daniel Flannery, Yusuke Miyao, Graham Neubig, and Shinsuke Mori. 2011. Training dependency parsers from partially annotated corpora. In *Proc. IJCNLP*, pages 776–784, Chiang Mai, Thailand, November.

Dmitriy Genzel. 2010. Automatically learning source-side reordering rules for large scale machine translation. In *Proc. COLING*.

Aria Haghighi, John Blitzer, John DeNero, and Dan Klein. 2009. Better word alignments with supervised ITG models. In *Proc. ACL*.

Hideki Isozaki, Tsutomu Hirao, Kevin Duh, Katsuhito Sudoh, and Hajime Tsukada. 2010a. Automatic evaluation of translation quality for distant language pairs. In *Proc. EMNLP*, pages 944–952.

Hideki Isozaki, Katsuhito Sudoh, Hajime Tsukada, and Kevin Duh. 2010b. Head finalization: A simple reordering rule for sov languages. In *Proc. WMT and MetricsMATR*.

Jason Katz-Brown, Slav Petrov, Ryan McDonald, Franz Och, David Talbot, Hiroshi Ichikawa, Masakazu Seno, and Hideto Kazawa. 2011. Training a parser for machine translation reordering. In *Proc. EMNLP*, pages 183–192.

Maurice G. Kendall. 1938. A new measure of rank correlation. *Biometrika*, 30(1/2):81–93.

Maxim Khalilov and Khalil Sima'an. 2011. Context-sensitive syntactic source-reordering by statistical transduction. In *Proc. IJCNLP*.

Dan Klein and Christopher D. Manning. 2003. Accurate unlexicalized parsing. In *Proc. ACL*, pages 423–430.

Phillip Koehn, Franz Josef Och, and Daniel Marcu. 2003. Statistical phrase-based translation. In *Proc. HLT*, pages 48–54.

Philipp Koehn, Amittai Axelrod, Alexandra Birch Mayne, Chris Callison-Burch, Miles Osborne, and David Talbot. 2005. Edinburgh system description for the 2005 IWSLT speech translation evaluation. In *Proc. IWSLT*.

Philipp Koehn, Hieu Hoang, Alexandra Birch, Chris Callison-Burch, Marcello Federico, Nicola Bertoldi, Brooke Cowan, Wade Shen, Christine Moran, Richard Zens, Chris Dyer, Ondrej Bojar, Alexandra Constantin, and Evan Herbst. 2007. Moses: Open source toolkit for statistical machine translation. In *Proc. ACL*, pages 177–180.

Philipp Koehn. 2004. Statistical significance tests for machine translation evaluation. In *Proc. EMNLP*.

Chi-Ho Li, Minghui Li, Dongdong Zhang, Mu Li, Ming Zhou, and Yi Guan. 2007. A probabilistic approach to syntax-based reordering for statistical machine translation. In *Proc. ACL*.

Percy Liang, Alexandre Bouchard-Côté, Dan Klein, and Ben Taskar. 2006. An end-to-end discriminative approach to machine translation. In *Proc. ACL*, pages 761–768.

Graham Neubig, Yosuke Nakata, and Shinsuke Mori. 2011. Pointwise prediction for robust, adaptable Japanese morphological analysis. In *Proc. ACL*, pages 529–533, Portland, USA, June.

Graham Neubig. 2011. The Kyoto free translation task. http://www.phontron.com/kftt.

Franz Josef Och. 1999. An efficient method for determining bilingual word classes. In *Proc. EACL*.

Kishore Papineni, Salim Roukos, Todd Ward, and Wei-Jing Zhu. 2002. BLEU: a method for automatic evaluation of machine translation. In *Proc. COLING*, pages 311–318.

Kay Rottmann and Stephan Vogel. 2007. Word reordering in statistical machine translation with a pos-based distortion model. In *Proc. of TMI-2007*.

Shai Shalev-Shwartz, Yoram Singer, and Nathan Srebro. 2007. Pegasos: Primal estimated subgradient solver for SVM. In *Proc. ICML*, pages 807–814.

Katsuhito Sudoh, Kevin Duh, Hajime Tsukada, Masaaki Nagata, Xianchao Wu, Takuya Matsuzaki, and Jun'ichi Tsujii. 2011a. NTT-UT statistical machine translation in NTCIR-9 PatentMT. In *Proc. NTCIR*.

Katsuhito Sudoh, Xianchao Wu, Kevin Duh, Hajime Tsukada, and Masaaki Nagata. 2011b. Post-ordering in statistical machine translation. In *Proc. MT Summit*.

David Talbot, Hideto Kazawa, Hiroshi Ichikawa, Jason Katz-Brown, Masakazu Seno, and Franz Och. 2011. A lightweight evaluation framework for machine translation reordering. In *Proc. WMT*.

Ben Taskar, Carlos Guestrin, and Daphne Koller. 2003. Max-margin Markov networks. *Proc. NIPS*, 16.

Roy Tromble and Jason Eisner. 2009. Learning linear ordering problems for better translation. In *Proc. EMNLP*.

Karthik Visweswariah, Rajakrishnan Rajkumar, Ankur Gandhe, Ananthakrishnan Ramanathan, and Jiri Navratil. 2011. A word reordering model for improved machine translation. In *Proc. EMNLP*.

Taro Watanabe, Jun Suzuki, Hajime Tsukada, and Hideki Isozaki. 2007. Online large-margin training for statistical machine translation. In *Proc. EMNLP*, pages 764–773.

Dekai Wu. 1997. Stochastic inversion transduction grammars and bilingual parsing of parallel corpora. *Computational Linguistics*, 23(3).

Fei Xia and Michael McCord. 2004. Improving a statistical MT system with automatically learned rewrite patterns. In *Proc. COLING*.

Peng Xu, Jaeho Kang, Michael Ringgaard, and Franz Och. 2009. Using a dependency parser to improve smt for subject-object-verb languages. In *Proc. NAACL*.

Kenji Yamada and Kevin Knight. 2001. A syntax-based statistical translation model. In *Proc. ACL*.

Chun-Nam John Yu and Thorsten Joachims. 2009. Learning structural SVMs with latent variables. In *Proc. ICML*, pages 1169–1176.

Yuqi Zhang, Richard Zens, and Hermann Ney. 2007. Chunk-level reordering of source language sentences with automatically learned rules for statistical machine translation. In *Proc. SSST*.

Andreas Zollmann and Ashish Venugopal. 2006. Syntax augmented machine translation via chart parsing. In *Proc. WMT*, pages 138–141.

Re-training Monolingual Parser Bilingually for Syntactic SMT

†Shujie Liu*, ‡Chi-Ho Li, ‡Mu Li and ‡Ming Zhou
†School of Computer Science and Technology
Harbin Institute of Technology, Harbin, China
shujieliu@mtlab.hit.edu.cn
‡Microsoft Research Asia, Beijing, China
{chl, muli, mingzhou}@microsoft.com

Abstract

The training of most syntactic SMT approaches involves two essential components, word alignment and monolingual parser. In the current state of the art these two components are mutually independent, thus causing problems like lack of rule generalization, and violation of syntactic correspondence in translation rules. In this paper, we propose two ways of re-training monolingual parser with the target of maximizing the consistency between parse trees and alignment matrices. One is targeted self-training with a simple evaluation function; the other is based on training data selection from forced alignment of bilingual data. We also propose an auxiliary method for boosting alignment quality, by symmetrizing alignment matrices with respect to parse trees. The best combination of these novel methods achieves 3 Bleu point gain in an IWSLT task and more than 1 Bleu point gain in NIST tasks.

1 Introduction

There are many varieties in syntactic statistical machine translation (SSMT). Apart from a few attempts to use synchronous parsing to produce the tree structure of both source language (SL) and target language (TL) simultaneously, most SSMT approaches make use of monolingual parser to produce the parse tree(s) of the SL and/or TL sentences, and then link up the information of the two languages through word alignment. In the current state of the art, word aligner and monolingual parser are trained and applied separately. On the one hand, an average word aligner does not consider the syntax information of both languages, and the output links may violate syntactic correspondence. That is, some SL words yielded by a SL parse tree node may not be traced to, via alignment links, some TL words with legitimate syntactic structure. On the other hand, parser design is a monolingual activity and its impact on MT is not well studied (Ambati, 2008). Many good translation rules may thus be filtered by a good monolingual parser.

In this paper we will focus on the translation task from Chinese to English, and the string-to-tree SSMT model as elaborated in (Galley et al., 2006). There are two kinds of translation rules in this model, minimal rules, and composed rules, which are composition of minimal rules. The minimal rules are extracted from a special kind of nodes, known as frontier nodes, on TL parse tree. The concept of frontier node can be illustrated by Figure 1, which shows two partial bilingual sentences with the corresponding TL sub-trees and word alignment links. The TL words yielded by a TL parse node can be traced to the corresponding SL words through alignment links. In the diagram, each parse node is represented by a rectangle, showing the phrase label, span, and complement span respectively. The span of a TL node N is defined as the minimal contiguous SL string that covers all the SL words reachable from N. The complement span of N is the union of spans of all the nodes that are neither descendants nor ancestors of N (c.f. Galley et al., 2006) . A frontier node is a node of which the span and the complement span do not overlap with each other. In the diagram, frontier nodes are grey in color. Frontier node is the key in the SSMT model, as it identifies the bilingual information which is consistent with both the parse tree and alignment matrix.

There are two major problems in the SSMT model. The first one is the violation of syntactic

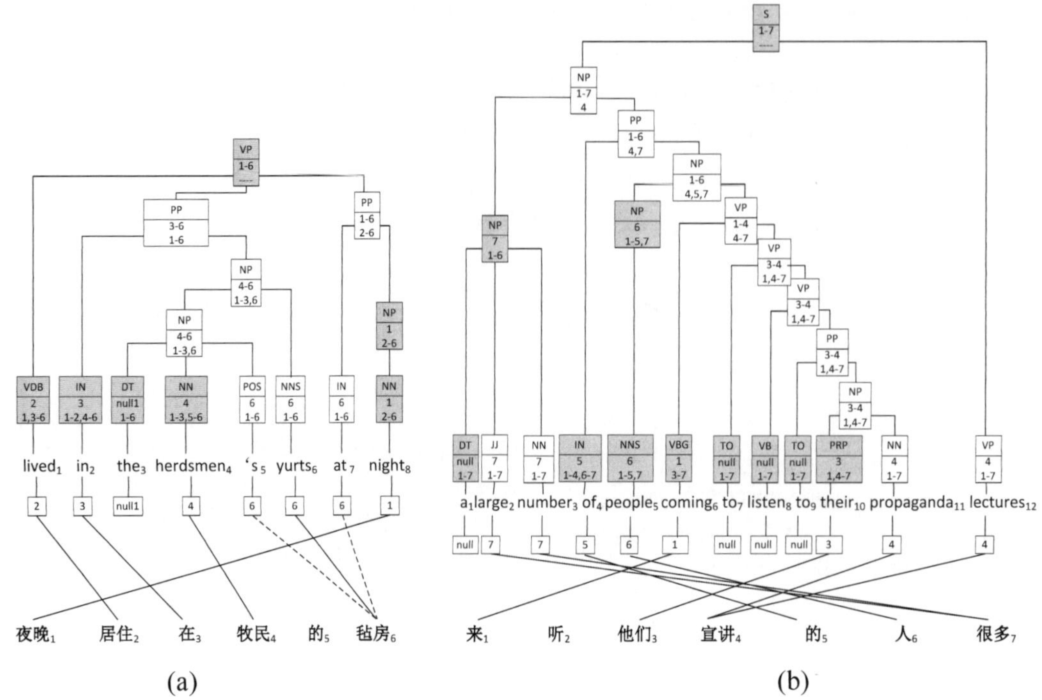

Figure 1. Two example partial bilingual sentences with word alignment and syntactic tree for the target sentence. All the nodes in gray are frontier nodes. Example (a) contains two error links (in dash line), and the syntactic tree for the target sentence of example (b) is wrong.

structure by incorrect alignment links, as shown by the two dashed links in Figure 1(a). These two incorrect links hinder the extraction of a good minimal rule "毡房→ NNS(yurts) " and that of a good composed rule "牧民, 的 → NP(DT(the), NN(herdsmen), POS('s)) ". By and large, incorrect alignment links lead to translation rules that are large in size, few in number, and poor in generalization ability (Fossum et al, 2008). The second problem is parsing error, as shown in Figure 1(b). The incorrect POS tagging of the word "lectures" causes a series of parsing errors, including the absence of the noun phrase "NP(NN(propaganda), NN(lectures))". These parsing errors hinder the extraction of good rules, such as " 宣讲 → NP(NN(propaganda), NN(lectures)) ".

Note that in Figure 1(a), the parse tree is correct, and the incorrect alignment links might be fixed if the aligner takes the parse tree into consideration. Similarly, in Figure 1(b) some parsing errors might be fixed if the parser takes into consideration the correct alignment links about "propaganda" and "lecture". That is, alignment errors and parsing might be fixed if word aligner and parser are not mutually independent.

In this paper, we emphasize more on the correction of parsing errors by exploiting alignment information. The general approach is to re-train a parser with parse trees which are the most consistent with alignment matrices. Our first strategy is to apply the idea of targeted self-training (Katz-Brown et al., 2011) with the simple evaluation function of frontier set size. That is to re-train the parser with the parse trees which give rise to the largest number of frontier nodes. The second strategy is to apply forced alignment (Wuebker et al., 2010) to bilingual data and select the parse trees generated by our SSMT system for re-training the parser. Besides, although we do not invent a new word aligner exploiting syntactic information, we propose a new method to symmetrize the alignment matrices of two directions by taking parse tree into consideration.

2 Parser Re-training Strategies

Most monolingual parsers used in SSMT are trained upon certain tree bank. That is, a parser is trained with the target of maximizing the agreement between its decision on syntactic structure and that decision in the human-annotated parse trees. As mentioned in Section 1, monolingual syntactic structure is not necessarily suitable for translation, and sometimes the bilingual information in word alignment may help the parser find out the correct structure. Therefore, it is desirable if there is a way to re-train a parser with bilingual information.

What is needed includes a framework of parser re-training, and a data selection strategy that maximizes the consistency between parse tree and alignment matrix. Our two solutions will be introduced in the next two subsections respectively.

2.1 Targeted Self-Training with Frontier Set Based Evaluation (TST-FS)

The first solution is based on targeted self-training (TST) (Katz-Brown et al., 2011). In standard self-training, the top one parse trees produced by the current parser are taken as training data for the next round, and the training objective is still the correctness of monolingual syntactic structure. In targeted self-training, the training objective shifts to certain external evaluation function. For each sentence, the n-best parse trees from the current parser are re-ranked in accordance with this external evaluation function, and the top one of the re-ranked candidates is then selected as training data for the next round. The key of targeted self-training is the definition of this external evaluation function.

As shown by the example in Figure 1(b), an incorrect parse tree is likely to hinder the extraction of good translation rules, because the number of frontier nodes in the incorrect tree is in general smaller than that in the correct tree. Consider the example in Figure 2, which is about the same partial bilingual sentence as in Figure 1(b). Although both parse trees do not have the correct syntactic structure, the tree in Figure 2 has more frontier nodes, leads to more valid translation rules, and is therefore more preferable.

This example suggests a very simple external evaluation function, viz. the size of frontier set. Given a bilingual sentence, its alignment matrix,

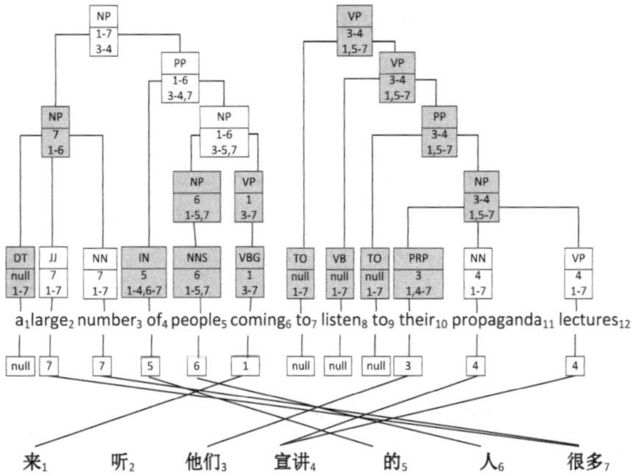

Figure 2. The parse tree selected by TST-FS for the example in Figure 1(b)

and the N-best parse trees of the TL sentence, we will calculate the number of frontier nodes for each parse tree, and re-rank the parse trees in its descending order. The new top one parse tree is selected as the training data for the next round of targeted self-training of the TL parser. In the following we will call this approach as targeted self-training with frontier set based evaluation (TST-FS).

Note that the size of the N-best list should be kept small. It is because sometimes a parse tree with an extremely mistaken structure happens to have perfect match with the alignment matrix, thereby giving rise to nearest the largest frontier set size. It is empirically found that a 5-best list of parse trees is already sufficient to significantly improve translation performance.

2.2 Forced Alignment-based Parser Re-Training (FA-PR)

If we doubt that the parse tree from a monolingual parser is not appropriate enough for translation purpose, then it seems reasonable to consider using the parse tree produced by an SSMT system to re-train the parser. A naïve idea is simply to run an SSMT system over some SL sentences and retrieve the by-product TL parse trees for re-training the monolingual parser. The biggest problem of this naïve approach is that the translation by an MT system is often a 'weird' TL sentence, and thus the associated parse tree is of little use in improving the parser.

Forced alignment (Wuebker et al., 2010) of bilingual data is a much more promising approach.

When applied to SSMT, given a bilingual sentence, it performs phrase segmentation of the SL side, parsing of the TL side, and word alignment of the bilingual sentence, using the full translation system as in decoding. It finds the best decoding path that generates the TL side of the bilingual sentence, and the parse tree of the TL sentence is also obtained as a by-product. The parse trees from forced alignment are suitable for re-training the monolingual parser.

Here is the simple iterative re-training algorithm. First we have a baseline monolingual parser and plug it into an SSMT system. Then perform forced alignment, using the SSMT system, of some bilingual data and obtain the parse trees as new training data for the parser. The new parser can then be applied again to do the second round of forced alignment. This iteration of forced alignment followed by parser re-training is kept going until some stopping criterion is met. In the following we will call this approach as forced alignment based parser re-training (FA-PR).

Algorithm 1 Forced Alignment Based Parser Re-Training (FA-PR)

- step1: $t = 0; Pars_0 = Pars_{init}$.
- step2: Use parser $Pars_t$ to parse target sentences of training data, and build a SSMT systems SYS_t.
- step3: Perform forced alignment on training data with SYS_t to get parse trees $Trees_{FAPR}$ for target sentence of training data.
- step4: Train a new parser $Pars_{FAPR}$ with $Trees_{FAPR}$.
- step5: $t = t + 1; Pars_t = Pars_{FAPR}$.
- Step6: Go to step 2, until performance of SYS_t on development data drops, or a preset limit is reached.

There are a few important implementation details of FA-PR. Forced alignment is guaranteed to obtain a parse tree if all translation rules are kept and no pruning is performed during decoding. Yet in reality an average MT system applies pruning during translation model training and decoding, and a lot of translation rules will then be discarded. In order to have more parse trees be considered by forced alignment, we keep all translation rules and relax pruning constraints in the decoder, viz.

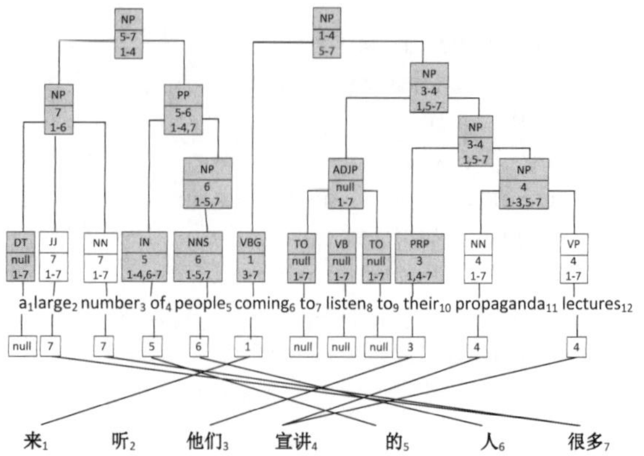

Figure 3. The parse tree selected by FA-PR for the example in Figure 1(b)

enlarge the stack size of each cell in the chart from 50 to 150.

Another measure to guarantee the existence of a decoding path in forced alignment is to allow part of a SL or TL sentence translate to null. Consider the example in Figure 1(b). We also add a null alignment for any span of the source and target sentences to handle the null translation scenario. It is easy to add a null translation candidate for a span of the source sentence during decoding, but not easy for target spans. For example, suppose the best translation candidate for the source span "来 $_1$ NP 的 $_5$ 人 $_6$ 很多 $_7$" is "a large number of people coming NP", and the best translation candidate for "听 $_2$ 他们 $_3$ 宣讲 $_4$" is "their propaganda lectures", there is no combination of candidates from two n-best translation lists which can match a sequence in the given target part, so we add a translation candidate ("to listen to ") generated from null, whose syntactic label can be any label (decided according to the translated context, which is "ADJP" here). The feature weights for the added null alignment are set to be very small, so as to avoid the competition with the normal candidates. In order to generate normal trees with not so many null alignment sub-trees for the target sentence (such trees are not suitable for parser re-training), only target spans with less than 4 words can align to null, and such null-aligned sub-tree can only be added no more than 3 times.

With all the mentioned modification of the forced alignment, the partial target tree generated using forced alignment for the example in Figure 1(b) is shown in Figure 3. We can see that even with an incorrect sub-tree, more useful rules can be extracted, compared with the baseline sub-tree and the sub-tree generated from TST-FS.

3 Word Alignment Symmetrization

The most widely used word aligners in MT, like HMM and IBM Models (Och and Ney, 2003), are directional aligners. Such aligner produces one set of alignment matrices for the SL-to-TL direction and another set for the TL-to-SL direction. Symmetrization refers to the combination of these two sets of alignment matrices.

The most popular method of symmetrization is intersect-diag-grow (IDG). Given a bilingual sentence and its two alignment matrices A_{ST} and A_{TS}, IDG starts with all the links in $A_{ST} \cap A_{TS}$. Then IDG considers each link in $A_{ST} \cup A_{TS} - (A_{ST} \cap A_{TS})$ in turn. A link is added if its addition does not make some phrase pairs overlap. Although IDG is simple and efficient, and has been shown to be effective in phrase-based SMT, it is problematic in SSMT, as illustrated by the example in section 1.

3.1 Intersect-Diag-Syntactic-Grow (IDSG)

We propose a new symmetrization method, Intersect-Diag-Syntactic-Grow (IDSG), which is an adaptation of IDG but also taking syntactic information in consideration. It is sketched in Algorithm 2.

Algorithm 2 Intersect-Diag-Syntactic-Grow

- step1: Generate all the candidate links A_{candi} using IDG.
- step2: Select the one which can generate the biggest frontier set:

$$l = \underset{l' \in A_{candi}}{\operatorname{argmax}}(frontierSize(A \cup l', Tree))$$

- step3: Add l to A, and repeat step 1, until no new link can be added.

Like IDG, IDSG starts with all the links in $A_{ST} \cap A_{TS}$ and its main task is to add links selected from $A_{candi} = A_{ST} \cup A_{TS} - (A_{ST} \cap A_{TS})$. IDSG is also subject to the constraints of IDG. The new criterion in link selection in IDSG is specified in Step 2. Given a parse tree of the TL side of the bilingual sentence, in each iteration IDSG considers the change of frontier set size caused by

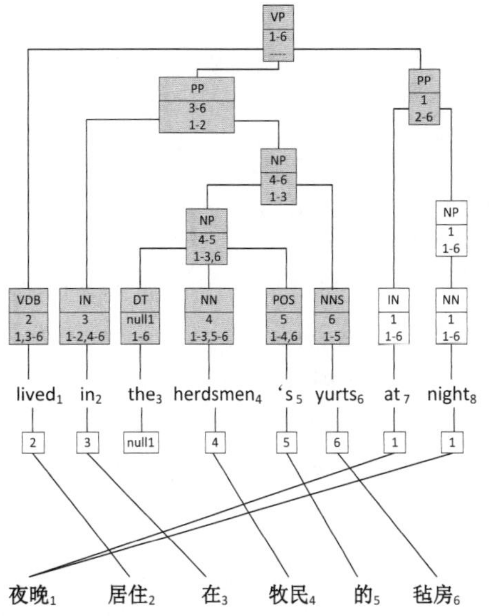

Figure 4, the alignment generated by IDSG for the example in Figure 1(a)

the addition of each link in A_{candi}. The link leading to the maximum number of frontier nodes is added (and removed from A_{candi}). This process continues until no more links can be added.

In sum, IDSG add links in an order which take syntactic structure into consideration, and the link with the least violation of the syntactic structure is added first.

For the example in Figure 1(a), IDSG succeeds in discarding the two incorrect links, and produces the final alignment and frontier set as shown in Figure 4. Note that IDSG still fails to produce the correct link (the$_3$, 牧民$_4$), since this link does not appear in A_{candi} at all.

3.2 Combining TST-FS/FA-PR and IDSG

Parser re-training aims to improve a parser with alignment matrix while IDSG aims to improve alignment matrix with parse tree. It is reasonable to combine them, and there are two alternatives of the combination, depending on the order of application. That is, we could either improve alignment matrix by IDSG and then re-train parser with the better alignment, or re-train parser and then improve alignment matrix with better syntactic information. Either alternative can be arranged into an iterative training routine, but empirically it is found that only one round of parser re-training before or after only one round of IDSG is already enough.

4 Experiment

In this section, we conduct experiments on Chinese to English translation task to test our proposed methods of parser re-training and word alignment symmetrization. The evaluation method is the case insensitive IBM BLEU-4 (Papineni et al., 2002). Significant testing is carried out using bootstrap re-sampling method proposed by Koehn (2004) with a 95% confidence level.

4.1 Parser and SMT Decoder

The syntactic parser we used in this paper is Berkley parser, with the grammar trained on WSJ corpus, and the training method follows Petrov and Klein (2007). Our SMT decoder is an in-house implementation of string-to-tree decoder. The features we used are standard used features, such as translation probabilities, lexical weights, language model probabilities and distortion probability. The feature weights are tuned using the minimum error rate training (MERT) (Och, 2003).

4.2 Experiment Data Setting and Baselines

We test our method with two data settings: one is IWSLT data set, the other is NIST data set.

	dev8+dialog	dev9
Baseline	50.58	49.85

Table 1. Baselines for IWSLT data set

	NIST'03	NIST'05	NIST'08
Baseline	37.57	36.44	24.87

Table 2. Baselines for NIST data set

Our IWSLT data is the IWSLT 2009 dialog task data set. The training data include the BTEC and SLDB training data. The training data contains 81k sentence pairs, 655k Chinese words and 806k English words. The language model is 5-gram language model trained with the English sentences in the training data. We use the combination of dev8 and dialog as development set, and dev9 as test set. The TL sentences of the training data with the selected/generated trees are used as the training data to re-train the parser. To get the baseline of this setting, we run IDG to combine the bi-direction alignment generated by Giza++ (Och Ney, 2003), and run Berkeley parser (Petrov and Klein, 2007) to parse the target sentences. With the baseline alignments and syntactic trees, we extract rules and calculate features. The baseline results are shown in Table 1.

For the NIST data set, the bilingual training data we used is NIST 2008 training set excluding the Hong Kong Law and Hong Kong Hansard. The training data contains 354k sentence pairs, 8M Chinese words and 10M English words, and is also the training data for our parser re-training. The language model is 5-gram language model trained with the Giga-Word corpus plus the English sentences in the training data. The development data to tune the feature weights of our decoder is NIST 2003 evaluation set, and test sets are NIST 2005 and 2008 evaluation sets. The baseline for NIST data is got in a similar way with for IWSLT, which are shown in Table 2 .

4.3 Results of TST-FS/ FA-PR

The parser re-training strategies TST-FS and FA-PR are tested with two baselines, one is the default parser without any re-training and another is standard self-training (SST). All three re-training approaches are based on the same bilingual datasets as used in translation model training. The MT performances on IWSLT and NIST by the four approaches are shown in Table 3 and 4 respectively.

It can be seen that just standard self-training does improve translation performance, as re-training on the TL side of bilingual data is a kind of domain adaptation (from WSJ to IWSLT/NIST). But targeted self-training achieves more noticeable improvement, almost twice as much as standard self-training. This confirms the value of word alignment information in parser re-training. Finally, the even larger improvement of FA-PR than TST-FS shows that merely increasing the number of frontier nodes is not enough. Some frontier nodes are of poor quality, and the frontier nodes found in forced alignment are more suitable.

It can also be seen that the improvement in IWSLT is larger than that in NIST. The first reason is that both WSJ and NIST are of the news domain and of formal writing style, whereas IWSLT is of the tourist domain and of colloquial style. Therefore any improvement from the default parser, which is trained on WSJ, is expected to be smaller in the NIST case. Another reason is that, since the

IWSLT dataset is much smaller, the impact of more and better rules is more obvious.

Note that the figures in Table 3 and 4 are about parser re-training for only one iteration. It is found that, more iteration do not lead to further significant improvement. The forced alignment of bilingual training data does not obtain a full decoding path for every bilingual sentence. It is because, although all translation rules are kept, there is still pruning during decoding. Only 64% of the IWSLT dataset and 53% of the NIST dataset can be successfully forced-aligned. In general, the longer the bilingual sentence, the less likely forced alignment is successful, and that is why a lower proportion of NIST can be forced-aligned.

4.4 Symmetrization

The new symmetrization method IDSG is compared with the baseline method IDG.

	dev8+dialog	dev9	# Rules
IDG	50.58	49.85	515K
IDSG	**52.71** (+2.31)	**51.80** (+2.05)	626K

Table 5. MT performance of symmetrization methods on IWSLT data set. The results in bold type are significantly better than the performance of IDG.

	NIST'03	NIST'05	NIST'08	#Rules
IDG	37.57	36.44	24.87	3,376K
IDSG	38.15 (+0.58)	**37.07** (+0.63)	**25.67** (+0.80)	4,109K

Table 6. MT performance of symmetrization methods on NIST data. The results in bold type are significantly better than the performance of IDG.

As shown by the results in Table 5 and 6, IDSG enlarges the set of translation rules by more than 20%, thereby improving translation performance significantly. As in parser re-training, the improvement in the IWSLT task is larger than that in the NIST task. Again, it is because the IWSLT dataset is very small and so the effect of rule table size is more obvious.

	dev8+dialog	dev9	# Rules
Baseline	50.58	49.85	515K
SST	**52.04** (+1.46)	**51.26** (+1.41)	574K
TST-FS	**52.75** (+2.17)	**52.51** (+2.66)	572K
FA-PR	**53.31** (+2.73)	**52.8** (+2.95)	591K

Table 3. MT performance of parser re-training strategies on IWSLT data set. The results in bold type are significantly better than the baseline.

	NIST'03	NIST'05	NIST'08	#Rules
Baseline	37.57	36.44	24.87	3,376K
SST	37.98 (+0.41)	36.79 (+0.35)	25.30 (+0.43)	3,462K
TST-FS	**38.42** (+0.85)	**37.39** (+0.95)	**25.79** (+0.92)	3,642K
FA-PR	**38.74** (+1.17)	**37.69** (+1.25)	**25.89** (+1.02)	3,976K

Table 4. MT performance of parser re-training strategies on NIST data set. The results in bold type are significantly better than the baseline.

4.5 Methods combined

As mentioned in section 3.2, parser re-training and the new symmetrization method can be combined in two different ways, depending on the order of application. Table 7 and 8 show the experiment results of combining FA-PR with IDSG.

It can be seen that either way of the combination is better than using FA-PR or IDSG alone. Yet there is no significant difference between the two kinds of combination.

The best result is a gain of more than 3 Bleu points on IWSLT and that of more than 1 Bleu point on NIST.

5 Related Works

There are a lot of attempts in improving word alignment with syntactic information (Cherry and Lin, 2006; DeNero and Klein, 2007; Hermjackob, 2009) and in improving parser with alignment information (Burkett and Klein, 2008). Yet strictly speaking all these attempts aim to improve the parser/aligner itself rather than the translation model.

To improve the performance of syntactic machine translation, Huang and Knight (2006) proposed a method incorporating a handful of relabeling strategies to modify the syntactic trees structures. Ambati and Lavie (2008) restructured target parse trees to generate highly isomorphic target trees that preserve the syntactic boundaries of constituents aligned in the original parse trees. Wang et al., (2010) proposed to use re-structuring and re-labeling to modify the parser tree. The re-structuring method uses a binarization method to enable the reuse of sub-constituent structures, and the linguistic and statistical re-labeling methods to handle the coarse nonterminal problem, so as to enhance generalization ability. Different from the previous work of modifying tree structures with post-processing methods, our methods try to learn a suitable grammar for string-to-tree SMT models, and directly produce trees which are consistent with word alignment matrices.

Instead of modifying the parse tree to improve machine translation performance, many methods were proposed to modify word alignment by taking syntactic tree into consideration, including deleting incorrect word alignment links by a discriminative model (Fossum et al., 2008), re-aligning sentence pairs using EM method with the rules extracted with initial alignment (Wang et al., 2010), and removing ambiguous alignment of functional words with constraint from chunk-level information during rule extraction (Wu et al., 2011). Unlike all these pursuits, to generate a consistent word alignment, our method modifies the popularly used IDG symmetrization method to make it suitable for string-to-tree rule extraction, and our method is much simpler and faster than the previous works.

6 Conclusion

In this paper we have attempted to improve SSMT by reducing the errors introduced by the mutual independence between monolingual parser and word aligner. Our major contribution is the strategies of re-training parser with the bilingual information in alignment matrices. Either of our proposals of targeted self-training with frontier set size as evaluation function and forced alignment based re-training is more effective than baseline parser or standard self-training of parser. As an auxiliary method, we also attempted to improve alignment matrices by a new symmetrization method.

In future, we will explore more alternatives in integrating parsing information and alignment information, such as discriminative word alignment using a lot of features from parser.

	dev8+dialog	dev9	# Rules
Baseline	50.58	49.85	515K
IDSG	**52.71** (+2.31)	**51.80** (+2.05)	626K
FA-PR	**53.31** (+2.73)	**52.8** (+2.95)	591K
IDSG then FA-PR	**53.64** (3.06)	**53.32** (+3.47)	602K
FA-PR then IDSG	**53.81** (+3.23)	**53.26** (+3.41)	597K

Table 7. MT performance of the new methods on IWSLT data set. The results in bold type are significantly better than the baseline.

	NIST'03	NIST'05	NIST'08	#Rules
Baseline	37.57	36.44	24.87	3,376K
IDSG	38.15 (+0.58)	**37.07** (+0.63)	**25.67** (+0.80)	4,109K
FA-PR	**38.74** (+1.17)	**37.69** (+1.25)	**25.89** (+1.02)	3,976K
IDSG then FA-PR	**38.97** (+1.40)	**37.95** (+1.51)	**26.74** (+1.87)	4,557K
FA-PR then IDSG	**38.90** (+1.33)	**37.94** (+1.50)	**26.52** (+1.65)	4,478K

Table 8. MT performance of the new methods on NIST data set. The results in bold type are significantly better than the baseline.

References

Vamshi Ambati and Alon Lavie. 2008. Improving syntax driven translation models by re-structuring divergent and non-isomorphic parse tree structures. In *Student Research Workshop of the Eighth Conference of the Association for Machine Translation in the Americas*, pages 235-244.

David Burkett and Dan Klein. 2008. Two languages are better than one (for syntactic parsing). In *Proceedings of the Conference on Empirical Methods on Natural Language Processing*, pages 877-886.

Colin Cherry and Dekang Lin. 2006. Soft syntactic constraints for word alignment through discriminative training. In *Proceedings of the 21st International Conference on Computational Linguistics and 44th Annual Meeting of the Association for Computational Linguistics*.

John DeNero and Dan Klein. 2007. Tailing word alignment to syntactic machine translation. In *Proceedings of the Association for Computational Linguistics*, pages 17-24.

Victoria Fossum, Kevin Knight, Steven Abney. 2008. Using syntax to improve word alignment precision for syntax-based machine translation. In *Proceedings of the Third Workshop on Statistical Machine Translation*, pages 44-52.

Michel Galley, Jonathan Graehl, Kevin Knight, Daniel Marcu, Steve Deneefe, Wei Wang and Ignacio Thayer. 2006. Scalable inference and training of context-rich syntactic translation models. In *Proceedings of the 21st International Conference on Computational Linguistics and 44th Annual Meeting of the Association for Computational Linguistics*, pages 961-968.

Ulf Hermjackob. Improved word alignment with statistics and linguistic heuristics. In *Proceedings of the Conference on Empirical Methods on Natural Language Processing*, pages 229-237.

Bryant Huang, Kevin Knight. 2006. Relabeling syntax trees to improve syntax-based machine translation quality. In *Proceedings of the Human Technology Conference of the North American Chapter of the ACL*, pages 240-247.

Jason Katz-Brown, Slav Petrov, Ryan McDonald, Franz Och, David Talbot, Hiroshi Ichikawa, Masakazu Seno, Hideto Kazawa. 2011. Training a parser for machine translation reordering. In *Proceedings of the Conference on Empirical Methods on Natural Language Processing*, pages 183-192.

Philipp Koehn. 2004. Statistical significance tests for machine translation evaluation. In *Proceedings of the Conference on Empirical Methods on Natural Language Processing*, pages 388-395.

Wei Wang, Jonathan May, Kevin Knight, Daniel Marcu. 2010. Re-structuring, re-labeling, and re-alignment for syntax-Based machine translation. *Computational Linguistics*, 36(2).

Xianchao Wu, Takuya Matsuzaki and Jun'ichi Tsujii. 2011. Effective use of function words for rule generalization in forest-based translation. In *Proceedings of the Association for Computational Linguistics*, pages 22-31.

Franz Josef Och. 2003. Minimum error rate training in statistical machine translation. In *Proceedings of the Association for Computational Linguistics*, pages 160-167.

Franz Josef Och and Hermann Ney. 2003. A systematic comparison of various statistical alignment models. *Computational Linguistics*, 29(1).

Joern Wuebker, Arne Mauser and Hermann Ney. 2010. Training phrase translation models with leaving-one-out. In *Proceedings of the Association for Computational Linguistics*, pages 475-484.

Kishore Papineni, Salim Roukos, Todd Ward and Wei-jing Zhu. 2002. BLEU: a method for automatic evaluation of machine translation. In *Proceedings of the Association for Computational Linguistics*, pages 311-318.

Slav Petrov and Dan Klein. 2007. Improved inference for unlexicalized parsing. In Proceedings of *Human Language Technologies: The Annual Conference of the North American Chapter of the Association for Computational Linguistics*, pages 404–411.

Transforming Trees to Improve Syntactic Convergence

David Burkett and **Dan Klein**
Computer Science Division
University of California, Berkeley
{dburkett,klein}@cs.berkeley.edu

Abstract

We describe a transformation-based learning method for learning a sequence of monolingual tree transformations that improve the agreement between constituent trees and word alignments in bilingual corpora. Using the manually annotated English Chinese Translation Treebank, we show how our method automatically discovers transformations that accommodate differences in English and Chinese syntax. Furthermore, when transformations are learned on automatically generated trees and alignments from the same domain as the training data for a syntactic MT system, the transformed trees achieve a 0.9 BLEU improvement over baseline trees.

1 Introduction

Monolingually, many Treebank conventions are more or less equally good. For example, the English WSJ treebank (Marcus et al., 1993) attaches verbs to objects rather than to subjects, and it attaches prepositional modifiers outside of all quantifiers and determiners. The former matches most linguistic theories while the latter does not, but to a monolingual parser, these conventions are equally learnable. However, once bilingual data is involved, such treebank conventions entail constraints on rule extraction that may not be borne out by semantic alignments. To the extent that there are simply divergences in the syntactic structure of the two languages, it will often be impossible to construct syntax trees that are simultaneously in full agreement with monolingual linguistic theories and with the alignments between sentences in both languages.

To see this, consider the English tree in Figure 1a, taken from the English side of the English Chinese Translation Treebank (Bies et al., 2007). The lowest VP in this tree is headed by 'select,' which aligns to the Chinese verb '挑选.' However, '挑选' also aligns to the other half of the English infinitive, 'to,' which, following common English linguistic theory, is outside the VP. Because of this violating alignment, many syntactic machine translation systems (Galley et al., 2004; Huang et al., 2006) won't extract any translation rules for this constituent. However, by applying a simple transformation to the English tree to set up the infinitive as its own constituent, we get the tree in Figure 1b, which may be less well-motivated linguistically, but which corresponds better to the Chinese-mediated semantics and permits the extraction of many more syntactic MT rules.

In this work, we develop a method based on *transformation-based learning* (Brill, 1995) for automatically acquiring a sequence of tree transformations of the sort in Figure 1. Once the transformation sequence has been learned, it can be deterministically applied to any parsed sentences, yielding new parse trees with constituency structures that agree better with the bilingual alignments yet remain consistent across the corpus. In particular, we use this method to learn a transformation sequence for the English trees in a set of English to Chinese MT training data. In experiments with a string-to-tree translation system, we show resulting improvements of up to 0.9 BLEU.

A great deal of research in syntactic machine translation has been devoted to handling the inherent syntactic divergence between source and target languages. Some systems attempt to model the differences directly (Yamada and Knight, 2001; Eisner, 2003), but most recent work focuses on reducing the sensitivity of the rule-extraction procedure to the constituency decisions made by 1-best syntactic parsers, either by using forest-based methods

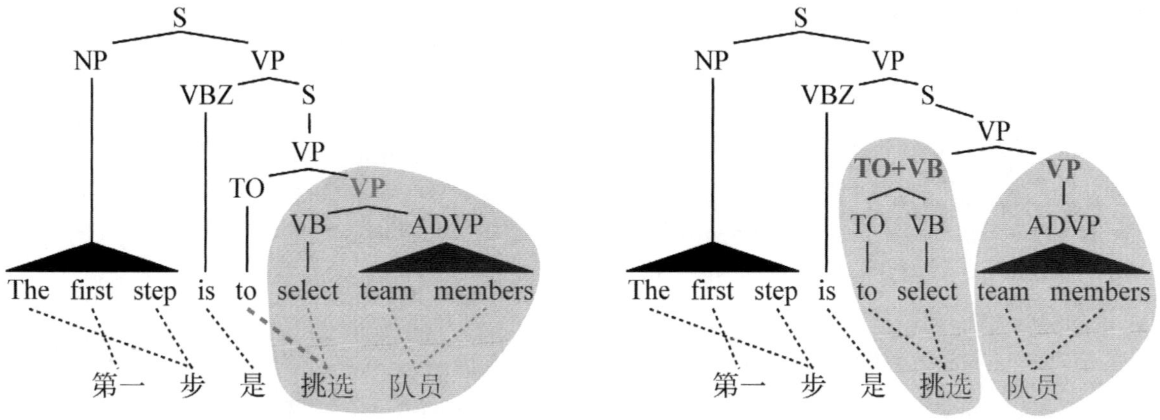

(a) Before

(b) After

Figure 1: An example tree transformation merging a VB node with the TO sibling of its parent VP. Before the transformation (a), the bolded VP cannot be extracted as a translation rule, but afterwards (b), both this VP and the newly created TO+VB node are extractable.

for learning translation rules (Mi and Huang, 2008; Zhang et al., 2009), or by learning rules that encode syntactic information but do not strictly adhere to constituency boundaries (Zollmann et al., 2006; Marton and Resnik, 2008; Chiang, 2010). The most closely related MT system is that of Zhao et al. (2011), who train a rule extraction system to transform the subtrees that make up individual translation rules using a manually constructed set of transformations similar to those learned by our system.

Instead of modifying the MT system to work around the input annotations, our system modifies the input itself in order to improve downstream translation. Most systems of this sort learn how to modify word alignments to agree better with the syntactic parse trees (DeNero and Klein, 2007; Fossum et al., 2008), but there has also been other work directly related to improving agreement by modifying the trees. Burkett et al. (2010) train a bilingual parsing model that uses bilingual agreement features to improve parsing accuracy. More closely related to the present work, Katz-Brown et al. (2011) retrain a parser to directly optimize a word reordering metric in order to improve a downstream machine translation system that uses dependency parses in a preprocessing reordering step. Our system is in the same basic spirit, using a proxy evaluation metric (agreement with alignments; see Section 2 for details) to improve performance on a downstream translation task. However, we are concerned more generally with the goal of creating trees that are more compatible with a wide range of syntactically-informed translation systems, particularly those that extract translation rules based on syntactic constituents.

2 Agreement

Our primary goal in adapting parse trees is to improve their agreement with a set of external word alignments. Thus, our first step is to define an *agreement score* metric to operationalize this concept.

Central to the definition of our agreement score is the notion of an *extractable node*. Intuitively, an extractable English[1] tree node (also often called a "frontier node" in the literature), is one whose span aligns to a contiguous span in the foreign sentence.

Formally, we assume a fixed word alignment $a = \{(i, j)\}$, where $(i, j) \in a$ means that English word i is aligned to foreign word j. For an English span $[k, \ell]$ (inclusive), the set of aligned foreign words is:

$$\textit{fset}([k, \ell]) = \{j \mid \exists\, i : k \leq i \leq \ell; (i, j) \in a\}$$

We then define the aligned foreign span as:

$$\textit{fspan}([k, \ell]) = [\min(\textit{fset}([k, \ell])), \max(\textit{fset}([k, \ell]))]$$

[1]For expositional clarity, we will refer to "English" and "foreign" sentences/trees, but our definitions are in no way language dependent and apply equally well to any language pair.

The aligned English span for a given foreign span $[s, t]$ is defined analogously:

$$eset([s,t]) = \{i \mid \exists\, j : s \leq j \leq t; (i,j) \in a\}$$
$$espan([s,t]) = [\min(eset([s,t])), \max(eset([s,t]))]$$

Finally, we define $[k, \ell]$ to be extractable if and only if it has at least one word alignment and its aligned foreign span aligns back to a subspan of $[k, \ell]$:

$$fset([k,\ell]) \neq \emptyset \wedge espan(fspan([k,\ell])) \subseteq [k,\ell]$$

With this definition of an extractable span, we can now define the agreement score $g_a(t)$ for an English tree t, conditioned on an alignment a:[2]

$$g_a(t) = \sum_{\substack{[k,\ell]\in t: \\ |[k,\ell]|>1}} sign([k,\ell]) \quad (1)$$

Where

$$sign([k,\ell]) = \begin{cases} 1 & [k,\ell] \text{ is extractable} \\ -1 & \text{otherwise} \end{cases}$$

Importantly, the sum in Equation 1 ranges over all *unique* spans in t. This is simply to make the metric less gameable, preventing degenerate solutions such as an arbitrarily long chain of unary productions over an extractable span. Also, since all individual words are generated by preterminal part-of-speech nodes, the sum skips over all length 1 spans.

As a concrete example of agreement score, we can return to Figure 1. The tree in Figure 1a has 6 unique spans, but only 5 are extractable, so the total agreement score is 5 - 1 = 4. After the transformation, though, the tree in Figure 1b has 6 extractable spans, so the agreement score is 6.

3 Transformation-Based Learning

Transformation-based learning (TBL) was originally introduced via the Brill part-of-speech tagger (Brill, 1992) and has since been applied to a wide variety of NLP tasks, including binary phrase structure bracketing (Brill, 1993), PP-attachment disambiguation (Brill and Resnik, 1994), base NP chunking (Ramshaw and Marcus, 1995), dialogue act tagging (Samuel et al., 1998), and named entity recognition (Black and Vasilakopoulos, 2002).

[2]Unextractable spans are penalized in order to ensure that space is saved for the formation of extractable ones.

The generic procedure is simple, and requires only four basic inputs: a set of training sentences, an initial state annotator, an inventory of atomic transformations, and an evaluation metric. First, you apply the initial state annotator (here, the source of original trees) to your training sentences to ensure that they all begin with a legal annotation. Then, you test each transformation in your inventory to see which one will yield the greatest improvement in the evaluation metric if applied to the training data. You greedily apply this transformation to the full training set and then repeat the procedure, applying transformations until some stopping criterion is met (usually either a maximum number of transformations, or a threshold on the marginal improvement in the evaluation metric).

The output of the training procedure is an ordered set of transformations. To annotate new data, you simply label it with the same initial state annotator and then apply each of the learned transformations in order. This process has the advantage of being quite fast (usually linear in the number of transformations and the length of the sentence; for parsing, the cost will typically be dominated by the cost of the initial state annotator), and, unlike the learned parameters of a statistical model, the set of learned transformations itself can often be of intrinsic linguistic interest.

For our task, we have already defined the evaluation metric (Section 2) and the initial state annotator will either be the gold Treebank trees or a Treebank-trained PCFG parser. Thus, to fully describe our system, it only remains to define the set of possible tree transformations.

4 Tree Transformations

The definition of an atomic transformation consists of two parts: a rewrite rule and the triggering environment (Brill, 1995). Tree transformations are best illustrated visually, and so for each of our transformation types, both parts of the definition are represented schematically in Figures 2-7. We have also included a real-world example of each type of transformation, taken from the English Chinese Translation Treebank.

Altogether, we define six types of tree transformations. Each class of transformation takes be-

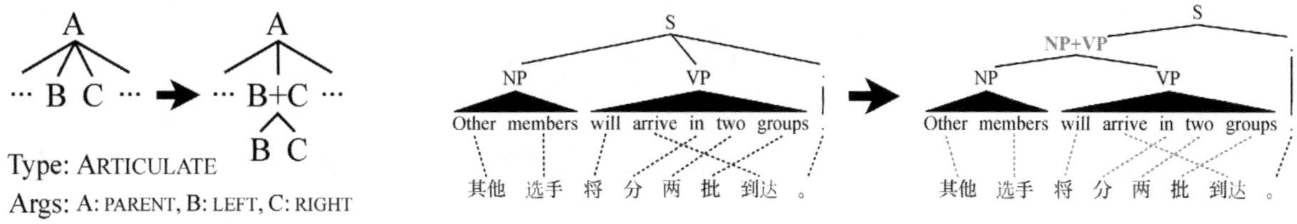

(a) Schematic

(b) Example: ARTICULATE⟨S, NP, VP⟩

Figure 2: ARTICULATE transformations.

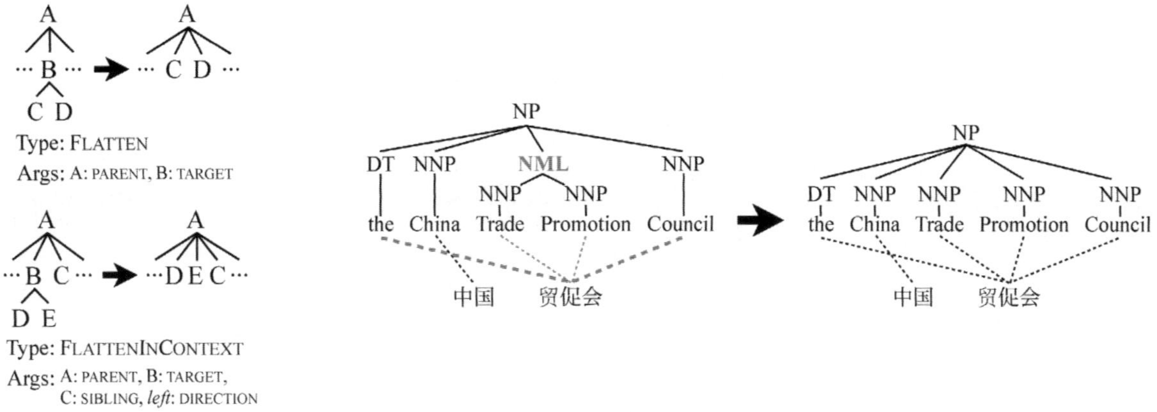

(a) Schematic

(b) Example: FLATTENINCONTEXT⟨NP, NML, NNP, *left*⟩

Figure 3: FLATTEN transformations.

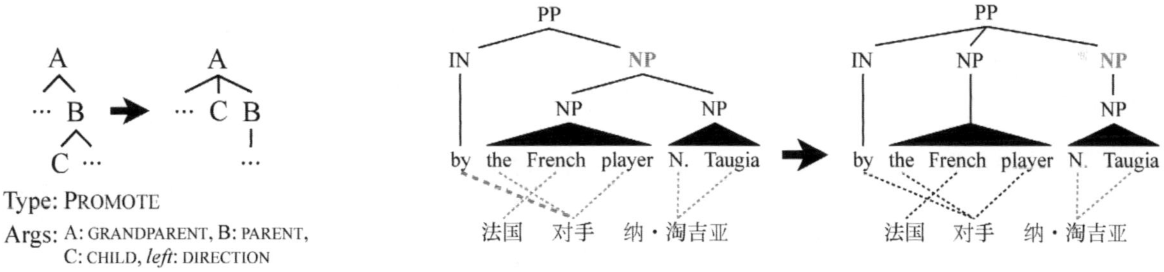

(a) Schematic

(b) Example: PROMOTE⟨PP, NP, NP, *left*⟩

Figure 4: PROMOTE transformations.

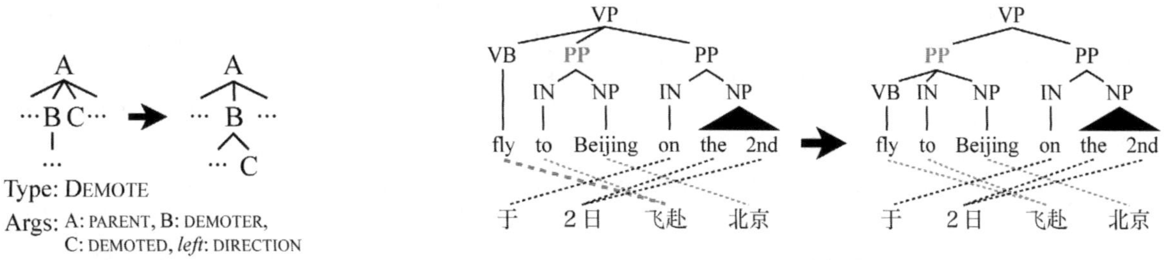

(a) Schematic

(b) Example: DEMOTE⟨VP, PP, VB, *right*⟩

Figure 5: DEMOTE transformations.

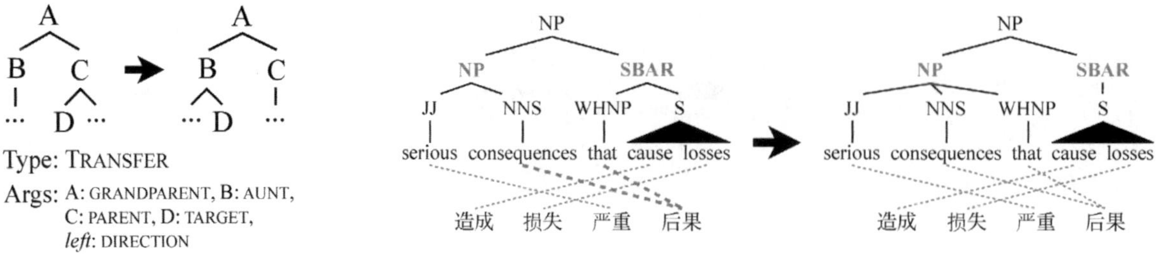

(a) Schematic

(b) Example: TRANSFER⟨NP, NP, SBAR, WHNP, *left*⟩

Figure 6: TRANSFER transformations.

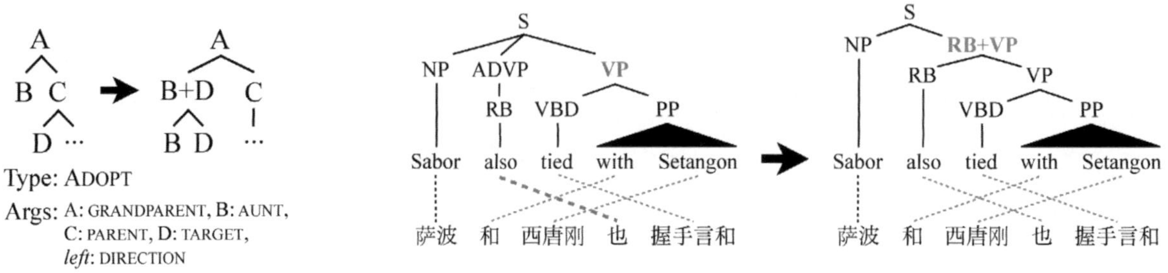

(a) Schematic

(b) Example: ADOPT⟨S, VP, ADVP, RB, *right*⟩

Figure 7: ADOPT transformations.

tween two and four syntactic category arguments, and most also take a DIRECTION argument that can have the value *left* or *right*.[3] We refer to the nodes in the schematics whose categories are arguments of the transformation definition as *participating* nodes. Basically, a particular transformation is triggered anywhere in a parse tree where all participating nodes appear in the configuration shown. The exact rules for the triggering environment are:

1. Each participating node must appear in the schematically illustrated relationship to the others. The non-participating nodes in the schematic do not have to appear. Similarly, any number of additional nodes can appear as siblings, parents, or children of the explicitly illustrated nodes.

2. Any node that will gain a new child as a result of the transformation must already have at least one nonterminal child. We have drawn the schematics to reflect this, so this condition is equivalent to saying that any participating node that is drawn with children must have a phrasal syntactic category (i.e. it cannot be a POS).

3. Repeated mergings are not allowed. That is, the newly created nodes that result from an ARTICULATE or ADOPT transformation cannot then participate as the LEFT or RIGHT argument of a subsequent ARTICULATE transformation or as the AUNT or TARGET argument of a subsequent ADOPT transformation. This is simply to prevent the unrestrained proliferation of new syntactic categories.

The rewrite rule for a transformation is essentially captured in the corresponding schematic. Additional nodes that do not appear in the schematic are generally handled in the obvious way: unillustrated children or parents of illustrated nodes remain in place, while unillustrated siblings of illustrated nodes are handled identically to their illustrated siblings. The only additional part of the rewrite that is not shown explicitly in the schematics is that if the node in the PARENT position of a TRANSFER or ADOPT transformation is left childless by the transformation (be-

[3]To save space, the schematic for each of these transformations is only shown for the *left* direction, but the *right* version is simply the mirror image.

cause the TARGET node was its only child), then it is deleted from the parse tree. In the case of a transformation whose triggering environment appears multiple times in a single tree, transformations are always applied leftmost/bottom-up and exhaustively.[4]

In principle, our transformation inventory consists of all possible assignments of syntactic categories to the arguments of each of the transformation types (subject to the triggering environment constraints). In practice, though, we only ever consider transformations whose triggering environments appear in the training corpus (including new triggering environments that appear as the result of earlier transformations). While the theoretical space of possible transformations is exponentially large, the set of transformations we actually have to consider is quite manageable, and empirically grows substantially sublinearly in the size of the training set.

5 Results and Analysis

There are two ways to use this procedure. One is to apply it to the entire data set, with no separate training phase. Given that the optimization has no notion of gold transformations, this procedure is roughly like an unsupervised learner that clusters its entire data. Another way is to learn annotations on a subset of data and apply it to new data. We choose the latter primarily for reasons of efficiency and simplicity: many common use cases are easiest to manage when annotation systems can be trained once offline and then applied to new data as it comes in.

Since we intend for our system to be used as a pre-trained annotator, it is important to ensure that the learned transformation sequence achieves agreement score gains that generalize well to unseen data. To minimize errors that might be introduced by the noise in automatically generated parses and word alignments, and to maximize reproducibility, we conducted our initial experiments on the English Chinese Translation Treebank. For this dataset, the initial state annotations (parse trees) were manually created by trained human annotators, as were the word alignments used to compute the agreement score.[5] The data was divided into training/dev/test using the standard Chinese parsing split; we trained the system on the training set (2261 sentences after filtering out sentences with missing annotations), and evaluated on the development set (223 sentences after filtering).

The improvements in agreement score are shown in Figure 8, with a slightly more detailed breakdown at a few fixed points in Table 1. While the system was able to find up to 2471 transformations that improved the training set agreement score, the majority of the improvement, and especially the majority of the improvement that generalized to the test set,

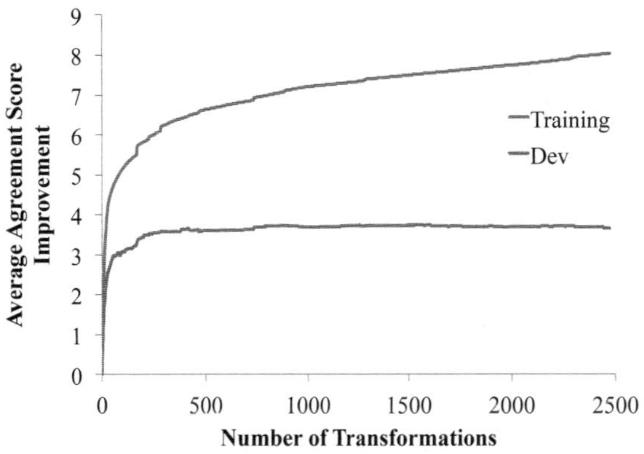

Figure 8: Transformation results on the English Chinese Translation Treebank. The value plotted is the average (per-sentence) improvement in agreement score over the baseline trees.

Transformations	Total Spans	Extractable Spans	Agreement Score
0	13.15	9.78	6.40
10	12.57	10.36	8.15
50	13.41	11.38	9.35
200	14.03	11.96	9.89
1584	14.58	12.36	10.15
2471	14.65	12.35	10.06

Table 1: Average span counts and agreement scores on the English Chinese Translation Treebank development set. The highest agreement score was attained at 1584 transformations, but most of the improvement happened much earlier.

[4] The transformation is repeatedly applied at the lowest, leftmost location of the parse tree where the triggering environment appears, until the triggering environment no longer appears anywhere in the tree.

[5] The annotation guidelines for the English side of this Treebank are similar, though not identical, to those for the WSJ Treebank.

1	ARTICULATE⟨S,NP,VP⟩
2	FLATTENINCONTEXT⟨PP,NP,IN,*right*⟩
3	PROMOTE⟨VP,VP,VBN,*left*⟩
4	ADOPT⟨VP,TO,VP,VB,*left*⟩
5	ADOPT⟨PP,VBG,PP,IN,*left*⟩
6	FLATTEN⟨VP,VP⟩
7	ARTICULATE⟨VP,VBD,NP⟩
8	FLATTENINCONTEXT⟨PP,NML,NNP,*left*⟩
9	ARTICULATE⟨NP,NNP,NNS⟩
10	ARTICULATE⟨S,NP,ADVP⟩
11	TRANSFER⟨NP,NP,SBAR,WHNP,*left*⟩
12	FLATTENINCONTEXT⟨NP,NML,NNP,*left*⟩
13	ARTICULATE⟨NP,NN,NNS⟩
14	TRANSFER⟨NP,NP+,,SBAR,WHNP,*left*⟩
15	ADOPT⟨PP,IN,PP,IN,*left*⟩
16	PROMOTE⟨S,VP,CC+VP,*right*⟩
17	ARTICULATE⟨VP,VBZ,VBN⟩
18	ARTICULATE⟨VP,VBD,PP⟩
19	ARTICULATE⟨VP,MD,ADVP⟩
20	ADOPT⟨PP,SYM,QP,CD,*right*⟩

Table 2: The first 20 learned transformations, excluding those that only merged punctuation or conjunctions with adjacent phrases. The first 5 are illustrated in Figure 9.

was achieved within the first 200 or so transformations. We also see from Table 1 that, though the first few transformations deleted many non-extractable spans, the overall trend was to produce more finely articulated trees, with the full transformation sequence increasing the number of spans by more than 10%.

As discussed in Section 3, one advantage of TBL is that the learned transformations can themselves often be interesting. For this task, some of the highest scoring transformations did uninteresting things like conjoining conjunctions or punctuation, which are often either unaligned or aligned monotonically with adjacent phrases. However, by filtering out all ARTICULATE transformations where either the LEFT or RIGHT argument is "CC", "-RRB-", ",", or "." and taking the top 20 remaining transformations, we get the list in Table 2, the first 5 of which are also illustrated in Figure 9. Some of these (e.g. #1, #7, #10) are additional ways of creating new spans when English and Chinese phrase structures roughly agree, but many others do recover known differences in English and Chinese syntax. For example, many of these transformations directly address compound verb forms in English, which tend to align to single words in Chinese: #3 (past participle constructions), #4 (infinitive), #6 (all), and #17 (present perfect). We also see differences between English and Chinese internal NP structure (e.g. #9, #12, #13).

6 Machine Translation

The ultimate goal of our system is to improve the agreement between the automatically generated parse trees and word alignments that are used as training data for syntactic machine translation systems. Given the amount of variability between the outputs of different parsers and word aligners (or even the same systems with different settings), the best way to improve agreement is to learn a transformation sequence that is specifically tuned for the same annotators (parsers and word aligners) we are evaluating with. In particular, we found that though training on the English Chinese Translation Treebank produces clean, interpretable rules, preliminary experiments showed little to no improvement from using these rules for MT, primarily because actual alignments are not only noisier but also systematically different from gold ones. Thus, all rules used for MT experiments were learned from automatically annotated text.

For our Chinese to English translation experiments, we generated word alignments using the Berkeley Aligner (Liang et al., 2006) with default settings. We used an MT pipeline that conditions on target-side syntax, so our initial state annotator was the Berkeley Parser (Petrov and Klein, 2007), trained on a modified English treebank that has been adapted to match standard MT tokenization and capitalization schemes.

As mentioned in Section 5, we could, in principle train on all 500k sentences of our MT training data. However, this would be quite slow: each iteration of the training procedure requires iterating through all n training sentences[6] once for each of the m candidate transformations, for a total cost of $O(nm)$ where m grows (albeit sublinearly) with n. Since the

[6]By using a simple hashing scheme to keep track of triggering environments, this cost can be reduced greatly but is still linear in the number of training sentences.

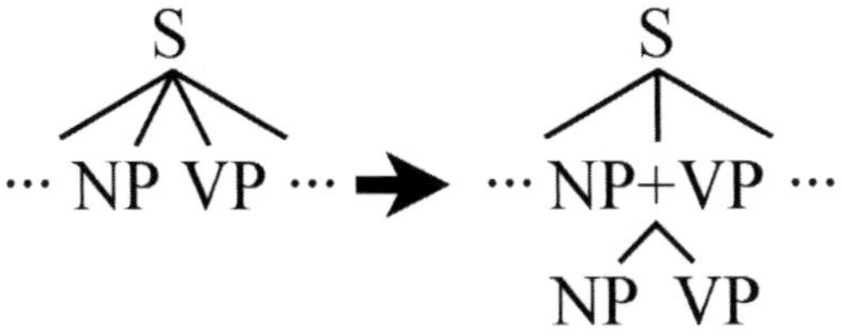

(a) ARTICULATE⟨S,NP,VP⟩

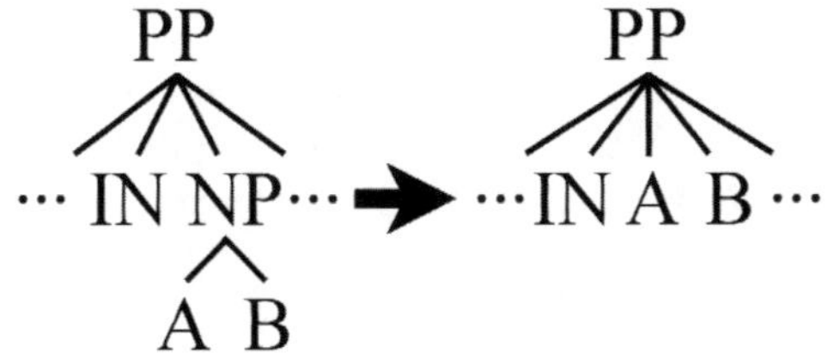

(b) FLATTENINCONTEXT⟨PP,NP,IN,*right*⟩

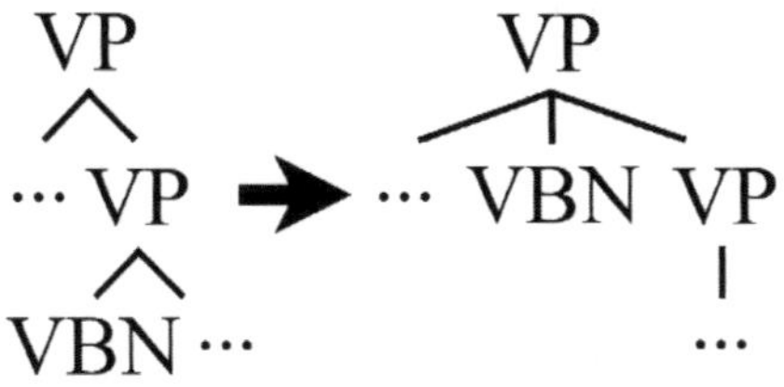

(c) PROMOTE⟨VP,VP,VBN,*left*⟩

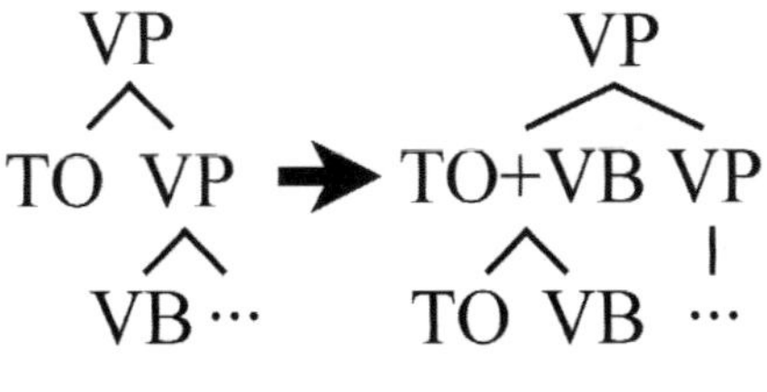

(d) ADOPT⟨VP,TO,VP,VB,*left*⟩

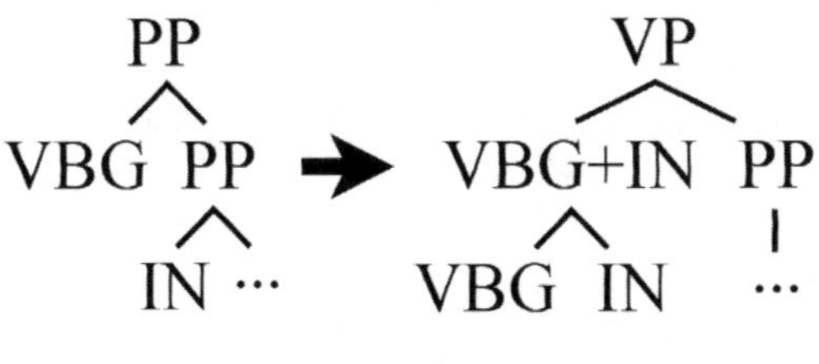

(e) ADOPT⟨PP,VBG,PP,IN,*left*⟩

Figure 9: Illustrations of the top 5 transformations from Table 2.

most useful transformations almost by definition are ones that are triggered the most frequently, any reasonably sized training set is likely to contain them, and so it is not actually likely that dramatically increasing the size of the training set will yield particularly large gains.

Thus, to train our TBL system, we extracted a random subset of 3000 sentences to serve as a training set.[7] We also extracted an additional 1000 sentence test set to use for rapidly evaluating agreement score generalization. Figure 10 illustrates the improvements in agreement score for the automatically annotated data, analogous to Figure 8. The same general patterns hold, although we do see that the automatically annotated data is more idiosyncratic and so more than twice as many transformations are learned before training set agreement stops improving, even though the training set sizes are roughly the same.[8] Furthermore, test set generalization in the automatic annotation setting is a little bit worse, with later transformations tending to actually hurt test set agreement.

For our machine translation experiments, we used the string-to-tree syntactic pipeline included in the current version of Moses (Koehn et al., 2007). Our training bitext was approximately 21.8 million words, and the sentences and word alignments were the same for all experiments; the only difference between each experiment was the English trees, for which we tested a range of transformation sequence prefixes (including a 0-length prefix, which just yields the original trees, as a baseline). Since the transformed trees tended to be more finely articulated, and increasing the number of unique spans often helps with rule extraction (Wang et al., 2007), we equalized the span count by also testing binarized versions of each set of trees, using the left-branching and right-branching binarization scripts included with Moses.[9]

We tuned on 1000 sentence pairs and tested on

[7] The sentences were shorter on average than those in the English Chinese Translation Treebank, so this training set contains roughly the same number of words as that used in the experiments from Section 5.

[8] Note that the training set improvement curves don't actually flatten out because training halts once no improving transformation exists.

[9] Binarized trees are guaranteed to have $k-1$ unique spans for sentences of length k.

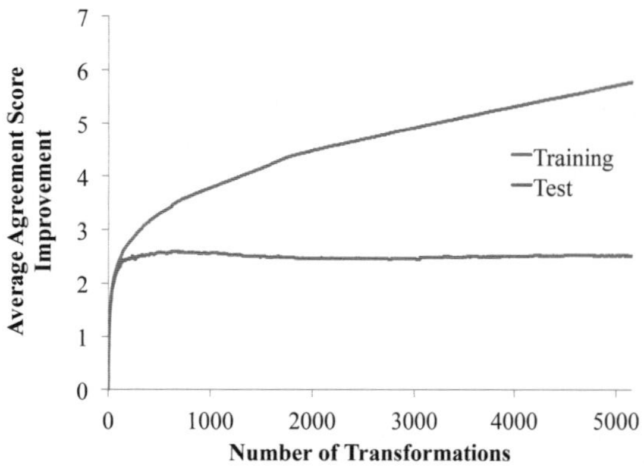

Figure 10: Transformation results on a subset of the MT training data. The training and test sets are disjoint in order to measure how well the learned transformation sequence generalizes. Once again, we plot the average improvement over the baseline trees. Though 5151 transformations were learned from the training set, the maximum test set agreement was achieved at 630 transformations, with an average improvement of 2.60.

642 sentence pairs from the NIST MT04 and MT05 data sets, using the BLEU metric (Papineni et al., 2001). As discussed by Clark et al. (2011), the optimizer included with Moses (MERT, Och, 2003) is not always particularly stable, and results (even on the tuning set) can vary dramatically across tuning runs. To mitigate this effect, we first used the Moses training scripts to extract a table of translation rules for each set of English trees. Then, for each rule table, we ran MERT 11 times and selected the parameters that achieved the maximum tuning BLEU to use for decoding the test set.

Table 3 shows the results of our translation experiments. The best translation results are achieved by using the first 139 transformations, giving a BLEU improvement of more than 0.9 over the strongest baseline.

7 Conclusion

We have demonstrated a simple but effective procedure for learning a tree transformation sequence that improves agreement between parse trees and word alignments. This method yields clear improvements in the quality of Chinese to English translation, showing that by manipulating English syntax to converge with Chinese phrasal structure, we improve our ability to explicitly model the types of

Transformations	Agrmnt Score	BLEU		
		None	Left	Right
0	5.36	31.66	31.81	31.84
32	7.17	32.41	32.17	32.06
58	7.42	32.18	32.68*	32.37
139	7.81	32.20	32.60*	**32.77***
630	7.96	32.48	32.06	32.22
5151	7.89	32.13	31.84	32.12

Table 3: Machine translation results. Agreement scores are taken from the test data used to generate Figure 10. Note that using 0 transformations just yields the original baseline trees. The transformation sequence cutoffs at 32, 58, and 139 were chosen to correspond to marginal training (total) agreement gain thresholds of 50, 25, and 10, respectively. The cutoff at 630 was chosen to maximize test agreement score and the cutoff at 5151 maximized training agreement score. Column headings for BLEU scores ("None," "Left," "Right") refer to the type of binarization used after transformations. Entries marked with a '*' show a statistically significant difference ($p < 0.05$) from the strongest (right-binarized) baseline, according to the paired bootstrap (Efron and Tibshirani, 1994).

structural relationships between languages that syntactic MT systems are designed to exploit, even if we lose some fidelity to the original monolingual annotation standards in the process.

Acknowledgements

This project is funded by an NSF graduate research fellowship to the first author and by BBN under DARPA contract HR0011-12-C-0014.

References

Ann Bies, Martha Palmer, Justin Mott, and Colin Warner. 2007. English Chinese translation treebank v 1.0. Web download. LDC2007T02.

William J. Black and Argyrios Vasilakopoulos. 2002. Language independent named entity classification by modified transformation-based learning and by decision tree induction. In *COLING*.

Eric Brill and Philip Resnik. 1994. A transformation-based approach to prepositional phrase attachment disambiguation. In *COLING*.

Eric Brill. 1992. A simple rule-based part of speech tagger. In *Proceedings of the workshop on Speech and Natural Language*.

Eric Brill. 1993. Automatic grammar induction and parsing free text: A transformation-based approach. In *ACL*.

Eric Brill. 1995. Transformation-based error-driven learning and natural language processing: a case study in part-of-speech tagging. *Computational Linguistics*, 21(4):543–565.

David Burkett, John Blitzer, and Dan Klein. 2010. Joint parsing and alignment with weakly synchronized grammars. In *NAACL:HLT*.

David Chiang. 2010. Learning to translate with source and target syntax. In *ACL*.

Jonathan H. Clark, Chris Dyer, Alon Lavie, and Noah A. Smith. 2011. Better hypothesis testing for statistical machine translation: controlling for optimizer instability. In *ACL:HLT*.

John DeNero and Dan Klein. 2007. Tailoring word alignments to syntactic machine translation. In *ACL*.

Bradley Efron and R. J. Tibshirani. 1994. *An Introduction to the Bootstrap (Chapman & Hall/CRC Monographs on Statistics & Applied Probability)*. Chapman and Hall/CRC.

Jason Eisner. 2003. Learning non-isomorphic tree mappings for machine translation. In *ACL*.

Victoria Fossum, Kevin Knight, and Steven Abney. 2008. Using syntax to improve word alignment for syntax-based statistical machine translation. In *ACL MT Workshop*.

Michel Galley, Mark Hopkins, Kevin Knight, and Daniel Marcu. 2004. What's in a translation rule? In *HLT-NAACL*.

Liang Huang, Kevin Knight, and Aravind Joshi. 2006. Statistical syntax-directed translation with extended domain of locality. In *HLT-NAACL*.

Jason Katz-Brown, Slav Petrov, Ryan McDonald, Franz Och, David Talbot, Hiroshi Ichikawa, Masakazu Seno, and Hideto Kazawa. 2011. Training a parser for machine translation reordering. In *EMNLP*.

Philipp Koehn, Hieu Hoang, Alexandra Birch, Chris Callison-Burch, Marcello Federico, Nicola Bertoldi, Brooke Cowan, Wade Shen, Christine Moran, Richard Zens, Chris Dyer, Ondrej Bojar, Alexandra Constantin, and Evan Herbst. 2007. Moses: Open source toolkit for statistical machine translation. In *ACL*.

Percy Liang, Ben Taskar, and Dan Klein. 2006. Alignment by agreement. In *HLT-NAACL*.

Mitchell P. Marcus, Mary Ann Marcinkiewicz, and Beatrice Santorini. 1993. Building a large annotated corpus of English: The Penn Treebank. *Computational Linguistics*, 19(2):313–330.

Yuval Marton and Philip Resnik. 2008. Soft syntactic constraints for hierarchical phrase-based translation. In *ACL:HLT*.

Haitao Mi and Liang Huang. 2008. Forest-based translation rule extraction. In *EMNLP*.

Franz Josef Och. 2003. Miminal error rate training in statistical machine translation. In *ACL*.

Kishore Papineni, Salim Roukos, Todd Ward, and Wei-Jing Zhu. 2001. Bleu: a method for automatic evaluation of machine translation. Research report, IBM. RC22176.

Slav Petrov and Dan Klein. 2007. Improved inference for unlexicalized parsing. In *HLT-NAACL*.

Lance A. Ramshaw and Mitchell P. Marcus. 1995. Text chunking using transformation-based learning. In *ACL Workshop on Very Large Corpora*.

Ken Samuel, Sandra Carberry, and K. Vijay-Shanker. 1998. Dialogue act tagging with transformation-based learning. In *COLING*.

Wei Wang, Kevin Knight, and Daniel Marcu. 2007. Binarizing syntax trees to improve syntax-based machine translation accuracy. In *EMNLP*.

Kenji Yamada and Kevin Knight. 2001. A syntax-based statistical translation model. In *ACL*.

Hui Zhang, Min Zhang, Haizhou Li, Aiti Aw, and Chew Lim Tan. 2009. Forest-based tree sequence to string translation model. In *ACL-IJCNLP*.

Bing Zhao, Young-Suk Lee, Xiaoqiang Luo, and Liu Li. 2011. Learning to transform and select elementary trees for improved syntax-based machine translations. In *ACL:HLT*.

Andreas Zollmann, Ashish Venugopal, Stephan Vogel, and Alex Waibel. 2006. The CMU-AKA syntax augmented machine translation system for IWSLT-06. In *IWSLT*.

Learning Constraints for Consistent Timeline Extraction

David McClosky and Christopher D. Manning
Natural Language Processing Group
Computer Science Department
Stanford University, Stanford, CA, USA
{mcclosky,manning}@stanford.edu

Abstract

We present a distantly supervised system for extracting the temporal bounds of *fluents* (relations which only hold during certain times, such as *attends school*). Unlike previous pipelined approaches, our model does not assume independence between each fluent or even between named entities with known connections (parent, spouse, employer, etc.). Instead, we model what makes timelines of fluents consistent by learning cross-fluent constraints, potentially spanning entities as well. For example, our model learns that someone is unlikely to start a job at age two or to marry someone who hasn't been born yet. Our system achieves a 36% error reduction over a pipelined baseline.

1 Introduction

Many information extraction (IE) systems traditionally extracted just relations, but a great many real world relations such as *attends school* or *has spouse* vary over time. To capture this, some recent IE systems have extended their focus from relations to *fluents* (relations combined with temporal bounds). This can be seen in the temporal slot filling track in the TAC-KBP 2011 shared task (Ji et al., 2011). A direct application of this work is the automatic improvement of online resources such as Freebase and Wikipedia infoboxes. Indirect applications include question answering systems.

Fluents can be grouped together to form timelines (see Figure 1 for an example) and provide easily capturable consistency constraints. Our goal is

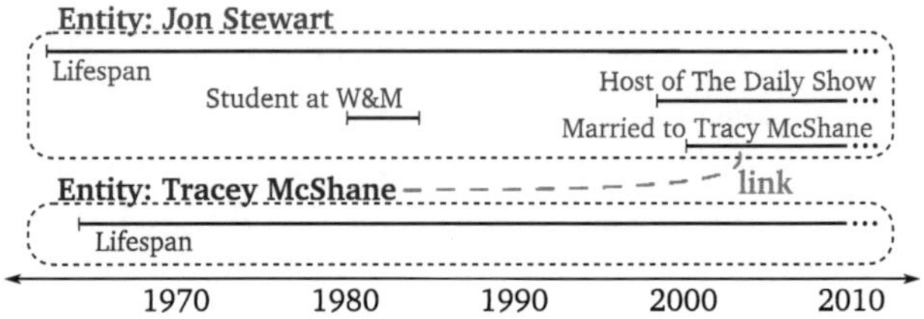

Figure 1: A timeline of two named entities. Each time span represents a *fluent* (a relation with temporal bounds). Temporal bounds are denoted by spans on the timeline. Fluents can create links between entities (e.g., marriage).

to learn these constraints and use them to produce more accurate timelines of significant events for people and organizations. For example, it is common knowledge that someone cannot attend a school if they haven't been born yet. Constraints on consistent timelines do not need to be hard constraints, though: it is rare, although possible, to become the CEO of a company at the age of 21.

Despite the rich constraints on valid timelines, there is relatively little work on exploiting these constraints for mutual disambiguation. Many existing systems extract different parts of a timeline separately and use heuristics to combine them. These heuristics tend to optimize only local consistency (within a single fluent) but ignore more global constraints across fluents (e.g., attending a school before being born) or across fluents of two linked entities (e.g., attending a school before the school was founded). In this work, we explore using joint inference to enforce these constraints. We show that these techniques can yield substantial improvements. Additionally, our general approach is not specific to extracting temporal boundaries of fluents. It could easily be applied to other IE systems which employ independent extractions followed by heuristics to improve consistency.

2 The timelining task

As a basis for our task, we first describe the Temporal KBP task (Ji et al., 2011). As input, one is given a list of *queries*, a database of example fluents, and source documents. Queries are named entities (people or organizations) with their gold relations but no temporal bounds. The database consists of training entities with their fluents, including known temporal bounds for each fluent. Example fluents can be seen in Table 1. Note that the database may be incomplete. In addition to missing fluents for an entity, some temporal bounds may be missing from the database; missing bounds are unfortunately indistinguishable from unbounded ranges. As a result, we can only trust concrete temporal boundaries in the database. Source documents consist of raw text from news, blogs, and Wikipedia articles. For each fluent, systems must output their predicted temporal bounds, along with references to source documents to provide provenance.

Our task is a variation of the Temporal KBP task. In our case, the database is a collection of Freebase[1] entities and their fluents, merged with Wikipedia infoboxes. Each entity has a unique ID, allowing us to avoid some coreference issues (though there can still be issues in document retrieval). In Temporal KBP, the temporal representation allows for upper and lower bounds on both the event start and end: $\langle s_l, s_u, e_l, e_u \rangle$ where $s_l \leq start \leq s_u$, $e_l \leq end \leq e_u$. However, it is difficult to obtain these bounds without manual annotation. As a result, we opted for the simpler representation which can be easily found in databases like Freebase. Our temporal representation is limited to bounds of the form $\langle start, end \rangle$ where either can be unbounded or unknown (both represented as $\pm\infty$).

Our set of fluents is closely related to those in the Temporal KBP task. Our goal was to use as much temporal information as possible, with the hope of each fluent providing additional potential constraints. While we omit the *resides in* and *member of* fluents,[2] we add several others. For people and organizations, we add a special fluent, *lifespan*, which doesn't take a slot value.[3] A list of fluents we use are listed in Table 3.

3 Model

To operate on a set of queries, we first collect candidate temporal expression mentions for each fluent from our source documents. This limits us to using temporal expression mentions which appear near fluent mentions in text. It also ensures that we can provide provenance for each temporal boundary assertion. This process is described in §3.1.

Our model contains two components, both of which assign probabilities to timelines. The *classifier component* determines how each candidate temporal expression mention connects to its fluent (§3.2). For example, the mention may indicate the START of the fluent, the END, both its START AND END (for instantaneous events), or be UNRELATED. These connections involve relations between temporal expression mentions and relations and we refer to them as *metarelations*.[4] For features, the classifier uses the surrounding textual and syntactic context of temporal expression and fluent mentions. Each classification decision is made independently, allowing for inconsistency at multiple levels (within a fluent, across fluents, or across entities). However, using joint inference, the classifier component can determine the best overall span for each fluent.

The *consistency component* learns what makes timelines consistent (§3.3). It is similar in nature to a language model for timelines instead of sentences. Given a candidate timeline, the consistency component estimates its probability of occurring. This is done by decomposing timelines into a series of *questions* (such as "did the entity go to school before starting a job?") and learning the probabilities of different answers from training data.

Unlike the classifier component, the consistency component is blind to the underlying text in the source documents. The two components work together to find a global timeline that is both based on textual evidence and coherent across entities using

[1] `http://freebase.org`

[2] This is because these fluents are rarely present in Freebase with temporal bounds.

[3] Note that this is a relation in the non-temporal KBP task.

[4] Other metarelations are possible under more complex temporal representations. For example, Artiles et al. (2011) uses the HOLDS metarelation.

Entity	Relation	Slot value	Temporal bounds
Jon Stewart `/en/jon_stewart`	*lifespan*	—	[1962-11-28, $+\infty$)
Jon Stewart `/en/jon_stewart`	*has parent*	Donald Leibowitz `/en/donald_leibowitz`	[1962-11-28, $+\infty$)
Jon Stewart `/en/jon_stewart`	*attends school*	College of William and Mary `/en/college_of_william_and_mary`	($-\infty$, 1984]
Jon Stewart `/en/jon_stewart`	*has spouse*	Tracey McShane `/en/tracy_mcshane`	[2000-11, $+\infty$)

Table 1: Example relations with their temporal bounds. Freebase IDs are shown in `monospace`. Note that temporal bounds differ in their resolution (some are days of the year, others are only years). Some bounds are unknown (e.g., the start of the *attends school* fluent) and indistinguishable from unbounded. The *lifespan* fluent is a unary relation.

joint inference (note that they are trained independently). The inference process is described in §3.4.

3.1 Temporal expression retrieval

Given a fluent, we search for all textual mentions of the fluent and collect nearby temporal expression mentions. These temporal expressions are used as candidate boundaries for the fluent in later steps. The search process assumes that if a fluent's entity and slot value co-occur in a sentence,[5] that sentence is typically a positive example of the fluent.[6] This is sometimes known as *distant supervision* (Craven and Kumlien, 1999; Mintz et al., 2009). We use the Stanford Core NLP suite (Toutanova et al., 2003; Finkel et al., 2005; Klein and Manning, 2003; Lee et al., 2011) to annotate each document with POS and NER tags, parse trees, and coreference chains. On top of this, we apply a rule-based temporal expression extractor (Chang and Manning, 2012). Since we have coreference links, we also search documents for anything coreferent with the fluent's entity.

The temporal expression extractor handles most standard date and time formats. For each document, one can provide an optional reference time. For underspecified dates, the reference time is used to resolve these dates to full expressions if possible. Some of our documents are news articles, where we use the publication date as the reference time. Other documents, e.g., Wikipedia articles, are undated and we typically omit a reference time for these. We exclude dates which are not uniquely resolvable (e.g., "September 15th," when the reference date is unknown) since our task requires us to output unambiguous dates.

We create training datums by computing the metarelation between each temporal expression and its gold fluent. For example, for the temporal expression mention "September 15th, 1981" and gold *lifespan* relation that spans [`1981-09-15`, $+\infty$), we would assign the START metarelation. As a heuristic, we allow for underspecified matches. Thus, both "1981" and "September 1981" would have the START metarelation but "September 2nd, 1981" would be assigned UNRELATED.

3.2 Classifier component

We use a classifier to determine the nature of the link between fluents and candidate temporal expression mentions. Our classifier (a standard multiclass maximum entropy classifier) learns a function $C : (t, f) \rightarrow \mathcal{M}$ where t is a temporal expression mention, $f = \langle$entity, relation name, slot value$\rangle$ is a fluent from the database, and $\mathcal{M}$ is the set of the four possible metarelations.

Features for the classifier include many of those in Artiles et al. (2011). These include standard relation extraction features such as the dependency paths between the temporal expression and the entity or slot value. We use both the original depen-

[5]While we limit our scope to sentences in this work, it is trivial to extend this to larger regions such as paragraphs.

[6]The *lifespan* fluent requires special handling. Ideally, its candidates would be provided by a relation extraction mention detector (e.g., a KBP system). For this work, we use the gold *lifespan* bounds as slot values for the purpose of document retrieval. While this does heavily bias the system towards using gold bounds, the system still must predict the correct associations (START, END, etc.) making the *lifespan* fluent non-trivial.

dency paths and their collapsed Stanford Dependencies forms (de Marneffe and Manning, 2008). We include the lengths of each path and, if the path is shorter than four edges, the grammatical relations, words, POS tags, and NER labels along the path. We extract the same sorts of features from surface paths (i.e., the words and tags between the entity and the temporal expression) if the path is five tokens or shorter. For temporal expressions, we include their century and decade as features. These features act as a crude prior over when valid temporal expressions occur. There are also features for the precision of the temporal expression (year only, has month, and has day). Lastly, we include the relation name itself as a feature.

Previous work (Artiles et al., 2011) heuristically aggregates the hard decisions from their classifier to create a locally consistent span. The *basic aggregation model* (described in §4.2) is similar to their method. In contrast, our method uses the likelihood of complete spans to ensure both boundaries are consistent with the text.

To calculate the likelihood of a specific temporal span for a fluent f, we represent the span as a series of metarelations and take the product of their probabilities. For example, if the candidate span is $[\texttt{1981-09-15}, +\infty)$ and we have two temporal expressions, "September 15th, 1981" and "2012":

$$\begin{aligned} &P\big(span(f) = [\texttt{1981-09-15}, +\infty) \mid f\big) = \\ &\quad P\big(C(\text{“September 15th, 1981”}, f) = \textsc{start}\big) \times \\ &\quad P\big(C(\text{“2012”}, f) = \textsc{unrelated}\big) \end{aligned}$$

This can easily be extended to calculating the joint probability of an entire timeline, represented as a list of $\langle \mathit{fluent}, \mathit{span} \rangle$ pairs:

$$P_{CC}\big(\langle f_1, s_1\rangle, \dots\big) = \prod_i P\big(span(f_i) = s_i \mid f_i\big)$$

We refer to this model as the Combined Classifier (CC) since it uses the probabilities of all timelines boundaries rather than aggregating hard local decisions.

3.3 Consistency component

While distant supervision can be used to create implicit negative examples for the classifier component (time expressions marked as UNRELATED), we do not have an equivalent technique to reliably create negative examples for the consistency component (examples of inconsistent timelines). Instead, we only have positive examples of consistent timelines from the database. As a result, we must treat predicting consistency as a density estimation rather than a classification problem.

Our consistency component is designed to be as general as possible – it does not even include basic constraints about timelines such as "starts are before ends." Instead, we provide several simple templates for temporal constraints to allow it to learn these basic tendencies as well as more complex ones. Examples include whether one typically goes to school first or starts their first job, how many jobs people typically have at one time, or if it is possible to marry someone who hasn't been born yet.

We achieve this by decomposing timelines into a series of probabilistic events, or *questions*. As an example, one question about the timeline shown in Table 1 is whether Jon Stewart graduated from the College of William and Mary BEFORE marrying Tracey McShane, i.e., *end*(*attends school*) < *start*(*has spouse*). In this case, the answer is "yes." More generally, we can apply the BEFORE template to all boundaries of all fluents: $boundary_1(\mathit{fluent}_1) < boundary_2(\mathit{fluent}_2)$. We use templates like these (denoted by SMALL CAPS) to generate all possible questions to ask about a specific entity.

Other questions can be asked at the fluent level rather than the boundary level (Allen, 1983). One set of fluent level questions asks whether two fluents' spans OVERLAP. For example, in Table 1, Jon Stewart's *lifespan* OVERLAPs with the span of his *has spouse* fluent. Other sets of fluent level questions ask whether the span of a fluent completely CONTAINS the span of another one, whether a fluent is COMPLETELY BEFORE another fluent, and whether two fluents TOUCH (the start of one fluent is the same as the end of another).

Since all of these questions involve ordering but ignore the actual differences in time, we create one more set of questions asking whether two boundaries are WITHIN a certain number of years:

$$|boundary_1(\mathit{fluent}_1) - boundary_2(\mathit{fluent}_2)| \leq K$$

for $K \in \{1, 2, 4, 8, 16\}$. The aim is to approximate the typical lengths of a single fluent or amount of time between boundaries from different fluents.

There is nothing which requires that the fluents in question come from a single entity. Thus, we can trivially ask questions about two entities which are linked by a fluent. For example, since Jon Stewart is linked to Tracey McShane by the *has spouse* fluent (Table 1), we could ask the question of whether Jon Stewart's *lifespan* OVERLAPS Tracey McShane's *lifespan*. We can ask any type of question about two linked entities and distinguish the questions by prefixing them with the nature of the link (*has spouse* in this case).

Note that not all questions can be answered since they may rely on comparing unknown values. This is because (for our setup) infinite values are indistinguishable from unknown values. For example, the start of the Jon Stewart's *attends school* fluent is undefined in the database, but clearly not actually $-\infty$. Thus, we add a third possible answer to each question: unknown. The answers to boundary level questions are defined only if both boundaries are finite. Fluent level questions have known answers as long as both fluents have at least one finite value.

To train our model, we gather the answers to questions over all the fluents from training entities. Each question forms a multinomial over the three possible values (yes, no, unknown). To determine the probability of a complete timeline:

$$P_{consistency}(timeline) = \prod_{(q,a)\in Q(timeline)} \begin{cases} (1-c)P_\theta(a \mid q) & q \text{ is old} \\ c & q \text{ is new} \end{cases}$$

where $Q(\cdot)$ generates all possible $\langle question, answer\rangle$ pairs which are consistent with the fluents in the timeline, θ is a vector of the model parameters, and c is a smoothing parameter (described below).

To learn the model parameters, we start by using maximum-likelihood estimation for these multinomials from training entities. However, some smoothing is required since new entities may contain previously unseen answers to existing questions. To address this, we apply add-λ smoothing to each multinomial, $P_\theta(a \mid q)$. Additionally, it is possible to see entirely new questions when we see a new combination of fluent types. We reserve an amount of probability mass for new questions, c. c and λ are estimated in turn by picking the value that maximizes the likelihood of the timeline made by the development entities.

To adjust the weight of the consistency component relative to the classifier component, we take the geometric mean of the likelihood using the total number of questions, $|Q(t)|$, as the exponent and raise the resulting mean to an exponent, β. This is necessary since the two components essentially operate on different scales. The Joint Classifier with Consistency (JCC) model calculates the score of a timeline, t, according to both components:

$$\text{score}_{JCC}(t) = P_{CC}(t)\left[P_{consistency}(t)^{\frac{\beta}{|Q(t)|}}\right]$$

3.4 Inference

Inference for the CC model is relatively simple: Simply pick the most likely span for each fluent. Since it assumes all fluents are independent, the bounds for each fluent can be inferred separately. To perform inference on a specific fluent, we consider all of its possible temporal spans, limited by the temporal expression mentions found by the retrieval system (§3.1). Each possible span assigns one of the four metarelations to each candidate temporal expression for the fluent. For example, if we found only the temporal expression mention "1981" for a specific fluent, there are four possible spans:

UNRELATED:	$(-\infty, +\infty)$
START:	$[$1981-01-01, $+\infty)$
END:	$(-\infty$, 1981-12-31$]$
START AND END:	[1981-01-01, 1981-12-31]

Note that when we assign "1981" as a start, we use the earliest possible time (January 1st) while when we assign it as an end, we use the latest possible time (December 31st). Of course, we typically have multiple candidate temporal expressions and thus potentially many more than four possible spans. All temporal expression mentions that resolve to the same time are grouped together, since it wouldn't make sense to assign "August 28th, 2010" one metarelation and a different one to "8/28/2010."

Joint inference for the JCC model is a little more involved since the consistency model does not assume independence across fluents. Thus, we need to apply techniques like Gibbs sampling or random-restart hillclimbing (RRHC) to determine the optimal temporal spans for each fluent. For our task, the two methods obtain similar performance while RRHC requires many fewer iterations so our discussion focuses on the latter. RRHC involves looping over all fluents in our testing entities, shuffling the order of the fluents at the beginning of each pass. We maintain a working timeline, t, with our current guesses of the spans for each fluent. For each fluent and span $\langle f, s \rangle \in t$, we pick the optimal span for f:

$$s^* = \arg\max_{s' \in S(f)} \text{score}_{JCC}(t_{s'})$$

where $S(f)$ determines all possible temporal spans for the fluent f and $t_{s'} = (t \cup \langle f, s' \rangle) - \langle f, s \rangle$ is a copy of t where s' is the span for f instead of s. After selecting s^*, we add it to our timeline: $t_{new} = (t \cup \langle f, s^* \rangle) - \langle f, s \rangle$. Rather than calculating the score of the full timeline, we can save time by using only the relevant fluents in $t_{s'}$. For example, if our fluent is the *has spouse* fluent for Jon Stewart, we include all the fluents involving Jon Stewart and any relevant linked entities. In this case, we also include all the fluents for Tracey McShane.

Each round of RRHC consists of two passes through the fluents we are inferring: An $\arg\max$ pass followed by a randomization pass where we randomly choose spans for a random fraction of the fluents. When finished, we return the highest scoring timeline seen during either of these passes.

4 Experiments

We evaluate our models (CC and JCC) according to their ability to predict the temporal bounds of fluents from Freebase. This is similar to the Diagnostic Track in the Temporal KBP task, where gold relations are provided as inputs. We provide three baselines for comparison, discussed further in §4.2. To form our database, we scraped a random sample of people and organization entities from Freebase using their API. Since our consistency model has limited effect if entities do not have any links to other entities, we restrict our attention to entities linked to at least one other entity – this eliminates a large portion of possible entities. Our corpus[7] consists of 8,450 entities for training, 1,072 for development, and 1,067 for test. Entities have approximately 2.0 fluents on average.

From experiments on the development set, we set the relative strength of the consistency component $\beta = 10$. For the JCC model, we perform three runs for each experiment with different random seeds. Each experiment performs 10 rounds of RRHC,[8] initializing from an empty timeline.

4.1 Evaluation metric

Our evaluation metric is adapted from the Temporal KBP metric (Ji et al., 2011) to work with 2-tuples for temporal representations rather than the 4-tuples in Temporal KBP. The metric favors tighter bounds on fluents while giving partial credit. All dates need to be given at day resolution. Thus, for gold fluents with only year- or month-level resolution, we treat them as their earliest (for starts) or latest (for ends) possible day. To score a boundary, we take the difference between the predicted and gold values: If they're both unbounded ($\pm\infty$), the boundary's score is 1. If only one is unbounded, the score is 0. If both are finite, the score is $1/(1 + |d|)$ where d is the difference between the values in years. To score a fluent, we average the scores of its start and end boundaries. In rare cases, we have multiple spans for the same relation (e.g., Elizabeth Taylor married Richard Burton twice). In these cases, we give systems the benefit of the doubt and greedily align fluents in such a way as to maximize the metric. The total metric computes the score of each fluent divided by the number of fluents. The official metric includes precision and recall components, but since our setup provides gold relations, our precision and recall are be equal. This allows us to report a single number.

4.2 Baselines and oracle

The simplest baseline is the *null* baseline, proposed in Surdeanu et al. (2011). This baseline assumes that all fluents are unbounded in their spans. The purpose

[7] `http://nlp.stanford.edu/~mcclosky/data/freebase-temporal-relations.tar.gz`

[8] There was no significant difference in accuracy between running 10 and 200 rounds of RRHC.

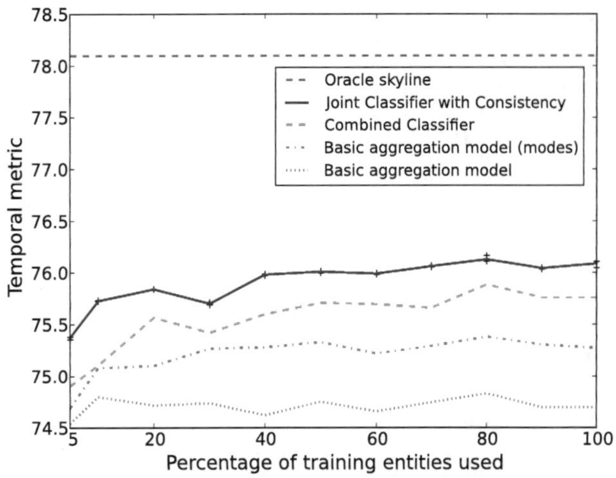

Figure 2: Performance of models and baselines on development data while varying amount of training data. Not pictured: The *null* baseline at 58.8%.

of this baseline is primarily to show the approximate minimal value for the temporal metric.

We provide two other baselines to describe heuristic methods of aggregating the hard decisions from the classifier function C learned in §3.2. These are unlike the CC model which uses the soft decisions of C. Both of these baselines maintain lists of possible starts and ends for each fluent. If the classifier assigns START AND END, we add the candidate temporal expression to both. The first baseline, *basic aggregation*, is along the same lines as the aggregation method used in Artiles et al. (2011), a state-of-the-art system. Our baseline assigns the earliest start and the latest end as the bounds for each fluent, assigning $\pm\infty$ for empty lists. The second baseline, *basic aggregation (modes)*, is the same except that it uses the mode from each list.

To determine the best possible score given our temporal expression retrieval system, we calculate the oracle score by assigning each fluent the span which maximizes the temporal metric. The oracle score can differ from a perfect score since we can only use candidate temporal expressions as values for a fluent if (a) mentions of the fluent are retrievable in our source documents, (b) the temporal expression mention appears nearby, and (c) our temporal expression extractor is able to recognize it correctly. Nevertheless, it is still a reasonable upper bound in our setting.

Model	Dev	Test
Oracle	78.1	75.2
Joint Classifier with Consistency	**76.1**	**72.2**
Combined Classifier	75.8	71.5
Basic aggregation (modes)	75.3	71.2
Basic aggregation	74.7	70.5
null baseline	58.8	55.6

Table 2: Performance of systems on development and test divisions. The Joint classifier with Consistency is the average of three runs with negligible variance ($\sigma \approx 0.02$).

4.3 Results

We present the performance of our models, baselines, and the oracle in Figure 2 while varying the percentage of training entities. The JCC model (76.1% on development with 100% training entities) is consistently the best non-oracle system. Its gains are larger when the amount of training data is low. This is presumably because the classifier suffers from insufficient data and the consistency component is able to learn consistency rules to recover from this. Both the CC and JCC models outperform the basic aggregation models. This shows the value of incorporating all marginal probabilities. On the test set (Table 2), the JCC model performs even better in comparison to the simple models, despite the test set being clearly more difficult than the development set. In this case, the JCC achieves a 36% error reduction over the basic aggregation model.[9] On the official KBP entities, the oracle score is 92%. Since we use a different set of entities, there is a mismatch between our entities and the source documents resulting in a lower oracle score. Addressing this is future work.

5 Discussion

Table 3 shows the performance of four systems and baselines on individual fluent types. The JCC model derives most of its improvement from the two *lifespan* fluents and other high frequency fluents. The *lifespan* fluents provide the most room for improvement since they tend to contain non-*null* values a reasonable amount of the time (note how these relations have a large gap between their ora-

[9]This counts errors relative to the oracle score since we treat the retrieval system as fixed in this work.

Fluent	Count	Model					
		null	Basic	Basic (modes)	CC	JCC	Oracle
organization: *lifespan*	266	49.2	71.0	70.7	71.1	71.7	73.4
organization: *top employees*	150	88.0	88.0	88.0	88.0	88.0	88.3
organization: *founders*	31	0.0	5.4	5.4	10.8	11.1	16.3
organization: *acquires company*	14	21.4	21.4	21.4	21.4	21.4	38.5
person: *lifespan*	806	28.6	63.1	64.6	65.6	66.1	69.1
person: *has spouse*	582	92.2	92.1	92.1	92.2	92.3	93.1
person: *attends school*	107	97.7	97.7	97.7	97.7	98.1	98.1
person: *has job*	85	78.8	79.4	79.4	78.8	78.8	80.3
person: *holds government position*	45	16.7	19.7	19.7	19.7	19.7	25.1
person: *romantic partner*	5	50.0	52.9	52.9	52.9	52.9	71.2

Table 3: Fluent-level performance of models and baselines on development data. Scores are calculated with the temporal metric. CC stands for Combined Classifier and JCC for Joint Classifier with Consistency. The JCC model obtains most of its benefits on the two *lifespan* relations. For *attends school*, it is the only system able to achieve oracle-level performance. The *null* baseline is especially strong for several fluents since these tend to be unbounded or (more likely) missing their values in Freebase. The two basic aggregation models differ primarily on their predictions for the *lifespan* fluents.

cle and *null* scores). Additionally, the *lifespan* fluent is always present for entities while other fluents are sparser. For *attends school*, JCC is the only system able to achieve oracle-level performance. No system improves on the *null* baseline for *acquires company*. This is likely due to its sparsity.

Inspecting the multinomials in the consistency component, we can see that the model learns reasonable answers to questions such as whether an entity "was born before getting married?" (yes: 14.8%, no: 0.04%),[10] "died before their parents were born?" (yes: 0.3%, no: 53.7%) and "finished a job before starting a job (not necessarily the same one)?" (yes: 72.5%, no: 20.5%). Despite some unavoidable noise in the data, it is clear these constraints are useful.

6 Related work

There is a large body of related work that focuses on ordering events or classifying temporal relations between them (Ling and Weld, 2010; Yoshikawa et al., 2009; Chambers and Jurafsky, 2008; Mani et al., 2006, *inter alia*). Much of this work uses the Allen interval relations (Allen, 1983) which richly describe partial orderings of fluents. We use several of these as fluent-level question templates.

Joint inference has been applied successfully to other NLP problems (Roth and Yih, 2004; Toutanova et al., 2008; Martins et al., 2009; Chang et al., 2010; Koo et al., 2010; Berant et al., 2011). Two recent examples in information extraction include using Markov Logic for temporal ordering (Ling and Weld, 2010) and using dual-decomposition for event extraction (Riedel and McCallum, 2011).

Our work is closest to Temporal KBP slot filling systems. The CUNY and UNED systems (Artiles et al., 2011; Garrido et al., 2011) for this task used classifiers to determine the relation between temporal expressions and fluents. These systems use the hard decisions from the classifier and combine the decisions by finding a span that includes all temporal expressions. In contrast, our system uses the classifier's marginal probabilities along with the consistency component to incorporate global consistency constraints. Other participants used rule-based and pattern matching approaches (Byrne and Dunnion, 2011; Surdeanu et al., 2011; Burman et al., 2011).

Outside of Temporal KBP, there are several works on the task of extracting fluents from text. Wang et al. (2011) which uses label propagation, a graph-based semi-supervised method to extend positive and negative seed examples over the graph. Talukdar et al. (2012) apply a similar approach by aggregating local classification decisions using tempo-

[10]Percentages for "unknown" are omitted here.

ral constraints (e.g., mutual exclusion, containment, and succession) and joint inference. One key difference is that their constraints are included as input rather than learned by the system.

7 Conclusion and future Work

Joint inference can be effectively applied to the task of inferring timelines about named entities. Rather than using hard coded heuristics, our model learns and applies consistency constraints which capture inter-entity and cross-entity rules. Simple inference techniques such as random-restart hillclimbing score well and run efficiently. Both of our models (CC and JCC) obtain a substantial error reductions over simpler heuristics-based consistency approaches.

The overall framework can easily be applied to other information extraction tasks. Rather than listing rules for consistency, these can be learned and enforced via joint inference. While simple joint inference methods such as random-restart hillclimbing and Gibbs sampling worked well in our case, more complex inference methods may be required with more elaborate constraints.

A prime direction for future work is combining our model with a probabilistic relation extraction system. This could be accomplished by using the marginal probabilities on the extracted relations and multiplying them with the probabilities from the classifier and consistency components. Inference would require an additional step which could add or drop candidate fluents. Furthermore, the consistency component can be extended with new question types to incorporate non-temporal constraints as well.

Acknowledgments

The authors would like to thank the Stanford NLP group (with special thanks to Gabor Angeli and Mihai Surdeanu), William Headden, Micha Elsner, Pontus Stenetorp, and our anonymous reviewers for their helpful comments and feedback.

We gratefully acknowledge the support of Defense Advanced Research Projects Agency (DARPA) Machine Reading Program under Air Force Research Laboratory (AFRL) prime contract no. FA8750-09-C-0181. Any opinions, findings, and conclusion or recommendations expressed in this material are those of the author(s) and do not necessarily reflect the view of the DARPA, AFRL, or the US government.

References

James F. Allen. 1983. Maintaining knowledge about temporal intervals. *Communications of the ACM*, 26(11):832–843.

Javier Artiles, Qi Li, Taylor Cassidy, Suzanne Tamang, and Heng Ji. 2011. CUNY BLENDER TAC-KBP2011 Temporal Slot Filling System Description. In *Proceedings of Text Analysis Conference (TAC)*, November.

Jonathan Berant, Ido Dagan, and Jacob Goldberger. 2011. Global learning of typed entailment rules. In *Proceedings of the 49th Annual Meeting of the Association for Computational Linguistics: Human Language Technologies*, pages 610–619, Portland, Oregon, USA, June. Association for Computational Linguistics.

Amev Burman, Arun Jayapal, Sathish Kannan, Madhu Kavilikatta, Ayman Alhelbawy, Leon Derczynski, and Robert Gaizauskas. 2011. USFD at KBP 2011: Entity Linking, Slot Filling and Temporal Bounding. In *Proceedings of Text Analysis Conference (TAC)*, November.

Lorna Byrne and John Dunnion. 2011. UCD IIRG at TAC 2011. In *Proceedings of Text Analysis Conference (TAC)*, November.

Nathanael Chambers and Dan Jurafsky. 2008. Jointly combining implicit constraints improves temporal ordering. In *Proceedings of the Conference on Empirical Methods in Natural Language Processing*, pages 698–706. Association for Computational Linguistics.

Angel X. Chang and Christopher D. Manning. 2012. SUTIME: A library for recognizing and normalizing time expressions. In *8th International Conference on Language Resources and Evaluation (LREC 2012)*, May.

Ming-Wei Chang, Dan Goldwasser, Dan Roth, and Vivek Srikumar. 2010. Discriminative learning over constrained latent representations. In *Human Language Technologies: The 2010 Annual Conference of the North American Chapter of the Association for Computational Linguistics*, pages 429–437. Association for Computational Linguistics.

Mark Craven and Johan Kumlien. 1999. Constructing biological knowledge bases by extracting information from text sources. In *Proceedings of the Seventh International Conference on Intelligent Systems for Molecular Biology*, pages 77–86. Heidelberg, Germany.

Marie-Catherine de Marneffe and Christopher D. Manning. 2008. The Stanford typed dependencies representation. In *Proceedings of the COLING Workshop on Cross-framework and Cross-domain Parser Evaluation*.

Jenny R. Finkel, Teg Grenager, and Christopher D. Manning. 2005. Incorporating non-local information into information extraction systems by Gibbs sampling. In *Proceedings of the 43rd Annual Meeting on Association for Computational Linguistics*, pages 363–370. Association for Computational Linguistics.

Guillermo Garrido, Bernardo Cabaleiro, Anselmo Pe nas, Alvaro Rodrigo, and Damiano Spina. 2011. A distant supervised learning system for the TAC-KBP Slot Filling and Temporal Slot Filling Tasks. In *Proceedings of Text Analysis Conference (TAC)*, November.

Heng Ji, Ralph Grishman, and Hoa Trang Dang. 2011. Overview of the TAC 2011 Knowledge Base Population track. In *Proceedings of Text Analysis Conference (TAC)*, November.

Dan Klein and Christopher D. Manning. 2003. Accurate unlexicalized parsing. In *Proceedings of the 41st Annual Meeting on Association for Computational Linguistics*, pages 423–430. Association for Computational Linguistics.

Terry Koo, Alexander M. Rush, Michael Collins, Tommi Jaakkola, and David Sontag. 2010. Dual decomposition for parsing with non-projective head automata. In *Proceedings of the 2010 Conference on Empirical Methods in Natural Language Processing*, pages 1288–1298. Association for Computational Linguistics.

Heeyoung Lee, Yves Peirsman, Angel X. Chang, Nathanael Chambers, Mihai Surdeanu, and Dan Jurafsky. 2011. Stanford's Multi-Pass Sieve Coreference Resolution System at the CoNLL-2011 Shared Task. In *CoNLL 2011*, page 28.

Xiao Ling and Daniel S. Weld. 2010. Temporal information extraction. In *Proceedings of the Twenty Fifth National Conference on Artificial Intelligence*.

Inderjeet Mani, Marc Verhagen, Ben Wellner, Chong Min Lee, and James Pustejovsky. 2006. Machine learning of temporal relations. In *Proceedings of the 21st International Conference on Computational Linguistics and the 44th Annual Meeting of the Association for Computational Linguistics*, pages 753–760. Association for Computational Linguistics.

André F. T. Martins, Noah A. Smith, and Eric P. Xing. 2009. Concise integer linear programming formulations for dependency parsing. In *Proceedings of the Joint Conference of the 47th Annual Meeting of the ACL and the 4th International Joint Conference on Natural Language Processing of the AFNLP*, pages 342–350. Association for Computational Linguistics.

Mike Mintz, Steven Bills, Rion Snow, and Dan Jurafsky. 2009. Distant supervision for relation extraction without labeled data. In *Proceedings of the Joint Conference of the 47th Annual Meeting of the ACL and the 4th International Joint Conference on Natural Language Processing of the AFNLP*, pages 1003–1011. Association for Computational Linguistics.

Sebastian Riedel and Andrew McCallum. 2011. Fast and robust joint models for biomedical event extraction. In *Proceedings of the Conference on Empirical Methods in Natural Language Processing (EMNLP '11)*, July.

Dan Roth and Wen-tau Yih. 2004. A linear programming formulation for global inference in natural language tasks. In Hwee Tou Ng and Ellen Riloff, editors, *HLT-NAACL 2004 Workshop: Eighth Conference on Computational Natural Language Learning (CoNLL-2004)*, pages 1–8, Boston, Massachusetts, USA, May 6 - May 7. Association for Computational Linguistics.

Mihai Surdeanu, Sonal Gupta, John Bauer, David McClosky, Angel X. Chang, Valentin I. Spitkovsky, and Christopher D. Manning. 2011. Stanford's Distantly-Supervised Slot-Filling System. In *Proceedings of Text Analysis Conference (TAC)*, November.

Partha Pratim Talukdar, Derry Wijaya, and Tom Mitchell. 2012. Coupled temporal scoping of relational facts. In *Proceedings of the Fifth ACM International Conference on Web Search and Data Mining*, pages 73–82. ACM.

Kristina Toutanova, Dan Klein, Christopher D. Manning, and Yoram Singer. 2003. Feature-rich part-of-speech tagging with a cyclic dependency network. In *Proceedings of the 2003 Conference of the North American Chapter of the Association for Computational Linguistics on Human Language Technology*, pages 173–180. Association for Computational Linguistics.

Kristina Toutanova, Aria Haghighi, and Christopher D. Manning. 2008. A global joint model for semantic role labeling. *Computational Linguistics*, 34(2):161–191.

Yafang Wang, Bing Yang, Lizhen Qu, Marc Spaniol, and Gerhard Weikum. 2011. Harvesting facts from textual web sources by constrained label propagation. In *Proceedings of the 20th ACM International Conference on Information and Knowledge Management*, pages 837–846. ACM.

Katsumasa Yoshikawa, Sebastian Riedel, Yuji Matsumoto, and Masayuki Asahara. 2009. Jointly identifying temporal relations with Markov Logic. In *Proceedings of the Joint Conference of the 47th Annual Meeting of the ACL and the 4th International Joint Conference on Natural Language Processing of the AFNLP*, pages 405–413. Association for Computational Linguistics.

Identifying Constant and Unique Relations by using Time-Series Text

Yohei Takaku*
Toyo Keizai Inc.
Chuo-ku, Tokyo 103-8345, Japan
takaku.yohei@gmail.com

Nobuhiro Kaji and **Naoki Yoshinaga**
Institute of Industrial Science,
University of Tokyo
Meguro-ku, Tokyo 153-8505, Japan
{kaji,ynaga}@tkl.iis.u-tokyo.ac.jp

Masashi Toyoda
Institute of Industrial Science,
University of Tokyo
Meguro-ku, Tokyo 153-8505, Japan
toyoda@tkl.iis.u-tokyo.ac.jp

Abstract

Because the real world evolves over time, numerous relations between entities written in presently available texts are already obsolete or will potentially evolve in the future. This study aims at resolving the intricacy in consistently compiling relations extracted from text, and presents a method for identifying constancy and uniqueness of the relations in the context of supervised learning. We exploit massive time-series web texts to induce features on the basis of time-series frequency and linguistic cues. Experimental results confirmed that the time-series frequency distributions contributed much to the recall of constancy identification and the precision of the uniqueness identification.

1 Introduction

We have witnessed a number of success stories in acquiring semantic relations between entities from ever-increasing text on the web (Pantel and Pennacchiotti, 2006; Banko et al., 2007; Suchanek et al., 2007; Wu et al., 2008; Zhu et al., 2009; Mintz et al., 2009; Wu and Weld, 2010). These studies have successfully revealed to us millions of relations between real-world entities, which have been proven to be beneficial in solving knowledge-rich problems such as question answering and textual entailment (Ferrucci et al., 2010).

There exists, however, a great challenge to compile consistently relations extracted from text by these methods, because they assume a simplifying assumption that relations are time-invariant. In other words, they implicitly disregard the fact that statements in texts actually reflect the state of the world at the time when they were written, which follows that relations extracted from such texts eventually become outdated as the real world evolves over time.

Let us consider that relations are extracted from the following sentences:[1]

(1) a. 1Q84 *is written by* Haruki Murakami.
  b. Moselle river *flows through* Germany.
  c. U.S.*'s president is* George Bush.
  d. Pentax *sells* K-5, a digital SLR.

Here, italicized predicates represent the relations, while underlined entities are their arguments. The relations in statements 1a and 1b are true across time, so we can simply accumulate all the relation instances. The relations in 1c and 1d in contrast evolve over time. The relation written in 1c becomes outdated when the other person takes the position, so we need to supersede it when a new relation is extracted from text (e.g., U.S*'s president is* Barack Obama). For the relation in 1d, we do not always need to supersede it with a new relation.

This study is motivated from the above consider-

*This work was conducted while the first author was a graduate student at University of Tokyo.

[1] Since our task settings are language-independent, we hereafter employ English examples as much as possible to widen the potential readership of the paper, although we conducted experiments with relations between entities in Japanese.

ations and proposes a method for identifying constancy and uniqueness of relations in order to select an appropriate strategy to maintain relation instances extracted from text. For example, the relations written in statements 1a and 1b are constant, while those in 1c and 1d are non-constant; the relation in 1c is unique,[2] whereas the relation in 1d is non-unique. With these properties of relations in mind, we can accumulate constant relations while appropriately superseding non-constant, unique relations with newly acquired relations.

We locate each identification task in the context of supervised classification. The key challenge in solving these classification tasks is how to induce an effective feature that identifies unique, non-constant relations (statement 1c) that seemingly appear as non-unique relations on text (statement 1b). We exploit massive time-series web text to observe actual evolutions of relation instances and induce features from the relation instances taken from a time sliding window and linguistic cues modifying the predicate and arguments of the target relation.

We evaluated our method on 1000 relations extracted from 6-year's worth of Japanese blog posts with 2.3-billion sentences. We have thereby confirmed that the features induced from this time-series text contributed much to improve the classification accuracy.

The main contributions of this paper are twofold:

- We have introduced a novel task for identifying constancy relations. Since most of the existing studies assume that relations are time-invariant as discussed by Weikum et al. (2011), non-constant relations prevalent in their outcome incur a serious problem in maintaining the acquired relations. The notion of constancy is meant to resolve this stalemate.

- We have for the first time demonstrated the usefulness of a time-series text in relation acquisition and confirmed its impact in the two relation classification tasks. The features induced from the time-series text have greatly contributed to the accuracy of the classification based on uniqueness as well as the recall of the classification based on constancy.

[2]This kind of relation is referred to as functional relation in the literature (Ritter et al., 2008; Lin et al., 2010).

Constant	Non-constant
arg1 *was born in* **arg2**	**arg1** *'s president is* **arg2**
arg1 *is a father of* **arg2**	**arg1** *belongs to* **arg2**
arg1 *is written by* **arg2**	**arg1** *lives in* **arg2**

Table 1: Examples of constant, non-constant relations.

The reminder of this paper is structured as follows. Section 2 introduces the two properties of relations (constancy and uniqueness) and then defines the task setting of this study. Sections 3 and 4 describe the features induced from time-series text for constancy and uniqueness classification, respectively. Section 5 reports experimental results. Section 6 addresses work related to this study. Section 7 concludes this study and mentions future work.

2 Classification of Relations based on Constancy and Uniqueness

2.1 Constancy and uniqueness

We introduce two properties of relations: *constancy* and *uniqueness*.

A relation is *constant* if, for most values of arg1, the value of arg2 is independent of time (Table 1). For example, ⟨**arg1** *was born in* **arg2**⟩ is a constant relation since one's birthplace never changes. On the other hand, ⟨**arg1** *'s president is* **arg2**⟩ is an example of non-constant relations. This can be checked by noting that, for example, the president of the United States was Barack Obama in 2011 but was previously George Bush and Bill Clinton before him.

A relation is *unique* if, for most values of arg1, there exists, at any given point in time, only one value of arg2 that satisfies the relation (Table 2). For example, ⟨**arg1** *was born in* **arg2**⟩ is obviously a unique relation. The relation ⟨**arg1** *is headquartered in* **arg2**⟩ is also unique, while it is non-constant. Notice that there is usually only one headquarters at any point in time, although the location of a headquarters can change. In contrast, the relation ⟨**arg1** *is funded by* **arg2**⟩ is a non-unique relation since it is likely that there exist more than one funder.

2.2 Discussion

Both constancy and uniqueness are properties that usually, not always, hold for most, not all, of the arg1's values. To see this, let us examine the relation ⟨**arg1** *'s president is* **arg2**⟩. Although this relation is

Unique	Non-unique
arg1 *was born in* **arg2**	**arg1** *is funded by* **arg2**
arg1 *is headquartered in* **arg2**	**arg1** *consists of* **arg2**
arg1 *'s president is* **arg2**	**arg1** *borders on* **arg2**

Table 2: Examples of unique and non-unique relations.

non-constant and unique (Table 1 and 2), it is still possible to find exceptional cases. For example, a country might exist in which the president has never changed; a country might have more than one president at the same time during civil war. However, since such situations are rare, the relation ⟨**arg1** *'s president is* **arg2**⟩ is considered as neither constant nor non-unique.

The above discussion implies that the constancy and uniqueness of relations can not be determined completely objectively. We, nevertheless, claim that these properties of relations are intuitively acceptable and thus they can be identified with moderate agreement by different people (see section 5).

2.3 Task and our approach

This paper explores classifying given relations on the basis of constancy and uniqueness. We treat the problem as two independent binary classification tasks, and train supervised classifiers.

The technical challenge we address in this paper is how to design features for the two tasks. Section 3 presents features based on time-series frequency and linguistic cues for classifying constant and non-constant relations. Similarly, section 4 presents analogous features for classifying unique and non-unique relations.

3 Features for Constancy Classification

3.1 Time-series frequency

It is intuitive to identify constant relations by comparing frequency distributions over arg2 in different time periods. This idea leads us to use frequency estimates from time-series text as features.

Time-series text For a time-series text, we used Japanese blog posts that had been gathered from Feb. 2006 to Sep. 2011 (68 months). These data include 2.3 billions of sentences. These posts were aggregated on a monthly basis by using time stamps attached with them, i.e., the unit of time is one month in our corpus.

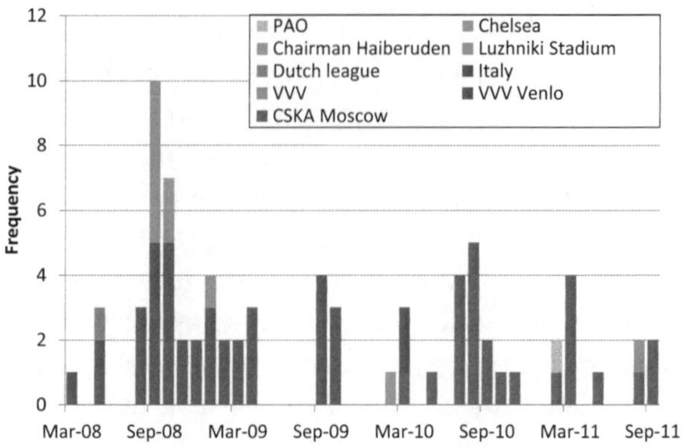

Figure 1: Time-series frequency distribution of ⟨**arg1** *belongs to* **arg2**⟩ when arg1 takes Keisuke Honda.

Basic idea For constant relations (e.g., ⟨**arg1** *was born in* **arg2**⟩), we can expect that the frequency distributions over arg2 for a given arg1 (e.g., *Mozart*) are similar to each other irrespective of the time windows that are used to estimate frequency.

In the case of non-constant relations (e.g., ⟨**arg1** *belongs to* **arg2**⟩), on the other hand, the frequency distributions over arg2 for a given arg1 significantly differ depending on the time window. For example, Figure 1 illustrates the frequency distributions of arg2s for ⟨**arg1** *belongs to* **arg2**⟩ in which arg1 takes Keisuke Honda, a famous football player. We can clearly observe that due to Keisuke Honda being sold from VVV Venlo to CSKA Moscow, the distributions differ greatly between 2008 and 2010.

As is evident from the above discussions, the stability/change in the distribution over arg2 is a good indicator of constant/non-constant relations. The following subsection addresses how to encode such information as features.

Feature computation Let us examine using as features the cosine similarity between frequency distributions over arg2. Averaging such similarities over representative values of arg1, we have

$$\frac{1}{N}\sum_{e\in\mathcal{E}_N(r)}\cos(F_{w_1}(r,e),F_{w_2}(r,e)),$$

where r is a relation (e.g., ⟨**arg1** *'s president is* **arg2**⟩), e is a named entity (e.g., *United States*) appearing in arg1, and $F_w(r,e)$ is the frequency distribution over arg2 when arg1 takes e. The subscripts

w_1 and w_2 denote the time window (e.g., from Jan. 2011 to Feb. 2011) used to estimate the frequency distribution. $\mathcal{E}_N(r)$ denotes a set of top N frequent entities appearing in arg1. We use the entire time-series text to obtain $\mathcal{E}_N(r)$.

Unfortunately, this idea is not suitable for our purpose. The problem is that it is not clear how to determine the two time windows, w_1 and w_2. To identify non-constant relations, arg2 must have different values in the two time periods. Such time windows are, however, impossible to know of in advance.

We propose avoiding this difficulty by using average, maximum and minimum similarity over all possible time windows:

$$\frac{1}{N}\sum_{e\in\mathcal{E}_N(r)} \underset{w_1,w_2\in\mathcal{W}_T}{\text{ave}} \cos(F_{w_1}(r,e), F_{w_2}(r,e)),$$

$$\frac{1}{N}\sum_{e\in\mathcal{E}_N(r)} \max_{w_1,w_2\in\mathcal{W}_T} \cos(F_{w_1}(r,e), F_{w_2}(r,e)),$$

$$\frac{1}{N}\sum_{e\in\mathcal{E}_N(r)} \min_{w_1,w_2\in\mathcal{W}_T} \cos(F_{w_1}(r,e), F_{w_2}(r,e)),$$

where $\mathcal{W}_T$ is a set of all time windows of the size T. For example, if we set T to 3 (months) in the 68-month's worth of blog posts, $\mathcal{W}_T$ consists of 66 ($=68-3+1$) time windows. Although we still have to specify the number of entities N and the window size T, this is not a serious problem in practice. We set N to 100. We use four window sizes (1, 3, 6, and 12 months) and induce different features for each window size. As a result, we have 12 real-valued features.

3.2 Linguistic cues

This subsection presents two types of linguistically-motivated features for discriminating between constant and non-constant relations.

Nominal modifiers We observe that non-constant relations could be indicated by some nominal modifiers:

(2) a. George Bush, *ex*-president of USA.

b. Lincoln is the *first* president of the USA.

The use of the prefix *ex-* and the adjective *first* implies that the president changes, and hence the relation ⟨**arg1** *'s president is* **arg2**⟩ is not constant.

前 (ex-), 現 (present), 次期 (next), 元 (former), 新 (new),	
旧 (old), 歴代 (successive), 初代 (first), 初 (first)	

Table 3: Japanese prefixes and adjectives indicating non-constant relations. The translations are provided in the parentheses.

We propose making use of such modifiers as features. Although the above examples are in English, we think modifiers also exist that have similar meanings in other languages including Japanese, our target language.

Our new features are induced as follows:

- First, we manually list eight nominal modifiers that indicate the non-constancy (Table 3).
- Next, we extract nouns from a relation to be classified (e.g., *president*), and count the frequency with which each modifier modifies those nouns. We use the same blog posts as in section 3.1 for counting the frequency. Since time information is not important in this case, the frequency is simply accumulated over the entire time span.
- We then generate eight features, one for each of the eight modifiers. The value of the features is one if the frequency exceeds threshold θ_1,[3] otherwise it is zero. Note that the value of this feature is always zero if the relation includes no nouns.

Tense and aspect Tense and aspect of verbs are also important indicators of the non-constancy:

(3) The U.S. president *was* George Bush.

If a relation, such as ⟨**arg1** *'s president is* **arg2**⟩, can often be rephrased in the past tense as in (3), it is likely to be, if not always, a non-constant relation.

It is, fortunately, straightforward to recognize tense and aspect in Japanese, because they are expressed by attaching suffixes to verbs. In this study, we use three common suffixes: "た", "ている", and "てる". The first suffix expresses past tense, while the other two express present continuous or progressive aspects depending on context.

[3] $\theta_1 = 10$ in our experiment.

A given relation is transformed into different forms by attaching the suffixes to a verb in the relation, and their frequencies are counted. By using the frequency estimates, we generate three new features, each of which corresponds to one of the three suffixes. The value of the new features is one if the frequency exceeds threshold θ_2,[4] otherwise it is zero.

The frequency is counted in the same way as in the case of the nominal modifiers. The value of this feature is always zero if the relation includes no verbs.

4 Features for Uniqueness Classification

This section provides features for identifying unique relations. These features are also based on the time-series text and linguistic cues, as in the case of constancy classification.

4.1 Time-series frequency

Number of entity types A straightforward approach to identifying unique relations is, for a given arg1, to count the number of entity types appearing in arg2 (Lin et al., 2010). For unique relations, the number of entity types should be one in an ideal noiseless situation. Even if the estimate is contaminated by noise, a small number of entity types can still be considered to indicate the uniqueness of the relation.

A shortcoming of such a simple approach is that it never considers the (non-)constancy of relations. Presume counting the number of entity types in arg2 of the relation ⟨**arg1** *is headquartered in* **arg2**⟩, which is non-constant and unique. If we use large size of time window to obtain counts, we will observe multiple types of entities in arg2, not because the relation is non-unique, but because it is non-constant. This problem cannot be resolved by trivially using very small windows, since a time window that is too small in turn causes a data sparseness problem.

This problem is attributed to the difficulty in determining the appropriate size of the time window. We tackle this problem by using the same technique presented in section 3.1. Specifically, we use the following three measures as features:

$$\frac{1}{N}\sum_{e\in\mathcal{E}_N(r)} \operatorname*{ave}_{w\in\mathcal{W}_T} \#\text{type}(F_w(r,e)),$$

$$\frac{1}{N}\sum_{e\in\mathcal{E}_N(r)} \max_{w\in\mathcal{W}_T} \#\text{type}(F_w(r,e)),$$

$$\frac{1}{N}\sum_{e\in\mathcal{E}_N(r)} \min_{w\in\mathcal{W}_T} \#\text{type}(F_w(r,e)),$$

where the function #type(·) denotes the number of entity types appearing in arg2.

Ratio of entity frequency Since it is not reliable enough to use only the number of entity types, we also exploit the frequency of the entity. Let e_{1st} and e_{2nd} be the most and the second most frequent entities found in arg2. If the frequency of e_{1st} is much larger than that of e_{2nd}, the relation is likely to be constant.

To encode this intuition, the following measures are used as features:

$$\frac{1}{N}\sum_{e\in\mathcal{E}_N(r)} \operatorname*{ave}_{w\in\mathcal{W}_T} \frac{f_w(e,r,e_{1st})}{f_w(e,r,e_{2nd})}$$

$$\frac{1}{N}\sum_{e\in\mathcal{E}_N(r)} \max_{w\in\mathcal{W}_T} \frac{f_w(e,r,e_{1st})}{f_w(e,r,e_{2nd})}$$

$$\frac{1}{N}\sum_{e\in\mathcal{E}_N(r)} \min_{w\in\mathcal{W}_T} \frac{f_w(e,r,e_{1st})}{f_w(e,r,e_{2nd})}$$

where the $f_w(e,r,e')$ is the frequency of the relation r in which arg1 and arg2 take e and e', respectively. The subscript w denotes the time window.

4.2 Linguistic cues

Coordination structures and some keywords indicate non-unique relations:

(4) a. France borders on *Italy and Spain.*

b. France borders on *Italy etc.*

The coordination structure in the first example implies an entity can border on more than one entity, and hence the relation ⟨**arg1** *borders on* **arg2**⟩ is not unique. The keyword *etc.* in the second example also indicates the non-uniqueness.

[4] $\theta_2 = 3000$ in our experiment.

と, とか, や, やら, だの, なり, か

Table 4: List of Japanese particles that are used to form coordination structures.

To capture this intuition, we introduce two types of linguistic features for classifying unique and non-unique relations. The first feature checks whether entities in arg2 form coordination structures. The feature is fired if the number of times that coordination structures are found in arg2 exceeds threshold θ_3.[5] Coordination structures are identified by a list of Japanese particles, which roughly correspond to *and* or *or* in English (Table 4). If two entities are connected by one of those particles, they are seen as forming a coordination structure.

The second feature exploits such keywords as *etc.* for identifying non-unique relations. We list four Japanese keywords that have similar meaning to the English word *etc.*, and induce another binary feature[6]. The feature is fired if the number of times that an entity in arg2 is followed by one of the four keywords exceeds threshold θ_3.

5 Experiments and discussions

We built labeled data and examine the classification performance of the proposed method. We also analyzed the influence of window size T on the performance, as well as major errors caused by our method.

5.1 Data

We built a dataset for evaluation by extracting relations from the time-series text (section 3.1) and then manually annotating 1000 relations. The detailed procedure is as follows.

First, we parsed the time-series text and extracted as relation dependency paths connecting two named entities. We used J.DepP,[7] an efficient shift-reduce parser with feature sequence trie (Yoshinaga and Kitsuregawa, 2009; Yoshinaga and Kitsuregawa, 2010), for parsing. All Japanese words that conjugate were normalized into standard forms.

[5] $\theta_3 = 10$ in our experiment.

[6] The keywords we used are 等, ら, たち, and 達.

[7] `http://www.tkl.iis.u-tokyo.ac.jp/~ynaga/jdepp/`

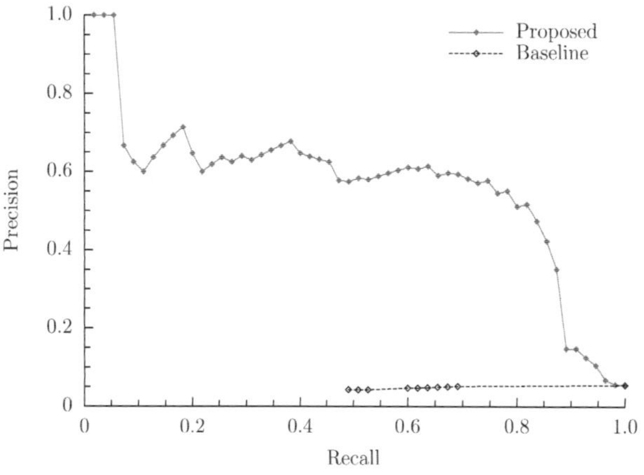

Figure 2: Recall-precision curve (constancy classification).

Then, annotators were asked to label 1000 relations as not only constant or non-constant but also unique or non-unique. Three annotators were assigned to each relation, and the goldstandard label is determined by majority vote. The Fleiss kappa (Fleiss, 1971) was 0.346 for constancy classification and was 0.428 for uniqueness classification. They indicate fair and moderate agreement, respectively (Landis and Koch, 1977).

We have briefly investigated the relations whose labels assigned by the annotators conflicted. The major cause was that the annotators sometimes assumed different types of named entities as values of arguments. A typical case in which this problem arises is that the relation has polysemous meanings, e.g., ⟨**arg1** *was born in* **arg2**⟩, or a vague meaning, e.g., ⟨**arg1** *makes* **arg2**⟩. For example, arg2 of ⟨**arg1** *was born in* **arg2**⟩ can be filled with different types of entities such as date and place. We can address this problem by typing arguments (Lin et al., 2010).

5.2 Result

Using the dataset, we performed 5-fold cross-validation for both classification tasks. We used the passive-aggressive algorithm for our classifier (Crammer et al., 2006).

Constancy classification Figure 2 illustrates the recall-precision curve in constancy classification. Because we are unaware of any previous methods for classifying constant and non-constant relations, a simple method based on the cosine similarity was

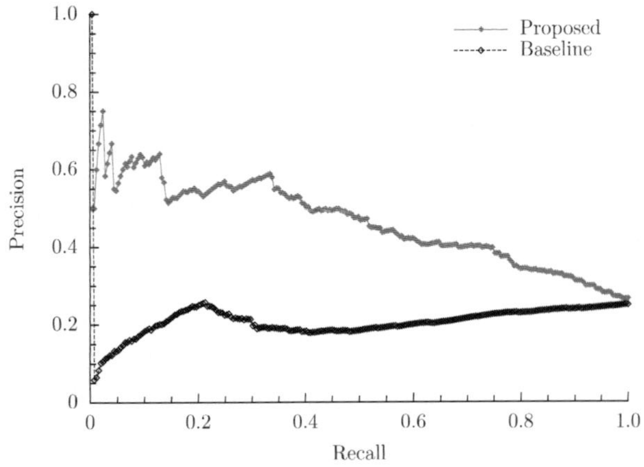

Figure 3: Recall-precision curve (uniqueness classification).

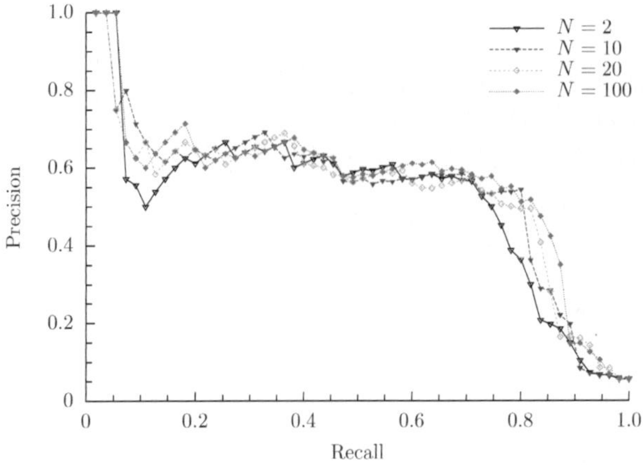

Figure 4: Comparison with the methods varying a value of N for constancy classification.

used as a baseline:

$$\frac{1}{N} \sum_{e \in \mathcal{E}_N(r)} \cos(F_{w_1}(r,e), F_{w_2}(r,e)),$$

where the time windows w_1 and w_2 are determined as the first and last month in which the relation r is observed. A given relation is classified as non-constant if the above similarity exceeds a threshold. The recall-precision curve was drawn by changing the threshold.

The results demonstrated that our method outperforms the baseline. This indicates the effectiveness of using time-series frequency and linguistic cues as features.

The poor performance of the baseline was mainly due to data sparseness. Since the baseline method is dependent on the frequency estimates obtained from only two months of texts, it is less reliable than the proposed method.

Uniqueness classification Figure 3 illustrates the recall-precision curve in uniqueness classification. As a baseline we implemented the method proposed by Lin et al. (2010). While they have presented three methods (KLFUNC, KLDIFF, and their average), we report the results of the last one because it performed the best among the three in our experiment.

From the figure, we can again see that the proposed method outperforms the baseline method. Lin's method is similar to ours, but differs in that they do not exploit time-series information at all.

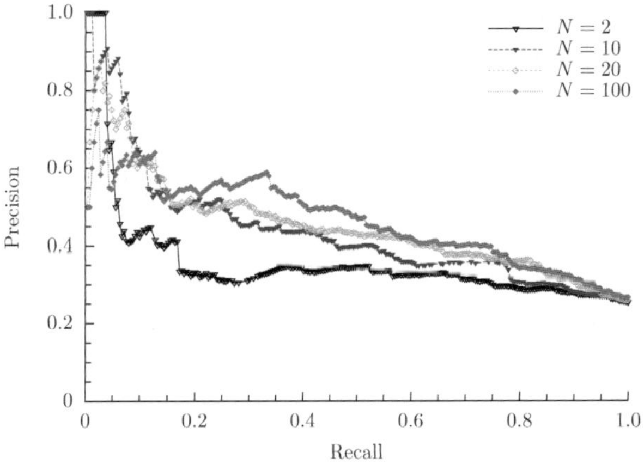

Figure 5: Comparison with the methods varying a value of N for uniqueness classification.

We hence conclude time-series information is useful for classifying not only constant but also unique relations.

5.3 Investigation into the number of entities, N

We ranged the value of N in $\{2, 10, 20, 100\}$. Setting N to a larger value yields the better recall for constancy classification and the better precision for uniqueness classification (Figures 4 and 5). These results meet our expectations, since features derived from frequency distributions of arg2 over various arg1s capture the generic nature of the target relation.

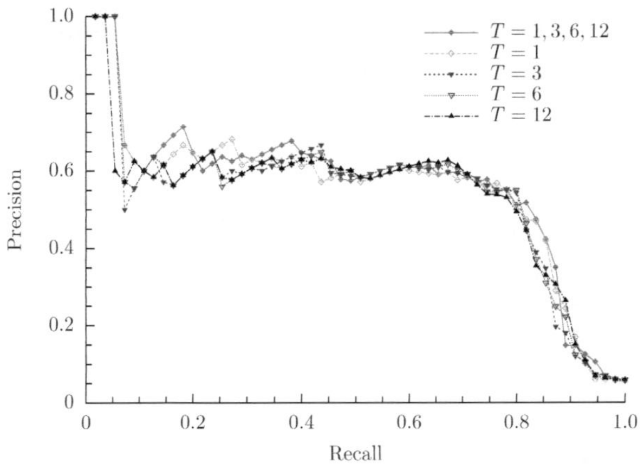

Figure 6: Comparison with the methods using only a single value of T for constancy classification.

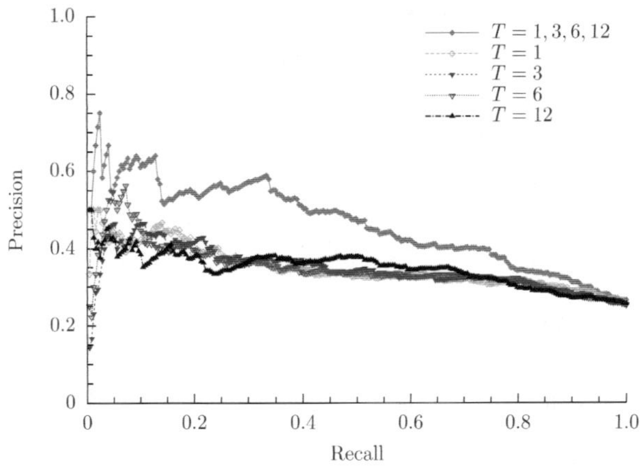

Figure 7: Comparison with the methods using only a single value of T for uniqueness classification.

5.4 Investigation into the window size, T

Our method uses multiple time windows of different sizes (i.e., different values of T) to induce features, as detailed in sections 3.1 and 4.1. To confirm the effect of this technique, we investigated the performance when we use only a single value of T (Figures 6 and 7).

The results in the uniqueness classification task demonstrated that our method achieves better overall results than the methods using a single value of T. We can therefore consider that using multiple values of T as features is a reasonable strategy. On the other hand, we could not confirm the effect of using multiple time windows of different sizes in the constancy classification task.

5.5 Error analysis

We randomly selected and analyzed 200 misclassified relations for both tasks. The analysis revealed four types of errors.

Paraphrases We observed that constant relations are prone to be miss-classified as non-constant when more than one paraphrase appear in arg2 and thus the value of arg2 is pretended to change. For example, America was also referred to as USA or United States of America. A similar problem was observed for unique relations as well.

Topical bias Topics mentioned in the blog posts are sometimes biased, and such bias can have a negative effect on classification, especially when a relation takes a small number of entity types in arg2 for given arg1. For example, Jaden Smith, who is one of Will Smith's sons, is frequently mentioned in our time-series text because he co-starred with his father in a movie, while Will Smith's other sons never appeared in our text. We consider this a possible reason for our method wrongly identifying ⟨**arg1** *'s son is* **arg2**⟩ as a unique relation.

Short-/Long-term evolution Since we have aggregated on a monthly basis the 6-year's worth of blog posts, the induced features cannot capture evolutions that occur in shorter or longer intervals. For example, consider relation ⟨**arg1** *beats* **arg2**⟩ taking Real Madrid as arg1. Since Real Madrid usually have more than one football match in a month, they can beat several teams in a month, which misleads the classifier to recognize the relation as non-unique. Similarly when a relation takes more than 6 years to evolve, it will be regarded as constant.

Reference to past, future, or speculative facts The blog authors sometimes refer to relations that do not occur around when they write their posts; such relations actually occurred in the past, will occur in the future, or even speculative. Since our method exploits the time stamps attached to the posts to associate the relations with time, those relations introduce noises in the frequency distributions. Although our robust feature induction could in most cases avoid an adverse effect caused by these noises, they sometimes leaded to misclassification.

6 Related Work

In recent years, much attention has been given to extracting relations from a massive amount of textual data, especially the web (cf. section 1). Most of those studies, however, explored just extracting relations from text. Only a few studies, as described below, have discussed classifying those relations.

There has been no previous work on identifying the constancy of relations. The most relevant research topic is the temporal information extraction (Verhagen et al., 2007; Verhagen et al., 2010; Ling and Weld, 2010; Wang et al., 2010; Hovy et al., 2012). This is the task of extracting from textual data an event and the time it happened, e.g., Othello was written by Shakespeare in 1602. Such temporal information alone is not sufficient for identifying the constancy of relations, while we think it would be helpful.

On the other hand, the uniqueness of relations has so far been discussed in some studies. Ritter et al. (2008) have pointed out the importance of identifying unique relations for various NLP tasks such as contradiction detection, quantifier scope disambiguation, and synonym resolution. They proposed an EM-style algorithm for scoring the uniqueness of relations. Lin et al. (2010) also proposed three algorithms for identifying unique relations. While those studies discussed the same problem as this paper, they did not point out the importance of the constancy in identifying unique relations (cf. section 4.1).

7 Conclusion

This paper discussed that the notion of constancy is essential in compiling relations between entities extracted from real-world text and proposed a method for classifying relations on the basis of constancy and uniqueness. The time-series web text was fully exploited to induce frequency-based features from time-series frequency distribution on relation instances as well as language-based features tailored for individual classification tasks. Experimental results confirmed that the frequency-based features contributed much to the precision and recall in both identification tasks.

We will utilize the identified properties of the relations to adopt an appropriate strategy to compile their instances. We also plan to start a spin-off research that acquires paraphrases by grouping values of arg2s for each value of arg1 in a constant, unique relation.

We consider that the notion of constancy will even be beneficial in acquiring world knowledge, other than relations between entities, from text; we aim at extending the notion of constancy to other types of knowledge involving real-world entities, such as concept-instance relations.

Acknowledgments

This work was supported by the Multimedia Web Analysis Framework towards Development of Social Analysis Software program of the Ministry of Education, Culture, Sports, Science and Technology, Japan. The authors thank the annotators for their hard work. The authors are also indebted to the three anonymous reviewers for their valuable comments.

References

Michele Banko, Michael J. Cafarella, Stephen Soderland, Matt Broadhead, and Oren Etzioni. 2007. Open information extraction from the web. In *Proceedings of IJCAI*, pages 2670–2676.

Koby Crammer, Ofer Dekel, Joseph Keshet, Shai Shalev-Shawartz, and Yoram Singer. 2006. Online passive-aggressive algorithms. *Journal of Machine Learning Research*, 7:551–583.

David Ferrucci, Eric Brown, Jennifer Chu-Carroll, James Fan, David Gondek, Aditya A. Kalyanpur, Adam Lally, J. William Murdock, Eric Nyberg, John Prager, Nico Schlaefer, and Chris Welty. 2010. Building Watson: An overview of the DeepQA project. *AI Magazine*, 31(3):59–79.

Joseph L. Fleiss. 1971. Measuring nominal scale agreement among many raters. *Psychological Bulletin*, 76(5):378–382.

Dirk Hovy, James Fan, Alfio Gliozzo, Siddharth Patwardhan, and Christopher Welty. 2012. When did that happen? — linking events and relations to timestamps. In *Proceedings of EACL*, pages 185–193.

Richard J. Landis and Gary G. Koch. 1977. The measurement of observer agreement for categorical data. *Biometrics*, 1(33):159–174.

Thomas Lin, Mausam, and Oren Etzioni. 2010. Identifying functional relation in web text. In *Proceedings of EMNLP*, pages 1266–1276.

Xiao Ling and Daniel S. Weld. 2010. Temporal information extraction. In *Proceedings of AAAI*, pages 1385–1390.

Mike Mintz, Steven Bills, Rion Snow, and Dan Jurafsky. 2009. Distant supervision for relation extraction without labeled data. In *Proceedings of ACL-IJCNLP*, pages 1003–1011.

Patrick Pantel and Marco Pennacchiotti. 2006. Espresso: Leveraging generic patterns for automatically harvesting semantic relations. In *Proceedings of ACL*, pages 113–120.

Alan Ritter, Doug Downey, Stephen Soderland, and Oren Etzioni. 2008. It's a contradiction—no, it's not: A case study using functional relations. In *Proceedings of EMNLP*, pages 11–20.

Fabian M. Suchanek, Gjergji Kasneci, and Gerhard Weikum. 2007. YAGO: A core of semantic knowledge unifying WordNet and Wikipedia. In *Proceedings of WWW*, pages 697–706.

Marc Verhagen, Robert Gaizauskas, Frank Schilder, Mark Hepple, Graham Katz, and James Pustejovsky. 2007. SemEval-2007 task 15: TempEval temporal relation identification. In *Proceedings of SemEval*, pages 75–80.

Marc Verhagen, Roser Sauri, Tommaso Caselli, and James Pustejovsky. 2010. SemEval-2010 task 13: TempEval-2. In *Proceedings of SemEval*, pages 57–62.

Yafang Wang, Mingjie Zhu, Lizhen Qu, Marc Spaniol, and Gerhard Weikum. 2010. Timely YAGO: harvesting, querying, and visualizing temporal knowledge from Wikipedia. In *Proceedings of EDBT*, pages 697–700.

Gerhard Weikum, Srikanta Bedathur, and Ralf Schenkel. 2011. Temporal knowledge for timely intelligence. In *Proceedings of BIRTE*, pages 1–6.

Fei Wu and Daniel S. Weld. 2010. Open information extraction using Wikipedia. In *Proceedings of ACL*, pages 118–127.

Fei Wu, Raphael Hoffmann, and Daniel S. Weld. 2008. Information extraction from Wikipedia: moving down the long tail. In *Proceedings of KDD*, pages 731–739.

Naoki Yoshinaga and Masaru Kitsuregawa. 2009. Polynomial to linear: Efficient classification with conjunctive features. In *Proceedings of EMNLP*, pages 1542–1551.

Naoki Yoshinaga and Masaru Kitsuregawa. 2010. Kernel slicing: Scalable online training with conjunctive features. In *Proceedings of COLING*, pages 1245–1253.

Jun Zhu, Zaiqing Nie, Xiaojiang Liu, Bo Zhang, and Ji-Rong Wen. 2009. StatSnowball: a statistical approach to extracting entity relationships. In *Proceedings of WWW*, pages 101–110.

No Noun Phrase Left Behind: Detecting and Typing Unlinkable Entities

Thomas Lin, Mausam, Oren Etzioni
Computer Science & Engineering
University of Washington
Seattle, WA 98195, USA
{tlin, mausam, etzioni}@cs.washington.edu

Abstract

Entity linking systems link noun-phrase mentions in text to their corresponding Wikipedia articles. However, NLP applications would gain from the ability to detect and type all entities mentioned in text, including the long tail of entities not prominent enough to have their own Wikipedia articles. In this paper we show that once the Wikipedia entities mentioned in a corpus of textual assertions are linked, this can further enable the detection and fine-grained typing of the unlinkable entities. Our proposed method for detecting unlinkable entities achieves 24% greater accuracy than a Named Entity Recognition baseline, and our method for fine-grained typing is able to propagate over 1,000 types from linked Wikipedia entities to unlinkable entities. Detection and typing of unlinkable entities can increase yield for NLP applications such as typed question answering.

1 Introduction

A key challenge in machine reading (Etzioni et al., 2006) is to identify the entities mentioned in text, and associate them with appropriate background information such as their type. Consider the sentence "Some people think that pineapple juice is good for vitamin C." To analyze this sentence, a machine should know that "pineapple juice" refers to a beverage, while "vitamin C" refers to a nutrient.

Entity linking (Bunescu and Paşca, 2006; Cucerzan, 2007) addresses this problem by linking noun phrases within the sentence to entries in a large, fixed entity catalog (almost always Wikipedia). Thus, entity linking has a limited and somewhat arbitrary range. In our example, systems by (Ferragina and Scaiella, 2010) and (Ratinov et al., 2011) both link "vitamin C" correctly, but link "pineapple juice" to "pineapple." "Pineapple juice" is not entity linked as a beverage because it is not prominent enough to have its own Wikipedia entry. As Table 1 shows, Wikipedia often has prominent entities, while missing tail and new entities of the same types.[1] (Wang et al., 2012) notes that there are more than 900 different active shoe brands, but only 82 exist in Wikipedia. In scenarios such as intelligence analysis and local search, non-Wikipedia entities are often the most important.

example noun phrases	status
"apple juice" "orange juice"	present
"prune juice" "wheatgrass juice"	**absent**
"radiation exposure" "workplace stress"	present
"asbestos exposure" "financial stress"	**absent**
"IJCAI" "OOPSLA"	present
"EMNLP" "ICAPS"	**absent**

Table 1: Wikipedia has entries for prominent entities, while missing tail and new entities of the same types.

Hence, we introduce the *unlinkable noun phrase problem*: Given a noun phrase that does not link into Wikipedia, return whether it is an entity, as well its fine-grained semantic types. Deciding if a non-Wikipedia noun phrase is an entity is challenging because many of them are not entities (e.g., "Some people," "an addition" and "nearly half"). Predict-

[1]The same problem occurs with Freebase, which is also missing the same Table 1 entities.

ing semantic types is a challenge because of the diversity of entity types in general text. In our experiments, we utilized the Freebase type system, which contains over 1,000 semantic types.

The first part of this paper proposes a novel method for detecting entities by observing that entities often have different usage-over-time characteristics than non-entities. Evaluation shows that our method achieves 24% relative accuracy gain over a NER baseline. The second part of this paper shows how instance-to-instance class propagation (Kozareva et al., 2011) can be adapted and scaled to semantically type general noun-phrase entities using types from linked entities, by leveraging over one million different possible textual relations.

Contributions of our research include:

- We motivate and introduce the *unlinkable noun phrase problem*, which extends previous work in entity linking.
- We propose a novel method for discriminating entities from arbitrary noun phrases, utilizing features derived from Google Books ngrams.
- We adapt and scale instance-to-instance class propagation in order to associate types with non-Wikipedia entities.
- We implement and evaluate our methods, empirically verifying improvement over appropriate baselines.

2 Background

In this section we provide an overview of entity linking, how we entity link our data set, and describe how our problem and approach differ from related areas such as NER and Web extraction.

2.1 Entity Linking

Given text, the task of entity linking (Bunescu and Paşca, 2006; Cucerzan, 2007; Milne and Witten, 2008; Kulkarni et al., 2009) is to identify the Wikipedia entities within the text, and mark them with which Wikipedia entity they correspond to. Entity linking elevates us from plain text into meaningful *entities* that have properties, semantic types, and relationships with each other. Other entity catalogs can be used in place of Wikipedia, especially in domain-specific contexts, but general purpose linking systems all use Wikipedia because of its broad general coverage, and to leverage its article texts and link structure during the linking process.

A problem we observed when using entity linking systems is that despite containing over 3 million entities, Wikipedia does not cover a significant number of entities. This occurs with entities that are not prominent enough to have their own dedicated article and with entities that are very new. For example, Facebook has over 600 million users, and each of them could be considered an entity. The REVERB extractor (Fader et al., 2011) on the ClueWeb09 Web corpus found over 1.4 billion noun phrases participating in textual relationships, and a sizable portion of these noun phrases are entities. While recent research has used NIL features to determine whether they are being asked to link an entity not in Wikipedia (Dredze et al., 2010; Ploch, 2011), there has been no research on whether given noun phrases that are *unlinkable* (for not being in Wikipedia) are entities, and how to make them usable if they are.

Our goal is to address this problem of learning whether non-Wikipedia noun phrases are entities, and assigning semantic types to them to make them useful. We begin with a corpus of 15 million "(noun phrase subject, textual relation, noun phrase object)" assertions from the Web that were extracted by REVERB (Fader et al., 2011).[2] REVERB already filters out relative pronouns, WHO-adverbs, and existential "there" noun phrases that do not make meaningful arguments. We then employ standard entity linking techniques including string matching, prominence priors (Fader et al., 2009), and context matching (Bunescu and Paşca, 2006) to link the noun phrase subjects into Wikipedia.

In this manner, we were able to entity link the noun phrase subject of 9,699,967 extractions, while the remaining 5,028,301 extractions had no matches (mostly due to no close string matches). There were 1,401,713 distinct noun phrase subjects in the 5 million extractions that had no matches. These are the *unlinkable* noun phrases we will study here.

2.2 Named Entity Recognition

Named Entity Recognition (NER) is the task of identifying named entities in text. A key difference between our final goals and NER is that in the con-

[2] available at http://reverb.cs.washington.edu

text of entity linking and Wikipedia, there are many more entities than just the *named* entities. For example, "apple juice" and "television" are Wikipedia entities (with Wikipedia articles), but are not traditional named entities. Still, as named entities do comprise a sizable portion of our *unlinkable* noun phrases, we compare against a NER baseline in our entity detection step.

Fine-grained NER (Sekine and Nobata, 2004; Lee et al., 2007) has studied scaling NER to up to 200 semantic types. This differs from our semantic typing of unlinked entities because our approach assumes access to corpora-level relationships between a large set of linked entities (with semantic types) and the unlinked entities. As a result we are able to propagate 1,339 Freebase semantic types from the linked entities to the unlinked entities, which is substantially more types than fine-grained NER.

2.3 Extracting Entity Sets

There is a line of research in using Web extraction (Etzioni et al., 2005) and entity set expansion (Pantel et al., 2009) to extract lists of typed entities from the Web (e.g., a list of every city). Our problem instead focuses on determining whether any individual noun phrase is an entity, and what semantic types it holds. Given a noun phrase representing a person name, we return that this is a person entity even if it is not in a list of people names harvested from the Web.

3 Architecture

Our goal is: given (1) a large set of linked assertions L and (2) a large set of unlinked assertions U, for each unlinkable noun phrase subject $n \in U$, predict: (1) whether n is an entity, and if so, then (2) the set of Freebase semantic types for n. For L we use the 9.7 million assertions whose *subject* argument we were able to link in Section 2.1, and for U we use the 5 million assertions that we could not link.

We divide the system into two components. The first component (described in Section 4) takes any unlinkable noun phrase and outputs whether it is an entity. All $n \in U$ classified as entities are placed in a set E. The second component (described in Section 5) uses L and U to predict the semantic types for each entity $e \in E$.

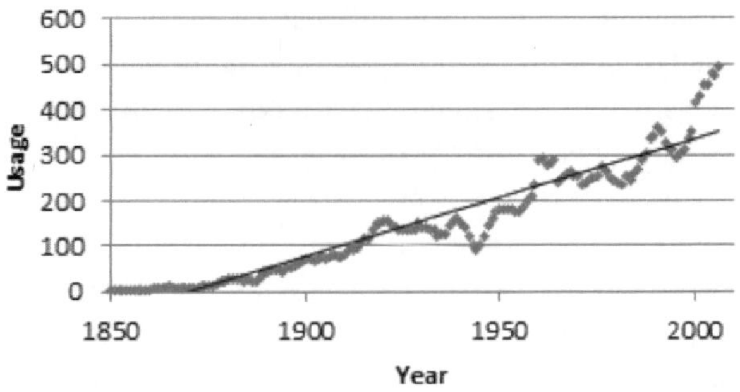

Figure 1: Usage over time in Google books for the noun phrase "Prices quoted" (e.g., from "Prices quoted are for 2 adults") which is not an entity.

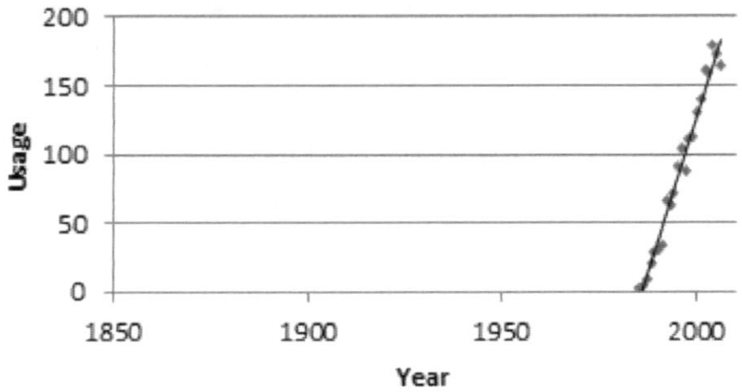

Figure 2: Usage over time for the unlinkable noun phrase "Soluble fibre," which is an entity. The best fit line has steeper slope compared to Figure 1.

4 Detecting Unlinkable Entities

This first task takes in any *unlinkable* noun phrase and outputs whether it is an entity. There is a long history of discussion in analytic philosophy literature on the question of what exists (e.g., (Quine, 1948)). We adopt a more pragmatic view, defining an "entity" as a noun phrase that could have a Wikipedia-style article if there were no notability or newness considerations, and which would have semantic types. We are interested in entities that could help populate an entity store. "EMNLP 2012" is an example of an entity, while "The method" and "12 cats" are examples of noun phrases that are not entities. This is challenging because at a surface level, many entities and non-entities look similar: "Sex and the City" is an entity, while "John and David" is not. "Eminem" is an entity, while "Youd" (a typo from "You'd") is not.

We address this task by training a classifier with features primarily derived from a timestamped corpus. An intuition here is that when considering only unlinkable noun phrases, usage patterns across

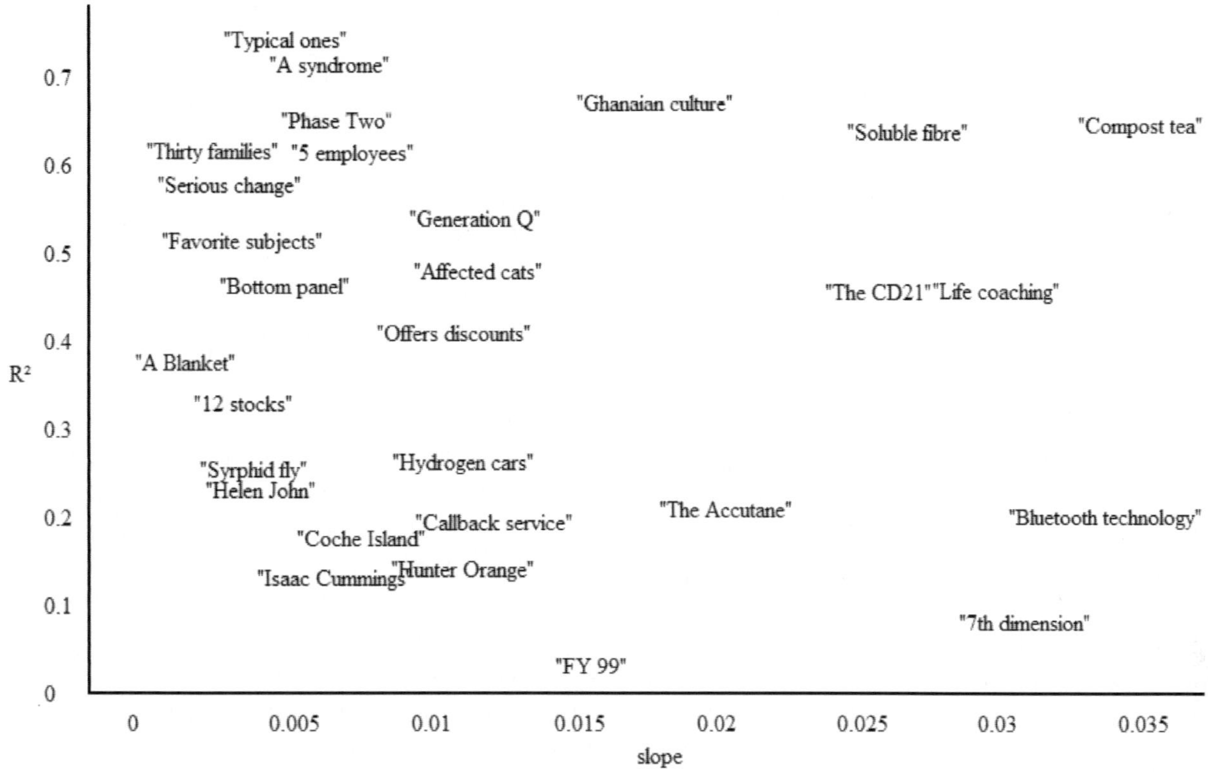

Figure 3: Plot of R^2 vs $Slope$ for the usage over time of a collection of noun phrases selected for illustrative purposes. Many of the non-entities occur at lower $Slope$ and higher R^2, while the entities often have higher slope and/or lower R^2. "Bluetooth technology" actually has even higher slope, but was adjusted left to fit in this figure.

time often differ for entities and non-entities. Noun phrase entities that are observed in text going back hundreds of years (e.g., "Europe") almost all have their own Wikipedia entries, so in unlinkable noun phrase space, the remaining noun phrases that are observed in text going back hundreds of years tend to be all the textual references and expressions that are not entities. We plan to use this signal to help separate the entities from the non-entities.

4.1 Classifier Features

We use the Google Books ngram corpus (Michel et al., 2010), which contains timestamped usage of 1-grams through 5-grams in millions of digitized books for each year from 1500 to 2007.[3] We use ngram match count values from case-insensitive matching. To avoid sparsity anomalies we observed in years before 1740, we use the data from 1740 onward. While it has not been used for our task before, this corpus is a rich resource that enables reasoning about knowledge (Evans and Foster, 2011) and understanding semantic changes of words over time (Wijaya and Yeniterzi, 2011). Talukdar et al. (2012) recently used it to effectively temporally scope relational facts.

Our first feature is the *slope* of the least-squares best fit line for usage over time. For example, if a term appears 25 times in books in 1950, 30 times in 1951, ..., 100 times in 2007, then we compute the straight line that best fits $\{(1950, 25), (1951, 31), ..., (2007, 100)\}$, and examine the slope. We have observed cases of non-entity noun phrases (e.g., Figure 1) having lower slopes than entity noun phrases (e.g., Figure 2). Note that we do not normalize match counts by yearly total frequency, but we do normalize counts for each term to range from 0 to 1 (setting the max count for each term to 1) to avoid bias from entity prominence. To capture the current usage, in cases where there exists a ≥ 5 year gap in usage of a term we only use the data after the gap.

Another feature is the R^2 fit of the best fit line. Higher R^2 indicates that the data is closer to a straight line. Figure 3 plots R^2 vs $Slope$ values

[3]available at http://books.google.com/ngrams/datasets

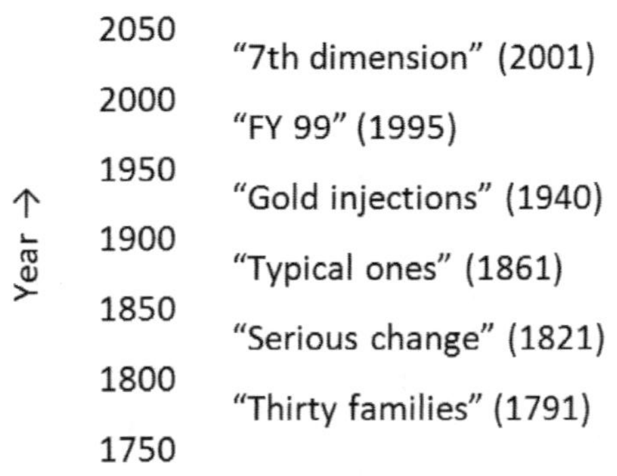

Figure 4: *UsageSinceYear* of example unlinked terms.

for some sample noun phrases. We observed that along with their lower *Slope*, the non-entities often also had higher R^2, indicating that their usage does not vary wildly from year to year. This contrasts with certain entities (e.g., "FY 99" for "Fiscal Year 1999") whose usage sometimes varied sharply from year to year based on their prominence in those specific years.

A third feature is *UsageSinceYear*, which finds the year from when a term last started continually being used. For example, a *UsageSinceYear* value of 1920 would indicate that the term was used in books every year from 1920 through 2007. Figure 4 shows examples of where various terms fall along this dimension.

From the books ngram corpus, we also calculate features for: *PercentProperCaps* - the percentage of case-insensitive matches for the term where all words began with a capital letter, *PercentExactMatch* - the percentage of case-insensitive matches for the term that matched the capitalization in the assertion exactly, and *Frequency* - the total number of case-insensitive occurrences of the term in the book ngrams data, summed across all years, which reflects prominence. Last, we also include a simple *numeric* feature to detect the presence of leading numeric words (e.g., "5" in "5 days" or "Three" in "Three choices").

4.2 Evaluation

From the corpus of 15 million ReVerb assertions, there were 1.4 million unlinked noun phrases including 17% unigrams, 51% bigrams, 21% trigrams, and 11% 4-grams or longer. Bigrams comprise over half the noun phrases and the books bigram data is a self-contained download that is easier to obtain and store than the full books ngram corpus, so we focus on bigrams in our evaluation. In a random sample of unlinked bigrams, we found that 73% were present in the books ngram data (65% exact match, 8% case-insensitive match only), while 27% were not (these were mostly entities or errors with non-alphabetic characters). Coverage is a greater issue with longer ngrams (e.g., there are many more possible 5-grams than bigrams, so any individual 5-gram is less likely to reach the minimum threshold to be included in the books data), but as mentioned earlier, only 11% of unlinkable noun phrases were 4-grams or longer.

system	correctly classified
Majority class baseline	50.4%
Named Entity Recognition	63.3%
Slope feature only	61.1%
PUF feature combination	69.1%
ALL features	78.4%

Table 2: Our classifier using all features (*ALL*) outperforms majority class and NER baselines.

We randomly sampled 250 unlinked bigrams that had books ngram data, and asked 2 annotators to label each as "entity," "non-entity," or "unclear." Our goal is to separate noun phrases that are clearly entities (e.g., "prune juice") from those that are clearly not entities (e.g., "prices quoted"), rather than to debate phrases that may be in some entity store definitions but not others, so we asked the annotators to choose "unclear" when there was any doubt. There were 151 bigrams that both annotators believed to be very clear labels, including 69 that both annotators labeled as entities, 70 that both annotators labeled as non-entities, and 12 with label disagreement. Cohen's kappa was 0.84, indicating excellent agreement. Our experiment is now to separate the 69 clear entities from the 70 clear non-entities.

For experiment baselines we use the majority class baseline *MAJ*, as well as a Named Entity Recognition baseline *NER*. For *NER* we used the Illinois Named Entity Tagger (Ratinov and Roth, 2009) on the highest setting (that achieved 90.5 F_1 score on the CoNLL03 shared task). *NER* expects a sentence, so we use the longest assertion in the corpus that the noun phrase was observed in. We evaluate several combinations of our features to test different aspects of our system: *Slope* uses only *Slope*, *PUF* uses *PercentProperCaps* + *UsageSinceYear* + *Frequency*, and *ALL* uses all features. We evaluate using the WEKA J48 Decision Tree on default settings, with leave-one-out cross validation.

Table 2 shows the results. *MAJ* correctly classifies 50.4% of instances, *NER* correctly classifies 63.3% and *ALL* correctly classifies 78.4%.

4.3 Analysis

Overall, 78.4% correctly classified instances is fairly strong performance on this task. By using the described features, our classifier was able to detect and filter many of the non-entity noun phrases in this scenario. Compared to the 63.3% of *NER*, it is an absolute gain of 15.1%, a relative gain of 24%, and a reduction in error of 41.1% (from 36.7% to 21.6%). Student's t-test at 95% confidence verified that the difference was significant.

We found that while low *Slope* (especially with higher R^2) often indicated non-entity, there were numerous cases where higher *Slope* did not necessarily indicate entity. For example, the noun phrase "several websites" has fairly sharp slope, but still does not denote a clear entity. In these cases, the addition of other features can serve as additional useful signal. One error from *ALL* is the term "Analyst estimates," which the annotators labeled as a non-entity, but which occasionally appears in text (especially titles) as "Analyst Estimates," and is a relatively recent phrase. *NER* misses entities such as "synthetic cubism" and "hunter orange" that occur in our data but are not traditional named entities. We observed that while none of our features achieves over 70% accuracy by themselves, they perform well in conjunction with each other.

5 Propagating Semantic Types

This second task uses a set of linked assertions L and set of unlinked assertions U to predict the semantic types for each entity $e \in E$. If the previous step output that "Sun Microsystems" is likely to be an entity, then the goal of this step is to further predict that it has the Freebase types such as *organization* and *software developer*.

From L we use the set of linked entities and the textual relations they occur with. For example, L might contain that the entity *Microsoft* links to a particular Wikipedia article, and also that it occurs with textual relations such as "has already announced" and "has released updates for." For each Wikipedia-linked entity in L, we further look up its exact set of Freebase types.[4] From U we obtain the set of textual relations that each $e \in E$ is in the domain of. We now have a large set of class-labeled instances (all entities in L), a large set of unlabeled instances (E), and a method to connect the unlabeled instances with the class-labeled instances (via any shared textual relations), so we cast this task as an instance-to-instance class propagation problem (Kozareva et al., 2011) for propagating class labels from labeled to unlabeled instances.

We build on the recent work of Kozareva et al. (2011), and adapt their approach to leverage the scale and resources of our scenario. While they use only one type of edge between instances, namely shared presence in the high precision *DAP* pattern (Hovy et al., 2009), our final system uses 1.3 million textual relations from $|L \cup U|$, corresponding to 1.3 million potential edge types. Their evaluation involved only 20 semantic classes, while we use all 1,339 Freebase types covered by our entities in L.

There is a rich history of other approaches for predicting semantic types. (Talukdar et al., 2008) and (Talukdar and Pereira, 2010) model relationships between instances and classes, but our unlinked entities do not come with any class information. Pattern-based approaches (Paşca, 2004; Pantel and Ravichandran, 2004) are popular, but (Kozareva et al., 2011) notes that they "are constraint to the information matched by the pattern and often suffer from recall," meaning that they do not cover many instances. Classifiers have also been trained for fine-grained semantic typing, but for noticeably fewer types than we work with. (Rahman and Ng, 2010) studied hierarchical and collective classification using 92 types, and FIGER (Ling and Weld, 2012) recently used an adapted perceptron for multi-class multi-label classification into 112 types.

5.1 Algorithm

Given an entity *e*, our algorithm involves: (1) finding the textual relations that *e* is in the domain of, (2)

[4] data available at http://download.freebase.com/wex

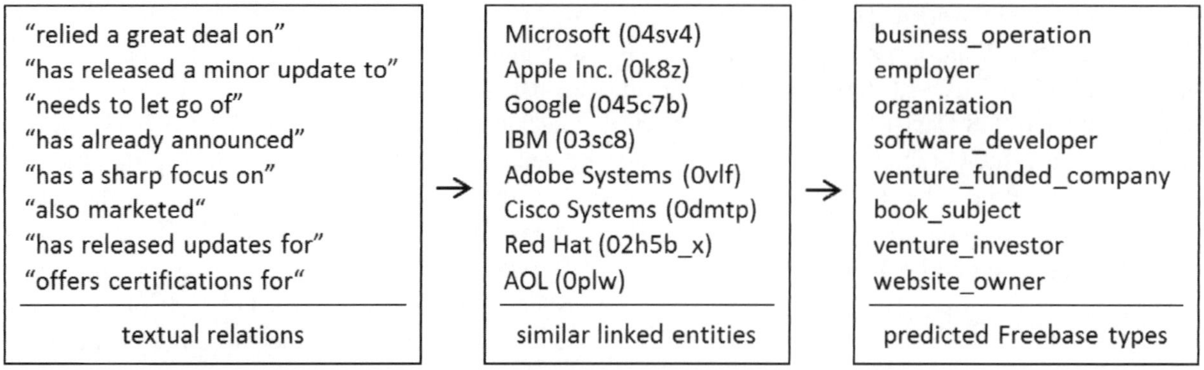

Figure 5: This example illustrates the set of Freebase type predictions for the noun phrase "Sun Microsystems." We predict the semantic type of a noun phrase by: (1) finding the textual relations it is in the domain of, (2) finding linked entities that are also in the domain of those textual relations, and (3) observing their semantic types.

finding linked entities that are also in the domain of those textual relations, and then (3) predicting types by observing the types of those linked entities. Figure 5 illustrates how we would predict the semantic types of the noun phrase "Sun Microsystems."

Find Relations: Obtain the set R of all textual relations in U that e is in the domain of. For example, if U contains the assertion "(Sun Microsystems, has released a minor update to, Java 1.4.2)," then the textual relation "has released a minor update to" should be added to R when typing "Sun Microsystems."

Find Similar Entities: Find the linked entities in L that are in the domain of the most relations in R. In our example, entities such as "Microsoft" and "Apple Inc." have the greatest overlap in textual relations because they are most often in the domain of the same textual relations, e.g., ("Microsoft, has released a minor update to, Windows Live Essentials"). Create a set S of the entities that share the most textual relations. We found keeping 10 similar entities ($|S|$ = 10) is generally enough to predict the original entity's types in the final step.

Predict Types: Return the most frequent Freebase types of the entities in S as the prediction. To avoid penalizing very small types, if there are n instances of semantic class C in S, then we rank C using a type score $T(n, C, S) = max(n/|S|, n/|C|)$, which we found to perform better than $T(n, C, S) = avg(n/|S|, n/|C|)$. For "Sun Microsystems," *business operation* was the top predicted type because all entities in S were observed to include *business operation* type.

5.2 Edge Validity

This algorithm will only be effective if entities that share textual relation strings are more likely to be of the same semantic types. To verify this, we sampled 30,000 linked entities from L that had at least 30 textual relations each, and associated each with their 30 most frequent relations. From the 900 million possible entity pairs, we then randomly sample 500 entity pairs that shared exactly *k* out of 30 relations, for each *k* from 0 to 15. At each *k* we then use our sampled pairs to estimate the probability that any two entities sharing exactly *k* relations (out of their 30 possible) will share at least one type.

The results are shown in Figure 6. We found that entities sharing more textual relations were in fact more likely to have semantic types in common. Two entities that shared exactly 0 of 30 textual relations were only 11% likely to share a semantic type, while two entities that shared exactly 10 of 30 relations were 80% likely to share a semantic type. This validates our use of textual relations as a signal-bearing edge in instance-to-instance class propagation.

5.3 Weighting Textual Relations

The algorithm as currently described treats all textual relations equally, when in reality some are stronger signal to entity type than others. For example, two entities in the domain of the "came with" relation often will not share semantic types, but two entities in the domain of the "autographed" relation will almost always share a type. To capture this intuition, we define relation weight $w(r)$ as the observed probability (among the linked entities) that two en-

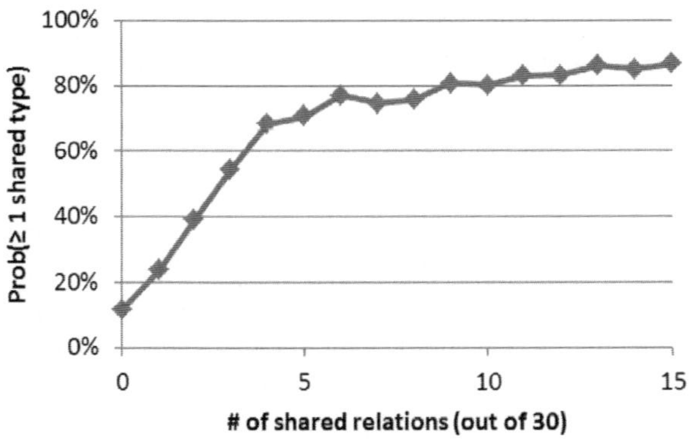

Figure 6: Entities that share more textual relations are more likely to have semantic types in common.

tities will share a Freebase type if they both occur in the domain of r. If $D(r)$ = all entities observed in the domain of relation r and $T(e)$ = all Freebase types listed for entity e, then weight $w(r)$ of a textual relation string r is:

$$w(r) = \sum_{e_1,e_2 \in D(r),\ e_1 \neq e_2} \frac{I(e_1,e_2)}{|D(r)| \cdot (|D(r)|-1)}$$

$$I(e_1,e_2) = \begin{cases} 1, & \text{if } |T(e_1) \cap T(e_2)| > 0 \\ 0, & \text{otherwise.} \end{cases}$$

Table 3 shows examples of high weight relations, and Table 4 shows low weight relations. We now modify the *Find Similar Entities* step such that if a linked entity shares a set of relations Q with the entity being typed, then it receives a score which considers all shared relations $q \in Q$ but uses the high weight relations more. On a development set we found that a score of $\sum_{q \in Q} 10^{4 \cdot w(q)}$ was effective, as higher weight signifies much stronger signal. This score then determines which entities to place in S.

5.4 Evaluation

The goal of the evaluation is to judge how well our method can predict the Freebase semantic types of entities in our scenario. Our linked entities covered 1,339 Freebase types, including many interesting types such as *computer operating system*, *religious text*, *airline* and *baseball team*. Human judges would have trouble manually annotating new entities with all these types because there are too many to keep in mind and understand the characteristics

"is a highway in"
"is a university located in"
"became the president of"
"turned down the role of"
"has an embassy in"

Table 3: Example relations found to have high weight.

"comes with"
"is a generic term for"
"works best on"
"can be made from"
"is almost identical to"

Table 4: Example relations found to have low weight.

of. Instead, we automatically generate testing data by sampling entities from L, and then test on ability to recover the actual Freebase types (which we know).

We sample a *HEAD* set of distinct 500 Freebase entities (drawn randomly from our set of linked extractions), and a *TAIL* set of 500 entities (drawn randomly from our set of linked entities). An entity that occurs in many extractions is more likely to be in *HEAD* than *TAIL*. Our sampling also picks only entities that occur with at least 10 relations, which is appropriate for the Web scenario where more instances can always be queried for.

For baselines we use random baseline B_{Random} and a frequency baseline $B_{Frequency}$ which always returns types in order of their frequency among all linked entities (e.g., always *person*, then *location*, etc). We evaluate our system without relation weighting ($S_{NoWeight}$) and also with relation weighting ($S_{Weighted}$). For $S_{Weighted}$ we leave all the test set entities out when calculating global relation weights. Our metrics are *Precision at 1* and *F_1 score*. Precision at 1 measures how often the top returned type is a correct type, and is useful for applications that want one type per entity. F_1 measures how well the method recovers the full set of Freebase types (for each test case we graph precision/recall and take the max F_1), and is useful for applications such as typed question answering.

Table 5 shows the results. B_{Random} performs poorly because there are so many semantic types, and very few of them are correct for each test case. $B_{Frequency}$ performs slightly better on *TAIL* than *HEAD* because *TAIL* contains more entities of the most frequent types. $S_{NoWeight}$ performance

	HEAD		TAIL	
	Prec@1	**F$_1$**	**Prec@1**	**F$_1$**
$\mathbf{B_{Random}}$	0.008	0.028	0.004	0.023
$\mathbf{B_{Frequency}}$	0.244	0.302	0.298	0.322
$\mathbf{S_{NoWeight}}$	0.542†	0.465†	0.510†	0.456†
$\mathbf{S_{Weighted}}$	0.610‡	0.521‡	0.598‡	0.522‡

Table 5: Evaluation on HEAD and TAIL, 500 elements each. † indicates statistical significance over $\mathbf{B_{Frequency}}$, and ‡ over both $\mathbf{B_{Frequency}}$ and $\mathbf{S_{NoWeight}}$. Significance is measured using the Student's t-test at 95% confidence. The top type predicted by our $\mathbf{S_{Weighted}}$ method is correct about 60% of the time, while the top type predicted by the $\mathbf{B_{Frequency}}$ baseline is correct under 30% of the time.

is statistically significant above all baselines, and $S_{Weighted}$ is statistically significant over $S_{NoWeight}$ on both test sets and metrics.

5.5 Analysis

$S_{Weighted}$ was successful at recovering the correct Freebase types of many entities. For example, it finds that "Atherosclerosis" is a *medical risk factor* by connecting it to "obesity" and "diabetes," that "Supernatural" is a *TV program* and a *Netflix title* by connecting it to "House" and "30 Rock," and that "America West" is an *aircraft owner* and an *airline* by connecting it to "Etihad Airways" and "China Eastern Airlines." While precision at 1 around 60% may not be high enough yet for certain applications, it is significantly better than competing approaches, which are under 30%, and we hope that our values can serve as a non-trivial baseline on this task for future systems.

One example where $S_{Weighted}$ made some mistakes is *fictional characters*. Many *fictional characters* participate in a textual relations that make them look like *people* (e.g., "was born on"), but predicting that they belong to *people* class is incorrect. Some performance hit was also due to entity linking errors. From an assertion like "The Four Seasons is located in Hamamatsu," our entity linker (and other entity linkers we tried) prefer linking "The Four Seasons" to Vivaldi's music composition rather than the hotel chain. We are then unable to recover *music composition* type from relations like "is located in." Our algorithm relies on accurate entity linking in L, but there is a precision/recall tradeoff to consider here because it also benefits from higher coverage of entities and relations in L.

As a general reference for performance of state-of-the-art fine-grained entity classification, the FIGER system (Ling and Weld, 2012) for classifying into 112 types reported F_1 scores ranging from 0.471 to 0.693 in their experiments. It is important to note that these numbers are not directly comparable to us because they used different data, different (and fewer) types, and different evaluation methodology.

6 Discussion

This paper presented an approach for working with non-Wikipedia entities in text. Consider the following possibilities for a noun phrase in a text corpus:

Wikipedia Entity: (e.g., "Computer Science," "South America," "apple juice") - Entity linking techniques can identify and type these.

Non-Wikipedia, Non-Entity: (e.g., "strange things," "Early studies," "A link") - Our classifier from Section 4 is able to filter these.

Non-Wikipedia, Entity: (e.g., "Safflower oil," "prune juice," "Amazon UK") - We identify these as entities, then propagate semantic types to them. Our technique finds that "Safflower oil" occurs with high weight relations such as "is sometimes used to treat" and "can be substituted for," making it similar to linked entities such as "Phentermine" and "Dandelion," and then correctly predicts semantic types including *food ingredient* and *medical treatment*.

6.1 Typed Question Answering

From our set of 15 million assertions, we found and typed many non-Wikipedia entities. In *food* while Wikipedia has "crab meat," we find it is missing others such as "rabbit meat" and "goat milk." In *job titles* it has "scientist" and "lawyer," but we find it is missing "PhD student," "fashion designer," and others. We find many of the *people* and *employers* not prominent enough for Wikipedia.

One application of this research is to increase the yield of applications such as Typed Question Answering (Buscaldi and Rosso, 2006). For example, consider the query "What *computer game* is a lot of fun?" A search for assertions matching "* is a lot of fun" in the data yields around 1,000 results such as "camping," "David Sedaris" and "Hawaii." Entity linking allows us to identify just the *computer games* in Wikipedia that match the query, such as "Civilization." However, around 400 query matches could not be entity linked. Our noun-phrase classifier filters out non-entities such as "actual play," "Just this" and "Two kids." After predicting types for the matches that did not get filtered, we find additional non-Wikipedia *computer games* that match the query, including "Cooking Dash," "Delicious Deluxe" and "Slingo Supreme."

7 Future Work

An area we are continuing to improve the system on is *textual ambiguity*. For example, an unlinkable noun phrase might simultaneously be the name of a *film*, a *car*, and a *person*. Instead of outputting that the noun phrase holds all of those types, a stronger output would be to realize that the noun phrase is ambiguous, determine how many senses it has, and determine which sense is being referred to in each instance. We have ideas for how to detect ambiguous entities using mutual exclusion (Carlson, 2010) and functional relations. For example, if we predict that a noun phrase has *film* and *car* types but we also observe in our linked instances that these types are mutually exclusive, then this is good evidence that the noun phrase refers to multiple terms.

We also plan to continue improving our techniques, as there is still plenty of room for improvement on both subtasks. For detecting new entities, we are interested in seeing if timestamped Twitter data could be analyzed to increase both recall and precision. For predicting semantic types, (Kozareva et al., 2011) proposed additional techniques which we have not fully explored. Also, we can incorporate additional signals such as shared term heads when they are available, in order to help find terms that are likely to share types. Last, we would like to feed back our system output to improve system performance. For example, non-entity noun phrases that make it to the typing step might lead to particular predicted type distributions that indicate an error occurred earlier in the process.

8 Conclusion

In this paper we showed that while entity linking cannot link to entities outside of Wikipedia, once a large text corpus has been entity linked, the presence and content of the existing links can be leveraged to help detect and semantically type the non-Wikipedia entities as well. We designed techniques for detecting whether unlinkable noun phrases are entities, and if they are, then propagating semantic types to them from the linked entities. In our evaluations, we showed that our techniques achieve statistically significant improvement over baseline methods.

Our research here takes initial steps toward a future where the vast universe of entities that are not prominent enough to include in manually-authored knowledge bases is analyzed automatically instead of being left behind.

Acknowledgements

We thank Stephen Soderland, Xiao Ling, and the three anonymous reviewers for their helpful feedback on earlier drafts. This research was supported in part by NSF grant IIS-0803481, ONR grant N00014-08-1-0431, and DARPA contract FA8750-09-C-0179, and carried out at the University of Washington's Turing Center.

References

Razvan Bunescu and Marius Paşca. 2006. Using encyclopedic knowledge for named entity disambiguation. In *Proceedings of the 11th Conference of the European Chapter of the Association of Computational Linguistics (EACL)*.

Davide Buscaldi and Paolo Rosso. 2006. Mining knowledge from wikipedia for the question answering task. In *Proceedings of the 5th International Conference on Language Resources and Evaluation (LREC)*.

Andrew Carlson. 2010. *Coupled Semi-Supervised Learning*. Ph.D. thesis, Carnegie Mellon University.

Silviu Cucerzan. 2007. Large-scale named entity disambiguation based on wikipedia data. In *Proceedings of EMNLP*.

Mark Dredze, Paul McNamee, Delip Rao, Adam Gerber, and Tim Finin. 2010. Entity disambiguation for knowledge base population. In *Proceedings of COLING*.

Oren Etzioni, Michael Cafarella, Doug Downey, Ana-Maria Popescu, Tal Shaked, Stephen Soderland, Daniel S. Weld, and Alexander Yates. 2005. Unsupervised named-entity extraction from the Web: An experimental study. In *Artificial Intelligence*.

Oren Etzioni, Michele Banko, and Michael J. Cafarella. 2006. Machine Reading. In *Proceedings of the 21st National Conference on Artificial Intelligence (AAAI)*.

James A. Evans and Jacob G. Foster. 2011. Metaknowledge. In *Science*.

Anthony Fader, Stephen Soderland, and Oren Etzioni. 2009. Scaling Wikipedia-based named entity disambiguation to arbitrary Web text. In *IJCAI-09 Workshop on User-contributed Knowledge and Artificial Intelligence (WikiAI09)*.

Anthony Fader, Stephen Soderland, and Oren Etzioni. 2011. Identifying relations for open information extraction. In *Proceedings of EMNLP*.

Paolo Ferragina and Ugo Scaiella. 2010. Tagme: On-the-fly annotation of short text fragments (by wikipedia entities). In *Proceedings of CIKM*.

Eduard Hovy, Zornitsa Kozareva, and Ellen Riloff. 2009. Toward completeness in concept extraction and classification. In *Proceedings of EMNLP*.

Zornitsa Kozareva, Konstantin Voevodski, and Shang-Hua Teng. 2011. Class label enhancement via related instances. In *Proceedings of EMNLP*.

Sayali Kulkarni, Amit Singh, Ganesh Ramakrishnan, and Soumen Chakrabarti. 2009. Collective annotation of wikipedia entities in text. In *Proceedings of KDD*.

Changki Lee, Yi-Gyu Hwang, and Myung-Gil Jang. 2007. Fine-grained named entity recognition and relation extraction for question answering. In *Proceedings of SIGIR*.

Xiao Ling and Daniel S. Weld. 2012. Fine-grained entity recognition. In *Proceedings of the 26th Conference on Artificial Intelligence (AAAI)*.

Jean-Baptiste Michel, Yuan Kui Shen, Aviva P. Aiden, Adrian Veres, Matthew K. Gray, The Google Books Team, Joseph P. Pickett, Dale Hoiberg, Dan Clancy, Peter Norvig, Jon Orwant, and Steven Pinker. 2010. Quantitative analysis of culture using millions of digitized books. In *Science*.

David Milne and Ian H. Witten. 2008. Learning to link with wikipedia. In *Proceedings of the 17h ACM International Conference on Information and Knowledge Management (CIKM)*.

Marius Paşca. 2004. Acquisition of categorized named entities for web search. In *Proceedings of the ACM International Conference on Information and Knowledge Management (CIKM)*.

Patrick Pantel and Deepak Ravichandran. 2004. Automatically labeling semantic classes. In *Proceedings of HLT-NAACL*.

Patrick Pantel, Eric Crestan, Arkady Borkovsky, Ana-Maria Popescu, and Vishnu Vyas. 2009. Web-scale distributional similarity and entity set expansion. In *Proceedings of EMNLP*.

Danuta Ploch. 2011. Exploring entity relations for named entity disambiguation. In *Proceedings of the Annual Meeting of the Association of Computational Linguistics (ACL)*.

Willard Van Orman Quine. 1948. On what there is. In *Review of Metaphysics*.

Altaf Rahman and Vincent Ng. 2010. Inducing fine-grained semantic classes via hierarchical and collective classification. In *Proceedings of COLING*.

Lev Ratinov and Dan Roth. 2009. Design challenges and misconceptions in named entity recognition. In *Proceedings of the Thirteenth Conference on Computational Natural Language Learning (CoNLL)*.

Lev Ratinov, Dan Roth, Doug Downey, and Mike Anderson. 2011. Local and global algorithms for disambiguation to wikipedia. In *Proceedings of the Annual Meeting of the Association of Computational Linguistics (ACL)*.

Satoshi Sekine and Chikashi Nobata. 2004. Definition, dictionaries and tagger for extended named entity hierarchy. In *Proceedings of the 4th International Conference on Language Resources and Evaluation (LREC)*.

Partha Pratim Talukdar and Fernando Pereira. 2010. Experiments in graph-based semi-supervised learning methods for class-instance acquisition. In *Proceedings of the Annual Meeting of the Association of Computational Linguistics (ACL)*.

Partha Pratim Talukdar, Joseph Reisinger, Marius Paşca, Deepak Ravichandran, Rahul Bhagat, and Fernando Pereira. 2008. Weakly supervised acquisition of labeled class instances using graph random walks. In *Proceedings of EMNLP*.

Partha Pratim Talukdar, Derry Tanti Wijaya, and Tom Mitchell. 2012. Coupled temporal scoping of relational facts. In *Proceedings of WSDM*.

Chi Wang, Kaushik Chakrabarti, Tao Cheng, and Surajit Chaudhuri. 2012. Targeted disambiguation of ad-hoc, homogeneous sets of named entities. In *Proceedings of the 21st International World Wide Web Conference (WWW)*.

Derry Tanti Wijaya and Reyyan Yeniterzi. 2011. Understanding semantic changes of words over centuries. In *Workshop on Detecting and Exploiting Cultural Diversity on the Social Web*.

A Novel Discriminative Framework for Sentence-Level Discourse Analysis

Shafiq Joty and Giuseppe Carenini and Raymond T. Ng
{rjoty, carenini, rng}@cs.ubc.ca
Department of Computer Science
University of British Columbia
Vancouver, BC, V6T 1Z4, Canada

Abstract

We propose a complete probabilistic discriminative framework for performing sentence-level discourse analysis. Our framework comprises a discourse segmenter, based on a binary classifier, and a discourse parser, which applies an optimal CKY-like parsing algorithm to probabilities inferred from a Dynamic Conditional Random Field. We show on two corpora that our approach outperforms the state-of-the-art, often by a wide margin.

1 Introduction

Automatic discourse analysis has been shown to be critical in several fundamental Natural Language Processing (NLP) tasks including text generation (Prasad et al., 2005), summarization (Marcu, 2000b), sentence compression (Sporleder and Lapata, 2005) and question answering (Verberne et al., 2007). Rhetorical Structure Theory (RST) (Mann and Thompson, 1988), one of the most influential theories of discourse, posits a tree representation of a discourse, known as a Discourse Tree (DT), as exemplified by the sample DT shown in Figure 1. The leaves of a DT correspond to contiguous atomic text spans, also called Elementary Discourse Units (EDUs) (three in the example). The adjacent EDUs are connected by a *rhetorical* relation (e.g., ELABORATION), and the resulting larger text spans are recursively also subject to this relation linking. A span linked by a rhetorical relation can be either a NUCLEUS or a SATELLITE depending on how central the message is to the author. Discourse analysis in RST involves two subtasks: (i) breaking the text into EDUs (known as *discourse segmentation*) and (ii) linking the EDUs into a labeled hierarchical tree structure (known as *discourse parsing*).

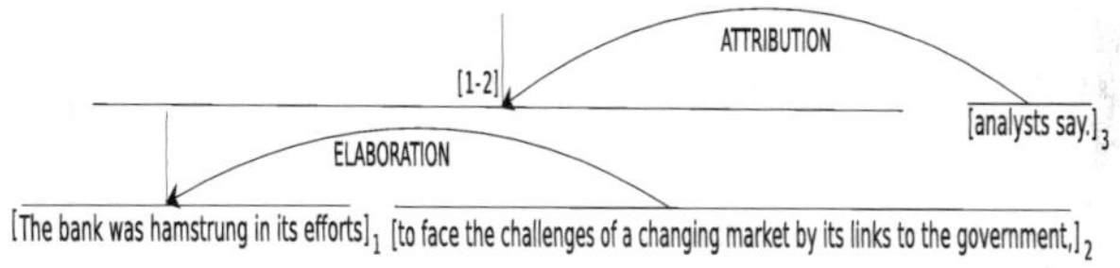

Figure 1: Discourse structure of a sentence in RST-DT.

Previous studies on discourse analysis have been quite successful in identifying what machine learning approaches and what features are more useful for automatic discourse segmentation and parsing (Soricut and Marcu, 2003; Subba and Eugenio, 2009; duVerle and Prendinger, 2009). However, all the proposed solutions suffer from at least one of the following two key limitations: first, they make strong independence assumptions on the structure and the labels of the resulting DT, and typically model the construction of the DT and the labeling of the relations separately; second, they apply a greedy, suboptimal algorithm to build the structure of the DT.

In this paper, we propose a new *sentence-level* discourse parser that addresses both limitations. The crucial component is a probabilistic discriminative parsing model, expressed as a Dynamic Conditional Random Field (DCRF) (Sutton et al., 2007). By representing the *structure* and the *relation* of each discourse tree constituent jointly and by explicitly capturing the *sequential* and *hierarchical* dependencies between constituents of a discourse tree, our DCRF model does not make any independence assumption among these properties. Furthermore, our parsing model supports a bottom-up parsing algorithm which is non-greedy and provably optimal.

The discourse parser assumes that the input text has been already segmented into EDUs. As an additional contribution of this paper, we propose a novel discriminative approach to discourse segmentation that not only achieves state-of-the-art performance, but also reduces the time and space complexities by using fewer features. Notice that the combination of our segmenter with our parser forms a complete probabilistic discriminative framework for performing sentence-level discourse analysis.

Our framework was tested in a series of experiments. The empirical evaluation indicates that our approach to discourse parsing outperforms the state-of-the-art by a wide margin. Moreover, we show this to be the case on two very different genres: news articles and instructional how-to-do manuals.

In the rest of the paper, after discussing related work, we present our discourse parser. Then, we describe our segmenter. The experiments and the corpora we used are described next, followed by a discussion of the key results and some error analysis.

2 Related work

Automatic discourse analysis has a long history; see (Stede, 2011) for a detailed overview. Soricut and Marcu (2003) present the publicly available SPADE[1] system that comes with probabilistic models for *sentence-level* discourse segmentation and parsing based on lexical and syntactic features derived from the lexicalized syntactic tree of a sentence. Their parsing algorithm finds the most probable DT for a sentence, where the probabilities of the constituents are estimated by their parsing model. A constituent (e.g., ATTRIBUTION-NS[(1,2),3] in Figure 1) in a DT has two components, first, the *label* denoting the relation and second, the *structure* indicating which spans are being linked by the relation. The nuclearity statuses of the spans are built into the relation labels (e.g., NS[(1,2),3] means that span (1,2) is the NUCLEUS and it comes before span 3 which is the SATELLITE). SPADE is limited in several ways. It makes an independence assumption between the label and the structure while modeling a constituent, and it ignores the sequential and hierarchical dependencies between the constituents in the parsing model. Furthermore, SPADE relies only on lexico-syntactic features, and it follows a *generative* approach to estimate the model parameters for the segmentation and the parsing models. SPADE was trained and tested on the RST-DT corpus (Carlson et al., 2002), which contains human-annotated discourse trees for news articles.

Subsequent research addresses the question of how much syntax one really needs in discourse analysis. Sporleder and Lapata (2005) focus on discourse chunking, comprising the two subtasks of segmentation and non-hierarchical nuclearity assignment. More specifically, they examine whether features derived via part of speech (POS) and chunk taggers would be sufficient for these purposes. Their results on RST-DT turn out to be comparable to SPADE without using any features from the syntactic tree. Later, Fisher and Roark (2007) demonstrate over 4% absolute "performance gain" in segmentation, by combining the features extracted from the syntactic tree with the ones derived via taggers. Using quite a large number of features in a binary log-linear model they achieve the state-of-the-art segmentation performance on the RST-DT test set.

On the different genre of *instructional manuals*, Subba and Eugenio (2009) propose a shift-reduce parser that relies on a classifier to find the appropriate relation between two text segments. Their classifier is based on Inductive Logic Programming (ILP), which learns first-order logic rules from a large set of features including the linguistically rich *compositional semantics* coming from a semantic parser. They show that the compositional semantics improves the classification performance. However, their discourse parser implements a greedy approach (hence not optimal) and their classifier disregards the sequence and hierarchical dependencies.

Using RST-DT, Hernault et al. (2010) present the HILDA system that comes with a segmenter and a parser based on Support Vector Machines (SVMs). The segmenter is a binary SVM classifier which relies on the same lexico-syntactic features used in SPADE, but with more context. The discourse parser builds a DT iteratively utilizing two SVM classifiers in each iteration: (i) a binary classifier decides which of the two adjacent spans to link, and (ii) a multi-class classifier then connects the se-

[1]http://www.isi.edu/licensed-sw/spade/

lected spans with the appropriate relation. They use a very large set of features in their parser. However, taking a radically-greedy approach, they model structure and relations separately, and ignore the sequence dependencies in their models.

Recently, there has been an explosion of interest in Conditional Random Fields (CRFs) (Lafferty et al., 2001) for solving structured output classification problems, with many successful applications in NLP including syntactic parsing (Finkel et al., 2008), syntactic chunking (Sha and Pereira, 2003) and discourse chunking (Ghosh et al., 2011) in Penn Discourse Treebank (Prasad et al., 2008). CRFs being a discriminative approach to sequence modeling (i.e., directly models the conditional $p(\mathbf{y}|\mathbf{x}, \Theta)$), have several advantages over its generative counterparts such as Hidden Markov Models (HMMs) and Markov Random Fields (MRFs), which first model the joint $p(\mathbf{y}, \mathbf{x}|\Theta)$, then infer the conditional $p(\mathbf{y}|\mathbf{x}, \Theta)$). Key advantages include the ability to incorporate arbitrary overlapping local and global features, and the ability to relax strong independence assumptions. It has been advocated that CRFs are generally more accurate since they do not "waste effort" modeling complex distributions (i.e., $p(\mathbf{x})$) that are not relevant for the target task (Murphy, 2012).

3 The Discourse Parser

Assuming that a sentence is already segmented into a sequence of EDUs $e_1, e_2, \ldots e_n$ manually or by an automatic segmenter (see Section 4), the discourse parsing problem is to decide which spans to connect (i.e., *structure* of the DT) and which relations (i.e., *labels* of the internal nodes) to use in the process of building the hierarchical DT. To build the DTs effectively, a common assumption is that they are *binary* trees (Soricut and Marcu, 2003; duVerle and Prendinger, 2009). That is, multi-nuclear relations (e.g., LIST, JOINT, SEQUENCE) involving more than two EDUs are mapped to a hierarchical right-branching binary tree. For example, a flat $LIST(e_1, e_2, e_3, e_4)$ is mapped to a right-branching binary tree $LIST(e_1, LIST(e_2, LIST(e_3, e_4)))$.

Our discourse parser has two components. The first component, the *parsing model*, assigns a probability to every possible DT. The second component, the *parsing algorithm*, finds the most probable DT among the candidate discourse trees.

3.1 Parsing Model

A DT can be represented as a set of constituents of the form $R[i, m, j]$, which denotes a rhetorical relation R that holds between the span containing EDUs i through m, and the span containing EDUs $m{+}1$ through j. For example, the DT in Figure 1 can be written as {ELABORATION-NS[1,1,2], ATTRIBUTION-NS[1,2,3]}. Notice that a relation R also indicates the nuclearity assignments of the spans being connected, which can be one of NUCLEUS-SATELLITE (NS), SATELLITE-NUCLEUS (SN) and NUCLEUS-NUCLEUS (NN).

Given the model parameters Θ and a candidate DT T, for all the constituents c in T, our parsing model estimates the *conditional probability* $P(c|C, \Theta)$, which specifies the joint probability of the relation R and the structure $[i, m, j]$ associated with the constituent c, given that c has a set of sub-constituents C. For instance, for the DT shown in Figure 1, our model would estimate $P(R'[1, 1, 2]|\Theta)$, $P(R'[2, 2, 3]|\Theta)$, $P(R'[1, 2, 3]|R''[1, 1, 2], \Theta)$ etc. for all R' and R'' ranging on the set of relations. In what follows we describe our probabilistic parsing model to compute all these conditional probabilities $P(c|C, \Theta)$. We will demonstrate how our approach not only models the structure and the relation jointly, but it also captures *linear sequence dependencies* and *hierarchical dependencies* between constituents of a DT.

Our novel parsing model is the Dynamic Conditional Random Field (DCRF) (Sutton et al., 2007) shown in Figure 2. A DCRF is a generalization of linear-chain CRFs to represent complex interaction between labels, such as when performing multiple labeling tasks on the same sequence. The *observed* nodes W_j in the figure are the text spans. A text span can be either an EDU or a concatenation of a sequence of EDUs. The *structure* nodes $S_j \in \{0, 1\}$ in the figure represent whether text spans W_{j-1} and W_j should be connected or not. The *relation* nodes $R_j \in \{1 \ldots M\}$ denote the discourse relation between spans W_{j-1} and W_j, given that M is the total number of relations in our relation set. Notice that we now model the structure and the relation jointly and also take the sequential dependencies between adjacent constituents into consideration.

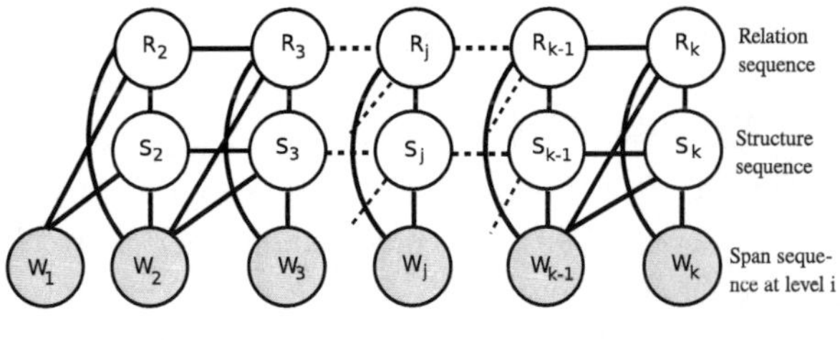

Figure 2: A Dynamic CRF as a discourse parsing model.

We can obtain the conditional probabilities of the constituents (i.e., $P(c|C, \Theta)$) of all candidate DTs for a sentence by applying the DCRF parsing model recursively at different levels, and by computing the posterior marginals of the relation-structure pairs. To illustrate, consider the example sentence in Figure 1 where we have three EDUs e_1, e_2 and e_3. The DCRF model for the first level is shown in Figure 3(a), where the (observed) EDUs are the spans in the span sequence. Given this model, we obtain the probabilities of the constituents $R[1, 1, 2]$ and $R[2, 2, 3]$ by computing the posterior marginals $P(R_2, S_2{=}1|e_1, e_2, e_3, \Theta)$ and $P(R_3, S_3{=}1|e_1, e_2, e_3, \Theta)$, respectively. At the second level (see Figure 3(b)), there are two possible span sequences $(e_{1:2}, e_3)$ and $(e_1, e_{2:3})$. In the first sequence, EDUs e_1 and e_2 are linked into a larger span, and in the second one, EDUs e_2 and e_3 are connected into a larger span. We apply our DCRF model to the two possible span sequences and obtain the probabilities of the constituents $R[1, 2, 3]$ and $R[1, 1, 3]$ by computing the posterior marginals $P(R_3, S_3{=}1|e_{1:2}, e_3, \Theta)$ and $P(R_{2:3}, S_{2:3}{=}1|e_1, e_{2:3}, \Theta)$, respectively.

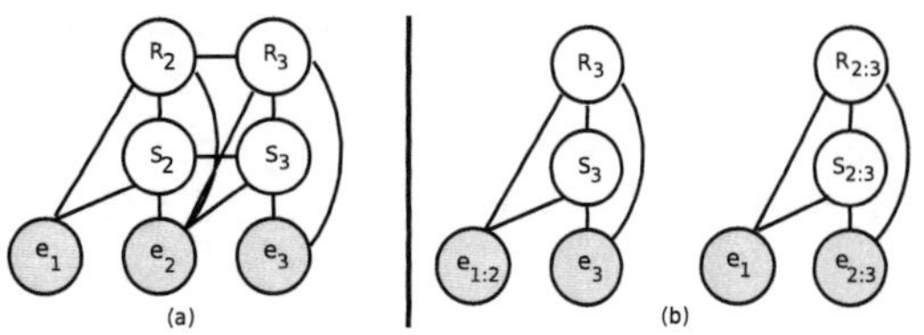

Figure 3: DCRF model applied to the sequences at different levels in the example in Fig. 1. (a) A sequence at the first level (b) Two possible sequences at the second level.

To further clarify the process, let us assume that the sentence contains four EDUs e_1, e_2, e_3 and e_4. At the first level (Figure 4(a)), there is only one possible span sequence to which we apply our DCRF model. We obtain the probabilities of the constituents $R[1, 1, 2]$, $R[2, 2, 3]$ and $R[3, 3, 4]$ by computing the posterior marginals $P(R_2, S_2{=}1|e_1, e_2, e_3, e_4, \Theta)$, $P(R_3, S_3{=}1|e_1, e_2, e_3, e_4, \Theta)$ and $P(R_4, S_4{=}1|e_1, e_2, e_3, e_4, \Theta)$, respectively. At the second level (Figure 4(b)), there are three possible sequences $(e_{1:2}, e_3, e_4)$, $(e_1, e_{2:3}, e_4)$ and $(e_1, e_2, e_{3:4})$. When the DCRF model is applied to the sequence $(e_{1:2}, e_3, e_4)$, we obtain the probabilities of the constituent $R[1, 2, 3]$ by computing the posterior marginal $P(R_3, S_3{=}1|e_{1:2}, e_3, e_4, \Theta)$. Likewise, the posterior marginals $P(R_{2:3}, S_{2:3}{=}1|e_1, e_{2:3}, e_4, \Theta)$ and $P(R_4, S_4{=}1|e_1, e_{2:3}, e_4, \Theta)$ in the DCRF model applied to the sequence $(e_1, e_{2:3}, e_4)$ represents the probabilities of the constituents $R[1, 1, 3]$ and $R[2, 3, 4]$, respectively. Similarly, we attain the probabilities of the constituent $R[2, 2, 4]$ from the DCRF model applied to the sequence $(e_1, e_2, e_{3:4})$ by computing the posterior marginal $P(R_{3:4}, S_{3:4}{=}1|e_1, e_2, e_{3:4}, \Theta)$. At the third level (Figure 4(c)), there are three possible sequences $(e_{1:3}, e_4)$, $(e_1, e_{2:4})$ and $(e_{1:2}, e_{3:4})$, to which we apply our model and acquire the probabilities of the constituents $R[1, 3, 4]$, $R[1, 1, 4]$ and $R[1, 2, 4]$ by computing their respective posterior marginals.

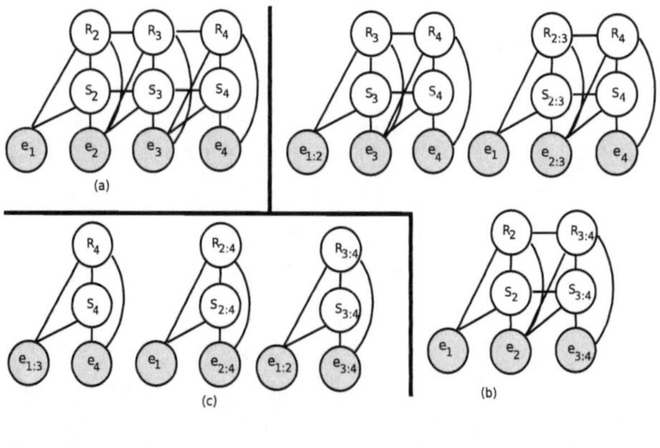

Figure 4: DCRF model applied to the sequences at different levels of a discourse tree. (a) A sequence at the first level, (b) Three possible sequences at the second level, (c) Two possible sequences at the third level.

Our DCRF model is designed using MALLET (McCallum, 2002). In order to avoid overfitting we regularize the DCRF model with l_2 regularization and learn the model parameters using the limited-memory BFGS (L-BFGS) fitting algorithm. Since exact inference can be intractable in DCRF models, we perform approximate inference (to compute the posterior marginals) using tree-based reparameterization (Wainwright et al., 2002).

3.1.1 Features Used in the Parsing Model

Crucial to parsing performance is the set of features used, as summarized in Table 1. Note that these features are defined on two consecutive spans W_{j-1} and W_j of a span sequence. Most of the features have been explored in previous studies. However, we improve some of these as explained below.

Organizational features encode useful information about the surface structure of a sentence as shown by (duVerle and Prendinger, 2009). We measure the length of the spans in terms of the number of *EDUs* and *tokens* in it. However, in order to better adjust to the length variations, rather than computing their absolute numbers in a span, we choose to measure their *relative numbers* with respect to their total numbers in the sentence. For example, in a sentence containing three EDUs, a span containing two of these EDUs will have a relative EDU number of 0.67. We also measure the *distances* of the spans from the beginning and to the end of the sentence in terms of the number of EDUs.

8 organizational features
Relative number of EDUs in *span 1* and *span 2*.
Relative number of tokens in *span 1* and *span 2*.
Distances of span 1 in EDUs to the *beginning* and to the *end*.
Distances of span 2 in EDUs to the *beginning* and to the *end*.
8 N-gram features
Beginning and *end* lexical N-grams in span 1.
Beginning and *end* lexical N-grams in span 2.
Beginning and *end* POS N-grams in span 1.
Beginning and *end* POS N-grams in span 2.
5 dominance set features
Syntactic labels of the *head* node and the *attachment* node.
Lexical heads of the *head* node and the *attachment* node.
Dominance relationship between the two text spans.
2 contextual features
Previous and *next* feature vectors.
2 substructure features
Root nodes of the *left* and *right* rhetorical subtrees.

Table 1: Features used in the DCRF parsing model.

Discourse connectives (e.g., *because, but*), when present, signal rhetorical relations between two text segments (Knott and Dale, 1994; Marcu, 2000a). However, previous studies (e.g., Hernault et al. (2010), Biran and Rambow (2011)) suggest that an empirically acquired lexical N-gram dictionary is more effective than a fixed list of connectives, since this approach is domain independent and capable of capturing non-lexical cues such as punctuations. To build the *lexical* **N-gram** dictionary empirically from the training corpus we consider the first and last N tokens ($N \in \{1, 2\}$) of each span and rank them according to their mutual information[2] with the two labels, *Structure* and *Relation*. Intuitively, the most informative cues are not only the most frequent, but also the ones that are indicative of the labels in the training data (Blitzer, 2008). In addition to the lexical N-grams we also encode *POS* tags of the first and last N tokens ($N \in \{1, 2\}$) as features.

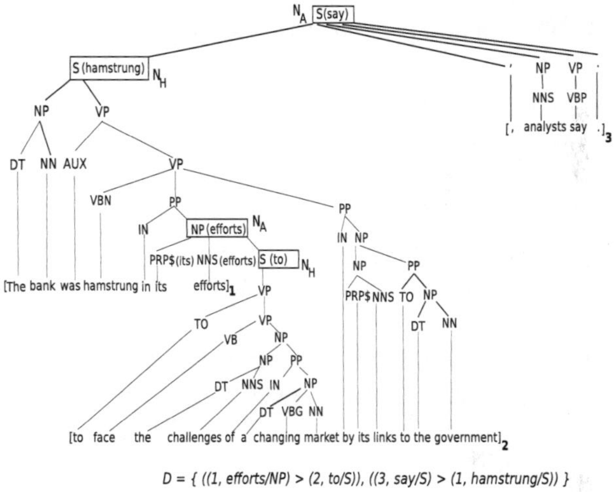

Figure 5: A discourse segmented lexicalized syntactic tree. Boxed nodes form the dominance set D.

Dominance set extracted from the Discourse Segmented Lexicalized Syntactic Tree (DS-LST) (Soricut and Marcu, 2003) has been shown to be a very effective feature in SPADE. Figure 5 shows the DS-LST for our running example (see Figure 1 and 3). In a DS-LST, each EDU except the one with the root node must have a *head node* N_H that is attached to an *attachment node* N_A residing in a separate EDU. A dominance set D (shown at the bottom of Figure 5 for our example) contains these *attachment* points of the EDUs in a DS-LST. In addition to the syntactic and lexical information of the head and attachment nodes, each element in D also represents a dominance relationship between the EDUs involved. The EDU with N_A dominates the EDU with N_H. In or-

[2]In contrast, HILDA ranks the N-grams by frequencies.

der to extract dominance set features for two consecutive spans $e_{i:j}$ and $e_{j+1:k}$, we first compute D from the DS-LST of the sentence. We then extract the element from D that holds across the EDUs j and $j+1$. In our running example, for the spans e_1 and e_2 (Figure 3(a)), the relevant dominance set element is *(1, efforts/NP)>(2, to/S)*. We encode the syntactic labels and lexical heads of N_H and N_A and the dominance relationship (i.e., which of the two spans is dominating) as features in our model.

We also incorporate more **contextual** information by including the above features computed for the neighboring span pairs in the current feature vector.

We incorporate *hierarchical dependencies* between constituents in a DT by means of the **substructure** features. For the two adjacent spans $e_{i:j}$ and $e_{j+1:k}$, we extract the roots of the rhetorical subtrees spanning over $e_{i:j}$ (left) and $e_{j+1:k}$ (right). In our example (see Figure 1 and Figure 3 (b)), the root of the rhetorical subtree spanning over $e_{1:2}$ is ELABORATION-NS. However, this assumes the presence of a labeled DT which is not the case when we apply the parser to a new sentence. This problem can be easily solved by looping twice through building the model and the parsing algorithm (described below). We first build the model without considering the substructure features. Then we find the optimal DT employing our parsing algorithm. This intermediate DT will now provide labels for the substructures. Next we can build a new, more accurate model by including the substructure features, and run again the parsing algorithm to find the final optimal DT.

3.2 Parsing Algorithm

Our parsing model above assigns a conditional probability to every possible DT constituent for a sentence, the job of the parsing algorithm is to find the most probable DT. Formally, this can be written as,

$$DT^* = argmax_{\ DT} P(DT|\Theta)$$

Our discourse parser implements a probabilistic CKY-like bottom-up algorithm for computing the most likely parse of a sentence using dynamic programming; see (Jurafsky and Martin, 2008) for a description. Specifically, with n number of EDUs in a sentence, we use the upper-triangular portion of the $n \times n$ Dynamic Programming Table (DPT). The cell $[i, j]$ in the DPT represents the span containing EDUs i through j and stores the probability of a constituent $R[i, m, j]$, where $m = argmax_{\ i \leq k \leq j} P(R[i, k, j])$.

In contrast to HILDA which implements a greedy algorithm, our approach finds a DT that is globally optimal. Our approach is also different from SPADE's implementation. SPADE first finds the *tree structure* that is globally optimal, then it assigns the most probable *relations* to the internal nodes. More specifically, the cell $[i, j]$ in SPADE's DPT stores the probability of a constituent $R[i, m, j]$, where $m = argmax_{\ i \leq k \leq j} P([i, k, j])$. Disregarding the relation label R while building the DPT, this approach may find a tree that is **not** globally optimal.

4 The Discourse Segmenter

Our discourse parser above assumes that the input sentences have been already segmented into EDUs. Since it has been shown that discourse segmentation is a primary source of inaccuracy for discourse parsing (Soricut and Marcu, 2003), we have developed our own segmenter, that not only achieves state-of-the-art performance as shown later, but also reduces the time complexity by using fewer features.

Our segmenter implements a binary classifier to decide for each word (except the last word) in a sentence, whether to put an EDU boundary *after* that word. We use a Logistic Regression (LR) (i.e., discriminative) model with l_2 regularization and learn the model parameters using the L-BFGS algorithm, which gives quadratic convergence rate. To avoid overfitting, we use 5-fold cross validation to learn the regularization strength parameter from the training data. We also use a simple *bagging* technique (Breiman, 1996) to deal with the sparsity of *boundary* tags. Note that, our first attempt at this task implemented a linear-chain CRF model to capture the sequence dependencies between the tags in a discriminative way. However, the binary LR classifier, using the same features, not only outperforms the CRF model, but also reduces the space complexity.

4.1 Features Used in the Segmentation Model

Our set of features for discourse segmentation are mostly inspired from previous studies but used in a novel way as we describe below.

Our first subset of features which we call *SPADE features*, includes the lexico-syntactic patterns extracted from the lexicalized syntactic tree for the given sentence. These features replicates the features used in SPADE, but used in a discriminative way. To decide on an EDU boundary after a token w_k, we find the lowest constituent in the lexicalized syntactic tree that spans over tokens $w_i \dots w_j$ such that $i \leq k < j$. The production that expands this constituent in the tree and its different variations, form the feature set. For example in Figure 5, the production *NP(efforts)→PRP$(its)NNS(efforts)↑S(to)* and its different variations depending on whether they include the lexical heads and how many nonterminals (up to two) to consider before and after the potential EDU boundary (↑), are used to determine the existence of a boundary after the word *efforts* (see (Fisher and Roark, 2007) for details). SPADE uses these features in a generative way, meaning that, it inserts an EDU boundary if the relative frequency (i.e., Maximum Likelihood Estimate (MLE)) of a potential boundary given the production in the training corpus is greater than 0.5. If the production has not been observed frequently enough, it uses its other variations to perform further smoothing. In contrast, we compute the MLE estimates for a production and its other variations, and use those as features with/without binarizing the values.

Shallow syntactic parse (or *Chunk*) and *POS* tags have been shown to possess valuable cues for discourse segmentation (Fisher and Roark, 2007). For example, it is less likely that an EDU boundary occurs within a chunk. We, therefore, annotate the tokens of a sentence with chunk and POS tags by a state-of-the-art tagger[3] and encode these as features.

EDUs are normally multi-word strings. Thus, a token near the beginning or end of a sentence is unlikely to be the end of a segment. Therefore, for each token we include its *relative position* in the sentence and *distances* to the beginning and end as features.

It is unlikely that two consecutive tokens are tagged with EDU boundaries. We incorporate *contextual* information for a token by including the above features computed for its neighboring tokens.

We also experimented with different N-gram ($N \in \{1, 2, 3\}$) features extracted from the token sequence, POS sequence and chunk sequence. However, since such features did not improve the segmentation accuracy on the development set, they were excluded from our final set of features.

5 Experiments

5.1 Corpora

To demonstrate the generality of our model, we experiment with two different genres. First, we use the standard *RST-DT* corpus (Carlson et al., 2002) that contains discourse annotations for 385 Wall Street Journal news articles from the Penn Treebank (Marcus et al., 1994). Second, we use the *Instructional* corpus developed by Subba and Eugenio (2009) that contains discourse annotations for 176 instructional how-to-do manuals on home-repair.

The RST-DT corpus is partitioned into a training set of 347 documents (7673 sentences) and a test set of 38 documents (991 sentences), and 53 documents (1208 sentences) have been (doubly) annotated by two human annotators, based on which we compute the human agreement. We use the human-annotated syntactic trees from Penn Treebank to train SPADE in our experiments using RST-DT as done in (Soricut and Marcu, 2003). We extracted a sentence-level DT from a document-level DT by finding the subtree that exactly spans over the sentence. By our count, 7321 sentences in the training set, 951 sentences in the test set and 1114 sentences in the doubly-annotated set have a well-formed DT in RST-DT. The Instructional corpus contains 3430 sentences in total, out of which 3032 have a well-formed DT. This forms our sentence-level corpora for discourse parsing. However, the existence of a well-formed DT in not a necessity for discourse segmentation, therefore, we do not exclude any sentence in our discourse segmentation experiments.

5.2 Experimental Setup

We perform our experiments on discourse parsing in RST-DT with the 18 coarser relations (see Figure 6) defined in (Carlson and Marcu, 2001) and also used in SPADE and HILDA. By attaching the nuclearity statuses (i.e., NS, SN, NN) to these relations we get 39 distinct relations[4]. Our experiments on the Instructional corpus consider the same 26 primary relations (e.g., GOAL:ACT, CAUSE:EFFECT, GENERAL-SPECIFIC) used in

[3]http://cogcomp.cs.illinois.edu/page/software

[4]Not all relations take all the possible nuclearity statuses.

(Subba and Eugenio, 2009) and also treat the reversals of non-commutative relations as separate relations. That is, PREPARATION-ACT and ACT-PREPARATION are two different relations. Attaching the nuclearity statuses to these relations gives 70 distinct relations in the Instructional corpus.

We use SPADE as our baseline model and apply the same modifications to its default setting as described in (Fisher and Roark, 2007), which delivers improved performance. Specifically, in testing, we replace the Charniak parser (Charniak, 2000) with a more accurate reranking parser (Charniak and Johnson, 2005). We use the reranking parser in all our models to generate the syntactic trees. This parser was trained on the sections of the Penn Treebank not included in the test set. For a fair comparison, we apply the same canonical lexical head projection rules (Magerman, 1995; Collins, 2003) to lexicalize the syntactic trees as done in SPADE and HILDA. Note that, all the previous works described in Section 2, report their models' performance on a particular test set of a specific corpus. To compare our results with the previous studies, we test our models on those specific test sets. In addition, we show more general performance based on 10-fold cross validation.

5.3 Parsing based on Manual Segmentation

First, we present the results of our discourse parser based on *manual* segmentation. The parsing performance is assessed using the unlabeled (i.e., span) and labeled (i.e., nuclearity, relation) precision, recall and F-score as described in (Marcu, 2000b, page 143). For brevity, we report only the F-scores in Table 2. Notice that, our parser (DCRF) consistently outperforms SPADE (SP) on the RST-DT test set[5]. Especially, on relation labeling, which is the hardest among the three tasks, we get an absolute F-score improvement of 9.5%, which represents a relative error rate reduction of 29.3%. Our F-score of 77.1 in relation labeling is also close to the human agreement (i.e., F-score of 83.0) on the doubly-annotated data. Our results on the RST-DT test set are consistent with the mean scores over 10-folds, when we perform 10-fold cross validation on RST-DT.

The improvement is even larger on the Instructional corpus, where we compare our mean results over 10-folds with the results reported in Subba and Eugenio (S&E) (2009) on a test set[6], giving absolute F-score improvements of 4.8%, 15.5% and 10.6% in span, nuclearity and relations, respectively. Our parser reduces the errors by 67.6%, 54.6% and 28.6% in span, nuclearity and relations, respectively.

	RST-DT				Instructional	
	Test set		10-fold	Doubly	S&E	10-fold
Scores	SP	DCRF	DCRF	Human	ILP	DCRF
Span	93.5	**94.6**	93.7	95.7	92.9	**97.7**
Nuc.	85.8	**86.9**	85.2	90.4	71.8	**87.2**
Rel.	67.6	**77.1**	75.4	83.0	63.0	**73.6**

Table 2: Parsing results using *manual* segmentation.

If we compare the performance of our model on the two corpora, we see that our model is more accurate in finding the right tree structure (see Span) on the Instructional corpus. This may be due to the fact that sentences in the Instructional domain are relatively short and contain fewer EDUs than sentences in the News domain, thus making it easier to find the right tree structure. However, when we compare the performance on the relation labeling task, we observe a decrease on the Instructional corpus. This may be due to the small amount of data available for training and the imbalanced distribution of a large number of discourse relations in this corpus.

To analyze the features, Table 3 presents the parsing results on the RST-DT test set using different subsets of features. Every new subset of features appears to improve the accuracy. More specifically, when we add the *organizational* features with the *dominance set* features (see S_2), we get about 2% absolute improvement in nuclearity and relations. With *N-gram* features (S_3), the gain is even higher; 6% in relations and 3.5% in nuclearity, demonstrating the utility of the N-gram features. This is consistent with the findings of (duVerle and Prendinger, 2009; Schilder, 2002). Including the *Contextual* features (S_4), we get further 3% and 2.2% improvements in nuclearity and relations, respectively. Notice that, adding the *substructure* features (S_5) does not help much in sentence-level parsing, giving only

[5]The improvements are statistically significant ($p < 0.01$).

[6]Subba and Eugenio (2009) report their results based on an arbitrary split between a training set and a test set. We asked the authors for their particular split. However, since we could not obtain that information, we compare our model's performance based on 10-fold cross validation with their reported results.

an improvement of 0.8% in relations. Therefore, one may choose to avoid using this computationally expensive feature in time-constrained scenarios. However, in the future, it will be interesting to see its importance in document-level parsing with large trees.

Scores	S_1	S_2	S_3	S_4	S_5
Span	91.3	92.1	93.3	94.6	94.6
Nuclearity	78.2	80.3	83.8	86.8	86.9
Relation	66.2	68.1	74.1	76.3	77.1

Table 3: Parsing results based on manual segmentation using different subsets of features on RST-DT test set. Feature subsets S_1 = {Dominance set}, S_2 = {Dominance set, Organizational}, S_3 = {Dominance set, Organizational, N-gram}, S_4 = {Dominance set, Organizational, N-gram, Contextual}, S_5 (all) = {Dominance set, Organizational, N-gram, Contextual, Substructure}.

5.4 Evaluation of the Discourse Segmenter

We evaluate the segmentation accuracy with respect to the intra-sentential segment boundaries following (Fisher and Roark, 2007). Specifically, if a sentence contains n EDUs, which corresponds to $n-1$ intra-sentence segment boundaries, we measure the model's ability to correctly identify these $n-1$ boundaries. Human agreement for this task is quite high (F-score of 98.3) on RST-DT.

Table 4 shows the results of different models in (P)recision, (R)ecall, and (F)-score on the two corpora. We compare our model's (LR) results with HILDA (HIL), SPADE (SP) and the results reported in Fisher and Roark (F&R) (2007) on the RST-DT test set. HILDA gives the weakest performance[7]. Our results are also much better than SPADE[8], with an absolute F-score improvement of 4.9%, and comparable to the results of F&R, even though we use fewer features. Furthermore, we perform 10-fold cross validation on both corpora and compare with SPADE. However, SPADE does not come with a training module for its segmenter. We reimplemented this module and verified it on the RST-DT test set. Due to the lack of human-annotated syntactic trees in the *Instructional* corpus, we train SPADE in this corpus using the syntactic trees produced by the reranking parser. Our model delivers absolute F-score improvements of 3.8% and 8.1% on the RST-DT and the Instructional corpora, respectively, which is statistically significant in both cases ($p < 3.0e-06$). However, when we compare our results on the two corpora, we observe a substantial decrease in performance on the Instructional corpus. This could be due to a smaller amount of data in this corpus and the inaccuracies in the syntactic parser and taggers, which are trained on news articles.

[7]Note that, the high segmentation accuracy reported in (Hernault et al., 2010) is due to a less stringent evaluation metric.

[8]The improvements are statistically significant (p<2.4e-06)

	RST-DT						Instructional	
	Test Set				10-fold		10-fold	10-fold
	HIL	SP	F&R	LR	SP	LR	SP	LR
P	77.9	83.8	**91.3**	88.0	83.7	**87.5**	65.1	**73.9**
R	70.6	86.8	89.7	**92.3**	86.2	**89.9**	82.8	**89.7**
F	74.1	85.2	**90.5**	90.1	84.9	**88.7**	72.8	**80.9**

Table 4: Segmentation results of different models.

5.5 Parsing based on Automatic Segmentation

In order to evaluate our full system, we feed our discourse parser the output of our discourse segmenter. Table 5 shows the F-score results. We compare our results with SPADE on the RST-DT test set. We achieve absolute F-score improvements of 3.6%, 3.4% and 7.4% in span, nuclearity and relation, respectively. These improvements are statistically significant ($p<0.001$). Our system, therefore, reduces the errors by 15.5%, 11.4%, and 17.6% in span, nuclearity and relations, respectively. These results are also consistent with the mean results over 10-folds.

	RST-DT			Instructional
	Test set		10-fold	10-fold
Scores	SPADE	DCRF	DCRF	DCRF
Span	76.7	**80.3**	78.7	71.9
Nuclearity	70.2	**73.6**	72.2	64.3
Relation	58.0	**65.4**	64.2	54.8

Table 5: Parsing results using *automatic* segmentation.

For the Instructional corpus, the last column of Table 5 shows the mean 10-fold cross validation results. We cannot compare with S&E because no results were reported using an automatic segmenter. However, it is interesting to observe how much our full system is affected by an automatic segmenter on both RST-DT and the Instructional corpus (see Table 2 and Table 5). Nevertheless, taking into account the segmentation results in Table 4, this is not surprising because previous studies (Soricut and Marcu, 2003) have already shown that automatic segmentation is the primary impediment to high accuracy discourse parsing. This demonstrates the need for a more accurate segmentation model in the Instructional genre. A promising future direction would be to apply effective domain adaptation methods (e.g., `easyadapt` (Daume, 2007)) to improve the segmentation performance in the Instructional domain by leveraging the rich data in RST-DT.

5.6 Error Analysis and Discussion

The results in Table 2 suggest that given a manually segmented discourse, our sentence-level discourse parser finds the unlabeled (i.e., span) discourse tree and assigns the nuclearity statuses to the spans at a performance level close to human annotators. We, therefore, look more closely into the performance of our parser on the hardest task of *relation labeling*.

Figure 6 shows the confusion matrix for the relation labeling task using manual segmentation on the RST-DT test set. The relation labels are ordered according to their frequency in the RST-DT training set and represented by their initial letters. For example, EL represents ELABORATION and CA represents CAUSE. In general, errors can be explained by two different phenomena acting together: (i) the frequency of the relations in the training data, and (ii) the semantic (or pragmatic) similarity between the relations. The most frequent relations (e.g., ELABORATION) tend to confuse the less frequent ones (e.g., SUMMARY), and the relations which are semantically similar (e.g., CAUSE, EXPLANATION) confuse each other, making it hard to distinguish for the computational models. Notice that, the confusions caused by JOINT appears to be high considering its frequency. The confusion between JOINT and TEMPORAL may be due to the fact that both of these coarser relations[9] contain finer relations (i.e., *list* in JOINT and *sequence* in TEMPORAL), which are semantically similar, as pointed out by Carlson and Marcu (2001). The confusion between JOINT and BACKGROUND may be explained by their different (semantic vs. pragmatic) interpretation in the RST theory (Stede, 2011, page 85).

[9]JOINT is actually not a relation, but is characterized by juxtaposition of two EDUs without a relation.

	TO	EV	SU	MA	COMP	EX	COND	TE	CA	EN	BA	CONT	JO	SA	AT	EL
TO	0	0	0	0	0	0	0	0	0	0	1	0	0	1	1	2
EV	0	0	0	0	0	0	0	0	0	0	0	0	1	1	3	2
SU	0	0	6	0	0	0	0	0	0	0	0	1	2	0	0	10
MA	0	0	0	10	0	1	0	1	0	0	0	0	2	0	1	7
COMP	0	0	0	1	1	1	0	0	2	0	3	2	1	0	0	6
EX	0	0	0	0	0	9	0	0	4	1	2	0	0	1	4	1
COND	0	0	0	0	0	0	20	3	0	1	1	1	1	2	6	7
TE	0	0	0	0	0	0	0	11	1	0	5	0	9	4	2	9
CA	0	0	0	1	0	4	0	1	5	4	1	1	6	1	6	3
EN	0	0	0	1	0	0	0	1	0	24	2	0	1	1	1	9
BA	0	0	0	0	1	1	2	7	1	0	15	2	7	4	6	15
CONT	0	0	0	0	1	1	2	1	0	0	4	26	4	6	5	6
JO	0	0	0	0	0	2	0	3	1	0	3	1	43	7	4	13
SA	0	0	2	0	0	0	3	2	0	3	0	0	0	80	3	31
AT	0	1	0	0	0	3	3	2	2	0	2	2	1	15	276	20
EL	1	0	1	3	2	3	2	5	5	11	5	6	14	9	19	295

Figure 6: Confusion matrix for the relation labels on the RST-DT test set. Y-axis represents *true* and X-axis represents *predicted* labels. The relation labels are **TO**PIC-COMMENT, **EV**ALUATION, **SU**MMARY, **MA**NNER-MEANS, **COMP**ARISON, **EX**PLANATION, **COND**ITION, **TE**MPORAL, **CA**USE, **EN**ABLEMENT, **BA**CKGROUND, **CONT**RAST, **JO**INT, **SA**ME-UNIT, **AT**TRIBUTION, **EL**ABORATION.

Based on these observations we will pursue two ways to improve our discourse parser. We need a more robust (e.g., *bagging*) method to deal with the imbalanced distribution of relations, along with a better representation of semantic knowledge. For example, *compositional semantics* (Subba and Eugenio, 2009) and *subjectivity* (Somasundaran, 2010) can be quite relevant for identifying relations.

6 Conclusion

In this paper, we have described a complete probabilistic discriminative framework for performing sentence-level discourse analysis. Experiments indicate that our approach outperforms the state-of-the-art on two corpora, often by a wide margin.

In ongoing work, we plan to generalize our DCRF-based parser to multi-sentential text and also verify to what extent parsing and segmentation can be jointly performed. A longer term goal is to extend our framework to also work with graph structures of discourse, as recommended by several recent discourse theories (Wolf and Gibson, 2005). Once we achieve similar performance on graph structures, we will perform extrinsic evaluation to determine their relative utility for various NLP tasks.

Acknowledgments

We are grateful to G. Murray, J. CK Cheung, the 3 reviewers and the NSERC CGS-D award.

References

Or Biran and Owen Rambow. 2011. Identifying Justifications in Written Dialogs by Classifying Text as Argumentative. *Int. J. Semantic Computing*, 5(4):363–381.

J. Blitzer, 2008. *Domain Adaptation of Natural Language Processing Systems*. PhD thesis, University of Pennsylvania.

L. Breiman. 1996. Bagging predictors. *Machine Learning*, 24(2):123–140, August.

L. Carlson and D. Marcu. 2001. Discourse Tagging Reference Manual. Technical Report ISI-TR-545, University of Southern California Information Sciences Institute.

L. Carlson, D. Marcu, and M. Okurowski. 2002. RST Discourse Treebank (RST-DT) LDC2002T07. *Linguistic Data Consortium, Philadelphia.*

E. Charniak and M. Johnson. 2005. Coarse-to-Fine n-Best Parsing and MaxEnt Discriminative Reranking. In *Proceedings of the 43rd Annual Meeting of the Association for Computational Linguistics*, pages 173–180, NJ, USA. ACL.

E. Charniak. 2000. A Maximum-Entropy-Inspired Parser. In *Proceedings of the 1st North American Chapter of the Association for Computational Linguistics Conference*, pages 132–139, Seattle, Washington. ACL.

M. Collins. 2003. Head-Driven Statistical Models for Natural Language Parsing. *Computational Linguistics*, 29(4):589–637, December.

H. Daume. 2007. Frustratingly Easy Domain Adaptation. In *Proceedings of the 45th Annual Meeting of the Association for Computational Linguistics*, pages 256–263, Prague, Czech Republic. ACL.

D. duVerle and H. Prendinger. 2009. A Novel Discourse Parser based on Support Vector Machine Classification. In *Proceedings of the Joint Conference of the 47th Annual Meeting of the ACL and the 4th International Joint Conference on Natural Language Processing of the AFNLP*, pages 665–673, Suntec, Singapore. ACL.

J. Finkel, A. Kleeman, and C. Manning. 2008. Efficient, Feature-based, Conditional Random Field Parsing. In *Proceedings of the 46th Annual Meeting of the Association for Computational Linguistics*, pages 959–967, Columbus, Ohio, USA. ACL.

S. Fisher and B. Roark. 2007. The Utility of Parse-derived Features for Automatic Discourse Segmentation. In *Proceedings of the 45th Annual Meeting of the Association for Computational Linguistics*, pages 488–495, Prague, Czech Republic. ACL.

S. Ghosh, R. Johansson, G. Riccardi, and S. Tonelli. 2011. Shallow Discourse Parsing with Conditional Random Fields. In *Proceedings of the 5th International Joint Conference on Natural Language Processing*, pages 1071–1079, Chiang Mai, Thailand. AFNLP.

H. Hernault, H. Prendinger, D. duVerle, and M. Ishizuka. 2010. HILDA: A Discourse Parser Using Support Vector Machine Classification. *Dialogue and Discourse*, 1(3):1–33.

D. Jurafsky and J. Martin, 2008. *Speech and Language Processing*, chapter 14. Prentice Hall.

A. Knott and R. Dale. 1994. Using Linguistic Phenomena to Motivate a Set of Coherence Relations. *Discourse Processes*, 18(1):35–62.

J. Lafferty, A. McCallum, and F. Pereira. 2001. Conditional Random Fields: Probabilistic Models for Segmenting and Labeling Sequence Data. In *Proceedings of the Eighteenth International Conference on Machine Learning*, pages 282–289, San Francisco, CA, USA. Morgan Kaufmann Publishers Inc.

D. Magerman. 1995. Statistical Decision-tree Models for Parsing. In *Proceedings of the 33rd annual meeting on Association for Computational Linguistics*, pages 276–283, Cambridge, Massachusetts. ACL.

W. Mann and S. Thompson. 1988. Rhetorical Structure Theory: Toward a Functional Theory of Text Organization. *Text*, 8(3):243–281.

D. Marcu. 2000a. The Rhetorical Parsing of Unrestricted Texts: A Surface-based Approach. *Computational Linguistics*, 26:395–448.

D. Marcu. 2000b. *The Theory and Practice of Discourse Parsing and Summarization*. MIT Press, Cambridge, MA, USA.

M. Marcus, B. Santorini, and M. Marcinkiewicz. 1994. Building a Large Annotated Corpus of English: The Penn Treebank. *Computational Linguistics*, 19(2):313–330.

A. McCallum. 2002. MALLET: A Machine Learning for Language Toolkit. http://mallet.cs.umass.edu.

K. Murphy. 2012. *Machine Learning A Probabilistic Perspective (Forthcoming, August 2012)*. MIT Press, Cambridge, MA, USA.

R. Prasad, A. Joshi, N. Dinesh, A. Lee, E. Miltsakaki, and B. Webber. 2005. The Penn Discourse TreeBank as a Resource for Natural Language Generation. In *Proceedings of the Corpus Linguistics Workshop on Using Corpora for Natural Language Generation*, pages 25–32, Birmingham, U.K.

R. Prasad, N. Dinesh, A. Lee, E. Miltsakaki, L. Robaldo, A. Joshi, and B. Webber. 2008. The Penn Discourse TreeBank 2.0. In *Proceedings of the Sixth International Conference on Language Resources and Evaluation (LREC)*, pages 2961–2968, Marrakech, Morocco. ELRA.

F. Schilder. 2002. Robust Discourse Parsing via Discourse Markers, Topicality and Position. *Natural Language Engineering*, 8(3):235–255, June.

F. Sha and F. Pereira. 2003. Shallow Parsing with Conditional Random Fields. In *Proceedings of the 2003 Conference of the North American Chapter of the Association for Computational Linguistics on Human Language Technology - Volume 1*, pages 134–141, Edmonton, Canada. ACL.

S. Somasundaran, 2010. *Discourse-Level Relations for Opinion Analysis*. PhD thesis, University of Pittsburgh.

R. Soricut and D. Marcu. 2003. Sentence Level Discourse Parsing Using Syntactic and Lexical Information. In *Proceedings of the 2003 Conference of the North American Chapter of the Association for Computational Linguistics on Human Language Technology - Volume 1*, pages 149–156, Edmonton, Canada. ACL.

C. Sporleder and M. Lapata. 2005. Discourse Chunking and its Application to Sentence Compression. In *Proceedings of the conference on Human Language Technology and Empirical Methods in Natural Language Processing*, pages 257–264, Vancouver, British Columbia, Canada. ACL.

M. Stede. 2011. *Discourse Processing*. Synthesis Lectures on Human Language Technologies. Morgan And Claypool Publishers, November.

R. Subba and B. Di Eugenio. 2009. An Effective Discourse Parser that Uses Rich Linguistic Information. In *Proceedings of Human Language Technologies: The 2009 Annual Conference of the North American Chapter of the Association for Computational Linguistics*, pages 566–574, Boulder, Colorado. ACL.

C. Sutton, A. McCallum, and K. Rohanimanesh. 2007. Dynamic Conditional Random Fields: Factorized Probabilistic Models for Labeling and Segmenting Sequence Data. *Journal of Machine Learning Research (JMLR)*, 8:693–723.

S. Verberne, L. Boves, N. Oostdijk, and P. Coppen. 2007. Evaluating Discourse-based Answer Extraction for Why-question Answering. In *Proceedings of the 30th annual international ACM SIGIR conference on Research and development in information retrieval*, pages 735–736, Amsterdam, The Netherlands. ACM.

M. Wainwright, T. Jaakkola, and A. Willsky. 2002. Tree-based Reparameterization for Approximate Inference on Loopy Graphs. In *Advances in Neural Information Processing Systems 14*, pages 1001–1008. MIT Press.

F. Wolf and E. Gibson. 2005. Representing Discourse Coherence: A Corpus-Based Study. *Computational Linguistics*, 31:249–288, June.

Using Discourse Information for Paraphrase Extraction

Michaela Regneri
Dept. of Computational Linguistics
Saarland University
Saarbrücken, Germany
regneri@coli.uni-saarland.de

Rui Wang
Language Technology Lab
DFKI GmbH
Saarbrücken, Germany
ruiwang@dfki.de

Abstract

Previous work on paraphrase extraction using parallel or comparable corpora has generally not considered the documents' discourse structure as a useful information source. We propose a novel method for collecting paraphrases relying on the sequential event order in the discourse, using multiple sequence alignment with a semantic similarity measure. We show that adding discourse information boosts the performance of sentence-level paraphrase acquisition, which consequently gives a tremendous advantage for extracting phrase-level paraphrase fragments from matched sentences. Our system beats an informed baseline by a margin of 50%.

1 Introduction

It is widely agreed that identifying paraphrases is a core task for natural language processing, including applications like document summarization (Barzilay et al., 1999), Recognizing Textual Entailment (Dagan et al., 2005), natural language generation (Zhao et al., 2010; Ganitkevitch et al., 2011), and machine translation (Marton et al., 2009). As a consequence, many methods have been proposed for generating large paraphrase resources (Lin and Pantel, 2001; Szpektor et al., 2004; Dolan et al., 2004). One of the intuitively appropriate data sources for such collections are parallel or comparable corpora: if two texts are translations of the same foreign document, or if they describe the same underlying scenario, they should contain a reasonable number of sentence pairs that convey the same meaning.

Most approaches that extract paraphrases from parallel texts employ some type of pattern matching: sentences with the same meaning are assumed to share many n-grams (Barzilay and Lee, 2003; Callison-Burch, 2008, among others), many words in their context (Barzilay and McKeown, 2001) or certain slots in a dependency path (Lin and Pantel, 2001; Szpektor et al., 2004). Discourse structure has only marginally been considered for this task: For example, Dolan et al. (2004) extract the first sentences from comparable articles and take them as paraphrases. Another approach (Deléger and Zweigenbaum, 2009) matches similar paragraphs in comparable texts, creating smaller comparable documents for paraphrase extraction.

We believe that discourse structure delivers important information for the extraction of paraphrases. Sentences that play the same role in a certain discourse and have a similar discourse context can be paraphrases, even if a semantic similarity model does not consider them very similar. This extends the widely applied distributional hypothesis to the discourse level: According to the distributional hypothesis, entities are similar if they share similar contexts. In our case, entities are whole sentences, and contexts are discourse units.

Based on this assumption, we propose a novel method for collecting paraphrases from parallel texts using discourse information. We create a new type of parallel corpus by collecting multiple summaries for several TV show episodes. The discourse structures of those summaries are easy to compare: they all contain the events in the same order as they have appeared on the screen. This allows us to take sentence order as event-based discourse structure, which is highly parallel for recaps of the same episode.

In its first step, our system uses a sequence alignment algorithm combined with a state-of-the-art similarity measure. The approach outperforms informed baselines on the task of sentential paraphrase identification. The usage of discourse information even contributes more to the final performance than the sentence similarity measure.

As second step, we extract phrase-level paraphrase fragments from the matched sentences. This step relies on the alignment algorithm's output, and we show that discourse information makes a big difference for the precision of the extraction. We then add more discourse-based information by preprocessing the text with a coreference resolution system, which results in additional performance improvement.

The paper is structured as follows: first we summarize related work (Sec. 2), and then we give an overview over our perspective on the task and sketch our system pipeline (Sec. 3). The following two sections describe the details of the sentence matching step (Sec. 4) and the subsequent paraphrase fragment extraction (Sec. 5). We present both automatic and manual evaluation of the two system components (Sec. 6). Finally, we conclude the paper and give some hints for future work (Sec. 7).

2 Related Work

Previous paraphrase extraction approaches can be roughly characterized under two aspects: 1) data source and 2) granularity of the output.

Both parallel corpora and comparable corpora have been quite well studied. Barzilay and McKeown (2001) use different English translations of the same novels (i.e., monolingual parallel corpora), while others (Quirk et al., 2004) experiment on multiple sources of the same news/events, i.e., monolingual comparable corpora. Commonly used (candidate) comparable corpora are news articles written by different news agencies within a limited time window (Wang and Callison-Burch, 2011). Other studies focus on extracting paraphrases from large bilingual parallel corpora, which the machine translation (MT) community provides in many varieties. Bannard and Callison-Burch (2005) as well as Zhao et al. (2008) take one language as the pivot and match two possible translations in the other languages as paraphrases if they share a common pivot phrase. As parallel corpora have many alternative ways of expressing the same foreign language concept, large quantities of paraphrase pairs can be extracted.

The paraphrasing task is also strongly related to cross-document event coreference resolution, which is tackled by similar techniques used by the available paraphrasing systems (Bagga and Baldwin, 1999; Tomadaki and Salway, 2005).

Most work in paraphrase acquisition has dealt with sentence-level paraphrases, e.g., (Barzilay and McKeown, 2001; Barzilay and Lee, 2003; Dolan et al., 2004; Quirk et al., 2004). Our approach for sentential paraphrase extraction is related to the one introduced by Barzilay and Lee (2003), who also employ multiple sequence alignment (MSA). However, they use MSA at the sentence level rather than at the discourse level.

We take some core ideas from our previous work on mining script information (Regneri et al., 2010). In this earlier work, we focused on event structures and their possible realizations in natural language. The corpus used in those experiments were short crowd-sourced descriptions of everyday tasks written in bullet point style. We aligned them with a hand-crafted similarity measure that was specifically designed for this text type. In this current work, we target the general task of extracting paraphrases for events rather than the much more specific script-related task. The current approach uses a domain-independent similarity measure instead of a specific hand-crafted similarity score and is thus applicable to standard texts.

From an applicational point of view, sentential paraphrases are difficult to use in other NLP tasks. At the phrasal level, interchangeable patterns (Shinyama et al., 2002; Shinyama and Sekine, 2003) or inference rules (Lin and Pantel, 2001) are extracted. In both cases, each pattern or rule contains one or several slots, which are restricted to certain type of words, e.g., named entities (NE) or content words. They are quite successful in NE-centered tasks, like information extraction, but their level of generalization or coverage is insufficient for applications like Recognizing Textual Entailment (Dinu and Wang, 2009).

The research on *general* paraphrase fragment extraction at the sub-sentential level is mainly based on phrase pair extraction techniques from the MT literature. Munteanu and Marcu (2006) extract sub-sentential translation pairs from comparable corpora using the log-likelihood-ratio of word translation probability. Quirk et al. (2007) extract fragments using a generative model of noisy translations. Our own work (Wang and Callison-Burch, 2011) extends the first idea to paraphrase fragment extraction on monolingual parallel and comparable corpora. Our current approach also uses word-word alignment, however, we use syntactic dependency trees to compute *grammatical* fragments. Our use of dependency trees is inspired by the constituent-tree-based experiments of Callison-Burch (2008).

3 Paraphrases and Discourse

Previous approaches have shown that comparable texts provide a good basis for paraphrase extraction. We want to show that discourse structure is highly useful for precise and high-yield paraphrase collection from such corpora. Consider the following (made-up) example:

(1) [House keeps focusing on his aching leg.$_{1.1}$.] [The psychiatrist suggests him to get a hobby $_{1.2}$.] [House joins a cooking class.$_{1.3}$]

(2) [He tells him that the Ibuprofen is not helping with the pain.$_{2.1}$.] [Nolan tells House to take up a hobby.$_{2.2}$] [Together with Wilson he goes to a cookery course.$_{2.3}$]

Read as a whole, it is clear that the two texts describe the same three events, in the same order, and thus, e.g., 1.2 and 2.2 are paraphrases. However, they share very few n-grams, nor named entities. We determine three factors that can help to identify such paraphrases:

1. Consider the **sequence of events**. A system which recognizes that the three sentence pairs occur in the same sequential event order would have a chance of actually matching the sentences.

2. Do **coreference resolution**. To determine which *sentence parts* actually carry the same meaning, pronoun resolution is essential (e.g., to match "suggest him" and "tells House").

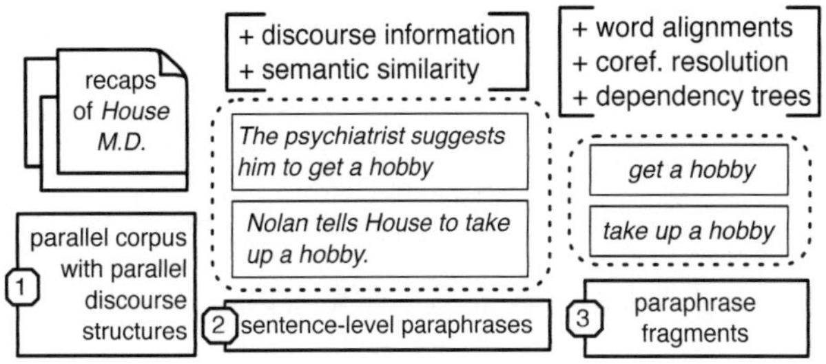

Figure 1: System pipeline

3. Try a generic **sentence similarity model**. Pattern matching or n-gram overlap might not be sufficient to solve this problem.

Our system pipeline is sketched in Fig. 1:

1. **Create a corpus:** First, we create a comparable corpus of texts with *highly comparable discourse structures*. Complete discourse structures like in the RST Discourse Treebank (Carlson et al., 2002) may be very useful for paraphrase computation, however, they are hard to obtain. Discourse annotation is difficult and work-intensive, and full-blown automatic discourse parsers are neither robust nor very precise. To circumvent this problem, we assemble documents that have parallel discourse structures by default: We compile multiple plot summaries of TV show episodes. The textual order of those summaries typically mirrors the underlying event order of the episodes, in the same sequence they happened on screen. We take sentence sequences of recaps as parallel discourse structures.

2. **Extract sentence-level paraphrases:** Our system finds sentence pairs that are either paraphrases themselves, or at least contain paraphrase fragments. This procedure crucially relies on discourse knowledge: A Multiple Sequence Alignment (MSA) algorithm matches sentences if both their inherent *semantic similarities* and the overall similarity score of their *discourse contexts* are high enough.

3. **Extract paraphrase fragments:** Sentence-level paraphrases may be too specific for further domain-independent applications, as they

row	recap 1	recap 2	recap 3	recap 4	recap 5
34	She gives Foreman one shot.	Cuddy tells Foreman he has one chance to prove to her he can run the team.	⊘	Cuddy agrees to give him one chance to prove himself.	Foreman insists he deserves a chance and Cuddy gives in, warning him he gets one shot.
35	⊘	⊘	⊘	Foreman, Hadley, and Taub get the conference room ready and Foreman explains that he'll be in charge.	Foreman gives the news to Thirteen and Taub and they unpack the conference room and go with a diagnosis of CRPS.
36	They decide that it might be CRPS and Foreman orders a spinal stimulation.	⊘	Foreman says to treat him for complex regional pain syndrome with a spinal stimulation.	⊘	⊘

Figure 2: Excerpt from an alignment table for 5 exemplary recaps of Episode 2 (Season 6).

contain specific NEs (e.g. "House") or time references. Thus we take a necessary second step and extract finer-grained paraphrase *fragments* from the sentence pairs matched in step 2. The resulting matched phrases should be grammatical and interchangeable regardless of context. We propose and compare different fragment extraction algorithms.

The remainder of the paper shows how both of the paraphrasing steps benefit from using a corpus with highly parallel discourse structures: The system components employ discourse information either directly by using MSA (step 1) or coreference resolution (step 2), or indirectly, because using MSA in step 1 results in a high precision gain for the subsequent second step.

4 Sentence Matching with MSA

This section explains how we apply MSA to extract sentence-level paraphrases from a comparable corpus. As our input data, we manually collect recaps for *House M.D.* episodes from different sources on the web[1]. *House* episodes have an intermediate length (~45 min), which results in recaps of a convenient size (40 to 150 sentences). The result is one comparable document collection per episode. We applied a sentence splitter (Gillick, 2009) to the documents and treat them as sequences of sentences for further processing.

Sequence alignment takes as its input two sequences consisting of elements of some alphabet, and an alphabet-specific score function c_m over pairs of sequence elements. For insertions and deletions, the algorithm additionally takes gap costs (c_{gap}). Multiple Sequence Alignment generalizes pairwise alignment to arbitrarily many sequences. MSA has its main application area in bioinformatics, where it is used to identify equivalent parts of DNA (Durbin et al., 1998). Our alphabet consists of sentences, and a sequence is an ordered sentence list constituting a recap.

A Multiple Sequence Alignment results in a table like Fig. 2. Each column contains the sentences of one recap, possibly intermitted with gaps ("⊘"), and each row contains at least one non-gap. If two sentences end up in the same row, they are *aligned*; we take aligned sentence to be paraphrases. Aligning a sentence with a gap can be thought of as an insertion or deletion. Each alignment has a *score* which is the sum of all scores for substitutions and all costs for insertions and deletions. Informally, the alignment

[1] e.g. `http://house.wikia.com` – for a detailed list of URLs, please check the supplementary material or contact the authors.

score is the sum of all scores for each pair of cells (c_1, c_2), if c_1 and c_2 are in the same row. If either c_1 or c_2 is a gap, the pair's score is c_{gap}. If both cells contain sentences, the score is $c_m(c_1, c_2)$.

Fern and Stevenson (2009) showed that sophisticated similarity measures improve paraphrasing, so we apply a state-of-the-art vector space model (Thater et al., 2011) as our score function. The vector space model provides contextualized similarities of words, i.e. the vector of each word is disambiguated by the context the current instance occurs in. $c_m(c_1, c_2)$ returns the model's similarity score for c_1 and c_2.

We re-implement a standard MSA algorithm (Needleman and Wunsch, 1970) which approximates the best MSA given the input sequences, c_m and c_{gap}. This algorithm recursively aligns two sequences at a time, treating the resulting alignment as a new sequence. This does not necessarily result in the globally optimal alignment, because the order in which sequences are aligned can change the final output. Given this constraint, the algorithm finds the best alignment, which - in our case - is the alignment with the maximal score. Intuitively, we are looking for the alignment where the most similar sentences with the most similar preceding and trailing contexts end up as paraphrases.

5 Paraphrase Fragment Extraction

Taking the output of the sentence alignment as input, we next extract shorter phrase-level paraphrases (*paraphrase fragments*) from the matched sentence pairs. We try different algorithms for this step, all relying on word-word alignments.

5.1 Preprocessing

Before extracting paraphrase fragments, we first preprocess all documents as follows:

Stanford CoreNLP [2] provides a set of natural language analysis tools. We use the part-of-speech (POS) tagger, the named-entity recognizer, the parser (Klein and Manning, 2003), and the coreference resolution system (Lee et al., 2011). In particular, the dependency structures of the parser's output are used for VP-fragment extraction (Sec. 5.3). The output from the coreference resolution system is used to cluster all mentions referring to the same entity and to select one as the *representative* mention. If the representative mention is not a pronoun, we modify the original texts by replacing all pronoun mentions in the cluster with the syntactic head of the representative mention. Note that the coreference resolution system is applied to each recap as a whole.

GIZA++ (Och and Ney, 2003) is a widely used word aligner for MT systems. We amend the input data by copying identical word pairs 10 times and adding them as additional 'sentence' pairs (Byrne et al., 2003), in order to emphasize the higher alignment probability between identical words. We run GIZA++ for bi-directional word alignment and obtain a lexical translation table.

5.2 Fragment Extraction

As mentioned in Sec. 2, we choose to use alignment-based approaches to this task, which allows us to use many existing MT techniques and tools. We mainly follow our previous approach (Wang and Callison-Burch, 2011), which is a modified version of an approach by Munteanu and Marcu (2006) on translation fragment extraction. We briefly review the three-step procedure here and refer the reader to the original paper for more details:

1. Establish word-word alignment between each sentence pair using GIZA++;
2. Smooth the alignment based on lexical occurrence likelihood;
3. Extract fragment pairs using different heuristics, e.g., non-overlapping n-grams, chunk boundaries, or dependency trees.

After obtaining a lexical translation table by running GIZA++, for each word pair, w_1 and w_2, we use both positive and negative lexical associations for the alignment, which are defined as the conditional probabilities $p(w_1|w_2)$ and $p(w_1|\neg w_2)$, respectively. The resulting alignment can be further constrained by a modified longest common substring (LCS) algorithm, which takes sequences of

[2] http://nlp.stanford.edu/software/corenlp.shtml

words instead of letters as input. Smoothing (step 2) is done for each word by taking the average score of it and its four neighbor words. All the word alignments (excluding stop-words) with positive scores are selected as candidate fragment elements.

Provided with the candidate fragment elements, we previously (Wang and Callison-Burch, 2011) used a chunker[3] to finalize the output fragments, in order to follow the linguistic definition of a *(para-) phrase*. We extend this step in the current system by applying a dependency parser to constrain the boundary of the fragments (Sec. 5.3). Finally, we filter out trivial fragment pairs, such as identical or the original sentence pairs.

5.3 VP-fragment Extraction

To obtain more grammatical output fragments, we add another layer of linguistic information to our input sentences. Based on the dependency parses produced during preprocessing, we extract phrases containing verbs and their complements. More precisely, we match two phrases if their respective subtrees t_1 and t_2 satisfy the following conditions:

- The subtrees mirror a complete subset of the GIZA++ word alignment, i.e., all words aligned to a given word in t_1 are contained in t_2, and vice versa. For empty alignments, we require an overlap of at least one lemma (ignoring stop words).
- The root nodes of t_1 and t_2 have the same roles within their trees, e.g., we match clauses with an `xcomp`-label only with other `xcomp`-labelled clauses.
- Both t_1 and t_2 contain at least one verb with at least one complement. To enhance recall, we additionally extract complete prepositional phrases.
- We exclude trivial fragment pairs that are prefixes or suffixes of each other (or identical).

The main advantage of this approach lies in the output's grammaticality, because the subtrees always match complete phrases. This method also functions as a filtering mechanism for mistakenly aligned sentences: If only the two sentence nodes are returned as possible matching partners, the pair is discarded from the results.

6 Evaluation

We evaluate both sentential paraphrase matching and paraphrase fragment extraction using manually labelled gold standards (provided in the supplementary material). We collect recaps for all 20 episodes of season 6 of *House M.D.*, taking 8 summaries per episode (the supplementary material contains a list of all URLs). This results in 160 documents containing 14735 sentences. For evaluation, we use all episodes except no. 2, which is held out for parameter optimizations and other development purposes.

6.1 Sentential Paraphrase Evaluation

To evaluate sentence matching, we adapt the baselines from our earlier work (Regneri et al., 2010) and create a new gold standard. We compute precision, recall and accuracy of our main system and suggest baselines that separately show the influence of both the MSA and the semantic scoring function.

Gold-Standard

We aim to create an evaluation set that contains a sufficient amount of genuine paraphrases. Finding such sentence pairs with random sampling and manual annotation is infeasible: There are more than $200,000,000$ possible sentence pairs, and we expect less than 1% of them to be paraphrases. We thus sample pairs that either the system or the baselines recognized as paraphrases and try to create an evaluation set that is not biased towards the actual system or any of the baselines. The evaluation set consists of 2000 sentence pairs: 400 that the system recognized as paraphrases, 400 positively labelled pairs for each of the three baselines (described in the following section) and 400 randomly selected pairs. For the final evaluation, we compute precision, recall, f-score and accuracy for our main system and each baseline on this set.

Two annotators labelled each sentence pair (S_1, S_2) with one of the following labels:

1. **paraphrases**: S_1 and S_2 refer to exactly the same event(s).
2. **containment**: S_1 contains all the event information mentioned in S_2, but refers to at least

[3]We use the same OpenNLP chunker (`http://opennlp.sourceforge.net/`) for consistency.

one additional event, or vice versa.

3. **related**: S_1 and S_2 overlap in at least one event reference, but both refer to at least one additional event.

4. **unrelated**: S_1 and S_2 do not overlap at all.

This scheme has a double purpose: The main objective is judging whether two sentences contain paraphrases (1-3) or if they are unrelated (4). We use this coarser distinction for system evaluation by collapsing the categories 1-3 in one $paraphrase_{coll}$ category. Secondly, the annotation shows how well the sentences fit each other's content (1 vs. 2&3), and how much work needs to be done to extract the sentence parts with the same meaning (2 vs. 3).

The inter-annotator agreement according to Cohen's Kappa (Cohen, 1960) is $\kappa = 0.55$ ("moderate agreement"). The distinction between *unrelated* cases and elements of $paraphrase_{coll}$ reaches $\kappa = 0.71$ ("substantial agreement"). For the final gold standard, a third annotator resolved all conflict cases.

Among all gold standard sentence pairs, we find 158 *paraphrases*, 238 *containment* cases, 194 *related* ones and 1402 *unrelated*. We had to discard 8 sentence pairs because one of the items was invalid or empty. The high proportion of 'unrelated' cases results from the 400 random pairs and the low precision of the baselines. Looking at the paraphrases, 27% of the 590 instances in the $paraphrase_{coll}$ category are proper paraphrases, and 73% of them contain additional information that does not belong to the paraphrased part.

Experimental Setup

We compute precision, recall and f-score with respect to the gold standard (paraphrases are members of $paraphrase_{coll}$), taking f-score as follows:

$$f\text{-}score = \frac{2 * precision * recall}{precision + recall}$$

We also compute accuracy as the overall fraction of correct labels (negative and positive ones).

Our main system uses MSA (denoted by MSA afterwards) with vector-based similarities (VEC) as a scoring function. The gap costs are optimized for f-score, resulting in $c_{gap} = 0$.[4]

To show the contribution of MSA's structural component and compare it to the vector model's contribution, we create a second MSA-based system that uses MSA with BLEU scores (Papineni et al., 2002) as scoring function (MSA+BLEU). BLEU establishes the average 1-to-4-gram overlap of two sentences. The gap costs for this baseline were optimized separately, ending up with $c_{gap} = 1$.

In order to quantify the contribution of the alignment, we create a discourse-unaware baseline by dropping the MSA and using a state-of-the-art clustering algorithm (Noack, 2007) fed with the vector space model scores (CLUSTER+VEC). The algorithm partitions the set of sentences into paraphrase clusters such that the most similar sentences end up in one cluster. This does not require any parameter tuning.

We also show a baseline that uses the clustering algorithm with BLEU scores (CLUSTER+BLEU). The comparison of this baseline with the other clustering-baseline that uses vector similarities helps to underline the sentence similarities' advantage compared to pure word overlap. Note that the CLUSTER+BLEU system resembles popular n-gram overlap measures for paraphrase classification.

We also show the results completely random label assignment, which constitutes a lower bound for the baselines and the system.

Results

Overall, our system extracts 20379 paraphrase pairs. Tab. 1 shows the evaluation results on our gold-standard.

The MSA based system variants outperform the two clustering baselines significantly (all levels refer to $p = 0.01$ and were tested with a resampling test (Edgington, 1986)).

The clustering baselines perform significantly better than a random baseline, especially considering recall. The more elaborated vector-space measure even gives 10% more in precision and accuracy, and overall 14% more in f-score. This is al-

[4] Gap costs directly influence precision and recall: "cheap" gaps lead to a more restrictive system with higher precision, and more expensive gaps give more recall. We chose f-score as our objective.

System	*Prec.*	*Recall*	*F-score*	Acc.
RANDOM	0.30	0.49	0.37	0.51
CLUSTER+BLEU	0.35	0.63	0.45	0.54
CLUSTER+VEC	0.40	0.68	0.51	0.61
MSA+BLEU	0.73	**0.74**	**0.73**	0.84
MSA+VEC	**0.79**	0.66	0.72	**0.85**

Table 1: Results for sentence matching.

ready a remarkable improvement compared to the random baseline, and still a significant one compared to CLUSTER+BLEU.

Adding structural knowledge with MSA improves the clustering's accuracy performance by 24% (CLUSTER+VEC vs. MSA+VEC), precision even goes up by 39%.

Intuitively we expected the MSA-based systems to end up with a higher recall than the clustering baselines, because sentences can be matched even if their similarity is moderate or low, but their discourse context is highly similar. However, this is only the case for the system using BLEU scores, but not for the system based on the vector space model. One possible explanation lies in picking f-score as objective for the optimization of the gap costs for MSA: For the naturally more restrictive word overlap measure, this leads to a more recall-oriented system with a low threshold for aligning sentences, whereas the gap costs for the vector-based system favors a more restrictive alignment with more precise results.

The comparison of the two MSA-based systems highlights the great benefit of using structural knowledge: Both MSA+BLEU and MSA+VEC have comparable f-scores and accuracy. The advantage from using the vector-space model that is still obvious for the clustering baselines is nearly evened out when adding discourse knowledge as a backbone. However, the vector model still results in nominally higher precision and accuracy.

It is hard to do a direct comparison with state-of-the-art paraphrase recognition systems, because most are evaluated on different corpora, e.g., the Microsoft paraphrase corpus (Dolan and Brockett, 2005, MSR). We cannot apply our system to the MSR corpus, because we take complete texts as input, while the MSR corpus solely delivers sentence pairs. While the MSR corpus is larger than our collection, the wording variations in its paraphrase pairs are usually lower than for our examples. Thus the final numbers of previous approaches might be vaguely comparable with our results: Das and Smith (2009) present two systems reaching f-scores of 0.82 and 0.83, with a precision of 0.75 and 0.80. Both precision and f-scores of our msa-based systems lie within the same range. Heilman and Smith (2010) introduce a recall-oriented system, which reaches an f-score of 0.81 by a precision of 0.76. Compared to this system, our approach results in better precision values.

All further computations bases on the system using MSA and the vector space model (MSA+VEC), because it achieves the highest precision and accuracy values.

6.2 Paraphrase Fragment Evaluation

We also manually evaluate precision on paraphrase fragments, and additionally describe the *productivity* of the different setups, providing some intuition about the methods' recall.

Gold-Standard

We randomly collect 150 fragment pairs for each of the five system configurations (explained in the following section). Each fragment pair (f_1, f_2) is annotated with one of the following categories:

1. **paraphrases**: f_1 and f_2 convey the same meaning, i.e., they are well-formed and good matches on the content level.
2. **related**: f_1 and f_2 overlap in their meaning, but one or both phrases have additional unmatched information.
3. **irrelevant**: f_1 and f_2 are unrelated.

This labeling scheme again assesses precision as well as paraphrase granularity. For precision rating, we collapse categories 1&2 into one $paraphrase_{coll}$ category. Each pair is labelled by two annotators, who were shown both the fragments and the whole sentences they originate from. Overall, the raters had an agreement of $\kappa = 0.67$ ("substantial agreement"), which suggests that the task was easier than sentence level annotation. The agreement for the distinction between the $paraphrase_{coll}$ categories and *irrelevant* instances reaches a level of $\kappa = 0.88$ (also "substantial agreement"). All conflicts were again adjudicated by a third annotator. Overall, the gold standard contains 190 paraphrases, 258 *related* pairs and 302 *irrelevant* instances. Unlike previous approaches to fragment extraction, we do not evaluate *grammaticality*, given that the VP-fragment method implicitly constrains the output fragments to be complete phrases.

Configurations & Results

We take the output of the sentence matching system MSA+VEC as input for paraphrase fragment extraction. As detailed in Sec. 5, our core fragment module uses the word-word alignments provided by GIZA++ and uses a chunker for fragment extraction. We successively enrich this core module with more information, either by longest common substring (LCS) matching or by operating on dependency trees (VP). In addition, we evaluate the influence of coreference resolution by preprocessing the input to the best performing configuration with pronoun resolution (COREF).

We mainly compute precision for this task, as the recall of paraphrase fragments is difficult to define. However, we do include a measure we call *productivity* to indicate the algorithm's completeness. It is defined as the ratio between the number of resulting fragment pairs and the number of sentence pairs used as input.

Extraction Method	*Precision*	*Productivity*
MSA	0.57	**0.76**
MSA+LCS	0.45	0.30
MSA+VP	0.81	0.42
MSA+VP+COREF	**0.84**	0.45

Table 2: Results of paraphrase fragment extraction.

Tab. 2 shows the evaluation results. We reach our best precision by using the VP-fragment heuristics, which is still more productive than the LCS method. The grammatical filter gives us a higher precision compared to the purely alignment-based approaches. Enhancing the system with coreference resolution raises the score even further. We cannot directly compare this performance to other systems, as all other approaches have different data sources. However, precision is usually manually evaluated, so the figures are at least indicative for a comparison with previous work: One state-of-the-art system introduced by Zhao et al. (2008) extracts paraphrase fragments from bilingual parallel corpora and reaches a precision of 0.67. We found the same number using our previous approach (Wang and Callison-Burch, 2011), which is roughly equivalent to our core module. Our approach outperforms both by 17% with similar estimated productivity.

As a final comparison, we show how the performance of the sentence matching methods directly affects the fragment extraction. We use the VP-based fragment extraction system (VP), and compare the performances by using either the outputs from our main system (MSA+VP) or alternatively the baseline that replaces MSA with a clustering algorithm (CLUSTER+VP). Both variants use the vector-based semantic similarity measure.

Sentence matching	*Precision*	*Productivity*
CLUSTER+VP	0.31	0.04
MSA+VP	**0.81**	**0.42**

Table 3: Impact of MSA on fragment extraction

As shown in Tab. 3, the precision gain from using MSA becomes tremendous during further processing: We beat the baseline by 50% here, and productivity increases by a factor of 10. This means that the baseline produces on average 0.01 good fragment pairs per matched sentence pair, and the final system extracts 0.3 of them. Those numbers show that for any application that acquires paraphrases of arbitrary granularity, sequential event information provides an invaluable source to achieve a lean paraphrasing method with high precision.

6.3 Example output

Fig. 3 shows exemplary results from our system pipeline, using the VP–FRAGMENTS method with full coreference resolution on the sentence pairs extracted by MSA. The results reflect the importance of discourse information for this task: Sentences are correctly matched in spite of not having common de-

	Sentence 1 [*with fragment 1*]	Sentence 2 [*with fragment 2*]
1	Taub meets House for dinner and claims [*that Rachel had a pottery class*].	Taub shows up for his dinner with House without Rachel, explaining [*that she's at a ceramics class*].
2	House doesn't want her to go and she doesn't want to go either, but [*she can't leave her family.*]	Lydia admits that she doesn't want to leave House but [*she has to stay with her family*].
3	Thirteen is in a cab to the airport when she finds out that [*her trip had been canceled*].	Hadley discovers that [*her reservation has been cancelled*].
4	Nash asks House [*for the extra morphine*].	The patient is ready [*for more morphine*].
5	House comes in to tell Wilson that Tucker has cancer and [*shows him the test results*].	House comes in and [*informs Wilson that the tests have proven positive*]: Tucker has cancer.
6	Foreman tells him [*to confide in Cameron*].	When Chase points out they can't move Donny without alerting Cameron, Foreman tells Chase [*to be honest with his wife*].
7	Thirteen breaks [*into the old residence*] and tells Taub that she realizes that he's been with Maya.	Taub and Thirteen break [*into Ted's former residence*].
8	He finds [*a darkened patch on his right foot near the big toe*].	House finally finds [*a tumorous mole on his toe*].

Figure 3: Example results; fragments extracted from aligned sentences are bracketed and *emphasized*.

pendency patterns (e.g., Example 4) or sharing many n-grams (6-8). Additionally, the coreference resolution allows us to match *Rachel* (1) and *Wilson* (5) to the correct corresponding pronouns. All examples show that this technique of matching sentence could even help to make coreference resolution better, because we can easily identify *Cameron* with *his wife*, *Lydia* with the respective pronouns, *Nash* with *The Patient* or the nickname *Thirteen* with *Hadley*, the character's actual name.

7 Conclusion and Future Work

We presented our work on paraphrase extraction using discourse information, on a corpus consisting of recaps of TV show episodes. Our approach first uses MSA to extract sentential paraphrases, which are then further processed to compute finer-grained paraphrase fragments using dependency trees and pronoun resolution. The experimental results show great advantages from using discourse information, beating informed baselines and performing competitively with state-of-the-art systems.

For future work, we plan to use MSA to align single clauses rather than whole sentences. This can also help to define the fragment boundaries more clearly. Additionally, we plan to generalize the method for other parallel texts by preprocessing them with a temporal classifier. In a more advanced step, we will also use the aligned paraphrases to help resolving discourse structure, e.g. for coreference resolution, which could lead to a high-performance bootstrapping system. In a long-term view, it would be interesting to see how aligned discourse trees could help to extract paraphrases from arbitrary parallel text.

Acknowledgements

The first author was funded by the Cluster of Excellence "Multimodal Computing and Interaction" in the German Excellence Initiative. The second Author was funded by the European Community's Seventh Framework Programme (FP7/2007-2013) under grant agreement No. 287923 (EXCITEMENT, `http://www.excitement-project.eu/`). – We want to thank Stefan Thater for supplying the semantic similarity scores of his algorithm for our data. We are grateful to Manfred Pinkal, Alexis Palmer and three anonymous reviewers for their helpful comments on previous versions of this paper.

References

Amit Bagga and Breck Baldwin. 1999. Cross-document event coreference: annotations, experiments, and observations. In *Proceedings of the Workshop on Coreference and its Applications*.

Colin Bannard and Chris Callison-Burch. 2005. Paraphrasing with bilingual parallel corpora. In *Proceedings of ACL 2005*.

Regina Barzilay and Lillian Lee. 2003. Learning to paraphrase: An unsupervised approach using multiple-sequence alignment. In *Proc. of HLT-NAACL 2003*.

Regina Barzilay and Kathleen R. McKeown. 2001. Extracting paraphrases from a parallel corpus. In *Proc. of ACL 2001*.

Regina Barzilay, Kathleen McKeown, and Michael Elhadad. 1999. Information fusion in the context of multi-document summarization. In *Proceedings of ACL 1999*.

W. Byrne, S. Khudanpur, W. Kim, S. Kumar, P. Pecina, P. Virga, P. Xu, and D. Yarowsky. 2003. The Johns Hopkins University 2003 Chinese-English machine translation system. In *Proceedings of the MT Summit IX*.

Chris Callison-Burch. 2008. Syntactic constraints on paraphrases extracted from parallel corpora. In *Proceedings of EMNLP 2008*.

Lynn Carlson, Daniel Marcu, and Mary Ellen Okurowski. 2002. RST Discourse Treebank. LDC.

J. Cohen. 1960. A Coefficient of Agreement for Nominal Scales. *Educational and Psychological Measurement*, 20(1):37.

Ido Dagan, Oren Glickman, and Bernardo Magnini. 2005. The pascal recognising textual entailment challenge. In *MLCW*, pages 177–190.

D. Das and N. A. Smith. 2009. Paraphrase identification as probabilistic quasi-synchronous recognition. In *Proceedings of ACL-IJCNLP 2009*.

Louise Deléger and Pierre Zweigenbaum. 2009. Extracting lay paraphrases of specialized expressions from monolingual comparable medical corpora. In *Proceedings of the ACL-IJCNLP BUCC-2009 Workshop*.

Georgiana Dinu and Rui Wang. 2009. Inference rules and their application to recognizing textual entailment. In *Proceedings of EACL 2009*.

W. B. Dolan and C. Brockett. 2005. Automatically constructing a corpus of sentential paraphrases. In *Proceedings of the third International Workshop on Paraphrasing*.

Bill Dolan, Chris Quirk, and Chris Brockett. 2004. Unsupervised construction of large paraphrase corpora: Exploiting massively parallel news sources. In *Proceedings of COLING 2004*.

Richard Durbin, Sean Eddy, Anders Krogh, and Graeme Mitchison. 1998. *Biological Sequence Analysis*. Cambridge University Press.

Eugene S Edgington. 1986. *Randomization tests*. Marcel Dekker, Inc., New York, NY, USA.

Samuel Fern and Mark Stevenson. 2009. A semantic similarity approach to paraphrase detection. In *Proceedings of the Computational Linguistics UK (CLUK 2008) 11th Annual Research Colloquium*.

Juri Ganitkevitch, Chris Callison-Burch, Courtney Napoles, and Benjamin Van Durme. 2011. Learning sentential paraphrases from bilingual parallel corpora for text-to-text generation. In *Proceedings of EMNLP 2011*.

Dan Gillick. 2009. Sentence boundary detection and the problem with the u.s. In *Proceedings of HLT-NAACL 2009: Companion Volume: Short Papers*.

Michael Heilman and Noah A. Smith. 2010. Tree edit models for recognizing textual entailments, paraphrases, and answers to questions. In *Proceedings of NAACL-HLT 2010*.

Dan Klein and Christopher D. Manning. 2003. Accurate unlexicalized parsing. In *Proceedings of ACL 2003*.

Heeyoung Lee, Yves Peirsman, Angel Chang, Nathanael Chambers, Mihai Surdeanu, and Dan Jurafsky. 2011. Stanford's multi-pass sieve coreference resolution system at the conll-2011 shared task. In *Proceedings of the CoNLL-2011 Shared Task*.

Dekang Lin and Patrick Pantel. 2001. DIRT - Discovery of Inference Rules from Text. In *Proceedings of the ACM SIGKDD*.

Yuval Marton, Chris Callison-Burch, and Philip Resnik. 2009. Improved Statistical Machine Translation Using Monolingually-Derived Paraphrases. In *Proceedings of EMNLP 2009*.

Dragos Stefan Munteanu and Daniel Marcu. 2006. Extracting Parallel Sub-Sentential Fragments from Non-Parallel Corpora. In *Proceedings of ACL 2006*.

Saul B. Needleman and Christian D. Wunsch. 1970. A general method applicable to the search for similarities in the amino acid sequence of two proteins. *Journal of molecular biology*, 48(3), March.

Andreas Noack. 2007. Energy models for graph clustering. *Journal of Graph Algorithms and Applications*, 11(2):453–480.

Franz Josef Och and Hermann Ney. 2003. A systematic comparison of various statistical alignment models. *Computational Linguistics*, 29(1).

Kishore Papineni, Salim Roukos, Todd Ward, and Wei-Jing Zhu. 2002. BLEU: a method for automatic evaluation of machine translation. In *Proceedings of ACL 2002*.

Chris Quirk, Chris Brockett, and William B. Dolan. 2004. Monolingual machine translation for paraphrase generation. In *Proceedings of EMNLP 2004*.

Chris Quirk, Raghavendra Udupa, and Arul Menezes. 2007. Generative models of noisy translations with applications to parallel fragment extraction. In *Proceedings of MT Summit XI*, Copenhagen, Denmark.

Michaela Regneri, Alexander Koller, and Manfred Pinkal. 2010. Learning Script Knowledge with Web Experiments. In *Proceedings of ACL 2010*.

Yusuke Shinyama and Satoshi Sekine. 2003. Paraphrase acquisition for information extraction. In *Proceedings of the ACL PARAPHRASE '03 Workshop*.

Yusuke Shinyama, Satoshi Sekine, and Kiyoshi Sudo. 2002. Automatic paraphrase acquisition from news articles. In *Proceedings of HLT 2002*.

Idan Szpektor, Hristo Tanev, Ido Dagan, and Bonaventura Coppola. 2004. Scaling Web-based Acquisition of Entailment Relations. In *Proceedings of EMNLP 2004*.

Stefan Thater, Hagen Fürstenau, and Manfred Pinkal. 2011. Word Meaning in Context: A Simple and Effective Vector Model. In *Proceedings of IJCNLP 2011*.

Eleftheria Tomadaki and Andrew Salway. 2005. Matching verb attributes for cross-document event coreference. In *Proc. of the Interdisciplinary Workshop on the Identification and Representation of Verb Features and Verb Classes*.

Rui Wang and Chris Callison-Burch. 2011. Paraphrase fragment extraction from monolingual comparable corpora. In *Proc. of the ACL BUCC-2011 Workshop*.

Shiqi Zhao, Haifeng Wang, Ting Liu, and Sheng Li. 2008. Pivot Approach for Extracting Paraphrase Patterns from Bilingual Corpora. In *Proceedings of ACL 2008*.

Shiqi Zhao, Haifeng Wang, Xiang Lan, and Ting Liu. 2010. Leveraging Multiple MT Engines for Paraphrase Generation. In *Proceedings of COLING 2010*.

Generating Non-Projective Word Order in Statistical Linearization

Bernd Bohnet **Anders Björkelund** **Jonas Kuhn** **Wolfgang Seeker** **Sina Zarrieß**
Institut für Maschinelle Sprachverarbeitung
University of Stuttgart
{bohnetbd,anders,jonas,seeker,zarriesa}@ims.uni-stuttgart.de

Abstract

We propose a technique to generate non-projective word orders in an efficient statistical linearization system. Our approach predicts *liftings* of edges in an unordered syntactic tree by means of a classifier, and uses a projective algorithm for tree linearization. We obtain statistically significant improvements on six typologically different languages: English, German, Dutch, Danish, Hungarian, and Czech.

1 Introduction

There is a growing interest in language-independent data-driven approaches to natural language generation (NLG). An important subtask of NLG is surface realization, which was recently addressed in the 2011 Shared Task on Surface Realisation (Belz et al., 2011). Here, the input is a linguistic representation, such as a syntactic dependency tree lacking all precedence information, and the task is to determine a natural, coherent linearization of the words.

The standard data-driven approach is to traverse the dependency tree deciding locally at each node on the relative order of the head and its children. The shared task results have proven this approach to be both effective and efficient when applied to English.

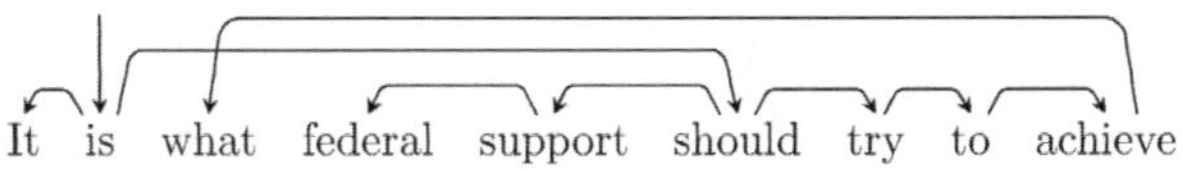

Figure 1: A non-projective example from the CoNLL 2009 Shared Task data set for parsing (Hajič et al., 2009).

However, the approach can only generate projective word orders (which can be drawn without any crossing edges). Figure 1 shows a non-projective word order: the edge connecting the extracted *wh*-pronoun with its head crosses another edge. Once *what* has been ordered relative to *achieve*, there are no ways of inserting intervening material. In this case, only ungrammatical linearizations can be produced from the unordered input tree:

(1) a. *It is federal support should try to what achieve
b. *It is federal support should try to achieve what
c. *It is try to achieve what federal support should

Although rather infrequent in English, non-projective word orders are quite common in languages with a less restrictive word order. In these languages, it is often possible to find a grammatically correct *projective* linearization for a given input tree, but discourse coherence, information structure, and stylistic factors will often make speakers prefer some non-projective word order.[1] Figure 2 shows an object fronting example from German where the edge between the subject and the finite verb crosses the edge between the object and the full verb. Various other constructions, such as extraposition of (relative) clauses or scrambling, can lead to non-projectivity. In languages where word order is driven to an even larger degree by information structure, such as Czech and Hungarian, non-projectivity can likewise result from various ordering decisions. These phenomena have been studied extensively in

[1] A categorization of non-projective edges in the Prague Dependency Treebank (Böhmová et al., 2000) is presented in Hajičová et al. (2004).

the linguistic literature, and for certain languages, work on rule-based generation has addressed certain aspects of the problem.

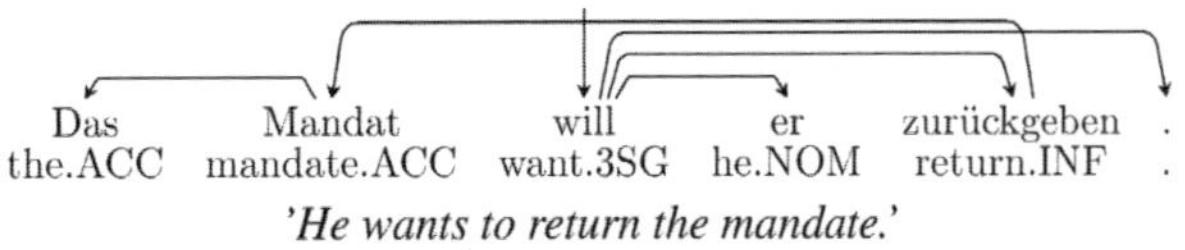

Figure 2: German object fronting with complex verb introducing a non-projective edge.

In this paper, we aim for a general data-driven approach that can deal with various causes for non-projectivity and will work for typologically different languages. Our technique is inspired by work in data-driven multilingual parsing, where non-projectivity has received considerable attention. In pseudo-projective parsing (Kahane et al., 1998; Nivre and Nilsson, 2005), the parsing algorithm is restricted to projective structures, but the issue is side-stepped by converting non-projective structures to projective ones prior to training and application, and then restoring the original structure afterwards.

Similarly, we split the linearization task in two stages: initially, the input tree is modified by lifting certain edges in such a way that new orderings become possible even under a projectivity constraint; the second stage is the original, projective linearization step. In parsing, projectivization is a deterministic process that lifts edges based on the linear order of a sentence. Since the linear order is exactly what we aim to produce, this deterministic conversion cannot be applied before linearization. Therefore, we use a statistical classifier as our initial lifting component. This classifier has to be trained on suitable data, and it is an empirical question whether the projective linearizer can take advantage of this preceding lifting step.

We present experiments on six languages with varying degrees of non-projective structures: English, German, Dutch, Danish, Czech and Hungarian, which exhibit substantially different word order properties. Our approach achieves significant improvements on all six languages. On German, we also report results of a pilot human evaluation.

2 Related Work

An important concept for tree linearization are *word order domains* (Reape, 1989). The domains are bags of words (constituents) that are not allowed to be discontinuous. A straightforward method to obtain the word order domains from dependency trees and to order the words in the tree is to use each word and its children as domain and then to order the domains and contained words recursively. As outlined in the introduction, the direct mapping of syntactic trees to domains does not provide the possibility to obtain all possible correct word orders.

Linearization systems can be roughly distinguished as either rule-based or statistical systems. In the 2011 Shared Task on Surface Realisation (Belz et al., 2011), the top performing systems were all statistical dependency realizers (Bohnet et al., 2011; Guo et al., 2011; Stent, 2011).

Grammar-based approaches map dependency structures or phrase structures to a tree that represents the linear precedence. These approaches are mostly able to generate non-projective word orders. Early work was nearly exclusively applied to phrase structure grammars (e.g. (Kathol and Pollard, 1995; Rambow and Joshi, 1994; Langkilde and Knight, 1998)). Concerning dependency-based frameworks, Bröker (1998) used the concept of word order domains to separate surface realization from linear precedence trees. Similarly, Duchier and Debusmann (2001) differentiate Immediate Dominance trees (ID-trees) from Linear Precedence trees (LP-trees). Gerdes and Kahane (2001) apply a hierarchical topological model for generating German word order. Bohnet (2004) employs graph grammars to map between dependency trees and linear precedence trees represented as hierarchical graphs. In the frameworks of HPSG, LFG, and CCG, a grammar-based generator produces word order candidates that might be non-projective, and a ranker is used to select the best surface realization (Cahill et al., 2007; White and Rajkumar, 2009).

Statistical methods for linearization have recently become more popular (Langkilde and Knight, 1998; Ringger et al., 2004; Filippova and Strube, 2009; Wan et al., 2009; He et al., 2009; Bohnet et al., 2010; Guo et al., 2011). They typically work by traversing the syntactic structure either bottom-up (Filippova and Strube, 2007; Bohnet et al., 2010) or top-down (Guo et al., 2011; Bohnet et al., 2011). These linearizers are mostly applied to English and do not deal with non-projective word orders. An exception is Filippova and Strube (2007), who contribute a study on the treatment of preverbal and postverbal constituents for German focusing on constituent order at the sentence level. The work most similar to ours is that of Gamon et al. (2002). They use machine-learning techniques to lift edges in a preprocessing step to a surface realizer. Their objective is the same as ours: by lifting, they avoid crossing edges. However, contrary to our work, they use phrase-structure syntax and focus on a limited number of cases of crossing branches in German only.

3 Lifting Dependency Edges

In this section, we describe the first of the two stages in our approach, namely the classifier that lifts edges in dependency trees. The classifier we aim to train is meant to predict liftings on a given unordered dependency tree, yielding a tree that, with a perfect linearization, would not have any non-projective edges.

3.1 Preliminaries

The dependency trees we consider are of the form displayed in Figure 1. More precisely, all words (or nodes) form a rooted tree, where every node has exactly one parent (or *head*). Edges point from head to dependent, denoted in the text by $h \rightarrow d$, where h is the head and d the dependent. All nodes directly or transitively depend on an artificial root node (depicted in Figure 1 as the incoming edge to *is*).

We say that a node a *dominates* a node d if a is an ancestor of d. An edge $h \rightarrow d$ is *projective* iff h dominates all nodes in the linear span between h and d. Otherwise it is *non-projective*. Moreover, a dependency tree is projective iff all its edges are projective. Otherwise it is non-projective.

A *lifting* of an edge $h \rightarrow d$ (or simply of the node d) is an operation that replaces $h \rightarrow d$ with $g \rightarrow d$, given that there exists an edge $g \rightarrow h$ in the tree, and undefined otherwise (i.e. the dependent d is reattached to the head of its head).[2] When the lifting operation is applied n successive times to the same node, we say the node was lifted n *steps*.

3.2 Training

During training we make use of the projectivization algorithm described by Nivre and Nilsson (2005). It works by iteratively lifting the shortest non-projective edges until the tree is projective. Here, shortest edge refers to the edge spanning over the fewest number of words. Since finding the shortest edge relies on the linear order, instead of lifting the shortest edge, we lift non-projective edges ordered by depth in the tree, starting with the deepest nested edge. A lifted version of the tree from Figure 1 is shown in Figure 3. The edge of *what* has been lifted three steps (the original edge is dotted), and the tree is no longer non-projective.

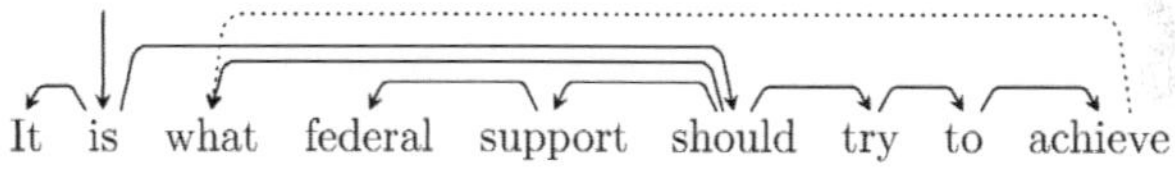

Figure 3: The sentence from Figure 1, where *what* has been assigned a new head (solid line). The original edge is dotted.

We model the edge lifting problem as a multi-class classification problem and consider nodes one at a time and ask the question "*How far should this edge be lifted?*", where classes correspond to lifting $0, 1, 2, ..., n$ steps. To create training instances we use the projectivization algorithm mentioned above. We traverse the nodes of the tree sorted by depth. For multiple nodes at the same depth, ties are broken by linear order, i.e. for multiple nodes at the same depth, the leftmost is visited first. When a node is visited, we create a training instance out of it. Its class is determined by the number of steps it would be lifted by the projectivization algorithm given the linear order (in most cases the class corresponds to no lifting, since most edges are projective). As we traverse the nodes, we also execute the liftings (if any) and update the tree on the fly.

The training instances derived are used to train a logistic regression classifier using the LIBLINEAR package (Fan et al., 2008). The features used for the lifting classifier are described in Table 1. Since we use linear classifiers, our feature set also contains conjunctions of atomic features. The features

[2]The undefined case occurs only when d depends on the root, and hence cannot be lifted further; but these edges are by definition projective, since the root dominates the entire tree.

Atomic features	
$\forall x \in \{w, w_p, w_{gp}, w_{ch}, w_s, w_{un}\}$	morph(x), label(x), lemma(x), PoS(x)
$\forall x \in \{w_{gc}, w_{ne}, w_{co}\}$	label(x), lemma(x), PoS(x)
Complex features	
$\forall x \in \{w, w_p, w_{gp}\}$	lemma(x)+PoS(x), label(x)+PoS(x), label(x)+lemma(x)
$\forall x \in \{w_{ch}, w_s, w_{un}\}, y = w$	lemma(x)+lemma(y), PoS(y)+lemma(x), PoS(y)+lemma(x)
$\forall x \in \{w, w_p, w_{gp}\}, y = \text{HEAD}(x)$	lemma(x)+lemma(y), lemma(x)+PoS(y), PoS(x)+lemma(y)
$\forall x \in \{w, w_p, w_{gp}\}, y = \text{HEAD}(x), z = \text{HEAD}(y)$	PoS(x)+PoS(y)+PoS(z), label(x)+label(y)+label(z)
$\forall x \in \{w_{ch}, w_s, w_{un}\}, y = \text{HEAD}(x), z = \text{HEAD}(y)$	PoS(x)+PoS(y)+PoS(z), label(x)+label(y)+label(z)
Non-binary features	
$\forall x \in \{w, w_p, w_{gp}\}$	SUBTREESIZE(x), RELSUBTREESIZE(x)

Table 1: Features used for lifting. w refers to the word (dependent) in question. And with respect to w, w_p is the parent; w_{gp} is the grandparent; w_{ch} are children; w_s are siblings; w_{un} are uncles (i.e. children of the grandparent, excluding the parent); w_{gc} are grandchildren; w_{ne} are nephews (i.e. grandchildren of the parent that are not children of w); w_{co} are cousins (i.e. grandchildren of the grandparent that are not w or siblings of w). The non-binary feature functions refer to: SUBTREESIZE – the absolute number of nodes below x, RELSUBTREESIZE – the relative size of the subtree rooted at x with respect to the whole tree.

involve the lemma, dependency edge label, part-of-speech tag, and morphological features of the node in question, and of several neighboring nodes in the dependency tree. We also have a few non-binary features that encode the size of the subtree headed by the node and its ancestors.

We ran preliminary experiments to determine the optimal architecture. First, other ways of modeling the liftings are conceivable. To find new reattachment points, Gamon et al. (2002) propose two other ways, both using a binary classifier: applying the classifier to each node x along the path to the root asking "*Should* d *be reattached to* x*?*"; or lifting one step at a time and applying the classifier iteratively until it says stop. They found that the latter outperformed the former. We tried this method, but found that it was inferior to the multi-class model and more frequently over- or underlifted.

Second, to avoid data sparseness for infrequent lifting distances, we introduce a maximum number of liftings. We found that a maximum of 3 gave the best performance. In the pseudocode below, we refer to this number as *maxsteps*.[3] This means that we are able to predict the correct lifting for most (but not all) of the non-projective edges in our data sets (cf. Table 3).

Third, as Nivre and Nilsson (2005) do for parsing, we experimented with marking edges that were lifted by indicating this on the edge labels. In the case of parsing, this step is necessary in order to reverse the liftings in the parser output. In our case, it could potentially be beneficial for both the lifting classifier, and for the linearizer. However, we found that marking liftings at best gave similar results as not marking, so we kept the original labels without marking.

3.3 Decoding

In the decoding stage, an unordered tree is given and the goal is to lift edges that would be non-projective with respect to the gold linear order. Similarly to how training instances are derived, the decoding algorithm traverses the tree bottom-up and visits every node once. Ties between nodes at the same depth are broken in an arbitrary but deterministic way. When a node is visited, the classifier is applied and the corresponding lifting is executed. Pseudocode is given in Algorithm 1.[4]

Different orderings of nodes at the same depth can lead to different lifts. The reason is that liftings are applied immediately and this influences the features when subsequent nodes are considered. For instance, consider two sibling nodes n_i and n_j. If n_i is visited before n_j, and n_i is lifted, this means

[3]During training, nodes that are lifted further than *maxsteps* are assigned to the class corresponding to *maxsteps*. This approach worked better than ignoring the training instance or treating it as a non-lifting (i.e. a lifting of 0 steps).

[4]The MIN function is used to guarantee that the edge is not lifted beyond the root node of the tree. This does not happen in practice though, since the feature set of the classifier include features that implicitly encode the proximity to the root node.

that at the time we visit n_j, n_i is no longer a sibling of n_j, but rather an uncle. An obvious extension of the decoding algorithm presented above is to apply beam search. This allows us to consider n_j both in the context where n_i has been lifted and when it has not been lifted.

```
N ← NODES(T)
SORT-BY-DEPTH-BREAK-TIES-ARBITRARILY(N, T)
foreach node ∈ N do
    feats ← EXTRACT-FEATURES(node, T)
    steps ← CLASSIFY(feats)
    steps ← MIN(steps,ROOT-DIST(node))
    LIFT(node, T, steps)
return T
```

Algorithm 1: Greedy decoding for lifting.

Pseudocode for the beam search decoder is given in Algorithm 2. The algorithm keeps an agenda of trees to explore as each node is visited. For every node, it clones the current tree and applies every possible lifting. Every tree also has an associated score, which is the sum of the scores of each lifting so far. The score of a lifting is defined to be the log probability returned from the logistic classifier. After exploring all trees in the agenda, the k-best new trees from the beam are extracted and put back into the agenda. When all nodes have been visited, the best tree in the agenda is returned. For the experiments the beam size (k in Algorithm 2) was set to 20.

```
N ← NODES(T)
SORT-BY-DEPTH-BREAK-TIES-ARBITRARILY(N, T)
T_score ← 0
Agenda ← {T}
foreach node ∈ N do
    Beam ← ∅
    foreach tree ∈ Agenda do
        feats ← EXTRACT-FEATURES(node, tree)
        m ← MIN(maxsteps,ROOT-DIST(node))
        foreach s ∈ 0 .. maxsteps do
            t ← CLONE(tree)
            score ← GET-LIFT-SCORE(feats, s)
            t_score = t_score + score
            LIFT(node, t, s)
            Beam ← Beam ∪ {t}
        Agenda ← EXTRACTKBEST(Beam, k)
return EXTRACTKBEST(Agenda, 1)
```

Algorithm 2: Beam decoding for lifting.

While beam search allows us to explore the search space somewhat more thoroughly, a large number of possibilities remain unaccounted for. Again, consider the sibling nodes n_i and n_j when n_i is visited before n_j. The beam allows us to consider n_j both when n_i is lifted and when it is not. However, the situation where n_j is visited *before* n_i is still never considered. Ideally, all permutations of nodes at the same depth should be explored before moving on. Unfortunately this leads to a combinatorial explosion of permutations, and exhaustive search is not tractable. As an approximation, we create two orderings and run the beam search twice. The difference between the orderings is that in the second one all ties are reversed. As this *bibeam* consistently improved over the beam in Algorithm 2, we only present these results in Section 5 (there denoted simply *Beam*).

4 Linearization

A linearizer searches for the optimal word order given an unordered dependency tree, where the optimal word order is defined as the single reference order of the dependency tree in the gold standard. We employ a statistical linearizer that is trained on a corpus of pairs consisting of unordered dependency trees and their corresponding sentences. The linearization method consists of the following steps:

Creating word order domains. In the first step, we build the word order domains d_h for all nodes $h \in y$ of a dependency tree y. A domain is defined as a node and all of its direct dependents. For example, the tree shown in Figure 3 has the following domains: {*it, be, should*}, {*what, support, should, try*}, {*federal, support*}, {*try, to*}, {*to, achieve*}

If an edge was lifted before the linearization, the lifted node will end up in the word order domain of its new head rather than in the domain of its original head. This way, the linearizer can deduce word orders that would result in non-projective structures in the non-lifted tree.

Ordering the words of the domains. In the second step, the linearizer orders the words of each domain. The position of a subtree is determined by the position of the head of the subtree in the enclosing domain. Algorithm 3 shows the tree linearization algorithm. In our implementation, the linearizer traverses the tree either top-down or bottom-up.

```
1  // T is the dependency tree with lifted nodes
2  beam-size ← 1000
3  for h ∈ T do
4      domain_h ← GET-DOMAIN(T,h)
5      // initialize the beam with a empty word list
6      Agenda_h ← (ε)
7      foreach w ∈ domain_h do
8          // beam for extending word order lists
9          Beam ← ()
10         foreach l ∈ Agenda_h do
11             // clone list l and append the word w
12             if w ∉ l then
13                 l' ← APPEND(l,m)
14                 Beam ← Beam ⊕ l'
15                 score[l'] ← COMPUTE-SCORE(l')
16         if | Beam | > beam-size then
17             SORT-LISTS-DESCENDING-TO-
               SCORE(Beam,score)
18             Agenda_h ← SUBLIST(0,beam-size,Beam)
19         else
20             Agenda_h ← Beam
21     foreach l ∈ Beam do
22         SCORE_g[l] ← SCORE[l] +
           GLOBAL-SCORE(l)
23     Agenda_h ← Beam
24 return Beam
```

Algorithm 3: Dependency Tree Linearization.

The linearization algorithm initializes the word order beam (*agenda*$_h$) with an empty order (ϵ) (line 6). It then iterates over the words of a domain (lines 7-20). In the first iteration, the algorithm clones and extends the empty word order list (ϵ) by each word of the sentence (line 12-15). If the beam (*beam*) exceeds a certain size (*beam-size*), it is sorted by score and pruned to maximum beam size (*beam-size*) (lines 16-20). The following example illustrates the extensions of the beam for the top domain shown in Figure 3.

Iter. agenda$_{be}$
0: (ϵ)
1: ((it) (be) (should))
2: ((it be) (it should) (be it) (be should) ...)

The beam enables us to apply features that encode information about the first tokens and the last token, which are important for generating, e.g. the word order of questions, i. e. if the last token is a question mark then the sentence should probably be a question (cf. feature set shown in Table 2). Furthermore, the beam enables us to generate alternative linearizations. For this, the algorithm iterates over the alternative word orders of the domains in order to assemble different word orders on the sentence level.[5] Finally, when traversing the tree bottom-up, the algorithm has to use the different orders of the already ordered subtrees as context, which also requires a search over alternative word orders of the domains.

Training of the Linearizer. We use MIRA (Crammer et al., 2006) for the training of the linearizer. The classifier provides a score that we use to rank the alternative word orders. Algorithm 3 calls two functions to compute the score: *compute-score* (line 15) for features based on pairs of words and trigrams and *compute-global-score* for features based on word patterns of a domain. Table 2 shows the feature set for the two functions. In the case that the linearization of a word order domain is incorrect the algorithm updates its weight vector w. The following equation shows the update function of the weight vector:

$$w = w + \tau_h(\phi(d_h, T, x_g) - \phi(d_h, T, x_p))$$

We update the weight vector w by adding the difference of the feature vector representation of the correct linearization x_g and the wrongly predicted linearization x_p, multiplied by τ. τ is the passive-aggressive update factor as defined below. The suffered $loss_h$ is $\phi(d_h, T, x_p) - \phi(d_h, T, x_g)$.

$$\tau = \frac{loss_h}{||\phi(d_h,T,x_g) - \phi(d_h,T,x_p)||^2}$$

Creating the word order of a sentence. The linearizer traverses the tree either top-down or bottom-up and assembles the results in the surface order. The bottom-up linearization algorithm can take into account features drawn from the already ordered subtrees while the top-down algorithm can employ as context only the unordered nodes. However, the bottom-up algorithm additionally has to carry out a search over the alternative linearization of the subdomains, as different orders of the subdomain provide different context features. This leads to a higher linearization time. We implemented both, but could only find a rather small accuracy difference. In the following, we therefore present results only for the top-down method.

[5] The beam also makes it possible to employ a generative language model to rerank alternative linearizations.

Atomic features		
For nodes $w \in domain_h$	lemma(w), label(w), PoS(w), num-children(w), num-grandchildren(w), label-children(w), PoS-children(w)	
For domain $domain_h$	head(w_1,w_2), head(w_1,w_2,w_3), label($head$), PoS($head$), PoS(w_1), label(w_n), label(w_{n-1}), contains-?($domain_h$)	
Complex features		
For bigrams $(w_1, w_2) \in domain_h$	feat$_2$:	label(w_1)+label(w_2), label(w_1)+lemma(w_2), lemma(w_1)+lemma(w_2), PoSw_1+PoSw_2
	feat$_3$:	label(w_1)+num-children(w_2)+num-children(w_1),PoS-child(w_1)+label(w_1)+label(w_2)
	feat$_4$:	label(w_1)+label(w_2)+lemma(w_2)+PoS(w_1), label(w_1)+label(w_2)+PoS($head$)+head(w_1,w_2)
	feat$_5$:	label(w_1)+label(w_2)+PoS($head$)+label($head$)+head(w_1,w_2)
For trigrams $(w_1, w_2, w_3) \in domain_h$	feat$_3$:	lemma(w_1)+lemma(w_2)+lemma(w_3)
	feat$_4$:	PoS(w_1)+PoS(w_2)+PoS(w_3)+head(w_1,w_2,w_3)
	feat$_5$:	label(w_1)+label(w_2)+label(w_3)+PoS(w_1)+head(w_1,w_2,w_3)
For sentence s	feat$_6$:	label(w_1)+label(w_{n-1})+lemma($head$)+lemma(w_1)+lemma(w_{n-1})
	feat$_7$:	PoS(w_1)+PoS(w_2)+PoS(w_3)+PoS(w_{n-1})+PoS(w_{n-2})+PoS(w_{n-3})+contains-?(s)

Table 2: Exemplified features used for scoring linearizations of a word order domain (see Algorithm 3). Atomic features which represent properties of a node or a domain are conjoined into feature vectors of different lengths. Linearizations are scored based on bigrams, trigrams, and global sentence-level features.

5 Experiments

We conduct experiments on six European languages with varying degrees of word order restrictions: While English word order is very restrictive, Czech and Hungarian exhibit few word order constraints. Danish, Dutch, and German (so-called V2, i. e. verb-second, languages) show a relatively free word order that is however more restrictive than in Hungarian or Czech. The English and the Czech data are from the CoNLL 2009 Shared Task data sets (Hajič et al., 2009). The Danish and the Dutch data are from the CoNLL 2006 Shared Task data sets (Buchholz and Marsi, 2006). For Hungarian, we use the Hungarian Dependency Treebank (Vincze et al., 2010), and for German, we use a dependency conversion by Seeker and Kuhn (2012).

	# sent's	np sent's	np edges	np $\leq$ 3 lifts
English	39,279	7.63 %	0.39%	98.39%
German	36,000	28.71%	2.34%	94.98%
Dutch	13,349	36.44%	5.42%	99.80%
Danish	5,190	15.62 %	1.00%	96.72%
Hungarian	61,034	15.81%	1.45%	99.82%
Czech	38,727	22.42%	1.86%	99.84%

Table 3: Size of training sets, percentage of non-projective (np) sentences and edges, percentage of np edges covered by 3 lifting steps.

Table 3 shows the sizes of the training corpora and the percentage of non-projective sentences and edges in the data. Note that the data sets for Danish and Dutch are quite small. English has the least percentage of non-projective edges. Czech, German, and Dutch show the highest percentage of non-projective edges. The last column shows the percentage of non-projective edges that can be made projective by at most 3 lifting steps.

5.1 Setup

In our two-stage approach, we first train the lifting classifier. The results for this classifier are reported in Section 5.2.

Second, we train the linearizer on the output of the lifting classifier. To assess the impact of the lifting technique on linearization, we built four systems on each language: (**a**) a linearizer trained on the original, non-lifted dependency structures (*No-lift*), two trained on the automatically lifted edges (comparing (**b**) the beam and (**c**) greedy decoding), (**d**) one trained on the oracle, i. e. gold-lifted structures, which gives us an upper bound for the lifting technique. The linearization results are reported in Section 5.3.

In this two-stage setup, we have the problem that, if we re-apply the lifting classifier on the data it was trained on, the input for the linearizer will be better during training than during testing. To provide realistic training data for the linearizer, we make a 10-fold cross-validation of the lifting classifier on the training set, and use this as training data for the linearizer. The lifting classifier that is applied to the test set is trained on the entire training set.

5.2 Lifting results

To evaluate the performance of the lifting classifier, we present precision, recall, and F-measure results for each language. We also compute the percentage of sentences that were handled perfectly by the lifting classifier. Precision and recall are defined the usual way in terms of true positives, false positives, and false negatives, where true positives are edges that should be lifted and were lifted correctly; false positives are edges that should not be lifted but were *and* edges that should be lifted and were lifted, but were reattached in the wrong place; false negatives are edges that should be lifted but were not.

The performance of both the greedy decoder and the bibeam decoder are shown in Table 4. The scores are taken on the cross-validation on the training set, as this provides more reliable figures. The scores are micro-averaged, i.e. all folds are concatenated and compared to the entire training set.

Although the major evaluation of the lifting is given by the performance of the linearizer, Table 4 gives us some clues about the lifting. We see that precision is generally much higher than recall. We believe this is related to the fact that some phenomena encoded by non-projective edges are more systematic and thus easier to learn than others (e. g. wh-extraction vs. relative clause extraposition). We also find that beam search consistently yields modest increases in performance.

	Greedy				Beam			
	P	R	F1	Perfect	P	R	F1	Perfect
Eng	77.31	50.45	61.05	95.76	78.85	50.63	61.66	95.83
Ger	72.33	63.59	67.68	81.91	72.05	64.41	68.02	81.97
Dut	76.66	74.89	75.77	79.28	78.07	76.49	77.27	80.34
Dan	85.90	58.55	69.64	92.76	85.90	58.55	69.64	92.74
Hun	72.60	61.61	66.66	88.46	73.06	64.77	68.67	88.73
Cze	77.79	55.00	64.44	86.28	77.31	55.68	64.74	86.33

Table 4: Precision, recall, F-measure and perfect projectivization results for the lifting classifier.

5.3 Linearization Results and Discussion

We evaluate the linearizer with standard metrics: n-gram overlap measures (BLEU, NIST), edit distance (Edit), and the proportion of exactly linearized sentences (Exact). As a means to assess the impact of lifting more precisely, we propose the word-based measure Exact_{lift} which only looks at the words with an incoming lifted edge. The Exact_{lift} score then corresponds to the percentage of these words that has been realized in the exact same position as in the original sentence.

Lang_{Lift}	BLEU	NIST	Edit	Exact	Exact_{lift}	N_{lift}
Eng_{Nolift}	0.911	15.09	0.922	56.40	0.00	0
Eng_{Greedy}	0.914	15.10	0.923	57.27	59.87	152
Eng_{Beam}	0.916	15.11	0.925	58.48	62.82	156
Eng_{Oracle}	0.923	15.14	0.928	60.73	70.42	240
Ger_{Nolift}	0.792	13.76	0.844	40.4	0.00	0
Ger_{Greedy}	0.811	13.86	0.864	42.9	55.21	480
Ger_{Beam}	0.813	13.86	0.866	43.3	56.47	487
Ger_{Oracle}	0.843	13.97	0.889	49.95	72.87	634
Dut_{Nolift}	0.743	11.31	0.796	30.05	0.00	0
Dut_{Greedy}	0.784	11.47	0.797	37.56	41.02	256
Dut_{Beam}	0.778	11.46	0.8	37.05	47.45	255
Dut_{Oracle}	0.825	11.63	0.848	44.82	70.55	292
Dan_{Nolift}	0.836	11.80	0.886	44.41	0.00	0
Dan_{Greedy}	0.852	11.88	0.90	45.96	67.65	34
Dan_{Beam}	0.858	11.90	0.90	48.76	67.65	34
Dan_{Oracle}	0.865	11.92	0.90	50.93	74.42	43
Hun_{Nolift}	0.755	15.70	0.839	30.71	0.00	0
Hun_{Greedy}	0.764	15.71	0.844	31.98	41,81	1,538
Hun_{Beam}	0.764	15.71	0.844	31.98	41.37	1,581
Hun_{Oracle}	0.777	15.79	0.849	34.30	57.53	1,933
Cze_{Nolift}	0.693	14.32	0.789	25.14	0.00	0
Cze_{Greedy}	0.711	14.45	0.797	26.85	42.04	923
Cze_{Beam}	0.712	14.45	0.795	26.37	41.34	941
Cze_{Oracle}	0.729	14.52	0.806	28.79	53.12	1,282

Table 5: Performance of linearizers using different liftings, Exact_{lift} is the exact match for words with an incoming lifted edge, N_{lift} is the total number of lifted edges.

The results are presented in Table 5. On each language, the predicted liftings significantly improve on the non-lifted baseline (except the greedy decoding in English).[6] The differences between the beam and the greedy decoding are not significant. The scores on the oracle liftings suggest that the impact of lifting on linearization is heavily language-dependent: It is highest on the V2-languages, and somewhat smaller on English, Hungarian, and Czech. This is not surprising since the V2-languages (especially German and Dutch) have the highest proportion of non-projective edges and sentences (see Table 3). On the other hand, English has a very small number of non-projective edges, such that the BLEU score (which captures the n-gram level) reflects the improvement by only

[6] We used a t-test, with $\alpha = 0.01$.

a small increase. However, note that, on the sentence level, the percentage of exactly regenerated sentences increases by 2 points which suggests that a non-negligible amount of non-projective sentences can now be generated more fluently.

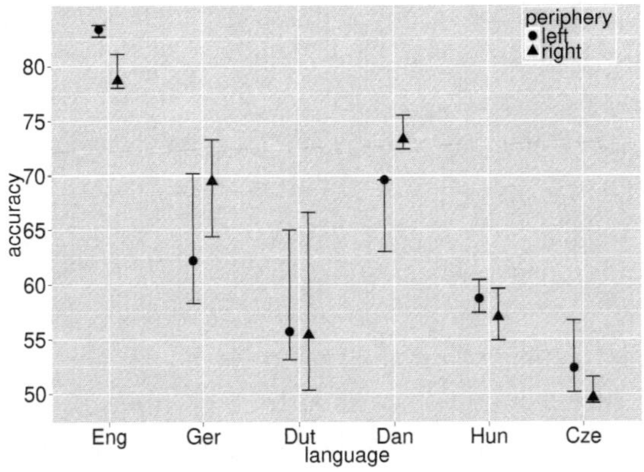

Figure 4: Accuracy for the linearization of the sentences' left and right periphery, the bars are upper and lower bounds of the non-lifted and the gold-lifted baseline.

The Exact_{lift} measure refines this picture: The linearization of the non-projective edges is relatively exact in English, and much less precise in Hungarian and Czech where Exact_{lift} is even low on the gold-lifted edges. The linearization quality is also quite moderate on Dutch where the lifting leads to considerable improvements. These tendencies point to some important underlying distinctions in the non-projective word order phenomena over which we are generalizing: In certain cases, the linearization seems to systematically follow from the fact that the edge has to be lifted, such as *wh*-extraction in English (Figure 1). In other cases, the non-projective linearization is just an alternative to other grammatical, but maybe less appropriate, realizations, such as the *prefield*-occupation in German (Figure 2).

Since a lot of non-projective word orders affect the clause-initial or clause-final position, we evaluate the exact match of the left periphery (first three words) and the right periphery (last three words) of the sentence. The accuracies obtained are plotted in Figure 4, where the lower and upper bars correspond to the lower and upper bound from the non-lifted and the gold-lifted baseline. It clearly emerges from this figure that the range of improvements obtainable from lifting is closely tied to the general linearization quality, and also to word order properties of the languages. Thus, the range of sentences affected by the lifting is clearly largest for the V2-languages. The accuracies are high, but the ranges are small for English, whereas the accuracies are low and the ranges quite small for Czech and Hungarian.

System	BLEU	NIST
(Bohnet et al., 2011) (ranked 1st)	0.896	13.93
(Guo et al., 2011) (ranked 2nd)	0.862	13.68
Baseline-Non-Lifted + LM	0.896	13.94
Beam-Lifted + LM	0.901	13.96

Table 6: Results on the development set of the 2011 Shared Task on Surface Realisation data, (the test set was not officially released).

We also evaluated our linearizer on the data of 2011 Shared Task on Surface Realisation, which is based on the English CoNLL 2009 data (like our previous evaluations) but excludes information on morphological realization. For training and evaluation, we used the exact set up of the Shared Task. For the morphological realization, we used the morphological realizer of Bohnet et al. (2010) that predicts the word form using shortest edit scripts. For the language model (LM), we use a 5-gram model with Kneser-Ney (Kneser and Ney, 1995) smoothing derived from 11 million sentences of the Wikipedia.

In Table 6, we compare our two linearizers (with and without lifting) to the two top systems of the 2011 Shared Task on Surface Realisation, (Bohnet et al., 2011) and (Guo et al., 2011). Without the lifting, our system reaches a score comparable to the top-ranked system in the Shared Task. With the lifting, we get a small[7] but statistically significant improvement in BLEU such that our system reaches a higher score than the top ranked systems. This shows that the improvements we obtain from the lifting carry over to more complex generation tasks which include morphological realization.

5.4 Human Evaluation

We have carried out a pilot human evaluation on the German data in order to see whether human judges prefer word orders obtained from the lifting-based

[7]Remember that English has the least percentage of non-projective edges in our data sets, which are however important to linearize correctly (see Figure 1).

linearizer. In particular, we wanted to check whether the lifting-based linearizer produces more natural word orders for sentences that had a non-projective tree in the corpus, and maybe less natural word orders on originally projective sentences. Therefore, we divided the evaluated items into originally projective and non-projective sentences.

We asked four annotators to judge 60 sentence pairs comparing the lifting-based against the non-lifted linearizer using the toolkit by Kow and Belz (2012). All annotators are students, two of them have a background in linguistics. The items were randomly sampled from the subset of the development set containing those sentences where the linearizers produced different surface realizations. The items are subdivided into 30 originally projective and 30 originally non-projective sentences.

For each item, we presented the original context sentence from the corpus and the pair of automatically produced linearizations for the current sentence. The annotators had to decide on two criteria: (i) which sentence do they prefer? (ii) how fluent is that sentence? In both cases, we used continuous sliders as rating tools, since humans seem to prefer them (Belz and Kow, 2011). For the first criterion, the slider positions were mapped to values from -50 (preference for left sentence) to 50 (preference for right sentence). If the slider position is zero, both sentences are equally preferred. For the second criterion, the slider positions were mapped to values from 0 (absolutely broken sentence) to 100 (perfectly fluent sentence).

Sentences	Scores	Equal	Lifted	Non-lifted
All	% selected	44.58%	35.0%	20.42%
	Fluency	56.14	75.77	72.78
	Preference	0	34.75	31.06
Non-Proj.	% selected	29.63%	58.33%	12.04%
	Fluency	43.06	76.27	68.85
	Preference	0	37.52	24.46
Proj.	% selected	56.82%	15.91%	27.27%
	Fluency	61.72	74.29	74.19
	Preference	0	26.43	33.44

Table 7: Results from human evaluation.

Table 7 presents the results averaged over all sentences, as well as for the subsets of non-projective and projective sentences. We report the percentage of items where the judges selected both, the lifted, or non-lifted sentence, alongside with the average fluency score (0-100) and preference strength (0-50).

On the entire set of items, the judges selected both sentences in almost half of the cases. However, on the subset of non-projective sentences, the lifted version is clearly preferred and has a higher average fluency and preference strength. The percentage of zero preference items is much higher on the subset of projective sentences. Moreover, the average fluency of the zero preference items is remarkably higher on the projective sentences than on the non-projective subset. We conclude that humans have a strong preference for lifting-based linearizations on non-projective sentences. We attribute the low fluency score on the non-projective zero preference items to cases where the linearizer did not get a correct lifting or could not linearize the lifting correctly such that the lifted and the non-lifted version were not appropriate. On the other hand, incorrect liftings on projective sentences do not necessarily seem to result in deprecated linearizations, which leads to the high percentage of zero preferences with a good average fluency on this subset.

6 Conclusion

We have presented a novel technique to linearize sentences for a range of languages that exhibit non-projective word order. Our approach deals with non-projectivity by lifting edges in an unordered input tree which can then be linearized by a standard projective linearization algorithm.

We obtain significant improvements for the lifting-based linearization on English, German, Dutch, Danish, Czech and Hungarian, and show that lifting has the largest impact on the V2-languages. In a human evaluation carried out on German we also show that human judges clearly prefer lifting-based linearizations on originally non-projective sentences, and, on the other hand, that incorrect liftings do not necessarily result in bad realizations of the sentence.

Acknowledgments

This work was funded by the Deutsche Forschungsgemeinschaft (DFG) via the SFB 732 "Incremental Specification in Context". We would also like to thank Anna Hätty and our four annotators for their contribution to the human evaluation.

References

A. Belz and E. Kow. 2011. Discrete vs. Continuous Rating Scales for Language Evaluation in NLP. In *Proceedings of the 49th Annual Meeting of the Association for Computational Linguistics: Human Language Technologies*, pages 230–235, Portland, Oregon, USA, June. Association for Computational Linguistics.

A. Belz, M. White, D. Espinosa, D. Hogan, E. Kow, and A. Stent. 2011. The First Surface Realisation Shared Task: Overview and Evaluation Results. In *ENLG'11*.

A. Böhmová, J. Hajič, E. Hajičová, and B. Hladká. 2000. The Prague Dependency Treebank: A Three-level annotation scenario. In A. Abeillé, editor, *Treebanks: Building and using syntactically annotated corpora.*, chapter 1, pages 103–127. Kluwer Academic Publishers, Amsterdam.

B. Bohnet, L. Wanner, S. Mille, and A. Burga. 2010. Broad coverage multilingual deep sentence generation with a stochastic multi-level realizer. In *Coling 2010*, pages 98–106.

B. Bohnet, S. Mille, B. Favre, and L. Wanner. 2011. <stumaba>: From deep representation to surface. In *Proceedings of the Generation Challenges Session at the 13th European Workshop on NLG*, pages 232–235, Nancy, France.

B. Bohnet. 2004. A Graph Grammar Approach to Map Between Dependency Trees and Topological Models. In *IJCNLP*, pages 636–645.

N. Bröker. 1998. Separating Surface Order and Syntactic Relations in a Dependency Grammar. In *COLING-ACL 98*.

S. Buchholz and E. Marsi. 2006. CoNLL-X shared task on multilingual dependency parsing. In *Proceedings of the Tenth Conference on Computational Natural Language Learning*, pages 149–164, Morristown, NJ, USA. Association for Computational Linguistics.

A. Cahill, M. Forst, and C. Rohrer. 2007. Stochastic realisation ranking for a free word order language. ENLG '07, pages 17–24.

K. Crammer, O. Dekel, S. Shalev-Shwartz, and Y. Singer. 2006. Online Passive-Aggressive Algorithms. *Journal of Machine Learning Research*, 7:551–585.

D. Duchier and R. Debusmann. 2001. Topological dependency trees: A constraint-based account of linear precedence. In *Proceedings of the ACL*.

R. Fan, K. Chang, C. Hsieh, X. Wang, and C. Lin. 2008. LIBLINEAR: A library for large linear classification. *Journal of Machine Learning Research*, 9:1871–1874.

K. Filippova and M. Strube. 2007. Generating constituent order in german clauses. In *ACL*, pages 320–327.

K. Filippova and M. Strube. 2009. Tree linearization in English: improving language model based approaches. In *NAACL*, pages 225–228, Morristown, NJ, USA. Association for Computational Linguistics.

M. Gamon, E. Ringger, R. Moore, S. Corston-Olivier, and Z. Zhang. 2002. Extraposition: A case study in German sentence realization. In *Proceedings of Coling 2002*. Association for Computational Linguistics.

K. Gerdes and S. Kahane. 2001. Word order in german: A formal dependency grammar using a topological hierarchy. In *Proceedings of the ACL*.

Y. Guo, D. Hogan, and J. van Genabith. 2011. Dcu at generation challenges 2011 surface realisation track. In *Proceedings of the Generation Challenges Session at the 13th European Workshop on NLG*, pages 227–229.

J. Hajič, M. Ciaramita, R. Johansson, D. Kawahara, M.-A. Martí, L. Màrquez, A. Meyers, J. Nivre, S. Padó, J. Stepánek, P. Stranák, M. Surdeanu, N. Xue, and Y. Zhang. 2009. The CoNLL-2009 shared task: Syntactic and Semantic dependencies in multiple languages. In *Proceedings of the 13th CoNLL Shared Task*, pages 1–18, Boulder, Colorado.

E. Hajičová, J. Havelka, P. Sgall, K. Veselá, and D. Zeman. 2004. Issues of projectivity in the prague dependency treebank. *Prague Bulletin of Mathematical Linguistics*, 81.

W. He, H. Wang, Y. Guo, and T. Liu. 2009. Dependency Based Chinese Sentence Realization. In *Proceedings of the ACL and of the IJCNLP*, pages 809–816.

S. Kahane, A. Nasr, and O. Rambow. 1998. Pseudo-projectivity: A polynomially parsable non-projective dependency grammar. In *COLING-ACL*, pages 646–652.

A. Kathol and C. Pollard. 1995. Extraposition via complex domain formation. In *Meeting of the Association for Computational Linguistics*, pages 174–180.

R. Kneser and H. Ney. 1995. In *In Proceedings of the IEEE International Conference on Acoustics, Speech and Signal Processing*, pages 181–184.

E. Kow and A. Belz. 2012. LGRT-Eval: A Toolkit for Creating Online Language Evaluation Experiments. In *Proceedings of the 8th International Conference on Language Resources and Evaluation (LREC'12)*.

I. Langkilde and K. Knight. 1998. Generation that exploits corpus-based statistical knowledge. In *COLING-ACL*, pages 704–710.

J. Nivre and J. Nilsson. 2005. Pseudo-projective dependency parsing. In *Proceedings of the 43rd Annual Meeting of the Association for Computational Linguistics (ACL'05)*, pages 99–106, Ann Arbor, Michigan, June. Association for Computational Linguistics.

O. Rambow and A. K. Joshi. 1994. A formal look at dependency grammars and phrase-structure grammars, with special consideration of word-order phenomena.

In Leo Wanner, editor, *Current Issues in Meaning-Text Theory*. Pinter, London, UK.

M. Reape. 1989. A logical treatment of semi-free word order and bounded discontinuous constituency. In *Proceedings of the EACL*, EACL '89, pages 103–110.

E. Ringger, M. Gamon, R. C. Moore, D. Rojas, M. Smets, and S. Corston-Oliver. 2004. Linguistically informed statistical models of constituent structure for ordering in sentence realization. In *COLING '04*, pages 673–679.

W. Seeker and J. Kuhn. 2012. Making Ellipses Explicit in Dependency Conversion for a German Treebank. In *Proceedings of LREC 2012*, Istanbul, Turkey. European Language Resources Association (ELRA).

A. Stent. 2011. Att-0: Submission to generation challenges 2011 surface realization shared task. In *Proceedings of the Generation Challenges Session at the 13th European Workshop on Natural Language Generation*, pages 230–231, Nancy, France, September. Association for Computational Linguistics.

V. Vincze, D. Szauter, A. Almási, G. Móra, Z. Alexin, and J. Csirik. 2010. Hungarian Dependency Treebank. In *Proceedings of the Seventh conference on International Language Resources and Evaluation (LREC 2010)*, pages 1855–1862, Valletta, Malta.

S. Wan, M. Dras, R. Dale, and C. Paris. 2009. Improving grammaticality in statistical sentence generation: Introducing a dependency spanning tree algorithm with an argument satisfaction model. In *EACL*, pages 852–860.

M. White and R. Rajkumar. 2009. Perceptron reranking for CCG realization. In *EMNLP'09*, pages 410–419, Singapore, August.

Learning Syntactic Categories Using Paradigmatic Representations of Word Context

Mehmet Ali Yatbaz **Enis Sert** **Deniz Yuret**
Artificial Intelligence Laboratory
Koç University, İstanbul, Turkey
{myatbaz,esert,dyuret}@ku.edu.tr

Abstract

We investigate paradigmatic representations of word context in the domain of unsupervised syntactic category acquisition. Paradigmatic representations of word context are based on potential substitutes of a word in contrast to syntagmatic representations based on properties of neighboring words. We compare a bigram based baseline model with several paradigmatic models and demonstrate significant gains in accuracy. Our best model based on Euclidean co-occurrence embedding combines the paradigmatic context representation with morphological and orthographic features and achieves 80% many-to-one accuracy on a 45-tag 1M word corpus.

1 Introduction

Grammar rules apply not to individual words (e.g. dog, eat) but to syntactic categories of words (e.g. noun, verb). Thus constructing syntactic categories (also known as lexical or part-of-speech categories) is one of the fundamental problems in language acquisition.

Syntactic categories represent groups of words that can be substituted for one another without altering the grammaticality of a sentence. Linguists identify syntactic categories based on semantic, syntactic, and morphological properties of words. There is also evidence that children use prosodic and phonological features to bootstrap syntactic category acquisition (Ambridge and Lieven, 2011). However there is as yet no satisfactory computational model that can match human performance. Thus identifying the best set of features and best learning algorithms for syntactic category acquisition is still an open problem.

Relationships between linguistic units can be classified into two types: syntagmatic (concerning positioning), and paradigmatic (concerning substitution). Syntagmatic relations determine which units can combine to create larger groups and paradigmatic relations determine which units can be substituted for one another. Figure 1 illustrates the paradigmatic vs syntagmatic axes for words in a simple sentence and their possible substitutes.

In this study, we represent the paradigmatic axis directly by building *substitute vectors* for each word position in the text. The dimensions of a substitute vector represent words in the vocabulary, and the magnitudes represent the probability of occurrence in the given position. Note that the substitute vector for a word position (e.g. the second word in Fig. 1) is a function of the context only (i.e. "the ___ cried"), and does not depend on the word that does actually appear there (i.e. "man"). Thus substi-

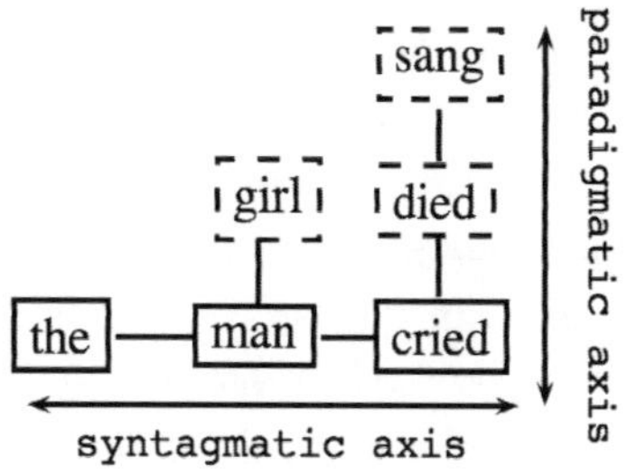

Figure 1: Syntagmatic vs. paradigmatic axes for words in a simple sentence (Chandler, 2007).

tute vectors represent *individual word contexts*, not word types. We refer to the use of features based on substitute vectors as *paradigmatic representations of word context*.

Our preliminary experiments indicated that using context information alone without the identity or the features of the target word (e.g. using dimensionality reduction and clustering on substitute vectors) has limited success and modeling the co-occurrence of word and context types is essential for inducing syntactic categories. In the models presented in this paper, we combine paradigmatic representations of word context with features of co-occurring words within the co-occurrence data embedding (CODE) framework (Globerson et al., 2007; Maron et al., 2010). The resulting embeddings for word types are split into 45 clusters using k-means and the clusters are compared to the 45 gold tags in the 1M word Penn Treebank Wall Street Journal corpus (Marcus et al., 1999). We obtain many-to-one accuracies up to .7680 using only distributional information (the identity of the word and a representation of its context) and .8023 using morphological and orthographic features of words improving the state-of-the-art in unsupervised part-of-speech tagging performance.

The high probability substitutes reflect both semantic and syntactic properties of the context as seen in the example below (the numbers in parentheses give substitute probabilities):

> *"Pierre Vinken, 61 years old, will join the board as a nonexecutive director Nov. 29."*
>
> **the:** its (.9011), the (.0981), a (.0006), . . .
> **board:** board (.4288), company (.2584), firm (.2024), bank (.0731), . . .

Top substitutes for the word "the" consist of words that can act as determiners. Top substitutes for "board" are not only nouns, but specifically nouns compatible with the semantic context.

This example illustrates two concerns inherent in all distributional methods: (i) words that are generally substitutable like "the" and "its" are placed in separate categories (DT and PRP$) by the gold standard, (ii) words that are generally not substitutable like "do" and "put" are placed in the same category (VB). Freudenthal et al. (2005) point out that categories with unsubstitutable words fail the standard linguistic definition of a syntactic category and children do not seem to make errors of substituting such words in utterances (e.g. *"What do you want?"* vs. **"What put you want?"*). Whether gold standard part-of-speech tags or distributional categories are better suited to applications like parsing or machine translation can be best decided using extrinsic evaluation. However in this study we follow previous work and evaluate our results by comparing them to gold standard part-of-speech tags.

Section 2 gives a detailed review of related work. Section 3 describes the dataset and the construction of the substitute vectors. Section 4 describes co-occurrence data embedding, the learning algorithm used in our experiments. Section 5 describes our experiments and compares our results with previous work. Section 6 gives a brief error analysis and Section 7 summarizes our contributions. All the data and the code to replicate the results given in this paper is available from the authors' website at `http://goo.gl/RoqEh`.

2 Related Work

There are several good reviews of algorithms for unsupervised part-of-speech induction (Christodoulopoulos et al., 2010; Gao and Johnson, 2008) and models of syntactic category acquisition (Ambridge and Lieven, 2011).

This work is to be distinguished from supervised part-of-speech disambiguation systems, which use labeled training data (Church, 1988), unsupervised disambiguation systems, which use a dictionary of possible tags for each word (Merialdo, 1994), or prototype driven systems which use a small set of prototypes for each class (Haghighi and Klein, 2006). The problem of induction is important for studying under-resourced languages that lack labeled corpora and high quality dictionaries. It is also essential in modeling child language acquisition because every child manages to induce syntactic categories without access to labeled sentences, labeled prototypes, or dictionary constraints.

Models of unsupervised part-of-speech induction fall into two broad groups based on the information they utilize. Distributional models only use word types and their context statistics. Word-feature models incorporate additional morphological and orthographic features.

2.1 Distributional models

Distributional models can be further categorized into three subgroups based on the learning algorithm. The first subgroup represents each word type with its context vector and clusters these vectors accordingly (Schütze, 1995). Work in modeling child syntactic category acquisition has generally followed this clustering approach (Redington et al., 1998; Mintz, 2003). The second subgroup consists of probabilistic models based on the Hidden Markov Model (HMM) framework (Brown et al., 1992). A third group of algorithms constructs a low dimensional representation of the data that represents the empirical co-occurrence statistics of word types (Globerson et al., 2007), which is covered in more detail in Section 4.

Clustering: Clustering based methods represent context using neighboring words, typically a single word on the left and a single word on the right called a "frame" (e.g., **the** *dog* **is**; **the** *cat* **is**). They cluster word types rather than word tokens based on the frames they occupy thus employing one-tag-per-word assumption from the beginning (with the exception of some methods in (Schütze, 1995)). They may suffer from data sparsity caused by infrequent words and infrequent contexts. The solutions suggested either restrict the set of words and set of contexts to be clustered to the most frequently observed, or use dimensionality reduction. Redington et al. (1998) define context similarity based on the number of common frames bypassing the data sparsity problem but achieve mediocre results. Mintz (2003) only uses the most frequent 45 frames and Biemann (2006) clusters the most frequent 10,000 words using contexts formed from the most frequent 150-200 words. Schütze (1995) and Lamar et al. (2010b) employ SVD to enhance similarity between less frequently observed words and contexts. Lamar et al. (2010a) represent each context by the currently assigned left and right tag (which eliminates data sparsity) and cluster word types using a soft k-means style iterative algorithm. They report the best clustering result to date of .708 many-to-one accuracy on a 45-tag 1M word corpus.

HMMs: The prototypical bitag HMM model maximizes the likelihood of the corpus $w_1 \ldots w_n$ expressed as $P(w_1|c_1)\prod_{i=2}^{n} P(w_i|c_i)P(c_i|c_{i-1})$ where w_i are the word tokens and c_i are their (hidden) tags. One problem with such a model is its tendency to distribute probabilities equally and the resulting inability to model highly skewed word-tag distributions observed in hand-labeled data (Johnson, 2007). To favor sparse word-tag distributions one can enforce a strict one-tag-per-word solution (Brown et al., 1992; Clark, 2003), use sparse priors in a Bayesian setting (Goldwater and Griffiths, 2007; Johnson, 2007), or use posterior regularization (Ganchev et al., 2010). Each of these techniques provide significant improvements over the standard HMM model: for example Gao and Johnson (2008) show that sparse priors can gain from 4% (.62 to .66 with a 1M word corpus) in cross-validated many-to-one accuracy. However Christodoulopoulos et al. (2010) show that the older one-tag-per-word models such as (Brown et al., 1992) outperform the more sophisticated sparse prior and posterior regularization methods both in speed and accuracy (the Brown model gets .68 many-to-one accuracy with a 1M word corpus). Given that close to 95% of the word occurrences in human labeled data are tagged with their most frequent part of speech (Lee et al., 2010), this is probably not surprising; one-tag-per-word is a fairly good first approximation for induction.

2.2 Word-feature models

One problem with the algorithms in the previous section is the poverty of their input features. Of the syntactic, semantic, and morphological information linguists claim underlie syntactic categories, context vectors or bitag HMMs only represent limited syntactic information in their input. Experiments incorporating morphological and orthographic features into HMM based models demonstrate significant improvements. (Clark, 2003; Berg-Kirkpatrick and Klein, 2010; Blunsom and Cohn, 2011) incorporate similar orthographic features and report improvements of 3, 7, and 10% respectively over the baseline Brown model. Christodoulopoulos et al. (2010) use prototype based features as described in (Haghighi and Klein, 2006) with automatically induced prototypes and report an 8% improvement over the baseline Brown model. Christodoulopoulos et al. (2011) define a type-based Bayesian multinomial mixture model in which each word instance is generated from the corresponding word type mixture component and word contexts are represented as features. They achieve a .728 MTO score by extending their model with additional morphological and alignment features gathered from parallel corpora. To our knowledge, nobody has yet tried to incorporate phonological or prosodic features in a computational model for syntactic category acquisition.

2.3 Paradigmatic representations

Sahlgren (2006) gives a detailed analysis of paradigmatic and syntagmatic relations in the context of word-space models used to represent word meaning. Sahlgren's paradigmatic model represents word types using co-occurrence counts of their frequent neighbors, in contrast to his syntagmatic model that represents word types using counts of contexts (documents, sentences) they occur in. Our substitute vectors do not represent word types at all, but *contexts of word tokens* using probabilities of likely substitutes. Sahlgren finds that in word-spaces built by frequent neighbor vectors, more nearest neighbors share the same part-of-speech compared to word-spaces built by context vectors. We find that representing the paradigmatic axis more directly using substitute vectors rather than frequent neighbors improve part-of-speech induction.

Our paradigmatic representation is also related to the second order co-occurrences used in (Schütze, 1995). Schütze concatenates the left and right context vectors for the target word type with the left context vector of the right neighbor and the right context vector of the left neighbor. The vectors from the neighbors include potential substitutes. Our method improves on his foundation by using a 4-gram language model rather than bigram statistics, using the whole 78,498 word vocabulary rather than the most frequent 250 words. More importantly, rather than simply concatenating vectors that represent the target word with vectors that represent the context we use S-CODE to model their co-occurrence statistics.

2.4 Evaluation

We report many-to-one and V-measure scores for our experiments as suggested in (Christodoulopoulos et al., 2010). The many-to-one (MTO) evaluation maps each cluster to its most frequent gold tag and reports the percentage of correctly tagged instances. The MTO score naturally gets higher with increasing number of clusters but it is an intuitive metric when comparing results with the same number of clusters. The V-measure (VM) (Rosenberg and Hirschberg, 2007) is an information theoretic metric that reports the harmonic mean of homogeneity (each cluster should contain only instances of a single class) and completeness (all instances of a class should be members of the same cluster). In Section 6 we argue that homogeneity is perhaps more important in part-of-speech induction and suggest MTO with a fixed number of clusters as a more intuitive metric.

3 Substitute Vectors

In this study, we predict the part of speech of a word in a given context based on its substitute vector. The dimensions of the substitute vector represent words in the vocabulary, and the entries in the substitute vector represent the probability of those words being used in the given context. Note that the substitute vector is a function of the context only and is indifferent to the target word. This section details the choice of the data set, the vocabulary and the estimation of substitute vector probabilities.

The Wall Street Journal Section of the Penn Treebank (Marcus et al., 1999) was used as the test corpus (1,173,766 tokens, 49,206 types). The treebank uses 45 part-of-speech tags which is the set we used as the gold standard for comparison in our experiments. To compute substitute probabilities we trained a language model using approximately 126 million tokens of Wall Street Journal data (1987-1994) extracted from CSR-III Text (Graff et al., 1995) (we excluded the test corpus). We used SRILM (Stolcke, 2002) to build a 4-gram language model with Kneser-Ney discounting. Words that were observed less than 20 times in the language model training data were replaced by UNK tags, which gave us a vocabulary size of 78,498. The perplexity of the 4-gram language model on the test corpus is 96.

It is best to use both left and right context when estimating the probabilities for potential lexical substitutes. For example, in *"He lived in San Francisco suburbs."*, the token *San* would be difficult to guess from the left context but it is almost certain looking at the right context. We define c_w as the $2n-1$ word window centered around the target word position: $w_{-n+1} \dots w_0 \dots w_{n-1}$ ($n = 4$ is the n-gram order). The probability of a substitute word w in a given context c_w can be estimated as:

$$\begin{aligned} P(w_0 = w|c_w) &\propto P(w_{-n+1} \dots w_0 \dots w_{n-1}) && (1) \\ &= P(w_{-n+1})P(w_{-n+2}|w_{-n+1}) \\ &\quad \dots P(w_{n-1}|w_{-n+1}^{n-2}) && (2) \\ &\approx P(w_0|w_{-n+1}^{-1})P(w_1|w_{-n+2}^{0}) \\ &\quad \dots P(w_{n-1}|w_0^{n-2}) && (3) \end{aligned}$$

where w_i^j represents the sequence of words $w_i w_{i+1} \dots w_j$. In Equation 1, $P(w|c_w)$ is proportional to $P(w_{-n+1} \dots w_0 \dots w_{n+1})$ because the words of the context are fixed. Terms without w_0 are identical for each substitute in Equation 2 therefore they have been dropped in Equation 3. Finally, because of the Markov property of n-gram language model, only the closest $n-1$ words are used in the experiments.

Near the sentence boundaries the appropriate terms were truncated in Equation 3. Specifically, at the beginning of the sentence shorter n-gram contexts were used and at the end of the sentence terms beyond the end-of-sentence token were dropped.

For computational efficiency only the top 100 substitutes and their unnormalized probabilities were computed for each of the 1,173,766 positions in the test set[1]. The probability vectors for each position were normalized to add up to 1.0 giving us the final substitute vectors used in the rest of this study.

[1]The substitutes with unnormalized log probabilities can be downloaded from `http://goo.gl/jzKH0`. For a description of the FASTSUBS algorithm used to generate the substitutes please see `http://arxiv.org/abs/1205.5407v1`. FASTSUBS accomplishes this task in about 5 hours, a naive algorithm that looks at the whole vocabulary would take more than 6 days on a typical 2012 workstation.

4 Co-occurrence Data Embedding

The general strategy we follow for unsupervised syntactic category acquisition is to combine features of the context with the identity and features of the target word. Our preliminary experiments indicated that using the context information alone (e.g. clustering substitute vectors) without the target word identity and features had limited success.[2] It is the co-occurrence of a target word with a particular type of context that best predicts the syntactic category. In this section we review the unsupervised methods we used to model co-occurrence statistics: the Co-occurrence Data Embedding (CODE) method (Globerson et al., 2007) and its spherical extension (S-CODE) introduced by (Maron et al., 2010).

Let X and Y be two categorical variables with finite cardinalities $|X|$ and $|Y|$. We observe a set of pairs $\{x_i, y_i\}_{i=1}^n$ drawn IID from the joint distribution of X and Y. The basic idea behind CODE and related methods is to represent (embed) each value of X and each value of Y as points in a common low dimensional Euclidean space $\mathbf{R}^d$ such that values that frequently co-occur lie close to each other. There are several ways to formalize the relationship between the distances and co-occurrence statistics, in this paper we use the following:

$$p(x,y) = \frac{1}{Z}\bar{p}(x)\bar{p}(y)e^{-d_{x,y}^2} \qquad (4)$$

where $d_{x,y}^2$ is the squared distance between the embeddings of x and y, $\bar{p}(x)$ and $\bar{p}(y)$ are empirical probabilities, and $Z = \sum_{x,y}\bar{p}(x)\bar{p}(y)e^{-d_{x,y}^2}$ is a normalization term. If we use the notation ϕ_x for the point corresponding to x and ψ_y for the point corresponding to y then $d_{x,y}^2 = \|\phi_x - \psi_y\|^2$. The log-likelihood of a given embedding $\ell(\phi, \psi)$ can be

[2]A 10-nearest-neighbor supervised baseline using cosine distance between substitute vectors gives .7213 accuracy. Clustering substitute vectors using various distance metrics and dimensionality reduction methods give results inferior to this upper bound.

expressed as:

$$\ell(\phi, \psi) = \sum_{x,y} \bar{p}(x,y) \log p(x,y) \tag{5}$$
$$= \sum_{x,y} \bar{p}(x,y)(-\log Z + \log \bar{p}(x)\bar{p}(y) - d_{x,y}^2)$$
$$= -\log Z + const - \sum_{x,y} \bar{p}(x,y) d_{x,y}^2$$

The likelihood is not convex in ϕ and ψ. We use gradient ascent to find an approximate solution for a set of ϕ_x, ψ_y that maximize the likelihood. The gradient of the $d_{x,y}^2$ term pulls neighbors closer in proportion to the empirical joint probability:

$$\frac{\partial}{\partial \phi_x} \sum_{x,y} -\bar{p}(x,y) d_{x,y}^2 = \sum_{y} 2\bar{p}(x,y)(\psi_y - \phi_x) \tag{6}$$

The gradient of the Z term pushes neighbors apart in proportion to the estimated joint probability:

$$\frac{\partial}{\partial \phi_x}(-\log Z) = \sum_{y} 2p(x,y)(\phi_x - \psi_y) \tag{7}$$

Thus the net effect is to pull pairs together if their estimated probability is less than the empirical probability and to push them apart otherwise. The gradients with respect to ψ_y are similar.

S-CODE (Maron et al., 2010) additionally restricts all ϕ_x and ψ_y to lie on the unit sphere. With this restriction, Z stays around a fixed value during gradient ascent. This allows S-CODE to substitute an approximate constant $\tilde{Z}$ in gradient calculations for the real Z for computational efficiency. In our experiments, we used S-CODE with its sampling based stochastic gradient ascent algorithm and smoothly decreasing learning rate.

5 Experiments

In this section we present experiments that evaluate substitute vectors as representations of word context within the S-CODE framework. Section 5.1 replicates the bigram based S-CODE results from (Maron et al., 2010) as a baseline. The S-CODE algorithm works with discrete inputs. The substitute vectors as described in Section 3 are high dimensional and continuous. We experimented with two approaches to use substitute vectors in a discrete setting. Section 5.2 presents an algorithm that partitions the high dimensional space of substitute vectors into small neighborhoods and uses the partition id as a discrete context representation. Section 5.3 presents an even simpler model which pairs each word with a random substitute. When the left-word – right-word pairs used in the bigram model are replaced with word – partition-id or word – substitute pairs we see significant gains in accuracy. These results support our running hypothesis that paradigmatic features, i.e. potential substitutes of a word, are better determiners of syntactic category compared to left and right neighbors. Section 5.4 explores morphologic and orthographic features as additional sources of information and its results improve the state-of-the-art in the field of unsupervised syntactic category acquisition.

Each experiment was repeated 10 times with different random seeds and the results are reported with standard errors in parentheses or error bars in graphs. Table 1 summarizes all the results reported in this paper and the ones we cite from the literature.

5.1 Bigram model

In (Maron et al., 2010) adjacent word pairs (bigrams) in the corpus are fed into the S-CODE algorithm as X, Y samples. The algorithm uses stochastic gradient ascent to find the ϕ_x, ψ_y embeddings for left and right words in these bigrams on a single 25-dimensional sphere. At the end each word w in the vocabulary ends up with two points on the sphere, a ϕ_w point representing the behavior of w as the left word of a bigram and a ψ_w point representing it as the right word. The two vectors for w are concatenated to create a 50-dimensional representation at the end. These 50-dimensional vectors are clustered using an instance weighted k-means algorithm and the resulting groups are compared to the correct part-of-speech tags. Maron et al. (2010) report many-to-one scores of .6880 (.0016) for 45 clusters and .7150 (.0060) for 50 clusters (on the full PTB45 tag-set). If only ϕ_w vectors are clustered without concatenation we found the performance drops significantly to about .62.

To make a meaningful comparison we re-ran the bigram experiments using our default settings and obtained a many-to-one score of .7314 (.0096) and the V-measure is .6558 (.0052) for 45 clusters. The following default settings were used: (i) each word

Distributional Models	MTO	VM	Models with Additional Features	MTO	VM
(Lamar et al., 2010a)	.708	-	(Clark, 2003)*	.712	.655
(Brown et al., 1992)*	.678	.630	(Christodoulopoulos et al., 2011)	.728	.661
(Goldwater et al., 2007)	.632	.562	(Berg-Kirkpatrick and Klein, 2010)	.755	-
(Ganchev et al., 2010)*	.625	.548	(Christodoulopoulos et al., 2010)	.761	.688
(Maron et al., 2010)	.688 (.0016)	-	(Blunsom and Cohn, 2011)	.775	.697
Bigrams (Sec. 5.1)	.7314 (.0096)	.6558 (.0052)	Substitutes and Features (Sec. 5.4)	.8023 (.0070)	.7207 (.0041)
Partitions (Sec. 5.2)	.7554 (.0055)	.6703 (.0037)			
Substitutes (Sec. 5.3)	.7680 (.0038)	.6822 (.0029)			

Table 1: Summary of results in terms of the MTO and VM scores. Standard errors are given in parentheses when available. Starred entries have been reported in the review paper (Christodoulopoulos et al., 2010). Distributional models use only the identity of the target word and its context. The models on the right incorporate orthographic and morphological features.

was kept with its original capitalization, (ii) the learning rate parameters were adjusted to $\varphi_0 = 50$, $\eta_0 = 0.2$ for faster convergence in log likelihood, (iii) the number of s-code iterations were increased from 12 to 50 million, (iv) k-means initialization was improved using (Arthur and Vassilvitskii, 2007), and (v) the number of k-means restarts were increased to 128 to improve clustering and reduce variance.

5.2 Random partitions

Instead of using left-word – right-word pairs as inputs to S-CODE we wanted to pair each word with a paradigmatic representation of its context to get a direct comparison of the two context representations. To obtain a discrete representation of the context, the random–partitions algorithm first designates a random subset of substitute vectors as centroids to partition the space, and then associates each context with the partition defined by the closest centroid in cosine distance. Each partition thus defined gets a unique id, and word (X) – partition-id (Y) pairs are given to S-CODE as input. The algorithm cycles through the data until we get approximately 50 million updates. The resulting ϕ_x vectors are clustered using the k-means algorithm (no vector concatenation is necessary). Using default settings (64K random partitions, 25 s-code dimensions, $Z = 0.166$) the many-to-one accuracy is .7554 (.0055) and the V-measure is .6703 (.0037).

To analyze the sensitivity of this result to our specific parameter settings we ran a number of experiments where each parameter was varied over a range of values.

Figure 2 gives results where the number of initial random partitions is varied over a large range and shows the results to be fairly stable across two orders of magnitude.

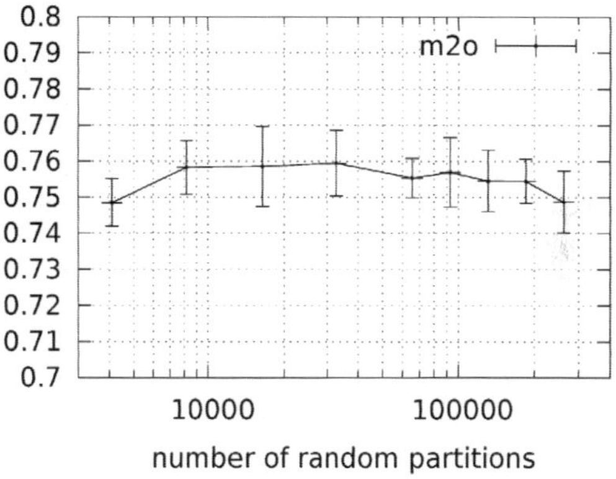

Figure 2: MTO is not sensitive to the number of partitions used to discretize the substitute vector space within our experimental range.

Figure 3 shows that at least 10 embedding dimensions are necessary to get within 1% of the best result, but there is no significant gain from using more than 25 dimensions.

Figure 4 shows that the constant $\tilde{Z}$ approximation can be varied within two orders of magnitude without a significant performance drop in the many-to-one score. For uniformly distributed points on a 25 dimensional sphere, the expected $Z \approx 0.146$. In the experiments where we tested we found the real Z always to be in the 0.140-0.170 range. When the constant $\tilde{Z}$ estimate is too small the attraction in Eq. 6 dominates the repulsion in Eq. 7 and all points tend to converge to the same location. When $\tilde{Z}$ is too high, it prevents meaningful clusters from coalesc-

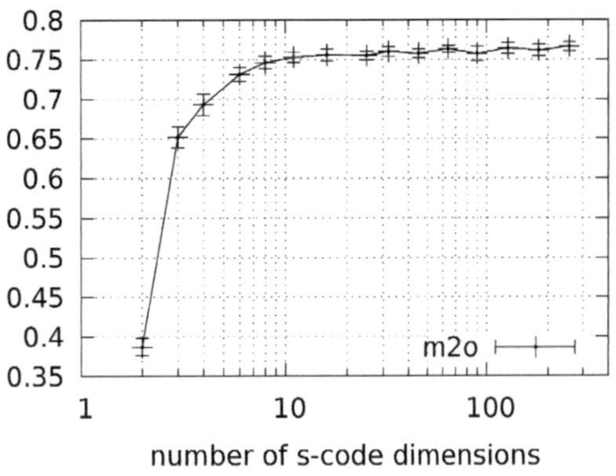

Figure 3: MTO falls sharply for less than 10 S-CODE dimensions, but more than 25 do not help.

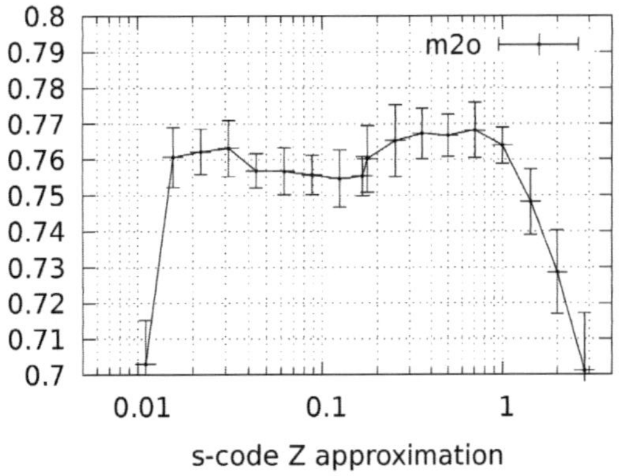

Figure 4: MTO is fairly stable as long as the $\tilde{Z}$ constant is within an order of magnitude of the real Z value.

ing.

We find the random partition algorithm to be fairly robust to different parameter settings and the resulting many-to-one score significantly better than the bigram baseline.

5.3 Random substitutes

Another way to use substitute vectors in a discrete setting is simply to sample individual substitute words from them. The random-substitutes algorithm cycles through the test data and pairs each word with a random substitute picked from the precomputed substitute vectors (see Section 3). We ran the random-substitutes algorithm to generate 14 million word (X) – random-substitute (Y) pairs (12 substitutes for each token) as input to S-CODE. Clustering the resulting ϕ_x vectors yields a many-to-one score of .7680 (.0038) and a V-measure of .6822 (.0029).

This result is close to the previous result by the random-partition algorithm, .7554 (.0055), demonstrating that two very different discrete representations of context based on paradigmatic features give consistent results. Both results are significantly above the bigram baseline, .7314 (.0096). Figure 5 illustrates that the random-substitute result is fairly robust as long as the training algorithm can observe more than a few random substitutes per word.

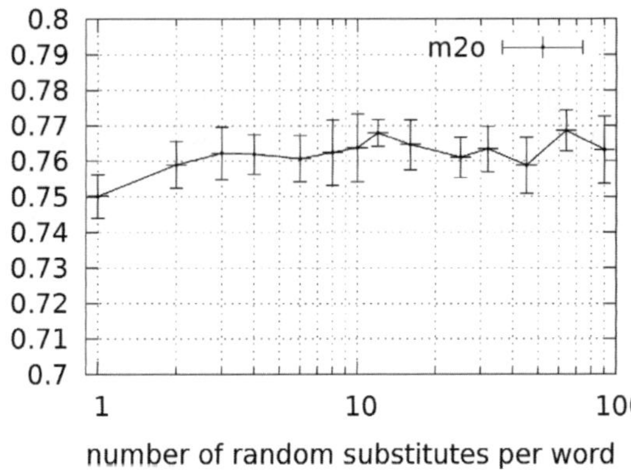

Figure 5: MTO is not sensitive to the number of random substitutes sampled per word token.

5.4 Morphological and orthographic features

Clark (2003) demonstrates that using morphological and orthographic features significantly improves part-of-speech induction with an HMM based model. Section 2 describes a number other approaches that show similar improvements. This section describes one way to integrate additional features to the random-substitute model.

The orthographic features we used are similar to the ones in (Berg-Kirkpatrick et al., 2010) with small modifications:

- Initial-Capital: this feature is generated for capitalized words with the exception of sentence initial words.
- Number: this feature is generated when the token starts with a digit.
- Contains-Hyphen: this feature is generated for lowercase words with an internal hyphen.

- Initial-Apostrophe: this feature is generated for tokens that start with an apostrophe.

We generated morphological features using the unsupervised algorithm Morfessor (Creutz and Lagus, 2005). Morfessor was trained on the WSJ section of the Penn Treebank using default settings, and a perplexity threshold of 300. The program induced 5 suffix types that are present in a total of 10,484 word types. These suffixes were input to S-CODE as morphological features whenever the associated word types were sampled.

In order to incorporate morphological and orthographic features into S-CODE we modified its input. For each word – random-substitute pair generated as in the previous section, we added word – feature pairs to the input for each morphological and orthographic feature of the word. Words on average have 0.25 features associated with them. This increased the number of pairs input to S-CODE from 14.1 million (12 substitutes per word) to 17.7 million (additional 0.25 features on average for each of the 14.1 million words).

Using similar training settings as the previous section, the addition of morphological and orthographic features increased the many-to-one score of the random-substitute model to .8023 (.0070) and V-measure to .7207 (.0041). Both these results improve the state-of-the-art in part-of-speech induction significantly as seen in Table 1.

6 Error Analysis

Figure 6 is the Hinton diagram showing the relationship between the most frequent tags and clusters from the experiment in Section 5.4. In general the errors seem to be the lack of completeness (multiple large entries in a row), rather than lack of homogeneity (multiple large entries in a column). The algorithm tends to split large word classes into several clusters. Some examples are:

- Titles like Mr., Mrs., and Dr. are split from the rest of the proper nouns in cluster (39).

- Auxiliary verbs (10) and the verb "say" (22) have been split from the general verb clusters (12) and (7).

- Determiners "the" (40), "a" (15), and capitalized "The", "A" (6) have been split into their own clusters.

- Prepositions "of" (19), and "by", "at" (17) have been split from the general preposition cluster (8).

Nevertheless there are some homogeneity errors as well:

- The adjective cluster (5) also has some noun members probably due to the difficulty of separating noun-noun compounds from adjective modification.

- Cluster (6) contains capitalized words that span a number of categories.

Most closed-class items are cleanly separated into their own clusters as seen in the lower right hand corner of the diagram. The completeness errors are not surprising given that the words that have been split are not generally substitutable with the other members of their Penn Treebank category. Thus it can be argued that metrics that emphasize homogeneity such as MTO are more appropriate in this context than metrics that average homogeneity and completeness such as VM as long as the number of clusters is controlled.

7 Contributions

Our main contributions can be summarized as follows:

- We introduced substitute vectors as paradigmatic representations of word context and demonstrated their use in syntactic category acquisition.

- We demonstrated that using paradigmatic representations of word context and modeling co-occurrences of word and context types with the S-CODE learning framework give superior results when compared to a baseline bigram model.

- We extended the S-CODE framework to incorporate morphological and orthographic features and improved the state-of-the-art in unsupervised part-of-speech induction to 80% many-to-one accuracy.

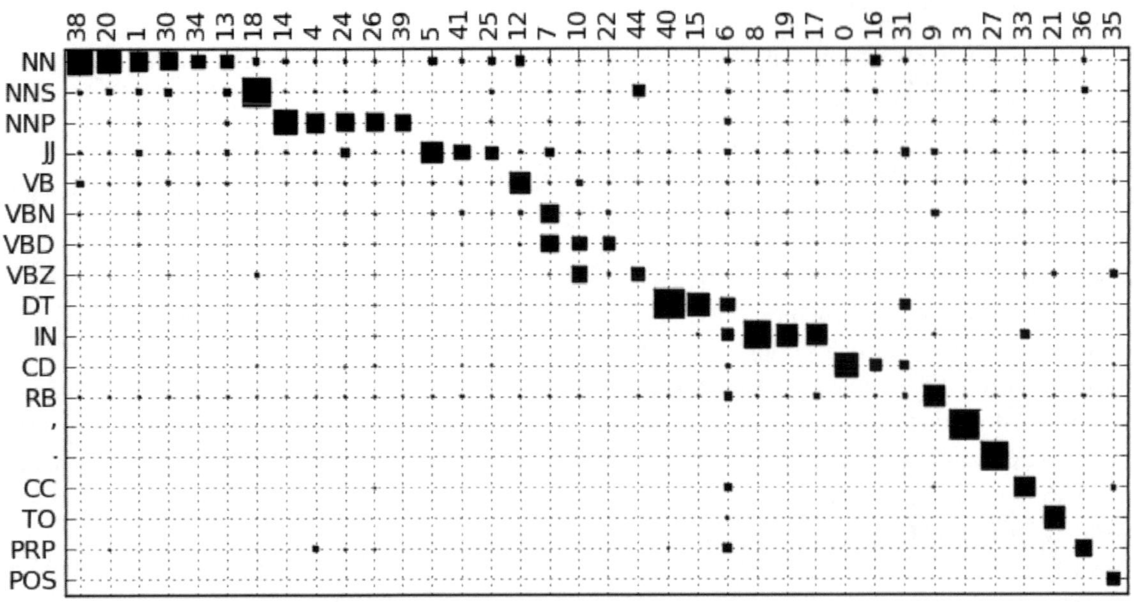

Figure 6: Hinton diagram comparing most frequent tags and clusters.

- All our code and data, including the substitute vectors for the one million word Penn Treebank Wall Street Journal dataset, is available at the authors' website at `http://goo.gl/RoqEh`.

References

B. Ambridge and E.V.M. Lieven, 2011. *Child Language Acquisition: Contrasting Theoretical Approaches*, chapter 6.1. Cambridge University Press.

D. Arthur and S. Vassilvitskii. 2007. k-means++: The advantages of careful seeding. In *Proceedings of the eighteenth annual ACM-SIAM symposium on Discrete algorithms*, pages 1027–1035. Society for Industrial and Applied Mathematics.

Taylor Berg-Kirkpatrick and Dan Klein. 2010. Phylogenetic grammar induction. In *Proceedings of the 48th Annual Meeting of the Association for Computational Linguistics*, pages 1288–1297, Uppsala, Sweden, July. Association for Computational Linguistics.

Taylor Berg-Kirkpatrick, Alexandre Bouchard-Côté, John DeNero, and Dan Klein. 2010. Painless unsupervised learning with features. In *Human Language Technologies: The 2010 Annual Conference of the North American Chapter of the Association for Computational Linguistics*, pages 582–590, Los Angeles, California, June. Association for Computational Linguistics.

C. Biemann. 2006. Unsupervised part-of-speech tagging employing efficient graph clustering. In *Proceedings of the 21st International Conference on computational Linguistics and 44th Annual Meeting of the Association for Computational Linguistics: Student Research Workshop*, pages 7–12. Association for Computational Linguistics.

Phil Blunsom and Trevor Cohn. 2011. A hierarchical pitman-yor process hmm for unsupervised part of speech induction. In *Proceedings of the 49th Annual Meeting of the Association for Computational Linguistics: Human Language Technologies*, pages 865–874, Portland, Oregon, USA, June. Association for Computational Linguistics.

Peter F. Brown, Peter V. deSouza, Robert L. Mercer, Vincent J. Della Pietra, and Jenifer C. Lai. 1992. Class-based n-gram models of natural language. *Comput. Linguist.*, 18:467–479, December.

D. Chandler. 2007. *Semiotics: the basics*. The Basics Series. Routledge.

Christos Christodoulopoulos, Sharon Goldwater, and Mark Steedman. 2010. Two decades of unsupervised pos induction: how far have we come? In *Proceedings of the 2010 Conference on Empirical Methods in Natural Language Processing*, EMNLP '10, pages 575–584, Stroudsburg, PA, USA. Association for Computational Linguistics.

Christos Christodoulopoulos, Sharon Goldwater, and Mark Steedman. 2011. A bayesian mixture model for pos induction using multiple features. In *Proceedings of the 2011 Conference on Empirical Methods in Natural Language Processing*, pages 638–647, Edinburgh, Scotland, UK., July. Association for Computational Linguistics.

Kenneth Ward Church. 1988. A stochastic parts program and noun phrase parser for unrestricted text. In *Proceedings of the second conference on Applied natural language processing*, ANLC '88, pages 136–143, Stroudsburg, PA, USA. Association for Computational Linguistics.

Alexander Clark. 2003. Combining distributional and morphological information for part of speech induction. In *Proceedings of the tenth conference on European chapter of the Association for Computational Linguistics - Volume 1*, EACL '03, pages 59–66, Stroudsburg, PA, USA. Association for Computational Linguistics.

Mathias Creutz and Krista Lagus. 2005. Inducing the morphological lexicon of a natural language from unannotated text. In *Proceedings of AKRR'05, International and Interdisciplinary Conference on Adaptive Knowledge Representation and Reasoning*, pages 106–113, Espoo, Finland, June.

D. Freudenthal, J.M. Pine, and F. Gobet. 2005. On the resolution of ambiguities in the extraction of syntactic categories through chunking. *Cognitive Systems Research*, 6(1):17–25.

Kuzman Ganchev, João Graça, Jennifer Gillenwater, and Ben Taskar. 2010. Posterior regularization for structured latent variable models. *J. Mach. Learn. Res.*, 99:2001–2049, August.

Jianfeng Gao and Mark Johnson. 2008. A comparison of bayesian estimators for unsupervised hidden markov model pos taggers. In *Proceedings of the Conference on Empirical Methods in Natural Language Processing*, EMNLP '08, pages 344–352, Stroudsburg, PA, USA. Association for Computational Linguistics.

Amir Globerson, Gal Chechik, Fernando Pereira, and Naftali Tishby. 2007. Euclidean embedding of co-occurrence data. *J. Mach. Learn. Res.*, 8:2265–2295, December.

Sharon Goldwater and Tom Griffiths. 2007. A fully bayesian approach to unsupervised part-of-speech tagging. In *Proceedings of the 45th Annual Meeting of the Association of Computational Linguistics*, pages 744–751, Prague, Czech Republic, June. Association for Computational Linguistics.

David Graff, Roni Rosenfeld, and Doug Paul. 1995. Csr-iii text. Linguistic Data Consortium, Philadelphia.

Aria Haghighi and Dan Klein. 2006. Prototype-driven learning for sequence models. In *Proceedings of the main conference on Human Language Technology Conference of the North American Chapter of the Association of Computational Linguistics*, HLT-NAACL '06, pages 320–327, Stroudsburg, PA, USA. Association for Computational Linguistics.

Mark Johnson. 2007. Why doesn't EM find good HMM POS-taggers? In *Proceedings of the 2007 Joint Conference on Empirical Methods in Natural Language Processing and Computational Natural Language Learning (EMNLP-CoNLL)*, pages 296–305, Prague, Czech Republic, June. Association for Computational Linguistics.

Michael Lamar, Yariv Maron, and Elie Bienenstock. 2010a. Latent-descriptor clustering for unsupervised pos induction. In *Proceedings of the 2010 Conference on Empirical Methods in Natural Language Processing*, EMNLP '10, pages 799–809, Stroudsburg, PA, USA. Association for Computational Linguistics.

Michael Lamar, Yariv Maron, Mark Johnson, and Elie Bienenstock. 2010b. Svd and clustering for unsupervised pos tagging. In *Proceedings of the ACL 2010 Conference Short Papers*, pages 215–219, Uppsala, Sweden, July. Association for Computational Linguistics.

Yoong Keok Lee, Aria Haghighi, and Regina Barzilay. 2010. Simple type-level unsupervised pos tagging. In *Proceedings of the 2010 Conference on Empirical Methods in Natural Language Processing*, EMNLP '10, pages 853–861, Stroudsburg, PA, USA. Association for Computational Linguistics.

Mitchell P. Marcus, Beatrice Santorini, Mary Ann Marcinkiewicz, and Ann Taylor. 1999. Treebank-3. Linguistic Data Consortium, Philadelphia.

Yariv Maron, Michael Lamar, and Elie Bienenstock. 2010. Sphere embedding: An application to part-of-speech induction. In J. Lafferty, C. K. I. Williams, J. Shawe-Taylor, R.S. Zemel, and A. Culotta, editors, *Advances in Neural Information Processing Systems 23*, pages 1567–1575.

Bernard Merialdo. 1994. Tagging english text with a probabilistic model. *Comput. Linguist.*, 20:155–171, June.

T.H. Mintz. 2003. Frequent frames as a cue for grammatical categories in child directed speech. *Cognition*, 90(1):91–117.

M. Redington, N. Crater, and S. Finch. 1998. Distributional information: A powerful cue for acquiring syntactic categories. *Cognitive Science*, 22(4):425–469.

A. Rosenberg and J. Hirschberg. 2007. V-measure: A conditional entropy-based external cluster evaluation measure. In *Proceedings of the 2007 Joint Conference on Empirical Methods in Natural Language Processing and Computational Natural Language Learning*, pages 410–420.

Magnus Sahlgren. 2006. *The Word-Space Model: Using distributional analysis to represent syntagmatic and paradigmatic relations between words in high-dimensional vector spaces*. Ph.D. thesis, Stockholm University.

Hinrich Schütze. 1995. Distributional part-of-speech tagging. In *Proceedings of the seventh conference on European chapter of the Association for Computational Linguistics*, EACL '95, pages 141–148, San Francisco, CA, USA. Morgan Kaufmann Publishers Inc.

Andreas Stolcke. 2002. Srilm-an extensible language modeling toolkit. In *Proceedings International Conference on Spoken Language Processing*, pages 257–286, November.

Exploring Topic Coherence over many models and many topics

Keith Stevens[1,2] **Philip Kegelmeyer**[3] **David Andrzejewski**[2] **David Buttler**[2]
[1]University of California Los Angeles; Los Angeles , California, USA
[2]Lawrence Livermore National Lab; Livermore, California, USA
[3]Sandia National Lab; Livermore, California, USA
{stevens35,andrzejewski1,buttler1}@llnl.gov
wpk@sandia.gov

Abstract

We apply two new automated semantic evaluations to three distinct latent topic models. Both metrics have been shown to align with human evaluations and provide a balance between internal measures of information gain and comparisons to human ratings of coherent topics. We improve upon the measures by introducing new aggregate measures that allows for comparing complete topic models. We further compare the automated measures to other metrics for topic models, comparison to manually crafted semantic tests and document classification. Our experiments reveal that LDA and LSA each have different strengths; LDA best learns descriptive topics while LSA is best at creating a compact semantic representation of documents and words in a corpus.

1 Introduction

Topic models learn bags of related words from large corpora without any supervision. Based on the words used within a document, they mine topic level relations by assuming that a single document covers a small set of concise topics. Once learned, these topics often correlate well with human concepts. For example, one model might produce topics that cover ideas such as government affairs, sports, and movies. With these unsupervised methods, we can extract useful semantic information in a variety of tasks that depend on identifying unique topics or concepts, such as distributional semantics (Jurgens and Stevens, 2010), word sense induction (Van de Cruys and Apidianaki, 2011; Brody and Lapata, 2009), and information retrieval (Andrzejewski and Buttler, 2011).

When using a topic model, we are primarily concerned with the degree to which the learned topics match human judgments and help us differentiate between ideas. But until recently, the evaluation of these models has been ad hoc and application specific. Evaluations have ranged from fully automated intrinsic evaluations to manually crafted extrinsic evaluations. Previous extrinsic evaluations have used the learned topics to compactly represent a small fixed vocabulary and compared this distributional space to human judgments of similarity (Jurgens and Stevens, 2010). But these evaluations are hand constructed and often costly to perform for domain-specific topics. Conversely, intrinsic measures have evaluated the amount of information encoded by the topics, where perplexity is one common example(Wallach et al., 2009), however, Chang et al. (2009) found that these intrinsic measures do not always correlate with semantically interpretable topics. Furthermore, few evaluations have used the same metrics to compare distinct approaches such as Latent Dirichlet Allocation (LDA) (Blei et al., 2003), Latent Semantic Analysis (LSA) (Landauer and Dutnais, 1997), and Non-negative Matrix Factorization (NMF) (Lee and Seung, 2000). This has made it difficult to know which method is most useful for a given application, or in terms of extracting useful topics.

We now provide a comprehensive and automated evaluation of these three distinct models (LDA, LSA, NMF), for automatically learning semantic topics. While these models have seen significant improvements, they still represent the core differences between each approach to modeling topics. For our evaluation, we use two recent automated coherence measures (Mimno et al., 2011; Newman et al., 2010) originally designed for LDA that bridge the gap between comparisons to human judgments and intrinsic measures such as perplexity. We consider several key questions:

1. How many topics should be learned?
2. How many learned topics are useful?
3. How do these topics relate to often used semantic tests?
4. How well do these topics identify similar documents?

We begin by summarizing the three topic models and highlighting their key differences. We then describe the two metrics. Afterwards, we focus on a series of experiments that address our four key questions and finally conclude with some overall remarks.

2 Topic Models

We evaluate three latent factor models that have seen widespread usage:

1. Latent Dirichlet Allocation
2. Latent Semantic Analysis with Singular Value Decomposition
3. Latent Semantic Analysis with Non-negative Matrix Factorization

Each of these models were designed with different goals and are supported by different statistical theories. We consider both LSA models as topic models as they have been used in a variety of similar contexts such as distributional similarity (Jurgens and Stevens, 2010) and word sense induction (Van de Cruys and Apidianaki, 2011; Brody and Lapata, 2009). We evaluate these distinct models on two shared tasks (1) grouping together similar words while separating unrelated words and (2) distinguishing between documents focusing on different concepts.

We distill the different models into a shared representation consisting of two sets of learned relations: how words interact with topics and how topics interact with documents. For a corpus with $\mathcal{D}$ documents and $\mathcal{V}$ words, we denote these relations in terms of $\mathcal{T}$ topics as

(1) a $\mathcal{V} \times \mathcal{T}$ matrix, W, that indicates the strength each word has in each topic, and

(2) a $\mathcal{T} \times \mathcal{D}$ matrix, H, that indicates the strength each topic has in each document.

$\mathcal{T}$ serves as a common parameter to each model.

2.1 Latent Dirichlet Allocation

Latent Dirichlet Allocation (Blei et al., 2003) learns the relationships between words, topics, and documents by assuming documents are generated by a particular probabilistic model. It first assumes that there are a fixed set of topics, $\mathcal{T}$ used throughout the corpus, and each topic z is associated with a multinomial distribution over the vocabulary Φ_z, which is drawn from a Dirichlet prior $Dir(\beta)$. A given document D_i is then generated by the following process

1. Choose $\Theta_i \sim Dir(\alpha)$, a topic distribution for D_i
2. For each word $w_j \in D_i$:
   (a) Select a topic $z_j \sim \Theta_i$
   (b) Select the word $w_j \sim \Phi_{z_j}$

In this model, the Θ distributions represent the probability of each topic appearing in each document and the Φ distributions represent the probability of words being used for each topic. These two sets of distributions correspond to our H and W matrices, respectively. The process above defines a generative model; given the observed corpus, we use collapsed Gibbs sampling implementation found in Mallet[1] to infer the values of the latent variables Φ and Θ (Griffiths and Steyvers, 2004). The model relies only on two additional hyper parameters, α and β, that guide the distributions.

2.2 Latent Semantic Analysis

Latent Semantic Analysis (Landauer and Dutnais, 1997; Landauer et al., 1998) learns topics by first forming a traditional term by document matrix used in information retrieval and then smoothing the counts to enhance the weight of informative words. Based on the original LSA model, we use the Log-Entropy transform. LSA then decomposes this smoothed, term by document matrix in order to generalize observed relations between words and documents. For both LSA models, we used implementations found in the S-Space package.[2]

Traditionally, LSA has used the Singular Value Decomposition, but we also consider Non-negative Matrix Factorization as we've seen NMF applied in similar situations (Pauca et al., 2004) and others

[1] http://mallet.cs.umass.edu/

[2] https://github.com/fozziethebeat/S-Space

Model	Label	Top Words	UMass	UCI
High Quality Topics				
LDA	interview	told asked wanted interview people made thought time called knew	-2.52	1.29
	wine	wine wines bottle grapes made winery cabernet grape pinot red	-1.97	1.30
NMF	grilling	grilled sweet spicy fried pork dish shrimp menu dishes sauce	-1.01	1.98
	cloning	embryonic cloned embryo human research stem embryos cell cloning cells	-1.84	1.46
SVD	cooking	sauce food restaurant water oil salt chicken pepper wine cup	-1.87	-1.21
	stocks	fund funds investors weapons stocks mutual stock movie film show	-2.30	-1.88
Low Quality Topics				
LDA	rates	10-yr rate 3-month percent 6-month bds bd 30-yr funds robot	-1.94	-12.32
	charity	fund contributions .com family apartment charities rent 22d children assistance	-2.43	-8.88
NMF	plants	stem fruitful stems trunk fruiting currants branches fence currant espalier	-3.12	-12.59
	farming	buzzards groundhog prune hoof pruned pruning vines wheelbarrow tree clematis	-1.90	-12.56
SVD	city	building city area buildings p.m. floors house listed eat-in a.m.	-2.70	-8.03
	time	p.m. system study a.m. office political found school night yesterday	-1.67	-7.02

Table 1: Top 10 words from several high and low quality topics when ordered by the UCI Coherence Measure. Topic labels were chosen in an ad hoc manner only to briefly summarize the topic's focus.

have found a connection between NMF and Probabilistic Latent Semantic Analysis (Ding et al., 2008), an extension to LSA. We later refer to these two LSA models simply as SVD and NMF to emphasize the difference in factorization method.

Singular Value Decomposition decomposes M into three smaller matrices

$$M = U\Sigma V^T$$

and minimizes Frobenius norm of M's reconstruction error with the constraint that the rows of U and V are orthonormal eigenvectors. Interestingly, the decomposition is agnostic to the number of desired dimensions. Instead, the rows and columns in U and V^T are ordered based on their descriptive power, i.e. how well they remove noise, which is encoded by the diagonal singular value matrix Σ. As such, reduction is done by retaining the first T rows and columns from U and V^T. For our generalization, we use $W = U\Sigma$ and $H = \Sigma V^T$. We note that values in U and V^T can be both negative and positive, preventing a straightforward interpretation as unnormalized probabilities

Non-negative Matrix Factorization also factorizes M by minimizing the reconstruction error, but with only one constraint: the decomposed matrices consist of only non-negative values. In this respect, we can consider it to be learning an unnormalized probability distributions over topics. We use the original Euclidean least squares definition of NMF[3]. Formally, NMF is defined as

$$M = WH$$

where H and W map directly onto our generalization. As in the original NMF work, we learn these unnormalized probabilities by initializing each set of probabilities at random and update them according to the following iterative update rules

$$W = W\frac{MH^T}{WHH^T} \quad H = H\frac{W^TM}{W^TWH}$$

3 Coherence Measures

Topic Coherence measures score a single topic by measuring the degree of semantic similarity between high scoring words in the topic. These measurements help distinguish between topics that are semantically interpretable topics and topics that are artifacts of statistical inference, see Table 1 for examples ordered by the UCI measure. For our evaluations, we consider two new coherence measures designed for LDA, both of which have been shown to match well with human judgements of topic quality: (1) The UCI measure (Newman et al., 2010) and (2) The UMass measure (Mimno et al., 2011).

Both measures compute the coherence of a topic as the sum of pairwise distributional similarity

[3]We note that the alternative KL-Divergence form of NMF has been directly linked to PLSA (Ding et al., 2008)

scores over the set of topic words, V. We generalize this as

$$coherence(V) = \sum_{(v_i,v_j)\in V} score(v_i, v_j, \epsilon)$$

where V is a set of word describing the topic and ϵ indicates a smoothing factor which guarantees that $score$ returns real numbers. (We will be exploring the effect of the choice of ϵ; the original authors used $\epsilon = 1$.)

The UCI metric defines a word pair's score to be the pointwise mutual information (PMI) between two words, i.e.

$$score(v_i, v_j, \epsilon) = \log \frac{p(v_i, v_j) + \epsilon}{p(v_i)p(v_j)}$$

The word probabilities are computed by counting word co-occurrence frequencies in a sliding window over an external corpus, such as Wikipedia. To some degree, this metric can be thought of as an external comparison to known semantic evaluations.

The UMass metric defines the score to be based on document co-occurrence:

$$score(v_i, v_j, \epsilon) = \log \frac{D(v_i, v_j) + \epsilon}{D(v_j)}$$

where $D(x, y)$ counts the number of documents containing words x and y and $D(x)$ counts the number of documents containing x. Significantly, the UMass metric computes these counts over the *original corpus* used to train the topic models, rather than an external corpus. This metric is more intrinsic in nature. It attempts to confirm that the models learned data known to be in the corpus.

4 Evaluation

We evaluate the quality of our three topic models (LDA, SVD, and NMF) with three experiments. We focus first on evaluating aggregate coherence methods for a complete topic model and consider the differences between each model as we learn an increasing number of topics. Secondly, we compare coherence scores to previous semantic evaluations. Lastly, we use the learned topics in a classification task and evaluate whether or not coherent topics are equally informative when discriminating between documents.

For all our experiments, we trained our models on 92,600 New York Times articles from 2003 (Sandhaus, 2008). For all articles, we removed stop words and any words occurring less than 200 times in the corpus, which left 35,836 unique tokens. All documents were tokenized with OpenNLP's MaxEnt[4] tokenizer. For the UCI measure, we compute the PMI between words using a 20 word sliding window passed over the WaCkypedia corpus (Baroni et al., 2009). In all experiments, we compute the coherence with the top 10 words from each topic that had the highest weight, in terms of LDA and NMF this corresponds with a high probability of the term describing the topic but for SVD there is no clear semantic interpretation.

4.1 Aggregate methods for topic coherence

Before we can compare topic models, we require an aggregate measure that represents the quality of a complete model, rather than individual topics. We consider two aggregates methods: (1) the average coherence of all topics and (2) the entropy of the coherence for all topics. The average coherence provides a quick summarization of a model's quality whereas the entropy provides an alternate summarization that differentiates between two interesting situations. Since entropy measures the complexity of a probability distribution, it can easily differentiate between uniform distributions and multimodal, distributions. This distinction is relevant when users prefer to have roughly uniform topic quality instead of a wide gap between high- and low-quality topics, or vice versa. We compute the entropy by dropping the log and ϵ factor from each scoring function.

Figure 1 shows the average coherence scores for each model as we vary the number of topics. These average scores indicate some simple relationships between the models: LDA and NMF have approximately the same performance and both models are consistently better than SVD. All of the models quickly reach a stable average score at around 100 topics. This initially suggests that learning more

[4]http://incubator.apache.org/opennlp/

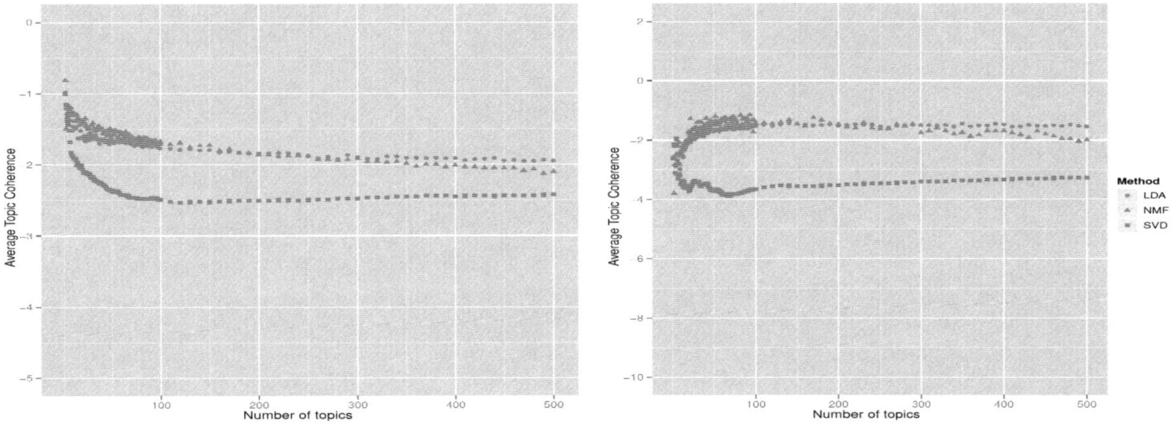

(a) UMass (b) UCI

Figure 1: Average Topic Coherence for each model

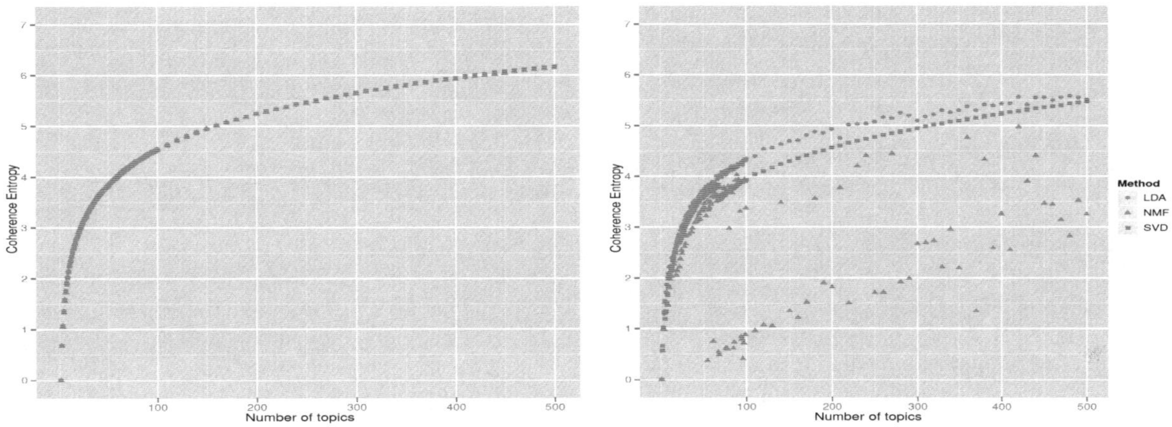

(a) UMass (b) UCI

Figure 2: Entropy of the Topic Coherence for each model

topics neither increases or decreases the quality of the model, but Figure 2 indicates otherwise. While the entropy for the UMass score stays stable for all models, NMF produces erratic entropy results under the UCI score as we learn more topics. As entropy is higher for even distributions and lower for all other distributions, these results suggest that the NMF is learning topics with drastically different levels of quality, i.e. some with high quality and some with very low quality, but the average coherence over all topics do not account for this.

Low quality topics may be composed of highly unrelated words that can't be fit into another topic, and in this case, our smoothing factor, ϵ, may be artificially increasing the score for unrelated words. Following the practice of the original use of these metrics, in Figures 1 and 2 we set $\epsilon = 1$. In Figure 3, we consider $\epsilon = 10^{-12}$, which should significantly reduce the score for completely unrelated words. Here, we see a significant change in the performance of NMF, the average coherence decreases dramatically as we learn more topics. Similarly, performance of SVD drops dramatically and well below the other models. In figure 4 we lastly compute the average coherence using only the top 10% most coherence topics with $\epsilon = 10^{-12}$. Here, NMF again performs on par with LDA. With the top 10% topics still having a high average coherence but the full set

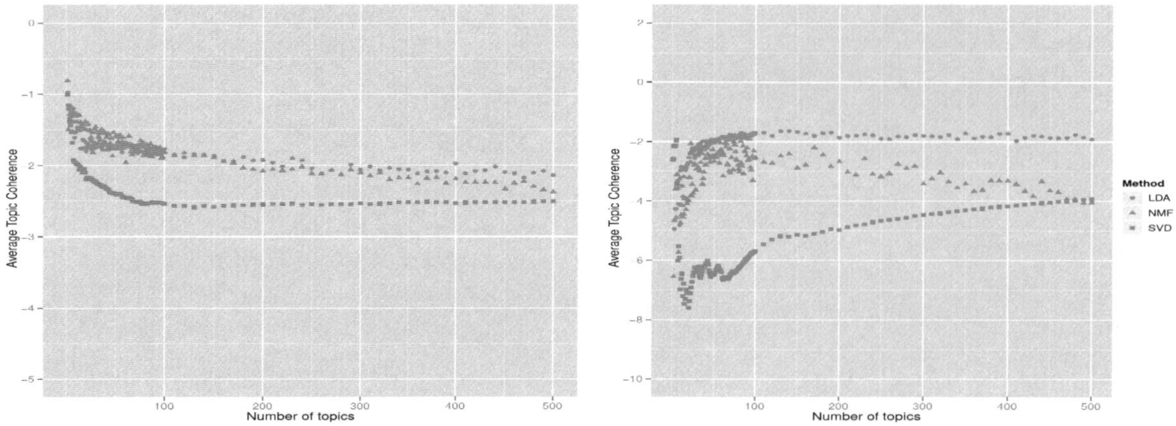

(a) UMass (b) UCI

Figure 3: Average Topic Coherence with $\epsilon = 10^{-12}$

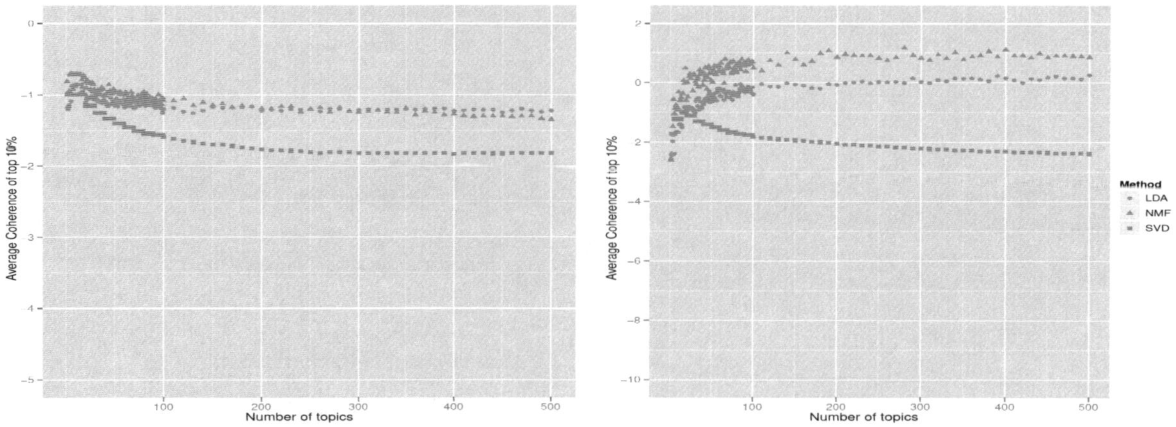

(a) UMass (b) UCI

Figure 4: Average Topic Coherence of the top 10% topics with $\epsilon = 10^{-12}$

of topics having a low coherence, NMF appears to be learning more low quality topics once it's learned the first 100 topics, whereas LDA learns fewer low quality topics in general.

4.2 Word Similarity Tasks

The initial evaluations for each coherence measure asked human judges to directly evaluate topics (Newman et al., 2010; Mimno et al., 2011). We expand upon this comparison to human judgments by considering word similarity tasks that have often been used to evaluate distributional semantic spaces (Jurgens and Stevens, 2010). Here, we use the learned topics as generalized semantics describing our knowledge about words. If a model's topics generalize the knowledge accurately, we would expect similar words, such as "cat" and "dog", to be represented with a similar set of topics. Rather than evaluating individual topics, this similarity task considers the knowledge within the entire set of topics, the topics act as more compact representation for the known words in a corpus.

We use the Rubenstein and Goodenough (1965) and Finkelstein et al. (2002) word similarity tasks. In each task, human judges were asked to evaluate the similarity or relatedness between different sets of word pairs. Fifty-One Evaluators for the Rubenstein and Goodenough (1965) dataset were given 65 pairs

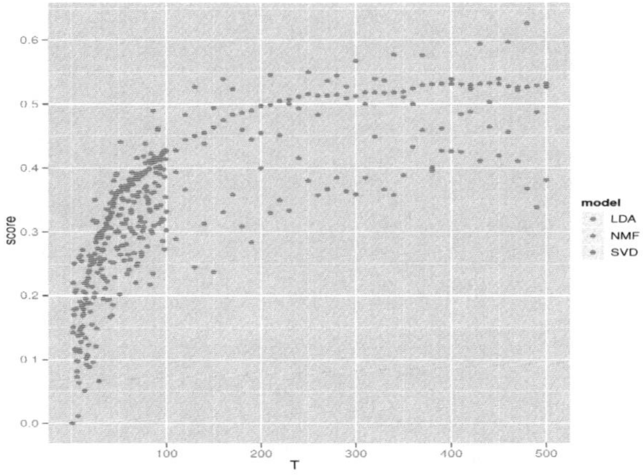

(a) Rubenstein & Goodenough

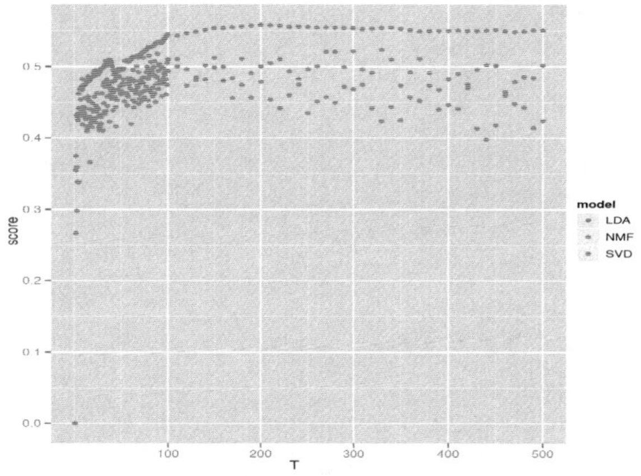

(b) Wordsim 353/Finklestein et. al.

Figure 5: Word Similarity Evaluations for each model

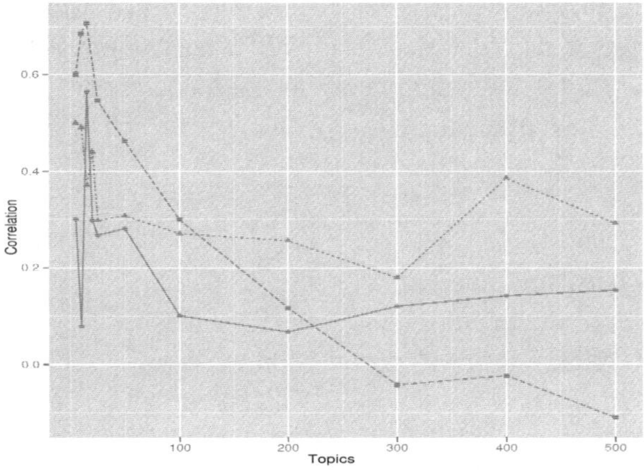

(a) UMass

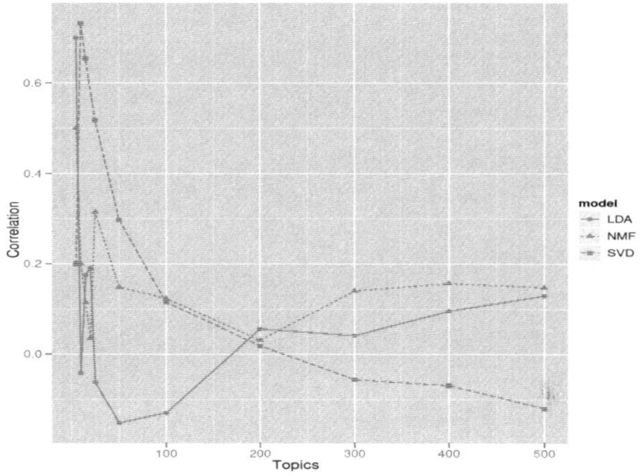

(b) UCI

Figure 7: Correlation between topic coherence and topic ranking in classification

of words and asked to rate their similarity on a scale from 0 to 4, where a higher score indicates a more similar word pair. Finkelstein et al. (2002) broadens the word similarity evaluation and asked 13 to 16 different subjects to rate 353 word pairs on a scale from 0 to 10 based on their relatedness, where relatedness includes similarity and other semantic relations. We can evaluate each topic model by computing the cosine similarity between each pair of words in the evaluate set and then compare the model's ratings to the human ratings by ranked correlation. A high correlation signifies that the topics closely model human judgments.

Figure 5 displays the results. SVD and LDA both surpass NMF on the Rubenstein & Goodenough test while SVD is clearly the best model on the Finklestein et. al test. While our first experiment showed that SVD was the worst model in terms of topic coherence scores, this experiment indicates that SVD provides an accurate, stable, and reliable approximation to human judgements of similarity and relatedness between word pairs in comparison to other topic models.

4.3 Coherence versus Classification

For our final experiment, we examine the relationship between topic coherence and classification accuracy for each topic model. We suspect that highly

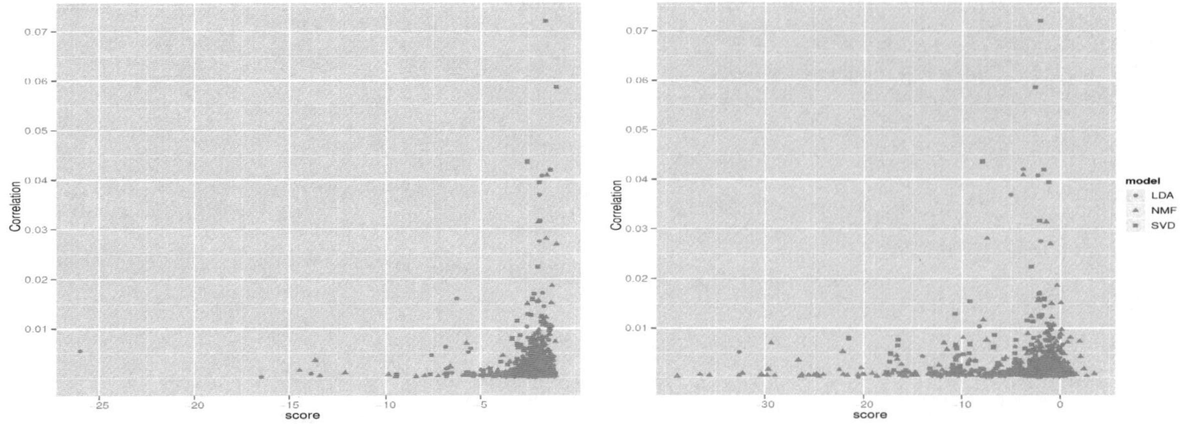

(a) UMass

(b) UCI

Figure 8: Comparison between topic coherence and topic rank with 500 topics

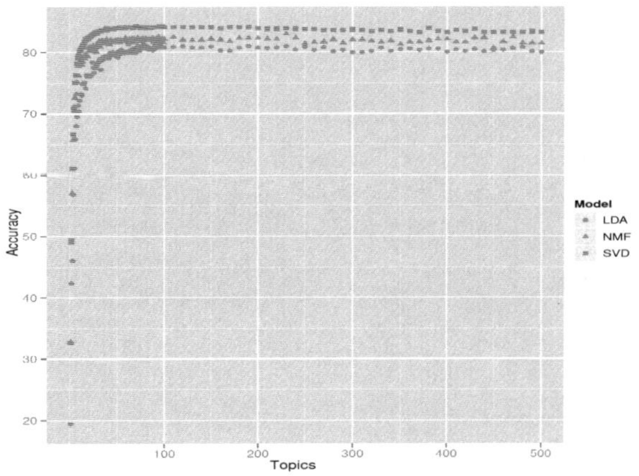

Figure 6: Classification accuracy for each model

coherent topics, and coherent topic models, will perform better for classification. We address this question by performing a document classification task using the topic representations of documents as input features and examine the relationship between topic coherence and the usefulness of the corresponding feature for classification.

We trained each topic model with all 92,600 New York Times articles as before. We use the section labels provided for each article as class labels, where each label indicates the on-line section(s) under which the article was published and should thus be related to the topics contained in each article. To reduce the noise in our data set we narrow down the articles to those that have only one label and whose label is applied to at least 2000 documents. This results in 57,696 articles with label distributions listed in Table 2. We then represent each document using columns in the topic by document matrix H learned for each topic model.

Label	Count	Label	Count
New York and Region	11219	U.S.	3675
Paid Death Notices	11152	Arts	3437
Opinion	8038	World	3330
Business	7494	Style	2137
Sports	7214		

Table 2: Section label counts for New York Times articles used for classification

For each topic model trained on N topics, we performed stratified 10-fold cross-validation on the 57,696 labeled articles. In each fold, we build an automatically-sized bagged ensemble of unpruned CART-style decision trees(Banfield et al., 2007) on 90% of the dataset[5], use that ensemble to assign labels to the other 10%, and measure the accuracy of that assignment. Figure 6 shows the average classification accuracy over all ten folds for each model. Interestingly, SVD has slightly, but statistically significantly, higher accuracy results than both NMF and LDA. Furthermore, performance quickly increases

[5]The precise choice of the classifier scheme matters little, as long as it is accurate, speedy, and robust to label noise; all of which is true of the choice here.

and plateaus with well under 50 topics.

Our bagged decision trees can also determine the importance of each feature during classification. We evaluate the strength of each topic during classification by tracking the number of times each node in our decision trees observe each topic, please see (Caruana et al., 2006) for more details. Figure 8 plot the relationship between this feature ranking and the topic coherence for each topic when training LDA, SVD, and NMF on 500 topics. Most topics for each model provide little classification information, but SVD shows a much higher rank for several topics with a relatively higher coherence score. Interestingly, for all models, the most coherent topics are not the most informative. Figure 7 plots a more compact view of this same relationship: the Spearman rank correlation between classification feature rank and topic coherence. NMF shows the highest correlation between rank and coherence, but none of the models show a high correlation when using more than 100 topics. SVD has the lowest correlation, which is probably due to the model's overall low coherence yet high classification accuracy.

5 Discussion and Conclusion

Through our experiments, we made several exciting and interesting discoveries. First, we discovered that the coherence metrics depend heavily on the smoothing factor ϵ. The original value, 1.0 created a positive bias towards NMF from both metrics even when NMF generated incoherent topics. The high smoothing factor also gave a significant increase to SVD scores. We suspect that this was not an issue in previous studies with the coherence measures as LDA prefers to form topics from words that co-occur frequently, whereas NMF and SVD have no such preferences and often create low quality topics from completely unrelated words. Therefore, we suggest a smaller ϵ value in general.

We also found that the UCI measure often agreed with the UMass measure, but the UCI-entropy aggregate method induced more separation between LSA, SVD, and NMF in terms of topic coherence. This measure also revealed the importance of the smoothing factor for topic coherence measures.

With respects to human judgements, we found that coherence scores do not always indicate a better representation of distributional information. The SVD model consistently out performed both LDA and NMF models, which each had higher coherence scores, when attempting to predict human judgements of similarity.

Lastly, we found all models capable of producing topics that improved document classification. At the same time, SVD provided the most information during classification and outperformed the other models, which again had more coherent topics. Our comparison between topic coherence scores and feature importance in classification revealed that relatively high quality topics, but not the most coherent topics, drive most of the classification decisions, and most topics do not affect the accuracy.

Overall, we see that each topic model paradigm has it's own strengths and weaknesses. Latent Semantic Analysis with Singular Value Decomposition fails to form individual topics that aggregate similar words, but it does remarkably well when considering all the learned topics as similar words develop a similar topic representation. These topics similarly perform well during classification. Conversely, both Non Negative Matrix factorization and Latent Dirichlet Allocation learn concise and coherent topics and achieved similar performance on our evaluations. However, NMF learns more incoherent topics than LDA and SVD. For applications in which a human end-user will interact with learned topics, the flexibility of LDA and the coherence advantages of LDA warrant strong consideration. All of code for this work will be made available through an open source project.[6]

6 Acknowledgments

This work was performed under the auspices of the U.S. Department of Energy by Lawrence Livermore National Laboratory under Contract DE-AC52-07NA27344 (LLNL-CONF-522871) and by Sandia National Laboratory under Contract DE-AC04-94AL85000.

References

David Andrzejewski and David Buttler. 2011. Latent topic feedback for information retrieval. In *Proceed-*

[6]https://github.com/fozziethebeat/TopicModelComparison

ings of the 17th ACM SIGKDD international conference on Knowledge discovery and data mining, KDD '11, pages 600–608, New York, NY, USA. ACM.

Robert E. Banfield, Lawrence O. Hall, Kevin W. Bowyer, and W. Philip Kegelmeyer. 2007. A comparison of decision tree ensemble creation techniques. *IEEE Transactions on Pattern Analysis and Machine Intelligence*, 29(1):173–180, January.

Marco Baroni, Silvia Bernardini, Adriano Ferraresi, and Eros Zanchetta. 2009. The WaCky wide web: A collection of very large linguistically processed web-crawled corpora. *Language Resources and Evaluation*, 43(3):209–226.

David M. Blei, Andrew Y. Ng, and Michael I. Jordan. 2003. Latent dirichlet allocation. *J. Mach. Learn. Res.*, 3:993–1022, March.

Samuel Brody and Mirella Lapata. 2009. Bayesian word sense induction. In *Proceedings of the 12th Conference of the European Chapter of the Association for Computational Linguistics*, EACL '09, pages 103–111, Stroudsburg, PA, USA. Association for Computational Linguistics.

Rich Caruana, Mohamed Elhawary, Art Munson, Mirek Riedewald, Daria Sorokina, Daniel Fink, Wesley M. Hochachka, and Steve Kelling. 2006. Mining citizen science data to predict orevalence of wild bird species. In *Proceedings of the 12th ACM SIGKDD international conference on Knowledge discovery and data mining*, KDD '06, pages 909–915, New York, NY, USA. ACM.

Jonathan Chang, Sean Gerrish, Chong Wang, and David M Blei. 2009. Reading tea leaves : How humans interpret topic models. *New York*, 31:1–9.

Chris Ding, Tao Li, and Wei Peng. 2008. On the equivalence between non-negative matrix factorization and probabilistic latent semantic indexing. *Comput. Stat. Data Anal.*, 52:3913–3927, April.

Lev Finkelstein, Evgeniy Gabrilovich, Yossi Matias, Ehud Rivlin, Zach Solan, Gadi Wolfman, and Eytan Ruppin. 2002. Placing search in context: the concept revisited. *ACM Trans. Inf. Syst.*, 20:116–131, January.

T. L. Griffiths and M. Steyvers. 2004. Finding scientific topics. *Proceedings of the National Academy of Sciences*, 101(Suppl. 1):5228–5235, April.

David Jurgens and Keith Stevens. 2010. The s-space package: an open source package for word space models. In *Proceedings of the ACL 2010 System Demonstrations*, ACLDemos '10, pages 30–35, Stroudsburg, PA, USA. Association for Computational Linguistics.

Thomas K Landauer and Susan T. Dutnais. 1997. A solution to platos problem: The latent semantic analysis theory of acquisition, induction, and representation of knowledge. *Psychological review*, pages 211–240.

Thomas K. Landauer, Peter W. Foltz, and Darrell Laham. 1998. An Introduction to Latent Semantic Analysis. *Discourse Processes*, (25):259–284.

Daniel D. Lee and H. Sebastian Seung. 2000. Algorithms for non-negative matrix factorization. In *In NIPS*, pages 556–562. MIT Press.

David Mimno, Hanna Wallach, Edmund Talley, Miriam Leenders, and Andrew McCallum. 2011. Optimizing semantic coherence in topic models. In *Proceedings of the 2011 Conference on Emperical Methods in Natural Language Processing*, pages 262–272, Edinburgh, Scotland, UK. Association of Computational Linguistics.

David Newman, Youn Noh, Edmund Talley, Sarvnaz Karimi, and Timothy Baldwin. 2010. Evaluating topic models for digital libraries. In *Proceedings of the 10th annual joint conference on Digital libraries*, JCDL '10, pages 215–224, New York, NY, USA. ACM.

V Paul Pauca, Farial Shahnaz, Michael W Berry, and Robert J Plemmons, 2004. *Text mining using nonnegative matrix factorizations*, volume 54, pages 452–456. SIAM.

Herbert Rubenstein and John B. Goodenough. 1965. Contextual correlates of synonymy. *Commun. ACM*, 8:627–633, October.

Evan Sandhaus. 2008. The New York Times Annotated Corpus.

Tim Van de Cruys and Marianna Apidianaki. 2011. Latent semantic word sense induction and disambiguation. In *Proceedings of the 49th Annual Meeting of the Association for Computational Linguistics: Human Language Technologies - Volume 1*, HLT '11, pages 1476–1485, Stroudsburg, PA, USA. Association for Computational Linguistics.

Hanna Wallach, Iain Murray, Ruslan Salakhutdinov, and David Mimno. 2009. Evaluation methods for topic models. In *Proceedings of the 26th International Conference on Machine Learning (ICML)*. Omnipress.

Entropy-based Pruning for Phrase-based Machine Translation

Wang Ling, João Graça, Isabel Trancoso, Alan Black
L[2]F Spoken Systems Lab, INESC-ID, Lisboa, Portugal
Language Technologies Institute, Carnegie Mellon University, Pittsburgh, PA, USA
{wang.ling,joao.graca,isabel.trancoso}@inesc-id.pt
awb@cs.cmu.edu

Abstract

Phrase-based machine translation models have shown to yield better translations than Word-based models, since phrase pairs encode the contextual information that is needed for a more accurate translation. However, many phrase pairs do not encode any relevant context, which means that the translation event encoded in that phrase pair is led by smaller translation events that are independent from each other, and can be found on smaller phrase pairs, with little or no loss in translation accuracy. In this work, we propose a relative entropy model for translation models, that measures how likely a phrase pair encodes a translation event that is derivable using smaller translation events with similar probabilities. This model is then applied to phrase table pruning. Tests show that considerable amounts of phrase pairs can be excluded, without much impact on the translation quality. In fact, we show that better translations can be obtained using our pruned models, due to the compression of the search space during decoding.

1 Introduction

Phrase-based Machine Translation Models (Koehn et al., 2003) model n-to-m translations of n source words to m target words, which are encoded in phrase pairs and stored in the translation model. This approach has an advantage over Word-based Translation Models (Brown et al., 1993), since translating multiple source words allows the context for each source word to be considered during translation. For instance, the translation of the English word "in" by itself to Portuguese is not obvious, since we do not have any context for the word. This word can be translated in the context of "in (the box)" to "dentro", or in the context of "in (China)" as "na". In fact, the lexical entry for "in" has more than 10 good translations in Portuguese. Consequently, the lexical translation entry for Word-based models splits the probabilistic mass between different translations, leaving the choice based on context to the language model. On the other hand, in Phrase-based Models, we would have a phrase pair $p(in\ the\ box, dentro\ da\ caixa)$ and $p(in\ china, na\ china)$, where the words "in the box" and "in China" can be translated together to "dentro da caixa" and "na China", which substantially reduces the ambiguity. In this case, both the translation and language models contribute to find the best translation based on the local context, which generally leads to better translations.

However, not all words add the same amount of contextual information. Using the same example for "in", if we add the context "(hid the key) in", it is still not possible to accurately identify the best translation for the word "in". The phrase extraction algorithm (Ling et al., 2010) does not discriminate which phrases pairs encode contextual information, and extracts all phrase pairs with consistent alignments. Hence, phrases that add no contextual information, such as, $p(hid\ the\ key\ in, escondeu\ a\ chave\ na)$ and $p(hid\ the\ key\ in, escondeu\ a\ chave\ dentro)$ are extracted. This is undesirable because we are populating translation models with redundant phrase pairs, whose translations can be obtained using combinations of other phrases with the same probabilities, namely $p(hid\ the\ key, escondeu\ a\ chave)$, $p(in, dentro)$ and $p(in, na)$. This is a problem that is also found in language modeling, where large amounts of redundant higher-order n-grams can make the model needlessly large. For backoff language models, multiple pruning strategies based on relative entropy have been proposed (Seymore and Rosenfeld, 1996) (Stolcke, 1998), where the objective is to prune n-grams in a way to minimize the relative entropy between the model before and after pruning.

While the concept of using relative entropy for pruning is not new and frequently used in backoff language models, there are no such models for machine translation. Thus, the main contribution of our work is to propose a relative entropy pruning model for translation models used in Phrase-based Machine Translation. It is shown that our pruning algorithm can eliminate phrase pairs with little or no impact in the predictions made in our translation model. In fact, by reducing the search space, less search errors are made during decoding, which leads to improvements in translation quality.

This paper is organized as follows. We describe and contrast the state of the art pruning algorithms in section 2. In section 3, we describe our relative-entropy model for machine translation. Afterwards, in section 4, we apply our model for pruning in Phrase-based Machine Translation systems. We perform experiments with our pruning algorithm based on phrase pair independence and analyse the results in section 5. Finally, we conclude in section 6.

2 Phrase Table Pruning

Phrase table pruning algorithms are important in translation, since they efficiently reduce the size of the translation model, without having a large negative impact in the translation quality. This is especially relevant in environments where memory constraints are imposed, such as translation systems for small devices like cellphones, and also when time constraints for the translation are defined, such as online Speech-to-Speech systems.

2.1 Significance Pruning

A relevant reference in phrase table pruning is the work of (Johnson and Martin, 2007), where it is shown that a significant portion of the phrase table can be discarded without a considerable negative impact on translation quality, or even positive one. This work computes the probability, named p-value, that the joint occurrence event of the source phrase s and target phrase t occurring in same sentence pair happens by chance, and are actually statistically independent. Phrase pairs that have a high p-value, are more likely to be spurious and more prone to be pruned. This work is followed in (Tomeh et al., 2009), where phrase pairs are treated discriminately based on their complexity. Significance-based pruning has also been successfully applied in language modeling in (Moore and Quirk, 2009).

Our work has a similar objective, but instead of trying to predict the independence between the source and target phrases in each phrase pair, we attempt to predict the independence between a phrase pair and other phrase pairs in the model.

2.2 Relevance Pruning

Another proposed approach (Matthias Eck and Waibel, 2007) consists at collecting usage statistics for phrase pairs. This algorithm decodes the training corpora and extracts the number of times each phrase pair is used in the 1-best translation hypothesis. Thus, phrase pairs that are rarely used during decoding are excluded first during pruning.

This method considers the relationship between phrase pairs in the model, since it tests whether the decoder is more prone to use some phrase pairs than others. However, it leads to some undesirable pruning choices. Let us consider a source phrase "the box in China" and 2 translation hypotheses, where the first hypothesis uses the phrase translation $p(the\ key\ in\ China, a\ chave\ na\ China)$ with probability 70%, and the second hypothesis uses two phrase translations $p(the\ key, a\ chave)$ and $p(in\ China, na\ China)$ with probability 65%. This approach will lean towards pruning the phrase pairs in the second hypothesis, since the decoder will use the first hypothesis. This is generally not desired, since the 2 smaller phrase pairs can be used to translate the same source sentence with a small probability loss (5%), even if the longer phrase is pruned. On the other hand, if the smaller phrases are pruned, the longer phrase can not be used to translate smaller chunks, such as "the key in Portugal". This matter is aggravated due to the fact that the training corpora is used to decode, so longer phrase pairs will be used more frequently than when translating unseen sentences, which will make the model more biased into pruning shorter phrase pairs.

3 Relative Entropy Model For Phrase-based Translation Models

In this section, we shall define our entropy model for phrase pairs. We start by introducing some notation to distinguish different types of phrase pairs and show why some phrase pairs are more redundant than others. Afterwards, we illustrate our notion of relative entropy between phrase pairs. Then, we describe our entropy model, its computation and its application to phrase table pruning.

3.1 Atomic and Composite Phrase Pairs

We discriminate between 2 types of phrase pairs: atomic phrase pairs and composite phrase pairs.

Atomic phrase pairs define the smallest translation units, such that given an atomic phrase pair that translates from s to t, the same translation cannot be obtained using any combination of other phrase pairs. Removing these phrase pairs reduces the range of translations that our model is capable of translating and also the possible translations.

Composite phrase pairs define translations of a given sequence of words that can also be obtained using atomic or other smaller composite phrase pairs. Each combination is called a derivation or translation hypothesis. Removing these phrase pairs does not change the amount of sentences that the model can translate, since all translations encoded in these phrases can still be translated using other phrases, but these will lead to different translation probabilities.

Considering table 1, we can see that atomic phrases encode one elementary translation event, while composite phrases encode joint events that are encoded in atomic phrase pairs. If we look at the source phrase "in", there is a multitude of possible translations for this word in most target languages. Taking Portuguese as the target language, the probability that "in" is translated to "em" is relatively low, since it can also be translated to "no", "na", "dentro", "dentro de" and many others.

However, if we add another word such as "Portugal" forming "in Portugal", it is more likely that "in" is translated to "em". Thus, we define the joint event of "in" translating to "em" (A_1) and "Portugal" to "Portugal" (B_1), denoted as $A_1 \cap B_1$, in the phrase pair $p(in\ Portugal, em\ Portugal)$. Without this phrase pair it is assumed that these are independent events with probability given by $P(A_1)P(B_1)$[1], which would be 10%, leading to a 60% reduction. In this case, it would be more likely, that $in\ Portugal$ is translated to $no\ Portugal$ or $na\ Portugal$, which would be incorrect.

Some words, such as "John", forming "John in", do not influence the translations for the word "in", since it can still be translated to "em", "no", "na", "dentro" or "dentro de" depending on the word that follows. By definition, if the presence of phrase $p(John, John)$ does not influence the translation of $p(in, em)$ and viceversa, we can say that probability of the joint event $P(A_1 \cap C_1)$ is equal to the product of the probabilities of the events $P(A_1)P(C_1)$.

If we were given a choice of pruning either the composite phrase pairs $p(John\ in, John\ em)$ or $p(in\ Portugal, em\ Portugal)$, the obvious choice would be the former, since the probability of the event encoded in that phrase pair is composed by 2 independent events, in which case the decoder will inherently consider the hypothesis that "John in" is translated to "John em" with the same probability. In another words, the model's predictions even, without this phrase pair will remain the same.

The example above shows an extreme case, where the event encoded in the phrase pair $p(John\ in, John\ em)$ is decomposed into independent events, and can be removed without changing the model's prediction. However, finding and pruning phrase pairs that are independent, based on smaller events is impractical, since most translation events are not strictly independent. However, many phrase pairs can be replaced with derivations using smaller phrases with a small loss in the model's pre-

[1]For simplicity, we assume at this stage that no reordering model is used

Phrase Pair	Prob	Event
Atomic Phrase Pairs		
in → em	10%	A_1
in → na	20%	A_2
in → no	20%	A_3
in → dentro	5%	A_4
in → dentro de	5%	A_5
Portugal → Portugal	100%	B_1
John → John	100%	C_1
Composite Phrase Pairs		
in Portugal → em Portugal	70%	$A_1 \cap B_1$
John in → John em	10%	$C_1 \cap A_1$
John in → John na	20%	$C_1 \cap A_2$
John in → John no	20%	$C_1 \cap A_3$
John in → John dentro	5%	$C_1 \cap A_4$
John in → John dentro de	5%	$C_1 \cap A_5$

Table 1: Phrase Translation Table with associated events

dictions.

Hence, we would like to define a metric for phrase pairs that allows us evaluate how discarding each phrase pair will affect the pruned model's predictions. By removing phrase pairs that can be derived using smaller phrase pairs with similar probability, it is possible to discard a significant portion of the translation model, while minimizing the impact on the model's predictions.

3.2 Relative Entropy Model for Machine Translation

For each phrase pair p_a, we define the supporting set $SP(p_a(s,t)) = S_1, ..., S_k$, where each element $S_i = p_i, ..., p_j$ is a distinct derivation of $p_a(s,t)$ that translates s to t, with probability $P(S_i) = P(p_i) \times ... \times P(p_j)$. A phrase pair can have multiple elements in its supporting set. For instance, the phrase pair $p(John\ in\ Portugal, John\ em\ Portugal)$, has 3 elements in the support set:

- $S_1 = \{p(John, John), p(in, em), p(Portugal, Portugal)\}$
- $S_2 = \{p(John, John), p(in\ Portugal, em\ Portugal)\}$
- $S_3 = \{p(John\ in, John\ em), p(Portugal, Portugal)\}$

S_1, S_2 and S_3 encode 3 different assumptions about the event of translating "John in Portugal" to "John em Portugal". S_1 assumes that the event is composed by 3 independent events A_1, B_1 and C_1, S_2 assumes that A_1 and B_1 are dependent, and groups them into a single composite event $A_1 \cap B_1$, which is independent from C_1, and S_3 groups A_1 and C_1 independently from B_1. As expected, the event encoded in the phrase pair p itself is $A_1 \cap B_1 \cap C_1$, which assumes that A_1, B_1 and C_1 are all dependent. We can see that if any of the events S_1, S_2 or S_3 has a "similar probability" as the event coded in the phrase pair, we can remove this phrase pair with a minimal impact in the phrase prediction.

To formalize our notion of "similar probability", we apply the relative entropy or the Kullback-Leibler divergence, and define the divergence between a pruned translation model $P_p(s,t)$ and the unpruned model $P(s,t)$ as:

$$D(P_p||P) = -\sum_{s,t} P(s,t) log \frac{P_p(t|s)}{P(t|s)} \quad (1)$$

Where $\frac{P_p(t|s)}{P(t|s)}$, measures the deviation from the probability emission from the pruned model and the original probability from the unpruned model, for each source-target pair s,t. This is weighted by the frequency that the pair s,t is observed, given by $P(s,t)$.

Our objective is to minimize $D(P_p||P)$, which can be done locally by removing phrase pairs $p(s,t)$ with the lowest values for $-P(s,t)log\frac{P_p(t|s)}{P(t|s)}$. Ideally, we would want to minimize the relative entropy for all possible source and target sentences, rather than all phrases in our model. However, minimizing such an objective function would be intractable due to reordering, since the probability assigned to a phrase pair in a sentence pair by each model would depend on the positioning of all other phrase pairs used in the sentence. Because of these dependencies, we would not be able to reduce this problem to a local minimization problem. Thus, we assume that all phrase pairs have the same probability regardless of their context in a sentence.

Thus, our pruning algorithm takes a threshold δ and prunes all phrase pairs that fail to meet the following criteria:

$$-P(s,t)log\frac{P_p(t|s)}{P(t|s)} > \delta \quad (2)$$

The main components of this function is the ratio between the emission from the pruned model and unpruned models given by $\frac{P_p(t|s)}{P(t|s)}$, and the weight given to each s, t pair given by $P(s, t)$. In the remainder of this section, we will focus on how to model each of these components in equation 2.

3.3 Computing $P(s, t)$

The term $P(s, t)$ can be seen as a weighting function for each s, t pair. There is no obvious optimal distribution to model $P(s, t)$. In this work, we apply 2 different distributions for $P(s, t)$. First, an uniform distribution, where all phrases are weighted equally. Secondly, a multinomial function defined as:

$$P(s,t) = \frac{N(s,t)}{N} \quad (3)$$

where N is the number of sentence pairs in the parallel data, and $N(s, t)$ is the number of sentence pairs where s was observed in the source sentence and t was observed in the target sentence. Using this distribution, the model is more biased in pruning phrase pairs with s, t pairs that do not occur frequently.

3.4 Computing $\frac{P_p(t|s)}{P(t|s)}$

The computation of $\frac{P_p(t|s)}{P(t|s)}$ depends on how the decoder adapts when a phrase pair is pruned from the model. In the case of back-off language models, this can be solved by calculating the difference of the logs between the n-gram estimate and the back-off estimate. However, a translation decoder generally functions differently. In our work, we will assume that the decoding will be performed using a Viterbi decoder, such as MOSES (Koehn et al., 2007), where the translation with the highest score is chosen.

In the example above, where s="John in Portugal" and t="John em Portugal", the decoder would choose the derivation with the highest probability from s to t. Using the unpruned model, the possible derivations are either using phrase $p(s, t)$ or one element of its support set S_1, S_2 or S_3. On the other hand, on the pruned model where $p(s, t)$ does not exist, only S_1, S_2 and S_3 can be used. Thus, given a s, t pair one of three situations may occur. First, if the probability of the phrase pair $p(s, t)$ is lower than the highest probability element in $SP(p(s, t))$, then both the models will choose that element, in which case, $\frac{P_p(t|s)}{P(t|s)} = 1$. This can happen, if we define features that penalize longer phrase pairs, such as lexical weighting, or if we apply smoothing (Foster et al., 2006). Secondly, if the probability of $p(s, t)$ is equal to the most likely element in $SP(p(s, t))$, regardless of whether the unpruned model choses to use $p(s, t)$ or that element, the probability emissions of the pruned and unpruned model will be identical. Thus, for this case $\frac{P_p(t|s)}{P(t|s)} = 1$. Finally, if the probability of $p(s, t)$ is higher than other possible derivations, the unpruned model will choose to emit the probability of $p(s, t)$, while the pruned model will emit the most likely element in $SP(p(s, t))$. Hence, the probability loss between the 2 models, will be the ratio between the probability of $p(s, t)$ and the probability of the most likely element in $SP(p(s, t))$.

From the example above, we can generalize the function for $\frac{P_p(t|s)}{P(t|s)}$ as:

$$\frac{\prod_{p' \in argmax(SP(p(s,t)))} P(p')}{P(p(s,t))} \quad (4)$$

Where $P(p(s, t))$ denotes the probability of $p(s, t)$ and $\prod_{p' \in argmax(SP(p(s,t)))} P(p')$ the most likely sequence of phrasal translations that translates s to t, with the probability equal to the product of all phrase translation probabilities in that sequence.

Replacing in equation 2, our final condition that must be satisfied for keeping a phrase pair is:

$$-P(s,t) log \frac{\prod_{p' \in argmax(SP(p(s,t)))} P(p')}{P(p(s,t))} > \delta \quad (5)$$

4 Application for Phrase-based Machine Translation

We will now show how we apply our entropy pruning model in the state-of-the-art phrase-based translation system MOSES and describe the problems that need to be addressed during the implementation of this model.

4.1 Translation Model

The translation model in Moses is composed by a phrase translation model and a phrase reordering model. The first one models, for each phrase pair $p(s, t)$, the probability of translating the s to t by combining multiple features ϕ_i, weighted by

w_i^T, as $P_T(p) = \prod_{i=1}^{n} \phi_i(p)^{w_i^T}$. The reordering model is similar, but models the local reordering between p, given the previous and next phrase according to the target side, p_P and p_N, or more formally, $P_R(p|p_P, p_N) = \prod_{i=1}^{m} \psi_i(p|p_P, p_P)^{w_i^R}$

4.2 Building the Support Set

Essentially, implementing our model is equivalent to calculating the components described in equation 5. These are $P(s,t)$, $P(p(s|t))$ and $argmax(SP(p(s,t)))$. Calculating the uniform distribution and multinomial distributions for $P(s,t)$ is simple, the uniform distribution just assumes the same value for all s and t, and the multinomial distribution can be modeled by extracting counts from the parallel corpora.

Calculating $P(s|t)$ is also trivial, since it only envolves calculating $P_T(p(s,t))$, which can be done by retrieving the translation features of p and applying the weights for each feature.

The most challenging task is to calculate $argmax(SP(p(s,t)))$, which is similar to the decoding task in machine translation, where we need to find the best translation $\hat{t}$ for a sentence s, that is, $\hat{t} = argmax_t P(s|t)P(t)$. In practice, we are not searching in the space of possible translations, but in the space of possible derivations, which are sequences of phrase translations $p_1(s_1,t_1), ..., p_n(s_n,t_n)$ that can be applied to s to generate an output t with the score given by $P(t) \prod_{i=1}^{n} P(s_i, t_i)$.

Our algorithm to determine $SP(p(s,t))$ can be described as an adaptation to the decoding algorithm in Moses, where we restrict the search space to the subspace $SP(p(s,t))$, that is, our search space is only composed by derivations that output t, without using p itself. This can be done using the forced decoding algorithm proposed in (Schwartz, 2008). Secondly, the score of a given translation hypothesis does not depend on the language model probability $P(t)$, since all derivations in this search space have the same t, thus we discard this probability from the score function. Finally, rather than using beam search, we exhaustively search all the search space, to reduce the hypothesis of incurring a search error at this stage. This is possible, since phrase pairs are generally smaller than text (less than 8 words), and because we are constraining the search space to t, which is an order of magnitude smaller than the regular search space with all possible translations.

4.3 Pruning Algorithm

The algorithm to generate a pruned translation model is shown in 1. We iterate over all phrase pairs $p_1(s_1,t_1), ..., p_n(s_n,t_n)$, decode using our forced decoding algorithm from s_i to t_i, to obtain the best path S. If no path is found then it means that the p_i is atomic. Then, we prune p_i based on condition 5.

Algorithm 1 Independence Pruning

Require: pruning threshold δ,
  unpruned model $\{p_1(s_1,t_1), ..., p_n(s_n,t_n)\}$
  for $p_i(s_i,t_i) \in \{p_1(s_1,t_1), ..., p_n(s_n,t_n)\}$ **do**
    $S := argmax(SP(p_i)) \setminus p_i$
    $score := \infty$
    if $S \neq \{\}$ **then**
      $score := -P(s,t) log \frac{\prod_{p'(s',t') \in S} P(s'|t')}{P(s|t)}$
    end if
    if $score \leq \delta$ **then**
      $prune(p_i)$
    end if
  end for
  return pruned model

The main bottle neck in this algorithm is finding $argmax(SP(p_i))$. While this appears relatively simple and similar to a document decoding task, the size of our task is on a different order of magnitude, since we need to decode every phrase pair in the translation model, which might not be tractable for large models with millions of phrase pairs. We address this problem in section 5.3.

Another problem with this algorithm is that the decision to prune each phrase pair is made assuming that all other phrase pairs will remain in the model. Thus, there is a chance a phrase pair p_1 is pruned because of a derivation using p_2 and p_3 that leads to the same translation. However, if p_3 also happens to be pruned, such a derivation will no longer be possible. One possible solution to address this problem is to perform pruning iteratively, from the smallest phrase pairs (number of words) and increase the size at each iteration. However, we find this undesirable, since the model will be biased into removing smaller phrase pairs, which are generally more useful, since they can be used in multiple derivation to replace larger phrase pairs. In the example above, the model would eliminate p_3 and keep p_1, yet the best decision could be to keep p_3 and remove p_1, if p_3 is also frequently used in derivations of other phrase pairs. Thus, we leave the problem of finding the best set of phrases to prune as future work.

5 Experiments

We tested the performance of our system under two different environments. The first is the small scale DIALOG translation task for IWSLT 2010 evaluation (Paul et al., 2010) using a small corpora for the Chinese-English language pair (henceforth referred to as "IWSLT"). The second one is a large scale test using the complete EUROPARL (Koehn, 2005) corpora for the Portuguese-English language pair, which we will denote by "EUROPARL".

5.1 Corpus

The IWSLT model was trained with 30K training sentences. The development corpus and test corpus were taken from the evaluation dataset in IWSLT 2006 (489 tuning and 500 test sentences with 7 references). The EUROPARL model was trained using the EUROPARL corpora with approximately 1.3M sentence pairs, leaving out 1K sentences for tuning and another 1K sentences for tests.

5.2 Setup

In the IWSLT experiment, word alignments were generated using an HMM model (Vogel et al., 1996), with symmetric posterior constraints (V. Graça et al., 2010), using the Geppetto toolkit[2]. This setup was used in the official evaluation in (Ling et al., 2010). For the EUROPARL experiment the word alignments were generated using IBM model 4. In both experiments, the translation model was built using the phrase extraction algorithm (Paul et al., 2010), with commonly used features in Moses (Ex: probability, lexical weighting, lexicalized reordering model). The optimization of the translation model weights was done using MERT tuning (Och, 2003) and the results were evaluated using BLEU-4.

5.3 Pruning Setup

Our pruning algorithm is applied after the translation model weight optimization with MERT. We generate multiple translation models by setting different values for δ, so that translation models of different sizes are generated at intervals of 5%. We also run the significance pruning (Johnson and Martin, 2007) algorithm in these conditions.

While the IWSLT translation model has only 88,424 phrase pairs, for the EUROPARL experiment, the translation model was composed by 48,762,372 phrase pairs, which had to be decoded. The average time to decode each phrase pair using the full translation model is 4 seconds per sentence, since the table must be read from disk due to its size. This would make translating 48M phrase pairs unfeasible. To address this problem, we divide the phrase pairs in the translation model into blocks of K phrase pairs, that are processed separately. For each block, we resort to the approach used in MERT tuning, where the model is filtered to only include the phrase pairs that are used for translating tuning sentences. We filter each block with phrase pairs from K to $2K$ with the source sentences $s_K, ..., s_{2K}$. Furthermore, since we are force decoding using the target sentences, we also filter the remaining translation models using the target sentences $t_K, ..., t_{2K}$. We used blocks of 10,000 phrase pairs and each filtered table was reduced to less than 1% of the translation table on average, reducing the average decoding time to 0.03 seconds per sentence. Furthermore, each block can be processed in parallel allowing multiple processes to be used for the task, depending on the resources that are available.

5.4 Results

Figure 1 shows the BLEU results for different sizes of the translation model for the IWSLT experiment using the uniform and multinomial distributions for $P(s,t)$. We observe that there is a range of values from 65% to 95% where we actually observe improvements caused by our pruning algorithm, with the peak at 85% for the uniform distribution, where we improve from 15.68 to 15.82 (0.9% improvement). Between 26% and 65%, the BLEU score is lower than the baseline at 100%, with the minimum at 26% with 15.54, where only atomic phrase pairs remain and both the multinomial and uniform distribution have the same performance, obviously. This is a considerable reduction in phrase table size by sacrificing 0.14 BLEU points. Regarding the com-

[2]http://code.google.com/p/geppetto/

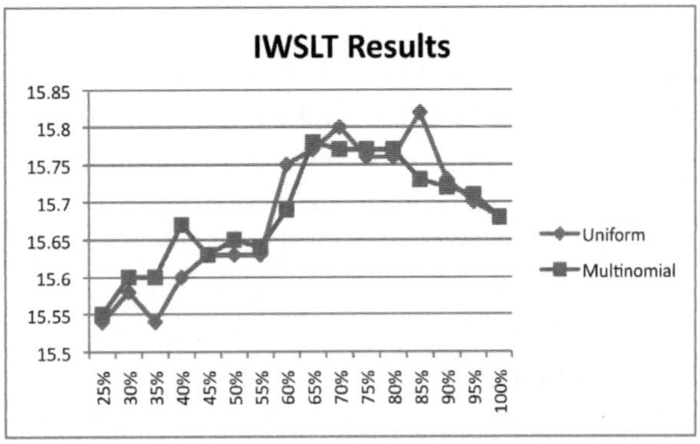

Figure 1: Results for the IWSLT experiment. The x-axis shows the percentage of the phrase table used. The BLEU scores are shown in the y-axis. Two distributions for $P(s,t)$ were tested Uniform and Multinomial.

Table size	Significance Pruning	Entropy (u) Pruning	Entropy (m) Pruning
IWSLT			
57K (65%)	14.82	15.77	**15.78**
71K (80%)	15.14	15.76	**15.77**
80K (90%)	15.31	**15.73**	15.72
88K (100%)	15.68	15.68	15.68
EUROPARL			
29M (60%)	28.64	28.82	**28.91**
34M (70%)	28.84	28.94	**28.99**
39M (80%)	28.86	**28.99**	**28.99**
44M (90%)	28.91	29.00	**29.02**
49M (100%)	29.18	29.18	29.18

Table 2: Comparison between Significance Pruning (Significance Pruning) and Entropy-based pruning using the uniform (Entropy (u) Pruning) and multinomial distributions (Entropy (m) Pruning).

parison between the uniform and multinomial distribution, we can see that both distributions yield similar results, specially when a low number of phrase pairs is pruned. In theory, the multinomial distribution should yield better results, since the pruning model will prefer to prune phrase pairs that are more likely to be observed. However, longer phrase pairs, which tend compete with other long phrase pairs on which get pruned first. These phrase pairs generally occur only once or twice, so the multinomial model will act similarly to the uniform model regarding longer phrase pairs. On the other hand, as the model size reduces, we can see that using multinomial distribution seems to start to improve over the uniform distribution.

The comparison between our pruning model and pruning based on significance is shown in table 2. These models are hard to compare, since not all phrase table sizes can be obtained using both metrics. For instance, the significance metric can either keep or remove all phrase pairs that only appear once, leaving a large gap of phrase table sizes that cannot be attained. In the EUROPARL experiment the sizes of the table suddenly drops from 60% to 8%. The same happens with our metric that cannot distinguish atomic phrase pairs. In the EUROPARL experiment, we cannot generate phrase tables with sizes smaller than 15%. Thus, we only show results at points where both algorithms can produce a phrase table.

Significant improvements are observed in the IWSLT experiment, where significance pruning does not perform as well. On the other hand, on the EUROPARL experiment, our model only achieves slightly higher results. We believe that this is related by the fact the EUROPARL corpora is generated from automatically aligning documents, which means that there are misaligned sentence pairs. Thus, many spurious phrase pairs are extracted. Significance pruning performs well under these conditions, since the measure is designed for this purpose. In our metric, we do not have any means for detecting spurious phrase pairs, in fact, spurious phrase pairs are probably kept in the phrase table, since each distinct spurious phrase pair is only extracted once, and thus, they have very few derivations in its support set. This suggests, that the significance score can be integrated in our model to improve our model, which we leave as future work.

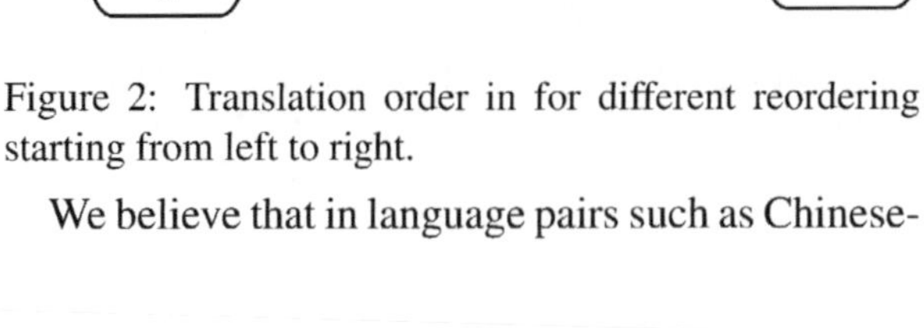

Figure 2: Translation order in for different reordering starting from left to right.

We believe that in language pairs such as Chinese-

English with large distance reorderings between phrases are more prone to search errors and benefit more from our pruning algorithm. To illustrate this, let us consider the source sentence "John married in Portugal", and translating either using the blocks "John", "married" and "in Portugal" or the blocks "John", "married in", "Portugal", the first hypothesis would be much more viable, since the word "Portugal" is more relevant as the context for the word "in". Thus, the key choice for the decoder is to decide whether to translate using "married" with or without "in", and it is only able to predict that it is better to translate "married" by itself until it finds that "in" is better translated with "Portugal". Thus, a search error occurs if the hypothesis where "married" is translated by itself is removed. In figure 2, we can see the order that blocks are considered for different reorderings, starting from left to right. In a), we illustrate the case for a monotonous translation. We observe that the correct decision between translating "married in" or just "married" is found immediately, since the blocks "Portugal" and "in Portugal" are considered right afterwards. In this case, it is unlikely that the hypothesis using "married" is removed. However, if we consider that due to reordering, "John" is translated after "married" and before "Portugal", which is shown in b). Then, the correct decision can only be found after considering "John". In this case, "John" does not have many translations, so the likelihood of eliminating the correct hypothesis. However, if there were many translations for John, it is highly likely that the correct partial hypothesis is eliminated. Furthermore, the more words exist between "married" and "Portugal", the more likely will the correct hypothesis not exist when we reach "Portugal". By pruning the hypothesis "married in" a priori, we contribute in preventing such search errors.

We observe that some categories of phrase pairs that are systematically pruned, but these cannot be generalized in rules, since there are many exceptions. The most obvious type of phrase pairs are phrases with punctuations, such as "谢谢." to "thanks ." and ". 谢谢" to "thanks .", since "." is translated independently from most contextual words. However, this rule should not be generalized, since in some cases "." is a relevant contextual marker. For instance, the word "please" is translated to "请" in the sentence 'open the door, please." and translated to "使高兴" in "please my advisors". Another example are sequences of numbers, which are generally translated literally. For instance, "八(8) 三(3) 八(8)" is translated to "eight three eight" (Ex: "room eight three eight"). Thus, phrase pairs for number sequences can be removed, since those numbers can be translated one by one. However, for sequences such as "一(1) 八(8)", we need a phrase pair to represent this specifically. This is because "一(1)" can be translated to "one", but also to "a", "an", "single". Other exceptions include "一(1) 一(1)", which tends to be translated as "eleven", and which tends to be translated to "o", rather than "zero" in sequences ("room eleven o five").

6 Conclusions

We present a pruning algorithm for Machine Translation based on relative entropy, where we assess whether the translation event encoded in a phrase pair can be decomposed into combinations of events encoded in other phrase pairs. We show that such phrase pairs can be removed from the translation model with little negative impact or even a positive one in the overall translation quality. Tests show that our method yields comparable or better results with state of the art pruning algorithms.

As future work, we would like to combine our approach with significance pruning, since both approaches are orthogonal and address different issues. We also plan to improve the pruning step of our algorithm to find the optimal set of phrase pairs to prune given the pruning threshold.

The code used in this work will be made available.

7 Acknowledgements

This work was partially supported by FCT (INESC-ID multiannual funding) through the PIDDAC Program funds, and also through projects CMU-PT/HuMach/0039/2008 and CMU-PT/0005/2007. The PhD thesis of Wang Ling is supported by FCT grant SFRH/BD/51157/2010. The authors also wish to thank the anonymous reviewers for many helpful comments.

References

Peter F. Brown, Vincent J. Della Pietra, Stephen A. Della Pietra, and Robert L. Mercer. 1993. The mathematics of statistical machine translation: parameter estimation. *Comput. Linguist.*, 19:263–311, June.

George Foster, Roland Kuhn, and Howard Johnson. 2006. Phrasetable smoothing for statistical machine translation. In *Proceedings of the 2006 Conference on Empirical Methods in Natural Language Processing*, EMNLP '06, pages 53–61, Stroudsburg, PA, USA. Association for Computational Linguistics.

J Howard Johnson and Joel Martin. 2007. Improving translation quality by discarding most of the phrasetable. In *In Proceedings of EMNLP-CoNLL'07*, pages 967–975.

Philipp Koehn, Franz Josef Och, and Daniel Marcu. 2003. Statistical phrase-based translation. In *Proceedings of the 2003 Conference of the North American Chapter of the Association for Computational Linguistics on Human Language Technology - Volume 1*, NAACL '03, pages 48–54, Morristown, NJ, USA. Association for Computational Linguistics.

Philipp Koehn, Hieu Hoang, Alexandra Birch, Chris Callison-burch, Richard Zens, Rwth Aachen, Alexandra Constantin, Marcello Federico, Nicola Bertoldi, Chris Dyer, Brooke Cowan, Wade Shen, Christine Moran, and Ondrej Bojar. 2007. Moses: Open source toolkit for statistical machine translation. In *Proceedings of the 45th Annual Meeting of the Association for Computational Linguistics Companion Volume Proceedings of the Demo and Poster Sessions*, pages 177–180, Prague, Czech Republic, June. Association for Computational Linguistics.

Philipp Koehn. 2005. Europarl: A Parallel Corpus for Statistical Machine Translation. In *Conference Proceedings: the tenth Machine Translation Summit*, pages 79–86, Phuket, Thailand. AAMT, AAMT.

Wang Ling, Tiago Luís, João Graça, Luísa Coheur, and Isabel Trancoso. 2010. Towards a general and extensible phrase-extraction algorithm. In *IWSLT '10: International Workshop on Spoken Language Translation*, pages 313–320, Paris, France.

Stephen Vogal Matthias Eck and Alex Waibel. 2007. Estimating phrase pair relevance for translation model pruning. *MTSummit XI.*

Robert C. Moore and Chris Quirk. 2009. Less is more: significance-based n-gram selection for smaller, better language models. In *Proceedings of the 2009 Conference on Empirical Methods in Natural Language Processing: Volume 2 - Volume 2*, EMNLP '09, pages 746–755, Stroudsburg, PA, USA. Association for Computational Linguistics.

Franz Josef Och. 2003. Minimum error rate training in statistical machine translation. In *Proceedings of the 41st Annual Meeting on Association for Computational Linguistics - Volume 1*, ACL '03, pages 160–167, Stroudsburg, PA, USA. Association for Computational Linguistics.

Michael Paul, Marcello Federico, and Sebastian Stüker. 2010. Overview of the iwslt 2010 evaluation campaign. In *IWSLT '10: International Workshop on Spoken Language Translation*, pages 3–27.

Lane Schwartz. 2008. Multi-source translation methods. In *Proceedings of AMTA*, pages 279–288.

Kristie Seymore and Ronald Rosenfeld. 1996. Scalable backoff language models. In *In Proceedings of ICSLP*, pages 232–235.

Andreas Stolcke. 1998. Entropy-based pruning of backoff language models. In *In Proc. DARPA Broadcast News Transcription and Understanding Workshop*, pages 270–274.

Nadi Tomeh, Nicola Cancedda, and Marc Dymetman. 2009. Complexity-based phrase-table filtering for statistical machine translation. *MTSummit XII*, Aug.

João V. Graça, Kuzman Ganchev, and Ben Taskar. 2010. Learning Tractable Word Alignment Models with Complex Constraints. *Comput. Linguist.*, 36:481–504.

S. Vogel, H. Ney, and C. Tillmann. 1996. Hmm-based word alignment in statistical translation. In *Proceedings of the 16th conference on Computational linguistics-Volume 2*, pages 836–841. Association for Computational Linguistics.

A Systematic Comparison of Phrase Table Pruning Techniques

Richard Zens and Daisy Stanton and Peng Xu

Google Inc.
{zens,daisy,xp}@google.com

Abstract

When trained on very large parallel corpora, the phrase table component of a machine translation system grows to consume vast computational resources. In this paper, we introduce a novel pruning criterion that places phrase table pruning on a sound theoretical foundation. Systematic experiments on four language pairs under various data conditions show that our principled approach is superior to existing ad hoc pruning methods.

1 Introduction

Over the last years, statistical machine translation has become the dominant approach to machine translation. This is not only due to improved modeling, but also due to a significant increase in the availability of monolingual and bilingual data. Here are just two examples of very large data resources that are publicly available:

- The Google Web 1T 5-gram corpus available from the Linguistic Data Consortium consisting of the 5-gram counts of about one trillion words of web data.[1]
- The 10^9-French-English bilingual corpus with about one billion tokens from the Workshop on Statistical Machine Translation (WMT).[2]

These enormous data sets yield translation models that are expensive to store and process. Even with modern computers, these large models lead to a long experiment cycle that hinders progress. The situation is even more severe if computational resources are limited, for instance when translating on handheld devices. Then, reducing the model size is of the utmost importance.

The most resource-intensive components of a statistical machine translation system are the language model and the phrase table. Recently, compact representations of the language model have attracted the attention of the research community, for instance in Talbot and Osborne (2007), Brants et al. (2007), Pauls and Klein (2011) or Heafield (2011), to name a few. In this paper, we address the other problem of any statistical machine translation system: large phrase tables.

Johnson et al. (2007) has shown that large portions of the phrase table can be removed without loss in translation quality. This motivated us to perform a systematic comparison of different pruning methods. However, we found that many existing methods employ ad-hoc heuristics without theoretical foundation.

The pruning criterion introduced in this work is inspired by the very successful and still state-of-the-art language model pruning criterion based on entropy measures (Stolcke, 1998). We motivate its derivation by stating the desiderata for a good phrase table pruning criterion:

- **Soundness**: The criterion should optimize some well-understood information-theoretic measure of translation model quality.

[1] LDC catalog No. LDC2006T13

[2] http://www.statmt.org/wmt11/translation-task.html

- **Efficiency**: Pruning should be fast, i. e., run linearly in the size of the phrase table.
- **Self-containedness**: As a practical consideration, we want to prune phrases from an existing phrase table. This means pruning should use only information contained in the model itself.
- **Good empirical behavior**: We would like to be able to prune large parts of the phrase table without significant loss in translation quality.

Analyzing existing pruning techniques based on these objectives, we found that they are commonly deficient in at least one of them. We thus designed a novel pruning criterion that not only meets these objectives, it also performs very well in empirical evaluations.

The **novel contributions** of this paper are:

1. a systematic description of existing phrase table pruning methods.
2. a new, theoretically sound phrase table pruning criterion.
3. an experimental comparison of several pruning methods for several language pairs.

2 Related Work

The most basic pruning methods rely on probability and count cutoffs. We will cover the techniques that are implemented in the Moses toolkit (Koehn et al., 2007) and the Pharaoh decoder (Koehn, 2004) in Section 3. We are not aware of any work that analyzes their efficacy in a systematic way. It is thus not surprising that some of them perform poorly, as our experimental results will show.

The work of Johnson et al. (2007) is promising as it shows that large parts of the phrase table can be removed without affecting translation quality. Their pruning criterion relies on statistical significance tests. However, it is unclear how this significance-based pruning criterion is related to translation model quality. Furthermore, a comparison to other methods is missing. Here we close this gap and perform a systematic comparison. The same idea of significance-based pruning was exploited in (Yang and Zheng, 2009; Tomeh et al., 2009) for hierarchical statistical machine translation.

A different approach to phrase table pruning was undertaken by Eck et al. (2007a; 2007b). They rely on usage statistics from translating sample data, so it is not self-contained. However, it could be combined with the methods proposed here.

Another approach to phrase table pruning is triangulation (Chen et al., 2008; Chen et al., 2009). This requires additional bilingual corpora, namely from the source language as well as from the target language to a third bridge language. In many situations this does not exist or would be costly to generate.

Duan et al. (2011), Sanchis-Trilles et al. (2011) and Tomeh et al. (2011) modify the phrase extraction methods in order to reduce the phrase table size. The work in this paper is independent of the way the phrase extraction is done, so those approaches are complementary to our work.

3 Pruning Using Simple Statistics

In this section, we will review existing pruning methods based on simple phrase table statistics. There are two common classes of these methods: absolute phrase table pruning and relative phrase table pruning.

3.1 Absolute pruning

Absolute pruning methods rely only on the statistics of a single phrase pair $(\tilde{f}, \tilde{e})$. Hence, they are independent of other phrases in the phrase table. As opposed to relative pruning methods (Section 3.2), they may prune all translations of a source phrase. Their application is easy and efficient.

- **Count-based pruning.** This method prunes a phrase pair $(\tilde{f}, \tilde{e})$ if its observation count $N(\tilde{f}, \tilde{e})$ is below a threshold τ_c:

$$N(\tilde{f}, \tilde{e}) < \tau_c \quad (1)$$

- **Probability-based pruning.** This method prunes a phrase pair $(\tilde{f}, \tilde{e})$ if its probability is below a threshold τ_p:

$$p(\tilde{e}|\tilde{f}) < \tau_p \quad (2)$$

Here the probability $p(\tilde{e}|\tilde{f})$ is estimated via relative frequencies.

3.2 Relative pruning

A potential problem with the absolute pruning methods is that it can prune all occurrences of a source phrase $\tilde{f}$.[3] Relative pruning methods avoid this by considering the full set of target phrases for a specific source phrase $\tilde{f}$.

- **Threshold pruning.** This method discards those phrases that are far worse than the best target phrase for a given source phrase $\tilde{f}$. Given a pruning threshold τ_t, a phrase pair $(\tilde{f}, \tilde{e})$ is discarded if:

$$p(\tilde{e}|\tilde{f}) < \tau_t \cdot \max_{\tilde{e}} \left\{ p(\tilde{e}|\tilde{f}) \right\} \quad (3)$$

- **Histogram pruning.** An alternative to threshold pruning is histogram pruning. For each source phrase $\tilde{f}$, this method preserves the K target phrases with highest probability $p(\tilde{e}|\tilde{f})$ or, equivalently, their count $N(\tilde{f}, \tilde{e})$.

Note that, except for count-based pruning, none of the methods take the frequency of the source phrase into account. As we will confirm in the empirical evaluation, this will likely cause drops in translation quality, since frequent source phrases are more useful than the infrequent ones.

4 Significance Pruning

In this section, we briefly review significance pruning following Johnson et al. (2007). The idea of significance pruning is to test whether a source phrase $\tilde{f}$ and a target phrase $\tilde{e}$ co-occur more frequently in a bilingual corpus than they should just by chance. Using some simple statistics derived from the bilingual corpus, namely

- $N(\tilde{f})$ the count of the source phrase $\tilde{f}$
- $N(\tilde{e})$ the count of the target phrase $\tilde{e}$
- $N(\tilde{f}, \tilde{e})$ the co-occurence count of the source phrase $\tilde{f}$ and the target phrase $\tilde{e}$
- N the number of sentences in the bilingual corpus

[3] Note that it has never been systematically investigated whether this is a real problem or just speculation.

we can compute the two-by-two contingency table in Table 1.

Following Fisher's exact test, we can calculate the probability of the contingency table via the hypergeometric distribution:

$$p_h(N(\tilde{f}, \tilde{e})) = \frac{\binom{N(\tilde{f})}{N(\tilde{f},\tilde{e})} \cdot \binom{N - N(\tilde{f})}{N(\tilde{e}) - N(\tilde{f},\tilde{e})}}{\binom{N}{N(\tilde{e})}} \quad (4)$$

The p-value is then calculated as the sum of all probabilities that are at least as extreme. The lower the p-value, the less likely this phrase pair occurred with the observed frequency by chance; we thus prune a phrase pair $(\tilde{f}, \tilde{e})$ if:

$$\left(\sum_{k=N(\tilde{f},\tilde{e})}^{\infty} p_h(k) \right) > \tau_F \quad (5)$$

for some pruning threshold τ_F. More details of this approach can be found in Johnson et al. (2007). The idea of using Fisher's exact test was first explored by Moore (2004) in the context of word alignment.

5 Entropy-based Pruning

In this section, we will derive a novel entropy-based pruning criterion.

5.1 Motivational Example

In general, pruning the phrase table can be considered as selecting a subset of the original phrase table. When doing so, we would like to alter the original translation model distribution as little as possible. This is a key difference to previous approaches: Our goal is to remove *redundant* phrases, whereas previous approaches usually try to remove low-quality or unreliable phrases. We believe this to be an advantage of our method as it is certainly easier to measure the redundancy of phrases than it is to estimate their quality.

In Table 2, we show some example phrases from the learned French-English WMT phrase table, along with their counts and probabilities. For the French phrase *le gouvernement français*, we have, among others, two translations: *the French government* and *the government of France*. If we have to prune one of those translations, we can ask ourselves: how would the translation cost change if the

$N(\tilde{f},\tilde{e})$	$N(\tilde{f})-N(\tilde{f},\tilde{e})$	$N(\tilde{f})$
$N(\tilde{e})-N(\tilde{f},\tilde{e})$	$N-N(\tilde{f})-N(\tilde{e})+N(\tilde{f},\tilde{e})$	$N-N(\tilde{f})$
$N(\tilde{e})$	$N-N(\tilde{e})$	N

Table 1: Two-by-two contingency table for a phrase pair $(\tilde{f},\tilde{e})$.

Source Phrase $\tilde{f}$	Target Phrase $\tilde{e}$	$N(\tilde{f},\tilde{e})$	$p(\tilde{e}\|\tilde{f})$
le	the	7.6 M	0.7189
gouvernement	government	245 K	0.4106
français	French	51 K	0.6440
	of France	695	0.0046
le gouvernement français	the French government	148	0.1686
	the government of France	11	0.0128

Table 2: Example phrases from the French-English phrase table (K=thousands, M=millions).

same translation were generated from the remaining, shorter, phrases? Removing the phrase *the government of France* would increase this cost dramatically. Given the shorter phrases from the table, the probability would be $0.7189 \cdot 0.4106 \cdot 0.0046 = 0.0014^*$, which is about an order of a magnitude smaller than the original probability of 0.0128.

On the other hand, composing the phrase *the French government* out of shorter phrases has probability $0.7189 \cdot 0.4106 \cdot 0.6440 = 0.1901$, which is very close to the original probability of 0.1686. This means it is safe to discard the phrase *the French government*, since the translation cost remains essentially unchanged. By contrast, discarding the phrase *the government of France* does not have this effect: it leads to a large change in translation cost.

Note that here the pruning criterion only considers redundancy of the phrases, not the quality. Thus, we are not saying that *the government of France* is a better translation than *the French government*, only that it is less redundant.

5.2 Entropy Criterion

Now, we are going to formalize the notion of redundancy. We would like the pruned model $p'(\tilde{e}|\tilde{f})$ to be as similar as possible to the original model $p(\tilde{e}|\tilde{f})$. We use conditional Kullback-Leibler divergence, also called conditional relative entropy (Cover and Thomas, 2006), to measure the model similarity:

$$D(p(\tilde{e}|\tilde{f})||p'(\tilde{e}|\tilde{f}))$$
$$= \sum_{\tilde{f}} p(\tilde{f}) \sum_{\tilde{e}} p(\tilde{e}|\tilde{f}) \log \left[\frac{p(\tilde{e}|\tilde{f})}{p'(\tilde{e}|\tilde{f})}\right] \quad (6)$$
$$= \sum_{\tilde{f},\tilde{e}} p(\tilde{e},\tilde{f}) \left[\log p(\tilde{e}|\tilde{f}) - \log p'(\tilde{e}|\tilde{f})\right] \quad (7)$$

Computing the best pruned model of a given size would require optimizing over all subsets with that size. Since that is computationally infeasible, we instead apply the equivalent approximation that Stolcke (1998) uses for language modeling. This assumes that phrase pairs affect the relative entropy roughly independently.

We can then choose a pruning threshold τ_E and prune those phrase pairs with a contribution to the relative entropy below that threshold. Thus, we

*We use the assumption that we can simply multiply the probabilities of the shorter phrases.

prune a phrase pair $(\tilde{f}, \tilde{e})$, if

$$p(\tilde{e}, \tilde{f}) \left[\log p(\tilde{e}|\tilde{f}) - \log p'(\tilde{e}|\tilde{f})\right] < \tau_E \quad (8)$$

We now address how to assign the probability $p'(\tilde{e}|\tilde{f})$ under the pruned model. A phrase-based system selects among different segmentations of the source language sentence into phrases. If a segmentation into longer phrases does not exist, the system has to compose a translation out of shorter phrases. Thus, if a phrase pair $(\tilde{f}, \tilde{e})$ is no longer available, the decoder has to use shorter phrases to produce the same translation. We can therefore decompose the pruned model score $p'(\tilde{e}|\tilde{f})$ by summing over all segmentations s_1^K and all reorderings π_1^K:

$$p'(\tilde{e}|\tilde{f}) = \sum_{s_1^K, \pi_1^K} p(s_1^K, \pi_1^K|\tilde{f}) \cdot p(\tilde{e}|s_1^K, \pi_1^K, \tilde{f}) \quad (9)$$

Here the segmentation s_1^K divides both the source and target phrases into K sub-phrases:

$$\tilde{f} = \bar{f}_{\pi_1} ... \bar{f}_{\pi_K} \text{ and } \tilde{e} = \bar{e}_1 ... \bar{e}_K \quad (10)$$

The permutation π_1^K describes the alignment of those sub-phrases, such that the sub-phrase $\bar{e}_k$ is aligned to $\bar{f}_{\pi_k}$. Using the normal phrase translation model, we obtain:

$$p'(\tilde{e}|\tilde{f}) = \sum_{s_1^K, \pi_1^K} p(s_1^K, \pi_1^K|\tilde{f}) \prod_{k=1}^{K} p(\bar{e}_k|\bar{f}_{\pi_k}) \quad (11)$$

Virtually all phrase-based decoders use the so-called maximum-approximation, i. e. the sum is replaced with the maximum. As we would like the pruning criterion to be similar to the search criterion used during decoding, we do the same and obtain:

$$p'(\tilde{e}|\tilde{f}) \approx \max_{s_1^K, \pi_1^K} \prod_{k=1}^{K} p(\bar{e}_k|\bar{f}_{\pi_k}) \quad (12)$$

Note that we also drop the segmentation probability, as this is not used at decoding time. This leaves the pruning criterion a function only of the model $p(\tilde{e}|\tilde{f})$ as stored in the phrase table. There is no need for a special development or adaptation set. We can determine the best segmentation using dynamic programming, similar to decoding with a phrase-based model. However, here the target side is constrained to the given phrase $\tilde{e}$.

It can happen that a phrase is not compositional, i. e., we cannot find a segmentation into shorter phrases. In these cases, we assign a small, constant probability:

$$p'(\tilde{e}|\tilde{f}) = p_c \quad (13)$$

We found that the value $p_c = e^{-10}$ works well for many language pairs.

5.3 Computation

In our experiments, it was more efficient to vary the pruning threshold τ_E without having to re-compute the entire phrase table. Therefore, we computed the entropy criterion in Equation (8) once for the whole phrase table. This introduces an approximation for the pruned model score $p'(\tilde{e}|\tilde{f})$. It might happen that we prune short phrases that were used as part of the best segmentation of longer phrases. As these shorter phrases should not be available, the pruned model score might be inaccurate. Although we believe this effect is minor, we leave a detailed experimental analysis for future work.

One way to avoid this approximation would be to perform entropy pruning with increasing phrase length. Starting with one-word phrases, which are trivially non-compositional, the entropy criterion would be straightforward to compute. Proceeding to two-word phrases, one would decompose the phrases into sub-phrases by looking up the probabilities of some of the unpruned one-word phrases. Once the set of unpruned two-word phrases was obtained, one would continue with three-word phrases, etc.

6 Experimental Evaluation

6.1 Data Sets

In this section, we describe the data sets used for the experiments. We perform experiments on the publicly available WMT shared translation task for the following four language pairs:

- German-English
- Czech-English
- Spanish-English

	Number of Words	
Language Pair	Foreign	English
German - English	42 M	45 M
Czech - English	56 M	65 M
Spanish - English	232 M	210 M
French - English	962 M	827 M

Table 3: Training data statistics. Number of words in the training data (M=millions).

- French-English

For each pair, we train two separate system, one for each direction. Thus it can happen that a phrase is pruned for X-to-Y, but not for Y-to-X.

These four language pairs represent a nice range of training corpora sizes, as shown in Table 3.

6.2 Baseline System

Pruning experiments were performed on top of the following baseline system. We used a phrase-based statistical machine translation system similar to (Zens et al., 2002; Koehn et al., 2003; Och and Ney, 2004; Zens and Ney, 2008). We trained a 4-gram language model on the target side of the bilingual corpora and a second 4-gram language model on the provided monolingual news data. All language models used Kneser-Ney smoothing.

The baseline system uses the common phrase translation models, such as $p(\tilde{e}|\tilde{f})$ and $p(\tilde{f}|\tilde{e})$, lexical models, word and phrase penalty, distortion penalty as well as a lexicalized reordering model (Zens and Ney, 2006).

The word alignment was trained with six iterations of IBM model 1 (Brown et al., 1993) and 6 iterations of the HMM alignment model (Vogel et al., 1996) using a symmetric lexicon (Zens et al., 2004).

The feature weights were tuned on a development set by applying minimum error rate training (MERT) under the Bleu criterion (Och, 2003; Macherey et al., 2008). We ran MERT once with the full phrase table and then kept the feature weights fixed, i. e., we did *not* rerun MERT after pruning to avoid adding unnecessary noise. We extract phrases up to a length of six words. The baseline system already includes phrase table pruning by removing singletons and keeping up to 30 target language phrases per source phrase. We found that this does not affect translation quality significantly[4]. All pruning experiments are done on top of this.

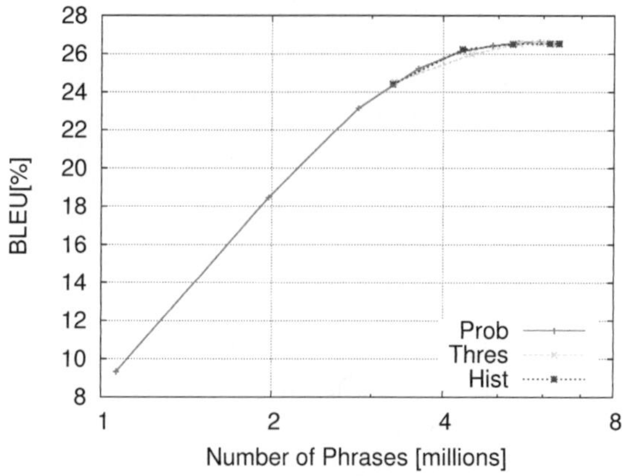

Figure 1: Comparison of probability-based pruning methods for German-English.

6.3 Results

In this section, we present the experimental results. Translation results are reported on the WMT'07 news commentary blind set.

We will show translation quality measured with the Bleu score (Papineni et al., 2002) as a function of the phrase table size (number of phrases). Being in the upper left corner of these figures is desirable.

First, we show a comparison of several probability-based pruning methods in Figure 1. We compare

- **Prob**. Absolute pruning based on Eq. (2).
- **Thres**. Threshold pruning based on Eq. (3).
- **Hist**. Histogram pruning as described in Section 3.2.[5]

We observe that these three methods perform equally well. There is no difference between absolute and relative pruning methods, except that the two relative methods (Thres and Hist) are limited by

[4]The Bleu score drops are as follows: English-French 0.3%, French-English 0.4%, Czech-English 0.3%, all other are less than 0.1%.

[5]Instead of using $p(\tilde{e}|\tilde{f})$ one could use the weighted model score including $p(\tilde{f}|\tilde{e})$, lexical weightings etc.; however, we found that this does not give significantly different results; but it does introduce a undesirable dependance between feature weights and phrase table pruning.

the number of source phrases. Thus, they reach a point where they cannot prune the phrase table any further. The results shown are for German-English; the results for the other languages are very similar. The results that follow use only the absolute pruning method as a representative for probability-based pruning.

In Figures 2 through 5, we show the translation quality as a function of the phrase table size. We vary the pruning thresholds to obtain different phrase table sizes. We compare four pruning methods:

- **Count**. Pruning based on the frequency of a phrase pair, c.f. Equation (1).
- **Prob**. Pruning based on the absolute probability of a phrase pair, c.f. Equation (2).
- **Fisher**. Pruning using significance tests, c.f. Equation (5).
- **Entropy**. Pruning using the novel entropy criterion, c.f. Equation (8).

Note that the x-axis of these figures is on a logarithmic scale, so the differences between the methods can be quite dramatic. For instance, entropy pruning requires less than a quarter of the number of phrases needed by count- or significance-based pruning to achieve a Spanish-English Bleu score of 34 (0.4 million phrases compared to 1.7 million phrases).

These results clearly show how the pruning methods compare:

1. Probability-based pruning performs poorly. It should be used only to prune small fractions of the phrase table.
2. Count-based pruning and significance-based pruning perform equally well. They are much better than probability-based pruning.
3. Entropy pruning consistently outperforms the other methods across translation directions and language pairs.

Figures 6 and 7 show compositionality statistics for the pruned Spanish-English phrase table (we observed similar results for the other language pairs).

Total number of phrases	4 137 M
Compositional	3 970 M
Non-compositional	167 M
of those: one-word phrases	85 M
no segmentation	82 M

Table 4: Statistics of phrase compositionality (M=millions).

Each figure shows the composition of the phrase table for a type of pruning for different phrase tables sizes. Along the x-axis, we plotted the phrase table size. These are the same phrase tables used to obtain the Bleu scores in Figure 2 (left). The different shades of grey correspond to different phrase lengths. For instance, in case of the smallest phrase table for count-based pruning, the 1-word phrases account for about 30% of all phrases, the 2-word phrases account for about 35% of all phrases, etc.

With the exception of the probability-based pruning, the plots look comparable. The more aggressive the pruning, the larger the percentage of short phrases. We observe that entropy-based pruning removes many more long phrases than any of the other methods. The plot for probability-based pruning is different in that the percentage of long phrases actually increases with more aggressive pruning (i. e. smaller phrase tables). A possible explanation is that probability-based pruning does *not* take the frequency of the source phrase into account. This difference might explain the poor performance of probability-based pruning.

To analyze how many phrases are compositional, we collect statistics during the computation of the entropy criterion. These are shown in Table 4, accumulated across all language pairs and all phrases, i. e., including singleton phrases. We see that 96% of all phrases are compositional (3 970 million out of 4 137 million phrases). Furthermore, out of the 167 million non-compositional phrases, more than half (85 million phrases), are trivially non-compositional: they consist only of a single source or target language word. The number of non-trivial non-compositional phrases is, with 82 million or 2% of the total number of phrases, very small.

In Figure 8, we show the effect of the constant

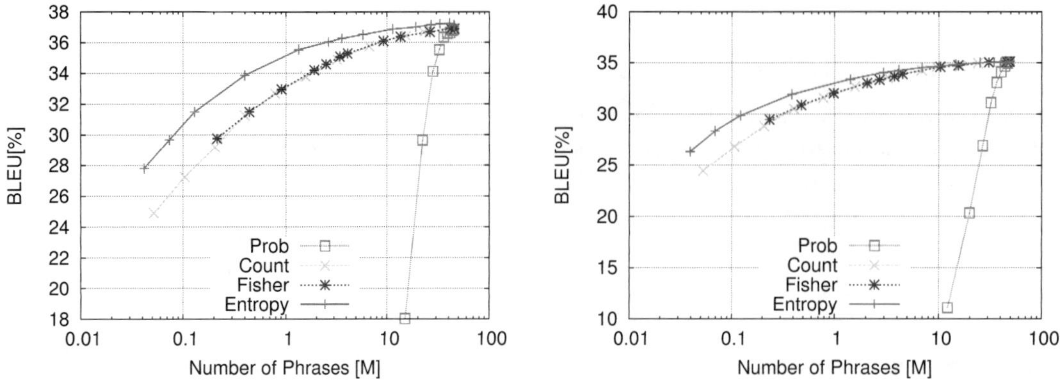

Figure 2: Translation quality as a function of the phrase table size for Spanish-English (left) and English-Spanish (right).

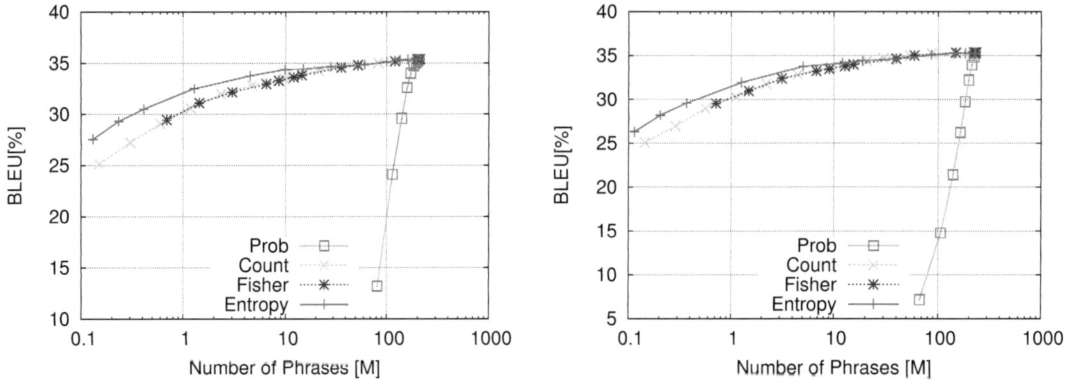

Figure 3: Translation quality as a function of the phrase table size for French-English (left) and English-French (right).

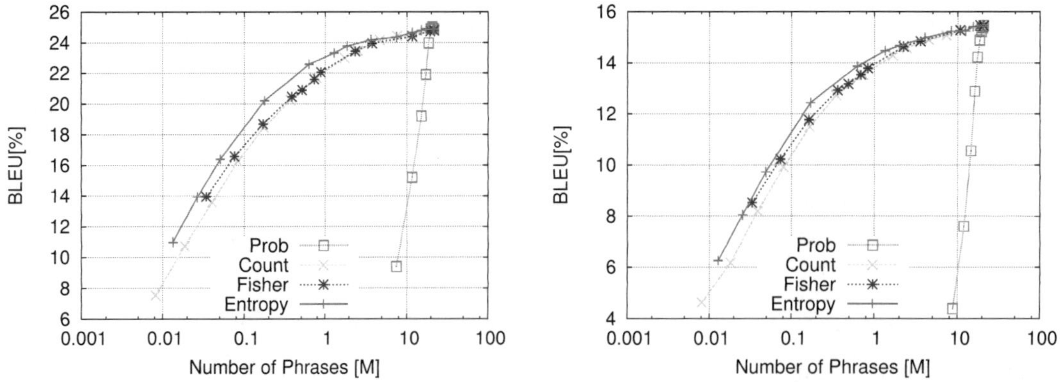

Figure 4: Translation quality as a function of the phrase table size for Czech-English (left) and English-Czech (right).

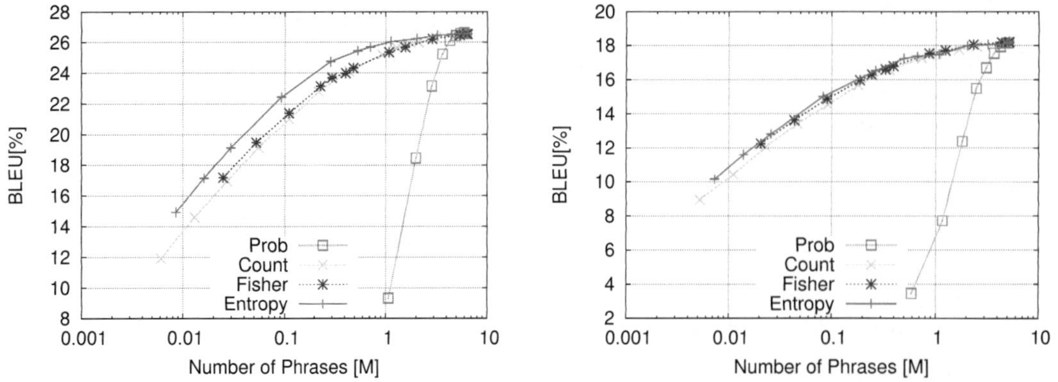

Figure 5: Translation quality as a function of the phrase table size for German-English (left) and English-German (right).

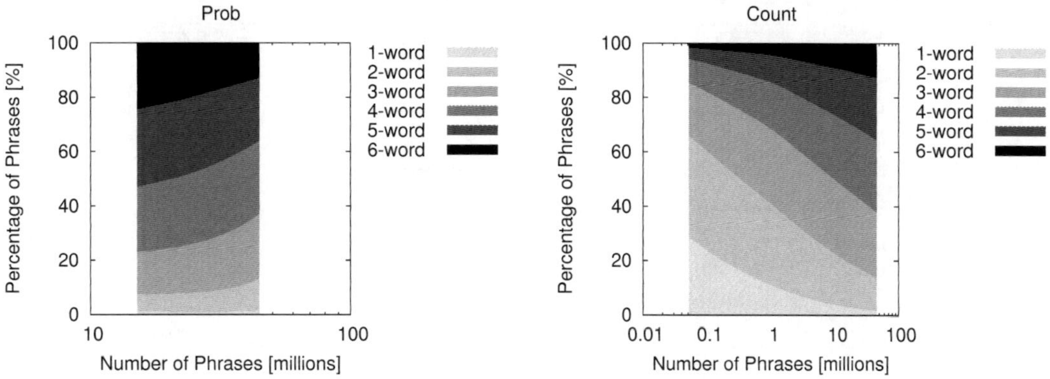

Figure 6: Phrase length statistics for Spanish-English for probability-based (left) and count-based pruning (right).

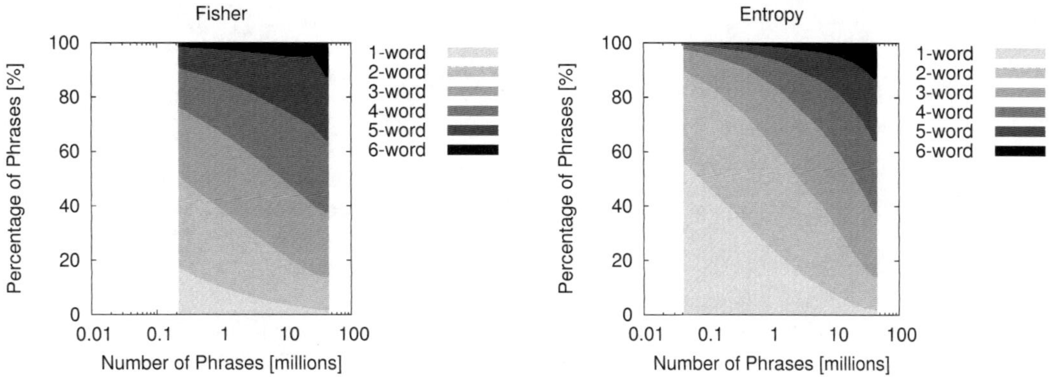

Figure 7: Phrase length statistics for Spanish-English for significance-based (left) and entropy-based pruning (right).

p_c for non-compositional phrases.[6] The results shown are for Spanish-English; additional experiments for the other languages and translation directions showed very similar results. Overall, there is no big difference between the values. Hence, we chose a value of 10 for all experiments.

The results in Figure 2 to Figure 5 show that entropy-based pruning clearly outperforms the alternative pruning methods. However, it is a bit hard to see from the graphs exactly how much additional savings it offers over other methods. In Table 5, we show how much of the phrase table we have to retain under various pruning criteria without losing more than one Bleu point in translation quality. We see that probability-based pruning allows only for marginal savings. Count-based and significance-based pruning results in larger savings between 70% and 90%, albeit with fairly high variability. Entropy-based pruning achieves consistently high savings between 85% and 95% of the phrase table. It always outperforms the other pruning methods and yields significant savings on top of count-based or significance-based pruning methods. Often, we can cut the required phrase table size in half compared to count or significance based pruning.

As a last experiment, we want to confirm that phrase-table pruning methods are actually better than simply reducing the maximum phrase length. In Figure 9, we show a comparison of different pruning methods and a length-based approach for Spanish-English. For the 'Length' curve, we first drop all 6-word phrases, then all 5-word phrases, etc. until we are left with only single-word phrases; the phrase length is measured as the number of source language words. We observe that entropy-based, count-based and significance-based pruning indeed outperform the length-based approach. We obtained similar results for the other languages.

[6]The values are in neg-log-space, i. e., a value of 10 corresponds to $p_c = e^{-10}$.

Method	ES-EN	EN-ES	DE-EN	EN-DE	FR-EN	EN-FR	CS-EN	EN-CS
Prob	77.3 %	82.7 %	61.2 %	67.3 %	84.8 %	94.1 %	85.6 %	86.3 %
Count	24.9 %	11.9 %	19.9 %	14.3 %	11.4 %	9.0 %	20.2 %	10.4 %
Fisher	23.5 %	12.6 %	21.7 %	14.0 %	14.5 %	13.6 %	31.9 %	9.9 %
Entropy	**7.2** %	**6.0** %	**10.2** %	**11.1** %	**7.1** %	**8.1** %	**14.8** %	**6.4** %

Table 5: To what degree can we prune the phrase table without losing more than 1 Bleu point? The table shows percentage of phrases that we have to retain. ES=Spanish, EN=English, FR=French, CS=Czech, DE=German.

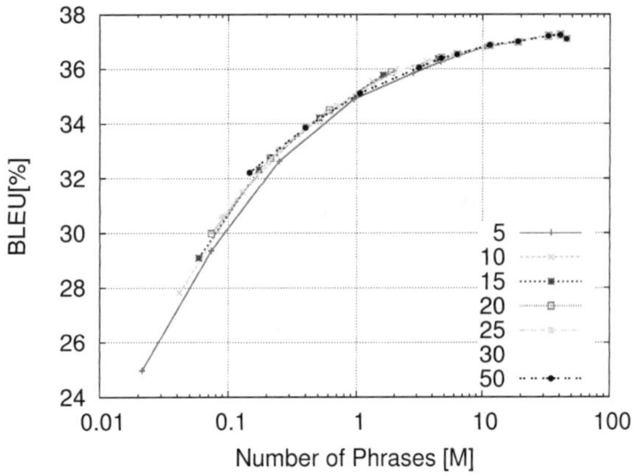

Figure 8: Translation quality (Bleu) as a function of the phrase table size for Spanish-English for entropy pruning with different constants p_c.

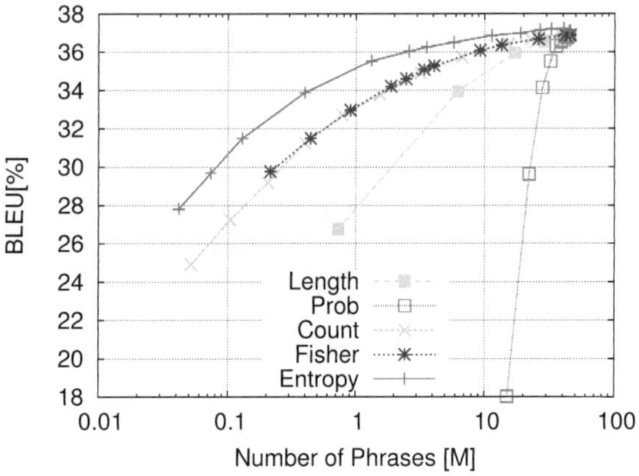

Figure 9: Translation quality (Bleu) as a function of the phrase table size for Spanish-English.

7 Conclusions

Phrase table pruning is often addressed in an ad-hoc way using the heuristics described in Section 3. We have shown that some of those do *not* work well. Choosing the wrong technique can result in significant drops in translation quality without saving much in terms of phrase table size. We introduced a novel entropy-based criterion and put phrase table pruning on a sound theoretical foundation. Furthermore, we performed a systematic experimental comparison of existing methods and the new entropy criterion. The experiments were carried out for four language pairs under small, medium and large data conditions. We can summarize our conclusions as follows:

- Probability-based pruning performs poorly when pruning large parts of the phrase table. This might be because it does not take the frequency of the source phrase into account.
- Count-based pruning performs as well as significance-based pruning.
- Entropy-based pruning gives significantly larger savings in phrase table size than any other pruning method.
- Compared to previous work, the novel entropy-based pruning often achieves the same Bleu score with only half the number of phrases.

8 Future Work

Currently, we take only the model $p(\tilde{e}|\tilde{f})$ into account when looking for the best segmentation. We might obtain a better estimate by also considering the distortion costs, which penalize reordering. We could also include other phrase models such as $p(\tilde{f}|\tilde{e})$ and the language model.

The entropy pruning criterion could be applied to hierarchical machine translation systems (Chiang, 2007). Here, we might observe even larger reductions in phrase table size as there are many more entries.

References

Thorsten Brants, Ashok C. Popat, Peng Xu, Franz J. Och, and Jeffrey Dean. 2007. Large language models in machine translation. In *Proceedings of the 2007 Joint Conference on Empirical Methods in Natural Language Processing and Computational Natural Language Learning (EMNLP-CoNLL)*, pages 858–867, Prague, Czech Republic, June. Association for Computational Linguistics.

Peter F. Brown, Stephen A. Della Pietra, Vincent J. Della Pietra, and Robert L. Mercer. 1993. The mathematics of statistical machine translation: Parameter estimation. *Computational Linguistics*, 19(2):263–311, June.

Yu Chen, Andreas Eisele, and Martin Kay. 2008. Improving statistical machine translation efficiency by triangulation. In *Proceedings of the Sixth International Conference on Language Resources and Evaluation (LREC'08)*, Marrakech, Morocco, May. European Language Resources Association (ELRA). http://www.lrec-conf.org/proceedings/lrec2008/.

Yu Chen, Martin Kay, and Andreas Eisele. 2009. Intersecting multilingual data for faster and better statistical translations. In *Proceedings of Human Language Technologies: The 2009 Annual Conference of the North American Chapter of the Association for Computational Linguistics*, pages 128–136, Boulder, Colorado, June. Association for Computational Linguistics.

David Chiang. 2007. Hierarchical phrase-based translation. *Computational Linguistics*, 33(2):201–228, June.

Thomas M. Cover and Joy A. Thomas. 2006. *Elements of information theory*. Wiley-Interscience, New York, NY, USA.

Nan Duan, Mu Li, and Ming Zhou. 2011. Improving phrase extraction via MBR phrase scoring and pruning. In *Proceedings of MT Summit XIII*, pages 189–197, Xiamen, China, September.

Matthias Eck, Stephan Vogel, and Alex Waibel. 2007a. Estimating phrase pair relevance for machine translation pruning. In *Proceedings of MT Summit XI*, pages 159–165, Copenhagen, Denmark, September.

Matthias Eck, Stephan Vogel, and Alex Waibel. 2007b. Translation model pruning via usage statistics for statistical machine translation. In *Human Language Technologies 2007: The Conference of the North American Chapter of the Association for Computational Linguistics; Companion Volume, Short Papers*, pages 21–24, Rochester, New York, April. Association for Computational Linguistics.

Kenneth Heafield. 2011. KenLM: Faster and smaller language model queries. In *Proceedings of the Sixth Workshop on Statistical Machine Translation*, pages 187–197, Edinburgh, Scotland, July. Association for Computational Linguistics.

Howard Johnson, Joel Martin, George Foster, and Roland Kuhn. 2007. Improving translation quality by discarding most of the phrasetable. In *Proceedings of the 2007 Joint Conference on Empirical Methods in Natural Language Processing and Computational Natural Language Learning (EMNLP-CoNLL)*, pages 967–975, Prague, Czech Republic, June. Association for Computational Linguistics.

Philipp Koehn, Franz Joseph Och, and Daniel Marcu. 2003. Statistical phrase-based translation. In *Human Language Technology Conf. / North American Chapter of the Assoc. for Computational Linguistics Annual Meeting (HLT-NAACL)*, pages 127–133, Edmonton, Canada, May/June.

Philipp Koehn, Hieu Hoang, Alexandra Birch, Chris Callison-Burch, Marcello Federico, Nicola Bertoldi, Brooke Cowan, Wade Shen, Christine Moran, Richard Zens, Chris Dyer, Ondřej Bojar, Alexandra Constantine, and Evan Herbst. 2007. Moses: Open source toolkit for statistical machine translation. In *45th Annual Meeting of the Assoc. for Computational Linguistics (ACL): Poster Session*, pages 177–180, Prague, Czech Republic, June.

Philipp Koehn. 2004. Pharaoh: a beam search decoder for phrase-based statistical machine translation models. In *6th Conf. of the Assoc. for Machine Translation in the Americas (AMTA)*, pages 115–124, Washington DC, September/October.

Wolfgang Macherey, Franz Och, Ignacio Thayer, and Jakob Uszkoreit. 2008. Lattice-based minimum error rate training for statistical machine translation. In *Proceedings of the 2008 Conference on Empirical Methods in Natural Language Processing*, pages 725–734, Honolulu, HI, October. Association for Computational Linguistics.

Robert C. Moore. 2004. On log-likelihood-ratios and the significance of rare events. In *Proceedings of the 2004 Conference on Empirical Methods in Natural Language Processing*, pages 333–340.

Franz Josef Och and Hermann Ney. 2004. The alignment template approach to statistical machine translation. *Computational Linguistics*, 30(4):417–449, December.

Franz Josef Och. 2003. Minimum error rate training in statistical machine translation. In *41st Annual Meeting of the Assoc. for Computational Linguistics (ACL)*, pages 160–167, Sapporo, Japan, July.

Kishore Papineni, Salim Roukos, Todd Ward, and Wei-Jing Zhu. 2002. Bleu: a method for automatic evaluation of machine translation. In *40th Annual Meeting of the Assoc. for Computational Linguistics (ACL)*, pages 311–318, Philadelphia, PA, July.

Adam Pauls and Dan Klein. 2011. Faster and smaller n-gram language models. In *Proceedings of the 49th Annual Meeting of the Association for Computational Linguistics: Human Language Technologies*, pages 258–267, Portland, Oregon, USA, June. Association for Computational Linguistics.

German Sanchis-Trilles, Daniel Ortiz-Martinez, Jesus Gonzalez-Rubio, Jorge Gonzalez, and Francisco Casacuberta. 2011. Bilingual segmentation for phrasetable pruning in statistical machine translation. In *Proceedings of the 15th Conference of the European Association for Machine Translation*, pages 257–264, Leuven, Belgium, May.

Andreas Stolcke. 1998. Entropy-based pruning of backoff language models. In *Proc. DARPA Broadcast News Transcription and Understanding Workshop*, pages 270–274.

David Talbot and Miles Osborne. 2007. Smoothed Bloom filter language models: Tera-scale LMs on the cheap. In *Proceedings of the 2007 Joint Conference on Empirical Methods in Natural Language Processing and Computational Natural Language Learning (EMNLP-CoNLL)*, pages 468–476, Prague, Czech Republic, June. Association for Computational Linguistics.

Nadi Tomeh, Nicola Cancedda, and Marc Dymetman. 2009. Complexity-based phrase-table filtering for statistical machine translation. In *Proceedings of MT Summit XII*, Ottawa, Ontario, Canada, August.

Nadi Tomeh, Marco Turchi, Guillaume Wisniewski, Alexandre Allauzen, and François Yvon. 2011. How good are your phrases? Assessing phrase quality with single class classification. In *Proceedings of the International Workshop on Spoken Language Translation*, pages 261–268, San Francisco, California, December.

Stephan Vogel, Hermann Ney, and Christoph Tillmann. 1996. HMM-based word alignment in statistical translation. In *16th Int. Conf. on Computational Linguistics (COLING)*, pages 836–841, Copenhagen, Denmark, August.

Mei Yang and Jing Zheng. 2009. Toward smaller, faster, and better hierarchical phrase-based SMT. In *Proceedings of the ACL-IJCNLP 2009 Conference Short Papers*, pages 237–240, Suntec, Singapore, August. Association for Computational Linguistics.

Richard Zens and Hermann Ney. 2006. Discriminative reordering models for statistical machine translation. In *Human Language Technology Conf. / North American Chapter of the Assoc. for Computational Linguistics Annual Meeting (HLT-NAACL): Workshop on Statistical Machine Translation*, pages 55–63, New York City, NY, June.

Richard Zens and Hermann Ney. 2008. Improvements in dynamic programming beam search for phrase-based statistical machine translation. In *Proceedings of the International Workshop on Spoken Language Translation*, pages 195–205, Honolulu, Hawaii, October.

Richard Zens, Franz Josef Och, and Hermann Ney. 2002. Phrase-based statistical machine translation. In M. Jarke, J. Koehler, and G. Lakemeyer, editors, *25th German Conf. on Artificial Intelligence (KI2002)*, volume 2479 of *Lecture Notes in Artificial Intelligence (LNAI)*, pages 18–32, Aachen, Germany, September. Springer Verlag.

Richard Zens, Evgeny Matusov, and Hermann Ney. 2004. Improved word alignment using a symmetric lexicon model. In *20th Int. Conf. on Computational Linguistics (COLING)*, pages 36–42, Geneva, Switzerland, August.

Probabilistic Finite State Machines for Regression-based MT Evaluation

Mengqiu Wang and **Christopher D. Manning**
Computer Science Department
Stanford University
Stanford, CA 94305 USA
{mengqiu,manning}@cs.stanford.edu

Abstract

Accurate and robust metrics for automatic evaluation are key to the development of statistical machine translation (MT) systems. We first introduce a new regression model that uses a probabilistic finite state machine (pFSM) to compute weighted edit distance as predictions of translation quality. We also propose a novel pushdown automaton extension of the pFSM model for modeling word swapping and cross alignments that cannot be captured by standard edit distance models. Our models can easily incorporate a rich set of linguistic features, and automatically learn their weights, eliminating the need for ad-hoc parameter tuning. Our methods achieve state-of-the-art correlation with human judgments on two different prediction tasks across a diverse set of standard evaluations (NIST OpenMT06,08; WMT06-08).

1 Introduction

Research in automatic machine translation (MT) evaluation metrics has been a key driving force behind the recent advances of statistical machine translation (SMT) systems. The early seminal work on automatic MT metrics (e.g., BLEU and NIST) is largely based on n-gram matches (Papineni et al., 2002; Doddington, 2002). Despite their simplicity, these measures have shown good correlation with human judgments, and enabled large-scale evaluations across many different MT systems, without incurring the huge labor cost of human evaluation (Callison-Burch et al. (2009; 2010; 2011), *inter alia*). Recent studies have also confirmed that tuning MT systems against better MT metrics — using algorithms like MERT (Och, 2003) — leads to better system performance (He and Way, 2009; Liu et al., 2011).

Later metrics that move beyond n-grams achieve higher accuracy and improved robustness from resources like WordNet synonyms (Miller et al., 1990), and paraphrasing (Snover et al., 2009; Denkowski and Lavie, 2010). But a common problem in these metrics is they typically resort to ad-hoc tuning methods instead of principled approaches to incorporate linguistic features. Recent models use linear or SVM regression and train them against human judgments to automatic learn feature weights, and have shown state-of-the-art correlation with human judgments (Kulesza and Shieber, 2004; Albrecht and Hwa, 2007a; Albrecht and Hwa, 2007b; Sun et al., 2008; Pado et al., 2009). The drawback, however, is they rely on time-consuming preprocessing modules to extract linguistic features (e.g., a full end-to-end textual entailment system was needed in Pado et al. (2009)), which severely limits their practical use. Furthermore, these models employ a large number of features (on the order of hundreds), and consequently make the model predictions opaque and hard to analyze.

In this paper, we propose a simple yet powerful probabilistic Finite State Machine (pFSM) for the task of MT evaluation. It is built on the backbone of weighted edit distance models, but learns to weight edit operations in a probabilistic regression framework. One of the major contributions of this paper is a novel extension of the pFSM model into a probabilistic Pushdown Automaton (pPDA), which enhances traditional edit-distance models with the ability to model phrase shift and word swapping. Furthermore, we give a new log-linear parameterization to the pFSM model, which allows it to easily incorporate rich linguistic features. We experiment with a set of simple features based on labeled head-modifier dependency structure, in order to test the hypothesis that modeling overall sentence structure can lead to more accurate evaluation measures.

We conducted extensive experiments on a diverse set of standard evaluation data sets (NIST OpenMT06, 08; WMT06, 07, 08). Our model achieves or surpasses state-of-the-art results on all test sets.

2 pFSMs for MT Regression

We start off by framing the problem of machine translation evaluation in terms of weighted edit distances calculated using probabilistic finite state machines (pFSMs). A FSM defines a language by accepting a string of input tokens in the language, and rejecting those that are not. A probabilistic FSM defines the probability that a string is in a language, extending on the concept of a FSM. Commonly used models such as HMMs, *n*-gram models, Markov Chains and probabilistic finite state transducers all fall in the broad family of pFSMs (Knight and Al-Onaizan, 1998; Eisner, 2002; Kumar and Byrne, 2003; Vidal et al., 2005). Unlike all the other applications of FSMs where tokens in the language are words, in our language tokens are edit operations. A string of tokens that our pFSM accepts is an edit sequence that transforms a reference translation (denoted as *ref*) into a system translation (*sys*).

Our pFSM has a unique start and stop state, and one state per edit operation (i.e., *Insert*, *Delete*, *Substitution*). The probability of an edit sequence $\mathbf{e}$ is generated by the model is the product of the state transition probabilities in the pFSM, formally described as:

$$w(\mathbf{e} \mid \mathbf{s}, \mathbf{r}) = \frac{\prod_{k=1}^{|\mathbf{e}|} \exp \theta \cdot \mathbf{f}(e_{k-1}, e_k, \mathbf{s}, \mathbf{r})}{Z} \qquad (1)$$

We featurize each of the state changes with a log-linear parameterization; $\mathbf{f}$ is a set of binary feature functions defined over pairs of neighboring states (by the Markov assumption) and the input sentences, and θ are the associated feature weights; r and s are shorthand for *ref* and *sys*; Z is a partition function. In this basic pFSM model, the feature functions are simply identity functions that emit the current state, and the state transition sequence of the previous state and the current state.

The feature weights are then automatically learned by training a global regression model where some translational equivalence judgment score (e.g., human assessment score, or HTER (Snover et al., 2006)) for each *sys* and *ref* translation pair is the regression target ($\hat{y}$). We introduce a new regression variable $y \in \mathbb{R}$ which is the log-sum of the unnormalized weights (Eqn. (1)) of all edit sequences, formally expressed as:

$$y = \log \sum_{\mathbf{e}' \subseteq \mathbf{e}^*} \prod_{k=1}^{|\mathbf{e}'|} \exp \theta \cdot \mathbf{f}(e_{k-1}, e_k, \mathbf{s}, \mathbf{r}) \qquad (2)$$

$\mathbf{e}^*$ denotes a valid edit sequence. Since the "gold" edit sequence are not given at training or prediction time, we treat the edit sequences as hidden variables and sum them out. The sum over an exponential number of edit sequences in $\mathbf{e}^*$ is solved efficiently using a forward-backward style dynamic program. Any edit sequence that does not lead to a complete transformation of the translation pair has a probability of zero in our model. Our regression target then seeks to minimize the least squares error with respect to $\hat{y}$, plus a $L2$-norm regularizer term parameterized by λ:

$$\theta^* = \min_{\theta} \{ \sum_{\mathbf{s_i}, \mathbf{r_i}} [\hat{y}_i - (\frac{y_i}{|\mathbf{s_i}| + |\mathbf{r_i}|} + \alpha)]^2 + \lambda \|\theta\|^2 \} \qquad (3)$$

The $|\mathbf{s_i}| + |\mathbf{r_i}|$ is a length normalization term for the ith training instance, and α is a scaling constant for adjusting to different scoring standards (e.g., 7-point scale vs. 5-point scale), whose value is automatically learned. At test time, $y/(|\mathbf{s}| + |\mathbf{r}|) + \alpha$ is computed as the predicted score.

We replaced the standard substitution edit operation with three new operations: S_{word} for same word substitution, S_{lemma} for same lemma substitution, and S_{punc} for same punctuation substitution. In other words, all but the three matching-based substitutions are disallowed. The start state can transition into any of the edit states with a constant unit cost, and each edit state can transition into any other edit state if and only if the edit operation involved is valid at the current edit position (e.g., the model cannot transition into *Delete* state if it is already at the end of *ref*; similarly it cannot transition into S_{lemma} unless the

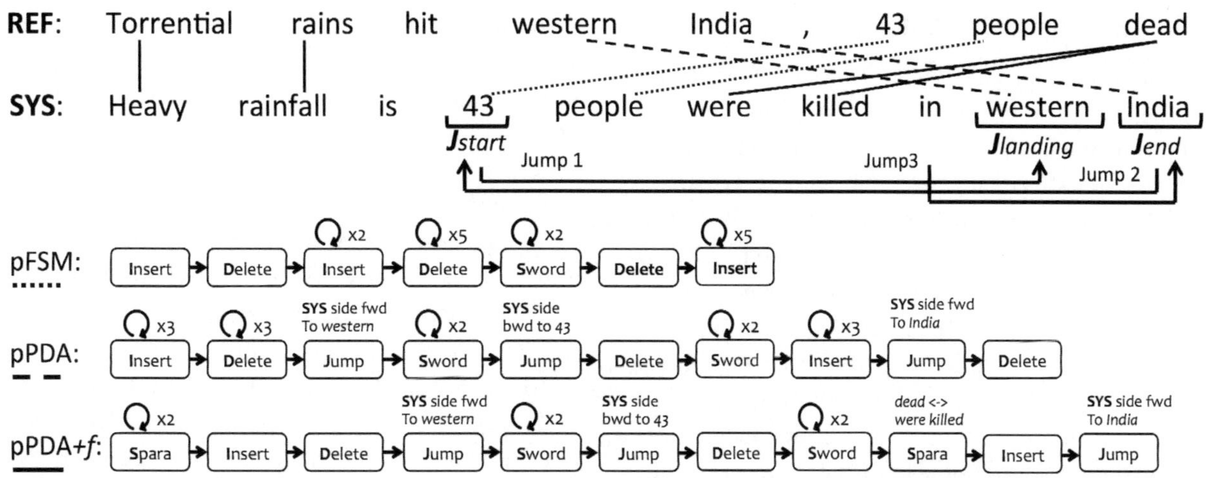

Figure 1: This diagram illustrates an example translation pair in the Chinese-English portion of OpenMT08 data set (Doc:AFP_CMN_20070703.0005, system09, sent 1). The three rows below are the best state transition sequences according to the three proposed models. The corresponding alignments generated by the models (pFSM, pPDA, pPDA+f) are shown with different styled lines, with later models in the order generating strictly more alignments than earlier ones. The gold human evaluation score is 6.5 (on a 7-point scale), and model predictions are: pPDA+f 5.5, pPDA 4.3, pFSM 3.1, METEORR 3.2, TERR 2.8.

lemma of the two words under edit in *sys* and *ref* match). When the end of both sentences are reached, the model transitions into the stop state and ends the edit sequence. The first row in Figure 1 starting with pFSM shows a state transition sequence for an example *sys*/*ref* translation pair. [1] There exists a one-to-one correspondence between substitution edits and word alignments. Therefore this example state transition sequence correctly generates an alignment for the word *43* and *people*.

It is helpful to compare with the TER metric (Snover et al., 2006), which is based on the idea of word error rate measured in terms of edit distance, to better understand the intuition behind our model. There are two major improvements in our model: 1) the edit operations in our model are weighted, as defined by the feature functions and weights; 2) the weights are automatically learned, instead of being uniform or manually set; and 3) we model state transitions, which can be understood as a bigram extension of the unigram edit distance model used in TER. For example, if in our learned model the feature for two consecutive S_{word} states has a positive weight, then our model would favor consecutive same word substitutions, whereas in the TER model the order of the substitution does not matter. The extended TER-plus (Snover et al., 2009) metric addresses the first problem but not the other two.

2.1 Soft-max Interpretation

There is also an alternative interpretation of the model as a simple soft-max approximation that is very intuitive and easy to understand. For ease of illustration, we introduce a quantity $Q(\mathbf{e} \mid \mathbf{s},\mathbf{r})$ to be the *score* of an edit sequence, defined simply as the sum of the dot product of feature values and feature weights:

$$Q(\mathbf{e} \mid \mathbf{s},\mathbf{r}) = \sum_{i=1}^{|\mathbf{e}|} \theta \cdot \mathbf{f}(e_{i-1}, e_i, \mathbf{s}, \mathbf{r})$$

For the regression task, the intuition is that we want y to take on the score (Q) of the **best** edit sequence:

$$y = \max_{\mathbf{e} \subseteq \mathbf{e}^*} Q(\mathbf{e} \mid \mathbf{s},\mathbf{r})$$

But since the *max* function is non-differentiable, we replace it with a *softmax*:

$$y = \underbrace{\log \sum_{\mathbf{e} \subseteq \mathbf{e}^*} \exp}_{softmax} Q(\mathbf{e} \mid \mathbf{s},\mathbf{r})$$

Substituting in Q, we arrive at the same objective function as (2).

[1] It is safe to ignore the second and third row in Figure 1 for now, their explanations are forthcoming in Section 2.2.

2.2 Restricted pPDA Extension

A shortcoming of edit distance models is that they cannot handle long-distance word swapping — a pervasive phenomenon found in most natural languages. [2] Edit operations in standard edit distance models need to obey strict incremental order in their edit position, in order to admit efficient dynamic programming solutions. The same limitation is shared by our pFSM model, where the Markov assumption is made based on the incremental order of edit positions. Although there is no known solution to the general problem of computing edit distance where long-distance swapping is permitted (Dombb et al., 2010), approximate algorithms do exist. We present a simple but novel extension of the pFSM model to a restricted probabilistic pushdown automaton (pPDA), to capture non-nested word swapping within limited distance, which covers a majority of word swapping in observed in real data (Wu, 2010).

A pPDA, in its simplest form, is a pFSM where each control state is equipped with a stack (Esparza and Kucera, 2005). The addition of stacks for each transition state endows the machine with memory, extending its expressiveness beyond that of context-free formalisms. By construction, at any stage in a normal edit sequence, the pPDA model can "jump" forward within a fixed distance (controlled by a max distance parameter) to a new edit position on either side of the sentence pair, and start a new edit subsequence from there. Assuming the jump was made on the *sys* side, [3] the machine remembers its current edit position in *sys* as J_{start}, and the destination position on *sys* after the jump as $J_{landing}$.

We constrain our model so that the only edit operations that are allowed immediately following a "jump" are from the set of substitution operations (e.g., S_{word}). And after at least one substitution has been made, the device can now "jump" back to J_{start}, remembering the current edit position as J_{end}. Another constraint here is that after the backward "jump", all edit operations are permitted except for *Insert*, which cannot take place until at least one substitution has been made. When the edit sequence advances to position $J_{landing}$, the only operation allowed at that point is another "jump" forward operation to position J_{end}, at which point we also clear all memory about jump positions and reset.

An intuitive explanation is that when pPDA makes the first forward jump, a gap is left in *sys* that has not been edited yet. It remembers where it left off, and comes back to it after some substitutions have been made to complete the edit sequence. The second row in Figure 1 (starting with pPDA) illustrates an edit sequence in a pPDA model that involves three "jump" operations, which are annotated and indexed by number 1-3 in the example. "Jump 1" creates an un-edited gap between word *43* and *western*, after two substitutions, the model makes "jump 2" to go back and edit the gap. The only edit permitted immediately after "jump 2" is deleting the comma in *ref*, since inserting the word *43* in *sys* before any substitution is disallowed. Once the gap is completed, the model resumes at position J_{end} by making "jump 3", and completes the jump sequence. The "jumps" allowed the model to align words such as *western India*, in addition to the alignments of *43 people* found by the pFSM.

In a general pPDA model without the limited distance and non-nestedness jump constraints, there could be recursive jump structures, which violates the finite state property that we are looking for. The constraints we introduced upper-bounds possible reordering, and the resulting model is finite state. In practice, we found that our extension gives a big boost to model performance (*cf.* Section 4.1), with only a modest increase in computation time. [4]

2.3 Parameter Estimation

Since the least squares operator preserves convexity, and the inner log-sum-exponential function is convex, the resulting objective function is also convex. For parameter learning, we used the limited memory quasi-newton method (Liu and Nocedal, 1989) to find the optimal feature weights and scaling constant for the objective. We initialized $\theta = \vec{0}$, $\alpha = 0$, and $\lambda = 5$. We also threw away features occurring fewer than five times in training corpus. Two variants of the

[2]The edit distance algorithm described in Cormen et al. (2001) can only handle adjacent word swapping (transposition), but not long-distance swapping.

[3]Recall that we transform *ref* into *sys*, and thus on the *sys* side, we can only insert but not delete. The argument applies equally to the case where the jump was made on the other side.

[4]The length of the longest edit sequence with jumps only increased by $0.5 * max(|\mathbf{s}|, |\mathbf{r}|)$ in the worst case, and on the whole swapping is rare in comparison to basic edits.

forward-backward style dynamic programming algorithm were used for computing gradients in the pFSM and pPDA models, similar to other sequence models such as HMMs and CRFs. Details are omitted here for brevity.

3 Rich Linguistic Features

In this section we will add new substitution operations beyond those introduced in Section 2, to capture various linguistic phenomena. These new substitution operations correspond to new transition states in the pPDA.

3.1 Synonyms

Our first set of features matches words that have synonym relations according to WordNet (Miller et al., 1990). Synonyms have been found to be very useful in METEOR and TERplus, and can be easily built into our model as a new substitution operation S_{syn}.

3.2 Paraphrasing

Newer versions of METEOR and TERplus both found that inclusion of phrase-based matching greatly improves model robustness and accuracy (Denkowski and Lavie, 2010; Snover et al., 2009). We add a substitution operator (S_{para}) that matches words that are paraphrases. To better take advantage of paraphrase information at the multi-word phrase level, we extended our substitution operations to match longer phrases by adding one-to-many and many-to-many n-gram block substitutions. In preliminary experiments, we found that most of the gain came from unigrams and bigrams, with little to no additional gains from trigrams. Therefore, we limited our experiments to bigram pFSM and pPDA models, and pruned the paraphrase table adopted from TERplus [5] to unigrams and bigrams, resulting in 2.5 million paraphrase pairs.

3.3 Sentence Structure

A problem that remains largely unaddressed by most popular MT evaluation metrics is the overall goodness of the translated sentence's structure (Liu et al., 2005; Owczarzak et al., 2008). Translations with good local n-gram coverage but horrible global syntactic ordering are not unusual in SMT outputs. Such translations usually score well with existing metrics but poorly among human evaluators.

In our model, when we detect consecutive bigram substitutions in the state transition, we examine the head-modifier dependency between the two words on each side of the sentence pair. A feature is triggered if and only if there is a head-modifier relation between the two words on each side, the labeled dependency on the two sides match, and it is one of subject, object or predicative relations. We deliberately left out features that model mismatches of dependency labels, because we found parsing output from translations to be usually very poor. Since parsing results are generally more reliable for more fluent translations, our hope is that by only modeling parse matches, our model will be able to pick them up as positive signals, indicating good translation quality.

4 Experiments

The goal of our experiments is to test both the accuracy and robustness of the proposed new models. We then show that modeling word swapping and rich linguistics features further improve our results.

To better situate our work among past research and to draw meaningful comparison, we use exactly the same standard evaluation data sets and metrics as Pado et al. (2009), which is currently the state-of-the-art result for regression-based MT evaluation. We consider four widely used MT metrics (BLEU, NIST, METEOR (v0.7), and TER) as our baselines. Since our models are trained to regress human evaluation scores, to make a direct comparison in the same regression setting, we also train a small linear regression model for each baseline metric in the same way as described in Pado et al. (2009). These regression models are strictly more powerful than the baseline metrics and show higher robustness and better correlation with human judgments. [6] We also compare our models with the state-of-the-art linear regression models reported in Pado et al. (2009) that

[5] Available from www.umiacs.umd.edu/~snover/terp.

[6] The baseline metric (e.g., BLEU) computes its raw score by taking the geometric mean of n-gram precision scores ($1 \leq n \leq 4$) scaled by a brevity penalty. The regression model learns to combine these fine-grained scores more intelligently, by optimizing their weights to regress human judgments. See Pado et al. (2009) for more discussion.

combine features from multiple MT evaluation metrics (MT), as well as rich linguistic features from a textual entailment system (RTE).

In all of our experiments, each reference and system translation sentence pair is tokenized using the Penn Treebank (Marcus et al., 1993) tokenization script, and lemmatized by the Porter Stemmer (Porter, 1980). For the overall sentence structure experiment, translations are additionally part-of-speech tagged with MXPOST tagger (Ratnaparkhi, 1996), and parsed with MSTParser (McDonald et al., 2005) [7] labeled dependency parser. Statistical significance tests are performed using the paired bootstrap resampling method (Koehn, 2004).

We divide our experiments into two sections, based on two different prediction tasks — predicting absolute scores and predicting pairwise preference.

4.1 Exp. 1: Predicting Absolute Scores

The first task is to evaluate a system translation on a seven point Likert scale against a single reference. Higher scores indicate translations that are closer to the meaning intended by the reference. Human ratings in the form of absolute scores are available for standard evaluation data sets such as NIST OpenMT06,08.[8] Since our model makes predictions at the granularity of a whole sentence, we focus on sentence-level evaluation. A metric's goodness is judged by how well it correlates with human judgments, and Spearman's rank correlation (ρ) is reported for all experiments in this section.

We used the NIST OpenMT06 corpus for development purposes, and reserved the NIST OpenMT08 corpus for post-development evaluation. The OpenMT06 data set contains 1,992 English translations of Arabic newswire text from 8 MT systems. For development, we used a 2-fold cross-validation scheme with splits at the first 1,000 and last 992 sentences. The OpenMT08 data set contains English translations of newswire text from three languages (Arabic has 2,769 pairs from 13 MT systems; Chinese has 1,815 pairs from 15; and Urdu has 1,519 pairs, from 7). We followed the same experimental setup as Pado et al. (2009), using a "round robin" training/testing scheme, i.e., we train a model on data from two languages, making predictions for the third. We also show results of models trained on the entire OpenMT08 data set and tested on OpenMT06.

4.1.1 pFSM vs. pPDA

Data Set		pFSM		pPDA			
tr	*te*	*n*1	*n*2	*j*1	*j*2	*j*5	*j*10
A+C	U	54.6	54.8	**55.6**	55.0	55.3	55.3
A+U	C	59.9	59.8	58.0	61.4	63.8	**64.0**
C+U	A	**61.2**	**61.2**	60.2	59.9	60.4	60.2

Table 1: pFSM vs. pPDA results for the round-robin approach on OpenMT08 data set over three languages (A=Arabic, C=Chinese, U=Urdu). Numbers in this table are Spearman's ρ for correlation between human assessment scores and model predictions; *tr* stands for training set, and *te* stands for test set. *nx* means the model has *x*-gram block edits. *jy* means the model has jump distance limit *y*. The Best result for each test set row is highlighted in bold.

The second and third columns under the pFSM label in Table 1 compares our bigram block edit extension for the pFSM model. Although we do not yet see a significant performance gain (or loss) from adding block edits, they will enable longer paraphrase matches in later experiments.

Columns 5 through 8 in Table 1 show experimental results validating the contribution of our pPDA extension to the pFSM model (*cf.* Section 2.2). We can see that the pPDA extension gave modest improvements on the Urdu test set, but at a small decrease in performance on the Arabic data. However, for Chinese, there is a substantial gain, particularly with jump distances of five or longer. This trend is even more pronounced at the long jump distance of 10, consistent with the observation that Chinese-English translations exhibit much more medium and long distance reordering than languages like Arabic (Birch et al., 2009).

4.1.2 Evaluating Linguistic Features

Experimental results evaluating the benefits of each linguistic feature set are presented in Table 3. The first row is the pPDA model with jump distance limit 5, without other additional features. The next three rows are the results of adding each of the three feature sets described in Section 3.

Overall, we observed that only paraphrase matching features gave a significant boost to performance.

[7] Trained on the entire Penn Treebank.

[8] Available from `http://www.nist.gov`.

Data Set		Our Metrics			Baseline Metrics					Combined Metrics	
train	test	pFSM	pPDA	pPDA+*f*	BLEUR	NISTR	TERR	METR	MTR	RTER	MT+RTER
A+C	U	54.6	55.3	**57.2**	49.9	49.5	50.1	49.1	50.1	54.5	55.6
A+U	C	59.9	63.8	**65.8**	53.9	53.1	50.3	61.1	57.3	58.0	62.7
C+U	A	**61.2**	60.4	59.8	52.5	50.4	54.5	60.1	55.2	59.9	**61.1**
MT08	MT06	**65.2**	63.4	64.5	57.6	55.1	63.8	62.1	62.6	62.2	**65.2**

Table 2: Overall Comparison: Results from OpenMT08 and OpenMT06 evaluation data sets. The R (as in BLEUR) refers to the regression model trained for each baseline metric, same as Pado et al. (2009). The first three rows are round-robin train/test results over three languages on OpenMT08 (A=Arabic, C=Chinese, U=Urdu). The last row are results trained on entire OpenMT08 (A+C+U) and tested on OpenMT06. Numbers in this table are Spearman's rank correlation ρ between human assessment scores and model predictions. The pPDA column describes our pPDA model with jump distance limit 5. METR is shorthand for METEORR. +*f* means the model includes synonyms, paraphrase and parsing features (*cf.* Section 3). Best results and scores that are not statistically significantly worse are highlighted in bold in each row.

	Urdu	Chinese	Arabic
pPDA	55.3	63.8	60.4
+Synonym	55.6	63.7	**60.7**
+Tree	55.3	63.8	60.3
+Paraphrase	57.1	65.4	60.0
+Syn+Tree+Para	**57.2**	**65.8**	59.8

Table 3: Results for OpenMT08 with linguistic features, using the same round robin scheme as in Table 1. Numbers in this table are Spearman's rank correlation ρ between human assessment scores and model predictions. Best results on each test set are highlighted in bold.

The row starting with pPDA+*f* in Figure 1 shows an example where adding paraphrase features allow pPDA+*f* to find more correct alignments and make better predictions than pPDA.

No significant improvements from synonym and dependency tree matching features are evident from the results. An examination of the feature statistics in training data showed that the parse tree features have very low occurrence counts. On the Chinese+Urdu training set, for example, the features for subject, object and predicative labeled dependency matches fired only 55, 784 and 13 times, respectively. As a reference point for the scale of feature counts, the "same word" match feature fired 875,375 times on the same data set. And our qualitative assessment of the labeled dependency parser outputs was that the quality is very poor on system translations. For future work, more elaborate parse feature engineering could be a promising direction, but is outside the scope of our study.

In combination, the joint feature set of synonym, paraphrase and parse tree features gave modest improvements over the paraphrase feature alone on the Chinese test set.

4.1.3 Overall Comparison

Results of our proposed models compared against the baseline models described in Pado et al. (2009) are shown in Table 2. The pPDA+*f* model has access to paraphrase information, which is not available to the baselines, so it should not be directly compared with. But the pFSM and pPDA models do not use any additional information other than words and lemmas, and thus make a fair comparison with the baseline metrics. [9] We can see from the table that pFSM significantly outperforms all baselines on Urdu and Arabic, but trails behind METEORR on Chinese by a small margin (1.2 point in Spearman's ρ). On Chinese data set, the pPDA extension gives results significantly better than the best baseline metrics for Chinese (2.7 better than METEORR). Both the pFSM and pPDA models also significantly outperform the MTR linear regression model that combines the outputs of all four baselines, on all three source languages. This demonstrates that our regression model is more robust and accurate than a state-of-the-art system combination linear-regression model. Both pFSM and pPDA learned to assign a lower negative feature weight for deletion than insertion (i.e., it is bad to insert an unseen word into system trans-

[9] METEORR actually has an unfair advantage in this comparison, since it uses synonym information from WordNet; TERR on the other hand has a disadvantage because it does not use lemmas. Lemma is added later in the TERplus extension (Snover et al., 2009).

lation, but worse if words from reference translation are deleted), which corresponds to the setting in METEOR where recall is given more importance than precision (Banerjee and Lavie, 2005).

The RTER and MT+RTER linear regression models benefit from the rich linguistic features in the textual entailment system's output. It has access to all the features in pPDA+*f* such as paraphrase and dependency parse relations, and many more (e.g., Norm Bank, part-of-speech, negation, antonyms). However, our pPDA+*f* model rivals the performance of RTER and MT+RTER on Arabic (with no statistically significant difference from RTER), and greatly improve over these two models on Urdu and Chinese. Most noticeably, pPDA+*f* is 7.7 points better than RTER on Chinese.

Consistent with our earlier observation on OpenMT08 data set that the pPDA model performs slightly worse than the pFSM model on Arabic, the same performance decrease is seen in OpenMT06 data set, which is also Arabic-to-English.

As shown earlier in Table 3, the combined set of paraphrase, parsing and synonym features in pPDA+*f* helps for Urdu and Chinese, but not for Arabic. Here we found that even though the pPDA+*f* model is still worse than pFSM on OpenMT06 tests, it did give a decent improvement to pPDA model, closing up the gap with pFSM.

Other than robustness and accuracy, simplicity is also an important trait we seek in good MT metrics. Our models only have a few tens of features (instead of hundreds of features as found in RTER and MT+RTER), which makes interpretation of the model's prediction relatively easy. On an important practical note, our model is much more lightweight than the RTER or MTR system. It runs at a much faster speed with a smaller memory footprint, hence potentially useable in MERT training.

4.2 Exp. 2: Predicting Pairwise Preferences

To further test our model's robustness, we evaluate it on WMT data sets with a different prediction task in which metrics make pairwise preference judgments between translation systems. The WMT06-08 data sets are much larger in comparison to the OpenMT06 and 08 data. They contain MT outputs of over 40 systems from five different source languages (French, German, Spanish, Czech, and Hungarian). The WMT06, 07 and 08 sets contains 10,159, 5,472 and 6,856 sentence pairs, respectively. We used portions of WMT 06 and 07 data sets [10] that are annotated with absolute scores on a five point scale for training, and the WMT08 data set annotated with pairwise preference for testing.

To generate pairwise preference predictions, we first predict an absolute score for each system translation, then compare the scores between each system pair, and give preference to the higher score. We adopt the sentence-level evaluation metric used in Pado et al. (2009), which measures the consistency (accuracy) of metric predictions with human preferences. The random baseline for this task on WMT08 data set is 39.8%. [11]

Models	WMT06	WMT07	WMT06+07
pPDA+*f*	51.6	**52.4**	52.0
BLEUR	49.7	49.5	49.6
METEORR	51.4	51.4	51.5
NISTR	50.0	50.3	50.2
TERR	50.9	51.0	51.2
MTR	50.8	51.5	51.5
RTER	51.8	50.7	51.9
MT+RTER	**52.3**	51.8	**52.5**

Table 4: Pairwise preference prediction results on WMT08 test set. Each column shows a different training data set. Numbers in this table are model's consistency with human pairwise preference judgments. Best result on each test set is highlighted in bold.

Results are shown in Table 4. Similar to the results on OpenMT experiments, our model consistently outperformed BLEUR, METEORR, NISTR and TERR. Our model also gives better performance than the MTR ensemble model on all three tests; and ties with RTER in two out of the three tests but performs significantly better on the other test. The MT+RTER ensemble model is better on two tests, but worse on the other. But overall the two systems are quite comparable, with less than 0.6% accuracy difference. The results also show that our method is stable across different training sets, with test accuracy differences less than 0.4%.

[10] Available from `http://www.statmt.org`.

[11] The random baseline is not 50% for two reasons: (1) human judgments include contradictory and tie annotations; (2) transitivity constraints need to be respected in total ordering. For details, see Pado et al. (2009).

4.3 Qualitative Analysis

Example (1) shows a system and reference translation pair in the Chinese test portion of OpenMT08.

(1) **REF:** Two Jordanese sentenced_1 for plotting_2 an attack_3 on Americans_4
SYS: The name of Jordan plotting_2 attacks_3 Americans_4 were sentenced_1 to death

Human annotators give this example a score of 4.0, but TERR and METEORR both assigned erroneously low scores (1.0 and 2.2, respectively). Words with the same subscript index were aligned by pPDA model. This example exhibits a word swapping phenomenon, and our model was able to capture it correctly. TERR clearly suffered from not being able to model word swapping in this case. It also missed out the word pair *attack* and *attacks* due to the lack of lemma support. The reason why METEORR assigned such a low score for this example is because none of the matched words in the reference were adjacent to each other, causing a high fragmentation penalty. The fragmentation penalty term has two parameters that need to be manually tuned, and has a high variance across examples and data sets. This example illustrates models that require ad-hoc tuning tend not to be robust. Our pPDA model (without linguistic feature) was able to make a prediction of 3.7, much closer to human judgment.

4.4 MetricsMATR10 and WMT12 Results

An earlier version of the pFSM model that was trained on the OpenMT08 data set was submitted to the single reference sentence level track at MetricsMATR10 (Peterson and Przybocki, 2010) NIST evaluation. Even though our system was not in the most ideal state at the time of the evaluation, [12] and was trained on a small amount of data, the pFSM model still performed competitively against other metrics. Noticeably, we achieved second best results for Human-targeted Translation Edit Rate (HTER) assessment, trailing behind TERplus with no statistically significant difference. On average, our system made 5th place among 15 different sites and 7th place among 25 different metrics, averaged across 9 assessment types.

[12] Unfortunately the version we submitted in 2010 was plagued with a critical bug. More general enhancements have been made to the model since.

We submitted the version of the pPDA+f model trained on the WMT07 dataset to the "into English" segment-leval track of the WMT 2012 Shared Evaluation Metrics Task (Callison-Burch et al., 2012). Our model achieved the highest score (measured by Kendall's tau correlation) on all four language pairs (Fr-En, De-En, Es-En and Cs-En), and tied for the first place with METEOR v1.3 on average correlation.

5 Related Work

Features and Representation

One of the findings in our experimentation is that paraphrasing helps boosting model accuracy, and the idea of using paraphrases in MT evaluation was first proposed by Zhou et al. (2006). Several recent studies have introduced metrics over dependency parses (Liu et al., 2005; Owczarzak et al., 2008; He et al., 2010), but their improvements over n-gram models at the sentence level are not always consistent (Liu et al., 2005; Peterson and Przybocki, 2010). Other than string-based methods, recent work has explored more alternative representations for MT evaluation, such as network properties (Amancio et al., 2011), semantic role structures (Lo and Wu, 2011), and the quality of word order (Birch and Osborne, 2011).

Modeling

The idea of using extended edit distance models with block movements was also explored in Leusch et al. (2003). However, their model is largely empirical and not in a probabilistic learning setting. The line of work on probabilistic tree-edit distance models bears a strong connection to this work (McCallum et al., 2005; Bernard et al., 2008; Wang and Manning, 2010; Emms, 2012). In particular, our pFSM model and the log-linear parameterization were inspired by Wang and Manning (2010). Another body of literature that is closely related to this work is FSM models for word alignment (Vogel et al., 1996; Saers et al., 2010; Berg-Kirkpatrick et al., 2010). The stochastic Inversion Transduction Grammar in Saers et al. (2010) for instance, is a pFSM with special constraints. More recently, Saers and Wu (2011) further explored the connection between Linear Transduction Grammars and FSMs. There is a close tie between our pFSM model and the HMM model in Berg-Kirkpatrick et al. (2010). Both models adopted a log-linear parameterization for the state transition distribution, [13] but in their case the HMM model and the pFSM arc weights are normalized locally, and the objective is non-convex.

6 Conclusion

We described a probabilistic finite state machine based on string edits and a novel pushdown automaton extension for the task of machine translation evaluation. The models admit a rich set of linguistic features, and are trained to learn feature weights automatically by optimizing a regression objective. The proposed models achieve state-of-the-art results on a wide range of standard evaluations, and are much more lightweight than previous regression models, making them suitable candidates to be used in MERT training.

Acknowledgements

We gratefully acknowledge the support of Defense Advanced Research Projects Agency (DARPA) Machine Reading Program under Air Force Research Laboratory (AFRL) prime contract no. FA8750-09-C-0181 and the support of the DARPA Broad Operational Language Translation (BOLT) program through IBM. Any opinions, findings, and conclusion or recommendations expressed in this material are those of the author(s) and do not necessarily reflect the view of the DARPA, AFRL, or the US government.

References

J. Albrecht and R. Hwa. 2007a. A re-examination of machine learning approaches for sentence-level MT evaluation. In *Proceedings of ACL*.

J. Albrecht and R. Hwa. 2007b. Regression for sentence-level MT evaluation with pseudo references. In *Proceedings of ACL*.

D.R. Amancio, M.G.V. Nunes, O.N. Oliveira Jr., T.A.S. Pardo, L. Antiqueira, and L. da F. Costa. 2011. Using metrics from complex networks to evaluate machine translation. *Physica A*, 390(1):131–142.

S. Banerjee and A. Lavie. 2005. Meteor: An automatic metric for MT evaluation with improved correlation with human judgments. In *Proceedings of ACL Workshop on Intrinsic and Extrinsic Evaluation Measures*.

T. Berg-Kirkpatrick, A. Bouchard-Cote, J. DeNero, and D. Klein. 2010. Painless unsupervised learning with features. In *Proceedings of NAACL*.

M. Bernard, L. Boyer, A. Habrard, and M. Sebban. 2008. Learning probabilistic models of tree edit distance. *Pattern Recognition*, 41(8):2611–2629.

A. Birch and M. Osborne. 2011. Reordering metrics for MT. In *Proceedings of ACL/HLT*.

A. Birch, P. Blunsom, and M. Osborne. 2009. A quantitative analysis of reordering phenomena. In *Proceedings of WMT 09*.

C. Callison-Burch, P. Koehn, C. Monz, and J. Schroeder. 2009. Findings of the 2009 Workshop on Statistical Machine Translation. In *Proceedings of the Fourth Workshop on Statistical Machine Translation*.

C. Callison-Burch, P. Koehn, C. Monz, K. Peterson, M. Przybocki, and O. Zaidan. 2010. Findings of the 2010 joint workshop on Statistical Machine Translation and metrics for Machine Translation. In *Proceedings of Joint WMT 10 and MetricsMatr Workshop at ACL*.

C. Callison-Burch, P. Koehn, C. Monz, and O. Zaidan. 2011. Findings of the 2011 workshop on statistical machine translation. In *Proceedings of the Sixth Workshop on Statistical Machine Translation*.

C. Callison-Burch, P. Koehn, C. Monz, M. Post, R. Soricut, and L. Specia. 2012. Findings of the 2012 workshop on Statistical Machine Translation. In *Proceedings of Seventh Workshop on Statistical Machine Translation at NAACL*.

T. Cormen, C. Leiserson, R. Rivest, and C. Stein. 2001. *Introduction to Algorithms, Second Edition*. MIT Press.

M. Denkowski and A. Lavie. 2010. Extending the METEOR machine translation evaluation metric to the phrase level. In *Proceedings of HLT/NAACL*.

G. Doddington. 2002. Automatic evaluation of machine translation quality using n-gram cooccurrence statistics. In *Proceedings of HLT*.

Y. Dombb, O. Lipsky, B. Porat, E. Porat, and A. Tsur. 2010. The approximate swap and mismatch edit distance. *Theoretical Computer Science*, 411(43).

J. Eisner. 2002. Parameter estimation for probabilistic finite-state transducers. In *Proceedings of ACL*.

M. Emms. 2012. On stochastic tree distances and their training via expectation-maximisation. In *Proceedings of International Conference on Pattern Recognition Application and Methods*.

J. Esparza and A. Kucera. 2005. Quantitative analysis of probabilistic pushdown automata: Expectations and variances. In *Proceedings of the 20th Annual IEEE Symposium on Logic in Computer Science*.

[13] Similar parameterization was also used in much previous work, such as Riezler et al. (2000).

Y. He and A. Way. 2009. Improving the objective function in minimum error rate training. In *Proceedings of MT Summit XII*.

Y. He, J. Du, A. Way, and J. van Genabith. 2010. The DCU dependency-based metric in WMT-MetricsMATR 2010. In *Proceedings of Joint WMT 10 and Metrics-Matr Workshop at ACL*.

K. Knight and Y. Al-Onaizan. 1998. Translation with finite-state devices. In *Proceedings of AMTA*.

P. Koehn. 2004. Statistical significance tests for machine translation evaluation. In *Proceedings of EMNLP*.

A. Kulesza and S. Shieber. 2004. Robust machine translation evaluation with entailment features. In *Proceedings of TMI*.

S. Kumar and W. Byrne. 2003. A weighted finite state transducer implementation of the alignment template model for statistical machine translation. In *Proceedings of HLT/NAACL*.

G. Leusch, N. Ueffing, and H. Ney. 2003. A novel string-to-string distance measure with applications to machine translation evaluation. In *Proceedings of MT Summit I*.

D. C. Liu and J. Nocedal. 1989. On the limited memory BFGS method for large scale optimization. *Math. Programming*, 45:503–528.

D. Liu, , and D. Gildea. 2005. Syntactic features for evaluation of machine translation. In *Proceedings of the ACL Workshop on Intrinsic and Extrinsic Evaluation Measures*.

C. Liu, D. Dahlmeier, and H. Ng. 2011. Better evaluation metrics lead to better machine translation. In *Proceedings of EMNLP*.

C. Lo and D. Wu. 2011. MEANT: An inexpensive, high-accuracy, semi-automatic metric for evaluating translation utility based on semantic roles. In *Proceedings of ACL/HLT*.

M. P. Marcus, M. A. Marcinkiewicz, and B. Santorini. 1993. Building a large annotated corpus of english: the Penn Treebank. *Computational Linguistics*, 19(2):313–330.

A. McCallum, K. Bellare, and F. Pereira. 2005. A conditional random field for discriminatively-trained finite-state string edit distance. In *Proceedings of UAI*.

R. McDonald, K. Crammer, and F. Pereira. 2005. Online large-margin training of dependency parsers. In *Proceedings of ACL*.

G. A. Miller, R. Beckwith, C. Fellbaum, D. Gross, and K. J. Miller. 1990. WordNet: an on-line lexical database. *International Journal of Lexicography*, 3(4).

F. Och. 2003. Minimum error rate training in statistical machine translation. In *Proceedings of ACL*.

K. Owczarzak, J. van Genabith, and A. Way. 2008. Evaluating machine translation with LFG dependencies. *Machine Translation*, 21(2):95–119.

S. Pado, M. Galley, D. Jurafsky, and C. D. Manning. 2009. A learning approach to improving sentence-level MT evaluation. In *Proceedings of ACL*.

K. Papineni, S. Roukos, T. Ward, and W. Zhu. 2002. BLEU: a method for automatic evaluation of machine translation. In *Proceedings of ACL*.

K. Peterson and M. Przybocki. 2010. NIST 2010 metrics for machine translation evaluation (MetricsMaTr10) official release of results.

M.F. Porter. 1980. An algorithm for suffix stripping. *Program*, 14(3):130–137.

A. Ratnaparkhi. 1996. A maximum entropy part-of-speech tagger. In *Proceedings of EMNLP*.

S. Riezler, D. Prescher, J. Kuhn, and M. Johnson. 2000. Lexicalized stochastic modeling of constraint-based grammars using log-linear measures and em training. In *Proceedings of ACL*.

M. Saers and D. Wu. 2011. Linear transduction grammars and zipper finite-state transducers. In *Proceedings of Recent Advances in Natural Language Processing*.

M. Saers, J. Nivre, and D. Wu. 2010. Word alignment with stochastic bracketing linear inversion transduction grammar. In *Proceedings of NAACL*.

M. Snover, B. Dorr, R. Schwartz, L. Micciulla, and J. Makhoul. 2006. A study of translation edit rate with targeted human annotation. In *Proceedings of AMTA*.

M. Snover, , N. Madnani, B. Dorr, and R. Schwartz. 2009. Fluency, adequacy, or HTER? exploring different human judgments with a tunable MT metric. In *Proceedings of WMT09 Workshop*.

S. Sun, Y. Chen, and J. Li. 2008. A re-examination on features in regression based approach to automatic MT evaluation. In *Proceedings of ACL*.

E. Vidal, F. Thollard, C. de la Higuera, F. Casacuberta, and R. C. Carrasco. 2005. Probabilistic finite-state machines part I. *IEEE Transactions on Pattern Analysis and Machine Intelligence*, 27(7):1013–1025.

S. Vogel, H. Ney, and C. Tillmann. 1996. HMM-based word alignment in statistical translation. In *Proceedings of COLING*.

M. Wang and C.D. Manning. 2010. Probabilistic tree-edit models with structured latent variables for textual entailment and question answering. In *Proceedings of COLING*.

D. Wu, 2010. *CRC Handbook of Natural Language Processing*, chapter Alignment, pages 367–408. CRC Press.

L. Zhou, C.Y. Lin, and E. Hovy. 2006. Re-evaluating machine translation results with paraphrase support. In *Proceedings of EMNLP*.

An Empirical Investigation of Statistical Significance in NLP

Taylor Berg-Kirkpatrick **David Burkett** **Dan Klein**
Computer Science Division
University of California at Berkeley
{tberg, dburkett, klein}@cs.berkeley.edu

Abstract

We investigate two aspects of the empirical behavior of paired significance tests for NLP systems. First, when one system appears to outperform another, how does significance level relate in practice to the magnitude of the gain, to the size of the test set, to the similarity of the systems, and so on? Is it true that for each task there is a gain which roughly implies significance? We explore these issues across a range of NLP tasks using both large collections of past systems' outputs and variants of single systems. Next, once significance levels are computed, how well does the standard i.i.d. notion of significance hold up in practical settings where future distributions are neither independent nor identically distributed, such as across domains? We explore this question using a range of test set variations for constituency parsing.

1 Introduction

It is, or at least should be, nearly universal that NLP evaluations include statistical significance tests to validate metric gains. As important as significance testing is, relatively few papers have empirically investigated its practical properties. Those that do focus on single tasks (Koehn, 2004; Zhang et al., 2004) or on the comparison of alternative hypothesis tests (Gillick and Cox, 1989; Yeh, 2000; Bisani and Ney, 2004; Riezler and Maxwell, 2005).

In this paper, we investigate two aspects of the empirical behavior of paired significance tests for NLP systems. For example, all else equal, larger metric gains will tend to be more significant. However, what does this relationship look like and how reliable is it? What should be made of the conventional wisdom that often springs up that a certain metric gain is roughly the point of significance for a given task (e.g. 0.4 F1 in parsing or 0.5 BLEU in machine translation)? We show that, with heavy caveats, there are such thresholds, though we also discuss the hazards in their use. In particular, many other factors contribute to the significance level, and we investigate several of them. For example, what is the effect of the similarity between the two systems? Here, we show that more similar systems tend to achieve significance with smaller metric gains, reflecting the fact that their outputs are more correlated. What about the size of the test set? For example, in designing a shared task it is important to know how large the test set must be in order for significance tests to be sensitive to small gains in the performance metric. Here, we show that test size plays the largest role in determining discrimination ability, but that we get diminishing returns. For example, doubling the test size will not obviate the need for significance testing.

In order for our results to be meaningful, we must have access to the outputs of many of NLP systems. Public competitions, such as the well-known CoNLL shared tasks, provide one natural way to obtain a variety of system outputs on the same test set. However, for most NLP tasks, obtaining outputs from a large variety of systems is not feasible. Thus, in the course of our investigations, we propose a very simple method for automatically generating arbitrary numbers of comparable system outputs and we then validate the trends revealed by our synthetic method against data from public competitions. This methodology itself could be of value in, for example, the design of new shared tasks.

Finally, we consider a related and perhaps even more important question that can only be answered empirically: to what extent is statistical significance on a test corpus predictive of performance on other test corpora, in-domain or otherwise? Focusing on constituency parsing, we investigate the relationship between significance levels and actual performance on data from outside the test set. We show that when the test set is (artificially) drawn i.i.d. from the same distribution that generates new data, then significance levels are remarkably well-calibrated. However, as the domain of the new data diverges from that of the test set, the predictive ability of significance level drops off dramatically.

2 Statistical Significance Testing in NLP

First, we review notation and standard practice in significance testing to set up our empirical investigation.

2.1 Hypothesis Tests

When comparing a new system A to a baseline system B, we want to know if A is better than B on some large population of data. Imagine that we sample a small test set $x = x_1, \ldots, x_n$ on which A beats B by $\delta(x)$. Hypothesis testing guards against the case where A's victory over B was an unlikely event, due merely to chance. We would therefore like to know how likely it would be that a new, independent test set x' would show a similar victory for A *assuming that A is no better than B on the population as a whole*; this assumption is the null hypothesis, denoted H_0.

Hypothesis testing consists of attempting to estimate this likelihood, written $p(\delta(X) > \delta(x)|H_0)$, where X is a random variable over possible test sets of size n that we could have drawn, and $\delta(x)$ is a constant, the metric gain we actually observed. Traditionally, if $p(\delta(X) > \delta(x)|H_0) < 0.05$, we say that the observed value of $\delta(x)$ is sufficiently unlikely that we should reject H_0 (i.e. accept that A's victory was real and not just a random fluke). We refer to $p(\delta(X) > \delta(x)|H_0)$ as p-value(x).

In most cases p-value(x) is not easily computable and must be approximated. The type of approximation depends on the particular hypothesis testing method. Various methods have been used in the NLP community (Gillick and Cox, 1989; Yeh, 2000; Riezler and Maxwell, 2005). We use the paired bootstrap[1] (Efron and Tibshirani, 1993) because it is one of the most widely used (Och, 2003; Bisani and Ney, 2004; Zhang et al., 2004; Koehn, 2004), and because it can be easily applied to any performance metric, even complex metrics like F1-measure or BLEU (Papineni et al., 2002). Note that we could perform the experiments described in this paper using another method, such as the paired Student's t-test. To the extent that the assumptions of the t-test are met, it is likely that the results would be very similar to those we present here.

```
1. Draw b bootstrap samples x^(i) of size n by
   sampling with replacement from x.
2. Initialize s = 0.
3. For each x^(i) increment s if δ(x^(i)) > 2δ(x).
4. Estimate p-value(x) ≈ s/b
```

Figure 1: The bootstrap procedure. In all of our experiments we use $b = 10^6$, which is more than sufficient for the bootstrap estimate of p-value(x) to stabilize.

2.2 The Bootstrap

The bootstrap estimates p-value(x) though a combination of simulation and approximation, drawing many simulated test sets $x^{(i)}$ and counting how often A sees an accidental advantage of $\delta(x)$ or greater. How can we get sample test sets $x^{(i)}$? We lack the ability to actually draw new test sets from the underlying population because all we have is our data x. The bootstrap therefore draws each $x^{(i)}$ from x itself, sampling n items from x with replacement; these new test sets are called *bootstrap samples.*

Naively, it might seem like we would then check how often A beats B by more than $\delta(x)$ on $x^{(i)}$. However, there's something seriously wrong with these $x^{(i)}$ as far as the null hypothesis is concerned: the $x^{(i)}$ were sampled from x, and so their average $\delta(x^{(i)})$ won't be zero like the null hypothesis demands; the average will instead be around $\delta(x)$. If we ask how many of these $x^{(i)}$ have A winning by $\delta(x)$, about half of them will. The solution is a recentering of the mean – we want to know how often A does *more than $\delta(x)$ better than expected.* We expect it to beat B by $\delta(x)$. Therefore, we count up how many of the $x^{(i)}$ have A beating B by at least $2\delta(x)$.[2] The pseudocode is shown in Figure 1.

[1]Riezler and Maxwell (2005) argue the benefits of approximate randomization testing, introduced by Noreen (1989). However, this method is ill-suited to the type of hypothesis we are testing. Our null hypothesis does not condition on the test data, and therefore the bootstrap is a better choice.

[2]Note that many authors have used a variant where the event tallied on the $x^{(i)}$ is whether $\delta(x^{(i)}) < 0$, rather than $\delta(x^{(i)}) > 2\delta(x)$. If the mean of $\delta(x^{(i)})$ is $\delta(x)$, and if the distribution of $\delta(x^{(i)})$ is symmetric, then these two versions will be equivalent.

As mentioned, a major benefit of the bootstrap is that any evaluation metric can be used to compute $\delta(x)$.[3] We run the bootstrap using several metrics: F1-measure for constituency parsing, unlabeled dependency accuracy for dependency parsing, alignment error rate (AER) for word alignment, ROUGE score (Lin, 2004) for summarization, and BLEU score for machine translation.[4] We report all metrics as percentages.

3 Experiments

Our first goal is to explore the relationship between metric gain, $\delta(x)$, and statistical significance, p-value(x), for a range of NLP tasks. In order to say anything meaningful, we will need to see both $\delta(x)$ and p-value(x) for many pairs of systems.

3.1 Natural Comparisons

Ideally, for a given task and test set we could obtain outputs from all systems that have been evaluated in published work. For each pair of these systems we could run a comparison and compute both $\delta(x)$ and p-value(x). While obtaining such data is not generally feasible, for several tasks there are public competitions to which systems are submitted by many researchers. Some of these competitions make system outputs publicly available. We obtained system outputs from the TAC 2008 workshop on automatic summarization (Dang and Owczarzak, 2008), the CoNLL 2007 shared task on dependency parsing (Nivre et al., 2007), and the WMT 2010 workshop on machine translation (Callison-Burch et al., 2010).

For cases where the metric linearly decomposes over sentences, the mean of $\delta(x^{(i)})$ is $\delta(x)$. By the central limit theorem, the distribution will be symmetric for large test sets; for small test sets it may not.

[3] Note that the bootstrap procedure given only approximates the true significance level, with multiple sources of approximation error. One is the error introduced from using a finite number of bootstrap samples. Another comes from the assumption that the bootstrap samples reflect the underlying population distribution. A third is the assumption that the mean bootstrap gain is the test gain (which could be further corrected for if the metric is sufficiently ill-behaved).

[4] To save time, we can compute $\delta(x)$ for each bootstrap sample without having to rerun the evaluation metric. For our metrics, sufficient statistics can be recorded for each sentence and then sampled along with the sentences when constructing each $x^{(i)}$ (e.g. size of gold, size of guess, and number correct are sufficient for F1). This makes the bootstrap very fast in practice.

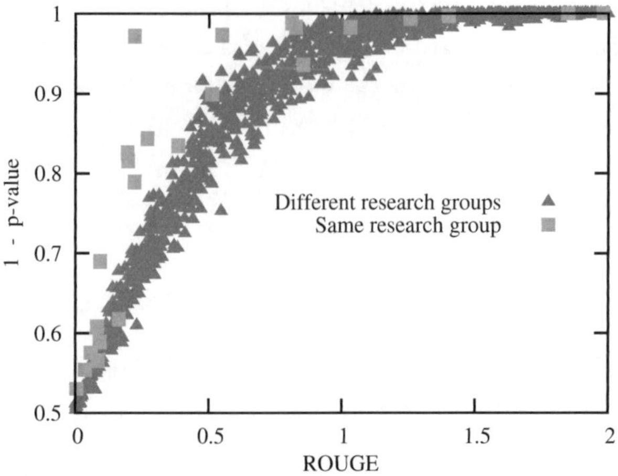

Figure 2: **TAC 2008 Summarization:** Confidence vs. ROUGE improvement on TAC 2008 test set for comparisons between all pairs of the 58 participating systems at TAC 2008. Comparisons between systems entered by the same research group and comparisons between systems entered by different research groups are shown separately.

3.1.1 TAC 2008 Summarization

In our first experiment, we use the outputs of the 58 systems that participated in the TAC 2008 workshop on automatic summarization. For each possible pairing, we compute $\delta(x)$ and p-value(x) on the non-update portion of the TAC 2008 test set (we order each pair so that the gain, $\delta(x)$, is always positive).[5] For this task, test instances correspond to document collections. The test set consists of 48 document collections, each with a human produced summary. Figure 2 plots the ROUGE gain against $1 -$ p-value, which we refer to as *confidence*. Each point on the graph corresponds to an individual pair of systems.

As expected, larger gains in ROUGE correspond to higher confidences. The curved shape of the plot is interesting. It suggests that relatively quickly we reach ROUGE gains for which, in practice, significance tests will most likely be positive. We might expect that systems whose outputs are highly correlated will achieve higher confidence at lower metric gains. To test this hypothesis, in Figure 2 we

[5] In order to run bootstraps between all pairs of systems quickly, we reuse a random sample counts matrix between bootstrap runs. As a result, we no longer need to perform quadratically many corpus resamplings. The speed-up from this approach is enormous, but one undesirable effect is that the bootstrap estimation noise between different runs is correlated. As a remedy, we set b so large that the correlated noise is not visible in plots.

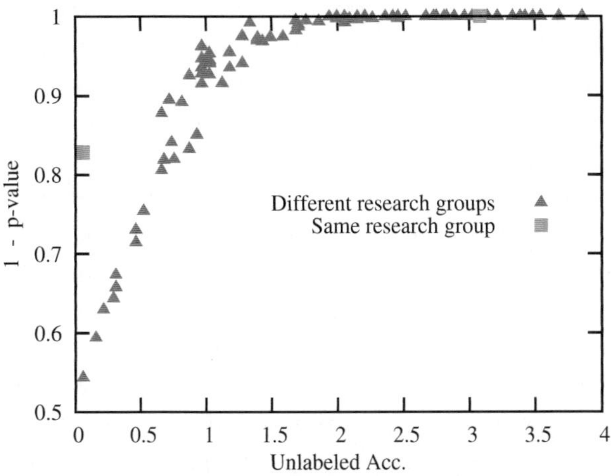

Figure 3: **CoNLL 2007 Dependency parsing:** Confidence vs. unlabeled dependency accuracy improvement on the Chinese CoNLL 2007 test set for comparisons between all pairs of the 21 participating systems in CoNLL 2007 shared task. Comparisons between systems entered by the same research group and comparisons between systems entered by different research groups are shown separately.

separately show the comparisons between systems entered by the same research group and comparisons between systems entered by different research groups, with the expectation that systems entered by the same group are likely to have more correlated outputs. Many of the comparisons between systems submitted by the same group are offset from the main curve. It appears that they do achieve higher confidences at lower metric gains.

Given the huge number of system comparisons in Figure 2, one obvious question to ask is whether we can take the results of all these statistical significance tests and estimate a ROUGE improvement threshold that predicts when future statistical significance tests will probably be significant at the p-value$(x) < 0.05$ level. For example, let's say we take all the comparisons with p-value between 0.04 and 0.06 (47 comparisons in all in this case). Each of these comparisons has an associated metric gain, and by taking, say, the 95th percentile of these metric gains, we get a potentially useful threshold. In this case, the computed threshold is 1.10 ROUGE.

What does this threshold mean? Well, based on the way we computed it, it suggests that if somebody reports a ROUGE increase of around 1.10 *on the exact same test set*, there is a pretty good chance that a statistical significance test would show significance at the p-value$(x) < 0.05$ level. After all, 95% of the borderline significant differences that we've already seen showed an increase of even less than 1.10 ROUGE. If we're evaluating past work, or are in some other setting where system outputs just aren't available, the threshold could guide our interpretation of reports containing only summary scores.

That being said, it is important that we don't overinterpret the meaning of the 1.10 ROUGE threshold. We have already seen that pairs of systems submitted by the same research group and by different research groups follow different trends, and we will soon see more evidence demonstrating the importance of system correlation in determining the relationship between metric gain and confidence. Additionally, in Section 4, we will see that properties of the test corpus have a large effect on the trend. There are many factors are at work, and so, of course, metric gain alone will not fully determine the outcome of a paired significance test.

3.1.2 CoNLL 2007 Dependency Parsing

Next, we run an experiment for dependency parsing. We use the outputs of the 21 systems that participated in the CoNLL 2007 shared task on dependency parsing. In Figure 3, we plot, for all pairs, the gain in unlabeled dependency accuracy against confidence on the CoNLL 2007 Chinese test set, which consists of 690 sentences and parses. We again separate comparisons between systems submitted by the same research group and those submitted by different groups, although for this task there were fewer cases of multiple submission. The results resemble the plot for summarization; we again see a curve-shaped trend, and comparisons between systems from the same group (few that they are) achieve higher confidences at lower metric gains.

3.1.3 WMT 2010 Machine Translation

Our final task for which system outputs are publicly available is machine translation. We run an experiment using the outputs of the 31 systems participating in WMT 2010 on the system combination portion of the German-English WMT 2010 news test set, which consists of 2,034 German sentences and English translations. We again run comparisons for pairs of participating systems. We plot gain in test BLEU score against confidence in Figure 4. In this experiment there is an additional class of compar-

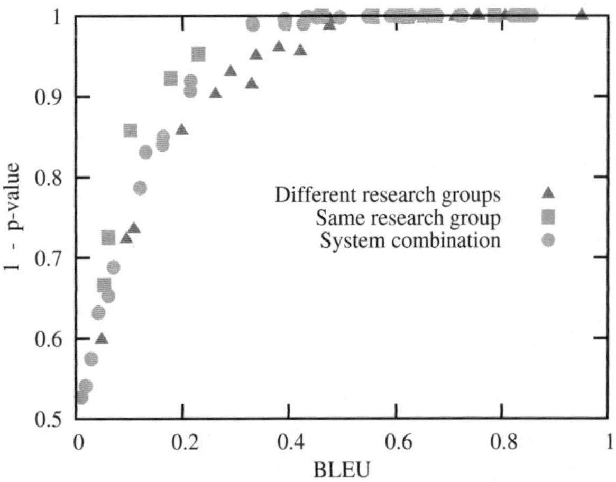

Figure 4: **WMT 2010 Machine translation:** Confidence vs. BLEU improvement on the system combination portion of the German-English WMT 2010 news test set for comparisons between pairs of the 31 participating systems at WMT 2010. Comparisons between systems entered by the same research group, comparisons between systems entered by different research groups, and comparisons between system combination entries are shown separately.

isons that are likely to have specially correlated systems: 13 of the submitted systems are system combinations, and each take into account the same set of proposed translations. We separate comparisons into three sets: comparisons between non-combined systems entered by different research groups, comparisons between non-combined systems entered by the same research group, and comparisons between system-combinations.

We see the same curve-shaped trend we saw for summarization and dependency parsing. Different group comparisons, same group comparisons, and system combination comparisons form distinct curves. This indicates, again, that comparisons between systems that are expected to be specially correlated achieve high confidence at lower metric gain levels.

3.2 Synthetic Comparisons

So far, we have seen a clear empirical effect, but, because of the limited availability of system outputs, we have only considered a few tasks. We now propose a simple method that captures the shape of the effect, and use it to extend our analysis.

3.2.1 Training Set Resampling

Another way of obtaining many different systems' outputs is to obtain implementations of a handful of systems, and then vary some aspect of the training procedure in order to produce many different systems from each implementation. Koehn (2004) uses this sort of amplification; he uses a single machine translation implementation, and then trains it from different source languages. We take a slightly different approach. For each task we pick some fixed training set. Then we generate resampled training sets by sampling sentences with replacement from the original. In this way, we can generate as many new training sets as we like, each of which is similar to the original, but with some variation. For each base implementation, we train a new system on each resampled training set. This results in slightly tweaked trained systems, and is intended to very roughly approximate the variance introduced by incremental system changes during research. We validate this method by comparing plots obtained by the synthetic approach with plots obtained from natural comparisons.

We expect that each new system will be different, but that systems originating from the same base model will be highly correlated. This provides a useful division of comparisons: those between systems built with the same model, and those between systems built with different models. The first class can be used to approximate comparisons of systems that are expected to be specially correlated, and the latter for comparisons of systems that are not.

3.2.2 Dependency Parsing

We use three base models for dependency parsing: MST parser (McDonald et al., 2005), Maltparser (Nivre et al., 2006), and the ensemble parser of Surdeanu and Manning (2010). We use the CoNLL 2007 Chinese training set, which consists of 57K sentences. We resample 5 training sets of 57K sentences, 10 training sets of 28K sentences, and 10 training sets of 14K sentences. Together, this yields a total of 75 system outputs on the CoNLL 2007 Chinese test set, 25 systems for each base model type. The score ranges of all the base models overlap. This ensures that for each pair of model types we will be able to see comparisons where the metric gains are small. The results of the pairwise comparisons of all 75 system outputs are shown in Figure 5, along with the results of the CoNLL 2007 shared task system comparisons from Figure 3.

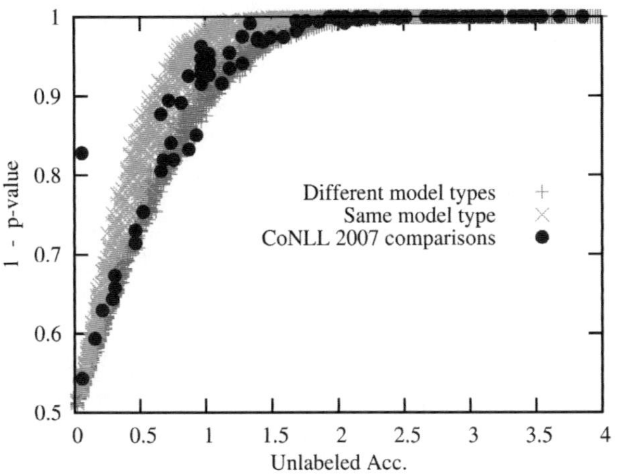

Figure 5: **Dependency parsing:** Confidence vs. unlabeled dependency accuracy improvement on the Chinese CoNLL 2007 test set for comparisons between all pairs of systems generated by using resampled training sets to train either MST parser, Maltparser, or the ensemble parser. Comparisons between systems generated using the same base model type and comparisons between systems generated using different base model types are shown separately. The CoNLL 2007 shared task comparisons from Figure 3 are also shown.

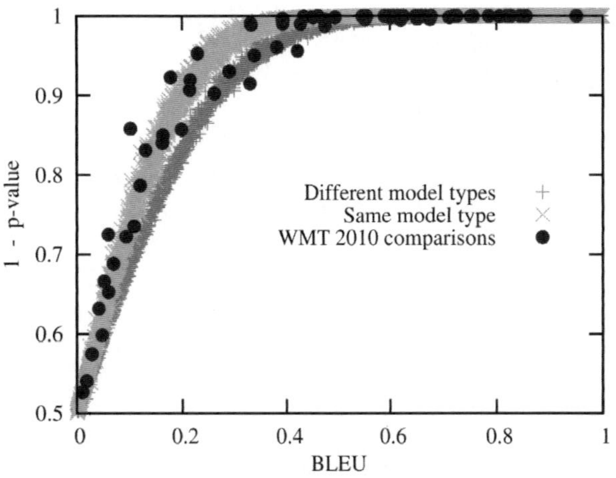

Figure 6: **Machine translation:** Confidence vs. BLEU improvement on the system combination portion of the German-English WMT 2010 news test set for comparisons between all pairs of systems generated by using resampled training sets to train either Moses or Joshua. Comparisons between systems generated using the same base model type and comparisons between systems generated using different base model types are shown separately. The WMT 2010 workshop comparisons from Figure 4 are also shown.

The overlay of the natural comparisons suggests that the synthetic approach reasonably models the relationship between metric gain and confidence. Additionally, the different model type and same model type comparisons exhibit the behavior we would expect, matching the curves corresponding to comparisons between specially correlated systems and standard comparisons respectively.

Since our synthetic approach yields a large number of system outputs, we can use the procedure described in Section 3.1.1 to compute the threshold above which the metric gain is probably significant. For comparisons between systems of the same model type, the threshold is 1.20 unlabeled dependency accuracy. For comparisons between systems of different model types, the threshold is 1.51 unlabeled dependency accuracy. These results indicate that the similarity of the systems being compared is an important factor. As mentioned, rules-of-thumb derived from such thresholds cannot be applied blindly, but, in special cases where two systems are known to be correlated, the former threshold should be preferred over the latter. For example, during development most comparisons are made between incremental variants of the same system. If adding a feature to a supervised parser increases unlabeled accuracy by 1.3, it is useful to be able to quickly estimate that the improvement is probably significant. This still isn't the full story; we will soon see that properties of the test set also play a major role. But first, we carry our analysis to several more tasks.

3.2.3 Machine Translation

Our two base models for machine translation are Moses (Koehn et al., 2007) and Joshua (Li et al., 2009). We use 1.4M sentence pairs from the German-English portion of the WMT-provided Europarl (Koehn, 2005) and news commentary corpora as the original training set. We resample 75 training sets, 20 of 1.4M sentence pairs, 29 of 350K sentence pairs, and 26 of 88K sentence pairs. This yields a total of 150 system outputs on the system combination portion of the German-English WMT 2010 news test set. The results of the pairwise comparisons of all 150 system outputs are shown in Figure 6, along with the results of the WMT 2010 workshop system comparisons from Figure 4.

The natural comparisons from the WMT 2010 workshop align well with the comparisons between synthetically varied models. Again, the different model type and same model type comparisons form distinct curves. For comparisons between systems

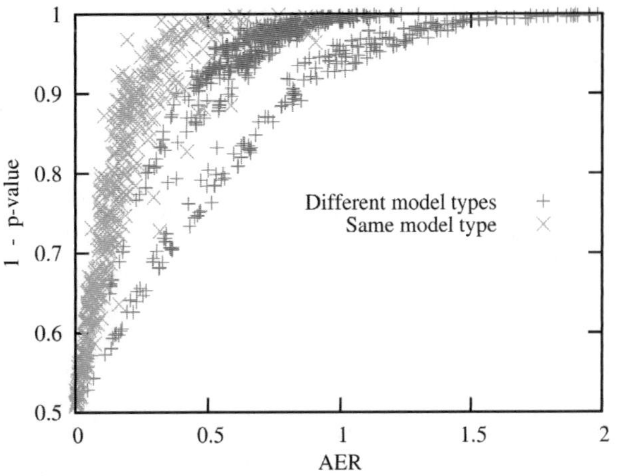

Figure 7: **Word alignment:** Confidence vs. AER improvement on the Hansard test set for comparisons between all pairs of systems generated by using resampled training sets to train either the ITG aligner, the joint HMM aligner, or GIZA++. Comparisons between systems generated using the same base model type and comparisons between systems generated using different base model types are shown separately.

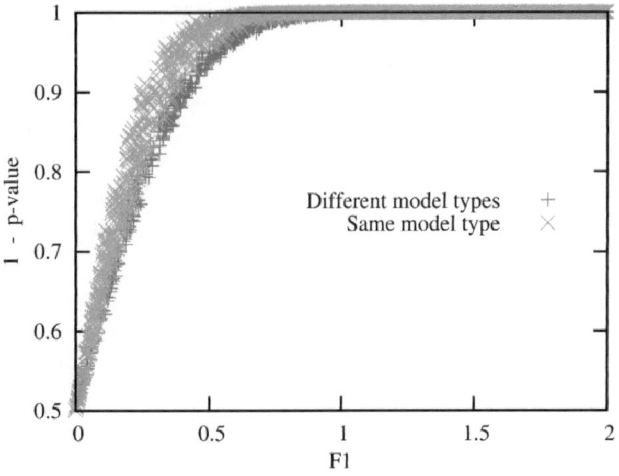

Figure 8: **Constituency parsing:** Confidence vs. F1 improvement on section 23 of the WSJ corpus for comparisons between all pairs of systems generated by using resampled training sets to train either the Berkeley parser, the Stanford parser, or the Collins parser. Comparisons between systems generated using the same base model type and comparisons between systems generated using different base model types are shown separately.

of the same model type the computed p-value < 0.05 threshold is 0.28 BLEU. For comparisons between systems of different model types the threshold is 0.37 BLEU.

3.2.4 Word Alignment

Now that we have validated our simple model of system variation on two tasks, we go on to generate plots for tasks that do not have competitions with publicly available system outputs. The first task is English-French word alignment, where we use three base models: the ITG aligner of Haghighi et al. (2009), the joint HMM aligner of Liang et al. (2006), and GIZA++ (Och and Ney, 2003). The last two aligners are unsupervised, while the first is supervised. We train the unsupervised word aligners using the 1.1M sentence pair Hansard training corpus, resampling 20 training sets of the same size.[6] Following Haghighi et al. (2009), we train the supervised ITG aligner using the first 337 sentence pairs of the hand-aligned Hansard test set; again, we resample 20 training sets of the same size as the original data. We test on the remaining 100 hand-aligned sentence pairs from the Hansard test set.

Unlike previous plots, the points corresponding to comparisons between systems with different base model types form two distinct curves. It turns out that the upper curve consists only of comparisons between ITG and HMM aligners. This is likely due to the fact that the ITG aligner uses posteriors from the HMM aligner for some of its features, so the two models are particularly correlated. Overall, the spread of this plot is larger than previous ones. This may be due to the small size of the test set, or possibly some additional variance introduced by unsupervised training. For comparisons between systems of the same model type the p-value < 0.05 threshold is 0.50 AER. For comparisons between systems of different model types the threshold is 1.12 AER.

3.2.5 Constituency Parsing

Finally, before we move on to further types of analysis, we run an experiment for the task of constituency parsing. We use three base models: the Berkeley parser (Petrov et al., 2006), the Stanford parser (Klein and Manning, 2003), and Dan Bikel's implementation (Bikel, 2004) of the Collins parser (Collins, 1999). We use sections 2-21 of the WSJ corpus (Marcus et al., 1993), which consists of 38K sentences and parses, as a training set. We resample 10 training sets of size 38K, 10 of size 19K, and 10 of size 9K, and use these to train systems. We test on section 23. The results are shown in Figure 8.

For comparisons between systems of the same

[6]GIZA++ failed to produce reasonable output when trained with some of these training sets, so there are fewer than 20 GIZA++ systems in our comparisons.

model type, the p-value < 0.05 threshold is 0.47 F1. For comparisons between systems of different model types the threshold is 0.57 F1.

4 Properties of the Test Corpus

For five tasks, we have seen a trend relating metric gain and confidence, and we have seen that the level of correlation between the systems being compared affects the location of the curve. Next, we look at how the size and domain of the test set play a role, and, finally, how significance level predicts performance on held out data. In this section, we carry out experiments for both machine translation and constituency parsing, but mainly focus on the latter because of the availability of large test corpora that span more than one domain: the Brown corpus and the held out portions of the WSJ corpus.

4.1 Varying the Size

Figure 9 plots comparisons for machine translation on variously sized initial segments of the WMT 2010 news test set. Similarly, Figure 10 plots comparisons for constituency parsing on initial segments of the Brown corpus. As might be expected, the size of the test corpus has a large effect. For both machine translation and constituency parsing, the larger the corpus size, the lower the threshold for p-value < 0.05 and the smaller the spread of the plot. At one extreme, the entire Brown corpus, which consists of approximately 24K sentences, has a threshold of 0.22 F1, while at the other extreme, the first 100 sentences of the Brown corpus have a threshold of 3.00 F1. Notice that we see diminishing returns as we increase the size of the test set. This phenomenon follows the general shape of the central limit theorem, which predicts that variances of observed metric gains will shrink according to the square root of the test size. Even using the entire Brown corpus as a test set there is a small range where the result of a paired significance test was not completely determined by metric gain.

It is interesting to note that for a fixed test size, the domain has only a small effect on the shape of the curve. Figure 11 plots comparisons for a fixed test size, but with various test corpora.

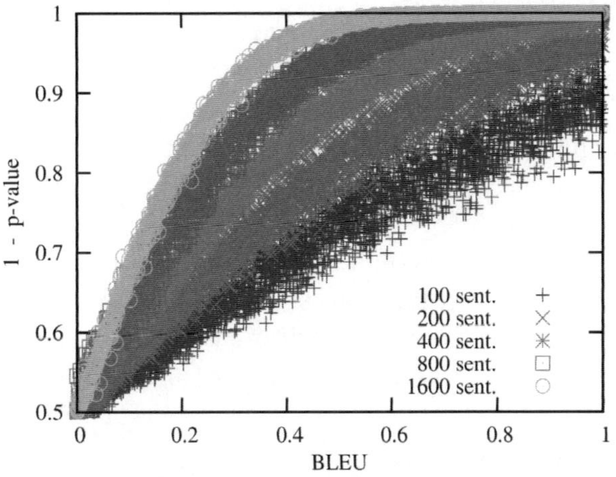

Figure 9: **Machine translation; varying test size:** Confidence vs. BLEU improvement on portions of the German-English WMT 2010 news test set.

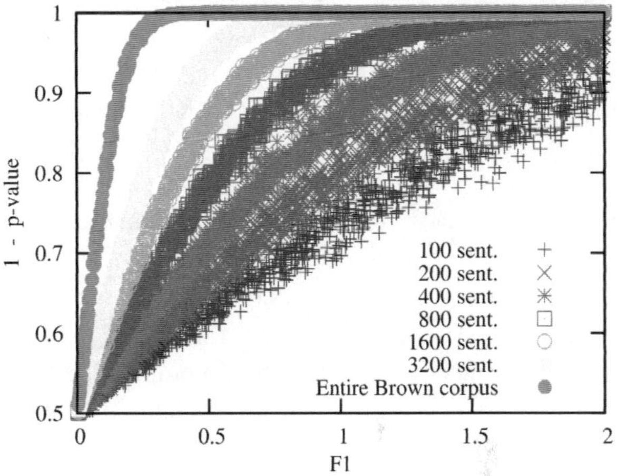

Figure 10: **Constituency parsing; varying test size:** Confidence vs. F1 improvement on portions of the Brown corpus.

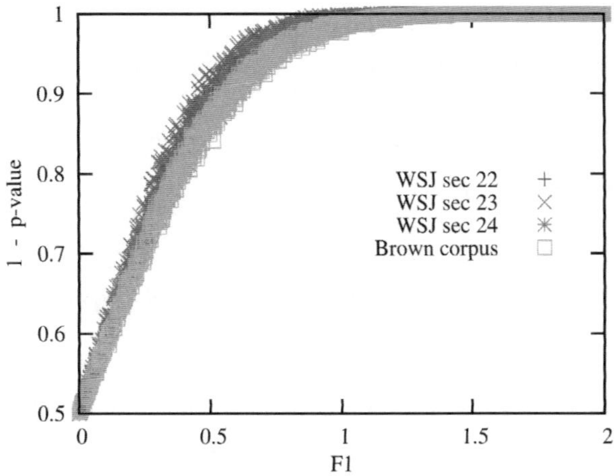

Figure 11: **Constituency parsing; varying domain:** Confidence vs. F1 improvement on the first 1,600 sentences of sections 22, 23, and 24 of the WSJ corpus, and the Brown corpus.

4.2 Empirical Calibration across Domains

Now that we have a way of generating outputs for thousands of pairs of systems, we can check empirically the practical reliability of significance testing. Recall that the bootstrap p-value(x) is an approximation to $p(\delta(X) > \delta(x)|H_0)$. However, we often really want to determine the probability that the new system is better than the baseline on the underlying test distribution or even the distribution from another domain. There is no reason a priori to expect these numbers to coincide.

In our next experiment, we treat the entire Brown corpus, which consists of 24K sentences, as the true population of English sentences. For each system generated in the way described in Section 3.2.5 we compute F1 on *all* of Brown. Since we are treating the Brown corpus as the actual population of English sentences, for each pair of parsers we can say that the sign of the F1 difference indicates which is the truly better system. Now, we repeatedly resample small test sets from Brown, each consisting of 1,600 sentences, drawn by sampling sentences with replacement. For each pair of systems, and for each resampled test set, we compute p-value(x) using the bootstrap. Out of the 4K bootstraps computed in this way, 942 had p-value between 0.04 and 0.06, 869 of which agreed with the sign of the F1 difference we saw on the entire Brown corpus. Thus, 92% of the significance tests with p-value in a tight range around 0.05 correctly identified the better system.

This result is encouraging. It suggests that statistical significance computed using the bootstrap is reasonably well calibrated. However, test sets are almost never drawn i.i.d. from the distribution of instances the system will encounter in practical use. Thus, we also wish to compute how calibration degrades as the domain of the test set changes. In another experiment, we look at how significance near p-value $= 0.05$ on section 23 of the WSJ corpus predicts performance on sections 22 and 24 and the Brown corpus. This time, for each pair of generated systems we run a bootstrap on section 23. Out of all these bootstraps, 58 system pairs had p-value between 0.04 and 0.06. Of these, only 83% had the same sign of F1 difference on section 23 as they did on section 22, 71% the had the same sign on section 23 as on section 24, and 48% the same sign on section 23 as on the Brown corpus. This indicates that reliability degrades as we switch the domain. In the extreme, achieving a p-value near 0.05 on section 23 provides no information about performance on the Brown corpus.

Sec. 23 p-value	% Sys. A > Sys. B		
	Sec. 22	Sec. 24	Brown
0.00125 - 0.0025	97%	95%	73%
0.0025 - 0.005	92%	92%	60%
0.005 - 0.01	92%	85%	56%
0.01 - 0.02	88%	92%	54%
0.02 - 0.04	87%	78%	51%
0.04 - 0.08	83%	74%	48%

Table 1: **Empirical calibration:** p-value on section 23 of the WSJ corpus vs. fraction of comparisons where system A beats system B on section 22, section 24, and the Brown corpus. Note that system pairs are ordered so that A always outperforms B on section 23.

If we intend to use our system on out-of-domain data, these results are somewhat discouraging. How low does p-value(x) have to get before we start getting good information about out-of-domain performance? We try to answer this question for this particular parsing task by running the same domain calibration experiment for several different ranges of p-value. The results are shown in Table 1. From these results, it appears that for constituency parsing, when testing on section 23, a p-value level below 0.00125 is required to reasonably predict performance on the Brown corpus.

It should be considered a good practice to include statistical significance testing results with empirical evaluations. The bootstrap in particular is easy to run and makes relatively few assumptions about the task or evaluation metric. However, we have demonstrated some limitations of statistical significance testing for NLP. In particular, while statistical significance is usually a minimum necessary condition to demonstrate that a performance difference is real, it's also important to consider the relationship between test set performance and the actual goals of the systems being tested, especially if the system will eventually be used on data from a different domain than the test set used for evaluation.

5 Conclusion

We have demonstrated trends relating several important factors to significance level, which include both properties of the systems being compared and properties of the test corpus, and have presented a simple approach to approximating the response of these factors for tasks where large numbers of system outputs are not available. Our results reveal that the relationship between metric gain and statistical significance is complex, and therefore simple thresholds are not a replacement for significance tests. Indeed, we strongly advocate the use of statistical significance testing to validate metric gains in NLP, but also note that informal rules-of-thumb do arise in popular discussion and that, for some settings when previous systems are unavailable, these empirical results can supplement less sensitive unpaired tests (e.g. bar-overlaps-point test) in evaluation of progress. Finally, even formal testing has its limits. We provide cautionary evidence to this effect, showing that the information provided by a test quickly degrades as the target corpus shifts domain.

Acknowledgements

This work was partially supported by NSF fellowships to the first and second authors and by the NSF under grant 0643742.

References

D.M. Bikel. 2004. Intricacies of collins' parsing model. *Computational Linguistics*.

M. Bisani and H. Ney. 2004. Bootstrap estimates for confidence intervals in asr performance evaluation. In *Proc. of ICASSP*.

C. Callison-Burch, P. Koehn, C. Monz, K. Peterson, M. Przybocki, and O.F. Zaidan. 2010. Findings of the 2010 joint workshop on statistical machine translation and metrics for machine translation. In *Proc. of the Joint Fifth Workshop on Statistical Machine Translation and MetricsMATR*.

M. Collins. 1999. *Head-driven statistical models for natural language parsing*. Ph.D. thesis, University of Pennsylvania.

H.T. Dang and K. Owczarzak. 2008. Overview of the tac 2008 update summarization task. In *Proc. of Text Analysis Conference*.

B. Efron and R. Tibshirani. 1993. *An introduction to the bootstrap*. Chapman & Hall/CRC.

L. Gillick and S.J. Cox. 1989. Some statistical issues in the comparison of speech recognition algorithms. In *Proc. of ICASSP*.

A. Haghighi, J. Blitzer, J. DeNero, and D. Klein. 2009. Better word alignments with supervised ITG models. In *Proc. of ACL*.

D. Klein and C.D. Manning. 2003. Accurate unlexicalized parsing. In *Proc. of ACL*.

P. Koehn, H. Hoang, A. Birch, C. Callison-Burch, M. Federico, N. Bertoldi, B. Cowan, W. Shen, C. Moran, R. Zens, et al. 2007. Moses: Open source toolkit for statistical machine translation. In *Proc. of ACL*.

P. Koehn. 2004. Statistical significance tests for machine translation evaluation. In *Proc. of EMNLP*.

P. Koehn. 2005. Europarl: A parallel corpus for statistical machine translation. In *MT summit*.

Z. Li, C. Callison-Burch, C. Dyer, J. Ganitkevitch, S. Khudanpur, L. Schwartz, W.N.G. Thornton, J. Weese, and O.F. Zaidan. 2009. Joshua: An open source toolkit for parsing-based machine translation. In *Proc. of the Fourth Workshop on Statistical Machine Translation*.

P. Liang, B. Taskar, and D. Klein. 2006. Alignment by agreement. In *Proc. of NAACL*.

C.Y. Lin. 2004. Rouge: A package for automatic evaluation of summaries. In *Proc. of the Workshop on Text Summarization*.

M.P. Marcus, M.A. Marcinkiewicz, and B. Santorini. 1993. Building a large annotated corpus of english: The penn treebank. *Computational linguistics*.

R. McDonald, F. Pereira, K. Ribarov, and J. Hajič. 2005. Non-projective dependency parsing using spanning tree algorithms. In *Proc. of EMNLP*.

J. Nivre, J. Hall, and J. Nilsson. 2006. Maltparser: A data-driven parser-generator for dependency parsing. In *Proc. of LREC*.

J. Nivre, J. Hall, S. Kübler, R. McDonald, J. Nilsson, S. Riedel, and D. Yuret. 2007. The conll 2007 shared task on dependency parsing. In *Proc. of the CoNLL Shared Task Session of EMNLP-CoNLL 2007*.

E.W. Noreen. 1989. *Computer Intensive Methods for Hypothesis Testing: An Introduction*. Wiley, New York.

F.J. Och and H. Ney. 2003. A systematic comparison of various statistical alignment models. *Computational linguistics*.

F.J. Och. 2003. Minimum error rate training in statistical machine translation. In *Proc. of ACL*.

K. Papineni, S. Roukos, T. Ward, and W.J. Zhu. 2002. Bleu: a method for automatic evaluation of machine translation. In *Proc. of ACL*.

S. Petrov, L. Barrett, R. Thibaux, and D. Klein. 2006. Learning accurate, compact, and interpretable tree annotation. In *Proc. of ACL*.

S. Riezler and J.T. Maxwell. 2005. On some pitfalls in automatic evaluation and significance testing for mt. In *Proc. of ACL Workshop on Intrinsic and Extrinsic Evaluation Measures for Machine Translation and/or Summarization*.

M. Surdeanu and C.D. Manning. 2010. Ensemble models for dependency parsing: cheap and good? In *Proc. of NAACL*.

A. Yeh. 2000. More accurate tests for the statistical significance of result differences. In *Proc. of ACL*.

Y. Zhang, S. Vogel, and A. Waibel. 2004. Interpreting bleu/nist scores: How much improvement do we need to have a better system. In *Proc. of LREC*.

Employing Compositional Semantics and Discourse Consistency in Chinese Event Extraction

Peifeng Li, Guodong Zhou, Qiaoming Zhu, Libin Hou
School of Computer Science & Technology
Soochow University, Suzhou, 215006, China
{pfli, gdzhou, qmzhu, 20094227021}@suda.edu.cn

Abstract

Current Chinese event extraction systems suffer much from two problems in trigger identification: unknown triggers and word segmentation errors to known triggers. To resolve these problems, this paper proposes two novel inference mechanisms to explore special characteristics in Chinese via compositional semantics inside Chinese triggers and discourse consistency between Chinese trigger mentions. Evaluation on the ACE 2005 Chinese corpus justifies the effectiveness of our approach over a strong baseline.

1 Introduction

Event extraction, a classic information extraction task, is to identify instances of a predefined event type and can be typically divided into four subtasks: trigger identification, trigger type determination, argument identification and argument role determination. In the literature, most studies focus on English event extraction and have achieved certain success (e.g. Grishman et al., 2005; Ahn, 2006; Hardy et al., 2006; Maslennikov and Chua, 2007; Finkel et al., 2005; Ji and Grishman, 2008; Patwardhan and Riloff, 2009, 2011; Liao and Grishman 2010; Hong et al., 2011).

In comparison, there are few successful stories regarding Chinese event extraction due to special characteristics in Chinese trigger identification. In particular, there are two major reasons for the low performance: unknown triggers [1] and word segmentation errors to known triggers. Table 1 gives the statistics of unknown triggers and word segmentation errors to known triggers in both the ACE 2005 Chinese and English corpora[2] using 10-fold cross-validation. In each validation, we leave 10% trigger mentions as the test set and the remaining ones as the training set. If a mention in the test set doesn't occurred in the training set, we regard it as an unknown trigger. It shows that these two cases cover almost 30% of Chinese trigger mentions while this figure reduces to only about 9% in English. It also shows that given the same number of event mentions, there are 30% more different triggers in Chinese than that in English. This justifies the low performance (specifically, the recall) of a Chinese event extraction system, which normally extracts those known triggers occurring in the training data as candidate instances and uses a classifier to distinguish correct triggers from wrong ones.

Language	Chinese	English
%unknown triggers	33.7%	18.5%
%unknown trigger mentions	20.9%	8.9%
%word segmentation errors to known trigger mentions	8.7%	0%
#triggers	763	586

Table 1. Statistics: a comparison between Chinese and English event extraction with regard to unknown triggers and word segmentation errors to known triggers. Note that word segmentation only applies to Chinese.

In this paper, we propose two novel inference mechanisms to Chinese trigger identification by employing compositional semantics inside Chinese triggers and discourse consistency between Chinese trigger mentions.

The first mechanism is motivated by the compositional nature of Chinese words, whose semantics can be often determined by the component characters. Hence, it is natural to infer

[1] In this paper, a trigger word/phrase occurring in the training data is called a known trigger and otherwise, an unknown trigger.

2 The whole Chinese ACE corpus has about 3300 event mentions. For the sake of fair comparison, we choose the same number of event mentions from the English corpus as the cross-validation data.

unknown triggers by employing compositional semantics inside Chinese triggers.

The second mechanism is enlightened by the wide use of discourse consistency in natural languages, particularly for Chinese, due to its discourse-driven nature (Zhu, 1980). Very often, distinguishing true trigger mentions from pseudo ones is only possible with contextual information.

The rest of this paper is organized as follows. Section 2 overviews the related work. Section 3 introduces a state-of-the-art baseline system for Chinese event extraction. Sections 4 and 5 describe two novel inference mechanisms to Chinese trigger identification by employing compositional semantics inside Chinese triggers and discourse consistency between Chinese trigger mentions. Section 6 presents the experimental results. Section 7 concludes the paper and points out future work.

2 Related Work

Almost all the existing studies on event extraction concern English. While earlier studies focus on sentence-level extraction (Grishman et al., 2005; Ahn, 2006; Hardy et al., 2006), later ones turn to employ high-level information, such as document (Maslennikov and Chua, 2007; Finkel et al., 2005; Patwardhan and Riloff, 2009), cross-document (Ji and Grishman, 2008), cross-event (Liao and Grishman, 2010; Gupta and Ji, 2009) and cross-entity (Hong et al., 2011) information.

2.1 Chinese Event Extraction

Compared with tremendous efforts in English event extraction, there are only a few studies on Chinese event extraction.

Tan et al. (2008) modeled event extraction as a pipeline of classification tasks. Specially, they used a local feature selection approach to ensure the performance of trigger classification (trigger identification + trigger type determination) and applied multiple levels of patterns to improve the coverage of patterns in argument classification (argument identification + argument role determination). Chen and Ji (2009a) proposed a bootstrapping framework, which exploited extra information captured by an English event extraction system. Chen and Ji (2009b) applied various kinds of lexical, syntactic and semantic features to address the specific issues in Chinese. They also constructed a global errata table to record the inconsistency in the training set and used it to correct the inconsistency in the test set. Ji (2009) extracted cross-lingual predicate clusters using bilingual parallel corpora and a cross-lingual information extraction system, and then used the derived clusters to improve the performance of Chinese event extraction.

2.2 Compositional Semantics

Almost all the related studies on compositional semantics focus on how to combine words together to convey complex meanings, such as semantic parser (Zettlemoyer and Collins, 2007; Wong and Mooney, 2007; Liang et al., 2011). However, the compositional semantics mentioned in this paper is more fined-grained and focuses on how to construct Chinese characters into a word and mine the semantics of words from the word structures, especially of verbs as event triggers.

To our knowledge, there is only one paper associated with compositional semantics inside Chinese words. Li (2011) discussed the internal structures inside Chinese nouns and used it in word segmentation.

2.3 Discourse Consistency

Discourse consistency is an important hypothesis in natural languages and has been applied to many natural language processing applications, such as named entity recognition and coreference resolution. Specially, several studies have successfully incorporated trigger or entity consistency constraint into event extraction.

Yarowsky (1995) and Yangarber et al. (Yangarber and Jokipii, 2005; Yangarber et al., 2007) applied cross-document inference to refine local extraction results for disease name, location and start/end time. Mann (2007) proposed some specific inference rules to improve extraction of personal information. Ji and Grishman (2008) employed a rule-based approach to propagate consistent triggers and arguments across topic-related documents. Gupta and Ji (2009) used a similar approach to recover implicit time information for events. Liao and Grishman (2011) also used a similar approach and a self-training strategy to extract events. Liao and Grishman (2010) employed cross-event consistency information to improve sentence-level event extraction. Hong et al. (2011) regarded entity type consistency as a key feature to predict event mentions and adopted this inference method to improve the traditional event extraction system.

3 Baseline

As a baseline, we re-implement a state-of-the-art system, which consists of four typical components (trigger identification, trigger type determination, argument identification and argument role determination), in a pipeline way and employ the same set of features as described in Chen and Ji (2009b).

Besides, the Maximum-Entropy (ME) model is employed to train individual component classifiers for the above four components. During testing, each word in the test set is first scanned for instances of known triggers from the training set. When an instance is found, the trigger identifier is applied to distinguish true trigger mentions from pseudo ones. If true, the trigger type determiner is then applied to recognize its event type. For any entity mentions in the sentence, the argument identifier is employed to assign possible arguments to them afterwards. Finally, the argument role determiner is introduced to assign a role to each argument.

One problem with Chen and Ji's system is its ignoring effective long-distance features. In order to resolve this problem and provide a stronger baseline, we introduce more refined and dependency features in four components:

- **Trigger Identification and Trigger Type Determination:** 1) syntactic features: path to the root of the governing clause, 2) nearest entity information: entity type of left syntactically/physically nearest entity to the trigger + entity, entity type of right syntactically/physically nearest entity to the trigger mention in the sentence + entity; 3) dependency features: the subject and the object of the trigger when they are entities.
- **Argument Identification and Argument Role Determination**: 1) basic features: POS of trigger; 2) neighboring words: left neighboring word of the entity + its POS, right neighbor word of the entity + its POS, left neighbor word of the trigger + its POS, right neighbor word of the trigger + its POS; 3) dependency feature: dependency path from the entity to the trigger; 4) semantic role features: Arg0 and Arg1 which tagged by semantic role labeling tool (Li, et al., 2010).

3.1 Experimental Setting

The ACE 2005 Chinese corpus (only the training data is available) is used in all our experiments. The corpus contains 633 Chinese documents annotated with 8 predefined event types and 33 predefined subtypes. Similar to previous studies, we treat these subtypes simply as 33 separate event types and do not consider the hierarchical structure among them.

Following Chen and Ji (2009b), we randomly select 567 documents as the training set and the remaining 66 documents as the test set. Besides, we reserve 33 documents in the training set as the development set, and follow the setting of ACE diagnostic tasks and use the ground truth entities, times and values for our training and testing.

For evaluation, we follow the standards as defined in Ji (2009):

- A trigger is *correctly* identified if its position in the document matches a reference trigger;
- A trigger type is *correctly* determined if its event type and position in the document match a reference trigger;
- An argument is *correctly* identified if its involved event type and position in the document match any of the reference argument mentions;
- An argument role is *correctly* determined if its involved event type, position in the document, and role match any of the reference argument mentions.

Finally, all sentences in the corpus are divided into words using a word segmentation tool ICTCLAS[3] with all entities annotated in the corpus kept. Besides, we use Stanford Parser (Levy and Manning, 2003, Chang, et al., 2009) to create the constituent and dependency parse trees and employ the ME model to train individual component classifiers.

3.2 Experimental Results

Table 2 and 3 show the Precision (P), Recall (R) and F1-Measure (F) on the held-out test set. It shows that our baseline system outperforms Chen and Ji (2009b) by 1.8, 2.2, 3.9 and 2.3 in F1-measure on trigger identification, trigger type

[3] http://ictclas.org/

determination, argument identification and argument role determination, respectively, with both gains in precision and recall. This is simply due to contribution of the newly-added refined and dependency features.

Performance / System	Trigger Identification			Trigger Type Determination		
	P(%)	R(%)	F	P(%)	R(%)	F
Chen and Ji (2009b)	71.5	51.2	59.7	66.5	47.7	55.6
Our Baseline	75.2	52.0	61.5	70.3	49.0	57.8

Table 2. Performance of trigger identification and trigger type determination

Performance / System	Argument Identification			Argument Role Determination		
	P(%)	R(%)	F	P(%)	R(%)	F
Chen and Ji (2009b)	56.1	38.2	45.4	53.1	36.2	43.1
Our Baseline	58.4	42.7	49.3	55.2	38.6	45.4

Table 3. Performance of argument identification and argument role determination

For our baseline system, given the small performance gaps between trigger identification and trigger type determination (3.7 in F1-measure: 61.5 vs. 57.8) and between argument identification and argument role determination (3.9 in F1-measure: 49.3 vs. 45.4), the performance bottlenecks of our baseline system mainly exist in trigger identification and argument identification, particularly for the former one. While argument identification has the performance gap of 8.5 in F1-measure compared to trigger type determination (49.3 vs. 57.8), the former one, trigger identification, can only achieve the performance of 61.5 in F1-measure (in particular the recall with only 52.0). In this paper, we will focus on trigger identification to improve its performance, particularly for the recall, via compositional semantics inside Chinese triggers and discourse consistency between Chinese trigger mentions.

4 Employing Compositional Semantics inside Chinese Triggers

Language is perhaps the only communicative system in nature, which compositionally builds structured meanings from smaller pieces, and this compositionality is the cognitive mechanism that allows for what Humboldt called language's "infinite use of finite means." As usual, the lexical semantics is the smallest piece in most Chinese language processing applications. In this section, we introduce a more fine-grained semantics - the compositional semantics in Chinese verb structure - and unveil its effect and usage in Chinese language processing by employing it into Chinese event extraction.

4.1 Compositional Semantics inside Chinese Triggers

In English, a component character is just the basic unit to form a word instead of a semantics unit. In comparison, almost all Chinese characters have their own meanings and can be formed as SCWs (Single Character Words) themselves. If a Chinese word contains more than one character, its meaning can be often inferred from the meanings of its component characters (Yuan, 1998). Actually, it is the normal way of understanding a new Chinese word in everyday life of a Chinese native speaker. A general method to this problem is to systematically explore the morphological structures in Chinese words. In this paper, compositional semantics provides a simple but effective compromise to the general method and we leave the general method in the future work. Table 4 shows samples of such compositional semantics in Chinese words. For example, "会见" is composed of two characters: "会" and "见" which have their own semantics and the semantics of "会见" comes from that of its component characters "会" and "见".

Words	Characters
会见 (interview[4])	会 (meet) 见(meet)
击毙 (shoot and kill)	击(shoot) 毙 (kill)
来到(come)	来 (come) 到 (to)
私信 (private letter)	私(private) 信(letter)

Table 4. Examples of compositional semantics in Chinese words

Therefore, it is natural to infer unknown triggers by employing compositional semantics inside Chinese triggers. Take following two sentences as examples:

(1) 4名学生被玻璃**划伤**。(Known trigger)

[4] Most Chinese words have more than one sense. Here, we just give the one when it acts as a trigger.

(Four students were scratched by the glass.)

(2) 1 名乘客被**刺伤**。(Unknown trigger)

(A passenger was stabbed.)

where "划伤" is a known trigger and "刺伤" is an unknown one.

In above examples, the semantics of "划伤" (injure by scratching) can be largely determined from those of its component characters "划" (scratch) and "伤" (injure) while the semantics of "刺伤" (injure by stabbing) from those of its component characters "刺" (stab) and "伤" (injure). Since these two triggers have similar internal structures, we can easily infer that "刺伤" is a trigger of *injure* event if "划伤" is known as a trigger of *injure* event. Similarly, we can infer more triggers for *injure* event, such as "灼伤" (injure by burning), "撞伤" (injure by hitting), "压伤" (injure by pressing), all with component character "伤" (injure) as the head and the other component character as the way of causing injury.

Since most triggers in Chinese event extraction are verbs [5], we focus on the compositional semantics in the verb structure. Statistics on the training set shows that 3.3% triggers (e.g. "公开信" (open letter), "事件" (event), "病情" (patient's condition), etc.) don't contain a BV and all of them are nouns. Normally, almost all verbs contain one or more single-character verbs as the basic element to construct a verb (we call it basic verb, shorted as BV) and the semantics of such a verb thus can be inferred from its BV. There are some studies on the Chinese verb structure in linguistics. However, their structures are much more complex and there are no annotated corpora available. We define following six main structures from our empirical observations:

(1) BV (e.g. "看" (see), "杀" (kill))
(2) BV + verb (e.g. "会见" (meet))
(3) verb + BV (e.g. "解雇" (fire))
(4) BV + complementation (e.g. "杀了" (kill))
(5) BV + noun/adj. (e.g. "回家" (go to home))
(6) noun/adj. +BV (e.g. "枪击" (shoot using gun)).

From above structures, a BV plays an important role in the verb structure and most of semantics of a verb can be interred from its contained BV and two words normally have very similar semantics if they have the same BV (e.g. "会见" (meet) and "会晤" (meet)). Actually, sometime the verb can be shortened to its contained BV (e.g. "我**见**王教授" and "我**会见**王教授" have the same semantics.).

4.2 Inferring via Compositional Semantics inside Chinese Triggers

Here a simple rule is employed to infer triggers via compositional semantics inside Chinese triggers: **a verb is a trigger if it contains a BV which occurs as a known trigger or is contained in a known trigger**. Table 5 shows the distribution of the set of triggers (contains the same BV [6]) classified by number of triggers.

From Table 5, we can find out that 85.3% of BVs occur in more than one trigger and 56.2% of them in more than 4 triggers. As for trigger mentions, these percentages become 89.1% and 65.2% respectively. A extreme example is that 85.2% (75/88) of triggers of *Trial-Hearing* event mentions contain "审" (trial) and 85.4% (117/138) of triggers of *injure* event mentions contains "伤" (injure).

Number	Distribution over Triggers	Distribution over Trigger Mentions
1	14.7%	10.9%
2~4	29.1%	23.9%
5~9	28.1%	32.9%
>=10	28.1%	32.3%

Table 5. Distribution of BVs in the number of triggers/trigger mentions

In this paper, the inference is done as follows:

- Add all single-character triggers into the BV set if it's a verb;
- Split all other triggers in the training set into a set of single characters and include all single characters into the BV set if it's a verb;
- For each word in the test set, it is identified as a trigger if it contains a BV.

It is worthwhile to note that such inference works for unknown triggers and word

[5] Actually, in the ACE 2005 Chinese (training) corpus, more than 90% of triggers are either verbs al or verbal nouns (those verbs which act as nouns). For simplicity, we don't differentiate these two types in this paper.

[6] We didn't tag BVs in the training set and regards all single-character verbs contained in triggers as BVs.

segmentation errors to known triggers since in both cases, their BVs will always exist as either a SCW or a component of a word.

4.3 Noise Filtering

One problem with above inference is that while it is able to recover some true triggers and increase the recall, it may introduce many pseudo ones and harm the precision. To filter out those pseudo triggers, we propose following rules according to our intuition and statistics over the training set.

Non-trigger Filtering

A Chinese word will not be a trigger if it appears in the training set but never trigger an event. Statistics on the training set shows that this rule applies at 99.7% of cases.

POS filtering

A Chinese word will not be a trigger if it has a different POS from that of the same known trigger or similar known triggers [7] in the training set. In Chinese, a single-character verb has very high probability of composing words (e.g. "到" (come), "为" (act as), "并" (combine), etc) with different POS from the single-character verb itself, such as preposition (e.g. "为了" (for)), conjunction (e.g. "并且" (and)), etc. Statistics on the training set shows that this rule applies at 97.3% of cases.

Verb structure filtering

A Chinese word will not be a trigger if its verb structure is different from that of the same known trigger or similar known triggers in the training set. Figure 1 shows different distributions of three BVs over six verb structures as described in subsection 4.1. For example, we can find that all triggers including "解" (unbind) (e.g. "解聘" (fire), "解雇" (fire), "解散" (disband)) just have one verb structure (BV + verb) and those of "杀" (kill) have 4 structures. Obviously, we can use such distribution information to filter out pseudo triggers. For example, although both word "劝解" (console) and "分解" (decompose) are constructed form verb "解", their verb structure (verb + BV) does not appear in the training set. Therefore, they will be filtered our via verb structure filtering. Statistics on the training set shows that this rule applies at 95.5% of cases.

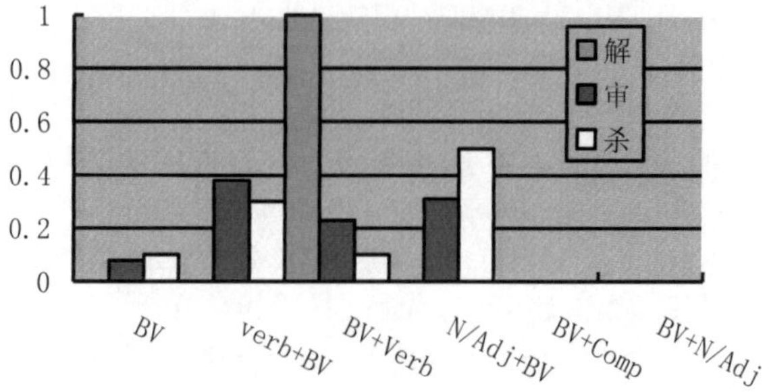

Figure 1. Distribution of three BVs ("解" (unbind), "审" (trial) and "杀" (kill)) over six verb structures in constructing triggers

5 Employing Discourse Consistency between Chinese Trigger Mentions

Chinese event extraction may suffer much from the errors propagated from upstream processing such as part-of-speech tagging and parsing, especially word segmentation. To alleviate word segmentation errors to known triggers, Chen and Ji (2009b) constructed a global errata table to record the inconsistency in the training set and proved its effectiveness. In this paper, a merge and split method is applied to recover those known triggers. In this way, word segmentation errors can be alleviated to certain extent.

For unknown triggers, we can merge two or more neighboring short words or single characters as a trigger candidate. In this paper, for each single-character verb in a document after word segmentation, this single-character verb can be merged with either previous SCW or next SCW to form a trigger candidate if this single-character verb has occurred in the training set with the same verb structure.

Given above recovered triggers for both known and unknown triggers, the key issue here is how to distinguish true triggers from pseudo ones. In this paper, we employ discourse consistency between Chinese trigger mentions for Chinese event extraction. Previous studies on English event extraction have proved the effectiveness of both cross-entity and cross-document consistency.

5.1 Discourse Consistency between Chinese Trigger Mentions

As a discourse-driven language, the syntax of

[7] Similar triggers are those ones which have the same BV and verb structure.

Chinese is not as strict as English and sometime we must infer from the discourse-level information to understand the meaning of a sentence. Kim (2000) compared the use of overt subjects in English and Chinese and he found that overt subjects occupy over 96% in English, while this percentage drops to only 64% in Chinese. Similarly, argument missing is another issue in Chinese event extraction and almost 55% of arguments are missing in the ACE 2005 Chinese corpus. Normally, using a feature-based approach to distinguish true triggers from pseudo ones is very difficult from the sentence level if some of related arguments are missing from the trigger-occurring sentence. Take following two contingent sentences as examples:

(3) 美国与北韩 3 号在吉隆坡结束飞弹**会谈。**
(The United States and the Democratic People's Republic of Korea finished missile **talks** in Kuala Lumpur.)

(4) **会谈**的气氛严肃。
(The **talks** are serious.)

While it is relatively easy to determine that mention "会谈" in sentence (3) indicates a *meet* event from the contained information in itself (there are many entities, such as agents, time and place in the sentence) and difficult to determine that mention "会谈" in sentence (4) is a *meet* event from the contained information in itself, we can easily infer from sentence (3) that sentence (4) also indicates a *meet* event, using discourse consistency: if one instance of a word is a trigger mention, other instances in the same discourse will be a trigger mention with high probability.

Language	Discourse-based	Instance-based
English	70.2%	87.5%
Chinese	90.5%	95.4%

Table 6. Comparison of discourse consistency between Chinese and English trigger mentions

Table 6 compares the probabilities of discourse consistency between Chinese and English trigger mentions in the ACE 2005 Chinese and English corpora. A trigger may appear many times in a discourse. It's considered discourse-consistent when all the appearances of a trigger have the same event type while instance-based consistency refers to pair-wired cases. It shows that within the discourse, there is a strong consistency in both Chinese and English between trigger mentions: if one instance of a word is a trigger, other instances in the same discourse will be a trigger of the same event type with very high probability.

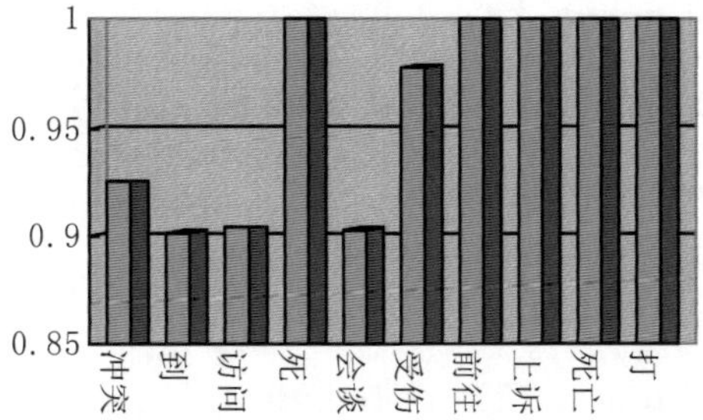

Figure 2. Probabilities of discourse-level consistency of top 10 frequent triggers

It also shows that discourse consistency in Chinese triggers holds much more likely than the English counterpart. Figure 2 give the probabilities of discourse-level consistency of top 10 frequent triggers, which occupy 18% of event mentions in the ACE 2005 Chinese corpus.

5.2 Inference via Discourse Consistency between Chinese Trigger Mentions

Given a discourse and different mentions of a trigger returned by the trigger identifier, we can simply accept those mentions with high probability as true mentions of the trigger and discard those with low probability[8]. However, for those mentions in-between, an additional discourse-level trigger identifier is further employed to determine whether a trigger mention is true or not from the discourse level by augmenting the normal trigger identifier with several features to explore the consistency information between trigger mentions in the discourse (first three features) and the related information returned from the trigger type identifier (last two features).

- Probability of the discourse consistency of the candidate trigger mention in the training set. If it doesn't exist in the training set, we infer its probability from that of all of its similar triggers
- Number of candidate trigger mentions being a trigger in the same discourse via trigger identification
- Number of candidate trigger mentions being a non-trigger in the same discourse via trigger identification

[8] The high and low probability thresholds are fine-tuned to 95% and 5% respectively, using the development set.

- Event type of candidate trigger mention via trigger type determination
- Confidence of trigger type determination

6 Experiments

In this section, we evaluate our two inference mechanisms in Chinese trigger identification and its application to overall Chinese event extraction, using the same experimental settings as described in Subsection 3.1.

6.1 Chinese Trigger Identification

Table 7 shows the impact of compositional semantics in trigger identification. Here, the baseline just extracts those triggers occurring in the training data. It justifies the effectiveness of our compositional semantics-based inference mechanism in recovering true triggers and its three filtering rules in removing pseudo triggers.

Approaches \ Numbers	Triggers	Non-triggers
Baseline	266	629
+Compositional semantics without filtering	334	1885
+ Non-trigger filtering	328	1062
+ POS filtering	325	974
+ Verb structure filtering	302	444
Gold	367	-

Table 7. Impact of compositional semantics in trigger identification

To reduce those pseudo triggers after above inference process, three rules are introduced.

The first rule, the non-trigger filtering rule, filters out those pseudo ones in the test set which do not frequently occur as trigger mentions in the training set. In particular, to keep true triggers in our candidate set as many as possible, we just filter out those candidates which occur as non-triggers more than 5 times in the training set according to our validation on the development set. Table 7 shows that 43.7% (823) of pseudo triggers are filtered out while only 1.8% (6) of true ones is wrongly filtered out.

The second rule, the POS filtering rule, just filters out 8.3% (88) of pseudo triggers, due to POS errors in word segmentation and constituent parsing (e.g. 9.4% of candidate triggers have wrong POS tags in the development set.). Manual inspection shows that if we correct those wrong POS tags, that percentage will be increased to 14.5%.

The third rule, the verb structure filtering rule, is deployed in following steps: 1) keeping all candidates if they act as a trigger in the training set; 2) if the candidate is a SCW, removing it when it does not occur as a BV in any triggers in the training set; 3) if the candidate is not a SCW, calculating the condition probability of its similar trigger words as triggers in the training set[9] and then deleting all candidates whose conditional probabilities are less than a threshold θ, which is fine-tuned to 0.5. Figure 3 shows the effect on precision, recall and F1-measure of varying the threshold θ on the development set.

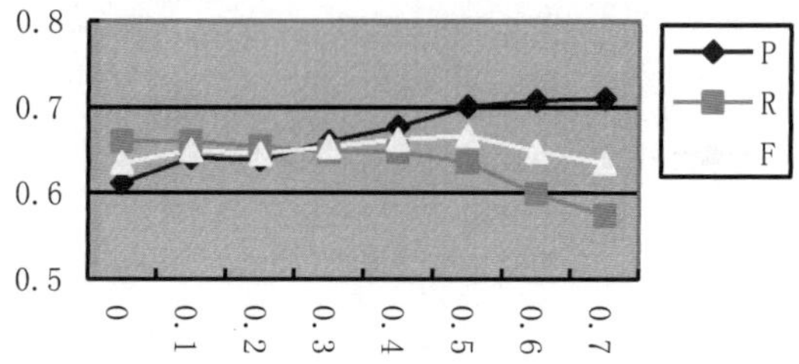

Figure 3. Effect of threshold θ on the development set

System \ Performance	Trigger Identification		
	P(%)	R(%)	F
Baseline	75.2	52.0	61.5
+Compositional semantics without filtering	34.8	66.8	45.8
+ Non-trigger filtering	49.4	66.5	56.7
+ POS filtering	50.2	65.9	57.0
+ Verb structure filtering	73.5	62.1	67.4
+Discourse consistency	**79.3**	**63.5**	**70.5**

Table 8. Contribution to Chinese triggers identification (incremental)

Table 8 shows the contribution of employing compositional semantics and discourse consistency to trigger identification on the held-out test set. We can find out that our approach dramatically enhances F1-measure by 9.0 units, largely due to a dramatic increase of 11.5% in recall, benefiting from both compositional semantics and discourse consistency mechanisms. We expect that the precision will also increase since our filtering approach successfully filters out almost 30% more

[9] If there are more than one BV in a candidate, we calculate the average one.

non-triggers and the number of non-trigger mentions is less than that of the baseline. Unfortunately, the resulting set of 444 non-trigger mentions (after all filtering) is not a subset of original 629 non-trigger ones. Our observation shows that our compositional semantics inference adds almost 10% new non-triggers into candidates which are very hard to distinguish.

Table 8 also justifies the impact of the discourse consistency between trigger mentions in trigger identification and the effect of the additional discourse-level trigger identifier, with a big gain of 5.8% in precision and a small gain of 1.4% in recall.

6.2 Chinese Event Extraction

Table 9 shows the contribution of trigger identification with compositional semantics and discourse consistency to overall event extraction on the held-out test set. In addition, we also report the performance of two human annotators (The human annotator 1 is a first year postgraduate student with no background to Chinese event extraction while the human annotator 2 is a third year postgraduate student working on Chinese event extraction) on 33 texts (a subset of the held-out test set). From the results presented in Table 9, we can find that our approach can improve the F1-measure for trigger identification by 9.0 units, trigger type determination by 9.1 units, argument identification by 6.0 units and argument role determination (i.e. overall event extraction) by 5.4 units, largely due to the dramatic increase in recall of 11.5%, 11.2%, 7.5% and 7.2%.

Performance / System/Human	Trigger Identification			Trigger Type Determination			Argument Identification			Argument Role Determination		
	P(%)	R(%)	F	P(%)	R(%)	F	P(%)	R(%)	F	P(%)	R(%)	F
Our Baseline	75.2	52.0	61.5	70.3	49.0	57.8	58.4	42.7	49.3	55.2	38.6	45.4
+Compositional semantics	73.5	62.1	67.4	70.2	59.1	64.2	58.0	48.9	53.0	54.7	44.5	49.1
+Discourse consistency	**79.3**	**63.5**	**70.5**	**75.2**	**60.2**	**66.9**	**61.6**	**50.2**	**55.3**	**56.9**	**45.8**	**50.8**
Human annotator1(blind)	63.3	62.9	63.1	61.7	59.5	60.6	64.6	54.1	58.9	60.9	48.2	53.8
Human annotator2(familiar)	72.6	74.3	73.4	69.1	70.2	69.6	71.5	65.9	68.6	66.4	54.6	59.9
Inter-Annotator Agreement	45.8	42.9	44.3	45.3	42.5	43.8	60.4	49.7	54.5	55.1	45.9	50.1

Table 9: Overall contribution to Chinese event extraction

In addition, the results of two annotators show that Chinese event extraction is really challenging even for a well-educated human being. As shown in Table 9, the inter-annotator agreement on trigger identification and trigger type determination is even less than 45%. Although this figure is very low, it is not surprising: the results on the English ACE 2005 corpus show that the inter-annotator agreement on trigger identification is only about 40% (Ji and Grishman, 2008). Detailed analysis shows that a human annotator tends to make more mistakes in trigger identification for two reasons. The first reason is that a human annotator always misses some event mentions when a sentence contains more than one event mention. The second reason is that it is hard to identify an event mention due to the failure of following specified annotation guidelines, as mentioned in Ji and Grishman (2008). Table 9 also shows the performance gaps of human annotators between trigger identification and trigger type determination is very small (2.5% and 3.8% in F1-measure). It ensures that trigger identification is the most important step in Chinese event extraction for a human being. For human annotators, it's much easier to determine the event type of a trigger, identify its arguments and determine the role of each argument, all with more than 90% in accuracy, once a trigger is identified correctly.

6.3 Discussion

Compared with English, the word structures in Chinese are much more complex and diverse, causing a lot of troubles in Chinese language processing. We ensure that compositional semantics in Chinese words is very useful for many Chinese language processing applications, such as machine translation, semantic parser, etc. For example, many actions (e.g. "砍" (hack), "咬" (bite), "踢" (kick), etc) can combine with "伤" (injure) to form words and most of those words have similar semantics. The results in table 8 show its contribution in Chinese event extraction. Although our approach is simple, the result is promising enough for further efforts in this direction.

This paper shows that the compositional semantics in the verb structure provides an ideal way to expand the coverage of triggers. As a discourse-driven language, ellipsis is very common in Chinese, causing inference from the discourse-level information is a fundamental requirement to understand the meaning of a clause, sentence or discourse.

7 Conclusion

In this paper we propose two novel inference mechanisms to Chinese trigger identification. In particular, compositional semantics inside Chinese triggers and discourse consistency between Chinese trigger mentions are used to resolve two critical issues in Chinese trigger identification: unknown triggers and word segmentation errors to known triggers. We give good reasons why this should be done, and present effective methods how this could be done. It shows that such novel inference mechanisms for Chinese event extraction are linguistically justified and pragmatically beneficial to real world applications.

In future work, we will focus on how to introduce the discourse information into the individual classifiers to capture those long-distance features and joint learning of subtasks in Chinese event extraction.

Acknowledgments

The authors would like to thank three anonymous reviewers for their comments on this paper. This research was supported by the National Natural Science Foundation of China under Grant No. 61070123 and No. 90920004, the National 863 Project of China under Grant No. 2012AA011102.

References

David Ahn. 2006. The Stages of Event Extraction. In Proc. COLING/ACL 2006 Workshop on Annotating and Reasoning about Time and Events. Pages 1-8, Sydney, Australia.

Pi-Chuan Chang, Huihsin Tseng, Dan Jurafsky, and Christopher Manning. 2009. Discriminative Reordering with Chinese Grammatical Relations Features. In Proc. Third Workshop on Syntax and Structure in Statistical Translation, pages 51-59.

Zheng Chen and Heng Ji. 2009a. Can One Language Bootstrap the Other: A Case Study on Event Extraction. In Proc. NAACL HLT Workshop on Semi-supervised Learning for Natural Language Processing, pages 66-74, Boulder, Colorado.

Zheng Chen and Heng Ji. 2009b. Language Specific Issue and Feature Exploration in Chinese Event Extraction. In Proc. NAACL HLT 2009, pages 209-212, Boulder, CO.

Jenny Rose Finkel, Trond Grenager and Christopher Manning. 2005. Incorporating Non-local Information into Information Extraction Systems by Gibbs Sampling. In Proc. ACL 2005, pages 363-370, Ann Arbor, MI.

Prashant Gupta and Heng Ji. 2009. Predicting Unknown Time Arguments based on Cross-Event Propagation. In Proc. ACL-IJCNLP 2009, pages 369-272, Suntec, Singapore.

Ralph Grishman, David Westbrook and Adam Meyers. 2005. NYU's English ACE 2005 System Description. In Proc. ACE 2005 Evaluation Workshop, Gaithersburg, MD.

Hilda Hardy, Vika Kanchakouskaya and Tomek Strzalkowski. 2006. Automatic Event Classification Using Surface Text Features. In Proc. AAAI 2006 Workshop on Event Extraction and Synthesis, pages 36-41, Boston, MA.

Yu Hong, Jianfeng Zhang, Bin Ma, Jianmin Yao, Guodong Zhou and Qiaoming Zhu. 2011. Using Cross-Entity Inference to Improve Event Extraction. In Proc. ACL 2011, pages 1127-1136, Portland, OR.

Heng Ji. 2009. Cross-lingual Predicate Cluster Acquisition to Improve Bilingual Event Extraction by Inductive Learning. In Proc. NAACL HLT Workshop on Unsupervised and Minimally Supervised Learning of Lexical Semantics, pages 27-35, Boulder, CO.

Heng Ji and Ralph Grishman. 2008. Refining Event Extraction through Cross-Document Inference. In Proc. ACL-08: HLT, pages 254-262, Columbus, OH.

Young-Joo Kim. 2000. Subject/object drop in the acquisition of Korean: A Cross-linguistic Comparison. Journal of East Asian Linguistics, 9(4): 325-351.

Roger Levy and Christopher D. Manning. 2003. Is it harder to parse Chinese, or the Chinese Treebank? In Proc. ACL 2003, pages 439-446, Sapporo, Japan.

Shasha Liao and Ralph Grishman. 2010. Using Document Level Cross-Event Inference to Improve Event Extraction. In Proc. ACL 2010, pages 789-797, Uppsala, Sweden.

Zhongguo Li. 2011. Parsing the Internal Structure of Words: A New Paradigm for Chinese Word Segmentation. In Proc. ACL 2011, pages 1405-1414, Portland, OR.

Percy Liang, Michael I. Joedan and Dan Klein. 2011. Learning Dependency-Based Compositional

Semantics. In Proc. ACL 2011, pages 590-599, Portland, OR.

Gideon Mann. 2007. Multi-document Relationship Fusion via Constraints on Probabilistic Databases. In Proc. HLT/NAACL 2007, pages 332-229, Rochester, NY.

Mstislav Maslennikov and Tat-Seng Chua. 2007. A Multi Resolution Framework for Information Extraction from Free Text. In Proc. ACL 2007, pages 592-599, Prague, Czech Republic.

Siddharth Patwardhan and Ellen Riloff. 2007. Effective Information Extraction with Semantic Affinity Patterns and Relevant Regions. In Proc. EMNLP/CoNLL 2007, pages 717-727, Prague, Czech Republic.

Siddharth Patwardhan and Ellen Riloff. 2009. A Unified Model of Phrasal and Sentential Evidence for Information Extraction. In Proc. EMNLP 2009, pages 151-160, Singapore.

Hongye Tan, Tiejun Zhao, Jiaheng Zheng. 2008. Identification of Chinese Event and Their Argument Roles. Proc. of the 2008 IEEE 8th International Conference on Computer and Information Technology Workshops, pages 14-19, Sydney, Australia.

Yuk Wah Wong and Raymond J. Mooney. 2007. Learning Synchronous Grammars for Semantic Parsing with Lambda Calculus. In Proc. ACL 2007, pages 960-967, Prague, Czech Republic.

Roman Yangarber, Clive Best, Peter von Etter, Flavio Fuart, David Horby and Ralf Steinberger. 2007. Combining Information about Epidemic Threats from Multiple Sources. In Proc. RANLP 2007 workshop on Multi-source, Multilingual Information Extraction and Summarization. Borovets, pages 41-48, Borovets, Bulgaria.

Roman Yangarber and Lauri Jokipii. 2005. Redundancy-based Correction of Automatically Extracted Facts. In Proc. EMNLP 2005, pages 57-64, Vancouver, Canada.

David Yarowsky. 1995. Unsupervised Word Sense Disambiguation Rivaling Supervised Methods. In Proc. ACL 1995, pages 189-196, Cambridge, MA.

Minglin Yuan. 1998. Studies on Valency in Modern Chinese. Chinese Commerce and Trade Press, Beijing, China.

Luke S. Zettlemoyer and Michael Collins. 2007. Online Learning of Relaxed CCG Grammars for Parsing to Logical Form. In EMNLP/CoNLL 2007, pages 678-687, Prague, Czech Republic.

Dexi Zhu. 1980. Research on Chinese Modern Grammars. Chinese Commerce and Trade Press, Beijing, China.

Reading The Web with Learned Syntactic-Semantic Inference Rules

Ni Lao[1]*, **Amarnag Subramanya**[2], **Fernando Pereira**[2], **William W. Cohen**[1]
[1]Carnegie Mellon University, 5000 Forbes Avenue, Pittsburgh, PA 15213, USA
[2]Google Research, 1600 Amphitheatre Parkway, Mountain View, CA 94043, USA
nlao@cs.cmu.edu, {asubram, pereira}@google.com, wcohen@cs.cmu.edu

Abstract

We study how to extend a large knowledge base (Freebase) by reading relational information from a large Web text corpus. Previous studies on extracting relational knowledge from text show the potential of syntactic patterns for extraction, but they do not exploit background knowledge of other relations in the knowledge base. We describe a distributed, Web-scale implementation of a path-constrained random walk model that learns syntactic-semantic inference rules for binary relations from a graph representation of the parsed text and the knowledge base. Experiments show significant accuracy improvements in binary relation prediction over methods that consider only text, or only the existing knowledge base.

1 Introduction

Manually-created knowledge bases (KBs) often lack basic information about some entities and their relationships, either because the information was missing in the initial sources used to create the KB, or because human curators were not confident about the status of some putative fact, and so they excluded it from the KB. For instance, as we will see in more detail later, many person entries in Freebase (Bollacker et al., 2008) lack nationality information. To fill those KB gaps, we might use general rules, ideally automatically learned, such as "if *person* was born in *town* and *town* is in *country* then the *person* is a national of the *country*." Of course, rules like this may be defeasible, in this case for example because of naturalization or political changes. Nevertheless, many such imperfect rules can be learned and combined to yield useful KB completions, as demonstrated in particular with the *Path-Ranking Algorithm* (PRA) (Lao and Cohen, 2010; Lao et al., 2011), which learns such rules on heterogenous graphs for link prediction tasks.

Alternatively, we may attempt to fill KB gaps by applying relation extraction rules to free text. For instance, Snow et al. (2005) and Suchanek et al. (2006) showed the value of syntactic patterns in extracting specific relations. In those approaches, KB tuples of the relation to be extracted serve as positive training examples to the extraction rule induction algorithm. However, the KB contains much more knowledge about other relations that could potentially be helpful in improving relation extraction accuracy and coverage, but that is not used in such purely text-based approaches.

In this work, we use PRA to learn weighted rules (represented as graph path patterns) that combine both semantic (KB) and syntactic information encoded respectively as edges in a graph-structured KB, and as syntactic dependency edges in dependency-parsed Web text. Our approach can easily incorporate existing knowledge in extraction tasks, and its distributed implementation scales to the whole of the Freebase KB and 60 million parsed documents. To the best of our knowledge, this is the first successful attempt to apply relational learning methods to heterogeneous data with this scale.

*This research was carried out during an internship at Google Research

1.1 Terminology and Notation

In this study, we use a simplified KB consisting of a set C of concepts and a set R of labels. Each label r denotes some binary relation partially represented in the KB. The concrete KB is a directed, edge-labeled graph $G = (C, T)$ where $T \subseteq C \times R \times C$ is the set of labeled edges (also known as *triples*) (c, r, c'). Each triple represents an instance $r(c, c')$ of the relation $r \in R$. The KB may be incomplete, that is, $r(c, c')$ holds in the real world but $(c, r, c') \notin T$. Our method will attempt to learn rules to infer such missing relation instances by combining the KB with parsed text.

We denote by r^{-1} the inverse relation of r: $r(c, c') \Leftrightarrow r^{-1}(c', c)$. For instance Parent^{-1} is equivalent to *Children*. It is convenient to take G as containing triple (c', r^{-1}, c) whenever it contains triple (c, r, c').

A *path type* in G is a sequence $\pi = \langle r_1, \ldots, r_m \rangle$. An *instance* of the path type is a sequence of nodes $c_0, \ldots, c_m$ such that $r_i(c_{i-1}, c_i)$. For instance, "the persons who were born in the same town as the query person", and "the nationalities of persons who were born in the same town as the query person" can be reached respectively through paths matching the following types

$$\pi_1 : \langle \mathit{BornIn}, \mathit{BornIn}^{-1} \rangle$$
$$\pi_2 : \langle \mathit{BornIn}, \mathit{BornIn}^{-1}, \mathit{Nationality} \rangle$$

1.2 Learning Syntactic-Semantic Rules with Path-Constrained Random Walks

Given a query concept $s \in C$ and a relation $r \in R$, PRA begins by enumerating a large set of bounded-length path types. These path types are treated as ranking "experts," each generating some random instance of the path type starting from s, and ranking end nodes t by their weights in the resulting distribution. Finally, PRA combines the weights contributed by different "experts" by using logistic regression to predict the probability that the relation $r(s, t)$ holds.

In this study, we test the hypothesis that PRA can be used to find useful "syntactic-semantic patterns" – that is, patterns that exploit both semantic and syntactic relationships, thereby using semantic knowledge as background in interpreting syntactic relationships. As shown in Figure 1, we extend the KB graph G with nodes and edges from text that has been syntactically analyzed with a dependency parser[1] and where pronouns and other anaphoric referring expressions have been clustered with their antecedents. The text nodes are word/phrase instances, and the edges are syntactic dependencies labeled by the corresponding dependency type. Mentions of entities in the text are linked to KB concepts by mention edges created by an entity resolution process.

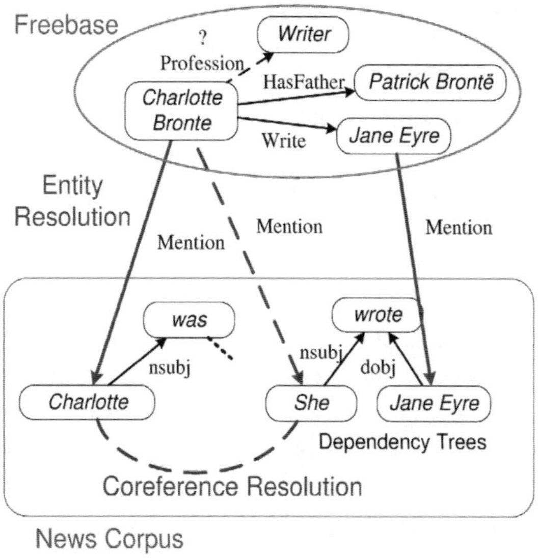

Figure 1: Knowledge base and parsed text as a labeled graph. For clarity, some word nodes are omitted.

Given for instance the query *Profession*(*CharlotteBronte*, ?), PRA produces a ranked list of answers that may have the relation *Profession* with the query node *CharlotteBronte*. The features used to score answers are the random walk probabilities of reaching a certain profession node from the query node by paths with particular path types. PRA can learn path types that combine background knowledge in the database with syntactic patterns in the text corpus. We now exemplify some path types involving relations described in Table 3. Type $\langle M, \mathit{conj}, M^{-1}, \mathit{Profession} \rangle$ is *active* (matches paths) for professions of persons who are mentioned in conjunction with the query person as in "collaboration between McDougall and Simon

[1]Stanford dependencies (de Marneffe and Manning, 2008).

Philips". For a somewhat subtler example, type $\langle M, TW, CW^{-1}, Profession^{-1}, Profession\rangle$ is active for persons who are mentioned by their titles as in "President Barack Obama". The type subsequence $\langle Profession^{-1}, Profession\rangle$ ensures that only profession concepts are activated. The features generated from these path types combine syntactic dependency relations (*conj*) and textual information relations (*TW* and *CW*) with semantic relations in the KB (*Profession*).

Experiments on three Freebase relations (profession, nationality and parents) show that exploiting existing background knowledge as path features can significantly improve the quality of extraction compared with using either Freebase or the text corpus alone.

1.3 Related Work

Information extraction from varied unstructured and structured sources involves both complex relational structure and uncertainty at all levels of the extraction process. Statistical Relational Learning (SRL) seeks to combine statistical and relational learning methods to address such tasks. However, most SRL approaches (Friedman et al., 1999; Richardson and Domingos, 2006) suffer the complexity of inference and learning when applied to large scale problems. Recently, Lao and Cohen (2010) introduced Path Ranking algorithm, which is applicable to larger scale problems such as literature recommendation (Lao and Cohen, 2010) and inference on a large knowledge base (Lao et al., 2011).

Much of the previous work on automatic relation extraction was based on certain lexico-syntactic patterns. Hearst (1992) first noticed that patterns such as "NP and other NP" and "NP such as NP" often imply hyponym relations (NP here refers to a noun phrase). However, such approaches to relation extraction are limited by the availability of domain knowledge. Later systems for extracting arbitrary relations from text mostly use shallow surface text patterns (Etzioni et al., 2004; Agichtein and Gravano, 2000; Ravichandran and Hovy, 2002). The idea of using sequences of dependency edges as features for relation extraction was explored by Snow et al. (2005) and Suchanek et al. (2006). They define features to be shortest paths on dependency trees which connect pairs of NP candidates.

This study is most closely related to work of Mintz et al. (2009), who also study the problem of extending Freebase with extraction from parsed text. As in our work, they use a logistic regression model with path features. However, their approach does not exploit existing knowledge in the KB. Furthermore, their path patterns are used as binary-values features. We show experimentally that fractional-valued features generated by random walks provide much higher accuracy than binary-valued ones.

Culotta et al. (2006)'s work is similar to our approach in the sense of relation extraction by discovering relational patterns. However while they focus on identifying relation mentions in text (microreading),this work attempts to infer new tuples by gathering path evidence over the whole corpus (macroreading). In addition, their work involves a few thousand examples, while we aim for Web-scale extraction.

Do and Roth (2010) use a KB (YAGO) to aid the generation of features from free text. However their method is designed specifically for extracting hierarchical taxonomic structures, while our algorithm can be used to discover relations for general general graph-based KBs.

In this paper we extend the PRA algorithm along two dimensions: combining syntactic and semantic cues in text with existing knowledge in the KB; and a distributed implementation of the learning and inference algorithms that works at Web scale.

2 Path Ranking Algorithm

We briefly review the Path Ranking algorithm (PRA), described in more detail by Lao and Cohen (2010). Each path type $\pi = \langle r_1, r_2, ..., r_\ell\rangle$ specifies a real-valued *feature*. For a given query-answer node pair (s, t), the value of the feature π is $P(s \to t; \pi)$, the probability of reaching t from s by a random walk that instantiates the type. More specifically, suppose that the random walk has just reached v_i by traversing edges labeled $r_1, \ldots, r_i$ with $s{=}v_0$. Then v_{i+1} is drawn at random from all nodes reachable from v_i by edges labeled r_{i+1}. A path type π is *active* for pair (s, t) if $P(s \to t; \pi) > 0$.

Let $B = \{\perp, \pi_1, ..., \pi_n\}$ be the set of all path types of length no greater than ℓ that occur in the graph together with the dummy type $\perp$, which represents the bias feature. For convenience, we set $P(s \to t; \perp) = 1$ for any nodes s, t. The score for whether query node s is related to another node t by relation r is given by

$$score(s,t) = \sum_{\pi \in B} P(s \to t; \pi)\theta_\pi \quad ,$$

where θ_π is the weight of feature π. The model parameters to be learned are the vector $\boldsymbol{\theta} = \langle \theta_\pi \rangle_{\pi \in B}$. The procedures used to discover B and estimate $\boldsymbol{\theta}$ are described in the following. Finally, note that we train a *separate* PRA model for each relation r.

Path Discovery: Given a graph and a target relation r, the total number of path types is an exponential function of the maximum path length ℓ and considering all possible paths would be computationally very expensive. As a result, B is constructed using only path types that satisfy the following two constraints:

1. the path type is active for more than K training query nodes, and

2. the probability of reaching any correct target node t is larger than a threshold α on average for the training query nodes s.

We will discuss how K, α and the training queries are chosen in Section 5. In addition to making the training more efficient, these constraints are also helpful in removing low quality path types.

Training Examples: For each relation r of interest, we start with a set of node pairs $S_r = \{(s_i, t_i)\}$. From S_r, we create the training set $D_r = \{(\mathbf{x}_i, y_i)\}$, where $\mathbf{x}_i = \langle P(s_i \to t_i; \pi) \rangle_{\pi \in B}$ is the vector of path feature values for the pair (s_i, t_i), and y_i indicates whether $r(s_i, t_i)$ holds.

Following previous work (Lao and Cohen, 2010; Mintz et al., 2009), node pairs that are in r in the KB are legitimate positive training examples[2]. One can generate negative training examples by considering all possible pairs of concepts whose type is compatible with r (as given by the schema) and are not present in the KB. However this procedure leads to a very large number of negative examples (e.g., for the parents relation, any pair of person concepts which are related by this relation would be valid negative examples) which not only makes training very expensive but also introduces an incorrect bias in the training set. Following Lao and Cohen (2010) we use a simple biased sampling procedure to generate negative examples: first, the path types discovered in the previous (path discovery) step are used to construct an initial PRA model (all feature weights are set to 1.0); then, for each query node s_i, this model is used to retrieve candidate answer nodes, which are then sorted in descending order by their scores; finally, nodes at the $k(k+1)/2$-th positions are selected as negative samples, where $k = 0, 1, 2, ...$

Logistic Regression Training: Given a training set D, we estimate parameters $\boldsymbol{\theta}$ by maximizing the following objective

$$\mathcal{F}(\boldsymbol{\theta}) = \frac{1}{|D|} \sum_{(\mathbf{x},y) \in D} f(\mathbf{x}, y; \boldsymbol{\theta}) - \lambda_1 \|\boldsymbol{\theta}\|_1 - \lambda_2 \|\boldsymbol{\theta}\|_2^2$$

where λ_1 and λ_2 control the strength of the L_1-regularization which helps with structure selection and L_2^2-regularization which prevents overfitting. The log-likelihood $f(\mathbf{x}, y; \boldsymbol{\theta})$ of example $(\mathbf{x}, y)$ is given by

$$f(\mathbf{x}, y, \boldsymbol{\theta}) = y \ln p(\mathbf{x}, \boldsymbol{\theta}) + (1-y) \ln(1 - p(\mathbf{x}, \boldsymbol{\theta}))$$
$$p(\mathbf{x}, \boldsymbol{\theta}) = \frac{\exp(\boldsymbol{\theta}^T \mathbf{x})}{1 + \exp(\theta^T \mathbf{x})} \quad .$$

Inference: After a model is trained for a relation r in the knowledge base, it can be used to produce new instances of r. We first generate unlabeled queries s which belong to the domain of r. Queries which appear in the training set are excluded. For each unlabeled query node s, we apply the trained PRA model to generate a list of candidate t nodes together with their scores. We then sort all the predictions (s, t) by their scores in descending order, and evaluate the top ones.

3 Extending PRA

As described in the previous section, the PRA model is trained on positive and negative queries generated from the KB. As Freebase contains millions of

[2] In our experiments we subsample the positive examples. See section 3.2 for more details.

concepts and edges, training on all the generated queries is computationally challenging. Further, we extend the Freebase graph with parse paths of mentions of concepts in Freebase in millions of Web pages. Yet another issue is that the training queries generated using Freebase are inherently biased towards the distribution of concepts in Freebase and may not reflect the distribution of mentions of these concepts in text data. As one of the goals of our approach is to learn relation instances that are missing in Freebase, training on such a set biased towards the distribution of concepts in Freebase may not lead to good performance. In this section we explain how we modified the PRA algorithm to address those issues.

3.1 Scaling Up

Most relations in Freebase have a large set of existing triples. For example, for the *profession* relation, there are around 2 million persons in Freebase, and about 0.3 million of them have known professions. This results in more than 0.3 million training queries (persons), each with one or more positive answers (professions), and many negative answers, which make training computationally challenging. Generating all the paths for millions of queries over a graph with millions of concepts and edges further complicates the computational issues. Incorporating the parse path features from the text only exacerbates the matter. Finally once we have trained a PRA model for a given relation, say *profession*, we would like to infer the professions for all the 1.7 million persons whose professions are not known to Freebase (and possibly predict changes to the profession information of the 0.3 million people whose professions were given).

We use distributed computing to deal with the large number of training and prediction queries over a large graph. A key observation is that the different stages of the PRA algorithm are based on independent computations involving individual queries. Therefore, we can use the MapReduce framework to distribute the computation (Dean and Ghemawat, 2008). For path discovery, we modify Lao et al.'s path finding (2011) approach to decouple the queries: instead of using one depth-first search that involves all the queries, we first find all paths up to certain length for each query node in the map stage, and then collect statistics for each path from all the query nodes in the reduce stage. We used a 500-machine, 8GB/machine cluster for these computations.

Another challenge associated with applying PRA to a graph constructed using a large amounts of text is that we cannot load the entire graph on a single machine. To circumvent this problem, we first index all parsed sentences by the concepts that they mention. Therefore, to perform a random walk for a query concept s, we only load the sentences which mention s.

3.2 Sampling Training Data

Using the r-edges in the KB as positive examples distorts the training set. For example, for the *profession* relation, there are 0.3 million persons for whom Freebase has profession information, and amongst these 0.24 million are either politicians or actors. This may not reflect the distribution of professions of persons mentioned in Web data. Using all of these as training queries will most certainly bias the trained model towards these professions as PRA is trained discriminatively. In other words, training directly with this data would lead to a model that is more likely to predict professions that are popular in Freebase. To avoid this distortion, we use stratified sampling. For each relation r and concept $t \in C$, we count the number of r edges pointing to t

$$N_{r,t} = |\{(s,r,t) \in T\}| \quad .$$

Given a training query (s,r,t) we sample it according to

$$P_{r,t} = \min\left(1, \frac{\sqrt{m + N_{r,t}}}{N_{r,t}}\right)$$

We fix $m = 100$ in our experiments. If we take the profession relation as an example, the above implies that for popular professions, we only sample about $\sqrt{N_{r,t}}$ out of the $N_{r,t}$ possible queries that end in t, whereas for the less popular professions we would accept all the training queries.

3.3 Text Graph Construction

As we are processing Web text data (see following section for more detail), the number of mentions of a concept follows a somewhat heavy-tailed distribution: there are a small number of very popular concepts (head) and a large number of not so popular concepts (tail). For instance the concept *BarackObama* is mentioned about 8.9 million times in our text corpus. To prevent the text graph from being dominated by the head concepts, for each sentence that mentions concept $c \in C$, we accept it as part of the text graph with probability:

$$P_c = \min\left(1, \frac{\sqrt{k + S_c}}{S_c}\right)$$

where S_c is the number of sentences in which c is mentioned in the whole corpus. In our experiments we use $k = 10^5$. This means that if $S_c \gg k$, then we only sample about $\sqrt{S_c}$ of the sentences that contain a mention of the concept, while if $S_c \ll k$, then all mentions of that concept will likely be included.

4 Datasets

We use Freebase as our knowledge base. Freebase data is harvested from many sources, including Wikipedia, AMG, and IMDB.[3] As of this writing, it contains more than 21 million concepts and 70 million labeled edges. For a large majority of concepts that appear both in Freebase and Wikipedia, Freebase maintains a link to the Wikipedia page of that concept.

We also collect a large Web corpus and identify 60 million pages that mention concepts relevant to this study. The free text on those pages are POS-tagged and dependency parsed with an accuracy comparable to that of the current Stanford dependency parser (Klein and Manning, 2003). The parser produces a dependency tree for each sentence with each edge labeled with a standard dependency tag (see Figure 1).

In each of the parsed documents, we use POS tags and dependency edges to identify potential referring noun phrases (NPs). We then use a within-document coreference resolver comparable to that of Haghighi and Klein (2009) to group referring NPs into co-referring clusters. For each cluster that contains a proper-name mention, we find the Freebase concept or concepts, if any, with a name or alias that matches the mention. If a cluster has multiple possible matching Freebase concepts, we choose a single sense based on the following simple model. For each Freebase concept $c \in C$, we compute $N(c, m)$, the number of times the concept c is referred by mention m by using both the alias information in Freebase and the anchors of the corresponding Wikipedia page for that concept. Based on $N(c, m)$ we can calculate the empirical probability $p(c|m) = N(c, m)/\sum_{c'} N(c', m)$. If u is a cluster with mention set $M(u)$ in the document, and $C(m)$ the set of concepts in KB with name or alias m, we assign u to concept $c^* = \underset{c \in C(m), m \in M(u)}{\operatorname{argmax}} p(c|m)$, provided that there exists at least one $c \in C(m)$ and $m \in M(u)$ such that $p(c|m) > 0$. Note that $M(c)$ only contains the proper-name mentions in cluster c.

[3] www.wikipedia.org, www.allmusic.com, www.imdb.com.

Table 1: Size of training and test sets for each relation.

Task	Training Set	Test Set
Profession	22,829	15,219
Nationality	14,431	9,620
Parents	21,232	14,155

5 Results

We use three relations *profession*, *nationality* and *parents* for our experiments. For each relation, we select its current set of triples in Freebase, and apply the stratified sampling (Section 3.2) to each of the three triple sets. The resulting triple sets are then randomly split into training (60% of the triples) and test (the remaining triples). However, the *parents* relation yields 350k triples after stratified sampling, so to reduce experimental effort we further randomly sub-sample 10% of that as input to the train-test split. Table 1 shows the sizes of the training and test sets for each relation.

To encourage PRA to find paths involving the text corpus, we do not count relation *M* (which connects concepts to their mentions) or M^{-1} when calculating path lengths. We use L_1/L_2^2-regularized logistic regression to learn feature weights. The PRA hyperparameters (α and K as defined in Section 2) and regularizer hyperparameters are tuned by threefold cross validation (CV) on the training set. We average the models across all the folds and choose the model that gives the best

Table 2: Mean Reciprocal Rank (MRR) for different approaches under closed-world assumption. Here KB, Text and KB+Text columns represent results obtained by training a PRA model with only the KB, only text, and both KB and text. KB+Text[b] is the binarized PRA approach trained on both KB and text. The best performing system (results shown in bold font) is significant at 0.0001 level over its nearest competitor according to a difference of proportions significance test.

Task	KB	Text	KB+Text	KB+Text[b]
Profession	0.532	0.516	**0.583**	0.453
Nationality	0.734	0.729	**0.812**	0.693
Parents	0.329	0.332	**0.392**	0.319

performance on the training set for each relation.

We report results of two evaluations. First, we evaluate the performance of the PRA algorithm when trained on a subset of existing Freebase facts and tested on the rest. Second, we had human annotators verify facts proposed by PRA that are not in Freebase.

5.1 Evaluation with Existing Knowledge

Previous work in relation extraction from parsed text (Mintz et al., 2009) has mostly used binary features to indicate whether a pattern is present in the sentences where two concepts are mentioned. To investigate the benefit of having fractional valued features generated by random walks (as in PRA), we also evaluate a *binarized PRA* approach, for which we use the same syntactic-semantic pattern features as PRA does, but binarize the feature values from PRA: if the original fractional feature value was zero, the feature value is set to zero (equivalent to not having the feature in that example), otherwise it is set to 1.

Table 2 shows a comparison of the results obtained using the PRA algorithm trained using only Freebase (**KB**), using only the text corpus graph (**Text**), trained with both Freebase and the text corpus (**KB+Text**) and the binarized PRA algorithm using both Freebase and the text corpus (**KB+Text[b]**). We report Mean Reciprocal Rank (MRR) where, given a set of queries Q,

$$\text{MRR} = \frac{1}{|Q|} \sum_{q \in Q} \frac{1}{\text{rank of } q\text{'s first correct answer}} .$$

Comparing the results of first three columns we see that combining Freebase and text achieves significantly better results than using either Freebase or text alone. Further comparing the results of last two columns we also observe a significant drop in MRR for the binarized version of PRA. This clearly shows the importance of using the random walk probabilities. It can also be seen that the MRR for the parents relation is lower than those for other relations. This is mainly because there are larger number of potential answers for each query node of *Parent* relation than for each query node of the other two relations – all persons in Freebase versus all professions or nationalities. Finally, it is important to point out that our evaluations are actually *lower bounds* of actual performance, because, for instance, a person might have a profession besides the ones in Freebase and in such cases, this evaluation does not give any credit for predicting those professions — they are treated as errors. We try to address this issue with the manual evaluations in the next section.

Table 2 only reports results for the maximum path length $\ell = 4$ case. We found that shorter maximum path lengths give worse results: for instance, with $\ell = 3$ for the profession relation, MRR drops to 0.542, from 0.583 for $\ell = 4$ when using both Freebase and text. This difference is significant at the 0.0001 level according to a difference of proportions test. Further we find that using longer path length takes much longer time to train and test, but does not lead to significant improvements over the $\ell = 4$ case. For example, for profession, $\ell = 5$ gives a MRR of 0.589.

Table 3 shows the top weighted features that involve text edges for PRA models trained on both Freebase and the text corpus. To make them easier to understand, we group them based on their functionality. For the profession and nationality tasks, the conjunction dependency relation (in group 1,4) plays an important role: these features first find persons mentioned in conjunction with the query

Table 3: Top weighted path types involving text edges for each task grouped according to functionality. *M* relations connect each concept in knowledge base to its mentions in the corpus. *TW* relations connect each token in a sentence to the words in the text representation of this token. *CW* relations connect each concept in knowledge base to the words in the text representation of this concept. We use lower case names to denote dependency edges, word capitalized names to denote KB edges, and "-1" to denote the inverse of a relation.

Profession	**Top Weighted Features**	**Comments**
1	$\langle M, conj, M^{-1}, Profession\rangle$ $\langle M, conj^{-1}, M^{-1}, Profession\rangle$	Professions of persons mentioned in conjunction with the query person: *"McDougall and Simon Phillips collaborated ..."*
2	$\langle M, TW, CW^{-1}, Profession^{-1}, Profession\rangle$	Active if a person is mentioned by his profession: *"The president said ..."*
3	$\langle M, TW, TW^{-1}, M^{-1}, Children, Profession\rangle$ $\langle M, TW, TW^{-1}, M^{-1}, Parents, Profession\rangle$ $\langle M, TW, TW^{-1}, M^{-1}, Advisors, Profession\rangle$	First find persons with similar names or mentioned in similar ways, then aggregate the professions of their children/parents/advisors: starting from the concept *BarackObama*, words such as *"Obama"*, *"leader"*, *"president"*, and *"he"* are reachable through path $\langle M, TW\rangle$
Nationality	**Top Weighted Features**	**Comments**
4	$\langle M, conj, TW, CW^{-1}, Nationality\rangle$ $\langle M, conj^{-1}, TW, CW^{-1}, Nationality\rangle$	The nationalities of persons mentioned in conjunction with the query person: *"McDougall and Simon Phillips collaborated ..."*
5	$\langle M, nc^{-1}, TW, CW^{-1}, Nationality\rangle$ $\langle M, tmod^{-1}, TW, CW^{-1}, Nationality\rangle$ $\langle M, nn, TW, CW^{-1}, Nationality\rangle$	The nationalities of persons mentioned close to the query person through other dependency relations.
6	$\langle M, poss, poss^{-1}, M^{-1}, PlaceOfBirth, ContainedBy\rangle$ $\langle M, title, title^{-1}, M^{-1}, PlaceOfDeath, ContainedBy\rangle$	The birth/death places of the query person with restrictions to different syntactic constructions.

Parents	**Top Weighted Features**	**Comments**
7	$\langle M, TW, CW^{-1}, Parents\rangle$	The parents of persons with similar names or mentioned in similar ways: starting from the concept *CharlotteBronte* words such as *"Bronte"*, *"Charlotte"*, *"Patrick"*, and *"she"* are reachable through path $\langle M, TW\rangle$.
8	$\langle M, nsubj, nsubj^{-1}, TW, CW^{-1}\rangle$ $\langle M, nsubj, nsubj^{-1}, M^{-1}, CW, CW^{-1}\rangle$ $\langle M, nc^{-1}, nc, TW, CW^{-1}\rangle$ $\langle M, TW, CW^{-1}\rangle$ $\langle M, TW, TW^{-1}, TW, CW^{-1}\rangle$	Persons with similar names or mentioned in similar ways to the query person with various restrictions or expansions. $\langle nsubj, nsubj^{-1}\rangle$ and $\langle nc^{-1}, nc\rangle$ require the query to be subject and noun compound respectively. $\langle TW^{-1}, TW\rangle$ expands further by word similarities.

person, and then find their professions or nationalities. The features in group 2 capture the fact that sometimes people are mentioned by their professions. The subpath $\langle \mathit{Profession}^{-1}, \mathit{Profession} \rangle$ ensures that only profession related concepts are activated. Features in group 3 first find persons with similar names or mentioned in similar ways to the query person, and then aggregate the professions of their children, parents, or advisors. Features in group 6 can be seen as special versions of feature $\langle \mathit{PlaceOfBirth}, \mathit{ContainedBy} \rangle$ and $\langle \mathit{PlaceOfDeath}, \mathit{ContainedBy} \rangle$. The subpaths $\langle M, poss, poss^{-1}, M^{-1} \rangle$ and $\langle M, title, title^{-1}, M^{-1} \rangle$ return the random walks back to the query node only if the mentions of the query node have *poss* (stands for *possessive modifier*, e.g. "Bill's clothes") or *title* (stands for *person's title*, e.g. "President Obama") edges in text; otherwise these features are inactive. Therefore, these features are active only for specific subsets of queries. Features in group 8 generally find persons with similar names or mentioned in similar ways to the query person. However, they further expand or restrict this person set in various ways.

Typically, each trained model includes hundreds of paths with non-zero weights, so the bulk of classifications are not based on a few high-precision-recall patterns, but rather on the combination of a large number of lower-precision high-recall or high-precision lower-recall rules.

5.2 Manual Evaluation

We performed two sets of manual evaluations. In each case, an annotator is presented with the triples predicted by PRA, and asked if they are correct. The annotator has access to the Freebase and Wikipedia pages for the concepts (and is able to issue search queries about the concepts).

In the first evaluation, we compared the performance of two PRA models, one trained using the stratified sampled queries and another trained using a randomly sampled set of queries for the profession relation. For each model, we randomly sample 100 predictions from the top 1000 predictions (sorted by the scores returned by the model). We found that the PRA model trained with stratified sampled queries has 0.92 precision, while the other model has only 0.84 precision (significant at the 0.02 level). This shows that stratified sampling leads to improved performance.

Table 4: Human judgement for predicted new beliefs.

Task	p@100	p@1k	p@10k
Profession	0.97	0.92	0.84
Nationality	0.98	0.97	0.90
Parents	0.86	0.81	0.79

We also evaluated the new beliefs proposed by the models trained for all the three relations using stratified sampled queries. We estimated precision for the top 100 predictions and randomly sampled 100 predictions each from the top 1,000 and 10,000 predictions. Here we use the PRA model trained using both KB and text. The results of this evaluation are shown in Table 4. It can be seen that the PRA model is able to produce very high precision predications even when one considers the top 10,000 predictions.

Finally, note that our model is inductive. For instance, for the profession relation, we are able to predict professions for the around 2 million persons in Freebase. The top 1000 profession facts extracted by our system involve 970 distinct people, the top 10,000 facts involve 8,726 distinct people, and the top 100,000 facts involve 79,885 people.

6 Conclusion

We have shown that path constrained random walk models can effectively infer new beliefs from a large scale parsed text corpus with background knowledge. Evaluation by human annotators shows that by combining syntactic patterns in parsed text with semantic patterns in the background knowledge, our model can propose new beliefs with high accuracy. Thus, the proposed random walk model can be an effective way to automate knowledge acquisition from the web.

There are several interesting directions to continue this line of work. First, bidirectional search from both query and target nodes can be an efficient way to discover long paths. This would especially useful for parsed text. Second, relation paths that contain constant nodes (lexicalized features) and conjunction of random walk features are potentially very useful for extraction tasks.

Acknowledgments

We thank Rahul Gupta, Michael Ringgaard, John Blitzer and the anonymous reviewers for helpful comments. The first author was supported by a Google Research grant.

References

Eugene Agichtein and Luis Gravano. 2000. Snowball: extracting relations from large plain-text collections. In *Proceedings of the fifth ACM conference on Digital libraries*, DL '00, pages 85–94, New York, NY, USA. ACM.

Kurt Bollacker, Colin Evans, Praveen Paritosh, Tim Sturge, and Jamie Taylor. 2008. Freebase: a collaboratively created graph database for structuring human knowledge. In *Proceedings of the 2008 ACM SIGMOD international conference on Management of data*, SIGMOD '08, pages 1247–1250, New York, NY, USA. ACM.

Aron Culotta, Andrew McCallum, and Jonathan Betz. 2006. Integrating probabilistic extraction models and data mining to discover relations and patterns in text. In *Proceedings of the Human Language Technology Conference of the NAACL, Main Conference*, pages 296–303, New York City, USA, June. Association for Computational Linguistics.

Marie-Catherine de Marneffe and Chris Manning. 2008. Stanford dependencies. `http://www.tex.ac.uk/cgi-bin/texfaq2html?label=citeURL`.

Jeffrey Dean and Sanjay Ghemawat. 2008. Mapreduce: simplified data processing on large clusters. *Commun. ACM*, 51(1):107–113, January.

Quang Do and Dan Roth. 2010. Constraints based taxonomic relation classification. In *Proceedings of the 2010 Conference on Empirical Methods in Natural Language Processing*, pages 1099–1109, Cambridge, MA, October. Association for Computational Linguistics.

Oren Etzioni, Michael Cafarella, Doug Downey, Stanley Kok, Ana-Maria Popescu, Tal Shaked, Stephen Soderland, Daniel S. Weld, and Alexander Yates. 2004. Web-scale information extraction in knowitall: (preliminary results). In *Proceedings of the 13th international conference on World Wide Web*, WWW '04, pages 100–110, New York, NY, USA. ACM.

Nir Friedman, Lise Getoor, Daphne Koller, and Avi Pfeffer. 1999. Learning Probabilistic Relational Models. In *IJCAI*, volume 16, pages 1300–1309.

Aria Haghighi and Dan Klein. 2009. Simple coreference resolution with rich syntactic and semantic features. In *Proceedings of the 2009 Conference on Empirical Methods in Natural Language Processing*, pages 1152–1161, Singapore, August. Association for Computational Linguistics.

Marti A. Hearst. 1992. Automatic acquisition of hyponyms from large text corpora. In *Proceedings of COLING-92*, pages 539–545. Association for Computational Linguistics, August.

Dan Klein and Christopher D. Manning. 2003. Accurate unlexicalized parsing. In Erhard Hinrichs and Dan Roth, editors, *Proceedings of the 41st Annual Meeting on Association for Computational Linguistics*, pages 423–430. Association for Computational Linguistics, July.

Ni Lao and William Cohen. 2010. Relational retrieval using a combination of path-constrained random walks. *Machine Learning*, 81:53–67.

Ni Lao, Tom Mitchell, and William W. Cohen. 2011. Random walk inference and learning in a large scale knowledge base. In *Proceedings of the 2011 Conference on Empirical Methods in Natural Language Processing*, pages 529–539, Edinburgh, Scotland, UK., July. Association for Computational Linguistics.

Mike Mintz, Steven Bills, Rion Snow, and Daniel Jurafsky. 2009. Distant supervision for relation extraction without labeled data. In *Proceedings of the Joint Conference of the 47th Annual Meeting of the ACL and the 4th International Joint Conference on Natural Language Processing of the AFNLP*, pages 1003–1011, Suntec, Singapore, August. Association for Computational Linguistics.

Deepak Ravichandran and Eduard Hovy. 2002. Learning surface text patterns for a question answering system. In *Proceedings of 40th Annual Meeting of the Association for Computational Linguistics*, pages 41–47, Philadelphia, Pennsylvania, USA, July. Association for Computational Linguistics.

Matthew Richardson and Pedro Domingos. 2006. Markov logic networks. *Machine Learning*, 62:107–136.

Rion Snow, Daniel Jurafsky, and Andrew Y. Ng. 2005. Learning syntactic patterns for automatic hypernym discovery. In Lawrence K. Saul, Yair Weiss, and Léon Bottou, editors, *Advances in Neural Information Processing Systems 17*, pages 1297–1304, Cambridge, MA. NIPS Foundation, MIT Press.

Fabian M. Suchanek, Georgiana Ifrim, and Gerhard Weikum. 2006. Combining linguistic and statistical analysis to extract relations from web documents. In *Proceedings of the 12th ACM SIGKDD international conference on Knowledge discovery and data mining*, KDD '06, pages 712–717, New York, NY, USA. ACM.

Ensemble Semantics for Large-scale Unsupervised Relation Extraction

Bonan Min[1*] **Shuming Shi**[2] **Ralph Grishman**[1] **Chin-Yew Lin**[2]

[1]New York University
New York, NY, USA
{min,grishman}@cs.nyu.edu

[2]Microsoft Research Asia
Beijing, China
{shumings,cyl}@microsoft.com

Abstract

Discovering significant types of relations from the web is challenging because of its open nature. Unsupervised algorithms are developed to extract relations from a corpus without knowing the relations in advance, but most of them rely on tagging arguments of predefined types. Recently, a new algorithm was proposed to jointly extract relations and their argument semantic classes, taking a set of relation instances extracted by an open IE algorithm as input. However, it cannot handle polysemy of relation phrases and fails to group many similar ("synonymous") relation instances because of the sparseness of features. In this paper, we present a novel unsupervised algorithm that provides a more general treatment of the polysemy and synonymy problems. The algorithm incorporates various knowledge sources which we will show to be very effective for unsupervised extraction. Moreover, it explicitly disambiguates polysemous relation phrases and groups synonymous ones. While maintaining approximately the same precision, the algorithm achieves significant improvement on recall compared to the previous method. It is also very efficient. Experiments on a real-world dataset show that it can handle 14.7 million relation instances and extract a very large set of relations from the web.

1 Introduction

Relation extraction aims at discovering semantic relations between entities. It is an important task that has many applications in answering factoid questions, building knowledge bases and improving search engine relevance. The web has become a massive potential source of such relations. However, its open nature brings an open-ended set of relation types. To extract these relations, a system should not assume a fixed set of relation types, nor rely on a fixed set of relation argument types.

The past decade has seen some promising solutions, unsupervised relation extraction (URE) algorithms that extract relations from a corpus without knowing the relations in advance. However, most algorithms (Hasegawa et al., 2004, Shinyama and Sekine, 2006, Chen et. al, 2005) rely on tagging predefined types of entities as relation arguments, and thus are not well-suited for the open domain.

Recently, Kok and Domingos (2008) proposed Semantic Network Extractor (SNE), which generates argument semantic classes and sets of synonymous relation phrases at the same time, thus avoiding the requirement of tagging relation arguments of predefined types. However, SNE has 2 limitations: 1) Following previous URE algorithms, it only uses features from the set of input relation instances for clustering. Empirically we found that it fails to group many relevant relation instances. These features, such as the surface forms of arguments and lexical sequences in between, are very sparse in practice. In contrast, there exist several well-known corpus-level semantic resources that can be automatically derived from a source corpus and are shown to be useful for generating the key elements of a relation: its 2 argument semantic classes and a set of synonymous phrases. For example, semantic classes can be derived from a source corpus with contextual distributional similarity and web table co-occurrences. The *"synonymy"* [1] problem for clustering relation instances

[*] Work done during an internship at Microsoft Research Asia

could potentially be better solved by adding these resources. 2) SNE assumes that each entity or relation phrase belongs to exactly one cluster, thus is not able to effectively handle *polysemy* of relation phrases[2]. An example of a polysemous phrase is *be the currency of* as in 2 triples <*Euro, be the currency of, Germany*> and <*authorship, be the currency of, science*>. As the target corpus expands from mostly news to the open web, polysemy becomes more important as input covers a wider range of domains. In practice, around 22% (section 3) of relation phrases are polysemous. Failure to handle these cases significantly limits its effectiveness.

To move towards a more general treatment of the *polysemy* and *synonymy* problems, we present a novel algorithm WEBRE for open-domain large-scale unsupervised relation extraction without predefined relation or argument types. The contributions are:

- WEBRE incorporates a wide range of corpus-level semantic resources for improving relation extraction. The effectiveness of each knowledge source and their combination are studied and compared. To the best of our knowledge, it is the first to combine and compare them for unsupervised relation extraction.
- WEBRE explicitly disambiguates polysemous relation phrases and groups synonymous phrases, thus fundamentally it avoids the limitation of previous methods.
- Experiments on the Clueweb09 dataset (lemurproject.org/clueweb09.php) show that WEBRE is effective and efficient. We present a large-scale evaluation and show that WEBRE can extract a very large set of high-quality relations. Compared to the closest prior work, WEBRE significantly improves recall while maintaining the same level of precision. WEBRE is efficient. To the best of our knowledge, it handles the largest triple set to date (7-fold larger than largest previous effort). Taking 14.7 million triples as input, a complete run with one CPU core takes about a day.

[1] We use the term *synonymy* broadly as defined in Section 3.

[2] A cluster of relation phrases can, however, act as a whole as the phrase cluster for 2 different relations in SNE. However, this only accounts for 4.8% of the polysemous cases.

2 Related Work

Unsupervised relation extraction (URE) algorithms (Hasegawa et al., 2004; Chen et al., 2005; Shinyama and Sekine, 2006) collect pairs of co-occurring entities as relation instances, extract features for instances and then apply unsupervised clustering techniques to find the major relations of a corpus. These UREs rely on tagging a predefined set of argument types, such as Person, Organization, and Location, in advance. Yao et al. 2011 learns fine-grained argument classes with generative models, but they share the similar requirement of tagging coarse-grained argument types. Most UREs use a quadratic clustering algorithm such as Hierarchical Agglomerate Clustering (Hasegawa et al., 2004, Shinyama and Sekine, 2006), K-Means (Chen et al., 2005), or both (Rosenfeld and Feldman, 2007); thus they are not scalable to very large corpora.

As the target domain shifts to the web, new methods are proposed without requiring predefined entity types. Resolver (Yates and Etzioni, 2007) resolves objects and relation synonyms. Kok and Domingos (2008) proposed Semantic Network Extractor (SNE) to extract concepts and relations. Based on second-order Markov logic, SNE used a bottom-up agglomerative clustering algorithm to jointly cluster relation phrases and argument entities. However, both Resolver and SNE require each entity and relation phrase to belong to exactly one cluster. This limits their ability to handle polysemous relation phrases. Moreover, SNE only uses features in the input set of relation instances for clustering, thus it fails to group many relevant instances. Resolver has the same sparseness problem but it is not affected as much as SNE because of its different goal (synonym resolution).

As the preprocessing instance-detection step for the problem studied in this paper, open IE extracts relation instances (in the form of triples) from the open domain (Etzioni et al., 2004; Banko et al., 2007; Fader et al., 2011; Wang et al. 2011). For efficiency, they only use shallow features. Reverb (Fader et al., 2011) is a state-of-the-art open domain extractor that targets verb-centric relations, which have been shown in Banko and Etzioni (2008) to cover over 70% of open domain relations. Taking their output as input, algorithms have been proposed to resolve objects and relation synonyms (Resolver), extract semantic networks

(SNE), and map extracted relations into an existing ontology (Soderland and Mandhani, 2007).

Recent work shows that it is possible to construct semantic classes and sets of similar phrases automatically with data-driven approaches. For generating semantic classes, previous work applies distributional similarity (Pasca, 2007; Pantel et al., 2009), uses a few linguistic patterns (Pasca 2004; Sarmento et al., 2007), makes use of structure in webpages (Wang and Cohen 2007, 2009), or combines all of them (Shi et al., 2010). Pennacchiotti and Pantel (2009) combines several sources and features. To find similar phrases, there are 2 closely related tasks: paraphrase discovery and recognizing textual entailment. Data-driven paraphrase discovery methods (Lin and Pantel, 2001; Pasca and Dienes, 2005; Wu and Zhou, 2003; Sekine, 2005) extends the idea of distributional similarity to phrases. The Recognizing Textual Entailment algorithms (Berant et al. 2011) can also be used to find related phrases since they find pairs of phrases in which one entails the other.

To efficiently cluster high-dimensional datasets, canopy clustering (McCallum et al., 2000) uses a cheap, approximate distance measure to divide data into smaller subsets, and then cluster each subset using an exact distance measure. It has been applied to reference matching. The second phase of WEBRE applies the similar high-level idea of partition-then-cluster for speeding up relation clustering. We design a graph-based partitioning subroutine that uses various types of evidence, such as shared hypernyms.

3 Problem Analysis

The basic input is a collection of relation instances (triples) of the form <*ent*$_1$, *ctx*, *ent*$_2$>. For each triple, *ctx* is a relational phrase expressing the relation between the first argument *ent*$_1$ and the second argument *ent*$_2$. An example triple is <*Obama, win in, NY*>. The triples can be generated by an open IE extractor such as TextRunner or Reverb. Our goal is to automatically build a list of relations $R = \{< \text{ent}_1, ctx, \text{ent}_2 >\} \approx$ [3] $< C_1, P, C_2 >$ where P is the set of relation phrases, and C_1 and C_2 are two argument classes. Examples of triples and relations R (as Type B) are shown in Figure 1.

[3] This approximately equal sign connects 2 possible representations of a relation: as a set of triple instances or a triple with 2 entity classes and a relation phrase class.

The first problem is the *polysemy* of relation phrases, which means that a relation phrase *ctx* can express different relations in different triples. For example, the meaning of *be the currency of* in the following two triples is quite different: <*Euro, be the currency of, Germany*> and <*authorship, be the currency of, science*>. It is more appropriate to assign these 2 triples to 2 relations "*a currency is the currency of a country*" and "*a factor is important in an area*" than to merge them into one. Formally, a relation phrase *ctx* is *polysemous* if there exist 2 different relations $< C_1, P, C_2 >$ and $< C_1^{'}, P^{'}, C_2^{'} >$ where $ctx \in P \cap P^{'}$. In the previous example, *be the currency of* is polysemous because it appears in 2 different relations.

Polysemy of relation phrases is not uncommon. We generate clusters from a large sample of triples with the assistance of a soft clustering algorithm, and found that around 22% of relation phrases can be put into at least 2 disjoint clusters that represent different relations. More importantly, manual inspection reveals that some common phrases are polysemous. For example, *be part of* can be put into a relation "a *city is located in a country*" when connecting *Cities* to *Countries*, and another relation *"a company is a subsidiary of a parent company"* when connecting *Companies* to *Companies.* Failure to handle polysemous relation phrases fundamentally limits the effectiveness of an algorithm. The WEBRE algorithm described later explicitly handles polysemy and synonymy of relation phrases in its first and second phase respectively.

The second problem is the *"synonymy"* of relation instances. We use the term *synonymy* broadly and we say 2 relation instances are synonymous if they express the same semantic relation between the same pair of semantic classes. For example, both <*Euro, be the currency used in, Germany*> and <*Dinar, be legal tender in, Iraq*> express the relation <*Currencies, be currency of, Countries*>. Solving this problem requires grouping synonymous relation phrases and identifying argument semantic classes for the relation.

Various knowledge sources can be derived from the source corpus for this purpose. In this paper we pay special attention to incorporating various semantic resources for relation extraction. We will show that these semantic sources can significantly improve the coverage of extracted relations and the

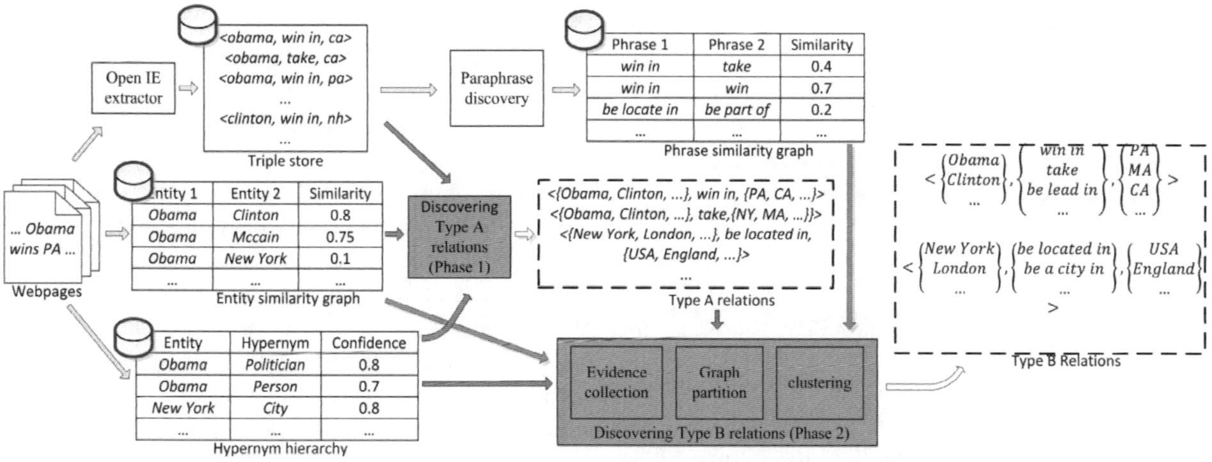

Figure 1. Overview of the WEBRE algorithm (Illustrated with examples sampled from experiment results). The tables and rectangles with a database sign show knowledge sources, shaded rectangles show the 2 phases, and the dotted shapes show the system output, a set of Type A relations and a set of Type B relations. The orange arrows denote resources used in phase 1 and the green arrows show the resources used in phase 2.

best performance is achieved when various resources are combined together.

4 Mining Relations from the Web

We first describe relevant knowledge sources, and then introduce the WEBRE algorithm, followed by a briefly analysis on its computational complexity.

4.1 Knowledge Sources

Entity similarity graph We build two similarity graphs for entities: a distributional similarity (DS) graph and a pattern-similarity (PS) graph. The DS graph is based on the distributional hypothesis (Harris, 1985), saying that terms sharing similar contexts tend to be similar. We use a text window of size 4 as the context of a term, use Pointwise Mutual Information (PMI) to weight context features, and use Jaccard similarity to measure the similarity of term vectors. The PS graph is generated by adopting both sentence lexical patterns and HTML tag patterns (Hearst, 1992; Kozareva et al., 2008; Zhang et al., 2009; Shi et al., 2010). Two terms (*T*) tend to be semantically similar if they co-occur in multiple patterns. One example of sentence lexical patterns is *(such as | including) T{,T}* (and|,|.)*. HTML tag patterns include tables, dropdown boxes, etc. In these two graphs, nodes are entities and the edge weights indicate entity similarity. In all there are about 29.6 million nodes and 1.16 billion edges.

Hypernymy graph Hypernymy relations are very useful for finding semantically similar term pairs. For example, we observed that a small city in UK and another small city in Germany share common hypernyms such as *city*, *location*, and *place*. Therefore the similarity between the two cities is large according to the hypernymy graph, while their similarity in the DS graph and the PS graph may be very small. Following existing work (Hearst, 1992, Pantel & Ravichandran 2004; Snow et al., 2005; Talukdar et al., 2008; Zhang et al., 2011), we adopt a list of lexical patterns to extract hypernyms. The patterns include *NP {,} (such as) {NP,}* {and|or} NP*, *NP (is|are|was|were|being) (a|an|the) NP*, etc. The hypernymy graph is a bipartite graph with two types of nodes: entity nodes and label (hypernym) nodes. There is an edge *(T, L)* with weight *w* if *L* is a hypernym of entity *T* with probability *w*. There are about 8.2 million nodes and 42.4 million edges in the hypernymy graph. In this paper, we use the terms *hypernym* and *label* interchangeably.

Relation phrase similarity: To generate the pairwise similarity graph for relation phrases with regard to the probability of expressing the same relation, we apply a variant of the DIRT algorithm (Lin and Pantel, 2001). Like DIRT, the paraphrase discovery relies on the distributional hypothesis, but there are a few differences: 1) we use stemmed lexical sequences (relation phrases) instead of dependency paths as phrase candidates because of the very large scale of the corpus. 2) We used ordered pairs of arguments as features of phrases while DIRT uses them as independent features. We empirically tested both feature schemes and found that using ordered pairs results in likely paraphrases but using independent features the result contains general inference rules[4].

4.2 WEBRE for Relation Extraction

WEBRE consists of two phases. In the first phase, a set of semantic classes are discovered and used as argument classes for each relation phrase. This results in a large collection of relations whose arguments are pairs of semantic classes and which have exactly one relation phrase. We call these relations the *Type A* relations. An example Type A relation is *<{New York, London...}, be locate in, {USA, England, ...}>*. During this phase, polysemous relation phrases are disambiguated and placed into multiple Type A relations. The second phase is an efficient algorithm which groups similar Type A relations together. This step enriches the argument semantic classes and groups synonymous relation phrases to form relations with multiple expressions, which we called *Type B* relations. Both Type A and Type B relations are system outputs since both are valuable resources for downstream applications such as QA and Web Search. An overview of the algorithm is shown in Figure 1. Here we first briefly describe a clustering subroutine that is used in both phases, and then describe the algorithm in detail.

To handle polysemy of objects (e.g., entities or relations) during the clustering procedure, a key building block is an effective Multi-Membership Clustering algorithm (*MMClustering*). For simplicity and effectiveness, we use a variant of Hierarchical Agglomerative Clustering (HAC), in which we first cluster objects with HAC, and then reassign each object to additional clusters when its similarities with these clusters exceed a certain threshold[5]. In the remainder of this paper, we use *{C} = MMClustering({object}, SimFunc, α)* to represent running *MMClustering* over a set of objects, with threshold α to generate a list of clusters *{C}* of the objects, given the pairwise object similarity function *SimFunc*. Our implementation uses HAC with average linkage since empirically it performs well.

Discovering Type A Relations The first phase of the relation extraction algorithm generates Type A relations, which have exactly one relation phrase and two argument entity semantic classes. For each relation phrase, we apply a clustering algorithm on each of its two argument sets to generate argument semantic classes. The *Phase 1* algorithm processes relation phrases one by one. For each relation phrase *ctx*, step 4 clusters the set $\{ent_1\}$ using *MMClustering* to find left-hand-side argument semantic classes $\{C_1\}$. Then for each cluster *C* in $\{C_1\}$, it gathers the right-hand-side arguments which appeared in some triple whose left hand-side-side argument is in *C*, and puts them into $\{ent_2'\}$. Following this, it clusters $\{ent_2'\}$ to find right-hand-side argument semantic classes. This results in pairs of semantic classes which are arguments of *ctx*. Each relation phrase can appear in multiple non-overlapping Type A relations. For example, *<Cities, be part of, Countries>* and *<Companies, be part of, Companies>* are different Type A relations which share the same relation phrase *be part of*. In the pseudo code, *SimEntFunc* is encoded in the entity similarity graphs.

Algorithm ***Phase 1: Discovering Type A relations***

Input: set of triples $T=\{<ent_1, ctx, ent_2>\}$
entity similarity function *SimEntFunc*
Similarity threshold α
Output: list of Type A relations $\{<C_1, ctx, C_2>\}$
Steps:
01. For each relation phrase *ctx*
02. $\{ent_1, ctx, ent_2\}$ = set of triples sharing *ctx*
03. $\{ent_1\}$ = set of ent_1 in $\{ent_1, ctx, ent_2\}$
04. $\{C_1\}$ = *MMClustering*($\{ent_1\}$, *SimEntFunc*, α)
05. For each *C* in $\{C_1\}$
06. $\{ent_2'\}$ = set of ent_2 s.t. $\exists < ent_1, ctx, ent_2 > \in T \wedge ent_1 \in C_1$
07. $\{C_2\}$ = *MMClustering*($\{ent_2'\}$, *SimEntFunc*, α)
08. For each C_2 in $\{C_2\}$
09. Add $<C_1, ctx, C_2>$ into $\{<C_1, ctx, C_2>\}$
10. Return $\{<C_1, ctx, C_2>\}$

Discovering Type B Relations The goal of *phase 2* is to merge similar Type A relations, such as *<Cities, be locate in, Countries>* and *<Cities, be city of, Countries>*, to produce Type B relations, which have a set of synonymous relation phrases and more complete argument entity classes. The challenge for this phase is to cluster a very large

[4] For example, *be part of* has ordered argument pairs *<A, B>* and *<C, D>*, and *be not part of* has ordered argument pairs *<A, D>* and *<B, C>*. If arguments are used as independent features, these two phrases shared the same set of features *{A, B, C, D}*. However, they are inferential (complement relationship) rather than being similar phrases.

[5] This threshold should be slightly greater than the clustering threshold for HAC to avoid generating duplicated clusters.

set of Type A relations, on which it is infeasible to run a clustering algorithm that does pairwise all pair comparison. Therefore, we designed an evidence-based partition-then-cluster algorithm.

The basic idea is to heuristically partition the large set of Type A relations into small subsets, and run clustering algorithms on each subset. It is based on the observation that most pairs of Type A relations are not similar because of the sparseness in the entity class and the relation semantic space. If there is little or no evidence showing that two Type A relations are similar, they can be put into different partitions. Once partitioned, the clustering algorithm only has to be run on each much smaller subset, thus computation complexity is reduced.

The 2 types of evidence we used are shared members and shared hypernyms of relation arguments. For example, 2 Type A relations r_1=*<Cities, be city of, Countries>* and r_2=*<Cities, be locate in, Countries>* share a pair of arguments *<Tokyo, Japan>*, and a pair of hypernyms <*"city"*, *"country"*>. These pieces of evidence give us hints that they are likely to be similar. As shown in the pseudo code, shared arguments and hypernyms are used as independent evidence to reduce sparseness.

Algorithm ***Phase 2: Discovering Type B relations***

Input:	Set of Type A relations $\{r\}=\{<C_1, ctx, C_2>\}$
	Relation similarity function *SimRelationFunc*
	Map from entities to their hypernyms: $M_{entity2label}$
	Similarity threshold α
	Edge weight threshold μ
Variables	$G(V, E)$ = weighted graph in which $V=\{r\}$
Output:	Set of Type B relations $\{<C_1, P, C_2>\}$
Steps:	
01.	$\{<ent, \{r'\}>\}$ = build inverted index from argument *ent* to set of Type A relations $\{r'\}$ on $\{<C_1, ctx, C_2>\}$
02	$\{<l, \{r'\}>\}$ = build inverted index from hypernym l of arguments to set of Type A relations $\{r'\}$ on $\{<C_1, ctx, C_2>\}$ with map $M_{entity2label}$
03.	For each *ent* in $\{<ent, \{r'\}>\}$
04.	For each pair of r_1 and r_2 s.t. $r_1 \in \{r'\} \wedge r_2 \in \{r'\}$
05.	$weight\_edge(<r_1, r_2>)$ += $weight(ent)$
06.	For each l in $\{<l, \{r'\}>\}$
07.	For each pair of r_1 and r_2 s.t. $r_1 \in \{r'\} \wedge r_2 \in \{r'\}$
08.	$weight\_edge(<r_1, r_2>)$ += $weight(l)$
09.	For each edge $<r_1, r_2>$ in G
10.	If $weight\_edge(<r_1, r_2>) < \mu$
11.	Remove edge $<r_1, r_2>$ from G
12.	$\{CC\}= DFS(G)$
13.	For each connected component CC in $\{CC\}$
14.	$\{<C_1, ctx, C_2>\}$ = vertices in CC
15.	$\{<C_1', P', C_2'>\} = MMClustering(\{<C_1, ctx, C_2>\}, SimRelationFunc, \alpha)$
16.	Add $\{<C_1', P', C_2'>\}$ into $\{<C_1, P, C_2>\}$
17.	Return $\{<C_1, P, C_2>\}$

Steps 1 and 2 build an inverted index from evidence to sets of Type A relations. On the graph G whose vertices are Type A relations, steps 3 to 8 set the value of edge weights based on the strength of evidence that shows the end-points are related. The weight of evidence E is calculated as follows:

$$weight(E) = \frac{\#\ shared\ tuples\ in\ which\ E\ appears\ in}{\max(\#\ classes\ E\ appears\ in)}$$

The idea behind this weighting scheme is similar to that of TF-IDF in that the weight of evidence is higher if it appears more frequently and is less ambiguous (appeared in fewer semantic classes during clustering of phase 1). The weighting scheme is applied to both shared arguments and labels.

After collecting evidence, we prune (steps 9 to 11) the edges with a weight less than a threshold μ to remove noise. Then a Depth-First Search (DFS) is called on G to find all Connected Components CC of the graph. These CCs are the partitions of likely-similar Type A relations. We run *MMClustering* on each CC in $\{CC\}$ and generate Type B relations (step 13 to step 16). The similarity of 2 relations (*SimRelationFunc*) is defined as follows:

$$sim(<C_1, P, C_2>, <C_1', P', C_2'>) = \begin{cases} 0, & if\ sim(P, P') < \sigma \\ \min(sim(C_1, C_1'), sim(C_2, C_2')), & else \end{cases}$$

4.3 Computational Complexity

WEBRE is very efficient since both phases decompose the large-clustering task into much smaller clustering tasks over partitions. Given n objects for clustering, a hierarchical agglomerative clustering algorithm requires $O(n^2)$ pairwise comparisons. Assuming the clustering task is split into subtasks of size n_1, n_2, ..., n_k, thus the computational complexity is reduced to $O(\sum_1^k n_i^2)$. Ideally each subtask has an equal size of n/k, so the computational complexity is reduced to $O(n^2/k)$, a factor of k speed up. In practice, the sizes of partitions are not equal. Taking the partition sizes observed in the experiment with 0.2 million Type A relations as input, the phase 2 algorithm achieves around a 100-fold reduction in pairwise comparisons compared to the agglomerative clustering algorithm. The combination of phase 1 and phase 2 achieves more than a 1000-fold reduction in pairwise comparison, compared to running an agglomerative clustering algorithm directly on 14.7 million triples. This reduction of computational complexity makes the unsupervised extraction of relations on a large dataset a reality. In the experiments with 14.7 million triples as input, phase 1 finished in 22 hours, and the phase 2 algorithm finished in 4 hours with one CPU core.

Furthermore, both phases can be run in parallel in a distributed computing environment because data is partitioned. Therefore it is scalable and efficient for clustering a very large number of relation instances from a large-scale corpus like the web.

5 Experiment

Data preparation We tested WEBRE on resources extracted from the English subset of the Clueweb09 Dataset, which contains 503 million webpages. For building knowledge resources, all webpages are cleaned and then POS tagged and chunked with in-house tools. We implemented the algorithms described in section 4.1 to generate the knowledge sources, including a hypernym graph, two entity similarity graphs and a relation phrase similarity graph.

We used Reverb Clueweb09 Extractions 1.1 (downloaded from *reverb.cs.washington.edu*) as the triple store (relation instances). It is the complete extraction of Reverb over Clueweb09 after filtering low confidence and low frequency triples. It contains 14.7 million distinct triples with 3.3 million entities and 1.3 million relation phrases. We choose it because 1) it is extracted by a state-of-the-art open IE extractor from the open-domain, and 2) to the best of our knowledge, it contains the largest number of distinct triples extracted from the open-domain and which is publicly available.

Evaluation setup The evaluations are organized as follows: we evaluate Type A relation extraction and Type B relation extraction separately, and then we compare WEBRE to its closest prior work SNE. Since both phases are essentially clustering algorithms, we compare the output clusters with human labeled gold standards and report performance measures, following most previous work such as Kok and Domingos (2008) and Hasegawa et al. (2004). Three gold standards are created for evaluating Type A relations, Type B relations and the comparison to SNE, respectively. In the experiments, we set $\alpha=0.6$, $\mu=0.1$ and $\sigma=0.02$ based on trial runs on a small development set of 10k relation instances. We filtered out the Type A relations and Type B relations which only contain 1 or 2 triples since most of these relations are not different from a single relation instance and are not very interesting. Overall, 0.2 million Type A relations and 84,000 Type B relations are extracted.

Evaluating Type A relations To understand the effectiveness of knowledge sources, we run *Phase 1* multiple times taking entity similarity graphs (matrices) constructed with resources listed below:

- **TS**: Distributional similarity based on the triple store. For each triple <ent_1, ctx, ent_2>, features of ent_1 are $\{ctx\}$ and $\{ctx\ ent_2\}$; features of ent_2 are $\{ctx\}$ and $\{ent_1\ ctx\}$. Features are weighted with PMI. Cosine is used as similarity measure.
- **LABEL:** The similarity between two entities is computed according to the percentage of top hypernyms they share.
- **SIM:** The similarity between two entities is the linear combination of their similarity scores in the distributional similarity graph and in the pattern similarity graph.
- **SIM+LABEL** SIM and LABEL are combined. Observing that SIM generates high quality but overly fine-grained semantic classes, we modify the entity clustering procedure to cluster argument entities based on SIM first, and then further clustering the results based on LABEL.

The outputs of these runs are pooled and mixed for labeling. We randomly sampled 60 relation phrases. For each phrase, we select the 5 most frequent Type A relations from each run ($4\times5=20$[6] Type A relations in all). For each relation phrase, we ask a human labeler to label the mixed pool of Type A relations that share the phrase: 1) The labelers[7] are asked to first determine the major semantic relation of each Type A relation, and then label the triples as *good*, *fair* or *bad* based on whether they express the major relation. 2) The labeler also reads all Type A relations and manually merges the ones that express the same relation. These 2 steps are repeated for each phrase. After labeling, we create a gold standard *GS1*, which contains roughly 10,000 triples for 60 relation phrases. On average, close to 200 triples are manu-

[6] Here 4 means the 4 methods (the bullet items above) of computing similarity.

[7] 4 human labelers perform the task. A portion of the judgments were independently dual annotated; inter-annotator agreement is 79%. Moreover, each judgment is cross-checked by at least one more annotator, further improving quality.

ally labeled and clustered for each phrase. This creates a large data set for evaluation.

We report micro-average of precision, recall and F1 on the 60 relation phrases for each method. Precision (P) and Recall (R) of a given relation phrase is defined as follows. Here R_A and R'_A represents a Type A relation in the algorithm output and *GS1*, respectively. We use *t* for triples and *s(t)* to represent the score of the labeled triple *t*. *s(t) is* set to *1.0, 0.5* or *0* for *t* labeled as good, fair and bad, respectively.

$$P = \frac{\sum_{R_A} \sum_{t \in R_A} s(t)}{\sum_{R_A} |R_A|}, R = \frac{\sum_{R_A} \sum_{t \in R_A} s(t)}{\sum_{R'_A} \sum_{t' \in R'_A} s(t')}$$

The results are in table 1. Overall, LABEL performs 53% better than TS in F-measure, and SIM+LABEL performs the best, 8% better than LABEL. Applying a simple sign test shows both differences are clearly significant (p<0.001). Surprisingly, SIM, which uses the similarity matrix extracted from full text, has a F1 of 0.277, which is lower than TS. We also tried combining TS and LABEL but did not find encouraging performance compared to SIM+LABEL.

Algorithm	Precision	Recall	F1
TS	0.842 (0.886)	0.266	0.388
LABEL	0.855 (0.870)	0.481	0.596
SIM	0.755 (**0.964**)	0.178	0.277
SIM+LABEL	0.843 (0.872)	**0.540**	**0.643**

Table 1. Phase 1 performance (averaged on multiple runs) of the 4 methods. The highest performance numbers are in bold. (The number in parenthesis is the micro-average when empty-result relation phrases are not considered for the method).

Among the 4 methods, SIM has the highest precision (0.964) when relation phrases for which it fails to generate any Type A relations are excluded, but its recall is low. Manual checking shows that SIM tends to generate overly fine-grained argument classes. If fine-grained argument classes or extremely high-precision Type A relations are preferred, SIM is a good choice. LABEL performs significantly better than TS, which shows that hypernymy information is very useful for finding argument semantic classes. However, it has coverage problems in that the hypernym finding algorithm failed to find any hypernym from the corpus for some entities. Following up, we found that SIM+LABEL has similar precision and the highest recall. This shows that the combination of semantic spaces is very helpful. The significant recall improvement from TS to SIM+LABEL shows that the corpus-based knowledge resources significantly reduce the data sparseness, compared to using features extracted from the triple store only. The result of the phase 1 algorithm with SIM+LABEL is used as input for phase 2.

Evaluating Type B relations The goal is 2-fold: 1) to evaluate the phase 2 algorithm. This involves comparing system output to a gold standard constructed by hand, and reporting performance; 2) to evaluate the quality of Type B relations. For this, we will also report triple-level precision.

We construct a gold standard *GS2*[8] for evaluating Type B relations as follows: We randomly sampled 178 Type B relations, which contain 1547 Type A relations and more than 100,000 triples. Since the number of triples is very large, it is infeasible for labelers to manually cluster triples to construct a gold standard. To report precision, we asked the labelers to label each Type A relation contained in this Type B relation as good, fair or bad based on whether it expresses the same relation. For recall evaluation, we need to know how many Type A relations are missing from each Type B relation. We provide the full data set of Type A relations along with three additional resources: 1) a tool which, given a Type A relation, returns a ranked list of similar Type A relations based on the pairwise relation similarity metric in section 4, 2) DIRT paraphrase collection, 3) WordNet (Fellbaum, 1998) synsets. The labelers are asked to find similar phrases by checking phrases which contain synonyms of the tokens in the query phrase. Given a Type B relation, ideally we expect the labelers to find all missing Type A relations using these resources. We report precision (P) and recall (R) as follows. Here R_B and R'_B represent Type B relations in the algorithm output and *GS2*, respectively. R_A and R'_A represent Type A relations. $s(R_A)$ denotes the score of R_A. It is set to 1.0, 0.5 and 0 for good, fair or bad respectively.

$$P = \frac{\sum_{R_B} \sum_{R_A \in R_B} |R_A| \cdot s(R_A)}{\sum_{R_B} \sum_{R_A \in R_B} |R_A|}, R = \frac{\sum_{R_B} \sum_{R_A \in R_B} |R_A| \cdot s(R_A)}{\sum_{R'_B} \sum_{R'_A \in R'_B} |R'_A|}$$

We also ask the labeler to label at most 50 randomly sampled triples from each Type B relation, and calculate triple-level precision as the ratio of the sum of scores of triples over the number of

[8] 3 human labelers performed the task. A portion of the judgments were independently dual annotated; inter-annotator agreement is 73%. Similar to labeling Type A relations, each judgment is cross-checked by at least one more annotator, further improving quality.

Argument 1	Relation phrase	Argument 2
marijuana, caffeine, nicotine...	*result in, be risk factor for, be major cause of...*	*insomnia, emphysema, breast cancer,...*
C# 2.0, php5, java, c++, ...	*allow the use of, also use, introduce the concept of...*	*destructors, interfaces, template,...*
clinton, obama, mccain, ...	*win, win in, take, be lead in,...*	*ca, dc, fl, nh, pa, va, ga, il, nc,...*

Table 3. Sample Type B relations extracted.

sampled triples. We use P_{ins} to represent the precision calculated based on labeled triples. Moreover, as we are interested in how many phrases are found by our algorithm, we also include R_{phrase}, which is the recall of synonymous phrases. Results are shown in Table 2.

Interval	P	R (R_{phrase})	$F1$	P_{ins}	count
[3, 5)	0.913	0.426 (0.026)	0.581	0.872	52149
[5, 10)	0.834	0.514 (0.074)	0.636	0.863	21981
[10, 20)	0.854	0.569 (0.066)	0.683	0.883	6277
[20, 50)	0.899	0.675 (0.406)	0.771	0.894	2630
[50, +∞)	0.922	0.825 (0.594)	0.871	0.929	1089
Overall	0.897	0.684 (0.324)	0.776	0.898	84126

Table 2. Performance for Type B relation extraction. The first column shows the range of the maximum sizes of Type A relations in the Type B relation. The last column shows the number of Type B relations that are in this range. The number in parenthesis in the third column is the recall of phrases.

The result shows that WEBRE can extract Type B relations at high precision (both P and P_{ins}). The overall recall is 0.684. Table 2 also shows a trend that if the maximum number of Type A relation in the target Type B relation is larger, the recall is better. This shows that the recall of Type B relations depends on the amount of data available for that relation. Some examples of Type B relations extracted are shown in Table 3.

Comparison with SNE We compare WEBRE's extracted Type B relations to the relations extracted by its closest prior work SNE[9]. We found SNE is not able to handle the 14.7 million triples in a foreseeable amount of time, so we randomly sampled 1 million (1M) triples[10] and test both algorithms on this set. We also filtered out result clusters which have only 1 or 2 triples from both system outputs. For comparison purposes, we constructed a gold standard *GS3* as follows: randomly select 30 clusters from both system outputs, and then find similar clusters from the other system output, followed by manually refining the clusters by merging similar ones and splitting non-coherent clusters. *GS3* contains 742 triples and 135 clusters. We report triple-level pairwise precision, recall and F1 for both algorithms against *GS3*, and report results in Table 4. We fine-tuned SNE (using grid search, internal cross-validation, and coarse-to-fine parameter tuning), and report its best performance.

Algorithm	Precision	Recall	F1
WEBRE	0.848	0.734	0.787
SNE	0.850	0.080	0.146

Table 4. Pairwise precision/recall/F1 of WEBRE and SNE.

Table 4 shows that WEBRE outperforms SNE significantly in pairwise recall while having similar precision. There are two reasons. First, WEBRE makes use of several corpus-level semantic sources extracted from the corpus for clustering entities and phrases while SNE uses only features in the triple store. These semantic resources significantly reduced data sparseness. Examination of the output shows that SNE is unable to group many triples from the same generally-recognized fine-grained relations. For example, SNE placed relation instances *<Barbara, grow up in, Santa Fe>* and *<John, be raised mostly in, Santa Barbara>* into 2 different clusters because the arguments and phrases do not share features nor could be grouped by SNE's mutual clustering. In contrast, WEBRE groups them together. Second, SNE assumes a relation phrase to be in exactly one cluster. For example, SNE placed *be part of* in the phrase cluster *be city of* and failed to place it in another cluster *be subsidiary of*. This limits SNE's ability to placing relation instances with polysemous phrases into correct relation clusters.

It should be emphasized that we use pairwise precision and recall in table 4 to be consistent with the original SNE paper. Pairwise metrics are much more sensitive than instance-level metrics, and penalize recall exponentially in the worst case[11] if an algorithm incorrectly splits a coherent cluster; therefore the absolute pairwise recall difference

[9] Obtained from alchemy.cs.washington.edu/papers/kok08

[10] We found that SNE's runtime on 1M triples varies from several hours to over a week, depending on the parameters. The best performance is achieved with runtime of approximately 3 days. We also tried SNE with 2M triples, on which many runs take several days and show no sign of convergence. For fairness, the comparison was done on 1M triples.

[11] Pairwise precision and recall are calculated on all pairs that are in the same cluster, thus are very sensitive. For example, if an algorithm incorrectly split a cluster of size N to a smaller main cluster of size $N/2$ and some constant-size clusters, pairwise recall could drop to as much as ¼ of its original value.

should not be interpreted as the same as the instance-level recall reported in previous experiments. On 1 million triples, WEBRE generates 12179 triple clusters with an average size[12] of 13 while SNE generate 53270 clusters with an average size 5.1. In consequence, pairwise recall drops significantly. Nonetheless, at above 80% pairwise precision, it demonstrates that WEBRE can group more related triples by adding rich semantics harvested from the web and employing a more general treatment of polysemous relation phrases. On 1M triples, WEBRE finished in 40 minutes, while the run time of SNE varies from 3 hours to a few days.

6 Conclusion

We present a fully unsupervised algorithm WEBRE for large-scale open-domain relation extraction. WEBRE explicitly handles polysemy relations and achieves a significant improvement on recall by incorporating rich corpus-based semantic resources. Experiments on a large data set show that it can extract a very large set of high-quality relations.

Acknowledgements

Supported in part by the Intelligence Advanced Research Projects Activity (IARPA) via Air Force Research Laboratory (AFRL) contract number FA8650-10-C-7058. The U.S. Government is authorized to reproduce and distribute reprints for Governmental purposes notwithstanding any copyright annotation thereon. The views and conclusions contained herein are those of the authors and should not be interpreted as necessarily representing the official policies or endorsements, either expressed or implied, of IARPA, AFRL, or the U.S. Government.

References

Michele Banko, Michael J. Cafarella, Stephen Soderland, Matt Broadhead, and Oren Etzioni. 2007. Open Information Extraction from the Web. In Proceedings of IJCAI 2007.

Michele Banko and Oren Etzioni. 2008. The Tradeoffs Between Open and Traditional Relation Extraction. In Proceedings of ACL 2008.

Jonathan Berant, Ido Dagan and Jacob Goldberger. 2011. Global Learning of Typed Entailment Rules. In Proceedings of ACL 2011.

Razvan Bunescu and Raymond J. Mooney. 2004. Collective Information Extraction with Relational Markov Networks. In Proceedings of ACL 2004.

Jinxiu Chen, Donghong Ji, Chew Lim Tan, Zhengyu Niu. 2005. Unsupervised Feature Selection for Relation Extraction. In Proceedings of IJCNLP 2005.

Oren Etzioni, Michael Cafarella, Doug Downey, Stanley Kok, Ana-Maria Popescu, Tal Shaked, Stephen Soderland, Daniel S. Weld, and Alexander Yates. 2004. Web-scale information extraction in KnowItAll (preliminary results). In Proceedings of WWW 2004.

Oren Etzioni, Michael Cafarella, Doug Downey, AnaMaria Popescu, Tal Shaked, Stephen Soderland, Daniel S. Weld and Alexander Yates. 2005. Unsupervised named-entity extraction from the Web: An Experimental Study. In Artificial Intelligence, 165(1):91-134.

Anthony Fader, Stephen Soderland, and Oren Etzioni. 2011. Identifying Relations for Open Information Extraction. In Proceedings of EMNLP 2011.

Christiane Fellbaum (Ed.). 1998. WordNet: An Electronic Lexical Database. Cambridge, MA: MIT Press.

Zelig S. Harris. 1985. Distributional Structure. The Philosophy of Linguistics. New York: Oxford University Press.

Takaaki Hasegawa, Satoshi Sekine, Ralph Grishman . 2004.Discovering Relations among Named Entities from Large Corpora. In Proceedings of ACL 2004.

Marti A. Hearst. 1992. Automatic Acquisition of Hyponyms from Large Text Corpora. In Proceedings of COLING 1992.

Stanley Kok and Pedro Domingos. 2008. Extracting Semantic Networks from Text via Relational Clustering. In Proceedings of ECML 2008.

Zornitsa Kozareva, Ellen Riloff, Eduard Hovy. 2008. Semantic Class Learning from the Web with Hyponym Pattern Linkage Graphs. In Proceedings of ACL 2008.

Dekang Lin and Patrick Pantel. 2001. DIRT – Discovery of Inference Rules from Text. In Proceedings of KDD 2001.

Andrew McCallum, Kamal Nigam and Lyle Ungar. 2000. Efficient Clustering of High-Dimensional Data Sets with Application to Reference Matching. In Proceedings of KDD 2000.

Patrick Pantel, Eric Crestan, Arkady Borkovsky, Ana-Maria Popescu and Vishnu Vyas. 2009. Web-Scale Distributional Similarity and Entity Set Expansion. In Proceedings of EMNLP 2009.

[12] The clusters which have only 1 or 2 triples are removed and not counted here for both algorithms.

Patrick Pantel and Dekang Lin. 2002. Discovering word senses from text. In Proceedings of KDD2002.

Patrick Pantel and Deepak Ravichandran. 2004. Automatically Labeling Semantic Classes. In Proceedings of HLT/NAACL-2004.

Marius Pasca. 2004. Acquisition of Categorized Named Entities for Web Search, In Proceedings of CIKM 2004.

Marius Pasca. 2007. Weakly-supervised discovery of named entities using web search queries. In Proceedings of CIKM 2007.

Marius Pasca and Peter Dienes. 2005. Aligning needles in a haystack: Paraphrase acquisition across the Web. In Proceedings of IJCNLP 2005.

Marco Pennacchiotti and Patrick Pantel. 2009. Entity Extraction via Ensemble Semantics. In Proceedings of EMNLP 2009.

Benjamin Rosenfeld and Ronen Feldman. 2007. Clustering for Unsupervised Relation Identification. In Proceedings of CIKM 2007.

Luis Sarmento, Valentin Jijkoun, Maarten de Rijke and Eugenio Oliveira. 2007. "More like these": growing entity classes from seeds. In Proceedings of CIKM 2007.

Satoshi Sekine. 2005. Automatic paraphrase discovery based on context and keywords between NE pairs. In Proceedings of the International Workshop on Paraphrasing, 2005.

Shuming Shi, Huibin Zhang, Xiaojie Yuan, Ji-Rong Wen. 2010. Corpus-based Semantic Class Mining: Distributional vs. Pattern-Based Approaches. In Proceedings of COLING 2010.

Yusuke Shinyama, Satoshi Sekine. 2006. Preemptive Information Extraction using Unrestricted Relation Discovery, In Proceedings of NAACL 2006.

Rion Snow, Daniel Jurafsky, and Andrew Y. Ng. 2005. Learning Syntactic Patterns for Automatic Hypernym Discovery. In Proceedings of In NIPS 17, 2005.

Stephen Soderland and Bhushan Mandhani. 2007. Moving from Textual Relations to Ontologized Relations. In Proceedings of the 2007 AAAI Spring Symposium on Machine Reading.

Partha Pratim Talukdar, Joseph Reisinger, Marius Pasca, Deepak Ravichandran, Rahul Bhagat and Fernando Pereira. 2008. Weakly-Supervised Acquisition of Labeled Class Instances using Graph Random Walks. In Proceedings of EMNLP 2008.

David Vickrey, Oscar Kipersztok and Daphne Koller. 2010. An Active Learning Approach to Finding Related Terms. In Proceedings of ACL 2010.

Vishnu Vyas and Patrick Pantel. 2009. SemiAutomatic Entity Set Refinement. In Proceedings of NAACL/HLT 2009.

Vishnu Vyas, Patrick Pantel and Eric Crestan. 2009, Helping Editors Choose Better Seed Sets for Entity Set Expansion, In Proceedings of CIKM 2009.

Richard C. Wang and William W. Cohen. 2007. Language- Independent Set Expansion of Named Entities Using the Web. In Proceedings of ICDM 2007.

Richard C. Wang and William W. Cohen. 2009. Automatic Set Instance Extraction using the Web. In Proceedings of ACL-IJCNLP 2009.

Wei Wang, Romaric Besançon and Olivier Ferret. 2011. Filtering and Clustering Relations for Unsupervised Information Extraction in Open Domain. In Proceedings of CIKM 2011.

Fei Wu and Daniel S. Weld. 2010. Open information extraction using Wikipedia. In Proceedings of ACL 2010.

Hua Wu and Ming Zhou. 2003. Synonymous collocation extraction using translation information. In Proceedings of the ACL Workshop on Multiword Expressions: Integrating Processing 2003.

Limin Yao, Aria Haghighi, Sebastian Riedel, Andrew McCallum. 2011. Structured Relation Discovery Using Generative Models. In Proceedings of EMNLP 2011.

Alexander Yates and Oren Etzioni. 2007. Unsupervised Resolution of Objects and Relations on the Web. In Proceedings of HLT-NAACL 2007.

Fan Zhang, Shuming Shi, Jing Liu, Shuqi Sun, Chin-Yew Lin. 2011. Nonlinear Evidence Fusion and Propagation for Hyponymy Relation Mining. In Proceedings of ACL 2011.

Huibin Zhang, Mingjie Zhu, Shuming Shi, and Ji-Rong Wen. 2009. Employing Topic Models for Pattern-based Semantic Class Discovery. In Proceedings of ACL 2009.

Forest Reranking through Subtree Ranking

Richárd Farkas, Helmut Schmid
Institute for Natural Language Processing
University of Stuttgart
{farkas,schmid}@ims.uni-stuttgart.de

Abstract

We propose the *subtree ranking* approach to *parse forest reranking* which is a generalization of current perceptron-based reranking methods. For the training of the reranker, we extract competing local subtrees, hence the training instances (candidate subtree sets) are very similar to those used during beam-search parsing. This leads to better parameter optimization. Another chief advantage of the framework is that arbitrary learning to rank methods can be applied. We evaluated our reranking approach on German and English phrase structure parsing tasks and compared it to various state-of-the-art reranking approaches such as the perceptron-based forest reranker. The subtree ranking approach with a Maximum Entropy model significantly outperformed the other approaches.

1 Introduction

Reranking has become a popular technique for solving various structured prediction tasks, such as phrase-structure (Collins, 2000) and dependency parsing (Hall, 2007), semantic role labeling (Toutanova et al., 2008) and machine translation (Shen et al., 2004). The idea is to (re)rank candidates extracted by a base system exploiting a rich feature set and operating at a global (usually sentence) level. Reranking achieved significant gains over the base system in many tasks because it has access to information/features which are not computable in the base system. Reranking also outperforms discriminative approaches which try to handle the entire candidate universe (cf. Turian et al. (2006)) because the base system effectively and efficiently filters out many bad candidates and makes the problem tractable.

The standard approach for reranking is the n-best list ranking procedure, where the base system extracts its top n global-level candidates with associated goodness scores that define an initial ranking. Then the task is to rerank these candidates by using a rich feature set. The bottleneck of this approach is the small number of candidates considered. Compared to n-best lists, packed parse forests encode more candidates in a compact way. **Forest reranking** methods have been proposed, which can exploit the richer set of candidates and they have been successfully applied for phrase-structure (Huang, 2008), dependency (Hayashi et al., 2011) parsing and machine translation (Li and Khudanpur, 2009) as well.

Huang (2008) introduced the **perceptron-based forest reranking** approach. The core of the algorithm is a beam-search based decoder operating on the packed forest in a bottom-up manner. It follows the assumption that the feature values of the whole structure are the sum of the feature values of the local elements and they are designed to the usage of the perceptron update. Under these assumptions a 1-best Viterbi or beam-search decoder can be efficiently employed at parsing and training time. During training, it decodes the 1-best complete parse then it makes the perceptron update against the oracle parse, i.e. the perceptron is trained at the global (sentence) level.

We propose here a **subtree ranker** approach which can be regarded as a generalization of this forest reranking procedure. In contrast to updating on a single (sub)tree per sentence using only the 1-best parse (perceptron-based forest reranking), the subtree ranker exploits subtrees of all sizes from a sentence and trains a (re)ranker utilising several derivations of the constituent in question. During parsing we conduct a beam-search extraction by asking the ranker to select the k best subtrees among the possible candidates of each forest node. The chief motivation for this approach is that in this way, training and prediction are carried out on similar local candidate lists which we expect to be favorable to the learning mechanism. We empirically prove that the trained discriminative rankers benefit from having access to a larger amount of subtree candidates. Moreover, in this framework any kind of learning to rank methods can be chosen as ranker, including pair-wise and list-wise classifiers (Li, 2011).

The contributions of this paper are the following:

- We extend the perceptron-based forest rerankers to the subtree ranker forest reranking framework which allows to replace the perceptron update by any kind of learning to rank procedure.
- We report experimental results on German and English phrase-structure parsing comparing subtree rerankers to various other rerankers showing a significant improvement over the perceptron-based forest reranker approach.

2 Related Work

Our method is closely related to the work of Huang (2008), who introduced forest-based reranking for phrase structure parsing. The proposed framework can be regarded as an extension of this approach. It has several advantages compared with the perceptron-based forest reranker. In this paper we focus on the most important one – and briefly discuss two others in Section 5 – which is enabling the use of any kind of learning to rank approaches. While the perceptron is fast to train, other machine learning approaches usually outperform it. Most of the existing learning to rank approaches are built on linear models and evaluate the candidates independently of each other (such as MaxEnt (Charniak and Johnson, 2005), SVMRank (Joachims, 2002), SoftRank (Guiver and Snelson, 2008)). Thus the choice of the learning method does not influence parsing time. We believe that the real bottleneck of parsing applications is parsing time and not training time. On the other hand, they can learn a better model (at the cost of higher training time) than the Perceptron. In theory, we can imagine learning to rank approaches which can not be reduced to the individual scoring of candidates at prediction time, for instance a decision tree-based pairwise ranker. Although such methods would also fit into the general subtree framework, they are not employed in practice (Li, 2011).

The subtree ranking approach is a generalization of the perceptron-based approach. If the ranking algorithm is the Averaged Perceptron, the parsing algorithm reduces to perceptron-based forest parsing. If the "selection strategy" utilizes the base system ranking and training starts with a filtering step which keeps only candidate sets from the root node of the forest we get the offline version of the training procedure of the perceptron-based forest reranker of Huang (2008).

As our approach is based on local ranking (local update in the online learning literature), it is highly related to early update which looks for the first local decision point where the oracle parse falls out from the beam. Early update was introduced by Collins and Roark (2004) for incremental parsing and adopted to forest reranking by Wang and Zong (2011).

Besides phrase structure parsing, the forest reranking approach was successfully applied for dependency parsing as well. Hayashi et al. (2011) introduced a procedure where the interpolation of a generative and a forest-based discriminative parser is exploited.

From the algorithmic point of view, our approach is probably most closely related to Searn (Daumé et al., 2009) and Magerman (1995) as we also employ a particular machine learned model for a sequence of local decisions. The topological order of the parse forest nodes can form the "sequence of choices" of Searn. The biggest differences between our approach and Searn are that we propose an approach employing beam search and the "policy" is a ranker in our framework instead of a multiclass classifier as there are no "actions" here, instead we have to choose from candidate sets in the forest reranking framework. In a wider sense, our approach can be regarded – like Searn – as an Inverse Reinforcement Learning approach where "one is given an environment and a set of trajectories and the problem is to find a reward function such that an agent acting optimally with respect to the reward function would follow trajectories that match those in the training set" (Neu and Szepesvári, 2009). Neu and Szepesvári (2009) introduced the top-down parsing Markov Decision Processes and experiment with several inverse reinforcement learning methods. The forest reranking approaches are bottom-up parsers which would require a new (non-straightforward) definition of a corresponding Markov Decision Process.

3 Subtree Ranking-based Forest Reranking

A **packed parse forest** is a compact representation of possible parses for a given sentence. A forest has the structure of a hypergraph, whose nodes V are the elementary units of the underlying structured prediction problem and the hyperedges E are the possible deductive steps from the nodes. In this paper we experimented with phrase-structure parse reranking. In this framework *nodes* correspond to constituents spanning a certain scope of the input sentence and a *hyperedge* e links a parent node $head(e)$ to its children $tails(e)$ (i.e. a hyperedge is a CFG rule in context).

The forest is extracted from the chart of a base PCFG parser, usually employing a heavy pruning strategy. Then the goal of a forest reranker is to find the best parse of the input sentence exploiting a feature representation of (sub)trees.

We sketch the **parsing** procedure of the subtree ranker in Algorithm 1. It is a bottom-up beam-search parser operating on the hypergraph. At each node v we store the k best subtrees $S(v)$ headed by the node. The $S(v)$ lists contain the k top-ranked subtrees by the ranker R among the candidates in the beam. The set of candidate subtrees at a node is the union of the candidates at the different hyperedges. The set of candidate subtrees at a certain hyperedge, in turn, is formed by the Cartesian product $\otimes S(v_i)$ of the k-best subtrees stored at the child nodes v_i. The final output of forest ranking is the 1-best subtree headed by the goal node $S_1(v_{goal})$.

Algorithm 1 Subtree Ranking

Require: $\langle V, E \rangle$ forest, R ranker
  for all $v \in V$ in bottom-up topological order **do**
    $C \leftarrow \emptyset$
    for all $e \in E, head(e) = v$ **do**
      $C \leftarrow C \cup (\otimes S(v_i)), v_i \in tails(e)$
    end for
    $S(v) \leftarrow R_k(C)$
  end for
  return $S_1(v_{goal})$

For **training** the ranker we propose to extract local candidate lists from the forests which share the characteristics of the candidates at parsing time. Algorithm 2 depicts the training procedure of the subtree ranker.

As forests sometimes do not contain the gold standard tree, we extract an oracle tree instead, which is the closest derivable tree in the forest to the gold standard tree (Collins, 2000). Then we optimize the parser for ranking the oracle tree at the top. This procedure is beneficial to training since the objective is a reachable state. In Algorithm 2, we extract the oracle tree from the parses encoded in the forest $\langle V, E \rangle_i$ for the ith training sentence, which is the tree with the highest F-score when compared to the gold standard tree y_i. For each of the training sentences we calculate the oracle subtrees for each node $\{O_v\}$ of the corresponding parse forest. We follow the dynamic programming approach of Huang (2008) for the extraction of the forest oracle. The goal of this algorithm is to extract the full oracle tree, but as a side product it calculates the best possible subtree for all nodes including the nodes outside of the full oracle tree as well.

After computing the oracle subtrees, we crawl the forests bottom-up and extract a training instance $\langle C, O_v \rangle$ at each node v which consists of the candidate set C and the oracle O_v at that node. The creation of candidate lists is exactly the same as it was at parsing time. Then we create training instances from each of the candidate lists and form the set of subtrees $S(v)$ which is stored for candidate extraction at the higher levels of the forest (later steps in the training instance extraction).

A crucial design question is how to form the $S(v)$ sets during training, which is the task of the *selection*

Algorithm 2 Subtree Ranker Training

Require: $\{\langle V, E\rangle_i, y_i\}_1^N$, SS selection strategy
  $T \leftarrow \emptyset$
  for all $i \leftarrow 1...N$ **do**
    $O \leftarrow$ oracle extractor($\langle V, E\rangle_i, y_i$)
    for all $v \in V_i$ in bottom-up topological order **do**
      $C \leftarrow \emptyset$
      for all $e \in E, head(e) = v$ **do**
        $C \leftarrow C \cup (\otimes S(v_j)), v_j \in tails(e)$
      end for
      $T \leftarrow T \cup \langle C, O_v\rangle$
      $S(v) \leftarrow SS(C, O_v)$
    end for
  end for
  $R \leftarrow$ train reranker(T)
  return R

strategy SS. One possible solution is to keep the k best oracle subtrees, i.e. the k subtrees closest to the gold standard parse, which is analogous to using the gold standard labels in Maximum Entropy Markov Models for sequence labeling problems (we refer this selection strategy as 'oracle subtree' later on). The problem with this solution is that if the rankers have been trained on the oracle subtrees potentially leads to a suboptimal performance as the outputs of the ranker at prediction time are noisy. Note that this approach is not a classical beam-based decoding anymore as the "beam" is maintained according to the oracle parses and there is no model which influences that. An alternative solution – beam-based decoding – is to use a ranker model to extract the $S(v)$ set in training time as well. In the general reranking approach, we assume that the ranking of the base parser is reliable. So we store the k best subtrees according to the base system in $S(v)$ (the 'base system ranking' selection strategy). Note that the general framework keeps this question open and lets the implementations define a selection strategy SS.

After extracting the training instances T we can train an arbitrary ranker R offline. Note that the extraction of candidate lists is exactly the same in Algorithm 1 and 2 while the creation of S_v can be different.

4 Experiments

We carried out experiments on English and German phrase-structure reranking. As evaluation metric, we used the standard `evalb` implementation of PARSEVAL on every sentence without length limitation and we start from raw sentences without gold standard POS tagging. As the grammatical functions of constituents are important from a downstream application point of view – especially in German – we also report PARSEVAL scores on the conflation of constituent labels and grammatical functions. These scores are shown in brackets in Table 2.

4.1 Datasets

We used the Wall Street Journal subcorpus of the Ontonotes v4.0 corpus (Weischedel et al., 2011)[1] for English. As usual sections 2-21, 23 and 24 served as training set (30,060 sentences), test set (1,640 sentences), and development set (1,336 sentences), respectively. Using the Ontonotes version enables us to assess parser robustness. To this end, we evaluated our models also on the weblog subcorpus of the Ontonotes v4.0 corpus which consists of 15,103 sentences.

For German we used the Tiger treebank (Brants et al., 2002). We take the first 40,474 sentences of the Tiger treebank as training data, the next 5,000 sentences as development data, and the last 5,000 sentences as test data.

4.2 Implementation of the Generic Framework

We investigate the Averaged Perceptron and a Maximum Entropy ranker as the reranker R in the subtree ranking framework. The Maximum Entropy ranker model is optimized with a loss function which is the negative log conditional likelihood of the oracle trees relative to the candidate sets. In the case of multiple oracles we optimize for the sum of the oracle trees' posterior probabilities (Charniak and Johnson, 2005).

In our setup the parsing algorithm is identical to the perceptron-based forest reranker of Huang (2008) because both the Averaged Perceptron and the Maximum Entropy rankers score the local subtree candidates independently of each other using

[1]Note that it contains less sentences and a slightly modified annotation schema than the Penn Treebank.

a linear model. There is no need to compute the global normalization constant of the Maximum Entropy model because we only need the ranking and not the probabilities. Hence the difference is in how to train the ranker model.

We experimented with both the 'oracle subtree' and the 'base system ranking' selection strategies (see Section 3).

4.3 Five Methods for Forest-based Reranking

We conducted comparative experiments employing the proposed subtree ranking approach and state-of-the-art methods for forest reranking. Note that they are equivalent in parsing time as each of them uses beam-search with a linear classifier, on the other hand they are radically different in their training.

- The original perceptron-based forest reranker of Huang (2008) ('perceptron with global training').
- The same method employing the early-update updating mechanism instead of the global update. Wang and Zong (2011) reported a significant gain using this update over the standard global update ('perceptron with early update').
- Similar to learning a perceptron at the global level and then applying it at local decisions, we can train a Maximum Entropy ranker at the global level utilizing the n-best full parse candidates of the base parser, then use this model for local decision making. So we train the standard n-best rerankers (Charniak and Johnson, 2005) and then apply them in the beam-search-based Viterbi parser ('n-best list training'). Applying the feature weights adjusted in this approach in the forest-based decoding outperforms the standard n-best list decoding by an F-score of 0.3 on the German dataset.
- The subtree ranker method using the Averaged Perceptron reranker. This is different from the 'perceptron with global training' as we conduct updates at every local decision point and we do offline training ('subtree ranking by AvgPer').
- The subtree ranker method using Maximum Entropy training ('subtree ranking by MaxEnt').

We (re)implemented these methods and used the same forests and the same feature sets for the comparative experiments.

4.4 Implementation Details

We used the first-stage **PCFG parser** of Charniak and Johnson (2005) for English and BitPar (Schmid, 2004) for German. BitPar employs a grammar engineered for German (for details please refer to Farkas et al. (2011)). These two parsers are state-of-the-art PCFG parsers for English and German, respectively. For German the base parser and the reranker operate on the conflation of constituent labels and grammatical functions. For English, we used the forest extraction and pruning code of Huang (2008). The pruning removes hyperedges where the difference between the cost of the best derivation using this hyperedge and the cost of the globally best derivation is above some threshold. For German, we used the pruned parse forest of Bitpar (Schmid, 2004). After computing the posterior probability of each hyperedge given the input sentence, Bitpar prunes the parse forest by deleting hyperedges whose posterior probability is below some threshold. (We used the threshold 0.01).

We employed an Averaged Perceptron (for 'perceptron with global training', 'perceptron with early update' and 'subtree ranking by AvgPer') and a Maximum Entropy **reranker** (for 'subtree ranking by MaxEnt' and 'n-best list training'). For the perceptron reranker, we used the Joshua implementation[2]. The optimal number of iterations was determined on the development set. For the Maximum Entropy reranker we used the `RankMaxEnt` implementation of the Mallet package (McCallum, 2002) modified to use the objective function of Charniak and Johnson (2005) and we optimized the L2 regularizer coefficient on the development set.

The beam-size were set to 15 (the value suggested by Huang (2008)) during parsing and the training of the 'perceptron with global training' and 'perceptron with early update' models. We used $k = 3$ for training the 'subtree ranking by AvgPer' and 'subtree ranking by MaxEnt' rankers (see Section 5 for a discussion on this).

In the English experiments, we followed (Huang,

[2]`http://joshua.sourceforge.net/Joshua/`

	Tiger test	WSJ dev	WSJ test	WB
base system (1-best)	76.84 (65.91)	89.29	88.63	81.86
oracle tree	90.66 (80.38)	97.31	97.30	94.18

Table 1: The lower and upper bounds for rerankers on the four evaluation datasets. The numbers in brackets refers to evaluation with grammatical function labels on the German dataset.

	Tiger test	WSJ dev	WSJ test	WB
perceptron with global training	78.39 (67.79)	90.58	89.60	82.87
perceptron with early update	78.83 (68.05)	90.81†	90.01	83.03†
n-best list training	78.75 (68.04)	90.89	90.11	83.55
subtree ranking by AvgPer	78.54† (67.97†)	90.65†	89.97	83.04†
subtree ranking by MaxEnt	79.36 (68.72)	91.14	90.32	83.83

Table 2: The results achieved by various forest rerankers. The difference between the scores marked by † and the 'perceptron with global training' were not statistically significant with $p < 0.005$ according to the the McNemar test. All other results are statistically different from this baseline.

2008) and selectively re-implemented **feature templates** from (Collins, 2000) and Charniak and Johnson (2005). For German we re-implemented the feature templates of Versley and Rehbein (2009) which is the state-of-the-art feature set for German. It consists of features constructed from the lexicalized parse tree and its typed dependencies along with features based on external statistical information (such as the clustering of unknown words according to their context of occurrence and PP attachment statistics gathered from the automatically POS tagged DE-WaC corpus, a 1.7G words sample of the German-language WWW). We filtered out rare features which occurred in less than 10 forests (we used the same non-tuned threshold for the English and German training sets as well).

We also re-implemented the oracle extraction procedure of Huang (2008) and extended its convolution and translation operators for using the base system score as tie breaker.

4.5 Results

Table 1 shows the results of the 1-best parse of the base system and the oracle scores – i.e. the **lower and upper bounds** for the rerankers – for the four evaluation datasets used in our experiments. The German and the weblog datasets are more difficult for the parsers.

The following table summarizes the characteristics of the subtree ranker's training sample of the German and English datasets by employing the 'oracle subtree' selection strategy:

	Tiger train	WSJ train
#candidate lists	266,808	1,431,058
avg. size of cand. lists	3.2	5.7
#features before filtering	2,683,552	22,164,931
#features after filtering	94,164	858,610

Table 3: The sizes of the subtree ranker training datasets at $k = 3$.

Using this selection strategy the training dataset is smaller than the training dataset of the n-best list rankers – where offline trainers are employed as well – as the total number of candidates is similar (and even less in the Tiger corpus) while there are fewer firing features at the subtrees than at full trees.

Table 2 summarizes the results achieved by various forest rerankers. Both subtree rankers used the oracle subtrees as the selection strategy of Algorithm 2. The 'subtree ranking by MaxEnt' method significantly outperformed the perceptron-based forest reranking algorithms at each of the datasets and seems to be more robust as its advantage on the outdomain data 'WB' is higher compared with the indomain 'WSJ' datasets. The early update improves the perceptron based forest rerankers which is in line with the results reported by Wang and Zong (2011). The 'n-best list training' method works surprisingly well. It outperforms both perceptron-based forest rerankers on the English datasets (while achieving a smaller F-score than the perceptron with early update on the Tiger corpus) which demonstrates the potential of utilizing larger candidate lists for discriminative training of rerankers. The comparison of the 'subtree ranking by AvgPer' row and the 'subtree ranking by MaxEnt' row shows a clear advantage of the Maximum Entropy training mechanism over the Averaged Perceptron.

Besides the 'oracle subtree' **selection strategy** we also experimented with the 'base system ranking' selection strategy with subtree Maximum Entropy ranker. Table 4 compares the accuracies of the two strategies. The difference between the two strategies varies among datasets. In the German dataset, they are competitive and the prediction of grammatical functions benefits from the 'base system ranking' strategy, while it performs considerably worse at the English datasets.

	Tiger test	WSJ test	WB
oracle SS	79.36 (68.72)	90.32	83.83
base sys SS	79.34 (68.84)	89.97	83.34

Table 4: The results of the two selection strategies. Using the oracle trees proved to be better on each of the datasets.

Extracting candidate lists from each of the local decision points might seem to be redundant. To gain some insight into this question, we investigated the effect of training instance filtering strategies on the Tiger treebank. We removed the training instances from the training sample T where the F-score of the oracle (sub)tree against the gold standard tree is less than a certain threshold (this data selection procedure was inspired by Li and Khudanpur (2008)). The idea behind this **data selection** is to eliminate bad training examples which might push the learner into the wrong direction. Figure 1 depicts the results on the Tiger treebank as a function of this data selection threshold.

With this data selection strategy we could further gain 0.22 F-score percentage points achieving 79.58 (68.87) and we can conclude that omitting candidate sets far from the gold-standard tree helps training. Figure 1 also shows that too strict filtering hurts the performance. The result with threshold=90 is worse than the result without filtering. We should note that similar data selection methods can be applied

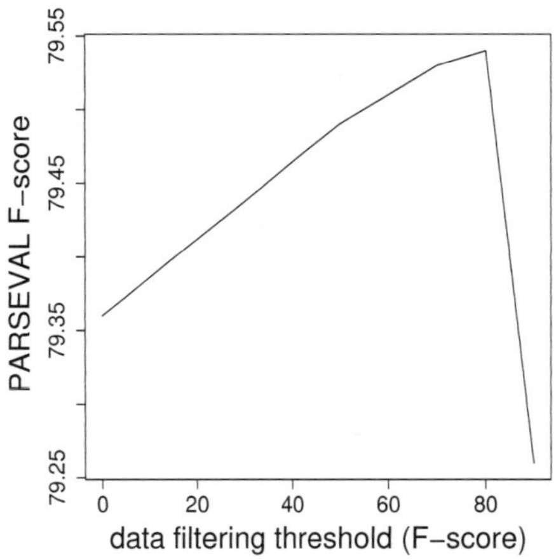

Figure 1: The effect of data selection on the Tiger test set.

to each of the baseline systems and the comparison to them would be fair with conducting that. Thus we consider our results without data selection to be final.

5 Discussion

We experimentally showed in the previous section that the subtree forest reranking approach with Maximum Entropy models significantly outperforms the perceptron-based forest reranking approach. This improvement must be the result of differences in the training algorithms because there is no difference between the two approaches at parse time, as we discussed in Section 4.2.

There are two sources of these improvements. (i) We use local subtrees as training instances instead of using the global parses exclusively. The most important difference between the training of the perceptron-based forest reranker and the subtree forest reranker is that we train on subtrees (extract candidate sets) outside of the Viterbi parses as well, i.e. our intuition is that the training of the discriminative model can benefit from seeing good and bad subtrees far from the best parses as well. (ii) The subtree ranker framework enables us to employ the Maximum Entropy ranker on multiple candidates, which usually outperforms the Averaged Perceptron.

The results of Table 2 can be considered as two paths from the 'perceptron with global training' to the 'subtree ranking by MaxEnt' applying these sources of improvements. If we use (i) and stay with the Averaged Perceptron as learning algorithm we get 'subtree ranking by AvgPer'. If we additionally replace the Averaged Perceptron by Maximum Entropy – i.e. follow (ii) – we arrive at 'subtree ranking by MaxEnt'. On the other hand, the 'n-best training' uses global trees and Maximum Entropy for training, so the reason of the difference between 'perceptron with global training' and 'n-best training' is (ii). Then we arrive at 'subtree ranking by MaxEnt' by (i). This line of thoughts and the figures of Table 2 indicate that the added value of (i) and (ii) are similar in magnitude.

5.1 Error Analysis

For understanding the added value of the proposed subtree ranking method, we manually investigated sentences from the German development set and compared the parses of the 'perceptron with global training' with the 'subtree ranking by MaxEnt'. We could not found any linguistic phenomena which was handled clearly better by the subtree ranker[3], but it made considerably more fixes than errors in the following cases:

- the attachment of adverbs,
- the unary branching verbal phrases and
- extremely short sentences which does not contain any verb (fragments).

5.2 Novel Opportunities with the Subtree Ranking Framework

A generalization issue of the subtree ranking approach is that it allows to use **any kind of feature representation and arbitrary aggregation** of local features. The basic assumption of training on the global (sentence) level in the perceptron reranking framework is that the feature vector of a subtree is the sum of the feature vectors of the children and the features extracted from the root of the subtree in question. This decomposability assumption provides a fine framework in the case of binary features which fire if a certain linguistic phenomenon occurs. On the other hand, this is not straightforward in the presence of real valued features. For example, Versley and Rehbein (2009) introduce real-valued features for supporting German PP-attachment recognition – the mutual information of noun and preposition co-occurrence estimated from a huge unlabeled corpus – and this single feature template (about 80 features) could achieve a gain of 1 point in phrase structure parsing accuracy while the same improvement can be achieved by several feature templates and millions of binary features. The aggregation of such feature values can be different from summing, for instance the semantics of the feature can demand averaging, minimum, maximum or introducing new features etc. Another opportunity for extending current approaches is to employ utility functions on top of the sum of the binary feature values. Each of these extensions fits into the proposed framework.

The subtree ranking framework also enables the usage of **different models at different kinds of nodes**. For example, different models can be trained for ranking subtress headed by noun phrases and for verb phrases. This is not feasible in the perceptron-based forest ranker which sums up features and updates feature weights at the sentence level while the ranker R in Algorithm 2 can refer to several models because we handle local decisions separately. This approach would not hurt parsing speed as one particular model is asked at each node, but it multiplies memory requirements. This is an approach which the subtree ranking framework allows, but which would not fit to the global level updates of the perceptron forest rerankers.

As a first step in this direction of research we experimented with training three different Maximum Entropy models using the same feature representation, the first only on candidate lists extracted from noun phrase nodes, the second on verb phrase nodes and the third on all nodes (i.e. the third model is equivalent to the 'subtree MaxEnt' model). Then at prediction time, we ask that model (out of the three) which is responsible for ranking the candidates of the current type of node. This approach performed worse than the single model approach achieving an F-scores of 79.24 (68.46) on the Tiger test dataset. This negative results – compared with 79.36 (68.72) achieved by a single model – is probably due to data sparsity problems. The amount of training samples for noun phrases is 6% of the full training sample

[3]We believe that this might be the case only if we would introduce new information (e.g. features) for the system.

and it seems that a better model can be learned from a much bigger but more heterogeneous dataset.

5.3 On the Efficiency of Subtree Ranking

In subtree ranking, we extract a larger number of training instances (candidate lists) than the perceptron-based approach which extracts exactly one instance from a sentence. Moreover, the candidate lists are longer than the perceptron-based approach (where 2 "candidates" are compared against each other). Training on this larger set (refer Table 3 for concrete figures) consumes more space and time.

In our implementation, we keep the whole training dataset in the memory. With this implementation the whole training process (feature extraction, candidate extraction and training the Maximum Entropy ranker) takes 3 hours and uses 10GB of memory at $k = 1$ and it takes 20 hours and uses 60GB of memory at $k = 3$ ((Huang, 2008) reported 5.3 and 27.3 hours at beam-sizes of 1 and 15 respectively but it used only 1.2GB of memory). The in-depth investigation of the effect of k is among our future plans.

6 Conclusions

We presented a subtree ranking approach to parse forest reranking, which is a generalization of current reranking methods. The main advantages of our approach are: (i) The candidate lists used during training are very similar to those used during parsing, which leads to better parameter optimization. (ii) Arbitrary ranking methods can be applied in our approach. (iii) The reranking models need not to be decomposable.

We evaluated our parse reranking approach on German and English phrase structure parsing tasks and compared it to various state-of-the-art reranking approaches such as the perceptron-based forest reranker (Huang, 2008). The subtree reranking approach with a Maximum Entropy model significantly outperformed the other approaches.

We conjecture two reasons for this result: (i) By training on all subtrees instead of Viterbi parses or n-best parses only, we use the available training data more effectively. (ii) The subtree ranker framework allows us to use a standard Maximum Entropy learner in parse-forest training instead of the Perceptron, which is usually superior.

Acknowledgements

We thank Liang Huang to provide us the modified version of the Charniak parser, which output a packed forest for each sentence along with his forest pruning code.

This work was founded by the Deutsche Forschungsgemeinschaft grant SFB 732, project D4.

References

Sabine Brants, Stefanie Dipper, Silvia Hansen, Wolfgang Lezius, and George Smith. 2002. The TIGER treebank. In *Proceedings of the Workshop on Treebanks and Linguistic Theories*, pages 24–41.

Eugene Charniak and Mark Johnson. 2005. Coarse-to-fine n-best parsing and maxent discriminative reranking. In *Proceedings of the 43rd Annual Meeting on Association for Computational Linguistics*, ACL '05, pages 173–180.

Michael Collins and Brian Roark. 2004. Incremental parsing with the perceptron algorithm. In *Proceedings of the 42nd Meeting of the Association for Computational Linguistics (ACL'04), Main Volume*, pages 111–118.

Michael Collins. 2000. Discriminative reranking for natural language parsing. In *Proceedings of the Seventeenth International Conference on Machine Learning*, ICML '00, pages 175–182.

Hal Daumé, III, John Langford, and Daniel Marcu. 2009. Search-based structured prediction. *Machine Learning*, 75(3):297–325, June.

Richárd Farkas, Bernd Bohnet, and Helmut Schmid. 2011. Features for phrase-structure reranking from dependency parses. In *Proceedings of the 12th International Conference on Parsing Technologies*, pages 209–214.

John Guiver and Edward Snelson. 2008. Learning to rank with softrank and gaussian processes. In *Proceedings of the 31st annual international ACM SIGIR conference on Research and development in information retrieval*, SIGIR '08, pages 259–266.

Keith Hall. 2007. K-best spanning tree parsing. In *Proceedings of the 45th Annual Meeting of the Association of Computational Linguistics*, pages 392–399, June.

Katsuhiko Hayashi, Taro Watanabe, Masayuki Asahara, and Yuji Matsumoto. 2011. Third-order variational reranking on packed-shared dependency forests. In *Proceedings of the 2011 Conference on Empirical Methods in Natural Language Processing*, pages 1479–1488.

Liang Huang. 2008. Forest reranking: Discriminative parsing with non-local features. In *Proceedings of ACL-08: HLT*, pages 586–594.

T. Joachims. 2002. Optimizing search engines using clickthrough data. In *ACM SIGKDD Conference on Knowledge Discovery and Data Mining (KDD)*, pages 133–142.

Zhifei Li and Sanjeev Khudanpur. 2008. Large-scale discriminative n-gram language models for statistical machine translation. In *Proceedings of the 8th AMTA conference*, pages 133–142.

Z. Li and S. Khudanpur, 2009. *GALE book chapter on "MT From Text"*, chapter Forest reranking for machine translation with the perceptron algorithm.

Hang Li. 2011. *Learning to Rank for Information Retrieval and Natural Language Processing*. Synthesis Lectures on Human Language Technologies. Morgan & Claypool Publishers.

David M. Magerman. 1995. Statistical decision-tree models for parsing. In *Proceedings of the 33rd Annual Meeting of the Association for Computational Linguistics*, pages 276–283, June.

Andrew Kachites McCallum. 2002. Mallet: A machine learning for language toolkit. http://mallet.cs.umass.edu.

Gergely Neu and Csaba Szepesvári. 2009. Training parsers by inverse reinforcement learning. *Machine Learning*, 77(2–3):303–337.

Helmut Schmid. 2004. Efficient parsing of highly ambiguous context-free grammars with bit vectors. In *Proceedings of Coling 2004*, pages 162–168.

Libin Shen, Anoop Sarkar, and Franz Josef Och. 2004. Discriminative reranking for machine translation. In Daniel Marcu Susan Dumais and Salim Roukos, editors, *HLT-NAACL 2004: Main Proceedings*, pages 177–184.

Kristina Toutanova, Aria Haghighi, and Christopher D. Manning. 2008. A global joint model for semantic role labeling. *Computational Linguistics*, 34(2):161–191.

Joseph P. Turian, Benjamin Wellington, and I. Dan Melamed. 2006. Scalable discriminative learning for natural language parsing and translation. In *NIPS*, pages 1409–1416.

Yannick Versley and Ines Rehbein. 2009. Scalable discriminative parsing for german. In *Proceedings of the 11th International Conference on Parsing Technologies (IWPT'09)*, pages 134–137.

Zhiguo Wang and Chengqing Zong. 2011. Parse reranking based on higher-order lexical dependencies. In *Proceedings of 5th International Joint Conference on Natural Language Processing*, pages 1251–1259.

Ralph Weischedel, Eduard Hovy, Martha Palmer, Mitch Marcus, Robert Belvin, Sameer Pradhan, Lance Ramshaw, and Nianwen Xue, 2011. *Handbook of Natural Language Processing and Machine Translation.*, chapter OntoNotes: A Large Training Corpus for Enhanced Processing.

Parser Showdown at the Wall Street Corral: An Empirical Investigation of Error Types in Parser Output

Jonathan K. Kummerfeld[†] **David Hall**[†] **James R. Curran**[‡] **Dan Klein**[†]

[†]Computer Science Division
University of California, Berkeley
Berkeley, CA 94720, USA
{jkk,dlwh,klein}@cs.berkeley.edu

[‡]ə-lab, School of IT
University of Sydney
Sydney, NSW 2006, Australia
james@it.usyd.edu.au

Abstract

Constituency parser performance is primarily interpreted through a single metric, F-score on WSJ section 23, that conveys no linguistic information regarding the remaining errors. We classify errors within a set of linguistically meaningful types using tree transformations that repair groups of errors together. We use this analysis to answer a range of questions about parser behaviour, including what linguistic constructions are difficult for state-of-the-art parsers, what types of errors are being resolved by rerankers, and what types are introduced when parsing out-of-domain text.

1 Introduction

Parsing has been a major area of research within computational linguistics for decades, and constituent parser F-scores on WSJ section 23 have exceeded 90% (Petrov and Klein, 2007), and 92% when using self-training and reranking (McClosky et al., 2006; Charniak and Johnson, 2005). While these results give a useful measure of overall performance, they provide no information about the nature, or relative importance, of the remaining errors.

Broad investigations of parser errors beyond the PARSEVAL metric (Abney et al., 1991) have either focused on specific parsers, e.g. Collins (2003), or have involved conversion to dependencies (Carroll et al., 1998; King et al., 2003). In all of these cases, the analysis has not taken into consideration how a set of errors can have a common cause, e.g. a single mis-attachment can create multiple node errors.

We propose a new method of error classification using tree transformations. Errors in the parse tree are repaired using subtree movement, node creation, and node deletion. Each step in the process is then associated with a linguistically meaningful error type, based on factors such as the node that is moved, its siblings, and parents.

Using our method we analyse the output of thirteen constituency parsers on newswire. Some of the frequent error types that we identify are widely recognised as challenging, such as prepositional phrase (PP) attachment. However, other significant types have not received as much attention, such as clause attachment and modifier attachment.

Our method also enables us to investigate where reranking and self-training improve parsing. Previously, these developments were analysed only in terms of their impact on F-score. Similarly, the challenge of out-of-domain parsing has only been expressed in terms of this single objective. We are able to decompose the drop in performance and show that a disproportionate number of the extra errors are due to coordination and clause attachment.

This work presents a comprehensive investigation of parser behaviour in terms of linguistically meaningful errors. By applying our method to multiple parsers and domains we are able to answer questions about parser behaviour that were previously only approachable through approximate measures, such as counts of node errors. We show which errors have been reduced over the past fifteen years of parsing research; where rerankers are making their gains and where they are not exploiting the full potential of k-best lists; and what types of errors arise when moving out-of-domain. We have released our system[1] to enable future work to apply our methodology.

[1]http://code.google.com/p/berkeley-parser-analyser/

2 Background

Most attempts to understand the behaviour of constituency parsers have focused on overall evaluation metrics. The three main methods are intrinsic evaluation with PARSEVAL, evaluation on dependencies extracted from the constituency parse, and evaluation on downstream tasks that rely on parsing.

Intrinsic evaluation with PARSEVAL, which calculates precision and recall over labeled tree nodes, is a useful indicator of overall performance, but does not pinpoint which structures the parser has most difficulty with. Even when the breakdown for particular node types is presented (e.g. Collins, 2003), the interaction between node errors is not taken into account. For example, a VP node could be missing because of incorrect PP attachment, a coordination error, or a unary production mistake. There has been some work that addresses these issues by analysing the output of constituency parsers on linguistically motivated error types, but only by hand on sets of around 100 sentences (Hara et al., 2007; Yu et al., 2011). By automatically classifying parse errors we are able to consider the output of multiple parsers on thousands of sentences.

The second major parser evaluation method involves extraction of grammatical relations (King et al., 2003; Briscoe and Carroll, 2006) or dependencies (Lin, 1998; Briscoe et al., 2002). These metrics have been argued to be more informative and generally applicable (Carroll et al., 1998), and have the advantage that the breakdown over dependency types is more informative than over node types. There have been comparisons of multiple parsers (Foster and van Genabith, 2008; Nivre et al., 2010; Cer et al., 2010), as well as work on finding relations between errors (Hara et al., 2009), and breaking down errors by a range of factors (McDonald and Nivre, 2007). However, one challenge is that results for constituency parsers are strongly influenced by the dependency scheme being used and how easy it is to extract the dependencies from a given parser's output (Clark and Hockenmaier, 2002). Our approach does not have this disadvantage, as we analyse parser output directly.

The third major approach involves extrinsic evaluation, where the parser's output is used in a downstream task, such as machine translation (Quirk and Corston-Oliver, 2006), information extraction (Miyao et al., 2008), textual entailment (Yuret et al., 2010), or semantic dependencies (Dridan and Oepen, 2011). While some of these approaches give a better sense of the impact of parse errors, they require integration into a larger system, making it less clear where a given error originates.

The work we present here differs from existing approaches by directly and automatically classifying errors into meaningful types. This enables the first very broad, yet detailed, study of parser behaviour, evaluating the output of thirteen parsers over thousands of sentences.

3 Parsers

Our evaluation is over a wide range of PTB constituency parsers and their variants from the past fifteen years. For all parsers we used the publicly available version, with the standard parameter settings.

Berkeley (Petrov et al., 2006; Petrov and Klein, 2007). An unlexicalised parser with a grammar constructed with automatic state splitting.

Bikel (2004) implementation of Collins (1997).

BUBS (Dunlop et al., 2011; Bodenstab et al., 2011). A 'grammar-agnostic constituent parser,' which uses a Berkeley Parser grammar, but parses with various pruning techniques to improve speed, at the cost of accuracy.

Charniak (2000). A generative parser with a maximum entropy-inspired model. We also use the reranker (Charniak and Johnson, 2005), and the self-trained model (McClosky et al., 2006).

Collins (1997). A generative lexicalised parser, with three models, a base model, a model that uses subcategorisation frames for head words, and a model that takes into account traces.

SSN (Henderson, 2003; Henderson, 2004). A statistical left-corner parser, with probabilities estimated by a neural network.

Stanford (Klein and Manning, 2003a; Klein and Manning, 2003b). We consider both the unlexicalised PCFG parser (-U) and the factored parser (-F), which combines the PCFG parser with a lexicalised dependency parser.

System	F	P	R	Exact	Speed
ENHANCED TRAINING / SYSTEMS					
Charniak-SR	92.07	92.44	91.70	44.87	1.8
Charniak-R	91.41	91.78	91.04	44.04	1.8
Charniak-S	91.02	91.16	90.89	40.77	1.8
STANDARD PARSERS					
Berkeley	90.06	90.30	89.81	36.59	4.2
Charniak	89.71	89.88	89.55	37.25	1.8
SSN	89.42	89.96	88.89	32.74	1.8
BUBS	88.50	88.57	88.43	31.62	27.6
Bikel	88.16	88.23	88.10	32.33	0.8
Collins-3	87.66	87.82	87.50	32.22	2.0
Collins-2	87.62	87.77	87.48	32.51	2.2
Collins-1	87.09	87.29	86.90	30.35	3.3
Stanford-L	86.42	86.35	86.49	27.65	0.7
Stanford-U	85.78	86.48	85.09	28.35	2.7

Table 1: PARSEVAL results on WSJ section 23 for the parsers we consider. The columns are F-score, precision, recall, exact sentence match, and speed (sents/sec). Coverage was left out as it was above 99.8% for all parsers. In the ENHANCED TRAINING / SYSTEMS section we include the Charniak parser with reranking (R), with a self-trained model (S), and both (SR).

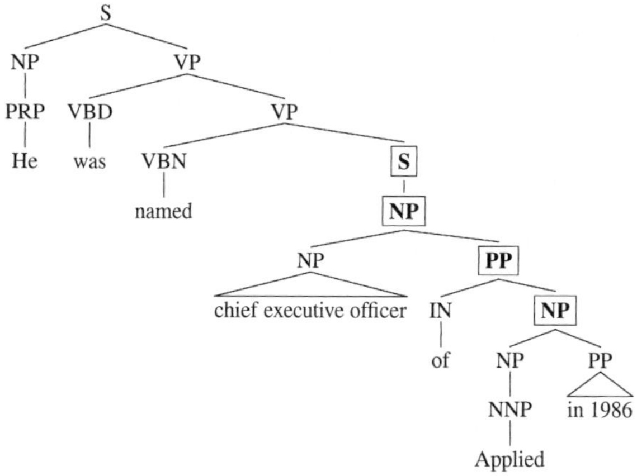

(a) Parser output

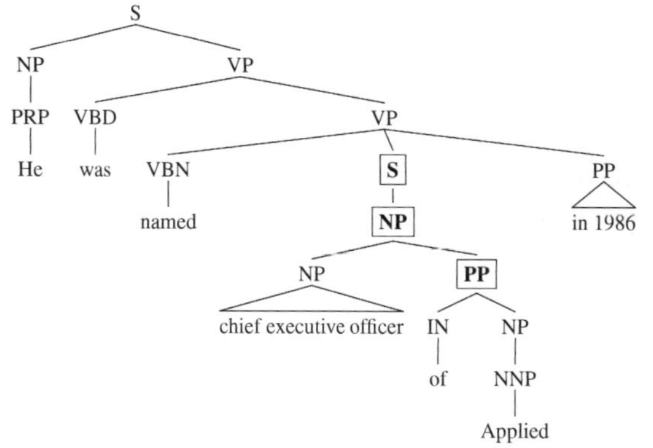

(b) Gold tree

Figure 1: Grouping errors by node type is of limited usefulness. In this figure and those that follow the top tree is the incorrect parse and the bottom tree is the correct parse. Bold, boxed nodes are either extra (marked in the incorrect tree) or missing (marked in the correct tree). This is an example of **PP Attachment** (*in 1986* is too low), but that is not at all clear from the set of incorrect nodes (extra S, NP, PP, and NP, missing S, NP, and PP).

Table 1 shows the standard performance metrics, measured on section 23 of the WSJ, using all sentences. Speeds were measured using a Quad-Core Xeon CPU (2.33GHz 4MB L2 cache) with 16GB of RAM. These results clearly show the variation in parsing performance, but they do not show which constructions are the source of those variations.

4 Error Classification

While the statistics in Table 1 give a sense of overall parser performance they do not provide linguistically meaningful intuition for the source of remaining errors. Breaking down the remaining errors by node type is not particularly informative, as a single attachment error can cause multiple node errors, many of which are for unrelated node types. For example, in Figure 1 there is a PP attachment error that causes seven bracket errors (extra S, NP, PP, and NP, missing S, NP, and PP). Determining that these correspond to a PP attachment error from just the labels of the missing and extra nodes is difficult. In contrast, the approach we describe below takes into consideration the relations between errors, grouping them into linguistically meaningful sets.

We classify node errors in two phases. First, we find a set of tree transformations that convert the output tree into the gold tree. Second, the transformation are classified into error types such as PP attachment and coordination. Pseudocode for our method is shown in Algorithm 1. The tree transformation stage corresponds to the main loop, while the second stage corresponds to the final loop.

4.1 Tree Transformation

The core of our transformation process is a set of operations that move subtrees, create nodes, and delete nodes. Searching for the shortest path to transform one tree into another is prohibitively slow.[2] We find

[2]We implemented various search procedures and found similar results on the sentences that could be processed in a reason-

Algorithm 1 Tree transformation error classification

```
U = initial set of node errors
Sort U by the depth of the error in the tree, deepest first
G = ∅
repeat
    for all errors e ∈ U do
        if e fits an environment template t then
            g = new error group
            Correct e as specified by t
            for all errors f that t corrects do
                Remove f from U
                Insert f into g
            end for
            Add g to G
        end if
    end for
until unable to correct any further errors
for all remaining errors e ∈ U do
    Insert a group into G containing e
end for
for all groups g ∈ G do
    Classify g based on properties of the group
end for
```

a path by applying a greedy bottom–up approach, iterating through the errors in order of tree depth.

We match each error with a template based on nearby tree structure and errors. For example, in Figure 1 there are four extra nodes that all cover spans ending at *Applied in 1986*: S, NP, PP, NP. There are also three missing nodes with spans ending between *Applied* and *in*: PP, NP, and S. Figure 2 depicts these errors as spans, showing that this case fits three criteria: (1) there are a set of extra spans all ending at the same point, (2) there are a set of missing spans all ending at the same point, and (3) the extra spans cross the missing spans, extending beyond their end-point. This indicates that the node starting after *Applied* is attaching too low and should be moved up, outside all of the extra nodes. Together, the criteria and transformation form a template.

Once a suitable template is identified we correct the error by moving subtrees, adding nodes and removing nodes. In the example this is done by moving the node spanning *in 1986* up in the tree until it is outside of all the extra spans. Since moving the PP leaves a unary production from an NP to an NP, we also collapse that level. In total this corrects seven

able amount of time.

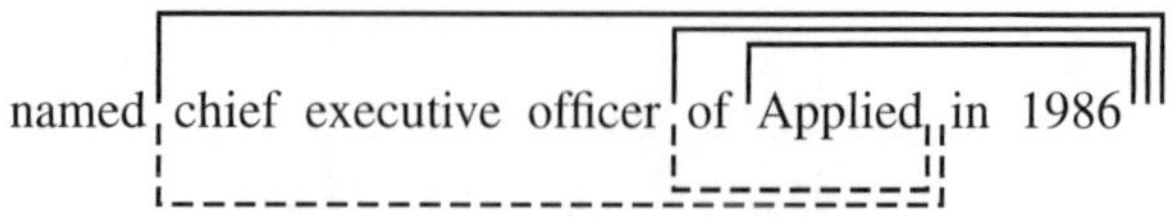

Figure 2: Templates are defined in terms of extra and missing spans, shown here with unbroken lines above and dashed lines below, respectively. This is an example of a set of extra spans that cross a set of missing spans (which in both cases all end at the same position). If the last two words are moved, two of the extra spans will match the two missing spans. The other extra span is deleted during the move as it creates an NP→NP unary production.

errors, as there are three cases in which an extra node is present that matches a missing node once the PP is moved. All of these errors are placed in a single group and information about the nearby tree structure before and after the transformation is recorded.

We continue to make passes through the list until no errors are corrected on a pass. For each remaining node error an individual error group is created.

The templates were constructed by hand based on manual analysis of parser output. They cover a range of combinations of extra and missing spans, with further variation for whether crossing is occurring and if so whether the crossing bracket starts or ends in the middle of the correct bracket. Errors that do not match any of our templates are left uncorrected.

4.2 Transformation Classification

We began with a large set of node errors, in the first stage they were placed into groups, one group per tree transformation used to get from the test tree to the gold tree. Next we classify each group as one of the error types below.

PP Attachment Any case in which the transformation involved moving a Prepositional Phrase, or the incorrect bracket is over a PP, e.g.
He was (VP *named chief executive officer of* (NP *Applied* (PP *in 1986*)))
where (PP *in 1986*) should modify the entire VP, rather than just *Applied*.

NP Attachment Several cases in which NPs had to be moved, particularly for mistakes in appositive constructions and incorrect attachments within a verb phrase, e.g.
The bonds (VP *go* (PP *on sale* (NP *Oct. 19*)))
where *Oct. 19* should be an argument of *go*.

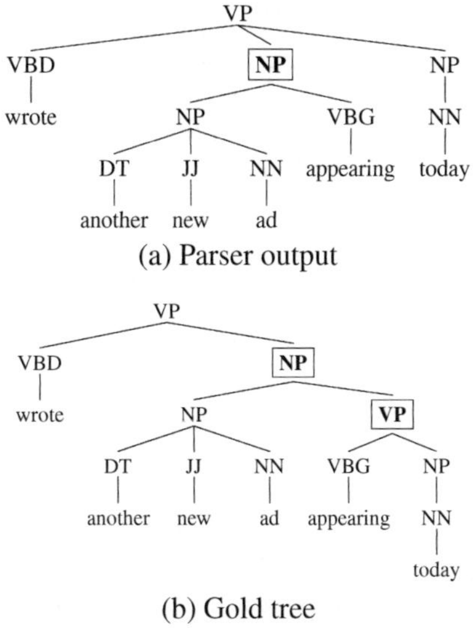

(a) Parser output

(b) Gold tree

Figure 3: **NP Attachment**: *today* is too high, it should be the argument of *appearing*, rather than *wrote*. This causes three node errors (extra NP, missing NP and VP).

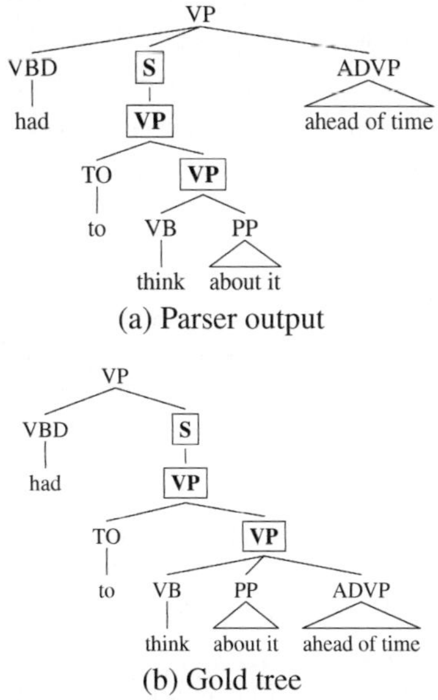

(a) Parser output

(b) Gold tree

Figure 4: **Modifier Attachment**: *ahead of time* is too high, it should modify *think*, not *had*. This causes six node errors (extra S, VP, and VP, missing S, VP, and VP).

Modifier Attachment Cases involving incorrectly placed adjectives and adverbs, including errors corrected by subtree movement and errors requiring only creation of a node, e.g. (NP (ADVP *even more*) *severe setbacks*) where there should be an extra ADVP node over *even more severe*.

Clause Attachment Any group that involves movement of some form of S node.

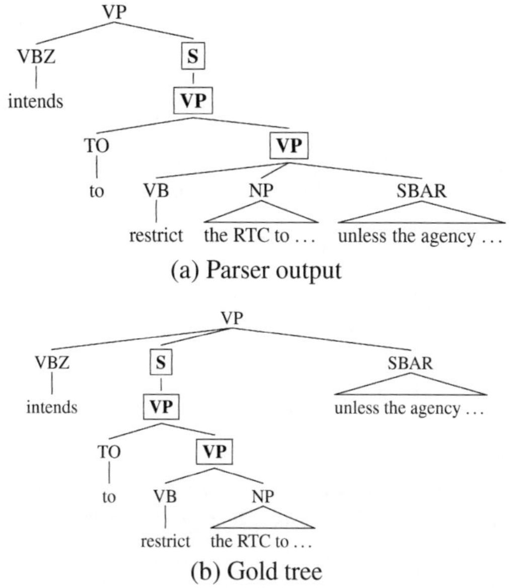

(a) Parser output

(b) Gold tree

Figure 5: **Clause Attachment**: *unless the agency receives specific congressional authorization* is attaching too low. This causes six node errors (extra S, VP, and VP, missing S, VP and VP).

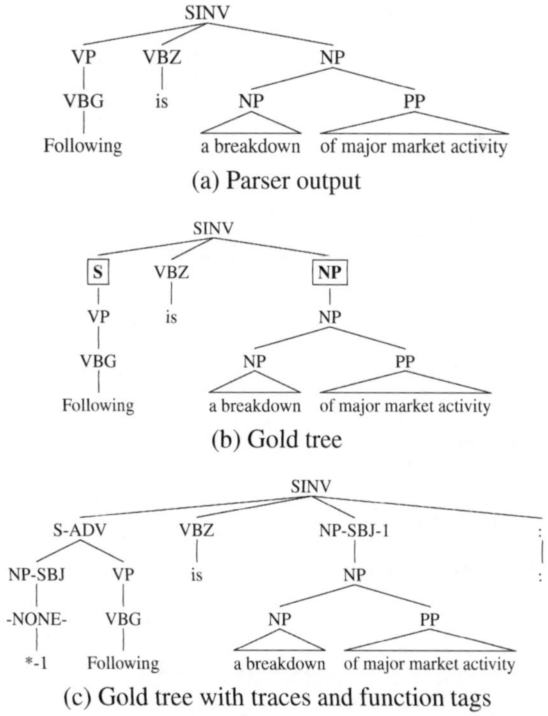

(a) Parser output

(b) Gold tree

(c) Gold tree with traces and function tags

Figure 6: Two **Unary** errors, a missing S and a missing NP. The third tree is the PTB tree before traces and function tags are removed. Note that the missing NP is over another NP, a production that does occur widely in the treebank, particularly over the word *it*.

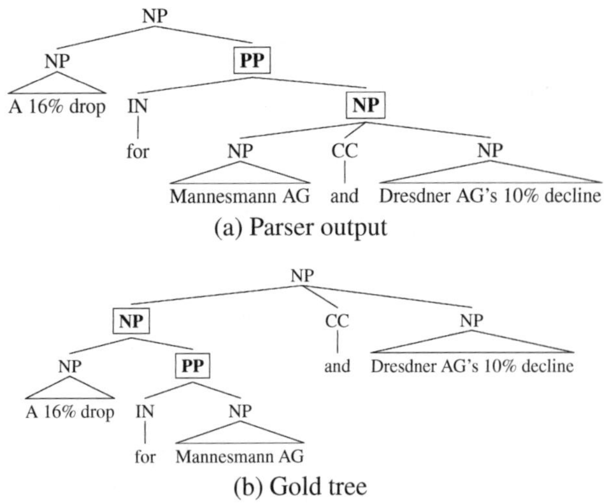

Figure 7: **Coordination**: *and Dresdner AG's 10% decline* is too low. This causes four node errors (extra PP and NP, missing NP and PP).

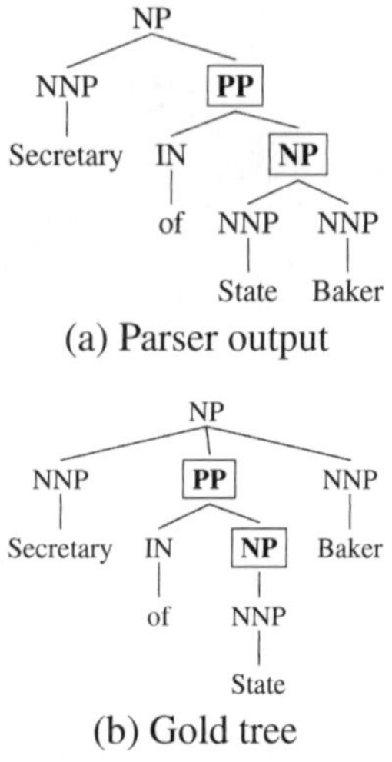

Figure 8: **NP Internal Structure**: *Baker* is too low, causing four errors (extra PP and NP, missing PP and NP).

Unary Mistakes involving unary productions that are not linked to a nearby error such as a matching extra or missing node. We do not include a breakdown by unary type, though we did find that clause labeling (S, SINV, etc) accounted for a large proportion of the errors.

Coordination Cases in which a conjunction is an immediate sibling of the nodes being moved, or is the leftmost or rightmost node being moved.

NP Internal Structure While most NP structure is not annotated in the PTB, there is some use of ADJP, NX, NAC and QP nodes. We form a single group for each NP that has one or more errors involving these types of nodes.

Different label In many cases a node is present in the tree that spans the correct set of words, but has the wrong label, in which case we group the two node errors, (one extra, one missing), as a single error.

Single word phrase A range of node errors that span a single word, with checks to ensure this is not linked to another error (e.g. one part of a set of internal noun phrase errors).

Other There is a long tail of other errors. Some could be placed within the categories above, but would require far more specific rules.

For many of these error types it would be difficult to extract a meaningful understanding from only the list of node errors involved. Even for error types that can be measured by counting node errors or rule production errors, our approach has the advantage that we identify groups of errors with a single cause. For example, a missing unary production may correspond to an extra bracket that contains a subtree that attached incorrectly.

4.3 Methodology

We used sections 00 and 24 as development data while constructing the tree transformation and error group classification methods. All of our examples in text come from these sections as well, but for all tables of results we ran our system on section 23. We chose to run our analysis on section 23 as it is the only section we are sure was not used in the development of any of the parsers, either for tuning or feature development. Our evaluation is entirely focused on the errors of the parsers, so unless there is a particular construction that is unusually prevalent in section 23, we are not revealing any information about the test set that could bias future work.

5 Results

Our system enables us to answer questions about parser behaviour that could previously only be probed indirectly. We demonstrate its usefulness by applying it to a range of parsers (here), to reranked K-best lists of various lengths, and to output for out-of-domain parsing (following sections).

In Table 2 we consider the breakdown of parser

Parser	F-score	PP Attach	Clause Attach	Diff Label	Mod Attach	NP Attach	Co-ord	1-Word Span	Unary	NP Int.	Other
Best		0.60	0.38	0.31	0.25	0.25	0.23	0.20	0.14	0.14	0.50
Charniak-RS	92.07										
Charniak-R	91.41										
Charniak-S	91.02										
Berkeley	90.06										
Charniak	89.71										
SSN	89.42										
BUBS	88.63										
Bikel	88.16										
Collins-3	87.66										
Collins-2	87.62										
Collins-1	87.09										
Stanford-F	86.42										
Stanford-U	85.78										
Worst		1.12	0.61	0.51	0.39	0.45	0.40	0.42	0.27	0.27	1.13

Table 2: Average number of bracket errors per sentence due to the top ten error types. For instance, Stanford-U produces output that has, on average, 1.12 bracket errors per sentence that are due to PP attachment. The scale for each column is indicated by the Best and Worst values.

Error Type	Occurrences	Nodes Involved	Ratio
PP Attachment	846	1455	1.7
Single word phrase	490	490	1.0
Clause Attachment	385	913	2.4
Modifier Attachment	383	599	1.6
Different Label	377	754	2.0
Unary	347	349	1.0
NP Attachment	321	597	1.9
NP Internal Structure	299	352	1.2
Coordination	209	557	2.7
Unary Clause Label	185	200	1.1
VP Attachment	64	159	2.5
Parenthetical Attachment	31	74	2.4
Missing Parenthetical	12	17	1.4
Unclassified	655	734	1.1

Table 3: Breakdown of errors on section 23 for the Charniak parser with self-trained model and reranker. Errors are sorted by the number of times they occur. Ratio is the average number of node errors caused by each error we identify (i.e. Nodes Involved / Occurrences).

errors on WSJ section 23. The shaded area of each bar indicates the frequency of parse errors (i.e. empty means fewest errors). The area filled in is determined by the expected number of node errors per sentence that are attributed to that type of error. The average number of node errors per sentence for a completely full bar is indicated by the Worst row, and the value for a completely empty bar is indicated by the Best row. Exact error counts are available at http://code.google.com/p/berkeley-parser-analyser/.

We use counts of node errors to make the contributions of each type of error more interpretable. As Table 3 shows, some errors typically cause only a single node error, where as others, such as coordination, generally cause several. This means that considering counts of error groups would over-emphasise some error types, e.g. single word phrase errors are second most important by number of groups (in Table 3), but seventh by total number of node errors (in Table 2).

As expected, PP attachment is the largest contributor to errors, across all parsers. Interestingly, coordination is sixth on the list, though that is partly due to the fact that there are fewer coordination decisions to be made in the treebank.[3]

By looking at the performance of the Collins parser we can see the development over the past fifteen years. There has been improvement across the board, but in some cases, e.g. clause attachment errors and different label errors, the change has been more limited (24% and 29% reductions respectively). We investigated the breakdown of the different label errors by label, but no particular cases of la-

[3]This is indicated by the frequency of CCs and PPs in sections 02–21 of the treebank, 16,844 and 95,581 respectively. These counts are only an indicator of the number of decisions as the nodes can be used in ways that do not involve a decision, such as sentences that start with a conjunction.

System	K	F-score	PP Attach	Clause Attach	Diff Label	Mod Attach	NP Attach	Co-ord	1-Word Span	Unary	NP Int.	Other
Best			0.08	0.04	0.08	0.05	0.06	0.04	0.08	0.04	0.04	0.11
	1000	98.30										
	100	97.54										
	50	97.18										
Oracle	20	96.40										
	10	95.66										
	5	94.61										
	2	92.59										
	1000	92.07										
	100	92.08										
	50	92.07										
Charniak	20	92.05										
	10	92.16										
	5	91.94										
	2	91.56										
	1	91.02										
Worst			0.66	0.43	0.33	0.26	0.28	0.26	0.23	0.16	0.19	0.60

Table 4: Average number of bracket errors per sentence for a range of K-best list lengths using the Charniak parser with reranking and the self-trained model. The oracle results are determined by taking the parse in each K-best list with the highest F-score.

bel confusion stand out, and we found that the most common cases remained the same between Collins and the top results.

It is also interesting to compare pairs of parsers that share aspects of their architecture. One such pair is the Stanford parser, where the factored parser combines the unlexicalised parser with a lexicalised dependency parser. The main sources of the 0.64 gain in F-score are PP attachment and coordination.

Another interesting pair is the Berkeley parser and the BUBS parser, which uses a Berkeley grammar, but improves speed by pruning. The pruning methods used in BUBS are particularly damaging for PP attachment errors and unary errors.

Various comparisons can be made between Charniak parser variants. We discuss the reranker below. For the self-trained model McClosky et al. (2006) performed some error analysis, considering variations in F-score depending on the frequency of tags such as PP, IN and CC in sentences. Here we see gains on all error types, though particularly for clause attachment, modifier attachment and coordination, which fits with their observations.

5.1 Reranking

The standard dynamic programming approach to parsing limits the range of features that can be employed. One way to deal with this issue is to modify the parser to produce the top K parses, rather than just the 1-best, then use a model with more sophisticated features to choose the best parse from this list (Collins, 2000). While re-ranking has led to gains in performance (Charniak and Johnson, 2005), there has been limited analysis of how effectively rerankers are using the set of available options. Recent work has explored this question in more depth, but focusing on how variation in the parameters impacts performance on standard metrics (Huang, 2008; Ng et al., 2010; Auli and Lopez, 2011; Ng and Curran, 2012).

In Table 4 we present a breakdown over error types for the Charniak parser, using the self-trained model and reranker. The oracle results use the parse in each K-best list with the highest F-score. While this may not give the true oracle result, as F-score does not factor over sentences, it gives a close approximation. The table has the same columns as Table 2, but the ranges on the bars now reflect the min and max for these sets.

While there is improvement on all errors when using the reranker, there is very little additional gain beyond the first 5-10 parses. Even for the oracle results, most of the improvement occurs within the first 5-10 parses. The limited utility of extra parses

Corpus	F-score	PP Attach	Clause Attach	Diff Label	Mod Attach	NP Attach	Co-ord	1-Word Span	Unary	NP Int.	Other
Best		0.022	0.016	0.013	0.011	0.011	0.010	0.009	0.006	0.005	0.021
WSJ 23	92.07										
Brown-F	85.91										
Brown-G	84.56										
Brown-K	84.09										
Brown-L	83.95										
Brown-M	84.65										
Brown-N	85.20										
Brown-P	84.09										
Brown-R	83.60										
G-Web Blogs	84.15										
G-Web Email	81.18										
Worst		0.040	0.035	0.053	0.020	0.034	0.023	0.046	0.009	0.029	0.073

Table 5: Average number of node errors per word for a range of domains using the Charniak parser with reranking and the self-trained model. We use per word error rates here rather than per sentence as there is great variation in average sentence length across the domains, skewing the per sentence results.

for the reranker may be due to the importance of the base parser output probability feature (which, by definition, decreases within the K-best list).

Interestingly, the oracle performance improves across all error types, even at the 2-best level. This indicates that the base parser model is not particularly biased against a single error. Focusing on the rows for $K = 2$ we can also see two interesting outliers. The PP attachment improvement of the oracle is considerably higher than that of the reranker, particularly compared to the differences for other errors, suggesting that the reranker lacks the features necessary to make the decision better than the parser. The other interesting outlier is NP internal structure, which continues to make improvements for longer lists, unlike the other error types.

5.2 Out-of-Domain

Parsing performance drops considerably when shifting outside of the domain a parser was trained on (Gildea, 2001). Clegg and Shepherd (2005) evaluated parsers qualitatively on node types and rule productions. Bender et al. (2011) designed a Wikipedia test set to evaluate parsers on dependencies representing ten specific linguistic phenomena.

To provide a deeper understanding of the errors arising when parsing outside of the newswire domain, we analyse performance of the Charniak parser with reranker and self-trained model on the eight parts of the Brown corpus (Marcus et al., 1993), and two parts of the Google Web corpus (Petrov and McDonald, 2012). Table 6 shows statistics for the corpora. The variation in average sentence lengths skew the results for errors per sentence. To handle this we divide by the number of words to determine the results in Table 5, rather than by the number of sentences, as in previous figures.

Corpus	Description	Sentences	Av. Length
WSJ 23	Newswire	2416	23.5
Brown F	Popular	3164	23.4
Brown G	Biographies	3279	25.5
Brown K	General	3881	17.2
Brown L	Mystery	3714	15.7
Brown M	Science	881	16.6
Brown N	Adventure	4415	16.0
Brown P	Romance	3942	17.4
Brown R	Humour	967	22.7
G-Web Blogs	Blogs	1016	23.6
G-Web Email	E-mail	2450	11.9

Table 6: Variation in size and contents of the domains we consider. The variation in average sentence lengths skews the results for errors per sentences, and so in Table 5 we consider errors per word.

There are several interesting features in the table. First, on the Brown datasets, while the general trend is towards worse performance on all errors, NP internal structure is a notable exception and in some cases PP attachment and unaries are as well.

In the other errors we see similar patterns across the corpora, except humour (Brown R), on which the parser is particularly bad at coordination and clause attachment. This makes sense, as the colloquial nature of the text includes more unusual uses of conjunctions, for example:

She was a living doll and no mistake – the ...

Comparing the Brown corpora and the Google Web corpora, there are much larger divergences. We see a particularly large decrease in NP internal structure. Looking at some of the instances of this error, it appears to be largely caused by incorrect handling of structures such as URLs and phone numbers, which do not appear in the PTB. There are also some more difficult cases, for example:

... going up for sale in the next month or do .

where *or do* is a QP. This typographical error is extremely difficult to handle for a parser trained only on well-formed text.

For e-mail there is a substantial drop on single word phrases. Breaking the errors down by label we found that the majority of the new errors are missing or extra NPs over single words. Here the main problem appears to be temporal expressions, though there also appear to be a substantial number of errors that are also at the POS level, such as when NNP is assigned to *ta* in this case:

... let you know that I 'm out ta here !

Some of these issues, such as URL handling, could be resolved with suitable training data. Other issues, such as ungrammatical language and unconventional use of words, pose a greater challenge.

6 Conclusion

The single F-score objective over brackets or dependencies obscures important differences between statistical parsers. For instance, a single attachment error can lead to one or many mismatched brackets.

We have created a novel tree-transformation methodology for evaluating parsers that categorises errors into linguistically meaningful types. Using this approach, we presented the first detailed examination of the errors produced by a wide range of constituency parsers for English. We found that PP attachment and clause attachment are the most challenging constructions, while coordination turns out to be less problematic than previously thought. We also noted interesting variations in error types for parsers variants.

We investigated the errors resolved in reranking, and introduced by changing domains. We found that the Charniak rerankers improved most error types, but made little headway on improving PP attachment. Changing domain has an impact on all error types, except NP internal structure.

We have released our system so that future constituent parsers can be evaluated using our methodology. Our analysis provides new insight into the development of parsers over the past fifteen years, and the challenges that remain.

Acknowledgments

We would like to thank the anonymous reviewers for their helpful suggestions. This research was partially supported by a General Sir John Monash Fellowship to the first author, the Office of Naval Research under MURI Grant No. N000140911081, an NSF Fellowship to the second author, ARC Discovery grant DP1097291, the Capital Markets CRC, and the NSF under grant 0643742.

References

S. Abney, S. Flickenger, C. Gdaniec, C. Grishman, P. Harrison, D. Hindle, R. Ingria, F. Jelinek, J. Klavans, M. Liberman, M. Marcus, S. Roukos, B. Santorini, and T. Strzalkowski. 1991. Procedure for quantitatively comparing the syntactic coverage of english grammars. In *Proceedings of the workshop on Speech and Natural Language*, pages 306–311, Pacific Grove, California, USA, February.

Michael Auli and Adam Lopez. 2011. A comparison of loopy belief propagation and dual decomposition for integrated ccg supertagging and parsing. In *Proceedings of ACL*, pages 470–480, Portland, Oregon, USA, June.

Emily M. Bender, Dan Flickinger, Stephan Oepen, and Yi Zhang. 2011. Parser evaluation over local and non-local deep dependencies in a large corpus. In *Proceedings of EMNLP*, pages 397–408, Edinburgh, United Kingdom, July.

Daniel M. Bikel. 2004. Intricacies of collins' parsing model. *Computational Linguistics*, 30(4):479–511.

Nathan Bodenstab, Aaron Dunlop, Keith Hall, and Brian Roark. 2011. Beam-width prediction for efficient context-free parsing. In *Proceedings of ACL*, pages 440–449, Portland, Oregon, USA, June.

Ted Briscoe and John Carroll. 2006. Evaluating the accuracy of an unlexicalized statistical parser on the PARC DepBank. In *Proceedings of ACL*, pages 41–48, Sydney, Australia, July.

Ted Briscoe, John Carroll, Jonathan Graham, and Ann Copestake, 2002. *Relational Evaluation Schemes*, pages 4–8. Las Palmas, Canary Islands, Spain, May.

John Carroll, Ted Briscoe, and Antonio Sanfilippo. 1998. Parser evaluation: a survey and a new proposal. In *Proceedings of LREC*, pages 447–454, Granada, Spain, May.

Daniel Cer, Marie-Catherine de Marneffe, Daniel Jurafsky, and Christopher D. Manning. 2010. Parsing to stanford dependencies: Trade-offs between speed and accuracy. In *Proceedings of LREC*, Valletta, Malta, May.

Eugene Charniak and Mark Johnson. 2005. Coarse-to-fine n-best parsing and maxent discriminative reranking. In *Proceedings of ACL*, pages 173–180, Ann Arbor, Michigan, USA, June.

Eugene Charniak. 2000. A maximum-entropy-inspired parser. In *Proceedings of NAACL*, pages 132–139, Seattle, Washington, USA, April.

Stephen Clark and Julia Hockenmaier. 2002. Evaluating a wide-coverage ccg parser. In *Proceedings of the LREC Beyond Parseval Workshop*, Las Palmas, Canary Islands, Spain, May.

Andrew B. Clegg and Adrian J. Shepherd. 2005. Evaluating and integrating treebank parsers on a biomedical corpus. In *Proceedings of the ACL Workshop on Software*, pages 14–33, Ann Arbor, Michigan, USA, June.

Michael Collins. 1997. Three generative, lexicalised models for statistical parsing. In *Proceedings of ACL*, pages 16–23, Madrid, Spain, July.

Michael Collins. 2000. Discriminative reranking for natural language parsing. In *Proceedings of ICML*, pages 175–182, Palo Alto, California, USA, June.

Michael Collins. 2003. Head-driven statistical models for natural language parsing. *Computational Linguistics*, 29(4):589–637.

Rebecca Dridan and Stephan Oepen. 2011. Parser evaluation using elementary dependency matching. In *Proceedings of IWPT*, pages 225–230, Dublin, Ireland, October.

Aaron Dunlop, Nathan Bodenstab, and Brian Roark. 2011. Efficient matrix-encoded grammars and low latency parallelization strategies for cyk. In *Proceedings of IWPT*, pages 163–174, Dublin, Ireland, October.

Jennifer Foster and Josef van Genabith. 2008. Parser evaluation and the bnc: Evaluating 4 constituency parsers with 3 metrics. In *Proceedings of LREC*, Marrakech, Morocco, May.

Daniel Gildea. 2001. Corpus variation and parser performance. In *Proceedings of EMNLP*, pages 167–202, Pittsburgh, Pennsylvania, USA, June.

Tadayoshi Hara, Yusuke Miyao, and Jun'ichi Tsujii. 2007. Evaluating impact of re-training a lexical disambiguation model on domain adaptation of an hpsg parser. In *Proceedings of IWPT*, pages 11–22, Prague, Czech Republic, June.

Tadayoshi Hara, Yusuke Miyao, and Jun'ichi Tsujii. 2009. Descriptive and empirical approaches to capturing underlying dependencies among parsing errors. In *Proceedings of EMNLP*, pages 1162–1171, Singapore, August.

James Henderson. 2003. Inducing history representations for broad coverage statistical parsing. In *Proceedings of NAACL*, pages 24–31, Edmonton, Canada, May.

James Henderson. 2004. Discriminative training of a neural network statistical parser. In *Proceedings of ACL*, pages 95–102, Barcelona, Spain, July.

Liang Huang. 2008. Forest reranking: Discriminative parsing with non-local features. In *Proceedings of ACL*, pages 586–594, Columbus, Ohio, USA, June.

Tracy H. King, Richard Crouch, Stefan Riezler, Mary Dalrymple, and Ronald M. Kaplan. 2003. The PARC 700 dependency bank. In *Proceedings of the 4th International Workshop on Linguistically Interpreted Corpora at EACL*, Budapest, Hungary, April.

Dan Klein and Christopher D. Manning. 2003a. Accurate unlexicalized parsing. In *Proceedings of ACL*, pages 423–430, Sapporo, Japan, July.

Dan Klein and Christopher D. Manning. 2003b. Fast exact inference with a factored model for natural language parsing. In *Proceedings of NIPS*, pages 3–10, Vancouver, British Columbia, Canada, December.

Dekang Lin. 1998. A dependency-based method for evaluating broad-coverage parsers. *Natural Language Engineering*, 4(2):97–114.

Mitchell P. Marcus, Mary Ann Marcinkiewicz, and Beatrice Santorini. 1993. Building a large annotated corpus of english: the penn treebank. *Computational Linguistics*, 19(2):313–330.

David McClosky, Eugene Charniak, and Mark Johnson. 2006. Effective self-training for parsing. In *Proceedings of NAACL*, pages 152–159, New York, New York, USA, June.

Ryan McDonald and Joakim Nivre. 2007. Characterizing the errors of data-driven dependency parsing models. In *Proceedings of EMNLP*, pages 122–131, Prague, Czech Republic, June.

Yusuke Miyao, Rune Sætre, Kenji Sagae, Takuya Matsuzaki, and Jun'ichi Tsujii. 2008. Task-oriented evaluation of syntactic parsers and their representations. In

Proceedings of ACL, pages 46–54, Columbus, Ohio, USA, June.

Dominick Ng and James R. Curran. 2012. N-best CCG parsing and reranking. In *Proceedings of ACL*, Jeju, South Korea, July.

Dominick Ng, Matthew Honnibal, and James R. Curran. 2010. Reranking a wide-coverage ccg parser. In *Proceedings of ALTA*, pages 90–98, Melbourne, Australia, December.

Joakim Nivre, Laura Rimell, Ryan McDonald, and Carlos Gómez-Rodríguez. 2010. Evaluation of dependency parsers on unbounded dependencies. In *Proceedings of Coling*, pages 833–841, Beijing, China, August.

Slav Petrov and Dan Klein. 2007. Improved inference for unlexicalized parsing. In *Proceedings of NAACL*, pages 404–411, Rochester, New York, USA, April.

Slav Petrov and Ryan McDonald. 2012. SANCL Shared Task. LDC2012E43. Linguistic Data Consortium. Philadelphia, Philadelphia, USA.

Slav Petrov, Leon Barrett, Romain Thibaux, and Dan Klein. 2006. Learning accurate, compact, and interpretable tree annotation. In *Proceedings of ACL*, pages 433–440, Sydney, Australia, July.

Chris Quirk and Simon Corston-Oliver. 2006. The impact of parse quality on syntactically-informed statistical machine translation. In *Proceedings of EMNLP*, pages 62–69, Sydney, Australia, July.

Kun Yu, Yusuke Miyao, Takuya Matsuzaki, Xiangli Wang, and Junichi Tsujii. 2011. Analysis of the difficulties in chinese deep parsing. In *Proceedings of IWPT*, pages 48–57, Dublin, Ireland, October.

Deniz Yuret, Aydin Han, and Zehra Turgut. 2010. Semeval-2010 task 12: Parser evaluation using textual entailments. In *Proceedings of the 5th International Workshop on Semantic Evaluation*, pages 51–56, Uppsala, Sweden, July.

Extending Machine Translation Evaluation Metrics with Lexical Cohesion To Document Level

Billy T. M. Wong and **Chunyu Kit**
Department of Chinese, Translation and Linguistics
City University of Hong Kong
83 Tat Chee Avenue, Kowloon, Hong Kong SAR, P. R. China
{tmwong,ctckit}@cityu.edu.hk

Abstract

This paper proposes the utilization of lexical cohesion to facilitate evaluation of machine translation at the document level. As a linguistic means to achieve text coherence, lexical cohesion ties sentences together into a meaningfully interwoven structure through words with the same or related meaning. A comparison between machine and human translation is conducted to illustrate one of their critical distinctions that human translators tend to use more cohesion devices than machine. Various ways to apply this feature to evaluate machine-translated documents are presented, including one without reliance on reference translation. Experimental results show that incorporating this feature into sentence-level evaluation metrics can enhance their correlation with human judgements.

1 Introduction

Machine translation (MT) has benefited a lot from the advancement of automatic evaluation in the past decade. To a certain degree, its progress is also confined to the limitations of evaluation metrics in use. Most efforts devoted to evaluate the quality of MT output so far have still focused on the sentence level without sufficient attention to how a larger text is structured. This is notably reflected in the representative MT evaluation metrics, such as BLEU (Papineni et al., 2002), METEOR (Banerjee and Lavie, 2005) and TER (Snover et al., 2006), that adopt a sentence-by-sentence fashion to score MT outputs. The evaluation result for a document by any of them is usually a simple average of its sentence scores. A drawback of this kind of sentence-based evaluation is the neglect of document structure. There is no guarantee for the coherence of a text if it is produced by simply putting together stand-alone sentences, no matter how well-translated, without adequate inter-sentential connection. As a consequence, MT system optimized this way to any of these metrics can only have a very dim chance of producing translated document that reads as natural as human writing.

The accuracy of MT output at the document level is particularly important to MT users, for they care about the overall meaning of a text in question more than the grammatical correctness of each sentence (Visser and Fuji, 1996). Post-editors particularly need to ensure the quality of a whole document of MT output when revising its sentences. The connectivity of sentences is surely a significant factor contributing to the understandability of a text as a whole.

This paper studies the inter-sentential linguistic features of cohesion and coherence and presents plausible ways to incorporate them into the sentence-based metrics to support MT evaluation at the document level. In the Framework for MT Evaluation in the International Standards of Language Engineering (FEMTI) (King et al., 2003), coherence is defined as "the degree to which the reader can describe the role of each individual sentence (or group of sentences) with respect to the text as a whole". The measurement of coherence has to rely on cohesion, referring to the "relations of meaning that exist within the text" (Halliday and Hasan, 1976). Cohesion is realized via the interlinkage of grammatical and lexical elements across sentences. *Grammatical* cohesion refers to the syntactic links between text items, while *lexical* cohesion is achieved through the word choices in a text. This paper focuses on the latter. A quantitative comparison of lexical cohesion devices between MT output and human translation is first conducted, to examine the weakness of current MT systems in handling this feature. Different ways of exploiting lexical cohesion devices for MT evaluation at the document level are then illustrated.

2 Related Works

Cohesion and coherence are both necessary monolingual features in a target text. They can hardly be evaluated in isolation and have to be conjoined with other quality criteria such as adequacy and fluency. A survey of MT post-editing (Vasconcellos, 1989) suggests that cohesion and coherence serve as higher level quality criteria beyond many others such as syntactic well-formedness. Post-editors tend to correct syntactic errors first before any amendment for improving the cohesion and coherence of an MT output. Also, as Wilks (1978)[1] noted, it is rather unlikely for a sufficiently large sample of translations to be coherent and totally wrong at the same time. Cohesion and coherence are appropriate to serve as criteria for the overall quality of MT output.

Previous researches in MT predominantly focus on specific types of cohesion devices. For grammatical cohesion, a series of works, including Nakaiwa and Ikehara (1992), Nakaiwa et al. (1995), and Nakaiwa and Shirai (1996), present approaches to resolving Japanese zero pronouns and to integrating them into a Japanese-English transferred-based MT system. Peral et al. (1999) propose an interlingual mechanism for pronominal anaphora generation by exploiting a rich set of lexical, syntactic, morphologic and semantic information. Murata and Nagao (1993) and Murata et al. (2001) develop a rule base to identify the referential properties of Japanese noun phrases, so as to facilitate anaphora resolution for Japanese and article generation for English during translation. A recent COMTIS project (Cartoni et al., 2011) begins to exploit inter-sentential information for statistical MT. A phase of its work is to have grammatical devices, such as verbal tense/aspect/mode, discourse connectives and pronouns, manually annotated in multilingual corpora, in hopes of laying a foundation for the development of automatic labelers for them that can be integrated into an MT model.

For lexical cohesion, it has been only partially and indirectly addressed in terms of translation consistency in MT output. Different approaches to maintaining consistency in target word choices are proposed (Itagaki et al., 2007; Gong et al., 2011; Xiao et al., 2011). Carpuat (2009) also observes a general tendency in human translation that a given sense is usually lexicalized in a consistent manner throughout the whole translation.

Nevertheless there are only a few evaluation methods explicitly targeting on the quality of a document. Miller and Vanni (2001) devise a human evaluation approach to measure the comprehensibility of a text as a whole, based on the Rhetorical Structure Theory (Mann and Thompson, 1988), a theory of text organization specifying coherence relations in an authentic text. Snover et al. (2006) proposes HTER to assess post-editing effort through human annotation. Its automatic versions TER and TERp (Snover et al., 2009), however, remain sentence-based metrics. Comelles et al. (2010) present a family of automatic MT evaluation measures, based on the Discourse Representation Theory (Kamp and Reyle, 1993), that generate semantic trees to put together different text entities for the same referent according to their contexts and grammatical connections. Apart from MT evaluation, automated essay scoring programs such as E-rater (Burstein, 2003) also employ a rich set of discourse features for assessment. However, the parsing process needed for these linguistic-heavy approaches may suffer seriously from grammatical errors, which are unavoidable in MT output. Hence their accuracy and reliability inevitably fluctuate in accord with different evaluation data.

Lexical cohesion has far been neglected in both MT and MT evaluation, even though it is the single most important form of cohesion devices, accounting for nearly half of the cohesion devices in English (Halliday and Hasan, 1976). It is also a significant feature contributing to translation equivalence of texts by preserving their texture (Lotfipour-Saedi, 1997). The lexical cohesion devices in a text can be

[1] As cited in van Slype (1979).

represented as lexical chains conjoining related entities. There are many methods of computing lexical chains for various purposes, e.g., Morris and Hirst (1991), Barzilay and Elhadad (1997), Chan (2004), Li et al. (2007), among many others. Contrary to grammatical cohesion highly depending on syntactic well-formedness of a text, lexical cohesion is less affected by grammatical errors. Its computation has to rely on a thesaurus, which is usually available for almost every language. In this research, a number of formulations of lexical cohesion, with or without reliance on external language resource, will be explored for the purpose of MT evaluation.

3 Lexical Cohesion in Machine and Human Translation

This section presents a comparative study of MT and human translation (HT) in terms of the use of lexical cohesion devices. It is an intuition that more cohesion devices are used by humans than machines in translation, as part of the superior quality of HT. Two different datasets are used to ensure the reliability and generality of the comparison. The results confirm the incapability of MT in handling this feature and the necessity of using lexical cohesion in MT evaluation.

3.1 Data

The MetricsMATR 2008 development set (Przybocki et al., 2009) and the Multiple-Translation Chinese (MTC) part 4 (Ma, 2006) are used for this study. They consist of MT outputs of different source languages in company with reference translations. The data of MetricsMATR is selected from the NIST Open MT 2006 evaluation, while MTC4 is from the TIDES 2003 MT evaluation. Both datasets include human assessments of MT output, from which the part of adequacy assessment is selected for this study. Table 1 provides overall statistics of the datasets.

	MetricsMATR	MTC4
Number of systems	8	6
Number of documents	25	100
Number of segments	249	919
Number of references	4	4
Source language	Arabic	Chinese
Genre	Newswire	Newswire

Table 1: Information about the datasets in use

3.2 Identification of Lexical Cohesion Devices

Lexical cohesion is achieved through word choices of two major types: reiteration and collocation. Reiteration can be realized in a continuum or a cline of specificity, with repetition of the same lexical item at one end and the use of a general noun to point to the same referent at the other. In between the two ends is to use a synonym (or near-synonym) and superordinate. Collocation refers to those lexical items that share the same or similar semantic relations, including complementarity, antonym, converse, coordinate term, meronym, troponym, and so on.

In this study, lexical cohesion devices are defined as content words (i.e., tokens after stopword having been removed) that reiterate once or more times in a document, including synonym, near-synonym and superordinate, besides those repetition and collocation. Repetition refers to the same words or stems in a document. Stems are identified with the aid of Porter stemmer (1980).

To classify the semantic relationships of words, WordNet (Fellbaum, 1998) is used as a lexical resource, which clusters words of the same sense (i.e., synonyms) into a semantic group, namely a synset. Synsets are interlinked in WordNet according to their semantic relationships. Superordinate and collocation are formed by words in a proximate semantic relationship, such as *bicycle* and *vehicle* (hypernym), *bicycle* and *wheel* (meronym), *bicycle* and *car* (coordinate term), and so on. They are defined as synset pairs with a distance of 1 in WordNet. The measure of semantic distance (Wu and Palmer, 1994) is also applied to identify near-synonyms, i.e., words that are synonyms in a broad sense but not grouped in the same synset. It quantifies the semantic similarity of word pairs as a real number in between 0 and 1 (the higher the more similar) as

$$sim(c_1, c_2) = \frac{2\,d(lcs(c_1, c_2))}{d(c_1) + d(c_2)}$$

where c_1 and c_2 are the concepts (synsets) that the two words in question belong to, d is the distance in terms of the shortest path from a concept to the

Word type	MetricsMATR			MTC4		
	MT	HT	Difference (%)	MT	HT	Difference (%)
Content word	4428	4636	208 (4.7)	16162	16982	830 (5.1)
- Not lexical cohesion device	2403	2381	-22 (-1.0)	8657	8814	157 (1.8)
- Lexical cohesion device	2025	2255	230 (11.4)	7505	8168	663 (8.9)
- Repetition	1297	1445	148 (11.4)	4888	5509	621 (12.7)
- Synonym and near-synonym	318	350	32 (10.1)	1323	1311	-12 (-0.9)
- Superordinate and collocation	410	460	50 (12.4)	1294	1348	54 (4.2)

Table 2: Statistics of lexical cohesion devices in machine versus human translation (average frequencies per version of MT/HT)

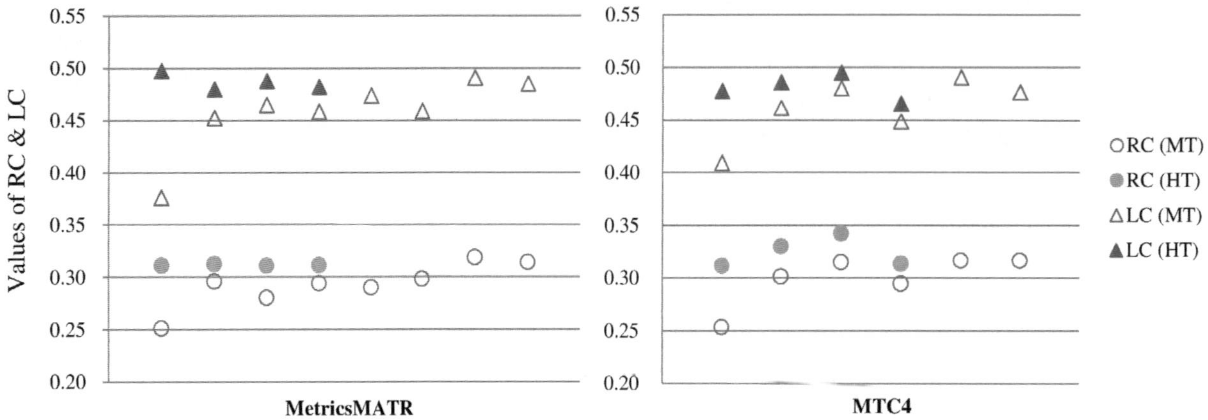

Figure 1: Use of lexical cohesion devices in machine versus human translation

global root node in WordNet, and lcs is the least common subsumer (i.e., the most specific ancestor concept) of c_1 and c_2. A threshold is set to 0.96 for words to be considered near-synonyms of each other, based on the empirical observation in a previous study (Wong, 2010).

3.3 Results

The difference between MT and HT (reference translation) in terms of the frequencies of lexical cohesion devices in MetricsMATR and MTC4 datasets is presented in Table 2. The frequencies are averaged by the number of MT/HT versions. A further categorization breaks down content words into lexical cohesion devices and those that are not. The count of each type of lexical cohesion device is also provided. In general the two datasets provide highly similar statistics. There are 4.7–5.1% more content words in HT than in MT. The numbers of ordinary content words (i.e., not lexical cohesion devices) are close in MT and HT. The difference of content words in HT and MT is mostly due to that of lexical cohesion devices, which are mostly repetition. 8.9–11.4% more lexical cohesion devices are found in HT than in MT in the datasets.

A further analysis is carried out to investigate into the use of lexical cohesion devices in each version of MT and HT in terms of the following two ratios,

LC = lexical cohesion devices / content words,

RC = repetition / content words.

A higher LC or RC ratio means that a greater proportion of content words are used as lexical cohesion devices.

Figure 1 illustrates the RC and LC ratios in the two datasets. The ratios of different MT systems are presented in an ascending order in each graph from left to right, according to their human assessment results. The distributions of these values show a strong similarity between the two datasets. First, most of the RC and LC ratios are within an observable range, i.e., 0.25–0.35 for the former and 0.40–0.50 for the latter, except a particularly low LC for

MT 1	
1	Chine scrambled research on 16 key *technical*
2	These techniques are from within headline everyones boosting science and *technology* and *achieving* goals and contend of delivered on time bound through *achieving* breakthroughs in essential *technology* and complimentarity resources . national
	BLEU: 0.224 (1-gram:7, 2-gram:0, 3-gram:2, 4-gram:1) LC: 0.107 (number of lexical cohesion devices: 5) Human assessment: 2.67
MT 2	
1	China is accelerating research 16 *main technologies*
2	These *technologies* are within the *important* realm to promote sciences and *technology* and *achieve* national goals and must be completed in a timely manner through *achieving main* discoveries in *technology* and integration of resources .
	BLEU: 0.213 (1-gram:5, 2-gram:3, 3-gram:2, 4-gram:1) LC: 0.231 (number of lexical cohesion devices: 9) Human assessment: 4.33
Reference	
1	China Accelerates Research on 16 Main Technologies
2	These technologies represent a significant part in the development of science and technology and the achievement of national goals. They must be accomplished within a fixed period of time by realizing breakthroughs in essential technologies and integration of resources.

Table 3: An example of MT outputs of different quality (underlined: matched n-grams; italic: lexical cohesion devices)

one MT system. Second, the ratios in those different HT versions are very stable in comparison with those of MT. Especially, all four HT versions in the MetricsMATR dataset share the same RC ratio 0.31. This shows a typical level of the use of lexical cohesion device. Third, the ratios in MT are lower than or at most equal to those in HT, suggesting their correlation with translation quality: the closer their RC and LC ratios to those in HT, the better the MT. These results verify our assumption that lexical cohesion can serve as an effective proxy of the level of translation quality.

4 MT Evaluation at Document Level

As a feature at the discourse level, lexical cohesion is a good complement to current evaluation metrics focusing on features at the sentence level. Table 3 illustrates an example selected from the MetricsMATR dataset, consisting two versions of MT output for a short document of two segments only. The n-grams matched with the reference are underlined, while the lexical cohesion devices are italicized. The two MT outputs have a similar number of matched n-grams and hence receive similar BLEU scores. These scores, however, do not reflect their real difference in quality: the second version is better, according to human assessment of adequacy. Instead, their LC ratios seem to represent such a variation more accurately. The theme of the second output is also highlighted through the lexical chains, including *main/important*, *technology/technologies* and *achieve/achieving*, which create a tight texture between the two sentences, a crucial factor of text quality.

To perform MT evaluation at the document level, the LC and RC ratios can be used alone or integrated into a sentence-level metric. The former way has an advantage that it does not have to rely on any reference translation. LC mainly requires a thesaurus for computing semantic relation, while RC only needs a morphological processor such as stemmer, both of which are available for most languages. Its drawback, however, lies in the risk of relying on a single discourse feature. Although lexical cohesion gives a strong indication of text coherence, it is not indispensable, because a text can be coherent without any surface cohesive clue. Furthermore, the quality of a document is also reflected in that of its sentences. A coherent translation may be mistranslated, and on the other hand, a text containing lots of sentence-level errors would make it difficult to determine its document-level quality. A previous study comparing MT evaluation at the sentence versus document level (Wong et al., 2011) reports a poor consistency in the evaluation results at these two levels when the sentence-level scores of MT output are low. In regard of these, how to integrate these two levels of MT evaluation is particularly worth studying.

5 Experiments

We examine, through experiments, the effectiveness of using LC and RC ratios alone and integrating them into other evaluation metrics for MT evaluation at the document and system levels. Three evaluation metrics, namely BLEU, TER and METEOR,[2] are selected for testing. They represent three distinctive types of evaluation metrics: n-gram, edit-distance, and unigram with external language resources, respectively. These metrics are evaluated in terms of their correlation with human assessments, using Pearson's r correlation coefficient. The MetricsMATR and MTC4 datasets and their adequacy assessments are used as evaluation data. Note that the adequacy assessment is in fact an evaluation method for the sentence level. We have to rely on an assumption that this evaluation data may emulate document-level quality, since its MT outputs were assessed sentence by sentence in sequence as in a document. All experiments are performed under a setting of multiple reference translations.

The integration of the two ratios into an evaluation metric follows a simple weighted average approach. A hybrid metric H is formulated as

$$H = \alpha\, m_{doc} + (1 - \alpha)\, m_{seg}$$

where m_{doc} refers to the document-level feature in use (i.e., LC or RC), m_{seg} to a sentence-level metric, and α to a weight controlling their proportion. The MetricsMATR dataset is used as training data to optimize the values of α for different metrics, while the MTC4 is used as evaluation data. Table 4 shows the optimized weights for the metrics for evaluation at the document level.

Metrics	RC	LC
BLEU	0.28	0.29
TER	0.40	0.38
METEOR	0.19	0.18

Table 4: Optimized weights for the integration of discourse feature into sentence-level metrics

Table 5 presents the correlation rates of evaluation metrics obtained in our experiments under different settings, with their 95% conference intervals (CI) provided. The LC and RC ratios are found to have strong correlations with human assessments at the system level even when used alone, highly comparable to BLEU and TER. At the document level, however, they are not as good as the others. They show their advantages when integrated into other metrics, especially BLEU and TER. LC raises the correlation of BLEU from 0.447 to 0.472 and from 0.861 to 0.905 at the document and system levels, respectively. It improves TER even more significantly, in that the correlation rates are boosted up from -0.326 to -0.390 at the document level, and even from -0.601 to -0.763 at the system level. Since there are only six systems in the MTC4 data, such a dramatic change may not be as meaningful as the smooth improvement at the document level. METEOR is a special case in this experiment. Its correlation cannot be improved by integrating LC or RC, and is even slightly dropped at the document level. The cause for this is yet to be identified. Nevertheless, these results confirm the close relationship of an MT system's capability to appropriately generate lexical cohesion devices with the quality of its output.

Table 6 presents the Pearson correlations between evaluation results at the document level using different evaluation metrics in the MTC4 data. It illustrates the homogeneity/heterogeneity of different metrics and helps explain the performance change

[2] METEOR 1.0 with default parameters optimized over the adequacy assessments.

	Document		System	
Metrics	Correlation	95% CI	Correlation	95% CI
RC	0.243	(0.167, 0.316)	0.873	(0.211, 0.985)
LC	0.267	(0.192, 0.339)	0.818	(0.020, 0.979)
BLEU	0.447	(0.381, 0.508)	0.861	(0.165, 0.984)
BLEU+*RC*	0.463	(0.398, 0.523)	0.890	(0.283, 0.987)
BLEU+*LC*	0.472	(0.408, 0.531)	0.905	(0.352, 0.989)
TER	-0.326	(-0.253, -0.395)	-0.601	(-0.411, -0.949)
TER+*RC*	-0.370	(-0.299, -0.437)	-0.740	(-0.179, -0.969)
TER+*LC*	-0.390	(-0.320, -0.455)	-0.763	(-0.127, -0.972)
METEOR	0.557	(0.500, 0.609)	0.961	(0.679, 0.995)
METEOR+*RC*	0.555	(0.498, 0.608)	0.960	(0.672, 0.995)
METEOR+*LC*	0.556	(0.499, 0.609)	0.962	(0.687, 0.995)

Table 5: Correlation of different metrics with adequacy assessment in MTC4 data

BLEU	1				
TER	-0.699	1			
METEOR	0.834	-0.510	1		
RC	0.287	-0.204	0.405	1	
LC	0.263	-0.097	0.437	0.736	1
	BLEU	TER	METEOR	*RC*	*LC*

Table 6: Correlation between the evaluation results of different metrics

by combining sentence- and document-level metrics. The table shows that the two ratios *LC* and *RC* highly correlate with each other, as if they are two variants of quantifying lexical cohesion devices. The three sentence-level metrics, BLEU, TER and METEOR, also show strong correlations with each other, especially between BLEU and METEOR. The correlations are generally weaker between sentence- and document-level metrics, for instance, 0.263 between BLEU and *LC* and only -0.097 between TER and *LC*, showing that they are quite heterogeneous in nature. This accounts for the significant performance gain from their combination: their difference allows them to complement each other. It is also worth noting that between METEOR and *LC* the correlation of 0.437 is mildly strong, explaining the negative result of their integration. On the one hand, lexical cohesion is word choice oriented, which is only sensitive to the reiteration and semantic relatedness of words in MT output. On the other hand, METEOR is strong in unigram matching, with multiple strategies to maximize the matching rate between MT output and reference translation. In this sense they are homogeneous to a certain extent, explaining the null effect of their combination.

6 Discussion and Conclusion

In this study we have attempted to address the problem that most existing MT evaluation metrics disregard the connectivity of sentences in a document. By focusing on a typical type of cohesion, i.e., lexical cohesion, we have shown that its use frequency is a significant factor to differentiate HT from MT and MT outputs of different quality from each other. The high correlation rate of its use with translation adequacy also suggests that the more lexical cohesion devices in use, the better the quality of MT output. Accordingly we have used two ratios, *LC* and *RC*, to capture such correlativity. Our experimental results have confirmed the effectiveness of this feature in accounting for the document-level quality of MT output. The performance of two evaluation metrics, BLEU and TER, is highly improved through incorporating this document-level feature, in terms of the change of their correlation with human assessments.

This finding is positive and sheds light on a region of MT research that is still severely under-explored. Our approach to extending the granularity of MT evaluation from sentence to document through lexical cohesion is highly applicable to different languages. It has a relatively weak demand for language resource in comparison with the processing of other discourse features like grammatical cohesion. It is also much unaffected by grammatical problems or errors commonly seen in natural languages and, in particular, MT outputs.

Our future work will continue to explore the relationship of lexical cohesion to translation quality, so as to identify, apart from its use frequency, other significant aspects for MT evaluation at the document level. A frequent use of cohesion devices in a text is not necessarily appropriate, because an excess of them may decrease the quality and readability of a text. Human writers can strategically change the ways of expression to achieve appropriate coherence and also avoid overuse of the same lexical item. To a certain extent, this is one of the causes for the unnaturalness of MT output: it may contain a large number of lexical cohesion devices which are simply direct translation of those in a source text that do not fit in the target context. How to use lexical cohesion devices appropriately instead of frequently is thus an important issue to tackle before we can adopt them in MT and MT evaluation by a suitable means.

Acknowledgments

The research described in this paper was substantially supported by the Research Grants Council (RGC) of Hong Kong SAR, P. R. China through GRF grant 144410.

References

Satanjeev Banerjee and Alon Lavie. 2005. METEOR: An automatic metric for MT evaluation with improved correlation with human judgments. In *Proceedings of the ACL Workshop on Intrinsic and Extrinsic Evaluation Measures for Machine Translation and/or Summarization*, pages 65–72, Ann Arbor, Michigan.

Regina Barzilay and Michael Elhadad. 1997. Using lexical chains for text summarization. In *Proceedings of the ACL Workshop on Intelligent Scalable Text Summarization*, pages 10–17.

Jill Burstein. 2003. The E-rater scoring engine: Automated essay scoring with natural language processing. In Mark D. Shermis and Jill Burstein, editors, *Automated Essay Scoring: A Cross-Disciplinary Perspective*, chapter 7, pages 113–122. Lawrence Erlbaum Associates.

Marine Carpuat. 2009. One translation per discourse. In *Proceedings of the NAACL HLT Workshop on Semantic Evaluations: Recent Achievements and Future Directions*, pages 19–27, Boulder, Colorado.

Bruno Cartoni, Andrea Gesmundo, James Henderson, Cristina Grisot, Paola Merlo, Thomas Meyer, Jacques Moeschler, Sandrine Zufferey, and Andrei Popescu-Belis. 2011. Improving MT coherence through text-level processing of input texts: The COMTIS project. In *Tralogy*, Paris.

Samuel W. K. Chan. 2004. Extraction of sailent textual patterns: Synergy between lexical cohesion and contextual coherence. *IEEE Transactions on Systems, Man and Cybernetics, Part A: Systems and Humans*, 34(2):205–218.

Elisabet Comelles, Jesus Giménez, Lluìs Márquez, Irene Castellòn, and Victoria Arranz. 2010. Document-level automatic MT evaluation based on discourse representations. In *Proceedings of the Joint Fifth Workshop on Statistical Machine Translation and Metrics-MATR*, pages 333–338, Uppsala.

Christiane Fellbaum. 1998. *WordNet: An Electronic Lexical Database*. MIT Press, Cambridge, MA.

Zhengxian Gong, Min Zhang, and Guodong Zhou. 2011. Cache-based document-level statistical machine translation. In *EMNLP 2011*, pages 909–919, Edinburgh, Scotland.

M. A. K. Halliday and Ruqaiya Hasan. 1976. *Cohesion in English*. London: Longman.

Masaki Itagaki, Takako Aikawa, and Xiaodong He. 2007. Automatic validation of terminology translation consistency with statistical method. In *MT Summit XI*, pages 269–274.

Hans Kamp and Uwe Reyle. 1993. *From Discourse to Logic: An Introduction to Modeltheoretic Semantics of Natural Language, Formal Logic and Discourse Representation Theory*. Dordrecht: Kluwer.

Margaret King, Andrei Popescu-Belis, and Eduard Hovy. 2003. FEMTI: Creating and using a framework for MT evaluation. In *MT Summit IX*, pages 224–231, New Orleans.

Jing Li, Le Sun, Chunyu Kit, and Jonathan Webster. 2007. A query-focused multi-document summarizer based on lexical chains. In *DUC 2007*, Rochester, New York.

Kazem Lotfipour-Saedi. 1997. Lexical cohesion and translation equivalence. *Meta*, 42(1):185–192.

Xiaoyi Ma. 2006. Multiple-Translation Chinese (MTC) part 4. Linguistic Data Consortium.

William C. Mann and Sandra A. Thompson. 1988. Rhetorical structure theory: Toward a functional theory of text organization. *Text*, 8(3):243–281.

Keith J. Miller and Michelle Vanni. 2001. Scaling the ISLE taxonomy: Development of metrics for the multi-dimensional characterisation of machine translation quality. In *MT Summit VIII*, pages 229–238.

Jane Morris and Graeme Hirst. 1991. Lexical cohesion computed by thesaural relations as an indicator of the structure of text. *Computational Linguistics*, 17(1):21–48.

Masaki Murata and Makoto Nagao. 1993. Determination of referential property and number of nouns in Japanese sentences for machine translation into English. In *TMI 1993*, pages 218–225, Kyoto.

Masaki Murata, Kiyotaka Uchimoto, Qing Ma, and Hitoshi Isahara. 2001. A machine-learning approach to estimating the referential properties of Japanese noun phrases. In *CICLING 2001*, pages 142–153, Mexico-City.

Hiromi Nakaiwa and Satoru Ikehara. 1992. Zero pronoun resolution in a machine translation system by using Japanese to English verbal semantic attributes. In *ANLP 1992*, pages 201–208.

Hiromi Nakaiwa and Satoshi Shirai. 1996. Anaphora resolution of Japanese zero pronouns with deictic reference. In *COLING 1996*, pages 812–817, Copenhagen.

Hiromi Nakaiwa, Satoshi Shirai, Satoru Ikehara, and Tsukasa Kawaok. 1995. Extrasentential resolution of Japanese zero pronouns using semantic and pragmatic constraints. In *Proceedings of the AAAI 1995 Spring Symposium Series: Empirical Methods in Discourse Interpretation and Generation*, pages 99–105, Stanford.

Kishore Papineni, Salim Roukos, Todd Ward, and Wei-Jing Zhu. 2002. BLEU: A method for automatic evaluation of machine translation. In *ACL 2002*, pages 311–318.

Jesús Peral, Manuel Palomar, and Antonio Ferràndez. 1999. Coreference-oriented interlingual slot structure and machine translation. In *Proceedings of the ACL Workshop on Coreference and its Applications*, pages 69–76, College Park, MD.

Martin F. Porter. 1980. An algorithm for suffix stripping. *Program*, 14(3):130–137.

Mark Przybocki, Kay Peterson, and Sébastien Bronsart. 2009. 2008 NIST metrics for machine translation (MetricsMATR08) development data. Linguistic Data Consortium.

Matthew Snover, Bonnie Dorr, Richard Schwartz, Linnea Micciulla, and John Makhoul. 2006. A study of translation edit rate with targeted human annotation. In *AMTA 2006*, pages 223–231.

Matthew Snover, Nitin Madnani, Bonnie J. Dorr, and Richard Schwartz. 2009. Fluency, adequacy, or HTER? Exploring different human judgments with a tunable MT metric. In *Proceedings of the 4th Workshop on Statistical Machine Translation*, pages 259–268, Athens.

Georges van Slype. 1979. Critical Study of Methods for Evaluating the Quality of Machine Translation. Technical report, Bureau Marcel van Dijk / European Commission, Brussels.

Muriel Vasconcellos. 1989. Cohesion and coherence in the presentation of machine translation products. In James E. Alatis, editor, *Georgetown University Round Table on Languages and Linguistics 1989: Language Teaching, Testing, and Technology: Lessons from the Past with a View Toward the Future*, pages 89–105. Georgetown University Press.

Eric M. Visser and Masaru Fuji. 1996. Using sentence connectors for evaluating MT output. In *COLING 1996*, pages 1066–1069.

Yorick Wilks. 1978. The Value of the Monolingual Component in MT Evaluation and its Role in the Battelle. Report on Systran, Luxembourg CEC Memorandum.

Billy T. M. Wong, Cecilia F. K. Pun, Chunyu Kit, and Jonathan J. Webster. 2011. Lexical cohesion for evaluation of machine translation at document level. In *NLP-KE 2011*, pages 238–242, Tokushima.

Billy Tak-Ming Wong. 2010. Semantic evaluation of machine translation. In *LREC 2010*, pages 2884–2888, Valletta.

Zhibiao Wu and Martha Palmer. 1994. Verb semantics and lexical selection. In *ACL 1994*, pages 133–138, Las Cruces.

Tong Xiao, Jingbo Zhu, Shujie Yao, and Hao Zhang. 2011. Document-level consistency verification in machine translation. In *MT summit XIII*, pages 131–138, Xiamen.

Fast Large-Scale Approximate Graph Construction for NLP

Amit Goyal and Hal Daumé III
Dept. of Computer Science
University of Maryland
College Park, MD
{amit,hal}@umiacs.umd.edu

Raul Guerra
Dept. of Computer Science
University of Maryland
College Park, MD
rguerra@cs.umd.edu

Abstract

Many natural language processing problems involve constructing large nearest-neighbor graphs. We propose a system called **FLAG** to construct such graphs approximately from large data sets. To handle the large amount of data, our algorithm maintains approximate counts based on sketching algorithms. To find the approximate nearest neighbors, our algorithm pairs a new distributed online-PMI algorithm with novel fast approximate nearest neighbor search algorithms (variants of PLEB). These algorithms return the approximate nearest neighbors quickly. We show our system's efficiency in both intrinsic and extrinsic experiments. We further evaluate our fast search algorithms both quantitatively and qualitatively on two NLP applications.

1 Introduction

Many natural language processing (NLP) problems involve graph construction. Examples include constructing polarity lexicons based on lexical graphs from WordNet (Rao and Ravichandran, 2009), constructing polarity lexicons from web data (Velikovich et al., 2010) and unsupervised part-of-speech tagging using label propagation (Das and Petrov, 2011). The later two approaches construct nearest-neighbor graphs between word pairs by computing nearest neighbors between word pairs from large corpora. These nearest neighbors form the edges of the graph, with weights given by the distributional similarity (Turney and Pantel, 2010) between terms. Unfortunately, computing the distributional similarity between all words in a large vocabulary is computationally and memory intensive when working with large amounts of data (Pantel et al., 2009). This bottleneck is typically addressed by means of commodity clusters. For example, Pantel et al. (2009) compute distributional similarity between 500 million terms over a 200 billion words in 50 hours using 100 quad-core nodes, explicitly storing a similarity matrix between 500 million terms.

In this work, we propose Fast Large-Scale Approximate Graph (**FLAG**) construction, a system that constructs a fast large-scale approximate nearest-neighbor graph from a large text corpus. To build this system, we exploit recent developments in the area of approximation, randomization and streaming for large-scale NLP problems (Ravichandran et al., 2005; Goyal et al., 2009; Levenberg et al., 2010). More specifically we exploit work on Locality Sensitive Hashing (LSH) (Charikar, 2002) for computing word-pair similarities from large text collections (Ravichandran et al., 2005; Van Durme and Lall, 2010). However, Ravichandran et al. (2005) approach stored an enormous matrix of all unique words and their contexts in main memory, which is infeasible for very large data sets. A more efficient online framework to locality sensitive hashing (Van Durme and Lall, 2010; Van Durme and Lall, 2011) computes distributional similarity in a streaming setting. Unfortunately, their approach can handle only additive features like raw-counts, and not non-linear association scores like pointwise mutual information (PMI), which generates better context vectors for distributional similarity (Ravichandran et al., 2005; Pantel et al., 2009; Turney and Pantel, 2010).

In **FLAG**, we first propose a *novel* distributed online-PMI algorithm (Section 3.1). It is a streaming method that processes large data sets in one pass while distributing the data over commodity clusters and returns context vectors weighted by pointwise mutual information (PMI) for all the words. Our distributed online-PMI algorithm makes use of the Count-Min (CM) sketch algorithm (Cormode and Muthukrishnan, 2004) (previously shown effective for computing distributional similarity in our earlier work (Goyal and Daumé III, 2011)) to store the counts of all words, contexts and word-context pairs using only $8GB$ of main memory. The main motivation for using the CM sketch comes from its linearity property (see last paragraph of Section 2) which makes CM sketch to be implemented in distributed setting for large data sets. In our implementation, **FLAG** scaled up to 110 GB of web data with 866 million sentences in less than 2 days using 100 quad-core nodes. Our intrinsic and extrinsic experiments demonstrate the effectiveness of distributed online-PMI.

After generating context vectors from distributed online-PMI algorithm, our goal is to use them to find fast approximate nearest neighbors for all words. To achieve this goal, we exploit recent developments in the area of existing randomized algorithms for random projections (Achlioptas, 2003; Li et al., 2006), Locality Sensitive Hashing (LSH) (Charikar, 2002) and improve on previous work done on PLEB (Point Location in Equal Balls) (Indyk and Motwani, 1998; Charikar, 2002). We propose novel variants of PLEB to address the issue of reducing the pre-processing time for PLEB. One of the variants of PLEB (FAST-PLEB) with considerably *less* pre-processing time has effectiveness comparable to PLEB. We evaluate these variants of PLEB both quantitatively and qualitatively on large data sets. Finally, we show the applicability of large-scale graphs built from **FLAG** on two applications: the Google-Sets problem (Ghahramani and Heller, 2005), and learning concrete and abstract words (Turney et al., 2011).

2 Count-Min sketch

The Count-Min (CM) sketch (Cormode and Muthukrishnan, 2004) belongs to a class of 'sketch' algorithms that represents a large data set with a compact summary, typically much smaller than the full size of the input by processing the data in one pass. The following surveys comprehensively review the streaming literature (Rusu and Dobra, 2007; Cormode and Hadjieleftheriou, 2008) and sketch techniques (Charikar et al., 2004; Li et al., 2008; Cormode and Muthukrishnan, 2004; Rusu and Dobra, 2007). In our another recent paper (Goyal et al., 2012), we conducted a systematic study and compare many sketch techniques which answer point queries with focus on large-scale NLP tasks. In that paper, we empirically demonstrated that CM sketch performs the best among all the sketches on three large-scale NLP tasks.

CM sketch uses hashing to store the approximate frequencies of all items from the large data set onto a small sketch vector that can be updated and queried in constant time. CM has two parameters ϵ and δ: ϵ controls the amount of tolerable error in the returned count and δ controls the probability with which the error exceeds the bound ϵ.

CM sketch with parameters (ϵ,δ) is represented as a two-dimensional array with width w and depth d; where w and d depends on ϵ and δ respectively. We set w=$\frac{2}{\epsilon}$ and d=$\log(\frac{1}{\delta})$. The depth d denotes the number of pairwise-independent hash functions employed by the CM sketch; and the width w denotes the range of the hash functions. Given an input stream of items of length N ($\mathrm{x}_1, \mathrm{x}_2 \ldots \mathrm{x}_N$), each of the hash functions h_k:$\{\mathrm{x}_1, \mathrm{x}_2 \ldots \mathrm{x}_N\} \rightarrow \{1 \ldots w\}, \forall 1 \leq k \leq d$, takes an item from the input stream and maps it into a position indexed by the corresponding hash function.

UPDATE: For each new item "x" with count c, the sketch is updated as:

$$\text{sketch}[k, h_k(\mathrm{x})] \leftarrow \text{sketch}[k, h_k(\mathrm{x})] + c, \ \ \forall 1 \leq k \leq d.$$

QUERY: Since multiple items can be hashed to the same index for each row of the array, hence the stored frequency in each row is guaranteed to *overestimate* the true count, which makes it a biased estimator. Therefore, to answer the point query (QUERY (x)), CM returns the minimum over all the d positions indexed by the hash functions.

$$\hat{c}(\mathrm{x}) = \min_k \ \text{sketch}[k, h_k(\mathrm{x})], \ \ \forall 1 \leq k \leq d.$$

All reported frequencies by CM exceed the true frequencies by at most ϵN with probability of at least $1 - \delta$. The space used by the algorithm is $O(\frac{1}{\epsilon} \log \frac{1}{\delta})$. Constant time of O(log($\frac{1}{\delta}$)) per each update and query operation.

CM sketch has a linearity property which states that: Given two sketches s_1 and s_2 computed (using the same parameters w and d, and the same set of d hash functions) over different input streams; the sketch of the combined data stream can be easily obtained by adding the individual sketches in $O(d \times w)$ time which is independent of the stream size. This property enables sketches to be implemented in distributed setting, where each machine computes the sketch over a small portion of the corpus and makes it *scalable* to large datasets.

The idea of conservative update (Estan and Varghese, 2002) is to only increase counts in the sketch by the minimum amount needed to ensure that the estimate remains accurate. We (Goyal and Daumé III, 2011) used CM sketch with conservative update (CM-CU sketch) to show that the update reduces the amount of over-estimation error by a factor of at least 1.5 on NLP data and showed the effectiveness of CM-CU on three important NLP tasks. The QUERY procedure for CM-CU is identical to Count-Min. However, to UPDATE an item "x" with frequency c, first we compute the frequency $\hat{c}(\mathrm{x})$ of this item from the existing data structure:

$(\forall 1 \leq k \leq d, \hat{c}(\mathrm{x}) = \min_k \text{ sketch}[k, h_k(\mathrm{x})])$

and the counts are updated according to:

$\text{sketch}[k, h_k(\mathrm{x})] \leftarrow \max\{\text{sketch}[k, h_k(\mathrm{x})], \hat{c}(\mathrm{x}) + c\}$.

The intuition is that, since the point query returns the minimum of all the d values, we will update a counter only if it is necessary as indicated by the above equation. This heuristic avoids the unnecessary updating of counter values to reduce the over-estimation error.

3 FLAG: Fast Large-Scale Approximate Graph Construction

We describe a system, **FLAG**, for generating a nearest neighbor graph from a large corpus. For every node (word), our system returns top l approximate nearest neighbors, which implicitly defines the graph. Our system operates in four steps. First, for every word "z", our system generates a sparse context vector $(\langle(\mathrm{c}_1, v_1); (\mathrm{c}_2, v_2) \ldots; (\mathrm{c}_d, v_d)\rangle)$ of size d where c_d denotes the context and v_d denotes the PMI (strength of association) between the context c_d and the word "z". The context can be lexical, semantic, syntactic, and/or dependency units that co-occur with the word "z". We compute this efficiently using a new distributed online Pointwise Mutual Information algorithm (Section 3.1). Second, we project all the words with context vector size d onto k random vectors and then binarize these random projection vectors (Section 3.2). Third, we propose novel variants of PLEB (Section 3.3) with less pre-processing time to represent data for fast query retrieval. Fourth, using the output of variants of PLEB, we generate a small set of potential nearest neighbors for every word "z" (Section 3.4). From this small set, we can compute the Hamming distance between every word "z" and its potential nearest neighbors to return the l nearest-neighbors for all unique words.

3.1 Distributed online-PMI

We propose a *new* distributed online Pointwise Mutual Information (PMI) algorithm motivated by the online-PMI algorithm (Van Durme and Lall, 2009b) (page 5). This is a streaming algorithm which processes the input corpus in one pass. After one pass over the data set, it returns the context vectors for all query words. The original online-PMI algorithm was used to find the top-d verbs for a query verb using the highest approximate online-PMI values using a Talbot-Osborne-Morris-Bloom[1] (TOMB) Counter (Van Durme and Lall, 2009a). Unfortunately, this algorithm is prohibitively slow when computing contexts for *all* words, rather than just a small query set. This motivates us to propose a distributed variant that enables us to scale to large data and large vocabularies.[2]

We make three modifications to the original online-PMI algorithm and refer to it as the "modified online-PMI algorithm" shown in Algorithm 1. First, we use Count-Min with conservative update (CM-CU) sketch (Goyal and Daumé III, 2011) instead of TOMB. We prefer CM because it enables distribution due to its linearity property (Section 2) and footnote #1. Distribution using TOMB is not known in literature and we will like to explore that direction in future. Second, we store the counts of words ("z"), contexts ("y") and word-context pairs all together in

[1]TOMB is a variant of CM sketch which focuses on reducing the bit size of each counter (in addition to the number of counters) at the cost of incurring more error in the counts.

[2]The serialized online-PMI algorithm took a week to generate context vectors for all the words from **GW** (Section 4.1).

Algorithm 1 Modified online-PMI

```
Require: Data set D, buffer size B
Ensure: context vectors V, mapping word z to d-best
    contexts in priority queue ⟨ y,PMI(z, y)⟩
initialize CM-CU sketch to store approximate counts
    of words, context and word-context pairs
for each buffer B in the data set D do
    initialize S to store ⟨z,y⟩ observed in B
    for ⟨z,y⟩ in B do
        set S (⟨z,y⟩) =1
        insert z, y and pair ⟨z,y⟩ in sketch
    end for
    for x in set S do
        recompute vectors V(x) using current contexts
        in priority queue and {y|S(⟨z,y⟩)=1}
    end for
end for
return context vectors V
```

the CM-CU sketch (in the original online-PMI algorithm, exact counts of words and contexts were stored in a hash table; only the pairs were stored in the TOMB data structure). Third, in the original algorithm, for each "z" a vector of top-d contexts are modified at the end of each buffer (refer Algorithm 1). However, in our algorithm, we only modify the list of those "z"'s which appeared in the recent buffer rather than modifying for all the "z"'s (Note, if "z" does not appear in the recent buffer, then its top-d contexts cannot be changed. Hence, we only modify those "z"'s which appear in the recent buffer).

In our distributed online-PMI algorithm, first we split the data into chunks of 10 million sentences. Second, we run the modified online-PMI algorithm on each chunk in distributed setting. This stores counts of all words ("z"), contexts ("y") and word-context pairs in the CM-CU sketch, and store top-d contexts for each word in priority queues. In third step, we merge all the sketches using linearity property to sum the counts of the words, contexts and word-context pairs. Additionally we merge the lists of top-d contexts for each word. In the last step, we use the single merged sketch and merged top-d contexts list to generate the final distributed online-PMI top-d contexts list.

It takes around one day to compute context vectors for all the words from a chunk of 10 million sentences using first step of distributed online-PMI. We generated context vectors for all the 87 chunks (110 GB data with 866 million sentences: see Table 1) in one day by running one process per chunk over a cluster. The first step of the algorithm involves traversing the data set and is the most time intensive step. For the second step, the merging of sketches is fast, since sketches are two dimensional array data structures (we used the sketch of size 2 billion counters with 3 hash functions). Merging the lists of top-d contexts for each word is embarrassingly parallel and fast. The last step to generate the final top-d contexts list is again embarrassingly parallel and fast and takes couple of hours to generate the top-d contexts for all the words from all the chunks. If implemented serially the "modified online-PMI algorithm" on 110 GB data with 866 million sentences would take approximately 3 months.

The downside of the distributed online-PMI is that it splits the data into small chunks and loses information about the global best contexts for a word over all the chunks. The algorithm locally computes the best contexts for each chunk, that can be bad if the algorithm misses out globally *good* contexts and that can affect the accuracy of downstream application. We will demonstrate in our experiments (Section 4.2) by using distributed online-PMI, we do not lose any significant information about global contexts and perform comparable to offline-PMI over an intrinsic and extrinsic evaluation.

3.2 Dimensionality Reduction from $\mathbb{R}^D$ to $\mathbb{R}^k$

We are given context vectors for Z words, our goal is to use k random projections to project the context vectors from $\mathbb{R}^D$ to $\mathbb{R}^k$. There are total D unique contexts ($D >> k$) for all Z words. Let $(\langle(c_1, v_1); (c_2, v_2) \ldots; (c_d, v_d)\rangle)$ be sparse context vectors of size d for Z words. For each word, we use hashing to project the context vectors onto k directions. We use k pairwise independent hash functions that maps each of the d context (c_d) dimensions onto $\beta_{d,k} \in \{-1, +1\}$; and compute inner product between $\beta_{d,k}$ and v_d. Next, $\forall k$, $\sum_d \beta_{d,k}.v_d$ returns the k random projections for each word "z". We store the k random projections for all words (mapped to integers) as a matrix A of size of $k \times Z$.

The mechanism described above generates random projections by implicitly creating a random projection matrix from a set of $\{-1, +1\}$. This idea of creating implicit random projection matrix

$$\begin{array}{c} \\ \mathbf{k_1} \\ \mathbf{k_2} \\ \vdots \\ \mathbf{k_K} \end{array} \begin{array}{c} \begin{array}{cccc} 1 & 2 & \cdots & Z \end{array} \\ \begin{pmatrix} \langle z_1, 26\rangle & \langle z_2, 80\rangle & \cdots & \langle z_Z, 3\rangle \\ \langle z_1, -28\rangle & \langle z_2, 6\rangle & \cdots & \langle z_Z, 111\rangle \\ \vdots & \vdots & \ddots & \vdots \\ \langle z_1, 78\rangle & \langle z_2, 69\rangle & \cdots & \langle z_Z, 92\rangle \end{pmatrix} \end{array}$$

(a) Matrix A

$$\overset{\text{Sort}}{\Longrightarrow} \begin{array}{c} \begin{array}{ccc} \textbf{Smallest} & \textbf{to} & \textbf{Largest} \end{array} \\ \begin{pmatrix} \langle z_Z, 3\rangle & \langle z_1, 26\rangle & \cdots & \langle z_m, 700\rangle \\ \langle z_r, -50\rangle & \langle z_2, 6\rangle & \cdots & \langle z_Z, 111\rangle \\ \vdots & \vdots & \ddots & \vdots \\ \langle z_1, 78\rangle & \langle z_Z, 92\rangle & \cdots & \langle z_u, 432\rangle \end{pmatrix} \end{array}$$

(b) Matrix A

$$\Rightarrow \begin{array}{c} \begin{array}{cccc} 1 & 2 & \cdots & Z \end{array} \\ \begin{pmatrix} z_Z & z_1 & \cdots & z_m \\ z_r & z_2 & \cdots & z_Z \\ \vdots & \vdots & \ddots & \vdots \\ z_1 & z_Z & \cdots & z_u \end{pmatrix} \end{array}$$

(c) Matrix A

$$\Rightarrow \begin{array}{c} \begin{array}{cccc} z_1 & z_2 & \cdots & z_Z \end{array} \\ \begin{pmatrix} 2 & 60 & \cdots & 1 \\ 55 & 2 & \cdots & Z \\ \vdots & \vdots & \ddots & \vdots \\ 1 & 90 & \cdots & 2 \end{pmatrix} \end{array}$$

(d) Matrix C

Figure 1: First matrix pairs the words $1 \cdots Z$ and their random projection values. Second matrix sorts each row by the random projection values from smallest to largest. Third matrix throws away the projection values leaving only the words. Fourth matrix maps the words $1 \cdots Z$ to their sorted position in the third matrix for each k. This allows constant query time for all the words.

is motivated by the work on stable random projections (Li et al., 2006; Li et al., 2008), Count sketch (Charikar et al., 2004), feature hashing (Weinberger et al., 2009) and online Locality Sensitive Hashing (LSH) (Van Durme and Lall, 2010). The idea of generating random projections from the set $\{-1, +1\}$ was originally proposed by Achlioptas (2003).

Next we create a binary matrix B using matrix A by taking sign of each of the entries of the matrix A. If $A(i, j) \geq 0$, then $B(i, j) = 1$; else $B(i, j) = 0$. This binarization creates Locality Sensitive Hash (LSH) function that preserves the cosine similarity between every pair of word vectors. This idea was first proposed by Charikar (2002) and used in NLP for large-scale noun clustering (Ravichandran et al., 2005). However, in large-scale noun clustering work, their approach had to store the random projection matrix of size $D \times k$; where D denotes the number of all unique contexts (which is generally large and $D >> Z$) and in this paper, we do not explicitly require storing a random projection matrix.

3.3 Representation for Fast-Search

We describe three approaches to represent the data (matrix A and B from Section 3.2) in such a manner that finding nearest neighbors is fast. These three approaches differ in amount of pre-processing time. First, we propose a naive baseline approach using random projections independently with the best pre-processing time. Second, we describe PLEB (Point Location in Equal Balls) (Indyk and Motwani, 1998; Charikar, 2002) with the worst pre-processing time. Third, we propose a variant of PLEB to reduce its pre-processing time.

3.3.1 Independent Random Projections (IRP)

Here, we describe a naive baseline approach to arrange nearest neighbors next to each other by using Independent Random Projections (IRP). In this approach, we pre-process the matrix A. First for matrix A, we pair the words $z_1 \cdots z_Z$ and their random projection values as shown in Fig. 1(a). Second, we sort the elements of each row of matrix A by their random projection values from smallest to largest (shown in Fig. 1(b)). The sorting step takes $O(ZlogZ)$ time (We can assume k to be a constant). The sorting operation puts all the nearest neighbor words (for each k independent projections) next to each other. After sorting the matrix A, we throw away the projection values leaving only the words (see Fig. 1(c)). To search for a word in matrix A in constant time, we create another matrix C of size $(k \times Z)$ (see Fig. 1(d)). Matrix C maps the words $z_1 \cdots z_Z$ to their sorted position in the matrix A (see Fig. 1(c)) for each k.

3.3.2 PLEB

PLEB (Point Location in Equal Balls) was first proposed by Indyk and Motwani (1998) and further improved by Charikar (2002). The improved PLEB algorithm puts in operation *all* k random projections together. It randomly permutes the ordering of k binary LSH bits (stored in matrix B) for all the words p times. For each permutation it sorts all the words lexicographically based on their permuted LSH representation of size k. The sorting operation puts all the nearest neighbor words (using k projections together) next to each other for all the permutations. In practice p is generally large, Ravichandran et al. (2005) used $p = 1000$ in their work.

In our implementation of PLEB, we have a matrix A of size $(p \times Z)$ similar to the first matrix in Fig. 1(a). The main difference to the first matrix in Fig. 1(a) is that bit vectors of size k are used for sorting rather than using scalar projection values. Similar to Fig. 1(c) after sorting, bit vectors are discarded and a matrix C of size $(p \times Z)$ is used to map the words $1 \cdots Z$ to their sorted position in the matrix A. Note, in IRP approach, the size of A and C matrix is $(k \times Z)$. In PLEB generating random permutations and sorting the bit vectors of size k involves worse pre-processing time than using IRP. However, spending more time in pre-processing leads to finding better approximate nearest neighbors.

3.3.3 FAST-PLEB

To reduce the pre-processing time for PLEB, we propose a variant of PLEB (FAST-PLEB). In PLEB, while generating random permutations, it uses all the k bits. In this variant, for each random permutation we randomly sample without replacement q ($q << k$) bits out of k. We use q bits to represent each permutation and sort based on these q bits. This makes pre-processing *faster* for PLEB. Section 4.3 shows that FAST-PLEB only needs $q = 10$ to perform comparable to PLEB with $q = 3000$ (that makes FAST-PLEB 300 times faster than PLEB). Here, again we store matrices A and C of size $(p \times Z)$.

3.4 Finding Approximate Nearest Neighbors

The goal here is to exploit three representations discussed in Section 3.3 to find approximate nearest neighbors quickly. For all the three methods (IRP, PLEB, FAST-PLEB), we can use the same fast approximate search which is simple and fast. To search a word "z", first, we can look up matrix C to locate the k positions where "z" is stored in matrix A. This can be done in constant time (Again assuming k (for IRP) and p (for PLEB and FAST-PLEB) to be a constant.). Once, we find "z" in each row, we can select b (beam parameter) neighbors ($b/2$ neighbors from left and $b/2$ neighbors from right of the query word.) for all the k or p rows. This can be done in constant time (Assuming k, p and b to be constants.). This search procedure produces a set of bk (IRP) or bp (PLEB and FAST-PLEB) potential nearest neighbors for a query word "z". Next, we compute Hamming distance between query word "z" and the set of potential nearest neighbors from matrix B to return l closest nearest neighbors. For computing hamming distance, all the approaches discussed in Section 3.3 require all k random projection bits.

4 Experiments

We evaluate our system **FLAG** for fast large-scale approximate graph construction. First, we show that using distributed online-PMI algorithm is as effective as offline-PMI. Second, we compare the approximate nearest neighbors lists generated by **FLAG** against the exact nearest neighbor lists. Finally, we show the quality of our approximate similarity lists generated by **FLAG** from the web corpus.

4.1 Experimental Setup

Data sets: We use two data sets: Gigaword (Graff, 2003) and a copy of news web (Ravichandran et al., 2005). For both the corpora, we split the text into sentences, tokenize and convert into lower-case. To evaluate our approximate graph construction, we evaluate on three data sets: Gigaword (**GW**), Gigaword + 50% of web data (**GWB50**) and Gigaword + 100% ((**GWB100**)) of web data. Corpus statistics are shown in Table 1. We define the context for a given word "z" as the surrounding words appearing in a window of 2 words to the left and 2 words to the right. The context words are concatenated along with their positions -2, -1, +1, and +2.

Corpus	GW	GWB50	GWB100
Unzipped Size (GB)	12	60	110
# of sentences (Million)	57	463	866
# of tokens (Billion)	2.1	10.9	20.0

Table 1: Corpus Description

4.2 Evaluating Distributed online-PMI

Experimental Setup: First we do an intrinsic evaluation to quantitatively evaluate the distributed online-PMI vectors against the offline-PMI vectors computed from Gigaword (**GW**). Offline-PMI computed from the sketches have been shown as effective as exact PMI by Goyal and Daumé III (2011). To compute offline-PMI vectors, we do two passes over the corpus. In the first pass, we store the counts of words, contexts and word-context pairs computed from **GW** in the Count-Min with conservative update (CM-CU) sketch. We use the CM-CU sketch of size 2 billion counters (bounded 8 GB memory) with 3 hash functions. In second pass, using the aggregated counts from the sketch, we generate the offline-PMI vectors of size $d = 1000$ for every word. For rest of this paper for distributed online-PMI, we set $d = 1000$ and the size of the buffer=$10,000$ and we split the data sets into small chunks of 10 million sentences.

Intrinsic Evaluation: We use four kinds of measures: precision (P), recall (R), f-measure (F1) and Pearson's correlation (ρ) to measure the overlap in the context vectors obtained using online and offline PMI. ρ is computed between contexts that are found in offline and online context vectors. We do this evaluation on 447 words selected from the concatenation of four test-sets mentioned in the next paragraph. On these 447 words, we achieve an average P of .97, average R of .96 and average F1 of .97 and a perfect average ρ of 1. This evaluation show that the vectors obtained using online-PMI are as effective as offline-PMI.

Extrinsic Evaluation: We also compare online-PMI effectiveness on four test sets which consist of word pairs, and their corresponding human rankings. We generate the word pair rankings using online-PMI and offline-PMI strategies. We report the Pearson's correlation (ρ) between the human and system generated similarity rankings. The four test sets are: **WS-353** (Finkelstein et al., 2002) is a set of 353 word pairs. **WS-203**: A subset of WS-353 with 203 word pairs (Agirre et al., 2009). **RG-65**: (Rubenstein and Goodenough, 1965) has 65 word pairs. **MC-30**: A subset of RG-65 dataset with 30 word pairs (Miller and Charles, 1991).

The results in Table 2 shows that by using distributed online-PMI (by making a single pass over the corpus) is comparable to offline-PMI (which is computed by making two passes over the corpus).

For generating context vectors from **GW**, for both offline-PMI and online-PMI, we use a frequency cutoff of 5 for word-context pairs to throw away the rare terms as they are sensitive to PMI (Church and Hanks, 1989). Next, **FLAG** generates online-PMI vectors from **GWB50** and **GWB100** and uses frequency cutoffs of 15 and 25. The higher frequency cutoffs are selected based on the intuition that, with more data, we get more noise, and hence not considering word-context pairs with frequency less than 25 will be better for the system. As **FLAG** is going to use the context vectors to find nearest neighbors, we also throw away all those words which have ≤ 50 contexts associated with them. This generates context vectors for $57,930$ words from **GW**; $95,626$ from **GWB50** and $106,733$ from **GWB100**.

Test Set	WS-353	WS-203	RG-65	MC-30
Offline-PMI	.41	.55	.40	.52
Online-PMI	.41	.56	.39	.51

Table 2: Evaluating word pairs ranking with online and offline PMI. Scores are evaluated using ρ metric.

	10		25		50		100	
	R	ρ	R	ρ	R	ρ	R	ρ
IRP	.40	.53	.38	.51	.35	.54	.34	.51
q=1	.24	.62	.20	.63	.18	.59	.17	.54
q=5	.47	.60	.43	.57	.40	.57	.37	.53
q=10	.53	.58	.49	.56	.45	.55	.42	.53
q=100	.53	.60	.50	.59	.46	.56	.43	.53
q=3000	.54	.58	.50	.59	.46	.56	.43	.54

Table 4: Varying parameter q for FAST-PLEB with fixed $p = 1000$, $k = 3000$ and $b = 40$. Results reported on recall and ρ.

4.3 Evaluating Approximate Nearest Neighbor

Experimental Setup: To evaluate approximate nearest neighbor similarity lists generated by **FLAG**, we conduct three experiments. We evaluate all the three experiments on 447 words (test set) as used in Section 4.2. For each word, both exact and approximate methods return $l = 100$ nearest neighbors. The exact similarity lists for 447 test words is computed by calculating cosine similarity between 447 test words with respect to all other words. We also compare the LSH (computed using Hamming distance between all words and test set.) approximate nearest neighbor similarity lists against the exact similarity lists. LSH provides an upper bound on the performance of our approximate search representations (IRP, PLEB, and FAST-PLEB) for fast-search from Section 3.3) . We set the number of projections $k = 3000$ for all three methods and for PLEB and FAST-PLEB, we set number of permutations $p = 1000$ as used in large-scale noun clustering work (Ravichandran et al., 2005).

Evaluation Metric: We use two kinds of measures, recall and Pearson's correlation to measure the overlap in the approximate and exact similarity lists. Intuitively, recall (R) captures the number of

	Irp								Pleb								Fast-Pleb							
	10		25		50		100		10		25		50		100		10		25		50		100	
	R	ρ	R	ρ	R	ρ	R	ρ	R	ρ	R	ρ	R	ρ	R	ρ	R	ρ	R	ρ	R	ρ	R	ρ
Lsh	.55	.57	.52	.56	.49	.54	.46	.52	.55	.57	.52	.56	.49	.54	.46	.52	.55	.57	.52	.56	.49	.54	.46	.52
20	.29	.50	.26	.55	.25	.54	.24	.50	.50	.59	.45	.60	.41	.57	.37	.55	.48	.58	.42	.58	.38	.58	.35	.55
30	.36	.55	.33	.56	.31	.55	.30	.52	.53	.59	.48	.59	.44	.56	.41	.54	.51	.57	.47	.57	.42	.56	.40	.54
40	.40	.53	.38	.51	.35	.54	.34	.51	.54	.58	.50	.59	.46	.56	.43	.54	.53	.58	.49	.56	.45	.55	.42	.53
50	.44	.56	.42	.54	.39	.54	.37	.52	.54	.58	.51	.57	.47	.56	.44	.53	.54	.58	.50	.56	.46	.55	.44	.53
100	.53	.59	.49	.54	.46	.55	.43	.53	.55	.56	.52	.56	.48	.54	.46	.53	.55	.57	.52	.56	.48	.54	.46	.53

Table 3: Evaluation results on comparing Lsh, Irp, Pleb, and Fast-Pleb with $k = 3000$ and $b = \{20, 30, 40, 50, 100\}$ with exact nearest neighbors over **GW** data set. For Pleb and Fast-Pleb, we set $p = 1000$ and for Fast-Pleb, we set $q = 10$. We report results on recall (R) and ρ metric. For Irp, we sample first p rows and only use p rows rather than k.

	GW								GWB50								GWB100							
	10		25		50		100		10		25		50		100		10		25		50		100	
	R	ρ	R	ρ	R	ρ	R	ρ	R	ρ	R	ρ	R	ρ	R	ρ	R	ρ	R	ρ	R	ρ	R	ρ
Lsh	.55	.57	.52	.56	.49	.54	.46	.52	.51	.55	.46	.54	.44	.52	.42	.48	.48	.58	.45	.52	.42	.49	.40	.47
Irp	.40	.53	.37	.53	.35	.54	.34	.51	.29	.50	.27	.51	.25	.51	.24	.47	.26	.57	.24	.49	.23	.48	.22	.45
Pleb	.54	.58	.50	.59	.46	.56	.43	.54	.46	.58	.42	.56	.38	.53	.36	.51	.44	.57	.40	.56	.36	.52	.33	.49
Fast-Pleb	.53	.58	.49	.56	.45	.55	.42	.53	.46	.56	.41	.56	.37	.54	.35	.51	.43	.57	.38	.55	.35	.52	.32	.50

Table 5: Evaluation results on comparing Lsh, Irp, Pleb, and Fast-Pleb with $k = 3000$, $b = 40$, $p = 1000$ and $q = 10$ with exact nearest neighbors across three different data sets: **GW**, **GWB50**, and **GWB100**. We report results on recall (R) and ρ metric. The gray color row is the system that we use for further evaluations.

nearest neighbors that are found in both the lists and then Pearson's (ρ) correlation captures if the relative order of these lists is preserved in both the similarity lists. We also compute R and ρ at various $l = \{10, 25, 50, 100\}$.

Results: For the first experiment, we evaluate Irp, Pleb, and Fast-Pleb against the exact nearest neighbor similarity lists. For Irp, we sample first p rows and only use p rather than k, this ensures that all the three methods (Irp, Pleb, and Fast-Pleb) take the same query time. We vary the approximate nearest neighbor beam parameter $b = \{20, 30, 40, 50, 100\}$ that controls the number of closest neighbors for a word with respect to each independent random projection. Note, with increasing b, our algorithm approaches towards Lsh (computing Hamming distance with respect to all the words). For Fast-Pleb, we set $q = 10$ ($q << k$) that is the number of random bits selected out of k to generate p permuted bit vectors of size q. The results are reported in Table 3, where the first row compares the Lsh approach against the exact similarity list for test set words. Across three columns we compare Irp, Pleb, and Fast-Pleb. For all methods, increasing b means better recall. If we move down the table, with $b = 100$, Irp, Pleb, and Fast-Pleb get results comparable to Lsh (reaches an upper bound). However, using large b implies generating a long potential nearest neighbor list close to the size of the unique context vectors. If we focus on the gray color row with $b = 40$ (This will have comparatively *small* potential list and return nearest neighbors in *less* time), Irp has worse recall with best pre-processing time. Fast-Pleb ($q = 10$) is comparable to Pleb (using all bits $q = 3000$) with pre-processing time 300 times faster than Pleb. For rest of this work, **FLAG** will use Fast-Pleb as it has best recall and pre-processing time with fixed $b = 40$.

For the second experiment, we vary parameter $q = \{1, 5, 10, 100, 3000\}$ for Fast-Pleb in Table 4. Table 4 demonstrates using $q = \{1, 5\}$ result in worse recall, however using $q = 5$ for Fast-Pleb is better than Irp. $q = 10$ has comparable recall to $q = \{100, 3000\}$. For rest of this work, we fix $q = 10$ as it has best recall and pre-processing time.

For the third experiment, we increase the size of the data set across the Table 5. With the increase in size of the data set, Lsh, Irp, Pleb, and Fast-Pleb ($q = 10$) have worse recall. The reason for such a behavior is that the number of unique context vectors is greater for big data sets. Across all the

jazz	yale	soccer	physics	wednesday
reggae	harvard	basketball	chemistry	tuesday
rockabilly	cornell	hockey	mathematics	thursday
rock	fordham	lacrosse	biology	monday
bluegrass	rutgers	handball	biochemistry	friday
indie	dartmouth	badminton	science	saturday
baroque	nyu	softball	microbiology	sunday
ska	ucla	football	geophysics	yesterday
funk	princeton	tennis	economics	tues
banjo	stanford	wrestling	psychology	october
blues	loyola	rugby	neuroscience	week

Table 6: Sample Top 10 similarity lists returned by FAST-PLEB with $k = 3000$, $p = 1000$, $b = 40$ and $q = 10$ from **GWB100**.

three data sets, FAST-PLEB has recall comparable to PLEB with best pre-processing time. Hence, for the next evaluation to show the quality of final lists we use FAST-PLEB with $q = 10$ for **GWB100** data set.

In Table 6, we list the top 10 most similar words for some words found by our system **FLAG** using **GWB100** data set. Even though **FLAG**'s approximate nearest neighbor algorithm has less recall with respect to exact but still the quality of these nearest neighbor lists is excellent.

For the final experiment, we demonstrate the pre-processing and query time results comparing LSH, IRP, PLEB, and FAST-PLEB with $k = 3000$, $p = 1000$, $b = 40$ and $q = 10$ parameter settings. For pre-processing timing results, we perform all the experiments (averaged over 5 runs) on **GWB100** data set with 106,733 words. The second pre-processing step of the system **FLAG** (Section 3.2) that is dimensionality reduction from $\mathbb{R}^D$ to $\mathbb{R}^k$ took 8.8 hours. The pre-processing time differences among IRP, PLEB, and FAST-PLEB from third step (Section 3.3) are shown in second column of Table 7. Experimental results show that the naive baseline IRP is the fastest and FAST-PLEB has 120 times *faster pre-processing time* compared to PLEB.

For comparing query time among several methods, we evaluate over 447 words (Section 4.2). We report average timing results (averaged over 10 runs and 447 words) to find top 100 nearest neighbors for single query word. The results are shown in third column of Table 7. Comparing first and second rows show that LSH is 87 times faster than computing exact top-100 (cosine similarity) nearest neighbors. Comparing second, third, fourth and fifth rows of the table demonstrate that IRP, PLEB and FAST-PLEB

Methods	Preprocessing	Query (seconds)
Exact	n/a	87
LSH	8.8 hours	0.59
IRP	7.5 minutes	0.28
PLEB	1.8 days	0.28
FAST-PLEB	22 minutes	0.26

Table 7: Preprocessing and query time results comparing exact, LSH, IRP, PLEB, and FAST-PLEB methods on **GWB100** data set.

Language	english	chinese	japanese	spanish	russian
Place	africa	america	washington	london	pacific
Nationality	american	european	french	british	western
Date	january	may	december	october	june
Organization	ford	microsoft	sony	disneyland	google

Table 8: Query terms for Google Sets Problem evaluation

methods are twice as fast as LSH.

5 Applications

We use the graph constructed by **FLAG** from **GWB100** data set (110 GB) by applying FAST-PLEB with parameters $k = 3000$, $p = 1000$, $q = 10$ and $b = 40$. The graph has 106,733 nodes (words), with each node having 100 edges that denote the top $l = 100$ approximate nearest neighbors associated with each node. However, **FLAG** applied FAST-PLEB (approximate search) to find these neighbors. Therefore many of these edges can be noisy for our applications. Hence for each node, we only consider top 10 edges. In general for graph-based NLP problems; for example, constructing web-derived polarity lexicons (Velikovich et al., 2010), top 25 edges were used, and for unsupervised part-of-speech tagging using label propagation (Das and Petrov, 2011), top 5 edges were used.

5.1 Google Sets Problem

Google Sets problem (Ghahramani and Heller, 2005) can be defined as: given a set of query words, return top t similar words with respect to query words. To evaluate the quality of our approximate large-scale graph, we return top 25 words which have best aggregated similarity scores with respect to query words. We take 5 classes and their query terms (McIntosh and Curran, 2008) shown in Table 8 and our goal is to learn 25 *new* words which are similar with these 5 query words.

Language: german, french, estonian, hungarian, bulgarian	
Place: scandinavia, mongolia, mozambique, zambia, namibia	
Nationality: german, hungarian, estonian, latvian, lithuanian	
Date: september, february, august, july, november	
Organization: looksmart, hotbot, lycos, webcrawler, alltheweb	

Table 9: Learned terms for Google Sets Problem

Concrete seeds	car, house, tree, horse, animal man, table, bottle, woman, computer
Abstract seeds	idea, bravery, deceit, trust, dedication anger, humour, luck, inflation, honesty

Table 10: Example seeds for bootstrapping.

We conduct a manual evaluation to directly measure the quality of returned words. We recruited 1 annotator and developed annotation guidelines that instructed each recruiter to judge whether learned values are similar to query words or not. Overall the annotator found almost all the learned words to be similar to the query words. However, the algorithm can not differentiate between different senses of the word. For example, "French" can be a language and a nationality. Table 9 shows the top ranked words with respect to query words.

5.2 Learning Concrete and Abstract Words

Our goal is to automatically learn concrete and abstract words (Turney et al., 2011). We apply bootstrapping (Kozareva et al., 2008) on the word graphs by manually selecting 10 seeds for concrete and abstract words (see Table 10). We use in-degree (sum of weights of incoming edges) to compute the score for each node which has connections with known (seeds) or automatically labeled nodes, previously exploited to learn hyponymy relations from the web (Kozareva et al., 2008). We learn concrete and abstract words together (known as mutual exclusion principle in bootstrapping (Thelen and Riloff, 2002; McIntosh and Curran, 2008)), and each word is assigned to only one class. Moreover, after each iteration, we harmonically decrease the weight of the in-degree associated with instances learned in later iterations. We add 25 new instances at each iteration and ran 100 iterations of bootstrapping, yielding 2506 concrete nouns and 2498 abstract nouns. To evaluate our learned words, we searched in WordNet whether they had 'abstraction' or 'physical' as their hypernym. Out of 2506 learned concrete nouns, 1655 were found in WordNet. According to WordNet, **74**% of those are *concrete* and 26% are abstract. Out of 2498 learned abstract nouns, 942 were found in WordNet. According to WordNet, 5% of those are concrete and **95**% are *abstract*. Table 11 shows the top ranked concrete and abstract words.

Concrete: girl, person, bottles, wife, gentleman, microcomputer, neighbor, boy, foreigner, housewives, texan, granny, bartender, tables, policeman, chubby, mature, trees, mainframe, backbone, truck
Abstract: perseverance, tenacity, sincerity, professionalism, generosity, heroism, compassion, commitment, openness, resentment, treachery, deception, notion, jealousy, loathing, hurry, valour

Table 11: Learned concrete/abstract words.

6 Conclusion

We proposed a system, **FLAG** which constructs fast large-scale approximate graphs from large data sets. To build this system we proposed a distributed online-PMI algorithm that scaled up to 110 GB of web data with 866 million sentences in less than 2 days using 100 quad-core nodes. Our both intrinsic and extrinsic experiments demonstrated that online-PMI algorithm not at all loses globally good contexts and perform comparable to offline-PMI. Next, we proposed FAST-PLEB (a variant of PLEB) and empirically demonstrated that it has recall comparable to PLEB with 120 *times faster* pre-processing time. Finally, we show the applicability of **FLAG** on two applications: Google-Sets problem and learning concrete and abstract words.

In future, we will apply **FLAG** to construct graphs using several kinds of contexts like lexical, semantic, syntactic and dependency relations or a combination of them. Moreover, we will apply graph theoretic models on graphs constructed using **FLAG** for solving a large variety of NLP applications.

Acknowledgments

This work was partially supported by NSF Award IIS-1139909. Thanks to Graham Cormode and Suresh Venkatasubramanian for useful discussions and the anonymous reviewers for many helpful comments.

References

Dimitris Achlioptas. 2003. Database-friendly random projections: Johnson-lindenstrauss with binary coins. *J. Comput. Syst. Sci.*, 66(4):671–687.

Eneko Agirre, Enrique Alfonseca, Keith Hall, Jana Kravalova, Marius Paşca, and Aitor Soroa. 2009. A study on similarity and relatedness using distributional and wordnet-based approaches. In *NAACL '09: Proceedings of HLT-NAACL*.

Moses Charikar, Kevin Chen, and Martin Farach-Colton. 2004. Finding frequent items in data streams. *Theor. Comput. Sci.*, 312:3–15, January.

Moses S. Charikar. 2002. Similarity estimation techniques from rounding algorithms. In *In Proc. of 34th STOC*, pages 380–388. ACM.

K. Church and P. Hanks. 1989. Word Association Norms, Mutual Information and Lexicography. In *Proceedings of ACL*, pages 76–83, Vancouver, Canada, June.

Graham Cormode and Marios Hadjieleftheriou. 2008. Finding frequent items in data streams. In *VLDB*.

Graham Cormode and S. Muthukrishnan. 2004. An improved data stream summary: The count-min sketch and its applications. *J. Algorithms*.

Dipanjan Das and Slav Petrov. 2011. Unsupervised part-of-speech tagging with bilingual graph-based projections. In *Proceedings of the 49th Annual Meeting of the Association for Computational Linguistics: Human Language Technologies*, pages 600–609, Portland, Oregon, USA, June. Association for Computational Linguistics.

Cristian Estan and George Varghese. 2002. New directions in traffic measurement and accounting. *SIGCOMM Comput. Commun. Rev.*, 32(4).

L. Finkelstein, E. Gabrilovich, Y. Matias, E. Rivlin, Z. Solan, G. Wolfman, and E. Ruppin. 2002. Placing search in context: The concept revisited. In *ACM Transactions on Information Systems*.

Zoubin Ghahramani and Katherine A. Heller. 2005. Bayesian Sets. In *in Advances in Neural Information Processing Systems*, volume 18.

Amit Goyal and Hal Daumé III. 2011. Approximate scalable bounded space sketch for large data NLP. In *Empirical Methods in Natural Language Processing (EMNLP)*.

Amit Goyal, Hal Daumé III, and Suresh Venkatasubramanian. 2009. Streaming for large scale NLP: Language modeling. In *NAACL*.

Amit Goyal, Graham Cormode, and Hal Daumé III. 2012. Sketch algorithms for estimating point queries in NLP. In *Empirical Methods in Natural Language Processing (EMNLP)*.

D. Graff. 2003. English Gigaword. Linguistic Data Consortium, Philadelphia, PA, January.

Piotr Indyk and Rajeev Motwani. 1998. Approximate nearest neighbors: towards removing the curse of dimensionality. In *Proceedings of the thirtieth annual ACM symposium on Theory of computing*, STOC '98, pages 604–613. ACM.

Zornitsa Kozareva, Ellen Riloff, and Eduard Hovy. 2008. Semantic class learning from the web with hyponym pattern linkage graphs. In *Proceedings of ACL-08: HLT*, pages 1048–1056, Columbus, Ohio, June. Association for Computational Linguistics.

Abby Levenberg, Chris Callison-Burch, and Miles Osborne. 2010. Stream-based translation models for statistical machine translation. In *Human Language Technologies: The 2010 Annual Conference of the North American Chapter of the Association for Computational Linguistics*, HLT '10, pages 394–402. Association for Computational Linguistics.

Ping Li, Trevor J. Hastie, and Kenneth W. Church. 2006. Very sparse random projections. In *Proceedings of the 12th ACM SIGKDD international conference on Knowledge discovery and data mining*, KDD '06, pages 287–296. ACM.

Ping Li, Kenneth Ward Church, and Trevor Hastie. 2008. One sketch for all: Theory and application of conditional random sampling. In *Neural Information Processing Systems*, pages 953–960.

Tara McIntosh and James R Curran. 2008. Weighted mutual exclusion bootstrapping for domain independent lexicon and template acquisition. In *Proceedings of the Australasian Language Technology Association Workshop 2008*, pages 97–105, December.

G.A. Miller and W.G. Charles. 1991. Contextual correlates of semantic similarity. *Language and Cognitive Processes*, 6(1):1–28.

Patrick Pantel, Eric Crestan, Arkady Borkovsky, Ana-Maria Popescu, and Vishnu Vyas. 2009. Web-scale distributional similarity and entity set expansion. In *Proceedings of EMNLP*.

Delip Rao and Deepak Ravichandran. 2009. Semi-supervised polarity lexicon induction. In *Proceedings of the 12th Conference of the European Chapter of the ACL (EACL 2009)*, pages 675–682, Athens, Greece, March. Association for Computational Linguistics.

Deepak Ravichandran, Patrick Pantel, and Eduard Hovy. 2005. Randomized algorithms and nlp: using locality sensitive hash function for high speed noun clustering. In *Proceedings of ACL*.

H. Rubenstein and J.B. Goodenough. 1965. Contextual correlates of synonymy. *Computational Linguistics*, 8:627–633.

Florin Rusu and Alin Dobra. 2007. Statistical analysis of sketch estimators. In *SIGMOD '07*. ACM.

M. Thelen and E. Riloff. 2002. A Bootstrapping Method for Learning Semantic Lexicons Using Extraction Pattern Contexts. In *Proceedings of the Empirical Methods in Natural Language Processing*, pages 214–221.

Peter D. Turney and Patrick Pantel. 2010. From frequency to meaning: Vector space models of semantics. *JOURNAL OF ARTIFICIAL INTELLIGENCE RESEARCH*, 37:141.

Peter Turney, Yair Neuman, Dan Assaf, and Yohai Cohen. 2011. Literal and metaphorical sense identification through concrete and abstract context. In *Proceedings of the 2011 Conference on Empirical Methods in Natural Language Processing*, pages 680–690. Association for Computational Linguistics.

Benjamin Van Durme and Ashwin Lall. 2009a. Probabilistic counting with randomized storage. In *IJCAI'09: Proceedings of the 21st international jont conference on Artifical intelligence*.

Benjamin Van Durme and Ashwin Lall. 2009b. Streaming pointwise mutual information. In *Advances in Neural Information Processing Systems 22*.

Benjamin Van Durme and Ashwin Lall. 2010. Online generation of locality sensitive hash signatures. In *Proceedings of the ACL 2010 Conference Short Papers*, pages 231–235, July.

Benjamin Van Durme and Ashwin Lall. 2011. Efficient online locality sensitive hashing via reservoir counting. In *Proceedings of the ACL 2011 Conference Short Papers*, June.

Leonid Velikovich, Sasha Blair-Goldensohn, Kerry Hannan, and Ryan McDonald. 2010. The viability of web-derived polarity lexicons. In *Human Language Technologies: The 2010 Annual Conference of the North American Chapter of the Association for Computational Linguistics*, pages 777–785, Los Angeles, California, June. Association for Computational Linguistics.

Kilian Weinberger, Anirban Dasgupta, John Langford, Alex Smola, and Josh Attenberg. 2009. Feature hashing for large scale multitask learning. In *Proceedings of the 26th Annual International Conference on Machine Learning*, ICML '09, pages 1113–1120. ACM.

Building a Lightweight Semantic Model for Unsupervised Information Extraction on Short Listings

Doo Soon Kim
Accenture Technology Lab
50 W San Fernando St.,
San Jose, CA, 95113

Kunal Verma
Accenture Technology Lab
50 W San Fernando St.,
San Jose, CA, 95113

Peter Z. Yeh
Accenture Technology Lab
50 W San Fernando St.,
San Jose, CA, 95113

{doo.soon.kim, k.verma, peter.z.yeh}@accenture.com

Abstract

Short listings such as classified ads or product listings abound on the web. If a computer can reliably extract information from them, it will greatly benefit a variety of applications. Short listings are, however, challenging to process due to their informal styles. In this paper, we present an unsupervised information extraction system for short listings. Given a corpus of listings, the system builds a semantic model that represents typical objects and their attributes in the domain of the corpus, and then uses the model to extract information. Two key features in the system are a semantic parser that extracts objects and their attributes and a listing-focused clustering module that helps group together extracted tokens of same type. Our evaluation shows that the semantic model learned by these two modules is effective across multiple domains.

1 Introduction

Short listings such as classified ads or product listings are prevalent on the web. These texts are generally concise – around 10 words in length. Fig. 1 shows some example listings. Due to the recent explosive growth of such listings, extracting information from them becomes crucial for tasks such as faceted search and reasoning. For example, consider an online shopping site on which information about merchandises for sale is posted. Detecting brands/styles/features that are frequently mentioned in the postings would allow a company to design a better marketing strategy.

Most Information Extraction (IE) techniques developed for formal texts, however, would be inapplicable to listings because of their informal and idiosyncratic styles. For example, typos, abbreviations and synonyms often appear and should be resolved (e.g., *apartment/apt*, *bike/bicycle*). Symbols could have the special meanings (e.g., x in *2x2* in Fig. 1 indicates number of bedrooms and bathrooms). Tokenization based only on space is insufficient (e.g., *RawlingBaseball* in Fig. 1). Multiwords such as *granite top* should also be detected. Applying off-the-shelf parsers is infeasible because of unusual phrasal forms in most listings, such as a long sequence of nouns/adjectives (e.g., *"New Paint Wood Floors New Windows Gated Complex"*)

To address these challenges, several approaches have applied machine learning algorithms (Ghani et al., 2006) (Putthividhya and Hu, 2011) or an external knowledge base (Michelson and Knoblock, 2005). These approaches, however, commonly require human supervision to produce training data or to build a knowledge base. This is expensive, requiring repeated manual effort whenever a new domain or a new set of information to be extracted is introduced.

In this paper, we present an unsupervised IE system for listings. The system extracts tokens from a corpus of listings and then clusters tokens of the same types, where each resulting cluster corresponds to an information type (e.g., size, brand, etc.). For formal texts, contexts (e.g., surrounding words) have been a major feature for word clustering (Turney and Pantel, 2010). This feature alone, however, is insufficient for short listings because of lack of contextual clues in short listings.

2x2 Charming Condo – 1515 Martin Avenue near Downtown (from Craigslist)	HousingType: *Condo*, BedroomNum: *2*, BathroomNum: *2*, Location: *1515 Martin Avenue*, Neighborhood: *Downtown*
RawlingsBaseball Gloves Pro Preferred Black 12" (from EBay)	ProductType: *Gloves*, Brand: *Rawlings*, Sport: *Baseball*, Color: *Black*, Size: *12"*, SeriesName: *Pro Preferred*
LG 32" 1080p LCD TV – \$329 @ BestBuy (from FatWallet)	Product Type: *TV*, Brand: *Panasonic*, Size: *32"*, Resolution : *1080P*, DisplayTechnology: *LCD*, Price *329\$*, Seller: *Best Buy*

Figure 1: Example short listings and the information extracted from them.

To address this limitation of context-based clustering, we first identify common types of information (main objects and their attributes) represented in listings and apply customized clustering for these types. Specifically, we define a semantic model to explicitly represent these information types, and based on the semantic model, develop two components to improve clustering – a shallow semantic parser and listing-focused clustering module. The semantic parser specifically focuses on extracting main objects and the listing-focused clustering module helps group together extracted tokens of the same type.

Our evaluation shows that our two main contributions (shallow semantic parser and listing-focused clustering) significantly improve performance across three different domains – Craigslist, EBay, and FatWallet. Our system achieves .50∼.65 F1-score for the EBay and the FatWallet datasets based on gold standards constructed by human annotators. For the Craigslist dataset, which is more difficult than the other two, F1-score is .35.

2 Related Work

IE on Listings. (Ghani et al., 2006) (Putthividhya and Hu, 2011) propose semi-supervised approaches to extract product types and their attributes from product listings. (Ghani et al., 2006) applies the EM (Expectation-Maximization) algorithm to incorporate unlabelled data. (Putthividhya and Hu, 2011) uses unlabelled data to build dictionaries of values to be extracted (e.g., brand or model names), which are then used as a feature for a machine learning system. (Michelson and Knoblock, 2005) uses a manually-crafted knowledge base called *reference set* to define standard forms of values to be extracted. Using a string edit function, the system then identifies tokens in listings that have a low distance score with the values defined in the reference set. They also propose a semi-supervised method to building reference sets (Michelson and Knoblock, 2009).Unlike these systems, our approach is unsupervised.

Unsupervised Information Extraction. Most unsupervised IE systems produce clusters for tokens of same type extracted from a corpus of unlabelled texts. (Chambers and Jurafsky, 2011) (Poon and Domingos, 2010) (Chen et al., 2011) focus on extracting frame-like structures (Baker et al., 1998) by defining two types of clusters, event clusters and role clusters. Event clusters define an event (a situation or a frame) such as BOMBING by clustering verbs/nominalized verbs such as {*kill*, *explosion*}. Role clusters define the semantic roles of the event (e.g., {*terrorist*, *gunman*} for the Perpetrator role in BOMBING). Similarly, our system defines two types of clusters – the main concept clusters (e.g., TV or book) and the attribute clusters (e.g., size, color). (Chambers and Jurafsky, 2011) is similar to our approach in that it learns a semantic model, called *template*, from unlabelled news articles and then uses the template to extract information.

Our system is different because it focuses on informal listings, which the components (such as a parser) used by these systems cannot handle.

Field Segmentation (Sequence Modelling). This task focuses on segmenting a short text, such as bibliographies or listings. (Grenager et al., 2005) presents an unsupervised HMM based on the observation that the segmented fields tend to be of multiple words length. (Haghighi and Klein, 2006) exploits prototype words (e.g., *close*, *near*, *shopping* for the NEIGHBORHOOD attribute) in an unsupervised setting. (Chang et al., 2007) incorporates domain specific constraints in semi-supervised learning. Our task is different than these systems because we focus on extracting information to enable a variety of automated applications such as business intelligence reporting, faceted search or automated reasoning, rather than segmenting the text. The segmented fields are often a long unstructured text (e.g., *2 bath 1 bed* for size rather than 2 for BathroomNum and 1 for BedroomNum).

IE on Informal Texts. IE on informal texts is getting much attention because of the recent explosive growth of these texts. The informal texts that are attempted for IE include online forums (Gruhl et al., 2009), SMS (Beaufort et al., 2010), twitter messages (Liu et al., 2011).

3 Our Approach

Given a corpus of listings for a domain of interest, our system constructs a semantic model that represents the types of information and their values to be extracted. Our system then uses the resulting model to extract both the type and value from the corpus [1].

We first describe the semantic model and then the two key steps for creating this model – shallow semantic parsing and listing-focused clustering. Fig. 3 illustrates these two steps with example listings.

3.1 Semantic Model

Our semantic model captures two important pieces of information – the main concept and its attributes. This representation is based on the observation that most listings (e.g. rentals, products) describe the attributes of a single object (i.e. the main concept in our model). Our system takes advantage of this observation by applying customized clustering for each type of information in the model, which results in better performance compared to a *one-size-fits-all* algorithm. Moreover, this model is general enough to be applicable across a wide range of domains. We quantitatively show both benefits in our evaluation.

Fig. 2 illustrates our model along with an instantiation for rental listings. The main concept is a cluster containing tokens referencing the main object in the listing. For example, in the rental listing, the main concept cluster includes tokens such as *house*, *condo*, and *townhouse*.

Each attribute of the main concept (e.g. Address, BedroomNum, etc.) is also a cluster, and two types

[1]To handle string variations (e.g., typos) during extraction, our system uses a string edit distance function, Jaro-Winkler distance (Winkler, 1990) with a threshold, 0.9.

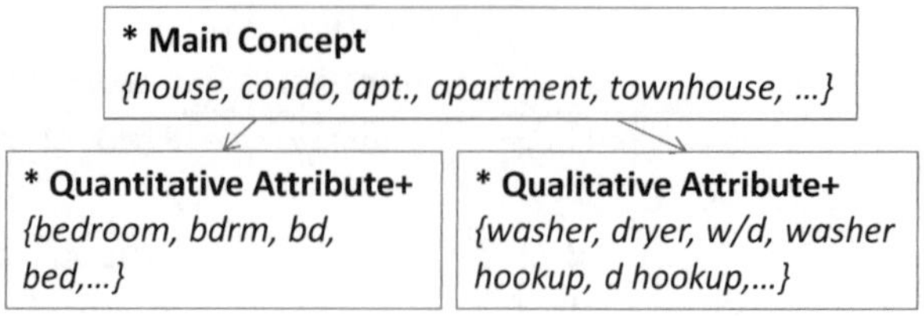

Figure 2: Semantic model and its instantiation for rental listings. + indicates multiple clusters can be created.

of attributes are defined in our model – quantitative attributes and qualitative ones. Quantitative attributes capture numeric values (e.g. *1 bedroom*, *150 Hz*, and *70 kg*), and are generally a number followed by a token indicating the attribute (e.g., unit of measurement). Hence, clusters for quantitative attributes include these indicator tokens (see Fig. 2).

Qualitative attributes capture descriptions about the main concept (e.g., address, shipping information, condition). The values of these attributes generally appear in listings without explicitly mentioning the names of these attributes. Hence, the clusters for qualitative attributes include tokens corresponding to the values themselves (e.g. *washer hookup*).

3.2 Shallow Semantic Parser

Our Shallow Semantic Parser (SSP) analyzes an input corpus to produce a partial semantic model. SSP first performs preprocessing and multiword detection. SSP then identifies which resulting tokens are the main concepts and which are their attributes.

3.2.1 Preprocessing and Multiword Detection

SSP preprocesses the corpus through three steps. (1) SSP cleans the corpus by removing duplicate listings and HTML expressions/tags. (2) SSP tokenizes each listing based on spaces along with custom heuristics – e.g., handling alpha-numeric tokens starting with numbers (e.g., *3bedroom* to *3 bedroom*) and mixed case tokens (e.g., *NikeShoes* to *Nike Shoes*). (3) SSP performs POS tagging using an off-the-shelf tagger (Tsuruoka and Tsujii, 2005). To improve accuracy, SSP assigns to a token the most frequent POS across all occurrences of that token. This heuristic works well because most tokens in focused domains, like listings, have only one POS.

SSP then detects multiword tokens based on the following rules:

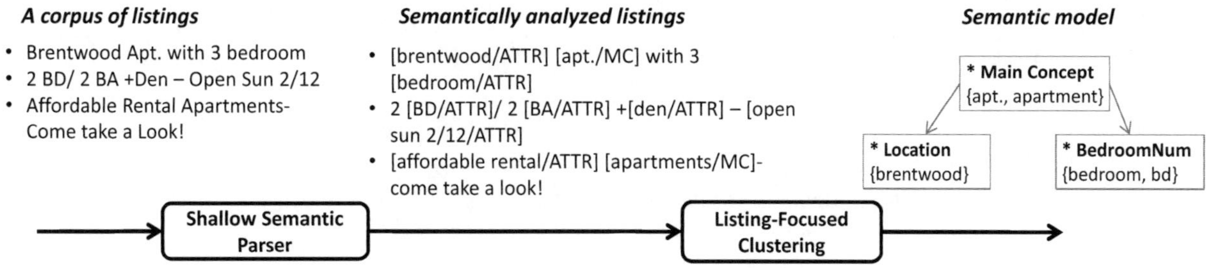

Figure 3: Steps of our system: The parser tokenizes listings (multiword detection) and then identifies main concepts and attributes (marked as MC and ATTR). The clustering module then clusters tokens of the same type. The tags (such as Location, BedroomNum) are included to help understand the figure. They are not produced by the system.

1. If a bigram (e.g., *top floor*) in a listing frequently appears as either a single or dashed token (e.g., *TopFloor* or *top-floor*) in other listings, then the bigram is regarded as a multiword.

2. For each bigram, w_1 w_2 (excluding symbols and numbers), if the conditional probability of the bigram given either w_1 or w_2 (i.e., $p(w_1 w_2 \mid w_1(or\ w_2))$ is high (over 0.75 in our system)), the bigram is considered as a candidate multiword. This rule tests the tendency of two tokens appearing together when either one appears.

However, this test alone is insufficient, as it often generates coarse-grained results – e.g., *baseball glove*, *softball glove*, and *Hi-Def TV* [2]. To prevent this problem, for each w_2, we measure the entropy over the distribution of the tokens in the w_1 position. Our intuition is that high variability in the w_1 position (i.e., high entropy) indicates that the multiword is likely a breakable phrase. Hence, those candidates with high entropy are removed.

SPP repeatedly applies the above rules to acquire multiwords of arbitrary length. In our implementation, we limit multiword detection up to four-gram.

3.2.2 Main Concept Identification

SSP then identifies the main concepts (*mc_words*) and their attributes (*attrs*) to produce a partial semantic model. This process is guided by the observation that main concepts tend to appear as head nouns in a listing and attributes as the modifiers of these head nouns (see the examples in Fig. 3).

[2]Even though these examples are legitimate multiwords, they overlook useful information such as baseball and softball are types of gloves and Hi-Def is an attribute of TV.

Algorithm 1 describes the discovery process of *mc_words* and *attrs*. First, SSP initializes *attrs* with tokens that are likely to be a modifier (line 2), by choosing tokens that frequently appear as the object of a preposition within the corpus – e.g., *for rent*, *with washer and dryer*, *for baseball*.

SSP then iteratively performs two steps – PARSE and EXPANDMODEL (lines 3 $\sim$ 6) – in a bootstrap manner (see Fig. 4). PARSE tags the noun tokens in each listing as either head nouns or modifiers. Specifically, PARSE first assesses if a listing is "hard" to parse (line 10) based on two criteria – (1) the listing contains a long sequence of nouns (seven words or longer in our system) without any prepositions (e.g., *worth shutout series 12" womens fastpitch softball fielders glove s0120 lefty*); and (2) the majority of these nouns do not appear in *mc_words* and *attrs* (e.g., over 70% in our system). The listings meeting these criteria are generally difficult to recognize the head noun without any semantic knowledge. PARSE will revisit these listings in the next round as more *mc_words* and *attrs* are identified.

If a listing does not meet these criteria, PARSE tags nouns appearing in *mc_words* and *attrs* as head nouns and modifiers respectively (line 11). If this step fails to recognize a head noun, a heuristic is used to identify the head noun – it identifies the first noun phrase by finding a sequence of nouns/adjectives/numbers, and then tags as the head noun the last noun in the phrase that is not tagged as a modifier (line 13). For example, in the first listing of Fig. 3, *brentwood apts.* is the first noun phrase that meets the condition above; and hence *apt.* is tagged as the head noun. The remaining untagged nouns in the listing are tagged as modifiers (line 15).

Algorithm 1 Extracting main concepts

```
Input: POS-tagged corpus, corp
Initialize attrs
repeat
    (hn,mod) = Parse(corp, mc_words, attrs)
    (mc_words,attrs) = ExpandModel(hn,mod)
until mc_words, attrs not changed

function PARSE(mc_words, attrs)
    for all each listing do
        if parsible then
            Parse with mc_words, attrs
            if headnoun is not tagged then
                Tag the last noun in the first noun phrase that are not a modifier as hn
            end if
            Tag the other nouns as mod
        end if
    end for
end function

function EXPANDMODEL(corp)
    For each token, calculate a ratio of as a head noun to as a modifier
    Add tokens with high ratio to mc_words
    Add tokens with low ratio to attrs
end function
```

EXPANDMODEL assigns tokens to either *mc_words* or *attrs* based on the tags generated by PARSE. For each token, EXPANDMODEL counts the frequency of the token being tagged as a head noun and as a modifier. If a token is predominately tagged as a head noun (or a modifier), the token is added to *mc_words* (or *attrs*) [3].

This bootstrap method is advantageous [4] because SSP can initially focus on easy cases – i.e., *mc_words* and *attrs* that can be detected with high confidence, such as *condo(mc_words)* and *bedroom(attrs)*, which often appear as a head noun and a modifier in the easy-to-parse listings. These results can help the system to parse more difficult listings. For example, identifying *condo(mc_words)* helps parsing the following more difficult listing, *"2 bedroom 1 bathroom condo large patio washer dryer available"* – *condo* would be tagged as a head noun and the rest of the nouns as modifiers.

The result of this step is a partial semantic model that contains a cluster for the main concept and a list of candidate attribute tokens.

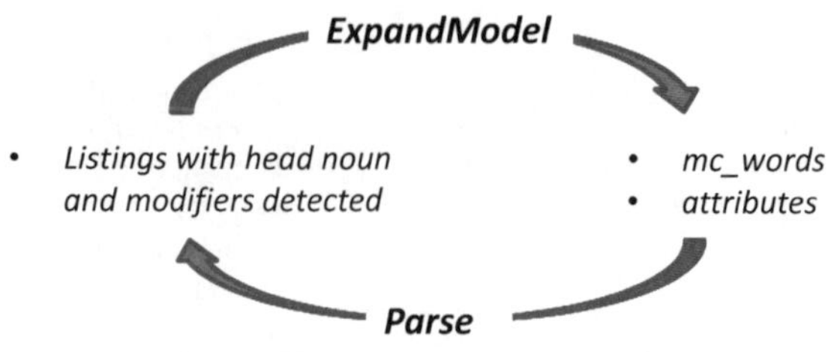

Figure 4: Bootstrapped PARSE and EXPANDMODEL

3.3 Listing-Focused Clustering

Listing-Focused Clustering (LFC) further expands the partial semantic model (constructed by SSP) by grouping the remaining candidate attribute tokens into attribute clusters – i.e. one cluster for each attribute of the main concept. LFC may also add a token to the main concept cluster if appropriate.

For formal texts, distributional similarity is widely used for clustering words because the contextual clues in these texts are sufficiently discriminative (Lin and Pantel, 2001). This feature alone, however, is insufficient for listings because they lack discriminative contexts due to the short length. Hence, our approach augments context-based similarity with the following rules (presented in order of precedence), based on general properties we observed from listing data across various domains.

- Two quantitative attribute tokens cannot be placed into the same cluster if they frequently appear together in a listing. For example, *bed* and *bath* should not be clustered because they frequently appear together (e.g. *2 bed / 2bath*). This rule is based on the observation that a quantitative attribute is likely to appear only once in a listing. To enforce this restriction, for all pairs of tokens, t_1 and t_2, LFC measures the conditional probability of the pair appearing together in a listing given the appearance of either

[3]In our system, if the ratio of the frequency of the head noun to the frequency of the modifier is over .55, the token is added to *mc_words*. If less than .35, it is added to *attrs*.

[4]The bootstrapping cycle generally ends within 3∼4 iterations.

t_1 and t_2. If any of these conditional probabilities are high, t_1 and t_2 are not clustered.

- Attribute types are strongly enforced by never clustering together a quantitative attribute token and a qualitative attribute token. The type of a token is determined by analyzing the immediate preceding tokens throughout the corpus. If the preceding tokens are generally numbers, then LFC regards the token as a quantitative attribute. Otherwise, the token is regarded as a qualitative attribute.
- Two tokens are similar if the characters in one token appear in the other, preserving the order (e.g., *bdrm* and *bedroom*)

If the above rules fail to determine the similarity between two tokens, LFC reverts to context-based similarity. For each token, LFC creates a context vector containing frequencies of the context words around the token with a window size of two. For example, in the first sentence in Fig. 3, the context words around *apts.* are *l-start* (beginning of the sentence), *l-brentwood*, *r-with*, and *r-3* [5]. The frequencies in these vectors are also weighted using PMI scores (pointwise mutual information) between a token and its context words, as suggested by (Turney and Pantel, 2010). The intuition is that a high PMI indicates a context word is strongly associated with a token and hence has high discriminative power. We also apply a smoothing function suggested in (Turney and Pantel, 2010) to mitigate PMI's bias towards infrequent events. The similarity score is based on a cosine similarity between the two weighted vectors.

Based on this similarity function, LFC applies agglomerative clustering (with average linkage) to produce attribute clusters (or to expand the main concept cluster). However, calculating similarity scores for all pairs of tokens is expensive. To address this problem, LFC performs clustering in two steps. First, LFC performs agglomerative clustering on all pairs of tokens with high frequency [6]. LFC then calculates the similarity between each low-frequency token and the clusters resulting from the previous step. If the similarity score is over a user-specified threshold, then LFC addes the token to the cluster. If the score is less than the threshold but the token still appears relatively frequently, then LFC creates a new cluster for the token.

[5] *l* and *r* indicates the left or right window.

[6] The threshold for stopping clustering is determined with the development dataset.

Dataset	Dev	Test	Avg word
Rent Ad	8,950	9,400	9.44
Glove	8,600	9,500	10.56
TV Deal	-	900	15.60

Table 1: **Dev/Test** indicates the number of listings used for development/testing. **Avg word** indicates the average number of words in a listing. The development dataset is used to tune the parameters.

4 Evaluation

We perform two evaluations to assess the performance of our approach. First, we evaluate how well our approach extracts the correct type (e.g., BedroomNum) and value (e.g., 2) across multiple domains. Next, we evaluate the contribution of each main component in our approach – i.e., shallow semantic parsing and listing-focused clustering – through an ablation study. We also provide an in-depth error analysis along with how our system's performance is affected by the corpus size.

4.1 Evaluation Setup

We first assemble three different listing datasets for our evaluation – housing rental advertisements from Craigslist (Rent Ad), auction listings of baseball gloves from EBay (Glove), and hot deal postings of TV/Projector from FatWallet (TV Deal) [7]. Table 1 shows the size of each dataset, and example listings are shown in Fig. 1 [8]. We also include example extractions for each domain in Table. 3.

We then construct a gold standard by employing two independent human annotators. To do this, we first define the information types (i.e. main concept and attribute) for each dataset (and hence the targets for extraction). We use attributes from EBay

[7] The datasets are available at `https://sites.google.com/site/2soonk/`

[8] The parameters were tuned by the development set. Our system is sensitive to the similarity score threshold in agglomerative clustering but less sensitive to the other parameters. Hence, we tuned the similarity threshold for each domain while fixing the values for the other parameters across different domains.

Rent Ad	housing_type (.70/.93), num_bedroom (.94/.99), num_bathroom (.97/1), location (-.64/.82), neighborhood (.55/.79), others(14 types)
Glove	product_type (.71/1.00), brand (.58/.98), sport (.71/1.00), size (.87/.99), series_name (.51/.77), others(10 types)
TV Deal	product_type (.98/1.00), size (.85/1.00), display_technology (.93/1.00), resolution (.89/.99), seller (.73/1.00), others(14 types)

Table 2: Information types for each domain. See Fig. 1 for the examples of each type. Due to space limitation, we show only top five types in terms of the number of extractions made by the annotators. The parentheses indicate inter-annotator agreement based on exact match between two annotators (first number) and partial match (second number). Exact agreement for qualitative attributes (e.g., location, neighborhood, series_name) is found to be difficult.

Rent Ad	housing_type	studio, townhome, condo, townhouse, cottage,
	num_bedroom	bd, bed, br, bedroom, bdrm, bedrooms
	neighborhood	downtown, San Francisco, china town
Glove	product_type	mitt, base mitt, glove, glove mitt
	size	", inch, in
	brand	rawlings, louisville slugger, mizuno, wilson
TV Deal	product_type	hdtv, wall mount, monitor
	size	", inch
	seller	wallmart, amazon, newegg, best buy

Table 3: Examples of positive extractions for the main concept attributes (e.g., housing_type, product_type), the qualitative attributes (e.g., num_bedroom, size) and the quantitative attributes (e.g., neighborhood, brand, seller) used in the experiment

as the starting point for Glove and TV Deal; and attributes from Rent.com[9] for Rent Ad. We review these attributes with two independent Subject Matter Experts (SMEs) to identify (and include) additional, missing attributes that are useful for analytics and reporting. In total, 19 types (Rent Ad), 15 types (Glove) and 19 types (TV Deal) are defined. For each dataset, we randomly select 100 listings from the *Test* listings, and instruct each annotator to extract values from these listings, based on the information types for the dataset. Table 2 shows the defined attributes of each data set and the inter-annotator agreement across the attributes [10].

Finally, we apply our system to the *Test* listings in each dataset; and evaluate the extraction results against the gold standards using the metrics of precision (P), recall (R), and F1-score (a harmonic mean of precision and recall). Each extraction result is a tuple (T_i, v_i) where T_i is the information type (e.g., BedroomNum) and v_i is the value (e.g. 2).

$$\text{P} = \frac{\text{\# correct extractions by our system}}{\text{Total \# extractions by our system}}$$

$$\text{R} = \frac{\text{\# correct extractions by our system}}{\text{Total \# extractions by an annotator}}$$

We say that an extraction result is correct if v_i matches exactly the value extracted by the annotator and T_i matches the information type assigned to v_i by the annotator. To enforce this criteria, we match the attribute clusters produced by our system to the information types. This matching step is needed because our approach is unsupervised and hence the clusters are unlabelled. We use two methods for this matching step – many-to-one mapping and one-to-one mapping. For many-to-one mapping (as used in (Chen et al., 2011)), we match an attribute cluster to the information type whose values (as extracted by the annotator) have the highest overlap with the

[9] `http://www.rent.com`

[10] We use Cohen's kappa, $\frac{P(a)-P(e)}{1-P(e)}$. P(a), the agreement probability, is calculated by the number of listings in which the two annotators agree divided by 100. P(e), the chance agreement probability, is calculated by $\sum_{(T_i,v_i)} P_1((T_i, v_i)) * P_2((T_i, v_i))$ in which $P_j((T_i, v_i))$ denotes a probability of extracting v_i of the type T_i by the annotator j. $P((T_i, v_i))$ is calculated by the frequency of (T_i, v_i) extracted divided by the frequency of T_i extracted.

values of the cluster. Hence, many attribute clusters can map to the same information type. This method, however, has one major disadvantage: high performance can be easily achieved by creating small-sized clusters – e.g., singleton clusters in the extreme case. To mitigate this problem, we also use a one-to-one mapping method – i.e. at most one attribute cluster (i.e. the one with the best overlap) can be mapped to one information type.

We report results for both methods. We also report results for partial matches using the same metrics above. We say that an extraction result is partially correct if v_i partially matches the value extracted by the annotator (*hardwood* vs. *hardwood floors*) and T_i matches the information type assigned to v_i by the annotator. [11]

4.2 Performance Across Multiple Domains

Table 4 shows the system performance result across the domains. Considering our approach is unsupervised, the result is encouraging. For the baseball glove and the TV dataset, F-score is .51 and .66 (in one-to-one mapping). For the rent ad, which is more difficult, F-score is .39. We hypothesize that the low F1-score in the rent ad dataset is the result of poor extraction due to spurious tokens (e.g., *our community, this weather*). To test this hypothesis, we measure the performance of our system only on the extraction task (i.e., excluding the information type assignment task). Table 5 shows that the performance on extraction for the rent ad dataset is the lowest, confirming our hypothesis.

We also measure the performance per each information type. Fig. 5 shows the result, revealing several facts. First, the main concept clusters (housing_type and product_type) achieve a high F1-score, showing the benefit of our semantic parser. Second, the quantitative attributes (e.g., num_bedroom, glove_size, screen_size) generally have a higher F1 than the qualitative attributes (e.g., location, neighborhood, series_name). These qualitative attributes, in fact, have a low inter-annotator agreement (e.g., -.64, .55 for location and neighborhood in Rent Ad and .51 for series_name in Glove), indicating the difficulty of exactly predicting the extractions made by the annotators. If we consider the partial match or the extraction only match (Ext) for those qualitative attributes, their F1-scores are significantly higher than the exact match in the Full task.

[11] We could not compare our system to other systems for several reasons. First, to the best of our knowledge, no unsupervised IE system has been built specifically for short listings. Second, semi-supervised systems such as (Putthividhya and Hu, 2011) (Michelson and Knoblock, 2005) require domain-specific dictionaries, which are expensive to build and scale. Third, even developing a supervised IE system is non-trivial. In our preliminary evaluation with the (linear chain) conditional random field (170/30 training/testing listings) using basic features (the lexemes and POS of the current word and words in the two left/right windows), precision/recall/F1-score are .5/.33/.4. This result is no better than our system. More training data and/or better features seem to be required.

	Full			Full(Par)		
	P	R	F	P	R	F
Rent Ad	0.3	0.41	0.35	0.43	0.55	0.48
(302/219)	0.34	0.46	0.39	0.65	0.69	0.67
Glove	0.54	0.48	0.51	0.72	0.58	0.64
(563/631)	0.57	0.51	0.54	0.81	0.65	0.72
TV Deal	0.7	0.63	0.66	0.81	0.7	0.75
(765/851)	0.74	0.67	0.7	0.86	0.74	0.79

Table 4: Performance based on one-to-one (first row) and many-to-one mappings (second row) combined across both annotators. Full indicates exact match between system's extraction and annotators' extraction. (Par) indicates partial match. The parentheses indicate the total number of extraction made by our system and the annotators (averaged) respectively.

	Full	Full(Par)	Ext	Ext(Par)
Rent Ad	0.35	0.48	0.42	0.58
Glove	0.51	0.64	0.62	0.69
TV Deal	0.66	0.75	0.75	0.77

Table 5: F1-score when considering only extraction task (Ext and Ext(Par)). Ext(Par) is based on partial match.

4.3 Ablation Study

To evaluate our semantic parser and listing-focused clustering module, we ablate these two components to create four versions of our system for comparison – Baseline, Baseline+LFC, Baseline+SSP and Full System. Baseline performs a space-based tokenization followed by clustering based only on the context feature. Baseline+LFC and Baseline+SSP add listing-focused clustering and shallow semantic parser features respectively. The Full system uses both features.

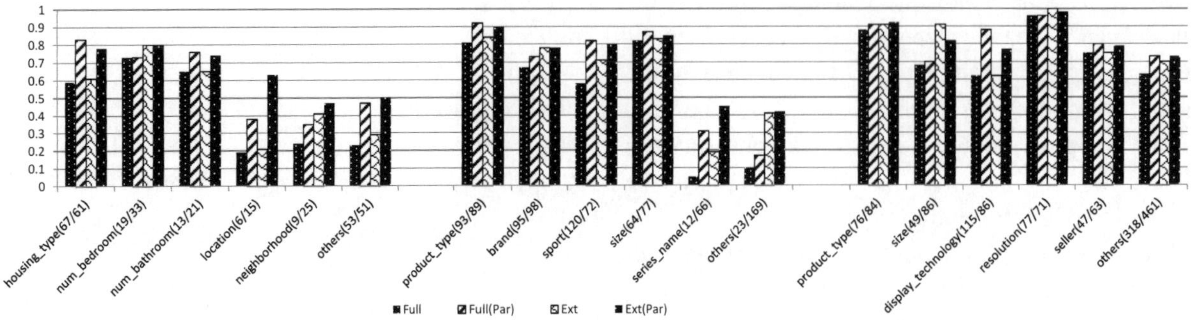

Figure 5: F1-score across the attribute types shown in Table 2. The parentheses indicate the number of extractions made by our system and the annotators respectively.

		Rent Ad			Glove			TV Deal		
		P	R	F	P	R	F	P	R	F
Full	Baseline	0.10	0.27	0.14	0.26	0.34	0.29	0.42	0.51	0.46
	Baseline+LFC	0.11	0.30	0.16	**0.30**†	**0.39**†	0.34	0.42	0.51	0.46
	Baseline+SSP	**0.21***	**0.37***	0.26	**0.46***	**0.47***	0.46	**0.65***	**0.59***	0.62
	Full System	**0.30** *	**0.41** *	0.35	**0.54** *	**0.48** *	0.51	**0.70** *	**0.63** *	0.66
Full(Par)	Baseline	0.15	0.40	0.22	0.37	0.50	0.42	0.59	0.69	0.63
	Baseline+SSP	0.15	0.43	0.22	**0.44***	**0.56***	0.49	0.59	0.69	0.63
	Baseline+LFC	**0.39***	**0.55***	0.46	0.37	*0.34*	0.35	**0.79***	0.69	0.73
	Full System	**0.43** *	**0.55** *	0.48	**0.72** *	**0.58** *	0.64	**0.81** *	0.70	0.75

Table 6: Based on one-to-one mapping. * indicates two-tail statistically significant difference ($p < 0.05$) against Baseline in Fisher's test. † indicates one-tail difference. The Fisher's test is inapplicable to F1-scores.

Rent Ad		Glove		TV Deal	
NOT IN MAPPING	0.42	NOT IN MAPPING	0.27	NOT_IN_MAPPING	0.33
WRONG EXT	0.25	WRONG EXT	0.16	WRONG EXT	0.20
TK-neighborhood	0.05	WRONG TYPE	0.15	TK-display_technology	0.13
TK-housing_type	0.05	TK-series_name	0.13	TK-shipping_info	0.07
TK-location	0.03	TK-dexterity	0.12	WRONG TYPE	0.07

Table 7: The top five errors based on the one-to-one mapping.

The results shown in Table 6 lead to the following observations. First, the use of SSP (Baseline+SSP) makes an improvement for all categories except Full(Par) in the glove dataset. This is because SSP identifies main concepts accurately. Second, while LFC by itself (Bseline+LFC) is effective only in the glove dataset, it has the best F1-score in all three domains when combined with SSP (Full System). The result also shows that the simple space-based tokenization and the context-based clustering (Baseline) is insufficient for handling short listings.

4.4 Error Analysis and Corpus Size Effect

We analyze the error types for the wrong extraction made by our system. Specifically, for each error, we assign it to one (or more) of the following causes: (1) a cluster (and hence attribute type) was excluded due to the 1-to-1 mapping methodology described above (NOT IN MAPPING); (2) the value extracted by the system was not extracted by any of the annotators (WRONG EXT); (3) wrong information type – i.e., the token belonged to a wrong cluster (WRONG TYPE); (4) incorrect tokenization for an information type (TK-<type name>).

Table 7 shows the result. In all three domains, NOT IN MAPPING is a major source of error, indicating the system's clusters are too fine-grained as compared to the gold standard. WRONG EXT is another source of error (especially in the housing rental), indicating the system should extract more informative tokens. Tokenization on the qualitative attributes (neighborhood, series name, display technology in Table 7) should be improved also.

Finally, we measure the effect of the corpus size on the system performance. Fig. 6 shows how the F1-score varies with the corpus size [12]. It shows that a small corpus size is sufficient for achieving good performance. We hypothesize that, for focused domains such as our dataset, only a couple of hundred listings are sufficient to acquire meaningful statistics.

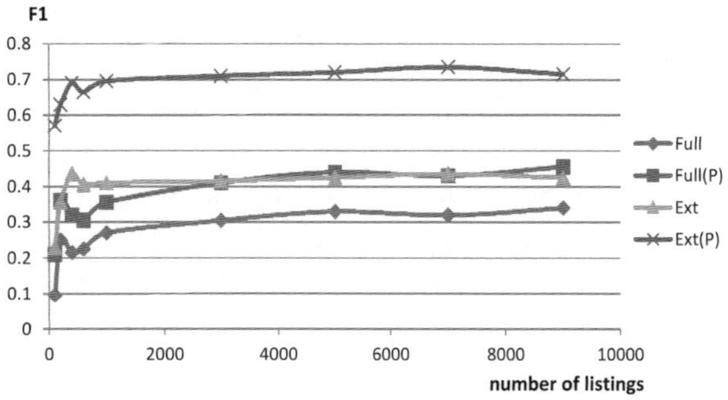

Figure 6: F1-score of our system over varying corpus size for the rent domain

5 Conclusion and Future Work

We presented an unsupervised IE system on short listings. The key features in our system are a shallow semantic parser and a listing-focused clustering module. Our evaluation shows the benefits of the two features across multiple domains. To improve our system further, we plan the following works.

First, we plan to compare our system with supervised systems to identify the gap between the two systems. Second, as in (Poon and Domingos, 2010), we plan to explore a joint learning method to combine the tasks of tokenization, forming the main concept cluster and forming the attribute clusters; these tasks depend on the outputs of one another. Finally, we plan to explore that external knowledge resources such as DBPedia (Auer et al., 2007) and FreeBase (Bollacker et al., 2008) can be used to further improve performance.

6 Acknowledgements

We would like to thank Colin Puri and Rey Vasquez for their contribution to this work. We also thank the anonymous reviewers for their helpful comments and suggestions for improving the paper.

References

Sören Auer, Christian Bizer, Georgi Kobilarov, Jens Lehmann, Richard Cyganiak, and Zachary Ives. 2007. Dbpedia: a nucleus for a web of open data. In *Proceedings of the 6th international The semantic web and 2nd Asian conference on Asian semantic web conference*, ISWC'07/ASWC'07, pages 722–735, Berlin, Heidelberg. Springer-Verlag.

Collin F. Baker, Charles J. Fillmore, and John B. Lowe. 1998. The berkeley framenet project. In *Proceedings of the 36th Annual Meeting of the Association for Computational Linguistics and 17th International Conference on Computational Linguistics - Volume 1*,

[12] Due to the space limitation, we include only the rent domain result. However, all three datasets follow a similar pattern.

ACL '98, pages 86–90, Stroudsburg, PA, USA. Association for Computational Linguistics.

Richard Beaufort, Sophie Roekhaut, Louise-Amélie Cougnon, and Cédrick Fairon. 2010. A hybrid rule/model-based finite-state framework for normalizing sms messages. In *Proceedings of the 48th Annual Meeting of the Association for Computational Linguistics*, ACL '10, pages 770–779, Stroudsburg, PA, USA. Association for Computational Linguistics.

Kurt Bollacker, Colin Evans, Praveen Paritosh, Tim Sturge, and Jamie Taylor. 2008. Freebase: a collaboratively created graph database for structuring human knowledge. In *Proceedings of the 2008 ACM SIGMOD international conference on Management of data*, SIGMOD '08, pages 1247–1250, New York, NY, USA. ACM.

Nathanael Chambers and Dan Jurafsky. 2011. Template-based information extraction without the templates. In *Proceedings of the 49th Annual Meeting of the Association for Computational Linguistics: Human Language Technologies - Volume 1*, HLT '11, pages 976–986, Stroudsburg, PA, USA. Association for Computational Linguistics.

Ming-Wei Chang, Lev Ratinov, and Dan Roth. 2007. Guiding semi-supervision with constraint-driven learning. In *Proceedings of the 45th Annual Meeting of the Association of Computational Linguistics*, pages 280–287, Prague, Czech Republic, June. Association for Computational Linguistics.

Harr Chen, Edward Benson, Tahira Naseem, and Regina Barzilay. 2011. In-domain relation discovery with meta-constraints via posterior regularization. In *Proceedings of the 49th Annual Meeting of the Association for Computational Linguistics: Human Language Technologies - Volume 1*, HLT '11, pages 530–540, Stroudsburg, PA, USA. Association for Computational Linguistics.

Rayid Ghani, Katharina Probst, Yan Liu, Marko Krema, and Andrew Fano. 2006. Text mining for product attribute extraction. *SIGKDD Explor. Newsl.*, 8(1):41–48, June.

Trond Grenager, Dan Klein, and Christopher D. Manning. 2005. Unsupervised learning of field segmentation models for information extraction. In *Proceedings of the 43rd Annual Meeting on Association for Computational Linguistics*, ACL '05, pages 371–378, Stroudsburg, PA, USA. Association for Computational Linguistics.

Daniel Gruhl, Meena Nagarajan, Jan Pieper, Christine Robson, and Amit Sheth. 2009. Context and domain knowledge enhanced entity spotting in informal text. In *Proceedings of the 8th International Semantic Web Conference*, ISWC '09, pages 260–276, Berlin, Heidelberg. Springer-Verlag.

Aria Haghighi and Dan Klein. 2006. Prototype-driven learning for sequence models. In *Proceedings of the main conference on Human Language Technology Conference of the North American Chapter of the Association of Computational Linguistics*, HLT-NAACL '06, pages 320–327, Stroudsburg, PA, USA. Association for Computational Linguistics.

Dekang Lin and Patrick Pantel. 2001. Dirt @sbt@discovery of inference rules from text. In *Proceedings of the seventh ACM SIGKDD international conference on Knowledge discovery and data mining*, KDD '01, pages 323–328, New York, NY, USA. ACM.

Xiaohua Liu, Shaodian Zhang, Furu Wei, and Ming Zhou. 2011. Recognizing named entities in tweets. In *Proceedings of the 49th Annual Meeting of the Association for Computational Linguistics: Human Language Technologies - Volume 1*, HLT '11, pages 359–367, Stroudsburg, PA, USA. Association for Computational Linguistics.

Matthew Michelson and Craig A. Knoblock. 2005. Semantic annotation of unstructured and ungrammatical text. In *Proceedings of the 19th international joint conference on Artificial intelligence*, IJCAI'05, pages 1091–1098, San Francisco, CA, USA. Morgan Kaufmann Publishers Inc.

Matthew Michelson and Craig A. Knoblock. 2009. Exploiting background knowledge to build reference sets for information extraction. In *Proceedings of the 21st international jont conference on Artifical intelligence*, IJCAI'09, pages 2076–2082, San Francisco, CA, USA. Morgan Kaufmann Publishers Inc.

Hoifung Poon and Pedro Domingos. 2007. Joint inference in information extraction. In *Proceedings of the 22nd national conference on Artificial intelligence - Volume 1*, AAAI'07, pages 913–918. AAAI Press.

Hoifung Poon and Pedro Domingos. 2010. Unsupervised ontology induction from text. In *Proceedings of the 48th Annual Meeting of the Association for Computational Linguistics*, ACL '10, pages 296–305, Stroudsburg, PA, USA. Association for Computational Linguistics.

Duangmanee (Pew) Putthividhya and Junling Hu. 2011. Bootstrapped named entity recognition for product attribute extraction. In *Proceedings of the Conference on Empirical Methods in Natural Language Processing*, EMNLP '11, pages 1557–1567, Stroudsburg, PA, USA. Association for Computational Linguistics.

Joseph Reisinger and Marius Paşca. 2011. Fine-grained class label markup of search queries. In *Proceedings of the 49th Annual Meeting of the Association for Computational Linguistics: Human Language Technologies - Volume 1*, HLT '11, pages 1200–1209,

Stroudsburg, PA, USA. Association for Computational Linguistics.

Sunita Sarawagi and William W. Cohen. 2004. Semi-markov conditional random fields for information extraction. In *In Advances in Neural Information Processing Systems 17*, pages 1185–1192.

Satoshi Sekine. 2006. On-demand information extraction. In *Proceedings of the COLING/ACL on Main conference poster sessions*, COLING-ACL '06, pages 731–738, Stroudsburg, PA, USA. Association for Computational Linguistics.

Yoshimasa Tsuruoka and Jun'ichi Tsujii. 2005. Bidirectional inference with the easiest-first strategy for tagging sequence data. In *Proceedings of the conference on Human Language Technology and Empirical Methods in Natural Language Processing*, HLT '05, pages 467–474, Stroudsburg, PA, USA. Association for Computational Linguistics.

Peter D. Turney and Patrick Pantel. 2010. From frequency to meaning: vector space models of semantics. *J. Artif. Int. Res.*, 37(1):141–188, January.

William E. Winkler. 1990. String comparator metrics and enhanced decision rules in the fellegi-sunter model of record linkage. In *Proceedings of the Section on Survey Research*, pages 354–359.

Sketch Algorithms for Estimating Point Queries in NLP

Amit Goyal and Hal Daumé III
University of Maryland
{amit,hal}@umiacs.umd.edu

Graham Cormode
AT&T Labs–Research
graham@research.att.com

Abstract

Many NLP tasks rely on accurate statistics from large corpora. Tracking complete statistics is memory intensive, so recent work has proposed using compact approximate "sketches" of frequency distributions. We describe 10 sketch methods, including existing and novel variants. We compare and study the errors (over-estimation and underestimation) made by the sketches. We evaluate several sketches on three important NLP problems. Our experiments show that *one* sketch performs best for all the three tasks.

1 Introduction

Since the emergence of the World Wide Web, social media and mobile devices, we have ever larger and richer examples of text data. Such vast corpora have led to leaps in the performance of many language-based tasks: the concept is that simple models trained on big data can outperform more complex models with fewer examples. However, this new view comes with its own challenges: principally, how to effectively represent such large data sets so that model parameters can be efficiently extracted? One answer is to adopt compact summaries of corpora in the form of probabilistic "sketches".

In recent years, the field of Natural Language Processing (NLP) has seen tremendous growth and interest in the use of approximation, randomization, and streaming techniques for large-scale problems (Brants et al., 2007; Turney, 2008). Much of this work relies on tracking very many statistics. For example, storing approximate counts (Talbot and Osborne, 2007; Van Durme and Lall, 2009a; Goyal and Daumé III, 2011a), computing approximate association scores like Pointwise Mutual Information (Li et al., 2008; Van Durme and Lall, 2009b; Goyal and Daumé III, 2011a), finding frequent items (like n-grams) (Goyal et al., 2009), building streaming language models (Talbot and Brants, 2008; Levenberg and Osborne, 2009), and distributional similarity (Ravichandran et al., 2005; Van Durme and Lall, 2010). All these problems ultimately depend on approximate counts of items (such as n-grams, word pairs and word-context pairs). Thus we focus on solving this central problem in the context of NLP applications.

Sketch algorithms (Charikar et al., 2004; Cormode, 2011) are a memory- and time-efficient solution to answering point queries. Recently in NLP, we (Goyal and Daumé III, 2011a) demonstrated that a version of the Count-Min sketch (Cormode and Muthukrishnan, 2004) accurately solves three large-scale NLP problems using small bounded memory footprint. However, there are several other sketch algorithms, and it is not clear why this instance should be preferred amongst these. In this work, we conduct a systematic study and compare many sketch techniques which answer point queries with focus on large-scale NLP tasks. While sketches have been evaluated within the database community for finding frequent items (Cormode and Hadjieleftheriou, 2008) and join-size estimation (Rusu and Dobra, 2007), this is the *first* comparative study for NLP problems.

Our work includes three contributions: (1) We propose novel variants of existing sketches by extending the idea of *conservative update* to them. We propose Count sketch (Charikar et al., 2004) with conservative update (COUNT-CU) and Count-mean-min sketch with conservative update

(CMM-CU). The motivation behind proposing new sketches is inspired by the success of Count-Min sketch with conservative update in our earlier work (Goyal and Daumé III, 2011a). (2) We empirically compare and study the errors in approximate counts for several sketches. Errors can be over-estimation, under-estimation, or a combination of the two. We also evaluate their performance via Pointwise Mutual Information and LogLikelihood Ratio. (3) We use sketches to solve three important NLP problems. Our experiments show that sketches can be very effective for these tasks, and that the best results are obtained using the "conservative update" technique. Across all the three tasks, *one* sketch (CM-CU) performs best.

2 Sketches

In this section, we review existing sketch algorithms from the literature, and propose novel variants based on the idea of conservative update (Estan and Varghese, 2002). The term 'sketch' refers to a class of algorithm that represents a large data set with a compact summary, typically much smaller than the full size of the input. Given an input of N items $(\mathrm{x}_1, \mathrm{x}_2 \ldots \mathrm{x}_N)$, each item x (where x is drawn from some domain U) is mapped via hash functions into a small sketch vector that records frequency information. Thus, the sketch does not store the items explicitly, but only information about the frequency distribution. Sketches support fundamental queries on their input such as point, range and inner product queries to be quickly answered approximately. In this paper, we focus on point queries, which ask for the (approximate) count of a given item.

The algorithms we consider are *randomized* and *approximate*. They have two user-chosen parameters ϵ and δ. ϵ controls the amount of tolerable error in the returned count and δ controls the probability with which the error exceeds the bound ϵ. These values of ϵ and δ determine respectively the width w and depth d of a two-dimensional array sk$[\cdot,\cdot]$ of count information. The depth d denotes the number of hash functions employed by the sketch algorithms.

Sketch Operations. Every sketch has two operations: UPDATE and QUERY to update and estimate the count of an item. They all guarantee essentially *constant time* operation (technically, this grows as $O(\log(\frac{1}{\delta})$ but in practice this is set to a constant) per UPDATE and QUERY. Moreover, sketches can be combined: given two sketches s_1 and s_2 computed (using the same parameters w and d, and same set of d hash functions) over different inputs, a sketch of the combined input is obtained by adding the individual sketches, entry-wise. The time to perform the COMBINE operation on sketches is $O(d \times w)$, independent of the data size. This property enables sketches to be implemented in distributed setting, where each machine computes the sketch over a small portion of the corpus and makes it *scalable* to large datasets.

2.1 Existing sketch algorithms

This section describes sketches from the literature:

Count-Min sketch (CM): The CM (Cormode and Muthukrishnan, 2004) sketch has been used effectively for many large scale problems across several areas, such as Security (Schechter et al., 2010), Machine Learning (Shi et al., 2009; Aggarwal and Yu, 2010), Privacy (Dwork et al., 2010), and NLP (Goyal and Daumé III, 2011a). The sketch stores an array of size $d \times w$ counters, along with d hash functions (drawn from a pairwise-independent family), one for each row of the array. Given an input of N items $(\mathrm{x}_1, \mathrm{x}_2 \ldots \mathrm{x}_N)$, each of the hash functions h_k:$U \rightarrow \{1 \ldots w\}, \forall 1 \leq k \leq d$, takes an item from the input and maps it into a counter indexed by the corresponding hash function.

UPDATE: For each new item "x" with count c, the sketch is updated as:

$$\mathrm{sk}[k, h_k(\mathrm{x})] \leftarrow \mathrm{sk}[k, h_k(\mathrm{x})] + c, \ \ \forall 1 \leq k \leq d.$$

QUERY: Since multiple items are hashed to the same index for each array row, the stored frequency in each row is guaranteed to *overestimate* the true count, making it a biased estimator. Therefore, to answer the point query (QUERY (x)), CM returns the minimum over all the d positions x is stored.

$$\hat{c}(\mathrm{x}) = \min_k \ \mathrm{sk}[k, h_k(\mathrm{x})], \ \ \forall 1 \leq k \leq d.$$

Setting w=$\frac{2}{\epsilon}$ and d=$\log(\frac{1}{\delta})$ ensures all reported frequencies by CM exceed the true frequencies by at most ϵN with probability of at least $1 - \delta$. This makes the space used by the algorithm $O(\frac{1}{\epsilon} \log \frac{1}{\delta})$.

Spectral Bloom Filters (SBF): Cohen and Matias (2003) proposed SBF, an extension to Bloom Filters (Bloom, 1970) to answer point queries. The

UPDATE and QUERY procedures for SBF are the same as Count-Min (CM) sketch, except that the range of all the hash functions for SBF are the full array: $h_k{:}U \rightarrow \{1 \dots w \times d\}, \forall 1 \leq k \leq d$. While CM and SBF are very similar, only CM provides guarantees on the query error.

Count-mean-min (CMM): The motivation behind the CMM (Deng and Rafiei, 2007) sketch is to provide an unbiased estimator for Count-Min (CM) sketch. The construction of CMM sketch is identical to the CM sketch, while the QUERY procedure differs. Instead of returning the minimum value over the d counters (indexed by d hash functions), CMM deducts the value of estimated noise from each of the d counters, and return the median of the d residues. The noise is estimated as $(N - \text{sk}[k, h_k(\text{x})])/(w-1)$. Nevertheless, the median estimate ($\hat{f}_1$) over the d residues can overestimate more than the original CM sketch min estimate ($\hat{f}_2$), so we return min ($\hat{f}_1$,$\hat{f}_2$) as the final estimate for CMM sketch. CMM gives the same theoretical guarantees as Count sketch (below).

Count sketch (COUNT) (Charikar et al., 2004): COUNT (aka Fast-AGMS) keeps two hash functions for each row, h_k maps items onto $[1, w]$, and g_k maps items onto $\{-1,+1\}$. UPDATE: For each new item "x" with count c:

$$\text{sk}[k, h_k(\text{x})] \leftarrow \text{sk}[k, h_k(\text{x})] + c \cdot g_k(\text{x}), \;\; \forall 1 \leq k \leq d.$$

QUERY: the median over the d rows is an unbiased estimator of the point query:

$$\hat{c(\text{x})} = \text{median}_{\text{k}} \;\; \text{sk}[k, h_k(\text{x})] \cdot g_k(\text{x}), \;\; \forall 1 \leq k \leq d.$$

Setting w=$\frac{2}{\epsilon^2}$ and d=$\log(\frac{4}{\delta})$ ensures that all reported frequencies have error at most $\epsilon(\sum_{i=1}^{N} f_i^2)^{1/2}$ $\leq \epsilon N$ with probability at least $1-\delta$. The space used by the algorithm is $O(\frac{1}{\epsilon^2} \log \frac{1}{\delta})$.

2.2 Conservative Update sketch algorithms

In this section, we propose novel variants of existing sketches (see Section 2) by combining them with the conservative update process (Estan and Varghese, 2002). The idea of conservative update (also known as Minimal Increase (Cohen and Matias, 2003)) is to only increase counts in the sketch by the minimum amount needed to ensure the estimate remains accurate. It can easily be applied to Count-Min (CM) sketch and Spectral Bloom Filters (SBF) to further improve the estimate of a point query. Goyal and Daumé III (2011a) showed that CM sketch with conservative update reduces the amount of over-estimation error by a factor of at least 1.5, and also improves performance on three NLP tasks.

Note that while conservative update for CM and SBF never increases the error, there is no guaranteed improvement. The method relies on seeing multiple updates in sequence. When a large corpus is being summarized in a distributed setting, we can apply conservative update on each sketch independently before combining the sketches together (see "Sketch Operations" in Section 2).

Count-Min sketch with conservative update (CM-CU): The QUERY procedure for CM-CU (Cormode, 2009; Goyal and Daumé III, 2011a) is identical to Count-Min. However, to UPDATE an item "x" with frequency c, we first compute the frequency $\hat{c}(\text{x})$ of this item from the existing data structure ($\forall 1 \leq k \leq d$, $\hat{c}(\text{x}) = \min_k \; \text{sk}[k, h_k(\text{x})]$) and the counts are updated according to:

$$\text{sk}[k, h_k(\text{x})] \leftarrow \max\{\text{sk}[k, h_k(\text{x})], \hat{c}(\text{x}) + \text{c}\} \qquad (*).$$

The intuition is that, since the point query returns the minimum of all the d values, we update a counter only if it is necessary as indicated by $(*)$. This heuristic avoids unnecessarily updating counter values to reduce the over-estimation error.

Spectral Bloom Filters with conservative update (SBF-CU): The QUERY procedure for SBF-CU (Cohen and Matias, 2003) is identical to SBF. SBF-CU UPDATE procedure is similar to CM-CU, with the difference that all d hash functions have the common range $d \times w$.

Count-mean-min with conservative update (CMM-CU): We propose a *new* variant to reduce the over-estimation error for CMM sketch. The construction of CMM-CU is identical to CM-CU. However, due to conservative update, each row of the sketch is not updated for every update, hence the sum of counts over each row ($\sum_i \text{sk}[k, i]$, $\forall 1 \leq k \leq d$) is not equal to input size N. Hence, the estimated noise to be subtracted here is $(\sum_i \text{sk}[k, i] - \text{sk}[k, h_k(\text{x})]) \,/\, (w-1)$. CMM-CU deducts the value of estimated noise from each of the d counters, and returns the median of the d residues as the point query.

Count sketch with conservative update (COUNT-CU): We propose a *new* variant to reduce over-estimation error for the COUNT sketch. The QUERY procedure for COUNT-CU is the same as

COUNT. The UPDATE procedure follows the same outline as CM-CU, but uses the current estimate $\hat{c}(\text{x})$ from the COUNT sketch, i.e.

$$\hat{c}(\text{x}) = \text{median}_k \ \text{sk}[k, h_k(\text{x})] \cdot g_k(\text{x}), \ \forall 1 \le k \le d.$$

Note, this heuristic is not as strong as for CM-CU and SBF-CU because COUNT can have both over-estimate and under-estimate errors.

Lossy counting with conservative update (LCU-WS): LCU-WS (Goyal and Daumé III, 2011b) was proposed to reduce the amount of over-estimation error for CM-CU sketch, without incurring too much under-estimation error. This scheme is inspired by lossy counting (Manku and Motwani, 2002). In this approach, the input sequence is conceptually divided into *windows*, each containing $1/\gamma$ items. The size of each window is equal to size of the sketch i.e. $d \times w$. Note that there are γN windows; let t denote the index of current window. At window boundaries, $\forall\ 1 \le i \le d$, $1 \le j \le w$, if (sk$[i, j] > 0$ and sk$[i, j] \le t$), then sk$[i, j] \leftarrow$ sk$[i, j] - 1$. The idea is to remove the contribution of small items colliding in the same entry, while not altering the count of frequent items. The current window index is used to draw this distinction. Here, all reported frequencies $\hat{f}$ have both under and over estimation error: $f - \gamma N \le \hat{f} \le f + \epsilon N$.

Lossy counting with conservative update II (LCU-SWS): This is a variant of the previous scheme, where the counts of the sketch are decreased more conservatively. Hence, this scheme has worse over-estimation error compared to LCU-WS, with better under-estimation. Here, only those counts are decremented which are at most the square root of current window index, t. At window boundaries, $\forall\ 1 \le i \le d$, $1 \le j \le w$, if (sk$[i, j] > 0$ and sk$[i, j] \le \lceil\sqrt{t}\rceil$), then sk$[i, j] \leftarrow$ sk$[i, j] - 1$. LCU-SWS has similar analytical bounds to LCU-WS.

3 Intrinsic Evaluations

We empirically compare and study the errors in approximate counts for all 10 sketches. Errors can be over-estimation, under-estimation, or a combination of the two. We also study the behavior of approximate Pointwise Mutual Information and Log Likelihood Ratio for the sketches.

3.1 Experimental Setup

DATA: We took 50 million random sentences from Gigaword (Graff, 2003). We split this data in 10 chunks of 5 million sentences each. Since all sketches have probabilistic bounds, we report average results over these 10 chunks. For each chunk, we generate counts of all word pairs within a window size 7. This results in an average stream size of 194 million word pair tokens and 33.5 million word pair types per chunk.

To compare error in various sketch counts, first we compute the exact counts of all the word pairs. Second, we store the counts of all the word pairs in all the sketches. Third, we query sketches to generate *approximate* counts of all the word pairs. Recall, we do not store the word pairs explicitly in sketches but only a compact summary of the associated counts.

We fix the size of each sketch to be $w = \frac{20 \times 10^6}{3}$ and $d = 3$. We keep the size of sketches equal to allow fair comparison among them. Prior work (Deng and Rafiei, 2007; Goyal and Daumé III, 2011a) showed with *fixed sketch size*, a small number of hash functions (d=number of hash functions) with large w (or range) give rise to small error over counts. Next, we group all word pairs with the same true frequency into a single bucket. We then compute the Mean Relative Error (MRE) in each of these buckets. Because different sketches have different accuracy behavior on low, mid, and high frequency counts, making this distinction based on frequency lets us determine the regions in which different sketches perform best. Mean Relative Error (MRE) is defined as the average of absolute difference between the predicted and the exact value divided by the exact value over all the word pairs in each bucket.

3.2 Studying the Error in Counts

We study the errors produced by all 10 sketches. Since various sketches result in different errors on low, mid, and high frequency counts, we plot the results with a linear error scale (Fig. 1(a)) to highlight the performance for low frequency counts, and with a log error scale (Fig. 1(b)) for mid and high frequency counts.

We make several observations on low frequency counts from Fig. 1(a). (1) Count-Min (CM) and

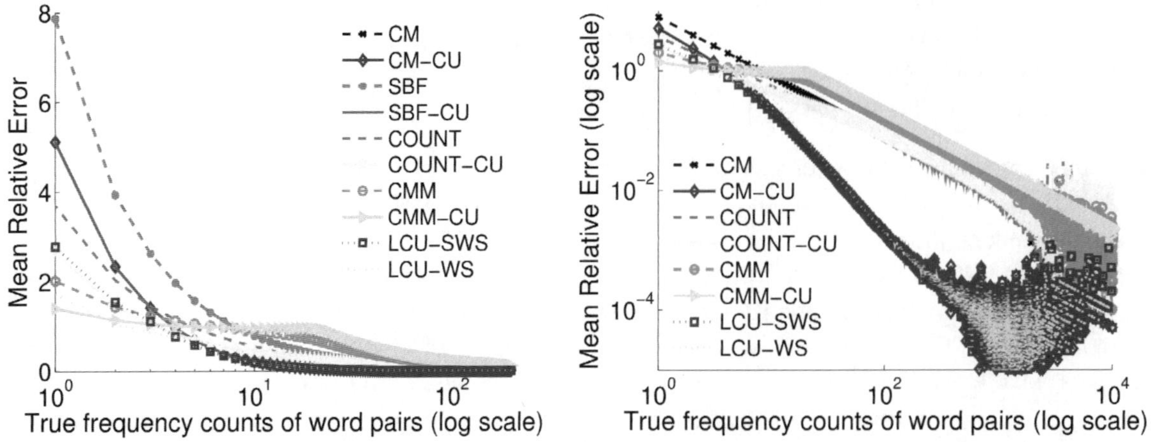

(a) Focusing on low frequency counts

(b) Focusing on mid and high frequency counts

Figure 1: Comparing several sketches for input size of 75 million word pairs. Size of each sketch: $w = \frac{20\times10^6}{3}$ and $d = 3$. All items with same exact count are put in one bucket and we plot Mean Relative Error on the y-axis with exact counts on the x-axis.

Spectral Bloom Filters (SBF) have identical MRE for word pairs. Using conservative update with CM (CM-CU) and SBF (SBF-CU) reduces the MRE by a factor of 1.5. MRE for CM-CU and SBF-CU is also identical. (2) COUNT has better MRE than CM-CU and using conservative update with COUNT (COUNT-CU) further reduces the MRE. (3) CMM has better MRE than COUNT and using conservative update with CMM (CMM-CU) further reduces the MRE. (4) Lossy counting with conservative update variants (LCU-SWS, LCU-WS) have comparable MRE to COUNT-CU and CMM-CU respectively.

In Fig. 1(b), we do not plot the SBF variants as SBF and CM variants had identical MRE in Fig. 1(a). From Figure 1(b), we observe that, CM, COUNT, COUNT-CU, CMM, CMM-CU sketches have worse MRE than CM-CU, LCU-SWS, and LCU-WS for mid and high frequency counts. CM-CU, LCU-SWS, and LCU-WS have zero MRE for all the counts > 1000.

To summarize the above observations, for those NLP problems where we cannot afford to make errors on mid and high frequency counts, we should employ CM-CU, LCU-SWS, and LCU-WS sketches. If we want to reduce the error on low frequency counts, LCU-WS generates least error. For NLP tasks where we can allow error on mid and high frequency counts but not on low frequency counts, CMM-CU sketch is best.

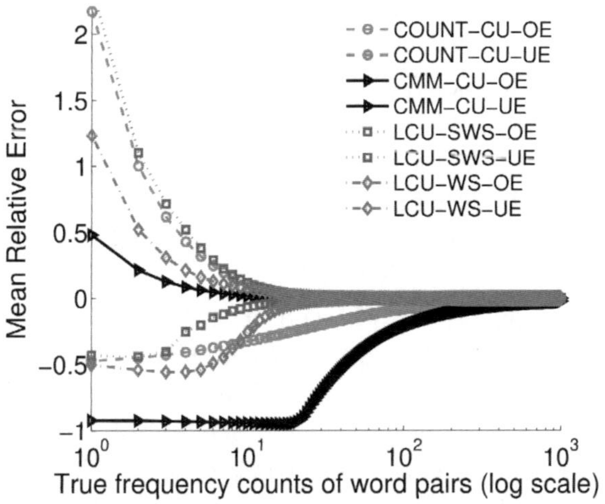

Figure 2: Compare several sketches on over-estimation and under-estimation errors with respect to exact counts.

3.3 Examining OE and UE errors

In many NLP applications, we are willing to tolerate either over-estimation or under-estimation errors. Hence we breakdown the error into over-estimation (OE) and under-estimation (UE) errors for the six best-performing sketches (COUNT, COUNT-CU, CMM, CMM-CU, LCU-SWS, and LCU-WS). To accomplish that, rather than using absolute error values, we divide the values into over-estimation (positive), and under-estimation (negative) error buck-

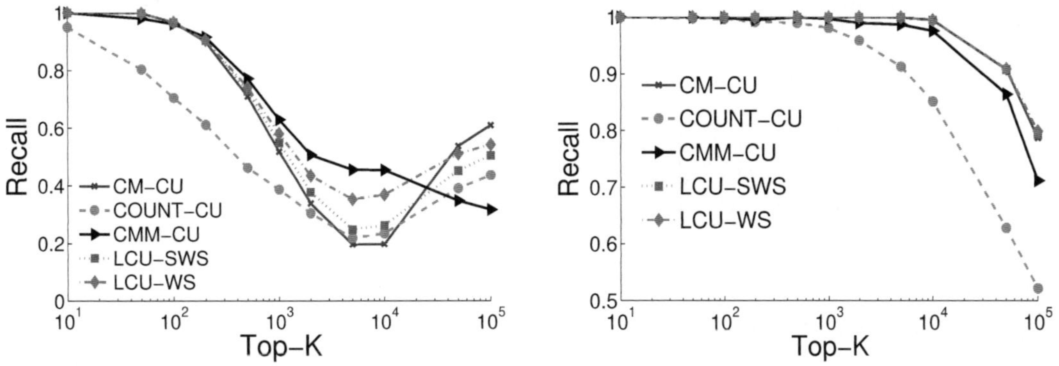

(a) PMI (b) LLR

Figure 3: Evaluate the approximate PMI and LLR rankings (obtained using various sketches) with the exact rankings.

ets. Hence, to compute the over-estimation MRE, we take the average of positive values over all the items in each bucket. For under-estimation, we take the average over the negative values. We can make several interesting observations from Figure 2: (1) Comparing COUNT-CU and LCU-SWS, we learn that both have the same over-estimation errors. However, LCU-SWS has less under-estimation error than COUNT-CU. Therefore, LCU-SWS is always better than COUNT-CU. (2) LCU-WS has less over-estimation than LCU-SWS but with more under-estimation error on mid frequency counts. LCU-WS has less under-estimation error than COUNT-CU. (3) CMM-CU has the least over-estimation error and most under-estimation error among all the compared sketches.

From the above experiments, we conclude that tasks sensitive to under-estimation should use the CM-CU sketch, which guarantees over-estimation. However, if we are willing to make some under-estimation error with less over-estimation error, then LCU-WS and LCU-SWS are recommended. Lastly, to have minimal over-estimation error with willingness to accept large under-estimation error, CMM-CU is recommended.

3.4 Evaluating association scores ranking

Last, in many NLP problems, we are interested in association rankings obtained using Pointwise Mutual Information (PMI) and Log Likelihood Ratio (LLR). In this experiment, we compare the word pairs association rankings obtained using PMI and LLR from several sketches and exact word pair counts. We use recall to measure the number of top-K sorted word pairs that are found in both the rankings.

In Figure 3(a), we compute the recall for CM-CU, COUNT-CU, CMM-CU, LCU-SWS, and LCU-WS sketches at several top-K thresholds of word pairs for approximate PMI ranking. We can make several observations from Figure 3(a). COUNT-CU has the worst recall for almost all the top-K settings. For top-K values less than 750, all sketches except COUNT-CU have comparable recall. Meanwhile, for K greater than 750, LCU-WS has the best recall. The is because PMI is sensitive to low frequency counts (Church and Hanks, 1989), over-estimation of the counts of low frequency word pairs can make their approximate PMI scores worse.

In Figure 3(b), we compare the LLR rankings. For top-K values less than 1000, all the sketches have comparable recall. For top-K values greater than 1000, CM-CU, LCU-SWS, and LCU-WS perform better. The reason for such a behavior is due to LLR favoring high frequency word pairs, and COUNT-CU and CMM-CU making under-estimation error on high frequency word pairs.

To summarize, to maintain top-K PMI rankings making over-estimation error is *not* desirable. Hence, LCU-WS is recommended for PMI rankings. For LLR, producing under-estimation error is *not* preferable and therefore, CM-CU, LCU-WS, and LCU-SWS are recommended.

Test Set	Random			Buckets			Neighbor		
Model	CM-CU	CMM-CU	LCU-WS	CM-CU	CMM-CU	LCU-WS	CM-CU	CMM-CU	LCU-WS
50M	87.2	74.3	86.5	83.9	72.9	83.2	71.7	64.7	72.1
100M	90.4	79.0	91.0	86.5	76.9	86.9	73.4	67.2	**74.7**
200M	**93.3**	83.1	92.9	**88.3**	80.1	**88.4**	**75.0**	69.0	**75.4**
500M	**94.4**	86.6	**94.1**	**89.3**	83.4	**89.3**	**75.7**	70.8	**75.5**
1B	**94.4**	88.7	**94.4**	**89.5**	85.1	**89.5**	**75.8**	71.9	**75.8**
Exact		**94.5**			**89.5**			**75.8**	

Table 1: Pseudo-words evaluation on accuracy metric for selectional preferences using several sketches of different sizes against the exact. There is *no* statistically significant difference (at $p < 0.05$ using bootstrap resampling) among bolded numbers.

4 Extrinsic Evaluation

4.1 Experimental Setup

We study three important NLP applications, and compare the three best-performing sketches: Count-Min sketch with conservative update (CM-CU), Count-mean-min with conservative update (CMM-CU), and Lossy counting with conservative update (LCU-WS). The above mentioned 3 sketches are selected from 10 sketches (see Section 2) considering these sketches make errors on different ranges of the counts: low, mid and, high frequency counts as seen in our intrinsic evaluations in Section 3. The goal of this experiment is to show the effectiveness of sketches on large-scale language processing tasks.

These adhere to the premise that simple methods using large data can dominate more complex models. We purposefully select simple methods as they use approximate counts and associations directly to solve these tasks. This allows us to have a fair comparison among different sketches, and to more directly see the impact of different choices of sketch on the task outcome. Of course, sketches are still broadly applicable to many NLP problems where we want to count (many) items or compute associations: e.g. language models, Statistical Machine Translation, paraphrasing, bootstrapping and label propagation for automatically creating a knowledge base and finding interesting patterns in social media.

Data: We use **Gigaword** (Graff, 2003) and a 50% portion of a copy of news web (**GWB50**) crawled by (Ravichandran et al., 2005). The raw size of **Gigaword (GW)** and **GWB50** is 9.8 GB and 49 GB with 56.78 million and 462.60 sentences respectively. For both the corpora, we split the text into sentences, tokenize and convert into lower-case.

4.2 Pseudo-Words Evaluation

In NLP, it is difficult and time consuming to create annotated test sets. This problem has motivated the use of pseudo-words to automatically create the test sets without human annotation. The pseudo-words are a common way to evaluate selectional preferences models (Erk, 2007; Bergsma et al., 2008) that measure the strength of association between a predicate and its argument filler, e.g., that the noun "song" is likely to be the object of the verb "sing".

A pseudo-word is the conflation of two words (e.g. song/dance). One word is the original in a sentence, and the second is the confounder. For example, in our task of selectional preferences, the system has to decide for the verb "sing" which is the correct object between "song"/"dance". Recently, Chambers and Jurafsky (2010) proposed a simple baseline based on co-occurrence counts of words, which has state-of-the-art performance on pseudo-words evaluation for selectional preferences.

We use a simple approach (without any typed dependency data) similar to Chambers and Jurafsky (2010), where we count all word pairs (except word pairs involving stop words) that appear within a window of size 3 from **Gigaword** (9.8 GB). That generates 970 million word pair tokens (stream size) and 94 million word pair types. Counts of all the 94 million unique word pairs are stored in CM-CU, CMM-CU, and LCU-WS. For a target verb, we return that noun which has higher co-occurrence count with it, as the correct selectional preference. We evaluate on Chambers and Jurafsky's three test sets[1] (excluding instances involving stop words) that are based on different strategies in selecting confounders: *Random* (4081 instances), *Buckets* (4028

[1] http://www.usna.edu/Users/cs/nchamber/data/pseudowords/

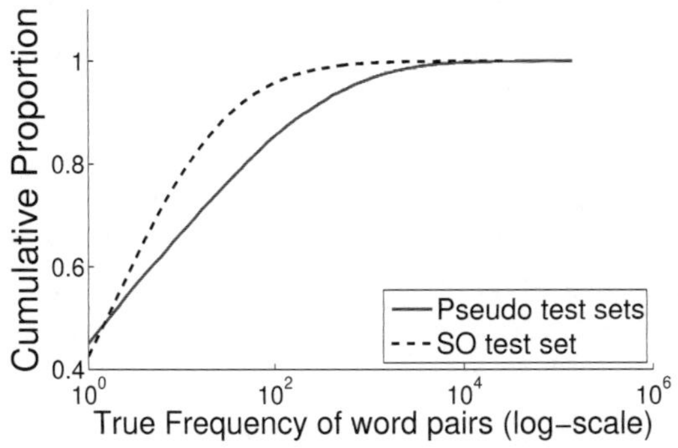

Figure 4: Determining the proportion of low, mid and high frequency test word pairs in **Gigaword** (**GW**).

instances), and *Neighbor* (3881 instances). To evaluate against the exact counts, we compute exact counts for only those word pairs that are present in the test sets. Accuracy is used for evaluation and is defined as the percentage of number of correctly identified pseudo words.

In Fig. 4, we plot the cumulative proportion of true frequency counts of all word pairs (from the three tests) in **Gigaword** (**GW**). To include unseen word pairs from test set in **GW** on log-scale in Fig. 4, we increment the true counts of all the word pairs by 1. This plot demonstrates that 45% of word-pairs are unseen in **GW**, and 67% of word pairs have counts less than 10. Hence, to perform better on this task, it is essential to *accurately maintain counts of rare word pairs*.

In Table 1, we vary the size of all sketches (50 million (M), $100M$, $200M$, $500M$ and 1 billion ($1B$) counters) with 3 hash functions to compare them against the exact counts. It takes 1.8 GB uncompressed space to maintain the exact counts on the disk. Table 1 shows that with sketches of size $> 200M$ on all the three test sets, CM-CU and LCU-WS are comparable to exact. However, the CMM-CU sketch performs less well. We conjecture the reason for such a behavior is due to loss of recall (information about low frequency word pairs) by under-estimation error. For this task CM-CU and LCU-WS scales to storing $94M$ unique word pairs using $200M$ integer (4 bytes each) counters (using 800 MB) $<$ 1.8 GB to maintain exact counts. Moreover, these results are comparable to Chambers and Jurafsky's state-of-the-art framework.

Data	Exact	CM-CU	CMM-CU	LCU-WS
GW	*74.2*	*74.0*	65.3	*72.9*
GWB50	**81.2**	**80.9**	74.9	78.3

Table 2: Evaluating Semantic Orientation on accuracy metric using several sketches of 2 billion counters against exact. Bold and italic numbers denote no statistically significant difference.

4.3 Finding Semantic Orientation of a word

Given a word, the task of finding its Semantic Orientation (SO) (Turney and Littman, 2003) is to determine if the word is more probable to be used in positive or negative connotation. We use Turney and Littman's (2003) state-of-the-art framework to compute the SO of a word. We use same seven positive words (good, nice, excellent, positive, fortunate, correct, and superior) and same seven negative words (bad, nasty, poor, negative, unfortunate, wrong, and inferior) from their framework as seeds. The SO of a given word is computed based on the strength of its association with the seven positive words and the seven negative words. Association scores are computed via Pointwise Mutual Information (PMI). We compute the SO of a word "w" as:

$$\mathrm{SO(w)} = \sum_{\mathrm{p}\in\mathrm{Pos}} PMI(\mathrm{p},\mathrm{w}) - \sum_{\mathrm{n}\in\mathrm{Neg}} PMI(\mathrm{n},\mathrm{w})$$

where, Pos and Neg denote the seven positive and negative seeds respectively. If this score is negative, we predict the word as negative; otherwise, we predict it as positive. We use the General Inquirer lexicon[2] (Stone et al., 1966) as a benchmark to evaluate the semantic orientation similar to Turney and Littman's (2003) work. Our test set consists of 1611 positive and 1987 negative words. Accuracy is used for evaluation and is defined as the percentage of number of correctly identified SO words.

We evaluate SO of words on two different sized corpora (see Section 4.1): **Gigaword** (**GW**) (9.8GB), and **GW** with 50% news web corpus (**GWB50**) (49GB). We fix the size of all sketches to 2 billion ($2B$) counters with 5 hash functions. We store exact counts of all words in a hash table for both **GW** and **GWB50**. We count all word pairs (except word pairs involving stop words) that appear within a window of size 7 from **GW** and **GWB50**. This yields 2.67 billion(B) tokens and $.19B$ types

[2]The General Inquirer lexicon is freely available at `http://www.wjh.harvard.edu/~inquirer/`

	Test Set	WS-203			MC-30		
	Model	CM-CU	CMM-CU	LCU-WS	CM-CU	CMM-CU	LCU-WS
PMI	10M	**.58**	.25	.28	**.67**	.20	.16
	50M	**.44**	.23	.41	**.61**	.22	.31
	200M	**.53**	**.44**	**.47**	**.57**	.28	**.43**
	Exact		**.52**			**.50**	
LLR	10M	*.47*	.27	.29	*.50*	.29	.10
	50M	*.42*	.31	.34	*.48*	.32	*.35*
	200M	*.41*	*.35*	*.39*	*.40*	*.31*	*.40*
	Exact		*.42*			*.41*	

Table 3: Evaluating distributional similarity using sketches. Scores are evaluated using rank correlation ρ. Bold and italic numbers denote no statistically significant difference.

from **GW** and $13.20B$ tokens and $0.8B$ types from **GWB50**. Next, we compare the sketches against the exact counts over two different size corpora.

Table 2 shows that increasing the amount of data improves the accuracy of identifying the SO of a word. We get an absolute increase of 7 percentage points (with exact counts) in accuracy (The 95% statistical significance boundary for accuracy is about $\pm$ 1.5.), when we add 50% web data (**GWB50**). CM-CU results are equivalent to exact counts for all the corpus sizes. These results are also comparable to Turney's (2003) accuracy of 82.84%. However, CMM-CU results are worse by absolute 8.7 points and 6 points on **GW** and **GWB50** respectively with respect to CM-CU. LCU-WS is better than CMM-CU but worse than CM-CU. Using $2B$ integer (4 bytes each) counters (bounded memory footprint of 8 GB), CM-CU scales to $0.8B$ word pair types (It takes 16 GB uncompressed disk space to store *exact* counts of all the unique word pair types.).

Figure 4 has similar frequency distribution of word pairs[3] in SO test set as pseudo-words evaluation test sets word pairs. Hence, CMM-CU again has substantially worse results than CM-CU due to loss of recall (information about low frequency word pairs) by under-estimation error. We can conclude that for this task CM-CU is best.

4.4 Distributional Similarity

Distributional similarity is based on the distributional hypothesis that similar terms appear in similar contexts (Firth, 1968; Harris, 1954). The context vector for each term is represented by the strength of association between the term and each of the lexical, semantic, syntactic, and/or dependency units that co-occur with it. For this work, we define context for a given term as the surrounding words appearing in a window of 2 words to the left and 2 words to the right. The context words are concatenated along with their positions -2, -1, +1, and +2. We use PMI and LLR to compute the association score (AS) between the term and each of the context to generate the context vector. We use the cosine similarity measure to find the distributional similarity between the context vectors for each of the terms.

We use two test sets which consist of word pairs, and their corresponding human rankings. We generate the word pair rankings using distributional similarity. We report the Spearman's rank correlation coefficient (ρ) between the human and distributional similarity rankings. We report results on two test sets: **WS-203**: A set of 203 word pairs marked according to similarity (Agirre et al., 2009). **MC-30**: A set of 30 noun pairs (Miller and Charles, 1991).

We evaluate distributional similarity on **Gigaword (GW)** (9.8GB) (see Section 4.1). First, we store exact counts of all words and contexts in a hash table from **GW**. Next, we count all the word-context pairs and store them in CM-CU, CMM-CU, and LCU-WS sketches. That generates a stream of size 3.35 billion ($3.35B$) word-context pair tokens and 215 million unique word-context pair types (It takes 4.6 GB uncompressed disk space to store *exact* counts of all these unique word-context pair types.). For every target word in the test set, we maintain top-1000 approximate AS scores contexts using a priority queue, by passing over the corpus a second time. Finally, we use cosine similarity with these approximate top-K context vectors to compute distributional similarity.

In Table 3, we vary the size of all sketches across 10 million (M), $50M$, and $200M$ counters with 3 hash functions. The results using PMI shows that CM-CU has best ρ on both **WS-203** and **MC-30** test sets. The results for LLR in Table 3 show similar trends with CM-CU having best results on small size sketches. Thus, CM-CU scales using $10M$ counters (using fixed memory of 40 MB versus 4.6 GB to store exact counts). These results are compa-

[3]Consider only those pairs in which one word appears in the seed list and the other word appears in the test set.

rable against the state-of-the-art results for distributional similarity (Agirre et al., 2009).

On this task CM-CU is best as it avoids loss of recall (information about low frequency word pairs) due to under-estimation error. For a target word that has low frequency, using CMM-CU will not generate any contexts for it, as it will have large under-estimation error for word-context pairs counts. This phenomenon is demonstrated in Table 3, where CMM-CU and LCU-WS have worse result with small size sketches.

5 Conclusion

In this work, we systematically studied the problem of estimating point queries using different sketch algorithms. As far as we know, this represents the *first* comparative study to demonstrate the relative behavior of sketches in the context of NLP applications. We proposed two novel sketch variants: Count sketch (Charikar et al., 2004) with conservative update (COUNT-CU) and Count-mean-min sketch with conservative update (CMM-CU). We empirically showed that CMM-CU has under-estimation error with small over-estimation error, CM-CU has only over-estimation error, and LCU-WS has more under-estimation error than over-estimation error. Finally, we demonstrated CM-CU has better results on all three tasks: pseudo-words evaluation for selectional preferences, finding semantic orientation task, and distributional similarity. This shows that maintaining information about low frequency items (even with over-estimation error) is better than throwing away information (under-estimation error) about rare items.

Future work is to reduce the bit size of each counter (instead of the number of counters), as has been tried for other summaries (Talbot and Osborne, 2007; Talbot, 2009; Van Durme and Lall, 2009a) in NLP. However, it may be challenging to combine this with conservative update.

Acknowledgments

This work was partially supported by NSF Award IIS-1139909. Thanks to Suresh Venkatasubramanian for useful discussions and the anonymous reviewers for many helpful comments.

References

Charu C. Aggarwal and Philip S. Yu. 2010. On classification of high-cardinality data streams. In *SDM'10*, pages 802–813.

Eneko Agirre, Enrique Alfonseca, Keith Hall, Jana Kravalova, Marius Paşca, and Aitor Soroa. 2009. A study on similarity and relatedness using distributional and wordnet-based approaches. In *NAACL '09: Proceedings of HLT-NAACL.*

Shane Bergsma, Dekang Lin, and Randy Goebel. 2008. Discriminative learning of selectional preference from unlabeled text. In *Proc. EMNLP*, pages 59–68, Honolulu, Hawaii, October.

Burton H. Bloom. 1970. Space/time trade-offs in hash coding with allowable errors. *Communications of the ACM*, 13:422–426.

Thorsten Brants, Ashok C. Popat, Peng Xu, Franz J. Och, and Jeffrey Dean. 2007. Large language models in machine translation. In *Proceedings of EMNLP-CoNLL.*

Nathanael Chambers and Dan Jurafsky. 2010. Improving the use of pseudo-words for evaluating selectional preferences. In *Proceedings of the 48th Annual Meeting of the Association for Computational Linguistics*, ACL '10, pages 445–453. Association for Computational Linguistics.

Moses Charikar, Kevin Chen, and Martin Farach-Colton. 2004. Finding frequent items in data streams. *Theor. Comput. Sci.*, 312:3–15, January.

K. Church and P. Hanks. 1989. Word Association Norms, Mutual Information and Lexicography. In *Proceedings of ACL*, pages 76–83, Vancouver, Canada, June.

Saar Cohen and Yossi Matias. 2003. Spectral bloom filters. In *Proceedings of the 2003 ACM SIGMOD international conference on Management of data*, SIGMOD '03, pages 241–252. ACM.

Graham Cormode and Marios Hadjieleftheriou. 2008. Finding frequent items in data streams. In *VLDB*.

Graham Cormode and S. Muthukrishnan. 2004. An improved data stream summary: The count-min sketch and its applications. *J. Algorithms*.

Graham Cormode. 2009. Encyclopedia entry on 'Count-Min Sketch'. In *Encyclopedia of Database Systems*, pages 511–516. Springer.

Graham Cormode. 2011. Sketch techniques for approximate query processing. Foundations and Trends in Databases. NOW publishers.

Fan Deng and Davood Rafiei. 2007. New estimation algorithms for streaming data: Count-min can do more. `http://webdocs.cs.ualberta.ca/`.

Cynthia Dwork, Moni Naor, Toniann Pitassi, Guy N. Rothblum, and Sergey Yekhanin. 2010. Pan-private streaming algorithms. In *Proceedings of ICS*.

Katrin Erk. 2007. A simple, similarity-based model for selectional preferences. In *Proceedings of the 45th Annual Meeting of the Association of Computational Linguistics*, volume 45, pages 216–223. Association for Computational Linguistics.

Cristian Estan and George Varghese. 2002. New directions in traffic measurement and accounting. *SIGCOMM Comput. Commun. Rev.*, 32(4).

J. Firth. 1968. A synopsis of linguistic theory 1930-1955. In F. Palmer, editor, *Selected Papers of J. R. Firth*. Longman.

Amit Goyal and Hal Daumé III. 2011a. Approximate scalable bounded space sketch for large data NLP. In *Empirical Methods in Natural Language Processing (EMNLP)*.

Amit Goyal and Hal Daumé III. 2011b. Lossy conservative update (LCU) sketch: Succinct approximate count storage. In *Conference on Artificial Intelligence (AAAI)*.

Amit Goyal, Hal Daumé III, and Suresh Venkatasubramanian. 2009. Streaming for large scale NLP: Language modeling. In *NAACL*.

D. Graff. 2003. English Gigaword. Linguistic Data Consortium, Philadelphia, PA, January.

Z. Harris. 1954. Distributional structure. *Word 10 (23)*, pages 146–162.

Abby Levenberg and Miles Osborne. 2009. Stream-based randomised language models for SMT. In *EMNLP*, August.

Ping Li, Kenneth Ward Church, and Trevor Hastie. 2008. One sketch for all: Theory and application of conditional random sampling. In *Neural Information Processing Systems*, pages 953–960.

G. S. Manku and R. Motwani. 2002. Approximate frequency counts over data streams. In *VLDB*.

G.A. Miller and W.G. Charles. 1991. Contextual correlates of semantic similarity. *Language and Cognitive Processes*, 6(1):1–28.

Deepak Ravichandran, Patrick Pantel, and Eduard Hovy. 2005. Randomized algorithms and nlp: using locality sensitive hash function for high speed noun clustering. In *Proceedings of ACL*.

Florin Rusu and Alin Dobra. 2007. Statistical analysis of sketch estimators. In *SIGMOD '07*. ACM.

Stuart Schechter, Cormac Herley, and Michael Mitzenmacher. 2010. Popularity is everything: a new approach to protecting passwords from statistical-guessing attacks. In *Proceedings of the 5th USENIX conference on Hot topics in security*, HotSec'10, pages 1–8, Berkeley, CA, USA. USENIX Association.

Qinfeng Shi, James Petterson, Gideon Dror, John Langford, Alex Smola, and S.V.N. Vishwanathan. 2009. Hash kernels for structured data. *Journal Machine Learning Research*, 10:2615–2637, December.

Philip J. Stone, Dexter C. Dunphy, Marshall S. Smith, and Daniel M. Ogilvie. 1966. *The General Inquirer: A Computer Approach to Content Analysis*. MIT Press.

David Talbot and Thorsten Brants. 2008. Randomized language models via perfect hash functions. In *Proceedings of ACL-08: HLT*.

David Talbot and Miles Osborne. 2007. Smoothed Bloom filter language models: Tera-scale LMs on the cheap. In *Proceedings of the 2007 Joint Conference on Empirical Methods in Natural Language Processing and Computational Natural Language Learning (EM NLP-CoNLL)*.

David Talbot. 2009. Succinct approximate counting of skewed data. In *IJCAI'09: Proceedings of the 21st international jont conference on Artifical intelligence*.

Peter D. Turney and Michael L. Littman. 2003. Measuring praise and criticism: Inference of semantic orientation from association. *ACM Trans. Inf. Syst.*, 21:315–346, October.

Peter D. Turney. 2008. A uniform approach to analogies, synonyms, antonyms, and associations. In *Proceedings of COLING 2008*.

Benjamin Van Durme and Ashwin Lall. 2009a. Probabilistic counting with randomized storage. In *IJCAI'09: Proceedings of the 21st international jont conference on Artifical intelligence*.

Benjamin Van Durme and Ashwin Lall. 2009b. Streaming pointwise mutual information. In *Advances in Neural Information Processing Systems 22*.

Benjamin Van Durme and Ashwin Lall. 2010. Online generation of locality sensitive hash signatures. In *Proceedings of the ACL 2010 Conference Short Papers*, pages 231–235, July.

Monte Carlo MCMC: Efficient Inference by Approximate Sampling

Sameer Singh
University of Massachusetts
140 Governor's Drive
Amherst MA
sameer@cs.umass.edu

Michael Wick
University of Massachsetts
140 Governor's Drive
Amherst, MA
mwick@cs.umass.edu

Andrew McCallum
University of Massachusetts
140 Governor's Drive
Amherst MA
mccallum@cs.umass.edu

Abstract

Conditional random fields and other graphical models have achieved state of the art results in a variety of tasks such as coreference, relation extraction, data integration, and parsing. Increasingly, practitioners are using models with more complex structure—higher treewidth, larger fan-out, more features, and more data—rendering even approximate inference methods such as MCMC inefficient. In this paper we propose an alternative MCMC sampling scheme in which transition probabilities are approximated by sampling from the set of relevant factors. We demonstrate that our method converges more quickly than a traditional MCMC sampler for both marginal and MAP inference. In an author coreference task with over 5 million mentions, we achieve a 13 times speedup over regular MCMC inference.

1 Introduction

Conditional random fields and other graphical models are at the forefront of many natural language processing (NLP) and information extraction (IE) tasks because they provide a framework for discriminative modeling while succinctly representing dependencies among many related output variables. Previously, most applications of graphical models were limited to structures where exact inference is possible, for example linear-chain CRFs (Lafferty et al., 2001). More recently, there has been a desire to include more factors, longer range dependencies, and more sophisticated features; these include skip-chain CRFs for named entity recognition (Sutton and McCallum, 2004), probabilistic DBs (Wick et al., 2010), higher-order models for dependency parsing (Carreras, 2007), entity-wise models for coreference (Culotta et al., 2007; Wick et al., 2009), and global models of relations (Hoffmann et al., 2011). The increasing sophistication of these individual NLP components compounded with the community's desire to model these tasks jointly across cross-document considerations has resulted in graphical models for which inference is computationally intractable. Even popular approximate inference techniques such as loopy belief propagation and Markov chain Monte Carlo (MCMC) may be prohibitively slow.

MCMC algorithms such as Metropolis-Hastings are usually efficient for graphical models because the only factors needed to score a proposal are those touching the changed variables. However, MCMC is slowed in situations where a) the model exhibits variables that have a high-degree (neighbor many factors), b) proposals modify a substantial subset of the variables to satisfy domain constraints (such as transitivity in coreference), or c) evaluating a single factor is expensive, for example when features are based on string-similarity. For example, the seemingly innocuous proposal changing the entity type of a single entity requires examining all its mentions, i.e. scoring a linear number of factors (in the number of mentions of that entity). Similarly, evaluating coreference of a mention to an entity also requires scoring factors to all the mentions of the entity. Often, however, the factors are somewhat *redundant*, for example, not all mentions of the "USA" entity need to be examined to confidently conclude that it is a COUNTRY, or that it is coreferent with "United

States of America".

In this paper we propose an approximate MCMC framework that facilitates efficient inference in high-degree graphical models. In particular, we approximate the acceptance ratio in the Metropolis Hastings algorithm by replacing the exact model score with a stochastic approximation that samples from the set of relevant factors. We explore two sampling strategies, a fixed proportion approach that samples the factors uniformly, and a dynamic alternative that samples factors until the method is confident about its estimate of the model score.

We evaluate our method empirically on both synthetic and real-world data. On synthetic classification data, our approximate MCMC procedure obtains the true marginals faster than a traditional MCMC sampler. On real-world tasks, our method achieves 7 times speedup on citation matching, and 13 times speedup on large-scale author disambiguation.

2 Background

2.1 Graphical Models

Factor graphs (Kschischang et al., 2001) succinctly represent the joint distribution over random variables by a product of factors that make the dependencies between the random variables explicit. A factor graph is a bipartite graph between the variables and factors, where each (log) factor $f \in \mathcal{F}$ is a function that maps an assignment of its neighboring variables to a real number. For example, in a linear-chain model of part-of-speech tagging, transition factors score compatibilities between consecutive labels, while emission factors score compatibilities between a label and its observed token.

The probability distribution expressed by the factor graph is given as a normalized product of the factors, which we rewrite as an exponentiated sum:

$$p(\mathbf{y}) = \frac{\exp \psi(\mathbf{y})}{Z} \quad (1)$$

$$\psi(\mathbf{y}) = \sum_{f \in \mathcal{F}} f(\mathbf{y}_f) \quad (2)$$

$$Z = \sum_{\mathbf{y} \in \mathcal{Y}} \exp \psi(\mathbf{y}) \quad (3)$$

Intuitively, the model favors assignments to the random variables that yield higher factor scores and will assign higher probabilities to such configurations.

The two common inference problems for graphical models in NLP are *maximum a posterior* (MAP) and marginal inference. For models without latent variables, the MAP estimate is the setting to the variables that has the highest probability under the model:

$$\mathbf{y}_{\text{MAP}} = \operatorname*{argmax}_{\mathbf{y}} p(\mathbf{y}) \quad (4)$$

Marginal inference is the problem of finding marginal distributions over subsets of the variables, used primarily in maximum likelihood gradients and for max marginal inference.

2.2 Markov chain Monte Carlo (MCMC)

Often, computing marginal estimates of a model is computationally intractable due to the normalization constant Z, while maximum a posteriori (MAP) is prohibitive due to the search space of possible configurations. Markov chain Monte Carlo (MCMC) is important tool for performing sample- and search-based inference in these models. A particularly successful MCMC method for graphical model inference is Metropolis-Hastings (MH). Since sampling from the true model $p(\mathbf{y})$ is intractable, MH instead uses a simpler distribution $q(\mathbf{y}'|\mathbf{y})$ that conditions on a current state $\mathbf{y}$ and proposes a new state $\mathbf{y}'$ by modifying a few variables. This new assignment is then accepted with probability α:

$$\alpha = \min\left(1, \frac{p(\mathbf{y}')}{p(\mathbf{y})} \frac{q(\mathbf{y}|\mathbf{y}')}{q(\mathbf{y}'|\mathbf{y})}\right) \quad (5)$$

Computing this acceptance probability is often highly efficient because the partition function cancels, as do all the factors in the model that do not neighbor the modified variables. MH can be used for both MAP and marginal inference.

2.2.1 Marginal Inference

To compute marginals with MH, the variables are initialized to an arbitrary assignment (i.e., randomly or with some heuristic), and sampling is run until the samples $\{\mathbf{y}_i | i = 0, \cdots, n\}$ become independent of the initial assignment. The ergodic theorem provides the MCMC analog to the law-of-large-numbers, justifying the use of the generated samples to compute the desired statistics (such as feature expectations or variable marginals).

2.2.2 MAP Inference

Since MCMC can efficiently explore the high density regions for a given distribution, the distribution p can be modified such that the high-density region of the new distribution represents the MAP configuration of p. This is achieved by adding a temperature term τ to the distribution p, resulting in the following MH acceptance probability:

$$\alpha = \min\left(1, \left(\frac{p(\mathbf{y}')}{p(\mathbf{y})}\right)^{\frac{1}{\tau}}\right) \tag{6}$$

Note that as $\tau \to 0$, MH will sample closer to the MAP configuration. If a cooling schedule is implemented for τ then the MH sampler for MAP inference can be seen as an instance of simulated annealing (Bertsimas and Tsitsiklis, 1993).

3 Monte Carlo MCMC

In this section we introduce our approach for approximating the acceptance ratio of Metropolis-Hastings that samples the factors, and describe two sampling strategies.

3.1 Stochastic Proposal Evaluation

Although one of the benefits of MCMC lies in its ability to leverage the locality of the proposal, for some information extraction tasks this can become a crucial bottleneck. In particular, evaluation of each sample requires computing the score of all the factors that are *involved* in the change, i.e. all factors that neighbor any variable in the set that has changed. This evaluation becomes a bottleneck for tasks in which a large number of variables is involved in each proposal, or in which the model contains a number of high-degree variables, resulting in a large number of factors, or in which computing the factor score involves an expensive computation, such as string similarity between mention text.

Instead of evaluating the log-score ψ of the model exactly, this paper proposes a Monte-Carlo estimation of the log-score. In particular, if the set of factors for a given proposal $\mathbf{y} \to \mathbf{y}'$ is $\mathcal{F}(\mathbf{y}, \mathbf{y}')$, we use a sampled subset of the factors $\mathcal{S} \subseteq \mathcal{F}(\mathbf{y}, \mathbf{y}')$ as an approximation of the model score. In the following we use $\mathcal{F}$ as an abbreviation for $\mathcal{F}(\mathbf{y}, \mathbf{y}')$. Formally,

$$\begin{aligned} \psi(\mathbf{y}) &= \sum_{f \in \mathcal{F}} f(\mathbf{y}_f) = |\mathcal{F}| \cdot \mathbb{E}_{\mathcal{F}}\left[f(\mathbf{y}_f)\right] \\ \psi_{\mathcal{S}}(\mathbf{y}) &= |\mathcal{F}| \cdot \mathbb{E}_{\mathcal{S}}\left[f(\mathbf{y}_f)\right] \end{aligned} \tag{7}$$

We use the sample log-score ($\psi_{\mathcal{S}}$) in the acceptance probability α to evaluate the samples. Since we are using a stochastic approximation to the model score, in general we need to take more MCMC samples before we converge, however, since evaluating each sample will be *much* faster ($O(|\mathcal{S}|)$ as opposed to $O(|\mathcal{F}|)$), we expect overall sampling to be faster.

In the next sections we describe several alternative strategies for sampling the set of factors $\mathcal{S}$. The primary restriction on the set of samples $\mathcal{S}$ is that their mean should be an unbiased estimator of $\mathbb{E}_{\mathcal{F}}[f]$. Further, time taken to obtain the set of samples should be negligible when compared to scoring all the factors in $\mathcal{F}$. Note that there is an implicit minimum of 1 to the number of the sampled factors.

3.2 Uniform Sampling

The most direct approach for subsampling the set of $\mathcal{F}$ is to perform uniform sampling. In particular, given a proportion parameter $0 < p \leq 1$, we select a random subset $\mathcal{S}_p \subseteq \mathcal{F}$ such that $|\mathcal{S}_p| = p \cdot |\mathcal{F}|$. Since this approach is agnostic as to the actual factors scores, $\mathbb{E}_{\mathcal{S}}[f] \equiv \mathbb{E}_{\mathcal{F}}[f]$. A low p leads to fast evaluation, however it may require a large number of samples due to the substantial approximation. On the other hand, although a higher p will converge with fewer samples, evaluating each sample is slower.

3.3 Confidence-Based Sampling

Selecting the best value for p is difficult, requiring analysis of the graph structure, and statistics on the distribution of the factors scores; often a difficult task in real-world applications. Further, the same value for p can result in different levels of approximation for different proposals, either unnecessarily accurate or problematically noisy. We would prefer a strategy that adapts to the distribution of the scores in $\mathcal{F}$.

Instead of sampling a fixed proportion of factors, we can sample until we are confident that the current set of samples $\mathcal{S}_c$ is an accurate estimate of the true mean of $\mathcal{F}$. In particular, we maintain a running count of the sample mean $\mathbb{E}_{\mathcal{S}_c}[f]$ and variance

$\sigma_{\mathcal{S}_c}$, using them to compute a confidence interval $I_{\mathcal{S}}$ around our estimate of the mean. Since the number of sampled factors $\mathcal{S}$ could be a substantial fraction of the set of factors $\mathcal{F}$,[1] we also incorporate *finite population control (fpc)* in our sample variance computation. We compute the confidence interval as follows:

$$\sigma_{\mathcal{S}}^2 = \frac{1}{|\mathcal{S}|-1}\sum_{f\in\mathcal{S}}(f-\mathbb{E}_S[f])^2 \quad (8)$$

$$I_{\mathcal{S}} = 2z\frac{\sigma_{\mathcal{S}}}{\sqrt{|\mathcal{S}|}}\sqrt{\frac{|\mathcal{F}|-|\mathcal{S}|}{|\mathcal{F}|-1}} \quad (9)$$

where we set the z to 1.96, i.e. the 95% confidence interval. This approach starts with an empty set of samples, $\mathcal{S} = \{\}$, and iteratively samples factors without replacement to add to $\mathcal{S}$, until the confidence interval around the estimated mean falls below a user specified maximum interval width threshold i. As a result, for proposals that contain high-variance factors, this strategy examines a large number of factors, while proposals that involve similar factors will result in fewer samples. Note that this user-specified threshold is agnostic to the graph structure and the number of factors, and instead directly reflects the score distribution of the relevant factors.

4 Experiments

In this section we evaluate our approach for both marginal and MAP inference.

4.1 Marginal Inference on Synthetic Data

Consider the task of classifying entities into a set of types, for example, POLITICIAN, VEHICLE, CITY, GOVERMENT-ORG, etc. For knowledge base construction, this prediction often takes place on the entity-level, as opposed to the mention-level common in traditional NLP. To evaluate the type at the entity-level, the scored factors examine features of all the entity mentions of the entity, along with the labels of all relation mentions for which it is an argument. See Yao et al. (2010) and Hoffmann et al. (2011) for examples of such models. Since a subset of the mentions can be sufficiently informative for the model, we expect our stochastic MCMC approach to work well.

[1]Specifically, the fraction may be higher than > 5%

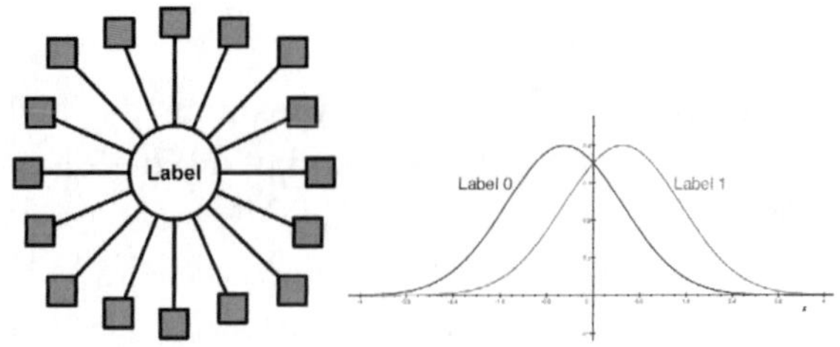

(a) Binary Classification Model ($n = 100$) (b) Distribution of Factor scores

Figure 1: Synthetic Model for Classification

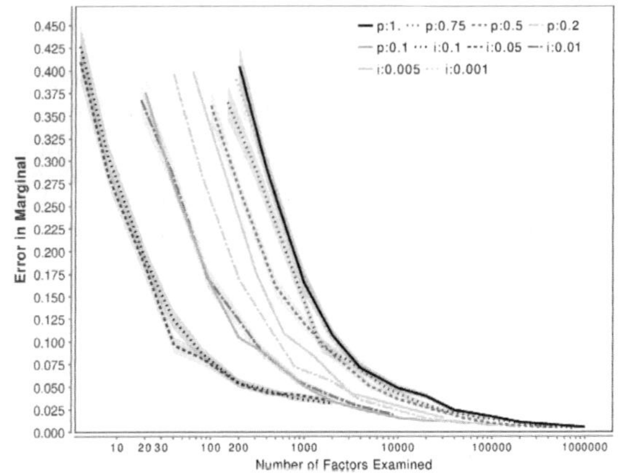

Figure 2: Marginal Inference Error for Classification on Synthetic Data

We use synthetic data for such a model to evaluate the quality of marginals returned by the Gibbs sampling form of MCMC. Since the Gibbs algorithm samples each variable using a fixed assignment of its neighborhood, we represent generating a single sample as classification. We create star-shaped models with a single unobserved variable (entity type) that neighbors many unary factors, each representing a single entity- or a relation-mention factor (See Figure 1a for an example). We generate a synthetic dataset for this model, creating 100 variables consisting of 100 factors each. The scores of the factors are generated from gaussians, $\mathcal{N}(0.5, 1)$ for the positive label, and $\mathcal{N}(-0.5, 1)$ for the negative label (note the overlap between the weights in Figure 1b). Although each structure contains only a single variable, and no cycles, it is a valid benchmark to test our sampling approach since the effects of the setting of burn-in period and the thinning samples are not a concern.

We perform standard Gibbs sampling, and compare the marginals obtained during sampling with the true marginals, computed exactly. We evaluate the previously described uniform sampling and confidence-based sampling, with several parameter values, and plot the L_1 error to the true marginals as more factors are examined. Note that here, and in the rest of the evaluation, we shall use the number of factors scored as a proxy for running time, since the effects of the rest of the steps of sampling are relatively negligible. The error in comparison to regular MCMC ($p = 1$) is shown in Figure 2, with standard error bars averaging over 100 models. Initially, as the sampling approach is made more stochastic (lowering p or increasing i), we see a steady improvement in the running time needed to obtain the same error tolerance. However, the amount of relative improvements slows as stochasticity is increased further; in fact for extreme values ($i = 0.05, p = 0.1$) the chains perform worse than regular MCMC.

4.2 Entity Resolution in Citation Data

To evaluate our approach on a real world dataset, we apply stochastic MCMC for MAP inference on the task of citation matching. Given a large number of citations (that appear at the end of research papers, for example), the task is to group together the citations that refer to the same paper. The citation matching problem is an instance of entity resolution, in which observed mentions need to be partitioned such that mentions in a set refer to the same underlying entity. Note that neither the identities, or the number of underlying entities is known.

In this paper, the graphical model of entity resolution consists of observed mentions (m_i), and pairwise binary variables between all pairs of mentions (y_{ij}) which represent whether the corresponding observed mentions are coreferent. There is a local factor for each coreference variable y_{ij} that has a high score if the underlying mentions m_i and m_j are similar. For the sake of efficiency, we only instantiate and incorporate the variables and factors when the variable is true, i.e. if $y_{ij} = 1$. Thus, $\psi(\mathbf{y}) = \sum_e \sum_{m_i, m_j \in e} f(y_{ij})$. The set of possible worlds consists of all settings of the $\mathbf{y}$ variables that are consistent with transitivity, i.e. the binary variables directly represent a valid clustering over the mentions. An example of the model defined over 5 mentions is given in Figure 3. This representation is equivalent to Model 2 as introduced in McCallum and Wellner (2004). As opposed to belief propagation and other approximate inference techniques, MCMC is especially appropriate for the task as it can directly enforce transitivity.

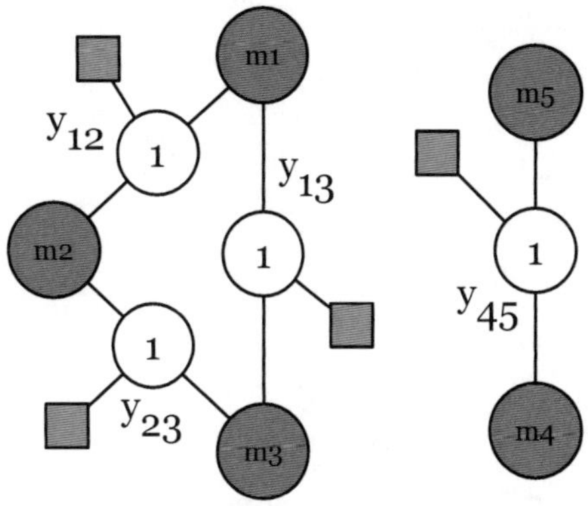

Figure 3: **Graphical Model for Entity Resolution:** defined over 5 mentions, with the setting of the variables resulting in 2 entities. For the sake of brevity, we've only included variables set to 1; binary variables between mentions that are not coreferent have been omitted.

When performing MCMC, each sample is a setting to all the $\mathbf{y}$ variables that is consistent with transitivity. To maintain transitivity during sampling, Metropolis Hastings is used to change the binary variables in a way that is consistent with moving individual mentions. Our proposal function selects a random mention, and moves it to a random entity, changing all the pairwise variables with mentions in its old entity, and the pairwise variables with mentions in its new entity. Thus, evaluation of such a proposal function requires scoring a number of factors linear in the size of the entities, which, for large datasets, can be a significant bottleneck. In practice, however, these set of factors are often highly redundant, as many of the mentions that refer to the same entity contain redundant information and features, and entity membership may be efficiently determined by observing a subset of its mentions.

We evaluate on the Cora dataset (McCallum et al., 1999), used previously to evaluate a number of information extraction approaches (Pasula et al., 2003), including MCMC based inference (Poon and Domingos, 2007; Singh et al., 2009). The dataset

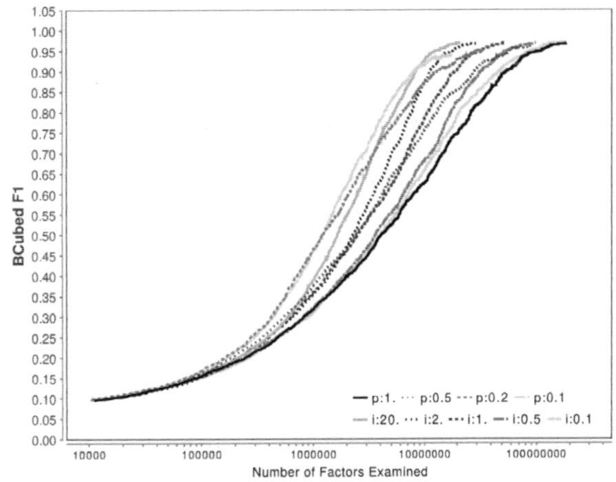

Figure 4: Citation Resolution Accuracy Plot for uniform and variance-based sampling compared to regular MCMC ($p = 1$)

consists of 1295 mentions, that refer to 134 true underlying entities. We use the same features for our model as (Poon and Domingos, 2007), using true *author*, *title*, and *venue* segmentation for features. Since our focus is on evaluating scalability of inference, we combine all the three folds of the data, and train the model using Samplerank (Wick et al., 2011).

We run MCMC on the entity resolution model using the proposal function described above, running our approach with different parameter values. Since we are interested in the MAP configuration, we use a temperature term for annealing. As inference progresses, we compute *BCubed*[2] F1 of the current sample, and plot it against the number of scored factors in Figure 4. We observe consistent speed improvements as stochasticity is improved, with uniform sampling and confidence-based sampling performing competitively. To compute the speedup, we measure the number of factors scored to obtain a desired level of accuracy (90% F1), shown for a diverse set of parameters in Table 1. With a very large confidence interval threshold ($i = 20$) and small proportion ($p = 0.1$), we obtain up to 7 times speedup over regular MCMC. Since the average entity size in this data set is < 10, using a small proportion (and a wide interval) is equivalent to picking a single mention to compare against.

[2] B^3 is a coreference evaluation metric, introduced by Bagga and Baldwin (1998)

Method	Factors Examined	Speedup
Baseline	57,292,700	1x
Uniform Sampling		
$p = 0.75$	34,803,972	1.64x
$p = 0.5$	28,143,323	2.04x
$p = 0.3$	17,778,891	3.22x
$p = 0.2$	12,892,079	4.44x
$p = 0.1$	7,855,686	7.29x
Variance-Based Sampling		
$i = 0.001$	52,522,728	1.09x
$i = 0.01$	51,547,000	1.11x
$i = 0.1$	47,165,038	1.21x
$i = 0.5$	32,828,823	1.74x
$i = 1$	18,938,791	3.02x
$i = 2$	11,134,267	5.14x
$i = 5$	9,827,498	5.83x
$i = 10$	8,675,833	6.60x
$i = 20$	8,295,587	6.90x

Table 1: Speedups on Cora to obtain 90% B^3 F1

4.3 Large-Scale Author Coreference

As the body of published scientific work continues to grow, author coreference, the problem of clustering mentions of research paper authors into the real-world authors to which they refer, is becoming an increasingly important step for performing meaningful bibliometric analysis. However, scaling typical pairwise models of coreference (e.g., McCallum and Wellner (2004)) is difficult because the number of factors in the model grows quadratically with the number of mentions (research papers) and the number of factors evaluated for every MCMC proposal scales linearly in the size of the clusters. For author coreference, the number of author mentions and the number of references to an author entity can often be in the millions, making the evaluation of the MCMC proposals computationally expensive.

We use the publicly available DBLP dataset[3] of BibTex entries as our unlabeled set of mentions, which contains nearly 5 million authors. For evaluation of accuracy, we also include author mentions from the Rexa corpus[4] that contains 2,833 mentions

[3] http://www.informatik.uni-trier.de/~ley/db/

[4] http://www2.selu.edu/Academics/Faculty/aculotta/data/rexa.html

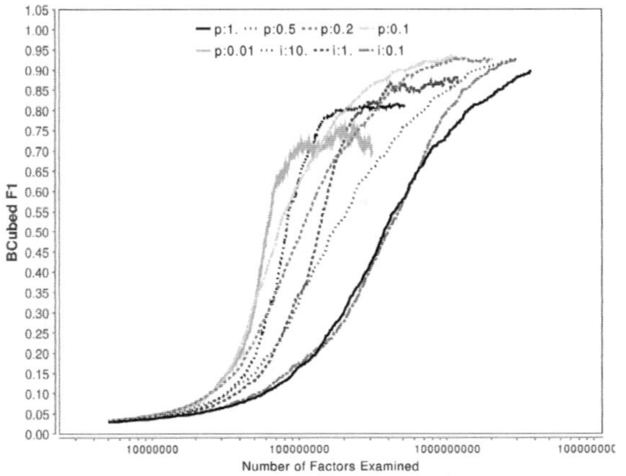

(a) Accuracy versus Number of Factors scored

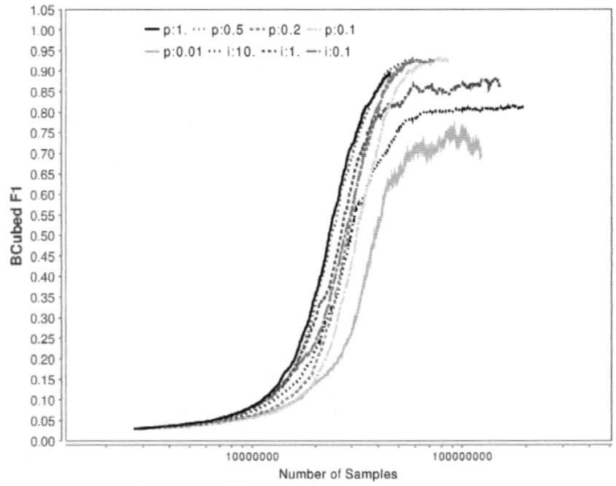

(b) Accuracy versus Number of Samples

Figure 5: Performance of Different Sampling Strategies and Parameters for coreference over 5 million mentions. Plot with p refer to uniform sampling with proportion p of factors picked, while plots with i sample till confidence intervals are narrower than i.

labeled for coreference.

We use the same Metropolis-Hastings scheme that we employ in the problem of citation matching. As before, we initialize to the singleton configuration and run the experiments for a fixed number of samples, plotting accuracy versus the number of factors evaluated (Figure 5a) as well as accuracy versus the number of samples generated (Figure 5b). We also tabulate the relative speedups to obtain the desired accuracy level in Table 2. Our proposed method achieves substantial savings on this task: speedups of 13.16 using the variance sampler and speedups of 9.78 using the uniform sampler. As expected, when we compare the performance using the number of generated samples, the approximate MCMC chains appear to converge more slowly; however, the overall convergence for our approach is substantially faster because evaluation of each sample is significantly cheaper. We also present results on using extreme approximations (for example, $p = 0.01$), resulting in convergence to a low accuracy.

Method	Factors Examined	Speedup
Baseline	1,395,330,603	1x
Uniform		
$p = 0.5$	689,254,134	2.02x
$p = 0.2$	327,616,794	4.26x
$p = 0.1$	206,157,705	6.77x
$p = 0.05$	152,069,987	9.17x
$p = 0.02$	142,689,770	9.78x
Variance		
$i = 0.00001$	1,442,091,344	0.96x
$i = 0.0001$	1,419,110,724	0.98x
$i = 0.001$	1,374,667,077	1.01x
$i = 0.1$	1,012,321,830	1.38x
$i = 1$	265,327,983	5.26x
$i = 10$	179,701,896	7.76x
$i = 100$	106,850,725	13.16x

Table 2: Speedups on DBLP to reach 80% B^3 F1

5 Discussion and Related Work

MCMC is a popular method for inference amongst researchers that work with large and dense graphical models (Richardson and Domingos, 2006; Poon and Domingos, 2006; Poon et al., 2008; Singh et al., 2009; Wick et al., 2009). Some of the probabilistic programming packages popular amongst NLP practitioners also rely on MCMC for inference and learning (Richardson and Domingos, 2006; McCallum et al., 2009). Although most of these methods apply MCMC directly, the rate of convergence of MCMC has become a concern as larger and more densely-factored models are being considered, motivating the need for more efficient sampling that uses parallelism (Singh et al., 2011; Gonzalez et al., 2011) and domain knowledge for blocking (Singh et al., 2010). Thus we feel providing a method to speed up MCMC inference can have a significant impact.

There has also been recent work in designing scalable approximate inference techniques. Belief propagation has, in particular, has gained some recent interest. Similar to our approach, a number of researchers propose modifications to BP that perform inference without visiting all the factors. Recent work introduces dynamic schedules to prioritize amongst the factors (Coughlan and Shen, 2007; Sutton and McCallum, 2007) that has been used to only visit a small fraction of the factors (Riedel and Smith, 2010). Gonzalez et al. (2009) utilize these schedules to facilitate parallelization.

A number of existing approaches in statistics are also related to our contribution. Leskovec and Faloutsos (2006) propose techniques to sample a graph to compute certain graph statistics with associated confidence. Christen and Fox (2005) also propose an approach to efficiently evaluate a proposal, however, once accepted, they score all the factors. Murray and Ghahramani (2004) propose an approximate MCMC technique for Bayesian models that estimates the partition function instead of computing it exactly.

Related work has also applied such ideas for robust learning, for example Kok and Domingos (2005), based on earlier work by Hulten and Domingos (2002), uniformly sample the groundings of an MLN to estimate the likelihood.

6 Conclusions and Future Work

Motivated by the need for an efficient inference technique that can scale to large, densely-factored models, this paper considers a simple extension to the Markov chain Monto Carlo algorithm. By observing that many graphical models contain substantial redundancy among the factors, we propose *stochastic* evaluation of proposals that subsamples the factors to be scored. Using two proposed sampling strategies, we demonstrate improved convergence for marginal inference on synthetic data. Further, we evaluate our approach on two real-world entity resolution datasets, obtaining a 13 times speedup on a dataset containing 5 million mentions.

Based on the ideas presented in the paper, we will consider additional sampling strategies. In particular, we will explore *dynamic* sampling, in which we sample fewer factors during the initial, burn-in phase, but sample more factors as we get close to convergence. Motivated by our positive results, we will also study the application of this approach to other approximate inference techniques, such as belief propagation and variational inference. Since training is often a huge bottleneck for information extraction, we will also explore its applications to parameter estimation.

Acknowledgements

This work was supported in part by the Center for Intelligent Information Retrieval, in part by ARFL under prime contract number is FA8650-10-C-7059, and the University of Massachusetts gratefully acknowledges the support of Defense Advanced Research Projects Agency (DARPA) Machine Reading Program under Air Force Research Laboratory (AFRL) prime contract no. FA8750-09-C-0181. The U.S. Government is authorized to reproduce and distribute reprint for Governmental purposes notwithstanding any copyright annotation thereon. Any opinions, findings and conclusions or recommendations expressed in this material are those of the authors and do not necessarily reflect those of the sponsor.

References

[Bagga and Baldwin1998] Amit Bagga and Breck Baldwin. 1998. Algorithms for scoring coreference chains. In *International Conference on Language Resources and Evaluation (LREC) Workshop on Linguistics Coreference*, pages 563–566.

[Bertsimas and Tsitsiklis1993] D. Bertsimas and J. Tsitsiklis. 1993. Simulated annealing. *Statistical Science*, pages 10–15.

[Carreras2007] Xavier Carreras. 2007. Experiments with a higher-order projective dependency parser. In *Proceedings of the CoNLL Shared Task Session of EMNLP-CoNLL 2007*, pages 957–961.

[Christen and Fox2005] J. Andrés Christen and Colin Fox. 2005. Markov chain monte carlo using an approximation. *Journal of Computational and Graphical Statistics*, 14(4):pp. 795–810.

[Coughlan and Shen2007] James Coughlan and Huiying Shen. 2007. Dynamic quantization for belief propagation in sparse spaces. *Computer Vision and Image Understanding*, 106:47–58, April.

[Culotta et al.2007] Aron Culotta, Michael Wick, and Andrew McCallum. 2007. First-order probabilistic models for coreference resolution. In *North American Chapter of the Association for Computational Linguistics - Human Language Technologies (NAACL HLT)*.

[Gonzalez et al.2009] Joseph Gonzalez, Yucheng Low, and Carlos Guestrin. 2009. Residual splash for optimally parallelizing belief propagation. In *Artificial Intelligence and Statistics (AISTATS)*.

[Gonzalez et al.2011] Joseph Gonzalez, Yucheng Low, Arthur Gretton, and Carlos Guestrin. 2011. Parallel gibbs sampling: From colored fields to thin junction trees. In *Artificial Intelligence and Statistics (AISTATS)*, Ft. Lauderdale, FL, May.

[Hoffmann et al.2011] Raphael Hoffmann, Congle Zhang, Xiao Ling, Luke Zettlemoyer, and Daniel S. Weld. 2011. Knowledge-based weak supervision for information extraction of overlapping relations. In *Annual Meeting of the Association for Computational Linguistics (ACL)*, pages 541–550, Portland, Oregon, USA, June. Association for Computational Linguistics.

[Hulten and Domingos2002] Geoff Hulten and Pedro Domingos. 2002. Mining complex models from arbitrarily large databases in constant time. In *International Conference on Knowledge Discovery and Data Mining (KDD)*, pages 525–531, New York, NY, USA. ACM.

[Kok and Domingos2005] Stanley Kok and Pedro Domingos. 2005. Learning the structure of markov logic networks. In *International Conference on Machine Learning (ICML)*, pages 441–448, New York, NY, USA. ACM.

[Kschischang et al.2001] Frank R. Kschischang, Brendan J. Frey, and Hans Andrea Loeliger. 2001. Factor graphs and the sum-product algorithm. *IEEE Transactions of Information Theory*, 47(2):498–519, Feb.

[Lafferty et al.2001] John D. Lafferty, Andrew McCallum, and Fernando Pereira. 2001. Conditional random fields: Probabilistic models for segmenting and labeling sequence data. In *International Conference on Machine Learning (ICML)*.

[Leskovec and Faloutsos2006] Jure Leskovec and Christos Faloutsos. 2006. Sampling from large graphs. In *International Conference on Knowledge Discovery and Data Mining (KDD)*, pages 631–636, New York, NY, USA. ACM.

[McCallum and Wellner2004] Andrew McCallum and Ben Wellner. 2004. Conditional models of identity uncertainty with application to noun coreference. In *Neural Information Processing Systems (NIPS)*.

[McCallum et al.1999] Andrew McCallum, Kamal Nigam, Jason Rennie, and Kristie Seymore. 1999. A machine learning approach to building domain-specific search engines. In *International Joint Conference on Artificial Intelligence (IJCAI)*.

[McCallum et al.2009] Andrew McCallum, Karl Schultz, and Sameer Singh. 2009. FACTORIE: Probabilistic programming via imperatively defined factor graphs. In *Neural Information Processing Systems (NIPS)*.

[Murray and Ghahramani2004] Iain Murray and Zoubin Ghahramani. 2004. Bayesian learning in undirected graphical models: Approximate MCMC algorithms. In *Uncertainty in Artificial Intelligence (UAI)*.

[Pasula et al.2003] H. Pasula, B. Marthi, B. Milch, S. Russell, and I. Shpitser. 2003. Identity uncertainty and citation matching. In *Neural Information Processing Systems (NIPS)*.

[Poon and Domingos2006] Hoifung Poon and Pedro Domingos. 2006. Sound and efficient inference with probabilistic and deterministic dependencies. In *AAAI Conference on Artificial Intelligence*.

[Poon and Domingos2007] Hoifung Poon and Pedro Domingos. 2007. Joint inference in information extraction. In *AAAI Conference on Artificial Intelligence*, pages 913–918.

[Poon et al.2008] Hoifung Poon, Pedro Domingos, and Marc Sumner. 2008. A general method for reducing the complexity of relational inference and its application to MCMC. In *AAAI Conference on Artificial Intelligence*.

[Richardson and Domingos2006] Matthew Richardson and Pedro Domingos. 2006. Markov logic networks. *Machine Learning*, 62(1-2):107–136.

[Riedel and Smith2010] Sebastian Riedel and David A. Smith. 2010. Relaxed marginal inference and its application to dependency parsing. In *North American Chapter of the Association for Computational Linguistics - Human Language Technologies (NAACL HLT)*, pages 760–768.

[Singh et al.2009] Sameer Singh, Karl Schultz, and Andrew McCallum. 2009. Bi-directional joint inference for entity resolution and segmentation using imperatively-defined factor graphs. In *Machine Learning and Knowledge Discovery in Databases (Lecture Notes in Computer Science) and European Conference on Machine Learning and Principles and Practice of Knowledge Discovery in Databases (ECML PKDD)*, pages 414–429.

[Singh et al.2010] Sameer Singh, Michael L. Wick, and Andrew McCallum. 2010. Distantly labeling data for large scale cross-document coreference. *Computing Research Repository (CoRR)*, abs/1005.4298.

[Singh et al.2011] Sameer Singh, Amarnag Subramanya, Fernando Pereira, and Andrew McCallum. 2011.

Large-scale cross-document coreference using distributed inference and hierarchical models. In *Association for Computational Linguistics: Human Language Technologies (ACL HLT)*.

[Sutton and McCallum2004] Charles Sutton and Andrew McCallum. 2004. Collective segmentation and labeling of distant entities in information extraction. Technical Report TR#04-49, University of Massachusetts, July.

[Sutton and McCallum2007] Charles Sutton and Andrew McCallum. 2007. Improved dynamic schedules for belief propagation. In *Uncertainty in Artificial Intelligence (UAI)*.

[Wick et al.2009] Michael Wick, Aron Culotta, Khashayar Rohanimanesh, and Andrew McCallum. 2009. An entity-based model for coreference resolution. In *SIAM International Conference on Data Mining (SDM)*.

[Wick et al.2010] Michael Wick, Andrew McCallum, and Gerome Miklau. 2010. Scalable probabilistic databases with factor graphs and mcmc. *International Conference on Very Large Databases (VLDB)*, 3:794–804, September.

[Wick et al.2011] Michael Wick, Khashayar Rohanimanesh, Kedar Bellare, Aron Culotta, and Andrew McCallum. 2011. Samplerank: Training factor graphs with atomic gradients. In *International Conference on Machine Learning (ICML)*.

[Yao et al.2010] Limin Yao, Sebastian Riedel, and Andrew McCallum. 2010. Collective cross-document relation extraction without labelled data. In *Empirical Methods in Natural Language Processing (EMNLP)*.

On Amortizing Inference Cost for Structured Prediction

Vivek Srikumar* and **Gourab Kundu*** and **Dan Roth**
University of Illinois, Urbana-Champaign
Urbana, IL. 61801
{vsrikum2, kundu2, danr}@illinois.edu

Abstract

This paper deals with the problem of predicting structures in the context of NLP. Typically, in structured prediction, an inference procedure is applied to each example independently of the others. In this paper, we seek to optimize the time complexity of inference over entire datasets, rather than individual examples. By considering the general inference representation provided by integer linear programs, we propose three exact inference theorems which allow us to re-use earlier solutions for certain instances, thereby completely avoiding possibly expensive calls to the inference procedure. We also identify several approximation schemes which can provide further speedup. We instantiate these ideas to the structured prediction task of semantic role labeling and show that we can achieve a speedup of over 2.5 using our approach while retaining the guarantees of exactness and a further speedup of over 3 using approximations that do not degrade performance.

1 Introduction

Typically, in structured prediction applications, every example is treated independently and an inference algorithm is applied to each one of them. For example, consider a dependency parser that uses the maximum spanning tree algorithm (McDonald et al., 2005) or its integer linear program variants (Riedel and Clarke, 2006; Martins et al., 2009) to make predictions. Given a trained model, the parser addresses each sentence separately and runs the inference algorithm to predict the parse tree. Thus, the time complexity of inference over the test set is linear in the size of the corpus.

In this paper, we ask the following question: *For a given task, since the inference procedure predicts structures from the same family of structures (dependency trees, semantic role structures, etc.), can the fact that we are running inference for a large number of examples help us improve the time complexity of inference?* In the dependency parsing example, this question translates to asking whether, having parsed many sentences, we can decrease the parsing time for the next sentence.

Since any combinatorial optimization problem can be phrased as an integer linear program (ILP), we frame inference problems as ILPs for the purpose of analysis. By analyzing the objective functions of integer linear programs, we identify conditions when two ILPs have the same solution. This allows us to reuse solutions of previously solved problems and theoretically guarantee the optimality of the solution. Furthermore, in some cases, even when the conditions are not satisfied, we can reuse previous solutions with high probability of being correct.

Given the extensive use of integer linear programs for structured prediction in Natural Language Processing over the last few years, these ideas can be applied broadly to NLP problems. We instantiate our improved inference approaches in the structured prediction task of semantic role labeling, where we use an existing implementation and a previous trained model that is based on the approach of (Punyakanok et al., 2008). We merely modify the inference pro-

* These authors contributed equally to this work.

cess to show that we can realize the theoretical gains by making fewer calls to the underlying ILP solver.

Algorithm	Speedup
Theorem 1	2.44
Theorem 2	2.18
Theorem 3	2.50

Table 1: The speedup for semantic role labeling corresponding to the three theorems described in this paper. These theorems guarantee the optimality of the solution, thus ensuring that the speedup is not accompanied by any loss in performance.

Table 1 presents a preview of our results, which are discussed in Section 4. All three approaches in this table improve running time, while guaranteeing optimum solutions. Allowing small violations to the conditions of the theorems provide an even higher improvement in speedup (over 3), without loss of performance.

The primary contributions of this paper are:

1. We pose the problem of optimizing inference costs over entire datasets rather than individual examples. Our approach is agnostic to the underlying models and allows us to use pre-trained scoring functions.

2. We identify equivalence classes of ILP problems and use this notion to prove exact conditions under which no inference is required. These conditions lead to algorithms that can speed up inference problem without losing the exactness guarantees. We also use these conditions to develop approximate inference algorithms that can provide a further speedup.

3. We apply our approach to the structured prediction task of semantic role labeling. By not having to perform inference on some of the instances, those that are equivalent to previously seen instances, we show significant speed up in terms of the number of times inference needs to be performed. These gains are also realized in terms of wall-clock times.

The rest of this paper is organized as follows: In section 2, we formulate the problem of amortized inference and provide motivation for why amortized gains can be possible. This leads to the theoretical discussion in section 3, where we present the meta-algorithm for amortized inference along with several exact and approximate inference schemes. We instantiate these schemes for the task of semantic role labeling (Section 4). Section 5 discusses related work and future research directions.

2 Motivation

Many NLP tasks can be phrased as structured prediction problems, where the goal is to jointly assign values to many inference variables while accounting for possible dependencies among them. This decision task is a combinatorial optimization problem and can be solved using a dynamic programming approach if the structure permits. In general, the inference problem can be formulated and solved as integer linear programs (ILPs).

Following (Roth and Yih, 2004) Integer linear programs have been used broadly in NLP. For example, (Riedel and Clarke, 2006) and (Martins et al., 2009) addressed the problem of dependency parsing and (Punyakanok et al., 2005; Punyakanok et al., 2008) dealt with semantic role labeling with this technique.

In this section, we will use the ILP formulation of dependency parsing to introduce notation. The standard approach to framing dependency parsing as an integer linear program was introduced by (Riedel and Clarke, 2006), who converted the MST parser of (McDonald et al., 2005) to use ILP for inference. The key idea is to build a complete graph consisting of tokens of the sentence where each edge is weighted by a learned scoring function. The goal of inference is to select the maximum spanning tree of this weighted graph.

2.1 Problem Formulation

In this work, we consider the general inference problem of solving a 0-1 integer linear program. To perform inference, we assume that we have a model that assigns scores to the ILP decision variables. Thus, our work is applicable not only in cases where inference is done after a separate learning phase, as in (Roth and Yih, 2004; Clarke and Lapata, 2006; Roth and Yih, 2007) and others, but also when inference is done during the training phase, for algorithms like the structured perceptron of (Collins, 2002), structured SVM (Tsochantaridis et al., 2005) or the constraints driven learning approach of (Chang et al., 2007).

Since structured prediction assigns values to a collection of inter-related binary decisions, we denote the ith binary decision by $y_i \in \{0, 1\}$ and the entire structure as $\mathbf{y}$, the vector composed of all the binary decisions. In our running example, each edge in the weighted graph generates a single decision variable (for unlabeled dependency parsing). For each y_i, let $c_i \in \Re$ denote the weight associated with it. We denote the entire collection of weights by the vector $\mathbf{c}$, forming the *objective* for this ILP.

Not all assignments to these variables are valid. Without loss of generality, these constraints can be expressed using linear inequalities over the inference variables, which we write as $\mathbf{M}^T\mathbf{y} \leq \mathbf{b}$ for a real valued matrix $\mathbf{M}$ and a vector $\mathbf{b}$. In dependency parsing, for example, these constraints ensure that the final output is a spanning tree.

Now, the overall goal of inference is to find the highest scoring structure. Thus, we can frame inference as an optimization problem $\mathbf{p}$ with n inference variables as follows:

$$\arg\max_{\mathbf{y}\in\{0,1\}^n} \quad \mathbf{c}^T\mathbf{y} \qquad (1)$$

$$\text{subject to} \quad \mathbf{M}^T\mathbf{y} \leq \mathbf{b}. \qquad (2)$$

For brevity, we denote the space of feasible solutions that satisfy the constraints for the ILP problem $\mathbf{p}$ as $K_\mathbf{p} = \{\mathbf{y} \in \{0,1\}^n | \mathbf{M}^T\mathbf{y} \leq \mathbf{b}\}$. Thus, the goal of inference is to find

$$\arg\max_{\mathbf{y}\in K_\mathbf{p}} \mathbf{c}^T\mathbf{y}.$$

We refer to $K_\mathbf{p}$ as the feasible set for the inference problem $\mathbf{p}$ and $\mathbf{y_p}$ as its solution.

In the worst case, integer linear programs are known to be NP-hard. Hence, solving large problems, (that is, problems with a large number of constraints and/or variables) can be infeasible.

For structured prediction problems seen in NLP, we typically solve many instances of inference problems. In this paper, we investigate whether an inference algorithm can use previous predictions to speed up inference time, thus giving us an *amortized gain* in inference time over the lifetime of the program. We refer to inference algorithms that have this capability as **amortized inference algorithms**.

In our running example, each sentence corresponds to a separate ILP. Over the lifetime of the dependency parser, we create one inference instance (that is, one ILP) per sentence and solve it. An amortized inference algorithm becomes *faster* at parsing as it parses more and more sentences.

2.2 Why can inference costs be amortized over datasets?

In the rest of this section, we will argue that the time cost of inference can be amortized because of the nature of inference in NLP tasks. Our argument is based on two observations, which are summarized in Figure (1): (1) Though the space of possible structures may be large, only a very small fraction of these occur. (2) The distribution of observed structures is heavily skewed towards a small number of them.

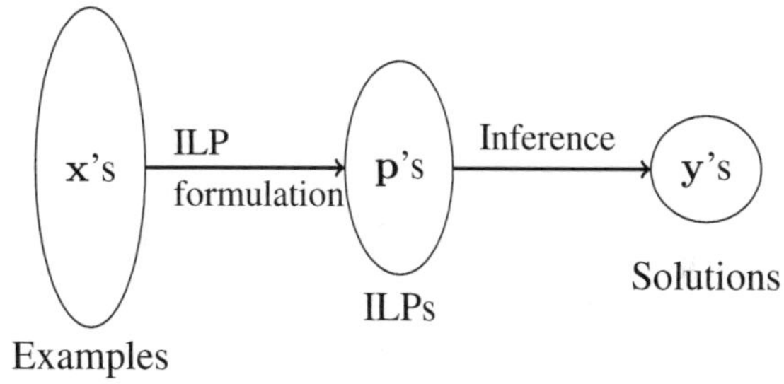

Figure 1: For a structured prediction task, the inference problem $\mathbf{p}$ for an example $\mathbf{x}$ needs to be formulated before solving it to get the structure $\mathbf{y}$. In structured prediction problems seen in NLP, while an exponential number of structures is possible for a given instance, in practice, only a small fraction of these ever occur. This figure illustrates the empirical observation that there are fewer inference problems $\mathbf{p}$'s than the number of examples and the number of observed structures $\mathbf{y}$'s is even lesser.

As an illustration, consider the problem of part-of-speech tagging. With the standard Penn Treebank tag set, each token can be assigned one of 45 labels. Thus, for a sentence of size n, we could have 45^n structures out of which the inference process needs to choose one. However, a majority of these structures never occur. For example, we cannot have a

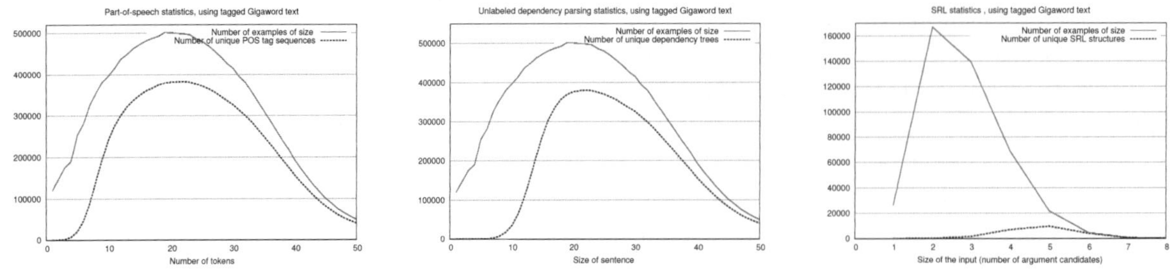

(a) Part-of-speech tagging (b) Unlabeled dependency parsing (c) Semantic role labeling

Figure 2: Number of inference instances for different input sizes (red solid lines) and the number of unique structures for each size (blue dotted lines). The x-axis indicates the size of the input (number of tokens for part of speech and dependency, and number of argument candidates for SRL.) Note that the number of instances is not the number of unique examples of a given length, but the number of times an inference procedure is called for an input of a given size.

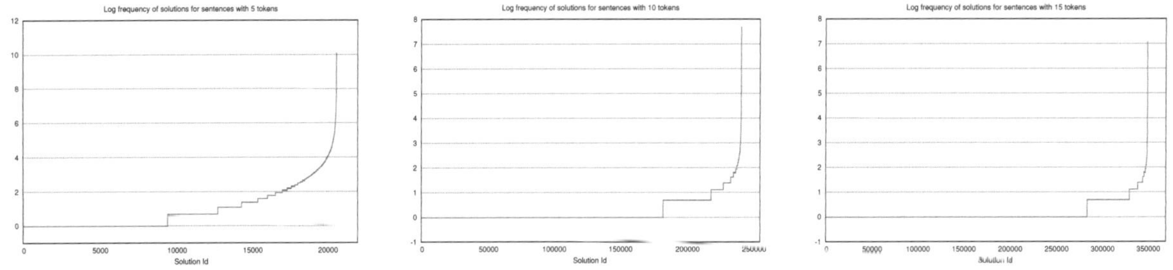

(a) Sentence length = 5 (b) Sentence length = 10 (c) Sentence length = 15

Figure 3: These plots show the log-frequencies of occurrences of part-of-speech sequences for sentences with five, ten and fifteen tokens. The x-axes list different unique part-of-speech tag sequences for the entire sentence. These plots show that for sentences of a given length, most structures (solutions) that are possible never occur, or occur very infrequently; only a few of the possible structures (solutions) actually occur frequently.

sentence where all the tokens are determiners.

Furthermore, many sentences of the same size share the same part-of-speech tag sequence. To quantify the redundancy of structures, we part-of-speech tagged the English Gigaword corpus (Graff and Cieri, 2003). Figure (2a) shows the number of sentences in the corpus for different sentence lengths. In addition, it also shows the number of unique part-of-speech tag sequences (over the entire sentence) for each size. We see that the number of structures is much fewer than the number of instances for any sentence size. Note that 45^n quickly outgrows the number of sentences as n increases. The figures (2b) and (2c) show similar statistics for unlabeled dependency parsing and semantic role labeling. In the former case, the size of the instance is the number of tokens in a sentence, while in the latter, the size is the number of argument candidates that need to be labeled for a given predicate. In both cases, we see that the number of empirically observed structures is far fewer than the number of instances to be labeled.

Thus, for any given input size, the number of instances of that size (over the lifetime of the program) far exceeds the number of observed structures for that size. Moreover, the number of observed structures is significantly smaller than the number of theoretically possible structures. Thus, we have a small number of structures that form optimum structures for many inference instances of the same size.

Our second observation deals with the distribution of structures for a given input size. Figure (3) shows the log frequencies of part-of-speech tagging sequences for sentences of lengths five, ten and fifteen. In all cases, we see that a few structures are most frequent. We observed similar distributions of structures for all input sizes for dependency parsing and semantic role labeling as well.

Since the number of structures for a given example size is small, many examples $\mathbf{x}$'s, and hence many inference problems $\mathbf{p}$'s, are associated with the same structure $\mathbf{y}$. These observations suggest the possibility of getting an amortized gain in inference time by characterizing the set of inference problems that produce the same structure. Then, for a new inference problem, if we can identify that it belongs to a known set, that is, will yield a solution that we have already seen, we do not have to run inference at all. The second observation also suggests that this characterization of sets of problems that have the same solution can be done in a data-driven way because characterizing a small number of structures can give us high coverage.

3 Amortizing inference costs

In this section, we present different schemes for amortized inference leading up to an inference meta-algorithm. The meta-algorithm is both agnostic to the underlying inference algorithm that is used by the problem and maintains the exactness properties of the underlying inference scheme. That is, if we have an exact/approximate inference algorithm with a certain guarantees, the meta-algorithm will have the same guarantees, but with a speedup.

3.1 Notation

For an integer linear program $\mathbf{p}$ with $n_{\mathbf{p}}$ variables, we denote its objective coefficients by $\mathbf{c_p}$ and its feasible set by $K_{\mathbf{p}}$. We denote its solution as as $\mathbf{y_p}$. We represent vectors by boldfaced symbols and their i^{th} component using subscripts.

We consider many instantiations of the inference problem and use superscripts to denote each individual instance. Thus, we have a large collection of inference instances $P = \{\mathbf{p}^1, \mathbf{p}^2, \cdots\}$ along with their respective solutions $\{\mathbf{y}_\mathbf{p}^1, \mathbf{y}_\mathbf{p}^2, \cdots\}$.

Definition 1 (Equivalence classes of ILPs)**.** *Two integer linear programs are said to be in the same equivalence class if they have the same number of inference variables and the same feasible set.*

We square brackets to denote equivalence classes. If $[P]$ is an equivalence class of ILPs, we use the notation $K_{[P]}$ to denote its feasible set and $n_{[P]}$ to denote the number of variables. Also, for a program $\mathbf{p}$, we use the notation $\mathbf{p} \sim [P]$ to indicate that it belongs to the equivalence class $[P]$.

3.2 Exact theorems

Our goal is to characterize the set of objective functions which will have the same solution for a given equivalence class of problems.

Suppose we have solved an ILP $\mathbf{p}$ to get a solution $\mathbf{y_p}$. For every inference variable that is active in the solution (i.e., whose value is 1), increasing the corresponding objective value will not change the optimal assignment to the variables. Similarly, for all other variables (whose value in the solution is 0), decreasing the objective value will not change the optimal solution. This intuition gives us our first theorem for checking whether two ILPs have the same solution by looking at the difference between their objective coefficients.

Theorem 1. *Let $\mathbf{p}$ denote an inference problem posed as an integer linear program belonging to an equivalence class $[P]$. Let $\mathbf{q} \sim [P]$ be another inference instance in the same equivalence class. Define $\delta\mathbf{c} = \mathbf{c_q} - \mathbf{c_p}$ to be the difference of the objective coefficients of the ILPs. Then, $\mathbf{y_p}$ is the solution of the problem $\mathbf{q}$ if for each $i \in \{1, \cdots, n_\mathbf{p}\}$, we have*

$$(2\mathbf{y}_{\mathbf{p},i} - 1)\delta\mathbf{c}_i \geq 0 \tag{3}$$

The condition in the theorem, that is, inequality (3), requires that the objective coefficients corresponding to values $\mathbf{y}_{\mathbf{p},i}$ that are set to 1 in $\mathbf{p}$ increase, and those that correspond to values of $\mathbf{y}_{\mathbf{p},i}$ set to 0, decrease. Under these conditions, if $\mathbf{y_p}$ is the maximizer of the original objective, then it maximizes the new objective too.

Theorem 1 identifies perturbations of an ILP's objective coefficients that will not change the optimal assignment. Next, we will characterize the sets of objective values that will have the same solution using a criterion that is independent of the actual solution. Suppose we have two ILPs $\mathbf{p}$ and $\mathbf{q}$ in an equivalence class $[P]$ whose objective values are $\mathbf{c_p}$ and $\mathbf{c_q}$ respectively. Suppose $\mathbf{y}^*$ is the solution to both these programs. That is, for every $\mathbf{y} \in K_{[P]}$, we have $\mathbf{c}_\mathbf{p}^T\mathbf{y} \leq \mathbf{c}_\mathbf{p}^T\mathbf{y}^*$ and $\mathbf{c}_\mathbf{q}^T\mathbf{y} \leq \mathbf{c}_\mathbf{q}^T\mathbf{y}^*$. Multiplying these inequalities by any two positive real numbers x_1 and x_2 and adding them shows us that $\mathbf{y}^*$ is also the solution for the ILP in $[P]$ which has the objective coefficients $x_1\mathbf{c}_\mathbf{p} + x_2\mathbf{c}_\mathbf{q}$. Extending this to an arbitrary number of inference problems gives us our next theorem.

Theorem 2. *Let P denote a collection $\{\mathbf{p}^1, \mathbf{p}^2, \cdots, \mathbf{p}^m\}$ of m inference problems in the same equivalence class $[P]$ and suppose that all the problems have the same solution, $\mathbf{y}_\mathbf{p}$. Let $\mathbf{q} \sim [P]$ be a new inference program whose optimal solution is $\mathbf{y}$. Then $\mathbf{y} = \mathbf{y}_\mathbf{p}$ if there is some $\mathbf{x} \in \Re^m$ such that $\mathbf{x} \geq \mathbf{0}$ and*

$$\mathbf{c}_\mathbf{q} = \sum_j \mathbf{x}_j \mathbf{c}_\mathbf{p}^j. \quad (4)$$

From the geometric perspective, the pre-condition of this theorem implies that if the new coefficients lie in the cone formed by the coefficients of the programs that have the same solution, then the new program shares the solution.

Theorems 1 and 2 suggest two different approaches for identifying whether a new ILP can use the solution of previously solved inference instances. These theorems can be combined to get a single criterion that uses the objective coefficients of previously solved inference problems *and* their common solution to determine whether a new inference problem will have the same solution. Given a collection of solved ILPs that have the same solution, from theorem 2, we know that an ILP with the objective coefficients $\mathbf{c} = \sum_j \mathbf{x}_j \mathbf{c}_\mathbf{p}^j$ will share the solution. Considering an ILP whose objective vector is $\mathbf{c}$ and applying theorem 1 to it gives us the next theorem.

Theorem 3. *Let P denote a collection $\{\mathbf{p}^1, \mathbf{p}^2, \cdots, \mathbf{p}^m\}$ of m inference problems belonging to the same equivalence class $[P]$. Furthermore, suppose all the programs have the same solution $\mathbf{y}_\mathbf{p}$. Let $\mathbf{q} \sim [P]$ be a new inference program in the equivalence class. For any $\mathbf{x} \in \Re^m$, define $\Delta\mathbf{c}(\mathbf{x}) = \mathbf{c}_\mathbf{q} - \sum_j \mathbf{x}_j \mathbf{c}_\mathbf{p}^j$. The assignment $\mathbf{y}_\mathbf{p}$ is the optimal solution of the problem $\mathbf{q}$ if there is some $\mathbf{x} \in \Re^m$ such that $\mathbf{x} \geq \mathbf{0}$ and for each $i \in \{1, n_\mathbf{p}\}$, we have*

$$(2\mathbf{y}_{\mathbf{p},i} - 1)\Delta\mathbf{c}_i \geq 0 \quad (5)$$

Theorem	Condition
Theorem 1	$\forall i \in \{1, \cdots, n_\mathbf{p}\}$, $(2\mathbf{y}_{\mathbf{p},i} - 1)\delta\mathbf{c}_i \geq 0;\ \forall i.$
Theorem 2	$\exists\, \mathbf{x} \in \Re^m$, such that $\mathbf{x} \geq 0$ and $\mathbf{c}_\mathbf{q} = \sum_j \mathbf{x}_j \mathbf{c}_\mathbf{p}^j$
Theorem 3	$\exists\, \mathbf{x} \in \Re^m$, such that $\mathbf{x} \geq \mathbf{0}$ and $(2\mathbf{y}_{\mathbf{p},i} - 1)\Delta\mathbf{c}_i \geq 0;\ \forall i.$

Table 2: Conditions for checking whether $\mathbf{y}_\mathbf{p}$ is the solution for an inference problem $\mathbf{q} \sim [P]$ according to theorems 1, 2 and 3. Please refer to the statements of the theorems for details about the notation.

3.3 Implementation

Theorems 1, 2 and 3 each specify a condition that checks whether a pre-existing solution is the optimal assignment for a new inference problem. These conditions are summarized in Table 2. In all cases, if the condition matches, the theorems guarantee that the two solutions will be the same. That is, applying the theorems will not change the performance of the underlying inference procedure. Only the number of inference calls will be decreased.

In our implementation of the conditions, we used a database[1] to cache ILPs and implemented the retrieval of equivalence classes and solutions as queries to the database. To implement theorem 1, we iterate over all ILPs in the equivalence class and check if the condition is satisfied for one of them. The conditions of theorems 2 and 3 check whether a collection of linear (in)equalities has a feasible solution using a linear program solver.

We optimize the wall-clock time of theorems 2 and 3 by making two observations. First, we do not need to solve linear programs for all possible observed structures. Given an objective vector, we only need consider the highest scoring structures within an equivalence class. (All other structures cannot be the solution to the ILP.) Second, since theorem 2 checks whether an ILP lies within a cone, we can optimize the cache for theorem 2 by only storing the ILPs that form on the boundary of the cone. A similar optimization can be performed for theorem 3 as well. Our implementation uses the following weaker version of this optimization: while caching ILPs, we

[1] We used the H2 database engine, which can be downloaded from `http://h2database.com`, for all caching.

do not add an instance to the cache if it already satisfies the theorem. This optimization reduces the size of the linear programs used to check feasibility.

3.4 Approximation schemes

So far, in the above three theorems, we retain the guarantees (in terms of exactness and performance) of the underlying inference procedure. Now, we will look at schemes for approximate inference. Unlike the three theorems listed above, with the following amortized inference schemes, we are not guaranteed an optimal solution.

3.4.1 Most frequent solution

The first scheme for approximation uses the observation that the most frequent solution occurs an overwhelmingly large number of times, compared to the others. (See the discussion in section 2.2 and figures 3a, 3b and 3c for part-of-speech tagging.) Under this approximation scheme, given an ILP problem, we simply pick the most frequent solution for that equivalence class as the solution, provided this solution has been seen a sufficient number of times. If the support available in the cache is insufficient, we call the underlying inference procedure.

3.4.2 Top-K approximation

The previous scheme for approximate amortized inference is agnostic to the objective coefficients of integer linear program to be solved and uses only its equivalence class to find a candidate structure. The top-K approach extends this by scoring the K most frequent solutions using the objective coefficients and selecting the highest scoring one as the solution to the ILP problem. As with the previous scheme, we only consider solutions that have sufficient support.

3.4.3 Approximations to theorems 1 and 3

The next approximate inference schemes relaxes the conditions in theorems 1 and 3 by allowing the inequalities to be violated by ϵ. That is, the inequality (3) from Theorem 1 now becomes

$$(2\mathbf{y}_{\mathbf{p},i} - 1)\delta\mathbf{c}_i + \epsilon \geq 0. \quad (6)$$

The inequality (5) from Theorem 3 is similarly relaxed as follows:

$$(2\mathbf{y}_{\mathbf{p},i} - 1)\Delta\mathbf{c}_i + \epsilon \geq 0 \quad (7)$$

3.5 Amortized inference algorithm

Each exact and approximate inference approach described above specifies a condition to check whether an inference procedure should be called for a new problem. This gives us the following meta-algorithm for amortized inference, parameterized by the actual scheme used: If the given input instance $\mathbf{p}$ satisfies the condition specified by the scheme, then use the cached solution. Otherwise, call the inference procedure and cache the solution for future use.

4 Experiments

In this section, we apply the theory from Section 3 to the structure prediction problem of semantic role labeling. Since the inference schemes presented above are independent of the learning aspects, we use an off-the-shelf implementation and merely modify the inference as discussed in Section 3.5.

The goal of the experiments is to show that using an amortized inference algorithm, we can make fewer calls to the underlying inference procedure. For the exact inference algorithms, doing so will not change the performance as compared to the underlying system. For the approximations, we can make a trade-off between the inference time and performance.

4.1 Experimental setup

Our goal is to simulate a long-running NLP process that can use a cache of already solved problems to improve inference time. Given a new input problem, our theorems require us to find all elements in the equivalence class of that problem along with their solutions. Intuitively, we expect a higher probability of finding members of an arbitrary equivalence class if the size of the cache is large. Hence, we processed sentences from the Gigaword corpus and cached the inference problems for our task.

The wall-clock time is strongly dependent on such specific implementation of the components, which are independent of the main contributions of this work. Also, in most interesting applications, the computation time for each step will be typically dominated by the number of inference steps, especially with efficient implementations of caching and retrieval. Hence, the number of calls to the underlying procedure is the appropriate complexity parameter. Let N_{Base} be the number of times we would need to call the underlying inference procedure had we not used an amortized algorithm. (This is the same as the number of inference problems.) Let N_A be the number of times the underlying inference procedure is actually called using an amortized algorithm A. We define the *speedup* of A as

$$Speedup(A) = \frac{N_{Base}}{N_A}. \tag{8}$$

We also report the *clock speedup* of our implementation for all algorithms, which is the ratio of the wall-clock time taken by the baseline algorithm to that of the amortized algorithm. For measuring time, we only measure the time for inference as the other aspects (feature extraction, scoring, etc.) are not changed.

4.2 Semantic Role Labeling

The goal of Semantic Role Labeling (SRL) (Palmer et al., 2010) is to identify and assign semantic roles to arguments of verb predicates in a sentence. For example, consider the the sentence *John gave the ball to Mary.* The verb *give* takes three arguments, *John*, *the ball* and *to Mary*, which are labeled A0, A1 and A2 respectively.

We used the system of (Punyakanok et al., 2008) as our base SRL system. It consists of two classifiers trained on the Propbank corpus. The first one, called the argument identifier, filters argument candidates which are generated using a syntactic parse-based heuristic. The second model scores each candidate that has not been filtered for all possible argument labels. The scores for all candidates of a predicate are combined via inference. As in the system of (Punyakanok et al., 2008), the softmax function is applied to the raw classifier scores to ensure that they are in the same numeric range.

Inference mandates that certain structural and linguistic constraints hold over the full predicate-argument structure for a verb. (Punyakanok et al., 2008) modeled inference via an integer linear program instance, where each assignment of labels to candidates corresponds to one decision variable. Given a set of argument candidates, the feasible set of decisions is dependent of the number of argument candidates and the verb predicate. Thus, in terms of the notation used in this paper, the equivalence classes are defined by the pair *(predicate, number of argument candidates)*.

We ran the semantic role labeler on 225,000 verb predicates from the Gigaword corpus and cached the equivalence classes, objective coefficients and solutions generated by the SRL system. We report speedup for the various amortized inference schemes on the standard Penn Treebank test set. On this data, the unaltered baseline system, processes 5127 integer linear programs and achieves an F1 of 75.85%.

Table 3 shows the speedup and performance for the various inference schemes. The most frequent and top-K systems are both naive solutions that take advantage of the cache of stored problems. In spite of their simplicity, they attain F1 scores of 62% and 70.06% because few structures occur most frequently, as described in section 2.2. We see that all the exact theorems attain a speedup higher than two without losing performance. (The variation in F1 between them is because of the existence of different equivalent solutions in terms of the objective value.) This shows us that we can achieve an amortized gain in inference. Note that a speedup of 2.5 indicates that the solver is called only for 40% of the examples. The approximate versions of theorems 1 and 3 (with $\epsilon = 0.3$ in both cases, which was not tuned) attain an even higher gain in speedup over the baseline than the base versions of the theorems. Interestingly, the SRL performance in both cases does not decline much even though the conditions of the theorems may be violated.

5 Related work and Future directions

In recent years, we have seen several approaches to speeding up inference using ideas like using the cutting plane approach (Riedel, 2009), dual decomposition and Lagrangian relaxation (Rush et al., 2010; Chang and Collins, 2011). The key difference between these and the work in this paper is that all these approaches solve one instance at a time. Since we can use any inference procedure as a underlying system, the speedup reported in this paper is applicable to all these algorithms.

Decomposed amortized inference In this paper, we have taken advantage of redundancy of structures that can lead to the re-use of solutions. In the

Type	Algorithm	# instances	# solver calls	Speedup	Clock speedup	F1
Exact	Baseline	5127	5217	1.0	1.0	75.85
Exact	Theorem 1	5127	2134	2.44	1.54	75.90
Exact	Theorem 2	5127	2390	2.18	1.14	75.79
Exact	Theorem 3	5127	2089	2.50	1.36	75.77
Approx.	Most frequent (Support = 50)	5127	2812	1.86	1.57	62.00
Approx.	Top-10 solutions (Support = 50)	5127	2812	1.86	1.58	70.06
Approx.	Theorem 1 (approx, $\epsilon = 0.3$)	5127	1634	3.19	1.81	75.76
Approx.	Theorem 3 (approx, $\epsilon = 0.3$)	5127	1607	3.25	1.50	75.46

Table 3: Speedup and performance for various inference methods for the task of Semantic Role Labeling. All the exact inference algorithms get a speedup higher than two. The speedup of the approximate version of the theorems is even higher without loss of performance. The clock speedup is defined as the ratio of the inference times of the baseline and the given algorithm. All numbers are averaged over ten trials.

part of speech example, we showed redundancy of structures at the sentence level (Figure 2a). However, for part-of-speech tagging, the decisions are rarely, if at all, dependent on a very large context. One direction of future work is to take advantage of the fact that the inference problem can be split into smaller sub-problems. To support this hypothesis, we counted the number of occurrences of ngrams of tokens (including overlapping and repeated mentions) for $n <= 10$ and compared this to the number of unique part-of-speech ngrams of this length. Figure 4 shows these two counts. Following the argument in Section 2.2, this promises a large amortized gain in inference time. We believe that such decomposition can also be applied to other, more complex structured prediction tasks.

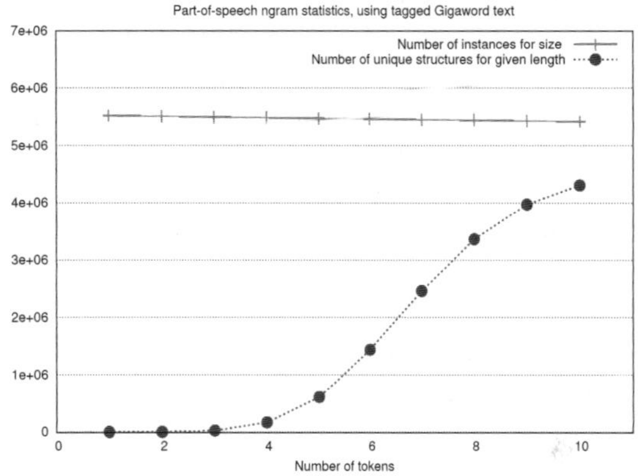

Figure 4: The red line shows the number of ngrams of tokens (including overlapping and repeated occurrences) in the Gigaword corpus and the blue line shows the number of unique POS tag sequences.

The value of approximate inference From the experiments, we see that the first two approximate inference schemes (most frequent solution and the top-K scheme) can speed up inference with the only computational cost being the check for preconditions of the exact theorems. Effectively, these algorithms have parameters (i.e., the support parameter) that allow us to choose between the inference time and performance. Figure 5 shows the performance of the most frequent and top-K baselines for different values of the support parameter, which indicates how often a structure must occur for it to be considered. We see that for lower values of support, we can get a very high speedup but pay with poorer performance.

However, the prediction of the approximate algorithms can be used to warm-start any solver that can accept an external initialization. Warm-starting a solver can give a way to get the exact solution and yet take advantage of the frequency of structures that have been observed.

Lifted inference The idea of amortizing inference time over the dataset is conceptually related to the idea of lifted inference (de Salvo Braz et al., 2005). We abstract many instances into equivalence classes and deal with the inference problem with respect to the equivalence classes in the same way as done in lifted inference algorithms.

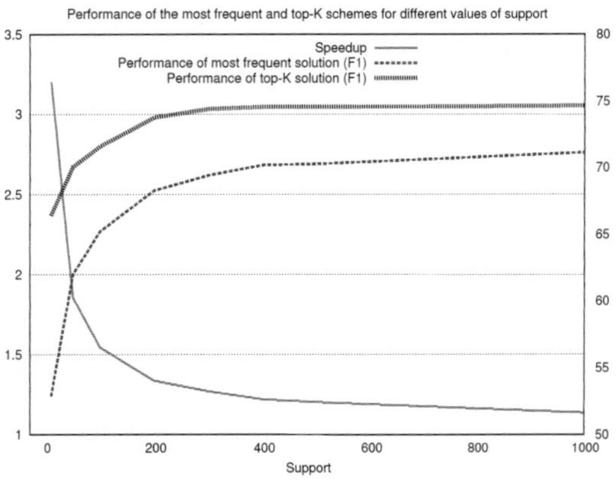

Figure 5: Most frequent solutions and top-K: Speedup and SRL performance (F1) for different values of the support parameter, using the most-frequent solutions (dashed blue line) and the top-K scheme (thick gray line). Support indicates how many times a structure should be seen for it to be considered. Note that the speedup values for both schemes are identical (red line).

6 Conclusion

In this paper, we addressed structured prediction in the context of NLP and proposed an approach to improve inference costs over an entire dataset, rather than individual instances. By treating inference problems as instances of integer linear programs, we proposed three exact theorems which identify examples for which the inference procedure need not be called at all and previous solutions can be re-used with the guarantee of optimality. In addition, we also proposed several approximate algorithms. We applied our algorithms, which are agnostic to the actual tasks, to the problem semantic role labeling, showing significant decrease in the number of inference calls without any loss in performance. While the approach suggested in this paper is evaluated in semantic role labeling, it is generally applicable to any NLP task that deals with structured prediction.

Acknowledgements

The authors wish to thank Sariel Har-Peled and the members of the Cognitive Computation Group at the University of Illinois for insightful discussions and the anonymous reviewers for their valuable feedback. This research is sponsored by the Army Research Laboratory (ARL) under agreement W911NF-09-2-0053. The authors also gratefully acknowledge the support of the Defense Advanced Research Projects Agency (DARPA) Machine Reading Program under Air Force Research Laboratory (AFRL) prime contract no. FA8750-09-C-0181. This work is also supported by the Intelligence Advanced Research Projects Activity (IARPA) Foresight and Understanding from Scientific Exposition (FUSE) Program via Department of Interior National Business Center contract number D11PC2015. Any opinions, findings, and conclusions or recommendations expressed in this material are those of the author(s) and do not necessarily reflect the view of ARL, DARPA, AFRL, IARPA, or the US government.

References

Y-W. Chang and M. Collins. 2011. Exact decoding of phrase-based translation models through lagrangian relaxation. EMNLP.

M. Chang, L. Ratinov, and D. Roth. 2007. Guiding semi-supervision with constraint-driven learning. In *ACL*.

J. Clarke and M. Lapata. 2006. Constraint-based sentence compression: An integer programming approach. In *ACL*.

M. Collins. 2002. Discriminative training methods for hidden Markov models: Theory and experiments with perceptron algorithms. In *EMNLP*.

R. de Salvo Braz, E. Amir, and D. Roth. 2005. Lifted first-order probabilistic inference. In *IJCAI*.

D Graff and C. Cieri. 2003. English gigaword.

A. Martins, N. A. Smith, and E. Xing. 2009. Concise integer linear programming formulations for dependency parsing. In *ACL*.

R. McDonald, F. Pereira, K. Ribarov, and J. Hajic. 2005. Non-projective dependency parsing using spanning tree algorithms. In *EMNLP*, pages 523–530, Vancouver, British Columbia, Canada, October. Association for Computational Linguistics.

M. Palmer, D. Gildea, and N. Xue. 2010. *Semantic Role Labeling*, volume 3. Morgan & Claypool Publishers.

V. Punyakanok, D. Roth, and W. Yih. 2005. The necessity of syntactic parsing for semantic role labeling. In *IJCAI*.

V. Punyakanok, D. Roth, and W. Yih. 2008. The importance of syntactic parsing and inference in semantic role labeling. *Computational Linguistics*.

S. Riedel and J. Clarke. 2006. Incremental integer linear programming for non-projective dependency parsing. In *EMNLP*.

S. Riedel. 2009. Cutting Plane MAP Inference for Markov Logic. *Machine Learning*.

D. Roth and W. Yih. 2004. A linear programming formulation for global inference in natural language tasks. In Hwee Tou Ng and Ellen Riloff, editors, *CoNLL*.

D. Roth and W. Yih. 2007. Global inference for entity and relation identification via a linear programming formulation. In Lise Getoor and Ben Taskar, editors, *Introduction to Statistical Relational Learning*.

A. M. Rush, D. Sontag, M. Collins, and T. Jaakkola. 2010. On dual decomposition and linear programming relaxations for natural language processing. In *EMNLP*.

I. Tsochantaridis, T. Joachims, T. Hofmann, and Y. Altun. 2005. Large margin methods for structured and interdependent output variables. *Journal of Machine Learning Research*.

Exact Sampling and Decoding in High-Order Hidden Markov Models

Simon Carter* | **Marc Dymetman** | **Guillaume Bouchard**

ISLA, University of Amsterdam
Science Park 904, 1098 XH Amsterdam,
The Netherlands
s.c.carter@uva.nl

Xerox Research Centre Europe
6, chemin de Maupertuis
38240 Meylan, France
{first.last}@xrce.xerox.com

Abstract

We present a method for exact optimization and sampling from high order Hidden Markov Models (HMMs), which are generally handled by approximation techniques. Motivated by adaptive rejection sampling and heuristic search, we propose a strategy based on sequentially refining a lower-order language model that is an upper bound on the true model we wish to decode and sample from. This allows us to build tractable variable-order HMMs. The ARPA format for language models is extended to enable an efficient use of the *max-backoff* quantities required to compute the upper bound. We evaluate our approach on two problems: a SMS-retrieval task and a POS tagging experiment using 5-gram models. Results show that the same approach can be used for exact optimization and sampling, while explicitly constructing only a fraction of the total implicit state-space.

1 Introduction

In NLP, sampling is important for many real tasks, such as: (i) diversity in language generation or machine translation (proposing multiple alternatives which are not clustered around a single maximum); (ii) Bayes error minimization, for instance in Statistical Machine Translation (Kumar and Byrne, 2004); (iii) learning of parametric and non-parametric Bayesian models (Teh, 2006).

However, most practical sampling algorithms are based on MCMC, i.e. they are based on local moves starting from an initial valid configuration. Often, these algorithms are stuck in local minima, i.e. in a basin of attraction close to the initialization, and the method does not really sample the whole state space. This is a problem when there are ambiguities in the distribution we want to sample from: by having a local approach such as MCMC, we might only explore states that are close to a given configuration.

The necessity of exact sampling can be questioned in practice. Approximate sampling techniques have been developed over the last century and seem sufficient for most purposes. However, the cases where one actually knows the quality of a sampling algorithm are very rare, and it is common practice to forget about the approximation and simply treat the result of a sampler as a set of i.i.d. data. Exact sampling provides a de-facto guarantee that the samples are truly independent. This is particularly relevant when one uses a cascade of algorithms in complex NLP processing chains, as shown by (Finkel et al., 2006) in their work on linguistic annotation pipelines.

In this paper, we present an approach for exact decoding and sampling with an HMM whose hidden layer is a high-order language model (LM), which innovates on existing techniques in the following ways. First, it is a *joint* approach to sampling and optimization (i.e. decoding), which is based on introducing a simplified, "optimistic", version $q(x)$ of the underlying language model $p(x)$, for which it is tractable to use standard dynamic programming techniques both for sampling and optimization. We then formulate the problem of sampling/optimization with the original model $p(x)$ in

*This work was conducted during an internship at XRCE.

terms of a novel algorithm which can be viewed as a form of *adaptive rejection sampling* (Gilks and Wild, 1992; Gorur and Teh, 2008), in which a low acceptance rate (in sampling) or a low ratio $p(x^*)/q(x^*)$ (in optimization, with x^* the argmax of q) leads to a refinement of q, i.e., a slightly more complex and less optimistic q but with a higher acceptance rate or ratio.

Second, it is the first technique that we are aware of which is able to perform *exact sampling* with such models. Known techniques for sampling in such situations have to rely on approximation techniques such as Gibbs or Beam sampling (see e.g. (Teh et al., 2006; Van Gael et al., 2008)). By contrast, our technique produces exact samples from the start, although in principle, the first sample may be obtained only after a long series of rejections (and therefore refinements). In practice, our experiments indicate that a good acceptance rate is obtained after a relatively small number of refinements. It should be noted that, in the case of exact optimization, a similar technique to ours has been proposed in an image processing context (Kam and Kopec, 1996), but without any connection to sampling. That paper, written in the context of image processing, appears to be little known in the NLP community.

Overall, our method is of particular interest because it allows for exact decoding and sampling from HMMs where the applications of existing dynamic programming algorithms such as Viterbi decoding (Rabiner, 1989) or Forward-Backward sampling (Scott, 2002) are not feasible, due to a large state space.

In Section 2, we present our approach and describe our joint algorithm for HMM sampling/optimization, giving details about our extension of the ARPA format and refinement procedure. In Section 3 we define our two experimental tasks, SMS-retrieval and POS tagging, for which we present the results of our joint algorithm. We finally discuss perspectives and conclude in Section 4.

2 Adaptive rejection sampling and heuristic search for high-order HMMs

Notation Let $x = \{x_1, x_2, ...x_\ell\}$ be a given hidden state sequence (e.g. each x_i is an English word) which takes values in $\mathcal{X} = \{1, \cdots, N\}^\ell$ where ℓ is the length of the sequence and N is the number of latent symbols. Subsequences $(x_a, x_{a+1}, \cdots, x_b)$ are denoted by x_a^b, where $1 \leq a \leq b \leq \ell$. Let $o = \{o_1, o_2, ...o_\ell\}$ be the set of observations associated to these words (e.g. o_i is an acoustic realization of x_i). The notations p, q and q' refer to unnormalized densities, i.e. non-negative measures on $\mathcal{X}$. Since only discrete spaces are considered, we use for short $p(x) = p(\{x\})$. When the context is not ambiguous, sampling according to p means sampling according to the distribution with density $\bar{p}(x) = \frac{p(x)}{p(\mathcal{X})}$, where $p(\mathcal{X}) = \int_\mathcal{X} p(x)dx$ is the total mass of the unnormalized distribution p.

Sampling The objective is to sample a sequence with density $\bar{p}(x)$ proportional to $p(x) = p_{\text{lm}}(x)p_{\text{obs}}(o|x)$ where p_{lm} is the probability of the sequence x under a n-gram model and $p_{\text{obs}}(o|x)$ is the probability of observing the noisy sequence o given that the correct/latent sequence is x. Assuming the observations depend only on the current state, this probability becomes

$$p(x) \quad = \quad \prod_{i=1}^{\ell} p_{\text{lm}}(x_i|x_{i-n+1}^{i-1})p_{\text{obs}}(o_i|x_i) \ . \quad (1)$$

To find the most likely sequence given an observation, or to sample sequences from Equation 1, standard dynamic programming techniques are used (Rabiner, 1989; Scott, 2002) by expanding the state space at each position. However, as the transition order n increases, or the number of latent tokens N that can emit to each observation o_l increases, the dynamic programming approach becomes intractable, as the number of operations increases exponentially in the order of $\mathcal{O}(\ell N^n)$.

If one can find a proposal distribution q which is an upper bound of p — i.e such that $q(x) \geq p(x)$ for all sequences $x \in \mathcal{X}$ — and which it is easy to sample from, the standard *rejection sampling* algorithm can be used:

1. Sample $x \sim q/q(\mathcal{X})$, with $q(\mathcal{X}) = \int_\mathcal{X} q(x)dx$;
2. Accept x with probability $p(x)/q(x)$, otherwise reject x;

To obtain multiple samples, the algorithm is repeated several times. However, for simple bounds,

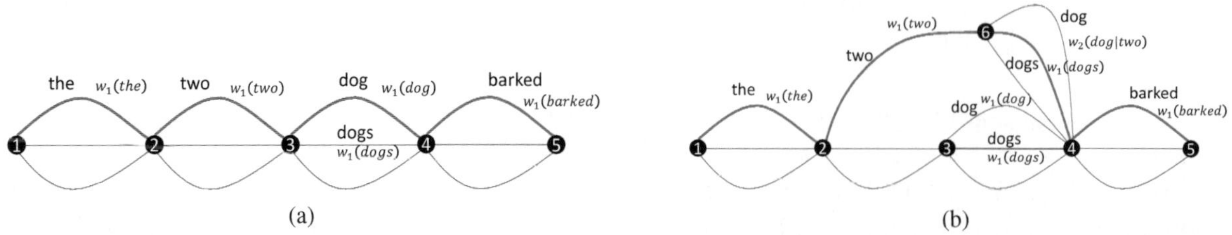

Figure 1: *An example of an initial q-automaton (a), and the refined q-automaton (b) Each state corresponds to a context (only state 6 has a non-empty context) and each edge represents the emission of a symbol. Thick edges are representing the path for the sampling/decoding of* `two dog(s) barked`*, thin edges corresponding to alternative symbols. By construction,* $w_1(dog) \geq w_2(dog\,|\,two)$ *so that the total weight of (b) is smaller than the total weight of (a).*

the average acceptance rate — which is equal to $p(\mathcal{X})/q(\mathcal{X})$ — can be so large that rejection sampling is not practical. In *adaptive rejection sampling* (ARS), the initial bound q is incrementally improved based on the values of the rejected elements. While often based on log-concave distributions which are easy to bound, ARS is valid for any type of bound, and in particular can be applied to the upper bounds on n-gram models introduced by (Kam and Kopec, 1996) in the context of optimization. When a sample is rejected, our algorithm assumes that a small set of refined proposals is available, say $q'_1, \cdots, q'_m$, where m is a small integer value. These refinements are *improved* versions of the current proposal q in the sense that they still upper-bound the target distribution p, but their mass is strictly smaller than the mass of q, i.e. $q'(\mathcal{X}) < q(\mathcal{X})$. Thus, each such refinement q', while still being optimistic relative to the target distribution p, has higher average acceptance rate than the previous upper bound q. A bound on the n-gram LM will be presented in Section 2.1.

Optimization In the case of optimization, the objective is to find the sequence maximizing $p(x)$. Viterbi on high-order HMMs is intractable but we have access to an upper bound q, for which Viterbi is tractable. Sampling from q is then replaced by finding the maximum point x of q, looking at the ratio $r(x) = p(x)/q(x)$, and accepting x if this ratio is equal to 1, otherwise refining q into q' exactly as in the sampling case. This technique is able to find the exact maximum of p, similarly to standard heuristic search algorithms based on optimistic bounds. We stop the process when q and p agree at the value maximizing q which implies that we have found the global maximum.

2.1 Upper bounds for n-gram models

To apply ARS on the target density given by Equation 1 we need to define a random sequence of proposal distributions $\{q^{(t)}\}_{t=1}^{\infty}$ such that $q^{(t)}(x) \geq p(x), \forall x \in \mathcal{X}, \forall t \in \{0, 1, \cdots\}$. Each n-gram $x_{i-n+1}, ..., x_i$ in the hidden layer contributes an n-th order factor $w_n(x_i|x_{i-n+1}^{i-1}) \equiv p_{\text{lm}}(x_i|x_{i-n+1}^{i-1})p_{\text{obs}}(o_i|x_i)$. The key idea is that these n-th order factors can be upper bounded by factors of order $n-k$ by maximizing over the head (i.e. prefix) of the context, as if part of the context was "forgotten". Formally, we define the *max-backoff weights* as:

$$w_{n-k}(x_i|x_{i-n+1+k}^{i-1}) \equiv \max_{x_{i-n+1}^{i-n+k}} w_n(x_i|x_{i-n+1}^{i-1}), \tag{2}$$

By construction, the max-backoff weights w_{n-k} are factors of order $n-k$ and can be used as surrogates to the original n-th order factors of Equation (1), leading to a nested sequence of upper bounds until reaching binary or unary factors:

$$\begin{aligned} p(x) &= \Pi_{i=1}^{\ell} w_n(x_i|x_{i-n+1}^{i-1}) & (3)\\ &\leq \Pi_{i=1}^{\ell} w_{n-1}(x_i|x_{i-n+2}^{i-1}) & (4)\\ &\cdots & \\ &\leq \Pi_{i=1}^{\ell} w_2(x_i|x_{i-1}) & (5)\\ &\leq \Pi_{i=1}^{\ell} w_1(x_i) := q^{(0)}(x)\ . & (6) \end{aligned}$$

Now, one can see that the loosest bound (6) based on unigrams corresponds to a completely factorized distribution which is straightforward to sample and optimize. The bigram bound (5) corresponds to a standard HMM probability that can be efficiently decoded (using Viterbi algorithm) and sampled (using backward filtering-forward sampling). [1] In the context of ARS, our initial proposal $q^{(0)}(x)$ is set to

[1]Backward filtering-forward sampling (Scott, 2002) refers to the process of running the Forward algorithm (Rabiner,

the unigram bound (6). The bound is then incrementally improved by adaptively refining the max-backoff weights based on the values of the rejected samples. Here, a refinement refers to the increase of the order of *some* of the max-backoff weights in the current proposal (thus most refinements consist of n-grams with heterogeneous max-backoff orders, not only those shown in equations (3)-(6)). This operation tends to tighten the bound and therefore increase the acceptance probability of the rejection sampler, at the price of a higher sampling complexity. The are several possible ways of choosing the weights to refine; in Section 2.2 different refinement strategies will be discussed, but the main technical difficulty remains in the efficient exact optimization and sampling of a HMM with n-grams of variable orders. The construction of the refinement sequence $\{q^{(t)}\}_{t \geq 0}$ can be easily explained and implemented through a Weighted Finite State Automaton (WFSA) referred as a *q-automaton*, as illustrated in the following example.

Example We give now a high-level description of the refinement process to give a better intuition of our method. In Fig. 1(a), we show a WFSA representing the initial proposal $q^{(0)}$ corresponding to an example with an acoustic realization of the sequence of words (`the`, `two`, `dogs`, `barked`). The weights on edges of this q-automaton correspond to the unigram max-backoffs, so that the total weight corresponds to Equation (6). Considering sampling, we suppose that the first sample from $q^{(0)}$ produces x_1 = (`the, two, dog, barked`), marked with bold edges in the drawing. Now, computing the ratio $p(x_1)/q^{(0)}(x_1)$ gives a result much below 1, because from the viewpoint of the full model p, the trigram (`the two dog`) is very unlikely; in other words the ratio $w_3(\texttt{dog}|\texttt{the two})/w_1(\texttt{dog})$ (and, in fact, already the ratio $w_2(\texttt{dog}|\texttt{two})/w_1(\texttt{dog})$) is very low. Thus, with high probability, x_1 is rejected. When this is the case, we produce a refined proposal $q^{(1)}$, represented by the WFSA in Fig. 1(b), which takes into account the more realistic weight $w_2(\texttt{dog}|\texttt{two})$ by adding a node (node 6) for the context `two`. We then perform a sampling trial with $q^{(1)}$, which this time tends to avoid producing `dog` in the context of `two`; if the new sample is rejected, the refinement process continues until we start observing that the acceptance rate reaches a fixed threshold value. The case of optimization is similar. Suppose that with $q^{(0)}$ the maximum is x_1, then we observe that $p(x_1)$ is lower than $q^{(0)}(x_1)$, reject suboptimal x_1 and refine $q^{(0)}$ into $q^{(1)}$.

Algorithm 1 ARS for HMM algorithm.

while not Stop(h) **do**
  if Optimisation **then**
    Viterbi $x \sim q$
  else
    Sample $x \sim q$
  $r \leftarrow p(x)/q(x)$
  Accept-or-Reject(x, r)
  Update(h, x)
  if Rejected(x) **then**
    for all $i \in \{2, \cdots, \ell\}$ **do**
      $q \leftarrow$ UpdateHMM (q, x, i)
return q along with accepted x's in h

Algorithm 2 UpdateHMM

Input: A triplet (q, x, i) where q is a WFSA, x is a sequence determining a unique path in the WFSA and i is a position at which a refinement must be done.

n :=ORDER$_i(x_1^i) + 1$ #implies $x_{i-n+2}^{i-1} \in S_{i-1}$
if $x_{i-n+1}^{i-1} \notin S_{i-1}$ **then**
  CREATE-STATE($x_{i-n+1}^{i-1}, i-1$)
  #move incoming edges, keeping WFSA deterministic
  for all s $\in$ SUF$_{i-2}(x_{i-n+1}^{i-2})$ **do**
    $e :=$ EDGE(s, x_{i-1})
    MOVE-EDGE-END(e,x_{i-n+1}^{i-1})
  #create outgoing edges
  for all $(s, l, \omega) \in T_i(x_{i-n+2}^{i-1})$ **do**
    CREATE-EDGE(x_{i-n+1}^{i-1},s,l,ω)
#update weights
for all s $\in$ SUF$_{i-1}(x_{i-n+1}^{i-1})$ **do**
  weight of EDGE$(s, x_i) := w_n(x_i|x_{i-n+1}^{i-1})$
return

2.2 Algorithm

We describe in detail the algorithm and procedure for updating a q-automaton with a max-backoff of longer context.

Algorithm 1 gives the pseudo-code of the sam-

1989), which creates a lattice of forward probabilities that contains the probability of ending in a latent state at a specific time t, given the subsequence of previous observations o_1^t, for all the previous latent sub-sequences x_1^{t-1}, and then recursively moving backwards, sampling a latent state based on these probabilities.

pling/optimization strategy. On line 1, h represents the history of all trials so far, where the stopping criterion for decoding is whether the last trial in the history has been accepted, and for sampling whether the ratio of accepted trials relative to all trials exceeds a certain threshold. The WFSA is initialized so that all transitions only take into account the $w_1(x_i)$ max-backoffs, i.e. the initial optimistic-bound ignores all contexts. Then depending on whether we are sampling or decoding, in lines 2-5, we draw an event from our automaton using either the Viterbi algorithm or Forward-Backward sampling. If the sequence is rejected at line 7, then the q-automaton is updated in lines 10 and 11. This is done by expanding all the factors involved in the sampling/decoding of the rejected sequence x to a higher order. That is, while sampling or decoding the automaton using the current proposal $q^{(t)}$, the contexts used in the path of the rejected sequence are replaced with higher order contexts in the new refined proposal $q^{t+1}(x)$.

The update process of the q-automaton represented as a WFSA is described in Algorithm 2. This procedure guarantees that a lower, more realistic weight is used in *all* paths containing the n-gram x_{i-n+1}^{i} while decoding/sampling the q-automaton, where n is the order at which x_{i-n+1}^{i} has been expanded so far. The algorithm takes as input a max-backoff function, and refines the WFSA such that any paths that include this n-gram have a smaller weight thanks to the fact that higher-order max-backoff have automatically smaller weights.

The algorithm requires the following functions:

- ORDER$_i(x)$ returns the order at which the n-gram has been expanded so far at position i.
- S_i returns the states at a position i.
- $T_i(s)$ returns end states, labels and weights of all edges that originate from this state.
- SUF$_i(x)$ returns the states at i which have a suffix matching the given context x. For empty contexts, all states at i are returned.
- EDGE(s, l) returns the edge which originates from s and has label l. Deterministic WFSA, such as those used here, can only have a single transition with a label l leaving from a state s.
- CREATE-STATE(s, i) creates a state with name s at position i, CREATE-EDGE(s_1, s_2, l, ω) creates an edge (s_1, s_2) between s_1 and s_2 with weight ω and label l, and MOVE-EDGE-END(e, s) sets the end of edge e to be the state s, keeping the same starting state, weight and label.

At line 1, the expansion of the current n-gram is increased by one so that we only need to expand contexts of size $n-2$. Line 2 checks whether the context state exists. If it doesn't it is created at lines 3-10. Finally, the weight of the edges that could be involved in the decoding of this n-gram are updated to a smaller value given by a higher-order max-backoff weight.

The creation of a new state in lines 3-10 is straightforward: At lines 5-7, incoming edges are moved from states at position $i-2$ with a matching context to the newly created edge. At lines 9-10 edges heading out of the context state are created. They are simply copied over from all edges that originate from the suffix of the context state, as we know these will be legitimate transitions (i.e we will always transition to a state of the same order or lower).

Note that we can derive many other variants of Algorithm 2 which also guarantee a smaller total weight for the q-automaton. We chose to present this version because it is relatively simple to implement, and numerical experiments comparing different refinement approaches (including replacing the max-backoffs with the highest-possible context, or picking a single "culprit" to refine) showed that this approach gives a good trade-off between model complexity and running time.

2.3 Computing Max-Backoff Factors

An interesting property of the max-backoff weights is that they can be computed recursively; taking a 3-gram LM as an example, we have:

$$\begin{aligned} w_1(x_i) &= \max_{x_i-1} w_2(x_i|x_{i-1}) \\ w_2(x_i|x_{i-1}) &= \max_{x_i-2} w_3(x_i|x_{i-2}^{i-1}) \\ w_3(x_i|x_{i-2}^{i-1}) &= p(x_i|x_{i-2}^{i-1})\, p(o_i|x_i). \end{aligned}$$

The final $w_3(x_i|x_{i-2}^{i-1})$ upper bound function is simply equal to the true probability (multiplied by the conditional probability of the observation), as any extra context is discarded by the 3-gram language model. It's easy to see that as we refine $q^{(t)}$ by replacing existing max-backoff weights with more specific contexts, the $q^{(t)}$ tends to p at t tends to infinity.

In the HMM formulation, we need to be able to efficiently compute at run-time the max-backoffs $w_1(\texttt{the})$, $w_2(\texttt{dog}|\texttt{the})$, $\cdots$, taking into account smoothing. To do so, we present a novel method for converting language models in the standard ARPA format used by common toolkits such as (Stolcke, 2002) into a format that we can use. The ARPA file format is a table T composed of three columns: (1) an n-gram which has been observed in the training corpus, (2) the log of the conditional probability of the last word in the n-gram given the previous words (log f(.)), and (3) a backoff weight (bow(.)) used when unseen $n-$grams 'backoff' to this n-gram. [2]

The probability of any n-gram x^i_{i-n} (in the previous sense, i.e. writing $p(x^i_{i-n})$ for $p(x_i|x^{i-1}_{i-n})$) is then computed recursively as:

$$p(x^i_{i-n}) = \begin{cases} \mathrm{f}(x^i_{i-n}) & \text{if } x^i_{i-n} \in T \\ \mathrm{bow}(x^{i-1}_{i-n})\, p(x^i_{i-n+1}) & \text{otherwise.} \end{cases} \quad (7)$$

Here, it is understood that if x^{i-1}_{i-n} is in T, then its bow(.) is read from the table, otherwise it is taken to be 1.

Different smoothing techniques will lead to different calculations of $\mathrm{f}(x^i_{i-n})$ and $\mathrm{bow}(x^{i-1}_{i-n})$, however both backoff and linear-interpolation methods can be formulated using the above equation.

Starting from the ARPA format, we pre-compute a new table MAX-ARPA, which has the same lines as ARPA, each corresponding to an n-gram x^i_{i-n} observed in the corpus, and the same f and bow, but with two additional columns: (4) a max log probability (log $\mathrm{mf}(x^i_{i-n})$), which is equal to the maximum log probability over all the n-grams extending the context of x^i_{i-n}, i.e. which have x^i_{i-n} as a suffix; (5) a "max backoff" weight ($\mathrm{mbow}(x^i_{i-n})$), which is a number used for computing the max log probability of an n-gram not listed in the table. From the MAX-ARPA table, the max probability w of any n-gram x^i_{i-n}, i.e the maximum of $p(x^i_{i-n-k})$ over all n-grams extending the context of x^i_{i-n}, can then be computed recursively (again very quickly) as:

$$w(x^i_{i-n}) = \begin{cases} \mathrm{mf}(x^i_{i-n}) & \text{if } x^i_{i-n} \in T \\ \mathrm{mbow}(x^{i-1}_{i-n})\, p(x^i_{i-n}) & \text{otherwise.} \end{cases} \quad (8)$$

Here, if x^{i-1}_{i-n} is in T, then its mbow(.) is read from the table, otherwise it is taken to be 1. Also note that the procedure calls p, which is computed as described in Equation 7. [3]

3 Experiments

In this section we empirically evaluate our joint, exact decoder and sampler on two tasks; SMS-retrieval (Section 3.1), and supervised POS tagging (Section 3.2).

3.1 SMS-Retrieval

We evaluate our approach on an SMS-message retrieval task. A latent variable $x \in \{1, \cdots, N\}^\ell$ represents a sentence represented as a sequence of words: N is the number of possible words in the vocabulary and ℓ is the number of words in the sentence. Each word is converted into a sequence of numbers based on a mobile phone numeric keypad. The standard character-to-numeric function num : $\{\texttt{a}, \texttt{b}, \cdots, \texttt{z}, ., \cdots, ?\} \rightarrow \{1, 2, \cdots, 9, 0\}$ is used. For example, the words `dog` and `fog` are represented by the sequence $(3, 6, 4)$ because num(d)=num(f)=3, num(o)=6 and num(g)=4. Hence, observed sequences are sequences of numeric strings separated by white spaces. To take into account typing errors, we assume we observe a noisy version of the correct numeric sequence $(\mathrm{num}(x_{i1}), \cdots, \mathrm{num}(x_{i|x_i|}))$ that encodes the word x_i at the i-th position of the sentence x. The noise model is:

$$p(o_i|x_i) \propto \prod_{t=1}^{|x_i|} \frac{1}{k * d(o_{it}, \mathrm{num}(x_{it})) + 1}, \quad (9)$$

where $d(a, b)$ is the physical distance between the numeric keys a and b and k is a user provided con-

[2] See www.speech.sri.com/projects/srilm/manpages/ngram-format.5.html, last accessed at 1/3/2012, for further details.

[3] In this discussion of the MAX-ARPA table we have ignored the contribution of the observation $p(o_i|x_i)$, which is a constant factor over the different max-backoffs for the same x_i and does not impact the computation of the table.

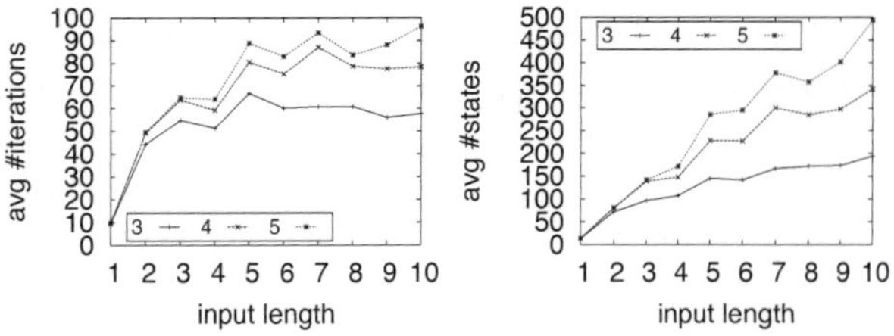

Figure 2: *On the left we report the average # of iterations taken to decode given different LMs over input sentences of different lengths, and on the right we show the average # of states in the final q-automaton once decoding is completed.*

stant that controls the ambiguity in the distribution; we use 64 to obtain moderately noisy sequences.

We used the English side of the Europarl corpus (Koehn, 2005). The language model was trained using SRILM (Stolcke, 2002) on 90% of the sentences. On the remaining 10%, we randomly selected 100 sequences for lengths 1 to 10 to obtain 1000 sequences from which we removed the ones containing numbers, obtaining a test set of size 926.

Decoding Algorithm 1 was run in the optimization mode. In the left plot of Fig. 2, we show the number of iterations (running Viterbi then updating q) that the different n-gram models of size 3, 4 and 5 take to do exact decoding of the test-set. For a fixed sentence length, we can see that decoding with larger n-gram models leads to a sub-linear increase w.r.t. n in the number of iterations taken. In the right plot of Fig. 2, we show the average number of states in our variable-order HMMs.

To demonstrate the reduced nature of our q-automaton, we show in Tab. 1 the distribution of n-grams in our final model for a specific input sentence of length 10. The number of n-grams in the full model is $\sim 3.0 \times 10^{15}$. Exact decoding here is not tractable using existing techniques. Our HMM has only 9008 n-grams in total, including 118 5-grams.

n:	1	2	3	4	5
q:	7868	615	231	176	118

Table 1: *# of n-grams in our variable-order HMM.*

Finally, we show in Tab. 2 an example run of our algorithm in the optimization setting for a given input. Note that the weight according to our q-automaton for the first path returned by the Viterbi algorithm is high in comparison to the true log probability according to p.

Sampling For the sampling experiments, we limit the number of latent tokens to 100. We refine our q-automaton until we reach a certain fixed cumulative acceptance rate (AR). We also compute a rate based only on the last 100 trials (AR-100), as this tends to better reflect the current acceptance rate.

In Fig. 3a, we plot a running average of the ratio at each iteration over the last 10 trials, for a single sampling run using a 5-gram model for an example input. The ratios start off at 10^{-20}, but gradually increase as we refine our HMM. After $\sim$ 500 trials, we start accepting samples from p. In Fig. 3b, we show the respective ARs (bottom and top curves respectively), and the cumulative # of accepts (middle curve), for the same input. Because the cumulative accept ratio takes into account all trials, the final AR of 17.7% is an underestimate of the true accept ratio at the final iteration; this final accept ratio can be better estimated on the basis of the last 100 trials, for which we read AR-100 to be at around 60%.

We note that there is a trade-off between the time needed to construct the forward probability lattice needed for sampling, and the time it takes to adapt the variable-order HMM. To resolve this, we propose to use batch-updates: making B trials from the same q-automaton, and then updating our model in one step. By doing this, we noted significant speed-ups in sampling times. In Tab. 3, we show various

input:	3637 843 66639 39478 *		
oracle:	does the money exist ?		
best:	does the money exist .		
Viterbi paths		log q(x)	log p(x)
q^1	does the money exist)	-0.11	-17.42
q^{50}	does the **owned** exist .	-11.71	-23.54
q^{100}	**ends** the money exist .	-12.76	-17.09
q^{150}	does **vis** money exist .	-13.45	-23.74
q^{170}	does the money exist .	-13.70	-13.70

Table 2: *Viterbi paths given different q^t. Here, for the given input, it took 170 iterations to find the best sequence according to p, so we only show every 50th path.*

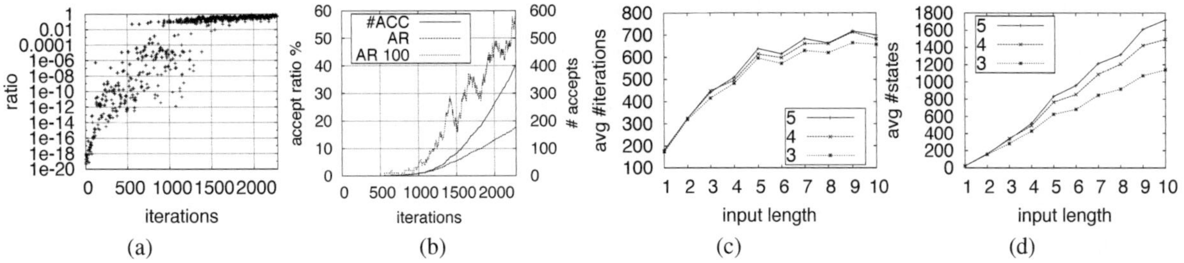

Figure 3: *In 3a, we plot the running average over the last 10 trials of the ratio. In 3b, we plot the cumulative # of accepts (middle curve), the accept rate (bottom curve), and the accept rate based on the last 100 samples (top curve). In 3c, we plot the average number of iterations needed to sample up to an AR of 20% for sentences of different lengths in our test set, and in 3d, we show the average number of states in our HMMs for the same experiment.*

B:	1	10	20	30	40	50	100
time:	97.5	19.9	15.0	13.9	12.8	12.5	11.4
iter:	453	456	480	516	536	568	700

Table 3: *In this table we show the average amount of time in seconds and the average number of iterations (iter) taken to sample sentences of length 10 given different values of* B.

input:	3637 843 66639 39478 *		
oracle:	does the money exist ?		
best:	does the money exist .		
samples	#	log q(x)	log p(x)
does the money exist .	429	-13.70	-13.70
does the money exist **?**	211	-14.51	-14.51
does the money exist **!**	72	-15.49	-15.49
does the **moody** exist .	45	-15.70	-15.70
does the money exist **:**	25	-16.73	-16.73

Table 4: *Top-5 ranked samples for an example input. We highlight in bold the words which are different to the Viterbi best of the model. The oracle and best are not the same for this input.*

statistics for sampling up to AR-100 $= 20$ given different values for B. We ran this experiment using the set of sentences of length 10. A value of 1 means that we refine our automaton after each rejected trial, a value of 10 means we wait until rejecting 10 trials before updating our automaton in one step. We can see that while higher values of B lead to more iterations, as we do not need to re-compute the forward trellis needed for sampling, the time needed to reach the specific AR threshold actually decreases, from 97.5 seconds to 11.4 seconds, an 8.5% speedup. Unless explicitly stated otherwise, further experiments use a $B = 100$.

We now present the full sampling results on our test-set in Fig. 3c and 3d, where we show the average number of iterations and states in the final models once refinements are finished (AR-100=20%) for different orders n over different lengths. We note a sub-linear increase in the average number of trials and states when moving to higher n; thus, for length=10, and for $n = 3, 4, 5$, # trials: 3-658.16, 4-683.3, 5-700.9, and # states: 3-1139.5, 4-1494.0, 5-1718.3.

Finally, we show in Tab. 4, the ranked samples drawn from an input sentence, according to a 5-gram LM. After refining our model up to AR-100 $= 20\%$, we continued drawing samples until we had 1000 exact samples from p (out of $\sim$ 4.7k trials). We show the count of each sequence in the 1000 samples, and the log probability according to p for that event. We only present the top-five samples, though in total there were 90 unique sequences sampled, 50 of which were only sampled once.

3.2 POS-tagging

Our HMM is the same as that used in (Brants, 2001); the emission probability of a word given a POS tag x_i is calculated using maximum likelihood techniques. That is, $p(o_i|x_i) = \frac{c(o_i,x_i)}{c(x_i)}$. Unseen words are handled by interpolating longer suffixes with shorter, more general suffixes. To train our language model, we use the SRILM toolkit (Stolcke, 2002) We build LMs of up to size 9. We present results on the WSJ Penn Treebank corpus (Marcus et al., 1993). We use sections 0-18 to train our emission and transitions probabilities, and report results on

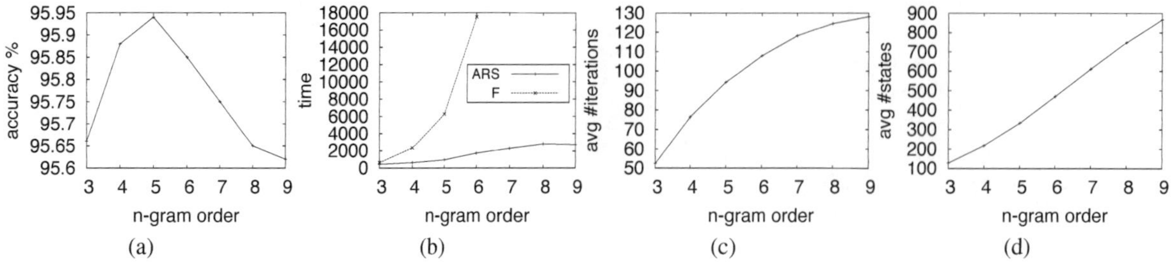

Figure 4: *In 4a, we report the accuracy results given different n-gram models on the WSJ test-set. In 4b, we show the time taken (seconds) to decode the WSJ test-set given our method (ARS), and compare this to the full model (F). In 4c, the average number of iterations needed to sample the test-set given different n-gram language models is given, and 4d shows the average number of states in the variable-order HMMs.*

sections 22-24.

We first present results for our decoding experiments. In Fig. 4a we show the accuracy results of our different models on the WSJ test-set. We see that the best result is achieved with the 5-gram LM giving an accuracy of 95.94%. After that, results start to drop, most likely due to over-fitting of the LM during training and an inability for the smoothing technique to correctly handle this.

In Fig. 4b, we compare the time it takes in seconds to decode the test-set with the full model at each n-gram size; that is a WFSA with all context states and weights representing the true language model log probabilities. We can see that while increasing the n-gram model size, our method (ARS) exhibits a linear increase in decoding time, in contrast to the exponential factor exhibited when running the Viterbi algorithm over the full WFSA (F). Note for n-gram models of order 7 and higher, we could not decode the entire test set as creating the full WFSA was taking too long.

Finally in both Figs 4c and 4d, we show the average number of iterations taken to sample from the entire test-test, and the average number of states in our variable-order HMMs, with AR-100=60%. Again we note a linear increase in both Fig., in contrast to the exponential nature of standard techniques applied to the full HMM.

4 Conclusion and Perspectives

We have presented a dual-purpose algorithm that can be used for performing exact decoding and sampling on high-order HMMs. We demonstrated the validity of our method on SMS-retrieval and POS examples, showing that the "proposals" that we obtain require only a fraction of the space that would result from explicitly representing the HMM. We believe that this ability to support exact inference (both approximation and sampling) at a reasonable cost has important applications, in particular when moving from inference to learning tasks, which we see as a natural extension of this work.

By proposing a common framework for sampling and optimization our approach has the advantage that we do not need separate skills or expertise to solve the two problems. In several situations, we might be interested not only in the most probable sequence, but also in the distribution of the sequences, especially when diversity is important or in the presence of underlying ambiguities.

The interplay between optimization and sampling is a fruitful area of research that can lead to state-of-the art performances on inference and decoding tasks in the special case of high-order HMM decoding, but the method is generic enough to be generalized to many others models of interest for NLP applications. One family of models is provided by agreement-based models, for example HMM+PCFG, where distribution p takes the form of a product: $p(x) = p_{\text{HMM}}(x)p_{\text{PCFG}}(x)$. Even if the factors $p_{\text{HMM}}(x)$ and $p_{\text{PCFG}}(x)$ can be decoded and sampled efficiently, the product of them is intractable. Dual decomposition is a generic method that has been proposed for handling decoding (i.e. optimization) with such models, by decoupling the problem into two alternating steps that can each be handled by dynamic programming or other polynomial-time algorithms (Rush et al., 2010), an approach that has been applied to Statistical Machine Translation (phrase-based (Chang and Collins,

2011) and hierarchical (Rush and Collins, 2011)) among others. However, sampling such distributions remains a difficult problem. We are currently extending the approach described in this paper to handle such applications. Again, using ARS on a sequence of upper bounds to the target distribution, our idea is to express one of the two models as a context free grammar and incrementally compute the intersection with the second model, maintaining a good trade-off between computational tractability of the refinement and a reasonable acceptance rate.

References

Thorsten Brants. 2001. Tnt - a statistical part-of-speech tagger. In *Proceedings of the Sixth conference of Applied Natural Language Processing (ANLP 2001)*, pages 224–231.

Yin-Wen Chang and Michael Collins. 2011. Exact decoding of phrase-based translation models through lagrangian relaxation. In *Proceedings of the Conference on Empirical Methods for Natural Language Processing (EMNLP 2011)*.

Jenny Rose Finkel, Christopher D. Manning, and Andrew Y. Ng. 2006. Solving the problem of cascading errors: approximate bayesian inference for linguistic annotation pipelines. In *Proceedings of the Conference on Empirical Methods in Natural Language Processing (EMNLP 2006)*, pages 618–626.

W. R. Gilks and P. Wild. 1992. Adaptive rejection sampling for gibbs sampling. *Applied Statistics*, 42(2):337–348.

Dilan Gorur and Yee Whye Teh. 2008. Concave convex adaptive rejection sampling. Technical report, Gatsby Computational Neuroscience Unit.

Anthony C. Kam and Gary E. Kopec. 1996. Document image decoding by heuristic search. *IEEE Transactions on Pattern Analysis and Machine Intelligence*, 18:945–950.

Philipp Koehn. 2005. Europarl: A parallel corpus for statistical machine translation. In *Proceedings of Machine Translation Summit (MT-Summit 2005)*, pages 79–86.

Shankar Kumar and William Byrne. 2004. Minimum bayes risk decoding for statistical machine translation. In *Joint Conference of Human Language Technologies and the North American chapter of the Association for Computational Linguistics (HLT-NAACL 2004)*.

Mitchell P. Marcus, Beatrice Santorini, and Mary Ann Marcinkiewicz. 1993. Building a large annotated corpus of english: the penn treebank. *Computional Linguistics*, 19:313–330.

Lawrence R. Rabiner. 1989. A tutorial on hidden markov models and selected applications in speech recognition. *Proceedings of the IEEE*, 77(2):257–286, February.

Alexander M. Rush and Michael Collins. 2011. Exact decoding of syntactic translation models through lagrangian relaxation. In *Proceedings of the Conference on Empirical Methods for Natural Language Processing (EMNLP 2011)*, pages 26–37.

Alexander M. Rush, David Sontag, Michael Collins, and Tommi Jaakkola. 2010. On dual decomposition and linear programming relaxations for natural language processing. In *Proceedings of the Conference on Empirical Methods for Natural Language Processing (EMNLP 2010)*.

Steven L. Scott. 2002. Bayesian methods for hidden markov models: Recursive computing in the 21st century. *Journal of the American Statistical Association*, 97:337–351.

Andreas Stolcke. 2002. Srilm - an extensible language modeling toolkit. In *Proceedings of the International Conference of Spoken Language Processing (INTERSPEECH 2002)*, pages 257–286.

Yee Whye Teh, Michael I. Jordan, Matthew J. Beal, and David M. Blei. 2006. Hierarchical dirichlet processes. *Journal of the American Statistical Association*, 101(476):1566–1581.

Yee Whye Teh. 2006. A hierarchical bayesian language model based on pitman-yor processes. In *Proceedings of the 21st International Conference on Computational Linguistics and the 44th annual meeting of the Association for Computational Linguistics (ACL 2006)*, pages 985–992.

Jurgen Van Gael, Yunus Saatci, Yee Whye Teh, and Zoubin Ghahramani. 2008. Beam sampling for the infinite hidden Markov model. In *Proceedings of the International Conference on Machine Learning (ICML 2008)*, volume 25.

PATTY: A Taxonomy of Relational Patterns with Semantic Types

Ndapandula Nakashole, Gerhard Weikum, Fabian Suchanek
Max Planck Institute for Informatics
Saarbrücken, Germany
{nnakasho,weikum,suchanek}@mpi-inf.mpg.de

Abstract

This paper presents PATTY: a large resource for textual patterns that denote binary relations between entities. The patterns are semantically typed and organized into a subsumption taxonomy. The PATTY system is based on efficient algorithms for frequent itemset mining and can process Web-scale corpora. It harnesses the rich type system and entity population of large knowledge bases. The PATTY taxonomy comprises 350,569 pattern synsets. Random-sampling-based evaluation shows a pattern accuracy of 84.7%. PATTY has 8,162 subsumptions, with a random-sampling-based precision of 75%. The PATTY resource is freely available for interactive access and download.

1 Introduction

Motivation. WordNet (Fellbaum 1998) is one of the most widely used lexical resources in computer science. It groups nouns, verbs, and adjectives into sets of synonyms, and arranges these synonyms in a taxonomy of hypernyms. WordNet is limited to single words. It does not contain entire *phrases* or *patterns*. For example, WordNet does not contain the pattern *X is romantically involved with Y*. Just like words, patterns can be synonymous, and they can subsume each other. The pattern *X is romantically involved with Y* is synonymous with the pattern *X is dating Y*. Both are subsumed by *X knows Y*. Patterns for relations are a vital ingredient for many applications, including information extraction and question answering. If a large-scale resource of relational patterns were available, this could boost progress in NLP and AI tasks.

Yet, existing large-scale knowledge bases are mostly limited to abstract binary relationships between entities, such as "bornIn" (Auer 2007; Bollacker 2008; Nastase 2010; Suchanek 2007). These do not correspond to real text phrases. Only the ReVerb system (Fader 2011) yields a larger number of relational textual patterns. However, no attempt is made to organize these patterns into synonymous patterns, let alone into a taxonomy. Thus, the patterns themselves do not exhibit semantics.

Goal. Our goal in this paper is to systematically compile relational patterns from a corpus, and to impose a semantically typed structure on them. The result we aim at is a WordNet-style taxonomy of binary relations. In particular, we aim at patterns that contain *semantic types*, such as ⟨*singer*⟩ *sings* ⟨*song*⟩. We also want to automatically generalize syntactic variations such as *sings her* ⟨*song*⟩ and *sings his* ⟨*song*⟩, into a more general pattern *sings [prp]* ⟨*song*⟩ with POS tag [prp]. Analogously but more demandingly, we want to automatically infer that the above patterns are semantically subsumed by the pattern ⟨*musician*⟩ *performs on* ⟨*musical composition*⟩ with more general types for the entity arguments in the pattern.

Compiling and organizing such patterns is challenging for the following reasons. 1) The number of possible patterns increases exponentially with the length of the patterns. For example, the string "Amy sings 'Rehab'" can give rise to the patterns ⟨*singer*⟩ *sings* ⟨*song*⟩, ⟨*person*⟩ *sings* ⟨*artifact*⟩, ⟨*person*⟩ *[vbz]* ⟨*entity*⟩, etc. If wildcards for multiple words are allowed (such as in ⟨*person*⟩ *sings* * ⟨*song*⟩), the number of possible patterns explodes. 2) A pattern can be semantically more general than another pattern (when one relation is implied by the other relation), and it can also be syntactically more general than another pattern (by the use of placeholders such as [vbz]). These two subsumption orders have a non-obvious interplay, and none can be analyzed without the other. 3) We have to handle pattern sparseness and coincidental matches. If the corpus is small, e.g., the patterns ⟨*singer*⟩ *later disliked her song* ⟨*song*⟩ and ⟨*singer*⟩ *sang* ⟨*song*⟩, may apply to the same set of entity pairs in the corpus. Still, the patterns are not synonymous. 4) Computing mutual subsumptions on a large set of patterns may be prohibitively slow. Moreover, due to noise and vague semantics, patterns may even not form a crisp taxonomy, but require a hierarchy in which subsumption relations have to be weighted by statistical confidence measures.

Contributions. In this paper, we present PATTY, a large resource of relational patterns that are arranged in a semantically meaningful taxonomy, along with entity-pair instances. More precisely, our contributions are as follows:

1) *SOL patterns:* We define an expressive family of relational patterns, which combines syntactic features (S), ontological type signatures (O), and lexical features (L). The crucial novelty is the addition of the ontological, semantic dimension to patterns. When compared to a state-of-the-art pattern language, we found that SOL patterns yield higher recall while achieving similar precision.

2) *Mining algorithms:* We present efficient and scalable algorithms that can infer SOL patterns and subsumptions at scale, based on instance-level overlaps and an ontological type hierarchy.

3) A large *Lexical resource:*. On the Wikipedia corpus, we obtained 350,569 pattern synsets with 84.7% precision. We make our pattern taxonomy available for further research at `www.mpi-inf.mpg.de/yago-naga/patty/`.

The paper is structured as follows. Section 2 discusses related work. Section 3 outlines the basic machinery for pattern extraction. Section 4 introduces our SOL pattern model. Sections 5 and 6 present the syntactic and semantic generalization of patterns. Section 7 explains how to arrange the patterns into a taxonomy. Section 8 reports our experimental findings.

2 Related Work

A wealth of taxonomic knowledge bases (KBs) about entities and their semantic classes have become available. These are very rich in terms of unary predicates (semantic classes) and their entity instances. However, the number of *binary relations* (i.e., relation types, not instances) in these KBs is usually small: Freebase (Bollacker 2008) has a few thousand hand-crafted relations. WikiNet (Nastase 2010) has automatically extracted ca. 500 relations from Wikipedia category names. DBpedia (Auer 2007) has automatically compiled ca. 8000 names of properties from Wikipedia infoboxes, but these include many involuntary semantic duplicates such as *surname* and *lastname*. In all of these projects, the resource contains the *relation names*, but not the *natural language patterns* for them. The same is true for other projects along these lines (Navigli 2010; Philpot 2008; Ponzetto 2007; Suchanek 2007).

In contrast, knowledge base projects that automatically populate relations from Web pages also learn *surface patterns* for the relations: examples are TextRunner/ReVerb (Banko 2007; Fader 2011), NELL (Carlson 2010; Mohamed11), Probase (Wu 2011), the dynamic lexicon approach by (Hoffmann 2010; Wu 2008), the LDA-style clustering approach by (Yao 2011), and projects on Web tables (Limaye 2010; Venetis 2011). Of these, only TextRunner/ReVerb and NELL have made large pattern collections publicly available.

ReVerb (Fader 2011) constrains patterns to verbs or verb phrases that end with prepositions, while PATTY can learn arbitrary patterns. More importantly, all methods in the TextRunner/ReVerb family are blind to the ontological dimension of the entities in the patterns. Therefore, there is no notion of semantic typing for relation phrases as in PATTY.

NELL (Carlson 2010) is based on a fixed set of prespecified relations with type signatures, (e.g., *personHasCitizenship:* ⟨*person*⟩ × ⟨*country*⟩), and learns to extract suitable noun-phrase pairs from a large Web corpus. In contrast, PATTY discovers patterns for relations that are a priori unknown.

In *OntExt* (Mohamed11), the NELL architecture was extended to automatically compute new relation types (beyond the prespecified ones) for a given type signature of arguments, based on a clustering technique. For example, the relation *musicianPlaysInstrument* is found by clustering pattern co-occurrences for the noun-phrase pairs that fall into the specific type signature $\langle musician \rangle \times \langle musicinstrument \rangle$. This technique works for one type signature at a time, and does not scale up to mining a large corpus. Also, the technique is not suitable for inferring semantic subsumptions. In contrast, PATTY efficiently acquires patterns from large-scale corpora and organizes them into a subsumption hierarchy.

Class-based *attribute discovery* is a special case of mining relational patterns (e.g., (Alfonseca 2010; Pasca 2007; Pasca 2008; Reisinger 2009)). Given a semantic class, such as *movies* or *musicians*, the task is to determine relevant attributes, such as *cast* and *budget* for movies, or *albums* and *biography* for musicians, along with their instances. Unlike PATTY's patterns, the attributes are not typed. They come with a prespecified type for the domain, but without any type for the range of the underlying relation.

There are further *relation-centric tasks in NLP and text mining* that have commonalities with our endeavor, but differ in fundamental ways. The SemEval-2010 task on classification of semantic relations between noun-phrase pairs (Hendrickx 2010) aimed at predicting the relation for a given sentence and pair of nominals, but used a fixed set of prespecified relations. Another task in this research avenue is to characterize and predict the argument types for a given relation or pattern (Kozareva 2010; Nakov 2008). This is closer to KB population and less related to our task of discovering relational patterns and systematically organizing them.

From a *linguistic perspective*, there is ample work on patterns for unary predicates of the form *class(entity)*. This includes work on entailment of classes, i.e., on *is-a* and *subclassOf* relationships. Entailment among binary predicates of the form *relation(entity1, entity2)* has received less attention (Lin 2001; Chklovski 2004; Hashimoto 2009; Berant 2011). These works focus solely on verbs, while PATTY learns arbitrary phrases for patterns.

Several lexical resources capture verb categories and entailment: WordNet 3.0 (Fellbaum 1998) contains about 13,000 verb senses, with troponymy and entailment relations; VerbNet (Kipper 2008) is a hierarchical lexicon with more than 5,000 verb senses in ca. 300 classes, including selectional preferences. Again, all of these resources focus solely on verbs.

ConceptNet 5.0 (Havasi 2007) is a thesaurus of commonsense knowledge built as a crowdsourcing endeavor. PATTY, in contrast, is constructed fully automatically from large corpora. Automatic learning of paraphrases and textual entailment has received much attention (see the survey of (Androutsopoulos 2010)), but does not consider fine-grained typing for binary relations, as PATTY does.

3 Pattern Extraction

This section explains how we obtain basic textual patterns from the input corpus. We first apply the Stanford Parser (Marneffe 2006) to the individual sentences of the corpus to obtain dependency paths. The dependency paths form a directed graph, with words being nodes and dependencies being edges. For example, the sentence *"Winehouse effortlessly performed her song Rehab."* yields the following dependency paths:

nsubj(performed-3, Winehouse-1)
advmod(performed-3, effortlessly-2)
poss(Rehab-6, her-4)
nn(Rehab-6, song-5)
dobj(performed-3, Rehab-6)

While our method also works with patterns obtained from shallow features such as POS tags, we found that dependency paths improve pattern extraction precision especially on long sentences.

We then detect mentions of named entities in the parsed corpus. For this purpose, we use a dictionary of entities. This can be any resource that contains named entities with their surface names and semantic types (Auer 2007; Suchanek 2007; Hoffart 2011; Bollacker 2008). In our experiments, we used the YAGO2 knowledge base (Hoffart 2011). We match noun phrases that contain at least one proper noun against the dictionary. For disamiguation, we use a simple context-similarity prior, as described in (Suchanek 2009). We empirically found that this technique has accuracy well above 80% (and higher for prominent and thus frequently occurring entities). In our example, the entity detection yields the entities *Amy Winehouse* and *Rehab (song)*.

Whenever two named entities appear in the same sentence, we extract a textual pattern. For this purpose, we traverse the dependency graph to get the shortest path that connects the two entities. In the example, the shortest path between "Winehouse" and "Rehab" is: Winehouse *nsubj* performed *dobj* Rehab. In order to capture only relations that refer to subject-relation-object triples, we only consider shortest paths that start with subject-like dependencies, such as *nsubj, rcmod and partmod*. To reflect the full meaning of the patterns, we expand the shortest path with adverbial and adjectival modifiers, for example the *advmod* dependency. The sequence of words on the expanded shortest path becomes our final textual pattern. In the example, the textual pattern is *Amy Winehouse effortlessly performed Rehab (song)*.

4 SOL Pattern Model

Textual patterns are tied to the particular surface form of the text. Therefore, we transform the textual patterns into a new type of patterns, called syntactic-ontologic-lexical patterns (SOL patterns). SOL patterns extend lexico-syntactic patterns by ontological type signatures for entities. The SOL pattern language is expressive enough to capture fine-grained relational patterns, yet simple enough to be dealt with by efficient mining algorithms at Web scale.

A SOL pattern is an abstraction of a textual pattern that connects two entities of interest. It is a sequence of words, POS-tags, wildcards, and ontological types. A POS-tag stands for a word of the part-of-speech class. We introduce the special POS-tag [word], which stands for any word of any POS class. A wildcard, denoted $*$, stands for any (possibly empty) sequence of words. Wildcards are essential to avoid overfitting of patterns to the corpus. An ontological type is a semantic class name (such as $\langle$*singer*$\rangle$) that stands for an instance of that class. Every pattern contains at least two types, and these are designated as *entity placeholders*.

A string and a pattern *match*, if there is an order-preserving bijection from sequences of words in the string to items in the pattern, so that each item can stand for the respective sequence of words. For example, the pattern $\langle$*person*$\rangle$*'s [adj] voice* * $\langle$*song*$\rangle$ matches the strings "Amy Winehouse's soft voice in 'Rehab'" and "Elvis Presley's solid voice in his song 'All shook up'". The *type signature* of a pattern is the pair of the entity placeholders. In the example, the type signature is $person \times song$. The *support set* of a pattern is the set of pairs of entities that appear in the place of the entity placeholders in all strings in the corpus that match the pattern. In the example, the support set of the pattern could be $\{(Amy, Rehab), (Elvis, AllShookUp)\}$. Each pair is called a *support pair* of the pattern.

Pattern B is *syntactically more general* than pattern A if every string that matches A also matches B. Pattern B is *semantically more general* than A if the support set of B is a superset of the support set of A. If A is semantically more general than B and B is semantically more general than A, the patterns are called *synonymous*. A set of synonymous patterns is called a *pattern synset*. Two patterns, of which neither is semantically more general than the other, are called *semantically different*.

To generate SOL patterns from the textual patterns, we decompose the textual patterns into n-grams (n consecutive words). A SOL pattern contains only the n-grams that appear frequently in the corpus and the remaining word sequences are replaced by wildcards. For example, in the sentence "was the first female to run for the governor of" might give rise to the pattern * *the first female* * *governor of*, if "the first female" and "governor of" are frequent in the corpus.

To find the frequent n-grams efficiently, we apply the technique of frequent itemset mining (Agrawal 1993; Srikant 1996): each sentence is viewed as a "shopping transaction" with a "purchase" of several n-grams, and the mining algorithm computes the n-gram combinations with large co-occurrence support[1]. These n-grams allow us to break down a sen-

[1]Our implementation restricts n-grams to length 3 and uses up to 4 n-grams per sentence

tence into wildcard-separated subsequences, which yields an SOL pattern. We generate multiple patterns with different types, one for each combination of types that the detected entities have in the underlying ontology.

We quantify the *statistical strength* of a pattern by means of its support set. For a given pattern p with type signature *t1* $\times$ *t2*, the *support* of p is the size of its support set. For confidence, we compare the support-set sizes of p and an untyped variant p^u of p, in which the types ⟨*t1*⟩ and ⟨*t2*⟩ are replaced by the generic type ⟨*entity*⟩. We define the *confidence* of p as the ratio of the support-set sizes of p and p^u.

5 Syntactic Pattern Generalization

Almost every pattern can be generalized into a syntactically more general pattern in several ways: by replacing words by POS-tags, by introducing wildcards (combining more n-grams), or by generalizing the types in the pattern. It is not obvious which generalizations will be reasonable and useful. We observe, however, that generalizing a pattern may create a pattern that subsumes two semantically different patterns. For example, the generalization ⟨*person*⟩ *[vb]* ⟨*person*⟩ subsumes the two semantically different patterns ⟨*person*⟩ *loves* ⟨*person*⟩ and ⟨*person*⟩ *hates* ⟨*person*⟩. This means that the pattern is semantically meaningless.

Therefore, we proceed as follows. For every pattern, we generate all possible generalizations. If a generalization subsumes multiple patterns with disjoint support sets, we abandon the generalized pattern. Otherwise, we add it to our set of patterns.

6 Semantic Pattern Generalization

The main difficulty in generating semantic subsumptions is that the support sets may contain spurious pairs or be incomplete, thus destroying crisp set inclusions. To overcome this problem, we designed a notion of a *soft set inclusion*, in which one set S can be a subset of another set B to a certain degree. One possible measure for this degree is the confidence, i.e., the ratio of elements in S that are in B, $deg(S \subseteq B) = |S \cap B|/|S|$. However, if a support set S has only few elements due to sparsity, it may become a subset of another support set B, even if the two patterns are semantically different. Therefore, one has to take into account also the *support*, i.e., the size of the set S. Traditionally, this is done through a weighted trade-off between confidence and support.

To avoid the weight tuning, we instead devised a probabilistic model. We interpret S as a *random sample* from the "true" support set S' that the pattern would have on an infinitely large corpus. We want to estimate the ratio of elements of S' that are in B. This ratio is a Bernoulli parameter that can be estimated from the ratio of elements of the sample S that are in B. We compute the Wilson score interval $[c-d, c+d]$ (Brown 2001) for the sample. This interval guarantees that with a given probability (set a priori, usually to $\alpha = 95\%$), the true ratio falls into the interval $[c-d, c+d]$. If the sample is small, d is large and c is close to 0.5. If the sample is large, d decreases and c approaches the naive estimation $|S \cap B|/|S|$. Thereby, the Wilson interval center naturally balances the trade-off between confidence and the support. Hence we define $deg(S \subset B) = c$. This estimator may degrade when the sample size is too small We can alternatively use a conservative estimator $deg(S \subset B) = c-d$, i.e., the lower bound of the Wilson score interval. This gives a low score to the case where $S \subset B$ if we have few samples (S is small).

7 Taxonomy Construction

We now have to arrange the patterns in a semantic taxonomy. A baseline solution would compare every pattern support set to every other pattern support set in order to determine inclusion, mutual inclusion, or independence. This would be prohibitively slow. For this reason, we make use of a prefix-tree for frequent patterns (Han 2005). The prefix-tree stores support sets of patterns. We then developed an algorithm for obtaining set intersections from the prefix-tree.

7.1 Prefix-Tree Construction

Suppose we have pattern synsets and their support sets as shown in Table 1. An entity pair in a support set is denoted by a letter. For example, in the support set for the pattern ⟨$Politican$⟩ *was governor of* ⟨$State$⟩, the entry ⟨*A,80*⟩ may denote the entity

ID	Pattern Synset & Support Sets
P_1	$\langle Politician \rangle$ was governor of $\langle State \rangle$ A,80 B,75 C,70
P_2	$\langle Politician \rangle$ *politician from* $\langle State \rangle$ A,80 B,75 C,70 D,66 E,64
P_3	$\langle Person \rangle$ *daughter of* $\langle Person \rangle$ F,78 G,75 H,66
P_4	$\langle Person \rangle$ *child of* $\langle Person \rangle$ I,88 J,87 F,78 G,75 K,64

Table 1: Pattern Synsets and their Support Sets

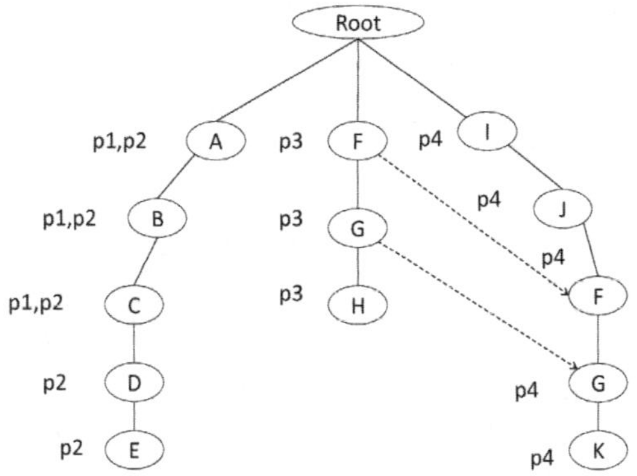

Figure 1: Prefix-Tree for the Synsets in Table 1.

pair *Arnold Schwarzenegger, California*, with an occurrence frequency *80*. The contents of the support sets are used to construct a prefix-tree, where nodes are entity pairs. If synsets have entity pairs in common, they share a common prefix; thus the shared parts can be represented by one prefix-path in the tree. This enables subsumptions to be directly "read off" from the tree, while representing the tree in a compact manner. To increase the chance of shared prefixes, entity pairs are inserted into the tree in decreasing order of occurrence frequency.

The prefix-tree of support sets is a prefix-tree augmented with synset information stored at the nodes. Each node (entity pair) stores the identifiers of the pattern sysnets whose support sets contain that entity pair. In addition, each node stores a link to the next node with the same entity pair.

Figure 1 shows the tree for the pattern synsets in Table 1. The left-most path contains synsets P_1 and P_2. The two patterns have a prefix in common, thus they share the same path. This is reflected by the synsets stored in the nodes in the path. Synsets P_2 and P_3 belong to two different paths due to dissimilar prefixes although they have common nodes. Instead, their common nodes are connected by the same-entity-pair links shown as dotted lines in Figure 1. These links are created whenever the entity pair already exists in the tree but with a prefix different from the prefix of the synset being added to the tree. The size of the tree is at most the total number of entity pairs making up the supports sets of the synsets. The height of the tree is at most the size of the the largest support set.

7.2 Mining Subsumptions from the Prefix-Tree

To efficiently mine subsumptions from the prefix-tree, we have to avoid comparing every path to every other path as this introduces the same inefficiencies that the baseline approach suffers from.

From the construction of the tree it follows that for any node N_i in the tree, all paths containing N_i can be found by following node N_i*'s* links including the same-entity-pair links. By traversing the entire path of a synset P_i, we can reach all the pattern synsets sharing common nodes with P_i. This leads to our main insight: if we start traversing the tree bottom up, starting at the last node in $P_i's$ support set, we can determine exactly which paths are subsumed by P_i. Traversing the tree this way for all patterns gives us the sizes of the support set intersection. The determined intersection sizes can then be used in the Wilson estimator to determine the degree of semantic subsumption and semantic equivalence of patterns.

7.3 DAG Construction

Once we have generated subsumptions between relational patterns, there might be cycles in the graph we generate. We ideally want to remove the minimal total number of subsumptions whose removal results in an a directed acyclic graph (DAG). This task is related to the minimum feedback-arc-set problem: given a directed graph, we want to remove the smallest set of edges whose removal makes the remaining graph acyclic. This is a well known NP-hard problem (Kann 1992). We use a greedy algorithm for removing cycles and eliminating redundancy in the subsumptions, thus effectively constructing a DAG. Starting with a list of subsumption edges ordered by decreasing weights, we construct the DAG bottom-up by adding the highest-weight subsumption edge. This step is repeated for all subsumptions, where we add a subsumption to the DAG only if it does not introduce cycles or redundancy. Redundancy occurs when there already exists a path, by transitivity of subsumptions, between pattern synsets linked by the subsumption. This process finally yields a DAG of pattern synsets – the PATTY taxonony.

8 Experimental Evaluation

8.1 Setup

The PATTY extraction and mining algorithms were run on two different input corpora: the New York Times archive (*NYT*) which includes about 1.8 Million newspaper articles from the years 1987 to 2007, and the English edition of Wikipedia (*WKP*), which contains about 3.8 Million articles (as of June 21, 2011). Experiments were carried out, for each corpus, with two different type systems: a) the type system of YAGO2, which consists of about 350,000 semantic classes from WordNet and the Wikipedia category system, and b) the two-level domain/type hierarchy of Freebase which consists of 85 domains and a total of about 2000 types within these domains.

All relational patterns and their respective entity pairs are stored in a MongoDB database. We evaluated PATTY along four dimensions: quality of patterns, quality of subsumptions, coverage, and design alternatives. These dimensions are discussed in the following four subsections. We also performed an extrinsic study to demonstrate the usefulness of PATTY for paraphrasing the relations of DBpedia and YAGO2. In terms of runtimes, he most expensive part is the pattern extraction, where we identify pattern candidates through dependency parsing and perform entity recognition on the entire corpus. This phase runs about a day for Wikipedia a cluster. All other phases of the PATTY system take less than an hour. All experimental data is available on our Web site at `www.mpi-inf.mpg.de/yago-naga/patty/`.

8.2 Precision of Relational Patterns

To assess the precision of the automatically mined patterns (patterns in this section always mean pattern synsets), we sampled the PATTY taxonomy for each combination of input corpus and type system. We ranked the patterns by their statistical strength (Section 4), and evaluated the precision of the *top 100* pattern synsets. Several human judges were shown a sampled pattern synset, its type signature, and a few example instances, and then stated whether the pattern synset indicates a valid relation or not. Evaluators checked the correctness of the type signature, whether the majority of patterns in the synset is reasonable, and whether the instances seem plausible. If so, the synset was flagged as meaningful. The results of this evaluation are shown in column four of Table 2, with a 0.9-confidence Wilson score interval (Brown 2001). In addition, the same assessment procedure was applied to *randomly sampled* synsets, to evaluate the quality in the long tail of patterns. The results are shown in column five of Table 2. For the top 100 patterns, we achieve above 90% precision for Wikipedia, and above 80% for 100 random samples.

Corpus	Types	Patterns	Top 100	Random
NYT	YAGO2	86,982	0.89±0.06	0.72±0.09
	Freebase	809,091	0.87 ±0.06	0.71±0.09
WKP	YAGO2	350,569	0.95±0.04	**0.85**±0.07
	Freebase	1,631,531	0.93±0.05	0.80±0.08

Table 2: Precision of Relational Patterns

From the results we make two observations. First, Wikipedia patterns have higher precision than those from the New York Times corpus. This is because some the language in the news corpus does not express relational information; especially the news on stock markets produced noisy patterns picked up by PATTY. However, we still manage to have a precision of close to 90% for the top 100 patterns and around 72% for random sample on the NYT corpus. The second observation is that the YAGO2 type system generally led to higher precision than the Freebase type system. This is because YAGO2 has finer grained, ontologically clean types, whereas Freebase has broader categories with a more liberal assignment of entities to categories.

8.3 Precision of Subsumptions

We evaluated the quality of the subsumptions by assessing 100 top-ranked as well as 100 randomly selected subsumptions. As shown in Table 3, a large number of the subsumptions are correct. The Wikipedia-based PATTY taxonomy has a random-sampling-based precision of 75%.

Corpus	Types	# Edges	Top 100	Random
NYT	YAGO2	12,601	0.86±0.07	0.68±0.09
	Freebase	80,296	0.89±0.06	0.41±0.09
WKP	YAGO2	**8,162**	0.83±0.07	**0.75**±0.07
	Freebase	20,339	0.85±0.07	0.62±0.09

Table 3: Quality of Subsumptions

Example subsumptions from Wikipedia are:

- ⟨*person*⟩ *nominated for* ⟨*award*⟩ ⊐ ⟨*person*⟩ *winner of* ⟨*award*⟩
- ⟨*person*⟩ *' s wife* ⟨*person*⟩ ⊐ ⟨*person*⟩ *'s widow* ⟨*person*⟩

8.4 Coverage

To evaluate the coverage of PATTY, we would need a complete ground-truth resource that contains all possible binary relations between entities. Unfortunately, there is no such resource[2]. We tried to approximate such a resource by manually compiling all binary relations between entities that appear in Wikipedia articles of a certain domain. We chose the domain of popular music, because it offers a plethora of non-trivial relations (such as *addictedTo(person,drug)*, *coveredBy(musician,musician)*, *dedicatedSongTo(musician,entity)*)). We considered the Wikipedia articles of five musicians (Amy Winehouse, Bob Dylan, Neil Young, John Coltrane, Nina Simone). For each page, two annotators hand-extracted all relationship types that they would spot in the respective articles. The annotators limited themselves to relations where at least one argument type is ⟨*musician*⟩. Then we formed the intersection of the two annotators' outputs (i.e., their agreement) as a reasonable gold standard for relations identifiable by skilled humans. In total, the gold-standard set contains 163 relations.

We then compared our relational patterns to the relations included in four major knowledge bases, namely, YAGO2, DBpedia (DBP), Freebase (FB), and NELL, limited to the specific domain of music. Table 4 shows the absolute number of relations covered by each resource. For PATTY, the patterns were derived from the Wikipedia corpus with the YAGO2 type system.

gold standard	PATTY	YAGO2	DBP	FB	NELL
163	**126**	31	39	69	13

Table 4: Coverage of Music Relations

PATTY covered 126 of the 163 gold-standard relations. This is more than what can be found in large semi-curated knowledge bases such as Freebase, and twice as much as Wikipedia-infobox-based resources such as DBpedia or YAGO offer. Some PATTY examples that do not appear in the other resources at all are:

- ⟨*musician*⟩ *PRP idol* ⟨*musician*⟩ for the relation *hasMusicalIdol*
- ⟨*person*⟩ *criticized by* ⟨*organization*⟩ for *critizedByMedia*
- ⟨*person*⟩ *headliner* ⟨*artifact*⟩ for *headlinerAt*
- ⟨*person*⟩ *successfully sued* ⟨*person*⟩ for *suedBy*
- ⟨*musician*⟩ *wrote hits for* ⟨*musician*⟩ for *wroteHitsFor*,

This shows (albeit anecdotically) that PATTY's patterns contribute added value beyond today's knowledge bases.

8.5 Pattern Language Alternatives

We also investigated various design alternatives to the PATTY pattern language. We looked at three main alternatives: the first is verb-phrase-centric patterns advocated by ReVerb (Fader 2011), the second is the PATTY language without type signatures (just using sets of n-grams with syntactic generalizations), and the third one is the full PATTY language. The results for the Wikipedia corpus and the

[2]Lexical resources such as WordNet contain only verbs, but not binary relations such as *is the president of*. Other resources are likely incomplete.

	Reverb-style patterns	PATTY without types	PATTY full
# Patterns	5,996	184,629	**350,569**
Patterns Precision	0.96±0.03	0.74±0.08	**0.95**±0.04
# Subsumptions	74	15,347	**8,162**
Subsumptions Precision	0.79 ±0.09	0.58±0.09	**0.83**±0.07
# Facts	192,144	6,384,684	**3,890,075**
Facts Precision.	0.86 ±0.07	0.64±0.09	**0.88** ±0.06

Table 5: Results for Different Pattern Language Alternatives

Relation	Paraphrases	Precision	Sample Paraphrases
DBPedia/artist	83	0.96±0.03	[adj] studio album of, [det] song by ...
DBPedia/associatedBand	386	0.74±0.11	joined band along, plays in ...
DBPedia/doctoralAdvisor	36	0.558±0.15	[det] student of, under * supervision ...
DBPedia/recordLabel	113	0.86±0.09	[adj] artist signed to, [adj] record label ...
DBPedia/riverMouth	31	0.83±0.12	drains into, [adj] tributary of ...
DBPedia/team	1,108	0.91±0.07	be * traded to, [prp] debut for ...
YAGO/actedIn	330	0.88±0.08	starred in * film, [adj] role for ...
YAGO/created	466	0.79±0.10	founded, 's book ...
YAGO/isLeaderOf	40	0.53±0.14	elected by, governor of ...
YAGO/holdsPoliticalPosition	72	0.73±0.10	[prp] tenure as, oath as ...

Table 6: Sample Results for Relation Paraphrasing

YAGO2 type system are shown in Table 5; precision figures are based on the respective top 100 patterns or subsumption edges. We observe from these results that the type signatures are crucial for precision. Moreover, the number of patterns, subsumptions and facts found by verb-phrase-centric patterns (ReVerb (Fader 2011)), are limited in recall. General pattern synsets with type signatures, as newly pursued in this paper, substantially outperform the verb-phrase-centric alternative in terms of pattern and subsumption recall while yielding high precision.

8.6 Extrinsic Study: Relation Paraphrasing

To further evaluate the usefulness of PATTY, we performed a study on relation paraphrasing: given a relation from a knowledge base, identify patterns that can be used to express that relation. Paraphrasing relations with high-quality patterns is important for populating knowledge bases and counters the problem of semantic drifting caused by ambiguous and noisy patterns.

We considered relations from two knowledge bases, DBpedia and YAGO2, focusing on relations that hold between entities and do not include literals. PATTY paraphrased 225 DBpedia relations with a total of 127,811 patterns, and 25 YAGO2 relations with a total of 43,124 patterns. Among these we evaluated a random sample of 1,000 relation paraphrases. Table 6 shows precision figures for some selected relations, along anecdotic example patterns.

Some relations are hard to capture precisely. For *DBPedia/doctoralAdvisor*, e.g., PATTY picked up patterns like "worked with" as paraphrases. These are not entirely wrong, but we evaluated them as false because they are too general to indicate the more specific doctoral advisor relation.

Overall, however, the paraphrasing precision is high. Our evaluation showed an average precision of **0.76**±0.03 across all relations.

9 Conclusion and Future Directions

This paper presented PATTY, a large resource of text patterns. Different from existing resources, PATTY organizes patterns into synsets and a taxonomy, similar in spirit to WordNet. Our evaluation shows that PATTY's patterns are semantically meaningful, and that they cover large parts of the relations of other knowledge bases. The Wikipedia-based version of PATTY contains 350,569 pattern synsets at a precision of 84.7%, with 8,162 subsumptions, at a precision of 75%. The PATTY resource is freely available for interactive access and download at www.mpi-inf.mpg.de/yago-naga/patty/.

Our approach harnesses existing knowledge bases for entity-type information. However, PATTY is not tied to a particular choice for this purpose. In fact, it would be straightforward to adjust PATTY to using surface-form noun phrases rather than disambiguated entities, as long as we have means to infer at least coarse-grained types (e.g., person, organization, location). An interesting future direction is to study this generalized setting. We would also like to investigate the enhanced interplay of information extraction and pattern extraction, and possible applications for question answering.

References

Ion Androutsopoulos, Prodromos Malakasiotis: A Survey of Paraphrasing and Textual Entailment Methods. Journal of Artificial Intelligence Research 38: 135–187, 2010

Rakesh Agrawal, Tomasz Imielinski, Arun N. Swami: Mining Association Rules between Sets of Items in Large Databases. SIGMOD Conference 1993

Enrique Alfonseca, Marius Pasca, Enrique Robledo-Arnuncio: Acquisition of instance attributes via labeled and related instances. SIGIR 2010

Sören Auer, Christian Bizer, Georgi Kobilarov, Jens Lehmann, Richard Cyganiak, Zachary G. Ives: DBpedia: A Nucleus for a Web of Open Data. ISWC 2007, data at http://dbpedia.org

Michele Banko, Michael J. Cafarella, Stephen Soderland, Matthew Broadhead, Oren Etzioni: Open Information Extraction from the Web. IJCAI 2007

Jonathan Berant, Ido Dagan, Jacob Goldberger: Global Learning of Typed Entailment Rules. ACL 2011

Kurt D. Bollacker, Colin Evans, Praveen Paritosh, Tim Sturge, Jamie Taylor: Freebase: a collaboratively created graph database for structuring human knowledge. SIGMOD Conference 2008, data at http://freebase.com

Lawrence D. Brown, T.Tony Cai, Anirban Dasgupta: Interval Estimation for a Binomial Proportion. Statistical Science 16: 101–133, 2001

Andrew Carlson, Justin Betteridge, Bryan Kisiel, Burr Settles, Estevam R. Hruschka Jr., Tom M. Mitchell. Toward an Architecture for Never-Ending Language Learning. AAAI 2010, data at http://rtw.ml.cmu.edu/rtw/

Timothy Chklovski, Patrick Pantel: VerbOcean: Mining the Web for Fine-Grained Semantic Verb Relations. EMNLP 2004; data available at http://demo.patrickpantel.com/demos/verbocean/

Anthony Fader, Stephen Soderland, Oren Etzioni: Identifying Relations for Open Information Extraction. EMNLP 2011, data at http://reverb.cs.washington.edu

Christiane Fellbaum (Editor): WordNet: An Electronic Lexical Database. MIT Press, 1998

Jiawei Han, Jian Pei , Yiwen Yin : Mining frequent patterns without candidate generation. SIGMOD 2000.

Chikara Hashimoto, Kentaro Torisawa, Kow Kuroda, Stijn De Saeger, Masaki Murata, Jun'ichi Kazama: Large-Scale Verb Entailment Acquisition from the Web. EMNLP 2009

Catherine Havasi, Robert Speer, and Jason Alonso. ConceptNet 3: a Flexible, Multilingual Semantic Network for Common Sense Knowledge, RANLP 2007; data available at http://conceptnet5.media.mit.edu/

Iris Hendrickx, Su Nam Kim, Zornitsa Kozareva, Preslav Nakov, Diarmuid O Seaghdha, Sebastian Pado, Marco Pennacchiotti, Lorenza Romano, Stan Szpakowicz: SemEval-2010 Task 8: Multi-Way Classification of Semantic Relations Between Pairs of Nominals, 5th ACL International Workshop on Semantic Evaluation, 2010; data available at http://www.isi.edu/~kozareva/downloads.html

Johannes Hoffart, Fabian Suchanek, Klaus Berberich, Edwin Lewis-Kelham, Gerard de Melo, Gerhard Weikum: YAGO2: Exploring and Querying World Knowledge in Time, Space, Context, and Many Languages. WWW 2011, data at http://yago-knowledge.org

Raphael Hoffmann, Congle Zhang, Daniel S. Weld: Learning 5000 Relational Extractors. ACL 2010

Vigo Kann: On the approximability of NP-complete optimization problems. PhD thesis, Department of Numerical Analysis and Computing Science, Royal Institute of Technology, Stockholm. 1992.

Karin Kipper, Anna Korhonen, Neville Ryant, Martha Palmer, A Large-scale Classification of English Verbs, Language Resources and Evaluation Journal, 42(1): 21-40, 2008, data available at http://verbs.colorado.edu/~mpalmer/projects/verbnet/downloads.html

Zornitsa Kozareva, Eduard H. Hovy: Learning Arguments and Supertypes of Semantic Relations Using Recursive Patterns. ACL 2010

Girija Limaye, Sunita Sarawagi, Soumen Chakrabarti: Annotating and Searching Web Tables Using Entities, Types and Relationships. PVLDB 3(1): 1338-1347 (2010)

Dekang Lin, Patrick Pantel: DIRT: discovery of inference rules from text. KDD 2001

Marie-Catherine de Marneffe, Bill MacCartney and Christopher D. Manning. Generating Typed Dependency Parses from Phrase Structure Parses. LREC 2006.

Thahir Mohamed, Estevam R. Hruschka Jr., Tom M. Mitchell: Discovering Relations between Noun Categories. EMNLP 2011

Ndapandula Nakashole, Martin Theobald, Gerhard Weikum: Scalable Knowledge Harvesting with High Precision and High Recall. WSDM 2011

Preslav Nakov, Marti A. Hearst: Solving Relational Similarity Problems Using the Web as a Corpus. ACL 2008

Vivi Nastase, Michael Strube, Benjamin Boerschinger, Căcilia Zirn, Anas Elghafari: WikiNet: A Very Large Scale Multi-Lingual Concept Network. LREC 2010, data at http://www.h-its.org/english/research/nlp/download/wikinet.php

Roberto Navigli, Simone Paolo Ponzetto: BabelNet: Building a Very Large Multilingual Semantic Network. ACL 2010 data at http://lcl.uniroma1.it/babelnet/

Marius Pasca, Benjamin Van Durme: What You Seek Is What You Get: Extraction of Class Attributes from Query Logs. IJCAI 2007

Marius Pasca, Benjamin Van Durme: Weakly-Supervised Acquisition of Open-Domain Classes and Class Attributes from Web Documents and Query Logs. ACL 2008

Andrew Philpot, Eduard Hovy, Patrick Pantel: The Omega Ontology, in: Ontology and the Lexicon, Cambridge University Press, 2008, data at http://omega.isi.edu/

Simone Paolo Ponzetto, Michael Strube: Deriving a Large-Scale Taxonomy from Wikipedia. AAAI 2007, data at http://www.h-its.org/english/research/nlp/download/wikitaxonomy.php

Joseph Reisinger, Marius Pasca: Latent Variable Models of Concept-Attribute Attachment. ACL/AFNLP 2009

Ramakrishnan Srikant, Rakesh Agrawal: Mining Sequential Patterns: Generalizations and Performance Improvements. EDBT 1996

Fabian M. Suchanek, Gjergji Kasneci, Gerhard Weikum: YAGO: a Core of Semantic Knowledge. WWW 2007

Fabian M. Suchanek, Mauro Sozio, Gerhard Weikum: SOFIE: a self-organizing framework for information extraction. WWW 2009

Lin Sun, Anna Korhonen: Hierarchical Verb Clustering Using Graph Factorization. EMNLP 2011

Petros Venetis, Alon Y. Halevy, Jayant Madhavan, Marius Pasca, Warren Shen, Fei Wu, Gengxin Miao, Chung Wu: Recovering Semantics of Tables on the Web. PVLDB 4(9): 528-538, 2011

Tom White: Hadoop: The Definitive Guide, 2nd Edition. O'Reilly, 2010.

Fei Wu, Daniel S. Weld: Automatically refining the wikipedia infobox ontology. WWW 2008

Wentao Wu, Hongsong Li, Haixun Wang, Kenny Q. Zhu: Towards a Probabilistic Taxonomy of Many Concepts. Technical Report MSR-TR-2011-25, Microsoft Research, 2011

Limin Yao, Aria Haghighi, Sebastian Riedel, Andrew McCallum: Structured Relation Discovery using Generative Models. EMNLP 2011

Jun Zhu, Zaiqing Nie, Xiaojiang Liu, Bo Zhang, Ji-Rong Wen: StatSnowball: a statistical approach to extracting entity relationships. WWW 2009

Training Factored PCFGs with Expectation Propagation

David Hall and **Dan Klein**
Computer Science Division
University of California, Berkeley
{dlwh,klein}@cs.berkeley.edu

Abstract

PCFGs can grow exponentially as additional annotations are added to an initially simple base grammar. We present an approach where multiple annotations coexist, but in a factored manner that avoids this combinatorial explosion. Our method works with linguistically-motivated annotations, induced latent structure, lexicalization, or any mix of the three. We use a structured expectation propagation algorithm that makes use of the factored structure in two ways. First, by partitioning the factors, it speeds up parsing exponentially over the unfactored approach. Second, it minimizes the redundancy of the factors during training, improving accuracy over an independent approach. Using purely latent variable annotations, we can efficiently train and parse with up to 8 latent bits per symbol, achieving F1 scores up to 88.4 on the Penn Treebank while using two orders of magnitudes fewer parameters compared to the naïve approach. Combining latent, lexicalized, and unlexicalized annotations, our best parser gets 89.4 F1 on all sentences from section 23 of the Penn Treebank.

1 Introduction

Many high-performance PCFG parsers take an initially simple base grammar over treebank labels like NP and enrich it with deeper syntactic features to improve accuracy. This broad characterization includes lexicalized parsers (Collins, 1997), unlexicalized parsers (Klein and Manning, 2003), and latent variable parsers (Matsuzaki et al., 2005). Figures 1(a), 1(b), and 1(c) show small examples of context-free trees that have been annotated in these ways.

When multi-part annotations are used in the same grammar, systems have generally multiplied these annotations together, in the sense that an NP that was definite, possessive, and VP-dominated would have a single unstructured PCFG symbol that encoded all three facts. In addition, modulo backoff or smoothing, that unstructured symbol would often have rewrite parameters entirely distinct from, say, the indefinite but otherwise similar variant of the symbol (Klein and Manning, 2003). Therefore, when designing a grammar, one would have to carefully weigh new contextual annotations. Should a definiteness annotation be included, doubling the number of NPs in the grammar and perhaps overly fragmenting statistics? Or should it be excluded, thereby losing important distinctions? Klein and Manning (2003) discuss exactly such trade-offs and omit annotations that were helpful on their own because they were not worth the combinatorial or statistical cost when combined with other annotations.

In this paper, we argue for grammars with *factored annotations*, that is, grammars with annotations that have structured component parts that are partially decoupled. Our annotated grammars can include both latent and explicit annotations, as illustrated in Figure 1(d), and we demonstrate that these factored grammars outperform parsers with unstructured annotations.

After discussing the factored representation, we describe a method for parsing with factored annotations, using an approximate inference technique called expectation propagation (Minka, 2001). Our algorithm has runtime linear in the number of annotation factors in the grammar, improving on the naïve algorithm, which has runtime exponential in the number of annotations. Our method, the Expectation Propagation for Inferring Constituency (*EPIC*) parser, jointly trains a model over factored annotations, where each factor naturally leverages information from other annotation factors and improves on their mistakes.

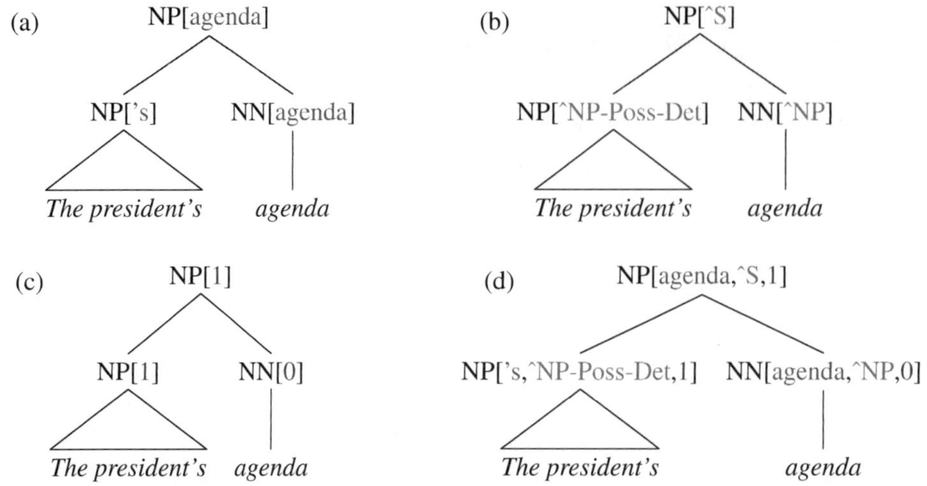

Figure 1: Parse trees using four different annotation schemes: (a) Lexicalized annotation like that in Collins (1997); (b) Unlexicalized annotation like that in Klein and Manning (2003); (c) Latent annotation like that in Matsuzaki et al. (2005); and (d) the factored, mixed annotations we argue for in our paper.

We demonstrate the empirical effectiveness of our approach in two ways. First, we efficiently train a latent-variable grammar with 8 disjoint one-bit latent annotation factors, with scores as high as 89.7 F1 on length $\leq$40 sentences from the Penn Treebank (Marcus et al., 1993). This latent variable parser outscores the best of Petrov and Klein (2008a)'s comparable parsers while using two orders of magnitude fewer parameters. Second, we combine our latent variable factors with lexicalized and unlexicalized annotations, resulting in our best F1 score of 89.4 on all sentences.

2 Intuitions

Modern theories of grammar such as HPSG (Pollard and Sag, 1994) and Minimalism (Chomsky, 1992) do not ascribe unstructured conjunctions of annotations to phrasal categories. Rather, phrasal categories are associated with sequences of metadata that control their function. For instance, an NP might have annotations to the effect that it is singular, masculine, and nominative, with perhaps further information about its animacy or other aspects of the head noun. Thus, it is appealing for a grammar to be able to model these (somewhat) orthogonal notions, but most models have no mechanism to encourage this. As a notable exception, Dreyer and Eisner (2006) tried to capture this kind of insight by allowing factored annotations to pass unchanged from parent label to child label, though they were not able to demonstrate substantial gains in accuracy.

Moreover, there has been to our knowledge no attempt to employ both latent and non-latent annotations at the same time. There is good reason for this: lexicalized or highly annotated grammars like those of Collins (1997) or Klein and Manning (2003) have a very large number of states and an even larger number of rules. Further annotating these rules with latent annotations would produce an infeasibly large grammar. Nevertheless, it is a shame to sacrifice expert annotation just to get latent annotations. Thus, it makes sense to combine these annotation methods in a way that does not lead to an explosion of the state space or a fragmentation of statistics.

3 Parsing with Annotations

Suppose we have a raw (binarized) treebank grammar, with productions of the form $A \to B\ C$. The typical process is to then annotate these rules with additional information, giving rules of the form $A[x] \to B[y]\ C[z]$. In the case of explicit annotations, an x might include information about the parent category, or a head word, or a combination of things. In the case of latent annotations, x will be an integer that may or may not correspond to some linguistic notion. We are interested in the specific case where each x is actually factored into M disjoint parts: $A[x_1, x_2, \ldots, x_M]$. (See Figure 1(d).) We call each component of x an *annotation factor* or an *annotation component*.

3.1 Annotation Classes

In this paper, we consider three kinds of annotation models, representing three of the major traditions in constituency parsing. Individually, none of our models are state-of-the-art, instead achieving F1 scores in the mid-80's on the Penn Treebank.

The first model is a relatively simple lexicalized parser. We are not aware of a prior discriminative lexicalized constituency parser, and it is quite different from the generative models of Collins (1997). Broadly, it considers features over a binary rule annotated with head words: $A[h] \rightarrow B[h]\ C[d]$ and $A[h] \rightarrow B[d]\ C[h]$, focusing on monolexical rule features and bilexical dependency features. It is our best individual model, scoring 87.3 F1 on the development set.

The second is similar to the unlexicalized model of Klein and Manning (2003). This parser starts from a grammar with labels annotated with sibling and parent information, and then adds specific annotations, such as whether an NP is possessive or whether a symbol rewrites as a unary. This parser gets 86.3, tying the original generative version of Klein and Manning (2003).

Finally, we use a straightforward *discriminative* latent variable model much like that of Petrov and Klein (2008a). Here, each symbol is given a latent annotation, referred to as a substate. Typically, these substates correlate at least loosely with linguistic phenomena. For instance, NP-1 might be associated with possessive NPs, while NP-3 might be for adjuncts. Often, these latent integers are considered as bit strings, with each bit indicating one latent annotation. Prior work in this area has considered the effect of splitting and merging these states (Petrov et al., 2006; Petrov and Klein, 2007), as well as "multiscale" grammars (Petrov and Klein, 2008b). With two states (or one bit of annotation), our version of this parser gets 81.7 F1, edging out the comparable parser of Petrov and Klein (2008a). On the other hand, our parser gets 83.2 with four states (two bits), short of the performance of prior work.[1]

[1]Much of the difference stems from the different binarization scheme we employ. We use head-outward binarization, rather than the left-branching binarization they employed. This change was to enable integrating lexicalization with our other models.

3.2 Model Representation

We employ a general exponential family representation of our grammar. This representation is fairly general, and—in its generic form—by no means new, save for the focus on annotation components.

Formally, we begin with a parse tree T over base symbols for some sentence $\mathbf{w}$, and we decorate the tree with annotations X, giving a parse tree $T[X]$. We focus on the case when X partitions into disjoint components $X = [X_1, X_2, \ldots, X_M]$. These components are decoupled in the sense that, conditioned on the coarse tree T, each column of the annotation is independent of every other column. However, they are crucially not independent conditioned only on the sentence $\mathbf{w}$. This model is represented schematically in Figure 2(a).

The conditional probability $\mathrm{P}(T[X]|\mathbf{w},\theta)$ of an annotated tree given words is:

$$\begin{aligned} \mathrm{P}&(T[X]|\mathbf{w},\theta) \\ &= \frac{\prod_m f_m(T[X_m];\mathbf{w},\theta_m)}{\sum_{T',X'}\prod_m f_m(T'[X'_m];\mathbf{w},\theta_m)} \\ &= \frac{1}{Z(\mathbf{w},\theta)}\prod_m f_m(T[X_m];\mathbf{w},\theta_m) \end{aligned} \quad (1)$$

where the factors f_m for each model take the form:

$$f_m(T[X_m];\mathbf{w},\theta_m) = \exp\left(\theta_m^T \varphi_m(T, X_m, \mathbf{w})\right)$$

Here, X_m is the annotation associated with a particular model m. φ is a feature function that projects the raw tree, annotations, and words into a feature vector. The features φ need to decompose into features for each factor f_m; we do not allow features that take into account the annotation from two different components.

We further add a pruning filter that assigns zero weight to any tree with a constituent that a baseline unannotated grammar finds sufficiently unlikely, and a weight of one to any other tree. This filter is similar to that used in Petrov and Klein (2008a) and allows for much more efficient training and inference.

Because our model is discriminative, training takes the form of maximizing the probability of the training trees given the words. This objective is convex for deterministic annotations, but non-convex for latent annotations. We (locally) optimize the

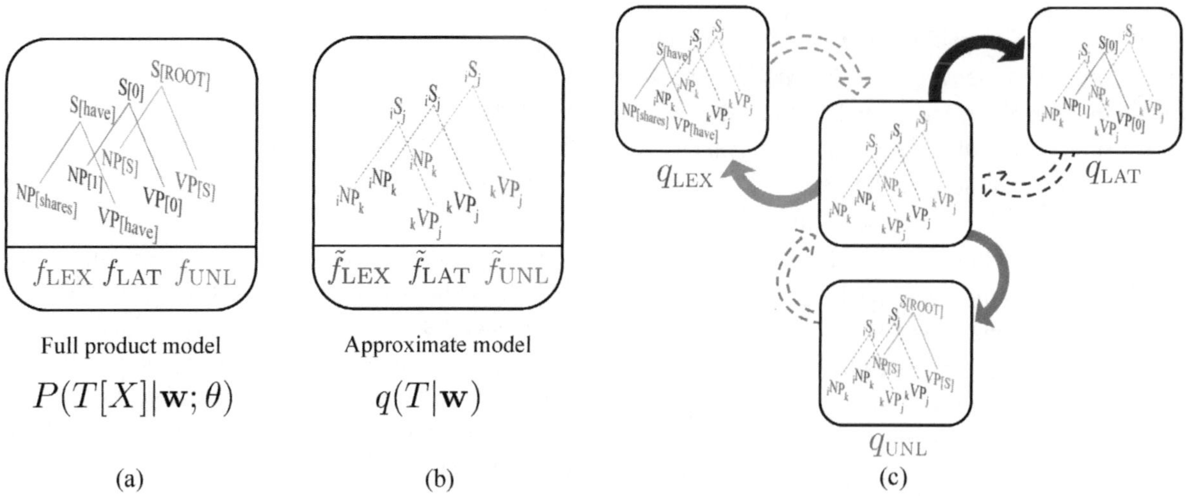

Figure 2: Schematic representation of our model, its approximation, and expectation propagation. (a) The full joint distribution consists of a product of three grammars with different annotations, here lexicalized, latent, and unlexicalized. This model is described in Section 3.2. (b) The core approximation is an anchored PCFG with one factor corresponding to each annotation component, described in Section 5.1. (c) Fitting the approximation with expectation propagation, as described in Section 5.3. At the center is the core approximation. During each step, an "augmented" distribution q_m is created by taking one annotation factor from the full grammar and the rest from the approximate grammar. For instance, in upper left hand corner the full f_{LEX} is substituted for $\tilde{f}_{\text{LEX}}$. This new augmented distribution is projected back to the core approximation. This process is repeated for each factor until convergence.

(non-convex) log conditional likelihood of the observed training data $(T^{(d)}, \mathbf{w}^{(d)})$:

$$\begin{aligned}\ell(\theta) &= \sum_d \log \mathrm{P}(T^{(d)}|\mathbf{w}^{(d)}, \theta) \\ &= \sum_d \log \sum_X \mathrm{P}(T^{(d)}[X]|\mathbf{w}^{(d)}, \theta)\end{aligned} \tag{2}$$

Using standard results, the derivative takes the form:

$$\begin{aligned}\nabla\ell(\theta) &= \sum_d E[\varphi(T, X, \mathbf{w})|T^{(d)}, \mathbf{w}^{(d)}] \\ &\quad - \sum_d E[\varphi(T, X, \mathbf{w})|\mathbf{w}^{(d)}]\end{aligned} \tag{3}$$

The first half of this derivative can be obtained by the forward/backward-like computation defined by Matsuzaki et al. (2005), while the second half requires an inside/outside computation (Petrov and Klein, 2008a). The partition function $Z(\mathbf{w}, \theta)$ is computed as a byproduct of the latter computation. Finally, this objective is regularized, using the L2 norm of θ as a penalty.

We note that we omit from our parser one major feature class found in other discriminative parsers, namely those that use features over the words in the span (Finkel et al., 2008; Petrov and Klein, 2008b). These features might condition on words on either side of the split point of a binary rule or take into account the length of the span. While such features have proven useful in previous work, they are not the focus of our current work and so we omit them.

4 The Complexity of Annotated Grammars

Note that the first term of Equation 3—which is conditioned on the coarse tree T—factors into M pieces, one for each of the annotation components. However, the second term does not factor because it is conditioned on just the words $\mathbf{w}$. Indeed, naïvely computing this term requires parsing with the fully articulated grammar, meaning that inference would be no more efficient than parsing with non-factored annotations.

Standard algorithms for parsing run in time $O(G|\mathbf{w}|^3)$, where $|\mathbf{w}|$ is the length of the sentence, and G is the size of the grammar, measured in the number of (binary) rules. Let G_0 be the number of binary rules in the unannotated "base" grammar.

Suppose that we have M annotation components. Each annotation component can have up to A primitive annotations per rule. For instance, a latent variable grammar will have $A = 8^b$ where b is the number of bits of annotation. If we compile all annotation components into unstructured annotations, we can end up with a total grammar size of $O(A^M G_0)$, and so in general parsing time scales exponentially with the number of annotation components. Thus, if we use latent annotations and the hierarchical splitting approach of Petrov et al. (2006), then the grammar has size $O(8^S G_0)$, where S is the number of times the grammar was split in two. Therefore, the size of annotated grammars can reach intractable levels very quickly, particularly in the case of latent annotations, where all combinations of annotations are possible.

Petrov (2010) considered an approach to slowing this growth down by using a set of M independently trained parsers P_m, and parsed using the product of the scores from each parser as the score for the tree. This approach worked largely because training was intractable: if the training algorithm could reach the global optimum, then this approach might have yielded no gain. However, because the optimization technique is local, the same algorithm produced multiple grammars.

In what follows, we propose another solution that exploits the factored structure of our grammar with expectation propagation. Crucially, we are able to jointly train and parse with all annotation factors, minimizing redundancy across the models. While not exact, we will see that expectation propagation is indeed effective.

5 Factored Inference

The key insight behind the approximate inference methods we consider here is that the full model is a product of complex factors that interact in complicated ways, and we will approximate it with a product of corresponding simple factors that interact in simple ways. Since each annotation factor is a reasonable model in both power and complexity on its own, we can consider them one at a time, replacing all others with their approximations, as shown in Figure 2(c).

The way we will build these approximations is with *expectation propagation* (Minka, 2001). Expectation propagation (EP) is a general method for approximate inference that generalizes belief propagation. We describe it here, but we first try to provide an intuition for how it functions in our system. We also describe a simplified version of EP, called *assumed density filtering* (Boyen and Koller, 1998), which is somewhat easier to understand and rhetorically convenient. For a more detailed introduction to EP in general, we direct the reader to either Minka (2001) or Wainwright and Jordan (2008). Our treatment most resembles the former.

5.1 Factored Approximations

Our goal is to build an approximation that takes information from all components into account. To begin, we note that each of these components captures different phenomena: an unlexicalized grammar is good at capturing structural relationships in a parse tree (e.g. subject noun phrases have different distributions than object noun phrases), while a lexicalized grammar captures preferred attachments for different verbs. At the same time, each of these component grammars can be thought of as a refinement of the raw unannotated treebank grammar. By itself, each of these grammars induces a different posterior distribution over *unannotated* trees for each sentence. If we can approximate each model's contribution by using only unannotated symbols, we can define an algorithm that avoids the exponential overhead of parsing with the full grammar, and instead works with each factor in turn.

To do so, we define a sentence specific *core approximation* over unannotated trees $q(T|\mathbf{w}) = \prod_m \tilde{f}_m(T, \mathbf{w})$. Figure 2(b) illustrates this approximation. Here, $q(T)$ is a product of M structurally identical factors, one for each of the annotated components. We will approximate each model f_m by its corresponding $\tilde{f}_m$. Thus, there is one color-coordinated approximate factor for each component of the model in Figure 2(a).

There are multiple choices for the structure of these factors, but we focus on *anchored PCFGs*. Anchored PCFGs have productions of the form ${}_iA_j \rightarrow {}_iB_k\ {}_kC_j$, where i, k, and j are indexes into the sentence. Here, ${}_iA_j$ is a symbol representing building the base symbol A over the span $[i, j]$.

Billott and Lang (1989) introduced anchored

CFGs as "shared forests," and Matsuzaki et al. (2005) have previously used these grammars for finding an approximate one-best tree in a latent variable parser. Note that, even though an anchored grammar is unannotated, because it is sentence specific it can represent many complex properties of the full grammar's posterior distribution for a given sentence. For example, it might express a preference for whether a PP token attaches to a particular verb or to that verb's object noun phrase in a particular sentence.

Before continuing, note that a pointwise product of anchored grammars is still an anchored grammar. The complexity of parsing with a product of these grammars is therefore no more expensive than parsing with just one. Indeed, anchoring adds no inferential cost at all over parsing with an unannotated grammar: the anchored indices i, j, k have to be computed just to parse the sentence at all. This property is crucial to EP's efficiency in our setting.

5.2 Assumed Density Filtering

We now describe a simplified version of EP: parsing with assumed density filtering (Boyen and Koller, 1998). We would like to train a sequence of M models, where each model is trained with knowledge of the posterior distribution induced by the previous models. Much as boosting algorithms (Freund and Schapire, 1995) work by focusing learning on as-yet-unexplained data points, this approach will encourage each model to improve on earlier models, albeit in a different formal way.

At a high level, assumed density filtering (ADF) proceeds as follows. First, we have an initially uninformative q: it assigns the same probability to all unpruned trees for a given sentence. Then, we factor in one of the annotated grammars and parse with this new augmented grammar. This gives us a new posterior distribution for this sentence over trees annotated with just that annotation component. Then, we can marginalize out the annotations, giving us a new q that approximates the annotated grammar as closely as possible without using any annotations. Once we have incorporated the current model's component, we move on to the next annotated grammar, augmenting it with the new q, and repeating. In this way, information from all grammars is incorporated into a final posterior distribution over trees using only unannotated symbols. The algorithm is then as follows:

- Initialize $q(T)$ uniformly.
- For each m in sequence:
  1. Create the augmented distribution $q_m(\mathbf{T}[X_m]) \propto q(\mathbf{T}) \cdot f_m(\mathbf{T}[X_m])$ and compute inside and outside scores.
  2. Minimize $\mathrm{D}_{\mathrm{KL}}\left(q_m(T) || \tilde{f}_m(T)q(T)\right)$ by fitting an anchored grammar $\tilde{f}_m$.
  3. Set $q(T) = \prod_{m'=1}^{m} \tilde{f}_{m'}(T)$.

Step 1 of the inner loop forms an approximate posterior distribution using f_m, which is the parsing model associated with component m, and q, which is the anchored core approximation to the posterior induced by the first $m-1$ models. Then, the marginals are computed, and the new posterior distribution is projected to an anchored grammar, creating $\tilde{f}_m$. More intuitively, we create an anchored PCFG that makes the approximation "as close as possible" to the augmented grammar. (We describe this procedure more precisely in Section 5.4.) Thus, each term f_m is approximated in the context of the terms that come before it. This contextual approximation is essential: without it, ADF would approximate the terms independently, meaning that no information would be shared between the models. This method would be, in effect, a simple method for parser combination, not all that dissimilar to the method proposed by Petrov (2010). Finally, note that the same inside and outside scores computed in the loop can be used to compute the expected counts needed in Equation 3.

Now we consider the runtime complexity of this algorithm. If the maximum number of annotations per rule for any factor is A, ADF has complexity $O\left(MAG_0|\mathbf{w}|^3\right)$ when using M factors. In contrast, parsing with the fully annotated grammar would have complexity $O\left(A^M G_0|\mathbf{w}|^3\right)$. Critically, for a latent variable parser with M annotation bits, the exact algorithm takes time exponential in M, while this approximate algorithm takes time linear in M.

It is worth pausing to consider what this algorithm does during training. At each step, we have in q an approximation to what the posterior distribution looks like with the first $m-1$ models. In some places, q will assign high probabilities to spans in the gold tree, and in some places it will not be so accurate. θ_m will be particularly motivated to correct the latter, because they are less like the gold tree. On the other hand, θ_m will ignore the other "correct" segments, because q has already sufficiently captured them.

5.3 Expectation Propagation

While this sequential algorithm gives us a way to efficiently combine many kinds of annotations, it is not a fully joint algorithm: there is no backward propagation of information from later models to earlier models. Ideally, no model should be privileged over any other. To correct that, we use EP, which is essentially the iterative generalization of ADF.

Intuitively, EP cycles among the models, updating the approximation for that model in turn so that it closely resembles the predictions made by f_m in the context of all other approximations, as in Figure 2(c). Thus, each approximate term $\tilde{f}_m$ is created using information from all other $\tilde{f}_{m'}$, meaning that the different annotation factors can still "talk" to each other. The product of these approximations q will therefore come to act as an approximation to the true posterior: it takes into account joint information about all annotation components, all within one tractable anchored grammar.

With that intuition in mind, EP is defined as follows:

- Initialize contributions $\tilde{f}_m$ to the approximate posterior q.

- At each step, choose m.
  1. Include approximations to all factors other than m: $q^{\backslash m}(T) = \prod_{\mathrm{m}' \neq \mathrm{m}} \tilde{f}_{m'}(T)$.
  2. Create the augmented distribution by including the actual factor for component m
  $$q_m(T[X_m]) \propto f_m(T[X_m]) q^{\backslash m}(T)$$
  and compute inside and outside scores.
  3. Create a new $\tilde{f}_m(T)$ that minimizes $\mathrm{D}_{\mathrm{KL}}\left(q_m(T) || \tilde{f}_m(T) q^{\backslash m}(T)\right)$.

- Finally, set $q(T) \propto \prod_m \tilde{f}_m(T)$.

Step 2 creates the augmented distribution q_m, which includes f_m along with the approximate factors for all models except the current model. Step 3 creates a new anchored $\tilde{f}_m$ that has the same marginal distribution as the true model f_m in the context of the other approximations, just as we did in ADF.

In practice, it is usually better to not recompute the product of all $\tilde{f}_m$ each time, but instead to maintain the full product $q(T) \propto \prod_m \tilde{f}_m$ and to remove the appropriate $\tilde{f}_m$ by division. This optimization is analogous to belief propagation, where messages are removed from beliefs by division, instead of recomputing beliefs on the fly by multiplying all messages.

Schematically, the whole process is illustrated in Figure 2(c). At each step, one piece of the core approximation is replaced with the corresponding component from the full model. This augmented model is then reapproximated by a new core approximation q after updating the corresponding $\tilde{f}_m$. This process repeats until convergence.

5.4 EPIC Parsing

In our parser, EP is implemented as follows. q and each of the $\tilde{f}_m$ are anchored grammars that assign weights to unannotated rules. The product of anchored grammars with the annotated factor f_m need not be carried out explicitly. Instead, note that an anchored grammar is just a function $q(A \to B\ C, i, k, j) \in \mathbb{R}^+$ that returns a score for every anchored binary rule. This function can be easily integrated into the CKY algorithm for a single annotated grammar by simply multiplying in the value of q whenever computing the score of the respective production over some span. The modified inside recurrence takes the form:

$$\begin{aligned}
&\textsc{inside}(A[x], i, j) \\
&\quad = \sum_{B,y,C,z} \theta^T \varphi(A[x] \to B[y]\ C[z], \mathbf{w}) \\
&\qquad \cdot \sum_{i<k<j} \textsc{inside}(B[y], i, k) \cdot \textsc{inside}(C[z], k, j) \\
&\qquad\quad \cdot q(A \to B\ C, i, k, j)
\end{aligned} \tag{4}$$

Thus, parsing with a pointwise product of an anchored grammar and an annotated grammar has no increased combinatorial cost over parsing with just the annotated grammar.

To actually perform the projection in step 3 of EP, we create an anchored grammar from inside and outside probabilities. First, we compute the expected number of times the rule ${}_iA_j \rightarrow {}_iB_k\, {}_kC_j$ occurs, and then then we locally normalize for each symbol ${}_iA_j$. This actually creates the new q distribution, and so we have to divide out $q^{\backslash m}$ This process minimizes KL divergence subject to the local normalization constraints.

All in all, this gives an algorithm that takes time $O\left(IMAG_0|\mathbf{w}|^3\right)$, where I is the maximum number of iterations, M is the number of models, and A is the maximum number of annotations for any given rule.

5.5 Other Inference Algorithms

To our knowledge, expectation propagation has been used only once in the NLP community; Daumé III and Marcu (2006) employed an unstructured version in a Bayesian model of extractive summarization. Therefore, it is worth describing how EP differs from more familiar techniques.

EP can be thought of as a more flexible generalization of belief propagation, which has been used several times in NLP (Smith and Eisner, 2008; Niehues and Vogel, 2008; Cromières and Kurohashi, 2009; Burkett and Klein, 2012). In particular, EP allows for the arbitrary choice of messages (the $\tilde{f}_m$), meaning that we can use structured messages like anchored PCFGs.

Mean field (Saul and Jordan, 1996) is another approximate inference technique that allows for structured approximations (Xing et al., 2003; Burkett et al., 2010), but here the natural version of mean field for our model would still be intractable. However, it is possible to adapt mean field into allowing for tractable updates that are similar to the ones we proposed. We do not pursue that approach here.

Dual decomposition (Dantzig and Wolfe, 1960; Komodakis et al., 2007) has recently become popular in the community (Rush et al., 2010; Koo et al., 2010). In fact, EP can be seen as a particular kind of dual decomposition of the log normalization constant $\log Z(\mathbf{w}, \theta)$ that is optimized with message passing rather than (sub-)gradient descent or LP relaxations. Indeed, Minka (2001) argues that the EP objective is more efficiently optimized with message passing than with gradient updates. This assertion should be examined for the structured models common in NLP, but that is beyond the scope of this paper.

Finally, note that EP, like belief propagation but unlike mean field, is not guaranteed to converge, though in practice it usually seems to. In our experiments, typically three or four iterations are enough for almost all sentences to reach convergence, and we found no loss in cutting off the number of iterations to four.

6 Experiments

In what follows, we describe three experiments. First, in a small experiment, we examine how effective the different inference algorithms are for both training and testing. Second, we scale up our latent variable model into successively larger products. Finally, we present a selection of the many possible model combinations, showing that combining latent and expert annotation can be quite effective.

6.1 Experimental Setup

For our experiments, we trained and tested on the Penn Treebank using the standard splits: sections 2-21 were training, 22 development, and 23 testing. In preliminary experiments, we report development set F1 on sentences up to length 40. For our final test set experiment, we report F1 on sentences from section 23 up to length 40, as well as all sentences from that section. Scores reported are computed using EVALB (Sekine and Collins, 1997). We binarize trees using Collins' head rules (Collins, 1997).

Each discriminative parser was trained using the Adaptive Gradient variant of Stochastic Gradient Descent (Duchi et al., 2010). Smaller models were seeded from larger models. That is, before training a grammar of 5 models with 1 latent bit each, we started with weights from a parser with 4 factored bits. Initial experiments suggested this step did not affect final performance, but greatly decreased total training time, especially for the latent variable parsers. For extracting a one-best tree, we use a version of the Max-Recall algorithm of Goodman (1996). When using EP or ADF, we initialized the core approximation q to the uniform distribution over unpruned trees.

	Parsing			
Training	ADF	EP	Exact	Petrov
ADF	84.3	84.5	84.5	82.5
EP	84.1	84.6	84.5	78.7
Exact	83.8	84.5	**84.9**	81.5
Indep.	82.3	82.1	82.2	82.6

Table 1: The effect of algorithm choice for training and parsing on a product of two 2-state parsers on F1. Petrov is the product parser of Petrov (2010), and Indep. refers to independently trained models. For comparison, a four-state parser achieves a score of 83.2.

When counting parameters, we consider the number of parameters per binary rule. Hence, a single four-state latent model would have 64 (= 4^3) parameters per rule, while a product of 5 two-state models would have just 40 (= $5 \cdot 2^3$).

6.2 Comparison of Inference Algorithms

In our first experiment, we test the relative performance of the various approximate inference methods at both train and test time. In order to include exact inference, we necessarily need to look at a smaller scale example for which exact inference is still feasible. We examined development performance for training and inference on a small product of two parsers, each with two latent states per symbol.

During training, we have several options. We can use exact training by parsing with the fully articulated product of both grammars, or, we can instead use EP, ADF, or independent training. At test time, we can parse using the full product of both grammars, or, we can instead use EP, ADF, or we can use the method of Petrov (2010) wherein we multiply the parsers together in an *ad hoc* fashion.

The results are in Table 1. The best reported score, unsurprisingly, is for using exact training and parsing, but using EP for training and parsing results in a relatively small loss of 0.3 F1. ADF, however, suffers a loss of 0.6 F1 over Exact when used for training and parsing. Otherwise, Exact and EP seem to perform fairly similarly at parse time for all training conditions.

In general, there seems to be a gain for using the same method for training and testing. Each testing method performs at its best when using models trained with the same method. Moreover, except for ADF, the converse holds true: the grammars trained with a given parsing method are best decoded using the same method.

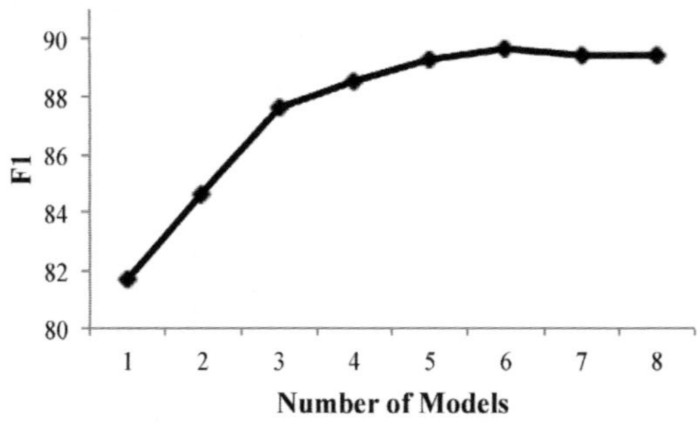

Figure 3: Development F1 plotted against the number M of one-bit latent annotation components. The best grammar has 6 one-bit annotations, with 89.7 F1.

Oddly, using Petrov (2010)'s method does not seem to work well at all for jointly trained models, except for ADF. Similarly, joint parsing underperforms Petrov (2010)'s method when using independently trained models. Likely, the joint parsing algorithms are miscalibrating the redundant information present in the two independently-trained models, while the two jointly-trained components come to depend on each other. In fact, the F1 scores for the two separate models of the EP parser are in the 60's.

As expected, ADF does not perform as well as EP. Therefore, we exclude it from our subsequent experiments, focusing exclusively on EP.

6.3 Latent Variable Experiments

Most of the previous work in latent variable parsing has focused on splitting smaller unstructured annotations into larger unstructured annotations. Here, we consider training a joint model consisting of a large number of disjoint one-bit (i.e. two-state) latent variable annotations. Specifically, we consider the performance of products of up to 8 one-bit annotations.

In Figure 3, we show development F1 as a function of the number of latent bits. Improvement is roughly linear up to 3 components. Performance levels off afterwards, with the top performing system scoring 89.7 F1. Nevertheless, these parsers outperform the comparable parsers of Petrov and Klein (2008a) (89.3), even though our six-bit parser has many fewer effective parameters per binary rule:

Models	F1, ≤ 40	F1, All
Lexicalized	87.3	86.5
Unlexicalized	86.3	85.4
3xLatent	88.6	87.6
Lex+Unlex	90.2	89.5
Lex+Lat	90.0	89.4
Unlex+Lat	90.0	89.4
Lex+Unlex+Lat	90.2	89.7

Table 2: Development F1 score for various model combinations for sentences less than length 40 and all sentences. 3xLatent refers to a latent annotation model with 3 factored latent bits.

48 instead of the 4096 in their best parser. We also ran our best system on Section 23, where it gets 89.1 and 88.4 on sentences less than length 40 and on all sentences, respectively. This result compares favorably to the 88.8/88.3 of Petrov and Klein (2008a).

6.4 Heterogeneous Models

We now consider factored models with different kinds of annotations. Specifically, we tested grammars comprising all subsets of {Lexicalized, Unlexicalized, Latent}. We used a model with 3 factored bits as our representative of the latent variable class, because it was closest in performance to the other models. Of course, other smaller and larger combinations are possible, but we found this selection to be representative.

The development results are in Table 2. Unsurprisingly, adding more kinds of annotations helps for the most part, though the combination of all three components is not much better than a combination of just the lexicalized and unlexicalized models. Indeed, our best systems involved combining the lexicalized model with some other model. This is probably because the lexicalized model can represent very different syntactic relationships than the latent and unlexicalized models, meaning there is more diversity in the joint model's capacity when using combinations involving the lexicalized annotations.

Finally, we ran our best system (the fully combined one) on Section 23 of the Penn Treebank. It scored 90.1/89.4 F1 on length 40 and all sentences respectively, slightly edging out the 90.0/89.3 F1 of Petrov and Klein (2008a). However, it is not quite as good at exact match: 37.7/35.3 vs 40.1/37.7. Note, though, that their parser makes use of span features, which deliver a gain of +0.3/0.2F1 respectively, while ours does not. We suspect that similar gains could be had by incorporating these features, but we leave that for future work.

7 Conclusion

Factored representations capture a fundamental linguistic insight: grammatical categories are not monolithic, unanalyzable entities. Instead, they are composed of numerous facets that together govern how categories combine into parse trees.

We have developed a new model for grammars with factored annotations and presented two methods for parsing with these grammars. Our experiments have demonstrated that our approach produces higher performance parsers with many fewer parameters. Moreover, our model works with both latent and explicit annotations, allowing us to combine linguistic knowledge with machine learning. Finally, our source code is available at `http://nlp.cs.berkeley.edu/Software.shtml`.

Acknowledgments

We would like to thank Slav Petrov, David Burkett, Adam Pauls, Greg Durrett and the anonymous reviewers for helpful comments. We would also like to thank Daphne Koller for originally suggesting the assumed density filtering approach. This work was partially supported by BBN under DARPA contract HR0011-12-C-0014, and by an NSF fellowship to the first author.

References

Sylvie Billott and Bernard Lang. 1989. The structure of shared forests in ambiguous parsing. In *Proceedings of the 27th Annual Meeting of the Association for Computational Linguistics*, pages 143–151, Vancouver, British Columbia, Canada, June.

Xavier Boyen and Daphne Koller. 1998. Tractable inference for complex stochastic processes. In *Proceedings of the 14th Conference on Uncertainty in Artificial Intelligence—UAI 1998*, pages 33–42. San Francisco: Morgan Kaufmann.

David Burkett and Dan Klein. 2012. Fast inference in phrase extraction models with belief propagation. In *NAACL*.

David Burkett, John Blitzer, and Dan Klein. 2010. Joint parsing and alignment with weakly synchronized grammars. In *NAACL*.

Noam Chomsky. 1992. *A minimalist program for linguistic theory*, volume 1. MIT Working Papers in Linguistics, MIT, Cambridge Massachusetts.

Michael Collins. 1997. Three generative, lexicalised models for statistical parsing. In *ACL*, pages 16–23.

Fabien Cromières and Sadao Kurohashi. 2009. An alignment algorithm using belief propagation and a structure-based distortion model. In *EACL*.

G. B. Dantzig and P. Wolfe. 1960. Decomposition principle for linear programs. *Operations Research*, 8:101–111.

Hal Daumé III and Daniel Marcu. 2006. Bayesian query-focused summarization. In *Proceedings of the Conference of the Association for Computational Linguistics (ACL)*, Sydney, Australia.

Markus Dreyer and Jason Eisner. 2006. Better informed training of latent syntactic features. In *EMNLP*, pages 317–326, July.

John Duchi, Elad Hazan, and Yoram Singer. 2010. Adaptive Subgradient Methods for Online Learning and Stochastic Optimization. *COLT*.

Jenny Rose Finkel, Alex Kleeman, and Christopher D. Manning. 2008. Efficient, feature-based, conditional random field parsing. In *ACL 2008*, pages 959–967.

Yoav Freund and Robert E. Schapire. 1995. A decision-theoretic generalization of on-line learning and an application to boosting.

Joshua Goodman. 1996. Parsing algorithms and metrics. In *ACL*, pages 177–183.

Dan Klein and Christopher D. Manning. 2003. Accurate unlexicalized parsing. In *ACL*, pages 423–430.

Nikos Komodakis, Nikos Paragios, and Georgios Tziritas. 2007. Mrf optimization via dual decomposition: Message-passing revisited. In *ICCV*, pages 1–8.

Terry Koo, Alexander M. Rush, Michael Collins, Tommi Jaakkola, and David Sontag. 2010. Dual decomposition for parsing with non-projective head automata. In *Proceedings of the 2010 Conference on Empirical Methods in Natural Language Processing (EMNLP)*.

Mitchell P. Marcus, Beatrice Santorini, and Mary Ann Marcinkiewicz. 1993. Building a large annotated corpus of English: The Penn Treebank. *Computational Linguistics*, 19(2):313–330.

Takuya Matsuzaki, Yusuke Miyao, and Jun'ichi Tsujii. 2005. Probabilistic CFG with latent annotations. In *ACL*, pages 75–82, Morristown, NJ, USA.

Thomas P. Minka. 2001. Expectation propagation for approximate Bayesian inference. In *UAI*, pages 362–369.

Jan Niehues and Stephan Vogel. 2008. Discriminative word alignment via alignment matrix modeling. In *Proceedings of the Third Workshop on Statistical Machine Translation*, pages 18–25, June.

Slav Petrov and Dan Klein. 2007. Improved inference for unlexicalized parsing. In *NAACL-HLT*, April.

Slav Petrov and Dan Klein. 2008a. Discriminative log-linear grammars with latent variables. In *NIPS*, pages 1153–1160.

Slav Petrov and Dan Klein. 2008b. Sparse multi-scale grammars for discriminative latent variable parsing. In *EMNLP*, pages 867–876, Honolulu, Hawaii, October.

Slav Petrov, Leon Barrett, Romain Thibaux, and Dan Klein. 2006. Learning accurate, compact, and interpretable tree annotation. In *Proceedings of the 21st International Conference on Computational Linguistics and 44th Annual Meeting of the Association for Computational Linguistics*, pages 433–440, Sydney, Australia, July.

Slav Petrov. 2010. Products of random latent variable grammars. In *Human Language Technologies: The 2010 Annual Conference of the North American Chapter of the Association for Computational Linguistics*, pages 19–27, Los Angeles, California, June.

Carl Pollard and Ivan A. Sag. 1994. *Head-Driven Phrase Structure Grammar*. University of Chicago Press, Chicago.

Alexander M Rush, David Sontag, Michael Collins, and Tommi Jaakkola. 2010. On dual decomposition and linear programming relaxations for natural language processing. In *EMNLP*, pages 1–11, Cambridge, MA, October.

Lawrence Saul and Michael Jordan. 1996. Exploiting tractable substructures in intractable networks. In *NIPS 1995*.

Satoshi Sekine and Michael J. Collins. 1997. Evalb – bracket scoring program.

David A. Smith and Jason Eisner. 2008. Dependency parsing by belief propagation. In *EMNLP*, pages 145–156, Honolulu, October.

Martin J Wainwright and Michael I Jordan. 2008. *Graphical Models, Exponential Families, and Variational Inference*. Now Publishers Inc., Hanover, MA, USA.

Eric P. Xing, Michael I. Jordan, and Stuart J. Russell. 2003. A generalized mean field algorithm for variational inference in exponential families. In *UAI*, pages 583–591.

A coherence model based on syntactic patterns

Annie Louis
University of Pennsylvania
Philadelphia, PA 19104, USA
lannie@seas.upenn.edu

Ani Nenkova
University of Pennsylvania
Philadelphia, PA 19104, USA
nenkova@seas.upenn.edu

Abstract

We introduce a model of coherence which captures the intentional discourse structure in text. Our work is based on the hypothesis that syntax provides a proxy for the communicative goal of a sentence and therefore the sequence of sentences in a coherent discourse should exhibit detectable structural patterns. Results show that our method has high discriminating power for separating out coherent and incoherent news articles reaching accuracies of up to 90%. We also show that our syntactic patterns are correlated with manual annotations of intentional structure for academic conference articles and can successfully predict the coherence of abstract, introduction and related work sections of these articles.

1 Introduction

Recent studies have introduced successful automatic methods to predict the structure and coherence of texts. They include entity approaches for local coherence which track the repetition and syntactic realization of entities in adjacent sentences (Barzilay and Lapata, 2008; Elsner and Charniak, 2008) and content approaches for global coherence which view texts as a sequence of topics, each characterized by a particular distribution of lexical items (Barzilay and Lee, 2004; Fung and Ngai, 2006). Other work has shown that co-occurrence of words (Lapata, 2003; Soricut and Marcu, 2006) and discourse relations (Pitler and Nenkova, 2008; Lin et al., 2011) also predict coherence.

Early theories (Grosz and Sidner, 1986) posited that there are three factors which collectively contribute to coherence: intentional structure (purpose of discourse), attentional structure (what items are discussed) and the organization of discourse segments. The highly successful entity approaches capture attentional structure and content approaches are related to topic segments but intentional structure has largely been neglected. Every discourse has a purpose: explaining a concept, narrating an event, critiquing an idea and so on. As a result each sentence in the article has a communicative goal and the sequence of goals helps the author achieve the discourse purpose. In this work, we introduce a model to capture coherence from the intentional structure dimension. Our key proposal is that syntactic patterns are a useful proxy for intentional structure.

This idea is motivated from the fact that certain sentence types such as questions and definitions have distinguishable and unique syntactic structure. For example, consider the opening sentences of two descriptive articles[1] shown in Table 1. Sentences (1a) and (2a) are typical instances of definition sentences. Definitions are written with the concept to be defined expressed as a noun phrase followed by a copular verb (is/are). The predicate contains two parts: the first is a noun phrase reporting the concept as part of a larger class (eg. an aqueduct is a water supply), the second component is a relative clause listing unique properties of the concept. These are examples of syntactic patterns related to the communicative goals of individual sentences. Similarly, sentences (1b) and (2b) which provide further details about the concept also have some distinguish-

[1]Wikipedia articles on "Aqueduct" and "Cytokine Receptors"

1a) An aqueduct is a water supply or navigable channel constructed to convey water. b) In modern engineering, the term is used for any system of pipes, canals, tunnels, and other structures used for this purpose.
2a) Cytokine receptors are receptors that binds cytokines. b) In recent years, the cytokine receptors have come to demand more attention because their deficiency has now been directly linked to certain debilitating immunodeficiency states.

Table 1: The first two sentences of two descriptive articles

ing syntactic features such as the presence of a topicalized phrase providing the focus of the sentence. The two sets of sentences have similar sequence of communicative goals and so we can expect the syntax of adjacent sentences to also be related.

We aim to characterize this relationship on a broad scale using a coherence model based entirely on syntax. The model relies on two assumptions which summarize our intuitions about syntax and intentional structure:

1. Sentences with similar syntax are likely to have the same communicative goal.
2. Regularities in intentional structure will be manifested in syntactic regularities between adjacent sentences.

There is also evidence from recent work that supports these assumptions. Cheung and Penn (2010) find that a better syntactic parse of a sentence can be derived when the syntax of adjacent sentences is also taken into account. Lin et al. (2009) report that the syntactic productions in adjacent sentences are powerful features for predicting which discourse relation (cause, contrast, etc.) holds between them. Cocco et al. (2011) show that significant associations exist between certain part of speech tags and sentence types such as explanation, dialog and argumentation.

In our model, syntax is represented either as parse tree productions or a sequence of phrasal nodes augmented with part of speech tags. Our best performing method uses a Hidden Markov Model to learn the patterns in these syntactic items. Sections 3 and 5 discuss the representations and their specific implementations and relative advantages. Results show that syntax models can distinguish coherent and incoherent news articles from two domains with 75-90% accuracies over a 50% baseline. In addition, the syntax coherence scores turn out complementary to scores given by lexical and entity models.

We also study our models' predictions on academic articles, a genre where intentional structure is widely studied. Sections in these articles have well-defined purposes and we find recurring sentence types such as motivation, citations, description, and speculations. There is a large body of work (Swales, 1990; Teufel et al., 1999; Liakata et al., 2010) concerned with defining and annotating these sentence types (called zones) in conference articles. In Section 6, we describe how indeed some patterns captured by the syntax-based models are correlated with zone categories that were proposed in prior literature. We also present results on coherence prediction: our model can distinguish the introduction section of conference papers from its perturbed versions with over 70% accuracy. Further, our model is able to identify conference from workshop papers with good accuracies, given that we can expect these articles to vary in purpose.

2 Evidence for syntactic coherence

We first present a pilot study that confirms that adjacent sentences in discourse exhibit stable patterns of syntactic co-occurrence. This study validates our second assumption relating the syntax of adjacent sentences. Later in Section 6, we examine syntactic patterns in individual sentences (assumption 1) using a corpus of academic articles where sentences were manually annotated with communicative goals.

Prior work has reported that certain grammatical productions are repeated in adjacent sentences more often than would be expected by chance (Reitter et al., 2006; Cheung and Penn, 2010). We analyze all co-occurrence patterns rather than just repetitions.

We use the gold standard parse trees from the Penn Treebank (Marcus et al., 1994). Our unit of analysis is a pair of adjacent sentences (S_1, S_2) and we choose to use Section 0 of the corpus which has 99 documents and 1727 sentence pairs. We enumerate all productions that appear in the syntactic parse of any sentence and exclude those that appear less than 25 times, resulting in a list of 197 unique productions. Then all ordered pairs[2] (p_1, p_2) of productions are formed. For each pair, we compute

[2] (p_1, p_2) and (p_2, p_1) are considered as different pairs.

p_1, p_2	Sentence 1	Sentence 2
NP → NP NP-ADV QP → CD CD	The two concerns said they entered into a definitive merger agreement under which Ratners will begin a tender offer for all of Weisfield's common shares for [\$57.50 each]$_{\text{NP}}$.	Also on the takeover front, Jaguar's ADRs rose 1/4 to 13 7/8 on turnover of [4.4 million]$_{\text{QP}}$.
VP → VB VP NP-SBJ → NNP NNP	"The refund pool may not [be held hostage through another" round of appeals]$_{\text{VP}}$," Judge Curry said.	[Commonwealth Edison]$_{\text{NP-SBJ}}$ said it is already appealing the underlying commission order and is considering appealing Judge Curry's order.
NP-LOC → NNP S-TPC-1 → NP-SBJ VP	"It has to be considered as an additional risk for the investor," said Gary P. Smaby of Smaby Group Inc., [Minneapolis]$_{\text{NP-LOC}}$.	["Cray Computer will be a concept" "stock,"]$_{\text{S-TPC-1}}$ he said.

Table 2: Example sentences for preferred production sequences. The span of the LHS of the corresponding production is indicated by [] braces.

the following: $c(p_1p_2)$ = number of sentence pairs where $p_1 \in S_1$ and $p_2 \in S_2$; $c(p_1\neg p_2)$ = number of pairs where $p_1 \in S_1$ and $p_2 \notin S_2$; $c(\neg p_1 p_2)$ and $c(\neg p_1 \neg p_2)$ are computed similarly. Then we perform a chi-square test to understand if the observed count $c(p_1p_2)$ is significantly (95% confidence level) greater or lesser than the expected value if occurrences of p_1 and p_2 were independent.

Of the 38,809 production pairs, we found that 1,168 pairs occurred in consecutive sentences significantly more often than chance and 172 appeared significantly fewer times than expected. In Table 2 we list, grouped in three simple categories, the 25 pairs of the first kind with most significant p-values.

Some of the preferred pairs are indeed repetitions as pointed out by prior work. But they form only a small fraction (5%) of the total preferred production pairs indicating that there are several other classes of syntactic regularities beyond priming. Some of these other sequences can be explained by the fact that these articles come from the finance domain: they involve productions containing numbers and quantities. An example for this type is shown in Table 2. Finally, there is also a class that is not repetitions or readily observed as domain-specific. The most frequent one reflects a pattern where the first sentence introduces a subject and predicate and the subject in the second sentence is pronominalized. Examples for two other patterns are given in Table 2. For the sequence (VP → VB VP | NP-SBJ → NNP NNP), a bare verb is present in S_1 and is often associated with modals. In the corpus, these statements often present hypothesis or speculation. The following sentence S_2 has an entity, a person or organization, giving an explanation or opinion on the statement. This pattern roughly correponds to a SPECULATE followed by ENDORSE sequence of intentions.

p_1	p_2	$c(p_1p_2)$
	— Repetition —	
VP → VBD SBAR	VP → VBD SBAR	83
QP → \$ CD CD	QP → \$ CD CD	18
NP → \$ CD -NONE-	NP → \$ CD -NONE-	16
NP → QP -NONE-	NP → QP -NONE-	15
NP-ADV → DT NN	NP-ADV → DT NN	10
NP → NP NP-ADV	NP → NP NP-ADV	7
	— Quantities/Amounts —	
NP → QP -NONE-	QP → \$ CD CD	16
QP → \$ CD CD	NP → QP -NONE-	15
NP → NP NP-ADV	NP → QP -NONE-	11
NP-ADV → DT NN	NP → QP -NONE-	11
NP → NP NP-ADV	NP-ADV → DT NN	9
NP → \$ CD -NONE-	NP-ADV → DT NN	8
NP-ADV → DT NN	NP → \$ CD -NONE-	8
NP-ADV → DT NN	NP → NP NP-ADV	8
NP → NP NP-ADV	QP → CD CD	6
	— Other —	
S → NP-SBJ VP	NP-SBJ → PRP	290
VP → VBD SBAR	PP-TMP → IN NP	79
S → NP-SBJ-1 VP	VP → VBD SBAR	43
VP → VBD NP	VP → VBD VP	31
VP → VB VP	NP-SBJ → NNP NNP	27
NP-SBJ-1 → NNP NNP	VP → VBD NP	13
VP → VBZ NP	S → PP-TMP , NP-SBJ VP .	8
NP-SBJ → JJ NNS	VP → VBP NP	8
NP-PRD → NP PP	NP-PRD → NP SBAR	7
NP-LOC → NNP	S-TPC-1 → NP-SBJ VP	6

Table 3: Top patterns in productions from WSJ

Similarly, in all the six adjacent sentence pairs from our corpus containing the items (NP-LOC → NNP | S-TPC-1 → NP-SBJ VP), p_1 introduces a location name, and is often associated with the title of a person or organization. The next sentence has a quote from that person, where the quotation forms the topicalized clause in p_2. Here the intentional structure is INTRODUCE X / STATEMENT BY X.

In the remainder of the paper we formalize our representation of syntax and the derived model of coherence and test its efficacy in three domains.

3 Coherence models using syntax

We first describe the two representations of sentence structure we adopted for our analysis.[3] Next, we

[3]Our representations are similar to features used for reranking in parsing. Our first representation corresponds to "rules" features (Charniak and Johnson, 2005; Collins and Koo, 2005), and our second representation is related to "spines" (Carreras et al., 2008) and edge annotation(Huang, 2008).

present two coherence models: a local model which captures the co-occurrence of structural features in adjacent sentences and a global one which learns from clusters of sentences with similar syntax.

3.1 Representing syntax

Our models rely exclusively on syntactic cues. We derive representations from constituent parses of the sentences, and terminals (words) are removed from the parse tree before any processing is done. The leaf nodes in our parse trees are part of speech tags.

Productions: In this representation we view each sentence as the set of grammatical productions, LHS $\rightarrow$ RHS, which appear in the parse of the sentence. As we already pointed out, the right-hand side (RHS) contains only non-terminal nodes. This representation is straightforward, however, some productions can be rather specific with long right hand sides. Another apparent drawback of this representation is that it contains sequence information only about nodes that belong to the same constituent.

***d*-sequence:** In this representation we aim to preserve more sequence information about adjacent constituents in the sentence. The simplest approach would be to represent the sentence as the sequence of part of speech (POS) tags but then we lose all the abstraction provided by higher level nodes in tree. Instead, we introduce a more general representation, *d-sequence* where the level of abstraction can be controlled using a parameter d. The parse tree is truncated to depth at most d, and the leaves of the resulting tree listed left to right form the d-sequence representation. For example, in Figure 1, the line depicts the cutoff at depth 2.

Next the representation is further augmented; all *phrasal* nodes in the d-sequence are annotated (concatenated) with the left-most leaf that they dominate in the full non-lexicalized parse tree. This is shown as suffixes on the S, NP and VP nodes in the figure. Such annotation conveys richer information about the structure of the subtree below nodes in the d-sequence. For example, "the chairs", "his chairs", "comfortable chairs" will be represented as NP_{DT}, $NP_{PRP\$}$ and NP_{JJ}. In the resulting representations, sentences are viewed as sequences of *syntactic words* (w_1,w_2...,w_k), $k \leq p$, where p is the length of the full POS sequence and each w_i is either POS tag or a phrasal node+POS tag combination.

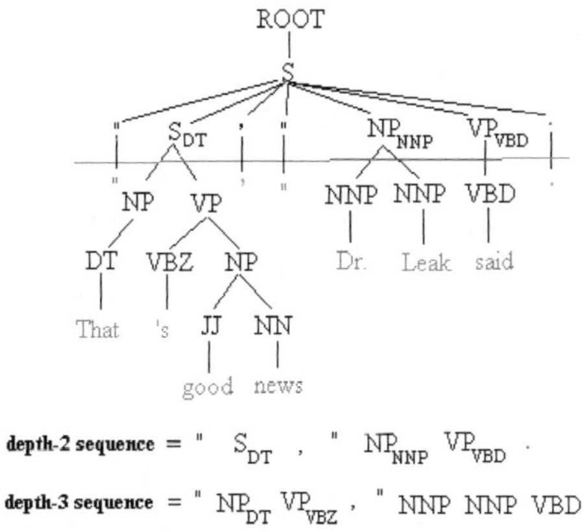

Figure 1: Example for d-sequence representation

In our example, at depth-2, the quotation sentence gets the representation (w_1=" , w_2=S_{DT} , w_3=, , w_4=" , w_5=NP_{NNP} , w_6=VP_{VBD} , w_7=.) where the actual quote is omitted. Sentences that contain attributions are likely to appear more similar to each other when compared using this representation in contrast to representations derived from word or POS sequence. The depth-3 sequence is also indicated in the figure.

The main verb of a sentence is central to its structure, so the parameter d is always set to be greater than that of the main verb and is tuned to optimize performance for coherence prediction.

3.2 Implementing the model

We adapt two models of coherence to operate over the two syntactic representations.

3.2.1 Local co-occurrence model

This model is a direct extension from our pilot study. It allows us to test the assumption that coherent discourse is characterized by syntactic regularities in adjacent sentences. We estimate the probabilities of pairs of syntactic items from adjacent sentences in the training data and use these probabilities to compute the coherence of new texts.

The coherence of a text T containing n sentences (S_1...S_n) is computed as:

$$P(T) = \prod_{i=2}^{n} \prod_{j=1}^{|S_i|} \frac{1}{|S_{i-1}|} \sum_{k=1}^{|S_{i-1}|} p(S_i^j | S_{i-1}^k)$$

where S_x^y indicates the yth item of S_x. Items are either productions or syntactic word unigrams depending on the representation. The conditional probabilities are computed with smoothing:

Cluster a	Cluster b
ADJP → JJ PP | VP → VBZ ADJP	VP → VB VP | VP → MD VP
[1] This method VP-[is ADJP-[capable of sequence-specific detection of DNA with high accuracy]-ADJP]-VP .	[1] Our results for the difference in reactivity VP-[can VP-[be linked to experimental observations]-VP]-VP .
[2] The same VP-[is ADJP-[true for synthetic polyamines such as polyallylamine]-ADJP]-VP .	[2] These phenomena taken together VP-[can VP-[be considered as the signature of the gelation process]-VP]-VP .

Table 4: Example syntactic similarity clusters. The top two descriptive productions for each cluster are also listed.

$$p(w_j|w_i) = \frac{c(w_i, w_j) + \delta_C}{c(w_i) + \delta_C * |V|}$$

where w_i and w_j are syntactic items and $c(w_i, w_j)$ is the number of sentences that contain the item w_i immediately followed by a sentence that contains w_j. $|V|$ is the vocabulary size for syntactic items.

3.2.2 Global structure

Now we turn to a global coherence approach that implements the assumption that sentences with similar syntax have the same communicative goal as well as captures the patterns in communicative goals in the discourse. This approach uses a Hidden Markov Model (HMM) which has been a popular implementation for modeling coherence (Barzilay and Lee, 2004; Fung and Ngai, 2006; Elsner et al., 2007). The hidden states in our model depict communicative goals by encoding a probability distribution over syntactic items. This distribution gives higher weight to syntactic items that are more likely for that communicative goal. Transitions between states record the common patterns in intentional structure for the domain.

In this syntax-HMM, states h_k are created by clustering the sentences from the documents in the training set by *syntactic similarity*. For the productions representation of syntax, the features for clustering are the number of times a given production appeared in the parse of the sentence. For the d-sequence approach, the features are n-grams of size one to four of syntactic words from the sequence. Clustering was done by optimizing for average cosine similarity and was implemented using the CLUTO toolkit (Zhao et al., 2005). C clusters are formed and taken as the states of the model. Table 4 shows sentences from two clusters formed on the abstracts of journal articles using the productions representation. One of them, cluster (a), appears to capture descriptive sentences and cluster (b) involves mostly speculation type sentences.

The emission probabilities for each state are modeled as a (syntactic) language model derived from the sentences in it. For productions representation, this is the unigram distribution of productions from the sentences in h_k. For d-sequences, the distribution is computed for bigrams of syntactic words. These language models use Lidstone smoothing with constant δ_E. The probability for a sentence S_l to be generated from state h_k, $p_E(S_l|h_k)$ is computed using these syntactic language models.

The transition probability p_M from a state h_i to state h_j is computed as:

$$p_M(h_j|h_i) = \frac{d(h_i, h_j) + \delta_M}{d(h_i) + \delta_M * C}$$

where $d(h_i)$ is the number of documents whose sentences appear in h_i and $d(h_i, h_j)$ is the number of documents which have a sentence in h_i which is immediately followed by a sentence in h_j. In addition to the C states, we add one initial h_S and one final h_F state to capture document beginning and end. Transitions from h_S to any state h_k records how likely it is for h_k to be the starting state for documents of that domain. δ_M is a smoothing constant.

The likelihood of a text with n sentences is given by $P(T) = \sum_{h_1...h_n} \prod_{t=1}^{n} p_M(h_t|h_{t-1}) p_E(S_t|h_t)$.

All model parameters—the number of clusters C, smoothing constants δ_C, δ_E, δ_M and d for d-sequences—are tuned to optimize how well the model can distinguish coherent from incoherent articles. We describe these settings in Section 5.1.

4 Content and entity grid models

We compare the syntax model with content model and entity grid methods. These approaches are the most popular ones from prior work and also allow us to test the complementary nature of syntax with lexical statistics and entity structure. This section explains how we implemented these approaches.

Content models introduced by Barzilay and Lee (2004) and Fung and Ngai (2006) use lexically driven HMMs to capture coherence. The hidden states represent the topics of the domain and encode a probability distribution over words. Transitions between states record the probable succession of topics. We built a content model using our HMM implementation. Clusters are created using word bigram features after replacing numbers and proper names with tags NUM and PROP. The emissions are given by a bigram language model on words from the clustered sentences. Barzilay and Lee (2004) also employ an iterative clustering procedure before finalizing the states of the HMM but our method only uses one-step clustering. Despite the difference, the content model accuracies for our implementation are quite close to that from the original.

For the entity grid model, we follow the generative approach proposed by Lapata and Barzilay (2005). A text is converted into a matrix, where rows correspond to sentences, in the order in which they appear in the article. Columns are created one for each entity appearing in the text. Each cell (i,j) is filled with the grammatical role $r_{i,j}$ of the entity j in sentence i. We computed the entity grids using the Brown Coherence Toolkit[4]. The probability of the text (T) is defined using the likely sequence of grammatical role transitions.

$$P(T) = \prod_{j=1}^{m} \prod_{i=1}^{n} p(r_{i,j} | r_{i-1,j} ... r_{i-h,j})$$

for m entities and n sentences. Parameter h controls the history size for transitions and is tuned during development. When $h = 1$, for example, only the grammatical role for the entity in the previous sentence is considered and earlier roles are ignored.

5 Evaluating syntactic coherence

We follow the common approach from prior work and use pairs of articles, where one has the original document order and the other is a random permutation of the sentences from the same document. Since the original article is always more coherent than a random permutation, a model can be evaluated using the accuracy with which it can identify the original article in the pair, i.e. it assigns higher probability to the original article. This setting is not ideal but has become the de facto standard for evaluation of coherence models (Barzilay and Lee, 2004; Elsner et al., 2007; Barzilay and Lapata, 2008; Karamanis et al., 2009; Lin et al., 2011; Elsner and Charniak, 2011). It is however based on a reasonable assumption as recent work (Lin et al., 2011) shows that people identify the original article as more coherent than its permutations with over 90% accuracy and assessors also have high agreement. Later, we present an experiment distinguishing conference from workshop articles as a more realistic evaluation.

We use two corpora that are widely employed for coherence prediction (Barzilay and Lee, 2004; Elsner et al., 2007; Barzilay and Lapata, 2008; Lin et al., 2011). One contains reports on airplane accidents from the National Transportation Safety Board and the other has reports about earthquakes from the Associated Press. These articles are about 10 sentences long. These corpora were chosen since within each dataset, the articles have the same intentional structure. Further, these corpora are also standard ones used in prior work on lexical, entity and discourse relation based coherence models. Later in Section 6, we show that the models perform well on the academic genre and longer articles too.

For each of the two corpora, we have 100 articles for training and 100 (accidents) and 99 (earthquakes) for testing. A maximum of 20 random permutations were generated for each test article to create the pairwise data (total of 1986 test pairs for the accident corpus and 1956 for earthquakes).[5] The baseline accuracy for random prediction is 50%. The articles were parsed using the Stanford parser (Klein and Manning, 2003).

5.1 Accuracy of the syntax model

For each model, the relevant parameters were tuned using 10-fold cross validation on the training data. In each fold, 90 documents were used for training and evaluation was done on permutations from the remaining articles. After tuning, the final model was trained on all 100 articles in the training set.

[4] http://www.cs.brown.edu/~melsner/manual.html

[5] We downloaded the permutations from `http://people.csail.mit.edu/regina/coherence/CLsubmission/`

Table 5 shows the results on the test set. The best number of clusters and depth for d-sequences are also indicated. Overall, the syntax models work quite well, with accuracies at least 15% or more absolute improvement over the baseline.

In the local co-occurrence approach, both productions and d-sequences provide 72% accuracy for the accidents corpus. For the earthquake corpus, the accuracies are lower and the d-sequence method works better. The best depth setting for d-sequence is rather small: depth of main verb (MVP) + 2 (or 1), and indicates that a fairly abstract level of nodes is preferred for the patterns. For comparison, we also provide results using just the POS tags in the model and this is worse than the d-sequence approach.

The global HMM model is better than the local model for each representation type giving 2 to 38% better accuracies. Here we see a different trend for the d-sequence representation, with better results for greater depths. At such depths (8 and 9) below the main verb, the nodes are mostly POS tags.

Overall both productions and d-sequence work competitively and give the best accuracies when implemented with the global approach.

Model	**Accidents**		**Earthquake**	
	Parameter	**Acc**	**Parameter**	**Acc**
A. Local co-occurrence				
Prodns		72.8		55.0
d-seq	dep. MVP+2	71.8	dep. MVP+1	65.1
POS		61.3		42.6
B. HMM-syntax				
Prodns	clus. 37	74.6	clus. 5	93.8
d-seq	dep. MVP+8 clus. 8	82.2	dep. MVP+9 clus. 45	86.5
C. Other approaches				
Egrid	history 1	67.6	history 1	82.2
Content	clus. 48	71.4	clus. 23	84.5

Table 5: Accuracies on accident and earthquake corpora

Model	**Accid.**	**Earthq.**
Content + Egrid	**76.8**	**90.7**
Content + HMM-prodn	74.2	**95.3**
Content + HMM-d-seq	82.1	**90.3**
Egrid + HMM-prodn	**79.6**	93.9
Egrid + HMM-d-seq	**84.2**	**91.1**
Egrid + Content + HMM-prodn	79.5	95.0
Egrid + Content + HMM-d-seq	84.1	92.3
Egrid + Content + HMM-prodn + HMM-d-seq	83.6	95.7

Table 6: Accuracies for combined approaches

5.2 Comparison with other approaches

For our implementations of the content and entity grid models, the best accuracies are 71% on the accidents corpus and 85% on the earthquakes one, similar to the syntactic models.

Ideally, we would like to combine models but we do not have separate training data. So we perform the following classification experiment which combines the predictions made by different models on the *test set*. Each test pair (article and permutation) forms one example and is given a class value of 0 or 1 depending on whether the first article in the pair is the original one or the second one. The example is represented as an n-dimensional vector, where n is the number of models we wish to combine. For instance, to combine content models and entity grid, two features are created: one of these records the difference in log probabilities for the two articles from the content model, the other feature indicates the difference in probabilities from the entity grid.

A logistic regression classifier is trained to predict the class using these features. The test pairs are created such that an equal number of examples have class 0 and 1, so the baseline accuracy is 50%. We run this experiment using 10-fold cross validation on the test set after first obtaining the log probabilities from individual models. In each fold, the training is done using the pairs from 90 articles and tested on permutations from the remaining 10 articles. These accuracies are reported in Table 6. When the accuracy of a combination is better than that using any of its smaller subsets, the value is bolded.

We find that syntax supplements both content and entity grid methods. While on the airplane corpus syntax only combines well with the entity grid, on the earthquake corpus, both entity and content approaches give better accuracies when combined with syntax. However, adding all three approaches does not outperform combinations of any two of them. This result can be due to the simple approach that we tested for combination. In prior work, content and entity grid methods have been combined generatively (Elsner et al., 2007) and using discriminative training with different objectives (Soricut and

Marcu, 2006). Such approaches might bring out the complementary strengths of the different aspects better and we leave such analysis for future work.

6 Predictions on academic articles

The distinctive intentional structure of academic articles has motivated several proposals to define and annotate the communicative purpose (argumentative zone) of each sentence (Swales, 1990; Teufel et al., 1999; Liakata et al., 2010). Supervised classifiers were also built to identify these zones (Teufel and Moens, 2000; Guo et al., 2011). So we expect that these articles form a good testbed for our models. In the remainder of the paper, we examine how unsupervised patterns discovered by our approach relate to zones and how well our models predict coherence for articles from this genre.

We employ two corpora of scientific articles.

ART Corpus: contains a set of 225 Chemistry journal articles that were manually annotated for intentional structure (Liakata and Soldatova, 2008). Each sentence was assigned one of 11 zone labels: *Result*, *Conclusion*, *Objective*, *Method*, *Goal*, *Background*, *Observation*, *Experiment*, *Motivation*, *Model*, *Hypothesis*. For our study, we use the annotation of the introduction and the abstract sections. We divide the data into training, development and test sets. For abstracts, we have 75, 50 and 100 for these sets respectively. For introductions, this split is 75, 31, 82.[6]

ACL Anthology Network (AAN) Corpus: Radev et al. (2009) provides the full text of publications from ACL venues. These articles do not have any zone annotations. The AAN corpus is produced from OCR analysis and no section marking is available. To recreate these, we use the Parscit tagger[7] (Councill et al., 2008). We use articles from years 1999 to 2011. For training, we randomly choose 70 articles from ACL and NAACL main conferences. Similarly, we obtain a development corpus of 36 ACL-NAACL articles. We create two test sets: one has 500 ACL-NAACL conference articles and another has 500 articles from ACL-sponsored workshops. We only choose articles in which all three sections—abstract, introduction and related work—could be successfully identified using Parscit.[8]

This data was sentence-segmented using MxTerminator (Reynar and Ratnaparkhi, 1997) and parsed with the Stanford Parser (Klein and Manning, 2003).

For each corpus and each section, we train all our syntactic models: the two local coherence models using the production and d-sequence representations and the HMM models with the two representations. These models are tuned on the respective development data, on the task of differentiating the original from a permuted section. For this purpose, we created a maximum of 30 permutations per article.

6.1 Comparison with ART Corpus zones

We perform this analysis using the ART corpus. The zone annotations present in this corpus allow us to directly test our first assumption in this work, that sentences with similar syntax have the same communicative goal.

For this analysis, we use the the HMM-prod model for abstracts and the HMM-d-seq model for introductions. These models were chosen because they gave the best performance on the ART corpus development sets.[9] We examine the clusters created by these models on the training data and check whether there are clusters which strongly involve sentences from some particular annotated zone.

For each possible pair of cluster and zone (C_i, Z_j), we compute $c(C_i, Z_j)$: the number of sentences in C_i that are annotated as zone Z_j. Then we use a chi-square test to identify pairs for which $c(C_i, Z_j)$ is significantly greater than expected (there is a "positive" association between C_i and Z_j) and pairs where $c(C_i, Z_j)$ is significantly less than chance (C_i is not associated with Z_j). A 95% confidence level was used to determine significance.

The HMM-prod model for abstracts has 9 clusters (named Clus0 to 8) and the HMM-d-seq model for introductions has 6 clusters (Clus0 to 5). The pairings of these clusters with zones which turned out to be significant are reported in Table 7. We also report for each positively associated cluster-zone pair, the following numbers: matches $c(C_i, Z_j)$, precision $c(C_i, Z_j)/|C_i|$ and recall $c(C_i, Z_j)/|Z_j|$.

[6]Some articles did not have labelled 'introduction' sections resulting in fewer examples for this setup.

[7]http://aye.comp.nus.edu.sg/parsCit/

[8]We also exclude introduction and related work sections longer than 50 sentences and those shorter than 4 sentences since they often have inaccurate section boundaries.

[9]Their test accuracies are reported in the next section.

Abstracts (HMM-prod 9 clusters)			
Positive associations	**matches**	**prec.**	**recall**
Clus5 - Model	7	17.1	43.8
Clus7 - Objective	27	27.6	32.9
Clus7 - Goal	16	16.3	55.2
Clus0 - Conclusion	15	50.0	12.1
Clus6 - Conclusion	27	51.9	21.8
Not associated: Clus7 - Conclusion, Clus8 - Conclusion			
Introductions (HMM-d-seq 6 clusters)			
Positive associations	**matches**	**prec.**	**recall**
Clus2-Background	161	64.9	14.2
Clus3-Objective	37	7.9	38.5
Clus4-Goal	29	9.8	32.6
Clus4-Hypothesis	12	4.1	52.2
Clus5-Motivation	61	12.9	37.4
Not associated: Clus1 - Motivation, Clus2 - Goal, Clus4 - Background, Clus 5 - Model			

Table 7: Cluster-Zone mappings on the ART Corpus

The presence of significant associations validate our intuitions that syntax provides clues about communicative goals. Some clusters overwhelmingly contain the same zone, indicated by high precision, for example 64% of sentences in Clus2 from introduction sections are background sentences. Other clusters have high recall of a zone, 55% of all goal sentences from the abstracts training data is captured by Clus7. It is particularly interesting to see that Clus7 of abstracts captures both objective and goal zone sentences and for introductions, Clus4 is a mix of hypothesis and goal sentences which intuitively are closely related categories.

6.2 Original versus permuted sections

We also explore the accuracy of the syntax models for predicting coherence of articles from the test set of ART corpus and the 500 test articles from ACL-NAACL conferences. We use the same experimental setup as before and create pairs of original and permuted versions of the test articles. We created a maximum of 20 permutations for each article. The baseline accuracy is 50% as before.

For the ART corpus, we also built an oracle model of annotated zones. We train a first order Markov Chain to record the sequence of zones in the training articles. For testing, we assume that the oracle zone is provided for each sentence and use the model to predict the likelihood of the zone sequence. Results from this model represent an upper bound because an accurate hypothesis of the communicative goal is available for each sentence.

The accuracies are presented in Table 8. Overall, the HMM-d-seq model provides the best accuracies. The highest results are obtained for ACL introduction sections (74%). These results are lower than that obtained on the earthquake/accident corpus but the task here is much harder: the articles are longer and the ACL corpus also has OCR errors which affect sentence segmentation and parsing accuracies. When the oracle zones are known, the accuracies are much higher on the ART corpus indicating that the intentional structure of academic articles is very predictive of their coherence.

6.3 Conference versus workshop papers

Finally, we test whether the syntax-based model can distinguish the structure of conference from workshop articles. Conferences publish more complete and tested work and workshops often present preliminary studies. Workshops are also venues to discuss a focused and specialized topic. So the way information is conveyed in the abstracts and introductions would vary in these articles.

We perform this analysis on the ACL corpus and no permutations are used, only the original text of the 500 articles each in the conference and workshop test sets. While permutation examples provide cheap training/test data, they have a few unrealistic properties. For example, both original and permuted articles have the same length. Further some permutations could result in an outstandingly incoherent sample which is easily distinguished from the original articles. So we use the conference versus workshop task as another evaluation of our model.

We designed a classification experiment for this task which combines features from the different syntax models that were trained on the ACL conference training set. We include four features indicating the perplexity of an article under each model (Local-prod, Local-d-seq, HMM-prod, HMM-d-seq). We use perplexity rather than probability because the length of the articles vary widely in contrast to the previous permutation-based tests, where both permutation and original article have the same length. We compute perplexity as $P(T)^{-1/n}$, where n is the number of words in the article. We also obtain the most likely state sequence for the article under

Data	Section	Test pairs	Local-prod	Local-d-seq	HMM-prod	HMM-d-seq	Oracle zones
ART Corpus	Abstract	1633	57.0	52.9	**64.1**	55.0	80.8
	Intro	1640	44.5	54.6	58.1	**64.6**	94.0
ACL Conference	Abstract	8815	44.0	47.2	58.2	**63.7**	
	Intro	9966	54.5	53.0	64.4	**74.0**	
	Rel. wk.	10,000	54.6	54.4	57.3	**67.3**	

Table 8: Accuracy in differentiating permutation from original sections on ACL and ART test sets.

HMM-prod and HMM-d-seq models using Viterbi decoding. Then the proportion of sentences from each state of the two models are added as features.

We also add some fine-grained features from the local model. We represent sentences in the training set as either productions or d-sequence items and compute pairs of associated items (x_i, x_j) from adjacent sentences using the same chi-square test as in our pilot study. The most significant (lowest p-values) 30 pairs (each for production and d-seq) are taken as features.[10] For a test article, we compute features that represent how often each pair is present in the article such that x_i is in S_m and x_j is in S_{m+1}.

We perform this experiment for each section and there are about 90 to 140 features for the different sections. We cast the problem as a binary classification task: conference articles belong to one class and workshop to the other. Each class has 500 articles and so the baseline random accuracy is 50%. We perform 10-fold cross validation using logistic regression. Our results were 59.3% accuracy for distinguishing abstracts of conference verus workshop, 50.3% for introductions and 55.4% for related work. For abstracts and related work, these accuracies are significantly better than baseline (95% confidence level from a two-sided paired t-test comparing the accuracies from the 10 folds). It is possible that introductions in either case, talk in general about the field and importance of the problem addressed and hence have similar structure.

Our accuracies are not as high as on permutations examples because the task is clearly harder. It may also be the case that the prediction is more difficult for certain papers than for others. So we also analyze our results by the confidence provided by the classifier for the predicted class. We consider only the examples predicted above a certain confidence level and compute the accuracy on these predictions.

[10]A cutoff is applied such that the pair was seen at least 25 times in the training data.

Conf.	Abstract	Intro	Rel wk
$>= 0.5$	59.3 (100.0)	50.3 (100.0)	55.4 (100.0)
$>= 0.6$	63.8 (67.2)	50.8 (71.1)	58.6 (75.9)
$>= 0.7$	67.2 (32.0)	54.4 (38.6)	63.3 (52.8)
$>= 0.8$	74.0 (10.0)	51.6 (22.0)	63.0 (25.7)
$>= 0.9$	91.7 (2.0)	30.6 (5.0)	68.1 (7.2)

Table 9: Accuracy (% examples) above each confidence level for the conference versus workshop task.

These results are shown in Table 9. The proportion of examples under each setting is also indicated.

When only examples above 0.6 confidence are examined, the classifier has a higher accuracy of 63.8% for abstracts and covers close to 70% of the examples. Similarly, when a cutoff of 0.7 is applied to the confidence for predicting related work sections, we achieve 63.3% accuracy for 53% of examples. So we can consider that 30 to 47% of the examples in the two sections respectively are harder to tell apart. Interestingly however even high confidence predictions on introductions remain incorrect.

These results show that our model can successfully distinguish the structure of articles beyond just clearly incoherent permutation examples.

7 Conclusion

Our work is the first to develop an unsupervised model for intentional structure and to show that it has good accuracy for coherence prediction and also complements entity and lexical structure of discourse. This result raises interesting questions about how patterns captured by these different coherence metrics vary and how they can be combined usefully for predicting coherence. We plan to explore these ideas in future work. We also want to analyze genre differences to understand if the strength of these coherence dimensions varies with genre.

Acknowledgements

This work is partially supported by a Google research grant and NSF CAREER 0953445 award.

References

Regina Barzilay and Mirella Lapata. 2008. Modeling local coherence: An entity-based approach. *Computational Linguistics*, 34(1):1–34.

Regina Barzilay and Lillian Lee. 2004. Catching the drift: Probabilistic content models, with applications to generation and summarization. In *Proceedings of NAACL-HLT*, pages 113–120.

Xavier Carreras, Michael Collins, and Terry Koo. 2008. Tag, dynamic programming, and the perceptron for efficient, feature-rich parsing. In *Proceedings of CoNLL*, pages 9–16.

Eugene Charniak and Mark Johnson. 2005. Coarse-to-fine n-best parsing and maxent discriminative reranking. In *Proceedings of ACL*, pages 173–180.

Jackie C.K. Cheung and Gerald Penn. 2010. Utilizing extra-sentential context for parsing. In *Proceedings of EMNLP*, pages 23–33.

Christelle Cocco, Raphaël Pittier, François Bavaud, and Aris Xanthos. 2011. Segmentation and clustering of textual sequences: a typological approach. In *Proceedings of RANLP*, pages 427–433.

Michael Collins and Terry Koo. 2005. Discriminative reranking for natural language parsing. *Computational Linguistics*, 31:25–70.

Isaac G. Councill, C. Lee Giles, and Min-Yen Kan. 2008. Parscit: An open-source crf reference string parsing package. In *Proceedings of LREC*, pages 661–667.

Micha Elsner and Eugene Charniak. 2008. Coreference-inspired coherence modeling. In *Proceedings of ACL-HLT, Short Papers*, pages 41–44.

Micha Elsner and Eugene Charniak. 2011. Extending the entity grid with entity-specific features. In *Proceedings of ACL-HLT*, pages 125–129.

Micha Elsner, Joseph Austerweil, and Eugene Charniak. 2007. A unified local and global model for discourse coherence. In *Proceedings of NAACL-HLT*, pages 436–443.

Pascale Fung and Grace Ngai. 2006. One story, one flow: Hidden markov story models for multilingual multidocument summarization. *ACM Transactions on Speech and Language Processing*, 3(2):1–16.

Barbara J. Grosz and Candace L. Sidner. 1986. Attention, intentions, and the structure of discourse. *Computational Linguistics*, 3(12):175–204.

Yufan Guo, Anna Korhonen, and Thierry Poibeau. 2011. A weakly-supervised approach to argumentative zoning of scientific documents. In *Proceedings of EMNLP*, pages 273–283.

Liang Huang. 2008. Forest reranking: Discriminative parsing with non-local features. In *Proceedings of ACL-HLT*, pages 586–594, June.

Nikiforos Karamanis, Chris Mellish, Massimo Poesio, and Jon Oberlander. 2009. Evaluating centering for information ordering using corpora. *Computational Linguistics*, 35(1):29–46.

Dan Klein and Christopher D. Manning. 2003. Accurate unlexicalized parsing. In *Proceedings of ACL*, pages 423–430.

Mirella Lapata and Regina Barzilay. 2005. Automatic evaluation of text coherence: Models and representations. In *Proceedings of IJCAI*.

Mirella Lapata. 2003. Probabilistic text structuring: Experiments with sentence ordering. In *Proceedings of ACL*, pages 545–552.

Maria Liakata and Larisa Soldatova. 2008. Guidelines for the annotation of general scientific concepts. *JISC Project Report*.

Maria Liakata, Simone Teufel, Advaith Siddharthan, and Colin Batchelor. 2010. Corpora for the conceptualisation and zoning of scientific papers. In *Proceedings of LREC*.

Ziheng Lin, Min-Yen Kan, and Hwee Tou Ng. 2009. Recognizing implicit discourse relations in the Penn Discourse Treebank. In *Proceedings of EMNLP*, pages 343–351.

Ziheng Lin, Hwee Tou Ng, and Min-Yen Kan. 2011. Automatically evaluating text coherence using discourse relations. In *Proceedings of ACL-HLT*, pages 997–1006.

Mitchell P. Marcus, Beatrice Santorini, and Mary Ann Marcinkiewicz. 1994. Building a large annotated corpus of english: The penn treebank. *Computational Linguistics*, 19(2):313–330.

Emily Pitler and Ani Nenkova. 2008. Revisiting readability: A unified framework for predicting text quality. In *Proceedings of EMNLP*, pages 186–195.

Dragomir R. Radev, Mark Thomas Joseph, Bryan Gibson, and Pradeep Muthukrishnan. 2009. A Bibliometric and Network Analysis of the field of Computational Linguistics. *Journal of the American Society for Information Science and Technology*.

David Reitter, Johanna D. Moore, and Frank Keller. 2006. Priming of Syntactic Rules in Task-Oriented Dialogue and Spontaneous Conversation. In *Proceedings of the 28th Annual Conference of the Cognitive Science Society*, pages 685–690.

Jeffrey C. Reynar and Adwait Ratnaparkhi. 1997. A maximum entropy approach to identifying sentence boundaries. In *Proceedings of the fifth conference on Applied natural language processing*, pages 16–19.

Radu Soricut and Daniel Marcu. 2006. Discourse generation using utility-trained coherence models. In *Proceedings of COLING-ACL*, pages 803–810.

John Swales. 1990. *Genre analysis: English in academic and research settings*, volume 11. Cambridge University Press.

Simone Teufel and Marc Moens. 2000. What's yours and what's mine: determining intellectual attribution in scientific text. In *Proceedings of EMNLP*, pages 9–17.

Simone Teufel, Jean Carletta, and Marc Moens. 1999. An annotation scheme for discourse-level argumentation in research articles. In *Proceedings of EACL*, pages 110–117.

Ying Zhao, George Karypis, and Usama Fayyad. 2005. Hierarchical clustering algorithms for document datasets. *Data Mining and Knowledge Discovery*, 10:141–168.

Language Model Rest Costs and Space-Efficient Storage

Kenneth Heafield[*,†] **Philipp Koehn**[†] **Alon Lavie**[*]

[*] Language Technologies Institute
Carnegie Mellon University
5000 Forbes Avenue
Pittsburgh, PA 15213, USA
{heafield,alavie}@cs.cmu.edu

[†] School of Informatics
University of Edinburgh
10 Crichton Street
Edinburgh EH8 9AB, UK
pkoehn@inf.ed.ac.uk

Abstract

Approximate search algorithms, such as cube pruning in syntactic machine translation, rely on the language model to estimate probabilities of sentence fragments. We contribute two changes that trade between accuracy of these estimates and memory, holding sentence-level scores constant. Common practice uses lower-order entries in an N-gram model to score the first few words of a fragment; this violates assumptions made by common smoothing strategies, including Kneser-Ney. Instead, we use a unigram model to score the first word, a bigram for the second, etc. This improves search at the expense of memory. Conversely, we show how to save memory by collapsing probability and backoff into a single value without changing sentence-level scores, at the expense of less accurate estimates for sentence fragments. These changes can be stacked, achieving better estimates with unchanged memory usage. In order to interpret changes in search accuracy, we adjust the pop limit so that accuracy is unchanged and report the change in CPU time. In a German-English Moses system with target-side syntax, improved estimates yielded a 63% reduction in CPU time; for a Hiero-style version, the reduction is 21%. The compressed language model uses 26% less RAM while equivalent search quality takes 27% more CPU. Source code is released as part of KenLM.

1 Introduction

Language model storage is typically evaluated in terms of speed, space, and accuracy. We introduce a fourth dimension, rest cost quality, that captures how well the model scores sentence fragments for purposes of approximate search. Rest cost quality is distinct from accuracy in the sense that the score of a complete sentence is held constant. We first show how to improve rest cost quality over standard practice by using additional space. Then, conversely, we show how to compress the language model by making a pessimistic rest cost assumption[1].

Language models are designed to assign probability to sentences. However, approximate search algorithms use estimates for sentence fragments. If the language model has order N (an N-gram model), then the first $N-1$ words of the fragment have incomplete context and the last $N-1$ words have not been completely used as context. Our baseline is common practice (Koehn et al., 2007; Dyer et al., 2010; Li et al., 2009) that uses lower-order entries from the language model for the first words in the fragment and no rest cost adjustment for the last few words. Formally, the baseline estimate for sentence fragment w_1^k is

$$\left(\prod_{n=1}^{N-1} p_N(w_n|w_1^{n-1})\right)\left(\prod_{n=N}^{k} p_N(w_n|w_{n-N+1}^{n-1})\right)$$

where each w_n is a word and p_N is an N-gram language model.

The problem with the baseline estimate lies in lower order entries $p_N(w_n|w_1^{n-1})$. Commonly used Kneser-Ney (Kneser and Ney, 1995) smoothing,

[1]Here, the term rest cost means an adjustment to the score of a sentence fragment but not to whole sentences. The adjustment may be good or bad for approximate search.

including the modified version (Chen and Goodman, 1998), assumes that a lower-order entry will only be used because a longer match could not be found[2]. Formally, these entries actually evaluate $p_N(w_n|w_1^{n-1}$, did not find $w_0^n)$. For purposes of scoring sentence fragments, additional context is simply indeterminate, and the assumption may not hold.

As an example, we built 5-gram and unigram language models with Kneser-Ney smoothing on the same data. Sentence fragments frequently begin with "the". Using a lower-order entry from the 5-gram model, $\log_{10} p_5(\text{the}) = -2.49417$. The unigram model does not condition on backing off, assigning $\log_{10} p_1(\text{the}) = -1.28504$. Intuitively, the 5-gram model is surprised, by more than an order of magnitude, to see "the" without matching words that precede it.

To remedy the situation, we train N language models on the same data. Each model p_n is an n-gram model (it has order n). We then use p_n to score the nth word of a sentence fragment. Thus, a unigram model scores the first word of a sentence fragment, a bigram model scores the second word, and so on until either the n-gram is not present in the model or the first $N-1$ words have been scored. Storing probabilities from these models requires one additional value per n-gram in the model, except for N-grams where this probability is already stored.

Conversely, we can lower memory consumption relative to the baseline at the expense of poorer rest costs. Baseline models store two entries per n-gram: probability and backoff. We will show that the probability and backoff values in a language model can be collapsed into a single value for each n-gram without changing sentence probability. This transformation saves memory by halving the number of values stored per entry, but it makes rest cost estimates worse. Specifically, the rest cost pessimistically assumes that the model will back off to unigrams immediately following the sentence fragment.

The two modifications can be used independently or simultaneously. To measure the impact of their different rest costs, we experiment with cube pruning (Chiang, 2007) in syntactic machine translation. Cube pruning's goal is to find high-scoring sentence fragments for the root non-terminal in the parse tree. It does so by going bottom-up in the parse tree, searching for high-scoring sentence fragments for each non-terminal. Within each non-terminal, it generates a fixed number of high-scoring sentence fragments; this is known as the *pop limit*. Increasing the pop limit therefore makes search more accurate but costs more time. By moderating the pop limit, improved accuracy can be interpreted as a reduction in CPU time and vice-versa.

[2]Other smoothing techniques, including Witten-Bell (Witten and Bell, 1991), do not make this assumption.

2 Related Work

Vilar and Ney (2011) study several modifications to cube pruning and cube growing (Huang and Chiang, 2007). Most relevant is their use of a class-based language model for the first of two decoding passes. This first pass is cheaper because translation alternatives are likely to fall into the same class. Entries are scored with the maximum probability over class members (thereby making them no longer normalized). Thus, paths that score highly in this first pass may contain high-scoring paths under the lexicalized language model, so the second pass more fully explores these options. The rest cost estimates we describe here could be applied in both passes, so our work is largely orthogonal.

Zens and Ney (2008) present rest costs for phrase-based translation. These rest costs are based on factors external to the sentence fragment, namely output that the decoder may generate in the future. Our rest costs examine words internal to the sentence fragment, namely the first and last few words. We also differ by focusing on syntactic translation.

A wide variety of work has been done on language model compression. While data structure compression (Raj and Whittaker, 2003; Heafield, 2011) and randomized data structures (Talbot and Osborne, 2007; Guthrie and Hepple, 2010) are useful, here we are concerned solely with the values stored by these data structures. Quantization (Whittaker and Raj, 2001; Federico and Bertoldi, 2006) uses less bits to store each numerical value at the expense of model quality, including scores of full sentences, and is compatible with our approach. In fact, the lower-order probabilities might be quantized further than normal since these are used solely for rest cost purposes. Our compression technique reduces storage from two values, probability and backoff, to one value, theoretically halving the bits per value (except N-grams which all have backoff 1). This makes the storage requirement for higher-quality modified Kneser-Ney smoothing comparable to stupid backoff (Brants et al., 2007). Whether to use one smoothing technique or the other then becomes largely an issue of training costs and quality after quantization.

3 Contribution

3.1 Better Rest Costs

As alluded to in the introduction, the first few words of a sentence fragment are typically scored using lower-order entries from an N-gram language model. However, Kneser-Ney smoothing (Kneser and Ney, 1995) conditions lower-order probabilities on backing off. Specifically, lower-order counts are adjusted to represent the number of unique extensions an n-gram has:

$$a(w_1^n) = \begin{cases} |\{w_0 : c(w_0^n) > 0\}| & \text{if } n < N \\ c(w_1^n) & \text{if } n = N \end{cases}$$

where $c(w_1^n)$ is the number of times w_1^n appears in the training data[3]. This adjustment is also performed for modified Kneser-Ney smoothing. The intuition is based on the fact that the language model will base its probability on the longest possible match. If an N-gram was seen in the training data, the model will match it fully and use the smoothed count. Otherwise, the full N-gram was not seen in the training data and the model resorts to a shorter n-gram match. Probability of this shorter match is based on how often the n-gram is seen in different contexts. Thus, these shorter n-gram probabilities are not representative of cases where context is short simply because additional context is unknown at the time of scoring.

In some cases, we are able to determine that the model will back off and therefore the lower-order probability makes the appropriate assumption. Specifically, if vw_1^n does not appear in the model for any word v, then computing $p(w_n|vw_1^{n-1})$ will always back off to w_1^{n-1} or fewer words[4]. This criterion is the same as used to minimize the length of left language model state (Li and Khudanpur, 2008) and can be retrieved for each n-gram without using additional memory in common data structures (Heafield et al., 2011).

Where it is unknown if the model will back off, we use a language model of the same order to produce a rest cost. Specifically, there are N language models, one of each order from 1 to N. The models are trained on the same corpus with the same smoothing parameters to the extent that they apply. We then compile these into one data structure where each n-gram record has three values:

1. Probability p_n from the n-gram language model
2. Probability p_N from the N-gram language model
3. Backoff b from the N-gram language model

For N-grams, the two probabilities are the same and backoff is always 1, so only one value is stored. Without pruning, the n-gram model contains the same n-grams as the N-gram model. With pruning, the two sets may be different, so we query the n-gram model in the normal way to score every n-gram in the N-gram model. The idea is that p_n is the average conditional probability that will be encountered once additional context becomes known. We also tried more complicated estimates by additionally interpolating upper bound, lower bound, and p_N with weights trained on cube pruning logs; none of these improved results in any meaningful way.

Formalizing the above, let w_1^k be a sentence fragment. Choose the largest s so that vw_1^s appears in the model for some v; equivalently w_1^s is the left state described in Li and Khudanpur (2008). The

[3] Counts are not modified for n-grams bound to the beginning of sentence, namely those with $w_1 =$ <s>.

[4] Usually, this happens because w_1^n does not appear, though it can also happen that w_1^n appears but all vw_1^n were removed by pruning or filtering.

baseline estimate is

$$p_b(w_1^k) = \left(\prod_{n=1}^{s} p_N(w_n|w_1^{n-1})\right) \cdot \left(\prod_{n=s+1}^{N+1} p_N(w_n|w_1^{n-1})\right) \cdot \left(\prod_{n=N}^{k} p_N(w_n|w_{n-N+1}^{n-1})\right) \quad (1)$$

while our improved estimate is

$$p_r(w_1^k) = \left(\prod_{n=1}^{s} p_n(w_n|w_1^{n-1})\right) \cdot \left(\prod_{n=s+1}^{N+1} p_N(w_n|w_1^{n-1})\right) \cdot \left(\prod_{n=N}^{k} p_N(w_n|w_{n-N+1}^{n-1})\right) \quad (2)$$

The difference between these equations is that p_n is used for words in the left state i.e. $1 \leq n \leq s$. We have also abused notation by using p_N to denote both probabilities stored explicitly in the model and the model's backoff-smoothed probabilities when not present. It is not necessary to store backoffs for p_n because s was chosen such that all queried n-grams appear in the model.

This modification to the language model improves rest costs (and therefore quality or CPU time) at the expense of using more memory to store p_n. In the next section, we do the opposite: make rest costs worse to reduce storage size.

3.2 Less Memory

Many language model smoothing strategies, including modified Kneser-Ney smoothing, use the backoff algorithm shown in Figure 1. Given an n-gram w_1^n, the backoff algorithm bases probability on as much context as possible. Equivalently, it finds the minimum f so that w_f^n is in the model then uses $p(w_n|w_f^{n-1})$ as a basis. Backoff penalties b are charged because a longer match was not found, forming the product

$$p(w_n|w_1^{n-1}) = p(w_n|w_f^{n-1}) \prod_{j=1}^{f-1} b(w_j^{n-1}) \quad (3)$$

Notably, the backoff penalties $\{b(w_j^{n-1})\}_{j=1}^{n-1}$ are independent of w_n, though which backoff penalties are charged depends on f and therefore w_n.

backoff $\leftarrow 1$
for $f = 1 \rightarrow n$ **do**
  if w_f^n is in the model **then**
    return $p(w_n|w_f^{n-1}) \cdot$ backoff
  else
    if w_f^{n-1} is in the model **then**
      backoff $\leftarrow$ backoff $\cdot\, b(w_f^{n-1})$
    end if
  end if
end for

Figure 1: The baseline backoff algorithm to compute $p(w_n|w_1^{n-1})$. It always terminates with a probability because even unknown words are treated as a unigram.

for $f = 1 \rightarrow n$ **do**
  if w_f^n is in the model **then**
    return $q(w_n|w_f^{n-1})$
  end if
end for

Figure 2: The run-time pessimistic backoff algorithm to find $q(w_n|w_1^{n-1})$. It assumes that q has been computed at model building time.

In order to save memory, we propose to account for backoff in a different way, defining q

$$q(w_n|w_1^{n-1}) = \frac{p(w_n|w_f^{n-1}) \prod_{j=f}^{n} b(w_j^n)}{\prod_{j=f}^{n-1} b(w_j^{n-1})}$$

where again w_f^n is the longest matching entry in the model. The idea is that q is a term in the telescoping series that scores a sentence fragment, shown in equation (1) or (2). The numerator pessimistically charges all backoff penalties, as if the next word w_{n+1} will only match a unigram. When w_{n+1} is scored, the denominator of $q(w_{n+1}|w_1^n)$ cancels out backoff terms that were wrongly charged. Once these terms are canceled, all that is left is p, the correct backoff penalties, and terms on the edge of the series.

Proposition 1. *The terms of q telescope. Formally, let w_1^k be a sentence fragment and f take the minimum value so that w_f^k is in the model. Then,*

$$q(w_1^k) = p(w_1^k) \prod_{j=f}^{k} b(w_j^k)$$

Proof. By induction on k. When $k = 1$, $f = 1$ since the word w_1 is either in the vocabulary or mapped to <unk> and treated like a unigram.

$$q(w_1) = \frac{p(w_1) \prod_{j=1}^{1} b(w_j^1)}{\prod_{j=1}^{0} b(w_j^0)} = p(w_1)b(w_1)$$

For $k > 1$,

$$\begin{aligned} q(w_1^k) &= q(w_1^{k-1})q(w_k|w_1^{k-1}) \\ &= \frac{q(w_1^{k-1})p(w_k|w_f^{k-1}) \prod_{j=f}^{k} b(w_j^k)}{\prod_{j=f}^{k-1} b(w_j^{k-1})} \end{aligned}$$

where f has the lowest value such that w_f^k is in the model. Applying the inductive hypothesis to expand $q(w_1^{k-1})$, we obtain

$$\frac{p(w_1^{k-1}) \left(\prod_{j=e}^{k-1} b(w_j^{k-1})\right) p(w_k|w_f^{k-1}) \prod_{j=f}^{k} b(w_j^k)}{\prod_{j=f}^{k-1} b(w_j^{k-1})}$$

where e has the lowest value such that w_e^{k-1} is in the model. The backoff terms cancel to yield

$$p(w_1^{k-1}) \left(\prod_{j=e}^{f-1} b(w_j^{k-1})\right) p(w_k|w_f^{k-1}) \prod_{j=f}^{k} b(w_j^k)$$

By construction of e, w_j^{k-1} is not in the model for all $j < e$. Hence, $b(w_j^{k-1}) = 1$ implicitly for all $j < e$. Multiplying by 1,

$$p(w_1^{k-1}) \left(\prod_{j=1}^{f-1} b(w_j^{k-1})\right) p(w_k|w_f^{k-1}) \prod_{j=f}^{k} b(w_j^k)$$

Recognizing the backoff equation (3) to simplify,

$$p(w_1^{k-1})p(w_k|w_1^{k-1}) \prod_{j=f}^{k} b(w_j^k)$$

Finally, the conditional probability folds as desired

$$q(w_1^k) = p(w_1^k) \prod_{j=f}^{k} b(w_j^k)$$

□

We note that entries ending in </s> have backoff 1, so it follows from Proposition 1 that sentence-level scores are unchanged.

$$q(\text{<s>}\ w_1^k\ \text{</s>}) = p(\text{<s>}\ w_1^k\ \text{</s>})$$

Proposition 1 characterizes q as a pessimistic rest cost on sentence fragments that scores sentences in exactly the same way as the baseline using p and b. To save memory, we simply store q in lieu of p and b. Compared with the baseline, this halves number of values from two to one float per n-gram, except N-grams that already have one value. The impact of this reduction is substantial, as seen in Section 4.3. Run-time scoring is also simplified as shown in Figure 2 since the language model locates the longest match w_f^n then returns the value $q(w_n|w_1^{n-1}) = q(w_n|w_f^{n-1})$ without any calculation or additional lookup. Baseline language models either retrieve backoffs values with additional lookups (Stolcke, 2002; Federico et al., 2008) or modify the decoder to annotate sentence fragments with backoff information (Heafield, 2011); we have effectively moved this step to preprocessing. The disadvantage is that q is not a proper probability and it produces worse rest costs than does the baseline.

Language models are actually applied at two points in syntactic machine translation: scoring lexical items in grammar rules and during cube pruning. Grammar scoring is an offline and embarrassingly parallel process where memory is not as tight (since the phrase table is streamed) and fewer queries are made, so slow non-lossy compression and even network-based sharding can be used. We therefore use an ordinary language model for grammar scoring and only apply the compressed model during cube pruning. Grammar scoring impacts grammar pruning (by selecting only top-scoring grammar rules) and the order in which rules are tried during cube pruning.

3.3 Combined Scheme

Our two language model modifications can be trivially combined by using lower-order probabilities on the left of a fragment and by charging all backoff penalties on the right of a fragment. The net result is a language model that uses the same memory as the baseline but has better rest cost estimates.

4 Experiments

To measure the impact of different rest costs, we use the Moses chart decoder (Koehn et al., 2007) for the WMT 2011 German-English translation task (Callison-Burch et al., 2011). Using the Moses pipeline, we trained two syntactic German-English systems, one with target-side syntax and the other hierarchical with unlabeled grammar rules (Chiang, 2007). Grammar rules were extracted from Europarl (Koehn, 2005) using the Collins parser (Collins, 1999) for syntax on the English side. The language model interpolates, on the WMT 2010 test set, separate models built on Europarl, news commentary, and the WMT news data for each year. Models were built and interpolated using SRILM (Stolcke, 2002) with modified Kneser-Ney smoothing (Kneser and Ney, 1995; Chen and Goodman, 1998) and the default pruning settings. In all scenarios, the primary language model has order 5. For lower-order rest costs, we also built models with orders 1 through 4 then used the n-gram model to score n-grams in the 5-gram model. Feature weights were trained with MERT (Och, 2003) on the baseline using a pop limit of 1000 and 100-best output. Since final feature values are unchanged, we did not re-run MERT in each condition. Measurements were collected by running the decoder on the 3003-sentence test set.

4.1 Rest Costs as Prediction

Scoring the first few words of a sentence fragment is a prediction task. The goal is to predict what the probability will be when more context becomes known. In order to measure performance on this task, we ran the decoder on the hierarchical system with a pop limit of 1000. Every time more context became known, we logged[5] the prediction error (estimated log probability minus updated log probability) for both lower-order rest costs and the baseline. Table 1 shows the results.

		Lower			Baseline		
n	**Mean**	**Bias**	**MSE**	**Var**	**Bias**	**MSE**	**Var**
1	-3.21	.10	.84	.83	-.12	.87	.86
2	-2.27	.04	.18	.17	-.14	.23	.24
3	-1.80	.02	.07	.07	-.09	.10	.09
4	-1.29	.01	.04	.04	-.10	.09	.08

Table 1: Bias (mean error), mean squared error, and variance (of the error) for the lower-order rest cost and the baseline. Error is the estimated log probability minus the final probability. Statistics were computed separately for the first word of a fragment ($n = 1$), the second word ($n = 2$), etc. The lower-order estimates are better across the board, reducing error in cube pruning. All numbers are in log base ten, as is standard for ARPA-format language models. Statistics were only collected for words with incomplete context.

Cube pruning uses relative scores, so bias matters less, though positive bias will favor rules with more arity. Variance matters the most because lower variance means cube pruning's relative rankings are more accurate. Our lower-order rest costs are better across the board in terms of absolute bias, mean squared error, and variance.

4.2 Pop Limit Trade-Offs

The cube pruning pop limit is a trade-off between search accuracy and CPU time. Here, we measure how our rest costs improve (or degrade) that trade-off. Search accuracy is measured by the average model score of single-best translations. Model scores are scale-invariant and include a large constant factor; higher is better. We also measure overall performance with uncased BLEU (Papineni et al., 2002). CPU time is the sum of user and system time used by Moses divided by the number of sentences (3003). Timing includes time to load, though files were forced into the disk cache in advance. Our test machine has 64 GB of RAM and 32 cores. Results are shown in Figures 3 and 4.

Lower-order rest costs perform better in both systems, reaching plateau model scores and BLEU with less CPU time. The gain is much larger for tar-

[5]Logging was only enabled for this experiment.

	Baseline			Lower Order			Pessimistic			Combined		
Pop	CPU	Model	BLEU	CPU	Model	BLEU	CPU	Model	BLEU	CPU	Model	BLEU
2	3.29	-105.56	20.45	3.68	-105.44	20.79	3.74	-105.62	20.01	3.18	-105.49	20.43
10	5.21	-104.74	21.13	5.50	-104.72	21.26	5.43	-104.77	20.85	5.67	-104.75	21.10
50	23.30	-104.31	21.36	23.51	-104.24	21.38	23.68	-104.33	21.25	24.29	-104.22	21.34
500	54.61	-104.25	21.33	55.92	-104.15	21.38	54.23	-104.26	21.31	55.74	-104.15	21.40
700	64.08	-104.25	21.34	87.02	-104.14	21.42	68.74	-104.25	21.29	78.84	-104.15	21.41

(a) Numerical results for select pop limits.

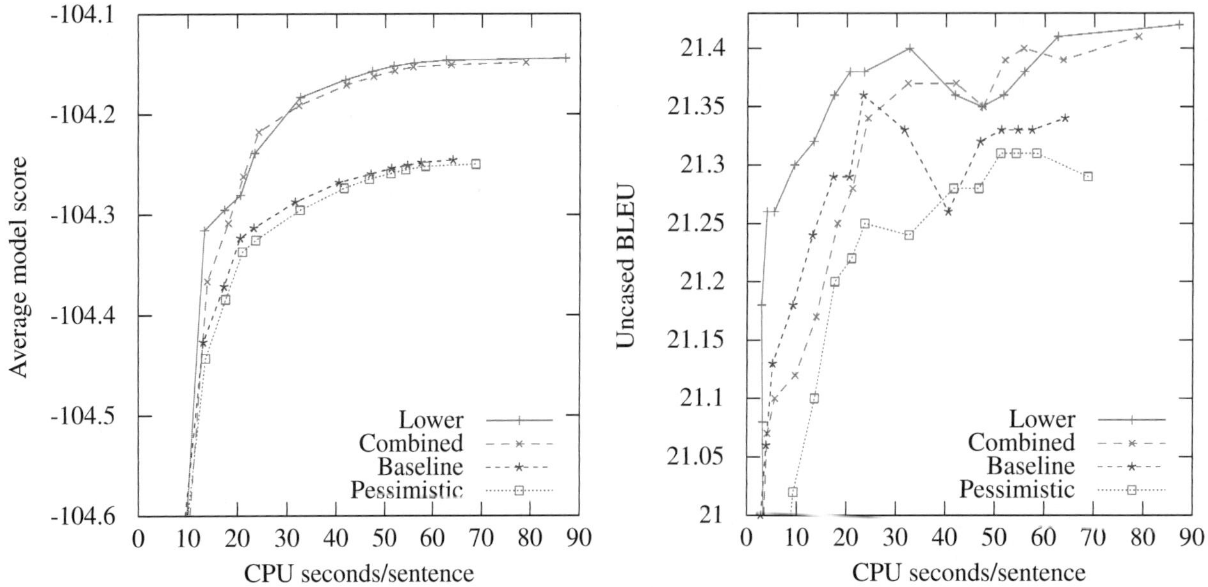

(b) Model and BLEU scores near the plateau.

Figure 3: Target-syntax performance. CPU time and model score are averaged over 3003 sentences.

get syntax, where a pop limit of 50 outperforms the baseline with pop limit 700. CPU time per sentence is reduced to 23.5 seconds from 64.0 seconds, a 63.3% reduction. The combined setting, using the same memory as the baseline, shows a similar 62.1% reduction in CPU time. We attribute this difference to improved grammar rule scoring that impacts pruning and sorting. In the target syntax model, the grammar is not saturated (i.e. less pruning will still improve scores) but we nonetheless prune for tractability reasons. The lower-order rest costs are particularly useful for grammar pruning because lexical items are typically less than five words long (and frequently only word).

The hierarchical grammar is nearly saturated with respect to grammar pruning, so improvement there is due mostly to better search. In the hierarchical system, peak BLEU 22.34 is achieved under the lower-order condition with pop limits 50 and 200, while other scenarios are still climbing to the plateau. With a pop limit of 1000, the baseline's average model score is -101.3867. Better average models scores are obtained from the lower-order model with pop limit 690 using 79% of baseline CPU, the combined model with pop limit 900 using 97% CPU, and the pessimistic model with pop limit 1350 using 127% CPU.

Pessimistic compression does worsen search, requiring 27% more CPU in the hierarchical system to achieve the same quality. This is worthwhile to fit large-scale language models in memory, especially if the alternative is a remote language model.

4.3 Memory Usage

Our rest costs add a value (for lower-order probabilities) or remove a value (pessimistic compression) for each n-gram except those of highest order ($n = N$). The combined condition adds one value

	Baseline			Lower Order			Pessimistic			Combined		
Pop	**CPU**	**Model**	**BLEU**	**CPU**	**Model**	**BLEU**	**CPU**	**Model**	**BLEU**	**CPU**	**Model**	**BLEU**
2	2.96	-101.85	21.19	2.44	-101.80	21.63	2.71	-101.90	20.85	3.05	-101.84	21.37
10	2.80	-101.60	21.90	2.42	-101.58	22.20	2.95	-101.63	21.74	2.69	-101.60	21.98
50	3.02	-101.47	22.18	3.11	-101.46	22.34	3.46	-101.48	22.08	2.67	-101.47	22.14
690	10.83	-101.39	22.28	11.45	-101.39	22.25	10.88	-101.40	22.25	11.19	-101.39	22.23
900	13.41	-101.39	22.27	14.00	-101.38	22.24	13.38	-101.39	22.25	14.09	-101.39	22.22
1000	14.50	-101.39	22.27	15.17	-101.38	22.25	15.09	-101.39	22.26	15.23	-101.39	22.23
1350	18.52	-101.38	22.27	19.16	-101.38	22.23	18.46	-101.39	22.25	18.61	-101.38	22.23
5000	59.67	-101.38	22.24	61.41	-101.38	22.22	59.76	-101.38	22.27	61.38	-101.38	22.22

(a) Numerical results for select pop limits.

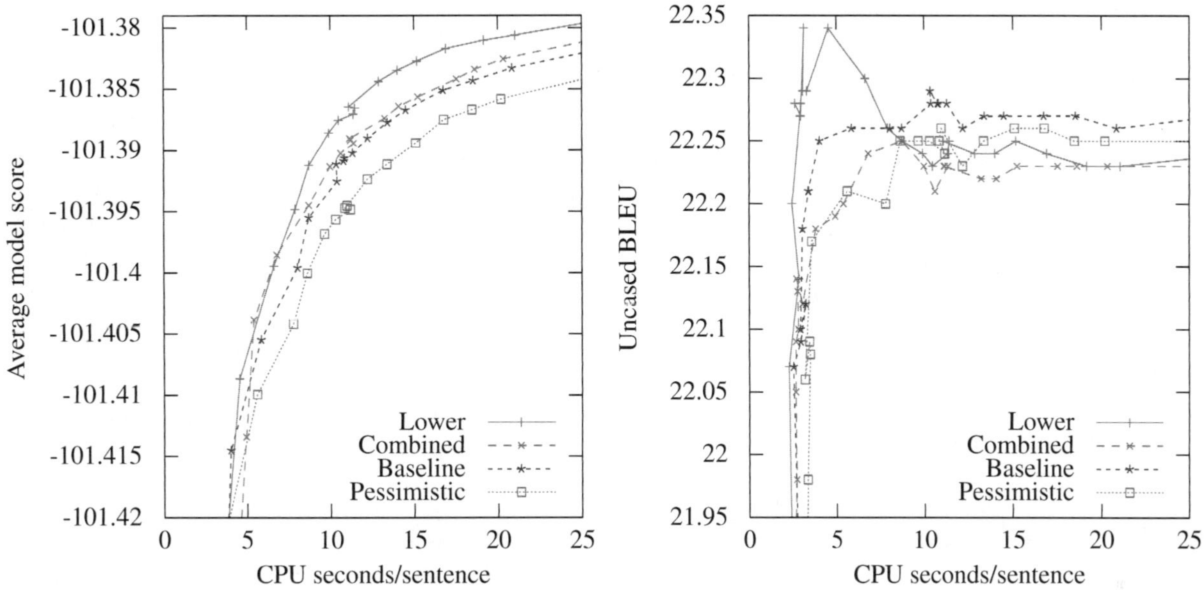

(b) Model and BLEU scores near the plateau.

Figure 4: Hierarchical system performance. All values are averaged over 3003 sentences.

and removes another, so it uses the same memory as the baseline. The memory footprint of adding or removing a value depends on the number of such n-grams, the underlying data structure, and the extent of quantization. Our test language model has 135 million n-grams for $n < 5$ and 56 million 5-grams. Memory usage was measured for KenLM data structures (Heafield, 2011) and minimal perfect hashing (Guthrie and Hepple, 2010). For minimal perfect hashing, we assume the Compress, Hash and Displace algorithm (Belazzougui et al., 2008) with 8-bit signatures and 8-bit quantization. Table 2 shows the results. Storage size of the smallest model is reduced by 26%, bringing higher-quality smoothed models in line with stupid backoff models that also store one value per n-gram.

Structure	**Baseline**	**Change**	**%**
Probing	4,072	517	13%
Trie	2,647	506	19%
8-bit quantized trie	1,236	140	11%
8-bit minimal perfect hash	540	140	26%

Table 2: Size in megabytes of our language model, excluding operating system overhead. Change is the cost of adding an additional value to store lower-order probabilities. Equivalently, it is the savings from pessimistic compression.

5 Conclusion

Our techniques reach plateau-level BLEU scores with less time or less memory. Efficiently storing lower-order probabilities and using them as rest costs improves both cube pruning (21% CPU reduction in a hierarchical system) and model filtering (net 63% CPU time reduction with target syntax) at the expense of 13-26% more RAM for the language model. This model filtering improvement is surprising both in the impact relative to changing the pop limit and simplicity of implementation, since it can be done offline. Compressing the language model to halve the number of values per n-gram (except N-grams) results in a 13-26% reduction in RAM with 26% over the smallest model, costing 27% more CPU and leaving overall sentence scores unchanged. This compression technique is likely to have more general application outside of machine translation, especially where only sentence-level scores are required. Source code is being released[6] under the LGPL as part of KenLM (Heafield, 2011).

Acknowledgements

This work was supported by the National Science Foundation under grants DGE-0750271, IIS-0713402, and IIS-0915327; by the EuroMatrixPlus project funded by the European Commission (7th Framework Programme), and by the DARPA GALE program. Benchmarks were run on Trestles at the San Diego Supercomputer Center under allocation TG-CCR110017. Trestles is part of the Extreme Science and Engineering Discovery Environment (XSEDE), which is supported by National Science Foundation grant number OCI-1053575.

References

Djamal Belazzougui, Fabiano C. Botelho, and Martin Dietzfelbinger. 2008. Hash, displace, and compress. In *Proceedings of the 35th international colloquium on Automata, Languages and Programming (ICALP '08)*, pages 385–396.

Thorsten Brants, Ashok C. Popat, Peng Xu, Franz J. Och, and Jeffrey Dean. 2007. Large language models in machine translation. In *Proceedings of the 2007 Joint Conference on Empirical Methods in Natural Language Processing and Computational Language Learning*, pages 858–867, June.

Chris Callison-Burch, Philipp Koehn, Christof Monz, and Omar Zaidan. 2011. Findings of the 2011 workshop on statistical machine translation. In *Proceedings of the Sixth Workshop on Statistical Machine Translation*, pages 22–64, Edinburgh, Scotland, July. Association for Computational Linguistics.

Stanley Chen and Joshua Goodman. 1998. An empirical study of smoothing techniques for language modeling. Technical Report TR-10-98, Harvard University, August.

David Chiang. 2007. Hierarchical phrase-based translation. *Computational Linguistics*, 33:201–228, June.

Michael Collins. 1999. *Head-Driven Statistical Models for Natural Language Parsing*. Ph.D. thesis, University of Pennsylvania.

Chris Dyer, Adam Lopez, Juri Ganitkevitch, Johnathan Weese, Ferhan Ture, Phil Blunsom, Hendra Setiawan, Vladimir Eidelman, and Philip Resnik. 2010. cdec: A decoder, alignment, and learning framework for finite-state and context-free translation models. In *Proceedings of the ACL 2010 System Demonstrations*, ACLDemos '10, pages 7–12.

Marcello Federico and Nicola Bertoldi. 2006. How many bits are needed to store probabilities for phrase-based translation? In *Proceedings of the Workshop on Statistical Machine Translation*, pages 94–101, New York City, June.

Marcello Federico, Nicola Bertoldi, and Mauro Cettolo. 2008. IRSTLM: an open source toolkit for handling large scale language models. In *Proceedings of Interspeech*, Brisbane, Australia.

David Guthrie and Mark Hepple. 2010. Storing the web in memory: Space efficient language models with constant time retrieval. In *Proceedings of EMNLP 2010*, Los Angeles, CA.

Kenneth Heafield, Hieu Hoang, Philipp Koehn, Tetsuo Kiso, and Marcello Federico. 2011. Left language model state for syntactic machine translation. In *Proceedings of the International Workshop on Spoken Language Translation*, San Francisco, CA, USA, December.

Kenneth Heafield. 2011. KenLM: Faster and smaller language model queries. In *Proceedings of the Sixth Workshop on Statistical Machine Translation*, Edinburgh, UK, July. Association for Computational Linguistics.

Liang Huang and David Chiang. 2007. Forest rescoring: Faster decoding with integrated language models. In *Proceedings of the 45th Annual Meeting of the Association for Computational Linguistics*, Prague, Czech Republic.

[6] http://kheafield.com/code/kenlm/

Reinhard Kneser and Hermann Ney. 1995. Improved backing-off for m-gram language modeling. In *Proceedings of the IEEE International Conference on Acoustics, Speech and Signal Processing*, pages 181–184.

Philipp Koehn, Hieu Hoang, Alexandra Birch, Chris Callison-Burch, Marcello Federico, Nicola Bertoldi, Brooke Cowan, Wade Shen, Christine Moran, Richard Zens, Chris Dyer, Ondrej Bojar, Alexandra Constantin, and Evan Herbst. 2007. Moses: Open source toolkit for statistical machine translation. In *Annual Meeting of the Association for Computational Linguistics (ACL)*, Prague, Czech Republic, June.

Philipp Koehn. 2005. Europarl: A parallel corpus for statistical machine translation. In *Proceedings of MT Summit*.

Zhifei Li and Sanjeev Khudanpur. 2008. A scalable decoder for parsing-based machine translation with equivalent language model state maintenance. In *Proceedings of the Second ACL Workshop on Syntax and Structure in Statistical Translation (SSST-2)*, pages 10–18, Columbus, Ohio, June.

Zhifei Li, Chris Callison-Burch, Chris Dyer, Sanjeev Khudanpur, Lane Schwartz, Wren Thornton, Jonathan Weese, and Omar Zaidan. 2009. Joshua: An open source toolkit for parsing-based machine translation. In *Proceedings of the Fourth Workshop on Statistical Machine Translation*, pages 135–139, Athens, Greece, March. Association for Computational Linguistics.

Franz Josef Och. 2003. Minimum error rate training in statistical machine translation. In *ACL '03: Proceedings of the 41st Annual Meeting on Association for Computational Linguistics*, pages 160–167, Morristown, NJ, USA. Association for Computational Linguistics.

Kishore Papineni, Salim Roukos, Todd Ward, and Wei-Jing Zhu. 2002. BLEU: A method for automatic evalution of machine translation. In *Proceedings 40th Annual Meeting of the Association for Computational Linguistics*, pages 311–318, Philadelphia, PA, July.

Bhiksha Raj and Ed Whittaker. 2003. Lossless compression of language model structure and word identifiers. In *Proceedings of IEEE International Conference on Acoustics, Speech and Signal Processing*, pages 388–391.

Andreas Stolcke. 2002. SRILM - an extensible language modeling toolkit. In *Proceedings of the Seventh International Conference on Spoken Language Processing*, pages 901–904.

David Talbot and Miles Osborne. 2007. Randomised language modelling for statistical machine translation. In *Proceedings of ACL*, pages 512–519, Prague, Czech Republic.

David Vilar and Hermann Ney. 2011. Cardinality pruning and language model heuristics for hierarchical phrase-based translation. *Machine Translation*, pages 1–38, November. DOI 10.1007/s10590-011-9119-4.

Ed Whittaker and Bhiksha Raj. 2001. Quantization-based language model compression. In *Proceedings of EUROSPEECH*, pages 33–36, September.

Ian H. Witten and Timothy C. Bell. 1991. The zero-frequency problem: Estimating the probabilities of novel events in adaptive text compression. *IEEE Transactions on Information Theory*, 37(4):1085–1094.

Richard Zens and Hermann Ney. 2008. Improvements in dynamic programming beam search for phrase-based statistical machine translation. In *Proceedings of the International Workshop on Spoken Language Translation (IWSLT)*, Honolulu, Hawaii, October.

Document-Wide Decoding for Phrase-Based Statistical Machine Translation

Christian Hardmeier   Joakim Nivre   Jörg Tiedemann
Uppsala University
Department of Linguistics and Philology
Box 635, 751 26 Uppsala, Sweden
firstname.lastname@lingfil.uu.se

Abstract

Independence between sentences is an assumption deeply entrenched in the models and algorithms used for statistical machine translation (SMT), particularly in the popular dynamic programming beam search decoding algorithm. This restriction is an obstacle to research on more sophisticated discourse-level models for SMT. We propose a stochastic local search decoding method for phrase-based SMT, which permits free document-wide dependencies in the models. We explore the stability and the search parameters of this method and demonstrate that it can be successfully used to optimise a document-level semantic language model.

1 Motivation

In the field of translation studies, it is undisputed that discourse-wide context must be considered carefully for good translation results (Hatim and Mason, 1990). By contrast, the state of the art in statistical machine translation (SMT), despite significant advances in the last twenty years, still assumes that texts can be translated sentence by sentence under strict independence assumptions, even though it is well known that certain linguistic phenomena such as pronominal anaphora cannot be translated correctly without referring to extra-sentential context. This is true both for the phrase-based and the syntax-based approach to SMT. In the rest of this paper, we shall concentrate on phrase-based SMT.

One reason why it is difficult to experiment with document-wide models for phrase-based SMT is that the dynamic programming (DP) algorithm which has been used almost exclusively for decoding SMT models in the recent literature has very strong assumptions of locality built into it. DP beam search for phrase-based SMT was described by Koehn et al. (2003), extending earlier work on word-based SMT (Tillmann et al., 1997; Och et al., 2001; Tillmann and Ney, 2003). This algorithm constructs output sentences by starting with an empty hypothesis and adding output words at the end until translations for all source words have been generated. The core models of phrase-based SMT, in particular the n-gram language model (LM), only depend on a constant number of output words to the left of the word being generated. This fact is exploited by the search algorithm with a DP technique called *hypothesis recombination* (Och et al., 2001), which permits the elimination of hypotheses from the search space if they coincide in a certain number of final words with a better hypothesis and no future expansion can possibly invert the relative ranking of the two hypotheses under the given models. Hypothesis recombination achieves a substantial reduction of the search space without affecting search optimality and makes it possible to use aggressive pruning techniques for fast search while still obtaining good results.

The downside of this otherwise excellent approach is that it only works well with models that have a local dependency structure similar to that of an n-gram language model, so they only depend on a small context window for each target word. Sentence-local models with longer dependencies can be added, but doing so greatly increases the risk for search errors by inhibiting hypothesis recombination. Cross-sentence dependencies cannot be directly integrated into DP SMT decoding in any obvious way, especially if joint optimisation of a number of interdependent decisions over an entire document is required. Research into models with a more varied, non-local dependency structure is to some extent stifled by the difficulty of decoding such models effectively, as can be seen by the problems some researchers encountered when they attempted to solve discourse-level problems. Consider, for instance, the work on cache-based language models by Tiedemann (2010) and Gong et al. (2011), where error propagation was a serious issue, or the works on pronominal anaphora by Le Nagard and Koehn (2010), who implemented cross-sentence dependencies with an ad-hoc two-pass decoding strategy, and Hardmeier and Federico (2010) with the use of an external decoder driver to manage backward-only dependencies between sentences.

In this paper, we present a method for decoding complete documents in phrase-based SMT. Our decoder uses a local search approach whose state consists of a complete translation of an entire document at any time. The initial state is improved by the application of a series of operations using a hill climbing strategy to find a (local) maximum of the score function. This setup gives us complete freedom to define scoring functions over the entire document. Moreover, by optionally initialising the state with the output of a traditional DP decoder, we can ensure that the final hypothesis is no worse than what would have been found by DP search alone. We start by describing the decoding algorithm and the state operations used by our decoder, then we present empirical results demonstrating the effectiveness of our approach and its usability with a document-level semantic language model, and finally we discuss some related work.

2 SMT Decoding by Hill Climbing

In this section, we formally describe the phrase-based SMT model implemented by our decoder as well as the decoding algorithm we use.

2.1 SMT Model

Our decoder is based on local search, so its state at any time is a representation of a complete translation of the entire document. Even though the decoder operates at the document level, it is important to keep track of sentence boundaries, and the individual operations that are applied to the state are still confined to sentence scope, so it is useful to decompose the state of a document into the state of its sentences, and we define the overall state S as a sequence of sentence states:

$$S = S_1 S_2 \dots S_N, \tag{1}$$

where N is the number of sentences. This implies that we constrain the decoder to emit exactly one output sentence per input sentence.

Let i be the number of a sentence and m_i the number of input tokens of this sentence, p and q (with $1 \leq p \leq q \leq m_i$) be positions in the input sentence and $[p;q]$ denote the set of positions from p up to and including q. We say that $[p;q]$ precedes $[p';q']$, or $[p;q] \prec [p';q']$, if $q < p'$. Let $\Phi_i([p;q])$ be the set of translations for the source phrase covering positions $[p;q]$ in the input sentence i as given by the phrase table. We call $A = \langle [p;q], \phi \rangle$ an *anchored phrase pair* with coverage $C(A) = [p;q]$ if $\phi \in \Phi_i([p;q])$ is a target phrase translating the source words at positions $[p;q]$. Then a sequence of n_i anchored phrase pairs

$$S_i = A_1 A_2 \dots A_{n_i} \tag{2}$$

is a valid sentence state for sentence i if the following two conditions hold:

1. The coverage sets $C(A_j)$ for j in $1, \dots, n_i$ are mutually disjoint, and
2. the anchored phrase pairs jointly cover the complete input sentence, or

$$\bigcup_{j=1}^{n_i} C(A_j) = [1; m_i]. \tag{3}$$

Let $f(S)$ be a scoring function mapping a state S to a real number. As usual in SMT, it is assumed that the scoring function can be decomposed into a linear combination of K feature functions $h_k(S)$, each with a constant weight λ_k, so

$$f(S) = \sum_{k=1}^{K} \lambda_k h_k(S). \tag{4}$$

The problem addressed by the decoder is the search for the state $\hat{S}$ with maximal score, such that

$$\hat{S} = \arg\max_S f(S). \tag{5}$$

The feature functions implemented in our baseline system are identical to the ones found in the popular Moses SMT system (Koehn et al., 2007). In particular, our decoder has the following feature functions:

1. phrase translation scores provided by the phrase table including forward and backward conditional probabilities, lexical weights and a phrase penalty (Koehn et al., 2003),

2. n-gram language model scores implemented with the KenLM toolkit (Heafield, 2011),

3. a word penalty score,

4. a distortion model with geometric decay (Koehn et al., 2003), and

5. a feature indicating the number of times a given distortion limit is exceeded in the current state.

In our experiments, the last feature is used with a fixed weight of negative infinity in order to limit the gaps between the coverage sets of adjacent anchored phrase pairs to a maximum value. In DP search, the distortion limit is usually enforced directly by the search algorithm and is not added as a feature. In our decoder, however, this restriction is not required to limit complexity, so we decided to add it among the scoring models.

2.2 Decoding Algorithm

The decoding algorithm we use (algorithm 1) is very simple. It starts with a given initial document state. In the main loop, which extends from line 3 to line 12, it generates a successor state S' for the current state S by calling the function `Neighbour`, which non-deterministically applies one of the operations described in section 3 of this paper to S. The score of the new state is compared to that of the previous one. If it meets a given acceptance criterion, S' becomes the current state, else search continues from the previous state S. For the experiments in this paper, we use the *hill climbing acceptance criterion*, which simply accepts a new state if its score is higher than that of the current state. Other acceptance criteria are possible and could be used to endow the search algorithm with stochastic behaviour.

The main loop is repeated until a maximum number of steps (*step limit*) is reached or until a maximum number of moves are rejected in a row (*rejection limit*).

Algorithm 1 Decoding algorithm

Input: an initial document state S;
search parameters *maxsteps* and *maxrejected*
Output: a modified document state
1: $nsteps \leftarrow 0$
2: $nrejected \leftarrow 0$
3: **while** $nsteps < maxsteps$ **and** $nrejected < maxrejected$ **do**
4: $S' \leftarrow$ `Neighbour(`S`)`
5: **if** `Accept(`$f(S')$`, `$f(S)$`)` **then**
6: $S \leftarrow S'$
7: $nrejected \leftarrow 0$
8: **else**
9: $nrejected \leftarrow nrejected + 1$
10: **end if**
11: $nsteps \leftarrow nsteps + 1$
12: **end while**
13: **return** S

A notable difference between this algorithm and other hill climbing algorithms that have been used for SMT decoding (Germann et al., 2004; Langlais et al., 2007) is its non-determinism. Previous work for sentence-level decoding employed a *steepest ascent* strategy which amounts to enumerating the complete neighbourhood of the current state as defined by the state operations and selecting the next state to be the best state found in the neighbourhood of the current one. Enumerating all neighbours of a given state, costly as it is, has the advantage that it makes it easy to prove local optimality of a state by recognising that all possible successor states have lower scores. It can be rather inefficient, since at every step only one modification will be adopted; many of the modifications that are discarded will very likely be generated anew in the next iteration.

As we extend the decoder to the document level, the size of the neighbourhood that would have to be explored in this way increases considerably. Moreover, the inefficiency of the steepest ascent approach potentially increases as well. Very likely, a promising move in one sentence will remain promising after a modification has been applied to another sentence, even though this is not guaranteed to be true in the presence of cross-sentence models. We therefore adopt a *first-choice hill climbing* strategy that non-deterministically generates successor states and accepts the first one that meets the acceptance criterion. This frees us from the necessity of generating the full set of successors for each state. On the downside, if the full successor set is not known, it is no longer possible to prove local optimality of a state, so we are forced to use a different condition for halting the search. We use a combination of two limits: The step limit is a hard limit on the resources the user is willing to expend on the search problem. The value of the rejection limit determines how much of the neighbourhood is searched for better successors before a state is accepted as a solution; it is related to the probability that a state returned as a solution is in fact locally optimal.

To simplify notations in the description of the individual state operations, we write

$$S_i \longrightarrow S'_i \tag{6}$$

to signify that a state operation, when presented with a document state as in equation 1 and acting on sentence i, returns a new document state of

$$S' = S_1 \dots S_{i-1}\, S'_i\, S_{i+1} \dots S_N. \tag{7}$$

Similarly,

$$S_i : A_j \dots A_{j+h-1} \longrightarrow A'_1 \dots A'_{h'} \tag{8}$$

is equivalent to

$$S_i \longrightarrow A_1 \dots A_{j-1}\, A'_1 \dots A'_{h'}\, A_{j+h} \dots A_{n_i} \tag{9}$$

and indicates that the operation returns a state in which a sequence of h consecutive anchored phrase pairs has been replaced by another sequence of h' anchored phrase pairs.

2.3 Efficiency Considerations

When implementing the feature functions for the decoder, we have to exercise some care to avoid recomputing scores for the whole document at every iteration. To achieve this, the scores are computed completely only once, at the beginning of the decoding run. In subsequent iterations, scoring functions are presented with the scores of the previous iteration and a list of modifications produced by the state operation, a set of tuples $\langle i, r, s, A'_1 \dots A'_{h'} \rangle$, each indicating that the document should be modified as described by

$$S_i : A_r \dots A_s \longrightarrow A'_1 \dots A'_{h'}. \tag{10}$$

If a feature function is decomposable in some way, as all the standard features developed under the constraints of DP search are, it can then update the state simply by subtracting and adding score components pertaining to the modified parts of the document. Feature functions have the possibility to store their own state information along with the document state to make sure the required information is available. Thus, the framework makes it possible to exploit decomposability for efficient scoring without imposing any particular decomposition on the features as beam search does.

To make scoring even more efficient, scores are computed in two passes: First, every feature function is asked to provide an upper bound on the score that will be obtained for the new state. In some cases, it is possible to calculate reasonable upper bounds much more efficiently than computing the exact feature value. If the upper bound fails to meet the acceptance criterion, the new state is discarded right away; if not, the full score is computed and the acceptance criterion is tested again.

Among the basic SMT models, this two-pass strategy is only used for the n-gram LM, which requires fairly expensive parameter lookups for scoring. The scores of all the other baseline models are fully computed during the first scoring pass. The n-gram model is more complex. In its state information, it keeps track of the LM score and LM library state for each word. The first scoring pass then identifies the words whose LM scores are affected by the current search step. This includes the words changed by the search operation as well as the words whose LM history is modified. The range of the history dependencies can be determined precisely by considering the "valid state length" information provided by the KenLM library. In the first pass, the LM scores of the affected words are subtracted from the total score. The model only looks up the new LM scores for the affected words and updates the total score if the new search state passes the first acceptance check. This two-pass scoring approach allows us to avoid LM lookups altogether for states that will be rejected anyhow because of low scores from the other models, e. g. because the distortion limit is violated.

Model score updates become more complex and slower as the number of dependencies of a model increases. While our decoding algorithm does not impose any formal restrictions on the number or type of dependencies that can be handled, there will be practical limits beyond which decoding becomes unacceptably slow or the scoring code becomes very difficult to maintain. These limits are however fairly independent of the types of dependencies handled by a model, which permits the exploration of more varied model types than those handled by DP search.

2.4 State Initialisation

Before the hill climbing decoding algorithm can be run, an initial state must be generated. The closer the initial state is to an optimum, the less work remains to be done for the algorithm. If the algorithm is to be self-contained, initialisation must be relatively uninformed and can only rely on some general prior assumptions about what might be a good initial guess. On the other hand, if optimal results are sought after, it pays off to invest some effort into a good starting point. One way to do this is to run DP search first.

For uninformed initialisation, we chose to implement a very simple procedure based only on the observation that, at least for language pairs involving the major European languages, it is usually a good guess to keep the word order of the output very similar to that of the input. We therefore create the initial state by selecting, for each sentence in the document, a sequence of anchored phrase pairs covering the input sentence in monotonic order, that is, such that for all pairs of adjacent anchored phrase pairs A_j and A_{j+1}, we have that $C(A_j) \prec C(A_{j+1})$.

For initialisation with DP search, we first run the Moses decoder (Koehn et al., 2007) with default search parameters and the same models as those used by our decoder. Then we extract the best output hypothesis from the search graph of the decoder and map it into a sequence of anchored phrase pairs in the obvious way. When the document-level decoder is used with models that are incompatible with beam search, Moses can be run with a subset of the models in order to find an approximation of the solution which is then refined with the complete feature set.

3 State Operations

Given a document state S, the decoder uses a neighbourhood function `Neighbour` to simulate a move in the state space. The neighbourhood function non-deterministically selects a type of state operation and a location in the document to apply it to and returns the resulting new state. We use a set of three operations that has the property that every possible document state can be reached from every other state in a sequence of moves.

Designing operations for state transitions in local search for phrase-based SMT is a problem that has been addressed in the literature (Langlais et al., 2007; Arun et al., 2010). Our decoder's first-choice hill climbing strategy never enumerates the full neighbourhood of a state. We therefore place less emphasis than previous work on defining a compact neighbourhood, but allow the decoder to make quite extensive changes to a state in a single step with a certain probability. Otherwise our operations are similar to those used by Arun et al. (2010).

All of the operations described in this paper make changes to a single sentence only. Each time it is called, the `Neighbour` function selects a sentence in the document with a probability proportional to the number of input tokens in each sentence to ensure a fair distribution of the decoder's attention over the words in the document regardless of varying sentence lengths.

3.1 Changing Phrase Translations

The `change-phrase-translation` operation replaces the translation of a single phrase with a random translation with the same coverage taken from the phrase table. Formally, the operation selects an anchored phrase pair A_j by drawing uniformly from the elements of S_i and then draws a new translation ϕ' uniformly from the set $\Phi_i(C(A_j))$. The new state is given by

$$S_i : A_j \longrightarrow \langle C(A_j), \phi' \rangle. \qquad (11)$$

3.2 Changing Word Order

The `swap-phrases` operation affects the output word order without changing the phrase translations.

It exchanges two anchored phrase pairs A_j and A_{j+h}, resulting in an output state of

$$S_i : A_j \dots A_{j+h} \longrightarrow A_{j+h}\, A_{j+1} \dots A_{j+h-1}\, A_j. \quad (12)$$

The start location j is drawn uniformly from the eligible sentence positions; the swap range h comes from a geometric distribution with configurable decay. Other word-order changes such as a one-way move operation that does not require another movement in exchange or more advanced permutations can easily be defined.

3.3 Resegmentation

The most complex operation is `resegment`, which allows the decoder to modify the segmentation of the source phrase. It takes a number of anchored phrase pairs that form a contiguous block both in the input and in the output and replaces them with a new set of phrase pairs covering the same span of the input sentence. Formally,

$$S_i : A_j \dots A_{j+h-1} \longrightarrow A'_1 \dots A'_{h'} \quad (13)$$

such that

$$\bigcup_{j'=j}^{j+h-1} C(A_{j'}) = \bigcup_{j'=1}^{h'} C(A'_{j'}) = [p;q] \quad (14)$$

for some p and q, where, for $j' = 1,\dots,h'$, we have that $A'_{j'} = \langle [p_{j'};q_{j'}], \phi_{j'} \rangle$, all $[p_{j'};q_{j'}]$ are mutually disjoint and each $\phi_{j'}$ is randomly drawn from $\Phi_i([p_{j'};q_{j'}])$.

Regardless of the ordering of $A_j \dots A_{j+h-1}$, the `resegment` operation always generates a sequence of anchored phrase pairs in linear order, such that $C(A'_{j'}) \prec C(A'_{j'+1})$ for $j' = 1,\dots,h'-1$.

As for the other operations, j is generated uniformly and h is drawn from a geometric distribution with a decay parameter. The new segmentation is generated by extending the sequence of anchored phrase pairs with random elements starting at the next free position, proceeding from left to right until the whole range $[p;q]$ is covered.

4 Experimental Results

In this section, we present the results of a series of experiments with our document decoder. The goal of our experiments is to demonstrate the behaviour of the decoder and characterise its response to changes in the fundamental search parameters.

The SMT models for our experiments were created with a subset of the training data for the English-French shared task at the WMT 2011 workshop (Callison-Burch et al., 2011). The phrase table was trained on Europarl, news-commentary and UN data. To reduce the training data to a manageable size, singleton phrase pairs were removed before the phrase scoring step. Significance-based filtering (Johnson et al., 2007) was applied to the resulting phrase table. The language model was a 5-gram model with Kneser-Ney smoothing trained on the monolingual News corpus with IRSTLM (Federico et al., 2008). Feature weights were trained with Minimum Error-Rate Training (MERT) (Och, 2003) on the news-test2008 development set using the DP beam search decoder and the MERT implementation of the Moses toolkit (Koehn et al., 2007). Experimental results are reported for the newstest2009 test set, a corpus of 111 newswire documents totalling 2,525 sentences or 65,595 English input tokens.

4.1 Stability

An important difference between our decoder and the classical DP decoder as well as previous work in SMT decoding with local search is that our decoder is inherently non-deterministic. This implies that repeated runs of the decoder with the same search parameters, input and models will not, in general, find the same local maximum of the score space. The first empirical question we ask is therefore how different the results are under repeated runs. The results in this and the next section were obtained with random state initialisation, i. e. without running the DP beam search decoder.

Figure 1 shows the results of 7 decoder runs with the models described above, translating the newstest2009 test set, with a step limit of 2^{27} and a rejection limit of 100,000. The x-axis of both plots shows the number of decoding steps on a logarithmic scale, so the number of steps is doubled between two adjacent points on the same curve. In the left plot, the y-axis indicates the model score optimised by the decoder summed over all 2525 sentences of the document. In the right plot, the case-sensitive BLEU score (Papineni et al., 2002) of the current decoder

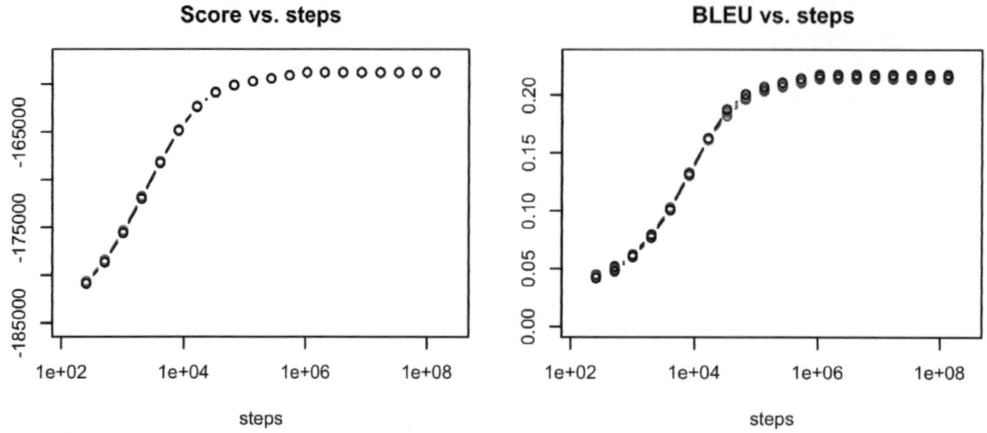

Figure 1: Score stability in repeated decoder runs

state against a reference translation is displayed.

We note, as expected, that the decoder achieves a considerable improvement of the initial state with diminishing returns as decoding continues. Between 2^8 and 2^{14} steps, the score increases at a roughly logarithmic pace, then the curve flattens out, which is partly due to the fact that decoding for some documents effectively stopped when the maximum number of rejections was reached. The BLEU score curve shows a similar increase, from an initial score below 5 % to a maximum of around 21.5 %. This is below the score of 22.45 % achieved by the beam search decoder with the same models, which is not surprising considering that our decoder approximates a more difficult search problem, from which a number of strong independence assumptions have been lifted, without, at the moment, having any stronger models at its disposal to exploit this additional freedom for better translation.

In terms of stability, there are no dramatic differences between the decoder runs. Indeed, the small differences that exist are hardly discernible in the plots. The model scores at the end of the decoding run range between -158767.9 and -158716.9, a relative difference of only about 0.03 %. Final BLEU scores range from 21.41 % to 21.63 %, an interval that is not negligible, but comparable to the variance observed when, e. g., feature weights from repeated MERT runs are used with one and the same SMT system. Note that these results were obtained with random state initialisation. With DP initialisation, score differences between repeated runs rarely exceed 0.02 absolute BLEU percentage points.

Overall, we conclude that the decoding results of our algorithm are reasonably stable despite the non-determinism inherent in the procedure. In our subsequent experiments, the evaluation scores reported are calculated as the mean of three runs for each experiment.

4.2 Search Algorithm Parameters

The hill climbing algorithm we use has two parameters which govern the trade-off between decoding time and the accuracy with which a local maximum is identified: The *step limit* stops the search process after a certain number of steps regardless of the search progress made or lack thereof. The *rejection limit* stops the search after a certain number of unsuccessful attempts to make a step, when continued search does not seem to be promising. In most of our experiments, we used a step limit of $2^{27} \approx 1.3 \cdot 10^8$ and a rejection limit of 10^5. In practice, decoding terminates by reaching the rejection limit for the vast majority of documents. We therefore examined the effect of different rejection limits on the learning curves. The results are shown in figure 2.

The results show that continued search does pay off to a certain extent. Indeed, the curve for rejection limit 10^7 seems to indicate that the model score increases roughly logarithmically, albeit to a higher base, even after the curve has started to flatten out at 2^{14} steps. At a certain point, however, the probability of finding a good successor state drops rather sharply by about two orders of magnitude, as

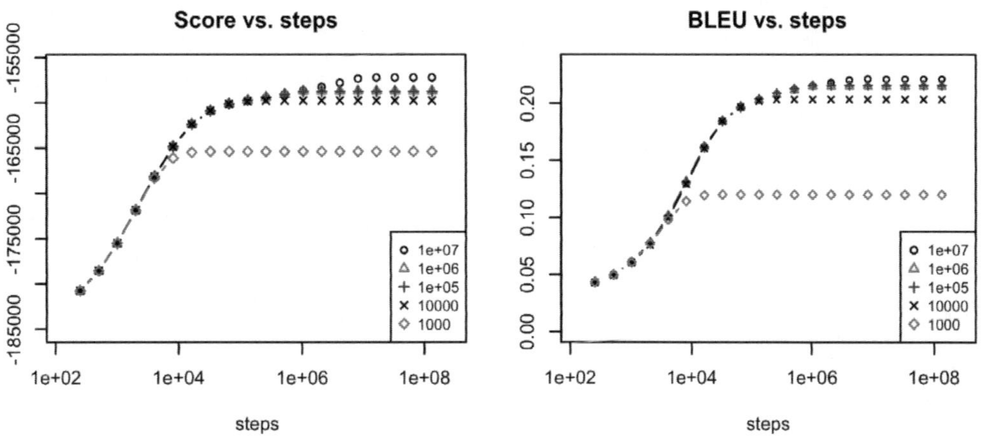

Figure 2: Search performance at different rejection limits

evidenced by the fact that a rejection limit of 10^6 does not give a large improvement over one of 10^5, while one of 10^7 does. The continued model score improvement also results in an increase in BLEU scores, and with a BLEU score of 22.1 % the system with rejection limit 10^7 is fairly close to the score of 22.45 % obtained by DP beam search.

Obviously, more exact search comes at a cost, and in this case, it comes at a considerable cost, which is an explosion of the time required to decode the test set from 4 minutes at rejection limit 10^3 to 224 minutes at rejection limit 10^5 and 38 hours 45 minutes at limit 10^7. The DP decoder takes 31 minutes for the same task. We conclude that the rejection limit of 10^5 selected for our experiments, while technically suboptimal, realises a good trade-off between decoding time and accuracy.

4.3 A Semantic Document Language Model

In this section, we present the results of the application of our decoder to an actual SMT model with cross-sentence features. Our model addresses the problem of *lexical cohesion*. In particular, it rewards the use of semantically related words in the translation output by the decoder, where semantic distance is measured with a word space model based on Latent Semantic Analysis (LSA). LSA has been applied to semantic language modelling in previous research with some success (Coccaro and Jurafsky, 1998; Bellegarda, 2000; Wandmacher and Antoine, 2007). In SMT, it has mostly been used for domain adaptation (Kim and Khudanpur, 2004; Tam et al., 2007), or to measure sentence similarities (Banchs and Costa-jussà, 2011).

The model we use is inspired by Bellegarda (2000). It is a Markov model, similar to a standard n-gram model, and assigns to each content word a score given a history of n preceding content words, where $n = 30$ below. Scoring relies on a 30-dimensional LSA word vector space trained with the S-Space software (Jurgens and Stevens, 2010). The score is defined based on the cosine similarity between the word vector of the predicted word and the mean word vector of the words in the history, which is converted to a probability by histogram lookup as suggested by Bellegarda (2000). The model is structurally different from a regular n-gram model in that word vector n-grams are defined over content words occurring in the word vector model only and can cross sentence boundaries. Stop words, identified by an extensive stop word list and amounting to around 60 % of the tokens, are scored by a different mechanism based on their relative frequency (undiscounted unigram probability) in the training corpus. In sum, the score produced by the semantic document LM has the following form:

$$h(w|h) = \begin{cases} p_{\text{unigr}}(w) & \text{if } w \text{ is a stop word, else} \\ \alpha p_{\cos}(w|h) & \text{if } w \text{ is known, else} \\ \varepsilon & \text{if } w \text{ is unknown,} \end{cases} \quad (15)$$

where α is the proportion of content words in the training corpus and ε is a small fixed probability. It is integrated into the decoder as an extra feature function. Since we lack an automatic method for training the feature weights of document-wide features, its weight was selected by grid search over a number of values, comparing translation performance for the newstest2009 test set.

In these experiments, we used DP beam search to initialise the state of our local search decoder. Three results are presented (table 1): The first table row shows the baseline performance using DP beam search with standard sentence-local features only. The scores in the second row were obtained by running the hill climbing decoder with DP initialisation, but without adding any models. A marginal increase in scores for all three test sets demonstrates that the hill climbing decoder manages to fix some of the search errors made by the DP search. The last row contains the scores obtained by adding in the semantic language model. Scores are presented for three publicly available test sets from recent WMT Machine Translation shared tasks, of which one (newstest2009) was used to monitor progress during development and select the final model.

Adding the semantic language model results in a small increase in NIST scores (Doddington, 2002) for all three test sets as well as a small BLEU score gain (Papineni et al., 2002) for two out of three corpora. We note that the NIST score turned out to react more sensitively to improvements due to the semantic LM in all our experiments, which is reasonable because the model specifically targets content words, which benefit from the information weighting done by the NIST score. While the results we present do not constitute compelling evidence in favour of our semantic LM in its current form, they do suggest that this model could be improved to realise higher gains from cross-sentence semantic information. They support our claim that cross-sentence models should be examined more closely and that existing methods should be adapted to deal with them, a problem addressed by our main contribution, the local search document decoder.

5 Related Work

Even though DP beam search (Koehn et al., 2003) has been the dominant approach to SMT decoding in recent years, methods based on local search have been explored at various times. For word-based SMT, greedy hill-climbing techniques were advocated as a faster replacement for beam search (Germann et al., 2001; Germann, 2003; Germann et al., 2004), and a problem formulation specifically targeting word reordering with an efficient word reordering algorithm has been proposed (Eisner and Tromble, 2006).

A local search decoder has been advanced as a faster alternative to beam search also for phrase-based SMT (Langlais et al., 2007; Langlais et al., 2008). That work anticipates many of the features found in our decoder, including the use of local search to refine an initial hypothesis produced by DP beam search. The possibility of using models that do not fit well into the beam search paradigm is mentioned and illustrated with the example of a reversed n-gram language model, which the authors claim would be difficult to implement in a beam search decoder. Similarly to the work by Germann et al. (2001), their decoder is deterministic and explores the entire neighbourhood of a state in order to identify the most promising step. Our main contribution with respect to the work by Langlais et al. (2007) is the introduction of the possibility of handling document-level models by lifting the assumption of sentence independence. As a consequence, enumerating the entire neighbourhood becomes too expensive, which is why we resort to a "first-choice" strategy that non-deterministically generates states and accepts the first one encountered that meets the acceptance criterion.

More recently, Gibbs sampling was proposed as a way to generate samples from the posterior distribution of a phrase-based SMT decoder (Arun et al., 2009; Arun et al., 2010), a process that resembles local search in its use of a set of state-modifying operators to generate a sequence of decoder states. Where local search seeks for the best state attainable from a given initial state, Gibbs sampling produces a representative sample from the posterior. Like all work on SMT decoding that we know of, the Gibbs sampler presented by Arun et al. (2010) assumes independence of sentences and considers the complete neighbourhood of each state before taking a sample.

6 Conclusion

In the last twenty years of SMT research, there has been a strong assumption that sentences in a text

	newstest2009		newstest2010		newstest2011	
	BLEU	NIST	BLEU	NIST	BLEU	NIST
DP search only	22.56	6.513	27.27	7.034	24.94	7.170
DP + hill climbing	22.60	6.518	27.33	7.046	24.97	7.169
with semantic LM	22.71	6.549	27.53	7.087	24.90	7.199

Table 1: Experimental results with a cross-sentence semantic language model

are independent of one another, and discourse context has been largely neglected. Several factors have contributed to this. Developing good discourse-level models is difficult, and considering the modest translation quality that has long been achieved by SMT, there have been more pressing problems to solve and lower hanging fruit to pick. However, we argue that the popular DP beam search algorithm, which delivers excellent decoding performance, but imposes a particular kind of local dependency structure on the feature models, has also had its share in driving researchers away from discourse-level problems.

In this paper, we have presented a decoding procedure for phrase-based SMT that makes it possible to define feature models with cross-sentence dependencies. Our algorithm can be combined with DP beam search to leverage the quality of the traditional approach with increased flexibility for models at the discourse level. We have presented preliminary results on a cross-sentence semantic language model addressing the problem of lexical cohesion to demonstrate that this kind of models is worth exploring further. Besides lexical cohesion, cross-sentence models are relevant for other linguistic phenomena such as pronominal anaphora or verb tense selection. We believe that SMT research has reached a point of maturity where discourse phenomena should not be ignored any longer, and we consider our decoder to be a step towards this goal.

References

Abhishek Arun, Chris Dyer, Barry Haddow, Phil Blunsom, Adam Lopez, and Philipp Koehn. 2009. Monte carlo inference and maximization for phrase-based translation. In *Proceedings of the Thirteenth Conference on Computational Natural Language Learning (CoNLL-2009)*, pages 102–110, Boulder, Colorado, June. Association for Computational Linguistics.

Abhishek Arun, Barry Haddow, Philipp Koehn, Adam Lopez, Chris Dyer, and Phil Blunsom. 2010. Monte Carlo techniques for phrase-based translation. *Machine translation*, 24(2):103–121.

Rafael E. Banchs and Marta R. Costa-jussà. 2011. A semantic feature for Statistical Machine Translation. In *Proceedings of Fifth Workshop on Syntax, Semantics and Structure in Statistical Translation*, pages 126–134, Portland, Oregon, USA, June. Association for Computational Linguistics.

Jerome R. Bellegarda. 2000. Exploiting latent semantic information in statistical language modeling. *Proceedings of the IEEE*, 88(8):1279–1296.

Chris Callison-Burch, Philipp Koehn, Christof Monz, and Omar Zaidan. 2011. Findings of the 2011 Workshop on Statistical Machine Translation. In *Proceedings of the Sixth Workshop on Statistical Machine Translation*, pages 22–64, Edinburgh, Scotland, July. Association for Computational Linguistics.

Noah Coccaro and Daniel Jurafsky. 1998. Towards better integration of semantic predictors in statistical language modeling. In *Proceedings of the 5th International Conference on Spoken Language Processing*, Sydney.

George Doddington. 2002. Automatic evaluation of machine translation quality using *n*-gram co-occurrence statistics. In *Proceedings of the second International conference on Human Language Technology Research*, pages 138–145, San Diego.

Jason Eisner and Roy W. Tromble. 2006. Local search with very large-scale neighborhoods for optimal permutations in machine translation. In *Proceedings of the HLT-NAACL Workshop on Computationally Hard Problems and Joint Inference in Speech and Language Processing*, pages 57–75.

Marcello Federico, Nicola Bertoldi, and Mauro Cettolo. 2008. IRSTLM: an open source toolkit for handling large scale language models. In *Interspeech 2008*, pages 1618–1621. ISCA.

Ulrich Germann, Michael Jahr, Kevin Knight, Daniel Marcu, and Kenji Yamada. 2001. Fast decoding and optimal decoding for machine translation. In *Proceedings of 39th Annual Meeting of the Association for Computational Linguistics*, pages 228–235, Toulouse, France, July. Association for Computational Linguistics.

Ulrich Germann, Michael Jahr, Kevin Knight, Daniel Marcu, and Kenji Yamada. 2004. Fast and optimal decoding for machine translation. *Artificial Intelligence*, 154(1–2):127–143.

Ulrich Germann. 2003. Greedy decoding for Statistical Machine Translation in almost linear time. In *Proceedings of the 2003 Human Language Technology Conference of the North American Chapter of the Association for Computational Linguistics*.

Zhengxian Gong, Min Zhang, and Guodong Zhou. 2011. Cache-based document-level Statistical Machine Translation. In *Proceedings of the 2011 Conference on Empirical Methods in Natural Language Processing*, pages 909–919, Edinburgh, Scotland, UK., July. Association for Computational Linguistics.

Christian Hardmeier and Marcello Federico. 2010. Modelling Pronominal Anaphora in Statistical Machine Translation. In *Proceedings of the seventh International Workshop on Spoken Language Translation (IWSLT)*, pages 283–289.

Basil Hatim and Ian Mason. 1990. *Discourse and the Translator*. Language in Social Life Series. Longman, London.

Kenneth Heafield. 2011. KenLM: faster and smaller language model queries. In *Proceedings of the Sixth Workshop on Statistical Machine Translation*, pages 187–197, Edinburgh, Scotland, July. Association for Computational Linguistics.

Howard Johnson, Joel Martin, George Foster, and Roland Kuhn. 2007. Improving translation quality by discarding most of the phrasetable. In *Proceedings of the 2007 Joint Conference on Empirical Methods in Natural Language Processing and Computational Natural Language Learning (EMNLP-CoNLL)*, pages 967–975, Prague, Czech Republic, June. Association for Computational Linguistics.

David Jurgens and Keith Stevens. 2010. The S-Space package: An open source package for word space models. In *Proceedings of the ACL 2010 System Demonstrations*, pages 30–35, Uppsala, Sweden, July. Association for Computational Linguistics.

Woosung Kim and Sanjeev Khudanpur. 2004. Cross-lingual latent semantic analysis for language modeling. In *IEEE international conference on acoustics, speech, and signal processing (ICASSP)*, volume 1, pages 257–260, Montréal.

Philipp Koehn, Franz Josef Och, and Daniel Marcu. 2003. Statistical phrase-based translation. In *Proceedings of the 2003 conference of the North American chapter of the Association for Computational Linguistics on Human Language Technology*, pages 48–54, Edmonton.

Philipp Koehn, Hieu Hoang, Alexandra Birch, et al. 2007. Moses: open source toolkit for Statistical Machine Translation. In *Annual meeting of the Association for Computational Linguistics: Demonstration session*, pages 177–180, Prague.

Philippe Langlais, Alexandre Patry, and Fabrizio Gotti. 2007. A greedy decoder for phrase-based statistical machine translation. In *TMI-2007: Proceedings of the 11th International Conference on Theoretical and Methodological Issues in Machine Translation*, pages 104–113, Skövde.

Philippe Langlais, Alexandre Patry, and Fabrizio Gotti. 2008. Recherche locale pour la traduction statistique par segments. In *TALN 2008*, pages 119–128, Avignon, France, June. ATALA.

Ronan Le Nagard and Philipp Koehn. 2010. Aiding pronoun translation with co-reference resolution. In *Proceedings of the Joint Fifth Workshop on Statistical Machine Translation and MetricsMATR*, pages 252–261, Uppsala, Sweden, July. Association for Computational Linguistics.

Franz Josef Och, Nicola Ueffing, and Hermann Ney. 2001. An efficient A* search algorithm for Statistical Machine Translation. In *Proceedings of the Data-Driven Machine Translation Workshop, 39th Annual Meeting of the Association for Computational Linguistics (ACL)*, pages 55–62, Toulouse.

Franz Josef Och. 2003. Minimum error rate training in Statistical Machine Translation. In *Proceedings of the 41st annual meeting of the Association for Computational Linguistics*, pages 160–167, Sapporo (Japan).

Kishore Papineni, Salim Roukos, Todd Ward, and Wei-Jing Zhu. 2002. BLEU: a method for automatic evaluation of Machine Translation. In *Proceedings of the 40th annual meeting of the Association for Computational Linguistics*, pages 311–318, Philadelphia. ACL.

Yik-Cheung Tam, Ian Lane, and Tanja Schultz. 2007. Bilingual LSA-based adaptation for Statistical Machine Translation. *Machine Translation*, 21(4):187–207.

Jörg Tiedemann. 2010. To cache or not to cache? Experiments with adaptive models in Statistical Machine Translation. In *Proceedings of the ACL 2010 Joint Fifth Workshop on Statistical Machine Translation and Metrics MATR*, pages 189–194, Uppsala, Sweden. Association for Computational Linguistics.

Christoph Tillmann and Hermann Ney. 2003. Word reordering and a Dynamic Programming beam search algorithm for Statistical Machine Translation. *Computational linguistics*, 29(1):97–133.

Christoph Tillmann, Stephan Vogel, Hermann Ney, and Alex Zubiaga. 1997. A DP-based search using monotone alignments in Statistical Translation. In *Proceedings of the 35th Annual Meeting of the Association for*

Computational Linguistics, pages 289–296, Madrid, Spain, July. Association for Computational Linguistics.

Tonio Wandmacher and Jean-Yves Antoine. 2007. Methods to integrate a language model with semantic information for a word prediction component. In *Proceedings of the 2007 Joint Conference on Empirical Methods in Natural Language Processing and Computational Natural Language Learning (EMNLP-CoNLL)*, pages 506–513, Prague, Czech Republic, June. Association for Computational Linguistics.

Left-to-Right Tree-to-String Decoding with Prediction

Yang Feng[†] **Yang Liu**[‡] **Qun Liu**[⋆] **Trevor Cohn**[†]

[†] Department of Computer Science
The University of Sheffield, Sheffield, UK
{y.feng, t.cohn}@sheffield.ac.uk

[‡] State Key Laboratory on Intelligent Technology and Systems
Tsinghua National Laboratory for Information Science and Technology
Department of Computer Sci. and Tech., Tsinghua University, Beijing, China
liuyang2011@tsinghua.edu.cn

[⋆]Key Laboratory of Intelligent Information Processing
Institute of Computing Technology
Chinese Academy of Sciences, Beijing, China
liuqun@ict.ac.cn

Abstract

Decoding algorithms for syntax based machine translation suffer from high computational complexity, a consequence of intersecting a language model with a context free grammar. Left-to-right decoding, which generates the target string in order, can improve decoding efficiency by simplifying the language model evaluation. This paper presents a novel left to right decoding algorithm for tree-to-string translation, using a bottom-up parsing strategy and dynamic future cost estimation for each partial translation. Our method outperforms previously published tree-to-string decoders, including a competing left-to-right method.

1 Introduction

In recent years there has been rapid progress in the development of tree-to-string models for statistical machine translation. These models use the syntactic parse tree of the source language to inform its translation, which allows the models to capture consistent syntactic transformations between the source and target languages, e.g., from subject-verb-object to subject-object-verb word orderings. Decoding algorithms for grammar-based translation seek to find the best string in the intersection between a weighted context free grammar (the translation mode, given a source string/tree) and a weighted finite state acceptor (an n-gram language model). This intersection is problematic, as it results in an intractably large grammar, and makes exact search impossible.

Most researchers have resorted to approximate search, typically beam search (Chiang, 2007). The decoder parses the source sentence, recording the target translations for each span.[1] As the partial translation hypothesis grows, its component ngrams are scored and the hypothesis score is updated. This decoding method though is inefficient as it requires recording the language model context ($n-1$ words) on the left and right edges of each chart cell. These contexts allow for boundary ngrams to be evaluated when the cell is used in another grammar production. In contrast, if the target string is generated in left-to-right order, then only one language model context is required, and the problem of language model evaluation is vastly simplified.

In this paper, we develop a novel method of left-to-right decoding for tree-to-string translation using a shift-reduce parsing strategy. A central issue in any decoding algorithm is the technique used for pruning the search space. Our left-to-right decoding algorithm groups hypotheses, which cover the same number of source words, into a bin. Pruning requires the evaluation of different hypotheses in the same bin, and elimating the least promising options. As each hypotheses may cover different sets of tree

[1]The process is analogous for tree-to-string models, except that only rules and spans matching those in the source trees are considered. Typically nodes are visited according to a post-order traversal.

nodes, it is necessary to consider the cost of uncovered nodes, i.e., the *future cost*. We show that a good future cost estimate is essential for accurate and efficient search, leading to high quality translation output.

Other researchers have also considered the left-to-right decoding algorithm for tree-to-string models. Huang and Mi (2010) developed an Earley-style parsing algorithm (Earley, 1970). In their approach, hypotheses covering the same number of tree nodes were binned together. Their method uses a top-down depth-first search, with a mechanism for early elimation of some rules which lead to dead-ends in the search. Huang and Mi (2010)'s method was shown to outperform the traditional post-order-traversal decoding algorithm, considering fewer hypotheses and thus decoding much faster at the same level of performance. However their algorithm used a very rough estimate of future cost, resulting in more search errors than our approach.

Our experiments show that compared with the Earley-style left-to-right decoding (Huang and Mi, 2010) and the traditional post-order-traversal decoding (Liu et al., 2006) algorithms, our algorithm achieves a significant improvement on search capacity and better translation performance at the same level of speed.

2 Background

A typical tree-to-string system (Liu et al., 2006; Huang et al., 2006) searches through a 1-best source parse tree for the best derivation. It transduces the source tree into a target-language string using a Synchronous Tree Substitution Grammar (STSG). The grammar rules are extracted from bilingual word alignments using the GHKM algorithm (Galley et al., 2004).

We will briefly review the traditional decoding algorithm (Liu et al., 2006) and the Earley-style top-down decoding algorithm (Huang and Mi, 2010) for the tree-to-string model.

2.1 Traditional Decoding

The traditional decoding algorithm processes source tree nodes one by one according to a post-order traversal. For each node, it applies matched STSG rules by substituting each non-terminal with its corresponding translation. For the derivation in Figure 1 (b), the traditional algorithm applies r_2 at node NN_2

$$r_2 : \text{NN}_2\ (jieguo) \rightarrow the\ result,$$

to obtain "the result" as the translation of NN_2. Next it applies r_4 at node NP,

$$r_4 : \text{NP}\ (\ \text{NN}_1\ (toupiao),\ x_1 : \text{NN}_2\ ) \rightarrow x_1\ of\ the\ vote$$

and replaces NN_2 with its translation "the result", then it gets the translation of NP as "the result of the vote".

This algorithm needs to contain boundary words at both left and right extremities of the target string for the purpose of LM evaluation, which leads to a high time complexity. The time complexity in theory and with beam search (Huang and Mi, 2010) is shown in Table 1.

	in theory	beam search
traditional	$O(nc\|V\|^{4(g-1)})$	$O(ncb^2)$
top-down	$O(c(cr)^d\|V\|^{g-1})$	$O(ncb)$
bottom-up	$O((cr)^d\|V\|^{g-1})$	$O(nub)$

Table 1: Time complexity of different algorithms. *traditional* : Liu et al. (2006), *top-down* : Huang and Mi (2010). n is the source sentence length, b is the beam width, c is the number of rules used for each node, V is the target word vocabulary, g is the order of the language model, d is the depth of the source parse tree, u is the number of viable prefixes for each node and r is the maximum arity of each rule.

2.2 Earley-style Top-down Decoding

The Earley-style decoding algorithm performs a top-down depth-first parsing and generates the target translation left to right. It applies Context-Free Grammar (CFG) rules and employs three actions: *predict*, *scan* and *complete* (Section 3.1 describes how to convert STSG rules into CFG rules). We can simulate its translation process using a stack with a dot **.** indicating which symbol to process next. For the derivation in Figure 1(b) and CFG rules in Figure 1(c), Figure 2 illustrates the whole translation process.

The time complexity is shown in Table 1 .

3 Bottom-Up Left-to-Right Decoding

We propose a novel method of left-to-right decoding for tree-to-string translation using a bottom-up parsing strategy. We use **viable prefixes** (Aho and Johnson, 1974) to indicate all possible target strings the translations of each node should starts with. Therefore, given a tree node to expand, our algorithm can drop immediately to target terminals no matter whether there is a **gap** or not. We say that there is a gap between two symbols in a derivation when there are many rules separating them, e.g. IP $\stackrel{r_6}{\rightarrow}$ ... $\stackrel{r_4}{\rightarrow}$ NN$_2$. For the derivation in Figure 1(b), our algorithm starts from the root node IP and applies r_2 first although there is a gap between IP and NN$_2$. Then it applies r_4, r_5 and r_6 in sequence to generate the translation "the result of the vote was released at night". Our algorithm takes the gap as a black-box and does not need to fix which partial derivation should be used for the gap at the moment. So it can get target strings as soon as possible and thereby perform more accurate pruning. A valid derivation is generated only when the source tree is completely matched by rules.

Our bottom-up decoding algorithm involves the following steps:

1. Match STSG rules against the source tree.
2. Convert STSG rules to CFG rules.
3. Collect the viable prefix set for each node in a post-order transversal.
4. Search bottom-up for the best derivation.

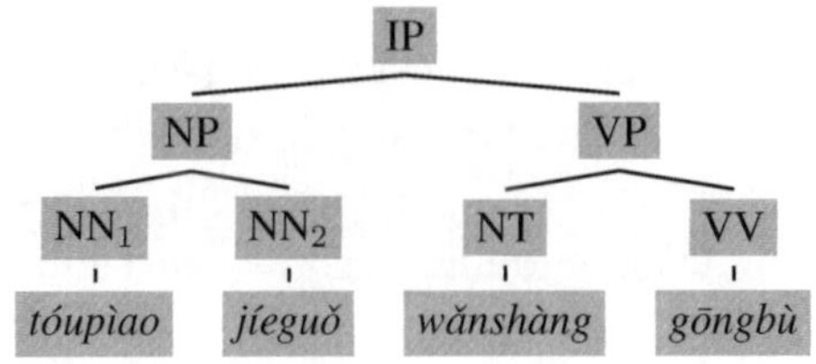

(a) Source parse tree

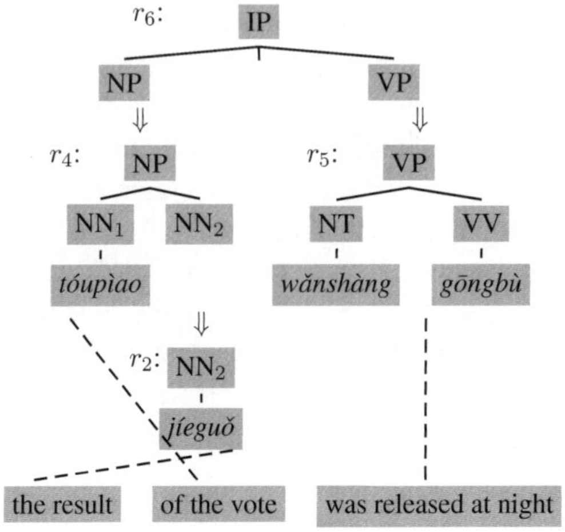

(b) A derivation

r_1:	NN$_1$ → *the vote*
r_2:	NN$_2$ → *the result*
r_3:	NP → NN$_2$ *of* NN$_1$
r_4:	NP → NN$_2$ *of the vote*
r_5:	VP → *was released at night*
r_6:	IP → NP VP
r_7:	IP → NN$_2$ of the vote VP
r_8:	IP → VP NP

(c) Target-side CFG rule set

Figure 1: A toy example.

3.1 From STSG to CFG

After rule matching, each tree node has its applicable STSG rule set. Given a matched STSG rule, our decoding algorithm only needs to consider the tree node the rule can be applied to and the target side, so we follow Huang and Mi (2010) to convert STSG rules to CFG rules. For example, an STSG rule

NP (NN$_1$ $(toupiao)$, x_1 : NN$_2$) $\rightarrow x_1$ $of\ the\ vote$

can be converted to a CFG rule

$$\text{NP} \rightarrow \text{NN}_2\ of\ the\ vote$$

The target non-terminals are replaced with corresponding source non-terminals. Figure 1 (c) shows all converted CFG rules for the toy example. Note that different STSG rules might be converted to the same CFG rule despite having different source tree structures.

3.2 Viable Prefix

During decoding, how do we decide which rules should be used next given a partial derivation, especially when there is a gap? A key observation is that some rules should be excluded. For example, any derivation for Figure 1(a) will never begin with r_1 as there is no translation starting with "the vote". In order to know which rules can be excluded for each node, we can recursively calculate the starting terminal strings for each node. For example,

NN_1:	{the vote}	NN_2:	{the result}
NT:	$\emptyset$	VV:	$\emptyset$
NP:	{the result}		
VP:	{was released at night}		
IP:	{the result, was released at night}		

Table 2: The Viable prefix sets for Figure 1 (c)

according to r_1, the starting terminal string of the translation for NN_1 is "the vote". According to r_2, the starting terminal string for NN_2 is "the result". According to r_3, the starting terminal string of NP must include that of NN_2. Table 2 lists the starting terminal strings of all nodes in Figure 1(a). As the translations of node IP should begin with either "the result" or "was released at night", the first rule must be either r_2 or r_5. Therefore, r_1 will never be used as the first rule in any derivation.

We refer to starting terminal strings of a node as a **viable prefixes**, a term borrowed from LR parsing (Aho and Johnson, 1974). Viable prefixes are used to decide which rule should be used to ensure efficient left-to-right target generation. Formally, assume that V_N denotes the set of non-terminals (i.e., source tree node labels), V_T denotes the set of terminals (i.e., target words), $v_1, v_2 \in V_N$, $w \in V_T$, $\pi \in \{V_T \cup V_N\}^*$, we say that w is a viable prefix of v_1 if and only if:

- $v_1 \rightarrow w$, or
- $v_1 \rightarrow w v_2 \pi$, or
- $v_1 \rightarrow v_2 \pi$, and w is a viable prefix of v_2.

Note that we bundle all successive terminals in one symbol.

3.3 Shift-Reduce Parsing

We use a shift-reduce algorithm to search for the best deviation. The algorithm maintains a stack of dotted rules (Earley, 1970). Given the source tree in Figure 1(a), the stack is initialized with a dotted rule for the root node IP:

[. IP].

Then, the algorithm selects one viable prefix of IP and appends it to the stack with the dot at the beginning (*predict*):

[. IP] [. the result][2].

Then, a *scan* action is performed to produce a partial translation "the result":

[. IP] [the result .].

Next, the algorithm searches for the CFG rules starting with "the result" and gets r_2. Then, it pops the rightmost dotted rule and append the left-hand side (LHS) of r_2 to the stack (*complete*):

[. IP] [NN_2 .].

Next, the algorithm chooses r_4 whose right-hand side "NN2 of the vote" matches the rightmost dotted rule in the stack[3] and *grows* the rightmost dotted rule:

[. IP] [NN_2 . of the vote].

Figure 3 shows the whole process of derivation generation.

Formally, we define four actions on the rightmost rule in the stack:

- *Predict.* If the symbol after the dot in the rightmost dotted rule is a non-terminal v, this action chooses a viable prefix w of v and generates a new dotted rule for w with the dot at the beginning. For example:

  [. IP] $\xrightarrow{predict}$ [. IP] [. the result]

- *Scan.* If the symbol after the dot in the rightmost dotted rule is a terminal string w, this action advances the dot to update the current partial translation. For example:

  [. IP] [. the result] $\xrightarrow{scan}$ [. IP] [the result .]

- *Complete.* If the rightmost dotted rule ends with a dot and it happens to be the right-hand side of a rule, then this action removes the right-most dotted rule. Besides, if the symbol after the dot in the new rightmost rule corresponds to the same tree node as the LHS non-terminal of the rule, this action advance the dot. For example,

  [. IP] [NP . VP] [was released at night .]
  $\xrightarrow{complete}$ [. IP] [NP VP .]

[2]There are another option: "was released at night"

[3]Here there is an alternative: r_3 or r_7

step	action	rule used	stack	hypothesis
0			[. IP]	
1	p	r_6	[. IP] [. NP VP]	
2	p	r_4	[. IP] [. NP VP] [. NN_2 of the vote]	
3	p	r_2	[. IP] [. NP VP] [. NN_2 of the vote] [. the result]	
4	s		[. IP] [. NP VP] [. NN_2 of the vote] [the result .]	the result
5	c		[. IP] [. NP VP] [NN_2 . of the vote]	the result
6	s		[. IP] [. NP VP] [NN_2 of the vote .]	the result of the vote
7	c		[. IP] [NP . VP]	the result of the vote
8	p	r_5	[. IP] [NP . VP] [. was released at night]	the result of the vote
9	s		[. IP] [NP . VP] [was released at night .]	the ... vote was ... night
10	c		[. IP] [NP VP .]	the ... vote was ... night
11	c		[IP .]	the ... vote was ... night

Figure 2: Simulation of top-down translation process for the derivation in Figure 1(b). Actions: p, predict; s, scan; c, complete. "the ... vote" and "was ... released" are the abbreviated form of "the result of the vote" and "was released at night", respectively.

step	action	rule used	stack	number	hypothesis
0			[. IP]	0	
1	p		[. IP] [. the result]	0	
2	s		[. IP] [the result .]	1	the result
3	c	r_2	[. IP] [NN_2 .]	1	the result
4	g	r_4 or r_7	[. IP] [NN_2 . of the vote]	1	the result
5	s		[. IP] [NN_2 of the vote .]	2	the result of the vote
6	c	r_4	[. IP] [NP .]	2	the result of the vote
7	g	r_6	[. IP] [NP . VP]	2	the result of the vote
8	p		[. IP] [NP . VP] [. was released at night]	2	the result of the vote
9	s		[. IP] [NP . VP] [was released at night .]	4	the ... vote was ... night
10	c	r_5	[. IP] [NP VP .]	4	the ... vote was ... night
11	c	r_6	[IP .]	4	the ... vote was ... night

Figure 3: Simulation of bottom-up translation process for the derivation in Figure 1(b). Actions: p, predict; s, scan; c, complete; g, grow. The column of *number* gives the number of source words the hypothesis covers.

If the string cannot rewrite on the frontier nonterminal, then we add the LHS to the stack with the dot after it. For example:

$$[.\ \text{IP}]\ [\text{the result}\ .] \xrightarrow{complete} [.\ \text{IP}]\ [\text{NN}_2\ .]$$

- *Grow.* If the right-most dotted rule ends with a dot and it happens to be the starting part of a CFG rule, this action appends one symbol of the remainder of that rule to the stack [4]. For example:

$$[.\ \text{IP}]\ [\text{NN}_2\ .] \xrightarrow{grow} [.\ \text{IP}]\ [\text{NN}_2\ .\ \text{of the vote}]$$

From the above definition, we can find that there may be an ambiguity about whether to use a complete action or a grow action. Similarly, predict actions must select a viable prefix form the set for a node. For example in step 5, although we select to perform complete with r_4 in the example, r_7 is applicable, too. In our implementation, if both r_4 and r_7 are applicable, we apply them both to generate two seperate hypotheses. To limit the exponential explosion of hypotheses (Knight, 1999), we use beam search over bins of similar partial hypotheses (Koehn, 2004).

[4] We bundle the successive terminals in one rule into a symbol

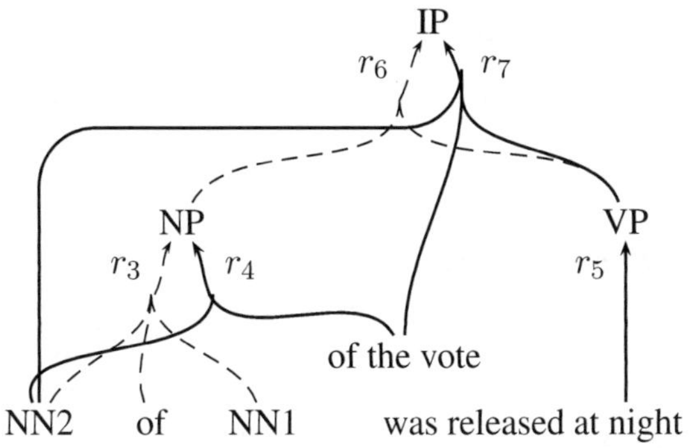

Figure 4: The translation forest composed of applicable CFG rules for the partial derivation of step 3 in Figure 3.

3.4 Future Cost

Partial derivations covering different tree nodes may be grouped in the same bin for beam pruning[5]. In order to perform more accurate pruning, we take into consideration **future cost**, the cost of the uncovered part. The **merit** of a derivation is the **covered cost** (the cost of the covered part) plus the future cost. We borrow ideas from the Inside-Outside algorithm (Charniak and Johnson, 2005; Huang, 2008; Mi et al., 2008) to compute the merit. In our algorithm, the merit of a derivation is just the Viterbi inside cost β of the root node calculated with the derivations continuing from the current derivation.

Given a partial derivation, we calculate its future cost by searching through the translation forest defined by all applicable CFG rules. Figure 4 shows the translation forest for the derivation of step 3. We calculate the future cost for each node as follows: given a node v, we define its cost function $f(v)$ as

$$f(v) = \begin{cases} 1 & v \text{ is completed} \\ lm(v) & v \text{ is a terminal string} \\ \max_{r \in \boldsymbol{R_v}} f(r) \prod_{\pi \in \text{rhs}(r)} f(\pi) & \text{otherwise} \end{cases}$$

where V_N is the non-terminal set, V_T is the terminal set, $v, \pi \in V_N \cup V_T{}^+$, R_v is the set of currently applicable rules for v, $rhs(r)$ is the right-hand symbol set of r, lm is the local language model probability, $f(r)$ is calculated using a linear model whose features are bidirectional translation probabilities and lexical probabilities of r. For the translation forest in Figure 4, if we calculate the future cost of NP with r_4, then

$$\begin{aligned} f(NP) &= f(r_4) \cdot f(NN_2) \cdot lm(of\ the\ vote) \\ &= f(r_4) \cdot 1 \cdot lm(of\ the\ vote) \end{aligned}$$

Note that we calculate lm(of the vote) locally and do not take "the result" derived from NN_2 as the context. The lm probability of "the result" has been included in the covered cost.

As a partial derivation grows, some CFG rules will conflict with the derivation (i.e. inapplicable) and the translation forest will change accordingly. For example, when we reach step 5 from step 3 (see Figure 4 for its translation forest), r_3 is inapplicable and thereby should be ruled out. Then the nodes on the path from the last covered node (it is "of the vote" in step 5) to the root node should update their future cost, as they may employ r_3 to produce the future cost. In step 5, NP and IP should be updated. In this sense, we say that the future cost is dynamic.

3.5 Comparison with Top-Down Decoding

In order to generate the translation "the result" based on the derivation in Figure 1(b), Huang and Mi's top-down algorithm needs to specify which rules to apply starting from the root node until it yields "the result". In this derivation, rule r_6 is applied to IP, r_4 to NP, r_2 to NN_2. That is to say, it needs to represent the partial derivation from IP to NN_2 explicitly. This can be a problem when combined with beam pruning. If the beam size is small, it may discard the intermediate hypotheses and thus never consider the string. In our example with a beam of 1, we must select a rule for IP among r_6, r_7 and r_8 although we do not get any information for NP and VP.

Instead, our bottom-up algorithm allows top-down and bottom-up information to be used together with the help of viable prefixes. This allows us to encode more candidate derivations than the purely top-down method. In the above example, our algorithm does not specify the derivation for the gap from IP and "the result". In fact, all derivations composed of currently applicable rules are allowed. When needed, our algorithm derives the derivation dynamically using applicable rules. So when our algorithm performs pruning at the root node, it has got much more information and consequently introduces fewer pruning errors.

[5]Section 3.7 will describe the binning scheme

3.6 Time Complexity

Assume the depth of the source tree is d, the maximum number of matched rules for each node is c, the maximum arity of each rule is r, the language model order is g and the target-language vocabulary is V, then the time complexity of our algorithm is $O((cr)^d|V|^{g-1})$. Analysis is as follows:

Our algorithm expands partial paths with terminal strings to generate new hypotheses, so the time complexity depends on the number of partial paths used. We split a path which is from the root node to a leaf node with a node on it (called the end node) and get the segment from the root node to the end node as a partial path, so the length of the partial path is not definite with a maximum of d. If the length is $d'(d' \leq d)$, then the number of partial paths is $(cr)^{d'}$. Besides, we use the rightest $g-1$ words to signature each partial path, so we can get $(cr)^{d'}|V|^{g-1}$ states. For each state, the number of viable prefixes produced by predict operation is $c^{d-d'}$, so the total time complexity is $f = O((cr)^{d'}|V|^{g-1}c^{d-d'}) = O(c^d r^{d'}|V|^{g-1}) = O((cr)^d|V|^{g-1})$.

3.7 Beam Search

To make decoding tractable, we employ beam search (Koehn, 2004) and choose "binning" as follows: hypotheses covering the same number of source words are grouped in a bin. When expanding a hypothesis in a beam (bin), we take series of actions until new terminals are appended to the hypothesis, then add the new hypothesis to the corresponding beam. Figure 3 shows the number of source words each hypothesis covers.

Among the actions, only the scan action changes the number of source words each hypothesis covers. Although the complete action does not change source word number, it changes the covered cost of hypotheses. So in our implementation, we take scan and complete as "closure" actions. That is to say, once there are some complete actions after a scan action, we finish all the compete actions until the next action is grow. The predict and grow actions decide which rules can be used to expand hypotheses next, so we update the applicable rule set during these two actions.

Given a source sentence with n words, we maintain n beams, and let each beam hold b hypotheses at most. Besides, we prune viable prefixes of each node up to u, so each hypothesis can expand to u new hypotheses at most, so the time complexity of beam search is $O(nub)$.

4 Related Work

Watanabe et al. (2006) present a novel Earley-style top-down decoding algorithm for hierarchical phrase-based model (Chiang, 2005). Their framework extracts Greibach Normal Form rules only, which always has at least one terminal on the left of each rule, and discards other rules.

Dyer and Resnik (2010) describe a translation model that combines the merits of syntax-based models and phrase-based models. Their decoder works in two passes: for first pass, the decoder collects a context-free forest and performs tree-based source reordering without a LM. For the second pass, the decoder adds a LM and performs bottom-up CKY decoding.

Feng et al. (2010) proposed a shift-reduce algorithm to add BTG constraints to phrase-based models. This algorithm constructs a BTG tree in a reduce-eager manner while the algorithm in this paper searches for a best derivation which must be derived from the source tree.

Galley and Manning (2008) use the shift-reduce algorithm to conduct hierarchical phrase reordering so as to capture long-distance reordering. This algorithm shows good performance on phrase-based models, but can not be applied to syntax-based models directly.

5 Experiments

In the experiments, we use two baseline systems: our in-house tree-to-string decoder implemented according to Liu et al. (2006) (denoted as *traditional*) and the Earley-style top-down decoder implemented according to Huang and Mi (2010) (denoted as *top-down*), respectively. We compare our bottom-up left-to-right decoder (denoted as bottom-up) with the baseline in terms of performance, translation quality and decoding speed with different beam sizes, and search capacity. Lastly, we show the influence of future cost. All systems are implemented in C++.

5.1 Data Setup

We used the FBIS corpus consisting of about 250K Chinese-English sentence pairs as the training set. We aligned the sentence pairs using the GIZA++ toolkit (Och and Ney, 2003) and extracted tree-to-string rules according to the GHKM algorithm (Galley et al., 2004). We used the SRILM toolkit (Stolcke, 2002) to train a 4-gram language model on the Xinhua portion of the GIGAWORD corpus.

We used the 2002 NIST MT Chinese-English test set (571 sentences) as the development set and the 2005 NIST MT Chinese-English test set (1082 sentences) as the test set. We evaluated translation quality using BLEU-metric (Papineni et al., 2002) with case-insensitive n-gram matching up to $n = 4$. We used the standard minimum error rate training (Och, 2003) to tune feature weights to maximize BLEU score on the development set.

5.2 Performance Comparison

Our bottom-up left-to-right decoder employs the same features as the traditional decoder: rule probability, lexical probability, language model probability, rule count and word count. In order to compare them fairly, we used the same beam size which is 20 and employed cube pruning technique (Huang and Chiang, 2005).

We show the results in Table 3. From the results, we can see that the bottom-up decoder out performs top-down decoder and traditional decoder by 1.1 and 0.8 BLEU points respectively and the improvements are statistically significant using the *sign-test* of Collins et al. (2005) ($p < 0.01$). The improvement may result from dynamically searching for a whole derivation which leads to more accurate estimation of a partial derivation. The additional time consumption of the bottom-up decoder against the top-down decoder comes from dynamic future cost computation.

Next we compare decoding speed versus translation quality using various beam sizes. The results are shown in Figure 5. We can see that our bottom-up decoder can produce better BLEU score at the same decoding speed. At small beams (decoding time around 0.5 second), the improvement of translation quality is much bigger.

System	BLEU(%)	Time (s)
Traditional	29.8	0.84
Top-down	29.5	0.41
Bottom-up	**30.6**	0.81

Table 3: Performance comparison.

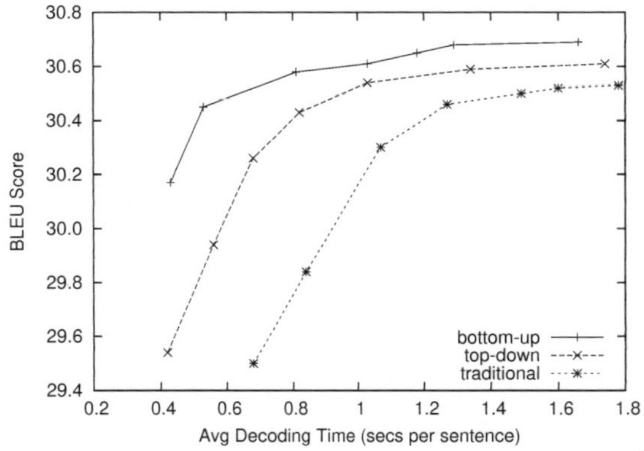

Figure 5: BLEU score against decoding time with various beam size.

5.3 Search Capacity Comparison

We also compare the search capacity of the bottom-up decoder and the traditional decoder. We do this in the following way: we let both decoders use the same weights tuned on the traditional decoder, then we compare their translation scores of the same test sentence.

From the results in Table 4, we can see that for many test sentences, the bottom-up decoder finds target translations with higher score, which have been ruled out by the traditional decoder. This may result from more accurate pruning method. Yet for some sentences, the traditional decoder can attain higher translation score. The reason may be that the traditional decoder can hold more than two nonterminals when cube pruning, while the bottom-up decoder always performs dual-arity pruning.

Next, we check whether higher translation scores bring higher BLEU scores. We compute the BLEU score of both decoders on the test sentence set on which bottom-up decoder gets higher translation scores than the traditional decoder does. We record the results in Figure 6. The result shows that higher score indeed bring higher BLEU score, but the improvement of BLEU score is not large. This is because the features we use don't reflect the real statis-

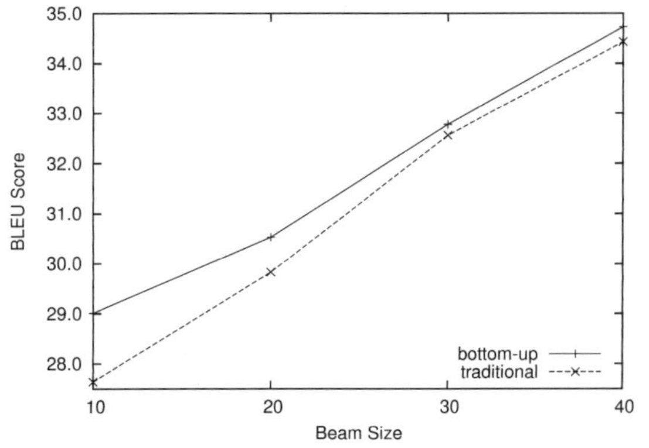

Figure 6: BLEU score with various beam sizes on the sub test set consisting of sentences on which the bottom-up decoder gets higher translation score than the traditional decoder does.

b	$>$		$=$		$<$	
10	728	67%	347	32%	7	1%
20	657	61%	412	38%	13	1%
30	615	57%	446	41%	21	2%
40	526	49%	523	48%	33	3%
50	315	29%	705	65%	62	6%

Table 4: Search capacity comparison. The first column is beam size, the following three columns denote the number of test sentences, on which the translation scores of the bottom-up decoder are greater, equal to, lower than that of the traditional decoder.

System	BLEU(%)	Time (s)
with	30.6	0.81
without	28.8	0.39

Table 5: Influence of future cost. The results of the bottom-up decoder with and without future cost are given in the second and three rows, respectively.

tical distribution of hypotheses well. In addition, the weights are tuned on the traditional decoder, not on the bottom-up decoder. The bottom-up decoder can perform better with weights tuned by itself.

5.4 Influence of Future Cost

Next, we will show the impact of future cost via experiments. We give the results of the bottom-up decoder with and without future cost in Table 5. From the result, we can conclude that future cost plays a significant role in decoding. If the bottom-up decoder does not employ future cost, its performance will be influenced dramatically. Furthermore, calculating dynamic future cost is time consuming. If the bottom-up decoder does not use future cost, it decodes faster than the top-down decoder. This is because the top-down decoder has $|T|$ beams, while the bottom-up decoder has n beams, where T is the source parse tree and n is the length of the source sentence.

6 Conclusions

In this paper, we describe a bottom-up left-to-right decoding algorithm for tree-to-string model. With the help of viable prefixes, the algorithm generates a translation by constructing a target-side CFG tree according to a post-order traversal. In addition, it takes into consideration a dynamic future cost to estimate hypotheses.

On the 2005 NIST Chinese-English MT translation test set, our decoder outperforms the top-down decoder and the traditional decoder by 1.1 and 0.8 BLEU points respectively and shows more powerful search ability. Experiments also prove that future cost is important for more accurate pruning.

7 Acknowledgements

We would like to thank Haitao Mi and Douwe Gelling for their feedback, and anonymous reviewers for their valuable comments and suggestions. This work was supported in part by EPSRC grant EP/I034750/1 and in part by High Technology R&D Program Project No. 2011AA01A207.

References

A. V. Aho and S. C. Johnson. 1974. Lr parsing. *Computing Surveys*, 6:99–124.

Eugene Charniak and Mark Johnson. 2005. Coarse-to-fine n-best parsing and maxent discriminative reranking. In *Proc. of ACL*, pages 173–180.

David Chiang. 2005. A hierarchical phrase-based model for statistical machine translation. In *Proc. of ACL*, pages 263–270.

David Chiang. 2007. Hierarchical phrase-based translation. *Computational Linguistics*, 33:201–228.

Michael Collins, Philipp Koehn, and Ivona Kucerova. 2005. Clause restructuring for statistical machine translation. In *Proc. of ACL*, pages 531–540.

Chris Dyer and Philip Resnik. 2010. Context-free reordering, finite-state translation. In *Proc. of NAACL*, pages 858–866, June.

Jay Earley. 1970. An efficient context-free parsing algorithm. *Communications of the ACM*, 13:94–102.

Yang Feng, Haitao Mi, Yang Liu, and Qun Liu. 2010. An efficient shift-reduce decoding algorithm for phrased-based machine translation. In *Proc. of Coling*, pages 285–293.

Michel Galley and Christopher D. Manning. 2008. A simple and effective hierarchical phrase reordering model. In *Proc. of EMNLP*, pages 848–856.

Michel Galley, Mark Hopkins, Kevin Knight, and Daniel Marcu. 2004. What's in a translation rule? In *Proc of NAACL*, pages 273–280.

Liang Huang and David Chiang. 2005. Better k-best parsing. In *Proc. of IWPT*, pages 53–64.

Liang Huang and Haitao Mi. 2010. Efficient incremental decoding for tree-to-string translation. In *Proc. of EMNLP*, pages 273–283.

Liang Huang, Kevin Knight, and Aravind Joshi. 2006. Statistical syntax-directed translation with extended domain of locality. In *Proceedings of AMTA*.

Liang Huang. 2008. Forest reranking: Discriminative parsing with non-local features. In *Proc. of ACL*, pages 586–594.

Kevin Knight. 1999. Decoding complexity in word-replacement translation models. *Computational Linguistics*, 25:607–615.

Philipp Koehn. 2004. Pharaoh: A beam search decoder for phrased-based statistical machine translation. In *Proc. of AMTA*, pages 115–124.

Yang Liu, Qun Liu, and Shouxun Lin. 2006. Tree-to-string alignment template for statistical machine translation. In *Proceedings of COLING-ACL*, pages 609–616, July.

Haitao Mi, Liang Huang, and Qun Liu. 2008. Forest-based translation. In *Proc. of ACL*, pages 192–199.

Frans J. Och and Hermann Ney. 2003. A systematic comparison of various statistical alignment models. *Computational Linguistics*, 29:19–51.

Frans J. Och. 2003. Minimum error rate training in statistical machine translation. In *Proc. of ACL*, pages 160–167.

Kishore Papineni, Salim Roukos, Todd Ward, and Wei-Jing Zhu. 2002. Bleu: a method for automatic evaluation of machine translation. In *Proceedings of ACL*, pages 311–318.

Andreas Stolcke. 2002. Srilm-an extensible language modeling toolkit. In *Proc. of ICSLP*.

Taro Watanabe, Hajime Tsukada, and Hideki Isozaki. 2006. Left-to-right target generation for hierarchical phrase-based translation. In *Proc. of COLING*, pages 777–784.

Semantic Compositionality through Recursive Matrix-Vector Spaces

Richard Socher Brody Huval Christopher D. Manning Andrew Y. Ng
richard@socher.org, {brodyh,manning,ang}@stanford.edu
Computer Science Department, Stanford University

Abstract

Single-word vector space models have been very successful at learning lexical information. However, they cannot capture the compositional meaning of longer phrases, preventing them from a deeper understanding of language. We introduce a recursive neural network (RNN) model that learns compositional vector representations for phrases and sentences of arbitrary syntactic type and length. Our model assigns a vector and a matrix to every node in a parse tree: the vector captures the inherent meaning of the constituent, while the matrix captures how it changes the meaning of neighboring words or phrases. This matrix-vector RNN can learn the meaning of operators in propositional logic and natural language. The model obtains state of the art performance on three different experiments: predicting fine-grained sentiment distributions of adverb-adjective pairs; classifying sentiment labels of movie reviews and classifying semantic relationships such as cause-effect or topic-message between nouns using the syntactic path between them.

1 Introduction

Semantic word vector spaces are at the core of many useful natural language applications such as search query expansions (Jones et al., 2006), fact extraction for information retrieval (Paşca et al., 2006) and automatic annotation of text with disambiguated Wikipedia links (Ratinov et al., 2011), among many others (Turney and Pantel, 2010). In these models the meaning of a word is encoded as a vector computed from co-occurrence statistics of a word and its neighboring words. Such vectors have been shown to correlate well with human judgments of word similarity (Griffiths et al., 2007).

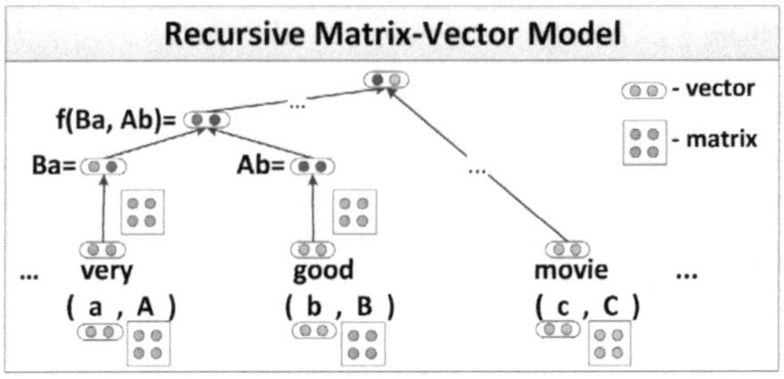

Figure 1: A recursive neural network which learns semantic vector representations of phrases in a tree structure. Each word and phrase is represented by a vector and a matrix, e.g., *very* = (a, A). The matrix is applied to neighboring vectors. The same function is repeated to combine the phrase *very good* with *movie*.

Despite their success, single word vector models are severely limited since they do not capture *compositionality*, the important quality of natural language that allows speakers to determine the meaning of a longer expression based on the meanings of its words and the rules used to combine them (Frege, 1892). This prevents them from gaining a deeper understanding of the semantics of longer phrases or sentences. Recently, there has been much progress in capturing compositionality in vector spaces, e.g., (Mitchell and Lapata, 2010; Baroni and Zamparelli, 2010; Zanzotto et al., 2010; Yessenalina and Cardie, 2011; Socher et al., 2011c) (see related work). We extend these approaches with a more general and powerful model of semantic composition.

We present a novel recursive neural network model for semantic compositionality. In our context, compositionality is the ability to learn compositional vector representations for various types of phrases and sentences of arbitrary length. Fig. 1 shows an illustration of the model in which each constituent (a word or longer phrase) has a matrix-vector (MV) representation. The vector captures the meaning of that constituent. The matrix captures how it modifies the meaning of the other word that it combines with. A representation for a longer phrase is computed bottom-up by recursively combining the words according to the syntactic structure of a parse tree. Since the model uses the MV representation with a neural network as the final merging function, we call our model a matrix-vector recursive neural network (MV-RNN).

We show that the ability to capture semantic compositionality in a syntactically plausible way translates into state of the art performance on various tasks. The first experiment demonstrates that our model can learn fine-grained semantic compositionality. The task is to predict a sentiment distribution over movie reviews of adverb-adjective pairs such as *unbelievably sad* or *really awesome*. The MV-RNN is the only model that is able to properly negate sentiment when adjectives are combined with *not*. The MV-RNN outperforms previous state of the art models on full sentence sentiment prediction of movie reviews. The last experiment shows that the MV-RNN can also be used to find relationships between words using the learned phrase vectors. The relationship between words is recursively constructed and composed by words of arbitrary type in the variable length syntactic path between them. On the associated task of classifying relationships between nouns in arbitrary positions of a sentence the model outperforms all previous approaches on the SemEval-2010 Task 8 competition (Hendrickx et al., 2010). It outperforms all but one of the previous approaches without using any hand-designed semantic resources such as WordNet or FrameNet. By adding WordNet hypernyms, POS and NER tags our model outperforms the state of the art that uses significantly more resources. The code for our model is available at `www.socher.org`.

2 MV-RNN: A Recursive Matrix-Vector Model

The dominant approach for building representations of multi-word units from single word vector representations has been to form a linear combination of the single word representations, such as a sum or weighted average. This happens in information retrieval and in various text similarity functions based on lexical similarity. These approaches can work well when the meaning of a text is literally "the sum of its parts", but fails when words function as operators that modify the meaning of another word: the meaning of "extremely strong" cannot be captured as the sum of word representations for "extremely" and "strong."

The model of Socher et al. (2011c) provided a new possibility for moving beyond a linear combination, through use of a matrix W that multiplied the word vectors (a, b), and a nonlinearity function g (such as a sigmoid or $\tanh$). They compute the parent vector p that describes both words as

$$p = g\left(W \begin{bmatrix} a \\ b \end{bmatrix}\right) \quad (1)$$

and apply this function recursively inside a binarized parse tree so that it can compute vectors for multiword sequences. Even though the nonlinearity allows to express a wider range of functions, it is almost certainly too much to expect a single fixed W matrix to be able to capture the meaning combination effects of all natural language operators. After all, inside the function g, we have the same linear transformation for all possible pairs of word vectors.

Recent work has started to capture the behavior of natural language operators inside semantic vector spaces by modeling them as matrices, which would allow a matrix for "extremely" to appropriately modify vectors for "smelly" or "strong" (Baroni and Zamparelli, 2010; Zanzotto et al., 2010). These approaches are along the right lines but so far have been restricted to capture linear functions of pairs of words whereas we would like nonlinear functions to compute compositional meaning representations for multi-word phrases or full sentences.

The MV-RNN combines the strengths of both of these ideas by (i) assigning a vector and a matrix to *every* word and (ii) learning an input-specific, nonlinear, compositional function for computing vector and matrix representations for multi-word sequences of any syntactic type. Assigning vector-matrix representations to all words instead of only to words of one part of speech category allows for greater flexibility which benefits performance. If a word lacks operator semantics, its matrix can be an identity matrix. However, if a word acts mainly as an operator, such as "extremely", its vector can become close to zero, while its matrix gains a clear operator meaning, here magnifying the meaning of the modified word in both positive and negative directions.

In this section we describe the initial word representations, the details of combining two words as well as the multi-word extensions. This is followed by an explanation of our training procedure.

2.1 Matrix-Vector Neural Word Representation

We represent a word as both a continuous vector and a matrix of parameters. We initialize all word vectors $x \in \mathbb{R}^n$ with pre-trained 50-dimensional word vectors from the unsupervised model of Collobert and Weston (2008). Using Wikipedia text, their model learns word vectors by predicting how likely it is for each word to occur in its context. Similar to other local co-occurrence based vector space models, the resulting word vectors capture syntactic and semantic information. Every word is also associated with a matrix X. In all experiments, we initialize matrices as $X = I + \epsilon$, i.e., the identity plus a small amount of Gaussian noise. If the vectors have dimensionality n, then each word's matrix has dimensionality $X \in \mathbb{R}^{n \times n}$. While the initialization is random, the vectors and matrices will subsequently be modified to enable a sequence of words to compose a vector that can predict a distribution over semantic labels. Henceforth, we represent any phrase or sentence of length m as an ordered list of vector-matrix pairs $((a, A), \ldots, (m, M))$, where each pair is retrieved based on the word at that position.

2.2 Composition Models for Two Words

We first review composition functions for two words. In order to compute a parent vector p from two consecutive words and their respective vectors a and b, Mitchell and Lapata (2010) give as their most general function: $p = f(a, b, R, K)$,where R is the a-priori known syntactic relation and K is background knowledge.

There are many possible functions f. For our models, there is a constraint on p which is that it has the same dimensionality as each of the input vectors. This way, we can compare p easily with its children and p can be the input to a composition with another word. The latter is a requirement that will become clear in the next section. This excludes tensor products which were outperformed by simpler weighted addition and multiplication methods in (Mitchell and Lapata, 2010).

We will explore methods that do not require any manually designed semantic resources as background knowledge K. No explicit knowledge about the type of relation R is used. Instead we want the model to capture this implicitly via the learned matrices. We propose the following combination function which is input dependent:

$$p = f_{A,B}(a, b) = f(Ba, Ab) = g\left(W \begin{bmatrix} Ba \\ Ab \end{bmatrix}\right), \quad (2)$$

where A, B are matrices for single words, the global $W \in \mathbb{R}^{n \times 2n}$ is a matrix that maps both transformed words back into the same n-dimensional space. The element-wise function g could be simply the identity function but we use instead a nonlinearity such as the sigmoid or hyperbolic tangent $\tanh$. Such a nonlinearity will allow us to approximate a wider range of functions beyond purely linear functions. We can also add a bias term before applying g but omit this for clarity. Rewriting the two transformed vectors as one vector z, we get $p = g(Wz)$ which is a single layer neural network. In this model, the word matrices can capture compositional effects specific to each word, whereas W captures a general composition function.

This function builds upon and generalizes several recent models in the literature. The most related work is that of (Mitchell and Lapata, 2010; Zanzotto et al., 2010) who introduced and explored the composition function $p = Ba + Ab$ for word pairs. This model is a special case of Eq. 2 when we set $W = [II]$ (i.e. two concatenated identity matrices) and $g(x) = x$ (the identity function). Baroni and Zamparelli (2010) computed the parent vector of adjective-noun pairs by $p = Ab$, where A is an adjective matrix and b is a vector for a noun. This cannot capture nouns modifying other nouns, e.g., *disk drive*. This model too is a special case of the above model with $B = 0_{n \times n}$. Lastly, the models of (Socher et al., 2011b; Socher et al., 2011c; Socher et al., 2011a) as described above are also special cases with both A and B set to the identity matrix. We will compare to these special cases in our experiments.

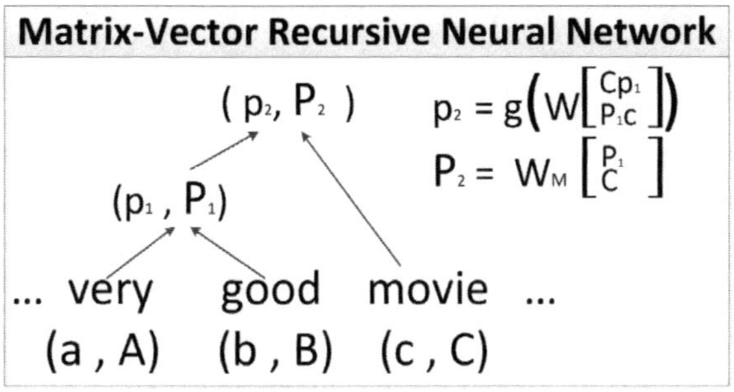

Figure 2: Example of how the MV-RNN merges a phrase with another word at a nonterminal node of a parse tree.

2.3 Recursive Compositions of Multiple Words and Phrases

This section describes how we extend a word-pair matrix-vector-based compositional model to learn vectors and matrices for longer sequences of words. The main idea is to apply the same function f to pairs of constituents in a parse tree. For this to work, we need to take as input a binary parse tree of a phrase or sentence and also compute matrices at each nonterminal parent node. The function f can be readily used for phrase vectors since it is recursively compatible (p has the same dimensionality as its children). For computing nonterminal phrase matrices, we define the function

$$P = f_M(A, B) = W_M \begin{bmatrix} A \\ B \end{bmatrix}, \tag{3}$$

where $W_M \in \mathbb{R}^{n \times 2n}$, so $P \in \mathbb{R}^{n \times n}$ just like each input matrix.

After two words form a constituent in the parse tree, this constituent can now be merged with another one by applying the same functions f and f_M. For instance, to compute the vectors and matrices depicted in Fig. 2, we first merge words a and b and their matrices: $p_1 = f(Ba, Ab), P_1 = f_M(A, B)$. The resulting vector-matrix pair (p_1, P_1) can now be used to compute the full phrase when combining it with word c and computing $p_2 = f(Cp_1, P_1c), P_2 = f_M(P_1, C)$. The model computes vectors and matrices in a bottom-up fashion, applying the functions f, f_M to its own previous output (i.e. recursively) until it reaches the top node of the tree which represents the entire sentence.

For experiments with longer sequences we will compare to standard RNNs and the special case of the MV-RNN that computes the parent by $p = Ab + Ba$, which we name the *linear Matrix-Vector Recursion* model (linear MVR). Previously, this model had not been trained for multi-word sequences. Sec. 6 talks about alternatives for compositionality.

2.4 Objective Functions for Training

One of the advantages of RNN-based models is that each node of a tree has associated with it a distributed vector representation (the parent vector p) which can also be seen as features describing that phrase. We train these representations by adding on top of each parent node a simple softmax classifier to predict a class distribution over, e.g., sentiment or relationship classes: $d(p) = \text{softmax}(W^{label}p)$. If there are K labels, then $d \in \mathbb{R}^K$ is a K-dimensional multinomial distribution. For the applications below (excluding logic), the corresponding error function $E(s, t, \theta)$ that we minimize for a sentence s and its tree t is the sum of cross-entropy errors at all nodes.

The only other methods that use this type of objective function are (Socher et al., 2011b; Socher et al., 2011c), who also combine it with either a score or reconstruction error. Hence, for comparisons to other related work, we need to merge variations of computing the parent vector p with this classifier. The main difference is that the MV-RNN has more flexibility since it has an input specific recursive function $f_{A,B}$ to compute each parent. In the following applications, we will use the softmax classifier to predict both sentiment distributions and noun-noun relationships.

2.5 Learning

Let $\theta = (W, W_M, W^{label}, L, L_M)$ be our model parameters and λ a vector with regularization hyperparameters for all model parameters. L and L_M are the sets of all word vectors and word matrices. The gradient of the overall objective function J becomes:

$$\frac{\partial J}{\partial \theta} = \frac{1}{N} \sum_{(x,t)} \frac{\partial E(x, t; \theta)}{\partial \theta} + \lambda\theta. \tag{4}$$

To compute this gradient, we first compute all tree nodes (p_i, P_i) from the bottom-up and then take derivatives of the softmax classifiers at each node in the tree from the top down. Derivatives are computed efficiently via backpropagation through structure (Goller and Küchler, 1996). Even though the objective is not convex, we found that L-BFGS run over the complete training data (batch mode) minimizes the objective well in practice and convergence is smooth. For more information see (Socher et al., 2010).

2.6 Low-Rank Matrix Approximations

If every word is represented by an n-dimensional vector and additionally by an $n \times n$ matrix, the dimensionality of the whole model may become too large with commonly used vector sizes of $n = 100$. In order to reduce the number of parameters, we represent word matrices by the following low-rank plus diagonal approximation:

$$A = UV + \text{diag}(a), \quad (5)$$

where $U \in \mathbb{R}^{n \times r}, V \in \mathbb{R}^{r \times n}, a \in \mathbb{R}^n$ and we set the rank for all experiments to $r = 3$.

2.7 Discussion: Evaluation and Generality

Evaluation of compositional vector spaces is a complex task. Most related work compares similarity judgments of unsupervised models to those of human judgments and aims at high correlation. These evaluations can give important insights. However, even with good correlation the question remains how these models would perform on downstream NLP tasks such as sentiment detection. We experimented with unsupervised learning of general vector-matrix representations by having the MV-RNN predict words in their correct context. Initializing the models with these general representations, did not improve the performance on the tasks we consider. For sentiment analysis, this is not surprising since antonyms often get similar vectors during unsupervised learning from co-occurrences due to high similarity of local syntactic contexts. In our experiments, the high prediction performance came from supervised learning of meaning representations using labeled data. While these representations are task-specific, they could be used across tasks in a multi-task learning setup. However, in order to fairly compare to related work, we use only the supervised data of each task. Before we describe our full-scale experiments, we analyze the model's expressive powers.

3 Model Analysis

This section analyzes the model with two proof-of-concept studies. First, we examine its ability to learn operator semantics for adverb-adjective pairs. If a model cannot correctly capture how an adverb operates on the meaning of adjectives, then there's little chance it can learn operators for more complex relationships. The second study analyzes whether the MV-RNN can learn simple boolean operators of propositional logic such as conjunctives or negation from truth values. Again, if a model did not have this ability, then there's little chance it could learn these frequently occurring phenomena from the noisy language of real texts such as movie reviews.

3.1 Predicting Sentiment Distributions of Adverb-Adjective Pairs

The first study considers the prediction of fine-grained sentiment distributions of adverb-adjective pairs and analyzes different possibilities for computing the parent vector p. The results show that the MV-RNN operators are powerful enough to capture the operational meanings of various types of adverbs. For example, *very* is an intensifier, *pretty* is an attenuator, and *not* can negate or strongly attenuate the positivity of an adjective. For instance *not great* is still *pretty good* and not *terrible*; see Potts (2010) for details.

We use a publicly available IMDB dataset of extracted adverb-adjective pairs from movie reviews.[1] The dataset provides the distribution over star ratings: Each consecutive word pair appears a certain number of times in reviews that have also associated with them an overall rating of the movie. After normalizing by the total number of occurrences, one gets a multinomial distribution over ratings. Only word pairs that appear at least 50 times are kept. Of the remaining pairs, we use 4211 randomly sampled ones for training and a separate set of 1804 for testing. We never give the algorithm sentiment distributions for single words, and, while single words overlap between training and testing, the test set consists of never before seen word pairs.

The softmax classifier is trained to minimize the cross entropy error. Hence, an evaluation in terms of KL-divergence is the most reasonable choice. It is

[1] *http://compprag.christopherpotts.net/reviews.html*

Method	Avg KL
Uniform	0.327
Mean train	0.193
$p = \frac{1}{2}(a+b)$	0.103
$p = a \otimes b$	0.103
$p = [a; b]$	0.101
$p = Ab$	0.103
RNN	0.093
Linear MVR	0.092
MV-RNN	**0.091**

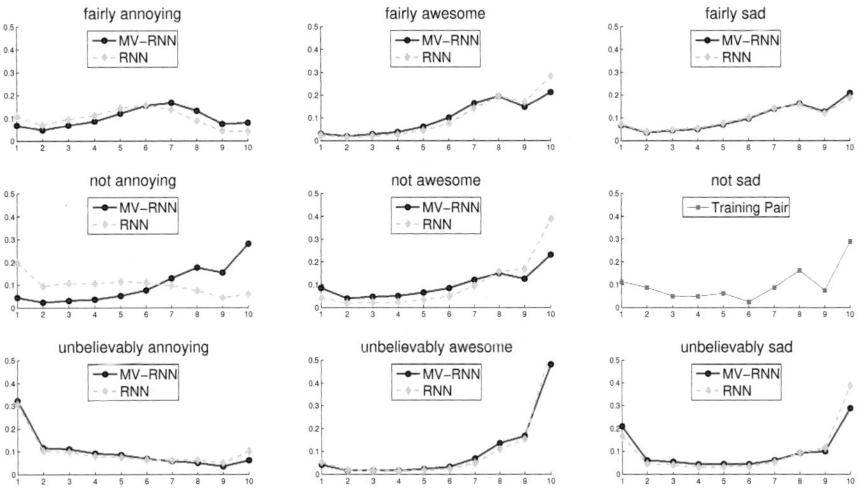

Figure 3: **Left**: Average KL-divergence for predicting sentiment distributions of unseen adverb-adjective pairs of the test set. See text for p descriptions. Lower is better. The main difference in the KL divergence comes from the few negation pairs in the test set. **Right**: Predicting sentiment distributions (over 1-10 stars on the x-axis) of adverb-adjective pairs. Each row has the same adverb and each column the same adjective. Many predictions are similar between the two models. The RNN and linear MVR are not able to modify the sentiment correctly: *not awesome* is more positive than *fairly awesome* and *not annoying* has a similar shape as *unbelievably annoying*. Predictions of the linear MVR model are almost identical to the standard RNN for these examples.

defined as $KL(g||p) = \sum_i g_i \log(g_i/p_i)$, where g is the gold distribution and p is the predicted one.

We compare to several baselines and ablations of the MV-RNN model. An (adverb,adjective) pair is described by its vectors (a, b) and matrices (A, B).

1 $p = 0.5(a + b)$, vector average
2. $p = a \otimes b$, element-wise vector multiplication
3. $p = [a; b]$, vector concatenation
4. $p = Ab$, similar to (Baroni and Lenci, 2010)
5. $p = g(W[a; b])$, RNN, similar to Socher et al.
6. $p = Ab + Ba$, Linear MVR, similar to (Mitchell and Lapata, 2010; Zanzotto et al., 2010)
7. $p = g(W[Ba; Ab])$, MV-RNN

The final distribution is always predicted by a $\mathrm{softmax}$ classifier whose inputs p vary for each of the models. This objective function (see Sec. 2.4) is different to all previously published work except that of (Socher et al., 2011c).

We cross-validated all models over regularization parameters for word vectors, the $\mathrm{softmax}$ classifier, the RNN parameter W and the word operators $(10^{-4}, 10^{-3})$ and word vector sizes ($n = 6, 8, 10, 12, 15, 20$). All models performed best at vector sizes of below 12. Hence, it is the model's power and not the number of parameters that determines the performance. The table in Fig. 3 shows the average KL-divergence on the test set. It shows that the idea of matrix-vector representations for all words and having a nonlinearity are both important. The MV-RNN which combines these two ideas is best able to learn the various compositional effects. The main difference in KL divergence comes from the few negation cases in the test set. Fig. 3 shows examples of predicted distributions. Many of the predictions are accurate and similar between the top models. However, only the MV-RNN has enough expressive power to allow negation to completely shift the sentiment with respect to an adjective. A negated adjective carrying negative sentiment becomes slightly positive, whereas *not awesome* is correctly attenuated. All three top models correctly capture the U-shape of *unbelievably sad*. This pair peaks at both the negative and positive spectrum because it is ambiguous. When referring to the performance of actors, it is very negative, but, when talking about the plot, many people enjoy sad and thought-provoking movies. The $p = Ab$ model does not perform well because it cannot model the fact that for an adjective like "sad," the operator of "unbelievably" behaves differently.

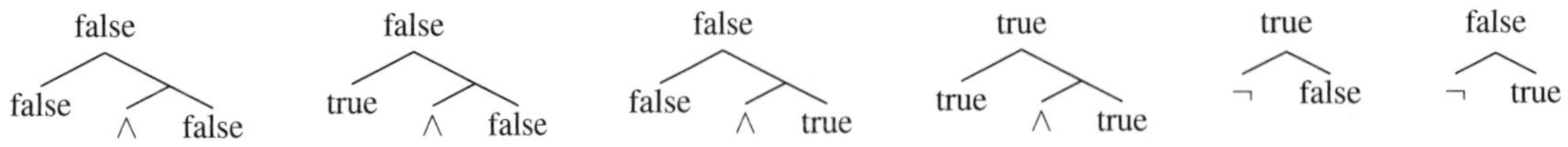

Figure 4: Training trees for the MV-RNN to learn propositional operators. The model learns vectors and operators for $\wedge$ (*and*) and $\neg$ (negation). The model outputs the exact representations of *false* and *true* respectively at the top node. Hence, the operators can be combined recursively an arbitrary number of times for more complex logical functions.

3.2 Logic- and Vector-based Compositionality

Another natural question is whether the MV-RNN can, in general, capture some of the simple boolean logic that is sometimes found in language. In other words, can it learn some of the propositional logic operators such as *and, or, not* in terms of vectors and matrices from a few examples. Answering this question can also be seen as a first step towards bridging the gap between logic-based, formal semantics (Montague, 1974) and vector space models.

The logic-based view of language accounts nicely for compositionality by directly mapping syntactic constituents to lambda calculus expressions. At the word level, the focus is on function words, and nouns and adjectives are often defined only in terms of the sets of entities they denote in the world. Most words are treated as atomic symbols with no relation to each other. There have been many attempts at automatically parsing natural language to a logical form using recursive compositional rules.

Conversely, vector space models have the attractive property that they can automatically extract knowledge from large corpora without supervision. Unlike logic-based approaches, these models allow us to make fine-grained statements about the semantic similarity of words which correlate well with human judgments (Griffiths et al., 2007). Logic-based approaches are often seen as orthogonal to distributional vector-based approaches. However, Garrette et al. (2011) recently introduced a combination of a vector space model inside a Markov Logic Network.

One open question is whether vector-based models can learn some of the simple logic encountered in language such as negation or conjunctives. To this end, we illustrate in a simple example that our MV-RNN model and its learned word matrices (operators) have the ability to learn propositional logic operators such as $\wedge, \vee, \neg$ (and, or, not). This is a necessary (though not sufficient) condition for the ability to pick up these phenomena in real datasets and tasks such as sentiment detection which we focus on in the subsequent sections.

Our setup is as follows. We train on 6 strictly right-branching trees as in Fig. 4. We consider the 1-dimensional case and fix the representation for *true* to $(t = 1, T = 1)$ and *false* to $(f = 0, F = 1)$. Fixing the operators to the 1×1 identity matrix 1 is essentially ignoring them. The objective is then to create a perfect reconstruction of (t, T) or (f, F) (depending on the formula), which we achieve by the least squares error between the top vector's representation and the corresponding truth value, e.g. for $\neg false$: $\min ||p_{top} - t||^2 + ||P_{top} - T||^2$.

As our function g (see Eq. 2), we use a linear threshold unit: $g(x) = \max(\min(x, 1), 0)$. Giving the derivatives computed for the objective function for the examples in Fig. 4 to a standard L-BFGS optimizer quickly yields a training error of 0. Hence, the output of these 6 examples has exactly one of the truth representations, making it recursively compatible with further combinations of operators. Thus, we can combine these operators to construct any propositional logic function of any number of inputs (including xor). Hence, this MV-RNN is complete in terms of propositional logic.

4 Predicting Movie Review Ratings

In this section, we analyze the model's performance on full length sentences. We compare to previous state of the art methods on a standard benchmark dataset of movie reviews (Pang and Lee, 2005; Nakagawa et al., 2010; Socher et al., 2011c). This dataset consists of 10,000 positive and negative single sentences describing movie sentiment. In this and the next experiment we use binarized trees from the Stanford Parser (Klein and Manning, 2003). We use the exact same setup and parameters (regularization, word vector size, etc.) as the published code of Socher et al. (2011c).[2]

[2] `www.socher.org`

Method	Acc.
Tree-CRF (Nakagawa et al., 2010)	77.3
RAE (Socher et al., 2011c)	77.7
Linear MVR	77.1
MV-RNN	**79.0**

Table 1: Accuracy of classification on full length movie review polarity (MR).

S.	C.	Review sentence
1	√	The film is bright and flashy in all the right ways.
0	√	Not always too whimsical for its own good this strange hybrid of crime thriller, quirky character study, third-rate romance and female empowerment fantasy never really finds the tonal or thematic glue it needs.
0	√	Doesn't come close to justifying the hype that surrounded its debut at the Sundance film festival two years ago.
0	x	Director Hoffman, his writer and Kline's agent should serve detention.
1	x	A bodice-ripper for intellectuals.

Table 2: Hard movie review examples of positive (1) and negative (0) sentiment (S.) that of all methods only the MV-RNN predicted correctly (C: √) or could not classify as correct either (C: x).

Table 1 shows comparisons to the system of (Nakagawa et al., 2010), a dependency tree based classification method that uses CRFs with hidden variables. The state of the art recursive autoencoder model of Socher et al. (2011c) obtained 77.7% accuracy. Our new MV-RNN gives the highest performance, outperforming also the linear MVR (Sec. 2.2).

Table 2 shows several hard examples that only the MV-RNN was able to classify correctly. None of the methods correctly classified the last two examples which require more world knowledge.

5 Classification of Semantic Relationships

The previous task considered global classification of an entire phrase or sentence. In our last experiment we show that the MV-RNN can also learn how a syntactic context composes an aggregate meaning of the semantic relationships between words. In particular, the task is finding semantic relationships between pairs of nominals. For instance, in the sentence "My [apartment]$_{e1}$ has a pretty large [kitchen]$_{e2}$.", we want to predict that the kitchen and apartment are in a *component-whole* relationship. Predicting such

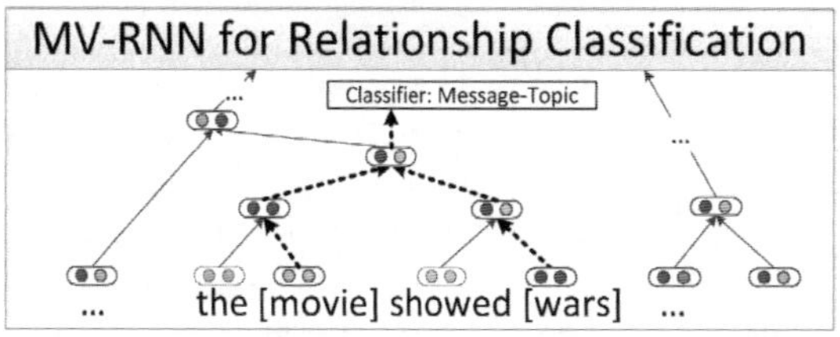

Figure 5: The MV-RNN learns vectors in the path connecting two words (dotted lines) to determine their semantic relationship. It takes into consideration a variable length sequence of various word types in that path.

semantic relations is useful for information extraction and thesaurus construction applications. Many approaches use features for all words on the path between the two words of interest. We show that by building a single compositional semantics for the minimal constituent including both terms one can achieve a higher performance.

This task requires the ability to deal with sequences of words of arbitrary type and length in between the two nouns in question.Fig. 5 explains our method for classifying nominal relationships. We first find the path in the parse tree between the two words whose relation we want to classify. We then select the highest node of the path and classify the relationship using that node's vector as features. We apply the same type of MV-RNN model as in sentiment to the subtree spanned by the two words.

We use the dataset and evaluation framework of SemEval-2010 Task 8 (Hendrickx et al., 2010). There are 9 ordered relationships (with two directions) and an undirected *other* class, resulting in 19 classes. Among the relationships are: message-topic, cause-effect, instrument-agency (etc. see Table 3 for list). A pair is counted as correct if the order of the words in the relationship is correct.

Table 4 lists results for several competing methods together with the resources and features used by each method. We compare to the systems of the competition which are described in Hendrickx et al. (2010) as well as the RNN and linear MVR. Most systems used a considerable amount of hand-designed semantic resources. In contrast to these methods, the MV-RNN only needs a parser for the tree structure and learns all semantics from unlabeled corpora and the training data. Only the SemEval training dataset is specific to this task, the re-

Relationship	Sentence with labeled nouns for which to predict relationships
Cause-Effect(e2,e1)	Avian [influenza]$_{e1}$ is an infectious disease caused by type a strains of the influenza [virus]$_{e2}$.
Entity-Origin(e1,e2)	The [mother]$_{e1}$ left her native [land]$_{e2}$ about the same time and they were married in that city.
Message-Topic(e2,e1)	Roadside [attractions]$_{e1}$ are frequently advertised with [billboards]$_{e2}$ to attract tourists.
Product-Producer(e1,e2)	A child is told a [lie]$_{e1}$ for several years by their [parents]$_{e2}$ before he/she realizes that ...
Entity-Destination(e1,e2)	The accident has spread [oil]$_{e1}$ into the [ocean]$_{e2}$.
Member-Collection(e2,e1)	The siege started, with a [regiment]$_{e1}$ of lightly armored [swordsmen]$_{e2}$ ramming down the gate.
Instrument-Agency(e2,e1)	The core of the [analyzer]$_{e1}$ identifies the paths using the constraint propagation [method]$_{e2}$.
Component-Whole(e2,e1)	The size of a [tree]$_{e1}$ [crown]$_{e2}$ is strongly correlated with the growth of the tree.
Content-Container(e1,e2)	The hidden [camera]$_{e1}$, found by a security guard, was hidden in a business card-sized [leaflet box]$_{e2}$ placed at an unmanned ATM in Tokyo's Minato ward in early September.

Table 3: Examples of correct classifications of ordered, semantic relations between nouns by the MV-RNN. Note that the final classifier is a recursive, compositional function of all the words in the syntactic path between the bracketed words. The paths vary in length and the words vary in type.

Classifier	Feature Sets	F1
SVM	POS, stemming, syntactic patterns	60.1
SVM	word pair, words in between	72.5
SVM	POS, WordNet, stemming, syntactic patterns	74.8
SVM	POS, WordNet, morphological features, thesauri, Google n-grams	77.6
MaxEnt	POS, WordNet, morphological features, noun compound system, thesauri, Google n-grams	77.6
SVM	POS, WordNet, prefixes and other morphological features, POS, dependency parse features, Levin classes, PropBank, FrameNet, NomLex-Plus, Google n-grams, paraphrases, TextRunner	82.2
RNN	-	74.8
Lin.MVR	-	73.0
MV-RNN	-	79.1
RNN	POS,WordNet,NER	77.6
Lin.MVR	POS,WordNet,NER	78.7
MV-RNN	POS,WordNet,NER	**82.4**

Table 4: Learning methods, their feature sets and F1 results for predicting semantic relations between nouns. The MV-RNN outperforms all but one method without any additional feature sets. By adding three such features, it obtains state of the art performance.

maining inputs and the training setup are the same as in previous sentiment experiments.

The best method on this dataset (Rink and Harabagiu, 2010) obtains 82.2% F1. In order to see whether our system can improve over this system, we added three features to the MV-RNN vector and trained another softmax classifier. The features and their performance increases were POS tags (+0.9); WordNet hypernyms (+1.3) and named entity tags (NER) of the two words (+0.6). Features were computed using the code of Ciaramita and Altun (2006).[3] With these features, the performance improved over the state of the art system. Table 3 shows random correct classification examples.

6 Related work

Distributional approaches have become omnipresent for the recognition of semantic similarity between words and the treatment of compositionality has seen much progress in recent years. Hence, we cannot do justice to the large amount of literature. Commonly, single words are represented as vectors of distributional characteristics – e.g., their frequencies in specific syntactic relations or their co-occurrences with given context words (Pado and Lapata, 2007; Baroni and Lenci, 2010; Turney and Pantel, 2010). These representations have proven very effective in sense discrimination and disambiguation (Schütze, 1998), automatic thesaurus extraction (Lin, 1998; Curran, 2004) and selectional preferences.

There are several sophisticated ideas for compositionality in vector spaces. Mitchell and Lapata (2010) present an overview of the most important compositional models, from simple vector addition and component-wise multiplication to tensor products, and convolution (Metcalfe, 1990). They measured the similarity between word pairs such as compound nouns or verb-object pairs and compared these with human similarity judgments. Simple vector averaging or multiplication performed best, hence our focus on related baselines above.

[3] sourceforge.net/projects/supersensetag/

Other important models are tensor products (Clark and Pulman, 2007), quantum logic (Widdows, 2008), holographic reduced representations (Plate, 1995) and the Compositional Matrix Space model (Rudolph and Giesbrecht, 2010). RNNs are related to autoencoder models such as the recursive autoassociative memory (RAAM) (Pollack, 1990) or recurrent neural networks (Elman, 1991). Bottou (2011) and Hinton (1990) discussed related models such as recursive autoencoders for text understanding.

Our model builds upon and generalizes the models of (Mitchell and Lapata, 2010; Baroni and Zamparelli, 2010; Zanzotto et al., 2010; Socher et al., 2011c) (see Sec. 2.2). We compare to them in our experiments. Yessenalina and Cardie (2011) introduce a sentiment analysis model that describes words as matrices and composition as matrix multiplication. Since matrix multiplication is associative, this cannot capture different scopes of negation or syntactic differences. Their model, is a special case of our encoding model (when you ignore vectors, fix the tree to be strictly branching in one direction and use as the matrix composition function $P = AB$). Since our classifiers are trained on the vectors, we cannot compare to this approach directly. Grefenstette and Sadrzadeh (2011) learn matrices for verbs in a categorical model. The trained matrices improve correlation with human judgments on the task of identifying relatedness of subject-verb-object triplets.

7 Conclusion

We introduced a new model towards a complete treatment of compositionality in word vector spaces. Our model builds on a syntactically plausible parse tree and can handle compositional phenomena. The main novelty of our model is the combination of matrix-vector representations with a recursive neural network. It can learn both the meaning vectors of a word and how that word modifies its neighbors (via its matrix). The MV-RNN combines attractive theoretical properties with good performance on large, noisy datasets. It generalizes several models in the literature, can learn propositional logic, accurately predicts sentiment and can be used to classify semantic relationships between nouns in a sentence.

Acknowledgments

We thank for great discussions about the paper: John Platt, Chris Potts, Josh Tenenbaum, Mihai Surdeanu, Quoc Le and Kevin Miller. The authors gratefully acknowledges the support of the Defense Advanced Research Projects Agency (DARPA) Machine Reading Program under Air Force Research Laboratory (AFRL) prime contract no. FA8750-09-C-0181, and the DARPA Deep Learning program under contract number FA8650-10-C-7020. Any opinions, findings, and conclusions or recommendations expressed in this material are those of the authors and do not necessarily reflect the view of DARPA, AFRL, or the US government.

References

M. Baroni and A. Lenci. 2010. Distributional memory: A general framework for corpus-based semantics. *Computational Linguistics*, 36(4):673–721.

M. Baroni and Roberto Zamparelli. 2010. Nouns are vectors, adjectives are matrices: Representing adjective-noun constructions in semantic space. In *EMNLP*.

L. Bottou. 2011. From machine learning to machine reasoning. *CoRR*, abs/1102.1808.

M. Ciaramita and Y. Altun. 2006. Broad-coverage sense disambiguation and information extraction with a supersense sequence tagger. In *EMNLP*.

S. Clark and S. Pulman. 2007. Combining symbolic and distributional models of meaning. In *Proceedings of the AAAI Spring Symposium on Quantum Interaction*, pages 52–55.

R. Collobert and J. Weston. 2008. A unified architecture for natural language processing: deep neural networks with multitask learning. In *ICML*.

J. Curran. 2004. *From Distributional to Semantic Similarity*. Ph.D. thesis, University of Edinburgh.

J. L. Elman. 1991. Distributed representations, simple recurrent networks, and grammatical structure. *Machine Learning*, 7(2-3).

G. Frege. 1892. Über Sinn und Bedeutung. In *Zeitschrift für Philosophie und philosophische Kritik, 100*.

D. Garrette, K. Erk, and R. Mooney. 2011. Integrating Logical Representations with Probabilistic Information using Markov Logic. In *Proceedings of the International Conference on Computational Semantics*.

C. Goller and A. Küchler. 1996. Learning task-dependent distributed representations by backpropagation through structure. In *Proceedings of the International Conference on Neural Networks (ICNN-96)*.

E. Grefenstette and M. Sadrzadeh. 2011. Experimental support for a categorical compositional distributional model of meaning. In *EMNLP*.

T. L. Griffiths, J. B. Tenenbaum, and M. Steyvers. 2007. Topics in semantic representation. *Psychological Review*, 114.

I. Hendrickx, S.N. Kim, Z. Kozareva, P. Nakov, D. Ó Séaghdha, S. Padó, M. Pennacchiotti, L. Romano, and S. Szpakowicz. 2010. Semeval-2010 task 8: Multi-way classification of semantic relations between pairs of nominals. In *Proceedings of the 5th International Workshop on Semantic Evaluation*.

G. E. Hinton. 1990. Mapping part-whole hierarchies into connectionist networks. *Artificial Intelligence*, 46(1-2).

R. Jones, B. Rey, O. Madani, and W. Greiner. 2006. Generating query substitutions. In *Proceedings of the 15th international conference on World Wide Web*.

D. Klein and C. D. Manning. 2003. Accurate unlexicalized parsing. In *ACL*.

D. Lin. 1998. Automatic retrieval and clustering of similar words. In *Proceedings of COLING-ACL*, pages 768–774.

E. J. Metcalfe. 1990. A compositive holographic associative recall model. *Psychological Review*, 88:627–661.

J. Mitchell and M. Lapata. 2010. Composition in distributional models of semantics. *Cognitive Science*, 34(8):1388–1429.

R. Montague. 1974. English as a formal language. *Linguaggi nella Societa e nella Tecnica*, pages 189–224.

T. Nakagawa, K. Inui, and S. Kurohashi. 2010. Dependency tree-based sentiment classification using CRFs with hidden variables. In *NAACL*, HLT.

M. Paşca, D. Lin, J. Bigham, A. Lifchits, and A. Jain. 2006. Names and similarities on the web: fact extraction in the fast lane. In *ACL*.

S. Pado and M. Lapata. 2007. Dependency-based construction of semantic space models. *Computational Linguistics*, 33(2):161–199.

B. Pang and L. Lee. 2005. Seeing stars: Exploiting class relationships for sentiment categorization with respect to rating scales. In *ACL*, pages 115–124.

T. A. Plate. 1995. Holographic reduced representations. *IEEE Transactions on Neural Networks*, 6(3):623–641.

J. B. Pollack. 1990. Recursive distributed representations. *Artificial Intelligence*, 46, November.

C. Potts. 2010. On the negativity of negation. In David Lutz and Nan Li, editors, *Proceedings of Semantics and Linguistic Theory 20*. CLC Publications, Ithaca, NY.

L. Ratinov, D. Roth, D. Downey, and M. Anderson. 2011. Local and global algorithms for disambiguation to wikipedia. In *ACL*.

B. Rink and S. Harabagiu. 2010. UTD: Classifying semantic relations by combining lexical and semantic resources. In *Proceedings of the 5th International Workshop on Semantic Evaluation*.

S. Rudolph and E. Giesbrecht. 2010. Compositional matrix-space models of language. In *ACL*.

H. Schütze. 1998. Automatic word sense discrimination. *Computational Linguistics*, 24:97–124.

R. Socher, C. D. Manning, and A. Y. Ng. 2010. Learning continuous phrase representations and syntactic parsing with recursive neural networks. In *Proceedings of the NIPS-2010 Deep Learning and Unsupervised Feature Learning Workshop*.

R. Socher, E. H. Huang, J. Pennington, A. Y. Ng, and C. D. Manning. 2011a. Dynamic Pooling and Unfolding Recursive Autoencoders for Paraphrase Detection. In *NIPS*. MIT Press.

R. Socher, C. Lin, A. Y. Ng, and C.D. Manning. 2011b. Parsing Natural Scenes and Natural Language with Recursive Neural Networks. In *ICML*.

R. Socher, J. Pennington, E. H. Huang, A. Y. Ng, and C. D. Manning. 2011c. Semi-Supervised Recursive Autoencoders for Predicting Sentiment Distributions. In *EMNLP*.

P. D. Turney and P. Pantel. 2010. From frequency to meaning: Vector space models of semantics. *Journal of Artificial Intelligence Research*, 37:141–188.

D. Widdows. 2008. Semantic vector products: Some initial investigations. In *Proceedings of the Second AAAI Symposium on Quantum Interaction*.

A. Yessenalina and C. Cardie. 2011. Compositional matrix-space models for sentiment analysis. In *EMNLP*.

F.M. Zanzotto, I. Korkontzelos, F. Fallucchi, and S. Manandhar. 2010. Estimating linear models for compositional distributional semantics. COLING.

Polarity Inducing Latent Semantic Analysis

Wen-tau Yih **Geoffrey Zweig** **John C. Platt**
Microsoft Research
One Microsoft Way
Redmond, WA 98052, USA
{scottyih,gzweig,jplatt}@microsoft.com

Abstract

Existing vector space models typically map synonyms and antonyms to similar word vectors, and thus fail to represent antonymy. We introduce a new vector space representation where antonyms lie on opposite sides of a sphere: in the word vector space, synonyms have cosine similarities close to one, while antonyms are close to minus one.

We derive this representation with the aid of a thesaurus and latent semantic analysis (LSA). Each entry in the thesaurus – a word sense along with its synonyms and antonyms – is treated as a "document," and the resulting document collection is subjected to LSA. The key contribution of this work is to show how to assign signs to the entries in the co-occurrence matrix on which LSA operates, so as to induce a subspace with the desired property.

We evaluate this procedure with the Graduate Record Examination questions of (Mohammed et al., 2008) and find that the method improves on the results of that study. Further improvements result from refining the subspace representation with discriminative training, and augmenting the training data with general newspaper text. Altogether, we improve on the best previous results by 11 points absolute in F measure.

1 Introduction

Vector space representations have proven useful across a wide variety of text processing applications ranging from document clustering to search relevance measurement. In these applications, text is represented as a vector in a multi-dimensional continuous space, and a similarity metric such as cosine similarity can be used to measure the relatedness of different items. Vector space representations have been used both at the document and word levels. At the document level, they are effective for applications including information retrieval (Salton and McGill, 1983; Deerwester et al., 1990), document clustering (Deerwester et al., 1990; Xu et al., 2003), search relevance measurement (Baeza-Yates and Ribiero-Neto, 1999) and cross-lingual document retrieval (Platt et al., 2010). At the word level, vector representations have been used to measure word similarity (Deerwester et al., 1990; Turney and Littman, 2005; Turney, 2006; Turney, 2001; Lin, 1998; Agirre et al., 2009; Reisinger and Mooney, 2010) and for language modeling (Bellegarda, 2000; Coccaro and Jurafsky, 1998). While quite successful, these applications have typically been consistent with a very general notion of similarity in which basic association is measured, and finer shades of meaning need not be distinguished. For example, latent semantic analysis might assign a high degree of similarity to opposites as well as synonyms (Landauer and Laham, 1998; Landauer, 2002).

Independent of vector-space representations, a number of authors have focused on identifying different kinds of relatedness. At the simplest level, we may wish to distinguish between synonyms and antonyms, which can be further differentiated. For example, in synonymy, we may wish to distinguish hyponyms and hypernyms. Moreover, Cruse (1986) notes that numerous kinds of antonymy are possible, for example *antipodal pairs* like "top-bottom" or *gradable opposites* like "light-heavy." Work in this area includes (Turney, 2001; Lin et al., 2003; Turney and Littman, 2005; Turney, 2006; Curran and Moens, 2002; van der Plas and Tiedemann, 2006; Mohammed et al., 2008; Mohammed et al., 2011). Despite the existence of a large amount of related work in the literature, distinguishing synonyms and antonyms is still considered as a difficult open problem in general (Poon and Domingos, 2009).

In this paper, we fuse these two strands of research in an attempt to develop a vector space representation in which the synonymy and antonymy are naturally differentiated. We follow Schwab et al. (2002) in requiring a representation in which two lexical items in an antonymy relation should lie at opposite ends of an axis. However, in contrast to the logical axes used previously, we desire that antonyms should lie at the opposite ends of a sphere lying in a continuous and automatically induced vector space. To generate this vector space, we present a novel method for assigning both *negative* and *positive* values to the TF-IDF weights used in latent semantic analysis.

To determine these signed values, we exploit the information present in a thesaurus. The result is a vector space representation in which synonyms cluster together, and the opposites of a word tend to cluster together at the opposite end of a sphere.

This representation provides several advantages over the raw thesaurus. First, by finding the items most and least similar to a word, we are able to discover new synonyms and antonyms. Second, as discussed in Section 5, the representation provides a natural starting point for gradient-descent based optimization. Thirdly, as we discuss in Section 6, it is straightforward to embed *new words* into the derived subspace by using information from a large unsupervised text corpus such as Wikipedia.

The remainder of this paper is organized as follows. Section 2 describes previous work. Section 3 presents the classical LSA approach and analyzes some of its limitations. In Section 4 we present our polarity inducing extension to LSA. Section 5 further extends the approach by optimizing the vector space representation with supervised discriminative training. Section 6 describes the proposed method of embedding new words in the thesaurus-derived subspace. The experimental results of Section 7 indicate that the proposed method outperforms previous approaches on a GRE test of closest-opposites (Mohammed et al., 2008). Finally, Section 8 concludes the paper.

2 Related Work

The detection of antonymy has been studied in a number of previous papers. Mohammed et al. (2008) approach the problem by combining information from a published thesaurus with corpus statistics derived from the Google n-gram corpus (Brants and Franz, 2006). Their method consists of two main steps: first, detecting contrasting word categories (e.g. "WORK" vs. "ACTIVITY FOR FUN") and then determining the degree of antonymy. Categories are defined by a thesaurus; contrasting categories are found by using affix rules (e.g., un- & dis-) and WordNet antonymy links. Words belonging to contrasting categories are treated as antonyms and the degree of contrast is determined by distributional similarity. Mohammed et al. (2008) also provides a publicly available dataset for detection of antonymy, which we have adopted. This work has been extended in (Mohammed et al., 2011) to include a study of antonymy based on crowd-sourcing experiments.

Turney (2008) proposes a unified approach to handling analogies, synonyms, antonyms and associations by transforming the last three cases into cases of analogy. A supervised learning method is then used to solve the resulting analogical problems. This is evaluated on a set of 136 ESL questions. Lin et al. (2003) builds on (Lin, 1998) and identifies antonyms as semantically related words which also happen to be found together in a database in pre-identified phrases indicating opposition. Lin et al. (2003) further note that whereas synonyms will tend to translate to the same word in another language, antonyms will not. This observation is used to select antonyms from amongst distributionally similar words. Antonymy is used in (de Simone and Kazakov, 2005) for document clustering and (Harabagiu et al., 2006) to find contradiction.

The automatic detection of synonyms has been more extensively studied. Lin (1998) presents a thorough comparison of word-similarity metrics based on distributional similarity, where this is determined from co-occurrence statistics in dependency triples extracted by parsing a large dataset. Related studies are described in (Curran and Moens, 2002; van der Plas and Bouma, 2005). Later, van der Plas and Tiedemann (2006) extend the use of multilingual data present in Lin et al. (2003) by measuring distributional similarity based on the contexts that a word occurs in *once translated* into a new language. This is used to improve the precision/recall characteristics on synonym pairs. Structured information can be important in determining relatedness, and thesauri and Wikipedia links have been studied in (Milne and Witten, 2008; Jarmasz and Szpakowicz, 2003). Combinations of approaches are studied in (Turney et al., 2003).

Vector-space models and latent semantic analysis in particular have a long history of use in synonym detection, which in fact was suggested in some of the earliest LSA papers. Deerwester et al. (1990) defines a metric for measuring word similarity based on LSA, and it has been used in (Landauer and Dumais, 1997; Landauer et al., 1998) to answer word similarity questions derived from the Test of English as a Foreign Language (TOEFL). Turney (2001) proposes the use of point-wise mutual information in conjunction with LSA, and again presents results on synonym questions derived from the TOEFL. Variants of vector space models are further analyzed in (Turney and Littman, 2005; Turney, 2006; Turney and Pantel, 2010).

3 Latent Semantic Analysis

Latent Semantic Analysis (Deerwester et al., 1990) is a widely used method for representing words and documents in a low dimensional vector space. The method is based on applying singular value decomposition (SVD) to a matrix W which indicates the occurrence of words in documents. To perform LSA, one proceeds as follows. The input is a collection of d documents which are expressed in terms of words from a vocabulary of size n. These documents may be actual documents such as newspaper articles, or simply notional documents such as sentences, or any other collection in which words are grouped together. Next, a $d \times n$ document-term matrix W is formed[1]. At its simplest form, the ij^{th} entry contains the number of times word j has occurred in document i – its *term frequency* or TF value. More conventionally, the entry is weighted by some notion of the importance of word j, for example the negative logarithm of the fraction of documents that contain it, resulting in a TF-IDF weighting (Salton et al., 1975). The similarity between two documents can be computed using the cosine similarity of their corresponding row vectors:

$$\mathtt{sim}(\mathbf{x},\mathbf{y}) = \frac{\mathbf{x}\cdot\mathbf{y}}{\|\mathbf{x}\|\|\mathbf{y}\|}$$

Similarly, the cosine similarity of two column vectors can be used to judge the similarity of the corresponding words. Finally, to obtain a subspace representation of dimension k, W is decomposed as

$$W \approx USV^T$$

where U is $d \times k$, V^T is $k \times n$, and S is a $k \times k$ diagonal matrix. In applications, $k \ll n$ and $k \ll d$; for example one might have a $50,000$ word vocabulary and $1,000,000$ documents and use a 300 dimensional subspace representation.

An important property of SVD is that the columns of SV^T – which now represent the words – behave similarly to the original columns of W, in the sense that the cosine similarity between two columns in SV^T approximates the cosine similarity between the corresponding columns in W. This follows from the observation that $W^TW = VS^2V^T$, and the fact that the ij^{th} entry of W^TW is the dot product of the ith and j^{th} columns (words) in W. We will use this observation subsequently in the derivation of polarity-inducing LSA. For efficiency, we normalize the columns of SV^T to unit length, allowing the cosine similarity between two words to be computed with a single dot-product; this also has the property of mapping each word to a point on a multi-dimensional sphere.

A second important property of LSA is that in the word representations which result can by viewed as the result of applying a projection matrix U to the original vectors as:

$$U^TW = SV^T$$

[1](Bellegarda, 2000) constructs the transpose of this, but we have found it convenient in data processing for documents to represent rows.

In Section 5, we will view U simply as a $d \times k$ matrix learned through gradient descent so as to optimize an objective function.

3.1 Limitation of LSA

Word similarity as determined by LSA assigns high values to words which tend to co-occur in documents. However, as noted by (Landauer and Laham, 1998; Landauer, 2002), there is no notion of antonymy; words with low or negative cosine scores are simply unrelated. In comparison, words with high cosine similarity scores are typically *semantically* related, which includes both synonyms and antonyms, as contrasting words often co-occur (Murphy and Andrew, 1993; Mohammed et al., 2008). To illustrate this, we have performed SVD with the aid of the Encarta thesaurus developed by Bloomsbury Publishing Plc. This thesaurus contains approximately 47k word senses and a vocabulary of 50k words and phrases. Each "document" is taken to be the thesaurus entry for a word-sense, including synonyms and antonyms. For example, the word "admirable" induces a document consisting of {admirable, estimable, commendable, venerable, good, splendid, worthy, marvelous, excellent, *unworthy*}. Note that the last word in this set is its antonym. Performing SVD on this set of thesaurus derived "meaning-documents" results in a subspace representation for each word. This form of LSA is similar to the use of Wikipedia in (Gabrilovich and Markovitch, 2007).

Table 1 shows some words, their original thesaurus documents, and the most and least similar words in the LSA subspace. Several properties are apparent:

- The vector-space representation of words is able to identify related words that are not explicitly present in the original thesaurus. For example, "meritorious" for "admirable" – arguably better than any of the words given in the thesaurus itself.
- Similarity is based on co-occurrence, so the co-occurrence of antonyms in the thesaurus-derived documents induces their presence as LSA-similar words. For example, "contemptible" is identified as similar to "admirable." In the case of "mourning," opposites such as "joy" and "elation" actually dominate the list of LSA-similar words.
- The LSA-least-similar words have no relationship at all to the word they are least-similar to. For example, the least-similar word to "considered" is "ready-made-meal."

In the next section, we will present a method for inducing polarity in LSA subspaces, where opposite words will tend to have negative cosine similarities, analogous to the positive similarities of synonyms. Thus, the least-similar words to a given word will be its opposites.

	acrimony	rancor	goodwill	affection
acrimony	1	1	1	1
affection	1	1	1	1

Table 2: The W matrix for two thesaurus entries in its original form. Rows represent documents; columns words.

	acrimony	rancor	goodwill	affection
acrimony	1	1	-1	-1
affection	-1	-1	1	1

Table 3: The W matrix for two thesaurus entries in its polarity-inducing form.

4 Polarity Inducing LSA

We modify LSA so that we may exploit a thesaurus to embed meaningful axes in the induced subspace representation. Words with opposite meaning will lie at opposite positions on a sphere. Recall that the cosine similarity between word-vectors in the original matrix W are preserved in the subspace representation of words. Thus, if we construct the original matrix so that the columns representing antonyms will tend to have negative cosine similarities while columns representing synonyms will tend to have positive similarities, we will achieve the desired behavior.

This can be achieved by negating the TF-IDF entries for the antonyms of a word when constructing W from the thesaurus, which is illustrated in Tables 2 and 3. The two rows in these tables correspond to thesaurus entries for the sense-categories

Word	Thesaurus Entry	LSA Most-Similar Words	LSA Least-Similar Words
admirable	estimable, commendable, venerable, good, splendid, worthy, marvelous, excellent, *unworthy*	commendable, creditable, laudable, praiseworthy, worthy, meritorious, scurvy, contemptible, despicable, estimable	easy-on-the-eye, peacekeeper, peace-lover, conscientious-objector, uninviting, dishy, dessert, pudding, seductive
considered	careful, measured, well-thought-out, painstaking, *rash*	calculated, premeditated, planned, tactical, strategic, thought-through, intentional, fortuitous, purposeful, unpremeditated	ready-made-meal, ready-meal, disposed-to, apt-to, wild-animals, big-game, game-birds, game-fish, rugger, rugby
mourning	grief, bereavement, sorrow, sadness, lamentation, woe, grieving, *exultation*	sorrowfulness, anguish, exultation, rejoicing, jubilation, glee, heartache, travail, joy, elation	muckiness, turn-the-corner, impassibility, filminess, pellucidity, limpidity, sheerness

Table 1: LSA on a thesaurus. Thesaurus entries include antonyms in italics.

"acrimony," and "affection." The thesaurus entries induce two "documents" containing the words and their synonyms and antonyms. The complete set of words is *acrimony, rancor, goodwill, affection*. For simplicity, we assume that all TF-IDF weights are 1. In the original LSA formulation, we have the representation of Table 2. "Rancor" is listed as a synonym of "acrimony," which has "goodwill" and "affection" as its antonyms. This results in the first row. Note that the cosine similarity between every pair of words (columns) is 1.

Table 3 shows the polarity-inducing representation. Here, the cosine similarity between synonymous words (columns) is 1, and the cosine similarity between antonymous words is -1. Since LSA tends to preserve cosine similarities between words, in the resulting subspace we may expect to find meaningful axes, where opposite senses map to opposite extremes. We refer to this as polarity-inducing LSA or PILSA.

In Table 4, we show the PILSA-similar and PILSA-least-similar words for the same words as in Table 1. We see now that words which are least similar in the sense of having the lowest cosine-similarity are indeed opposites. In this table generally the most similar words have similarities in the range of 0.7 to 1.0 and the least similar in the range of -0.7 to -1.0.

5 Discriminative Training

Although the cosine similarity of LSA-derived word vectors are generally very effective in applications such as judging the relevance of words or documents, or detecting antonyms as in our construction, the process of singular value decomposition in LSA does not explicitly try to achieve such goals. In this section, we see that when supervised training data is available, the projection matrix of LSA can be enhanced through a discriminative training technique explicitly designed to create a representation suited to a specific task.

Bccause LSA is closely related to principle component analysis (PCA), extensions of PCA such as canonical correlation analysis (CCA) and oriented principle component analysis (OPCA) can leverage the labeled data and produce the projection matrix through general eigen-decomposition (Platt et al., 2010). Along this line of work, Yih et al. (2011) proposed a Siamese neural network approach called *S2Net*, which tunes the projection matrix directly through gradient descent, and has shown to outperform other methods in several tasks. Below we describe briefly this technique and explain how we adopt it for the task of antonym detection.

The goal of S2Net is to learn a concept vector representation of the original sparse term vectors. Although such transformation can be non-linear in general, its current design chooses the model form to be a linear projection matrix, which is identical to

Word	PILSA-Similar Words	PILSA-Least-Similar Words
admirable	commendable, creditable, laudable, praiseworthy, worthy, meritorious, estimable, deserving, tiptop, valued	scurvy, contemptible, despicable, lamentable, shameful, reprehensible, unworthy, disgraceful, discreditable, undeserving
considered	calculated, premeditated, planned, tactical, strategic, thought-through, intentional, purposeful, intended, psychological	fortuitous, unpremeditated, unconsidered, off-your-own-bat, unintended, undirected, objectiveless, hit-and-miss, unforced, involuntary
mourning	sorrowful, doleful, sad, miserable, wistful, pitiful, wailing, sobbing, heavy-hearted, forlorn	smiley, happy, blissful, wooden, mirthful, joyful, deadpan, fulfilled, straight-faced, content

Table 4: PILSA on a thesaurus. Thesaurus entries are as in Table 1.

that of LSA, PCA, OPCA or CCA. Given a d-by-1 input vector $\mathbf{f}$, the model of S2Net is a d-by-k matrix $\mathbf{A} = [a_{ij}]_{d \times k}$, which maps $\mathbf{f}$ to a k-by-1 output vector $\mathbf{g} = \mathbf{A}^T\mathbf{f}$. The fact that the transformation can be viewed as a two-layer neural network leads to the method's name.

What differentiates S2Net from other approaches is its loss function and optimization process. In the "parallel text" setting, the labeled data consists of pairs of *similar* text objects such as documents. The objective of the training process is to assign higher cosine similarities to these pairs compared to others. More specifically, suppose the training set consists of m pairs of raw input vectors $\{(\mathbf{f}_{p_1}, \mathbf{f}_{q_1}), (\mathbf{f}_{p_2}, \mathbf{f}_{q_2}), \cdots, (\mathbf{f}_{p_m}, \mathbf{f}_{q_m})\}$. Given a projection matrix $\mathbf{A}$, the similarity score of any pair of objects is $sim_{\mathbf{A}}(\mathbf{f}_{p_i}, \mathbf{f}_{q_j}) = cosine(\mathbf{A}^T\mathbf{f}_{p_i}, \mathbf{A}^T\mathbf{f}_{q_j})$. Let $\Delta_{ij} = sim_{\mathbf{A}}(\mathbf{f}_{p_i}, \mathbf{f}_{q_i}) - sim_{\mathbf{A}}(\mathbf{f}_{p_i}, \mathbf{f}_{q_j})$ be the difference of the similarity scores of $(\mathbf{f}_{p_i}, \mathbf{f}_{q_i})$ and $(\mathbf{f}_{p_i}, \mathbf{f}_{q_j})$. The learning procedure tries to increase Δ_{ij} by using the following logistic loss:

$$L(\Delta_{ij}; \mathbf{A}) = \log(1 + exp(-\gamma\Delta_{ij})),$$

where γ is a scaling factor that adjusts the loss function[2]. The loss of the whole training set is thus:

$$\frac{1}{m(m-1)} \sum_{1 \le i,j \le m, i \ne j} L(\Delta_{ij}; \mathbf{A})$$

Parameter learning (i.e., tuning $\mathbf{A}$) can be done by standard gradient-based methods, such as L-BFGS (Nocedal and Wright, 2006).

The original setting of S2Net can be directly applied to finding synonymous words, where the training data consists of pairs of vectors representing two synonyms. It is also easy to modify the loss function to apply it to the antonym detection problem. We first sample pairs of antonyms from the thesaurus to create the training data. The raw input vector $\mathbf{f}$ of a selected word is its corresponding column vector of the document-term matrix W (Section 3) after inducing polarity (Section 4). When each pair of vectors in the training data represents two antonyms, we can redefine Δ_{ij} by flipping the sign: $\Delta_{ij} = sim_{\mathbf{A}}(\mathbf{f}_{p_i}, \mathbf{f}_{q_j}) - sim_{\mathbf{A}}(\mathbf{f}_{p_i}, \mathbf{f}_{q_i})$, and leave others unchanged. As the loss function encourages Δ_{ij} to be larger, an antonym pair will tend to have a smaller cosine similarity than other pairs. Because S2Net uses a gradient descent technique and a non-convex objective function, it is sensitive to initialization, and we have found that the PILSA projection matrix U (Section 3) provides an excellent starting point. As illustrated in Section 7, learning the word vectors with S2Net produces a significant improvement over PILSA alone.

6 Extending PILSA to Out-of-thesaurus Words

While PILSA is effective at representing synonym and antonym information, in its pure form, it is limited to the vocabulary of the thesaurus. In order to extend PILSA to operate on out-of-thesaurus words,

[2]As suggested in (Yih et al., 2011), γ is set to 10 in our experiments.

we employ a two-stage strategy. We first conduct some lexical analysis and try to match an unknown word to one or more in-thesaurus words in their lemmatized forms. If no such match can be found, we then attempt to find semantically related in-thesaurus words by leveraging co-occurrence statistics from general text data. These two steps are described in detail below.

6.1 Matching via Lexical Analysis

When a target word is not included in a thesaurus, it is quite often that some of its morphological variations are covered. For example, although the Encarta thesaurus does not have the word "corruptibility," it does contain other forms like "corruptible" and "corruption." Replacing the out-of-thesaurus target word with these morphological variations may alter the part-of-speech but typically does not change the meaning[3].

Given an out-of-thesaurus target word, we first apply a morphological analyzer for English developed by Minnen et al. (2001), which removes the inflectional affixes and returns the lemma. If the lemma still does not exist in the thesaurus, we then apply Porter's stemmer (Porter, 1980) and check whether the target word can match any of the in-thesaurus words in their stemmed forms. A simple rule that checks whether removing hyphens from words can lead to a match and whether the target word occurs as part of a compound word in the thesaurus is applied when both morphological analysis and stemming fail to find a match. When there are more than one matched words, the centroid of their PILSA vectors is used to represent the target word. When there is only one matched word, the matched word is treated as the target word.

6.2 Leveraging General Text Data

If no words in the thesaurus can be linked to the target word through the simple lexical analysis procedure, we try to find matched words by creating a *context* vector space model from a large document collection, and then mapping from this space to the PILSA space. We use contexts because of the *distributional hypothesis* – words that occur in the same *contexts* tend to have similar meaning (Harris, 1954). When a word is not in the thesaurus but appears in the corpus, we predict its PILSA vector representation from the context vector space model by using its k-nearest neighbors which are in the thesaurus and *consistent* with each other.

[3]The rules we use based on lexical analysis are moderately conservative to avoid mistakes like mapping *hopeless* to *hope*.

6.2.1 Context Vector Space Model

Given a corpus of documents, we construct the raw context vectors as follows. For each target word, we first create a bag of words by collecting all the terms within a window of [-10,+10] centered at each occurrence of the target word in the corpus. The non-identical terms form a term-vector, where each term is weighted using its TF-IDF value. We then perform LSA on the context-word matrix. The semantic similarity/relatedness of two words can then be determined using the cosine similarity of their corresponding LSA word vectors. In the following text, we refer to this LSA context vector space model as the *corpus* space, in contrast to the PILSA *thesaurus* space.

6.2.2 Embedding Out-of-Vocabulary Words

Given the context space model, we may use a linear regression or a k-nearest neighbors approach to embed out-of-thesaurus words into the thesaurus-space representation. However, as near words in the context space may be synonyms in addition to other semantically related words (including antonyms), such approaches can potentially be noisy. For example, words like "hot" and "cold" may be close to each other in the context space due to their similar usage in text. An affine transform cannot "tear space" and map them to opposite poles in the thesaurus space.

Therefore, we propose a revised k-nearest neighbors approach. Suppose we are interested in an out-of-thesaurus word w. We first find K-nearest in-thesaurus neighbors to w in the context space. We then select a subset of k members of these K words such that the pairwise similarity of each of the k members with every other member is positive. The thesaurus-space centroid of these k items is computed as w's representation. This procedure has the property that the k nearby words used to form the embedding of a non-thesaurus word are selected to be consistent with each other. In practice, we used $K = 10$ and $k = 3$, which requires only around

1000 pairwise computations even done in a brute-force way. To provide a concrete example, if we had the out-of-thesaurus word "sweltering" with in-thesaurus neighbors "hot, cold, burning, scorching, ..." the procedure would return the centroid of "hot, burning, scorching" and exclude "cold."

7 Experimental Validation

In this section, we present our experimental results on applying PILSA and its extensions to answering the closest-opposite GRE questions.

7.1 Data Resources

The primary thesaurus we use is the Encarta Thesaurus developed by Bloomsbury Publishing Plc[4]. Our version of this has approximately 47k word senses and a vocabulary of 50k words, and contains 125,724 pairs of antonyms. To experiment with the effect of using a different thesaurus, we used WordNet as an information source. Each *synset* in WordNet maps to a row in the document-term matrix; synonyms in a synset are weighted with positive TFIDF values, and antonyms are weighted negative TFIDF values. Entries corresponding to other words in the vocabulary are 0. WordNet provides significantly greater coverage with approximately 227k synsets involving multiple words, and a vocabulary of about 190k words. However, it is also much sparser, with 5.3 words per sense on average as opposed to 10.3 in the thesaurus, and has only 62,821 pairs of antonyms. As general text data for use in embedding out-of-vocabulary words, we used a Nov-2010 dump of English Wikipedia, which contains approximately 917M words.

7.2 Development and Test Data

For testing, we use the closest-opposite questions from GRE tests provided by (Mohammed et al., 2008). Each question contains a target word and five choices, and asks which of the choice words has the most opposite meaning to the target word. Two datasets are made publicly available by Mohammad et al. (2008): the *development set*, which consists of 162 questions, and the *test set*, which has 950 questions[5]. We considered making our own, more extensive, test – for example one which would require the use of sentence context to choose between related yet distributionally different antonyms (e.g. "little, small" as antonyms of "big") but chose to stick to a previously used benchmark. This allows the direct comparison with previously reported methods.

[4]http://www.bloomsbury.com/

[5]http://www.umiacs.umd.edu/~saif/WebDocs/LC-data/{devset,testset}.txt

Dimensions	Bloomsbury Prec.	WordNet Prec.
50	0.778	0.475
100	0.850	0.563
200	0.856	0.569
300	**0.863**	**0.625**
400	0.843	**0.625**
500	0.843	0.613
750	0.830	0.613
1000	0.837	0.544
2000	0.784	0.519
3000	0.778	0.494

Table 5: The performance of PILSA vs. the number of dimensions when applied to the closest-opposite questions from the GRE development set. Out of the 162 questions, using the Bloomsbury thesaurus data we are able to answer 153 of them. Using 300 dimensions gives the best precision (132/153 = 0.863). This dimension setting is also optimal when using the WordNet data, which answers 100 questions correctly out of the 160 attempts (100/160 = 0.625).

Some of these questions contain very rarely used target or choice words, which are not included in the thesaurus vocabulary. In order to provide a fair comparison to existing methods, we do not try to randomly answer these questions. Instead, when the target word is out of vocabulary, we skip the whole question. When the target word is in vocabulary but one or more choices are unknown words, we ignore those unknown words and pick the word with the lowest cosine similarity from the rest as the answer. The results of our methods are reported in *precision* (the number of questions answered correctly divided by the number of questions attempted), *recall* (the number of questions answered correctly divided by the number of all questions) and F_1 (the harmonic mean of precision and recall)[6]. We now turn to an in-depth evaluation.

[6]Precision/recall/F_1 were used in (Mohammed et al., 2008) as when their system "did not find any evidence of antonymy between the target and any of its alternatives, then it refrained from attempting that question." We adopt this convention to provide a fair comparison to their system.

	Dev. Set			Test Set		
	Prec	Rec	F_1	Prec	Rec	F_1
WordNet lookup	0.40	0.40	0.40	0.42	0.41	0.42
WordNet signed-TFIDF w/o LSA	0.41	0.41	0.41	0.43	0.42	0.43
WordNet PILSA	0.63	0.62	0.62	0.60	0.60	0.60
Bloomsbury lookup	0.65	0.61	0.63	0.61	0.56	0.59
Bloomsbury signed TFIDF w/o LSA	0.68	0.64	0.66	0.63	0.57	0.60
Bloomsbury PILSA	0.86	0.81	0.84	0.81	0.74	0.77
Bloomsbury PILSA + S2Net	**0.89**	0.84	0.86	**0.84**	0.77	0.80
Bloomsbury PILSA + S2Net + Embedding	0.88	**0.87**	**0.87**	0.81	**0.80**	**0.81**
(Mohammed et al., 2008)	0.76	0.66	0.70	0.76	0.64	0.70

Table 6: The overall results. PILSA performs LSA on the signed TF-IDF vectors.

7.3 Basic PILSA

When applying PILSA, we need to determine the number of dimensions in the projected space. Evaluated on the GRE development set, Table 5 shows the precision of PILSA, using two different training datasets, Bloomsbury and WordNet, at different dimensions.

The Bloomsbury-based system is able to answer 153 questions, and the best dimension setting is 300, which answers 132 questions correctly and thus archives 0.863 in precision. In contrast, the larger vocabulary in WordNet helps the system answer 160 questions but the quality is not as good. We find dimensions 300 and 400 are equally good, where both answer 100 questions correctly (0.625 in precision)[7]. Because a lower number of dimensions is preferred for saving storage space and computing time, we choose 300 as the number of dimensions in PILSA.

We now compare the proposed methods. All results are summarized in Table 6. When evaluated on the GRE test set, the Bloomsbury thesaurus-based methods (Lines 4–7) attempted 865 questions. The precision, recall and F_1 of the Bloomsbury-based PILSA model (Line 6) are 0.81, 0.74 and 0.77, which are all better than the best reported method in (Mohammed et al., 2008)[8]. In contrast, the WordNet-based methods (Lines 1–3) attempted 936 questions. However, consistent with what we observed on the development set, the WordNet-based model is inferior. Its precision, recall and F_1 on the test set are 0.60, 0.60 and 0.60 (Line 3). Although the quality of the data source plays an important role, we need to emphasize that performing LSA using our polarity inducing construction is in fact a critical step in enhancing the model performance. For example, directly using the antonym sets in the Bloomsbury thesaurus gives 0.59 in F_1 (Line 4), while using cosine similarity on the signed vectors prior to LSA only reaches 0.60 in F_1 (Line 5).

7.4 Improving Precision with Discriminative Training

Building on the success of the unsupervised PILSA model, we refine the projection matrix. As described in Section 5, we take the PILSA projection matrix as the initial model in S2Net and train the model using 20,517 pairs of antonyms sampled from the Bloomsbury thesaurus. A separate sample of 5,000 antonym pairs is used as the validation set for hyper-parameter tuning in regularization. Encouragingly, we found that the already strong results of PILSA can indeed be improved, which gives 3 more points in both precision (0.84), recall (0.77) and F_1 (0.80).

7.5 Improving Recall with Unsupervised Data

We next evaluate our approach of extending the word coverage with the help of an external text corpus, as well as the lexical analysis procedure. Using the Bloomsbury PILSA-S2Net thesaurus space and the Wikipedia corpus space, our method increases

[7]Note that the number of questions attempted is not a function of the number of dimensions.

[8]We take a conservative approach and assume that skipped questions are answered incorrectly. The difference is statistically significant at 99% confidence level using a binomial test.

recall by 3 points on the test set. Compared to the in-vocabulary only setting, it attempted 75 more questions (865 → 940) and had 33 of them correctly answered.

While the accuracy on these questions is much higher than random, the fact that it is substantially below the precision of the original indicates some room for improvement. We notice that the out-of-thesaurus words are either offensive words excluded in the thesaurus (e.g., *moronic*) or some very rarely used words (e.g., *froward*). When the lexical analysis procedure fails to match the target word to some in-thesaurus words, the context vector embedding approach solves the former case, but has difficulty in handling the latter. The main reason is that such words occur very infrequently in a general corpus, which result in significant uncertainty in their semantic vectors. Other than using a much larger corpus, approaches that leverage character n-grams may help. We leave this as future work.

8 Conclusion

In this paper we have tackled the problem of finding a vector-space representation of words where, by construction, synonyms and antonyms are easy to distinguish. Specifically, we have defined a way of assigning sign to the entries in the co-occurrence matrix on which LSA operates, such that synonyms will tend to have positive cosine similarity, and antonyms will tend to have negative similarities. To the best of our knowledge, our method of inducing polarity to the document-term matrix *before* applying LSA is novel and has shown to effectively preserve and generalize the synonymous/antonymous information in the projected space. With this vector space representation, we were able to bring to bear the machinery of discriminative training in order to further optimize the word representations. Finally, by using the notion of closeness in this space, we were able to embed new out-of-vocabulary words into the space. On a standard test set, the proposed methods improved the F measure by 11 points absolute over previous results.

Acknowledgments

We thank Susan Dumais for her thoughtful comments, Silviu-Petru Cucerzan for preparing the Wikipedia data, and Saif Mohammed for sharing the GRE datasets. We are also grateful to the anonymous reviewers for their useful suggestions.

References

Eneko Agirre, Enrique Alfonseca, Keith Hall, Jana Kravalova, Marius Paşca, and Aitor Soroa. 2009. A study on similarity and relatedness using distributional and wordnet-based approaches. In *Proceedings of HLT-NAACL*, pages 19–27.

Ricardo Baeza-Yates and Berthier Ribiero-Neto. 1999. *Modern Information Retrieval*. Addison-Wesley.

J. Bellegarda. 2000. Exploiting latent semantic information in statistical language modeling. *Proceedings of the IEEE*, 88(8).

Thorsten Brants and Alex Franz. 2006. *Web 1T 5-gram Version 1*. Linguistic Data Consortium.

N. Coccaro and D. Jurafsky. 1998. Towards better integration of semantic predictors in statistical language modeling. In *Proceedings, International Conference on Spoken Language Processing (ICSLP-98)*.

D. A. Cruse. 1986. *Lexical Semantics*. Cambridge University Press.

James R. Curran and Marc Moens. 2002. Improvements in automatic thesaurus extraction. In *Proceedings of the ACL-02 workshop on Unsupervised lexical acquisition - Volume 9*, pages 59–66. Association for Computational Linguistics.

Thomas de Simone and Dimitar Kazakov. 2005. Using wordnet similarity and antonymy relations to aid document retrieval. In *Recent Advances in Natural Language Processing (RANLP)*.

S. Deerwester, S.T. Dumais, G.W. Furnas, T.K. Landauer, and R. Harshman. 1990. Indexing by latent semantic analysis. *Journal of the American Society for Information Science*, 41(96).

E. Gabrilovich and S. Markovitch. 2007. Computing semantic relatedness using wikipedia-based explicit semantic analysis. In *AAAI Conference on Artificial Intelligence (AAAI)*.

Sanda Harabagiu, Andrew Hickl, and Finley Lacatusu. 2006. Negation, contrast and contradiction in text processing. In *AAAI Conference on Artificial Intelligence (AAAI)*.

Zelig Harris. 1954. Distributional structure. *Word*, 10(23):146–162.

Mario Jarmasz and Stan Szpakowicz. 2003. Rogets thesaurus and semantic similarity. In *Proceedings of the International Conference on Recent Advances in Natural Language Processing (RANLP-2003)*.

Thomas Landauer and Susan Dumais. 1997. A solution to plato's problem: The latent semantic analysis theory of the acquisition, induction, and representation of knowledge. *Psychological Review, 104(2)*, pages 211–240.

T.K. Landauer and D. Laham. 1998. Learning human-like knowledge by singular value decomposition: A progress report. In *Neural Information Processing Systems (NIPS)*.

Thomas K. Landauer, Peter W. Foltz, and Darrell Laham. 1998. An introduction to latent semantic analysis. *Discourse Processes, 25*, pages 259–284.

T.K. Landauer. 2002. On the computational basis of learning and cognition: Arguments from lsa. *Psychology of Learning and Motivation*, 41:43–84.

Dekang Lin, Shaojun Zhao, Lijuan Qin, and Ming Zhou. 2003. Identifying synonyms among distributionally similar words. In *International Joint Conference on Artificial Intelligence (IJCAI)*.

Dekang Lin. 1998. Automatic retrieval and clustering of similar words. In *Proceedings of the 36th Annual Meeting of the Association for Computational Linguistics and 17th International Conference on Computational Linguistics - Volume 2*, ACL '98, pages 768–774, Stroudsburg, PA, USA. Association for Computational Linguistics.

David Milne and Ian H. Witten. 2008. An effective low-cost measure of semantic relatedness obtained from wikipedia links. In *Proceedings of the AAAI 2008 Workshop on Wikipedia and Artificial Intelligence*.

G. Minnen, J. Carroll, and D. Pearce. 2001. Applied morphological processing of english. *Natural Language Engineering*, 7(3):207–223.

Saif Mohammed, Bonnie Dorr, and Graeme Hirst. 2008. Computing word pair antonymy. In *Empirical Methods in Natural Language Processing (EMNLP)*.

Saif M. Mohammed, Bonnie J. Dorr, Graeme Hirst, and Peter D. Turney. 2011. Measuring degrees of semantic opposition. Technical report, National Research Council Canada.

Gregory L. Murphy and Jane M. Andrew. 1993. The conceptual basis of antonymy and synonymy in adjectives. *Journal of Memory and Language*, 32(3):1–19.

Jorge Nocedal and Stephen Wright. 2006. *Numerical Optimization*. Springer, 2nd edition.

John Platt, Kristina Toutanova, and Wen-tau Yih. 2010. Translingual document representations from discriminative projections. In *Proceedings of EMNLP*, pages 251–261.

Hoifung Poon and Pedro Domingos. 2009. Unsupervised semantic parsing. In *Empirical Methods in Natural Language Processing (EMNLP)*.

Martin F. Porter. 1980. An algorithm for suffix stripping. *Program*, 14(3):130–137.

Joseph Reisinger and Raymond J. Mooney. 2010. Multi-prototype vector-space models of word meaning. In *Proceedings of HLT-NAACL*, pages 109–117.

Gerard Salton and Michael J. McGill. 1983. *Introduction to Modern Information Retrieval*. McGraw Hill.

G. Salton, A. Wong, and C. S. Yang. 1975. A Vector Space Model for Automatic Indexing. *Communications of the ACM*, 18(11).

D. Schwab, M. Lafourcade, and V. Prince. 2002. Antonymy and conceptual vectors. In *International Conference on Computational Linguistics (COLING)*.

Peter Turney and Michael Littman. 2005. Corpus-based learning of analogies and semantic relations. *Machine Learning, 60 (1-3)*, pages 251–278.

Peter D. Turney and Patrick Pantel. 2010. From frequency to meaning: Vector space models of semantics. *Journal of Artificial Intelligence Research*, (37).

Peter D. Turney, Michael L. Littman, Jeffrey Bigham, and Victor Shnayder. 2003. Combining independent modules to solve multiple-choice synonym and analogy problems. In *Recent Advances in Natural Language Processing (RANLP)*.

Peter D. Turney. 2001. Mining the web for synonyms: Pmi-ir versus lsa on toefl. In *European Conference on Machine Learning (ECML)*.

P. D. Turney. 2006. Similarity of semantic relations. *Computational Linguistics*, 32(3):379–416.

Peter Turney. 2008. A uniform approach to analogies, synonyms, antonyms, and associations. In *International Conference on Computational Linguistics (COLING)*.

Lonneke van der Plas and Gosse Bouma. 2005. Syntactic contexts for finding semantically similar words. In *Proceedings of the Meeting of Computational Linguistics in the Netherlands 2004 (CLIN)*.

Lonneke van der Plas and Jörg Tiedemann. 2006. Finding synonyms using automatic word alignment and measures of distributional similarity. In *Proceedings of the COLING/ACL on Main conference poster sessions*, COLING-ACL '06, pages 866–873. Association for Computational Linguistics.

Wei Xu, Xin Liu, and Yihong Gong. 2003. Document clustering based on non-negative matrix factorization. In *Proceedings of the 26th annual international ACM SIGIR conference on Research and development in informaion retrieval*, pages 267–273, New York, NY, USA. ACM.

Wen-tau Yih, Kristina Toutanova, John C. Platt, and Christopher Meek. 2011. Learning discriminative projections for text similarity measures. In *Proceedings of the Fifteen Conference on Computational Natural Language Learning (CoNLL)*, pages 247–256, Portland, Oregon, USA.

First-order vs. higher-order modification in distributional semantics

Gemma Boleda
Linguistics Department
University of Texas at Austin
gemma.boleda@utcompling.com

Eva Maria Vecchi
Center for Mind/Brain Sciences
University of Trento
evamaria.vecchi@unitn.it

Miquel Cornudella and **Louise McNally**
Departament de Traducció i Ciències del Llenguatge
Universitat Pompeu Fabra
miquel.cornudellagaya@gmail.com, louise.mcnally@upf.edu

Abstract

Adjectival modification, particularly by expressions that have been treated as higher-order modifiers in the formal semantics tradition, raises interesting challenges for semantic composition in distributional semantic models. We contrast three types of adjectival modifiers – intersectively used color terms (as in ***white*** *towel*, clearly first-order), subsectively used color terms (***white*** *wine*, which have been modeled as both first- and higher-order), and intensional adjectives (***former*** *bassist*, clearly higher-order) – and test the ability of different composition strategies to model their behavior. In addition to opening up a new empirical domain for research on distributional semantics, our observations concerning the attested vectors for the different types of adjectives, the nouns they modify, and the resulting noun phrases yield insights into modification that have been little evident in the formal semantics literature to date.

1 Introduction

One of the most appealing aspects of so-called distributional semantic models (see Turney and Pantel (2010) for a recent overview) is that they afford some hope for a non-trivial, computationally tractable treatment of the context dependence of lexical meaning that might also approximate in interesting ways the psychological representation of that meaning (Andrews et al., 2009). However, in order to have a complete theory of natural language meaning, these models must be supplied with or connected to a compositional semantics; otherwise, we will have no account of the recursive potential that natural language affords for the construction of novel complex contents.

In the last 4-5 years, researchers have begun to introduce compositional operations on distributional semantic representations, for instance to combine verbs with their arguments or adjectives with nouns (Erk and Padó, 2008; Mitchell and Lapata, 2010; Baroni and Zamparelli, 2010; Grefenstette and Sadrzadeh, 2011; Socher et al., 2011)[1]. Although the proposed operations have shown varying degrees of success in a number of tasks such as detecting phrase similarity and paraphrasing, it remains unclear to what extent they can account for the full range of meaning composition phenomena found in natural language. Higher-order modification (that is, modification that cannot obviously be modeled as property intersection, in contrast to first-order modification, which can) presents one such challenge, as we will detail in the next section.

The goal of this paper is twofold. First, we examine how the properties of different types of adjectival modifiers, both in isolation and in combination with nouns, are represented in distributional models. We take as a case study three groups of adjectives: 1) color terms used to ascribe true color properties (referred to here as **intersective** color terms), as prototypical representative of first-order modifiers; 2) color terms used to ascribe properties other than simple color (here, **subsective** color terms), as representatives of expressions that could in principle

[1]In a complementary direction, Garrette et al. (2011) connect distributional representations of lexical semantics to logic-based compositional semantics.

be given a well-motivated first-order or higher-order analysis; and 3) **intensional** adjectives (e.g. *former*), as representative of modifiers that arguably require a higher-order analysis. Formal semantic models tend to group the second and third groups together, despite the existence of some natural language data that questions this grouping. However, our results show that all three types of modifiers behave differently from each other, suggesting that their semantic treatment needs to be differentiated.

Second, we test how five different composition functions that have been proposed in recent literature fare in predicting the attested properties of nominals modified by each type of adjective. The model by Baroni and Zamparelli (2010) emerges as a suitable model of adjectival composition, while multiplication and addition shed mixed results.

The paper is structured as follows. Section 2 provides the necessary background on the semantics of adjectival modification. Section 3 presents the methods used in our study. Section 4 describes the characteristics of the different types of adjectival modification, and Section 5, the results of the composition operations. The paper concludes with a general discussion of the results and prospects for future work.

2 The semantics of adjectival modification

Accounting for inference in language is an important concern of semantic theory. Perhaps for this reason, within the formal semantics tradition the most influential classification of adjectives is based on the inferences they license (see (Parsons, 1970) and (Kamp, 1975) for early discussion). We very briefly review this classification here.

First, so called intersective adjectives, such as (the literally used) *white* in *white dress*, yield the inference that both the property contributed by the adjective and that contributed by the noun hold of the individual described; in other words, a white dress is white and is a dress. The semantics for such modifiers is easily characterized in terms of the intersection of two first-order properties, that is, properties that can be ascribed to individuals.

On the other extreme, intensional adjectives, such as *former* or *alleged* in *former/alleged criminal*, do not license the inference that either of the properties holds of the individual to which the modified nominal is ascribed. Indeed, such adjectives cannot be used as predicates at all:

(1) ??The criminal was former/alleged.

The infelicity of (1) is generally attributed to the fact that these adjectives do not describe individuals directly but rather effect more complex operations on the meaning of the modified noun. It is for this reason that these adjectives can be considered higher-order modifiers: they behave as properties of properties. Though rather abstract, the higher-order analysis is straightforwardly implementable in formal semantic models and captures a range of linguistic facts successfully.

Finally, subsective adjectives such as (the non-literally-used) *white* in *white wine*, consitute an intermediate case: they license the inference that the property denoted by the noun holds of the individual being described, but not the property contributed by the adjective. That is, white wine is not white but rather a color that we would probably call some shade of yellow. This use of color terms, in general, is distinguished primarily by the fact that color serves as a proxy for another property that is related to color (e.g. type of grape), though the color in question may or may not match the color identified by the adjective on the intersective use (see (Gärdenfors, 2000) and (Kennedy and McNally, 2010) for discussion and analysis). The effect of the adjective, rather than to identify a value for an incidental COLOR attribute of an object, is often to characterize a subclass of the class described by the noun (white wine is a kind of wine, brown rice a kind of rice, etc.).

This use of color terms can be modeled by property intersection in formal semantic models only if the term is previously disambiguated or allowed to depend on context for its precise denotation. However, it is easily modeled if the adjective denotes a (higher-order) function from properties (e.g. that denoted by *wine*) to properties (that denoted by *white wine*), since the output of the function denoted by the color term can be made to depend on the input it receives from the noun meaning. Nonetheless, there is ample evidence in natural language that a first-order analysis of the subsective color terms would be preferable, as they share more features with predicative adjectives such as *happy* than they do with adjectives such as *former*.

The trio of intersective color terms, subsective color terms, and intensional adjectives provides fertile ground for exploring the different composition functions that have been proposed for distributional semantic representations. Most of these functions start from the assumption that composition takes pairs of vectors (e.g. a verb vector and a noun vector) and returns another vector (e.g. a vector for the verb with the noun as its complement), usually by some version of vector addition or multiplication (Erk and Padó, 2008; Mitchell and Lapata, 2010; Grefenstette and Sadrzadeh, 2011). Such functions, insofar as they yield representations which strengthen distributional features shared by the component vectors, would be expected to model intersective modification.

Consider the example of *white dress*. We might expect the vector for *dress* to include non-zero frequencies for words such as *wedding* and *funeral*. The vector for *white*, on the other hand, is likely to have higher frequencies for *wedding* than for *funeral*, at least in corpora obtained from the U.S. and the U.K. Combining the two vectors with an additive or multiplicative operation should rightly yield a vector for *white dress* which assigns a higher frequency to *wedding* than to *funeral*.

Additive and multiplicative functions might also be expected to handle subsective modification with some success because these operations provide a natural account for how polysemy is resolved in meaning composition. Thus, the vector that results from adding or multiplying the vector for *white* with that for *dress* should differ in crucial features from the one that results from combining the same vector for *white* with that for *wine*. For example, depending on the details of the algorithm used, we should find the frequencies of words such as *snow* or *milky* weakened and words like *straw* or *yellow* strengthened in combination with *wine*, insofar as the former words are less likely than the latter to occur in contexts where *white* describes wine than in those where it describes dresses. In contrast, it is not immediately obvious how these operations would fare with intensional adjectives such as *former*. In particular, it is not clear what specific distributional features of the adjective would capture the effect that the adjective has on the meaning of the resulting modified nominal.

Interestingly, recent approaches to the semantic composition of adjectives with nouns such as Baroni and Zamparelli (2010) and Guevara (2010) draw on the classical analysis of adjectives within the Montagovian tradition of formal semantic theory (Montague, 1974), on which they are treated as higher order predicates, and model adjectives as matrices of weights that are applied to noun vectors. On such models, the distributional properties of observed occurrences of adjective-noun pairs are used to induce the effect of adjectives on nouns. Insofar as it is grounded in the intuition that adjective meanings should be modeled as mappings from noun meanings to adjective-noun meanings, the matrix analysis might be expected to perform better than additive or multiplicative models for adjective-noun combinations when there is evidence that the adjective denotes only a higher-order property. There is also no *a priori* reason to think that it would fare more poorly at modeling the intersective and subsective adjectives than would additive or multiplicative analyses, given its generality.

In this paper, we present the first studies that we know of that explore these expectations.

3 Method

We built a semantic space and tested the composition functions as specified in what follows.

3.1 Semantic space

The semantic space we used for our experiments consists of a matrix where each row vector represents an adjective, noun or adjective-noun phrase (henceforth, AN). We first introduce the source corpus, then the vocabulary that we represent in the space, and finally the procedure to build the vectors representing the vocabulary items from corpus data.

3.1.1 Source corpus

Our source corpus is the concatenation of the ukWaC corpus[2], a mid-2009 dump of the English Wikipedia[3] and the British National Corpus[4]. The corpus is tokenized, POS-tagged and lemmatized

[2]`http://wacky.sslmit.unibo.it/`

[3]`http://en.wikipedia.org`

[4]`http://www.natcorp.ox.ac.uk/`

with TreeTagger (Schmid, 1995) and contains about 2.8 billion tokens. We extracted all statistics at the lemma level, ignoring inflectional information.

3.1.2 Vocabulary

The core vocabulary of the semantic space consists of the 8K most frequent nouns and the 4K most frequent adjectives from the corpus. By crossing the set of 700 most frequent adjectives (reduced to 663 after removing questionable items like *above*, *less* and *very*) and the 4K most frequent nouns and selecting those ANs that occured at least 100 times in the corpus, we obtained a set of 179K ANs that we added to the semantic space, for a total of 191K rows. These ANs were used for training the linear models as well as for providing a basis for the analysis of the results.

3.1.3 Semantic space parameters

The dimensions (columns) of our semantic space are the top 10K most frequent content words in the corpus (nouns, adjectives, verbs and adverbs), excluding the 300 most frequent words of *all* parts of speech.

For each word or AN, we collected raw co-occurrence counts by recording their sentence-internal co-occurrence with each of words in the dimensions. The counts were then transformed into Local Mutual Information (LMI) scores, an association measure that closely approximates the commonly used Log-Likelihood Ratio but is simpler to compute (Evert, 2005). Specifically, given a row element r, a column element c and a counting function $C(r, c)$, then

$$LMI = C(r, c) \cdot \log \frac{C(r, c)C(*, *)}{C(r, *)C(*, c)} \quad (1)$$

where $C(r, c)$ is how many times r cooccurs with c, $C(r, *)$ is the total count of r, $C(*, c)$ is the total count of c, and $C(*, *)$ is the cumulative co-occurrence count of any r with any c.

The dimensionality of the space was reduced using Singular Value Decomposition (SVD), as in Latent Semantic Analysis and related distributional semantic methods (Landauer and Dumais, 1997; Rapp, 2003; Schütze, 1997). Both LMI and SVD were used for the core vocabulary, and the AN vectors were computed based on the values for the core vocabulary. All of the results discussed in the article are based on the SVD-reduced space, because it yielded consistently better results, except for those involving multiplicative composition, which was carried out on the non-reduced model because SVD reduction introduces negative values for the latent dimensions used for the reduced space.

Some of the parameters of the space and composition functions were set based on performance on independent word similarity and AN similarity tasks (Rubenstein and Goodenough, 1965; Mitchell and Lapata, 2010). In addition to LMI, we tested the performance using log-transformed frequencies and found very poor performance in the aforementioned tasks. The number of latent dimensions for the SVD-reduced space was set at 300 after testing the performance using 300, 600 and 900 latent dimensions.

In the discussion, we use the cosine of two vectors as a measure of similarity. This is the most common choice in related work, as it has shown to be robust across different tasks and settings, though other options (in particular, measures that are not symmetric or do not normalize) could be explored (Widdows, 2004).

3.2 Composition models

The experiments described below were carried out using five compositional methods that have been explored in recent studies of compositionality in distributional semantic spaces (Mitchell and Lapata, 2010; Guevara, 2010; Baroni and Zamparelli, 2010). For each function, we define $\mathbf{p}$ as the composition of the adjective vector, $\mathbf{u}$, and the noun vector, $\mathbf{v}$, a nomenclature that follows Mitchell and Lapata (2010).

Additive (*add*) AN vectors were obtained by summing the corresponding adjective and noun vectors. We also explored the effects of the additive model with normalized component adjective and noun vectors (add_n).

$$\mathbf{p} = \mathbf{u} + \mathbf{v} \quad (2)$$

Multiplicative (*mult*) AN vectors were obtained by component-wise multiplication of the adjective and noun vectors in the non-reduced semantic space.

$$\mathbf{p} = \mathbf{u} \odot \mathbf{v} \quad (3)$$

Dilation (*dl*) AN vectors were obtained by calculating the dot products of $\mathbf{u} \cdot \mathbf{u}$ and $\mathbf{u} \cdot \mathbf{v}$ and stretching $\mathbf{v}$ by a factor λ (in our case, 16.7) in the direction of $\mathbf{u}$ (Clark et al., 2008; Mitchell and Lapata, 2010). The effect of this operation is to "stretch" the head vector $\mathbf{v}$ (noun, in our case) in the direction of the modifying vector $\mathbf{u}$ (adjective).

$$\mathbf{p} = (\mathbf{u} \cdot \mathbf{u})\mathbf{v} + (\lambda - 1)(\mathbf{u} \cdot \mathbf{v}) \quad (4)$$

The factor λ was selected based on the optimal parameters presented in Mitchell and Lapata (2010). We tested both reported values (16.7 and 2.2) and found $\lambda = 16.7$ to perform better in terms of rank of observed equivalent (see Section 5).

The preceding functions produce an AN vector from the component A and N vectors. The remaining two functions do not use the vector for the adjective, but learn a matrix representation for it. The composed AN vector is obtained by multiplying the matrix by the noun vector. The general equation for the two functions is the following, where $\mathbf{B}$ is a matrix of weights that is multiplied by the noun vector $\mathbf{v}$ to produce the AN vector $\mathbf{p}$.

$$\mathbf{p} = \mathbf{B}\mathbf{v} \quad (5)$$

In the **linear map** (*lim*) approach proposed by Guevara (2010), one single matrix $\mathbf{B}$ is learnt that represents all adjectives. An AN vector is obtained by multiplying the weight matrix by the concatenation of the adjective and noun vectors, so that each dimension of the generated AN vector is a linear combination of dimensions of the corresponding adjective and noun vectors. In our implementation, $\mathbf{B}$ is an 300 x 300 weight matrix representing an adjective, and $\mathbf{v}$ is a 300-dimension noun vector. Following Guevara (2010), we estimate the coefficients of the equation using (multivariate) partial least squares regression (PLSR) as implemented in the R `pls` package (Mevik and Wehrens, 2007), setting the latent dimension parameter of PLSR to 300. This value was chosen after testing values 100, 200 and 300 on the AN similarity tasks (Mitchell and Lapata, 2010). Coefficient matrix estimation is performed by feeding PLSR a set of input-output examples, where the input is given by concatenated adjective and noun vectors, and the output is the vector of the corresponding AN directly extracted from our semantic space. The matrix is estimated using a random sample of 2.5K adjective-noun-AN tuples.[5]

In the **adjective-specific linear map** (*alm*) model, proposed by Baroni and Zamparelli (2010), a different matrix $\mathbf{B}$ is learnt for each adjective. The weights of each of the rows of the weight matrix are the coefficients of a linear equation predicting the values of one of the dimensions of the normalized AN vector as a linear combination of the dimensions of the normalized component noun. The linear equation coefficients are estimated again using PLSR, and in the present implementation we use ridge regression generalized cross-validation (GCV) to automatically choose the optimal ridge parameter for each adjective (Golub et al., 1979). This procedure drastically outperforms setting a fixed number of dimensions. The model is trained on all N-AN vector pairs available in the semantic space for each adjective, and range from 100 to over 1K items across the adjectives we tested.

3.3 Datasets

We built two datasets of adjective-noun phrases for the present research, one with color terms and one with intensional adjectives.[6]

Color terms. This dataset is populated with a randomly selected set of adjective-noun pairs from the space presented above. From the 11 colors in the basic set proposed by Berlin and Kay (1969), we cover 7 (*black*, *blue*, *brown*, *green*, *red*, *white*, and *yellow*), since the remaining (*grey*, *orange*, *pink*, and *purple*) are not in the 700 most frequent set of adjectives in the corpora used. From an original set of 412 ANs, 43 were manually removed because of suspected parsing errors (e.g. *white photograph*, for *black and white photograph*) or because the head noun was semantically transparent (*white variety*). The remaining 369 ANs were tagged independently by the second and fourth authors of this paper, both native English speaker linguists, as **intersective** (e.g. *white towel*), **subsective** (e.g. *white wine*), or **idiomatic**, i.e. compositionally non-transparent (e.g. *black hole*). They were allowed the assignment of at

[5] 2.5K ANs is the upper bound of the software package used.

[6] Available at `http://dl.dropbox.com/u/513347/resources/data-emnlp2012.zip`. See Bruni et al. (to appear) for an analysis of the color term dataset from a multimodal perspective.

most two labels in case of polysemy, for instance for *black staff* for the person vs. physical object senses of the noun or *yellow skin* for the race vs. literally painted interpretations of the AN. In this paper, only the first label (most frequent interpretation, according to the judges) has been used. The κ coefficient of the annotation on the three categories (first interpretation only) was 0.87 (conf. int. 0.82-0.92, according to Fleiss et al. (1969)), observed agreement 0.96.[7] There were too few instances of idioms (17) for a quantitative analysis of the sort presented here, so these are collapsed with the subsective class in what follows.[8] The dataset as used here consists of 239 intersective and 130 subsective ANs.

Intensional adjectives. The intensional dataset contains all ANs in the semantic space with a preselected list of 10 intensional adjectives, manually pruned by one of the authors of the paper to eliminate erroneous examples and to ensure that the adjective was being intensionally used. Examples of the ANs eliminated on these grounds include *past twelve* (cp. accepted *past president*), *former girl* (probably *former girl friend* or similar), *false rumor* (which is a real rumor that is false, vs. e.g. *false floor*, which is not a real floor), or *theoretical work* (which is real work related to a theory, vs. e.g. *theoretical speed*, which is a speed that should have been reached in theory). Other AN pairs were excluded on the grounds that the noun was excessively vague (e.g. *past one*) or because the AN formed a fixed expression (e.g. *former USSR*). The final dataset contained 1,200 ANs, distributed as follows: *former* (300 examples), *possible* (244), *future* (243), *potential* (183), *past* (87), *false* (44), *apparent* (39), *artificial* (36), *likely* (18), *theoretical* (6).[9]

Table 1 contains examples of each type of AN we are considering.

Intersective	*Subsective*	*Intensional*
white towel	white wine	artificial leg
black sack	black athlete	former bassist
green coat	green politics	likely suspect
red disc	red ant	possible delay
blue square	blue state	theoretical limit

Table 1: Example ANs in the datasets.

4 Observed vectors

We began by exploring the empirically **observed vectors** for the adjectives (A), nouns (N), and adjective-noun phrases (AN) in the datasets, as they are represented in the semantic space. Note that we are working with the AN vectors directly harvested from the corpora (that is, based on the co-occurrence of, say, the phrase *white towel* with each of the 10K words in the space dimensions), without doing any composition. AN vectors obtained by composition will be examined in the following section. Though observed AN vectors should not be regarded as a gold standard in the sense of, for instance, Machine Learning approaches, because they are typically sparse[10] and thus the vectors of their component adjective and noun will be richer, they are still useful for exploration and as a comparison point for the composition operations (Baroni and Lenci, 2010; Guevara, 2010).

Figure 1 shows the distribution of the cosines between A, N, and AN vectors with intensional adjectives (I, white box), intersective uses of color terms (IE, lighter gray box), and subsective uses of color terms (S, darker gray box).

In general, the similarity of the A and N vectors is quite low (cosine < 0.2, left graph of Figure 1), and much lower than the similarities between both the AN and A vectors and the AN and N vectors. This is not surprising, given that adjectives and nouns describe rather different sorts of things.

We find significant differences between the three types of adjectives in the similarity between AN and A vectors (middle graph of Figure 1). The adjective and adjective-noun phrase vectors are nearer for

[7]Code for the computation of inter-annotator agreement by Stefan Evert, available at `http://www.collocations.de/temp/kappa_example.zip`.

[8]An alternative would have been to exclude idiomatic ANs from the analysis.

[9]*Alleged*, one of the most prototypical intensional adjectives, is not considered here because it was not among the 700 most frequent adjectives in the space. We will consider it in future work.

[10]The frequency of the adjectives in the datasets range from 3.5K to 3.7M, with a median frequency of 109,114. The nouns range from 4.9K to 2.5M, with a median frequency of 148,459. While the frequency of the ANs range from 100 to 18.5K, with a median frequency of 239.

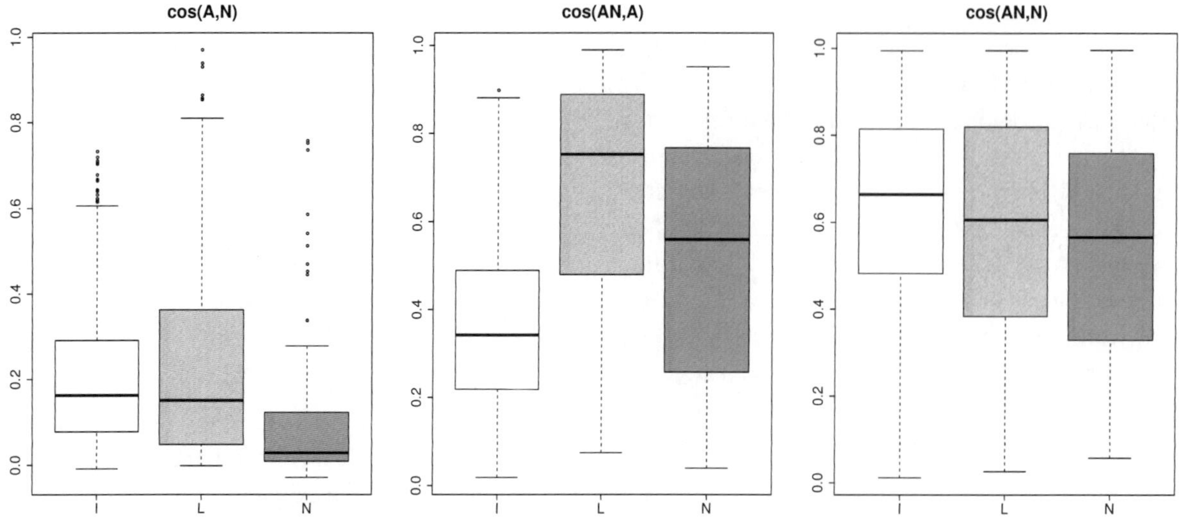

Figure 1: Cosine distance distribution in the different types of AN. We report the cosines between the component adjective and noun vectors (cos(A,N)), between the observed AN and adjective vectors (cos(AN,A)), and between the observed AN and noun vectors (cos(AN,N)). Each chart contains three boxplots with the distribution of the cosine scores (y-axis) for the intensional (I), intersective (IE), and subsective (S) types of ANs. The boxplots represent the value distribution of the cosine between two vectors. The horizontal lines in the rectangles represent the first quartile, median, and third quartile. Larger rectangles correspond to a more spread distribution, and their (a)symmetry mirrors the (a)symmetry of the distribution. The lines above and below the rectangle stretch to the minimum and maximum values, at most 1.5 times the length of the rectangle. Values outside this range (outliers) are represented as points.

intersective uses than for subsective uses of color terms, a pattern that parallels the difference in the distance between component A and N vectors. Since intersective uses correspond to the prototypical use of color terms (a *white dress* is the color white, while *white wine* is not), the greater similarity for the intersective cases is unsurprising – it suggests that in the case of subsective adjectival modifiers, the noun "pulls" the AN further away from the adjective than happens with the cases of intersective modification. This is compatible with the intuition (manifest in the formal semantics tradition in the treatment of subsective adjectives as higher-order rather than first-order, intersective modifiers) that the adjective's effect on the AN in cases of subsective modification depends heavily on the interpretation of the noun with which the adjective combines, whereas that is less the case when the adjective is used intersectively.

As for intensional adjectives, the middle graph shows that their AN vectors are quite distant from the corresponding A vectors, in sharp contrast to what we find with both intersective and subsective color terms. We hypothesize that the results for the intensional adjectives are due to the fact that they cannot plausibly be modeled as first order attributes (i.e. being *potential* or *apparent* is not a property in the same sense that being *white* or *yellow* is) and thus typically do not restrict the nominal description *per se*, but rather provide information about whether or when the nominal description applies. The result is that intensional adjectives should be even weaker than subsectively used adjectives, in comparison with the nouns with which they combine, in their ability to "pull" the AN vector in their direction. Note, incidentally, that an alternative explanation, namely that the effect mentioned could be due to the fact that most nouns in the intensional dataset are abstract and that adjectives modifying abstract nouns might tend to be further away from their nouns altogether, is ruled out by the comparison between the A and N vectors: the A-N cosines of the intensional and intersective ANs are similar. We thus conclude that here we see an effect of the *type of modification* involved.

An examination of the average distances among

the nearest neighbors of the intensional and of the color adjectives in the distributional space supports our hypothesized account of their contrasting behaviors. We predict that the nearest neighbors are more dispersed for adjectives that cannot be modeled as first-order properties (i.e., intensional adjectives), than for those that can (here, the color terms). We find that the average cosine distance among the nearest ten neighbors of the intensional adjectives is 0.74 with a standard deviation of 0.13, which is significantly lower (t-test, $p<0.001$) than the average similarity among the nearest neighbors of the color adjectives, 0.96 with astandard deviation of 0.04.

Finally, with respect to the distances between the adjective-noun and head noun vectors (right graph of Figure 1), there is no significant difference for the intersective vs. subsective color terms. This can be explained by the fact that both kinds of modifiers are subsective, that is, the fact that a white dress is a dress and that white wine is wine.

In contrast, intensional ANs are closer to their component Ns than are color ANs (the difference is qualitatively quite small, but significant even for the intersective vs. intensional ANs according to a t-test, p-value = 0.015). This effect, the inverse of what we find with the AN-A vectors, can similarly be explained by the fact that intensional adjectives do not restrict the descriptive content of the noun they modify, in contrast to both the intersective and subsective color ANs. Restriction of the nominal description may lead to significantly restricted distributions (e.g. the phrase *red button* may appear in distinctively different contexts than does *button*; similarly for *green politics* and *politics*), while we do not expect the contexts in which *former bassist* and *bassist* appear to diverge in a qualitatively different way because the basic nominal descriptions are identical, though further research will be necessary to confirm these explanations.

Finally, note that, contrary to predictions from some approaches in formal semantics, subsective color ANs and intensional ANs do not pattern together: subsective ANs are closer to their component As, and intensional ANs closer to their component Ns. This unexpected behavior underscores the fact highlighted in the previous paragraph: that the distributional properties of modified expressions are more sensitive to whether the modification restricts the nominal description than to whether the modifier is intersective in the strictest sense of term.

We now discuss the extent to which the different composition functions account for these patterns.

5 Composed vectors

Since intersective modification is the point of comparison for both subsective and intensional modification, we first discuss the composed vectors for the intersective vs. subsective uses of color terms, and then turn to intersective vs. intensional modification.

5.1 Intersective and subsective modification with color terms

To adequately model the differences between intersective and subsective modification observed in the previous section, a successful composition function should yield a significantly smaller distance between the adjective and AN vectors for intersectively used adjectives, whereas it should yield no significant difference for the distances between the noun and AN vectors.

Table 2 provides a summary of the results with the observed data (*obs*) and the composition functions discussed in Section 3.2. The median rank of observed equivalent (ROE) is provided as a general measure of the quality of the composition function. It is computed by finding the cosine between the composed AN vectors and all rows in the semantic space and then determining the rank in which the observed ANs are found.[11] The remaining columns report the differences in standardized (z-score) cosines between the vector built with each of the composition functions and the observed AN, A, and N vectors. A positive value means that the cosines for intersective uses are higher, while a negative value means that the cosines for subsective uses are higher. The first row (*obs*) contains a numerical summary of the tendencies for observed ANs explained in the previous section. This is the behavior that we expect to model.

Two composition functions come close to modeling the observed behavior: *alm* and *mult*, though *alm* is better in terms of ROE, consistent with the

[11]The ROE is provided as a general guide; however, recall that the ROE was taken into account to tune the λ parameter in the dilation model, and that the ANs of the color dataset were included when training the matrices for the *alm* model.

model	*ROE*	Δ:*AN*		Δ:*A*		Δ:*N*	
obs	-	-		.54	***	.10	
add	286	.40	***	.14		.15	
add_n	11	.40	***	.65	***	.65	***
mult	111	.40	***	.74	***	.29	*
dl	298	.63	***	.85	***	-.66	***
lim	1,940	.46	***	.20		.38	**
alm	1	.16		.52	***	.27	*

Table 2: Intersective vs. subsective uses of color terms. The first column reports the rank of the observed equivalent (ROE), the rest report the differences (Δ) betwen the intersective and subsective uses of color terms when comparing the composed AN with the observed vectors for: AN, adjective (A), noun (N). See text for details. Significances according to a t-test: *** for $p < 0.001$, ** < 0.01, * < 0.05.

results reported in Baroni and Zamparelli (2010). In both cases, we find that these functions yield higher similarities for AN-A for the intersective than for the subsective uses of color terms, and a very slight (though still mildly significant) difference for the distance to the head noun. The add_n function performs very good in terms of ROE (median 11). This suggests that, for adjectival modification, providing a vector that is in the middle of the two component vectors (which is what normalized addition does) is a reasonable approximation of the observed vectors. However, precisely because the resulting vector is in the middle of the two component vectors, this function cannot account for the asymmetries in the distances found in the observed data. The non-normalized version also cannot account for these effects because the adjective vector, being much longer (as color terms are very frequent), totally dominates the AN, which results in no difference across uses when comparing to the adjective or to the noun.

The dilation model shows a strange pattern, as it yields a strongly significant negative difference in the AN-N distance. The *lim* function exhibits the opposite pattern as predicted, yielding no difference for the AN-A similarities and a difference for the AN-N similarities. A possible explanation for the AN-A results is that *lim* learns from such a broad range of AN pairs that the impact of the distance between intersective vs. subsective uses of color terms from their component adjectives is dampened. Moreover, *lim* is by far the worst function in terms of ROE.

All composition functions except for *alm* find intersective uses easier to model. This is shown in the positive values in column Δ:AN, which mean that the similarity between observed and composed AN vectors is greater for intersective than for subsective ANs. This is consistent with expectations. The subsective uses are specific to the nouns with which the color terms combine, and the exact interpretation of the adjective varies across those nouns. In contrast, the interpretation associated with intersective use is consistent across a larger variety of nouns, and in that sense should be predominantly reflected in the adjective's vector. The exception in this respect is the *alm* function, since the weights for each adjective matrix are estimated in relation to the noun vectors with which the adjective combines, on the one hand, and the related observed AN vectors, on the other; thus, the basic lexical representation of the adjective is inherently reflective of the distributions of the ANs in which it appears in a way that is not the case for the adjective representations used in the other composition models. And indeed, *alm* is the only function that shows no difference in difficulty (distance) between the predicted and observed AN vectors for intersective vs. subsective ANs.

Both *mult* and *alm* seem to account for the observed patterns in color terms. However, an examination of the nearest neighbors of the composed ANs suggest that *alm* captures the semantics of adjective composition in this case to a larger extent than *mult*. For instance, the NN for *blue square* (intersective) are the following according to *mul*: *blue, red, official colour, traditional colour, blue number, yellow*; while *alm* yields the following: *blue square, red square, blue circle, blue triangle, blue pattern, yellow circle*. Similarly, for *green politics* (subsective) *mul* yields: *pleasant land, green business, green politics, green issue, green strategy, green product*, while *alm* yields *green politics, green movement, political agenda, environmental movement, progressive government, political initiative*.

5.2 Intensional modification

Table 3 contains the results of the composition functions comparing the behavior of intersective color ANs and intensional ANs. The tendencies in the ROE are as in Table 2, so we will not comment on

model	*ROE*	Δ:*AN*		Δ:*A*		Δ:*N*	
obs	-	-		1.39	***	-.27	***
add	198	.66	***	.71	***	-.81	***
add_n	40	.93	***	.20	*	.20	*
mult	110	.58	***	1.09	***	-.25	***
dl	354	.97	***	-.27	**	.47	***
lim	7,943	.27	***	.65	***	-.47	***
alm	1	.81	***	1.43	***	-.59	***

Table 3: Intersective vs. intensional ANs. Information as in Table 2.

them further (note the very poor performance of *lim*, though). As noted above, we expect more difficulty in modeling intensional modification vs. other kinds of modification, and this is verified in the results (cf. the positive values in second column). The difference with the results in the previous subsection is that in this case the *alm* function does present a higher difficulty in modeling intensional ANs, unlike with the color terms. This points to a qualitative difference between subsective and intensional adjectives that could be evidence for a first-order analysis of subsective color terms.

A good composition function should provide a large positive difference when comparing the AN to the A, and a small negative difference (because the effect is very small in the observed data) when comparing the AN to the N. The functions that best match the observed data are again *alm* and *mult*. *Add* and *lim* show the predicted pattern, but to a much lesser degree (cf. smaller differences in column Δ:A). *Dl* yields the exact opposite effect and add_n, though good in terms of ROE, is subject to the problems discussed in the previous section.

Again, *alm* seems to be capturing relevant semantic aspects of composition with intensional adjectives. For instance, the nearest neighbors of *artificial leg* according to *alm* are *artificial leg*, *artificial limb*, *artificial joint*, *artificial hip*, *scar*, *small wound*.

6 Discussion and conclusions

The present research provides some evidence for treating adjectives as matrices or functions, rather than vectors, although simple operations on vectors such as addition (for its excellent approximation to observed vectors) and multiplication (for its ability to reproduce the observed trends in the data) still account for some aspects of adjectival modification. The dilation model, in contrast, is not suitable for adjectival modification.

Our results also show that *alm* performs better than *lim*, but it is worth observing that it does so at the expense of modeling each adjective as a completely different function. We consider *lim* very attractive in principle because it generalizes across adjectives and is thus more parsimonious. Part of the poor results on *lim* were due to limitations of our implementation, as we trained the matrices on only 2.5K ANs, while our semantic space contains more than 170K ANs. However, the linguistic literature and the present results suggest that it might be useful to try a compromise between *alm* and *lim*, training one matrix for each subclass of adjectives under analysis.

Beyond the new data it offers regarding the comparative ability of the different composition functions to account for different kinds of adjectival modification, the study presented here underscores the complexity of modification as a semantic phenomenon. The role of adjectival modifiers as restrictors of descriptive content is reflected differently in distributional data than is their role in providing information about whether or when a description applies to some individual. Formal semantic models, thanks to their abstractness, are able to handle these two roles with little difficulty, but also with limited insight. Distributional models, in contrast, offer the promise of greater insight into each of these roles, but face serious challenges in handling both of them in a unified manner.

Acknowledgments

This research was funded by the Spanish MICINN (FFI2010-09464-E, FFI2010-15006, TIN2009-14715-C04-04), the Catalan AGAUR (2010BP-A00070), and the EU (PASCAL2; FP7-ICT-216886). Eva Maria Vecchi was partially funded by ERC Starting Grant 283554. We thank Marco Baroni, Roberto Zamparelli, and six anonymous reviewers for valuable feedback, and Yao-zhong Zhang for the code for the *alm* function.

References

Mark Andrews, Gabriella Vigliocco, and David Vinson. 2009. Integrating experiential and distributional data to learn semantic represenations. *Psychological Review*, 116(3):463–498.

Marco Baroni and Alessandro Lenci. 2010. Distributional Memory: A general framework for corpus-based semantics. *Computational Linguistics*, 36(4):673–721.

Marco Baroni and Roberto Zamparelli. 2010. Nouns are vectors, adjectives are matrices: Representing adjective-noun constructions in semantic space. In *Proceedings of EMNLP*, pages 1183–1193, Boston, MA.

Brent Berlin and Paul Kay. 1969. *Basic Color Terms: Their Universality an Evolution*. University of California Press, Berkeley and Los Angeles, CA.

E. Bruni, G. Boleda, M. Baroni, and N. K. Tran. to appear. Distributional semantics in technicolor. In *Proceedings of ACL 2012*.

Stephen Clark, Bob Coecke, and Mehrnoosh Sadrzadeh. 2008. A compositional distributional model of meaning. In *Proceedings of the AAAI Spring Symposium on Quantum Interaction*, pages 52–55, Stanford, CA.

Katrin Erk and Sebastian Padó. 2008. A structured vector space model for word meaning in context. In *Proceedings of EMNLP*, pages 897–906, Honolulu, HI, USA.

Stefan Evert. 2005. *The Statistics of Word Cooccurrences*. Dissertation, Stuttgart University.

Joseph L. Fleiss, Jacob Cohen, and B. S. Everitt. 1969. Large sample standard errors of kappa and weighted kappa. *Psychological Bulletin*, 72(5):323–327.

Peter Gärdenfors. 2000. *Conceptual Spaces: The Geometry of Thought*. MIT Press, Cambridge, MA.

Dan Garrette, Katrin Erk, and Raymond Mooney. 2011. Integrating logical representations with probabilistic information using markov logic. In *Proceedings of IWCS 2011*.

G.H. Golub, M. Heath, and G. Wahba. 1979. Generalized cross-validation as a method for choosing a good ridge parameter. *Technometrics*, pages 215–223.

Edward Grefenstette and Mehrnoosh Sadrzadeh. 2011. Experimenting with transitive verbs in a discocat. In *Proceedings of the GEMS 2011 Workshop on GEometrical Models of Natural Language Semantics*.

Emiliano Guevara. 2010. A regression model of adjective-noun compositionality in distributional semantics. In *Proceedings of the ACL GEMS Workshop*, pages 33–37, Uppsala, Sweden.

H. Kamp. 1975. Two theories about adjectives. *Formal semantics of natural language*, pages 123–155.

Christopher Kennedy and Louise McNally. 2010. Color, context, and compositionality. *Synthese*, 174:79–98.

Thomas Landauer and Susan Dumais. 1997. A solution to Plato's problem: The latent semantic analysis theory of acquisition, induction, and representation of knowledge. *Psychological Review*, 104(2):211–240.

Björn-Helge Mevik and Ron Wehrens. 2007. The pls package: Principal component and partial least squares regression in R. *Journal of Statistical Software*, 18(2). Published online: `http://www.jstatsoft.org/v18/i02/`.

Jeff Mitchell and Mirella Lapata. 2010. Composition in distributional models of semantics. *Cognitive Science*, 34(8):1388–1429.

Richard Montague. 1974. *Formal philosophy: Selected Papers of Richard Montague*. Yale University Press, New Haven.

Terence Parsons. 1970. Some problems concerning the logic of grammatical modifiers. *Synthese*, 21:320–334.

Reinhard Rapp. 2003. Word sense discovery based on sense descriptor dissimilarity. In *Proceedings of the 9th MT Summit*, pages 315–322, New Orleans, LA, USA.

Herbert Rubenstein and John Goodenough. 1965. Contextual correlates of synonymy. *Communications of the ACM*, 8(10):627–633.

Helmut Schmid. 1995. Improvements in part-of-speech tagging with an application to German. In *Proceedings of the EACL-SIGDAT Workshop*, Dublin, Ireland.

Hinrich Schütze. 1997. *Ambiguity Resolution in Natural Language Learning*. CSLI, Stanford, CA.

R. Socher, J. Pennington, E.H. Huang, A.Y. Ng, and C.D. Manning. 2011. Semi-supervised recursive autoencoders for predicting sentiment distributions. In *Proceedings of the Conference on Empirical Methods in Natural Language Processing*, pages 151–161, Edinburgh, UK.

Peter Turney and Patrick Pantel. 2010. From frequency to meaning: Vector space models of semantics. *Journal of Artificial Intelligence Research*, 37:141–188.

Dominic Widdows. 2004. *The Geometry of Meaning*. CSLI Publications, Stanford, CA.

Learning-based Multi-Sieve Co-reference Resolution with Knowledge*

Lev Ratinov
Google Inc.†
ratinov@google.com

Dan Roth
University of Illinois at Urbana-Champaign
danr@illinois.edu

Abstract

We explore the interplay of knowledge and structure in co-reference resolution. To inject knowledge, we use a state-of-the-art system which cross-links (or "grounds") expressions in free text to Wikipedia. We explore ways of using the resulting grounding to boost the performance of a state-of-the-art co-reference resolution system. To maximize the utility of the injected knowledge, we deploy a learning-based multi-sieve approach and develop novel entity-based features. Our end system outperforms the state-of-the-art baseline by 2 B^3 F1 points on non-transcript portion of the ACE 2004 dataset.

1 Introduction

Co-reference resolution is the task of grouping mentions to entities. For example, consider the text snippet in Fig. 1[1]. The correct output groups the mentions $\{m_1, m_2, m_5\}$ to one entity while leaving m_3 and m_4 as singletons. Resolving co-reference is fundamental for understanding natural language. For example in Fig. 1, to infer that Kusrk has suffered a torpedo detonation, we have to understand that $\{[\textit{vessel}]\}_{m1}$ refers to $\{[\textit{Kursk}]\}_{m2}$.

> *"After the $\{[\text{vessel}]\}_{m_1}$ suffered a catastrophic torpedo detonation, $\{[\text{Kursk}]\}_{m_2}$ sank in the waters of $\{[\text{Barents Sea}]\}_{m_3}$ with all hands lost. Though rescue attempts were offered by a nearby $\{\text{Norwegian [ship]}\}_{m_4}$, Russia declined initial rescue offers, and all 118 sailors and officers aboard $\{[\text{Kursk}]\}_{m_5}$ perished."*

Figure 1: Example illustrating the challenges in co-reference resolution.

This inference is typically trivial for humans, but proves extremely challenging for state-of-the-art co-reference resolution systems. We believe that it is world knowledge that gives people the ability to understand text with such ease. A human reader can infer that since Kursk sank, it must be a vessel and vessels which suffer catastrophic torpedo detonations can sink. Moreover, some readers might *just know* that *Kursk* is a Russian submarine named after the city of Kursk, where the largest tank battle in history took place in 1943. In this work we are using Wikipedia as a source of encyclopedic knowledge. The key contributions of this work are:

(1) Using Wikipedia to assign a set of knowledge attributes to mentions in a context-sensitive way. For example, for the text in Fig. 1, our system assigns to the mention *"Kursk"* the nationalities: *Russian, Soviet* and the attributes *ship, incident, submarine, shipwreck* (as opposed to *city* or *battle*). We are using a publicly available system for context-

* We thank Nicholas Rizzolo and Kai Wei Chang for their invaluable help with modifying the baseline co-reference system. We thank the anonymous EMNLP reviewers for constructive comments. This research was supported by the Army Research Laboratory (ARL) under agreement W911NF-09-2-0053 and by the Defense Advanced Research Projects Agency (DARPA) Machine Reading Program under Air Force Research Laboratory (AFRL) prime contract no. FA8750-09-C-0181. Any opinions, findings, conclusions or recommendations are those of the authors and do not necessarily reflect the view of the ARL, DARPA, AFRL, or the US government.

† The majority of this work was done while the first author was at the University of Illinois.

1 Throughout this paper, curly brackets {} denote the extent and square brackets [] denote the head.

sensitive disambiguation to Wikipedia. We then extract attributes from the cross-linked Wikipedia pages (described in Sec. 3.1), assign these attributes to the document mentions (Sec. 3.2) and develop knowledge-rich compatibility metric between mentions (Sec. 3.3)[2].

(2) Integrating the strength of rule-based systems such as (Haghighi and Klein, 2009; Raghunathan et al., 2010) into a machine learning framework. We are using a multi-sieve approach (Raghunathan et al., 2010), which splits pairwise "co-reference" vs. "non-coreference" decisions to different types and attempts to make the easy decisions first (Goldberg and Elhadad, 2010). Our multi-sieve approach is different from (Raghunathan et al., 2010) in several respects: (a) our sieves are machine-learning classifiers, (b) the same pair of mentions can fall into multiple sieves, (c) later sieves can override the decisions made by earlier sieves, allowing to recover from errors as additional evidence becomes available. In our running example, the decision of whether $\{[\textit{vessel}]\}_{m1}$ refers to $\{[\textit{Kursk}]\}_{m2}$ is made before the decision of whether $\{[\textit{vessel}]\}_{m1}$ refers to $\{\textit{Norwegian}\ [\textit{ship}]\}_{m_4}$ since decisions in the same sentence are believed to be easier than cross-sentence ones. We describe our learning-based multi-sieve approach in Sec. 4.

(3) A novel approach for entity-based features. As sieves of classifiers are applied, our system attempts to model entities and share the attributes between the mentions belonging to the same entity. Once the decision that $\{[\textit{vessel}]\}_{m1}$ and $\{[\textit{Kursk}]\}_{m2}$ co-refer is made, we want the two mentions to share the *Russian* nationality. This allows us to avoid erroneously linking $\{[\textit{vessel}]\}_{m1}$ to $\{\textit{Norwegian}\ [\textit{ship}]\}_{m_4}$ despite *vessel* and *ship* being synonyms in WordNet. However, in this work we allow the sieves to make conflicting decisions on the same pair of mentions. Hence, obtaining entities and their attributes by straightforward transitive closure of co-reference predictions is impossible. We describe our approach for leveraging possibly contradicting predictions in Sec. 5.

(4) By adding word-knowledge features and using learning-based multi-sieve approach, we improve the performance of the state-of-the-art system of (Bengtson and Roth, 2008) by 3 MUC, 2 B^3 and 2 CEAF F1 points on the non-transcript portion of the ACE 2004 dataset. We report our experimental results in Sec. 6 and conclude with discussion in Sec. 7.

We conclude the introduction by giving a high-level overview of our system in Fig. 2.

[2]The extracted attributes and the related resources are available for public download at `http://cogcomp.cs.illinois.edu/Data/Ace2004CorefWikiAttributes.zip`

> Input: document d; mentions $M = \{m_1, \ldots, m_N\}$
> 1) For each $m_i \in M$, assign it a Wikipedia page p_i in a context-sensitive way (p_i may be $null$).
> - If $p_i \neq null$: extract knowledge attributes from p_i and assign to m.
> - Else extract knowledge attributes directly from m via noun-phrase parsing techniques (Vadas and Curran, 2008).
> 3) Let $Q = \{(m_i, m_j)\}_{i \neq j}$, be the queue of mention pairs *approximately* sorted by "easy-first" (Goldberg and Elhadad, 2010).
> 4) Let G be a partial clustering graph.
> 5) While Q is not empty
> - Extract a pair $p = (m_i, m_j)$ from Q.
> - Using the knowledge attributes of m_i and m_j as well as the structure of G, classify whether p is co-referent.
> - Update G with the classification decision.
> 6) Construct an end clustering from G.

Figure 2: High-level system architecture.

2 Baseline System

In this work, we are using the state-of-the-art system of (Bengtson and Roth, 2008), which relies on a pairwise scoring function pc to assign an ordered pair of mentions a probability that they are coreferential. It uses a rich set of features including: string edit distance, gender match, whether the mentions appear in the same sentence, whether the heads are synonyms in WordNet etc. The function pc is modeled using regularized averaged perceptron for a tuned number of training rounds, learning rate and margin. For the end system, we keep these parameters intact, our only modifications will be adding knowledge-rich features and adding intermediate classification sieves to the training and the inference, which we will discuss in the following sections.

At inference time, given a document d and a pairwise co-reference scoring function pc, (Bengtson and Roth, 2008) generate a graph G_d according to the Best-Link decision model (Ng and Cardie, 2002) as follows. For each mention m in document d, let B_m be the set of mentions appearing before m in d. Let a be the highest scoring antecedent: $a = \text{argmax}_{b \in B_m}(pc(b, m))$. We will add the edge (a, m) to G_d if $pc(a, m)$ predicts the pair to be co-referent with a confidence exceeding a chosen threshold, then we take the transitive closure[3].

The properties of the Best-Link inference are illustrated in Fig. 3. At this stage, we ask the reader to ignore the knowledge attributes at the bottom of the figure. Let us assume that the pairwise classifier labeled the mentions (m_2, m_5) co-referent because they have identical surface form; mentions (m_1, m_4) are co-referred because the heads are synonyms in WordNet. Let us assume that since m_1 and m_2 appear in the same sentence, the pairwise classifier managed to leverage the dependency parse tree to correctly co-ref the pair (m_1, m_2). The transitive closure would correctly link (m_1, m_5) despite the incorrect prediction of the pairwise classifier on (m_1, m_5), and would incorrectly link m_4 with all other mentions because of the incorrect pairwise prediction on (m_1, m_4) and despite the correct predictions on (m_2, m_4) and (m_4, m_5).

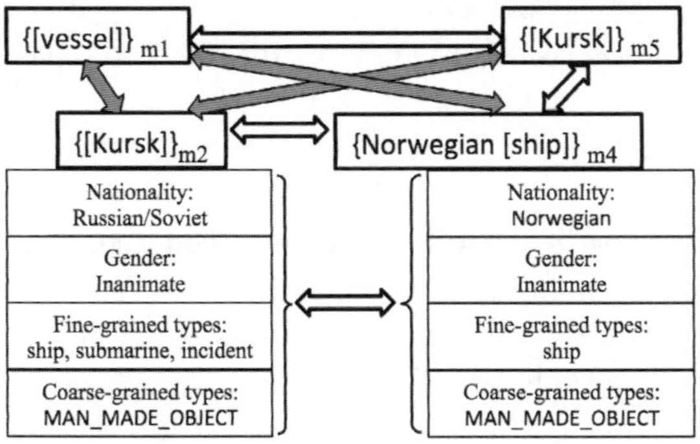

Figure 3: A sample output of a pairwise co-reference classifier. The full edges represent a co-ref prediction and the empty edges represent a non-coref prediction. A set of knowledge attributes for selected mentions is shown as well.

3 Wikipedia as Knowledge

In this section we describe our methodology for using Wikipedia as a knowledge resource. In Sec. 3.1 we cover the process of knowledge extraction from Wikipedia pages. We describe how to inject this knowledge into mentions in Sec. 3.2. The bottom part of Fig. 3 illustrates the knowledge attributes our system injects to two sample mentions at this stage. Finally, in Sec. 3.3 we describe a compatibility metric our system learns over the injected knowledge.

3.1 Wikipedia Knowledge Attributes

Our goal in this section is to extract from Wikipedia pages a compact and highly-accurate set of **knowledge attributes**, which nevertheless possesses discriminative power for co-reference[4]. We concentrate on three types of knowledge attributes: fine-grained semantic categories, gender information and nationality where applicable.

Each Wikipedia page is assigned a set of categories. There are over 100K categories in Wikipedia, many are extremely fine-grained and contain very few pages. The value of the Wikipedia category structure for knowledge acquisition has long been noticed in several influential works, such as (Suchanek et al., 2007; Nastase and Strube, 2008) to name a few. However, while the recall of the above resources is excellent, we found their precision insufficient for our purposes. We have implemented a simple high-precision low-recall heuristic for extracting the head words of Wikipedia categories as follows.

We noticed that Wikipedia categories have a simple structure of either *<noun-phrase>* or *<noun-phrase><relation-token><noun-phrase>*, where in the second case the category information is always on the left. Therefore, we first remove the text succeeding a set of carefully chosen relation tokens[5]. With this heuristic *"Recipients of the Gold Medal of the Royal Astronomical Society"* becomes just *"Recipients"*; *"Populated places in Africa"* becomes *"places"*; however *"Institute for Advanced Study faculty"* becomes *"Institute"* (rather than *"faculty"*). At the second step, we apply the Illinois POS tagger and keep only the tokens labeled as NNS. This step allows us to exclude singular nouns incorrectly identified as heads, such as *"Institute"* above. To further reduce the noise in the category

[3]We use Platt Scaling while (Bengtson and Roth, 2008) used the raw output value of *pc*.

[4]We justify the reasons for our choice of high-precision low-recall knowledge extraction in Sec. 3.2.

[5]The selected set was: {of, in, with, from, ",", at, who, which, for, and, by}

extraction, we also remove all rare category tokens which appeared in less than 100 titles ending up with 2088 fine-grained entity types. We manually map popular fine-grained categories to coarser-grained ones, more consistent with ACE entity typing. A sample of the mapping is shown in the table below:

Fine-grained	Coarse-grained
departments, organizations, banks, ...	ORG
venues, trails, areas, buildings, ...	LOC
countries, towns, villages, ...	GPE
churches, highways, schools, ...	FACILITY

Manual inspection of the extracted category keywords has led us to believe that this heuristic achieves a higher precision at a considerable loss of recall when compared to the more sophisticated approach of (Nastase and Strube, 2008), which correctly identifies *"faculty"* as the head of *"Institute for Advanced Study faculty"*, but incorrectly identifies *"statistical organizations"* as the head of *"Presidents of statistical organizations"* in about half the titles containing the category[6].

We assign gender to the titles using the following simple heuristic. The first paragraph of each Wikipedia article provides a very brief summary of the entity in focus. If the first paragraph of a Wikipedia page contains the pronoun "she", but not "he", the article is considered to be about a female (and vice-versa). However, when the page is assigned a non-person-related fine-grained NE type (e.g. school) and at the same time is not assigned a person-related fine-grained NE type (e.g. novelist), we mark the page as inanimate regardless of the presence of he/she pronouns. The nationality is assigned by matching the tokens in the original (unprocessed) categories of the Wikipedia page to a list of countries. We assign nationality not only to the Wikipedia titles, but also to single tokens. For each token, we track the list of titles it appears in, and if the union of the nationalities assigned to the titles it appears in is less than 7, we mark the token compatible with these nationalities. This allows us to identify Ivan Lebedev as Russian and Ronen Ben-Zohar as Israeli, even though Wikipedia may not contain pages for these specific people.

[6] (Nastase and Strube, 2008) analyze a set of categories S assigned to Wikipedia page p jointly, hence the same category expression can be interpreted differently, depending on S.

3.2 Injecting Knowledge Attributes

Once we have extracted the knowledge attributes of Wikipedia pages, we need to inject them into the mentions. (Rahman and Ng, 2011) used YAGO for similar purposes, but noticed that knowledge injection is often noisy. Therefore they used YAGO only for mention pairs where one mention was an NE of type PER/LOC/ORG and the other was a common noun. This implies that all MISC NEs were discarded, and all NE-NE pairs were discarded as well. We also note that (Rahman and Ng, 2011) reports low utility of FrameNet-based features. In fact, when incrementally added to other features in cluster-ranking model the FrameNet-based features sometimes led to performance drops. This observation has motivated our choice of high-precision low-recall heuristic in Sec. 3.1 and will motivate us to add features conservatively when building attribute compatibility metric in Sec. 3.3.

Additionally, while (Rahman and Ng, 2011) uses the union of all possible meanings a mention may have in Wikipedia, we deploy GLOW (Ratinov et al., 2011)[7], a context-sensitive system for disambiguation to Wikipedia. Using context-sensitive disambiguation to Wikipedia as well as high-precision set of knowledge attributes allows us to inject the knowledge to more mention pairs when compared to (Rahman and Ng, 2011). Our exact heuristic for injecting knowledge attributes to mentions is as follows:

Named Entities with Wikipedia Disambiguation
If the mention head is an NE matched to a Wikipedia page p by GLOW, we import all the knowledge attributes from p. GLOW allows us to map *"***Eph***raim Sneh"* to *http://en.wikipedia.org/wiki/***Ef***raim_Sneh* and to assign it the *Israeli* nationality, *male* gender, and the fine-grained entity types: {*member, politician, person, minister, alumnus, physician, general*}.

Head and Extent Keywords
If the mention head is not mapped to Wikipedia by GLOW and the head contains keywords which appear in the list of 2088 fine-grained entity types, then the rightmost such keyword is added to the list of mention knowledge attributes. If the head does

[7] Available at: `http://cogcomp.cs.illinois.edu/page/software_view/Wikifier`

not contain any entity-type keywords but the extent does, we add the rightmost such keyword of the extent. In both cases, we apply the heuristic of removing clauses starting with a select set of punctuations, prepositions and pronouns, annotating what is left with POS tagger and restricting to noun tokens only[8]. This allows us to inject knowledge to mentions unmapped to Wikipedia, such as: *"{current Cycle World publisher [Larry Little]}"*, which is assigned the attribute *publisher* but not *world* or *cycle*. Likewise, *"{[Joseph Conrad Parkhurst], who founded the motorcycle magazine Cycle World in 1962 }"*, is not assigned the attribute *magazine*, since the text following *"who"* is discarded.

3.3 Learning Attributes Compatibility

In the previous section we have assigned knowledge attributes to the mentions. Some of this information, such as gender and coarse-grained entity types are also modeled in the baseline system of (Bengtson and Roth, 2008). Our goal is to build a compatibility metric on top of this redundant, yet often inconsistent information.

The majority of the features we are using are straightforward, such as: (1) whether the two mentions mapped to the same Wikipedia page, (2) gender agreement (both Wikipedia and dictionary-based), (3) nationality agreement (here we measure only whether the sets intersect, since mentions can have multiple nationalities in the real world), (4) coarse-grained entity type match, etc.

The only non-trivial feature is measuring compatibility between sets of fine-grained entity types, which we describe below. Let us assume that mention m_1 was assigned the set of fine-grained entity types S_1 and the mention m_2 was assigned the set of fine-grained entity types S_2. We record whether S_1 and S_2 share elements. If they do, than, in addition to the Boolean feature, the list of the shared elements also appears as a list of discrete features. We do the same for the most similar and most dissimilar elements of S_1 and S_2 (along with their discretized similarity score) according to a WordNet-based similarity metric of (Do et al., 2009). The reason for explicitly listing the shared, the most similar and dissimilar elements is that the WordNet similarity does not always correspond to co-reference compatibility. For example, the pair $(company, rival)$ has a low similarity score according to WordNet, but characterizes co-referent mentions. On the other hand, the pair $(city, region)$ has a high WordNet similarity score, but characterizes non-coreferent mentions. We want to allow our system to "memorize" the discrepancy between the WordNet similarity and co-reference compatibility of specific pairs.

We also note that we generate a set of selected conjunctive features, most notably of fine-grained categories with NER predictions. The reason is that the pair of mentions *"(Microsoft, Google)"* are not co-referent despite the fact that they both have the *company* attribute. On the other hand *"(Microsoft, Redmond-based company)"* is a co-referent pair. To capture this difference, we generate the feature *ORG-ORG&&share_attribute* for the first pair, and *ORG-O&&share_attribute* for the second pair[9]. These features are also used in conjunction with string edit distance. Therefore, if our system sees two named entities which share the same fine-grained type but have a large string edit distance, it will label the pair as non-coref.

4 Learning-based Multi-Sieve Aproach

State-of-the-art machine-learning co-ref systems, e.g. (Bengtson and Roth, 2008; Rahman and Ng, 2011) train a single model for predicting co-reference of all mention pairs. However, rule-based systems, e.g. (Haghighi and Klein, 2009; Raghunathan et al., 2010) characterize mention pairs by discourse structure and linguistic properties and apply rules in a prescribed order (high-precision rules first). Somewhat surprisingly, such hybrid approach of applying rules on top of structures produced by statistical tools (such as dependency parse trees) performs better than pure machine-learning approach[10].

In this work, we attempt to integrate the strength of linguistically motivated rule-based systems with the robustness of a machine learning approach. We started with a hypothesis that different types of men-

[8]This heuristic is similar to the one we used for extracting Wikipedia category headwords and seems to be a reasonable baseline for parsing noun structures (Vadas and Curran, 2008).

[9]The head of *"Redmond-based company"* is *"company"*, which is not a named entity, and is marked O.

[10](Raghunathan et al., 2010) recorded the best result on CoNLL 2011 shared task.

tion pairs may require a different co-ref model. For example, consider the text below:

> *Queen Rania of Jordan , Egypt's [Suzanne Mubarak]$_{m_1}$ and others were using their charisma and influence to campaign for equality of the sexes. [Mubarak]$_{m_2}$, wife of Egyptian President [Hosni Mubarak]$_{m_3}$, and one of the conference organizers, said they must find ways to ...*

There is a subtle difference between mention pairs (m_1, m_2) and (m_2, m_3). One of the differences is purely structural. The first pair appears in different sentences, while the second pair – in the same sentence. It turns out that string edit distance feature between two named entities has different "semantics" depending on whether the two mentions appear in the same sentence. The reason is that to avoid redundancy, humans refer to the same entity differently within the sentence, preferring titles, nicknames and pronouns. Therefore, when a similar-looking named entities appear in the same sentence, they are actually likely to refer to different entities. On the other hand, in the sentence *"Reggie Jackson, nicknamed Mr. October ... "* we have to rely heavily on sentence structure rather than string edit distance to make the correct co-ref prediction.

Sieve	Trained on All Data	Sieve-specific Training
AllSentencePairs	61.37	67.46
ClosestNonProDiffSent	60.71	63.33
NonProSameSentence	62.97	63.80
NerMentionsDiffSent	86.44	87.12
SameSentenceOneNer	64.10	68.88
Adjacent	71.00	78.80
SameSenBothNer	75.30	73.75
Nested	76.11	79.00

Table 1: F1 performance on co-referent mention pairs by sieve type when trained with all data versus sieve-specific data only.

Our second intuition is that "easy-first" inference is necessary to effectively leverage knowledge. For example, in Fig. 3, our goal is to link *vessel* to *Kursk* and assign it the *Russian/Soviet* nationality prior to applying the pairwise co-reference classifier on (*vessel*, *Norwegian ship*). Therefore, our goal is to apply the pairwise classifier on pairs in *prescribed order* and to propagate the knowledge across mentions. The ordering should be such that (a) maximum amount of information is injected at early stages (b) the precision at the early stages is as high as possible (Raghunathan et al., 2010). Hence, we divide the mention pairs as follows:

Nested: are pairs such as "{{[*city*]$_{m_1}$} *of* [*Jerusalem*]$_{m_2}$}" where the extent of one of the mentions contains the extent of the other. For some mentions, the extent is the entire clause, so we also added a requirement that mention heads are at most 7 tokens apart. Intuitively, it is the easiest case of co-reference. There are 5,804 training samples and 992 testing samples, out of which 208 are co-referent.

SameSenBothNer: are pairs of named entities which appear in the same sentence. We already saw an example for this case involving [Mubarak]$_{m2}$ and [Hosni Mubarak]$_{m3}$. There are 13,041 training samples and 1,746 testing samples, out of which 86 are co-referent.

Adjacent: are pairs of mentions which appear closest to each other on the dependency tree. We note that most of the nested pairs are also adjacent. There are training 5,872 samples and 895 testing samples, out of which 219 are co-referent.

SameSentenceOneNer: are pairs which appear in the same sentence and exactly one of the mentions is a named entity, and the other is not a pronoun. Typical pairs are *"Israel-country"*, as opposed to *"Bill Clinton - reporter"*. This type of pairs is fairly difficult, but our hope is to use encyclopedic knowledge to boost the performance. There are 15,715 training samples and 2,635 testing samples, out of which 207 are co-referent.

NerMentionsDiffSent: are pairs of mentions in different sentences, both of which are named entities. There are 189,807 training samples and 24,342 testing samples, out of which 1,628 are co-referent.

NonProSameSentence: are pairs in the same sentence, where both mentions are non-pronouns. This sieve includes all the pairs in the SameSentenceOneNer sieve. Typical pairs are *"city-capital"* and *"reporter-celebrity"*. *There are 33,895 training samples and 5,393 testing samples, out of which 336 are co-referent..*

ClosestNonProDiffSent: are pairs of mentions in different sentences with no other mentions between the two. 3,707 training samples and 488 testing samples, out of which 38 are co-referent.

AllSentencePairs: All mention pairs within same sentence. There are 49,953 training samples and 7,809 testing samples, out of which 846 are co-referent.

TopSieve: The set of mention pairs classified by the baseline system. 525,398 training samples and 85,358 testing samples, out of which 1,387 are co-referent.

In Tab. 1 we compare the performance at each sieve in two scenarios[11]. First, we train with the entire 525,398 training samples, and then we train on

[11]The data is described in Sec. 6.1.

whatever training data is available for the specific sieve[12]. We were surprised to see that the F1 on the nested mentions, when trained on the 5,804 sieve-specific samples improves to 79.00 versus 76.11 when trained on the 525,398 top sieve samples.

There are several things to note when interpreting the results in Tab 1. First, the sheer ratio of positive to negative samples fluctuates drastically. For example, 208 out of the 992 testing samples at the nested sieve are positive, while there are only 86 positive samples out of 1,746 testing samples in the SameSenBothNer sieve. It seems unreasonable to use the same model for inference at both sieves. Second, the data for intermediate sieves is not always a subset of the top sieve. The reason is that top sieve extracts a positive instance only for the closest co-referent mentions, while sieves such as AllSentencePairs extract samples for all co-referent pairs which appear in the same sentence. Third, while our division to sieves may resemble witchcraft, it is motivated by the intuition that mentions appearing close to one another are easier instances of co-ref as well as linguistic insights of (Raghunathan et al., 2010).

5 Entity-Based Features

In this section we describe our approach for building entity-based features. Let $\{C_1, C_2, \ldots C_N\}$ be the set of sieve-specific classifiers. In our case, C_1 is the nested mention pairs classifier, C_2 is the SameSenBothNer classifier, and C_9 is the top sieve classifier. We design entity-based features so that the subsequent sieves "see" the decisions of the previous sieves and use entity-based features based on the intermediate clustering. However, unlike (Raghunathan et al., 2010), we allow the subsequent sieves to change the decisions made by the lower sieves (since additional information becomes available).

5.1 Intermediate Clustering Features (IC)

Let $R_i(m)$ be the set of all mentions which, when paired with the mention m, form valid sample pairs for sieve i. E.g. in our running example of Fig. 1, $R_2([Kursk]_{m_2}) = \{[\textit{Barents Sea}]_{m_3}\}$, since both m_1 and m_2 are NEs and appear in the same sentence. Let $R_i^+(m)$ be the set of all mentions which were labeled as co-referent to the mention m by the classifier C_i (including m, which is co-referent to itself). We define $R_i^-(m)$ similarly. We denote the union of mentions co-refed to m during inference up to sieve i as $E_i^+(m) = \cup_{j=1}^{i-1} R_j^+(m)$. Similarly, $E_i^-(m) = \cup_{j=1}^{i-1} R_j^-(m)$. Using these definitions we can introduce entity-based prediction features which allow subsequent sieves to use information aggregated from previous sieves:

$$IC_i^R(m_j, m_k) = \begin{cases} -1 & m_j \in R_{i-1}^-(m_k) \\ +1 & m_j \in R_{i-1}^+(m_k) \\ 0 & \text{Otherwise} \end{cases}$$

$$IC_i^E(m_j, m_k) = \begin{cases} -1 & m_j \in E_{i-1}^-(m_k) \\ +1 & m_j \in E_{i-1}^+(m_k) \\ 0 & \text{Otherwise} \end{cases}$$

IC_i^R stores the pairwise prediction history, thus when classifying a pair (m_j, m_k) at sieve i, a classifier can see the predictions of all the previous sieves applicable on that pair. IC_i^E stores the transitive closures of the sieve-specific predictions. We note that both IC_i^R and IC_i^E can have the values +1 and -1 active at the same time if intermediate sieve classifiers generated conflicting predictions. However, a classifier at sieve i will use as features both $IC_1^R, \ldots IC_{i-1}^R$ and $IC_1^E, \ldots IC_{i-1}^E$, thus it will know the lowest sieve at which the conflicting evidence occurs. The classifier at sieve i also uses set identity, set containment, set overlap and other set comparison features between $E_{i-1}^{+/-}(m_j)$ and $E_{i-1}^{+/-}(m_k)$. We check whether the sets have symmetric difference, whether the size of the intersection between the two sets is at least half the size of the smallest set etc. We also generate subtypes of set comparison features when restricting the elements to NE-mentions and non-pronominal mentions (e.g "what percent of named entities do the sets have in common?").

5.2 Surface Form Compatibility (SFC)

The intermediate clustering features do not allow us to generalize predictions from pairs of mentions to pairs of surface strings. For example, if we have three mentions: $\{[\textit{vessel}]_{m_1}, [\textit{Kursk}]_{m_2}, [\textit{Kursk}]_{m_5}\}$, then the prediction on the pair (m_1, m_2) will not be

[12] We report *pairwise* performance on mention pairs because it is the more natural metric for the intermediate sieves. We report only performance on co-referent pairs, because for many sieves, such as the top sieve, 99% of the mention pairs are non-coreferent, hence the baseline of labeling all samples as non-coreferent would result in 99% accuracy. We are interested in a more challenging baseline, the co-referent pairs.

	(B)aseline	(B)+Knowledge	(B)+Predictions	(B)+Knowledge+Predictions
TopSieve	66.58	69.08	68.77	**70.43**
AllSentencePairs	67.46	71.79	69.59	**73.50**
ClosestNonProDiffSent	63.33	65.62	65.57	**70.76**
NonProSameSentence	63.80	69.62	67.03	**71.11**
NerMentionsDiffSent	87.12	88.23	88.68	**89.07**
SameSentenceOneNer	68.88	70.58	67.89	**73.17**
Adjacent	78.80	81.32	80.00	**81.79**
SameSenBothNer	73.75	80.50	77.21	**80.98**
Nested	79.00	83.59	80.65	**83.37**

Table 2: Utility of knowledge and prediction features (F1 on co-referent mention pairs) by inference sieves. Both knowledge and entity-based features significantly and independently improve the performance for all sieves. The goal of entity-based features is to propagate knowledge effectively, thus it is encouraging that the combination of entity-based and knowledge features performed significantly better than any of the approaches individually at the top sieve.

used for the prediction on the pair (m_1, m_5), even though in both pairs we are asking whether *Kursk* can be referred to as *vessel*. The surface form compatibility features mirror the intermediate clustering features, but relax mention IDs and replace them by surface forms. Similarly to intermediate clustering features, both +1 and -1 values can be active at the same time. We also generate subtypes of set-comparison features for NE-mentions and optionally stemmed non-pronominal mentions. For example, in a text discussing *President Clinton* and *President Putin*, some instances of the surface from *president* will refer to *Putin* but not *Clinton* and vice-versa. Therefore, both for *(Putin, president)* and for *(Clinton, president)*, the surface from compatibility will be +1 and -1 simultaneously. This indicates to the system that *Putin* can be referred to as *president*, but *president* can refer to other entities in the document as well.

6 Experiments and Results

6.1 Data

We use the official ACE 2004 English training data (NIST, 2004). We started with the data split used in (Culotta et al., 2007), which used 336 documents for training and 107 documents for testing. We note that ACE data contains both newswire text and transcripts. In this work, we are using NLP tools such as POS tagger, named entity recognizer, shallow parser, and a disambiguation to Wikipedia system to inject expressive features into a co-reference system.

Unfortunately, current state-of-the-art NLP tools do not work well on transcribed text. Therefore, we discard all the transcripts. Our criteria was simple. The ACE annotators have marked the named entities both in newswire and in the transcripts. We kept only those documents which contained named entities (according to manual ACE annotation) and at least $1/3$ of the named entities started with a capital letter. After this pre-processing step, we were left with 275 out of the original 336 training documents, and 42 out of the 107 testing documents.

For the experiments throughout this paper, following Culotta et al. (Culotta et al., 2007) and much other work, to make experiments more comparable across systems, we assume that perfect mention boundaries and mention type labels are given. However, we do not use the gold named entity types such as person/location/facility etc. available in the data. In all experiments we automatically split words and sentences, and annotate the text with part-of-speech tags, named entities and cross-link concepts from the text to Wikipedia using publicly available tools.

6.2 Ablation Study

In Tab. 2 we report the pairwise F1 scores on co-referent mention pairs broken down by sieve and using different components. This allows us to see, for example, that adding only the knowledge attributes improved the performance at *NonProSame-Sentence* sieve from 63.80 to 69.62. We have ordered the sieves according to our initial intuition of "easy first". We were surprised to see that co-ref resolution for named entities in the same sentence was harder than cross-sentence (73.75 vs. 87.12 base-

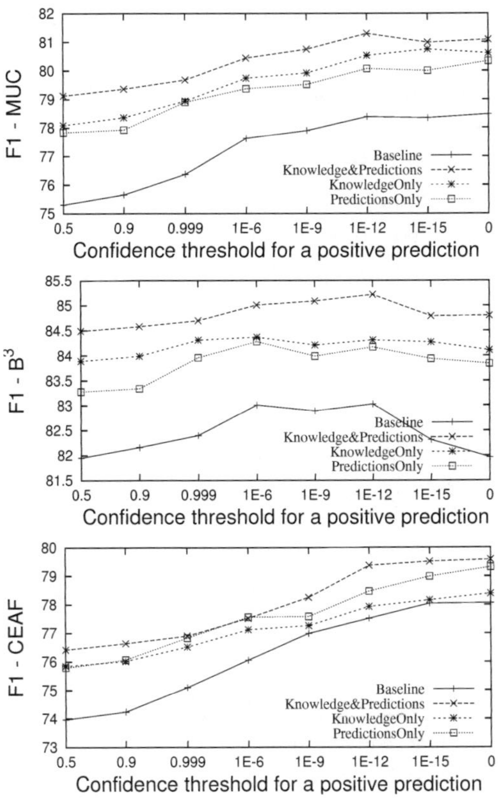

Figure 4: End performance for various systems.

line F1). We were also surprised to see that resolving all mention pairs within sentence when including pronouns was easier than resolving pairs where both mentions were non-pronouns (67.46 vs. 63.80 baseline F1).

We note that conceptually, the nested (B)+Predictions sieve should be identical to the baseline. However, in practice, the surface form compatibility (SFC) features are generated for the nested sieve as well. Given two mentions m_1 and m_2, the SFC features capture how many surface forms $E^+(m_1)$ and $E^+(m_2)$ share. At the nested sieve, $E^+(m)$ and $R^+(m)$ are just m, which is identical to string comparison features already existing in the baseline system. While the SFC features do not add new information, they influence the weight the features get (essentially leading to a different regularization), which in turn leads to slightly different results.

6.3 End system performance

Recall that the Best-Link algorithm applies transitive closure on the graph generated by thresholding the pairwise co-reference scoring function pc. The lower the threshold on the positive prediction, the lower is the precision and the higher is the recall. In Fig. 4 we compare the end clustering quality across a variety of thresholds and for various system flavors using three metrics: MUC (Vilain et al., 1995), B^3 (Bagga and Baldwin, 1998) and CEAF (Luo, 2005)[13]. The purpose of this comparison is to see the impact of the knowledge and the prediction features on the final output and to see whether the performance gains are due to (mis-)tuning of one of the systems or are they consistent across a variety of thresholds.

The end performance of the baseline system on our training/testing split peaks at around 78.39 MUC, 83.03 B^3 and 77.52 CEAF, which is higher (e.g. 3 B^3 F1 points) than the originally reported result on the entire dataset (which includes the transcripts). This is expected, since well-formed text is easier to process than transcripts. We note that our baseline is a state-of-the art system which recorded the highest B^3 and BLANC scores at CoNLL 2011 shared task and took the third place overall. Fig. 4 shows a minimum improvement of 3 MUC, 2 B^3 and 1.25 CEAF F1 points across all thresholds when comparing the baseline to our end system. Surprisingly, the knowledge features outperformed prediction features on pairwise, MUC and B^3 metrics, but not on the CEAF metric. This shows that pairwise performance is not always indicative of cluster-level performance for all metrics.

7 Conclusions and Related Work

To illustrate the strengths of our approach, let us consider the following text:

Another terminal was made available in $\{[\textit{Jiangxi}]_{m_1}\}$*, an* $\{$*inland* $[\textit{province}]_{m_2}\}$*. ...The previous situation whereby large amount of goods for* $\{$*Jiangxi* $[\textit{province}]_{m_3}\}$ *had to be re-shipped through Guangzhou and Shanghai will be changed completely.*

The baseline system assigns each mention to a separate cluster. The pairs (m_1, m_2) and (m_1, m_3)

[13] In the interest of space, we refer the reader to the literature for details about the different metrics.

are misclassified because the baseline classifier does not know that *Jiangxi* is a *province* and the preposition *an* before m_2 is interpreted to mean it is a previously unmentioned entity. The pair (m_2, m_3) is misclassified because identical heads have different modifiers, as in *(big province, small province)*. Our end system first co-refs (m_1, m_2) at the *AllSameSentence* sieve due to the knowledge features, and then co-refs (m_1, m_3) at the top sieve due to surface form compatibility features indicating that *province* was observed to refer to *Jiangxi* in the document. The transitivity of Best-Link takes care of (m_2, m_3).

However, our approach has multiple limitations. Entity-based features currently do not propagate knowledge attributes directly, but through aggregating pairwise predictions at knowledge-infused intermediate sieves. We rely on gold mention boundaries and exhaustive gold co-reference annotation. This prevented us from applying our approach to the Ontonotes dataset where singleton clusters and co-referent nested mentions are removed. Therefore the gold annotation for training several sieves of our scheme is missing (e.g. nested mentions). Another limitation is our somewhat preliminary division to sieves. (Vilalta and Rish, 2003) have experimented with approaches for automatic decomposition of data to subclasses and learning multiple models to improve data separability. We hope that similar approach would be useful for co-reference resolution. Ideally, we want to make "simple decisions" first, similarly to what was done in (Goldberg and Elhadad, 2010) for dependency parsing, and model clustering as a structured problem, similarly to (Joachims et al., 2009; Wick et al., 2011). However, our experience with multi-sieve approach with classifiers suggests that a single model would not perform well for both lower sieves with little entity-based information and higher sieves with a lot of entity-based features. Addressing the aforementioned challenges is a subject for future work.

There has been an increasing interest in knowledge-rich co-reference resolution (Ponzetto and Strube, 2006; Haghighi and Klein, 2010; Rahman and Ng, 2011). We use Wikipedia differently from (Ponzetto and Strube, 2006) who focus on using WikiRelate, a Wikipedia-based relatedness metric (Strube and Ponzetto, 2006). (Rahman and Ng, 2011) used the union of all possible interpretations a mention may have in YAGO, which means that *Michael Jordan* could be co-refed both to a *scientist* and *basketball player* in the same document. Additionally, (Rahman and Ng, 2011) use exact word matching, relying on YAGO's ability to extract a comprehensive set of facts offline[14]. We are the first to use context-sensitive disambiguation to Wikipedia, which received a lot of attention recently (Bunescu and Pasca, 2006; Cucerzan, 2007; Mihalcea and Csomai, 2007; Milne and Witten, 2008; Ratinov et al., 2011). We extract context-sensitive, high-precision knowledge attributes from Wikipedia pages and apply (among other features) WordNet similarity metric on pairs of knowledge attributes to determine attribute compatibility.

We have integrated the strengths of rule-based systems such as (Haghighi and Klein, 2009; Raghunathan et al., 2010) into a multi-sieve machine learning framework. We show that training sieve-specific models significantly increases the performance on most intermediate sievesieves.

We develop a novel approach for entity-based inference. Unlike (Rahman and Ng, 2011) who construct entities left-to-right, and similarly to (Raghunathan et al., 2010) we resolve easy instances of coref to reduce error propagation in entity-based features. Unlike (Raghunathan et al., 2010), we allow later stages of inference to change the decisions made at lower stages as additional entity-based evidence becomes available.

By adding word-knowledge features and refining the inference, we improve the performance of a state-of-the-art system of (Bengtson and Roth, 2008) by 3 MUC, 2 B^3 and 2 CEAF F1 points on the non-transcript portion of the ACE 2004 dataset.

References

A. Bagga and B. Baldwin. 1998. Algorithms for scoring coreference chains. In *MUC7*.

E. Bengtson and D. Roth. 2008. Understanding the value of features for coreference resolution. In *EMNLP*.

[14] YAGO uses WordNet to expand its set of facts. For example, if *Martha Stewart* is assigned the meaning *personality* from category head words analysis, YAGO adds the meaning *celebrity* because *personality* is a direct hyponym of *celebrity* in WordNet. However, this is done offline in a context-insensitive way, which is inherently limited.

R. C. Bunescu and M. Pasca. 2006. Using encyclopedic knowledge for named entity disambiguation. In *EACL*.

S. Cucerzan. 2007. Large-scale named entity disambiguation based on Wikipedia data. In *EMNLP-CoNLL*.

A. Culotta, M. Wick, R. Hall, and A. McCallum. 2007. First-order probabilistic models for coreference resolution. In *HLT/NAACL*, pages 81–88.

Q. Do, D. Roth, M. Sammons, Y. Tu, and V. Vydiswaran. 2009. Robust, light-weight approaches to compute lexical similarity. Technical report, University of Illinois at Urbana-Champaign.

A. Fader, S. Soderland, and O. Etzioni. 2009. Scaling wikipedia-based named entity disambiguation to arbitrary web text. In *WikiAI (IJCAI workshop)*.

Y. Goldberg and M. Elhadad. 2010. An efficient algorithm for easy-first non-directional dependency parsing. In *NAACL*.

A. Haghighi and D. Klein. 2009. Simple coreference resolution with rich syntactic and semantic features. In *EMNLP*.

A. Haghighi and D. Klein. 2010. Coreference resolution in a modular, entity-centered model. In *HLT-ACL*. Association for Computational Linguistics.

T. Joachims, T. Hofmann, Y. Yue, and C. Yu. 2009. Predicting structured objects with support vector machines. *Communications of the ACM, Research Highlight*, 52(11):97–104, November.

X. Luo. 2005. On coreference resolution performance metrics. In *HLT*.

R. Mihalcea and A. Csomai. 2007. Wikify!: linking documents to encyclopedic knowledge. In *CIKM*.

D. Milne and I. H. Witten. 2008. Learning to link with wikipedia. In *CIKM*.

V. Nastase and M. Strube. 2008. Decoding wikipedia categories for knowledge acquisition. In *AAAI*.

V. Ng and C. Cardie. 2002. Improving machine learning approaches to coreference resolution. In *ACL*.

NIST. 2004. The ace evaluation plan. www.nist.gov/speech/tests/ace/index.htm.

S. P. Ponzetto and M. Strube. 2006. Exploiting semantic role labeling, wordnet and wikipedia for coreference resolution. In *HLT-ACL*.

K. Raghunathan, H. Lee, S. Rangarajan, N. Chambers, M. Surdeanu, D. Jurafsky, and C. Manning. 2010. A multi-pass sieve for coreference resolution. In *EMNLP*.

A. Rahman and V. Ng. 2011. Coreference resolution with world knowledge. In *HLT-ACL*.

L. Ratinov, D. Downey, M. Anderson, and D. Roth. 2011. Local and global algorithms for disambiguation to wikipedia. In *ACL*.

M. Strube and S. P. Ponzetto. 2006. WikiRelate! Computing Semantic Relatedness Using Wikipedia. In *Proceedings of the Twenty-First National Conference on Artificial Intelligence*, July.

F. M. Suchanek, G. Kasneci, and G. Weikum. 2007. Yago: A core of semantic knowledge. In *WWW*.

D. Vadas and J. R. Curran. 2008. Parsing noun phrase structure with CCG. In *ACL*.

M. Vilain, J. Burger, J. Aberdeen, D. Connolly, and L. Hirschman. 1995. A model-theoretic coreference scoring scheme. In *MUC6*, pages 45–52.

R. Vilalta and I. Rish. 2003. A decomposition of classes via clustering to explain and improve naive bayes. In *ECML*.

M. Wick, K. Rohanimanesh, K. Bellare, A. Culotta, and A. McCallum. 2011. Samplerank: Training factor graphs with atomic gradients. In *ICML*.

Joint Learning for Coreference Resolution with Markov Logic

Yang Song[1], Jing Jiang[2], Wayne Xin Zhao[3], Sujian Li[1], Houfeng Wang[1]
[1]Key Laboratory of Computational Linguistics (Peking University) Ministry of Education,China
[2]School of Information Systems, Singapore Management University, Singapore
[3]School of Electronics Engineering and Computer Science, Peking University, China
{ysong, lisujian, wanghf}@pku.edu.cn, jingjiang@smu.edu.sg, batmanfly@gmail.com

Abstract

Pairwise coreference resolution models must merge pairwise coreference decisions to generate final outputs. Traditional merging methods adopt different strategies such as the best-first method and enforcing the transitivity constraint, but most of these methods are used independently of the pairwise learning methods as an isolated inference procedure at the end. We propose a joint learning model which combines pairwise classification and mention clustering with Markov logic. Experimental results show that our joint learning system outperforms independent learning systems. Our system gives a better performance than all the learning-based systems from the CoNLL-2011 shared task on the same dataset. Compared with the best system from CoNLL-2011, which employs a rule-based method, our system shows competitive performance.

1 Introduction

The task of noun phrase coreference resolution is to determine which mentions in a text refer to the same real-world entity. Many methods have been proposed for this problem. Among them the mention-pair model (McCarthy and Lehnert, 1995) is one of the most influential ones and can achieve the state-of-the-art performance (Bengtson and Roth, 2008). The mention-pair model splits the task into three parts: mention detection, pairwise classification and mention clustering. Mention detection aims to identify anaphoric noun phrases, including proper nouns, common noun phrases and pronouns. Pairwise classification takes a pair of detected anaphoric noun phrase candidates and determines whether they refer to the same entity. Because these classification decisions are local, they do not guarantee that candidate mentions are partitioned into clusters. Therefore a mention clustering step is needed to resolve conflicts and generate the final mention clusters.

Much work has been done following the mention-pair model (Soon et al., 2001; Ng and Cardie, 2002). In most work, pairwise classification and mention clustering are done sequentially. A major weakness of this approach is that pairwise classification considers only local information, which may not be sufficient to make correct decisions. One way to address this weakness is to jointly learn the pairwise classification model and the mention clustering model. This idea has been explored to some extent by McCallum and Wellner (2005) using conditional undirected graphical models and by Finley and Joachims (2005) using an SVM-based supervised clustering method.

In this paper, we study how to use a different learning framework, Markov logic (Richardson and Domingos, 2006), to learn a joint model for both pairwise classification and mention clustering under the mention-pair model. We choose Markov logic because of its appealing properties. Markov logic is based on first-order logic, which makes the learned models readily interpretable by humans. Moreover, joint learning is natural under the Markov logic framework, with local pairwise classification and global mention clustering both formulated as weighted first-order clauses. In fact, Markov logic has been previously used by Poon and Domingos (2008) for coreference resolution and achieved good results, but it was used for unsupervised coreference resolution and the method was based on a different model, the entity-mention model.

More specifically, to combine mention clustering with pairwise classification, we adopt the commonly used strategies (such as best-first clustering and transitivity constraint), and formulate them as first-order logic formulas under the Markov logic framework. Best-first clustering has been previously studied by Ng and Cardie (2002) and Bengtson and Roth (2008) and found to be effective. Transitivity constraint has been applied to coreference resolution by Klenner (2007) and Finkel and Manning (2008), and also achieved good performance.

We evaluate Markov logic-based method on the dataset from CoNLL-2011 shared task. Our experiment results demonstrate the advantage of joint learning of pairwise classification and mention clustering over independent learning. We examine best-first clustering and transitivity constraint in our methods, and find that both are very useful for coreference resolution. Compared with the state of the art, our method outperforms a baseline that represents a typical system using the mention-pair model. Our method is also better than all learning systems from the CoNLL-2011 shared task based on the reported performance. Even with the top system from CoNLL-2011, our performance is still competitive.

In the rest of this paper, we first describe a standard pairwise coreference resolution system in Section 2. We then present our Markov logic model for pairwise coreference resolution in Section 3. Experimental results are given in Section 4. Finally we discuss related work in Section 5 and conclude in Section 6.

2 Standard Pairwise Coreference Resolution

In this section, we describe standard learning-based framework for pairwise coreference resolution. The major steps include mention detection, pairwise classification and mention clustering.

2.1 Mention Detection

For mention detection, traditional methods include learning-based and rule-based methods. Which kind of method to choose depends on specific dataset. In this paper, we first consider all the noun phrases in the given text as candidate mentions. Without gold standard mention boundaries, we use a well-known preprocessing tool from Stanford's NLP group[1] to extract noun phrases. After obtaining all the extracted noun phrases, we also use a rule-based method to remove some erroneous candidates based on previous studies (e.g. Lee et al. (2011), Uryupina et al. (2011)). Some examples of these erroneous candidates include stop words (e.g. *uh*, *hmm*), web addresses (e.g. `http://www.google.com`), numbers (e.g. $9,000) and pleonastic "it" pronouns.

2.2 Pairwise Classification

For pairwise classification, traditional learning-based methods usually adopt a classification model such as maximum entropy models and support vector machines. Training instances (i.e. positive and negative mention pairs) are constructed from known coreference chains, and features are defined to represent these instances.

In this paper, we build a baseline system that uses maximum entropy models as the classification algorithm. For generation of training instances, we follow the method of Bengtson and Roth (2008). For each predicted mention m, we generate a positive mention pair between m and its closest preceding antecedent, and negative mention pairs by pairing m with each of its preceding predicted mentions which are not coreferential with m. To avoid having too many negative instances, we impose a maximum sentence distance between the two mentions when constructing mention pairs. This is based on the intuition that for each anaphoric mention, its preceding antecedent should appear quite near it, and most coreferential mention pairs which have a long sentence distance can be resolved using string matching. During the testing phase, we generate mention pairs for each mention candidate with each of its preceding mention candidates and use the learned model to make coreference decisions for these mention pairs. We also impose the sentence distance constraint and use string matching for mention pairs with a sentence distance exceeding the threshold.

[1] http://nlp.stanford.edu/software/corenlp.shtml

2.3 Mention Clustering

After obtaining the coreferential results for all mention pairs, some clustering method should be used to generate the final output. One strategy is the single-link method, which links all the mention pairs that have a prediction probability higher than a threshold value. Two other alternative methods are the best-first clustering method and clustering with the transitivity constraint. Best-first clustering means that for each candidate mention m, we select the best one from all its preceding candidate mentions based on the prediction probabilities. A threshold value is given to filter out those mention pairs that have a low probability to be coreferential. Transitivity constraint means that if a and b are coreferential and b and c are coreferential, then a and c must also be coreferential. Previous work has found that best-first clustering and transitivity constraint-based clustering are better than the single-link method. Finally we remove all the singleton mentions.

3 Markov Logic for Pairwise Coreference Resolution

In this section, we present our method for joint learning of pairwise classification and mention clustering using Markov logic. For mention detection, training instance generation and postprocessing, our method follows the same procedures as described in Section 2. In what follows, we will first describe the basic Markov logic networks (MLN) framework, and then introduce the first-order logic formulas we use in our MLN including local formulas and global formulas which perform pairwise classification and mention clustering respectively. Through this way, these two isolated parts are combined together, and joint learning and inference can be performed in a single framework. Finally we present inference and parameter learning methods.

3.1 Markov Logic Networks

Markov logic networks combine Markov networks with first-order logic (Richardson and Domingos, 2006; Riedel, 2008). A Markov logic network consists of a set of first-order clauses (which we will refer to as *formulas* in the rest of the paper) just like in first-order logic. However, different from first-order logic where a formula represents a hard constraint, in an MLN, these constraints are softened and they can be violated with some penalty. An MLN $\mathcal{M}$ is therefore a set of *weighted* formulas $\{(\phi_i, w_i)\}_i$, where ϕ_i is a first order formula and w_i is the penalty (the formula's weight). These weighted formulas define a probability distribution over sets of ground atoms or so-called possible worlds. Let y denote a possible world, then we define $p(\mathbf{y})$ as follows:

$$p(\mathbf{y}) = \frac{1}{Z} exp\left(\sum_{(\phi_i, w_i) \in M} w_i \sum_{\mathbf{c} \in C^{n_{\phi_i}}} f_{\mathbf{c}}^{\phi_i}(\mathbf{y}) \right). \quad (1)$$

Here each $\mathbf{c}$ is a binding of free variables in ϕ_i to constants. Each $f_{\mathbf{c}}^{\phi_i}$ represents a binary feature function that returns 1 if the ground formula we get by replacing the free variables in ϕ_i with the constants in $\mathbf{c}$ under the given possible world $\mathbf{y}$ is true, and 0 otherwise. n_{ϕ_i} denotes the number of free variables of a formula ϕ_i. $C^{n_{\phi_i}}$ is the set of all bindings for the free variables in ϕ_i. Z is a normalization constant. This distribution corresponds to a Markov network where nodes represent ground atoms and factors represent ground formulas.

Each formula consists of a set of first-order predicates, logical connectors and variables. Take the following formula as one example:

$$(\phi_i, w_i) : \mathit{headMatch}(a, b) \wedge (a \neq b) \Rightarrow \mathit{coref}(a, b).$$

The formula above indicates that if two different candidate mentions a and b have the same head word, then they are coreferential. Here a and b are variables which can represent any candidate mention, *headMatch* and *coref* are observed predicate and hidden predicate respectively. An observed predicate is one whose value is known from the observations when its free variables are assigned some constants. A hidden predicate is one whose value is not known from the observations. From this example, we can see that *headMatch* is an observed predicate because we can check whether two candidate mentions have the same head word. *coref* is a hidden predicate because this is something we would like to predict.

3.2 Formulas

We use two kinds of formulas for pairwise classification and mention clustering, respectively. For

describing the attributes of $\mathbf{m_i}$	
mentionType(i,t)	m_i has mention type NAM(named entities), NOM(nominal) or PRO(pronouns).
entityType(i,e)	m_i has entity type PERSON, ORG, GPE or UN...
genderType(i,g)	m_i has gender type MALE, FEMALE, NEUTRAL or UN.
numberType(i,n)	m_i has number type SINGULAR, PLURAL or UN.
hasHead(i,h)	m_i has head word h, here h can represent all possible head words.
firstMention(i)	m_i is the first mention in its sentence.
reflexive(i)	m_i is reflexive.
possessive(i)	m_i is possessive.
definite(i)	m_i is definite noun phrase.
indefinite(i)	m_i is indefinite noun phrase.
demonstrative(i)	m_i is demonstrative.
describing the attributes of relations between $\mathbf{m_j}$ and $\mathbf{m_i}$	
mentionDistance(j,i,m)	Distance between m_j and m_i in mentions.
sentenceDistance(j,i,s)	Distance between m_j and m_i in sentences.
bothMatch(j,i,b)	Gender and number of both m_j and m_i match: AGREE_YES, AGREE_NO and AGREE_UN).
closestMatch(j,i,c)	m_j is the first agreement in number and gender when looking backward from m_i: CAGREE_YES, CAGREE_NO and CAGREE_UN.
exactStrMatch(j,i)	Exact strings match between m_j and m_i.
pronounStrMatch(j,i)	Both are pronouns and their strings match.
nopronounStrMatch(j,i)	Both are not pronouns and their strings match.
properStrMatch(j,i)	Both are proper names and their strings match.
headMatch(j,i)	Head word strings match between m_j and m_i.
subStrMatch(j,i)	Sub-word strings match between m_j and m_i.
animacyMatch(j,i)	Animacy types match between m_j and m_i.
nested(j,i)	$m_{j/i}$ is included in $m_{i/j}$.
c_command(j,i)	$m_{j/i}$ C-Commands $m_{i/j}$.
sameSpeaker(j,i)	m_j and m_i have the same speaker.
entityTypeMatch(j,i)	Entity types match between m_j and m_i.
alias(j,i)	$m_{j/i}$ is an alias of $m_{i/j}$.
srlMatch(j,i)	m_j and m_i have the same semantic role.
verbMatch(j,i)	m_j and m_i have semantic role for the same verb.

Table 1: Observed predicates.

pairwise classification, because the decisions are local, we use a set of *local* formulas. For mention clustering, we use *global* formulas to implement best-first clustering or transitivity constraint. We naturally combine pairwise classification with mention clustering via local and global formulas in the Markov logic framework, which is the essence of "joint learning" in our work.

3.2.1 Local Formulas

A local formula relates any observed predicates to exactly one hidden predicate. For our problem, we define a list of observed predicates to describe the properties of individual candidate mentions and the relations between two candidate mentions, shown in Table 1. For our problem, we have only one hidden predicate, i.e. *coref*. Most of our local formulas are from existing work (e.g. Soon et al. (2001), Ng and Cardie (2002), Sapena et al. (2011)). They are listed in Table 2, where the symbol "+" indicates that for every value of the variable preceding "+" there is a separate weight for the corresponding formula.

3.2.2 Global Formulas

Global formulas are designed to add global constraints for hidden predicates. Since in our problem there is only one hidden predicate, i.e. *coref*, our global formulas incorporate correlations among different ground atoms of the *coref* predicates. Next we will show the best-first and transitivity global constraints. Note that we treat them as hard constraints so we do not set any weights for these global formulas.

Lexical Features
mentionType(j,t_1+) $\wedge$ mentionType(i,t_2+) $\wedge$ exactStrMatch(j,i) $\wedge$ j$\neq$ i $\Rightarrow$ coref(j,i)
mentionType(j,t_1+) $\wedge$ mentionType(i,t_2+) $\wedge$ pronounStrMatch (j,i) $\wedge$ j$\neq$ i $\Rightarrow$ coref(j,i)
mentionType(j,t_1+) $\wedge$ mentionType(i,t_2+) $\wedge$ properStrMatch(j,i) $\wedge$ j$\neq$ i $\Rightarrow$ coref(j,i)
mentionType(j,t_1+) $\wedge$ mentionType(i,t_2+) $\wedge$ nopronounStrMatch(j,i) $\wedge$ j$\neq$ i $\Rightarrow$ coref(j,i)
mentionType(j,t_1+) $\wedge$ mentionType(i,t_2+) $\wedge$ headMatch(j,i) $\wedge$ j$\neq$ i $\Rightarrow$ coref(j,i)
mentionType(j,t_1+) $\wedge$ mentionType(i,t_2+) $\wedge$ subStrMatch(j,i) $\wedge$ j$\neq$ i $\Rightarrow$ coref(j,i)
hasHead(j,h_1+) $\wedge$ hasHead(i,h_2+) $\wedge$ j$\neq$ i $\Rightarrow$ coref(j,i)
Grammatical Features
mentionType(j,t_1+) $\wedge$ mentionType(i,t_2+) $\wedge$ genderType(j,g_1+) $\wedge$ genderType(i,g_2+) $\wedge$ j$\neq$ i $\Rightarrow$ coref(j,i)
mentionType(j,t_1+) $\wedge$ mentionType(i,t_2+) $\wedge$ numberType(j,n_1+) $\wedge$ numberType(i,n_2+) $\wedge$ j$\neq$ i $\Rightarrow$ coref(j,i)
mentionType(j,t_1+) $\wedge$ mentionType(i,t_2+) $\wedge$ bothMatch(j,i,b+) $\wedge$ j$\neq$ i $\Rightarrow$ coref(j,i)
mentionType(j,t_1+) $\wedge$ mentionType(i,t_2+) $\wedge$ closestMatch(j,i,c+) $\wedge$ j$\neq$ i $\Rightarrow$ coref(j,i)
mentionType(j,t_1+) $\wedge$ mentionType(i,t_2+) $\wedge$ animacyMatch(j,i) $\wedge$ j$\neq$ i $\Rightarrow$ coref(j,i)
mentionType(j,t_1+) $\wedge$ mentionType(i,t_2+) $\wedge$ nested(j,i) $\wedge$ j$\neq$ i $\Rightarrow$ coref(j,i)
mentionType(j,t_1+) $\wedge$ mentionType(i,t_2+) $\wedge$ c_command(j,i) $\wedge$ j$\neq$ i $\Rightarrow$ coref(j,i)
(mentionType(j,t_1+) $\vee$ mentionType(i,t_2+)) $\wedge$ j$\neq$ i $\Rightarrow$ coref(j,i)
(reflexive(j) $\vee$ reflexive(i)) $\wedge$ j$\neq$ i $\Rightarrow$ coref(j,i)
(possessive(j) $\vee$ possessive(i)) $\wedge$ j$\neq$ i $\Rightarrow$ coref(j,i)
(definite(j) $\vee$ definite(i)) $\wedge$ j$\neq$ i $\Rightarrow$ coref(j,i)
(indefinite(j) $\vee$ indefinite(i)) $\wedge$ j$\neq$ i $\Rightarrow$ coref(j,i)
(demonstrative(j) $\vee$ demonstrative(i)) $\wedge$ j$\neq$ i $\Rightarrow$ coref(j,i)
Distance and position Features
mentionType(j,t_1+) $\wedge$ mentionType(i,t_2+) $\wedge$ sentenceDistance(j,i,s+) $\wedge$ j$\neq$ i $\Rightarrow$ coref(j,i)
mentionType(j,t_1+) $\wedge$ mentionType(i,t_2+) $\wedge$ mentionDistance (j,i,m+) $\wedge$ j$\neq$ i $\Rightarrow$ coref(j,i)
(firstMention(j) $\vee$ firstMention(i)) $\wedge$ j$\neq$ i $\Rightarrow$ coref(j,i)
Semantic Features
mentionType(j,t_1+) $\wedge$ mentionType(i,t_2+) $\wedge$ alias(j,i) $\wedge$ j$\neq$ i $\Rightarrow$ coref(j,i)
mentionType(j,t_1+) $\wedge$ mentionType(i,t_2+) $\wedge$ sameSpeaker(j,i) $\wedge$ j$\neq$ i $\Rightarrow$ coref(j,i)
mentionType(j,t_1+) $\wedge$ mentionType(i,t_2+) $\wedge$ entityTypeMatch(j,i) $\wedge$ j$\neq$ i $\Rightarrow$ coref(j,i)
mentionType(j,t_1+) $\wedge$ mentionType(i,t_2+) $\wedge$ srlMatch(j,i) $\wedge$ j$\neq$ i $\Rightarrow$ coref(j,i)
mentionType(j,t_1+) $\wedge$ mentionType(i,t_2+) $\wedge$ verbMatch(j,i) $\wedge$ j$\neq$ i $\Rightarrow$ coref(j,i)
(entityType(j,e_1+) $\vee$ entityType(i,e_2+)) $\wedge$ j$\neq$ i $\Rightarrow$ coref(j,i)

Table 2: Local Formulas.

Best-First constraint:

$$coref(j,i) \Rightarrow \neg coref(k,i) \quad \forall j,k < i (k \neq j) \quad (2)$$

Here we assume that *coref(j,i)* returns true if candidate mentions j and i are coreferential and false otherwise. Therefore for each candidate mention i, we should only select at most one candidate mention j to return true for the predicate *coref(j,i)* from all its preceding candidate mentions.

Transitivity constraint:

$$coref(j,k) \wedge coref(k,i) \wedge j < k < i \Rightarrow coref(j,i) \quad (3)$$

$$coref(j,k) \wedge coref(j,i) \wedge j < k < i \Rightarrow coref(k,i) \quad (4)$$

$$coref(j,i) \wedge coref(k,i) \wedge j < k < i \Rightarrow coref(j,k) \quad (5)$$

With the transitivity constraint, it means for given mentions j, k and i, if any two pairs of them are coreferential, then the third pair of them should be also coreferential.

We use best-first clustering and transitivity constraint in our joint learning model respectively. Detailed comparisons between them will be shown in Section 4.

3.3 Inference

We use MAP inference which is implemented by Integer Linear Programming (ILP). Its objective is to maximize a posteriori probability as follows. Here we use x to represent all the observed ground atoms and y to represent the hidden ground atoms. Formally, we have

$$\hat{y} = \arg\max_y \, p(y|x) \simeq \arg\max_y s(y,x),$$

where

$$s(y,x) = \sum_{(\phi_i,w_i)\in M} w_i \sum_{\mathbf{c}\in C^{n_{\phi_i}}} f_{\mathbf{c}}^{\phi_i}(y,x). \quad (6)$$

Each hidden ground atom can only takes a value of either 0 or 1. And global formulas should be satisfied as hard constraints when inferring the best $\hat{y}$. So the problem can be easily solved using ILP. Detailed introduction about transforming ground Markov networks in Markov logic into an ILP problem can be found in (Riedel, 2008).

3.4 Parameter Learning

For parameter learning, we employ the online learner MIRA (Crammer and Singer, 2003), which establishes a large margin between the score of the gold solution and all wrong solutions to learn the weights. This is achieved by solving the quadratic program as follows

$$\min \parallel \mathbf{w}_t - \mathbf{w}_{t-1} \parallel . \tag{7}$$

$$s.t. \quad s(y_i, x_i) - s(y', x_i) \geq L(y_i, y')$$
$$\forall y' \neq y_i, \quad (y_i, x_i) \in D$$

Here $D = \{(y_i, x_i)\}_{i=1}^{N}$ represents N training instances (each instance represents one single document in the dataset) and t represents the number of iterations. In our problem, we adopt 1-best MIRA, which means that in each iteration we try to find $\mathbf{w}_t$ which can guarantee the difference between the right solution y_i and the best solution y' (i.e. the one with the highest score s(y', x_i), equivalent to $\hat{y}$ in Section 3.3)) is at least as big as the loss $L(y_i, y')$, while changing $\mathbf{w}_{t-1}$ as little as possible. The number of false ground atoms of *coref* predicate is selected as loss function in our experiments. Hard global constraints (i.e. best-first clustering or transitivity constraint) must be satisfied when inferring the best y' in each iteration, which can make learned weights more effective.

4 Experiments

In this section, we will first describe the dataset and evaluation metrics we use. We will then present the effect of our joint learning method, and finally discuss the comparison with the state of the art.

4.1 Data Set

We use the dataset from the CoNLL-2011 shared task, "Modeling Unrestricted Coreference in OntoNotes" (Pradhan et al., 2011)[2]. It uses the English portion of the OntoNotes v4.0 corpus. There are three important differences between OntoNotes and another well-known coreference dataset from ACE. First, OntoNotes does not label any singleton entity cluster, which has only one reference in the text. Second, only identity coreference is tagged in OntoNotes, but not appositives or predicate nominatives. Third, ACE only considers mentions which belong to ACE entity types, whereas OntoNotes considers more entity types. The shared task is to automatically identify both entity coreference and event coreference, although we only focus on entity coreference in this paper. We don't assume that gold standard mention boundaries are given. So we develop a heuristic method for mention detection. See details in Section 2.1.

The training set consists of 1674 documents from newswire, magazine articles, broadcast news, broadcast conversations and webpages, and the development set consists of 202 documents from the same source. For training set, there are 101264 mentions from 26612 entities. And for development set, there are 14291 mentions from 3752 entities (Pradhan et al., 2011).

4.2 Evaluation Metrics

We use the same evaluation metrics as used in CoNLL-2011. Specifically, for mention detection, we use precision, recall and the F-measure. A mention is considered to be correct only if it matches the exact same span of characters in the annotation key. For coreference resolution, MUC (Vilain et al., 1995), B-CUBED (Bagga and Baldwin, 1998) and CEAF-E (Luo, 2005) are used for evaluation. The unweighted average F score of them is used to compare different systems.

4.3 The Effect of Joint Learning

To assess the performance of our method, we set up several variations of our system to compare with the joint learning system. The *MLN-Local* system uses only the local formulas described in Table 2 without any global constraints under the MLN framework. By default, the *MLN-Local* system uses the single-link method to generate clustering results. The *MLN-Local+BF* system replaces the single-link method with best-first clustering to infer mention clustering results after learning the weights for all the local formulas. The *MLN-Local+Trans* system replaces the best-first clustering with transitivity

[2] http://conll.cemantix.org/2011/

System	Mention Detection			MUC			B-cube			CEAF			Avg
	R	P	F	R	P	F	R	P	F	R	P	F	F
MLN-Local	62.52	74.75	68.09	56.07	65.55	60.44	65.67	72.95	69.12	45.55	37.19	40.95	56.84
MLN-Local+BF	65.74	73.2	69.27	56.79	64.08	60.22	65.71	74.18	69.69	47.29	40.53	43.65	57.85
MLN-Local+Trans	**68.49**	70.32	69.40	**57.16**	60.98	59.01	**66.97**	72.90	69.81	46.96	**43.34**	**45.08**	57.97
MLN-Joint(BF)	64.36	75.25	69.38	55.47	66.95	60.67	64.14	77.75	70.29	50.47	39.85	44.53	58.50
MLN-Joint(Trans)	64.46	**75.37**	**69.49**	55.48	**67.15**	**60.76**	64.00	**78.11**	**70.36**	**50.63**	39.84	44.60	**58.57**

Table 3: Comparison between different MLN-based systems, using 10-fold cross validation on the training dataset.

constraint. The *MLN-Joint* system is a joint model for both pairwise classification and mention clustering. It can combine either best-first clustering or enforcing transitivity constraint with pairwise classification, and we denote these two variants of *MLN-Joint* as *MLN-Joint(BF)* and *MLN-Joint(Trans)* respectively.

To compare the performance of the various systems above, we use 10-fold cross validation on the training dataset. We empirically find that our method has a fast convergence rate, to learn the MLN model, we set the number of iterations to be 10.

The performance of these compared systems is shown in Table 3. To provide some context for the performance of this task, we report the median average F-score of the official results of CoNLL-2011, which is 50.12 (Pradhan et al., 2011). We can see that *MLN-Local* achieves an average F-score of 56.84, which is well above the median score. When adding best-first or transitivity constraint which is independent of pairwise classification, *MLN-Local+BF* and *MLN-Local+Trans* achieve better results of 57.85 and 57.97. Most of all, we can see that the joint learning model (*MLN-Joint(BF)* or *MLN-Joint(Trans)*) significantly outperforms independent learning model (*MLN-Local+BF* or *MLN-Local+Trans*) no matter whether best-first clustering or transitivity constraint is used (based on a paired 2-tailed t-test with $p < 0.05$) with the score of 58.50 or 58.57, which shows the effectiveness of our proposed joint learning method.

Best-first clustering and transitivity constraint are very useful in Markov logic framework, and both *MLN-Local* and *MLN-Joint* benefit from them. For *MLN-Joint*, these two clustering methods result in similar performance. But actually, transitivity is harder than best-first, because it significantly increases the number of formulas for constraints and slows down the learning process. In our experiments, we find that *MLN-Joint(Trans)*[3] is much slower than *MLN-Joint(BF)*. Overall, *MLN-Joint(BF)* has a good trade-off between effectiveness and efficiency.

4.4 Comparison with the State of the Art

In order to compare our method with the state-of-the-art systems, we consider the following systems. We implemented a traditional pairwise coreference system using Maximum Entropy as the base classifier and best-first clustering to link the results. We used the same set of local features in *MLN-Joint*. We refer to this system as *MaxEnt+BF*. To replace best-first clustering with transitivity constraint, we have another system named as *MaxEnt+Trans*. We also consider the best 3 systems from CoNLL-2011 shared task. Chang's system uses ILP to perform best-first clustering after training a pairwise coreference model. Sapena's system uses a relaxation labeling method to iteratively perform function optimization for labeling each mention's entity after learning the weights for features under a C4.5 learner. Lee's system is a purely rule-based one. They use a battery of sieves by precision (from highest to lowest) to iteratively choose antecedent for each mention. They obtained the highest score in CoNLL-2011.

Table 4 shows the comparisons of our system with the state-of-the-art systems on the development set of CoNLL-2011. From the results, we can see that our joint learning systems are obviously better than

[3]For MLN-Joint(Trans), not all training instances can be learnt in a reasonable amount of time, so we set up a time out threshold of 100 seconds. If the model cannot response in 100 seconds for some training instance, we remove it from the training set.

System	Mention Detection			MUC			B-cube			CEAF			Avg
	R	P	F	R	P	F	R	P	F	R	P	F	F
MLN-Joint(BF)	67.33	72.94	**70.02**	**58.03**	64.05	60.89	67.11	73.88	70.33	47.6	41.92	44.58	58.60
MLN-Joint(Trans)	67.28	72.88	69.97	58.00	64.10	**60.90**	67.12	74.13	**70.45**	47.70	41.96	44.65	**58.67**
MaxEnt+BF	60.54	**76.64**	67.64	52.20	**68.52**	59.26	60.85	80.15	69.18	51.6	37.05	43.13	57.19
MaxEnt+Trans	61.36	76.11	67.94	51.46	68.40	58.73	59.79	**81.69**	69.04	**53.03**	37.84	44.17	57.31
Lee's System	-	-	-	57.50	59.10	58.30	**71.00**	69.20	70.10	48.10	**46.50**	**47.30**	58.60
Sapena's System	**92.45**	27.34	42.20	54.53	62.25	58.13	63.72	73.83	68.40	47.20	40.01	43.31	56.61
Chang's System	-	-	64.69	-	-	55.8	-	-	69.29	-	-	43.96	56.35

Table 4: Comparisons with state-of-the-art systems on the development dataset.

MaxEnt+BF and *MaxEnt+Trans*. They also outperform the learning-based systems of Sapena et al. (2011) and Chang et al. (2011), and perform competitively with Lee's system (Lee et al., 2011). Note that Lee's system is purely rule-based, while our methods are developed in a theoretically sound way, i.e., Markov logic framework.

5 Related Work

Supervised noun phrase coreference resolution has been extensively studied. Besides the mention-pair model, two other commonly used models are the entity-mention model (Luo et al., 2004; Yang et al., 2008) and ranking models (Denis and Baldridge, 2008; Rahman and Ng, 2009). Interested readers can refer to the literature review by Ng (2010).

Under the mention-pair model, Klenner (2007) and Finkel and Manning (2008) applied Integer Linear Programming (ILP) to enforce transitivity on the pairwise classification results. Chang et al. (2011) used the same ILP technique to incorporate best-first clustering and generate the mention clusters. In all these studies, however, mention clustering is combined with pairwise classification only at the inference stage but not at the learning stage.

To perform joint learning of pairwise classification and mention clustering, in (McCallum and Wellner, 2005), each mention pair corresponds to a binary variable indicating whether the two mentions are coreferential, and the dependence between these variables is modeled by conditional undirected graphical models. Finley and Joachims (2005) proposed a general SVM-based framework for supervised clustering that learns item-pair similarity measures, and applied the framework to noun phrase coreference resolution. In our work, we take a different approach and apply Markov logic. As we have shown in Section 3, given the flexibility of Markov logic, it is straightforward to perform joint learning of pairwise classification and mention clustering.

In recent years, Markov logic has been widely used in natural language processing problems (Poon and Domingos, 2009; Yoshikawa et al., 2009; Che and Liu, 2010). For coreference resolution, the most notable one is unsupervised coreference resolution by Poon and Domingos (2008). Poon and Domingos (2008) followed the entity-mention model while we follow the mention-pair model, which are quite different approaches. To seek good performance in an unsupervised way, Poon and Domingos (2008) highly rely on two important strong indicators: appositives and predicate nominatives. However, OntoNotes corpus (state-of-art NLP data collection) on coreference layer for CoNLL-2011 has excluded these two conditions of annotations (appositives and predicate nominatives) from their judging guidelines. Compared with it, our methods are more applicable for real dataset. Huang et al. (2009) used Markov logic to predict coreference probabilities for mention pairs followed by correlation clustering to generate the final results. Although they also perform joint learning, at the inference stage, they still make pairwise coreference decisions and cluster mentions sequentially. Unlike their method, We formulate the two steps into a single framework.

Besides combining pairwise classification and mention clustering, there has also been some work that jointly performs mention detection and coreference resolution. Daumé and Marcu (2005) developed such a model based on the Learning as

Search Optimization (LaSO) framework. Rahman and Ng (2009) proposed to learn a cluster-ranker for discourse-new mention detection jointly with coreference resolution. Denis and Baldridge (2007) adopted an Integer Linear Programming (ILP) formulation for coreference resolution which models anaphoricity and coreference as a joint task.

6 Conclusion

In this paper we present a joint learning method with Markov logic which naturally combines pairwise classification and mention clustering. Experimental results show that the joint learning method significantly outperforms baseline methods. Our method is also better than all the learning-based systems in CoNLL-2011 and reaches the same level of performance with the best system.

In the future we will try to design more global constraints and explore deeper relations between training instances generation and mention clustering. We will also attempt to introduce more predicates and transform structure learning techniques for MLN into coreference problems.

Acknowledgments

Part of the work was done when the first author was a visiting student in the Singapore Management University. And this work was partially supported by the National High Technology Research and Development Program of China(863 Program) (No.2012AA011101), the National Natural Science Foundation of China (No.91024009, No.60973053, No.90920011), and the Specialized Research Fund for the Doctoral Program of Higher Education of China (Grant No. 20090001110047).

References

Amit Bagga and Breck Baldwin. 1998. Algorithms for scoring coreference chains. In *The First International Conference on Language Resources and Evaluation Workshop on Linguistics Coreference*, pages 563–566.

Eric Bengtson and Dan Roth. 2008. Understanding the value of features for coreference resolution. In *EMNLP*.

K. Chang, R. Samdani, A. Rozovskaya, N. Rizzolo, M. Sammons, and D. Roth. 2011. Inference protocols for coreference resolution. In *CoNLL Shared Task*, pages 40–44, Portland, Oregon, USA. Association for Computational Linguistics.

Wanxiang Che and Ting Liu. 2010. Jointly modeling wsd and srl with markov logic. In Chu-Ren Huang and Dan Jurafsky, editors, *COLING*, pages 161–169. Tsinghua University Press.

Koby Crammer and Yoram Singer. 2003. Ultraconservative online algorithms for multiclass problems. *Journal of Machine Learning Research*, 3:951–991.

III Hal Daumé and Daniel Marcu. 2005. A large-scale exploration of effective global features for a joint entity detection and tracking model. In *HLT '05: Proceedings of the conference on Human Language Technology and Empirical Methods in Natural Language Processing*, pages 97–104, Morristown, NJ, USA. Association for Computational Linguistics.

Pascal Denis and Jason Baldridge. 2007. Joint determination of anaphoricity and coreference resolution using integer programming. In *Human Language Technologies 2007: The Conference of the North American Chapter of the Association for Computational Linguistics; Proceedings of the Main Conference*, pages 236–243, Rochester, New York, April. Association for Computational Linguistics.

Pascal Denis and Jason Baldridge. 2008. Specialized models and ranking for coreference resolution. In *EMNLP*, pages 660–669.

Jenny Rose Finkel and Christopher D. Manning. 2008. Enforcing transitivity in coreference resolution. In *ACL (Short Papers)*, pages 45–48. The Association for Computer Linguistics.

T. Finley and T. Joachims. 2005. Supervised clustering with support vector machines. In *International Conference on Machine Learning (ICML)*, pages 217–224.

Shujian Huang, Yabing Zhang, Junsheng Zhou, and Jiajun Chen. 2009. Coreference resolution using markov logic networks. In *Proceedings of Computational Linguistics and Intelligent Text Processing: 10th International Conference, CICLing 2009*.

M. Klenner. 2007. Enforcing consistency on coreference sets. In *RANLP*.

Heeyoung Lee, Yves Peirsman, Angel Chang, Nathanael Chambers, Mihai Surdeanu, and Dan Jurafsky. 2011. Stanford's multi-pass sieve coreference resolution system at the conll-2011 shared task. In *Proceedings of the Fifteenth Conference on Computational Natural Language Learning: Shared Task*, pages 28–34, Portland, Oregon, USA, June. Association for Computational Linguistics.

Xiaoqiang Luo, Abe Ittycheriah, Hongyan Jing, A Kambhatla, and Salim Roukos. 2004. A mention-synchronous coreference resolution algorithm based on the bell tree. In *Proc. of the ACL*, pages 135–142.

Xiaoqiang Luo. 2005. On coreference resolution performance metrics. In *Proc. of HLT/EMNLP*, pages 25–32.

Andrew McCallum and Ben Wellner. 2005. Conditional models of identity uncertainty with application to noun coreference. In *Advances in Neural Information Processing Systems*, pages 905–912. MIT Press.

J. McCarthy and W. Lehnert. 1995. Using decision trees for coreference resolution. In *Proceedings of the 14th International Joint Conference on Artificial Intelligence*.

Vincent Ng and Claire Cardie. 2002. Improving machine learning approaches to coreference resolution. In *Proceedings of the ACL*, pages 104–111.

Vincent Ng. 2010. Supervised noun phrase coreference research: The first fifteen years. In *ACL*, pages 1396–1411. The Association for Computer Linguistics.

Hoifung Poon and Pedro Domingos. 2008. Joint unsupervised coreference resolution with markov logic. In *EMNLP*, pages 650–659.

Hoifung Poon and Pedro Domingos. 2009. Unsupervised semantic parsing. In *EMNLP*, pages 1–10.

Sameer Pradhan, Lance Ramshaw, Mitchell Marcus, Martha Palmer, Ralph Weischedel, and Nianwen Xue. 2011. Conll-2011 shared task: Modeling unrestricted coreference in ontonotes. In *Proceedings of the Fifteenth Conference on Computational Natural Language Learning: Shared Task*, pages 1–27, Portland, Oregon, USA, June. Association for Computational Linguistics.

Altaf Rahman and Vincent Ng. 2009. Supervised models for coreference resolution. In *Proceedings of EMNLP*, pages 968–977.

Matthew Richardson and Pedro Domingos. 2006. Markov logic networks. *Machine Learning*, 62(1-2):107–136.

Sebastian Riedel. 2008. Improving the accuracy and efficiency of map inference for markov logic. In *UAI*, pages 468–475. AUAI Press.

Emili Sapena, Lluís Padró, and Jordi Turmo. 2011. Relaxcor participation in conll shared task on coreference resolution. In *Proceedings of the Fifteenth Conference on Computational Natural Language Learning: Shared Task*, pages 35–39, Portland, Oregon, USA, June. Association for Computational Linguistics.

Wee Meng Soon, Hwee Tou Ng, and Chung Yong Lim. 2001. A machine learning approach to coreference resolution of noun phrases. *Computational Linguistics*, 27(4):521–544.

Olga Uryupina, Sriparna Saha, Asif Ekbal, and Massimo Poesio. 2011. Multi-metric optimization for coreference: The unitn / iitp / essex submission to the 2011 conll shared task. In *Proceedings of the Fifteenth Conference on Computational Natural Language Learning: Shared Task*, pages 61–65, Portland, Oregon, USA, June. Association for Computational Linguistics.

Marc B. Vilain, John D. Burger, John S. Aberdeen, Dennis Connolly, and Lynette Hirschman. 1995. A model-theoretic coreference scoring scheme. In *MUC*, pages 45–52.

Xiaofeng Yang, Jian Su, Jun Lang, Chew Lim Tan, Ting Liu, and Sheng Li. 2008. An entity-mention model for coreference resolution with inductive logic programming. In *ACL*, pages 843–851. The Association for Computer Linguistics.

Katsumasa Yoshikawa, Sebastian Riedel, Masayuki Asahara, and Yuji Matsumoto. 2009. Jointly identifying temporal relations with markov logic. In *ACL/AFNLP*, pages 405–413. The Association for Computer Linguistics.

Resolving "This-issue" Anaphora

Varada Kolhatkar
Department of Computer Science
University of Toronto
Toronto, ON, M5S 3G4, Canada
varada@cs.toronto.edu

Graeme Hirst
Department of Computer Science
University of Toronto
Toronto, ON, M5S 3G4, Canada
gh@cs.toronto.edu

Abstract

We annotate and resolve a particular case of abstract anaphora, namely, *this-issue* anaphora. We propose a candidate ranking model for *this-issue* anaphora resolution that explores different *issue*-specific and general abstract-anaphora features. The model is not restricted to nominal or verbal antecedents; rather, it is able to identify antecedents that are arbitrary spans of text. Our results show that (a) the model outperforms the strong adjacent-sentence baseline; (b) general abstract-anaphora features, as distinguished from *issue*-specific features, play a crucial role in *this-issue* anaphora resolution, suggesting that our approach can be generalized for other NPs such as *this problem* and *this debate*; and (c) it is possible to reduce the search space in order to improve performance.

1 Introduction

Anaphora in which the anaphoric expression refers to an abstract object such as a proposition, a property, or a fact is known as *abstract object anaphora*. This is seen in the following examples.

(1) [**Be careful what you wish... because wishes sometimes come true.**]$_i$ [**That**]$_i$ is what the Semiconductor Industry Association, which represents U.S. manufacturers, has been learning. (from Asher (1993))

(2) This prospective study suggested [**that oral carvedilol is more effective than oral metoprolol in the prevention of AF after on-pump CABG**]$_i$. It is well tolerated when started before and continued after the surgery. However, further prospective studies are needed to clarify [**this issue**]$_i$.

(3) In principle, he said, airlines should be allowed [**to sell standing-room-only tickets for adults**]$_i$ — as long as [**this decision**]$_i$ was approved by their marketing departments.

These examples highlight a difficulty not found with nominal anaphora. First, the anaphors refer to abstract concepts that can be expressed with different syntactic shapes which are usually not nominals. The anaphor *That* in (1) refers to the proposition in the previous utterance, whereas the anaphor *this issue* in (2) refers to a clause from the previous text. In (3), the anaphoric expression *this decision* refers to a verb phrase from the same sentence. Second, the antecedents do not always have precisely defined boundaries. In (2), for example, the whole sentence containing the marked clause could also be thought to be the correct antecedent. Third, the actual referents are not always the precise textual antecedents. The actual referent in (2), the issue to be clarified, is <u>whether</u> *oral carvedilol is more effective than oral metoprolol in the prevention of AF after on-pump CABG* <u>or not</u>, a variant of the antecedent text.

Generally, abstract anaphora, as distinguished from *nominal anaphora*, is signalled in English by pronouns *this*, *that*, and *it* (Müller, 2008). But in abstract anaphora, English prefers demonstratives to personal pronouns and definite articles (Passonneau, 1989; Navarretta, 2011).[1] Demonstra-

[1]This is not to say that personal pronouns and definite articles do not occur in abstract anaphora, but they are not common.

tives can be used in isolation (*That* in (1)) or with *nouns* (e.g., *this issue* in (2)). The latter follows the pattern *demonstrative* $\{modifier\}*$ *noun*. The demonstrative acts as a determiner and the noun following the demonstrative imposes selectional constraints for the antecedent, as in examples (2) and (3). Francis (1994) calls such nouns *label nouns*, which "serve to encapsulate or package a stretch of discourse". Schmid (2000) refers to them as *shell nouns*, a metaphoric term which reflects different functions of these nouns such as encapsulation, pointing, and signalling.

Demonstrative nouns, along with pronouns like *both* and *either*, are referred to as *sortal anaphors* (Castaño et al., 2002; Lin and Liang, 2004; Torii and Vijay-Shanker, 2007). Castaño et al. observed that sortal anaphors are prevalent in the biomedical literature. They noted that among 100 distinct anaphors derived from a corpus of 70 Medline abstracts, 60% were sortal anaphors. But how often do demonstrative nouns refer to abstract objects? We observed that from a corpus of 74,000 randomly chosen Medline[2] abstracts, of the first 150 most frequently occurring distinct demonstrative nouns (frequency > 30), 51.3% were abstract, 41.3% were concrete, and 7.3% were discourse deictic. This shows that abstract anaphora resolution is an important component of general anaphora resolution in the biomedical domain. However, automatic resolution of this type of anaphora has not attracted much attention and the previous work for this task is limited.

The present work is a step towards resolving abstract anaphora in written text. In particular, we choose the interesting abstract concept *issue* and demonstrate the complexities of resolving *this-issue* anaphora manually as well as automatically in the Medline domain. We present our algorithm, results, and error analysis for *this-issue* anaphora resolution.

The abstract concept *issue* was chosen for the following reasons. First, it occurs frequently in all kinds of text from newspaper articles to novels to scientific articles. There are 13,489 *issue* anaphora instances in the New York Times corpus and 1,116 instances in 65,000 Medline abstracts. Second, it is abstract enough that it can take several syntactic and semantic forms, which makes the problem interesting and non-trivial. Third, *issue* referents in scientific literature generally lie in the previous sentence or two, which makes the problem tractable. Fourth, *issues* in Medline abstracts are generally associated with clinical problems in the medical domain and spell out the motivation of the research presented in the article. So extraction of this information would be useful in any biomedical information retrieval system.

2 Related Work

Anaphora resolution has been extensively studied in computational linguistics (Hirst, 1981; Mitkov, 2002; Poesio et al., 2011). But CL research has mostly focused on nominal anaphora resolution (e.g., resolving multiple ambiguous mentions of a single entity representing a person, a location, or an organization) mainly for two reasons. First, nominal anaphora is the most frequently occurring anaphora in most domains, and second, there is a substantial amount of annotated data available for this kind of anaphora.

Besides pronominal anaphora, some work has been done on complement anaphora (Modjeska, 2003) (e.g., *British and **other** European steelmakers*). There is also some research on resolving sortal anaphora in the medical domain using domain knowledge (Castaño et al., 2002; Lin and Liang, 2004; Torii and Vijay-Shanker, 2007). But all these approaches focus only on the anaphors with nominal antecedents.

By contrast, the area of abstract object anaphora remains relatively unexplored mainly because the standard anaphora resolution features such as agreement and apposition cannot be applied to abstract anaphora resolution. Asher (1993) built a theoretical framework to resolve abstract anaphora. He divided discourse abstract anaphora into three broad categories: event anaphora, proposition anaphora, and fact anaphora, and discussed how abstract entities can be resolved using discourse representation theory. Chen et al. (2011) focused on a subset of event anaphora and resolved event coreference chains in terms of the representative verbs of the events from the OntoNotes corpus. Our task differs from their work as follows. Chen et al. mainly

[2] `http://www.nlm.nih.gov/bsd/pmresources.html`

focus on events and actions and use verbs as a proxy for the non-nominal antecedents. But *this-issue* antecedents cannot usually be represented by a verb. Our work is not restricted to a particular syntactic type of the antecedent; rather we provide the flexibility of marking arbitrary spans of text as antecedents.

There are also some prominent approaches to abstract anaphora resolution in the spoken dialogue domain (Eckert and Strube, 2000; Byron, 2004; Müller, 2008). These approaches go beyond nominal antecedents; however, they are restricted to spoken dialogues in specific domains and need serious adaptation if one wants to apply them to arbitrary text.

In addition to research on resolution, there is also some work on effective annotation of abstract anaphora (Strube and Müller, 2003; Botley, 2006; Poesio and Artstein, 2008; Dipper and Zinsmeister, 2011). However, to the best of our knowledge, there is currently no English corpus annotated for *issue* anaphora antecedents.

3 Data and Annotation

To create an initial annotated dataset, we collected 188 *this* {*modifier*}* *issue* instances along with the surrounding context from Medline abstracts.[3] Five instances were discarded as they had an unrelated (publication related) sense. Among the remaining 183 instances, 132 instances were independently annotated by two annotators, a domain expert and a non-expert, and the remaining 51 instances were annotated only by the domain expert. We use the former instances for training and the latter instances (unseen by the developer) for testing. The annotator's task was to mark arbitrary text segments as antecedents (without concern for their linguistic types). To make the task tractable, we assumed that an antecedent does not span multiple sentences but lies in a single sentence (since we are dealing with singular *this-issue* anaphors) and that it is a continuous span of text.

[3]Although our dataset is rather small, its size is similar to other available abstract anaphora corpora in English: 154 instances in Eckert and Strube (2000), 69 instances in Byron (2003), 462 instances annotated by only one annotator in Botley (2006), and 455 instances restricted to those which have only nominal or clausal antecedents in Poesio and Artstein (2008).

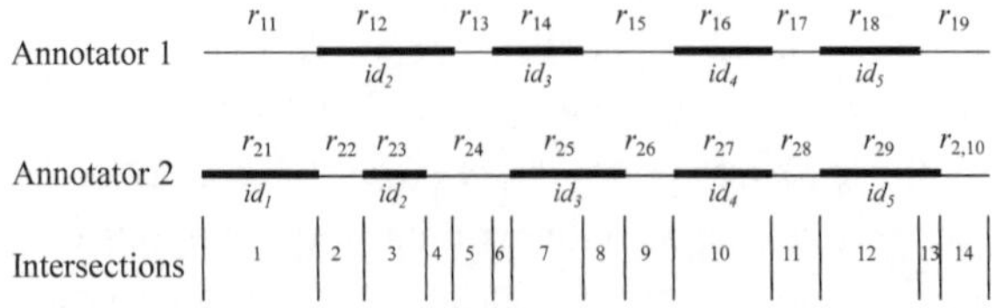

Figure 1: Example of annotated data. Bold segments denote the marked antecedents for the corresponding anaphor *ids*. r_{hj} is the jth section identified by the annotator *h*.

3.1 Inter-annotator Agreement

This kind of annotation — identifying and marking arbitrary units of text that are not necessarily constituents — requires a non-trivial variant of the usual inter-annotator agreement measures. We use Krippendorff's *reliability coefficient for unitizing* (α_u) (Krippendorff, 1995) which has not often been used or described in CL. In our context, *unitizing* means marking the spans of the text that serve as the antecedent for the given anaphors within the given text. The coefficient α_u assumes that the annotated sections do not overlap in a single annotator's output and our data satisfies this criterion.[4] The general form of coefficient α_u is:

$$\alpha_u = 1 - \frac{_uD_o}{_uD_e} \tag{1}$$

where $_uD_o$ and $_uD_e$ are observed and expected disagreements respectively. Both disagreement quantities express the average squared differences between the mismatching pairs of values assigned by annotators to given units of analysis. $\alpha_u = 1$ indicates perfect reliability and $\alpha_u = 0$ indicates the absence of reliability. When $\alpha_u < 0$, the disagreement is systematic. Annotated data with reliability of $\alpha_u \geq 0.80$ is considered reliable (Krippendorff, 2004).

Krippendorff's α_u is non-trivial, and explaining it in detail would take too much space, but the general idea, in our context, is as follows. The annotators mark the antecedents corresponding to each anaphor in their respective copies of the text, as shown in Figure 1. The marked antecedents are mutually exclusive sections *r*; we denote the jth section identified

[4]If antecedents overlap with each other in a single annotator's output (which is a rare event) we construct data that satisfies the non-overlap criterion by creating different copies of the same text corresponding to each anaphor instance.

Antecedent type	Distribution	Example
clause	37.9%	There is a controversial debate (**SBAR** *whether back school program might improve quality of life in back pain patients*). This study aimed to address **this issue**.
sentence	26.5%	(**S** *Reduced serotonin function and abnormalities in the hypothalamic-pituitary-adrenal axis are thought to play a role in the aetiology of major depression.*) We sought to examine **this issue** in the elderly ...
mixed	18.2%	(S (PP Given these data) (, ,) (**NP** *decreasing HTD to < or = 5 years*) (**VP** *may have a detrimental effect on patients with locally advanced prostate cancer*) (. .)) Only a randomized trial will conclusively clarify **this issue**.
nominalization	17.4%	As (**NP** *the influence of estrogen alone on breast cancer detection*) is not established, we examined **this issue** in the Women's Health Initiative trial...

Table 1: Antecedent types. In examples, the antecedent type is in **bold** and the marked antecedent is in *italics*.

by the annotator h by r_{hj}. In Figure 1, annotators 1 and 2 have reached different conclusions by identifying 9 and 10 sections respectively in their copies of the text. Annotator 1 has not marked any antecedent for the anaphor with $id = 1$, while annotator 2 has marked r_{21} for the same anaphor. Both annotators have marked exactly the same antecedent for the anaphor with $id = 4$. The difference between two annotated sections is defined in terms of the square of the distance between the non-overlapping parts of the sections. The distance is 0 when the sections are unmarked by both annotators or are marked and exactly same, and is the summation of the squares of the unmatched parts if they are different. The coefficient is computed using intersections of the marked sections. In Figure 1, annotators 1 and 2 have a total of 14 intersections. The observed disagreement $_uD_o$ is the weighted sum of the differences between all mismatching intersections of sections marked by the annotators, and the expected disagreement is the summation of all possible differences of pairwise combinations of all sections of all annotators normalized by the length of the text (in terms of the number of tokens) and the number of pairwise combinations of annotators.

For our data, the inter-annotator agreement was $\alpha_u = 0.86$ ($_uD_o = 0.81$ and $_uD_e = 5.81$) despite the fact that the annotators differed in their domain expertise, which suggests that abstract concepts such as *issue* can be annotated reliably.

3.2 Corpus Statistics

A gold standard corpus was created by resolving the cases where the annotators disagreed. Among 132 training instances, the annotators could not resolve 6 instances and we broke the tie by writing to the authors of the articles and using their response to resolve the disagreement. In the gold standard corpus, 95.5% of the antecedents were in the current or previous sentence and 99.2% were in the current or previous two sentences. Only one antecedent was found more than two sentences back and it was six sentences back. One instance was a cataphor, but the antecedent occurred in the same sentence as the anaphor. This suggests that for an automatic *this-issue* resolution system, it would be reasonable to consider only the previous two sentences along with the sentence containing the anaphor.

The distribution of the different linguistic forms that an antecedent of *this-issue* can take in our data set is shown in Table 1. The majority of antecedents are clauses or whole sentences. A number of antecedents are noun phrases, but these are generally nominalizations that refer to abstract concepts (e.g., *the influence of estrogen alone on breast cancer detection*). Some antecedents are not even well-defined syntactic constituents[5] but are combinations of several well-defined constituents. We denote the type of such antecedents as *mixed*. In the corpus, 18.2% of the antecedents are of this type, suggesting that it is not sufficient to restrict the antecedent search space to well-defined syntactic constituents.[6]

In our data, we did not find anaphoric chains for any of the *this-issue* anaphor instances, which indicates that the antecedents of *this-issue* anaphors are

[5]We refer to every syntactic constituent identified by the parser as a *well-defined syntactic constituent*.

[6]Indeed, many of mixed type antecedents (nearly three-quarters of them) are the result of parser attachment errors, but many are not.

in the reader's local memory and not in the global memory. This observation supports the THIS-NPs hypothesis (Gundel et al., 1993; Poesio and Modjeska, 2002) that *this*-NPs are used to refer to entities which are *active* albeit not in *focus*, i.e., they are not the center of the previous utterance.

4 Resolution Algorithm

4.1 Candidate Extraction

For correct resolution, the set of extracted candidates must contain the correct antecedent in the first place. The problem of candidate extraction is non-trivial in abstract anaphora resolution because the antecedents are of many different types of syntactic constituents such as clauses, sentences, and nominalizations. Drawing on our observation that the mixed type antecedents are generally a combination of different well-defined syntactic constituents, we extract the set of candidate antecedents as follows. First, we create a set of candidate sentences which contains the sentence containing the *this-issue* anaphor and the two preceding sentences. Then, we parse every candidate sentence with the Stanford Parser[7]. Initially, the set of candidate constituents contains a list of well-defined syntactic constituents. We require that the node type of these constituents be in the set {S, SBAR, NP, SQ, SBARQ, S+V}. This set was empirically derived from our data. To each constituent, there is associated a set of mixed type constituents. These are created by concatenating the original constituent with its sister constituents. For example, in (4), the set of well-defined eligible candidate constituents is $\{\text{NP}, \text{NP}_1\}$ and so NP_1 PP_1 is a mixed type candidate.

(4)

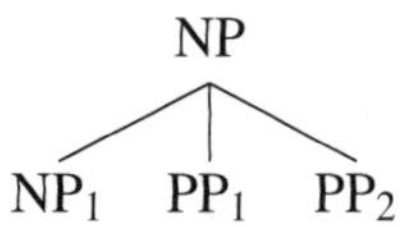

The set of candidate constituents is updated with the extracted mixed type constituents. Extracting mixed type candidate constituents not only deals with mixed type instances as shown in Table 1, but as a side effect it also corrects some attachment errors made by the parser. Finally, the constituents having a number of leaves (words) less than a threshold[8] are discarded to give the final set of candidate constituents.

4.2 Features

We explored the effect of including 43 automatically extracted features (12 feature classes), which are summarized in Table 2. The features can also be broadly divided into two groups: *issue*-specific features and general abstract-anaphora features. *Issue*-specific features are based on our common-sense knowledge of the concept of *issue* and the different semantic forms it can take; e.g., controversy (*X is controversial*), hypothesis (*It has been hypothesized X*), or lack of knowledge (*X is unknown*), where *X* is the issue. In our data, we observed certain syntactic patterns of issues such as *whether X or not* and *that X* and the IP feature class encodes this information. Other *issue*-specific features are IVERB and IHEAD. The feature IVERB checks whether the governing verb of the candidate is an issue verb (e.g., *speculate*, *hypothesize*, *argue*, *debate*), whereas IHEAD checks whether the candidate head in the dependency tree is an issue word (e.g., *controversy*, *uncertain*, *unknown*). The general abstract-anaphora resolution features do not make use of the semantic properties of the word *issue*. Some of these features are derived empirically from the training data (e.g., ST, L, D). The EL feature is borrowed from Müller (2008) and encodes the embedding level of the candidate within the candidate sentence. The MC feature tries to capture the idea of the THIS-NPs hypothesis (Gundel et al., 1993; Poesio and Modjeska, 2002) that the antecedents of *this*-NP anaphors are not the center of the previous utterance. The general abstract-anaphora features in the SR feature class capture the semantic role of the candidate in the candidate sentence. We used the Illinois Semantic Role Labeler[9] for SR features. The general abstract-anaphora features also contain a few lexical features (e.g., M, SC). But these features are independent of the semantic properties of the word *issue*. The general abstract-anaphora resolution features also contain dependency-tree features, lexical-

[7] http://nlp.stanford.edu/software/lex-parser.shtml

[8] The threshold 5 was empirically derived. Antecedents in our training data had on average 17 words.

[9] http://cogcomp.cs.illinois.edu/page/software_view/SRL

ISSUE PATTERN (IP)	
ISWHETHER	1 iff the candidate follows the pattern `SBAR` → `(IN whether) (S ...)`
ISTHAT	1 iff the candidate follows the pattern `SBAR` → `(IN that) (S ...)`
ISIF	1 iff the candidate follows the pattern `SBAR` → `(IN iff) (S ...)`
ISQUESTION	1 iff the candidate node is `SBARQ` or `SQ`
SYNTACTIC TYPE (ST)	
ISNP	1 iff the candidate node is of type NP
ISS	1 iff the candidate node is a sentence node
ISSBAR	1 iff the candidate node is an SBAR node
ISSQ	1 iff the candidate node is an SQ or SBARQ node
MIXED	1 iff the candidate node is of type *mixed*
EMBEDDING LEVEL (EL) (Müller, 2008)	
TLEMBEDDING	level of embedding of the given candidate in its top clause (the root node of the syntactic tree)
ILEMBEDDING	level of embedding of the given candidate in its immediate clause (the closest parent of type S or SBAR)
MAIN CLAUSE (MC)	
MCLAUSE	1 iff the candidate is in the main clause
DISTANCE (D)	
ISSAME	1 iff the candidate is in the same sentence as anaphor
SADJA	1 iff the candidate is in the adjacent sentence
ISREM	1 iff the candidate occurs 2 or more sentences before the anaphor
POSITION	1 iff the antecedent occurs before anaphor
SEMANTIC ROLE LABELLING (SR)	
IVERB	1 iff the governing verb of the given candidate is an *issue* verb
ISA0	1 iff the candidate is the *agent* of the governing verb
ISA1	1 iff the candidate is the *patient* of the governing verb
ISA2	1 iff the candidate is the *instrument* of the governing verb
ISAM	1 iff the candidate plays the role of *modification*
ISNOR	1 iff the candidate plays no well-defined semantic role in the sentence
DEPENDENCY TREE (DT)	
IHEAD	1 iff the candidate head in the dependency tree is an issue word (e.g., *controversial*, *unknown*)
ISSUBJ	1 iff the dependency relation of the candidate to its head is of type *nominal, controlling* or *clausal subject*
ISOBJ	1 iff the dependency relation of the candidate to its head is of type *direct object* or *preposition obj*
ISDEP	1 iff the dependency relation of the candidate to its head is of type *dependent*
ISROOT	1 iff the candidate is the root of the dependency tree
ISPREP	1 iff the dependency relation of the candidate to its head is of type *preposition*
ISCONT	1 iff the dependency relation of the candidate to its head is of type *continuation*
ISCOMP	1 iff the dependency relation of the candidate to its head is of type *clausal* or *adjectival complement*
ISSENT	1 iff candidate's head is the root node
PRESENCE OF MODALS (M)	
MODAL	1 iff the given candidate contains a modal verb
PRESENCE OF SUBORDINATING CONJUNCTION (SC)	
ISCONT	1 iff the candidate starts with a contrastive subordinating conjunction (e.g., *however*, *but*, *yet*)
ISCAUSE	1 iff the candidate starts with a causal subordinating conjunction (e.g., *because*, *as*, *since*)
ISCOND	1 iff the candidate starts with a conditional subordinating conjunction (e.g., *if*, *that*, *whether or not*)
LEXICAL OVERLAP (LO)	
TOS	normalized ratio of the overlapping words in candidate and the title of the article
AOS	normalized ratio of the overlapping words in candidate and the anaphor sentence
DWS	proportion of domain-specific words in the candidate
CONTEXT (C)	
ISPPREP	1 iff the preceding word of the candidate is a preposition
ISFPREP	1 iff the following word of the candidate is a preposition
ISPPUNCT	1 iff the preceding word of the candidate is a punctuation
ISFPUNCT	1 iff the following word of the candidate is a punctuation
LENGTH (L)	
LEN	length of the candidate in words

Table 2: Feature sets for *this-issue* resolution. All features are extracted automatically.

overlap features, and context features.

4.3 Candidate Ranking Model

Given an anaphor a_i and a set of candidate antecedents $C = \{C_1, C_2, ..., C_k\}$, the problem of anaphora resolution is to choose the best candidate antecedent for a_i. We follow the candidate-ranking model proposed by Denis and Baldridge (2008). The advantage of the candidate-ranking model over the mention-pair model is that it overcomes the strong independence assumption made in mention-pair models and evaluates how good a candidate is relative to *all* other candidates.

We train our model as follows. If the anaphor is a *this-issue* anaphor, the set C is extracted using the candidate extraction algorithm from Section 4.1. Then a corresponding set of feature vectors, $C_f = \{C_{f1}, C_{f2}, ..., C_{fk}\}$, is created using the features in Table 2. The training instances are created as described by Soon et al. (2001). Note that the instance creation is simpler than for general coreference resolution because of the absence of anaphoric chains in our data. For every anaphor a_i and eligible candidates $C_f = \{C_{f1}, C_{f2}, ..., C_{fk}\}$, we create training examples $(a_i, C_{fi}, label), \forall C_{fi} \in C_f$. The label is 1 if C_i is the true antecedent of the anaphor a_i, otherwise the label is -1. The examples with label 1 get the rank of 1, while other examples get the rank of 2. We use SVM^{rank} (Joachims, 2002) for training the candidate-ranking model. During testing, the trained model is used to rank the candidates of each test instance of *this-issue* anaphor.

5 Evaluation

In this section we present the evaluation of each component of our resolution system.

5.1 Evaluation of Candidate Extraction

The set of candidate antecedents extracted by the method from Section 4.1 contained the correct antecedent 92% of the time. Each anaphor had, on average, 23.80 candidates, of which only 5.19 candidates were nominal type. The accuracy dropped to 84% when we did not extract mixed type candidates. The error analysis of the 8% of the instances where we failed to extract the correct antecedent revealed that most of these errors were parsing errors which could not be corrected by our candidate extraction method.[10] In these cases, the parts of the antecedent had been placed in completely different branches of the parse tree. For example, in (5), the correct antecedent is a combination of the NP from the $S \rightarrow VP \rightarrow NP \rightarrow PP \rightarrow$ **NP** branch and the PP from $S \rightarrow VP \rightarrow$ **PP** branch. In such a case, concatenating sister constituents does not help.

(5) The data from this pilot study (VP (VBP provide) (NP (NP no evidence) (PP (IN for) (NP **a difference in hemodynamic effects between pulse HVHF and CPFA**))) (PP **in patients with septic shock already receiving CRRT**)). A larger sample size is needed to adequately explore **this issue**.

5.2 Evaluation of *this-issue* Resolution

We propose two metrics for abstract anaphora evaluation. The simplest metric is the percentage of antecedents on which the system and the annotated gold data agree. We denote this metric as *EXACT-M* (Exact Match) and compute it as the ratio of number of correctly identified antecedents to the total number of marked antecedents. This metric is a good indicator of a system's performance; however, it is a rather strict evaluation because, as we noted in section 1, issues generally have no precise boundaries in the text. So we propose another metric called RLL, which is similar to the ROUGE-L metric (Lin, 2004) used for the evaluation of automatic summarization. Let the marked antecedents of the gold corpus for k anaphor instances be $G = \langle g_1, g_2, ..., g_k \rangle$ and the system-annotated antecedents be $A = \langle a_1, a_2, ..., a_k \rangle$. Let the number of words in G and A be m and n respectively. Let $LCS(g_i, a_i)$ be the the number of words in the longest common subsequence of g_i and a_i. Then the precision (P_{RLL}) and recall (R_{RLL}) over the whole data set are computed as shown in equations (2) and (3). P_{RLL} is the total number of word overlaps between the gold and system-annotated antecedents normalized by the number of words in system-annotated antecedents and R_{RLL} is the total number of such word overlaps normalized by the number of words in the gold antecedents. If the system picks too much text for antecedents, R_{RLL} is high but P_{RLL} is low. The F-score,

[10]Extracting candidate constituents from the dependency trees did not add any new candidates to the set of candidates.

		5-fold Cross-Validation				Test			
		P_{RLL}	R_{RLL}	F_{RLL}	EX-M	P_{RLL}	R_{RLL}	F_{RLL}	EX-M
1	Adjacent sentence	66.47	86.16	74.93	22.93	61.73	87.69	72.46	24.00
2	Random	50.71	32.84	39.63	8.40	43.75	35.00	38.89	15.69
3	{IP, D, C, LO, EL, M, MC, L, SC, SR, DT}	79.37	83.66	81.11	59.80	71.89	85.74	78.20	58.82
4	{IP, D, C, LO, M, MC, L, SC, DT}	78.71	83.86	81.14	59.89	70.64	88.09	78.40	54.90
5	{IP, D, C, EL, L, SC, SR, DT}	77.95	83.06	80.33	57.41	72.03	84.85	77.92	**60.78**
6	{IP, D, EL, MC, L, SR, DT}	80.00	84.75	**82.24**	**59.91**	68.88	85.29	76.22	56.86
7	{IP, D, M, L, SR}	73.42	83.16	77.90	52.31	70.74	91.03	**79.61**	50.98
8	{D, C, LO, L, SC, SR, DT}	79.15	85.28	82.04	56.07	67.39	86.32	75.69	52.94
9	*issue*-specific features	74.66	45.70	56.57	41.42	64.20	45.88	53.52	41.38
10	non-*issue* features	76.39	79.39	77.82	51.48	71.19	83.24	76.75	58.82
11	All	78.22	82.92	80.41	56.75	71.28	83.24	76.80	56.86
12	Oracle candidate extractor + row 3	79.63	82.26	80.70	58.32	74.65	87.06	80.38	**64.71**
13	Oracle candidate sentence extractor + row 3	86.67	92.12	**89.25**	**63.72**	79.71	91.49	**85.20**	62.00

Table 3: *this-issue* resolution results with SVM^{rank}. *All* means evaluation using all features. *Issue*-specific features = {IP, IVERB, IHEAD}. EX-M is EXACT-M.

F_{RLL}, combines these two scores.

$$P_{RLL} = \frac{1}{n}\sum_{i=1}^{k} LCS(g_i, a_i) \quad (2)$$

$$R_{RLL} = \frac{1}{m}\sum_{i=1}^{k} LCS(g_i, a_i) \quad (3)$$

$$F_{RLL} = \frac{2 \times P_{RLL} \times R_{RLL}}{P_{RLL} + R_{RLL}} \quad (4)$$

The lower bound of F_{RLL} is 0, where no true antecedent has any common substring with the predicted antecedents and the upper bound is 1, where all the predicted and true antecedents are exactly the same. In our results we represent these scores in terms of percentage.

There are no implemented systems that resolve *issue* anaphora or abstract anaphora signalled by label nouns in arbitrary text to use as a comparison. So we compare our results against two baselines: *adjacent sentence* and *random*. The adjacent sentence baseline chooses the previous sentence as the correct antecedent. This is a high baseline because in our data 84.1% of the antecedents lie within the adjacent sentence. The random baseline chooses a candidate drawn from a uniform random distribution over the set of candidates.[11]

[11] Note that our F_{RLL} scores for both baselines are rather high because candidates often have considerable overlap with one another; hence a wrong choice may still have a high F_{RLL} score.

We carried out two sets of systematic experiments in which we considered all combinations of our twelve feature classes. The first set consists of 5-fold cross-validation experiments on our training data. The second set evaluates how well the model built on the training data works on the unseen test data.

Table 3 gives results of our system. The first two rows are the baseline results. Rows 3 to 8 give results for some of the best performing feature sets. All systems based on our features beat both baselines on F-scores and EXACT-M. The empirically derived feature sets IP (issue patterns) and D (distance) appeared in almost all best feature set combinations. Removing D resulted in a 6 percentage points drop in F_{RLL} and a 4 percentage points drop in EXACT-M scores. Surprisingly, feature set ST (syntactic type) was not included in most of the best performing set of feature sets. The combination of syntactic and semantic feature sets {IP, D, EL, MC, L, SR, DT} gave the best F_{RLL} and EXACT-M scores for the cross-validation experiments. For the test-data experiments, the combination of semantic and lexical features {D, C, LO, L, SC, SR, DT} gave the best F_{RLL} results, whereas syntactic, discourse, and semantic features {IP, D, C, EL, L, SC, SR, DT} gave the best EXACT-M results. Overall, row 3 of the table gives reasonable results for both cross-validation and test-data experiments with no statistically significant difference to the corresponding best

EXACT-M scores in rows 6 and 5 respectively.[12]

To pinpoint the errors made by our system, we carried out three experiments. In the first experiment, we examined the contribution of *issue*-specific features versus non-*issue* features (rows 9 and 10). Interestingly, when we used only non-*issue* features, the performance dropped only slightly. The F_{RLL} results from using only *issue*-specific features were below baseline, suggesting that the more general features associated with abstract anaphora play a crucial role in resolving *this-issue* anaphora.

In the second experiment, we determined the error caused by the candidate extractor component of our system. Row 12 of the table gives the result when an oracle candidate extractor was used to add the correct antecedent in the set of candidates whenever our candidate extractor failed. This did not affect cross-validation results by much because of the rarity of such instances. However, in the test-data experiment, the EXACT-M improvements that resulted were statistically significant. This shows that our resolution algorithm was able to identify antecedents that were arbitrary spans of text.

In the last experiment, we examined the effect of the reduction of the candidate search space. We assumed an oracle candidate sentence extractor (Row 13) which knows the exact candidate sentence in which the antecedent lies. We can see that both RLL and EXACT-M scores markedly improved in this setting. In response to these results, we trained a decision-tree classifier to identify the correct antecedent sentence with simple location and length features and achieved 95% accuracy in identifying the correct candidate sentence.

6 Discussion and Conclusions

We have demonstrated the possibility of resolving complex abstract anaphora, namely, *this-issue* anaphora having arbitrary antecedents. The work takes the annotation work of Botley (2006) and Dipper and Zinsmeister (2011) to the next level by resolving *this-issue* anaphora automatically. We proposed a set of 43 automatically extracted features that can be used for resolving abstract anaphora.

Our results show that general abstract-anaphora resolution features (i.e., other than *issue*-specific features) play a crucial role in resolving *this-issue* anaphora. This is encouraging, as it suggests that the approach could be generalized for other NPs — especially NPs having similar semantic constraints such as *this problem*, *this decision*, and *this conflict*.

The results also show that reduction of search space markedly improves the resolution performance, suggesting that a two-stage process that first identifies the broad region of the antecedent and then pinpoints the exact antecedent might work better than the current single-stage approach. The rationale behind this two-stage process is twofold. First, the search space of abstract anaphora is large and noisy compared to nominal anaphora.[13] And second, it is possible to reduce the search space and accurately identify the broad region of the antecedents using simple features such as the location of the anaphor in the anaphor sentence (e.g., if the anaphor occurs at the beginning of the sentence, the antecedent is most likely present in the previous sentence).

We chose scientific articles over general text because in the former domain the actual referents are seldom discourse deictic (i.e., not present in the text). In the news domain, for instance, which we have also examined and are presently annotating, a large percentage of *this-issue* antecedents lie outside the text. For example, newspaper articles often quote sentences of others who talk about the issues in their own world, as shown in example (6).

(6) As surprising and encouraging to organizers of the movement are the Wall Street names added to their roster. Prominent among them is Paul Singer, a hedge fund manager who is straight and chairman of the conservative Manhattan Institute. He has donated more than $8 million to various same-sex marriage efforts, in states including California, Maine, New Hampshire, New Jersey, New York and Oregon, much of it since 2007.

"It's become something that gradually peo-

[12] We performed a simple one-tailed, k-fold cross-validated paired t-test at significance level $p = 0.05$ to determine whether the difference between the EXACT-M scores of two feature classes is statistically significant.

[13] If we consider all well-defined syntactic constituents of a sentence as issue candidates, in our data, a sentence has on average 43.61 candidates. Combinations of several well-defined syntactic constituents only add to this number. Hence if we consider the antecedent candidates from the previous 2 or 3 sentences, the search space can become quite large and noisy.

ple like myself weren't afraid to fund, weren't afraid to speak out on," Mr. Singer said in an interview. "I'm somebody who is philosophically very conservative, and on **this issue** I thought that this really was important on the basis of liberty and actual family stability."

In such a case, the antecedent of *this issue* is not always in the text of the newspaper article itself, but must be inferred from the context of the quotation and the world of the speaker quoted. That said, we do not use any domain-specific information in our *this-issue* resolution model. Our features are solely based on distance, syntactic structure, and semantic and lexical properties of the candidate antecedents which could be extracted for text in any domain.

Issue anaphora can also be signalled by demonstratives other than *this*. However, for our initial study, we chose *this issue* for two reasons. First, in our corpus as well as in other general corpora such as the New York Times corpus, *issue* occurs much more frequently with *this* than other demonstratives. Second, we did not want to increase the complexity of the problem by including the plural *issues*.

Our approach needs further development to make it useful. Our broad goal is to resolve abstract anaphora signalled by label nouns in all kinds of text. At present, the major obstacle is that there is very little annotated data available that could be used to train an abstract anaphora resolution system. And the understanding of abstract anaphora itself is still at an early stage; it would be premature to think about unsupervised approaches. In this work, we studied the narrow problem of resolution of *this-issue* anaphora in the medical domain to get a good grasp of the general abstract-anaphora resolution problem.

A number of extensions are planned for this work. First, we will extend the work to resolve other abstract anaphors (e.g., *this decision*, *this problem*). Second, we will experiment with a two-stage resolution approach. Third, we would like to explore the effect of including serious discourse structure features in our model. (The feature sets SC and C encode only shallow discourse information.) Finally, during annotation, we noted a number of *issue* patterns (e.g., *An open question is X*, *X is under debate*); a possible extension is extracting issues and problems from text using these patterns as seed patterns.

7 Acknowledgements

We thank Dr. Brian Budgell from the Canadian Memorial Chiropractic College for annotating our data and for helpful discussions. We also thank the anonymous reviewers for their detailed and constructive comments. This research was financially supported by the Natural Sciences and Engineering Research Council of Canada and by the University of Toronto.

References

Nicholas Asher. 1993. *Reference to Abstract Objects in Discourse*. Kluwer Academic Publishers, Dordrecht, Netherlands.

Philip Simon Botley. 2006. Indirect anaphora: Testing the limits of corpus-based linguistics. *International Journal of Corpus Linguistics*, 11(1):73–112.

Donna K. Byron. 2003. Annotation of pronouns and their antecedents: A comparison of two domains. *Technical Report, University of Rochester.*

Donna K. Byron. 2004. *Resolving pronominal reference to abstract entities*. Ph.D. thesis, Rochester, New York: University of Rochester.

José Castaño, Jason Zhang, and James Pustejovsky. 2002. Anaphora resolution in biomedical literature. In *Proceedings of the International Symposium on Reference Resolution for NLP*, Alicante, Spain, June.

Bin Chen, Jian Su, Sinno Jialin Pan, and Chew Lim Tan. 2011. A unified event coreference resolution by integrating multiple resolvers. In *Proceedings of 5th International Joint Conference on Natural Language Processing*, Chiang Mai, Thailand, November.

Pascal Denis and Jason Baldridge. 2008. Specialized models and ranking for coreference resolution. In *Proceedings of the 2008 Conference on Empirical Methods in Natural Language Processing*, pages 660–669, Honolulu, Hawaii, October. Association for Computational Linguistics.

Stefanie Dipper and Heike Zinsmeister. 2011. Annotating abstract anaphora. *Language Resources and Evaluation*, 69:1–16.

Miriam Eckert and Michael Strube. 2000. Dialogue acts, synchronizing units, and anaphora resolution. *Journal of Semantics*, 17:51–89.

Gill Francis. 1994. Labelling discourse: an aspect of nominal group lexical cohesion. In Malcolm Coulthard, editor, *Advances in written text analysis*, pages 83–101, London. Routledge.

Jeanette K. Gundel, Nancy Hedberg, and Ron Zacharski. 1993. Cognitive status and the form of referring expressions in discourse. *Language*, 69(2):274–307, June.

Graeme Hirst. 1981. *Anaphora in Natural Language Understanding: A Survey*, volume 119 of *Lecture Notes in Computer Science*. Springer.

Thorsten Joachims. 2002. Optimizing search engines using clickthrough data. In *ACM SIGKDD Conference on Knowledge Discovery and Data Mining (KDD)*, pages 133–142.

Klaus Krippendorff. 1995. On the reliability of unitizing contiguous data. *Sociological Methodology*, 25:47–76.

Klaus Krippendorff. 2004. *Content Analysis: An Introduction to Its Methodology*. Sage, Thousand Oaks, CA, second edition.

Yu-Hsiang Lin and Tyne Liang. 2004. Pronominal and sortal anaphora resolution for biomedical literature. In *Proceedings of ROCLING XVI: Conference on Computational Linguistics and Speech Processing*, Taiwan, September.

Chin-Yew Lin. 2004. ROUGE: A package for automatic evaluation of summaries. In *Text Summarization Branches Out: Proceedings of the ACL-04 Workshop*, pages 74–81, Barcelona, Spain, July. Association for Computational Linguistics.

Ruslan Mitkov. 2002. *Anaphora Resolution*. Longman.

Natalia N. Modjeska. 2003. *Resolving Other-Anaphora*. Ph.D. thesis, School of Informatics, University of Edinburgh.

Christoph Müller. 2008. *Fully Automatic Resolution of It, This and That in Unrestricted Multi-Party Dialog*. Ph.D. thesis, Universität Tübingen.

Costanza Navarretta. 2011. Antecedent and referent types of abstract pronominal anaphora. In *Proceedings of the Workshop Beyond Semantics: Corpus-based investigations of pragmatic and discourse phenomena*, Göttingen, Germany, February.

Rebecca Passonneau. 1989. Getting at discourse referents. In *Proceedings of the 27th Annual Meeting of the Association for Computational Linguistics*, pages 51–59, Vancouver, British Columbia, Canada, June. Association for Computational Linguistics.

Massimo Poesio and Ron Artstein. 2008. Anaphoric annotation in the ARRAU corpus. In *Proceedings of the Sixth International Conference on Language Resources and Evaluation (LREC'08)*, Marrakech, Morocco, May.

Massimo Poesio and Natalia N. Modjeska. 2002. The THIS-NPs hypothesis: A corpus-based investigation. In *Proceedings of the 4th Discourse Anaphora and Anaphor Resolution Conference (DAARC 2002)*, pages 157–162, Lisbon, Portugal, September.

Massimo Poesio, Simone Ponzetto, and Yannick Versley. 2011. Computational models of anaphora resolution: A survey. Unpublished.

Hans-Jörg Schmid. 2000. *English Abstract Nouns As Conceptual Shells: From Corpus to Cognition*. Topics in English Linguistics. De Gruyter Mouton, Berlin.

Wee Meng Soon, Hwee Tou Ng, and Chung Yong Lim. 2001. A machine learning approach to coreference resolution of noun phrases. *Computational Linguistics*, 27(4):521–544.

Michael Strube and Christoph Müller. 2003. A machine learning approach to pronoun resolution in spoken dialogue. In *Proceedings of the 41st Annual Meeting of the Association for Computational Linguistics*, pages 168–175, Sapporo, Japan, July. Association for Computational Linguistics.

Manabu Torii and K. Vijay-Shanker. 2007. Sortal anaphora resolution in Medline abstracts. *Computational Intelligence*, 23(1):15–27.

Entity based Q&A retrieval

Amit Singh
IBM Research
Bangalore, India
amising3@in.ibm.com

Abstract

Bridging the lexical gap between the user's question and the question-answer pairs in the Q&A archives has been a major challenge for Q&A retrieval. State-of-the-art approaches address this issue by implicitly expanding the queries with additional words using statistical translation models. While useful, the effectiveness of these models is highly dependant on the availability of quality corpus in the absence of which they are troubled by noise issues. Moreover these models perform word based expansion in a context agnostic manner resulting in translation that might be mixed and fairly general. This results in degraded retrieval performance. In this work we address the above issues by extending the lexical word based translation model to incorporate semantic concepts (entities). We explore strategies to learn the translation probabilities between words and the concepts using the Q&A archives and a popular entity catalog. Experiments conducted on a large scale real data show that the proposed techniques are promising.

1 Introduction

Over the past few years community-based question answering (CQA) portals like Naver, Yahoo! Answers, Baidu Zhidao and WikiAnswers have attracted great attention from both academia and industry (Adamic et al., 2008; Singh and Visweswariah, 2011). These portals foster collaborative creation of content by allowing the users to both submit questions to be answered and answer questions asked by other users. These portals aim to provide highly focused access to this information by directly returning pertinent question and answer (Q&A) pairs to the users questions, instead of a long list of ranked URLs. This is in noted contrast to the usual search paradigm, where the question is used to search the database of potential answers, in this case the question is used to search the database of previous questions, which in turn are associated with answers. This involves addressing the word mismatch problem between the users question and the question-answer pairs in the archive. This is the major challenge for Q&A retrieval.

Researchers have proposed the use of translation models (Berger and Lafferty, 1999; Jeon et al., 2005; Xue et al., 2008) to solve this problem. As a principled approach to capturing semantic word relations, statistical translation language models are built by using the IBM model 1 (Brown et al., 1993) and have been shown to outperform traditional document language models on Q&A retrieval task. The basic idea is to estimate the likelihood of translating a document[1] to a query by exploiting the dependencies that exists between query words and document words. For example the document containing the word `Wheezing` may well answer the question containing the term `Asthma`. They learn the these dependencies (encoded as translation probabilities) between words using parallel mono-lingual corpora created from the Q&A pairs. While useful, the effectiveness of these models is highly dependant on the availability of quality corpus (Lee et al.,

[1] we will use (Q&A, document), (word, term) and (user query, question) interchangeably

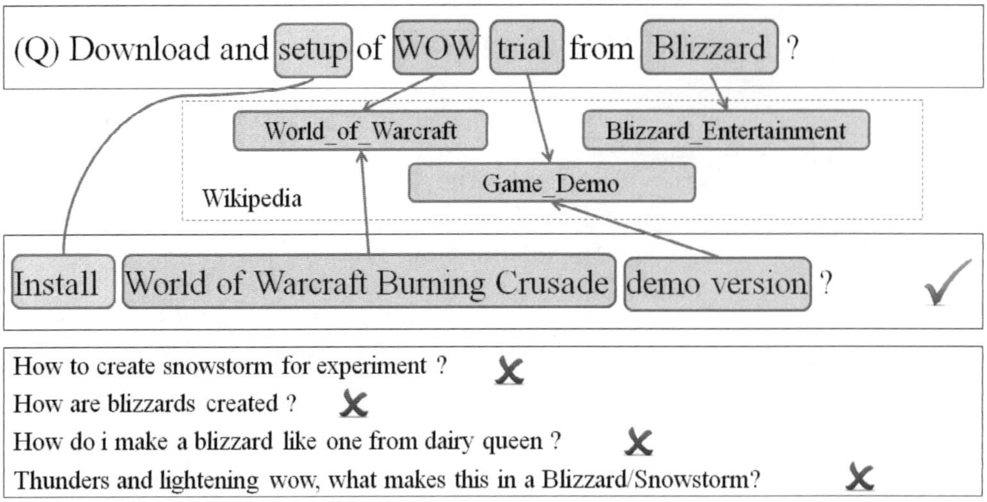

Figure 1: Need for entity based expansions

2008). Also these models only capture shallow semantics between words via the co-occurrence statistics, while some of the more explicit relationships between words and entities is freely available externally. Being context agnostic (Zhou et al., 2007) is another very common criticism hailed on translation models as it results in noisy and generic translations.

Example shown in Figure 1 captures these problems. Specifically, the word `Blizzard` can refer to an American game development company that develops World of Warcraft game or it could refer to a severe snowstorm. Expanding query without taking the gaming context established by the word `WOW` (acronym for World of Warcraft) into account would lead to topic drift. Also it would be difficult to learn relationships between `World of Warcraft Burning Crusade` and `Blizzard` from the Q&A corpus alone due to the sparsity of co-occurance counts as these can be expressed in several lexical forms, some of which are multi word phrases.

In this paper we argue that solution to all the above problems lies in a unified model in which entities are a primary citizen. The guiding hypothesis being, an entity based representation provides a less ambiguous representation of the users question and provides for a more semantically accurate expansion if the relationship between entities and words can be estimated more reliably. Our main contributions are

1. We propose Entity based Translation Language Model (ETLM) for Q&A retrieval that accommodates semantic information associated between entities and words. Being closely related to the general source-channel framework (Berger and Lafferty, 1999), the model enjoys its benefits, while mitigating some of its shortcomings. Specifically it provides for context aware expansions of the query by exploiting entity annotations on both, the document and the query side. Entity annotations also provide a means to handle the "many-to-one" (Moore, 2004) translation limitation in the IBM model, due to which each word in the target document can be generated by at most one word in the question[2]. For the same reasons, it also alleviates another related limitation by enabling translation between contiguous words across the query and documents (Moore, 2004).

2. We learn relationships between entities and terms by proposing new ways of organizing monolingual parallel corpus and simultaneously leveraging external resources like Wikipedia from which one can derive these relationships reliably. This helps alleviate the noise problem associated with learning translation models on Q&A archive described above. An important point to note is that, our technique has merits independent to the choice of the entity catalog. In this work we use

[2]entity mentions can be of more than unit word length

D	original Q&A collection
E	set of all entities in catalog
$d(e)$	description of entity e
C	D annotated with $e \in E$
q_{user}	users question
q	q_{user} annotated with $e \in E$
t	token span
t_q, t_d	token span in q and d
V	word vocabulary

Table 1: Notation.

Wikipedia, as it is a popular choice due to its large and ever expanding coverage and its ability to keep up with world events on a timely basis.

3. We provide detailed evaluation of impact of modelling assumptions and model components on retrieval performance on a large scale real data from Yahoo Answers comprising ~5 million Q&A pairs.

Rest of the paper is organized as follows: In the next section, we define ETLM and outline its details. This is followed by Section 3 which gives the details of entity annotators and its performance. Section 4 describes our experiments on the retrieval method used Q&A retrieval. In Section 5 we compare and contrast related literature. Finally, we conclude in Section 6.

2 Our Approach

Problem Definition: Let $D = d_1, d_2, ..., d_n$ denote the Q&A collection. Here d_i refers to the i-th Q&A data consisting of a question q_i and its answer a_i. Given the user question q_{user}, the task of Q&A retrieval is to rank d_i according to $score(q_{user}, d_i)$. Figure 2 outlines the approach to compute this score in the ETLM framework.

Offline processing: Using the entity catalog E, we learn the entity annotation models EA$_{offline}$ and EA$_{online}$ for annotation of entities in the Q&A corpus and the query respectively. Refer Section 3 for details. For each $d_i \in D$, we then annotate references to entities in Wikipedia using EA$_{offline}$ resulting in annotated Q&A corpus C. We then compute relationships between entities and words using C and E. These relationships are used to learn our ETLM model.

Online processing: At runtime, annotate the user query q_{user} with entities using EA$_{online}$to create an enriched question q. Issue this query over the annotated corpus C and rank the candidates as per the ETLM model described below.

2.1 ETLM Model

Let the annotated query q (and similarly annotated Q&A pair d) be composed of sequence of token spans T_q (and T_d). Each token span t_q (similarly t_d) corresponds to sequence of contiguous words occurring in the running text. These t_q's can correspond to entity mentions, phrases or words. Let e_q denote the tokens spans that are annotated and ne_q that are not ($T_q = e_q \cup ne_q$). For example, in the query , $\underbrace{\texttt{What}}_{ne_q}\underbrace{\texttt{is}}_{ne_q}\underbrace{\texttt{a}}_{ne_q}\underbrace{\texttt{Quadratic Formula}}_{e_q}$?, token span `Quadratic Formula` is linked to an entity corresponding to Quadratic Equation[3], while all other token spans are marked as ne_q .

For the sake of simplicity, in this work we do not identify phrases i.e. ne_q is always of unit word length[4]. In the ETLM framework, the similarity between a query q and a document d within a collection C is given by the probability

$$\begin{aligned} score(q,d) \quad \sim \quad P(q|d) &= \prod_{\substack{t_q \in q \\ t_q = e_q \cup ne_q}} P(t_q|d) \\ P(t_q|d) &= (1-\lambda)P_{ml}(t_q|d) + \lambda P_{ml}(t_q|C) \\ P_{ml}(t_q|d) &= \sum_{t_d \in d} T(t_q|t_d)P_{ml}(t_d|d) \end{aligned} \quad (1)$$

Intuitively this indicates a generative process for creating q from d. Ideally both q and d are "only" composed of e i.e. $\forall t_q \in q;\ t_q \in E_U$, where E_U is the universal set of entities [5] (similarly for all t_d). This is because when the document was created, each and every $t_d \in d$ had a sense attached to it. however in reality, for various reasons, set of target entities are clearly a subset of E_U (for e.g. E: set of all entities

[3]http://en.wikipedia.org/wiki/Quadratic_equation

[4]its not a restriction as the model is valid for ne_q consisting of more than one word.

[5]language for creating q and d

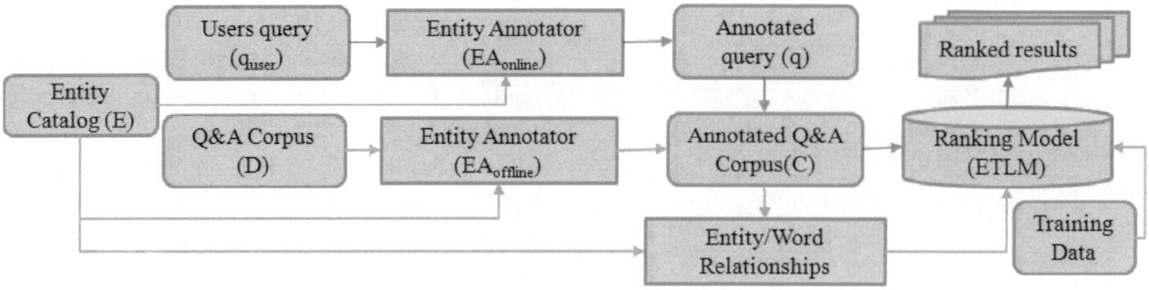

Figure 2: ETLM Architecture (gray and brown arrows indicate offline and online processes respectively

in the catalog) also not all of them may be recognized by the annotation system.

$T(t_q|t_d)$ in Equation 1 denotes the probability that a token span t_q is the translation of token span t_d. This induces the desired query expansion effect. The key task is to estimate $P_{ml}(t_q|C)$, $T(t_q|t_d)$ and $P_{ml}(t_d|d)$; $t_q \in e_q \cup ne_q$ and $t_d \in e_d \cup ne_d$

2.2 Estimating Model Parameters

We adopt 2 different approach for estimating $T(t_q|t_d)$, leading to 2 different configurations of ETLM system . As the name suggests, ETLM$_{qa}$ is estimated from Q&A data (C and D) while we leverage the entity catalog (in our case it is Wikipedia) for ETLM$_{wiki}$.

2.3 ETLM$_{qa}$: Estimate from parallel corpus

Following (Xue et al., 2008) we pool the question and answers from D to create a master parallel corpus $P = (q_1, a_1), .., (q_n, a_n) \cup (a_1, q_1), ., (a_n, q_n)$. This is used for learning $T(ne|ne')$[6]. Similarly we create P^* from C. We then derive 2 different parallel corpora from P and P^* as follows

P_{entity} We remove all non linked tokens ne from P^* thereby reducing it to parallel corpus over e. This is used for learning $T(e|e')$ i.e. translation probabilities between two entities e and e' in E.

P_{hybrid} This is hybrid of P_{entity} and P where in one part of Q&A pair consists on only ne while other consists of only e. This is used for learning $T(ne|e)$ and $T(e|ne)$.

To handle entities e, we introduce special id's in the ne space. Thus our universal token span set is given by $V \cup E$. This is done so that $T(t_q|t_d)$ is learnt from P, P_{entity} and P_{hybrid}, w/o any modification to the corresponding translation algorithm (Brown et al., 1993). Lets call this approach ETLM$_{qa'}$.

We explored another intuitive approach ETLM$_{qa}$, to learn $T(e|e')$, $T(e|ne)$, $T(ne|e)$ and $T(ne|ne')$ directly by using only P^* as our parallel corpus. We do so by redistributing the probability mass i.e. when calculating $T(e|e')$, we redistribute probability mass spread over all the ne to e given by Equation 2 and 3. Similar process is followed for $T(e|ne)$, $T(ne|e)$ and $T(ne|nc')$.

$$S(e|e') = \frac{T(e|e')}{\sum_{t \in V} T(t|e')} \quad (2)$$

$$T(e|e') = \frac{S(e|e')}{\sum_{t \in E} T(t|e')} \quad (3)$$

Remaining model components are calculated using Equation 4 and 5. Here d refers to question part of the Q&A pair.

$$P_{ml}(t_q|C) = \frac{tf_{t_q,C} + 1}{\sum_{t' \in C} tf_{t',C} + |C|} \quad (4)$$

$$P_{ml}(t_q|d) = \frac{tf_{t_q,d}}{\sum_{t' \in d} tf_{t',d}} \quad (5)$$

2.4 ETLM$_{wiki}$: Estimating from Wikipedia

Number of symmetric measures have been proposed (Medelyan et al., 2009) to measure semantic relationships between entities and words using Wikipedia. For our problem we need an asymmetric measure. We use co-citation information in Wikipedia to detect relatedness between entities ($T(e|e')$) and co-occurrence counts to estimate

[6]subscript of q and d has been dropped as translation probability learnt agnostic to it, due to pooling.

$T(ne|ne')$ as follows: .

$$T(e|e') = \frac{co(e,e')}{\sum_{e''} co(e'',e')} \quad (6)$$

$$T(ne|ne') = \frac{cf(ne,ne')}{\sum_{ne''} cf(ne'',ne')} \quad (7)$$

$$T(ne|e) = \frac{tf_{ne,D(e)}+1}{|D(e)|+|V|} \quad (8)$$

$$T(e|ne) = \frac{tf_{ne,D(e)}+1}{\sum_{e'\in E} tf_{ne,D(e')}+|E|} \quad (9)$$

Here $d(e)$ represents the page corresponding to entity e. $D(e)$ represents concatenation of $d(e)$ and all context of size 5 surrounding anchor text in Wikipedia that link to e. $cf(ne, ne')$ is the number context windows of fixed size containing both ne and ne' in Wikipedia. In our case, we set the window size at 10 (because this size turned out to be reasonable in our pilot experiments). $tf_{t,d(e)}$ is the frequency of t in $d(e)$; $co(e, e')$ indicates number of entities in Wikipedia that have a hyperlink to both e and e'. As links from pages with a small number of outgoing links are generally considered to be more valuable than links from pages with a high outgoing link degree, we tried with weighted version of 6 where the co-citations are weighted by the outdegree of Wikipedia page corresponding to entity s that link to e and e'. Lets denote the weighted version by ETLM$_{wiki}$ and unweighted version by ETLM$_{wiki'}$. $P_{ml}(t_q|C)$ and $P_{ml}(t_q|d)$ are estimated as per Equation 4 and 5 respectively.

2.5 Self translation probability

To make sure self translation probability is not underestimated i.e. $T(t|t) \geq T(t'|t)$ always holds true, we introduce new parameter γ as $T(t|t') = \gamma + (1-\gamma)T(t|t')$; $\gamma = 0$ when $t \neq t'$ and $\gamma > 0.5$ otherwise.

2.6 ETLM$_{combo}$: Combining ETLM$_{qa}$ and ETLM$_{wiki}$

Often, combining language models yields better results than any of the individual language models themselves. Linear interpolation is often the technique of choice in language modelling for combining models to exploit complementary features of the component models. It involves taking a weighted sum of the probabilities given by the component language models. An advantage of the linear interpolation is that it is simple and fast to calculate. If the inputs are probability estimates, also the output is a probability estimate. The mixture translation model $T_{combo}(e|e')$ over M component models is given by Equation 10.

$$T_{combo}(t|t') = \sum_{j=1}^{M} \alpha_j T_j(t|t') \qquad t \in E \cup V; \quad \sum_{j=1}^{M} \alpha_j = 1; \quad \alpha_j \geq 0 \quad (10)$$

One can immediately notice that $T_{combo}(t|t')$ has one global weight for each of the M component models which might not be ideal. With access to large training data one could employ more powerful context dependent interpolation techniques (Liu et al., 2008). In our case we have 2 components T$_{qa}$ and T$_{wiki}$ and four classes for each ; $\alpha_{wiki}^{(e,e')}$[7], $\alpha_{wiki}^{(e,ne)}$, $\alpha_{wiki}^{(ne,ne')}$ and $\alpha_{wiki}^{(ne,e)}$), one corresponding to each class of $T(t|t')$. respectively.

3 Entity Annotation

In this section we describe our entity annotation system. Recently there has been lot of work addressing the problem of annotating text with links to Wikipedia entities (Mihalcea and Csomai, 2007; Bunescu and Pasca, 2006; Milne and Witten, 2008; Kulkarni et al., 2009; Ratinov et al., 2011; Ferragina and Scaiella, 2010). We adopt a similar approach, wherein we first find the best disambiguation (BESTDISAMBIGUATION) for a given mention and then decide to prune it (PRUNE), via the dummy mapping NA (similar to "no assignment" (Kulkarni et al., 2009)).

3.1 BESTDISAMBIGUATION

As defined earlier, $e \in E$ represent an entity corresponding to URN of a Wikipedia article. Let $E_m = \{e_{m,1}, e_{m,2}, \cdots, e_{m,|E_m|}\}$ $e_{m,i} \in E$ represent the set of possible disambiguations for a mention m (m is an index over all mentions in the corpus). Given a mention m, task is to find best disambiguation e from Wikipedia. Without loss of gener-

[7] $\alpha_{qa}^{(e,e')} = 1 - \alpha_{wiki}^{(e,e')}$

ality, we consider $e_{m,*} \in E_m$ as the correct answer. Let $\phi(m, e_{m,j})$ represent the mapping onto features between an entity mention m and the Wikipedia entity $e_{m,j}$ and $\overrightarrow{\omega}$ be the corresponding weight vector and $D(e_{m,j}) = \overrightarrow{\omega}\phi(m, e_{m,j})$ represent the disambiguation score. The task is to learn $\overrightarrow{\omega}$ such that $\underset{e_{m,j}}{\text{argmax}}\ D(e_{m,j})$ gives the best disambiguation for the mention m.

We pose this as a ranking problem and solve it using max-margin technique (Joachims, 2002; Joachims, 2006) as follows

$$\begin{aligned} &\underset{\overrightarrow{\omega},\xi}{\text{minimize}} \quad \frac{1}{2}\overrightarrow{\omega}\cdot\overrightarrow{\omega} + C\sum \xi_{i,j} \\ &\text{subject to} \\ &\forall m, \forall e_{m,j} \in E_m - e_{m,*} : \\ &\overrightarrow{\omega}\phi(m, e_{m,*}) > \overrightarrow{\omega}\phi(m, e_{m,j}) + \xi_{i,j} \\ &\qquad \forall i, \forall j : \xi_{i,j} \geq 0 \end{aligned} \tag{11}$$

where $\sum \xi_{i,j}$ is the total training error that upper bounds the number of pair preferences violations. This is controlled by adjusting the parameter C. Note that Equation 11 means pairwise comparison between the correct disambiguation $e_{m,*}$ and other disambiguation candidates $e_{m,j}$ such that $j \neq$ index corresponding to $*$.

3.2 PRUNE

The disambiguation phase produces one candidate disambiguation per mention. To discard any unmeaningful annotations a simple strategy similar to LOCAL (Kulkarni et al., 2009) is followed where the $D(e_{m,*})$ is compared against a predefined threshold ρ_{na}, so that if $D(e_{m,*}) < \rho_{na}$ then that annotation for menton m is discarded by linking m to NA. The parameter ρ_{na} allows the algorithm to back-off when short of evidence.

3.3 FEATUREMAP $\phi(m, e_{m,j})$

Sense probability prior (SP): It represents the prior probability that a mention name s points to a specific entity in Wikipedia. For example, without any other information, mention name "tree" will more likely refer to the entity woody plant[8], rather than the less popular notion related to graphs [9].

Entity Probability prior (EP): It captures the popularity knowledge as a distribution of entities, i.e., the $EP(e_i)$ should be larger than $EP(e_j)$ if e_i is more popular than e_j. This score is independent of the mention name.

Context specific features: It captures the textual similarity between weighted word vectors corresponding to the context of the mention (window around the mention) and textual description associated with the entity (Wikipedia page).

Let EA_{online} and $\text{EA}_{offline}$ represent configurations for annotating user question and corpus respectively. For EA_{online}, user question represents the document from which context specific features are computed. For $\text{EA}_{offline}$, question and the answer(best) is concatenated to represents the document. Based on the "one sense per discourse" assumption, one additional heuristic is used in $\text{EA}_{offline}$ where, for the same Q&A pair, if same name mention is repeated multiple times across the question and the answer then one with the maximum $D(c_{m,*}) > \rho_{na}$ is annotated for all instances.

3.4 Annotation Experiments

We used 2010 version of Wikipedia as our knowledge base. It contains more than 2.5 million entities. Annotations were done by volunteers fluent in english. Volunteers were told to be as exhaustive as possible and tag all possible name mentions, even if to mark them as "NA". Inter-annotator agreement=92.1%; Kappa coefficient = 0.72. As our corpus, we collected 8.3K manual annotations spanning 1315 Q&A pairs. 2.8K of the annotations were assigned to NA. 2.1K annotations (out of 8.3K) were made in the question of which 551 were assigned to NA. We use Precision, Recall and F_1 score micro-averaged across documents as the evaluation measures. We do a linear scan of data to identify entity mentions by first tokenizing and then identifying token sequences that maximally match an entity ID in the entity name dictionary (constructed using Wikipedia anchor text, redirect pages). Figure 3 outlines the performance of $\text{EA}_{offline}$ and EA_{online}. We measured $\text{EA}_{offline}$ in 3 test data configurations; (1) $\text{EA}_{offline}$: measured over entire

[8]en.wikipedia.org/wiki/Tree

[9]en.wikipedia.org/wiki/Tree_(data_structure)

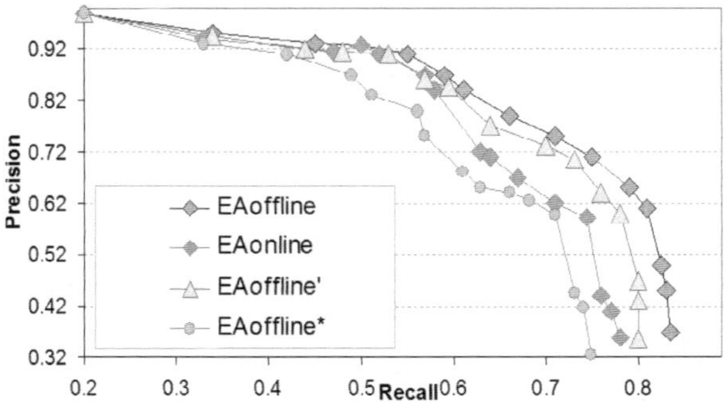

Figure 3: Precision v/s Recall

annotation set; 2) EA$_{offline'}$ is measured only on annotations made in question. this is done to compare it with EA$_{online}$; 3) EA$_{offline^*}$ is similar to (2), only difference is that for (2) entire Q&A pair is the context, while here only question part is the context. This is done to check if separate annotators are required for online and online phase. As seen in Figure 3, this indeed is necessary as EA$_{offline^*}$ performs worse than EA$_{online}$. Closer look at the feature weights revealed that in EA$_{offline}$ context specific features have much more weightage when compared to its weight in EA$_{online}$, on the contrary EA$_{online}$ weighs SP significantly higher.

4 Evaluation

We now describe the empirical evaluation where we compare our techniques against the baseline techniques. We use several standard measures (R-Precision, MAP, MRR, Precision@k) in evaluation. We first describe the dataset used followed by describing an exhaustive set of results across techniques and performance measures.

4.1 Dataset

We crawled a dataset of ~5 million questions and answers from Yahoo! Answers spanning all the leaf level categories. Tokenization and stop word removal were the only preprocessing steps performed. We have used a stoplist[10] having a vocabulary of 429 common words to remove the stopwords.

In our retrieval experiments we used 339 queries (average length 5.6 words). We employed pooling technique used in the TREC conference series. We pooled the top 25 Q&A pairs from retrieval results generated by varying the retrieval algorithms and the search field. Relevance judgments were marked by human annotators without disclosing the identity of method used for retrieval. The annotators were asked to label candidate as "relevant" or "irrelevant" based on semantic similarity with the query. Answer quality/correctness was not a criteria. In case of disagreement between two volunteers, authors made the final judgment. Inter-annotator agreement was 87.9% and Kappa coefficient = 0.68. Over all we had collected more than 12K relevance judgements corresponding to these queries, of which >2.3K were marked as relevant.

[10]http://truereader.com/manuals/onix/stopwords1.html

4.2 Baselines

To evaluate the effectiveness of our models we compared them against the following baselines

Traditional models: VSM (Zobel and Moffat, 2006) and OKAPI BM25 (Robertson et al., 1996) (k1, b, and k3 are parameters that are set to 1.2, 0.75 and ∞ respectively).
Translation based language models: TLM (Jeon et al., 2005), TransLM (using answers) (Xue et al., 2008) and CTM (Lee et al., 2008).

For our experiments we used a set of 50 queries to select the model parameters. Translation based language model use 2 parameters; smoothing parameter λ in the Language Model and β to control the self-translation impact in the TransLM. Final values of parameters used in our experiments were $\lambda = 0.2$ (Zhai and Lafferty, 2004) and $\beta = 0.75$ (Xue et al., 2008). For CTM, we used *tf-idf* based weighing scheme (Lee et al., 2008) to remove words from the (Q||A) corpus P. Word elimination threshold of 20% was selected based on the above 50 queries. Final values of ETLM parameters used in our experiments were $\lambda = 0.18$ and $\gamma = 0.65$.

4.3 Result Analysis

Table 2 presents the performance of the various techniques. Under each measure, we highlight the best performing technique. Performance of all the translation based models is better than VSM and OKAPI thereby confirming the importance of addressing the lexical gap. Using high confidence annotations for

	MAP	%chg	MRR	%chg	R-Prec	%chg	Prec@5	%chg	Prec@10	%chg
VSM	0.221		0.421		0.21		0.202		0.15	
OKAPI	0.298		0.532		0.271		0.264		0.214	
TLM	0.337		0.583		0.318		0.297		0.239	
TransLM	0.352		0.612		0.347		0.332		0.261	
CTM	0.361		0.641		0.351		0.341		0.279	
ETLM_{qa}	$0.390^{\dagger}$	8.03	$0.699^{\dagger}$	9.05	$0.379^{\dagger}$	7.98	$0.367^{\dagger}$	7.62	$0.302^{\dagger}$	8.24
ETLM_{wiki}	$0.413^{\dagger}$	14.40	$0.719^{\dagger}$	12.17	$0.399^{\dagger}$	13.68	$0.391^{\dagger}$	14.66	$0.323^{\dagger}$	15.77
ETLM_{combo}	**0.427**†	18.28	**0.726**†	13.26	**0.413**†	17.66	**0.407**†	19.35	**0.331**†	18.64

Table 2: Comparisons of retrieval models. † indicate a statistically significant improvement over the CTM using paired t-test with p-value < 0.05. %chg indicates change over CTM as it is the most competitive baseline

query expansion in ETLM, leads to an improved performance as compared to the all the baseline methods that do not consider this signal. This is validated by the fact that ETLM_{qa} and ETLM_{wiki} can achieve statistically significant improvements in terms of all the measures. The reason for this improvement is the context sensitive computation of $T(t|t')$ leading to reduced spurious expansions and improved top expansions, this is made possible because of entity disambiguation. This computation in baselines happens on word by word basis without exploiting contextual information. ETLM_{qa} performs worse than ETLM_{wiki}. On close inspection of failure cases and translation probability tables we found that $T(e|e')$ for ETLM_{qa} was much worse than ETLM_{wiki}. This is because for getting good estimates of $T(e|e')$, we need enough instances where both e and e' need to be correctly annotated in the same Q&A pair. Failure in this leads to sparse counts thereby reducing the gap in $T(e|e')$ scores for related and unrelated e. Figure 4 shows the impact of choices made for learning the translation probabilities $T(t|t')$. We found that ETLM_{wiki} performs slightly better than $\text{ETLM}_{wiki'}$, indicating the utility of weighted co-citation measure for computing $T(e|e')$. We believe that embedding other measures that are better in capturing relationships from Wikipedia, should improve the performance. Similarly ETLM_{qa} also performs better than $\text{ETLM}_{qa'}$. This is because for creating P_{entity} all ne are removed. This leads to count sparsity problem discussed above, but slightly worse. Due to absence of ne, in $\text{ETLM}_{qa'}$ e' in d are thought be being generated "only" from e in q. On the contrary in ETLM_{qa}, e' had an option of mapping to ne in q. An interesting observation is that while the performances of different configurations vary, all of them perform better than CTM which is the best baseline.

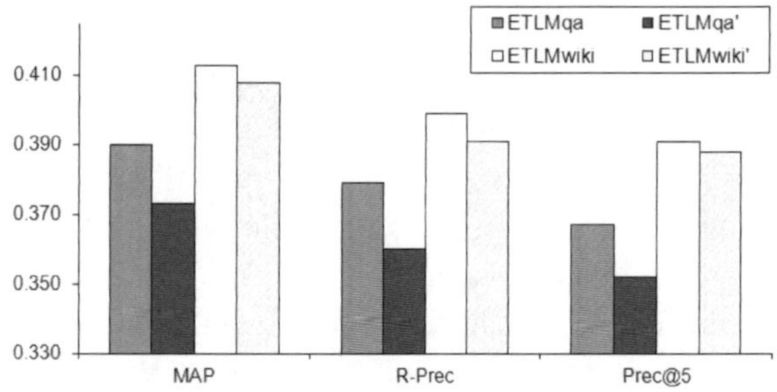

Figure 4: Performance of ETLM configurations

4.4 Impact of Annotations on retrieval

Since entities are central in our model, impact of entity annotation on q_{user} is one of the most important aspect to be studied. Figure 5 shows the plot of retrieval measures obtained by varying ρ_{na} in EA_{online}. CTM is shown by horizontal lines. As explained in Section 3, value of ρ_{na} is inversely proportional to aggressiveness of annotation. Which implies for high values, EA_{online} will annotate only those mentions in query that its highly confident about. Beyond a value no annotations are made.

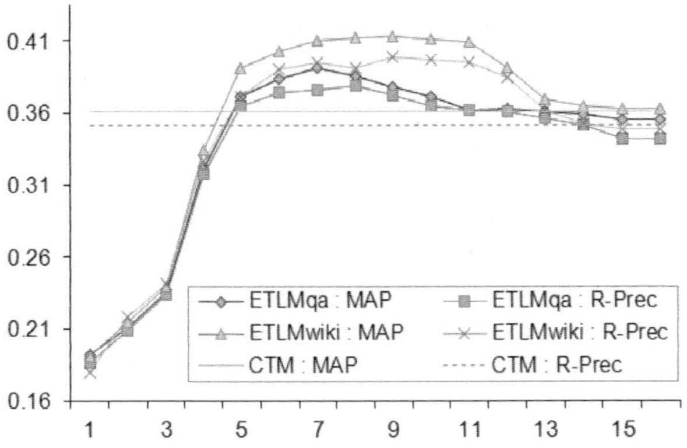

Figure 5: Impact of query annotation on retrieval. x-axis represents value of ρ_{na} used to control annotation

This is represented on the extreme right in Figure 5. One important observation is that, even with no annotations made in query, performance of ETLM_{qa} and ETLM_{wiki} is competitive to CTM. This is evidence for addressing the noise related issue for which CTM is designed. For large range of values, all ETLM configurations are above CTM. As we decrease ρ_{na} performance increases smoothly and then after a certain point ($\rho_{na} = 5$) is starts decreasing.

4.5 ETLM$_{combo}$

We believe that $T(t|t')$ learnt from one source would encode word association characteristics which might not be exactly the same across sources.ETLM_{combo} tries to address this by combining the two models. Values for mixing parameters are : $\alpha_{wiki}^{(e,e')} = 0.95$[11], $\alpha_{wiki}^{(e,ne)} = 0.75$, $\alpha_{wiki}^{(ne,ne')} = 0.7$ and $\alpha_{wiki}^{(ne,e)} = 0.75$). The interpolation weights were obtained by optimizing the retrieval performance by doing a using grid search over the parameter space. Same 50 queries were used for tuning. As seen entity relationships obtained from Wikipedia are far superior to one from Q&A corpus. As seen in Table 2 combining the two models improves the performance.

5 Related Work

Recently Q&A retrieval has been garnering lot of attention. Translation model (TLM) (Jeon et al., 2005) has been extensively employed in question search and has been shown to outperform the traditional IR methods significantly (VSM, BM25, LM). Existing work can be broadly grouped under the following topics:

(a) *Improved training of translation models by exploiting answer content/inter-word co-occurrence relations and restriction to reliable parallel corpora:* Translation-based language model (TRLM) (Xue et al., 2008) improved stability of TLM by providing better probability estimates and also exploited answers for question retrieval. It further improved the retrieval results and obtained the state-of-the-art performance. Another line of work on translation models focused on providing suitable parallel data to learn the translation probabilities. Compact translation models (CTM) (Lee et al., 2008) tried to further improve the translation probabilities based on question-answer pairs by selecting the most important terms to build compact translation models. We show that such special-purpose models to control noisy translations may not be necessary because models learnt using entity annotations are robust to noise in Q&A data.

Instead of using noisy Q&A data, new approach (Bernhard and Gurevych, 2009) to build parallel corpus from reliable sources has showed improvements. They proposed to use as a parallel training data comprising of set the definitions and glosses provided for the same term by different lexical semantic resources. We move beyond terms and capture relationships between entities and terms using the page contents and link structure in Wikipedia.

Apart from translation models there are other approaches (Gao et al., 2004) that try to extend the existing language models for adhoc retrieval by incorporating term relationships or dependencies. Some expand queries using word relationships derived from co-occurrence thesaurus (Bai et al., 2005; Qiu and Frei, 1993), hand-crafted thesaurus (Liu et al., 2004; Voorhees, 1994) and combination of both (Cao et al., 2005).

(b) *Incorporation of query context information in translation models using latent factor modeling and smoothing approaches:* All these existing approaches mentioned above are considered to be context independent, in that they do not take into account any contextual information in modeling word word relationships. Topic signature model (Zhou et al., 2007) exploited contextual information

[11] $\alpha_{qa}^{(e,e')} = (1 - 0.95)$

by decomposing a document into a set of weighted topic signatures and use it for model smoothing. This model turns out to be inefficient when confronted with ambiguous words and phrases because it is unable to disambiguate the sense of topic signatures. Others (Liu and Croft, 2004) perform semantic smoothing by means of clustering. Recently (Tu et al., 2010; Cai et al., 2011; Zhou et al., 2011) showed improved performance by performing sense based smoothing for document retrieval, latent topic mining and phase based retrieval respectively. Contrary to these approaches we used entity disambiguation to capture contextual information for improving Q&A retrieval.

(c) *Complementary ideas for improving retrieval performance that can be used alongside translation models:* Other work on question retrieval include the use of category information available (Cao et al., 2010), learning-to-rank techniques (Bian et al., 2008; Surdeanu et al., 2008; Bunescu and Huang, 2010), proposed a syntactic tree matching ((Wang et al., 2009) or question structure for important phrase matching (Duan et al., 2008)). These methods seem orthogonal to ours, in some cases complementary and can be leveraged to get an even better performance

There also exists work where exploiting entity based representation has been found helpful in information retrieval (Singh et al., 2009; Egozi et al., 2011; Meij et al., 2008; Grootjen and van der Weide, 2006). In our work we use entity annotations in Q&A retrieval context. There is also some work on using Wikipedia in general web search (Xu et al., 2009).

6 Conclusion

In this work we extend word based model to incorporate semantic concepts for addressing the lexical gap issue in retrieval models for large online Q&A collections. Compared to the existing translation based model, our model is more robust and effective in that it can perform context aware expansions. We proposed ways to embed rich information freely available in Wikipedia into our models and combine it one learnt from Q&A corpus. Experiments performed on a large real Q&A data demonstrate that all configurations of ETLM significantly outperforms existing models for Q&A retrieval.

Acknowledgments

Thanks to Srujana Merugu for helpful discussions. Thanks to the anonymous reviewers for helping us improve the presentation.

References

Lada A. Adamic, Jun Zhang, Eytan Bakshy, and Mark S. Ackerman. 2008. Knowledge sharing and yahoo answers: everyone knows something. In *Proceedings of the 17th international conference on World Wide Web*, WWW '08, pages 665–674, New York, NY, USA. ACM.

Jing Bai, Dawei Song, Peter Bruza, Jian-Yun Nie, and Guihong Cao. 2005. Query expansion using term relationships in language models for information retrieval. In *Proceedings of the 14th ACM international conference on Information and knowledge management*, CIKM '05, pages 688–695, New York, NY, USA. ACM.

Adam Berger and John Lafferty. 1999. Information retrieval as statistical translation. In *Proceedings of the 22nd annual international ACM SIGIR conference on Research and development in information retrieval*, SIGIR '99, pages 222–229, New York, NY, USA. ACM.

Delphine Bernhard and Iryna Gurevych. 2009. Combining lexical semantic resources with question & answer archives for translation-based answer finding. In *ACL-IJCNLP '09: Proceedings of the Joint Conference of the 47th Annual Meeting of the ACL and the 4th International Joint Conference on Natural Language Processing of the AFNLP: Volume 2*, pages 728–736, Morristown, NJ, USA. Association for Computational Linguistics.

Jiang Bian, Yandong Liu, Eugene Agichtein, and Hongyuan Zha. 2008. Finding the right facts in the crowd: factoid question answering over social media. In *WWW '08: Proceeding of the 17th international conference on World Wide Web*, pages 467–476, New York, NY, USA. ACM.

Peter F. Brown, Vincent J. Della Pietra, Stephen A. Della Pietra, and Robert L. Mercer. 1993. The mathematics of statistical machine translation: parameter estimation. *Comput. Linguist.*, 19:263–311, June.

Razvan Bunescu and Yunfeng Huang. 2010. Learning the relative usefulness of questions in community qa. In *Proceedings of the 2010 Conference on Empirical Methods in Natural Language Processing*, EMNLP

'10, pages 97–107, Stroudsburg, PA, USA. Association for Computational Linguistics.

R. Bunescu and M. Pasca. 2006. Using encyclopedic knowledge for named entity disambiguation. In *Proceedings of EACL*, volume 6, pages 9–16.

Li Cai, Guangyou Zhou, Kang Liu, and Jun Zhao. 2011. Learning the latent topics for question retrieval in community qa. In *Proceedings of 5th International Joint Conference on Natural Language Processing*, pages 273–281, Chiang Mai, Thailand, November. Asian Federation of Natural Language Processing.

Guihong Cao, Jian-Yun Nie, and Jing Bai. 2005. Integrating word relationships into language models. In *Proceedings of the 28th annual international ACM SIGIR conference on Research and development in information retrieval*, SIGIR '05, pages 298–305, New York, NY, USA. ACM.

Xin Cao, Gao Cong, Bin Cui, and Christian S. Jensen. 2010. A generalized framework of exploring category information for question retrieval in community question answer archives. In *WWW '10: Proceedings of the 19th international conference on World wide web*, pages 201–210, New York, NY, USA. ACM.

Huizhong Duan, Yunbo Cao, Chin yew Lin, and Yong Yu. 2008. Searching questions by identifying question topic and question focus. In *In Proceedings of 46th Annual Meeting of the Association for Computational Linguistics: Human Language Tchnologies (ACL:HLT)*.

Ofer Egozi, Shaul Markovitch, and Evgeniy Gabrilovich. 2011. Concept-based information retrieval using explicit semantic analysis. *ACM Trans. Inf. Syst.*, 29(2):8:1–8:34, April.

Paolo Ferragina and Ugo Scaiella. 2010. Tagme: on-the-fly annotation of short text fragments (by wikipedia entities). In *Proceedings of the 19th ACM international conference on Information and knowledge management*, CIKM '10, pages 1625–1628, New York, NY, USA. ACM.

Jianfeng Gao, Jian-Yun Nie, Guangyuan Wu, and Guihong Cao. 2004. Dependence language model for information retrieval. In *Proceedings of the 27th annual international ACM SIGIR conference on Research and development in information retrieval*, SIGIR '04, pages 170–177, New York, NY, USA. ACM.

F. A. Grootjen and Th. P. van der Weide. 2006. Conceptual query expansion. *Data Knowl. Eng.*, 56(2):174–193, February.

Jiwoon Jeon, W. Bruce Croft, and Joon Ho Lee. 2005. Finding similar questions in large question and answer archives. In *Proceedings of the 14th ACM international conference on Information and knowledge management*, CIKM '05, pages 84–90, New York, NY, USA. ACM.

Thorsten Joachims. 2002. Optimizing search engines using clickthrough data. In *Proceedings of the eighth ACM SIGKDD international conference on Knowledge discovery and data mining*, KDD '02, pages 133–142, New York, NY, USA. ACM.

Thorsten Joachims. 2006. Training linear svms in linear time. In *Proceedings of the 12th ACM SIGKDD international conference on Knowledge discovery and data mining*, KDD '06, pages 217–226, New York, NY, USA. ACM.

S. Kulkarni, A. Singh, G. Ramakrishnan, and S. Chakrabarti. 2009. Collective annotation of wikipedia entities in web text. In *Proceedings of the 15th ACM SIGKDD international conference on Knowledge discovery and data mining*, pages 457–466. ACM.

Jung-Tae Lee, Sang-Bum Kim, Young-In Song, and Hae-Chang Rim. 2008. Bridging lexical gaps between queries and questions on large online q&a collections with compact translation models. In *Proceedings of the Conference on Empirical Methods in Natural Language Processing*, EMNLP '08, pages 410–418, Stroudsburg, PA, USA. Association for Computational Linguistics.

Xiaoyong Liu and W. Bruce Croft. 2004. Cluster-based retrieval using language models. In *Proceedings of the 27th annual international ACM SIGIR conference on Research and development in information retrieval*, SIGIR '04, pages 186–193, New York, NY, USA. ACM.

Shuang Liu, Fang Liu, Clement Yu, and Weiyi Meng. 2004. An effective approach to document retrieval via utilizing wordnet and recognizing phrases. In *Proceedings of the 27th annual international ACM SIGIR conference on Research and development in information retrieval*, SIGIR '04, pages 266–272, New York, NY, USA. ACM.

Xunying Liu, Mark J. F. Gales, and Philip C. Woodland. 2008. Context dependent language model adaptation. In *INTERSPEECH 2008, 9th Annual Conference of the International Speech Communication Association, Brisbane, Australia, September 22-26, 2008*, pages 837–840. ISCA.

Olena Medelyan, David Milne, Catherine Legg, and Ian H. Witten. 2009. Mining meaning from wikipedia. *Int. J. Hum.-Comput. Stud.*, 67:716–754, September.

Edgar Meij, Dolf Trieschnigg, Maarten de Rijke, and Wessel Kraaij. 2008. Parsimonious concept modeling. In *Proceedings of the 31st annual international ACM SIGIR conference on Research and development in information retrieval*, SIGIR '08, pages 815–816, New York, NY, USA. ACM.

R. Mihalcea and A. Csomai. 2007. Wikify!: linking

documents to encyclopedic knowledge. In *CIKM*, volume 7, pages 233–242.

D. Milne and I.H. Witten. 2008. Learning to link with wikipedia. In *Proceeding of the 17th ACM conference on Information and knowledge management*, pages 509–518. ACM.

Robert C. Moore. 2004. Improving ibm word-alignment model 1. In *Proceedings of the 42nd Annual Meeting on Association for Computational Linguistics*, ACL '04, Stroudsburg, PA, USA. Association for Computational Linguistics.

Yonggang Qiu and Hans-Peter Frei. 1993. Concept based query expansion. In *Proceedings of the 16th annual international ACM SIGIR conference on Research and development in information retrieval*, SIGIR '93, pages 160–169, New York, NY, USA. ACM.

Lev Ratinov, Dan Roth, Doug Downey, and Mike Anderson. 2011. Local and global algorithms for disambiguation to wikipedia. In *Proceedings of the 49th Annual Meeting of the Association for Computational Linguistics: Human Language Technologies - Volume 1*, HLT '11, pages 1375–1384, Stroudsburg, PA, USA. Association for Computational Linguistics.

S.E. Robertson, S. Walker, S. Jones, M.M. Hancock-Beaulieu, and M. Gatford. 1996. Okapi at trec-3. pages 109–126.

Amit Singh and Karthik Visweswariah. 2011. CQC: classifying questions in cqa websites. In *Proceedings of the 20th ACM international conference on Information and knowledge management*, CIKM '11, pages 2033–2036, New York, NY, USA. ACM.

Amit Singh, Sayali Kulkarni, Somnath Banerjee, Ganesh Ramakrishnan, and Soumen Chakrabarti. 2009. Curating and searching the annotated web. In *In SIGKDD Conference, 2009*. ACM.

Mihai Surdeanu, Massimiliano Ciaramita, and Hugo Zaragoza. 2008. Learning to rank answers on large online qa collections. In *In Proceedings of the 46th Annual Meeting for the Association for Computational Linguistics: Human Language Technologies (ACL-08: HLT*, pages 719–727.

Xinhui Tu, Tingting He, Long Chen, Jing Luo, and Maoyuan Zhang. 2010. Wikipedia-based semantic smoothing for the language modeling approach to information retrieval. In *Proceedings of the 32nd European conference on Advances in Information Retrieval*, ECIR'2010, pages 370–381, Berlin, Heidelberg. Springer-Verlag.

Ellen M. Voorhees. 1994. Query expansion using lexical-semantic relations. In *Proceedings of the 17th annual international ACM SIGIR conference on Research and development in information retrieval*, SIGIR '94, pages 61–69, New York, NY, USA. Springer-Verlag New York, Inc.

Kai Wang, Zhaoyan Ming, and Tat-Seng Chua. 2009. A syntactic tree matching approach to finding similar questions in community-based qa services. In *Proceedings of the 32nd international ACM SIGIR conference on Research and development in information retrieval*, SIGIR '09, pages 187–194, New York, NY, USA. ACM.

Yang Xu, Gareth J.F. Jones, and Bin Wang. 2009. Query dependent pseudo-relevance feedback based on wikipedia. In *Proceedings of the 32nd international ACM SIGIR conference on Research and development in information retrieval*, SIGIR '09, pages 59–66, New York, NY, USA. ACM.

Xiaobing Xue, Jiwoon Jeon, and W. Bruce Croft. 2008. Retrieval models for question and answer archives. In *Proceedings of the 31st annual international ACM SIGIR conference on Research and development in information retrieval*, SIGIR '08, pages 475–482, New York, NY, USA. ACM.

Chengxiang Zhai and John Lafferty. 2004. A study of smoothing methods for language models applied to information retrieval. *ACM Trans. Inf. Syst.*, 22(2):179–214, April.

Xiaohua Zhou, Xiaohua Hu, and Xiaodan Zhang. 2007. Topic signature language models for ad hoc retrieval. *IEEE Trans. on Knowl. and Data Eng.*, 19(9):1276–1287, September.

Guangyou Zhou, Li Cai, Jun Zhao, and Kang Liu. 2011. Phrase-based translation model for question retrieval in community question answer archives. In *Proceedings of the 49th Annual Meeting of the Association for Computational Linguistics: Human Language Technologies - Volume 1*, HLT '11, pages 653–662, Stroudsburg, PA, USA. Association for Computational Linguistics.

Justin Zobel and Alistair Moffat. 2006. Inverted files for text search engines. *ACM Comput. Surv.*, 38, July.

Constructing Task-Specific Taxonomies for Document Collection Browsing

Hui Yang
Department of Computer Science
Georgetown University
37th and O street, NW
Washington, DC, 20057
huiyang@cs.georgetown.edu

Abstract

Taxonomies can serve as browsing tools for document collections. However, given an arbitrary collection, pre-constructed taxonomies could not easily adapt to the specific topic/task present in the collection. This paper explores techniques to *quickly* derive *task-specific* taxonomies supporting browsing in arbitrary document collections. The supervised approach directly learns semantic distances from users to propose meaningful task-specific taxonomies. The approach aims to produce globally optimized taxonomy structures by incorporating path consistency control and user-generated task specification into the general learning framework. A comparison to state-of-the-art systems and a user study jointly demonstrate that our techniques are highly effective.

1 Introduction

Taxonomies are widely used for knowledge standardization, knowledge sharing, and inferencing in natural language processing (NLP) tasks (Harabagiu et al., 2003; Szpektor et al., 2004). However, another common function of taxonomies, *browsing*, has received little attention in the NLP community. Browsing is the task of exploring and accessing information through a structure, e.g. a hierarchy, built upon a given document collection. In fact, taxonomies serve as browsing tools in many venues, including the Library of Congress Subject Headings (LCSH, 2011) for the U.S. Library of Congress and the Open Directory Project (ODP, 2011) for about 5% of the entire Web. We call taxonomies supporting browsing as *browsing taxonomies*.

When used for browsing, concepts[1] in taxonomies are linked to documents containing them and taxonomic structures are navigated to find particular documents. Users can navigate through a browsing taxonomy to explore the documents in the collection. A browsing taxonomy benefits information access by providing corpus overview for a document collection and allowing more focused reading by presenting together documents about the same concept.

Most existing browsing taxonomies, such as LCSH and ODP, are manually constructed to support large collections in general domains. Not only their constructions are expensive and slow, but also their structures are static and difficult to adapt to specific tasks. In situations where document collections are given ad-hoc, such as search result organization (Carpineto et al., 2009), email collection exploration (Yang and Callan, 2008), and literature investigation (Chau et al., 2011), existing taxonomies may even not be able to provide the right coverage of concepts. It is necessary to explore *ad-hoc* (semi-)automatic techniques to *quickly* derive *task-specific* browsing taxonomies for arbitrary document collections.

(Hovy, 2002) pointed out that one key challenge in taxonomy construction is multiple perspectives embedded in concepts and relations. One cause for multiple perspectives is the inherent facets in concepts, e.g., *jewelries* can be organized by *price* or by *gemstone types*. Another cause is task specification or even personalization. For example, when building a taxonomy for search results of query *trip to*

[1]English terms or entities; usually nouns or noun phrases.

DC, Jane may organize the concepts based on *places of interests* while Tom may organize them based on *dates in visit*. Typically, a taxonomy only conveys one or two perspectives from many choices. It is difficult to decide which perspective should be present. One realistic solution is to leave the decision to the constructor independent of the confusion that comes from facets, task specification or personalization.

When multiple perspectives present in the same taxonomy, it is not uncommon that the perspectives are mixed. For example, along a path *financial institute→bank→river bank*, *financial institute→bank* shows one perspective and *bank→river bank* shows another. We call this problem *path inconsistency*. Many approaches on automatic taxonomy construction suffer from this problem because their foci are on accurately identifying local relations between concept pairs (Etzioni et al., 2005; Pantel and Pennacchiotti, 2006) instead of on global control over the entire taxonomic structure. More recently, approaches attempted to build the full taxonomy structure (Snow et al., 2006; Yang and Callan, 2009; Kozareva and Hovy, 2010), however, few have looked into how to incorporate task specifications into taxonomy construction.

In this paper, we extended an existing taxonomy construction approach (Yang and Callan, 2009) to build task-specific taxonomies for document collection browsing. The extension comes in two parts: handling path consistency and incorporating specifications from users. We uniquely employ pairwise semantic distance as an entry point to incrementally build browsing taxonomies. A supervised distance learning algorithm not only allows us to incorporate multiple semantic features to evaluate the proximity between concepts, but also allows us to learn the metric function from personal preferences. Users can thus manually modify the taxonomies and to some extent teach the algorithm to predict his/her way to organize the concepts. Moreover, by minimizing the overall semantic distances among concepts and restricting minimal semantic distances along a path, we find the best hierarchical structure as the browsing taxonomy.

Our contributions include:

- A supervised learning mechanism to capture task-specific or personalized requirements for organizing a browsing taxonomy;

- A strategy to address path inconsistency due to word sense ambiguity and/or mixed perspectives;

- A general scheme to capture user inputs in taxonomy construction;

- A user study to evaluate the effectiveness of task-specific taxonomies for browsing activities.

2 Related Work

Document collection browsing has been studied as an alternative to the ranked list representation for search results by the Information Retrieval (IR) community. The popular IR approaches include clustering (Cutting et al., 1992) and monothetic concept hierarchies (Sanderson and Croft, 1999; Lawrie et al., 2001; Kummamuru et al., 2004; Carpineto et al., 2009). Clustering approaches hierarchically cluster documents in a collection and label the clusters. Monothetic approaches organize the concepts into hierarchies and link documents to related concepts. Both approaches are mainly based on pure statistics, such as document frequency (Sanderson and Croft, 1999) and conditional probability (Lawrie et al., 2001). The major drawback of these pure statistical approaches is their neglect of semantics among concepts. As an consequence, they often fail to produce semantically meaningful taxonomies.

The NLP community has extensively studied automatic taxonomy construction. Although traditional research on taxonomy construction focuses on extracting local relations between concept pairs (Hearst, 1992; Berland and Charniak, 1999; Ravichandran and Hovy, 2002; Girju et al., 2003; Etzioni et al., 2005; Pantel and Pennacchiotti, 2006; Kozareva et al., 2008), more recent efforts has been made in building full taxonomies. For example, (Snow et al., 2006) proposed to estimate taxonomic structure via maximizing the overall likelihood of a taxonomy. (Kozareva and Hovy, 2010) proposed to connect local concept pairs by finding the longest path in a subsumption graph. Yang and Callan proposed the Minimum Evolution (ME) framework to model the semantic distance $d(c_x, c_y)$ between concepts c_x and c_y as a weighted combination of various lexical, statistical, and semantic features: $\sum_j \text{weight}_j * \text{feature}_j(c_x, c_y)$ and estimate the taxonomic structure by minimizing the overall semantic distances.

Researcher also attempted to carve out taxonomies from existing ones. For example, Stoica et al. (Stoica and Hearst, 2007) managed to extract a browsing taxonomy from hypernym relations within WordNet (Fellbaum, 1998).

To support browsing in arbitrary collections, in this paper, we propose to incorporate task specification in a taxonomy. One way to achieve it is to define task-specific distances among concepts. Moreover, through controlling distance scores among concepts, we can enforce path consistency in taxonomies. For example, when the distance between *financial institute* and *river bank* is big, the path *financial institute→bank→river bank* will be pruned and the concepts will be repositioned. Inspired by ME, we take a distance learning approach to deal with path consistency (Section 3) and task specification (Section 4) in taxonomy construction.

3 Build Structure-Optimized Taxonomies

This section presents how to automatically build taxonomies. We take two steps to build browsing taxonomy for a given document collection. The first step is to extract the concepts and the second is to organize the concepts. For concept extraction, we take a simple but effective approach: (1) We first parse the document collection and exhaustively extract nouns, noun phrases, and named entities that occur >5 times in the collection. (2) We then filter out part-of-speech errors and typos by a Web-based frequency test. In the test, we search each candidate concept in the Google search engine and remove a candidate if it appears <4 times within the top 10 Google snippets. (3) We finally cluster similar concept candidates into groups by Latent Semantic Analysis (Bellegarda et al., 1996) and select the candidate with the highest $tfidf$ value within a group to form the concept set C. Although our extraction algorithm is very effective with 95% precision and 80% recall in a manual evaluation, sometimes C may still miss some important concepts for the collection. This can be later corrected by users interactively through adding new concepts (Section 4).

To organize the concepts in C into taxonomic structures, we extend the incremental clustering framework proposed by ME (Yang and Callan, 2009). In ME, concepts are inserted one at a time. At each insertion, a concept c_z is at the parent (or child) position for every existing node in the current taxonomy. The evaluation of the best position depends on the semantic distance between c_z and its temporary child (or parent) node and the semantic distance among all other concepts in the taxonomy. An advantage in ME is that it allows incorporating various constraints to the taxonomic structure. For example, ME can handle concept generality-specificity by learning different semantic distance functions for general concepts which are located at upper levels and specific concepts which are located at lower levels in a taxonomy.

In this section, we introduce a new semantic distance learning method (Section 3.1) and extend ME by controlling path consistency (Section 3.2).

3.1 Estimating Semantic Distances

Pair-wise semantic distances among concepts build the foundation for taxonomy construction. ME models the semantic distance $d(c_x, c_y)$ between concepts c_x and c_y as a linear combination of underlying feature functions. Similar to ME, we also assume that "there are some underlying feature functions that measure semantic dissimilarity for concepts and a good semantic distance is a combination of these features". Different from ME, we model the semantic distance $d(c_x, c_y)$ between concepts (c_x, c_y) as a Mahalanobis distance (Mahalanobis, 1936): $d_{c_x,c_y} = \sqrt{\Phi(c_x, c_y)^T W^{-1} \Phi(c_x, x_y)}$, where $\Phi(c_x, c_y)$ is the set of underlying feature functions $\{\phi_k : (c_x, c_y)\}$ with k=1,...,$|\Phi|$. W is the weight matrix, whose diagonal values weigh the various feature functions. We use the same set of features as proposed in ME.

Mahalanobis distance is a general parametric function widely used in distance metric learning (Yang, 2006). It measures the dissimilarity between two random vectors of the same distribution with a covariance matrix W, which scales the data points from their original values by $W^{1/2}$. When only diagonal values of W are taken into account, W is equivalent to assigning weights to different axes in the random vectors.

We choose Mahalanobis distance for two reasons. (1) It is in a parametric form so that it allows us to learn a distance function by supervised learning and provides an opportunity to assign different weights for each type of semantic features. (2) When W is properly constrained to be positive semi-definite (PSD) (Bhatia, 2006), a Mahalanobis-formatted distance will be guaranteed to satisfy non-negativity and triangle inequality, which was not addressed in ME. As long as these two conditions are satisfied, one may learn other forms of distance functions to represent a semantic distance.

We can estimate W by minimizing the squared errors between training semantic distances d and the expected value $\hat{d}$. We also need to constrain W to be PSD to satisfy triangle inequality and non-negativity. The objective function for semantic distance estimation is:

$$\min_{W} \sum_{x=1}^{|\mathbf{C}|} \sum_{y=1}^{|\mathbf{C}|} \left(d_{c_x,c_y} - \sqrt{\Phi(c_x,c_y)^T W^{-1} \Phi(c_x,c_y)} \right)^2 \quad (1)$$
$$\text{subject to } W \succeq 0$$

In this implementation, we used (Sedumi, 2011) and (Yalmip, 2011) to solve the semi-definite programming (SDP).

To generate the training semantic distances, we collected 100 hypernym taxonomy fragments from WordNet (Fellbaum, 1998) and ODP. The semantic distance for a concept pair (c_x, c_y) in a training taxonomy fragment is generated by assuming every edge is weighted as 1 and summing up the edge weights along the shortest path from c_x to c_y in the taxonomy fragment. In Section 4, we will show how to use user inputs as training data to capture task-specifications in taxonomy construction.

3.2 Enforcing Path Consistency

In ME, the main taxonomy structure optimization framework is based on minimization of overall semantic distance among all concepts in the taxonomy and the minimum evolution assumption. We extend the framework by introducing another optimization objective to the framework: path consistency objective. The idea is that in any root-to-leaf path in a taxonomy, all concepts on the path should be about the same topic or the same perspective. Within a root-to-leaf path, the concepts need to be coherent no matter how far away they are apart. It suggests that a good path's sum of the semantic distances should be small.

Algorithm: Automatic Taxonomy Optimization.
$W = \min_W \sum_{x=1} \sum_{y=1}^{|N(c_{tr_x})|} ((d_{c_{tr_x}, c_{tr_y}} - \sqrt{\Phi(c_{tr_x}, c_{tr_y})^T W^{-1} \Phi(c_{tr_x}, c_{tr_y})})^2;$
foreach $c_z \in C \setminus S$
  $S \leftarrow S \cup \{c_z\};$
  if $W \succeq 0$
    $d(c_z, .) = \sqrt{\Phi(c_z, .)^T W^{-1} \Phi(c_z,)};$
  $R \leftarrow R \cup \{\arg\min_{R_{(c_z,.)}} (\lambda \, \text{obj}_{ME} + (1-\lambda) \, \text{obj}_{path})\};$
Output $T(S, R)$

Figure 1: An algorithm for taxonomy structure optimization with path consistency control. C denotes the entire concept set, S the current concept set, and R the current relation set. $N(c_{tr_x})$ is the neighborhood of a training concept c_{tr_x}, including its parent and child(ren). $R(c_z, .)$ indicates the set of relations between a new concept c_z and all other existing concepts. T is the taxonomy with concept set S and relation set R.

Therefore, we propose to minimize the sum of semantic distances along a root-to-leaf path. Particularly, when adding a new concept c_z into an existing browsing hierarchy T, we try it at different positions in T. At each temporary position, we can calculate the sum of the semantic distances along the root-to-leaf path P_{c_z} that contains the new concept c_x. The path consistency objective is given by:

$$\text{obj}_{path} = \min_{P_{c_z}} \sum_{c_x, c_y \in P_{c_z}, x<y} d(c_x, c_y) \quad (2)$$

where $x < y$ defines the order of the concepts to avoid counting the same pair of pair-wise distances twice.

Towards modeling path consistency in taxonomy construction, we introduce a Pareto co-efficient $\lambda \in [0, 1]$ to control the contributions from obj_{ME}, the overall semantic distance minimization objective as proposed in ME, and obj_{path}, the path distance minimization objective. The optimization is:

$$\min \lambda \, \text{obj}_{ME} + (1-\lambda) \, \text{obj}_{path} \quad (3)$$

where $\text{obj}_{ME} = |\sum_{c_x, c_y \in C^n \cup \{c_z\}, x<y} d(c_x, c_y) - \sum_{c_x, c_y \in C^n, x<y} d(c_x, c_y)|$, $0 \leq \lambda \leq 1$, and C^n is the concept set after n^{th} concept is added. Empirically, we set $\lambda = 0.8$.

The algorithm shown in Figure 1 outlines our greedy algorithm to build taxonomies with path consistency control. Each time when a new concept arrives, the algorithm first estimates its semantic distances based on W learned from the training data, then finds the optimal position for the concept by minimizing overall semantic distances and path inconsistency, and gradually grows the structure into a full taxonomy.

The order of adding concepts may affect the final taxonomy structure. We hence insert concepts in an arbitrary order with 10 random restarts with different initial concepts and pick the taxonomy that minimizes both objectives among all candidate structures.

Algorithm: Interactive Taxonomy Construction.
1. $T(S, R)$ =CreateInitialTaxonomy();
2. $U^{(0)}$={Unmodified Concepts}=$C \setminus S$,
   $G^{(0)}$={Modified concepts}=S, $M^{(0)} = \emptyset$, $i = 0$;
3. **while** (not Satisfied) or $U^{(i)} \neq \emptyset$
4. $M^{(i)}$=CollectManualGuidance($G^{(i)}$,$U^{(i)}$);
5. $W^{(i)}$=LearnDistanceMetricFunction($M^{(i)}$);
6. $D^{(i)}$=PredictDistanceScores($W^{(i)}$,$U^{(i)}$);
7. ($G^{(i+1)}$, $U^{(i+1)}$) = UpdateTaxonomy($D^{(i)}$,$U^{(i)}$,$G^{(i)}$);
8. $i = i + 1$;
9. **Output** $G^{(i)}$ as the taxonomy.

Figure 2: Interactive taxonomy construction procedure.

4 Incorporating Task Specification

This section studies how to incorporate user-defined task specifications in taxonomy construction. Although the automatic algorithm proposed in Section 3 is able to well-organize most concepts for a given document collection, it has not yet addressed the issue of mixed perspective in taxonomy construction. For concepts with multiple perspectives, we need to decide which perspective is more appropriate for the browsing taxonomy. This task-specific requirement can only be captured by the user/constructor who builds and uses the browsing taxonomy. Moreover, the automatic algorithm relies on training data from WordNet and ODP, which are known for imperfect term organizations such as unbalanced granularity among terms at the same level. To correct the wrong relations learned from imperfect training data, we propose to utilize user inputs in the learning process.

Particularly, we formulate taxonomy construction as a user-teaching-machine-learning process. To guide how to organize the concepts, a user trains the supervised distance learning model via a taxonomy construction interface that allows the user to intuitively modify a taxonomy. The interface supports editing actions such as dragging and dropping, adding, deleting, and renaming nodes. When a user put c_x under c_y, i.e. $c_x \rightarrow c_y$, this action indicates that the user wants a relation represented by $c_x \rightarrow c_y$ to be true in this taxonomy. We did not expect users to make all the edits. In a human-computer-interaction cycle, a user is not restricted to give a certain number of edits. Based on a user study (Section 5.5), an average number of edits per interaction is 3.6, which can be achieved with ease by most users.

The algorithm shown in Figure 2 provides the pseudo code for the interactive taxonomy construction procedure. It starts with automatic construction of initial taxonomies using the techniques presented in Section 3 (Line 1). We then capture the user inputs as *manual guidance* (Line 4) and make use of it to adjust the distance learning model (Line 5), make new predictions for semantic distances of other concepts (Line 6), and organize those concepts to agree with the user and update the taxonomy accordingly (Line 7). Line 2 initiates three variables, the unmodified concepts U, the modified concepts G, and the manual guidance M, indexed by the iteration number i. The process iterates until the user is satisfied with the taxonomy's organization (Line 3).

Learning and predicting distances have been presented in Section 3.1. In this section, we present how to capture manual guidance (Section 4.1) and update the taxonomies accordingly (Section 4.2).

4.1 Manual Guidance as the Training Data

Taxonomies are tree-structured. It is not trivial to model a taxonomy, especially changes in a taxonomy, and feed that into a learning algorithm. In this section, we propose a general scheme to capture changes, i.e., user inputs during interactions, in taxonomy construction.

We propose to convert a taxonomy into matrices of neighboring nodes. We compare the changes between a series of snapshots of the changing taxonomy to identify the user inputs. Specifically, before a user starts editing in an interaction cycle, we represent the organization of concepts as a *before matrix*; likewise, after the user finishes all edits in one cycle, we represent the new organization of concepts as an *after matrix*. For both matrices, the $(x, y)^{th}$ entry indicates whether (or how confident) a relation $r(c_x, c_y)$ is true. r could be any type of relation

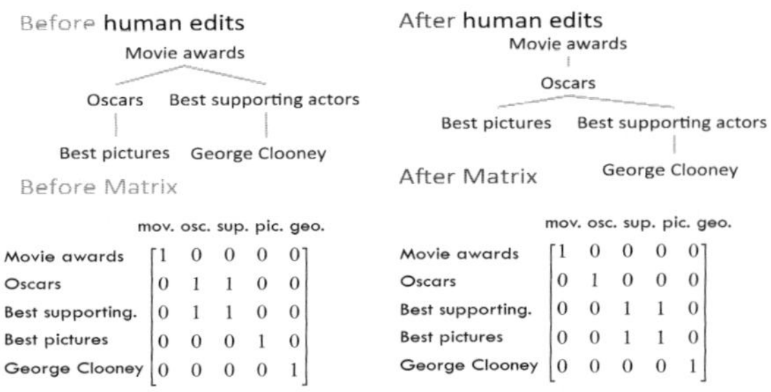

Figure 3: An example taxonomy before and after human edits (Concepts unchanged; relation type = $sibling$).

between the concepts. Figure 3 shows an example taxonomy's before and after matrices.

We define *manual guidance* M as a submatrix which consists of entries in the *after matrix* B; at these entries, there exist differences between the *before matrix* A and the *after matrix* B. Formally,

$$\begin{aligned} M &= B[r;c] \\ r &= \{i : b_{ij} - a_{ij} \neq 0\} \\ c &= \{j : b_{ij} - a_{ij} \neq 0\} \end{aligned} \tag{4}$$

where a_{ij} is the $(i,j)^{th}$ entry in A, b_{ij} is the $(i,j)^{th}$ entry in B, r indicates the rows and c indicates the columns.

Note that manual guidance is not simply the matrix difference between A and B. It is part of the after matrix because it is the after matrix that indicates where the user wants the concept hierarchy to develop. The manual guidance for the example shown in Figure 3 is: $M = B[2,3,4;2,3,4] =$

	$Oscars$	$Best\ supporting$	$Best\ picture$
$Oscars$	1	0	0
$Best\ supporting$	0	1	1
$Best\ picture$	0	1	1

When the user adds or deletes concepts, we expand rows and columns in A and B by filling 0 for non-diagonal entries and 1 for diagonal entries. The expanded before and after matrices A' and B' are used in the calculation.

For taxonomies with concept changes, we define *manual guidance with concept set change* M_{change} as a submatrix which consists of some entries of the *after matrix* B; at these entries, there exist differences from the *expanded before matrix* A' to the *expanded after matrix* B'. Note that the concepts corresponding to these entries should exist in the unexpanded set of concepts. Formally, manual guidance with concept set change

$$\begin{aligned} M_{change} &= B[r';c'] \\ r' &= \{i : b'_{ij} - a'_{ij} \neq 0, \text{ concept } c_i \in C_B\} \\ c' &= \{j : b'_{ij} - a'_{ij} \neq 0, \text{ concept } c_j \in C_B\} \end{aligned} \tag{5}$$

where a'_{ij} is the $(i,j)^{th}$ entry in A', b'_{ij} is the $(i,j)^{th}$ entry in B', C_B is the set of concepts in the unexpanded after matrix B, r indicates the rows and c indicates the columns.

Based on manual guidance M, we can create training data for the supervised distance learning algorithm (Section 3.1). In particular, we transform the manual guidance into a distance matrix $D = 1 - M$, which is used as the training data. The learning algorithm is then able to learn a good model which best preserves the regularity defined by the task and the user. The difference is that the training data here is derived from manual guidance while in the automatic algorithm we use training data from WordNet and ODP.

4.2 Update the Taxonomy

According to the algorithm shown in Figure 2, after learning $W^{(i)}$, the weight matrix at the ith iteration, from the manual guidance, we can use it to predict the pair-wise semantic distances for the unmodified concepts and further group them in the taxonomy.

When the pair-wise distance score for a concept pair (c_l, c_m) is small (<0.5), we consider the relation between the concept pair is true; when it is big ($\geq$0.5), false. How to organize concepts whose relations are true, is decided again by the relation type in the distance matrix. If r is "sibling", c_l and c_m are put under the same parent. If r is "is-a", c_m is put under c_l as one of c_l's children. The user interface then presents the updated taxonomy to the user and waits for the next round of manual guidance.

Since only a few changes are made during each human-computer interaction, the learning model may suffer from overfitting and the taxonomic structure may change too rapidly. To avoid such issues caused by too few manual guidance, we employ background training taxonomy fragments from WordNet and ODP, to smooth the learning models and achieve less variance.

5 Evaluation

We conduct experiments and a user study to evaluate the effectiveness of our approach. We have two goals for the evaluation. One is to evaluate how the browsing taxonomies constructed by our approach compare with those constructed by other baseline systems. Another is to investigate how well our system can learns from task-specifications based on user supervision.

5.1 Datasets

The datasets we used in the evaluation are collections of Web documents crawled for complex search tasks. For each task, we created the dataset by submitting 4 to 5 queries to and collecting the returned Web documents from two search engines *bing.com* and *google.com*. For example, queries "trip to DC", "Washington DC", "DC", and "Washington" were submitted for the task "planning a trip to DC". In total, we created 50 Web datasets on the topics such as *find a good kindergarten*, *purchase a used car*, *plan a trip to DC*, *how to make a cake*, *find a good wedding videographer*, *write a survey paper for health care systems*, *find the best deals for a Mother's day gift*, *write a survey paper for social network*, *write a survey paper for EU's finance*, and *write a survey paper for information technology*.

Around 1000 Web documents are collected for each dataset. We filter out spams and advertisements and then search for more relevant Web documents to make the total number 1000. However, not all topics can retrieve 1000 documents. Among all 50 datasets, the average number of documents is 988.5. The average number of unique words in a dataset is 698,875.

5.2 Comparing with Baseline Systems

We compare the following 5 systems.

- Subsumption: the automatic algorithm proposed by (Sanderson and Croft, 1999), the most effective state-of-the-art browsing hierarchy construction technique as reported by (Lawrie et al., 2001).
- KH: the automatic taxonomy construction algorithm proposed by (Kozareva and Hovy, 2010).
- ME: the automatic taxonomy construction algorithm proposed by (Yang and Callan, 2009). This framework does not perform path consistency control nor learning from users.
- DistOpt: our automatic taxonomy construction algorithm with path consistency control.
- PDistOpt: our interactive approach with human supervision. The process starts from a flat list of concepts. The user built the browsing taxonomy from the list in a user study (Section 5.5).

5.3 Browsing Effectiveness

A popular measure to evaluate the quality of the browsing taxonomies is the expected mutual information measure (EMIM (Lawrie et al., 2001)). It calculates the mutual information between the language model in a taxonomy T and the language model in a document collection Z. It is defined as:

$$I(C;V) = \sum_{c \in C, v \in V} P(c,v) log \frac{P(c,v)}{P(c)P(v)},$$

where $P(c,v) = \sum_{d \in Z} P(d)P(c|d)P(v|d)$, C is the set of concepts in T, V is the set of non-stopwords in Z, and d is a document in Z. EMIM only evaluates the content of a browsing taxonomy, not its structure. However, it is still popularly used to indicate how representative a browsing taxonomy is for a document collection.

Table 1 shows the EMIM of the browsing taxonomies constructed by the five systems under evaluation. Based on the mean EMIM over the 50 datasets, we can rank the systems in terms of EMIM in the descending order as PDistOpt $>>$ DistOpt $>>$ ME $>$ KH $>>$ Subsumption.[2] It shows that DistOpt is the best performing *automatic* algorithm to generate browsing taxonomies. DistOpt is 109% and statistically significantly more effective than ME (p-value$<.001$, t-test), 159% and statistically significantly more effective than KH (p-value$<.001$, t-test), and 17 times and statistically significantly more effective than Subsumption (p-value$<.001$, t-test). It strongly suggests that our techniques are

[2] $>>$ indicates statistically significant difference between the left and the right hand sides ($p < .001$, t-test) and $>$ indicates moderate statistical significance between the left and the right hand sides ($p < .05$, t-test). We will use the same symbols throughout the remainder of this paper.

Table 1: Expected Mutual Information (in 1000*EMIM).

Example dataset	Subs.	KH	ME	DistOpt	PDistOpt
kindergarten	0.4	3.8	3.9	5.6	7.3
health care	0.5	2.8	3.1	7.8	8.3
used car	0.1	0.2	0.1	2.8	3.6
trip to DC	0.2	4.3	4.5	6.4	6.8
finance	0.01	0.01	0.1	0.6	0.6
gift	0.2	1.2	1.2	3.8	4.7
social network	0.1	1.5	1.3	2.4	3.2
information	0.3	1.9	2.3	3.5	4.9
cake	0.2	1.2	3.1	6.6	6.8
videographer	0.4	1.8	1.6	4.9	5.6
Mean of 50 sets	**0.24**	**1.7**	**2.1**	**4.4**	**5.2**

Table 2: Reach time.

Example dataset	Subs.	KH	ME	DistOpt	PDistOpt
kindergarten	14.4	9.8	9.9	8.7	4.3
health care	12.3	9.8	6.8	4.5	3.3
used car	15.4	12.4	10.2	8.7	7.6
trip to DC	11.2	10.3	9,8	8.7	5.8
finance	24.5	18.3	19.7	18.7	15.6
gift	11.2	8.4	7.7	5.6	5.4
social network	14.3	9.8	7.8	7.6	6.8
information	10.6	9.5	8.8	8.9	6.7
cake	8.9	4.8	4.5	3.4	3.2
videographer	9.5	8.8	7.6	6.9	4.5
Mean of 50 sets	**14.2**	**12.2**	**9.8**	**7.2**	**5.2**

more effective than the state-of-the-art systems in constructing browsing taxonomies.

Moreover, Table 1 shows that the PDistOpt taxonomies is 18% more effective than the DistOpt taxonomies in terms of EMIM. The result is also statistically significant (p-value<.01, t-test). It indicates that incorporating user preferences in browsing taxonomy construction is able to produce even more effective browsing taxonomies than all automated methods.

Another popular evaluation measure[3] for browsing effectiveness is reach time (Carpineto et al., 2009). It is defined as:

$$t_{reach} = \frac{1}{|R|} \sum_{d_i \in R} L(c_i) + p_i,$$

where R is the relevant documents, c_i is the concept that connects to a relevant document d_i, $L(c_i)$ is the path length from the root to reach c_i, and p_i is the position that d_i appears in the document cluster associated with c_i. Reach time evaluates both the content and the structure of a browsing taxonomy. This measure needs relevance judgements about a query for the documents organized by the taxonomies. We obtained the relevance judgements by using the majority votes from a user study involving 29 subjects followed by expert reviews. Three experts manually examined the majority votes and reached agreements on all relevance judgements.

Table 2 elaborates reach time for the systems. Based on the mean reach time over 50 datasets, we obtain a similar ranking of the systems as suggested by EMIM. The ranking based on reach time is: PDistOpt >> DistOpt >> ME > KH >> Subsumption. It shows that the best performing *automatic* system is DistOpt, which on average can produce taxonomies to reach a relevant document by visiting only 7.2 nodes, including 5.2 non-leaf concepts and 2 documents in the leaf cluster on average. To find all relevant documents in a collection sized around 1000, this reach time is very fast. The interactive PDistOpt unsurprisingly gives even better reach time, 5.2 nodes on average.

[3]Other proposed measures include coverage and compactness (Kummamuru et al., 2004).

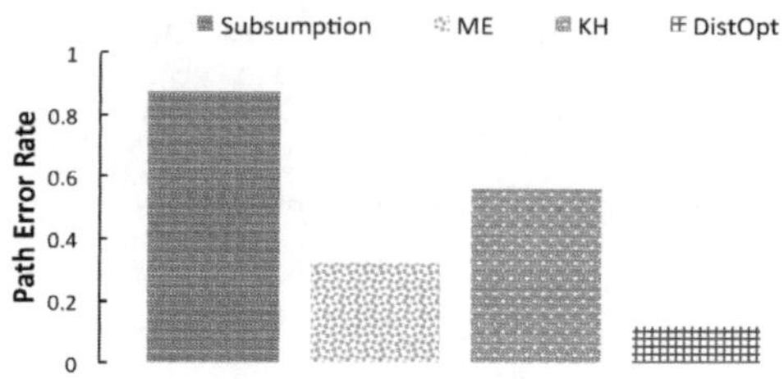

Figure 4: Path error rate.

5.4 Path Consistency

To evaluate how well path consistency is handled, we compare the *path error rate* generated by our approach and by other baseline systems. This evaluation is only applied to automatic algorithms.

The path error is defined as the average number of wrong ancestor-descendant pairs in a taxonomy. It is only applied for concepts are *not* immediately connected. It can be judged and calculated as follows. Three human assessors manually evaluated the path errors by (1) gathering the paths by performing a depth-first traverse in the taxonomy from the root concept; (2) along each path, counting the number of wrong ancestor-descendant pairs; (3) summing up

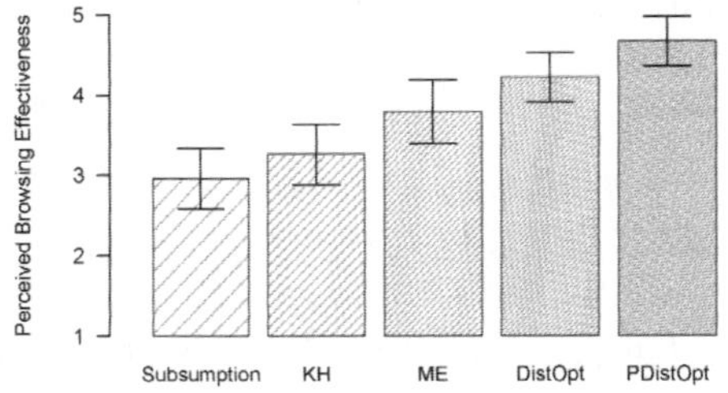

Figure 5: Perceived browsing effectiveness.

the errors that all assessors agree on and normalizing the sum by the taxonomy size.

Figure 4 shows the path error rate generated by all the automated algorithms under evaluation. We can see that DistOpt produces the least path error. The algorithms can be ranked in terms of the ability to handle path consistency as DistOpt >> ME >> KH >> Subsumption. DistOpt statistically significantly reduces path errors from not using the path consistency control (ME) by 500% (p-value<.001, t-test). It strongly indicates that our technique is effective to maintain path consistency. We conclude that DistOpt best handles path consistency among all the system under evaluation.

5.5 User Study

Besides objective evaluations, we conducted an user study consisting of two parts: qualitative comparison of the systems under evaluation, and using our taxonomy construction user interface to interactively construct personalized browsing taxonomies.

Twenty-nine (Thirty subjects initially, one was excluded because of incomplete data entry) graduate and undergraduate students from various majors in two universities participated in the study. They were all familiar with use of computers and highly proficient in English. Each user study lasted for 4 hours.

In the first half of the user study, the participants were first introduced to the taxonomy construction user interface for about 10 minutes to get familiar with its functions. After that, the participants performed an exercise task which lasted about 5 minutes and then started the real tasks. For each dataset, the participants were asked to interactively work with PDistOpt to build browsing taxonomies. Once the real tasks were done, the participants spend 5 minutes to answer a questionnaire regarding their experience and opinions.

In the second half of the user study, we asked the participants to use and compare the provided browsing taxonomies with the following task in mind.

> Imagine your have a task [task name]. You use a browsing taxonomy designed for the collection of Web documents about this task. Use the browsing taxonomy to find all useful topics for your task. Identify at least one document for each topic.

For each dataset, we asked the participants to rate the browsing taxonomies built by the systems under evaluation by answering the following question about *perceived browsing effectiveness* - *"How well did the browsing taxonomy help you to complete the task?"*. Ratings in the 5-point Likert-type scale, ranging from "very good"(5), "good"(4), "fair"(3), "bad"(2), to "trash"(1), are used to rate browsing effectiveness perceived by the participants.

5.5.1 Perceived Browsing Effectiveness

Figure 5 shows the mean and 95% confidence interval for the *perceived browsing effectiveness* for browsing taxonomies constructed by the systems under evaluation. These perceived browsing effectiveness can be ranked in descending order as PDistOpt >> DistOpt > ME >> KH > Subsumption. PDistOpt shows the highest mean perceived browsing effectiveness, which is as high as 4.4. Such high rating shows that browsing taxonomy with personalization could well satisfy users' information needs and are perceived as very effective in browsing by the users.

5.5.2 Accuracy of System Predictions

When a user provided manual guidance to the interactive system, during each human-computer interaction cycle, the system made predictions based on the user's edits. He or she could directly judge the correctness of these machine-predicted modifications on-the-fly by selecting an option "yes" or "no" from the "Accept the change?" menu. Note that these were personalized tasks and the predictions were evaluated by the user according

Table 3: Accuracy of system predictions.

	Max	Min	Avg
accuracy of system predictions	0.98	0.92	0.94

Table 4: Perceived learning ability.

	Max	Min	Avg
perceived learning ability	4.2	2.8	3.61
which dataset	health care	finance	-

to his/her own standard. We calculate the accuracy of system predictions as: $\text{Accuracy} = \frac{1}{I}\sum_{i=1}^{I}\frac{\text{number of accepted predictions in } i^{th} \text{ cycle}}{\text{number of predictions in } i^{th} \text{ cycle}}$, where I is the total number of human-computer interaction cycles when constructing a browsing taxonomy. A high accuracy indicates that the system learns well from user edits. This evaluation is only applied to PDistOpt.

Table 3 shows that for all datasets, the mean accuracy of the system predictions is above 0.92. The average value is 0.94. This high accuracy clearly demonstrates that the system successfully learns from a user and makes highly accurate predictions on how the user would organize the concepts.

5.5.3 Perceived Learning Ability

After completing constructing a browsing taxonomy, a participant was asked immediately to rate how well the system learned from his/her edits. The question was *"How well did the system appear to learn your method of organizing the concepts?"*. We also used the 5-point Likert-type scale to rate this *perceived system learning ability*. This evaluation is only applied to PDistOpt.

Table 4 shows the max, min, and average responses of perceived system learning ability. The mean perceived learning ability is 3.61, with a standard derivation of 0.45. It suggests that the learning ability of the system was only perceived as moderately good. This result contradicts with the conclusion that we drew based on the more objective measure, accuracy of system prediction (Section 5.5.2).

We further investigate why the participants were only moderately satisfied with the system's learning ability. From the after session questionnaire, we found that participants thought that some datasets such as "finance" were more difficult than other datasets such as "health care". For example, the dataset "finance" was considered by all participants as "very difficult" while "health care" was considered as "very easy". The participants also complained that they were not familiar with the difficult datasets. It is interesting that when a dataset is less familiar for the users, the system was perceived performing badly too. It may suggest that when people are not familiar with the tasks, they provide less promising edits, the system learns from the lower quality training data, and in the end the users perceive the output as poor system learning ability.

6 Conclusion

Document collection browsing is another common use of taxonomies. Given an arbitrary collection, a taxonomy must suit the specific domain in order to support browsing. This paper explores techniques to *quickly* derive *task-specific* taxonomies supporting browsing in arbitrary document sets. In particular, we uniquely employ pair-wise semantic distance as an entry point to incrementally build browsing taxonomies. The supervised distance learning algorithm not only allows us to incorporate multiple semantic features to evaluate the proximity between concepts, but also allows us to learn the metric function from personal preferences. Users can thus manually modify the taxonomies and to some extent teach the algorithm to predict his/her way to organize the concepts. Moreover, by minimizing the overall semantic distances among concepts and restricting minimal semantic distances along a path, we find the best hierarchical structure as the browsing hierarchy. It guarantees that semantically close concepts are put together so that users will have a good idea about why the concepts are put together. This greatly increases the interpretability of a constructed browsing hierarchy than the existing approaches. This makes our approach more flexible and more general to effectively creating browsing taxonomies to support more complicated and more realistic tasks such as Web information triage.

Acknowledgments

The author sincerely thanks Prof. Jamie Callan for in-depth discussions about the research and anonymous reviewers for valuable comments to this paper.

References

J. R. Bellegarda, J. W. Butzberger, Yen-Lu Chow, N. B. Coccaro, and D. Naik. 1996. A novel word clustering algorithm based on latent semantic analysis. In *Proceedings of the Acoustics, Speech, and Signal Processing, 1996. on Conference Proceedings., 1996 IEEE International Conference - Volume 01*, ICASSP '96, pages 172–175, Washington, DC, USA. IEEE Computer Society.

Matthew Berland and Eugene Charniak. 1999. Finding parts in very large corpora. In *Proceedings of the 27th Annual Meeting for the Association for Computational Linguistics (ACL 1999)*.

Rajendra Bhatia. 2006. *Positive definite matrices (princeton series in applied mathematics)*. Princeton University Press, December.

Claudio Carpineto, Stefano Mizzaro, Giovanni Romano, and Matteo Snidero. 2009. Mobile information retrieval with search results clustering: Prototypes and evaluations. *Journal of American Society for Information Science and Technology (JASIST)*, pages 877–895.

Duen Horng Chau, Aniket Kittur, Jason I. Hong, and Christos Faloutsos. 2011. Apolo: making sense of large network data by combining rich user interaction and machine learning. In *CHI*, pages 167–176.

Gouglass R. Cutting, David R. Karger, Jan R. Petersen, and John W. Tukey. 1992. Scatter/Gather: A cluster-based approach to browsing large document collections. In *Proceedings of the fifteenth Annual ACM Conference on Research and Development in Information Retrieval (SIGIR 1992)*.

Oren Etzioni, Michael Cafarella, Doug Downey, Ana-Maria Popescu, Tal Shaked, Stephen Soderland, Daniel S. Weld, and Alexander Yates. 2005. Unsupervised named-entity extraction from the web: an experimental study. In *Artificial Intelligence, 165(1):91-134, June*.

Christiane Fellbaum. 1998. *WordNet: an electronic lexical database*. MIT Press.

Roxana Girju, Adriana Badulescu, and Dan Moldovan. 2003. Learning semantic constraints for the automatic discovery of part-whole relations. In *Proceedings of the Human Language Technology Conference/Annual Conference of the North American Chapter of the Association for Computational Linguistics (HLT/NAACL 2003)*.

Sanda M. Harabagiu, Steve J. Maiorano, and Marius A. Pasca. 2003. Open-domain textual question answering techniques. In *Natural Language Engineering 9 (3): 1-38*.

Marti A. Hearst. 1992. Automatic acquisition of hyponyms from large text corpora. In *Proceedings of the 14th International Conference on Computational Linguistics (COLING 1992)*.

E. H. Hovy. 2002. Comparing Sets of Semantic Relations in Ontologies. In R. Green, C. A. Bean, and Myaeng S. H. (eds), editors, *The Semantics of Relationships: An Interdisciplinary Perspective*. Dordrecht: Kluwer.

Zornitsa Kozareva and Eduard Hovy. 2010. A semi-supervised method to learn and construct taxonomies using the web. In *Proceedings of the 2010 Conference on Empirical Methods in Natural Language Processing*, pages 1110–1118, Cambridge, MA, October. Association for Computational Linguistics.

Zornitsa Kozareva, Ellen Riloff, and Eduard Hovy. 2008. Semantic class learning from the web with hyponym pattern linkage graphs. In *Proceedings of the 46th Annual Meeting for the Association for Computational Linguistics (ACL 2008)*.

Krishna Kummamuru, Rohit Lotlikar, Shourya Roy, Karan Singal, and Raghu Krishnapuram. 2004. A hierarchical monothetic document clustering algorithm for summarization and browsing search results. *Proceedings of the 13th conference on World Wide Web WWW 04*, page 658.

Dawn Lawrie, W. Bruce Croft, and Arnold Rosenberg. 2001. Finding topic words for hierarchical summarization. In *Proceedings of the 24th Annual ACM Conference on Research and Development in Information Retrieval (SIGIR 2001)*, pages 349–357.

LCSH. 2011. Library of congress subject headings. `http://www.loc.gov/`.

P. C. Mahalanobis. 1936. On the generalised distance in statistics. In *Proceedings of the National Institute of Sciences of India 2 (1): 495*.

ODP. 2011. Open directory project. `http://www.dmoz.org/`.

Patrick Pantel and Marco Pennacchiotti. 2006. Espresso: Leveraging generic patterns for automatically harvesting semantic relations. In *Proceedings of the 44th Annual Meeting for the Association for Computational Linguistics (ACL 2006)*.

Deepak Ravichandran and Eduard Hovy. 2002. Learning surface text patterns for a question answering system. In *Proceedings of the 40th Annual Meeting for the Association for Computational Linguistics (ACL 2002)*.

Mark Sanderson and W. Bruce Croft. 1999. Deriving concept hierarchies from text. In *Proceedings of the 22nd Annual International ACM SIGIR Conference on Research and Development in Information Retrieval (SIGIR 1999)*.

Sedumi. 2011. `http://sedumi.mcmaster.ca`.

Rion Snow, Daniel Jurafsky, and Andrew Y. Ng. 2006. Semantic taxonomy induction from heterogenous evidence. In *Proceedings of the 21st International Conference on Computational Linguistics and 44th Annual Meeting of the Association for Computational Linguistics (ACL/COLING 2006)*.

Emilia Stoica and Marti A. Hearst. 2007. Automating Creation of Hierarchical Faceted Metadata Structures. In *Proceedings of the Human Language Technology Conference (NAACL-HLT)*.

Idan Szpektor, Hristo Tanev, Ido Dagan, and Bonaventura Coppola. 2004. Scaling web-based acquisition of entailment relations. In *Proceedings of the Conference on Empirical Methods in Natural Language Processing (EMNLP 2004)*.

Yalmip. 2011. http://users.isy.liu.se/johanl/yalmip.

Hui Yang and Jamie Callan. 2008. Ontology generation for large email collections. In *Proceedings of the 8th National Conference on Digital Government Research (Dg.O 2008)*.

Hui Yang and Jamie Callan. 2009. A metric-based framework for automatic taxonomy induction. In *Proceedings of the 47th Annual Meeting for the Association for Computational Linguistics (ACL 2009)*.

Liu Yang. 2006. Distance metric learning: A comprehensive survey. http://www.cs.cmu.edu/~liuy/frame_survey_v2.pdf.

Ka-Ping Yee, Kirsten Swearingen, Kevin Li, and Marti Hearst. 2003. Faceted metadata for image search and browsing. In *Human factors in computing systems*. ACM.

Besting the Quiz Master: Crowdsourcing Incremental Classification Games

Jordan Boyd-Graber
iSchool and UMIACS
University of Maryland
jbg@umiacs.umd.edu

Brianna Satinoff, He He, and Hal Daumé III
Department of Computer Science
University of Maryland
{bsonrisa, hhe, hal}@cs.umd.edu

Abstract

Cost-sensitive classification, where the *features* used in machine learning tasks have a cost, has been explored as a means of balancing knowledge against the expense of incrementally obtaining new features. We introduce a setting where humans engage in classification with incrementally revealed features: the collegiate trivia circuit. By providing the community with a web-based system to practice, we collected tens of thousands of implicit word-by-word ratings of how useful features are for eliciting correct answers. Observing humans' classification process, we improve the performance of a state-of-the art classifier. We also use the dataset to evaluate a system to compete in the incremental classification task through a reduction of reinforcement learning to classification. Our system learns **when** to answer a question, performing better than baselines and most human players.

1 Introduction

A typical machine learning task takes as input a set of features and learns a mapping from features to a label. In such a setting, the objective is to minimize the error of the mapping from features to labels. We call this traditional setting, where all of the features are consumed, *rapacious* machine learning.[1]

This not how humans approach the same task. They do not exhaustively consider every feature. After a certain point, a human has made a decision and no longer needs additional features. Even indefatigable computers cannot always exhaustively consider every feature. This is because the result is time sensitive, such as in interactive systems, or because processing time is limited by the sheer quantity of data, as in sifting e-mail for spam (Pujara et al., 2011). In such settings, often the best solution is incremental: allow a decision to be made without seeing all of an instance's features. We discuss the incremental classification framework in Section 2.

Our understanding of how humans conduct incremental classification is limited. This is because complicating an already difficult annotation task is often an unwise tradeoff. Instead, we adapt a real world setting where humans are already engaging (eagerly) in incremental classification—trivia games—and develop a cheap, easy method for capturing human incremental classification judgments.

After qualitatively examining how humans conduct incremental classification (Section 3), we show that knowledge of a human's incremental classification process improves state-of-the-art *rapacious* classification (Section 4). Having established that these data contain an interesting signal, we build Bayesian models that, when embedded in a Markov decision process, can engage in effective incremental classification (Section 5), and develop new hierarchical models combining local and thematic content to better capture the underlying content (Section 7). Finally, we conclude in Section 8 and discuss extensions to other problem areas.

2 Incremental Classification

In this section, we discuss previous approaches that explore how much *effort* or resources a classifier needs to come to a decision, a problem not as thoroughly examined as the question of whether the decision is right or not.[2] Incremental classification is

[1] Earlier drafts called this "batch" machine learning, which confused the distinction between batch and online learning. We gladly adopt "rapacious" to make this distinction clearer and to cast traditional machine learning—that always examines all features—as a resource hungry approach.

[2] When have an *externally* interrupted feature stream, the setting is called "any time" (Boddy and Dean, 1989; Horsch and Poole, 1998). Like "budgeted" algorithms (Wang et al., 2010), these are distinct but related problems.

not equivalent to *missing* features, which have been studied at training time (Cesa-Bianchi et al., 2011), test time (Saar-Tsechansky and Provost, 2007), and in an online setting (Rostamizadeh et al., 2011). In contrast, incremental classification allows the learner to decide whether to acquire additional features.

A common paradigm for incremental classification is to view the problem as a Markov decision process (MDP) (Zubek and Dietterich, 2002). The incremental classifier can either request an additional feature or render a classification decision (Chai et al., 2004; Ji and Carin, 2007; Melville et al., 2005), choosing its actions to minimize a known cost function. Here, we assume that the *environment* chooses a feature in contrast to a learner, as in some active learning settings (Settles, 2011). In Section 5, we use a MDP to decide whether additional features need to be processed in our application of incremental classification to a trivia game.

2.1 Trivia as Incremental Classification

A real-life setting where humans classify documents incrementally is quiz bowl, an academic competition between schools in English-speaking countries; hundreds of teams compete in dozens of tournaments each year (Jennings, 2006). Note the distinction between quiz bowl and Jeopardy, a recent application area (Ferrucci et al., 2010). While Jeopardy also uses signaling devices, these are only usable *after a question is completed* (interrupting Jeopardy's questions would make for bad television). Thus, Jeopardy is *rapacious* classification followed by a race to see—among those who know the answer—who can punch a button first. Moreover, buzzes *before* the question's end are penalized.

Two teams listen to the same question.[3] In this context, a question is a series of clues (features) referring to the same entity (for an example question, see Figure 1). We assume a fixed feature ordering for a test sequence (i.e., you cannot request specific features). Teams interrupt the question at any point by "buzzing in"; if the answer is correct, the team gets points and the next question is read. Otherwise, the team loses points and the other team can answer.

[3]Called a "starter" (UK) or "tossup" (US) in the lingo, as it often is followed by a "bonus" given to the team that answers the starter; here we only concern ourselves with tossups answerable by both teams.

After losing a race for the Senate, this politician edited the Omaha World-Herald. This man resigned ◇ from one of his posts when the President sent a letter to Germany protesting the Lusitania ◇ sinking, and ◇ he advocated ◇ coining ◇ silver at a 16 ◇ to 1 ◇◇ rate ◇ compared to ◇ gold. He was the ◇ three-time Democratic ◇ Party ◇◇◇ nominee for ◇ President ◇ but ◇◇◇ lost to McKinley twice ◇◇ and then Taft, although he served as Secretary of State ◇◇ under Woodrow Wilson, ◇ and he later argued ◇ against Clarence Darrow ◇ in the Scopes ◇◇ Monkey Trial. For ten points, name this ◇ man who famously declared that "we shall not be crucified on a Cross of ◇ Gold". ◇

Figure 1: Quiz bowl question on William Jennings Bryan, a late nineteenth century American politician; obscure clues are at the beginning while more accessible clues are at the end. Words (excluding stop words) are shaded based on the number of times the word triggered a buzz from any player who answered the question (darker means more buzzes; buzzes contribute to the shading of the previous five words). Diamonds (◇) indicate buzz positions.

The answers to quiz bowl questions are well-known entities (e.g., scientific laws, people, battles, books, characters, etc.), so the answer space is relatively limited; there are no open-ended questions of the form "why is the sky blue?" However, there are no multiple choice questions—as there are in Who Wants to Be a Millionaire (Lam et al., 2003)—or structural constraints—as there are in crossword puzzles (Littman et al., 2002).

Now that we introduced the concepts of questions, answers, and buzzes, we pause briefly to define them more formally and explicitly connect to machine learning. In the sequel, we will refer to: **questions**, sequences of words (tokens) associated with a single answer; **features**, inputs used for decisions (derived from the tokens in a question); **labels**, a question's correct response; **answers**, the responses (either correct or incorrect) provided; and **buzzes**, positions in a question where users halted the stream of features and gave an answer.

Quiz bowl is not a typical problem domain for natural language processing; why should we care about it? First, it is a real-world instance of incremental classification that happens hundreds of thousands of times most weekends. Second, it is a classification problem intricately intertwined with core computational linguistics problems such as anaphora resolution, online sentence processing, and semantic priming. Finally, quiz bowl's inherent fun makes it easy to acquire human responses, as we describe in the next section.

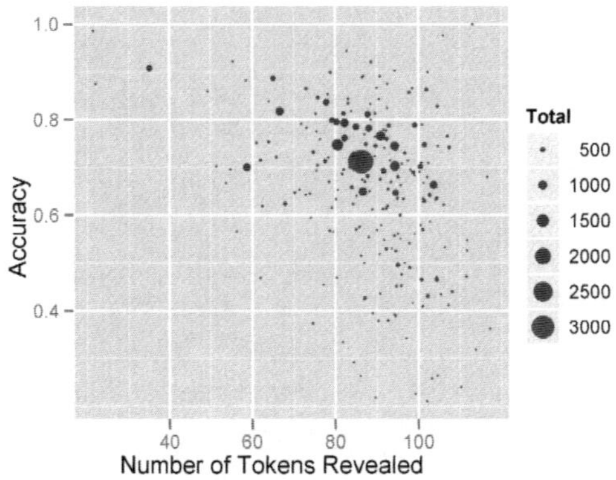

Figure 2: Users plotted based on *accuracy* vs. the *number of tokens*—on average—the user took to give an answer. Dot size and colour represent the *total* number of questions answered. Users that answered questions later in the question had higher accuracy. However, there were users that were able to answer questions relatively early without sacrificing accuracy.

3 Getting a Buzz through Crowdsourcing

We built a corpus with 37,225 quiz bowl questions with 25,498 distinct labels from 121 tournaments written for tournaments between 1999 and 2010. We created a webapp[4] that simulates the experience of playing quiz bowl. Text is incrementally revealed (at a pace adjustable by the user) until users press the space bar to "buzz". Users then answer, and the webapp judges correctness using a string matching algorithm. Players can override the automatic check if the system mistakenly judged an answer incorrect. Answers of previous users are displayed after answering a question; this enhances the sense of community and keeps users honest (e.g., it's okay to say that "wj bryan" is an acceptable answer for the label "william jennings bryan", but "asdf" is not). We did not see examples of nonsense answers from malicious users; in contrast, users were stricter than we expected, perhaps because protesting required effort.

To collect a set of labels with many buzzes, we focused on the 1186 labels with more than four distinct questions. Thus, we shuffled the labels into a canonical order shown to all users (e.g., everyone saw a question on "Jonathan Swift" and then a question on "William Jennings Bryan", but because these labels have many questions the specific questions

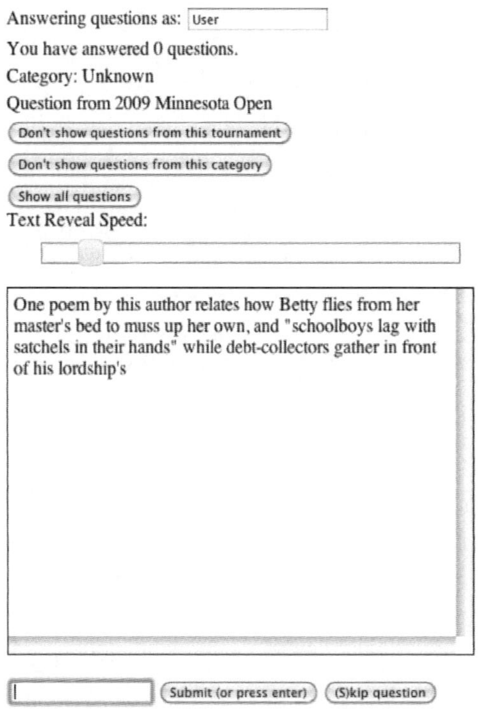

Figure 3: A screenshot of the webapp used to collect data. Users see a question revealed one word at a time. They signal buzzes by clicking on the answer button and input an answer.

were different for each user). Participants were eager to answer questions; over 7000 questions were answered in the first day, and over 43000 questions were answered in two weeks by 461 users.

To represent a "buzz", we define a function $b(q, f)$ ("b" for buzz) as the number of times that feature f occurred in question q at most five tokens before a user correctly buzzed on that question.[5] Aggregating buzzes across questions (summing over q) shows different features useful for eliciting a buzz (Figure 4(a)). Some features coarsely identify the type of answer sought, e.g., "author", "opera", "city", "war", or "god". Other features are relational, connecting the answer to other clues, e.g., "namesake", "defeated", "husband", or "wrote". The set of buzzes help narrow which words are important for matching a question to its answer; for an example, see how the word cloud for all of the buzzes on "Wuthering

[4]Play online or download the datasets at `http://umiacs.umd.edu/~jbg/qb`.

[5]This window was chosen qualitatively by examining the patterns of buzzes; this is person-dependent, based on reading comprehension, reaction time, and what reveal speed the user chose. We leave explicitly modeling this for future work.

(a) Buzzes over all Questions (b) Wuthering Heights Question Text (c) Buzzes on Wuthering Heights

Figure 4: Word clouds representing all words that were a part of a buzz (a), the original text appearing in seven questions on the book "Wuthering Heights" by Emily Brönte (b), and the buzzes of users on those questions (c). The buzzes reflect what users remember about the work and is more focused than the complete question text.

Heights" (Figure 4(c)) is much more focused than the word cloud for *all* of the words from the questions with that label (Figure 4(b)).

4 Buzzes Reveal Useful Features

If we restrict ourselves to a finite set of labels, the process of answering questions is a multiclass classification problem. In this section, we show that information gleaned from humans making a similar decision can help improve rapacious machine learning classification. This validates that our crowdsourcing technique is gathering useful information.

We used a state-of-the-art maximum entropy classification model, MEGAM (Daumé III, 2004), that accepts a per-class mean prior for feature weights and applied MEGAM to the 200 most frequent labels (11,663 questions, a third of the dataset). The prior mean of the feature weight is a convenient, simple way to incorporate human feature utility; apart from the mean, all default options are used.

Specifying the prior requires us to specify a weight for each pair of label and feature. The weight combines buzz information (described in Section 3) and tf-idf (Salton, 1968). The tf-idf value is computed by treating the training set of questions with the same label as a single document.

Buzzes and tf-idf information were combined into the prior μ for label a and feature f as $\mu_{a,f} =$

$$\left[\beta b(a,f) + \alpha \mathbb{I}\left[b(a,f) > 0\right] + \gamma\right] \text{tf-idf}(a,f). \quad (1)$$

We describe our weight strategies in increasing order of human knowledge. If α, β, and γ are zero, this is a naïve **zero** prior. If γ only is nonzero, this is a linear transformation of features' **tf-idf**. If only α is nonzero, this is a linear transformation of buzzed words' tf-idf weights. If only β is non-zero, *number* of buzzes is now a linear multiplier of the tf-idf weight (**buzz-linear**). Finally we allow unbuzzed words to have a separate linear transformation if both β and γ are non-zero (**buzz-tier**).

Weighting	α	β	γ	Error
zero	-	-	-	0.37
tf-idf	-	-	3.5	0.14
buzz-binary	7.1	-	-	0.10
buzz-linear	-	1.5	-	0.16
buzz-tier	-	1.1	0.1	**0.09**

Table 1: Classification error of a rapacious classifier able to draw on human incremental classification. The best weighting scheme for each dataset is in **bold**. Missing parameter values (-) mean that the parameter is fixed to zero for that weighting scheme.

Grid search (width of 0.1) on development set error was used to set parameters. Table 1 shows test error for weighting schemes and demonstrates that adding human information as a prior improves classification error, leading to a 36% error reduction over tf-idf alone. While not directly comparable (this classifier is rapacious, not incremental, and has a predefined answer space), the average user had an error rate of 16.7%.

5 Building an Incremental Classifier

In the previous section we improved rapacious classification using humans' incremental classification. A more interesting problem is how to compete against humans in incremental classification. While in the previous section we used human data for a *training* set, here we use human data as an *evaluation* set. Doing so requires us to formulate an incremental representation of the contents of questions and to learn a strategy to decide when to buzz.

Because this is the first machine learning algorithm for quiz bowl, we attempt to provide reasonable rapacious baselines and compare against our new strategies. We believe that our attempts represent a reasonable explanation of the problem space, but additional improvements could improve performance, as discussed in Section 8.

A common way to represent state-dependent strategies is via a Markov decision process (MDP). The most salient component of a MDP is the policy, i.e., a mapping from the state space to an action. In our context, a state is a sequence of (thus far revealed) tokens, and the action is whether to buzz or not. To learn a policy, we use a standard reinforcement learning technique (Langford and Zadrozny, 2005; Abbeel and Ng, 2004; Syed et al., 2008): given a representation of the state space, learn a classifier that can map from a state to an action. This is also a common paradigm for other incremental tasks, e.g., shift-reduce parsing (Nivre, 2008).

Given examples of the correct answer given a configuration of the state space, we can learn a MDP without explicitly representing the reward function. In this section, we define our method of defining actions and our representation of the state space.

5.1 Action Space

We assume that there are only two possible actions: buzz now or wait. An alternative would be a more expressive action space (e.g., an action for every possible answer). However, this conflates the question of *when* to buzz with *what* to answer. Instead, we call the distinct component that provides *what to answer* the **content model**. We describe an initial content model in Section 5.2, below, and improve the models further in Section 7. For the moment, assume that a content model maintains a posterior distribution over labels and when needed can provide its best guess (e.g., given the features seen, the best answer is "William Jennings Bryan").

Given the action space, we need to specify where examples of state space and action come from. In the language of classification, we need to provide (x, y) pairs to learn a mapping $x \mapsto y$. The classifier attempts to learn that action y is ("buzz") in all states where the content model gave a correct response given state x. Negative examples ("wait") are applied to states where the content model gave a wrong answer. Every token in our training set corresponds to a classification example; both states are prevalent enough that we do not to explicitly need to address class imbalance. This resembles approaches that merge different classifiers (Riedel et al., 2011) or attempt to estimate confidence of models (Blatz et al., 2004). However, here we use *partial* observations.

This is a simplification of the problem and corresponds to a strategy of "buzz as soon as you know the answer", ignoring all other factors. While reasonable, this is not always optimal. For example, if you know your opponent is unlikely to answer a question, it is better to wait until you are more confident. Incorrect answers might also help your opponent, e.g., by eliminating an incorrect answer. Moreover, strategies in a game setting (rather than a single question) are more complicated. For example, if a right answer is worth $+10$ points and the penalty for an incorrect question is -5, then a team leading by 15 points on the last question should never attempt to answer. Investigating such gameplay strategies would require a "roll out" of game states (Tesauro and Galperin, 1996) to explore the efficacy of such strategies. While interesting, we leave these issues to future work.

We also investigated learning a policy directly from users' buzzes directly (Abbeel and Ng, 2004), but this performed poorly because the content model is incompatible with the players' abilities and the high variation in players' ability and styles (compare Figure 2).

5.2 State Space

Recall that our goal is to learn a classifier that maps states to actions; above, we defined the action space (the classifier's output) but not the state space, the classifier's input. The straightforward parameterization of the state space would be all of the words that have been revealed. However, such a feature set is very sparse.

We use three components to form the state space: what information has been observed, what the content model believes is the correct answer, how confident the content model is, and whether the content model's confidence is changing. We describe each in more detail below.

Text In addition to the obvious, sparse parameterization that contains all of the features thus far observed, we also include the total number of tokens revealed and whether the phrase "for ten points" has appeared.[6]

Guess An additional feature that we used to represent the state space is the current guess of the content model; i.e., the argmax of the posterior.

Posterior The posterior feature (**Pos** for short) captures the shape of the posterior distribution: the probability of the current guess (the max of the posterior), the difference between the top two probabilities and the probabilities associated with the fifteen most probable labels under the posterior.

Change As features are revealed, there is often a rapid transition from a state of confusion—when there are many candidates with no clear best choice—to a state of clarity with the posterior pointing to only one probable label. To capture when this happens, we add a binary feature to reflect when the best guess has changed when a single feature has been revealed.

Other Features We thought that other features would be useful. While useful on their own, no features that we tried were useful when the content model's **posterior** was also used as a feature. Features that we attempted to use were: a logistic regression model attempting to capture the probability that any player would answer (Silver et al., 2008), a regression predicting how many individuals would buzz in the next n words, the year the question was written, the category of the question, etc.

5.3 Naïve Content Model

The action space is only deciding *when* to answer, having abdicated responsibility for *what* to answer. So where does do the answers come from? We assume that at any point we can ask "what is the highest probability label given my current feature observations?" We call the component of our model that answers this question the *content model*.

Our first content model is a naïve Bayes model (Lewis, 1998) trained over a text collection. This generative model assumes labels for questions come from a multinomial distribution $\phi \sim \text{Dir}(\alpha)$ and assumes that label l has a word distribution $\theta_l \sim \text{Dir}(\lambda)$. Each question n has a label z_n and its words are generated from θ_{z_n}. Given labeled observations, we use the *maximum a posteriori* (MAP) estimate of θ_l.

Why use a generative model when a discriminative classifier could use a richer feature space? The most important reason is that, by definition, it makes sense to ask a generative model the probability of a label given a *partial* observation; such a question is not well-formed for discriminative models, which expect a complete feature set. Another important consideration is that generative models can predict future, unrevealed features (Chai et al., 2004); however, we do not make use of that capability here.

In addition to providing our answers, the content model also provides an additional, critically important feature for our state space: its **posterior** (**pos** for short) probability. With every revealed feature, the content model updates its posterior distribution over labels given that t tokens have been revealed in question n,

$$p(z_n \mid w_1 \dots w_t, \phi, \boldsymbol{\theta}). \tag{2}$$

To train our naïve Bayes model, we semi-automatically associate labels with a Wikipedia page (correcting mistakes manually) and then form the MAP estimate of the class multinomial distribution from the Wikipedia page's text. We did this for the 1065 labels that had at least three human answers, excluding ambiguous labels associated with multiple concepts (e.g., "europa", "steppenwolf", "georgia", "paris", and "v").

Features were taken to be the 25,000 most frequent tokens and bigrams[7] that were not stop words; features were extracted from the Wikipedia text in the same manner as from the question tokens.[8]

After demonstrating our ability to learn an incremental classifier using this simple content model, we extend the content model to capture local context and correlations between similar labels in Section 7.

[6] The phrase "for ten points" (abbreviated FTP) appears in all quiz bowl questions to signal the question's last sentence or clause. It is a signal to answer soon, as the final "giveaway" clue is next.

[7] We used NLTK (Loper and Bird, 2002) to filter stop words and we used a χ^2 test to identify bigrams with that rejected the null hypothesis at the 0.01 level.

[8] The Dirichlet scaling parameter λ was set to 10,000 given our relatively large vocabulary (25,000) and to not penalize a label's posterior probability if there were unseen features; this corresponds to a pseudocount of 0.4. α was set to 1.0.

6 Pitting the Algorithm Against Humans

With a state space and a policy, we now have all the necessary ingredients to have our algorithm compete against humans. Classification, which allows us to learn a policy, was done using the default settings of LIBLINEAR (Fan et al., 2008). To determine where the algorithm buzzes, we provide a sequence of state spaces until the policy classifier determines that it is time to buzz.

We simulate competition by taking the human answers and buzzes as a given and ask our algorithm (independently) to provide its decision on when to buzz on a test set. We compare the two buzz positions. If the algorithm buzzed earlier with the right answer, we consider it to have "won" the question; equivalently, if the algorithm buzzed later, we consider it to have "lost" that question. Ties are rare (less than 1% of cases), as the algorithm had significantly different behavior from humans; in the case where there was a tie, ties were broken in favor of the machine.

Because we have a large, diverse population answering questions, we need aggregate measures of human performance to get a comprehensive view of algorithm performance. We use the following metrics for each question in the test set:

- **best**: the earliest *anyone* buzzed correctly
- **median**: the first buzz after 50% of human buzzes
- **mean**: for each recorded buzz compute a reward and we average over all rewards

We compare the algorithm against baseline strategies:

- **rap** The rapacious strategy waits until the end of the question and answers the best answer possible.
- **ftp** Waiting until when "for 10 points" is said, then giving the best answer possible.
- **index**$_n$ Waiting until the first feature after the nth token has been processed, then giving the best answer possible. The indices were chosen as the quartiles for question length (by convention, most questions are of similar length).

We compare these baselines against policies that decide *when* to buzz based on the state.

Recall that the non-oracle algorithms were unaware of the true reward function. To best simulate conventional quiz bowl settings, a correct answer was $+10$ and the incorrect answer was -5. The full payoff matrix for the computer is shown in Table 2. Cases where the opponent buzzes first but is wrong are equivalent to rapacious classification, as there is no longer any incentive to answer early. Thus we exclude such situations (Outcomes 3, 5, 6 in Table 2) from the dataset to focus on the challenge of processing clues incrementally.

	Computer	Human	Payoff
1	first and wrong	right	-15
2	—	first and correct	-10
3	first and wrong	wrong	-5
4	first and correct	—	$+10$
5	wrong	first and wrong	$+5$
6	right	first and wrong	$+15$

Table 2: Payoff matrix (from the computer's perspective) for when agents "buzz" during a question. To focus on incremental classification, we exclude instances where the human interrupts with an *incorrect* answer, as after an opponent eliminates themselves, the answering reduces to rapacious classification.

Table 3 shows the algorithm did much better when it had access to the posterior. While incremental algorithms outperform rapacious baselines, they lose to humans. Against the median and average players, they lose between three and four points per question, and nearly twice that against the best players.

Although the content model is simple, this poor performance is not from the content model never producing the correct answer. To see this, we also computed the optimal actions that could be executed. We called this strategy the oracle strategy; it was able to consistently win against its opponents. Thus, while the content model was able to come up with correct answers often enough to on average win against opponents (even the best human players), we were unable to consistently learn winning policies.

There are two ways to solve this problem: create deeper, more nuanced policies (or the features that feed into them) or refine content models that provide the signal needed for our policies to make sound decisions. We chose to refine the content model, as we felt we had added all of the obvious features for learning effective policies.

7 Expanding the Content Model

When we asked quiz bowlers how they answer questions, they said that they first determine the category

Strategy	Features	Mean	Best	Median	Index
Classify	text	-8.72	-10.04	-6.50	40.36
	+guess	-5.71	-8.40	-3.95	66.02
	+pos	-4.13	-7.56	-2.70	67.97
	+change	**-4.02**	**-7.41**	**-2.63**	77.33
Oracle	text	3.36	0.61	4.35	49.90
Rapacious Baseline	all	-6.61	-9.03	-4.42	100.19
	ftp	-5.22	-8.62	-4.23	88.65
	index_{30}	-7.89	-8.71	-6.41	32.23
	index_{60}	-5.16	**-7.56**	-3.71	61.90
	index_{90}	**-5.02**	-8.62	**-3.50**	87.13

Table 3: Performance of strategies against users. The human scoring columns show the average points per question (positive means winning on average, negative means losing on average) that the algorithm would expect to accumulate per question versus each human amalgam metric. The index column notes the average index of the token when the strategy chose to buzz.

of a question, which substantially narrows the answer space. Ideally, the content model should conduct the same calculus—if a question seems to be about mathematics, all answers related with mathematics should be more likely in the posterior. This was consistent with our error analysis; many errors were non-sensical (e.g., answering "entropy" for "Johannes Brahms", when an answer such as "Robert Schumann", another composer, would be better).

In addition, assuming independence between features given a label causes us to ignore potentially informative multiword expressions such as quotations, titles, or dates. Adding a language model to our content model allows us to capture some of these phenomena.

To create a model that jointly models categories and local context, we propose the following model:

1. Draw a distribution over labels $\phi \sim \text{Dir}(\alpha)$
2. Draw a background distribution over words $\theta_0 \sim \text{Dir}(\lambda_0 \vec{1})$
   (a) For each category c of questions, draw a distribution over words $\theta_c \sim \text{Dir}(\lambda_1 \theta_0)$.
      i. For each label l in category c, draw a distribution over words $\theta_{l,c} \sim \text{Dir}(\lambda_2 \theta_c)$
         A. For each type v, draw a bigram distribution $\theta_{l,c,v} \sim \text{Dir}(\lambda_3 \theta_{l,c})$
3. Draw a distribution over labels $\phi \sim \text{Dir}(\alpha)$.
4. For each question with category c and N words, draw answer $l \sim \text{Mult}(\phi)$:
   (a) Assume $w_0 \equiv \text{START}$
   (b) Draw $w_n \sim \text{Mult}(\theta_{l,c,w_{n-1}})$ for $n \in \{1 \ldots N\}$

This creates a language model over categories, labels, and observed words (we use "words" loosely, as bigrams replace some word pairs). By constructing the word distributions using hierarchical distributions based on domain and ngrams (a much simpler parametric version of more elaborate methods (Wood and Teh, 2009)), we can share statistical strength across related contexts. We assume that labels are (only) associated with their majority category as seen in our training data and that category assignments are observed. All scaling parameters λ were set to 10,000, α was 1.0, and the vocabulary was still 25,000.

We used the maximal seating assignment (Wallach, 2008) for propagating counts through the Dirichlet hierarchy. Thus, if the word v appeared $B_{l,u,v}$ times in label l following a preceding word u, $S_{l,v}$ times in label l, $T_{c,v}$ times in category c, and G_v times in total, we estimate the probability of a word v appearing in label k, category t, and after word u as $p(w_n = v \,|\, \text{lab} = l, \text{cat} = c, w_{n-1} = u; \vec{\lambda}) =$

$$\frac{B_{l,u,v} + \lambda_3 \frac{S_{l,v} + \lambda_2 \frac{T_{c,v} + \lambda_1 \frac{G_v + \lambda_0 / V}{G_{\cdot} + \lambda_0}}{T_{c,\cdot} + \lambda_2}}{S_{l,\cdot} + \lambda_2}}{B_{l,u,\cdot} + \lambda_3}, \tag{3}$$

where we use $\cdot$ to represent marginalization, e.g. $T_{c,\cdot} = \sum_{v'} T_{c,v'}$. As with naïve Bayes, Bayes' rule provides posterior label probabilities (Equation 2).

We compare the naïve model with models that capture more of the content in the text in Table 4; these results also include intermediate models between naïve Bayes and the full content model: "cat" (omit 2.a.i.A) and "bigram" (omit 2.a). These models perform much better than the naïve Bayes models seen in Table 3. They are about even against the mean and median players and lose four points per question against top players.

7.1 Qualitative Analysis

In this section, we explore what defects are preventing the model presented here from competing with top players, exposing challenges in reinforcement learning, interpreting pragmatic cues, and large data. Three examples of failures of the model are in Figure 5. This model is the best performing model of the previous section.

Too Slow The first example is a question on Maurice Ravel, a French composer known for *Boléro*. The question leads off with Ravel's orchestral version of

Strategy	Model	Mean	Best	Median	Index
Classify	naïve	-4.02	-7.41	-2.63	77.33
	cat	-1.69	-5.22	0.12	67.97
	bigram	-3.80	-7.66	-2.51	78.69
	bgrm+cat	**-0.86**	**-4.46**	**0.83**	63.42
Oracle	naive	3.36	0.61	4.35	49.90
	cat	4.48	1.64	5.47	47.88
	bigram	3.58	0.87	4.61	49.34
	bgrm+cat	**4.67**	**1.99**	**5.74**	46.49

Table 4: As in Table 3, performance of strategies against users, but with enhanced content models. Modeling both bigrams and label categories improves overall performance.

Mussorgsky's piano piece "Pictures at an Exhibition". Based on that evidence, the algorithm considers "Pictures at an Exhibition" the most likely but does not yet buzz. When it receives enough information to be sure about the correct answer, over half of the players had already buzzed. Correcting this problem would require a more aggressive strategy, perhaps incorporating the identity of the opponent or estimating the difficulty of the question.

Mislead by the Content Model The second example is a question on Enrico Fermi, an Italian-American physicist. The first clues are about magnetic fields near a Fermi surface, which causes the content model to view "magnetic field" as the most likely answer. The question's text, however, has pragmatic cues "this man" and "this Italian" which would have ruled out the abstract answer "magnetic field". Correcting this would require a model that jointly models content and bigrams (Hardisty et al., 2010), has a coreference system as its content model (Haghighi and Klein, 2007), or determines the correct question type (Moldovan et al., 2000).

Insufficient Data The third example is where our approach had no chance. The question is a very difficult question about George Washington, America's first president. As a sign of its difficulty, only half the players answered correctly, and only near the end of the question. The question concerns lesser known episodes from Washington's life, including a mistress caught in the elements. To the content model, of the several hypotheses it considers, the closest match it can find is "Yasunari Kawabata", who wrote the novel *Snow Country*, whose plot matches some of these keywords. To answer these types of question,

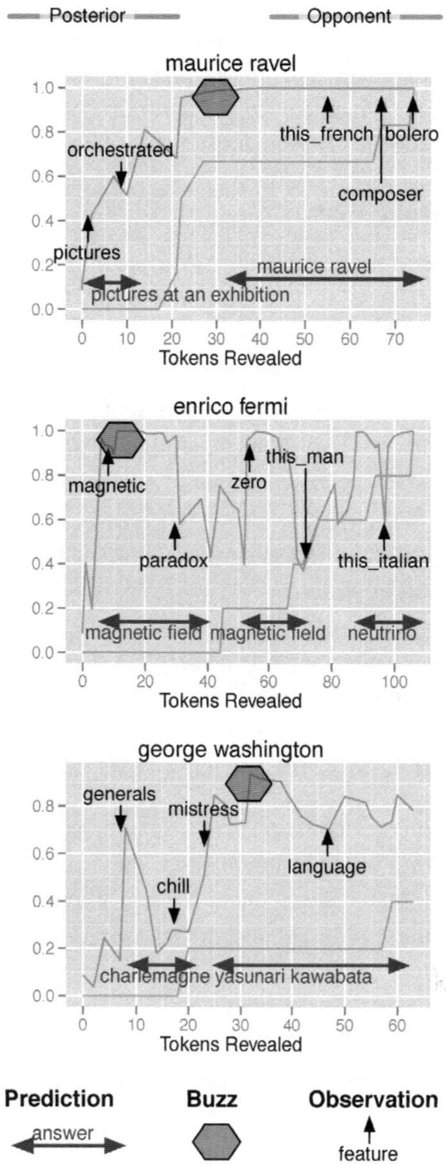

Figure 5: Three questions where our algorithm performed poorly. It gets "Maurice Ravel" (top) right but only after over half the humans had answered correctly (i.e., the buzz's hexagon appears when the cyan line is above 0.6); on "Enrico Fermi" (middle) it confuses the correct type of answer (person vs. concept); on "George Washington" (bottom) it lacks information to answer correctly. Lines represent the current estimate posterior probability of the answer (red) and the proportion of opponents who have answered the question correctly (cyan). The label of each of the three questions is above each chart. Words are in black with arrows and arrows, and the current argmax answer is at the bottom of the graph in red. The buzz location is the hexagon.

the repository used to train the content model would have to be orders of magnitude larger to be able to link the disparate clues in the question to a consistent target. The content model would also benefit from weighting later (more informative) features higher.

7.2 Assumptions

We have made assumptions to solve a problem that is subtly different that the game of quiz bowl that a human would play. Some of these were simplifying assumptions, such as our assumption that the algorithm has a closed set of possible answers (Section 5.3). Even with this advantage, the algorithm is unable to compete with human players, who choose answers from an unbounded set. On the other hand, to focus on incremental classification, we idealized our human opponents so that they never give incorrect answers (Section 6). This causes our estimates of our performance to be lower than they would be against real players.

8 Conclusion and Future Work

We make three contributions. First, we introduce a new setting for exploring the problem of incremental classification: trivia games. This problem is intrinsically interesting because of its varied topics and competitive elements, has a great quantity of standardized, machine-readable data, and also has the boon of being cheaply and easily annotated. We took advantage of that ease and created a framework for quickly and efficiently gathering examples of humans doing incremental classification.

There are other potential uses for the dataset; the progression of clues from obscure nuggets to could help determine how "known" a particular aspect of an entity is (e.g., that William Jennings Bryant gave the "Cross of Gold" speech is better known his resignation after the Lusitania sinking, Figure 1). Which could be used in educational settings (Smith et al., 2008) or summarization (Das and Martins, 2007).

The second contribution shows that humans' incremental classification improves state-of-the-art rapacious classification algorithms. While other frameworks (Zaidan et al., 2008) have been proposed to incorporate user clues about features, the system described here provides analogous features without the need for explicit post-hoc reflection, has faster annotation throughput, and is much cheaper.

The problem of answering quiz bowl questions is itself a challenging task that combines issues from language modeling, large data, coreference, and reinforcement learning. While we do not address all of these problems, our third contribution is a system that learns a policy in a MDP for incremental classification even in very large state spaces; it can successfully compete with skilled human players.

Incorporating richer content models is one of our next steps. This would allow us to move beyond the closed-set model and use a more general coreference model (Haghighi and Klein, 2007) for identifying answers and broader corpora for training. In addition, using larger corpora would allow us to have more comprehensive doubly-hierarchical language models (Wood and Teh, 2009). We are also interested in adding richer models of opponents to the state space that would adaptively adjust strategies as it learned more about the strengths and weaknesses of its opponent (Waugh et al., 2011).

Further afield, our presentation of sentences closely resembles paradigms for cognitive experiments in linguistics (Thibadeau et al., 1982) but are much cheaper to conduct. If online processing effects (Levy et al., 2008; Levy, 2011) could be observed in buzzing behavior; e.g., if a confusingly worded phrase depresses buzzing probability, it could help validate cognitively-inspired models of online sentence processing.

Incremental classification is a natural problem, both for humans and resource-limited machines. While our data set is trivial (in a good sense), learning how humans process data and make decisions in a cheap, easy crowdsourced application can help us apply new algorithms to improve performance in settings where features aren't free, either because of computational or annotation cost.

Acknowledgments

We thank the many players who played our online quiz bowl to provide our data (and hopefully had fun doing so) and Carlo Angiuli, Arnav Moudgil, and Jerry Vinokurov for providing access to quiz bowl questions. This research was supported by NSF grant #1018625. Jordan Boyd-Graber is also supported by the Army Research Laboratory through ARL Cooperative Agreement W911NF-09-2-0072. Any opinions, findings, conclusions, or recommendations expressed are the authors' and do not necessarily reflect those of the sponsors.

References

Pieter Abbeel and Andrew Y. Ng. 2004. Apprenticeship learning via inverse reinforcement learning. In *Proceedings of International Conference of Machine Learning*.

J. Blatz, E. Fitzgerald, G. Foster, S. Gandrabur, C. Goutte, A. Kulesza, A. Sanchis, and N. Ueffing. 2004. Confidence estimation for machine translation. In *Proceedings of the Association for Computational Linguistics*.

Mark Boddy and Thomas L. Dean. 1989. Solving time-dependent planning problems. In *International Joint Conference on Artificial Intelligence*, pages 979–984. Morgan Kaufmann Publishers, August.

Nicolò Cesa-Bianchi, Shai Shalev-Shwartz, and Ohad Shamir. 2011. Efficient learning with partially observed attributes. *Journal of Machine Learning Research*, 12:2857–2878.

Xiaoyong Chai, Lin Deng, Qiang Yang, and Charles X. Ling. 2004. Test-cost sensitive naive bayes classification. In *IEEE International Conference on Data Mining*.

Dipanjan Das and Andre Martins. 2007. A survey on automatic text summarization. *Engineering and Technology*, 4:192–195.

Hal Daumé III. 2004. Notes on CG and LM-BFGS optimization of logistic regression. Paper available at `http://pub.hal3.name/~daume04cg-bfgs`, implementation available at `http://hal3.name/megam/`.

Rong-En Fan, Kai-Wei Chang, Cho-Jui Hsieh, Xiang-Rui Wang, and Chih-Jen Lin. 2008. LIBLINEAR: A library for large linear classification. *Journal of Machine Learning Research*, 9:1871–1874.

David Ferrucci, Eric Brown, Jennifer Chu-Carroll, James Fan, David Gondek, Aditya A. Kalyanpur, Adam Lally, J. William Murdock, Eric Nyberg, John Prager, Nico Schlaefer, and Chris Welty. 2010. Building Watson: An Overview of the DeepQA Project. *AI Magazine*, 31(3).

Aria Haghighi and Dan Klein. 2007. Unsupervised coreference resolution in a nonparametric bayesian model. In *Proceedings of the Association for Computational Linguistics*.

Eric Hardisty, Jordan Boyd-Graber, and Philip Resnik. 2010. Modeling perspective using adaptor grammars. In *Proceedings of Emperical Methods in Natural Language Processing*.

Michael C. Horsch and David Poole. 1998. An anytime algorithm for decision making under uncertainty. In *Proceedings of Uncertainty in Artificial Intelligence*.

Ken Jennings. 2006. *Brainiac: adventures in the curious, competitive, compulsive world of trivia buffs*. Villard.

Shihao Ji and Lawrence Carin. 2007. Cost-sensitive feature acquisition and classification. *Pattern Recognition*, 40:1474–1485, May.

Shyong K. Lam, David M. Pennock, Dan Cosley, and Steve Lawrence. 2003. 1 billion pages = 1 million dollars? mining the web to play "who wants to be a millionaire?". In *Proceedings of Uncertainty in Artificial Intelligence*.

John Langford and Bianca Zadrozny. 2005. Relating reinforcement learning performance to classification performance. In *Proceedings of International Conference of Machine Learning*.

Roger P. Levy, Florencia Reali, and Thomas L. Griffiths. 2008. Modeling the effects of memory on human online sentence processing with particle filters. In *Proceedings of Advances in Neural Information Processing Systems*.

Roger Levy. 2011. Integrating surprisal and uncertain-input models in online sentence comprehension: formal techniques and empirical results. In *Proceedings of the Association for Computational Linguistics*.

David D. Lewis. 1998. Naive (Bayes) at forty: The independence assumption in information retrieval. In Claire Nédellec and Céline Rouveirol, editors, *Proceedings of European Conference of Machine Learning*, number 1398.

Michael L. Littman, Greg A. Keim, and Noam Shazeer. 2002. A probabilistic approach to solving crossword puzzles. *Artif. Intell.*, 134(1-2):23–55, January.

Edward Loper and Steven Bird. 2002. NLTK: the natural language toolkit. In *Tools and methodologies for teaching*.

Prem Melville, Maytal Saar-Tsechansky, Foster Provost, and Raymond J. Mooney. 2005. An expected utility approach to active feature-value acquisition. In *International Conference on Data Mining*, November.

Dan Moldovan, Sanda Harabagiu, Marius Pasca, Rada Mihalcea, Roxana Girju, Richard Goodrum, and Vasile

Rus. 2000. The structure and performance of an open-domain question answering system. In *Proceedings of the Association for Computational Linguistics*.

Joakim Nivre. 2008. Algorithms for deterministic incremental dependency parsing. *Comput. Linguist.*, 34(4):513–553, December.

Jay Pujara, Hal Daume III, and Lise Getoor. 2011. Using classifier cascades for scalable e-mail classification. In *Collaboration, Electronic Messaging, Anti-Abuse and Spam Conference*, ACM International Conference Proceedings Series.

Sebastian Riedel, David McClosky, Mihai Surdeanu, Andrew McCallum, and Christopher D. Manning. 2011. Model combination for event extraction in bionlp 2011. In *Proceedings of the BioNLP Workshop*.

Afshin Rostamizadeh, Alekh Agarwal, and Peter L. Bartlett. 2011. Learning with missing features. In *Proceedings of Uncertainty in Artificial Intelligence*.

Maytal Saar-Tsechansky and Foster Provost. 2007. Handling missing values when applying classification models. *Journal of Machine Learning Research*, 8:1623–1657, December.

Gerard. Salton. 1968. *Automatic Information Organization and Retrieval.* McGraw Hill Text.

Burr Settles. 2011. Closing the loop: Fast, interactive semi-supervised annotation with queries on features and instances. In *Proceedings of Emperical Methods in Natural Language Processing*.

David Silver, Richard S. Sutton, and Martin Müller. 2008. Sample-based learning and search with permanent and transient memories. In *International Conference on Machine Learning*.

Noah A. Smith, Michael Heilman, and Rebecca Hwa. 2008. Question generation as a competitive undergraduate course project. In *Proceedings of the NSF Workshop on the Question Generation Shared Task and Evaluation Challenge*.

Umar Syed, Michael Bowling, and Robert E. Schapire. 2008. Apprenticeship learning using linear programming. In *Proceedings of International Conference of Machine Learning*.

Gerald Tesauro and Gregory R. Galperin. 1996. On-line policy improvement using monte-carlo search. In *Proceedings of Advances in Neural Information Processing Systems*.

Robert Thibadeau, Marcel A. Just, and Patricia A. Carpenter. 1982. A model of the time course and content of reading. *Cognitive Science*, 6.

Hanna M Wallach. 2008. *Structured Topic Models for Language*. Ph.D. thesis, University of Cambridge.

Lidan Wang, Donald Metzler, and Jimmy Lin. 2010. Ranking Under Temporal Constraints. In *Proceedings of the ACM International Conference on Information and Knowledge Management*.

Kevin Waugh, Brian D. Ziebart, and J. Andrew Bagnell. 2011. Computational rationalization: The inverse equilibrium problem. In *Proceedings of International Conference of Machine Learning*.

F. Wood and Y. W. Teh. 2009. A hierarchical nonparametric Bayesian approach to statistical language model domain adaptation. In *Proceedings of Artificial Intelligence and Statistics*.

Omar F. Zaidan, Jason Eisner, and Christine Piatko. 2008. Machine learning with annotator rationales to reduce annotation cost. In *Proceedings of the NIPS*2008 Workshop on Cost Sensitive Learning*.

Valentina Bayer Zubek and Thomas G. Dietterich. 2002. Pruning improves heuristic search for cost-sensitive learning. In *International Conference on Machine Learning*.

Multi-Domain Learning: When Do Domains Matter?

Mahesh Joshi
School of Computer Science
Carnegie Mellon University
Pittsburgh, PA, 15213, USA
maheshj@cs.cmu.edu

Mark Dredze
Human Language Technology Center of Excellence
Johns Hopkins University
Baltimore, Maryland 21211
mdredze@cs.jhu.edu

William W. Cohen
School of Computer Science
Carnegie Mellon University
Pittsburgh, PA, 15213, USA
wcohen@cs.cmu.edu

Carolyn P. Rosé
School of Computer Science
Carnegie Mellon University
Pittsburgh, PA, 15213, USA
cprose@cs.cmu.edu

Abstract

We present a systematic analysis of existing multi-domain learning approaches with respect to two questions. First, many multi-domain learning algorithms resemble ensemble learning algorithms. (1) Are multi-domain learning improvements the result of ensemble learning effects? Second, these algorithms are traditionally evaluated in a balanced class label setting, although in practice many multi-domain settings have domain-specific class label biases. When multi-domain learning is applied to these settings, (2) are multi-domain methods improving because they capture domain-specific class biases? An understanding of these two issues presents a clearer idea about where the field has had success in multi-domain learning, and it suggests some important open questions for improving beyond the current state of the art.

1 Introduction

Research efforts in recent years have demonstrated the importance of domains in statistical natural language processing. A mismatch between training and test domains can negatively impact system accuracy as it violates a core assumption in many machine learning algorithms: that data points are independent and identically distributed (*i.i.d.*). As a result, numerous domain adaptation methods (Chelba and Acero, 2004; Daumé III and Marcu, 2006; Blitzer et al., 2007) target settings with a training set from one domain and a test set from another.

Often times the training set itself violates the *i.i.d.* assumption and contains multiple domains. In this case, training a single model obscures domain distinctions, and separating the dataset by domains reduces training data. Instead, multi-domain learning (MDL) can take advantage of these domain labels to improve learning (Daumé III, 2007; Dredze and Crammer, 2008; Arnold et al., 2008; Finkel and Manning, 2009; Zhang and Yeung, 2010; Saha et al., 2011). One such example is sentiment classification of product reviews. Training data is available from many product categories and while all data should be used to learn a model, there are important differences between the categories (Blitzer et al., 2007)[1].

While much prior research has shown improvements using MDL, this paper explores what properties of an MDL setting matter. Are previous improvements from MDL algorithms discovering important distinctions between features in different domains, as we would hope, or are other factors contributing to learning success? The key question of this paper is: when do domains matter?

Towards this goal we explore two issues. First, we explore the question of whether domain distinctions are used by existing MDL algorithms in meaningful ways. While differences in feature behaviors between domains will hurt performance (Blitzer et al., 2008; Ben-David et al., 2009), it is not clear if the improvements in MDL algorithms can be attributed to correcting these errors, or whether they are benefiting from something else. In particular, there are many similarities between MDL and ensemble methods, with connections to instance bag-

[1] Blitzer et al. (2007) do not consider the MDL setup, they consider a single source domain, and a single target domain, with little or no labeled data available for the target domain.

ging, feature bagging and classifier combination. It may be that gains in MDL are the usual ensemble learning improvements.

Second, one simple way in which domains can change is the distribution of the prior over the labels. For example, reviews of some products may be more positive on average than reviews of other product types. Simply capturing this bias may account for significant gains in accuracy, even though nothing is learned about the behavior of domain-specific features. Most prior work considers datasets with balanced labels. However, in real world applications, where labels may be biased toward some values, gains from MDL could be attributed to simply modeling domain-specific bias. A practical advantage of such a result is ease of implementation and the ability to scale to many domains.

Overall, irrespective of the answers to these questions, a better understanding of the performance of existing MDL algorithms in different settings will provide intuitions for improving the state of the art.

2 Multi-Domain Learning

In the multi-domain learning (MDL) setting, examples are accompanied by both a class label and a domain indicator. Examples are of the form $(\boldsymbol{x}_i, y, d_i)$, where $\boldsymbol{x}_i \in \mathbb{R}^N$, d_i is a domain indicator, $\boldsymbol{x}_i$ is drawn according to a fixed domain-specific distribution D_{d_i}, and y_i is the label (e.g. $y_i \in \{-1, +1\}$ for binary labels). Standard learning ignores d_i, but MDL uses these to improve learning accuracy.

Why should we care about the domain label? Domain differences can introduce errors in a number of ways (Ben-David et al., 2007; Ben-David et al., 2009). First, the domain-specific distributions D_{d_i} can differ such that they favor different features, i.e. $p(\boldsymbol{x})$ changes between domains. As a result, some features may only appear in one domain. This aspect of domain difference is typically the focus of unsupervised domain adaptation (Blitzer et al., 2006; Blitzer et al., 2007). Second, the features may behave differently with respect to the label in each domain, i.e. $p(y|\boldsymbol{x})$ changes between domains. As a result, a learning algorithm cannot generalize the behavior of features from one domain to another. The key idea behind many MDL algorithms is to target one or both of these properties of domain difference to improve performance.

Prior approaches to MDL can be broadly categorized into two classes. The first set of approaches (Daumé III, 2007; Dredze et al., 2008) introduce parameters to capture domain-specific behaviors while preserving features that learn domain-general behaviors. A key of these methods is that they do not explicitly model any relationship between the domains. Daumé III (2007) proposes a very simple "easy adapt" approach, which was originally proposed in the context of adapting to a specific target domain, but easily generalizes to MDL. Dredze et al. (2008) consider the problem of learning how to combine different domain-specific classifiers such that behaviors common to several domains can be captured by a shared classifier, while domain-specific behavior is still captured by the individual classifiers. We describe both of these approaches in § 3.2.

The second set of approaches to MDL introduce an explicit notion of relationship between domains. For example, Cavallanti et al. (2008) assume a fixed task relationship matrix in the context of online multi-task learning. The key assumption is that instances from two different domains are half as much related to each other as two instances from the same domain. Saha et al. (2011) improve upon the idea of simply using a fixed task relationship matrix by instead *learning* it adaptively. They derive an online algorithm for updating the task interaction matrix.

Zhang and Yeung (2010) derive a convex formulation for adaptively learning domain relationships. We describe their approach in § 3.2. Finally, Daumé III (2009) proposes a joint task clustering and multi-task/multi-domain learning setup, where instead of just learning pairwise domain relationships, a hierarchical structure among them is inferred. Hierarchical clustering of tasks is performed in a Bayesian framework, by imposing a hierarchical prior on the structure of the task relationships.

In all of these settings, the key idea is to learn both domain-specific behaviors and behaviors that generalize between (possibly related) domains.

3 Data

To support our analysis we develop several empirical experiments. We first summarize the datasets and methods that we use in our experiments, then proceed to our exploration of MDL.

3.1 Datasets

A variety of multi-domain datasets have been used for demonstrating MDL improvements. In this paper, we focus on two datasets representative of many of the properties of MDL.

Amazon (AMAZON) Our first dataset is the Multi-Domain Amazon data (version 2.0), first introduced by Blitzer et al. (2007). The task is binary sentiment classification, in which Amazon product reviews are labeled as positive or negative. Domains are defined by product categories. We select the four domains used in most studies: `books`, `dvd`, `electronics` and `kitchen appliances`.

The original dataset contained 2,000 reviews for each of the four domains, with 1,000 positive and 1,000 negative reviews per domain. Feature extraction follows Blitzer et al. (2007): we use case insensitive unigrams and bigrams, although we remove rare features (those that appear less than five times in the training set). The reduced feature set was selected given the sensitivity to feature size of some of the MDL methods.

ConVote (CONVOTE) Our second dataset is taken from segments of speech from United States Congress floor debates, first introduced by Thomas et al. (2006). The binary classification task on this dataset is that of predicting whether a given speech segment supports or opposes a bill under discussion in the floor debate. We select this dataset because, unlike the AMAZON data, CONVOTE can be divided into domains in several ways based on different metadata attributes available with the dataset. We consider two types of domain divisions: the bill identifier and the political party of the speaker. Division based on the bill creates domain differences in that each bill has its own topic. Division based on political party implies preference for different issues and concerns, which manifest as different language. We refer to these datasets as BILL and PARTY.

We use Version 1.1 of the CONVOTE dataset, available at `http://www.cs.cornell.edu/home/llee/data/convote.html`. More specifically, we combine the training, development and test folds from the `data_stage_three/` version, and sub-sample to generate different versions of the dataset required for our experiments. For BILL we randomly sample speech segments from three different bills. The three bills and the number of instances for each were chosen such that we have sufficient data in each fold for every experiment. For PARTY we randomly sample speech segments from the two major political parties (Democrats and Republicans). Feature processing was identical to AMAZON, except that the threshold for feature removal was two.

3.2 Learning Methods and Features

We consider three MDL algorithms, two are representative of the first approach and one of the second approach (learning domain similarities) (§2). We favored algorithms with available code or that were straightforward to implement, so as to ensure reproducibility of our results.

FEDA Frustratingly easy domain adaptation (`FEDA`) (Daumé III, 2007; Daumé III et al., 2010b; Daumé III et al., 2010a) is an example of a classifier combination approach to MDL. The feature space is a cross-product of the domain and input features, augmented with the original input features (shared features). Prediction is effectively a linear combination of a set of domain-specific weights and shared weights. We combine `FEDA` with both the SVM and logistic regression algorithms described below to obtain `FEDA-SVM` and `FEDA-LR`.

MDR Multi-domain regularization (`MDR`) (Dredze and Crammer, 2008; Dredze et al., 2009) extends the idea behind classifier combination by explicitly formulating a classifier combination scheme based on Confidence-Weighted learning (Dredze et al., 2008). Additionally, classifier updates (which happen in an online framework) contain an explicit constraint that the combined classifier should perform well on the example. Dredze et al. (2009) consider several variants of `MDR`. We select the two best performing methods: `MDR-L2`, which uses the underlying algorithm of Crammer et al. (2008), and `MDR-KL`, which uses the underlying algorithm of Dredze et al. (2008). We follow their approach to classifier training and parameter optimization.

MTRL The multi-task relationship learning (`MTRL`) approach proposed by Zhang and Yeung

(2010) achieves states of the art performance on many MDL tasks. This method is representative of methods that learn similarities between domains and in turn regularize domain-specific parameters accordingly. The key idea in their work is the use of a matrix-normal distribution $p(\boldsymbol{X}|\boldsymbol{M},\boldsymbol{\Omega},\boldsymbol{\Sigma})$ as a prior on the matrix $\boldsymbol{W}$ created by column-wise stacking of the domain-specific classifier weight vectors. $\boldsymbol{\Omega}$ represents the covariance matrix for the variables along the columns of $\boldsymbol{X}$. When used as a prior over $\boldsymbol{W}$ it models the covariance between the domain-specific classifiers (and therefore the tasks). $\boldsymbol{\Omega}$ is learned jointly with the domain-specific classifiers. This method has similar benefits to `FEDA` in terms of classifier combination, but also attempts to model domain relationships. We use the implementation of `MTRL` made available by the authors[2]. For parameter tuning, we perform a grid search over the parameters λ_1 and λ_2, using the following values for each (a total of 36 combinations): $\{0.00001, 0.0001, 0.001, 0.01, 0.1, 1\}$.

In addition to these multi-task learning methods, we consider a common baseline: ignoring the domain distinctions and learning a single classifier over all the data. This reflects single-domain learning, in which no domain knowledge is used and will indicate baseline performance for all experiments. While some earlier research has included a separate *one classifier per domain* baseline, it almost always performs worse, since splitting the domains provides much less data to each classifier (Dredze et al., 2009). So we omit this baseline for simplicity.

To obtain a single classifier we use two classification algorithms: SVMs and logistic regression.

Support Vector Machines A single SVM run over all the training data, ignoring domain labels. We use the SVM implementation available in the LIBLINEAR package (Fan et al., 2008). In particular, we use the L_2-regularized L_2-loss SVM (option `-s 1` in version 1.8 of LIBLINEAR, and also option `-B 1` for including a standard bias feature). We tune the SVM using five-fold stratified cross-validation on the training set, using the following values for the trade-off parameter C: $\{0.0001, 0.001, 0.01, 0.1, 0.2, 0.3, 0.5, 1\}$.

[2] `http://www.cse.ust.hk/~zhangyu/codes/MTRL.zip`

Logistic Regression (LR) A single logistic regression model run over all the training data, ignoring domain labels. Again, we use the L_2-regularized LR implementation available in the LIBLINEAR package (option `-s 0`, and also option `-B 1`). We tune the LR model using the same strategy as the one used for SVM above, including the values of the trade-off parameter C.

For all experiments, we measure average accuracy over K-fold cross-validation, using 10 folds for AMAZON, and 5 folds for both BILL and PARTY.

4 When Do Domains Matter?

We now empirically explore two questions regarding the behavior of MDL.

4.1 Ensemble Learning

Question: *Are MDL improvements the result of ensemble learning effects?*

Many of the MDL approaches bear a striking resemblance to ensemble learning. Traditionally, ensemble learning combines the output from several different classifiers to obtain a single improved model (Maclin and Opitz, 1999). It is well established that ensemble learning, applied on top of a diverse array of quality classifiers, can improve results for a variety of tasks. The key idea behind ensemble learning, that of combining a diverse array of models, has been applied to settings in which data preprocessing is used to create many different classifiers. Examples include instance bagging and feature bagging (Dietterich, 2000).

The core idea of using diverse inputs in making classification decisions is common in the MDL literature. In fact, the top performing and only successful entry to the 2007 CoNLL shared task on domain adaptation for dependency parsing was a straightforward implementation of ensemble learning by creating variants of parsers (Sagae and Tsujii, 2007). Many MDL algorithms, among them Dredze and Crammer (2008), Daumé III (2009), Zhang and Yeung (2010) and Saha et al. (2011), all include some notion of learning domain-specific classifiers on the training data, and combining them in the best way possible. To be clear, we *do not* claim that these approaches can be reduced to an existing ensemble learning algorithm. There are crucial elements in each of these algorithms that separate them from existing ensemble learning algorithms. One example of such a distinction is the learning of domain relationships by both Zhang and Yeung (2010) and Saha et al. (2011). However, we argue that their core approach, that of combining parameters that are trained on variants of the data (all data or individual domains), is an ensemble learning idea.

Consider instance bagging, in which multiple classifiers are each trained on random subsets of the data. The resulting classifiers are then combined to form a final model. In MDL, we can consider each domain a subset of the data, albeit non-random and non-overlapping. The final model combines the domain-specific parameters and parameters trained on other instances, which in the case of `FEDA` are the shared parameters. In this light, these methods are a complex form of instance bagging, and their development could be justified from this perspective.

However, given this justification, are improvements from MDL simply the result of standard ensemble learning effects, or are these methods really learning something about domain behavior? If knowledge of domain was withheld from the algorithm, could we expect similar improvements? As we will do in each empirical experiment, we propose a contrarian hypothesis:

Hypothesis: *Knowledge of domains is irrelevant for MDL.*

Empirical Evaluation We evaluate this hypothesis as follows. We begin by constructing a true MDL setting, in which we attempt to improve accuracy through knowledge of the domains. We will apply three MDL algorithms (`FEDA`, `MDR`, and `MTRL`) to our three multi-domain datasets (AMAZON, BILL, and PARTY) and compare them against a single classifier baseline. We will then withhold knowledge of the true domains from these algorithms and instead provide them with random "pseudo-domains," and then evaluate the change in their behavior. The question is whether we can obtain similar benefits by ignoring domain labels and relying strictly on an ensemble learning motivation (instance bagging).

For the "True Domain" setting, we apply the MDL algorithms as normal. For the "Random Domain" setting, we randomly shuffle the domain labels within a given class label within each fold, thus maintaining the same number of examples for each domain label, and also retaining the same class distribution within each randomized domain. The resulting "pseudo-domains" are then similar to random subsets of the data used in ensemble learning.

Following the standard practice in previous work, for this experiment we use a balanced number of examples from each domain and a balanced number of positive and negative labels (no class bias). For AMAZON (4 domains), we have 10 folds of 400 examples per fold, for BILL (3 domains) 5 folds of 60 examples per fold, and for PARTY (2 domains) 5 folds of 80 examples per fold. In the "Random Domain" setting, since we are randomizing the domain labels, we increase the number of trials. We repeat each cross-validation experiment 5 times with different randomization of the domain labels each time.

Results Results are shown in Table 1. The first row shows absolute (average) accuracy for a single classifier trained on all data, ignoring domain distinctions. The remaining cells indicate absolute improvements against the baseline.

First, we note for the well-studied AMAZON dataset that our results with true domains are consistent with the previous literature. `FEDA` is known to not improve upon a single classifier baseline for that dataset (Dredze et al., 2009). Both `MDR-L2` and `MDR-KL` improve upon the single classifier baseline, again as per Dredze et al. (2009). And finally, `MTRL` also improves upon the single classifier baseline. Although the `MTRL` improvement is not as dramatic as in the original paper[3], the average accuracy that we achieve for `MTRL` (84.2%) is better than the best average accuracy in the original paper (83.65%).

The main comparison to make in Table 1 is between having knowledge of true domains or not. "Random Domain" in the table is the case where domain identifiers are randomly shuffled within a given fold. Ignoring the significance test results for now, overall the results indicate that knowing the true domains is useful for MDL algorithms. Randomizing the domains does not work better than knowing true domains in any case. However, in all except one case, the improvements of MDL algorithms are

[3]This might be due to a different version of the dataset being used in a cross-validation setup, rather than their train/test setup, and also because of differences in baseline approaches.

	AMAZON		BILL		PARTY	
	SVM	**LR**	**SVM**	**LR**	**SVM**	**LR**
	Single Classifier					
	83.93%	83.78%	66.67%	68.00%	62.75%	64.00%
	FEDA					
True Domain	-0.35	-0.10	+2.33	+ 1.00	+4.25 ▲	+1.25
Random Domain	-1.30 ▼	-1.02 ▼	-1.20	-2.07	-2.05	-2.10
	MDR-L2					
True Domain	+1.87 ▲	+2.02 ▲	+0.00	-1.33	+2.25	+1.00
Random Domain	+0.91 ▲	+1.07 ▲	-2.67	-4.00	-2.80	-4.05
	MDR-KL					
True Domain	+1.85 ▲	+2.00 ▲	+1.00	-0.33	+3.00	+1.75
Random Domain	+1.36 ▲	+1.51 ▲	+0.60	-0.73	-1.30	-2.55 ▼
	MTRL					
True Domain	+0.27	+0.42	+0.67	-0.67	+1.50	+0.25
Random Domain	-0.37	-0.21	-1.47	-2.80	-3.55	-4.80

Table 1: A comparison between MDL methods with access to the "True Domain" labels and methods that use "Random Domain" information, essentially ensemble learning. The first row has raw accuracy numbers, whereas the remaining entries are absolute improvements over the baseline. ▲: Significantly better than the corresponding SVM or LR baseline, with $p < 0.05$, using a paired t-test. ▼: Significantly worse than corresponding baseline, with $p < 0.05$, using a paired t-test.

significantly better only for the AMAZON dataset[4]. And interestingly, exactly in the same case, randomly shuffling the domains also gives significant improvements compared to the baseline, showing that there is an ensemble learning effect in operation for MDR-L2 and MDR-KL on the AMAZON dataset. For FEDA, randomizing the domains significantly hurts its performance on the AMAZON data, as is the case for MDR-KL on the PARTY data. Therefore, while our contrarian hypothesis about irrelevance of domains is not completely true, it is indeed the case that some MDL methods benefit from the ensemble learning effect.

A second observation to be made from these results is that, while all of empirical research on MDL assumes the definition of domains as a given, the question of how to split a dataset into domains given various metadata attributes is still open. For example, in our experiments, in general, using the political party as a domain distinction gives us more improvements over the corresponding baseline approach[5].

We provide a detailed comparison of using true vs. randomized domains in Table 6, after presenting the second set of experimental results.

[4]Some numbers in Table 1 might appear to be significant, but are not. That is because of high variance in the performance of the methods across the different folds.

[5]The BILL and the PARTY datasets are not directly comparable to each other, although the prediction task is the same.

4.2 Domain-specific Class Bias

Question: *Are MDL methods improving because they capture domain-specific class biases?*

In previous work, and the above section, experiments have assumed a balanced dataset in terms of class labels. It has been in these settings that MDL methods improve. However, this is an unrealistic assumption. Even in our datasets, the original versions demonstrated class bias: Amazon product reviews are generally positive, votes on bills are rarely tied, and political parties vote in blocs. While it is common to evaluate learning methods on balanced data, and then adjust for imbalanced real world datasets, it is unclear what effect *domain-specific* class bias will have on MDL methods. Domains can differ in their proportion of examples of different classes. For example, it is quite likely that less controversial bills in the United States Congress will have more yes votes than controversial bills. Similarly, if instead of the category of a product, its brand is considered as a domain, it is likely that some brands receive a higher proportion of positive reviews than others.

Improvements from MDL in such settings may simply be capturing domain-specific class biases.

domain	class	cb1	cb2	cb3	cb4
AMAZON					
b	–	20	80	60	40
	+	80	20	40	60
d	–	40	20	80	60
	+	60	80	20	40
e	–	60	40	20	80
	+	40	60	80	20
k	–	80	60	40	20
	+	20	40	60	80
BILL					
031	N	16	4	8	12
	Y	4	16	12	8
088	N	12	16	4	8
	Y	8	4	16	12
132	N	8	12	16	4
	Y	12	8	4	16
PARTY					
D	N	10	30	15	25
	Y	30	10	25	15
R	N	30	10	25	15
	Y	10	30	15	25

Table 2: The table shows the distribution of instances across domains and class labels *within one fold* of each of the datasets, for four different class bias trials. These datasets with varying class bias across domains were used for the experiments described in §4.2

Consider two domains, where each domain is biased towards the opposite label. In this case, domain-specific parameters may simply be capturing the bias towards the class label, increasing the weight uniformly of features predictive of the dominant class. Similarly, methods that learn domain similarity may be learning class bias similarity.

Why does the effectiveness of these domain-specific bias parameters matter? First, if capturing domain-specific class bias is the source of improvement, there are much simpler methods for learning that can be just as effective. This would be especially important in settings where we have many domains, and learning domain-specific parameters for each feature becomes infeasible. Second, if class bias accounted for most of the improvement in learning, it suggests that such settings could be amenable to unsupervised adaptation of the bias parameters.

Hypothesis: *MDL largely capitalizes on domain-specific class bias.*

Empirical Evaluation To evaluate our hypothesis, for each of our three datasets we create 4 random versions, each with some domain-specific class-bias. A summary of the dataset partitions is shown in Table 2. For example, for the AMAZON dataset, we create 4 versions (cb1 ... cb4), where each domain has 100 examples *per fold* and each domain has a different balance between positive and negative classes. For each of these settings, we conduct a 10-fold cross validation experiment, then average the CV results for each of the 4 settings. The resulting accuracy numbers therefore reflect an average across many types of bias, each evaluated many times. We do a similar experiment for the BILL and PARTY datasets, except we use 5-fold CV.

In addition to the multi-domain and baseline methods, we add a new baseline: DOM-ID. In this setting, we augment the baseline classifier (which ignores domain labels) with a new feature that indicates the domain label. While we already include a general bias feature, as is common in classification tasks, these new features will capture domain-specific bias. This is the only change to the baseline classifier, so improvements over the baseline are indicative of the change in domain-bias that can be captured using these simple features.

Results Results are shown in Table 3. The table follows the same structure as Table 1, with the addition of the results for the DOM-ID approach. We first examine the efficacy of MDL in this setting. An observation that is hard to miss is that MDL results in these experiments show significant improvements in almost all cases, as compared to only a few cases in Table 1, despite the fact that even the baseline approaches have a higher accuracy. This shows that MDL results can be highly influenced by systematic differences in class bias across domains. Note that there is also a significant negative influence of class bias on MTRL for the AMAZON data.

A comparison of the MDL results on true domains to the DOM-ID baseline gives us an idea of how much MDL benefits purely from class bias differences across domains. We see that in most cases, about half of the improvement seen in MDL is accounted for by a simple baseline of using the domain identifier as a feature, and all but one of the improvements from DOM-ID are significant. This

	AMAZON		BILL		PARTY	
	SVM	**LR**	**SVM**	**LR**	**SVM**	**LR**
	Single Classifier					
	85.52%	85.46%	70.50%	70.67%	65.44%	65.81%
	FEDA					
True Domain	+0.11	+0.31	+4.25 ▲	+4.00 ▲	+4.81 ▲	+4.69 ▲
Random Domain	+0.94 ▲	+1.03 ▲	+3.68 ▲	+4.03 ▲	+4.24	+3.73
	MDR-L2					
True Domain	+0.92 ▲	+0.98 ▲	+4.42 ▲	+4.25 ▲	+1.31	+0.94
Random Domain	+1.86 ▲	+1.92 ▲	+3.93 ▲	+3.77 ▲	+0.65	+0.28
	MDR-KL					
True Domain	+1.54 ▲	+1.59 ▲	+5.17 ▲	+5.00 ▲	+4.25 ▲	+3.88 ▲
Random Domain	+2.84 ▲	+2.90 ▲	+4.13 ▲	+3.97 ▲	+3.81 ▲	+3.44
	MTRL					
True Domain	-1.22 ▼	-1.17 ▼	+4.50 ▲	+4.33 ▲	+6.44 ▲	+6.06 ▲
Random Domain	-0.69 ▼	-0.63 ▼	+3.53 ▲	+3.37 ▲	+4.87 ▲	+4.50 ▲
	DOM-ID					
True Domain	+0.36	+0.38 ▲	+2.83 ▲	+2.75 ▲	+3.75 ▲	+4.00 ▲
Random Domain	+1.73 ▲	+1.76 ▲	+4.50 ▲	+4.98 ▲	+5.24 ▲	+5.31 ▲

Table 3: A comparison between MDL methods with class biased data. Similar to the setup where we evaluate the ensemble learning effect, we have a setting of using randomized domains. ▲: Significantly better than the corresponding SVM or LR baseline, with $p < 0.05$, using a paired t-test. ▼: Significantly worse than corresponding baseline, with $p < 0.05$, using a paired t-test.

suggests that in a real-world scenario where difference in class bias across domains is quite likely, it is useful to consider DOM-ID as a simple baseline that gives good empirical performance. To our knowledge, using this approach as a baseline is not standard practice in MDL literature.

Finally, we also include the "Random Domain" evaluation in the our class biased version of experiments. Each "Random Domain" result in Table 3 is an average over 20 cross-validation runs (5 randomized trials for each of the four class biased trials cb1 ... cb4). This setup combines the effects of ensemble learning and bias difference across domains. As seen in the table, for MDL algorithms the results are consistently better as compared to knowing the true domains for the AMAZON dataset. For the other datasets, the performance after randomizing the domains is still significantly better than the baseline. This evaluation on randomized domains further strengthens the conclusion that differences in bias across domains play an important role, even in the case of noisy domains. Looking at the performance of DOM-ID with randomized domains, we see that in all cases the DOM-ID baseline performs *better* with randomized domains. While the difference is significant mostly only on the AMAZON dataset (details in Table 6, columns under "**Varying Class Bias**,") this trend is still counter-intuitive. We suspect this might be because randomization creates a noisy version of the domain labels, which helps learners to avoid over-fitting that single feature.

domain	**class**	**cb5**	**cb6**	**cb7**	**cb8**
		AMAZON			
b	−	20	40	60	80
	+	80	60	40	20
d	−	20	40	60	80
	+	80	60	40	20
e	−	20	40	60	80
	+	80	60	40	20
k	−	20	40	60	80
	+	20	40	60	80

Table 4: The table shows the distribution of instances across domains and class labels *within one fold* of the AMAZON dataset, for four different class bias trials. For the BILL and PARTY datasets, similar folds with consistent bias were created (number of examples used was different). These datasets with *consistent class bias* across domains were used for the experiments described in §4.2.1

4.2.1 Consistent Class Bias

We also performed a set of experiments that apply MDL algorithms to a setting where the datasets have different class biases (unlike the experiments reported in Table 1, where the classes are balanced), but, unlike the experiments reported in Table 3, the class bias is the *same* within each of the domains. We refer to this as the case of *consistent class bias* across domains. The distribution of classes within each domain within each fold is shown in Table 4. The results for this set of experiments are reported in Table 5. The structure of Table 5 is identical to that of Table 1. Comparing these results to those in Table 1, we can see that in most cases the improvements seen using MDL algorithms are lower than those seen in Table 1. This is likely due to the higher baseline performance in the *consistent class bias* case. A notable difference is in the performance of `MTRL` — it is significantly worse for the AMAZON dataset, and significantly better for the PARTY dataset. For the AMAZON dataset, we believe that the domain distinctions are less meaningful, and hence forcing `MTRL` to learn the relationships results in lower performance. For the PARTY dataset, in the case of a class-biased setup, knowing the party is highly predictive of the vote (in the original CONVOTE dataset, Democrats mostly vote "no" and Republicans mostly vote "yes"), and this is rightly exploited by `MTRL`.

4.2.2 True vs. Randomized Domains

In Table 6 we analyze the difference in performance of MDL methods when using true vs. randomized domain information. For the three sets of results reported earlier, we evaluated whether using true domains as compared to randomized domains gives significantly **better**, significantly **worse** or **equal** performance. Significance testing was done using a paired t-test with $\alpha = 0.05$ as before. As the table shows, for the first set of results where the class labels were balanced (overall, as well as within each domain), using true domains was significantly better mostly only for the AMAZON dataset. `FEDA-SVM` was the only approach that was consistently better with true domains across all datasets. Note, however, that it was significantly better than the baseline approach only for PARTY.

For the second set of results (Table 3) where the class bias varied across the different domains, using true domains was either no different from using randomized domains, or it was significantly worse. In particular, it was consistently significantly worse to use true domains on the AMAZON dataset. This questions the utility of domains on the AMAZON dataset in the context of MDL in a domain-specific class bias scenario. Since randomizing the domains works better for all of the MDL methods on AMAZON, it suggests that an ensemble learning effect is primarily responsible for the significant improvements seen on the AMAZON data, when evaluated in a domain-specific class bias setting.

Finally, for the case of consistent class bias across domains, the trend is similar to the case of no class bias — using true domains is useful. This table further supports the conclusion that domain-specific class bias highly influences multi-domain learning.

5 Discussion and Open Questions

Our analysis of MDL algorithms revealed new trends that suggest further avenues of exploration. We suggest three open questions in response.

Question: *When are MDL methods most effective?*

Our empirical results suggest that MDL can be more effective in settings with domain-specific class biases. However, we also saw differences in improvements for each method, and for different domains. Differences emerge between the AMAZON and CONVOTE datasets in terms of the ensemble learning hypothesis. While there has been some theoretical analyses on the topic of MDL (Ben-David et al., 2007; Ben-David et al., 2009; Mansour et al., 2009; Daumé III et al., 2010a), our results suggest performing new analyses that relate ensemble learning results with the MDL setting. These analyses could provide insights into new algorithms that can take advantage of the specific properties of each multi-domain setting.

Question: *What makes a good domain for MDL?*

To the best of our knowledge, previous work has assumed that domain identities are provided to the learning algorithm. However, in reality, there may be many ways to split a dataset into domains. For example, consider the CONVOTE dataset, which we split both by BILL and PARTY. The choice of splits

	AMAZON		BILL		PARTY	
	SVM	**LR**	**SVM**	**LR**	**SVM**	**LR**
	Single Classifier					
	86.06%	86.22%	76.42%	75.58%	69.31%	68.38%
	FEDA					
True Domain	-0.25	-0.33	-0.83	+0.25	+0.88	+1.25
Random Domain	-1.17 ▼	-1.26 ▼	-1.33	-0.82	-0.55	-0.04
	MDR-L2					
True Domain	+0.39 ▲	+0.23	-0.42	+0.42	-2.12	-1.19
Random Domain	-0.38	-0.53 ▼	-3.57	-2.73	-4.30 ▼	-3.36 ▼
	MDR-KL					
True Domain	+0.81 ▲	+0.65 ▲	-0.83	+0.00	+1.31	+2.25 ▲
Random Domain	+0.22	+0.06	-1.90	-1.07	-0.60	+0.34
	MTRL					
True Domain	-1.52 ▼	-1.68 ▼	-1.92	-1.08	+3.12 ▲	+4.06 ▲
Random Domain	-2.12 ▼	-2.28 ▼	-0.95	-0.12	+0.19	+1.12 ▲

Table 5: A comparison between MDL methods with data that have a *consistent class bias* across domains. Similar to the setup where we evaluate the ensemble learning effect, we have a setting of using randomized domains. ▲: Significantly better than the corresponding SVM or LR baseline, with $p < 0.05$, using a paired t-test. ▼: Significantly worse than corresponding baseline, with $p < 0.05$, using a paired t-test.

MDL Method	**No Class Bias (Tab. 1)**			**Varying Class Bias (Tab. 3)**			**Consistent Class Bias (Tab. 5)**		
	better	**worse**	**equal**	**better**	**worse**	**equal**	**better**	**worse**	**equal**
FEDA-SVM	AM, BI, PA				AM	BI, PA	AM, PA		BI
FEDA-LR	AM		BI, PA		AM	BI, PA	AM, BI		PA
MDR-L2	AM		BI, PA		AM	BI, PA	AM, BI	PA	
MDR-KL	PA		AM, BI		AM	BI, PA	AM, PA		BI
MTRL	AM		BI, PA		AM	BI, PA	AM, PA	BI	
DOM-ID-SVM	–	–	–		AM	BI, PA	–	–	–
DOM-ID-LR	–	–	–		AM, BI	PA	–	–	–

Table 6: The table shows the datasets (AM:AMAZON, BI:BILL, PA:PARTY) for which a given MDL method using true domain information was significantly **better**, significantly **worse**, or not significantly different (**equal**) as compared to using randomized domain information with the same MDL method.

impacted MDL. This poses new questions: what makes a good domain? How should we choose to divide data along possible metadata properties? If we can gain improvements simply by randomly creating new domains ("Random Domain" setting in our experiments) then there may be better ways to take advantage of the provided metadata for MDL.

Question: *Can we learn class-bias for unsupervised domain adaptation?*

Experiments with domain-specific class biases revealed that a significant part of the improvements could be achieved by adding domain-specific bias features. Limiting the multi-domain improvements to a small set of parameters raises an interesting question: can these parameters be adapted to a new domain without labeled data? Traditionally, domain adaptation without target domain labeled data has focused on learning the behavior of new features; beliefs about existing feature behaviors could not be corrected without new training data. However, by collapsing the adaptation into a single bias parameter, we may be able to learn how to adjust this parameter in a fully unsupervised way. This would open the door to improvements in this challenging setting for real world problems where class bias was a significant factor.

Acknowledgments

Research presented here is supported by the Office of Naval Research grant number N000141110221.

References

Andrew Arnold, Ramesh Nallapati, and William W. Cohen. 2008. Exploiting Feature Hierarchy for Transfer Learning in Named Entity Recognition. In *Proceedings of ACL-08: HLT*, pages 245–253.

Shai Ben-David, John Blitzer, Koby Crammer, and Fernando Pereira. 2007. Analysis of representations for domain adaptation. In *Proceedings of NIPS 2006*.

Shai Ben-David, John Blitzer, Koby Crammer, Alex Kulesza, Fernando Pereira, and Jennifer Wortman Vaughan. 2009. A theory of learning from different domains. *Machine Learning*.

John Blitzer, Ryan McDonald, and Fernando Pereira. 2006. Domain Adaptation with Structural Correspondence Learning. In *Proceedings of the 2006 Conference on Empirical Methods in Natural Language Processing*, pages 120–128.

John Blitzer, Mark Dredze, and Fernando Pereira. 2007. Biographies, Bollywood, Boom-boxes and Blenders: Domain Adaptation for Sentiment Classification. In *Proceedings of the 45th Annual Meeting of the Association of Computational Linguistics*, pages 440–447.

John Blitzer, Koby Crammer, Alex Kulesza, Fernando Pereira, and Jennifer Wortman. 2008. Learning Bounds for Domain Adaptation. In *Advances in Neural Information Processing Systems (NIPS 2007)*.

Giovanni Cavallanti, Nicolò Cesa-Bianchi, and Claudio Gentile. 2008. Linear Algorithms for Online Multitask Classification. In *Proceedings of COLT*.

Ciprian Chelba and Alex Acero. 2004. Adaptation of Maximum Entropy Capitalizer: Little Data Can Help a Lot. In Dekang Lin and Dekai Wu, editors, *Proceedings of EMNLP 2004*, pages 285–292.

Koby Crammer, Mark Dredze, and Fernando Pereira. 2008. Exact convex confidence-weighted learning. In *Advances in Neural Information Processing Systems (NIPS)*.

Hal Daumé III and Daniel Marcu. 2006. Domain adaptation for statistical classifiers. *Journal of Artificial Intelligence Research*, 26(1):101–126.

Hal Daumé III, Abhishek Kumar, and Avishek Saha. 2010a. A Co-regularization Based Semi-supervised Domain Adaptation. In *Neural Information Processing Systems*.

Hal Daumé III, Abhishek Kumar, and Avishek Saha. 2010b. Frustratingly Easy Semi-Supervised Domain Adaptation. In *Proceedings of the ACL 2010 Workshop on Domain Adaptation for Natural Language Processing*, pages 53–59.

Hal Daumé III. 2007. Frustratingly Easy Domain Adaptation. In *Proceedings of the 45th Annual Meeting of the Association of Computational Linguistics*, pages 256–263.

Hal Daumé III. 2009. Bayesian multitask learning with latent hierarchies. In *Proceedings of the Twenty-Fifth Conference on Uncertainty in Artificial Intelligence*.

Thomas G. Dietterich. 2000. An experimental comparison of three methods for constructing ensembles of decision trees: Bagging, boosting, and randomization. *Machine Learning*, 40:139–157.

Mark Dredze and Koby Crammer. 2008. Online methods for multi-domain learning and adaptation. *Proceedings of the Conference on Empirical Methods in Natural Language Processing - EMNLP '08*.

Mark Dredze, Koby Crammer, and Fernando Pereira. 2008. Confidence-weighted linear classification. *Proceedings of the 25th international conference on Machine learning - ICML '08*.

Mark Dredze, Alex Kulesza, and Koby Crammer. 2009. Multi-domain learning by confidence-weighted parameter combination. *Machine Learning*, 79(1-2).

Rong-En Fan, Kai-Wei Chang, Cho-Jui Hsieh, Xiang-rui Wang, and Chih-Jen Lin. 2008. LIBLINEAR : A Library for Large Linear Classification. *Journal of Machine Learning Research*, 9:1871–1874.

Jenny R. Finkel and Christopher D. Manning. 2009. Hierarchical Bayesian Domain Adaptation. In *Proceedings of Human Language Technologies: The 2009 Annual Conference of the North American Chapter of the Association for Computational Linguistics*, pages 602–610.

Richard Maclin and David Opitz. 1999. Popular Ensemble Methods: An Empirical Study. *Journal of Artificial Intelligence Research*, 11:169–198.

Yishay Mansour, Mehryar Mohri, and Afshin Rostamizadeh. 2009. Domain Adaptation with Multiple Sources. In *Proceedings of NIPS 2008*, pages 1041–1048.

Kenji Sagae and Jun'ichi Tsujii. 2007. Dependency parsing and domain adaptation with lr models and parser ensembles. In *Conference on Natural Language Learning (Shared Task)*.

Avishek Saha, Piyush Rai, Hal Daumé III, and Suresh Venkatasubramanian. 2011. Online learning of multiple tasks and their relationships. In *Proceedings of AISTATS 2011*.

Matt Thomas, Bo Pang, and Lillian Lee. 2006. Get out the vote: Determining support or opposition from Congressional floor-debate transcripts. In *Proceedings of EMNLP*, pages 327–335.

Yu Zhang and Dit-Yan Yeung. 2010. A Convex Formulation for Learning Task Relationships in Multi-Task Learning. In *Proceedings of the Proceedings of the Twenty-Sixth Conference Annual Conference on Uncertainty in Artificial Intelligence (UAI-10)*.

Biased Representation Learning for Domain Adaptation

Fei Huang , Alexander Yates
Temple University
Computer and Information Sciences
324 Wachman Hall
Philadelphia, PA 19122
{fhuang,yates}@temple.edu

Abstract

Representation learning is a promising technique for discovering features that allow supervised classifiers to generalize from a source domain dataset to arbitrary new domains. We present a novel, formal statement of the representation learning task. We argue that because the task is computationally intractable in general, it is important for a representation learner to be able to incorporate expert knowledge during its search for helpful features. Leveraging the Posterior Regularization framework, we develop an architecture for incorporating biases into representation learning. We investigate three types of biases, and experiments on two domain adaptation tasks show that our biased learners identify significantly better sets of features than unbiased learners, resulting in a relative reduction in error of more than 16% for both tasks, with respect to existing state-of-the-art representation learning techniques.

1 Introduction

Supervised natural language processing (NLP) systems have been widely used and have achieved impressive performance on many NLP tasks. However, they exhibit a significant drop-off in performance when tested on domains that differ from their training domains. (Gildea, 2001; Sekine, 1997; Pradhan et al., 2007) One major cause for poor performance on out of-domain texts is the traditional representation used by supervised NLP systems (Ben-David et al., 2007). Most systems depend on lexical features, which can differ greatly between domains, so that important words in the test data may never be seen in the training data. The connection between words and labels may also change across domains. For instance, "signaling" appears only as a present participle (VBG) in WSJ text (as in, "signaling that..."), but predominantly as a noun (as in "signaling pathway") in biomedical text.

Recently, several authors have found that learning new features based on distributional similarity can significantly improve domain adaptation (Blitzer et al., 2006; Huang and Yates, 2009; Turian et al., 2010; Dhillon et al., 2011). This framework is attractive for several reasons: experimentally, learned features can yield significant improvements over standard supervised models on out-of-domain tests. Moreover, since the representation-learning techniques are unsupervised, they can easily be applied to arbitrary new domains. There is no need to supply additional labeled examples for each new domain.

Traditional representations still hold one significant advantage over representation-learning, however: because features are hand-crafted, these representations can readily incorporate the linguistic or domain expert knowledge that leads to state-of-the-art in-domain performance. In contrast, the only guide for existing representation-learning techniques is a corpus of unlabeled text.

To address this shortcoming, we introduce representation-learning techniques that incorporate a domain expert's preferences over the learned features. For example, out of the set of all possible distributional-similarity features, we might prefer those that help predict the labels in a labeled training data set. To capture this preference, we might bias a representation-learning algorithm towards features with low joint entropy with the labels in the training data. This particular biased form of representation learning is a type of semi-supervised learning that allows our system to learn *task-specific* representations from a source domain's training data, rather than the single representation for all tasks produced by current, unsupervised representation-learning techniques.

We present a novel formal statement of representation learning, and demonstrate that it is computationally intractable in general. It is therefore critical for representation learning to be flexible enough to incorporate the intuitions and knowledge of human experts, to guide the search for representations efficiently and effectively. Leveraging the Posterior Regularization framework (Ganchev et al., 2010), we present an architecture for learning representations for sequence-labeling tasks that allows for biases. In addition to a bias towards task-specific representations, we investigate a bias towards representations that have similar features across domains, to improve domain-independence; and a bias towards multi-dimensional representations, where different dimensions are independent of one another. In this paper, we focus on incorporating the biases with HMM-type representations (Hidden Markov Model). However, this technique can also be applied to other graphical model-based representations with little modification. Our experiments show that on two different domain-adaptation tasks, our biased representations improve significantly over unbiased ones. In a part-of-speech tagging experiment, our best model provides a 25% relative reduction in error over a state-of-the-art Chinese POS tagger, and a 19% relative reduction in error over an unbiased representation from previous work.

The next section describes background and previous work. Section 3 introduces our framework for learning biased representations. Section 4 describes how we estimate parameters for the biased objective functions efficiently. Section 5 details our experiments and results, and section 6 concludes and outlines directions for future work.

2 Background and Previous Work

2.1 Terminology and Notation

A *representation* is a set of features that describe data points. Formally, given an instance set $\mathcal{X}$, it is a function $\mathcal{R} : \mathcal{X} \rightarrow \mathcal{Y}$ for some suitable space $\mathcal{Y}$ (often $\mathbf{R}^d$), which is then used as the input space for a classifier. For instance, a traditional representation for POS tagging over vocabulary V would include (in part) $|V|$ dimensions, and would map a word to a binary vector with a 1 in only one of the dimensions. By a *structured representation*, we mean a function R that incorporates some form of joint inference. In this paper, we use Viterbi decoding of variants of Hidden Markov Models (HMMs) for our structured representations, although our techniques are applicable to arbitrary (Dynamic) Bayes Nets. A *domain* is a probability distribution D over the instance set $\mathcal{X}$; $R(D)$ denotes the induced distribution over $\mathcal{Y}$. In *domain adaptation* tasks, a learner is given samples from a *source* domain D_S, and is evaluated on samples from a *target* domain D_T.

2.2 Theoretical Background

Ben-David *et al.* (2010) give a theoretical analysis of domain adaptation which shows that the choice of representation is crucial. A good choice is one that minimizes error on the training data, but equally important is that the representation must make data from the two domains look similar. Ben-David *et al.* show that for every hypothesis h, we can provably bound the error of h on the target domain by its error on the source domain plus a measure of the distance between D_S and D_T:

$$\mathrm{E}_{x \sim D_T} \mathcal{L}(x, R, f, h) \leq \mathrm{E}_{x \sim D_S} \mathcal{L}(x, R, f, h) + d_1(R(D_S), R(D_T))$$

where $\mathcal{L}$ is a loss function, f is the target function, and the variation divergence d_1 is given by

$$d_1(D, D') = 2 \sup_{B \in \mathcal{B}} |Pr_D[B] - Pr_{D'}[B]| \quad (1)$$

where $\mathcal{B}$ is the set of measurable sets under D, D'.

2.3 Problem Formulation

Ben-David *et al.*'s theory provides learning bounds for domain adaptation under a fixed R. We now reformulate this theory to define the task of representation learning for domain adaptation as the following optimization problem: given a set of unlabeled instances U_S drawn from the source domain and unlabeled instances U_T from the target domain, as well as a set of labeled instances L_S drawn from the source domain, identify a function R^* from the space of possible representations $\mathcal{R}$:

$$R^* = \underset{R \in \mathcal{R}}{\text{argmin}}\{ \min_{h \in \mathcal{H}} (\text{E}_{x \sim D_S} \mathcal{L}(x, R, f, h)) \\ + d_1(R(D_S), R(D_T))\} \quad (2)$$

Unlike most learning problems, where the representation R is fixed, this problem formulation involves a search over the space of representations and hypotheses. The equation also highlights an important underlying tension: the best representation for the source domain would naturally include domain-specific features, and allow a hypothesis to learn domain-specific patterns. We are aiming, however, for the best *general* classifier, that happens to be trained on training data from one or a few domains. Domain-specific features would contribute to distance between domains, and to classifier errors on data taken from unseen domains. By optimizing for this combined objective function, we allow the optimization method to trade off between features that are best for classifying source-domain data and features that allow generalization to new domains.

Naturally, the objective function in Equation 2 is completely intractable. Just finding the optimal hypothesis for a fixed representation of the training data is intractable for many hypothesis classes. And the d_1 metric is intractable to compute from samples of a distribution, although Ben-David *et al.* propose some tractable bounds (2007; 2010). We view Equation 2 as a high-level goal rather than a computable objective. We leverage prior knowledge to bias the representation learner towards attractive regions of the representations space $\mathcal{R}$, and we develop efficient, greedy optimization techniques for learning effective representations.

2.4 Previous Work

There is a long tradition of research on representations for NLP, mostly falling into one of three categories: 1) vector space models and dimensionality reduction techniques (Salton and McGill, 1983; Turney and Pantel, 2010; Sahlgren, 2005; Deerwester et al., 1990; Honkela, 1997) 2) using structured representations to identify clusters based on distributional similarity, and using those clusters as features (Lin and Wu, 2009; Candito and Crabbé, 2009; Huang and Yates, 2009; Ahuja and Downey, 2010; Turian et al., 2010; Huang et al., 2011); 3) and structured representations that induce multi-dimensional real-valued features (Dhillon et al., 2011; Emami et al., 2003; Morin and Bengio, 2005). Our work falls into the second category, but builds on the previous work by demonstrating how to improve the distributional-similarity clusters with prior knowledge. To our knowledge, we are the first to apply semi-supervised representation learning techniques for structured NLP tasks.

Most previous work on domain adaptation has focused on the case where some labeled data is available in both the source and target domains (Daumé III, 2007; Jiang and Zhai, 2007; Daumé III et al., 2010). Learning bounds are known (Blitzer et al., 2007; Mansour et al., 2009). A few authors have considered domain adaptation with no labeled data from the target domain (Blitzer et al., 2006; Huang et al., 2011) by using features based on distributional similarity. We demonstrate empirically that incorporating biases into this type of representation-learning process can significantly improve results.

3 Biased Representation Learning

As before, let U_S and U_T be unlabeled data, and L_S be labeled data from the source domain only. Previous work on representation learning with Hidden Markov Models (HMMs) (Huang and Yates, 2009) has estimated parameters θ for the HMM from unlabeled data alone, and then determined the Viterbi-optimal latent states for training and test data to produce new features for a supervised classifier. The objective function for HMM learning in this case is marginal log-likelihood, optimized using the Baum-Welch algorithm:

$$\mathcal{L}(\theta) = \sum_{\mathbf{x} \in U_S \cup U_T} \log \sum_{\mathbf{y}} p(\mathbf{x}, \mathbf{Y} = \mathbf{y} | \theta) \quad (3)$$

where $\mathbf{x}$ is a sentence, $\mathbf{Y}$ is the sequence of latent random variables for the sentence, and $\mathbf{y}$ is an instance of the latent sequence. The joint distribution in an HMM factors into observation and transition distributions, typically mixtures of multinomials:

$$p(\mathbf{x}, \mathbf{y}|\theta) = P(y_1)P(x_1|y_1) \prod_{i \geq 2} P(y_i|y_{i-1})P(x_i|y_i)$$

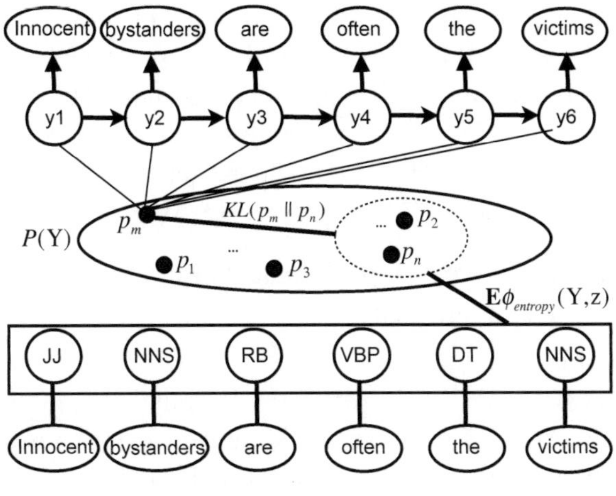

Figure 1: Illustration of how the entropy bias is incorporated into HMM learning. The dotted oval shows the space of desired distributions in the hidden space, which have small or zero entropy with the real labels. The learning algorithm aims to maximize the log-likelihood of the unlabeled data, and to minimize the KL divergence between the real distribution, p_m, and the closest desired distribution, p_n.

Intuitively, this form of representation learning identifies clusters of distributionally-similar words: those words with the same Viterbi-optimal latent state. The Viterbi-optimal latent states are then used as features for the supervised classifier. Our previous work (2009) has shown that the features from the learned HMM significantly improve the accuracy of POS taggers and chunkers on benchmark domain adaptation datasets.

We use the HMM model from our previous work (2009) as our baseline. Our techniques follow the same general setup, as it provides an efficient and empirically-proven starting point for exploring (one part of) the space of possible representations. Note, however, that the HMM on its own does not provide even an approximate solution to the objective function in our problem formulation (Eqn. 2), since it makes no attempt to find the representation that minimizes loss on labeled data. To address this and other concerns, we modify the objective function for HMM training. Specifically, we encode biases for representation learning by defining a set of *properties* ϕ that we believe a good representation function would minimize. One possible bias is that the HMM states should be predictive of the labels in labeled training data. We can encode this as a property that computes the entropy between the HMM states and the labels. For example, in Figure 1, we want to learn the best HMM distribution for the sentence "Innocent bystanders are often the victims" for POS tagging task. The hidden sequence $y_1, y_2, y_3, y_4, y_5, y_6$ can have any distribution $p_1, p_2, p_3, ..., p_m, ..., p_n$ from the latent space $\mathcal{Y}$. Since we are doing POS tagging, we want the distribution to learn the information encoded in the original POS labels "JJ NNS RB VBP DT NNS". Therefore, by calculating the entropy between the hidden sequence and real labels, we can identify a subset of desired distributions that have low entropy, shown in the dotted oval. By minimizing the KL divergence between the learned distribution and the set of desired distributions, we can find the best distribution which is the closest to our desire.

The following subsections describe the specific properties we investigate; here we show how to incorporate them into the objective function. Let $\mathbf{z}$ be the sequence of labels in L_S, and let $\phi(\mathbf{x}, \mathbf{y}, \mathbf{z})$ be a property of the completed data that we wish the learned representation to minimize, based on our prior beliefs. Let Q be the subspace of the possible distributions over $\mathbf{Y}$ that have a small expected value for ϕ: $Q = \{q(\mathbf{Y}) | \mathbf{E}_{\mathbf{Y}\sim q}[\phi(\mathbf{x}, \mathbf{Y}, \mathbf{z})] \leq \xi\}$, for some constant ξ. We then add penalty terms to the objective function (3) for the divergence between the HMM distribution p and the "good" distributions q, as well as for ξ:

$$\mathcal{L}(\theta) - \min_{q,\xi} [\mathbf{KL}(q(\mathbf{Y}) || p(\mathbf{Y}|\mathbf{x}, \theta)) + \sigma|\xi|] \quad (4)$$

$$\text{s.t. } \mathbf{E}_{\mathbf{Y}\sim q}[\phi(\mathbf{x}, \mathbf{Y}, \mathbf{z})] \leq \xi \quad (5)$$

where $\mathbf{KL}$ is the Kullback-Leibler divergence, and σ is a free parameter indicating how important the bias is compared with the marginal log likelihood.

To incorporate multiple biases, we define a vector of properties ϕ, and we constrain each property $\phi_i \leq \xi_i$. Everything else remains the same, except that in the penalty term $\sigma|\xi|$, the absolute value is replaced with a suitable norm: $\sigma \, \|\xi\|$. To allow ourselves to place weights on the relative importance of the different biases, we use a norm of the form $\|\mathbf{x}\|_A = \sqrt{(\mathbf{x}^t A \mathbf{x})}$, where A is a diagonal matrix whose diagonal entries A_{ii} are free parameters that provide weights on the different properties. For our experiments, we set the free parameters σ and A_{ii} using a grid search over development data, as described in Section 5.[1]

3.1 A Bias for Task-specific Representations

Current representation learning techniques are unsupervised, so they will generate the exact same representation for different tasks. Yet it is exceedingly rare that two state-of-the-art NLP systems for different tasks share the same feature set, even if they do tend to share some core set of lexical features.

Traditional non-learned (*i.e.*, manually-engineered) representations essentially always include task-specific features. In response, we propose to bias our representation learning such that the learned representations are optimized for a specific task. In particular, we propose a property that measures how difficult it is to predict the labels in training data, given the learned latent states. Our *entropy property* uses conditional entropy of the labels given the latent state as the measure of unpredictability:

$$\phi^{entropy}(\mathbf{y}, \mathbf{z}) = -\sum_i \tilde{P}(y_i, z_i) \log \tilde{P}(z_i|y_i) \quad (6)$$

where $\tilde{P}$ is the empirical probability and i indicates the ith position in the data. We can plug this feature into Equation 5 to obtain a new version of Equation 4 as an objective function for task-specific representations. We refer to this model as **HMM+E**. Unlike previous formulations for supervised and semi-supervised dimensionality reduction (Zhang et al., 2007; Yang et al., 2006), our framework works efficiently for structured representations.

3.2 A Bias for Domain-Independent Features

Following the theory in Section 2.2, we devise a biased objective to provide an explicit mechanism for minimizing the distance between the source and target domain. As before, we construct a property of the completed data:

$$\phi^{distance}(\mathbf{y}) = d_1(\tilde{P}_S, \tilde{P}_T)$$

where $\tilde{P}_S(Y)$ is the empirical distribution over latent state values estimated from source-domain latent states, and similarly for $\tilde{P}_T(Y)$. Essentially, minimizing this property will bias the the representation towards features that appear approximately as often in the source domain as the target domain. We refer to the model trained with a bias of minimizing $\phi^{distance}$ as **HMM+D**, and the model with both $\phi^{distance}$ and $\phi^{entropy}$ biases as **HMM+D+E**.

3.3 A Bias for Multi-Dimensional Representations

Words are multidimensional objects. In English, words can be nouns or verbs, singular or plural, count or mass, just to name a few dimensions along which they may vary. Factorial HMMs (FHMMs) (Ghahramani and Jordan, 1997) can learn multi-dimensional models, but inference and learning are complex and computationally expensive even in supervised settings. Our previous work (2010) created a multi-dimensional representation called an "I-HMM" by training several HMM layers independently; we showed that by finding several latent categories for each word, this representation can provide useful and domain-independent features for supervised learners. In this work, we also learn a similar multi-dimensional model (**I-HMM+D+E**), but within each layer we add in the two biases described above. While more efficient than FHMMs, the drawback of these I-HMM-based models is that there is no mechanism to encourage the different HMM models to learn different things. As a result, the layers may produce similar or equivalent features describing the dominant aspect of distributional similarity in the data, but miss features that are less strong, but still important, in the data.

To encourage learning a truly multi-dimensional representation, we add a bias towards I-HMM models in which each layer is different from all previous layers. We define an entropy-based *predictability* property that measures how predictable each previous layer is, given the current one. Formally, let y_i^l denote the hidden state at the ith position in layer l of the model. For a given layer l, this property measures the conditional entropy of $\mathbf{y}_m$ given $\mathbf{y}_l$, summed over layers $m < l$, and subtracts this from the maximum possible entropy:

$$\phi_l^{predict}(\mathbf{y}) = MAX + \sum_{i;m<l} \tilde{P}(y_i^l, y_i^m) \log \tilde{P}(y_i^m | y_i^l)$$

The entropy between layer l and the previous layer-

[1]Note that ξ, unlike A and σ, is not a free parameter. It is explicitly minimized in the modified objective function.

s m measures how unpredictable the previous layers are, given layer l. By biasing the model such that MAX minus the entropy approaches zero, we encourage layer l towards completely different features from previous layers. We call the model with this bias **P-HMM+D+E**.

4 Efficient Parameter Estimation

Several machine learning paradigms have been developed recently for incorporating biases and constraints into parameter estimation (Liang et al., 2009; Chang et al., 2007; Mann and McCallum, 2007). We leverage the Posterior Regularization (PR) framework for our problem because of its flexibility in handling different kinds of biases; we provide a brief overview of the technique here, but see (Ganchev et al., 2010) for full details.

4.1 Overview of PR

PR introduces a modified EM algorithm to handle constrained objectives, like Equation 4. The modified E-step estimates a distribution $q(\mathbf{Y})$ that is close to the current estimate of $p(\mathbf{Y}|\mathbf{x}, \theta)$, but also close to the ideal set of distributions that (in expectation) have $\phi = 0$ for each property ϕ. The M step remains the same, except that it re-estimates parameters with respect to expected latent states computed with q rather than p.

E step:

$$q^{t+1} = \arg\min_{q} \min_{\xi} \mathbf{KL}(q(\mathbf{Y})||p(\mathbf{Y}|\mathbf{x}, \theta^t)) + \sigma \, ||\xi|| \quad \text{s.t. } \mathbf{E}_q[\phi(\mathbf{x}, \mathbf{Y}, \mathbf{z})] \leq \xi$$

M step:

$$\theta^{t+1} = \operatorname*{argmax}_{\theta} \mathbf{E}_{q^{t+1}}[\log p(\mathbf{x}, \mathbf{Y}|\theta^t))]$$

To make the optimization task in the E-step more tractable, PR transforms it to a dual problem:

$$\max_{\lambda \geq 0, ||\lambda||_* \leq \sigma} \; -\log \sum_{\mathbf{Y}} p(\mathbf{Y}|\mathbf{x}, \theta) \exp\{-\lambda \cdot \phi(\mathbf{x}, \mathbf{Y}, \mathbf{z})\}$$

where $||\cdot||_*$ is the dual norm of $||\cdot||$. The gradient of this dual objective is $-\mathbf{E}_q[\phi(\mathbf{x}, \mathbf{Y}, \mathbf{z})]$. A projected subgradient descent algorithm is used to perform the optimization.

4.2 Modifying ϕ for Tractability

In unstructured settings, this optimization problem is relatively straightforward. However, for structured representations, we need to ensure that the dynamic programming algorithms needed for inference remain tractable for the biased objectives. For efficient PR over structured models, the properties ϕ need to be decomposed as a sum over the cliques in the structured model. Unfortunately, the properties we mention above do not decompose so nicely, so we must resort to approximations.

In order to efficiently compute the expected value of the entropy property with respect to $\mathbf{Y} \sim q$, we need to be able to compute each component $\mathbf{E}_{Y_i \sim q}[\phi^{entropy}(Y_i, z_i)]$ separately. Yet $\tilde{P}$ depends on the setting of other latent states Y_j in the corpus. To avoid this problem, we pre-compute the expected empirical distributions over the completed data. For each specific value y and z:

$$\tilde{P}_q(y, z) = \frac{1}{|L_S|} \sum_{x} \sum_{i=1}^{|x|} \mathbf{1}[z_i = z] q(Y_i = y)$$

$$\tilde{P}_q(y) = \frac{1}{|L_S|} \sum_{x} \sum_{i=1}^{|x|} q(Y_i = y)$$

These expected empirical distributions $\tilde{P}_q$ can be computed efficiently using standard inference algorithms, such as the forward algorithm for HMMs. Note that $\tilde{P}_q$ depends on q, but unlike the original $\tilde{P}$ from Equation 6, they do not depend on the data completions $\mathbf{y}$. Thus we can compute $\tilde{P}_q$ once for each q^t, and then substitute it for $\tilde{P}$ for all values of $\mathbf{Y}$ in the computation of $\mathbf{E}_{\mathbf{Y} \sim q} \phi^{entropy}(\mathbf{Y}, \mathbf{z})$, making this computation tractable. For the entropy-based predictability properties, the calculation is similar, but instead of using the label z, we use the decoded states y_i^l from previous layers.

For the distance property, Ben-David *et al.*'s analysis depends on a particular notion of distance (Eqn. 1) that is computationally intractable. They also propose more tractable lower bounds, but these are again incompatible with the PR framework. Since no computationally feasible exact algorithm exists for this distance feature, we resort to a crude but efficient approximation of this measure: for each possible value y of the latent states, we define:

$$\phi_y^{dist}(\mathbf{y}) = \sum_{i|x_i \in U_S} \frac{\mathbf{1}[y_i = y]q(Y_i = y)}{|U_S|} - \sum_{i|x_i \in U_T} \frac{\mathbf{1}[y_i = y]q(Y_i = y)}{|U_T|}$$

Each of these individual properties is tractable for structured models. Combining these properties using the $||\cdot||_A$ norm results in a Euclidean distance (weighted by A) between the frequencies of features in each domain, rather than d_1 distance.

5 Experiments

We tested the structured representations with biases on two NLP tasks: Chinese POS tagging and English NER. In both cases, we use a domain adaptation setting where no labeled data is available for the target domain — a particularly difficult setting, but one that provides a strong test for an NLP system's ability to generalize . In our work (Huang and Yates, 2009), we used a plain HMM for domain adaptation tasks in which there is labeled source data and unlabeled source and target data, but no labeled target data for training. Therefore, here, we use the HMM technique as a baseline, and build on it by including biases.

5.1 Chinese POS tagging

We use the UCLA Corpus of Written Chinese, which is a part of The Lancaster Corpus of Mandarin Chinese (LCMC). The UCLA Corpus consists of 11,192 sentences of word-segmented and POS-tagged text in 13 genres. We use gold-standard word segmentation labels during training and testing. The LCMC tagset consists of 50 Chinese POS tags. Each genre averages 5284 word tokens, for a total of 68,695 tokens among all genres. We use the 'news' genre as our source domain and randomly select 20% of every other genre as labeled test data. To train our representation models, we use the 'news' text, plus the remaining 80% of the texts from the other genres. We use 90% of the labeled news text for training, and 10% for development. We replace *hapax legomena* in the unlabeled data with the special symbol *UNKNOWN*, and also do the same for word types in the labeled test sets that never appear in our unlabeled training texts.

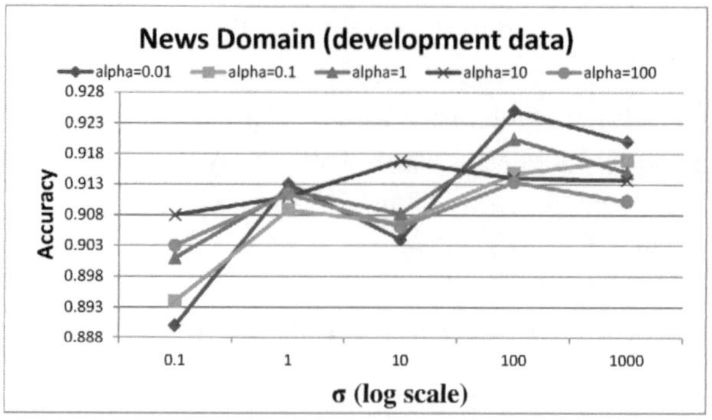

Figure 2: Grid search for parameters on news text

Following our previous HMM setup in (Huang and Yates, 2009) for consistency, we use an HMM with 80 latent states. For our multi-layer models, we use 7 layers of HMMs. We tuned the free parameters σ and A on development data. We varied σ from 0.1 to 1000. To tune A, we start by setting the diagonal entry for $\phi^{entropy}$ to 1, without loss of generality. We then tie all the entries in A for ϕ_y^{dist} to a single parameter α, and tie all of the entries for $\phi_y^{predict}$ to a parameter β. We vary α and β over the set $\{0.01,0.1,1,10,100\}$. Figure 2 shows our results for σ and α on news development data. A setting of $\alpha = 0.01$ and $\sigma = 100$ performs best, with all $\sigma = 100$ doing reasonably well. Results for each of these models on the general fiction test text confirm the general trends seen on development data — a comforting sign, since this indicates we can optimize the free parameters on in-domain development data, rather than requiring labeled data from the target domain. Our models tended to perform better with increasing β on development data, though with diminishing returns. We pick the largest setting tested, $\beta = 100$, for our final models.

We use a linear-chain Conditional Random Field (CRF) for our supervised classifier. To incorporate the learned representations, we use the Viterbi Algorithm to find the optimal latent state sequence from each HMM-based model and then use the optimal states as features in the CRF. Table 1 presents the full list of features in the CRF. To handle Chinese, we add in two features introduced in previous work (Wang et al., 2009): radical features and repeated characters. A *radical* is a portion of a Chinese character that consists of a small number of pen or brush strokes in a regular pattern.

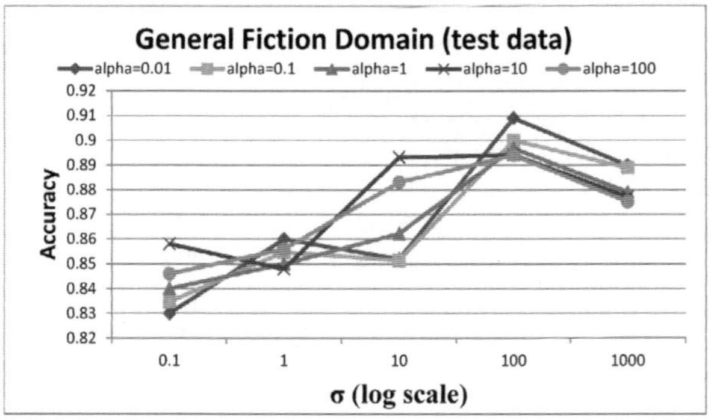

Figure 3: Validating parameter settings on fiction text

CRF Feature Set
Transition
$\forall_z \mathbf{1}[z_j = z]$
$\forall_{z,z'} \mathbf{1}[z_j = z \text{ and } z_{j-1} = z']$
Word
$\forall_{w,z} \mathbf{1}[x_j = w \text{ and } z_j = z]$
Radical
$\forall_{z,r} \mathbf{1}[\exists_{c \in x_j} radical(c) = r \text{ and } z_j = z]$
Repeated Words
$\forall_{A,B,z} \mathbf{1}[x_j = AABB \text{ and } z_j = z]$
$\forall_{A,z} \mathbf{1}[(x_j = AA\text{的} \text{or } x_j = AA\text{地}) \text{ and } z_j = z]$
$\forall_{A,B,z} \mathbf{1}[x_j = ABAB \text{ and } z_j = z]$
Features from Representation Learning
$\forall_{y,l,z} \mathbf{1}[y_j^l = y \text{ and } z_j = z]$

Table 1: **Features used in our Chinese POS tagging CRF systems.** c represents a character within a word.

Table 2 shows our results. We compare against the Baseline CRF without any additional representations and the unbiased HMM, a state-of-the-art domain adaptation technique from previous work, over all 13 domains (source and target). We also compare against a state-of-the-art Chinese POS tagger for in-domain text, the CRF-based Stanford tagger (Tseng et al., 2005), retrained for this corpus. H-MM+D+E outperforms the Stanford tagger on 10 out of 12 target domains and the unbiased HMM on all domains, while the P-HMM+D+E outperforms the Stanford tagger (2.6% average improvement) and HMM (1.7%) on all 12 target domains. The I-HMM+D+E is slightly better than the HMM+D+E (.3%), but incorporating the multi-dimensional bias (P-HMM+D+E) adds an additional 0.6% improvement.

Our interpretation for the success of I-HMM+D+E and P-HMM+D+E is that the increase in the state space of the models yields improved performance. Because P-HMM+D+E biases against redundant states found in I-HMM+D+E, it effectively increases the state space beyond I-HMM+D+E. Ahuja and Downey (2010) and our own work with HMMs as representations (2010) have previously shown that increasing the state space of the HMM can significantly improve the representation, but memory constraints eventually prevent further progress this way. The I-HMM+D+E and P-HMM+D+E models can provide similar benefits, but because they split parameters across multiple HMMs, they can accommodate much greater state spaces in the same amount of memory.

We also tested the entropy and distance biases separately. Figure 4 shows the result of the distance-biased HMM+D on the general-fiction test text, as we vary σ over the set $\{0.1,1,10,100,1000\}$ (we observed similar results for other domains). For all values of σ, the biased representation outperforms the unbiased HMM. There is also a strong negative correlation between the expected value of $||\phi_{distance}||$ and the resulting accuracy, as expected from Ben-David *et al.*'s theoretical analysis. The HMM+E model outperforms the HMM on the (source) news domain by 0.3%, but actually performs worse for most target domains. We suspect that the entropy feature, which is learned only from labeled source-domain data, makes the representation biased towards features that are important in the source domain only. However, after we add in the distance bias and a parameter to balance the weights from both biases, the representation is able to capture the label information as well as the target domain features. Thus, the representation won't solely depend on source data. HMM+D+E, which combines both biases, outperforms HMM+D, suggesting that task-specific features for domain adaptation can be helpful, but only if there is some control for the domain-independence of the features.

5.2 English Named Entity Recognition

To evaluate on a second task, we turn to Named Entity Recognition. We use the training data from the

	news (source)	lore	reli	humour	gen-fic	essay	mystery	romance	sci-fi	skill	science	adv-fic	report	avg
words	9774	5428	3248	3326	4913	5214	5774	5489	3070	5464	5262	5071	6662	5284
CRF w/o HMM	93.8	85.0	80.0	85.4	85.0	83.8	84.7	86.0	82.8	78.2	82.2	77.1	85.3	84.5
HMM+E	97.1	88.2	83.1	87.5	87.4	89.2	89.5	87.1	86.7	82.1	87.2	79.4	91.7	88.3
Stanford	**98.8**	88.4	83.5	89.0	87.5	88.4	87.4	87.5	88.6	82.7	86.0	82.1	91.7	88.7
HMM	96.9	89.7	85.2	89.6	89.4	89.0	90.1	89.0	87.0	84.9	87.8	80.0	91.4	89.2
HMM+D	97.4	89.9	85.4	89.4	89.6	89.9	90.1	88.6	87.9	85.3	87.9	80.0	92.0	89.5
HMM+D+E	97.7	90.1	86.1	**89.8**	90.9	89.7	**90.3**	89.8	88.4	85.6	**87.9**	81.2	92.0	89.9
I-HMM+D+E	97.8	90.5	87.0	89.1	91.1	90.2	90.0	90.5	89.8	86.0	87.1	82.2	92.1	90.2
P-HMM+D+E	98.2	**91.5**	**87.7**	89.0	**91.8**	**91.0**	89.9	**91.4**	**90.4**	**87.0**	87.7	**83.4**	**92.4**	**90.8**

Table 2: **POS tagging accuracy: The P-HMM+D+E tagger outperforms the unbiased HMM tagger and the Stanford tagger on all target domains.** The 'avg' column includes source-domain development data results. Differences between the P-HMM+D+E and the Stanford tagger are statistically significant at $p < 0.01$ on average and on 11 out of 12 target domain. We used the two-tailed Chi-square test with Yates' correction.

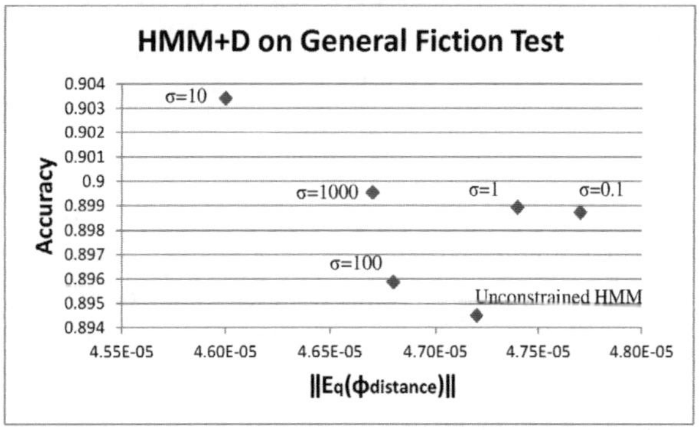

Figure 4: Greater distance between domains correlates with worse target-domain tagging accuracy.

System	F1
CRF without HMM	66.15
HMM+E	74.25
HMM	75.06
HMM+D	75.75
HMM+D+E	76.03
I-HMM+D+E	77.04
P-HMM+D+E	78.62

Table 3: English Named Entity recognition results

CoNLL 2003 shared task for our labeled training set, consisting of 204k tokens from the newswire domain. We tested the system on the MUC7 formal run test data, consisting of 59k tokens of stories on the telecommunications and aerospace industries.

To train our representations, we use the CoNLL training data and the MUC7 training data without labels. We again use a CRF, with features introduced by Zhang and Johnson (2003) for our baseline. We use the same setting of free parameters from our POS tagging experiments.

Results are shown in Table 3. Our best biased representation P-HMM+D+E outperformed the unbiased HMM representation by 3.6%, and beats the I-HMM+D+E by 1.6%. The domain-distance and multi-dimensional biases help most, while the task-specific bias helps somewhat, but only when the domain-distance bias is included. The best system tested on this dataset achieved a slightly better F1 score (78.84) (Turian et al., 2010), but used a much larger training corpus (they use RCV1 corpus which contains approximately 63 million tokens). Other studies (Turian et al., 2010; Huang et al., 2011) have performed a detailed comparison between these types of systems, so we concentrate on comparisons between biased and unbiased representations here.

5.3 Does the task-specific bias actually help?

In this section, we test whether the task-specific bias (entropy bias) actually learns something task-specific. We learn the entropy-biased representations for two tasks on the same set of sentences, labeled differently for the two tasks: English POS tagging and Named Entity Recognition. Then we switch the representations to see whether they will help or hurt the performance on the other task. We randomly picked 500 sentences from WSJ section

Representation/Task	POS Accuracy	NER F1
HMM	88.5	66.3
HMM+E(POS labels)	89.7	64.5
HMM+E(NER labels)	86.5	68.0

Table 4: Results of POS tagging and Named Entity recognition tasks with different representations. With the entropy-biased representation, the system has better performance on the task which the bias is trained for, but worse performance on the other task.

0-18 as our labeled training data and 500 sentences from WSJ section 20-23 as testing data. Because WSJ data does not have gold standard NER tags, we manually labeled these sentences with NER tags. For simplicity, we only use three types of NER tags: person, organization and location. The result is shown in Table 4. When the entropy bias uses labels from the same task as the classifier, the performance is improved: about 1.2% in accuracy on POS tagging and 1.7% in F1 score on NER. Switching the representations for the tasks actually hurts the performance compared with the unbiased representation. The results suggest that the entropy bias does indeed yield a task-specific representation.

6 Conclusion and Future Work

We introduce three types of biases into representation learning for sequence labeling using the PR framework. Our experiments on POS tagging and NER indicate domain-independent biases and multi-dimensional biases significantly improve the representations, while the task-specific bias improves performance on out-of-domain data if it is combined with the domain-independent bias. Our results indicate the power of representation learning in building domain-agnostic classifiers, but also the complexity of the task and the limitations of current techniques, as even the best models still fall significantly short of in-domain performance. Important considerations for future work include identifying further effective and tractable biases, and extending beyond sequence-labeling to other types of NLP tasks.

Acknowledgments

This research was supported in part by NSF grant IIS-1065397.

References

Arun Ahuja and Doug Downey. 2010. Improved extraction assessment through better language models. In *Proceedings of the Annual Meeting of the North American Chapter of the Association of Computational Linguistics (NAACL-HLT)*.

Shai Ben-David, John Blitzer, Koby Crammer, and Fernando Pereira. 2007. Analysis of representations for domain adaptation. In *Advances in Neural Information Processing Systems 20*, Cambridge, MA. MIT Press.

Shai Ben-David, John Blitzer, Koby Crammer, Alex Kulesza, Fernando Pereira, and Jennifer Wortman Vaughan. 2010. A theory of learning from different domains. *Machine Learning*, 79:151–175.

John Blitzer, Ryan McDonald, and Fernando Pereira. 2006. Domain adaptation with structural correspondence learning. In *EMNLP*.

John Blitzer, Koby Crammer, Alex Kulesza, Fernando Pereira, and Jenn Wortman. 2007. Learning bounds for domain adaptation. In *Advances in Neural Information Processing Systems*.

M. Candito and B. Crabbé. 2009. Improving generative statistical parsing with semi-supervised word clustering. In *IWPT*, pages 138–141.

M. Chang, L. Ratinov, and D. Roth. 2007. Guiding semi-supervision with constraint-driven learning. In *Proceedings of the ACL*.

Hal Daumé III, Abhishek Kumar, and Avishek Saha. 2010. Frustratingly easy semi-supervised domain adaptation. In *Proceedings of the ACL Workshop on Domain Adaptation (DANLP)*.

Hal Daumé III. 2007. Frustratingly easy domain adaptation. In *ACL*.

S. C. Deerwester, S. T. Dumais, T. K. Landauer, G. W. Furnas, and R. A. Harshman. 1990. Indexing by latent semantic analysis. *Journal of the American Society of Information Science*, 41(6):391–407.

Paramveer S. Dhillon, Dean Foster, and Lyle Ungar. 2011. Multi-view learning of word embeddings via cca. In *Neural Information Processing Systems (NIPS)*.

A. Emami, P. Xu, and F. Jelinek. 2003. Using a connectionist model in a syntactical based language model. In *Proceedings of the International Conference on Spoken Language Processing*, pages 372–375.

Kuzman Ganchev, João Graça, Jennifer Gillenwater, and Ben Taskar. 2010. Posterior regularization for structured latent variable models. *Journal of Machine Learning Research*, 11:10–49.

Zoubin Ghahramani and Michael I. Jordan. 1997. Factorial hidden markov models. *Machine Learning*, 29(2-3):245–273.

Daniel Gildea. 2001. Corpus Variation and Parser Performance. In *Conference on Empirical Methods in Natural Language Processing*.

T. Honkela. 1997. Self-organizing maps of words for natural language processing applications. In *In Proceedings of the International ICSC Symposium on Soft Computing*.

Fei Huang and Alexander Yates. 2009. Distributional representations for handling sparsity in supervised sequence labeling. In *Proceedings of the Annual Meeting of the Association for Computational Linguistics (ACL)*.

Fei Huang and Alexander Yates. 2010. Exploring representation-learning approaches to domain adaptation. In *Proceedings of the ACL 2010 Workshop on Domain Adaptation for Natural Language Processing (DANLP)*.

Fei Huang, Alexander Yates, Arun Ahuja, and Doug Downey. 2011. Language models as representations for weakly supervised nlp tasks. In *Conference on Natural Language Learning (CoNLL)*.

Jing Jiang and ChengXiang Zhai. 2007. Instance weighting for domain adaptation in NLP. In *ACL*.

P. Liang, M. I. Jordan, and D. Klein. 2009. Learning from measurements in exponential families. In *International Conference on Machine Learning (ICML)*.

D. Lin and X Wu. 2009. Phrase clustering for discriminative learning. In *ACL-IJCNLP*, pages 1030–1038.

G. S. Mann and A. McCallum. 2007. Simple, robust, scalable semi-supervised learning via expectation regularization. In *In Proc. ICML*.

Y. Mansour, M. Mohri, and A. Rostamizadeh. 2009. Domain adaptation with multiple sources. In *Advances in Neural Information Processing Systems*.

F. Morin and Y. Bengio. 2005. Hierarchical probabilistic neural network language model. In *Proceedings of the International Workshop on Artificial Intelligence and Statistics*, pages 246–252.

Sameer Pradhan, Wayne Ward, and James H. Martin. 2007. Towards robust semantic role labeling. In *Proceedings of NAACL-HLT*, pages 556–563.

M. Sahlgren. 2005. An introduction to random indexing. In *In Methods and Applications of Semantic Indexing Workshop at the 7th International Conference on Terminology and Knowledge Engineering (TKE)*.

G. Salton and M.J. McGill. 1983. *Introduction to Modern Information Retrieval*. McGraw-Hill.

Satoshi Sekine. 1997. The domain dependence of parsing. In *Proc. Applied Natural Language Processing (ANLP)*, pages 96–102.

Huihsin Tseng, Daniel Jurafsky, and Christopher Manning. 2005. Morphological features help pos tagging of unknown words across language varieties. In *Proceedings of the Fourth SIGHAN Workshop on Chinese Language Processing*.

Joseph Turian, Lev Ratinov, and Yoshua Bengio. 2010. Word representations: A simple and general method for semi-supervised learning. In *Proceedings of the Annual Meeting of the Association for Computational Linguistics (ACL)*, pages 384–394.

P. D. Turney and P. Pantel. 2010. From frequency to meaning: Vector space models of semantics. *Journal of Artificial Intelligence Research*, 37:141–188.

Lijie Wang, Wanxiang Che, and Ting Liu. 2009. An svmtool-based chinese pos tagger. In *Journal of Chinese Information Processing*.

X. Yang, H. Fu, H. Zha, and J. Barlow. 2006. Semi-supervised nonlinear dimensionality reduction. In *Proceedings of the 23rd International Conference on Machine Learning*.

T. Zhang and D. Johnson. 2003. A robust risk minimization based named entity recognition system. In *CoNLL*.

D. Zhang, Z.H. Zhou, and S. Chen. 2007. Semi-supervised dimensionality reduction. In *Proceedings of the 7th SIAM International Conference on Data Mining*.

Unambiguity Regularization for Unsupervised Learning of Probabilistic Grammars

Kewei Tu*
Departments of Statistics and Computer Science
University of California, Los Angeles
Los Angeles, CA 90095, USA
tukw@ucla.edu

Vasant Honavar
Department of Computer Science
Iowa State University
Ames, IA 50011, USA
honavar@cs.iastate.edu

Abstract

We introduce a novel approach named *unambiguity regularization* for unsupervised learning of probabilistic natural language grammars. The approach is based on the observation that natural language is remarkably unambiguous in the sense that only a tiny portion of the large number of possible parses of a natural language sentence are syntactically valid. We incorporate an inductive bias into grammar learning in favor of grammars that lead to unambiguous parses on natural language sentences. The resulting family of algorithms includes the expectation-maximization algorithm (EM) and its variant, Viterbi EM, as well as a so-called softmax-EM algorithm. The softmax-EM algorithm can be implemented with a simple and computationally efficient extension to standard EM. In our experiments of unsupervised dependency grammar learning, we show that unambiguity regularization is beneficial to learning, and in combination with annealing (of the regularization strength) and sparsity priors it leads to improvement over the current state of the art.

1 Introduction

Machine learning offers a potentially powerful approach to learning probabilistic grammars from data. Because of the high cost of manual sentence annotation, there is substantial interest in unsupervised grammar learning, i.e., the induction of a grammar from a corpus of unannotated sentences. The simplest such approaches attempt to maximize the likelihood of the grammar given the training data, typically using expectation-maximization (EM) (Baker, 1979; Lari and Young, 1990; Klein and Manning, 2004). More recent approaches incorporate additional prior information of the target grammar into learning. For example, Kurihara and Sato (2004) used Dirichlet priors over rule probabilities to obtain smoothed estimates of the probabilities. Johnson et al. (2007) used Dirichlet priors with hyperparameters set to values less than 1 to encourage sparsity of grammar rules. Finkel et al. (2007) and Liang et al. (2007) proposed to use the hierarchical Dirichlet process prior to bias learning towards concise grammars without the need to pre-specify the number of nonterminals. Cohen et al. (2008) and Cohen and Smith (2009) employed the logistic normal prior to model the correlations between grammar symbols. Gillenwater et al. (2010) incorporated a sparsity bias on grammar rules into learning by means of posterior regularization.

More recently, Spitkovsky et al. (2010) and Poon and Domingos (2011) observed that the use of Viterbi EM (also called hard EM) in place of standard EM can lead to significantly improved results in unsupervised learning of probabilistic grammars from natural language and image data respectively, even if no prior information is used. This finding is surprising because Viterbi EM is a degenerate case of standard EM and is therefore generally considered to be less effective in locating the optimum of the objective function. Spitkovsky et al. (2010) speculated that the observed advantage of Viterbi EM over standard EM is due to standard EM reserving too much probability mass to spurious parses in

*Part of the work was done while at Iowa State University.

the E-step. However, it is still unclear as to why Viterbi EM can avoid this problem.

Against this background, we propose the use of a novel type of prior information for unsupervised learning of probabilistic natural language grammars, namely the syntactic unambiguity of natural language. Although it is often possible to correctly parse a natural language sentence in more than one way, natural language is remarkably unambiguous in the sense that the number of plausible parses of a natural language sentence is rather small in comparison with the total number of possible parses. Thus, we incorporate into learning an inductive bias in favor of grammars that lead to unambiguous parses on natural language sentences, by using the posterior regularization framework (Ganchev et al., 2010). We name this approach *unambiguity regularization*. The resulting family of algorithms includes standard EM and Viterbi EM, as well as an algorithm that falls between standard EM and Viterbi EM which we call softmax-EM. The softmax-EM algorithm can be implemented with a simple and computationally efficient extension to standard EM. The fact that Viterbi EM is a special case of our approach also gives an explanation of the advantage of Viterbi EM observed in previous work: it is because Viterbi EM implicitly utilizes unambiguity regularization. In our experiments of unsupervised dependency grammar learning, we show that unambiguity regularization is beneficial to learning, and in combination with annealing (of the regularization strength) and sparsity priors it leads to improvement over the current state of the art.

It should be noted that our approach is closely related to the deterministic annealing (DA) technique studied in the optimization literature (Rose, 1998). However, DA has a very different motivation than ours and differs from our approach in a few important algorithmic details, as will be discussed in section 5. When applied to unsupervised grammar learning, DA has been shown to lead to worse parsing accuracy than standard EM (Smith and Eisner, 2004); in contrast, we show that our approach leads to significantly higher parsing accuracy than standard EM in unsupervised dependency grammar learning.

The rest of the paper is organized as follows. Section 2 analyzes the degree of unambiguity of natural language grammars. Section 3 introduces the unambiguity regularization approach and shows that standard EM, Viterbi EM and softmax-EM are its special cases. We show the experimental results in section 4, discuss related work in section 5 and conclude the paper in section 6.

2 The (Un)ambiguity of Natural Language Grammars

A grammar is said to be ambiguous on a sentence if the sentence can be parsed in more than one way by the grammar. It is widely acknowledged that natural language grammars are ambiguous on a significant proportion of natural language sentences. For example, Manning and Schütze (1999) show that a sentence randomly chosen from the Wall Street Journal — "The post office will hold out discounts and service concessions as incentives" — has at least five plausible syntactic parses. When we parse this sentence using the Berkeley parser (Petrov et al., 2006), one of the state-of-the-art English language parsers, we find many alternative parses in addition to the parses shown in (Manning and Schütze, 1999). Indeed, with a probabilistic context-free grammar of only 26 nonterminals (as used in the Berkeley parser), the estimated total number of possible parses[1] of the example sentence is 2×10^{37}. However, upon closer examination, we find that among this very large number of possible parses, only a few have significant probabilities. Figure 1 shows the probabilities of the 100 best parses of the example sentence. We can see that most of the parses have probabilities that are negligible compared with the probability of the best parse (i.e., the parse with the largest probability). Quantitatively, we find that the probabilities of the parses decrease roughly exponentially as we go from the best parse to the less likely parses. We confirmed this observation by examining the parses of many other natural language sentences obtained using the Berkeley parser. This observation suggests that natural language grammars are indeed remarkably unambiguous on natural language sentences, in the sense that for a typical

[1]Given a sentence of length m and a complete Chomsky normal form grammar with n nonterminals, the number of all possible parses is $C_{m-1} \times n^{2m-1}$, where C_{m-1} is the $(m-1)$-th Catalan number. This number is further increased if there are unary rules between nonterminals in the grammar.

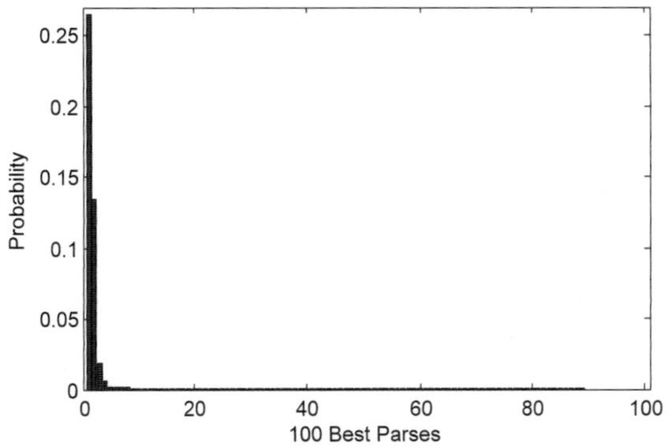

Figure 1: The probabilities of the 100 best parses of the example sentence.

natural language sentence, the probability mass of the parses is concentrated to a tiny portion of all possible parses. This is not surprising in light of the fact that the main purpose of natural language is communication and in the course of language evolution the selection pressure for more efficient communication would favor unambiguous languages.

To highlight the unambiguity of natural language grammars, here we compare the parse probabilities shown in Figure 1 with the parse probabilities produced by two other probabilistic context-free grammars. In figure 2(a) we show the probabilities of the 100 best parses of the example sentence produced by a random grammar. The random grammar has a similar number of nonterminals as in the Berkeley parser, and its grammar rule probabilities are sampled from a uniform distribution and then normalized. It can be seen that unlike the natural language grammar, the random grammar produces a very uniform probability distribution over parses. Figure 2(b) shows the probabilities of the 100 best parses of the example sentence produced by a maximum-likelihood grammar learned from the unannotated Wall Street Journal corpus of the Penn Treebank using the EM algorithm. An exponential decrease can be observed in the probabilities, but the probability mass is still much less concentrated than in the case of the natural language grammar. Again, we confirmed this observation by repeating the experiments on many other natural language sentences. This suggests that both the random grammar and the maximum-likelihood grammar are far more ambiguous on natural language sentences than true natural language grammars.

3 Learning with Unambiguity Regularization

Motivated by the preceding observation, we want to incorporate into learning an inductive bias in favor of grammars that are unambiguous on natural language sentences. First of all, we need a precise definition of the ambiguity of a grammar on a sentence. Assume a grammar with a fixed set of grammar rules and let θ be the rule probabilities. Let x represent a sentence and let z represent the parse of x. One natural measurement of the ambiguity is the information entropy of z conditioned on x and θ:

$$H(z|x,\theta) = -\sum_{z} p_\theta(z|x) \log p_\theta(z|x)$$

The lower the entropy is, the less ambiguous the grammar is on sentence x. When the entropy reaches 0, the grammar is strictly unambiguous on sentence x, i.e., sentence x has a unique parse according to the grammar.

Now we need to modify the objective function of grammar learning to favor low ambiguity of the learned grammar in parsing natural langauge sentences. One approach is to use a prior distribution that favors grammars with low ambiguity on the sentences that they generate. Since the likelihood term in the objective function would ensure that the learned grammar will have high probability of generating natural language sentences, combining the likelihood and the prior would lead to low ambiguity of the learned grammar on natural language sentences. Unfortunately, adding this prior to the objective function makes learning intractable. Hence, here we adopt an alternative approach using the posterior regularization framework (Ganchev et al., 2010). Posterior regularization biases learning in favor of solutions with desired behavior by constraining the model posteriors on the unlabeled data. In our case, we use the constraint that the probability distributions on the parses of the training sentences given the learned grammar must have low entropy, which is equivalent to requiring the learned grammar to have low ambiguity on the training sentences.

Let $\mathbf{X} = \{x_1, x_2, \ldots, x_n\}$ denote the set of training sentences, $\mathbf{Z} = \{z_1, z_2, \ldots, z_n\}$ denote the set

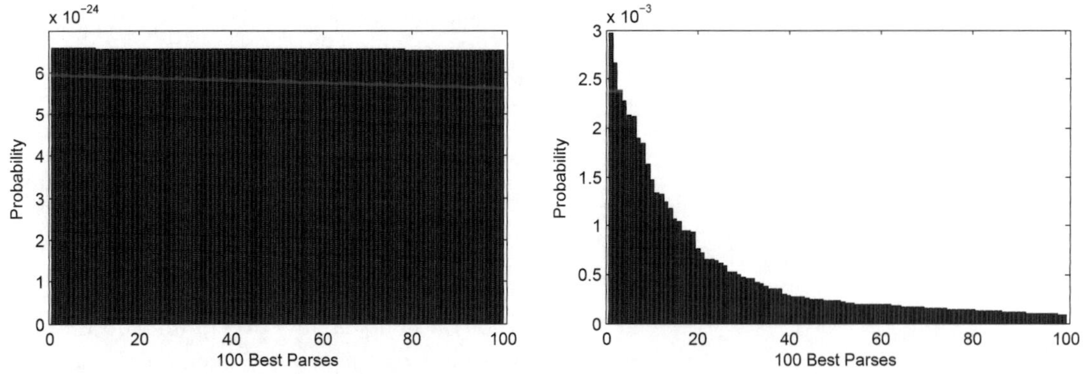

(a) (b)

Figure 2: The probabilities of the 100 best parses of the example sentence produced by (a) a random grammar and (b) a maximum-likelihood grammar learned by the EM algorithm.

of parses of the training sentences, and θ denote the rule probabilities of the grammar. We use the slack-penalized version of the posterior regularization objective function:

$$J(\theta) = \log p(\theta|\mathbf{X}) - \min_{q,\xi}\left(\mathbf{KL}(q(\mathbf{Z})||p_\theta(\mathbf{Z}|\mathbf{X})) + \sigma\sum_i \xi_i\right)$$
$$\text{s.t. } \forall i, H(z_i) = -\sum_{z_i} q(z_i)\log q(z_i) \le \xi_i$$

where σ is a nonnegative constant that controls the strength of the regularization term; q is an auxiliary distribution such that $q(\mathbf{Z}) = \prod_i q(z_i)$. The first term in the objective function is the log posterior probability of the grammar parameters given the training corpus, and the second term minimizes the KL-divergence between the auxiliary distribution q and the posterior distribution on $\mathbf{Z}$ while constrains q to have low entropy. We can incorporate the constraint into the objective function, so we get

$$J(\theta) = \log p(\theta|\mathbf{X}) - \min_{q}\left(\mathbf{KL}(q(\mathbf{Z})||p_\theta(\mathbf{Z}|\mathbf{X})) + \sigma\sum_i H(z_i)\right)$$

To optimize this objective function, we can perform coordinate ascent on a two-variable function:

$$F(\theta, q) = \log p(\theta|\mathbf{X}) - \left(\mathbf{KL}(q(\mathbf{Z})||p_\theta(\mathbf{Z}|\mathbf{X})) + \sigma\sum_i H(z_i)\right)$$

There are two steps in each coordinate ascent iteration. In the first step, we fix q and optimize θ. It can be shown that

$$\begin{aligned}\theta^* &= \arg\max_\theta F(\theta, q)\\ &= \arg\max_\theta \mathbf{E}_q[\log(p_\theta(\mathbf{X}, \mathbf{Z})p(\theta))]\end{aligned}$$

This is equivalent to the M-step in the EM algorithm. The second step fixes θ and optimizes q.

$$q^* = \arg\max_q F(\theta, q) = \arg\min_q\left(\mathbf{KL}(q(\mathbf{Z})||p_\theta(\mathbf{Z}|\mathbf{X})) + \sigma\sum_i H(z_i)\right)$$

It is different from the E-step of the EM algorithm in that it contains an additional regularization term $\sigma\sum_i H(z_i)$. Ganchev et al. (2010) propose to use the projected subgradient method to solve this optimization problem in the general case of posterior regularization. In our case, however, it is possible to obtain an analytical solution as shown below.

First, note that the optimization objective of this step can be rewritten as the sum over functions of individual training sentences.

$$\mathbf{KL}(q(\mathbf{Z})||p_\theta(\mathbf{Z}|\mathbf{X})) + \sigma\sum_i H(z_i) = \sum_i f_i(q)$$

where

$$\begin{aligned}f_i(q) &= \mathbf{KL}(q(z_i)||p_\theta(z_i|x_i)) + \sigma H(z_i)\\ &= \sum_{z_i}\left(q(z_i)\log\frac{q(z_i)^{1-\sigma}}{p_\theta(z_i|x_i)}\right)\end{aligned}$$

So we can optimize $f_i(q)$ for each training sentence x_i. The optimum of $f_i(q)$ depends on the value of the constant σ.

Case 1: $\sigma = 0$**.**

$f_i(q)$ contains only the KL-divergence term, so the second step in the coordinate ascent iteration becomes the standard E-step of the EM algorithm.

$$q^*(z_i) = p_\theta(z_i|x_i)$$

Case 2: $0 < \sigma < 1$**.**

The space of valid assignments of the distribution $q(z_i)$ is a unit $(m-1)$-simplex, where m is the number of valid parses of sentence x_i. Denote this space by Δ.

Theorem 1. *$f_i(q)$ is strictly convex on the unit simplex Δ when $0 < \sigma < 1$.*

Proof Sketch. Define $g(x) = x \log x$, where $g(0)$ is defined to be 0. For any $t \in (0,1)$, for any two points q_1 and q_2 in the unit simplex Δ, we can show that

$$\begin{aligned} & tf_i(q_1) + (1-t)f_i(q_2) - f_i(tq_1 + (1-t)q_2) \\ = \;& (1-\sigma)\sum_{z_i} \left[\begin{array}{l} tg(q_1(z_i)) + (1-t)g(q_2(z_i)) \\ -\, g(tq_1(z_i) + (1-t)q_2(z_i)) \end{array} \right] \end{aligned}$$

It is easy to prove that $g(x)$ is strictly convex on the interval $[0,1]$. Because $\forall z_i, 0 \le q_1(z_i), q_2(z_i) \le 1$, we have

$$\begin{aligned} & tg(q_1(z_i)) + (1-t)g(q_2(z_i)) \\ & > \; g(tq_1(z_i) + (1-t)q_2(z_i)) \end{aligned}$$

Because $1 - \sigma > 0$, we have

$$tf_i(q_1) + (1-t)f_i(q_2) - f_i(tq_1 + (1-t)q_2) > 0$$

□

By applying the Lagrange multiplier, we get the stationary point of $f_i(q)$ on the unit simplex Δ:

$$q^*(z_i) = \alpha_i p_\theta(z_i|x_i)^{\frac{1}{1-\sigma}} \quad (1)$$

where α_i is the normalization factor

$$\alpha_i = \frac{1}{\sum_{z_i} p_\theta(z_i|x_i)^{\frac{1}{1-\sigma}}}$$

Because $f_i(q)$ is strictly convex on the unit simplex Δ, this stationary point is the global minimum. Note that because $\frac{1}{1-\sigma} > 1$, $q^*(z_i)$ can be seen as the result of applying a variant of the softmax function to $p_\theta(z_i|x_i)$. To compute q^*, note that $p_\theta(z_i|x_i)$ is the product of a set of grammar rule probabilities, so we can raise all the rule probabilities of the grammar to the power of $\frac{1}{1-\sigma}$ and then run the normal E-step of the EM algorithm. The normalization of q^* is included in the normal E-step.

With q^*, the objective function becomes

$$\begin{aligned} F(\theta, q^*) \;=\; & (1-\sigma)\sum_i \log \sum_{z_i} p(z_i, x_i|\theta)^{\frac{1}{1-\sigma}} \\ & + \log p(\theta) - \log p(\mathbf{X}) \end{aligned}$$

The first term is proportional to the log "likelihood" of the corpus computed with the exponentiated rule probabilities. So we can use the parsing algorithm to efficiently compute the value of the objective function (on the training corpus or on a separate development set) to determine when the coordinate ascent iteration shall be terminated.

Case 3: $\sigma = 1$

We need to minimize

$$f_i(q) = -\sum_{z_i} \left(q(z_i) \log p_\theta(z_i|x_i)\right)$$

Because $\log p_\theta(z_i|x_i) \le 0$ for any z_i, the minimum of $f_i(q)$ is reached at

$$q^*(z_i) = \begin{cases} 1 & \text{if } z_i = \arg\max_{z_i} p_\theta(z_i|x_i) \\ 0 & \text{otherwise} \end{cases}$$

Case 4: $\sigma > 1$

Theorem 2. *$f_i(q)$ is strictly concave on the unit simplex Δ when $\sigma > 1$.*

The proof is the same as that of theorem 1, except that $1 - \sigma$ is now negative which reverses the direction of the last inequality in the proof.

Theorem 3. *The minimum of $f_i(q)$ is attained at a vertex of the unit simplex Δ.*

Proof. Assume the minimum of $f_i(q)$ is attained at q^* that is not a vertex of the unit simplex Δ, so there are at least two assignments of z_i, say z^1 and z^2, such that $q^*(z^1)$ and $q^*(z^2)$ are nonzero.

Let q' be the same distribution as q^* except that $q'(z^1) = 0$ and $q'(z^2) = q^*(z^1) + q^*(z^2)$. Let q'' be the same distribution as q^* except that $q''(z^1) = q^*(z^1) + q^*(z^2)$ and $q''(z^2) = 0$. Obviously, both q' and q'' are in the unit simplex Δ and $q' \neq q''$. Let $t = \frac{q^*(z^2)}{q^*(z^1)+q^*(z^2)}$, and obviously we have $0 < t < 1$. So we get $q^* = tq' + (1-t)q''$. According to Theorem 2, $f_i(q)$ is strictly concave on the unit simplex Δ, so we have $f_i(q^*) > tf_i(q') + (1-t)f_i(q'')$. Without loss of generality, suppose $f_i(q') \geq f_i(q'')$. So we have $tf_i(q') + (1-t)f_i(q'') \geq f_i(q'')$ and therefore $f_i(q^*) > f_i(q'')$, which means $f_i(q)$ does not attain the minimum at q^*. This contradicts the assumption. □

Now we need to find out at which of the vertices of the unit simplex Δ is the minimum of $f_i(q)$ attained. At the vertex where the probability mass is concentrated at the assignment z, the value of $f_i(q)$ is $-\log p_\theta(z|x_i)$. So the minimum is attained at

$$q^*(z_i) = \begin{cases} 1 & \text{if } z_i = \arg\max_{z_i} p_\theta(z_i|x_i) \\ 0 & \text{otherwise} \end{cases}$$

It can be seen that the minimum in the case of $\sigma > 1$ is attained at the same point as in the case of $\sigma = 1$, at which all the probability mass is assigned to the best parse of the sentence. So q^* can be computed using the E-step of the Viterbi EM algorithm. Denote the best parse by z_i^*. With q^*, the objective function becomes

$$\begin{aligned} F(\theta, q^*) &= \sum_i \log p(z_i^*, x_i|\theta) \\ &\quad + \log p(\theta) - \log p(\mathbf{X}) \end{aligned}$$

The first term is the sum of the log probabilities of the best parses of the corpus. So again we can use the parsing algorithm to efficiently compute it to decide when to terminate the iterative algorithm.

Summary

Our unambiguity regularization approach is an extension of the EM algorithm. The behavior of our approach is controlled by the value of the nonnegative parameter σ. A larger value of σ corresponds to a stronger bias in favor of an unambiguous grammar. When $\sigma = 0$, our approach reduces to the standard EM algorithm. When $\sigma \geq 1$, our approach reduces to the Viterbi EM algorithm, which considers only the best parses of the training sentences in the E-step. When $0 < \sigma < 1$, our approach falls between standard EM and Viterbi EM: it applies a softmax function (Eq.1) to the distributions of parses of the training sentences in the E-step. The softmax function can be computed by simply exponentiating the grammar rule probabilities before the standard E-step, which does not increase the time complexity of the E-step. We refer to the algorithm in the case of $0 < \sigma < 1$ as the *softmax-EM* algorithm.

3.1 Annealing the Strength of Regularization

In unsupervised learning of probabilistic grammars, the initial grammar is typically very ambiguous (e.g., a random grammar). So we need to set σ to a value that is large enough to induce unambiguity. On the other hand, natural language grammars do contain some degree of ambiguity, so if the value of σ is too large, then the learned grammar might be excessively unambiguous and thus not a good model of natural languages. Hence, it is unclear how to choose an optimal value of σ.

One way to avoid choosing a fixed value of σ is to anneal its value. We start learning with a large value of σ (e.g., $\sigma = 1$) to strongly push the learner away from the highly ambiguous initial grammar; then we gradually reduce the value of σ, possibly ending with $\sigma = 0$, to avoid inducing excessive unambiguity in the learned grammar. Note that if the value of σ is annealed to 0, then our approach can be seen as providing an unambiguous initialization for standard EM.

3.2 Unambiguity Regularization with Mean-field Variational Inference

Variational inference approximates the posterior of the model given the data. It typically leads to more accurate predictions than the maximum a posteriori (MAP) estimation. In addition, for certain types of prior distributions (e.g., a Dirichlet prior with hyperparameters set to values less than 1), variational inference is able to find a solution when MAP estimation fails. Here we incorporate unambiguity regularization into mean-field variational inference.

The objective function with unambiguity regularization for mean-field variational inference is:

$$F(q(\theta), q(\mathbf{Z})) = \log p(\mathbf{X}) - \left(\mathbf{KL}(q(\theta)q(\mathbf{Z})||p(\theta, \mathbf{Z}|\mathbf{X})) + \sigma \sum_i H(z_i) \right)$$
$$\text{where } \forall i, H(z_i) = -\sum_{z_i} q(z_i) \log q(z_i)$$

We can perform coordinate ascent that alternately optimizes $q(\theta)$ and $q(\mathbf{Z})$. Since the regularization term does not contain $q(\theta)$, the optimization of $q(\theta)$ is exactly the same as in the standard mean-field variational inference. To optimize $q(\mathbf{Z})$, we have

$$q^*(\mathbf{Z}) = \arg\min_{q(\mathbf{Z})} \left(\mathbf{KL}(q(\mathbf{Z})||\widetilde{p}(\mathbf{X}, \mathbf{Z})) + \sigma \sum_i H(z_i) \right)$$

where $\widetilde{p}(\mathbf{X}, \mathbf{Z})$ is defined as

$$\log \widetilde{p}(\mathbf{X}, \mathbf{Z}) = E_{q(\theta)}[\log p(\theta, \mathbf{Z}, \mathbf{X})] + \text{const}$$

Now we can follow a derivation similar to that in the setting of MAP estimation with unambiguity regularization, and we can obtain a similar result but with $p_\theta(z_i|x_i)$ replaced with $\widetilde{p}(x_i, z_i)$ in each of the four cases.

Note that if Dirichlet priors are used over grammar rule probabilities θ, then $\widetilde{p}(x_i, z_i)$ can be represented as the product of a set of weights in mean-field variational inference (Kurihara and Sato, 2004). Therefore in order to compute $q^*(z_i)$, when $0 < \sigma < 1$, we simply need to raise all the weights to the power of $\frac{1}{1-\sigma}$ before running the normal step of computing $q^*(z_i)$ in standard mean-field variational inference; and when $\sigma \geq 1$, we can simply use the weights to find the best parse of the training sentence and assign probability 1 to it.

4 Experiments

We tested the effectiveness of unambiguity regularization in unsupervised learning of a type of dependency grammar called the dependency model with valence (DMV) (Klein and Manning, 2004). We report the results on the Wall Street Journal corpus (with section 2-21 for training and section 23 for testing) in section 4.1–4.3, and the results on the corpora of eight additional languages in section 4.4. On each corpus, we trained the learner on the gold-standard part-of-speech tags of the sentences of length ≤ 10 with punctuation stripped off. We started our algorithm with the informed initialization proposed in (Klein and Manning, 2004), and terminated the algorithm when the increase in the value of the objective function fell below a threshold of 0.001%. To evaluate a learned grammar, we used the grammar to parse the testing corpus and computed the dependency accuracy which is the percentage of the dependencies that are correctly matched between the parses generated by the grammar and the gold standard parses. We report the dependency accuracy on subsets of the testing corpus corresponding to sentences of length ≤ 10, length ≤ 20, and the entire testing corpus.

Value of σ	Testing Accuracy ≤ 10	≤ 20	All
0 (standard EM)	46.2	39.7	34.9
0.25	53.7	44.7	**40.3**
0.5	51.9	42.9	38.8
0.75	51.6	43.1	38.8
1 (Viterbi EM)	**58.3**	**45.2**	39.4

Table 1: The dependency accuracies of grammars learned by our approach with different values of σ.

4.1 Results with Different Values of σ

We compared the performance of our approach with five different values of the parameter σ: 0 (i.e., standard EM), 0.25, 0.5, 0.75, 1 (i.e., Viterbi EM). Table 1 shows the experimental results. It can be seen that learning with unambiguity regularization (i.e., with $\sigma > 0$) consistently outperforms learning without unambiguity regularization (i.e., $\sigma = 0$). The grammar learned by Viterbi EM has significantly higher dependency accuracy in parsing short sentences. We speculate that this is because short sentences are less ambiguous and therefore a strong unambiguity regularization is especially helpful in learning the grammatical structures of short sentences. On the testing sentences of all lengths, $\sigma = 0.25$ achieves the best dependency accuracy, which suggests that controlling the strength of unambiguity regularization can contribute to improved performance.

	Testing Accuracy		
	≤ 10	≤ 20	All
DMV Model			
UR-Annealing	63.6	53.1	47.9
UR-Annealing&Prior	**66.6**	**57.7**	**52.3**
PR-S (Gillenwater et al., 2010)	62.1	53.8	49.1
SLN TieV&N (Cohen and Smith, 2009)	61.3	47.4	41.4
LN Families (Cohen et al., 2008)	59.3	45.1	39.0
Extended Models			
UR-Annealing on E-DMV(2,2)	**71.4**	**62.4**	**57.0**
UR-Annealing on E-DMV(3,3)	71.2	61.5	56.0
L-EVG (Headden et al., 2009)	68.8	-	-
LexTSG-DMV (Blunsom and Cohn, 2010)	67.7	-	55.7

Table 2: The dependency accuracies of grammars learned by our approach (denoted by "UR") with annealing and prior, compared with previous published results.

4.2 Results with Annealing and Prior

We annealed the value of σ from 1 to 0 when running our approach. We reduced the value of σ at a constant speed such that it reaches 0 at iteration 100. The results of this experiment (shown as "UR-Annealing" in Table 2) suggest that annealing the value of σ not only helps circumvent the problem of choosing an optimal value of σ, but may also lead to substantial improvements over the results of learning using any fixed value of σ.

Dirichlet priors with the hyperparameter α set to a value less than 1 are often used to induce parameter sparsity. We added Dirichlet priors over grammar rule probabilities and ran the variational inference version of our approach. The value of α was set to 0.25 as suggested by previous work (Cohen et al., 2008; Gillenwater et al., 2010). When tested with different values of σ, adding Dirichlet priors with $\alpha = 0.25$ consistently boosted the dependency accuracy of the learned grammar by 1–2%. When the value of σ was annealed during variational inference with Dirichlet priors, the dependency accuracy was further improved (shown as "UR-Annealing&Prior" in Table 2).

The first part of Table 2 also compares our results with the best results that have been published in the literature for unsupervised learning of the DMV model (with different priors or regularizations than ours). It can be seen that our best result (unambiguity regularization with annealing and prior) clearly outperforms previous results. Furthermore, we expect our approach to be more computationally efficient than the other approaches, because our approach only inserts an additional parameter exponentiation step into each iteration of standard EM or variational inference, in contrast to the other three approaches all of which involve additional gradient descent optimization steps in each iteration.

4.3 Results on Extended Models

It has been pointed out that the DMV model is very simplistic and cannot capture many linguistic phenomena; therefore a few extensions of DMV have been proposed, which achieve significant improvement over DMV in unsupervised grammar learning (Headden et al., 2009; Blunsom and Cohn, 2010). We examined the effect of unambiguity regularization on E-DMV, an extension of DMV (with two different settings: (2,2) and (3,3)) (Headden et al., 2009; Gillenwater et al., 2010). As shown in the second part of Table 2, unambiguity regularization with annealing on E-DMV achieves better dependency accuracies than the state-of-the-art approaches to unsupervised parsing with extended dependency models. Addition of Dirichlet priors, however, did not further improve the accuracies in this setting. Note that E-DMV is an unlexicalized extension of DMV that is relatively simple. We speculate that the performance of unambiguity regularization can be further improved if applied to more advanced models like LexTSG-DMV (Blunsom and Cohn, 2010).

4.4 Results on More Languages

We examined the effect of unambiguity regularization with the DMV model on the corpora of eight additional languages[2]. The experimental results of all the nine languages are summarized in Table 3. It can be seen that learning with unambiguity regularization (i.e., with $\sigma > 0$) outperforms learning without unambiguity regularization (i.e., $\sigma = 0$) on eight out of the nine languages, but the optimal value of σ is very different across languages. Annealing the value of σ from 1 to 0 does not always lead to further improvement over using the optimal value of σ

[2]The corpora are from the PASCAL Challenge on Grammar Induction (`http://wiki.cs.ox.ac.uk/InducingLinguisticStructure/SharedTask`).

for each language, but on average it has better performance than using any fixed value of σ and hence is useful when the optimal value of σ is hard to identify.

5 Related Work

Deterministic annealing (DA) (Rose, 1998; Smith and Eisner, 2004) also extends the standard EM algorithm by exponentiating the posterior probabilities of the hidden variables in the E-step. However, the goal of DA is to improve the optimization of a non-concave objective function, which is achieved by setting the exponent in the E-step to a value *close to 0*, so that the distribution of the hidden variables becomes *nearly uniform* and the objective function becomes almost concave and therefore easy to optimize; this exponent is then gradually *increased to 1* to optimize the original objective function. In contrast, the goal of unambiguity regularization is to bias learning in favor of unambiguous grammars, which is achieved by setting the exponent in the E-step (i.e., $\frac{1}{1-\sigma}$ in Eq.1) to a value *larger than 1*, so that the distribution of the hidden variables becomes *less uniform* (i.e., parses become less ambiguous); in our annealing approach, the exponent is *initialized to a very large value* (positive infinity in our experiment) to push the learner away from the ambiguous initial grammar, and then gradually *decreased to 1* to avoid inducing excessive unambiguity in the learned grammar. The empirical results of Smith and Eisner (2004) show that DA resulted in lower parsing accuracy compared with standard EM in unsupervised constituent parsing; and a "skew" posterior term had to be inserted into the E-step formulation of DA to boost its accuracy over that of standard EM. In contrast, the results of our experiments show that unambiguity regularization leads to significantly higher parsing accuracy than standard EM.

Unambiguity regularization is also related to the minimum entropy regularization framework for semi-supervised learning (Grandvalet and Bengio, 2005; Smith and Eisner, 2007), which tries to minimize the entropy of the class label or hidden variables on unlabeled data in addition to maximizing the likelihood of labeled data. However, entropy regularization is either motivated by the theoretical result that unlabeled data samples are informative when classes are well separated (Grandvalet and Bengio, 2005), or derived from the expected conditional log-likelihood (Smith and Eisner, 2007). In contrast, our approach is motivated by the observed unambiguity of natural language grammars. One implication of this difference is that if our approach is applied to semi-supervised learning, the regularization term would be applied to labeled sentences as well (by ignoring the labels) because the target grammar shall be unambiguous on all the training sentences.

The sparsity bias, which favors a grammar with fewer grammar rules, has been widely used in unsupervised grammar learning (Chen, 1995; Johnson et al., 2007; Gillenwater et al., 2010). Although a more sparse grammar is often less ambiguous, in general that is not always the case. We have shown that unambiguity regularization could lead to better performance than approaches utilizing the sparsity bias, and that the two types of biases can be applied together for further improvement in the learning performance.

6 Conclusion

We have introduced unambiguity regularization, a novel approach to unsupervised learning of probabilistic natural language grammars. It is based on the observation that natural language grammars are remarkably unambiguous in the sense that in parsing natural language sentences they tend to concentrate the probability mass to a tiny portion of all possible parses. By using posterior regularization, we incorporate an inductive bias into learning in favor of grammars that are unambiguous on natural language sentences. The resulting family of algorithms includes standard EM and Viterbi EM, as well as the softmax-EM algorithm which falls between standard EM and Viterbi EM. The softmax-EM algorithm can be implemented by adding a simple parameter exponentiation step into standard EM. In our experiments of unsupervised dependency grammar learning, we show that unambiguity regularization is beneficial to learning, and by incorporating regularization strength annealing and sparsity priors our approach outperforms the current state-of-the-art grammar learning algorithms. For future work, we plan to combine unambiguity regularization with

	Arabic	Basque	Czech	Danish	Dutch	English	Portuguese	Slovene	Swedish
$\sigma = 0$ (standard EM)	27.4	32.1	27.8	35.6	29.4	34.9	23.7	**30.6**	31.9
$\sigma = 0.25$	30.6	39.3	27.2	35.2	30.9	**40.3**	**27.7**	23.8	**42.0**
$\sigma = 0.5$	**32.6**	40.6	**33.0**	**37.4**	32.7	38.8	27.5	15.3	29.3
$\sigma = 0.75$	31.6	**41.8**	16.1	36.0	**35.1**	38.8	26.2	15.1	32.7
$\sigma = 1$ (Viterbi EM)	29.6	39.8	28.6	33.6	28.0	39.4	27.3	14.6	37.2
UR-Annealing	26.7	41.6	**39.3**	34.1	**43.1**	**47.8**	26.4	16.4	**46.0**

Table 3: The dependency accuracies (on sentences of all lengths in the testing corpus) of grammars learned by our approach from the corpora of the following languages: Arabic (Hajič et al., 2004), Basque (Aduriz et al., 2003), Czech (Hajič et al., 2000), Danish (Buch-Kromann et al., 2007), Dutch (Beek et al., 2002), English, Portuguese (Afonso et al., 2002), Slovene (Erjavec et al., 2010), Swedish (Nivre et al., 2006).

other types of priors and regularizations for unsupervised grammar learning, to apply it to more advanced grammar models, and to explore alternative formulations of unambiguity regularization.

Acknowledgement

The work of Kewei Tu was supported at Iowa State University in part by a research assistantship from the Iowa State University Center for Computational Intelligence, Learning, and Discovery, and at University of California, Los Angeles by the DARPA grant FA 8650-11-1-7149. The work of Vasant Honavar was supported by the National Science Foundation, while working at the Foundation. Any opinion, finding, and conclusions contained in this article are those of the authors and do not necessarily reflect the views of the National Science Foundation.

References

I. Aduriz, M. J. Aranzabe, J. M. Arriola, A. Atutxa, A. Diaz de Ilarraza, A. Garmendia, , and M. Oronoz. 2003. Construction of a basque dependency treebank. In *Proc. of the 2nd Workshop on Treebanks and Linguistic Theories (TLT)*.

Susana Afonso, Eckhard Bick, Renato Haber, and Diana Santos. 2002. "floresta sintá(c)tica": a treebank for Portuguese. In *Proceedings of the 3rd Intern. Conf. on Language Resources and Evaluation (LREC)*, pages 1968–1703.

J. K. Baker. 1979. Trainable grammars for speech recognition. In *Speech Communication Papers for the 97th Meeting of the Acoustical Society of America*.

Van Der Beek, G. Bouma, R. Malouf, G. Van Noord, and Rijksuniversiteit Groningen. 2002. The alpino dependency treebank. In *In Computational Linguistics in the Netherlands (CLIN*, pages 1686–1691.

Phil Blunsom and Trevor Cohn. 2010. Unsupervised induction of tree substitution grammars for dependency parsing. In *Proceedings of the 2010 Conference on Empirical Methods in Natural Language Processing*, EMNLP '10, pages 1204–1213, Stroudsburg, PA, USA. Association for Computational Linguistics.

Matthias Buch-Kromann, Jürgen Wedekind, , and Jakob Elming. 2007. The copenhagen danish-english dependency treebank v. 2.0. http://www.buch-kromann.dk/matthias/cdt2.0/.

Stanley F. Chen. 1995. Bayesian grammar induction for language modeling. In *Proceedings of the 33rd annual meeting on Association for Computational Linguistics*.

Shay B. Cohen and Noah A. Smith. 2009. Shared logistic normal distributions for soft parameter tying in unsupervised grammar induction. In *HLT-NAACL*, pages 74–82.

Shay B. Cohen, Kevin Gimpel, and Noah A. Smith. 2008. Logistic normal priors for unsupervised probabilistic grammar induction. In *NIPS*, pages 321–328.

Tomaz Erjavec, Darja Fiser, Simon Krek, and Nina Ledinek. 2010. The jos linguistically tagged corpus of slovene. In *LREC*.

Jenny Rose Finkel, Trond Grenager, and Christopher D. Manning. 2007. The infinite tree. In *Proceedings of the 45th Annual Meeting of the Association of Computational Linguistics*, pages 272–279. Association for Computational Linguistics, June.

Kuzman Ganchev, João Graça, Jennifer Gillenwater, and Ben Taskar. 2010. Posterior regularization for structured latent variable models. *Journal of Machine Learning Research*, 11:2001–2049.

Jennifer Gillenwater, Kuzman Ganchev, João Graça, Fernando Pereira, and Ben Taskar. 2010. Sparsity in dependency grammar induction. In *ACL '10: Proceedings of the ACL 2010 Conference Short Papers*, pages 194–199, Morristown, NJ, USA. Association for Computational Linguistics.

Yves Grandvalet and Yoshua Bengio. 2005. Semi-supervised learning by entropy minimization. In

Lawrence K. Saul, Yair Weiss, and Léon Bottou, editors, *Advances in Neural Information Processing Systems 17*, pages 529–536. MIT Press, Cambridge, MA.

Jan Hajič, Alena Böhmová, Eva Hajičová, and Barbora Vidová-Hladká. 2000. The Prague Dependency Treebank: A Three-Level Annotation Scenario. In A. Abeillé, editor, *Treebanks: Building and Using Parsed Corpora*, pages 103–127. Amsterdam:Kluwer.

Jan Hajič, Otakar Smrž, Petr Zemánek, Jan Šnaidauf, and Emanuel Beška. 2004. Prague arabic dependency treebank: Development in data and tools. In *In Proc. of the NEMLAR Intern. Conf. on Arabic Language Resources and Tools*, pages 110–117.

William P. Headden, III, Mark Johnson, and David McClosky. 2009. Improving unsupervised dependency parsing with richer contexts and smoothing. In *HLT-NAACL*, pages 101–109.

Mark Johnson, Thomas L. Griffiths, and Sharon Goldwater. 2007. Bayesian inference for pcfgs via markov chain monte carlo. In *HLT-NAACL*, pages 139–146.

Dan Klein and Christopher D. Manning. 2004. Corpus-based induction of syntactic structure: Models of dependency and constituency. In *Proceedings of ACL*.

Kenichi Kurihara and Taisuke Sato. 2004. An application of the variational Bayesian approach to probabilistic contextfree grammars. In *IJCNLP-04 Workshop beyond shallow analyses*.

K. Lari and S. Young. 1990. The estimation of stochastic context-free grammars using the inside-outside algorithm. *Computer Speech and Language*, 4:35–36.

Percy Liang, Slav Petrov, Michael I. Jordan, and Dan Klein. 2007. The infinite pcfg using hierarchical Dirichlet processes. In *Proceedings of EMNLP-CoNLL*, pages 688–697.

Christopher D. Manning and Hinrich Schütze. 1999. *Foundations of statistical natural language processing*. MIT Press, Cambridge, MA, USA.

Joakim Nivre, Jens Nilsson, and Johan Hall. 2006. Talbanken05: A Swedish Treebank with Phrase Structure and Dependency Annotation. In *Proceedings of the fifth international conference on Language Resources and Evaluation (LREC2006), May 24-26, 2006, Genoa, Italy*, pages 1392–1395. European Language Resource Association, Paris.

Slav Petrov, Leon Barrett, Romain Thibaux, and Dan Klein. 2006. Learning accurate, compact, and interpretable tree annotation. In *ACL-44: Proceedings of the 21st International Conference on Computational Linguistics and the 44th annual meeting of the Association for Computational Linguistics*, pages 433–440, Morristown, NJ, USA. Association for Computational Linguistics.

Hoifung Poon and Pedro Domingos. 2011. Sum-product networks : A new deep architecture. In *Proceedings of the Twenty-Seventh Conference on Uncertainty in Artificial Intelligence (UAI)*.

Kenneth Rose. 1998. Deterministic annealing for clustering, compression, classification, regression, and related optimization problems. In *Proceedings of the IEEE*, pages 2210–2239.

Noah A. Smith and Jason Eisner. 2004. Annealing techniques for unsupervised statistical language learning. In *Proceedings of the 42nd Annual Meeting on Association for Computational Linguistics*, ACL '04, Stroudsburg, PA, USA. Association for Computational Linguistics.

David A. Smith and Jason Eisner. 2007. Bootstrapping feature-rich dependency parsers with entropic priors. In *Proceedings of the 2007 Joint Conference on Empirical Methods in Natural Language Processing and Computational Natural Language Learning (EMNLP-CoNLL)*, pages 667–677, Prague, June.

Valentin I. Spitkovsky, Hiyan Alshawi, Daniel Jurafsky, and Christopher D. Manning. 2010. Viterbi training improves unsupervised dependency parsing. In *Proceedings of the Fourteenth Conference on Computational Natural Language Learning*, CoNLL '10, pages 9–17, Stroudsburg, PA, USA. Association for Computational Linguistics.

Extracting Opinion Expressions with semi-Markov Conditional Random Fields

Bishan Yang
Department of Computer Science
Cornell University
bishan@cs.cornell.edu

Claire Cardie
Department of Computer Science
Cornell University
cardie@cs.cornell.edu

Abstract

Extracting opinion expressions from text is usually formulated as a token-level sequence labeling task tackled using Conditional Random Fields (CRFs). CRFs, however, do not readily model potentially useful segment-level information like syntactic constituent structure. Thus, we propose a semi-CRF-based approach to the task that can perform sequence labeling at the segment level. We extend the original semi-CRF model (Sarawagi and Cohen, 2004) to allow the modeling of arbitrarily long expressions while accounting for their likely syntactic structure when modeling segment boundaries. We evaluate performance on two opinion extraction tasks, and, in contrast to previous sequence labeling approaches to the task, explore the usefulness of segment-level syntactic parse features. Experimental results demonstrate that our approach outperforms state-of-the-art methods for both opinion expression tasks.

1 Introduction

Accurate opinion expression identification is crucial for tasks that benefit from fine-grained opinion analysis (Wiebe et al., 2005): e.g., it is a first step in characterizing the sentiment and intensity of the opinion; it provides a textual anchor for identifying the opinion holder and the target or topic of an opinion; and these, in turn, form the basis of opinion-oriented question answering and opinion summarization systems. In this paper, we focus on opinion expressions as defined in Wiebe et al. (2005) — subjective expressions that denote emotions, sentiment, beliefs, opinions, judgments, or other *private states* (Quirk et al., 1985) in text. These include *direct subjective expressions* (DSEs): explicit mentions of private states or speech events expressing private states; and *expressive subjective expressions* (ESEs): expressions that indicate sentiment, emotion, etc. without explicitly conveying them. Following are two example sentences labeled with DSEs and ESEs.

(1) The International Committee of the Red Cross, [as usual]$_{[ESE]}$, [has refused to make any statements]$_{[DSE]}$.

(2) The Chief Minister [said]$_{[DSE]}$ that [the demon they have reared will eat up their own vitals]$_{[ESE]}$.

As a type of information extraction task, opinion expression extraction has been successfully tackled in the past via sequence tagging methods: Choi et al. (2006) and Breck et al. (2007), for example, apply conditional random fields (CRFs) (Lafferty et al., 2001) using sophisticated token-level features. In token-level sequence labeling, labels are assigned to single tokens, and the label of each token depends on the current token and the label of the previous token (we consider the usual first-order assumption). Segment-based features — features that describe a set of related contiguous tokens, e.g., a phrase or constituent — might provide critical information for identifying opinion expressions; they cannot, however, be readily and naturally represented in the CRF model.

Our goal in this work is to extract opinion expressions at the segment level with semi-Markov conditional random fields (semi-CRFs). Semi-CRFs (Sarawagi and Cohen, 2004) are more powerful than CRFs in that they allow one to construct features to capture characteristics of the subsequences of a sentence. They are defined on semi-Markov chains where labels are attached to segments instead of tokens and label dependencies are modeled at the segment-level. Previous work has shown that semi-CRFs outperform CRFs on named entity recognition (NER) tasks (Sarawagi and Cohen, 2004; Okanohara et al., 2006). However, to the best of our knowledge, semi-CRF techniques have not been investigated for opinion expression extraction.

The contribution of this paper is a semi-CRF-based approach for opinion expression extraction that leverages parsing information to provide better modeling of opinion expressions. Specifically, possible segmentations are generated by taking into account likely syntactic structure during learning and inference. As a result, arbitrarily long expressions can be modeled and their boundaries can be influenced by probable syntactic structure. We also explore the impact of syntactic features for extracting opinion expressions.

We evaluate our model on two opinion extraction tasks: identifying direct subjective expressions (DSEs) and expressive subjective expressions (ESEs). Experimental results show that our approach outperforms the state-of-the-art approach for the task by a large margin. We also identify useful syntactic features for the task.

2 Related Work

Previous research to extract direct subjective expressions exists, but is mainly focused on single-word expressions (Wiebe et al., 2005; Wilson et al., 2005; Munson et al., 2005). More recent studies tackle opinion expression extraction at the expression level. Breck et al. (2007) formulate the problem as a token-level sequence labeling problem; their CRF-based approach was shown to significantly outperform two subjectivity-clue-based baselines. Others extend the token-level approach to jointly identify opinion holders (Choi et al., 2006), and to determine the polarity and intensity of the opinion expressions (Choi and Cardie, 2010). Reranking the output of a simple sequence labeler has been shown to further improve the extraction of opinion expressions (Johansson and Moschitti, 2010; Johansson and Moschitti, 2011); importantly, their reranking approach relied on features that encoded syntactic structure. All of the above approaches, however, are based on token-level sequence labeling, which ignores potentially useful phrase-level information.

Semi-CRFs (Sarawagi and Cohen, 2004) are general CRFs that relax the Markovian assumptions to allow sequence labeling at the segment level. Previous work has shown that semi-CRFs are superior to CRFs for NER and Chinese word segmentation (Sarawagi and Cohen, 2004; Okanohara et al., 2006; Andrew, 2006). The task of opinion expression extraction is known to be harder than traditional NER since subjective expressions exhibit substantial lexical variation and their recognition requires more attention to linguistic structure.

Parsing has been leveraged to improve performance for numerous natural language tasks. In opinion mining, numerous studies have shown that syntactic parsing features are very helpful for opinion analysis. A lot of work uses syntactic features to identify opinion holders and opinion topics (Bethard et al., 2005; Kim and Hovy, 2006; Kobayashi et al., 2007; Joshi and Carolyn, 2009; Wu et al., 2009; Choi et al., 2005). Jakob et al. (2010) recently employed dependency path features for the extraction of opinion targets. Johansson and Moschitti (2010; Johansson and Moschitti (2011) also successfully employed syntactic features that indicate dependency relations between opinion expressions for the task of opinion expression extraction. However, as their approach is based on the output of a sequence labeler, these features cannot be encoded to help the learning of the sequence labeler.

3 Approach

We formulate the extraction of opinion expressions as a sequence labeling problem. Unlike previous sequence-labeling approaches to the task (e.g., Breck et al. (2007)), however, we aim to model segment-level, rather than token-level, information. As a result, we explore the use of semi-CRFs, which can assign labels to segments instead of tokens; hence, features can be defined at the segment level. For example, features like $[\![X \text{ is a verb phrase}]\!]$ can be easily encoded in the model. In the following subsections, we first introduce standard semi-CRFs and then describe our semi-CRF-based approach for opinion expression extraction.

3.1 Semi-CRFs

In semi-CRFs, each observed sentence x is represented as a sequence of consecutive segments $s = \langle s_1, ..., s_n \rangle$, where s_i is a triple $s_i = (t_i, u_i, y_i)$, t_i denotes the start position of segment s_i, u_i denotes the end position, and y_i denotes the label of the segment. Segments are restricted to have positive length less than or equal to a maximum length of L that has been seen in the corpus ($1 \le u_i - t_i + 1 \le L$).

Features in semi-CRFs are defined at the segment level rather than the word level. The feature function $g(i, x, s)$ is a function of x, the current segment s_i, and the label y_{i-1} of the previous segment s_{i-1} (we consider the usual first-order Markovian assumption). It can also be written as $g(x, t_i, u_i, y_i, y_{i-1})$. The conditional probability of a segmentation s given a sequence x is defined as

$$p(s|x) = \frac{1}{Z(x)} \exp \left\{ \sum_i \sum_k \lambda_k g_k(i, x, s) \right\} \quad (1)$$

where

$$Z(x) = \sum_{s' \in S} \exp \left\{ \sum_i \sum_k \lambda_k g_k(i, x, s') \right\}$$

and the set S contains all possible segmentations obtained from segment candidates with length ranging from 1 to the maximum length L.

The correct segmentation s of a sentence is defined as a sequence of entity segments (i.e., the entities to be extracted) and non-entity segments. For example, the correct segmentation of sentence (2) in Section 1 is ⟨(The,NONE),(Chief,NONE),(Minister,NONE), (said,DSE),(that,NONE),(the demon they have reared will eat up their own vitals,ESE),(.,NONE)⟩. Here, non-entity segments are represented as unit-length segments.

3.2 Semi-CRF-based Approach for Opinion Expression Extraction

In this section, we present an extended version of semi-CRFs in which we can make use of parsing information in learning entity boundaries and labels for opinion expression extraction.

As discussed in Section 3.1, the maximum entity length L is fixed during training to generate segment candidates in the standard semi-CRFs. In opinion expression extraction, L is unbounded since opinion expressions may be clauses or whole sentences, which can be arbitrarily long. Thus, fixing an upper bound on segment length based on the observed entities may lead to an incorrect removal of segments during inference. Also note that possible segment candidates are generated based on the length constraint, which means any span of the text consisting of no more than L words would be considered as a possible segment. This would lead to the consideration of implausible segments, e.g., "The Chief" in sentence (2) is an incorrect segment within the multi-word expression "The Chief Minister".

To address these problems, we propose techniques to incorporate parsing information into the modeling of segments in semi-CRFs. More specifically, we construct segment units from the parse tree of each sentence[1], and then build up possible segment candidates based on those units. In the parse tree, each leaf phrase or leaf word is considered to be a segment unit. Each segment unit performs as the smallest unit in the model (words within a segment unit will be automatically assigned the same label). The segment units are highlighted in rectangles in the parse tree example in Figure 1. As the segment units are not separable, we avoid implausible segments, which truncate multi-word expressions. For example, "both ridiculous and", would not be considered a possible segment in our model.

To generate segment candidates for the model, we consider meaningful combinations of consecutive segment units. Intuitively, a sentence is made up of several parts, and each has its own grammatical role or meaning. We define the boundary of these parts based on the parse tree structure. Specifically,

[1]We use the Stanford Parser `http://nlp.stanford.edu/software/lex-parser.shtml` to generate the parse trees.

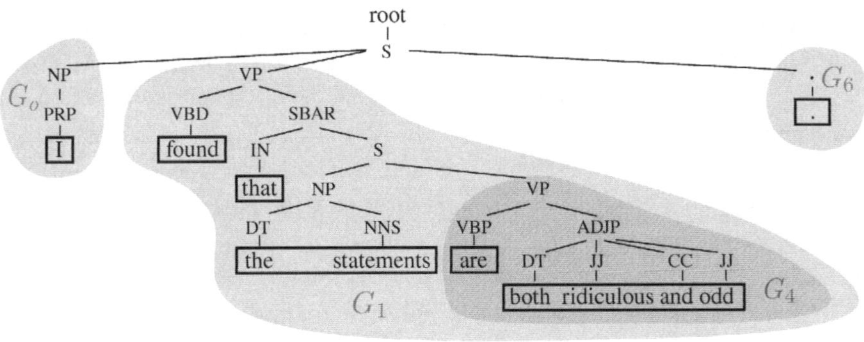

Figure 1: A parse tree example. There are seven segment units in the sentence. The shaded regions correspond to segment groups, where G_i represents the segment group starting from segment unit U_i.

we consider each segment unit to belong to a meaningful group defined by the span of its parent node. Two consecutive segment units are considered to belong to the same group if the subtrees rooted in their parent nodes have the same rightmost child. For example, in Figure 1, segment units "are" and "both ridiculous and odd" belong to the same group, while "I" and "found" belong to different groups.

Algorithm 1 Construction of segment candidates

Input: A training sentence x
Output: A set of segment candidates S

```
Obtain the segment units U = (U_1, ..., U_m) by
   preorder traversal of the parse tree T, each U_i
   corresponds to a node in T
for i = 1 to m do
   j ← i − 1
   while j < m − 1 and
         commonGroup(U_i, ..., U_{j+1}) do
      j ← j + 1
   for k = i to j do
      for t = 0 to j − k do
         s ← segment(U_k, ..., U_{k+t})
         S ← S ∪ s
Return S
```

Following this idea, we generate possible segment candidates by Algorithm 1. Starting from each segment unit U_i, we first find the rightmost segment unit U_j that belongs to the same group as U_i. Function $\text{commonGroup}(U_i, ..., U_j)$ returns True if $U_i, ..., U_j$ are within the same group (the parent nodes of U_i,...,U_j have the same rightmost child in their subtrees), otherwise it returns False. Then we enumerate all possible combinations of segment units $U_i, ..., U_k$ where $i \leq k \leq j$. $\text{segment}(U_i, ..., U_j)$ denotes the segment obtained by concatenating words in the consecutive segment units U_i,...,U_j. This way, segment candidates are generated without constraints on length and are meaningful for learning entity boundaries.

Based on the generated segment candidates, the correct segmentation for each training sentence can be obtained as follows. For opinion expressions that do not match any segment candidate, we break them down into smaller segments using a greedy matching process. Starting from the start position of the expression, we search for the longest candidate that is contained in the expression, add it to the correct segmentation for the sentence, set the start position to be the next position, and repeat the process. Using this process, the correct segmentation of sentence (2) would be $s = \langle$(The Chief Minister,NONE),(said,DSE),(that,NONE),(the demon they have reared,ESE), (will eat up their own vitals,ESE),(.)$\rangle$. Note that here non-entities correspond to segment units instead of single-word segments in the original semi-CRF model.[2]

After obtaining the set of possible segment candidates and the correct segmentation s for each training sentence, the semi-CRF model can be trained. The goal of learning is to find the optimal parameter λ by maximizing log-likelihood. We use the limited-

[2]There are cases where words within a segment unit have different labels. This may be due to errors by the human annotators or the errors in the parser. In such cases, we consider each word within the segment unit as a segment.

memory BFGS algorithm (Liu and Nocedal, 1989) for optimization in our implementation, where the gradient of the log-likelihood L (corresponding to one instance x) is computed:

$$\frac{\partial L}{\partial \lambda_k} = \sum_i g_k(x, t_i, u_i, y_i, y_{i-1}) - \sum_{s' \in S} \sum_{y,y'} \sum_j g_k(x, t'_j, u'_j, y, y') p(y, y'|x) \quad (2)$$

where S is all possible segmentations consisting of the generated segment candidates, $p(y, y'|x)$ is the probability of having label y for the current segment s'_j (with boundary (t'_j, u'_j)) and label y' for the previous segment s'_{j-1}.

We use a forward-backward algorithm to compute the marginal distribution $p(y, y'|x)$ and the normalization factor $Z(x)$ efficiently. For inference we seek the best segmentation $s^* = \arg\max_s p(s|x)$, where $p(s|x)$ is defined by Equation 1. We implement efficient inference using an extension of Viterbi algorithm to segments. In particular, define $V(j, y)$ as the largest unnormalized probability of $p(s_{1:j}|x)$ with label y at the ending position j. Then we have

$$V(j, y) = \max_{(i,j) \in s_{:,j}} \max_{y'} \phi(x, i, j, y, y') V(i-1, y')$$

where

$$\phi(x, i, j, y, y') = \exp\left\{\sum_k \lambda_k g_k(x, i, j, y, y')\right\}$$

and $s_{:,j}$ denotes the set of the generated segment candidates ending at position j. The best segmentation can be obtained from tracing the path of $\max_y V(n, y)$.

3.3 Features

Here we described the features used in our model. Very generally, we include CRF-style features that are segment-level extensions of the token-level features. We also include new segment-level features that can be naturally represented in semi-CRFs but not CRFs.

For CRF-style features, we consider the string representation of the current word, its part-of-speech, and a dictionary-derived feature, which is based on a subjectivity lexicon provided by Wilson et al. (2005). The lexicon consists of a set of words that can act as strong or weak cues to subjectivity. If the current word appears as an entry in the lexicon, then a feature *strong* or *weak* will be fired if the entry is of that strength. These features have been successfully employed in previous work (Breck et al., 2007). To employ them in our model, we simply extend the feature definition to the segment level. For example, a token-level feature $[\![x$ is *great* $]\!]$ will be extended to a segment-level feature $[\![s$ contains *great* $]\!]$.

Previous work on semi-CRFs has explored features such as the length of the segment, the position of the segment in the current segmentation (at the beginning or at the end), indicators for the start word and end word within the segment, and indicators for words before and after the segment. These features have been shown useful for the task of NE recognition (Sarawagi and Cohen, 2004; Okanohara et al., 2006). However, we only found the position of the segment to be helpful for the extraction of opinion expressions, probably due to the lack of patterns in the length distribution and word choices of opinion expressions.

Besides the above features, we design new segment-level syntactic features to capture the syntactic patterns of opinion expressions. Syntactic patterns are often used to identify useful information in information extraction tasks. In our task, we found that the majority of opinion expressions involve verb phrases.[3] For example, "was encouraged", "expressed goodwill", "cannot accept" are all within a VP constituent. To capture such structural preferences, we define several syntax-based parse features for VP-related constituents.[4]

Let VPROOT denote a VP constituent whose parent node is not VP, and let VPLEAF denote a VP constituent whose children nodes are non-VP. Denote the head of VPLEAF as the predicate, and its next segment unit as the argument. If a segment consists of words in the VP nodes visited by the preorder

[3]The percentages of opinion expressions involving VP/NP/PP are 64.13%/18.43%/5.92% for DSEs and 43.22%/24.99%/11.77% for ESEs in the data set we used.

[4]We also conducted experiments with NP and PP-related features, and could not find any performance improvement for the tasks.

traversal from a VPROOT to a VPLEAF, then we refer to it as a verb-cluster segment. If a segment consists of a verb cluster and the argument in VPLEAF, we consider it as a VP segment. The following features are defined for verb-cluster segments and VP segments.

VPcluster: Indicates whether or not the segment matches the verb-cluster structure.

VPpred: A feature of the syntactic category and the word of the head of VPLEAF. The head of VPLEAF is the predicate of the verb phrase, which may encode some intention of opinions in the verb phrase. For example, if "warned" is the head of VPLEAF rather than "informed", the chance of the segment being an opinion expression increases.

VParg: A feature of the syntactic category and the head word of the argument in VPLEAF. For example, the noun phrase "a negative stand" is the argument of the predicate "take" in the verb phrase "take a negative stand". The argument in the verb phrase (could be a noun phrase, adjectival phrase or prepositional phrase) may convey some relevant information for identifying opinion expressions.

VPsubj: Whether the verb clusters or the argument in the segment contains an entry from the subjectivity lexicon. For example, the word "negative" is in the lexicon, so the segment "take a negative stand" has a feature ISVPSUBJ.

4 Experiments

For evaluation, we use the MPQA 1.2 corpus (Wiebe et al., 2005)[5], a widely used data set for fine-grained opinion analysis. It contains 535 news articles, a total of 11,114 sentences with subjectivity-related annotations at the phrase level. We focus on the task of extracting two types of opinion expressions: direct subjective expressions (DSEs) and expressive subjective expressions (ESEs). Table 1 shows some statistics of the corpus. As in prior research that uses the corpus, we set aside the standard 135 documents as a development set and use 400 documents as the evaluation set. All experiments employ 10-fold cross validation on the evaluation set, and the average over all runs is reported.

[5]Available at http://www.cs.pitt.edu/mpqa/.

	DSEs	ESEs
Sentences with opinions(%)	55.89	57.93
TotalNum	9746	11730
MaxLength	15	40
Length ≥ 1 (%)	43.38	71.65
Length ≥ 4 (%)	9.44	35.01

Table 1: Statistics of opinion expressions in the MPQA Corpus.

4.1 Evaluation Metrics

We use precision, recall, and F-measure to evaluate the quality of the model. Precision is defined as $\frac{|C \cap P|}{|P|}$ and recall, as $\frac{|C \cap P|}{|C|}$, where C and P are the sets of correct and predicted expression spans, respectively. F-measure is computed as $\frac{2PR}{P+R}$. Because the boundaries of opinion expressions are hard to define even for human annotators (Wiebe et al., 2005), previous research mainly focused on soft precision and recall measures for performance evaluation. Breck et al. (2007) introduced an overlap measure, which considers a predicted expression to be correct if it overlaps with a correct expression. We refer to this metric as *Binary Overlap*. Johansson and Moschitti (2010) provides a stricter measure that computes the proportion of overlapping spans: if a correct expression s overlaps with a predicted expression s', the overlap contributes value $\frac{|s \cap s'|}{|s'|}$ to $|C \cap P|$ instead of value 1. We refer to this metric as *Proportional Overlap*. To compare with previous work, we present our results according to both metrics.

4.2 Baseline Methods

As a baseline, we use the token-level CRF-based approach of Breck et al. (2007) applied to the MPQA dataset. We employ a very similar, but not identical set of features: indicators for specific words at the current location and neighboring words in a $[-4, +4]$ window, part-of-speech features, and opinion lexicon features for tokens that are contained in the subjectivity lexicon (see Section 3.3). We do not include WordNet, Levin's verb categorization, and FrameNet features.

We also include two variants of standard CRFs as baselines: segment-CRF and syntactic-CRF. They incorporate segmentation information into standard CRFs without modifying the Markovian assump-

	DSE Extraction			ESE Extraction		
Method	**Precision**	**Recall**	**F-measure**	**Precision**	**Recall**	**F-measure**
CRF	82.83	49.38	61.87	78.56	43.57	56.05
segment-CRF	82.52	51.48	63.41	78.90	44.46	56.88
syntactic-CRF	82.48	49.09	61.55	78.41	43.39	55.95
semi-CRF	66.67	74.13	70.20	71.21	57.41	63.57
new-semi-CRF	67.72**	74.33	70.87*	73.57***	57.63	64.74**
semi-CRF(w/ syn)	64.86	74.10	69.17	70.68	56.61	62.87
new-semi-CRF(w/ syn)	70.12***	74.74*	**72.36*****	73.61***	59.27***	**65.67*****

Table 2: Results for extracting opinion expressions with Binary-Overlap metric. (w/ syn) indicates the inclusion of syntactic parse features VPpre, VParg and VPsubj. Results of new-semi-CRF that are statistically significantly greater than semi-CRF according to a two-tailed t-test are indicated with *($p < 0.1$), **($p < 0.05$), ***($p < 0.005$). T-test results are also shown for new-semi-CRF(w/ syn) versus semi-CRF(w/ syn).

	DSE Extraction			ESE Extraction		
Method	**Precision**	**Recall**	**F-measure**	**Precision**	**Recall**	**F-measure**
CRF	77.91	46.45	58.20	67.72	37.55	48.31
segment-CRF	77.86	48.58	59.83	68.03	38.34	49.04
syntactic-CRF	77.73	46.27	58.01	67.80	37.60	48.37
semi-CRF	60.38	68.34	64.11	57.30	46.20	51.16
new-semi-CRF	62.50**	68.59*	65.41*	61.69***	47.44**	53.63***
semi-CRF(w/ syn)	58.69	67.80	62.92	57.09	45.63	50.72
new-semi-CRF(w/ syn)	65.52***	68.91***	**67.17*****	61.66***	48.77***	**54.47*****

Table 3: Results for extracting opinion expressions with Proportional-Overlap metric. Notation is the same as above.

tion. Segment-CRF treats segment units obtained from the parser as word tokens. For example, in Figure 1, the segment units *the statement* and *both ridiculous and odd* will be treated as word tokens. Syntactic-CRF encodes segment-level syntactic information in a standard token-level CRF as input features. We consider the VP-related segment features introduced in Section 3.3. VPPRE and VPARG are added to the head word of the corresponding verb phrase, and VPSUBJ and VPCLUSTER are added to each token within the corresponding segment.

Another baseline method is the original semi-CRF model (Sarawagi and Cohen, 2004). To the best of our knowledge, our work is the first to explore the use of semi-CRFs on the extraction of opinion expressions. They are considered to be more powerful than CRFs since they allow information to be represented at the expression level. The model requires an input of the maximum entity length. We set it to 15 for DSE and 40 for ESE. For segment features, we used the same features as in our approach (see Section 3.3).

4.3 Results

Table 2 and Table 3 show the results of DSE and ESE extraction using two different metrics. The standard token-based CRF baseline of Breck et al. (2007) is labeled **CRF**; the original semi-CRF baseline is labeled **semi-CRF**; and our extended semi-CRF approach is labeled **new-semi-CRF**. For semi-CRF and new-semi-CRF, the results were obtained using two different settings of features: the basic feature set includes features described in Section 3.3 excluding the segment-level syntactic features. In the second feature setting (labeled as **w/ syn** in the tables), we further augment the basic features with the syntactic parse features.

Using the basic features, we observe that semi-CRF-based approaches significantly outperform CRF and its two variants segment-CRF and syntactic-CRF in F-Measure on both DSE and ESE extraction, and new-semi-CRF achieves the best results. By simply incorporating the segmentation prior into the standard CRF, segment-CRF achieves a slight improvement over standard CRF, but the results are still worse than those of semi-CRF and new-semi-CRF. However, adding segment-level

	DSE Extraction			ESE Extraction		
Feature set	**Precision**	**Recall**	**F-measure**	**Precision**	**Recall**	**F-measure**
Basic	67.72	74.33	70.87	73.57	57.63	64.74
Basic+VPpre	70.88	71.44	71.16	73.20	58.20	64.85
Basic+VParg	70.12	74.03	72.02	73.05	58.20	64.79
Basic+VPcluster	70.08	72.94	71.48	73.06	58.45	64.94
Basic+VPsubj	70.04	72.34	71.17	73.31	58.53	65.09
Basic+VPpre+VPsubj	70.91	72.54	71.72	73.61	58.29	65.07
Basic+VParg+VPsubj	70.45	73.53	71.96	74.45	57.80	65.07
Basic+VPpre+VParg+VPsubj	70.12	74.74	**72.36**	73.61	59.27	**65.67**
Basic+VPcluster+VPpre+VParg+VPsubj	70.91	72.54	71.72	72.84	58.45	64.86

Table 4: Effect of syntactic features on extracting opinion expressions with Binary-Overlap metric

syntactic features into standard CRF yields slightly reduced performance. This is not surprising as encoding segment-level information into the token-level CRF is not natural. These experiments indicate that simply encoding segmentation information into standard CRF cannot result in large performance gains. The promising F-measure results obtained by semi-CRF and new-semi-CRF confirm that relaxing the Markovian assumption on segments leads to better modeling of opinion expressions. We can also see that new-semi-CRF consistently outperforms the original semi-CRF model. This further confirms the benefit of taking into account syntactic parsing information in modeling segments. In Table 3, we observe the same general results trend as in Table 2. The scores are generally lower since the metric *Proportional Overlap* is stricter than *Binary Overlap*.

We also study the impact of syntactic parse features on the semi-Markov CRF models. Here we consider the combination of VPPRE, VPARG and VPSUBJ since they turned out to be the most helpful features for our tasks. Interestingly, we found that after incorporating the syntactic parse features, performance decreases on semi-CRF. This indicates that syntactic information does not help if learning and inference take place on segment candidates generated without accounting for parse information. In contrast, our approach incorporates syntactic parsing information in modeling segments and meaningful segmentations. We can see in Tables 2 and 3 that adding syntactic features successfully boosts the performance of our approach.

To further explore the effect of the syntactic features, we include the results of our model with different configurations of syntactic features in Table 4 (here we focus on the *Binary Overlap* metric as the results with *Proportional Overlap* demonstrate a similar conclusion). We can see that using the basic features and the combination of VPPRE, VPARG and VPSUBJ yields the best results for both DSE and ESE extraction. For DSE extraction, combining these three features improves the precision noticeably from 67.72% to 70.12% while the recall slightly improves. This indicates that VP-related structural information is very helpful for modeling segments as DSEs. However, this trend is not so clear for ESE extraction. This may be due to the fact that DSEs often involve verb phrases while ESEs are represented via a variety of syntactic structures.

Comparison with previous work. In Table 5, we compare our results to the previous work on opinion expression extraction (here we also focus on the *Binary Overlap* metric due to the similar trend demonstrated by the *Proportional Overlap* metric). Breck et al. (2007) presents the state-of-the-art sequence labeling approach on the tasks of DSE and ESE extraction. Their best results are shown as **Breck et al. Baseline** in the table. Johansson and Moschitti (2010) use a reranking technique on the best k outputs of a sequence labeler to further improve their sequence labeling results on the task of extracting DSEs, ESEs and OSEs (Objective Speech Events) (we don't consider OSEs here). Results using our re-implementation of their approach using SVM^{struct} (Tsochantaridis et al., 2004) on the output of CRF are labeled **CRF+Reranking Baseline** in the table. We use the same features and parameter settings as in their approach. **Our approach+Reranking** are results obtained by applying the reranking step on the output of our new-semi-CRF approach.

We can see that our approach outperforms the Breck et al. Baseline on both DSE extraction and ESE extraction in spite of the fact that we do not use their WordNet, Levin's verb categorization, and FrameNet features. The CRF+Reranking Baseline does provide a performance increase over the the baseline CRF results, but overall it cannot beat the other methods since the CRF baseline is very low. As one might expect, reranking also succeeds in boosting the performance of new-semi-CRF, achieving the best performance on F-measure for both DSE and ESE extraction. Note that the interannotator agreement results for these two tasks are 75% for DSE and 72% for ESE using a similar metric to *Binary Overlap*. Our results are much closer to these interannotator scores than previous systems especially for DSEs.

Task	Method	F-measure
DSE Extraction	Breck et al. Baseline	70.65
	CRF+Reranking Baseline	63.87
	Our approach	72.36
	Our approach+Reranking	**73.12**
ESE Extraction	Breck et al. Baseline	63.43
	CRF+Reranking Baseline	58.21
	Our approach	65.67
	Our approach+Reranking	**67.01**

Table 5: Comparison of our work with previous work on opinion expression extraction using the Binary-Overlap metric

4.4 Discussion

We note that our new-semi-CRF approach outperforms the original semi-CRF w.r.t. both precision and recall, but compared to CRF, our approach yields a clear improvement on recall but not on precision. An error analysis helps explain why. We found that our semi-CRF approach predicted almost the same number of DSEs as the gold standard labels while CRF only predicted half of them (for ESE extraction, the trend is similar). With more predicted entities, the precision is sacrificed but recall is boosted substantially, and overall we see an increase in F-measure.

Looking further into the errors, we found several mistakes that could potentially be fixed to yield better a precision score. Some errors were due to the false prediction of speech events like "said" or "told" as DSEs in cases where they actually just introduced statements of fact without expressing any private state. Adding features to distinguish such cases should help improve performance. Other errors were due to inadequate modeling of the context surrounding the expressions. For example, "enjoy a relative advantage" was falsely predicted as an ESE. If incorporating information about the subject of this verb phrase which is "products", this mistake could be avoided since "products" cannot hold or express private state. We also noticed some errors caused by inaccurate parsing and hope to study ways to account for these in our approach as future work.

By comparing the extraction results across different methods, we see that full parsing provides many benefits for modeling segment boundaries and improving the prediction precision for opinion expression extraction. For example, given the sentence, "... who are living [a lot better]$_{\text{[ESE]}}$ ...", both CRF and the original semi-CRF extract "lot better" as an ESE, while our approach correctly extracts "a lot better" as an ESE. And we also found many cases where the original semi-CRF cannot extract the opinion expressions while our approach can. Another benefit of utilizing parsing is to speed up learning and inference. Although in theory, the computational cost of parsing is $O(g \times n^3)$ where g is the grammar size and n is the sentence length while the cost of semi-CRFs is $O(K^2 \times L \times n)$ where K is the number of labels and L is the maximum entity length, feature extraction overhead and the potentially large number of learning iterations in parameter optimization may lead to a long training time for semi-CRFs. In our experiments on the MPQA data set, our machine with Intel Core 2 Duo CPU and 4GB RAM took 2 hours to fully parse 11,114 sentences using the Stanford Parser, and also 2 hours to train the standard semi-CRF. With the parsing information, our semi-CRF-based approach is able to finish training in 15 minutes. As full parsing would be expensive when the average sentence length is very large, it would be interesting to study how to utilize parsing with less cost in our task.

5 Conclusion

In this paper we propose a semi-CRF-based approach for extracting opinion expressions that takes into account during learning and inference the structural information available from syntactic parsing. Our approach allows opinion expressions to be identified at the segment level and their boundaries to be influenced by their probable syntactic structure. Experimental evaluations show that our model outperforms the best existing approaches on two opinion extraction tasks. In addition, we identify useful syntactic parse features for these tasks that have not been explored in previous work. Our error analysis indicates that adding additional features that account for subjectivity cues in the local context might further improve the performance. In future work, we hope to explore better ways of utilizing parsing information with less cost. Also, we will apply our model to additional opinion analysis tasks such as fine-grained opinion summarization and relation extraction.

6 Acknowledgement

This work was supported in part by National Science Foundation Grants IIS-1111176 and IIS-0968450, and by a gift from Google. We thank Nikos Karampatziakis, Igor Labutov, Veselin Stoyanov, Ainur Yessenalina and Jason Yosinski for their helpful comments.

References

Galen Andrew. 2006. A hybrid Markov/semi-Markov conditional random field for sequence segmentation. In Proceedings of EMNLP '06.

Steven Bethard, Hong Yu, Ashley Thornton, Vasileios Hatzivassiloglou, and Dan Jurafsky. 2005. Extracting opinion propositions and opinion holders using syntactic and lexical cues. In Shanahan, James G., Yan Qu, and Janyce Wiebe, editors, Computing Attitude and Affect in Text: Theory and Applications.

Eric Breck, Yejin Choi, and Claire Cardie. 2007. Identifying expressions of opinion in context. IJCAI'07.

Yejin Choi, Claire Cardie, Ellen Riloff, and Siddharth Patwardhan. 2005. Identifying sources of opinions with conditional random fields and extraction patterns. In Proceedings of HLT '05.

Yejin Choi, Eric Breck, and Claire Cardie. 2006. Joint extraction of entities and relations for opinion recognition. In Proceedings of EMNLP '06.

Yejin Choi and Claire Cardie. 2010. Hierarchical sequential learning for extracting opinions and their attributes. In Proceedings of ACL 2010, Short Papers.

Richard Johansson and Alessandro Moschitti. 2010. Syntactic and semantic structure for opinion expression detection. In Proceedings of CoNLL '10.

Niklas Jakob and Iryna Gurevych. Extracting opinion targets in a single- and cross-domain setting with conditional random fields. In Proceedings of EMNLP' 10.

Mahesh Joshi and Penstein-Ros'e Carolyn. 2009. Generalizing dependency features for opinion mining. In Proceedings of ACL/IJCNLP 2009, Short Papers Track.

Dan Klein and Christopher D. Manning. 2003. Accurate unlexicalized parsing. In Proceedings of ACL '03.

Soo-Min Kim and Eduard Hovy. 2006. Extracting opinions, opinion holders, and topics expressed in online news media text. In Proceedings of the ACL Workshop on Sentiment and Subjectivity in Text.

Nozomi Kobayashi, Kentaro Inui, and Yuji Matsumoto. 2007. Extracting aspect-evaluation and aspect-of relations in opinion mining. In Proceedings of EMNLP-CoNLL-2007.

John D. Lafferty, Andrew McCallum, and Fernando C. N. Pereira. 2001. Conditional Random Fields: Probabilistic Models for Segmenting and Labeling Sequence Data. In Proceedings of ICML '01.

Dong C. Liu and Jorge Nocedal. 1989. On the limited memory BFGS method for large scale optimization. Mathematical Programming B 45(3): 503-528.

M Arthur Munson, Claire Cardie, and Rich Caruana. Optimizing to arbitrary NLP metrics using ensemble selection. In HLT-EMNLP05, 2005.

Daisuke Okanohara, Yusuke Miyao, Yoshimasa Tsuruoka, and Jun'ichi Tsujii. Improving the scalability of semi-Markov conditional random fields for named entity recognition. In Proceedings of ACL'06.

Randolph Quirk, Sidney Greenbaum, Geoffrey Leech, and Jan Svartvik. A comprehensive grammar of the English language. New York: Longman, 1985.

Richard Johansson and Alessandro Moschitti. Extracting Opinion Expressions and Their Polarities - Exploration of Pipelines and Joint Models. In Proceedings of ACL '11, Short Paper.

Ellen Riloff and Janyce M Wiebe. Learning extraction patterns for subjective expressions. In Proceedings of EMNLP 2003.

Sunita Sarawagi and William W. Cohen. 2004. Semi-Markov Conditional Random Fields for Information Extraction. In Proceedings of NIPS 2004.

Charles Sutton and Andrew McCallum. An Introduction to Conditional Random Fields. Foundations and Trends in Machine Learning (FnT ML), 2010.

Janyce Wiebe, Theresa Wilson , and Claire Cardie. 2005. Annotating expressions of opinions and emotions in language. Language Resources and Evaluation, volume 39, issue 2-3, pp. 165-210.

Theresa Wilson, Janyce Wiebe, and Paul Hoffmann. 2005. Recognizing contextual polarity in phrase-level sentiment analysis. In Proceedings of HLT '05.

Theresa Wilson, Paul Hoffmann, Swapna Somasundaran, Jason Kessler, Janyce Wiebe, Yejin Choi, Claire Cardie, Ellen Riloff, and Siddharth Patwardhan. OpinionFinder: A system for subjectivity analysis. EMNLP 2005. Demo abstract.

Yuanbin Wu, Qi Zhang, Xuanjing Huang, and Lide Wu. Phrase dependency parsing for opinion mining. In Proceedings of EMNLP 2009.

Ioannis Tsochantaridis, Thomas Hofmann, Thorsten Joachims, and Yasemi Altun. Support Vector Learning for Interdependent and Structured Output Spaces. In Proceedings of ICML 2004.

Opinion Target Extraction Using Word-Based Translation Model

Kang Liu, Liheng Xu, Jun Zhao

National Laboratory of Pattern Recognition,
Institute of Automation, Chinese Academy of Sciences, Beijing, 100190, China
{kliu, lhxu, jzhao}@nlpr.ia.ac.cn

Abstract

This paper proposes a novel approach to extract opinion targets based on word-based translation model (WTM). At first, we apply WTM in a monolingual scenario to mine the associations between opinion targets and opinion words. Then, a graph-based algorithm is exploited to extract opinion targets, where candidate opinion relevance estimated from the mined associations, is incorporated with candidate importance to generate a global measure. By using WTM, our method can capture opinion relations more precisely, especially for long-span relations. In particular, compared with previous syntax-based methods, our method can effectively avoid noises from parsing errors when dealing with informal texts in large Web corpora. By using graph-based algorithm, opinion targets are extracted in a global process, which can effectively alleviate the problem of error propagation in traditional bootstrap-based methods, such as *Double Propagation*. The experimental results on three real world datasets in different sizes and languages show that our approach is more effective and robust than state-of-art methods.

1 Introduction

With the rapid development of e-commerce, most customers express their opinions on various kinds of entities, such as products and services. These reviews not only provide customers with useful information for reference, but also are valuable for merchants to get the feedback from customers and enhance the qualities of their products or services. Therefore, mining opinions from these vast amounts of reviews becomes urgent, and has attracted a lot of attentions from many researchers.

In opinion mining, one fundamental problem is opinion target extraction. This task is to extract items which opinions are expressed on. In reviews, opinion targets are usually nouns/noun phrases. For example, in the sentence of "*The phone has a colorful and even amazing screen*", "*screen*" is an opinion target. In online product reviews, opinion targets often are products or product features, so this task is also named as product feature extraction in previous work (Hu et al., 2004; Ding et al., 2008; Liu et al., 2005; Popescu et al., 2005; Wu et al., 2005; Su et al., 2008).

To extract opinion targets, many studies regarded opinion words as strong indicators (Hu et al., 2004; Popescu et al., 2005; Liu et al., 2005; Qiu et al., 2011; Zhang et al., 2010), which is based on the observation that opinion words are usually located around opinion targets, and there are associations between them. Therefore, most pervious methods iteratively extracted opinion targets depending upon the associations between opinion words and opinion targets (Qiu et al., 2011; Zhang et al., 2010). For example, "*colorful*" and "*amazing*" is usually used to modify "*screen*" in reviews about cell phone, so there are strong associations between them. If "*colorful*" and "*amazing*" had been known to be opinion words, "*screen*" is likely to be an opinion target in this domain. In addition, the extracted opinion targets can be used to expand more opinion words according to their associations. It's a mutual reinforcement procedure.

Therefore, mining associations between opinion targets and opinion words is a key for opinion target extraction (Wu et al., 2009). To this end, most previous methods (Hu et al., 2004; Ding et al., 2004; Wang et al., 2008), named as *adjacent methods*, employed the *adjacent rule*, where an opinion target was regarded to have opinion relations with the surrounding opinion words in a given window. However, because of the limitation of window size, opinion relations cannot be captured precisely, especially for long-span relations, which would hurt estimating associations between opinion targets and opinion words. To resolve this problem, several studies exploited syntactic information such as dependency trees (Popescu et al., 2005; Qiu et al., 2009; Qiu et al., 2011; Wu et al., 2009; Zhang et al., 2010). If the syntactic relation between an opinion word and an opinion target satisfied a designed pattern, then there was an opinion relation between them. Experiments consistently reported that *syntax-based methods* could yield better performance than *adjacent methods* for small or medium corpora (Zhang et al., 2010). The performance of *syntax-based methods* heavily depends on the parsing performance. However, online reviews are often informal texts (including grammar mistakes, typos, improper punctuations etc.). As a result, parsing may generate many mistakes. Thus, for large corpora from Web including a great deal of informal texts, these *syntax-based methods* may suffer from parsing errors and introduce many noises. Furthermore, this problem maybe more serious on non-English language reviews, such as Chinese reviews, because that the performances of parsing on these languages are often worse than that on English.

To overcome the weakness of the two kinds of methods mentioned above, we propose a novel unsupervised approach to extract opinion targets by using word-based translation model (WTM). We formulate identifying opinion relations between opinion targets and opinion words as a word alignment task. We argue that an opinion target can find its corresponding modifier through monolingual word alignment. For example in Figure 1, the opinion words "*colorful*" and "*amazing*" are aligned with the target "*screen*" through word alignment. To this end, we use WTM to perform monolingual word alignment for mining associations between opinion targets and opinion words. In this process, several factors, such as word co-occurrence frequencies, word positions etc., can be considered globally. Compared with *adjacent methods*, WTM doesn't identify opinion relations between words in a given window, so long-span relations can be effectively captured (Liu et al., 2009). Compared with *syntax-based methods*, without using parsing, WTM can effectively avoid errors from parsing informal texts. So it will be more robust. In addition, by using WTM, our method can capture the "one-to-many" or "many-to-one" relations ("one-to-many" means that, in a sentence one opinion word modifies several opinion targets, and "many-to-one" means several opinion words modify one opinion target). Thus, it's reasonable to expect that WTM is likely to yield better performance than traditional methods for mining associations between opinion targets and opinion words.

Based on the mined associations, we extract opinion targets in a ranking framework. All nouns/noun phrases are regarded as opinion target candidates. Then a graph-based algorithm is exploited to assign confidences to each candidate, in which candidate opinion relevance and importance are incorporated to generate a global measure. At last, the candidates with higher ranks are extracted as opinion targets. Compared with most traditional methods (Hu et al. 2004; Liu et al., 2005; Qiu et al., 2011), we don't extract opinion targets iteratively based on the bootstrapping strategy, such as *Double Propagation* (Qiu et al., 2011), instead all candidates are dynamically ranked in a global process. Therefore, error propagation can be effectively avoided and the performance can be improved.

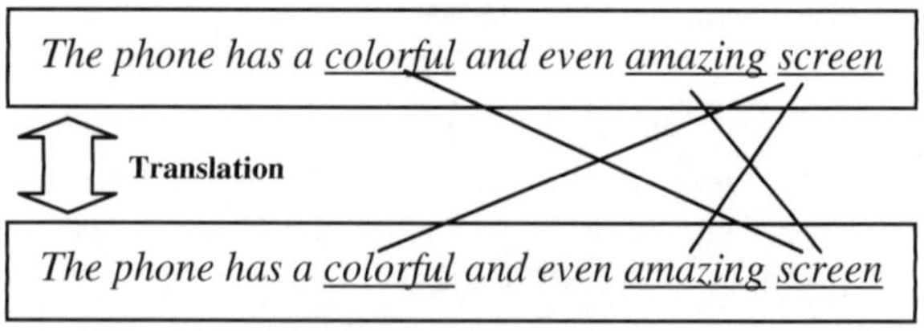

Figure 1: Word-based translation model for opinion relation identification

The main contributions of this paper are as follows.

1) We formulate the opinion relation identification between opinion targets and opinion words as a word alignment task. To our best knowledge, none of previous methods deal with this task using monolingual word alignment model (in Section 3.1).

2) We propose a graph-based algorithm for opinion target extraction in which candidate opinion relevance and importance are incorporated into a unified graph to estimate candidate confidence. Then the candidates with higher confidence scores are extracted as opinion targets (in Section 3.2).
3) We have performed experiments on three datasets in different sizes and languages. The experimental results show that our approach can achieve performance improvement over the traditional methods. (in Section 4).

The rest of the paper is organized as follows. In the next section, we will review related work in brief. Section 3 describes our approach in detail. Then experimental results will be given in Section 4. At the same time, we will give some analysis about the results. Finally, we give the conclusion and the future work.

2 Related Work

Many studies have focused on the task of opinion target extraction, such as (Hu et al., 2004; Ding et al., 2008; Liu et al., 2006; Popescu et al., 2005; Wu et al., 2005; Wang et al., 2008; Li et al., 2010; Su et al., 2008; Li et al., 2006). In general, the existing approaches can be divided into two main categories: supervised and unsupervised methods.

In supervised approaches, the opinion target extraction task was usually regarded as a sequence labeling task (Jin et al. 2009; Li et al. 2010; Wu et al., 2009; Ma et al. 2010; Zhang et al., 2009). Jin et al. (2009) proposed a lexicalized HMM model to perform opinion mining. Li et al. (2010) proposed a Skip-Tree CRF model for opinion target extraction. Their methods exploited three structures including linear-chain structure, syntactic structure, and conjunction structure. In addition, Wu et al. (2009) utilized a SVM classifier to identify relations between opinion targets and opinion expressions by leveraging phrase dependency parsing. The main limitation of these supervised methods is that labeling training data for each domain is impracticable because of the diversity of the review domains.

In unsupervised methods, most approaches regarded opinion words as the important indicators for opinion targets (Hu et al., 2004; Popsecu et al., 2005; Wang et al., 2008; Qiu et al., 2011; Zhang et al., 2010). The basic idea was that reviewers often use the same opinion words when they comment on the similar opinion targets. The extraction procedure was often a bootstrapping process which extracted opinion words and opinion targets iteratively, depending upon their associations. Popsecu et al. (2005) used syntactic patterns to extract opinion target candidates. After that they computed the point-wise mutual information (PMI) score between a candidate and a product category to refine the extracted results. Hu et al. (2004) exploited an association rule mining algorithm and frequency information to extract frequent explicit product features. The adjective nearest to the frequent explicit feature was extracted as an opinion word. Then the extracted opinion words were used to extract infrequent opinion targets. Wang et al. (2008) adopted the similar idea, but their method needed a few seeds to weakly supervise the extraction process. Qiu et al. (2009, 2011) proposed a *Double Propagation* method to expand a domain sentiment lexicon and an opinion target set iteratively. They exploited direct dependency relations between words to extract opinion targets and opinion words iteratively. The main limitation of Qiu's method is that the patterns based on dependency parsing tree may introduce many noises for the large corpora (Zhang et al., 2010). Meanwhile, *Double Propagation* is a bootstrapping strategy which is a greedy process and has the problem of error propagation. Zhang et al. (2010) extended Qiu's method. Besides the patterns used in Qiu's method, they adopted some other patterns, such as phrase patterns, sentence patterns and "no" pattern, to increase recall. In addition they used the HITS (Klernberg et al., 1999) algorithm to compute the feature relevance scores, which were simply multiplied by the log of feature frequencies to rank the extracted opinion targets. In this way, the precision of result can be improved.

3 Opinion Target Extraction Using Word-Based Translation Model

3.1 Method Framework

As mentioned in the first section, our approach for opinion target extraction is composed of the following two main components:

1) ***Mining associations between opinion targets and opinion words***: Given a collection of reviews, we adopt a word-based translation

model to identify potential opinion relations in all sentences, and then the associations between opinion targets and opinion words are estimated.

2) ***Candidate confidence estimation***: Based on these associations, we exploit a graph-based algorithm to compute the confidence of each opinion target candidate. Then the candidates with higher confidence scores are extracted as opinion targets.

3.2 Mining associations between opinion targets and opinion words using Word-based Translation Model

This component is to identify potential opinion relations in sentences and estimate associations between opinion targets and opinion words. We assume opinion targets and opinion words respectively to be nouns/noun phrases and adjectives, which have been widely adopted in previous work (Hu et al., 2004; Ding et al., 2008; Wang et al., 2008; Qiu et al., 2011). Thus, our aim is to find potential opinion relations between nouns/noun phrases and adjectives in sentences, and calculate the associations between them. As mentioned in the first section, we formulate opinion relation identification as a word alignment task. We employ the word-based translation model (Brown et al. 1993) to perform monolingual word alignment, which has been widely used in many tasks, such as collocation extraction (Liu et al., 2009), question retrieval (Zhou et al., 2011) and so on. In our method, every sentence is replicated to generate a parallel corpus, and we apply the bilingual word alignment algorithm to the monolingual scenario to align a noun/noun phase with its modifier.

Given a sentence with n words $S=\{w_1,w_2,...,w_n\}$, the word alignment $A=\{(i,a_i)\,|\,i\in[1,n]\}$ can be obtained by maximizing the word alignment probability of the sentence as follows.

$$\hat{A}=\arg\max_{A} P(A\,|\,S) \qquad (1)$$

where (i,a_i) means that a noun/noun phrase at position i is aligned with an adjective at position a_i. If we directly use this alignment model to our task, a noun/noun phrase may align with the irrelevant words other than adjectives, like prepositions or conjunctions and so on. Thus, in the alignment procedure, we introduce some constrains: 1) nouns/noun phrases (adjectives) must be aligned with adjectives (nouns/noun phrases) or null words; 2) other words can only align with themselves. Totally, we employ the following 3 WTMs (IBM 1~3) to identify opinion relations.

$$P_{IBM-1}(A\,|\,S)\propto\prod_{j=1}^{n}t(w_j\,|\,w_{a_j})$$

$$P_{IBM-2}(A\,|\,S)\propto\prod_{j=1}^{n}t(w_j\,|\,w_{a_j})d(j\,|\,a_j,n)$$

$$P_{IBM-3}(A\,|\,S)\propto\prod_{i=1}^{n}n(\phi_i\,|\,w_i)\prod_{j=1}^{n}t(w_j\,|\,w_{a_j})d(j\,|\,a_j,n) \qquad (2)$$

There are three main factors: $t(w_j\,|\,w_{a_j})$, $d(j\,|\,a_j,n)$ and $n(\phi_i\,|\,w_i)$, which respectively models different information.

1) $t(w_j\,|\,w_{a_j})$ models the co-occurrence information of two words in corpora. If an adjective co-occurs with a noun/noun phrase frequently in the reviews, this adjective has high association with this noun/noun phrase. For example, in reviews of cell phone, "*big*" often co-occurs with "*phone's size*", so "*big*" has high association with "*phone's size*".

2) $d(j\,|\,a_j,l)$ models word position information, which describes the probability of a word in position a_j aligned with a word in position j.

3) $n(\phi_i\,|\,w_i)$ models the fertility of words, which describe the ability of a word for "one-to-many" alignment. ϕ_i denotes the number of words that are aligned with w_i. For example, "*Iphone4 has amazing screen and software*". In this sentence, "*amazing*" is used to modify two words: "*screen*" and "*software*". So ϕ equals to 2 for "*amazing*".

Therefore, in Eq. (2), $P_{IBM-1}(A\,|\,S)$ only models word co-occurrence information. $P_{IBM-2}(A\,|\,S)$ additionally employs word position information. Besides these two information, $P_{IBM-3}(A\,|\,S)$ considers the ability of a word for "one-to-many" alignment. In the following experiments section, we will discuss the performance difference among these models in detail. Moreover, these models may capture "one-to-many" or "many-to-one" opinion relations (mentioned in the first section). In our knowledge, it isn't specifically considered by previous methods including *adjacent methods* and *syntax-based methods*. Meanwhile, the alignment results may contain empty-word alignments, which means a noun/noun phrase has no modifier or an adjective modify nothing in the sentence.

After gathering all word pairs from the review sentences, we can estimate the translation probabilities between nouns/noun phrases and adjectives as follows.

$$p(w_N \mid w_A) = \frac{Count(w_N, w_A)}{Count(w_A)} \tag{3}$$

where $p(w_N \mid w_A)$ means the translation probabilities from adjectives to nouns/noun phrases. Similarly, we can obtain translation probability $p(w_A \mid w_N)$. Therefore, similar to (Liu et al. 2009), the association between a noun/noun phrase and an adjective is estimated as follows.

$$Association(w_N, w_A) = (t/p(w_N \mid w_A) + (1-t)/p(w_A \mid w_N))^{-1} \tag{4}$$

where t is the harmonic factor to combine these two translation probabilities. In this paper, we set $t = 0.5$. For demonstration, we give some examples in Table 1. We can see that our method using WTM can successfully capture associations between opinion targets and opinion words.

	battery life	sound	software
wonderful	0.000	0.042	0.000
poor	0.032	0.000	0.026
long	0.025	0.000	0.000

Table 1: Examples of associations between opinion targets and opinion words.

3.3 Candidate Confidence Estimation

In this component, we compute the confidence of each opinion target candidate and rank them. The candidates with higher confidence are regarded as the opinion targets. We argue that the confidence of a candidate is determined by two factors: 1) *Opinion Relevance*; 2) *Candidate Importance*.

Opinion Relevance reflects the degree that a candidate is associated to opinion words. If an adjective has higher confidence to be an opinion word, the noun/noun phrase it modifies will have higher confidence to be an opinion target. Similarly, if a noun/noun phrase has higher confidence to be an opinion target, the adjective which modifies it will be highly possible to be an opinion word. It's an iterative reinforcement process, which indicates that existing graph-based algorithms are applicable.

Candidate Importance reflects the salience of a candidate in the corpus. We assign an importance score to an opinion target candidate f according to its $tf\text{-}idf$ score, which is further normalized by the sum of $tf\text{-}idf$ scores of all candidates.

$$Importance(c) = \frac{tf\text{-}idf(c)}{\sum_c tf\text{-}idf(c)} \tag{5}$$

where c represents a candidate, tf is the term frequency in the dataset, and df is computed by using the Google n-gram corpus[1].

To model these two factors, a bipartite graph is constructed, the vertices of which include all nouns/noun phrases and adjectives. As shown in Figure 2, the white vertices represent nouns/noun phrases and the gray vertices represent adjectives. An edge between a noun/noun phrase and an adjective represents that there is an opinion relation between them. The weight on the edges represents the association between them, which are estimated by using WTM, as shown in Eq. (4).

To estimate the confidence of each candidate on this bipartite graph, we exploit a graph-based algorithm, where we use C to represent candidate confidence vector, a $n \times 1$ vector. We set the candidate initial confidence with candidate importance score, i.e. $C^0 = S$, where S is the candidate initial confidence vector and each item in S is computed using Eq. (5).

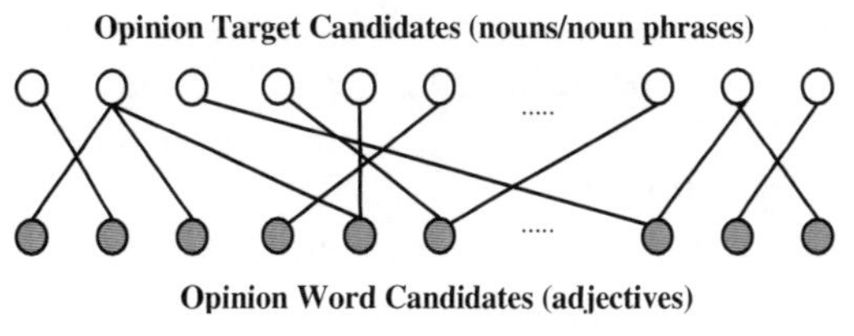

Figure 2: Bipartite graph for modeling relations between opinion targets and opinion words

[1] http://books.google.com/ngrams/datasets

Then we compute the candidate confidence by using the following iterative formula.

$$C^{t+1} = M^T \times M \times C^t \quad (6)$$

where C^t is the candidate confidence vector at time t, and C^{t+1} is the candidate confidence vector at time $t+1$. M is an opinion relevance matrix, a $m \times n$ matrix, where $M_{i,j}$ is the associated weight between a noun/noun phrase i and an adjective j.

To consider the candidate importance scores, we introduce a reallocate condition: combining the candidate opinion relevance with the candidate importance at each step. Thus we can get the final recursive form of the candidate confidence as follows.

$$C^{t+1} = (1-\lambda) \times M^T \times M \times C^t + \lambda \times S \quad (7)$$

where $\lambda \in [0,1]$ is the proportion of candidate importance in the candidate confidence. When $\lambda = 1$, the candidate confidence is completely determined by the candidate importance; and when $\lambda = 0$, the candidate confidence is determined by the candidate opinion relevance. We will discuss its effect in the section of experiments.

To solve Eq. (7), we rewrite it as the following form.

$$C = \lambda \times (I - (1-\lambda) \times M^T \times M)^{-1} \times S \quad (8)$$

where I is an identity matrix. To handle the inverse of the matrix, we expand the Eq. (8) as a power series as following.

$$C = \lambda \times [I + B + \ldots + B^k] \times S \quad (9)$$

where $B = (1-\lambda) \times M^T \times M$ and $k \in [0, \infty)$ is an approximate factor. In experiments, we set $k = 100$. Using this equation, we estimate confidences for opinion target candidates. The candidates with higher confidence scores than the threshold will be extracted as the opinion targets.

4 Experiments

4.1 Datasets and Evaluation Metrics

In our experiments, we select three real world datasets to evaluate our approach. The first dataset is *COAE2008 dataset2*[2], which contains Chinese reviews of four different products. The detailed information can be seen in Table 2. Moreover, to evaluate our method comprehensively, we collect a larger collection named by *Large*, which includes three corpora from three different domains and different languages. The detailed statistical information of this dataset is also shown in Table 2. Restaurant is crawled from the Chinese Web site: www.dianping.com. The Hotel and MP3[3] were used in (Wang et al., 2011), which are respectively clawed from www.tripadvisor.com and www.amazon.com. For each collection, we perform random sampling to generate testing dataset, which include 6,000 sentences for each domain. Then the opinion targets in *Large* were manually annotated as the gold standard for evaluations. Three annotators are involved in the annotation process as follows. First, every noun/noun phrase and its contexts in review sentences are extracted. Then two annotators were required to judge whether every noun/noun phrase is opinion target or not. If a conflict happens, a third annotator will make judgment for finial results. The inter-agreement was 0.72. In total, we respectively obtain 1,112, 1,241 and 1,850 opinion targets in Hotel, MP3 and Restaurant. The third dataset is Customer Review Datasets[4] (English reviews of five products), which was also used in (Hu et al., 2004; Qiu et al., 2011). They have labeled opinion targets. The detailed information can be found in (Hu et al., 2004).

Domain	Language	#Sentence	#Reviews
Camera	Chinese	2075	137
Car	Chinese	4783	157
Laptop	Chinese	1034	56
Phone	Chinese	2644	123

(a) *COAE2008 dataset2*

Domain	Language	#Sentence	#Reviews
Hotel	English	1,855,351	185,829
MP3	English	289,931	30,837
Restaurant	Chinese	1,683,129	395,124

(b) *Large*

Table 2: Experimental Data Sets, # denotes the size of the reviews/sentences

In experiments, each review is segmented into sentences according to punctuations. Then sentences are tokenized and the part-of-speech of

[2] http://ir-china.org.cn/coae2008.html

[3] http://sifaka.cs.uiuc.edu/~wang296/Data/index.html

[4] http://www.cs.uic.edu/~liub/FBS/sentiment-analysis.html

Methods	Camera			Car			Laptop			Phone		
	P	R	F	P	R	F	P	R	F	P	R	F
Hu	0.63	0.65	0.64	0.62	0.58	0.60	0.51	0.67	0.58	0.69	0.60	0.64
DP	0.71	0.70	0.70	0.72	0.65	0.68	0.58	0.69	0.63	0.78	0.66	0.72
Zhang	0.71	0.78	0.74	0.69	0.68	0.68	0.57	0.80	0.67	0.80	0.71	0.75
Ours	0.75	0.81	0.78	0.71	0.71	0.71	0.61	0.85	0.71	0.83	0.74	0.78

Table 3: Experiments on *COAE2008 dataset2*

Methods	Hotel			MP3			Restaurant		
	P	R	F	P	R	F	P	R	F
Hu	0.60	0.65	0.62	0.61	0.68	0.64	0.64	0.69	0.66
DP	0.67	0.69	0.68	0.69	0.70	0.69	0.74	0.72	0.73
Zhang	0.67	0.76	0.71	0.67	0.77	0.72	0.75	0.79	0.77
Ours	0.71	0.80	0.75	0.70	0.82	0.76	0.80	0.84	0.82

Table 4: Experiments on *Large*

Methods	D1			D2			D3			D4			D5		
	P	R	F	P	R	F	P	R	F	P	R	F	P	R	F
Hu	0.75	0.82	0.78	0.71	0.79	0.75	0.72	0.76	0.74	0.69	0.82	0.75	0.74	0.80	0.77
DP	0.87	0.81	0.84	0.90	0.81	0.85	0.90	0.86	0.88	0.81	0.84	0.82	0.92	0.86	0.89
Zhang	0.83	0.84	0.83	0.86	0.85	0.85	0.86	0.88	0.87	0.80	0.85	0.83	0.86	0.86	0.86
Ours	0.84	0.85	0.84	0.87	0.85	0.86	0.88	0.89	0.88	0.81	0.85	0.83	0.89	0.87	0.88

Table 5: Experiments on *Customer Review Dataset*

each word is assigned. Stanford NLP tool[5] is used to perform POS-tagging and dependency parsing. The method in (Zhu et al., 2009) is used to identify noun phrases. We select precision, recall and F-measure as the evaluation metrics. We also perform a significant test, i.e., a t-test with a default significant level of 0.05.

4.2 Our Methods vs. State-of-art Methods

To prove the effectiveness of our method, we select the following state-of-art unsupervised methods as baselines for comparison.

1) ***Hu*** is the method described in (Hu et al., 2004), which extracted opinion targets by using adjacent rule.

2) ***DP*** is the method described in (Qiu et al., 2011), which used *Double Propagation* algorithm to extract opinion targets depending on syntactic relations between words.

3) ***Zhang*** is the method described in (Zhang et al., 2010), which is an extension of *DP*. They extracted opinion targets candidates using syntactic patterns and other specific patterns. Then HITS (Kleinberg 1999) algorithm combined with candidate frequency is employed to rank the results for opinion target extraction.

Hu is selected to represent *adjacent* methods for opinion target extraction. And ***DP*** and ***Zhang*** are selected to represent *syntax-based* methods. The parameter settings in these three baselines are the same as the original papers. In special, for *DP* and *Zhang*, we used the same patterns for different language reviews. The overall performance results are shown in Table 3, 4 and 5, respectively, where "P" denotes precision, "R" denotes recall and "F" denotes F-measure. *Ours* denotes full model of our method, in which we use IBM-3 model for identifying opinion relations between words. Moreover, we set $\phi_{max} = 2$ in Eq. (2) and $\lambda = 0.3$ in Eq. (7). From results, we can make the following observations.

1) *Ours* achieves performance improvement over other methods. This indicates that our method based on word-based translation model is effective for opinion target extraction.
2) The graph-based methods (*Ours* and *Zhang*) outperform the methods using *Double Propagation* (*DP*). Similar observations have been made by Zhang et al. (2010). The reason is that graph-based methods extract opinion targets in a global framework and they can effectively avoid the error propagation made by traditional methods based on *Double Propagation*. Moreover, *Ours* outperforms *Zhang*. We believe the reason is that *Ours* consider the opinion relevance and the candidate importance in a unified graph-based framework. By contrast, Zhang only simply

[5] http://nlp.stanford.edu/software/tagger.shtml

plus opinion relevance with frequency to determine the candidate confidence.

3) In Table 4, the improvement made by *Ours* on Restaurant (Chinese reviews) is larger than that on Hotel and MP3 (English reviews). The same phenomenon can be found when we compare the improvement made by *Ours* in Table 3 (Chinese reviews) with that in Table 5 (English reviews). We believe that reason is that syntactic patterns used in *DP* and *Zhang* were exploited based on English grammar, which may not be suitable to Chinese language. Moreover, another reason is that the performance of parsing on Chinese texts is not better than that on English texts, which will hurt the performance of *syntax-based methods* (*DP* and *Zhang*).
4) Compared the results in Table 3 with the results in Table 4, we can observe that *Ours* obtains larger improvements with the increase of the data size. This indicates that our method is more effective for opinion target extraction than state-of-art methods, especially for large corpora. When the data size increase, the methods based on syntactic patterns will introduce more noises due to the parsing errors on informal texts. On the other side, *Ours* uses WTM other than parsing to identify opinion relations between words, and the noises made by inaccurate parsing can be avoided. Thus, *Ours* can outperform baselines.
5) In Table 5, *Ours* makes comparable results with baselines in *Customer Review Datasets*, although there is a little loss in precision in some domains. We believe the reason is that the size of *Customer Review Datasets* is too small. As a result, WTM may suffer from data sparseness for association estimation. Nevertheless, the average recall is improved.

An Example In Table 6, we show top 10 opinion targets extracted by *Hu, DP*, *Zhang* and *Ours* in MP3 of *Large*. In *Hu* and *DP*, since they didn't rank the results, their results are ranked according to frequency in this experiment. The errors are marked in bold face. From these examples, we can see *Ours* extracts more correct opinion targets than others. In special, *Ours* outperforms *Zhang*. It indicates the effectiveness of our graph-based method for candidate confidence estimation. Moreover, *Ours* considers candidate importance besides opinion relevance, so some specific opinion targets are ranked to the fore, such as "voice recorder", "fm radio" and "lcd screen".

4.3 Effect of Word-based Translation Model

In this subsection, we aim to prove the effectiveness of our WTM for estimating associations between opinion targets and opinion words. For comparison, we select two baselines for comparison, named as *Adjacent* and *Syntax*. These baselines respectively use adjacent rule (Hu et al. 2004; Wang et al., 2008) and syntactic patterns (Qiu et al., 2009) to identify opinion relations in sentences. Then the same method (Eq.3 and Eq.4) is used to estimate associations between opinion targets and opinion words. At last the same graph-based method (in Section 3.3) is used to extract opinion targets. Due to the limitation of the space, the experimental results only on *COAE2008 dataset2* and *Large* are shown in Figure 3.

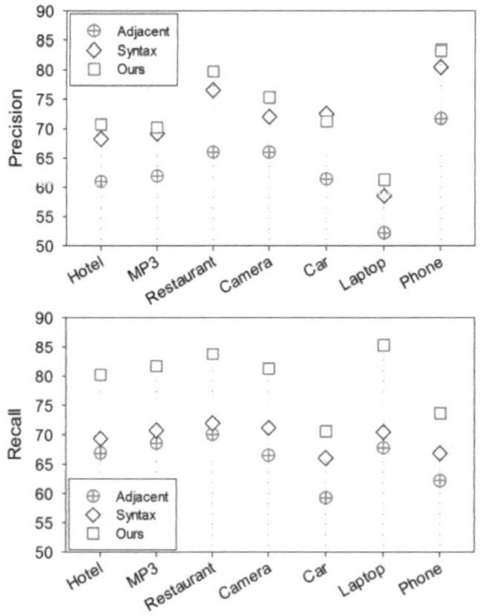

Figure 3: Experimental comparison among different relation identification methods

Hu	quality, **thing**, drive, feature, battery, sound, **time**, music, price
DP	quality, battery, software, device, screen, file, **thing**, feature, battery life
Zhang	quality, size, battery life, **hour**, version, function, upgrade, **number**, music
Ours	quality, battery life, voice recorder, video, fm radio, battery, file system, screen, lcd screen

Table 6: Top 10 opinion targets extracted by different methods.

In Figure 3, we observe that *Ours* using WTM makes significant improvements compared with two baselines, both on precision and recall. It indicates that WTM is effective for identifying opinion relations, which makes the estimation of the associations be more precise.

4.4 Effect of Our Graph-based Method

In this subsection, we aim to prove the effectiveness of our graph-based method for opinion target extraction. We design two baselines, named as *WTM_DP* and *WTM_HITS*. Both *WTM_DP* and *WTM_HITS* use WTM to mine associations between opinion targets and opinion words. Then, *WTM_DP* uses *Double Propagation* adapted in (Wang et al. 2008; Qiu et al. 2009) to extract opinion targets, which only consider the candidate opinion relevance. *WTM_HITS* uses a graph-based method of Zhang et al. (2010) to extract opinion targets, which consider both candidate opinion relevance and frequency. Figure 4 gives the experimental results on *COAE2008 dataset2* and *Large*. In Figure 4, we can observe that our graph-based algorithm outperforms not only the method based on *Double Propagation,* but also the previous graph-based approach.

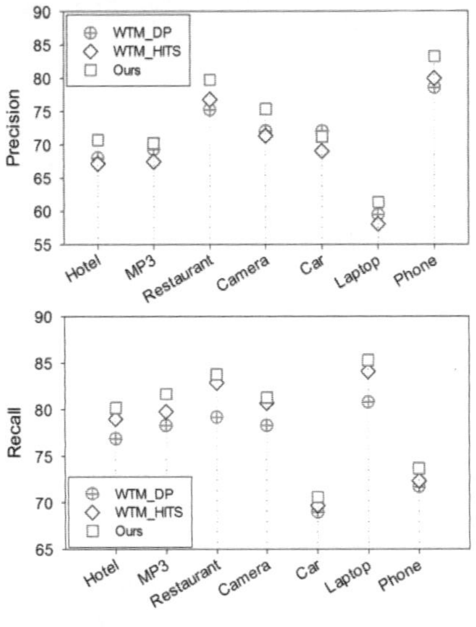

Figure 4: Experimental Comparison between different ranking algorithms

4.5 Parameter Influences

4.5.1 Effect of Different WTMs

In section 3, we use three different WTMs in Eq. (2) to identify opinion relations. In this subsection, we make comparison among them. Experimental results on *COAE2008 dataset2* and *Large* are shown in Figure 5. *Ours_1*, *Ours_2* and *Ours_3* respectively denote our method using different WTMs (IBM 1~3). From the results in Figure 5, we observe that *Ours_2* outperforms *Ours_1*, which indicates that word position is useful for identifying opinion relations. Furthermore, *Ours_3* outperforms other models, which indicates that considering the fertility of a word can produce better performance.

4.5.2 Effect of λ

In our method, when we employ Eq. (7) to assign confidence score to each candidate, $\lambda \in [0,1]$ decides the proportion of candidate importance in our method. Due to the limitation of space, we only show the F-measure of *Ours* on COAE2008 dataset2 and *Large* when varying λ in Figure 6.

In Figure 6, curves increase firstly, and decrease with the increase of λ. The best performance is obtained when λ is around 0.3. It indicates that candidate importance and candidate opinion relevance are both important for candidate confidence estimation. The performance of opinion target extraction benefits from their combination.

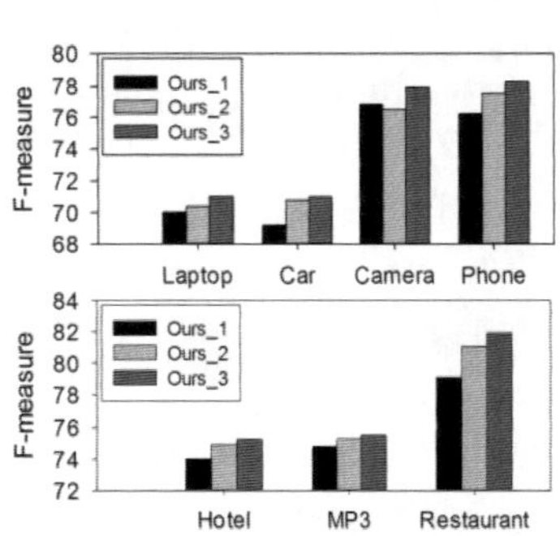

Figure 5. Experimental results by using different word-based translation model.

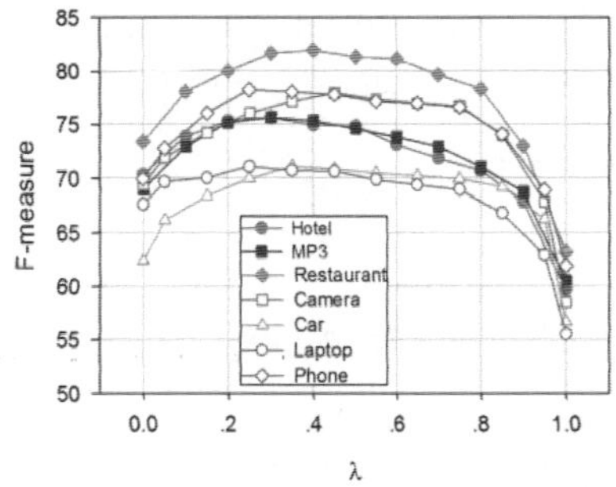

Figure 6. Experimental results when varying λ

5 Conclusions and Future Work

This paper proposes a novel graph-based approach to extract opinion targets using WTM. Compared with previous *adjacent methods* and *syntax-based methods*, by using WTM, our method can capture opinion relations more precisely and therefore be more effective for opinion target extraction, especially for large informal Web corpora.

In future work, we plan to use other word alignment methods, such as discriminative model (Liu et al., 2010) for this task. Meanwhile, we will add some syntactic information into WTM to constrain the word alignment process, in order to identify opinion relations between words more precisely. Moreover, we believe that there are some verbs or nouns can be opinion words and they may be helpful for opinion target extraction. And we think that it's useful to add some prior knowledge of opinion words (sentiment lexicon) in our model for estimating candidate opinion relevance.

Acknowledgements

The work is supported by the National Natural Science Foundation of China (Grant No. 61070106), the National Basic Research Program of China (Grant No. 2012CB316300), Tsinghua National Laboratory for Information Science and Technology (TNList) Cross-discipline Foundation and the Opening Project of Beijing Key Laboratory of Internet Culture and Digital Dissemination Research (Grant No. 5026035403). We thank the anonymous reviewers for their insightful comments.

References

Peter F. Brown, Stephen A. Della Pietra, Vincent J. Della Pietra, and Robert L. Mercer. 1993. *The Mathematics of Statistical Machine Translation: Parameter Estimation. Computational Linguistics*, 19(2): 263-311.

Xiaowen Ding, Bing Liu and Philip S. Yu. 2008. A Holistic Lexicon-Based Approach to Opinion Mining. In *Proceedings of WSDM 2008*.

Xiaowen Ding and Bing Liu. 2010. Resolving Object and Attribute Reference in Opinion Mining. In *Proceedings of COLING 2010*.

Mingqin Hu and Bing Liu. 2004. Mining and Summarizing Customer Reviews. In *Proceedings of KDD 2004*

Minqing Hu and Bing Liu. 2004. Mining Opinion Features in Customer Reviews. In *Proceedings of AAAI-2004*, San Jose, USA, July 2004.

Wei Jin and Huang Hay Ho. A Novel Lexicalized HMM-based Learning Framework for Web Opinion Mining. In *Proceedings of ICML 2009*.

Jon Klernberg. 1999. Authoritative Sources in Hyperlinked Environment. *Journal of the ACM* 46(5): 604-632

Zhuang Li, Feng Jing, Xiao-yan Zhu. 2006. Movie Review Mining and Summarization. In *Proceedings of CIKM 2006*

Fangtao Li, Chao Han, Minlie Huang and Xiaoyan Zhu. 2010. Structure-Aware Review Mining and Summarization. In *Proceedings of COLING 2010*.

Zhichao Li, Min Zhang, Shaoping Ma, Bo Zhou, Yu Sun. Automatic Extraction for Product Feature Words from Comments on the Web. In *Proceedings of AIRS 2009*.

Bing Liu, Hu Mingqing and Cheng Junsheng. 2005. Opinion Observer: Analyzing and Comparing Opinions on the Web. In *Proceedings of WWW 2005*

Bing Liu. 2006. Web Data Mining: Exploring Hyperlinks, contents and usage data. *Springer*, 2006

Bing Liu. 2010. Sentiment analysis and subjectivity. *Handbook of Natural Language Processing, second edition*, 2010.

Yang Liu, Qun Liu, and Shouxun Lin. 2010. Discriminative word alignment by linear modeling. *Computational Linguistics*, 36(3):303–339.

Zhanyi Liu, Haifeng Wang, Hua Wu and Sheng Li. 2009. Collocation Extraction Using Monolingual Word Alignment Model. In *Proceedings of EMNLP 2009*.

Tengfei Ma and Xiaojun Wan. 2010. Opinion Target Extraction in Chinese News Comments. In *Proceedings of COLING 2010*.

Popescu, Ana-Maria and Oren, Etzioni. 2005. Extracting produt fedatures and opinions from reviews. In *Proceedings of EMNLP 2005*

Guang Qiu, Bing Liu., Jiajun Bu and Chun Che. 2009. Expanding Domain Sentiment Lexicon through Double Popagation. In *Proceedings of IJCAI 2009*

Guang Qiu, Bing Liu, Jiajun Bu and Chun Chen. 2011. Opinion Word Expansion and Target Extraction through Double Propagation. *Computational Linguistics*, March 2011, Vol. 37, No. 1: 9.27

Qi Su, Xinying Xu., Honglei Guo, Zhili Guo, Xian Wu, Xiaoxun Zhang, Bin Swen and Zhong Su. 2008. Hidden Sentiment Association in Chinese Web Opinion Mining. In *Proceedings of WWW 2008*

Bo Wang, Houfeng Wang. Bootstrapping both Product Features and Opinion Words from Chinese Customer Reviews with Cross-Inducing. In *Proceedings of IJCNLP 2008*.

Hongning Wang, Yue Lu and Chengxiang Zhai. 2011. Latent Aspect Rating Analysis without Aspect Keyword Supervision. In *Proceedings of KDD 2011*.

Yuanbin Wu, Qi Zhang, Xuangjing Huang and Lide Wu, 2009, Phrase Dependency Parsing For Opinion Mining, In *Proceedings of EMNLP 2009*

Lei Zhang, Bing Liu, Suk Hwan Lim and Eamonn O'Brien-Strain. 2010. Extracting and Ranking Product Features in Opinion Documents. *In Proceedings of COLING 2010.*

Qi Zhang, Yuanbin Wu, Tao Li, Mitsunori Ogihara, Joseph Johnson, Xuanjing Huang. 2009. Mining Product Reviews Based on Shallow Dependency Parsing, In Proceedings of SIGIR 2009.

Guangyou Zhou, Li Cai, Jun Zhao and Kang Liu. 2011. Phrase-based Translation Model for Question Retrieval in Community Question Answer Archives. In Proceedings of ACL 2011.

Jingbo Zhu, Huizhen Wang, Benjamin K. Tsou and Muhua Zhu. 2009. Multi-aspect Opinion Polling from Textual Reviews. *In Proceedings of CIKM 2009*.

Word Salad: Relating Food Prices and Descriptions

Victor Chahuneau **Kevin Gimpel**
Language Technologies Institute
Carnegie Mellon University
Pittsburgh, PA 15213, USA
{vchahune,kgimpel}@cs.cmu.edu

Bryan R. Routledge
Tepper School of Business
Carnegie Mellon University
Pittsburgh, PA 15213, USA
routledge@cmu.edu

Lily Scherlis
Phillips Academy
Andover, MA 01810, USA
lily.scherlis@gmail.com

Noah A. Smith
Language Technologies Institute
Carnegie Mellon University
Pittsburgh, PA 15213, USA
nasmith@cs.cmu.edu

Abstract

We investigate the use of language in food writing, specifically on restaurant menus and in customer reviews. Our approach is to build predictive models of concrete external variables, such as restaurant menu **prices**. We make use of a dataset of menus and customer reviews for thousands of restaurants in several U.S. cities. By focusing on prediction tasks and doing our analysis at scale, our methodology allows quantitative, objective measurements of the words and phrases used to describe food in restaurants. We also explore interactions in language use between menu prices and **sentiment** as expressed in user reviews.

1 Introduction

What words might a menu writer use to justify the high price of a steak? How does describing an item as *chargrilled* vs. *charbroiled* affect its price? When a customer writes an unfavorable review of a restaurant, how is her word choice affected by the restaurant's prices? In this paper, we explore questions like these that relate restaurant menus, prices, and customer sentiment. Our goal is to understand how language is used in the food domain, and we direct our investigation using external variables such as restaurant menu **prices**.

We build on a thread of NLP research that seeks linguistic understanding by predicting real-world quantities from text data. Recent examples include prediction of stock volatility (Kogan et al., 2009) and movie revenues (Joshi et al., 2010). There, prediction tasks were used for quantitative evaluation and objective model comparison, while analysis of learned models gave insight about the social process behind the data.

We echo this pattern here as we turn our attention to language use on restaurant menus and in user restaurant reviews. We use data from a large corpus of restaurant menus and reviews crawled from the web and formulate several prediction tasks. In addition to predicting menu prices, we also consider predicting **sentiment** along with price.

The relationship between language and sentiment is an active area of investigation (Pang and Lee, 2008). Much of this research has focused on customer-written reviews of goods and services, and perspectives have been gained on how sentiment is expressed in this type of informal text. In addition to sentiment, however, other variables are reflected in a reviewer's choice of words, such as the price of the item under consideration. In this paper, we take a step toward joint modeling of multiple variables in review text, exploring connections between price and sentiment in restaurant reviews.

Hence this paper contributes an exploratory data

analysis of language used to describe food (by its purveyors and by its consumers). While our primary goal is to understand the language used in our corpus, our findings bear relevance to economics and hospitality research as well. This paper is a step on the way to the eventual goal of using linguistic analysis to understand social phenomena like sales and consumption.

2 Related Work

There are several areas of related work scattered throughout linguistics, NLP, hospitality research, and economics.

Freedman and Jurafsky (2011) studied the use of language in food advertising, specifically the words on potato chip bags. They argued that, due to the ubiquity of food writing across cultures, ethnic groups, and social classes, studying the use of language for describing food can provide perspective on how different socioeconomic groups self-identify using language and how they are linguistically targeted. In particular, they showed that price affects how "authenticity" is realized in marketing language, a point we return to in §5. This is an example of how price can affect how an underlying variable is expressed in language. Among other explorations in this paper, we consider how price interacts with expression of sentiment in user reviews of restaurants.

As mentioned above, our work is related to research in predicting real-world quantities using text data (Koppel and Shtrimberg, 2006; Ghose et al., 2007; Lerman et al., 2008; Kogan et al., 2009; Joshi et al., 2010; Eisenstein et al., 2010; Eisenstein et al., 2011; Yogatama et al., 2011). Like much of this prior work, we aim to learn how language is used in a specific context while building models that achieve competitive performance on a quantitative prediction task.

Along these lines, there is recent interest in exploring the relationship between product sales and user-generated text, particularly online product reviews. For example, Ghose and Ipeirotis (2011) studied the sales impact of particular properties of review text, such as readability, the presence of spelling errors, and the balance between subjective and objective statements. Archak et al. (2011) had a similar goal but decomposed user reviews into parts describing particular aspects of the product being reviewed (Hu and Liu, 2004). Our paper differs from price modeling based on product reviews in several ways. We consider a large set of weakly-related products instead of a homogeneous selection of a few products, and the reviews in our dataset are not product-centered but rather describe the overall experience of visiting a restaurant. Consequently, menu items are not always mentioned in reviews and rarely appear with their exact names. This makes it difficult to directly use review features in a pricing model for individual menu items.

Menu planning and pricing has been studied for many years by the culinary and hospitality research community (Kasavana and Smith, 1982; Kelly et al., 1994), often including recommendations for writing menu item descriptions (Miller and Pavesic, 1996; McVety et al., 2008). Their guidelines frequently include example menus from successful restaurants, but typically do not use large corpora of menus or automated analysis, as we do here. Other work focused more specifically on particular aspects of the language used on menus, such as the study by Zwicky and Zwicky (1980), who made linguistic observations through manual analysis of a corpus of 200 menus.

Relatedly, Wansink et al. (2001; 2005) showed that the way that menu items are described affects customers' perceptions and purchasing behavior. When menu items are described evocatively, customers choose them more often and report higher satisfaction with quality and value, as compared to when they are given the same items described with conventional names. Wansink et al. did not use a corpus, but rather conducted a small-scale experiment in a working cafeteria with customers and collected surveys to analyze consumer reaction. While our goals are related, our experimental approach is different, as we use automated analysis of thousands of restaurant menus and rely on a set of one million reviews as a surrogate for observing customer behavior.

Finally, the connection between products and prices is also a central issue in economics. However, the stunning heterogeneity in products makes empirical work challenging. For example, there are over 50,000 menu items in New York that include

City	# Restaurants			# Menu Items			# Reviews		
	train	dev.	test	train	dev.	test	train	dev.	test
Boston	930	107	113	63,422	8,426	8,409	80,309	10,976	11,511
Chicago	804	98	100	51,480	6,633	6,939	73,251	9,582	10,965
Los Angeles	624	80	68	17,980	2,938	1,592	75,455	13,227	5,716
New York	3,965	473	499	365,518	42,315	45,728	326,801	35,529	37,795
Philadelphia	1,015	129	117	83,818	11,777	9,295	52,275	7,347	5,790
San Francisco	1,908	255	234	103,954	12,871	12,510	499,984	59,378	67,010
Washington, D.C.	773	110	121	47,188	5,957	7,224	71,179	11,852	14,129
Total	10,019	1,252	1,252	733,360	90,917	91,697	1,179,254	147,891	152,916

Table 1: Dataset statistics.

the word *chicken*. What is the price of chicken? This is an important practical and daunting matter when measuring inflation (e.g., Consumer Price Index is measured with a precisely-defined basket of goods). Price dispersion across goods and the variation of the goods is an important area of industrial organization economic theory. For example, economists are interested in models of search, add-on pricing, and obfuscation (Baye et al., 2006; Ellison, 2005).

3 Data

We crawled Allmenus.com (`www.allmenus.com`) to gather menus for restaurants in seven U.S. cities: Boston, Chicago, Los Angeles, New York, Philadelphia, San Francisco, and Washington, D.C. Each menu includes a list of item names with optional text descriptions and prices. Most Allmenus restaurant pages contain a link to the corresponding page on Yelp (`www.yelp.com`) with metadata and user reviews for the restaurant, which we also collected.

The metadata consist of many fields for each restaurant, which can be divided into three categories: location (city, neighborhood, transit stop), services available (take-out, delivery, wifi, parking, etc.), and ambience (good for groups, noise level, attire, etc.). Also, the category of food and a price range ($ to $$$$, indicating the price of a typical meal at the restaurant) are indicated. The user reviews include a star rating on a scale of 1 to 5.

The distribution of prices of individual menu items is highly skewed, with a mean of $9.22 but a median of $6.95. On average, a restaurant has 73 items on its menu with a median price of $8.69 and 119 Yelp reviews with a median rating of 3.55 stars. The star rating and price range distributions are shown in Figure 1.

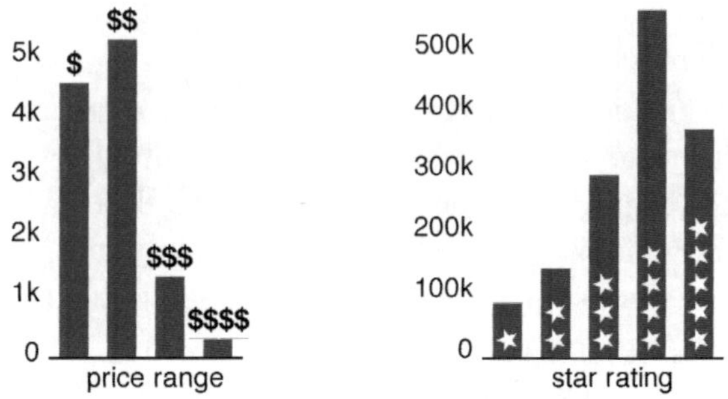

Figure 1: Frequency distributions of restaurant price ranges (left) and review ratings (right).

The set of restaurants was randomly split into three parts (80% for training, 10% for development, 10% for evaluation), independently for each city. The sizes of the splits and the full set of dataset statistics are provided in Table 1.

4 Predictive Tasks

We consider several prediction tasks using the dataset just described. These include predicting **individual menu item prices** (§5), predicting the **price range** for each restaurant (§6), and finally jointly predicting **median price and sentiment** for each restaurant (§7). To do this, we use two types of models: linear regression (§5 and §6) and logistic regression (§7), both with ℓ_1 regularization when sparsity is desirable. We tune the regularization coefficient by choosing the value that minimizes development set loss (mean squared error and log loss, respectively).

For evaluation, we use mean absolute error (MAE) and mean relative error (MRE). Given a dataset $\langle \boldsymbol{x}_i, y_i \rangle_{i=1}^N$ with inputs $\boldsymbol{x}_i$ and outputs y_i, and denoting predicted outputs by $\hat{y}_i$, these are defined as follows:

$$\text{MAE} = \frac{1}{N}\sum_{i=1}^{N}|y_i - \hat{y}_i|$$

$$\text{MRE} = \frac{1}{N}\sum_{i=1}^{N}\left|\frac{y_i - \hat{y}_i}{y_i}\right|$$

In practice, since we model log-prices but evaluate on real prices, the final prediction is often a non-linear transformation of the output of the linear classifier of weight vector $\boldsymbol{w}$, which we denote by: $\hat{y}_i = f(\boldsymbol{w}^\top \boldsymbol{x}_i)$.

We also frequently report the total number of features available in the training set for each model (nf) as well as the number of non-zero feature weights following learning (nnz).

5 Menu Item Price Prediction

We first consider the problem of predicting the **price** of each item on a menu. In this case, every instance $\boldsymbol{x}_i$ corresponds to a single item in the menu parametrized by the features detailed below and y_i is the item's price. In this section, our models always use the logarithm of the price[1] as output values and therefore: $\hat{y}_i = e^{\boldsymbol{w}^\top \boldsymbol{x}_i}$.

Baselines We evaluate several baselines which make independent predictions for each distinct item name. The first two predict the mean or the median of the prices in the training set for a given item name, and use the overall price mean or median when a name is missing in the training set. The third baseline is an ℓ_1-regularized linear regression model trained with a single binary feature for each item name in the training data. These baselines are shown as the first three rows in Table 2.

We note that there is a wide variation of menu item names in the dataset, with more than 400,000 distinct names. Although we address this issue later by introducing local text features, we also performed simple normalization of the item names for all of the baselines described above. To do this normalization, we first compiled a stop word list based on the most frequent words in the item names.[2] We removed stop words and then ordered the words in each item name lexicographically, in order to collapse together items such as *coffee black* and *black coffee*. This normalization reduced the unique item name count by 40%, strengthening the baselines.

5.1 Features

We use ℓ_1-regularized linear regression for feature-rich models. We now introduce several sets of features that we add to the normalized item names:[3]

I. METADATA: Binary features for each restaurant metadata field mentioned above, excluding price range. A separate binary feature is included for each unique ⟨field, value⟩ tuple.
II. MENUNAMES: n-grams in menu item names. We used binary features for unique unigrams, bigrams, and trigrams. Here, stop words were retained as they can be informative (e.g., *with* and *large* correlate with price).
III. MENUDESC: n-grams in menu item descriptions, as in MENUNAMES.

Review Features In addition to these features, we consider leveraging the large amount of text present in user reviews to improve predictions. We attempted to find mentions of menu items in the reviews and to include features extracted from the surrounding words in the model. Perfect item mentions being relatively rare, we consider inexact matches weighted by a coefficient measuring the degree of resemblance: we used the Dice similarity between the set of words in the sentence and in the item name. We then extracted n-gram features from this sentence, and tried several ways to use them for price prediction.

Given a review sentence, one option is to add the corresponding features to every item matching this sentence, with a value equal to the similarity coefficient. Another option is to select the best matching item and use the same real-valued features but only for this single item. Binary feature values can be used instead of the real-valued similarity coefficient. We also experimented with the use of part-of-speech tags in order to restrict our features to adjective and adverb n-grams instead of the full vocabulary. All of

[1] The price distribution is more symmetric in the log domain.
[2] This list can be found in the supplementary material.

[3] The normalized item names are present as binary features in all of our regression models

	MAE	MRE	nf	nnz
Predict mean	3.70	43.32	n/a	n/a
Predict median	3.67	43.93	n/a	n/a
Regression	3.66	45.64	267,945	240,139
METADATA	3.55	43.11	268,450	258,828
$\widehat{\text{PR}}$	3.47	43.11	267,946	205,176
MENUNAMES	3.23	38.33	896,631	230,840
+ MENUDESC	3.19	36.23	1,981,787	151,785
+ $\widehat{\text{PR}}$	3.08	34.51	1,981,788	140,954
+ METADATA	3.08	34.97	1,982,363	148,774
+ MENTIONS	3.06	34.37	4,959,488	458,462

Table 2: Results for menu item price prediction. MAE = mean absolute error ($), MRE = mean relative error (%), nf = total number of features, nnz = number of features with non-zero weight.

these attempts yielded negative or only slightly positive results, of which we include only one example in our experiments: the MENTIONS feature set consists of n-grams for the best matching item with the Dice coefficient as the feature value.

We also tried to incorporate the reviews by using them in aggregate via predictions from a separate model; we found this approach to work better than the methods described above which all use features from the reviews directly in the regression model. In particular, we use the review features in a separate model that we will describe below (§6) to predict the price range of each restaurant. The model uses unigrams, bigrams, and trigrams extracted from the reviews. We use the estimated price range (which we denote $\widehat{\text{PR}}$) as a single additional real-valued feature for individual item price prediction.

5.2 Results

Our results are shown in Table 2. We achieve a final reduction of 50 cents in MAE and nearly 10% in MRE compared with the baselines. Using menu name features (MENUNAMES) brings the bulk of the improvement, though menu description features (MENUDESC) and the remaining features also lead to small gains. Interestingly, as the MENUDESC and $\widehat{\text{PR}}$ features are added to the model, the regularization favors more general features by selecting fewer and fewer non-zero weights.

While METADATA features improve over the baselines when used alone, they do not lead to improved performance over the MENU* + $\widehat{\text{PR}}$ features, suggesting that the text features may be able to substitute for the information in the metadata, at least for prediction of individual item prices.

The MENTIONS features resulted in a small improvement in MAE and MRE, but at the cost of expanding the model size significantly. A look at the learned feature weights reveals that most of the selected features seem more coincidental than generic (*rachel's*, highly negative) when not totally unintuitive (*those suicide*, highest positive). This suggests that our method of extracting features from mentions is being hampered by noise. We suspect that these features could be more effective with a better method of linking menu items to mentions in review text.

5.3 Analysis

We also inspected the feature weights of our learned models. By comparing the weights of related features, we can see the relative differences in terms of contribution to menu item prices. Table 3 shows example feature weights, manually arranged into several categories (taken from the model with MENUNAMES + MENUDESC + $\widehat{\text{PR}}$ + METADATA).

Table 3(a) shows selected features for the "ambience" field in the Yelp restaurant metadata and pane (b) lists some unigrams related to cooking methods. Pane (c) shows feature weights for n-grams often used to market menu items; we see larger weights for words targeting those who want to eat organically- or locally-grown food (*farmhouse*, *heirloom*, *wild*, and *hormone*), compared to those looking for comfort food (*old time favorite*, *traditional*, *real*, and *fashioned*). This is related to observations made by Freedman and Jurafsky (2011) that cheaper food is marketed by appealing to tradition and historicity, with more expensive food described in terms of naturalness, quality of ingredients, and the preparation process (e.g., *hand picked*, *wild caught*, etc.). Relatedly, in pane (e) we see that *real* mashed potatoes are expected to be cheaper than those described as *creamy* or *smooth*.

Pane (d) shows feature weights for trigrams containing units of chicken; we can see an ordering in terms of size (*bits* < *cubes* < *strips* < *cuts*) as well as the price increase associated with the use of the word *morsels* in place of less refined units. We also see a difference between *pieces* and *pcs*, with the latter being frequently used to refer to entire cuts of

(a) METADATA: ambience	
dive-y	-0.015
intimate	-0.013
trendy	-0.012
casual	-0.005
romantic	-0.004
classy	-7e-6
touristy	0.058
upscale	0.099

(c) MENUDESC: descriptors	
old time favorite	-0.112
fashioned	-0.034
line caught	-0.028
all natural	-0.028
traditional	-0.009
natural	3e-4
classic	0.002
free range	0.004
real	0.004
fresh	0.006
homemade	0.010
authentic	0.012
organic	0.020
specialty	0.025
special	0.033
locally	0.037
natural grass fed	0.038
artisanal	0.064
raised	0.066
heirloom	0.083
wild	0.084
hormone	0.085
farmed	0.099
hand picked	0.101
wild caught	0.116
farmhouse	0.133

(b) MENUDESC: cooking	
panfried	-0.094
chargrilled	-0.029
cooked	-0.012
boiled	-0.006
fried	-0.005
steamed	0.011
charbroiled	0.015
grilled	0.022
simmered	0.025
roasted	0.034
sauteed	0.034
broiled	0.053
seared	0.066
braised	0.068
stirfried	0.071
flamebroiled	0.106

(d) MENUDESC: _ = "of chicken"	
slices _	-0.102
bits _	-0.032
cubes _	-0.030
pieces _	-0.024
strips _	-0.001
chunks _	0.015
morsels _	0.025
pcs _	0.040
cuts _	0.042

(e) MENUDESC: _ = "potatoes"	
real mashed _	-0.028
mashed _	-0.005
creamy mashed _	-5e-9
smashed _	0.018
smooth mashed _	0.129

(f) MENUDESC: _ = "potato"	
mash _	-0.022
mashed _	-0.019

(g) MENUDESC: "crisp" vs. "crispy"			
crisp	-0.022	crispy bacon	0.008
crispy	-0.011	crisp bacon	0.033

(h) MENUDESC: "roast" vs. "roasted"			
roasted	0.034	roasted potatoes	0.026
roast	0.040	roast potatoes	0.110
roasted chicken	-0.041	roasted salmon	0.091
roast chicken	-0.012	roast salmon	0.151
roast pork	-0.038	roasted tomato	0.010
roasted pork	0.055	roast tomato	0.026

Table 3: Selected features from model for menu item price prediction. See text for details.

chicken (e.g., wings, thighs, etc.) and the former more often used as a synonym for *chunks*.

Panes (f), (g), and (h) reveal price differences due to slight variations in word form. We find that, even though *crispy* has a higher weight than *crisp*, *crisp bacon* is more expensive than *crispy bacon*. We also find that food items prefixed with *roast* lead to more expensive prices than the similar *roasted*, except in the case of *pork*, though here the different forms may be evoking two different preparation styles.

Also of note is the slight difference between the nonstandard *mash potato* and *mashed potato*. We observed lower weights with other nonstandard spellings, notably *portobella* having lower weight than each of the more common spellings *portabella*, *portobello*, and *portabello*.

6 Restaurant Price Range Prediction

In addition to predicting the prices of individual menu items, we also considered the task of predicting the **price range** listed for each restaurant on its Yelp page. The values for this field are integers from 1 to 4 and indicate the price of a typical meal from the restaurant.

For this task, we again train an ℓ_1-regularized linear regression model with integral price ranges as the true output values y_i. Each input $\boldsymbol{x}_i$ corresponds to the feature vector for an entire restaurant. For evaluation, we round the predicted values to the nearest integer: $\hat{y}_i = \text{ROUND}(\boldsymbol{w}^\top \boldsymbol{x}_i)$ and report the corresponding mean absolute error and accuracy.

We compared this simple approach with an ordinal regression model (McCullagh, 1980) trained with the same ℓ_1 regularizer and noted very little improvement (77.32% vs. 77.15% accuracy for METADATA). Therefore, we only report in this section results for the linear regression model.

In addition to the feature sets used for individual menu item price prediction, we used features on reviews (REVIEWS). Specifically, we used binary features for unigrams, bigrams, and trigrams in the full set of reviews for each restaurant. A stopword list was derived from the training data.[4] Bigrams and trigrams were filtered if they ended with stopwords. Additionally, features occurring fewer than three times in the training set were discarded.

[4]This list is included in the supplementary material.

Features	MAE	Acc.	nf	nnz
Predict mode	0.5421	48.22	n/a	n/a
MENU*	0.3875	66.29	1,910,622	995
METADATA	0.2372	77.15	591	219
REVIEWS	0.2172	79.76	3,027,470	1,567
+METADATA	0.2111	80.36	3,027,943	1,376

Table 4: Results for restaurant price range prediction. MAE = mean absolute error, Acc = classification accuracy (%), nf = total number of features, nnz = number of features with non-zero weight.

6.1 Results

Our results for price range prediction are shown in Table 4. Predicting the most frequent price range gave us an accuracy of 48.22%. Performance improvements were obtained by separately adding menu (MENU*), metadata (METADATA), and review features (REVIEWS). Unlike individual item price prediction, the reviews were more helpful than the menu features for predicting overall price range. This is not surprising, since reviewers will often generally discuss price in their reviews. We combined metadata and review features to get our best accuracy, exceeding 80%.

We also wanted to perform an analysis of sentiment in the review text. To do this, we trained a logistic regression model predicting polarity for each review; we used the REVIEWS feature set, but this time considering each review as a single training instance. The polarity of a review was determined by whether or not its star rating was greater than the average rating across all reviews in the dataset (3.7 stars). We achieved an accuracy of 87% on the test data. We omit full details of these models because the polarity prediction task for user reviews is well-known in the sentiment analysis community and our model is not an innovation over prior work (Pang and Lee, 2008). However, our purpose in training the model was to use the learned weights for understanding the text in the reviews.

6.2 Interpreting Reviews

Given learned models for predicting a restaurant's price range from its set of reviews as well as polarity for each review, we can turn the process around and use the feature weights to analyze the review text. Restricting our attention to reviews of 50–60 words, Table 5 shows sample reviews from our test set that lead to various predictions of price range and sentiment.[5]

This technique can also be useful when trying to determine the "true" star rating for a review (if provided star ratings are noisy), or to show the most positive and most negative reviews for a product within a particular star rating. The 5-point scale is merely a coarse approximation to the reviewer's mental state; using fitted models can provide additional clues to decode the reviewer's sentiment.

We can also do a more fine-grained analysis of review text by noting the contribution to the price range prediction of each position in the text stream. This is straightforward because our features are simply n-grams of the review text. In Figure 2, we show the influence of each word in a review sentence on the predicted polarity (brown) and price range (yellow). The height of a bar at a given position is proportional to the sum of the feature weights for every unigram, bigram, and trigram containing the token at that position (there are at most 6 active n-grams at a position).

The first example shows the smooth shift in expressed sentiment from the beginning of the sentence to the end. The second sentence is a difficult example for sentiment analysis, since there are several positive words and phrases early but the sentiment is chiefly expressed in the final clause. Our model noted the steady positive sentiment early in the sentence but identified the crucial negation due to strong negative weight on bigrams *fresh but*, *left me*, and *me yearning*. In both examples, the yellow bars show that price estimates are reflected mainly through isolated mentions of offerings and amenities (*drinks*, *atmosphere*, *security*, *good service*).

7 Joint Prediction of Price and Sentiment

Although we observe no interesting correlation ($r = 0.06$) between median star rating and median item price in our dataset, this does not imply that senti-

[5]To choose the 9 reviews in the table, we took the reviews from our test set in the desired length range and computed predicted sentiment and price range for each; then we scaled the predicted price range so that its range matched that of predicted sentiment, and maximized various linear combinations of the two. This accounts for the four corners. The others were found by maximizing a linear combination of one (possibly negated) prediction minus the absolute value of the other.

	← cheap		expensive →
↑ ⊕	i love me a cheap vietnamese sandwich . mmm , pate . this place has the best ones i 've had in the city , and i conveniently live a few blocks away . the ladies behind the counter are always courteous and fast , and who can beat a $ 3 sandwich ?! crazy ass deli .	this place is tiny ! the pork buns are so tender and flavorful . i dream about these things . manila clams were awesome , not the biggest clam fan either , but i loved it . mmm 7 spice chips . i ca n't wait to go back !	amazing service and desserts . nice wine list and urban decor . i went with a girlfriend and we split an entree , appetizer and dessert and they happily brought us separate portions which were just the right size . the bread is awesome , too . definitely a bit of a splurge , but worth it in moderation .
	great place to get fast food that tastes good . paneer and chicken are both good . i would prefer to go thursday thru saturday night . thats when they have their good shift working . also it stays open late until 4 am on weekends . really enjoyable !	had some solid thai here for lunch last week . ordered the special of the day , a chicken curry . quick service and nice interior . only issue was , had a bit of a stomach ache afterwards ? prefer their sister restaurant , citizen thai and the monkey , in north beach .	weekday evening was quiet , not every table was filled . our waiter was amicable and friendly , which is always a plus . the coconut bread pudding was ok and very sweet . it 's definitely a dessert plate that can be shared with a glass of wine .
⊖ ↓	for some reason my friend wanted me to go here with him . it was a decent standard greasy slice of pizza . it was n't bad by any means , but it was nothing special at all . on the plus side , cheap and fast . so in summary : cheap , fast , greasy , average .	ugh ! the salt ! all 5 dishes we ordered were so unbearably salty , i 'd rather just have the msg . greasy , oily , salty - there is much better chinese food to be had in sf than here . i was very disappointed and wo n't be back .	downhill alert ... had a decent lunch at dragon well this week marred by pretty spotty service . our waiter just did n't have it together , forgetting to bring bowls for our split soup , our beverages , etc. . food was good but pretty pricey for what we got .

Table 5: Reviews from the test set deemed by our model to have particular values of sentiment and price.

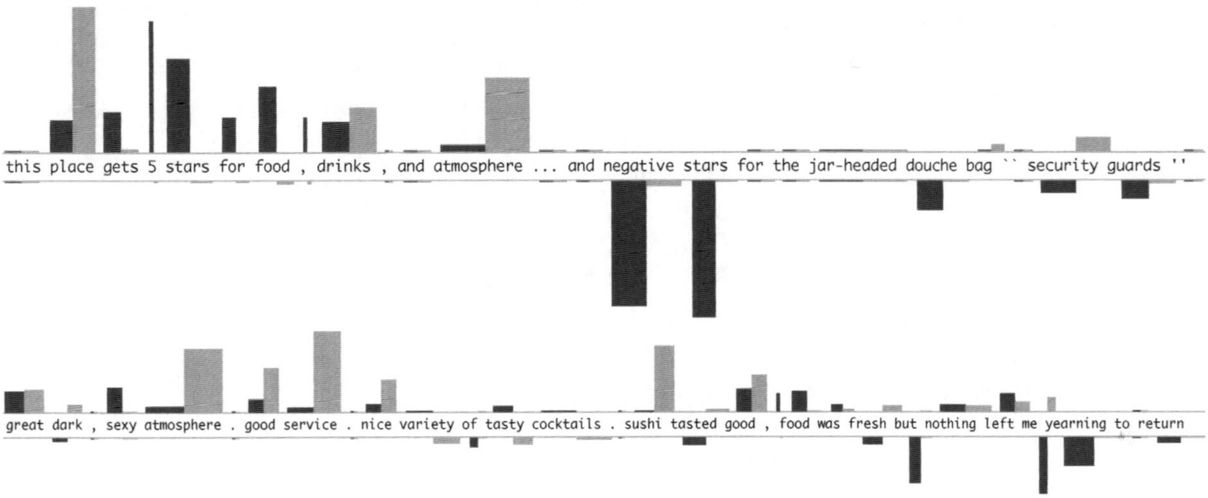

Figure 2: Local (position-level) sentiment (brown) and price (yellow) estimates for two sentences in the test corpus.

ment and price are independent of each other.[6] We try to capture this interaction by modeling at the same time review polarity and item price: we consider the task of jointly predicting **aggregate sentiment and price** for a restaurant.

For every restaurant in our dataset, we compute its median item price $\bar{p}$ and its median star rating $\bar{r}$. The average of these two values for the entire dataset ($8.69 and 3.55 stars) split the plane $(\bar{p}, \bar{r})$ in four sections: we assign each restaurant to one of these quadrants which we denote $\downarrow \ominus$, $\downarrow \oplus$, $\uparrow \ominus$ and $\uparrow \oplus$. This allows us to train a 4-class logistic regression model using the REVIEWS feature set for each restaurant. We achieve an accuracy of 65% on the test data, but we are mainly interested in interpreting the estimated feature weights.

7.1 Analysis

To visualize the top feature weights learned by the model, we have to map the four weight vectors learned by the model back to the underlying two-dimensional sentiment/price space. Therefore, we compute the following values:

$$\boldsymbol{w}_{\$} = (\boldsymbol{w}_{\uparrow\oplus} + \boldsymbol{w}_{\uparrow\ominus}) - (\boldsymbol{w}_{\downarrow\oplus} + \boldsymbol{w}_{\downarrow\ominus})$$
$$\boldsymbol{w}_{\bigstar} = (\boldsymbol{w}_{\uparrow\oplus} + \boldsymbol{w}_{\downarrow\oplus}) - (\boldsymbol{w}_{\uparrow\ominus} + \boldsymbol{w}_{\downarrow\ominus})$$

[6]Price and sentiment are both endogenous outcomes reflecting the characteristics of the restaurant. E.g., "better" restaurants can charge higher prices.

We then select for display the features which are the furthest from the origin ($\max w_{\$}^2 + w_{\bigstar}^2$) and represent the selected n-grams as points in the sentiment/price space to obtain Figure 3.

We notice that the spread of the sentiment values is larger, which suggests that reviews give stronger clues about consumer experience than about the cost of a typical meal. However, obvious price-related adjectives (*inexpensive* vs. *expensive*) appear in this limited selection, as well as certain phrases indicating both sentiment and price (*overpriced* vs. *very reasonable*). Other examples of note: *gem* is used in strongly-positive reviews of cheap restaurants; for expensive restaurants, reviewers use *highly recommended* or *amazing*. Also, phrases like *no flavor* and *manager* appear in negative reviews of more expensive restaurants, while *dirty* appears more often in negative reviews of cheaper restaurants.

8 Conclusion

We have explored linguistic relationships between food prices and customer sentiment through quantitative analysis of a large corpus of menus and reviews. We have also proposed visualization techniques to better understand what our models have learned and to see how they can be applied to new data. More broadly, this paper is an example of using extrinsic variables to drive model-building for linguistic data, and future work might explore richer extrinsic variables toward a goal of task-driven notions of semantics.

Acknowledgments

We thank Julie Baron, Ric Crabbe, David Garvett, Laura Gimpel, Chenxi Jiao, Elaine Lee, members of the ARK research group, and the anonymous reviewers for helpful comments that improved this paper. This research was supported in part by the NSF through CAREER grant IIS-1054319 and Sandia National Laboratories (fellowship to K. Gimpel).

References

N. Archak, A. Ghose, and P. G. Ipeirotis. 2011. Deriving the pricing power of product features by mining consumer reviews. *Management Science*, 57(8).

M. R. Baye, J. Morgan, and P. Scholten. 2006. Economics and information systems; handbooks in information systems. In T. Hendershott, editor, *Judgement under Uncertainty: Heuristics and Biases*. Elsevier, Amsterdam.

J. Eisenstein, B. O'Connor, N. A. Smith, and E. P. Xing. 2010. A latent variable model for geographic lexical variation. In *Proc. of EMNLP*.

J. Eisenstein, N. A. Smith, and E. P. Xing. 2011. Discovering sociolinguistic associations with structured sparsity. In *Proc. of ACL*.

G. Ellison. 2005. A model of add-on pricing. *Quarterly Journal of Economics*, 120(2):585–637, May.

J. Freedman and D. Jurafsky. 2011. Authenticity in America: Class distinctions in potato chip advertising. *Gastronomica*, 11(4):46–54.

A. Ghose and P. G. Ipeirotis. 2011. Estimating the helpfulness and economic impact of product reviews: Mining text and reviewer characteristics. *IEEE Transactions on Knowledge and Data Engineering*, 23(10).

A. Ghose, P. G. Ipeirotis, and A. Sundararajan. 2007. Opinion mining using econometrics: A case study on reputation systems. In *Proc. of ACL*.

M. Hu and B. Liu. 2004. Mining opinion features in customer reviews. In *Proc. of AAAI*.

M. Joshi, D. Das, K. Gimpel, and N. A. Smith. 2010. Movie reviews and revenues: An experiment in text regression. In *Proc. of NAACL*.

M. L. Kasavana and D. I. Smith. 1982. *Menu Engineering: A Practical Guide to Menu Analysis*. Hospitality Publications.

T. J. Kelly, N. M. Kiefer, and K. Burdett. 1994. A demand-based approach to menu pricing. *Cornell Hotel and Restaurant Administrative Quarterly*, 35(1).

S. Kogan, D. Levin, B. R. Routledge, J. Sagi, and N. A. Smith. 2009. Predicting risk from financial reports with regression. In *Proc. of NAACL*.

M. Koppel and I. Shtrimberg. 2006. Good news or bad news? let the market decide. *Computing Attitude and Affect in Text: Theory and Applications*.

K. Lerman, A. Gilder, M. Dredze, and F. Pereira. 2008. Reading the markets: Forecasting public opinion of political candidates by news analysis. In *Proc. of COLING*.

P. McCullagh. 1980. Regression models for ordinal data. *Journal of the royal statistical society. Series B (Methodological)*, pages 109–142.

P. J. McVety, B. J. Ware, and C. L. Ware. 2008. *Fundamentals of Menu Planning*. John Wiley & Sons.

J. E. Miller and D. V. Pavesic. 1996. *Menu: Pricing & Strategy*. Hospitality, Travel, and Tourism Series. John Wiley & Sons.

B. Pang and L. Lee. 2008. Opinion mining and sentiment analysis. *Foundations and Trends in Information Retrieval*, 2(1-2):1–135.

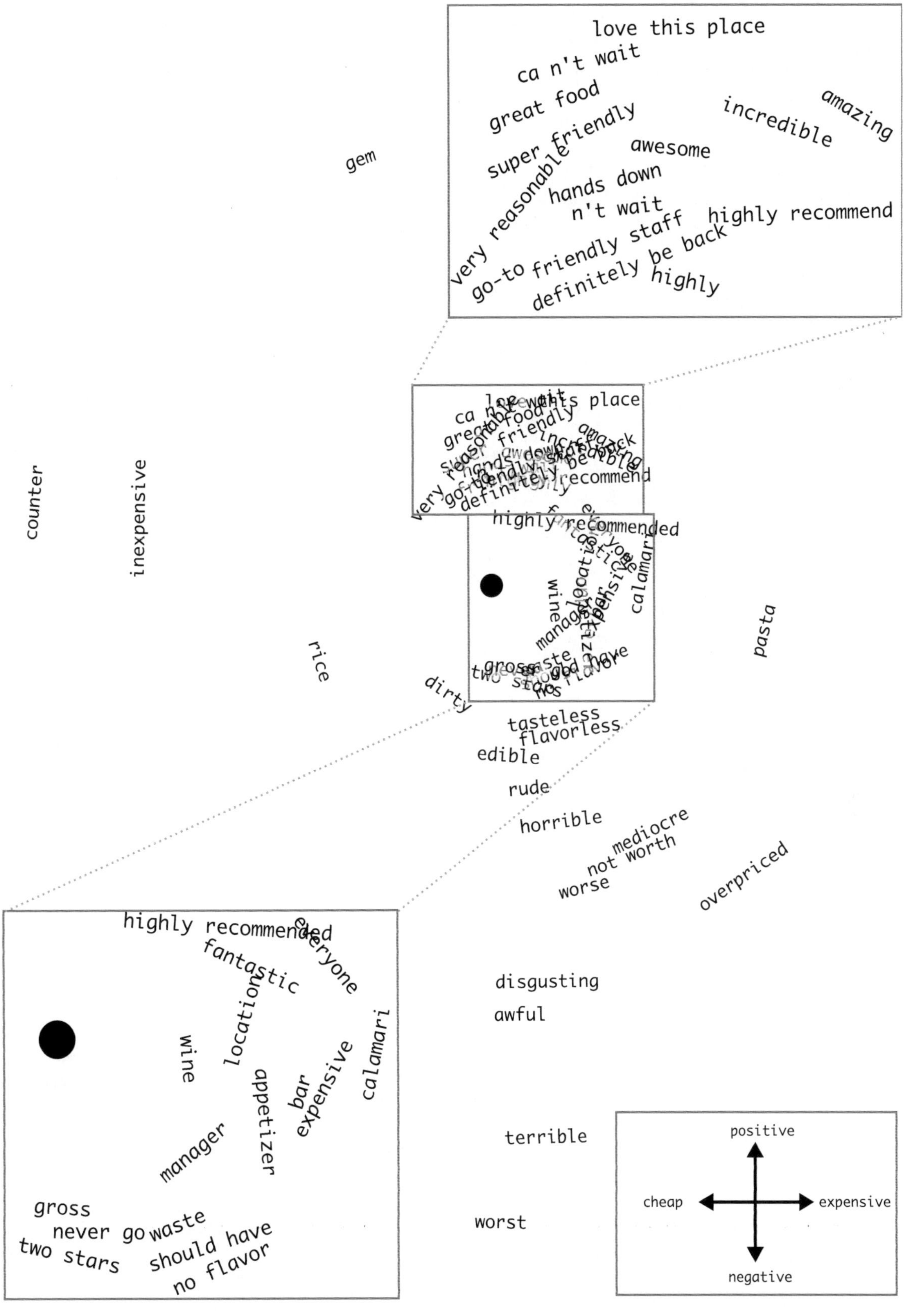

Figure 3: Top 50 features from joint prediction of price and sentiment. The black circle is the origin. See text for details on how the coordinates for each feature were computed. Insets show enlargements of dense areas of the graph.

B. Wansink, J. E. Painter, and K. van Ittersum. 2001. Descriptive menu labels' effect on sales. *Cornell Hotel and Restaurant Administrative Quarterly*, 42(6).

B. Wansink, K. van Ittersum, and J. E. Painter. 2005. How descriptive food names bias sensory perceptions in restaurants. *Food Quality and Preference*, 16(5).

D. Yogatama, M. Heilman, B. O'Connor, C. Dyer, B. R. Routledge, and N. A. Smith. 2011. Predicting a scientific community's response to an article. In *Proc. of EMNLP*.

A. D. Zwicky and A. M. Zwicky. 1980. America's national dish: The style of restaurant menus. *American Speech*, 55(2):83–92.

Learning to Map into a Universal POS Tagset

Yuan Zhang, Roi Reichart, Regina Barzilay
Massachusetts Institute of Technology
{yuanzh, roiri, regina}@csail.mit.edu

Amir Globerson
The Hebrew University
gamir@cs.huji.ac.il

Abstract

We present an automatic method for mapping *language-specific* part-of-speech tags to a set of *universal tags*. This unified representation plays a crucial role in cross-lingual syntactic transfer of multilingual dependency parsers. Until now, however, such conversion schemes have been created manually. Our central hypothesis is that a valid mapping yields POS annotations with coherent linguistic properties which are consistent across source and target languages. We encode this intuition in an objective function that captures a range of distributional and typological characteristics of the derived mapping. Given the exponential size of the mapping space, we propose a novel method for optimizing over soft mappings, and use entropy regularization to drive those towards hard mappings. Our results demonstrate that automatically induced mappings rival the quality of their manually designed counterparts when evaluated in the context of multilingual parsing.[1]

1 Introduction

In this paper, we explore an automatic method for mapping *language-specific* part-of-speech tags to a *universal tagset*. In multilingual parsing, this unified input representation is required for cross-lingual syntactic transfer. Specifically, the universal tagset annotations enable an unlexicalized parser to capitalize on annotations from one language when learning a model for another.

While the notion of a universal POS tagset is widely accepted, in practice it is hardly ever used for annotation of monolingual resources. In fact, available POS annotations are designed to capture language-specific idiosyncrasies and therefore are substantially more detailed than a coarse universal tagset. To reconcile these cross-lingual annotation differences, a number of mapping schemes have been proposed in the parsing community (Zeman and Resnik, 2008; Petrov et al., 2011; Naseem et al., 2010). In all of these cases, the conversion is performed manually and has to be repeated for each language and annotation scheme anew.

Despite the apparent simplicity, deriving a mapping is by no means easy, even for humans. In fact, the universal tagsets manually induced by Petrov et al. (2011) and by Naseem et al. (2010) disagree on 10% of the tags. An example of such discrepancy is the mapping of the Japanese tag "PVfin" to the universal tag "particle" according to one scheme, and to "verb" according to another. Moreover, the quality of this conversion has a direct implication on the parsing performance. In the Japanese example above, this difference in mapping yields a 6.7% difference in parsing accuracy.

The goal of our work is to induce the mapping for a new language, utilizing existing manually-constructed mappings as training data. The existing mappings developed in the parsing community rely on gold POS tags for the target language. A more realistic scenario is to employ the mapping technique to resource-poor languages where gold POS annotations are lacking. In such cases, a mapping algorithm has to operate over automatically in-

[1]The source code and data for the work presented in this paper is available at http://groups.csail.mit.edu/rbg/code/unitag/emnlp2012

duced clusters on the target language (e.g., using the Brown algorithm) and convert them to universal tags. We are interested in a mapping approach that can effectively handle both gold tags and induced clusters.

Our central hypothesis is that a valid mapping yields POS annotations with coherent linguistic properties which are consistent across languages. Since universal tags play the same linguistic role in source and target languages, we expect similarity in their *global distributional statistics*. Figure 1a shows statistics for two close languages, English and German. We can see that their unigram frequencies on the five most common tags are very close. Other properties concern *POS tag per sentence statistics* – e.g., every sentence has to have at least one verb. Finally, the mappings can be further constrained by *typological properties* of the target language that specify likely tag sequences. This information is readily available even for resource poor language (Haspelmath et al., 2005). For instance, since English and German are prepositional languages, we expect to observe adposition-noun sequences but not the reverse (see Figure 1b for sample sentences). We encode these heterogeneous properties into an objective function that guides the search for the optimal mapping.

Having defined a quality measure for mappings, our goal is to find the optimal mapping. However, such partition optimization problems[2] are NP hard (Garey and Johnson, 1979). A naive approach to the problem is to greedily improve the map, but it turns out that this approach yields poor quality mappings. We therefore develop a method for optimizing over soft mappings, and use entropy regularization to drive those towards hard mappings. We construct the objective in a way that facilitates simple monotonically improving updates corresponding to solving convex optimization problems.

We evaluate our mapping approach on 19 languages that include representatives of Indo-European, Semitic, Basque, Japonic and Turkic families. We measure mapping quality based on the target language parsing accuracy. In addition to considering gold POS tags for the target language, we also evaluate the mapping algorithm on automatically induced POS tags. In all evaluation scenarios, our model consistently rivals the quality of manually induced mappings. We also demonstrate that the proposed inference procedure outperforms greedy methods by a large margin, highlighting the importance of good optimization techniques. We further show that while all characteristics of the mapping contribute to the objective, our largest gain comes from distributional features that capture global statistics. Finally, we establish that the mapping quality has a significant impact on the accuracy of syntactic transfer, which motivates further study of this topic.

2 Related Work

Multilingual Parsing Early approaches for multilingual parsing used parallel data to bridge the gap between languages when modeling syntactic transfer. In this setup, finding the mapping between various POS annotation schemes was not essential; instead, the transfer algorithm could induce it directly from the parallel data (Hwa et al., 2005; Xi and Hwa, 2005; Burkett and Klein, 2008). However, more recent transfer approaches relinquish this data requirement, learning to transfer from non-parallel data (Zeman and Resnik, 2008; McDonald et al., 2011; Cohen et al., 2011; Naseem et al., 2010). These approaches assume access to a common input representation in the form of universal tags, which enables the model to connect patterns observed in the source language to their counterparts in the target language.

Despite ongoing efforts to standardize POS tags across languages (e.g., EAGLES initiative (Eynde, 2004)), many corpora are still annotated with language-specific tags. In previous work, their mapping to universal tags was performed manually. Yet, even though some of these mappings have been developed for the same CoNLL dataset (Buchholz and Marsi, 2006; Nivre et al., 2007), they are not identical and yield different parsing performance (Zeman and Resnik, 2008; Petrov et al., 2011; Naseem et al., 2010). The goal of our work is to automate this process and construct mappings that are optimized for performance on downstream tasks (here we focus on parsing). As our results show, we achieve this goal

[2]Instances of related hard problems are 3-partition and subset-sum.

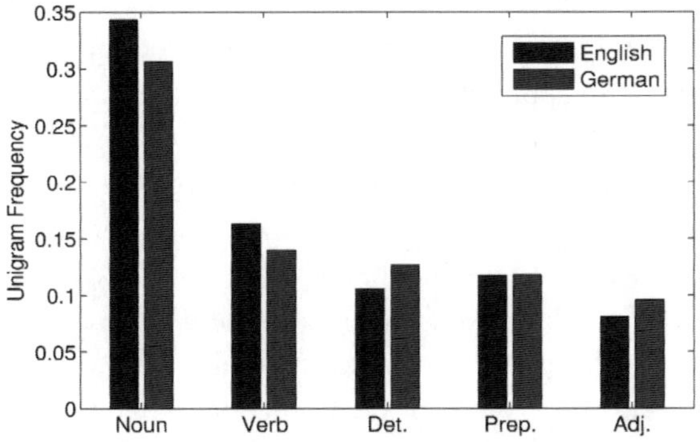

(a)

-Investors [are appealing] to the Securities and Exchange Commission not to [limit] their access to information [*about* stock purchases] and sales [*by* corporate insiders]

-Einer der sich [*für* den Milliardär] [ausspricht] [ist] Steve Jobs dem Perot [*für* den aufbau] der Computerfirma Next 20 Millionen Dollar [bereitstellte]

(b)

Figure 1: Illustration of similarities in POS tag statistics across languages. (a) The unigram frequency statistics on five tags for two close languages, English and German. (b) Sample sentences in English and German. Verbs are shown in blue, prepositions in red and noun phrases in green. It can be seen that noun phrases follow prepositions.

on a broad range of languages and evaluation scenarios.

Syntactic Category Refinement Our work also relates to work in syntactic category refinement in which POS categories and parse tree non-terminals are refined in order to improve parsing performance (Finkel et al., 2007; Klein and Manning, 2003; Matsuzaki et al., 2005; Petrov et al., 2006; Petrov and Klein, 2007; Liang et al., 2007). Our work differs from these approaches in two ways. First, these methods have been developed in the monolingual setting, while our mapping algorithm is designed for multilingual parsing. Second, these approaches are trained on the syntactic trees of the target language, which enables them to directly link the quality of newly induced categories with the quality of syntactic parsing. In contrast, we are not given trees in the target language. Instead, our model is informed by mappings derived for other languages.

3 Task Formulation

The input to our task consists of a *target* corpus written in a language T, and a set of non-parallel *source* corpora written in languages $\{S_1, \ldots, S_n\}$. In the source corpora, each word is annotated with both a language-specific POS tag and a universal POS tag (Petrov et al., 2011). In the target corpus each word is annotated only with a language-specific POS tag, either gold or automatically induced.

Our goal is to find a map from the set of L_T target language tags to the set of K universal tags. We assume that each language-specific tag is only mapped to one universal tag, which means we never split a language-specific tag and $L_T \geq K$ holds for every language. We represent the map by a matrix A of size $K \times L_T$ where $A(c|f) = 1$ if the target language tag f is mapped to the universal tag c, and $A(c|f) = 0$ otherwise.[3] Note that each column of A should contain a single value of 1. We will later relax the requirement that $A(c|f) \in \{0, 1\}$. A candidate mapping A can be applied to the target language to produce sentences labeled with universal tags.

4 Model

In this section we describe an objective that reflects the quality of an automatic mapping.

Our key insight is that for a good mapping, the statistics over the universal tags should be similar for source and target languages because these tags play the same role cross-linguistically. For example, we should expect the frequency of a particular universal tag to be similar in the source and target languages.

One choice to make when constructing an objective is the source languages to which we want to be similar. It is clear that choosing all languages is not a good idea, since they are not all expected to have distributional properties similar to the target language. There is strong evidence that projecting from single languages can lead to good parsing performance

[3]We use c and f to reflect the fact that universal tags are a coarse version (hence c) of the language specific fine tags (hence f).

(McDonald et al., 2011). Therefore, our strategy is to choose a single source language for comparison. The choice of the source language is based on similarity between typological properties; we describe this in detail in Section 5.

We must also determine which statistical properties we expect to be preserved across languages. Our model utilizes three linguistic phenomena which are consistent across languages: POS tag global distributional statistics, POS tag per sentence statistics, and typology-based ordering statistics. We define each of these below.

4.1 Mapping Characterization

We focus on three categories of mapping properties. For each of the relevant statistics we define a function $F_i(A)$ that has low values if the source and target statistics are similar.

Global distributional statistics: The unigram and bigram statistics of the universal tags are expected to be similar across languages with close typological profiles. We use $p_S(c_1, c_2)$ to denote the bigram distribution over universal tags in the source language, and $p_T(f_1, f_2)$ to denote the bigram distribution over language specific tags in the target language. The bigram distribution over universal tags in the target language depends on A and $p_T(f_1, f_2)$ and is given by:

$$p_T(c_1, c_2; A) = \sum_{f_1, f_2} A(c_1|f_1)A(c_2|f_2)p_T(f_1, f_2) \tag{1}$$

To enforce similarity between source and target distributions, we wish to minimize the KL divergence between the two: [4]

$$F_{bi}(A) = D_{KL}[p_S(c_1, c_2)|p_T(c_1, c_2; A)] \tag{2}$$

We similarly define $F_{uni}(A)$ as the distance between unigram distributions.

Per sentence statistics: Another defining property of POS tags is their average count per sentence. Specifically, we focus on the verb count per sentence, which we expect be similar across languages. To express this constraint, we use $n_v(s, A)$ to denote the number of verbs (i.e., the universal tags corresponding to verbs according to A) in sentence s. This is a linear function of A. We also use $E[n_v(s, A)]$ to denote the average number of verbs per sentence, and $V[n_v(s, A)]$ to denote the variance. We estimate these two statistics from the source language and denote them by E_{Sv}, V_{Sv}. Good mappings are expected to follow these patterns by having a variance upper bounded by V_{Sv} and an average lower bounded by E_{Sv}.[5] This corresponds to minimizing the following objectives:

$$\begin{aligned} F_{Ev}(A) &= \max\left[0, E_{Sv} - E[n_v(s, A)]\right] \\ F_{Vv}(A) &= \max\left[0, V[n_v(s, A)] - V_{Sv}\right] \end{aligned}$$

Note that the above objectives are convex in A, which will make optimization simpler. We refer to the two terms jointly as $F_{verb}(A)$.

Typology-based ordering statistics: Typological features can be useful for determining the relative order of different tags. If we know that the target language has a particular typological feature, we expect its universal tags to obey the given relative ordering. Specifically, we expect it to agree with ordering statistics for source languages with a similar typology. We consider two such features here. First, in pre-position languages the preposition is followed by the noun phrase. Thus, if T is such a language, we expect the probability of a noun phrase following the adposition to be high, i.e., cross some threshold. Formally, we define $C_1 = \{\text{noun, adj, num, pron, det}\}$ and consider the set of bigram distributions $\mathcal{S}_{\text{pre}}$ that satisfy the following constraint:

$$\sum_{c \in C_1} p_T(\text{adp,}c) \geq a_{\text{pre}} \tag{3}$$

where $a_{\text{pre}} = \sum_{c \in C_1} p_S(\text{adp,}c)$ is calculated from the source language. This constraint set is non-convex in A due to the bilinearity of the bigram term. To simplify optimization[6] we take an

[4]We use the KL divergence because it assigns low weights to infrequent universal tags. Furthermore, this choice results in a simple, EM-like parameter estimation algorithm as discussed in Section 5.

[5]The rationale is that we want to put a lower bound on the number of verbs per sentence, and induce it from the source language. Furthermore, we expect the number of verbs to be well concentrated, and we induce its maximal variance from the source language.

[6]In Section 5 we shall see that this makes optimization easier.

approach inspired by the posterior regularization method (Ganchev et al., 2010) and use the objective:

$$F_{\text{C}}(A) = \min_{r(c_1,c_2)\in\mathcal{S}_{\text{pre}}} D_{KL}[r(c_1,c_2)|p_T(c_1,c_2;A)] \tag{4}$$

The above objective will attain lower values for A such that $p_T(c_1,c_2;A)$ is close to the constraint set. Specifically, it will have a value of zero when the bigram distribution induced by A has the property specified in $\mathcal{S}_{\text{pre}}$. We similarly define a set $\mathcal{S}_{\text{post}}$ for post-positional languages.

As a second typological feature, we consider the Demonstrative-Noun ordering. In DN languages we want the probability of a determiner to come before $C_2 = \{\text{noun, adj, num}\}$, (i.e., frequent universal noun-phrase tags), to cross a threshold. This constraint translates to:

$$\sum_{c\in C_2} p_T(\text{det}, c) \geq a_{\text{det}} \tag{5}$$

where $a_{\text{det}} = \sum_{c\in C_2} p_S(\text{det}, c)$ is a threshold determined from the source language. We denote the set of distributions that have this property by $\mathcal{S}_{\text{DN}}$, and add them to the constraint in (4). The overall constraint set is denoted by $\mathcal{S}$.

4.2 The Overall Objective

We have defined a set of functions $F_i(A)$ that are expected to have low values for good mappings. To combine those, we use a weighted sum: $F_\alpha(A) = \sum_i \alpha_i \cdot F_i(A)$. (The weights in this equation are learned; we discussed the procedure in Section 5)

Optimizing over the set of mappings is difficult since each mapping is a discrete set whose size is exponential size in L_T. Technically, the difficulty comes from the requirement that elements of A are integral and its columns sum to one. To relax this restriction, we will allow $A(c|f) \in [0,1]$ and encourage A to correspond to a mapping by adding an entropy regularization term:

$$H[A] = -\sum_f \sum_c A(c|f) \log A(c|f) \tag{6}$$

This term receives its minimal value when the conditional probability of the universal tags given a language-specific tag is 1 for one universal tag and zero for the others.

The overall objective is then: $F(A) = F_\alpha(A) + \lambda \cdot H[A]$, where λ is the weight of the entropy term.[7] The resulting optimization problem is:

$$\min_{A\in\Delta} F(A) \tag{7}$$

where Δ is the set of non-negative matrices whose columns sum to one:

$$\Delta = \left\{ A : \begin{array}{ll} A(c|f) \geq 0 & \forall c, f \\ \sum_{c=1}^{K} A(c|f) = 1 & \forall f \end{array} \right\} \tag{8}$$

5 Parameter Estimation

In this section we describe the parameter estimation process for our model. We start by describing how to optimize A. Next, we discuss the weight selection algorithm, and finally the method for choosing source languages.

5.1 Optimizing the Mapping A

Recall that our goal is to solve the optimization problem in Eq. (7). This objective is non convex since the function $H[A]$ is concave, and the objective $F(A)$ involves bilinear terms in A and logarithms of their sums (see Equations (1) and (2)).

While we do not attempt to solve the problem globally, we do have a simple update scheme that monotonically decreases the objective. The update can be derived in a similar manner to expectation maximization (EM) (Neal and Hinton, 1999) and convex concave procedures (Yuille and Rangarajan, 2003). Figure 2 describes our optimization algorithm. The key ideas in deriving it are using posterior distributions as in EM, and using a variational formulation of entropy. The term $F_c(A)$ is handled in a similar way to the posterior regularization algorithm derivation. A detailed derivation is provided in the supplementary file. [8]

The kth iteration of the algorithm involves several steps:

- In step 1, we calculate the current estimate of the bigram distribution over tags, $p_T(c_1,c_2;A^k)$.

[7] Note that as $\lambda \to \infty$, only valid maps will be selected by the objective.

[8] The supplementary file is available at `http://groups.csail.mit.edu/rbg/code/unitag/emnlp2012`.

- In step 2, we find the bigram distribution in the constraint set $\mathcal{S}$ that is closest in KL divergence to $p_T(c_1, c_2; A^k)$, and denote it by $r^k(c_1, c_2)$. This optimization problem is convex in $r(c_1, c_2)$.

- In step 3, we calculate the bigram posterior over language specific tags given a pair of universal tags. This is analogous to the standard E-step in EM.

- In step 4, we use the posterior in step 3 and the bigram distributions $p_S(c_1, c_2)$ and $r^k(c_1, c_2)$ to obtain joint counts over language specific and universal bigrams.

- In step 5, we use the joint counts from step 4 to obtain counts over pairs of language specific and universal tags.

- In step 6, analogous to the M-step in EM, we optimize over the mapping matrix A. The objective is similar to the Q function in EM, and also includes the $F_{verb}(A)$ term, and a linear upper bound on the entropy term. The objective can be seen to be convex in A.

As mentioned above, each of the optimization problems in steps 2 and 6 is convex, and can therefore be solved using standard convex optimization solvers. Here, we use the CVX package (Grant and Boyd, 2008; Grant and Boyd, 2011). It can be shown that the algorithm improves $F(A)$ at every iteration and converges to a local optimum.

The above algorithm generates a mapping A that may contain fractional entries. To turn it into a *hard* mapping we round A by mapping each f to the c that maximizes $A(c|f)$ and then perform greedy improvement steps (one f at a time) to further improve the objective. The regularization constant λ is tuned to minimize the $F_\alpha(A)$ value of the rounded A.

5.2 Learning the Objective Weights

Our $F_\alpha(A)$ objective is a weighted sum of the individual $F_i(A)$ functions. In the following, we describe how to learn the α_i weights for every target language. We would like $F_\alpha(A)$ to have low values when A is a *good* map. Since our performance goal is parsing accuracy, we consider a map to be good

Initialize A^0.
Repeat

Step 1 (calculate current bigram estimate):

$$p_T(c_1, c_2; A^k) = \sum_{f_1, f_2} A^k(c_1|f_1) A^k(c_2|f_2) p_T(f_1, f_2)$$

Step 2 (incorporate constraints):

$$r^k(c_1, c_2) = \arg\min_{r \in \mathcal{S}} D_{KL}[r(c_1, c_2) | p_T(c_1, c_2; A^k)]$$

Step 3 (calculate model posterior):

$$p(f_1, f_2 | c_1, c_2; A^k) \propto A^k(c_1|f_1) A^k(c_2|f_2) p_T(f_1, f_2)$$

Step 4: (complete joint counts):

$$N^k(c_1, c_2, f_1, f_2) = p(f_1, f_2 | c_1, c_2; A^k) \left(r^k(c_1, c_2) + p_S(c_1, c_2) \right)$$

Step 5 (obtain pairwise):

$$M^k(c, f) = N_1^k(c, f) + N_2^k(c, f)$$

where $N_1^k(c, f) = \sum_{c_2, f_2} N^k(c, c_2, f, f_2)$ and similarly for $N_2^k(c, f)$.
Step 6 (M step with entropy linearization): Set A^{k+1} to be the solution of

$$\min_{A \in \Delta} - \sum_{c,f} \left[M^k(c, f) \log A(c|f) + A(c|f) \log A^k(c|f) \right] + F_{verb}(A)$$

Until Convergence of A^k

Figure 2: An iterative algorithm for minimizing our objective in Eq. (7). For simplicity we assume that all the weights α_i and λ are equal to one. It can be shown that the objective monotonically decreases in every iteration.

if it results in high parsing accuracy, as measured when projecting a parser from to S to T.

Since we do not have annotated parses in T, we use the other source languages $S = \{S_1, \ldots, S_n\}$ to learn the weight. For each S_i as the target, we first train a parser for each language in $S \setminus \{S_i\}$ as if it was the source, using the map of Petrov et al. (2011), and choose $S_i^* \in S \setminus \{S_i\}$ which gives the highest parsing accuracy on S_i. Next we generate 7000 candidate mappings for S_i by randomly perturbing the map of (Petrov et al., 2011). We evaluate the quality of each candidate A by projecting the parser of S_i^* to S_i, and recording the parsing accuracy. Among all the candidates we choose the highest accuracy one and denote it by $A^*(S_i)$. We now want the score $F(A^*(S_i))$ to be lower than that of all other candidates. To achieve this, we train a ranking SVM whose inputs are pairs of maps $A^*(S_i)$ and another *worse* $A(S_i)$. These map pairs are taken from many different traget languages, i.e. many different S_i. The features given to the SVM are the terms of the score $F_i(A)$. The goal of the SVM is to weight these terms such that the better map $A^*(S_i)$ has a lower score. The weights assigned by the SVM are taken as α_i.

5.3 Source Language Selection

As noted in Section 4 we construct $F(A)$ by choosing a single source language S. Here we describe the method for choosing S. Our goal is to choose S that is closest to T in terms of typology. Assume that languages are described by binary typological vectors $\mathbf{v}_L$. We would like to learn a diagonal matrix D such that $d(S, T; D) = (\mathbf{v}_S - \mathbf{v}_T)^T D(\mathbf{v}_S - \mathbf{v}_T)$ reflects the similarity between the languages. In our context, a good measure of similarity is the performance of a parser trained on S and projected on T (using the optimal map A). We thus seek a matrix D such that $d(S, T; D)$ is ranked according to the parsing accuracy. The matrix D is trained using an SVM ranking algorithm that tries to follow the ranking of parsing accuracy. Similar to the technique for learning the objective weights, we train across many pairs of source languages.[9]

The typological features we use are a subset of the features described in "The World Atlas of Languages Structure" (WALS, (Haspelmath et al., 2005)), and are shown in Table 1.

6 Evaluation Set-Up

Datasets We test our model on 19 languages: Arabic, Basque, Bulgarian, Catalan, Chinese, Czech, Danish, Dutch, English, German, Greek, Hungarian, Italian, Japanese, Portuguese, Slovene, Spanish, Swedish, and Turkish. Our data is taken from the CoNLL 2006 and 2007 shared tasks (Buchholz and Marsi, 2006; Nivre et al., 2007). The CoNLL datasets consist of manually created dependency trees and language-specific POS tags. Following Petrov et al. (2011), our model maps these language-specific tags to a set of 12 universal tags: noun, verb, adjective, adverb, pronoun, determiner, adposition, numeral, conjunction, particle, punctuation mark and X (a general tag).

[9]Ties are broken using the $F(A)$ objective.

Evaluation Procedure We perform a separate experiment for each of the 19 languages as the target and a source language chosen from the rest (using the method from Section 5.3). For the selected source language, we assume access to the mapping of Petrov et al. (2011).

Evaluation Measures We evaluate the quality of the derived mapping in the context of the target language parsing accuracy. In both the training and test data, the language-specific tags are replaced with universal tags: Petrov's tags for the source languages and learned tags for the target language. We train two non-lexicalized parsers using source annotations and apply them to the target language. The first parser is a non-lexicalized version of the MST parser (McDonald et al., 2005) successfully used in the multilingual context (McDonald et al., 2011). In the second parser, parameters of the target language are estimated as a weighted mixture of parameters learned from supervised source languages (Cohen et al., 2011). For the parser of Cohen et al. (2011), we trained the model on the four languages used in the original paper — English, German, Czech and Italian. When measuring the performance on each of these four languages, we selected another set of four languages with a similar level of diversity.[10]

Following the standard evaluation practice in parsing, we use directed dependency accuracy as our measure of performance.

Baselines We compare mappings induced by our model against three baselines: the manually constructed mapping of Petrov et al. (2011), a randomly constructed mapping and a greedy mapping. The greedy mapping uses the same objective as our full model, but optimizes it using a greedy method. In each iteration, this method makes $|L_T|$ passes over the language-specific tags, selecting a substitution that contributes the most to the objective.

Initialization To reduce the dimension of our algorithm's search space and speed up our method, we start by clustering the language-specific POS tags of the target into $|K| = 12$ clusters using an unsuper-

[10]We also experimented with a version of the Cohen et al. (2011) model trained on all the source languages. This set-up resulted in decreased performance. For this reason, we chose to train the model on the four languages.

ID	Feature Description	Values
81A	Order of Subject, Object and Verb	SVO, SOV, VSO, VOS, OVS, OSV
85A	Order of Adposition and Noun	Postpositions, Prepositions, Inpositions
86A	Order of Genitive and Noun	Genitive-Noun, Noun-Genitive
87A	Order of Adjective and Noun	Adjective-Noun, Noun-Adjective
88A	Order of Demonstrative and Noun	Demonstrative-Noun, Noun-Demonstrative, before and after

Table 1: The set of typological features that we use for source language selection. The first column gives the ID of the feature as listed in WALS. The second column describes the feature and the last column enumerates the allowable values for each feature; besides these values each feature can also have a value of 'No dominant order'.

vised POS induction algorithm (Lee et al., 2010).[11] Our mapping algorithm then learns the connection between these clusters and universal tags.

For initialization, we perform multiple random restarts and select the one with the lowest final objective score.

7 Results

We first present the results of our model using the gold POS tags for the target language. Table 2 summarizes the performance of our model and the baselines.

Comparison against Baselines On average, the mapping produced by our model yields parsers with higher accuracy than all of the baselines. These results are consistent for both parsers (McDonald et al., 2011; Cohen et al., 2011). As expected, random mappings yield abysmal results — 20.2% and 12.7% for the two parsers. The low accuracy of parsers that rely on the *Greedy* mapping — 29.9% and 25.4% — show that a greedy approach is a poor strategy for mapping optimization.

Surprisingly, our model slightly outperforms the mapping of (Petrov et al., 2011), yielding an average accuracy of 56.7% as compared to the 55.4% achieved by its manually constructed counterpart for the direct transfer method (McDonald et al., 2011). Similar results are observed for the mixture weights parser (Cohen et al., 2011). The main reason for these differences comes from mistakes introduced in the manual mapping. For example, in Czech tag "R" is labeled as "pronoun", while actually it should be mapped to "adposition". By correcting this mistake, we gain 5% in parsing accuracy for the direct transfer parser.

[11]This pre-clustering results in about 3% improvement, presumably since it uses contextual information beyond what our algorithm does.

Overall, the manually constructed mapping and our model's output disagree on 21% of the assignments (measured on the token level). However, the extent of disagreement is not necessarily predictive of the difference in parsing performance. For instance, the manual and automatic mappings for Catalan disagree on 8% of the tags and their parsing accuracy differs by 5%. For Greek on the other hand, the disagreement between mappings is much higher — 17%, yet the parsing accuracy is very close. This phenomenon shows that not all mistakes have equal weight. For instance, a confusion between "pronoun" and "noun" is less severe in the parsing context than a confusion between "pronoun" and "adverb".

Impact of Language Selection To assess the quality of our language selection method, we compare the model against an oracle that selects the best source for a given target language. As Table 2 shows our method is very close to the oracle performance, with only 0.7% gap between the two. In fact, for 10 languages our method correctly predicts the best pairing. This result is encouraging in other contexts as well. Specifically, McDonald et al. (2011) have demonstrated that projecting from a single oracle-chosen language can lead to good parsing performance, and our technique may allow such projection without an oracle.

Relations between Objective Values and Optimization Performance The suboptimal performance of the Greedy method shows that choosing a good optimization strategy plays a critical role in finding the desired mapping. A natural question to ask is whether the objective value is predictive of the end goal parsing performance. Figure 3 shows the objective values for the mappings computed by our method and the baselines for four languages. Over-

	Direct Transfer Parser (Accuracy)					Mixture Weight Parser (Accuracy)				Tag Diff.
	Random	Greedy	Petrov	Model	Best Pair	Random	Greedy	Petrov	Model.	
Catalan	15.9	32.5	74.8	**79.3**	79.3	12.6	24.6	65.6	**73.9**	8.8
Italian	16.4	41.0	**68.7**	68.3	71.4	11.7	33.5	**64.2**	61.9	6.7
Portuguese	15.8	24.6	72.0	**75.1**	75.1	10.7	14.1	70.4	**72.6**	12.2
Spanish	11.5	27.4	**72.1**	68.9	68.9	6.4	26.5	58.8	**62.8**	7.5
Danish	35.5	23.7	**46.6**	46.5	49.2	4.2	23.7	51.4	**51.7**	5.0
Dutch	18.0	22.1	**58.2**	56.8	57.3	7.1	15.3	**54.9**	53.2	4.9
English	14.7	19.0	**51.6**	49.0	49.0	13.3	15.1	**47.5**	41.8	17.7
German	15.8	24.3	**55.7**	50.4	51.6	20.9	18.7	**52.4**	51.8	15.0
Swedish	15.1	26.3	63.1	**63.1**	63.1	9.1	36.5	55.7	**55.9**	8.2
Bulgarian	17.4	28.0	51.6	**63.4**	63.4	22.6	39.9	**64.6**	60.4	35.7
Czech	19.0	34.4	47.7	**57.3**	57.3	12.7	26.2	48.3	**55.7**	28.5
Slovene	15.6	21.8	43.5	**51.4**	52.8	11.3	20.7	42.2	**53.0**	38.8
Greek	17.3	19.5	**62.3**	59.7	59.8	22.0	15.2	56.2	**57.0**	17.0
Hungarian	28.4	44.1	**53.8**	52.3	52.3	4.0	43.8	46.4	**51.7**	18.1
Arabic	22.1	45.4	**51.5**	51.2	52.9	3.9	40.9	48.3	**51.1**	15.7
Basque	18.0	19.2	27.9	**33.1**	35.1	6.3	8.3	**32.3**	30.6	43.8
Chinese	22.4	34.1	46.0	**47.6**	49.5	17.7	34.9	**44.0**	40.4	38.1
Japanese	36.5	46.2	51.4	**53.6**	53.6	15.4	18.0	25.7	**28.7**	73.8
Turkish	28.8	34.9	**53.2**	49.8	49.8	19.7	20.3	**27.7**	27.5	9.9
Average	20.2	29.9	55.4	**56.7**	57.4	12.7	25.4	50.8	**51.7**	21.3

Table 2: Directed dependency accuracy of our model and the baselines using gold POS tags for the target language. The first section of the table is for the direct transfer of the MST parser (McDonald et al., 2011). The second section is for the weighted mixture parsing model (Cohen et al., 2011). The first two columns (Random and Greedy) of each section present the parsing performance with a random or a greedy mapping. The third column (Petrov) shows the results when the mapping of Petrov et al. (2011) is used. The fourth column (Model) shows the results when our mapping is used and the fifth column in the first section (Best Pair) shows the performance of our model when the best source language is selected for every target language. The last column (Tag Diff.) presents the difference between our mapping and the mapping of Petrov et al. (2011) by showing the percentage of target language tokens for which the two mappings select a different universal tag.

all, our method and the manual mappings reach similar values, both considerably better than other baselines. While the parsing performance correlates with the objective, the correlation is not perfect. For instance, on Greek our mapping has a better objective value, but lower parsing performance.

Ablation Analysis We next analyze the contribution of each component of our objective to the resulting performance.[12] The strongest factor in our objective is the distributional features capturing global statistics. Using these features alone achieves an average accuracy of 51.1%, only 5.6% less than the full model score. Adding just the verb-related constraints to the distributional similarity objectives improves the average model performance by 2.1%. Adding just the typological constraints yields a very modest performance gain of 0.5%. This is not surprising — the source language is selected to be typologically similar to the target language, and thus its distributional properties are consistent with typological features. However, adding both the verb-related constraints and the typological constraints results in a synergistic performance gain of 5.6% over the distributional similarity objective, a gain which is much better than the sum of the two individual gains.

Application to Automatically Induced POS Tags A potential benefit of the proposed method is to relate automatically induced clusters in the target language to universal tags. In our experiments, we induce such clusters using Brown clustering,[13] which

[12] The results are consistent for both parsers, here we report the accuracy for the direct transfer method (McDonald et al., 2011).

[13] In our experiments, we employ Liang's implementation http://cs.stanford.edu/∼pliang/software/. The number of clusters is set to 30.

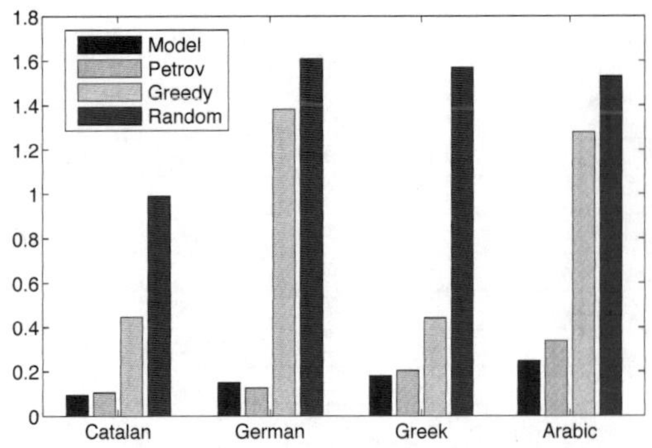

Figure 3: Objective values for the different mappings used in our experiments for four languages. Note that the goal of the optimization procedure is to minimize the objective value.

has been successfully used for similar purposes in parsing research (Koo et al., 2008). We then map these clusters to the universal tags using our algorithm.

The average parsing accuracy on the 19 languages is 45.5%. Not surprisingly, automatically induced tags negatively impact parsing performance, yielding a decrease of 11% when compared to mappings obtained using manual POS annotations (see Table 2). To further investigate the impact of inaccurate tags on the mapping performance, we compare our model against the oracle mapping model that maps each cluster to the most common universal tag of its members. Parsing accuracy obtained using this method is 45.1%, closely matching the performance of our mapping algorithm.

An alternative approach to mapping words into universal tags is to directly partition words into K clusters (without passing through language specific tags). In order for these clusters to be meaningful as universal tags, we can provide several prototypes for each cluster (e.g., "walk" is a verb etc.). To test this approach we used the prototype driven tagger of Haghighi and Klein (2006) with 15 prototypes per universal tag.[14] The resulting universal tags yield an average parsing accuracy of 40.5%. Our method (using Brown clustering as above) outperforms this baseline by about 5%.

8 Conclusions

We present an automatic method for mapping *language-specific* part-of-speech tags to a set of *universal tags*. Our work capitalizes on manually designed conversion schemes to automatically create mappings for new languages. Our experimental results demonstrate that automatically induced mappings rival the quality of their hand-crafted counterparts. We also establish that the mapping quality has a significant impact on the accuracy of syntactic transfer, which motivates further study of this topic. Finally, our experiments show that the choice of mapping optimization scheme plays a crucial role in the quality of the derived mapping, highlighting the importance of optimization for the mapping task.

Acknowledgments

The authors acknowledge the support of the NSF (IIS-0835445), the MURI program (W911NF-10-1-0533) and the DARPA BOLT program. We thank Tommi Jaakkola, the members of the MIT NLP group and the ACL reviewers for their suggestions and comments. Any opinions, findings, conclusions, or recommendations expressed in this paper are those of the authors, and do not necessarily reflect the views of the funding organizations.

References

Sabine Buchholz and Erwin Marsi. 2006. CoNLL-X shared task on multilingual dependency parsing. In *Proceedings of CoNLL*, pages 149–164.

David Burkett and Dan Klein. 2008. Two languages are better than one (for syntactic parsing). In *Proceedings of EMNLP*, pages 877–886.

Shay B. Cohen, Dipanjan Das, and Noah A. Smith. 2011. Unsupervised structure prediction with non-parallel multilingual guidance. In *Proceedings of EMNLP*, pages 50–61.

Frank Van Eynde. 2004. Part of speech tagging en lemmatisering van het corpus gesproken nederlands. In *Technical report*.

Jenny Rose Finkel, Trond Grenager, and Christopher D. Manning. 2007. The infinite tree. In *Proceedings of ACL*, pages 272–279.

Kuzman Ganchev, Joao Graca, Jennifer Gillenwater, and Ben Taskar. 2010. Posterior regularization for structured latent variable models. *JMLR*, 11:2001–2049.

[14] Oracle prototypes were obtained by taking the 15 most frequent words for each universal tag. This yields almost the same total number of prototypes as those in the experiment of (Haghighi and Klein, 2006).

Michael Garey and David S. Johnson. 1979. *Computers and Intractability: A Guide to the Theory of NP-Completeness*. W. H. Freeman & Co.

Michael C. Grant and Stephen P. Boyd. 2008. Graph implementations for nonsmooth convex programs. In *Recent Advances in Learning and Control*, Lecture Notes in Control and Information Sciences, pages 95–110. Springer-Verlag Limited.

Michael C. Grant and Stephen P. Boyd. 2011. CVX: Matlab software for disciplined convex programming, version 1.21.

Aria Haghighi and Dan Klein. 2006. Prototype-driven learning for sequence models. In *Proceedings of NAACL*, pages 320–327.

Martin Haspelmath, Matthew S. Dryer, David Gil, and Bernard Comrie, editors. 2005. *The World Atlas of Language Structures*. Oxford University Press.

Rebecca Hwa, Philip Resnik, Amy Weinberg, Clara Cabezas, and Okan Kolak. 2005. Bootstrapping parsers via syntactic projection across parallel texts. *Journal of Natural Language Engineering*, 11:311–325.

Dan Klein and Christopher Manning. 2003. Accurate unlexicalized parsing. In *Proceedings of ACL*, pages 423–430.

Terry Koo, Xavier Carreras, and Michael Collins. 2008. Simple semi-supervised dependency parsing. In *Proceedings of ACL*, pages 595–603.

Yoong Keok Lee, Aria Haghighi, and Regina Barzilay. 2010. Simple type-level unsupervised pos tagging. In *Proceedings of EMNLP*, pages 853–861.

Percy Liang, Slav Petrov, Michael I. Jordan, and Dan Klein. 2007. The infinite pcfg using hierarchical dirichlet processes. In *Proceedings of EMNLP-CoNLL*, pages 688–697.

Takuya Matsuzaki, Yusuke Miyao, and Jun'ichi Tsujii. 2005. Probabilistic cfg with latent annotations. In *Proceedings of ACL*, pages 75–82.

Ryan McDonald, Fernando Pereira, Kiril Ribarov, and Jan Hajic. 2005. Non-projective dependency parsing using spanning tree algorithms. In *Proceedings of EMNLP*, pages 523–530.

Ryan McDonald, Slav Petrov, and Keith Hall. 2011. Multi-source transfer of delexicalized dependency parsers. In *Proceedings of EMNLP*, pages 62–72.

Tahira Naseem, Harr Chen, Regina Barzilay, and Mark Johnson. 2010. Using universal linguistic knowledge to guide grammar induction. In *Proceedings of EMNLP*, pages 1234–1244.

Radford M. Neal and Geoffrey E. Hinton. 1999. A view of the em algorithm that justifies incremental, sparse, and other variants. In Michael I. Jordan, editor, *Learning in Graphical Models*, pages 355–368. MIT Press.

Joakim Nivre, Johan Hall, Sandra Kübler, Ryan McDonald, Jens Nilsson, Sebastian Riedel, and Deniz Yuret. 2007. The CoNLL 2007 shared task on dependency parsing. In *Proceedings of the CoNLL Shared Task Session of EMNLP-CoNLL 2007*, pages 915–932.

Slav Petrov and Dan Klein. 2007. Improved inference for unlexicalized parsing. In *Proceedings of NAACL*, pages 404–411.

Slav Petrov, Leon Barrett, Romain Thibaux, and Dan Klein. 2006. Learning accurate, compact, and interpretable tree annotation. In *Proceedings of ACL-COLING*, pages 433–440.

Slav Petrov, Dipanjan Das, and Ryan McDonald. 2011. A universal part-of-speech tagset. In *ArXiv*, April.

Chenhai Xi and Rebecca Hwa. 2005. A backoff model for bootstrapping resources for non-english languages. In *Proceedings of EMNLP*, pages 851–858.

Alan Yuille and Anand Rangarajan. 2003. The concave-convex procedure (cccp). In *Proceedings of Neural Computation*, volume 15, pages 915–936.

Daniel Zeman and Philip Resnik. 2008. Cross-language parser adaptation between related languages. In *Proceedings of IJCNLP-08 Workshop on NLP for Less Privileged Languages*, pages 35–42.

Part-of-Speech Tagging for Chinese-English Mixed Texts with Dynamic Features

Jiayi Zhao[†] **Xipeng Qiu**[‡] **Shu Zhang**[§] **Feng Ji**[‡] **Xuanjing Huang**[‡]
School of Computer Science, Fudan University, Shanghai, China [†] [‡]
Fujitsu Research and Development Center, Beijing, China[§]
zjy.fudan@gmail.com[†]
{xpqiu,fengji,xjhuang}@fudan.edu.cn[‡]
zhangshu@cn.fujitsu.com [§]

Abstract

In modern Chinese articles or conversations, it is very popular to involve a few English words, especially in emails and Internet literature. Therefore, it becomes an important and challenging topic to analyze Chinese-English mixed texts. The underlying problem is how to tag part-of-speech (POS) for the English words involved. Due to the lack of specially annotated corpus, most of the English words are tagged as the oversimplified type, "foreign words". In this paper, we present a method using dynamic features to tag POS of mixed texts. Experiments show that our method achieves higher performance than traditional sequence labeling methods. Meanwhile, our method also boosts the performance of POS tagging for pure Chinese texts.

1 Introduction

Nowadays, Chinese-English mixed texts are prevalent in modern articles or emails. More and more English words are used in Chinese texts as names of organizations, products, terms and abbreviations, such as "eBay", "iPhone", "GDP", "Android" etc. On the other hand, it is also a common phenomenon to use Chinese-English mixed texts in daily conversation, especially in communication among employers in large international corporations.

There are some challenges for analyzing Chinese-English mixed texts:

1. How to define the POS tags for English words in these mixed texts. Since the standard of POS tags for English and Chinese are different, we cannot use English POS to tag the English words in mixed texts.

2. Due to lack of annotated corpus for mixed texts, most of the English words are tagged as "foreign words", which is oversimplified. So we cannot use them in further processing for the syntactic and semantic analysis.

3. Most English words used in mixed texts are often out-of-vocabulary (OOV), which thus increases the difficulties to tag them.

Currently, the mainstream method of Chinese POS tagging is joint segmentation & tagging with cross-labels, which can avoid the problem of error propagation and achieve higher performance on both subtasks(Ng and Low, 2004). Each label is the cross-product of a segmentation label and a tagging label, e.g. {B-NN, I-NN, E-NN, S-NN, ...}. The features are generated by position-based templates on character-level.

Since the main part of mixed texts is in Chinese and the role of English word is more like Chinese, we use Chinese POS tags (Xia, 2000) to tag English words. Since the categories of the most commonly used English words are nouns, verbs and adjectives, we can use "NN", "NR", "VV", "VA", "JJ" to label their POS tags.

For the English proper nouns and verbs, there are no significant differences in Chinese and English POS tags except that English features plural and tense forms.

For the English nouns, these are some English nouns used as verbs, such as "我很 [fan/VV] 他。(*I adore him very much.*)" where "fan" means "adore" and is used as a verb.

For the English adjectives, there are two corresponding Chinese POS tags "VA" and "JJ". For example, the roles of some English words in Table 1,

Table 1: The POS tags of English Adjectives in Mixed Texts

Chinese	English
我 非 常 [professional/VA]。	I am very professional.
感觉很 [high/VA]。	Feel very high.
他是 [super/JJ] [star/NN]	He is a super star.

such as "professional" and "high", are different with their original ones.

Therefore, the POS tagging for mixed texts cannot be settled with simple methods, such as looking up in a dictionary.

One of the main differences between Chinese and English in POS tagging is that the two languages have character-based features and word-based features respectively. To ensure the consistency of tagging models, we prefer to use word-level information in Chinese, which is both useful for Chinese-English mixed texts and Chinese-only texts. For instance, in a sentence "X 或者 Y ... (X or Y ...)", the word Y ought to have the same POS tag as the word X. Another example is that the word following a pronoun is usually a verb, and adjectives often describe nouns. Some related works show that word-level features can improve the performance of Chinese POS tagging (Jiang et al., 2008; Sun, 2011).

In this paper, we propose a method to tag mixed texts with dynamic features. Our method combines these dynamic features, which are dynamically generated at the decoding stage, with traditional static features. For Chinese-English mixed texts, the traditional features cannot yield a satisfied result due to lack of training data. The proposed dynamic features can improve the performance by using the information of a word, such as POS tag or length of the whole word, which is proven effective by experiments.

The rest of the paper is organized as follows: In section 2, we introduce the sequence labeling models, then we describe our method of dynamic features in section 3 and analyze its complexity in section 4. Section 5 describes the training method. The experimental results are manifested in section 6. Finally, We review the relevant research works in section 7 and conclude our work in section 8.

2 Sequence Labeling Models

Sequence labeling is the task of assigning labels $\mathbf{y} = y_1, \ldots, y_n$ to an input sequence $\mathbf{x} = x_1, \ldots, x_n$. Given a sample $\mathbf{x}$, we define the feature $\Phi(\mathbf{x}, \mathbf{y})$. Thus, we can label $\mathbf{x}$ with a score function,

$$\hat{\mathbf{y}} = \arg\max_{\mathbf{y}} F(\mathbf{w}, \Phi(\mathbf{x}, \mathbf{y})), \quad (1)$$

where $\mathbf{w}$ is the parameter of function $F(\cdot)$.

For sequence labeling, the feature can be denoted as $\phi_k(y_i, y_{i-1}, \mathbf{x}, i)$, where i stands for the position in the sequence and k stands for the number of feature templates.

we use online Passive-Aggressive (PA) algorithm (Crammer and Singer, 2003; Crammer et al., 2006) to train the model parameters. Following (Collins, 2002), the average strategy is used to avoid the overfitting problem.

3 Dynamic Features

The form of traditional features is shown in Table 2, where C represents a Chinese character, and T represents the character-based tag. The subscript i indicates its position related to the current character.

Table 2: Traditional Feature Templates

$C_i, T_0 (i = -2, -1, 0, 1, 2)$
$C_i, C_j, T_0 (i, j = -2, -1, 0, 1, 2 \text{ and } i \neq j)$
T_{-1}, T_0

Traditional features are generated by position-fixed templates. Since the length of Chinese word is unfixed, their meanings are incomplete. We categorize them as "static" features since they can be calculated before tagging (except "T_{-1}, T_0").

The form of dynamic features is shown in Table 3, where $WORD$ represents a Chinese word, and POS (LEN) is the POS tag (length) of the word. The subscript of dynamic feature template indicates its position related to the current word.

Table 4 shows an example. If the current position is " Apple", then $\{POS_{-1}$=CC, POS_{-2}=NR, $WORD_{-1}$="和", LEN_{-2}=2$\}$. Since these features are unavailable before tagging, we call them "dynamic" features.

Table 3: Examples of Dynamic Feature Templates

$POS_i, POS_j, T_0(i, j = -2, -1, 0 \text{ and } i \neq j)$
$POS_i, WORD_j, T_0(i, j = -2, -1, 0)$
$WORD_i, LEN_j, POS_k, T_0(i, j, k = -2, -1, 0)$
...

Dynamic features are more flexible because the number of involved characters is dependent on the length of previous words. Unlike static features, dynamic features do not merely rely on the input sequence $C_{1:n}$, so the weights of dynamic features, in which POS/LEN are involved, can be trained by Chinese-only texts and used by mixed texts, which resolve the problem of the lack of training data.

4 Tagging with Dynamic Features

In the tagging stage, we use the current best result to approximately calculate the unknown tag information. For an input sequence $C_{1:n}$, the current best tags from index 0 to $i-1$ can be calculated by Viterbi algorithm and they can be used to generate dynamic features for index i. The specific algorithm is shown in Algorithm 1.

Here is an example to explain the time complexity of the dynamic features. Normal template $x_{i-2}x_{i-1}y_i$ requires to look for the positions of $i-2$ and $i-1$ related to the current character x_i, but dynamic template $pos_{i-2}pos_{i-1}y_i$ needs to know the pos tags of two words. If the length of $word_{i-1}/word_{i-2}$ is 2, then the positions of $i-4, i-3, i-2, i-1$ are needed to generate the dynamic features.

For all dynamic features, it is unnecessary to repetitively calculate the $POS/WORD/LEN$ array. Apart from that one time calculation of the array, no distinction can be found between the time complexity of the dynamic features and the traditional features. For input $C_{1:n}$, the time complexity is $O(n*[O(op.2)+(T_s.num+T_d.num)*O(op.1)+O(op.4)])$, n.b. $O(op.1) = O(op.3)$. Universally the dynamic features only require the information of position $i-2$ and $i-1$, so the time complexity of calculating the $POS/WORD/LEN$ array can be ignored as compared with the complexity of Viterbi algorithm and feature extraction. The approximate algorithm is thus faster than the Brute-Force way by using word-level information.

input : character sequence $C_{1:n}$
static templates T_s
dynamic templates T_d
number of labels m
trans matrix M
output: results Max & V_p
Initialize: weight matrix W $(n \times m)$
viterbi score matrix V_s $(n \times m)$
viterbi path matrix V_p $(n \times m)$
the index of current best label Max
for $i = 1 \cdots n$ **do**
  for t_s *in* T_s **do**
    // create feature string F_s $(Op.1)$
    F_s = createFeature($C_{1:n}$, t_s);
    $W[i]$ += getWeightVector(F_s);
  end
  // create a list of $<pos_k, word_k, len_k>$
  // $(k = 0, -1, -2 \ldots)$ $(Op.2)$
  $dList$ = getCurrentBestPath(Max, V_p);
  for t_d *in* T_d **do**
    // create dynamic features string F_d
    // $(Op.3)$
    F_d = createFeature($C_{1:n}$, t_d, $dList$);
    $W[i]$ += getWeightVector(F_d);
  end
  // Update $V_s[i]$, $V_p[i]$ $(Op.4)$
  viterbi_OneStep($V_s[i-1]$, $W[i]$, M);
  $Max = \arg\max_{\mathbf{i}}(V_s[i])$;
end

Algorithm 1: Tagging Algorithm with Dynamic Features

5 Training

Given an example $(\mathbf{x}, \mathbf{y})$, $\hat{\mathbf{y}}$ are denoted as the incorrect labels with the highest score

$$\hat{\mathbf{y}} = \arg\max_{\mathbf{z} \neq \mathbf{y}} \mathbf{w}^T \Phi(\mathbf{x}, \mathbf{z}). \quad (2)$$

The **margin** $\gamma(\mathbf{w}; (\mathbf{x}, \mathbf{y}))$ is defined as

$$\gamma(\mathbf{w}; (\mathbf{x}, \mathbf{y})) = \mathbf{w}^T \Phi(\mathbf{x}, \mathbf{y}) - \mathbf{w}^T \Phi(\mathbf{x}, \hat{\mathbf{y}}). \quad (3)$$

Thus, we calculate the **hinge loss** $\ell(\mathbf{w}; (\mathbf{x}, \mathbf{y}))$, (abbreviated as ℓ_w) by

Table 4: Example for Chinese-English Mixed POS Tagging

微	软	和	Apple	的	OS	风	格	不	同	。
B-NR	E-NR	S-CC	S-NR	S-DEG	S-NN	B-NN	E-NN	B-VA	E-VA	S-PU

$$\ell_w = \begin{cases} 0, & \gamma(\mathbf{w};(\mathbf{x},\mathbf{y})) > 1 \\ 1 - \gamma(\mathbf{w};(\mathbf{x},\mathbf{y})), & \text{otherwise} \end{cases} \quad (4)$$

In round k, the new weight vector $\mathbf{w}_{k+1}$ is calculated by

$$\mathbf{w}_{k+1} = \arg\min_{\mathbf{w}} \frac{1}{2}||\mathbf{w} - \mathbf{w}_k||^2 + \mathcal{C}\cdot\xi, \\ \textbf{s.t. } \ell(\mathbf{w};(\mathbf{x}_k,\mathbf{y}_k)) <= \xi \textbf{ and } \xi >= 0 \quad (5)$$

where ξ is a non-negative slack variable, and $\mathcal{C}$ is a positive parameter which controls the influence of the slack term on the objective function.

Following the derivation in PA (Crammer et al., 2006), we can get the update rule,

$$\mathbf{w}_{k+1} = \mathbf{w}_k + \tau_k(\Phi(\mathbf{x}_k,\mathbf{y}_k) - \Phi(\mathbf{x}_k,\hat{\mathbf{y}_k})), \quad (6)$$

where

$$\tau_k = \min(\mathcal{C}, \frac{\ell_{w_k}}{\|\Phi(\mathbf{x}_k,\mathbf{y}_k) - \Phi(\mathbf{x}_k,\hat{\mathbf{y}_k})\|^2}) \quad (7)$$

Our algorithm based on PA algorithm is shown in Algorithm 2.

```
input  : training data sets:
         (x_i, y_i), i = 1, ..., N, and parameters:
         C, K
output: w_K
Initialize: wTemp <- 0, w <- 0;
for k = 0 ... K-1 do
    for i = 1 ... N do
        receive an example (x_i, y_i);
        predict: ŷ_i = argmax_y <w_k, Φ(x_i, y)>;
        if ŷ_i ≠ y_i then
            update w_{k+1} with Eq. 6;
        end
    end
    wTemp = wTemp + w_{k+1} ;
end
w_K = wTemp/K ;
```

Algorithm 2: Training Algorithm

Table 5: Feature Templates

Static	$x_{i-2}y_i, x_{i-1}y_i, x_iy_i, x_{i+1}y_i, x_{i+2}y_i$
	$x_{i-1}x_iy_i, x_{i+1}x_iy_i, x_{i-1}x_{i+1}y_i,$
	$y_{i-1}y_i$
Dynamic	$pos_{i-2}pos_{i-1}y_i, pos_{i-1}pos_iy_i$
	$pos_{i-2}word_{i-1}y_i, pos_{i-1}word_iy_i$
	$pos_{i-1}word_{i-1}y_i, pos_iword_iy_i$
	$word_{i-2}word_{i-1}y_i, word_{i-1}word_iy_i$
	$word_ilen_iy_i$

6 Experiments

We implement our system based on FudanNLP[1]. We employ the commonly used label set {B, I, E, S} for the segmentation part of cross-labels. {B, I, E} represent *Begin*, *Inside*, *End* of a multi-node segmentation respectively, and S represents a *Single* node segmentation.

The $F1$ score is used for evaluation, which is the harmonic mean of precision P (percentage of predict phrases that exactly match the reference phrases) and recall R (percentage of reference phrases that returned by system).

The feature templates, which are used to extract features, are listed in Table 5. We set traditional method (static features) as the baseline. The detailed experimental settings and results are reported in the following subsections.

6.1 POS Tagging for Chinese-only Texts

Before the experiments on Chinese-English mixed texts, we evaluate the performance of our method on Chinese-only texts. We use the CTB dataset from the POS tagging task of the Fourth International Chinese Language Processing Bakeoff (SIGHAN Bakeoff 2008)(Jin and Chen, 2008). The details are shown in Table 6.

The performance comparison on joint segmentation & POS tagging is shown in Table 7. Our method obtains an error reduction of 6.7% over the baseline. The reason is that our dynamic features can utilize

[1] Available at http://code.google.com/p/fudannlp/

Table 6: POS Tagging Dataset in SIGHAN Bakeoff 2008

		Train Set (number)	Test Set (number)
Sentence		23444	2079
Word	Total	642246	59955
	NN	168896	16793
	NR	42906	3970
	VV	92887	8641
	VA	9106	649
	JJ	15640	1581

word-level information effectively and the feature templates are more flexible.

Table 7: Performances of POS Tagging on Chinese-only Texts with Static and Dynamic Features

Method	P	R	F1
Baseline	89.68	89.60	89.64
Our	**90.35**	**90.31**	**90.33**

6.2 POS Tagging for Chinese-English Mixed Texts

Without annotated corpus for Chinese-English mixed texts, we use synthetic data as the alternative. In Chinese-English mixed texts, English words of noun(NN/NR), verb(VV/VA) and adjective(JJ) categories are the most commonly used, so we randomly transform a certain percentage of Chinese words with these POS tags in the SIGHAN Bakeoff 2008 dataset(Jin and Chen, 2008) into their English counterparts.

6.2.1 Synthetic Data

Before trying out an experiment, we first study how to generate the data of mixed texts.

We use two ways to produce the synthetic data: "Respective Replacement" and "Unified Replacement".

Respective Replacement We replace the selected Chinese words into their corresponding English counterparts.

Unified Replacement We replace the selected Chinese words with a unified label ENG. The reason we use the label ENG instead of real words is that we want to consider the context of these words but not the words themselves and overcome the problem of out-of-vocabulary (OOV) English words.

For our experiments, we just select 5% of the Chinese nouns and verbs from SIGHAN dataset, and replace them in the above two ways. After replacement, the training and test data have 12780 and 1254 English words, respectively. 5189 words are generated by way of "Respective Replacement". In the test data, 326 words are OOV, which comprises 25% of the whole vocabulary. The information of generated data is shown in Table 8.

Table 8: The Synthetic Chinese-English Mixed Dataset H

Dataset		Numbers of ENG	
		NN	VV
H	Train Set	8191	4589
	Test Set	842	412

We use H_1 to represent the dataset generated by way of "Respective Replacement", and H_2 for the dataset by way of with "Unified Replacement". The experimental results on these two datasets are shown in Table 9.

Table 9: Performances of POS Tagging on Dataset H_1 and H_2

Method	Dataset	ENG	OOV	Total
		F1	$F1_{oov}$	F1
Baseline	H_1	73.60	54.91	88.93
	H_2	77.59	73.93	89.11
Our	H_1	75.60	54.60	89.79
	H_2	**79.82**	**77.61**	**89.81**

From Table 9, we can see that the "Unified Replacement" way is better than the "Respective Replacement" way for both the baseline and our method. The main reason is that the "Unified Replacement" way can greatly improve the tagging performance of OOV words.

6.2.2 Detail Comparisons

For detail comparisons of all situations of mixed texts, we design six synthetic datasets, $A/B/C/D_1/D_2/E$ by randomly selecting 10% or 15% of Chinese words ("NN/NR/VV/VA/JJ") in the above SIGHAN Bakeoff 2008 dataset, and replacing them with English label ENG.

The differences of these datasets are as following:

- Dataset A only contains English words with tags "NN/VV".
- Dataset B contains English words with tags "NN/VV/VA".
- Dataset C contains one more tag "NR" than Dataset B.
- Datasets D_1 and D_2 contain one more tag "JJ" than Dataset B. The difference between D_1 and D_2 is that D_2 has about 50% more English words than D_1 in training set.
- Dataset E contains English words with all the tags "NN/NR/VV/VA/JJ".

The detailed information of datasets $A/B/C/D_1/D_2/E$ is shown in Table 10.

Table 10: The Synthetic Chinese-English Mixed Dataset

Dataset		Numbers of ENG				
		NN	NR	VV	VA	JJ
A	Train	16302	0	9007	0	0
	Test	1675	0	841	0	0
B	Train	16116	0	8882	906	0
	Test	1573	0	830	58	0
C	Train	16312	4057	9067	899	0
	Test	1549	400	795	61	0
D_1	Train	16042	0	8957	855	1539
	Test	1588	0	845	58	150
D_2	Train	23705	0	13154	1300	2211
	Test	1588	0	845	58	150
E	Train	16066	4162	9156	886	1547
	Test	1647	415	809	57	141

The results are shown in Table 11. On dataset E, our method achieves 6.78% higher performance on tagging ENG labels than traditional static features. This result is reasonable because our model can use more flexible feature templates to extract features and reduce the problem of being dependent on specific English words.

Tables 12/13/14/15/16/17 show the detailed results on datasets $A/B/C/D_1/D_2/E$.

Table 11: Performances of POS Tagging on Datasets $A/B/C/D_1/D_2/E$

Dataset	Method	ENG labels	Total
		F1	F1
A	Baseline	80.25	88.74
	Our	**83.03**	**89.72**
B	Baseline	76.72	88.51
	Our	**80.54**	**89.55**
C	Baseline	68.16	88.13
	Our	**70.34**	**88.99**
D_1	Baseline	71.30	88.33
	Our	**74.02**	**89.15**
D_2	Baseline	69.59	88.09
	Our	**74.10**	**89.15**
E	Baseline	61.58	87.71
	Our	**68.36**	**88.83**

Experiment on dataset A gets the best result because "NN" and "VV" can be easily distinguished by its context. Sometimes, "VA" has the similar context with "VV", experiment on dataset B shows its influence. The performances on datasets $B/C/E$ descend in turn. The reason is that words with tag "NN" or "NR/JJ" have the similar usage/contexts in Chinese. Since we use the same form ENG instead of real words, there are no differences between these words, which leads to some errors. Though the datasets is generated randomly, we can see our method perform better on every dataset than the baseline.

Table 12: Performances on Dataset A

POS tag	Method	P	R	F1
NN	Baseline	84.36	86.33	85.33
	Our	85.37	89.91	**87.58**
VV	Baseline	71.45	68.13	69.75
	Our	77.53	69.32	**73.20**

Table 13: Performances on Dataset B

POS tag	Method	P	R	F1
NN	Baseline	84.89	80.36	82.56
	Our	83.51	88.87	**86.11**
VV	Baseline	65.90	72.65	69.11
	Our	75.75	67.35	**71.30**
VA	Baseline	36.84	36.21	36.52
	Our	51.02	43.10	**46.73**

Table 14: Performances on Dataset C

POS tag	Method	P	R	F1
NN	Baseline	73.77	78.24	75.94
	Our	76.84	77.99	**77.41**
VV	Baseline	61.67	66.79	64.13
	Our	64.94	67.80	**66.34**
NR	Baseline	55.22	37.00	44.31
	Our	55.65	50.50	**52.95**
VA	Baseline	63.64	34.43	44.68
	Our	60.00	39.34	**47.52**

Table 15: Performances on Dataset D_1

POS tag	Method	P	R	F1
NN	Baseline	77.15	81.42	79.23
	Our	76.70	88.54	**82.20**
VV	Baseline	67.53	64.50	65.98
	Our	79.65	59.76	**68.29**
JJ	Baseline	25.00	18.00	**20.93**
	Our	22.92	14.67	17.89
VA	Baseline	36.00	31.03	**33.33**
	Our	28.57	37.93	32.59

Table 16: Performances on Dataset D_2

POS tag	Method	P	R	F1
NN	Baseline	79.11	74.87	76.93
	Our	79.29	82.68	**80.95**
VV	Baseline	55.77	72.78	65.64
	Our	69.17	70.89	**70.02**
JJ	Baseline	27.27	12.00	16.67
	Our	34.38	22.00	**26.83**
VA	Baseline	37.21	27.59	**31.68**
	Our	52.17	20.69	29.63

6.3 POS Tagging for Mixed Texts with a Real Dataset

To investigate the actual performance, we collect a real dataset from Web, which consists of 142 representative Chinese-English mixed sentences. This dataset contains $4,238$ Chinese characters and 275 English words. Since we focus on the performance for English words, we only label the POS tags of the English words. Table 18 shows some examples in the real dataset of mixed texts.

Table 17: Performances on Dataset E

POS tag	Method	P	R	F1
NN	Baseline	72.41	68.85	70.59
	Our	71.18	84.88	**77.43**
VV	Baseline	63.65	59.09	61.28
	Our	76.19	55.38	**64.14**
JJ	Baseline	28.57	25.53	**26.97**
	Our	30.21	20.57	24.47
VA	Baseline	44.83	45.61	45.22
	Our	60.42	50.88	**55.24**
NR	Baseline	38.03	52.05	43.95
	Our	52.01	46.75	**49.24**

Table 18: Examples in Real Dataset of Mixed Texts

通过 [Ninja Cloud/NR] 的云服务，[Ninja Blocks/NR] 能与 [Facebook/NR]、[Twitter/NR]、[Dropbox/NR] 等无缝连接。
By using [Ninja Cloud/NR], [Ninja Blocks/NR] can connect to [Facebook/NR], [Twitter/NR], [Dropbox/NR].
你去 [follow/VV] 一下这个人的工作。
You should [follow/VV] this man's work.
强烈的视觉震撼！！很 [COOL/VA]！
... very [COOL/VA]!

The information of the real dataset is shown in Table 19. If all involved English words are tagging as "NN", the precision is just 56%.

Table 19: The Numbers of English Words with Different Tags in Dataset R

Dataset	NN	VV	VA	NR
R	154	58	28	35

Since there is no noun-modifier "JJ" in our collected data. We use the models trained on dataset B and C to tag the real data. The results are shown in Table 20. The difference between model B and C is that model B regards all words with tag "NR" as "NN". Since it is difficult to distinguish between "NR" and "NN" merely according to the context, model B performs better than model C.

The detail results of model B and C are shown in Table 21 and 22.

Table 20: Performances of POS Tagging on R

Model	Method	ENG
		F1
B	Baseline	74.91
	Our	**82.55**
C	Baseline	70.91
	Our	**74.91**

Table 21: Performances of Model B on Dataset R

POS tag	Method	P	R	F1
NN	Baseline	88.62	78.31	83.15
	Our	91.67	87.30	**89.43**
VV	Baseline	48.31	74.14	58.50
	Our	60.53	79.31	**68.66**
VA	Baseline	78.95	53.57	63.83
	Our	84.21	57.14	**68.09**

Table 22: Performances of Model C on Dataset R

POS tag	Method	P	R	F1
NN	Baseline	80.25	81.82	81.03
	Our	84.56	81.82	**83.17**
VV	Baseline	54.88	77.59	64.29
	Our	61.25	84.48	**71.01**
VA	Baseline	84.62	39.29	53.66
	Our	88.24	53.57	**66.67**
NR	Baseline	56.52	37.14	44.83
	Our	55.17	45.71	**50.00**

7 Related Works

In recent years, POS tagging has undergone great development. The mainstream method is to regard POS tagging as sequence labeling problems (Rabiner, 1990; Xue, 2003; Peng et al., 2004; Ng and Low, 2004).

However, the analysis of Chinese-English mixed texts is rarely involved in previous literature. In the aspect of the general multilingual POS tagging, most works focus on modeling cross-lingual correlations and tagging multilingual POS on respective monolingual texts, not on mixed texts (Cucerzan and Yarowsky, 2002; Yarowsky et al., 2001; Naseem et al., 2009).

Since we choose to use dynamic word-level features to improve the performance of POS tagging, we also review some works on word-level features.

Semi-Markov Conditional Random Fields (semi-CRF) (Sarawagi and Cohen, 2004) is a model in which segmentation task is implicitly included into the decoding algorithm. In this model, feature representation would be more flexible than traditional CRFs, since features can be extracted from the previous/the next segmentation within a window of variable size. The problem of this approach lies in that the decoding algorithm depends on the predefined window size to exploit the boundaries of segmentations but not the real length of words.

Bunescu (2008) presents an improved pipeline model in which the output of the previous subtasks are considered as hidden variables, and the hidden variables together with their probabilities denoting the confidence are used as probabilistic features in the next subtasks. One shortcoming of this method is inefficiency caused by the calculation of marginal probabilities of features. The other disadvantages of the pipeline method are error propagation and the need of separate training of different subtasks in the pipeline. Another disadvantage of pipeline method is error propagation.

Jiang et al. (2008) proposes a cascaded linear model for joint Chinese word segmentation and POS tagging. With a character-based perceptron as the core, combined with real-valued features such as language models, the cascaded model can efficiently utilize knowledge sources that are inconvenient to incorporate into the perceptron directly. However, they use POS tags or word information in a Brute-Force way, which may suffer from the problem of time complexity.

Sun (2011) presents a stacked sub-word model for joint Chinese word segmentation and POS tagging. By merging the outputs of the three predictors (including one word-based segmenter) into sub-word sequences, rich contextual features can be approximately derived. The experiments are conducted to show the effectiveness of using word-based information.

The difference between the above methods and ours is that our word-level features are dynamically generated in the decoding stage without exhaustive or preprocessed word segmentation.

8 Conclusion

In this paper, we focus on Chinese-English mixed texts and use dynamic features for POS tagging. To overcome the problem of the lack of annotated corpus on mixed texts, our features use both local and non-local information and take advantage of the characteristics of Chinese-English mixed texts. The experiments demonstrate the effectiveness of our method. It should be noted that our method is also effective for the mixed texts of Chinese and any foreign languages since we use "Unified Replacement".

For future works, we plan to improve our approximate tagging algorithm to reduce error propagation. In addition, we will refer to an English dictionary to generate some useful features to distinguish between "NR" and "NN" in Chinese-English mixed texts and add some statistical features derived from English resources, such as the most common tag of each English word. We would also like to investigate these features in more applications of natural language processing, such as name entity recognition, information extraction, etc.

Acknowledgements

We would like to thank the anonymous reviewers for their valuable comments. We also thanks Amy Zhou for her help in spell and grammar checking. This work was funded by NSFC (No.61003091 and No.61073069), 863 Program (No.2011AA010604) and 973 Program (No.2010CB327900).

References

Razvan C. Bunescu. 2008. Learning with probabilistic features for improved pipeline models. In *EMNLP*, pages 670–679. ACL.

Michael Collins. 2002. Discriminative training methods for hidden markov models: theory and experiments with perceptron algorithms. In *Proceedings of the ACL-02 conference on Empirical methods in natural language processing - Volume 10*, EMNLP '02, pages 1–8, Stroudsburg, PA, USA. Association for Computational Linguistics.

Koby Crammer and Yoram Singer. 2003. Ultraconservative online algorithms for multiclass problems. *J. Mach. Learn. Res.*, 3:951–991, March.

Koby Crammer, Ofer Dekel, Joseph Keshet, Shai Shalev-Shwartz, and Yoram Singer. 2006. Online passive-aggressive algorithms. *J. Mach. Learn. Res.*, 7:551–585, December.

Silviu Cucerzan and David Yarowsky. 2002. Bootstrapping a multilingual part-of-speech tagger in one person-day. In *proceedings of the 6th conference on Natural language learning - Volume 20*, COLING-02, pages 1–7, Stroudsburg, PA, USA. Association for Computational Linguistics.

Wenbin Jiang, Liang Huang, Qun Liu, and Yajuan Lü. 2008. A cascaded linear model for joint chinese word segmentation and part-of-speech tagging. In Kathleen McKeown, Johanna D. Moore, Simone Teufel, James Allan, and Sadaoki Furui, editors, *ACL*, pages 897–904. The Association for Computer Linguistics.

C. Jin and X. Chen. 2008. The fourth international chinese language processing bakeoff: Chinese word segmentation, named entity recognition and chinese pos tagging. In *Sixth SIGHAN Workshop on Chinese Language Processing*, page 69.

T. Naseem, B. Snyder, J. Eisenstein, and R. Barzilay. 2009. Multilingual part-of-speech tagging: Two unsupervised approaches. *Journal of Artificial Intelligence Research*, 36(1):341–385.

H.T. Ng and J.K. Low. 2004. Chinese part-of-speech tagging: One-at-a-time or all-at-once? word-based or character-based. In *Proceedings of EMNLP*, volume 2004, page 277.

Fuchun Peng, Fangfang Feng, and Andrew McCallum. 2004. Chinese segmentation and new word detection using conditional random fields. In *Proceedings of the 20th international conference on Computational Linguistics*, COLING '04, Stroudsburg, PA, USA. Association for Computational Linguistics.

Lawrence R. Rabiner. 1990. Readings in speech recognition. chapter A tutorial on hidden Markov models and selected applications in speech recognition, pages 267–296. Morgan Kaufmann Publishers Inc., San Francisco, CA, USA.

Sunita Sarawagi and William W. Cohen. 2004. Semi-markov conditional random fields for information extraction. In *NIPS*.

Weiwei Sun. 2011. A stacked sub-word model for joint chinese word segmentation and part-of-speech tagging. In Dekang Lin, Yuji Matsumoto, and Rada Mihalcea, editors, *ACL*, pages 1385–1394. The Association for Computer Linguistics.

F. Xia. 2000. The part-of-speech tagging guidelines for the Penn Chinese Treebank (3.0).

N. Xue. 2003. Chinese word segmentation as character tagging. *Computational Linguistics and Chinese Language Processing*, 8(1):29–48.

D. Yarowsky, G. Ngai, and R. Wicentowski. 2001. Inducing multilingual text analysis tools via robust projection across aligned corpora. In *Proceedings of the first international conference on Human language technology research*, pages 1–8. Association for Computational Linguistics.

Wiki-ly Supervised Part-of-Speech Tagging

Shen Li
Computer & Information Science
University of Pennsylvania
shenli@seas.upenn.edu

João V. Graça
L[2]F INESC-ID
Lisboa, Portugal
javg@l2f.inesc-id.pt

Ben Taskar
Computer & Information Science
University of Pennsylvania
taskar@cis.upenn.edu

Abstract

Despite significant recent work, purely unsupervised techniques for part-of-speech (POS) tagging have not achieved useful accuracies required by many language processing tasks. Use of parallel text between resource-rich and resource-poor languages is one source of weak supervision that significantly improves accuracy. However, parallel text is not always available and techniques for using it require multiple complex algorithmic steps. In this paper we show that we can build POS-taggers exceeding state-of-the-art bilingual methods by using simple hidden Markov models and a freely available and naturally growing resource, the Wiktionary. Across eight languages for which we have labeled data to evaluate results, we achieve accuracy that significantly exceeds best unsupervised and parallel text methods. We achieve highest accuracy reported for several languages and show that our approach yields better out-of-domain taggers than those trained using fully supervised Penn Treebank.

1 Introduction

Part-of-speech categories are elementary building blocks that play an important role in many natural language processing tasks, from machine translation to information extraction. Supervised learning of taggers from POS-annotated training text is a well-studied task, with several methods achieving near-human tagging accuracy (Ratnaparkhi, 1996; Toutanova et al., 2003; Shen et al., 2007). However, while English and a handful of other languages are fortunate enough to have comprehensive POS-annotated corpora such as the Penn Treebank (Marcus et al., 1993), most of the world's languages have no labeled corpora. The annotated corpora that do exist were costly to build (Abeillé, 2003), and are often not freely available or restricted to research-only use. Furthermore, much of the annotated text is of limited genre, normally focusing on newswire or literary text. Performance of treebank-trained systems degrades significantly when applied to new domains (Blitzer et al., 2006).

Unsupervised induction of POS taggers offers the possibility of avoiding costly annotation, but despite recent progress, the accuracy of unsupervised POS taggers still falls far behind supervised systems, and is not suitable for most applications (Berg-Kirkpatrick et al., 2010; Graça et al., 2011; Lee et al., 2010). Using additional information, in the form of tag dictionaries or parallel text, seems unavoidable at present. Early work on using tag dictionaries used a labeled corpus to extract all allowed word-tag pairs (Merialdo, 1994), which is quite an unrealistic scenario. More recent work has used a subset of the observed word-tag pairs and focused on generalizing dictionary entries (Smith and Eisner, 2005; Haghighi and Klein, 2006; Toutanova and Johnson, 2007; Goldwater and Griffiths, 2007). Using corpus-based dictionaries greatly biases the test results, and gives little information about the capacity to generalize to different domains.

Recent work by Das and Petrov (2011) builds a dictionary for a particular language by transferring annotated data from a resource-rich language through the use of word alignments in parallel text.

The main idea is to rely on existing dictionaries for some languages (e.g. English) and use parallel data to build a dictionary in the desired language and extend the dictionary coverage using label propagation. However, parallel text does not exist for many pairs of languages and the proposed bilingual projection algorithms are fairly complex.

In this work we use the Wiktionary, a freely available, high coverage and constantly growing dictionary for a large number of languages. We experiment with a very simple second-order Hidden Markov Model with feature-based emissions (Berg-Kirkpatrick et al., 2010; Graça et al., 2011). We outperform best current results using parallel text supervision across 8 different languages, even when the word type coverage is as low as 20%. Furthermore, using the Brown corpus as out-of-domain data we show that using the Wiktionary produces better taggers than using the Penn Treebank dictionary (88.5% vs 85.9%). Our empirical analysis and the natural growth rate of the Wiktionary suggest that free, high-quality and multi-domain POS-taggers for a large number of languages can be obtained by standard and efficient models.

The source code, the dictionary mappings and the trained models described in this work are available at `http://code.google.com/p/wikily-supervised-pos-tagger/`.

2 Related Work

The scarcity of labeled corpora for resource poor languages and the challenges of domain adaptation have led to several efforts to build systems for unsupervised POStagging.

Several lines of research have addressed the fully unsupervised POS-tagging task: mutual information clustering (Brown et al., 1992; Clark, 2003) has been used to group words according to their distributional context. Using dimensionality reduction on word contexts followed by clustering has led to accuracy gains (Schütze, 1995; Lamar et al., 2010). Sequence models, HMMs in particular, have been used to represent the probabilistic dependencies between consecutive tags. In these approaches, each observation corresponds to a particular word and each hidden state corresponds to a cluster. However, using maximum likelihood training for such models does not achieve good results (Clark, 2003): maximum likelihood training tends to result in very ambiguous distributions for common words, in contradiction with the rather sparse word-tag distribution. Several approaches have been proposed to mitigate this problem, including Bayesian approaches using an improper Dirichlet prior to favor sparse model parameters (Johnson, 2007; Gao and Johnson, 2008; Goldwater and Griffiths, 2007), or using the Posterior Regularization to penalize ambiguous posteriors distributions of tags given tokens (Graça et al., 2009). Berg-Kirkpatrick et al. (2010) and Graça et al. (2011) proposed replacing the multinomial emission distributions of standard HMMs by maximum entropy (ME) feature-based distributions. This allows the use of features to capture morphological information, and achieves very promising results. Despite these improvements, fully unsupervised systems require an oracle to map clusters to true tags and the performance still fails to be of practical use.

In this paper we follow a different line of work where we rely on a prior tag dictionary indicating for each word type what POS tags it can take on (Merialdo, 1994). The task is then, for each word token in the corpus, to disambiguate between the possible POS tags. Even when using a tag dictionary, disambiguating from all possible tags is still a hard problem and the accuracy of these methods is still fall far behind their supervised counterparts. The scarcity of large, manually-constructed tag dictionaries led to the development of methods that try to generalize from a small dictionary with only a handful of entries (Smith and Eisner, 2005; Haghighi and Klein, 2006; Toutanova and Johnson, 2007; Goldwater and Griffiths, 2007), however most previous works build the dictionary from the labeled corpus they learn on, which does not represent a realistic dictionary. In this paper, we argue that the Wiktionary can serve as an effective and much less biased tag dictionary.

We note that most of the previous dictionary based approaches can be applied using the Wiktionary and would likely lead to similar accuracy increases that we show in this paper. For example, the work if Ravi and Knight (2009) minimizes the number of possible tag-tag transitions in the HMM via a integer program, hence discarding unlikely transitions that would confuse the model. Models can also be trained jointly using parallel corpora in several languages, exploiting the fact that different languages present different ambiguities (Snyder et al., 2008).

The Wiktionary has been used extensively for other tasks such as domain specific information retrieval (Müller and Gurevych, 2009), ontology matching (Krizhanovsky and Lin, 2009), synonymy detection (Navarro et al., 2009), sentiment classification (Chesley et al., 2006). Recently, Ding (2011) used the Wiktionary to initialize an HMM for Chinese POS tagging combined with label propagation.

3 The Wiktionary and tagged corpora

The Wiktionary[1] is a collaborative project that aims to produce a free, large-scale multilingual dictionary. Its goal is to describe all words from all languages (currently more than 400) using definitions and descriptions in English. The coverage of the Wiktionary varies greatly between languages: currently there are around 75 languages for which there exists more than 1000 word types, and 27 for which there exists more than 10,000 word types. Nevertheless, the Wiktionary has been growing at a considerable rate (see Figure 1), and the number of available words has almost doubled in the last three years. As more people use the Wiktionary, it is likely to grow. Unlike tagged corpora, the Wiktionary provides natural incentives for users to contribute missing entries and expand this communal resource akin to Wikipedia. As with Wikipedia, the questions of accuracy, bias, consistency across languages, and selective coverage are paramount. In this section, we explore these concerns by comparing Wiktionary to dictionaries derived from tagged corpora.

3.1 Labeled corpora and Universal tags

We collected part-of-speech tagged corpora for 9 languages, from CoNLL-X and CoNLL-2007 shared tasks on dependency parsing (Buchholz and Marsi, 2006; Nivre et al., 2007). In this work we use the Universal POS tag set (Petrov et al., 2011) that defines 12 universal categories with a relatively stable functional definition across languages. These categories include NOUN, VERB, ADJ = adjective, ADV = adverb, NUM = number, ADP = adposition, CONJ = conjunction, DET = determiner, PRON = pronoun, PUNC = punctuation, PRT = particle, and X = residual (a category for language-specific categories which defy cross-linguistic classification). We found several small problems with the mapping[2] which we corrected as follows. In Spanish, the fine-level tag for date ("w") is mapped to universal tag NUM, while it should be mapped to NOUN. In Danish there were no PRT, NUM, PUNC, or DET tags in the mapping. After examining the corpus guidelines and the mapping more closely, we found that the tag AC (Cardinal numeral) and AO (Ordinal numeral) are mapped to ADJ. Although the corpus guidelines indicate the category SsCatgram 'adjective' that encompasses both 'normal' adjectives (AN) as well as cardinal numeral (AC) and ordinal numerals (AO), we decided to tag AC and AO as NUM, since this assignment better fits the existing mapping. We also reassigned all punctuation marks, which were erroneously mapped to X, to PUNC and the tag U which is used for words *at, de* and *som*, to PRT.

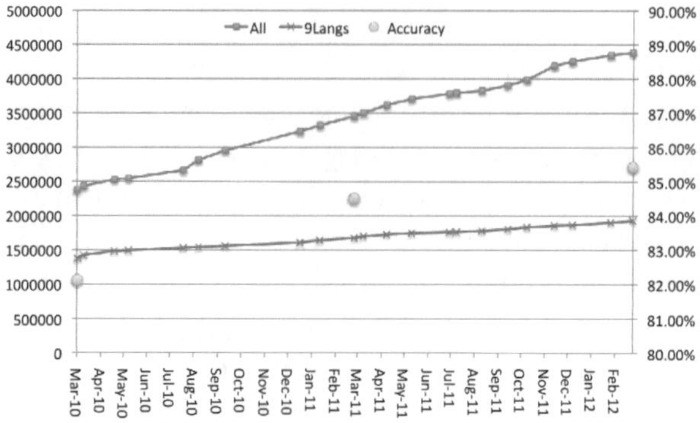

Figure 1: Growth of the Wiktionary over the last three years, showing total number of entries for all languages and for the 9 languages we consider (left axis). We also show the corresponding increase in average accuracy (right axis) achieved by our model across the 9 languages (see details below).

3.2 Wiktionary to Universal tags

There are a total of 330 distinct POS-type tags in Wiktionary across all languages which we have mapped to the Universal tagset. Most of the mapping was straightforward since the tags used in the Wiktionary are in fact close to the Universal tag set. Some exceptions like "Initialism", "Suffix"

[1] http://www.wiktionary.org/

[2] http://code.google.com/p/universal-pos-tags/

were discarded. We also mapped relatively rare tags such as "Interjection", "Symbol" to the "X" tag. A example of POS tags for several words in the Wiktionary is shown in Table 1. All the mappings are available at http://code.google.com/p/wikily-supervised-pos-tagger/.

3.3 Wiktionary coverage

There are two kinds of coverage of interest: type coverage and token coverage. We define type coverage as the proportion of word types in the corpus that simply appear in the Wiktionary (accuracy of the tag sets are considered in the next subsection). Token coverage is defined similarly as the portion of all word tokens in the corpus that appear in the Wiktionary. These statistics reflect two aspects of the usefulness of a dictionary that affect learning in different ways: token coverage increases the density of supervised signal while type coverage increases the diversity of word shape supervision. At one extreme, with 100% word and token coverage, we recover the POS tag disambiguation scenario and, on the other extreme of 0% coverage, we recover the unsupervised POS induction scenario.

The type and token coverage of Wiktionary for each of the languages we are using for evaluation is shown in Figure 2. We plot the coverage bar for three different versions of Wiktionary (v20100326, v20110321, v20120320), arranged chronologically. We chose these three versions of the Wiktionary simply by date, not any other factors like coverage, quality or tagging accuracy.

As expected, the newer versions of the Wiktionary generally have larger coverage both on type level and token level. Nevertheless, even for languages whose type coverage is relatively low, such as Greek (el), the token level coverage is still quite good (more than half of the tokens are covered). The reason for this is likely the bias of the contributors towards more frequent words. This trend is even more evident when we break up the coverage by frequency of the words. Since the number of words varies from corpus to corpus, we normalize the word counts by the count of the most frequent word(s) in its corpus and group the normalized frequency into three categories labeled as "low", "medium" and "high" and for each category, we calculate the word type coverage, shown in Figure 3.

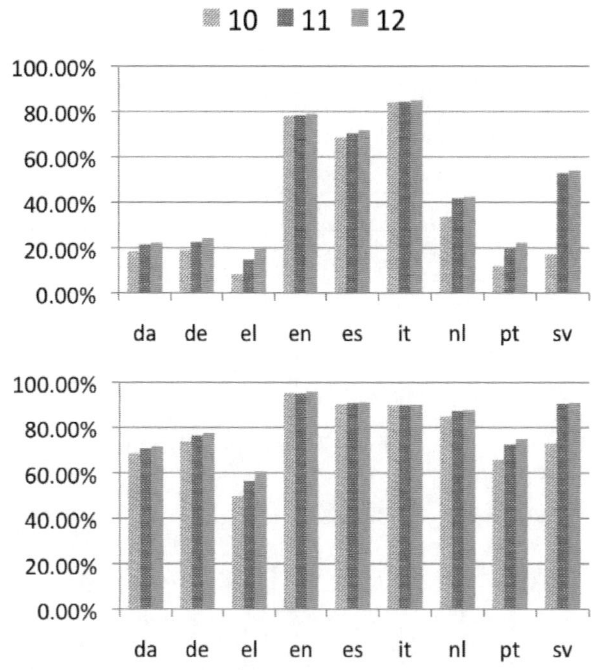

Figure 2: Type-level (top) and token-level (bottom) coverage for the nine languages in three versions of the Wiktionary.

We also compared the coverage provided by the Wiktionary versus the Penn Treebank (PTB) extracted dictionary on the Brown corpus. Figure 4 shows that the Wiktionary provides a greater coverage for all sections of the Brown corpus, hence being a better dictionary for tagging English text in general. This is also reflected in the gain in accuracy on Brown over the taggers learned from the PTB dictionary in our experiments.

3.4 Wiktionary accuracy

A more refined notion of quality is the accuracy of the tag sets for covered words, as measured against dictionaries extracted from labeled tree bank corpora. We consider word types that are in both the Wiktionary (W) and the tree bank dictionaries (T). For each word type, we compare the two tag sets and distinguish five different possibilities:

1. Identical: $W = T$
2. Superset: $W \supset T$
3. Subset: $W \subset T$
4. Overlap: $W \cap T \neq \emptyset$

<table>
<tr><th colspan="4">Wiktionary Entries</th><th rowspan="2">Universal POS Set</th></tr>
<tr><th>Language</th><th>Word</th><th>POS</th><th>Definition</th></tr>
<tr><td>English</td><td>today</td><td>Adverb</td><td># In the current [[era]]; nowadays.</td><td rowspan="3">{ADV, NOUN}</td></tr>
<tr><td>English</td><td>today</td><td>Adverb</td><td># On the current [[day]] or [[date]].</td></tr>
<tr><td>English</td><td>today</td><td>Noun</td><td># A current day or date.</td></tr>
<tr><td>German</td><td>achtzig</td><td>Numeral</td><td># [[eighty]]</td><td>{NUM}</td></tr>
<tr><td>Swedish</td><td>SCB</td><td>Acronym</td><td># [[statistiska]] ...</td><td>{NOUN}</td></tr>
<tr><td>Portuguese</td><td>nessa</td><td>Contraction</td><td># {{contraction ...</td><td>discard entry</td></tr>
</table>

Table 1: Examples of constructing Universal POS tag sets from the Wiktionary.

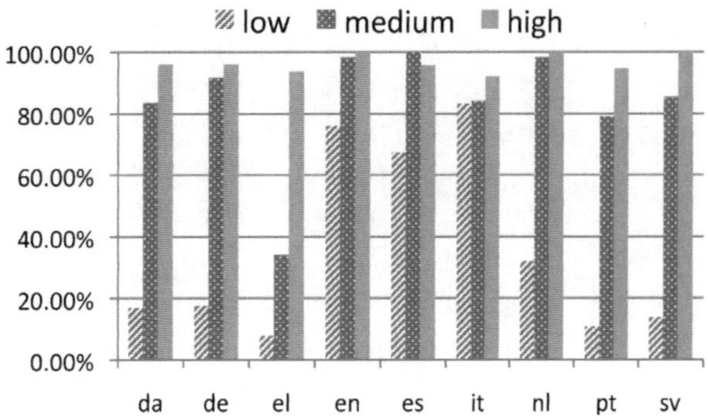

Figure 3: Word type coverage by normalized frequency: words are grouped by word count / highest word count ratio: low [0, 0.01), medium [0.01, 0.1), high [0.1, 1].

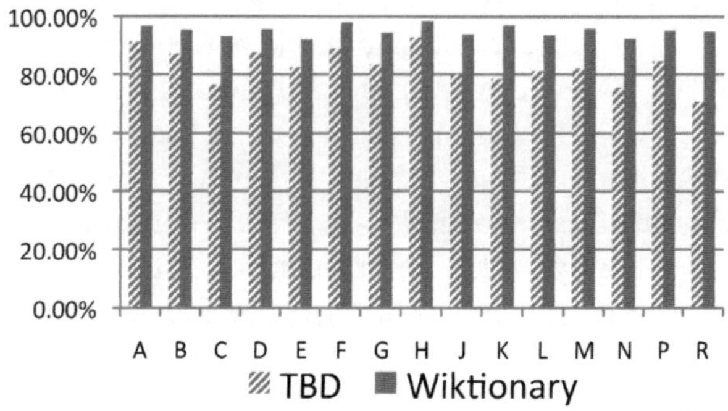

Figure 4: PTB vs. Wiktionary type coverage across sections of the Brown corpus.

5. Disjoint: $W \cap T = \emptyset$.

In Figure 5, the word types are grouped into the categories described above. Most of the tag sets (around 90%) in the Wiktionary are identical to or supersets of the tree bank tag sets for our nine languages, which is surprisingly accurate. About 10% of the Wiktionary tag sets are subsets of, partially overlapping with, or disjoint from the tree bank tag sets. Our learning methods, which assume the given tag sets are correct, may be somewhat hurt by these word types, as we discuss in Section 5.6.

4 Models

Our basic models are first and second order Hidden Markov Models (HMM and SHMM). We also used feature-based max-ent emission models with both (HMM-ME and SHMM-ME). Below, we denote the sequence of words in a sentence as boldface $\mathbf{x}$ and the sequence of hidden states which correspond to part-of-speech tags as boldface $\mathbf{y}$. To simplify notation, we assume that every tag sequence is prefixed with two conventional start tags $y_0 = \texttt{start}, y_{-1} = \texttt{start}$, allowing us to write as $p(y_1|y_0, y_{-1})$ the initial state probability of the SHMM.

The probability of a sentence $\mathbf{x}$ along with a particular hidden state sequence $\mathbf{y}$ in the SHMM is given by:

$$p(\mathbf{x}, \mathbf{y}) = \prod_{i=1}^{\text{length}(\mathbf{x})} p_t(y_i \mid y_{i-1}, y_{i-2}) p_o(x_i \mid y_i), \tag{1}$$

where $p_o(x_i \mid y_i)$ is the probability of observing word x_i in state y_i (emission probability), and $p_t(y_i \mid y_{i-1}, y_{i-2})$ is the probability of being in state y_i, given two previous states y_{i-1}, y_{i-2} (transition probability).

In this work, we compare multinomial and maximum entropy (log-linear) emission models. Specifically, the max-ent emission model is:

$$p_o(x|y) = \frac{\exp(\theta \cdot \mathbf{f}(x, y))}{\sum_{x'} \exp(\theta \cdot \mathbf{f}(x', y))} \tag{2}$$

where $\mathbf{f}(x, y)$ is a feature function, x ranges over all

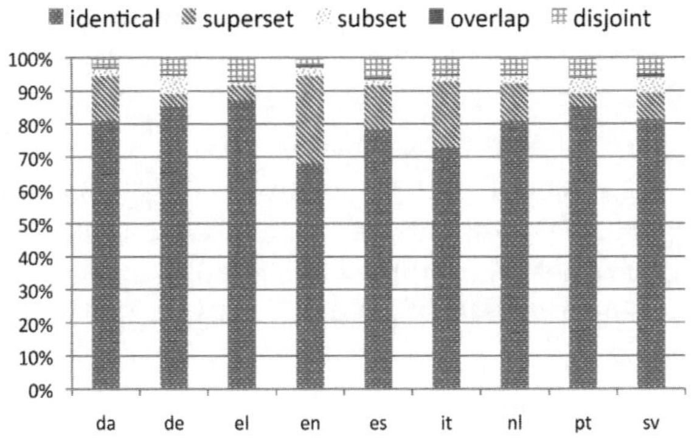

Figure 5: The Wiktionary vs. tree bank tag sets. Around 90% of the Wiktionary tag sets are identical or subsume tree bank tag sets. See text for details.

word types, and θ are the model parameters. We use the following feature templates:

- Word identity - lowercased word form if the word appears more than 10 times in the corpus.
- Hyphen - word contains a hyphen
- Capital - word is uppercased
- Suffix - last 2 and 3 letters of a word if they appear in more than 20 different word types.
- Number - word contains a digit

The idea of replacing the multinomial models of an HMM by maximum entropy models has been applied before in different domains (Chen, 2003), as well as in POS induction (Berg-Kirkpatrick et al., 2010; Graça et al., 2011).

We use the EM algorithm to learn the models, restricting the tags of each word to those specified by the dictionary. For each tag y, the observations probabilities $p_o(x \mid y)$ were initialized randomly for every word type that allows tag y according to the Wiktionary and zero otherwise. For the M-step in max-ent models, there is no closed form solution so we need to solve an unconstrained optimization problem. We use L-BFGS with Wolfe's rule line search (Nocedal and Wright, 1999). We found that EM achieved higher accuracy across languages compared to direct gradient approach (Berg-Kirkpatrick et al., 2010).

5 Results

We evaluate the accuracy of taggers trained using the Wiktionary using the 4 different models: A first order Hidden Markov Model (HMM), a second order Hidden Markov Model (SHMM), a first order Hidden Markov Model with Maximum Entropy emission models (HMM-ME) and a second order Hidden Markov Model with Maximum Entropy emission models (SHMM-ME). For each model we ran EM for 50 iterations, which was sufficient for convergence of the likelihood. Following previous work (Graça et al., 2011), we used a Gaussian prior with variance of 10 for the max-ent model parameters. We obtain hard assignments using posterior decoding, where for each position we pick the label with highest posterior probability: this produces small but consistent improvements over Viterbi decoding.

5.1 Upper and lower bounds

We situate our results against several upper bounds that use more supervision. We trained the SHMM-ME model with a dictionary built from the training and test tree bank (ALL TBD) and also with tree bank dictionary intersected with the Wiktionary (Covered TBD). The Covered TBD dictionary is more supervised than the Wiktionary in the sense that some of the tag set mismatches of the Wiktionary are cleaned using the true corpus tags. We also report results from training the SHMM-ME in the standard supervised fashion, using 50 (50 Sent.), 100 (100 Sent.) and all sentences (All Sent.).

As a lower bound we include the results for unsupervised systems: a regular HMM model trained with EM (Johnson, 2007) and an HMM model using a ME emission model trained using direct gradient (Berg-Kirkpatrick et al., 2010)[3].

5.2 Bilingual baselines

Finally, we also compare our system against a strong set of baselines that use bilingual data. These approaches build a dictionary by transferring labeled data from a resource rich language (English) to a resource poor language (Das and Petrov, 2011). We compare against two such methods. The first, *projection*, builds a dictionary by transferring the pos

[3]Values for these systems where taken from the D&P paper.

tags from English to the new language using word alignments. The second method, *D&P*, is the current state-of-the-art system, and runs label propagation on the dictionary resulting from the *projected* method. We note that both of these approaches are orthogonal to ours and could be used simultaneously with the Wiktionary.

5.3 Analysis

Table 2 shows results for the different models across languages. We note that the results are not directly comparable since both the Unsupervised and the Bilingual results use a different setup, using the number of fine grained tags for each language as hidden states instead of 12 (as we do). This greatly increases the degrees of freedom of the model allowing it to capture more fine grained distinctions.

The first two observations are that using the ME entropy emission model always improves over the standard multinomial model, and using a second order model always performs better. Comparing with the work of *D&P*, we see that our model achieves better accuracy on average and on 5 out of 8 languages.

The most common errors are due to tag set idiosyncrasies. For instance, for English the symbol % is tagged as NUM by our system while in the Penn treebank it is tagged as Noun. Other common mistakes for English include tagging *to* as an adposition (preposition) instead of particle and tagging *which* as a pronoun instead of determiner. In the next subsections we analyze the errors in more detail.

Finally, for English we also trained the SHMM-ME model using the Celex2 dictionary available from LDC[4]. Celex2 coverage for the PTB corpus is much smaller than the coverage provided by the Wiktionary (43.8% type coverage versus 80.0%). Correspondingly, the accuracy of the model trained using Celex2 is 75.5% compared 87.1% when trained using the Wiktionary.

5.4 Performance vs. Wiktionary ambiguity

While many words overwhelmingly appear with one tag in a given genre, in the Wiktionary a large proportion of words are annotated with several tags, even when those are extremely rare events. Around 35% of word types in English have more than one tag according to the Wiktionary. This increases the difficulty of predicting the correct tag as compared to having a corpus-based dictionary, where words have a smaller level of ambiguity. For example, in English, for words with one tag, the accuracy is 95% (the reason it is not 100% is due to a discrepancy between the Wiktionary and the tree bank.) For words with two possible tags, accuracy is 81% and for three tags, it drops to 63%.

5.5 Generalization to unknown words

Comparing the performance of the proposed model for words in the Wiktionary against words not in the Wiktionary, we see an average drop from 89% to 63% for out-of-vocabulary words across nine languages. Table 2 shows that the average loss of accuracy between All TBD and Covered TBD of 4.5% (which is due purely to decrease in coverage) is larger than the loss between Covered TBD and the best Wiktionary model, of 3.2% (which is due to tag set inconsistency).

One advantage of the Wiktionary is that it is a general purpose dictionary and not tailored for a particular domain. To illustrate this we compared several models on the Brown corpus: the SHMM-ME model using the Wiktionary (Wik), against using a model trained using a dictionary extracted from the PTB corpus (PTBD), or trained fully supervised using the PTB corpus (PTB). We tested all these models on the 15 different sections of the Brown corpus. We also compare against a state-of-the-art POS-tagger tagger (ST)[5].

Figure 6 shows the accuracy results for each model on the different sections. The fully supervised SHMM-ME model did not perform as well as the the Stanford tagger (about 3% behind on average), most likely because of generative vs. discriminate training of the two models and feature differences. However, quite surprisingly, the Wiktionary-tag-set-trained model performs much better not only than the PTB-tag-set-trained model but also the supervised model on the Brown corpus.

[4] http://www.ldc.upenn.edu/Catalog/catalogEntry.jsp?catalogId=LDC96L14

[5] Available at http://nlp.stanford.edu/software/tagger.shtml

		Danish	Dutch	German	Greek	English	Italian	Portuguese	Spanish	Swedish	*avg.*
Unsupervised	HMM	68.7	57.0	75.9	65.8		63.7	62.9	71.5	68.4	*66.7*
	HMM-ME	69.1	65.1	81.3	71.8		68.1	78.4	80.2	70.1	*73.0*
Bilingual	Projection	73.6	77.0	83.2	79.3		79.7	82.6	80.1	74.7	*78.8*
	D&P	83.2	79.5	82.8	**82.5**		**86.8**	**87.9**	84.2	80.5	*83.4*
Wiktionary	HMM	71.8	80.8	77.1	73.1	85.4	84.6	79.1	83.9	76.7	*78.4*
	HMM-ME	82.8	86.1	81.2	80.1	86.1	85.4	83.7	84.6	85.9	*83.7*
	SHMM	74.5	81.6	81.2	73.1	85.0	85.2	79.9	84.5	78.7	*79.8*
	SHMM-ME	**83.3**	**86.3**	**85.8**	79.2	**87.1**	86.5	84.5	**86.4**	**86.1**	***84.8***
Supervised	Covered TBD	90.1	91.4	89.4	79.7	92.7	86.3	91.5	85.1	91.0	*88.6*
	All TBD	93.6	91.2	95.6	87.9	90.6	92.9	91.2	92.1	83.8	*91.0*
	50 Sent.	65.3	48.5	74.5	74.2	70.2	76.2	79.2	76.2	54.7	*68.6*
	100 Sent.	73.9	52.3	80.9	81.6	77.3	75.3	82.0	80.1	64.8	*73.9*
	All Sent.	93.9	90.9	97.4	95.1	95.8	93.8	95.5	93.8	95.5	*94.5*

Table 2: Accuracy for Unsupervised, Bilingual, Wiktionary and Supervised models. Avg. is the average of all languages except English. Unsupervised models are trained without dictionary and use an oracle to map tags to clusters. Bilingual systems are trained using a dictionary transferred from English into the target language using word alignments. The *Projection* model uses a dictionary build directly from the part-of-speech projection. The *D&P* model extends the *Projection* model dictionary by using Label Propagation. Supervised models are trained using tree bank information with SHMM-ME: Covered TBD used tree bank tag set for the words only if they are also in the Wiktionary and All TBD uses tree bank tag sets for all words. 50, 100 and All Sent. models are trained in a supervised manner using increasing numbers of training sentences.

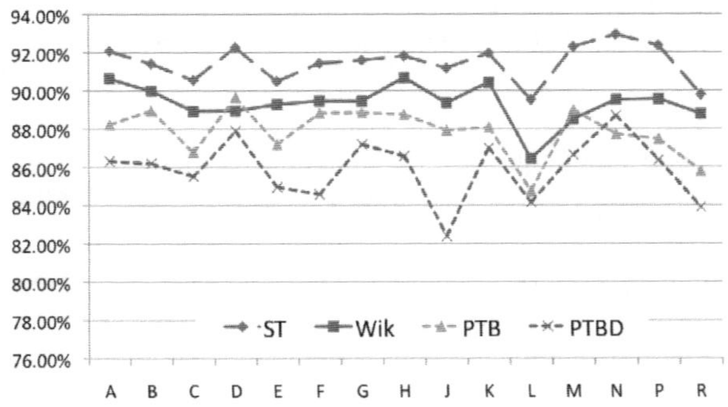

Figure 6: Model accuracy across the Brown corpus sections. ST: Stanford tagger, Wik: Wiktionary-tag-set-trained SHMM-ME, PTBD: PTB-tag-set-trained SHMM-ME, PTB: Supervised SHMM-ME. Wik outperforms PTB and PTBD overall.

5.6 Error breakdown

In Section 3.4 we discussed the accuracy of the Wiktionary tag sets and as Table 2 shows, a dictionary with better tag set quality generally (except for Greek) improves the POS tagging accuracy. In Figure 7, we group actual errors by the word type classified into the five cases discussed above: identical, superset, subset, overlap, disjoint. We also add oov – out-of-vocabulary word types. The largest source of error across languages are out-of-vocabulary (oov) word types at around 45% of the errors, followed by tag set mismatch types: subset, overlap, disjoint, which together comprise another 50% of the errors. As Wiktionary grows, these types of errors will likely diminish.

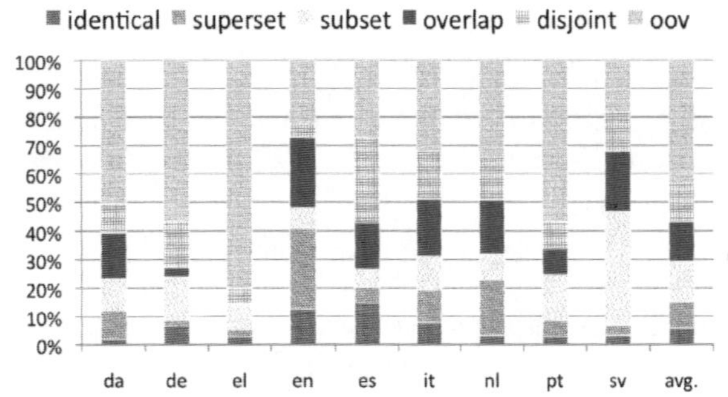

Figure 7: Tag errors broken down by the word type classified into the six classes: oov, identical, superset, subset, overlap, disjoint (see text for detail). The largest source of error across languages are out-of-vocabulary (oov) word types, followed by tag set mismatch types: subset, overlap, disjoint.

6 Conclusion

We have shown that the Wiktionary can be used to train a very simple model to achieve state-of-art weakly-supervised and out-of-domain POS taggers. The methods outlined in the paper are standard and easy to replicate, yet highly accurate and should serve as baselines for more complex proposals. These encouraging results show that using free, collaborative NLP resources can in fact produce results of the same level or better than using expensive annotations for many languages. Furthermore, the Wiktionary contains other possibly useful information, such as glosses and translations. It would be very interesting and perhaps necessary to incorporate this additional data in order to tackle challenges that arise across a larger number of language types, specifically non-European languages.

Acknowledgements

We would like to thank Slav Petrov, Kuzman Ganchev and André Martins for their helpful feedback in early versions of the manuscript. We would also like to thank to our anonymous reviewers for their comments and suggestions. Ben Taskar was partially supported by a Sloan Fellowship, ONR 2010 Young Investigator Award and NSF Grant 1116676.

References

A. Abeillé. 2003. *Treebanks: Building and Using Parsed Corpora*. Springer.

Taylor Berg-Kirkpatrick, Alexandre Bouchard-Côté, John DeNero, and Dan Klein. 2010. Painless unsupervised learning with features. In *Proc. NAACL*, June.

John Blitzer, Ryan McDonald, and Fernando Pereira. 2006. Domain adaptation with structural correspondence learning. In *Conference on Empirical Methods in Natural Language Processing*, Sydney, Australia.

Peter F. Brown, Peter V. deSouza, Robert L. Mercer, Vincent J. Della Pietra, and Jenifer C. Lai. 1992. Class-based n-gram models of natural language. *Computational Linguistics*, 18:467–479.

S. Buchholz and E. Marsi. 2006. Conll-x shared task on multilingual dependency parsing. In *Proceedings of the Tenth Conference on Computational Natural Language Learning*, pages 149–164. Association for Computational Linguistics.

S.F. Chen. 2003. Conditional and joint models for grapheme-to-phoneme conversion. In *Proc. ECSCT*.

P. Chesley, B. Vincent, L. Xu, and R.K. Srihari. 2006. Using verbs and adjectives to automatically classify blog sentiment. *Training*, 580(263):233.

Alexander Clark. 2003. Combining distributional and morphological information for part of speech induction. In *Proc. EACL*.

Dipanjan Das and Slav Petrov. 2011. Unsupervised part-of-speech tagging with bilingual graph-based projections. In *Proceedings of the 49th Annual Meeting of the Association for Computational Linguistics: Human Language Technologies*, pages 600–609, Portland, Oregon, USA, June. Association for Computational Linguistics.

Weiwei Ding. 2011. Weakly supervised part-of-speech tagging for chinese using label propagation. Master's thesis, University of Texas at Austin.

Jianfeng Gao and Mark Johnson. 2008. A comparison of Bayesian estimators for unsupervised hidden Markov model POS taggers. In *In Proc. EMNLP*, pages 344–352, Honolulu, Hawaii, October. ACL.

S. Goldwater and T. Griffiths. 2007. A fully Bayesian approach to unsupervised part-of-speech tagging. In *In Proc. ACL*, volume 45, page 744.

J.V. Graça, K. Ganchev, L. Coheur, F. Pereira, and B. Taskar. 2011. Controlling complexity in part-of-speech induction. *Journal of Artificial Intelligence Research*, 41(2):527–551.

J. Graça, K. Ganchev, F. Pereira, and B. Taskar. 2009. Parameter vs. posterior sparisty in latent variable models. In *Proc. NIPS*.

A. Haghighi and D. Klein. 2006. Prototype-driven learning for sequence models. In *Proc. HTL-NAACL*. ACL.

M Johnson. 2007. Why doesn't EM find good HMM POS-taggers. In *In Proc. EMNLP-CoNLL*.

AA Krizhanovsky and F. Lin. 2009. Related terms search based on wordnet/wiktionary and its application in ontology matching. *Arxiv preprint arXiv:0907.2209*.

Michael Lamar, Yariv Maron, Mark Johnson, and Elie Bienenstock. 2010. SVD and clustering for unsupervised POS tagging. In *Proceedings of the ACL 2010 Conference: Short Papers*, pages 215–219, Uppsala, Sweden, July. Association for Computational Linguistics.

Yoong Keok Lee, Aria Haghighi, and Regina Barzilay. 2010. Simple type-level unsupervised POS tagging. In *Proceedings of the 2010 Conference on Empirical Methods in Natural Language Processing*, pages 853–861, Cambridge, MA, October. Association for Computational Linguistics.

M.P. Marcus, M.A. Marcinkiewicz, and B. Santorini. 1993. Building a large annotated corpus of English: The Penn Treebank. *Computational linguistics*, 19(2):313–330.

B. Merialdo. 1994. Tagging English text with a probabilistic model. *Computational linguistics*, 20(2):155–171.

C. Müller and I. Gurevych. 2009. Using wikipedia and wiktionary in domain-specific information retrieval.

Evaluating Systems for Multilingual and Multimodal Information Access, pages 219–226.

E. Navarro, F. Sajous, B. Gaume, L. Prévot, H. ShuKai, K. Tzu-Yi, P. Magistry, and H. Chu-Ren. 2009. Wiktionary and nlp: Improving synonymy networks. In *Proceedings of the 2009 Workshop on The People's Web Meets NLP: Collaboratively Constructed Semantic Resources*, pages 19–27. Association for Computational Linguistics.

J. Nivre, J. Hall, S. Kübler, R. McDonald, J. Nilsson, S. Riedel, and D. Yuret. 2007. The conll 2007 shared task on dependency parsing. In *Proceedings of the CoNLL Shared Task Session of EMNLP-CoNLL 2007*. Association for Computational Linguistics.

J. Nocedal and Stephen J. Wright. 1999. *Numerical optimization*. Springer.

S. Petrov, D. Das, and R. McDonald. 2011. A universal part-of-speech tagset. *Arxiv preprint ArXiv:1104.2086*.

A. Ratnaparkhi. 1996. A maximum entropy model for part-of-speech tagging. In *Proc. EMNLP*. ACL.

Sujith Ravi and Kevin Knight. 2009. Minimized models for unsupervised part-of-speech tagging. In *In Proc. ACL*.

H. Schütze. 1995. Distributional part-of-speech tagging. In *Proc. EACL*, pages 141–148.

Libin Shen, Giorgio Satta, and Aravind Joshi. 2007. Guided learning for bidirectional sequence classification. In *Proc. ACL*, Prague, Czech Republic, June.

N. Smith and J. Eisner. 2005. Contrastive estimation: Training log-linear models on unlabeled data. In *Proc. ACL*. ACL.

B. Snyder, T. Naseem, J. Eisenstein, and R. Barzilay. 2008. Unsupervised multilingual learning for POS tagging. In *Proceedings of the Conference on Empirical Methods in Natural Language Processing*, pages 1041–1050. Association for Computational Linguistics.

K. Toutanova and M. Johnson. 2007. A Bayesian LDA-based model for semi-supervised part-of-speech tagging. *In Proc. NIPS*, 20.

K. Toutanova, D. Klein, C. Manning, and Y. Singer. 2003. Feature-rich part-of-speech tagging with a cyclic dependency network. In *In Proc. HLT-NAACL*.

Joining Forces Pays Off: Multilingual Joint Word Sense Disambiguation

Roberto Navigli and **Simone Paolo Ponzetto**
Dipartimento di Informatica
Sapienza Università di Roma
{navigli,ponzetto}@di.uniroma1.it

Abstract

We present a multilingual joint approach to Word Sense Disambiguation (WSD). Our method exploits BabelNet, a very large multilingual knowledge base, to perform graph-based WSD across different languages, and brings together empirical evidence from these languages using ensemble methods. The results show that, thanks to complementing wide-coverage multilingual lexical knowledge with robust graph-based algorithms and combination methods, we are able to achieve the state of the art in both monolingual and multilingual WSD settings.

1 Introduction

Nowadays the textual information needed by a user accessing websites for content such as news reports, commentaries and encyclopedic knowledge is provided in an increasingly wide range of languages. For example, even though English is still the majority language of the Web, the Chinese and Spanish languages are moving fast to capture their "juicy share", and more languages are about to join them in the near future. This language explosion clearly forces researchers to focus on the challenging problem of being able to analyze and understand text written in any language. However, it also opens up novel perspectives for multilingual Natural Language Processing (NLP) such as, for instance, the development of approaches aimed at "joining forces" and taking advantage of the lexico-semantic knowledge provided in the different languages to improve text understanding. These two aspects are strongly intertwined: on the one hand, enabling language-independent text understanding would allow for the harvesting of more knowledge in arbitrary languages, while, on the other hand, bringing together the lexical and semantic information available in different languages would improve the quality of text understanding in arbitrary languages.

However, these two goals have hitherto never been achieved, as is attested to by the fact that research in a core language understanding task such as Word Sense Disambiguation (Navigli, 2009, WSD) has always been focused mostly on English. Historically, English became established as the language used and understood by the scientific community and, consequently, most resources were developed for it, including large-scale computational lexicons like WordNet (Fellbaum, 1998) and sense-tagged corpora like SemCor (Miller et al., 1993). As a result WSD in other languages was hindered by a lack of resources, which in turn led to poor results or low involvement on the part of the research community (Magnini et al., 2004; Màrquez et al., 2004; Orhan et al., 2007; Okumura et al., 2010). Nonetheless, already in the 1990s it had been remarked that WSD could be improved by means of multilingual information: a recurring idea proposed by several researchers was that plausible translations of a word in context would restrict its possible senses to a manageable subset of meanings (Dagan et al., 1991; Gale et al., 1992; Resnik and Yarowsky, 1999). While the lack of resources at that time hampered the development of effective multilingual approaches to WSD, recently this idea has been revamped with the organization of SemEval tasks dealing with cross-lingual WSD (Lefever and Hoste, 2010) and cross-lingual lexical substitution (Mihalcea et al., 2010). At the same time, new research on the topic has been done, including the use of statistical translations of sentences into many languages as features for supervised models (Banea and Mihalcea, 2011; Lefever et al., 2011), and the projection of monolingual knowledge onto another language (Khapra et al., 2011).

Yet the above two goals, i.e., disambiguating in an arbitrary language and using lexical and semantic knowledge from many languages in a joint way to improve the WSD task, have not hitherto been attained. In this paper, we address both objectives and propose a graph-based approach to multilingual joint Word Sense Disambiguation. Our proposal brings together the lexical knowledge from different languages by exploiting empirical evidence for disambiguation from each of them, and then combining this information in a synergistic way: each language provides a piece of sense evidence for the meaning of a target word in context, and subsequent integration of these various pieces enables them to (soft) constrain each other. The results show that this way we are able to improve over previous, high-performing graph-based methods in both a monolingual and multilingual setting, thus showing for the first time the beneficial effects of exploiting multilingual knowledge in a joint fashion.

2 Related Work

Parallel corpora have been used in the literature for the automatic creation of a sense-tagged dataset for supervised WSD in different languages (Gale et al., 1992; Chan and Ng, 2005; Zhong and Ng, 2009). Other approaches include the use of a coherence index for identifying the tendency to lexicalize senses differently across languages (Ide, 2000) and the clustering of source words which translate into the same target word, then used to perform WSD using a similarity measure (Diab, 2003). A historical approach (Brown et al., 1991) uses bilingual corpora to perform unsupervised word alignment and determine the most appropriate translation for a target word from a set of contextual features.

All the above approaches to multilingual or cross-lingual WSD rely on bilingual corpora, including those which exploit existing multilingual WordNet-like resources (Ide et al., 2002), or use automatically induced multilingual co-occurrence graphs (Silberer and Ponzetto, 2010). However, this requirement is often very hard to satisfy, especially if we need wide coverage. To overcome this limitation, in this work we make use of BabelNet (Navigli and Ponzetto, 2010), a very large multilingual lexical knowledge base. This resource – complementary in nature to other recent efforts presented by de Melo and Weikum (2010), Nastase et al. (2010) and Meyer and Gurevych (2012), *inter alia* – provides a truly multilingual semantic network by combining Wikipedia's multilinguality with the output of a state-of-the-art machine translation system to achieve high coverage for all languages. The key insight here is that Word Sense Disambiguation and Machine Translation (MT) are highly intertwined tasks, as previously shown by Carpuat and Wu (2007) and Chan et al. (2007), who successfully used sense information to boost state-of-the-art statistical MT. In this work we focus instead on the benefits of using multilingual information for WSD by exploiting the structure of a multilingual semantic network.

3 Multilingual Joint WSD

We present our methodology for multilingual WSD: we first introduce BabelNet, the resource used in our work (Section 3.1) and then present our algorithm for multilingual joint WSD (Section 3.2), including its main components, namely graph-based WSD, ensemble methods and translation weighting (sections 3.3, 3.4 and 3.5).

3.1 BabelNet

BabelNet (Navigli and Ponzetto, 2010) follows the structure of a traditional lexical knowledge base and, accordingly, consists of a labeled directed graph whose nodes represent concepts and named entities, and whose edges express semantic relations between them. Concepts and relations are harvested from the largest available semantic lexicon of English, i.e., WordNet, and a wide-coverage collaboratively-edited encyclopedia, i.e., Wikipedia[1], thus making BabelNet a multilingual 'encyclopedic dictionary' which combines lexicographic information with encyclopedic knowledge on the basis of an unsupervised mapping framework. In addition to a core

[1] `http://www.wikipedia.org`. In the following, we refer to Wikipedia pages and senses using SMALL CAPS.

semantic network, BabelNet provides a multilingual lexical dimension. Each of its nodes, called *Babel synsets*, contains a set of lexicalizations of the concept for different languages, e.g., { $\textsf{bank}_n^{\text{EN}}$, $\textsf{Bank}_n^{\text{DE}}$, $\textsf{banca}_n^{\text{IT}}$, ..., $\textsf{banco}_n^{\text{ES}}$ }[2]. Multilingual lexicalizations for all concepts are collected from Wikipedia's inter-language links (e.g., the English Wikipedia page BANK links to the Italian BANCA), as well as by acquiring missing translations by means of a statistical machine translation system applied to sense-tagged data from SemCor and Wikipedia itself – for instance, most occurrences of $\textsf{bank}_n^1$ in SemCor[3] are translated into German and Italian as Ufer and riva, respectively. As a result of combining human-edited translations from Wikipedia and automatically generated ones from sense-labeled data, BabelNet is able to achieve wide coverage for all its languages (Catalan, English, French, German, Italian and Spanish): accordingly, we chose it to perform graph-based WSD in a multilingual setting since it is specifically focused on lexical knowledge. In addition, BabelNet is available for any language required to perform standard SemEval cross-lingual disambiguation tasks (e.g., Spanish, in order to perform cross-lingual lexical substitution). Since previous work in knowledge-based WSD shows the benefits of using rich lexical resources (Navigli and Lapata, 2010; Ponzetto and Navigli, 2010), BabelNet is a suitable choice for performing graph-based multilingual WSD.

3.2 Exploiting multilingual information in a knowledge-based WSD framework

We present a multilingual approach to WSD which exploits three main factors:

i) the fact that translations of a target word provide complementary information on the range of its candidate senses in context;

ii) the wide-coverage, multilingual lexical knowledge stored in BabelNet;

iii) the support for disambiguation from different languages in a synergistic, unified way.

Algorithm 1 Multilingual joint WSD

Input: a word sequence $\sigma = (w_1, \ldots, w_n)$
a target word $w \in \sigma$
BabelNet BN
an ensemble method M

Output: a distribution of scores for the senses of w

($\triangleright$ indicates a comment)

$S \leftarrow Synsets_{BN}(w)$
$T \leftarrow \{w\}$
for each $s \in S$
  $T \leftarrow T \cup getTranslations(s)$
$ctx \leftarrow \sigma - \{w\}$
$\triangleright$ $LScore := \{lScore_{i,j}\}_{i=1,\ldots,|T|,\ j=1,\ldots,|S|}$
for each $t_i \in T$
  $\sigma' \leftarrow \{t_i\} \cup ctx$
  $\triangleright$ $G_i := (V_i, E_i)$
  $G_i \leftarrow createGraph(\sigma', BN)$
  for each $s_j \in S \cap V_i$
    $lScore_{i,j} \leftarrow score(G_i, s_j)$
$\triangleright$ $Score := (score_1, \ldots, score_{|S|})$
$Score \leftarrow M(LScore)$
return $Score$

We call this approach *multilingual joint WSD*, since disambiguation is performed by exploiting different languages *together at the same time*. To this end, we first perform graph-based WSD using the target word in context as input, and then combine sense evidence from its translations using an ensemble method. The key idea of our joint approach is that sense evidence from different translations provides complementary views for the senses of a target word in context. Therefore, combining such evidence should produce more accurate sense predictions. We view WSD as a sense ranking problem. Given a word sequence $\sigma = (w_1, \ldots, w_n)$, we disambiguate a target word $w \in \sigma$ by scoring each of its senses and selecting the highest-ranking one:

$$\hat{s} = \operatorname*{arg\,max}_{s \,\in\, Synsets_{BN}(w)} score(s)\ , \qquad (1)$$

where $Synsets_{BN}(w)$ is the set of Babel synsets containing the different senses for w.[4] We score these

[2] BabelNet senses are referred to with $\textsf{w}_p^l$, namely the sense of a word w in a language l with part of speech p.

[3] We denote WordNet senses with $\textsf{w}_p^i$, namely the i-th sense of a word w with part of speech p.

[4] Babel synsets unambiguously identify different senses of the target word, e.g., { $\textsf{bank}_n^{\text{EN}}$, $\textsf{Bank}_n^{\text{DE}}$, $\textsf{banco}_n^{\text{ES}}$ ..., $\textsf{banca}_n^{\text{IT}}$ } corresponds to the 'financial institute' sense of $\textsf{bank}_n^{\text{EN}}$ (i.e., $\textsf{bank}_n^2$ in WordNet).

synsets using Algorithm 1, which we illustrate in the following by means of the example sentence '*bank bonuses are paid in stock*', where we focus on $\text{bank}_n^{\text{EN}}$ as the target word and { $\text{bonus}_n^{\text{EN}}$, pay_v^{EN}, $\text{stock}_n^{\text{EN}}$ } as its context. The following steps are performed:

Initialization. We start by gathering the data required for disambiguation (lines 1–5). First, we collect in line 1 the set S of Babel synsets corresponding to the different senses of the target word w – namely, the synsets containing the 'financial institution', 'money container', 'building' senses of $\text{bank}_n^{\text{EN}}$, among others. Next, we obtain the multilingual lexicalizations of the target word: to this end, we first include in T the word w itself (line 2), and then iterate through each synset $s \in S$ to collect the translations of each of its senses in the languages of interest (lines 3–4). For instance, given the English word $\text{bank}_n^{\text{EN}}$, we collect its sense-specific German, Italian and Spanish translations and obtain a set of multilingual terms T = { $\text{bank}_n^{\text{EN}}$, ..., $\text{Bank}_n^{\text{DE}}$, $\text{Sparbüchse}_n^{\text{DE}}$, $\text{Bankgebäude}_n^{\text{DE}}$, ..., $\text{banca}_n^{\text{IT}}$, $\text{salvadanaio}_n^{\text{IT}}$, ..., $\text{banco}_n^{\text{ES}}$, $\text{hucha}_n^{\text{ES}}$ }. Finally, we create a disambiguation context ctx by taking the word sequence σ and removing w from it (line 5, as a result, e.g., ctx = { $\text{bonus}_n^{\text{EN}}$, pay_v^{EN}, $\text{stock}_n^{\text{EN}}$ }).

Collecting sense distributions. In the next phase (lines 6–12), we collect a scoring distribution over the different synsets S of w for each term $t_i \in T$. Each distribution quantifies the empirical support for the different senses of the target word, obtained using t_i and the context ctx: we store this information in a $|T| \times |S|$ matrix $LScore$, where each cell $lScore_{i,j}$ quantifies the support for synset $s_j \in S$, computed using the term in $t_i \in T$. We calculate the scores as follows:

- We select at each step an element t_i from T (line 7), for instance $\text{banco}_n^{\text{ES}}$.
- Next, we create a multilingual context σ' by combining t_i with the words in ctx (line 8, e.g., we set σ' = { $\text{banco}_n^{\text{ES}}$, $\text{bonus}_n^{\text{EN}}$, pay_v^{EN}, $\text{stock}_n^{\text{EN}}$ }.
- We use σ' to build a graph $G_i = (V_i, E_i)$ by computing the paths in BabelNet which connect the synsets of t_i with those of the other words in σ' (line 10, see Section 3.3 for details on the $createGraph$ function). Note that by selecting at each step a different element from T we create a new graph where different sets of Babel synsets get activated by the context words in ctx. In our example, Figures 1(a)–(c) show the graphs obtained by setting at different steps t_i to $\text{bank}_n^{\text{EN}}$, $\text{banco}_n^{\text{ES}}$ and $\text{Bank}_n^{\text{DE}}$, respectively (we show excerpts by using only $\text{stock}_n^{\text{EN}}$ as context word for ease of readability).
- Finally, we compute the support from term t_i for each synset $s_j \in S$ of the target word by applying a graph connectivity measure to G_i and store the result in $lScore_{i,j}$ (lines 11–12). For instance, using degree as graph measure, we can compute the following scores from the graph in Figure 1(b):

	bank_n^2	bank_n^8	bank_n^9
$\text{banco}_n^{\text{ES}}$	2	0	1

By repeating the process for each term in T (lines 7–12) we compute all values in the matrix $LScore$. For instance, given $T = \{\text{bank}_n^{\text{EN}}, \text{banco}_n^{\text{ES}}, \text{Bank}_n^{\text{DE}}\}$, we create the set of graphs in Figures 1(a)–(c), and compute from each of them the following scores (again, using degree as scoring measure):

$$LScore = \begin{array}{c} \\ \text{bank}_n^{\text{EN}} \\ \text{banco}_n^{\text{ES}} \\ \text{Bank}_n^{\text{DE}} \end{array} \begin{array}{c} \begin{array}{ccc} \text{bank}_n^2 & \text{bank}_n^8 & \text{bank}_n^9 \end{array} \\ \begin{bmatrix} 2 & 2 & 1 \\ 2 & 0 & 1 \\ 2 & 0 & 0 \end{bmatrix} \end{array}$$

Combining sense distributions. In the last step (line 14) we aggregate the scores associated with each term of T using an ensemble method M (see Section 3.4 for details). For instance, M could simply consist of summing the scores associated with each sense over all distributions and thus return a score of 6, 2, and 2 for bank_n^2, bank_n^8 and bank_n^9, respectively. As a result of the execution of Algorithm 1, the combined scoring distribution is returned (line 15). This sense distribution in turn can be used to select the best sense using Equation 1.

The main hunch behind our approach is that using information from different languages improves disambiguation performance, as in the example of Figure 1 where more accurate disambiguation is performed by combining scores computed from translations in different languages, as opposed to using

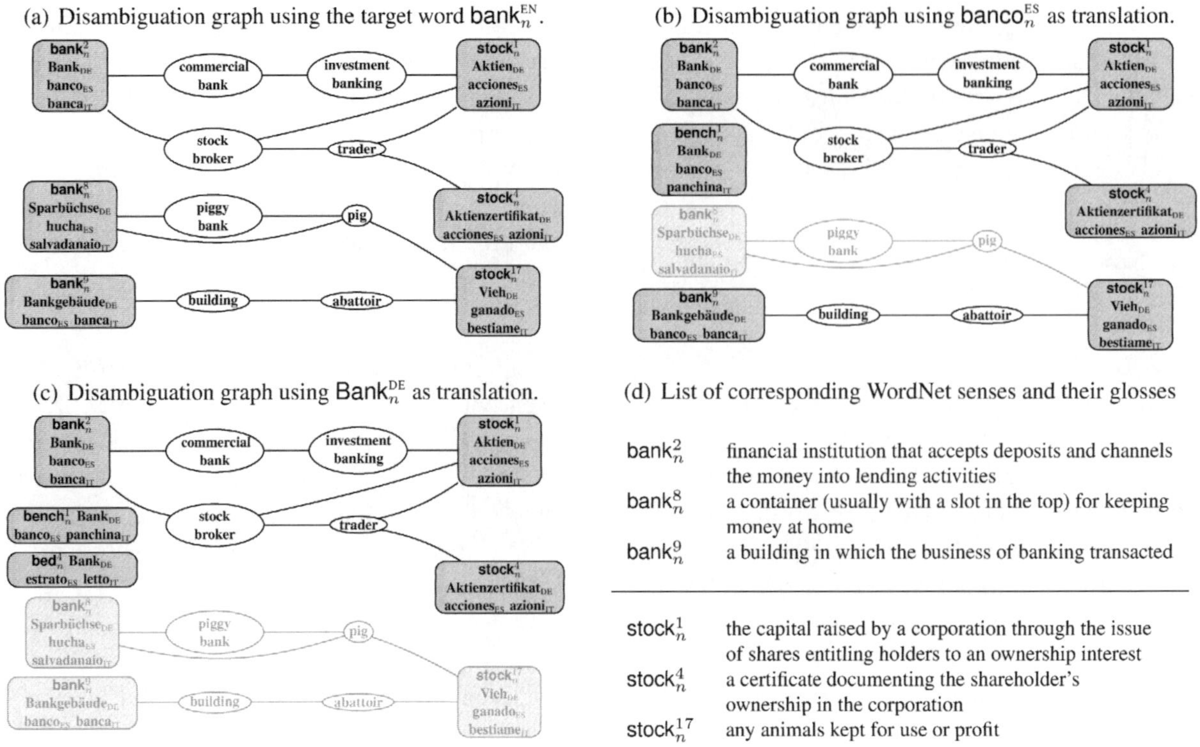

Figure 1: Multilingual graph construction for the input sentence '*bank bonuses are paid in stock*'. We show excerpts using only stock$_n^{EN}$ as context word for ease of readability.

monolingual sense evidence only. Figure 1(a) shows the graph created to disambiguate the English target word bank$_n^{EN}$ in our example sentence. In the graph, some of the possible senses of this word are activated, including the correct one (bank$_n^2$) but also related, yet incorrect ones such as bank$_n^8$ and bank$_n^9$. Figure 1(b) and 1(c) show instead the graphs obtained from replacing the target word with its Spanish and German translations, respectively. In these graphs, different subsets of the senses of bank$_n^{EN}$ are activated, together with others pertaining to the translations only (e.g., the meaning of banco$_n^{ES}$ corresponding to the English bench$_n^1$). However, the sense that is consistently activated across all graphs is the correct one – i.e., bank$_n^{EN}$ as financial institution – which is in fact the sense selected by our multilingual approach by means of combining the scoring distributions from all these graphs.

3.3 Graph-based WSD

We use graph-based algorithms to exploit multilingual knowledge from BabelNet for WSD. These are a natural choice for our approach, since BabelNet is a semantic network, and such algorithms have been shown to achieve high performance across domains (Agirre et al., 2009; Navigli et al., 2011), as well as to compete with supervised methods on a variety of lexical disambiguation tasks (Ponzetto and Navigli, 2010). To this end, we use the method of Navigli and Lapata (2010) and construct a directed graph $G = (V, E)$ for an input word sequence $\sigma = (w_1, \ldots, w_n)^5$ using the lexical and semantic relations found in BabelNet. The result of this procedure is a subgraph of BabelNet containing (1) the senses of the words in context, (2) all edges and intermediate senses found in BabelNet along all paths that connect them. Given G, a target word $w \in \sigma$ and its set of senses in BabelNet $S \subseteq V$, we compute a score distribution $(score_1, \ldots, score_{|S|})$ over S, where $score_j$ refers to the confidence score for the j-th sense of w, e.g. bank$_n^2$, based on some connectivity measure applied to G. In this paper, we specifically focus on two such measures.

[5]In our experiments we always take σ to be a single sentence, thus disambiguating on a sentence-by-sentence basis.

Degree Centrality (Degree): The first measure ranks the senses of a given word in the graph based on the number of their incident edges, namely:

$$score_j = |\{\{s_j, v\} \in E : v \in V\}| \, .$$

This standard connectivity measure weights a sense as more appropriate if it has a higher degree. We chose context-based Degree since, albeit simple, it had previously been shown to yield a highly competitive performance on various WSD tasks (Navigli and Lapata, 2010; Ponzetto and Navigli, 2010).

Inverse path length sum (PLength): We then developed a graph connectivity measure which scores each sense by summing over the inverse length of all paths which connect it to other senses in the graph:

$$score_j = \sum_{p \in paths(s_j)} \frac{1}{e^{length(p)-1}} \, ,$$

where $paths(s_j)$ is the set of simple paths connecting s_j to the senses of other context words, $length(p)$ is the number of edges in the path p and each path is scored with the exponential inverse decay of the path length. This measure overcomes the locality of Degree by aggregating over all paths between a sense of the target word and those of the context words, thus being able to capture the richness of the BabelNet subgraph and the semantic density of the underlying knowledge base.

3.4 Ensemble methods for multilingual WSD

At the core of our algorithm lies the combination of the scores generated using the different translations of the target word w. For this purpose, we apply so-called *ensemble* methods, which have been shown to improve the performance of both supervised (Florian et al., 2002) and unsupervised WSD systems (Brody et al., 2006). Given $|T|$ lexicalizations and $|S|$ senses for w, the input to the combination component consists of a $|T| \times |S|$ matrix $LScore$, where each cell $lScore_{i,j}$ quantifies the empirical support for sense s_j from a term $t_i \in T$ (see Section 3.2 for an example). The ensemble method computes from this translation-sense matrix a combined scoring, expressing the *joint* confidence across terms in different languages over the set of senses S. In this work, we use the 'Probability Mixture' (PMixture) method proposed by Brody et al. (2006), which they show to be the best performing for WSD. This method takes the scores associated with each term, normalizes and combines them by summing across distributions. Formally, it computes the score for the j-th sense of w as follows:

$$score_j = \sum_{i=1}^{|T|} p(s_{i,j}), \; p(s_{i,j}) = \frac{lScore_{i,j}}{\sum_{s=1}^{|S|} lScore_{i,s}} \, .$$

For instance, using the (normalized) sense distributions from our example, the ensemble distribution will be the following:

	bank_n^2	bank_n^8	bank_n^9
$\text{bank}_n^{\text{EN}}$	0.40	0.40	0.20
$\text{banco}_n^{\text{ES}}$	0.67	0.00	0.33
$\text{Bank}_n^{\text{DE}}$	1.00	0.00	0.00
PMixture	2.07	0.40	0.53

3.5 Weighting multilingual sense distribution

Computing a sense distribution for each translation using the same graph connectivity measure assumes that all translations are equal. However, a *leitmotif* of multilingual WSD research is that translations restrict the set of candidate senses of the target word in the source language. In our example of Figure 1, for instance, $\text{Bank}_n^{\text{DE}}$ provides structural support only for the financial sense of English bank, since this is the only sense it covers. Within our framework this can potentially lead to skewed sense distributions when only some senses of the target word have a translation. In such cases, in fact, scores tend to be concentrated mostly on the senses covered by the translations, with the result that sense evidence for uncovered English senses is disregarded. In order to cope with this issue, we weight the elements of each sense distribution $lScore_i$ for the i-th translation $t_i \in T$ by a factor of $1+\log_2 cov(t_i, w)$, where $cov(t_i, w)$ is the number of Babel synsets where t_i co-occurs with the target word w – i.e., the number of senses of w that it covers (we use the log function to dampen the effect of high coverage values). This is to say, in order to level off the effects of unbalanced sense coverage we assume that, all things being equal, the more senses a translation covers, the stronger the disambiguation evidence it provides in context for specific senses. As a result, the contributions of each translation are weighted differently and we are thus able to dampen the effects of a highly skewed distribution like, for instance, that of $\text{Bank}_n^{\text{DE}}$:

	bank_n^2	bank_n^8	bank_n^9
$\text{bank}_n^{\text{EN}}$	1.72	1.72	0.86
$\text{banco}_n^{\text{ES}}$	1.34	0.00	0.66
$\text{Bank}_n^{\text{DE}}$	1.00	0.00	0.00
Weighted PMixture	4.04	1.70	1.52

4 Experiments

We evaluate our approach in two different settings, namely a monolingual all-words WSD task in Section 4.1, as well as two different cross-lingual disambiguation gold standards in Section 4.2.

4.1 Monolingual WSD

Experimental setting. We first evaluate the performance of multilingual joint WSD on a standard monolingual dataset, namely the SemEval-2010 domain WSD task 17 (Agirre et al., 2010), since it provides the latest dataset for fine-grained WSD in English. We opt for an English all-words task for two main reasons: first, it is a well-established and widely-participated task in the WSD community – thus ensuring a comparison of our method with a wide range of state-of-the-art approaches, including other graph-based techniques (e.g., Personalized PageRank), as well as weakly-supervised and supervised approaches (see Agirre et al. (2010) for details on the participating systems); second, we want to assess whether a multilingual approach benefits lexical disambiguation in *all* settings, namely *even* in a standard monolingual one. We use in our experiments the dataset's nouns-only subset (1032 instances), since BabelNet currently contains multilingual lexicalizations for nouns only (and thus no multilingual strategy can be applied to other parts of speech). We perform graph-based WSD with BabelNet in two different configurations, namely a monolingual and multilingual setting. The multilingual system performs WSD by means of the full joint multilingual approach described in Algorithm 1. The monolingual approach, instead, simply uses the English input sentence for disambiguation – that is, we skip lines 3–4 of Algorithm 1. Knowledge-based systems typically suffer from a low recall – i.e., they cannot provide an answer if no information can be found with senses of the context words. To overcome this issue, in both settings we use a type-based fallback strategy which assigns to the target word the sense which has been most frequently assigned by the system to other instances of the word in the dataset.

	Algorithm	P	R	F_1
Monolingual graph	Degree	50.6	45.2	47.7
	PLength	51.0	47.3	49.1
Multilingual ensemble	Degree†	53.9	48.6	51.1
	PLength†	**54.3**	50.2	**52.2**
	SemCor MFS	51.9	**51.2**	51.5
	Random	25.3	25.3	25.3

Table 1: Performance on SemEval-2010 all-words domain WSD (nouns only subset). Best results for each measure are bolded. † indicates statistically significant differences with respect to the monolingual setting.

Results and discussion. We report our results in terms of precision (P), recall (R) and F_1 measure in Table 1, where we compare the monolingual variant (rows 1–2 of the table) with our multilingual approach (rows 3–4). Following standard practice, (1) we benchmark our method against two baselines, namely a random sense assignment and the most frequent sense (MFS) from SemCor; (2) we test for statistical significance by computing a 95% confidence interval on the recall score (i.e., the main evaluation measure for the WSD task) using bootstrap resampling (Noreen, 1989).

The results show that our multilingual approach improves over the monolingual one by a substantial (i.e., statistically significant) margin. Combining multilingual information from different languages yields a higher precision (+3.3 for both graph algorithms) and recall (+3.4 and +2.9 for Degree and PLength, respectively). Manual inspection of the output reveals that these increases in precision are due to translations in different languages constraining each other – e.g., an implausible English sense is 'ruled out' from the sense distributions of the other languages (cf. the example in Figure 1). The increases in recall, instead, indicate that using translations triggers responses in those cases where no sense of the English target word can be connected to the senses of the context words – i.e., some trans-

	Algorithm	P	R	F_1
Monolingual graph	Degree	52.0	51.3	51.6
	PLength	55.0	54.2	54.6
Multilingual ensemble	Degree†	61.6	59.5	60.5
	PLength†	**62.5**	**60.4**	**61.4**
	CFILT	61.4	59.4	60.4
	IIITH	56.4	55.3	55.8

Table 2: Performance on SemEval-2010 all-words domain WSD (nouns only subset) using the most frequent sense assigned by the system as back-off strategy when no sense assignment is attempted.

lations activate senses in the knowledge base which are closer to the senses of the context words. The result is an overall increase in F_1 measure of 3.4 and 3.1 points for Degree and PLength, respectively, which makes it possible for us to beat the MFS baseline (notably a difficult competitor for WSD systems). Among the different graph algorithms, PLength consistently outperforms Degree: however, the differences are not statistically significant.

In order to better understand the impact of our approach we follow previous work (e.g., Navigli and Lapata (2010)) and explore a weakly-supervised setting where the system attempts no sense assignment if the highest score among those assigned to the senses of a target word is below a certain threshold. If this is the case, in order to provide an answer for all items, we output the most frequent sense assigned by the system to other instances of the target word, and fall back to SemCor's MFS if no assignment has been attempted. We estimate the optimal value for the threshold by maximizing F_1 on a development set obtained by combining the Senseval-2 (Palmer et al., 2001) and Senseval-3 (Snyder and Palmer, 2004) English all-words datasets. The results for this setting are shown in Table 2, where we also compare with the top-performing systems from the SemEval competition, namely CFILT (Kulkarni et al., 2010) and IIITH (Reddy et al., 2010).

By complementing our multilingual method with the MFS heuristic we achieve a performance comparable with the state of the art on this task. Again, the multilingual ensemble approach consistently outperforms the monolingual one and enables us to achieve the best overall results for this dataset: without multilingual information, in fact, we achieve only average performance above the MFS level, whereas by effectively combining sense evidence from multilingual translations we are able to boost the F_1 measure by a 6-8 point margin, and thus outperform the top-ranking SemEval systems. While differences with CFILT are not statistically significant, we still take this to be good news, since our system is general purpose in nature and, accordingly, does not use any domain information such as manually-labeled examples for the most frequent domain words (CFILT) or a domain-specific sense ranking (IIITH).

4.2 Cross-lingual lexical disambiguation

Using a multilingual lexical resource makes it possible to perform WSD in any of its languages. Accordingly, we complement our evaluation on English texts with a second set of experiments where we quantify the impact of our approach on a lexical disambiguation task in a multilingual setting. To this end, we use the SemEval-2010 cross-lingual lexical substitution (Mihalcea et al., 2010, CL-LS, henceforth) and WSD (Lefever et al., 2011, CL-WSD) tasks and evaluate our methodology on performing disambiguation across different languages. Both cross-lingual WSD tasks cast disambiguation as a word translation problem: given an English polysemous noun in context as input, the system disambiguates it by providing a translation into another language (translations are deemed correct if they preserve the meaning of the source word in the target language). Their main difference, instead, lies in the range of translations which are assumed to be valid: that is, while CL-LS assumes no predefined sense inventory (i.e., any translation can be potentially correct), CL-WSD makes use of a sense inventory built on the basis of the Europarl corpus (Koehn, 2005).

Our approach to lexical disambiguation involves two steps: first, given a target word in context, we disambiguate it as usual to the highest-ranked Babel synset; next, given the translations in the selected synset, we return the most suitable lexicalization in the language of interest. Since the selected synset can contain multiple translations in a target language for the input English word, we explore using an unsupervised strategy to select the most reliable translation from multiple candidates. To this end, we return for each test instance only the

	Algorithm	P/R/F_1
	Baseline	23.80
Monolingual graph	Degree	30.52
	PLength	30.64
Multilingual ensemble	Degree	32.21
	PLength	**32.47**
	UBA-T	32.17

Table 3: Performance on SemEval-2010 lexical substitution (best results are bolded).

most frequent translation found in the Babel synset. Given that the two tasks make different assumptions on the sense inventory (no fixed inventory for CL-LS vs. Europarl-based for CL-WSD), the frequency of a translation is calculated as either the number of Babel synsets in which it occurs (CL-LS), or its frequency of alignment with the target word, as obtained by applying GIZA++ (Och and Ney, 2003) to Europarl (CL-WSD). To provide an answer for all instances, we return this most frequent translation even when no sense assignment is attempted – i.e., no sense of the target word is connected to any other sense of the context words – or a tie occurs.

Results and discussion. We report our results for CL-LS and CL-WSD in Tables 3 and 4. We evaluate using the nouns-only subset of the CL-LS dataset and the full CL-WSD dataset, consisting of 300 and 1,000 instances of nouns in context, respectively. The evaluation scheme is based on the SemEval-2007 English lexical substitution task (McCarthy and Navigli, 2009), and consists of an adaptation of the metrics of precision and recall for the translation setting. For each task, we compare our monolingual and multilingual approaches against the best performing SemEval systems for these tasks, namely UBA-T (Basile and Semeraro, 2010) and UVT-v (van Gompel, 2010) for CL-LS and CL-WSD, respectively, as well as a recent supervised proposal that exploits automatically generated multilingual features from parallel text and translated contexts (Lefever et al., 2011, Parasense). For each task we also report its official baseline, namely the first translation from an online-dictionary[6] for CL-LS, and the most frequent word alignment obtained by applying GIZA++ to the Europarl data for CL-WSD.

[6] www.spanishdict.com

Our cross-lingual results confirm all trends of the English monolingual evaluation, namely that: a) our joint multilingual approach substantially improves over the simple monolingual graph-based approach; b) it enables us to achieve state-of-the-art performance for these tasks. In the case of both CL-LS and CL-WSD, using a rich multilingual knowledge base like BabelNet makes it possible to achieve a respectable performance already with the simple monolingual approach, thus indicating the viability of a knowledge-rich approach to sense-driven word translation. The use of multilingual ensembles always improves the monolingual setting for all languages, and allows us to achieve the best overall results for both CL-LS and CL-WSD. Similarly to the case of monolingual WSD, manual inspection of the output reveals that translations help us rule out incorrect senses and let the disambiguation algorithm focus on the more coherent set of senses for the input context in a way similar to the one highlighted by the example in Figure 1. As a result of this we are able to improve the performance of both monolingual Degree and PLength, and compete with the state of the art on all disambiguation tasks.

5 Conclusions

In this paper we presented a multilingual joint approach to WSD. Key to our methodology is the effective use of a wide-coverage multilingual knowledge base, BabelNet, which we exploit to perform graph-based WSD across languages and combine complementary sense evidence from translations in different languages using an ensemble method. This is the first proposal to exploit structured multilingual information within a joint, knowledge-rich framework for WSD. The APIs to perform multilingual WSD using BabelNet are freely available for research purposes (Navigli and Ponzetto, 2012b).

Thanks to multilingual joint WSD we achieve state-of-the-art performance on three different gold standards. The good news about these results is that not only can further advances be achieved by using multilingual lexical knowledge, but, more importantly, that combining multilingual sense evidence from different languages at the same time yields consistent improvements over a monolingual ap-

		French $P/R/F_1$	German $P/R/F_1$	Italian $P/R/F_1$	Spanish $P/R/F_1$
	Baseline	21.25	13.16	15.18	19.74
	UvT-v	N/A	N/A	N/A	23.39
	Parasense	24.54	16.88	18.03	22.80
Monolingual graph	Degree	22.94	17.15	18.03	22.48
	PLength	23.42	17.72	18.19	22.76
Multilingual ensemble	Degree	24.02	18.07	18.93	23.51
	PLength	**24.61**	**18.26**	**19.05**	**23.65**

Table 4: Results on the SemEval-2010 cross-lingual WSD dataset (best results are bolded).

proach in both monolingual and cross-lingual lexical disambiguation tasks – that is, 'joining forces pays off'. Effectively leveraging multilingual knowledge for WSD helps overcome the shortcomings of the underlying resource (noise, coverage, etc.), thus indicating that further performance boosts can come in the future from even better multilingual lexical resources. Moreover, our methodology is general-purpose and can be adapted to tasks other than WSD: in fact, we have already taken the first steps in this direction by showing the beneficial effects of a joint multilingual approach to computing semantic relatedness (Navigli and Ponzetto, 2012a). In addition, we plan in the very near future to generalize our multilingual joint approach and apply it to high-end tasks such as multilingual textual entailment (Mehdad et al., 2011) and sentiment analysis (Lu et al., 2011) – so as to provide a general framework for knowledge-rich multilingual NLP.

Acknowledgments

The authors gratefully acknowledge the support of the ERC Starting Grant MultiJEDI No. 259234.

BabelNet and its API are available for download at `http://lcl.uniroma1.it/babelnet`.

References

Eneko Agirre, Oier Lopez de Lacalle, and Aitor Soroa. 2009. Knowledge-based WSD on specific domains: performing better than generic supervised WSD. In *Proceedings of the 21st International Joint Conference on Artificial Intelligence (IJCAI-09)*, pages 1501–1506.

Eneko Agirre, Oier López de Lacalle, Christiane Fellbaum, Shu-Kai Hsieh, Maurizio Tesconi, Monica Monachini, Piek Vossen, and Roxanne Segers. 2010. Semeval-2010 task 17: All-words Word Sense Disambiguation on a specific domain. In *Proceedings of the 5th International Workshop on Semantic Evaluations (SemEval-2010)*, pages 75–80.

Carmen Banea and Rada Mihalcea. 2011. Word Sense Disambiguation with multilingual features. In *Proceedings of the 9th International Conference on Computational Semantics (IWCS 2011)*, pages 25–34.

Pierpaolo Basile and Giovanni Semeraro. 2010. UBA: Using automatic translation and Wikipedia for cross-lingual lexical substitution. In *Proceedings of the 5th International Workshop on Semantic Evaluations (SemEval-2010)*, pages 242–247.

Samuel Brody, Roberto Navigli, and Mirella Lapata. 2006. Ensemble methods for unsupervised WSD. In *Proceedings of the 21st International Conference on Computational Linguistics and 44th Annual Meeting of the Association for Computational Linguistics (COLING-ACL-06)*, pages 97–104.

Peter F. Brown, Stephen A. Della Pietra, Vincent J. Della Pietra, and Robert L. Mercer. 1991. Word-sense disambiguation using statistical methods. In *Proceedings of the 29th Annual Meeting of the Association for Computational Linguistics (ACL-91)*, pages 264–270.

Marine Carpuat and Dekai Wu. 2007. Improving Statistical Machine Translation using Word Sense Disambiguation. In *Proceedings of the 2007 Joint Conference on Empirical Methods in Natural Language Processing and Computational Language Learning (EMNLP-CoNLL-07)*, pages 61–72.

Yee Seng Chan and Hwee Tou Ng. 2005. Scaling up Word Sense Disambiguation via parallel texts. In *Proceedings of the 20th National Conference on Artificial Intelligence (AAAI-05)*, pages 1037–1042.

Yee Seng Chan, Hwee Tou Ng, and David Chiang. 2007. Word Sense Disambiguation improves Statistical Machine Translation. In *Proceedings of the 45th Annual Meeting of the Association for Computational Linguistics (ACL-07)*, pages 33–40.

Ido Dagan, Alon Itai, and Ulrike Schwall. 1991. Two languages are more informative than one. In *Proceedings of the 29th Annual Meeting of the Association for Computational Linguistics (ACL-91)*, pages 130–137.

Gerard de Melo and Gerhard Weikum. 2010. MENTA: Inducing multilingual taxonomies from Wikipedia. In *Proceedings of the 19th ACM Conference on Information and Knowledge Management (CIKM-10)*, pages 1099–1108.

Mona Diab. 2003. *Word Sense Disambiguation within a Multilingual Framework*. Ph.D. thesis, University of Maryland, College Park, Maryland.

Christiane Fellbaum, editor. 1998. *WordNet: An Electronic Database*. MIT Press, Cambridge, MA.

Radu Florian, Silviu Cucerzan, Charles Schafer, and David Yarowsky. 2002. Combining classifiers for Word Sense Disambiguation. *Natural Language Engineering*, 8(4):1–14.

William A. Gale, Kenneth Church, and David Yarowsky. 1992. Using bilingual materials to develop Word Sense Disambiguation methods. In *Proceedings of the Fourth International Conference on Theoretical and Methodological Issues in Machine Translation*, pages 101–112.

Nancy Ide, Tomaz Erjavec, and Dan Tufiş. 2002. Sense discrimination with parallel corpora. In *Proceedings of the ACL-02 Workshop on WSD: Recent Successes and Future Directions*, pages 54–60.

Nancy Ide. 2000. Cross-lingual sense determination: Can it work? *Computers and the Humanities*, 34:223–234.

Mitesh M. Khapra, Salil Joshi, Arindam Chatterjee, and Pushpak Bhattacharyya. 2011. Together we can: Bilingual bootstrapping for WSD. In *Proceedings of the 49th Annual Meeting of the Association for Computational Linguistics, (ACL-11)*, pages 561–569.

Philipp Koehn. 2005. Europarl: A parallel corpus for statistical machine translation. In *Proceedings of Machine Translation Summit X*.

Anup Kulkarni, Mitesh Khapra, Saurabh Sohoney, and Pushpak Bhattacharyya. 2010. CFILT: Resource conscious approaches for all-words domain specific WSD. In *Proceedings of the 5th International Workshop on Semantic Evaluations (SemEval-2010)*, pages 421–426.

Els Lefever and Veronique Hoste. 2010. SemEval-2010 task 3: Cross-lingual Word Sense Disambiguation. In *Proceedings of the 5th International Workshop on Semantic Evaluations (SemEval-2010)*, pages 15–20.

Els Lefever, Véronique Hoste, and Martine De Cock. 2011. Parasense or how to use parallel corpora for Word Sense Disambiguation. In *Proceedings of the 49th Annual Meeting of the Association for Computational Linguistics, (ACL-11)*, pages 317–322.

Bin Lu, Chenhao Tan, Claire Cardie, and Benjamin K. Tsou. 2011. Joint bilingual sentiment classification with unlabeled parallel corpora. In *Proceedings of the 49th Annual Meeting of the Association for Computational Linguistics, (ACL-11)*, pages 320–330.

Bernardo Magnini, Danilo Giampiccolo, and Alessandro Vallin. 2004. The Italian lexical sample task at Senseval-3. In *Proceedings of the 3rd International Workshop on the Evaluation of Systems for the Semantic Analysis of Text (SENSEVAL-3)*, pages 17–20.

Lluis Màrquez, Mariona Taulé, Antonia Martí, Núria Artigas, Mar García, Francis Real, and Dani Ferrés. 2004. Senseval-3: The Spanish lexical sample task. In *Proceedings of the 3rd International Workshop on the Evaluation of Systems for the Semantic Analysis of Text (SENSEVAL-3)*, pages 21–24.

Diana McCarthy and Roberto Navigli. 2009. The English lexical substitution task. *Language Resources and Evaluation*, 43(2):139–159.

Yashar Mehdad, Matteo Negri, and Marcello Federico. 2011. Using bilingual parallel corpora for cross-lingual textual entailment. In *Proceedings of the 49th Annual Meeting of the Association for Computational Linguistics, (ACL-11)*, pages 1336–1345.

Christian M. Meyer and Iryna Gurevych. 2012. Ontowiktionary – Constructing an ontology from the collaborative online dictionary Wiktionary. In Maria Teresa Pazienza and Armando Stellato, editors, *Semi-Automatic Ontology Development: Processes and Resources*. IGI Global, Hershey, Penn.

Rada Mihalcea, Ravi Sinha, and Diana McCarthy. 2010. Semeval-2010 task 2: Cross-lingual lexical substitution. In *Proceedings of the 5th International Workshop on Semantic Evaluations (SemEval-2010)*, pages 9–14.

George A. Miller, Claudia Leacock, Randee Tengi, and Ross Bunker. 1993. A semantic concordance. In *Proceedings of the 3rd DARPA Workshop on Human Language Technology*, pages 303–308.

Vivi Nastase, Michael Strube, Benjamin Börschinger, Caecilia Zirn, and Anas Elghafari. 2010. WikiNet: A very large scale multi-lingual concept network. In *Proceedings of the 7th International Conference on Language Resources and Evaluation, (LREC '10)*.

Roberto Navigli and Mirella Lapata. 2010. An experimental study on graph connectivity for unsupervised Word Sense Disambiguation. *IEEE Transactions on Pattern Anaylsis and Machine Intelligence*, 32(4):678–692.

Roberto Navigli and Simone Paolo Ponzetto. 2010. BabelNet: Building a very large multilingual semantic network. In *Proceedings of the 48th Annual Meeting of the Association for Computational Linguistics, (ACL-10)*, pages 216–225.

Roberto Navigli and Simone Paolo Ponzetto. 2012a. BabelRelate! A joint multilingual approach to computing semantic relatedness. In *Proceedings of the 26th Conference on Artificial Intelligence (AAAI-12)*.

Roberto Navigli and Simone Paolo Ponzetto. 2012b. Multilingual WSD with just a few lines of code: The BabelNet API. In *Proceedings of the 50th Annual Meeting of the Association for Computational Linguistics, (ACL-12). System Demonstrations*.

Roberto Navigli, Stefano Faralli, Aitor Soroa, Oier Lopez de Lacalle, and Eneko Agirre. 2011. Two birds with one stone: Learning semantic models for Text Categorization and Word Sense Disambiguation. In *Proceedings of the 20th ACM Conference on Information and Knowledge Management (CIKM-11)*, pages 2317–2320.

Roberto Navigli. 2009. Word Sense Disambiguation: A survey. *ACM Computing Surveys*, 41(2):1–69.

Eric W. Noreen, editor. 1989. *Computer-intensive methods for testing hypotheses: an introduction*. New York, N.Y.: John Wiley.

Franz Josef Och and Hermann Ney. 2003. A systematic comparison of various statistical alignment models. *Computational Linguistics*, 29(1):19–51.

Manabu Okumura, Kiyoaki Shirai, Kanako Komiya, and Hikaru Yokono. 2010. SemEval-2010 task: Japanese WSD. In *Proceedings of the 5th International Workshop on Semantic Evaluations (SemEval-2010)*, pages 69–74.

Zeynep Orhan, Emine Çelik, and Demirgüç Neslihan. 2007. SemEval-2007 task 12: Turkish lexical sample task. In *Proceedings of the 4th International Workshop on Semantic Evaluations (SemEval-2007)*, pages 59–63.

Martha Palmer, Christiane Fellbaum, Scott Cotton, Lauren Delfs, and Hoa Trang Dang. 2001. English tasks: All-words and verb lexical sample. In *Proceedings of the 2nd International Workshop on Evaluating Word Sense Disambiguation Systems (SENSEVAL-2)*, pages 21–24.

Simone Paolo Ponzetto and Roberto Navigli. 2010. Knowledge-rich Word Sense Disambiguation rivaling supervised system. In *Proceedings of the 48th Annual Meeting of the Association for Computational Linguistics, (ACL-10)*, pages 1522–1531.

Siva Reddy, Abhilash Inumella, Diana McCarthy, and Mark Stevenson. 2010. IIITH: Domain specific Word Sense Disambiguation. In *Proceedings of the 5th International Workshop on Semantic Evaluations (SemEval-2010)*, pages 387–391.

Philip Resnik and David Yarowsky. 1999. Distinguishing systems and distinguishing senses: new evaluation methods for Word Sense Disambiguation. *Journal of Natural Language Engineering*, 5(2):113–133.

Carina Silberer and Simone Paolo Ponzetto. 2010. UHD: Cross-lingual Word Sense Disambiguation using multilingual co-occurrence graphs. In *Proceedings of the 5th International Workshop on Semantic Evaluations (SemEval-2010)*, pages 134–137.

Benjamin Snyder and Martha Palmer. 2004. The English all-words task. In *Proceedings of the 3rd International Workshop on the Evaluation of Systems for the Semantic Analysis of Text (SENSEVAL-3)*, pages 41–43.

Maarten van Gompel. 2010. UvT-WSD1: A cross-lingual word sense disambiguation system. In *Proceedings of the 5th International Workshop on Semantic Evaluations (SemEval-2010)*, pages 238–241.

Zhi Zhong and Hwee Tou Ng. 2009. Word Sense Disambiguation for all words without hard labor. In *Proceedings of the 21st International Joint Conference on Artificial Intelligence (IJCAI-09)*, pages 1616–1622.

A New Minimally-Supervised Framework for Domain Word Sense Disambiguation

Stefano Faralli and **Roberto Navigli**
Dipartimento di Informatica
Sapienza Università di Roma
{faralli,navigli}@di.uniroma1.it

Abstract

We present a new minimally-supervised framework for performing domain-driven Word Sense Disambiguation (WSD). Glossaries for several domains are iteratively acquired from the Web by means of a bootstrapping technique. The acquired glosses are then used as the sense inventory for fully-unsupervised domain WSD. Our experiments, on new and gold-standard datasets, show that our wide-coverage framework enables high-performance results on dozens of domains at a coarse and fine-grained level.

1 Introduction

Domain information pervades most of the text we read every day. If we just think of the Web, the vast majority of its textual content is domain oriented. A case in point is Wikipedia, which provides encyclopedic coverage for a huge number of knowledge domains (Medelyan et al., 2009), but most blogs, Web sites and newspapers also provide a great deal of information focused on specific areas of knowledge. When it comes to automatic text understanding, then, it is crucial to take into account the domain specificity of a piece of text, so as to perform a focused and as-precise-as-possible analysis which, in its turn, can enable domain-aware applications such as question answering and information extraction. Domain knowledge also has the potential to improve open-text applications such as summarization (Ceylan et al., 2010) and machine translation (Foster et al., 2010).

Research in Word Sense Disambiguation (Navigli, 2009, WSD), the task aimed at the automatic labeling of text with word senses, has been oriented towards domain text understanding for several years now. Many approaches have been devised, including the identification of domain-specific predominant senses (McCarthy et al., 2007; Lapata and Keller, 2007), the development of domain resources (Magnini and Cavaglià, 2000; Magnini et al., 2002), their application to WSD (Gliozzo et al., 2004), and the effective use of link analysis algorithms such as Personalized PageRank (Agirre et al., 2009; Navigli et al., 2011). More recently, semi-supervised approaches to domain WSD have been proposed which aim at decreasing the amount of supervision needed to carry out the task (Khapra et al., 2010).

High-performance domain WSD, however, has been hampered by the widespread use of a general-purpose sense inventory, i.e., WordNet (Miller et al., 1990; Fellbaum, 1998). Unfortunately WordNet does not contain many specialized terms, making it difficult to use it in work on arbitrary specialized domains. While Wikipedia has recently been considered a valid alternative (Mihalcea, 2007), it is mainly focused on covering named entities and, strictly speaking, does not contain a formal wide-coverage sense inventory (not even in disambiguation pages, which are often incomplete, especially in the lexicographic sense).

In this paper we provide three main contributions:

- We tackle the above issues by introducing a new framework based on the minimally-supervised acquisition of specialized glossaries for dozens of domains.

- In turn, we use the acquired domain glossaries as a sense inventory for domain WSD. As a result, we redefine the domain WSD task as one of picking out the most appropriate gloss (fine-grained setting) or domain (coarse-grained setting) from a multi-domain glossary.

- We show that our framework represents a considerable departure from the common usage of a general-purpose sense inventory such as WordNet, in that, thanks to the wide coverage of domain meanings, it enables high-performance unsupervised WSD on many domains in the range of 69-80% F1.

Furthermore, our approach can be customized to any set of domains of interest, and new senses, i.e., glosses, can be added at any time (either manually or automatically) to the multi-domain sense inventory.

2 Related Work

Domain WSD has been the focus of much interest in the last few years. An important research direction identifies distributionally similar neighbors in raw text as cues for determining the predominant sense of a target word by means of a semantic similarity measure (McCarthy et al., 2004; Koeling et al., 2005; McCarthy et al., 2007). Other distributional methods include the use of a word-category cooccurrence matrix, where categories are coarse senses obtained from an existing thesaurus (Mohammad and Hirst, 2006), and synonym-based word occurrence counts (Lapata and Keller, 2007). Domain-informed methods have also been proposed which make use of domain labels as cues for disambiguation purposes (Gliozzo et al., 2004).

Domain-driven approaches have been shown to obtain the best performance among the unsupervised alternatives (Strapparava et al., 2004), especially when domain kernels are coupled with a syntagmatic one (Gliozzo et al., 2005). However, their performance is typically lower than supervised systems. On the other hand, supervised systems fall short of carrying out high-performance WSD within domains, the main reason being the need for retraining on each new specific knowledge domain. Nonetheless, the knowledge acquisition bottleneck can be relieved by means of domain adaptation (Chan and Ng, 2006; Chan and Ng, 2007; Agirre and de Lacalle, 2009) or by effectively injecting a general-purpose corpus into a smaller domain-specific training set (Khapra et al., 2010).

However, as mentioned above, most work on domain WSD uses WordNet as a sense inventory. But even if WordNet senses have been enriched with topically-distinctive words and concepts (Agirre and de Lacalle, 2004; Cuadros and Rigau, 2008), manually-developed domain labels (Magnini et al., 2002), and disambiguated semantic relations (Navigli, 2005), the main obstacle of being stuck with an open-ended fine-grained sense inventory remains. Recent results on the SPORTS and FINANCE gold standard dataset (Koeling et al., 2005) show that domain WSD can achieve accuracy in the 50-60% ballpark when a state-of-the-art algorithm such as Personalized PageRank is paired with a distributional approach (Agirre et al., 2009) or with semantic model vectors acquired for many domains (Navigli et al., 2011).

In this paper, we take domain WSD to the next level by proposing a new framework based on the minimally-supervised acquisition of large domain sense inventories thanks to which high performance can be attained on virtually any domain using unsupervised algorithms. Glossary acquisition approaches in the literature are mostly focused on pattern-based definition extraction (Fujii and Ishikawa, 2000; Hovy et al., 2003; Fahmi and Bouma, 2006, among others) and lattice-based supervised models (Navigli and Velardi, 2010) starting from an initial terminology, while we jointly bootstrap the lexicon and the definitions for several domains with minimal supervision and without the requirement of domain-specific corpora. To do so, we adapt bootstrapping techniques (Brin, 1998; Agichtein and Gravano, 2000; Pasca et al., 2006) to the novel task of domain glossary acquisition from the Web.

Approaches to domain sense modeling have already been proposed which go beyond the WordNet sense inventory (Duan and Yates, 2010). Distinctive collocations are extracted from corpora and used as features to bootstrap a supervised WSD system. Experiments in the biomedical domain show good performance, however only in-domain ambiguity is addressed. In contrast, our approach tackles cross-

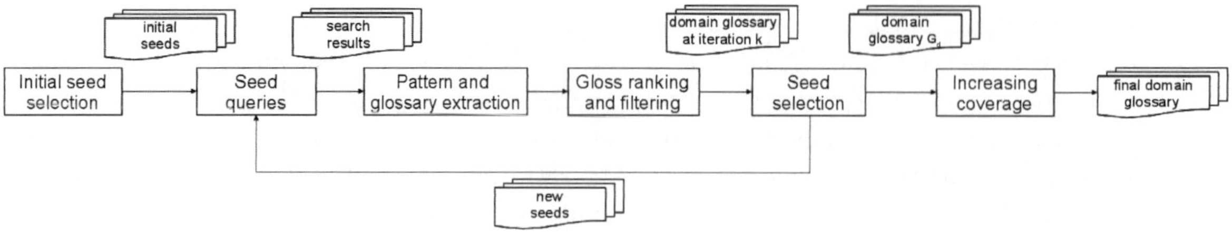

Figure 1: The bootstrapping process for glossary acquisition.

domain ambiguity, by working with virtually any set of domains and minimizing the requirements by harvesting domain terms and definitions from the Web, bootstrapped using a small number of seeds.

The existing approach closest to ours is that of Huang and Riloff (2010), who devised a bootstrapping approach to induce semantic class taggers from domain text. The semantic classes are associated with arbitrary NPs and must be established beforehand. Our objective, instead, is to perform domain disambiguation at the word level. To do this, we redefine the domain WSD problem as one of selecting the most suitable gloss from those available in our full-fledged multi-domain glossary.

3 A Minimally-Supervised Framework for Domain WSD

In this section we present our new framework for performing domain WSD. The framework consists of two phases: glossary bootstrapping (Section 3.1) and domain WSD (Section 3.2).

3.1 Phase 1: Bootstrapping Domain Glossaries

The objective of the first phase is to acquire a multi-domain glossary from the Web with minimal supervision. We initially select a set D of domains of interest. For each individual domain $d \in D$ we start with an empty set of HTML patterns P_d (i.e., $P_d := \emptyset$), used for gloss harvesting. During this phase we iteratively populate the pattern set by means of six steps, described in the next six subsections and depicted in Figure 1. The final output of this phase will be a glossary G_d consisting of domain terms and their automatically-harvested glosses.

3.1.1 Step 1: Initial seed selection

First, given the domain d, we manually pick out K hypernymy relation seeds $S_d = \{(t_1, h_1), \ldots, (t_K, h_K)\}$, where the pair (t_i, h_i) contains a domain term t_i and its generalization h_i (e.g., (*firewall*, *security system*)). The only constraint we impose is that the selected relations must be distinctive for the domain d of interest. The chosen hypernymy relations have to be as topical and representative as possible for the given domain (e.g., (*compiler*, *computer program*) is an appropriate pair for computer science, while (*byte*, *unit of measurement*) is not, as it might cause the extraction of several glossaries of various units and measures). Note that this is the only human intervention in the entire glossary acquisition process.

We now set the iteration counter k to 1 and start the first iteration of the process (steps 2-5). After each iteration k, we keep track of the set of glosses G_d^k, acquired during iteration k.

3.1.2 Step 2: Seed queries

For each seed pair (t_i, h_i), we submit the following three queries to a Web search engine: "t_i" "h_i" `glossary`[1], "t_i" "h_i" `definition`, "t_i" "h_i" `dictionary` and collect the 64 top-ranking results for each query[2]. Each resulting page is a candidate glossary for the domain d identified by our relation seeds S_d.

3.1.3 Step 3: Pattern and glossary extraction

We initialize the glossary for iteration k as follows: $G_d^k := \emptyset$. Next, from each resulting page, we harvest all the text snippets s starting with t_i and ending with h_i (e.g., *firewall*`</b> -- a <i>`*security system*), i.e., $s = t_i \ldots h_i$. For each such text snippet s, we perform five substeps:

a) **extraction of the term/gloss separator:** we

[1]In what follows, we use the `typewriter font` for keywords and term/gloss separators.

[2]We use the Google AJAX API, which returns 64 results.

Term	Gloss	Hypernym	# seeds	Gloss score
dynamic packet filter	A **firewall** facility that monitors the state of connections and uses this information to determine which network packets to allow through the **firewall**	firewall	2	0.75
peripheral	Hardware that extends the capabilities of the computer, such as a printer, modem, or **scanner**.	hardware	1	0.83
die	An integrated circuit **chip** cut from a finished wafer.	integrated circuit	1	0.75
constructor	a method used to help create a new object and initialise its data	method	0	1.00
schema	In database terminology, a schema is the organization of the tables, the fields in each table, and the relationships between fields and tables.	database	0	0.78

Table 1: Examples of extracted terms, glosses and hypernyms (seeds are in bold, domain terms are underlined).

start from t_i and move right until we extract the longest sequence p_M of HTML tags and non-alphanumeric characters, which we call the *term/gloss separator*, between t_i and the glossary definition (e.g., "</b> --" between "firewall" and "a" in the above example);

b) **gloss extraction:** we expand the snippet s to the right of h_i in search of the entire gloss of t_i, i.e., until we reach a non-formatting tag element (e.g., <span>, <p>, <div>), while ignoring formatting elements such as <b>, <i> and <a> which are typically included within a definition sentence. As a result, we obtain the sequence $t_i\ p_M\ gloss_s(t_i)\ p_R$, where $gloss_s(t_i)$ is our gloss for seed term t_i in snippet s (which includes h_i by construction) and p_R is the non-formatting HTML tag element to the right of the extracted gloss. For example, we extend the above definition for *firewall* to: "a <i>*security system*</i> for protecting against illegal entry to a local area network.".

c) **pattern instance extraction:** we extract the following pattern instance:

$$p_L\ t_i\ p_M\ gloss_s(t_i)\ p_R,$$

where p_L and p_R are, respectively, the left boundary of t_i and the right boundary of $gloss_s(t_i)$, and p_M is the term/gloss separator extracted at step 3(a). The two boundaries p_L and p_R are obtained by extracting the longest sequence of HTML tags and non-alphanumeric characters obtained when moving to the left of t_i and the right of $gloss_s(t_i)$, respectively[3]. For the above example, we extract the following pattern instance: p_L = "<p><b>", t_i = "*firewall*", p_M = "</b> --", $gloss_s(t_i)$ = "a <i>*security system*</i> for protecting against illegal entry to a local area network.", p_R ="</p>".

d) **pattern extraction:** we generalize the above pattern instance to the following pattern:

$$p_L\ *\ p_M\ *\ p_R,$$

i.e., we replace t_i and $gloss_s(t_i)$ with *. In the above example, we obtain the following pattern:

<p><b> * </b> -- * </p>.

Finally, we add the generalized pattern to the set of patterns P_d, i.e., we set $P_d := P_d \cup \{p_L\ *\ p_M\ *\ p_R\}$. We also add the first sentence of the retrieved definition $gloss_s(t_i)$ to our glossary G_d^k, i.e., $G_d^k := G_d^k \cup \{(t_i, first(gloss_s(t_i)))\}$, where $first(g)$ returns the first sentence of gloss g.

e) **pattern matching:** we look for additional pairs of terms/glosses in the Web page containing the snippet s by matching the page against the generalized pattern $p_L\ *\ p_M\ *\ p_R$. We then add to G_d^k the new (term, gloss) pairs matching the generalized pattern.

As a result of this step, we obtain a glossary G_d^k for the terms discovered at iteration k.

3.1.4 Step 4: Gloss ranking and filtering

Importantly not all the extracted definitions pertain to the domain of interest. In order to rank by domain pertinence the glosses obtained at iteration k, we define the terminology T_1^{k-1} of the terms accumulated up until iteration $k-1$ as follows: $T_1^{k-1} := \bigcup_{i=1}^{k-1} T^i$, where $T^i := \{t : \exists(t, g) \in G_d^i\}$.

[3]The minimum and maximum length of both p_L and p_R are set to 4 and 50 characters, respectively, as a result of a tuning phase described in Section 4.1.

Gloss	Domain
Measures undertaken to return a degraded ecosystem's functions and values, including its hydrology, plant and...	BIOLOGY
The renewing or repairing of a natural system so that its functions and qualities are comparable to its original...	GEOGRAPHY
The reign of Charles II in England.	ROYALTY
A goal of criminal sentencing that attempts to make the victim "whole again."	LAW
The process and work of improving the degraded quality of the sound or image in terms of video and audio preservation.	MEDIA
A process used by radio astronomers to eliminate the smoothing effect observed in radio maps that is caused by...	PHYSICS

Table 2: Examples of glosses harvested for the term *restoration*.

For the base step $k = 1$, we define $T_1^0 := T^1$, i.e., we use the first-iteration terminology itself. To rank the glosses, we first transform each acquired gloss g to its bag-of-words representation $Bag(g)$, which contains all the single- and multi-word expressions in g. We then score each gloss g by the ratio of domain terms found in its bag of words:

$$score(g) = \frac{|Bag(g) \cap T_1^{k-1}|}{|Bag(g)|}. \quad (1)$$

In Table 1 we show some glosses in the computer science domain (second column, domain terms are underlined) together with their score (last column). Next, we use a threshold θ (tuned on a held-out domain, described in Section 4.1) to remove from G_d^k those glosses g whose $score(g) < \theta$.

3.1.5 Step 5: Seed selection for next iteration

We now aim at selecting the new set of hypernymy relation seeds to be used to start the next iteration. We perform three substeps:

a) **Hypernym extraction:** for each newly-acquired term/gloss pair $(t, g) \in G_d^k$, we automatically extract a candidate hypernym h from the textual gloss g. To do this we use a simple unsupervised heuristic which just selects the first term in the gloss. More sophisticated, supervised approaches could have been used for hypernym extraction from glosses (Navigli and Velardi, 2010). However, note that, for the purposes of our glossary extraction task, it is not crucial to extract accurate hypernyms, but rather to harvest terms h which are very likely to occur in the glosses of t. We show an example of hypernym extraction for some terms in Table 1 (we report the term in column 1, the gloss in column 2 and the hypernyms extracted by our hypernym extraction technique in column 3).

b) **(Term, Hypernym)-ranking:** we sort all the glosses in G_d^k by the number of seed terms found in each gloss. In the case of ties (i.e., glosses with the same number of seed terms), we further sort the glosses by the score shown in Formula 1. We show the number of seed terms and the scores for some glosses in Table 1 (columns 4 and 5, respectively), where seed terms are in bold and domain terms (i.e., in T_1^{k-1}) are underlined.

c) **New seed selection:** as new seeds we select the (term, hypernym) pairs corresponding to the K top-ranking glosses.

If k equals the maximum number of iterations, we stop. Else, we increment the iteration counter (i.e., $k := k + 1$) and jump to step (2) of our glossary bootstrapping algorithm after replacing S_d with the new set of seeds.

The output of the glossary bootstrapping phase is a domain glossary $G_d := \bigcup_{i=1,\ldots,max} G_d^i$, where max is the total number of iterations.

3.1.6 Step 6: Increasing Coverage

Given the nature of Web domain glossaries one can rarely find terms and definitions for general terms (e.g., *jurisprudence* for the LAW domain). In order to cover this gap, we apply domain filtering (see Section 3.1.4) to all the glosses contained in a general-purpose dictionary (we use WordNet). We then add the surviving term/gloss pairs to G_d.

3.2 Phase 2: Domain WSD

Now that we have acquired a glossary for each domain in our set D, we can create a multi-domain glossary $\mathcal{G} := \{((t, g), d) : d \in D, (t, g) \in G_d\}$. Our glossary $\mathcal{G}$ is thus a set of term/gloss pairs for many domains. Note that one pair might individually belong to more than one domain, as glossary bootstrapping is performed separately for each domain. In Table 2 we show an example of the glosses acquired for the term *restoration*. We observe that 5 out of 6 senses are not available in WordNet (namely: the BIOLOGY, GEOGRAPHY, LAW, MEDIA and PHYSICS senses). Many of them are domain-specific meanings for the general concept of "the act of restoring", with the BIOLOGY and GEOGRAPHY senses being very similar. However, this is a perfectly acceptable phenomenon as any of the two senses, i.e., glosses, would be equally valid when disambiguating a domain text dealing with ecosystem restoration.

3.2.1 Gloss-driven WSD

We redefine the task of domain WSD as one of selecting the most suitable gloss, if one exists, for an input term t. For instance, consider the sentence: "He performed the *restoration* of heavily corrupted images". An appropriate option for this occurrence would be the MEDIA sense of *restoration* in Table 2.

Our gloss-driven WSD paradigm has the desirable property of automatically providing two levels of sense granularity: a domain, coarse-grained level, similar in spirit to Word Domain Disambiguation (Sanfilippo et al., 2006), in which the sense inventory of a term t is just the set of domains for which t is covered (e.g., BIOLOGY, GEOGRAPHY, ROYALTY, LAW, MEDIA, PHYSICS in the example of Table 2), and a fine-grained level, which requires the selection of the gloss which best describes the sense denoted by the given word occurrence. A second desirable property of our gloss-driven WSD paradigm is that it relies on a flexible framework, which allows for the bootstrapping of new domain glossaries or the expansion of existing ones. However, while these two properties – i.e., double level of granularity distinctions and flexibility – are naturally inherent in the gloss-driven paradigm, the same cannot be said for mainstream open-text WSD in which general-purpose static dictionaries are typically used.

In order to evaluate our framework for domain WSD, we propose two fully unsupervised algorithms for gloss-driven domain WSD. Ideally, high performance could be obtained using state-of-the-art supervised WSD systems. However, in order to train such systems, a wide-coverage sense-labeled corpus should be available for each domain, a heavy task which we leave to future work. Instead, our objective is to show that high-performance domain WSD can be enabled with little effort by our framework.

3.2.2 Algorithm 1: WSD with Personalized PageRank

Domain Glossaries as Graphs For each domain $d \in D$, we create an undirected graph $N_d = (V_d, E_d)$ as follows: V_d is the set of concepts identified by term/gloss pairs in the domain glossary G_d, i.e., $V_d := G_d$; E_d is the set of edges between pairs of concepts, where an edge $\{(t,g),(t',g')\}$ exists if and only if t' is such that $t' \neq t$ and t' occurs in the bag of words of the gloss g of t. In other words, t is connected to all the domain senses of words used in its definition g.

Graph-based WSD Given an input text, for each domain $d \in D$, we produce its bag of domain content words $C_d = \{w_1, w_2, \dots, w_n\}$ by performing tokenization, lemmatization and compounding based on the lexicon of domain d. Then, given a target word t, we use $C_d \setminus \{t\}$ as the context to disambiguate t within the domain d. In order to carry out domain WSD, i.e., to pick out the most suitable sense of t across domains, we apply a state-of-the-art graph-based algorithm, namely Personalized PageRank (Haveliwala, 2002, PPR), to each domain graph N_d. PPR is a variant of the popular PageRank algorithm (Brin and Page, 1998) in which the damping probability mass is concentrated on a selected number of graph nodes, instead of being uniformly distributed across all nodes. Specifically, following Agirre and Soroa (2009) we concentrate the probability mass on the nodes $(t',g') \in V_d$ for which the term t' is a context word, i.e., $t' \in C_d$. Next, for each domain $d \in D$, we run PPR for a given number of iterations and obtain as output a probability distribution PPV_d over the graph nodes. Finally, we select the most suitable gloss of t as follows:

$$Sense_{PPR}(t) = \underset{g:\exists d \in D,(t,g)\in V_d}{\arg\max} PPV_d(t,g) \quad (2)$$

where $PPV_d(t,g)$ is the PPR probability for the term/gloss pair (t,g) and $Sense_{PPR}(t)$ contains the best interpretation of t across all the domains D.

3.2.3 Algorithm 2: PPR Boosted with Domain Distribution Information

The words in a given text do not typically deal with a single domain. Instead, they touch different

ART	BIOLOGY	BUSINESS	CHEMISTRY	COMPUTING	EDUCATION	ENGINEERING	ENVIRONMENT	FOOD & DRINK	GEOGRAPHY
GEOLOGY	HEALTH	HISTORY	LANGUAGE	LAW	LITERATURE	MATHS	MEDIA	METEOROLOGY	MUSIC
PHILOSOPHY	PHYSICS	POLITICS	PSYCHOLOGY	RELIGION	ROYALTY	SPORTS	TOURISM	VIDEOGAMES	WARFARE

Table 3: List of the 30 domains used in our experiments.

COMPUTING		FOOD		ENVIRONMENT		BUSINESS	
chip	circuit	timbale	dish	sewage	waste	eurobond	bond
destructor	method	brioche	bread	acid rain	rain	asset play	stock
compiler	program	macaroni	pasta	ecosystem	system	income stock	security
html	language	pizza	dish	air monitoring	sampling	financial intermediary	institution
firewall	security system	ice cream	dessert	global warming	temperature	derivative	financial product
remote lan access	process	pasteurized milk	milk	fermentation	decomposition	arbitrage pricing theory	economic theory
relational database	tabular database	salted butter	butter	attainment area	area	banker's draft	bill of exchange
admin console	user interface	prosecco	wine	fugitive dust	matter	working capital	cash

Table 4: Hypernymy relation seeds used to bootstrap glossary acquisition in four of the 30 domains.

areas of knowledge which are intertwined with each other within the discourse. For example, a text dealing with VIDEOGAMES will often concern domains such as BUSINESS, COMPUTING, SPORTS, etc. Given an input text, we can capture its relevance for each domain by calculating the following domain score:

$$\beta_d = \frac{|C_d|}{\sum_{d' \in D} |C_{d'}|} \qquad (3)$$

where, as above, C_d is the set of content words from the input text which are covered by domain d. We thus propose a second algorithm which synergistically combines the spreading effect of PPR with the domain distribution information. The best sense for a given term t is calculated as follows:

$$Sense_{DomPPR}(t) = \underset{g:\exists d \in D, (t,g) \in V_d}{\arg\max} \beta_d PPV_d(t, g) \qquad (4)$$

that is, we select as the most suitable gloss for t the one which maximizes the product of its domain relevance score by its domain PPV_d value. Note that the same gloss can occur in multiple domains and that it might obtain different scores depending on the domain. Again, since the approach is gloss-driven, we do not see this as a problem, but rather as a natural characteristic of our framework.

4 Experimental Setup

4.1 Domains

We selected 30 domains starting from the Wikipedia featured articles[4]. We show the domain labels in Table 3 (some labels have been conveniently shortened, e.g., PHYSICS should read PHYSICS & ASTRONOMY). We manually identified 8 hypernym/hyponym seeds for each domain, totalizing 240 seeds. We used two criteria for selecting a seed: i) it covers a separate segment of the domain, and ii) it has to be specialized enough to avoid ambiguity. We show the seeds used in four of our domains in Table 4. We bootstrapped our glossary acquisition technique (cf. Section 3.1) on each domain and performed 5 iterations. For increasing the coverage of domain terms we used WordNet glosses (see Section 3.1.6). As a result, we obtained 30 domain glossaries. We also kept aside a 31st domain, namely FASHION, which we employed for tuning the minimum and maximum length of both p_L and p_R in Section 3.1.3 and the threshold θ used to filter out non-domain glosses in Section 3.1.4.

[4]http://en.wikipedia.org/wiki/Wikipedia:Featured_articles

Table 5: Statistics on the multi-domain acquired glossary.

	From the Web	From WordNet	From both	Total
Terms	74,295	83,904	18,313	176,512
Glosses	153,920	68,731	596	223,247

In Table 5 we show the statistics for the acquired multi-domain glossary by distinguishing Web-derived and WordNet terms and glosses.

4.2 Sense Inventory

Our sense inventory is given by the 30-domain glossary obtained as a result of our glossary bootstrapping phase. Overall we collected 176,512 and 223,247 distinct terms and glosses, respectively, with an important contribution from both the Web and WordNet (see Table 5). The average number of glosses per term in our inventory is 1.9 (3.6 glosses on polysemous terms). However, note that a monosemous word in our domain sense inventory does not necessarily make disambiguation easier, as i) we might have missed other domain-specific senses, ii) an uncovered, non-domain sense might fit a word occurrence (in this case, the domain WSD algorithms might be (wrongly) biased towards returning the only possible choice if a non-zero disambiguation score is calculated for it).

In order to determine the suitability of our multi-domain sense inventory, we compared it with the latest version of WordNet Domains (Magnini et al., 2002, WND 3.2), a well-known resource which provides domain labels for almost 65,000 nominal WordNet synsets (we removed all the synsets tagged with the FACTOTUM label, which indicates no domain specificity). Since WND uses about 160 finer-grained domain labels, we manually mapped them to our 30 labels when possible (e.g. SOCCER and SWIMMING were mapped to SPORTS), totalizing 62,100 domain-labeled synsets.

We calculated the coverage of our sense inventory against WND at the synset and the sense level, for each non-FACTOTUM synset. Given a WordNet synset S, let $d = \bigcup_{s \in S} d_s$ be the union of the domains d_s provided for each synonym $s \in S$ by our sense inventory ($d_s = \emptyset$ if not present), and let d' be the domain labels assigned to S by WND. A synset is covered if d and d' intersect. At the sense level, instead, we consider a synonym $s \in S$ to be covered if d_s and d' intersect. Our synset and sense coverage is 65.9% (40,969/62,100) and 63.7% (71,950/112,875), respectively. We also calculated an extra-coverage of 203.2% (229,384/112,875), that is the fraction of domain senses which are not available in WND, but we are able to provide in our sense inventory (see e.g. the example in Table 2) over the total number of senses in WND. While coverage and extra-coverage provide a good indicator of the completeness of our sense inventory, we need to calculate its precision to determine its correctness. To do so, we randomly sampled 500 domain glosses of terms for which no WordNet sense was tagged with the same domain in WND. A manual validation of this sample resulted in an 87.0% (435/500) estimate of the precision of our sense inventory.

4.3 Datasets

A dataset for 30 domains We used the Gigaword corpus (Graff and Cieri, 2003) to extract a 6-paragraph text snippet for each of the 30 domains. As a result, we obtained a domain dataset made up of 180 paragraphs to which we applied tokenization, lemmatization and compounding, totaling 1432 domain content words overall (47.7 content words per domain on average). The average polysemy of the words in the dataset was of 9.7 glosses and 4.4 domains per word. Each content word was manually tagged with the most suitable glosses from our multi-domain glossary (3.9 glosses, i.e., senses per word were assigned on average). The annotation task was performed by two annotators with adjudication.

Sports and Finance We also experimented with the gold standard produced by Koeling et al. (2005). The dataset covers two domains: SPORTS and FINANCE. The dataset comprises 41 ambiguous words (with an average polysemy of 6.7 senses), many of which express different meanings in the two domains. In each domain, and for each word, around 100 sentences were sense-annotated with WordNet.

Environment Finally, we also carried out an experiment on the ENVIRONMENT dataset from the Semeval-2010 domain WSD task (Agirre et al., 2010). The dataset includes 1,398 content words (of which 1,032 content nouns) tagged with WordNet senses.

4.4 Systems

We applied the two algorithms proposed in Section 3.2, namely vanilla PPR and domain-boosted PPR. For both versions of PPR we employed UKB, a readily-available implementation of PPR for WSD[5], successfully experimented by Agirre and Soroa (2009) and Agirre et al. (2009).

4.5 Baselines

Random baseline We compared our algorithms with the random baseline, which associates a random gloss among those available for each word occurrence according to a uniform distribution.

[5]http://ixa2.si.ehu.es/ukb/

Predominant domain We also compared our algorithms with a predominant sense baseline which assigns to each word occurrence the domain label with the highest domain score β_d among those available for the word (cf. Formula 3). Note that this is a strong baseline, because it aims at identifying the domain covered by the majority of terms in the input text, however it can disambiguate only at a coarse-grained level, i.e., at the domain level.

	Coarse-grained			Fine-grained		
	P	R	F1	P	R	F1
Vanilla PPR	76.7	74.3†	75.5	66.1	64.1†	65.1
Domain PPR	81.2	78.7†	79.9	69.7	67.6†	68.6
Predom. domain	77.9	76.8	77.3	-	-	-
Random baseline	42.5	42.5	42.5	44.1	44.1	44.1

Table 6: Performance results on the 30-domain dataset († differences between the two systems are statistically significant using a χ^2 test, $p < 0.05$).

5 Experimental Results

30 domains We ran our WSD systems and the baselines on our 30-domain dataset, on a sentence-by-sentence basis. We calculated results at the two levels of granularity enabled by our WSD framework: a coarse-grained setting where systems output the most appropriate domain label for each word item to be disambiguated; a fine-grained setting where systems are required to output the most suitable gloss for the input word. The results are shown in Table 6. Domain PPR outperforms Vanilla PPR by some points in precision, recall and F1 in both the coarse-grained and the fine-grained setting, achieving an F1 around 80% and 69%, respectively (differences in recall performance are statistically significant using a χ^2 test). The predominant domain baseline, available only in the coarse-grained setting, lags behind Domain PPR by more than 3 points in precision and 2 in recall. While these differences are not statistically significant, the variance across domains is much higher, thus suggesting lower reliability of the method.

These results were obtained in a fully unsupervised setting in which no structured knowledge was provided, unlike previous applications of PPR to WSD (Agirre et al., 2009; Agirre and Soroa, 2009) which relied on the underlying WordNet graph, a manually created resource. Furthermore, our graph contains "noisy" semantic relations, as we connect each gloss to all the senses of its gloss words (cf. Section 3.2.2). Finally, we note that the results shown in Table 6 could never have been obtained with WordNet. In fact, drawing on our domain mapping, we calculated that the correct domain sense is not in WordNet for about 68% of the words in the dataset. Instead, the results in Table 6 show that our framework enables high-performance unsupervised WSD thanks to the wide coverage of domain meanings.

As regards the random baseline, this performs 42.5% and 44.1% in the two settings. Despite the higher polysemy of glosses (9.7 glosses vs. 4.4 domains per word in the dataset), the performance is higher in the fine-grained setting because often there is more than one gloss covering the same meaning of a domain word.

Sports, Finance and Environment For the SPORTS, FINANCE and ENVIRONMENT datasets (cf. Section 4.3) we did not have gloss-based sense annotations, so we could not perform a fine-grained evaluation. Therefore, we first studied the different systems at a coarse level on the basis of the domain distribution of the senses returned for the word items in the dataset. We show the 3 most frequent domain labels for each system and each dataset in Figure 2. The figure seems to confirm our results showing Domain PPR as being more robust than its Vanilla version. Next, to get a more accurate evaluation, we randomly sampled 200 sentences from each dataset and manually validated the coarse-grained senses, i.e., domain assignments, output by each system on this set of sentences. We remark that several words in the datasets did not pertain to the domain of interest. For instance, *will* and *share* do not have any sports sense in WordNet, while the same applies to *half* and *chip* for the business domain. Table 7 shows the results of our validation, where a domain output by a system was considered correct if a suitable gloss existed for that domain in our inventory.

The results show that our framework enables coarse-grained recall in the 70-80% ballpark even on difficult gold standard datasets for which fine-grained recall with WordNet struggles to surpass the 50-60% range. For instance, the best performance

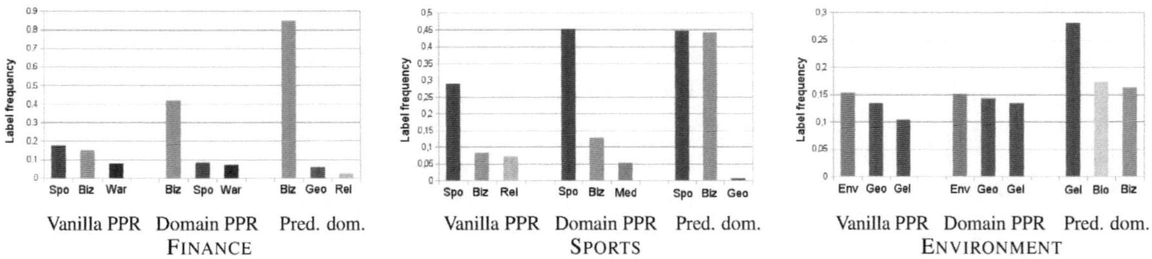

Figure 2: Frequency of the most common domain labels returned by our 3 systems on standard domain datasets.

	FINANCE			SPORTS			ENVIRONMENT		
	P	R	F1	P	R	F1	P	R	F1
Vanilla PPR	57.8	56.5	57.1	65.5	63.2	64.3	81.5	77.9	79.7
Domain PPR	77.8	76.1	76.9	72.1	71.3	71.7	83.1	79.4	81.2
Predom. domain	80.0	78.3	79.1	72.6	70.1	71.3	72.7	70.6	71.6

Table 7: Coarse-grained performance results on gold-standard domain datasets.

on the ENVIRONMENT dataset was around 60% recall (Kulkarni et al., 2010) using a semi-supervised WSD system, trained on the domain. Similarly, both the FINANCE and SPORTS datasets are notoriously difficult gold standards on which state-of-the-art recall using WordNet is lower than 60% (Navigli et al., 2011).

Interestingly, the predominant domain baseline shows a bias towards BUSINESS, thus performing best on the FINANCE dataset. This is because of the large number of terms covered in our domain glossary, and consequently the high overlap with cue words in context. On the other two domains, we observe performance in line with our 30-domain experiment.

6 Conclusion

We have here presented a new framework for domain Word Sense Disambiguation. We depart from the use of general-purpose sense inventories like WordNet and propose a bootstrapping approach to the acquisition of sense inventories for virtually any domain. While we selected 30 domains for this study, nothing would prevent us from using a smaller or larger set of these domains, or a set of completely different domains.

Our work provides three main contributions:

i) we propose a new, flexible approach to glossary bootstrapping which harvests hundreds of thousands of term/gloss pairs; the resulting multi-domain glossary is shown to have wide coverage across domains and to include a large amount of terms not available in WordNet;

ii) we propose a novel framework for fully-unsupervised domain WSD which uses the multi-domain glossary as our sense inventory;

iii) we show that high performance can be achieved by means of simple, unsupervised WSD algorithms (around 80% and 69% in a coarse- and fine-grained setting, respectively).

Note that our aim here has not been to determine which system performs best, but rather to show that a reliable, full-fledged framework for domain WSD can be set up with minimal supervision. Additionally, our framework can be applied to any language of interest, provided enough glossaries are available online, by simply translating the keywords used for our queries.

The multi-domain glossary (and sense inventory) together with the seeds used for bootstrapping are available from `http://lcl.uniroma1.it/dwsd`.

Acknowledgments

The authors gratefully acknowledge the support of the ERC Starting Grant MultiJEDI No. 259234.

References

Eugene Agichtein and Luis Gravano. 2000. Snowball: extracting relations from large plain-text collections. In *Proceedings of the fifth ACM conference on Digital Libraries (DL 2000)*, pages 85–94, San Antonio, Texas, United States.

Eneko Agirre and Oier Lopez de Lacalle. 2004. Publicly available topic signatures for all WordNet nominal senses. In *Proceedings of the 4th International Conference on Language Resources and Evaluation*, LREC 2004, pages 1123–1126, Lisbon, Portugal.

Eneko Agirre and Oier Lopez de Lacalle. 2009. Supervised domain adaption for WSD. In *Proceedings of the 12th Conference of the European Chapter of the Association for Computational Linguistics*, EACL 2009, pages 42–50, Athens, Greece.

Eneko Agirre and Aitor Soroa. 2009. Personalizing PageRank for Word Sense Disambiguation. In *Proceedings of the 12th Conference of the European Chapter of the Association for Computational Linguistics*, EACL 2009, pages 33–41, Athens, Greece.

Eneko Agirre, Oier Lopez de Lacalle, and Aitor Soroa. 2009. Knowledge-based WSD on specific domains: performing better than generic supervised WSD. In *Proceedings of the 21st International Joint Conference on Artificial Intelligence (IJCAI)*, pages 1501 1506, Pasadena, California.

Eneko Agirre, Oier López de Lacalle, Christiane Fellbaum, Shu-Kai Hsieh, Maurizio Tesconi, Monica Monachini, Piek Vossen, and Roxanne Segers. 2010. Semeval-2010 task 17: All-words word sense disambiguation on a specific domain. In *Proceedings of the 5th International Workshop on Semantic Evaluation*, pages 75–80, Uppsala, Sweden.

Sergey Brin and Michael Page. 1998. Anatomy of a large-scale hypertextual web search engine. In *Proceedings of the 7th Conference on World Wide Web*, WWW 2007, pages 107–117, Brisbane, Australia.

Sergey Brin. 1998. Extracting patterns and relations from the world wide web. In *Proceedings of the International Workshop on The World Wide Web and Databases (WebDB 1998)*, pages 172–183, London, UK.

Hakan Ceylan, Rada Mihalcea, Umut Özertem, Elena Lloret, and Manuel Palomar. 2010. Quantifying the limits and success of extractive summarization systems across domains. In *Human Language Technologies: The 2010 Annual Conference of the North American Chapter of the Association for Computational Linguistics*, pages 903–911, Los Angeles, California.

Yee Seng Chan and Hwee Tou Ng. 2006. Estimating class priors in domain adaptation for word sense disambiguation. In *Proceedings of the 21st International Conference on Computational Linguistics and the 44th annual meeting of the Association for Computational Linguistics*, ACL 2006, pages 89–96, Sydney, Australia.

Yee Seng Chan and Hwee Tou Ng. 2007. Domain adaptation with active learning for word sense disambiguation. In *Proceedings of the 45th Annual Meeting of the Association of Computational Linguistics*, ACL 2007, pages 49–56, Prague, Czech Republic.

Montse Cuadros and German Rigau. 2008. KnowNet: building a large net of knowledge from the Web. In *Proceedings of the 22nd International Conference on Computational Linguistics*, COLING 2008, pages 161–168, Manchester, U.K.

Weisi Duan and Alexander Yates. 2010. Extracting glosses to disambiguate word senses. In *Proceedings of Human Language Technologies: Conference of the North American Chapter of the Association of Computational Linguistics*, NAACL 2010, pages 627–635, Los Angeles, California, USA.

Ismail Fahmi and Gosse Bouma. 2006. Learning to identify definitions using syntactic features. In *Proceedings of the EACL 2006 workshop on Learning Structured Information in Natural Language Applications*, pages 64–71, Trento, Italy.

Christiane Fellbaum, editor. 1998. *WordNet: An Electronic Database*. MIT Press, Cambridge, MA.

George Foster, Cyril Goutte, and Roland Kuhn. 2010. Discriminative instance weighting for domain adaptation in statistical machine translation. In *Proceedings of the 2010 Conference on Empirical Methods in Natural Language Processing (EMNLP 2010)*, pages 451–459, Cambridge, Massachusetts.

Atsushi Fujii and Tetsuya Ishikawa. 2000. Utilizing the world wide web as an encyclopedia: extracting term descriptions from semi-structured texts. In *Proceedings of the 38th Annual Meeting on Association for Computational Linguistics*, ACL 2000, pages 488–495, Hong Kong.

Alfio Gliozzo, Carlo Strapparava, and Ido Dagan. 2004. Unsupervised and supervised exploitation of semantic domains in lexical disambiguation. *Computer Speech and Language*, 18(3):275–299.

Alfio Gliozzo, Claudio Giuliano, and Carlo Strapparava. 2005. Domain kernels for word sense disambiguation. In *Proceedings of the 43rd Annual Meeting on Association for Computational Linguistics*, ACL 2005, pages 403–410, Ann Arbor, Michigan.

David Graff and Christopher Cieri. 2003. English Gigaword, LDC2003T05. In *Linguistic Data Consortium*, Philadelphia.

Taher H. Haveliwala. 2002. Topic-sensitive PageRank. In *Proceedings of 11th International Conference on World Wide Web*, WWW 2002, pages 517–526, Honolulu, Hawaii.

Eduard Hovy, Andrew Philpot, Judith Klavans, Ulrich Germann, and Peter T. Davis. 2003. Extending metadata definitions by automatically extracting and organizing glossary definitions. In *Proceedings of the 2003 Annual National Conference on Digital Government Research*, pages 1–6, Boston, MA.

Ruihong Huang and Ellen Riloff. 2010. Inducing domain-specific semantic class taggers from (almost) nothing. In *Proceedings of the 48th Annual Meeting of the Association for Computational Linguistics*, ACL 2010, pages 275–285, Uppsala, Sweden.

Mitesh Khapra, Anup Kulkarni, Saurabh Sohoney, and Pushpak Bhattacharyya. 2010. All words domain adapted WSD: Finding a middle ground between supervision and unsupervision. In *Proceedings of the 48th Annual Meeting of the Association for Computational Linguistics*, pages 1532–1541, Sweden.

Rob Koeling, Diana McCarthy, and John Carroll. 2005. Domain-specific sense distributions and predominant sense acquisition. In *Proceedings of the Human Language Technology Conference and the 2005 Conference on Empirical Methods in Natural Language Processing*, pages 419–426, Vancouver, B.C., Canada.

Anup Kulkarni, Mitesh Khapra, Saurabh Sohoney, and Pushpak Bhattacharyya. 2010. CFILT: Resource conscious approaches for all-words domain specific WSD. In *Proceedings of the 5th International Workshop on Semantic Evaluation (Semeval-2010)*, pages 421–426, Stroudsburg, PA, USA.

Mirella Lapata and Frank Keller. 2007. An information retrieval approach to sense ranking. In *Proceedings of Human Language Technologies 2007: The Conference of the North American Chapter of the Association for Computational Linguistics*, HLT-NAACL 2007, pages 348–355, Rochester, USA.

Bernardo Magnini and Gabriela Cavaglià. 2000. Integrating subject field codes into WordNet. In *Proceedings of the 2nd Conference on Language Resources and Evaluation*, LREC 2000, pages 1413–1418, Athens, Greece.

Bernardo Magnini, Carlo Strapparava, Giovanni Pezzulo, and Alfio Gliozzo. 2002. The role of domain information in word sense disambiguation. *Natural Language Engineering*, 8:359–373.

Diana McCarthy, Rob Koeling, Julie Weeds, and John Carroll. 2004. Finding predominant senses in untagged text. In *Proceedings of the 42nd Annual Meeting of the Association for Computational Linguistics*, ACL 2004, pages 280–287, Barcelona, Spain.

Diana McCarthy, Rob Koeling, Julie Weeds, and John Carroll. 2007. Unsupervised acquisition of predominant word senses. *Computational Linguistics*, 33(4):553–590.

Olena Medelyan, David Milne, Catherine Legg, and Ian H. Witten. 2009. Mining meaning from Wikipedia. *Int. J. Hum.-Comput. Stud.*, 67(9):716–754.

Rada Mihalcea. 2007. Using Wikipedia for automatic Word Sense Disambiguation. In *Proceedings of Human Language Technologies 2007: The Conference of the North American Chapter of the Association for Computational Linguistics*, HLT-NAACL, pages 196–203, Rochester, N.Y.

George A. Miller, R.T. Beckwith, Christiane D. Fellbaum, D. Gross, and K. Miller. 1990. WordNet: an online lexical database. *International Journal of Lexicography*, 3(4):235–244.

Saif Mohammad and Graeme Hirst. 2006. Determining word sense dominance using a thesaurus. In *Proceedings of the 11th Conference of the European Chapter of the Association for Computational Linguistics*, EACL 2006, pages 121–128, Trento, Italy.

Roberto Navigli and Paola Velardi. 2010. Learning Word-Class Lattices for definition and hypernym extraction. In *Proceedings of the 48th Annual Meeting of the Association for Computational Linguistics*, ACL 2010, pages 1318–1327, Uppsala, Sweden.

Roberto Navigli, Stefano Faralli, Aitor Soroa, Oier de Lacalle, and Eneko Agirre. 2011. Two birds with one stone: Learning semantic models for text categorization and Word Sense Disambiguation. In *Proceedings of the 20th ACM Conference on Information and Knowledge Management*, CIKM 2011, pages 2317–2320, Glasgow, UK.

Roberto Navigli. 2005. Semi-automatic extension of large-scale linguistic knowledge bases. In *Proceedings of the 18th Internationa Florida AI Research Symposium Conference (FLAIRS)*, 15–17 May 2005, pages 548–553, Clearwater Beach, Florida.

Roberto Navigli. 2009. Word Sense Disambiguation: A survey. *ACM Computing Surveys*, 41(2):1–69.

Marius Pasca, Dekang Lin, Jeffrey Bigham, Andrei Lifchits, and Alpa Jain. 2006. Organizing and searching the world wide web of facts - step one: the one-million fact extraction challenge. In *Proceedings of the 21st National Conference on Artificial intelligence (AAAI 2006)*, pages 1400–1405, Boston, MA.

Antonio Sanfilippo, Stephen Tratz, and Michelle Gregory. 2006. Word domain disambiguation via word sense disambiguation. In *Proceedings of the Human Language Technology Conference of the NAACL, Companion Volume: Short Papers*, NAACL 2006, pages 141–144, New York, USA.

Carlo Strapparava, Alfio Gliozzo, and Claudio Giuliano. 2004. Pattern abstraction and term similarity for Word Sense Disambiguation: IRST at Senseval-3. In *Proceedings of the 3rd International Workshop on the Evaluation of Systems for the Semantic Analysis of Text (SENSEVAL-3)*, pages 229–234, Barcelona, Spain.

Grounded Models of Semantic Representation

Carina Silberer and **Mirella Lapata**
Institute for Language, Cognition and Computation
School of Informatics, University of Edinburgh
10 Crichton Street, Edinburgh EH8 9AB
c.silberer@ed.ac.uk, mlap@inf.ed.ac.uk

Abstract

A popular tradition of studying semantic representation has been driven by the assumption that word meaning can be learned from the linguistic environment, despite ample evidence suggesting that language is *grounded* in perception and action. In this paper we present a comparative study of models that represent word meaning based on linguistic and perceptual data. Linguistic information is approximated by naturally occurring corpora and sensorimotor experience by feature norms (i.e., attributes native speakers consider important in describing the meaning of a word). The models differ in terms of the mechanisms by which they integrate the two modalities. Experimental results show that a closer correspondence to human data can be obtained by uncovering latent information shared among the textual and perceptual modalities rather than arriving at semantic knowledge by concatenating the two.

1 Introduction

Distributional models of lexical semantics have seen considerable success at accounting for a wide range of behavioral data in tasks involving semantic cognition (Landauer and Dumais, 1997; Griffiths et al., 2007). These models have also enjoyed lasting popularity in natural language processing. Examples involve information retrieval (Salton et al., 1975), word sense discrimination (Schütze, 1998), text segmentation (Choi et al., 2001), and numerous studies of lexicon acquisition (Grefenstette, 1994; Lin, 1998). Despite their widespread use, distributional models have been criticized as "disembodied" in that they learn exclusively from linguistic information but are not *grounded* in perception and action (Perfetti, 1998; Barsalou, 1999; Glenberg and Kaschak, 2002).

This lack of grounding contrasts with many experimental studies suggesting that word meaning is acquired not only from exposure to the linguistic environment but also from our interaction with the physical world (Landau et al., 1998; Bornstein et al., 2004). Beyond language acquisition, there is considerable evidence across both behavioral experiments and neuroimaging studies that the perceptual associates of words play an important role in language processing (for a review see Barsalou (2008)).

It is thus no surprise that recent years have witnessed the emergence of perceptually grounded distributional models. An important question in the formulation of such models concerns the provenance of perceptual information. A few models use feature norms as a proxy for sensorimotor experience (Howell et al., 2005; Andrews et al., 2009; Steyvers, 2010; Johns and Jones, 2012). These are obtained by asking native speakers to write down attributes they consider important in describing the meaning of a word. The attributes represent perceived physical and functional properties associated with the referents of words. For example, *apples* are typically green or red, round, shiny, smooth, crunchy, tasty, and so on; *dogs* have four legs and bark, whereas *chairs* are used for sitting. Other models focus solely on the visual modality under the assumption that it represents a major source of data from which humans can learn semantic representations of both linguistic and non-linguistic communicative actions (Regier, 1996). For example, Feng and Lapata (2010) learn semantic representations from corpora of texts paired with naturally co-occurring images (e.g., news articles and their associated pictures), whereas Bruni et al. (2011) learn textual and visual representations independently from distinct data sources.

Aside from the type of data used to capture perceptual information, another important issue concerns how the two modalities (perceptual and textual) are integrated. A simple solution would be to learn both modalities independently (Bruni et al., 2011) or to infer one modality by means of the other (Johns and Jones, 2012) and to arrive at a grounded representation simply by concatenating the two. An alternative is to learn from both modalities *jointly* (Andrews et al., 2009; Feng and Lapata, 2010; Steyvers, 2010). According to this view, semantic knowledge is gained by simultaneously learning from the statistical structure within each modality assuming both data sources have been generated by a shared set of meanings or topics.

In this paper we undertake the first comparative study of perceptually grounded distributional models. We examine three models with different assumptions regarding the integration of perceptual and linguistic data. The first model, originally proposed by Andrews et al. (2009), is an extension of latent Dirichlet allocation (LDA, Blei et al. (2003)). It simultaneously considers the distribution of words across contexts in a text corpus and the distribution of words across perceptual features and extracts joint information from both data sources. Our second model is based on Johns and Jones (2012) who represent the meaning of a word as the concatenation of its textual and its perceptual vector. Interestingly, their model allows to infer a perceptual vector for words without feature norms, simply by taking into account similar words for which perceptual information is available.

Finally, we propose Canonical Correlation Analysis (Hotelling, 1936; Hardoon et al., 2004) as our third model. CCA is a data analysis and dimensionality reduction method similar to PCA. While PCA deals with only one data space, CCA is a technique for joint dimensionality reduction across two (or more) spaces that provide heterogeneous representations of the same objects. The assumption is that the representations in these two spaces contain some joint information that is reflected in correlations between them.

Features	table	dog	apple
has_4_legs	.28	.60	0
used_for_eating	.50	0	0
a_pet	0	.40	0
is_brown	0	0	0
is_crunchy	0	0	.58
is_round	.22	0	.42
has_fangs	0	0	0

Table 1: Feature norms for the nouns *table*, *dog*, and *apple* shown as a distribution.

In all three models we use feature norms as a proxy for perceptual information. Despite their shortcomings (e.g., they often cover a small fraction of the vocabulary of an adult speaker due to the effort involved in eliciting them), feature norms provide detailed knowledge about meaning representations and are a useful starting point for studying the integration of perceptual and textual information without being susceptible to the effects of noise, e.g., coming from image processing. In other words, feature norms can serve as an upper bound of what can be achieved when integrating detailed perceptual information with vanilla text-based distributional models.

Our experimental results demonstrate that joint models give a better fit to human word similarity and association data than a model that considers only one data source, or the simple concatenation of the two sources.

2 Perceptually Grounded Models

In this study we examine semantic representation models that rely on linguistic and perceptual data. The linguistic environment is approximated by corpora such as the British National Corpus (BNC). As mentioned earlier, we resort to feature norms as proxy for perceptual information. In our experiments, we relied on the norming study of McRae et al. (2005), in which a large number of human participants were presented with a series of words and asked to list relevant features of the words' referents. Table 1 presents examples of features participants listed for the nouns *apple*, *dog*, and *table*. The number of participants listing a certain feature for a word can be used to compute a probability distribution over features given the word:

$$P(f_k|w) = \frac{f(f_k, w)}{\sum_{m=1}^{F} f(f_m, w)} \quad (1)$$

where $f(f_k, w)$ is the number of participants who listed feature f_k for word w and F is the total number of features.

In the remainder of this section we will describe our models and how they arrive at an integrated perceptual and linguistic representation.

2.1 Feature-topic Model

Andrews et al. (2009) present an extension of LDA (Blei et al., 2003) where words in documents as well as their associated features are treated as observed variables that are explained by a generative process. The underlying training data consists of a corpus $\mathcal{D}$ where each document is represented by words and their frequency of occurrence within the document. In addition, those words of a document that are also included in the feature norms are paired with one of their features, where a feature is sampled according to the feature distribution given that word. For example, suppose a document d_j consists of the sentence *Mix in the apple, celery, raisins, and apple juice.* Suppose further that all content words except of *mix* and *juice* are included in the feature norms. Then, a representation for d_j is *mix*:1, *apple*;is_red:2, *celery*;has_leaves:1, *raisin*;is_edible:1, *juice*:1.

The plate diagram in Figure 1 illustrates the graphical model in detail. Each document d_j in $\mathcal{D}$ is generated by a mixture of components $\{x_1, ..., x_c, ..., x_C\} \in \mathcal{C}$; a component x_c comprises a latent discourse topic coupled with a feature cluster originating from the feature norms. A discourse topic belonging to x_c, in turn, is a distribution $\phi_c \in \phi = \{\phi_1, ..., \phi_C\}$ over words, and a feature cluster is a distribution $\psi_c \in \psi = \{\psi_1, ..., \psi_C\}$ over features.

In order to create document d_j, a distribution π_j over components is sampled from a Dirichlet distribution parametrized by α. To generate each word $w_{ji} \in \{w_{j1}, ..., w_{jn_j}\}$, a component $x_c = x_{ji}$ is drawn from π_j; w_{ji} is then drawn from the corresponding distribution ϕ_c. If w_{ji} is in the feature norms, it is coupled with a feature f_{ji} which is correspondingly drawn from ψ_c. A symmetric Dirichlet prior with hyperparameters β and γ is placed on ϕ and ψ, respectively. The probability of the corpus $\mathcal{D}$ is defined as:

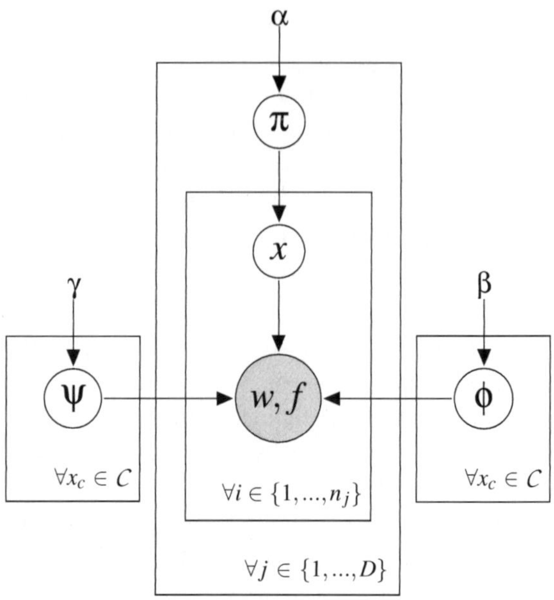

Figure 1: Feature-topic model. The components x_{ji} of a document d_j are sampled from π_j. For each $x_c = x_{ji}$, a word w_{ji} is drawn from distribution ϕ_c and a feature f_{ji} is drawn from distribution ψ_c.

$$P((w \cup f)_{1:D}|\phi, \psi, \alpha) = \prod_{j=1}^{D} \int d\pi_j \prod_{i=1}^{n_j} P(\pi_j|\alpha) \sum_{c=1}^{C} P(w_{ji}|x_{ji} = x_c, \phi) P(f_{ji}|x_{ji} = x_c, \psi) P(x_{ji} = x_c|\pi_j) \quad (2)$$

where D is the number of documents and C the predefined number of components. Computing the posterior distribution $P(\phi, \psi, \alpha, \beta, \gamma|(w \cup f)_{1:D})$ of the hidden variables given the data is generally intractable:

$$P(\phi, \psi, \alpha, \beta, \gamma|(w \cup f)_{1:D}) \propto P((w \cup f)_{1:D}|\phi, \psi, \alpha) P(\phi|\beta) P(\psi|\gamma) P(\alpha) P(\beta) P(\gamma) \quad (3)$$

Equation (3) may be approximated using the Gibbs

	x_1	x_2	x_{12}	...	x_{28}	x_{75}	x_{107}	x_{119}	x_{125}	x_{148}	x_{182}	...	x_{266}	x_{326}	x_{349}	x_{350}
apple	3e-5	3e-5	0	...	5e-4	9e-4	.09	.002	7.6e-5	2e-4	.003	...	0	0	3e-6	0

Figure 2: Example of the representation of the meaning of *apple* with the model of (Andrews et al., 2009) .

	...	d_{16}	...	d_{322}	...	d_{2469}	d_{2470}	...	d_D	*a_fruit*	*has_fangs*	*is_crunchy*	...	*is_yellow*	*is_red*	*is_green*	*is_round*
apple	...	1	...	1	...	0	1	...	0	0	0	0	...	0	0	0	0
apple	...	1	...	1	...	0	1	...	0	.006	1.8e-5	8e-4	...	.004	.004	.006	.02

Figure 3: Example representation for *apple* before (first row) and after (second row) applying the perceptual inference method of Johns and Jones (2012).

sampling procedure described in Andrews et al. (2009).

Inducing feature-topic components from a document collection $\mathcal{D}$ with the extended LDA model just described gives two sets of parameters: word probabilities given components $P_W(w_i|X = x_c)$ for w_i, $i = 1,...,N$, and feature probabilities given components $P_F(f_k|X = x_c)$ for f_k, $k = 1,...,F$. For example, most of the probability mass of component x_{107} would be reserved for the words apple, fruit, lemon, orange, tree and the features is_red, tastes_sweet, is_round and so on.

Word meaning in this model is represented by the distribution $P_{X|W}$ over the learned components (see Figure 2 for an example). Assuming a uniform distribution over components x_c in $\mathcal{D}$, $P_{X|W}$ can be approximated as:

$$P_{X=x_c|W=w_i} = \frac{P(w_i|x_c)P(x_c)}{P(w_i)} \approx \frac{P(w_i|x_c)}{\sum_{l=1}^{C} P(w_i|x_l)} \quad (4)$$

where C is the total number of components. The model can be also used to infer features for words that were not originally included in the feature norms. The probability distribution $P_{F|W}$ over features given a word w_i is simply inferred by summing over all components x_c for each feature f_k:

$$P_F(f_k|W = w_i) = \sum_{c=1}^{C} P(f_k|x_c)P(x_c|w_i) \quad (5)$$

2.2 Global Similarity Model

Johns and Jones (2012) propose an approach for generating perceptual representations for words by means of global lexical similarity. Their model does not place so much emphasis on the integration of perceptual and linguistic information, rather its main focus is on inducing perceptual representations for words with no perceptual correlates. Their idea is to assume that lexically similar words also share perceptual features and hence it should be possible to transfer perceptual information onto words that have none from their linguistically similar neighbors.

Let $T \in \{1,0\}^{N\times D}$ denote a binary term-document matrix, where each cell records the presence or absence of a term in a document. Let $P \in [0,1]^{N\times F}$ denote a perceptual matrix, representing a probability distribution over features for each word (see Table 1). A word's meaning is represented by the concatenation of its textual and perceptual vectors (see Figure 3). If a word has not been normed, its perceptual vector will be all zeros. Johns and Jones (2012) propose a two-step estimation process for words without perceptual vectors. Initially, a perceptual vector is constructed based on the word's weighted similarity to other words that have non-zero perceptual vectors:

$$\mathbf{p}_{inf} = \sum_{i=1}^{N} \mathbf{t_i} * sim(\mathbf{t_i}, \mathbf{p})^{\lambda} \quad (6)$$

where $\mathbf{p}$ is the representation of a word with a textual vector but an empty perceptual vector, $\mathbf{t}$s are composite representations consisting of textual and perceptual vectors, *sim* is a measure of distributional similarity such as cosine, λ a weighting parameter, and $\mathbf{p}_{inf}$ the resulting inferred representation of the word. The process is repeated a second time, so as to incorporate the inferred perceptual vector in the computation of the inferred vectors of all other words. An example of this inference procedure is illustrated in Figure 3.

	...	d_{16}	...	d_{322}	...	d_{2470}	...	d_D	*a_fruit*	*has_fangs*	*is_crunchy*	...	*is_yellow*	*is_red*	*is_green*	*is_round*
apple	...	.006	...	.003	...	.1e-6	...	0	.13	0	.06	...	.04	.14	.09	.04

	k_1	k_2	k_3	...	k_{409}	k_{410}	k_1	k_2	k_3	...	k_{409}	k_{410}
apple	−.003	−.01	.002	...	−.002	−.01	.008	−.03	−.008	...	−.02	−.07

Figure 4: Example representation for *apple* before (first row) and after (second row) applying CCA.

2.3 Canonical Correlation Analysis

Our third model uses Canonical Correlation Analysis (CCA, Hardoon et al. (2004)) to learn a joint semantic representation from the textual and perceptual views. Given two random variables **x** and **y** (or two sets of vectors), CCA can be seen as determining two sets of basis vectors in such a way, that the correlation between the projections of the variables onto these bases is mutually maximized (Borga, 2001). In effect, the representation-specific details pertaining to the two views of the same phenomenon are discarded and the underlying hidden factors responsible for the correlation are revealed.

In our case the linguistic view is represented by a term-document matrix, $T \in \mathbb{R}^{N \times D}$, containing information about the occurrence of each word in each document. The perceptual view is captured by a perceptual matrix, $P \in [0,1]^{N \times F}$, representing words as a probability distribution over normed features. CCA is concerned with describing linear dependencies between two sets of variables of relatively low dimensionality. Since the correlation between the linguistic and perceptual views may exist in some nonlinear relationship, we used a kernelized version of CCA (Hardoon et al., 2004) which first projects the data into a higher-dimensional feature space and then performs CCA in this new feature space. The two kernel matrices are $K_T = TT'$ and $K_P = PP'$. After applying CCA we obtain two matrices projected onto L basis vectors, $C_t \in \mathbb{R}^{N \times L}$, resulting from the projection of the textual matrix T onto the new basis and $C_p \in \mathbb{R}^{N \times L}$, resulting from the projection of the corresponding perceptual feature matrix. The meaning of a word can thus be represented by its projected textual vector in C_T, its projected perceptual vector in C_P or their concatenation. Figure 4 shows an example of the textual and perceptual vectors for the word *apple* which were used as input for CCA (first row) and their new representation after the projection onto new basis vectors (second row).

The CCA model as sketched above will only obtain full representations for words with perceptual features available. One solution would be to apply the method from Johns and Jones (2012) to infer the perceptual vectors and then perform CCA on the inferred vectors. Another approach which we assess experimentally (see Section 4) is to create a perceptual vector for a word that has none from its k-most (textually) similar neighbors, simply by taking the average of their perceptual vectors. This inference procedure can be applied to the original vectors or the projected vectors in C_T and C_P, respectively, once CCA has taken place.

2.4 Discussion

Johns and Jones (2012) primarily present a model of perceptual inference, where textual data is used to infer perceptual information for words not included in feature norms. There is no means in this model to obtain a joint representation resulting from the mutual influence of the perceptual and textual views. As shown in the example in Figure 3 the textual vector on the left-hand side does not undergo any transformation whatsoever. The generative model put forward by Andrews et al. (2009) learns meaning representations by simultaneously considering documents and features. Rather than simply adding perceptual information to textual data it integrates both modalities jointly in a *single* representation which is desirable, at least from a cognitive perspective. It is unlikely that we have separate representations for different aspects of word meaning (Rogers et al., 2004). Similarly to Johns and Jones (2012), Andrews et al's (2009) feature-topic model can also infer perceptual representations for words that have none. The inference is performed automatically in an implicit manner during component induction.

In CCA, textual and perceptual data represent two different views of the same objects and the model operates on these views *directly* without combining or manipulating any of them a priori. Instead, the combination of the two modalities is realized via correlating the linear relationships between them. A drawback of the model lies in the need of additional methods for inferring perceptual representations for words not available in feature norms.

3 Experimental Setup

Data All our experiments used a lemmatized version of the British National Corpus (BNC) as a source of textual information. The feature norms of McRae et al. (2005) were used as a proxy for perceptual information. The BNC comprises 4,049 texts totalling approximately 100 million words. McRae et al.'s feature norms consist of 541 words and 2,526 features; 824 of these features occur with at least two different words.

Evaluation Tasks Our evaluation experiments compared the models discussed above on three tasks. Two of them have been previously used to evaluate semantic representation models, namely word association and word similarity. In order to simulate word association, we used the human norms collected by (Nelson et al., 1998).[1] These were established by presenting a large number of participants with a cue word (e.g., *rice*) and asking them to name an associate word in response (e.g., *Chinese, wedding, food, white*). For each cue word, the norms provide a set of associates and the frequencies with which they were named. We can thus compute the probability distribution over associates for each cue. Analogously, we can estimate the degree of similarity between a cue and its associates using our models (see the following section for details on the similarity measures we employed). The norms contain 63,619 unique normed cue-associate pairs in total. Of these, 25,968 pairs were covered by all models and 520 appeared in McRae et al.'s (2005) norms. Using correlation analysis, we examined the degree of linear relationship between the human cue-associate probabilities and the automatically derived similarity values.

Our word similarity experiments used the WordSimilarity-353 test collection (Finkelstein et al., 2002)[2] which consists of relatedness judgments for word pairs. For each pair, a similarity judgment (on a scale of 0 to 10) was elicited from 13 or 16 human subjects (e.g., *tiger-cat* are very similar, whereas *delay–racism* are not). The average rating for each pair represents an estimate of the perceived similarity of the two words. The task varies slightly from word association. Here, participants are asked to rate perceived similarity rather than to generate the first word that came to mind in response to a cue word. The collection contains similarity ratings for 353 word pairs. Of these, 76 pairs appeared in our corpus and 3 in McRae et al.'s (2005) norms. Again, we evaluated how well model produced similarities correlate with human ratings. Throughout this paper we report correlation coefficients using Pearson's r.

Our third task assessed the models' ability to infer perceptual vectors for words that have none. To do this, we conducted 10-fold cross-validation on McRae et al.'s (2005) norms. We treated the perceptual vectors in each test fold as unseen, and used the data in the corresponding training fold together with the models presented in Section 2 to infer them. Then, for each word, we examined how close the inferred vector was to the actual one, via correlation analysis.

Model Parameters The feature-topic model has a few parameters that must be instantiated. These include, C, the number of predefined components and the priors α, β, and γ. Following Andrews et al. (2009), the components C were set to 350.[3] A vague inverse gamma prior was placed on α, β, and γ.[4] To measure word similarity within this model, we adopt Griffiths et al.'s (2007) definition. The underlying idea is that word association can be expressed as a conditional distribution. If we have seen word w_1, then we can determine the probability that w_2 will be also generated by computing $P(w_2|w_1)$. Assuming that both w_1 and w_2 came from a single component, $P(w_2|w_1)$ can be estimated as:

$$P(w_2|w_1) = \sum_{c=1}^{C} P(w_2|x_c)P(x_c|w_1) \qquad (7)$$

$$P(x_c|w_1) \propto P(w_1|x_c)P(x_c)$$

[1] Available at http://www.usf.edu/Freeassociation.

[2] Available at http://www.cs.technion.ac.il/~gabr/resources/data/wordsim353/.

[3] As we explain in Section 4 the feature-topic model was compared to a vanilla LDA model trained on the BNC only. For that model, C was set to 250.

[4] That is $P(\bullet) = exp(-\frac{1}{\bullet})\bullet^{-2}$.

where $P(x_c)$ is uniform, a single component x_c is sampled from the distribution $P(x_c|w_1)$, and an overall estimate is obtained by averaging over all C components.

Johns and Jones' (2012) model uses binary textual vectors to represent word meaning. If the word is present in a given document, that vector element is coded as one; if it is absent, it is coded as zero. We built a binary term-document matrix from the BNC over 14,000 lemmas. The value of the similarity weighting parameter λ was set to the same values reported by Johns and Jones (λ_1=3 for Step 1 and $\lambda_2 = 13$ for Step 2).

For the CCA model, we represented the textual view with a term-document co-occurrence matrix. Matrix cells were set to their tf-idf values.[5] The textual and perceptual matrices were projected onto 410 vectors. As mentioned in Section 2.3, CCA does not naturally lend itself to inferring perceptual vectors, yet a perceptual vector for a word can be created from its k-nearest neighbors. We inferred a perceptual vector by averaging over the perceptual vectors of the word's k most similar words; textual similarity between two words was measured using the cosine of the angle of the two vectors representing them. To find the optimal value for k, we used one third of Nelson's (1998) cues as development set. The highest correlation was achieved with $k = 2$ when the perceptual vectors were created prior to CCA and $k = 8$ when they were inferred on the projected textual and perceptual matrices.

4 Results

Our experiments were designed to answer three questions: (1) Does the integration of perceptual and textual information yield a better fit with behavioral data compared to a model that considers only one data source? (2) What is the best way to integrate the two modalities, e.g., via simple concatenation or jointly? (3) How accurately can we approximate the perceptual information when the latter is absent?

To answer the first question, we assessed the models' performance when textual and perceptual information are both available. The results in Table 2 are thus computed on the subset of Nelson's (1998) norms (520 cue-associate pairs) that also appeared in McRae et al. (2005) and for which a perceptual vector was present. The table shows different instantiations of the three models depending on the type of modality taken into account: textual, perceptual or both.

Models	Modality		Pearson's r
Feature-topic	+t	+p	.35
Feature-topic	+t	−p	.12
Feature-topic	−t	+p	.22
Global similarity	+t	+p	.23
Global similarity	+t	−p	.11
Global similarity	−t	+p	.22
CCA	+t	+p	.32
CCA	+t	−p	.14
CCA	−t	+p	.29
Upper Bound	—		.91

Table 2: Performance of feature-topic, global similarity, and CCA models on a subset of the Nelson et al. (1998) norms when taking into account the textual and perceptual modalities on their own (+t−p and −t+p) and in combination (+t+p). All correlation coefficients are statistically significant ($p < 0.01$).

As can be seen, Andrews et al.'s (2009) feature-topic model provides a better fit with the association data when both modalities are taken into account (+t+p). A vanilla LDA model constructed solely on the BNC (+t−p) or McRae et al.'s (2005) feature norms (−t+p) yields substantially lower correlations. We observe a similar pattern with Johns and Jones' (2012) global similarity model. Concatenation of perceptual and textual vectors yields the best fit with the norming data, relying on perceptual information alone (−t+p) comes close, whereas textual information on its own seems to have a weaker effect (+t−p).[6] The CCA model takes perceptual and textual information as input in order to find a projection onto basis vectors that are maximally correlated. Although by definition the CCA model must operate on the two views, we can nevertheless isolate the contribution of each modality by considering the vectors resulting from the projection of the tex-

[5] Experiments with a binarized version of the term-document matrix consistently performed worse.

[6] In this evaluation setting, the model does not infer any perceptual representations; perceptual vectors are taken directly from McRae et al. (2005).

tual matrix (+t−p), the perceptual matrix (−t+p) or their concatenation (+t+p). We obtain best results with the latter representation; again we observe that the perceptual information is more dominant.

Overall we find that the feature-topic model and CCA perform best. In fact the correlations achieved by the two models do not differ significantly, using a t-test (Cohen and Cohen, 1983). The performance of the global similarity model is significantly worse than the feature-topic model and CCA ($p < 0.01$). Recall that the feature-topic model (+t+p) represents words as distributions over components, whereas the global similarity model simply concatenates the textual and perceptual vectors. The same input is also given to CCA which in turn attempts to interpret the data by inferring common relationships between the two views. In sum, we can conclude that the higher correlation with human judgments indicates that integrating textual and perceptual modalities jointly is preferable to concatenation.

However, note that all models in Table 2 fall short of the human upper bound which we measured by calculating the *reliability* of Nelson et al.'s (1998) norms. Reliability estimates the likelihood of a similarly-composed group of participants presented with the same task under the same circumstances producing identical results. We split the collected cue-associate pairs randomly into two halves and computed the correlation between them; this correlation was averaged across 200 random splits. These correlations were adjusted by applying the Spearman-Brown prediction formula (Voorspoels et al., 2008).

The results in Table 2 are computed on a small fraction of Nelson et al.'s (1998) norms. One might even argue that the comparison is slightly unfair as the global similarity model is more geared towards inferring perceptual vectors rather than integrating the two modalities in the best possible way. To gain a better understanding of the models' behavior and to allow comparisons on a larger dataset and more equal footing, we also report results on the entire dataset (20,556 cue-associate pairs).[7] This entails that the models will infer perceptual vectors for the

Models	Pearson's r
Feature-topic	.15
Global similarity	.03
Global similarity $\ll$ CCA	.12
k-NN $\ll$ CCA	.11
CCA $\ll$ k-NN	.12
Upper Bound	.96

Table 3: Performance of the feature-topic, global similarityand CCA models on the Nelson et al. (1998) norms (entire dataset). All correlation coefficients are statistically significant ($p < 0.01$).

words that are not attested in McRae et al.'s norms. Recall from Section 2.3 that CCA does not have a dedicated inference mechanism. We thus experimented with three options (a) interfacing the inference method of Johns and Jones (2012) with CCA (global similarity $\ll$ CCA) (b) creating a perceptual vector from the words' k-nearest neighbors before (k-NN $\ll$ CCA) or (c) after CCA takes place (CCA $\ll$ k-NN).

Our results are summarized in Table 3. The upper bound was estimated in the same fashion as for the smaller dataset. Despite being statistically significant ($p < 0.01$), the correlation coefficients are lower. This is hardly surprising as perceptual information is approximate and in several cases likely to be wrong. Interestingly, we observe similar modeling trends, irrespective of whether the models are performing perceptual inference or not. The feature-topic model achieves the best fit with the data, followed by CCA. The inference method here does not seem to have much of an impact: CCA $\ll$ k-NN does as well as global similarity $\ll$ CCA. This is perhaps expected as the inference procedure adopted by Johns and Jones (2012) is a generalization of our k-nearest neighbor approach. The global similarity model performs worst; we conjecture that this is due to the way semantic information is integrated rather than the inference method itself. CCA works with similar input, yet achieves better correlations with the human data, due to its ability to represent the commonalities shared by the two modalities. Taken together the results in Tables 2 and 3 provide an answer to our second question. Models that capture latent information shared between the two modalities

[7]This excludes the data used as development set for tuning the k-nearest neighbors for CCA.

Models	Pearson's r
Feature-topic	.17
Global similarity	.25
Global similarity $\ll$ CCA	.21
k-NN $\ll$ CCA	.19
CCA $\ll$ k-NN	.13

Table 4: Mean correlation coefficients between original and inferred feature vectors in McRae et al.'s (2005) norms.

Models	Pearson's r
Feature-topic	.35
Global similarity	.08
Global similarity $\ll$ CCA	.38
k-NN $\ll$ CCA	.39
CCA $\ll$ k-NN	.28
Upper Bound	.98

Table 5: Model performance on predicting word similarity. All correlation coefficients are statistically significant ($p < 0.01$), except for the global similarity model.

create more accurate semantic representations compared to simply treating the two as independent data sources.

In order to isolate the influence of the inference method from the resulting semantic representation we evaluated the inferred perceptual vectors on their own by computing their correlation with the original feature distributions in McRae et al.'s (2005) norms. The correlation coefficients are reported in Table 4 and were computed by averaging the coefficients obtained for individual words. Here, the global similarity model achieves the highest correlation, and for a good reason. It is the only model with an emphasis on inference, the other two models do not have such a dedicated mechanism. CCA has in fact none, whereas in the feature-topic model the inference of missing perceptual information is a by-product of the generative process. The results in Table 4 indicate that the perceptual vectors are not reconstructed very accurately (the highest correlation coefficient is .25) and that better inference mechanisms are required for perceptual information to have a positive impact on semantic representation.

In Table 5 we examine the models' performance on semantic similarity rather than association using the WordSimilarity-353 dataset (Finkelstein et al., 2002). The models were evaluated on 76 word pairs that appeared in the BNC. We inferred the perceptual vectors for 51 words. We computed the upper bound using the reliability method described earlier. Again, the joint models achieve better results than the simple concatenation model. The feature-topic and CCA models perform comparably, with the global similarity model lagging substantially behind. In sum, our results indicate that the issue of how to best integrate the two modalities has a greater impact on the resulting semantic representations compared to the mechanism by which missing perceptual information is inferred.

5 Conclusions

In this paper, we have presented a comparative study of semantic representation models which compute word meaning on the basis of linguistic and perceptual information. The models differ in terms of the mechanisms by which they integrate the two modalities. In the feature-topic model (Andrews et al., 2009), the textual and perceptual views are integrated via a set of latent components that are inferred from the *joint* distribution of textual words and perceptual features. The model based on Canonical Correlation Analysis (Hardoon et al., 2004) integrates the two views by deriving a *consensus* representation based on the correlation between the linguistic and perceptual modalities. Johns and Jones' (2012) similarity-based model simply concatentates the two representations. In addition, it uses the linguistic representations of words to infer perceptual information when the latter is absent.

Experiments on word association and similarity show that all models benefit from the integration of perceptual data. We also find that joint models are superior as they obtain a closer fit with human judgments compared with an approach that simply concatenates the two views. We have also examined how these models perform on the perceptual inference task which has implications for the wider applicability of grounded semantic representation models. Johns and Jones' (2012) inference mechanism goes some way towards reconstructing the information contained in the feature norms, however, further work is needed to achieve representations accurate enough to be useful in semantic tasks.

In this paper we have used McRae et al.'s (2005) norms without any extensive feature engineering other than applying a frequency cut-off. In the future we plan to experiment with feature selection methods in an attempt to represent perceptual information more succinctly. For example, it may be that different features are appropriate for different word classes (e.g., color versus event denoting nouns). Although feature norms are a useful first approximation of perceptual data, the effort involved in eliciting them limits the scope of any computational model based on normed data. A natural avenue for future work would be to develop semantic representation models that exploit perceptual data that is both naturally occurring and easily accessible (e.g., images, physical simulations).

Acknowledgments We are grateful to Brendan Johns for his help with the re-implementation of his model. Thanks to Frank Keller and Michael Roth for their input on earlier versions of this work, Ioannis Konstas for his help with the final version, and members of the ILCC at the School of Informatics for valuable discussions and comments. We acknowledge the support of EPSRC through project grant EP/I032916/1.

References

M. Andrews, G. Vigliocco, and D. Vinson. 2009. Integrating Experiential and Distributional Data to Learn Semantic Representations. *Psychological Review*, 116(3):463–498.

Lawrence Barsalou. 1999. Perceptual Symbol Systems. *Behavioral and Brain Sciences*, 22:577–609.

Lawrence W. Barsalou. 2008. Grounded Cognition. *Annual Review of Psychology*, 59:617–845.

David M. Blei, Andrew Y. Ng, and Michael I. Jordan. 2003. Latent Dirichlet Allocation. *Journal of Machine Learning Research*, 3:993–1022, March.

Magnus Borga. 2001. Canonical Correlation - a Tutorial, January.

M. H. Bornstein, L. R. Cote, S. Maital, K. Painter, S.-Y. Park, and L. Pascual. 2004. Cross-linguistic Analysis of Vocabulary in Young Children: Spanish, Dutch, French, Hebrew, Italian, Korean, and American English. *Child Development*, 75(4):1115–1139.

Elia Bruni, Giang Binh Tran, and Marco Baroni. 2011. Distributional Semantics from Text and Images. In *Proceedings of the GEMS 2011 Workshop on GEometrical Models of Natural Language Semantics*, pages 22–32, Edinburgh, UK, July. Association for Computational Linguistics.

Freddy Choi, Peter Wiemer-Hastings, and Johanna Moore. 2001. Latent Semantic Analysis for Text Segmentation. In *Proceedings of the 6th EMNLP*, pages 109–117, Seattle, WA.

J Cohen and P Cohen. 1983. *Applied Multiple Regression/Correlation Analysis for the Behavioral Sciences*. Hillsdale, NJ: Erlbaum.

Yansong Feng and Mirella Lapata. 2010. Visual Information in Semantic Representation. In *Human Language Technologies: The 2010 Annual Conference of the North American Chapter of the Association for Computational Linguistics*, pages 91–99, Los Angeles, California, June. Association for Computational Linguistics.

Lev Finkelstein, Evgeniy Gabrilovich, Yossi Matias, Ehud Rivlin, Zach Solan, Gadi Wolfman, and Eytan Ruppin. 2002. Placing Search in Context: The Concept Revisited. *ACM Transactions on Information Systems*, 20(1):116–131, January.

Arthur M. Glenberg and Michael P. Kaschak. 2002. Grounding Language in Action. *Psychonomic Bulletin and Review*, 9(3):558–565.

Gregory Grefenstette. 1994. *Explorations in Automatic Thesaurus Discovery*. Kluwer Academic Publishers.

T. L. Griffiths, M. Steyvers, and J. B. Tenenbaum. 2007. Topics in Semantic Representation. *Psychological Review*, 114(2):211–244.

David R. Hardoon, Sandor R. Szedmak, and John R. Shawe-Taylor. 2004. Canonical Correlation Analysis: An Overview with Application to Learning Methods. *Neural Computation*, 16(12):2639–2664.

H Hotelling. 1936. Relations between Two Sets of Variates. *Biometrika*, 28:312–377.

Steve R. Howell, Damian Jankowicz, and Suzanna Becker. 2005. A Model of Grounded Language Acquisition: Sensorimotor Features Improve Lexical and Grammatical Learning. *Journal of Memory and Language, 53(2), 258-276*, 53(2):258–276.

Brendan T. Johns and Michael N. Jones. 2012. Perceptual Inference through Global Lexical Similarity. *Topics in Cognitive Science*, 4(1):103–120.

B. Landau, L. Smith, and S. Jones. 1998. Object Perception and Object Naming in Early Development. *Trends in Cognitive Science*, 27:19–24.

T. Landauer and S. T. Dumais. 1997. A Solution to Plato's Problem: the Latent Semantic Analysis Theory of Acquisition, Induction, and Representation of Knowledge. *Psychological Review*, 104(2):211–240.

Dekang Lin. 1998. Automatic Retrieval and Clustering of Similar Words. In *Proceedings of the joint Annual Meeting of the Association for Computational Linguistics and International Conference on Computational Linguistics*, pages 768–774, Montréal, Canada.

K. McRae, G. S. Cree, M. S. Seidenberg, and C. McNorgan. 2005. Semantic Feature Production Norms for a Large Set of Living and Nonliving Things. *Behavior Research Methods*, 37(4):547–559, November.

D. L. Nelson, C. L. McEvoy, and T. A. Schreiber. 1998. The University of South Florida Word Association, Rhyme, and Word Fragment Norms.

C. Perfetti. 1998. The Limits of Co-occurrence: Tools and Theories in Language Research. *Discourse Processes*, (25):363–377.

Terry Regier. 1996. *The Human Semantic Potential*. MIT Press, Cambridge, MA.

T. T. Rogers, M. A. Lambon Ralph, P. Garrard, S. Bozeat, J. L. McClelland, J. R. Hodges, and K. Patterson. 2004. Structure and Deterioration of Semantic Memory: A Neuropsychological and Computational Investigation. *Psychological Review*, 111(1):205–235.

G Salton, A Wang, and C Yang. 1975. A Vector-space Model for Information Retrieval. *Journal of the American Society for Information Science*, 18:613–620.

Hinrich Schütze. 1998. Automatic Word Sense Discrimination. *Computational Linguistics*, 24(1):97–124.

Mark Steyvers. 2010. Combining Feature Norms and Text Data with Topic Models. *Acta Psychologica*, 133(3):234–342.

Wouter Voorspoels, Wolf Vanpaemel, and Gert Storms. 2008. Exemplars and Prototypes in Natural Language Concepts: A Typicality-based Evaluation. *Psychonomic Bulletin & Review*, 15:630–637.

Improved Parsing and POS Tagging Using Inter-Sentence Consistency Constraints

Alexander M. Rush[1*] **Roi Reichart**[1*] **Michael Collins**[2] **Amir Globerson**[3]

[1]MIT CSAIL, Cambridge, MA, 02139, USA
{srush|roiri}@csail.mit.edu

[2]Department of Computer Science, Columbia University, New-York, NY 10027, USA
mcollins@cs.columbia.edu

[3]School of Computer Science and Engineering, The Hebrew University, Jerusalem, 91904, Israel
gamir@cs.huji.ac.il

Abstract

State-of-the-art statistical parsers and POS taggers perform very well when trained with large amounts of in-domain data. When training data is out-of-domain or limited, accuracy degrades. In this paper, we aim to compensate for the lack of available training data by exploiting similarities between test set sentences. We show how to augment sentence-level models for parsing and POS tagging with inter-sentence consistency constraints. To deal with the resulting global objective, we present an efficient and exact dual decomposition decoding algorithm. In experiments, we add consistency constraints to the MST parser and the Stanford part-of-speech tagger and demonstrate significant error reduction in the domain adaptation and the lightly supervised settings across five languages.

1 Introduction

State-of-the-art statistical parsers and POS taggers perform very well when trained with large amounts of data from their test domain. When training data is out-of-domain or limited, the performance of the resulting model often degrades. In this paper, we aim to compensate for the lack of available training data by exploiting similarities between test set sentences. Most parsing and tagging models are defined at the sentence-level, which makes such inter-sentence information sharing difficult. We show how to augment sentence-level models with inter-sentence constraints to encourage consistent descisions in similar contexts, and we give an efficient algorithm with formal guarantees for decoding such models.

In POS tagging, most taggers perform very well on word types that they have observed in training data, but they perform poorly on unknown words. With a global objective, we can include constraints that encourage a consistent tag across all occurrences of an unknown word type to improve accuracy. In dependency parsing, the parser can benefit from surface-level features of the sentence, but with sparse or out-of-domain training data these features are very noisy. Using a global objective, we can add constraints that encourage similar surface-level contexts to exhibit similar syntactic behaviour.

The first contribution of this work is the use of Markov random fields (MRFs) to model global constraints between sentences in dependency parsing and POS tagging. We represent each word as a node, the tagging or parse decision as its label, and add constraints through edges. MRFs allow us to include global constraints tailored to these problems, and to reason about inference in the corresponding global models.

The second contribution is an efficient dual decomposition algorithm for decoding a global objective with inter-sentence constraints. These constraints generally make direct inference challenging since they tie together the entire test corpus. To alleviate this issue, our algorithm splits the global inference problem into subproblems - decoding of individual sentences, and decoding of the global MRF. These subproblems can be solved efficiently through known methods. We show empirically that by iteratively solving these subproblems, we can find the

[*] Both authors contributed equally to this work.

exact solution to the global model.

We experiment with domain adaptation and lightly supervised training. We demonstrate that global models with consistency constraints can improve upon sentence-level models for dependency parsing and part-of-speech tagging. For domain adaptation, we show an error reduction of up to 7.7% when adapting the second-order projective MST parser (McDonald et al., 2005) from newswire to the QuestionBank domain. For lightly supervised learning, we show an error reduction of up to 12.8% over the same parser for five languages and an error reduction of up to 10.3% over the Stanford trigram tagger (Toutanova et al., 2003) for English POS tagging. The algorithm requires, on average, only 1.7 times the costs of sentence-level inference and finds the exact solution on the vast majority of sentences.

2 Related Work

Methods that combine inter-sentence information with sentence-level algorithms have been applied to a number of NLP tasks. The most similar models to our work are skip-chain CRFs (Sutton and Mccallum, 2004), relational markov networks (Taskar et al., 2002), and collective inference with symmetric clique potentials (Gupta et al., 2010). These models use a linear-chain CRF or MRF objective modified by potentials defined over pairs of nodes or clique templates. The latter model makes use of Lagrangian relaxation. Skip-chain CRFs and collective inference have been applied to problems in IE, and RMNs to named entity recognition (NER) (Bunescu and Mooney, 2004). Finkel et al. (2005) also integrated non-local information into entity annotation algorithms using Gibbs sampling.

Our model can be applied to a variety of off-the-shelf structured prediction models. In particular, we focus on dependency parsing which is characterized by a more complicated structure compared to the IE tasks addressed by previous work.

Another line of work that integrates corpus-level declarative information into sentence-level models includes the posterior regularization (Ganchev et al., 2010; Gillenwater et al., 2010), generalized expectation (Mann and McCallum, 2007; Mann and McCallum,), and Bayesian measurements (Liang et al., 2009) frameworks. The power of these methods has been demonstrated for a variety of NLP tasks, such as unsupervised and semi-supervised POS tagging and parsing. The constraints used by these works differ from ours in that they encourage the posterior label distribution to have desired properties such as sparsity (e.g. a given word can take a small number of labels with a high probability). In addition, these methods use global information during training as opposed to our approach which applies test-time inference global constraints.

The application of dual decomposition for inference in MRFs has been explored by Wainwright et al. (2005), Komodakis et al. (2007), and Globerson and Jaakkola (2007). In NLP, Rush et al. (2010) and Koo et al. (2010) applied dual decomposition to enforce agreement between different sentence-level algorithms for parsing and POS tagging. Work on dual decomposition for NLP is related to the work of Smith and Eisner (2008) who apply belief propagation to inference in dependency parsing, and to constrained conditional models (CCM) (Roth and Yih, 2005) that impose inference-time constraints through an ILP formulation.

Several works have addressed semi-supervised learning for structured prediction, suggesting objectives based on the max-margin principles (Altun and Mcallester, 2005), manifold regularization (Belkin et al., 2005), a structured version of co-training (Brefeld and Scheffer, 2006) and an entropy-based regularizer for CRFs (Wang et al., 2009). The complete literature on domain adaptation is beyond the scope of this paper, but we refer the reader to Blitzer and Daume (2010) for a recent survey.

Specifically for parsing and POS tagging, self-training (Reichart and Rappoport, 2007), co-training (Steedman et al., 2003) and active learning (Hwa, 2004) have been shown useful in the lightly supervised setup. For parser adaptation, self-training (McClosky et al., 2006; McClosky and Charniak, 2008), using weakly annotated data from the target domain (Lease and Charniak, 2005; Rimell and Clark, 2008), ensemble learning (McClosky et al., 2010), hierarchical bayesian models (Finkel and Manning, 2009) and co-training (Sagae and Tsujii, 2007) achieve substantial performance gains. For a recent survey see Plank (2011). Constraints similar to those we use for POS tagging were used by Subramanya et al. (2010) for POS tagger adaptation.

Their work, however, does not show how to decode a global, corpus-level, objective that enforces these constraints, which is a major contribution of this paper.

Inter-sentence syntactic consistency has been explored in the psycholinguistics and NLP literature. Phenomena such as parallelism and syntactic priming – the tendency to repeat recently used syntactic structures – have been demonstrated in human language corpora (e.g. WSJ and Brown) (Dubey et al., 2009) and were shown useful in generative and discriminative parsers (e.g. (Cheung and Penn, 2010)). We complement these works, which focus on consistency between consecutive sentences, and explore corpus level consistency.

3 Structured Models

We begin by introducing notation for sentence-level dependency parsing as a structured prediction problem. The goal of dependency parsing is to find the best parse y for a tagged sentence $x = (w_1/t_1, \ldots, w_n/t_n)$ with words w and POS tags t. Define the *index set* for dependency parsing as

$$\mathcal{I}(x) = \{(m,h) \ : \ m \in \{1 \ldots n\}, \ h \in \{0 \ldots n\}, m \neq h\}$$

where $h = 0$ represents the root word. A dependency parse is a vector $y = \{y(m,h) : (m,h) \in \mathcal{I}(x)\}$ where $y(m,h) = 1$ if m is a modifier of the head word h. We define the set $\mathcal{Y}(x) \subset \{0,1\}^{|\mathcal{I}(x)|}$ to be the set of all valid dependency parses for a sentence x. In this work, we use projective dependency parses, but the method also applies to the set of non-projective parse trees.

Additionally, we have a scoring function $f : \mathcal{Y}(x) \rightarrow \mathbb{R}$. The optimal parse y^* for a sentence x is given by, $y^* = \arg\max_{y \in \mathcal{Y}(x)} f(y)$. This sentence-level decoding problem can often be solved efficiently. For example in commonly used projective dependency parsing models (McDonald et al., 2005), we can compute y^* efficiently using variants of the Viterbi algorithm.

For this work, we make the assumption that we have an efficient algorithm to find the argmax of

$$f(y) + \sum_{(m,h) \in \mathcal{I}(x)} u(m,h) y(m,h) = f(y) + u \cdot y$$

where u is a vector in $\mathbb{R}^{|\mathcal{I}(x)|}$. In practice, u will be a vector of Lagrange multipliers associated with the dependencies of y in our dual decomposition algorithm given in Section 6.

We can construct a very similar setting for POS tagging where the goal is to find the best tagging y for a sentence $x = (w_1, \ldots, w_n)$. We skip the formal details here.

We next introduce notation for Markov random fields (MRFs) (Koller and Friedman, 2009). An MRF consists of an undirected graph $G = (V, E)$, a set of possible labels for each node L_i for $i \in \{1, \ldots, |V|\}$, and a scoring function g. The index set for MRFs is

$$\begin{aligned} \mathcal{I}^{\text{MRF}} &= \{(i,l) : i \in \{1 \ldots |V|\}, l \in L_i\} \\ &\cup \ \{((i,j), l_i, l_j) : \ (i,j) \in E, l_i \in L_i, l_j \in L_j\} \end{aligned}$$

A label assignment in the MRF is a binary vector z with $z(i,l) = 1$ if the label l is selected at node i and $z((i,j), l_i, l_j) = 1$ if the labels l_i, l_j are selected for the nodes i, j.

In applications such as parsing and POS tagging, some of the label assignments are not allowed. For example, in dependency parsing the resulting structure must be a tree. Consequently, if every node in the MRF corresponds to a word in a document and its label corresponds to the index of its head word, the resulting dependency structure for each sentence must be acyclic. The set of all valid label assignments (one label per node) is given by $\mathcal{Z} \subset \{0,1\}^{|\mathcal{I}^{\text{MRF}}|}$.

We score label assignments in the MRF with a scoring function $g : \mathcal{Z} \rightarrow \mathbb{R}$. The best assignment z^* in an MRF is given by, $z^* = \arg\max_{z \in \mathcal{Z}} g(z)$. We focus on pairwise MRFs where this function g is a linear function of z whose parameters are denoted by θ

$$g(z) = z \cdot \theta = \sum_{(i,l) \in \mathcal{I}^{\text{MRF}}} z(i,l)\theta(i,l) + \sum_{((i,j),l_i,l_j) \in \mathcal{I}^{\text{MRF}}} z((i,j), l_i, l_j)\theta((i,j), l_i, l_j)$$

As in parsing, we make the assumption that we have an efficient algorithm to find the argmax of

$$g(z) + \sum_{(i,l) \in \mathcal{I}^{\text{MRF}}(x)} u(i,l) z(i,l)$$

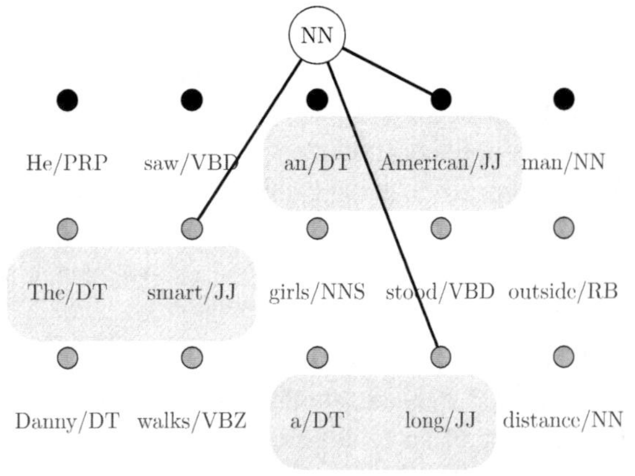

Figure 1: An example constraint from dependency parsing. The black nodes are modifiers observed in the training data. Each gray node corresponds to a possible modifier in the test corpus. The constraint applies to all modifiers in the context `DT JJ`. The white node corresponds to the consensus POS tag of the head word of these modifiers.

4 A Parsing Example

In this section we give a detailed example of global constraints for dependency parsing. The aim is to construct a global objective that encourages similar contexts across the corpus to exhibit similar syntactic behaviour. We implement this objective using an MRF with a node for each word in the test set. The label of each node is the index of the word it modifies. We add edges to this MRF to reward consistency among similar contexts. Furthermore, we add nodes with a fixed label to incorporate contexts seen in the training data.

Specifically, we say that the context of a word is its POS tag and the POS tags of some set of the words around it. We expand on this notion of context in Section 8; for simplicity we assume here that the context includes only the previous word's POS tag. Our constraints are designed to bias words in the same context to modify words with similar POS tags.

Figure 1 shows a global MRF over a small parsing example with one training sentence and two test sentences. The MRF contains a node associated with each word instance, where the label of the node is the index of the word it modifies. In this corpus, the context `DT JJ` appears once in training and twice in testing. We hope to choose head words with similar POS tags for these two test contexts biased by the observed training context.

More concretely, for each context $c \in \{1, \ldots, C\}$, we have a set S_c of associated word indices (s, m) that appear in the context, where s is a sentence index and m is a position in that sentence. For instance, in our example $S_1 = \{(1, 2), (2, 4)\}$ consists of all positions in the test set where we see `JJ` preceded by `DT`. Futhermore, we have a set O_c of indices (s, m, TR) of observed instances of the context in the training data where TR denotes a training index. In our example $O_1 = \{(1, 4, \mathrm{TR})\}$ consists of the one training instance. We associate each word instance with a single context c.

We then define our MRF to include one consensus node for each set S_c as well as a word node for each instance in the set $S_c \cup O_c$. Thus the set of variables corresponds to $V = \{1, \ldots, C\} \cup (\bigcup_{c=1}^{C} S_c \cup O_c)$. Additionally, we include an edge from each node $i \in S_c \cup O_c$ to its consensus node c, $E = \{(i, c) : c \in \{1, \ldots, C\}, i \in S_c \cup O_c\}$. The word nodes from S_c have the label set of possible head indices $L_{(s,m)} = \{0, \ldots, n_s\}$ where n_s is the length of the sentence s. The observed nodes from O_c have a singleton label set $L_{(s,m,\mathrm{TR})}$ with the observed index. The consensus nodes have the label set $L_c = \mathcal{T} \cup \{\mathrm{NULL}\}$ where $\mathcal{T}$ is the set of POS tags and the NULL symbol represents the constraint being turned off.

We can now define the scoring function g for this MRF. The scoring function aims to reward consistency among the head POS tag at each word and the consensus node

$$\theta((i, c), l_i, l_c) = \begin{cases} \delta_1 & \text{if } pos(l_i) = l_c \\ \delta_2 & \text{if } pos(l_i) \text{ is close to } l_c \\ \delta_3 & l_c = \mathrm{NULL} \\ 0 & \text{otherwise} \end{cases}$$

where pos maps a word index to its POS tag. The parameters $\delta_1 \geq \delta_2 \geq \delta_3 \geq 0$ determine the bonus for identical POS tags, similar POS tags, and for turning off the constraint .

We construct a similar model for POS tagging. We choose sets T_c corresponding to the c'th unknown word type in the corpus. The MRF graph is identical to the parsing case with T_c replacing S_c and we no longer have O_c. The label sets for the word nodes are now $L_{(s,m)} = \mathcal{T}$ where the label is the POS tag chosen at that word, and the label set for the consensus node is $L_c = \mathcal{T} \cup \{\text{NULL}\}$. We use the same scoring function as in parsing to enforce consistency between word nodes and the consensus node.

5 Global Objective

Recall the definition of sentence-level parsing, where the optimal parse y^* for a single sentence x under a scoring function f is given by: $y^* = \arg\max_{y \in \mathcal{Y}(x)} f(y)$. We apply this objective to a set of sentences, specified by the tuple $X = (x_1, ..., x_r)$, and the product of possible parses $\mathcal{Y}(X) = \mathcal{Y}(x_1) \times \ldots \times \mathcal{Y}(x_r)$. The sentence-level decoding problem is to find the optimal dependency parses $Y^* = (Y_1^*, ..., Y_r^*) \in \mathcal{Y}(X)$ under a global objective

$$Y^* = \arg\max_{Y \in \mathcal{Y}(X)} F(Y) = \arg\max_{Y \in \mathcal{Y}(X)} \sum_{s=1}^{r} f(Y_s)$$

where $F : \mathcal{Y}(X) \to \mathbb{R}$ is the global scoring function.

We now consider scoring functions where the global objective includes inter-sentence constraints. Objectives of this form will not factor directly into individual parsing problems; however, we can choose to write them as the sum of two convenient terms: (1) A simple sum of sentence-level objectives; and (2) A global MRF that connects the local structures.

For convenience, we define the following index set.

$$\mathcal{J}(X) = \{(s, m, h) : \quad s \in \{1, \ldots, r\}, \quad (m, h) \in \mathcal{I}(x_s)\}$$

This set enumerates all possible dependencies at each sentence in the corpus. We say the parses Y_s are consistent with a label assignment z if for all $(s, m, h) \in \mathcal{J}(X)$ we have that $z((s, m), h) = Y_s(m, h)$. In other words, the labels in z match the head words chosen in parse Y_s.

With this notation we can write the full global decoding objective as

$$(Y^*, z^*) = \arg\max_{Y \in \mathcal{Y}(X),\, z \in \mathcal{Z}} F(Y) + g(z) \quad (1)$$

$$\text{s.t. } \forall (s, m, h) \in \mathcal{J}(X),\ z((s, m), h) = Y_s(m, h)$$

The solution to this objective maximizes the local models as well as the global MRF, while maintaining consistency among the models. Specifically, the MRF we use in the experiments has a simple naive Bayes structure with the consensus node connected to all relevant word nodes.

The global objective for POS tagging has a similar form. As before we add a node to the MRF for each word in the corpus. We use the POS tag set as our labels for each of these nodes. The index set contains an element for each possible tag at each word instance in the corpus.

Set $u^{(1)}(s, m, h) \leftarrow 0$ for all $(s, m, h) \in \mathcal{J}(X)$
for $k = 1$ to K **do**
  $z^{(k)} \leftarrow \arg\max_{z \in \mathcal{Z}} \ (g(z) + \sum_{(s,m,h) \in \mathcal{J}(X)} u^{(k)}(s, m, h) z((s, m), h))$
  $Y^{(k)} \leftarrow \arg\max_{Y \in \mathcal{Y}(X)} (F(Y) - \sum_{(s,m,h) \in \mathcal{J}(X)} u^{(k)}(s, m, h) Y_s(m, h))$
  if $Y_s^{(k)}(m, h) = z^{(k)}((s, m), h)$
    for all $(s, m, h) \in \mathcal{J}(X)$ **then**
    return $(Y^{(k)}, z^{(k)})$
  for all $(s, m, h) \in \mathcal{J}(X)$,
    $u^{(k+1)}(s, m, h) \leftarrow u^{(k)}(s, m, h) + \alpha_k(z^{(k)}((s, m), h) - Y_s^{(k)}(m, h))$
return $(Y^{(K)}, z^{(K)})$

Figure 2: The global decoding algorithm for dependency parsing models.

6 A Global Decoding Algorithm

We now consider the decoding question: how to find the structure Y^* that maximizes the global objective. We aim for an efficient solution that makes use of the individual solvers at the sentence-level. For this work, we make the assumption that the graph chosen for the MRF has small tree-width, e.g. our naive Bayes constraints, and can be solved efficiently using dynamic programming.

Before we describe our dual decomposition algorithm, we consider the difficulty of solving the global objective directly. We have an efficient dynamic programming algorithm for solving dependency parsing at the sentence-level, and efficient algorithms for solving the MRF. It follows that we could construct an intersected dynamic programming algorithm that maintains the product of states over both models. This algorithm is exact, but it is very inefficient. Solving the intersected dynamic program requires decoding simultaneously over the entire corpus, with an additional multiplicative factor for solving the MRF. On top of this cost, we need to alter the internal structure of the sentence-level models.

In contrast, we can construct a dual decomposition algorithm which is efficient, produces a certificate when it finds an exact solution, and directly uses the sentence-level parsing models. Considering again the global objective of equation 1, we note that the difficulty in decoding this objective comes entirely from the constraints $z((s,m),h) = Y_s(m,h)$. If these were not there, the problem would factor into two parts, an optimization of F over the test corpus $\mathcal{Y}(X)$ and an optimization of g over possible MRF assignments $\mathcal{Z}$. The first problem factors naturally into sentence-level parsing problems and the second can be solved efficiently given our assumptions on the MRF topology G.

Recent work has shown that a relaxation based on dual decomposition often produces an exact solution for such problems (Koo et al., 2010). To apply dual decomposition, we introduce Lagrange multipliers $u(s,m,h)$ for the agreement constraints between the sentence-level models and the global MRF. The Lagrangian dual is the function $L(u) = \max_z g(z,u) + \max_y F(y,u)$ where

$$g(z,u) = g(z) + \sum_{(s,m,h)\in\mathcal{J}(X)} u(s,m,h) z((s,m),h)),$$

$$F(y,u) = F(Y) - \sum_{(s,m,h)\in\mathcal{J}(X)} u(s,m,h) Y_s(m,h)$$

In order to find $\min_u L(u)$, we use subgradient descent. This requires computing $g(z,u)$ and $F(y,u)$ for fixed values of u, which by our assumptions from Section 3 are efficient to calculate.

The full algorithm is given in Figure 2. We start with the values of u initialized to 0. At each iteration k, we find the best set of parses $Y^{(k)}$ over the entire corpus and the best MRF assignment $z^{(k)}$. We then update the value of u based on the difference between $Y^{(k)}$ and $z^{(k)}$ and a rate parameter α. On the next iteration, we solve the same decoding problems modified by the new value of u. If at any point the current solutions $Y^{(k)}$ and $z^{(k)}$ satisfy the consistency constraint, we return their current values. Otherwise, we stop at a max iteration K and return the values from the last iteration.

	≥ 0.7	≥ 0.8	≥ 0.9	1.0
All Contexts	66.8	57.9	46.8	33.3
Head in Context	76.0	67.9	57.2	42.3

Table 1: Exploratory statistics for constraint selection. The table shows the percentage of context types for which the probability of the most frequent head tag is at least p. Head in Context refers to the subset of contexts where the most frequent head is within the context itself. Numbers are based on Section 22 of the Wall Street Journal and are given for contexts that appear at least 10 times.

We now give a theorem for the formal guarantees of this algorithm.

Theorem 1 *If for some $k \in \{1 \dots K\}$ in the algorithm in Figure 2, $Y_s^{(k)}(m,h) = z^{(k)}(s,m,h)$ for all $(s,m,h) \in \mathcal{J}$, then $(Y^{(k)}, z^{(k)})$ is a solution to the maximization problem in equation 1.*

We omit the proof for brevity. It is a slight variation of the proof given by Rush et al. (2010).

7 Consistency Constraints

In this section we describe the consistency constraints used for the global models of parsing and tagging.

Parsing Constraints. Recall from Section 4 that we choose parsing constraints based on the word context. We encourage words in similar contexts to choose head words with similar POS tags.

We use a simple procedure to select which constraints to add. First define a context template to be a set of offsets $\{r, \dots, s\}$ with $r \leq 0 \leq s$ that specify the neighboring words to include in a context. In the example of Figure 1, the context template $\{-1, 0, 1, 2\}$ applied to the word `girls/NNS` would produce the context `JJ NNS VBD RB`. For each word in the corpus, we consider all possible templates with $s - r < 4$. We use only contexts that predict the head POS of the context in the training data with probability 1 and prefer long over short contexts. Once we select the context of each word, we add a consensus node for each context type in the corpus. We connect each word node to its corresponding consensus node.

Local context does not fully determine the POS tag of the head word, but for certain contexts it provides a strong signal. Table 1 shows context statistics for English. For 46.8% of the contexts, the most frequent head tag is chosen $\geq 90\%$ of the time. The pattern is even stronger for contexts where the most frequent head tag is within the context itself. In this case, for 57.2% of the contexts the most frequent head tag is chosen $\geq 90\%$ of the time. Consequently, if more than one context can be selected for a word, we favor the contexts where the most frequent head POS is inside the context.

POS Tagging Constraints. For POS tagging, our constraints focus on words not observed in the training data. It is well-known that each word type appears only with a small number of POS tags. In Section 22 of the WSJ corpus, 96.35% of word types appear with a single POS tag.

In most test sets we are unlikely to see an unknown word more than once or twice. To fix this sparsity issue, we import additional unannotated sentences for each unknown word from the New York Times Section of the NANC corpus (Graff, 1995). These sentences give additional information for unknown word types.

Additionally, we note that morphologically related words often have similar POS tags. We can exploit this relationship by connecting related word types to the same consensus node. We experimented with various morphological variants and found that connecting a word type with the type generated by appending the suffix "s" was most beneficial. For each unknown word type, we also import sentences for its morphologically related words.

8 Experiments and Results

We experiment in two common scenarios where parsing performance is reduced from the fully supervised, in-domain case. In domain adaptation, we train our model completely in one source domain and test it on a different target domain. In lightly supervised training, we simulate the case where only a limited amount of annotated data is available for a language.

	Base	ST	Model	ER
WSJ $\rightarrow$ QTB	89.63	89.99	90.43	7.7
QTB $\rightarrow$ WSJ	74.89	74.97	75.76	3.5

Table 2: Dependency parsing UAS for domain adaptation. WSJ is the Penn TreeBank. QTB is the QuestionBank. ER is error reduction. Results are significant using the sign test with $p \leq 0.05$.

Data for Domain Adaptation We perform domain adaptation experiments in English using the WSJ PennTreebank (Marcus et al., 1993) and the QuestionBank (QTB) (Judge et al., 2006). In the WSJ $\rightarrow$ QTB scenario, we train on sections 2-21 of the WSJ and test on the entire QTB (4000 questions). In the QTB $\rightarrow$ WSJ scenario, we train on the entire QTB and test on section 23 of the WSJ.

Data for Lightly Supervised Training For all English experiments, our data was taken from the WSJ PennTreebank: training sentences from Section 0, development sentences from Section 22, and test sentences from Section 23. For experiments in Bulgarian, German, Japanese, and Spanish, we use the CONLL-X data set (Buchholz and Marsi, 2006) with training data taken from the official training files. We trained the sentence-level models with 50-500 sentences. To verify the robustness of our results, our test sets consist of the official test sets augmented with additional sentences from the official training files such that each test file consists of 25,000 words. Our results on the official test sets are very similar to the results we report and are omitted for brevity.

Parameters The model parameters, δ_1, δ_2, and δ_3 of the scoring function (Section 4) and α of the Lagrange multipliers update rule (Section 6), were tuned on the English development data. In our dual decomposition inference algorithm, we use $K = 200$ maximum iterations and tune the decay rate following the protocol described by Koo et al. (2010).

Sentence-Level Models For dependency parsing we utilize the second-order projective MST parser (McDonald et al., 2005)[1] with the gold-standard POS tags of the corpus. For POS tagging we use the Stanford POS tagger (Toutanova et al., 2003)[2].

[1] http://sourceforge.net/projects/mstparser/

[2] http://nlp.stanford.edu/software/tagger.shtml

	50			100			200			500		
	Base	ST	Model (ER)	Base	ST	Model (ER)	Base	ST	Model (ER)	Base	ST	Model (ER)
Jap	79.10	80.19	81.78 (12.82)	81.53	81.59	83.09 (8.45)	84.84	85.05	85.50 (4.35)	87.14	87.24	87.44 (2.33)
Eng	69.60	69.73	71.62 (6.64)	73.97	74.01	75.27 (4.99)	77.67	77.68	78.69 (4.57)	81.83	81.90	82.18 (1.93)
Spa	71.67	71.72	73.19 (5.37)	74.53	74.63	75.41 (3.46)	77.11	77.09	77.44 (1.44)	79.97	79.88	80.04 (0.35)
Bul	71.10	70.59	72.13 (3.56)	73.35	72.96	74.61 (4.73)	75.38	75.54	76.17 (3.21)	81.95	81.75	82.18 (1.27)
Ger	68.21	68.28	68.83 (1.95)	72.19	72.29	72.76 (2.05)	74.34	74.45	74.95 (2.4)	77.20	77.09	77.51 (1.4)

Table 3: Dependency parsing UAS by size of training set and language. English data is from the WSJ. Bulgarian, German, Japanese, and Spanish data is from the CONLL-X data sets. Base is the second-order, projective dependency parser of McDonald et al. (2005). ST is a self-training model based on Reichart and Rappoport (2007). Model is the same parser augmented with inter-sentence constraints. ER is error reduction. Using the sign test with $p \leq 0.05$, all 50, 100, and 200 results are significant, as are Eng and Ger 500.

	50		100		200		500	
	Base	Model (ER)	Base	Model (ER)	Base	Model (ER)	Base	Model (ER)
Acc	79.67	81.77 (10.33)	85.42	86.37 (6.52)	88.63	89.37 (6.51)	91.59	91.98 (4.64)
Unk	62.88	67.16 (11.53)	71.10	73.32 (7.68)	75.82	78.07 (9.31)	80.67	82.28 (8.33)

Table 4: POS tagging accuracy. Stanford POS tagger refers to the maximum entropy trigram tagger of Toutanova et al. (2003). Our inter-sentence POS tagger augments this baseline with global constraints. ER is error reduction. All results are significant using the sign test with $p \leq 0.05$.

Evaluation and Baselines To measure parsing performance, we use unlabeled attachment score (UAS) given by the CONLL-X dependency parsing shared task evaluation script (Buchholz and Marsi, 2006). We compare the accuracy of dependency parsing with global constraints to the sentence-level dependency parser of McDonald et al. (2005) and to a self-training baseline (Steedman et al., 2003; Reichart and Rappoport, 2007). The parsing baseline is equivalent to a single round of dual decomposition. For the self-training baseline, we parse the test corpus, append the labeled test sentences to the training corpus, train a new parser, and then re-parse the test set. We run this procedure for a single iteration.

For POS tagging we measure token level POS accuracy for all the words in the corpus and also for unknown words (words not observed in the training data). We compare the accuracy of POS tagging with global constraints to the accuracy of the Stanford POS tagger [3].

Domain Adaptation Accuracy Results are presented in Table 2. The constrained model reduces the error of the baseline on both cases. Note that when the base parser is trained on the WSJ corpus its UAS performance on the QTB is 89.63%. Yet, the constrained model is still able to reduce the baseline error by 7.7%.

[3] We do not run self-training for POS tagging as it has been shown unuseful for this application (Clark et al., 2003).

Lightly Supervised Accuracy The parsing results are given in Table 3. Our model improves over the baseline parser and self-training across all languages and training set sizes. The best results are for Japanese and English with error reductions of 2.33 – 12.82% and 1.93 – 6.64% respectively. The self-training baseline achieves small gains on some languages, but generally performs similarly to the standard parser.

The POS tagging results are given in Table 4. Our model improves over the baseline tagger for the entire training size range. For 50 training sentences we reduce 10.33% of the overall error, and 11.53% of the error on unknown words. Although the tagger performance substantially improves when the training set grows to 500 sentences, our model still provides an overall error reduction of 4.64% and of 8.33% for unknown words.

9 Discussion

Efficiency Since dual decomposition often requires hundreds of iterations to converge, a naive implementation would be orders of magnitude slower than the underlying sentence-level model. We use two techniques to speed-up the algorithm.

First, we follow Koo et al. (2010) and use lazy decoding as part of dual decomposition. At each iteration k, we cache the result of the MRF $z^{(k)}$ and set of parse tree $Y^{(k)}$. In the next iteration, we only

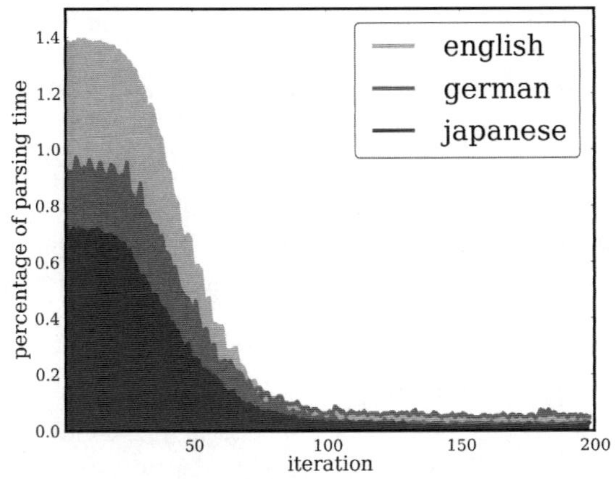

Figure 3: Efficiency of dependency parsing decoding for three languages. The plot shows the speed of each iteration of the subgradient algorithm relative to a round of unconstrained parsing.

Most Effective Contexts	
WSJ → QTB	QTB → WSJ
WRB VBP	VBD NN **NN** ,
DT JJS NN **IN**	IN PRP **VBZ**
VBP PRP **VB**	**JJ** JJ NN ,
DT **NN** NN VB	IN **JJ** JJ NN
RBS JJ NN **IN**	**NN** POS NN NN

Table 5: The five most effective constraint contexts from the domain adaptation experiments. The bold POS tag indicates the modifier word of the context.

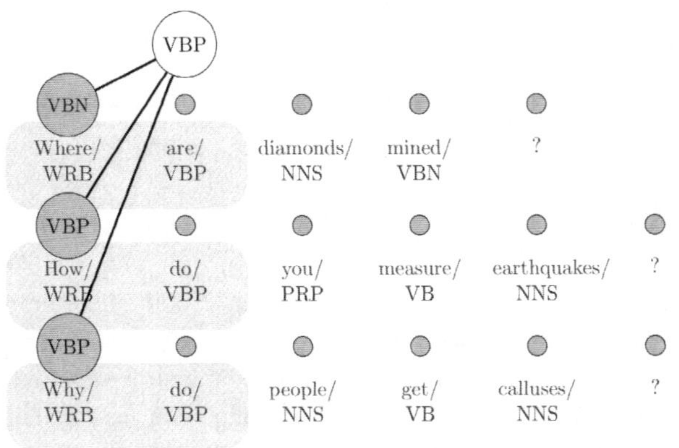

Figure 4: Subset of sentences with the context **WRB** VBP from WSJ → QTB domain adaptation. In the first round, the parser chooses VBN for the first sentence, which is inconsistent with similar contexts. The constraints correct this choice in later rounds.

recompute the solution Y_s^* for a sentence s if the weight $u(s, m, h)$ for some m, h was updated. A similar technique is applied to the MRF.

Second, during the first iteration of the algorithm we apply max-marginal based pruning using the threshold defined by Weiss and Taskar (2010). This produces a pruned hypergraph for each sentence, which allows us to avoid recomputing parse features and to solve a simplified search problem.

To measure efficiency, we compare the time spent in dual decomposition to the speed of unconstrained inference. Across experiments, the mean dual decomposition time is 1.71 times the cost of unconstrained inference. Figure 3 shows how this time is spent after the first iteration. The early iterations are around 1% of the total cost, and because of lazy decoding this quickly drops to almost nothing.

Exactness To measure exactness, we count the number of sentences for which we should remove the constraints in order for the model to reach convergence. For dependency parsing, across languages removing constraints on 0.6% of sentences yields exact convergence. Removing these constraints has very little effect on the final outcome of the model. For POS tagging, the algorithm finds an exact solution after removing constraints from 0.2% of the sentences.

Constraint Analysis We can also look at the number, size, and outcome of the constraints chosen in the experiments. In the lightly supervised experiments, the average number of constraints is 3298 for 25000 tokens, where the median constraint connects 19 different tokens. Of these constraints around 70% are active (non-NULL). The domain adaptation experiments have a similar number of constraints with around 75% of constraints active. In both experiments many of the constraints are found to be consistent after the first iteration, but as Figure 3 implies, other constraints take multiple iterations to converge.

Qualitative Analysis In order to understand why these simple consistency constraints are effective, we take a qualitative look at the the domain adaptation experiments on the QuestionBank. Table 5 ranks the five most effective contextual constraints from both experiments. For the WSJ → QTB experiment, the most effective constraint relates the inital question word with an adjacent verb. Figure 4 shows sentences where this constraint applies in the QuestionBank. For the QTB → WSJ experiment, the effective contexts are mostly long base noun phrases. These occur often in the WSJ but are rare in the simpler QuestionBank sentences.

10 Conclusion

In this work we experiment with inter-sentence consistency constraints for dependency parsing and POS tagging. We have proposed a corpus-level objective that augments sentence-level models with such constraints and described an exact and efficient dual decomposition algorithm for its decoding. In future work, we intend to explore efficient techniques for joint parameter learning for both the global MRF and the local models.

Acknowledgments Columbia University gratefully acknowledges the support of the Defense Advanced Research Projects Agency (DARPA) Machine Reading Program under Air Force Research Laboratory (AFRL) prime contract no. FA8750-09-C-0181. Any opinions, findings, and conclusions or recommendations expressed in this material are those of the author(s) and do not necessarily reflect the view of DARPA, AFRL, or the US government. Alexander Rush was supported by a National Science Foundation Graduate Research Fellowship.

References

Y. Altun and D. Mcallester. 2005. Maximum margin semi-supervised learning for structured variables. In *NIPS*.

M. Belkin, P. Niyogi, and V. Sindhwani. 2005. On manifold regularization. In *AISTATS*.

John Blitzer and Hal Daume. 2010. Icml 2010 tutorial on domain adaptation. In *ICML*.

U. Brefeld and T. Scheffer. 2006. Semi-supervised learning for structured output variables. In *ICML*.

S. Buchholz and E. Marsi. 2006. CoNLL-X shared task on multilingual dependency parsing. In *CoNLL*.

R.C. Bunescu and R.J. Mooney. 2004. Collective information extraction with relational markov networks. In *ACL*.

J.C.K Cheung and G. Penn. 2010. Utilizing extra-sentential context for parsing. In *EMNLP*.

Stephen Clark, James Curran, and Miles Osborne. 2003. Bootstrapping pos taggers using unlabelled data. In *CoNLL*.

A. Dubey, F. Keller, and P. Sturt. 2009. A probabilistic corpus-based model of parallelism. *Cognition*, 109(2):193–210.

Jenny Rose Finkel and Christopher Manning. 2009. Hierarchical bayesian domain adaptation. In *NAACL*.

J.R. Finkel, T. Grenager, and C. Manning. 2005. Incorporating non-local information into information extraction systems by gibbs sampling. In *ACL*.

K. Ganchev, J. Graça, J. Gillenwater, and B. Taskar. 2010. Posterior Regularization for Structured Latent Variable Models. *Journal of Machine Learning Research*, 11:2001–2049.

J. Gillenwater, K. Ganchev, J. Graça, F. Pereira, and B. Taskar. 2010. Sparsity in dependency grammar induction. In *Proceedings of the ACL Conference Short Papers*.

A. Globerson and T. Jaakkola. 2007. Fixing max-product: Convergent message passing algorithms for map lp-relaxations. In *NIPS*.

D. Graff. 1995. North american news text corpus. *Linguistic Data Consortium*, LDC95T21.

Rahul Gupta, Sunita Sarawagi, and Ajit A. Diwan. 2010. Collective inference for extraction mrfs coupled with symmetric clique potentials. *JMLR*.

R. Hwa. 2004. Sample selection for statistical parsing. *Computational Linguistics*, 30(3):253–276.

John Judge, Aoife Cahill, and Josef van Genabith. 2006. Questionbank: Creating a corpus of parse-annotated questions. In *ACL-COLING*.

D. Koller and N. Friedman. 2009. *Probabilistic Graphical Models: Principles and Techniques*. MIT Press.

N. Komodakis, N. Paragios, and G. Tziritas. 2007. MRF optimization via dual decomposition: Message-passing revisited. In *ICCV*.

T. Koo, A.M. Rush, M. Collins, T. Jaakkola, and D. Sontag. 2010. Dual decomposition for parsing with non-projective head automata. In *EMNLP*.

Matthew Lease and Eugene Charniak. 2005. Parsing biomedical literature. In *IJCNLP*.

P. Liang, M. I. Jordan, and D. Klein. 2009. Learning from measurements in exponential families. In *ICML*.

G.S. Mann and A. McCallum. Generalized expectation criteria for semi-supervised learning with weakly labeled data. *Journal of Machine Learning Research*, 11:955–984.

G.S. Mann and A. McCallum. 2007. Simple, robust, scalable semi-supervised learning via expectation regularization. In *ICML*.

M.P. Marcus, M.A. Marcinkiewicz, and B. Santorini. 1993. Building a large annotated corpus of english: The penn treebank. *Computational linguistics*, 19(2):313–330.

David McClosky and Eugene Charniak. 2008. Self-training for biomedical parsing. In *ACL, sort papers*.

David McClosky, Eugene Charniak, and Mark Johnson. 2006. Reranking and self-training for parser adaptation. In *ACL*.

David McClosky, Eugene Charniak, and Mark Johnson. 2010. Automatic domain adapatation for parsing. In *NAACL*.

R.T. McDonald, F. Pereira, K. Ribarov, and J. Hajic. 2005. Non-projective dependency parsing using spanning tree algorithms. In *HLT/EMNLP*.

Barbara Plank. 2011. *Domain Adaptation for Parsing*. Ph.d. thesis, University of Groningen.

R. Reichart and A. Rappoport. 2007. Self-training for enhancement and domain adaptation of statistical parsers trained on small datasets. In *ACL*.

Laura Rimell and Stephen Clark. 2008. Adapting a lexicalized-grammar parser to contrasting domains. In *EMNLP*.

D. Roth and W. Yih. 2005. Integer linear programming inference for conditional random fields. In *ICML*.

A.M. Rush, D. Sontag, M. Collins, and T. Jaakkola. 2010. On dual decomposition and linear programming relaxations for natural language processing. In *EMNLP*.

Kenji Sagae and Junichi Tsujii. 2007. Dependency parsing and domain adaptation with lr models and parser ensembles. In *EMNLP-CoNLL*.

D.A. Smith and J. Eisner. 2008. Dependency parsing by belief propagation. In *EMNLP*.

M. Steedman, M. Osborne, A. Sarkar, S. Clark, R. Hwa, J. Hockenmaier, P. Ruhlen, S. Baker, and J. Crim. 2003. Bootstrapping statistical parsers from small datasets. In *EACL*.

Amarnag Subramanya, Slav Petrov, and Fernando Pereira. 2010. Efficient graph-based semi-supervised learning of structured tagging models. In *EMNLP*.

C. Sutton and A. Mccallum. 2004. Collective segmentation and labeling of distant entities in information extraction. In *In ICML Workshop on Statistical Relational Learning and Its Connections*.

B. Taskar, P. Abbeel, and d. Koller. 2002. Discriminative probabilistic models for relational data. In *UAI*.

K. Toutanova, D. Klein, C.D. Manning, and Y. Singer. 2003. Feature-rich part-of-speech tagging with a cyclic dependency network. In *HLT-NAACL*.

M. Wainwright, T. Jaakkola, and A. Willsky. 2005. MAP estimation via agreement on trees: message-passing and linear programming. In *IEEE Transactions on Information Theory*, volume 51, pages 3697–3717.

Y. Wang, G. Haffari, S. Wang, and G. Mori. 2009. A rate distortion approach for semi-supervised conditional random fields. In *NIPS*.

D. Weiss and B. Taskar. 2010. Structured prediction cascades. In *Proc. of AISTATS*, volume 1284.

Unified Dependency Parsing of Chinese Morphological and Syntactic Structures

Zhongguo Li **Guodong Zhou**
Natural Language Processing Laboratory
School of Computer Science and Technology
Soochow University, Suzhou, Jiangsu Province 215006, China
{lzg, gdzhou}@suda.edu.cn

Abstract

Most previous approaches to syntactic parsing of Chinese rely on a preprocessing step of word segmentation, thereby assuming there was a clearly defined boundary between morphology and syntax in Chinese. We show how this assumption can fail badly, leading to many out-of-vocabulary words and incompatible annotations. Hence in practice the strict separation of morphology and syntax in the Chinese language proves to be untenable. We present a unified dependency parsing approach for Chinese which takes unsegmented sentences as input and outputs both morphological and syntactic structures with a single model and algorithm. By removing the intermediate word segmentation, the unified parser no longer needs separate notions for words and phrases. Evaluation proves the effectiveness of the unified model and algorithm in parsing structures of words, phrases and sentences simultaneously. [1]

1 Introduction

The formulation of the concept of words has baffled linguists from ancient to modern times (Hockett, 1969). Things are even worse for Chinese, partly due to the fact that its written form does not delimit words explicitly. While we have no doubt that there are linguistic units which are definitely words (or phrases, for that matter), it's a sad truth that in many cases we cannot manage to draw such a clear boundary between morphology and syntax, for which we now give two arguments.

The first argument is that many sub-word linguistic units (such as suffixes and prefixes) are so productive that they can lead to a huge number of out-of-vocabulary words for natural language processing systems. This phenomenon brings us into an awkward situation if we adhere to a rigid separation of morphology and syntax. Consider character 者 'someone' as an example. On the one hand, there is strong evidence that it's not a word as it can never be used alone. On the other hand, taking it as a mere suffix leads to many out-of-vocabulary words because of the productivity of such characters. For instance, Penn Chinese Treebank (CTB6) contains 失败者 'one that fails' as a word but not 成功者 'one that succeeds', even with the word 成功 'succeed' appearing 207 times. We call words like 成功者 'one that succeeds' *pseudo* OOVs. By definition, pseudo OOVs are OOVs since they do not occur in the training corpus, though their components are frequently-seen words. Our estimation is that over 60% of OOVs in Chinese are of this kind (Section 2).

Of course, the way out of this dilemma is to parse the internal structures of these words. That is to say, we can still regard characters like 者 as suffixes, taking into account the fact that they cannot be used alone. Meanwhile, pseudo OOVs can be largely eliminated through analyzing their structures, thus greatly facilitating syntactic and semantic analysis of sentences. In fact, previous studies have revealed other good reasons for parsing internal structures of words (Zhao, 2009; Li, 2011).

The second argument is that in Chinese many linguistic units can form both words and phrases with exactly the same meaning and part-of-speech, which

[1] Corresponding author is Guodong Zhou.

Figure 1: Unified parsing of words and phrases.

causes lots of *incompatible annotations* in currently available corpora. Take character 法 'law' as an example. It is head of both 刑法 'criminal law' and 环境保护法 'environmental protection law', but CTB treat it as a suffix in the former (with the annotation being 刑法_NN) and a word in the later (the annotation is 环境_NN 保护_NN 法_NN). These annotations are incompatible since in both cases the character 法 'law' bears exactly the same meaning and usage (e.g. part-of-speech). We examined several widely used corpora and found that about 90% of affixes were annotated incompatibly (Section 2). Incompatibility can be avoided through parsing structures of both words and phrases. Figure 1 conveys this idea. A further benefit of unified parsing is to reduce data sparseness. As an example, in CTB6 器 'machine' appears twice in phrases but 377 times in words (e.g. 加速器 'accelerator'). Word structures in Chinese can be excellent guide for parsing phrase structures, and vice versa, due to their similarity.

The present paper makes two contributions in light of these issues. Firstly, in order to get rid of pseudo OOVs and incompatible annotations, we have annotated structures of words in CTB6, after which statistical models can learn structures of words as well as phrases from the augmented treebank (Section 4). Although previous authors have noticed the importance of word-structure parsing (Li, 2011; Zhao, 2009), no detailed description about annotation of word structures has been provided in the literature. Secondly, we designed a unified dependency parser whose input is unsegmented sentences and its output incorporates both morphological and syntactic structures with a single model and algorithm (Section 5). By removing the intermediate step of word segmentation, our unified parser no longer depends on the unsound notion that there is a clear boundary between words and phrases. Evaluation (Section 6) shows that our unified parser achieves satisfactory accuracies in parsing both morphological and syntactic structures.

corpus	OOV	pseudo	percent
CTB6	158	112	70.9
MSR	1,783	1,307	73.3
PKU	2,860	1,836	64.2
AS	3,020	2,143	71.0
CITYU	1,665	1,100	66.0

Table 1: Statistics of pseudo OOVs for five corpora.

2 Pseudo OOVs and Incompatible Annotations

In this section we show the surprisingly pervasive nature of pseudo OOVs and incompatible annotations through analysis of five segmented corpora, which are CTB6 and corpus by MSR, PKU, AS and CITYU provided in SIGHAN word segmentation Bakeoffs [2].

First we use the standard split of training and testing data and extract all OOVs for each corpus, then count the number of pseudo OOVs. Table 1 gives the result. It's amazing that for every corpus, over 60% of OOVs are pseudo, meaning they can be avoided if their internal structures were parsed. Reduction of OOVs at such a large scale can benefit greatly downstream natural language processing systems.

We then sample 200 word types containing a productive affix from each corpus, and check whether the affix also occurs somewhere else in a phrase, i.e, the affix is annotated as a word in the phrase. The results are in Table 2. It's clear and somewhat shocking that most affixes are annotated incompatibly. We believe it is not the annotators to blame, rather the root cause lies deeply in the unique characteristics of the Chinese language. This becomes obvious in comparison with English, where suffix like '-ism' in 'capitalism' cannot be used alone as a word in phrases. [3] Incompatible annotations can be removed only through unified parsing of word and phrase structures, as mentioned earlier and illustrated in Figure 1.

[2] http://www.sighan.org/bakeoff2005/

[3] Actually English allows examples like "pre- and post-war imperialism" where a prefix like "pre" can appear on its own as long as the hyphen is present and it is in a coordination structure. Note that such examples are much rarer than what we discuss in this paper for Chinese. We thank the reviewer very much for pointing this out and providing this example for us.

corpus	incompatible	percent
CTB6	190	95
MSR	178	89
PKU	192	96
AS	182	91
CITYU	194	97

Table 2: Statistics of incompatibly annotated affixes in 200 sampled words for five segmented corpora.

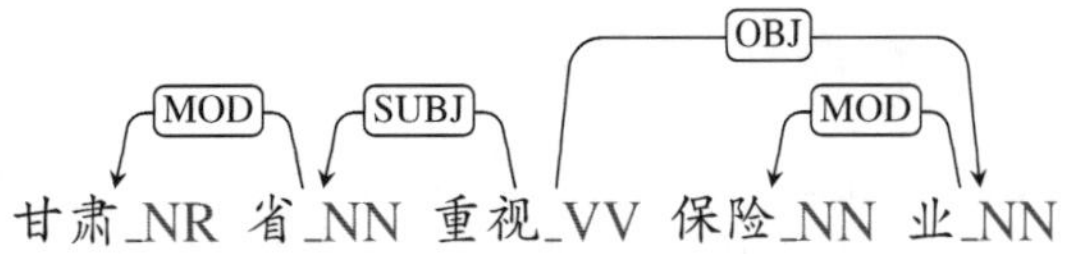

Figure 2: Example output of unified dependency parsing of Chinese morphological and syntactic structures.

3 Unified Parsing Defined

Given an unsegmented sentence 甘肃省重视保险业 'Gansu province attaches great importance to insurance industry', the output of unified dependency parser is shown in Figure 2. As can be seen, this output contains information about word (such as 重视_VV) as well as phrase structures (such as 重视_VV 保险_NN 业_NN), which is what we mean by 'unified' parsing. Now, it's no longer vital to differentiate between morphology and syntax for Chinese. People could regard 保险业 'insurance industry' as a word or phrase, but either way, there will be no disagreements about its internal structure. From the perspective of the unified parser, linguistic units are given the same labels as long as they function similarly (e.g, they have the same parts-of-speech).

As a bonus, output of unified parsing incorporates Chinese word segmentation, part-of-speech tagging and dependency parsing. To achieve these goals, previous systems usually used a pipelined approach by combining several statistical models, which was further complicated by different decoding algorithms for each of these models. The present paper shows that a single model does all these jobs. Besides being much simpler in engineering such a parser, this approach is also a lot more plausible for modeling human language understanding.

4 Annotation of Word Structures

Unified parsing requires a corpus annotated with both morphological and syntactic structures. Such a corpus can be built with the least effort if we begin with an existing treebank such as CTB6 already annotated with syntactic structures. It only remains for us to annotate internal structures of words in this treebank.

4.1 Scope of Annotation

In order to get rid of pseudo OOVs and incompatible annotations, internal structures are annotated for two kinds of words. The first kind contains words with a productive component such as suffix or prefix. One example is 陈述人 'speaker' whose suffix is the very productive 人 'person' (e.g, in CTB6 there are about 400 words having this suffix). The second kind includes words with compositional semantics. Examples are 星期一 'Monday' and 星期天 'Sunday'. Though 星期 'week' is not very productive, the meaning of words with this prefix is deducible from semantics of their components.

Other compound words such as 研究 'research' have no productive components and are not a cause of pseudo OOVs. They are universally considered as words instead of phrases due to their non-compositional semantics. Hence their structures are not annotated in the present research. Meanwhile, for single-morpheme words with no structures whatsoever, like 伊拉克 'Iraq' and 蝙蝠 'bat', annotation of internal structures is of course unnecessary either.

Of all the 54, 214 word types in CTB6, 35% are annotated, while the percentage is 24% for the 782, 901 word tokens. Around 80% of sentences contain words whose structures need annotation. Our annotations will be made publicly available for research purposes.

4.2 From Part-of-speeches to Constituents

Of all 33 part-of-speech tags in CTB, annotation of word structures is needed for nine tags: NN, VV, JJ, CD, NT, NR, AD, VA and OD. Since part-of-speech tags are preterminals and can only have one terminal word as its child, POS tags of words become constituent labels after annotation of word structures. The mapping rules from POS tags to constituent labels are listed in Table 3. Readers should note that

POS tags	constituent label
NR, NN, NT	NP
JJ	ADJP
AD	ADVP
CD, OD	QP
VV, VA	VP

Table 3: Correspondence between POS tags and constituent labels after annotation.

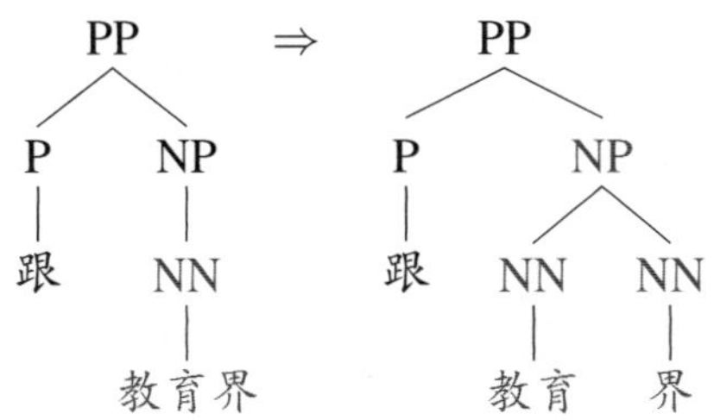

Figure 3: Example annotation for the word 教育界_NN in CTB6: POS tag NN changes to constituent label NP after annotation.

such mapping is not arbitrary. The constraint is that in the treebank the POS tag must somewhere be the unique child of the constituent label. Figure 3 depicts an example annotation, in which we also have an example of NP having a tag NN as its only child.

4.3 Recursive Annotation

Some words in CTB have very complex structures. Examples include 原子核物理学家 'physicist majoring in nuclear physics', 反托拉斯法 'anti-trust laws' etc. Structures of these words are annotated to their full possible depth. Existence of such words are characteristic of the Chinese language, since they are further demonstrations of the blurred boundary between morphology and syntax. A full-fledged parser is needed to analyze structures of these words, which incidentally provides us with another motivation for unified morphological and syntactic parsing of Chinese.

5 Unified Dependency Parsing

All previous dependency parsers for Chinese take it for granted that the input sentence is already segmented into words (Li et al., 2011). Most systems even require words to be tagged with their part-of-speeches (Zhang and Nivre, 2011). Hence current off-the-shelf algorithms are inadequate for parsing unsegmented sentences. Instead, a new unified parsing algorithm is given in this section.

5.1 Transitions

To map a raw sentence directly to output shown in Figure 2, we define four transitions for the unified dependency parser. They act on a stack containing the incremental parsing results, and a queue holding the incoming Chinese characters of the sentence:

SHIFT: the first character in the queue is shifted into the stack as the start of a new word. The queue should not be empty.

LEFT: the top two words of the stack are connected with an arc, with the top one being the head. There should be at least two elements on the stack.

RIGHT: the top two words of the stack are connected, but with the top word being the child. The precondition is the same as that of LEFT.

APPEND: the first character in the queue is appended to the word at the top of the stack. There are two preconditions. First, the queue should not be empty. Second, the top of the stack must be a word with no arcs connected to other words (i.e, up to now it has got neither children nor parent).

We see that these transitions mimic the general arc-standard dependency parsing models. The first three of them were used, for example, by Yamada and Matsumoto (2003) to parse English sentences. The only novel addition is APPEND, which is necessary because we are dealing with raw sentences. Its sole purpose is to assemble characters into words with no internal structures, such as 西雅图 'Seattle'. Thus this transition is the key for removing the need of Chinese word segmentation and parsing unsegmented sentences directly.

To also output part-of-speech tags and dependency labels, the transitions above can be augmented accordingly. Hence we can change SHIFT to SHIFT·X where X represents a certain POS tag. Also, LEFT and RIGHT should be augmented with appropriate dependency relations, such as LEFT·SUBJ for a dependency between verb and subject.

As a demonstration of the usage of these transitions, consider sentence 我喜欢西雅图 "I love Seattle". Table 4 lists all steps of the parsing process. Readers interested in implementing their own

step	stack	queue	action
1		我喜欢西雅图	SHIFT·PN
2	我_PN	喜欢西雅图	SHIFT·VV
3	我_PN 喜_VV	欢西雅图	APPEND
4	我_PN 喜欢_VV	西雅图	LEFT·SUBJ
5	我_PN $\xleftarrow{\text{SUBJ}}$ 喜欢_VV	西雅图	SHIFT·NR
6	我_PN $\xleftarrow{\text{SUBJ}}$ 喜欢_VV 西_NR	雅图	APPEND
7	我_PN $\xleftarrow{\text{SUBJ}}$ 喜欢_VV 西雅_NR	图	APPEND
8	我_PN $\xleftarrow{\text{SUBJ}}$ 喜欢_VV 西雅图_NR		RIGHT·OBJ
9	我_PN $\xleftarrow{\text{SUBJ}}$ 喜欢_VV $\xrightarrow{\text{OBJ}}$ 西雅图_NR		STOP

Table 4: Parsing process of a short sentence with the four transitions defined above.

unified dependency parsers are invited to study this example carefully.

5.2 Model

Due to structural ambiguity, there might be quite a lot of possibilities for parsing a given raw sentence. Hence at each step in the parsing process, all four transitions defined above may be applicable. To resolve ambiguities, each candidate parse is scored with a global linear model defined as follows.

For an input sentence x, the parsing result $F(x)$ is the one with the highest score in all possible structures for this x:

$$F(x) = \underset{y \in \text{GEN}(x)}{\arg\max}\ \text{Score}(y) \quad (1)$$

Here $\text{GEN}(x)$ is a set of all possible parses for sentence x, and $\text{Score}(y)$ is a real-valued linear function:

$$\text{Score}(y) = \Phi(y) \cdot \vec{w} \quad (2)$$

where $\Phi(y)$ is a global feature vector extracted from parsing result y, and $\vec{w}$ is a vector of weighting parameters. Because of its linearity, $\text{Score}(y)$ can be computed incrementally, following the transition of each parsing step. Parameter vector $\vec{w}$ is trained with the generalized perceptron algorithm of Collins (2002). The early-update strategy of Collins and Roark (2004) is used so as to improve accuracy and speed up the training.

5.3 Feature Templates

For a particular parse y, we now describe the way of computing its feature vector $\Phi(y)$ in the linear model of Equation (2). If S denotes the stack holding the partial results, and Q the queue storing the incoming Chinese characters of a raw sentence, then transition-based parsing features are extracted from S and Q according to those feature templates in Table 5.

	Description	Feature Templates
1	top of S	S0wt; S0w; S0t
2	next top of S	S1wt; S1w; S1t
3	S0 and S1	S1wtS0wt; S1wtS0w S1wS0wt; S1wtS0t S1tS0wt; S1wS0w; S1tS0t
4	char unigrams	Q0; Q1; Q2; Q3
5	char bigrams	Q0Q1; Q1Q2; Q2Q3
6	char trigrams	Q0Q1Q2; Q1Q2Q3
7	ST+unigrams	STwtQ0; STwQ0; STtQ0
8	ST+bigrams	STwtQ0Q1; STwQ0Q1 STtQ0Q1
9	ST+trigrams	STwtQ0Q1Q2 STwQ0Q1Q2; STtQ0Q1Q2
10	parent P of ST	PtSTtQ0; PtSTtQ0Q1 PtSTtQ0Q1Q2
11	leftmost child LC and rightmost child RC	STtLCtQ0; STtLCtQ0Q1 STtLCtQ0Q1Q2 STtRCtQ0; STtRCtQ0Q1 STtRCtQ0Q1Q2

Table 5: Transition-based feature templates. Q0 is the first character in Q, etc. w = word, t = POS tag.

Although we employ transition-based parsing, nothing prevents us from using graph-based features. As shown by Zhang and Clark (2011), depen-

	Description	Feature Templates
1	parent word	Pwt; Pw; Pt
2	child word	Cwt; Cw; Ct
3	P and C	PwtCwt; PwtCw; PwCwt PtCwt; PwCw; PtCt PwtCt
4	neighbor word of P and C left (L) or right (R)	PtPLtCtCLt; PtPLtCtCRt PtPRtCtCLt; PtPRtCtCRt PtPLtCLt; PtPLtCRt PtPRtCLt; PtPRtCRt PLtCtCLt; PLtCtCRt PRtCtCLt; PRtCtCRt PtCtCLt; PtCtCRt PtPLtCt; PtPRtCt
5	sibling(S) of C	CwSw;CtSt; CwSt CtSw; PtCtSt
6	leftmost and rightmost child	PtCtCLCt PtCtCRCt
7	left (la) and right (ra) arity of P	Ptla; Ptra Pwtla; Pwtra Pwla; Pwra

Table 6: Graph-based feature templates for the unified parser. Most of these templates are adapted from those used by Zhang and Clark (2011). w = word; t = POS tag.

dency parsers using both transition-based and graph-based features tend to achieve higher accuracy than parsers which only make use of one kind of features. Table 6 gives the graph-based feature templates used in our parser. All such templates are instantiated at the earliest possible time, in order to reduce as much as possible situations where correct parses fall out of the beam during decoding.

5.4 Decoding Algorithm

We use beam-search to find the best parse for a given raw sentence (Algorithm 1). This algorithm uses double beams. The first beam contains unfinished parsing results, while the second holds completed parses. Double beams are necessary because the number of transitions might well be different for different parses, and those parses that finished earlier are not necessarily better parses. During the searching process, correct parse could fall off the beams, resulting in a search error. However, in practice beam search decoding algorithm works quite well. In addition, it's not feasible to use dynamic programming because of the complicated features used in the model.

The B in Algorithm 1 is the width of the two beams. In our experiments we set B to 64. This value of B was determined empirically by using the standard development set of the data, with the goal of achieving the highest possible accuracy within reasonable time. Note that in line 20 of the algorithm, the beam for completed parsers are pruned at each iteration of the parsing process. The purpose of this action is to keep this beam from growing too big, resulting in a waste of memory space.

Algorithm 1 Beam Search Decoding

```
1: candidates ← {STARTITEM()}
2: agenda ← ϕ
3: completed ← ϕ
4: loop
5:   for all candidate in candidates do
6:     for all legal action of candidate do
7:       newc ← EXPAND(candidate, action)
8:       if COMPLETED(newc) then
9:         completed.INSERT(newc)
10:      else
11:        agenda.INSERT(newc)
12:      end if
13:    end for
14:  end for
15:  if EMPTY(agenda) then
16:    return TOP(completed)
17:  end if
18:  candidates ← TOPB(agenda, B)
19:  agenda ← ϕ
20:  completed ← TOPB(completed, B)
21: end loop
```

6 Experiments and Evaluation

We describe the experiments carried out and our method of evaluation of the unified dependency parser. We used Penn2Malt [4] to convert constituent trees of CTB to dependency relations. The head rules for this conversion was given by Zhang and Clark (2008). In all experiments, we followed the stan-

[4]http://w3.msi.vxu.se/~nivre/research/Penn2Malt.html

	P	R	F
our method, labeled	78.54	80.93	79.72
our method, unlabeled	81.01	83.77	82.37
ZC2011, unlabeled	N/A	N/A	75.09

Table 7: Evaluation results on the original CTB5. N/A means the value is not available to us. ZC2011 is Zhang and Clark (2011).

	P	R	F
original dependencies in CTB5	82.13	84.49	83.29
ZN2011 with Gold segmentation & POS	N/A	N/A	84.40
original dependencies plus word structures	85.71	87.18	86.44

Table 8: Evaluation results on CTB5 with word structures annotated. All results are labeled scores.

dard split of the data into training, testing and development data (Zhang and Clark, 2011). Though we annotated structures of words in CTB6, most previously results were on CTB5, a subset of the former treebank. Hence we report our results of evaluation on CTB5 for better comparability.

6.1 Dependency Parsing of Morphological and Syntactic Structures

If we look back at the Figure 2, it's clear that a dependency relation is correctly parsed if and only if three conditions are met: Firstly, words at both ends of the dependency are correctly segmented. Secondly, part-of-speech tags are correct for both words. Thirdly, the direction of the dependency relation are correct. Of course, if labeled precision and recall is to be measured, the label of the dependency relation should also be correctly recovered. Let nc be the number of dependencies correctly parsed with respect to these criterion, no be the total number of dependencies in the output, and nr the number of dependencies in the reference. Then precision is defined to be $p = nc/no$ and recall is defined to be $r = nc/nr$.

6.1.1 Results on the Original CTB5

We first train our unified dependency parser with the original treebank CTB5. In this case, all words are considered to be flat, with no internal structures. The result are shown in Table 7. Note that on exactly the same testing data, i.e, the original CTB5, unified parser performs much better than the result of a pipelined approach reported by Zhang and Clark (2011). There are about 30% of relative error reduction for the unlabeled dependency parsing results. This is yet another evidence of the advantage of joint modeling in natural language processing, details of which will be discussed in Section 7.

6.1.2 Results on CTB with Structures of Words Annotated

Then we train the parser with CTB5 augmented with our annotations of internal structures of words. For purpose of better comparability, we report results on both the original dependencies of CTB5 and on the dependencies of CTB5 plus those of the internal structures of words. The results are shown in Table 8. First, note that compared to another result by Zhang and Nivre (2011), whose input were sentences with gold standard word segmentation and POS tags, our F-score is only slightly lower even with input of unsegmented sentences. This is understandable since gold-standard segmentation and POS tags greatly reduced the uncertainty of parsing results.

For the unified parser, the improvement of F-score from 79.72% to 83.29% is attributed to the fact that with internal structures of words annotated, parsing of syntactic structures is also improved due to the similarity of word and phrase structures mentioned in Section 1, and also due to the fact that many phrase level dependencies are now facing a much less severe problem of data sparsity. The improvement of F-score from 83.29% to 86.44% is attributed to the annotation of word structures. Internal structures of words are be mostly local in comparison with phrase and sentence structures. Therefore, with the addition of word structures, the overall dependency parsing accuracy naturally can be improved.

6.2 Chinese Word Segmentation

From the example in Figure 2, it is clear that output of unified parser contains Chinese word segmentation information. Therefore, we can get results of word segmentation for each sentence in the test sets,

	P	R	F
K2009	N/A	N/A	97.87
This Paper	97.63	97.38	97.50

Table 9: Word segmentation results of our parser and the best performance reported in literature on the same dataset. K2009 is the result of Kruengkrai et al. (2009).

	P	R	F
K2009	N/A	N/A	93.67
ZC2011	N/A	N/A	93.67
This Paper	93.42	93.20	93.31

Table 10: Joint word segmentation and POS tagging scores. K2009 is result of Kruengkrai et al. (2009). ZC2011 is result of Zhang and Clark (2011).

and evaluate their accuracies. For maximal comparability, we train the unified parser on the original CTB5 data used by previous studies. The result is in Table 9. Despite the fact that the performance of our unified parser does not exceed the best reported result so far, which probably might be caused by some minute implementation specific details, it's fair to say that our parser performs at the level of state-of-the-art in Chinese word segmentation.

6.3 Joint Word Segmentation and POS Tagging

From Figure 2 we see that besides word segmentation, output of the unified parser also includes part-of-speech tags. Therefore, it's natural that we evaluate the accuracy of joint Chinese word segmentation and part of speech tagging, as reported in previous literature (Kruengkrai et al., 2009). The results are in Table 10, in which for ease of comparison, again we train the unified parser with the vanilla version of CTB5. We can see that unified parser performs at virtually the same level of accuracy compared with previous best systems.

7 Related Work

Researchers have noticed the necessity of parsing the internal structures of words in Chinese. Li (2011) gave an method that could take raw sentences as input and output phrase structures and internal structures of words. This paper assumes that the input are unsegmented, too, and our output also includes both word and phrase structures. There are

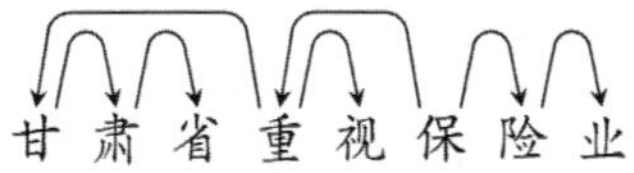

Figure 4: Example output of Zhao's parser.

two key differences, though. The first is we output dependency relations instead of constituent structures. Although dependencies can be extracted from the constituent trees of Li (2011), the time complexity of their algorithm is $O(n^5)$ while our parser runs in linear time. Secondly, we specify the details of annotating structures of words, with the annotations being made publicly available.

Zhao (2009) presented a dependency parser which regards each Chinese character as a word and then analyzes the dependency relations between characters, using ordinary dependency parsing algorithms. Our parser is different in two important ways. The first is we output both part-of-speech tags and labeled dependency relations, both of which were absent in Zhao's parser. More importantly, the APPEND transition for handling flat words were unseen in previous studies as far as we know. The difference can best be described with an example: For the sentence in Section 3, Zhao's parser output the result in Figure 4 while in contrast our output is Figure 2.

In recent years, considerable efforts have been made in joint modeling and learning in natural language processing (Lee et al., 2011; Sun, 2011; Li et al., 2011; Finkel and Manning, 2009; Kruengkrai et al., 2009; Jiang et al., 2008; Goldberg and Tsarfaty, 2008). Joint modeling can improve the performance of NLP systems due to the obvious reason of being able to make use of various levels of information simultaneously. However, the thesis of this paper, i.e, unified parsing of Chinese word and phrase structures, bears a deeper meaning. As demonstrated in Section 1 and by Li (2011), structures of words and phrases usually have significant similarity, and the distinction between them is very difficult to define, even for expert linguists. But for real world applications, such subtle matters can safely be ignored if we could analyzed morphological and syntactic structures in a unified framework. What applications really cares is structures instead of whether a linguistic unit is a word or phrase.

Another notable line of research closely related to the present work is to annotate and parse the flat structures of noun phrases (NP) (Vadas and Curran, 2007; Vadas and Curran, 2011). This paper differs from those previous work on parsing NPs in at least two significant ways. First, we aim to parse all kinds of words (e.g, nouns, verbs, adverbs, adjectives etc) whose structures are not annotated by CTB, and whose presence could cause lots of pseudo OOVs and incompatible annotations. Second, the problem we are trying to solve is a crucial observation specific to Chinese language, that is, in lots of cases forcing a separation of words and phrases leads to awkward situations for NLP systems. Remember that in Section 2 we demonstrated that all corpora we examined had the problem of pseudo OOVs and incompatible annotations. In comparison, the problem Vadas and Curran (2007) tried to solve is a lack of annotation for structures of NPs in currently available treebanks, or to put it in another way, a problem more closely related to treebanks rather than certain languages.

8 Discussion and Conclusion

Chinese word segmentation is an indispensable step for traditional approaches to syntactic parsing of Chinese. The purpose of word segmentation is to decide what goes to words, with the remaining processing (e.g, parsing) left to higher level structures of phrases and sentences. This paper shows that it could be very difficult to make such a distinction between words and phrases. This difficulty cannot be left unheeded, as we have shown quantitatively that in practice it causes lots of real troubles such as too many OOVs and incompatible annotations. We showed how these undesirable consequences can be resolved by annotation of the internal structures of words, and by unified parsing of morphological and syntactic structures in Chinese.

Unified parsing of morphological and syntactic structures of Chinese can also be implemented with a pipelined approach, in which we first segment input sentences into words or affixes (i.e, with the finest possible granularity), and then we do part-of-speech tagging followed by dependency (or constituent) parsing. However, a unified parsing approach using a single model as presented in this paper offers several advantages over pipelined approaches. The first one is that joint modeling tends to result in higher accuracy and suffer less from error propagation than do pipelined methods. Secondly, both the unified model and the algorithm are conceptually much more simpler than pipelined approaches. We only need one implementation of the model and algorithm, instead of several ones in pipelined approaches. Thirdly, our model and algorithm might comes closer to modeling the process of human language understanding, because human brain is more likely a parallel machine in understanding languages than an alternative pipelined processor. Hence this work, together with previous studies by other authors like Li (2011) and Zhao (2009), open up a possibly new direction for future research efforts in parsing the Chinese language.

Acknowledgments

Reviewers of this paper offered many detailed and highly valuable suggestions for improvement in presentation. The authors are supported by NSFC under Grant No. 90920004 and National 863 Program under Grant No. 2012AA011102.

References

Michael Collins and Brian Roark. 2004. Incremental parsing with the perceptron algorithm. In *Proceedings of the 42nd Meeting of the Association for Computational Linguistics (ACL'04), Main Volume*, pages 111–118, Barcelona, Spain, July.

Michael Collins. 2002. Discriminative training methods for hidden markov models: Theory and experiments with perceptron algorithms. In *Proceedings of the 2002 Conference on Empirical Methods in Natural Language Processing*, pages 1–8. Association for Computational Linguistics, July.

Jenny Rose Finkel and Christopher D. Manning. 2009. Joint parsing and named entity recognition. In *Proceedings of Human Language Technologies: The 2009 Annual Conference of the North American Chapter of the Association for Computational Linguistics*, pages 326–334, Boulder, Colorado, June. Association for Computational Linguistics.

Yoav Goldberg and Reut Tsarfaty. 2008. A single generative model for joint morphological segmentation and syntactic parsing. In *Proceedings of ACL-08: HLT*, pages 371–379, Columbus, Ohio, June. Association for Computational Linguistics.

C. F. Hockett. 1969. *A Course in Modern Linguistics*. Macmillan.

Wenbin Jiang, Liang Huang, Qun Liu, and Yajuan Lü. 2008. A cascaded linear model for joint Chinese word segmentation and part-of-speech tagging. In *Proceedings of ACL-08: HLT*, pages 897–904, Columbus, Ohio, June. Association for Computational Linguistics.

Canasai Kruengkrai, Kiyotaka Uchimoto, Jun'ichi Kazama, Yiou Wang, Kentaro Torisawa, and Hitoshi Isahara. 2009. An error-driven word-character hybrid model for joint Chinese word segmentation and POS tagging. In *Proceedings of the Joint Conference of the 47th Annual Meeting of the ACL and the 4th International Joint Conference on Natural Language Processing of the AFNLP*, pages 513–521, Suntec, Singapore, August. Association for Computational Linguistics.

John Lee, Jason Naradowsky, and David A. Smith. 2011. A discriminative model for joint morphological disambiguation and dependency parsing. In *Proceedings of the 49th Annual Meeting of the Association for Computational Linguistics: Human Language Technologies*, pages 885–894, Portland, Oregon, USA, June. Association for Computational Linguistics.

Zhenghua Li, Min Zhang, Wanxiang Che, Ting Liu, Wenliang Chen, and Haizhou Li. 2011. Joint models for Chinese POS tagging and dependency parsing. In *Proceedings of the 2011 Conference on Empirical Methods in Natural Language Processing*, pages 1180–1191, Edinburgh, Scotland, UK., July. Association for Computational Linguistics.

Zhongguo Li. 2011. Parsing the internal structure of words: A new paradigm for Chinese word segmentation. In *Proceedings of the 49th Annual Meeting of the Association for Computational Linguistics: Human Language Technologies*, pages 1405–1414, Portland, Oregon, USA, June. Association for Computational Linguistics.

Weiwei Sun. 2011. A stacked sub-word model for joint chinese word segmentation and part-of-speech tagging. In *Proceedings of the 49th Annual Meeting of the Association for Computational Linguistics: Human Language Technologies*, pages 1385–1394, Portland, Oregon, USA, June. Association for Computational Linguistics.

David Vadas and James Curran. 2007. Adding noun phrase structure to the penn treebank. In *Proceedings of the 45th Annual Meeting of the Association of Computational Linguistics*, pages 240–247, Prague, Czech Republic, June. Association for Computational Linguistics.

David Vadas and James R. Curran. 2011. Parsing noun phrases in the penn treebank. *Computational Linguistics*, 37(4):753–809.

Hiroyasu Yamada and Yuji Matsumoto. 2003. Statistical dependency analysis with support vector machines. In *Proceeding of the 8th International Workshop of Parsing Technologies (IWPT)*, pages 195–206, Nancy, France.

Yue Zhang and Stephen Clark. 2008. A tale of two parsers: Investigating and combining graph-based and transition-based dependency parsing. In *Proceedings of the 2008 Conference on Empirical Methods in Natural Language Processing*, pages 562–571, Honolulu, Hawaii, October. Association for Computational Linguistics.

Yue Zhang and Stephen Clark. 2011. Syntactic processing using the generalized perceptron and beam search. *Computational Linguistics*, 37(1):105–151.

Yue Zhang and Joakim Nivre. 2011. Transition-based dependency parsing with rich non-local features. In *Proceedings of the 49th Annual Meeting of the Association for Computational Linguistics: Human Language Technologies*, pages 188–193, Portland, Oregon, USA, June. Association for Computational Linguistics.

Hai Zhao. 2009. Character-level dependencies in Chinese: Usefulness and learning. In *Proceedings of the 12th Conference of the European Chapter of the ACL (EACL 2009)*, pages 879–887, Athens, Greece, March. Association for Computational Linguistics.

A Transition-Based System for Joint Part-of-Speech Tagging and Labeled Non-Projective Dependency Parsing

Bernd Bohnet
Institute for Natural Language Processing
University Stuttgart
bohnet@ims.uni-stuttgart.de

Joakim Nivre
Department of Linguistics and Philology
Uppsala University
joakim.nivre@lingfil.uu.se

Abstract

Most current dependency parsers presuppose that input words have been morphologically disambiguated using a part-of-speech tagger before parsing begins. We present a transition-based system for joint part-of-speech tagging and labeled dependency parsing with non-projective trees. Experimental evaluation on Chinese, Czech, English and German shows consistent improvements in both tagging and parsing accuracy when compared to a pipeline system, which lead to improved state-of-the-art results for all languages.

1 Introduction

Dependency-based syntactic parsing has been the focus of intense research efforts during the last decade, and the state of the art today is represented by globally normalized discriminative models that are induced using structured learning. Graph-based models parameterize the parsing problem by the structure of the dependency graph and normally use dynamic programming for inference (McDonald et al., 2005; McDonald and Pereira, 2006; Carreras, 2007; Koo and Collins, 2010; Bohnet, 2010), but other inference methods have been explored especially for non-projective parsing (Riedel and Clarke, 2006; Smith and Eisner, 2008; Martins et al., 2009; Martins et al., 2010; Koo et al., 2010). Transition-based models parameterize the problem by elementary parsing actions and typically use incremental beam search (Titov and Henderson, 2007; Zhang and Clark, 2008; Zhang and Clark, 2011). Despite notable differences in model structure, graph-based and transition-based parsers both give state-of-the-art accuracy with proper feature selection and optimization (Koo and Collins, 2010; Zhang and Nivre, 2011; Bohnet, 2011).

It is noteworthy, however, that almost all dependency parsers presuppose that the words of an input sentence have been morphologically disambiguated using (at least) a part-of-speech tagger. This is in stark contrast to the best parsers based on PCFG models, such as the Brown parser (Charniak and Johnson, 2005) and the Berkeley parser (Petrov et al., 2006; Petrov and Klein, 2007), which not only can perform their own part-of-speech tagging but normally give better parsing accuracy when they are allowed to do so. This suggests that joint models for tagging and parsing might improve accuracy also in the case of dependency parsing.

It has been argued that joint morphological and syntactic disambiguation is especially important for richly inflected languages, where there is considerable interaction between morphology and syntax such that neither can be fully disambiguated without considering the other. Thus, Lee et al. (2011) show that a discriminative model for joint morphological disambiguation and dependency parsing outperforms a pipeline model in experiments on Latin, Ancient Greek, Czech and Hungarian. However, Li et al. (2011) and Hatori et al. (2011) report improvements with a joint model also for Chinese, which is not a richly inflected language but is nevertheless rich in part-of-speech ambiguities.

In this paper, we present a transition-based model for joint part-of-speech tagging and labeled dependency parsing with non-projective trees. Experiments show that joint modeling improves both tagging and parsing accuracy, leading to state-of-the-art accuracy for richly inflected languages like Czech and German as well as more configurational languages like Chinese and English. To our knowledge, this is the first joint system that performs labeled dependency parsing. It is also the first joint system that achieves state-of-the-art accuracy for non-projective dependency parsing.

2 Transition-Based Tagging and Parsing

Transition-based dependency parsing was pioneered by Yamada and Matsumoto (2003) and Nivre et al. (2004), who used classifiers trained to predict individual actions of a deterministic shift-reduce parser. Recent research has shown that better accuracy can be achieved by using beam search and optimizing models on the entire sequence of decisions needed to parse a sentence instead of single actions (Zhang and Clark, 2008; Huang and Sagae, 2010; Zhang and Clark, 2011; Zhang and Nivre, 2011; Bohnet, 2011). In addition, a number of different transition systems have been proposed, in particular for dealing with non-projective dependencies, which were beyond the scope of early systems (Attardi, 2006; Nivre, 2007; Nivre, 2009; Titov et al., 2009).

In this section, we start by defining a transition system for joint tagging and parsing based on the non-projective transition system proposed in Nivre (2009). We then show how to perform beam search and structured online learning with this model, and conclude by discussing feature representations.

2.1 Transition System

Given a set P of part-of-speech tags and a set D of dependency labels, a *tagged dependency tree* for a sentence $x = w_1, \ldots, w_n$ is a directed tree $T = (V_x, A)$ with labeling functions π and δ such that:

1. $V_x = \{0, 1, \ldots, n\}$ is a set of nodes,
2. $A \subseteq V_x \times V_x$ is a set of arcs,
3. $\pi : V_x \rightarrow P$ is a labeling function for nodes,
4. $\delta : A \rightarrow D$ is a labeling function for arcs,
5. 0 is the root of the tree.

The set V_x of *nodes* is the set of positive integers up to and including n, each corresponding to the linear position of a word in the sentence, plus an extra artificial root node 0. The set A of *arcs* is a set of pairs (i, j), where i is the *head* node and j is the *dependent* node. The functions π and δ assign a unique part-of-speech label to each node/word and a unique dependency label to each arc, respectively. This notion of dependency tree differs from the standard definition only by including part-of-speech labels as well as dependency labels (Kübler et al., 2009).

Following Nivre (2008), we define a *transition system* for dependency parsing as a quadruple $S = (C, T, c_s, C_t)$, where

1. C is a set of *configurations*,
2. T is a set of *transitions*, each of which is a (partial) function $t : C \rightarrow C$,
3. c_s is an *initialization function*, mapping a sentence x to a configuration $c \in C$,
4. $C_t \subseteq C$ is a set of *terminal configurations*.

A transition sequence for a sentence x in S is a sequence of configuration-transition pairs $C_{0,m} = [(c_0, t_0), (c_1, t_1), \ldots, (c_m, t_m)]$ where $c_0 = c_s(x)$, $t_m(c_m) \in C_t$ and $t_i(c_i) = c_{i+1}$ $(0 \leq i < m)$.[1]

In this paper, we take the set C of configurations to be the set of all 5-tuples $c = (\Sigma, B, A, \pi, \delta)$ such that Σ (the stack) and B (the buffer) are disjoint sublists of the nodes V_x of some sentence x, A is a set of dependency arcs over V_x, and π and δ are labeling functions as defined above. We take the initial configuration for a sentence $x = w_1, \ldots, w_n$ to be $c_s(x) = ([0], [1, \ldots, n], \{\}, \bot, \bot)$, where $\bot$ is the function that is undefined for all arguments, and we take the set C_t of terminal configurations to be the set of all configurations of the form $c = ([0], [\,], A, \pi, \delta)$ (for any A, π and δ). The tagged dependency tree defined for x by $c = (\Sigma, B, A, \pi, \delta)$ is the tree (V_x, A) with labeling functions π and δ, which we write TREE(x, c).

The set T of transitions is shown in Figure 1. The LEFT-ARC$_d$ and RIGHT-ARC$_d$ transitions both add an arc (with dependency label d) between the two nodes on top of the stack and replaces these nodes by the head node of the new arc (which is the rightmost node for LEFT-ARC$_d$ and the leftmost node for RIGHT-ARC$_d$). The SHIFT$_p$ transition extracts the

[1] This definition of transition sequence differs from that of Nivre (2008) but is equivalent and suits our presentation better.

Transition		Condition
LEFT-ARC$_d$	$([\sigma\|i,j],B,A,\pi,\delta) \Rightarrow ([\sigma\|j],B,A\cup\{(j,i)\},\pi,\delta[(j,i)\rightarrow d])$	$i \neq 0$
RIGHT-ARC$_d$	$([\sigma\|i,j],B,A,\pi,\delta) \Rightarrow ([\sigma\|i],B,A\cup\{(i,j)\},\pi,\delta[(i,j)\rightarrow d])$	
SHIFT$_p$	$(\sigma,[i\|\beta],A,\pi,\delta) \Rightarrow ([\sigma\|i],\beta,A,\pi[i\rightarrow p],\delta)$	
SWAP	$([\sigma\|i,j],\beta,A,\pi,\delta) \Rightarrow ([\sigma\|j],[i\|\beta],A,\pi,\delta)$	$0 < i < j$

Figure 1: Transitions for joint tagging and dependency parsing extending the system of Nivre (2009). The stack Σ is represented as a list with its head to the right (and tail σ) and the buffer B as a list with its head to the left (and tail β). The notation $f[a \rightarrow b]$ is used to denote the function that is exactly like f except that it maps a to b.

first node in the buffer, pushes it onto the stack and labels it with the part-of-speech tag p. The SWAP transition extracts the second topmost node from the stack and moves it back to the buffer, subject to the condition that the two top nodes on the stack are still in the order given by the sentence.

Except for the addition of a tag parameter p to the SHIFT transition, this is equivalent to the system described in Nivre (2009), which thanks to the SWAP transition can handle arbitrary non-projective trees. The soundness and completeness results given in that paper trivially carry over to the new system. The only thing to note is that, before a terminal configuration can be reached, every word has to be pushed onto the stack in a SHIFT$_p$ transition, which ensures that every node/word in the output tree will be tagged.

```
PARSE(x, w, b1, b2)
1  h0.c ← cs(x)
2  h0.s ← 0.0
3  h0.f ← {0.0}^dim(w)
4  BEAM ← [h0]
5  while ∃h ∈ BEAM : h.c ∉ Ct
6      TMP ← [ ]
7      foreach h ∈ BEAM
8          foreach t ∈ T : PERMISSIBLE(h.c, t)
9              h.f ← h.f + f(h.c, t)
10             h.s ← h.s + f(h.c, t) · w
11             h.c ← t(h.c)
12             TMP ← INSERT(h, TMP)
13     BEAM ← PRUNE(TMP, b1, b2)
14 h ← TOP(BEAM)
15 y ← TREE(x, h.c)
16 return y
```

Figure 2: Beam search algorithm for joint tagging and dependency parsing of input sentence x with weight vector $\mathbf{w}$ and beam parameters b_1 and b_2. The symbols $h.c$, $h.s$ and $h.\mathbf{f}$ denote, respectively, the configuration, score and feature representation of a hypothesis h; $h.c.A$ denotes the arc set of $h.c$.

2.2 Inference and Learning

While early transition-based parsers generally used greedy best-first inference and locally trained classifiers, recent work has shown that higher accuracy can be obtained using beam search and global structure learning to mitigate error propagation. In particular, it seems that the globally learned models can exploit a much richer feature space than locally trained classifiers, as shown by Zhang and Nivre (2011). Since joint tagging and parsing increases the size of the search space and is likely to require novel features, we use beam search in combination with structured perceptron learning.

The beam search algorithm used to derive the best parse y for a sentence x is outlined in Figure 2. In addition to the sentence x, it takes as input a weight vector $\mathbf{w}$ corresponding to a linear model for scoring transitions out of configurations and two pruning parameters b_1 and b_2. A parse hypothesis h is represented by a configuration $h.c$, a score $h.s$ and a feature vector $h.\mathbf{f}$ for the transition sequence up to $h.c$. Hypotheses are stored in the list BEAM, which is sorted by descending scores and initialized to hold the hypothesis h_0 corresponding to the initial configuration $c_s(x)$ with score 0.0 and all features set to 0.0 (lines 1–4). In the main loop (lines 5–13), a set of new hypotheses is derived and stored in the list TMP, which is finally pruned and assigned as the new value of BEAM. The main loop terminates when all hypotheses in BEAM contain terminal configurations, and the dependency tree extracted from the top scoring hypothesis is returned (lines 14–16).

The set of new hypotheses is created in two nested loops (lines 7–12), where every hypothesis h in BEAM is updated using every permissible transition t for the configuration $h.c$. The feature representation of the new hypothesis is obtained by adding the feature vector $\mathbf{f}(t, h.c)$ for the current configuration-transition pair to the feature vector of the old hypothesis (line 9). Similarly, the score of the new hypothesis is the sum of the score $\mathbf{f}(t, h.c) \cdot \mathbf{w}$ of the current configuration-transition pair and the score of the old hypothesis (line 10). The feature representation/score of a complete parse y for x with transition sequence $C_{0,m}$ is thus the sum of the feature representations/scores of the configuration-transition pairs in $C_{0,m}$:

$$\mathbf{f}(x, y) = \sum_{(c,t) \in C_{0,m}} \mathbf{f}(c, t)$$

$$s(x, y) = \sum_{(c,t) \in C_{0,m}} \mathbf{f}(c, t) \cdot \mathbf{w}$$

Finally, the configuration of the new hypothesis is obtained by evaluating $t(h.c)$ (line 11). The new hypothesis is then inserted into TMP in score-sorted order (line 12).

The pruning parameters b_1 and b_2 determine the number of hypotheses allowed in the beam and at the same time control the tradeoff between syntactic and morphological ambiguity. First, we extract the b_1 highest scoring hypotheses with distinct dependency trees. Then we extract the b_2 highest scoring remaining hypotheses, which will typically be tagging variants of dependency trees that are already in the beam. In this way, we prevent the beam from getting filled up with too many tagging variants of the same dependency tree, which was found to be harmful in preliminary experiments.

One final thing to note about the inference algorithm is that the notion of permissibility for a transition t out of a configuration c can be used to capture not only formal constraints on transitions – such as the fact that it is impossible to perform a SHIFT$_p$ transition with an empty buffer or illegal to perform a LEFT-ARC$_d$ transition with the special root node on top of the stack – but also to filter out unlikely dependency labels or tags. Thus, in the experiments later on, we will typically constrain the parser so that SHIFT$_p$ is permissible only if p is one of the k best part-of-speech tags with a score no more than α below the score of the 1-best tag, as determined by a preprocessing tagger. We also filter out instances of LEFT-ARC$_d$ and RIGHT-ARC$_d$, where d does not occur in the training data for the predicted part-of-speech tag combination of the head and dependent. This procedure leads to a significant speed up.

In order to learn a weight vector $\mathbf{w}$ from a training set $\{(x_j, y_j)\}_{j=1}^{\mathcal{T}}$ of sentences with their tagged dependency trees, we use a variant of the structured perceptron, introduced by Collins (2002), which makes N iterations over the training data and updates the weight vector for every sentence x_j where the highest scoring parse y^* is different from y_j. More precisely, we use the passive-aggressive update of Crammer et al. (2006):

$$\mathbf{w}^{i+1} = \mathbf{w}^i + \tau(\mathbf{f}(x_j, y_j) - \mathbf{f}(x_j, y^*))$$

where

$$\tau = \frac{\mathbf{f}(x_j, y_j) - \mathbf{f}(x_j, y^*)}{||\mathbf{f}(x_j, y_j) - \mathbf{f}(x_j, y^*)||^2}$$

We also use the early update strategy found beneficial for parsing in several previous studies (Collins and Roark, 2004; Zhang and Clark, 2008; Huang and Sagae, 2010), which means that, during learning, we terminate the beam search as soon as the hypothesis corresponding to the gold parse y_j falls out of the beam and update with respect to the partial transition sequence constructed up to that point. Finally, we use the standard technique of averaging over all weight vectors, as originally proposed by Collins (2002).

2.3 Feature Representations

As already noted, the feature representation $\mathbf{f}(x, y)$ of an input sentence x with parse y decomposes into feature representations $\mathbf{f}(c, t)$ for the transitions $t(c)$ needed to derive y from $c_s(x)$. Features may refer to any aspect of a configuration, as encoded in the stack Σ, the buffer B, the arc set A and the labelings π and δ. In addition, we assume that each word w in the input is assigned up to k candidate part-of-speech tags $\pi_i(w)$ with corresponding scores $s(\pi_i(w))$.

Features involving word prefixes and suffixes
$\pi_i(B_0)p_2(B_0)$, $\pi_i(B_0)s_2(B_0)$, $\pi_i(B_0)p_1(B_0)p_1(\Sigma_0)$
$\pi_i(\Sigma_0)p_1(\Sigma_0)p_1(\Sigma_1)$, $\pi_i(\Sigma_0)s_1(\Sigma_0)s_1(\Sigma_0)$
$\pi_i(\Sigma_0)p_2(\Sigma_0)s_3(\Sigma_1)$,$\pi_i(\Sigma_0)s_3(\Sigma_0)p_2(\Sigma_1)$
$\pi_i(\Sigma_0)w(B_0)s_1(\Sigma_0)$, $\pi_i(\Sigma_0)w(B_0)s_2(\Sigma_0)$
Features involving tag score differences and ranks
$\pi_i(B_0)[s(\pi_1(B_0)) - s(\pi_i(B_0))]$
$\pi_i(B_0)\pi_i(\Sigma_0)[s(\pi_1(B_0)) - s(\pi_i(B_0))]\ i$
$\pi_i(B_0)[s(\pi_1(B_0)) - s(\pi_i(B_0))]\pi(\Sigma_0)$
$w(B_0)[s(\pi_1(B_0)) - s(\pi_i(B_0))]\pi(\Sigma_0)$

Figure 3: Specialized feature templates for tagging. We use Σ_i and B_i to denote the ith token in the stack Σ and buffer B, respectively, with indexing starting at 0, and we use the following functors to extract properties of a token: $\pi_i()$ = ith best tag; $s(\pi_i())$ = score of ith best tag; $\pi()$ = finally predicted tag; $w()$ = word form; $p_i()$ = word prefix of i characters; $s_i()$ = word suffix of i characters. Score differences are binned in discrete steps of 0.05.

The bulk of features used in our system are taken from Zhang and Nivre (2011), although with two important differences. First of all, like Hatori et al. (2011), we have omitted all features that presuppose an arc eager parsing order, since our transition system defines an arc-standard order. Secondly, any feature that refers to the part-of-speech tag of a word w in the buffer B will in our system refer to the top-scoring tag $\pi_1(w)$, rather than the finally predicted tag. By contrast, for a word in the stack Σ, part-of-speech features refer to the tag $\pi(w)$ chosen when shifting w onto the stack (which may or may not be the same as $\pi_1(w)$).

In addition to the standard features for transition-based dependency parsing, we have added features specifically to improve the tagging step in the joint model. The templates for these features, which are specified in Figure 3, all involve the ith best tag assigned to the first word of the buffer B (the next word to be shifted in a SHIFT_p transition) in combination with neighboring words, word prefixes, word suffixes, score differences and tag rank.

Finally, in some experiments, we make use of two additional feature sets, which we call graph features (G) and cluster features (C), respectively. Graph features are defined over the factors of a graph-based dependency parser, which was shown to improve the accuracy of a transition-based parser by Zhang and Clark (2008). However, while their features were limited to certain first- and second-order factors, we use features over second- and third-order factors as found in the parsers of Bohnet and Kuhn (2012). These features are scored as soon as the factors are completed, using a technique that is similar to what Hatori et al. (2011) call delayed features, although they use it for part-of-speech tags in the lookahead while we use it for subgraphs of the dependency tree. Cluster features, finally, are features over word clusters, as first used by Koo et al. (2008), which replace part-of-speech tag features.[2]

We use a hash kernel to map features to weights. It has been observed that most of the computing time in feature-rich parsers is spent retrieving the index of each feature in the weight vector (Bohnet, 2010). This is usually done via a hash table, but significant speedups can be achieved by using a hash kernel, which simply replaces table lookup by a hash function (Bloom, 1970; Shi et al., 2009; Bohnet, 2010). The price to pay for these speedups is that there may be collisions, so that different features are mapped to the same index, but this is often compensated by the fact that the lower time and memory requirements of the hash kernel enables the use of negative features, that is, features that are never seen in the training set but occur in erroneous hypotheses at training time and can therefore be helpful also at inference time. As a result, the hash kernel often improves accuracy as well as efficiency compared to traditional techniques that only make use of features that occur in gold standard parses (Bohnet, 2010).

3 Experiments

We have evaluated the model for joint tagging and dependency parsing on four typologically diverse languages: Chinese, Czech, English, and German.

3.1 Setup

Most of the experiments use the CoNLL 2009 data sets with the training, development and test split used in the Shared Task (Hajič et al., 2009), but for better comparison with previous work we also report results for the standard benchmark data sets for Chinese and English. For Chinese, this is the Penn Chinese Treebank 5.1 (CTB5), converted

[2]For replicability, a complete description of all features can be found at http://stp.lingfil.uu.se/~nivre/exp/emnlp12.html.

Parser		Chinese				Czech				English				German			
k	α	TLAS	LAS	UAS	POS	TLAS	LAS	UAS	POS	TLAS	LAS	UAS	POS	TLAS	LAS	UAS	POS
1	0.0	73.85	76.12	80.01	92.78	82.36	82.65	88.03	93.26	85.82	87.17	90.41	97.32	85.08	86.60	89.17	97.24
2	0.1	74.39	76.52	80.41	93.37	82.74	83.01	88.34	99.39	**86.43**	87.79	91.02	97.49	86.12	87.22	89.69	97.85
3	0.1	**74.47**	76.63	80.50	93.38	82.76	82.97	88.33	99.40	86.40	87.78	90.99	97.43	86.03	87.27	89.60	97.74
3	0.2	74.35	76.48	80.38	93.43	**82.85**	83.11	88.44	99.32	86.35	87.79	91.01	97.52	86.24	87.37	89.72	97.90
3	0.3	74.18	76.33	80.28	93.48	82.78	83.05	88.38	99.33	85.94	87.57	90.87	96.97	**86.35**	87.46	89.86	97.90
3	0.4													86.14	87.23	89.66	97.79

Table 1: Accuracy scores for the CoNLL 2009 shared task development sets as a function of the number of tags k and the score threshold α. Beam parameters fixed at $b_1 = 40$, $b_2 = 4$.

with the head-finding rules and conversion tools of Zhang and Clark (2008), and with the same split as in Zhang and Clark (2008) and Li et al. (2011).[3] For English, this is the WSJ section of the Penn Treebank, converted with the head-finding rules of Yamada and Matsumoto (2003) and the labeling rules of Nivre (2006).[4]

In order to assign k-best part-of-speech tags and scores to words in the training set, we used a perceptron tagger with 10-fold jack-knifing. The same type of tagger was trained on the entire training set in order to supply tags for the development and test sets. The feature set of the tagger was optimized for English and German and provides state-of-the-art accuracy for these two languages. The 1-best tagging accuracy for section 23 of the Penn Treebank is 97.28, which is on a par with Toutanova et al. (2003). For German, we obtain a tagging accuracy of 97.24, which is close to the 97.39 achieved by the RF-Tagger (Schmid and Laws, 2008), which to our knowledge is the best tagger for German.[5] The results are not directly comparable to the RF-Tagger as it was evaluated on a different part of the Tiger Treebank and trained on a larger part of the Treebank. We could not use the larger training set as it contains the test set of the CoNLL 2009 data that we use to evaluate the joint model. For Czech, the 1-best tagging accuracy is 99.11 and for Chinese 92.65 on the CoNLL 2009 test set.

We trained parsers with 25 iterations and report results for the model obtained after the last iteration. For cluster features, available only for English and German, we used standard Brown clusters based on the English and German Gigaword Corpus. We restricted the vocabulary to words that occur at least 10 times, used 800 clusters, and took cluster prefixes of length 6 to define features.

We report the following evaluation metrics: part-of-speech accuracy (POS), unlabeled attachment score (UAS), labeled attachment score (LAS), and tagged labeled attachment score (TLAS). TLAS is a new metric defined as the percentage of words that are assigned the correct part-of-speech tag, the correct head and the correct dependency label. In line with previous work, punctuation is included in the evaluation for the CoNLL data sets but excluded for the two benchmark data sets.

3.2 Results

Table 1 presents results on the development sets of the CoNLL 2009 shared task with varying values of the two tag parameters k (number of candidates) and α (maximum score difference to 1-best tag) and beam parameters fixed at $b_1 = 40$ and $b_2 = 4$. We use the combined TLAS score on the development set to select the optimal settings for each language. For Chinese, we obtain the best result with 3 tags and a threshold of 0.1.[6] Compared to the baseline, we observe a POS improvement of 0.60 and a LAS improvement of 0.51. For Czech, we get the best TLAS with $k = 3$ and $\alpha = 0.2$, where POS improves by 0.06 and LAS by 0.46. For English, the best setting is $k = 2$ and $\alpha = 0.1$ with a POS improvement of 0.17 and a LAS improvement of 0.62. For German, finally, we see the greatest improvement with $k = 3$

[3]Training: 001–815, 1001–1136. Development: 886–931, 1148–1151. Test: 816–885, 1137–1147..

[4]Training: 02-21. Development: 24. Test: 23.

[5]The RF-Tagger can take advantage of an additional lexicon and then reaches 97.97. The lexicon supplies entries for additional words that are not found in the training corpus and additional tags for words that do occur in the training data (Schmid and Laws, 2008).

[6]While tagging accuracy (POS) increases with larger values of α, TLAS decreases because of a drop in LAS.

Parser	Chinese				Czech				English				German			
	TLAS	LAS	UAS	POS	TLAS	LAS	UAS	POS	TLAS	LAS	UAS	POS	TLAS	LAS	UAS	POS
Gesmundo et al. (2009)		76.11		92.37		80.38		99.33		88.79		97.48		87.28		95.46
Bohnet (2010)		76.99		92.37		80.96		99.33		90.33		97.48		88.06		95.46
Baseline ($k = 1$), $b_1 = 40$	73.66	76.55	80.77	92.65	82.07	82.44	87.83	99.11	87.89	89.19	91.74	97.57	86.11	87.78	90.13	97.24
Best dev setting, $b_1 = 40$	74.72	77.00	81.18	93.06	82.56	82.70	88.07	99.32	88.26	89.54	92.06	97.77	86.91	88.23	90.43	97.63
Adding G, $b_1 = 80$	75.84	78.51	82.52	93.19	83.38	83.73	88.82	99.33	88.92	90.20	92.60	97.77	87.86	89.05	91.16	97.78
Adding G+C, $b_1 = 80$									89.22	90.60	92.87	97.84	88.31	89.38	91.37	98.05

Table 2: Accuracy scores for the CoNLL 2009 shared task test sets. Rows 1–2: Top performing systems in the shared CoNLL Shared Task 2009; Gesmundo et al. (2009) was placed first in the shared task; for Bohnet (2010), we include the updated scores later reported due to some improvements of the parser. Rows 3–4: Baseline ($k = 1$) and best settings for k and α on development set. Rows 5–6: Wider beam ($b_1 = 80$) and added graph features (G) and cluster features (C). Second beam parameter b_2 fixed at 4 in all cases.

and $\alpha = 0.3$, where POS improves by 0.66 and LAS by 0.86.

Table 2 shows the results on the CoNLL 2009 test sets. For all languages except English, we obtain state-of-the-art results already with $b_1 = 40$ (row 4), and for all languages both tagging and parsing accuracy improve compared to the baseline (row 3). The improvement in TLAS is statistically significant with $p < 0.01$ for all languages (paired t-test). Row 5 shows the scores with a beam of 80 and the additional graph features. Here the LAS scores for Chinese, Czech and German are higher than the best results on the CoNLL 2009 data sets, and the score for English is highly competitive. For Chinese, we achieve 78.51 LAS, which is 1.5 percentage points higher than the reference score, while the POS score is 0.54 higher than our baseline. For Czech, we get 83.73 LAS, which is by far the highest score reported for this data set, together with state-of-the-art POS accuracy. For German, we obtain 89.05 LAS and 97.78 POS, which in both cases is substantially better than in the CoNLL shared task. We believe it is also the highest POS accuracy ever reported for a tagger/parser trained only on the Tiger Treebank. Row 6, finally, presents results with added cluster features for English and German, which results in additional improvements in all metrics.

Table 3 gives the results for the Penn Treebank converted with the head-finding rules of Yamada and Matsumoto (2003) and the labeling rules of Nivre (2006). We use $k = 3$ and $\alpha = 0.4$, which gave the best results on the development set. The UAS improves by 0.24 when we do joint tagging and parsing. The POS accuracy improves slightly by 0.12

Parser	TLAS	UAS	LAS	POS
McDonald et al. (2005)		90.9		
McDonald and Pereira (2006)		91.5		
Zhang and Clark (2008)		92.1		
Huang and Sagae (2010)		92.1		
Koo and Collins (2010)		93.04		
Zhang and Nivre (2011)		92.9		
Martins et al. (2010)		93.26		
Koo et al. (2008) †		93.16		
Carreras et al. (2008) †		93.5		
Suzuki et al. (2009) †		93.79		
Baseline ($k = 1$), $b_1 = 40$	89.42	92.79	91.71	97.28
Best dev setting, $b_1 = 40$	89.75	93.03	91.92	97.40
Adding G, $b_1 = 40$	90.12	93.38	92.44	97.33
Adding G+C, $b_1 = 80$ †	90.41	93.67	92.68	97.42

Table 3: Accuracy scores for WSJ-PTB converted with head rules of Yamada and Matsumoto (2003) and labeling rules of Nivre (2006). Best dev setting: $k = 3$, $\alpha = 0.4$. Results marked with † use additional information sources and are not directly comparable to the others.

but to a lower degree than for the English CoNLL data where we observed an improvement of 0.20. Nonetheless, the improvement in the joint TLAS score is statistically significant at $p < 0.01$ (paired t-test). Our joint tagger and dependency parser with graph features gives very competitive unlabeled dependency scores for English with 93.38 UAS. To the best of our knowledge, this is the highest score reported for a (transition-based) dependency parser that does not use additional information sources. By adding cluster features and widening the beam to $b_1 = 80$, we achieve 93.67 UAS. We also obtain a POS accuracy of 97.42, which is on a par with the best results obtained using semi-supervised taggers

Parser	TLAS	UAS	LAS	POS
MSTParser1		75.56		93.51
MSTParser2		77.73		93.51
Li et al. (2011) 3rd-order		80.60		92.80
Li et al. (2011) 2nd-order		80.55		93.08
Hatori et al. (2011) HS		79.60		94.01
Hatori et al. (2011) ZN		81.20		93.94
Baseline (k = 1), b_1 = 40	61.95	80.33	76.79	92.81
Best dev setting, b_1 = 40	62.54	80.59	77.06	93.11
Adding G, b_1 = 80	63.20	81.42	77.91	93.24

Table 4: Accuracy scores for Penn Chinese Treebank converted with the head rules of Zhang and Clark (2008). Best dev setting: $k = 3$, $\alpha = 0.1$. MSTParser results from Li et al. (2011). UAS scores from Li et al. (2011) and Hatori et al. (2011) recalculated from the separate accuracy scores for root words and non-root words reported in the original papers.

Confusion	Baseline		Joint	
	Freq	F-score	Freq	F-score
VVINF → VVFIN	28	91.1	2	97.7
VVINF → VVPP|ADJ*|NN	5		9	
VVFIN → VVINF	43	94.2	5	98.5
VVFIN → VVPP	20		2	
VAINF → VAFIN	10	99.1	1	99.9
NE → NN	184	90.7	128	92.4
NE → ADJ*|ADV|FM	24		18	
NE → XY	12		21	
NN → NE	85	97.5	67	98.1
NN → ADJ*|XY|ADV|VV*	39		29	
PRELS → ART	13	92.9	5	95.4
PRELS → PWS	0		2	

Table 5: Selected entries from the confusion matrix for parts of speech in German with F-scores for the left-hand-side category. ADJ* (ADJD or ADJA) = adjective; ADV = adverb; ART = determiner; APPR = preposition; NE = proper noun; NN = common noun; PRELS = relative pronoun; VVFIN = finite verb; VVINF = non-finite verb; VAFIN = finite auxiliary verb; VAINF = non-finite auxiliary verb; VVPP = participle; XY = not a word. We use $\alpha*$ to denote the set of categories with α as a prefix.

(Søgaard, 2011).

Table 4 shows the results for the Chinese Penn Treebank CTB 5.1 together with related work. In experiments with the development set, we could confirm the results from the Chinese CoNLL data set and obtained the best results with the same settings ($k = 3$, $\alpha = 0.1$). With $b_1 = 40$, UAS improves by 0.25 and POS by 0.30, and the TLAS improvement is again highly significant ($p < 0.01$, paired t-test). We get the highest UAS, 81.42, with a beam of 80 and added graph features, in which case POS accuracy increases from 92.81 to 93.24. Since our tagger was not optimized for Chinese, we have lower baseline results for the tagger than both Li et al. (2011) and Hatori et al. (2011) but still manage to achieve the highest reported UAS.

The speed of the joint tagger and dependency parser is quite reasonable with about 0.4 seconds per sentence on the WSJ-PTB test set, given that we perform tagging and labeled parsing with a beam of 80 while incorporating the features of a third-order graph-based model. Experiments were performed on a computer with an Intel i7-3960X CPU (3.3 GHz and 6 cores). These performance values are preliminary since we are still working on the speed-up of the parser.

3.3 Analysis

In order to better understand the benefits of the joint model, we performed an error analysis for German and English, where we compared the baseline and the joint model with respect to F-scores for individual part-of-speech categories and dependency labels. For the part-of-speech categories, we found an improvement across the board for both languages, with no category having a significant decrease in F-score, but we also found some interesting patterns for categories that improved more than the average.

Table 5 shows selected entries from the confusion matrix for German, where we see substantial improvements for finite and non-finite verbs, which are often morphologically ambiguous but which can be disambiguated using syntactic context. We also see improved accuracies for common and proper nouns, which are both capitalized in standard German orthography and therefore often mistagged, and for relative pronouns, which are less often confused for determiners in the joint model.

Table 6 gives a similar snapshot for English, and we again see improvements for verb categories that are often morphologically ambiguous, such as past participles, which can be confused for past tense verbs, and present tense verbs in third person singular, which can be confused for nouns. We also see some improvement for the singular noun catego-

Confusion	Baseline		Joint	
	Freq	F-score	Freq	F-score
VBN → VBD	40	90.5	19	91.5
VBN → JJ|VB|VBP|NN	13		18	
VBZ → NN|NNS	19	97.8	13	98.3
VBZ → POS|JJ|RB	6		6	
NN → VBG|VB|VBN|VBD	72		58	
NN → JJ|JJR	79	96.8	69	97.2
NN → NN*|RB|IN|DT	58		57	
RB → IN	126	92.4	93	92.9
RB → JJ*|RP|NN*|RBR|UH	86		89	

Table 6: Selected entries from the confusion matrix for parts of speech in English with F-scores for the left-hand-side category. DT = determiner; IN = preposition or subordinating conjunction; JJ = adjective; JJR = comparative adjective; NN = singular or mass noun; NNS = plural noun; POS = possessive clitic; RB = adverb; RBR = comparative adverb; RP = particle; UH = interjection; VB = base form verb; VBD = past tense verb; VBG = gerund or present participle; VBN = past participle; VBP = present tense verb, not 3rd person singular; VBZ = present tense verb, 3rd person singular. We use $\alpha*$ to denote the set of categories with α as a prefix.

ry and for adverbs, which are less often confused for prepositions or subordinating conjunctions thanks to the syntactic information in the joint model.

For dependency labels, it is hard to extract any striking patterns and it seems that we mainly see an improvement in overall parsing accuracy thanks to less severe tagging errors. However, it is worth observing that, for both English and German, we see significant F-score improvements for the core grammatical functions subject (91.3 → 92.1 for German, 95.6 → 96.1 for English) and object (86.9 → 87.9 for German, 90.2 → 91.9 for English).

4 Related Work

Our work is most closely related to Lee et al. (2011), Li et al. (2011) and Hatori et al. (2011), who all present discriminative models for joint tagging and dependency parsing. However, all three models only perform unlabeled parsing, while our model incorporates dependency labels into the parsing process. Whereas Lee et al. (2011) and Li et al. (2011) take a graph-based approach to dependency parsing, Hatori et al. (2011) use a transition-based model similar to ours but limited to projective dependency trees. Both Li et al. (2011) and Hatori et al. (2011) only evaluate their model on Chinese, and of these only Hatori et al. (2011) report consistent improvements in both tagging and parsing accuracy. Like our system, the parser of Lee et al. (2011) can handle non-projective trees and experimental results are presented for four languages, but their graph-based model is relatively simple and the baselines therefore well below the state of the art. We are thus the first to show consistent improvements in both tagging and (labeled) parsing accuracy across typologically diverse languages at the state-of-the-art level. Moreover, the capacity to handle non-projective dependencies, which is crucial to attain good performance on Czech and German, does not seem to hurt performance on English and Chinese, where the benchmark sets contain only projective trees.

The use of beam search in transition-based dependency parsing in order to mitigate the problem of error propagation was first proposed by Johansson and Nugues (2006), although they still used a locally trained model. Globally normalized models were first explored by Titov and Henderson (2007), who were also the first to use a parameterized SHIFT transition like the one found in both Hatori et al. (2011) and our own work, although Titov and Henderson (2007) used it to define a generative model by parameterizing the SHIFT transition by an input word. Zhang and Clark (2008) was the first to combine beam search with a globally normalized discriminative model, using structured perceptron learning and the early update strategy of Collins and Roark (2004), and also explored the addition of graph-based features to a transition-based parser. This approach was further pursued in Zhang and Clark (2011) and was used by Zhang and Nivre (2011) to achieve state-of-the-art results in dependency parsing for both Chinese and English through the addition of rich non-local features. Huang and Sagae (2010) combined structured perceptron learning and beam search with the use of a graph-structured stack to allow ambiguity packing in the beam, a technique that was reused by Hatori et al. (2011).

Finally, as noted in the introduction, although joint tagging and parsing is rare in dependency parsing, most state-of-the-art parsers based on PCFG models naturally incorporate part-of-speech tagging and usually achieve better parsing accuracy (albeit not always tagging accuracy) with a joint model than with a pipeline approach (Collins, 1997; Charniak, 2000; Charniak and Johnson, 2005; Petrov et al., 2006). Models that in addition incorporate morphological analysis and segmentation have been explored by Tsarfaty (2006), Cohen and Smith (2007), and Goldberg and Tsarfaty (2008) with special reference to Hebrew parsing.

5 Conclusion

We have presented the first system for joint part-of-speech tagging and labeled dependency parsing with non-projective dependency trees. Evaluation on four languages shows consistent improvements in both tagging and parsing accuracy over a pipeline system with state-of-the-art results across the board. The error analysis reveals improvements in tagging accuracy for syntactically central categories, mainly verbs, with improvement in syntactic accuracy for core grammatical functions as a result. In future work we intend to explore joint models that incorporate not only basic part-of-speech tags but also more fine-grained morphological features.

References

Giuseppe Attardi. 2006. Experiments with a multilanguage non-projective dependency parser. In *Proceedings of CoNLL*, pages 166–170.

Burton H. Bloom. 1970. Space/time trade-offs in hash coding with allowable errors. *Communications of the ACM*, 13:422–426.

Bernd Bohnet and Jonas Kuhn. 2012. The best of both worlds – a graph-based completion model for transition-based parsers. In *Proceedings of EACL*, pages 77–87.

Bernd Bohnet. 2010. Top accuracy and fast dependency parsing is not a contradiction. In *Proceedings of COLING*, pages 89–97.

Bernd Bohnet. 2011. Comparing advanced graph-based and transition-based dependency parsers. In *Proceedings of the International Conference on Dependency Linguistics (Depling)*, pages 282–289.

Xavier Carreras, Michael Collins, and Terry Koo. 2008. Tag, dynamic programming, and the perceptron for efficient, feature-rich parsing. In *Proceedings of CoNLL*, pages 9–16.

Xavier Carreras. 2007. Experiments with a higher-order projective dependency parser. In *Proceedings of the CoNLL Shared Task of EMNLP-CoNLL 2007*, pages 957–961.

Eugene Charniak and Mark Johnson. 2005. Coarse-to-fine n-best parsing and MaxEnt discriminative reranking. In *Proceedings of ACL*, pages 173–180.

Eugene Charniak. 2000. A maximum-entropy-inspired parser. In *Proceedings of NAACL*, pages 132–139.

Shay B. Cohen and Noah A. Smith. 2007. Joint morphological and syntactic disambiguation. In *Proceedings of EMNLP-CoNLL*, pages 208–217.

Michael Collins and Brian Roark. 2004. Incremental parsing with the perceptron algorithm. In *Proceedings of ACL*, pages 112–119.

Michael Collins. 1997. Three generative, lexicalised models for statistical parsing. In *Proceedings of ACL-EACL*, pages 16–23.

Michael Collins. 2002. Discriminative training methods for hidden markov models: Theory and experiments with perceptron algorithms. In *Proceedings of EMNLP*, pages 1–8.

Koby Crammer, Ofer Dekel, Joseph Keshet, Shai Shalev-Shwartz, and Yoram Singer. 2006. Online passive-aggressive algorithms. *Journal of Machine Learning Research*, 7:551–585.

Andrea Gesmundo, James Henderson, Paola Merlo, and Ivan Titov. 2009. A latent variable model of synchronous syntactic-semantic parsing for multiple languages. In *Proceedings of the 2009 CoNLL Shared Task*, pages 37–42.

Yoav Goldberg and Reut Tsarfaty. 2008. A single generative model for joint morphological segmentation and syntactic parsing. In *Proceedings of ACL*, pages 371–379.

Jan Hajič, Massimiliano Ciaramita, Richard Johansson, Daisuke Kawahara, Maria Antònia Martí, Lluís Màrquez, Adam Meyers, Joakim Nivre, Sebastian Padó, Jan Štěpánek, Pavel Straňák, Mihai Surdeanu, Nianwen Xue, and Yi Zhang. 2009. The conll-2009 shared task: Syntactic and semantic dependencies in multiple languages. In *Proceedings of the 2009 CoNLL Shared Task*, pages 1–18.

Jun Hatori, Takuya Matsuzaki, Yusuke Miyao, and Jun'ichi Tsujii. 2011. Incremental joint pos tagging and dependency parsing in chinese. In *Proceedings of IJCNLP*, pages 1216–1224.

Liang Huang and Kenji Sagae. 2010. Dynamic programming for linear-time incremental parsing. In *Proceedings of ACL*, pages 1077–1086.

Richard Johansson and Pierre Nugues. 2006. Investigating multilingual dependency parsing. In *Proceedings of CoNLL*, pages 206–210.

Terry Koo and Michael Collins. 2010. Efficient third-order dependency parsers. In *Proceedings of ACL*, pages 1–11.

Terry Koo, Xavier Carreras, and Michael Collins. 2008. Simple semi-supervised dependency parsing. In *Proceedings of ACL*, pages 595–603.

Terry Koo, Alexander M. Rush, Michael Collins, Tommi Jaakkola, and David Sontag. 2010. Dual decomposition for parsing with non-projective head automata. In *Proceedings of EMNLP*, pages 1288–1298.

Sandra Kübler, Ryan McDonald, and Joakim Nivre. 2009. *Dependency Parsing*. Morgan and Claypool.

John Lee, Jason Naradowsky, and David A. Smith. 2011. A discriminative model for joint morphological disambiguation and dependency parsing. In *Proceedings of ACL*, pages 885–894.

Zhenghua Li, Min Zhang, Wanxiang Che, Ting Liu, Wenliang Chen, and Haizhou Li. 2011. Joint models for chinese POS tagging and dependency parsing. In *Proceedings of EMNLP*, pages 1180–1191.

Andre Martins, Noah Smith, and Eric Xing. 2009. Concise integer linear programming formulations for dependency parsing. In *Proceedings of ACL-IJCNLP*, pages 342–350.

Andre Martins, Noah Smith, Eric Xing, Pedro Aguiar, and Mario Figueiredo. 2010. Turbo parsers: Dependency parsing by approximate variational inference. In *Proceedings of EMNLP*, pages 34–44.

Ryan McDonald and Fernando Pereira. 2006. Online learning of approximate dependency parsing algorithms. In *Proceedings of EACL*, pages 81–88.

Ryan McDonald, Koby Crammer, and Fernando Pereira. 2005. Online large-margin training of dependency parsers. In *Proceedings of ACL*, pages 91–98.

Joakim Nivre, Johan Hall, and Jens Nilsson. 2004. Memory-based dependency parsing. In *Proceedings of CoNLL*, pages 49–56.

Joakim Nivre. 2006. *Inductive Dependency Parsing*. Springer.

Joakim Nivre. 2007. Incremental non-projective dependency parsing. In *Proceedings of NAACL HLT*, pages 396–403.

Joakim Nivre. 2008. Algorithms for deterministic incremental dependency parsing. *Computational Linguistics*, 34:513–553.

Joakim Nivre. 2009. Non-projective dependency parsing in expected linear time. In *Proceedings of ACL-IJCNLP*, pages 351–359.

Slav Petrov and Dan Klein. 2007. Improved inference for unlexicalized parsing. In *Proceedings of NAACL HLT*, pages 404–411.

Slav Petrov, Leon Barrett, Romain Thibaux, and Dan Klein. 2006. Learning accurate, compact, and interpretable tree annotation. In *Proceedings of COLING/ACL*, pages 433–440.

Sebastian Riedel and James Clarke. 2006. Incremental integer linear programming for non-projective dependency parsing. In *Proceedings of EMNLP*, pages 129–137.

Helmut Schmid and Florian Laws. 2008. Estimation of conditional probabilities with decision trees and an application to fine-grained POS tagging. In *Proceedings of COLING*, pages 777–784.

Qinfeng Shi, James Petterson, Gideon Dror, John Langford, Alex Smola, Alex Strehl, and S V N Vishwanathan. 2009. Hash Kernels for Structured Data. In *Journal of Machine Learning*.

David Smith and Jason Eisner. 2008. Dependency parsing by belief propagation. In *Proceedings of EMNLP*, pages 145–156.

Anders Søgaard. 2011. Semi-supervised condensed nearest neighbor for part-of-speech tagging. In *Proceedings of ACL*, pages 48–52.

Jun Suzuki, Hideki Isozaki, Xavier Carreras, and Michael Collins. 2009. An empirical study of semi-supervised structured conditional models for dependency parsing. In *Proceedings of EMNLP*, pages 551–560.

Ivan Titov and James Henderson. 2007. A latent variable model for generative dependency parsing. In *Proceedings of IWPT*, pages 144–155.

Ivan Titov, James Henderson, Paola Merlo, and Gabriele Musillo. 2009. Online graph planarization for synchronous parsing of semantic and syntactic dependencies. In *Proceedings of IJCAI*.

Kristina Toutanova, Dan Klein, Christopher D. Manning, and Yoram Singer. 2003. Feature-rich part-of-speech tagging with a cyclic dependency network. In *Proceedings of NAACL*, pages 252–259.

Reut Tsarfaty. 2006. Integrated morphological and syntactic disambiguation for modern hebrew. In *Proceedings of the COLING/ACL 2006 Student Research Workshop*, pages 49–54.

Hiroyasu Yamada and Yuji Matsumoto. 2003. Statistical dependency analysis with support vector machines. In *Proceedings of IWPT*, pages 195–206.

Yue Zhang and Stephen Clark. 2008. A tale of two parsers: Investigating and combining graph-based and transition-based dependency parsing. In *Proceedings of EMNLP*, pages 562–571.

Yue Zhang and Stephen Clark. 2011. Syntactic processing using the generalized perceptron and beam search. *Computational Linguistics*, 37:105–151.

Yue Zhang and Joakim Nivre. 2011. Transition-based parsing with rich non-local features. In *Proceedings of ACL*.

Identifying Event-related Bursts via Social Media Activities

Wayne Xin Zhao[†], **Baihan Shu**[†], **Jing Jiang**[‡], **Yang Song**[†], **Hongfei Yan**[†*] **and Xiaoming Li**[†]
[†]School of Electronics Engineering and Computer Science, Peking University
[‡]School of Information Systems, Singapore Management University
{batmanfly,baihan.shu,yhf1029}@gmail.com,ysong@pku.edu.cn
jingjiang@smu.edu.sg, lxm@pku.edu.cn

Abstract

Activities on social media increase at a dramatic rate. When an external event happens, there is a surge in the degree of activities related to the event. These activities may be temporally correlated with one another, but they may also capture different aspects of an event and therefore exhibit different bursty patterns. In this paper, we propose to identify event-related bursts via social media activities. We study how to correlate multiple types of activities to derive a global bursty pattern. To model smoothness of one state sequence, we propose a novel function which can capture the state context. The experiments on a large Twitter dataset shows our methods are very effective.

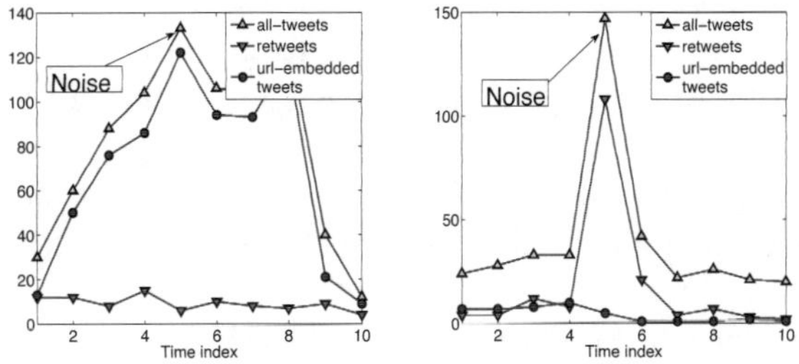

(a) Query="Amazon." (b) Query="Eclipse".

Figure 1: The amount of activities within a 10-hour window for two queries. Three types of activities are considered: (1) posting a tweet (upward triangle), (2) retweet (downward triangle), (3) posting a URL-embedded tweet (excluding retweet) (filled circle). As explained in Table 1, both bursts above are noisy.

1 Introduction

Online social networks (e.g., Twitter, Facebook, Myspace) significantly influence the way we live. Activities on social media increase at a dramatic rate. Millions of users engage in a diverse range of routine activities on social media such as posting blog messages, images, videos or status messages, as well as interacting with items generated by others such as forwarding messages. When an event interesting to a certain group of individuals takes place, there is usually a surge in the degree of activities related to the event (e.g., a sudden explosion of tweets). Since social media activities may indicate the happenings of external events, can we leverage on the rich social media activities to help identify meaningful external events? This is the research problem we study in this paper. By external events, we refer to real-world events that happen external to the online space.

Mining events from text streams is usually achieved by detecting bursty patterns (Swan and Allan, 2000; Kleinberg, 2003; Fung et al., 2005). However, previous work has mostly focused on traditional text streams such as scientific publications and news articles. There is still a lack of systematic investigations into the problem of identifying event-related bursty patterns via social media activities. There are at least two basic characteristics of social media that make the problem more interesting and challenging.

First, social media involve various types of activities taking place in real time. These activities may be temporally correlated with one another, but they may also capture different aspects of an event and therefore exhibit different bursty patterns. Most of previous methods (Swan and Allan, 2000; Kleinberg, 2003; Fung et al., 2005) deal with a single type of textual activities. When applied to social media, they oversimplify the complex nature of online so-

*Corresponding author.

Bursty Activity	Time	# in $\mathcal{S}_r$	# in $\mathcal{S}_u$	# in $\mathcal{S}_t$	Noisy?
$\mathcal{S}_r, \mathcal{S}_t$ See Fig. 1(b)	23:00~23:59, Nov. 23, 2009	**108**	5	147	**Y**
	[Query=**eclipse**] major bursty reason: The tweet from Robert Pattinson "@twilight: from rob cont . - i hope you are looking forward to **eclipse** as much as i am ." has been retweeted many times.				
$\mathcal{S}_u, \mathcal{S}_t$ See Fig. 1(a)	07:00~07:59, Jul. 25, 2009	6	**122**	133	**Y**
	[Query=**Amazon**] major bursty reason: Advertisement tweets like "@fitnessjunkies **amazon**.com deals : http://tinyurl.com/lakz3h." have been posted many times.				
$\mathcal{S}_t, \mathcal{S}_u, \mathcal{S}_r$	09:00~9:59, Oct. 9, 2009	1562	423	2848	**N**
	[Query=**Nobel**] major bursty reason: The news "Obama won **Nobel** Peace Prize" flood Twitter.				

Table 1: Examples of bursts. The first two bursts are judged as noise since they do not correspond to any meaningful external events. In fact, the reasons why a burst appears in social media can be quite diverse. In this paper, we only focus on event-related bursts. $\mathcal{S}_t$ denotes posting a tweet, $\mathcal{S}_u$ denotes posting a url-embedded tweet, and $\mathcal{S}_r$ denotes retweet.

cial activities, and therefore they may not be well suitable to social media. Let us consider a motivating example. Figure 1 shows the change of the amount of activities of three different types over a 10-hour time window for two queries. If we consider only the total number of tweets, we can see that for both queries there is a burst. However, neither of the two bursts corresponds to a real-world event. The first burst was caused by the broadcast of an advertisement from several Twitter bots, and the second burst was caused by numerous retweets of a status update of a movie star[1]. The detailed explanations of why the two bursts are noisy are also shown in Table 1. On the other hand, interestingly, we can see that not all the activity streams display noisy bursty patterns at the same time. It indicates that we may make use of multiple views of different activities to detect event-related bursts. The intuition is that using multiple types of activities may help learn a better global picture of event-related bursty patterns. Learning may also be more resistant to noisy bursts.

Second, in social media, burst detection is challenged by irregular, unpredictable and spurious noisy bursts. To overcome this challenge, a reasonable assumption is that a burst corresponding to a real event should not fluctuate too much within a relatively short time window. To illustrate it, we present an example in Figure 2, in which we first use a simple threshold method to detect bursts and then analyze the effect of local smoothness. In particular, if the amount of activities at a certain time is above a pre-defined threshold, we set its state to 1, which indicates a bursty state. Otherwise, we set the state to 0. Figure 2(a) shows that for the query "Eclipse," with a threshold of 50, the state sequence for the time window we consider is "0000100000."

[1]The reasons for these bursts were revealed by manually checking the tweets during the corresponding periods.

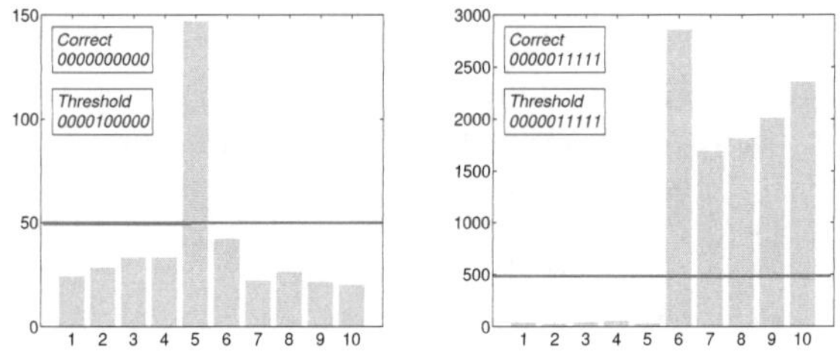

(a) Query="Eclipse". (b) Query="Nobel".

Figure 2: Analysis of the effect of local smoothness on threshold method. It shows two examples of threshold methods for burst detection in a 10-hour window. The red line denotes the bursty threshold. If the number of activities is above the threshold in one time interval, the state of this time interval is judge as bursty. Detailed descriptions of these cases are shown in Table 1.

Although there is a burst in this sequence, its duration is very short. In fact, this is the first example shown in Table 1, which is a noisy burst. In contrast, in Figure 2(b), the state sequence for the query "Nobel" is "0000011111," in which the longer and smoother burst corresponds to a true event. A good function for evaluating the smoothness of a state sequence should be able to discriminate these cases and model the context of state sequences effectively.

With its unique characteristics and challenges, there is an emergent need to deeply study the problem of event-related burst detection via social media activities. In this paper, we conduct a systematic investigation on this problem. We formulate this problem as burst detection from time series of social media activities. We develop an optimization model to learn bursty patterns based on multiple types of activities. We propose to detect bursts by considering both local state smoothness and correlation across multiple streams. We define a function to quantitatively measure local smoothness of one single state sequence. We systematically evaluate three types of activities for burst detection on a large Twitter dataset and analyze different properties of these three streams for burst detection.

2 Problem Definition

Before formally introducing our problems, we first define some basic concepts.

Activity: An activity refers to some type of action that users perform when they are interested in some topic or event.

Activity Stream: An activity stream of length N and type m is a sequence of numbers $(n_1^m, n_2^m, ..., n_N^m)$, where each n_i^m denotes the amount of activities of type m that occur during the ith time interval.

Query: A query Q is a sequence of terms $q_1, ..., q_{|Q|}$ which can represent the information needs of users. For example, an example query related to President Obama is "barack obama."

Event-related Burst: Given a query Q, an event-related burst is defined as a period $[t_s, t_e]$ in which some event related with Q takes place, where t_s and t_e are the start timestamp and end timestamp of the event period respectively. During the event period the amount of activities is significantly higher than average.

Based on these definitions, our task is to try to identify event-related bursts via multiple social media activity streams.

3 Identifying Event-related Bursts from Social Media

In this section, we discuss how to identify event-related bursts via social media activities. Formally, given a query Q, we first build M activity streams related with Q on T timestamps: $\{(n_1^m, ..., n_T^m)\}_{m=1}^M$. The definition of *activity* in our methods is very general; it includes various types of social media activities, including textual and non-textual activities, e.g., a click on a shared photo and a link formation between two users.

Given the input, we try to infer a state sequence over these T timestamps: $\boldsymbol{z} = (z_1, ..., z_T)$, where z_i is 1 or 0. 1 indicates a time point within a burst while 0 indicates a non-bursty time point.

3.1 Modeling a Single Activity Stream

3.1.1 Generation function

In probability theory and statistics, the Poisson distribution[2] is a discrete probability distribution that can measure the probability of a given number of "activities" occurring in a fixed time interval. We use the Poisson distribution to study the probability of observing the number of social media activities, and we treat one hour as one time interval in this paper.

Homogeneous Poisson Distribution The generative probability of the ith number in one activity stream of type m is defined as $f(n_i^m, i, z_i^m) = \frac{(\lambda_{z_i^m})^{n_i^m} \exp(-\lambda_{z_i^m})}{n_i^m!}$, where λ_0 is the (normal) expectation of the number of activities in one time interval. If one state is bursty, it would emit activities with a faster rate and result in a larger expectation λ_1. We can set $\lambda_1 = \lambda_0 \times \rho$, where $\rho > 1$.

Heterogeneous Poisson Distribution The two-state machine in (Kleinberg, 2003) used two global references for all the time intervals: one for bursty and the other for non-bursty. In our experiments, we observe temporal patterns of user behaviors, i.e., activities in some hours are significantly more than those in the others. Instead of using fixed global rates λ_0 and λ_1, we try to model temporal patterns of user behaviors by parameterizing $\lambda_{(\cdot)}$ with the time index. By following (Ihler et al., 2006), we use a set of hour-specific rates $\{\lambda_{1,h}\}_{h=1}^{24}$ and $\{\lambda_{0,h}\}_{h=1}^{24}$.[3] Given a time index h, we set $\lambda_{0,h}$ to be the expectation of the number of activities in hth time interval every day, then we have $\lambda_{1,h} = \lambda_{0,h} \times \rho$. In this paper, ρ is empirally set as 1.5.

3.1.2 Smoothness of a State Sequence

For burst detection, the major aim is to identify steady and meaningful bursts and to discard transient and spurious bursts. Given a state sequence $z_1 z_2 ... z_T$, to quantitatively measure the smoothness and compactness of it, we introduce some measures.

One simple method is to count the number of change in the state sequence. Formally, we use the following formula:

$$g_1(\boldsymbol{z}) = T - \sum_{i=1}^{T-1} \mathcal{I}(z_i \neq z_{i+1}), \quad (1)$$

[2] http://en.wikipedia.org/wiki/Poisson_distribution

[3] We can also make the rates both day-specific and hour-specific, i.e., $\{\lambda_{(\cdot),d,h}\}_{h \in \{1,...,24\}, d \in \{1,...,7\}}$.

where T is length of the state sequence and $\mathcal{I}(\cdot)$ is an indicator function which returns 1 only if the statement is true. Let us take the state sequence "0000100000" (shown in Figure 2(a)) as an example to see how g_1 works. State changes $0_{\text{pos}=4} \rightarrow 1_{\text{pos}=5}$ and $1_{\text{pos}=5} \rightarrow 0_{\text{pos}=6}$ each incur a cost of 1, therefore $g_1(0000100000) = 10 - 2 = 8$. Similarly, we can get $g_1(0000000000) = 10$. There is a cost difference between these two sequences, i.e., $\Delta_{g_1} = 2$. Kleinberg (2003) uses state transition probabilities to model the smoothness of state sequences. With simple derivations, we can show that Kleinberg's model essentially also uses a cost function that is linear in terms of the number of state changes in a sequence, and therefore similar to g_1.

In social media, very short noisy bursts like "0000100000" are very frequent. To discard such noises, we may multiply g_1 by a big cost factor to punish short-term fluctuations. However, it is not sensitive to the state context[4] and may affect the detection of meaningful bursts. For example, state change $0_{\text{pos}=4} \rightarrow 1_{\text{pos}=5}$ in "0000111100" would receive the same cost as that of $0_{\text{pos}=4} \rightarrow 1_{\text{pos}=5}$ in "0000100000" although the later is more like a noise.

To better measure the smoothness of a state sequence , we propose a novel context-sensitive function, which sums the square of the length of the maximum subsequences in which all states are the same. Formally, we have

$$g_2(z_1, z_2, ..., z_T) = \sum_{s_i < e_i} (e_i - s_i + 1)^2, \quad (2)$$

where s_i and e_i are the start index and end index of the ith subsequence respectively. To define "maximum", we have the constraints $z_{s_i} = z_{s_i+1} = ... = z_{e_i}, z_{s_i-1} \neq z_{s_i}, z_{e_i} \neq z_{e_i+1}$. For example, $g_2(0000000000) = 10^2 = 100$, $g_2(0000100000) = 4^2 + 1^2 + 5^2 = 42$, we can see that $\Delta_{g_2} = 100 - 42 = 58$, which is significantly larger than $\Delta_{g_1} (= 2)$. g_2 rewards the continunity of state sequences while punish the fluctuating changes, and it is context-sensitive. State change $0_{\text{pos}=4} \rightarrow 1_{\text{pos}=5}$ in "0000111100" receives a cost of 4,[5] which is much smaller than that of $0_{\text{pos}=4} \rightarrow 1_{\text{pos}=5}$ in "0000100000". g_2 is also sensitive to the position of state changes, e.g., $g_2(0000100000) \neq g_2(0100000000)$.

3.2 Burst Detection from a Single Activity Stream

Given an activity stream $(n_1^m, ..., n_T^m)$, we would like to infer a state sequence over these T timestamps, i.e., to find out the most possible state sequence $\boldsymbol{z} = (z_1^m, ..., z_T^m)$ based on the data, where $z_i^m = 1$ or 0. We formulate this problem as an optimization problem. The cost of a state sequence includes two parts: generation of activities and smoothness of the state sequence. The objective function is to find a state sequence which incurs the minimum cost. Formally, we define the total cost function as

$$Cost(\boldsymbol{z}) = \underbrace{-\sum_{i=1}^{T} \log f(n_i^m, i, z_i^m)}_{\text{generating cost}} + \underbrace{\Big(- \Phi(z_1^m, ..., z_T^m) \times \gamma_1 \Big)}_{\text{smoothness cost}}, \quad (3)$$

where $\gamma_1 > 0$ is a scaling factor which balance these two parts. $\Phi(\cdot)$ function is the smoothness function, and we can set it as either $g_1(\cdot)$ or $g_2(\cdot)$.

To seek the optimal state sequence, we can minimize Equation 3. However, exact inference is hard due to the exponential search space. Instead of examining the smoothness of the whole state sequence, we propose to measure the smoothness of all the L-length subsequences, so called "local smoothness". The assumption is that the states in a relatively short time window should not change too much. The new objective function is defined as

$$\begin{aligned} Cost(\boldsymbol{z}) \quad = \quad & -\sum_{i=1}^{T} \log f(n_i^m, i, z_i^m) \\ & -\Big(\sum_{i \geq L} \Phi(z_i^m, ..., z_{i+L-1}^m) \Big) \times \gamma_1. \end{aligned} \quad (4)$$

The objective function in Equation 4 can be solved efficiently by a dynamic programming algorithm shown in Algorithm 1. The time complexity of this algorithm is $\mathcal{O}(T \cdot 2^L)$. Note that the methods we present in Equation 4 and Algorithm 1 are quite general. They are independent of the concrete forms of $f(\cdot)$ and $\Phi(\cdot)$, which leaves room for flexible adaptation or extension in specific tasks. In previous methods (Kleinberg, 2003), L is often fixed as

[4] Here *context* refers to the window of hidden state sequences.

[5] Indeed, g_2 is not designed for a single state change but for the overall smoothness patterns, so we choose a referring sequence generated by making the corresponding state negative to compute the cost, i.e., $|g_2(0000\underline{1}1110) - g_2(0000\underline{0}1110)| = 4$.

2. Indeed, as shown in Figure 2, in some cases, we may need a longer window to infer the global patterns. In our model, L can be tuned based on real datasets. We can seek a trade-off between efficiency and length of context windows.

Algorithm 1: Dynamic Programming for Equation 4.

$d[i][s][z_i...z_{i-L+1}]$ denotes the minimum cost of the first i timestamps with the state subsequence: $z_i...z_{i-L+1}$ and $z_i = s$;
set $d[0][\cdot][\cdot] = 0$;
set $c_1[i] = \log f(n_i^m, i, z_i^m)$;
set $c_2[i] = \Phi(z_i, ..., z_{i-L+1})$;
b, b': previous and current state window are represented as L-bit binary numbers;
for $i = 1$ **to** T **do**
  for $s = 0$ **to** 1 **do**
    for $b = 0$ **to** $2^L - 1$ **do**
      $b' = (b << 1|s)\&(1 << L - 1)$;
      $d[i][s][b'] \longleftarrow \min(d[i][s][b'], d[i-1][s][b] + c_1[i] + c_2[i])$;
    end
  end
end

3.3 Correlating Multiple Activity Streams

In this section, we discuss how to correlate multiple activity streams to learn a global bursty patterns. The hidden state sequences corresponding to these activity streams are not fully independent. An external event may intricate surges in multiple activity streams simultaneously.

We propose to correlate multiple activity streams in an optimization model. The idea is that activity streams related with one query might be dependent, i.e., the states of multiple activity streams on the same timestamp tend to be the same[6]; if not, it would incur a cost. To implement this idea, we develop an optimization model. For convenience, we call the states of each activity stream as "local states" while the overall states learnt from multiple activity streams as "global states".

The idea is that although various activity streams are different in the scale of frequencies, they tend to share similar trend patterns. We incorporate the correlation between local states on the same timestamp.

[6]In our experiments, we compute the cross correlation between different streams with a lag factor δ, we find the cross correlation achieves maximum consistantly when $\delta = 0$.

Formally, we have

$$Cost(\boldsymbol{Z}) = \sum_{m=1}^{M} \left\{ -\sum_{i=1}^{T} \log f(n_i^m, i, z_i^m) - \sum_{i \geq L} \Phi(z_i^m, ..., z_{i+L-1}^m) \times \gamma_1 \right\} + \sum_{i=1}^{T} \sum_{m_1, m_2} \mathcal{I}(z_i^{m_1} \neq z_i^{m_2}) \times \gamma_2, \quad (5)$$

where $\mathcal{I}(\cdot)$ is indicator function, and γ_2 is the cost when a pair of states are different across multiple streams on the same timestamp.

The objective function in Equation 5 can be solved by a dynamic programming algorithm presented in Algorithm 2. The time complexity of this algorithm is $\mathcal{O}(T \cdot 2^{M \cdot L + M})$. Generally, L can be set as one small value, e.g., L =2 to 6, and we can select just a few representative activity streams, i.e., M =2 to 6. In this case, the algorithm can be efficient.

Algorithm 2: Dynamic Programming for Equation 5.

$d[i][z_i^1...z_{i-L+1}^1; ...; z_i^M...z_{i-L+1}^M]$ denotes the minimum cost of the first i timestamps with the local state subsequence $z_i^m...z_{i-L+1}^m$ in the mth stream;
set $d[0][...] = 0$;
$b^l, b^{l'}$: previous and current state windows represented as $M \cdot L$-bit binary numbers;
$c[i, b^l, b^{l'}]$ denotes all the cost in the tth timestamp;
for $i = 1$ **to** T **do**
  for $b_l = 0$ **to** $2^{M \cdot L} - 1$ **do**
    deriving current local state sequences $b^{l'}$ from b^l;
    $d[i][b_l'] \longleftarrow \min(d[i][b^{l'}], d[i-1][b^l] + c[i, b^l, b^{l'}])$;
  end
end

Given M types of activity streams, we can get M (local) state sequences $\{(z_1^m, ..., z_T^m)\}_{m=1}^M$. The next question is how to learn a global state sequence $(z_1^G, ..., z_T^G)$ based on local state sequences. Here we give a few options:

CONJUNCT: we set a global state z_i as bursty if all local states are bursty, i.e., $z_i^G = \cap_{m=1}^M z_i^m$.

DISJUNCT: we set a global state z_i as bursty if one of the local states is bursty, i.e., $z_i^G = \cup_{m=1}^M z_i^m$.

BELIEF: we set a global state z_i as the most confident local state, i.e., $z_i^G = \text{argmax}_m \text{belief}(z_i^m)$. The belief$(\cdot)$ function can be defined as the ratio between generating costs from states z_i^m and $1 - z_i^m$: $\text{belief}(z_i^m) = \frac{f(n_i^m, i, z_i^m)}{f(n_i^m, i, 1 - z_i^m)}$.

Table 2: Basic statistics of our golden test collection.

# of queries	17
Aver. # of event-related bursts per query	19
Min. bursty interval	3 hours
Max. bursty interval	163 hours
Aver. bursty interval	17.8 hours

L2G: we treat the states of one local stream as the global states.

4 Experiments

4.1 Construction of Test Collection

We test our algorithms on a large Twitter dataset, which contains about 200 million tweets and ranges from July, 2009 to December 2009. We manually constructed a list of 17 queries that have high volumes of relevant tweets during this period. These queries have a very broad coverage of topics. Example queries are "Barack Obama", "Apple", "Earthquake", "F1" and "Nobel Prize". For each query, we invite two senior graduate students to manually identify their golden bursty intervals, and each bursty interval is represented as a pair of timestamps in terms of hours. Specifically, to generate the golden standard, given a query, the judges first manually generate a candidate list of external events[7]; then for each event, they look into the tweets within the corresponding period and check whether there is a surge on the frequency of tweets. If so, the judges further determine the start timepoint and end timepoint of it. If there is a conflict, a third judge will make the final decision. We used Cohen's kappa coefficient to measure the agreement of between the first two judges, which turned out to be 0.67, indicating a good level of agreement[8]. We present basic statistics of the test collection in Table 2.

4.2 Evaluation Metrics

Before introducing our evaluation metrics, we first define the Bursty Interval Overlap Ratio (BIOR)

$$\text{BIOR}(f, \mathcal{X}) = \frac{\sum_{f' \in \mathcal{X}} \Delta l(f, f')}{L(f)},$$

f is a bursty interval, $\Delta l(f, f')$ is the length of overlap between f' and f, $L(f)$ is the length of bursty period of f. $\mathcal{X}$ is a set of bursty intervals, BIOR measures the proportion of the timestamps in f which are covered by one of bursty intervals in $\mathcal{X}$. We use BIOR to measure partial match of intervals, because a system may not return all the exact bursty intervals[9]. We show some examples of BIOR in Figure 3.

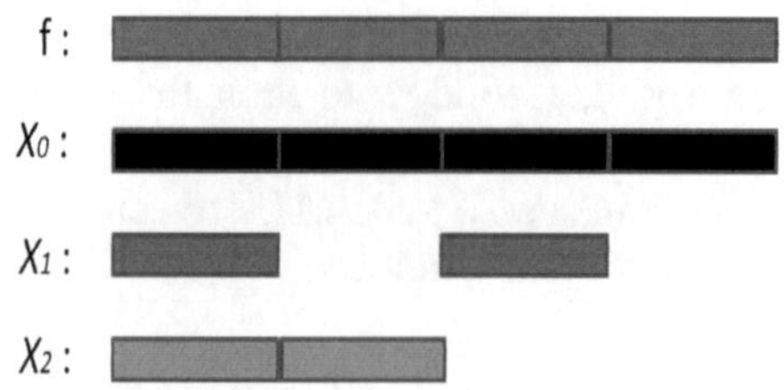

Figure 3: Examples to illustrate BIOR. X_0, X_1 and X_2 are three sets of bursty intervals. X_0 and X_2 consist of one interval, and X_1 consists of two intervals. BIOR(f, X_0)=1, BIOR(f, X_1)=0.5 and BIOR(f, X_2)=0.5.

We use modified Precision, Recall and F as basic measures. Given one query, P, R and F can be defined as follows

$$R = \frac{\sum_{f \in \mathcal{B}} \mathcal{I}\left(\frac{1}{|\mathcal{M}_f|}\text{BIOR}(f, \mathcal{M}) > 0.5\right)}{|\mathcal{B}|},$$

$$P = \frac{1}{|\mathcal{M}|} \sum_{f' \in \mathcal{M}} (\text{BIOR}(f', \mathcal{B})),$$

$$F = \frac{2 \times P \times R}{P + R},$$

where $\mathcal{M}$ is the set of bursty intervals identified by one candidate method, $\mathcal{B}$ is the set of bursty intervals in golden standards, and $\mathcal{M}_f$ is the set of intervals which overlap with f in $\mathcal{M}$. We incorporate the factor $\frac{1}{|\mathcal{M}_f|}$ in Recall to penalize the incontinuous coverage of the golden interval, and we also require that the overlap ratio with penalized factor is higher than a threshold of 0.5. Given two sets of bursty intervals which have the same value of BIOR, we prefer the one with fewer intervals. In Figure 3, we can easily derive X_1 and X_2 have the same value

[7]We refer to some gold news resources, e.g., Google News and Yahoo! News.

[8]http://en.wikipedia.org/wiki/Cohen's_kappa

[9]A simple evaluation method is that we label each one hour time slot as being part of a burst or not and compare with the gold standard. However, in our experiments, we find that some methods tend to break one meaningful burst into small parts and easier to be affected by small fluctuations although they may have a good coverage of bursty points. This is why we adopt a different evaluation approach.

Table 3: Average cross-correlation between different streams.

	$\mathcal{S}_t$	$\mathcal{S}_r$	$\mathcal{S}_u$
$\mathcal{S}_t$	1	0.830235	0.851514
$\mathcal{S}_r$	0.830235	1	0.59905
$\mathcal{S}_u$	0.851514	0.59905	1

of BIOR, when computing Recall, we prefer X_2 to X_1 since X_2 consists of only one complete interval while X_1 consists of two inconsecutive intervals. $\mathcal{I}(\cdot)$ is an indicator function which returns 1 only if the statement if true. In our experiments, we use the average of R, P and F over all test queries.

4.3 Experiment Setup

Selecting activity streams

We consider three types of activity streams in Twitter: 1) posting a tweet, denoted as $\mathcal{S}_t$; 2) forwarding a tweet (retweet), denoted as $\mathcal{S}_r$; 3) posting a URL-embedded tweet, denoted as $\mathcal{S}_u$. It is natural to test the performance of $\mathcal{S}_t$ in discovering bursty patterns, while $\mathcal{S}_u$ and $\mathcal{S}_r$ measure the influence of external events on users in Twitter in two different aspects. $\mathcal{S}_r$: An important convention in Twitter is the "retweeting" mechanism, through which users can actively spread the news or related information; $\mathcal{S}_u$: Another characteristic of Twitter is that the length of tweets is limited to 140 characters, which constrains the capacity of information. Users often embed a URL link in the tweets to help others know more about the corresponding information.

We compute the average cross correlation between different activity streams for these 17 queries in our test collection, and we summarize the results in Table 3. We can see that both $\mathcal{S}_r$ and $\mathcal{S}_u$ have a high correlation with $\mathcal{S}_t$, and $\mathcal{S}_r$ has a relatively low correlation with $\mathcal{S}_u$. [10]

Methods for comparisons

$S_{(\cdot)}$: using Equation 4 and considers a single activity stream, namely S_t, S_u and S_r.

$MBurst_{(\cdot)}$: using Equation 5 and considers multiple activity streams.

To compare our methods with previous methods, we adopt the following baselines:

StateMachine: This is the method proposed in (Kleinberg, 2003). We use heterogeneous Poisson function as generating functions instead of binomial function C_k^n because sometimes it is difficult to get the exact total number n in social media.

Threshold: If we find that the count in one time interval is higher than a predefined threshold, it is treated as a burst. The threshold is set as 1.5 times of the average number.

PeakFinding: This is the method proposed in (Marcus et al., 2011), which aims to automatically discover peaks from tweets.

Binomial: This is the method proposed in (Fung et al., 2007a), which uses a cumulative binomial distribution with a base probability estimated by removing abnormal frequencies.

As for multiple-stream burst detection, to the best of our knowledge, the only existing work is proposed by (Yao et al., 2010), which is supervised and requires a considerable amount of training time, so we do not compare our work with it. We compare our method with the following heuristic baselines:

SimpleConjunct: we first find the optimal state sequences for each single activity stream. We then derive a global state sequence by taking the conjunction of all local states.

SimpleDisjunct: we first find the optimal state sequences for each single activity stream, and then we derive a global state sequence by take the disjunction of all local states.

Another possible baseline is that we first merge all the activities, then apply the single-stream algorithm. However, in our data set, we find that the number of activities in S_t is significantly larger than that of the two types. S_t dominantly determines the final performance, so we do not incorporate it here as a comparison.

4.4 Experimental Results

Preliminary results on a single stream

We first examine the performance of our proposed method on a single stream. Note that, our method in Equation 4 has two merits: 1) the length of local window can be tuned on different datasets; 2) a novel state smoothness function is adopted.

We set the Φ function in Equation 4 respectively as g_1 and g_2, and apply our proposed methods to three streams $(\mathcal{S}_t, \mathcal{S}_r, \mathcal{S}_u)$ mentioned above. Note that, when $L = 2$ and $\Phi = g_1$, our method becomes the algorithm in (Kleinberg, 2003). We tune the parameter γ_1 in Equation 4 from 2 to 20 with a step of 2. We record the best F performance and compute

[10] We also consider the frequencies of unique users by hours, however, we find it has a extremely high correlation coefficient with $\mathcal{S}_t$, about 0.99, so we do not incorporate it.

the corresponding standard deviation. In Table 5, we can observe that 1) streams $\mathcal{S}_t$ and $\mathcal{S}_r$ perform better than $\mathcal{S}_u$; 2) the length of local window significantly affects the performance; 3) g_2 is much better than g_1 in our proposed burst detection algorithm; 4) generally speaking, a longer window size ($L = 3, 4$) performs better than the most common used size 2 in (Kleinberg, 2003).

We can see that our proposed method is more effective than the other baselines. The major reason is that none of these methods consider state smoothness in a systematic way. In our preliminary experiments, we find that these baselines usually output a lot of bursts, most of which are broken meaningful bursts. To overcome this, baseline method StateMachine ($g_1 + L = 2$) requires larger ρ and γ_1, which may discard relatively small meaningful bursts; while our proposed single stream method ($g_2 + L = 3, 4$) tends to identify steady and consecutive bursts through the help of longer context window and context sensitive smoothness function g_2, it is more suitable to be applied to social media for burst detection.

Compared with the other baselines, (Kleinberg, 2003) is still one good and robust baseline since it models the state smoothness partially. These preliminary findings indicate that state smoothness is very important for burst detection, and the length of state context window will affect the performance significantly.

To get a deep analysis of the performance of different streams, we set up three classes, and each class corresponds to a single stream. Since for each query, we can obtain multiple results in different activity streams, we further categorize the 17 annotated queries to the stream which leads to the optimal performance on that query. Interestingly, we can see: 1) the *url* stream gives better performance on queries about big companies because users in Twitter usually talk about the release of new products or important evolutionary news via url-embedded tweets; 2) the *retweet* stream gives better performance on queries which correspond to unexpected or significant events, e.g., diasters. It is consistent with our intuitions that users in Twitter do actively spread such information. Combining previous analysis of Table 5, overall we find the *retweet* stream is more capable to identify bursts which correspond to significant events.

Table 4: Categorization of 17 queries according to the optimal performance.

Streams	Queries
url	*Apple*,*Microsoft*,*Nokia*, climate
retweet	*bomb*,*crash*,*earthquake*,*typhoon*, F1,Google,Olympics
all_tweet	Amazon, eclipse, Lakers, NASA, Nobel Prize, Barack Obama

Table 5: Performance (average F) on a single stream. "⋆⋆" indicates that the improvement our proposed single-stream method$_{g_2,L=4}$ over all the other baselines is accepted at the confidence level of 0.95, i.e., StateMachine, PeakingFinding, Binomial and Threshold.

Φ	L	$\mathcal{S}_t$	$\mathcal{S}_r$	$\mathcal{S}_u$
g_2	4	0.545/0.015	0.543/0.037	0.451/0.036
	3	0.536/0.013	**0.549****/0.019	0.464/0.025
	2	0.468/0.055	0.542/0.071	0.455/0.045
g_1	4	0.513/0.059	0.546/0.058	0.465/0.047
	3	0.469/0.055	0.542/0.071	0.455/0.045
	2	0.396/0.043	0.489/0.074	0.374/0.035
StateMachine		0.396	0.489	0.374
PeakFinding		0.410	0.356	0.302
Binomial		0.315	0.420	0.341
Threshold		0.195	0.181	0.175

Preliminary results on multiple streams

After examining the basic results on a single stream, we continue to evaluate the performance of our proposed models on multiple activity streams. For $MBurst$ in Equation 5, we have three parameters to set, namely L, γ_1 and γ_2. We do a grid search for both γ_1 and γ_2 from 1 to 12 with a step of 1, and we also examine the performance when $L = 2, 3, 4$. We can see that $MBurst$ has four candidate methods to derive global states from local states; for *L2G*, we use the states of $\mathcal{S}_t$ as the final states, and we empirically find that it performs best compared with the other two streams in *L2G*.

Recall that our proposed single-stream method is better than all the other single-stream baselines, so here single-best denotes our method in Equation 4 ($\Phi = g_2, L = 4$) on $\mathcal{S}_r$. For *SimpleConjunct* and *SimpleDisjunct*, we first find the optimal state sequences for each single activity stream using our proposed method in Equation 4 ($\Phi = g_2, L = 4$), and then we derive a global state sequence by take the conjunction or disjunction of all local states respectively.

Besides the best performance, we further compute the average of the top 10 results of each method by tuning parameters to check the average perfor-

Table 6: Performance (average F) on multiple streams. "$\star$" indicates that the improvement our proposed multiple-stream method over our proposed single-stream method at the confidence level of 0.9 in terms of average performance.

Methods	best	average
single-best ($g_2 + \mathcal{S}_r$)	0.549	0.526
SimpleConjunct	0.548	-
SimpleDisjunct	0.465	-
$MBurst$+**CONJUNCT**$_{r,t,u}$	0.555	0.548
$MBurst$+**DISJUNCT**$_{r,t,u}$	**0.576**	**0.570***
$MBurst$+**BELIEF**$_{r,t,u}$	0.568	0.561
$MBurst$+**L2G**$_{r,t,u}(t)$	0.574	0.567
$MBurst$+**L2G**$_{r,t,u}(r)$	0.560	0.558

mance. The average performance can show the stability of models in some degree. If one model outputs the maximum in a very limited set of parameters, it may not work well in real data, especially in social media.

In Table 6, we can see $MBurst$+**DISJUNCT**$_{r,t,u}$ gives the best performance. $MBurst$ performs consistently better than *single-best* which is a very strong single-stream method, especially for average performance. $MBurst$+**DISJUNCT**$_{r,t,u}$ has an improvement of average performance over *single-best* by 8.4%. And simply combining three different streams may hit results (*SimpleConjunct* and *SimpleDisjunct*). It indicates that $MBurst$ is more stable and shows a higher performance.

For different methods to derive global bursty patterns, we can see that $MBurst$+**DISJUNCT** performs best while $MBurst$+**CONJUNCT** performs worst. Interestingly, however, *SimpleConjunct* is better than *SimpleDisjunct*, the major reason is that $MBurst$ performs a local-state correlation of multiple activity streams to correct possible noisy fluctuations from single streams before the conjunction or disjunction of local states. After such correlation, the performance of each activity stream should improve. To see this, we present the optimal results of a single stream without/with local-state correlation in Table 7. Local-state correlation significantly boosts the performance of a single stream. Indeed, we find that the step of local-state correlation is more important for our multiple stream algorithm than the step of how to derive global states based on local states.

We test our $MBurst$ algorithm with the setting: $T = 4416$, $L = 4$ and $M = 3$, and for all the test

Table 7: Comparison between the optimal results of a single stream with/without local-state correlation.

	all_retweet	retweet	url
without	0.536	0.549	0.464
with	0.574	0.560	0.547

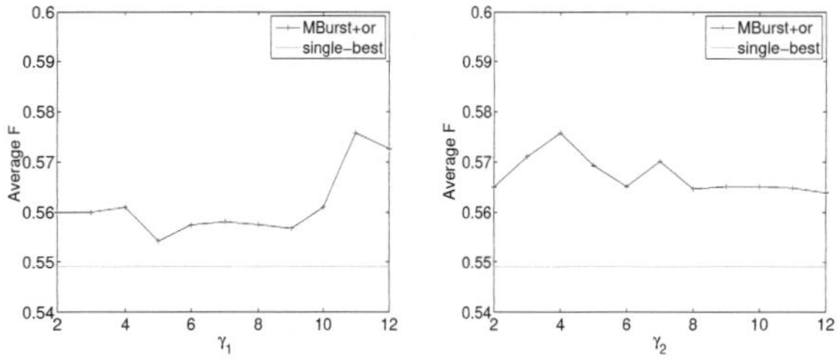

(a) $\gamma_2 = 4$, varying γ_1. (b) $\gamma_1 = 11$, varying γ_2.

Figure 4: Parameter sensitivity of $MBurst$ + **DISJUNCT**.

queries, our algorithm can respond in 2 seconds [11], which is efficient to be deployed in social media.

Parameter sensitivity

We have shown the performance of different parameter settings for single stream algorithm in Table 5. Next, we check parameter sensitivity in $MBurst$. In our experiments, we find a longer local window ($L = 3, 4$) is better than $L = 2$, so we first set $L = 4$, then we select parameter settings of $\gamma_2 = 4$ and $\gamma_1 = 11$, which give best performance for $MBurst$+**DISJUNCT**. We vary one with the other fixed to see how one single parameter affects the performance. The results are shown in Figure 4, and we can see $MBurst$+**DISJUNCT** is consistently better than single-best.

5 Related Work

Our work is related to burst detection from text streams. Pioneered by the automaton model proposed in (Kleinberg, 2003), many techniques have been proposed for burst detection such as the χ^2-test based method (Swan and Allan, 2000), the parameter-free method (Fung et al., 2005) and moving average method (Vlachos et al., 2004). Our work is related to the applications of these burst detection algorithms for event detection (He et al., 2007; Fung et al., 2007b; Shan et al., 2012; Zhao et al., 2012).

[11] All experiments are tested in a Mac PC, 2.4GHz Intel Core 2 Duo.

Some recent work try to identify hot trends (Mathioudakis and Koudas, 2010; Zubiaga et al., 2011; Budak et al., 2011; Naaman et al., 2011) or make use of the burstiness (Sakaki et al., 2010; Aramki et al., 2011; Marcus et al., 2011) in social media. However, few of these methods consider modeling the local smoothness of one state sequence in a systematic way and often use a fixed window length of 2.

Little work considers making use of different types of social media activities for burst detection. (Yao et al., 2010; Kotov et al., 2011; Wang et al., 2007; Wang et al., 2009) conducted some preliminary studies of mining correlated bursty patterns from multiple sources. However, they either highly relies on high-quality training datasets or require a considerable amount of training time. Online social activities are dynamic, with a large number of new items generated continuously. In such a dynamic setting, burst detection algorithms should effectively collect evidence, efficiently adjust prediction models and respond to the users as social media activities evolve. Therefore it is not suitable to deploy such algorithms in social media.

Our work is also similar to studies which aim to mine and leverage knowledge from social media (Mathioudakis et al., 2010; Ruiz et al., 2012; Morales et al., 2012). We share the common point with these studies that we try to utilize the underlying rich knowledge in social media, while our focus of this work is quite different from theirs, i.e., to identify event-related bursts.

Another line of related research is Twitter related studies (Kwak et al., 2010; Sakaki et al., 2010). Our proposed methods can provide event-related bursts for downstream applications.

6 Conclusion

In this paper, we propose to identify event-related bursts via social media activities. We propose one optimization model to correlate multiple activity streams to learn the bursty patterns. To better measure local smoothness of the state sequence, we propose a novel state cost function. We test our methods in a large Twitter dataset. The experiment results show that our methods are both effective and efficient. Our work can provide a preliminary understanding of the correlation between the happenings of events and the degree of online social media activities.

Finally, we present a few promising directions which may potentially improve or enrich current work.

1) **Variable-length context.** In this paper, L is a pre-determined parameter which controls the size of context window. It cannot be modified when the algorithm runs. A large L will significantly increases the algorithm complexity, and we may not need a large L for all the states in a Markov chain. This problem can be addressed by using the variable-length hidden Markov model (Wang et al., 2006), which is able to learn the "minimum" context length for accurately determining each state.

2) **Incorporation of more useful features.** Our current model mainly considers temporal variations of streaming data and searches the surge patterns existing in it. In some cases, simple frequency information may not be capable to identify all the meaningful bursts. It can be potentially useful to leverage up more features to help filter out noisy bursts, e.g., semantic information (Zhao et al., 2010).

3) **Modeling multi-modality data.** We have examined our multi-stream algorithm by using three different activity streams. These streams are textual-based. It will be interesting to check our algorithm in multi-modality data streams. E.g., in Facebook, we may collect a stream consisting of the daily frequencies of photo sharing and another stream consisting of the daily frequencies of text status updates.

4) **Evaluation of the identified bursts.** In most of previous work, they seldom construct a gold standard for quantitative test, instead they qualitatively evaluate their methods. In our work, we invite human judges to generate the gold standard. It is time-consuming, and the bias from human judges cannot be completely eliminated although more judges can be invited. A possible evaluation method is to examine the identified bursts in downstream applications, e.g., event detection.

Acknowledgement

This work is partially supported by NSFC Grant 61073082, 60933004 and 70903008. Xin Zhao is supported by Google PhD Fellowship (China). We thank the insightful comments from Junjie Yao and the anonymous reviewers.

References

Eiji Aramki, Sachiko Maskawa, and Mizuki Morita. 2011. Twitter catches the flu: Detecting influenza epidemics using twitter. In *Proceedings of the 2011 Conference on Empirical Methods in Natural Language Processing*, pages 1568–1576, Edinburgh, Scotland, UK., July. Association for Computational Linguistics.

Ceren Budak, Divyakant Agrawal, and Amr El Abbadi. 2011. Structural trend analysis for online social networks. *Proc. VLDB Endow.*, 4, July.

Gabriel Pui Cheong Fung, Jeffrey Xu Yu, Philip S. Yu, and Hongjun Lu. 2005. Parameter free bursty events detection in text streams. In *VLDB*.

Gabriel Pui Cheong Fung, Jeffrey Xu Yu, Huan Liu, and Philip S. Yu. 2007a. Time-dependent event hierarchy construction. In *Proceedings of the 13th ACM SIGKDD international conference on Knowledge discovery and data mining*, KDD '07.

Gabriel Pui Cheong Fung, Jeffrey Xu Yu, Huan Liu, and Philip S. Yu. 2007b. Time-dependent event hierarchy construction. In *SIGKDD*.

Qi He, Kuiyu Chang, and Ee-Peng Lim. 2007. Analyzing feature trajectories for event detection. In *SIGIR*.

Alexander Ihler, Jon Hutchins, and Padhraic Smyth. 2006. Adaptive event detection with time-varying poisson processes. In *Proceedings of the 12th ACM SIGKDD international conference on Knowledge discovery and data mining*, KDD, pages 207–216, New York, NY, USA. ACM.

J. Kleinberg. 2003. Bursty and hierarchical structure in streams. *Data Mining and Knowledge Discovery*.

Alexander Kotov, ChengXiang Zhai, and Richard Sproat. 2011. Mining named entities with temporally correlated bursts from multilingual web news streams. In *Proceedings of the fourth ACM international conference on Web search and data mining*, WSDM, pages 237–246.

Haewoon Kwak, Changhyun Lee, Hosung Park, and Sue Moon. 2010. What is Twitter, a social network or a news media? In *WWW '10: Proceedings of the 19th international conference on World wide web*, pages 591–600.

Adam Marcus, Michael S. Bernstein, Osama Badar, David R. Karger, Samuel Madden, and Robert C. Miller. 2011. Twitinfo: aggregating and visualizing microblogs for event exploration. In *Proceedings of the 2011 annual conference on Human factors in computing systems*, CHI '11.

Michael Mathioudakis and Nick Koudas. 2010. Twittermonitor: trend detection over the twitter stream. In *Proceedings of the 2010 international conference on Management of data*, SIGMOD '10, pages 1155–1158.

Michael Mathioudakis, Nick Koudas, and Peter Marbach. 2010. Early online identification of attention gathering items in social media. In *Proceedings of the third ACM international conference on Web search and data mining*, WSDM '10, pages 301–310, New York, NY, USA. ACM.

Gianmarco De Francisci Morales, Aristides Gionis, and Claudio Lucchese. 2012. From chatter to headlines: harnessing the real-time web for personalized news recommendation. In *WSDM*, pages 153–162.

Mor Naaman, Hila Becker, and Luis Gravano. 2011. Hip and trendy: Characterizing emerging trends on twitter. *JASIST*, 62(5):902–918.

Eduardo J. Ruiz, Vagelis Hristidis, Carlos Castillo, Aristides Gionis, and Alejandro Jaimes. 2012. Correlating financial time series with micro-blogging activity. pages 513–522.

Takeshi Sakaki, Makoto Okazaki, and Yutaka Matsuo. 2010. Earthquake shakes twitter users: real-time event detection by social sensors. WWW, pages 851–860, New York, NY, USA. ACM.

Dongdong Shan, Wayne Xin Zhao, Rishan Chen, Shu Baihan, Hongfei Yan, and Xiaoming Li. 2012. Eventsearch: A system for event discovery and retrieval on multi-type historical data. In *KDD'12*, Demostration.

Russell Swan and James Allan. 2000. Automatic generation of overview timelines. In *SIGIR*.

Michail Vlachos, Christopher Meek, Zografoula Vagena, and Dimitrios Gunopulos. 2004. Identifying similarities, periodicities and bursts for online search queries. In *SIGMOD*.

Yi Wang, Lizhu Zhou, Jianhua Feng, Jianyong Wang, and Zhi-Qiang Liu. 2006. Mining complex time-series data by learning markovian models. In *Proceedings of the Sixth International Conference on Data Mining*, ICDM, pages 1136–1140, Washington, DC, USA. IEEE Computer Society.

Xuanhui Wang, ChengXiang Zhai, Xiao Hu, and Richard Sproat. 2007. Mining correlated bursty topic patterns from coordinated text streams. In *Proceedings of the 13th ACM SIGKDD international conference on Knowledge discovery and data mining*.

Xiang Wang, Kai Zhang, Xiaoming Jin, and Dou Shen. 2009. Mining common topics from multiple asynchronous text streams. In *Proceedings of the Second ACM International Conference on Web Search and Data Mining*, WSDM, pages 192–201.

Junjie Yao, Bin Cui, Yuxin Huang, and Xin Jin. 2010. Temporal and social context based burst detection from folksonomies. In *AAAI*.

Wayne Xin Zhao, Jing Jiang, Jing He, Dongdong Shan, Hongfei Yan, and Xiaoming Li. 2010. Context modeling for ranking and tagging bursty features in text streams. In *Proceedings of the 19th ACM international conference on Information and knowledge management*, CIKM '10.

Wayne Xin Zhao, Rishan Chen, Kai Fan, Hongfei Yan, and Xiaoming Li. 2012. A novel burst-based text representation model for scalable event detection. In *ACL'12*.

Arkaitz Zubiaga, Damiano Spina, Víctor Fresno, and Raquel Martínez. 2011. Classifying trending topics: a typology of conversation triggers on twitter. In *Proceedings of the 20th ACM international conference on Information and knowledge management*, CIKM.

User Demographics and Language in an Implicit Social Network

Katja Filippova
Google Inc.
Brandschenkestr. 110
Zürich, 8004 Switzerland
katjaf@google.com

Abstract

We consider the task of predicting the gender of the YouTube[1] users and contrast two information sources: the comments they leave and the social environment induced from the affiliation graph of users and videos. We propagate gender information through the videos and show that a user's gender can be predicted from her social environment with the accuracy above 90%. We also show that the gender can be predicted from language alone (89%). A surprising result of our study is that the latter predictions correlate more strongly with the gender predominant in the user's environment than with the sex of the person as reported in the profile. We also investigate how the two views (linguistic and social) can be combined and analyse how prediction accuracy changes over different age groups.

1 Introduction

Over the past decade the web has become more and more social. The number of people having an identity on one of the Internet social networks (Facebook[2], Google+[3], Twitter[4], etc.) has been steadily growing, many users communicate online on a daily basis. Their interactions open new possibilities for social sciences, and linguistics is no exception. For example, with the development and growth of Web 2.0, it has become possible to get access to masses of text data labeled with respect to different social parameters such as country, age, gender, profession or religion. The study of language varieties between groups separated by a certain social variable belongs to the field of sociolinguistics which more generally investigates the effect of society on how language is used (Coulmas, 1998). Historically, sociolinguistics is connected to dialectology whose focus has been primarily on the phonetic aspect of the regional dialects but was later extended to sociolects (Chambers & Trudgill, 1998). A usual study would involve sampling speakers from a population, interviewing them and analyzing the linguistic items with respect to social variables (Hudson, 1980).

The last decade has seen several studies investigating the relationship between the language and the demographics of the users of blogs or Twitter (see Sec. 2 for references). Most of those studies used social network sites to collect labeled data–samples of text together with the demographics variable. However, they did not analyse how social environment affects language, although very similar questions have been recently posed (but not yet answered) by Ellist (2009). In our work we attempt to address precisely this issue. In particular, we consider the task of user gender prediction on YouTube and contrast two information sources: (1) the comments written by the user and (2) her social neighborhood as defined by the bipartite user-video graph. We use the comments to train a gender classifier on a variety of linguistic features. We also introduce a simple gender propagation procedure to predict person's gender from the user-video graph.

In what follows we will argue that although language does provide us with signals indicative of the

[1] www.youtube.com
[2] www.facebook.com
[3] www.plus.google.com
[4] www.twitter.com

user's gender[5] (as reported in the user's profile), it is in fact more indicative of a socially defined gender. Leaving aside the debate on the intricate relationship between language and gender (see Eckert & McConnell-Ginet (2003) for a thorough discussion of the subject), we simply demonstrate that a classifier trained to predict the predominant gender in the user's social environment, as approximated by the YouTube graph of users and videos, achieves higher accuracy for both genders than the one trained to predict the user's inborn gender. We also investigate ways of how the language-based and the social views can be combined to improve prediction accuracy. Finally, we look at three age groups – teenagers, people in their twenties and people over thirty – and show that gender identity is more evident in the language of younger people but also that there is a higher correlation between their inborn gender and the predominant gender in their social environment.

The paper is organized as follows: we first review related work on the language of social media and user demographics (Sec. 2) and elaborate on the goals of our research (Sec. 3). Then we describe our data (Sec. 4), introduce the demographics propagation experiments (Sec. 5) and the experiments on supervised learning gender from language (Sec. 6).

2 Related work

Previous studies on language and demographics which looked at online data can be distinguished with respect to their aims. (1) Studies coming from the sociolinguistic community aim at empirically confirming hypotheses, such as that female speakers use more pronouns, or that males tend to use longer words. (2) A standard goal of an NLP study is to build an automatic system which accurately solves a given task which in the case of demographics is predicting user age, gender or country of origin. In this section we start by reviewing the first kind of studies, which are about data analysis and hypotheses checking. These are relevant for our choice of features. Then we briefly summarize a selection of studies on demographics prediction to better situate and motivate our approach.

[5] Although it might be more correct to talk about the user's sex in place of gender (Eckert & McConnell-Ginet, 2003), we stick to the terminology adopted in previous NLP research on gender prediction.

2.1 Language and demographics analysis

Previous sociolinguistic studies mostly checked hypotheses formulated before the widespread use of the Internet, such as that women use hedges more often (Lakoff, 1973) or that men use more negations (Mulac et al., 2000), or looked at specific words or word classes. Newman et al. (2008) provide a comprehensive review of such work and a description of the non-web corpora used therein. Some of those hypotheses were confirmed by empirical evidence, some not.

For example, Herring & Paolillo (2006) analyse gender- and genre-specific use of language in online communication on a sample of about 130 blog entries. Looking at a number of stylistic features which had previously been claimed to be predictive of gender (Argamon et al., 2003; Koppel et al., 2004), such as personal pronouns, determiners and other function words, they find no gender effect. Unlike them, Kapidzic & Herring (2011) analyse recent chat communications and find that they are gendered. Similarly, Huffaker & Calvert (2005) investigate the question of identity of teenager bloggers (e.g., age, gender, sexuality) and find language features indicative of gender (e.g., use of emoticons by males). Burger & Henderson (2006) consider the relationship between different linguistic (e.g., text length, use of capital and punctuation letters) and non-linguistic (e.g., interests, mood) features and blogger's age and location. They find that many features correlate with the age and run an experiment with the goal of predicting whether the blog author is over 18.

2.2 Demographics prediction from language

The studies we review here used supervised machine learning to obtain models for predicting gender or age. Other demographic attributes, like location, ethnicity, or educational level, have also been predicted automatically (Gillick, 2010; Rao & Yarowsky, 2011, inter alia). Also, generative approaches have been applied to discover associations between language and demographics of social media users (Eisenstein et al., 2011, inter alia) but these are of less direct relevance for the present work. For supervised approaches, major feature sources are the text the user has written and also her profile which may list the name, interests, friends, etc. There have also been studies which did not look at the language at all but considered the social environment only. For example, MacKinnon & Warren (2006) aim at predicting the age and the location of the LiveJournal[6] users. What they found is that there is a remarkable correlation between the age and the location of the user and those of her friends, although there are interesting exceptions.

Burger et al. (2011) train a gender classifier on tweets with word and character-based ngram features achieving accuracy of 75.5%. Adding the full name feature alone gives a boost to 89.1%, further features like self-written description and screen name further help to get 92%. Also, a self-training method exploring unlabeled data is described but its performance is worse. Other kinds of sociolinguistic features and a different classifier have been applied to gender prediction on tweets by Rao & Yarowsky (2010).

Nowson & Oberlander (2006) achieve 92% accuracy on the gender prediction task using ngram features only. Their corpus consist of 1,400/450 posts written by 47 females and 24 males, respectively. However, the ngram features were preselected based on whether they occurred with significant relative frequency in the language of one gender over the other. Since the complete dataset was used to preselect features, the results are inconclusive.

Yan & Yan (2006) train a Naive Bayes classifier to predict the gender of a blog entry author. In total they looked at 75,000 individual blog entries authored by 3,000 bloggers, all of them posted their genders on the profile page. They measure precision and recall w.r.t. the minority class (males) and get the best f-measure of 0.64 (precision and recall are 65% and 71%, respectively).

Rosenthal & McKeown (2011) predict the age of a blogger, most features they use are extracted from the blog posts, other features include blogger's interests, the number of friends, the usual time of posting, etc. Similarly to Schler et al. (2006), they run a classification experiment with three age classes removing intermediate ages and use the majority-class baseline for comparison. In their other experiment they experiment with a binary classifier for age distinguishing between the pre- and post-social media generations and using the years from 1975-1988 as a boundary. The prediction accuracy increases as later years are taken.

Interestingly, it has been shown that demographics can be predicted in more restricted genres than the personal blog or tweets and from text fragments even shorter than tweets (Otterbacher, 2010; Popescu & Grefenstette, 2010).

3 Motivation for the present study

Similarly to previous NLP studies, our starting goal is to predict the self-reported user gender. The first novelty of our research is that in doing so we contrast two sources of information: the user's social environment and the text she has written. Indeed, a topic which has not yet been investigated much in the reviewed studies on language and user demographics is the relationship between the language of the user and her social environment. The data analysis studies (Sec. 2.1) verified hypotheses concerning the dependency between a language trait (e.g., average sentence length) and a demographic parameter (e.g., gender). The demographics prediction studies (Sec. 2.2) mostly relied on language and user profile features and considered users in isolation. An exception to this is Garera & Yarowsky (2009) who showed that, for gender prediction in a dialogue, it helps to know the interlocutor's gender. However, we aim at investigating the impact of the social environment in a much broader sense than the immediate interlocutors and in a much broader context than a conversation.

Language is a social phenomenon, and it is this fact that motivates all the sociolinguistic research. Many if not most language traits are not hard-wired or inborn but can be explained by looking at who the person interacts most with. Since every language speaker can be seen as a member of multiple overlapping communities (e.g., computer scientists, French, males, runners), the language of the person may reflect her membership in different communities to various degrees. Repeated interactions with other language speakers influence the way the person speaks (Baxter et al., 2006; Bybee, 2010), and

[6] www.livejournal.com

the influence is observable on all the levels of the language representation (Croft, 2000). For example, it has been shown that the more a person is integrated in a certain community and the tighter the ties of the social network are, the more prominent are the representative traits of that community in the language of the person (Milroy & Milroy, 1992; Labov, 1994). In our study we adopt a similar view and analyse the implications it has for gender prediction. Given its social nature, does the language reflect the norms of a community the user belongs to or the actual value of a demographic variable?

In our study we address this issue with a particular modeling technique: we assume that the observed online behavior adequately reflects the offline life of a user (more on this in Sec. 4 and 5) and based on this assumption make inferences about the user's social environment. We use language-based features and a supervised approach to gender prediction to analyse the relationship between the language and the variable to be predicted. To our knowledge, we are the first to question whether it is really the inborn gender that language-based classifiers learn to predict. More concrete questions we are going to suggest answers to are as follows:

1. Previous studies which looked at online data relied on self-reported demographics. The profile data are known to be noisy, although it is hard to estimate the proportion of false profiles (Burger et al., 2011). Concerning the prediction task, how can we make use of what we know about the user's social environment to reduce the effect of noise? How can we benefit from the language samples from the users whose gender we do not know at all?

2. When analyzing the language of a user, how much are its gender-specific traits due to the user's inborn gender and to which extent can they be explained by her social environment? Using our modeling technique and a language-based gender classifier, how is its performance affected by what we know about the online social environment of the user?

3. Concerning gender predictions across different age groups, how does classifier performance change? Judging from the online communication, do teenagers signal their gender identity more than older people? In terms of classifier accuracy, is it easier to predict a teenager's gender than the gender of an adult?

The final novelty of our study is that we are the first to demonstrate how YouTube can be used as a valuable resource for sociolinguistic research. In the following section we highlight the points which make YouTube interesting and unique.

4 Data

Most social networks strive to protect user privacy and by default do not expose profile information or reveal user activity (e.g., posts, comments, votes, etc.). To obtain data for our experiments we use YouTube, a video sharing site. Most of the YouTube registered users list their gender, age and location on their profile pages which, like their comments, are publicly available. YouTube is an interesting domain for sociolinguistic research for several reasons:

High diversity: it is not restricted to any particular topic (e.g., like political blogs) but covers a vast variety of topics attracting a very broad audience, from children interested in cartoons to academics watching lectures on philosophy[7].

Spontaneous speech: the user comments are arguably more spontaneous than blogs which are more likely to conform to the norms of written language. At the same time they are less restricted than tweets written under the length constraint which encourages highly compressed utterances.

Data availability: all the comments are publicly available, so we have do not get a biased subset of what a user has written for the public. Moreover, we observe users' interactions in different environments because every video targets particular groups of people who may share origin (e.g., *elections in Greece*) or possession (e.g., *how to unlock iPhone*) or any other property. Some videos attract a well-defined group of people (e.g., *the family of a newborn child*), whereas some videos appeal to a very broad audience (e.g., *a kitten video*).

[7]For more information and statistics see the official YouTube demographics on `http://www.youtube.com/yt/advertise/affinities.html`.

female	male	nn
26%	62%	12%

Table 1: Gender distribution for the extracted 6.9M users.

From the users, videos and the comment relationship we build an affiliation graph (Easley & Kleinberg, 2010): a user and a video are connected if the user commented on the video (Fig. 1(a)). Our graph is unweighted although the number of comments could be used to weight edges. The co-comment graph is a stricter version of a more popular co-view graph used in, e.g., video recommendation studies (Baluja et al., 2008, inter alia).

We obtained a random sample of videos by considering all the videos whose YouTube ID has a specific prefix[8]. From those, we collected the profiles of the users whose commented on the videos. In total, we extracted about 6.9M profiles of users who have written at least 20 comments, not more than 30 comments were collected for every user. The threshold on the minimum number of comments is set in order to reduce the proportion of users who have used YouTube only a few times and possibly followed the suggestions of the site in their video choice. The users' gender distributions is presented in Table 1. Although females, in particular teenagers, have been reported to be more likely to blog than males (Herring et al., 2004), males are predominant in our dataset. A random sample from a pool of users without the 20-comments threshold showed that there are more male commenters overall, although the difference is less remarkable for teenagers: 58% of the teenagers with known gender are male as opposed to 74% and 79% for the age groups 20-29 and 30+. Teenagers are also more numerous accounting for about 35% in our data.

Although we did not filter users based on their location or mother tongue as many users comment in multiple languages, the comment set is overwhelmingly English.

[8]The YouTube API (`http://code.google.com/apis/youtube/getting_started.html`) can be used to retrieve user profiles and video metadata as well as the comments.

5 Gender propagation

We first consider the user's social environment to see whether there is any correlation between the gender of a user and the gender distribution in her vicinity, independent of the language. We use a simple propagation procedure to reach the closest neighbors of a user, that is, other users "affiliated" with the same videos. Specifically, we perform the following two steps:

1. We send the gender information (female, male or unknown) to all the videos the user has commented on. This way for every video we obtain a multinomial distribution over three classes (see Fig. 1(b)).

2. We send the gender distributions from every video back to all the users who commented on it and average over all the videos the user is connected with (see Fig. 1(c)). However, in doing so we adjust the distribution for every user so that her own demographics is excluded. This way we have a fair setting where the original gender of the user is never included in what she gets back from the connected videos. Thus, the gender of a user contributes to the vicinity distributions of all the neighbors but not to her own final gender distribution.

In line with our motivation and modeling technique, we chose such a simple method (and not, say, classification) in order to approximate the offline encounters of the user: does she more often meet women or men? The way we think of the videos is that they correspond to places (e.g., a cinema, a cosmetic shop, a pub) visited by the user where she is unintentionally or deliberately exposed to how other speakers use the language. Similar to Baxter et al. (2006), we assume that these encounters influence the way the person speaks. Note that if the user's gender has no influence on her choice of videos, then, on average, we would expect every video to have the same distribution as in our data overall: 62% male, 26% female and 12% unknown (Table 1).

To obtain a single gender prediction from the propagated distribution, for a given user we select the gender class (female or male) which got more

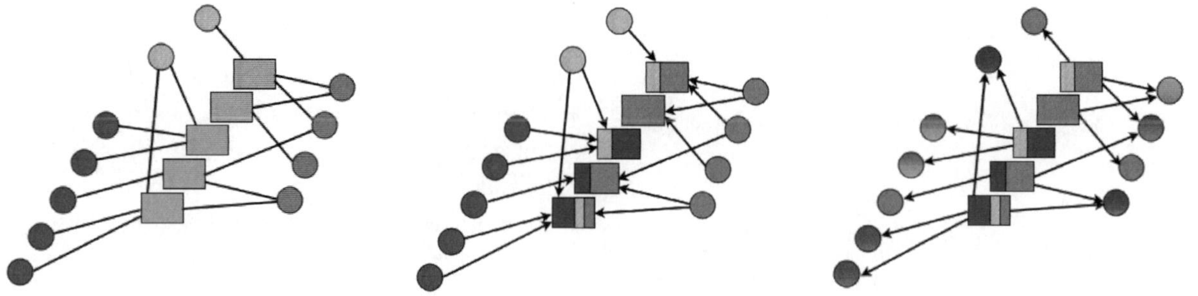

(a) Color represents gender information: *blue*=male, *red*=female, *grey*=unknown.

(b) Propagating gender from users to videos.

(c) Propagating gender distribution from videos to users.

Figure 1: Affiliation graph of users (circles) and videos (rectangles).

of the distribution mass. The exact procedure is as follows: given user *u* connected with videos $V_u = \{v_1, ..., v_m\}$, there are *m* gender distributions sent to *u*: $P_V(u) = \{p(g|v_i) : 1 \leq i \leq m, g \in \{f, m, n\}\}$. A single distribution is obtained from $P_V(u)$: $\hat{p}(g|u) = \sum_i p(g|v_i)/m$.

To address the skewness in the data, i.e., the fact that 70% of our users $(62/(26+62))$ with known gender are male, we select the female gender if (a) it got more than zero mass and at least as much mass as male: $\hat{p}(f) > 0 \wedge \hat{p}(f) \geq \hat{p}(m)$, or (b) it got at least τ of the mass: $\hat{p}(f) \geq \tau$. We set $\tau = 0.26$ initially because it corresponds to the expected proportion of females (26%) but further experimented with different τ values in the range of 0.25-0.4. We obtained best accuracy and f-measures with the threshold of 0.33, the difference in accuracy from the initial threshold of 0.26 being less than 2%. The fact that the optimal τ value is different from the overall proportion of females (26%) is not surprising given that we aggregate per video distributions and not raw user counts.

The predictions obtained with the described propagation method are remarkably accurate, reaching 90% accuracy (Table 2). The baseline of assigning all the users the majority class (*all male*) provides us with the accuracy of 70% – the proportion of males among the users with known gender.

Although the purpose of this section is not to present a gender prediction method, we find it worth emphasizing that 90% accuracy is remarkable given that we only look at the immediate user vicinity. In the following section we are going to investigate how this social view on demographics can help us in predicting gender from language.

	Acc%	P%	R%	F1
Baseline	70	-	-	-
all	90	-	-	-
fem	-	84.3	80.8	83
male	-	92.2	93.8	93

Table 2: Precision and recall for propagated gender.

6 Supervised learning of gender

In this section we start by describing our first gender prediction experiment and several extensions to it and then turn to the results.

6.1 Experiments

Similar to previous studies on demographics prediction, we start with a supervised approach and only look at the text (comments) written by the user. We do not rely on any information from the social environment of the user and do not use any features extracted from the user profile, like name, which would make the gender prediction task considerably easier (Burger et al., 2011). Finally, we do not extract any features from the videos the user has commented on because our goal here is to explore the language as a sole source of information. Here we simply want to investigate the extent to which the language of the user is indicative of her gender which is found in the profile and which, ignoring the noise, corresponds to the inborn gender.

In our experiments we use a distributed implementation of the maximum entropy learner (Berger et al., 1996; McDonald et al., 2010) which outputs a distribution over the classes, the final prediction is the class with the greater probability. We take 80% of the users for training and generate a training instance for every user who made her gender visible on the profile page (4.9M). The remaining 20% of the data are used for testing (1.2M). We use the following three groups of features: (1) *character-based:* average comment length, ratio of capital letters to the total number of letters, ratio of punctuation to the total number of characters; (2) *token-based:* average comment length in words, ratio of unique words to the total tokens, lowercase unigrams with total count over all the comments (10K most frequent unigrams were used, the frequencies were computed on a separate comment set), use of pronouns, determiners, function words; (3) *sentence-based:* average comment length in sentences, average sentence length in words.

Enhancing the training set. The first question we consider is how the affiliation graph and propagated gender can be used to enhance our data for the supervised experiments. One possibility would be to train a classifier on a refined set of users by eliminating all those whose reported gender did not match the gender predicted by the neighborhood. This would presumably reduce the amount of noise by discarding the users who intentionally provided false information on their profiles. Another possibility would be to extend the training set with the users who did not make their gender visible to the public but whose gender we can predict from their vicinity. The idea here is similar to co-training where one has two independent views on the data. In this case a social graph view would be combined with the language-based view.

Profile vs. vicinity gender prediction. The next question posed in the motivation section is as follows: Does the fact that language is a social phenomenon and that it is being shaped by the social environment of the speaker impact our gender classifier? If there are truly gender-specific language traits and they are reflected in our features, then we should not observe any significant difference between the prediction results on the users whose gender matches the gender propagated from the vicinity and those whose gender does not match. A contrary hypothesis would be that what the classifier actually learns to predict is not as much the inborn but a social gender. In this case, the classifier trained on the propagated gender labels should be more accurate than the one trained on the labels extracted from the profiles.

To address these questions we contrast two classifiers: (1) the one described in the beginning of the section which is trained on the gender labels collected from the user profiles; (2) a classifier trained on the vicinity gender, that is the dominating gender of the environment of a speaker as obtained with the procedure described in Section 5.

Age groups and gender prediction. Finally, we look at how gender predictions change with age and train three age-specific models to predict gender for teenagers (*13-19*), people in their twenties (*20-29*) and people over thirty (*30+*), the age is also extracted from the profiles. These groups are identified in order to check whether teenagers tend to signalize their gender identity more than older people, a hypothesis investigated earlier on a sample of blog posts (Huffaker & Calvert, 2005).

6.2 Results

We report the results of the supervised experiments for all the settings described above. As an estimate of the lowest bound we also give the results of the majority class baseline (*all male*) which guarantees 70% accuracy. For the supervised classifiers we report accuracy and per-gender precision, recall and f-measure. Table 3 presents the results for the starting classifier trained to predict profile gender.

	Acc%	P%	R%	F1	Total
Baseline	70	-	-	-	619K
all	89	-	-	-	619K
fem	-	83	78	80	182K
male	-	91	94	93	437K

Table 3: Results on the test set.

In order to investigate the relationship between the social environment of a person, her gender and the language, we split the users from the test set into two groups: those whose profile gender matched the gender propagated from the vicinity and those for whom there was a mismatch. Thus Table 4 presents the same results as Table 3 but separated for these two groups of users. It also gives user counts w.r.t. the profile gender.

	Acc%	P%	R%	F1	Total
all (same)	94	-	-	-	557K
fem (same)	-	89	87	88	147K
male (same)	-	95	96	96	410K
all (diff)	47	-	-	-	62K
fem (diff)	-	54	39	45	35K
male (diff)	-	42	56	48	27K

Table 4: Results for users whose profile gender matches/differs from the vicinity gender.

Enhanced training set. In the next experiment we refined the training set by removing all the users whose vicinity gender did not match the gender reported in the profile. The evaluation was done on the unmodified set (Table 5). The predictions made by the model trained on a refined set of users turned out to be slightly less accurate than those made by the model trained on the full training set (Table 3). The refined model performed slightly ($<$ 1%) better than the starting one on the users whose vicinity and the profile genders matched but got very poor results on the users with a gender mismatch, the accuracy being as low as 37%. The accuracy of the starting model on those users is 47% (Table 4).

	Acc%	P%	R%	F1
all	88	-	-	-
fem	-	83	76	79
male	-	90	94	92

Table 5: Results of the models trained on the refined training set.

In another experiment we extended the training data with the users whose gender was unknown but was predicted with the propagation method. However, a larger training set makes a difference only if there is a substantial performance gain over the increasing size of the training set. We observed only a minor gain in performance ($<$ 1%) when the training data size was increased by an order of magnitude. Given that, it is not surprising that adding 12% did not affect the results.

Language, the vicinity and the profile genders. The gap in accuracies of predictions for the two user groups in Table 4 is remarkable: 47% vs. 94%. If we extrapolate what we observe in the affiliation graph to other online and offline life, then this result may suggest that gender traits are more prominent in the language of people spending more time with the people of their gender than in that of the people who spend more time with the people of the opposite gender. Given the remarkable difference, a further question arises whether the classifier actually learns to predict a kind of socially rather than the profile gender. To investigate this, we looked at the results of the model which knew nothing about the profile gender but was trained to predict the vicinity gender instead (Table 6). This model relied on the exact same set of features but both for training and testing it used the gender labels obtained from the propagation procedure described in Section 5.

	Acc%	P%	R%	F1
all	91	-	-	-
fem	-	86	80	83
male	-	92	95	94

Table 6: Results of the models trained and tested on the propagated gender.

According to all the evaluation metrics, for both genders the performance of the classifier trained and tested on the propagated gender is higher (cf. Table 3): the differences in f-measure for female and male are four and two points respectively, both statistically significant. This indicates that it is the predominant *environment* gender that a language-based classifier is better at learning rather than the inborn gender.

Predictions across age groups. Finally, to address the question of whether gender differences are more prominent and thus easer to identify in the language of younger people, we looked at the accuracy of gender predictions across three age groups. Table 7 summarizes the results and gives the accuracy of the all male baseline as well as of the propagation procedure (*Prop-acc*). Although the overall accuracy over the three groups does not degrade much, from 89% to 87%, both precision and recall do decrease significantly for females. This is not directly reflected in the accuracy because the number of females drops dramatically from 42% among teenagers to 26% and then 21% in the latter groups. For a comparison, the accuracy of the propagated gender (*Prop-acc*) also decreases from younger to older age groups although it is slightly higher than that of language-based predictions. One conclusion we can make at this point is that a teenager's gender is easier to predict from the language which is in line with the hypothesis that younger people signalize their gender identities more than older people. Another observation is that, as the person gets older, we can be less sure about her gender by looking at her social environment. This in turn might be an explanation of why there are less gender signals in the language of a person: the environment becomes more mixed, and the influence of both genders becomes more balanced.

	13-19	20-29	30+	Overall
Base-acc%	58	74	79	70
Prop-acc%	91	90	88	90
Accuracy%	89	89	87	89
Fem-P%	87	81	74	83
Fem-R%	87	76	62	78
Fem-F1	87	78	68	80
Male-P%	90	92	90	91
Male-R%	90	94	94	94
Male-F1	90	93	92	93

Table 7: Results across the age groups.

7 Conclusions

In our study we addressed the gender prediction task from two perspectives: (1) the social one where we looked at an affiliation graph of users and videos and propagated gender information between users, and (2) the language one where we trained a classifier on features which have been claimed to be indicative of gender. We demonstrated that both perspectives provide us with comparably accurate predictions (around 90%) but that they are far from being independent. We also investigated a few ways of how the performance of a language-based classifier can be enhanced by the social aspect, compared the accuracy of predictions across different age groups and found support for hypotheses made in earlier sociolinguistic studies.

We are not the first to predict gender from language features with online data. However, to our knowledge, we are the first to contrast the two views, social and language-based, using online data and to question whether there is a clear understanding of what gender classifiers actually learn to predict from language. Our results indicate that from the standard language cues we are better at predicting a social gender, that is the gender defined by the environment of a person, rather than the inborn gender.

The theoretical significance of this result is that it provides support for the usage-based view on language (Bybee, 2010), namely that the person's language is largely shaped by the interactions with her social environment. On the practical side, it may have implications for targeted advertisement as it enriches the understanding of what gender classifiers predict.

Acknowledgements: I am thankful to Enrique Alfonseca, Keith Hall and the EMNLP reviewers for their feedback.

References

Argamon, S., M. Koppel, J. Fine & A. R. Shimoni (2003). Gender, genre, and writing style in formal written texts. *Text*, 23(3).

Baluja, S., R. Seth, D. Sivakumar, Y. Jing, J. Yagnik, S. Kumar, D. Ravichandran & M. Aly (2008). Video suggestion and discovery for YouTube: Taking random walks through the view graph. In *Proc. of WWW-08*, pp. 895–904.

Baxter, G. J., R. A. Blythe, W. Croft & A. J. McKane (2006). Utterance selection model of language change. *Physical Review*, E73.046118.

Berger, A., S. A. Della Pietra & V. J. Della Pietra (1996). A maximum entropy approach to natural language processing. *Computational Linguistics*, 22(1):39–71.

Burger, J. D., J. Henderson, G. Kim & G. Zarrella (2011). Discriminating gender on Twitter. In *Proc. of EMNLP-11*, pp. 1301–1309.

Burger, J. D. & J. C. Henderson (2006). An exploration of observable features related to blogger age. In *Proceedings of the AAAI Spring Symposium on Computational Approaches for Analyzing Weblogs,* Stanford, CA, 27-29 March 2006, pp. 15–20.

Bybee, J. (2010). *Language, Usage and Cognition.* Cambridge University Press.

Chambers, J. & P. Trudgill (1998). *Dialectology.* Cambridge University Press.

Coulmas, F. (Ed.) (1998). *The Handbook of Sociolinguistics.* Blackwell.

Croft, W. (2000). *Explaining Language Change: An Evolutionary Approach.* London: Longman.

Easley, D. & J. Kleinberg (2010). *Network, crowds, and markets: Reasoning about a highly connected world.* Cambridge University Press.

Eckert, P. & S. McConnell-Ginet (2003). *Language and Gender.* Cambridge University Press.

Eisenstein, J., N. A. Smith & E. P. Xing (2011). Discovering sociolinguistic associations with structured sparsity. In *Proc. of ACL-11*, pp. 1365–1374.

Ellist, D. (2009). Social (distributed) language modeling, clustering and dialectometry. In *Proc. of TextGraphs at ACL-IJCNLP-09*, pp. 1–4.

Garera, N. & D. Yarowsky (2009). Modeling latent biographic attributes in conversational genres. In *Proc. of ACL-IJCNLP-09*, pp. 710–718.

Gillick, D. (2010). Can conversational word usage be used to predict speaker demographics? In *Proceedings of Interspeech,* Makuhari, Japan, 26-30 September 2010.

Herring, S. C. & J. C. Paolillo (2006). Gender and genre variation in weblogs. *Journal of Sociolinguistics*, 10(4):439–459.

Herring, S. C., L. A. Scheidt, S. Bonus & E. Wright (2004). Bridging the gap: A genre analysis of weblogs. In *HICSS-04*.

Hudson, R. A. (1980). *Sociolinguistics.* Cambridge University Press.

Huffaker, D. A. & S. L. Calvert (2005). Gender, identity and language use in teenager blogs. *Journal of Computer-Mediated Communication*, 10(2).

Kapidzic, S. & S. C. Herring (2011). Gender, communication, and self-presentation in teen chatrooms revisited: Have patterns changed? *Journal of Computer-Mediated Communication*, 17(1):39–59.

Koppel, M., S. Argamon & A. R. Shimoni (2004). Automatically categorizing written text by author gender. *Literary and Linguistic Computing*, 17(4):401–412.

Labov, W. (1994). *Principles of Linguistic Change: Internal Factors.* Blackwell.

Lakoff, R. (1973). Language and woman's place. *Language in Society*, 2(1):45–80.

MacKinnon, I. & R. Warren (2006). Age and geographic inferences of the LiveJournal social network. In *Statistical Network Analysis: Models, Issues, and New Directions Workshop at ICML-2006,* Pittsburgh, PA, 29 June, 2006.

McDonald, R., K. Hall & G. Mann (2010). Distributed training strategies for the structured perceptron. In *Proc. of NAACL-HLT-10*, pp. 456–464.

Milroy, L. & J. Milroy (1992). Social network and social class: Toward an integrated sociolinguistic model. *Language in Society*, 21:1–26.

Mulac, A., D. R. Seibold & J. R. Farris (2000). Female and male managers' and professionals' criticism giving: Differences in language use and effects. *Journal of Language and Social Psychology*, 19(4):389–415.

Newman, M. L., C. J. Groom, L. D. Handelman & J. W. Pennebaker (2008). Gender differences in language use: An analysis of 14,000 text samples. *Discourse Processes*, 45:211–236.

Nowson, S. & J. Oberlander (2006). The identity of bloggers: Openness and gender in personal weblogs. In *Proceedings of the AAAI Spring Symposium on Computational Approaches for Analyzing Weblogs,* Stanford, CA, 27-29 March 2006, pp. 163–167.

Otterbacher, J. (2010). Inferring gender of movie reviewers: Exploiting writing style, content and metadata. In *Proc. of CIKM-10*.

Popescu, A. & G. Grefenstette (2010). Mining user home location and gender from Flickr tags. In *Proc. of ICWSM-10*, pp. 1873–1876.

Rao, D. & D. Yarowsky (2010). Detecting latent user properties in social media. In *Proc. of the NIPS MLSN Workshop*.

Rao, D. & D. Yarowsky (2011). Typed graph models for semi-supervised learning of name ethnicity. In *Proc. of ACL-11*, pp. 514–518.

Rosenthal, S. & K. McKeown (2011). Age prediction in blogs: A study of style, content, and online behavior in pre- and post-social media generations. In *Proc. of ACL-11*, pp. 763–772.

Schler, J., M. Koppel, S. Argamon & J. Pennebaker (2006). Effects of age and gender on blogging. In *Proceedings of the AAAI Spring Symposium on Computational Approaches for Analyzing Weblogs,* Stanford, CA, 27-29 March 2006, pp. 199–205.

Yan, X. & L. Yan (2006). Gender classification of weblogs authors. In *Proceedings of the AAAI Spring Symposium on Computational Approaches for Analyzing Weblogs,* Stanford, CA, 27-29 March 2006, pp. 228–230.

Revisiting the Predictability of Language: Response Completion in Social Media

Bo Pang **Sujith Ravi**
Yahoo! Research
4401 Great America Parkway
Santa Clara, CA 95054, USA
bopang42@gmail.com sujith_ravi@yahoo.com

Abstract

The question "how predictable is English?" has long fascinated researchers. While prior work has focused on formal English typically used in news articles, we turn to texts generated by users in online settings that are more informal in nature. We are motivated by a novel application scenario: given the difficulty of typing on mobile devices, can we help reduce typing effort with message completion, especially in conversational settings? We propose a method for automatic response completion. Our approach models both the language used in responses and the specific context provided by the original message. Our experimental results on a large-scale dataset show that both components help reduce typing effort. We also perform an information-theoretic study in this setting and examine the entropy of user-generated content, especially in conversational scenarios, to better understand predictability of user generated English.

1 Introduction

How predictable is language? As early as 1951, long before large quantities of texts (or the means to process them) were easily available, Shannon had raised this question and proceeded to answer it with a set of clever analytical estimations. He studied the predictability of printed English, or "how well can the next letter of a text be predicted when the preceding N letters are known" (Shannon, 1951). This was quantified as the conditional entropy, which measures the amount of information conveyed from statistics over the preceding *context*. In this paper, we discuss a novel application setting which mirrors the predictability study as defined by Shannon.

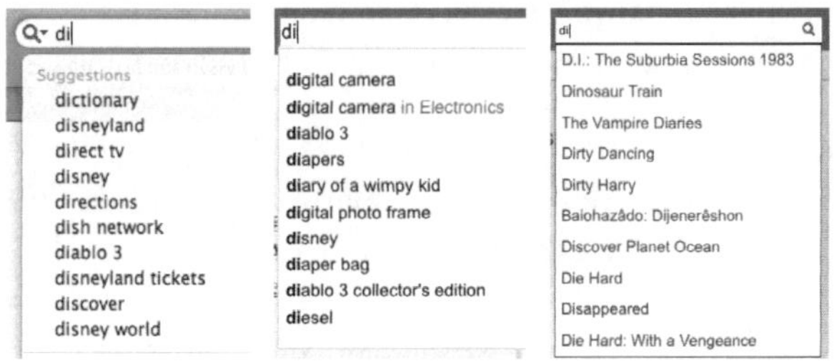

(a) Google (b) Amazon (c) Netflix

Figure 1: Query completion as users type into the "Search using Google" box on a browser, as well as the search box in Amazon and Netflix.

Text completion for user-generated texts: Consider a user who is chatting with her contact or posting to a social media site using a mobile device. If we can predict the next word given the preceding words that were already typed in, we can help reduce the typing cost by offering users suggestions of possible completions of their partially typed messages (e.g., in a drop-down list). If the intended word is ranked reasonably high, the user can select the word instead of typing it. Assuming a lower cost associated with selections, this could lead to less typing effort for the user.

An interface like this would be quite familiar to Web users today. Providing suggestions of possible completions to partially typed queries, which we will refer to as *query completion*,[1] is a common feature of search boxes (Figure 1). In spite of the similarity in the interface, the underlying technical challenge can be quite different. Query completion does not necessarily rely on language models: can-

[1]Note that this feature is often tagged as "query suggestion" in the user interface; we avoid that terminology since it is often used to refer to query re-formulation (of a completely entered query) in the literature, which is a very different task.

didate completions can be limited to popular queries that were previously submitted to the site or entries in a closed database of available objects, and ranking can be done by overall popularity. In contrast, our scenario requires generation of unseen texts.

Given the difficulty of generating full-length text, we consider a more realistic setting, where we perform completion on a word-by-word basis. Each time, we propose candidate completions at the word-level when the user is about to start a new word, or has partially entered the first few letters; once this word is successfully completed, we move on to the next one. This predict-verify-predict process exactly mirrors the human experiment described by Shannon (1951), except we do this at the word-level rather than the letter-level: having the user examine and verify predictions at the letter level would not be a practical solution for the intended application.

The response completion task: In addition, our task has another interesting difference from Shannon's human experiment. Consider the mobile-device user mentioned previously. If the user is *replying* to a piece of text (e.g., an instant message sent by a contact), we have an additional source of contextual information in the *stimulus*, or the text which triggered the *response* that the user is trying to type. Can we learn from previously observed stimulus-response pairs (which we will refer to as *exchanges*)? That is, can we take advantage of this conversational setting and effectively use the information provided by stimulus to better predict the next word in the response? We refer to this task as the *response completion* task.

Our task is different from "chatter-bots" (Weizenbaum, 1966), where the goal is to generate a response to an input that would resemble a human conversation partner. Instead, we want to complete a response as the replier intends to. Recently, Ritter et. al (2011) experimented with automatic response generation in social media. They had a similar conversational setting, but instead of completion based on partial input, they attempted to generate a response in its entirety given only the stimulus. While many of the generated responses are deemed possible replies to the stimulus, they have a low chance of actually matching the real response given by the user: they reported BLEU scores between 0 and 2 for various systems. This clearly shows the difficulty of the task. While we are addressing a more modest setting, would the problem prove to be too difficult even in this case?

In this paper, we propose a method for automatic response completion. Our approach models the generic language used in responses, as well as the contextual information provided by the stimulus. We construct a large-scale dataset of user-generated textual exchanges, and our experimental results show that both components help reduce typing effort. In addition, to better understand predictability of user generated English, we perform an information-theoretic study in this conversational setting to investigate the entropy of user-generated content.

2 Related work

There has been previous work in the area of human-computer interaction that examined text entry for mobile devices (MacKenzie and Soukoreff, 2002). In particular, one line of work looked into *predictive text input*, which examined input effort reduction by language prediction. Previous work in predictive text input had very different focus from our study. Oftentimes, the focus was to model actual typing efforts using mobile device keypads, examine the speed and cognitive load of different input methods, and evaluate with emprical user studies in lab settings (James and Reischel, 2001; How and Kan, 2005), where the underlying technique for language prediction can be as simple as unigram frequency (James and Reischel, 2001), or restricted to narrow domains such as grocery shopping lists (Nurmi et al., 2009). In addition, to the best of our knowledge, no previous work in predictive text input addressed the conversationl setting.

As discussed in Section 1, the response generation task (Ritter et al., 2011) also considered the converstational setting, but the MT-based technique was not well-suited to produce responses as intended by the user. There has been extensive previous research in language modeling (Rosenfeld, 2000). While previous work has explored Web text sources that are "better matched to a conversational speaking style" (Bulyko et al., 2003), we are not aware of much previous work that has taken advantage of information in the stimulus for word predictions in responses.

Previous work on entropy of language stems from the field of information theory (Shannon, 1948), starting with Shannon (1951). An extensive bibliography covering early related work (e.g., insights into the structure of language via information theory, entropy estimates via other techniques and/or for different languages, as well as a broad range of applications of such estimates) can be found in (Cover and King, 1978). More recently, Brown et. al (1992) computed an upper bound for the entropy of English with a trigram model, using the Brown corpus. Some other related works on this topic include (Teahan and Cleary, 1996; Moradi et al., 1998). There was also a recent study using entropy in the context of Web search (Mei and Church, 2008). In other settings, entropy has also been employed as a tool for studying the linguistic properties of ancient scripts (e.g., Indus Script) (Rao et al., 2009). While this seems like an interesting application of information theory for linguistic studies, it has also generated some controversies (Farmer et al., 2004).

In contrast, our work departs from traditional scenarios significantly. We perform entropy studies over texts generated in online settings which are more informal in nature. Additionally, we utilize the properties of language predictability within a novel application for automatically completing responses in conversational settings. Also, in our case we do not have to worry about issues like *"is this a language or not?"* because we work with real English news data which include articles written by professional editors and comments generated by users reading those articles.

3 Model

In this section, we first state our problem more formally, followed by descriptions of the basic N-gram language model we use, as well as two approaches that model both stimulus and preceding words in response as the context for the next-word generation. Given the intended application, we hope to achieve better prediction without incurring significant increase in model size.

3.1 Problem definition

Consider a stimulus-response pair, where the stimulus is a sequence of tokens $\mathbf{s} = (s_1, s_2, ..., s_m)$, and the response is a sequence of tokens $\mathbf{r} = (r_1, r_2, ..., r_n)$. Let $\mathbf{r_{1..i}} = (r_1, r_2, ..., r_i)$, our task is to generate and rank candidates for r_{i+1} given s and $\mathbf{r_{1..i}}$.

Note the models described in this section do not assume any knowledge of partial input for r_{i+1}. For the setting where the first c characters of r_{i+1} were also entered, we can restrict the candidate list to the subset with the matching prefix, and use the same ranking function.

3.2 Generic Response Language Model

First, we consider an N-gram language model trained on all responses in the training data as our generic response language model. Here we consider $N = 3$. Normally, trigram models use back-off to both bigrams and unigrams; in order to compare the effectiveness of trigram models vs. bigram models under comparable model size, we use back-off only to unigrams in both cases:

trigram: $$P(r_{i+1} \mid \mathbf{r_{1..i}}) = \lambda_1 * P_3(r_{i+1} \mid r_i, r_{i-1}) + (1 - \lambda_1) * P_1(r_{i+1})$$

bigram: $$P(r_{i+1} \mid \mathbf{r_{1..i}}) = \lambda_1 * P_2(r_{i+1} \mid r_i) + (1 - \lambda_1) * P_1(r_{i+1})$$

If we ignore the context provided by texts in the stimulus, we can simply generate and rank candidate words from the dictionary according to the generic response LM: $P(r_{i+1} \mid \mathbf{r_{1..i}})$.

As we will discuss in more detail in Section 6.2, modeling s and $\mathbf{r_{1..i}}$ jointly in the prediction of r_{i+1} would be rather expensive. In the following sections, we follow two main approaches to break this down into separate components: $P(r_{i+1} \mid \mathbf{r_{1..i}})$ and $P(r_{i+1} \mid \mathbf{s})$, and model each one separately.

3.3 Translating Stimuli to Responses

As mentioned in Section 1, Ritter et. al (2011) have considered a related task of generating a response in its entirety given only the text in the stimulus. They cast the problem as a translation task, where the stimulus is considered as the source language and the response is considered as the target language. We can adapt this approach for our response completion task.

Consider the noisy channel model used in statistical machine translation: $P(\mathbf{r}|\mathbf{s}) \propto P(\mathbf{r}) * P(\mathbf{s}|\mathbf{r})$. In order to predict r_{i+1} given $\mathbf{r_{1..i}}$ and $\mathbf{s}$, for each candidate r_{i+1}, in principle one can marginalize over all possible completions of $\mathbf{r_{1..i+1}}$, and rank candidate r_{i+1} by that. That is, let P(n) be the distribution of response length, let $\mathbf{r}'$ be a possible completion of $\mathbf{r_{1..i+1}}$ (i.e., a response whose first $i+1$ tokens match $\mathbf{r_{1..i+1}}$). For each possible $n > i$, we need to marginalize over all possible $\mathbf{r}'$ of length n, and rank r_{i+1} according to

$$P(\mathbf{r_{1..i+1}} \mid \mathbf{s}) = \sum_{n>i} P(n) \cdot \sum_{|\mathbf{r}'|=n} P(\mathbf{r}' \mid \mathbf{s})$$

Clearly this will be computationally expensive. Instead, we take a greedy approach, and choose r_{i+1} which yields the optimal partial response (without looking ahead):

$$P(\mathbf{r_{1..i+1}} \mid \mathbf{s}) \propto P(\mathbf{r_{1..i+1}}) * P(\mathbf{s} \mid \mathbf{r_{1..i+1}})$$

which is equivalent to ranking candidate r_{i+1} by

$$P(r_{i+1} \mid \mathbf{r_{1..i}}) * P(\mathbf{s} \mid \mathbf{r_{1..i+1}}) \qquad (1)$$

Since the first component is our LM model, and the second component is a translation model, we denote this as the *LM+TM model*. We use IBM Model-1 to learn the translation table on the training data. At test time, equal number of candidates are generated by each component, and combined to be ranked by Eq. 1.

3.4 Mixture Model

One potential concern over applying the translation model is that the response can often contain novel information not implied by the stimulus. While technically this could be generated from the so-called *null* token used in machine translation (added to the source text to account for target text with no clear alignment in the source text), significant amount of text corresponding to new information not in the source text is not what null tokens are meant to be capturing. In general, our problem here is a lack of clear word-to-word or phrase-to-phrase mapping in a stimulus-response pair, at least not what one would expect in clean parallel data.

Alternatively, one can model the response generation process with a mixture model: with probability λ_s, we generate a word according to a distribution over $\mathbf{s}$ ($P(w \mid \mathbf{s})$), and with probability $1 - \lambda_s$, we generate a word using the response language model:

$$\begin{aligned} P(r_{i+1} \mid \mathbf{s}, \mathbf{r_{1..i}}) &= \lambda_s \cdot P(r_{i+1} \mid \mathbf{s}) \\ &+ (1 - \lambda_s) \cdot P(r_{i+1} \mid \mathbf{r_{1..i}}) \end{aligned} \qquad (2)$$

We examine two concrete ways of exploiting the context provided by $\mathbf{s}$.

Model 1 — LM + Selection model First, we examine a very simple instantiation of $P(w \mid \mathbf{s})$ where we select a token in $\mathbf{s}$ uniformly at random. This is based on the intuition that to be semantically coherent, a reply often needs to repeat certain content words in the stimulus. (Similar intuition has been explored in the context of text coherency (Barzilay and Lapata, 2005).) This is particularly useful for words that are less frequently used: they may not be able to receive enough statistics to be promoted otherwise. More specifically,

$$P(r_{i+1} \mid \mathbf{s}) = \frac{\mathbf{1}_{r_{i+1} \in \mathbf{s}}}{|\mathbf{s}|}$$

We can take λ_s to be a constant λ_{select}, which can be estimated in the training data as the probability of a response token being a repetition of a token in the corresponding stimulus.

Model 2 — LM + Topic model Another way to incorporate information provided in $\mathbf{s}$ is to use it to constrict the topic in $\mathbf{r}$. We can learn a topic model over conversations in the training data using Latent Dirchlet Allocation (LDA) (Blei et al., 2003). At test time, we identify the most likely topic of the conversation based on $\mathbf{s}$, and expect r_{i+1} to be generated from this topic. That is,

$$P(r_{i+1} \mid \mathbf{s}) = P(r_{i+1} \mid t^*)$$

$$\text{where } t^* = \text{argmax}_t P(\text{topic} = t \mid \mathbf{s})$$

More specifically, we first train a topic model on ($\mathbf{s}$, $\mathbf{r}$) pairs from the training data. Given a new stimulus $\mathbf{s}$, we then select the highest ranked topic as being representative of $\mathbf{s}$. Note that alternatively we could consider all possible topic assignments; in that case we would have had to sum probabilities over all topics, and that could also introduce noise. A similar strategy has been previously employed for other topic modeling applications in information retrieval, where documents are smoothed with their highest ranked topic (Yi and Allan, 2009). We lower the weight λ_s if $P(t^* \mid \mathbf{s})$ is low. That is, we use $\lambda_s = \lambda_{topic} * P(t^* \mid \mathbf{s})$ in Eq. 2.

4 Data

In order to investigate text completion in a conversational setting, we need to construct a large-scale dataset with textual exchanges among users. An ideal dataset would have been a collection of instant messages, but these type of datasets are difficult to obtain given privacy concerns. To the best of our knowledge, existing SMS (short message service) datasets only contain isolated text spans and do not provide enough information to reconstruct the conversations. There are, however, a high volume of textual exchanges taking places in public forums. Many sites with a user comment environment allow other users to reply to existing comments, where the original comment and its reply can form a (stimulus, response) pair for our purposes.

To this end, we extracted (comment, reply) pairs from Yahoo! News[2], where under each news article, a user can post a new comment or reply to an existing comment. In fact, a popular comment can have a long thread of replies where multi-party discussions take place. To ensure the reply is a direct response to the original comment, we took only the first reply to a comment, and consider the resulting pair as a textual exchange in the form of a (stimulus, response) pair. We gathered data from a period of 14 weeks between March and May, 2011. A random sample yielded a total of 1,487,995 exchanges, representing 237,040 unique users posting responses to stimuli comments authored by 357,811 users. In the raw dataset (i.e., before tokenization), stimuli average at 59 tokens (332 characters), and responses average at 26 tokens (144 characters).

We took the first 12 weeks of data as training data (1,269,732 exchanges) and the rest 2 weeks of data as test data (218,263 exchanges).

[2]Note that previous work has used a dataset with 1 million Twitter conversations extracted from a scraping of the site (Ritter et al., 2011), where a status update and its replies in Twitter form "conversations". This dataset is no longer publicly available. At the time of this writing, we were not able to identify a data source to re-construct a dataset like that.

5 Experiments

5.1 Evaluation measures

Recall@k : Here, we follow a standard evaluation strategy used to assess ranking quality in information retrieval applications. For each word, we check if the correct answer is one of the top-k tokens being suggested. We then compute the recall at different values of k. While this is a straight-forward measure to assess the overall quality of different top-k lists, it is not tailored to suit our specific task of response completion. In particular, this measure (a) does not distinguish between (typing) savings for a short word versus a long one, and (b) does not distinguish between the correct answer being higher up in the list versus lower as long as the word is present in the top-k list.

TypRed : Our main evaluation measure is based on "reduction in typing effort for a user of the system", which is a more informative measure for our task. We estimate the typing reduction via a hypothetical typing model[3] in the following manner:

Suppose we show top k predictions for a given setting. Now, there are two possible scenarios:

1. if the user does not find the correct answer in the top-k list, he/she gives up on this word and will have to type the entire word. The typing cost is then estimated to be the number of characters in the word l_w;
2. if the user spots the correct answer in the list, the cost for choosing the word is proportional to the rank of the word $rank_w$, with a fixed cost ratio c_0. Suppose the user scrolls down the list using the down-arrow (↓) to reach the intended word (instead of typing), then $rank_w \cdot c_0$ reflects the scrolling effort required, where c_0 is the relative cost of scrolling down versus typing a character.

In general, pressing a fixed key can have a lower cost than typing a new one, in addition, we can imagine a virtual keyboard where navigational keys occupy bigger real-estate, and thus incur less cost to press. As a result, it's reasonable to assume c_0 value that is smaller than 1. In all our experiments, $c_0 = 0.5$ unless otherwise noted. Note that if the

[3]More accurate measures can be be developed by observing user behavior in a lab setting. We leave this as future work.

System	TypRed ($c = 0$)	TypRed ($c = 1$)	TypRed ($c = 2$)
1. Generic Response LM (trigram)	15.10	22.57	14.29
2. Generic Response LM (trigram) + TM	9.03	17.53	11.56
3. Mixture Model 1: Generic Response LM (trigram) + Selection	**15.18***	**23.43***	**15.13***
4. Mixture Model 2: Generic Response LM (trigram) + Topic Model	15.10	22.57	14.33

Table 1: Comparison of various prediction models (in terms of TypRed score @ rank 5) on all (stimulus,response) pairs from a large test collection (218,263 exchanges) when the first c characters of each word are typed in by the user. A higher score indicates better performance. * indicates statistical significance ($p < 0.05$) over the baseline score.

typing model assumes a user selects the intended word using an interface that is similar to a mousing device, the cost may increase with $rank_w$ at a sub-linear rate; in that case, our measure will be over-estimating the cost.

In order to have a consistent measure that always improves as the ranking improves, we assume a clever user who will choose to finish the word by typing or by selecting, depending on which cost is lower. Combining these two cases under the clever-user model, we estimate the reduction in typing cost for every word as follows:

$$TypRed(w, rank_w) = 100 \cdot [1 - \frac{min(l_w, rank_w \cdot c_0)}{l_w}]$$

where w is the correct word, l_w is the length of w, and $rank_w$ is the rank of w in the top-k list. A higher value of TypRed implies higher savings achieved in typing cost and thereby better prediction performance.

5.2 Experimental setup

We run experiments using the models described in Section 3 under two different settings: (1) *previous words* from the response are provided, and (2) *previous words from response + first c characters of the current word* are provided.

During the candidate generation phase, for every position in the response message we present the top 1,000 candidates (as scored by the generic response language model or mixture models). We reserve a small subset of ($\sim$1,000) exchanges as development data for tuning parameters from our models.

For the generic response language models, we set the interpolation weight $\lambda_1 = 0.9$. For the selection-based mixture model, we estimate the mixture weights on the training data and set λ_{select} (0.09). For the topic-based mixture model, we ran a grid search with different parameter settings for λ_{topic} on the held-out development set and chose the value (0.01) that gave the best performance (in terms of TypRed).

5.3 Results

Previous words from response observed: We first present results for the setting where only previous words from the response are provided as context. We use TypRed scores as our evaluation measure here (higher TypRed implies more savings in typing effort). Even with a unigram LM we achieve a small but non-negligible reduction (TypRed=2.15) in the typing cost. But a bigram LM significantly improves performance (TypRed=11.91), and with trigram LM we observe even better performance (TypRed=15.10). Since the trigram LM yields a high performance, we set this as our default LM for all other models.

Recall that in all experiments, we set c_0, the cost ratio of selecting a candidate from the ranked top-k list (via scrolling) versus typing a character to a value of 0.5. But we also experimented with a hypothetical setting where $c_0 = 1$ and noticed that the trigram LM achieves a slightly lower but still significant typing reduction (TypRed score of 9.58 versus 15.10 for the earlier case).

The first column of Table 1 ($c = 0$) compares the performance of other models for this setting. We find that adding a translation model (LM+TM) does not help for this task; in fact, it results in lower scores than using the LM alone. This suggests that a translation-based generative approach may not be suitable, if the goal is to predict text as intended by the user. This is consistent with previous observations on a related task (Ritter et al., 2011), as we discussed in Section 1.

In contrast, the mixture models do much better. In fact, LM+Selection model produces better results than trigram LM alone. We also note that estimating the mixture parameter on the training data rather than using a fixed value increases TypRed scores: 14.02 with a fixed λ_{select} = 0.5 versus 15.18 with $\lambda^*_{select} = 0.09$. This comparison also holds for $c > 0$ — that is, a naive version of LM+Selection that selects a word from the stimulus whenever the prefix allows would not have worked well.

In principle the LM+Topic model is potentially more powerful in that $P(w \mid \mathrm{s})$ is not limited to the words in s. However, in our experiments it does not yield any considerable improvement over the original LM. We postulate that this could be due to the following reason: once the context provided by s is reduced to the topic level, it is not specific enough to provide additional information over proceding words in the response.

Previous words from response + first c characters of current word observed: Table 1 also compares the TypRed performance of all the models under settings where $c > 0$. We notice striking improvements in performance for $c = 1$ which is consistent across all models. Our best model is able to save the user approximately 23% in terms of typing effort (according to TypRed scores). Interestingly a lot less reduction was observed for $c = 2$: the second character, on average, does not improve the ranking enough to justify the cost of typing this extra character.

Next, we pick our best model (Mixture Model 1) and perform some further analysis. We examine the effect of providing longer list (shown in Table 2) and notice little further improvement beyond $k = 10$. We also note that the TypRed improvement achieved over the baseline (LM) model at rank 10 is more than twice the gain achieved at rank 5.

We also evaluated its performance using a standard measure (Recall@k). Figure 2 plots the recall achieved by the system at different ranks k. An increasing recall at even high ranks ($k = 100$) suggests that the quality of the candidate list retrieved by this model is good. This also suggests that there is still room for improvements, and we leave that as interesting future work.

Rank (k)	TypRed score
1	9.02
5	15.18
10	16.14
15	16.28
20	16.29
25	16.29

Table 2: Comparison of typing reductions achieved over the entire test data when top k list is provided to the user.

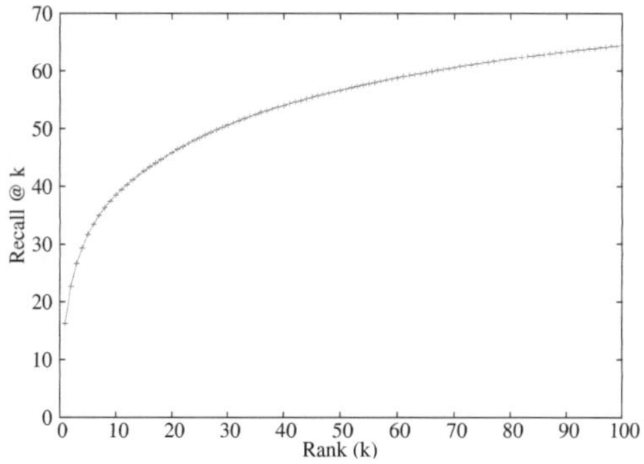

Figure 2: Recall @ rank k for Mixture Model 1 on the entire test data.

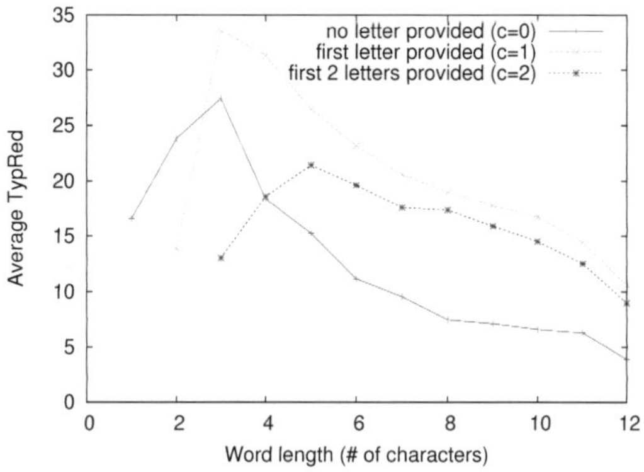

Figure 3: Average TypRed score versus Word length (# of characters) for Mixture Model 1 when the first c characters of the word is typed in by the user.

Finally, in Figure 3, we plot the average TypRed scores against individual token (word) length. Figure 3 indicates that the model is able to achieve a higher reduction for shorter words compared to very long ones. This demonstrates the utility of such a response completion system, especially since shorter words are predominant in conversational settings. We also compared the average reduction achieved on messages of different lengths (number of words). Overall we observe consistent reduction for different message lengths. This suggests our system can

Source	Top translations				
:)	:)	!	you	?	:D
lmao	lol	lmao	u	...	i
feeling	feeling	feel	better	!	you
question	.	question	the	,	to
Are	I	.	,	are	yes

Table 3: Examples of a few stimulus/response translations learned using IBM Model-1.

OBAMA, USA, Fact, Meghan, GIVE, PRESIDENT, Canadian, Mitch, Jon, Kerry, TODAY, Justice, Liberalism, ...
President, Notice, Tax, LMAO, Hmmm, Trump, people, OBAMA, common, Aren, WAIT, Bachman, mon, McCain, ...
Great, Cut, Release, Ummm, Rest, Mark, isnt, YAHOO, Sad, END, RON, jesus, Ugh, TRUMP, ...
Nice, Navy, Make, Interesting, Remember, Excuse, WAKE, Hooray, Birth, mon, Yeah, Dumb, Michael, geronimo, ...

Table 4: Examples of top representative words for a few topics generated by the LDA topic model trained on news comment data.

be useful for both Tweet-like short messages as well as more lengthy exchanges in detailed discussions.

5.4 Discussion

Table 3 displays some sample translations learned using the TM model described in Section 3.3. Interestingly, emoticons and informal expressions like `:)` or `lmao` in the stimulus tend to evoke similar type of expressions in the response (as seen in Table 3). Some translations (e.g., *feeling* $\rightarrow$ *better*) are indicative of question/answer type of exchanges in our data. But most of the other translations are noisy or uninformative (e.g., *Are* $\rightarrow$.). This provides further evidence as to why a translation-based approach is not well suited for this particular task and hence does not perform as well as other methods.

Finally, in Table 4, we provide a few sample topics generated by the LDA topic model (which is used by Mixture Model 2 described in Section 3.4). We find that while a few topics display some semantic coherence (e.g., political figures), many of them are noisy (or too generic) which further supports our earlier observation that they are not useful enough to help in the prediction task.

6 Entropy of user comments

We adapt the notion of predictability of English as examined by Shannon (1951) from letter-prediction to token-prediction, and define the predictability of English as how well can the next token be predicted when the preceding N tokens are known. How much does the immediate context in the response help reduce the uncertainty? How does user-generated content compare with more formal English in this respect? And how about the corresponding stimuli — given the preceding N tokens, does the knowledge of stimulus further reduce the uncertainty? These questions motivated a series of studies over entropy in different datasets.[4]

6.1 Comparison of N-gram entropy

Following Shannon (1951), we consider the following function F_N, which can be called the N-gram entropy, as the measure of predictability:

$$F_N = -\sum_{i,j} p(b_i, j) \log_2 p(j \mid b_i)$$

where b_i is a block of $N-1$ tokens, j is an arbitrary token following b_i, and $p(j \mid b_i)$ is the conditional probability of j given b_i. This conditional entropy reflects how much is the uncertainty of the next token reduced by knowing the preceding $N-1$ tokens.

Under this measure, is user-generated content more predictable or less predictable than the more formal "printed" English examined by Shannon? Maybe it is more predictable, since most users in informal settings use simpler English, which may contain fewer variations than the complex structures observed in more formal English. Or perhaps it is less predictable — variations among different users (who may not follow proper grammar) may lead to more uncertainty in the prediction of "the next word". Which would be the case?

To answer this question empirically, we construct a reference dataset written in more formal English (D_f) to be compared against the user comments dataset described in Section 4 (D_u). If D_f covers very different topics from D_u, then even if we do observe differences in entropy, it could be due to topical differences. A standard mixed-topic dataset like

[4]Note that our findings are not to be interpreted as prediction performance over unseen texts. For that, one needs to compute cross-entropy between training and test corpora. Since Section 5 is already addressing this question with proper training / test split, in this section, we focus on the variability of language usage in a corpus. This also avoids having to control for "comparable" training/test splits in different types of datasets.

the Brown Corpus (Kucera and Francis, 1967) may not be ideal in this sense (e.g., it contains fiction categories such as "Romance and Love Story", which may not be represented in our D_u). Instead, we obtained a sample of news articles on Yahoo! News during March - May, 2011, and extracted unique sentences from these articles. This yields a D_f with more comparable subject matters to D_u.[5]

Next, we compare both the entropy over unigrams and N-gram entropy in three datasets: the news article dataset described above, and comments data (Section 4) separated into stimuli and responses. We also report corresponding numbers computed on the Brown Corpus as references. Note that datasets with different vocabulary size can lead to different entropy: the entropy of picking a word from the vocabulary uniformly at random would have been different. Thus, we sample each dataset at different rates, and plot the (conditional) entropy in the sample against the corresponding vocabulary size.

As shown in Figure 4(a), the entropy of unigrams in D_u (both stimuli and responses) is consistently lower than in D_f.[6] On the other hand, both stimuli and responses exhibit higher uncertainty in bigram entropy (Figure 4(b)) and trigram entropy (Figure 4(c)). That is, when no contexts are provided, word choices (from similarly-sized vocabularies) in D_f is more evenly distributed than in D_u; but once the proceeding words are given, the next word is more predictable in D_f than in D_u. We postulate that the difference in unigram entropy could be due to (a) more balanced topic coverage in D_f vs. more skewed topic coverage in D_u, or (b) professional reporters mastering a more balanced use of the vocabulary. If (b) is the main reason, however, the lower trigram entropy in D_f would seem unexpected — shouldn't professional journalists also have a more balanced use of different phrases? Upon further contemplation, what we hypothesized earlier could be true: professional writers use the "proper" English expected in news coverage, which could limit

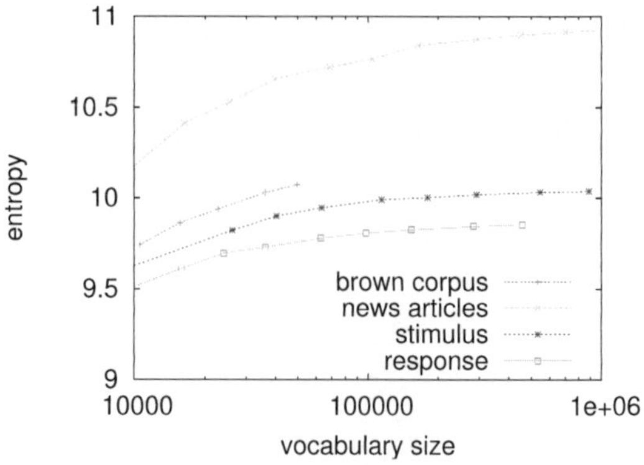

(a) Entropy of unigrams

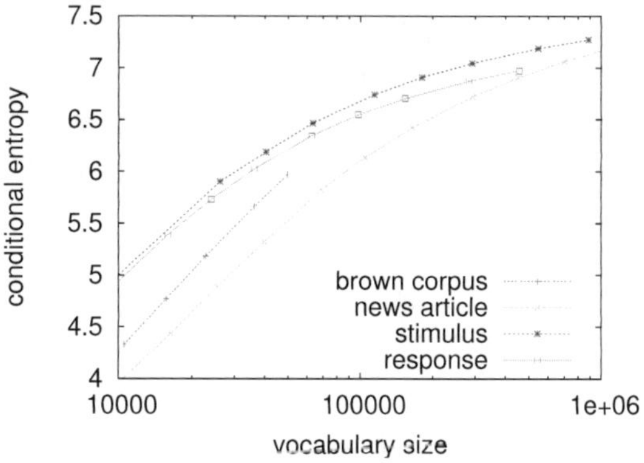

(b) Bigram entropy (F_2)

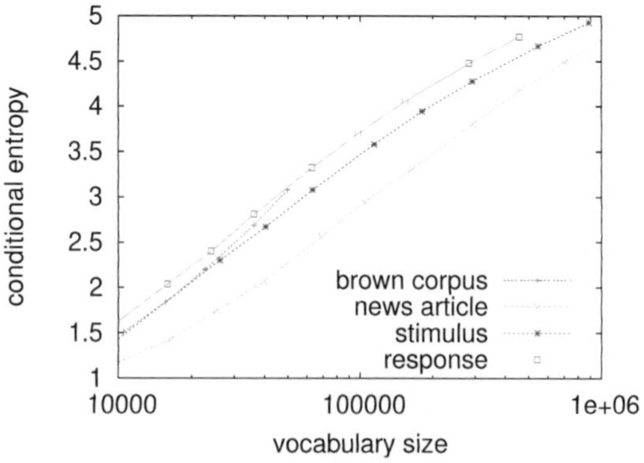

(c) Trigram entropy (F_3)

Figure 4: Entropy of unigrams and N-gram entropy.

their trigram uncertainties; on the other hand, users are not bound by conventions (or even grammars), which could lead to higher variations.

Interestingly, distributions in the stimulus dataset are closer to news articles: they have a higher unigram entropy than responses, but a lower trigram entropy at comparable vocabulary sizes. In particular, recall from Section 4 that our comments dataset contains roughly 237K repliers and 357K original com-

[5]We note that this does not guarantee the exact same topic distribution as in the comment data.

[6]For reference, Shannon (1951) estimated the entropy of English to be 11.82 bits per word, due to an incorrect calculation of a 8727-word vocabulary given Zipf distribution. The correct number should be 9.27 bits per word for a vocabulary size of 12,366 (Yavuz, 1978).

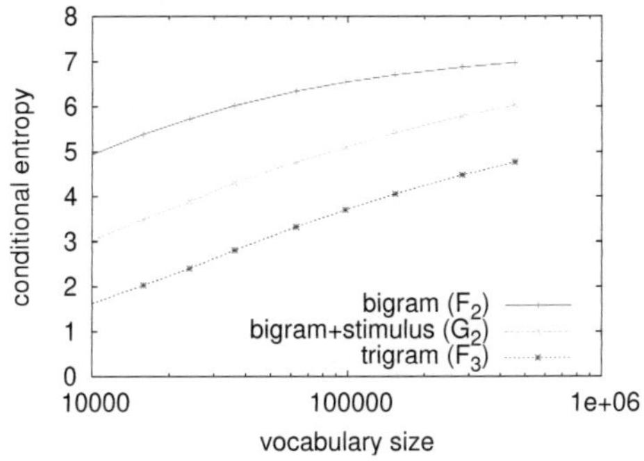

Figure 5: Predicting the next word in responses: bigram entropy vs. bigram+stimulus entropy vs. trigram entropy.

menters. If higher trigram entropy is due to variance among different users, the stimulus dataset should have had a higher trigram entropy. We leave an explanation of this interesting behavior as future work.

6.2 Information in stimuli

We now examine the next question: does knowing words in the stimulus further reduce the uncertainty of the next word in the response? For simplicity, we model the stimulus as a collection of unigrams. Consider the following conditional entropy:

$$G_N = -\sum_{i,k,j} p(b_i, j, s_k) \log_2 p(j \mid b_i, s_k)$$

where b_i is a block of $N-1$ tokens in a *response* $\mathbf{r}$, j is an arbitrary token following b_i, and s_k is an arbitrary token in the corresponding stimulus $\mathbf{s}$ for $\mathbf{r}$. Note that for each b_i, we consider every token in the corresponding $\mathbf{s}$. That is, a (stimulus, response) pair with m and n tokens respectively generates $m*(n-N+1)$ observations of (b_i, j, s_k) tuples. We refer to this as the N-gram+stimulus entropy. If knowing s_k in addition to b_i does not provide extra information, then $p(j \mid b_i, s_k) = p(j \mid b_i)$, and $G_N = F_N$.

Figure 5 plots G_N for $N = 2$. Interestingly, we observe $F_2 > G_2 > F_3$ (this trend holds for larger values of N, omitted here for clarity). That is, knowing both the preceding $N-1$ tokens and tokens in the stimulus results lowers the uncertainty over the next token in response (bigram+stimulus entropy < bigram entropy); on the other hand, this is not as effective as knowing one more token in the preceding block (trigram entropy < bigram+stimulus entropy).

Note that from the model size perspective, modeling $p(j \mid b_i, s_k)$ as in G_N would have been much more expensive than $p(j \mid b_i)$ in F_{N+1}. Take the case of G_2 vs. F_3. Let V be the vocabulary of user comments (ignore for now differences in responses and stimuli). While both seem to require computations over $V \times V \times V$, the number of unique observed (b_i, j, s_k) tuples for G_2 (i.e., number of unique bigrams in responses paired up with unigrams in corresponding stimuli) is 725,458,892, whereas the number of unique observed (b_i, j) pairs for F_3 (i.e., number of unique trigrams) is only 14,692,952. This means modeling trigrams would result in a model 2% the size of bigram+stimulus, yet it could achieve better reduction in uncertainty.

Note that in order to reduce model complexity, the models proposed in Section 3 all broke down $P(r_{i+1} \mid \mathbf{s}, \mathbf{r_{1..i}})$ into independent components $P(r_{i+1} \mid \mathbf{s})$ and $P(r_{i+1} \mid \mathbf{r_{1..i}})$, rather than modeling the effect of $\mathbf{s}$ and $\mathbf{r_{1..i}}$ jointly as the underlying model corresponding to G_N. Indeed, it would have been impractical to model $p(j \mid b_i, s_k)$ directly. Our studies confirmed the validity of this choice: even if we look at the performance on the training data itself (i.e., igoring data sparseness issues), the smaller trigram model would have yielded better results than the significantly more expensive bigram+stimulus model. Still, since G_N shows a consistent improvement over F_N, there could be more information in the stimulus that we are not yet fully utilizing, which can be interesting future work.

7 Conclusions

In this paper, we examined a novel application: automatic response completion in conversational settings. We investigated the effectiveness of several models that incorporate contextual information provided by the partially typed response as well as the stimulus. We found that the partially typed response provides strong signals. In addition, using a mixture model which also incorporates stimulus content yielded the best overall result. We also performed empirical studies to examine the predictability of user-generated content. Our analysis (entropy estimates along with upper-bound numbers observed from experiments) suggest that there can be interesting future work to explore the contextual information provided by the stimulus more effectively and further improve the response completion task.

References

Regina Barzilay and Mirella Lapata. 2005. Modeling local coherence: An entity-based approach. In *Proceedings of the 43rd Annual Meeting on Association for Computational Linguistics, ACL'05*.

David M. Blei, Andrew Y. Ng, and Michael I. Jordan. 2003. Latent dirichlet allocation. *Journal of Machine Learning Research*, 3:993–1022.

Peter F. Brown, Vincent J. Della Pietra, Robert L. Mercer, Stephen A. Della Pietra, and Jennifer C. Lai. 1992. An estimate of an upper bound for the entropy of English. *Comput. Linguist.*, 18:31–40.

Ivan Bulyko, Mari Ostendorf, and Andreas Stolcke. 2003. Getting more mileage from web text sources for conversational speech language modeling using class-dependent mixtures. In *Proceedings of the 2003 Conference of the North American Chapter of the Association for Computational Linguistics on Human Language Technology: companion volume of the Proceedings of HLT-NAACL 2003–short papers - Volume 2*, NAACL-Short '03, pages 7–9.

Thomas M. Cover and Roger C. King. 1978. A convergent gambling estimate of the entropy of English. *IEEE Transactions on Information Theory*, 24:413–421.

Steve Farmer, Richard Sproat, and Michael Witzel. 2004. The collapse of the Indus-script thesis: The myth of a literate Harappan civilization. *Electronic Journal of Vedic Studies*, 11:379–423 and 623–656.

Yijue How and Min-Yen Kan. 2005. Optimizing predictive text entry for short message service on mobile phones. In *Proceedings of the Human Computer Interfaces International (HCII)*.

Christina L. James and Kelly M. Reischel. 2001. Text input for mobile devices: comparing model prediction to actual performance. In *Proceedings of the SIGCHI conference on Human factors in computing systems*, CHI '01, pages 365–371, New York, NY, USA. ACM.

Henry Kucera and W. Nelson Francis. 1967. *Computational analysis of present-day American English*. Brown University Press.

I. Scott MacKenzie and R. William Soukoreff. 2002. Text entry for mobile computing: Models and methods,theory and practice. *Human-Computer Interaction*, 17(2-3):147–198.

Qiaozhu Mei and Kenneth Church. 2008. Entropy of search logs: how hard is search? with personalization? with backoff? In *Proceedings of the international conference on Web search and web data mining*, WSDM '08, pages 45–54.

Hamid Moradi, Jerzy W. Grzymala-busse, and James A. Roberts. 1998. Entropy of english text: experiments with humans and a machine learning system based on rough sets. *Information Sciences*, 104:31–47.

Petteri Nurmi, Andreas Forsblom, Patrik Floréen, Peter Peltonen, and Petri Saarikko. 2009. Predictive text input in a mobile shopping assistant: methods and interface design. In *Proceedings of the 14th international conference on Intelligent user interfaces*, IUI '09, pages 435–438, New York, NY, USA. ACM.

Rajesh P. N. Rao, Nisha Yadav, Mayank N. Vahia, Hrishikesh Joglekar, R. Adhikari, and Iravatham Mahadevan. 2009. Entropic evidence for linguistic structure in the Indus script. *Science*.

Alan Ritter, Colin Cherry, and William B. Dolan. 2011. Data-driven response generation in social media. In *Proceedings of the Conference on Empirical Methods in Natural Language Processing*, pages 583–593.

Ronald Rosenfeld. 2000. Two decades of statistical language modeling: Where do we go from here? *Proceedings of the IEEE*, 88.

Claude E. Shannon. 1948. A mathematical theory of communication. *Bell System Technical Journal*, 27:379–423 and 623–656.

Claude E. Shannon. 1951. Prediction and entropy of printed English. *Bell System Technical Journal*, 30:50–64.

W. J. Teahan and John G. Cleary. 1996. The entropy of English using PPM-based models. In *In Data Compression Conference*, pages 53–62. IEEE Computer Society Press.

Joseph Weizenbaum. 1966. Eliza: a computer program for the study of natural language communication between man and machine. *Commun. ACM*, 9:36–45.

D. Yavuz. 1978. Zipf's law and entropy (Corresp.). *IEEE Transactions on Information Theory*, 20:650.

Xing Yi and James Allan. 2009. A comparative study of utilizing topic models for information retrieval. In *Proceedings of the European Conference on IR Research on Advances in Information Retrieval*, pages 29–41.

Supervised Text-based Geolocation Using Language Models on an Adaptive Grid

Stephen Roller[†] **Michael Speriosu**[‡] **Sarat Rallapalli**[†]
Benjamin Wing[‡] **Jason Baldridge**[‡]
[†]Department of Computer Science, University of Texas at Austin
[‡]Department of Linguistics, University of Texas at Austin
{roller, sarat}@cs.utexas.edu, {speriosu, jbaldrid}@utexas.edu, ben@benwing.com

Abstract

The geographical properties of words have recently begun to be exploited for geolocating documents based solely on their text, often in the context of social media and online content. One common approach for geolocating texts is rooted in information retrieval. Given training documents labeled with latitude/longitude coordinates, a grid is overlaid on the Earth and *pseudo-documents* constructed by concatenating the documents within a given grid cell; then a location for a test document is chosen based on the most similar pseudo-document. Uniform grids are normally used, but they are sensitive to the dispersion of documents over the earth. We define an alternative grid construction using k-d trees that more robustly adapts to data, especially with larger training sets. We also provide a better way of choosing the locations for pseudo-documents. We evaluate these strategies on existing Wikipedia and Twitter corpora, as well as a new, larger Twitter corpus. The adaptive grid achieves competitive results with a uniform grid on small training sets and outperforms it on the large Twitter corpus. The two grid constructions can also be combined to produce consistently strong results across all training sets.

1 Introduction

The growth of the Internet in recent years has provided unparalleled access to informational resources. It is often desirable to extract summary metadata from such resources, such as the date of writing or the location of the author – yet only a small portion of available documents are explicitly annotated in this fashion. With sufficient training data, however, it is often possible to infer this information directly from a document's text. For example, clues to the geographic location of a document may come from a variety of word features, e.g. toponyms (*Toronto*), geographic features (*mountain*), culturally local features (*hockey*), and stylistic or dialectical differences (*cool* vs. *kewl* vs. *kool*).

This article focuses on text-based document geolocation, the prediction of the latitude and longitude of a document. Among the uses for this are region-based search engines; tracing the sources of historical documents; location attribution while summarizing large documents; tailoring of ads while browsing; phishing detection when a user account is accessed from an unexpected location; and "activist mapping" (Cobarrubias, 2009), as in the Ushahidi project.[1] Geolocation has also been used as a feature in automatic news story identification systems (Sankaranarayanan et al., 2009).

One of the first works on document geolocation is Ding et al. (2000), who attempt to automatically determine the geographic scope of web pages. They focus on named locations, e.g. cities and states, found in gazetteers. Locations are predicted based on toponym detection and heuristic resolution algorithms. A related, recent effort is Cheng et al. (2010), who geolocate Twitter users by resolving their profile locations against a gazetteer of U.S. cities and training a classifier to identify geographically local words.

An alternative to using a discrete set of locations from a gazetteer is to use information retrieval (IR) techniques on a set of geolocated training documents. A new test document is compared with each

[1] `http://ushahidi.com/`

training document and a location chosen based on the location(s) of the most similar training document(s). For image geolocation, Chen and Grauman (2011) perform mean-shift clustering over training images to discretize locations, then estimate a test image's location with weighted voting from the k most similar documents. For text, both Serdyukov et al. (2009) and Wing and Baldridge (2011) use a similar approach, but compute document similarity based on language models rather than image features. Additionally, they group documents via a uniform geodesic grid rather than a clustered set of locations. This reduces the number of similarity computations and removes the need to perform location clustering altogether, but introduces a new parameter controlling the granularity of the grid. Kinsella et al. (2011) predict the locations of tweets and users by comparing text in tweets to language models associated with zip codes and broader geopolitical enclosures. Sadilek et al. (2012) discretize by simply clustering data points within a small distance threshold, but only perform geolocation within fixed city limits.

While the above approaches discretize the continuous surface of the earth, Eisenstein et al. (2010) predict locations based on Gaussian distributions over the earth's surface as part of a hierarchical Bayesian model. This model has many advantages (e.g. the ability to compute a complete probability distribution over locations), but we suspect it will be difficult to scale up to the large document collections needed for high accuracy.

We build on the IR approach with grids while addressing some of the shortcomings of a uniform grid. Uniform grids are problematic in that they ignore the geographic dispersion of documents and forgo the possibility of greater-granularity geographic resolution in document-rich areas. Instead, we construct a grid using a k-d tree, which adapts to the size of the training set and the geographic dispersion of the documents it contains. This can better benefit from more data, since it enables the training set to support more pseudo-documents when there is sufficient evidence to do so, while still ensuring that all pseudo-documents contain comparable amounts of data. It also has the desirable property of generally requiring fewer active cells than a uniform grid, drastically reducing the computation time required to label a test document.

We show that consistently strong results, robust across both Wikipedia and Twitter datasets, are obtained from the union of the pseudo-documents from a uniform and adaptive grid. In addition, a simple difference in the choice of location for a given grid cell – the centroid of the training documents in the cell, rather than the cell midpoint – results in across-the-board improvements. We also construct and evaluate on a much larger dataset of geolocated tweets than has been used in previous papers, demonstrating the scalability and robustness of our methods and confirming the ability of the adaptive grid to more effectively use larger datasets.

2 Data

We work with three datasets: a corpus of geotagged Wikipedia articles and two corpora of geotagged tweets.

GEOWIKI is a collection of 1,019,490 geotagged English articles from Wikipedia. The dump from Wikimedia requires significant processing to obtain article text and location, so we rely on the preprocessed data used by Wing and Baldridge (2011).

GEOTEXT is a small dataset consisting of 377,616 messages from 9,475 users tweeting across 48 American states, compiled by Eisenstein et al. (2010). A document in this dataset is the concatenation of all tweets by a single user, with a location derived from the earliest tweet with specific, GPS-assigned latitude/longitude coordinates.

UTGEO2011 is a new dataset designed to address the sparsity problems resulting from the size of the previous dataset. It is based on 390 million tweets collected across the entire globe between September 4th and November 29th, 2011, using the publicly available Twitter Spritzer feed and global search API. Not all collected tweets were geotagged. To be comparable to GEOTEXT, we discarded tweets outside of North America (outside of the bounding box with latitude/longitude corners at $(25, -126)$ and $(49, -60)$). Following Eisenstein et al. (2010), we consider all tweets of a user concatenated as a single document, and use the earliest collected GPS-assigned location as the gold location. Users without a gold location were discarded. To remove many spammers and robots, we only kept users following 5 to 1000 people, followed by at least 5 users, and authoring no more than 1000 tweets in the three month period. The resulting dataset contains 38 million tweets from 449,694 users, or roughly 85 tweets per user on average. We randomly selected 10,000 users each for development and held-out test evaluation. The remaining 429,694 users serve as a training set termed **UTGEO2011-LARGE**. We also randomly selected a 10,000 user training subset (**UTGEO2011-SMALL**) to facilitate comparisons with GEOTEXT and allow us to investigate the relative improvements for different models with more training data.

Our code and the UTGEO2011 data set are both available for download.[2]

3 Model

Assume we have a collection $\mathbf{d}$ of documents and their associated location labels $\mathbf{l}$. These documents may be actual texts, or they can be pseudo-documents comprised of a number of texts grouped via some algorithm (such as the grids discussed in the next section).

For a test document d_i, its similarity to each labeled document is computed, and the location of the most similar document assigned to d_i. Given an abstract function sim that can be instantiated with an appropriate similarity function (e.g. cosine distance or Kullback-Leibler divergence),

$$loc(d_i) = loc(\arg\max_{d_j \in \mathbf{d}} sim(d_i, d_j)).$$

This is a winner-takes-all strategy, which we follow in this paper. In related work on image geolocation, Hays and Efros (2008) use the same general framework, but compute the location based on the k-nearest neighbors (kNN) rather than the top one. They compute a distribution from the 120 nearest neighbors using mean shift clustering (Comaniciu and Meer, 2002) and choose the cluster with the most members. This produced slightly better results than choosing only the closest image. In future work, we will explore the kNN approach to see if it is more effective for text geolocation.

[2] https://github.com/utcompling/textgrounder/wiki/RollerEtAl_EMNLP2012

Following previous work in document geolocation, particularly Serdyukov et al. (2009) (henceforth SMvZ) and Wing and Baldridge (2011) (henceforth W&B), we geolocate texts using a language modeling approach to information retrieval (Ponte and Croft, 1998; Zhai and Lafferty, 2001). For each document d_i, we construct a unigram probability distribution θ_{d_i} over the vocabulary.

We smooth documents using the pseudo-Good-Turing method of W&B, a nonparametric discounting model that backs off from the unsmoothed distribution $\tilde{\theta}_{d_i}$ of the document to the unsmoothed distribution $\tilde{\theta}_D$ of all documents. A general discounting model is as follows:

$$P(w|\theta_{d_i}) = \begin{cases} (1-\lambda_{d_i})P(w|\tilde{\theta}_{d_i}), & \text{if } P(w|\tilde{\theta}_{d_i}) > 0 \\ \lambda_{d_i} \frac{P(w|\tilde{\theta}_D)}{U_{d_i}}, & \text{otherwise,} \end{cases}$$

where $U_{d_i} = 1 - \sum_{w \in d_i} P(w|\tilde{\theta}_D)$ is a normalization factor that is precomputed when the distribution for d_i is constructed. The discount factor λ_{d_i} indicates how much probability mass to reserve for unseen words. For pseudo-Good-Turing, it is

$$\lambda_{d_i} = \frac{|w \in d_i \text{ s.t. count}(w \in d_i) = 1|}{|w \in d_i|},$$

i.e. the fraction of words seen once in d_i.

We experimented with other smoothing methods, including Jelinek-Mercer and Dirichlet smoothing. A disadvantage of these latter two methods is that they have an additional tuning parameter to which their performance is highly sensitive, and even with optimal parameter settings neither consistently outperformed pseudo-Good-Turing. We also found no consistent improvement from using interpolation in place of backoff.

We also follow W&B in using Kullback-Leibler (KL) divergence as the similarity metric, since it outperformed both naive Bayes classification probability and cosine similarity:

$$KL(\theta_{d_i}||\theta_{d_j}) = \sum_k \theta_{d_i}(k) \log \frac{\theta_{d_i}(k)}{\theta_{d_j}(k)}.$$

The motivation for computing similarity with KL is that it is a measure of how well each document in the labeled set explains the word distribution found in the test document.

4 Collapsing Documents with an Adaptive Grid

In the previous section, we used the term "document" loosely when speaking of training documents. A simplistic approach might indeed involve comparing a test document to each training document. However, in the winner-takes-all model described above, we can rely only on the result of comparing with the single best training document, which may not contain enough information to make a good prediction.

A standard strategy to deal with this problem is to collapse groups of geographically nearby documents into larger pseudo-documents. This also has the advantage of reducing the computation time, as fewer training documents need to be compared against. Formally, this involves partitioning the training documents into a set of sets of documents $G = \{g_1 \dots g_n\}$. A collection $\tilde{\mathbf{d}}$ of pseudo-documents is formed from this set, such that the pseudo-document for a particular group g_i is simply the concatenation of the documents in the group:

$$\tilde{d}_{g_i} = \bigcup_{d_j \in g_i} d_j.$$

A location must be associated with each pseudo-document. This can be chosen based on the partitioning function itself or the locations of the documents in each group.

Both W&B and SMvZ use *uniform* grids consisting of cells of equal degree size to partition documents. We explore an alternative that uses k-d (k-dimensional) trees to construct a non-uniform grid that *adapts* to training sets of different sizes more gracefully. It ensures a roughly equal number of documents in each cell, which means that all pseudo-documents compete on similar footing with respect to the amount of training data.

W&B define the location for a cell to be its geographic *center*, while SMvZ only perform error analysis in terms of choosing the correct cell. We obtain consistently improved results using the *centroid* of the cell's documents, which takes into account where the documents are concentrated.

4.1 *k*-d Trees

A k-d tree is a space-partitioning data structure for storing points in k-dimensional space, which groups nearby points into buckets. As one moves down the tree, the space is split into smaller regions along chosen dimensions. In this way, it is a generalization of a binary search tree to multiple dimensions. The k-d tree was first introduced by Bentley (1975) and has since been applied to numerous problems, e.g. Barnes-Hut simulation (Anderson, 1999) and nearest-neighbors search (Friedman et al., 1977).

Partitioning geolocated documents using a k-d tree provides finer granularity in dense regions and coarser granularity elsewhere. For example, documents from Queens and Brooklyn may show significant cultural distinctions, while documents separated by the same distance in rural Montana may appear culturally identical. A uniform grid with large cells will mash Queens and Brooklyn together, while small cells will create unnecessarily sparse regions in Montana.

An important parameter for a k-d tree is its *bucket size*, which determines the maximum number of points (documents in our case) that a cell may contain. By varying the bucket size, the cells can be made fine- or coarse-grained.

4.2 Partitioning with a *k*-d Tree

For geolocation, we consider the surface of earth to be a 2-dimensional space (k=2) over latitude, longitude pairs. We form a k-d tree by a recursive procedure over the training data. Initially, all documents are placed in the root node of the tree. If the number of documents in the node exceeds the bucket size, the node is split into two nodes along a chosen split dimension and point. This procedure is recursively called on each of the new child nodes, and repeats until no node is overflowing. The resulting leaves of the k-d tree form a patchwork of rectangles which cover the entire earth.[3]

When splitting an overflowing node, the choice of splitting dimension and point can greatly impact the structure of the resulting k-d tree. Following Friedman et al. (1977), we choose to always split a node

[3]We note that the grid "rectangles" are actually trapezoids due to the nature of the latitude/longitude coordinate system. We assume the effect of this is negligible, since most documents are away from the poles, where distortion is the most extreme.

Figure 1: View of North America showing *k*-d leaves created from GEOWIKI with a bucket size of 600 and the MIDPOINT method, as visualized in Google Earth.

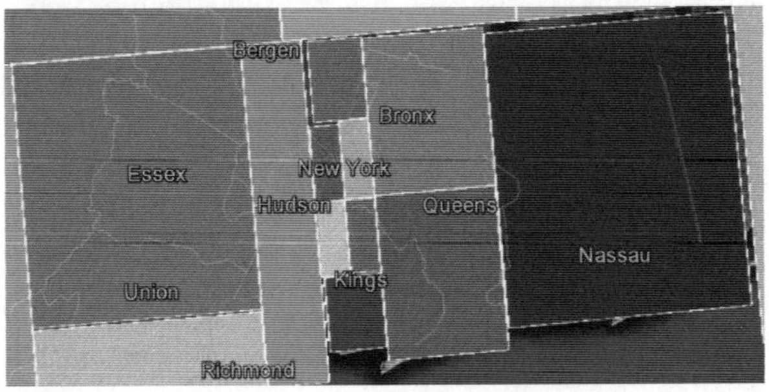

Figure 2: *k*-d leaves over the New York City and nearby areas from the same dataset and parameter settings as in Figure 1.

along the dimension exhibiting the greatest range of values. However, there still exist multiple methods for determining the split point, i.e. the point separating documents into "left" and "right" nodes. In this paper, we consider two possibilities for selecting this point: the **MIDPOINT** method, and the **FRIEDMAN** method. The latter splits at the median of all the points, resulting in an equal number of points in both the left and right nodes and a perfectly balanced *k*-d tree. The former splits at the midpoint between the two furthest points, allowing for a greater difference in the number of points in each bin. For geolocation, the FRIEDMAN splitting method will likely lead to less sparsity, and therefore more accurate cell selection. On the other hand, the MIDPOINT method is likely to draw more geographically desirable boundaries.

Figure 1 shows the leaves of the *k*-d tree formed over North America using the GEOWIKI dataset, the MIDPOINT node division method, and a bucket size of 600. Figure 2 shows the leaves over New York City and its surrounding area for the same dataset and settings. More densely populated areas of the earth (which in turn tend to have more Wikipedia documents associated with them) contain smaller and more numerous leaf cells. The cells over Manhattan are significantly smaller than those of Queens, the Bronx, and East Jersey, even at such a coarse bucket size. Though the leaves of the *k*-d tree implicitly cover the entire surface of the earth, our illustrations limit the size of each box by its data, leaving gaps where no training documents exist.

4.3 Selecting a Representative Location

W&B use the geographic **center** of a cell as the geolocation for the pseudo-document it represents. However, this ignores the fact that many cells will have imbalances in the dispersion of the documents they contain – typically, they will be clumpy, with documents clustering around areas of high population or activity. An alternative is to select the **centroid** of the locations of all the documents contained within a cell. Uniform grids with small cells are not especially sensitive to this choice since the absolute distance between a center or centroid prediction will not be great, and empty cells are simply discarded. Nonetheless, using the centroid has the benefit of making a uniform grid less sensitive to cell size, such that larger cells can be used more reliably – especially important when there are few training documents.

In contrast, when choosing representative locations for the leaves of a *k*-d tree, it is quite important to use the centroid because the leaves necessarily span the entire earth and none are discarded (since all have a roughly similar number of documents in them). Some areas with low document density are thus assigned very large cells, such as those over the oceans, as seen in Figures 1 and 2. Using the centroid allows these large leaves to be in the mix, while still predicting the locations in them that have the greatest document density.

5 Experimental Setup

Configurations. We experiment with several configurations of grids and representative locations.

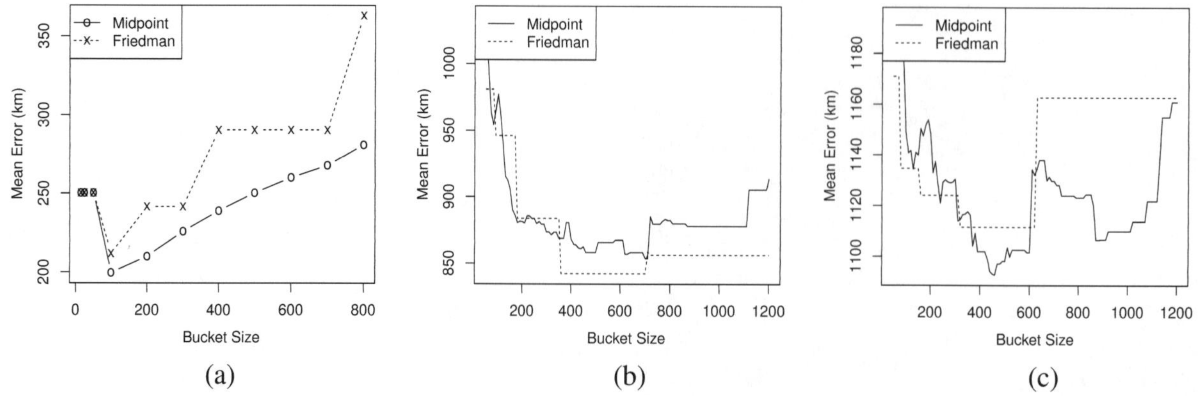

Figure 3: Development set comparisons for (a) GEOWIKI, (b) GEOTEXT, and (c) UTGEO2011-SMALL.

W&B refers to a uniform grid and geographic-center location selection, **UNIFCENTROID** to a uniform grid with centroid location selection, **KDCENTROID** to a k-d tree grid with centroid location selection, and **UNIFKDCENTROID** to the union of pseudo-documents constructed by UNIFCENTROID and KDCENTROID.

We also provide two baselines, both of which are based on a uniform grid with centroid location selection. **RANDOM** predicts a grid cell chosen at random uniformly; **MOSTCOMMONCELL** always predicts the grid cell containing the most training documents. Note that a most-common k-d leaf baseline does not make sense, as all k-d leaves contain approximately the same number of documents.

Evaluation. We use three metrics to measure geolocation performance. The output of each experiment is a predicted coordinate for each test document. For each prediction, we compute the error distance along the surface of the earth to the gold coordinate. We report the **mean** and **median** of all such distances as in W&B and Eisenstein et al. (2011). We also report the **fraction of error distances less than 161 km**, corresponding to Cheng et al. (2010)'s measure of predictions within 100 miles of the true location. This third measure can reveal differences between models not obvious from just mean and median.

6 Results

This section provides results for the datasets described previously: GEOWIKI, GEOTEXT, UTGEO2011-LARGE and UTGEO2011-SMALL. We first give details for how we tuned parameters and algorithmic choices using the development sets, and then provide performance on the test sets based on these determinations.

6.1 Tuning

The specific parameters are (1) the partition location method; (2) the bucket size for k-d partitioning; (3) the node division method for k-d partitioning; (4) the degree size for uniform grid partitioning. We tune with respect to mean error, like W&B.

Partition Location Method. Development set results show that the centroid always performs better than the center for all datasets, typically by a wide margin (especially for large partition sizes). To save space, we do not provide details, but point the reader to the differences in test set results between W&B and UNIFCENTROID (which are identical except that the former uses the center and the latter uses the centroid) in Tables 1 and 2. All further parameter tuning is done using the centroid method.

***k*-d Tree Bucket Size.** Bucket size should not be too large as a proportion of the total number of training documents. Larger bucket sizes tend to produce larger leaves, so documents in a partition will have a higher average distance to the center or centroid point. This will result in predictions being made at too coarse a granularity, greatly limiting obtainable precision even when the correct leaf is chosen.

Conversely, small bucket sizes lead to fewer training documents per partition. A bucket size of one reduces to the situation where no pseudo-documents are used. While this might work well if location prediction is done using the kNNs for a test document, it

Test dataset	GEOWIKI				GEOTEXT			
Method	Parameters	Mean	Med.	Acc.	Parameters	Mean	Med.	Acc.
RANDOM	0.1°	7056	7145	0.3	5°	2008	1866	1.6
MOSTCOMMONCELL	0.1°	4265	2193	5.0	5°	1158	757	31.3
Eisenstein et al.	-	-	-	-	-	**845**	501	-
Wing & Baldridge	0.1°	221	11.8	-	5°	967	479	-
UNIFCENTROID	0.1°	181	**11.0**	**90.3**	5°	897	**432**	**35.9**
KDCENTROID	B100, MIDPT.	192	22.5	87.9	B530, FRIED.	958	549	35.3
UNIFKDCENTROID	0.1°, B100, MIDPT.	**176**	13.4	90.3	5°, B530, FRIED.	890	473	34.1

Table 1: Performance on the held-out test sets of GEOWIKI and GEOTEXT, comparing to the results of Wing and Baldridge (2011) and Eisenstein et al. (2011).

is likely to perform very poorly for the 1NN rule we adopt. It would also require efficient similarity comparisons, using techniques such as locality-sensitive hashing (Kulis and Grauman, 2009).

The graphs in Figure 3 show development set performance when varying bucket size. For GEOWIKI and UTGEO2011-LARGE (not shown), increments of 100 were used, but for the smaller GEOTEXT and UTGEO2011-SMALL, more fine-grained increments of 10 were used. In the case of plateaus, as was common with the FRIEDMAN method, we chose the middle of the plateau as the bucket size. Overall, we found optimal bucket sizes of 100 for GEOWIKI, 530 for GEOTEXT, 460 for UTGEO2011-SMALL, and 1050 for UTGEO2011-LARGE. That the Wikipedia data requires a smaller bucket size is unsurprising: the documents themselves are generally longer and there are many more of them, so a small bucket size provides good coverage and granularity without sacrificing the ability to estimate good language models for each partition.

Node Division Method. The graphs in Figure 3 also display the difference between the two splitting methods. MIDPOINT is clearly better for GEOWIKI, while FRIEDMAN is better for GEOTEXT in the range of bucket sizes producing the best results. FRIEDMAN is best for UTGEO2011-LARGE (not shown), but MIDPOINT is best for UTGEO2011-SMALL.

These results only partly confirm our expectations. We expected FRIEDMAN to perform better on smaller datasets, as it distributes the documents evenly and avoids many sparsity issues. We expected MIDPOINT to win on larger datasets, where all nodes receive plentiful data and the *k*-d tree would choose more representative geographical boundaries.

Cell Size. Following W&B, we choose a cell degree size of 0.1° for GEOWIKI, and a cell degree size of 5.0° for GEOTEXT. For UTGEO2011-LARGE and UTGEO2011-SMALL, we follow the procedure of W&B, trying sizes 0.1°, 0.5°, 1.0°, 5.0°, and 10.0°, selecting the one which performed best on the development set. For UTGEO2011-SMALL, this resulted in coarse cells of 10.0°, while for UTGEO2011-LARGE, cell sizes of 0.1° were best.

With these tuned parameters, the average number of training tokens per *k*-d leaf was approximately 26k for GEOWIKI, 197k for GEOTEXT, 250k for UTGEO2011-SMALL, and 954k for UTGEO2011-LARGE.

6.2 Held-out Test Sets

Table 1 shows the performance on the test sets of GEOWIKI and GEOTEXT of the different configurations, along with that of W&B and Eisenstein et al. (2011) where possible. The results obtained by W&B on GEOWIKI are already very strong, but we do see a clear improvement by changing from the center-based locations for pseudo-documents they used to the centroid-based locations we employ: mean error drops from 221 km to 181 km, and median error from 11.8 km to 11.0 km. Also, we reduce the mean error further to 176 km for the configuration that combines the uniform grid and the *k*-d partitions, though at the cost of increasing median error somewhat. The 161 km accuracy is around 90% for all configurations, indicating that the general language modeling approach we employ is very

Test dataset	UTGEO2011							
Training dataset	UTGEO2011-SMALL				UTGEO2011-LARGE			
Method	Parameters	Mean	Med.	Acc.	Parameters	Mean	Med.	Acc.
RANDOM	10°	1975	1833	2.3	0.1°	1627	1381	2.0
MOSTCOMMONCELL	10°	1522	1186	9.3	0.1°	1525	1185	11.8
Wing & Baldridge	10°	1223	825	3.4	0.1°	956	570	30.9
UNIFCENTROID	10°	1147	782	12.3	0.1°	956	570	30.9
KDCENTROID	B460, MIDPT.	1098	733	**18.1**	B1050, FRIED.	**860**	**463**	**34.6**
UNIFKDCENTROID	10°, B460, MIDPT.	**1080**	**723**	**18.1**	0.1°, B1050, FRIED.	913	532	33.0

Table 2: Performance on the held-out test set of UTGEO2011 for different configurations trained on UTGEO2011-SMALL (comparable in size to GEOTEXT) and UTGEO2011-LARGE. The numbers given for W&B were produced from their implementation, and correspond to uniform grid partitioning with locations from centers rather than centroids.

robust for fact-oriented texts that are rich in explicit toponyms and geographically relevant named entities.

For GEOTEXT, the results show that the uniform grid with centroid locations is the most effective of our configurations. It improves on Eisenstein et al. (2011) by 69 km with respect to median error, but has 52 km worse performance than their model with respect to mean error. This indicates that our model is generally more accurate, but that it is comparatively more wildly off on some documents. Their model is a sophisticated one that attempts to build detailed models of the geographic linguistic variation found in the dataset. Dialectal cues are actually the most powerful ones in the GEOTEXT dataset, and it seems our general approach of winner-takes-all (1NN) hurts performance in this respect, especially with a very small training set.

Table 2 shows the performance on the test set of UTGEO2011 with the UTGEO2011-SMALL and UTGEO2011-LARGE training sets. (Performance for W&B is obtained from their code.[4]) With the small training set, error is worse than with GEOTEXT, reflecting the wider geographic scope of UTGEO2011. KDCENTROID is much more effective than the uniform grids, but combining it with the uniform grid in UNIFKDCENTROID edges it out by a small amount. More interestingly, KDCENTROID is the strongest on all measures when using the large training set, beating UNIFCENTROID by an even larger margin for mean and median error than with the small training set. The bucket size used with the large training set is double that for the small one, but there are many more leaves created since there are 42 times more training documents. With the extra data, the model is able to adapt better to the dispersion of documents and still have strong language models for each leaf that work well even with our greedy winner-takes-all decision method.

Note that the accuracy measurements for all UTGEO2011 experiments are substantially lower than those reported by Cheng et al. (2010), who report a best accuracy within 100 miles of 51%. While UTGEO2011-LARGE contains a substantially larger number of tweets, Cheng et al. (2010) limit themselves to users with at least 1,000 tweets, while we have an average of 85 tweets per user. Their reported mean error distance of 862 km (versus our best mean of 860 km on UTGEO2011-LARGE) indicates that their performance is hurt by a relatively small number of extremely incorrect guesses, as ours appears to be.

Figure 4 provides a learning curve on UTGEO2011's development set for KDCENTROID. Performance improves greatly with more data, indicating that GEOTEXT performance would also improve with more training data. Parameters, especially bucket size, need retuning as data increases, which we hope to estimate automatically in future work

Finally, we note that the KDCENTROID method was faster than other methods. While UNIFCENTROID took nearly 19 hours to complete the test run on GEOWIKI (approximately

[4]https://bitbucket.org/utcompling/textgrounder/wiki/WingBaldridge2011

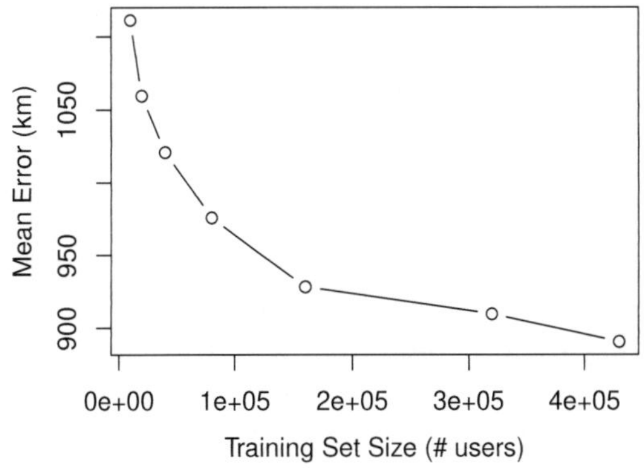

Figure 4: Learning curve of KDCENTROID on the UTGEO2011 development set.

1.38 seconds per test document), KDCENTROID took only 80 minutes (.078 s/doc). Similarly, UNIFCENTROID took about 67 minutes to run on UTGEO2011-LARGE (0.34 s/doc), but KDCENTROID took only 27 minutes (0.014 s/doc). Generally, the KDCENTROID partitioning results in fewer cells, and therefore fewer KL-divergence comparisons. As expected, the UNIFKDCENTROID model needs as much time as the two together, taking roughly 21 hours for GEOWIKI (1.52 s/doc) and 85 minutes for UTGEO2011-LARGE (0.36 s/doc).

7 Discussion

7.1 Error Analysis

We examine some of the greatest error distances to better understand and improve our models. In many cases, landmarks in Australia or New Zealand are predicted in European locations with similarly-named landmarks, or vice versa — e.g. the *Theatre Royal, Hobart* in Australia is predicted to be in London's theater district, and the *Embassy of Australia, Paris* is predicted to be in the capital city of Australia. Thus, our model may be inadvertently capturing what Clements et al. (2010) call *wormholes*, places that are related but not necessarily adjacent.

Some of the other large errors stem from incorrect gold labels, in particular due to sign errors in latitude or longitude, which can place documents 10,000 or more km from their correct locations.

Word	Error	Word	Error
paramus	78	6100	130
ludlow	79	figueroa	133
355	99	dundas	138
ctfuuu	101	120th	139
74th	105	mississauga	140
5701	105	pulaski	144
bloomingdale	122	cucina	146
covina	133	56th	153
lawrenceville	122	403	157
ctfuuuu	124	428	161

Table 3: The 20 words with least average error (km) in the UTGEO2011 development set, trained on the UTGEO2011-SMALL training set, using the KDCENTROID approach with our best parameters. Only words that occur in at least 10 documents are shown.

Word	Error	Word	Error
seniorpastor	1.1	KS01	2.4
prebendary	1.6	Keio	2.5
Wornham	1.7	Vrah	2.5
Owings	1.9	overspill	2.5
Londoners	2.0	Oriel	2.5
Sandringham	2.1	Holywell	2.6
Sheffield's	2.2	\'vr&h	2.6
Oxford's	2.2	operetta	2.6
Belair	2.3	Supertram	2.6
Beckton	2.4	Chanel	2.7

Table 4: Top 20 words with the least average error (km) in the GEOWIKI development set, using the UNIFKDCENTROID approach with our best parameters. Only words occurring in at least 10 documents are shown.

7.2 Most Predictive Words

Our approach relies on the idea that the use of certain words correlates with a Twitter user or Wikipedia article's location. To investigate which words tend to be good indicators of location, we computed, for each word in a development set, the average error distance of documents containing that word. Table 3 gives the 20 words with the least error, among those that occur in at least 10 documents (users), for the UTGEO2011 development set, trained on UTGEO2011-SMALL.

Many of the best words are town names (*paramus, ludlow, bloomingdale*), street names (*74th, figueroa,*

120th), area codes (*403*), and street numbers (*5701*, *6100*). All are highly locatable terms, as we would expect. Many of the street addresses are due to check-ins with the location-based social networking service Foursquare (e.g. the tweet *I'm at Starbucks (7301 164th Ave NE, Redmond Town Center, Redmond)*), where the user is literally broadcasting his or her location. The token *ctfuuu(u)*—an elongation of the internet abbreviation *ctfu*, or *cracking the fuck up*—is a dialectal or stylistic feature highly indicative of the Washington, D.C. area.

Similarly, several place names (*Wornham*, *Belair*, *Holywell*) appear in GEOWIKI. *Operetta*s are a cultural phenomenon largely associated with France, Germany, and England and particularly with specific theaters in these countries. However, other highly specific tokens such as *KS01* have a very low average error because they occur in few documents and are thus highly unambiguous indicators of location. Other terms, like *seniorpastor* and *\'vr&h*, are due to extraction errors in the dataset created by W&B, and are carried along because of a high correlation with specific documents.

8 Conclusion

We have shown how to construct an adaptive grid with k-d trees that enables robust text geolocation and scales well to large training sets. It will be interesting to consider how it interacts with other strategies for improving the IR-based approach. For example, the pseudo-document word distributions can be smoothed based on nearby documents or on the structure of the k-d tree itself. Integrating our system with topic models or Bayesian methods would likely provide more insight with regard to the most discriminative and geolocatable words. We also expect predicting locations based on multiple most similar documents (kNN) to be more effective in predicting document location, as the second and third most similar training documents together may sometimes be a better estimation of its distribution than just the first alone. Employing k Nearest Neighbors also allows for more sophisticated methods of location estimation than a single leaf's centroid. Other possibilities include constructing multiple k-d trees using random subsets of the training data to reduce sensitivity to the bucket size.

In this article, we have considered each user in isolation. However, Liben-Nowell et al. (2005) show that roughly 70% of social network links can be described using geographic information and that the probability of a social link is inversely proportional to geographic distance. Backstrom et al. (2010) verify these results on a much larger scale using geolocated Facebook profiles: their algorithm geolocates users with only the social graph and significantly outperforms IP-based geolocation systems. Given that both Twitter and Wikipedia have rich, linked document/user graphs, a natural extension to our work here will be to combine text and network prediction for geolocation. Sadilek et al. (2012) also show that a combination of textual and social data can accurately geolocate individual tweets when scope is limited to a single city.

Tweets are temporally ordered and the geographic distance between consecutive tweeting events is constrained by the author's movement. For tweet-level geolocation, it will be useful to build on work in geolocation that considers the temporal dimension (Chen and Grauman, 2011; Kalogerakis et al., 2009; Sadilek et al., 2012) to make better predictions for documents/images that are surrounded by others with excellent cues, but which are hard to resolve themselves.

9 Acknowledgments

We would like to thank Matt Lease and the three anonymous reviewers for their feedback. This research was supported by a grant from the Morris Memorial Trust Fund of the New York Community Trust.

References

Richard J. Anderson. 1999. Tree data structures for n-body simulation. *SIAM Journal on Computing*, 28(6):1923–1940.

Lars Backstrom, Eric Sun, and Cameron Marlow. 2010. Find me if you can: improving geographical prediction with social and spatial proximity. In *Proceedings of the 19th International Conference on World Wide Web*, pages 61–70.

Jon Louis Bentley. 1975. Multidimensional binary search trees used for associative searching. *Communications of the ACM*, 18(9):509–517.

Chao-Yeh Chen and Kristen Grauman. 2011. Clues from the beaten path: Location estimation with bursty sequences of tourist photos. In *Proceedings of the IEEE Conference on Computer Vision and Pattern Recognition*, pages 1569–1576.

Zhiyuan Cheng, James Caverlee, and Kyumin Lee. 2010. You are where you tweet: A content-based approach to geo-locating twitter users. In *Proceedings of the 19th ACM International Conference on Information and Knowledge Management*, pages 759–768.

Martin Clements, Pavel Serdyukov, Arjen P. de Vries, and Marcel J.T. Reinders. 2010. Finding wormholes with flickr geotags. In *Proceedings of the 32nd European Conference on Information Retrieval*, pages 658–661.

Sebastian Cobarrubias. 2009. *Mapping machines: activist cartographies of the border and labor lands of Europe*. Ph.D. thesis, University of North Carolina at Chapel Hill.

Dorin Comaniciu and Peter Meer. 2002. Mean shift: a robust approach toward feature space analysis. *IEEE Transactions on Pattern Analysis and Machine Intelligence*, 24(5):603–619.

Junyan Ding, Luis Gravano, and Narayanan Shivakumar. 2000. Computing geographical scopes of web resources. In *Proceedings of the 26th International Conference on Very Large Data Bases*, pages 545–556.

Jacob Eisenstein, Brendan O'Connor, Noah A. Smith, and Eric P. Xing. 2010. A latent variable model for geographic lexical variation. In *Proceedings of the 2010 Conference on Empirical Methods in Natural Language Processing*, pages 1277–1287.

Jacon Eisenstein, Ahmed Ahmed, and Eric P. Xing. 2011. Sparse additive generative models of text. In *Proceedings of the 28th International Conference on Machine Learning*, pages 1041–1048.

Jerome H. Friedman, Jon Louis Bentley, and Raphael Ari Finkel. 1977. An algorithm for finding best matches in logarithmic expected time. *ACM Transactions on Mathematical Software*, 3:209–226.

James Hays and Alexei A. Efros. 2008. im2gps: estimating geographic information from a single image. In *Proceedings of the IEEE Conference on Computer Vision and Pattern Recognition*, pages 1–8.

Evangelos Kalogerakis, Olga Vesselova, James Hays, Alexei Efros, and Aaron Hertzmann. 2009. Image sequence geolocation with human travel priors. In *Proceedings of the IEEE 12th International Conference on Computer Vision*, pages 253–260.

Sheila Kinsella, Vanessa Murdock, and Neil O'Hare. 2011. "I'm eating a sandwich in Glasgow": Modeling locations with tweets. In *Proceedings of the 3rd International Workshop on Search and Mining User-generated Contents*, pages 61–68.

Brian Kulis and Kristen Grauman. 2009. Kernelized locality-sensitive hashing for scalable image search. In *Proceedings of the 12th International Conference on Computer Vision*, pages 2130–2137.

David Liben-Nowell, Jasmine Novak, Ravi Kumar, Prabhakar Raghavan, and Andrew Tomkins. 2005. Geographic routing in social networks. *Proceedings of the National Academy of Sciences of the United States of America*, 102(33):11623–11628.

Jay M. Ponte and W. Bruce Croft. 1998. A language modeling approach to information retrieval. In *Proceedings of the 21st Annual International ACM SIGIR Conference on Research and Development in Information Retrieval*, pages 275–281.

Adam Sadilek, Henry Kautz, and Jeffrey P. Bigham. 2012. Finding your friends and following them to where you are. In *Proceedings of the 5th ACM International Conference on Web Search and Data Mining*, pages 723–732.

Jagan Sankaranarayanan, Hanan Samet, Benjamin E. Teitler, Michael D. Lieberman, and Jon Sperling. 2009. Twitterstand: news in tweets. In *Proceedings of the 17th ACM SIGSPATIAL International Conference on Advances in Geographic Information Systems*, pages 42–51.

Pavel Serdyukov, Vanessa Murdock, and Roelof van Zwol. 2009. Placing flickr photos on a map. In *Proceedings of the 32nd International ACM SIGIR Conference on Research and Development in Information Retrieval*, pages 484–491.

Benjamin Wing and Jason Baldridge. 2011. Simple supervised document geolocation with geodesic grids. In *Proceedings of the 49th Annual Meeting of the Association for Computational Linguistics: Human Language Technologies*, pages 955–964.

Chengxiang Zhai and John Lafferty. 2001. A study of smoothing methods for language models applied to ad hoc information retrieval. In *Proceedings of the 24th Annual International ACM SIGIR Conference on Research and Development in Information Retrieval*, pages 334–342.

A Discriminative Model for Query Spelling Correction with Latent Structural SVM

Huizhong Duan, Yanen Li, ChengXiang Zhai and Dan Roth
University of Illinois at Urbana-Champaign
201 N Goodwin Ave
Urbana, IL 61801
{duan9, yanenli2, czhai, danr}@illinois.edu

Abstract

Discriminative training in query spelling correction is difficult due to the complex internal structures of the data. Recent work on query spelling correction suggests a two stage approach a noisy channel model that is used to retrieve a number of candidate corrections, followed by discriminatively trained ranker applied to these candidates. The ranker, however, suffers from the fact the low recall of the first, suboptimal, search stage.

This paper proposes to directly optimize the search stage with a discriminative model based on latent structural SVM. In this model, we treat query spelling correction as a multiclass classification problem with structured input and output. The latent structural information is used to model the alignment of words in the spelling correction process. Experiment results show that as a standalone speller, our model outperforms all the baseline systems. It also attains a higher recall compared with the noisy channel model, and can therefore serve as a better filtering stage when combined with a ranker.

1 Introduction

Query spelling correction has become a crucial component in modern information systems. Particularly, search engine users rely heavily on the query correction mechanism to formulate effective queries. Given a user query q, which is potentially misspelled, the goal of query spelling correction is to find a correction of the query c that could lead to a better search experience. A typical query spelling correction system employs a noisy channel model (Kernighan et al., 1990). The model assumes that the correct query c is formed in the user's mind before entering the noisy channels, e.g., typing, and get misspelled. Formally, the model maximizes the posterior probability $p(c|q)$:

$$\hat{c} = \arg\max_c p(c|q). \quad (1)$$

Applying Bayes rule, the formulation can be rewritten as:

$$\begin{aligned} \hat{c} &= \arg\max_c p(q|c)p(c) \\ &= \arg\max_c [\log p(q|c) + \log p(c)]. \end{aligned} \quad (2)$$

The model uses two probabilities. The prior probability $p(c)$ represents how likely it is that c is the original correct query in the user's mind. The probability is usually modeled by a language model estimated from a sizable corpus. The transformation probability $p(q|c)$ measures how likely it is that q is the output given that c has been formed by the user. This probability can be either heuristic-based (edit distance) or learned from samples of well aligned corrections. One problem with the noisy channel model is that there is no weighting for the two kinds of probabilities, and since they are estimated from different sources, there are usually issues regarding their scale and comparability, resulting in suboptimal performance (Gao et al., 2010). Another limitation of this generative model is that it is not able to take advantage of additional useful features.

A discriminative model may solve these problems by adding the flexibility of using features and applying weights. But training such a model is not easy. The difficulty is that the output space of query correction is enormous, as the candidate corrections for each a query term could be the entire vocabulary. This is even worse when word boundary errors (i.e. merging and splitting of words) exist. The problem is intractable with standard discriminative models as we cannot enumerate every candidate correction.

To solve the problem, (Gao et al., 2010) proposed a two stage approach. In this approach, a ranker is trained to score each candidate correction of a query. When a query is issued, the system first uses the noisy channel model with a standard search algorithm to find the 20 best candidates. Then the ranker is used to re-rank these candidates and find the best correction for the query. This ranker based system has one critical limitation, though. Since the ranking stage is decoupled from the search, it relies on the outsourced search algorithm to find the candidates. Because query spelling correction is an online operation, only a small number of candidates can enter the ranker due to efficiency concerns, thus limiting the ability of the ranker to the ceiling of recall set by the suboptimal search phase.

The research question we address here is whether we can directly optimize the search phase of query spelling correction using a discriminative model without loss of efficiency. More specifically, we want 1) a learning process that is aware of the search phase and interacts with its result; 2) an efficient search algorithm that is able to incorporate the learned model and guide the search to the target spelling correction.

In this paper, we propose a new discriminative model for query correction that maintains the advantage of a discriminative model in accommodating flexible combination of features and naturally incorporates an efficient search algorithm in learning and inference. Similarly to (Chang et al., 2010) we collapse a two stage process into a single discriminatively trained process, by considering the output of the first stage as an intermediate latent representation for the joint learning process. Specifically, we make use of the latent structural SVM (LS-SVM) (Yu and Joachims, 2009) formulation. We formulate the problem query spelling correction as a multi-class classification problem on structured inputs and outputs. The advantage of the structural SVM model is that it allows task specific, customizable solutions for the inference problem. This allows us to adapt the model to make it work directly with the search algorithm we use for finding the best correction of the query. To account for word boundary errors, we model the word alignment between the query and the correction as a latent structural variable. The LS-SVM model allows us to jointly search over the output space and the latent structure space.

As the inference algorithm in the proposed discriminative model we use an algorithm that resembles a traditional noisy channel model. To adapt the LS-SVM model to enable the efficient search of query spelling correction, we study how features can be designed. We analyze the properties of features that can be used in the search algorithm and propose a criteria for selecting and designing new features. We demonstrate the use of the criteria by designing separate features for different types of spelling errors (e.g. splitting, merging). With the proposed discriminative model, we can directly optimize the search phase of query spelling correction without loss of efficiency. Our model can be used not only as a standalone speller with high accuracy, but also as a high recall candidate generation stage for a ranker based system.

Experiments verify the effectiveness of the discriminative model, as the accuracy of correction can be improved significantly over baseline systems including an award winning query spelling system. Even though the optimization is primarily based on the top correction, the weights trained by LS-SVM can be used to search for more candidate corrections. The improvement in recall at different levels over the noisy channel model demonstrates that our model is superior even when used in the two-stage approach..

2 Related Work

Spelling correction has a long history (Levenshtein, 1966). Traditional techniques were on small scale and depended on having a small trusted lexicons (Kukich, 1992). Later, statistical generative models were shown to be effective in spelling correction, where a source language model and an error model were identified as two major components

(Brill and Moore, 2000). Note that we are not dealing here with the standard models in context sensitive spelling (Golding and Roth, 1999) where the set of candidate correction is a known "confusion set". Query spelling correction, a special form of the problem, has received much attention in recent years. Compared with traditional spelling correction task, query spelling deals with more complex types of misspellings and a much larger scale of language. Research in this direction includes utilizing large web corpora and query log (Chen et al., 2007; Cucerzan and Brill, 2004; Ahmad and Kondrak, 2005), employing large-scale n-gram models, training phrase-based error model from clickthrough data (Sun et al., 2010) and developing additional features (Gao et al., 2010).

Query alteration/refinement is a very relevant topic to query spelling correction. The goal of query alteration/refinement is to modify the ineffective query so that it could . Researches on this track include query expansion (Xu and Croft, 1996; Qiu and Frei, 1993; Mitra et al., 1998), query contraction(Kumaran and Allan, 2008; Bendersky and Croft, 2008; Kumaran and Carvalho, 2009) and other types of query reformulations for bridging the vocabulary gap (Wang and Zhai, 2008). (Guo et al., 2008) proposed a unified model to perform a broad set of query refinements including correction, segmentation and stemming. However, it has very limited ability in query correction. In this paper, we study the discriminative training of query spelling correction, which is potentially beneficial to many existing studies.

Noisy channel model (or source channel model) has been widely used in NLP. Many approaches have been proposed to perform discriminative training of the model (McCallum et al., 2000; Lafferty, 2001). However, these approaches mostly deal with a relatively small search space where the number of candidates at each step is limited (e.g. POS tagging). A typically used search algorithm is dynamic programming. In spelling correction, however, the search space is much bigger and the existing approaches featuring dynamic programming are difficult to be applied.

Structural learning and latent structural learning has been studied a lot in NLP in recent years(Chang et al., 2010; Dyer et al., 2011), and has been shown to be useful in a range of NLP applications from Textual Entailment, Paraphrasing and Transliteration (Chang et al., 2010) to sentiment analysis (Yessenalina et al., 2010).

Work has also been done on integrating discriminative learning in search. Freitag and Khadivi used a perceptron algorithm to train for sequence alignment problem. A beam search algorithm was utilized in the search (Freitag and Khadivi, 2007). Daume et al. proposed the Searn framework for search based structural prediction (Daume et al., 2009). Our model differs from the Searn framework in that it learns to make global decisions rather than accumulating local decisions. The global decision was made possible by an efficient search algorithm.

Query spelling correction also shares many similarities with statistical machine translation (SMT). Sun et al. (2010) has formulated the problem within an SMT framework. However, SMT usually involves more complex alignments, while in query spelling correction search is the more challenging part. Our main contribution in this paper is a novel unified way to directly optimize the search phase of query spelling correction with the use of LS-SVM.

3 Discriminative Model for Query Spelling Correction Based on LS-SVM

In this section, we first present the discriminative formulation of the problem of query spelling correction. Then we introduce in detail the model we use for solving the problem.

3.1 The Discriminative Form of Query Spelling Correction

In query spelling correction, given a user entered query q, which is potentially misspelled, the goal is to find a correction c, such that it could be a more effective query which improves the quality of search results. A general discriminative formulation of the problem is of the following form:

$$f(q) = \arg\max_{c \in \mathcal{V}*} [w \cdot \Psi(q, c)], \quad (3)$$

where $\Psi(q, c)$ is a vector of features and w is the model parameter. This discriminative formulation is more general compared to the noisy channel model. It has the flexibility of using features and applying weights. The noisy channel model is a special case of the discriminative form where only two features, the source probability and the transformation probability, are used and uniform weightings are applied. However, this problem formulation does not give us much insight on how to proceed to design the model. Especially, it is unclear how $\Psi(q, c)$ can be computed.

To enhance the formulation, we explore the fact that spelling correction follows a word-by-word procedure. Let us first consider a scenario where word boundary errors does not exist. In this scenario, each query term matches and only matches to a single term in the correction. Formally, let us denote $q = q_1, ..., q_n$ and $c = c_1, ..., c_m$ as structured objects from the space of $\mathcal{V}^*$, where $\mathcal{V}$ is our vocabulary of words and $\mathcal{V}^*$ is all possible phrases formed by words in $\mathcal{V}$. Both q and c have an intrinsic sequential structure. When no word boundary error exists, $|c| = |q|$ holds for any candidate correction c. q_i and c_i establish a one-to-one mapping. In this case, we have a more detailed discriminative form:

$$f(q) = \arg\max_{c \in \mathcal{V}^{|q|}} [w \cdot (\Psi_0 + \sum_{i=1}^{|q|} \Psi_1(q_i, c_i))], \quad (4)$$

where Ψ_0 is a vector of normalizing factors, $\Psi_1(q_i, c_i)$ is the decomposed computation of $\Psi(q, c)$ for each query term q_i and c_i, for $i = 1$ to $|q|$.

Equation 4 is a clearer formulation. The major challenge of solving this discriminative problem is the complexity. Theoretically, each term has $|\mathcal{V}|$ candidates and it is impossible to enumerate over all possible combinations. To make it even worse, merging and splitting errors are quite common in misspelling. As a result, the assumption of one-to-one mapping does not hold in practice.

To account for these word boundary errors and enhance the discriminative formulation, we introduce a latent variable a to model the unobserved structural information. More specifically, $a = a_1, a_2, ...a_{|a|}$ is the alignment between q and c. Each alignment node a_t is a represented by a quadruple $(q_{start}, q_{end}, c_{start}, c_{end})$. Figure 1 shows a common merge error and its best alignment. The phrase "credit card", in this case, is incorrectly merged into one word "creditcard" by the user. Figure 2 shows the best alignment for a common split error, where the word "gamespot" is incorrectly split into a two word phrase "game spot".

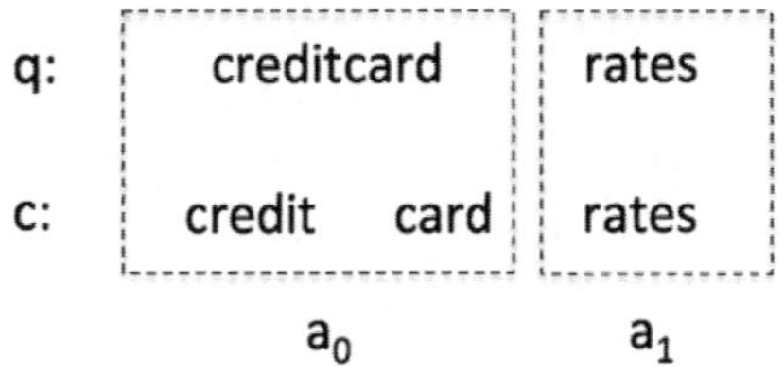

Figure 1: Example of Merge Error and Alignment

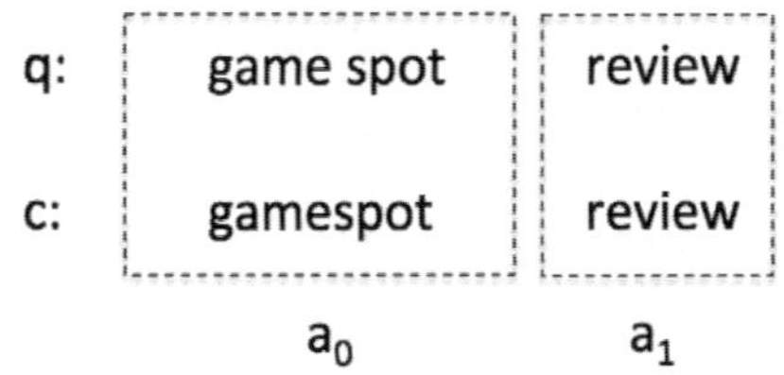

Figure 2: Example of Split Error and Alignment

Taking into consideration the latent variable, we arrive at our final discriminative form of query spelling correction:

$$\begin{aligned} f(q) &= \arg\max_{(c,a) \in \mathcal{V}^n \times \mathcal{A}} [w \cdot \Psi(q, c, a)] \\ &= \arg\max_{(c,a) \in \mathcal{V}^* \times \mathcal{A}} [w \cdot (\Psi_0 \\ &\quad + \textstyle\sum_{t=0}^{|a|} \Psi_1(q_{a_t}, c_{a_t}, a_t))], \end{aligned} \quad (5)$$

The challenges of successfully applying a discriminative model to this problem formulation are 1) how can we design a learning algorithm to learn the model parameter w to directly optimize the maximization problem; 2) how can we solve the maximization efficiently without having to enumerate all candidates; 3) how can we design features to guarantee the correctness of the search algorithm. In the following subsections we introduce our solutions to the three challenges in detail.

3.2 Latent Structural SVM

We employ the latent structural SVM (LS-SVM) model for learning the discriminative model of query spelling correction. LS-SVM is a large margin method that deals with structured prediction problems with latent structural information (Yu and Joachims, 2009). LS-SVM has the merit of allowing task specific, customizable solutions for the inference problem. This makes it easy to adapt to learning the model parameters for different problems. The following is a brief introduction of LS-SVM that largely mirrors the work by (Yu and Joachims, 2009).

Without loss of generality, let us aim at learning a prediction function $f : \mathcal{X} \rightarrow \mathcal{Y}$ that maps input $x \in \mathcal{X}$ to an output $y \in \mathcal{Y}$ with latent structural information $h \in \mathcal{H}$. The decision function is of the following form:

$$f(x) = \underset{(y,h) \in \mathcal{Y} \times \mathcal{H}}{\arg\max}\, [w \cdot \Psi(x, y, h)], \qquad (6)$$

where $\Psi(x, y, h)$ is the set of feature functions defined jointly over the input x, the output y and the latent variable h. w is the parameter of the model. Given a set of training examples that consist of input and output pairs $\{(x_1, y_1), ...(x_n, y_n)\} \in (\mathcal{X} \times \mathcal{Y})^n$, the LS-SVM method solves the following optimization problem:

$$\begin{aligned} & min_w \frac{1}{2}\|w\|^2 \\ & +C \sum_{i=1}^{n} \max_{(\hat{y},\hat{h}) \in \mathcal{Y} \times \mathcal{H}} [w \cdot \Psi(x_i, \hat{y}, \hat{h}) + \Delta(y_i, \hat{y})] \\ & -C \sum_{i=1}^{n} \max_{h \in \mathcal{H}} [w \cdot \Psi(x_i, y_i, h)], \end{aligned} \qquad (7)$$

where $\Delta(y_i, \hat{y})$ is the loss function for the ith example. The details of the derivation is omitted in this paper. Readers who are interested can read more from (Yu and Joachims, 2009).

There are two maximization problems that are essential in Equation 7. The first one is the loss augmented decision function:

$$\max_{(\hat{y},\hat{h}) \in \mathcal{Y} \times \mathcal{H}} [w \cdot \Psi(x_i, \hat{y}, \hat{h}) + \Delta(y_i, \hat{y})], \qquad (8)$$

and the second is the inference of latent variable given the label of the training data:

$$\max_{h \in \mathcal{H}} [w \cdot \Psi(x_i, y_i, h)]. \qquad (9)$$

The Latent Structural SVM framework does not specify how the maximization problems in Equation 8 and Equation 9 are solved, as well as the inference problem in 6. These maximization problems are task dependent. Being able to efficiently solve them is the key to successfully applying the Latent Structural SVM method. We will show in detail how we solve these maximization problems to make LS-SVM work for query spelling correction in the following subsection.

For training the LS-SVM model, a Concave-Convex Procedure (CCCP) was proposed to solve this optimization problem (Yu and Joachims, 2009). The method resembles the Expect-Maximization (EM) training method as it updates the model by iteratively recomputing the latent variable. However, rather than performing "sum-product" training as in EM where a distribution over the hidden variable is maintained, the CCCP method used for LS-SVM is more similar to the "max-product" paradigm where we "guess" the best hidden variable in each iteration, except here we "guess" by minimizing a regularized loss function instead of maximizing the likelihood.

3.3 Solving the Inference Problems

The essential inference problem is to find the correction that maximizes the scoring function according to the model (i.e., the decision function in Equation 6). For this purpose we design a best first search algorithm similar to the standard search algorithm in the noisy channel model. The essence of the search algorithm is to bound the score of each candidate so that we could evaluate the most promising candidates first. The algorithm is given in Algorithm 1.

Essentially, the algorithm maintains a priority queue of all search paths. Each time the best path is de-queued, it is expanded with up to $m - 1$ words in q by searching over a vocabulary trie of up to m-gram. Each path is represented as a quadruple (pos, str, sc, a), representing the current term position in query, the string of the path, the path's score and the alignment so far. The priority queue is sorted according to the score of each path in descending order. The $GetSuggestions()$ function retrieves the top n similar words to the given word with a vocabulary trie according to an error model.

Splitting errors are dealt with in Algorithm 1 by "looking forward" m words in the query when generating candidate words. Merging errors are accounted for by including up to m-gram in the vocabulary trie. It is worth mentioning that performance of Algorithm 1 could be further improved by computing heuristic scores for each path.

Algorithm 1: Best First Search Algorithm

```
Input: Vocabulary Trie V, query q, output size k,
       max order m, candidate pool size n
Output: List l of top k corrections for q
Initialize List l;
Initialize PriorityQueue pq;
Enqueue to pq a start path with position set to 0,
string set to empty string, score set to w · Ψ_0, and
path alignment set to empty set;
while pq is not Empty do
    Path π ← pq.Dequeue();
    if π.pos < q.terms.length then
        for i ← 0 to m do
            ph ← q.terms[π.pos + 1...π.pos + i];
            sug ← GetSuggestions(ph, V, n);
            foreach s in sug do
                pos' ← π.pos + i;
                str' ← concat(π.str, s.str);
                a' ← π.a ∪ s.a;
                sc' ← π.sc + w · Ψ_1(q_{s.a}, c_{s.a}, s.a);
                Enqueue pq with the new path
                (pos', str', sc', a');
    else
        Add suggestion string π.str to l;
        if l.Count > k then return l;
return l;
```

As Algorithm 1 originates from the noisy channel model, the two known features that work with the algorithm are $\log p(c)$ and $\log p(q|c)$ from the noisy channel model. However, it is unknown whether other features can work with the search algorithm and how we can develop new features to ensure it. After analyzing the properties of the features and the search algorithm, we find that a feature ψ has to satisfy the following monotonicity constraint in order to be used in Algorithm 1.

Monotonicity Property. Given query q, for any alignment $A_t = A_{t-1} \cup \{a_t\}$ at time t, $\psi(q_{A_t}, c_{A_t}, A_t) \leq \psi(q_{A_{t-1}}, c_{A_{t-1}}, A_{t-1})$, where q_{A_t} is the concatenation of q_{a_0} to q_{a_t} and c_{A_t} is the concatenation of c_{a_0} to c_{a_t}.

That is, the value of the feature (which is computed in an accumulative manner) cannot increase as the candidate is extended with a new term at any search step. This ensures that the score of the best candidate at any search step is guaranteed to be higher than the score of any future candidates. It also implies $\psi_t(q_{a_t}, c_{a_t}, a_t) \leq 0$ for any $t \in T$. The monotonicity feature ensures the correctness of Algorithm 1. We show how we design features with the guidance of the monotonicity constraint in Section 4.

The solution to to the loss augmented inference depends on the loss function we use. In spelling correction, usually only one correction is valid for an input query. Therefore, we apply the 0-1 loss to our model:

$$\Delta(c, \hat{c}) = \begin{cases} 0 & c = \hat{c} \\ 1 & c \neq \hat{c} \end{cases} \tag{10}$$

Given this loss function, the loss augmented inference problem can be solved easily with an algorithm similar to Algorithm 1. This is done by initializing the loss to be 1 at the beginning of each search path. During the search procedure, we check if the loss decreases to 0 given the correction string so far. If this is the case, we decreases the score by 1 and add the path back to the priority queue. More advanced functions may also be used (Dreyer et al., 2006), which may lead to better training performance. We plan to further study different loss functions in our future work.

The inference of the latent alignment variable can be solved with dynamic programming, as the number of possible alignments is limited given the query and the correction.

4 Features

In the following discussions, we will describe how the features in our discriminative model are developed under the guidance of the monotonicity constraint.

4.1 Source Probability and Transformation Probability

We know from empirical experience that the source probability and the transformation probability are the two most important features in query spelling correction. We include them in our model in a normalized form. Taking the source probability for example, we define the following feature:

$$\psi(q,c,a) = \frac{\mu+\sum_1^{|a|}\log p(c)}{\mu} = 1+\sum_1^{|a|}\frac{\log p(c)}{\mu}, \tag{11}$$

where μ is a normalizing factor computed as:

$$\mu = -|q|\log p_{min}, \tag{12}$$

where p_{min} is the smallest probability we use in practice.

The formula fits the general form we define in 5 in that $\psi_0 = 1$ and $\psi_1(q_{a_t}, c_{a_t}, a_t) = \frac{\log p(c)}{\mu}$ for any $t = 1$ to $|a|$.

Similarly, we have the follow feature for the transformation probability:

$$\psi'(q,c,a) = \frac{\mu+\sum_1^{|a|}\log p(q|c)}{\mu} = 1+\sum_1^{|a|}\frac{\log p(q|c)}{\mu}. \tag{13}$$

We use the web Microsoft n-gram model[1] to compute source model $p(c)$. We train the unigram transformation model for the transformation probability $p(q|c)$ according to (Duan and Hsu, 2011).

In generative models, we treat transformation probabilities from merging and splitting errors in the same way as single word errors. In our discriminative model we can assign separate weight to the transformation probabilities resulted from different types of errors. This allows fine tuning of the query spelling correction system, making it more adaptive to environments where the ratio of different types of errors may vary. Moreover, the model also allows us to include language models trained over different resources, such as query log, title of webpages or anchor texts.

4.2 Local Heuristic Features

Despite the goal of query spelling correction is to deal with misspellings, in real world most queries are correctly spelled. A good query spelling correction system shall prevent as much as possible from misjudging an correctly spelled query as misspelled. With this idea in mind, we invent some heuristic functions to avoid misjudging.

[1]http://research.microsoft.com/en-us/collaboration/focus/cs/web-ngram.aspx

Local Heuristic 1. When a query term is matched against trustable vocabulary, it increases the chance that the term is already in its correct form. For example, we extract a reliable vocabulary from the title field of Wikipedia[2]. We therefore design the following feature:

$$\phi(q,c,a) = 1 + \sum_{t=1}^{|a|}\phi_1(q_{a_t}, c_{a_t}, a_t), \tag{14}$$

where $\phi_1(q_{a_t}, c_{a_t}, a_t)$ is defined as:

$$\phi_1(q_{a_t}, c_{a_t}, a_t) = \begin{cases} 0 & q_{a_t} \notin \mathcal{W} \\ 0 & q_{a_t} \in \mathcal{W}, q_{a_t} = c_t \\ -\frac{1}{|q|} & q_{a_t} \in \mathcal{W}, q_{a_t} \neq c_{a_t} \end{cases} \tag{15}$$

where $\mathcal{W}$ is the vocabulary of Wikipedia titles. Since $|q| > |a|$ always holds, the feature is normalized between 0 and 1.

Local Heuristic 2. Another heuristic is that words with numbers in it, despite usually not included in any vocabulary, should be treated carefully as they tend to be correct words. Such words could be a model, a serial number or a special entity name. Since the number keys on keyboard are away from the letter keys, they are more likely to be intentionally typed in if found in user queries. Similar to Heuristic 1, we design the following feature to capture this heuristic:

$$\phi'(q,c,a) = 1 + \sum_{t=1}^{|a|}\phi'_1(q_{a_t}, c_{a_t}, a_t), \tag{16}$$

where $\phi'_1(q_{a_t}, c_{a_t}, a_t)$ is defined as:

$$\phi'_1(q_{a_t}, c_{a_t}, a_{a_t}) = \begin{cases} 0 & [0...9] \notin q_{a_t} \\ 0 & [0...9] \in q_{a_t}, q_{a_t} = c_{a_t} \\ -\frac{1}{|q|} & [0...9] \in q_{a_t}, q_{a_t} \neq c_{a_t} \end{cases} \tag{17}$$

4.3 Global Heuristic Features

Some global heuristics are also important in query spelling correction. For instance, the total number

[2]http://www.wikipedia.org

of words being corrected in the query may be an indicator of whether the system has leaned towards overcorrecting. To account for this global heuristic, we design the following feature:

$$\varphi(q, c, a) = \begin{cases} 1 & wc(q, c, a) < wc_{max} \\ 0 & otherwise \end{cases} \quad (18)$$

where $wc(q, c, a)$ is the number of word changes at step t, wc_{max} is the maximum number of word changes we allow in our system (in a soft way). Similarly, other thresholded features can be designed such as the number of total edit operations. The use of global features is similar to the use of loss function in the search algorithm.

5 Experiments

In order to test the effectiveness and efficiency of our proposed discriminative training method, in this section we conduct extensive experiments on two web query spelling datasets. Below we first present the dataset and evaluation metrics, followed by the experiment results on query spelling correction.

5.1 Dataset Preparation

The experiments are conducted on two query spelling correction datasets. One is the TREC dataset based on the publicly available TREC queries (2008 Million Query Track). This dataset contains 5892 queries and the corresponding corrections annotated by the MSR Speller Challenge [3] organizers. There could be more than one plausible corrections for a query. In this dataset only 5.3% of queries are judged as misspelled.

We have also annotated another dataset that contains 4926 MSN queries, where for each query there is at most one correction. Three experts are involved in the annotation process. For each query, we consult the speller from two major search engines (i.e. Google and Bing). If they agree on the returned results (including the case if the query is just unchanged), we take it as the corrected form of the input query. If the results are not the same from the two, as least one human expert will manually annotate the most likely corrected form of the query. Finally, about 13% of queries are judged as misspelled in this dataset, which is close to the error rate of real web queries. We've made this dataset publicly available to all researchers[4].

Both the two datasets are split randomly into two equal subsets for training and testing.

5.2 Evaluation Metrics

We evaluate our system based on the evaluation metrics proposed in Microsoft Speller Challenge, including expected precision, expected recall and expected F1 measure.

Let q be a user query and $C(q) = (c^1, c^2, , c^k)$ be the set of system output with posterior probabilities $P(c^i|q)$. Let $S(q)$ denote the set of plausible spelling variations annotated by the human experts for q. Expected Precision is computed as:

$$Precision = \frac{1}{|Q|} \sum_{q \in Q} \sum_{c \in C(q)} I_p(c, q) P(c|q), \quad (19)$$

where $I_p(c, q) = 1$ if $c \in S(q)$, and 0 otherwise. And expected recall is defined as:

$$Recall = \frac{1}{|Q|} \sum_{q \in Q} \sum_{a \in S(q)} I_r(C(q), a)/|S(q)|, \quad (20)$$

where $I_r(C(q), a) = 1$ if $a \in C(q)$ for $a \in S(q)$, and 0 otherwise. We use R@N to denote recall for systems limited to output top N corrections.

Expected F1 measure can be computed as:

$$F1 = \frac{2 \cdot precision \cdot recall}{precision + recall} \quad (21)$$

5.3 Experiment Results

Table 1 compares the performance of our LS-SVM based model with two strong baseline systems. The first baseline system is an Echo system which simply echos the input. The echo system is usually considered as a strong baseline in query spelling correction as the majority of the queries are correctly spelled queries. The second baseline Lueck-2011 we use is a award winning speller system[5] (Luec, 2011), which was ranked at the first place in Microsoft Spelling Challenge 2011.

[3] http://web-ngram.research.microsoft.com/spellerchallenge/

[4] http://times.cs.uiuc.edu/duan9/msn_speller.tar.gz

[5] http://www.phraselink.com

Table 1: LSSVM vs Baselines Serving as Standalone Speller

		All Queries			Misspelled Queries		
Dataset	Method	Precision	R@10	F1	Precision	R@10	F1
TREC	Echo	0.949	0.876	0.911	0	0	0
	Lueck-2011	**0.963**	0.932	0.947	**0.391**	0.479	0.430
	LS-SVM	0.955	**0.944**	**0.949**	0.331	**0.678**†	**0.445**†
MSN	Echo	0.869	0.869	0.869	0	0	0
	Lueck-2011	0.896	0.921	0.908	0.334	0.397	0.363
	LS-SVM	**0.903**	**0.953**	**0.928**	**0.353**†	**0.662**†	**0.461**†

We show performances for the entire query sets as well as the query sets consisting only the misspelled queries. As we can see, our system outperforms both baseline systems on almost all metrics, except the precision of Lueck-2011 is better than ours on TREC dataset. We perform statistical test and measures where our system shows statistical significant improvement over both baseline systems are noted by †. It is theoretically impossible to achieve statistical significance in the entire query set as majority queries have almost identical performance in different systems due to the large amount of correct queries. But our method shows significant improvement in the dealing with the misspelled queries. This experiment verified the effectiveness of our proposed discriminative model. As a standalone speller, our system achieves very high accuracy.

Despite we are primarily focused on optimizing the top correction in our discriminative model, we can also use the trained system to output multiple candidate corrections. Table 2 compare our system with the noisy channel model (N-C) in terms of recall at different levels of cutoff. For all levels, we see that our system achieves higher recall than the noisy channel model. This indicates that when used together with a secondary ranker, our system serves as a better filtering method than the unoptimized noisy channel model. Since the ranker makes use of arbitrary features, it has the potential of further improving the accuracy of query spelling correction. We plan to further explore this idea as a future work.

In Table 3 we study the effect of treating the transformation probability of merging and splitting errors as separate features and including the local and global heuristic features (rich features). We see that the precision of query spelling correction can benefits from the use of rich features. However, it does not result in much improvement in recall. This is reasonable as the additional features are primarily designed to improve the accuracy of the top correction generated by the system. In doing so, it actually regularizes the ability of the system in retrieving diversified results. For instance, the global heuristic feature on the number of word change tries to prevent the system from returning candidates having more than a certain number of changed words. For the TREC collection where more than one corrections can be labeled for a query, this phenomena is aggravated.

Table 2: LS-SVM vs Noisy Channel Model Serving as Filtering Method

Dataset	Method	R@5	R@10	R@20
TREC	N-C	0.896	0.899	0.901
	LS-SVM	**0.923**	**0.944**	**0.955**
MSN	N-C	0.870	0.873	0.876
	LS-SVM	**0.950**	**0.953**	**0.960**

Table 3: LSSVM w/ and w/o Rich Features

Dataset	Method	Precision	R@10	F1
TREC	w/o	0.942	**0.946**	0.944
	w/	**0.955**	0.944	**0.949**
MSN	w/o	0.898	0.952	0.924
	w/	**0.903**	**0.953**	**0.928**

6 Conclusions

In this paper, we present a novel discriminative model for query spelling correction. The paper made the following contributions:

First, to the best of our knowledge, this is a novel exploration of directly optimizing the search phase in query spelling correction with a discriminative model. By modeling word alignment as the latent structural information, our formulation also deals with word boundary errors. We propose to use LS-SVM for learning the discriminative model which naturally incorporates search in the learning process. Second, we develop an efficient search algorithm that solves the inference problems in the LS-SVM based model. We analyze the criteria for selecting and designing features to ensure the correctness and efficiency of the search algorithm. Third, we explore effective features to improve the accuracy of the model. Finally, experiments are conducted to verify the effectiveness of the proposed model. It is shown that as a standalone speller our system achieves high accuracy. When used in a two stage approach, it attains higher recall than the noisy channel model and can thus serve as a superior method for candidate generation. We also verify that through the use of rich features, we can further improve the accuracy of our query spelling correction system.

7 Acknowledgments

This paper is based upon work supported in part by MIAS, the Multimodal Information Access and Synthesis center at UIUC, part of CCICADA, a DHS Center of Excellence, and by the National Science Foundation under grant CNS-1027965, and by a Microsoft grant.

References

F. Ahmad and G. Kondrak. 2005. Learning a spelling error model from search query logs. In *HLT/EMNLP*. The Association for Computational Linguistics.

M. Bendersky and W. B. Croft. 2008. Discovering key concepts in verbose queries. In *Proceedings of the 31st annual international ACM SIGIR conference on Research and development in information retrieval*, SIGIR '08. ACM, New York, NY, USA, 491-498.

E. Brill and R. Moore. 2000. An improved error model for noisy channel spelling correction. In *Proceedings of the 38th Annual Meeting of the Association for Computational Linguistics*, Hong Kong.

M. Chang, D. Goldwasser, D. Roth and V. Srikumar. 2010. Discriminative Learning over Constrained Latent Representations. In *Proceedings of NAACL*.

Q. Chen, M. Li, and M. Zhou. 2007. Improving query spelling correction using web search results. In *EMNLP-CoNLL*, pages 181–189.

S. Cucerzan and E. Brill. 2004. Spelling correction as an iterative process that exploits the collective knowledge of web users. In *Proceedings of the Conference on Empirical Methods in Natural Language Processing (EMNLP)*.

H. Daume, J. Langford and D. Marcu. 2009. Search-based Structured Prediction. Machine Learning Journal (MLJ).

M. Dreyer, D. Smith and N. Smith. 2006. Vine parsing and minimum risk reranking for speed and precision. In *Proceedings of the Tenth Conference on Computational Natural Language Learning*. 201-205.

H. Duan and B.-J. P. Hsu. 2011. Online spelling correction for query completion. In *Proceedings of the 20th international conference on World wide web*, WWW '11, pages 117–126, New York, NY, USA.

C. Dyer, J. H. Clark, A. Lavie, and N. A. Smith. 2011. Unsupervised Word Alignment with Arbitrary Features. In *Proceedings of ACL*.

D. Freitag, S. Khadivi. 2007. A Sequence Alignment Model Based on the Averaged Perceptron. In *Proceedings of the 2007 Joint Conference on Empirical Methods in Natural Language Processing and Computational Natural Language Learning*. 238-247.

J. Gao, X. Li, D. Micol, C. Quirk, and X. Sun. 2010. A large scale ranker-based system for search query spelling correction. In *COLING*, pages 358–366.

A. R. Golding and D. Roth 1999. A Winnow based approach to Context-Sensitive Spelling Correction. In *Machine Learning*, vol 34, pages 107–130.

J. Guo, G. Xu, H. Li, and X. Cheng. 2008. A unified and discriminative model for query refinement. In *Proceedings of the 31st annual international ACM SIGIR*, SIGIR '08, pages 379–386, New York, NY, USA.

C. John Yu and T. Joachims. 2009. Learning structural SVMs with latent variables. In *Proceedings of the 26th Annual International Conference on Machine Learning* (ICML '09). ACM, New York, NY, USA, 1169-1176.

M. D. Kernighan , K. W. Church , W. A. Gale. 1990. A spelling correction program based on a noisy channel model. In *Proceedings of the 13th conference on Computational linguistics*. 205-210. August 20-25, 1990, Helsinki, Finland.

K. Kukich. 1992. Techniques for automatically correcting words in text. *ACM computing surveys*, 24(4).

G. Kumaran and J. Allan. 2008. Effective and efficient user interaction for long queries. In *Proceedings of the 31st annual international ACM SIGIR conference on Research and development in information retrieval*, SIGIR '08. ACM, New York, NY, USA.

G. Kumaran and V. R. Carvalho. 2009. Reducing long queries using query quality predictors. In *Proceedings of the 32nd international ACM SIGIR conference on Research and development in information retrieval*, SIGIR '09. ACM, New York, NY, USA, 564-571.

J. Lafferty. 2001. Conditional random fields: Probabilistic models for segmenting and labeling sequence data. In *Proceedings of the Eighteenth International Conference on Machine Learning* (ICML '01). 282–289.

V. I. Levenshtein. 1966. Binary codes capable of correcting deletions, insertions, and reversals. In *Soviet Physics Doklady, 10(8), 707-710.*

G. Luec. 2011. A data-driven approach for correcting search quaries. In *Spelling Alteration for Web Search Workshop.*

A. McCallum, D. Freitag, and F. Pereira. 2000. Maximum Entropy Markov Models for Information Extraction and Segmentation. In *Proceedings of the Seventeenth International Conference on Machine Learning* (ICML '00). 591-598.

M. Mitra, A. Singhal, and C. Buckley. 1998. Improving automatic query expansion. In *Proceedings of the 21st annual international ACM SIGIR conference on Research and development in information retrieval*, SIGIR '98.

Y. Qiu and H. Frei. 1993. Concept based query expansion. In *Proceedings of the 16th annual international ACM SIGIR conference on Research and development in information retrieval*, SIGIR '93. ACM, New York, NY, USA, 160-169.

X. Sun, J. Gao, D. Micol, and C. Quirk. 2010. Learning phrase-based spelling error models from clickthrough data. In *Proceedings of the 48th Annual Meeting of the Association for Computational Linguistics*, ACL '10, pages 266–274, Stroudsburg, PA, USA.

X. Wang, C. Zhai. 2008. Mining Term Association Patterns from Search Logs for Effective Query Reformulation. In *Proceedings of the 17th ACM International Conference on Information and Knowledge Management 2008*, CIKM'08. 479-488.

J. Xu and W. B. Croft. 1996. Query expansion using local and global document analysis. In *Proceedings of the 19th annual international ACM SIGIR conference on Research and development in information retrieval*, SIGIR '96. ACM, New York, NY.

A. Yessenalina, Y. Yue, C. Cardie. 2010. Multi-level Structured Models for Document-level Sentiment Classification. In *Proceedings of the 2010 Conference on Empirical Methods in Natural Language Processing* (EMNLP '10). 10461056.

Characterizing Stylistic Elements in Syntactic Structure

Song Feng **Ritwik Banerjee** **Yejin Choi**
Department of Computer Science
Stony Brook University
NY 11794, USA
songfeng, rbanerjee, ychoi@cs.stonybrook.edu

Abstract

Much of the writing styles recognized in rhetorical and composition theories involve deep syntactic elements. However, most previous research for *computational* stylometric analysis has relied on shallow lexico-syntactic patterns. Some very recent work has shown that PCFG models can detect distributional difference in syntactic styles, but without offering much insights into exactly what constitute salient stylistic elements in sentence structure characterizing each authorship. In this paper, we present a comprehensive exploration of syntactic elements in writing styles, with particular emphasis on *interpretable characterization* of stylistic elements. We present analytic insights with respect to the authorship attribution task in two different domains.

1 Introduction

Much of the writing styles recognized in rhetorical and composition theories involve deep syntactic elements in style (e.g., Bain (1887), Kemper (1987) Strunk and White (2008)). However, previous research for automatic authorship attribution and computational stylometric analysis have relied mostly on shallow lexico-syntactic patterns (e.g., Mendenhall (1887), Mosteller and Wallace (1984), Stamatatos et al. (2001), Baayen et al. (2002), Koppel and Schler (2003), Zhao and Zobel (2007), Luyckx and Daelemans (2008)).

Some very recent works have shown that PCFG models can detect distributional difference in sentence structure in gender attribution (Sarawgi et al., 2011), authorship attribution (Raghavan et al., 2010), and native language identification (Wong and Dras, 2011). However, still very little has been understood exactly what constitutes salient stylistic elements in sentence structures that characterize each author. Although the work of Wong and Dras (2011) has extracted production rules with highest information gain, their analysis stops short of providing insight any deeper than what simple n-gram-level analysis could also provide.[1] One might even wonder whether PCFG models are hinging mostly on leaf production rules, and whether there are indeed deep syntactic differences at all. This paper attempts to answer these questions.

As an example of syntactic stylistic elements that have been much discussed in rhetorical theories, but have not been analyzed computationally, let us consider two contrasting sentence styles: *loose (cumulative)* and *periodic*:[2] a *loose* sentence places the main clause at the beginning, and then appends subordinate phrases and clauses to develop the main message. In contrast, a *periodic* sentence starts with subordinate phrases and clauses, suspending the most

[1] For instance, missing determiners in English text written by Chinese speakers, or simple n-gram anomaly such as frequent use of "according to" by Chinese speakers (Wong and Dras, 2011).

[2] *Periodic* sentences were favored in classical times, while *loose* sentences became more popular in the modern age.

Hobbs	Joshi	Lin	McDon
S^ROOT → S , CC S	PP^PRN → IN NP	NP^S → NN CD	NP^NP → DT NN POS
NP^PP → DT	NP^PP → NP PRN SBAR	NP^NP → DT NN NNS	WHNP^SBAR → IN
VP^VP → TO VP	S^ROOT → PP NP VP .	S^ROOT → SBAR , NP VP .	NP^PP → NP SBAR
PP^PP → IN S	PRN^NP → -LRB- PP -RRB-	NP^PP → NP : NP	SBAR^PP → WHADVP S
NP^PP → NP , PP	NP^NP → NNP	S^ROOT → PP , NP VP .	SBAR^S → WHNP S
VP^S → VBZ ADJP S	S^SBAR → PP NP VP	NP^NP → PDT DT NNS	PP^NP → IN SBAR
VP^SINV → VBZ	S^ROOT → LST NP VP .	NP^VP → DT NN SBAR	SBAR^NP → WHNP S
VP^S → VBD S	CONJP^NP → RB RB IN	SBAR^S → WHADVP S	SBAR^PP → SBAR CC SBAR
VP^S → VBG PP	NP^PP → NP PRN PP	PRN^NP → -LRB- NP -RRB-	PP^VP → IN
ADVP^VP → RB PP	NP^NP → NP , NP	NP^PP → NN NN	S^SBAR → VP

Table 1: Top 10 most discriminative production rules for each author in the scientific domain.

LOOSE	*Christopher Columbus finally reached the shores of San Salvador* after months of uncertainty at sea, the threat of mutiny, and a shortage of food and water.
PERIODIC	After months of uncertainty at sea, the threat of mutiny, and a shortage of food and water, *Christopher Columbus finally reached the shores of San Salvador.*

Table 2: Loose/Periodic sentence with identical set of words and POS tags

important part to the end. The example in Table 2 highlights the difference:
Notice that these two sentences comprise of an identical set of words and part-of-speech. Hence, shallow lexico-syntactic analysis will not be able to catch the pronounced stylistic difference that is clear to a human reader.

One might wonder whether we could gain interesting insights simply by looking at the most discriminative production rules in PCFG trees. To address this question, Table 1 shows the top ten most discriminative production rules for authorship attribution for scientific articles,[3] ranked by LIBLINEAR (Fan et al., 2008).[4] Note that terminal production rules are excluded so as to focus directly on syntax.

It does provide some insights, but not to a satisfactory degree. For instance, Hobbs seems to favor inverted declarative sentences (SINV) and adverbs with prepositions (RB PP). While the latter can be easily obtained by simple part-of-speech analysis, the former requires using parse trees. We can also observe that none of the top 10 most discriminative production rules for Hobbs includes SBAR tag, which represents subordinate clauses. But examining discriminative rules alone is limited in providing more comprehensive characterization of idiolects.

Can we unveil something more in deep syntactic structure that can characterize the collective syntactic difference between any two authors? For instance, what can we say about distributional difference between loose and periodic sentences discussed earlier for each author? As can be seen in Table 1, simply enumerating most discriminative rules does not readily answer questions such as above.

In general, production rules in CFGs do not directly map to a wide variety of stylistic elements in rhetorical and composition theories. This is only as expected however, partly because CFGs are not designed for stylometric analysis in the first place, and also because some syntactic elements can go beyond the scope of context free grammars.

As an attempt to reduce this gap between modern statistical parsers and cognitively recognizable stylistic elements, we explore two complementary approaches:

1. Translating some of the well known stylistic elements of rhetorical theories into PCFG analysis (Section 3).

2. Investigating different strategies of analyzing PCFG trees to extract author characteristics that are interesting as well as *interpretable* (Sections 4 & 5).

[3]See Section 2 for the description of the dataset.

[4]We use Berkeley PCFG parser (Petrov and Klein, 2007) for all experiments.

Algorithm 1 Sentence Type-1 Identification

Input: Parse tree $t(N_r)$ of sentence s
Output: Type of s.
```
if S ∈ L^top then
  if SBAR ∉ Ω(N_r) then
    return COMPOUND
  else
    return COMPLEX-COMPOUND
else
  if VP ∈ L^top then
    if SBAR ∉ Ω(N_r) then
      return SIMPLE
    else
      return COMPLEX
return OTHER
```

We present analytic insights with respect to the authorship attribution task in two distinct domains.

2 Data

For the empirical analysis of authorship attribution, we use two different datasets described below. Sections 3, 4 & 5 provide the details of our stylometric analysis.

Scientific Paper We use the ACL Anthology Reference Corpus (Bird et al., 2008). Since it is nearly impossible to determine the gold-standard authorship of a paper written by multiple authors, we select 10 authors who have published at least 8 single-authored papers. We include 8 documents per author, and remove citations, tables, formulas from the text using simple heuristics.[5]

Novels We collect 5 novels from 5 English authors: Charles Dickens, Edward Bulwer-Lytton, Jane Austen, Thomas Hardy and Walter Scott. We select the first 3000 sentences from each novel and group every 50 consecutive sentences into 60 documents per novel per author.

[5] Some might question whether the size of the dataset used here is relatively small in comparison to typical dataset comprised of thousands of documents in conventional text categorization. We point out that authorship attribution is fundamentally different from text categorization in that it is often practically impossible to collect more than several documents for each author. Therefore, it is desirable that the attribution algorithms to detect the authors based on very small samples.

Algorithm 2 Sentence Type-II Identification

Input: Parse tree $t(N_r)$ of sentence s
Output: Type of s.
```
k ← 1
while k ≤ λ do
  if L_k^top ≠ VP then
    if S ∈ Ω(L_k^top) or SBAR ∈ Ω(L_k^top) then
      return PERIODIC
  else
    if S ∈ Ω(L_k^top) or SBAR ∈ Ω(L_k^top) then
      return LOOSE
return OTHER
```

3 Sentence Types

In this section, we examine well-known sentence types that are recognized in the literature, but have not been analyzed computationally.

Type-I Identification – Simple/Complex/Compound/Complex-Compound: PCFG trees do not provide this information directly, hence we must construct an algorithm to derive it. The key to identifying these sentences is the existence of *dependent* and *independent* clauses. For the former, we rely on the SBAR tag, while for the latter, we first define the sequence of nodes right below the root (e.g., [NP VP .] shown in the horizontal box in Figure 1). We call this the *top structural level.* We then check whether S (in addition to the root S) appears in this sequence.

Formally, let $L^{top} = \{N_i\}$ be the set of nodes in the top structural level, and $\lambda = |L^{top}|$. Let $t(N_r)$ be the tree rooted at N_r, and $\Omega(N_r)$ denote the set of nodes in $t(N_r)$. Algorithm 1 shows the procedure to determine the type-I class of a sentence based on its PCFG tree.[6]

Type-II Identification – Loose/Periodic: A sentence can also be classified as loose or periodic, and we present Algorithm 2 for this identification. We perform a mini-evaluation on 20 previously unseen sentences for each type[7]. Our algorithm was able to perform type-I identification on all sentences correctly. In type-II

[6] Note that Algorithm 1 & 2 rely on the use of Berkeley parser (Petrov and Klein, 2007).

[7] These were gathered from several online quizzes for English learners. E.g., `http://grammar.about.com`, `http://a4esl.org`

TYPE	HOBBS	JOSHI	LIN	MCDON
SIMPLE	40.0	41.7	50.2	27.9
CPLEX	40.8	40.7	37.6	48.4
CPND	7.9	5.6	3.9	5.5
CPXND	8.5	9.2	7.7	15.5
OTHER	2.8	2.8	0.6	2.7
LOOSE	27.6	26.4	26.9	30.8
PERIO	11.1	11.7	15.2	16.4
OTHER	61.3	61.9	57.9	52.8

Table 3: Sentence Types (%) in scientific data.

TYPE	DICKENS	B-LYT	AUSTEN	HARDY	SCOTT
SIMPLE	26.0	21.2	23.9	25.6	17.5
CPLEX	24.4	21.8	24.8	25.6	31.8
CPND	15.3	15.2	12.6	16.3	11.7
CPXND	20.8	23.3	31.1	18.9	28.7
OTHER	13.5	18.5	7.6	13.6	10.3
LOOSE	11.5	10.8	17.9	14.5	15.3
PERIO	19.5	13.6	14.0	16.2	18.0
OTHER	69.0	75.6	68.1	69.3	66.7

Table 4: Sentence Types (%) in Novels

identification, it labeled all loose sentences correctly, and achieved 90% accuracy on periodic sentences.

Discussion Tables 3 & 4 show the sentence type distribution in scientific data and novels, respectively.[8] We see that different authors are characterized by different distribution of sentence types. For instance, in Table 3, Lin is a prolific user of simple sentences while McDon prefers employing complex sentences. McDon also uses complex-compound sentences quite often (15.5%), more than twice as frequently as Lin. Notice that all authors use loose sentences much more often than periodic sentences, a known trend in modern English.

In Table 4, we see the opposite trend among 19th-century novels: with the exception of Jane Austen, all authors utilize periodic sentences comparatively more often. We also notice that complex and complex-compound sentences abound, as expected from classic literary proses.

Can we determine authorship solely based on the distribution of sentence types?

We experiment with a SVM classifier using just 6 features (one feature for each sentence type in Table 3), and we achieve accuracy 36.0% with the scientific data. Given that a random baseline would achieve only about 10% accuracy, this demonstrates that the distribution of sentence types does characterize an idiolect to some degree.

[8]Due to space limitation, we present analyses based on 4 authors from the scientific data.

4 Syntactic Elements Based on Production Rules

In this section, we examine three different aspects of syntactic elements based on production rules.

4.1 Syntactic Variations

We conjecture that the *variety* of syntactic structure, which most previous research in computational stylometry has not paid much attention to, provides an interesting insight into authorship. One way to quantify the degree of syntactic variations is to count the unique production rules. In Tables 5, we show the extent of syntactic variations employed by authors using the standard deviation σ and the *coverage* of an author:

$$\mathcal{C}(a) := \frac{|\mathcal{R}(a)|}{|\cup_a \mathcal{R}(a)|} \times 100$$

where $\mathcal{R}(a)$ denotes the set of unique production rules used by author a, and $\cup_a$ iterates over all authors. In order to compare among authors, we also show these parameters normalized with respect to the highest value. Our default setting is to exclude all lexicalized rules in the productions to focus directly on the syntactic variations. In our experiments (Section 6), however, we do augment the rules with (a) ancestor nodes to capture deeper syntactic structure and (b) lexical (*leaf*) nodes.

As hypothesized, these statistics provide us new insights into the authorship. For instance, we find that McDon employs a wider variety of syntactic structure than others, while Lin's writing exhibits relatively the least variation. Moreover, comparing Joshi and Hobbs, it is interesting to see the standard deviation differ a lot

	HOBBS	JOSHI	LIN	MCDON	DICKENS	B-LYT	AUSTEN	HARDY	SCOTT
$\mathcal{C}$	36.0	37.6	32.8	42.6	30.9	28.8	36.2	30.0	24.1
$\mathcal{C}_{\text{norm}}$	0.84	0.88	0.77	1.0	0.85	0.79	1.0	0.83	0.67
σ	51.5	39.2	63.3	44.4	88.3	81.6	98.0	125.3	114.7
σ_{norm}	0.81	0.62	1.0	0.7	0.7	0.65	0.78	1.0	0.92

Table 5: Syntactic variations of different authors in the scientific domain.

HOBBS	JOSHI	LIN	MCDON
# 136	# 142	# 124	# 161
S → S CC S .	S → ADVP PP NP VP .	S → SBAR NP VP .	S → S NP VP .
S → CC NP VP .	S → PP NP ADVP VP .	FRAG → NP : S .	S → S : S .
S → S VP .	S → NP VP	S → NP VP .	S → SBAR VP .
S → NP NP VP .	S → S S CC S .	S → PP VP .	S → SBAR S CC S .
S → PP NP VP .	S → ADVP NP VP .	S → NP ADVP VP .	S → NP PP VP .

Table 6: Most discriminative sentence outlines in the scientific data. $\#N$ shows the number of unique sentence outlines of each author.

(51.5 and 39.2), in spite of their $\mathcal{C}$ scores being similar: 36.0% and 37.6%, respectively. This indicates that Hobbs tends to use a certain subset production rules much more frequently than Joshi. Lin exhibits the highest standard deviation in spite of having least syntactic variation, indicating that he uses a much smaller subset of productions regularly, while ocassionally deviating to other rules.

Similarly, among novels, Jane Austen's writing has the highest amount of variation, while Walter Scott's writing style is the least varied. Even though authors from both datasets display similar $\mathcal{C}$ scores (Table 5), the difference in σ is noteworthy. The significantly higher linguistic variation is to be expected in creative writing of such stature. It is interesting to note that the authors with highest coverage – Austen and Dickens – have much lower deviation in their syntactic structure when compared to Hardy and Scott. This indicates that while Austen and Dickens consistently employ a wider variety of sentence structures in their writing, Hardy and Scott follow a relatively more uniform style with sporadic forays into diverse syntactic constructs.

4.2 Sentence Outlines

Although the approach of Section 4.1 give us a better and more general insight into the characteristics of each author, its ability to provide insight on *deep* syntactic structure is still limited, as it covers production rules at all levels of the tree. We thus shift our focus to the top level of the trees, e.g., the second level (marked in a horizontal box) in TREE (1) of Figure 1, which gives us a better sense of sentence outlines.

Tables 6 and 7 present the most discriminative sentence outlines of each author in the scientific data and novels, respectively. We find that McDon is a prolific user of subordinate clauses, indicating his bias towards using complex sentences. The rule "S → SBAR S CC S" shows his inclination towards complex-compound sentences as well. These inferences are further supported by the observations in Table 3. Another observation of possible interest is the tendency of Joshi and Lin to begin sentences with prepositional phrases.

In comparing Table 6 and Table 7, notice the significantly higher presence of complex and compound-complex structures in the latter[9]. The most discriminating sentence outlines for Jane Austen, for instance, are all indicative of complex-compound sentences. This is further supported by Table 4.

5 Syntactic Elements Based on Tree Topology

In this section, we investigate quantitative techniques to capture stylistic elements in the tree

[9]The presence of "FRAG" is not surprising. Intentional use of verbless sentence fragments, known as *scesis onomaton*, was often employed by authors such as Dickens and Bulwer-Lytton (Quinn, 1995).

DICKENS	BULWER-LYTTON	AUSTEN	HARDY	SCOTT
# 1820	# 1696	# 2137	# 1772	# 1423
SQ → NNP .	SBARQ → WHNP S .	S → S : CC S .	S → S NP VP .	S → NP PRN VP .
FRAG → NP .	FRAG → INTJ NP .	S → S CC S : CC S .	S → ADVP NP VP .	S → PP NP VP .
SINV → NP VP NP .	S → S : S CC S .	S → S : CC S : CC S .	S → FRAG : S .	S → S S : S .
INTJ → UH .	FRAG → CC NP .	S → S : S : CC S .	S → INTJ NP VP .	S → NP PP VP .
SBARQ → WHNP SQ .	FRAG → NP ADJP .	S → SBAR S : CC S .	S → NP VP .	S → ADVP PRN NP VP .

Table 7: Most discriminative sentence outlines in the novel data. #N shows the number of unique sentence outlines of each author.

METRICS	SCIENTIFIC DATA				NOVELS				
	HOBBS	JOSHI	LIN	MCDON	DICKENS	B-LYT	AUSTEN	HARDY	SCOTT
sen-len $\overline{avg}$	23.7	26.0	21.0	32.2	24.1	26.7	31.4	21.5	34.1
$h^{\mathcal{T}}\ \overline{avg}$	5.8	5.3	5.9	4.8	4.7	5.0	5.4	4.9	5.9
$h^{\mathcal{F}}\ \overline{avg}$	2.4	2.1	2.5	1.9	1.9	1.9	2.1	1.9	2.1
$w^{L}\ \overline{avg}$	5.0	4.8	5.5	4.2	4.1	4.4	4.7	3.8	4.9
$\sigma^{H}\ \overline{avg}$	1.2	1.1	1.1	1.0	1.1	1.1	1.3	1.2	1.4
$\sigma^{S}\ \overline{avg}$	1.9	1.8	1.8	1.7	1.0	1.1	1.2	1.0	1.4

Table 8: Tree topology metrics for scientific data and novels.

topology. Figure 1 shows three different parse trees to accompany our discussion.[10] Notice that sentence (1) is a loose sentence, and sentence (2) is periodic. In general, loose sentences grow deep and unbalanced, while periodic sentences are relatively more balanced and wider.

For a tree t rooted at N_R with a height n, let $\mathcal{T}$ be the set of leaf nodes, and let $\mathcal{F}$ be the set of furcation nodes, and let $\xi(N_i, N_j)$ denote the length of the shortest path from N_i to N_j. Inspired by the work of Shao (1990), we analyze tree topology with the following four measurements:

- LEAF HEIGHT ($h^{\mathcal{T}} = \{h_i^{\mathcal{T}}, N_i \in \mathcal{T}\}$), where $h_i^{\mathcal{T}} = \xi(N_i, N_R)\ N_i \in \mathcal{T}$. For instance, the leaf height of "free" of TREE (2) in Fig. 1 is 6.
- FURCATION HEIGHT ($h^{\mathcal{F}} = \{h_i^{\mathcal{F}}, N_i \in \mathcal{F}\}$), where $h_i^{\mathcal{F}}$ is the maximum leaf height within the subtree rooted at N_i. In Figure 1, for example, the furcation height of the VP in TREE (2) (marked in triangle) is 3.
- LEVEL WIDTH ($w^{L} = \{w_l, 1 \leq l \leq n\}$), where $w_l = |\{N_i : \xi(N_i, N_R) = l\}|$. E.g., w_4 of TREE (1) in Figure 1 is 6.
- HORIZONTAL $\sigma^H = \{\sigma_i^H, N_i \in \mathcal{F}\}$, and VERTICAL IMBALANCE $\sigma^S = \{\sigma_i^S, N_i \in \mathcal{F}\}$. Let $\mathcal{C}$ be the set of child nodes of N_k. If $|\mathcal{C}| \geq 2$, then

$$\sigma_k^H = \sqrt{\frac{1}{n}\sum_{i=1}^{|\mathcal{C}|}(h_i^{\mathcal{F}} - H)^2}$$

where $H = \frac{1}{|\mathcal{C}|}\sum_{i=1}^{|\mathcal{C}|} h_i^{\mathcal{F}}$. Similarly,

$$\sigma_k^S = \sqrt{\frac{1}{n}\sum_{i=1}^{|\mathcal{C}|}(s(N_i) - S)^2}$$

where $S = \frac{1}{|\mathcal{C}|}\sum_{i=1}^{|\mathcal{C}|} s(N_i)$ and $s(N_i)$ is the number of leaf nodes of tree rooted at N_i. As shown in Figure 1, the imbalance of the internal node VP in TREE (2) (marked in triangle) is 0.5 horizontally, and 0.5 vertically.

To give an intuition on the relation between these measurements and different tree structures, Table 9 provides the measurements of the three trees shown in Figure 1.

Note that all three sentences are of similar length but show different tree structures. TREE (1) and TREE (2) differ in that TREE (1) is highly unbalanced and grows deep, while TREE

[10] Example sentences are taken from Lin (1997), Joshi (1992), and Lin (1995).

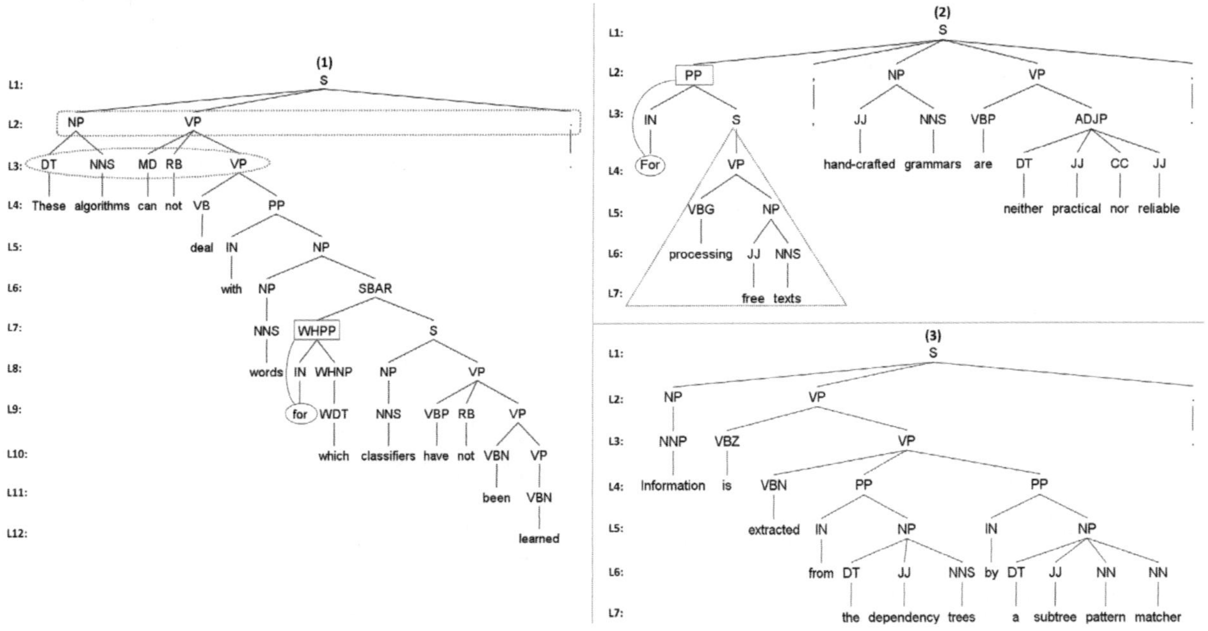

Figure 1: Parsed trees

METRICS	TREE (1)	TREE (2)	TREE (3)
# of tokens	15	13	13
$\max_i \{h_i^T\}$	11	6	6
$\max_i \{w_i^L\}$	6	9	9
$\max_i \{\sigma_i^H\}$	4.97	1.6	1.7
$\max_i \{\sigma_i^S\}$	4	1.5	4.7

Table 9: Tree Topology Statistics for Figure 1.

(2) is much better balanced and grows shorter but wider. Comparing TREE (2) and TREE (3), they have the same max LEAF HEIGHT, LEVEL WIDTH, and HORIZONTAL IMBALANCE, but the latter has bigger VERTICAL IMBALANCE, which requantifies the imbalance in terms of the text span covered by subtrees.

We provide these topological metrics for authors from both datasets in Table 8.

6 Experiments & Evaluation

In our experiments, we utilize a set of features motivated by PCFG trees. These consist of simple production rules and other syntactic features based on tree-traversals. Table 10 describes these features with examples from TREE (2), using the portion marked by the triangle.

These sets of production rules and syntax features are used to build SVM classifiers using LIBLINEAR (Fan et al., 2008), wherein all feature values are encoded as term-frequencies normalized by document size. We run 5-fold cross-validation with training and testing split first as 80%/20%, and then as 20%/80%.

We would like to point out that the latter configuration is of high practical importance in authorship attribution, since we may not always have sufficient training data in realistic situations, e.g., forensics (Luyckx and Daelemans, 2008).

Lexical tokens provide strong clues by creating features that are specific to each author: research topics in the scientific data, and proper nouns such as character names in novels. To lessen such topical bias, we lemmatize and rank words according to their frequency (in the entire dataset), and then consider the top 2,000 words only. Leaf-node productions with words outside this set are disregarded.

Our experimental results (Tables 11 & 12) show that not only do deep syntactic features perform well on their own, but they also significantly improve over lexical features. We also show that adding the STYLE$_{11}$ features further improves performance.

Features	
pr	Rules *excluding* terminal productions. E.g., **VP** → VBG NP
syn_v	Traversal from a non-leaf node to its grandparent (embedded rising). E.g., **VP**ˆS → PP
syn_h	Left-to-right traversal in the set of all non-leaf children of a node. E.g., VBG → NP (for node **VP**)
syn_{v+h}	$syn_v \cup syn_h$
syn_0	No tree traversal. Feature comprises interior nodes only.
$syn_\downarrow$	Union of all edges to child nodes, except when child is a leaf node. E.g., {**VP** → VBG, **VP** → NP}
$syn_\updownarrow$	$syn_\downarrow \cup$ { edge to parent node}
STYLE$_{11}$	The set of 11 extra stylistic features. 6 values from the distribution of sentence types (Section 3), and 5 topological metrics (Section 5) characterizing the height, width and imbalance of a tree.
Variations	
$\hat{pr}$	Each production rule is augmented with the grandparent node.
$*$	Terminal (*leaf*) nodes are included.

Table 10: Features and their lexico-syntactic variations. *Illustration*: $\hat{pr}^*$ denotes the set of production rules pr (including terminal productions) that are augmented with their grandparent nodes.

Features	Scientific		Novels	
		+STYLE$_{11}$		+STYLE$_{11}$
STYLE$_{11}$	20.6	–	43.1	–
Unigram	56.9	–	69.3	–
syn_h	53.7	53.7	68.3	67.9
syn_0	22.9	**31.1**	57.8	**62.5**
$syn_\downarrow$	43.4	**44.0**	63.6	**65.7**
$syn_\updownarrow$	51.1	**51.7**	71.3	**72.8**
syn_{v+h}	54.0	**55.7**	72.0	**73.2**
syn_h^*	63.1	**64.0**	72,1	**73.2**
syn_0^*	56.6	56.0	73.1	**74.1**
$syn_\downarrow^*$	56.3	**57.2**	74.0	**74.9**
$syn_\updownarrow^*$	64.6	**65.4**	**74.9**	**75.3**
syn_{v+h}^*	64.0	**67.7**	74.0	**74.7**
pr	50.3	**53.4**	67.0	66.7
$\hat{pr}$	59.1	**60.6**	69.7	68.7
$pr*$	63.7	**65.1**	71.5	**73.2**
$\hat{pr}*$	66.3	**69.4**	73.6	**74.9**

Table 11: Authorship attribution with **20% training data**. Improvement with addition of STYLE$_{11}$ shown in bold.

To quantify the amount of authorship information carried in the set STYLE$_{11}$, we experiment with a SVM classifier using only 11 features (one for each metric), and achieve accuracy of 42.0% and 52.0% with scientific data and novels, respectively. Given that a random-guess baseline would achieve only 10% and 20% (resp.), and that the classification is based on just 11 features, this experiment demonstrates how effectively the tree topology statistics capture idiolects. In general, lexicalized features yield higher performance even after removing topical words. This is expected since tokens such as function words play an important role in determining authorship (e.g., Mosteller and Wallace (1984), Garcia and Martin (2007), Argamon et al. (2007)).

A more important observation, however, is that even after removing the leaf production rules, accuracy as high as 93% (scientific) and 92.2% (novels) are obtained using syntactic features, which demonstrates that there are syntactic patterns unique to each author. Also notice that using only production rules, we achieve higher accuracy in novels (90.1%), but the addition of STYLE$_{11}$ features yields better results with scientific data (93.0%).

Using different amounts of training data provides insight about the influence of lexical clues. In the scientific dataset, increasing the amount of training data decreases the average performance difference between lexicalized and unlexicalized features: 13.5% to 11.6%. In novels, however, we see the opposite trend: 6.1% increases to 8.1%.

We further observe that with scientific data, increasing the amount of training data improves the average performance across all unlexicalized feature-sets from 50.0% to 82.9%, an improvement of 32.8%. For novels, the corresponding improvement is small in comparison: 17.0%.

This difference is expected. While authors such as Dickens or Hardy have their unique writing styles that a classifier can learn based on few documents, capturing idiolects in the more rigid domain of scientific writing is far from obvious with little training data.

FEATURES	SCIENTIFIC		NOVELS	
		+STYLE11		+STYLE11
STYLE11	42.0	–	52.0	–
Unigram	88.0	–	92.7	–
syn_h	85.0	85.0	87.6	**88.9**
syn_0	40.0	**53.0**	66.4	**72.3**
$syn_\downarrow$	78.0	**82.0**	80.3	**82.3**
$syn_\updownarrow$	85.0	**92.0**	89.3	**92.2**
syn_{v+h}	89.0	**93.0**	90.1	**91.2**
syn^*_h	93.0	93.0	93.7	**93.9**
syn^*_0	92.0	**94.0**	92.1	**93.2**
$syn^*_\downarrow$	93.0	**94.0**	93.4	**94.5**
$syn^*_\updownarrow$	93.0	**95.0**	94.9	**95.2**
syn^*_{v+h}	94.0	**96.0**	94.7	**94.8**
pr	85.0	**86.0**	86.7	86.7
$\hat{pr}$	87.0	**89.0**	88.2	**89.3**
$pr*$	93.0	**94.0**	92.1	**93.2**
$\hat{pr}*$	94.0	**95.0**	94.5	**95.1**

Table 12: Authorship attribution with **80% training data**.

Turning to lexicalized features, we note that with more training data, lexical cues perform better in scientific domain than in novels. With 80% data used for training, the average performance of lexicalized feature-sets with science data is 94.4%, and slightly lower at 94.3% for novels. With less training data, however, these figures are 63.5% and 74.3% respectively.

Finally, we point out that adding the style features derived from sentence types and tree topologies almost always improves the performance. In scientific data, syn^*_{v+h} with STYLE11 features shows the best performance (96%), while $syn^*_\updownarrow$ yields the best results for novels (95.2%). For unlexicalized features, adding STYLE11 to syn_{v+h} and $syn_\updownarrow$ yields respective improvements of 4.0% and 2.9% in the two datasets.

7 Related Work

There are several hurdles in authorship attribution. First and foremost, writing style is extremely domain-dependent. Much of previous research has focused on several domains of writing, such as informal modern writing in blogs and online messages (Zheng et al., 2006), relatively formal contemporary texts such as news articles (Raghavan et al., 2010), or classical literature like novels and proses (e.g., (Burrows, 2002), (Hoover, 2004)).

The nature of these features have also varied considerably. Character level n-grams have been used by several researchers; most notably by Peng et al. (2003), by Houvardas and Stamatatos (2006) for feature selection, and by Stamatatos (2006) in ensemble learning. Keselj et al. (2003) employed frequency measures on n-grams for authorship attribution.

Others, such as Zhao and Zobel (2005), Argamon and Levitan (2004), Garcia and Martin (2007), have used word-level approaches instead, incorporating the differential use of function words by authors.

More sophisticated linguistic cues have been explored as well: parts-of-speech n-grams (Diederich et al., 2003), word-level statistics together with POS-sequences (Luyckx and Daelemans, 2008), syntactic labels from partial parsing (Hirst and Feiguina, 2007), etc. The use of syntactic features from parse trees in authorship attribution was initiated by Baayen et al. (1996), and more recently, Raghavan et al. (2010) have directly employed PCFG language models in this area.

Syntactic features from PCFG parse trees have also been used for gender attribution (Sarawgi et al., 2011), genre identification (Stamatatos et al., 2000), native language identification (Wong and Dras, 2011) and readability assessment (Pitler and Nenkova, 2008). The primary focus of most previous research, however, was to attain better classification accuracy, rather than providing linguistic interpretations of individual authorship and their stylistic elements.

Our work is the first to attempt authorship attribution of scientific papers, a contemporary domain where language is very formal, and the stylistic variations have limited scope. In addition to exploring this new domain, we also present a comparative study expounding the role of syntactic features for authorship attribution in classical literature. Furthermore, our work is also the first to utilize tree topological features (Chan et al., 2010) in the context of stylometric analysis.

8 Conclusion

In this paper, we have presented a comprehensive exploration of syntactic elements in writing styles, with particular emphasis on interpretable characterization of stylistic elements, thus distinguishing our work from other recent work on syntactic stylometric analysis. Our analytical study provides novel statistically supported insights into stylistic elements that have not been computationally analyzed in previous literature. In the future, we plan to investigate the use of syntactic feature generators for text categorization (e.g., Collins and Duffy (2002), Moschitti (2008), Pighin and Moschitti (2009)) for stylometry analysis.

Acknowledgments Yejin Choi is partially supported by the Stony Brook University Office of the Vice President for Research. We thank reviewers for many insightful and helpful comments.

References

Shlomo Argamon and Shlomo Levitan. 2004. Measuring the usefulness of function words for authorship attribution. *Literary and Linguistic Computing*, pages 1–3.

Shlomo Argamon, Casey Whitelaw, Paul Chase, Sobhan Raj Hota, Navendu Garg, and Shlomo Levitan. 2007. Stylistic text classification using functional lexical features: Research articles. *J. Am. Soc. Inf. Sci. Technol.*, 58(6):802–822.

H. Baayen, H. Van Halteren, and F. Tweedie. 1996. Outside the cave of shadows: Using syntactic annotation to enhance authorship attribution. *Literary and Linguistic Computing*, 11(3):121.

H. Baayen, H. van Halteren, A. Neijt, and F. Tweedie. 2002. An experiment in authorship attribution. In *6th JADT*. Citeseer.

A. Bain. 1887. *English Composition and Rhetoric: Intellectual elements of style*. D. Appleton and company.

S. Bird, R. Dale, B.J. Dorr, B. Gibson, M.T. Joseph, M.Y. Kan, D. Lee, B. Powley, D.R. Radev, and Y.F. Tan. 2008. The acl anthology reference corpus: A reference dataset for bibliographic research in computational linguistics. In *Proc. of the 6th International Conference on Language Resources and Evaluation Conference (LREC08)*, pages 1755–1759.

J. Burrows. 2002. Delta: A measure of stylistic difference and a guide to likely authorship. *Literary and Linguistic Computing*, 17(3):267–287.

Samuel W. K. Chan, Lawrence Y. L. Cheung, and Mickey W. C. Chong. 2010. Tree topological features for unlexicalized parsing. In *Proceedings of the 23rd International Conference on Computational Linguistics: Posters*, COLING '10, pages 117–125, Stroudsburg, PA, USA. Association for Computational Linguistics.

Michael Collins and Nigel Duffy. 2002. New ranking algorithms for parsing and tagging: kernels over discrete structures, and the voted perceptron. In *Proceedings of the 40th Annual Meeting on Association for Computational Linguistics*, ACL '02, pages 263–270, Stroudsburg, PA, USA. Association for Computational Linguistics.

J. Diederich, J. Kindermann, E. Leopold, and G. Paass. 2003. Authorship attribution with support vector machines. *Applied Intelligence*, 19(1):109–123.

Rong-En Fan, Kai-Wei Chang, Cho-Jui Hsieh, Xiang-Rui Wang, and Chih-Jen Lin. 2008. LIBLINEAR: A library for large linear classification. *Journal of Machine Learning Research*, 9:1871–1874.

Antonion Miranda Garcia and Javier Calle Martin. 2007. Function words in authorship attribution studies. *Literary and Linguistic Computing*, 22(1):49–66.

Graeme Hirst and Olga Feiguina. 2007. Bigrams of syntactic labels for authorship discrimination of short texts. *Literary and Linguistic Computing*, 22(4):405–417.

D. L. Hoover. 2004. Testing burrow's delta. *Literary and Linguistic Computing*, 19(4):453–475.

J. Houvardas and E. Stamatatos. 2006. N-gram feature selection for author identification. In *Proc. of the* 12th *International Conference on Artificial Intelligence: Methodology, Systems and Applications*, volume 4183 of *LNCS*, pages 77–86, Varna, Bulgaria. Springer.

Aravind K. Joshi. 1992. Statistical language modeling. In *Proceedings of a Workshop Held at Harriman, New York, February 23-26, 1992*. Association for Computational Linguistics.

S. Kemper. 1987. Life-span changes in syntactic complexity. *Journal of gerontology*, 42(3):323.

Vlado Keselj, Fuchun Peng, Nick Cercone, and Calvin Thomas. 2003. N-gram-based author profiles for authorship attribution. In *Proc. of the*

Pacific Association for Computational Linguistics, pages 255–264.

M. Koppel and J. Schler. 2003. Exploiting stylistic idiosyncrasies for authorship attribution. In *Proceedings of IJCAI*, volume 3, pages 69–72. Citeseer.

D. Lin. 1995. University of manitoba: description of the pie system used for muc-6. In *Proceedings of the 6th conference on Message understanding*, pages 113–126. Association for Computational Linguistics.

D. Lin. 1997. Using syntactic dependency as local context to resolve word sense ambiguity. In *Proceedings of the 35th Annual Meeting of the Association for Computational Linguistics and Eighth Conference of the European Chapter of the Association for Computational Linguistics*, pages 64–71. Association for Computational Linguistics.

Kim Luyckx and Walter Daelemans. 2008. Authorship attribution and verification with many authors and limited data. In *COLING '08*, pages 513–520.

T.C. Mendenhall. 1887. The characteristic curves of composition. *Science*, ns-9(214S):237–246.

Alessandro Moschitti. 2008. Kernel methods, syntax and semantics for relational text categorization. In *Proceedings of the 17th ACM conference on Information and knowledge management*, CIKM '08, pages 253–262, New York, NY, USA. ACM.

Frederick Mosteller and David L. Wallace. 1984. *Applied Bayesian and Classical Inference: The Case of the Federalist Papers.* Springer-Verlag.

Fuchun Peng, Dale Schuurmans, Shaojun Wang, and Vlado Keselj. 2003. Language independent authorship attribution using character level language models. In *Proceedings of the tenth conference on European chapter of the Association for Computational Linguistics - Volume 1*, EACL '03, pages 267–274, Stroudsburg, PA, USA. Association for Computational Linguistics.

S. Petrov and D. Klein. 2007. Improved inference for unlexicalized parsing. In *Proceedings of NAACL HLT 2007*, pages 404–411.

Daniele Pighin and Alessandro Moschitti. 2009. Reverse engineering of tree kernel feature spaces. In *Proceedings of the 2009 Conference on Empirical Methods in Natural Language Processing: Volume 1 - Volume 1*, EMNLP '09, pages 111–120, Stroudsburg, PA, USA. Association for Computational Linguistics.

Emily Pitler and Ani Nenkova. 2008. Revisiting readability: a unified framework for predicting text quality. In *Proceedings of the Conference on Empirical Methods in Natural Language Processing*, EMNLP '08, pages 186–195, Stroudsburg, PA, USA. Association for Computational Linguistics.

Arthus Quinn. 1995. *Figures of Speech: 60 Ways To Turn A Phrase.* Routledge.

Sindhu Raghavan, Adriana Kovashka, and Raymond Mooney. 2010. Authorship attribution using probabilistic context-free grammars. In *Proceedings of the ACL 2010 Conference Short Papers*, pages 38–42, Uppsala, Sweden. Association for Computational Linguistics.

Ruchita Sarawgi, Kailash Gajulapalli, and Yejin Choi. 2011. Gender attribution: tracing stylometric evidence beyond topic and genre. In *Proceedings of the Fifteenth Conference on Computational Natural Language Learning*, CoNLL '11, pages 78–86, Stroudsburg, PA, USA. Association for Computational Linguistics.

K.T. Shao. 1990. Tree balance. *Systematic Biology*, 39(3):266.

Efstathios Stamatatos, George Kokkinakis, and Nikos Fakotakis. 2000. Automatic text categorization in terms of genre and author. *Comput. Linguist.*, 26(4):471–495.

E. Stamatatos, N. Fakotakis, and G. Kokkinakis. 2001. Computer-based authorship attribution without lexical measures. *Computers and the Humanities*, 35(2):193–214.

E. Stamatatos. 2006. Ensemble-based author identification using character n-grams. *ReCALL*, page 4146.

W. Strunk and E.B. White. 2008. *The elements of style.* Penguin Group USA.

Sze-Meng Jojo Wong and Mark Dras. 2011. Exploiting parse structures for native language identification. In *Proceedings of the Conference on Empirical Methods in Natural Language Processing*, EMNLP '11, pages 1600–1610, Stroudsburg, PA, USA. Association for Computational Linguistics.

Ying Zhao and Justin Zobel. 2005. Effective and scalable authorship attribution using function words. In *Proceedings of the Second Asia conference on Asia Information Retrieval Technology*, AIRS'05, pages 174–189, Berlin, Heidelberg. Springer-Verlag.

Y. Zhao and J. Zobel. 2007. Searching with style: Authorship attribution in classic literature. In *Proceedings of the thirtieth Australasian conference on Computer science-Volume 62*, pages 59–68. Australian Computer Society, Inc.

Rong Zheng, Jiexun Li, Hsinchun Chen, and Zan Huang. 2006. A framework for authorship identification of online messages: Writing-style features and classification techniques. *J. Am. Soc. Inf. Sci. Technol.*, 57(3):378–393.

Author Index